# CRUDEN'S COMPACT CONCORDANCE

# CRUDEN'S
# COMPACT CONCORDANCE

ZondervanPublishingHouse
*Academic and Professional Books*
*Grand Rapids, Michigan*
*A Division of* HarperCollins*Publishers*

Requests for information should be addressed to:
Zondervan Publishing House
Academic and Professional Books
Grand Rapids, Michigan 49530

ISBN 0-310-48971-7

*Cover design by Art Jacobs*
*Cover photos by Ben Chapman*

*Printed in the United States of America*

94 95 96 97 98 99 00 01 02 /BP/ 10 9 8 7 6 5 4 3 2 1

# CRUDEN'S COMPACT CONCORDANCE

# CRUDEN'S COMPACT CONCORDANCE

Based on the Famous Work of Alexander Cruden
as Edited by John Eadie

# A

**AARON.**
*Luke* 1:5 wife of daughters of A.
*Acts* 7:40 saying to A. make gods
*Heb.* 5:4 called of God, as was A.
7:11 not called after order of A.
9:4 A's rod that budded
AARONITES. 1 *Chr.* 12:27; 27:17
ABADDON. *Rev.* 9:11
ABAGTHA. *Est.* 1:10
ABANA. 2 *K.* 5:12

**ABASE.**
*Job* 40:11 Behold proud, and *a.*
*Is.* 31:4 lion will not *a.* himself
*Eze.* 21:26 and *a.* him that is high
*Dan.* 4:37 in pride is able to *a.*

**ABASED.**
*Mat.* 23:12 exalt, shall be *a.*
*Luke* 14:11; 18:14
*Phil.* 4:12 I know how to be *a.*

**ABASING.**
2 *Cor.* 11:7 offence in *a.* myself

**ABATED.**
*Gen.* 8:3 waters were *a.* 8:11
*Lev.* 27:18 be *a.* from thy estim.
*Deut.* 34:7 was Moses' force *a.*
*Jud.* 8:3 their anger was *a.*

**ABBA.**
*Mark* 14:36 *a.* Father, all things
*Rom.* 8:15 we cry, *a.* Father
*Gal.* 4:6 crying *a.* Father
ABDA. 1 *K.* 4:6; *Neh.* 11:17
ABDI. 2 *Chr.* 29:12; *Ezr.* 10:26
ABDIEL. 1 *Chr.* 5:15
ABDON. *Jud.* 12:13; 2 *Chr.* 34:20
ABED-NEGO. *Dan.* 1:7; 2:49; 3:23

**ABEL, person, *or* place.**
1 *Sam.* 6:18 stone of A. they set
2 *Sam.* 20:18 ask counsel at A.
*Mat.* 23:35 blood of A. *Luke* 11:51
*Heb.* 11:4 by faith A. offered
12:24 things than blood of A.
ABEL-BETH-MAACHAH. 1 *K.* 15:20; 2 *K.* 15:29
ABEL-MAIM. 2 *Chr.* 16:4
ABEL-MEHOLAH. *Jud.* 7:22; 1 *K.* 19:16
ABEL-MIZRAIM. *Gen.* 50:11

**ABHOR.**
*Lev.* 26:11 soul shall not *a.* you
15 your soul *a.* my judgments
30 my soul shall *a.* you
44 nor will I *a.* them
*Deut.* 7:26 shalt utterly *a.* it
23:7 not *a.* Edomite, Egyptian
1 *Sam.* 27:12 his people to *a.* him
*Job* 9:31 clothes shall *a.* me
30:10 they *a.* me, they flee far
42:6 I *a.* myself and repent in
*Ps.* 5:6 Lord will *a.* bloody man
119:163 I hate and *a.* lying
*Prov.* 24:24 nations shall *a.* him
*Jer.* 14:21 do not *a.* us
*Amos* 5:10 they *a.* him
6:8 I *a.* the excellency of Jacob
*Mic.* 3:9 ye that *a.* judgment
*Rom.* 12:9 *a.* that which is evil

**ABHORRED.**
*Ex.* 5:21 made savor to be *a.*
*Lev.* 20:23 therefore I *a* them
26:43 their soul *a* my statutes
*Deut.* 32:19 saw it, he *a* them
1 *Sam.* 2:17 men *a.* the offering
2 *Sam.* 16:21 art *a.* of thy father
*Job* 19:19 inward friends *a.* me
*Ps.* 22:24 nor *a.* affliction
78:59 he greatly *a.* Israel
89:38 thou hast cast off and *a.*
106:40 that he *a.* inherit.
*Prov.* 22:14 *a.* of the Lord
*Lam.* 2:7 hath *a.* his sanctuary
*Ezek.* 16:25 beauty to be *a.*
*Zec.* 11:8 their soul also *a.* me

**ABHORREST.**
*Is.* 7:16 thou *a.* shall be forsa.
*Rom.* 2:22 thou that *a.* idols

**ABHORRETH.**
*Job* 33:20 so life *a.* bread
*Ps.* 10:3 whom the Lord *a.*
36:4 mischief on bed, he *a.* not
107:18 their soul *a.* meat
*Is.* 49:7 to him whom nation *a.*

**ABHORRING.**
*Is.* 66:24 an *a.* to all flesh

**ABIAH.**
1 *Sam.* 8:2 sec. son was A.
1 *Chr.* 2:24 A. Hezron's wife
7:8 son of Becher, A.
3:10 son of R. was A. *Mat.* 1:7
ABI-ALBON. 2 *Sam.* 23:31

**ABIATHAR.**
1 *Sam.* 22:20 A. escaped and fled
23:6 when A. son of Ahimelech
9 David said to A. bring, 30:7
2 *Sam.* 8:17 Zadok and A. 20:25; 1 *K.* 4:4
1 *K.* 2:22 king. for him and A.
27 so Solomon thrust out A.
*Mark* 2:26 in days of A.

**ABIB.**
*Ex.* 13:4 out in A. 34:18
23:15 unleav. bread in month A. 34:18; *Deut.* 16:1

**ABIDAN.**
*Num.* 1:11 A. son of Gid. 2:22
7:60 A. of Benjamin offered, 65

**ABIDE.**
*Gen.* 22:5 *a.* you here with
*Ex.* 16:29 *a.* every man in
*Lev.* 8:35 *a.* at door of tabernacle
1 *Sam.* 5:7 ark shall not *a.* with
22:23 *a.* thou with me, fear not
2 *Sam.* 16:18 with him will I *a.*
*Job* 24:13 nor *a.* in paths of light

Ps. 15:1 shall a. in tabernacle?
61:4 I will a. in thy tabernacle
7 he shall a. before God
91:1 shall a. under the shadow
Prov. 7:11 her feet a. not in
19:23 shall a. satisfied
Ec. 8:15 shall a. of his labor
Jer. 10:10 not a. his indigna.
49:18 no man a. there, 33; 50:40
Joel 2:11 terrible, who can a. it?
Mic. 5:4 they shall a. for now
Nah. 1:6 can a. in his anger?
Mal. 3:2 whom may a. day of
Mat. 10:11 there a. Mark 6:10; Luke 9:4
Luke 19:5 I must a. at thy house
24:29 a. with us
John 12:46 not a. in darkness
14:16 Comforter that he may a.
15:4 a. in me, except ye a. 7
6 if a man a. not in me
10 a. in my love, a. in his love
Acts 27:31 these a. in ship
1 Cor. 3:14 if any man's work a.
7:8 good if they a. even as I
20 let every man a. in same
40 happier if she so a.
Phil. 1:24 to a. in the flesh
1 John 2:24 let that a. in you
27 ye shall a.; 28 children a.

**ABIDETH.**

2 Sam. 16:3 he a. at Jerus.
Ps. 49:12 man in honor, a. not
55:19 even he that a. of old
119:90 earth, and it a.
125:1 Zion, which a. ever
Prov. 15:31 a. among the wise
Ec. 1:4 the earth a. for ever
John 3.36 wrath of God a on
8:35 servant a. not, son a.
12:34 heard that Christ a.
15:5 he that a. in me bringeth
1 Cor. 13:13 now a. faith, hope
2 Tim. 2:13 yet he a. faithful
Heb. 7:3 Melchizedek a. a priest
1 Pet. 1:23 word of God which a.
1 John 2:6 he a. in him ought
10 loveth his brother a. in the
14 the word of God a. in you
17 doeth will of God a. for ever
27 the anointing a. in you
3:6 whosoever a. in him
3:14 loveth not brother a. in
24 we know that he a. in us
2 John 9 whoso a. not in the

**ABIDING.**

1 Sam. 26:19 from a. in inherit.
1 Chr. 29:15 here is done a.
Luke 2:8 shepherds a. in the field
John 5:38 his word a. in you
1 John 3:15 mur. hath eter. life a.

**ABIEZER.**

Jos. 17:2 for children of A.
Jud. 6:34 and A. was gathered
8:2 better than the vintage of A.
2 Sam. 23:27 A. one of David's

ABI-EZRITE. Jud. 6:11

**ABIGAIL.**

1 Sam. 25:3 Nabal's wife A.
27:3 dwelt at Gath with Ahi and A. 30:5; 2 Sam. 2:2
1 Chr. 2:16 sists. Zeruiah and A.

**ABIHAIL.**

2 Chr. 11:18 Rehoboam took A.
Est. 2:15 daughter of A. 9:29

**ABIHU.**

Ex. 6:23 Aaron's sons Nadab and A. 28:1; Lev. 10:1; Num. 3:2; 26:60; 1 Chr. 6:3; 24:1
24:1 come up A.; 9 A. went up
Num. 3:4 A. died bef. Lord, 26:61

**ABIJAH, ABIJAM.**

1 K. 14:1 A. son of Jero.
31 A. son of Reho. 15:1, 7
1 Chr. 24:10 eighth lot came to A.
2 Chr. 29:1 mother's name A.

**ABILITY.**

Ezr. 2:69 gave after their a.
Neh. 5:8 after our a. redeemed
Dan. 1:4 had a. to stand in pal.
Mat. 25:15 each accord. to his a.
Acts 11:29 according to a. to send
1 Pet. 4:11 as of the a. God giv.

**ABIMELECH.**

Gen. 20:2 A. king of Gerar sent
21:22 A. and Phichol spake
26:1 Isaac went unto A.
16 A. said unto Isaac, go
Jud. 8:31 Gideon's con. bare A.
2 Sam. 11:21 smote A. son of Jer.
1 Chr. 18:16 Zadok and A.

**ABINADAB.**

1 Sam. 7:1 into the house of A.
16:8 Jesse called A. made him
2 Sam. 6:3 out of house of A. 1 Chr. 13:7
1 K. 4:11 A. had Sol. daughter

ABINOAM. See BARAK.

**ABIRAM.**

Num. 16:1 Dathan and A. 26:9
12 sent to call Dath. and A.
Deut. 11:6 did to Dathan and A.
1 K. 16:34 laid founda. in A.
Ps. 106:17 company of A.

ABISHAG. 1 K. 1:15; 2:22

**ABISHAI.**

1 Sam. 26:6 A. said, I will go
2 Sam. 2:18 three sons, Joab, A. and Asahel, 1 Chr. 2:16
23:18 A. was chief, 1 Chr. 11:20
1 Chr. 18:12 A. slew of Edomites

ABIUD. Mat. 1:13

**ADJECTS.**

Ps. 35:15 the a. gathered

**ABLE.**

Ex. 18:21 provide a. men
Num. 1:3 a. to go to war, 26:2
13:30 well a. to overcome it
Deut. 16:17 man give as he is a.
Jos. 23:9 man been a. to stand
1 Sam. 6:20 who a. to stand
1 K. 3:9 who is a. to judge
2 Chr 2:6 who is a. to build
20:6 none is a. to withstand thee
25:9 Lord is a. to give
Job 41:10 who a. to stand
Prov. 27:4 who a. to stand bef.
Dan. 3:17 our God is a. to deliv.
6:20 God is a. to deliver from
Mat. 3:9 God is a. of these stones to raise up, Luke 3:8
9:28 believe ye I am a. to do
19:12 he that is a. to receive it
20:22 are ye a. to drink
22:46 no man was a. to answer
Mark 4:33 as they were a. to hear
John 10:29 no man is a. to pluck
Acts 15:10 yoke fathers nor we a.
20:32 word of grace, a. to build
Rom. 4:21 he was a. to perform
11:23 for God is a. to graff them
14:4 God is a. to make him
15:14 ye are a. also to admonish
1 Cor. 3:2 ye were not a. nor yet
10:13 above that ye are a.
2 Cor. 3:6 made us a. ministers of
9:8 God is a. to make all grace
Eph. 3:20 that is a. to do
Phil. 3:21 he is a. to subdue all
2 Tim. 1:12 he is a. to keep that I
3:7 never a. to come to the know.
15 scriptures a. to make wise.
Heb. 2:18 he is a. to succor them
5:7 to him that was a. to save
7:25 is a. to save to uttermost
11:19 that God was a. to raise
Jam. 1:21 which is a. to save
3:2 a. to bridle the whole body
4:12 one lawgiver a. to save and
Jude 24 to him that is a. to keep
Rev. 5:3 no man was a. to open
13:4 who is a. to make war with
15:18 no man was a. to enter

**Be ABLE.**

Jos. 1:5 any man be a. to stand
Deut. 7:24 no man be a. to, 11:25
2 Chr. 32:14 should be a. to deliv.
Is. 47:12 thou shalt be a. to profit
Eze. 33:12 righteous be a. to live
Luke 14:31 he be a. with 10,000
Rom. 8:39 be a. to separate us
1 Cor. 10:13 may be a. to bear
Eph. 3:18 be a. to comprehend
6:11 that ye may be a. to stand
16 ye shall be a. to quench
2 Tim. 2:2 who shall be a. to t.
Tit. 1:9 may be a. by sound
2 Pet. 1:15 be a. after my decease
Rev. 6:17 who shall be a. to stand

**Not be ABLE.**

2 K. 18:29 n. be a. to de. Is. 36:14
Ps. 36:12 shall not be a. to rise
Ec. 8:17 yet not be a. to find it
Is. 47:11 shall not be a. to put
Jer. 11:11 to escape; 49:10 to hide
Ezek. 7:19 gold shall not be a. to
Luke 13:24 seek, n. be a.; 21:15 to

**Not ABLE.**

Num. 13:31 we be not a. to go up
14:16 Lord was n. a. Deut. 9:28
Ezr. 10:13 we are not a. to stand
Neh. 4:10 we are not a. to build
Ps. 18:38 wounded not a. to rise
21:11 are not a. to perform
40:12 I am not a. to look up
Amos 7:10 land is not a. to bear
Luke 12:26 not a. to do that is l.
14:29 laid found. and not a. to
John 21:6 not a. to draw for the f.
Acts 6:10 not a. to resist the w.

**ABNER.**

1 Sam. 14:51 Ner father of A.
17:55 said to A. whose son?
26:7 but A. and the people lay
14 cried answer thou not A.
2 Sam. 2:14 A. said, let your men
3:25 A. the s. of Ner. 30,32,33,37
4:1 Saul's son heard A. was d.
12 Ish-bosheth in A. sepul.
1 K. 2:5 what Joab did to A.
1 Chr. 26:28 all that A. dedicated
27:21 Jaasiel son of A. rul. of B.

**ABOARD.**

Acts 21:2 went a. and set forth

**ABODE, Substantive.**

2 K. 19:27 I know thy a. Is. 37:28
John 14:23 come and make our a.

**ABODE, Verb.**

Gen. 29:14 Jacob a. with him
49:24 but his bow a. in strength
Ex. 24:16 glory of God a. on Si.
Num. 9:17 cloud a. 18
20 they a. in their tents, 22
11:35 the people a. at Hazeroth
Num. 20:1 the p. a. Jud. 11:17
22:8 princes of Moab, a. with B.
Deut. 1:46 so ye a. in Kadesh
3:29 we a. in the valley
9:9 I a. in the mount
Jos. 5:8 they a. in their places
8:9 they a. between Bethel
Jud. 5:17 Gilead a. beyond Jor.
Asher a. in his breaches
19:4 Levite a. with him 3 days
20:47 and a. in the rock Rim.
1 Sam. 1:23 the woman a. and g.
7:2 while the ark a. in Kirjath
13:16 Saul and Jona. a. in Gib.
22:6 Saul a.; 23:14, Dav. a. 25; 26:3
23:18 a. in wood; 2 Sam. 1:1 Zik.
2 Sam. 14:12 Uriah a. in Jerusa.
15:8 vowed while I a. at
1 K. 17:19 a loft where he a.

*Jer.* 38:28 Jeremiah *a.* in the ct.
*Mat.* 17:22 while they *a.* in Gal.
*Luke* 1:56 Mary *a.* with her a.
8:27 nor *a.* in any house, but
*John* 1:32 Spirit and it *a.* on him
39 they came and *a.* with him
7:9 he *a.* in Galilee
8:44 murderer and *a.* not in t.
11:6 he *a.* two days still
*Acts* 1:13 room where *a.* Peter
14:3 long time *a.* they speaking
18:3 Paul *a.* with them and w.
21:7 came and *a.* with brethren
8 house of Philip and *a.* with
*Gal.* 1:18 and *a.* with Peter

**ABODE there, *or* there ABODE.**

*Jud.* 21:2 people *a. there* till e.
*Ezr.* 8:15 *there a.* we in tents
*John* 4:40 Jesus *a. there* two d.
10:40 John bapt. and *there a.*
*Acts* 14:28 *there* they *a.* long t.
17:14 Silas and Tim. *a. there*

**ABODEST.**

*Jud.* 5:16 why *a.* among the sh.

**ABOLISH.**

*Is.* 2:18 idols he shall utterly *a.*

**ABOLISHED.**

*Is.* 51:6 right shall not be *a.*
*Ezek.* 6:6 your works may be *a.*
2 *Cor.* 3:13 that which is *a.*
*Eph.* 2:15 having *a.* in his flesh
2 *Tim.* 1:10 C. who hath *a.* death

**ABOMINABLE.**

*Lev.* 7:21 touch any *a.* thing
11:43 make yourselves *a.* with
18:30 commit not these *a.* cus.
19:7 on the third day, it is *a.*
20:25 make souls *a.* by beast
*Deut.* 14:3 eat any *a.* thing
1 *Chr.* 21:6 king's word was *a.* to
2 *Chr.* 15:8 Asa put away *a.* idols
*Job.* 15:16 much more *a.* is man
*Ps.* 14:1 have done *a.* works
53:1 have done *a.* iniquity
*Is.* 14:19 like an *a.* branch
65:4 broth of *a.* things is in
*Jer.* 16:18 carcasses of their *a.*
44:4 this *a.* thing I hate
*Ezek.* 4:14 came *a.* flesh into my
8:10 and behold *a.* beasts
16:52 sins committed more *a.*
*Mic.* 6:10 scant measure that is *a.*
*Nah.* 3:6 I will cast *a.* filth on
*Tit.* 1:16 deny him being *a.*
1 *Pet.* 4:3 walked in *a.* idolatries
*Rev.* 21:8 unbelieving and the *a.*

**ABOMINABLY.**

1 *K.* 21:26 Ahab did very *a.*

**ABOMINATION.**

*Gen.* 43:32 is an *a.* to Egyptians
46:34 shepherds is *a.* to Egyp.
*Ex.* 8:26 sacrifice the *a.* of Egyp.
*Lev.* 7:18 be an *a.* to you, 12.20.23
11:10 be an *a.* to you, 12, 20, 23
18:22 womankind it is *a.* 20:13
*Deut.* 7:25 it is *a.* to the Ld. 17:1
26 bring an *a.* into thy house
12:31 every *a.* they have done
13:14 such *a.* is wrought, 17:4
18:12 that do these are *a.* 22:5
23:18 these are an *a.* to God
24:4 is an *a.* before the Lord
25:16 that do unright. are *a.*
27:15 that maketh *a.* to Lord
1 *K.* 11:5 Milcom the *a.* of Am.
7 Chemosh the *a.* of Moab
2 *K.* 23:13 Ashtoreth *a* of Zid.
*Ps.* 88:8 thou hast made me an *a.*
*Prov.* 3:32 froward is an *a.*
6:16 seven things are an *a.*
8:17 wickedness is an *a.*
11:1 a false balance is *a.* to Lord
20 froward heart are *a.*
12:22 lying lips are *a.* to
13:19 *a.* to fools to depart
*Prov.* 15:8 sacrifi. of w. is *a.* 21:27
9 of the wicked is an *a.*
26 of wicked are *a.* to L.
16:5 one proud in heart is *a.*
12 *a.* to kings to commit
17:15 both are an *a.* to the Lord
20:10 both of them are alike *a.*
23 weights are an *a.* to Lord
24:9 the scorner is an *a.* to men
28:9 even his prayer shall be *a.*
29:27 unjust man is *a.* to just, upright in the way *a.* to
*Is.* 1:13 incense is an *a.* to me
41:24 an *a.* is he that
44:19 residue thereof an *a.*?
66:17 eating swine's flesh an *a.*
*Jer.* 2:7 my heritage an *a.*
6:15 they committed *a.* 8:12
32:35 that they should do this *a.*
*Ezek.* 16:50 and committed *a.*
18:12 to idols and committed *a.*
22:11 *a.* with neighbor's wife
33:26 and ye work *a.*
*Dan.* 11:31 *a.* that maketh
12:11 *a.* that maketh desolate
*Mal.* 2:11 an *a.* is committed
*Mat.* 24:15 *a.* of desol. *Mar.* 13:14
*Luke* 16:15 is *a.* with God
*Rev.* 21:27 enter that worketh *a.*

**ABOMINATIONS.**

*Deut.* 18:9 not learn to do after *a.*
32:16 with *a.* provoked they him
1 *K.* 14:24 did all *a.* of nations
2 *K.* 21:2 *a.* of heathen, 2 *Chr.* 33:2.
23:24 *a.* Jos. put away, 2 *Chr.* 34:2
2 *Chr.* 36:8 Jehoiakim and his *a.*
14 transgressed after all *a.*
*Prov.* 26:25 seven *a.* in his heart
*Jer.* 44:22 L. could not bear for *a.*
*Ezek.* 6:11 alas for all the evil *a.*
8:6 shalt see greater *a.* 13, 15
9 wicked *a.* that they do here
17 light thing to commit *a.*
9:4 that sigh and cry for the *a.*
11:18 take away all *a.* thereof
14:6 your faces from your *a.*
16:2 Jerusa. to know her *a.*
18:24 when righteous doth *a*
20:4 the *a.* of their fathers
7 cast ye away *a.* of eyes
22:2 show her all her *a.*
36:31 loathe yourselves for *a.*
44:6 O Israel, let it suffice of *a.*
*Dan.* 9:27 overspreading of *a.*
*Zec.* 9:7 *a.* from between
*Rev.* 17:4 golden cup full of *a.*
5 harlots and *a.* of earth

**Their ABOMINATIONS.**

*Deut.* 20:18 not after *t. a.*
*Ezr.* 9:11 *t. a.* which have
*Is.* 66:3 delighteth in *their a.*
*Jer.* 7:30 set *t. a.* in the, 32:34
*Ezek.* 11:21 walketh after *t. a.*
12:16 declare all *t. a.*
16:47 done after *t. a.*
23:36 declare to them *t. a.*
33:29 desolate because of *t. a.*
43:8 holy name by *t. a.*
44:13 bear their shame and *t. a.*
*Hos.* 9:10 *t. a.* were as they loved

**These ABOMINATIONS.**

*Lev.* 18:26 not com. any of *t. a.*
*Deut.* 18:12 bec. of *t. a.* L. doth
2 *K.* 21:11 hath done *t. a.*
*Ezr.* 9:14 with people of *t. a.*
*Jer.* 7:10 to do all *these a.*
*Ezek.* 18:13 done *t. a.* shall

**Thine ABOMINATIONS.**

*Jer.* 4:1 wilt put away *thine a.*
13:27 I have seen *t. a.* on hills
*Ezek.* 5:9 not because of *t. a.*
11 my sanctuary with *t. a.*
7:3 recompense all *t. a.* 4, 8, 9
16:36 the idols of *thine a.*
43 lewdness above all *t. a.*
51 multiplied *t. a.* more
58 hast borne *t. a.* saith

**ABOVE.**

*Deut.* 28:13 shalt be *a.* only
*Jos.* 3:13 that came from *a.* 16
2 *Sam.* 22:17 sent from *a.* *Ps.* 18:16
*John* 8:23 I am from *a.* ye of
19:11 were given from *a.*
*Col.* 3:1 seek things which are *a.*
2 set your affection on things *a.*

**ABOVE all.**

*John* 3:31 from heaven is *a. all*
*Eph.* 3:20 *a. all* that we ask
4:6 one God *a. all*
*Col.* 3:14 *a. all* these put on
2 *Thes.* 2:4 exalteth *a. all* called
*Jam.* 5:12 *a. all* things, swear not
1 *Pet.* 4:8 *a. all* things have ch.

ABOVE *all* GODS. *See* GODS.
ABOVE *heaven.* *See* HEAVEN.
*Stood* ABOVE. *See* STOOD.

**ABOUND.**

*Prov.* 28:20 faithful *a.* with
*Mat.* 24:12 iniquity shall *a.*
*Rom.* 5:20 the offence might *a.*
6:1 in sin, that grace may *a.*!
15:13 that ye may *a.* in hope
2 *Cor.* 1:5 as sufferings *a.* so
8:7 as ye *a.* in every thing, see
9:8 make all grace *a.* to you
*Phil.* 1:9 love may *a.* more
4:12 I know how to *a.* both to *a.*
17 may *a.* to your account
18 I have all and *a.* I am full
1 *Thes.* 3:12 make you to *a.* in love
4:1 would *a.* more and more
2 *Pet.* 1:8 things be in you and *a.*

**ABOUNDED, ETH, ING.**

*Prov.* 8:24 no fount. *a.* with
29:22 furious man *a.* in
*Rom.* 3:7 of God hath more *a.*
5:15 grace by J. C. hath *a.* to
20 sin *a.* grace did more *a.*
1 *Cor.* 15:58 always *a.* in the
2 *Cor.* 8:2 poverty *a.* to riches
*Eph.* 1:8 he hath *a.* toward
*Col.* 2:7 *a.* therein with thanksg.
2 *Thes.* 1:3 charity to ea. other *a.*

**ABOUT.**

*John* 7:19 go yet *a.* to kill me?
*See* GONE, ROUND, STOOD, TIME, WENT.

**ABRAHAM *with* father.**

*Gen.* 26:3 the oath to A. thy *f*
24 God of A. thy *f.* 28:13
32:9 G. of *f.* A. and God of
*Jos.* 24:3 took *f.* A. from
*Is.* 51:2 look to A. your *f.*
*Mat.* 3:9 A. to our *f.*, *Luke* 3:8
*Luke* 1:73 he sware to *f.* A.
16:24 *f.* A. have mercy on me
30 nay, *f.* A. but if one from
*John* 8:39 A. is our *f.*
53 greater than *f.* A.?
56 *f.* A. rejoiced to see
*Acts* 7:2 appeared to *f.* A.
*Rom.* 4:1 that A. our *f.* hath
12 in the steps of faith of *f.* A.
16 of A. who is *f.* of us all
*Jam.* 2:21 A. our *f.* justified by

**ABRAHAM *joined with* seed.**

2 *Chr.* 20:7 gavest it to *seed* of A.
*Ps.* 105:6 O ye *s.* of A. his
*Is.* 41:8 thou Israel, the *s.* of A.
*Jer.* 33:26 rulers over *s.* of A.
*Luke* 1:55 spake to A. and his *s.*
*John* 8:33 A.'s *s.* never in bond.
37 A. *s.* but ye seek to kill me
*Rom.* 4:13 promise not to A. or *s.*
9:7 they are the *seed* of A.
11:1 of the *s.* of A. 2 *Cor.* 11:22
*Gal.* 3:16 to A. and *s.* prom.

3:29 then A. *s.* and heirs
*Heb.* 2:16 on him the *s.* of A.

**ABROAD.**

*Ex.* 12:46 aught of flesh *a.*
*Lev.* 18:9 born at home or *a.*
*Jud.* 12:9 daughters from *a.*
2 *K.* 4:3 borrow thee vessels *a.*
2 *Chr.* 31:5 as com. came *a.*
*Job* 15:23 wandereth *a.* for bread
*Ps.* 41:6 he goeth *a.* telleth it
*Prov.* 5:16 be dispersed *a.*
*Is.* 44:24 spreadeth *a.* the earth
*Jer.* 6:11 on children *a.*
*Lam.* 1:20 *a.* the sword
*Mark* 1:45 blaze *a.* the matter
4:22 it should come *a.*
*Luke* 1:65 sayings were noised *a.*
2:17 *a.* the saying about
*Acts* 2:6 noised *a.* the multitude
*Rom.* 5:5 love of God shed *a* in
16:19 your obedience is come *a.*
*See* CAST, SPREAD, STAND, SCATTER, WENT.

**ABSENCE.**

*Luke* 22:6 betray him in *a.* of
*Phil.* 2:12 much more in my *a.*

**ABSENT.**

*Gen.* 31:49 we are *a.* one from
1 *Cor* 5:3 verily as *a.* in body
2 *Cor.* 5:6 at home in body are *a.*
8 willing to be *a.* from body
9 present or *a.* accepted
10:1 being *a.* am bold
11 by letters when *a.* such
13:2 being *a.* now I write, 10
*Phil.* 1:27 I come, or else *a.*
*Col.* 2:5 I be *a.* in the flesh

**ABSTAIN.**

*Acts* 15:20 *a.* from pollutions
29 that ye *a.* from meats
1 *Thes.* 4:3 *a.* from fornication
1 *Thes.* 5:22 *a.* from all appear.
1 *Tim.* 4:3 com. to *a.* from meats
1 *Pet.* 2:11 *a.* from fleshly lusts

**ABSTINENCE.**

*Acts* 27:21 after long *a.* Paul stood

**ABUNDANCE.**

*Deut.* 33:19 suck of the *a.* of the
1 *Sam.* 1:16 out of *a.* of my
1 *K.* 18:41 sound of *a.* of rain
2 *Chr.* 9:9 spices great *a.*
*Job* 22:11 *a.* waters cover, 38:34
*Ps.* 72:7 shall be *a.* of peace
*Ec.* 5:10 that loveth *a.* with
12 *a.* of the rich not suffer
*Is.* 15:7 the *a.* they have gotten
47:9 *a.* of thy enchantments
60:5 the *a.* of the sea
66:11 with the *a.* of her glory
*Jer.* 33:6 reveal *a.* of peace
*Ezek.* 16:49 *a.* of idleness was
*Zec.* 14:14 apparel in great *a.*
*Mat.* 12:34 *a.* of heart, *Luke* 6:45
13:12 have more *a.* 25:29
*Mark* 12:44 of their *a.* *Luke* 21:4
*Rom.* 5:17 receive *a.* of grace
2 *Cor.* 8:2 *a.* of their joy
14 your *a.* a supply, their *a.*
12:7 *a.* of the revelations
*Rev.* 18.3 thro' *a.* of delicacies

**In ABUNDANCE.**

*Ps.* 37:11 delight *in a.* of peace
52:7 *in* the *a.* of his riches
*Luke* 12:15 consisteth not *in a.*
2 *Cor.* 8:20 blame us *in* this *a.*

**ABUNDANT.**

*Ex.* 34:6 God *a.* in goodness
*Is.* 56:12 this day and more *a.*
1 *Cor.* 12:23 bestow more *a.* hon.
24 more *a.* honor to that part
2 *Cor.* 4:15 *a.* grace might
7:15 inward affection is more *a.*
9:12 the administration is *a.*
11:23 labors more *a.* in stripes
*Phil.* 1:26 rejoicing be more *a.*
1 *Tim.* 1:14 was exceeding *a.*
1 *Pet.* 1:3 his *a.* mercy

**ABUNDANTLY.**

*Gen.* 1:20 waters bring forth *a.* 21
8:17 that they may breed *a.*
9:7 multiply, bring forth *a.*
*Ex.* 1:7 Israel increased *a.*
*Num.* 20:11 water came out *a.*
1 *Chr.* 22:5 so David prepared *a.*
8 thou hast shed blood *a.*
*Job* 12:6 whose hand G. bring *a.*
36:28 distil upon man *a.*
*Ps.* 36:8 *a.* satisfied with fatness
65:10 thou waterest the ridges *a.*
132:15 I will *a.* bless her
145:7 shall *a.* utter the memory
*Cant.* 5:1 yea drink *a.* O beloved
*Is.* 15:3 shall howl, weeping *a.*
35:2 blossom *a.* and rejoice
55:7 for he will *a.* pardon
*John* 10:10 have life more *a.*
1 *Cor.* 15:10 I labored more *a.*
2 *Cor.* 1:12 and more *a.* to you
2:4 love I have more *a.* to you
10:15 according to our rule *a.*
12:15 though the more *a.* I love
*Eph.* 3:20 able to do exceeding *a.*
1 *Thes.* 2:17 more *a.* to see your
*Tit.* 3:6 he shed *a.* through
*Heb.* 6:17 God willing more *a.* to
2 *Pet.* 1:11 be ministered *a.*

**ABUSE, ED.**

*Jud.* 19:25 *a.* her all the night
1 *Sam.* 31:4 lest uncircum. *a.* me
1 *Chr.* 10:4
1 *Cor.* 9:18 I *a.* not my power

**ABUSERS, ING.**

1 *Cor.* 6:9 nor *a.* of themselves
71:31 use this world as not *a.* it

**ACCEPT.**

*Deut.* 33:11 and *a.* the work
1 *Sam.* 26:19 him *a.* an offering
2 *Sam.* 24:23 the L. thy God *a.*
*Job.* 13:8 will ye *a.* his person?
10 if ye do secretly *a.* persons
32:21 not *a.* any man's per.
42:8 shall pray, him will I *a.*
*Ps.* 20:3 and *a.* thy burnt-sac.
82:2 *a.* the persons of the wick.
119:108 *a.* freewill-offerings
*Prov.* 18:5 not good to *a.* the
*Jer.* 14:10 Lord doth not *a.* them
12 not *a.* them, *Amos* 5:22
*Ezek.* 20:40 there will I *a.* them
41 will *a.* you with sweet savor
43:27 and I will *a.* you, saith L.
*Mal.* 1:8 pleased, or *a.* thy
10 nor will I *a.* an offering
13 should I *a.* this of your h.?
*Acts* 24:3 we *a.* it always and

**ACCEPTABLE.**

*Deut.* 33:24 be *a.* to his brethren
*Ps.* 19:14 med. of my heart be *a.*
69:13 my prayer is in an *a.* time
*Prov.* 10:32 know what is *a.*
21:3 to do justice is more *a.*
*Ec.* 12:10 sought *a.* words
*Is.* 49:8 in an *a* time have I
58:5 call this an *a.* day
61:2 to proclaim the *a.* yr. of L.
*Jer.* 6:20 burnt-offerings are n. *a.*
*Dan.* 4:27 let my counsel be *a.*
*Luke* 4:19 to preach the *a.* year
*Rom.* 12:1 holy, *a.* to God
2 that good and *a.* will of God
14:18 is *a.* to God and approved
15:16 of Gentiles might be *a.*
*Eph.* 5:10 proving what is *a* unto
*Phil.* 4:18 sac. *a.* well-pleasing
1 *Tim.* 2:3 *a.* in the sight of God
5:4 good and *a.* before God
1 *Pet.* 2:5 sacrifices *a.* to God
20 this is *a.* with God

**ACCEPTABLY.**

*Heb.* 12:28 we may serve God *a.*

**ACCEPTANCE.**

*Is.* 60:7 with *a.* on mine altar

**ACCEPTATION.**

1 *Tim.* 1:15 worthy of all *a.* 4:9

**ACCEPTED.**

*Gen.* 4:7 shalt thou not be *a.*
19:21 I have *a.* thee concerning
*Ex.* 28:38 may be *a.* before
*Lev.* 1:4 offering shall be *a.* 22:27
7:18 not be *a.* 19:7; 22:23, 25
10:19 should it have been *a.* in
22:21 offering perfect, to be *a.*
1 *Sam.* 18:5 he was *a.* in the sight
25:35 see I have *a.* thy person
*Est.* 10:3 *a.* of his brethren
*Job* 42:9 the Lord also *a.* Job
*Is.* 56:7 their sacrifice shall be *a.*
*Jer.* 37:20 let supplication be *a.*
42:2 let our supplication be *a.*
*Luke* 4:24 no prophet is *a.* in his
*Acts* 10:35 righteousness is *a.*
*Rom.* 15:31 service may be *a.*
2 *Cor.* 5:9 or pres. we may be *a.*
6:2 in a time *a.* now is *a.* time
8:12 *a.* according to that a man
17 indeed he *a.* the exhortation
11:4 gospel which ye have not *a.*
*Eph.* 1:6 us *a.* in the Beloved

**ACCEPTEST.**

*Luke* 20:21 neither *a.* thou

**ACCEPTETH.**

*Job* 34:19 *a.* not persons of prin.
*Ec.* 9:7 for God now *a.* thy works
*Hos.* 8:13 Lord *a.* them not
*Gal.* 2:6 God *a.* no man's person

ACCEPTING. *See* DELIVERANCE

**ACCESS.**

*Rom.* 5:2 also we have *a.*
*Eph.* 2:18 have *a.* to the Father
3:12 boldness and *a.* by faith

ACCHO. *Jud.* 1:31
ACCOMPANY. *See* SALVATION.

**ACCOMPANIED.**

*Acts* 10:23 breth. from Joppa *a.*
11:12 these six brethren *a.* me
20:4 Sopater *a.* Paul into Asia
38 and they *a.* him to the ship

ACCOMPANYING. *See* ARK *of God.*

**ACCOMPLISH.**

*Job* 14:6 shall *a.* as hireling
*Ps.* 64:6 they *a.* a diligent
*Is.* 55:11 it shall *a.* that I please
*Jer.* 44:25 surely *a.* your vows
*Ezek.* 6:12 will I *a.* my fury
7:8 will I *a.* mine anger on thee
13:15 *a.* my wrath on the wall
20:8 fury to *a.* my anger, 21
*Dan.* 9:2 he would *a.* 70 years
*Luke* 9:31 should *a.* at Jerusalem

**ACCOMPLISHED.**

*Est.* 2:12 da. of puri. *a.* *Luke* 2:22
*Job* 15:32 shall be *a.* before
*Prov.* 13:19 desire *a.* is sweet
*Is.* 40:2 her warfare is *a.*
*Jer.* 25:12 70 years are *a.* 29:10
39:16 my words shall be *a.*
*Lam.* 4:11 Lord hath *a.* his fury
22 punish. of thine iniq. is *a.*
*Ezek.* 5:13 shall mine anger be *a.*
*Dan.* 11:36 indignation be *a.*
12:7 *a.* to scatter the power
*Luke* 1:23 his ministration *a.*
2:6 the days were *a.* that she
21 when eight days were *a.*
12:50 am I straitened till it be *a.*
18:31 concerning Son shall be *a.*
22:37 must yet be *a.* in me
*John* 19:28 things were now *a.*
*Acts* 21:5 had *a.* those days
1 *Pet.* 5:9 same afflictions are *a.*

ACCOMPLISHING. *See* SERVICE.

**ACCOMPLISHMENT.**
*Acts* 21:26 *a.* of days of purifica.

**ACCORD.**
*Lev.* 25:5 groweth of its own *a.*
*Acts* 1:14 with one *a.* in prayer
2:1 all with one *a.* in one place
46 daily with one *a.* in temple
4:24 voice to God with one *a.*
5:12 one *a.* in Solomon's porch
7:57 upon Stephen with one *a.*
8:6 with one *a.* gave heed
12:10 opened of his own *a.*
20 but they came with one *a.*
15:25 assembled with one *a.*
18:12 with one *a.* made insur.
19:29 one *a.* into the theatre
2 *Cor.* 8:17 forward of his own *a.*
*Phil.* 2:2 of one *a.* of one mind

**ACCORDING.**
*Ps.* 7:8 judge *a.* to my righteous.
17 praise *a.* to his righteous.
25:7 *a.* to thy mercy remember, 51:1; 106:45; 109:26; 119:124
28:4 give them *a.* to their deeds
33:22 *a.* as we hope in thee
35:24 judge *a.* to thy right.
48:10 *a.* to thy name, so
62:12 to every man *a.* to his work, *Prov.* 24:12, 29
79:11 *a.* to greatness of
90:11 *a.* to thy fear, so is
103:10 rewarded us *a.* to iniq.
119:25 *a.* to thy word, 28, 41, 58, 65, 76, 107, 116, 154, 169, 170
159 *a.* to thy kindness, *Is.* 63:7
150:2 praise him *a.* to his
*Is.* 8:20 speak not *a.* to this

ACCORDING *to all.* *See* ALL.

**ACCORDING to that.**
2 *Cor.* 8:12 *a. to that* a man hath

ACCORDINGLY. *See* REPAY.

**ACCOUNT, Substantive.**
*Job* 33:13 giveth not *a.* of his
*Ps.* 144:3 son of man that thou makest *a.* of him
*Ec.* 7:27 to find the *a.*
*Dan.* 6:2 princes might give *a.*
*Mat.* 12:36 give *a.* thereof
18:23 take *a.* of his servants
*Luke* 16:2 an *a.* of stewardship
*Acts* 19:40 give an *a.* of this
*Rom.* 14:12 give *a.* of himself
*Phil.* 4:17 abound to your *a.*
*Phile.* 18 put that on mine *a.*
*Heb.* 13:17 that must give *a.*
1 *Pet.* 4:5 *a.* to him that judgeth

**ACCOUNT, ED, ING.**
1 *K.* 1:21 shall be *a.* offenders
10:21 silver noth. *a.* 2 *Chr.* 9:20
*Ps.* 22:30 *a.* for a generation
*Is.* 2:22 is he to be *a.* of?
*Mark* 10:42 *a.* to rule over
*Luke* 20:35 be *a.* worthy
22:24 should be *a.* greatest
*Rom.* 8:36 we are *a.* as sheep
1 *Cor.* 4:1 man so *a.* of us as
*Gal.* 3:6 *a.* to him for right.
*Heb.* 11:19 *a.* that God was able
2 *Pet.* 3:15 *a.* that the long-suff.

**ACCURSED.**
*Deut.* 21:23 hanged is *a.* of G.
*Jos.* 6:17 shall be *a.* it and
18 keep from *a.* thing
7:1 trespass in the *a.* thing
11 taken of the *a.* thing
12 because they were *a.* destroy the *a.* from
13 there is an *a.* thing in
15 that is taken with *a.* thing
22:20 trespass in *a.* thing
1 *Chr.* 2:7 transgressed in thing *a.*
*Is.* 65:20 100 years old shall be *a.*
*Rom.* 9:3 could wish myself *a.*
1 *Cor.* 12:3 spirit calleth Jesus *a.*
*Gal.* 1:8 gospel, let him be *a.* 9

**ACCUSATION.**
*Ezr.* 4:6 an *a.* against Judah
*Mat.* 27:37 head his *a.* *Mark* 15:26
*Luke* 6:7 find an *a.* against
19:8 any thing by false *a.*
*John* 18:29 what *a.* bring ye
*Acts* 25:18 they brought no *a.*
1 *Tim.* 5:19 receive not an *a.*
2 *Pet.* 2:11 bring not a railing *a.*
*Jude* 9 durst not bring a railg. *a.*

**ACCUSE.**
*Prov.* 30:10 *a.* not a servant to
*Mat.* 12:10 might *a.* him; *Mar.* 3:2; *Luke* 11:54
*Luke* 3:14 nor *a.* any falsely
23:2 and they began to *a.* him
14 things whereof ye *a.* him
*John* 5:45 that I will *a.* you to F.
8:6 might have to *a.* him
*Acts* 24:2 Tertullus began to *a.*
8 all things whereof we *a.*
13 prove whereof they *a.* me
25:5 with me, and *a.* this man
11 if none, whereof these *a.* me
28:19 aught to *a.* my nation
1 *Pet.* 3:16 falsely *a.* your good

**ACCUSED.**
*Dan.* 3:8 Chaldeans *a.* the Jews
6:24 them which had *a.* Daniel
*Mat.* 27:12 *a.* answered nothing
*Mark* 15:3 priests *a.* *Luke* 23:10
*Luke* 16:1 *a.* that he had wasted
*Acts* 22:30 certainty wherefore *a.*
23:28 cause whereof they *a.* him
29 perceived to be *a.* of qu.
25:16 before he which is *a.* have
26:2 things whereof I am *a.*
7 for which hope's sake I am *a.*
*Tit.* 1:6 not *a.* of riot, or unruly
*Rev.* 12:10 who *a.* them before

ACCUSER. *See* CAST *down.*

**ACCUSERS.**
*John* 8:10 those thine *a.*
*Acts* 23:30 com. to his *a.* also
35 when thine *a.* are come
24:8 commanding his *a.* to come
25:16 he have the *a.* face to face
18 against whom, when *a.* stood
2 *Tim.* 3:3 affection, false *a.*
*Tit.* 2:3 not false *a.* not given to

**ACCUSETH, ING.**
*John* 5:45 there is one that *a.* you
*Rom.* 2:15 thoughts *a.* or exc.

ACCUSTOMED. *See Do* EVIL.

ACELDAMA. *See* FIELD.

**ACHAIA.**
*Acts* 18:12 Gallio was dep. of A.
27 Apollos to pass into A.
*Rom.* 15:26 them of A. to make
16:5 Epenetus, first-fruits of A.
1 *Cor.* 16:15 Steph., first-fr. of A.
2 *Cor.* 9:2 A. ready a year ago
11:10 in the regions of A
1 *Thes.* 1:7 ensamples to all in A.
8 sounded not only in A.

ACHAICUS. 1 *Cor.* 16:17

ACHAN, *or* ACHAR. *Jos.* 7. 22:20; 1 *Chr.* 2:7

ACHIM. *Mat.* 1:14

**ACHISH.**
1 *Sam.* 21:10 David fled to A. 27:2
12 David was sore afraid of A.
27:6 A. gave him Ziklag
29:2 in the rereward with A.
1 *Kings* 2:40 went to Gath to A.

ACHMETHA. *Ezr.* 6:2

**ACHOR.**
*Jos.* 7:26 valley of A. to this
*Is.* 65:10 valley of A. place for
*Hos.* 2:15 A. for a door of hope

ACHSAH. *Jos.* 15:16; *Jud.* 1:12

**ACHSHAPH.**
*Jos.* 11:1 sent to the king of A.
12:20 king of A. one, 19:25

ACHZIB. *Jos.* 19:29; *Mic.* 1:14

**ACKNOWLEDGE, ED.**
*Deut.* 21:17 *a.* son of hated
33:9 nor did he *a.* his brethren
*Ps.* 32:5 I *a.* my sin; 51:3 *a.* trans.
*Prov.* 3:6 in all thy ways *a.* him
*Is.* 33:13 are near, *a.* my might
61:9 all that see shall *a.* them
63:16 Father, tho' Israel *a.* us
*Jer.* 3:13 only *a.* thine iniquity
14:20 we *a.* our wickedness
*Dan.* 11:39 god, he shall *a.*
*Hos.* 5:15 they *a.* their offence
1 *Cor.* 14:37 let him *a.* the things
16:18 therefore *a.* ye them that
2 *Cor.* 1:13 *a.* and I trust shall *a.*
14 you have *a.* us in part

**ACKNOWLEDGING, ETH.**
2 *Tim.* 2:25 repentance to the *a.*
*Tit.* 1:1 to the *a.* the truth which
*Philem.* 6 by the *a.* every good
1 *John* 2:23 he that *a.* the Son

**ACKNOWLEDGMENT.**
*Col.* 2:2 to the *a.* of the mystery

**ACQUAINT, ED, ING.**
*Job* 22:21 *a.* thyself with him
*Ps.* 139:3 *a.* with all my ways
*Ec.* 2:3 *a.* my heart with
*Is.* 53:3 sorrows, and *a.* with

**ACQUAINTANCE.**
2 *K.* 12:5 every man of his *a.*
7 no more money of your *a.*
*Job* 19:13 mine *a.* are estranged
42:11 all that had been of his *a.*
*Ps.* 31:11 a reproach to mine *a.*
55:13 mine equal, and mine *a.*
88:8 hast put away mine *a.* far
18 and my *a.* into darkness
*Luke* 2:44 sought among their *a.*
23:49 all his *a.* stood afar off
*Acts* 24:23 forbid none of his *a.* to

**ACQUIT.**
*Job* 10:14 not *a.* me from mine
*Nah.* 1:3 L. not at all *a.* wicked

**ACRE, S.**
1 *Sam.* 14:14 half an *a.* of land
*Is.* 5:10 ten *a.* of vineyard

**ACT.**
*Is.* 28:21 his *a.* his strange *a.*
59:6 and the *a.* of violence
*John* 8:4 adultery, in the very *a.*

**ACTS.**
*Deut.* 11:7 seen the great *a.* of
*Jud.* 5:11 the righteous *a.*
1 *Sam.* 12:7 all righteous *a.*
2 *Sam.* 23:20 Benaiah who had done many *a.* 1 *Chr.* 11:22
1 *K.* 10:6 true report of thy *a.*
11:41 the *a.* of Solomon, 2 *Chr.* 9:5
2 *K.* 10:34 the *a.* of Jehu
23:28 the *a.* of Josiah
1 *Chr.* 29:29 the *a.* of David
2 *Chr.* 16:11 the *a.* of Asa
20:34 the *a.* of Jehoshaphat
32:32 *a.* of Hezekiah, 2 *K.* 20:20
*Est.* 10:2 all the *a.* of his power
*Ps.* 103:7 his *a.* to the children
106:2 can utter the mighty *a.*
145:4 declare thy mighty *a.* 6:12
150:2 praise him for mighty *a.*

**ACTIONS.**
1 *Sam.* 2:3 by L. *a.* are weighed

**ACTIVITY.**
*Gen.* 47:6 knowest any man of *a.*

**ADAM.**
*Gen.* 2:20 A. gave names to all
5:2 and called their name A.
*Deut.* 32:8 separated sons of A.
*Job* 31:33 transgressions as A.
*Rom.* 5:14 death reigned from A.

1 *Cor.* 15:22 for as in A. all die
45 first man A. the last A.
1 *Tim.* 2:13 A. was first formed
14 and A. was not deceived
*Jude* 14 Enoch the 7th from A.

ADAM. *Jos.* 3:16 the city A.

**ADAMANT.**
*Ezek.* 3:9 as an *a.* have I made
*Zec.* 7:12 heart as an *a.* stone

**ADAR.**
*Ezr.* 6:15 finished on 3d day of A.
*Est.* 3:7 twelfth month A.
13 day of month A. 8:12; 9:1,17
9:15 gathered on 14th day of A.

**ADD.**
*Gen.* 30:24 L. shall *a.* to me
*Deut.* 4:2 not *a.* to, 12:32
29:19 to *a.* drunkenness
2 *K.* 20:6 I *a.* 15 years, *Is.* 38:5
1 *Chr.* 22:14 mayest *a.* thereto
2 *Chr.* 28:13 to *a.* more to sins
*Ps.* 69:27 *a.* iniquity to iniquity
*Prov.* 3:2 long life shall they *a.*
30:6 *a.* thou not to his words
*Is.* 29:1 *a.* ye year to year
30:1 may *a.* sin to sin
*Mat.* 6:27 can *a.* one cub., *Lu.* 12:25
*Phil.* 1:16 supposing to *a.* afflict.
2 *Pet.* 1:5 *a.* to your faith virtue
*Rev.* 22:18 G. shall *a.* to him

**ADDED.**
*Deut.* 5:22 and he *a.* no more
1 *Sam.* 12:19 *a.* to all our sins
*Jer.* 36:32 there were *a.* besides
45:3 Lord hath *a.* grief
*Dan.* 4:36 majesty was *a.* to me
*Mat.* 6:33 shall be *a.* to you
*Luke* 3:20 Herod *a.* yet this
19:11 he *a.* and spake a parable
*Acts* 2:41 were *a.* 3,000 souls
47 *a.* to the church daily such
5:14 believers were the more *a.*
11:24 people was *a.* to the L.
*Gal.* 2:6 *a.* nothing to me.
3:19 the law was *a.* because of

**ADDER.**
*Gen.* 49:17 Dan shall be an *a.*
*Ps.* 58:4 the deaf *a.* that stops
91:13 thou shalt tread on the *a.*
140:3 *a.*'s poison is under
*Prov.* 23:32 stingeth like an *a.*

**ADDETH.**
*Job* 34:37 he *a.* rebellion
*Prov.* 10:22 he *a.* no sorrow
16:23 wise *a.* learning
*Gal.* 3:15 disannulleth or *a.*

**ADDICTED.**
1 *Cor.* 16:15 *a.* themselves

**ADJURE, ED.**
*Jos.* 6:26 Joshua *a.* them
1 *Sam.* 14:24 Saul had *a.*
1 *K.* 22:16 how many times shall
I *a.* thee, 2 *Chr.* 18:15
*Mat.* 26:63 I *a.* thee by the living
*Mark* 5:7 I *a.* thee by God
*Acts* 19:13 we *a.* you by Jesus

**ADMAH.**
*Gen.* 14:2 Shinab king of A.
*Deut.* 29:23 the overthrow of A.
*Hos.* 11:8 make thee as A.

**ADMINISTERED.**
2 *Cor.* 8:19 *a.* by us to the glory
20 this abundance which is *a.*

**ADMINISTRATION, S.**
1 *Cor.* 12:5 differences of *a.*
2 *Cor.* 9:12 *a.* of this service

**ADMIRATION.**
*Jude* 16 men's persons in *a.*
*Rev.* 17:6 wondered with great *a.*

**ADMIRED.**
2 *Thes.* 1:10 to be *a.* in all

**ADMONISH, ED.**
*Ec.* 4:13 will no more be *a.*
12:12 by these, my son, be *a.*
*Jer.* 42:19 certainly I have *a.*
*Acts* 27:9 Paul *a.* them
*Rom.* 15:14 to *a.* one another
*Col.* 3:16 *a.* one another
1 *Thes.* 5:12 over you and *a.* you
2 *Thes.* 3:15 *a.* him as a brother
*Heb.* 8:5 as Moses was *a.* of God

**ADMONITION.**
1 *Cor.* 10:11 are written for our *a.*
*Eph.* 6:4 bring them up in the *a.*
*Tit.* 3:10 after first and second *a.*

**ADO.**
*Mark* 5:39 why make ye this *a.*

ADONI-BEZEK. *Jud.* 1:5

**ADONIJAH.**
2 *Sam.* 3:4 A. son of Haggith
1 *K.* 1:5 A. exalted himself
25 God save king A.
2:21 let Abishag be given to A.
2 *Chron.* 17:8 sent Lev. to teach A.
*Neh.* 10:16 the people sealed, A.

ADONIKAM. *Ezr.* 2:13; *Neh.* 7:18

**ADOPTION.**
*Rom.* 8:15 received the spirit of *a.*
23 waiting for the *a.*
9:4 to whom pertaineth the *a.*
*Gal.* 4:5 receive the *a.* of sons
*Eph.* 1:5 predestinated us to *a.*

**ADORN, ED, ETH, ING.**
*Is.* 61:10 as a bride *a.* herself
*Jer.* 31:4 again *a.* with tabrets
*Luke* 21:5 temple *a.* with goodly
1 *Tim.* 2:9 women *a.* in modest
*Tit.* 2:10 *a.* the doctrine of God
1 *Pet.* 3:3 whose *a.* not outward *a.*
5 women *a.* themselves
*Rev.* 21:2 prepared as a bride *a.*

**ADRAMMELECH.**
2 *K.* 17:31 burnt children to A.
19:37 A. and Sharezer, *Is.* 37:38

ADRAMYTTIUM. *Acts* 27:2
ADRIA. *Acts* 27:27

**ADULLAM.**
1 *Sam.* 22:1 cave A. 1 *Chr.* 11:15
2 *Sam.* 23:13 came to David to A.
*Mic.* 1:15 he shall come to A.

**ADULTERER, S.**
*Lev.* 20:10 *a.* put to death
*Job* 24:15 the eye of *a.* waiteth
*Ps.* 50:18 partaker with *a.*
*Is.* 57:3 seed of *a.* and the whore
*Jer.* 9:2 for they be all *a.*
23:10 the land is full of *a.*
*Hos.* 7:4 all *a.* as an oven
*Mal.* 3:5 witness against the *a.*
*Luke* 18:11 I am not as others, *a.*
1 *Cor.* 6:9 neither *a.* shall inherit
*Heb.* 13:4 *a.* God will judge
*Jam.* 4:4 ye *a.* know ye not that

**ADULTERESS, ES.**
*Lev.* 20:10 the *a.* put to death
*Prov.* 6:26 the *a.* will hunt
*Ezek.* 23:45 judge them as *a.*
*Hos.* 3:1 a woman yet an *a.*
*Rom.* 7:3 no *a.* though married

**ADULTEROUS.**
*Prov.* 30:20 the way of *a.* wom.
*Mat.* 12:39 an *a.* generation, 16:4
*Mark* 8:38 ashamed in this *a.*

**ADULTERY, IES.**
*Ex.* 20:14 thou shalt not com. *a.*
*Deut.* 5:18; *Mat.* 5:27; 19:18;
*Rom.* 13:9
*Prov.* 6:32 commits *a.* lacketh
*Jer.* 3:8 backsliding Israel com. *a.*
9 committed *a.* with stones
5:7 then they committed *a.*
7:9 will ye steal and commit *a.*
13:27 I have seen thine *a.*
23:14 they commit *a.* and walk
29:23 they committed *a.*
*Ezek.* 16:32 a wife that com. *a.*
23:37 with their idols com. *a.*
43 said I to her old in *a.*
*Hos.* 2:2 *a.* between her breasts
4:2 committing *a.* they break
13 spouses shall commit *a.*
*Hos.* 4:14 punish when com. *a.*
*Mat.* 5:28 *a.* in his heart
32 marry her divorced committeth *a.* 19:9; *Luke* 16:18
15:19 heart proceed *a.* *Mark* 7:21
*Mark* 10:11 his wife and marry another com. *a.* *Luke* 16:18
19 not com. *a.* *Lu.* 18:20; *Jas.* 2:11
*John* 8:3 woman taken in *a.* 4
*Rom.* 2:22 should not commit *a.*
*Gal.* 5:19 flesh manifest *a.*
2 *Pet.* 2:14 having eyes full of *a.*
*Rev.* 2:22 cast them that com. *a.*

**ADVANTAGE, ED, ETH.**
*Job* 35:3 what *a.* will it be
*Luke* 9:25 a man *a.* if he gain
*Rom.* 3:1 what *a.* then hath Jew
1 *Cor.* 15:32 what *a.* if the dead
2 *Cor.* 2:11 Satan get an *a.* of us
*Jude* 16 admiration because of *a.*

**ADVENTURE, ED.**
*Deut.* 28:56 not *a.* to set the sole
*Jud.* 9:17 father *a.* his life far
*Acts* 19:31 not *a.* into the theatre

**ADVERSARY.**
*Ex.* 23:22 be an *a.* to thine
*Num.* 22:22 angel *a.* against Bal.
1 *Sam.* 1:6 her *a.* provoked her
29:4 lest in battle he be an *a.*
1 *K.* 5:4 there is neither *a.* nor
11:14 an *a.* to Solomon, 23
25 was an *a.* to Israel
*Est.* 7:6 *a.* is wicked Haman
*Job* 31:35 *a.* had written a book
*Ps.* 74:10 shall *a.* reproach
*Is.* 50:8 who is mine *a.* let him
*Lam.* 1:10 the *a.* hath spread out
2:4 with his right hand as an *a.*
4:12 *a.* have entered the gates
*Amos* 3:11 *a.* be round about
*Mat.* 5:25 *a.* quickly lest *a.* deliv.
*Luke* 12:58 goest with thine *a.*
18:3 avenge me of mine *a.*
1 *Tim.* 5:14 give no occas. to *a.*
1 *Pet.* 5:8 your *a.* the devil

**ADVERSARIES.**
*Deut.* 32:27 *a.* behave strangely
43 render vengeance to his *a.*
*Jos.* 5:13 for us, or for our *a.*?
1 *Sam.* 2:10 *a.* of L. shall be
*Ezr.* 4:1 *a.* of Judah heard
*Neh.* 4:11 *a.* said, they shall not
*Ps.* 38:20 evil for good are my *a.*
69:19 mine *a.* are all before thee
71:13 that are *a.* to my soul
81:14 my hand against their *a.*
89:42 the right hand of his *a.*
109:4 for my love they are *a.*
20 be the reward of my *a.*
29 *a.* be clothed with shame
*Is.* 1:24 I will ease me of my *a.*
9:11 shall set up the *a.* of Rezin
11:13 *a.* of Judah shall be cut off
59:18 he will repay fury to his *a.*
63:18 our *a.* have trodden down
64:2 name known to thine *a.*
*Jer.* 30:16 *a.* shall go into cap.
46:10 may avenge him of his *a.*
50:7 their *a.* said, we offend not
*Lam.* 1:5 her *a.* are the chief
7 *a.* saw her, and did mock
17 his *a.* should be round abt.
2:17 set up the horn of thine *a.*
*Mic.* 5:9 hand lifted up on *a.*
*Nah.* 1:2 vengeance on his *a.*
*Luke* 13:17 *a.* were ashamed

21:15 your *a.* not able to gainsay
1 *Cor.* 16:9 and there are many *a.*
*Phil.* 1:28 nothing terrified by *a.*
*Heb.* 10:27 shall devour the *a.*

**ADVERSITY, IES.**
1 *Sam.* 10:19 saved you of all *a.*
2 *Sam.* 4:9 my soul out of all *a.*
2 *Chr.* 15:6 vex them with all *a.*
*Ps.* 10:6 I shall never be in *a.*
31:7 known my soul in *a.*
35:15 in my *a.* they rejoiced
94:13 rest from the days of *a.*
*Prov.* 17:17 brother born for *a.*
24:10 if thou faint in day of *a*
*Ec.* 7:14 day of *a.* consider
*Is.* 30:20 tho' L. give bread of *a.*
*Heb.* 13:3 remem. them suffer *a.*

**ADVERTISE.**
*Num.* 24:14 I will *a.* thee
*Ruth* 4:4 I thought to *a.* thee

**ADVICE.**
*Jud.* 20:7 your *a.* and counsel
1 *Sam.* 25:33 blessed be thy *a.*
2 *Sam.* 19:43 our *a.* not be first
2 *Chr.* 10:14 after *a.* of young
*Prov.* 20:18 good *a.* make war
2 *Cor.* 8:10 herein I give my *a.*

**ADVISE, ED.**
2*Sam.*24:13*a.* and see,1 *Chr.*21:12
1 *K.* 12:6 how do ye *a.* that I
*Prov.* 13:10 well *a.* is wisdom
*Acts* 27:12 more part *a.* to depart

ADVISEMENT. 1 *Chr.* 12:19

**ADVOCATE.**
1 *John* 2:1 have an *a.* with the

**AFAR, AFAR OFF.**
*Gen.* 37:18 saw Joseph *a. off.*
*Ex.* 24:1 worship ye *a. off.*
*Ezr.* 3:13 noise was heard *a. off.*
*Neh.* 12:43 Jeru. heard *a. off*
*Job* 36:3 my knowledge from *a.*
25 man may behold it *a. off*
39:29 her eyes behold *a. off*
*Ps.* 65:5 are *a. off* on the sea
138:6 proud he knoweth *a. off*
139:2 my thoughts *a. off*
*Prov.* 31:14 bringeth food from *a.*
*Is.* 23:7 shall carry her *a. off*
66:19 escape to the isles *a. off*
*Jer.* 23:23 am I not a God *a. off*
30:10 save thee from *a.* 46:27
31:10 declare in isles *a. off*
51:50 remember the Lord *a. off*
*Mic.* 4:3 strong nations *a. off*
*Mat.* 26:58 Peter followed *a. off*
*Mark* 14:54 ; *Luke* 22:54
27:55 wom.behold*a.off*,*Ma.*15:40
*Mark* 5:6 he saw Jesus *a. off*
*Luke* 16:23 seeth Abraham *a. off*
*Acts* 2:39 promise is to all *a. off*
*Eph.* 2:17 peace to you *a. off*
*Heb.* 11:13 seen promises *a. off*
2 *Pet.* 1:9 and cannot see *a. off*
*See* FAR, STAND, STOOD.

**AFFAIRS.**
*Ps.* 112:5 guide *a.* with discr.
*Eph.* 6:21 ye may know my *a.*
22 that ye might know our *a.*
*Phil.* 1:27 I may hear of your *a.*
2 *Tim.* 2:4 entangleth with *a.*

**AFFECT, ED, ETH.**
*Lam.* 3:51 eye *a.* my heart
*Acts* 14:2 their minds evil *a.*
*Gal.* 4:17 zealously *a.* you
18 good to be zealously *a.*

**AFFECTION.**
1 *Chr.* 29:3 *a.* to house of God
*Rom.* 1:31 without natural *a.* 2 *Tim.* 3:3
2 *Cor.* 7:15 his inward *a.* is more
*Col.* 3:2 your *a.* on things above
5 mortify inordinate *a.*

**AFFECTIONS.**
*Rom.* 1:26 G. gave up to vile *a.*
*Gal.* 5:24 crucified flesh with *a.*

**AFFECTIONATELY.**
1 *Thes.* 2:8 *a.* desirous of you

**AFFECTIONED.**
*Rom.* 12:10 kindly *a.* one to

**AFFINITY.**
*Ezr.* 9:14 join in *a.* with

**AFFIRM.**
*Rom.* 3:8 and as some *a.* we say
1 *Tim.* 1:7 nor whereof they *a.*
*Tit.* 3:8 things *a.* constantly

**AFFIRMED.**
*Luke* 22:59 hour after another *a.*
*Acts* 12:15 Rhoda constantly *a.*
25:19 whom Paul *a.* alive

**AFFLICT.**
*Gen.* 15:13 shall *a.* them 400 yrs.
31:50 if thou *a.* my daughters
*Ex.* 1:11 taskmasters to *a.*
22:22 shall not *a.* any widow
*Lev.* 16:29 shall *a.* your souls, 31 ; 23:27, 32 ; *Num.* 29:7
*Num.* 24:24 ships shall *a.* Ashur
*Jud.* 16:19 *a* him, his strength
2*Sam.* 7:10 ch'n of wickedness *a.*
1 *K.* 11:39 *a.* seed of David
2 *Chr.* 6:26 turn when thou dost *a.* 1 *K.* 8:35.
*Ezr.* 8:21 *a.* ours. before God
*Job* 37:23 Almighty, he not *a.*
*Ps.* 44:2 thou didst *a.* the peo.
55:19 God shall hear and *a.*
89:22 son of wickedness *a.*
94:5 they *a.* thy heritage
143:12 all that *a.* my soul
*Is.* 9:1 grievously *a.* her
51:23 them that *a.* thee
58:5 for a man to *a.* his soul
64:12 wilt thou *a.* us very sore?
*Jer.* 31:28 as I watched to *a.*
*Lam.* 3:33 Lord not *a.* willingly
*Amos* 5:12 they *a.* the just, they
*Nah.* 1:12 I will *a.* thee no more
*Zep.* 3:19 I will undo all that *a.*

**AFFLICTED.**
*Ex.* 1:12 more *a.* more grew
2 *Sam.* 22:28 *a.* people wilt save
1 *K.* 2:26 *a.* in all father was *a.*
*Job* 6 14 to *a.* pity should be
30:11 loosed cord, and *a.* me
34:28 heareth cry of the *a.*
*Ps.* 18:27 save the *a.* people
22:24 abhorred affliction of *a.*
25:16 I am desolate and *a.*
82:3 do justice to the *a.*
88:7 hast *a.* me with waves
15 I am *a.* and ready to die
90:15 wherein thou hast *a.* us
107:17 fools because of iniq. *a.*
116:10 I was greatly *a.*
119:67 before I was *a.*
71 good that I have been *a.*
75 in faithfulness hast *a.* me
107 am *a.* very much, quicken
128:1 have *a.* me from youth, 2
140:12 L. maintain cause of *a.*
*Prov.* 15:15 days of the *a.* are evil
22:22 neither oppress *a.* in gate
26:28 lying tongue hateth *a.*
31:5 lest pervert judgment of *a.*
*Is.* 9:1 lightly *a.* the land
49:13 L. have mercy on his *a.*
51:21 hear now this, thou *a.*
53:4 smitten of God and *a.*
7 and was *a.* yet he opened not
54:11 O thou *a.* tossed with
58:3 have we *a.* our souls
10 if thou satisfy the *a.* soul
60:14 sons of them that *a.* thee
63:9 their affliction he was *a.*
*Lam.* 1:12 sorrow wherew. L. *a.*
*Mic.* 4:6 gather her that I have *a.*
*Nah.* 1:12 *a.* afflict no more
*Zep.* 3:12 leave an *a.* people
*Mat.* 24:9 deliver you up to be *a.*
2 *Cor.* 1:6 whether we be *a.* it is
1 *Tim.* 5:10 if she relieved the *a.*
*Heb.* 11:37 being destitute, *a.*
*Jam.* 4:9 *a.* and mourn and weep
5:13 is any among you *a.*? let

**AFFLICTION.**
*Gen.* 41:52 fruitful in land of *a.*
*Ex.* 3:17 *a.* of my p. *Acts* 7:34
3:17 out of the *a.* of Egypt
*Deut.* 16:3 shalt eat bread of *a.* 1 *K.* 22:27 ; 2 *Chr.* 18:26
26:7 L. heard and looked on *a.*
2 *Sam.* 16:12 L. look on my *a.*
2 *K.* 14:26 Lord saw *a.* of Israel
2 *Chr.* 20:9 cry in *a.* wilt hear
33:12 Manasseh was in *a.*
*Neh.* 1:3 remnant are in great *a.*
*Job* 5:6 *a.* cometh not forth
10:15 confusion see mine *a.*
30:16 days of *a.* have taken hold
27 the days of *a.* prevented me
36:8 holden in cords of *a.*
15 delivereth poor in his *a.*
21 chosen rather than *a.*
*Ps.* 25:18 my *a.* and pain
44:24 and forgettest our *a.*
66:11 laidst *a.* upon our loins
88:9 mourneth by reason of *a.*
106:44 regarded their *a.* when
107:10 bound in *a.* and iron
39 low through *a.* and sorrow
41 setteth poor on high from *a.*
119:50 comfort in my *a.*
92 perished in mine *a.*
153 mine *a.* deliver me
*Is.* 30:20 L. give water of *a.*
48:10 chosen in furnace of *a.*
63:9 their *a.* he was afflicted
*Jer.* 16:19 refuge in days of *a.*
30:15 criest thou for thine *a.*
*Lam.* 1:7 Jerusa. remem'd in *a.*
3:1 that hath seen *a.* by the rod
19 remembering my *a.* and
*Hos.* 5:15 in *a.* seek me early
*Amos* 6:6 grieved for *a.* of Jos.
*Nah.* 1:9 *a.* not rise second time
*Zec.* 1:15 helped forward the *a.*
10:11 pass thro' sea with *a.*
*Mark* 4:17 *a.* ariseth
13:19 shall be *a.* such
*Acts* 7:11 a dearth and great *a.*
2 *Cor.* 2:4 out of much *a.* I wrote
4:17 light *a.* which is but for
8:2 in a great trial of *a.*
*Phil.* 1:16 to add *a.* to my
4:14 communicate with in *a.*
1 *Thes.* 1:6 word in much *a.*
3:7 comforted in all our *a.*
*Heb.* 11:25 rather to suffer *a.*
*Jam.* 1:27 to visit fatherless in *a.*
5:10 an example of suffering *a.*

**AFFLICTIONS.**
*Ps.* 34:19 the *a.* of righteous
132:1 rememb. David and his *a.*
*Acts* 7:10 deliver out of all his *a.*
20:23 bonds and *a.* abide me
2 *Cor.* 6:4 approving in *a.*
*Col.* 1:24 behind of *a.* of Christ
1 *Thes.* 3:3 be moved by these *a.*
2 *Tim.* 1:8 of the *a.* of the gospel
3:11 *a.* which came at Antioch
4:5 watch in all, endure *a.*
*Heb.* 10:32 great fight of *a.*
33 made a gazing-stock by *a.*
1 *Pet.* 5:9 *a.* accomplished in

**AFFRIGHT, ED.**
*Job* 18:20 that went before *a.*
39:22 mocketh at fear and not *a.*
*Is.* 21:4 fearfulness *a.* me
*Mark* 16:5 were *a.* *Luke* 24:37
6 be not *a.* ye seek Jesus
*Rev.* 11:13 remnant *a.* gave glo.

**AFOOT.**
*Mark* 6:33 many ran *a.* thither
*Acts* 29:13 Paul minding to go *a.*

**AFORETIME.**
*Jer.* 30:20 their children as *a*
*Dan.* 6:10 he prayed as he did *a.*
*Rom.* 15:4 things were written *a.*

**AFRAID.**
*Ex.* 34:30 were *a.* to come nigh
*Lev.* 26:6 none make *a. Job* 11:19
*Num.* 12:8 why not *a.* to speak
1 *Sam.* 4:7 Philistines were *a.*
18:29 yet more *a.* of David
2 *Sam.* 1:14 not *a.* to destroy
22:5 ungodly men made me *a.* *Ps.* 18:4
*Neh.* 6:9 all made us *a.*
*Job* 9:28 *a.* of all my sorrows
11:19 none make thee *a.*
13:11 excellency make you *a.*
21 not thy dread make me *a.*
15:24 anguish make him *a.*
18:11 terrors make him *a.*
21:6 when I remember, I am *a.*
23:15 consider, I am *a* of him
33:7 terror not make thee *a.*
41:25 raiseth hims. mighty *a.*
*Ps.* 56:3 what time I am *a.*
65:8 dwell are *a.* at thy tokens
77:16 saw thee and were *a.*
83:15 *a.* with thy storm
119:120 *a.* of thy judgments
*Is.* 17:2 none make them *a. Ezek.* 34:28; *Mic.* 4:4; *Zep.* 3:13.
33:14 sinners in Zion are *a.*
41:5 ends of the earth were *a.*
*Jer.* 30:10 none make him *a.*
*Ezek.* 39:26 none made them *a.* *Nah.* 2:11.
*Dan.* 4:5 dream made me *a.*
*Jon.* 1:5 mariners were *a.* 10
*Mark* 5:15 in right mind were *a.* *Luke* 8:35
9:32 and were *a.* to ask him
10:32 as they followed were *a.*
16:8 said any thing, were *a.*
*Luke* 8:25 being *a.* wondered
*Acts* 9:26 were all *a.* of Saul
22:9 saw the light and were *a.*
*Gal.* 4:11 I am *a.* of you lest
1 *Pet.* 3:6 not *a.* with amazem.
2 *Pet.* 2:10 *a.* to speak evil of dig.

**Be AFRAID.**
*Deut.* 1:29 nei. *be a.* of them, 31:6
2 *Sam.* 22:46 *be a.* out of close *Ps.* 18:45
*Job* 5:21 nor *be a.* of destruction
19:29 *be* ye *a.* of the sword, for
*Ps.* 27:1 of whom shall I *be a.?*
*Is.* 8:12 nor fear nor *be a.* 44:8
19:17 shall *be a.* in himself
51:12 shouldest *be a.* of a man
*Rom.* 13:4 if thou do evil, *be a.*

**Not be AFRAID.**
*Deut.* 1:17 *not be a.* of face
7:18 shall *not be a.* of, 18:22
*Ps.* 3:6 *not be a.* of ten thous.
56:11 *not be a.* what man can do
91:5 *not be a.* for terror by night
*Ps.* 112:7 *not be a.* of evil tidings
8 estab'd, he shall *not be a.*
*Prov.* 3:24 liest down *not be a.*
*Is.* 12:2 trust and *not be a.*
31:4 *not be a.* of their voice
*Amos* 3:6 blown, people *not be a.*
*Rom.* 13:3 *not be a.* of the power

**Be not AFRAID.**
*Deut.* 20:1 *be not a.* of them, *Jos.* 11:6; *Neh.* 4:14; *Jer.* 10:5; *Ezek.* 2:6; *Luke* 12:4
1 *Sam.* 28:13 *be not a.* what saw.
*Ps.* 49:16 *be not a.* when one is
*Prov.* 3:25 *be not a.* of sudden
*Is.* 40:9 up thy voice, *be not a.*
*Jer.* 1:8 *be not a.* of their faces
*Mat.* 14:27 it is I, *be not a. Mark* 6:50; *John* 6:20
17:7 Jesus said, Arise, *be not a.*
28:10 *be not a.* go tell brethren
*Mark* 5:36 ruler, *be not a.* only
*Acts* 18:9 *be not a.* but speak
1 *Pet.* 3:14 *be not a.* of their

**Sore AFRAID.**
*Num.* 22:3 Moab *s. a.* of people
*Jos.* 9:24 *s. a.* of our lives
1 *Sam.* 17:24 from Goliah *s. a.*
28:20 Saul fell along *sore a.*
31:4 armor-bearer *s. a.* 1 *Chr.* 10:4
*Mark* 9:6 for they were *sore a.*
*Luke* 2:9 and they were *sore a.*

**Was AFRAID.**
*Gen.* 3:10 thy voice and *w. a.*
*Ex.* 3:6 Moses *w. a.* to look
*Deut.* 9:19 I *was a.* of the anger
1 *Sam.* 18:12 *was a.* of David, 15
28:5 saw Philistines, he *was a.*
2 *Sam.* 6:9 David *was a.* of the L. 1 *Chr.* 13:12
*Job* 3:25 that I *was a.* is come
32:6 I *was a.* and durst not
*Dan.* 8:17 *was a.* and fell
*Hab.* 3:2 thy speech and *was a.*
*Mal.* 2:5 feared me and *was a.*
*Mat.* 2:22 *was a.* to go thither
14:30 saw wind boisterous, *w.a.*
25:25 *was a.* and hid thy talent
*John* 19:8 *was* the more *a.*
*Acts* 10:4 Corn's looked, he *w.a.*

**AFRESH.**
*Heb.* 6:6 crucify Son of God *a.*

**AFTER.**
*Jos.* 10:14 no day like that *a.* it

**AFTER that.**
*Luke* 12:4 *a. t.* have no more that
1 *Cor.* 15:6 *a. t.* was seen of 500

**AFTERNOON.**
*Jud.* 19:8 they tarried till *a.*

**AFTERWARD, S.**
*Ps.* 73:24 *a.* receive me to glory
*Prov.* 29:11 keepeth it in till *a.*
*John* 13:36 shalt follow me *a.*
1 *Cor.* 15:23 *a.* that are Christ's
*Heb.* 12:11 *a.* yieldeth fruit

AGABUS. *Acts* 11:28; 21:10

**AGAG.**
*Num.* 24:7 be higher than A.
1 *Sam.* 15:9 the people spared A.
33 Samuel hewed A. in pieces

AGAGITE. *See* HAMAN.

**AGAINST.**
*Gen.* 16:12 hand will be *a.* every
*Mat.* 10:35 man *a.* his f. *Lu.* 12:53
12:30 he not with me, is *a.* me
*Luke* 2:34 for a sign spoken *a.*
14:31 cometh *a.* him with 20,000
*Acts* 19:36 cannot be spoken *a.*
28:22 sect everywh. spoken *a.*

*See* ANOTHER, GOD, JERUSALEM, ISRAEL, LORD, OVER.

AGAR. *Gal.* 4:24, 25

**AGATE, S.**
*Ex.* 28:19 third row, an *a.* 39:12
*Is.* 54:12 thy windows of *a.*
*Ezek.* 27:16 Syria occup. with *a.*

**AGE.**
*Gen.* 47:28 *a.* of Jacob 147 years
48:10 eyes of Israel dim for *a.*
*Num.* 8:25 *a.* of fifty cease
1 *Sam.* 2:33 flower of their *a.*
1 *K.* 14:4 set by reason of *a.*
2 *Chr.* 36:17 that stooped for *a.*
*Job* 5:26 come to grave in a full *a.*
8:8 inquire of the former *a.*
11:17 thy *a* clearer than
*Ps.* 39:5 my *a.* is as nothing
*Is.* 38:12 my *a.* is departed
*Zec.* 8:4 with his staff for *a.*
*Mark* 5:42 *a.* of 12 years, *Lu.* 8:42
*Luke* 2:36 Anna of a great *a.*
3:23 Jesus about 30 years of *a.*
*John* 9:21 he is of *a.* ask him, 23
1 *Cor.* 7:36 pass flower of *a.*
*Heb.* 5:14 strong meat to full *a.*

*See* OLD, STRICKEN.

**AGES.**
*Eph* 2:7 *a.* to come he might
3:5 other *a.* not made known
21 in church through all *a.*
*Col.* 1:26 mystery hid from *a.*

**AGED.**
2 *Sam.* 19:32 Barzillai very *a.*
*Job* 12:20 the understanding of *a.*
15:10 grey-headed and very *a.*
29:8 the *a.* arose and stood up
32:9 do the *a.* understand
*Jer.* 6:11 *a.* with him full of days
*Tit.* 2:2 that the *a.* men be sober
3 the *a.* women be in behavior
*Phile.* 9 such a one as Paul the *a.*

**AGO.**
1 *Sam.* 9:20 asses lost 3 days *a.*
1 *K.* 19:25 long *a. Is.* 37:26
*Ezr.* 5:11 builded many years *a.*
*Mat.* 11:21 long *a. Luke* 10:13
*Mark* 9:21 how long *a.* since this
*Acts* 10:30 four days *a.* I was
15:7 a good while *a.*
2 *Cor.* 8:10 be forward a year *a.*
9:2 Achaia was ready a year *a.*
12:2 above fourteen years *a.*

**AGONE.**
1 *Sam.* 30:13 three days *a.* I fell

**AGONY.**
*Luke* 22:44 in an *a.* he prayed

**AGREE, ED, ETH.**
*Amos* 3:3 walk except they be *a.*
*Mat.* 5:25 *a.* with adversary
18:19 if two shall *a.* on earth
20:2 had *a.* with laborers
13 not *a.* with me for a penny?
*Mark* 14:56 witness *a.* not, 59
70 Galilean, and thy speech *a.*
*Luke* 5:36 out of new, *a.* not
*John* 9:22 Jews had *a.* already
*Acts* 5:9 ye have *a.* to tempt
40 and to him they *a.* and
15:15 to this *a.* words of proph.
23:20 Jews have *a.* to desire
28:25 *a.* not among themselves
1 *John* 5:8 blood, these *a.* in one
*Rev.* 17:17 *a.* to give their kingd.

**AGREEMENT.**
2 *K.* 18:31 *a.* by a pres. *Is.* 36:16
*Is.* 28:15 with hell are we at *a.*
18 *a.* with hell shall not stand
*Dan.* 11:6 of north, to make *a.*
2 *Cor.* 6:16 what *a.* hath the

**AGRIPPA.**
*Acts.* 25:13 A. and Bernice came
22 A. said, I would also hear
26:7 which hope's sake, king A.
28 A. said, almost thou per.

**AGROUND.**
*Acts* 27:41 they ran the ship *a.*

**AGUE.**
*Lev.* 26:16 appoint burning *a.*

AGUR. *Prov.* 30:1

**AH.**
*Ps.* 35:25 *a.* so would we have it
*Is.* 1:4 *a.* sinful nation, a people
24 *a.* I will ease me of
*Jer.* 1:6 *a.* Lord God, I cannot
4:10 *a.* Lord thou hast
22:18 *a.* brother, *a.* sister, *a.* L.
32:17 *a.* Lord, thou made
34:5 lament thee, saying *a.* L.
*Ezek.* 9:8 *a.* Lord, wilt thou
*Mark* 15:29 *a.* thou that

**AHA.**
*Ps.* 35:21 *a.* our eye hath seen
40:15 that say unto me *a.*
70:3 turned back that say *a. a.*
*Is.* 44:16 *a.* I am warm, I have

Ezek. 25:3 saidst a. against sanc.
26:2 Tyrus said, a. she is brok.
36:2 a. the ancient places

**AHAB.**

1 K. 16:30, 33; 18:6, 9, 42, 46;
20:13; 21:4, 21, 25, 29; 22:20
2 K. 1:1; 3:5; 8:18, 27; 9:7, 8, 25;
10:11; 21:3, 13
2 Chr. 21:13 whored. of ho. of A.
Jer. 29:21 saith the Lord of A.
22 the L. make thee like A.
Mic. 6:16 works of house of A.

**AHASUERUS.**

Ezr. 4:6 reign of A. wrote
Est. 1:1 is A. which reigned
Dan. 9:1 of Darius, son of A.

AHAVAH. Ezr. 8:15, 21, 31

**AHAZ.**

2 K. 16:2 A. was 20 years
1 Chr. 8:35 Mic. Pithon, A. 9:41
2 Chr. 28:19 Judah low, bec. of A.
Is. 1:1 the vision in days of A.
Hos. 1:1; Mic. 1:1.
7:3 go forth to meet A. 10

**AHAZIAH.**

1 K. 22:40 A. his son, 2 K. 8:24
K. 1:2 A. fell through
8:29 A. king of Judah, went
10:13 the brethren of A.
2 Chr. 20:35 Jehosh. join with A.
22:7 destruction of A. was of

AHIAH. 1 Sam. 14:3; 1 K. 4:3

**AHIJAH.**

1 K. 11:29; 12:15; 14:2, 4, 6
15:27 Baasha, son of A.
1 Chr. 2:25 sons of Jerahmeel, A.

**AHIKAM.**

2 K. 22:12 Josiah commanded A.
to inquire, 2 Chr. 34:20
25:22 Gedaliah the son of A.
Jer. 26:24 hand of A. was with
40:6 Gedaliah the son of A.

See GEDALIAH.

**AHIMAAZ.**

1 Sam. 14:50 the daughter of A.
2 Sam. 17:17 Jonathan and A.
18:27 is like the running of A.
1 K. 4:15 A. in Naphtali
1 Chr. 6:8 and Zadok begat A.

**AHIMAN.**

Num. 13:22 A. of the children
Jud. 1:10 Judah slew A.
1 Chr. 9:17 and the porters, A.

**AHIMELECH.**

1 Sam. 21:1 A. was afraid at the
22:9 son of Jesse coming to A.
16 thou shalt surely die A.
26:6 David said to A. who
2 Sam. 8:17 Zadok and A. 1 Chr.
18:16
1 Chr. 24:3 A. of the sons of, 6, 31

AHINOAM. 1 Sam. 14:50; 25:43
AHIO. 2 Sam. 6:3; 1 Chr. 13:7
AHISAMACH. Ex. 35:34

**AHITHOPHEL.**

2 Sam. 15:12 Absalom sent for A.
16:15 came to Jerusal. and A.
23 counsel of A. was as if a
17:7 counsel of A. is not good
15 thus did A. counsel, 23
1 Chr. 27:33 A. was the king's

**AHITUB.**

1 Sam. 22:12 thou son of A.
2 Sam. 8:17 Zadok the son of A.
1 Chr. 18:16

**AHOLAH, AHOLIBAH.**

Ezek. 23:4 Sama. is A. Jerus. A.
36 wilt thou judge A. and A.?

AHOLIAB. Ex. 36:1
AHOLIBAMAH. Gen. 36:2, 5

**AI, or HAI.**

Gen. 13:3 betw. Beth-el and A.
Jos. 7:4 before the men of A.
8:1 up to A. 10:2 greater than A.
Ezr. 2:28 the men of Beth-el and
A. Neh. 7:32
Jer. 49.3 howl, O Heshbon, for A.

AIATH. Is. 10:28

**AILED, ETH.**

Gen. 21:17 what a. thee, Hagar?
Jud. 18:23 Micah, what a. thee?
1 Sam. 11:5 what a. the people
2 Sam. 14:5 the king said unto
her, what a. thee? 2 K. 6:28
Ps. 114:5 what a. thee, O sea
Is. 22:1 what a. thee now that

**AIR.**

2 Sam. 21:10 birds of the a.
Job 41:16 no a. can come bet.
Prov. 30:19 an eagle in the a.
Ec. 10:20 bird of the a. carry
Mat. 8:20 birds of a. have nests
13:32 birds of the a. lodge in the
Mark 4:32; Luke 9:58
Acts 22:23 threw dust into the a.
1 Cor. 9:26 one that beateth a.
14:9 ye shall speak into the a.
Eph. 2:2 prince of power of the a.
1 Thes. 4:17 meet the L. in the a.
Rev. 9:2 sun and a. were dark
16:17 poured out vial into the a.

See FOWLS.

AJALON. Jos. 10:12

**ALARM.**

Num. 10:5 when ye blow an a. 6
7 blow, but not sound an a.
9 if ye go to war, blow an a.
2 Chr. 13:12 trumpets to cry an a.
Jer. 4:19 O my soul, a. of war
49:21 will cause an a. of war
Joel 2:1 an a. in my holy mount.
Zep. 1:16 a. against fenced cities

**ALAS.**

Num. 24:23 a. who shall live
Jud. 6:22 a. I have seen an angel
11:35 a. daughter thou hast
1 K. 13:30 a. my brother
2 K. 6:5 a. master, for it was
15 a. master, how shall we do?
Ezek. 6:11 stamp with foot, say a.
Joel 1:15 a. for the day of the L.
Amos 5:16 say in highways, a. a.
Rev. 18:10 a. a. that great, 16, 19

**ALBEIT.**

Eze. 13:7 L. saith, a. I have not
Phile. 19 a. I say not, how thou

**ALEXANDER.**

Mark 15:21 Simon, father of A.
Acts 4:6 Annas, Caiaphas, A.
19:33 they drew A. out of the
1 Tim. 1:20 Hymeneus and A.
2 Tim. 4:14 A. the coppersmith

**ALEXANDRIA, ANS.**

Acts 6:9 of the Libertines and A.
18:24 nam. Apollos, born at A.
27:6 centurion found ship of A.

**ALIEN, S.**

Ex. 18:3 been a. in a strange
Deut. 14:21 mayest sell to an a.
Job 19:15 am an a. in their sight
Ps. 69:8 a. to my mother's child.
Is. 61:5 of a. your ploughmen
Lam. 5:2 our houses turned to a.
Eph. 2:12 a. from commonwealth
Heb. 11:34 flight the armies of a.

**ALIENATE, ED.**

Eze. 23:17 her mind was a. from
18 my mind was a. from her as
22 from whom thy mind is a. 28
48:14 not a. first-fruits of land
Eph. 4:18 a. from life of G. thro'
Col. 1:21 that were sometime a.

**ALIKE.**

1 Sam. 30:24 they shall part a.
Job 21:26 lie down a. in dust
Ps. 33:15 fashion. their hearts a.
139:12 darkn. and light both a.
Ec. 9:2 all things come a. to all
11:6 whe. both shall be a. good
Rom. 14:5 esteemeth ev day a.

**ALIVE.**

Gen. 7:23 Noah remained a. and
12:12 kill me, and save thee a.
50:20 to save much people a.
Ex. 1:17 men-children a. 18
22 daughter ye shall save a.
22:4 if the theft be found a.
Lev. 10:16 he was angry with
Aaron's sons left a.
Num. 16:33 went down a. into pit
22:33 slain thee, and sav. her a.
31:15 ye saved all the women a.
Deut. 4:4 a. every one this day
5:3 all of us a. here this day
6:24 might pres. us a. this day.
20:16 save a. noth. that breath.
32:39 and I make a. 1 Sam. 2:6
Jos. 2:13 ye save a. my father
14:10 the Lord hath kept me a.
Jud. 8:19 saved them a. I would
1 Sam. 15:8 he took Agag a.
27:9 left man nor woman a.
1 K. 20:18 peace or war take a.
21:15 Naboth is not a. but dead
2 K. 5:7 G. to kill and make a.?
7:4 if they save us a. we live
12 we shall catch them a.
10:14 and they took them a.
2 Chr. 25:12 other 10,000 left a.
Ps. 30:3 L. thou hast kept me a.
Prov. 1:12 swal. a. as the grave
Jer. 49:11 I will preserve a.
Eze. 13:18 the souls a. that come
19 souls a. that should not live
18:27 he shall save his soul a.
Dan. 5:19 whom would, kept a.
Mark 16:11 heard that he was a.
Luke 15:24 was dead and is a. 32
24:23 angels who said he was a.
Acts 1:3 a. after his passion
9:41 widows, presented her a.
20:12 brought the young man a.
25:19 whom P. affirmed to be a.
Rom. 6:11 a. to God through C.
13 as those a. from the dead
7:9 for I was a. without the law
1 Cor. 15:22 Christ all be made a.
1 Thes. 4:15 are a. and remain, 17
Rev. 1:18 I am a. forevermore
2:8 which was dead, and is a.
19:20 cast a. into lake of fire

Keep ALIVE. See KEEP.

**Yet ALIVE.**

Gen. 43:7 is your father yet a.?
Gen. 43:27 he yet a.? 28 is yet a.
45:26 Joseph is yet a. 28
46:30 bec. thou art yet a.
Ex. 4:18 see they be yet a.
Deut. 31:27 I am yet a. with you
2 Sam. 12:18 child yet a. 21, 22
18:14 yet a. in midst of the oak
1 K. 20:32 he yet a.? he is my bro.
Ec. 4:2 than the living yet a.
Ezek. 7:13 sold, although yet a.
Mat. 27:63 said while yet a.

**ALL.**

Gen. 24:36 given a. that he hath
1 Sam. 9:19 tell thee a. in thy h.
30:8 and without fail recover a.
1 K. 20:4 I am thine, and a. I
Neh. 9:6 L. preservest them a.
Job 34:19 they a. are works of his
Ps. 14:3 are a. gone aside, a.
34:19 deliv. him out of them a.
44:17 a. this is come upon us
Prov. 22:2 L. is maker of them a.
Ezek. 20:40 a. of them shall serve
37:22 shall be king to them a.
Dan. 1:19 among a. none like D.
Hos. 5:2 a rebuker of them a.
Mal. 2:10 have we not a. one F.

*Mat.* 13:56 sisters, are they not *a.*
22:28 for they *a.* had her
*Mark* 12:44 *a.* she had, *Lu.* 21:4
*Luke* 4:7 if thou worship me, *a.*
15:31 son, *a.* that I have is thine
17:10 when ye have done *a.* say
*John* 4:39 told me *a.* ever I did
13:10 ye are clean, but not *a.*
17:21 that they *a.* may be one
*Acts* 4:33 great grace was on *a.*
16:28 thyself no harm, we are *a.*
1 *Cor.* 3:22 *a.* are yours, ye are
*Phil* 4:18 I have *a.* and abound
2 *Tim.* 3:11 out of them *a.* the L.
1 *Pet.* 3:8 be ye *a.* of one mind
1 *John* 2:19 were not *a.* of us

*Above* ALL. *See* ABOVE.

**According to ALL.**

*Gen.* 6:22 N. did *accor. to a.* 7:5
*Ex.* 31:11 *ac. to a.* L. commanded 36:1; 39:32, 42; 40:16; *Num.* 2:34; 8:20; 9:5; 29:40; *Deut.* 1:3, 41
*Jos.* 11:23 took the land *ac. to a.*
1 *K.* 8:56 given rest *ac. to a.*
11:37 shalt reign *ac. to a.* thy
22:53 *ac. to a.* his father had d. 2 *K.* 23:32, 37; 24:9, 19; 2 *Chr.* 26:4; 27:2
2 *K.* 10:30 *ac. to a.* in my heart
18:3 *ac. to a.* David, 2 *Chr.* 29:2
1 *Chr.* 17:15 *ac. to a.* these words
*Neh.* 5:19 for good, *ac. to a.* I h.
*Jer.* 42:20 *ac. to a.* L. shall say
50:29 *ac. to a.* Babyl. hath done
*Eze.* 24:24 *ac. to a.* he hath done

**Before ALL.**

*Gal.* 2:14 Peter *bef.* them *a.*

**For ALL.**

*Phil.* 2:21 *for a.* seek their own
*Heb.* 8:11 *for a.* shall know me
10:10 offering of Ch. once *for a.*

**In ALL.**

*Gen.* 21:12 *in a.* Sarah hath said
22 God with thee *in a.* thou
*Deut.* 29:9 prosp. *in a.* that ye do
1 *K.* 2:3 mayest prosper *in a.*
1 *Cor.* 12:6 God worketh all *in a.*
15:28 that God may be all *in a.*
*Eph.* 1:23 him that fill. all *in a.*
*Col.* 3:11 Christ is all *in a.*

ALL *Night* *See* NIGHT.

**Over ALL.**

2 *Sam.* 3:21 mayest reign *over a.*
1 *Chr.* 29:12 thou reignest *over a.*
*Ps.* 103:19 kingdom ruleth *over a.*
*Mat.* 24:47 ruler *over a.* *Lu.* 12:44
*John* 17:2 giv. him power *over a.*
*Rom.* 9:5 *over a.* God blessed for
10:12 Lord *over a.* is rich to all

**To *or* Unto ALL.**

*Ps.* 145:9 the Lord is good *to a.*
*Ec.* 2:14 one event *to a.* 9:3, 11
9:2 all things come alike *to a.*
*Is.* 36:6 Pharaoh *to a.* that trust
*Mark* 13:37 I say *unto a.* watch
*Luke* 12:41 speakest to us, *to a.*?
*Acts* 2:39 promise is *to a.* afar off
4:16 manifest *to a.* that dwell
*Rom.* 10:12 rich *unto a.* that call
13:7 render *to a.* their dues
1 *Cor.* 9:19 a servant *unto a.*
1 *Tim.* 4:15 profit. may app. *to a.*

**Upon ALL.**

*Rom.* 3:22 *upon a.* them that be.

**ALL these.**

*Gen.* 15:10 took to him *a. these*
*Gen.* 42:36 *a. these* are against me
*Ex.* 10:1 G. spake *a. these* words
*Job* 12:9 know. not that in *a. t.*
*Hab.* 2:6 shall not *a. t.* take up
*Mat.* 6:33 *a. t.* shall be, *Lu.* 12:31

**ALL this.**

*Gen.* 41:39 God showed thee *a. t.*
*Deut.* 32:27 hath not done *a. this*
*Jud.* 6:13 *a. this* befallen us!
1 *Sam.* 22:15 k. nothing of *a. t.*
2 *Sam.* 14: 19 of Joab in *a. this*?
*Job* 1:22 *a. t.* J. sinned not, 2:10
13:1 mine eye hath seen *a. this*
*Ps.* 44:17 *a. this* is come upon us
78:32 for *a. this* they sinned still
*Ec.* 8:9 *a. this* have I seen and
9:1 *a. this* I considered in heart
*Is.* 5:25 for *a. this* his anger is not turned 9:12, 17, 21; 10:4
48:6 thou hast heard, see *a. this*
*Dan.* 5:22 thou knewest *a. this*
7:16 asked h. the truth of *a. t.*
*Hos.* 7:10 nor seek him for *a. t.*
*Mic.* 1:5 transgress. of Jac. is *a. t.*
*Mat.* 1:22 *a. t.* was done that prophets be fulfilled 21:4; 26:56
*Luke* 16:26 *a. t.* there is a gulf
24:21 *a. t.* to-day is the third d.

**ALL that he had.**

*Gen.* 12:20 P. and *a. t. h. h.*
13:1 A. out of E. and *a. t. h. h.*
25:5 Abr. gave *a. t. h. h.* to
31:21 Jacob fled with *a. t. h. h.*
39:4 *a. t. h. h.* into Joseph's 6
5 bl. of the L. was on *a. t. h. h.*
*Mat.* 18:25 he sold *a. t. he had*
*Mark* 5:26 she spent *a. t. she had*
12:44 cast in *a. t. s. h.* *Lu.* 21:4

**ALL the while.**

*Job* 27:3 *a. the w.* my breath

*See further other usual Substantives:*

CONGREGATION DAY, EARTH, ISRAEL, MEN, PEOPLE, THINGS, *etc.*

**ALLEGING.**

*Acts* 17:3 *a.* C. must have suf.

**ALLEGORY.**

*Gal.* 4:24 which things are an *a*

**ALLELUIAH.**

*Rev.* 19:1 great voice say *a.* 3, 4, 6

**ALLOW.**

*Luke* 11:48 that ye *a.* the deeds
*Acts* 24:15 themselves also *a.* that
*Rom.* 7:15 which I do, I *a.* not

**ALLOWED, ETH.**

*Rom.* 14:22 that thing wh. he *a.*
1 *Thes.* 2:4 as were *a.* of God

**ALLOWANCE.**

2 *K.* 25:20 his *a.* was continual *a.*

**ALLURE.**

*Hos.* 2:14 *a.* her into the wild.
2 *Pet.* 2:18 they *a.* through lusts

**ALMIGHTY.**

*Gen.* 17:1 I am the *a.* God, walk
28:3 God *a.* bless thee and make
35:11 I am God *a.* be fruitful
43:14 God *a.* give you mercy
49:25 by *a.* who shall bless thee
*Ex.* 6:3 appeared by name God *a.*
*Num.* 24:4 saw the vision of *a.* 16
*Ruth* 1:20 *a.* hath dealt bitterly
21 the *a.* hath afflicted me
*Job* 5:17 desp. not chasten. of a.
6:4 arrows of the *a.* are with. me
14 forsaketh the fear of the *a.*
8:3 doth the *a.* pervert justice?
5 thy supplication to the *a.*
11:7 find out *a.* to perfection?
13:3 surely I would speak to *a.*
15:25 strengtheneth ag. the *a.*
21:15 *a.* we should serve him
20 shall drink the wrath of *a.*
22:3 pleasure to *a.* thou art
17 what the *a.* do for them?
23 if thou return to the *a.* thou
25 the *a.* shall be thy defence
26 have thy delight in the *a.*
23:16 and the *a.* troubleth me
24:1 are not hid from the *a.*
27:2 *a.* who hath vexed my soul
10 delight himself in the *a.*
11 is with *a.* will I not conceal
29:5 w. the *a.* was yet with me
31:2 inheritance of *a.*
35 that the *a.* would answer me
32:8 inspiration of the *a.* giveth
33:4 breath of *a.* hath given me
34:10 far from *a.* to com. iniq.
12 neither will the *a.* pervert
35:13 the *a.* will not regard
37:23 the *a.* we cannot find him
40:2 contendeth with *a.* instruct
*Ps.* 68:14 when *a.* scattereth k.
*Ps.* 91:1 the shadow of the *a.*
*Is.* 13:6 destruction from the *a.*
*Ezek.* 1:24 voice of the *a.* 10:5
*Joel* 1:15 destruction from the *a.*
2 *Cor.* 6:18 my sons, saith L. *a.*
*Rev.* 1:8 was and is to come, *a.*
4:8 L. God *a.* which was, 11:17
15:3 Lord *a.* just and true, 16:7
21:22 G. *a.* and Lamb temple of

**ALMOND, S.**

*Gen.* 43:11 myrrh, nuts, and *a.*
*Ex.* 25:33 like to *a.* 34; 37:19, 20
*Num.* 17:8 rod of Aaron yield. *a.*
*Ec.* 12:5 *a.* tree shall flourish
*Jer.* 1:11 I see a rod of an *a.* tree

**ALMOST.**

*Ps.* 73:2 my feet were *a.* gone
94:17 my soul *a.* dwelt in silence
119:87 *a.* consumed me upon e.
*Prov.* 5:14 I was *a.* in all evil
*Acts* 13:44 came *a.* the whole city
19:26 but *a.* through all Asia
26:28 *a.* thou almost persuadest
29 were both *a.* and altogether
*Heb.* 9:22 *a.* all things by the law

**ALMS.**

*Mat.* 6:1 do not your *a.* before
2 doest thine *a.* do not sound
4 that thine *a.* may be in secret
*Luke* 11:41 give *a.* of such things
12:33 and give *a.* provide bags.
*Acts* 3:3 seeing P. and J. ask. *a.*
10:2 Cornelius gave much *a.*
4 thine *a.* for a memorial, 31
24:17 to bring *a.* to my nation

**ALMSDEEDS.**

*Acts* 9:36 Dorcas full of *a.*

**ALMUG-TREES.**

1 *K.* 10:11 fr. Ophir plenty of *a-t.*
12 made of *a-t.* pillars

**ALOES.**

*Ps.* 45:8 garments smell of *a.*
*Prov.* 7:17 perf. my bed with *a.*
*Cant.* 4:14 myrrh, *a.* with spices
*John* 19:39 brought a mix. of *a.*

**ALONE.**

*Gen.* 2:18 good man should be *a.*
*Ex.* 18:18 not able thyself *a.*
24:2 Moses *a.* shall come near
*Num.* 11:14 not able to bear all this people *a.* *Deut.* 1:9, 12
23:9 the people shall dwell *a.*
*Deut.* 32:12 as Lord *a.* did lead h.
33:28 Isr. shall dwell in safety *a.*
2 *Sam.* 18:24 a man run. *a.* 26
1 *K.* 11:29 they two *a.* in field
2 *K.* 19:15 art God *a.* *Is.* 37:16; *Ps.* 86:10
*Job* 1:15 escaped *a.* to t. 16, 17, 19
9:8 *a.* spreadeth out the heavens
15:19 to whom *a.* earth was giv.
31:17 have I eaten my morsel *a.*
*Ps.* 83:18 whose name *a.* is Jeh.
136:4 who *a.* doeth great wond.
148:13 his name *a.* is excellent
*Ec.* 4:8 one *a.* and not a second
10 that is *a.* when he falleth
*Is.* 2:11 L. *a.* shall be exalted, 17
14:31 none *a.* in appointed times
51:2 I called him *a.* and blessed
63:3 trodden the wine-press *a.*
*Lam.* 3:28 sitteth *a.* and keepeth
*Mat.* 4:4 live by bread *a.* *Lu.* 4:4
14:23 he was *a.* *Luke* 9:18
18:15 between thee and him *a.*

*Mark* 4:34 were *a*. he expounded
6:47 sea, and he *a*. on the land
*Luke* 5:21 forgive sins but G. *a*
6:4 but for the priests *a*.
9:18 as Jesus was *a*. praying
36 voice past, Jes. was found *a*.
*John* 6:15 into a mountain *a*.
22 discip. were gone away *a*.
8:16 for I am not *a*. but, 16:32
17:20 neither pray I for these *a*.
*Acts* 19:26 that not *a*. at Ephesus
*Rom*. 4:23 written for his sake *a*.
*Gal*. 6:4 rejoicing in himself *a*
*Heb*. 9:7 went high-priest *a*. once
*Jam*. 2:17 faith is dead, being *a*.

**Left ALONE.**

*Is*. 49:21 I was *left a*. these where
*John* 8:9 Jesus was *left a*. and w.
29 Father hath not *left* me *a*.
*Rom*. 11:3 I am *left a*. and they

**Let ALONE.**

*Job* 10:20 *let* me *a*. that I take
*Hos*. 4:17 join. to idols, *l*. him *a*.
*Mat*. 15:14 *let* them *a*. blind lead
*Mark* 1:24 *let* us *a*. what have we to do with thee, *Luke* 4:34
14:6 Jesus said, *let* her *a*.
*Luke* 13:8 *let* it *a*. this year also
*John* 11:48 if we *let* him *a*. all m.
12:7 *let* her *a*. against the day
*Acts* 5:38 refr. from these m. *l*. *a*.

**ALOOF.**

*Ps*. 38:11 my friends stand *a*.

ALOUD. *See* CRY, CRIED, SING.

**ALPHA.**

*Rev*. 1:8 I am *a*. 11; 21:6; 22:13

**ALPHEUS.**

*Mat*. 10:3 James, the son of A. *Mark* 3:18; *Luke* 6:15; *Acts* 1:13
*Mark* 2:14 saw Levi the son of A.

**ALREADY.**

*Ec*. 1:10 it hath been *a*. of old
*Mat*. 17:12 Elias is come *a*.
*John* 3:18 condemned *a*.
*Phil*. 3:16 we have *a*. attained
*Rev*. 2:25 that ye have *a*. hold f.

**ALSO.**

*Gen*. 6:3 for that he *a*. is flesh
1 *Sam*. 14:44 S. answ. God do so, and m. *a*. 2 *Sam*. 3:35; 19:13
*Ps*. 68:18 gifts for rebellious *a*.
*Zec*. 8:21 to seek Lord I will go *a*.
*Mat*. 6:21 w. heart be *a*. *Lu*. 12:34
26:73 thou art *a*. one of them
*John* 5:19 these *a*. doth the Son
12:26 where I am, there shall *a*.
14:3 where I am, ye may be *a*.
1 *Cor*. 15:8 he was seen of me *a*.
2 *Tim*. 1:5 persuaded in thee *a*.

**ALTAR.**

*Gen*. 8:20 Noah builded an *a*.
12:7 Abraham built an *a*. 22:9
35:1 Beth-el, make there an *a*.
*Ex*. 17:15 Moses built an *a*.
20:24 an *a*. of earth make to me
29:37 sanctify it, *a*. most holy
44 I will sanctify the *a*.
30:27 *a*. of incense
40:10 *a*. of burnt-offering
*Lev*. 6:9 fire of *a*. shall be burn.
*Num*. 7:84 dedication of the *a*.
18:3 shall not come nigh the *a*.
*Jos*. 22:34 called the *a*. Ed.
*Jud*. 6:25 throw down *a*. of B.
2 *Sam*. 24:18 rear an *a*. to the L.
1 *K*. 13:2 cried against the *a*. O *a*.
18:30 Elijah repaired the *a*.
35 the water ran about the *a*.
2 *K*. 18:22 shall worship before this *a*. *Is*. 36:7
*Ps*. 26:6 will I compass thine *a*.
43:4 then will I go to *a*. of God
*Is*. 19:19 an *a*. in midst of Egypt
27:9 stones of *a*. as chalk-sto.
56:7 sacri. accepted on mine *a*.
*Lam*. 2:7 Lord h. cast off his *a*.
*Ezek*. 8:16 between porch and *a*.
*Joel* 1:13 howl, ye minist. of *a*.
2:17 priests weep b. porch and *a*.
*Amos* 2:8 to pledge by every *a*.
*Mal*. 1:7 polluted bread on, *a*.
10 fire on mine *a*. for naught
2:13 covering *a*. with tears
*Mat*. 5:23 thou bring gift to the *a*.
23:18 swear by the *a*. it is n.
35 ye slew between the temple and *a*. *Luke* 11:51
*Acts* 17:23 *a*. with this inscript.
1 *Cor*. 9:13 partak. with *a*. 10:18
*Heb*. 7:13 attendance at the *a*.
13:10 we have an *a*. whereof
*Rev*. 6:9 under the *a*. souls of
8:3 prayers on the golden *a*.
9:13 from horns of golden *a*.
*See* BUILT.

**ALTARS.**

1 *K*. 19:10 thrown down *a*. 14
*Ps*. 84:3 even thine *a*. O Lord.
*Is*. 17:8 shall not look to the *a*.
*Jer*. 17:1 sin graven on horns of *a*.
2 their children remem. *a*.
*Ezek*. 6:4 your *a*. shall be desol.
*Hos*. 8:11 *a*. to sin, *a*. shall be
12:11 *a*. as heaps in the furrows
*Amos* 3:14 visit the *a*. of Beth-el
*Rom*. 11:3 digged down thine *a*.

**ALTER.**

*Ezr*. 6:11 whoso. shall *a*. this
*Ps*. 89:34 not *a*. the thing gone

**ALTERED.**

*Luke* 9:29 countenance was *a*.

**ALTOGETHER.**

*Ps*. 14:3 *a*. filthy, *Ps*. 53:3
19:9 judgments are righteous *a*.
50:21 *a*. such a one as thyself
139:4 lo, thou knowest it *a*.
*Cant*. 5:16 yea, he is *a*. lovely
*John* 9:34 wast *a*. born in sins
*Acts* 26:29 alm. and *a*. such as I

**ALWAY, S.**

*Job*. 7:16 I would not live *a*.
27:10 will he *a*. call upon God?
*Ps*. 16:8 have set L. *a*. before me
*Ps*. 103:9 he will not *a*. chide
*Mat*. 28:20 I am with you *a*.
*Mark* 14:7 ye have not *a*. *Jn*. 12:8
*John* 8:29 I do *a*. those things
11:42 thou hearest me *a*.
*Phil*. 1:4 *a*. in every prayer
20 as *a*. so now Christ shall
4:4 rejoice in the Lord *a*.
1 *Thes*. 2:16 fill up their sins *a*.

**AM I.**

*Mat*. 18:20 there *am I* in the m.

**I AM, I AM that I AM.**

*Ex*. 3:14 *I am that I am* hath
*Job* 9:32 he is not a man as *I am*
*Is*. 44:6 *I am* the first, *I am* the last, 48:12; *Rev*. 1:11
47:8 *I am*, none else, *Zep*. 2:15
*Luke* 22:70 ye say that *I am*
*John* 8:58 before Abr. was, *I am*
12:26 where *I am* there shall my
17:24 with me where *I am*
*Acts* 26:29 altog. such as *I am*
1 *Cor*. 15:10 of G. *I am* what *I am*
*Gal*. 4:12 be as *I am*, for *I am* as

**Here AM I, *or* Here I AM.**

*See* HERE.

**AMALEK.**

*Gen*. 36:12 T. bare to Eliphaz A.
*Ex*. 17:8 then came A. and f.
14 the remembrance of A. 16
*Num*. 24:20 looked on A. he took up his p. and said A. was
*Deut*. 25:17 A. did, 1 *Sam*. 15:2
19 out the remembrance of A.
*Jud*. 5:14 was a root against A.
1 *Sam*. 15:3 smite A.; 5 city of A.
28:18 exec. his wrath on A.
*Ps*. 83:7 Gebal, Ammon, A. are

AMANA. *Cant*. 4:8.

**AMASA.**

2 *Sam*. 17:25 A. capt. of the host
1 *K*. 2:5 what J. did to A. 32
1 *Chr*. 2:17 Abigail bare A.
2 *Chr*. 28:12 A. s. of H. stood up

**AMAZED.**

*Job* 32:15 *a*. answered no more
*Is*. 13:8 be *a*. one at another
*Ezek*. 32:10 people *a*. at thee
*Mat*. 19:25 the disciples were *a*.
*Mark* 2:12 were all *a*, *Luke* 5:26
14:33 he began to be sore *a*.
*Luke* 4:36 all *a*. and spake among
9:43 were all *a*. at mighty pow.
*Acts* 9:21 all that heard S. were *a*.

**AMAZEMENT.**

*Acts* 3:10 filled with *a*. at what
1 *Pet*. 3:6 not afraid with any *a*.

**AMAZIAH.**

2 *K*. 12:21 A. reign., 2 *Ch*. 24:27
13:12 fought against A. 14:15
14:11 but A. would not hear
15:3 A. had done, 2 *Chr*. 26:4
1 *Chr*. 6:45 A. son of Hilkiah
2 *Chr*. 25:27 A. did turn the L.
*Amos* 7:10 A. priest of Beth-el

**AMBASSADOR.**

*Prov*. 13:17 a faithful *a*. is health
*Jer*. 49:14 *a*. sent to heath. *Ob*. 1
*Eph*. 6:20 I am an *a*. in bonds

**AMBASSADORS.**

*Jos*. 9:4 as if they had been *a*.
2 *Chr*. 35:21 he sent *a*. saying
*Is*. 18:2 sendeth *a*. by the sea
30:4 his *a*. came to Hanes
33:7 *a*. of peace shall weep
*Ezek*. 17:15 rebelled in sending *a*.
2 *Cor*. 5:20 we are *a*. for Christ.

**AMBASSAGE.**

*Luke* 14:32 sendeth an *a*.

AMBER. *See* COLOR.

**AMBUSH, ES.**

*Jos*. 8:2 an *a*. for the city.
*Jer*. 51:12 prepare the *a*.

**AMBUSHMENT, S.**

2 *Chr*. 13:13 Jerob. caused an *a*.
20:22 Lord set *a*. against Am.

**AMEN.**

*Num*. 5:22 woman shall say *a*. *a*.
*Deut*. 27:15 people shall say *a*.
1 *K*. 1:36 Benaiah answered *a*.
1 *Chr*. 16:36 people said *a*. and
*Ps*. 41:13 everlasting, *a*. and *a*.
72:19 with his glory, *a*. and *a*.
89:52 blessed evermore, *a*. and *a*.
106:48 let all the people say *a*.
*Jer*. 28:6 even Jeremiah said *a*.
*Mat*. 6:13 the glory for ever, *a*.
1 *Cor*. 14:16 unlearned say *a*.
2 *Cor*. 1:20 in him yea and *a*.
*Rev*. 1:18 alive for evermore *a*.
3:14 these things saith the *a*.
5:14 the four beasts said *a*. 19:4
22:20 *a*. even so, come, L. Jesus

**AMEND, S.**

*Lev*. 5:16 he shall make *a*.
*Jer*. 7:3 *a*. ways, 5; 26:13; 35:15
*John* 4:52 when he began to *a*.

**AMERCE.**

*Deut*. 22:19 *a*. him in 100 shekels

AMETHYST. *See* AGATE *and* JACINTH.

**AMIABLE.**

*Ps*. 84:1 how *a*. are thy taber.

**AMISS.**

2 *Chr*. 6:37 done *a*.
*Dan*. 3:29 speak any thing *a*.
*Luke* 23:41 hath done nothing *a*.
*Jam*. 4:3 because ye ask *a*.

AMMAH. 2 *Sam.* 2:24
AMMI. *Hos.* 2:1

**AMMINADAB.**

*Ex.* 6:23 Aaron took daugh. of A.
*Ruth* 4:20 A. begat N. *Mat.* 1:4

AMMI-NADIB. *Cant.* 6:12

**AMMON.**

*Gen.* 19:38 f. of children of A.

**AMMONITE, S.**

*Deut.* 23:3 A. not enter congreg.
1 *Sam.* 11:11 slew A. till heat of
1 *K.* 11:1 S. loved women of A.
2 *Chr.* 26:8 A. gifts to Uzziah
*Ezr.* 9:1 the abomination of A.

**AMNON.**

2 *Sam.* 3:2 D's first-born was A.
13:2, 26, 28; 1 *Chr.* 3:1; 4:20

**AMON.**

1 *K.* 22:26 back to A.
2 *K.* 21:18 A. reigned; 23 slain
2 *Chr.* 33:22 A. sacrificed to img.
*Neh.* 7:59 out of capt. child. of A.
*Mat.* 1:10 Manasses begat A.

**AMORITE, S.**

*Gen.* 15:16 iniq. of A. not full.
48:22 I took fr. A. with my sw.
*Deut.* 20:17 utterly destroy the A.
*Jos.* 10:12 L. delivered up A.
*Jud.* 11:23 L. dispossessed the A.
1 *Sam.* 7:14 bet. Israel and A.
2 *Sam.* 21:2 Gibeonites were of A.
*Ezek.* 16:3 fath. an A. moth., 45

**AMOS, *or* AMOZ.**

2 *K.* 19:2 Is. the son of A. 20; 20:1; 2 *Chr.* 26:22; 32:20, 32; *Is.* 1:1; 2:1; 13:1; 20:2; 37:2, 21; 38:1
*Amos* 7:14 A. said I was no prop.
*Luke* 3:25 Matta. was son of A.

AMPHIPOLIS. *Acts* 17:1
AMPLIAS. *Rom.* 16:8

**AMRAM.**

*Ex.* 6:18 sons of Kohath, A.
1 *Chr.* 1:41 sons of Dishon, A.
6:3 children of A. Aaron
*Ezr.* 10:34 sons of B., Maadi, A.

ANAH. *Gen.* 36:24

**ANAK.**

*Num.* 13:28 children of A. 33
*Deut.* 9:2 bef. the children of A.?
*Jos.* 15:14 sons of A. *Jud.* 1:20

**ANAKIM.**

*Deut.* 2:10 people tall as A. 9:2
*Jos.* 11:22 none of the A. were
14:15 Arba was great among A.

ANAMMELECH. 2 *K.* 17:31.

**ANANIAS.**

*Acts* 5:5 A. hearing fell down
9:12 vision A. coming, 22:12
23:2 A. commanded to smite
24:1 A. descended

**ANATHEMA.**

1 *Cor.* 16:22 be *a.* maran-atha

**ANATHOTH.**

*Jos.* 21:18 A. with her suburbs
1 *K.* 2:26 to A. to thine own
1 *Chr.* 7:8 sons of Becher, A. and
*Neh.* 10:19 A. sealed the cov.
*Is.* 10:30 thy voice, O poor A.
*Jer.* 11:23 evil on the men of A.
29:27 reproved Jeremiah of A.
32:7 my field that is in A. 8.

**ANCESTORS.**

*Lev.* 26:45 covenant of their *a.*

**ANCHOR, S.**

*Acts* 27:30 would have cast *a.*
*Heb.* 6:19 hope we have as an *a.*

**ANCIENT.**

*Deut.* 33:15 things of *a.* moun.
*Jud.* 5:21 that *a.* river, Kishon
2 *K.* 19:25 *a.* times *Is.* 37:26
1 *Chr.* 4:22 these are *a.* things
*Ezr.* 3:12 *a.* men that had seen
*Job.* 12:12 with the *a.* is wisdom
*Prov.* 22:28 rem. not *a.* landmark
*Is.* 3:2 *a.* the Lord doth take
9:15 the *a.* and honorable he is
19:11 I am the son of *a.* kings
23:7 antiquity is of *a.* days
44:7 I appointed the *a.* people
47:6 the *a.* laid thy yoke
51:9 awake as in the *a* days
*Jer.* 18:15 stumble from *a.* paths
*Ezek.* 9:6 began at the *a.* men
*Dan.* 7:9 the *a.* of days did sit
13 like Son of man came to *a.*
22 till the *a.* of days came

**ANCIENTS.**

1 *Sam.* 24:13 proverb of the *a.*
*Ps.* 119:100 more than the *a.*
*Is.* 3:14 into judgment with *a.*
24:23 L. shall reign bef. his *a.*
*Jer.* 19:1 of *a.* of people and *a.*
*Ezek.* 7:26 shall per. from the *a.*
8:12 hast seen what the *a.* do?
27:9 *a.* of Gebal thy calkers

**ANCLE-BONES.**

*Acts* 3:7 *a.-b.* received strength.

**ANCLES.**

*Ezek.* 47:3 waters were to the *a.*

**ANDREW.**

*Mark* 13:3 A. asked privately
*John* 1:40 which heard was A.

ANDRONICUS. *Rom.* 16:7
ANER. *Gen.* 14:24; 1 *Chr.* 6:70

**ANGEL.**

*Gen.* 22:11 *a.* said, Abraham
24:7 send his *a.* before thee. 40
48:16 the *a.* who redeemed me
*Ex.* 23:20 send *a.* before thee, 23; 32:34; 33:2
*Num.* 20:16 sent an *a.*
*Jud.* 13:19 *a.* did wondrously
2 *Sam.* 24:16 the *a.* stretched out his hand, the *a.* 1 *Chr.* 21:15
17 he saw the *a.* that smote
1 *K.* 13:18 *a.* spake by the word
19:5 an *a.* touched Elijah
1 *Chr.* 21:15 G. sent an *a.* to Jeru.
20 Ornan turned and saw the *a.*
27 Lord com. *a.* and he put up
2 *Chr.* 32:21 an *a.* which cut off
*Ec.* 5:6 bef. *a.* it was an error
*Is.* 63:9 the *a.* of his presence
*Dan.* 3:28 God who hath sent *a.*
6:22 sent his *a.* and shut up
*Hos.* 12:4 had power over the *a.*
*Zec.* 1:9 *a.* that talked, 4:5
3:4 stood before *a.*
*Mat.* 28:5 *a.* answer. the women
*Luke* 1:13 *a.* said, fear not, Zach.
19 *a.* answered, I am Gabriel
26 in sixth month the *a.* Gab'l
30 the *a.* said, Fear not, Mary
35 *a.* answ., Holy Ghost shall
2:10 *a.* said to the shepherds
13 suddenly with *a.* a multit.
21 so named of the *a.*
22:43 an *a.* strengthening him
*John* 5:4 *a.* went down at a c. s.
12:29 an *a.* spake to him
*Acts* 6:15 as the face of an *a.*
7:35 *a.* that appear. in the bush
38 in wilderness with the *a.*
10:7 *a.* which spake to Cornel.
22 warned by a holy *a.* to send
11:13 he had seen *a.* in house
12:8 the *a.* said to Peter, bind
9 true which was done by *a.*
10 the *a.* departed from him
11 sent his *a.* and delivered me
15 then said they, it is his *a.*
23:8 say, neither *a.* nor spirit
9 if an *a.* hath spoken to him
2 *Cor.* 11:14 transf. into *a.* of l.
*Gal.* 1:8 though we or an *a.*
*Rev.* 1:1 sig. it by *a.* to John
2:1 *a.* of ch., 8, 12, 18; 3:1, 7, 14
5:2 I saw strong *a.* proclaiming
7:2 *a.* ascending from the east
8:3 *a.* came and stood at the al.
4 ascended out of the *a.* hand
5. *a.* took the censer
7 first *a.* sounded: 8 second *a.*
8:10 third *a.*; 12 fourth *a.*
13 I heard an *a.* flying through
9:1 fifth *a.* s. 13 sixth *a.*
11 the *a.* of the bottomless pit
14 sixth *a.* loose the four angs.
10:1 *a.* come down, 18:1; 20:1
5 *a.* which I saw stand on sea
7 in days of voice of seventh *a.*
8 take the book in hand of *a.*
11:15 seventh *a.* sounded
14:6 *a.* fly in the midst of heav.
8 another *a.* saying, Babylon is
19 the *a.* thrust in his sickle
16:1 *a.* poured out vial, 3, 4, etc.
5 *a.* of the waters
17:7 *a.* said, wherefore marvel?
18:21 mighty *a.* took up a stone
*Rev.* 19:17 an *a.* standing in the
21:17 of a man, that is of the *a.*
22:16 I Jesus have sent mine *a.*

**ANGEL of God.**

*Ex.* 14:19 *a. of God* removed
*Jud.* 13:6 counten. of *a. of God*
1 *Sam.* 29:9 good as an *a. of God*
2 *Sam.* 14:17 an *a. of God*, 19:27
20 accord. to wisd. of *a. of G.*
*Acts* 27:23 by me the *a. of G.*
*Gal.* 4:14 rec. me as an *a. of God*

**ANGEL of the Lord.**

*Gen.* 16:7 *a. of the L.* found Hag.
22:11 *a. of the L.* called 15
*Num.* 22:23 *a. of the L.* 25, 27
31 Balaam saw *a. of Lord*
*Jud.* 5:23 Meroz, said *a. of L.*
6:11 *a. of the Lord* sat under
12 *a. of the L.* appeared to G.
21 *a. of L.* put forth end of st.
13:3 *a. of L.* appeared to woman
16 he was an *a. of L.* 21
20 *a. of the L.* ascended
2 *Sam.* 24:16 *a. of the L.* was by the thresh-pl. 1 *Chr.* 21:15
2 *K.* 19:35 *a. of the L.* smote in camp, *Is.* 37:36
1 *Chr.* 21:12 *a. of the L.* destroy.
18 *a. of the L.* commanded G.
30 because of s. of *a. of the L.*
*Ps.* 34:7 *a. of the L.* encampeth
35:5 let *a. of the L.* chase them
6 let *a. of the L.* perse. them
*Zec.* 1:12 *a. of the L.* answered
3:5 *a. of the L.* stood by Joshua
6 *a. of the L.* protested
12:8 as the *a. of the L.* before
*Mat.* 1:20 *a. of L.* ap. in dm. 2:13, 9
24 Jos. did as *a. of L.* had bid.
28:2 *a. of L.* descended
*Luke* 1:11 Zacharias an *a of L.*
2:9 *a. of L.* came upon them
*Acts* 5:19 *a. of L.* opened prison
8:26 *a. of the L.* spake to Philip
12:23 *a. of the L.* smote Herod.

**ANGELS.**

*Gen.* 19:1 came two *a.* to Sodom
*Ps.* 8:5 low. than *a.* *Heb.* 2:7, 9
68:17 are thousands of *a.*
78:25 man did eat *a.*'s food
49 sending evil *a.* among them
*Mat.* 4:11 *a.* ministered, *Mk.* 1:13
13:39 the reapers are the *a.*
49 the *a.* shall sever the wick.
18:10 their *a.* behold face of G.
24:36 *a.* of heaven, *Mark* 13:32
25:31 all the holy *a.* with him
26:53 twelve legions of *a.*
*Mark* 8:38 Son of man cometh with the holy *a.* *Luke* 9:26
12:25 are as the *a.* in heaven
*Luke* 2:15 as the *a.* were gone
16:22 was carried by the *a.*

20:36 equal unto the a.
24:23 also seen a vision of a.
*John* 20:12 seeth two a. in white
*Acts* 7:53 by disposition of a.
*Rom.* 8:38 nor a. able to separate
1 *Cor.* 4:9 spect. to world, to a.
6:3 that we shall judge a.?
11:10 power because of the a.
13:1 tongues of men and a.
*Gal.* 3:19 ordained by a.
*Col.* 2:18 in worship. of a.
2 *Thes.* 1:7 rev. with mighty a.
1 *Tim.* 3:16 of a. preached to Ge.
5:21 before G. and the elect a.
*Heb.* 1:4 much better than the a.
5 to which of the a. said he, 13
7 who maketh his a. spirits
2:2 word spoken by a. steadfast
5 to the a. not put in subject.
16 not nature of a. but seed
12:22 innum. company of a.
13:2 entertained a. unawares
1 *Pet.* 1:12 a. desire to look into
3:22 a. and powers being subj.
2 *Pet.* 2:4 if God spared not the a.
11 whereas a greater in power
*Jude* 6 a. kept not first estate
*Rev.* 1:20 stars a. of churches
5:11 voice of many a. about th.
7:1 four a. on the four corners
2 with loud voice to the four a.
11 the a. stood round the th.
8:13 trumpet of a. yet to sound
9:14 loose the four a. bound
15 the a. were loosed
14:10 torment. in pres. of h. a.
21:12 and the gates twelve a.

**ANGELS of God.**

*Gen.* 28:12 a. *of G.* asc. *John* 1:51
32:1 Jacob went his way, and a. *of God* met him
*Mat.* 22:30 but as a. *of God* in heaven, *Mark* 12:25
*Luke* 12:8 him shall the Son confess before a. *of God*
9 be denied before the a. *of G.*
15:10 in presence of a. *of God*
*Heb.* 1:6 the a. *of God* worship

**His ANGELS.**

*Job* 4:18 *his* a. charged with
*Ps.* 91:11 give *his* a. charge, *Mat.* 4:6; *Luke* 4:10
103:20 ye *his* a. that excel
104:4 *his* a. spirits, *Heb.* 1:7
148:2 praise ye him all *his* a.
*Mat.* 13:41 shall send forth *his* a.
16:27 glory of his F. with *his* a.
24:31 *his* a. with s., *Mark* 13:27
25:41 fire for devil and *his* a.
*Rev.* 3:5 will confess before *his* a.
12:7 M. and *his* a. the dragon
9 drag. was cast out, and *his* a.

**ANGER, Verb.**

*Rom.* 10:19 fool. nation I will a.

**ANGER.**

*Gen.* 27:45 thy brother's a. turn
44:18 let not thine a. burn
49:7 cursed be their a.
*Ex.* 32:19 Moses' a. waxed hot
*Deut.* 9:19 I was afraid of the a.
13:17 the fierceness of his a.
29:24 the heat of this great a.?
*Jud.* 8:3 their a. was abated
*Job* 9:13 G. will not withdraw a.
*Ps.* 21:9 oven in time of thine a.
30:5 his a. endureth but a mom.
37:8 cease from a. and forsake
38:3 no soundness because of a.
69:24 wrathful a. take hold
74:1 why doth thy a. smoke
78:21 a. came up against Israel
38 many a time turn. he his a.
49 cast the fierceness of his a.
50 he made a way to his a.
85:3 turned from fierceness of a.
4 cause a. towards us to cease
5 out a. to all generations
90:7 consumed by thine a.
11 knoweth power of thine a.
103:9 his a. for ever, *Jer.* 3:5
*Prov.* 15:1 griev. words stir up a.
19:11 discretion deferreth his a.
21:14 a gift in secret pacifieth a.
22:8 the rod of his a. shall fail
27:4 and a. is outrageous
*Ec.* 7:9 a. resteth in bosom
*Is.* 5:25 his a. is not turned away, 9:12, 17, 21; 10:4
7:4 fear not for the a. of Resin
10:5 the rod of mine a. and staff
25 my a. in their destruction
12:1 angry, thine a. is turned
13:9 cometh with fierce a.
13 day of fierce a. *Lam.* 1:12
30:27 name of L. burn. with a.
30 the indignation of his a.
42:25 on him fury of his a.
48:9 will I defer mine a.
66:15 come to render his a.
*Jer.* 2:35 his a. shall turn
3:12 cause mine a. to fall on you, I will not keep mine a.
4:26 cities brok. down by his a.
7:20 a. be poured on this place
18:23 deal with them in thine a.
25:38 desolate because of his a.
32:31 city, provocat. of mine a.
36:7 great is the a. L. hath pron.
42:18 as mine a. on Jerusalem
44:6 mine a. was poured forth
49:37 evil on them, my fierce a.
*Lam.* 2:1 his footstool in day of a.
6 in the indignation of his a.
21 hast slain them in thine a.
22 the Lord's a. none escaped
3:43 thou hast covered with a.
4:11 poured out his fierce a.
*Ezek.* 5:13 thus a. be accompl.
7:3 send mine a. upon thee
8 accomp. a. on thee, 20:8, 21
35:11 will do accord. to thine a.
*Dan.* 9:16 let thine a. be turned
*Hos.* 11:9 not execute mine a.
14:4 for mine a. is turned away
*Amos* 1:11 his a. did tear
*Jon.* 3:9 God turn from fierce a.
*Mic.* 7:18 his a. for ever
*Nah.* 1:6 who can abide his a.?
*Hab.* 3:8 thine a. ag. the rivers
*Zep.* 3:8 to pour all my fierce a.
*Mark* 3:5 looked on them with a.
*Eph.* 4:31 a. be put, *Col.* 3:8

**ANGER of the Lord.**

*Num.* 25:4 fierce a. *of the L.*
32:14 to augment a. *of the L.*
*Deut.* 29:20 a. *of the L.* shall s.
*Jud.* 2:14 a. *of the L.* against Israel, 20; 3:8; 10:7
2 *K.* 24:20 thro' the a. *of the L.* it came to pass, *Jer.* 52:3
*Jer.* 4:8 a. *of the Lord* is not t.
12:13 fierce a. *of the L.* 25:37
23:20 a. *of the L.* shall not, 30:24
51:45 from a. *of the L.*
*Lam.* 4:16 a. *of the L.* hath
*Zep.* 2:2 before a. *of the L.* come
3 hid in day of a. *of the L.*

**In ANGER.**

*Gen.* 49:6 *in* a. they slew a man
*Deut.* 29:23 L. overthrew *in* a.
28 the L. rooted them out *in* a.
*Job* 9:5 overturn. them *in* his a.
18:4 he teareth hims. *in* his a.
21:17 distributeth sorrows *in* a.
35:15 he hath visited *in* his a.
*Ps.* 6:1 not *in* a. *Jer.* 10:24
7:6 *in* thine a. lift up thyself
27:9 put not thy serv. away *in* a.
56:7 *in* a. cast down the people
77:9 *in* a. shut up his mercies?
*Is.* 13:3 called mighty ones *in* a.
14:6 he that ruled nations *in* a.
63:3 I will tread them *in* a. 6
*Jer.* 21:5 against you, even *in* a.
32:37 driven them *in* mine a.
33:5 I have slain *in* mine a.
*Lam.* 2:1 Lord covered Zion with a cloud *in* his a.
3 cut off *in* a. horn of Israel
3:66 destroy them *in* a.
*Ezek.* 5:15 execute judgm. *in* a.
13:13 shower *in* mine a.
22:20 I gather you *in* a.
43:8 consumed them *in* mine a.
*Dan.* 11:20 destro'd, neither *in* a.
*Hos.* 13:11 gave a king *in* mine a.
*Mic.* 5:15 execute veng. *in* a.
*Hab.* 3:12 thresh heathen *in* a.

**ANGER kindled.**

*Ex.* 4:14 a. of L. *k.* against M.
*Num.* 11:1 a. of the Lord was *k.* 10; 12:9; 22:22
25:3 a. of the L. was *k.* against Israel. 32:13; *Jos.* 7:1; 2 *Sam.* 24:1; 2 *Kings* 13:3
*Deut.* 6:15 lest a. be *k.* against
7:4 so will a. be *k.* against you
29:27 a. of the L. *k.* against this
31:17 a. be *k.* in that day, *Jos.* 23:16
32:22 *k.* in mine a. *Jer.* 15:14
2 *Sam.* 6:7 a. of the Lord was *k.* against Uzziah, 1 *Chr.* 13:10
12:5 David's a. *k.* against
*Is.* 5:25 a. of L. *k.* against
*Jer.* 17:4 have *k.* a fire in mine a.
*Zec.* 10:3 a. *k.* ag. the shepherds

**Provoke *or* Provoked to ANGER.**

*Deut.* 32:16 abominations *p. t.* a.
21 they have *provoked* me *to* a.
*Jud.* 2:12 and *pr.* L. *to* a.
1 *K.* 16:2 *pr.* me *to* a. with sins, 2 *K.* 17:11; *Jer.* 11:17; 32:29, 32; *Ezek.* 16:26
2 *K.* 21:15 *pr. to* a. since day
22:17 forsaken me that they might *pro.* me *to* a. 2 *Chr.* 34:25; *Jer.* 25:7
*Ps.* 78:58 *pro.* him *to* a. with high places, 106:29
*Prov.* 20:2 whoso *pro. to* a.
*Is.* 1:4 *pro.* Holy One of Is. *to* a.
65:3 a people that *pro.* me *to* a.
*Hos.* 12:14 Ephr. *pro.* him *to* a.
*Col.* 3:21 *pro.* not your chil. *to* a.

**Slow to ANGER.**

*Neh.* 9:17 pardon, *slow to* a.
*Ps.* 103:8 *slow to* a. 145:8
*Prov.* 15:18 he *s. to* a. appeaseth
16:32 *s. to* a. better than mighty
*Joel* 2:13 *slow to* a. of great kindness, *Jon.* 4:2
*Nah.* 1:3 Lord is *sl. to* a.

**ANGERED.**

*Ps.* 106:32 a. him at waters

**ANGLE.**

*Is.* 19:8 all they that cast a.
*Hab.* 1:15 they take up with a.

**ANGRY.**

*Gen.* 18:30 let not L. be a. 32
45:5 be not a. that ye sold me
*Lev.* 10:16 Moses a. with Eleazar
*Deut.* 1:37 L. a. with me 4:21
9:20 L. was very a. with Aaron
*Jud.* 18:25 lest a. fellows run on
1 *K.* 8:46 thou be a. 2 *Chr.* 6:36
11:9 L. was a. with Solomon
2 *K.* 17:18 was a. with Israel
*Ezr.* 9:14 wouldst be a. with us
*Ps.* 2:12 kiss the S., lest he be a.
7:11 God is a. with the wicked
76:7 when thou art a.
*Ps.* 79:5 how long a.? 80:4; 85:5
*Prov.* 14:17 soon a. dealeth fool
21:19 than with an a. woman

22:24 friendship with an a. man
25:23 so doth an a. countenance
29:22 a. man stirreth up strife
Ec. 5:6 God be a. at thy voice?
7:9 be not hasty in spirit to be a.
Cant. 1:6 children were a.
Is. 12:1 thou wast a. with me
Ezek. 16:42 will be no more a.
Jon. 4:1 Jonah was very a.
4:4 doest thou well to be a.?
9 I do well to be a. unto death
Mat. 5:22 is a. with brother
Luke 14:21 master of h. being a.
15:28 a. and would not
John 7:23 are ye a. at me bec.
Eph. 4:26 be a. and sin not
Tit. 1:7 a bishop not soon a.
Rev. 11:18 the nations were a.

**ANGUISH.**

Ex. 6:9 not to M. for a.
Deut. 2:25 tremble, and be in a.
2 Sam. 1:9 slay me, for a. is come
Job 7:11 I will speak in a. of spir.
15:24 a. shall make him afraid
Ps. 119:143 and a. have taken
Prov. 1:27 when distress and a.
Is. 8:22 and behold dimness of a.
30:6 into land of trouble and a.
Jer. 4:31 the a. as of her that
John 16:21 no more her a. for joy
Rom. 2:9 tribulation and a. upon
2 Cor. 2:4 out of a. of heart

**ANISE.**

Mat. 23:23 pay tithe of mint, a.

ANNA. Luke 2:36
ANNAS. Lu. 3:2; John 18:13, 24

**ANOINT.**

Ex. 28:41 shalt a. 30:30; 40:15
29:7 take oil and a. him, 40:13
36 shalt a. the altar, 40:10
30:26 a. the tabernacle, 40:9
Lev. 16:32 whom he shall a.
Deut. 28:40 shalt not a. thyself
Jud. 9:8 trees went to a. a king
15 if in truth ye a. me king
1 Sam. 9:16 a. him captain
15:1 sent me to a. thee king
16:3 a. him whom I name
12 L. said, Arise, a. him
2 Sam. 14:2 a. not thys. with oil
1 K. 1:34 Zadok a. him king
19:15 a. Hazael king
16 a. Jehu, a. Elisha
Is. 21:5 princes, a. the shield
Dan. 9:24 and a. the most Holy
10:3 neither did I a. myself
Amos 6:6 a. themselves
Mic. 6:15 the olives, but not a.
Mat. 6:17 when thou fastest a.
Mark 14:8 is come to a. my body
16:1 spices that they might a.
Luke 7:46 head thou didst not a.
Rev. 3:18 a. thine eyes

**ANOINTED.**

Lev. 8:10 a. the tabernacle
11 a. the altar, Num. 7:1
12 A.'s head, and a. him
1 Sam. 10:1 the L. a. thee capt.
15:17 a. Saul
16:13 a. David, 2 Sam. 2:4, 7; 5:3, 17; 12:7; 2 K. 9:3, 6, 12; 1 Chr. 11:3; 14:8
2 Sam. 2:7 Judah have a. me k.
3:39 I am weak, though a. king
12:20 David arose, and a. hims.
23:1 David the a. of God said
Is. 61:1 a. me to preach, Lu. 4:18
Ezek. 28:14 a. cherub that covers
Luke 7:38 kissed his feet and a.
46 this woman hath a. my feet
John 9:6 he a. the eyes with clay
11:2 Mary which a. the Lord
12:3 Mary a. feet of Jesus
Acts 4:27 child J. thou hast a.
10:38 God a. Jesus of Nazar.
2 Cor. 1:21 hath a. us is God

**ANOINTED Ones.**

Zec. 4:14 a. ones which stand

**His ANOINTED.**

1 Sam. 2:10 exalt horn of his a.
12:3 against the L. and his a.
5 the L. and his a. is witness
2 Sam. 22:51 showeth mercy to his a. Ps. 18:50
Ps. 2:2 and against his a.
20:6 the Lord saveth his a.
28:8 saving strength of his a.
Is. 45:1 saith L. to his a. to C.

**Lord's ANOINTED.**

1 Sam. 16:6 Lord's a. is before
24:6 my master, the Lord's a.
10 my hand against Lord's a.
1 Sam. 26:9 L. a. and the guiltl.
16 have not kept the Lord's a.
2 Sam. 1:14 to destroy L. a.
19:21 he cursed L. a.
Lam. 4:20 a. of L. taken

**Mine ANOINTED.**

1 Sam. 2:35 walk before mine a.
1 Chr. 16:22 touch not mine a. Ps. 105:15
Ps. 132:17 a lamp for mine a.

**ANOINTED with Oil.**

2 Sam. 1:21 though not a. with o.
Ps. 45:7 a. w. o. of glad. Heb. 1:9
89:20 with holy oil have I a.
92:10 I shall be a. with fresh o.
Mark 6:13 a. with oil many sick

**Thine ANOINTED.**

2 Chr. 6:42 turn not away the face of thine a. Ps. 132:10
Ps. 84:9 look on face of thine a.
89:38 been wroth with thine a.
51 footsteps of thine a.
Hab. 3:13 salvation with thine a.

**ANOINTEST.**

Ps. 23:5 a. my head with oil

**ANOINTING.**

Ex. 40:15 a. everlast. priesthood
Is. 10:27 destroyed bec. of a.
1 John 2:27 a. teacheth all things

**ANOINTING Oil.**

Ex. 37:29 made the holy a. oil
Lev. 8:12 a. oil on Aaron's head
10:7 a. oil of the L. is upon you
Num. 4:16 Elea. pertaineth a. oil
Jam. 5:14 a. with o. in name of L.

**ANON.**

Mat. 13:20 a. with joy receiv. it
Mark 1:30 mother lay sick and a.

**ANOTHER.**

1 Sam. 10:6 shalt be turned to a.
Job 19:27 shall behold and not a.
Ps. 109:8 let a. take, Acts 1:20
Prov. 25:9 dis. not a secret to a.
27:2 let a. praise thee, and not
Is. 42:8 my glory not to a. 48:11
65:15 his servants by a. name
Hos. 3:3 shalt not be for a. man
4:4 let no man reprove a.
Mat. 11:3 or do we look for a.?
Mark 14:19 a. said, Is it I?
Luke 16:7 to a. How much owest
2 Cor. 11:4 a. Jesus, a. spirit, or a.
Gal. 1:7 which is not a. but
6:4 rejoic. in himself, not in a.
Heb. 3:13 exhort one a. 10:25

One ANOTHER. See LOVE.

**One against ANOTHER.**

1 Sam. 2:25 if one man sin a. a.
Jer. 13:14 dash them one a. a.
1 Cor. 4:6 puffed up one a. a.
Jam. 5:9 grudge not one a. a.

**One for ANOTHER.**

1 Cor. 11:33 tarry one for a.
Jam. 5:16 pray one for a. that ye

**ANSWER.**

Gen. 41:16 Phar. an a. of peace
Deut. 20:11 if city make a.
2 Sam. 24:13 see what a. I ret'rn
Job 19:16 and he gave me no a.
32:3 found no a. and condem'd
35:12 cry, but none giveth a.
Prov. 15:1 soft a. turneth away
23 hath joy by the a. of his
16:1 a. of the tongue is from L.
24:26 lips that giveth right a.
Cant. 5:6 he gave no a.
Mic. 3:7 for there is no a. of God
Luke 20:26 marvelled at his a.
John 1:22 that we may give a.
19:9 Jesus gave him no a.
Rom. 11:4 what saith a. of God?
1 Cor. 9:3 mine a. is this
2 Tim. 4:16 at my first a.
1 Pet. 3:15 be ready to give an a.
21 the a. of a good conscience

**ANSWERS.**

Job 21:34 in your a. remaineth
34:36 his a. for wicked men
Luke 2:47 were aston. at his a.

**ANSWER, Verb.**

Gen. 30:33 righteousn. a. for me
Deut. 27:15 people shall a. amen
1 K. 18:29 voice, nor any to a.
Job 13:22 call thou, and I will a.
23:5 the words he would a. me
31:14 he visiteth what a. him?
33:12 will a. G. is greater, 35:4
40:2 reproveth God, let him a.
Ps. 27:7 have mercy and a. me
65:5 in right, wilt thou a. us?
86:7 will call, thou wilt a. me
102:2 when I call a. me speedily
108:6 thy right hand, and a. me
Ps. 143:1 in thy faithful. a. me
Prov. 15:28 heart studieth to a.
22:21 mightest a. words of truth
26:5 a. a fool accord. to his folly
Is. 14:32 what a. the messengers
50:2 was there none to a.? 66:4
58:9 shalt thou call, L. will a.
Dan. 3:16 not careful to a. thee
Hab. 2:1 what a. when reproved
Mat. 22:46 no man was able to a.
Mark 11:30 heaven or of men? a.
14:40 wist they what to a.
Luke 11:7 from within shall a.
12:11 ye shall a. or say
13:25 he shall a. I know you not
21:14 not to meditate what ye a.
2 Cor. 5:12 somewhat to a. them
Col. 4:6 how to a. every man

**I will ANSWER.**

Job 13:22 call, I will a. 14:15; Ps. 91:15; Jer. 33:3
Is. 65:24 they call I will a.

**Not ANSWER.**

2 K. 18:36 king's commandment was a. him not, Is. 36:21
Job 9:3 a. him one of a thousand
Prov. 1:28 they shall call I not a.
26:4 a. not a fool accord. to his
29:19 understand, he will not a.
Is. 65:12 I called, ye did not a.
Jer. 7:27 they will not a. thee
Luke 14:6 they could not a. him
22:68 will not a. nor let me go

**ANSWERED.**

Jud. 8:8 a. as men of Succoth a.
1 Sam. 3:4 he a. Here am I, 16
1 K. 12:13 the king a. roughly, 2 Chr. 10:13
18:26 voice, nor any that a.
2 Chr. 25:9 a. the Lord is able
Job 11:2 multit. of words be a.?
Ezek. 37:3 I a. O L. thou knowest
Dan. 2:14 D. a. with counsel
Mat. 27:12 he a. nothing 14; Mark 14:61; 15:3, 5; Luke 23:9
Mark 12:28 perceiv. he a. well
34 Jesus saw he a. discreetly
Acts 22:8 I a. Who art thou, L.?
25:8 he a. for himself, 26:1

**ANSWERED,** *meant of God.*
*Gen.* 35:3 *a.* me in my distress
*Ex.* 19:19 M. spake, and G. *a.*
2 *Sam.* 21:1 L. *a.* It is for Saul
1 *Chr.* 21:26 *a.* from heaven
28 David saw Lord had *a.* him
*Ps.* 81:7 I *a.* thee in the secret
99:6 on the L., and he *a.* them
118:5 the L. *a.* me and set me
*Jer.* 23:35 hath the Lord *a.* 37

**ANSWERED not.**
1 *Sam.* 4:20 *a. not* nor did regard
2 *Sam.* 22:42 looked, but *a.* them *not*, *Ps.* 18:41
1 *K.* 18:21 people *a.* him *not*
2 *K.* 18:36; *Is.* 36:21
*Jer.* 7:13 called, ye *a. not*, 35:17
*Mat.* 15:23 he *a.* her *not* a word

**ANSWEREDST.**
*Ps.* 99:8 thou *a.* them, O Lord
138:3 when I cried thou *a.* me

**ANSWEREST.**
1 *Sam.* 26:14 *a.* thou not, Abner?
*Job* 16:3 embold. that thou *a.*?
*Mat.* 26:62 *a.* thou nothing? *Mark* 14:60; 15:4
*John* 18:22 *a.* thou the h.-p. so?

**ANSWERETH.**
1 *Sam.* 28:15 God *a.* me no more
1 *K.* 18:24 God that *a.* by fire
*Job* 12:4 on God and he *a.* him
*Prov.* 18:13 that *a.* a matter
23 but the rich *a.* roughly
27:19 as face *a.* to face, so
*Ec.* 5:20 God *a.* him in the joy
10:19 but money *a.* all things
*Gal.* 4:25 and *a.* to Jerusalem

**ANSWERING.**
*Luke* 23:40 the other *a.* rebuked
*Tit.* 2:9 obedient, not *a.* again

**ANT, S.**
*Prov.* 6:6 the *a.* thou sluggard
30:25 *a.* are a people not strong

**ANTICHRIST, S.**
1 *John* 2:18 there are many *a.*
22 *a.* denieth Father and Son
4:3 spir. of *a.* whereof ye heard
2 *John* 7 is a deceiver and an *a.*

**ANTIOCH.**
*Acts* 11:19 as far as A. 22
26 called Christians first in A.
*Gal.* 2:11 Peter to A. I withstood

ANTIPAS. *See* MARTYR.
ANTIPATRIS. *Acts* 23:31

**ANTIQUITY.**
*Is.* 23:7 joyous city, whose *a.*

**ANVIL.**
*Is.* 41:7 him that smote *a.*

**ANY.**
*Deut.* 32:39 nor *a.* that can del.
1 *K.* 18:26 nor *a.* that answered
*Job* 33:27 if *a.* say, I have sinned
*Ps.* 4:6 who will show us *a.* good?
*Is.* 44:8 is no God, I know not *a.*
*Amos* 6:10 is there yet *a.*
*Mark* 8:26 nor tell it to *a.* in t.
11:25 have aught against *a.*
*Acts* 9:2 if he found *a.*
*See* FURTHER, GOD, MAN, MORE, THING, TIME, WISE.
ANY *while.* *See* DEAD.
APACE. *See* FLEE, FLED.

**APART.**
*Ex.* 13:12 *a.* all that open
*Lev.* 15:19 she shall be put *a.*
18:19 as long as she is *a.*
*Ps.* 4:3 Lord hath set *a.* godly
*Zec.* 12:12 every family *a.* 14
*Mat.* 14:13 into a desert place *a.*
23 mountain *a.* 17:1; *Mark* 9:2
17:19 came the disciples to J. *a.*
*Mark* 6:31 come ye yourselves *a.*
*Jam.* 1:21 lay *a.* filthiness

APELLES. *Rom.* 16:10
APES. *See* PEACOCKS.

**APHEK.**
1 *Sam.* 4:1 pitched in A. 29:1
1 *K.* 20:30 the rest fled to A.
2 *K.* 13:17 the Syrians in A.

**APIECE.**
*Num.* 3:47 five shekels *a.*
17:6 gave him a rod *a.*
*Luke* 9:3 nor have two coats *a.*
*John* 2:6 two or three firkins *a.*

APOLLONIA. *Acts* 17:1

**APOLLOS.**
*Acts* 18:24 A. came to Ephesus
1 *Cor.* 1:12 and I of A. 3:4; 3:5
3:6 I planted, A. watered
4:6 in a figure transferred to A.
*Tit.* 3:13 bring Zenas and A.

APOLLYON. *Rev.* 9:11.

**APOSTLE.**
*Rom.* 1:1 Paul, called to be an *a.* 1 *Cor.* 1:1
11:13 am the *a.* of the Gentiles
1 *Cor.* 9:1 am I not an *a.*? 2
15:9 not meet to be called an *a.*
2 *Cor.* 1:1 Paul an *a.* *Eph.* 1:1; *Col.* 1:1; 1 *Tim.* 1:1; 2 *Tim.* 1:1; *Gal.* 1:1
12:12 the signs of an *a.*
1 *Tim.* 2:7 whereto I am ordained an *a.* 2 *Tim.* 1:11
*Tit.* 1:1 a servant of G. and *a.*
*Heb.* 3:1 *a.* and high-priest of our

**APOSTLES.**
*Mat.* 10:2 names of the twelve *a.*
*Mark* 6:30 the *a.* gathered
*Luke* 6:13 whom he named *a.*
9:10 the *a.* when they returned
11:49 will send prophets and *a.*
17:5 the *a.* said, Increase
22:14 down, and the twelve *a.*
24:10 told these things to *a.*
*Acts* 1:26 with the eleven *a.*
2:43 signs by the *a.* 5:12
4:35 them at *a.* feet, 37; 5:2
5:18 laid their hands on the *a.*
8:1 all scattered except the *a.*
*Rom.* 16:7 of note among the *a.*
1 *Cor.* 4:9 set forth us the *a.* last
12:28 set first *a.* 29 are all *a.*
15:9 for I am the least of the *a.*
2 *Cor.* 11:5 chiefest *a.* 12:11
13 such are false *a.*
*Gal.* 1:17 to them *a.* before me
19 other of the *a.* saw I none
*Eph.* 3:5 revealed to his holy *a.*
4:11 he gave some *a.*
1 *Thes.* 2:6 burdensome as the *a.*
2 *Pet.* 3:2 command. of us the *a.*
*Jude* 17 words spoken bef. of *a.*
*Rev.* 2:2 which they say are *a.*
18:20 rejoice over her, ye holy *a.*

**APOSTLESHIP.**
*Acts* 1:25 take part of this *a.*
*Rom.* 1:5 received grace and *a.*
1 *Cor.* 9:2 the seal of mine *a.*
*Gal.* 2:8 effectually in P. to the *a.*

**APOTHECARY.**
*Ex.* 30:25 after art of *a.*
35 conf. after art of *a.* 37:29
*Ec.* 10:1 flies cause oint of *a.*

**APPAREL.**
2 *Sam.* 12:20 D. changed his *a.*
1 *K.* 10:5 attend. of his ministers and their *a.* 2 *Chr.* 9:4
*Is.* 3:22 changeable suits of *a.*
4:1 we will wear our own *a.*
63:1 who this glorious in his *a.*
*Zep.* 1:8 clothed in strange *a.*
*Acts* 1:10 men stood in white *a.*
20:33 no man's silver or *a.*
1 *Tim.* 2:9 women in modest *a.*
*Jam.* 2:2 man come in goodly *a.*
1 *Pet.* 3:3 or putting on *a.*
*See* ROYAL.

**APPARELLED.**
2 *Sam.* 13:18 daughters were *a.*
*Luke* 7:25 are gorgeously *a.*

**APPARENTLY.**
*Num* 12:8 will I speak *a.*

**APPEAL, ED.**
*Acts* 25:11 I *a.* unto Cesar, 21
26:32 at liberty, if he had not *a.*
28:19 constrained to *a.* to Cesar

**APPEAR.**
*Gen.* 1:9 let the dry land *a.*
*Ex.* 23:15 none *a.* before me empty, 34:20; *Deut.* 16:16
34:24 when thou shalt go to *a.*
*Deut.* 31:11 Israel *a.* before L.
*Ps.* 42:2 shall I come and *a.*
90:16 work *a.* to thy servants
*Cant.* 2:12 flowers *a.* on earth
4:1 flock of goats that *a.* 6:5
*Is.* 1:12 ye come to *a.* before me
*Jer.* 13:26 that thy shame may *a.*
*Ezek.* 21:24 doings, your sins *a.*
*Mat.* 6:16 may *a.* to men to fast
23:28 ye outwardly *a.* righteous
24:30 *a.* the sign of the Son
*Luke* 11:44 as graves which *a.*
19:11 kingdom of God should *a.*
*Acts* 26:16 in which I will *a*
*Rom.* 7:13 that it might *a.* sin
2 *Cor.* 5:10 *a.* before judg.-seat
*Col.* 3:4 Christ our life shall *a.*
1 *Tim.* 4:15 profiting may *a.*
*Heb.* 9:24 to *a.* in the presence
28 *a.* the second time
11:3 of things which do *a.*
1 *Pet.* 4:18 where shall ungod. *a.*?
5:4 when chief Sheph. shall *a.*
1 *John* 2:28 when he shall *a.*
3:2 not yet *a.* what we shall be, when he shall *a.* we shall
*Rev.* 3:18 nakedness do not *a.*

**APPEAR,** *referred to God.*
*Lev.* 9:4 to-day L. will *a.* 6
16:2 I will *a.* in the cloud
1 *Sam.* 2:27 *a.* to the house
2 *Chr.* 1:7 did God *a.* to Solomon
*Ps.* 102:16 shall *a.* in his glory
*Is.* 66:5 he shall *a.* to your joy
*Acts* 26:16 in which I will *a.*

**APPEARANCE.**
*Num.* 9:15 as the *a.* of fire, 16
1 *Sam.* 16:7 looketh on outw. *a.*
*Dan.* 8:15 the *a.* of a man, 10:18
10:6 his face as *a.* of lightning
*John* 7:24 accord. to the *a.*
2 *Cor.* 5:12 which glory in *a.*
10:7 things after the outward *a.*
1 *Thes.* 5:22 abstain from all *a.*

**APPEARED.**
*Ex.* 4:1 L. hath not *a.* to thee
6:3 I *a.* by name of G. Almighty
1 *K.* 11:9 had *a.* to Solomon
*Jer.* 31:3 the L. hath *a.* of old
*Mat.* 2:7 what time the star *a.*
13:26 then *a.* the tares also
17:3 *a.* Moses and E. *Mark* 9:4
27:53 holy city, and *a.* to many
*Mark* 16:9 Jesus *a.* first to Mary
12 he *a.* in another form
14 after he *a.* to the eleven
*Luke* 1:11 there *a.* to him
9:31 who *a.* in glory, and spake
22:43 *a.* an angel, strengthening
24:34 L. is risen, *a.* to Simon
*Acts* 7:2 God *a.* to father Abra.
9:17 Jesus, that *a.* to thee in
26:16 I have *a.* for this purpose
27:20 neither sun nor stars *a.*
*Tit* 2:11 grace of God hath *a.*
3:4 after the love of God *a.*
*Heb.* 9:26 he *a.* to put away sin
*Rev.* 12:1 there *a.* a great w. 3

**APPEARETH.**
*Ps.* 84:7 in Zion *a.* before God
*Prov.* 27:25 the hay *a.*

*Jer.* 6:1 evil *a.* out of the north
*Mal.* 3:2 shall stand when he *a.*
*Jam.* 4:14 life as a vapor that *a.*

**APPEARING.**
1 *Tim.* 6:14 keep com. till *a.* L.
2 *Tim.* 1:10 manifest by the *a.*
4:1 quick and dead at his *a.*
8 to them also that love his *a.*
*Tit.* 2:13 looking for glorious *a.*
1 *Pet.* 1:7 to praise at the *a.* of J.

**APPEASE.**
*Gen.* 32:20 I will *a.* him

**APPEASED, ETH.**
*Est.* 2:1 Ahasuerus *a.*
*Prov.* 15:18 s. to anger, *a.* strife
*Acts* 19:35 town-clerk had *a.*

**APPERTAIN.**
*Num.* 16:30 swallow them, with all that *a.*
*Jer.* 10:7 for to thee doth it *a.*
*See* PERTAIN.

**APPERTAINED.**
*Num.* 16:32 that *a.* to Korah, 33

**APPERTAINETH, ING.**
*Lev.* 6:5 give it to whom it *a.*
*Rom.* 4:1 Abr. our father, as *a.*

**APPETITE.**
*Job* 38:39 fill the *a.* of lions
*Prov.* 23:2 a man given to *a.*
*Ec.* 6:7 yet *a.* not filled
*Is.* 29:8 and his soul hath *a.*

APPII-FORUM. *Acts* 28:15

**APPLE of the eye.**
*Deut.* 32:10 kept him as *a. of h. e.*
*Ps.* 17:8 keep me as *a. of eye*
*Prov.* 7:2 law as *a. of thine eye.*
*Lam.* 2:18 let not *a. of thine eye*
*Zec.* 2:8 toucheth *a. of his eye.*

**APPLE-TREE.**
*Cant.* 2:3 as *a.-tree* among trees
8:5 raised thee up under *a.-tree*
*Joel* 1:12 and *a.-tree* are withered

**APPLES.**
*Prov.* 25:11 like *a.* of gold in pic.
*Cant.* 2:5 comfort me with *a.*
7:8 smell of thy nose like *a.*

**APPLIED.**
*Ec.* 7:25 I *a.* my heart to know
8:9 I *a.* my heart to every work
16 I *a.* heart to know wisdom

**APPLY.**
*Ps.* 90:12 *a.* our hearts to wisd.
*Prov.* 2:2 *a.* heart to understand
22:17 *a.* thy heart to my know.
23:12 *a* thy heart to instruction

**APPOINT.**
*Lev.* 26:16 will *a.* over you terror
2 *Sam.* 6:21 to *a.* me ruler
7:10 *a.* a place for my people
*Job* 14:13 *a.* me a set time
*Is.* 26:1 will God *a.* for walls
61:3 to *a.* them that mourn in Z.
*Jer.* 15:3 *a.* over them four kinds
49:19 who is a chosen man, I may *a.* Who will *a.* me the time? 50:44
*Ezek.* 21:19 *a.* thee two ways
20 *a.* a way that the sword
*Hos.* 1:11 they shall *a.* one head
*Mat.* 24:51 *a.* his portion
*Luke* 12:46 *a.* his portion
22:29 I *a.* you a kingdom
*Acts* 6:3 seven men whom we *a.*

**APPOINTED.**
*Num.* 9:2 passover in *a.* sea. 3
7 offering of L. in his *a.* season
1 *Sam.* 13:11 not within days *a.*
1 *K.* 1:35 *a.* him to be ruler.
20:42 a man *a.* to destruction
*Neh.* 6:7 thou hast *a.* prophets
9:17 *a.* a captain to return, but
*Job* 7:3 wearisome nights are *a.*
14:5 thou hast *a.* his bounds
20:29 the heritage *a.* to him
30:23 the house *a.* for all living
*Ps.* 44:11 like sheep *a.* for meat
78:5 *a.* a law in Israel
79:11 preserve those *a.* to die
102:20 to loose those *a.* to death
*Prov.* 7:20 come home at day *a.*
8:29 he *a.* the foundations
31:8 as are *a.* to destruction
*Is.* 1:14 your *a.* feasts my soul
44:7 I *a.* the ancient people
*Jer.* 5:24 reserveth the *a.* weeks
47:7 sea-shore, there hath he *a.*
*Ezek.* 4:6 *a.* each day for a year
*Mic.* 6:9 and who hath *a.*
*Luke* 3:13 exact what is *a.* you
10:1 Lord *a.* other seventy
22:29 as Father *a.* me
*Acts* 1:23 they *a.* two, Joseph and
17:31 he hath *a.* a day in which
1 *Cor.* 4:9 apostles last, *a.* to d.
1 *Thes.* 3:3 that we are *a.* thereto
5:9 God hath not *a.* us to wrath
2 *Tim.* 1:11 I am *a.* a preacher
*Heb.* 3:2 faithful to him that *a.*
9:27 *a.* to men once to die
1 *Pet.* 2:8 whereunto they were *a.*

**APPOINTED, time *and* times.**
1 *Sam.* 13:8 to set *time* Sam. *a.*
*Job* 7:1 an *a. time* to man
14:14 all the days of my *a. time.*
*Ps.* 81:3 trumpet in *time a.*
*Is.* 14:31 be alone in his *a. time*
*Jer.* 8:7 knoweth her *a. times*
*Dan.* 8:19 at *time a.* the end
10:1 but the *time a.* was long
11:27 end be at the *time a.*
29 at the *time a.* shall return
35 it is yet for a *time a.*
*Hab.* 2:3 is yet for an *a. time*
*Acts* 17:26 determ. *times* bef. *a.*
*Gal.* 4:2 until *time a.*

**APPOINTETH.**
*Ps.* 104:19 *a.* moons for seasons
*Dan.* 5:21 *a* whomsoever he will

**APPOINTMENT.**
*Job* 2:11 made *a.* together to c.

**APPREHEND.**
2 *Cor.* 11:32 garrison desir. to *a.*
*Phil.* 3:12 may *a.* that for which

**APPREHENDED.**
*Acts* 12:4 when he *a.* Peter
*Phil.* 3:12 I am *a.* of Christ J.
13 count not myself to have *a.*

**APPROACH.**
*Deut.* 31:14 thy days *a.* that thou
*Job* 40:19 his sword to *a.* to him
*Ps.* 65:4 whom thou causest to *a.*
*Jer.* 30:21 engaged heart to *a.*
1 *Tim.* 6:16 in light no man c. *a.*

**APPROACHETH, ING.**
*Is.* 58:2 take delight in *a.* God
*Luke* 12:33 where no thief *a.*
*Heb.* 10:25 as ye see the day *a.*

**APPROVE.**
*Ps.* 49:13 posterity *a.* their say.
1 *Cor.* 16:3 shall *a.* by your let.
*Phil.* 1:10 that ye may *a.* things

**APPROVED.**
*Acts* 2:22 Jesus, a man *a.* of God
*Rom.* 14:18 accept to G. *a.* of m.
16:10 Apelles *a.* in Christ
1 *Cor.* 11:19 they *a.* be made m.
2 *Cor.* 7:11 all things you have *a.*
10:18 commendeth himself is *a.*
13:7 that we should appear *a.*
2 *Tim.* 2:15 thyself *a.* unto God

**APPROVEST, ETH.**
*Lam.* 3:36 subvert a man, *a.* not
*Rom.* 2:18 *a.* things more excel.

**APPROVING.**
2 *Cor.* 6:4 in all things *a.* oursel.

**APRON, S.**
*Gen.* 3:7 fig-leaves, made *a.*
*Acts* 19:12 brought to the sick *a.*

**APT.**
1 *Tim.* 3:2 *a.* teach, 2 *Tim.* 2:24

AQUILA. *Acts* 18:2, 26; *Rom.* 16:3; 1 *Cor.* 16:19; 2 *Tim.* 4:19

AR. *Num.* 21:28; *Deut.* 2:9; *Is.* 15:1

**ARABIA.**
1 *K.* 10:15 had kings of A.
*Is.* 21:13 the burden upon A.
*Jer.* 25:24 the cup to kings of A.
*Gal.* 1:17 I went into A. 4:25

**ARABIAN, S.**
2 *Chr.* 17:11 the A. brought Jeh.
26:7 helped Uzziah ag. the A.
*Is.* 13:20 nor shall A. pitch tent
*Jer.* 3:2 as A. in the wilderness
*Acts* 2:11 Cretes and A. we hear

**ARAM.**
*Gen.* 10:22 sons of Sh. Lud, A.
*Num.* 23:7 B. brought me fr. A.
*Mat.* 1:3 Esrom begat A. 4
*Luke* 3:33 Aminadab son of A.
*See* PADAN.

ARARAT. *Gen.* 8:4; *Jer.* 51:27
ARAUNAH. 2 *Sam.* 24:16, 23
ARBA. *Jos.* 14:15; 21:11

**ARCHANGEL.**
1 *Thes.* 4:16 with voice of *a.*
*Jude* 9 Michael the *a.* contend.

ARCHELAUS. *Mat.* 2:22

**ARCHER, S.**
*Gen.* 21:20 Ishmael became an *a.*
49:23 the *a.* sorely grieved him
1 *Sam.* 31:3 *a.* hit him, 1 *Chr.* 10:3
*Job* 16:13 his *a.* comp. me round
*Is.* 22:3 rulers are bound by *a.*
*Jer.* 51:3 bendeth let *a.* bend bow

**ARCHES.**
*Ezek.* 40:16 windows to the *a.*

ARCHIPPUS. *Col.* 4:17; *Phile.* 2
ARCTURUS. *Job* 9:9; 38:32

**ARE.**
*Num.* 15:15 as ye *a.* so stranger
*Job* 38:35 say to thee, here we *a.*
*Lam.* 5:7 sinned, and *a.* not
*Mat.* 2:18 not comf. bec. they *a.*
*Luke* 13:25 whence you *a.* 27
18:11 I am not as other men *a.*
*John* 17:11 may be one as we *a.*
1 *Cor.* 1:28 things which *a.* not
*Rev.* 1:19 the things which *a.*

AREOPAGITE. *Acts* 17:34
AREOPAGUS. *Acts* 17:19
ARETAS. 2 *Cor.* 11:32
ARGOB. *Deut.* 3:4, 13, 14; 1 *K.* 4:13

**ARGUING.**
*Job* 6:25 what doth your *a.* rep.

**ARGUMENTS.**
*Job* 23:4 fill my mouth with *a.*

**ARIEL.**
*Ezr.* 8:16 I sent for E. and A.
*Is.* 29:1 woe to A. the city, 2, 7

**ARIGHT.**
*Ps.* 50:23 ord. his conversa. *a.*
78:8 that set not their heart *a.*
*Prov.* 15:2 wise useth know. *a.*
23:31 when it moveth itself *a.*
*Jer.* 8:6 I heark. they spake not *a.*

**ARIMATHEA.**
*Mat.* 27:57 Joseph of A. who was, *Mark* 15:43; *Luke* 23:51; *John* 19:38

**ARIOCH.**
*Gen.* 14:1 in the days of A. king
*Dan.* 2:25 A. brought Daniel

**ARISE.**
Jos. 1:2 a. go over this Jordan
Jud. 5:12 a. Barak, lead
2 Sam. 2:14 young men a.
1 K. 3:12 any a. like thee
1 Chr. 22:16 a. be doing
Job 7:4 I a. and night be gone?
25:3 doth not his light a.?
Ps. 3:7 a. O Lord, save me
7:6 a. O Lord, in thine anger
12:5 will I a. saith the Lord
44:26 a. for help, and redeem
68:1 let God a. let his enemies
88:10 shall dead a. praise thee?
89:9 waves of sea a. thou stil.
102:13 a. and have mercy on Z.
Prov. 6:9 a. out of thy sleep?
Cant. 2:13 a. my love, fair one
Is. 21:5 a. ye princes
26:19 my dead body shall a.
49:7 kings shall a. princes wor.
60:1 a. shine, thy light is come
60:2 Lord shall a. upon thee
Jer. 2:27 in trouble will say, a.
8:4 shall they fall, and not a.?
31:6 a. ye, let us go up to Zion
Lam. 2:19 a. cry out in the night
Dan. 2:39 shall a. another kingd.
Amos 7:2 whom shall Jacob a. 5
Mic. 2:10 a. this is not your rest
4:13 a. and thresh, O daughter
7:8 enemy, I fall I shall a.
Hab. 2:19 to the dumb stone a.
Mal. 4:2 Sun of righteousness a.
Mat. 9:5 easier to say a. Mark 2:9
24:24 shall a. false Christs
Mark 7:41 damsel, a. Luke 8:54
Luke 7:14 L. said, young man a.
15:18 I will a. and go to my f.
24:38 thoughts a. in your hearts
John 14:31 a. let us go hence
Acts 9:40 said, Tabitha, a.
20:30 own selves shall men a.
22:16 a. and be baptized
Eph. 5:14 a. from the dead
2 Pet. 1:19 till the day-star a.

*See* RISE.

**ARISETH.**
1 K. 18:44 a. little cloud
Ps. 112:4 to the upright a. light
Is. 2:19 a. to shake terribly, 21
Mat. 13:21 persec. a. Mark 4:17
John 7:52 out of Galilee a.
Heb. 7:15 similitude of Melch. a.

*See* SUN

**ARISTARCHUS.**
Acts 19:29 caught Gaius and A.
20:4 A. accompanied Paul
27:2 one A. a Macedonian
Col. 4:10 A. f.-prisoner, Phile. 24

ARISTOBULUS. Rom. 16:10

**ARK.**
Gen. 6:14 an a. of gopher-wood
7:18 a. went on face of waters
Ex. 2:3 took an a. of bulrush.
25:16 put into the a. the testimony, 21; 40:3, 20
37:1 made the a. of shittim-w.
Num. 3:31 charge shall be the a
Jos. 4:11 a. of Lord, 6:12; 1 Sam. 4:6; 6:1; 2 Sam. 6:9
1 Sam. 6:19 looked into a.
2 Sam. 11:11 a. and Israel abide
1 K. 2:26 bec. thou barest the a.
8:9 nothing in a. save the two
1 Chr. 6:31 the a. had rest
13:3 let us bring again the a.
9 put forth hand to hold the a.
15:1 D. prepared a place for a.
2 Chr. 6:41 a. of thy strength, Ps. 132:8
8:11 whereunto a. hath come
Mat. 24:38 Noah ent. a. Lu. 17:27
Heb. 11:7 Noah prepared an a.
1 Pet. 3:20 G. waited while the a.
Rev. 11:19 in his temple the a.

**Before the ARK.**
Ex. 40:5 set altar of gold a.
Jos. 4:7 w. of Jordan cut off a.
7:6 J. fell on his face be. the a.
1 Sam. 5:3 D. was fallen be. the a.
1 Chr. 16:37 left before the a. A.
2 Chr. 5:6 S. and congr. be. the a.

**ARK of the Covenant.**
Num. 10:33 a. c. of L. went bef.
Deut. 31:26 inside of a. c.
Jos. 4:7 waters cut off before a. c.
Jud. 20:27 a. c. of God was there
1 Sam. 4:3 let us fetch the a. c.
2 Sam. 15:24 Levites bearing a. c.
1 Chr. 17:1 a. c. under curtains
Jer. 3:16 shall say no more, a. c.
Heb. 9:4 tabern. which had a. c.

**ARK of God.**
1 Sam. 3:3 where a. of G. was
4:11 a. of G. was taken, 17, 22
6:3 if ye send away the a.
2 Sam. 6:7 there he died before a.
7:2 a. dwelleth within
15:25 a. of God into the city
1 Chr. 13:12 bring the a. home
15:2 none carry a. of G. but L.

**ARM.**
Ex. 15:16 greatness of thine a.
Deut. 33:20 teareth the a. with
1 Sam. 2:31 I will cut off thy a. and the a. of thy father's h.
2 Chr. 32:8 with him is a. of flesh
Job 26:2 savest a. that hath
31:22 a. fall from my shoulder
35:9 cry out by reason of the a.
38:15 high a. shall be broken
40:9 hast thou an a. like God?
Ps. 10:15 the a. of the wicked
44:3 nor their own a. save them
77:15 with thy a. red. thy peo.
89:13 thou hast a mighty a.
21 mine a. shall strengthen
98:1 his holy a. hath gotten him
Cant. 8:6 as a seal on thine a.
Is. 9:20 the flesh of his a.
33:2 be their a. every morning
40:10 his a. shall rule for him
11 gather the lambs with a.
51:5 shall wait upon me, on mine a. shall they trust
9 put on strength, O a. of Lord
52:10 hath made bare his holy a.
53:1 to whom is the a. of the L. revealed? John 12:38
59:16 his a. brought salv. 63:5
62:8 hath sworn by the a.
63:12 with his glorious a.
Jer. 17:5 that maketh flesh his a.
21:5 I will fight with strong a.
Ezek. 4:7 thine a. shall be unc.
30:21 broken a. of Pharaoh
31:17 into hell that were his a.
Dan. 11:6 retain power of the a.
Zec. 11:17 on his a. his a.
Luke 1:51 showed str. with his a.
Acts 13:17 with a high a. brought

**ARM, Verb.**
1 Pet. 4:1 a. yours. with same m.

**Stretched-out ARM.**
Ex. 6:6 with a s.-out a.
Deut. 4:34 assayed to take nation by a stretched-out a.
5:15 out thence with a a. 7:19; 26:8; Jer. 32:21
2 Chr. 6:32 thy stretched-out a.
Ps. 136:12 a a. for his mercy
Jer. 27:5 made earth by a. 32:17
Ezek. 20:33 with a a. will I rule
34 I will gather you with a a.

**ARMS.**
Gen. 49:24 a. of his hands
Deut. 33:27 the everlasting a.
2 Sam. 22:35 bow of steel is brok. by mine a. Ps. 18:34
Job 22:9 the a. of the fatherless
Ps. 37:17 a. of wicked broken
Prov. 31:17 strengtheneth her a.
Is. 44:12 with strength of a.
49:22 bring thy sons in their a.
51:5 my a. shall judge the peo.
Ezek. 13:20 tear from your a.
30:22 break Pharaoh's a. 24
24 strength. a. of king of B. 25
Dan. 2:32 and his a. of silver
10:6 his a. like polished brass
11:15 a. of south shall not
22 with the a. of a flood shall
31 a. shall stand on his part
Hos. 7:15 strengthened their a.
11:3 taking them by their a.
Mark 9:36 taken him in his a.
10:16 took them up in his a.
Luke 2:28 S. took C. in his a.

ARMAGEDDON. Rev. 16:16

**ARMED.**
Job 39:21 goeth on to meet a. m.
Ps. 78:9 children of E. being a.
Prov. 6:11 as an a. man, 24:34
Luke 11:21 a strong man a.

ARMENIA. 2 K. 19:37; Is. 37:38

**ARMHOLES.**
Jer. 38:12 rotten rags under thy a.
Ezek. 13:18 sew pillows to a.

**ARMIES.**
Ex. 12:17 your a. out of E.
Num. 33:1 their a. under Mos.
1 Sam. 17:10 defy the a. of Israel
16 should defy the a. of God
45 name of God of a. of Israel
Job 25:3 any number of his a.?
Ps. 44:9 forth with our a.
68:12 kings of a. did flee apace
Cant. 6:13 company of two a.
Is. 34:2 fury upon all their a.
Mat. 22:7 he sent forth his a.
Luke 21:20 Jerus. compa. with a.
Heb. 11:34 to flight a.
Rev. 19:14 a. in heaven followed
19 kings and their a. gathered

**ARMOR.**
1 Sam. 17:54 Goliah's a. in his
1 K. 22:38 washed his a.
2 K. 3:21 all able to put on a.
10:2 a fenced city also and a.
20:13 Hez. showed his precious things, h. of his a. Is. 39:2
Is. 22:8 look in that day to a.
Luke 11:22 his a. wherein he
Rom. 13:12 put on a. of light
2 Cor. 6:7 approv. by a. of right
Eph. 6:11 put on the a. of God
13 take the whole a. of God

**ARMOR-BEARER.**
Jud. 9:54 Abim. called his a.-b.
1 Sam. 14:7 a.-b. said, do all that
16:21 David became his a.-b.
31:6 Saul died, and his a.-b.

**ARMORY.**
Cant. 4:4 builded for an a.
Jer. 50:25 L. hath opened his a.

**ARMY.**
Deut. 11:4 he did to the a. of E.
Jud. 9:29 increase thine a.
1 K. 20:25 a. like the a. lost
2 Chr. 20:21 praise before a.
Job 29:25 dw. as a king in the a.
Cant. 6:4 as a. with banners, 10
Jer. 37:11 fear of Pharaoh's a.
Ezek. 29:18 a. to serve a great
37:10 an exceeding great a.
Dan. 4:35 according to his will in the a. of heaven
Joel 2:11 his voice before his a.
Zec. 9:8 encamp bec. of the a.
Acts 23:27 came I with an a.
Rev. 9:16 of a. of horsemen
19:19 sat on horse and his a.

**ARNON.**
Num. 21:14 brooks of A. 22:36
Deut. 2:24 over the river of A.
Jud. 11:26 by the coasts of A.
Is. 16:2 shall be at fords of A.
Jer. 48:20 tell ye it in A.

**AROER.**
Num. 32:34 child. of G. built A.
1 Sam. 30:28; 2 Sam. 24:5; 1 Chr. 5:8
Is. 17:2 cities of A. are forsaken
Jer. 48:19 inhabitant of A. stand

**AROSE.**
Gen. 37:7 and lo, my sheaf a.
Ex. 1:8 a. a new king over Eg. who knew not J. Acts 7:18
Jud. 2:10 a. a generation that knew not the Lord
5:7 till I Deborah a. a mother
20:8 the people a. as one man
1 Sam. 9:26 a. early, Is. 37:36
17:35 he a. against me
2 K. 23:25 aft. him a. there any
2 Chr. 36:16 wrath of the Lord a.
Job 29:8 aged a. and stood up
Ps. 76:9 God a. to judgment
Ec. 1:5 sun hasteth where he a.
Dan. 6:19 the king a. early
Mat. 2:14 he a. and took child, 21
8:15 a. and ministered, Lu. 4:39
26 he a. and rebuked winds, Mark 4:39; Luke 8:24
9:9 a. and follow. 19; Mark 2:14
25 the hand, and the maid a.
27:52 saints which slept a.
Mark 9:27 J. lifted him up, he a.
Luke 6:48 when the flood a.
15:20 he a. and came to his f.
Acts 11:19 persec. which a. about
19:23 there a. no small stir
23:7 so said a. a dissension, 10
See ROSE.

**AROSE and went.**
1 Sam. 3:6 Samuel a. to Eli
1 K. 19:21 Elisha a. after Elijah
Jon. 3:3 so Jonah a. to Nineveh
Acts 9:39 Peter a. and went

**ARPAD, ARPHAD.**
2 K. 18:34 gods of A. Is. 36:19
19:13 king of A.? Is. 37:13
Is. 10:9 is not Hamath as A.?
Jer. 49:23 is confounded, and A.

**ARPHAXAD.**
Gen. 10:22 s. of Shem, A. 11:10
Luke 3:36 was the son of A.

**ARRAY.**
Job 6:4 terrors of God set in a.
Jer. 50:14 yourselves in a. ag. B.
See BATTLE.

**ARRAY, Verb.**
Est. 6:9 they may a. the man
Job 40:10 a. thyself with glory
Jer. 43:12 a. himself with land
1 Tim. 2:9 not with costly a.

**ARRAYED.**
Gen. 41:42 Pharaoh a. Joseph
2 Chr. 28:15 captives with sp. a.
Mat. 6:29 was not a. like one of these, Luke 12:27
Luke 23:11 Herod a. Christ
Acts 12:21 Herod a. in royal app.
Rev. 7:13 these a. in white
17:4 woman was a. in purple
19:8 to her was granted to be a.

**ARROGANCY.**
1 Sam. 2:3 let not a. come out
Prov. 8:13 pride and a. do I hate
Is. 13:11 cause a. of the proud
Jer. 48:29 M. his loftiness, his a.

**ARROW.**
1 Sam. 20:36 Jonathan shot a.
2 K. 9:24 a. went out at his h.
13:17 a. of Lord's deliverance
19:32 nor shoot an a. there, Is. 37:33
Job 41:28 a. cannot make him
Ps. 11:2 their a. on the string
64:7 an a. sudd. be wounded
91:5 nor afraid for a. that flieth
Prov. 25:18 witness is a sharp a.
Jer. 9:8 tongue as an a. shot out
Lam. 3:12 as a mark for the a.
Zec. 9:14 his a. go forth

**ARROWS.**
Num. 24:8 through with a.
Deut. 32:23 mine a. upon them
42 mine a. drunk with blood
1 Sam. 20:20 will shoot three a.
2 Sam. 22:15 sent out a. and scattered them, Ps. 18:14
2 K. 13:15 take bow and a.
18 take the a. and smite
Job 6:4 a. of Almighty are
Ps. 7:13 ordaineth a. against
21:12 thine a. against them
38:2 thine a. stick fast in me
45:5 a. sharp in heart of enem.
57:4 teeth are spears and a.
58:7 his bow to shoot his a.
64:3 their a. even bitter
76:3 brake he the a. of bow
77:17 thine a. also went abroad
120:4 sharp a. of the mighty
127:4 as a. in hand of a mighty
144:6 shoot thine a. and destroy
Prov. 26:18 man who cast a.
Is. 5:28 whose a. are sharp
7:24 with a. and bows shall m.
Jer. 50:9 a. as of expert man
14 at Babylon spare no a.
51:11 make bright the a.
Lam. 3:13 caused a. of his quiv.
Ezek. 5:16 send evil a. of fami.
21:21 he made his a. bright
39:3 cause thine a. to fall
9 Israel shall burn bows and a.
Hab. 3:11 light of thine a.

**ART, Verb.**
Gen. 32:17 whose a. thou?
Jud. 8:18 as thou a.
1 K. 22:4 as thou a. 2 K. 3:7
Jer. 14:22 a. not thou he, O L.
Luke 7:19 a. he that should
Rev. 11:17 a. and w. and a. 16:5

**ART, S, Substantive.**
Ex. 30:25 ointment after the a.
2 Chr. 16:14 spices prep. by a.
Acts 17:29 stones graven by a.
19:19 which used curious a.

**ARTAXERXES.**
Ezr. 4:7; 6:14; 7:1, 11, 21
Neh. 2:1 in 20th year of A. wine
5:14 from 20th to 32d year of A.

ARTEMAS. Tit. 3:12

**ARTIFICER, S.**
Gen. 4:22 T.-Cain an instr. of a.
1 Chr. 29:5 works made by a.
2 Chr. 34:11 to a. gave they m.
Is. 3:3 away the cunning a.

**ARTILLERY.**
1 Sam. 20:40 Jonath. gave his a.

**ASA.**
1 K. 15:11 A. did right, 2 Chr. 14:2, 12, 13; 2 Chr. 15:2, 17; 16:2
1 Chr. 9:16 Berechiah, son of A.
2 Chr. 14:11 A. cried to the Lord

**ASAHEL.**
2 Sam. 2:18, 21, 32; 1 Chr. 2:16
3:27 Abner died for blood of A.
23:24 A. was one, 1 Chr. 11:26

**ASAIAH.**
1 Chr. 4:36 Jeshohaiah and A.
6:30 sons of Merari, A. 9:5
2 Chr. 34:20 king Josiah sent A.

**ASAPH.**
2 K. 18:18 Joab the son of A. the recorder, 37; Is. 36:3, 22
1 Chr. 6:39 A. son of, 9:15; 15:17
16:7 delivered this psalm to A.
25:1 of the sons of A. 2; 26:1; 2 Chr. 5:12; 20:14; 29:13; 35:15; Ezr. 2:41; 3:10; Neh. 7:44; 11:17, 22; 12:35

**ASCEND.**
Jos. 6:5 people shall a. up
Ps. 24:3 a. into hill, Rom. 10:6
135:7 vap. to a. Jer. 10:13; 51:16
139:8 if I a. up into heaven
Is. 14:13 I will a. to heaven, 14
Ezek. 38:9 a. and come
John 6:62 Son of man a. up
20:17 I a. to my Father
Rev. 17:8 shall a. out of pit

**ASCENDED.**
Jud. 13:20 angel a. in the
Ps. 68:18 thou hast a. on high
Prov. 30:4 hath a. into heaven
John 3:13 no man hath a.
20:17 not yet a. to my Father
Acts 2:34 D. is not a. into the h
Eph. 4:8 when he a. up
9 that he a. 10 same that a.
Rev. 8:4 smoke of the incense a.
11:12 a. up to heaven

**ASCENDETH.**
Rev. 11:7 the beast that a. out
14:11 smoke of their torment a.

**ASCENDING.**
Gen. 28:12 the angels of God a.
1 Sam. 28:13 I saw gods a. out
Luke 19:28 before a. up to Jeru.
John 1:51 angels of God a. and
Rev. 7:2 angel a. from the east

**ASCENT.**
2 Sam. 15:30 Dav. went up by the a. of Olivet
1 K. 10:5 and his a. by which he went up, 2 Chr. 9:4

**ASCRIBE.**
Deut. 32:3 a. ye greatness
Job 36:3 I will a. to my Maker
Ps. 68:34 a. ye strength to God

**ASCRIBED.**
1 Sam. 18:8 a. to David 10,000

ASENATH. Gen. 41:45, 50; 46:20

**ASH.**
Is. 44:14 he planteth an a.

**ASHAMED.**
Gen. 2:25 m. and w. were not a.
2 Sam. 10:5 men were greatly a. 1 Chr. 19:5
19:3 as people being a.
2 K. 2:17 till he was a.
8:11 countenance until a.
2 Chr. 30:15 the priests were a.
Ezr. 9:6 I am a. to lift up
Job 6:20 came, and were a.
11:3 shall no man make a.?
19:3 not a. to make
Ps. 34:5 and their faces not a.
Ps. 74:21 not oppressed turn a.
Prov. 12:4 she that maketh a.
Is. 20:5 be a. of Ethiopia
24:23 the sun shall be a. when
30:5 a. of a people that could
33:9 L. is a. and hewn down
Jer. 2:26 as thief is a.
6:15 they a.? at all a. 8:12
8:9 the wise men are a.
14:4 ploughmen were a.
48:13 a. of C. as Is. was a.
Ezek. 16:27 daughters of P. are a.
32:30 terror a. of their might
Luke 13:17 adversaries were a.
16:3 to beg I am a.
Rom. 1:16 not a. of the gospel
5:5 hope maketh not a.
6:21 whereof ye are now a.?
2 Cor. 7:14 I am not a.
2 Tim. 1:12 neverth. I am not a.

16 O. was not *a.* of my chain
*Heb.* 2:11 not *a.* to call them
11:16 not *a.* to be called

ASHAMED *and confounded. See* CONFOUNDED.

**Be ASHAMED.**

*Ps.* 6:10 let my enemies *be a.*
25:3 that wait on thee *be a.*
let them *be a.* who transgress
31:1 let me never *be a.*
17 not *be a.* wicked *be a.* 35:26
69:6 wait *be a.* for my sake
86:17 wh. hate me, may *be a.*
109:28 let them *be a.*
119:78 let proud *be a.*
*Is.* 1:29 shall *be a.* of the oaks
23:4 *be* thou *a.* O Zidon
26:11 and *be a.* for their envy
42:17 *be* greatly *a.* that trust in
44:9 know, that they may *be a.*
11 all his fellows shall *be a.*
45:24 against him shall *be a.*
65:13 rejoice, ye shall *be a.*
66:5 and they shall *be a.*
*Jer.* 2:36 shalt *be a.* of Egypt
3:3 refusedst to *be a.*
12:13 shall *be a.* of your rev.
17:13 forsake thee shall *be a*
20:11 my persecutors shall *be a.*
48:13 Moab shall *be a.* of C.
50:12 your mother shall *be a.*
*Ezek.* 16:61 and *be a.*
43:10 they may *be a.* of their
*Hos.* 4:19 *be a.* bec. of their sac.
10:6 Is. *be a.* of his own counsel
*Joel* 1:11 *be* ye *a.* O ye husbandm.
2:26 shall never *be a.* 27
*Zec.* 9:5 expectation shall *be a.*
13:4 every one *be a.* of his vis.
*Mark* 8:38 *be a.* of me, *Luke* 9:26
2 *Cor.* 9:4 we (that we say not you) should *be a.*
*Phil.* 1:20 in nothing I shall *b. a.*
2 *Thes.* 3:14 that may *be a.*
*Tit.* 2:8 contrary part may *be a.*
1 *Pet.* 3:16 may *be a.* that falsely

**Not be, *or* Be not ASHAMED.**

*Num.* 12:14 she *b. a.* seven days?
*Ps.* 25:2 in thee, let me *n. b. a.*
31:17 let me *n. b. a.* 119:116
37:19 shall *n. b. a.* in the evil
119:6 *a.* when I have respect
46 testimonies, and *n. be a.*
80 be sound, that I *be n. a.*
127:5 shall *n. be a.* but speak
*Is.* 29:22 Jacob shall *not be a.*
45:17 *a.* world without end
49:23 shall *not be a.* that wait
50:7 like a flint, I shall *n. be a.*
54:4 for thou shalt *not be a.*
*Zep.* 3:11 that day shalt thou *a.*
*Rom.* 9:33 believ. shall *a.* 10:11
2 *Cor.* 10:8 I should *not be a.*
2 *Tim.* 1:8 *a.* of testimony of L.
2:15 that needeth *not be a.*
1 *Pet.* 4:16 as a Chr. let him *a.*
1 *John* 2:28 *a.* before him

**ASHDOD.**

1 *Sam.* 5:1 the ark to A. 6
2 *Chr.* 26:6 wall of A. cit. ab. A.
*Neh.* 13:23 mar. wives of A. 24
*Amos* 1:8; 3:9; *Zep.* 2:4; *Zec.* 9:6

**ASHER**

*Gen.* 30:13 L. called his name A.
49:20 out of A. his bread fat
*Deut.* 33:24 of A. he said A.
*Jud.* 5:17 A. on the sea-shore

**Tribe of ASHER.**

*Num.* 1:41 the *tribe of* A. 41,500
2:27 the *tribe of* A. shall
10:26 the host of *tribe of* A.
13:13 *tribe of* A. to spy, 34:27
*Jos.* 19:24 lot for *tribe of* A. 31
21:6 out of the *tribe of* A. 30
1 *Chr.* 6:62,74; *Luke* 2:36; *Rev.* 7:6

**ASHES.**

*Gen.* 18:27 am but dust and *a.*
*Lev.* 6:11 the *a.* without camp
*Num.* 19:9 gather the *a.*
1 *K.* 13:3 and *a.* poured out
20:38 disguised himself with *a.*
*Est.* 4:3 lay in sackcloth and *a.*
*Job* 2:8 sat down among the *a.*
13:12 your rememb. like *a.*
30:19 become like dust and *a.*
42:6 and repent in dust and *a.*
*Ps.* 102:9 eaten *a.* like bread
147:16 the hoar-frost like *a.*
*Is.* 44:20 he feedeth on *a.*
58:5 to spread *a.* under him
61:3 to give them beauty for *a.*
*Jer.* 6:26 daughter, wallow in *a.*
*Lam.* 3:16 covered me with *a.*
*Ezek.* 28:18 bring thee to *a.* on
*Dan.* 9:3 to seek in sack. and *a.*
*Jon.* 3:6 king sat in *a.*
*Mal.* 4:3 wicked be *a.* under
*Mat.* 11:21 repented long ago in sackcloth and *a.* *Luke* 10:13
*Heb.* 9:13 if the *a.* of a heifer
2 *Pet.* 2:6 cities of Sodom into *a.*

**ASHTAROTH.**

*Deut.* 1:4 at A. *Jos.* 9:10; 12:4
*Jud.* 2:13 Is. served A. 10:6
1 *Sam.* 7:3 strange gods and A. 4
12:10 because we have served A.
31:10 S.'s armor in house of A.
1 *K.* 11:33 have worshipped A.
1 *Chr.* 6:71 Gershom was giv. A.

**ASHUR, *or* ASSUR.**

*Gen.* 10:11 A. went forth, 22
*Num.* 24:22 A. shall carry, 24
1 *Chr.* 2:24 H. wife bare him A.
4:5 A. had two wives, H. and
*Ezr.* 4:2 Esar-haddon, king of A.
*Ps.* 83:8 A. also is joined with
*Ezek.* 27:23 A. and Chil. 32:22
*Hos.* 14:3 A. shall not save us

**ASIA.**

*Acts* 6:9 of A. disputing Stephen
19:10 all they in A. heard
27 whom all A. worshippeth
1 *Pet.* 1:1 to strangers scat. in A.

**ASIDE.**

2 *K.* 4:4 set *a.* that which
*Mark* 7:33 *a.* from the multitude
*John* 13:4 laid *a.* his garments
*Heb.* 12:1 lay *a.* every weight

*See* GO, GONE, TURN, WENT, LAY.

**ASK.**

*Gen.* 32:29 w. *a.* after my name
34:12 *a.* me never so much dowry and gift, and I will give
*Deut.* 4:32 *a.* of the days that are
32:7 *a.* thy father
*Jud.* 18:5 *a.* counsel of God
1 *Sam.* 12:19 this evil to *a.* us
28:16 why dost thou *a.* of me
1 *K.* 3:5 God said, *a.* what I shall give thee, 2 *Chr.* 1:7
2 *K.* 2:9 *a.* what I shall do
2 *Chr.* 20:4 J. gathered to *a.* help
*Job* 12:7 *a.* the beasts
*Ps.* 2:8 *a.* of me, and I will give
*Is.* 7:11 *a.* thee a sign of L. *a*
12 I will not *a.* neither tempt
45:11 L. *a.* of things to come
58:2 they *a.* ordinances
*Jer.* 6:16 *a.* for the old paths
15:5 aside to *a.* how thou doest
18:13 *a.* among the heathen
38:14 I will *a.* thee a thing
48:19 *a.* him that fleeth
50:5 shall *a.* the way to Zion
*Lam.* 4:4 children *a.* bread
*Dan.* 6:7 shall *a.* a petition
*Hos.* 4:12 people *a.* counsel
*Hag.* 2:11 *a.* priests concerning
*Zec.* 10:1 *a.* rain in time
*Mat.* 6:8 need of, before ye *a.*
7:7 *a.* and it shall be. *Luke* 11:9
9 his son *a.* bread, *Luke* 11:11
11 good things to them that *a.*
14:7 whatsoever she would *a.*
18:19 touch. any thing they *a.*
20:22 what ye *a.* *Mark* 10:38
21:22 whatsoever ye *a.*
22:46 *a.* him more questions, *Mark* 12:34; *Luke* 20:40
*Mark* 6:22 *a.* what thou wilt. 23
9:32 afraid to *a.* him, *Luke* 9:45
*Luke* 6:30 goods, *a.* them not
11:13 Holy S. to them that *a.*
12:48 of him they will *a.*
*John* 1:19 sent priests to *a.* him
9:21 he is of age, *a.* him, 23
11:22 whatsoever thou *a.* of G.
14:13 ye *a.* in my name, 15:16
14 if ye *a.* in my name I will
15:7 abide in me, *a.* what ye
16:19 they were desirous to *a.*
*John* 16:23 ye shall *a.* me nothing
24 *a.* and receive that your joy
30 that any should *a.*
18:21 *a.* them which heard me
*Acts* 10:29 I *a.* for what intent
1 *Cor.* 14:35 *a.* their husbands
*Eph.* 3:20 above all we can *a.*
*Jam.* 1:5 lack wisdom, let him *a.*
6 but let him *a.* in faith
4:2 ye have not, bec. ye *a.* not
3 ye *a.* and rec. not, bec. ye *a.*
1 *John* 3:22 we *a.* we receive
5:14 we *a.* according to his will
15 heareth us, whatever we *a.*
16 not unto death, he shall *a.*

*See* COUNSEL.

**ASKED.**

*Jud.* 5:25 he *a.* water
13:6 I *a.* not whence he was
1 *Sam.* 1:17 petition thou *a.*
1 *K.* 3:11 thou *a.* this thing
2 *K.* 2:10 hast *a.* hard thing
*Ezr.* 5:10 we *a.* their names
*Job* 21:29 *a.* them that go by
*Ps.* 21:4 he *a.* life of thee
105:40 people *a.* he brought
*Is.* 30:2 not *a.* at my mouth
41:28 when I *a.* of them, could
65:1 sought of them that *a.* not
*Dan.* 2:10 no king that *a.*
7:16 *a.* him the truth
*Mat.* 16:13 he *a.* his disciples, *Mark* 8:27; *Luke* 9:18
22:23 Sadducees *a.* him, 35; *Mark* 9:11; 10:2; 12:18
*Luke* 18:40 when near he *a.*
*John* 4:10 wouldest have *a.*
16:24 have ye *a.* nothing
*Rom.* 10:20 to them that *a.* not

**ASKELON, *or* ASHKELON.**

*Jud.* 1:18 Judah took G. and A.
14:19 Samson went down to A.
1 *Sam.* 6:17 for A. one, for Gath
2 *Sam.* 1:20 in the streets of A.
*Jer.* 25:20 I made A. and Azzah
47:5 A. is cut off with rem. 7
*Amos* 1:8 holds sceptre from A.
*Zep.* 2:4 A. a desolation, 7
*Zec.* 9:5 A. shall see; A. shall

**ASKEST.**

*Jud.* 13:18 why *a.* after my name?
*John* 4:9 *a.* drink of me
18:21 why *a.* thou me?

**ASKETH.**

*Ex.* 13:14 thy son *a.* *Deut.* 6:20
*Mic.* 7:3 prince *a.* for a reward
*Mat.* 5:42 him that *a.* *Luke* 6:30
7:8 that *a.* receiv. *Luke* 11:10
*John* 16:5 none *a.* whither goest
1 *Pet.* 3:15 *a.* you a reason of

**ASKING.**

*Ps.* 78:18 tempting God by *a.*
*Luke* 2:46 *a.* them questions
*John* 8:7 they continued *a*
1 *Cor.* 10:25 *a.* no question, 27

**ASLEEP.**
*Jud.* 4:21 Sisera was fast *a.*
*Cant.* 7:9 lips of those *a.* to speak
*Jon.* 1:5 Jonah was fast *a.*
*Mat.* 8:24 he was *a.* *Mark* 4:38
26:40 disciples *a.* *Mark* 14:40
*Acts* 7:60 Stephen fell *a.*
1 *Cor.* 15:6 but some are fallen *a.*
18 which are fallen *a.* in C.
1 *Thes.* 4:13 concerning them *a.*
15 prevent them that are *a.*
2 *Pet.* 3:4 since fathers fell *a.* all

ASNAPPAR. *Ezr.* 4:10

**ASP, S.**
*Deut.* 32:33 wine is venom of *a.*
*Job* 20:14 meat is the gall of *a.*
16 he shall suck poison of *a.*
*Is.* 11:8 on the hole of the *a.*
*Rom.* 3:13 poison of *a.*

**ASSAULT, ED.**
*Acts* 14:5 and *a.* made of the G.
17:5 they *a.* the house of Jason

**ASSAY, ED, ING.**
*Deut.* 4:34 hath God *a.* to take
1 *Sam.* 17:39 David *a.* to go
*Job* 4:2 if we *a.* to commune
*Acts* 9:26 Saul *a.* to join himself
16:7 they *a.* to go to Bithynia
*Heb.* 11:29 the Egyptians *a.*

**ASS.**
*Gen.* 22:3 Abrah. saddled his *a.*
5 abide you here with the *a.*
49:14 Issachar is a strong *a.*
*Ex.* 13:13 firstling of an *a.*
23:4 if thou meet enemy's *a.*
12 thine ox and thine *a.*
*Num.* 16:15 not taken one *a.*
22:23 *a.* saw the angel, 25, 27
28 opened the mouth of *a.* 30
*Deut.* 22:10 with ox and *a.*
*Jos.* 15:18 lighted off her *a.* *Jud.* 1:14; 1 *Sam.* 25:23
*Jud.* 15:16 jawbone of an *a.*
1 *K.* 13:28 had not torn the *a.*
2 *K.* 6:25 *a.* head sold for 80 p.
*Job* 24:3 the *a.* of the fatherless
*Prov.* 26:3 a bridle for the *a.*
*Is.* 1:3 the *a.* his master's crib
32:20 send feet of the ox and *a.*
*Jer.* 22:19 the burial of an *a.*
*Zec.* 9:9 cometh lowly riding on *a.* the foal of an *a.* *Mat.* 21:5
14:15 so be the plague of the *a.*
*Mat.* 21:2 shall find an *a.* tied
*Luke* 13:15 each loose his *a.*
14:5 have an *a.* fallen into pit
*John* 12:14 had found a young *a.*
2 *Pet.* 2:16 dumb *a.* speaking
*See* SADDLE.

**ASS'S COLT.**
*Gen.* 49:11 binding his *a. c.*
*Job* 11:12 born like a wild *a. c.*
*John* 12:15 sitting on an *a. c.*

**Wild ASS.**
*Job* 6:5 *a.* bray when he hath g.
39:5 sent out *w. a.* free
*Jer.* 2:24 *w. a.* used to the w'ness
*Hos.* 8:9 *w. a.* alone by himself

**ASSES.**
*Jud.* 5:10 ride on w. *a.*
1 *Sam.* 8:16 will take your *a.*
9:3 *a.* of Kish were lost, 10:2
2 *Sam.* 16:2 *a.* for k. household
1 *Chr.* 27:30 over *a.* was Jehd.
2 *Chr.* 28:15 carried feeble on *a.*
*Job* 42:12 J. had a thousand she *a.*
*Is.* 21:7 he saw a chariot of *a.*
*Ezek.* 23:20 flesh as flesh of *a.*

**Wild ASSES.**
*Job* 24:5 as *wild a.* go they forth
*Ps.* 104:11 *w. a.* quench
*Is.* 32:14 shall be a joy of *w. a.*
*Jer.* 14:6 *wild a* snuffed wind
*Dan.* 5:21 dwell. was with *w. a.*

**Young ASSES.**
*Is.* 30:6 riches on *young a.*
24 *y. a* that ear the ground

**ASSEMBLE.**
*Is.* 11:12 he shall *a.* outcasts
45:20 *a.* and come, and draw n
48:14 all ye *a.* yourselves
*Jer.* 4:5 *a.* and let us go
8:14 why sit still? *a.* let us
*Ezek.* 11:17 I will *a.* you out of
39:17 *a.* gather to my sacrifice
*Hos.* 7:14 *a.* for corn and wine
*Joel* 2:16 *a.* elders, gather
3:11 *a.* and come, all ye heathen
*Amos* 3:9 *a.* on mt. Samaria
*Mic.* 2:12 I will surely *a.* O J.
4:6 I will *a.* her that halteth
*Zep.* 3:8 I will *a.* the kingdoms

**ASSEMBLED.**
1 *Sam.* 2:22 lay with w. that *a.*
*Ezr.* 9:4 *a.* every one that trem.
*Neh.* 9:1 ch. of Is. *a.* with fast.
*Ps.* 48:4 lo the kings were *a.*
*Is.* 43:9 let the people be *a.* who
*Jer.* 5:7 *a.* by troops in harlot's h.
*Mat.* 28:12 when *a.* gave large
*John* 20:19 disciples *a.* for fear of
*Acts* 1.4 being *a.* not to depart
4:31 where they were *a.*
11:26 w. year *a.* with church
15:25 it seemed good to us *a.*

**ASSEMBLING.**
*Heb.* 10:25 forsake not the *a.*

**ASSEMBLY.**
*Gen.* 49:6 their *a.* mine honor
*Ex.* 16:3 kill *a.* with hunger
*Lev.* 4:13 from the eyes of the *a.*
*Deut.* 9:10 L. spake out of fire in day of *a.* 10:4; 18:16
1 *Sam.* 17:47 *a.* shall know Lord
2 *Chr.* 30:23 *a.* took counsel
*Ps.* 22:16 the *a.* of the wicked
89:7 feared in *a.* of the saints
107:32 praise him in *a.*
111:1 I will praise him in *a.*
*Prov.* 5:14 was in all evil in *a.*
*Jer.* 6:11 on *a.* of young men
9:2 an *a.* of treacherous men
15:17 sat not in *a.* of mockers
*Lam.* 2:6 dest. places of the *a.*
*Ezek.* 13:9 shall not be in the *a.*
*Acts* 19:32 the *a.* was confused
39 deter in a lawful *a.* 41
*Heb.* 12:23 to the general *a.*
*Jam.* 2:2 come to your *a.* a man

**Solemn ASSEMBLY.**
*Lev.* 23:36 eighth day is *a s. a.* *Num.* 29:35; *Neh.* 8:18
*Deut.* 16:8 seventh day *s. a.* to L.
2 *K.* 10:20 a *s. a.* for Baal
2 *Chr.* 7:9 eighth d. made a *s. a.*
*Joel* 1:14 called a *s. a.* 2:15
*Zep.* 3:18 sorrowful for the *s. a.*

**ASSEMBLIES.**
*Ps.* 86:14 *a.* of violent men
*Ec.* 12:11 fas. by masters of *a.*
*Is.* 1:13 calling of *a.*
4:5 create on her *a.* a cloud
*Ezek.* 44:24 in all mine *a.*
*Amos* 5:21 not smell in your *a.*

**ASSENTED.**
*Acts* 24:9 Jews also *a.*

**ASSOCIATE.**
*Is.* 8:9 *a.* and be broken in p.

**ASSUAGE, ED.**
*Gen.* 8:1 and the waters *a.*
*Job* 16:5 mov. of lips should *a.*
6 my grief is not *a.*

**ASSURANCE.**
*Deut.* 28:66 shalt have none *a.*
*Is.* 32:17 effect of righteous. *a.*
*Acts* 17:31 he hath given *a.*
*Col.* 2:2 full *a* of understanding
1 *Thes.* 1:5 came in much *a.*
*Heb.* 6:11 to the full *a.* of hope
10:22 draw near in full *a.*

**ASSURE.**
1 *John* 3:19 shall *a.* our hearts

**ASSURED.**
*Jer.* 14:13 give you *a.* peace
2 *Tim.* 3:14 thou hast been *a.*

**ASSUREDLY.**
*Acts* 2:36 house of Israel know *a.*
16:10 *a.* gathering, L. called us

**ASSYRIA.**
*Gen.* 2:14 toward the east of A.
25:18 dwelt as thou goest to A.
2 *K.* 15:29 cap. to A. 17:6; 18:11
*Is.* 7:18 that is a land of A.
11:11 recover people from A. 16
19:23 out of Egypt to A. 24, 25
27:13 were ready to perish in A.
*Jer.* 2:18 in the way of A.? 36
*Ezek.* 23:7 with men of A.
*Hos.* 7:11 to A. 8:9 up to A.
9:3 eat unclean things in A.
10:6 carried to A. for a present
11:11 dove out of the land of A.
*Mic.* 5:6 waste the land of A.
7:12 come to thee from A.
*Zep.* 2:13 destroy A. and Nin.
*Zec.* 10:10 g. them out of A. 11
*See* KING, KINGS.

**ASTONISHED.**
*Lev.* 26:32 enemies shall be *a.*
1 *K.* 9:8 shall be *a.* *Jer.* 18:16; 19:8; 49:17; 50:13
*Ezr.* 9:3 and sat down *a.*
*Job* 17:8 upright shall be *a.*
18:20 come after shall be *a.*
26:11 pillars of heaven are *a.*
*Is.* 52:14 many were *a.* at thee
*Jer.* 2:12 be *a.* O ye heavens
4:9 the priests shall be *a.*
14:9 why be as a man *a.*
*Ezek.* 3:15 I remained *a.* seven d.
4:17 *a.* one with another
26:16 shall tremble and be *a.*
28:19 know thee shall be *a.*
*Dan.* 3:24 Nebuchadnez. was *a.*
4:19 Daniel was *a.* for one hour
5:9 his lords *a.*
8:27 Daniel was *a.* at the vision
*Mat.* 7:28 *a.* at his, 22:33; *Mark* 1:22; 6:2; 11:18; *Luke* 4:32
*Mark* 5:42 *a.* with great astonish.
7:37 beyond measure *a.* 10:26
10:24 disciples were *a.*
*Luke* 2:47 *a.* at his answers
5:9 was *a.* at draught of fishes
8:56 her parents were *a.* but he
24:22 certain women made us *a.*
*Acts* 9:6 Saul trembling and *a.*
10:45 which believed were *a.*
12:16 saw Peter, they were *a.*
13:12 deputy believed, being *a.*

**ASTONISHMENT.**
*Deut.* 28:28 shall smite with *a.*
37 become an *a.* and a proverb
2 *Chr.* 7:21 shall be an *a.*
29:8 hath delivered them to *a.*
*Ps.* 60:3 to drink the wine of *a.*
*Jer.* 8:21 I am black, *a.* hath
25:9 I will make them an *a.* 18
11 land be a desolation and *a.*
29:18 deliver them to be an *a.*
42:18 execra. and an *a.* 44:12
44:22 theref. is your land an *a.*
51:37 Babyl. shall become an *a.*
*Ezek.* 4:16 drink w. with *a.* 12:19
5:15 an *a.* to the nations
23:33 be filled with cup of *a.*
*Zec.* 12:4 smite horse with *a.*

ASTRAY. *See* WENT, GO, GONE.

**ASTROLOGERS.**
*Is.* 47:13 let now *a.* star-gazers
*Dan.* 1:20 ten times better th. *a.*
2:27 cannot the *a.* show
4:7 came in magicians and *a.*

5:7 king cried to bring in the *a.*

ASUNDER. *See* CLEAVE, CUT, DIVIDE, PUT.

ASYNCRITUS. *Rom.* 16:14

ATAD. *Gen.* 50:10, 11

### ATE.
*Ps.* 106:28 *a.* sacrifi. of the dead
*Dan.* 10:3 I *a.* no pleasant bread
*Rev.* 10:10 book, and *a.* it up

### ATHALIAH.
2 *K.* 8:26 Ahaz. mother was A.
11:1 A. destroyed, 2 *Chr.* 22:10
2 hid Joash from A. 20
1 *Chr.* 8:26 Ben. Shehari. and A.
2 *Chr.* 24:7 the sons of A. 22:11
*Ezr.* 8:7 Jeshaiah son of A.

ATHENIANS. *Acts* 17:21

### ATHENS.
*Acts* 17:15 bro't Paul to A. 16, 22
18:1 Paul departed from A.
1 *Thes.* 3:1 good to be left at A.

### ATHIRST.
*Mat.* 25:44 when saw we thee *a.*
*Rev.* 21:6 give to him that is *a.*
22:17 let him that is *a.* come

### ATONEMENT.
*Ex.* 30:16 shalt take *a.* money
*Lev.* 4:20 *a.* for them, 26, 31, 35; 5:6; 6:7; 8:34; 12:8; 14:18; *Num.* 15:25
9:7 make *a.* for thyself, 16:24
16:10 the scape-goat to make *a.*
17 there, when maketh *a.*
34 to make *a.* once a year
23:28 no work, it is a day of *a.*
25:9 day of *a.* make trumpet
*Num.* 16:46 make *a.* for wrath
31:50 ear-rings to make an *a.*
2 *Sam.* 21:3 wherewith make *a.*
*Rom.* 5:11 we have rec. *a.*

### ATTAIN.
*Ps.* 139:6 I cannot *a.* unto it
*Prov.* 1:5 man of u. *a.* wisdom
*Hos.* 8:5 they *a.* to innocency?
*Phil.* 3:11 might *a.* to resurrec.

### ATTAINED.
*Gen.* 47:9 not *a.* to days of fath.
*Rom.* 9:30 G. have *a.* to right.
31 Is. hath not *a.* to law
*Phil.* 3:12 I had already *a.*
16 already *a.* let us walk
1 *Tim.* 4:6 whereto thou *a.*

ATTALIA. *Acts* 14:25

### ATTEND.
*Ps.* 17:1 *a.* to my c. 61:1; 142:6
55:2 *a.* to me, I mourn
86:6 *a.* to the voice
*Prov.* 4:1 *a.* to know understand.
20 son, *a.* to my words, 7:24
5:1 my son, *a.* to my wisdom
1 *Cor.* 7:35 *a.* on Lord

### ATTENDANCE.
1 *Tim.* 4:13 give *a.* to reading
*Heb.* 7:13 gave *a.* at altar

### ATTENDED.
*Job* 32:12 I *a.* none convinced J.
*Ps.* 66:19 hath *a.* to my prayer
*Acts* 16:14 she *a.* to things spok.

### ATTENDING.
*Rom.* 13:6 ministers *a.* contin.

### ATTENT.
2 *Chr.* 6:40 let thine ears be *a.*
7:15 shall be *a.* to the prayer

### ATTENTIVE.
*Neh.* 1:6 let thine ear now be *a.* 11; *Ps.* 130:2
8:3 people were *a.* *Luke* 19:48

### ATTENTIVELY.
*Job* 37:2 hear *a.* noise of his v.

### ATTIRE.
*Prov.* 7:10 with *a.* of harlot
*Jer.* 2:32 a bride forget her *a.*?
*Ezek.* 23:15 exceeding in dyed *a.*

### AUDIENCE.
*Ex.* 24:7 and read in *a.*
1 *Chr.* 28:8 in *a.* of our God
*Neh.* 13:1 they read in the *a.*
*Luke* 7:1 his sayings in the *a.*
20:45 in *a.* of the people
*Acts* 13:16 ye that fear G. give *a.*
15:12 multitude gave *a.* 22:22

AUGHT. *See* OUGHT.

### AUGMENT.
*Num.* 32:14 to *a.* fierce anger

### AUGUSTUS.
*Luke* 2:1 decree from Cesar A.
*Acts* 25:21 P. appealed to A. 25
27:1 Julius, a centurion of A.

### AUNT.
*Lev.* 18:14 his wife, she is thy *a.*

### AUSTERE.
*Luke* 19:21 thou art an *a.* man

### AUTHOR.
1 *Cor.* 14:33 not *a.* of confusion
*Heb.* 5:9 became *a.* of salvation
12:2 Jesus, the *a.* and finisher

### AUTHORITY, IES.
*Prov.* 29:2 righteous are in *a.*
*Mat.* 7:29 having *a.* *Mark* 1:22
8:9 a man under *a.* *Luke* 7:8
20:25 exercise *a.* *Mark* 10:42
21:23 by what *a.* *Mark* 11:28
*Mark* 1:27 for with *a.* com. unclean spirits, *Luke* 4:36.
13:34 gave *a.* to his servants
*Luke* 9:1 power and *a.* over
19:17 have thou *a.* over
20:20 deliver him to *a.*
22:25 exercise *a.* called benef.
*John* 5:27 *d.* to execute judgm.
*Acts* 8:27 eunuch of great *a.*
9:14 hath *a.* to bind, 26:10, 12
1 *Cor.* 15:24 put down all *a.*
2 *Cor.* 10:8 boast more of *a.*
1 *Tim.* 2:2 suppli. for all in *a.*
12 women to usurp *a.* over
*Tit.* 2:15 rebuke with all *a.*
1 *Pet.* 3:22 and *a.* made subject to
*Rev.* 13:2 gave him great *a.*

### AVAILETH.
*Gal.* 5:6 Christ cir. *a.* not, 6:15
*Jam.* 5:16 prayer of right *a.*

### AVEN.
*Ezek.* 30:17 men of A. fall
*Hos.* 10:8 high of A. *Amos* 1:5

### AVENGE.
*Lev.* 19:18 thou shalt not *a.*
26:25 *a.* the quarrel of my cov.
*Num.* 31:2 *a.* Is. of Midianites, 3
*Deut.* 32:43 *a.* blood of servants
1 *Sam.* 24:12 Lord *a.* me of thee
*Isa.* 1:24 *a.* me of mine enemies
*Jer.* 46:10 that he may *a.*
*Hos.* 1:4 will *a.* blood of Jezreel
*Luke* 18:3 *a.* me of mine adver.
7 shall not God *a.* his own el.
8 he will *a.* them speedily
*Rom.* 12:19 *a.* not yourselves
*Rev.* 6:10 dost thou not *a.* our

### AVENGED.
*Gen.* 4:24 Cain be *a.* seven-fold
*Jos.* 10:13 stayed till peo. had *a.*
*Jud.* 15:7 yet I will be *a.*
16:28 *a.* of Philis. of my
1 *Sam.* 14:24 that I may be *a.*
18:25 foreskins to be *a.*
25:31 my Lord hath *a.* himself
2 *Sam.* 4:8 hath *a.* my lord
18:19 the Lord hath *a.* him
*Jer.* 5:9 my soul be *a.* 29; 9:9
*Acts* 7:24 *a.* him oppressed
*Rev.* 18:20 God hath *a.* you
19:2 *a.* blood of his servants

### AVENGER.
*Num.* 35:12 from *a.* *Jos.* 20:3
*Deut.* 19:6 lest *a.* pursue
12 the elders deliver him to *a.*
*Jos.* 20:5 if the *a.* pursue
*Ps.* 8:2 mightest still the *a.*
44:16 by re. of the enemy and *a.*
1 *Thes.* 4:6 Lord is *a.* of all such

### AVENGETH.
2 *Sam.* 22:48 G. *a.* me, *Ps.* 18:47

### AVENGING.
*Jud.* 5:2 praise L. for *a.* of Isra.

### AVERSE.
*Mic.* 2:8 as men *a.* from war

### AVOID.
*Prov.* 4:15 *a.* it, pass not by it
*Rom.* 16:17 divisions, and *a.*
2 *Tim.* 2:23 unl. questions *a.*
*Tit.* 3:9 *a.* foolish questions

### AVOIDING.
2 *Cor.* 8:20 *a.* this, that no man
1 *Tim.* 6:20 *a.* profane babblings

### AVOUCHED.
*Deut.* 26:17 *a.* the Lord to be
18 *a.* thee to be his people

### AWAKE.
*Jud.* 5:12 *a.* *a.* Deb., *a.* *a.* utter
*Job* 8:6 he would *a.* for thee
14:12 be no more not *a.*
*Ps.* 7:6 *a.* for me, 35:23
17:15 I *a.* with thy likeness
44:23 *a.* why sleepest thou
57:8 *a.* my glory, I w. *a.* 108:2
59:4 they prepare, *a.* to help
*Ps.* 59:5 O L. *a.* to visit all the
*Prov.* 23:35 when shall I *a.*
*Cant.* 2:7 *a.* my love, 3:5; 8:4
4:16 *a.* O north wind
*Is.* 26:19 *a.* ye that dwell
51:9 *a.* *a.* put on strength, O arm of the Lord *a.* 52:1
17 *a.* stand up, O Jerusalem
*Jer.* 51:57 perp. sleep, and not *a.*
*Dan.* 12:2 in the dust shall *a.*
*Joel* 1:5 *a.* ye drunkards, weep
*Hab.* 2:7 *a.* that shall vex thee
19 that saith to the wood, *a.*
*Zec.* 13:7 *a.* O sword ag. my
*Mark* 4:38 and they *a.* him
*Luke* 9:32 when *a.* saw his glory
*John* 11:11 that I may *a.* him
*Rom.* 13:1 it is high time to *a.*
1 *Cor.* 15:34 *a.* to righteousness
*Eph.* 5:14 *a.* thou that sleepest

### AWAKED.
1 *Sam.* 26:12 knew it, neither *a.*
1 *K.* 18:27 and must be *a.*
2 *K.* 4:31 the child is not *a.*
*Ps.* 3:5 I *a.* for L. sustained me
78:65 L. *a.* as one out of sleep
*Jer.* 31:26 I *a.* and behold

### AWAKEST.
*Ps.* 73:20 when thou *a.* shalt
*Prov.* 6:22 when thou *a.* it shall

**AWAKETH, ING.**
*Ps.* 73:20 dream when one *a.*
*Is.* 29:8 he *a.* and his soul
*Acts* 16:27 keeper of the prison *a.*

**AWARE.**
*Cant.* 6:12 I was *a.* my soul
*Jer.* 50:24 O, and was not *a.*
*Luke* 11:44 over them not *a.*

**AWAY.**
*Is.* 1:13 I cannot *a.* with
*Luke* 23:18 *a.* with this man
*John* 19:15 *a.* with h. *Acts* 21:36
*Acts* 22:22 *a.* with such a fellow

**AWE.**
*Ps.* 4:4 stand in *a.* and sin not
33:8 inhab. of world stand in *a.*
119:161 my heart standeth in *a.*

**AWL.**
*Ex.* 21:6 bore his ear with an *a.*
*Deut.* 15:17 thou shalt take an *a.*

**AWOKE.**
*Mat.* 8:25 discip. *a.* h. *Luke* 8:24

**AXE.**
*Deut.* 20:19 destroy trees by *a.*
*Jud.* 9:48 Abimelech took an *a*
1 *Sam.* 13:20 went to sharp. *a.*
1 *K.* 6:7 hammer nor *a.* was h.
2 *K.* 6:5 *a.*-head fell into w.
*Is.* 10:15 shall the *a.* boast
*Jer.* 10:3 cuts a tree with the *a*
51:20 thou art my battle-*a.*
*Mat.* 3:10 *a.* is laid, *Luke* 3:9

**AXES.**
1 *Sam.* 13:21 had a file for the *a.*
2 *Sam.* 12:31 he put them under *a.* of iron, 1 *Chr.* 20:3
*Ps.* 74:5 fam. as he lifted up *a.*
6 break carved work with *a.*
*Jer.* 46:22 against her with *a.*
*Ezek.* 26:9 with *a.* break down

# B

BAALAH. *Jam.* 15:9
BAAL-GAD. *Jos.* 11:17
BAAL-HERMON. *Jud.* 3:3

**BAAL.**
*Num.* 22:41 to high places of B.
*Jud.* 2:13 Is. served B. and Ash.
6:25 down the altar of B. 31
1 *K.* 16:31 B. and worshipped
18:21 if B. be God, follow him
19:18 7,000 in Israel which have not bowed to B. *Rom.* 11:4
2 *K.* 10:19 sac. to do to B. 20
11:18 brake down house of B.
17:16 host of heaven served B.
21:3 Manas. reared altars for B.
23:4 bring all the vessels for B.
*Jer.* 2:8 proph. prophesied by B.
7:9 inc. to B. ? 11:13, 17; 32:29
12:16 to swear by B.
19;5 built high places of B.
23:13 prophesied in B. 27
*Hos.* 2:8 silver and gold for B.
13:1 Ephraim offended in B.
*Zep.* 1:4 cut off remnant of B.
BAAL-BERITH. *Jud.* 8:33
BAAL-HAMON. *Cant.* 8:11
BAALI. *Hos.* 2:16

**BAALIM.**
*Jud.* 2:11 Is. s. B. 3:7; 10:6, 10
8:33 Isr. went whoring after B.
1 *Sam.* 7:4 Israel put away B.
1 *K.* 18:18 hast followed B.
2 *Chr.* 17:3 J. sought not to B.
24:7 dedic. things on B. 28:2
33:3 M. reared altars for B.
34:4 brake the altars of B.
*Jer.* 2:23 have not gone after B.
9:14 have walked after B.
*Hos.* 2:13 on her days of B. 17
BAALIS. *Jer.* 40:14
BAAL-MEON. *Ezek.* 25:9

**BAAL-PEOR.**
*Num.* 25:3 Is. joined himself to B. 5; *Ps.* 106:28; *Hos.* 9:10
*Deut.* 4:3 Lord did because of B.
BAAL-PERAZIM. 2 *Sam.* 5:20; 1 *Chr.* 14:11
BAAL-SHALISHA. 2 *K.* 4:42
BAAL-TAMAR. *Jud.* 20:33
BAAL-ZEBUB. 2 *K.* 1:2, 16
BAAL-ZEPHON. *Ex.* 14:2; *Num.* 33:7

**BAANAH.**
2 *Sam.* 4:6 Rechab and B. esc.
23:29 Heleb the son of B.
1 *K.* 4:16 B. the son of H.
*Ezr.* 2:2 B. c. to. *Neh.* 7:7; 10:27

**BAASHA.**
1 *K.* 15:16, 19, 27; 16:1, 6, 11, 12; 21:22; 2 *K.* 9:9; 2 *Chr.* 16:3; *Jer.* 41:9

**BABBLER.**
*Ec.* 10:11 and a *b.* is no better
*Acts* 17:18 what will this *b.* say?

**BABBLING, S.**
*Prov.* 23:29 who hath *b.*?
1 *Tim.* 6:20 avoiding vain *b.*
2 *Tim.* 2:16 profane and vain *b.*

**BABE, S.**
*Ex.* 2:6 behold the *b.* wept
*Luke* 1:41 *b.* leaped in her womb
44 *b.* leaped in my womb
2:12 find *b.* wrapped in swad.
16 the *b.* lying in a manger
*Heb.* 5:13 for he is a *b.*
*Ps.* 8:2 mouth of *b.* *Mat.* 21:16
17:14 leave substance to their *b.*
*Is.* 3:4 princes and *b.* shall rule
*Mat.* 11:25 rev. t. to *b.* *Luke* 10:21
*Rom.* 2:20 a teacher of *b.*
1 *Cor.* 3:1 as unto *b.* in Christ
1 *Pet.* 2:2 as new-born *b.* desire
BABEL. *Gen.* 10:10; 11:9

**BABYLON.**
*Mat.* 1:17 the carrying into B.
*Acts* 7:43 carry away beyond B.
1 *Pet.* 5:13 church at B. saluteth
*Rev.* 14:8 B. is fallen, is fallen
16:19 B. came in remembrance
17:5 B. the mother of harlots
18:10 alas, that city B. 21
*See* DAUGHTER.
BABYLONIANS. *Ezek.* 23:15, 17
BABYLONISH. *Jos.* 7:21
BACA. *Ps.* 84:6

**BACK.**
1 *K.* 14:9 behind t. *b.* *Ezek.* 23:35
*Ps.* 21:12 turn their *b.*
129:3 ploughed on my *b.*
*Prov.* 10:13 rod for *b.* 19:29; 26:3
*Is.* 38,17 my sins behind thy *b.*
50:6 my *b.* to the smiters
*Jer.* 2:27 have turned *b.* unto me
18:17 will show *b.* not the face
32:33 turned to me *b.* and not
48:39 turned the *b.* with shame
*Rom.* 11:10 bow down their *b.*

**BACK, Adjective.**
*Ex.* 33:23 shalt see my *b.* parts

**BACKS.**
*Neh.* 9:26 thy law behind their *b.*
*Ezek.* 8:16 their *b.* toward the
10:12 body, and *b.* full of
*See* TURNED.

**BACKBITERS.**
*Rom.* 1:30 *b.* haters of God

**BACKBITETH.**
*Ps.* 15:3 that *b.* not with his

**BACKBITING, S.**
*Prov.* 25:23 a *b.* tongue
2 *Cor.* 12:20 there be debates, *b.*

**BACKSLIDER.**
*Prov.* 14:14 *b.* in heart be filled

**BACKSLIDING, S.**
*Jer.* 2:19 thy *b.* shall reprove
3:6 what *b.* Israel hath done
8 whereby *b.* Israel com. ad.
3:11 *b.* Is. hath justified herself
12 return thou *b.* Israel,
14 O *b.* children, saith L. 22
5:6 because their *b.* increased
8:5 back by a perpetual *b.*
*Jer.* 14:7 for our *b.* are many
31:22 O *b.* daughter, 49:4
*Hos.* 4:16 Is. slideth back as a *b.*
11:7 are bent to *b.* from me
14:4 I will heal their *b.* I will

**BACKWARD.**
*Gen.* 9:23 *b.* their faces were *b.*
49:17 his rider shall fall *b.*
2 *K.* 20:10 return *b.* *Is.* 38:8
*Job* 23:8 *b.* I cannot perceive h.
*Ps.* 40:14 driven *b.* that wish me
70:2 turned *b.* that desire
*Is.* 1:4 they are gone away *b.*
28:13 they might go and fall *b.*
44:25 that turneth wise men *b.*
59:14 judgm. is turned away *b.*
*Jer.* 7:24 went *b.* not forward
15:6 thou art gone *b.* therefore
*Lam.* 1:8 sigheth and turn. *b.*
*John* 18:6 went *b.* and fell to

**BAD.**
*Gen.* 24:50 speak *b.* or good
31:24 to Jacob good or *b.* 29
*Lev.* 27:10 a good for a *b.* or a *b.*
*Num.* 13:9 land if good or *b.*
24:13 to do either good or *b.*
2 *Sam.* 13:22 spake good nor *b.*
14:17 to discern good or *b.*
1 *K.* 3:9 discern good and *b.*
*Mat.* 13:48 but cast the *b.* away
22:10 good and *b.* and the wed.
2 *Cor.* 5:10 whether good or *b.*

**BADNESS.**
*Gen.* 41:19 never saw in E. for *b.*

**BADE, EST.**
*Gen.* 27:19 have done as thou *b.*
*Luke* 14:9 he that *b.* thee, 10
16 a supper, and *b.* many
*Acts* 11:12 Spirit *b.* me go
18:21 but *b.* them farewell

**BADGERS.**
*Ex.* 26:14 cov. above of *b.* skins
35:7 skins dyed red, *b.* skins
*Ezek.* 16:10 I shod thee w. *b.* sk.

**BAG.**
*Deut.* 25:13 in thy *b.* div. weig.
1 *Sam.* 17:40 sm. stones in a *b.*
*Job* 14:17 trans. is sealed in a *b.*
*Prov.* 7:20 taken a *b.* of money
16:11 weights of *b.* are his w.
*Is.* 46:6 lavish gold out of the *b.*
*Mic.* 6:11 *b.* of deceitful weights
*Hag.* 1:6 wages to put in a *b.* w.
*John* 12:6 a thief, and had the *b.*
13:29 because Judas had the *b.*

**BAGS.**
2 *K.* 5:23 two talents in two *b.*
12:10 they put up in *b.*
*Luke* 12:33 prov. *b.* that wax not

**BAHURIM.**
2 *Sam.* 3:16 behind her to B.
16:5 when David came to B.
17:18 came to a house in B.
19:16 a Benj. of B. 1 *K.* 2:8

**BAJITH.**
*Is.* 15:2 he is gone up to B.

**BAKE.**
*Ex.* 16:23 *b.* that you will *b.*
*Lev.* 24:5 and *b.* twelve cakes
26:26 ten women shall *b.*
1 *Sam.* 28:24 woman at E. did *b.*
*Ezek.* 4:12 shall *b.* it with

**BAKE-MEATS.**
*Gen.* 40:17 *b.-meats* for Pharaoh

**BAKEN.**
1 *K.* 19:6 was *b.* on the coals

**BAKER.**
*Gen.* 40:1 *b.* had offended the k.
22 hanged *b.* as Jo. interpreted
41:10 in ward me and chief *b.*
*Hos.* 7:4 oven heated by the *b.*
6 their *b.* sleepeth all the n.

**BAKERS.**
*Gen.* 40:2 wroth ag. chief of *b.*
1 *Sam.* 8:13 daughters to be *b.*
*Jer.* 37:21 bread out of *b.* street

**BAKETH.**
*Is.* 44:15 he *b.* bread, yea, he

**BALAAM.**
*Num.* 22:5, 9, 14, 25, 31, 35; 23:4, 30; 24:2, 3, 25; 31:8, 16
*Deut.* 23:4 hired B. 5; *Neh.* 13:2
*Jos.* 24:9 B. sent and called B.
*Mic.* 6:5 rem. what B. answ.
2 *Pet.* 2:15 fol. the way of B.
*Jude* 11 greedily after error of B.
*Rev.* 2:14 hold the doctrine of B.

**BALAK.**
*Num.* 22:4, 16; 23:2, 7, 18; 24:13
*Jos.* 24:9 B. arose and warred
*Jud.* 11:25 better than B.?
*Mic.* 6:5 remember what B. k.
*Rev.* 2:14 who taught B. to cast

**BALD.**
*Lev.* 13:40 he is *b.* yet clean, 41
2 *K.* 2:23 go up thou *b.* head
*Jer.* 16:6 make themselves *b.*
48:37 every head shall be *b.*
*Ezek.* 27:31 make themselves *b.*
29:18 every head was made *b.*
*Mic.* 1:16 make thee *b.* and poll

**BALD-LOCUST.**
*Lev.* 11:22 ye may eat the *b.-l*

**BALDNESS.**
*Lev.* 21:5 make *b.* on their head
*Deut.* 14:1 *b.* between your eyes
*Is.* 3:24 inst. of well-set hair, *b.*
15:2 on heads *b.* and beard cut
22:12 the Lord did call to *b.*
*Jer.* 47:5 *b.* is come upon Gaza.
*Ezek.* 7:18 *b.* on their h. *Am.* 8:10
*Mic.* 1:16 enlarge thy *b.*

**BALANCE.**
*Job* 31:6 be weighed in even *b.*
*Ps.* 62:9 laid in the *b.* are van.
*Prov.* 11:1 a false *b.* 20:23
16:11 just w. and *b.* are Lord's
*Is.* 40:12 weighed hills in a *b.*
15 as small dust of the *b.*
46:6 and weighs silver in the *b.*

**BALANCES.**
*Lev.* 19:36 just *b.* *Ezek.* 45:10
*Job* 6:2 calamity laid in the *b.*
*Ezek.* 5:1 take *b.* to weigh
*Dan.* 5:27 in the *b.* and found
*Hos.* 12:7 *b.* of deceit
*Amos* 8:5 falsifying the *b.*
*Mic.* 6:11 pure with wicked *b.*?
*Rev.* 6:5 he that sat on h. had *b.*

**BALANCINGS.**
*Job* 37:16 kn. the *b.* of t. clouds

**BALL.**
*Is.* 22:18 will toss thee like a *b.*

**BALM.**
*Gen.* 37:25 Ishmaelites bearing *b.*
43:11 take a little *b.* and honey
*Jer.* 8:22 is there no *b.* in Gilead?
46:11 to Gilead and take *b.* O
51:8 howl take *b.* for her pain
*Ezek.* 27:17 J. traded in honey *b.*

BAMAH. *Ezek.* 20:29

**BAND, S.**
*Lev.* 26:13 the *b.* of your yoke
*Jud.* 15:14 *b.* loosed off h. hands
2 *K.* 23:33 Phar. put Jeh. in *b.*
*Job* 38:9 darkness a swaddling *b.*
31 or loose the *b.* of Orion?
39:5 the *b.* of the wild ass?
10 the unicorn with his *b.*?
*Ps.* 2:3 break their *b.* asunder
73:4 there are no *b.*
107:14 brake their *b.* in sunder
*Ec.* 7:26 snares, hands as *b.*
*Is.* 28:22 lest *b.* be made strong
52:2 loose from *b.* of thy neck
58:6 loose the *b.* of wickedness
*Jer.* 2:20 I have burst thy *b*
*Ezek.* 3:25 shall put *b.* on thee
4:8 I will lay *b.* upon thee
34:27 broken the *b.* of their y.
*Dan.* 4:15 with a *b.* of iron, 23
*Hos.* 11:4 drew them with *b.*
*Zec.* 11:7 staves, beauty and *b.*
14 mine other staff, even *b.*
*Luke* 8:29 he brake *b.*
*Acts* 16:26 every one's *b.* were lo.
22:30 loosed Paul from his *b.*
*Col.* 2:19 all the body by *b.*
*See* BONDS.

**BAND, S—*companies.***
*Gen.* 32:10 I am become two *b.*
1 *Sam.* 10:26 went with him a *b.*
2 *K.* 13:21 a man, spied a *b.*
24:2 L. sent *b.* of Chaldeans, *b.*
1 *Chr.* 12:18 made them cap. of *b.*
21 David ag. the *b.* of rovers
*Job* 1:17 Chald. made three *b.*
*Ps.* 119:61 *b.* of wicked robbed
*Prov.* 30:27 the locusts go by *b.*
*Ezek.* 12:14 will scatter all his *b.*
38:22 rain on him and his *b.*
*Mat.* 27:27 whole *b.* *Mark* 15:16
*John* 18:3 Judas having re. *b.*
12 the *b.* took Jesus
*Acts* 10:1 *b.* called the Italian *b.*
21:31 tid. came to cap. of the *b.*
27:1 to Jul. cent. of Augustus' *b.*

**BANDED.**
*Acts* 23:12 certain of the Jews *b.*

**BANK.**
*Gen.* 41:17 I stood on the *b.*
*Deut.* 4:48 Aroer by the *b.* of Arnon, *Jos.* 12:2; 13:9, 16
2 *Sam.* 20:15 a *b.* ag. the city
2 *K.* 2:13 E. stood by the *b.*
19:32 not cast a *b.* *Is.* 37:33
*Ezek.* 47:7 at *b.* of river
*Dan.* 12:5 one on this side, other on that side of the *b.*
*Luke* 19:23 money into the *b.*?

**BANKS.**
*Jos.* 3:15 Jord. overfl. his *b.* 4:18

**BANNER.**
*Ps.* 60:4 a *b.* to them that fear
*Cant.* 2:4 his *b.* over me was
*Is.* 13:2 lift ye up a *b.*

**BANNERS.**
*Ps.* 20:5 n. of G. set up our *b.*
*Cant.* 6:4 terr. as an army w. *b.*

**BANISHED.**
2 *Sam.* 14:13 fetch home his *b.*
14 that his *b.* be not expelled

**BANISHMENT.**
*Ezr.* 7:26 whether to death or *b.*
*Lam.* 2:14 have seen causes of *b.*

**BANQUET.**
*Est.* 5:4 Haman come to *b.* 5, 8
6 to Esther at *b.* of wine, 7:2
*Job* 41:6 make a *b.* of him
*Amos* 6:7 *b.* of them that

**BANQUET-HOUSE.**
*Dan.* 5:10 came into the *b.-h.*

**BANQUETING, S.**
*Cant.* 2:4 brought me to the *b.*
1 *Pet.* 4:3 we walked in lusts, *b.*

**BAPTISM, S.**
*Mat.* 3:7 Pharisees come to his *b.*
20:22 bap. with *b.* *Mark* 10:38
21:25 the *b.* of J., whence was it? *Mark* 11:30; *Luke* 20:4
*Mark* 1:4 J. did baptize, and pre. the *b.* of repent., *Luke* 3:3
*Luke* 7:29 publicans with *b.* of J.
12:50 a *b.* to be baptiz. with
*Acts* 1:22 beginning from *b.* of J.
10:37 after *b.* which J. preached
13:24 J. prea. *b.* of repentance
18:25 Apollos knowing only *b.*
19:3 they said unto John's *b.*
4 John bap. with *b.* of repent.
*Rom.* 6:4 buried with him by *b.*
*Eph.* 4:5 one L., one faith, one *b.*
*Col.* 2:12 buried with him in *b.*
*Heb.* 6:2 doctrine of *b.* and lay'g.
1 *Pet.* 3:21 whereunto, even *b.*

**BAPTIST.**
*Mat.* 3:1 came John *b.* preaching
11:11 hath not risen a greater than J. the *b.* *Luke* 7:28
12 the days of John the *b.*
14:2 this is J. the *b.* he is risen
8 give me John the *b.* head
16:14 art John *b.* *Mark* 8:28
17:13 he spake of John the *b.*
*Mark* 6:14 John the *b.* was risen
25 give me head of John the *b.*
*Luke* 7:20 John the *b.* hath sent
33 J. the *b.* eating nor drink.
9:19 answering said, J. the *b.*

**BAPTIZE.**
*Mat.* 3:11 I *b.* with w., he shall *b.* with Holy Ghost, *Mark* 1:8; *Luke* 3:16; *John* 1:26
*Mark* 1:4 J. did *b.* in wilderness
*John* 1:33 he that sent me to *b.*
1 *Cor.* 1:17 Ch. sent me not to *b.*

**BAPTIZED.**
*Mat.* 3:6 were *b.* in J. *Mark* 1:5
13 then cometh Jesus to be *b.*
14 I have need to be *b.* of thee
16 J. when he was *b.* went up
*Mark* 1:9 Jesus was *b.* of John
10:39 baptism I am *b.* withal
16:16 believeth and is *b.* shall
*Luke* 3:7 mult. came to be *b.*
12 came publicans to be *b.* 7:29
21 Jesus being *b.* and praying
7:30 lawyers, being not *b.*
*John* 3:22 he tarried, and *b.*
23 and they were *b.*
4:1 J. made and *b.* more disci.
2 though Jesus himself *b.* not
10:40 place where J. at first *b.*
*Acts* 1:5 J. *b.* with water, but ye shall be *b.* with H. G. 11:16
2:38 be *b.* every one of you
41 received his word were *b.*
8:12 were *b.* both men and w.
13 Simon, and when he was *b.*
16 were *b.* in the name of J.
36 w. doth hinder me to be *b.*?
38 P. and eunuch, and he *b.*
9:18 Saul arose and was *b.*
10:47 these should not be *b.*
48 P. commanded them to be *b.*
16:15 Lydia when she was *b.*
33 jailer was *b.* and all his
18:8 C. believed, and were *b.*

*Acts* 19:3 to what were ye *b*.
5 w. they heard this, were *b*.
22:16 arise, and be *b*. and wash
*Rom*. 6:3 *b*. into Jesus, *b*. into
1 *Cor*. 1:13 *b*. in the name of P.?
14 thank God that I *b*. none
16 I *b*. household of S. not *b*.
10:2 and were all *b*. to Moses
12:13 one Spirit *b*. into one body
15:29 are they *b*. for the dead
*Gal*. 3:27 as many as *b*. into Ch.

**BAPTIZEST.**
*John* 1:25 why *b*. thou

**BAPTIZETH.**
*John* 1:33 who *b*. with the H. G.
3:26 the same *b*. all men come

**BAPTIZING.**
*Mat*. 28:19 t. all nations, *b*. them
*John* 1:28 Jordan where J. was *b*.
31 am I come *b*. with water
3:23 John was also *b*. in Enon

**BAR.**
*Neh*. 7:3 shut the doors, *b*. them

**BAR, Substantive.**
*Jud*. 16:3 took doors, posts, *b*.
*Amos* 1:5 break *b*. of Damas

**BARS.**
*Deut*. 3:5 cit. fenced w. gates and *b*. 2 *K*. 4:13; 2 *Chr*. 8:5; 14:7
1 *Sam*. 23:7 a town that hath *b*.
*Job* 17:16 to the *b*. of the pit
38:10 and set *b*. for the sea
40:18 Beh. his bones *b*. of iron
*Ps*. 107:16 *b*. of iron, *Is*. 45:2
147:13 strength, *b*. of thy gates
*Prov*. 18:19 cont. are like the *b*.
*Jer*. 49:31 neither gates nor *b*.
51:30 Babylon, her *b*. are brok.
*Lam*. 2:9 he hath broken her *b*.
*Ezek*. 38:11 having gates nor *b*.
*Jon*. 2:6 the earth with her *b*.
*Nah*. 3:13 fire shall dev. thy *b*.

BARACHEL. *Job* 32:2
BARABBAS. *Mat*. 27; *Mark* 15; *Luke* 23; *John* 18
BARACHIAS. *Mat*. 23:35
BARAK. *Jud*. 4:6, 9; 5:1, 12; *Heb*. 11:32

**BARBARIAN.**
1 *Cor*. 14:11 a *b*. and he a *b*.
*Col*. 3:11 nei. Greek nor Jew, *b*.

**BARBARIANS.**
*Acts* 28:4 *b*. saw venomous beast
*Rom*. 1:14 both to Greeks and *b*.

**BARBAROUS.**
*Acts* 28:2 *b*. people showed kind

**BARBED.**
*Job* 41:7 his skin with *b*. irons

**BARBER.**
*Ezek*. 5:1 take thee a *b*. razor

**BARE**—*carried*.
*Ex*. 19:4 I *b*. you on eagle's w.
*Deut*. 1:31 thy God *b*. thee as
*Is*. 53:12 he *b*. the sin of many
63:9 he *b*. them all the days
*Mat*. 8:17 *b*. our sicknesses
*Luke* 7:14 they that *b*. him stood
*John* 12:6 bag, *b*. what put th.
1 *Pet*. 2:24 his own self *b*. our s.

**BARE.**
*Gen*. 31:8 the cattle *b*. speckled
44:27 my wife *b*. me two sons
*Ex*. 6:20 Jochebed *b*. Moses
*Jud*. 13:2 Manoah's wife *b*. not
1 *Chr*. 4:9 Jabez, I *b*. him
*Prov*. 17:25 bitt. to her that *b*.
23:25 that *b*. thee shall rejoice
*Cant*. 6:9 ch. one of her that *b*.
8:5 that *b*. thee
*Is*. 51:2 look unto S. that *b*. you
*Jer*. 16:3 mother that *b*. them
20:14 the day my mother *b*. me
22:26 cast our mother that *b*.
50:12 *b*. you shall be ashamed
*Luke* 11:27 blessed is w. that *b*.
23:29 the wombs that never *b*.

**BARE fruit.**
*Luke* 8:8 and *b*. *f*. a hundred-fold
*Rev*. 22:2 tree of life *b*. *f*. twelve

**BARE rule.**
*Neh*. 5:15 their servants *b*. *r*. over

**BARE witness,** *and* **record.**
*Mark* 14:56 *b*. f. *w*. ag. him, 57
*Luke* 4:22 all *b*. him *w*. and won.
*John* 1:15 *b*. *w*. of him, 32, 34
5:33 John *b*. *witness* to the truth
12:17 the people with h. *b*. *rec*.
19:35 he that saw it *b*. *record*
*Acts* 15:8 kn. the hearts, *b*. *w*.
*Rev*. 1:2 *b*. *r*. of the word of God

**BAREST.**
*Is*. 63:19 thou never *b*. rule over
*John* 3:26 to whom thou *b*. witn.

**BARE, Adjective.**
*Lev*. 13:45 cl. rent, head *b*. 55
*Is*. 32:11 strip ye, make ye *b*.
47:2 make *b*. the leg, uncover
52:10 made *b*. his holy arm
*Jer*. 13:22 thy heels made *b*.
49:10 I have made Esau *b*.
*Ezek*. 16:7 wast naked and *b*. 22
39 naked and *b*. 23:29
*Joel* 1:7 my fig-tree clean *b*.
1 *Cor*. 15:37 shall be, but *b*. grain

**BAREFOOT.**
2 *Sam*. 15:30 went *b*. and the p.
*Is*. 20:2 Is. did so, walking *b*. 3
4 the Egyptians, naked and *b*.

BAR-JESUS. *Acts* 13:6
BAR-JONA. *Mat*. 16:17

**BARK.**
*Is*. 56:10 dumb dogs cannot *b*.

**BARLEY.**
*Ex*. 9:31 *b*. was smitten, for *b*.
*Deut*. 8:8 a land of wheat and *b*.
*Jud*. 7:13 a cake of *b*. tumbled
*Ruth* 1:22 begin. of *b*. harvest
3:2 B. winnoweth *b*. to-night
2 *Sam*. 14:30 Joab's field, *b*. there
17:28 Barzillai brought beds, *b*.
2 *K*. 4:42 brought 20 loaves of *b*.
7:1 two meas. of *b*. for sh. 16, 18
2 *Chr*. 2:10 20,000 measures of *b*.
15 wheat, and *b*. let him send
27:5 Am. gave 10,000 me. of *b*.
*Job* 31:40 let co. grow inst. of *b*.
*Is*. 28:25 wheat, and appointed *b*.
*Jer*. 41:8 we have treasures of *b*.
*Ezek*. 4:9 take to thee wh. and *b*.
12 shalt eat it as *b*. cakes
13:19 handfuls of *b*.
*Hos*. 3:2 for a homer of *b*.
*Joel* 1:11 howl for wheat and *b*.
*John* 6:9 hath five *b*. loaves
13 frag. of the five *b*. loaves
*Rev* 6:6 meas. of *b*. for a penny

**BARN.**
2 *K*. 6:27 out of the *b*. floor?
*Job* 39:12 g. thy seed into the *b*.
*Hag*. 2:19 is seed yet in *b*. vine
*Mat*. 13:30 g. wheat into my *b*.
*Luke* 12:24 no storehouse nor *b*.

**BARNS.**
*Prov*. 3:10 shall thy *b*. be filled
*Joel* 1:17 the *b*. are broken down
*Mat*. 6:26 nor gather into
*Luke* 12:18 will pull down my *b*.

**BARNABAS.**
*Acts* 4:36; 11:22, 25, 30; 12:25; 13:1, 2, 50; 14:12; 15:2, 12, 37
1 *Cor*. 9:6 or I only and B. have
*Gal*. 2:1 I went up with B. 9, 13
*Col*. 4:10 Marc. sister's son to B.

**BARREL, S.**
1 *K*. 17:14 the *b*. of meal shall
18:33 fill four *b*. with water

**BARREN.**
*Gen*. 11:30 but Sarai was *b*.
25:21 Reb. *b*. 29:31 Rachel *b*.
*Ex*. 23:26 cast young nor be *b*.
*Deut*. 7:14 male or female *b*.
*Jud*. 13:2 Man.'s wife was *b*. 3
1 *Sam*. 2:5 the *b*. hath borne sev.
2 *K*. 2:19 and the ground *b*.
21 shall not be death, or *b*.
*Job* 24:21 evil entreateth the *b*.
39:6 the *b*. land his dwellings
*Ps*. 113:9 the *b*. woman to keep
*Prov*. 30:16 *b*. womb not satis.
*Cant*. 4:2 and none is *b*. 6:6
*Is*. 54:1 sing, O *b*. that didst not
*Joel* 2:20 drive him into a land *b*.
*Luke* 1:7 bec. Elizabeth was *b*.
36 with her, who was called *b*.
23:29 blessed are the *b*. and
*Gal*. 4:27 written, Rejoice thou *b*.
2 *Pet*. 1:8 neither *b*. nor unfruitful

**BARRENNESS.**
*Ps*. 107:34 fruitful land into *b*.

BARSABAS. *Acts* 1:23; 15:22
BARTHOLOMEW. *Mat*. 10:3; *Mar*. 3:18; *Lu*. 6:14; *Acts* 1:13
BARTIMEUS. *Mark* 10:46

**BARUCH.**
*Neh*. 3:20 B. son of Zab. repair.
*Jer*. 32:12; 36:4, 26; 43:3; 45:1

BARZILLAI. 2 *Sam*. 17:27; 19:32, 39; 21:8; 1 *K*. 2:7; *Ezr*. 2:61

**BASE.**
*Zec*. 5:11 upon her own *b*.

**BASE, Adjective.**
2 *Sam*. 6:22 *b*. in mine own sight
*Job* 30:8 were children of *b*. men
*Is*. 3:5 *b*. against the honorable
*Ezek*. 17:14 kingdom might be *b*.
29:14 shall be a *b*. kingdom
*Mal*. 2:9 I have made you *b*.
1 *Cor*. 1:28 *b*. things G. hath ch.
2 *Cor*. 10:1 who in presence am *b*.

**BASER.**
*Acts* 17:5 fellows of the *b*. sort

**BASEST.**
*Ezek*. 29:15 Patros *b*. of kingd.
*Dan*. 4:17 set. over it *b*. of men

**BASHAN.**
*Num*. 21:33; 32:33; *Deut*. 1:4; 3:1, 3, 4, 10, 11; 4:47; *Jos*. 13:12
*Ps*. 22:12 strong bulls of B.
68:15 B. a h. hill, B. why leap, 22
*Is*. 33:9 B. and Carmel shake
*Jer*. 22:20 lift up thy voice in B.
50:19 feed on Carmel and B.
*Ezek*. 39:18 fatlings of B.
*Amos* 4:1 ye kine of B.
*Mic*. 7:14 let them feed in B.
*Nah*. 1:4 B. languished, Carmel

**BASHEMATH.**
*Gen*. 26:34 to wife B. 36:3

**BASIN.**
1 *Chr*. 28:17 gold for every *b*.
*John* 13:5 he poureth w. into a *b*.

**BASINS.**
2 *Sam*. 17:28 Barzillai brought *b*.
*Jer*. 52:19 *b*. captain took away

**BASKET.**
*Gen*. 40:17 in the *b*. all manner of bake-meats
*Ex*. 29:23 *b*. of unleavened bread, *Lev*. 8:2, 26; *Num*. 6:15, 17
*Lev*. 8:31 *b*. of consecrations
*Deut*. 28:5 blessed shall be thy *b*.
17 cursed shall be thy *b*.
*Jud*. 6:19 Gid. put flesh in a *b*.

*Jer.* 24:2 one *b.* had good figs
*Amos* 8:1 a *b.* of summer fruit, 2
*Acts* 9:25 w. in a *b.* 2 *Cor.* 11:33

**BASKETS.**

*Gen.* 40:16 I had three white *b.*
18 the three *b.* are three days
2 *K.* 10:7 their heads in *b.*
*Jer.* 6:9 as g.-gatherer into the *b.*
24:1 *b.* of figs before the temple
*Mat.* 14:20 twelve *b.* *Mark* 6:43; *Luke* 9:17; *John* 6:13
15:37 brok. meat 7 *b.* *Mark* 8:8
16:9 not rememb. how many *b.?* 10; *Mark* 8:9, 20

**BASTARD, S.**

*Deut.* 23:2 a *b.* shall not enter
*Zec.* 9:6 and a *b.* in Ashdod
*Heb.* 12:8 w. chast. them are *b.*

**BAT, S.**

*Lev.* 11:19 *b.* unclean. *Deut.* 14:18
*Is.* 2:20 idols to moles and *b.*

**BATH.**

*Is.* 5:10 ten a. shall yield one *b.*
*Ezek.* 45:10 a just ephah, a j. *b.*
11 ephah and *b.* of one meas.
14 offer the tenth part of a *b.*

**BATHED.**

*Is.* 34:5 my sword shall be *b.*

**BATHS.**

1 *K.* 7:26 molt. sea cont. 2,000 *b.*
38 one laver contained 40 *b.*
2 *Chr.* 2:10 give 2,000 *b.* of wine
4:5 the sea held 3,000 *b.*
*Ezr.* 7:22 *b.* of wine, 100 *b.* oil
*Ezek.* 45:14 ten *b.* are a homer

BATH-SHEBA. 2 *Sam.* 11:3; 12:24; 1 *K.* 1:15, 31; 2:13

**BATTLE.**

*Deut.* 20:3 O Israel you ap. to *b.*
5 lest he die in the *b.* 6, 7
*Jud.* 20:28 shall I yet go to *b.?*
1 *Sam.* 17:28 art come to see *b.*
47 *b.* is the L.'s, 2 *Chr.* 20:15
26:10 descend into *b.* and perish
28:1 thou shalt go with me to *b.*
2 *Sam.* 11:1 when kings go forth to *b.* 1 *Chr.* 20:1
15 set Uriah in forefront of *b.*
19:10 Absalom is dead in *b.*
1 *K.* 8:44 thy people go to *b.*
20:39 thy serv. into midst of *b.*
22:4 go with me to *b.?* 2 *K.* 3:7
1 *Chr.* 5:20 cried to God in the *b.*
12:8 Gadites men fit for the *b.*
*Job* 15:24 a king ready to the *b.*
39:25 he smelleth the *b.* afar off
41:8 remem. the *b.* do no more
*Ps.* 18:39 girded with str. to *b.*
24:8 the Lord mighty in *b.*
55:18 deliv. my soul from the *b.*
76:3 br. the shield, and the *b.*
*Ps.* 89:43 not made to st. in the *b.*
*Ec.* 9:11 nor *b.* to the strong
*Is.* 9:5 every *b.* of the warrior
13:4 L. must. the host of the *b.*
22:2 slain are not dead in *b.*
27:4 set briars ag. me in *b.*
28:6 turn the *b.* to the gate
42:25 the strength of the *b.*
*Jer.* 8:6 horse rusheth into the *b.*
18:21 young men be slain in *b.*
50:22 a sound of *b.* is in land
*Ezek.* 7:14 none goeth to the *b.*
13:5 in the *b.* in the day of L.
*Hos.* 1:7 not save them by *b.*
2:18 break *b.* out of the earth
10:9 *b.* in Gibeah not overtake
*Joel* 2:5 strong people in *b.* array
*Zec.* 10:3 goodly horse in the *b.*
5 tread their enemies in the *b.*
14:2 all nations against J. to *b.*
1 *Cor.* 14:8 shall prep. to the *b.*
*Rev.* 9:7 like horses prepare to *b.*
9 chariots running to *b.*
16:14 *b.* of that great day, 20:8

**Day of BATTLE.**

*Job* 38:23 reserved ag. *d. of b.*
*Ps.* 78:9 Eph. turned in *d. of b.*
140:7 covered my head in *d. of b.*
*Prov.* 21:31 horse is prep. ag. *b.*

BATTLE-AXE. *See* AXE.

**BATTLE-BOW.**

*Zec.* 9:10 the *b.-bow* shall be cut
10:4 out of him came the *b.-b.*

**BATTLES.**

1 *Sam.* 18:17 fight the Lord's *b.*
25:28 my lord fighteth *b.* of L.
1 *Chr.* 26:27 spoils won in *b.* ded.
2 *Chr.* 32:8 is God, to fight our *b.*
*Is.* 30:32 and in *b.* of shaking

**BATTERING.**

*Ezek.* 4:2 and set *b.* rams round
21:22 to ap. *b.* rams ag. gates

**BATTLEMENT, S.**

*Deut.* 22:8 a *b.* for thy roof
*Jer.* 5:10 take away her *b.*

**BAY.**

*Zec.* 6:3 in fourth chariot *b.* h.
7 the *b.* went forth and sought

**BAY-TREE.**

*Ps.* 37:35 w. like a green *b.-t.*

**BDELLIUM.**

*Gen.* 2:12 in Havilah there is *b.*
*Num.* 11:7 color of manna as *b.*

**BE.**

*Jud.* 6:13 the Lord *be* with us
2 *Chr.* 36:23 L. *be* w. him, *Ezr.* 1:3
*John* 3:9 can these things *be?*
*Rom.* 4:17 things which *be* not
8:31 if G. *be* for us, who can *be*
*Gal.* 4:12 *be* as I am, for I am

**Shall BE, *or* shalt BE.**

*Ec.* 1:9 is that which *shall be*
*Mat.* 24:21 ever *sh. be*, *Mark* 13:19
*Mark* 9:19 how long *shall* I *be* with you, *Luke* 9:41
*John* 14:17 with you, and *sh. be*
1 *John* 3:2 appear what we *sh. be*
*Rev.* 16:5 and wast, and *shalt be*

**Shall not, *or* shalt not BE.**

*Ps.* 37:10 *shall not be*. *Jer.* 48:30; *Dan.* 11:29; *Amos* 7:3, 6
*Hos.* 3:3 *shalt not be* for another
*Mat.* 16:22 *shall not be* to thee
20:26 *shall not be* so among you, *Mark* 10:43; *Luke* 22:26

**To BE.**

*Ec.* 3:15 that *to be* hath already

BEEN. *See after* BEE.

**BEACON.**

*Is.* 30:17 left as a *b.* on the top

**BEAM.**

*Jud.* 16:14 went away with the *b.*
1 *Sam.* 17:7 spear was like a weaver's *b.* 1 *Chr.* 11:23; 20:5
2 *K.* 6:2 J., and take thence a *b.*
5 was felling a *b.* axe-head
*Hab.* 2:11 the *b.* shall answer
*Mat.* 7:3 not *b.* *Luke* 6:41, 42
4 a *b.* is in thine own eye
5 cast out the *b.* *Luke* 6:42

**BEAMS.**

*Ps.* 104:3 layeth the *b.* in waters
*Cant.* 1:17 the *b.* of our house

**BEANS.**

2 *Sam.* 17:28 Barzillai brought *b.*
*Ezek.* 4:9 t. unto thee wheat *b.*

**BEAR—carry, *or* endure.**

*Gen.* 4:13 is greater than I can *b.*
13:6 not able to *b.* them, 36:7
43:9 let me *b.* the blame, 44:32
49:15 bowed his shoulder to *b.*
*Ex.* 18:22 shall *b.* the burden
25:27 to *b.* the table, 27:7; 30:4; 37:5; *Deut.* 10:8; *Jos.* 3:8, 13; 4:16; 2 *Sam.* 15:24
28:12 A. shall *b.* their names
*Num.* 11:14 *b.* all this, *Deut.* 1:9
14:27 how long *b.* with this
33 children shall *b.* your whoredoms, *Ezek.* 23:35
*Deut.* 1:31 a man doth *b.* his son
2 *K.* 18:14 put. on me, I will *b.*
*Ps.* 75:3 I *b.* pillars of the earth
89:50 how I do *b.* the reproach
91:12 *b.* thee up, *Mat.* 4:6; *Lu.* 4:11
*Prov.* 9:12 thou shalt *b.* it
18:14 w. spirit who can *b.?*
30:21 for four which it cannot *b.*
*Is.* 1:14 feasts, I am weary to *b.*
46:4 I have made and will *b.* you
7 *b.* him upon the shoulder
52:11 clean that *b.* vessels of L.
*Jer.* 10:19 and I must *b.* it
17:21 *b.* no burden on Sab. 27
31:19 *b.* the reproach of my y.
44:22 Lord could no longer *b.*
*Lam.* 3:27 good he *b.* yoke
*Ezek.* 12:6 in their sight shalt *b.*
16:52 *b.* own shame, 54
34:29 *b.* shame of heath. 36:15
*Mic.* 6:16 *b.* rep. of my people
7:9 I will *b.* indignation of L.
*Zec.* 5:10 whither *b.* the ephah?
6:13 he shall *b.* glory, and rule
*Mat.* 3:11 shoes not worthy to *b.*
27:32 Simon to *b.* his cross, *Mar.* 15:21; *Luke* 23:26
*Luke* 14:27 doth not *b.* his cross
18:7 av. his elect, though he *b.*
*John* 16:12 ye cannot *b.* them
*Acts* 9:15 vessel to *b.* my name
15:10 nor we were able to *b.*
18:14 reason would I should *b.*
*Rom.* 15:1 *b.* infirm. of the weak
1 *Cor.* 3:2 hitherto not able to *b.*
10:13 that ye may be able to *b.*
15:49 *b.* the image
2 *Cor.* 11:1 would to G. ye could *b.*
4 ye might well *b.* with him
*Gal.* 6:2 *b.* one another's burd.
5 shall *b.* his own burden
17 *b.* in my body the marks
*Jam.* 3:12 fig-tree *b.* ol.-berries?
*Rev.* 2:2 canst not *b.* them

**BEAR**—*bring forth.*

*Gen.* 17:17 S. 90 years old *b.?*
18:13 shall I *b.* a child
*Jud.* 13:3 conceive and *b.* a son
1 *K.* 3:21 not my son I did *b.*
*Cant.* 4:2 ev. one *b.* twins, 6:6
*Is.* 7:14 a virgin shall con. and *b*
54:1 sing, thou that didst not *b.*
*Jer.* 29:6 that they may *b.* sons
*Luke* 1:13 Elisab. shall *b.* a son
1 *Tim.* 5:14 marry, *b.* children

BEAR *fruit.* *See* FRUIT.

**BEAR iniquity.**

*Ex.* 28:38 A. may *b. in.* of holy
43 A. and his sons *b.* not *in.*
*Lev.* 5:1 he shall *b.* his *iniq.* 17; 7:18; 17:16; 19:8; 20:17
10:17 given to *b. in.* of the cong.
16:22 shall *b.* all their *in.*
20:19 shall *b.* their *in.* *Num.* 18:1, 23; *Ezek.* 44:10, 12
*Num.* 14:34 ye shall *b.* your *in.*
*Is.* 53:11 my righteous servant shall *b.* their *in.*
*Ezek.* 4:4 shalt *b.* their *in.* 5, 6
18:20 son shall not *b. in.* of the

**BEAR judgment.**

*Ex.* 28:30 A. shall *b. j.*
*Gal.* 5:10 troub. you shall *b.* his *j.*

BEAR *record.* *See* RECORD.

**BEAR rule.**

*Est.* 1:22 every man should *b. r.* in his own house
*Prov.* 12:24 of diligent *b. r.*
*Jer.* 5:31 priests *b. r.* by their m.

**BEAR sin.**
*Lev.* 24:15 shall *b.* his *sin.*
*Ezek.* 13:49 *b.* the *s.* of your idols
*Heb.* 9:28 once offered to *b. sin*

**BEAR witness.**
*Ex.* 20:16 not. *b.* false *w.* ag. thy.
*Deut.*5:20; *Mat.*19:18; *Rom.*13:9
1 *K.* 21:10 sons of B. to *b. wit.*
*Mark* 10:19 not *b.* f. *w. Luke* 18:20
*Luke* 11:48 ye *b. wit.* that
*John* 1:7 came for a wit. to *b. w.*
8 to *b. witness* of that light
3:28 ye *b.* me *w.* that I said
5:31 if I *b. wit.* of myself
36 *b. witness* of me, 10:25
8:18 I am one that *b. witness*
15:27 ye shall also *b. witness*
*John* 18:23 *b. witness* of the evil
37 that I should *b. witness*
*Acts* 22:5 h.-priest doth *b.* me *w.*
23:11 so must thou *b. w.* at R.
1 *John* 1:2 have seen it, and *b. w.*
5:8 three that *b. witness*

**BEAREST.**
*Ps.* 106:4 favor thou *b.* to thy
*John* 8:13 *b.* record of thyself
*Rom.* 11:18 *b.* not the root,
*Gal.* 4:27 rej. barren that *b.* not

**BEARETH.**
*Num.* 11:12 a nursing father *b.*
*Deut.* 29:18 a root that *b.* gall
23 it is not sown, nor *b.* nor
32:11 as an eagle *b.* her young
*Job* 24:21 entreateth barren th. *b.*
*Cant.* 6:6 every one *b.* twins
*Joel* 2:22 for the tree *b.* her fruit
*Mat.* 13:23 which also *b.* fruit
*John* 15:2 ev. branch that *b.* not
*Rom.* 13:4 *b.* not the sword
1 *Cor.* 13:7 charity *b.* all things
*Heb.* 6:8 which *b.* thorns

**BEARETH rule.**
*Prov.* 29:2 wicked *b. r.* people m.

**BEARETH witness.**
*Job* 16:8 my leanness *b. witness*
*Prov.* 25:18 that *b.* false *witness*
*John* 5:32 another that *b. wit.*
8:18 the Father *b. witness*
*Rom.* 8:16 S. *b. w.* with our sp.
1 *John* 5:6 it is the S. that *b. w.*

**BEARING.**
*Gen.* 1:29 every herb *b.* seed
16:2 hath restrained me from *b.*
*Jos.* 3:3 *b.* the ark, 14; 2*Sam.*15:24
*Ps.* 126:6 forth *b.* precious seed
*Mark* 14:13 *b.* a pitcher of water,
*Luke* 22:10
*John* 19:17 he *b.* his cross, went
*Rom.* 2:15 their conscience *b.* w.
9:1 my con. also *b.* me witness
2 *Cor.* 4:10 *b.* in the body
*Heb.* 2:4 G. also *b.* them witness
13:13 *b.* his reproach
1 *Tim.* 2:15 be saved in child-*b.*

**BEAR, S.**
1 *Sam.* 17:34 came a lion and a *b.*
36 thy servant slew lion and *b.*
2 *Sam.* 17:8 chafed as a *b.* robbed
2 *K.* 2:24 came f. two she-*b.*
*Prov.* 17:12 a *b.* robbed of whelps
28:15 and a ranging *b.*
*Is.* 11:7 cow and *b.* shall feed
59:11 we roar all like *b.*
*Lam.* 3:10 he was to me as a *b.*
*Dan.* 7:5 a second like to a *b.*
*Hos.* 13:8 as a *b.* bereaved
*Amos* 5:19 a man did flee fr. a *b.*
*Rev.* 13:2 his feet were as of a *b.*

**BEARD, S.**
*Lev.* 13:29 plague on head or *b.*
14:9 his hair off his head and *b.*
19:27 mar corners of *b.* 21:5
1 *Sam.* 17:35 caught him by *b.*
21:13 let his spittle fall on *b.*
2 *Sam.* 10:5 tarry till *b.* be gr.
1 *Chr.* 19:5
19:24 M. trimmed not his *b.*
20:9 A. by the *b.* to kiss him
*Ezr.* 9:3 hair off my *b.*
*Ps.* 133:2 on the *b.* even A.'s *b.*
*Is.* 7:20 shall also consume *b.*
15:2 and every *b.* cut off
*Jer.* 41:5 men *b.* shaven
48:37 every head bald, *b.* clip.
*Ezek.* 5:1 to pass on thy *b.*

**BEAST.**
*Gen.* 1:24 earth bring forth *b.*
3:1 more subtle than any *b.*
37:20 evil *b.* hath devoured, 33
*Ex.*13:12 firstling of a *b.*
22:5 put his *b.* in another
10 deliver any *b.* to keep
19 lieth with a *b. Lev.* 18:23;
20:15, 16; *Deut.* 27:21
23:29 the *b.* multiply
*Lev.* 11:47 *b.* that may be eaten
*Deut.* 4:17 the likeness of any *b.*
*Neh.* 2:12 save the *b.* I rode on
*Ps.* 73:22 as a *b.* before thee
147:9 giveth to the *b.* his food
*Prov.* 12:10 regards life of his *b.*
*Ec.* 3:19 pre-eminence above *b.*
*Is.* 43:20 the *b.* shall honor me
63:14 as a *b.* that goeth
*Dan.* 4:16 let a *b.* heart be given
7:11 till the *b.* was slain
19 the truth of the fourth *b.*
*Luke* 10:34 on his own *b.*
*Acts* 28:5 Paul shook off the *b.*
*Heb.* 12:20 if so much as a *b.*
*Rev.* 4:7 first *b.* like a lion, sec. *b.*
6:3 second *b.* say, Come
*Rev.* 11:7 *b.* that ascendeth out of
13:1 a *b.* rise up out of the sea
11 *b.* coming out of the earth
15:2 got the victory over the *b.*
16:13 unclean spirits out of *b.*
17:8 *b.* that was, and is not, 11
19:19 saw the *b.* and the kings
20:10 the *b.* and false prophet

**Every BEAST.**
*Gen.* 1:30 to *ev. b.* I have given
2:19 God formed *ev. b.*
20 Adam gave names to *ev. b.*
3:14 art cursed above *every b.*
7:2 *every* clean *b.* by sevens, 8
14 and *every b.* after his kind
8:19 *every b.* went out
20 of *every* clean *b.* he offered
9:2 shall be on *every b.*
5 blood at hand of *every b.*
10 *every b.* I estab. covenant
34:23 shall not *ev. b.* of theirs
*Lev.* 11:26 *ev. b.* which divideth
the hoof, *Deut.* 14:6
*Ps.* 50:10 *every b.* of the forest
104:11 give drink to *every b.*
*Ezek* 34:8 flock meat to *every b.*
39:17 speak to *every b.*

**BEAST,** *joined with* **Man.**
*Gen.* 6:7 destroy both *m.* and *b.*
*Ex.* 11:7 move tongue a. *m.* or *b.*
12:12 smite first-born of *m.* and
*b.* 13:15; *Ps.* 135:8
13:2 first-born of *m.* and *b.* is
mine, *Num.* 8:17
19:13 *m.* or *b.* it shall not live
*Ps.* 36:6 preservest *m.* and *b.*
*Jer.* 7:20 fury on *m.* and *b.* 21:6
36:29; *Ezek.* 14:13, 17, 19, 21;
25:13; 29:8; *Zep.* 1:3
27:5 I have made *man* and *b.*
31:27 sow J. with seed of *m.* a. *b.*
32:43 without *m.* or *b.* 33:10, 12;
36:29; 51:62
50:3 shall depart *m.* and *b.*
*Ezek.* 36:11 mul. on you *m.* and *b.*
*Jon.* 3:7 let not *m.* or *b.* taste

**Unclean BEAST.**
*Lev.* 5:2 touch any *u. b.* 7:21
27:11 if it be *u. b.* of which, 27

**Wild BEAST.**
2 *K.* 14:9 *w. b.* in L. 2 *Chr.* 25:18
*Job* 39:15 forgetteth *w. b.*
*Ps.* 80:13 *w. b.* doth devour it
*Hos.* 13:8 the *w. b.* shall tear

**BEASTS.**
*Gen.* 31:39 torn of *b. Ex.* 22:31;
*Lev.* 7:24; 17:15; 22:8
36:6 Esau took all his *b.*
45:17 lade your *b.* and go
*Ex.* 11:5 the first-b. of *b.*
*Lev.* 11:2 *b.* eat, *Deut.* 14:4
3 chew cud among *b. Deut.*14:6
26:6 will rid evil *b.* out of land
*Deut.* 32:24 will send teeth of *b.*
1 *K.* 4:33 Solomon spake of *b.*
*Ezr.* 1:4 help him with gold, *b.*
*Job* 12:7 ask the *b.* they teach
18:3 are we counted as *b.*
37:8 then the *b.* go into dens
*Ps.* 49:12 the *b.* that perish, 20
104:20 wherein *b.* of forest creep
25 sea, both small and great *b.*
148:10 *b.* and all cattle, praise
*Prov.* 9:2 hath killed her *b.*
30:30 lion strongest among *b.*
*Ec.* 3:18 themselves are *b.*
19 befalleth men, before *b.*
*Is.* 30:6 of *b.* of the south
40:16 nor *b.* thereof a burnt-off.
46:1 idols on the *b.* and cattle
66:20 upon swift *b.* to my holy
*Jer.* 9:10 *b.* fled, 12:4 consumed
*Ezek.* 5:17 send evil *b.* 14:15
32:4 fill *b.* of whole earth
13 destroy all the *b.* 34:25, 28
*Dan.* 4:14 *b.* get away
15 his portion be with the *b.*
7:17 four great *b.* are kings
8:4 no *b.* might stand before h.
*Joel* 1:18 how do the *b.* groan
*Hab.* 2:17 spoil of *b.*
*Zep.* 2:15 become a place for *b.*
*Zec.* 14:15 plague of all the *b.*
*Acts* 7:42 offered to me slain *b.?*
23:24 *b.* that ye may set Paul
*Rom.*1:23 image made like to *b.*
1 *Cor.*15:32 I have fought with *b.*
*Jam.* 3:7 *b.* is tamed, but tongue
2 *Pet.* 2:12 as natural brute *b.*
*Jude* 10 naturally as brute *b.*
*Rev.* 4:6 four *b.* full of eyes
8 four *b.* had each six wings
9 when those *b.* give glory
5:6 in midst of four *b.* stood a L.
14 the four *b.* said, Amen
6:1 *b.* saying, Come, 15:7
*Rev.* 7:11 stood about four *b.*
14:3 song before the four *b.*
19:4 and four *b.* fell down

**BEASTS of the Earth.**
*Deut.* 28:26 carc. meat to all *b.*
1 *Sam.* 17:46 carcasses of P. to *b.*
*Job* 5:22 nor be afraid of the *b.*
35:11 teacheth us more than *b.*
*Ps.* 79:2 flesh of thy saints to *b.*
*Is.* 18:6 they shall be left to *b.*
*Jer.* 7:33 carc. of peop. meat for *b.*
*of the earth,* 16:4; 19:7; 34:20
15:3 I will appoint over them *b.*
*Acts* 10:12 of four-footed *b.* 11:6
*Rev.* 6:8 kill with hunger and *b.*

**BEASTS of the Field.**
*Ex.* 23:11 leave, *b.* may eat
*Deut.* 7:22 lest *b.* increase
1 *Sam.* 17:44 give thy flesh to *b.*
2 *Sam.* 21:10 nor *b. of the field*
*Job* 5:23 *b.* shall be at peace
40:20 mountains where *b.* play
*Ps.* 8:7 put *b.* under his feet
*Is.* 56:9 ye *b.* come to devour
*Jer.* 12:9 assem. all *b. of the field*
27:6 *b.* given, 28:14; *Dan.* 2:38

Ezek. 29:5 I have given thee for meat to the b. 34:5; 39:4
31:6 under branches b. bring
13 b. shall be on his branches
38:20 b. shall shake
Dan. 4:12 the b. had shadow
25 thy dwelling with b. 32
Hos. 2:18 cov. for them with b.
4:3 shall land mourn with b.
Joel 1:20 b. cry also to thee
2:22 ye b. pastures

**Wild BEASTS.**
Lev. 26:22 I will send w. b.
1 Sam. 17:46 carc. of Phil. to w. b.
Ps. 50:11 the w. b. are mine
Is. 13:21 w. b. shall lie there
22 wild b. of the islands
34:14 w.b. of des. shall meet with w. b. of the island, Jer. 50:39
Mark 1:13 C. was with the w. b.
Acts 10:12 wh. were all w. b. 11:6

**BEAT.**
Jud. 9:45 A. b. down the city
19:22 sons of B. b. at the door
2 Sam. 22:43 I b. them, Ps. 18:42
Ps. 89:23 will b. down his foes
Prov. 23:14 b. him with the rod
Is. 2:4 b. their swords, Mic. 4:3
3:15 that ye b. my people
27:12 b. off from the channel
41:15 mountains, b. them small
Joel 3:10 b. your ploughshares
Mic. 4:13 shalt b. in pieces
Mat. 7:25 b. on house, 27; Luke 6:48, 49
21:35 his servants and b. one, Mark 12:3; Luke 20:10, 11
Mark 4:37 waves b. into the ship
Luke 12:45 begin to b.
Acts 16:22 commanded to b. them
18:17 took Sosthenes and b. him
22:19 b. in every synagogue

**BEATEN.**
2 Chr. 34:7 b. images to powder
Prov. 23:35 they have b. me
Is. 28:27 fitches are b. with staff
Jer. 46:5 mighty ones are b. down
Mic. 1:7 images shall be b.
Mark 13:9 synag. ye shall be b.
Luke 12:47 did not shall be b.
Acts 5:40 apostles and b. them
16:37 have b. us openly
2 Cor. 11:25 thrice was I b.

**BEATEN Oil.**
Ex. 27:20 oil b. Lev. 24:2
29:40 hin of b. oil, Num. 28:5

**BEATEST.**
Deut. 24:20 when thou b. thy ol.
Prov. 23:13 if thou b. him

**BEATETH.**
1 Cor. 9:26 as one that b. the air

**BEATING.**
1 Sam. 14:16 b. down one anoth
Mark 12:5 b. some and killing

**BEAUTY.**
Ex. 28:2 for glory and b.
2 Sam. 1:19 the b. of Israel
14:25 praised as Absalom for b.
1 Chr. 16:29 b. of hol. Ps. 29:2; 96:9
2 Chr. 20:21 praise b. of holiness
Est. 1:11 the people her b.
Job 40:10 array thyself with b.
Ps. 27:4 behold the b. of the L.
39:11 made his b. to consume
45:11 king greatly desire thy b.
49:14 their b. shall consume
50:2 the perfection of b.
90:17 the b. of Lord be on us
Ps. 96:6 and b. in sanctuary
Prov. 6:25 lust not after her b.
20:29 the b. of old is gray head
31:30 favor is deceitful, b. is v.
Is. 3:24 burning instead of b.
13:19 Babylon the b. of the C
28:1 b. is a fading flower. 4
5 a diadem of b. to residue
33:17 see the King in his b.
44:13 according to the b.
53:2 no b. that we should desire
61:3 that mourn b. for ashes
Lam. 1:6 Zion all her b. is dep.
2:1 from heaven the b. of Israel
15 men call perfection of b.?
Ezek. 7:20 b. of his ornament
16:14 renown am. heath. for b.
15 didst trust in thine own b.
25 made thy b. to be abhorred
27:3 I am of perfect b. 28:12
4 builders perfected thy b. 11
28:7 swords ag. the b. of thy
17 lifted up because of thy b.
31:8 no tree like Assyrian in b.
32:19 whom dost pass in b.
Hos. 14:6 Israel's b. shall be
Zec. 9:17 how great is his b.
11:7 staves, one I called b. 10

**BEAUTIES.**
Ps. 110:3 in the b. of holiness

**BEAUTIFY.**
Ezr. 7:27 king's heart, to b.
Ps. 149:4 b. the meek with salv.
Is. 60:13 b. place of my sanctu.

**BEAUTIFUL.**
Gen. 29:17 Rachel was b.
Deut. 21:11 am. cap. a b. woman
1 Sam. 16:12 was of a b. country
25:3 Abigail was of a b. count.
2 Sam. 11:2 Bath. was very b.
Est. 2:7 Esther was fair and b.
Ps. 48:2 b. for situation is Zion
Ec. 3:11 every thing b.
Cant. 6:4 thou art b. O my love
7:1 how b. thy feet with shoes
Is. 4:2 the branch of L. be b.
52:1 O Zion, put on thy b. gar.
7 how b. the feet, Rom. 10:15
64:11 and b. house is burnt up
Jer. 13:20 where is thy b. flock?
48:17 broken, and the b. rod
Ezek. 16:12 b. crown on thy head
13 thou wast exceeding b.
23:42 Sabeans put b. crowns
Mat. 23:27 sepulch. which ap. b.
Acts 3:2 at the gate called b. 10

**BECAME.**
1 Cor. 9:20 to the Jews I b. a Jew
Heb. 7:26 such a High-priest b. us

**BECAMEST.**
1 Chr. 17:22 thou L. b. their God
Ezek. 16:8 and thou b. mine

**BECKONED.**
Luke 1:22 Zacharias b. speechl.
5:7 they b. to their partners
John 13:24 Peter b. he should ask
Acts 19:33 Alex. b. and would
21:40 P. stood on stairs, and b.

**BECKONING.**
Acts 12:17 Peter b. unto them
13:16 Paul b. with his hand

**BECOME.**
Gen. 3:22 man is b. as one of us
Ex. 15:2 is b. my salvation, Ps. 118:14; Is. 12:2
32:1 as for M. we wot not what is b. of him, 23; Acts 7:40
Deut. 27:9 art b. the people
Mat. 21:42 is b. the head, Mark 12:10; Luke 20:17; Acts 4:11
John 1:12 to b. the sons of God
2 Cor. 5:17 all things are b. new
Rev. 11:15 b. the kingd. of our L.

**BECOMETH.**
Ps. 93:5 holiness b. thy house
Prov. 10:4 b. poor that dealeth
17:7 excell. speech b. not a fool
18 void of understand. b. surety
Ec. 4:14 born in his kingd. b.
Mat. 3:15 it b. us to fulfil
13:22 choketh the word, and he b. unfruitful, Mark 4:19
Rom. 16:2 receive P. as b. saints
Phil. 1:27 as b. gospel
1 Tim. 2:10 as b. women
Tit. 2:3 women as b. holiness

**BED.**
Gen. 47:31 bow. on b. 1 K. 1:47
49:4 thy father's b. 1 Chr. 5:1
Ex. 21:18 but keepeth b.
1 Sam. 19:13 and laid it in b.
2 Sam. 4:5 who lay on b.
11:2 David arose from his b.
2 K. 1:4 from that b. 6, 16
2 K. 4:10 set there for him a b.
Job 7:13 my b. shall comfort me
17:13 my b. in the darkness
33:15 slumberings upon the b.
Ps. 4:4 com. with heart on b.
36:4 devis. mischief on his b.
41:3 his b. in his sickness
63:6 I rem. thee upon my b.
132:3 into my b. till I find
139:8 if I make my b. in hell
Prov. 7:16 decked my b. 17
22:27 why take b. from under
26:14 the slothful on his b.
Cant. 1:16 our b. is green
3:1 on my b. I sought him
7 his b. which is Solomon's
Is. 28:20 b. is shorter
57:7 on mountain set thy b.
Amos 3:12 in the corner of a b.
Mat. 9:6 thy b. Mark 2:9, 11; John 5:11, 12
Mark 4:21 under a b. Luke 8:16
Luke 11:7 child. with me in b.
17:34 two men in one b.
Rev. 2:22 will cast her into a b.

**BED of love.**
Ezek. 23:17 came to her in b.

**BED of spices.**
Cant. 5:13 his cheeks are as a b.
6:2 my beloved is gone to the b.

**BED undefiled.**
Heb. 13:4 honorable and the b.

BEDAD. Gen. 36:35
BEDAN. 1 Sam. 12:11; 1 Chr. 7:17

**BEDCHAMBER.**
Ex. 8:3 frogs come into thy b.
2 Sam. 4:7 Ish. lay in his b.
2 K. 6:12 thou speakest in b.
11:2 hid him in b. 2 Chr. 22:11
Ec. 10:20 the rich in b.

**BEDS.**
Ps. 149:5 sing aloud on b.
Is. 57:2 rest in their b. each
Hos. 7:14 they howled on b.
Amos 6:4 lie on b. of ivory
Mic. 2:1 that work evil on b.

**BEDSTEAD.**
Deut. 3:11 b. was a b. of iron

**BEE, S.**
Deut. 1:44 as b. in Seir
Jud. 14:8 swarm of b. in the lion
Ps. 118:12 me about like b.
Is. 7:18 hiss for the b. in As.

BEELZEBUB. Mat. 10:25; 12:24; Mark 3:22; Luke 11:15

**Hath BEEN.**
Ec. 3:15 which h. been is now

**Have BEEN.**
Job 10:19 h. b. as if I had not b.
Is. 66:2 all those things h. b.

**Not BEEN.**
Ob. 16 though they had n. b.

BEER. Num. 21:16
BEER-LAHAI-ROI. Gen. 16:14
BEERSHEBA. Gen. 21:14, 33; 22:19; 26:33; 28:10; 1 K. 19:3

**BEETLE.**
Lev. 11:22 ye may eat, the b.

**BEEVES.**
Lev. 22:19 the b. of sheep
Num. 31:28 a tribute of the b.

**BEFALL.**
*Gen.* 42:4 lest mischief *b.* him
38 if mischief *b.* him, 44:29
49:1 what shall *b.* you, *Deut.* 31:29; *Dan.* 10:14
*Deut.* 31:17 evils shall *b.* them
*Ps.* 91:10 there shall no evil *b.*
*Acts* 20:22 things that shall *b.*

**BEFALLEN.**
*Lev.* 10:19 such things have *b.*
*Num.* 20:14 travail that hath *b.*
*Deut.* 31:21 when troubles are *b.*
*Jud.* 6:13 why is all this *b.*
1 *Sam.* 20:26 something had *b.*
*Mat.* 8:33 what was *b.*

**BEFALLETH.**
*Ec.* 3:19 *b.* men, *b.* beasts

**BEFELL.**
2 *Sam.* 19:7 than all that *b.* thee
*Acts* 20:19 *b.* me by lying in wait

**BEFORE.**
*Jos.* 10:14 like that *b.* it, or
*Ps.* 39:13 spare me *b.* I go
139:5 beset me behind and *b.*
*Is.* 43:13 *b.* the day was, I am
*Mat.* 24:25 I have told you *b.*
*John* 13:19 I tell you *b.* 14:29
*Phil.* 3:13 to things that are *b.*
1 *Thes.* 3:4 with you we told *b.*
*Heb.* 7:18 command going *b.*
*Heb.* 10:15 aft. that he had said *b.*
2 *Pet.* 3:17 know these things *b.*

**Come BEFORE.**
*Ps.* 100:2 *c. b.* presence
*Mic.* 6:6 shall I *c. b.* L?

**BEFORE the people.**
*Ex.* 13:22 pillar of fire from *b.*
17:5 L. said to Moses, go on *b.*
34:10 *b.* all *thy p.* I will do
1 *Sam.* 18:13 went out and in *b.*
*Mark* 8:6 discip. did set them *b.*
*Luke* 20:26 hold of his words *b.*
*Rev.* 10:11 prophesy *b. people*

**BEFORE whom.**
1 *K.* 17:1 as the Lord God of Isr. liveth, *b. whom* I stand, 18:15; 2 *K.* 3:14; 5:16
*Acts* 26:26 king *b. w.* I speak
*See further,* ALL, ARK, GOD, LORD, MOUNT, STAND, STOOD, WENT.

**BEFOREHAND.**
*Mark* 13:11 take no thought *b.*
2 *Cor.* 9:5 make up *b.* your boun.
1 *Tim.* 5:24 men's s. are open *b.*
25 good works of some mani. *b.*
1 *Pet.* 1:11 testified *b.* sufferings

**BEFORETIME.**
*Jos.* 20:5 he hated him not *b.*
2 *Sam.* 7:10 nor afflict them as *b.*
*Is.* 41:26 *b.* that we may say
*Acts* 8:9 Simon which *b.* used

**BEGAN.**
*Gen.* 4:26 *b.* men call on name
2 *K.* 10:32 *b.* to cut Israel short
2 *Chr.* 34:3 *b.* to seek after God
*Mat.* 4:17 Jesus *b.* to preach
*Luke* 1:70 been since world *b.*
14:30 this man *b.* to build
*John* 4:52 when he *b.* to amend
9:32 since the world *b. Acts* 3:21; *Rom.* 16:25
2 *Tim.* 1:9 in Christ before the world *b.* *Tit.* 1:2
*Heb.* 2:3 at first *b.* to be spoken

**BEGAT.**
*Prov.* 23:22 to thy father that *b.*
*Jer.* 16:3 their father that *b.* them
*Dan.* 11:6 and he that *b.* her
*Zec.* 13:3 and m. that *b.* him
*Jam.* 1:18 his own will *b.* he us
1 *John* 5:1 loveth him that *b.*

**BEGET.**
*Gen.* 17:20 princes shall he *b.*
*Deut.* 4:25 thou shalt *b.* children
28:41 *b.* sons
2 *K.* 20:18 sons thou shalt *b.* shall they make eunuchs, *Is.* 39:7
*Ec.* 6:3 if a man *b.* 100 children
*Jer.* 29:6 take wives, and *b.* sons
*Ezek.* 18:10 if he *b.* a son
14 if he *b.* a son that seeth

**BEGETTEST.**
*Gen.* 48:6 issue which thou *b.*
*Is.* 45:10 to his father, what *b.*

**BEGETTETH.**
*Prov.* 17:21 *b.* a fool, doeth it
23:24 he that *b.* a wise child
*Ec.* 5:14 he *b.* a son

**BEG.**
*Ps.* 109:10 let his children *b.*
*Prov.* 20:4 sluggard *b.* in harvest
*Luke* 16:3 to *b.* I am ashamed

**BEGGAR, LY.**
1 *Sam.* 2:8 lifted *b.* from dungh.
*Luke* 16:20 a *b.* named Lazarus
22 the *b.* died and was carried
*Gal.* 4:9 to the *b.* elements

**BEGGED.**
*Mat.* 27:58 *b.* body of J. *Lu.* 23:52
*John* 9:8 he that sat and *b.*

**BEGGING.**
*Ps.* 37:25 seen his seed *b.* bread
*Mark* 10:46 Bart. sat *b. Lu.* 18:35

**BEGIN.**
*Gen.* 11:6 this they *b.* to do, and
*Jos.* 3:7 will I *b.* to magnify
1 *Sam.* 3:12 I *b.* I will make
22:15 did I then *b.* to inquire
*Neh.* 11:17 Mattan. to *b.* thanks.
*Jer.* 25:29 I *b.* to bring evil
*Luke* 3:8 *b.* not to say within
13:26 *b.* to say we have eaten
14:29 behold it, *b.* to mock him
21:28 things *b.* to come to pass
2 *Cor.* 3:1 do we *b.* to commend
1 *Pet.* 4:17 judgment must *b.* at house of G., and if it first *b.*

**BEGINNING, Part.**
*Mat.* 14:30 *b.* to sink, L. save me
20:8 *b.* from last to first
*Luke* 24:47 all nations, *b.* at J.
*John* 8:9 *b.* at eldest
*Acts* 1:22 *b.* from baptism of J.

**BEGINNING, Substantive.**
*Gen.* 49:3 Reuben, *b.* of my st.
*Ex.* 12:2 the *b.* of months
*Deut.* 21:17 is *b.* of his strength
*Job* 8:7 thy *b.* was small
42:12 end of Job more than *b.*
*Ps.* 111:10 *b.* of wis. *Prov.* 9:10
*Prov.* 1:7 fear of L. *b.* of knowl.
17:14 *b.* of strife, as when one
*Ec.* 7:8 end of a thing than *b.*
10:13 *b.* of words is foolishness
*Is.* 64:4 since *b.* of world, men
*Mic.* 1:13 is *b.* of sin to daughter
*Mat.* 24:8 *b.* of sor. *Mark* 13:8
21 as was not since *b.*
*Mark* 1:1 the *b.* of the gospel
*John* 2:11 this *b.* of miracles
*Col.* 1:18 who is the *b.* the first-b.
*Heb.* 3:14 *b.* of our confidence
7:3 having neither *b.* of days
2 *Pet.* 2:20 is worse than the *b.*
*Rev.* 1:8 I am *b.* 21:6; 22:13
3:14 saith the *b.* of the creation

**At the BEGINNING.**
*Ruth* 3:10 kindness than *at b.*
1 *Chr.* 17:9 wicked. waste as *b.*
*Prov.* 20:21 in. gotten hastily *b.*
*Is.* 1:26 counsellors as *at the b.*
*Dan.* 9:23 *a. b.* of thy supplica.
*Mat.* 19:4 *at the b.* made them
*John* 16:4 I said not to you *b.*
*Acts* 11:15 H. G. as on us *a. t. b.*

**From the BEGINNING.**
*Deut.* 11:12 eyes of L. on it *b.*
*Ps.* 119:160 true *from the begin.*
*Prov.* 8:23 I was set up *f. b.*
*Ec.* 3:11 no man can find out the work God maketh *f. t. b.*
*Is.* 18:2 peop. terrible *f. t. b.* 7
40:21 been told *f. t. b.?*
41:26 hath declared *f. t. b.?*
46:10 declaring the end *f. t. b.*
48:16 not spoken in secret *f. t. b.*
*Jer.* 17:12 high throne *f. t. b.*
*Mat.* 19:8 *fr. the b.* it was not so
*Luke* 1:2 *f. b.* were eye-wit.
*John* 6:64 knew *f. b.* who believ.
8:25 same I said to you *f. b.*
44 a murderer *from the begin.*
15:27 have been with me *f. b.*
*Eph.* 3:9 *f. t. b.* of the world
2 *Thes.* 2:13 God hath *f. t. begin.* chosen you to salvation
2 *Pet.* 3:4 continue as *fr. t. begin.*
1 *John* 2:7 ye have heard *b.* 3:11
13 known him that is *f. t. b.*
3:8 the devil sinneth *from t. b.*
2 *John* 5 that which we had *f. t. b*

**In the BEGINNING.**
*Gen.* 1:1 *i. t. b.* God created h.
*Prov.* 8:22 the Lord possessed me *in the begin.* of his way
*John* 1:1 *in the b.* was the Word
2 the same was *in the b.*
*Phil.* 4:15 know *b.* of the gospel
*Heb.* 1:10 L. *b.* hast laid founda.

**BEGINNINGS.**
*Num.* 10:10 *b.* of your m. 28:11
*Ezek.* 36:11 bet. than at your *b.*

**BEGINNEST.**
*Deut.* 16:9 thou *b.* to put sickle

**BEGOTTEN.**
*Num.* 11:12 have I *b.* them?
*Deut.* 23:8 children *b.* of them
*Jud.* 8:30 Gideon had 70 sons *b.*
*Job* 38:28 hath *b.* drops of dew
*Ps.* 2:7 this day have I *b.* thee, *Acts* 13:33; *Heb.* 1:5; 5:15
*Is.* 49:21 hath *b.* me these?
*Hos.* 5:7 have *b.* strange children
*John* 1:14 the only *b.* of the F.
18 only *b.* Son, he hath declar.
3:16 he gave his only *b.* Son
18 not believed in only *b.* Son
1 *Cor.* 4:15 *b.* you through gospel
*Phile.* 10 Onesi. whom I have *b.*
*Heb.* 11:17 A. offered only *b.* Son
1 *Pet.* 1:3 *b.* us again
1 *John* 4:9 sent his only *b.* Son
5:1 loveth him *b.* of him
18 he that is *b.* of God

**First-BEGOTTEN.**
*Heb.* 1:6 he bringeth in *first-b.*
*Rev.* 1:5 who is *f.-b.* of the dead

**BEGUILE.**
*Col.* 2:4 lest any *b.* you
18 let no man *b.* you

**BEGUILED, ING.**
*Gen.* 3:13 serpent *b.* me
29:25 wherefore hast thou *b.*
*Num.* 25:18 they have *b.* you in the matter of Peor
*Jos.* 9:22 wherefore have ye *b.*
2 *Cor.* 11:3 as the serpent *b.* Eve
2 *Pet.* 2:14 cannot cease from sin, *b.* unstable souls

**BEGUN.**
*Deut.* 3:24 *b.* to show thy great.
*Mat.* 18:24 he had *b.* to reckon
2 *Cor.* 8:6 had *b.* so would finish
10 for you who have *b.* before
*Gal.* 3:3 having *b.* in the Spirit
*Phil.* 1:6 hath *b.* a good work
1 *Tim.* 5:11 *b.* to wax wanton

**BEHALF.**
Ex. 27:21 a statute on b. of Is.
2 Sam. 3:12 Abner sent on his b.
2 Chr. 16:9 sh. hims. strong in b.
Job 36:2 yet to speak on God's b.
Dan. 11:18 prince for his own b.
Rom. 16:19 I am glad on your b.
1 Cor. 1:4 I thank God on your b.
2 Cor. 1:11 th. be given on our b.
5:12 to glory on our b.
Phil. 1:29 given in b. of Christ
1 Pet. 4:16 glorify God on this b.

**BEHAVE.**
Deut. 32:27 lest adversaries b.
1 Chr. 19:13 let us b. valiantly
Ps. 101:2 I will b. wisely
Is. 3:5 child shall b. proudly
1 Cor. 13:5 not b. unseemly
1 Tim. 3:15 how thou oughtest to b. in the house of God

**BEHAVED.**
1 Sam. 18:5 D. b. wisely, 14, 15, 30
Ps. 35:14 I b. as he had been f.
131:2 have b. as child weaned
Mic. 3:4 as they have b. ill
1 Thes. 2:10 unblamably we b.
2 Thes. 3:7 b. not disorderly

**BEHAVETH.**
1 Cor. 7:36 think he b. uncomely

**BEHAVIOR.**
1 Sam. 21:13 D. changed his b.
1 Tim. 3:2 a bishop of good b.
Tit. 2:3 women in b. as becom.

**BEHEADED.**
2 Sam. 4:7 Ish. and b. him
Mat. 14:10 b. John, Mark. 6:16, 27; Luke 9:9
Rev. 20:4 I saw the souls of b.

**BEHELD.**
Num. 21:9 b. serpent of brass
23:21 hath not b. iniquity in J.
1 Chr. 21:15 destroying, the L. b.
Job 31:26 if I b. the sun when
Ps. 119:158 I b. transgressors
142:4 I b. but there was no man
Prov. 7:7 b. among the simple
Ec. 8:17 I b. all the work of God
Is. 41:28 I b. and there was no man, Jer. 4:25
Jer. 4:23 I b. the earth
Mark 15:47 b. where he was laid, Luke 23:55
Luke 10:18 I b. Satan as light.
19:41 he b. the city and wept
John 1:14 we b. his glory
Acts 1:9 they b. J. was taken up
17:23 and b. your devotions
Rev. 5:6 I b. and lo, a lamb
11:12 their enemies b. them

**BEHEMOTH.**
Job 40:15 behold now b.

**BEHIND.**
Is. 38:17 all my sins b. thy back
1 Cor. 1:7 ye come b. in no gift
2 Cor. 11:5 whit b. chiefest, 12:11
Phil. 3:13 forgetting things b.
Col. 1:24 fill up what is b.
See BEFORE.

**BEHOLD.**
Gen. 28:15 b. I am with thee
Job 1:12 b. all he hath
28:28 b. the fear of the Lord
40:4 b. I am vile what shall I
Ps. 139:8 bed in hell, b. thou
Is. 8:18 b. I and chil. Heb. 2:13
12:2 b. God is my salvation
41:27 say to Zion, b. b. them
65:1 I said, b. me, to a nation
Lam. 1:12 b. and see if any sor.
Zec. 9:9 b. thy King cometh, Mat. 21:5; John 12:15
Mark 16:6 b. place where they
Luke 24:39 b. my hands and feet
49 b. I send prom. of my Fath.
John 1:29 b. the Lamb of God
19:5 Pilate saith, b. the man
Acts 9:11 Saul, for b. he prayeth
1 John 3:1 b. what manner of love
Rev. 3:20 b. I stand at the door
16:15 b. I come as a thief
22:7 b. I come quickly, 12

**BEHOLD it is.**
Is. 52:6 I speak, b. it is I
Ezek. 7:10 b. the day, b. it is come
39:8 b. it is come, and it is

**Now BEHOLD, or BEHOLD now.**
Job 16:19 n. b. my witness is in
Jer. 40:4 now b. I loose thee
Mat. 26:65 b. n. ye heard
Acts 13:11 n. b. hand of Lord
20:22 now b. I go bound
2 Cor. 6:2 b. n. is the accepted t.

**BEHOLD it was, BEHOLD there was.**
See WAS.

**BEHOLD, Verb.**
Num. 12:8 simil. of L. shall he b.
23:9 from the hills I b. him
24:17 shall b. him, but not nigh
Deut. 3:27 b. it with thine eyes
Job 19:27 shall b. and not anoth.
20:9 his place any more b. him
23:9 work, but I cannot b. him
34:29 his face, who can b.?
36:24 magnify his work men b.
Ps. 11:4 his eyes b. his eyelids
7 doth b. the upright
17:2 let thine eyes b. things
15 I will b. thy face in right.
27:4 to b. the beauty of the L.
37:37 perfect, b. the upright
46:8 b. the works of the Lord
59:4 awake to help me, and b.
66:7 his eyes b. the nations
80:14 look from heaven, b.
91:8 eyes shalt thou b. and see
102:19 from heaven did L. b.
113:6 he humbleth hims. to b.
119:18 mine eyes, that I may b.
Prov. 23:33 b. strange women
Ec. 11:7 pleasant it is to b.
Is. 26:10 will not b. the majesty
38:11 I shall b. man no more
41:23 do good or evil that we b.
63:15 b. from habita. of thy holi.
Jer. 20:4 thine eyes shall b.
29:32 nor b. the good I will do
32:4 his eyes shall b. 34:3
42:2 as thine eyes do b. us
Lam. 1:18 and b. my sorrow
3:50 till Lord b. from heaven
5:1 consider and b. our reproach
Ezek. 8:9 b. wicked abomina.
28:17 that they may b.
18 in sight of all that b.
40:4 Son of man, b. 44:5
Dan. 9:18 and b. our desolations
Mic. 7:9 I shall b. his righteous.
mine eyes shall b. her
Hab. 1:3 why cause me to b.
13 purer eyes than to b. evil
Mat. 18:10 their angels b. face
Luke 14:29 all that b. it mock
21:6 as for these ye b. the days
John 17:24 they may b. my glory
Acts 7:31 he drew near to b. it
32 Moses durst not b.
2 Cor. 3:7 Is. could not b. face
1 Pet. 2:12 works they shall b.
3:2 b. your chaste conversation
Rev. 17:8 when they b. the beast

**BEHOLDEST.**
Ps. 10:14 thou b. all mischief
Mat. 7:3 w. b. mote? Luke 6:41
Luke 6:42 b. not the beam

**BEHOLDETH.**
Job 24:18 he b. not the way
Ps. 33:13 Lord b. all the sons
Jam. 1:24 b. himself and goeth

**BEHOLDING.**
Ps. 119:37 mine eyes from b.
Prov. 15:3 b. the evil and good
Ec. 5:11 saving the b. of them
Mat. 27:55 women b. Luke 23:49
Mark 10:21 Jesus b. him, loved
Luke 23:35 people stood b.
48 b. things done, smote breasts
Acts 4:14 and b. man healed
23:1 and Paul b. the council
2 Cor. 3:18 b. as in a glass the g.
Col. 2:5 joying, and b. your order
Jam. 1:23 b. his natural face

**BEHOVED.**
Luke 24:46 thus it b. Christ
Heb. 2:17 b. him to be made

**BEING.**
Ps. 104:33 I have b. 146:2
Acts 17:28 move, and have our b.

BEKAH. Ex. 38:26
BEL. Is. 46:1; Jer. 50:2; 51:44

**BELCH.**
Ps. 59:7 behold they b. out

**BELIAL.**
Deut. 13:13 children of B.
Jud. 19:22 certain sons of B.
20:13 the children of B.
1 Sam. 1:16 a daughter of B.
2:12 sons of Eli were sons of B
10:27 children of B. said, how
25:17 is such a son of B. 25
30:22 then answ. the men of B.
2 Sam. 16:7 come out, man of B.
20:1 a man of B.
23:6 sons of B. shall be as th.
1 K. 21:10 two sons of B. 13
2 Chr. 13:7 Jerob. children of B.
2 Cor. 6:15 hath Christ with B.?

**BELIED.**
Jer. 5:12 they have b. the L.

**BELIEF.**
2 Thes. 2:13 of Spirit and b.

**BELIEVE.**
Ex. 4:5 may b. L. hath appeared
19:9 may b. thee for ever
Num. 14:11 ere they b. me?
2 Chr. 20:20 b. in the L. his p.
Is. 43:10 may know and b. me.
Mat. 9:28 b. I am able to do this?
18:6 ones which b. Mark 9:42
21:32 that ye might b. him
27:42 and we will b. him
Mark 1:15 repent and b. gospel.
5:36 be not af. only b. Lu. 8:50
9:23 if thou canst b. all things
24 L. I b. help unb. John 9:38
11:23 b. things he saith
24 b. ye receive them, and ye
15:32 descend, that we may b.
16:17 signs fol. them which b.
Luke 8:12 the word lest they b.
13 which for a while b.
24:25 and slow of heart to b.
John 1:7 all thro' him might b.
12 them that b. on his name
3:12 shall ye b. if I tell you
4:21 woman b. me
42 we b. not bec. of thy saying
5:44 can ye b. which receive
47 how shall ye b. my words?
6:29 that ye b. on him he sent
7:5 did his brethren b. in him
39 Spirit, which they that b.
9:35 dost thou b. on S. of God?
36 who is he that I might b.
10:38 b. the w. that ye may b.
11:15 to the intent ye may b.
27 I b. thou art the Christ
40 said I not, if wouldest b.
42 may b. thou hast sent me
48 let him alone all will b.

12:36 ye have light, b. in the l.
13:19 ye may b. I am he
14:1 ye b. in God, b. also in me
11 or b. for the work's sake
29 come to pass, ye might b.
16:30 we b. thou camest from G.
31 J. answered, Do ye now b.?
17:20 for them which shall b.
21 world may b. thou sent me
19:35 that ye might b.
20:31 written that ye might b.
Acts 8:37 I b. J. C. is the S. of G.
13:39 by him all that b.
41 you shall in no wise b.
15:7 Gentiles by me should b.
11 b. thro' grace we sh. be sav.
16:31 b. on Jes. shalt be saved
19:4 b. on him that should come
21:20 seest how many Jews b.
25 touching Gentiles which b.
27:25 I b. God that it shall be
Rom. 3:22 on all that b.
4:11 of all that b.
24 if we b. on him
6:8 we b. we shall also live
10:9 shalt b. that G. raised him
14 how shall they b. in him
1 Cor. 1:21 to save that b.
14:22 tongues a sign, not to th. that b. but prophesying
2 Cor. 4:13 we b. therefore speak
Gal. 3:22 promise to them that b.
Eph. 1:19 to us who b.
Phil. 1:29 given not only to b.
1 Thes. 1:7 ensamples to all th. b.
2:10 behaved am. you that b.
13 worketh in you that b.
4:14 if we b. Jesus died
2 Thes. 1:10 admi. in all that b.
2:11 that they should b. a lie
1 Tim. 1:16 pat. to them that b.
4:3 thanksg. of them that b.
10 Saviour, spec. of th. that b.
Heb. 10:39 b. to saving of soul
11:6 to God must b. that he is
Jam. 2:19 devils also b.
Pet. 1:21 by him do b. in God
2:7 to you wh. b. he is precious
John 3:23 com. that we b.
5:13 to you that b. ye may b.

**BELIEVE not, or not BELIEVE.**
Ex. 4:1 they will not b. me
Deut. 1:32 ye did not b. the Lord
2 K. 17:14 fathers did not b. in L.
Job 9:16 I not b. he had heark.
Prov. 26:25 fair, b. him not
Is. 7:9 will not b. not be esta.
Jer. 12:6 b. not tho' they speak
Hab. 1:5 ye will not b.
Mat. 21:25 not b. him Mark 11:31
24:23 h. is C. b. n. 26; Mark 13:21
Luke 22:67 you will not b.
John 3:12 earthly th. and ye b. n.
4:48 ex. ye see signs will not b.
5:38 he hath sent, him ye b. n.
47 how shall ye b. my words?
6:36 ye have seen me and b. not
64 some of you which b. not
8:24 if ye b. n. I am he, die
45 tell the truth, ye b. me not
46 say the truth, why n. b. me
10:26 ye b. n. bec. not of my s.
37 do not works of F. b. me n.
38 ye b. not me, be. the works
12:30 could not b. because Isa.
47 hear words, and b. not
16:9 bec. they b. not on me
20:25 into his side, I will n. b.
Rom. 3:3 if some did not b.
15:31 from them that do not b.
1 Cor. 10:27 that b. not bid to a f.
14:22 sign to them that b. not
2 Cor. 4:4 blinded th. b. not
2 Tim. 2:13 if we b. not, he abid.
1 John 4:1 b. not every spirit

**BELIEVED.**
Gen. 15:6 he b. counted it, Rom. 4:3; Gal. 3:6; Jam. 2:23
Ex. 4:31 A. spake, people b.
14:31 they b. the L. and Moses
Ps. 27:13 fainted, unless I b.
106:12 then b. they his words
116:10 I b. therefore have I spoken, 2 Cor. 4:13
119:66 I have b. thy command.
Is. 53:1 who hath b. our report? John 12:38; Rom. 10:16
Dan. 6:23 bec. he b. in G.
Jon. 3:5 peo. of Nineveh b. G.
Mat. 8:13 b. so be it done to thee
21:32 publicans and harlots b.
Mark 16:13 neither b. they
Luke 1:1 things most surely b.
45 blessed is she that b. for
John 2:11 his disciples b. on him
22 they b. the scripture
4:50 the man b. word J. spoke
53 the father himself b.
5:46 had ye b. Moses
7:48 have Pharisees b. on him?
8:31 said Jesus to Jews that b.
11:45 seen things Jesus did, b.
12:11 many of the Jews b. on J.
16:27 loveth you, bec. you b.
17:8 have b. thou didst send me
20:8 other disciple, saw and b.
29 have not seen, and yet b.
Acts 2:44 all that b. were togeth.
4:4 many wh. h. the word b.
32 that b. were of one heart
8:12 b. Phil. preaching things
13 then Simon himself b.
10:45 who b. were astonished
11:17 like gift as to us who b.
21 a great number b. turned
13:12 then deputy b.
48 ordained to eternal life b.
14:1 both Jews and Greeks b.
23 to Lord on whom they b.
17:4 b. and consorted with Paul
34 certain clave to him and b.
18:8 Crispus ch. ruler of syn. b.
27 had b. through grace
19:2 rec. ye H. G. since ye b.?
22:19 I beat them that b.
27:11 centur. b. master of ship
28:24 some b. and some b. not
Rom. 4:18 against hope b. in h.
13:11 nearer than when we b.
1 Cor. 3:5 minis. by whom ye b.
15:2 unless ye have b. in vain
11 so we preach, and so ye b.
Gal. 2:16 we have b. in Jesus C.
Eph. 1:13 after ye b. ye were
2 Thes. 1:10 our testim. was b.
1 Tim. 3:16 b. on in the world
2 Tim. 1:12 whom I have b.
Tit. 3:8 which have b. in God
Heb. 4:3 we which b. do enter
1 John 4:16 b. the love of God.

**Many BELIEVED.**
John 2:23 at the pass. many b.
4:39 many of the Samaritans b.
11:45 m. Jews wh. came to M. b.
12:42 chief rulers also many b.
Acts 18:8 m. Corinth. hearing b.
Acts 19:18 m. b. confess. their d.

**BELIEVED not, or not BELIEVED.**
Gen. 45:26 h. fainted, he b. not
Num. 20:12 ye b. me not
Deut. 9:23 and b. him not
Job 29:24 they b. it not
Ps. 78:22 they b. not in God
32 b. not for his wond. works
106:24 despised land, b. n. his w.
Jer. 40:14 but G. b. them not
Lam. 4:12 world would n. have b.
Mat. 21:32 J. came, ye b. him not
Mark 16:11 he was alive, b. not
14 upbr. because they b. not

Luke 20:5 say, Why b. ye not?
24:41 while they b. not for joy
John 3:18 because he hath not b.
6:64 Jesus knew who b. not
10:25 I told you, and ye b. not
12:37 miracles, yet they b. not
Acts 9:26 b. not he was a disc.
17:5 Jews wh. b. not
19:9 were hardened, b. not
Rom. 10:14 they have not b.
11:30 times past have not b. G.
31 these also now not b.
2 Thes. 2:12 damned who b. not
Heb. 3:18 his rest that b. not
11:31 R. per. not with them b. n.
Jude 5 destroyed them that b. n.

**BELIEVERS.**
Acts 5:14 b. were the more added
1 Tim. 4:12 an example of the b.

**BELIEVEST.**
Luke 1:20 dumb, bec. thou b. not
John 1:50 under the fig tree, b.
11:26 never die, b. thou this?
14:10 b. thou not I am in the F.
Acts 8:37 b. with all thy heart
26:27 b. thou the prophets?
Jam. 2:19 thou b. there is one God

**BELIEVETH.**
Job 15:22 b. not he shall return
Prov. 14:15 simple b. every word
Is. 28:16 that b. not make haste
Mark 9:23 possible to him that b.
16:16 he that b. shall be saved, he th. b. not shall be damn.
John 3:15 b. in him, 16
18 b. not is condemned already
36 b. hath everlasting life, 6:47
5:24 b. on him that sent me
6:35 b. on me shall never thirst
40 Son, and b. on him, hath l.
7:38 b. on me, out of his belly
11:25 b. though dead, yet shall
26 b. in me shall never die
12:44 b. not on me, but on him
46 whoso b. not abide in dark.
14:12 b. on me the works
Acts 10:43 b. receive remission
Rom. 1:16 of G. to ev. that b.
3:26 justifier of him that b. in J.
4:5 that worketh not, but b. on
9:33 whoso b. not be asha. 10:11
10:4 end of law to ev. one th. b.
10 the heart man b. to right.
14:2 one b. he may eat
1 Cor. 7:12 a wife that b. not
13:7 love b. all things
14:24 come in one that b. not
2 Cor. 6:15 hath he that b.
1 Tim. 5:16 if any that b.
1 Pet. 2:6 b. shall not be conf.
1 John 5:1 whoso b. J. is the C.
5 overcometh, but he that b.
10 b. on the Son; he that b. n. G. bec. he b. not the record

**BELIEVING.**
Mat. 21:22 ask b. ye shall receive
John 20:27 not faithless, but b.
31 that b. ye might have life
Acts 16:34 b. in God
24:14 b. all things written
Rom. 15:13 joy and peace in b.
1 Tim. 6:2 that have b. masters
1 Pet. 1:8 yet b. ye rejoice

**BELL, S.**
Ex. 28:34 golden b. 39:26
Zec. 14:20 upon the b. of horses

BELLOW. See BULLS.

**BELLOWS.**
Jer. 6:29 the b. are burnt

**BELLY.**
Gen. 3:14 on thy b. shalt thou go
Lev. 11:42 goeth on the b.
Num. 5:21 and thy b. to swell
25:8 man and wom. through b.
Jud. 3:21 dag. thrust it in his b.

1 *K.* 7:20 pomeg. over against *b.*
*Job* 3:11 when I came out of *b.*
15:2 fill his *b.* with east wind
35 their *b.* prepareth deceit
20:15 G. shall cast out of his *b.*
*Job* 20:20 not feel quietness in *b.*
23 when about to fill his *b.*
32:19 my *b.* is as wine which
*Ps.* 17:14 whose *b.* fillest
22:10 from my mother's *b.*
44:25 our *b.* cleaveth to earth
*Prov.* 13:25 *b.* of wicked
18:8 innermost parts of *b.* 26:22
20 a man's *b.* shall be satisfied
20:27 inward parts of *b.*
30 stripes inward parts of *b.*
*Cant.* 5:14 his *b.* is as br. ivory
7:2 thy *b.* is like wheat
*Is.* 46:3 borne by me from the *b.*
*Jer.* 1:5 formed thee in *b.* I k.
51:34 his *b.* with my delicates
*Ezek.* 3:3 cause thy *b.* to eat
*Dan.* 2:32 image's *b.* of brass
*Jon.* 1:17 in *b.* of fish, *Mat.* 12:40
2:2 out of the *b.* of hell cried I
*Hab.* 3:16 my *b.* trembled
*Mat.* 15:17 into the *b.* and is cast out, *Mark* 7:19
*Luke* 15:16 his *b.* with the husks
*John* 7:38 out of his *b.* flow riv.
*Rom.* 16:18 serve their own *b.*
1 *Cor.* 6:13 meats for the *b.*
*Phil.* 3:19 whose God is their *b.*
*Rev.* 10:9 shall make thy *b.* bit.
10 eaten it, my *b.* was bitter.

**BELLIES.**

*Tit.* 1:12 the Cretians are slow *b.*

**BELONG.**

*Lev.* 27:24 to whom it did *b.*
*Deut.* 29:29 secret things *b.* to G.
*Ps.* 47:9 shields of earth *b.* to G.
68:20 to our God *b.* the issues
*Prov.* 24:2 these *b.* to the wise
*Dan.* 9:9 to the Lord *b.* mercies
*Mark* 9:41 bec. ye *b.* to Christ
*Luke* 19:42 which *b.* to thy p.
1 *Cor.* 7:32 things *b.* to Lord

**BELONGED, EST.**

1 *Sam.* 30:13 to whom *b.* thou?
*Luke* 23:7 *b.* to Herod's jurisd.

**BELONGETH.**

*Deut.* 32:35 to me *b.* vengeance, *Ps.* 94:1; *Heb.* 10:30
*Ps.* 3:8 salvation *b.* unto the L.
62:11 power *b.* unto God
12 unto thee, O Lord, *b.* mercy
*Dan.* 9:7 righteousness *b.* to thee
8 to us *b.* confusion of face
*Heb.* 5:14 strong meat *b.*

**BELONGING.**

*Prov.* 26:17 strife *b.* not to him

**BELOVED.**

*Deut.* 21:15 two wives, the one *b.*
33:12 *b.* of Lord dwell in safety
*Neh.* 13:26 Solomon, *b.* of his G.
*Ps.* 60:5 thy *b.* may be d. 108:6
127:2 so he giveth his *b.* sleep
*Prov.* 4:3 only *b.* in sight of m.
*Cant.* 5:1 drink abundantly, O *b.*
9 thy *b.* more than another *b.*?
61: whither is thy *b.* gone?
8:5 cometh leaning on her *b.*?
*Dan.* 9:23 greatly *b.* 10:11, 19
*Hos.* 31 a woman *b.* of her. fr.
9:16 I will slay the *b.* fruit
*Acts* 15:25 with *b.* B. and Paul
*Rom.* 1:7 all in Rome *b.* of God
9:25 call her *b.* wh. was not *b.*
11:28 are *b.* for Father's sake
16:12 *b.* Persis who labored
*Eph.* 1:6 accepted in the *b.*
6:21 T. a *b.* brother, *Col.* 4:7
*Col.* 3:12 elect of G. holy and *b.*
4:9 Onesimus, a *b.* brother
14 Luke the *b.* physician
1 *Thes.* 1:4 kn. *b.* your election
1 *Tim.* 6:2 serv. bec. they are *b.*
*Phile.* 16 a servant a brother *b.*
*Heb.* 6:9 *b.* we are persuaded
2 *Pet.* 3:8 *b.* be not ignorant
15 even as our *b.* brother Paul
1 *John* 3:2 *b.* now we are the sons
21 *b.* if our heart condemn
4:1 *b.* believe not every spirit
7 *b.* let us love one another
11 *b.* if God so loved us, we
3 *John* 11 *b.* follow not evil,
*Jude* 20 but ye *b.* building up
*Rev.* 20:9 they compassed *b.* city

*Dearly* BELOVED. *See* DEARLY.

**My BELOVED.**

*Cant.* 1:14 *my b.* is to me a clus.
16 art fair, *my b.* yea, pleasant
2:3 the apple-tree, so is *my b.*
9 *my b.* is like a roe or a hart
16 *my b.* is mine, 6:3
17 *my b.* and be like a roe
4:16 let *my b.* come into his g.
5:2 voice of *my b.* 2:8
5 to open to *my b.* 6 I opened
*Cant.* 5:10 *my b.* is, 16 is *my b.*
6:2 *my b.* is gone
3 I am *my b.* *my b.* mine, 7:10
7:13 laid up for thee, O *my b.*
*Is.* 5:1 song of *my b.* touching
*Jer.* 11:15 *my b.* to do in my h.
*Mat.* 3:17 this is *my b.* Son, 17:5; *Mark* 1:11; 9:7; *Luke* 3:22; 9:35; 2 *Pet.* 1:17
12:18 *my b.* in whom my soul
*Luke* 20:13 will send *my b.* Son
*Rom.* 16:8 greet Amplias *my b.*
1 *Cor.* 4:14 as *my b.* sons I warn
17 Tim. *my b.* son, 2 *Tim.* 1:2
*Jam.* 1:16 do not err, *my b.* breth.

BELSHAZZAR. *Dan.* 5:1, 2, 9, 22, 29, 30; 7:1; 8:1
BELTESHAZZAR. *Dan.* 1:7; 2:26; 4:8, 18, 19; 5:12; 10:1

**BEMOAN, ED, ING.**

*Job* 42:11 *b.* Job, and comfort.
*Jer.* 15:5 who shall *b.* thee, O J.
16:5 neither lament, nor *b.*
22:10 w. ye not for dead, nor *b.*
31:18 heard Eph. *b.* himself
48:17 all ye about him *b.* him
*Nah.* 3:7 N. who will *b.* her?

BENAIAH. 2 *Sam.* 23:22; 1 *Chr.* 11:24; *Ezek.* 11:1
BEN-AMMI. *Gen.* 19:38

**BENCHES.**

*Ezek.* 27:6 made thy *b.* of ivory

**BEND.**

*Ps.* 11:2 wicked *b.* their bow
64:3 *b.* their bows to shoot
*Jer.* 9:3 they *b.* their tongue
46:9 Lydians, that *b.* the bow
50:14 *b.* bow shoot at her, 29
51:3 bendeth, let the archer *b.*
*Ezek.* 17:7 vine did *b.* her roots

**BENDETH, ING.**

*Ps.* 58:7 when he *b.* his bow
*Is.* 60:14 that afflicted thee shall come *b.* to thee
*Jer.* 51:3 against him that *b.*

**BENEATH.**

*Ex.* 20:4 the earth *b.* *Deut.* 5:8
*Deut.* 4:39 earth *b.* there is none
28:13 above only, and not be *b.*
*Is.* 51:6 look on the earth *b.*
*John* 8:23 ye are from *b.* I above

**BENEFACTORS.**

*Luke* 22:25 exer. auth. are call. *b.*

**BENEFIT, Verb.**

*Jer.* 18:10 wherewith I *b.* them

**BENEFIT, S.**

2 *Chr.* 32:25 Hezekiah rendered not according to *b.*
*Ps.* 68:19 loadeth us with *b.*
103:2 forget not all his *b.*
116:12 render for all his *b.*?
2 *Cor.* 1:15 have a second *b.*
1 *Tim.* 6:2 partakers of the *b.*
*Phile.* 14 *b.* not be of necessity

**BENEVOLENCE.**

1 *Cor.* 7:3 render to the w. due *b.*

BEN-HADAD. 1 *K.* 15:18; 20:2; 2 *K.* 6:24; 8:7; 13:3; *Jer.* 49:27

**BENJAMIN.**

*Gen.* 35:18 his f. called him B.
42:36 J. and will ye take B.
46:21 the sons of B. *Num.* 26:38; 1 *Chr.* 7:6; 8:1, 40; 9:7; *Neh.* 11:7
49:27 B. shall ravin as a wolf
*Deut.* 33:12 of B. Moses said, The beloved of the Lord
*Jud.* 20:20 went to battle ag't B.
*Ps.* 68:27 B. with their ruler
80:2 before B. and Manasseh

*See* CHILDREN.

**BENJAMIN** *with* **Judah.**

*Jud.* 10:9 to fight J. and B.
1 *K.* 12:23 speak to the house of J. and B. 2 *Chr.* 11:3
1 *Chr.* 12:16 came of B. and J.
2 *Chr.* 15:2 Asa all J. and B.
31:1 the altars out of J. and B.
*Ezr.* 1:5 fathers of J. and B.

**Land of BENJAMIN.**

*Jud.* 21:21 go into *l. of* B.
1 *Sam.* 9:16 out of the *l. of* B.
2 *Chr.* 15:8 idols out of *l. of* B.
*Jer.* 17:26 come from *l. of* B.

**Tribe of BENJAMIN.**

*Num.* 1:37 of the *t. of* B.
*Jos.* 18:11 lot of *t. of* B. 21
*Jud.* 20:12 men thro' all *t. of* B.
1 *Sam.* 10:20 came near, *t. of* B.
*Rom.* 11:1 of *t. of* B. *Phil.* 3:5
*Rev.* 7:8 *t. of* B. sealed, 12,000

**BENJAMITES.**

*Jud.* 19:16 men of pl. were B.
20:35 destroyed of the B.
1 *Sam.* 22:7 Hear now, ye B.

BENONI. *Gen.* 35:18

**BENT.**

*Ps.* 7:12 *b.* his *b.* *Lam.* 2:4; 3:12
37:14 *b.* their bow to cast down
*Is.* 5:28 and all their bows *b.*
21:15 for they fled from *b.* bow
*Hos.* 11:7 my people are *b.*
*Zec.* 9:13 when I have *b.* Judah

BEOR. *Gen.* 36:32; *Num.* 22:5; 24:3; 31:8; *Deut.* 23:4; *Jos.* 13:22; 24:9; 1 *Chr.* 1:43; *Mic.* 6:5

BERACHAH. 1 *Chr.* 12:3; 2 *Chr.* 20:26
BEREA. *Acts* 17:10, 13; 20:4

**BEREAVE.**

*Ec.* 4:8 and *b.* my soul of good
*Jer.* 15:7 I will *b.* them, 18:21
*Ezek.* 5:17 send evil beasts, and they shall *b.* thee
36:12 no more *b.* them, 14
*Hos.* 9:12 yet will I *b.* them

**BEREAVED.**

*Gen.* 42:36 ye have *b.* of my ch.
43:14 *b.* of my children, I am *b.*
*Ezek.* 36:13 thou land hast *b.*
*Hos.* 13:8 meet them as a bear *b.*

**BEREAVETH.**

*Lam.* 1:20 abroad the sword *b.*

BERITH. *Jud.* 9:46
BERNICE. *Acts* 25:13, 23; 26:30

**BERRIES.**

*Is.* 17:6 two or three *b.*
*Jam.* 3:12 fig-tree bear olive *b.*

**BERYL.**
*Dan.* 10:6 his body like the *b.*
*Rev.* 21:20 foundation was *b.*

**BESEECH.**
*Ex.* 33:18 I *b.* show me
*Num.* 12:13 her now, I *b.* thee
*Ps.* 80:14 return, we *b.* O God
116:4 O L. I *b.* thee, deliver
118:25 save, I *b.* thee
119:108 accept, I *b.* thee
*Jer.* 38:20 obey, I *b.* thee
*Amos* 7:2 forgive I *b.* thee
*Jon.* 1:14 we *b.* thee O Lord
4:3 take, I *b.* thee, my life
*Mal.* 1:9 *b.* God, he be gracious
*Luke* 8:28 J. I *b.* thee tor. me not
9:38 I *b.* thee look on my s.
*Acts* 26:3 I *b.* thee to hear me
*Rom.* 12:1 I *b.* you by mercies
1 *Cor.* 4:16 I *b.* be ye followers
2 *Cor.* 2:8 I *b.* you confirm
5:20 as tho' God did *b.* you
6:1 we *b.* you rec. not the grace
10:1 I Paul *b.* you by the meek
*Gal.* 4:12 I *b.* you, be as I am
*Eph.* 4:1 pris. of L. *b.* you walk
*Phile.* 9 yet for love's sake I *b.*
10 I *b.* thee for my son Onesi.
*Heb.* 13:19 I *b.* you the rather
1 *Pet.* 2:11 I *b.* you as strangers
2 *John* 5 now I *b.* thee, lady
*See* BRETHREN.

**BESEECHING.**
*Mat.* 8:5 centurion *b.* *Luke* 7:3
*Mark* 1:40 leper to him, *b.* him

**BESET.**
*Jud.* 19:22 sons of Bel. *b.* 20:5
*Ps.* 22:12 bulls of B. have *b.* me
139:5 *b.* me behind and before
*Hos.* 7:2 doings have *b.* them
*Heb.* 12:1 which doth so easily *b.*

**BESIDE, S.**
*Gen.* 19:12 hast thou here any *b.*
*Luke* 16:26 *b.* all this
24:21 *b.* all this
*Phile.* 19 thine own self *b.*

**BESIDE,** *with* **self.**
*Mark* 3:21 said he is *b.* himself
*Acts* 26:24 P. thou art *b.* thyself
2 *Cor.* 5:13 whether we be *b.*

**BESIEGE.**
*Deut.* 28:52 *b.* thee in thy gates
1 *K.* 8:37 enemies *b.* 2 *Chr.* 6:28
*Is.* 21:2 O Elam, *b.* O Media

**BESIEGED.**
2 *K.* 19:24 rivers of *b.* pl. *Is.* 37:25
*Ec.* 9:14 a great king and *b.* it
*Is.* 1:8 Zion is left as a *b.* city
*Ezek.* 6:12 *b.* shall die by famine

**BESOM.**
*Is.* 14:23 the *b.* of destruction

BESOR. 1 *Sam.* 30:9

**BESOUGHT.**
*Gen.* 42:21 *b.* us, we would not
*Ex.* 32:11 Moses *b.* L. *Deut.* 3:23
2 *Sam.* 12:16 *b.* G. for the child
1 *K.* 13:6 man of God *b.* the L.
2 *K.* 13:4 Jehoahaz *b.* the Lord
2 *Chr.* 33:12 Manasseh in affl. *b.*
*Ezr.* 8:23 *b.* our God for this
*Jer.* 26:19 Hezekiah *b.* the Lord
*Mat.* 8:31 the devils *b.* him, *Mark* 5:10, 12; *Luke* 8:31, 32
34 *b.* him to depart, *Luke* 8:37
*Mark* 5:23 Jairus *b.* *Luke* 8:41
*John* 4:40 S. *b.* he would tarry
47 nobleman of Caper. *b.* him
19:38 *b.* he might take the body
*Acts* 13:42 *b.* that these words
16:15 Lydia *b.* us saying
39 magistrates *b.* them
21:12 we *b.* him not to go to J.
2 *Cor.* 12:8 for this I *b.* the Lord

**BEST.**
*Ps.* 39:5 man at his *b.* state
*Luke* 15:22 bring forth the *b.*
1 *Cor.* 12:31 covet the *b.* gifts

**BESTEAD.**
*Is.* 8:21 pass thro' it hardly *b.*

**BESTIR.**
2 *Sam.* 5:24 hearest the sound *b.*

**BESTOW.**
*Ex.* 32:29 may *b.* on you
*Deut.* 14:26 *b.* money for what
2 *Chr.* 24:7 they did *b.* on Baalim
*Ezr.* 7:20 *b.* it out of k.'s treas.
*Luke* 12:17 to *b.* my fruits
1 *Cor.* 12:23 on these we *b.* more
13:3 though I *b.* all my goods

**BESTOWED.**
*Is.* 63:7 ac. to all Lord *b.* on us
*John* 4:38 to reap whereon ye *b.*
*Rom.* 16:6 Mary, who *b.* much
1 *Cor.* 15:10 grace *b.* not in vain
2 *Cor.* 1:11 gift *b.* on us by many
8:1 grace *b.* on the churches
*Gal.* 4:11 lest I *b.* labor in vain
1 *John* 3:1 manner of love F. *b.*

BETHABARA. *John* 1:28

**BETHANY.**
*Mat.* 21:17 went into B. 26:6
*Mark* 11:12; 14:3; *Luke* 19:29
*Luke* 24:50 led out as far as B.
*John* 11:1 Lazarus of B. 12:1

**BETH-AVEN.**
*Jos.* 7:2 Ai, which is beside B.
1 *Sam.* 14:23 passed over to B.
*Hos.* 4:15 nor go ye up to B.
5:8 cry aloud at B. after thee
10:5 because of the calves of B.

BETH-CAR. 1 *Sam.* 7:11
BETH-DAGON. *Jos.* 19:27
BETH-DIBLATHAIM. *Jer.* 48:22

**BETH-EL.**
*Gen.* 28:19 c. the place B. 35:15
31:13 I am God of B.
35:1 up to B. 3; 6 came to B.
*Amos* 3:14 will visit altars of B.
4:4 come to B. and transgress
5:5 B. shall come to naught, 6
7:13 proph. not any more at B.

BETH-ELITE. 1 *K.* 16:34
BETHER. *Cant.* 2:17
BETHESDA. *John* 5:2
BETH-EZEL. *Mic.* 1:11
BETH-GAMUL. *Jer.* 48:23
BETH-HACCEREM. *Jer.* 6:1

**BETH-HORON.**
*Jos.* 10:11 going down to B.
21:22 gave Lev. B. 1 *Chr.* 6:68
1 *Sam.* 13:18 comp. turned to B.
1 *K.* 9:17 S. built B. 2 *Chr.* 8:5
1 *Chr.* 7:24 Sherah built B.

**BETHINK.**
1 *K.* 8:47 *b.* them. 2 *Chr.* 6:37

**BETH-LEHEM.**
2 *Sam.* 23:15 well of B. 1 *Ch.* 11:17
*Mat.* 2:1 Jesus born in B. 6, 16

**BETH-LEHEM EPHRATAH.**
*Mic.* 5:2 B. E. though thou be

BETH-LEHEM JUDAH. *Jud.* 17:7; 19:1, 18; *Ruth* 1:1

**BETH-LEHEMITE.**
1 *Sam.* 16:1 J. the B. 18; 17:58
2 *Sam.* 21:19 B. slew G. brother

**BETH-PEOR.**
*Deut.* 3:29 valley over ag'st B.
4:46 statutes over against B.
34:6 buried Moses over ag'st B.

BETHPHAGE. *Mat.* 21:1; *Mark* 11:1; *Luke* 19:29

**BETHSAIDA.**
*Mat.* 11:21 thee, B. 1 *Luke* 10:13
*Mark* 6:45 disciples go to B. 8:22
*Luke* 9:10 a desert belong. to B.
*John* 1:44 Phil. was of B. 12:21

BETH-SHAN. 1 *Sam.* 31:10
BETH-SHEMESH. *Jud.* 1:33; 1 *Sam.* 6:9, 12, 19; 2 *K.* 14:11
BETHUEL. *Gen.* 22:22, 23; 24:24; 28:2

**BETIMES.**
*Gen.* 26:31 rose up *b.* and sware
2 *Chr.* 36:15 his messen. rising *b.*
*Job* 8:5 wouldest seek unto G. *b.*
24:5 as wild asses rising *b.*
*Prov.* 13:24 chasteneth him *b.*

**BETRAY.**
1 *Chr.* 12:17 come to *b.* me
*Mat.* 24:10 shall *b.* one another
26:16 sought opportunity to *b.* *Mark* 14:11; *Luke* 22:6
21 one of you shall *b.* me, *Mark* 14:18; *John* 13:21
46 he is at hand that doth *b.*
*Mark* 13:12 brother shall *b.* bro.
*John* 6:64 should *b.* him, 13:11
13:2 into heart of Judas to *b.*

**BETRAYED.**
*Mat.* 10:4 J. who *b.* him, *Mark* 3:19
17:22 S. of m. shall be *b.* 20:18; 26:2, 45; *Mark* 14:41
26:24 Son of man is *b.* *Mark* 14:21; *Luke* 22:22
48 he that *b.* *Mark* 14:44
27:4 I *b.* innocent blood
*Luke* 21:16 be *b.* both by parents
*John* 18:2 *b.* him knew the place
1 *Cor.* 11:23 same night he was *b.*

**BETRAYERS.**
*Acts* 7:52 of whom ye the *b.*

**BETRAYEST, ETH.**
*Mark* 14:42 he that *b.* me
*Luke* 22:21 hand that *b.* me
48 *b.* Son of man with a kiss?
*John* 21:20 is he that *b.* thee?

**BETROTH.**
*Deut.* 28:30 shalt *b.* a wife
*Hos.* 2:19 *b.* thee to me
20 *b.* to me in faithfulness

**BETROTHED.**
*Ex.* 22:16 entice a maid not *b.* *Deut.* 22:28
*Lev.* 19:20 lieth with a woman *b.*
*Deut.* 20:7 who hath *b.* a wife
22:23 find a virgin *b.* and lie
27 *b.* damsel cried, none to save

**BETTER.**
*Gen.* 29:19 *b.* I give her to thee
*Ex.* 14:12 *b.* serv. the Egyptians
*Num.* 14:3 *b.* to return to E.?
*Jud.* 8:2 gleanings *b.* than vint.
11:25 art thou *b.* than Balak
1 *Sam.* 1:8 am not I *b.* than ten s.
27:1 nothing *b.* than go
1 *K.* 1:47 made name of k. Sol. *b.*
2:32 two men *b.* than he
19:4 am not *b.* than my fathers
21:2 give thee a *b.* vineyard
2 *K.* 5:12 rivers of Damascus *b.*
2 *Chr.* 21:13 slain brethren *b.* than
*Ps.* 69:31 please *b.* than ox
*Ec.* 2:24 nothing *b.* than to eat
3:22 nothing *b.* than rejoice
4:3 *b.* is he than both they
9 two are *b.*
6:11 what is man *b.*?
7:10 former days were *b.*
10:11 and a babbler is no *b.*
*Is.* 56:5 a name *b.* than of sons
*Lam.* 4:9 that be slain are *b.*
*Ezek.* 36:11 settle you and do *b.*
*Dan.* 1:20 ten times *b.*
*Hos.* 2:7 then was it *b.* with me
*Amos* 6:2 be they *b.* than these
*Nah.* 3:8 *b.* than populous No?
*Mat.* 6:26 f. of the air, are ye not *b.* than they? *Luke* 12:24

12:12 a man *b.* than a sheep?
18:6 *b.* that a millstone, *Mark* 9:42; *Luke* 17:2
*Rom.* 3:9 are we *b.* than they?
1 *Cor.* 7:38 marriage, doth *b.*
8:8 neither if we eat are we *b.*
9:15 *b.* for me to die
11:17 come together not for *b.*
*Phil.* 2:3 esteem other *b.* than
*Heb.* 1:4 much *b.* than the angels
6:9 persuaded *b.* things of you
7:7 the less is blessed of the *b.*
19 bringing in of a *b.* hope did
22 a surety of a *b.* testament
8:6 Mediator of a *b.* covenant, established on *b.* promises
9:23 things with *b.* sacrifices
10:34 a *b.* and enduring sub.
11:16 desire a *b.* country
*Heb.* 11:35 obtain a *b.* resurrec.
40 some *b.* thing for us
12:24 *b.* things than that of A.
2 *Pet.* 2:21 *b.* not to have known

**BETTER is.**

*Prov.* 15:16 *b. is* little with f. of L.
17 *b. is* dinner of herbs
16:8 *b. is* a little with right.
16 *b. is* it to get wisdom
17:1 *b. is* a dry morsel
19:1 *b. is* poor 28:6
27:10 *b. is* a neighbor near
*Ec.* 4:6 *b. is* handful with quiet
13 *b. is* a poor wise child than
6:9 *b. is* the sight of the eyes
7:8 *b. is* the end than the beg.
*Cant.* 4:10 *b. is* thy love

**Is BETTER, *or* is it BETTER.**

*Jud.* 9:2 whether *is b.* all reign
18:19 *is it b.* to be a priest
*Ruth* 4:15 thy daughter *is b.*
1 *Sam.* 15:22 to obey *is b.*
28 neighbor that *is b.*
2 *Sam.* 17:14 counsel of H. *is b.*
*Est.* 1:19 another that *is b.*
*Ps.* 37:16 righteous hath *is b.*
63:3 thy loving-kind. *is b.*
84:10 a day in thy courts *is b.*
119:72 *is b.* to me than gold
*Prov.* 3:14 wisdom *is b.*
8:11 wisdom *is b.* than rubies
19 my fruit *is b.* than gold
12:9 *is b.* than he that honoreth
16:32 that is slow to anger *is b.*
19:22 poor man *is b.* than a liar
27:5 rebuke *is b.* than secret l.
*Ec.* 6:3 an untimely birth *is b.*
7:1 a good name *is b.* than oint.
3 sorrow *is b.* than laughter, by sad. of coun. h. *is* made *b.*
8 the patient in spirit *is b.*
9:4 a liv. dog *is b.* than a d. lion
16 wisdom *is b.* than strength
18 wisd. *is b.* than w. of war
*Cant.* 1:2 love *is b.* than wine
*Luke* 5:39 he saith, the old *is b.*
*Phil.* 1:23 with C. wh. *is* far *b.*

**It is BETTER, *or* BETTER it is.**

*Ps.* 118:8 *it is b.* to trust in L. 9
*Prov.* 16:19 *b.* to be of humble
21:9 *b.* to dwell in a, 25:24
19 *it is b.* to dwell in the wild.
25:7 *b. it is* it be said, Come up
*Ec.* 5:5 *b. it is* thou sh. not vow
7:2 *it is b.* to go to house of m.
5 *b.* to hear reb. of wise men
*Jon.* 4:3 *it is b.* for me, 8
*Mat.* 18:8 *it is b.* to enter into life halt, 9; *Mark* 9:43, 45, 47
1 *Cor.* 7:9 *b.* to marry than to b.
1 *Pet.* 3:17 *b.* ye suffer for well-d.

**BETTERED.**

*Mark* 5:26 she was nothing *b.*

**BETWIXT.**

*Phil.* 1:23 I am in a strait *b.* two

BEULAH. *Is.* 62:4

**BEWAIL.**

*Lev.* 10:6 *b.* the burning L. kind.
*Deut.* 21:13 and *b.* her father
*Jud.* 11:37 *b.* my virginity, 38
*Is.* 16:9 will *b.* with the weep.
2 *Cor.* 12:21 *b.* many who have s.
*Rev.* 18:19 shall *b.* her

**BEWAILED, ETH.**

*Jer.* 4:31 daughter of Zion that *b.*
*Luke* 8:52 and all wept and *b.*
23:27 of women which also *b.*

**BEWARE.**

*Gen.* 24:6 *b.* bring not my son
*Ex.* 23:21 *b.* of him, obey his v.
*Deut.* 6:12 *b.* thou forget L. 8:11
15:9 *b.* there be not a thought
*Jud.* 13:4 *b.* drink no wine, 13
2 *Sam.* 18:12 *b.* none t. y. man
2 *K.* 6:9 *b.* thou pass not
*Job* 36:18 *b.* lest he take thee a.
*Prov.* 19:25 the simple will *b.*
*Is.* 36:18 *b.* lest H. persuade
*Mat.* 7:15 *b.* of false prophets
10:17 *b.* of men
16:6 *b.* of the leaven, 11; *Mark* 8:15; *Luke* 12:1
*Mark* 12:38 *b.* of s. *Luke* 20:46
*Luke* 12:15 *b.* of covetousness
*Acts* 13:40 *b.* lest that come
*Phil.* 3:2 *b.* of dogs, *b.* of evil w.
*Col.* 2:8 *b.* lest any man spoil
2 *Pet.* 3:17 *b.* lest being led

**BEWITCHED.**

*Acts* 8:9 Simon *b.* the people, 11
*Gal.* 3:1 who hath *b.* you?

**BEWRAY.**

*Is.* 16:3 *b.* not him that wand.

**BEWRAYETH.**

*Prov.* 27:16 oint. of right h. *b.*
29:24 cursing, and *b.* it not
*Mat.* 26:73 thy speech *b.* thee

**BEYOND.**

*Num.* 22:18 B. said, I cannot go *b.* the word of the L. 24:13
*Deut.* 30:13 nor is it *b.* the sea
2 *Sam.* 10:16 *b.* the river, 1 *K.* 14:15; 1 *Chr.* 19:16; *Ezr.* 4:17, 20; 6:6, 8; 7:21, 25; *Neh.* 2:7, 9; *Is.* 7:20; 18:1; *Zep.* 3:10
*Mark* 6:51 amazed *b.* meas. 7:37
2 *Cor.* 8:3 *b.* their power willing
10:14 stretch not *b.* our meas.
*Gal.* 1:13 *b.* measure I persecut.
1 *Thes.* 4:6 that no man go *b.*

BEYOND *Jordan. See* JORDAN.

BEZALEEL. *Ex.* 31:2; 36:1; 38:22

**BEZEK.**

*Jud.* 1:4 slew in B. 10,000 men, 5
1 *Sam.* 11:8 Is. in B. 300,000

BIBBER. *See* WINE.

BICHRI. 2 *Sam.* 20:1, 2, 6, 22

**BID.**

1 *Sam.* 9:27 *b.* the servant pass
2 *Sam.* 2:26 *b.* the people return
2 *K.* 5:13 *b.* thee do great thing
10:5 all that thou shalt *b.* us
*Zep.* 1:7 L. hath *b.* his guests
*Mat.* 14:28 *b.* me come on the w.
22:9 find *b.* to the marriage
23:3 what they *b.* you observe
*Luke* 9:61 first *b.* farewell
10:40 *b.* her that she help me
14:12 they also *b.* thee again
1 *Cor.* 10:27 any that bel. not *b.*
2 *John* 10 nor *b.* him God speed

**BIDDEN.**

1 *Sam.* 9:13 they eat that be *b.*
2 *Sam.* 16:11 for the L. hath *b.*
*Mat.* 1:24 as angel had *b.* him
22:3 to call them that were *b.*
4 tell them *b.* I have prepared
8 they *b.* were not worthy

*Luke* 7:39 Pharisee who had *b.*
14:7 to those who were *b.*
8 art *b.* lest a more hon. be *b.*
10 art *b.* sit in lowest room
24 none of those men *b.*

**BIDDETH, ING.**

1 *Sam.* 22:14 goeth at thy *b.*
2 *John* 11 that *b.* him God speed

**BIDE.**

*Rom.* 11:23 *b.* not still in unb.

BIDKAR. 2 *K.* 9:25

**BIER.**

2 *Sam.* 3:31 David followed the *b.*
*Luke* 7:14 and touched the *b.*

BIGTHAN. *Est.* 2:21; 6:2

BILDAD. *Job* 2:11; 8:1; 18:1; 25:1; 42:9

BILHAH. *Gen.* 29:29; 35:22, 25

**BILL.**

*Luke* 16:6 thy *b.* and write, 7
*See* DIVORCE.

**BILLOWS.**

*Ps.* 42:7 *b.* are gone over, *Jon.* 2:3

**BIND.**

*Num.* 30:2 an oath to *b.* his soul
*Deut.* 6:8 *b.* them for a sign
*Jud.* 15:10 to *b.* Samson
16:5 *b.* Samson to afflict him
*Job* 31:36 I will *b.* it as a crown
38:31 *b.* influence of Pleiades
39:10 canst thou *b.* the unicorn
40:13 *b.* their faces in secret
41:5 wilt thou *b.* Leviathan
*Ps.* 105:22 to *b.* his princes
118:27 *b.* the sacrifice
149:8 to *b.* their kings
*Prov.* 3:3 *b.* them about thy neck
6:21 *b.* them upon thy heart
7:3 *b.* them on thy fingers
*Is.* 8:16 *b.* up the testimony
49:18 *b.* them on thee as a bride
61:1 to *b.* up the broken-hearted
*Ezek.* 34:16 I will *b.* up broken
*Hos.* 6:1 smitten and will *b.* us
*Mic.* 1:13 *b.* the chariot
*Mat.* 12:29 first *b.* the strong man, *Mark* 3:27
13:30 *b.* tares to burn them
16:19 shall *b.* on earth, 18:18
22:13 *b.* him hand and foot
23:4 *b.* heavy burdens grievous
*Mark* 5:3 no man could *b.* him
*Acts* 9:14 authority to *b.* all that
12:8 angel said *b.* on sandals
21:11 so shall the Jews *b.*

**BINDETH.**

*Job* 5:18 maketh sore and *b.* up
26:8 he *b.* up the waters
28:11 he *b.* floods from overfl.
30:18 *b.* me about as the collar
36:13 hyp. cry not when he *b.*
*Ps.* 129:7 he that *b.* sheaves
147:3 he healeth and *b.* up
*Prov.* 26:8 *b.* a stone in a sling
*Is.* 30:26 Lord *b.* up breach

**BINDING.**

*Gen.* 49:11 *b.* his foal to the vine
*Acts* 22:6 *b.* and delivering men

**BIRD.**

*Gen.* 7:14 every *b.* went into
*Lev.* 14:52 cleanse with living *b.*
*Job* 41:5 play as with a *b.*
*Ps.* 11:1 as a *b.* to mountain
124:7 our soul is escaped as a *b.*
*Prov.* 1:17 in sight of any *b.*
6:5 as a *b.* from the fowler
7:23 as a *b.* hasteth to the snare
26:2 as the *b.* by wandering
27:8 as a *b.* that wandereth
*Ec.* 10:20 *b.* shall tell the matter
12:4 rise at the voice of the *b.*

*Is.* 16:2 as a wandering *b.*
46:11 ravenous *b.* from the east
*Jer.* 12:9 heritage as a speck. *b.*
*Lam.* 3:52 chased me like a *b.*
*Hos.* 9:11 fly away like a *b.*
11:11 they shall tremble as a *b.*
*Amos* 3:5 a *b.* fall where no gin
*Rev.* 18:2 every unclean *b.*

**BIRDS.**

*Gen.* 15:10 the *b.* divided he not
40:19 the *b.* shall eat thy flesh
*Lev.* 14:4 to take two *b.* alive
*Deut.* 14:11 clean *b.* shall eat
2 *Sam.* 21:10 *b.* to rest by day
*Ps.* 104:17 the *b.* make nests
*Ec.* 9:12 as *b.* caught
*Cant.* 2.12 time of singing of *b.*
*Is.* 31:5 as *b.* flying
*Jer.* 4:25 *b.* of heaven were fled
5:27 as a cage full of *b.* so are
12:4 are consumed and the *b.*
9 the *b.* round about
*Ezek.* 30:4 will gi. thee to rav. *b.*
*Dan.* 4:33 nails like *b.* claws
*Mat.* 8:20 *b.* have n. *Luke* 9:58
13:32 *b.* lodge in the branches
*Rom.* 1:23 an image like to *b.*
1 *Cor.* 15:39 another of *b.*
*Jam.* 3:7 every kind of *b.* is tam.

BIRSHA. *Gen.* 14:2

**BIRTH.**

2 *K.* 19:3 children are come to the *b.* *Is.* 37:3
*Job* 3:16 as a hidden untimely *b.*
*Ps.* 58:8 like the untimely *b.*
*Ec.* 6:3 untimely *b.* is better
7:1 better than day of one's *b.*
*Is.* 66:9 shall I bring to the *b.*
*Ezek.* 16:3 thy *b.* is of Canaan
*Hos.* 9:11 shall fly from the *b.*
*Mat.* 1:18 the *b.* of Jesus Christ
*Luke* 1:14 shall rejoice at his *b.*
*Gal.* 4:19 I travail in *b.*
*Rev.* 12:2 she cried, trav. in *b.*

**BIRTHDAY.**

*Gen.* 40:20 which was Ph.'s *b.*
*Mat.* 14:6 Herod's *b.* *Mark* 6:21

**BIRTHRIGHT.**

*Gen.* 25:31 this day thy *b.*
33 sold his *b.* to Jacob
34 thus Esau despised his *b.*
27:36 took away my *b.*
43:33 first-born ac. to his *b.*
1 *Chr.* 5:1 R.'s *b.* to sons of Jos.
*Heb.* 12:16 for morsel sold his *b.*

**BISHOP, S.**

*Phil.* 1:1 saints at Philippi, *b.*
1 *Tim.* 3:1 desire the office of a *b.*
2 *b.* must be blamel. *Tit.* 1:7.
1 *Pet.* 2:25 to the *b.* of your souls

**BISHOPRICK.**

*Acts* 1:20 his *b.* let another take

**BIT, S.**

*Ps.* 32:9 must be held in with *b.*
*Jam.* 3:3 we put *b.* in horses' m.

**BIT, Verb.**

*Num.* 21:6 they *b.* people.
*Amos* 5:19 and a serpent *b.* him

**BITE.**

*Ec.* 10:8 a serpent shall *b.*
11 *b.* without enchantment
*Jer.* 8:17 serpents, they shall *b.*
*Amos* 9:3 serp, and he shall *b.*
*Mic.* 3:5 the prophets that *b.*
*Hab.* 2:7 rise up that shall *b.*
*Gal.* 5:15 if ye *b.* and devour

**BITETH.**

*Gen.* 49:17 Dan an adder, that *b.*
*Prov.* 23:32 it *b.* like a serpent

**BITHYNIA.**

*Acts* 16:7 assayed to go into B.
1 *Pet.* 1:1 through Asia and B.

**BITTEN.**

*Num.* 21:8 is *b.* when he looks

**BITTER.**

*Gen.* 27:34 E. cried with *b.* cry
*Ex.* 1:14 made their lives *b.*
12:8 with *b.* herbs, *Num.* 9:11
15:23 waters, for they were *b.*
*Deut.* 32:24 dev. with *b.* destru.
32 their clusters are *b.*
2 *K.* 14:26 affl. of Isr. it was *b.*
*Job* 3:20 why is life given to *b.*?
13:26 writest *b.* things
23:2 to-day is my complaint *b.*
*Ps.* 64:3 arrows, even *b.* words
*Prov.* 5:4 *b.* as wormwood
27:7 to hungry soul *b.* thing
*Ec.* 7:26 more *b.* than death
*Is.* 5:20 that put *b.* for sweet
24:9 strong drink shall be *b.*
*Jer.* 2:19 an evil thing and *b.*
4:18 thy wickedness, it is *b.*
6:26 make most *b.* lamentation
31:15 in Ramah, *b.* weeping
*Amos* 8:10 the end, as a *b.* day
*Hab.* 1:6 *b.* and hasty nation
*Col.* 3:19 be not *b.* against them
*Jam.* 3:14 if ye have *b.* envying
*Rev.* 8:11 men died of waters *b.*
10:9 it shall make thy belly *b.*

**BITTER *with* Water.**

*Num.* 5:18 *b.* *w.* that causeth
*Jam.* 3:11 send sweet *w.* and *b.*?

**BITTERLY.**

*Jud.* 5:23 curse ye *b.* the inhab.
*Ruth* 1:20 Almighty hath dealt *b.*
*Is.* 22:4 I will weep *b.*
33:7 amb. of peace shall weep *b.*
*Ezek.* 27:30 the pilots shall cry *b.*
*Hos.* 12:14 Eph. provoked him *b.*
*Zep.* 1:14 the mighty shall cry *b.*
*Mat.* 26:75 P. wept *b.* *Luke* 22:62

**BITTERN.**

*Is.* 14:23 posses. for the *b.* 34:11
*Zep.* 2:14 the *b.* shall lodge

**BITTERNESS.**

1 *Sam.* 1:10 Hannah was in *b.*
15:32 the *b.* of death is past
2 *Sam.* 2:26 sword will be *b.*
*Job* 7:11 I will complain in the *b.*
9:18 but filleth me with *b.*
10:1 I will speak in *b.* of soul
21:25 another dieth in *b.* of soul
*Prov.* 14:10 heart knoweth his *b.*
17:25 a foolish son is *b.* to her.
*Is.* 38:15 softly in *b.* of my soul.
17 for peace I had great *b.*
*Lam.* 1:4 afflic., and she is in *b.*
3:15 he hath filled me with *b.*
*Ezek.* 3:14 and I went in *b.*
21:6 *b.* sigh before their eyes
27:31 weep for thee with *b.*
*Zec.* 12:10 in *b.* for him as one that is in *b.* for his first-born
*Acts* 8:23 art in the gall of *b.*
*Rom.* 3:14 full of cursing and *b.*
*Eph.* 4:31 let all *b.* be put away
*Heb.* 12:15 lest any root of *b.*

**BLACK.**

*Lev.* 13:31 there is no *b.* hair in it
1 *K.* 18:45 the heaven was *b.*
*Job* 30:30 my skin is *b.* upon me
*Prov.* 7:9 in the *b.* and dark n.
*Cant.* 1:5 I am *b.* but comely
6 look not on me, I am *b.*
5:11 his locks are *b* as a raven
*Jer.* 4:28 shall heavens be *b.*
8:21 I am hurt, I am *b.*
14:2 the gates thereof are *b.*
*Lam.* 5:10 our skin was *b.*
*Zec.* 6:2 in second chariot *b.* h.
6 *b.* horses go forth into north
*Mat.* 5:36 one hair white or *b.*
*Rev.* 6:5 and lo, a *b.* horse
12 the sun became *b.*

**BLACKER.**

*Lam.* 4:8 visage is *b.* than coal

**BLACKISH.**

*Job* 6:16 *b.* by reason of the ice

**BLACKNESS.**

*Job* 3:5 let *b.* of the day
*Is.* 50:3 clothe heavens with *b.*
*Joel* 2:6 shall gath. *b.* *Nah.* 2:10
*Heb.* 12:18 ye are not come to *b.*
*Jude* 13 to whom is reserved *b.*

**BLADE.**

*Jud.* 3:22 went in after the *b.*
*Job* 31:22 from my shoulder-*b.*
*Mat.* 13:26 *b.* was spr. *Mark* 4:28

**BLAINS.**

*Ex.* 9:9 a boil with *b.* 10

**BLAME.**

*Gen.* 43:9 bear the *b.* 44:32
2 *Cor.* 8:20 no man should *b.* us
*Eph.* 1:4 holy and without *b.*

**BLAMED.**

2 *Cor.* 6:3 the ministry be not *b.*
*Gal.* 2:11 bec. he was to be *b.*

**BLAMELESS.**

*Jos.* 2:17 be *b.* of thine oath
*Mat.* 12:5 prof. Sab. and are *b.*
*Luke* 1:6 in ordin. of the L. *b.*
1 *Cor.* 1:8 *b.* in the day of our L.
*Phil.* 2:15 be *b.* and harmless
3:6 in the law *b.*
1 *Thes.* 5:23 body be preserved *b.*
1 *Tim.* 3:2 bishop be *b.* *Tit.* 1:7
10 use office of deacon being *b.*
5:7 give in charge, they be *b.*
*Tit.* 1:6 if any be *b.* the husband
2 *Pet.* 3:14 ye may be found *b.*

**BLASPHEME.**

2 *Sam.* 12:14 enemies to *b.*
1 *K.* 21:10 didst *b.* God, 13
*Ps.* 74:10 shall the enemy *b.*
*Mark* 3:28 they shall *b*
29 that shall be ag. Holy G.
*Acts* 26:11 I compelled them to *b.*
1 *Tim.* 1:20 may learn not to *b.*
*Jam.* 2:7 *b.* that worthy name
*Rev.* 13:6 to *b.* his name

**BLASPHEMED.**

*Lev.* 24:11 Israelitish wom. son *b.*
2 *K.* 19:6 servants of king of Assyria *b.* me, 22; *Is.* 37:6, 23
*Ps.* 74:18 have *b.* thy name
*Is.* 52:5 my name every day is *b.*
65:7 and *b.* me on the hills
*Ezek.* 20:27 your fathers have *b.*
*Acts* 18:6 op. themselves and *b.*
*Rom.* 2:24 name of God is *b.*
1 *Tim.* 6:1 his doctrine be not *b.*
*Tit.* 2:5 that the word be not *b.*
*Rev.* 16:9 were scorched and *b.*
11 *b.* because of their pains
21 *b.* God because of the hail

**BLASPHEMEST, ETH.**

*Lev.* 24:16 whoso *b.* the Lord
*Ps.* 44:16 voice of him that *b.*
*Mat.* 9:3 scribes said, This m. *b.*
*John* 10:36 F. sanctified thou *b.*

**BLASPHEMING.**

*Acts* 13:45 J. contradicting and *b.*

**BLASPHEMER, S.**

*Acts* 19:37 are not *b.* of your god.
1 *Tim.* 1:13 who was before a *b.*
2 *Tim.* 3:2 men shall be *b.*

**BLASPHEMY.**

2 *K.* 19:3 a day of *b.* *Is.* 37:3
*Mat.* 12:31 all manner of *b.* shall be forgiven, but *b.* against
26:65 heard his *b.* *Mark* 14:64
*Mark* 7:22 out of heart proceed *b.*
*John* 10:33 st. thee not but for *b.*
*Col.* 3:8 now ye also put off *b.*
*Rev.* 2:9 the *b.* of them that
13:1 and upon his heads *b.*
6 opened his mouth in *b.*

**BLASPHEMIES.**
Ezek. 35:12 have heard all thy b.
Mat. 15:19 out of the heart b.
Mark 2:7 man thus speak b.?
3:28 b. they shall blaspheme
Luke 5:21 who is this speak. b.?
Rev. 13:5 speaking b.

**BLASPHEMOUS.**
Acts 6:11 heard him speak b. w.
13 ceaseth not to speak b. w.

**BLASPHEMOUSLY.**
Luke 22:65 other things b. spake

**BLAST.**
Ex. 15:8 b. of thy nostrils
Jos. 6:5 a long b. with horns
2 Sam. 22:16 the b. of the breath of his nostrils, Ps. 18:15
2 K. 19:7 b. on Sen. Is. 37:7
Job 4:9 by b. of God they perish
Is. 25:4 the b. of the terrible

**BLASTED.**
Gen. 41:6 thin ears b. 23:27
2 K. 19:26 as corn b. Is. 37:27

**BLASTING.**
Deut. 28:22 smite thee with b.
1 K. 8:37 there be b. 2 Chr. 6:28
Amos 4:9 smitten you with b.
Hag. 2:17 I smote you with b.

BLASTUS. Acts 12:20

**BLAZE.**
Mark 1:45 b. abroad the matter

**BLEATING, S.**
Jud. 5:16 to hear b. of flocks
1 Sam. 15:14 this b. of sheep

**BLEMISH.**
Ex. 12:5 without b. Lev. 9:3; 14:10; 23:12; Num. 6:14
29:1 two rams with b. Lev. 5:15, 18; 6:6; 9:12; Ezek. 46:4
Lev. 1:3 male without b. 10; 4:23; 22:19
21:17 hath b. not appr. 21:23
22:20 hath a b. Deut. 15:21
21 freewill-offering no b.
24:19 cause a b. in his neighbor
Num. 19:2 a red heifer with. b.
29:2 seven lambs without b.
2 Sam. 14:25 no b. in Absalom
Dan. 1:4 in whom was no b.
Eph. 5:27 holy and without b.
1 Pet. 1:19 of a lamb without b.

**BLEMISHES.**
Lev. 22:25 b. in them not accept.
2 Pet. 2:13 spots they are and b.

**BLESS.**
1 Cor. 10:16 cup of bless. we b.

**BLESS,** *God being agent.*
Gen. 12:2 I will b. thee, 16:3, 24
3 I will b. them that b. thee
17:16 will b. her, and give thee
22:17 I will b. Heb. 6:14
28:3 b. thee, and multiply thee
32:26 except thou b. me
48:16 b. the lads
49:25 by Alm. who shall b. thee
Ex. 20:24 and I will b. thee
23:25 he shall b. thy bread
Num. 6:24 Lord b. and keep thee
27 on Israel, and I will b. them
24:1 pleased the L. to b. Israel
Deut. 7:13 b. the fruit of thy w.
15:4 no poor, for L. shall b. t.
18 God shall b. thee, 30:16
16:15 bec. Lord shall b. thee
26:15 look down and b. Israel
28:8 b. thee in the land
12 b. all the work of thy hand
33:11 b. Lord, his substance
2 Sam. 7:29 to b. the house of thy servant, 1 Chr. 17:27
1 Chr. 4:10 wouldst b. me indeed
Ps. 5:12 wilt b. the righteous
28:9 b. thine inheritance
29:11 b. his people with peace
67:6 our own God shall b. us, 7
115:12 L. will b. us, he will b. the house of Israel, of Aaron
13 he will b. them that fear L.
128:5 shall b. thee out of Zion
132:15 abundantly b. her prov.
134:3 the Lord b. thee out of Z.
Is. 19:25 L. of hosts shall b.
Hag. 2:19 from this day will I b.
Acts 3:26 sent him to b. you

**BLESS,** *God being the object.*
Deut. 8:10 art full, shall b. Lord
Jud. 5:9 b. the L. Ps. 103:21; 134:1
1 Chr. 29:20 Dav. said, now b. L.
Neh. 9:5 stand up and b. L. for
Ps. 16:7 b. L. who hath given
26:12 in the cong. will I b. Lord
34:1 b. the Lord at all times
63:4 will I b. thee while I live
66:8 O b. our God
68:26 b. ye God in congregations
96:2 sing to the L. b. his name
100:4 b. his name, 103:1
103:1 b. L. O my soul, 2,22; 104:1, 35
20 b. ye his ang. 21 b. h. hosts
22 b. the Lord all his works
115:18 will b. L. from this time
134:2 lift up your h. b. the L.
135:19 b. the L. O house of Is.
20 O Levi, b. the Lord
145:1 will b. thy name forever
2 every day will I b. thee
10 thy saints shall b. thee
21 let all flesh b. his holy n.
Jam. 3:9 therewith b. we God

**BLESS,** *Man agent and object.*
Gen. 27:4 b. thee before I die, 25
34 b. me, O my father, 38
48:9 bring them to me, I will b.
20 in thee shall Israel b. saying
Ex. 12:32 begone, and b. me also
Num. 6:23 on this wise b. Israel
23:20 I have received com. to b.
25 curse them nor b. them
Deut. 10:8 separ. Levi to b. 21:5
27:12 stand on Gerizim, to b.
29:19 heareth curse, he b. him
1 Sam. 9:13 doth b. the sacrifice
2 Sam. 6:20 David returned to b. his household, 1 Chr. 16:43
8:10 Joram his son to b. David
21:3 that ye b. inh. of the Lord
1 K. 1:47 came to b. our lord k. D.
1 Chr. 23:13 to b. in his name
Ps. 62:4 b. with their mouth
109:28 let them curse, but b.
129:8 b. you in the name of L.
Prov. 30:11 doth not b. their m.
Is. 65:16 b. himself in God
Jer. 4:2 nations shall b. them
Mat. 5:44 b. that curse, Luke 6:28
Rom. 12:14 b. and curse not
1 Cor. 4:12 being reviled we b.
14:16 shall b. with the spirit

**BLESSED,** *Man agent and object.*
Gen. 14:19 Melchized. b. Abra.
24:60 they b. Rebekah
27:23 so Isaac b. Jacob, 27
29 b. be he that blesseth thee
33 have b. him, he shall be b.
41 his father b. him
28:1 Isaac called Jacob, b. him
30:13 daughters will call me b.
31:55 kissed his sons, and b.
47:7 b. Phar. 10; 48:15 Joseph
48:20 Jacob b. M. Heb. 11:21
49:28 Jacob b. his sons
Ex. 39:43 M. b. them, Deut. 33:1
Lev. 9:22 Aaron b. them
23 M. and A. b. the people
Num. 22:6 w. thou blesseth is b.
23:11 hast b. altogether, 24:10
Deut. 33:20 b. that enlargeth G.
24 Asher be b. with children
Jos. 22:6 b. sent them away, 7
24:10 Balaam b. you still
Jud. 5:24 b. above women J. be
1 Sam. 2:20 Eli b. Elkanah
25:33 b. be thy advice
26:25 Saul said b. be thou
2 Sam. 13:25 but b. him
19:39 kissed Barzillai, and b.
1 K. 2:45 Solomon shall be b.
8:14 Solomon b. congreg. 55
66 congreg. b. Sol. 2 Chr. 6:3
Job 29:11 ear heard me, b. me
31:20 his loins have not b. me
Ps. 49:18 lived he b. his soul
72:17 men be b. in him
118:26 b. be he that cometh in name of the L. we ha. b. you
Prov. 31:28 children call her b.
Ec. 10:17 b. art thou, O land
Cant. 6:9 the daughters b. her
Is. 66:3 as if he b. an idol
Jer. 20:14 let not the day be b.
Mal. 3:12 all nations call you b.
Mark 11:10 b. be king. of our f.
Luke 1:48 gen. shall call me b.
2:34 Simeon b. them, and said
Acts 20:35 it is more b. to give
Tit. 2:13 looking for that b. hope
Heb. 7:1 met Abraham b. him, 6
7 the less is b. of the better.

**BLESSED,** *God the agent.*
Gen. 1:22 b. Be fruitful, 28; 5:2
2:3 b. seventh day, Ex. 20:11
12:3 in thee shall all families be b. 18:18; 22:18; 26:4; 28:14; Acts 3:25; Gal. 3:8
17:20 b. Ish. 24:1 b. Abraham
24:31 thou b. of the Lord
25:11 God b. Isaac, 26:12
26:29 thou art now the b. of L.
27:27 which the Lord hath b.
30:27 hath b. me for thy sake
30 L. b. thee since my coming
32:29 b. J. there, 35:9; 48:3
39:5 Lord b. Egyptian's house
Num. 22:12 for the people are b.
23:20 b. I cannot reverse it
Deut. 2:7 thy God hath b. thee, 12:7; 15:14; 16:10
7:14 shalt be b. above all people
28:3 b. shalt thou be in city, b.
4 b. be fruit of body, 5 basket
33:13 of Joseph he said, b. of L.
Jos. 17:14 the Lord hath b. me
Jud. 13:24 Lord b. Samson
Ruth 3:10 b. be thou my daught.
1 Sam. 23:21 b. be ye, 2 Sam. 2:5
2 Sam. 6:11 b. Obed-edom, 12; 1 Chr. 13:14; 26:5
7:29 house of thy servant be b.
1 Chr. 17:27 blessest, it shall be b.
2 Chr. 31:10 hath b. his people
Job 1:10 b. the work of his hands
42:12 Lord b. latter end of Job
Ps. 21:6 hast made him most b.
33:12 b. is the nation whose God
37:22 as be b. of him shall inh.
26 lendeth, and his seed is b.
41:2 and he shall be b.
45:2 therefore God hath b. thee
89:15 b. is the people that know
112:2 gen. of upright shall be b.
115:15 you are b. of the Lord
119:1 b. are the undefiled
Ps. 128:1 b. is every one that fear.
4 man be b. that fear. the L.
147:13 he hath b. thy children
Prov. 5:18 let thy fountain be b.
10:7 memory of the just is b.
20:7 just man's children are b.
21 end thereof shall not be b.
22:9 bountiful eye shall be b.
Is. 19:25 b. be Egypt my people
51:2 I called him alone and b.
61:9 seed Lord hath b. 65:23
Mat. 5:3 b. poor in spirit, 5 meek
7 merciful, 8 pure in heart

9 peacemakers, 10 persecuted
13:16 b. are y. eyes, Luke 10:23
14:19 b. and br. 26:26; Mark 6:41; 14:22; Luke 9:16; 24:30
16:17 b. art thou, S. Bar-jona
24:46 b. is that serv. Luke 12:43
25:34 come, ye b. of my Father
Mark 10:16 in his arms and b.
14:61 thou Christ, son of the b.
Luke 1:28 b. among women, 42
45 b. is she that believed
6:20 b. be ye poor
11:27 b. is womb that bare thee
12:37 b. are serv. watching, 38
14:14 thou shalt be b. not rec.
19:38 b. be the king that com.
23:29 b. are the barren
24:50 he b. them, 51 while he b.
Gal. 3:9 b. with faithful Abrah.
Eph. 1:3 b. us with spiritual bl.
Jam. 1:25 shall be b. in his deed
Rev. 14:13 b. are the dead

**BLESSED, God the object.**

Gen. 14:20 b. be most high God
Jos. 22:33 children of Is. b. God
2 Sam. 22:47 b. be my r. Ps. 18:46
1 Chr. 29:10 D. b. the L. b. be L.
20 all the cong. b. the Lord God
2 Chr. 20:26 for there they b. L.
Neh. 9:5 b. be thy glo. n. Ps. 72:19
Job 1:21 b. be name, Ps. 113:2
Ps. 66:20 b. be G. 68:35; 2 Cor. 1:3
119:12 b. art thou, O Lord
Ezek. 3:12 saying, b. the glory
Dan. 2:19 b. the G. of heaven, 20
4:34 Nebuch. b. the Most High
Luke 2:28 in his arms and b. God
John 12:13 b. is the King of Is.
Rom. 1:25 who is b. for ever
9:5 over all, God b. for ever
2 Cor. 11:31 is b. for evermore
Eph. 1:3 b. be the F. 1 Pet. 1:3
1 Tim. 1:11 gospel of the b. God
6:15 b. and only Potentate

**BLESSED are they.**

Ps. 2:12 b. a. t. that trust
84:4 b. a. t. that dwell in thy h.
106:3 b. a. they that keep judg.
119:2 b. a. t. that keep his testi.
Prov. 8:32 b. a. t. that keep my w.
Is. 30:18 b. are t. that wait for h.
Mat. 5:4 b. are they that mourn
6 b. who hunger, 10 persecuted
Luke 11:28 rather b. hear the w.
John 20:29 b. have not seen
Rom. 4:7 b. are they whose iniq.
Rev. 19:19 b. called to mar. sup.
22:14 b. a. t. do his command.

**BLESSED are ye.**

Is. 32:20 b. a. ye sow beside w.
Mat. 5:11 b. when m. shall revile
Luke 6:21 b. are ye that hunger, be filled; b. a. ye that weep
22 b. a. ye when men shall hate

**BLESSED is he.**

Num. 24:9 b. is he that blesseth
Ps. 32:1 b. is he who transg.
41:1 b. is he that considereth p.
Dan. 12:12 b. is he that waiteth
Mat. 11:6 b. is he whoso. shall not be offended, Luke 7:23
21:9 b. is he that cometh in the name of the Lord, 23:39; Mark 11:9; Luke 13:35
Luke 14:15 b. shall eat bread
Rev. 1:3 b. is he that readeth
16:15 b. is he that watcheth
20:6 b. that hath part in first res.
22:7 b. keepeth sayings

**BLESSED is the man.**

Ps. 1:1 b. is the m. that walk. not
32:2 b. is the m. to whom the L. impu. not iniquity, Rom. 4:8
34:8 b. is the m. trusteth in him, 84:12; Jer. 17:7
40:4 b. m. that maketh Lord
65:4 b. is t. m. whom thou ch.
84:5 b. m. whose str. is in thee
94:12 b. is m. whom thou chast.
112:1 b. is th. m. that feareth L.
Prov. 8:34 b. m. that heareth me
Is. 56:2 b. is th. m. that doeth this
Jam. 1:12 b. that end. temptation

**BLESSEDNESS.**

Rom. 4:6 as D. describeth the b.
9 cometh this b. on cir. only
Gal. 4:15 the b. ye spake of

**BLESSEST.**

Num. 22:6 whom thou b. is bl.
1 Chr. 17:27 thou b. O Lord
Ps. 65:10 thou b. the springing

**BLESSETH.**

Gen. 27:29 that b. thee, Num. 24:9
Deut. 15:6 b. thee as he promised
Ps. 10:3 b. covetous
107:38 he b. they are multiplied
Prov. 3:33 b. habita. of the just
27:14 b. his friend with a loud
Is. 65:16 b. himself in the earth

**BLESSING, Substantive.**

Gen. 12:2 thou shalt be a b.
22:17 in b. I will bl. Heb. 6:14
27:12 a curse on me, not a b.
35 thy brother taken thy b.
38 but one b. my father?
28:4 give thee b. of Abraham
33:11 my b. that is brought
39:5 b. was on all he had
49:28 ev. one ac. to his b. he bl.
Ex. 32:29 bestow on you a b.
Lev. 25:21 I com. my b. on you
Deut. 11:26 before you a b. 30:19
27 a b. if ye obey the com.
29 shalt put the b. on Gerizim
12:15 ac. to b. of the L. 16:17
23:5 turned the curse into a b.
28:8 com. a b. on storehouse
33:1 b. wherewith Moses bl. 7
16 let the b. come upon Joseph
23 Naphtali full with the b.
Jos. 15:19 g. me a b. Jud. 1:15
1 Sam. 25:27 this b. thy handm.
2 Sam. 7:29 thy b. let the house
2 K. 5:15 take a b. of thy serv.
Neh. 9:5 exalted above all b.
13:2 God turned curse into a b.
Job 29:13 b. of him ready to per.
Ps. 3:8 thy b. is on thy people
24:5 shall receive b. from Lord
109:17 he delighteth not in b.
129:8 b. of the L. be upon you
133:3 L. comm. the b. even life
Prov. 10:22 b. of L. maketh rich
11:11 by the b. of the upright
26 a b. on him that selleth it
24:25 a good b. on them
Is. 19:24 a b. in midst of the l.
44:3 my b. on thy offspring
65:8 destroy it not, a b. is in it
Ezek. 34:26 about my hill a b. there shall be showers of b.
44:30 b. to rest in thy house
Joel 2:14 leave a b. behind him
Zec. 8:13 and ye shall be a b.
Mal. 3:10 and pour you out a b.
Luke 24:53 in the temple b. God
Rom. 15:29 fulness of the b.
1 Cor. 10:16 the cup of b. we bless
Gal. 3:14 b. of Ab. might come
Heb. 6:7 earth receiveth b.
12:17 have inherited the b.
Jam. 3:10 same mouth b. cursing
1 Pet. 3:9 but contrariwise b. that ye should inherit a b.
Rev. 5:12 worthy to receive b.
13 b. to him that sitteth on th.
7:12 b. and glory to our God

**BLESSINGS.**

Gen. 49:25 b. of the heav. above, b. of the deep, b. of t. breasts
26 b. of thy fath. above b. of my
Deut. 28:2 all these b. shall come
Jos. 8:34 he read the b. and curs.
Ps. 21:3 prev. him with the b.
Prov. 10:6 b. are upon the just
28:20 shall abound with b.
Mal. 2:2 and will curse your b.
Eph. 1:3 with all spiritual b.

**BLEW.**

Jos. 6:8 priests passed and b.
Jud. 3:27 Ehud b. a trumpet
6:34 Gideon, b. a trumpet
7:19 b. the trumpets, 20, 22
1 Sam. 13:3 Saul b. let Hebrews
2 Sam. 2:28 Joab b. 18:16; 20:22
20:1 Sheba a Benjamite b.
1 K. 1:39 b. people said, God save king Sol. 2 K. 9:13; 11:14
Mat. 7:25 b. on that house, 27
John 6:18 a great wind that b.
Acts 27:13 south-wind b. 28:13

**BLIND, Adjective.**

Ex. 4:11 who maketh the b.?
Lev. 19:14 stumb.-block before b.
21:18 a b. man shall not app.
22:22 offer the b. Deut. 15:21
Deut. 27:18 maketh b. to wander
28:29 as b. gropeth in darkness
2 Sam. 5:6 ex. thou take away b.
2 Sam. 5:8 b. hated of D. b. not
Job 29:15 I was eyes to the b.
Ps. 146:8 openeth the eyes of b.
Is. 29:18 eyes of b. shall see, 35:5
42:7 light to open the b. eyes
16 b. by a way they knew not
18 look, ye b. that ye may see
19 who is b.? who is b. as he that is perfect, and b.
43:8 b. people that have eyes
56:10 his watchmen are b.
59:10 we grope for wall like b.
Jer. 31:8 the b. and lame
Lam. 4:14 wandered as b. men
Zep. 1:17 walk like b. men
Mal. 1:8 b. for sacrifice
Mat. 9:27 two b men, 20:30
11:5 b. rec. sight, 12:22; Luke 7:22
15:14 b. leaders of b. if the b. lead the b. Luke 6:39
23:16 woe to you, ye b. guides
17 ye b. whether is greater, 19
26 thou b. Pharisee
Mark 8:23 took b. man by the h.
10:46 b. Bartimeus sat begging
Luke 4:18 recovery of sight to b.
7:21 to many b. he gave sight
14:13 makest a feast call the b.
John. 5:3 a great multitude of b.
9:1 he saw a man that was b.
39 which see might be made b.
40 are we b. 41 if ye were b.
10:21 can a d. open eyes of b.?
Acts 13:11 thou shalt be b.
Rom. 2:19 art a guide to the b.
2 Pet. 1:9 lack. these things is b.
Rev. 3:17 knowest not thou art b.

**BLIND, Verb.**

Deut. 16:19 gift doth b. the eyes
1 Sam. 12:3 a bribe to b.

**BLINDED, ETH.**

Ex. 23:8 for a gift b. the wise
John 12:40 he hath b. their eyes
Rom. 11:7 the rest were b.
2 Cor. 3:14 their minds were b.
4:4 god of this world hath b.
1 John 2:11 dark. hath b. his eyes

**BLINDFOLDED.**

Luke 22:64 when they had b. him

**BLINDNESS.**

Gen. 19:11 at the door with b.
Deut. 28:28 smite thee with b.
2 K. 6:18 E. prayed, Smite this people, I pray thee, with b.
Zec. 12:4 every horse with b.
Rom. 11:25 b. in part has hap.
Eph. 4:18 because of b. of their h.

BLOCK. See STUMBLING.

**BLOOD.**
*Where marked with † it is in the original* BLOODS.
Gen. 4:10† thy brother's b.
9:4 life which is the b. not eat
5 b. of your lives will I require
37:31 and dipped the coat in b.
Ex. 4:9 water shall become b.
7:17 waters be turned into b.
12:13 b. a token, when I see b.
23:18 the b. with leaven, 34:25
Lev. 15:19 in her flesh be b.
17:4 b. imputed unto that man
11 it is b. maketh atonement
19:16 stand ag. b. of neighbor
Num. 23:24 and drink b. of slain
35:33 by b. of him that shed it
Deut. 17:8 b. and b. 2 Chr. 19:10
21:8 b. shall be forgiven them
32:43 avenge b. of his servants
Jud. 9:24 their b. on Abimelech
1 Sam. 26:20 my b. fall to the e.
2 Sam. 1:16 thy b. be on thy h.
22 from the b. of the slain
16:7† come out, thou man of b.
8 returned upon thee all the b.
20:12 Amasa wallowed in b.
23:17 b. of the m. 1 Chr. 11:19
1 K. 2:5 b. of war on his girdle
18:28 till the b. gushed out
2 K. 3:22 saw the water red as b.
23 said, This is b. the kings
9:26† I have seen b. of Naboth
Job 16:18 earth, cover not my b.
39:30 eagles' young suck up b.
Ps. 30:9 what profit in my b.?
50:13 will I drink b. of goats?
58:10 wash his feet in b. of w.
68:23 dipped in b. of thine ene.
72:14 precious their b.
Prov. 28:17 violence to b. of any
Is. 1:15† hands are full of b.
4:4 L. purge b. of Jerusalem
9:5 and garments rolled in b.
15:9 waters of Dimon full of b.
26:21† earth shall disclose her b.
33:15† his ear from hearing b.
34:3 mount. melted with their b.
Jer. 2:34 b. of the poor innocents
18:21 pour out their b. by force
48:10 keepeth his sword from b.
51:35 my b. be on the inh. of C.
Lam. 4:14 pol. thems. with b.
Ezek. 5:17 pestilence and b. pass
9:9 the land is full of b.
14:19 my fury upon it in b.
16:6 when thou wast in thy b.
9† I washed away thy b.
38 I will give thee b. in fury
18:10 son that is a shedder of b.
13† he shall die, his b. shall be
19:10 a vine in thy b.
21:32 thy b. in midst, 22:13
22:3 sheddeth b. in midst of it
23:37 b. is in their hands, 45
24:8 her b. on the top of a rock
28:23 send b. into her streets
32:6 water with thy b. the land
35:6 to b. thou hast not hated b.
even b. shall pursue thee
44:7 the fat and the b. 15
Hos. 1:4 avenge the b. of Jezreel
4:2† and b. toucheth b.
Joel 2:30 b. fire, pillars of smoke
31 moon turn. into b. Acts 2:20
3:21 I will cleanse their b.
Zep. 1:17 their b. poured out
Mat. 9:20 w. with an issue of b.
12 yrs. Mark 5:25; Luke 8:43
16:17 b. hath not revealed it
23:30 in the b. of prophets
35 b. of right. Abel, Luke 11:51
26:28 b. of new test. Mark 14:24
27:6 because it is price of b.
8 called the field of b. Acts 1:19
24 inn. of b. of this just pers.
Luke 13:1 whose b. P. mingled
22:20 test. in my b. 1 Cor. 11:25
44 sweat as great drops of b.
John 1:13 born not of b.
6:54 and drinketh my b. 56
55 and my b. is drink indeed
19:34 forth. came there out b.
Acts 5:28 to bring this man's b.
15:20 abstain from b. 29; 21:25
17:26 made of one b. all nations
18:6 b. be on your own heads
20:26 pure from b. of all men
Cor. 11:27 the body and b.
15:50 flesh and b. cannot inherit
Eph. 6:12 against flesh and b.
Col. 1:20 through b. of his cross
Heb. 2:14 partak. of flesh and b.
9:7 without b. which he offered
12 b. of goats, but by his own b.
13 if the b. of bulls sanctifieth
20 the b. of the testament
22 without shedding of b.
10:19 holiest by the b. of Jesus
11:28 and sprinkling of b.
12:4 not yet resisted unto b.
24 b. of sprinkling that speak.
13:11 whose b. is brought into
1 Pet. 1:2 sprinkling of the b.
1 John 1:7 b. of J. C. cleanseth
5:6 came by water and b.
8 the Spirit, water, and b.
Rev. 5:9 redeemed us by thy b.
6:10 avenge our b.
12 and the moon became as b.
7:14 in the b. of the Lamb
8:8 part of sea became b. 16:3
11:6 to turn the waters into b.
12:11 overcame by b. of the L.
14:20 b. came out of wine-press
16:6 hast given them b. to drink
18:24 the b. of the prophets
19:2 avenged the b. of his serv.
13 with a vesture dipped in b.

See AVENGER, REVENGER.

**BLOOD be upon.**
Lev. 20: 9 curs. father, his b. him
11 incest, 13 sodomy, 16 bestiality, 27 wizard, their b. be u. them
Ezek. 18:13 abom. his b. be upon
33:5 his b. shall be upon him

**BLOOD, *with* bullock.**
Is. 1:11 I del. not in b. of bull.

**BLOOD of Christ.**
1 Cor. 10:6 com. of b. of C.
Eph. 2:13 made nigh by b. of C.
Heb. 9:14 shall b. purge?
1 Pet. 1:19 with precious b. of C.
1 John 1:7 the b. of C. cleanseth

**BLOOD of the Covenant.**
Ex. 24:8 M. said Behold the b.
Zec. 9:11 for thee also by b. of c.
Heb. 10:29 b. of cov. unholy thing
13:20 b. of the everlasting cov.

**BLOOD, *with* eat.**
Lev. 3:17 eat neither fat nor b.
7:26 eat no manner of b. 27; 17:14; Deut. 12:16, 23; 15:23
27 eateth b. soul cut off, 17:10
1 Sam. 14:32 eat them with the b.
Ezek. 33:25 ye eat with b.

**For BLOOD.**
2 Chr. 24:25 for the b. of sons
Ps. 9:12 maketh inquis. for b.
Prov. 1:11 lay wait for b. 18
12:6 are to lie in wait for b.
Mic. 7:2 lie in wait for b.

**His BLOOD.**
Gen. 37:26 and conceal his b.
42:22 behold his b. is required
Jos. 2:19 his b. be upon his head
2 Sam. 4:11 shall I not req. his b.
1 K. 2:32 shall return his b.
Ezek. 3:18 his b. will I require at thy hand, 20; 33:4, 6, 8
Hos. 12:14 leave his b. on him
Mat. 27:25 his b. be on us
Acts 20:28 ch. purchased with h. b.
Rom. 3:25 thro' faith in his b.
5:9 justified by his b.
Eph. 1:7 red. thro' his b. Col. 1:14
Heb. 9:12 by his own b. he ent.
13:12 sanct. the people with h. b.
Rev. 1:5 and washed us in his b.

**Innocent BLOOD.**
Deut. 19:10 that in. b. be not shed
13 put away guilt of in. b. 21:9
21:8 in. b. to thy people's ch.
1 Sam. 19:5 sin against in. b.
1 K. 2:31 take away in. b.
2 K. 21:16 Man. shed in. b. 24:4
Ps. 94:21 they condemn in. b.
106:38 in. b. even b. of sons
Prov. 6:17 hateth hands sh. in. b.
Is. 59:7 haste to shed in. b.
Jer. 7:6 shed not innocent b.
22:17 are to shed innocent b.
26:15 shall surely bring inno. b.
Joel 3:19 bec. they shed inno. b.
Jon. 1:14 L. lay not on us inno. b.
Mat. 27:4 I betrayed innocent b.

**Shed BLOOD.**
Gen. 9:6 m's b. by m. h. b. be s.
37:22 Reuben said, shed no b.
Lev. 17:4 shed b. shall be cut off
Num. 35:33 cl. of b. s. but by b.
Deut. 21:7 hands not shed this b.
1 K. 2:5 shed b. of war in peace
1 Chr. 22:8 shed b. much b. 28:3
Ps. 79:3 their b. shed like water
10 reveng. b. of thy servants sh.
Prov. 1:16 h. to shed b. Rom. 3:15
Lam. 4:13 shed the b. of the just
Ezek. 16:38 women that s. b. 23:45
22:4 guilty in b. th. hast shed, 6
33:25 ye s. b. and shall ye pos.
36:18 for the b. shed
Mat. 23:35 the righteous b. s.
Mark 14:24 this is my b. which is shed, Luke 22:20
Luke 11:50 b. of all the proph. s.
Acts 22:20 when b. of S. was s.
Rev. 16:6 s. the b. of the saints.

**Sprinkle BLOOD.**
Ex. 29:20 sprinkle b. on altar, Lev. 1:5, 11; 3:2, 8, 13; 7:2; 17:6; Num. 18:17.

**BLOOD sprinkled.**
Ex. 24:8 M. sp. b. on the people
Is. 63:3 their b. shall be sprinkled on my garment
Heb. 9:21 he sp. with b.

**With BLOOD.**
Ex. 30:10 A. make atone. with b.
Lev. 19:26 not eat any th. with b.
1 K. 2:9 bring thou down with b.
Ps. 106:38 land was pol. with b.
Is. 34:6 sword of L. filled with b.
7 land shall be soaked with b.
49:26 drunken with their own b.
59:3 hands are defiled with b.
Jer. 19:4 this place w. b. of innoc.
46:10 drunk with their b.
Lam. 4:14 pol. thems. with b.
Ezek. 38:22 plead ag. him with b.
Hos. 6:8 Gilead polluted with b.
Mic. 3:10 build up Zion with b.
Hab. 2:12 build. a town with b.
Gal. 1:16 I conferred not with b.
Heb. 9:22 the law purged with b.
Rev. 8:7 fire, mingled with b.
17:6 the woman drunken w. b.

**BLOOD-GUILTINESS.**
Ps. 51:14 deliver me from b.-g.

**BLOOD-THIRSTY.**
Prov. 29:10 b.-th. hate upright

**BLOODY.**
Ex. 4:25 a b. husb. art thou, 26
2 Sam. 16:7 Sh. said, Thou b. man
21:1 famine is for S. his b. house
Ps. 5:6 L. will abhor the b. man
26:9 gather not my life with b. m.

*Ps.* 55:23 *b.* m. not live half th. d.
59:2 and save me from *b.* men
139:19 depart from me, ye *b.* m.
*Ezek.* 7:23 full of *b.* crimes
22:2 wilt thou judge the *b.* city?
24:6 the *b.* city, 9; *Nah.* 3:1
*Acts* 28:8 lay sick of a *b.* flux

**BLOOMED.**

*Num.* 17:8 A. rod *b.* blossoms.

**BLOSSOM, S.**

*Gen.* 40:10 her *b.* shot forth
*Is.* 5:25 *b.* shall go up as dust

**BLOSSOM, ED.**

*Num.* 17:5 the man's rod shall *b.*
*Is.* 27:6 Israel shall *b.* and bud
35:1 desert shall *b.* as the rose
2 it shall *b.* abundantly
*Ezek.* 7:10 the rod hath *b.*
*Hab.* 3:17 fig-tree shall not *b.*

**BLOT.**

*Job* 31:7 if any *b.* hath cleaved
*Prov.* 9:7 wicked, getteth a *b.*

**BLOT out.**

*Ex.* 32:32 *b.* me *out* of thy b.
33 him will I *b. out*
*Deut.* 9:14 alone that I *b. out*
25:19 *b. out* reme. of Amalek
29:20 *b. out* his name
2 *K.* 14:27 would *b. out* name
*Ps.* 51:1 *b. out* transgress.
9 *b. out* all my iniquity
*Jer.* 18:23 nor *b. out* their sin
*Rev.* 3:5 not *b.* his name *out*

**BLOTTED.**

*Neh.* 4:5 let not their sin be *b.*
*Ps.* 69:28 *b.* out of book of the l.
109:13 let their name be *b.* out
14 sin of his mother be *b.* out
*Is.* 44:22 *b.* out as a thick cloud
*Acts* 3:19 that your sins be *b.* out

**BLOTTETH, ING.**

*Is.* 43:25 *b.* out thy transgress.
*Col.* 2:14 *b.* out the handwriting

**BLOW, Substantive.**

*Ps.* 39:10 consumed by the *b.*
*Jer.* 14:17 with a grievous *b.*

**BLOW, Verb.**

*Ex.* 15:10 *b.* with thy wind
*Jud.* 7:18 when I *b.* then *b.* ye
*Ps.* 78:26 caused east-wind to *b.*
147:18 causeth his wind to *b.*
*Cant.* 4:16 come, thou south, *b.*
*Is.* 40:24 *b.* upon them
*Ezek.* 21:31 will *b.* ag. thee, 22:21
*Hos.* 5:8 *b.* cornet in Gibeah
*Hag.* 1:9 I did *b.* upon it
*Luke* 12:55 see the south-wind *b.*
*Rev.* 7:1 that wind should not *b.*

*See* TRUMPET.

**BLOWETH.**

*Is.* 40:7 S. of the Lord *b.* on it
54:16 created the smith that *b.*
*John* 3:8 wind *b.* where it listeth

**BLOWN.**

*Job* 20:26 fire not *b.* consume

**BLUE.**

*Ex.* 25:4 *b.* 26:1, 31, 36; 27:16
2 *Chr.* 2:7 cunning to w. in *b.* 14
*Est.* 1:6 *b.* hangings, *b.* marble
8:15 Mordecai in apparel of *b.*
*Ezek.* 23:6 Assyr. clothed with *b.*

*See* PURPLE, CLOTH, LACE, LOOPS.

**BLUENESS.**

*Prov.* 20:30 *b.* of a wound

**BLUNT.**

*Ec.* 10:10 if iron be *b.* and he

**BLUSH.**

*Ezr.* 9:6 I *b.* to lift up my face
*Jer.* 6:15 nor could they *b.* 8:12

BOANERGES. *Mark* 3:17

**BOAR.**

*Ps.* 80:13 *b.* out of the wood

**BOARDS.**

*Cant* 8:9 inclose her with *b.*
*Acts* 27:44 on *b.* came to land

**BOAST, Substantive.**

*Ps.* 34:2 shall make her *b.*
*Rom.* 2:17 makest thy *b.* of God
23 makest thy *b.* of the law

**BOAST, Verb.**

1 *K.* 20:11 not *b.* as he
2 *Chr.* 25:19 lifteth thee up to *b.*
*Ps.* 44:8 in God we *b.* all the day
49:6 *b.* themselves
94:4 workers of iniquity *b.*
97:7 confounded that *b.* of idols
*Prov.* 27:1 *b.* not of to-morrow
*Is.* 10:15 shall the axe *b.* itself
61:6 in their glory shall you *b.*
*Rom.* 11:18 *b.* not ag. branches
2 *Cor.* 9:2 I *b.* to them of Maced.
10:13 *b.* without our measure
16 to *b.* in another man's line
11:16 receive me that I may *b.*
*Eph.* 2:9 of works, lest any *b.*

**BOASTED.**

*Ezek.* 35:13 with mouth ye h. *b.*
2 *Cor.* 7:14 if I have *b.* any thing

**BOASTERS.**

*Rom.* 1:30 *b.* inventors of evil th.
2 *Tim.* 3:2 covetous, *b.* proud

**BOASTEST, ETH.**

*Ps.* 10:3 wicked *b.* of his heart's
52:1 why *b.* thyself in mischief
*Prov.* 20:14 then he *b.*
25:14 whoso *b.* of a false gift
*Jam.* 3:5 tongue *b.* great things

**BOASTING, Participle.**

*Acts* 5:36 Theudas *b.* himself
2 *Cor.* 10:15 not *b.* without meas.

**BOASTING, Substantive.**

*Rom.* 3:27 where is *b.* then?
2 *Cor.* 7:14 our *b.* before Titus
8:24 show ye the proof of our *b.*
9:3 lest our *b.* of you be in vain
4 in this same confident *b.*
11:10 no man stop me of this *b.*
17 in this confidence of *b.*
*Jam.* 4:16 ye rejoice in your *b.*

**BOAT, S.**

*John* 6:22 no other *b.* there, Jesus went not into the *b.*
23 came other *b.* from Tiberias
*Acts* 27:16 work to come by the *b.*
30 they had let down the *b.*
32 cut off the ropes of the *b.*

BOAZ. 1 *K.* 7:21; 2 *Chr.* 3:17; *Ruth* 2:1, 19; 3:2; 4:1; *Lu.* 3:32

**BOCHIM.**

*Jud.* 2:1 angel came up to B. 5

**BODY.**

*Ex.* 24:10 as the *b.* of heaven
1 *Sam.* 31:12 *b.* of S. 1 *Chr.* 10:12
*Job* 19:17 child.'s sake of my *b.*
26 worms destroy *b.*
20:25 and cometh out of the *b.*
*Prov.* 5:11 flesh and *b.* are cons.
*Is.* 10:18 consume soul and *b.*
51:23 hast laid thy *b.* as ground
*Ezek.* 10:12 whole *b.* full of eyes
*Dan.* 7:15 in midst of my *b.*
*Mat.* 5:29 *b.* be cast into hell, 30
6:22 light of *b.* *Luke* 11:34; *b.* full of light. *Luke* 11:34, 36
23 *b.* shall be full of darkness
25 thought for *b.* *Luke* 12:22
10:28 kill the *b.* *Luke* 12:4
14:12 John's discip. took the *b.*
26:12 this ointment on my *b.*
26 this is my *b.* *Mark* 14:22; *Luke* 22:19; 1 *Cor.* 11:24
27:58 Joseph begged the *b.* of J. *Mark* 15:43; *Luke* 23:52

*Mark* 5:29 she felt in her *b.*
14:8 aforehand to anoint my *b.*
51 linen cloth cast about his *b.*
15:45 P. gave the *b.* *Mat.* 27:58
*Luke* 12:23 *b.* more than raiment
17:37 *b.* is, thither the eagles
24:3 found not the *b.* of Lord
*John* 20:12 *b.* of Jesus had lain
*Rom.* 6:6 *b.* of sin be destroyed
7:4 dead to the law by *b.* of C.
24 from the *b.* of this death
8:10 *b.* is dead because of sin
13 Spirit mortify deeds of *b.*
23 the redemption of our *b.*
1 *Cor.* 6:13 *b.* is not for fornication, but for L. and L. for *b.*
18 every sin is without the *b.*
6:19 your *b.* is the temple
7:4 no power over her own *b.*
9:27 I keep under my *b.* and
10:16 communion of the *b.* of C.
11:27 guilty of the *b.* and blood
29 not discerning the Lord's *b.*
12:14 the *b.* is not one member
15 therefore not of the *b.*? 16
17 if whole *b.* were an eye
19 wh. were the *b.*? 20 one *b.*
27 now ye are the *b.* of Christ
13:3 I give my *b.* to be burned
15:35 w. what *b.* do dead come?
37 sowest not that *b.* that shall
38 God giveth a *b.* as it hath
44 sown a nat. *b.* raised spir. *b.*
2 *Cor.* 5:8 to be absent from *b.*
*Eph.* 3:6 heirs of the same *b.*
4:12 the edifying of *b.* of Christ
16 from whom the whole *b.*
5:23 he is the Saviour of the *b.*
*Phil.* 3:21 shall change vile *b.*
*Col.* 1:18 head of the *b.* the ch.
2:11 in putting off the *b.* of sins
*Col.* 2:17 shadow, the *b.* is of Ch.
19 from which the *b.* by joints
23 a show of wisdom in neg. *b.*
1 *Thes.* 5:23 your soul and *b.*
*Heb.* 10:5 a *b.* hast thou prepared
10 offering of the *b.* of Jesus
*Jam.* 2:16 things needful to *b.*
26 the *b.* without the spirit
3:2 to bridle the whole *b.*
3 we turn about their whole *b.*
6 tongue defileth the whole *b.*
*Jude* 9 disputed about *b.* of M.

**Dead BODY.**

*Num.* 19:11 *d. b.* unclean, 16
2 *K.* 8:5 he had restored *d. b.*
*Is.* 26:19 my *d. b.* sh. they arise
*Jer.* 26:23 cast his *d. b.* into gra.
36:30 *dead b.* shall be cast out

**Fruit of the BODY.**

*Deut.* 28:4 blessed be *f. of thy b.*
18 cursed shall be *fr. of thy b.*
53 shalt eat the *fr. of thy b.*
*Ps.* 132:11 *f. b.* will I set on thy
*Mic.* 6:7 *f. of* my *b.* for sin of soul

**His BODY.**

1 *Sam.* 31:10 fast. *his b.* to wall
*Dan.* 4:33 *his b.* wet w. dew, 5:21
7:11 beast was slain, and *his b.*
10:6 *his b.* was like the beryl
*Luke* 23:55 b. how *his b.* was laid
24:23 they found not *his b.*
*John* 2:21 temple of *his b.*
*Acts* 19:12 from *his b.* were br.
*Rom.* 4:19 con. not *h. b.* now d.
1 *Cor.* 6:18 sinneth against *his b.*
7:4 power of *his* own *b.*
2 *Cor.* 5:10 things done in *his b.*
*Eph.* 1:23 which is *his b.* fulness
*Phil.* 3:21 like *his* glorious *b.*
*Col.* 1:24 for *his b.* sake
1 *Pet.* 2:24 bare our sins in *his b.*

**In BODY.**

*Lam.* 4:7 *in b.* than rubies
*Rom.* 6:12 *in* your mortal *b.*
1 *Cor.* 5:3 I verily as absent *in b.*

6:20 glorify God *in* your *b.*
7:34 that she may be holy *in b.*
12:18 members every one *in b.*
25 no schism *in* the *b.*
2 *Cor.* 4:10 *in b.* the dy. of the L. that life be manif. *in* our *b.*
5:6 whilst we are at home *in b.*
12:2 whether *in b.* or out of *b.*
*Gal.* 6:17 I bear *in b.* the marks
*Phil.* 1:20 be magnified *in* my *b.*
*Col.* 1:22 *in b.* of his flesh
*Heb.* 13:3 being yours. *in* the *b.*

**One BODY.**

*Rom.* 12:4 members in *one b.*
5 are *one b.* in C. 1 *Cor.* 10:17
1 *Cor.* 6:16 joined to a h. is *one b.*
12:12 as the *b.* is *one*, and hath
13 we are baptized into *one b.*
20 many members, yet *one b.*
*Eph.* 2:16 rec. both to G. in *one b.*
4:4 there is *one b.* and one S.
*Col.* 3:15 also called in *one b.*

**BODIES.**

*Job* 13:12 your *b.* like *b.* of clay
*Ezek.* 1:11 wings covered *b.* 23
*Dan.* 3:27 on *b.* fire had no power
*Mat.* 27:52 *b.* of saints arose
*John* 19:31 *b.* should not remain
*Rom.* 1:24 dishonor their own *b.*
8:11 quicken your mortal *b.*
12:1 your *b.* a living sacrifice
1 *Cor.* 6:15 your *b.* members
15:40 celestial *b.* and *b.*
*Eph.* 5:28 love wives as own *b.*
*Heb.* 10:22 *b.* washed with pure
13:11 *b.* of beasts, whose blood

**Dead BODIES.**

2 *Chr.* 20:24 were *d. b.* fallen
*Ps.* 79:2 *d. b.* of thy servants
110:6 fill places with *d. b.*
*Jer.* 31:40 valley of *dead b.*
33:5 to fill them with *d. b.*
34:20 *d. b.* shall be for meat
41:9 Ishm. cast *dead b.* of men
*Amos* 8:3 *d. b.* in every place
*Rev.* 11:8 *dead b.* in the street
9 their *dead b.* three days and a half, nor suffer *d. b.*

**BODILY.**

*Luke* 3:22 desc. in a *b.* shape
2 *Cor.* 10:10 *b.* presence is weak
*Col.* 2:9 fulness of the Godh. *b.*
1 *Tim.* 4:8 *b.* exer. profiteth little

**BOIL, S, Substantive.**

*Ex.* 9:10 it became a *b.*
2 *K.* 20:7 figs on *b.* *Is.* 38:21
*Job* 2:7 Satan smote Job with *b.*

**BOIL.**

*Job* 41:31 the deep to *b.* like a pot
*Is.* 64:2 fire causeth waters to *b.*
*Ezek.* 24:5 make it *b.* well. 46:20

**BOILED.**

1 *K.* 19:21 yoke of oxen and *b.*
2 *K.* 6:29 so we *b.* my son
*Job* 30:27 my bowels *b.*

**BOISTEROUS.**

*Mat.* 14:30 he saw the wind *b.*

**BOLD.**

*Prov.* 28:1 right. are *b.* as a lion
*Acts* 13:46 P. and Bar. waxed *b.*
*Rom.* 10:20 Esaias is very *b.*
2 *Cor.* 10:1 being absent, am *b.*
2 wherewith I think to be *b.*
11:21 any is *b.* I am *b.* also
*Phil.* 1:14 are much more *b.*
1 *Thes.* 2:2 we were *b.* in our G.
*Phile.* 8 I might be much *b.* in C.

**BOLDLY.**

*Mark* 15:43 Joseph went in *b.*
*John* 7:26 he speaketh *b.*
*Acts* 9:27 preached *b.* at Dam.
29 he spake *b.* in name of L. J.
14:3 abode they, speaking *b.*
18:26 Apollos began to speak *b.*
19:8 spake *b.* for three months
*Rom.* 15:15 written more *b.*
*Eph.* 6:19 open my mouth *b.*
20 I may speak *b.* as I ought
*Heb.* 4:16 *b.* to the thr. of grace
13:6 *b.* say, Lord is my helper

**BOLDNESS.**

*Ec.* 8:1 *b.* of his face be changed
*Acts* 4:13 *b.* of Peter and John
29 with all *b.* they may speak
31 spake word of God with *b.*
2 *Cor.* 7:4 great is my *b.* of speech
*Eph.* 3:12 we have *b.* and access
*Phil.* 1:20 with all *b.* as always
1 *Tim.* 3:13 they purchase gr. *b.*
*Heb.* 10:19 *b.* to enter into holiest
1 *John* 4:17 may have *b.* in judg.

**BOLSTER.**

1 *Sam.* 19:13 goats' hair for *b.* 16
26:7 spear at *b.* 11, 12; 16 water

**BOND, Adjective.**

1 *Cor.* 12:13 one body, *b.* or free
*See* FREE.

**BOND.**

*Ezek.* 20:37 bring you into *b.*
*Luke* 13:16 from his *b.* on sab.
*Acts* 8:23 art in the *b.* of iniquity
*Eph.* 4:3 Spirit, in *b.* of peace
*Col.* 3:14 charity, *b.* of perfect.

**BONDS.**

*Job* 12:18 looseth the *b.* of kings
*Ps.* 116:16 hast loosed my *b.*
*Jer.* 5:5 the yoke, and burst the *b.*
27:2 make thee *b.* and yokes
30:8 his yoke, and burst thy *b.*
*Nah.* 1:13 I will burst thy *b.*
*Acts* 20:23 that *b.* and aff. abide
23:29 wor. of death or *b.* 26:31
25:14 a certain man left in *b.*
26:29 as I am, except these *b.*
*Eph.* 6:20 am an ambassa. in *b.*
*Phil.* 1:7 in *b.* ye are all partak.
13 so my *b.* in C. are manifest
14 waxing confident by my *b.*
16 to add affliction to my *b.*
*Col.* 4:3 in *b.*; 18 rem. my *b.*
2 *Tim.* 2:9 suffer trouble even to *b.*
*Phile.* 10 begotten in my *b.*
13 in the *b.* of the gospel
*Heb.* 10:34 compassion of me in *b.*
11:36 others had trial of *b.* and
13:3 rem. them in *b.* as bound

**BONDAGE.**

*Ex.* 1:14 bitter with hard *b.*
2:23 Israel sighed by reason of *b.*
13:14 Lord brought us out of the house of *b.* 20:2; *Deut.* 5:6; 6:12; 8:14; 13:5, 10; *Jos.* 24:17; *Jud.* 6:8
*Deut.* 26:6 E. laid on us hard *b.*
*Neh.* 9:17 captain to return to *b.*
*Is.* 14:3 rest from thy hard *b.*
*Rom.* 8:15 received spirit of *b.*
21 from *b.* of corruption
*Gal.* 4:24 which gendereth to *b.*
5:1 not entangled with y. of *b.*
*Heb.* 2:15 lifetime subject to *b.*

**In, into, *or* under BONDAGE.**

*Ezr.* 9:8 reviving *in* our *b.*
9 God hath not fors. us *in b.*
*John* 8:33 never *in b.* to any
*Acts* 7:6 bring them *into b.*
7 to whom they shall be *in b.*
1 *Cor.* 7:15 is not *under b.*
2 *Cor.* 11:20 man bring you *into b.*
*Gal.* 2:4 might bring us *into b.*
4:3 *in b.* under the elements
9 ye desire to be *in b.*
*Gal.* 4:25 answ. to J. which is *in b.*
2 *Pet.* 2:19 is he brought *into b.*

**BONDMAID.**

*Gal.* 4:22 one by a *b.* the other

**BONDMAN.**

*Deut.* 15:15 wast a *b.* in Egypt, L. red. thee, 16:12; 24:18, 22
*Rev.* 6:15 every *b.* hid themselves

**BONDMEN.**

*Lev.* 25:44 *b.* shall ye be of the h.
*Deut.* 28:68 ye sh. be sold for *b.*
2 *K.* 4:1 my two sons to be *b.*
2 *Chr.* 28:10 children of J. for *b.*
*Ezr.* 9:9 we were *b.* yet God
*Est.* 7:4 had been sold for *b.*
*Jer.* 34:13 out of the house of *b.*

**BONDSERVICE.**

1 *K.* 9:21 a tribute of *b.*

**BONDWOMAN.**

*Gen.* 21:10 cast out this *b.* and her son, *Gal.* 4:30
13 son of *b.* will I make a nat.
*Gal.* 4:23 son of *b.* born
31 are not children of the *b.*

BONDWOMEN. *See* BONDMEN.

**BONE.**

*Gen.* 2:23 this is *b.* of my bones
29:14 art my *b.* and my flesh
*Ex.* 12:46 neither shall ye break a *b.* *Num.* 9:12
2 *Sam.* 5:1 are thy *b.* 1 *Chr.* 11:1
*Job* 2:5 touch his *b.* and flesh
19:20 my *b.* cleav. to my skin
31:22 my arm be bro. from the *b.*
*Prov.* 25:15 tongue break. the *b.*
*Ezek.* 37:7 together, *b.* to his *b.*
*John* 19:36 a *b.* of him sh. n. be b.

**BONES.**

*Ex.* 13:19 M. took *b.* of Joseph
*Jos.* 24:32 *b.* of Joseph buried
2 *Sam.* 21:12 took *b.* of Saul
1 *K.* 13:2 men's *b.* shall be burnt
2 *K.* 13:21 touched *b.* of Elisha
23:20 burnt men's *b.*
2 *Chr.* 34:5 burnt *b.* of the priests
*Job* 10:11 hast fenced me with *b.*
*Ps.* 51:8 *b.* thou hast broken
53:5 G. scattereth the *b.* of him
141:7 *b.* are scat. at grave's m.
*Prov.* 3:8 marrow to thy *b.*
14:30 the rottenness of the *b.*
15:30 good report maketh *b.* fat
16:24 pleas. words health to *b.*
17:22 broken spirit drieth the *b.*
*Ec.* 11:5 how the *b.* do grow
*Is.* 58:11 shall make fat thy *b.*
66:14 your *b.* shall flourish
*Jer.* 8:1 *b.* of the kings, priests, prophets, inhabitants
*Ezek.* 6:5 scat. your *b.* about
24:4 choice *b.*; 5 burn *b.* 10
37:1 valley full of *b.*; 3 *b.* live?
4 prophesy and say, O ye dry *b.*
11 *b.* are house of Isr. our *b.*
*Amos* 6:10 to bring out the *b.*
*Zep.* 3:3 they gnaw not the *b.*
*Mat.* 23:27 full of dead men's *b.*
*Luke* 24:39 a spirit hath not *b.*

**His BONES.**

1 *K.* 13:31 lay my *b.* beside *his b.*
2 *K.* 23:18 no man move *his b.*
*Job* 20:11 *his b.* are full
21:24 *his b.* moistened
33:19 *his b.* with strong pain
21 and *his b.* stick out
40:18 *his b.* as br. *his b.* as iron
*Ps.* 34:20 he keepeth all *his b.*
109:18 come like oil into *his b.*
*Prov.* 12:4 rottenness in *his b.*
*Eph.* 5:30 members of *his b.*
*Heb.* 11:22 com. concern. *his b.*

**My BONES.**

*Gen.* 50:25 up *my b.* *Ex.* 13:19
2 *Sam.* 19:12 are *my b.* and flesh
1 *K.* 13:31 *my b.* beside his *b.*
*Job* 4:14 made all *my b.* to shake
30:17 *my b.* are pierced in me
30 and *my b.* burnt with heat

Ps. 6:2 heal me, my b. are vexed
22:14 all my b. are out of joint
17 I may tell all my b.
31:10 my b. are consumed
32:3 my b. waxed old
35:10 my b. shall say, Lord
38:3 neither any rest in my b.
42:10 as with a sword in my b.
102:3 my b. are burnt as a hearth
5 my b. cleave to my skin
Is. 38:13 will he break all my b.
Jer. 20:9 a burning fire in my b.
23:9 all my b. shake
Lam. 1:13 sent fire into my b.
3:4 he hath broken my b.
Hab. 3:16 entered into my b.

**Their BONES.**

Num. 24:8 Is. shall break their b.
1 Sam. 31:13 their b. buried them
Lam. 4:8 skin cleaveth to their b.
Ezek. 32:27 iniquity on their b.
Dan. 6:24 lions brake all their b.
Mic. 3:2 flesh from their b.

**BONNETS.**

Is. 3:20 L. will take away the b.
Ezek. 44:18 shall have linen b.

**BOOK.**

Ex. 17:14 memorial in a b.
32:32 blot me out of thy b.
33 will I blot out of my b.
Num. 21:14 b. of the wars
Deut. 17:18 of this law in a b.
Jos. 10:13 b. of J. 2 Sam. 1:18
1 Sam. 10:25 S. wrote it in a b.
1 K. 11:41 b. of acts of Solomon
2 K. 22:8 Hilk. gave b. to Shap.
23:24 perform words in b.
Ezr. 4:15 s. may be made in b.
Neh. 8:5 Ezra opened the b.
Job 19:23 they were prin. in a b.
31:35 adver. had written a b.
Ps. 40:7 vol. of the b. Heb. 10:7
56:8 are they not in thy b.?
69:28 blotted out of b.
139:16 in thy b. all my members
Is. 29:11 as words of a b. sealed
12 b. is deliv. to him not learn.
18 shall hear words of the b.
30:8 now go and note it in a b.
34:16 seek ye out of the b. of L.
Jer. 30:2 write the words in a b.
36:2 roll of a b.; 10 read in b.
45:1 words in a b. from Jerem.
Ezek. 2:9 roll of a b. was therein
Dan. 12:1 ev. one writ. in the b.
4 O Daniel, seal the b.
Nah. 1:1 b. of vision of Nahum
Mal. 3:16 a b. of remembrance
Mat. 1:1 b. of the gen. of Jesus
Luke 3:4 written in the b. of E.
4:17 deliv. to J. the b. of Esaias, when he opened the b.
20 he closed the b. and gave it
20:42 in b. of Psalms, Acts 1:20
Acts 7:42 in b. of the prophets
Heb. 9:19 sprinkled the b. and
Rev. 1:11 write in a b.
5:1 a b. written within, on the
2 is worthy to open the b. 3
10:2 in his hand a little b. open
9 little b.; 10 I took the b.
20:12 b. was opened, b. of life
22:19 if any take from w. of b.

See COVENANT.

**BOOK of the Law.**

Deut. 31:26 b. of l. put it in ark
Jos. 1:8 b. of law shall not depart
2 K. 22:8 I have found b. of law
Neh. 8:8 read in the b. of law
Gal. 3:10 in b. of l. to do them

**BOOK of Life.**

Phil. 4:3 writ. in the b. of life
Rev. 3:5 name out of b. of l.
13:8 not writ. in b. of life, 17:8
20:12 an. b. opened, b. of life
15 not written in b. of life
21:27 written in L.'s b. of life
22:19 part out of the b. of life

**BOOK of Moses.**

2 Chr. 25:4 as in b. of M. 35:12
Ezr. 6:18
Neh. 13:1 read in the b. of M.
Mark 12:26 ye not read in b.

**This BOOK.**

Deut. 28:58 it t. b. 2 Chr. 34:21
2 K. 22:13 to the words of t. b.
23:3 perf. the words in this b.
Jer. 25:13 all that is in this b.
51:63 an end of reading this b.
John 20:30 not written in this b.
Rev. 22:9 keep the say. of this b.
10 the sayings of this b.
18 plagues in this b.
19 things in this b.

**BOOKS.**

Ec. 12:12 of making b.
Dan. 7:10 b. were op. Rev. 20:12
John 21:25 could not cont. the b.
Acts 19:19 their b. and burned
2 Tim. 4:13 bring the b. espec.
Rev. 20:12 out of things in b.

**BOOTH.**

Job 27:18 as a b. the keeper
Jon. 4:5 Jonah made him a b.

**BOOTHS.**

Gen. 33:17 and Jacob made b.
Lev. 23:42 dwell in b. seven days
43 I made Is. dwell in b.
Neh. 8:14 Isr. should dwell in b.

**BOOTY, IES.**

Jer. 49:32 camels shall be a b.
Hab. 2:7 be for b. unto them
Zep. 1:13 goods shall bec. a b.

**BORDER.**

Ex. 19:12 touch b. of mount
Deut. 12:20 w. L. enlarge thy b.
1 K. 4:21 Solomon reigned unto b. of Egypt, 2 Chr. 9:26
Ps. 78:54 b. of his sanctuary
Prov. 15:25 establish b. of widow
Is. 37:24 the height of his b.
Jer. 31:17 chil. again to their b.
Joel 3:6 remove them from b.
Amos 1:13 enlarge their b.
6:2 their b. great. than your b.
Ob. 7 even to the b.
Zep. 2:8 magnified ag. their b.
Mal. 1:4 the b. of wickedness
5 L. will be mag. fr. b. of Isr.
Mark 6:56 if it were but b.
Luke 8:44 touched b. of garment

See EAST, SOUTH.

**BORDER, Verb.**

Zec. 9:2 H. shall b. thereby

**BORDERS.**

Ex. 16:35 come to b. Canaan
34:24 I will enlarge thy b.
2 K. 19:23 enter lodg. of his b.
Ps. 74:17 set the b. of the earth
147:14 maketh peace in thy b.
Cant. 1:11 will make b. of gold
Is. 54:12 b. of pleasant stones
Jer. 15:13 thy sins in all thy b.
Ezek. 45:1 be holy in all the b.
Mic. 5:6 treadeth within our b.
Mat. 4:13 in the b. of Zebulun
23:5 enlarge b. of their garments

**BORE.**

Ex. 21:6 master shall b. his ear
Job 41:2 b. his jaw with thorn?

**BORN,** *for brought forth.*

Gen. 17:17 b. him 100 yrs. old, 21:5
Ex. 1:22 every son b. into river
Lev. 19:34 as one b. among
Num. 15:29 one law for him b.
Jos. 8:33 the stranger as he b.
Jud. 13:8 child that shall be b.
2 Sam. 12:14 the child b. shall die
1 K. 13:2 a child shall be b. to the house of David
1 Chr. 22:9 son shall be b. to thee
Job 3:3 day perish wh. I was b.
5:7 yet man is b. to trouble
11:12 b. like a wild ass's colt
15:7 first man that was b.?
38:21 bec. thou wast then b.?
Ps. 22:31 people that shall be b.
58:3 as soon as they be b.
78:6 children that should be b.
87:4 b. there, 6; 5 that man b.
Prov. 17:17 a brother is b.
Ec. 3:2 a time to be b.
4:14 b. in his kingdom
Is. 9:6 unto us a child is b.
66:8 shall a nat. be b. at once?
Jer. 16:3 con. sons and daugh. b.
20:14 cursed be day I was b.
22:26 where not b. shall ye die
Ezek. 16:4 the day thou wast b.
5 loath. of thy person in day b.
Mat. 2:2 is b. king of the Jews
4 where Christ should be b.
19:12 some eunuchs were so b.
26:24 good if not b. Mark 14:21
Luke 1:35 thing that shall be b.
2:11 to you is b. this day
John 3:4 be b. when he is old?
5 except a man be b. of water
6 b. of flesh is flesh, that b.
8 so is every one b. of the Sp.
8:41 we be not b. of fornication
9:2 did sin, that he was b. blind
34 wast altogether b. in sins
16:21 for joy that a man is b.
18:37 to this end was I b.
Acts 2:8 wherein we were b.
7:20 which time Moses was b.
22:3 b. in T.; 28 I was free b.
Rom. 9:11 chil. being not yet b.
1 Cor. 15:8 b. out of due time
Gal. 4:23 b. after the flesh, 29
Heb. 11:23 by faith M. when b.
1 Pet. 2:2 as new b. babes desire
1 John 2:29 righte. is b. of him
Rev. 12:4 dev. child as soon as b.

**BORN again.**

John 3:3 except a man be b. a. 5
7 ye must be b. again
1 Pet. 1:23 b. a. not of corruptible

See FIRST-BORN, WITNESS.

**BORN of God.**

John 1:13 b. n. of blood, but of G.
1 John 3:9 b. of God not com. sin
1 John 4:7 one that lov. b. of G.
5:1 Jesus is Christ is b. of God
4 whatsoever is b. of God
18 whosoever is b. of God

**BORN in the house.**

Gen. 15:3 b. in my h. is my heir
Ec. 2:7 had serv. b. in my h.

**BORN in the land.**

Ex. 12:48 stran. as one b. in l.
Num. 9:14 one ordin. for b. in l.

**BORN of a woman,** *or* **women.**

Job 14:1 man b. of a w.
15:14 b. of a w. that he
25:4 that is b. of a w.?
Mat. 11:11 are b. of w. Luke 7:28

**BORNE,** *brought forth.*

Gen. 21:7 b. him son in old age
29:34 I have b. three sons
30:20 because I have b. six sons
1 Sam. 2:5 barren hath b. seven
4:20 thou hast b. a son
Jer. 15:9 b. seven languisheth
10 that thou hast b. me
Ezek. 16:20 thy sons b. to me

**BORNE,** *carried.*

Is. 46:3 b. by me from the belly
66:12 be b. upon her sides
Jer. 10:5 they must be b. because
Amos 5:26 have b. tab. of Moloch
Mark 2:3 one sick of palsy was b.

*John* 20:15 *b.* him hence tell me
*Acts* 21:35 was *b.* of the soldiers
1 *Cor.* 15:49 *b.* image of the e.

**BORNE,** *endured*
*Job* 34:31 I have *b.* chastisement
*Ps.* 55:12 then I could have *b.*
69:7 thy sake I have *b.* reproach
*Is.* 53:4 surely he hath *b.* griefs
*Lam.* 3:28 hath *b.* it upon him
5:7 we have *b.* their iniquities
*Ezek.* 16:58 hast *b.* thy lewd.
32:24 *b.* shame, 36:6; 39:26
*Mat.* 20:12 *b.* burden and heat
23:4 griev. to be *b.* *Luke* 11:46
*Rev.* 2:3 hast *b.* and hast patience

**BORROW.**
*Ex.* 3:22 ev. wom. shall *b.* 11:2
22:14 if a man *b.* aught
*Deut.* 15:6 shalt not *b.* 28:12
2 *K.* 4:3 E. said, Go *b.* vessels
*Mat.* 5:42 him that would *b.*

**BORROWED.**
*Ex.* 12:35 *b.* of Egyptians
2 *K.* 6:5 master, for it was *b.*

**BORROWER.**
*Prov.* 22:7 *b.* is servant to lender
*Is.* 24:2 with lender, so with *b.*

**BORROWETH.**
*Ps.* 37:21 *b.* and payeth not

**BOSOM.**
*Gen.* 16:5 my maid into thy *b.*
*Ex.* 4:6 put hand into thy *b.* 7
*Num.* 11:12 carry th. in thy *b.*
*Ruth* 4:16 Naomi laid it in her *b.*
2 *Sam.* 12:3 and lay in his *b.*
8 master's wives into thy *b.*
1 *K.* 1:2 let her lie in thy *b.*
3:20 laid it in her *b.* and laid her dead child in my *b.*
17:19 E. took him out of her *b.*
*Job* 31:33 hiding iniq. in my *b.*
*Ps.* 35:13 returned to my *b.*
74:11 thy right hand out of *b.*
79:12 sevenfold into their *b.*
89:50 I do bear in my *b.*
129:7 bindeth sheaves, his *b.*
*Prov.* 5:20 emb. *b.* of stranger?
6:27 man take fire in his *b.*?
17:23 a gift out of the *b.*
19:24 his hand in *b.* 26:15
21:14 a reward in the *b.*
*Ec.* 7:9 resteth in *b.* of fools
*Is.* 40:11 the lambs in his *b.*
65:6 recompense into their *b.*
7 former work into their *b.*
*Jer.* 32:18 iniq. of fathers into *b.*
*Lam.* 2:12 soul into mother's *b.*
*Mic.* 7:5 lieth in thy *b.*
*Luke* 6:38 good m. into your *b.*
16:22 by angel's into Ab.'s *b.*
23 Abrah. and Laz. in his *b.*
*John* 1:18 the *b.* of the Father
13:23 leaning on Jesus' *b.*

**BOSSES.**
*Job* 15:26 thick *b.* of his bucklers

**BOTCH.**
*Deut.* 28:27 smite with the *b.* 35

**BOTTLE.**
*Gen.* 21:14 *b.* of water gave it H.
15 w. spent in *b.*; 19 filled *b.*
*Jud.* 4:19 opened a *b.* of milk
1 *Sam.* 1:24 H. took *b.* of wine
10:3 another carrying *b.* of w.
1 *Sam.* 16:20 Jesse took a *b.* of w.
*Ps.* 56:8 my tears into thy *b.*
119:83 like a *b.* in the smoke
*Jer.* 13:12 every *b.* filled with w.
19:1 a potter's *b.*; 10 break *b.*
*Hab.* 2:15 puttest thy *b.* to him

**BOTTLES.**
*Jos.* 9:4 Gibeonites took wine *b.*
13 these *b.* of wine were new
*Job* 32:19 to burst like new *b.*
38:37 can stay *b.* of heaven?
*Hos.* 7:5 sick with *b.* of wine
*Mat.* 9:17 new wine into old *b.* else *b.* break, *Mark* 2:22; *Luke* 5:37, 38

**BOTTOM.**
*Ex.* 15:5 they sank into the *b.*
*Job* 36:30 covereth *b.* of the sea
*Cant.* 3:10 made the *b.* of gold
*Dan.* 6:24 they came at *b.*
*Amos* 9:3 from my sight in *b.*
*Jon.* 2:6 to *b.* of the mount.
*Zec.* 1:8 myrtle-trees in *b.*
*Mat.* 27:51 veil rent from top to *b.* *Mark* 15:38

**BOTTOMLESS.**
*Rev.* 9:1 to him key of the *b.* pit
2 he opened *b.* pit, arose smoke
11 had a king, angel of *b.* pit
11:7 that ascend. out of *b.* pit
17:8 ascend out of the *b.* pit
20:1 an angel hav. key of *b.* pit
3 cast him into the *b.* pit

**BOUGH.**
*Gen.* 49:22 Joseph is fruitful *b.*
*Jud.* 9:48 Abim. cut down a *b.*
49 cut down every man his *b.*
*Is.* 10:33 Lord shall lop *b.*
17:6 in top of uppermost *b.*
9 cities be as a forsaken *b.*

**BOUGHS.**
*Lev.* 23:40 *b.* of goodly trees, *b.* of
*Deut.* 24:20 go over the *b.*
2 *Sam.* 18:9 mule went under *b.*
*Job* 14:9 brought forth *b.*
*Ps.* 80:10 *b.* like goodly cedars
11 sent out her *b.* to the sea
*Cant.* 7:8 take hold of the *b.*
*Is.* 27:11 when the *b.* are with.
*Ezek.* 17:23 it shall bring forth *b.*
31:3 his top among thick *b.* 14
6 nests in his *b.* *Dan.* 4:12

**BOUGHT.**
*Gen.* 33:19 J. *b.* field, *Jos.* 24:32
39:1 Potiphar *b.* Joseph
47:20 Joseph *b.* all land of E. 23
49:30 Abr. *b.* 50:13; *Acts* 7:16
*Lev.* 27:24 of whom it was *b.*
*Deut.* 32:6 father that *b.* thee?
2 *Sam.* 12:3 ewe-lamb he had *b.*
24:24 David *b.* threshing-floor
1 *K.* 16:24 O. *b.* hill Samaria
*Neh.* 5:16 nor *b.* we any land
*Jer.* 32:9 I *b.* field of Hanameel
*Hos.* 3:2 so I *b.* her for fifteen p.
*Mat.* 13:46 sold all, *b.* that field
21:12 sold and *b.* in the temple, *Mark* 11:15; *Luke* 19:45
27:7 *b.* with them potter's field
*Mark* 15:46 Joseph *b.* fine linen
16:1 *b.* sweet spices to anoint
*Luke* 14:18 have *b.* a piece of gro.
19 I have *b.* five yoke of oxen
17:28 drank, they *b.* and sold
1 *Cor.* 6:20 ye are *b.* 7:23
2 *Pet.* 2:1 deny. L. that *b.* them

**BOUND,** *actively*
*Gen.* 22:9 *b.* Isaac his son
42:24 took Simeon, and *b.* him
*Num.* 30:4 had *b.* her soul, 11
*Jud.* 15:13 *b.* Samson with new
16:8 withs; 12 ropes; 21 fetters
2 *K.* 5:23 he *b.* two talents
17:4 he shut up Hoshea and *b.*
25:7 *b.* Zedekiah with fetters
2 *Chr.* 33:11 *b.* Manasseh
36:6 *b.* Jehoiakim
*Prov.* 30:4 *b.* waters in a garm.
*Hos.* 7:15 I have *b.* their arms
*Mat.* 14:3 H. *b.* John, *Mark* 6:17
27:2 *b.* J. *Mark* 15:1; *John* 18:12
*Luke* 13:16 daughter S. hath *b.*
*Acts* 21:11 Agabus *b.* his hands
22:25 as they *b.* Paul, 29
23:12 *b.* them under, 14:21
*Rev.* 20:2 *b.* S. a thousand years

**BOUND,** *passively.*
*Gen.* 39:20 king's pris. are *b.*
42:19 one of your brethren be *b.*
*Jud.* 16:6 mightest be *b.* 10, 13
1 *Sam.* 25:29 soul of my lord be *b.*
2 *Sam.* 3:34 thy hands were not *b.*
*Job* 36:8 if they be *b.* in fetters
*Ps.* 107:10 being *b.* in affliction
*Prov.* 22:15 foolish. is *b.* in heart
*Is.* 22:3 *b.* by archers, all are *b.*
61:1 opening of pris. to them *b.*
*Lam.* 1:14 yoke of my tran. is *b.*
*Dan.* 3:21 *b.* in their coats
24 three men *b.* into furnace?
*Mat.* 16:19 *b.* in heaven, 18:18
*Mark* 15:7 Barabbas which lay *b.*
*John* 11:44 *b.* h. and foot, face *b.*
18:24 Annas had sent him *b.*
*Acts* 9:2 bring them *b.* 21; 22:5
12:6 Peter *b.*; 24:27 left Paul *b.*
20:22 I go *b.* in the Spirit to J.
21:13 I am ready not to be *b.*
*Rom.* 7:2 is *b.* by the law to her husband, 1 *Cor.* 7:39
1 *Cor.* 7:27 *b.* unto a wife
2 *Thes.* 1:3 *b.* to thank God, 2:13
2 *Tim.* 2:9 word of God is not *b.*
*Heb.* 13:3 in bonds, as *b.* with
*Rev.* 9:14 loose the angels *b.*

**BOUND with chains.**
*Ps.* 68:6 G. bring. out th. *b. w. c.*
*Jer.* 39:7 *b.* Zed. *with c.* 52:11
40:1 Jeremiah *b. with c.*
*Nah.* 3:10 her great men *b. w. c.*
*Mark* 5:4 had been often *b. w. c.*
*Luke* 8:29 was kept *b. with c.*
*Acts* 21:33 com. P. to be *b. w.* 2 *c.*
28:20 for hope of Israel I am *b.*

**BOUND up.**
*Gen.* 44:30 life is *b. up* in lad's
*Is.* 1:6 have not been *b. up*
*Jer.* 30:13 none to plead, that thou mayest be *b. up*
*Ezek.* 30:21 be *b. up* to be healed
34:4 have ye *b. up* that broken
*Hos.* 4:19 wind hath *b.* her *up*
13:12 iniq. of Ephraim is *b. up*
*Luke* 10:34 he *b. up* his wounds

**BOUND, Substantive.**
*Gen.* 49:26 *b.* of the everlasting
*Job* 38:20 take it to the *b.* there.
*Ps.* 104:9 the waters set a *b.*
*Jer.* 5:22 sand for *b.* of the sea
*Hos.* 5:10 them that remove *b.*

**BOUNDS.**
*Ex.* 19:23 *b.* about the mount
23:31 thy *b.* from the Red sea
*Deut.* 32:8 set *b.* of the people
*Job* 14:5 *b.* that he cannot pass
26:10 comp. the waters with *b.*
*Is.* 10:13 rem. *b.* of the people
*Acts* 17:26 hast determined the *b.*

**BOUNTY.**
2 *Cor.* 9:5 make up before h. y. *b.*

**BOUNTIFUL.**
*Prov.* 22:9 hath a *b.* eye
*Is.* 32:5 churl be said to be *b.*

**BOUNTIFULNESS.**
2 *Cor.* 9:11 enriched to all *b.*

**BOUNTIFULLY.**
*Ps.* 13:6 hath dealt *b.* with me
116:7 Lord hath dealt *b.*
119:17 deal *b.* with thy servant
142:7 shalt deal *b.* with me
2 *Cor.* 9:6 soweth *b.* shall reap *b.*

**BOW, Substantive.**
*Gen.* 9:13 set my *b.* in the cloud
27:3 take thy quiver and *b.*
48:22 I took of Amorite with *b.*
49:24 his *b.* abode in strength
*Jos.* 24:12 but not with thy *b.*
2 *Sam.* 1:22 *b.* of Jon. turned not

1 *K.* 22:34 a certain man drew a *b.* at a venture, 2 *Chr.* 18:33
2 *K.* 13:15 take *b.* and ar. took *b.*
*Job* 29:20 my *b.* was renewed
*Ps.* 44:6 will not trust in my *b.*
46:9 he breaketh the *b.* cutteth
76:3 there brake he arrows of *b.*
78:57 aside like a deceitful *b.*
*Is.* 41:2 as stubble to his *b.*
*Jer.* 6:23 shall lay hold on *b.*
49:35 I will break the *b.* of E.
*Lam.* 2:4 bent his *b.*
*Ezek.* 1:28 as the *b.* in the cloud
*Hos.* 1:5 I will break *b.* of Israel
7 will not save them by *b.*
2:18 I will break the *b.*
7:16 they are like a deceitful *b.*
*Amos* 2:15 he that handleth *b.*
*Hab* 3:9 *b.* made quite naked
*Zec.* 9:13 filled the *b.* with Eph.
*Rev.* 6:2 sat on wh. horse had *b.*

*See* BEND, BENT, BATTLE-BOW.

**BOWS.**

1 *Sam.* 2:4 the *b.* of mighty
*Neh.* 4:16 half of them held *b.*
*Ps.* 37:15 *b.* shall be broken
*Is.* 7:24 with *b.* shall men come
13:18 their *b.* shall dash young
*Jer.* 51:56 every one of their *b.*
*Ezek.* 39:9 they shall burn the *b.*

**BOW-SHOT.**

*Gen.* 21:16 as it were a *b.-s.*

**BOW, Verb.**

*Jos.* 23:7 nor *b.* yourselves to their gods, 2 *K.* 17:35
2 *K.* 5:18 I *b.* in house of Rim.
*Job* 39:3 *b.* themselves
*Ps.* 22:29 to the dust shall *b.*
72:9 in wilder. sh. *b.* before him
144:5 *b.* thy heavens, O Lord
*Prov.* 5:1 *b.* thine ear
14:19 evil *b.* before the good
*Ec.* 12:3 strong men shall *b.*
*Mic.* 6:6 *b.* myself bef. high G.?
*Hab.* 3:6 perpetual hills did *b.*
*Eph.* 3:14 *b.* my knees to the F.

**BOW down.**

*Gen.* 27:29 nations *b. down*
37:10 mother, brethren *b. down*
49:8 father's children shall *b. d.*
*Ex.* 11:8 serv. shall *b. d.* to me
20:5 not *b. d. Deut.* 5:9
23:24 shalt not *b. d.* to their g.
*Lev.* 26:1 any image to *b. d.* to it
*Jud.* 2:19 other gods to *b. d.*
2 *K.* 5:18 *b. d.* in house of Rim.
19:16 L. *b. d.* thine ear, *Ps.* 86:1
*Job* 31:10 others *b. d.* upon her
*Ps.* 31:2 *b. d.* th. ear, *Prov.* 22:17
95:6 worship and *b. down*
*Is.* 10:4 without me *b. down*
46:2 they stoop, they *b. down*
49:23 kings and queens sh. *b. d.*
51:23 *b. d.* that we may go over
58:5 to *b. d.* head as a bulrush?
60:14 despised thee shall *b. d.*
65:12 all *b. d.* to slaughter
*Rom.* 11:10 *b. d.* their back

**BOW knee.**

*Gen.* 41:43 before him *b.* the *k.*
*Is.* 45:23 *k.* shall *b. Rom.* 14:11
*Eph.* 3:14 I *b.* my *knee* to F.
*Phil.* 2:10 every *knee* shall *b.*

**BOWED.**

*Gen.* 43:26 Jos. brethren *b.*
49:15 Issachar *b.* shoulder
*Jos.* 23:16 served other gods, and *b.* to them, *Jud.* 2:12, 17
*Jud.* 5:27 at her feet he *b.*
2 *Sam.* 19:14 David *b.*
22:10 he *b.* heavens, *Ps.* 18:9
1 *K.* 19:18 not *b.* to B. *Rom.* 11:4
2 *K.* 2:15 prophets *b.* before E.
2 *Chr.* 7:3 *b.* upon the pavement
29:29 king and all present *b.*
*Est.* 3:5 Mordecai *b.* not
*Mat.* 27:29 *b.* the knee
*Luke* 13:11 spirit of infir. and *b.*

**BOWED down.**

*Gen.* 42:6 J. brethren *b. d.* 43:28
*Jud.* 7:6 rest of the people *b. d.*
*Ps.* 35:14 I *b. d.* heavily as one
38:6 I am *b. d.* greatly,
44:25 soul is *b. d.* to the dust
57:6 my soul is *b. d.*
145:14 rais. up all *b. d.* 146:8
*Is.* 2:11 haught. of men be *b. d.*
17 lofti. of man shall be *b. d.*
21:3 was *b. d.* at hearing of it
*Luke* 24:5 and *b. d.* their faces

**BOWED head.**

*Gen.* 43:28 they *b.* their *heads*
*Ex.* 4:31 they *b.* their *heads* and worship. 12:27; *Neh.* 8:6
34:8 Mos. made haste and *b. h.*
*Num.* 22:31 Balaam *b.* his *head*
1 *Chr.* 29:20 *b.* down their *head*
2 *Chr.* 20:18 Jehosh. *b.* his *head*
29:30 praises and *b.* their *head*
*John* 19:30 Jesus *b.* his *head*

**BOWED himself.**

*Gen.* 18:2 A. *b. himself,* 23:7, 12
19:1 Lot *b. himself*
33:3 Jacob *b. himself* 47:31
48:12 Joseph *b. himself*
*Jud.* 16:30 S. *b. h.* with might
2 *Sam.* 24:20 A. *b. h.* 1 *Chr.* 21:21
1 *K.* 1:23 N. *b. h.*; 47 king *b. h.*
43 Adonijah *b. h.* to king Sol.
2:19 Solomon *b. h.* to his mother

**BOWETH.**

*Jud.* 7:5 that *b.* on knees
*Is.* 2:9 m. man *b.*; 46:1 Bel. *b.*

**BOWING.**

*Gen.* 24:52 Eliezer *b.* h. to earth
*Ps.* 17:11 set their eyes, *b.* down
62:3 as a *b.* wall shall ye be
*Mark* 15:19 spit on him, *b.* knees

**BOWELS.**

*Gen.* 15:4 out of own *b.* thy heir
25:23 manner of people from *b.*
43:30 *b.* did yearn on brother
2 *Sam.* 7:12 which pro. out of *b.*
16:11 which came forth of my *b.*
2 *Sam.* 20:10 Jo. sh. Amasa's *b.*
1 *K.* 3:26 *b.* yearned on her son
2 *Chr.* 21:15 sick. by disease of *b.*
21:18 smote him in *b.* 19
32:21 of his own *b.* slew him
*Job* 20:14 meat in his *b.* is turn.
30:27 *b.* boiled, and rested not
*Ps.* 22:14 it is melted in my *b.*
71:6 out of my mother's *b.*
109:18 come into his *b.*
*Cant.* 5:4 *b.* were moved for him
*Is.* 16:11 *b.* sound like a harp
48:19 the offspring of thy *b.*
49:1 from *b.* of my mother
63:15 sounding of thy *b.*
*Jer.* 4:19 my *b.* I am pained
31:20 my *b.* are troubled
*Lam.* 1:20 *b.* are troubled, 2:11
*Ezek.* 3:3 fill thy *b.* with this roll
7:19 their souls, nor fill their *b.*
*Acts* 1:18 J. burst, and all his *b.*
2 *Cor.* 6:12 strait. in your own *b.*
*Phil.* 1:8 in *b.* of Christ
2:1 if there be any *b.*
*Col.* 3:12 put on *b.* of mercies
*Phile.* 7 *b.* of saints are refreshed
12 rec. him that is my own *b.*
20 refresh my *b.* in the Lord
1 *John* 3:17 shut. up *b.* of comp.

**BOWL.**

*Jud.* 6:38 a *b.* full of water
*Ec.* 12:6 or golden *b.* be broken
*Zec.* 4:2 candlestick with a *b.*

**BOWLS.**

*Amos* 6:6 that drink wine in *b.*
*Zec.* 9:15 shall be filled like *b.*
14:20 the pots shall be like *b.*

**BOWMEN.**

*Jer.* 4:29 for the noise of the *b.*

**BOX.**

2 *K.* 9:1 take this *b.* of oil, 3
*Mat.* 26:7 alaba. *b. Mark* 14:3
*Mark* 14:3 brake the *b. Luke* 7:37

**BOX-TREE.**

*Is.* 41:19 set in the desert *b.-tree*
60:13 glory of Lebanon *b.-tree*

**BOY, S.**

*Gen.* 25:27 the *b.* grew
*Joel* 3:3 given a *b.* for a harlot
*Zec.* 8:5 shall be full of *b.*

**BOZRAH.**

*Is.* 34:6 hath a sacrifice in B.
63:1 dyed garments from B.
*Jer.* 48:24 judg. is come upon B.
48:13 B. shall bec. desolation, 22
*Amos* 1:12 dev. the palaces of B.
*Mic.* 2:12 put as the sheep of B.

**BRACELET, S.**

*Gen.* 24:30 *b.* on sister's hands
38:18 signet, *b.* and staff, 25
*Ex.* 35:22 brought *b. Num.* 31:50
2 *Sam.* 1:10 the *b.* on his arm
*Is.* 3:19 I will take away the *b.*
*Ezek.* 16:11 I put *b.* on thy hands

**BRAKE.**

*Ex.* 32:19 tables out of his hands and *b.* them, *Deut.* 9:17
*Jud.* 7:19 they *b.* pitchers, 20
16:9 *b.* withs, 12 *b.* new ropes
1 *Sam.* 4:18 Eli fell, his neck *b.*
1 *K.* 19:11 a strong wind *b.* in pieces the rocks
2 *K.* 11:18 Baal's images *b.* they
18:4 *b.* images, *b.* brazen serp.
23:14 Josi. *b.* images, 2 *Chr.* 34:4
2 *Chr.* 21:17 Arabians *b.* into J.
*Job* 38:8 shut sea wh. it *b.* forth?
10 *b.* up for it my decreed place
*Ps.* 76:3 there *b.* he the arrows
105:16 *b.* the whole staff of bread
33 *b.* trees of their coast
106:29 plague *b.* in upon them
107:14 *b.* their bands in sunder
*Jer.* 28:10 yoke from Jer. *b.* it
31:32 my covenant they *b.*
*Ezek.* 17:16 and covenant he *b.*
*Dan.* 2:1 sleep *b.* from him 34
6:24 the lions *b.* all their bones
7:7 fourth beast *b.* in pieces
8:7 ram, and *b.* his two horns
*Mat.* 14:19 he blessed and *b.* and gave the loaves, 15:36; 26:26; *Mark* 6:41; 8:6; 14:22; *Luke* 9:16; 22:19; 24:30; 1 *Cor.* 11:24
*Mark* 8:19 I *b.* the five loaves
14:3 she *b.* the box, and poured
*Luke* 5:6 net *b.*; 8:29 *b.* the bands
*John* 19:32 soldiers *b.* legs
33 they *b.* not his legs

**BRAKE down.**

2 *K.* 10:27 *b. down* image of Baal, 2 *Chr.* 23:17
11:18 *b. down* the house of Baal
2 *K.* 14:13 *b. down* w. of J. 2 *Chr.* 25:23; 36:19; *Jer.* 39:8; 52:14
23:7 *b. d.* houses of Sodomites
2 *Chr.* 26:6 Uzziah *b. d.* wall of G.
34:4 *b. down* altars of Baalim

**BRAKEST.**

*Ex.* 34:1 first table *b. Deut.* 10:2
*Ps.* 74:13 *b.* heads of dragons, 14
*Ezek.* 29:7 leaned on thee, thou *b.*

**BRAMBLE, S.**

*Jud.* 9:14 said trees to the *b.*
15 let fire come out of the *b.*
*Is.* 34:13 *b.* shall come up
*Luke* 6:44 of a *b.*-bush grapes

**BRANCH.**
*Num.* 13:23 cut a *b.*
*Job* 8:16 his *b.* shooteth forth
14:7 tender *b.* thereof not cease
15:32 his *b.* shall not be green
18:16 shall his *b.* be cut off
29:19 lay all night on my *b.*
*Ps.* 80:15 *b.* thou madest strong
*Prov.* 11:28 shall flour. as a *b.*
*Is.* 4:2 shall *b.* of the L. be beau.
9:14 Lord will cut off *b.*
11:1 a *b.* shall grow out
14:19 cast out like abomina. *b.*
17:9 cities as an uppermost *b.*
19:15 work, *b.* or rush may do
25:5 the *b.* of terrible ones low
60:21 the *b.* of my planting
*Jer.* 23:5 to David a righteous *b.*
33:15 cause *b.* of righteousness
*Ezek.* 8:17 put *b.* to their nose
15:2 more than any *b.?*
17:3 took the highest *b.* 22
*Dan.* 11:7 a *b.* of her roots
*Zec.* 3:8 forth my servant the *b.*
6:12 man whose name is the *b.*
*Mal.* 4:1 it shall leave root nor *b.*
*Mat.* 24:32 *b.* yet t. *Mark* 13:28
*John* 15:2 every *b.* that beareth
4 as *b.* cannot bear fruit
6 he is cast forth as a *b.*

**BRANCHES.**
*Gen.* 40:12 the three *b.* are three
49:22 bough, whose *b.* run over
*Lev.* 23:40 *b.* of tree, *Neh.* 8:15
*Job* 15:30 shall dry up his *b.*
*Ps.* 80:11 sent out her *b.* to river
104:12 sing among the *b.*
*Is.* 16:8 Moab's *b.* are stretched
17:6 four or five in outmost *b.*
18:5 he shall cut down the *b.*
27:10 there lie and consume *b.*
*Jer.* 11:16 and *b.* of it are broken
*Ezek.* 17:6 spread. vine whose *b.*
19:10 fruitful and full of *b.*
14 fire out of a rod of her *b.*
31:8 not like the Assyrian's *b.*
36:8 O mount. ye shall shoot *b.*
*Dan.* 4:14 cut off his *b.*
*Hos.* 11:6 consume Ephraim's *b.*
14:6 his *b.* shall spread, and
*Joel* 1:7 *b.* thereof are m. white
*Nah.* 2:2 marred their vine *b.*
*Zec.* 4:12 these two olive *b.?*
*Mat.* 13:32 lodge in *b.* *Luke* 13:19
21:8 cut *b.* *Mark* 11:8; *John* 12:13
*Mark* 4:32 shooteth *b.*
*John* 15:5 the vine, ye the *b.*
*Rom.* 11:16 if root be holy so *b.*
17 if some *b.* be broken off, 19
18 boast not against the *b.*
21 spared not the natural *b.*

**BRAND, S.**
*Jud.* 15:5 had set the *b.* on fire
*Zec.* 3:2 *b.* plucked out of fire?

**BRANDISH.**
*Ezek.* 32:10 when I *b.* my sword.

**BRASS.**
*Ex.* 38:29 *b.* of offer. 70 talents
*Num.* 21:9 serpent of *b.* when he beheld serpent of *b.* he lived
*Deut.* 8:9 thou mayest dig *b.*
28:23 the heaven shall be *b.*
1 *Sam.* 17:6 greaves of *b.* on legs
2 *Sam.* 8:8 David took much *b.* 1 *Chr.* 18:8
1 *K.* 7:14 Hiram worker in *b.*
2 *K.* 25:7 Zed. with fetters of *b.*
13 *b.* to Babylon, *Jer.* 52:17
1 *Chr.* 15:19 with cymbals of *b.*
22:3 David prepared *b.* 29:7
29:2 prepared *b.* for things of *b.*
*Job* 6:12 or is my flesh *b.?*
40:18 as strong pieces of *b.*
41:27 esteemeth *b.* as rotten
*Ps.* 107:16 broken the gates of *b.*
*Is.* 45:2 in pieces the gates of *b.*
60:17 for wood *b.* for *b.* gold
*Ezek.* 24:11 the *b.* may be hot
*Dan.* 2:32 his thighs were of *b.*
39 third kingdom of *b.*
7:19 the fourth beast nails of *b.*
*Dan.* 10:6 like in color to pol. *b.*
*Mic.* 4:13 will make thy hoofs *b.*
*Zec.* 6:1 were mountains of *b.*
*Mat.* 10:9 neither gold nor *b.*
1 *Cor.* 13:1 I am as sounding *b.*
*Rev.* 1:15 feet like fine *b.* 2:18
9:20 not worship idols of *b.*

**Iron and BRASS.**
*Gen.* 4:22 T.-cain instruc. in *b.*
*Lev.* 26:19 heaven *iron*, earth *b.*
*Num.* 31:22 *b. i.* may abide fire
*Deut.* 33:25 shall be *iron and b.*
*Jos.* 22:8 ret. with *b. and iron*
1 *Chr.* 22:14 *b. i* with. weight, 16
2 *Chr.* 2:7 a cun. man in *b. ir.* 14
24:12 such as wrought in *ir. b.*
*Job* 28:2 *iron* taken out *b.*
*Is.* 48:4 neck *ir.* sin. *and* brow *b.*
60:17 for *b.* gold, for *iron* silver
*Jer.* 6:28 they are *b. i.* *Ezek.* 22:18
*Ezek.* 22:20 gather *iron and b.*
*Dan.* 2:35 was *iron b.* broken, 45
4:15 with hand of *iron and b.* 23
5:4 praised gods of silver, *b. i.*

**Vessels of BRASS.**
*Jos.* 6:19 all *v. of b.* are consec.
2 *K.* 25:16 the *b.* of all these *ves.* was with. w. *Jer.* 52:20
*Ezek.* 27:13 in *v. of b.* *Rev.* 18:12

**BRAVERY.**
*Is.* 3:18 will take away their *b.*

**BRAWLER, S.**
1 *Tim.* 3:3 bishop must be no *b.*
*Tit.* 3:2 to be no *b.*

**BRAWLING.**
*Prov.* 25:24 a *b.* woman, 21:19

**BRAY, ED, ETH.**
*Job* 6:5 doth the wild ass *b.*
30:7 among the bushes they *b.*
*Prov.* 27:22 *b.* a fool in a mortar

**BRAZEN.**
2 *K.* 18:4 brake the *b.* serpent
25:13 *b.* sea Chal. *Jer.* 52:17
2 *Chr.* 6:13 Sol. made a *b.* scaf.
*Jer.* 1:18 made thee this day *b.*
15:20 make thee a fenced *b.* wall
52:20 *b.* bulls; *Mark* 7:4 *b.* ves.
*See* ALTAR.

**BREACH.**
*Gen.* 38:29 midwife said, this *b.*
*Lev.* 24:20 *b.* for *b.* eye for eye.
*Num.* 14:34 my *b.* of promise
*Jud.* 21:15 a *b.* in the tribes
2 *Sam.* 5:20 forth as *b.* of waters
6:8 *b.* on Uzzah, 1 *Chr.* 13:11
2 *K.* 12:5 wheresoever any *b.*
1 *Chr.* 15:13 L. made a *b.* on us
*Neh.* 6:1 and there was no *b.*
*Job* 16:14 with *b.* upon *b.*
*Ps.* 106:23 not Moses stood in *b.*
*Prov.* 15:4 perverseness is a *b.*
*Is.* 7:6 a *b.* for us,
30:13 this iniq. shall be as a *b.*
26 in the day L. bindeth up *b.*
58:12 called the repairer of the *b.*
*Jer.* 14:17 is broken with a *b.*
*Lam.* 2:13 thy *b.* is great
*Ezek.* 26:10 city wherein a *b.*

**BREACHES.**
*Jud.* 5:17 Asher abode in his *b.*
1 *K.* 11:27 rep. *b.* of city of Dav.
2 *K.* 12:5 let them repair the *b.*
6 priests had not repaired the *b.*
*Ps.* 60:2 heal the *b.* for it shaketh
*Is.* 22:9 have seen *b.* of the city
*Amos* 4:3 shall go out at the *b.*
6:11 smite great house with *b.*
9:11 close up the *b.* thereof

**BREAD.**
*Gen.* 14:18 king of S. brought *b.*
18:5 will fetch a morsel of *b.*
21:14 Abraham took *b.* gave H.
25:34 then Jacob gave Esau *b.*
27:17 savory meat and *b.* to J.
41:54 in Egypt there was *b.*
55 cried to Pharaoh for *b.*
43:31 set on *b.*; 45:23 *b.* for f.
47:15 give us *b.*; 17 *b.* for h.
19 buy us and our land for *b.*
49:20 out of Asher his *b.* be fat
*Ex.* 16:4 I will rain *b.* from heav.
8 in morning *b.* to the full. 12
29 sixth day the *b.* of two days
32 may see the *b.* I fed you
23:25 he shall bless thy *b.*
40:23 he set the *b.* in order
*Lev.* 8:32 what remaineth of *b.*
21:6 *b.* of their G. 8, 17, 21, 22
26:26 ten women shall bake *b.*
*Num.* 4:7 continual *b.* be thereon
14:9 people of the land are *b.*
21:5 soul loatheth this light *b.*
*Deut.* 8:3 man doth not live by *b.* only, *Mat.* 4:4; *Luke* 4:4
*Deut.* 23:4 met you not with *b.*
29:6 ye have not eaten *b.* nor
*Jos.* 9:5 *b.* was dry and mouldy
12 this our *b.* we took hot
*Jud.* 7:13 a cake of *b.* tumbled
8:6 give *b.* to thy army, 15
19:5 comfort thy heart with *b.*
19 there is *b.* and wine also
*Ruth* 1:6 in giving them *b.*
1 *Sam.* 2:5 hired out them. for *b.*
36 crouch for a morsel of *b.*
9:7 the *b.* is spent in our vessels
21:4 hallowed *b.*; 5 *b.* is com.
6 priest gave him hallowed *b.*
22:13 hast given him *b.* and
28:22 let me set a morsel of *b.*
2 *Sam.* 3:29 J. one that lacketh *b.*
35 taste *b.* till sun be down
6:19 to every one a cake of *b*
1 *K.* 13:22 back and hast eaten *b.*
17:6 ravens brought *b.* and flesh
11 bring me a morsel of *b.*
2 *K.* 4:42 brought man of God *b.*
18:32 a land of *b.* *Is.* 36:17
*Neh.* 5:14 *b.* of governor
9:15 gavest them *b.* from h.
13:2 they met not Israel with *b.*
*Job* 15:23 wand. abroad for *b.*
22:7 withholden *b.* from hungry
27:14 not be satisfied with *b.*
28:5 out of it cometh *b.*
33:20 his life abhorreth *b.*
*Ps.* 37:25 his seed begging *b.*
78:20 can he give *b.?*
80:5 with *b.* of tears
102:9 eaten ashes like *b.*
104:15 *b.* which stren. man's h.
105:40 satisfied them with *b.*
109:10 seek their *b.*
132:15 satisfy her poor with *b.*
*Prov.* 9:17 *b.* eaten in secret
12:9 hon. hims. and lacketh *b.*
11 land satisfied with *b.* 28:19
20:13 shalt be satisfied with *b.*
17 *b.* of deceit is sweet
22:9 he giveth of his *b.*
31:27 eateth not *b.* of idleness
*Ec.* 9:11 nor *b.* to wise
11:1 cast thy *b.* upon the waters
*Is.* 3:1 away the whole stay of *b.*
7 in my house is neither *b.* nor
21:14 with their *b.* him that
30:20 Lord give *b.* of adversity
33:16 his *b.* shall be given him
44:15 baketh *b.* on the coals, 19
51:14 nor that his *b.* should fail
55:2 that which is not *b.*
10 that it may give *b.* to eater
58:7 deal thy *b.* to hungry?
*Jer.* 42:14 nor have hunger of *b.*

*Lam.* 1:11 they seek *b.*
4:4 young children ask *b.*
5:6 Egyptians to be sat. with *b.*
9 we gat our *b.* with peril
*Ezek.* 4:15 prep. thy *b.* therewith
17 they may want *b.* and water
16:49 pride, fulness of *b.* and
18:7 his *b.* to the hungry, 16
44:7 strang. when ye offer my *b.*
*Hos.* 2:5 lovers that give me *b.*
9:4 sacrifices as *b.* of mourners
*Amos* 4:6 given you want of *b.*
8:11 not famine of *b.*
*Hag.* 2:12 his skirt do touch *b.*
*Mal.* 1:7 ye offer polluted *b.*
*Mat.* 4:3 st. be made *b.* *Luke* 4:3
6:11 our daily *b.* *Luke* 11:11
7:9 if his son ask *b.* will he give
15:26 children's *b.* *Mark* 7:27
33 so much *b.*? *Mark* 8:4
16:5 forgot. to take *b.* *Mark* 8:14
11 spake it not concerning *b.*
12 not beware of leaven of *b.*
26:26 Jesus took *b.* *Mark* 14:22
*Luke* 7:33 Bapt. neither eating *b.*
9:3 for your journey, neither *b.*
15:17 servants have *b.* enough
22:19 took *b.* gave thanks, 24:30
24:35 in breaking *b.*
*John* 6:7 two hun. pennyw. of *b.*
32 M. gave you not that *b.* from h. my F. giveth true *b.*
33 the *b.* of God is he
34 Lord, give us this *b.*
35 I am the *b.* of life, 48
41 *b.* which came down, 50
58 eateth of this *b.* shall live
13:18 eateth *b.* hath lifted
21:9 fish laid thereon and *b.*
13 J. then taketh *b.* and giveth
*Acts* 2:42 con. in breaking of *b.*
46 break. *b.* from house to ho.
20:7 disciples came to break *b.*
11 when he had broken *b.*
27:35 he took *b.* and gave tha.
1 *Cor.* 10:16 *b.* we break is it not
17 being many are one *b.*
11:23 in wh. he was bet. took *b.*
2 *Cor.* 9:10 min. *b.* to your food
*See* AFFLICTION.

**BREAD-CORN.**
*Is.* 28:28 *b.-c.* is bruised because

**BREAD, *with* eat.**
*Gen.* 3:19 in sweat of face *e. b.*
28:20 if L. give me *b.* to *eat*
31:54 Jacob called breth. to *e. b.*
37:25 J.'s brethren sat to *e. b.*
39:6 save *b.* he *eat*
43:32 Egyptians not *e. b.* w. H.
*Ex.* 2:20 that he may *e. b.*
16:3 when we *eat b.* to the ful.
15 *b.* L. ha. giv. you to *e.*
18:12 to *e. b.* with M.s' f-in law
34:28 *e. b.* 40 da. *Deut.* 9:9, 18
*Lev.* 21:22 shall *e.* the *b.* of God
26:5 ye shall *eat b.* to the full
*Deut.* 8:9 *eat b.* without scarce.
*Ruth* 2:14 meal-time come *eat b.*
2 *Sam.* 9:7 *eat b.* at my table, 10
12:21 didst rise and *eat b.*
1 *K.* 13:8 nor will I *eat b.*
15 come home with me *eat b.*
2 *K.* 4:8 const. Elisha to *e. b.*
6:22 set *b.* and w. they may *e.*
25:29 did *e. b.* bef. h. *Jer.* 52:33
*Job* 42:11 and did *eat b.* with Job
*Ps.* 14:4 people as they *e. b.* 53:4
41:9 *eat* of my *b.* hath lift. heel
102:4 I forgot to *eat* my *b.*
127:2 to *eat* the *b.* of sorrows
*Prov.* 4:17 *e. b.* of wickedness
9:5 come *eat* of my *b.* and drink
23:6 *e.* not *b.* of him hath evil
25:21 if thy en. hunger give *b.*
*Ec.* 9:7 go *eat* thy *b.* with joy
*Is.* 4:1 we will *eat* our *b.*

*Jer.* 5:17 they shall eat up thy *b.*
41:1 I did *eat b.* together in Mi.
*Ezek.* 4:13 shall *eat* defiled *b.*
16 they shall *eat b.* by weight
12:18 *e. b.* with quaking; 19 care
24:17 and *eat* not *b.* of men, 22
44:3 prince sit in it to *eat b.*
*Amos* 7:12 flee into J. there *e. b.*
*Ob.* 7 *eat* thy *b.* have laid a w.
*Mat.* 15:2 w. not when they *e. b.*
*Mark* 3:20 not so much as *e. b.*
6:36 buy *b.* have nothing to *e.*
7:2 discip. *eat b.* with defiled, 5
*Luke* 14:1 to Phar.'s house to *e. b.*
15 he shall *e. b.* in kingdom
*John* 6:5 whence shall we buy *b.*
23 place where they did *eat b.*
31 gave them *b.* from hea. to *e.*
51 if any *e.* of this *b.* he shall l.
1 *Cor.* 11:26 often as ye *e.* this *b.*
27 whosoever shall *eat* this *b.*
2 *Thes.* 3:8 we eat *b.* for naught?
12 with quietness they *eat b.*

**Leavened BREAD.**
*Ex.* 13:3 shall no *l. b.* eaten
7 no *leav. b.* *Deut.* 16:3, 4
*Lev.* 7:13 he shall offer *leavened b.*

**Loaf, *or* Loaves of BREAD.**
*Jud.* 8:5 give *l. of b.* to people
1 *Sam.* 10:3 ano. car three *l. of b.*
4 will give thee two *l. of b.*
21:3 five *l. of b.* in my hand
*Chr.* 16:3 to every one *l. of b.*

**No BREAD.**
*Gen.* 47:13 *no b.* in all the land
*Num.* 21:5 *no b.* and our soul
1 *Sam.* 21:4 there is *no* com. *b.*
6 *no b.* there but showbread
28:20 S. had eaten *no b.* all day
30:12 Egyp. had eat *no b.* 3 days
1 *K.* 13:9 eat *no b.* 17:22
2 *K.* 25:3 *no b.* for peo. *Jer.* 52:6
*Jer.* 38:9 there is *no* more *b.*
*Dan.* 10:3 I ate *no* pleasant *b.*
*Mat.* 16:7 because we have taken *no b.* 8; *Mark* 8:16, 17
*Mark* 6:8 take no scrip, *no b.*

**Piece, *or* Pieces of BREAD.**
1 *Sam.* 2:36 I may eat a *p. of b.*
*Prov.* 6:26 to a *piece of b.*
28:21 for a *p. of b.* that man
*Jer.* 37:21 Jerem. daily a *p. of b.*
*Ezek.* 13:19 ye pollute me for *p. b*
SHOWBREAD. *See* SHOW.

**Staff of BREAD.**
*Lev.* 26:26 I have broken *st. b.*
*Ps.* 105:16 he brake whole *st. of b.*
*Ezek.* 4:16 break *st. b.* 5:16; 14:13

**Unleavened BREAD.**
*Ex.* 12:18 eat w. *u. b.* *Num.* 9:11
15 sev. days eat *unl. b.* 13:6, 7; 23:15; 34:18; *Lev.* 23:6; *Num.* 28:17; *Deut.* 16:3
*Deut.* 16:8 six days sh. eat *un. b.*
1 *Sam.* 28:24 witch of E. b. *u. b.*
*Ezek.* 45:21 passover of *un. b.*
*Mark* 14:12 first day of *un. b.*
*Luke* 22:7 day of *u. b.* *Acts* 12:3
*Acts* 20:6 after days of *u. b.*
1 *Cor.* 5:8 with *u. b.* of sincerity
*See* BASKET, FEAST.

**BREADTH.**
*Gen.* 13:7 through land in *b.* of it
*Deut.* 2:5 so much as a foot *b.*
*Jud.* 20:16 could sling at a h. *b.*
*Job* 37:10 *b.* of waters is strait.
38:18 perceived *b.* of the earth?
*Is.* 8:8 his wings shall fill the *b.*
*Hab.* 1:6 march through *b.* of la.
*Zec.* 2:2 measure J. to see the *b.*
5:2 I see a flying roll, the *b.*
*Eph.* 3:18 the *b.* and length
*Rev.* 20:9 up on *b.* of the earth
21:16 length of city is as the *b.*

**BREAK, Substantive.**
2 *Sam.* 2:32 J. came at *b.* of day
*Acts* 20:11 talked till *b.* of day

**BREAK.**
*Gen.* 27:40 *b.* his yoke off thy n.
*Ex.* 12:46 *b.* a bone, *Num.* 9:12
34:13 ye shall *b.* their images
*Lev.* 26:19 I will *b.* pride
*Num.* 24:8 Is. shall *b.* their bones
30:2 if a man vow, not *b.* word
*Deut.* 12:3 shall *b.* their pillars
1 *Sam.* 25:10 *b.* eve. man from m.
*Ezr.* 9:14 should we again *b.*
*Job* 13:25 wilt *b.* a leaf driven
39:15 t. wild beast may *b.* them
*Ps.* 2:3 let us *b.* their bands
9 *b.* them with rod of iron
10:15 *b.* the arm of the wicked
58:6 *b.* their teeth, O God
89:31 if they *b.* my statutes
141:5 which shall not *b.* my head
*Cant.* 2:17 until day *b.* 4:6
*Is.* 14:25 I will *b.* the Assyrian
28:24 *b.* the clods; 28 nor *b.* it
30:14 *b.* it as of the potters' ves.
38:13 as a lion so will he *b.* all
42:3 reed not *b.* *Mat.* 12:20
58:6 that ye *b.* every yoke?
*Jer.* 15:12 iron *b.* the north. iron
19:10 *b.* bottle, so will I *b.* 11
28:4 *b.* yoke 11; 30:8
49:35 I will *b.* the bow of Elam
*Ezek.* 4:16 I will *b.* the staff of bread, 5:16; 14:13
16:38 as a woman that *b.* wed.
23:34 shalt *b.* the sherds
29:7 hold of thee thou didst *b.*
30:18 when I *b.* yokes of Egypt
22 will *b.* Pharaoh's arms, 24
*Hos.* 1:5 will *b.* the bow of Israel
2:18 I will *b.* the bow
10:11 Jacob shall *b.* his clods
*Joel* 2:7 and not *b.* their ranks
*Amos* 1:5 *b.* the bar of Damascus
*Mic.* 3:3 who *b.* their bones
*Nah.* 1:13 will I *b.* his yoke off
*Zec.* 11:14 *b.* the brotherhood
*Mat.* 5:19 *b.* one of least com.
9:17 the bottles *b.* and the wine
*Acts* 20:7 came tog. to *b.* bread
21:13 mean ye to *b.* my heart?
1 *Cor.* 10:16 bread we *b.* is it not

**BREAK covenant.**
*Lev.* 26:44 I will not *b.* my *cov.*
*Deut.* 31:16 will *b.* my *c.* 20
*Jud.* 2:1 I will never *b.* my *c.*
*Ps.* 89:34 my *cov.* will I not *b.*
*Jer.* 14:21 *b.* not thy *cov.* with us
33:20 if ye can *b.* my *c.*
*Ezek.* 17:15 *b. cov.* and be deliv.
*Zec.* 11:10 I might *b.* my *cov.*

**BREAK down.**
*Ex.* 23:24 quite *b. d.* *Deut.* 7:5
*Jud.* 8:9 I will *b. down* tower
*Neh.* 4:3 shall *b. d.* stone wall
*Ps.* 74:6 *b. down* carved work
*Ec.* 3:3 a time to *b. d.*
*Is.* 5:5 I will *b. d.* wall of vine.
*Jer.* 31:28 over them to *b. d.*
45:4 I have built will I *b. down*
*Ezek.* 13:14 so will I *b. down* w.
26:4 shall *b. down* towers of T.
*Hos.* 10:2 he shall *b. d.* their al.

**BREAK forth.**
*Ex.* 19:22 L. *b. f.* on them, 24
*Is.* 14:7 they *b. forth* into singing, 44:23; 49:13; 54:1
52:9 *b. f.* into joy ye w. places
54:3 shalt *b. f.* on the right hand
55:12 hills shall *b. f.* into sing.
58:8 light *b. f.* as the morning
*Jer.* 1:14 an evil shall *b. forth*
*Gal.* 4:27 *b. forth* that trav. not

**BREAK off.**
*Gen.* 27:40 *b.* his y. *off* the neck
*Dan.* 4:27 O king, *b. off* thy sins

**BREAK out.**
Ps. 58:6 b. out the great teeth
Is. 35:6 shall waters b. out
Hos. 4:2 they b. out and blood, 4
Amos 5:6 lest he b. out like fire

**BREAK in pieces.**
Job. 19:2 b. me in pieces
34:24 b. in pieces mighty men
Ps. 72:4 he shall b. in p. the op.
94:5 they b. in p. thy people
Is. 45:2 I will b. in p. gates of b.
Jer. 51:20 will I b. in p. nations
21 with thee b. in p. horse a. r.
22 b. in p. man, woman
Dan. 2:40 shall it b. in pieces and bruise kingdoms, 44
7:23 shall b. in p. whole earth

**BREAK through.**
Ex. 19:21 b. th. to gaze, 24
2 K. 3:26 b. th. to king of Edom
Mat. 6:19 th. b. th.; 20 b. not th.

**BREAK up.**
Jer. 4:3 b. u. yo. f.-gr. Hos. 10:12

**BREAKER, S.**
Mic. 2:13 b. is come up before
Rom. 1:31 covenant-breakers
2:25 if thou be a b. of the law

**BREAKEST, ETH.**
Gen. 32:26 let me go, for day b.
Job 9:17 he b. me with tempest
12:14 he b. it cannot be built
16:14 he b. me with breach
28:4 flood b. out from inhabit.
Ps. 29:5 b. the ced.; 46:9 b. bow
48:7 thou b. ships of Tarshish
119:20 my soul b. for longing
Prov. 25:15 a soft tongue b. the
Ec. 10:8 b. a hedge, a serpent
Is. 59:5 crushed b. into a viper
Jer. 19:11 as one b. potter's ves.
23:29 a hammer that b. rock?
Lam. 4:4 ask bread, no man b.
Dan. 2:40 for as much as iron b.

**BREAKING.**
Gen. 32:24 wrestled till b. of day
1 Chr. 14:11 like b. forth of wa.
Job 30:14 as a wide b. in of wat.
41:25 by reason of b. they purify
Ps. 144:14 that there be no b. in
Is. 22:5 b. down walls, of crying
30:13 whose b. cometh suddenly
14 as b. of the potter's vessel
Ezek. 16:59 oath in b. cov. 17:18
21:6 with the b. of thy loins
Hos. 13:13 place of b. forth
Luke 24:35 known in b. of bread
Acts 2:42 continued in b. of bre.
46 b. bread from house to h.
Rom. 2:23 through b. law.

**BREAST.**
Job 24:9 pluck fatherless from b.
Is. 60:16 shall suck b. of kings
Lam. 4:3 monsters draw out b.
Dan. 2:32 head of gold, his b.
Luke 18:13 publican smote his b.
John 13:25 lying on J.'s b. 21:20

**BREASTS.**
Gen. 49:25 with blessings of b.
Job 3:12 b. that I should suck
21:24 his b. full of milk
Ps. 22:9 when on mother's b.
Prov. 5:19 let her b. satisfy thee
Cant. 1:13 all night bet. my b.
4:5 thy two b. like roes, 7:3
7:7 b. like clusters of grapes
8 thy b. as clusters of the vine
8:1 sucked the b. of my mother
8 little sister, she hath no b.
10 and my b. like towers
Is. 28:9 weaned from m. from b.
66:11 with b. of her consolations
Ezek. 16:7 thy b. are fashioned
23:3 there were their b. pressed
8 bruised the b. of her virgin.
34 shalt pluck off thine own b.
Hos. 2:2 adulterers from b. her b.
9:14 give them dry b.
Joel 2:16 gather those suck the b.
Nah. 2:7 doves taber. on their b.
Luke 23:48 people smote their b.
Rev. 15:6 having their b. girded

**BREASTPLATE.**
Ex. 25:7 sto. to be set in b. 35:9
28:4 shall make a b. 15; 39:8
29 the names of Israel in b.
30 put in b. the Urim, Lev. 8:8
Is. 59:17 he put on right. as a b.
Eph. 6:14 the b. of righteousness
1 Thes. 5:8 the b. of faith and lo.
Rev. 9:9 b. as it were b. of iron.
17 having b. of fire, of jacinth

**BREATH.**
Gen. 2:7 into his nostrils b. of l.
6:17 to destroy all flesh whose b.
7:15 wherein is b.
22 all in whose nostrils was b.
2 Sam. 22:16 found. discov. at b. of his nostrils, Ps. 18:15
1 K. 17:17 no b. left in him
Job 4:9 by b. of his nostrils
9:18 not suffer me to take my b.
12:10 in whose hand is b. of all
15:30 b. of his mouth go away
17:1 my b. is corrupt, my days
19:17 b. is strange to my wife
27:3 while my b. is in me
33:4 the b. of Alm. hath given
34:14 gather his spirit and b.
37:10 by b. of God frost is given
41:21 his b. kindleth coals
Ps. 33:6 made by the b. of his
104:29 takest away b. they die
135:17 any b. in their mouths
146:4 his b. goeth forth
150:6 that hath b. praise the L.
Ec. 3:19 they have all one b
Is. 2:22 b. in his nostrils
11:4 with b. of lips slay wicked
30:8 his b. as overflowing str.
33 b. of L. like stream of brim.
33:11 your b. as fire shall devour
42:5 giveth b. to people upon it
Jer. 10:14 no b. in them, 51:17
Lam. 4:20 the b. of our nostrils
Ezek. 37:5 b. to enter you
6 with skin, and put b. in you
8 no b. in them; 9 come, O b.
10 the b. came they lived
Dan. 5:23 in whose hand thy b.
10:17 neither is b. left in me
Hab. 2:19 b. in midst of image
Acts 17:25 giv. to all life and b.

**BREATHE.**
Jos. 11:11 not any left to b. 14
Ps. 27:12 such as b. out cruelty
Ezek. 37:9 O breath, b. on these

**BREATHED.**
Gen. 2:7 b. into nostrils b. of life
Jos. 10:40 destroyed all that b.
John 20:22 b. on them.

**BREATHETH, ING.**
Deut. 20:16 save alive n. that b.
Lam. 3:56 hide not ear at my b.
Acts 9:1 Saul yet b. threatenings

**BRED.**
Ex. 16:20 and it b. worms

**BREECHES.**
Ex. 28:42 make linen b. 39:28
Ezek. 44:18 shall have linen b.

**BREED.**
Deut. 32:14 rams of b. of Bashan

**BREED, ING.**
Gen. 8:17 may b. abundantly
Zep. 2:9 as Sodom b. of nettles

**BRETHREN.**
Gen. 13:8 no strife, for we be b.
19:7 Lot said, b. do not so wick.
24:27 Lord led me to master's b.
34:25 D.'s b. took each his sword
42:6 b. bowed; 13 twelve b. 32
45:16 b. are c.; 49:5 b. of cruel.
Num. 27:7 posses. am. father's b.
10 no b. give it to his fath.'s b.
Deut. 25:5 if b. dwell together
Jos. 6:23 brought out Rahab b.
17:4 inheritance among the b.
Jud. 9:1 A. went to mother's b.
2 K. 10:13 we are b. of Ahaziah
2 Chr. 21:2 had b. sons of Jehos.
Ps. 133:1 b. to dwell in unity
Prov. 6:19 soweth discord am. b.
17:2 shall have part among b.
19:7 b. of the poor to hate
Mat. 4:18 Jesus saw two b. 21
19:29 hath forsaken houses, b.
24:24 indignation ag'st two b.
22:25 seven b. Mark 12:20
23:8 one is Master, ye are b.
Mark 10:29 no man hath left b. for my sake, Luke 18:29
30 shall receive houses, b.
Luke 14:26 hate not children b.
16:28 for I have five b.
21:16 ye shall be betrayed by b.
John 21:23 went among the b.

Acts 3:17 b. I wot through ignor.
6:3 b. look out seven men
7:26 sirs, ye are b.; 9:30 b. knew
10:23 b. from Joppa accom. him
11:12 six b. accompanied me
29 to send relief to the b.
12:17 show these things to t. b.
14:2 evil affected against the b.
15:1 men from Judea taught b.
3 caused great joy to all the b.
22 and Silas chief among the b.
23 and b. send greeting to the b. of the Gentiles in Antioch
32 exhorted the b. 1 Thes. 5:14
33 let go in peace from b.
Acts 15:40 re. by b. to grace of G.
16:2 Tim. well reported of by b.
40 had seen b. they comfort.
17:6 drew Jason and certain b.
10 b. im. sent away Paul, 14
18:18 Paul took leave of the b.
27 b. wrote to receive Apollos
20:32 b. I commend you to God
21:7 Ptolemais, saluted the b.
16 to Jerus. b received us
22:5 I received letters to the b.
23:5 I wist not, b. he was h.-pri.
28:14 where we found b.
15 b. heard of us
21 any of the b. spake harm

Rom. 1:13 not have you ignor. b. 11:25; 1 Cor. 10:1; 12:1; 1 Thes. 4:13
7:1 know ye not, b. law hath
8:12 b. we are debtors
29 first-born among many b.
10:1 b. my prayer to God for Is.
12:1 b. by the mercies of God, 15:30; 16:17; 1 Cor. 1:10; 16:15; Gal. 4:12; Heb. 13:22

1 Cor. 1:26 see your calling, b.
2:1 I, b. when I came to you
3:1 I, b. could not speak to you
4:6 these things, b.
7:29 b. the time is short, 15:50
8:12 ye sin so against the b.
9:5 b. of the Lord and Cephas
11:2 b. that ye remember me
14:26 b. when ye come together
15:6 he was seen of above 500 b.
58 b. be steadfast, Jam. 2:5
16:11 I look for him with b.
20 the b. greet you, Phil. 4:21
2 Cor. 9:3 I sent b. lest our boast.
5 necessary to exhort the b.
11:9 b. from Macedonia supplied
26 been in perils among false b.
13:11 finally, b. farewell

*Gal.* 1:2 *b.* with me to churches
2:4 because of false *b.* brought
*Eph.* 6:23 peace be to the *b.* and
*Phil.* 1:14 *b.* waxing confident
*Col.* 1:2 to faithful *b.* in Christ
1 *Thes.* 4:1 we beseech you *b.* 10; 5:12; 2 *Thes.* 2:1
10 to all *b.* in Macedonia
5:15 *b.* pray for us, 2 *Thes.* 3:1
26 greet *b.* with a holy kiss
27 this epistle be read to *b.*
1 *Tim.* 4:6 put the *b.* in remem.
5:1 entreat younger men as *b.*
6:2 because they are *b.*
*Heb.* 2:11 not ash. to call them *b.*
3:1 holy *b.* consider the apostle
1 *Pet.* 1:22 unfeigned love of *b.*
3:8 love as *b.* be pitiful
1 *John* 3:14 because we love *b.*
16 to lay down our lives for *b.*
3 *John* 3 rej. when *b.* tes. of tru.
5 whatso. thou doest to the *b.*
10 neit. doth he receive the *b.*

**His BRETHREN.**

*Gen.* 9:25 servant of serv. to *h. b.*
16:12 he shall dwell in presence of *his b.* 25:18
27:37 *his b.* to him for servants
37:5 a dream and told it to *his b.*
11 *his b.* envied him, his father
38:11 lest he die also as *his b.*
47:12 Joseph nourished *his b.*
49:26 sep. from *b.* *Deut.* 33:16
*Ex.* 2:11 smiting one of *his b.*
*Num.* 25:6 to *h. b.* a Midian. w.
27:9 give his inheritance to *h. b.*
*Deut.* 10:9 L. no part with *his b.*
17:20 not lifted above *his b.*
20:8 lest *his b.* heart faint as
24:7 stealing any of *his b.*
33:9 nor did he acknow. *his b.*
24 let A. be acceptable to *his b.*
*Jud.* 9:5 Abimelech slew *his b.*
11:3 Jephthah fled from *his b.*
*Ruth* 4:10 not cut off from *b.*
1 *Sam.* 16:13 anointed in m. of
22:1 *his b.* and father heard it
2 *K.* 9:2 rise up from among *h. b.*
1 *Chr.* 4:9 J. more hon. than *h. b.*
5:2 Judah prevailed above *his b.*
7:22 Ephraim mourned *his b.*
25:9 *his b.* and sons twelve
2 *Chr.* 21:4 Jehor. slew all *his b.*
*Est.* 10:3 Mord. accepted of *his b.*
*Hos.* 13:15 fruitful among *his b.*
*Mic.* 5:3 rem. of *h. b.* return to I.
*Mat.* 12:46 *his b.* stood without, *Mark* 3:31; *Luke* 8:19
*John* 7:5 *his b.* believe in him
*Acts* 7:13 was made known to *h. b.*
23 into M.'s heart to visit *h. b.*
25 supposed *his b.* understood
1 *Cor.* 6:5 judge between *his b.*
*Heb.* 2:17 beh. to be like to *his b.*

**Men and BRETHREN.**

*Acts* 1:16 *m. b.* this scripture
2:29 *m. b.* let me fr. speak
37 *m. and b.* what shall we do?
7:2 *m. b.* and fathers, hearken
13:15 *m. and b.* if ye have any
26 *m. b.* children of stock of A.
38 *m. and b.* through this man
15:7 *m. and b.* God made choice
13 James answered, *m. and b.*
22:1 *m. and b.* and fathers
23:1 *m. b.* I have lived in all g.
6 *men and b.* I am a Pharisee
28:17 *m. and b.* though I have committed nothing

**My BRETHREN.**

*Gen.* 29:4 *my b.* whence be ye?
37:16 I seek *my b.* tell me
46:31 *my b.* are come, 47:1
*Ex.* 4:18 let me return to *my b.*
*Jos.* 2:13 will save alive *my b.*
*Jud.* 8:19 they were *my b.*
19:23 *my b.* do not so wickedly
1 *Sam.* 20:29 let me see *my b.*
30:23 ye shall not do so, *my b.*
2 *Sam.* 19:12 ye are *my b.*
1 *Chr.* 28:2 Hear me, *my b.*
*Neh.* 4:23 *my b.* put off clothes
*Job* 6:15 *my b.* have dealt deceit.
19:13 put *my b.* far from me
*Ps.* 22:22 to *my b.* *Heb.* 2:12
69:8 I am a stranger to *my b.*
122:8 for *my b.* sake, I will say
*Mat.* 12:48 are *my b.* *Mark* 3:33
49 m. and *my b.* *Mark* 3:34
25:40 to least of these *my b.*
28:10 tell *my b.* go into Galilee
*Luke* 8:21 *my b.* are which hear
*John* 20:17 *my b.* and say
*Rom.* 9:3 ac. from C. for *my b.*
*Jam.* 5:10 take *my b.* the prop.

**Our BRETHREN.**

*Num.* 20:3 when *our b.* died
1 *Chr.* 13:2 let us send to *our b.*
*Neh.* 5:5 as flesh of *our b.*
8 have redeemed *our b.* the J.
*Acts* 15:36 *our b.* in every city
2 *Cor.* 8:23 *our b.* be inquired of
*Rev.* 10:12 accuser of *our b.*

**Their BRETHREN.**

*Deut.* 18:18 a prophet from *th. b.*
*Jud.* 21:22 *th. b.* come to comp.
2 *Sam.* 2:26 from following *th. b.*
1 *Chr.* 12:32 *th. b.* at their com.
2 *Chr.* 28:15 brought them to *th. b.*
*Neh.* 13:13 to distribute to *th. b.*
*Job* 42:15 inheritance am. *th. b.*
*Jer.* 41:8 sl. them not am. *th. b.*
*Heb.* 7:5 people that is of *their b.*
*Rev.* 6:11 *th. b.* should be killed

**Thy BRETHREN.**

*Gen.* 27:29 be lord over *thy b.*
37:10 I and *thy b.* come to bow
13 do not *thy b.* feed the flock?
14 whet. it be well with *thy b.*
48:22 one portion above *thy b.*
49:8 whom *thy b.* shall praise
*Deut.* 15:7 a poor man of *thy b.*
17:15 from among *t. b.* set king
18:15 raise up a proph. of *thy b.*
24:14 not oppress poor of *thy b.*
*Jos.* 2:18 bring *thy b.* home
1 *Sam.* 17:17 to camp to *thy b.*
2 *Sam.* 15:20 take back *thy b.*
2 *Chr.* 21:13 hast slain *thy b.* better than thyself
*Jer.* 12:6 *thy b.* have dealt treac.
*Ezek.* 11:15 *thy b.* even *thy b.*
*Mat.* 12:47 mother and *thy b.* st. with. *Mark* 3:32; *Luke* 8:20
*Luke* 14:12 call not *thy b.*
22:32 strengthen *thy b.*
*Rev.* 19:10 I am of *thy b.* 22:9

**Your BRETHREN.**

*Gen.* 42:33 leave one of *your b.*
*Lev.* 10:4 carry *y. b.* from sanct.
6 let *your b.* bewail the burn.
25:46 *your b.* ye shall not rule
*Num.* 32:6 *your b.* go to war
*Deut.* 1:16 causes between *y. b.*
3:20 rest to *your b.* *Jos.* 1:15
*Jos.* 22:4 given rest to *your b.*
8 divide the spoil with *your b.*
1 *K.* 12:24 not fl. *y. b.* 2 *Chr.* 11:4
2 *Chr.* 19:10 *your b.* and so wrath come upon you and *your b.*
28:11 deliver captives of *your b.*
30:7 be not like *y. b.* which tres.
9 if ye turn, *y. b.* shall find
*Neh.* 4:14 fight for *your b.* sons
5:8 will you even sell *your b.*
*Is.* 66:5 *your b.* that hated you
20 *your b.* for an offering to L.
*Jer.* 7:15 have cast out all *y. b.*
*Hos.* 2:1 say to *your b.* Ammi
*Mat.* 5:47 if ye salute *your b.*
*Acts* 3:22 proph. of *your b.* 7:37
1 *Cor.* 6:8 defraud that *your b.*
1 *Pet.* 5:9 same afflic. in *your b.*

**BRIBE, S.**

1 *Sam.* 8:3 Samuel's sons took *b.*
12:3 hand have I received any *b.*
*Ps.* 26:10 right hand full of *b.*
*Is.* 33:15 hands from holding *b.*
*Amos* 5:12 they take a *b.* and

**BRIBERY.**

*Job* 15:34 consume taber. of *b.*

**BRICK, S.**

*Gen.* 11:3 make *b.* had *b.* for st
*Ex.* 1:14 their lives bitter in *b.*
5:7 give straw to make *b.* 16
8 tale of *b.* lay on them
18 yet deliver the tale of *b.* 19
*Is.* 9:10 the *b.* are fallen down
65:3 incense on altars of *b.*

**BRICKKILN.**

2 *Sam.* 12:31 make pass thro' *b.*
*Jer.* 43:9 hide stones in clay in *b.*
*Nah.* 3:14 make strong the *b.*

**BRIDE.**

*Is.* 49:18 bind them, as a *b.* doth
61:10 as a *b.* adorn. with jewels
62:5 bridegroom rejoic. over *b.*
*Jer.* 2:32 can a *b.* forget?
7:34 voice of the *b.* 16:9; 25:10
33:11 shall be heard voice of *b.*
*Joel* 2:16 *b.* go out of her closet
*John* 3:29 he that hath the *b.* is
*Rev.* 18:23 voice of *b.* heard
21:2 *b.* adorned for her husband
9 show the *b.* the Lamb's wife
22:17 Sp. and the *b.* say, Come

**BRIDECHAMBER.**

*Mat.* 9:15 can children *b.* mourn
*Mark* 2:19 child. of *b.* f. *Luke* 5:34

**BRIDEGROOM.**

*Ps.* 19:5 as a *b.* coming out
*Is.* 61:10 as a *b.* decketh himself
62:5 as *b.* rejoiceth over bride
*Mat.* 9:15 while the *b.* is with them, *Mark* 2:19; *Luke* 5:34
25:1 ten virgins to meet the *b.*
5 *b.* tarried; 6 *b.* cometh, 10
*John* 2:9 governor called the *b.*
3:29 friend of the *b.* rejoiceth greatly because of the *b.* voi.

*See* BRIDE.

**BRIDLE.**

2 *K.* 19:28 *b.* in thy lips, *Is.* 37:29
*Job* 30:11 have let loose the *b.*
41:13 to him with his double *b.*
*Ps.* 32:9 must be held with the *b.*
39:1 keep my mouth with a *b.*
*Prov.* 26:3 a *b.* for the ass
*Is.* 30:28 a *b.* in jaws of people
*Jam.* 1:26 and *b.* not his tongue
3:2 able also to *b.* whole body
*Rev.* 14:20 blood to the horse *b.*

**BRIEFLY.**

*Rom.* 13:9 it is *b.* comprehended
1 *Pet.* 5:12 by Sylv. I have writ. *b.*

**BRIER.**

*Is.* 55:13 instead of the *b.*
*Ezek.* 28:24 no more a pricking *b.*
*Mic.* 7:4 best of them is as a *b.*

**BRIERS.**

*Jud.* 8:7 tear your flesh with *b.*
16 he took the elders and *b.*
*Is.* 5:6 there shall come up *b.*
7:23 shall even be for *b.* and
24 shall become *b.* and thorns
25 come thither the fear of *b.*
9:18 wicked. shall devour the *b.*
10:17 devour his *b.* in one day
27:4 set *b.* against me in battle?
32:13 on land shall come up *b.*
*Ezek.* 2:6 though *b.* be with thee
*Heb.* 6:8 which beareth *b.* is rej.

**BRIGANDINE.**

*Jer.* 46:4 and put on the *b.*
51:3 lifteth up himself in his *b.*

**BRIGHT.**

*Job* 37:11 scattereth his *b.* cloud
21 see not *b.* light in the clouds

Cant. 5:14 his belly is as b. ivory
Jer. 51:11 make b. the arrows
Ezek. 1:13 fire was b. and out
21:15 the sword is made b.
21 made his arrows b.
27:19 b. iron in thy market
32:8 b. lights I will make dark
Nah. 3:3 lifteth up the b. sword
Zec. 10:1 shall make b. clouds
Mat. 17:5 a b. cloud overshad.
Luke 11:36 b. shining of a candle
Acts 10:30 stood in b. clothing
Rev. 22:16 b. and morning star

**BRIGHTNESS.**

2 Sam. 22:13 thro' b. before him were coals kindled, Ps. 18:12
Job 31:26 moon walking in b.
Is. 59:9 we wait for b. but walk
60:3 kings to the b. of thy rising
19 for b. the moon give light
62:1 righteousness go forth as b.
Ezek. 1:4 and b. was about it, 27
28 so appearance of the b. 8:2
10:4 court full of the b. of glory
28:7 strangers shall defile thy b.
17 hast corrupted by thy b.
Dan. 2:31 image, b. was excell.
4:36 my b. returned unto me
12:3 shine as b. of firmament
Amos 5:20 day of L. no b. in it
Hab. 3:4 his b. was as the light
Acts 26:13 above b. of the sun
2 Thes. 2:8 the b. of his coming
Heb. 1:3 being the b. of his glory

**BRIM.**

Jos. 3:15 dipped in b. of water
John 2:7 filled them to the b.

**BRIMSTONE.**

Gen. 19:24 on G. b. Luke 17:29
Deut. 29:23 the whole land is b.
Job 18:15 b. scattered on his hab.
Ps. 11:6 on the wicked snares, fire and b. Ezek. 38:22
Is. 30:33 like a stream of b.
34:9 dust thereof into b.
Rev. 9:17 out of their mouths b.
18 third part killed by the b.
14:10 shall be tormented with b.
19:20 burning with b. 20:10
21:8 part in the lake which burneth with fire and b.

**BRING.**

Gen. 6:17 b. a flood on the earth
19 two of every sort b. into ark
9:14 I b. a cloud over earth
18:16 Abra. did b. on their way
19 b. on A. what he hath spo.
27:12 I shall b. a curse on me
42:20 b. youngest brother, 34
37 if I b. him not, 43:9; 44:32
43:16 b. these men home
45:19 take wag. and b. your fa.
48:9 b. them, and I will bless
Ex. 13:5 L. shall b. thee, 11
18:19 mayest b. the causes to G.
21:6 master b. him to judges
23:19 first of first-fruits b. 34:26
23:20 send an angel to b. thee
35:5 a willing heart, let him b.
36:5 people b. more than enough
Num. 14:8 if L. del. in us, will b.
14:16 able to b. Deut. 9:28
24 Caleb will I b. into the land
20:12 ye shall not b. this cong.
Deut. 1:17 cause too hard, b.
7:1 Lord shall b. thee into land
21:12 shalt b. her to thy house
30:12 b. it to us that we may, 13
33:7 b. Judah to his people
1 Sam. 1:22 weaned, I will b. him
9:7 said Saul, what b. the man?
23 b. the portion I gave thee
20:8 why b. thee to thy father
2 Sam. 3:12 to b. all Israel to thee
13 except thou b. Michal when
14:10 saith aught, b. him to me
19:11 last to b. the king back
1 K. 8:32 b. his way on his head
13:18 b. him back to thy house
17:11 b. me a morsel of bread
20:33 he said, Go ye, b. him
2 K. 2:20 b. me a new cruse
6:19 b. you to whom ye seek
2 Chr. 16:29 b. an offering
Neh. 13:18 our God b. this evil
Job 6:22 did I say, b. unto me
10:9 wilt thou b. me into dust
14:4 who can b. a clean thing
18:14 b. him to king of terrors
30:23 thou wilt b. me to death
33:30 b. back his soul from pit
Ps. 43:3 b. me to thy holy hill
60:9 b. me into a str. city, 108:10
72:3 shall b. peace to people
94:23 b. on them their own
Prov. 29:8 scornful b. a city
Ec. 3:22 shall b. him to see
11:9 God will b. thee into judg.
12:14 b. every work into judg.
Cant. 8:2 b. thee into my m.
Is. 7:17 Lord shall b. on thee
14:2 b. them to their place
15:9 for I will b. more upon D.
25:12 shall b. to the ground
45:21 tell ye and b. them near
46:13 I b. near my righteousn.
56:7 will I b. to my holy moun.
58:7 b. the poor to thy house
60:17 for brass b. gold, for iron b.
66:4 b. their fears upon them
Jer. 3:14 I will b. you to Zion
10:24 lest thou b. me to nothing
Jer. 11:8 I will b. words of this
17:18 b. on them day of evil
31:8 b. them from the north
32:42 b. on them all the good
33:6 I will b. it health and cure
11 shall b. sacrifice of praise
49:5 I will b. a fear upon them
Ezek. 6:3 b. a sword upon you
11:9 b. you out of the midst
20:15 I would not b. them
21:29 will b. on necks of them
23:22 b. them against thee on
34:13 b. to own, 36:24; 37:21
38:17 b. thee against them
Hos. 2:14 and b. her to wildern.
Amos 4:1 b. and let us drink, 4
Mic. 1:15 will I b. an heir to thee
Zec. 8:8 I will b. them, and they
Mat. 2:13 be there till I b. word
5:23 b. thy gift to the altar
17:17 b. him to me, Mark 9:19
21:2 b. them to me, Mark 11:2; Luke 19:30
Mark 7:32 b. to him one deaf
Luke 2:10 I b. good tidings
8:14 b. no fruit to perfection
12:11 b. you into the synagog.
John 10:16 other sheep I must b.
14:26 b. all things to rememb.
18:29 what accusation b. you?
Acts 5:28 to b. this man's blood
7:6 should b. them into bondage
9:2 he might b. them bound, 21
22:5 I went to b. them bound
23:10 to b. Paul into the castle
17 b. this young man to capt.
1 Cor. 1:19 I will b. to nothing
28 to b. to naught
4:17 b. you into remembrance
9:27 body, I b. into subjection
16:6 may b. me on my journey
2 Cor. 11:20 if a man b. you
Gal. 3:24 schoolm. to b. us to C.
1 Thes. 4:14 sleep, will God b.
1 Pet. 3:18 he might b. us to G.
2 John 10 if any b. not this doc.
3 John 6 if thou b. on journey
Rev. 21:24 do b. their glory to it
26 b. the glory of nations into

See HOME, HITHER.

**BRING again.**

Gen. 24:6 b. not my son again, 8
28:15 b. thee a. into land, 48:21
42:37 I will b. him again
Ex. 23:4 b. it back to him again
Num. 22:8 I will b. word again
Deut. 1:22 b. us word again what
28:68 L. shall b. thee into E. a.
Jud. 11:9 if ye b. me home a.
19:3 her husb. went to b. her a.
2 Sam. 12:23 can I b. him again
14:21 b. the young man Ab. a.
15:8 if Lord b. me a. to Jerus.
25 b. me again and show me
1 K. 8:34 forg. and b. a. 2 Chr. 6:25
1 Chr. 13:3 let us b. a. the ark
21:12 what word I shall b. a.
2 Chr. 24:19 proph. to b. them a.
Neh. 9:29 mightest b. again
Ps. 68:22 b. again from B. I will b. my people from depths of
Prov. 19:24 as b. it to mouth a.
26:15 grieveth to b. it again
Is. 38:8 b. again shadow
46:8 b. it again to mind
49:5 saith Lord to b. Jac. again
52:8 Lord shall b. again Zion
Jer. 12:15 will b. them a. 50:19
15:19 will I b. thee again
16:15 b. a. to their l. 24:6; 32:37
23:3 b. again into their folds
28:4 I will b. again Jeconiah, 6
30:3 b. again the captivity, 18; 31:23; Ezek. 39.25; Amos 9:14
48:47 b. a. captivity of Moab
49:6 of Ammon; 39 of Elam
Ezek. 16:53 when I b. a. their
29:14 I will b. again captivity
34:16 will b. again that driven
Zep. 3:20 at that time b. you a.
Zec. 10:6 b. them again to place
10 I will b. them a. out of E.
Mat. 2:8 b. word a. that I may

See CAPTIVITY.

**BRING down.**

Gen. 42:38 b. d. gray h. 44:29, 31
43:7 say, b. brother down, 44:21
45:13 and b. down my father
Deut. 9:3 b. them down before
2 Sam. 22:28 on haughty to b. d.
1 K. 1:33 Solomon, b. d. to G.
2:9 his hoar head b. thou d.
Ps. 18:27 b. down high looks
55:23 shalt b. d. to pit of dest.
Is. 25:5 shalt b. d. the noise
11 he shall b. d. their pride
Is. 25:12 high fort shall he b. d.
63:6 b. d. their strength to earth
Jer. 49:16 b. thee d. from th. Ob. 4
51:40 will b. them d. like lambs
Ezek. 26:20 shall b. thee down
28:8 shall b. thee d. to the pit
Hos. 7:12 b. them d. as fowls
Joel 3:2 b. d. to valley of Jehosh.
Amos 3:11 he shall b. d. thy str.
9:2 climb to heaven, b. them d.
Ob. 3 Who shall b. me down
Acts 23:15 that he b. him down
20 thou wouldest b. down Paul
Rom. 10:6 to b. Christ down

See EVIL.

**BRING forth.**

Gen. 1:11 earth b. f. 24; 20 waters
3:16 in sor. shall b. f. children
18 th. and thist. sh. it b. f.
8:17 b. f. every living thing
9:7 b. f. abundantly in the earth
38:24 b. her f. let her be burnt
Ex. 3:10 may. b. f. my people Is.
11 who am I that sh. b. f. Is.
7:4 I may b. forth my armies
Lev. 26:10 b. f. old, bec. of new
Num. 20:8 b. f. w. out of the ro.
Jos. 2:3 b. f. men that are come
Jud. 6:18 I b. forth my present
19:22 b. f. man came to thy h.

2 K. 19:3 no str. to b. f. Is. 37:3
Job 14:9 b. f. boughs like a plant
15:35 conc. mischief, b. f. vanity
38:32 canst thou b. f. Mazzaroth
39:1 the wild goats b. f. 2, 3
40:20 mountains b. him f. food
Ps. 37:6 he shall b. f. thy right.
92:14 shall b. f. fruit in old age
104:14 b. f. food out of earth
144:13 our sheep may b. f.
Prov. 27:1 what a day may b. f.
Is. 5:2 should b. f. grapes, 4
3:4 I, nor b. f. children
33:11 conceive chaff, and b. f.
41:21 b. forth your strong reas.
42:1 he shall b. f. judg. to Gen.
3 he shall b. f. judgment
43:8 b. f. the blind
9 let them b. f. their witnesses
45:8 and let them b. f. salvation
55:10 water. maketh it b. forth
59:4 conceive mischief and b. f.
65:9 I will b. f. seed out of J.
23 nor b. forth for trouble
66:8 earth to b. f. in one day?
9 and not cause to b. f.?
Jer. 12:2 grow, yea b. f. fruit
51:44 I will b. f. what he swal.
Ezek. 12:4 shalt b. f. thy stuff.
17:23 it shall b. forth boughs
20:6 to b. them f. of land of E.
38 b. them f. out of country
47:12 it shall b. f. new fruit
Hos. 9:13 Eph. sh. b. f. his chil.
16 though they b. f. yet will I
Mic. 4:10 labor to b. f. O Zion
7:9 he will b. me f. to the light
Zep. 2:2 before decree b. f.
Zec. 3:8 b. f. my servant
4:7 b. f. headstone with shout.
5:4 b. f. a curse, it shall enter
Mat. 1:23 virg. sh. b. f. a son, 21
3:8 b. f. fruits meet, Luke 3:8
7:18 cannot b. f. evil, Luke 6:43
Mark 4:20 b. f. fruit
Luke 1:31 b. f. a son shalt call J.
8:15 having heard word, b. f.
15:22 b. f. best robe
John 15:2 it may b. f. more fruit
16 I ord. you, should b. f. fruit
19:4 I b. him f. that ye may
Acts 12:4 after Easter to b. him f.
Rom. 7:4 that we shall b. f. fruit
5 motions of sin to b. f.

**BRING in.**

Ex. 6:8 b. you into land
15:17 shalt b. in and plant them
23:23 my Angel shall b. thee in
Num. 14:31 lit. ones, will I b. in
Jer. 17:24 b. in no burden on sab.
Dan. 2:24 b. me in before the k.
9:24 to b. in everlasting right.
Hag. 1:6 s. much and b. in little
Luke 5:18 means to b. him in
14:21 b. in hither the poor
2 Pet. 2:1 b. in damnable here.

**BRING out.**

Gen. 40:14 b. me out of this ho.
50:24 G. will b. you out of this l.
Ex. 6:6 b. you out from under
13 b. chil. of Is. out of E. 26:27;
7:5; 12:51; Jer. 31:32
Deut. 22:21 b. o. d.; 24 b. both o.
Jos. 6:22 b. o. thence Rahab
Jud. 6:30 b. o. thy son
Ps. 25:17 O b. me o. of my dis.
Ps. 142:7 b. my soul o. of prison
143:11 b. my soul out of trou.
Is 42:7 to b. o. the prisoners
Ezek. 11:7 b. you out of midst
20:34 b. you o. from peo. 34:13
41 ac. you, when I b. you out
24:6 b. it out piece by piece
Acts 17:5 sought to b. them out

**BRING to pass.**

Gen. 41:32 God will b. it to p.
50:20 to b. t. p. as at this day
Ps. 37:5 he shall b. it t. p.
Is. 28:21 b. to p. his act
46:11 I will also b. it to p.

**BRING up.**

Gen. 46:4 I will b. thee up again
Ex. 3:17 I will b. you up out of
33:12 sayest, b. up this people
Num. 20:25 b. up Aaron to m. H.
Jud. 6:13 did not L. b. us up
1 Sam. 19:15 b. him up in the b.
28:11 he said, b. me up Samuel
2 Sam. 6:2 to b. up ark of G. 1 K.
8:1, 4; 1 Chr. 13:6; 15:3, 12,
14, 25; 2 Chr. 5:2, 5
1 Chr. 17:5 since I b. up Israel
Is. 23:4 nor b. up virgins
Jer. 27:22 then will I b. them up
Ezek. 16:40 b. up a company ag.
23:46 I will b. up a company
37:6 I will b. up flesh on you
Hos. 9:12 they b. up children
Rom. 10:7 to b. up C. from the d.
Eph. 6:4 b. them up in nurture

**BRINGERS.**

2 K. 10:5 b. up of chil. sent to J.

**BRINGEST.**

Job 14:3 b. me into judgment
Is. 40:9 O Jer. that b. good tid.
Acts 17:20 b. strange things

**BRINGETH.**

Ex. 6:7 b. you from under burd.
Lev. 11:45 L. that b. you out
Deut. 8:7 L. b. thee into a good
1 Sam. 2:6 he b. down to the gr.
7 Lord b. low, and lifteth up
2 Sam. 22:48 b. the people under
49 b. me forth from mine ene.
Job 12:6 into whose hand G. b.
22 b. to light shadow of death
19:29 wrath b. punis. of the sw.
28:11 thing hid b. he to light
Ps. 1:3 b. forth his fruit
14:7 when L. b. back cap. 53:6
33:10 b. coun. of hea. to naught
37:7 b. wicked devices to pass
68:6 b. out them that are bound
107:28 b. them out of their dist.
30 b. them to desired haven
135:7 b. wind, Jer. 10:3; 51:16
Prov. 10:31 mouth of just b. wis.
16:30 moving his lips, he b. evil
18:16 b. him before great men
19:26 son that b. reproach
20:26 king b. wheel over them
29:15 b. mother to shame
21 delicately b. up his servant
25 the fear of man b. a snare
31:14 she b. her food from afar
Is. 8:7 L. b. on them the waters
26:5 b. down them dwell on h.
40:23 b. the princes to nothing
26 b. out their host by number
43:17 b. forth chariot and horse
54:16 the smith that b. forth
61:11 the earth b. forth her bud
Jer. 4:31 b. forth her first child
Ezek. 29:16 b. iniquity to rem.
Hos. 10:1 Is. b. forth fruit to him.
Hag. 1:11 which ground b. forth
Mat. 3:10 every tree that b. not
forth g. fruit, 7:19; Luke 3:9
7:17 good tree b. forth g. fruit
12:35 a good man b. forth good,
evil b. evil things, Luke 6:45
13:23 b. forth some a h.-fold
52 b. out of treas. things new
17:1 Jesus b. them to high m.
Mark 4:28 the earth b. forth fr.
Luke 6:43 good tree b. not cor.
John 12:24 if it die it b. 15:5
Col. 1:6 gospel b. forth fruit
Tit. 2:11 grace of G. that b. sal.
Heb. 1:6 b. first-begot. into world
6:7 the earth b. forth herbs
Jam. 1:15 b. forth sin, and sin b.
See TIDINGS.

**BRINGING.**

Ex. 12:42 observed for b. them
36:6 were restrained from b.
Num. 14:36 by b. up a slander
2 Sam. 19:10 of b. the king, 43
2 K. 21:12 I am b. such evil
Ps. 126:6 rejoic. b. his sheaves
Ezek. 20:9 known in b. them
Dan. 9:12 b. upon us great evil
Mat. 21:43 a nation b. forth fruit
Rom. 7:23 b. me into captivity
2 Cor. 10:5 b. into capti. ev. tho.
Heb. 2:10 in b. many sons.
7:19 b. in of a better hope did
2 Pet. 2:5 b. in the flood on world

**BRINK.**

Ex. 2:3 laid the ark by river's b.
Jos. 3:8 when come to b. of J.
Ezek. 47:6 caused me return to b.

**BROAD.**

Neh. 3:8 they fortified Jerusalem
to the b. wall, 12:38
Job 36:16 out of strait into b. pl.
Ps. 119:96 thy com. is exceed. b.
Cant. 3:2 in b. ways I will seek
Is. 33:21 be a place of b. rivers
Jer. 5:1 seek in b. places thereof
51:58 b. walls of Babylon
Nah. 2:4 chariots justle in b. w.
Mat. 7:13 b. way to destruction
23:5 make b. their phylacteries

**BROADER.**

Job 11:9 meas. is b. than the sea

**BROIDERED.**

Ezek. 16:13 raim. was of b. work
18 b. garments and coveredst
27:7 with b. work to be thy sail
16 in thy fairs with b. work
24 thy merchants in b. work
1 Tim. 2:9 nor with b. hair

**BROILED.**

Luke 24:42 a piece of a b. fish

**BROKEN.**

Gen. 17:14 b. my cov. Ps. 55:20;
Is. 24:5; 33:8; Jer. 11:10
Lev. 21:19 m. b. footed, b. hand.
20 hath his stones b. not offer
22:22 b. ye shall not offer, 24
26:13 b. the hands of your yoke
26 when I have b. staff of bread
Jud. 5:22 the horse-hoofs b. by
1 Sam. 2:4 bows of mighty are b.
2 Sam. 22:35 b. of st. b. Ps. 18:34
1 Chr. 14:11 b. in upon mine ene.
2 Chr. 20:37 b. thy works, sh. b.
32:5 he built up all the wall b.
Job 4:10 teeth of y. lions are b.
7:5 skin is b. and loathsome
16:12 he hath b. me asunder
22:9 arms of fatherless been b.
24:20 wickedness shall be b.
31:22 arm be b. from the bone
38:15 the high arm shall be b.
Ps. 3:7 b. teeth of the ungodly
31:12 I am like a b. vessel
34:18 them of a b. heart, 51:17
20 not one of them is b.
37:15 their bows be b.; 17 arms
38:8 I am feeble and sore b.
44:19 b. us in place of dragons
51:8 bones thou hast b. may rej.
17 sacrifices of G. are a b. spi.
60:2 earth to tremble hast b.
69:20 repr. hath b. my heart
107:16 b. the gates of brass
109:16 slay the b. in heart
124:7 snare is b. we are escaped
147:3 he healeth the b. in heart
Prov. 6:15 suddenly sh. he be b.
15:13 by sor. of heart spirit is b.
17:22 b. spirit drieth the bones
25:19 is like a b. tooth
Ec. 4:12 threefold cord is not b.
12:6 or the golden bowl be b.
Is. 5:27 latchet of their shoes b.
7:8 shall Eph. be b.

8:15 among them shall be *b.*
9:4 *b.* the yoke of his burden
14:5 *b.* the staff of the wicked
29 rod of him smote thee is *b.*
19:10 shall be *b.* in purposes
21:9 all the images he hath *b.*
28:13 fall backward and be *b.*
33:8 *b.* the covenant
10 any of the cords be *b.*
36:6 trustest in staff of *b.* reed
*Jer.* 2:13 *b.* cisterns that hold no
16 *b.* the crown of thy head
20 of old I have *b.* thy yoke
5:5 these have *b.* the yoke and
10:20 all my cords are *b.*
11:16 the branches of it are *b.*
14:17 virgin of my people is *b.*
22:28 is this man C. a *b.* idol?
23:9 my heart is *b.*
28:2 *b.* yoke of king of Babylon
33:21 then may also my covenant be *b.* with David
48:17 how is the strong staff *b.*
38 I have *b.* Moab like a vessel
50:17 Nebuch. *b.* Israel's bones
23 hammer of whole earth *b.*
51:58 broad walls of B. sh. be *b.*
*Lam.* 2:9 he hath *b.* her bars
3:4 hath *b.* my bones; 16 teeth
*Ezek.* 6:9 *b.* with their wh. heart
17:19 covenant that he hath *b.*
19:12 her strong rods were *b.*
26:2 Aha, she is *b.*
27:26 east wind *b.* thee
34 shalt be *b.* by the seas
30:21 *b.* the arm of Pharaoh
22 break the strong and that *b.*
31:12 his boughs are *b.* by rivers
32:28 be *b.* in midst of uncir.
34:4 nor have ye bound up *b.*
16 and I will bind up that *b.*
27 *b.* the bands of their yoke
44:7 they have *b.* my covenant
*Dan.* 2:42 kingdom partly *b.*
8:8 the great horn was *b.* 22
25 he shall be *b.* without hand
11:4 his kingdom shall be *b.*
22 with arms of a flood be *b.*
*Hos.* 5:11 Eph. is *b.* in judgment
*Zec.* 11:11 it was *b.* in that day
16 shep. shall not heal that *b.*
*Mat.* 15:37 *b.* meat, *Mark* 8:8
21:44 fall on this stone, shall be *b. Luke* 20:18
*Luke* 12:39 suff. house to be *b.*
*John* 5:18 not only *b.* the Sab.
7:23 law of M. should not be *b.*
10:35 the scripture cannot be *b.*
19:31 their legs might be *b.*
36 bone of him shall not be *b.*
21:11 yet was not the net *b.*
*Acts* 20:11 *b.* bread and talked
27:35 had *b.* it, he began to eat
1 *Cor.* 11:24 my body *b.* for you
*Rev.* 2:27 as ves. shall they be *b.*

**BROKEN down.**

2 *K.* 11:6 that it be not *b. d.*
*Neh.* 2:13 I viewed the walls *b. d.*
*Ps.* 80:12 why *b. d.* her hedges?
89:40 has *b. d.* all his hedges
*Prov.* 24:31 wall was *b. down*
25:28 is like a city *b. down*
*Is.* 16:8 *b. d.* principal plants
22:10 houses *b. d.* to fortify wall
24:10 city of confusion is *b. d.*
19 is utterly *b. down.*
*Jer.* 4:26 cities *b. d.*; 48:20 M. 39
*Ezek.* 30:4 foundation sh. be *b. d.*
*Joel* 1:17 the barns are *b. d.*
*Eph.* 2:14 *b. d.* middle wall

**BROKEN forth.**

*Gen.* 38:29 how hast thou *b. forth*
2 *Sam.* 5:20 L. *b. f.* on mine ene.

**BROKEN in.**

1 *Chr.* 14:11 *b. in* on mine ene.

**BROKEN off.**

*Job* 17:11 my purposes are *b. off*
*Is.* 27:11 boughs withered *b. off*
*Rom.* 11:17 and if some be *b. off*
20 bec. of unbelief, *b. off*, 19

**BROKEN in, *or* to pieces.**

1 *Sam.* 2:10 adv. shall be *b. to p.*
2 *Chr.* 25:12 from rock, were *b.*
*Ps.* 89:10 thou has *b.* R. *in p.*
*Is.* 8:9 ye shall *b. in p.*
30:14 as a potter's ves. *b. in p.*
*Hos.* 8:6 calf of Sam. shall *b. p.*

**BROKEN up.**

*Gen.* 7:11 fount. of deep *b. up*
2 *K.* 25:4 J. *b. up*, *Jer.* 39:2; 52:7
2 *Chr.* 24:7 *b. up* house of God
*Prov.* 3:20 depths *b. up*
*Mat.* 24:43 house to be *b. up*
*Mark* 2:4 they had *b.* roof *up*
*Acts* 13:43 when cong. was *b. up*

**BROKEN-HEARTED.**

*Is.* 61:1 to bind up the *b.-h.*
*Luke* 4:18 to heal the *b.-h.*

**BROOD.**

*Luke* 13:34 hen doth gather *b.*

**BROOK.**

*Gen.* 32:23 sent them over the *b.*
*Lev.* 23:40 take willows of the *b.*
*Num.* 13:23 to *b.* Eschol. cut br.
*Deut.* 2:13 over the *b.* Zered, 14
9:21 cast the dust into the *b.*
1 *Sam.* 17:40 stones out of the *b.*
2 *Sam.* 15:23 passed *b.* Kidron
17:20 they be gone over the *b.*
1 *K.* 2:37 day thou passest ov. *b.*
17:3 hide by the *b.* Cherith, 5
6 he drank of the *b.*
18:40 Elijah brought to *b.* Kish.
2 *Chr.* 20:16 find them at e. of *b.*
29:16 carried it to the *b.* Kidron
32:4 gathered and stopped the *b.*
*Neh.* 2:15 by *b.* and viewed the
*Job* 6:15 dealt deceitfully as a *b.*
40:22 willows of *b.* compass him
*Ps.* 83:9 as to Jabin at the *b.* K.
110:7 drink of the *b.* in way
*Prov.* 18:4 wisdom as a *b.*
*Is.* 15:7 carry to *b.* of willows
*Jer.* 31:40 fields to *b.* Kid. holy
*John* 18:1 went over *b.* Cedron

**BROOKS.**

*Num.* 21:14 in the *b.* of Arnon
*Deut.* 8:7 a land of *b.* of water
2 *Sam.* 23:30 *b.* of G. 1 *Chr.* 11:32
1 *K.* 18:5 A. said, Go unto all *b.*
*Job* 6:15 as stream of *b.* pass
20:17 shall not see the *b.*
22:24 gold as stones of *b.*
*Ps.* 42:1 hart pant. after wat.-*b.*
*Is.* 19:6 *b.* of defence be emptied
7 paper-reeds by the *b.* shall
8 cast angle into *b.* shall lam.

**BROTH.**

*Jud.* 6:19 G. put the *b.* in a pot
*Is.* 65:4 *b.* of abominable things

**BROTHER.**

*Gen.* 9:5 of every man's *b.*
29:12 he was her father's *b.*
43:6 ye had a *b.* the man asked, have ye another *b.* 44:19
*Deut.* 25:5 husb. *b.* shall go in
*Jud.* 21:6 I. repen. for B. their *b.*
*Job* 1:13 in the eldest *b.* ho. 18
30:29 I am a *b.* to dragons
*Prov.* 17:17 a *b.* is born for adv.
18:9 slothful is *b.* to him
19 a *b.* offended is harder
24 sticketh closer than a *b.*
27:10 better a neigh. than *b.* far
*Ec.* 4:8 hath neither child nor *b.*
*Jer.* 9:4 tr. not in any *b.* for ev. *b.*
*Ezek.* 44:25 for *b.* they may defile
*Mal.* 1:2 was not E. Jacob's *b.?*
*Mat.* 10:21 *b.* de. up *b. Mark* 13:12
*Mark* 12:19 if m.'s *b.* die, *Luke* 20:28
*John* 11:19 J. came to co. con. *b.*
*Acts* 9:17 *b.* Saul receiv. 22:13
12:2 killed James the *b.* of John
21:20 *b.* how many thous. bel.
1 *Cor.* 5:11 called a *b.* be a forn.
6:6 *b.* goeth to law with *b.*
7:12 *b.* hath a wife
15 a *b.* is not under bondage
8:11 thy know. weak *b.* perish
2 *Cor.* 8:18 sent with him the *b.*
2 *Thes.* 3:6 withdraw from ev. *b.*
15 but admonish him as a *b.*
*Phile.* 7 saints refresh. by thee, *b.*
16 above a servant a *b.* beloved

**His BROTHER.**

*Gen.* 25:26 after that came *his b.*
42:38 *his b.* is dead, 44:20
*Ex.* 32:27 slay ev. man *his b.*
*Deut.* 19:19 to have done to *b.*
28:54 eye be evil toward *his b.*
*Neh.* 5:7 usury ev. one of *his b.*
*Ps.* 49:7 by any means red. *his b.*
*Is* 3:6 shall take hold of *his b.*
9:19 no man shall spare *his b.*
19:2 fight every one ag. *his b.*
41:6 to *his b.* be of good cour.
*Jer.* 31:34 teach no more every man *his b. Heb.* 8:11
34:9 serve himself of a J. *his b.*
17 liberty every one to *his b.*
*Ezek.* 18:18 spoiled *his b.* by vio.
33:30 every one to *his b.*
*Hos.* 12:3 *b.* by the heel in the w.
*Amos* 1:11 he did pursue *h. b.*
*Mic.* 7:2 hunt every man *his b.*
*Hag.* 2:22 by sword of *his b.*
*Zec.* 7:9 mercy ev. man to *h. b.*
10 imagine evil against *his b.*
*Mal.* 2:10 treacherously ag'st *b.*
*Mat.* 5:22 sayeth Raca to *his b.*
18:35 if ye forgive not every one *his b.* their trespasses
22:24 seed to *b. Mark* 12:19; *Luke* 20:28
25 left his wife to *his b.*
*John* 1:41 he findeth *his b.* Simon
*Rom.* 14:13 to fall in *his b.* way
1 *Thes.* 4:6 no man def. *his b.*
*Jam.* 4:11 evil of and jud. *his b.*
1 *John* 2:9 and hateth *his b.* 11
10 loveth *his b.* abideth in lig.
3:10 that loveth not *his b.* 14
12 not as Cain, who sle. *his b.*
15 hateth *his b.* is a murd. 4:20
4:21 love God, love *his b.* also
5:16 if any see *his b.* sin a sin

**My BROTHER.**

*Gen.* 4:9 C. said, Am I *my b.* kee.
20:5 he is *my b.* 13; 1 *K.* 20:32
27:41 will I slay *my b.* Jacob
29:15 because thou art *my b.*
2 *Sam.* 1:26 *my b.* Jonathan
1 *K.* 13:30 saying, Alas, *my b.*
*Ps.* 35:14 tho. he had been *my b.*
*Cant.* 8:1 wert as *my b.*
*Jer.* 22:18 saying, Ah, *my b.*
*Mat.* 12:50 is *my b. Mark* 3:35
18:21 how oft shall *my b.* sin
*Luke* 12:13 speak to *my b.*
*John* 11:21 *my b.* had not died
1 *Cor.* 8:13 if meat make *my b.*
2 *Cor.* 2:13 found not Tit. *my b.*

**Our BROTHER.**

*Gen.* 37:26 wh. profit if sl. *our b.*
27 for he is *our. b. Jud.* 9:3
42:21 guilty concerning *our b.*
2 *Cor.* 8:22 sent with them *our b*
*Phile.* 1 Tim. *our b.* to Philem.

**Thy BROTHER.**

*Gen.* 4:9 Where is Abel *thy b.*
10 voice of *thy b.* blood crieth
27:40 and shalt serve *thy b.*
38:8 *b.* wife r. up seed to *thy b*
*Ex.* 4:14 is not Aaron *thy b.?*

Lev. 19:17 shalt not hate thy b.
25:36 that thy b. may live
Deut. 13:6 if thy b. entice secretly
15:11 open thy h. wide to thy b.
12 thy b. a Heb. be sold to thee
22:3 all lost things of thy b.
23:7 not abhor Edom. he is t. b.
2 Sam. 2:22 my face to J. thy b.
13:20 h. thy peace, he is thy b.
1 K. 20:33 said, thy b. Benhadad
Job 22:6 pledge from thy b.
Ps. 50:20 speakest against thy b.
Prov. 27:10 into thy b. house
Ob. 10 violence against t. b. J.
Mat. 5:23 that t. b. hath aught
24 first be reconciled to thy b.
7:3 in t. b. eye, 5; Luke 6:41, 42
18:15 gained t. b. Luke 17:3
John 11:23 thy b. shall rise
Rom. 14:10 set at naught thy b.

**Your BROTHER.**

Gen. 42:34 will I deliver you y. b.
45:4 I am Joseph, your b.
Jud. 9:18 Abim. bec. he is y. b.
Rev. 1:9 I John who also am y. b.

**BROTHERHOOD.**

Zec. 11:14 break b. between J.
1 Pet. 2:17 love the b. fear God

**BROTHERLY.**

Amos 1:9 remember not b. cove.
Rom. 12:10 affect. with b. love
1 Thes. 4:9 as touching b. love
Heb. 13:1 let b. love continue
2 Pet. 1:7 to godliness b. kindness

**BROUGHT.**

Gen. 20:9 b. on me a great sin
27:20 Lord thy God b. it to me
Ex. 18:26 hard causes they b.
19:4 how I b. you to myself
32:1 that b. us up out, 23
21 thou hast b. so great a sin
Num. 14:3 b. us to this land
16:10 hath b. thee near to him
27:5 M. b. their cause before L.
Deut. 5:15 b. thee out thence
26:13 b. away the hal. things
Jos. 7:24 b. them to valley of A.
24:7 Lord b. the sea upon them
Jud. 2:1 b. you unto the land
18:3 who b. thee hither?
1 Sam. 1:24 b. Sam. to house of L.
10:27 and b. him no presents
15:35 D. received what she b.
2 Sam. 7:18 that thou hast b. me
hitherto, 1 Chr. 17:16
1 K. 9:9 b. this evil, 2 Chr. 7:22
17:20 b. evil upon the widow?
2 K. 5:20 in not receiv. what he b.
17:4 Hoshea b. no present
20:11 b. the shadow backward
1 Chr. 11:19 with jeop. of lives b.
14:17 L. b. fear of him on all
2 Chr. 13:18 chil. of Isr. were b.
22:9 b. Ahaziah to Jehu
32:23 many b. gifts to L. to Jer.
Ezra 8:18 b. us a man of underst.
Neh. 4:15 b. their counsel
9:33 in all that is b. upon us
13:12 Judah b. tithe of corn
Job 4:12 was secretly b. to me
21:32 yet shall he be b. to grave
Ps. 35:4 be b. to confusion, 26
45:15 with gladness shall he b.
71:24 b. to shame seek my hurt
Prov. 6:26 a man is b. to piece
Cant. 2:4 b. me to banquet-house
Is. 15:1 Ar b. Kir b. to silence
23:13 b. the land of C. to ruin
29:20 terrible one is b. to naught
43:23 b. me the small cattle, 24
48:15 called him, I have b. him
53:7 he is b. as a lamb
59:16 his arm b. salvation, 63:5
60:11 that their kings may be b.
62:9 they that b. it shall drink it
Jer. 15:8 I have b. on them
32:42 as I have b. all this evil on
40:3 now the Lord hath b. it
Ezek. 14:22 comf. concer. evil I b.
29:5 shalt not be b. together
40:4 art thou b. hither
Dan. 7:13 b. him near Ancient
9:14 watched evil and b. it on
11:6 and they that b. her
Hag. 1:9 ye b. it home
Mat. 10:18 shall be b. before kings,
Mark 13:9, Luke 21:12
12:25 is b. to desol. Luke 11:17
17:16 b. him to disciples
18:24 was b. owed 10,000 talents
19:13 b. little chil. Mark 10:13
Mark 10:13 rebuked those b. them
Luke 2:22 b. him to Jerusalem
10:34 b. him to an inn
John 7:45 have ye not b. him?
Acts 5:21 prison to have them b.
9:27 b. him to apostles
15:3 b. on their way
16:20 b. them to the magistrates
19:37 b. these men, no robbers
20:12 b. the young man alive
21:5 they all b. us on our way
25:6 commanded Paul to be b.
27:24 must be b. before Cesar
Rom. 15:24 to be b. thither
1 Cor. 6:12 not be b. under power
2 Cor. 1:16 be b. on my way to J.
2 Tim. 1:10 b. life and immortal.
1 Pet. 1:13 grace that is b. to you
2 Pet. 2:19 of same is he b.

**BROUGHT again.**

Gen. 14:16 Abram b. again Lot
Ex. 15:19 L. b. a. waters of sea
Deut. 1:25 b. us word again
Ruth 1:21 L. b. me home again
1 Sam. 6:21 Philistines b. again
2 Chr. 33:13 L. b. Manas. a. to J.
Ezek. 34:4 b. a. what was driven
39:27 b. them ag. from the peo.
Heb. 13:20 b. ag. from the dead

**BROUGHT back.**

1 K. 13:23 prophet he had b. back
2 Chr. 19:4 Jehos. b. them b. to L.
Ps. 85:1 b. back the captivity
Ezek. 38:8 land b. b. from the sw.

**BROUGHT down.**

Gen. 39:1 was b. d. into Egypt
1 Sam. 30:16 b. him d. they were
Ps. 20:8 they are b. d. and fallen
107:12 he b. d. their heart
Is. 5:15 mean man shall be b. d.
14:11 thy pomp is b. down
15 shall be b. down to hell
29:4 shall be b. d. speak out
43:14 b. down all the nobles
Lam. 2:2 b. them d. to the gro.
Ezek. 17:24 have b. d. high tree
31:18 be b. d. with trees of Eden
Zec. 10:11 pride of Assy. be b. d.
Mat. 11:23 Capern. b. d. to hell
Acts 9:30 brethren b. him d. to C.

**BROUGHT forth.**

Gen. 1:12 the earth b. forth grass
21 waters b. forth abundantly
14:18 king of Salem b. f. bread
15:5 Lord b. forth Abram
19:16 angels b. Lot forth
41:47 the earth b. forth by hand.
Ex. 3:12 thou hast b. f. peop.
16:3 ye have b. us f. into wild.
29:46 I am L. b. them f. Lev.
25:38; 26:13, 45
Num. 24:8 God b. him f.
Deut. 6:12 Lord b. thee f. 8:14
9:12 people b. f. have corrupted
26:8 L. b. us f. with a mighty h.
33:14 fruits b. forth by sun
Jud. 6:8 b. you f. out of house
2 Sam. 22:20 b. me forth into a
large place, Ps. 18:19
1 K. 9:9 forsook Lord who b. f.
their fathers, 2 Chr. 7:22
Job 10:18 hast thou b. me f.
21:30 be b. f. to day of wrath
Ps. 7:14 b. forth falsehood
90:2 before mountains were b. f.
105:30 their land b. f. frogs
43 b. forth his people with joy
Prov. 8:24 no depths, I was b. f.
25 before the hills was I b. f.
Cant. 8:5 thy mother b. thee f.
Is. 5:2 it b. forth wild grapes
26:18 b. f. wind; 45:10 w. b. f.
51:18 among sons she hath b. f.
66:7 before she trav. she b. f.
8 as soon as Z. trav. she b. f.
Jer. 2:27 thou hast b. me f.
11:4 I b. them forth, 34:13
20:3 Pashur b. f. J. out of stocks
32:21 b. forth Israel with signs
50:25 Lord b. f. weap. of indig.
51:10 L. hath b. f. our right.
Ezek. 12:7 I b. f. my stuff by day
14:22 a remnant b. f. sons
Mic. 5:3 which trav. hath b. f.
Hag. 2:19 olive-tree hath not b. f.
Mat. 1:25 she had b. f. first-born
Mat 13:8 good gr. b. f. Mark 4:8
Luke 1:57 Elizabeth b. f. a son
2:7 she b. f. her first-born son
12:16 ground of a rich man b. f.
John 19:13 Pilate b. forth Jesus
Acts 5:19 doors and b. them f.
12:6 Herod would have b. him f.
25:17 com. the man to be b. f.
Jam. 5:18 earth b. forth fruit
Rev. 12:5 she b. f. a man-child
13 persecuted woman wh. b. f.

**BROUGHT in.**

Gen. 39:14 b. in a Hebrew
47:7 Jos. b. in Jacob his father
Deut. 9:4 my right L. b. me in
11:29 L. hath b. in unto land
Neh. 13:19 no burden b. in
Ps. 78:26 b. in the south wind
Acts 7:45 b. in with Jesus
Gal. 2:4 brethren unawares b. in

**BROUGHT into.**

Num. 16:14 not b. us into a land
1 Sam. 20:8 b. thy serv. into a cov.
Ps. 22:15 b. me into dust
Cant. 1:4 king b. me i. his cham.
Jer. 2:7 b. you i. a plen. country
Lam. 3:2 b. me into darkness
Ezek. 44:7 b. in. my sanctuary
Acts 9:8 b. him into Damascus
21:28 b. Greeks into the temple
1 Tim. 6:7 b. nothing into world
Heb. 13:11 whose blood is b. into

**BROUGHT low.**

Jud. 11:35 dau. b. me very low
2 Chr. 28:19 Lord b. Judah low
Job 14:21 they are b. low
24:24 are gone and b. low
Ps. 79:8 for we are b. very low
106:43 b. low for their iniquity
107:39 b. low thro' oppression
116:6 I was b. low, he helped
142:6 for I am b. very low
Ec. 12:4 daug. of music be b. low
Is. 2:12 shall be b. low
25:5 of terrible ones b. low
Luke 3:5 every mountain and hill
b. low, Is. 40:4

**BROUGHT out.**

Gen. 15:7 b. thee o. of Ur of Cha.
43:23 he b. S. out unto them
Ex. 13:3 L. b. you out, 9, 14, 16
20:2 L. b. thee out, Lev. 19:36;
Num. 15:41; Deut. 5:6; Ps. 81:10
Lev. 23:43 I b. them o. 1 K. 8:21
Deut. 5:15 that L. b. thee out
9:28 b. out to slay them
Jos. 6:23 b. out Rahab and all
24:5 and afterward I b. you out
2 Sam. 13:18 b. her o. and bolted
2 Chr. 23:11 b. out the king's son

Ps. 78:16 he b. str. out of rock
80:8 hast b. a vine out of Egypt
107:14 b. them out of darkness
136:11 b. out Isr. from among
Jer. 7:22 in the day I b. them out
Dan. 5:13 king b. o. of Jewry?
Hos. 12:13 prophet L. b. Isr. out
Acts 7:40 M. wh. b. us out of Eg.
12:17 L. b. him out of prison
13:17 a high arm b. them out
16:30 b. o. and said, wh. m. I do?
39 bes. them and b. them out

**BROUGHT to pass.**

2 K. 19:25 I b. it to p. Is. 37:26
Ezek. 21:7 and shall be b. to p.
1 Cor. 15:54 then be b. to p.

**BROUGHT up.**

Ex. 17:3 wh. b. us up, Num. 21:5
32:1 as for M. that b. us up, 23
4 thy gods b. th. up, 8; 1 K. 12:28
Num. 16:13 hast b. us up
20:4 why have ye b. up
Deut. 20:1 with thee b. thee up
Jos. 24:17 he it is that b. us up
Jud. 6:8 b. you u. 1 Sam. 10:18
15:13 b. Samson u.; 16:31
1 Sam. 8:8 since the day I b. up; 2 Sam. 7:6; 1 Chr. 17:5
12:6 L. that b. your fathers up
2 Sam. 6:12 b. up the ark, 15; 1 K. 8:4; 1 Chr. 15:28; 2 Chr. 1:4
21:13 b. up the bones of Saul
2 K. 17:7 sin. ag. L. b. them up
36 Lord who b. you up
25:6 b. up Z. to king, Jer. 39:5
2 Chr. 8:11 Sol. b. up dau. of P.
10:8 men b. up with him, 10
Neh. 9:18 is thy God b. thee up
Est. 2:7 he b. up Esther
20 like as when b. up with him
Job 31:18 he was b. up with me
Ps. 30:3 b. up my soul
40:2 b. me up out of horrible pit
Prov. 8:30 one b. up with him
Is. 1:2 nourished and b. up chil.
49:21 who hath b. up these
Is. 51:18 her of sons she b. up
63:11 he b. them up, Jer. 2:6
Jer. 11:7 in day I b. them up
16:14 L. that b. u. Israel, 23:7
15 b. up Israel from the n. 23:8
Lam. 2:22 those I b. up my en.
4:5 b. up in scarlet, embrace
Ezek. 19:3 b. up one of her whelps
37:13 b. you up out of your gr.
Amos 2:10 I b. you u. 3:1; 9:7; Mic. 6:4
Jon. 2:6 b. up my life from cor.
Luke 4:16 N. where he been b. u.
Acts 13:1 I been b. up with Herod
22:3 b. up at the feet of Gamal.
1 Tim. 5:10 widow, if she b. up

**BROUGHTEST.**

Ex. 32:7 people b. out have cor.
Num. 14:13 b. up this people
Deut. 9:28 lest land whence b. us
29 inherit. b. out, 1 K. 8:51
2 Sam. 5:2 he b. in Isr. 1 Chr. 11:2
1 K. 8:53 when b. our fathers out
Neh. 9:7 b. him forth out of Ur.
15 b. forth water out of rock
23 b. them into the land
Ps. 66:11 thou b. us into the net
12 b. us out into a wealthy pl.

**BROW.**

Is. 48:4 thy neck iron, b. brass
Luke 4:29 led him to b. of the hill

**BROWN.**

Gen. 30:32 all b. cattle, 35, 40
33 every o. not b. accounted st.

**BRUISE, Substantive.**

Jer. 30:12 L. thy b. is incurable
Nah. 3:19 no healing of thy b

**BRUISES.**

Is. 1:6 but wounds and b.

**BRUISE, Verb.**

Gen. 3:15 b. thy head, b. his heel
Is. 28:28 nor b. it with horsemen
53:10 pleased the Lord to b. him
Dan. 2:40 as iron shall it b.
Rom. 16:20 G. of peace shall b. S.

**BRUISED.**

Lev. 22:24 not offer what is b.
2 K. 18:21 trustest this b. reed
Is. 42:3 a b. reed shall he not break, Mat. 12:20
53:5 he was b. for our iniquities
Ezek. 23:3 in Egypt b. the teats
8 b. the breasts of her virginity
Luke 4:18 set at liberty them b.

**BRUISING.**

Ezek. 23:21 in b. thy teats by E.
Luke 9:39 the spirit b. him

**BRUIT.**

Jer. 10:22 noise of the b. is come
Nah. 3:19 all that hear b. of thee

BRUTE. See BEASTS.

**BRUTISH.**

Ps. 49:10 fool and b. person
92:6 a b. man knoweth not
94:8 underst. ye b. am. the peo.
Prov. 12:1 hateth reproof is b.
30:2 I am more b. than any
Is. 19:11 the counsel of the counsellors of Phar. is become b.
Jer. 10:8 they are altogether b.
14 man is b. 51:17; 21 pastors
Ezek. 21:31 into the hand of b.

**BUCKET, S.**

Num. 24:7 water out of his b.
Is. 40:15 nat. are as drop of a b.

**BUCKLER.**

2 Sam. 22:31 a b. to all that trust in him, Ps. 18:30
1 Chr. 5:18 men able to bear a b.
12:8 Gadites that could h. b.
Ps. 18:2 Lord is my God, my b.
35:2 take hold of shield and b.
91:4 his truth shall be thy b.
Prov. 2:7 b. to them walk upr.
Jer. 46:3 order ye b. and shield
Ezek. 23:24 set against thee b.
26:8 he shall lift up b. against

**BUCKLERS.**

2 Chr. 23:9 Jehoiada delivered b.
Job 15:26 run. on bosses of his b.
Cant. 4:4 there hanged 1,000 b.
Ezek. 38:4 great company with b.
39:9 they shall set on fire b.

**BUD, Substantive.**

Job 38:27 b. of tender herb
Is. 18:5 when the b. is perfect
61:11 as earth bringeth forth b.
Ezek. 16:7 multiply as b. of field
Hos. 8:7 b. shall yield no meal

**BUDS.**

Num. 17:8 Aaron's rod b. forth b.

**BUD, Verb.**

Job 14:9 thr. scent of water, b.
Ps. 132:17 horn of David to b.
Cant. 7:12 see if pomegranates b.
Is. 27:6 Is. shall blossom and b.
55:10 maketh the earth to b.
Ezek. 29:21 cause horn of Is. to b.

**BUDDED.**

Gen. 40:10 was as though it b.
Num. 17:8 A. rod for house of L. b.
Cant. 6:11 to see whether pom. b.
Ezek. 7:10 pride hath b.
Heb. 9:4 ark wherein rod that b.

**BUFFET.**

2 Cor. 12:7 mes. of Satan to b. me

**BUFFETED.**

Mat. 26:67 b. him, Mark 14:65
1 Cor. 4:11 to present hour b.
1 Pet. 2:20 when b. for your f.

**BUILD, referred to God.**

1 Sam. 2:35 b. him a sure h. 2 Sam. 7:27; 1 K. 11:38
1 Chr. 17:10 will b. thee a house
25 told wilt b. him a house
Ps. 28:5 and not b. them up
51:18 b. thou the walls of Jer.
69:35 will b. the cities of Judah
89:4 b. up thy throne to all gen.
102:16 when L. shall b. up Zion
127:1 except the L. b. the house
147:2 Lord doth b. up Jerusalem
Jer. 18:9 con. a nation to b. it
24:6 I will b. not pull d. 31:28
31:4 I will b. thee, O virgin
33:7 I will b. Judah and Israel
42:10 if ye abide, I will b. you
Ezek. 36:36 that I b. ruined pl.
Amos 9:11 b. it as in days of old
Mat. 16:18 on this rock b. my ch.
26:61 b. it in three d. Mark 14:58
Acts 15:16 b. again tabernacle

**BUILD, Man the Agent.**

Gen. 11:4 go to, let us b. a city
Num. 32:24 b. ye cities
Deut. 20:20 shalt b. bulwarks
1 K. 9:24 then did b. Millo
11:7 Solom. did b. a high place
16:34 did Hiel b. Jericho
1 Chr. 22:19 b. ye the sanctuary
29:19 give Sol. a heart to b.
2 Chr. 14:7 let us b. these cities
Ezr. 4:2 let us b. with you
Neh. 2:17 let us b. the wall
4:3 which they b. if a fox go up
10 so we are not able to b.
Ec. 3:3 a time to b. up
Cant. 8:9 we will b. on her
Is. 9:10 fallen, but we will b.
45:13 he shall b. my city
58:12 b. old waste places, 61:4
60:10 sons of strangers, b. walls
65:22 not b. and another inhabit
Jer. 1:10 set over nations to b.
Ezek. 4:2 b. a fort against, 21:22
Dan. 9:25 to b. Jerusalem
Amos 9:11 I will b. as in days
14 Isr. shall b. the waste cities
Mic. 3:10 b. Zion with blood
Zec. 6:12 shall b. the temple, 13
15 they far off sh. b. in temple
9:3 Tyrus did b. a stronghold
Mal. 1:4 b. but I will throw d.
Mat. 23:29 ye b. tombs of proph. Luke 11:47, 48
Luke 12:18 barns and b. greater
14:28 intending to b. a tower
30 to b. and not able to finish
Acts 20:32 word of his grace able to b. you up
Rom. 15:20 lest I b. on ano. man's
1 Cor. 3:12 b. on this foundation
Gal. 2:18 if I b. again things

**BUILD altar, s.**

Ex. 20:25 b. altar of hewn stone
Num. 23:1 b. me here sev. a. 29
Deut. 27:5 there b. an altar to L.
6 shalt b. the a. of whole st.
Jos. 22:29 God forbid we sh. b. a.

See BEGAN.

**BUILD, joined with House, s.**

Deut. 25:9 will not b. brother's h.
28:30 b. a h. Zep. 1:13
Ruth 4:11 which two did b. h.
2 Sam. 7:5 b. me h. to dwell in
7 why b. ye not me a h.
13 thy seed shall b. a h. 1 K. 5:5; 8:19; 1 Chr. 17:12; 22:10
1 K. 2:36 b. thee a h. in Jerus.
5:3 D. not b. a h. for the wars
5 I purp. to b. a h. to L. 2 Chr. 2:1
8:16 no city to b. h. 2 Chr. 6:5
17 it was in heart of D. to b. a h. 1 Chr. 28:2; 2 Chr. 6:7
1 Chr. 17:12 shall b. a h. 2 Chr. 6:9
22:8 not b. a h. thou shed blood

1 *Chr.* 22:11 son, *b.* the *h.* of the L.
28:6 Sol. shall *b.* my *h.*
2 *Chr.* 2:4 behold, I *b.* a *h.*
5 *h.* I *b.* is great, for great is G.
6 who able to *b.* him a *h.*
36:23 ch. me to *b.* a *h.* *Ezr.* 1:2
*Ezr.* 1:3 go to Jerusalem *b.* *h.*
5:3 comman. you to *b.* this *h.* 9
6:7 let governor of Jews *b.* *h.*
*Ps.* 127:1 labor in vain that *b.* *h.*
*Prov.* 24:27 afterwards *b.* thy *h.*
*Is.* 65:21 shall *b.* *h.* and inhabit
66:1 where is *h.* ye *b.* unto me?
*Jer.* 22:14 I will *b.* me a wide *h.*
29:5 *b.* *h.* and dwell in them, 28
35:7 nei. shall ye *b.* *h.* nor sow
*Ezek.* 11:3 is not near, let us *b.* *h.*
28:26 and shall *b.* *h.*
*Hag.* 1:8 bring wood, *b.* the *h.*
*Zec.* 5:11 to *b.* it a *h.* in Shinar
*Acts* 7:49 what *h.* will ye *b.* me

**BUILDED.**

*Gen.* 4:17 C. *b.* city called Enoch
8:20 Noah *b.* an altar to the L.
10:11 Ashur *b.* Nineveh and
11:5 L. come to see tower men *b.*
*Jos.* 22:16 you *b.* an altar
1 *K.* 8:27 house I have *b.* 43
15:22 stones wh. Baasha had *b.*
2 *K.* 23:13 Solo. *b.* for Ashtoreth
1 *Chr.* 22:5 *b.* must be magnifical
*Ezr.* 4:13 if city be *b.* 16
5:8 to the house of great God *b.*
11 we build house *b.* years ago
15 let the house of G. be *b.* 6:3
6:14 elders of Jews *b.* and pros.
*Job* 20:19 a house he *b.* not
*Ps.* 122:3 J. is *b.* a city compact
*Prov.* 9:1 wisdom hath *b.* her h.
24:3 thr. wisdom is a house *b.*
*Ec.* 2:4 I *b.* me houses, I planted
*Cant.* 4:4 David *b.* for an armory
*Jer.* 30:18 city be *b.* on her heap
*Lam.* 3:5 he hath *b.* against me
*Ezek.* 36:10 wastes shall be *b.* 33
*Luke* 17:28 they planted, they *b.*
*Eph.* 2:22 in whom ye are *b.* tog.
*Heb.* 3:3 *b.* house hath more hon.
4 every house is *b.* by some m.

**BUILDEDST.**

*Deut.* 6:10 cities thou *b.* not

**BUILDER, S.**

1 *K.* 5:18 Solomon's and H.'s *b.*
2 *K.* 22:6 give it to *b.* 2 *Chr.* 34:11
*Ezr.* 3:10 when *b.* laid found.
*Neh.* 4:5 to anger before the *b.*
*Ps.* 118:22 stone *b.* refu. *Mat.* 21:42; *Mark* 12:10; *Luke* 20:17; *Acts* 4:11
*Ezek.* 27:4 thy *b.* have perfected
*Heb.* 11:10 city whose *b.* is God
1 *Pet.* 2:7 the stone *b.* disallowed

**Master-BUILDER.**

1 *Cor.* 3:10 as a wise *m.-b.* I have

**BUILDEST.**

*Deut.* 22:8 *b.* a new house
*Neh.* 6:6 for wh. cause *b.* the wall
*Ezek.* 16:31 *b.* thine eminent place
*Mat.* 27:40 that destroyest the temple and *b.* it, *Mark* 15:29

**BUILDETH.**

*Jos.* 6:26 cursed be man *b.* this c.
*Job* 27:18 *b.* his house as a moth
*Prov.* 14:1 wise woman *b.* her h.
*Jer.* 22:13 woe to him *b.* by un.
*Hos.* 8:14 for. maker, *b.* temples
*Amos* 9:6 *b.* his stories in heaven
*Hab.* 2:12 *b.* a town with blood
1 *Cor.* 3:10 another *b.* thereon

**BUILDING, Participle.**

1 *K.* 3:1 end of *b.* his own house
6:7 no tool of iron heard wh. *b.*
38 seven years in *b.* it
*Ezr.* 4:12 *b.* the rebellious city
*Ezek.* 17:17 *b.* forts to cut off
*John* 2:20 temple was 46 y. in *b.*
*Jude* 20 *b.* up on most holy faith

**BUILDING, Substantive.**

1 *K.* 9:1 when Sol. finished the *b.*
1 *Chr.* 28:2 made ready for the *b.*
2 *Chr.* 3:3 instructed for the *b.*
*Ec.* 10:18 slothful. *b.* decayeth
*Ezek.* 40:5 measured *b.* 41:15
46:23 a row of *b.* round about
1 *Cor.* 3:9 ye are God's *b.*
2 *Cor.* 5:1 we have a *b.* of God
*Eph.* 2:21 in whom *b.* fitly fra.
*Heb.* 9:11 tabernacle not of th. *b.*
*Rev.* 21:18 *b.* of wall was jasper

**BUILDINGS.**

*Mat.* 24:1 show him *b.* of temple
*Mark* 13:1 see what *b.* are here, 2

**BUILT.**

*Deut.* 13:16 it shall not be *b.*
1 *K.* 22:39 cities that Ahab *b.*
2 *Chr.* 14:7 they *b.* and prospered
20:8 *b.* thee a sanctuary therein
26:9 Uzziah *b.* towers in Jer. 10
27:4 Joth. *b.* castles and towers
*Job* 3:14 who *b.* desolate places
12:14 and it cannot be *b.* again
22:23 if return shalt be *b.* up
*Ps.* 78:69 *b.* his sanc. like high p.
89:2 mercy shall be *b.* up
*Is.* 5:2 *b.* a tower in the midst
44:28 to Jeru. thou shalt be *b.*
*Jer.* 12:16 then shall they be *b.*
31:4 thou shalt be *b.* O virgin
32:31 prov. from day they *b.* it
45:4 which I *b.* will break d.
*Ezek.* 16:24 hast *b.* eminent place
26:14 thou shalt be *b.* no more
*Dan.* 4:30 gr. Babylon I have *b.*?
9:25 street shall be *b.* again
*Zec.* 8:9 that temple be *b.*
*Mat.* 21:33 *b.* a tower, *Mark* 12:1
*Luke* 7:5 hath *b.* us a synagogue
1 *Cor.* 3:14 abide wh. he hath *b.*
*Eph.* 2:20 *b.* on found. of apost.
*Col.* 2:7 rooted and *b.* up in him
*Heb.* 3:4 that *b.* all things is God

**BUILT altar.**

*Ex.* 17:15 *b.* *a.* 24:4; 32:5 Aaron
*Jos.* 8:30 I *b.* *a.*; 22:10 half tr.
*Jud.* 6:24 G. *b.* *a.*; 21:4 peo. *b.* *a.*
1 *Sam.* 7:17 S. *b.* *a.*; 14:35 Saul *b.*
2 *Sam.* 24:25 D. *b.* *a.* to the Lord
1 *K.* 9:25 Solo. offered on *a.* he *b.*
18:32 with stones Elijah *b.* *a.*
2 *K.* 16:11 Urijah the priest *b.* *a.*

**BUILT altars.**

*Num.* 23:14 Balak *b.* seven *a.*
2 *K.* 21:4 he *b.* *a* in house of L.
5 *b.* *a.* for host of h. 2 *Chr.* 33:5
2 *Chr.* 33:15 away *a.* he had *b.* in

**BUILT city.**

*Num.* 21:27 let *city* of Sihon be *b.*
*Jos.* 19:50 Joshua *b.* *c.* and dwelt
1 *Chr.* 11:8 David *b.* *c.* from Millo
*Is.* 25:2 to be no *c.* never be *b.*
*Jer.* 31:38 *city* shall be *b.* to Lord
*Luke* 4:29 hill whereon *c.* was *b.*

**BUILT cities.**

*Ex.* 1:11 *b.* for Phar. treasure-*cit.*
*Jos.* 24:13 *cities* which ye *b.* not
2 *Chr.* 14:6 Asa *b.* fenced *c.* in J.
17:12 Jehosh. *b.* *cities* of store
27:4 Jotham *b.* *c.* in mountains
*Is.* 44:26 *c.* of J. ye shall be *b.*

**BUILT house, *or* houses.**

*Deut.* 8:12 when hast *b.* goodly *h.*
20:5 what man hath *b.* new *h.*
1 *K.* 3:2 no *h.* *b.* to name of Lord
6:9 Sol. *b.* *h.* 14; 8:13 *b.* th. a *h.*
8:20 have *b.* a *h.* for name of L.
44 toward the *h.* I have *b.* 48; 2 *Chr.* 6:34, 38
1 *Chr.* 17:6 why not *b.* me a *h.*?
2 *Chr.* 6:18 less this *h.* I have *b.*?
*Amos* 5:11 ye *b.* *h.* of hewn stone
*Hag.* 1:2 Lord's *h.* should be *b.*
*Zec.* 1:16 my *h.* shall be *b.* in it
*Mat.* 7:24 *b.* *h.* on a r. *Luke* 6:48
26 *b.* his *h.* on sand, *Luke* 6:49
*Acts* 7:47 Solomon *b.* him a *h.*
1 *Pet.* 2:5 *b.* up a spiritual *house*

**BUILT high places.**

1 *K.* 14:23 Jud. *b.* *h.* *p.* and ima.
2 *K.* 17:9 chil. of Israel *b.* *h.* *p.*
*Jer.* 7:31 *b.* *h.* *p.* of Tophet; 19:5 of Baal, 32:35

**BUILT wall, *or* walls.**

2 *Chr.* 27:3 on *w.* of O. *b.* much
32:5 Hezekiah *b.* up *w.* broken
33:14 Manas. *b.* *w.* without city
*Neh.* 4:6 so *b.* we the *w.* 7:1
*Ezek.* 13:10 one *b.* up the *w.*
*Dan.* 9:25 street *b.* ag. and the *w.*
*Mic.* 7:11 thy *walls* are to be *b.*

BUL. 1 *K.* 6:38

**BULL.**

*Job* 21:10 their *b.* gendereth
*Is.* 51:20 as a wild *b.* in a net

**BULLS.**

*Ps.* 22:12 many *b.* have compassed me, strong *b.*
50:13 will I eat the flesh of *b.*
68:30 rebuke the multitude of *b.*
*Is.* 34:7 with *b.* shall come down
*Jer.* 50:11 because ye bellow as *b.*
52:20 brazen *b.* under the bases
*Heb.* 9:13 if blood of *b.* and goats
10:4 blood of *b.* take away sins

**BULLOCK.**

*Ex.* 29:11 kill the *b.* *Lev.* 1:5; 9:18
*Deut.* 33:17 like firstling of *b.*
*Jud.* 6:25 take the young *b.* 26
1 *K.* 18:23 choose one *b.* 25
1 *K.* 18:33 E. cut the *b.* in pieces
*Ps.* 50:9 no *b.* out of thy house
69:31 than a *b.* that hath hor.
*Is.* 65:25 lion eat straw like *b.*
*Jer.* 31:18 a *b.* unaccus. to yoke

**BULLOCK *with* Sin-offering.**

*Ex.* 29:36 eve. day a *b.* for *sin-o.*
*Ezek.* 45:22 prepare a *b.* for *sin-o.*

*See* BLOOD.

**Young BULLOCK.**

*Lev.* 16:3 holy place with a *y.* *b.*
*Num.* 7:15 one *y.* *b.* 21, etc. to 81
2 *Chr.* 13:9 consecrate with *y.* *b.*
*Ezek.* 45:18 *y.* *b.* and clea. sanct.
46:6 day of new moon a *y.* *b.*

**BULLOCKS.**

1 *Chr.* 29:21 offered a thousand *b.*
*Ezr.* 6:17 the dedication 100 *b.*
*Ps.* 51:19 offer *b.* on thy altar
66:15 I will offer unto thee *b.*
*Is.* 1:11 I delight not in bl. of *b.*
34:7 the *b.* shall come down
*Jer.* 46:21 hired men like fatted *b.*
50:27 slay all her *b.* let them go
*Ezek.* 39:18 drink the blood of *b.*
*Hos.* 12:11 they sacrifice *b.* in G.

*See* SEVEN.

**BULRUSH, ES.**

*Ex.* 2:3 an ark of *b.*
*Is.* 18:2 ambas. in vessels of *b.*
58:5 to bow his head like a *b.*?

**BULWARKS.**

*Deut.* 20:20 *b.* against the city
2 *Chr.* 26:15 engines on the *b.*
*Ps.* 48:13 mark well her *b.*
*Ec.* 9:14 a great king built *b.*
*Is.* 26:1 salvation appoint for *b.*

**BUNCH, ES.**

*Ex.* 12:22 take a *b.* of hyssop
1 *Chr.* 12:40 Zebulun brought *b.*
*Is.* 30:6 treas. upon *b.* of camels

**BUNDLE, S.**

Gen. 42:35 every man's b.
1 Sam. 25:29 bound in b. of life
Cant. 1:13 a b. of myrrh is my b.
Mat. 13:30 bind the tares in b.
Acts 28:3 P. gathered a b. of s.

**BURDEN, Substantive.**

Ex. 18:22 b. with th. Num. 11:17
23:5 ass lying under b.
Num. 4:19 appoint each to his b.
11:11 b. of all this people on me
Deut. 1:12 can I bear alone b.?
2 Sam. 15:33 shalt be a b. to me
19:35 thy servant be a b.?
2 K. 8:9 forty camels b. to Elisha
2 Chr. 35:3 not be a b.
Neh. 13:19 no b. on the Sabbath
Job 7:20 I am a b. to myself
Ps. 38:4 as a b. they are too h.
55:22 cast thy b. on the Lord
81:6 rem. his shoulder from b.
Ec. 12:5 grasshop. shall be a b.
Is. 9:4 broken the yoke of his b.
10:27 b. taken off thy shoulder
13:1 b. of Babylon
14:25 his b. depart off
28 year Ahaz died, was this b.
15:1 b. of Moab; 17:1 Damascus
19:1 b. of Egypt; 23:1 b. of T.
21:1 b. of the desert of the sea
11 b. of Du. 13 b. on Arabia
22:1 b. of the valley of vision
25 b. upon it shall be cut off
30:6 b. of beasts of the south
27 the b. thereof is heavy
46:1 a b. to weary beast
2 they could not deliver the b.
Jer. 17:21 no b. on Sabbath, 22, 27
23:33 what is the b. of the L.?
36 b. of the Lord
38 but since ye say, b. of the L.
Ezek. 12:10 b. concerning prince
Hos. 8:10 for b. of the king
Nah. 1:1 the b. of Nineveh
Zep. 3:18 rep. of it was a b.
Mat. 11:30 and my b. is light
20:12 the b. and heat of the day
Acts 15:28 to lay no greater b.
21:3 ship was to unlade her b.
Gal. 6:5 man bear his own b.
Rev. 2:24 upon you none other b.

**BURDEN, ED.**

Zec. 12:3 b. thems. be cut in p.
2 Cor. 5:4 we groan being b.
8:13 others be eased, and you b.
12:16 be it so, I did not b. you

**BURDENS.**

Gen. 49:14 couching bet. two b.
Ex. 2:11 M. looked on their b.
5:4 king said, get you to your b.
6:6 under b. of Egyptians, 7
Num. 4:27 appoint all their b.
Neh. 4:17 bare b. held a weapon
Is. 58:6 to undo the heavy b.
Lam. 2:14 seen for thee false b.
Mat. 23:4 heavy b. Luke 11:46
Gal. 6:2 bear ye one another's b.

**BURDENSOME.**

Zec. 12:3 Jerusalem a b. stone
2 Cor. 11:9 kept from being b.
12:13 that I was not b. to you
14 I will not be b. to you
1 Thes. 2:6 might been b.

**BURIAL.**

Ec. 6:3 also that he have no b.
Is. 14:20 not j. with them in b.
Jer. 22:19 with the b. of an ass
Mat. 26:12 she did it for my b.
Acts 8:2 carried Stephen to his b.

**BURIED.**

Gen. 25:10 there was Abraham b.
49:31 there they b. Abra., Sarah, Isaac, Rebekah, there I b. L.
Num. 11:34 b. the people
20:1 Miriam died, was b. there
33:4 Egyptians b. all first-born
Deut. 10:6 Aaron, there he was b.
Jos. 24:32 bones of J. b. in She.
Ruth 1:17 and there will I be b.
2 Sam. 4:12 b. head of Ish-bosh.
21:14 bones of Saul b. in Zelah
1 K. 13:31 wherein man of G. b.
Ec. 8:10 so I saw the wicked b.
Jer. 8:2 nor b. 16:6; 20:6; 25:33
16:4 shall not be lamented nor b.
22:19 be b. with burial of an ass
Ezek. 39:15 till buriers have b.
Mat. 14:12 took body and b. it
Luke 16:22 died and was b.
Acts 2:29 D. is both dead and b.
5:9 feet of them which b.
Rom. 6:4 b. with him by baptism
1 Cor. 15:4 that he was b. and r.
Col. 2:12 b. with him in baptism

**BURIED him.**

Deut. 34:6 he b. him in val. in M.
2 Sam. 2:5 blessed be ye b. Saul
1 K. 14:18 b. h. all Isr. mourned
Acts 5:6 the young men b. him

**BURIED in.**

Gen. 15:15 b. in a good old age
1 K. 2:10 D. was b. in city of D.
Job 27:15 shall be b. in death.

**BURIERS.**

Ezek. 39:15 till b. have buried

**BURN.**

Gen. 44:18 let not thine anger b.
Ex. 27:20 lamp to b. Lev. 24:2
2 Chr. 2:6 save only to b. sacrif.
13:11 b. to Lord every morning
Is. 1:31 shall both b. together
10:17 b. and devour his thorns
27:4 I would b. them together
40:16 Lebanon is not suf. to b.
44:15 shall it be for man to b.
Jer. 7:20 my fury shall b.
34:5 so shall they b. odors
36:25 king would not b. roll
Ezek. 24:5 b. also bones under it
11 that the brass of it may b.
39:9 and b. the weapons
Nah. 2:13 I will b. her chariots
Mal. 4:1 that shall b. as oven
Mat. 13:30 in bundles to b. them
Luke 3:17 the chaff he will b.
24:32 did not our hearts b. in us
1 Cor. 7:9 bet. to marry than to b.
2 Cor. 11:29 offend. and I b. not?

**BURN** *joined with* **fire.**

Deut. 5:23 mount. did b. with f.
32:22 a f. shall b. to the lowest hell, Jer. 17:4
Jos. 11:6 b. chariots with fire
Jud. 9:52 to b. it with fire
12:1 b. h. with f.; 14:15 b. thee f.
Ps. 79:6 thy jealousy b. like f.?
89:46 thy wrath b. like fire?
Is. 47:14 as stubble f. shall b.
Jer. 4:4 like f. and b. 21:12
7:31 b. sons and dau. in f. 19:5
21:10 N. b. this city with fire, 32:29; 34:2, 22; 37:8, 10; 38:18
Ezek. 5:2 b. with fire a third part
16:41 b. thy h. with fire. 23:47
Mat. 3:12 b. up the chaff with unquench. fire, Luke 3:17
Rev. 17:16 and b. her with fire

**BURN incense.**

Ex. 30:7 A. shall b. sweet i. 8.
1 K. 13:1 Jeroboam stood to b. i.
2 K. 18:4 chil. of Is. did b. i. to
1 Chr. 23:13 for ever to b. i.
2 Chr. 2:4 to b. sweet incense
13:11 b. every morn. sweet inc.
26:16 U. went to b. incense, 19
29:11 L. hath chosen you to b. i.
32:12 one altar and b. inc. on it
Jer. 7:9 b. i. to Baal? 11:13
44:17 b. i. to queen of heaven
Hos. 4:13 b. incense on hills
Hab. 1:16 b. i. to their dragon
Luke 1:9 Zach. his lot to b. inc.

**BURNED.**

Ex. 3:2 bush b. was not cons.
Deut. 9:15 the mount b. with fire
Jos. 7:25 b. them with fire
2 Chr. 34:25 forsaken me b. inc.
Est. 1:12 king's anger b. in him
Ps. 39:3 while musing the fire b.
Is. 24:6 inhab. of the earth are b.
42:25 it b. him, laid it not to h.
Lam. 2:3 b. ag. J. like flaming
John 15:6 withered branches b.
Acts 19:19 books, and b. them
Rom. 1:27 b. in their lust
1 Cor. 13:3 th. I give body to b.
Heb. 6:8 whose end is to be b.
12:18 not come to mount that b.
Rev. 1:15 his feet as if they b.

**BURNETH.**

Ps. 46:9 b. chariot in the fire
83:14 as the fire b. the wood
97:3 a fire b. up his enemies
Is. 9:18 wickedness b. as the fire
44:16 he b. part thereof in fire
62:1 salvation as a lamp that b.
64:2 as when melting fire b.
65:5 these are a fire b. all day
66:3 b. incense as if he blessed
Jer. 48:35 him that b. incense
Joel 2:3 behind them a flame b.
Rev. 21:8 lake which b. with fire

**BURNING.**

Gen. 15:17 a b. lamp passed bet.
Lev. 26:16 will appoint b. ague
Deut. 28:22 with extreme b.
32:24 he devoured with b. heat
Job 41:19 out of mo. go b. lamps
Ps. 140:10 b. coals fall upon them
Prov. 16:27 in his lips as b. fire
26:21 as coals to b. coals
23 b. lips and a wicked heart
Is. 30:27 name of L. com. far, b.
34:9 land shall become b. pitch
Jer. 20:9 his word was as a b. fire
Ezek. 1:13 appearance like b. c.
Dan. 3:6 cast into b. furnace, 11
7:9 and his wheels were as b. f.
Hab. 3:5 b. coals forth at his feet
Luke 12:35 loins girded, lights b.
John 5:35 John b. and shin. light
Rev. 4:5 lamps b. before throne
8:8 great mountain b. with fire
10 there fell a great star b.
19:20 cast alive into a lake b.

**BURNING, Substantive.**

Ex. 21:25 b. for b. wound for w.
Lev. 10:6 bewail b. which Lord
Deut. 29:23 brimstone, salt, b.
2 Chr. 16:14 great b. for him
21:19 people made no b. like b.
Is. 3:24 be b. instead of beauty
4:4 purged Jeru. by spirit of b.
9:5 this shall be with b. and f.
10:16 under his glory kindle b.
33:12 people as the b. of lime
Amos 4:11 a firebrand out of b.
Rev. 18:9 see smoke of her b.

**BURNINGS.**

Is. 33:14 dwell with everla. b.?
Jer. 34:5 with b. of thy fathers

**BURNISHED.**

Ezek. 1:7 like color of b. brass

**BURNT.**

Gen. 38:24 let her be b.
Ex. 3:3 why the bush is not b.
Deut. 32:24 be b. with hunger
1 K. 13:2 men's bones be b.
15:13 b. her idol, 2 Chr. 15:16
2 K. 23:16 out of sepulc. b. them
25:9 b. house of the L. 2 Chr. 36:19; Jer. 52:13
Job 30:30 my bones are b.
Ps. 102:3 my bones b. as hearth
Prov. 6:27 his clothes not be b.?
28 and his feet not be b.?

Jer. 2:15 cities b.; 6:29 bellows b.
36:28 in the roll Jehoiakim b.
51:25 make thee a b. mountain
Ezek. 20:47 all faces be b. therein
24:10 and let the bones be b.
Joel 1:19 the flame b. all the trees
Amos 2:1 bec. he b. bones of k.
Nah. 1:5 earth is b. at his pres.
1 Cor. 3:15 man's work be b.
Heb. 13:11 b. without the camp

**BURNT joined with fire.**

Lev. 6:30 sin-offer. b. in the fire
20:14 if a man take a wife and her mother, shall be b. w. f.
21:9 if daughter of any priest pro. herself, be b. with fire
Num. 11:1 fl. of L. b. 3
Deut. 4:11 mountain b. with fire
12:31 sons and d. they b. in fire
Jos. 7:15 he taken with accursed thing be b. with fire
Jud. 15:6 b. her and fath. with fl.
14 cords bec. as flax b. with fl.
2 Sam. 23:7 shall be b. with fire
1 K. 16:18 b. king's house with f.
2 K. 1:14 fire b. up two captains
17:31 Seph. b. children in fire
23:11 b. chariots of sun with fl.
25:9 great man's house b. w. fl.
1 Chr. 14:12 gods were b. with fl.
2 Chr. 28:3 A. b. his child. in fl.
Neh. 1:3 gates b. with fl. 2:17
Ps. 80:16 it is b. with fire
Is. 1:7 cities are b. with fire
43:2 walkest thr. fire not be b.
64:11 house is b. with fire
Jer. 38:17 city not be b. with fl.
49:2 her dau. shall be b. with fl.
51:32 reeds may have b. with fl.
58 high gates be b. with fire
Rev. 18:8 utterly b. with fire

**BURNT incense.**

Ex. 40:27 he b. sweet incense
1 K. 9:25 Solomon b. i. upon alt.
12:33 Jerob. offered, and b. i.
22:43 people yet b. i. 2 K. 12:3; 14:4; 15:4, 35
2 Chr. 29:7 and have not b. i.
Is. 65:7 b. i. on the mountains
Jer. 18:15 my people b. i.
44:15 that their wives had b. i.
Hos. 2:13 she b. i. to them
11:2 and b. i. to graven images

**BURNT-OFFERING.**

Gen. 22:7 where is l. for a b.-o.?
8 G. will provide lamb for b.-o.
Lev. 6:9 law of the b.-o. 7:37
9:2 ram for b.-o. 16:3, 5; 23:18
Num. 7:15 one lamb for b.-o. 21 to 81; Ezek. 45:15
23:3 stand by thy b.-o. 15
28:10 the b.-o. of every sabbath
Jos. 22:26 altar not for a b.-o.
Jud. 13:23 not have rec. a b.-o.
1 Sam. 7:10 as S. was off. b.-o.
13:12 forced myself and off. b.-o.
2 K. 3:27 offered him for a b.-o.
2 Chr. 7:1 fire consumed the b.-o.
29:24 the b.-o. sh. be made
Ps. 40:6 b.-o. hast thou not req.
51:16 delightest not in b.-o.
19 pl. with b.-o. whole b.-o.
Is. 40:16 nor beasts th. for b.-o.
61:8 L. hate robbery for b.-o.
Ezek. 46:13 daily prepare a b.-o.

**Continual BURNT-OFFERING.**

Ex. 29:42 a con. b.-o. Num. 28:3, 6, 10, 15, 24, 31; 29:11, 16, 19, 22; Ezr. 3:5; Neh. 10:33; Ezek. 46:15

**Offer BURNT-OFFERING.**

Gen. 22:2 take I. o. for b.-o.
Jud. 11:31 o. it up for b.-o.
13:16 b.-o offer it to the Lord
1 Sam. 6:14 offer kine for b.-o.
7:9 off. sucking lamb for b.-o.
2 Chr. 29:27 Hez. com. to o. b.-o.
Job 42:8 o. for yourselves a b.-o.

**BURNT-OFFERINGS.**

Gen. 8:20 N. offered b.-o. on altar
Num. 10:10 trumpets over b.-o.
1 Sam. 15:22 delight in b.-o.
1 K. 3:15 Solomon offered b.-o.
2 Chr. 2:4 b. a house for b.-o.
29:34 not slay all the b.-o.
35:14 busied in offering b.-o.
Ezr. 6:9 have need for b.-o.
Job 1:5 off. b.-o. accor. to num.
Ps. 50:8 not re. thee for b.-o.
66:13 into thy house with b.-o.
Is. 1:11 full of b.-o. of rams
43:23 small cattle of thy b.-o.
56:7 b.-o. shall be accepted
Jer. 6:20 b.-o. are not acceptable
7:21 put your b.-o. to your sacri.
17:26 from south bringing b.-o.
19:5 burn sons for b.-o. to Baal
Hos. 6:6 know. of G. m. than b.-o.
Mic. 6:6 before him with b.-o.?
Mark 12:33 to love neighbor is more than b.-o.
Heb. 10:6 in b.-o. for sin

**Offer BURNT-OFFERINGS.**

2 Sam. 24:24 o. b.-o. of that cost me nothing, 1 Chr. 21:24
1 K. 3:4 1000 b.-o. did Solomon of.
Jer. 33:18 want man to o. b.-o.
Amos 5:22 ye offer me b.-o.

**BURNT-SACRIFICE.**

Num. 23:6 he stood by his b.-s.
Deut. 33:10 shall put whole b.-s.
2 Sam. 24:22 oxen for b.-s.
1 K. 18:38 fire fell and c. b.-s.
Ps. 20:3 accept thy b.-s.

**BURNT-SACRIFICES.**

1 Chr. 23:31 to offer all b.-s.
2 Chr. 13:11 morn. and eve. b.-s.
Ps. 66:15 I will offer b.-s.

**BURNT up.**

Jud. 15:5 foxes b. up the shocks
2 K. 1:14 fire b. up two captains
Job 1:16 fire of God b. up sheep
Ps. 74:8 have b. up synagogue
106:18 flame b. up the wicked
Is. 64:11 beautiful house b. up
Jer. 9:10 b. up none can pass, 12
Mat. 22:7 king b. up their city
2 Pet. 3:10 earth and w. be b. up
Rev. 8:7 third part of trees and all green grass was b. up

**BURST.**

Job 32:19 I am ready to b. like
Prov. 3:10 b. with new wine
Jer. 2:20 I have b. thy bands, 5:5; 30:8; Nah. 1:13
Mark 2:22 wine b. bot. Lu. 5:37
Acts 1:18 he b. asunder in midst

**BURSTING.**

Is. 30:14 in the b. of it a sherd

**BURY.**

Gen. 23:4 b. my d.; 6 b. dead, 11:15
47:29 b. me not in Egypt, 49:29
50:5 let me go and b. my father
1 K. 2:31 fall on Joab and b. him
13:29 old proph. came to b. him
31 b. me in the sepulchre
14:13 Israel shall b. him
2 K. 9:10 shall be none to b. her
34 this cursed woman b. her
35 went to b. her
Ps. 79:3 was none to b. them
Jer. 7:32 shall b. in Tophet, 19:11
14:16 shall have none to b. them
Ezek. 39:11 there shall they b. G.
13 all the people shall b. them
Hos. 9:6 Memphis shall b. them
Mat. 8:21 go b. father, Lu. 9:59
22 dead b. their dead, Lu. 9:60
27:7 potter's field, to b. strang.
John 19:40 manner of J. is to b.

**BURYING.**

Gen. 23:4 b. pl. 9; 49:30; 50:13
2 K. 13:21 as they were b.
Ezek. 39:12 sev. mon. b. of them
Mark 14:8 anoint my body to b.
John 12:7 against my b. she kept

**BUSH, ES.**

Ex. 3:2 in the b. Acts 7:30
4 God called to him out of b.
Deut. 33:16 good-w. of him in b.
Job 30:4 cut mallows by the b.
7 among the b. they brayed
Is. 7:19 and rest upon all b.
Mark 12:26 how in b. God spake
Luke 6:44 nor of bramble-b.
20:37 dead r. Moses showed at b.
Acts 7:35 angel which app. in b.

**BUSHEL.**

Mat. 5:15 a candle and put it under a b. Mark 4:21; Lu. 11:33

**BUSHY.**

Cant. 5:11 his locks are b.

**BUSINESS.**

Gen. 39:11 J. went to do his b.
Deut. 24:5 nor be charged with b.
Jos. 2:14 utter not this our b.
Jud. 18:7 had no b. with any, 28
1 Sam. 20:19 hide wh. b. in hand
21:2 let no man know of the b.
8 the king's b. required haste
2 Chr. 13:10 wait on their b.
32:31 in b. of the ambassadors
Neh. 13:30 every man in his b.
Est. 3:9 that have charge of b.
Ps. 107:23 do b. in great waters
Prov. 22:29 a man dilig. in his b.
Ec. 5:3 through mult. of b.
Dan. 8:27 did the king's b.
Luke 2:49 about my Father's b.
Acts 6:3 may appoint over this b.
Rom. 12:11 not slothful in b.
16:2 assist in b. she hath need
1 Thes. 4:11 to do your own b.

**BUSY, IED.**

1 K. 20:40 as thy serv. was busy
2 Chr. 35:14 sons of Aaron b.

**BUSYBODY, IES.**

2 Thes. 3:11 are b. 1 Tim. 5:13
1 Pet. 4:15 let none suffer as a b.

**BUTLER, S.**

Gen. 40:9 b. told dream to Jos.
21 restored the chief b. to his
41:9 b. said, I remem. my faults

**BUTTER.**

Gen. 18:8 Abra. took b. and milk
Deut. 32:14 b. of kine
Jud. 5:25 bro. b. in lordly dish
2 Sam. 17:29 Barzillai brought b.
Job 20:17 brooks of honey and b.
29:6 I washed my steps with b.
Ps. 55:21 smoother than b.
Prov. 30:33 churn. of milk bri. b.
Is. 7:15 b. shall he eat, 22

**BUTTOCKS.**

2 Sam. 10:4 garm. to b. 1 Ch. 19:4
Is. 20:4 b. uncov. to shame of E.

**BUY.**

Gen. 42:7 fr. Can. to b. food, 43:20
47:19 b. us and our land
Ex. 21:2 if b. Hebrew servant
Lev. 25:44 shall b. bondmen, 45
Deut. 2:6 ye shall b. meat
28:68 and no man shall b you
Ruth 4:5 must b. it also of Ruth
2 Sam. 24:21 D. said, to b. the thresh.-floor, 24; 1 Chr. 21:24
Neh. 10:31 not b. it on sabbath
Is. 55:1 b. eat, b. wine and milk
Jer. 32:7 b. my field in Anathoth
44 men shall b. fields for money

*Mat.* 14:15 *b.* victuals, *Mark* 6:36
25:9 go to them that sell, and *b.*
10 went to *b.* bridegroom came
*Mark* 6:37 sh. we *b.* 200 p. worth
*Luke* 9:13 *b.* meat for this peo.
22:36 let him sell garm. and *b.*
*John* 4:8 were gone to *b.* meat
6:5 whence shall we *b.* bread
13:29 *b.* things we have need of
1 *Cor.* 7:30 *b.* as though they pos.
*Jam.* 4:13 *b.* and sell and get gain
*Rev.* 3:18 to *b.* of me gold tried
13:17 no man might *b.* or sell

**BUY corn.**

*Gen.* 41:57 all came to Jos. to *b. c.*
42:3 Joseph's brethren to *b. c.* 5
*Neh.* 5:3 mort. our lands to *b. c.*

**BUY poor.**

*Amos* 8:6 may *b.* the *poor* for sil.

**BUY truth.**

*Prov.* 23:23 *b. truth*, sell it not

**BUYER.**

*Prov.* 20:14 it is naught, saith *b.*
*Is.* 24:2 as with the *b.* so the s.
*Ezek.* 7:12 let not *b.* rejoice, nor

**BUYEST.**

*Lev.* 25:14 and if thou *b.* aught
*Ruth* 4:5 day *b.* field of Naomi

**BUYETH.**

*Prov.* 31:16 consider. field, *b.* it
*Mat.* 13:44 he selleth all, *b.* field
*Rev.* 18:11 no man *b.* her mer.

**BUZ.**

*Gen.* 22:21 M. bare to Nahor B.
1 *Chr.* 5:14 Jahdo, the son of B
*Jer.* 25:23 B. to drink the cup

BUZI. *Ezek.* 1:3.
BUZITE. *Job* 32:2, 6

**BY and BY.**

*Mat.* 13:21 *b. and b.* he is off.
*Mark* 6:25 give me *b. and b.* head
*Luke* 17:7 *b. and b.* sit down
21:9 the end is not *b. and b.*

**BY-WAYS.**

*Jud.* 5:6 walked through *b.-w.*

**BYWORD.**

*Deut.* 28:37 a *b.* among nations
1 *K.* 9:7 be *b.* among all people
2 *Chr.* 7:20 make this house a *b.*
*Job* 17:6 made me a *b.* of the
30:9 yea I am their *b.*
*Ps.* 44:14 a *b.* among heathen

# C

**CABINS.**

*Jer.* 37:16 when J. entered into *c.*

CABUL. 1 *K.* 9:13.

**CAGE.**

*Jer.* 5:27 as a *c.* is full of birds
*Rev.* 18:2 *c.* of every uncl. bird

CAIAPHAS. *Mat.* 26:3, 7; *John* 11:49; 18:14, 28.

**CAIN.**

*Gen.* 4:2, 5, 15, 25; *Jos.* 15:57.
*Heb.* 11:4 excel. sacrifice than C.
1 *John* 3:12 not as C. who was of
*Jude* 11 gone in the way of C.

**CAINAN.**

*Luke* 3:36 the son of C. 37

**CAKE, S.**

*Lev.* 24:5 bake twelve *c.* thereof
*Jud.* 7:13 a *c.* tumbled into host
2 *Sam.* 6:19 D. dealt to each a *c.*
2 *Sam.* 13:6 Tam. m. couple of *c.*
1 *K.* 17:12 I have not a *c.*
19:6 there was a *c.* baken
*Ezek.* 4:12 shalt eat it as barley *c.*
*Hos.* 7:8 Ephr. is a *c.* not turned
*See* FIGS, UNLEAVENED.

CALAH. *Gen.* 10:12.

**CALAMITY, IES.**

*Deut.* 32:35 their *c.* is at hand
2 *Sam.* 22:19 day of *c.* *Ps.* 18:18
*Job* 6:2 my *c.* laid in balances
30:13 they set forward my *c.*
*Ps.* 57:1 until these *c.* be overp.
141:5 my prayer be in their *c.*
*Prov.* 1:26 I will laugh at your *c.*
6:15 his *c.* shall come suddenly
17:5 he glad at *c.* not be unpun.
19:13 foolish son is *c.* of father
24:22 *c.* shall rise suddenly
27:10 nor go to brother's h. in *c.*
*Jer.* 18:17 the back in day of *c.*
46:21 day of their *c.* was come
48:16 *c.* of Moab is near to come
49:8 bring *c.* of Esau upon him
32 bring their *c.* from all sides
*Ezek.* 35:5 shed blood of Israel by sword in day of their *c.*
*Ob.* 13 sub. in day of their *c.*

**CALAMUS.**

*Ex.* 30:23 sweet *c.* 250 shekels
*Cant.* 4:14 spikenard, saffron, *c.*
*Ezek.* 27:19 *c.* in market of Tyrus

**CALDRON.**

1 *Sam.* 2:14 he struck it into *c.*
*Job* 41:20 smoke, as out of a *c.*
*Ezek.* 11:3 this city is the *c.* 7
*Mic.* 3:3 chop them as flesh in *c.*

**CALDRONS.**

2 *Chr.* 35:13 offering sod in *c.*
*Jer.* 52:18 *c.* took they away, 19

**CALEB.**

*Num.* 13:6, 30; 14:24, 38; 34:19
*Jos.* 14:13 Josh. gave C. Hebron
15:14 C. drove sons of Anak, 16
1 *Sam.* 25:3 N. was of house of C.
30:14 south of C. burnt Ziklag

CALEB-EPHRATAH. 1 *Chr.* 2:24

**CALF.**

*Gen.* 18:7 Abraham fetched a *c.*
*Ex.* 32:20 Moses burnt *c.*
*Deut.* 9:16 made you a molten *c.* *Neh.* 9:18; *Ps.* 106:19
*Job* 21:10 their cow casteth not *c.*
*Ps.* 29:6 maketh to skip like a *c.*
*Is.* 11:6 *c.* and young lion
27:10 there sh. *c.* feed and lie
*Jer.* 34:18 when cut *c.* in twain
*Ezek.* 1:7 their feet like *c.* foot
*Hos.* 8:5 thy *c.* O S. cast thee off
6 *c.* of Samaria shall be broken
*Luke* 15:23 bring hither fatted *c.*
27 killed fatted *c.* 30
*Acts* 7:41 make a *c.* in those days
*Rev.* 4:7 second beast like a *c.*

**CALKERS.**

*Ezek.* 27:9 ancients of Geb. thy *c.*
27 thy *c.* shall fall into seas

**CALL.**

*Gen.* 2:19 what A. would *c.* them
*Num.* 22:20 if the men *c.* thee
*Deut.* 4:7 God is in all we *c.* for
26 I *c.* heaven and earth to wit. ag. you, 30:19; 31:28
*Jud.* 21:13 to *c.* peaceably
1 *Sam.* 3:6 thou didst *c.* me, 8
1 *K.* 8:52 hearken in all they *c.*
18:24 *c.* ye on your gods
*Job* 5:1 *c.* now if any
13:22 *c.* I will answer, 14:15
*Ps.* 4:1 hear when I *c.* O God
3 the Lord will hear when I *c.*
14:4 who eat my peo. and *c.* not
20:9 let king hear us when we *c.*
49:11 *c.* lands after their names
77:6 I *c.* to rem. my song in n.
86:5 plen. in m. to all *c.* on thee
99:6 among them *c.* on name
102:2 when I *c.* answer me sp.
145:18 L. is nigh all that *c.*
*Prov.* 8:4 to you, O men, I *c.*
9:15 *c.* passengers who go right
31:28 her children *c.* her blessed
*Is.* 5:20 them that *c.* evil good
45:3 *c.* thee by thy name
48:2 *c.* themselves of holy city
13 when I *c.* they stand up
55:6 *c.* on him while he is near
58:5 wilt thou *c.* this a fast
13 *c.* the sabbath a delight
65:15 *c.* his serv. by ano. name
24 before they *c.* I will answer
*Jer.* 33:3 *c.* to me, I will ans. thee
*Lam.* 2:15 men *c.* perfection
*Hos.* 1. 4 L. said, *c.* his n. Jezreel
6 *c.* his name Lo-ruhamah
9 *c.* his name Lo-ammi
7:11 *c.* to Egypt, go to Assy.
*Joel* 1:14 *c.* a sol. assembly, 2:15
*Jon.* 1:6 sleeper *c.* on thy God
*Zec.* 3:10 *c.* ev. man his neighbor
*Mal.* 3:15 we *c.* the proud happy
*Mat.* 9:13 not come to *c.* righteous, *Mark* 2:17; *Luke* 5:32
22:3 servants to *c.* them bidden
43 D. in spirit *c.* him Lord
23:9 *c.* no man father on earth
*Luke* 6:46 why *c.* me Lord
14:13 makest feast *c.* the poor
*John* 13:13 ye *c.* me Master
*Acts* 9:14 all *c.* on thy name
19:3 to *c.* over them had evil spi.
24:14 after way they *c.* heresy
*Rom.* 10:12 to all that *c.* on him
2 *Cor.* 1:23 I *c.* God for a record
2 *Tim.* 2:22 peace wi. th. *c.* on L.
*Heb.* 2:11 not asha. to *c.* them
10:32 *c.* to remem. former days
*Jam.* 5:14 let him *c.* the elders
1 *Pet.* 1:17 if ye *c.* on the Father

**CALL on the name of the Lord.**

*Gen.* 4:26 began men to *c. on L.*
1 *K.* 18:24 I will *c. L.* *Ps.* 116:17
2 *K.* 5:11 will come and *c. on L.*
1 *Chr.* 16:8 *c.* upon his name, *Ps.* 105:1; *Is.* 12:4
*Joel* 2:32 whosoever shall *c. on L.* *Acts* 2:21; *Rom.* 10:13
*Zep.* 3:9 they may all *c. on L.*
1 *Cor.* 1:2 in every place *c. L.*

**Not CALL.**

*Ruth* 1:20 *c.* me *not* N. *c.* me M.
*Ps.* 14:4 *c. not* upon the Lord
*Is.* 31:2 will *not c.* back his w.
*Jer.* 10:25 fury upon the families that *c. not* on thy name
*Luke* 14:12 *c. not* thy friends nor
*John* 15:15 I *c.* you *not* servants
*Acts* 10:15 *c. not* common, 11:9
28 *not* to *c.* any man common

**Shall, *or* shalt CALL.**

*Deut.* 30:1 *shalt c.* them to mind
33:19 *shall c.* people to moun.
*Job* 14:15 *shalt c.* I will answer
*Ps.* 50:4 *shall c.* to the heavens
72:17 nations *s. c.* him blessed

*Is.* 7:14 *s. c.* Imman. *Mat.* 1:23
41:25 rising of sun *shall* he *c.*
44:5 *s. c.* himself by name of J.
7 and who, as I, *shall c.* and
55:5 *shall c.* a nation
58:9 *shalt c.* and L. shall answer
60:14 *shall c.* thee city of Lord
18 *shalt c.* thy walls salvation
61:6 men *s. c.* you min. of our G.
62:12 *shall c.* them holy people
*Jer.* 3:17 *s. c.* Jer. throne of Lord
19 thou *shalt c.* me, my father
7:27 *shalt c.* to them, not answ.
*Hos.* 2:16 *shalt c.* me no more B.
*Joel* 2:32 the remnant L. *shall c.*
*Zec.* 13:9 they *shall c.* I will hear
*Mal.* 1:4 *s. c.* them bord. of wick.
3:12 nations *shall c.* you blessed
*Mat.* 1:21 *shalt c.* his name Jesus
10:25 much more *s. c.* them
*Luke* 1:13 *shalt c.* his name John
48 generations *s. c.* me blessed
*Acts* 2:39 as many as the L. *s. c.*
*Rom.* 10:14 how *s.* they *c.* on him

**Will CALL.**

1 *Sam.* 12:17 I *will c.* to Lord.
2 *Sam.* 22:4 I *will c.* Lord, *Ps.* 18:3
*Job* 27:10 *will* hypocrite *c.* on G.
*Ps.* 55:16 I *will c.* on God, 86:7
80:18 quicken us, we *will c.*
116:2 *w.* I *c.* on him
*Is.* 22:20 that I *w. c.* my ser. E.
*Jer.* 1:15 I *will c.* fam. of north
*Rom.* 9:25 I *w. c.* them my peo.

**CALL upon me.**

*Ps.* 50:15 *c. u. m.* in d. of trouble
91:15 he shall *c. upon me*
*Prov.* 1:28 *c. u. m.* but I will
*Jer.* 29:12 then shall ye *c. u. m.*

**CALLED.**

*Gen.* 11:9 name of it *c.* Babel
21:17 *c.* to Hagar out of heaven
22:11 *c.* to Abrah. out of heaven
35:10 not be *c.* any more Jacob
18 his father *c.* him Benjamin
*Ex.* 8:8 Pharaoh *c.* for Moses, 25;
9:27; 10:16, 24; 12:31
*Deut.* 5:1 Moses *c.* all Israel, 29:2
15:2 it is *c.* the Lord's release
28:10 thou art *c.* by name of L.
*Jud.* 14:15 S. wife, have ye *c.* us
15:17 cast away jawb. *c.* place
*Jud.* 15:18 w. athirst, and *c.* on L.
16:28 Samson *c.* to the Lord
1 *Sam.* 9:9 now *c.* a proph. was *c.*
2 *Sam.* 6:2 name is *c.* by name
12:28 city be *c.* after my name
1 *K.* 1:9 Adonijah *c.* breth. 19, 25
18:3 Ahab *c.* Obadiah the gov.
26 they *c.* on the name of Baal
1 *Chr.* 4:10 Jabez *c.* on God
13:6 whose name is *c.* on it
21:26 David *c.* on Lord
*Est.* 2:14 except that she were *c.*
4:11 I have not been *c.* to come
*Ps.* 53:4 they have not *c.* on G.
79:6 kingd. not *c.* on thy name
*Is.* 43:22 hast not *c.* on me, O J.
48:1 ye. *c.* by the name of Israel
12 O Jacob, my *c.*
61:3 be *c.* trees of righteousness
*Lam.* 1:21 bring day thou hast *c.*
2:22 thou hast *c.* my terrors
*Ezek.* 20:29 name is *c.* Bamah
*Dan.* 5:12 now let Daniel be *c.*
*Mat.* 1:16 Jesus who is *c.* Christ
13:55 is not his mother *c.* Mary?
18:2 *c.* a little child unto him
20:16 many be *c.* few cho. 22:14
32 Jesus stood still and *c.* them
23:8 be not ye *c.* Rabbi, 10
27:17 shall I release J. *c.* C. 22
*Mark* 10:49 J. com. him to be *c.*
14:72 P. *c.* to mind word J. said
*Luke* 1:61 none of thy kind. is *c.*
62 how he would have him *c.*
15:19 worthy to be *c.* thy son, 21
19:15 he com. servants to be *c.*
23:33 place that is *c.* Calvary
*John* 1:48 before Philip *c.* thee I
4:25 cometh which is *c.* Christ
9:11 a man *c.* Jesus made clay
*Acts* 9:11 go into str. *c.* Straight
11:26 disciples first *c.* Christians
13:7 *c.* for Barnabas and Saul
15:17 on whom my name is *c.*
19:40 *c.* in quest. for this day's
23:6 I am *c.* in question, 24:21
18 Paul the prisoner *c.* me
*Rom.* 1:1 P. *c.* to be apos. 1 *Cor.* 1:1
6 are ye also the *c.* of Jesus
7 *c.* to be saints, 1 *Cor.* 1:2
2:17 thou art *c.* a Jew
8:28 the *c.* acc. to his purpose
1 *Cor.* 1:9 were *c.* to fellowship
24 *c.* both Jews and Greeks
26 not many noble are *c.*
5:11 *c.* a brother be a fornicator
7:18 *c.* being circum.? is any *c.*
21 art thou *c.* being a servant?
24 wherein he is *c.*
*Gal.* 1:6 removed from him *c.* you
5:13 ye have been *c.* to liberty
*Eph.* 2:11 *c.* uncircum. by that *c.*
4:1 vocation wherew. ye are *c.*
4 even as ye are *c.* in one hope
*Col.* 3:15 to the which ye are *c.*
2 *Thes.* 2:4 exalteth above all *c.*
1 *Tim.* 6:12 et. life, wher. art *c.*
20 science falsely so *c.*
*Heb.* 3:13 while it is *c.* to-day
9:15 they *c.* might rec. promise
11:16 not ash. to be *c.* their G.
24 to be *c.* son of Phar. daught.
*Jam.* 2:7 name by wh. ye are *c.*
1 *Pet.* 2:9 *c.* you out of darkness
21 even hereunto were ye *c.*
3:9 that ye are thereunto *c.*
2 *Pet.* 1:3 that hath *c.* us to glory
1 *John* 3:1 sh. be *c.* the sons of G.
*Jude* 1 preserved in J. Ch. and *c.*
*Rev.* 8:11 star is *c.* Wormwood
11:8 city spiritually *c.* Sodom
17:18 they with him are *c.*
19:9 blessed are *c.* to mar. sup.

**CALLED,** *joined with* **God** *or* **Lord.**

*Gen.* 1:5 God *c.* the light Day
5:2 and *c.* their name Adam
*Ex.* 3:4 God *c.* to him
19:3 L. *c.* to him out of mount.
20 L. *c.* Moses to top of mount
*Num.* 12:5 L. *c.* Aaron and Mir.
1 *Sam.* 3:4 L. *c.* Samuel, 6, 8, 10
*Ps.* 50:1 *c.* earth from the rising
*Is.* 41:2 Lord *c.* him to his foot
42:6 I have *c.* thee in righteous.
49:1 L. hath *c.* me
54:6 *c.* thee as a woman fors.
*Jer.* 11:16 *c.* name green olive-t.
20:3 not *c.* thy name Pashur
*Amos* 7:4 God *c.* to contend
*Acts* 16:10 gath. that Lord *c.* us
1 *Cor.* 7:15 G. hath *c.* us to peace
17 L. hath *c.* every one, so let
*Gal.* 1:15 who *c.* me by grace
1 *Thes.* 2:12 *c.* you to his kingd.
4:7 hath not *c.* us to unclean.
2 *Thes.* 2:14 God *c.* you
2 *Tim.* 1:9 *c.* us with a holy call.
*Heb.* 5:4 *c.* of God as was Aaron
10 *c.* of God a high-priest after
1 *Pet.* 5:10 G. who hath *c.* us

**He CALLED.**

*Gen.* 26:18 *c.* names as hi[illegible] f. *c.*
35:10 *he c.* his name Isr[illegible]
*Ex.* 24:16 *c.* to M. out of [illegible]oud
2 *K.* 4:36 *c.* to Gehazi, s[illegible]e *c.*
*Ps.* 105:16 *he c.* for a fam[illegible]e on
*Lam.* 1:15 *c.* an assembly
*Mat.* 10:1 *c.* twelve; 15:10 mult.
*Mark* 1:20 *he c.* them
*Luke* 13:12 Jesus saw her, *he c.*
*John* 10:35 if *he c.* them gods
*Acts* 9:41 had *c.* saints and wid.
10:23 *c. he* them in, and lodged
23:23 *he c.* unto him two centur.
*Rom.* 8:30 *he* also *c.* whom he *c.*
9:24 even us whom *he* hath *c.*
1 *Pet.* 1:15 hath *c.* you is holy

*See* CALLED *the name.*

**I CALLED,** *or* **I have CALLED.**

*Num.* 24:10 *I c.* thee to curse
1 *Sam.* 3:5 Eli said, *I c.* not, 6
28:15 therefore *I have c.* thee
2 *Sam.* 22:7 in my distress *I c.*
*Ps.* 18:6; 118:5
*Job* 9:16 if *I* had *c.* and he answ.
19:16 *I c.* my servant, no answ.
*Ps.* 17:6 *I have c.* on thee, for
31:17 not be ashamed, *I have c.*
88:9 *I have c.* daily upon thee
116:4 then *c. I* on name of Lord
*Prov.* 1:24 *I have c.* and ye ref.
*Cant.* 5:6 *I c.* him
*Is.* 13:3 *I have c.* my mighty
41:9 *I have c.* thee from chief
43:1 *I c.* thee by thy name, 45:4
48:15 yea, *I have c.* him
50:2 *I c.* was there none to ans.
51:2 for *I c.* him alone
65:12 *I c.* ye did not a. *Jer.* 7:13
66:4 when *I c.* none did answer
*Jer.* 35:17 *I have c.* to them, but
*Lam.* 1:19 *I c.* for my lovers, but
3:55 *I c.* out of the low dungeon
57 drewest near in day *I c.* on
*Hos.* 11:1 then *I c.* my son out of
Egypt, *Mat.* 2:15
*Zec.* 11:7 one *I c.* b. other *I c.*
*John* 15:15 *I have c.* you friends
*Acts* 13:2 work wh. *I have c.* them
28:20 *have I c.* for you, to see

**CALLED by my name.**

2 *Chr.* 7:14 if my people which
are *c. by my name* humble
*Is.* 43:7 even every one *c. n.*
65:1 to nation not *c. my n.*
*Jer.* 7:10 this house *c. b. m. name,*
11, 14, 30; 32:34; 34:15
25:29 evil on city *c. by n.*
*Amos* 9:12 remnant of heath. *c. n.*

**CALLED by thy name.**

1 *K.* 8:43 house *c. b. t. n.* 2 *Chr.* 6:33
*Is.* 4:1 let us be *c. by t. n.* to take
43:1 I have *c.* thee *by t. n.* 45:4
63:19 were not *c. by thy name*
*Jer.* 14:9 we are *c. by thy n.*
15:16 am *c. t. n.* O L. G. of hosts
*Dan.* 9:18 the city *c. by thy n.*
19 for thy people are *c. n.*

**CALLED his name.**

*Gen.* 35:10 *c. n.* Is.; 18 Benoni
1 *Chr.* 4:9 Jabez; 7:16 Peresh; 23 Ber.
*Mat.* 1:25 he *c. his name* Jesus
*Rev.* 19:13 *n.* is *c.* the word of G.

**Sent and CALLED.**

*Acts* 20:17 *s.* to Ephesus *c.* elders

**Shall be CALLED.**

*Gen.* 2:23 *s. c.* Woman, because
17:5 name *shall be c.* Abraham
21:12 in Isaac *shall* thy seed *be c.* *Rom.* 9:7; *Heb.* 11:18
32:28 *shall be c.* no more Jacob
48:6 issue *s. c.* after their breth.
*Prov.* 16:21 wise in heart *s. c.*
24:8 deviseth evil *s. c.* mischiev.
*Is.* 4:3 remain. in Jer. *s. c.* holy
9:6 his name *s. be c.* Wonderful
32:5 no more *shall be c.* liberal
35:8 *s. be c.* the way of holiness
54:5 G. of whole earth *s.* he *be c.*
56:7 *s. c.* h. of prayer, *Mat.* 21:13
*Jer.* 23:6 *s. c.* L. our right. 33:16
*Zec.* 8:3 J. *s. be c.* city of truth
*Mat.* 2:23 *shall be c.* a Nazarene
5:9 peacemakers *s. c.* child. of G.
19 *s. be c.* least in kingdom

Luke 1:32 s. c. Son of the Highest
35 holy thing s. be c. the Son
60 but he shall be c. John
2:23 every male shall be c. holy
Rom. 9:26 s. be c. children of G.

**Shalt be CALLED.**

Is. 1:26 s. c. city of righteousness
47:1 shalt be c. no more tender
5 s. no more be c. a lady of k.
58:12 s. be c. repairer of the br.
62:2 s. be c. by a new name
4 s. c. Hephzi-bah, thy land B.
12 s. be c. Sought out, A city n.
Luke 1:76 s. c. proph. of Highest
John 1:42 thou shalt be c. Cephas

**They CALLED.**

Num. 25:2 t. c. people to sacrifices
Est. 9:26 they c. these days Pur.
Ps. 99:6 t. c. upon the Lord, and
Jer. 12:6 t. c. a multitude
30:17 bec. t. c. thee an outcast
Hos. 11:2 as they c. them, so they
7 t. c. them to Most High
Mat. 10:25 t. c. master Beelzebub
Luke 1:59 t. c. him Zacharias
John 9:18 t. c. parents of him
24 c. they man that was blind
Acts 4:18 t. c. com. not to speak
5:40 when t. had c. the apostles
14:12 they c. Barnabas Jupiter

**Was CALLED.**

Is. 48:8 was c. a transgressor
Luke 2:21 his name was c. Jesus
John 2:2 J. w. c. and his discip.
Acts 24:2 he w. c. forth, Tertullus
1 Cor. 7:20 calling wh. he w. c.
Heb. 11:8 A. wh. he w. c. obeyed
Jam. 2:23 w. c. the friend of God
Rev. 19:11 sat on him w. c. faith.

**CALLEDST, EST.**

Jud. 8:1 c. us not when wentest
1 Sam. 3:5 here am I, thou c. me
Ps. 81:7 thou c. in trouble
Mat. 19:17 w. c. thou me good?
Mark 10:18; Luke 18:19

**CALLETH.**

1 K. 8:43 do accor. to all stranger
c. to thee for, 2 Chr. 6:33
Job 12:4 c. on God, and he ans.
Ps. 42:7 deep c. unto deep
147:4 c. them, Is. 40:26
Prov. 18:6 mouth c. for strokes
Is. 21:11 he c. to me out of Seir
59:4 none c. for justice, nor any
64:7 none that c. on thy name
Hos. 7:7 none that c. to me
Amos 5:8 c. for waters of sea, 9:6
Mat. 27:47 c. for E. Mark 15:35
Mark 3:13 c. to him whom he w.
6:7 c. to him the twelve
8:1 Jesus c. his disciples
10:49 arise, he c. thee
12:37 David c. him L. Luke 20:44
Lu. 15:6 he c. together his friends
9 c. her friends and neighbors
20:37 when he c. L. the G. of A.
John 10:3 c. his sheep by name
11:28 the Master c. for thee
Rom. 4:17 c. things which be not
9:11 election m. stand of him c.
1 Cor. 12:3 by Spirit c. Jesus
Gal. 5:8 not of him that c.
1 Thes. 5:24 faithful is he c. you
Rev. 2:20 c. herself a prophetess

**CALLING, Substantive.**

Is. 1:13 c. of assemblies I cannot
Ezek. 23:19 c. to rem. her youth
Rom. 11:29 c. of God without
1 Cor. 1:26 ye see your c. breth.
7:20 ev. man abide in same c.
Eph. 1:18 the hope of his c.
4:4 called in one hope of your c.
Phil. 3:14 the high c. of God
2 Thes. 1:11 worthy of this c.
2 Tim. 1:9 called us w. a holy c.
Heb. 3:1 partakers of heavenly c.
2 Pet. 1:10 your c. and election

**CALLING, Participle.**

Is. 41:4 c. gen. from beginning
46:11 c. ravenous bird from east
Mat. 11:16 c. to fell. Luke 7:32
Mark 11:21 P. c. to remembrance
Acts 7:59 stoned Stephen c. on G.
22:16 thy sins, c. on Lord
1 Pet. 3:6 S. obeyed A. c. him lord

**CALM.**

Ps. 107:29 maketh storm a c.
Jon. 1:11 sea may be c. unto us
12 cast me forth, so sea be c.
Mat. 8:26 gr. c. Mark 4:39; Lu. 8:24

**CALNEH.**

Gen. 10:10 Babel and C. in land
Amos 6:2 pass ye unto C. from

CALNO. Is. 10:9
CALVARY. Luke 23:33

**CALVE, ED, ETH.**

Job 21:10 their cow c. casteth n.
39:1 mark when hinds do c.
Ps. 29:9 make hinds to c.
Jer. 14:5 the hind c. in the field

**CALVES.**

1 Sam. 6:7 bring c. home
1 K. 12:28 king made 2 c. of gold
32 sacrificing to c. he had m.
2 K. 10:29 dep. not from gold. c.
2 Chr. 11:15 ord. priests for the c.
13:8 there be with you golden c.
Ps. 68:30 rebuke bulls with the c.
Hos. 10:5 because of c. of Beth.
13:2 that sacrifice kiss the c.
14:2 render the c. of our lips
Amos 6:4 eat c. out of the stall
Mic. 6:6 with c. of a year old?
Mal. 4:2 ye shall grow up as c.
Heb. 9:12 nor by the blood of c.
19 blood of c. and sprinkled

**CAME.**

Gen. 27:35 brother c. w. subtilty
32:6 we c. to thy brother Esau
Num. 22:9 God c. to Balaam, 20
24:2 spirit of God c. upon him,
Jud. 3:10; 1 Sam. 10:10
Deut. 33:2 Lord c. from Sinai
Jud. 13:10 man that c. other day
1 Sam. 2:27 c. a man of G. to Eli
4:1 word of Samuel c. to all Isr.
2 Sam. 20:12 every one that c.
1 K. 1:42 while he spake Jon. c.
4:34 c. of all people to hear Sol.
13:10 returned not by way he c.
2 K. 6:32 ere the messe. c. he s.
10:21 all worshippers of Baal c.
17:28 one of priests c. to Bethel
19:33 by the way he c. return
24:3 at com. of Lord c. this on J.
1 Chr. 5:2 of Judah c. chief ruler
2 Chr. 11:14 Levites c. to Judah
14:14 fear of L. c. upon them
25:20 A. not hear, for it c. of G.
Est. 1:17 but Vashti c. not
Job 3:26 yet trouble c.
29:13 him ready to perish c.
30:26 I looked for good, evil c.
Ps. 18:6 my cry c. before him
27:2 when my foes c. upon me
78:31 wrath of G. c. upon them
88:17 they c. about me daily
105:19 until the time his w. c.
Ec. 5:15 to go as he c. 16
Is. 41:5 ends of earth were af. c.
Jer. 7:31 nor c. it into my mind,
19:5; 32:35
8:15 for peace, but no good c.
44:21 c. it not into his mind?
Ezek. 33:22 afore he that esc. c.
43:2 glory of G. c. from east
Dan. 4:28 all this c. on Nebuch.
Amos 6:1 to whom house of Is. c.
Hab. 3:3 G. c. from Teman, and
Mat. 3:1 in those days c. J. B.
9:1 and c. into his own city
20:28 c. not to be ministered to
21:30 he c. to second, said lik.
32 John c. in way of right.
25:36 in prison, ye c. to me
28:13 disciples c. by night
Mark 9:21 since this c. to him?
Luke 9:35 c. a voice out of cloud
15:17 when c. to himself, he said
20 he arose and c. to his father
John 1:11 he c. to his own
17 grace and truth c. by J. Chr.
3:2 same c. to Jesus, 7:50; 19:39
4:27 upon this c. his disciples
12:30 voice c. not because of me
20:19 at even c. J. in the midst
Acts 9:21 c. hither for that intent
19:18 many that believed c. and
Rom. 5:18 free gift c. on all men
7:9 when com. c. sin revived
9:5 whom con. the flesh C. c.
1 Cor. 15:21 since by man c. death
Gal. 2:12 certain c. from James
1 Thes. 1:5 gospel c. not in word
1 Tim. 1:15 that J. C. c. to save
2 Pet. 1:17 c. such a voice to him
18 this voice c. from heaven
21 proph. c. not by will of man
1 John 5:6 that c. by water and

See Spirit of the LORD.

**CAME again.**

Jud. 13:9 angel c. a. to the wom.
15:19 spirit c. a. 1 Sam. 30:12
1 K. 17:22 soul of the child c. a.
19:7 angel c. a. the second time
Luke 8:55 her spirit c. again
John 8:2 he c. a. into temple

**CAME down.**

Gen. 11:5 L. c. down to see tower
Ex. 19:20 L. c. d. on mount Sinai
34:29 Moses c. d. from mount S.
2 Sam. 22:10 bowed the heavens
and c. down, Ps. 18:9
Lam. 1:9 she c. down wonderf.
Dan. 4:13 holy one c. d. from h.
Mic. 1:12 evil c. down from the L.
Mat. 17:9 as c. d. fr. m. Mark 9:9
John 3:13 he that c. d. fr. heav.
6:38 I c. down from heaven
41 bread which c. d. 51, 58
Acts 15:1 which c. down from J.

**CAME forth.**

Num. 11:20 c. we f. out of Eg.?
Jud. 14:14 out of eater c. f. meat,
out of strong c. f. sweetness
2 Sam. 16:11 son which c. f. of
my bowels seeketh my life
2 Chr. 32:21 c. f. of his bowels
Prov. 7:15 c. I forth to meet thee
Ec. 5:15 as he c. f. naked
Jer. 20:18 c. I f. out of womb?
Zec. 10:4 of him c. f. the corner
Mark 1:38 for therefore c. I f.
John 16:28 I c. f. from the Father
19:5 J. c. f. wearing the crown

**I CAME.**

Gen. 30:30 thou hadst before I c.
1 K. 10:7 I believed not till I c.
half was not told, 2 Chr. 9:6
Is. 50:2 I c. was there no man?
Ezek. 3:15 I c. to them of capt.
Mat. 10:34 I c. not to send peace
Mark 2:17 I c. not to call, Lu. 5:32
John 8:14 I know whence I c.
42 I c. from G. nor c. I of mys.
12:27 for this cause c. I
47 I c. not to judge the world
18:37 for this cause c. I into w.
Acts 10:29 c. I, as soon as sent f.
20:18 from first day I c. into A.
22:11 I c. into Damascus
1 Cor. 2:1 I c. not with excellency
2 Cor. 1:23 to spare you I c. not
2:3 when I c. I sh. have sorrow

**CAME in.**
*Gen.* 6:4 sons of God *c. in*
19:5 where men *c. in* to thee
38:18 Judah *c. in* unto her
1 *Sam.* 18:13 David went out and *c. in* before the people, 16
2 *Sam.* 11:4 she *c. in* to him
2 *Chr.* 15:5 no p. to him that went out nor him *c. in*, *Zec.* 8:10
*Est.* 2:14 *c. in* to king no more
*Jer.* 37:4 Jer. *c. in* and went out
*Mat.* 22:10 k. *c. in* to see guests
*Luke* 1:28 angel *c. in* to Mary
7:45 since I *c. in* kissed my feet
*Gal.* 2:4 who *c. in* privily

**CAME near.**
*Ex.* 14:20 *c.* not *n.* other all night
*Deut.* 1:22 ye *c. n.* to me, 5:23
*Jos.* 17:4 they *c. n.* bef. El. 21:1
1 *K.* 18:36 Elijah *c. n.* and said
*Jer.* 42:1 least to the greatest *c. n.*
*Acts* 9:3 as he *c. n.* Damascus

**CAME nigh.**
*Mat.* 15:29 Jesus *c. n.* to sea of G.
*Mark* 11:1 when they *c. n.* to J.
*Luke* 7:12 when he *c. n.* to gate

**CAME out.**
*Gen.* 38:28 m. said this *c. o.* first
*Ex.* 13:3 remember day ye *c. o.* 4
*Num.* 16:27 Dathan and Ab. *c. o.*
2 *Sam.* 6:20 Michal *c. o.* to meet D.
18:4 people *c. out* by hundreds
*Job* 1:21 naked *c.* I *out* of womb
3:11 when I *c. out* of the belly
*Jer.* 17:16 which *c. o.* of my lips
*Mat.* 8:34 whole city *c. o.*
12:44 return to m. house whence I *c. out*, *Luke* 11:24
27:32 they *c. out* found Simon
53 *c. o.* of graves after his res.
*Mark* 1:26 unc. spirit *c. out*, 9:26
9:7 a voice *c. out* of the cloud
*Luke* 1:22 he *c. o.* could not speak
4:35 *c. out* of him, hurt him not
*John* 16:27 because ye believed I *c. out* from God
17:8 that I *c. out* from thee
19:34 forthwith *c. o.* blood
*Acts* 8:7 uncl. spir. *c. o.* of many
16:18 spirit *c. o.* the same hour
1 *Cor.* 14:36 *c.* word of G. *o.* from
*Heb.* 3:16 not all that *c. o.* of Eg.
*Rev.* 7:14 these *c. o.* of great trib.

**CAME over.**
*Jos.* 4:22 Is. *c. o.* J. on dry land
*Mark* 5:1 *c. over* to other side

**CAME to pass.**
*Ex.* 12:41 it *c. to p.* at end of 430 years, self-s. day it *c. to p.* 51
*Deut.* 2:16 *c. to p.* 1 *Sam.* 13:22; 2 *K.* 15:12; *Est.* 2:8; *Acts* 27:44
*Jos.* 21:45 L. had spoken all *c. p.*
1 *Sam.* 1:20 it *c. p.* wh. time was
10:9 all those signs *c. to pass*
2 *Sam.* 2:1 it *c. to p.* after, 8:1; 10:1; 2 *K.* 6:24; 2 *Chr.* 20:1
2 *K.* 8:15 it *c. to p.* on the morrow, 1 *Chr.* 10:8; *Jer.* 20:3; *Acts* 4:5
*Is.* 48:3 and they *c. to pass*
5 before it *c. to p.* I showed it
1 *Thes.* 3:4 as it *c. to pass.*

**Then CAME.**
2 *Sam.* 5:1 *then c.* all the tribes
2 *Chr.* 12:5 *t. c.* Shemaiah to R.
*Job* 30:26 for good *then* evil *c.*
*Jer.* 19:14 *t. c.* Jer. from Tophet
38:27 *t. c.* all the princes to Jer.
*Mat.* 9:14 *t. c.* disciples of John
15:1 *t. c.* to Jesus scribes and
12 *then c.* his disciples, 17:19
18:21 *then c.* Peter to him
*John* 7:45 *t. c.* officers to ch. pri.
12:28 *t. c.* a voice from heaven
20:26 *t. c.* Jesus, doors being

**They CAME, *or* CAME they.**
*Gen.* 11:31 *they c.* to Haran
12:5 into land of Canaan *they c.*
22:9 *t. c.* to place G. told him of
*Ex.* 16:35 till *t. c.* to a land
1 *K.* 2:7 so *t. c.* to me when I
2 *K.* 20:14 men wh. *c. t. Is.* 39:3
2 *Chr.* 20:4 *t. c.* to seek the Lord
*Neh.* 13:21 *c. t.* no more on sab.
*Job* 6:20 *t. c.* thither
30:14 *t. c.* as a wide breaking
*Ps.* 88:17 *t. c.* round me like w.
*Jer.* 43:7 thus *c. t.* to Tahpanhes
*Ezek.* 23:40 and lo, *they c.*
*Mat.* 1:18 before *they c.* together
14:34 *t. c.* into l. of Gennesaret
26:73 after a while *c. they*
*Mark* 1:45 *t. c.* from every quar.
3:13 whom he would and *t. c.*
*Luke* 2:16 *t. c.* with haste found
*John* 12:9 *t. c.* not for Jes. sake
*Acts* 12:20 *t. c.* with one accord
17:13 *they c.* thither also
23:14 *they c.* to the chief priests
*Rev.* 7:13 whence *c. they?*

**Word of the Lord CAME.**
*Gen.* 15:1 the *w. L. c.* to Abr. 4
1 *Sam.* 15:10 *w. L. c.* to Samuel
2 *Sam.* 24:11 Gad; 1 *K.* 6:11 Solo. 16:1 Jehu, 7; 17:2 Elijah, 8; 18:1; 19:9; 21:17, 28 ——
18:31 to whom *word of the L. c.* saying, Israel be thy name
1 *K.* 12:22 Shema. 2 *Chr.* 11:2; 12:7
2 *K.* 20:4 Isaiah, *Is.* 38:4
1 *Chr.* 17:3 Nathan; 22:8 David
*Jer.* 1:2 *w. L. c.* to Jere. 4; 2:1; 14:1; 29:30; 33:1, 19; *Dan.* 9:2
*Ezek.* 1:3 expressly to Ezek. 3:16
*Hos.* 1:1 Hosea; *Joel* 1:1 Joel
*Jon.* 1:1 Jon. 3:1; *Mic.* 1:1 Mic.
*Zep.* 1:1 Zeph.; *Hag.* 1:1 Hag.
*Zec.* 7:4 *c. w. L.* of hosts, 8:1

**CAMEL.**
*Gen.* 24:64 Reb. lighted off the *c.*
*Lev.* 11:4 not e. the *c. Deut.* 14:7
1 *Sam.* 15:3 slay infant, ox, and *c*
*Zec.* 14:15 so be plague of *c.*
*Mat.* 19:24 is easier for a *c. Mark* 10:25; *Luke* 18:25
23:24 strain at a gnat, swallow *c*

**CAMELS.**
*Gen.* 12:16 Abram had *c.*
24:19 draw water for thy *c.* 44
30:43 J. had much cattle, *c.*
31:34 put them in *c.* furniture
37:25 Ishmaelites came with *c.*
*Ex.* 9:3 hand of the L. on the *c.*
*Jud.* 6:5 *c.* without number, 7:12
8:21 took ornam. on *c.* necks, 26
1 *Sam.* 27:9 David took away *c.*
30:17 save 400 which rode on *c.*
1 *K.* 10:2 to Jer. with *c.* 2 *Chr.* 9:1
2 *K.* 8:9 a present forty *c.* burden
1 *Chr.* 5:21 Reu. took of *c.* 50,000
12:40 brought bread on *c.*
27:30 over the *c.* was Obil
*Ezr.* 2:67 their *c.* 435, *Neh.* 7:69
*Est.* 8:10 letters by post on *c.* 14.
*Job* 1:3 his substance was 3,000 *c.*
17 Chaldeans fell upon the *c.*
*Is.* 21:7 he saw a chariot of *c.*
30:6 treasures on bunches of *c.*
60:6 mult. of *c.* shall cover thee
*Jer.* 49:29 shall take their *c.*
32 their *c.* shall be a booty
*Ezek.* 25:5 Rabbah a stable for *c.*
*Mat.* 3:4 raim. of *c.* hair, *Mark* 1:6

**CAMEST.**
*Gen.* 16:8 Hagar, whence *c.* thou
27:33 eaten of all before thou *c.*
*Num.* 22:37 wherefore *c.* thou not
*Deut.* 16:3 rem. day *c.* out of Eg.
1 *Sam.* 13:11 *c.* not within days
17:28 why *c.* thou down hither
2 *Sam.* 15:20 whereas *c.* but yes.
1 *K.* 13:9 nor return by way *c.* 17
14 man of God that *c.* from J.?
2 *K.* 19:28 I will turn thee back by way thou *c. Is.* 37:29
*Neh.* 9:13 *c.* down also on M. Si.
*Is.* 64:3 *c.* down, mount. flowed
*Jer.* 1:5 before thou *c.* forth out of the womb I sancti. thee
*Ezek.* 32:2 *c.* forth with thy rivers
*Mat.* 22:12 friend, how *c.* in hit.
*John* 6:25 Rabbi, when *c.* hither
16:30 we believe thou *c.* from G.
*Acts* 9:17 in the way as thou *c.*

CAMON. *Jud.* 10:5

**CAMP.**
*Ex.* 14:19 ang. of L. went bef. *c.*
32:17 a noise of war in *c.*
27 *c.* slay every man brother
36:6 proclaimed through the *c.*
*Lev.* 24:10 strove together in *c.*
*Num.* 4:5 when *c.* setteth forw.
11:1 con. in utmost parts of *c.*
26 Eld. and Med. prophes. in *c.*
*Deut.* 23:14 in midst of thy *c.*
*Jos.* 6:18 made *c.* of Isr. a curse
*Jud.* 13:25 spirit of God began to move Samson in the *c.*
21:8 none to the *c.* from Jabesh
1 *Sam.* 4:6 noise of shout in the *c.*
17:17 run to *c.* to thy brethren
2 *K.* 6:8 in such a place be my *c.*
7:7 left *c.* as it was, fled for life
8 when these lepers came to *c.*
19:35 angel of L. smote in *c.* of Assyr. 185,000, *Is.* 37:36
*Ps.* 78:28 let it fall in midst of *c.*
106:16 envied M. also in the *c.*
*Ezek.* 4:2 set the *c.* also against it
*Joel* 2:11 for his *c.* is very great
*Rev.* 20:9 compassed *c.* of saints

**CAMP, Verb.**
*Is.* 29:3 I will *c.* against thee
*Jer.* 50:29 bend the bow *c. ag.* it
*Nah.* 3:17 *c.* in hedges in cold day

**CAMPED.**
*Ex.* 19:2 Israel *c.* before mount

**Into the CAMP.**
1 *Sam.* 4:7 God is come *into c.*

**Out of the CAMP.**
*Ex.* 19:17 M. brought people *o. c.*
*Lev.* 10:4 your brethren *out c.*
24:23 had cursed *out c.*
*Num.* 14:44 M. departed not *o. c.*
*Deut.* 23:10 unclean shall go *o. c.*
1 *Sam.* 13:17 spoilers *o. c.* of Phil.
2 *Sam.* 1:2 came *o. c.* from Saul

**Round about the CAMP.**
*Num.* 11:31 quails *r. a. c.* 32

**Without the CAMP.**
*Ex.* 29:14 bullock burn *w. c. Lev.* 8:17; 9:11; 16:27
33:7 sought the L. went *w. t. c.*
*Deut.* 23:12 have a place *w. c.*
*Jos.* 6:23 R. left kindred *w. t. c.*
*Heb.* 13:11 beasts burnt *w. the c.*
13 go forth to him *w. the c.*

**CAMPS.**
*Num.* 10:2 trum. for journey of *c.*
*Amos* 4:10 stink of your *c.* come

**CAMPHIRE.**
*Cant.* 1:14 my beloved is as *c.*
4:13 thy plants an orchard of *c.*

**CAN.**
*Mat.* 27:65 as sure as you *c.*
*John* 15:4 no more *c.* ye except
*Rom.* 8:7 subject to law, nor *c.* be

**How CAN.**
*John* 3:9 said, *h. c.* these th. be?
*Acts* 8:31 *h. c.* I exc. some guide?

**CANA.**
*John* 2:1 marriage in C. 11
4:46 Jesus came again into C.
21:2 Thomas and Nath. of C.

**CANAAN.**
*Gen.* 9:18, 22, 25; 10:15; 28:1
*Ex.* 15:15 the inhabitants of C.
*Jud.* 3:1; 4:2, 23; 5:19
*Ps.* 106:38 to the idols of C.
135:11 smote all kingdoms of C.
*Is.* 19:18 speak language of C.
*Zep.* 2:5 C. I will destroy thee
*Mat.* 15:22 a woman of C. cried

**Land of CANAAN.**
*Gen.* 12:5 to go into *land of* C.

**CANAANITE.**
*Gen.* 12:6; 15:21; 24:3; 34:30
*Ex.* 23:28 drive out C. 33:2; 34:11
*Num.* 21:3 deliv. up C. *Neh.* 9:24
*Mat.* 10:4 Simon the C. *Mark* 3:18

CANAANITESS. 1 *Chr.* 2:3
CANDACE. *Acts* 8:27

**CANDLE.**
*Job* 18:6 his *c.* be put out
21:17 *c.* of wicked put out?
29:3 his *c.* shined on my head
*Ps.* 18:28 thou wilt light my *c.*
*Prov.* 20:27 spirit of man is *c.*
24:20 *c.* of wicked be put out
31:18 *c.* goeth not out by night
*Jer.* 25:10 from them light of *c.*
*Mat.* 5:15 put *c.* under a bushel, *Mark* 4:21; *Luke* 8:16; 11:33
*Luke* 11:36 bright shining of a *c.*
15:8 a *c.* and sweep the house
*Rev.* 18:23 *c.* shine no more
22:5 need no *c.* nor light of sun

**CANDLES.**
*Zep.* 1:12 will search Jer. with *c.*

**CANDLESTICK.**
*Ex.* 25:31 make *c.* 37:17; *Num.* 8:4
40:24 put *c.* in tent of congreg.
*Lev.* 24:4 lamps on *c.* continually
*Num.* 3:31 their charge shall be *c.*
2 *K.* 4:10 let us set for him a *c.*
1 *Chr.* 28:15 gold for every *c.*
2 *Chr.* 13:11 set they in order *c.*
*Dan.* 5:5 wrote over ag. the *c.*
*Zec.* 4:2 behold a *c.* all of gold
11 olive-trees on right side of *c.*
*Mat.* 5:15 on a *c.* and it giveth light to all, *Luke* 8:16; 11:33
*Mark* 4:21 not be set on *c.*?
*Heb.* 9:2 first wherein was the *c.*
*Rev.* 2:5 else I will remove thy *c.*

**CANDLESTICKS.**
1 *K.* 7:49 *c.* of p. gold, 2 *Chr.* 4:7
*Jer.* 52:19 he took away the *c.*
*Rev.* 11:4 two *c.* standing bef. G.
*See* SEVEN.

**CANE.**
*Is.* 43:24 brought me no sweet *c.*
*Jer.* 6:20 *c.* from far country

**CANKER, ED.**
2 *Tim.* 2:17 will eat as *c.*
*Jam.* 5:3 your gold and silver is *c.*

**CANKER-WORM.**
*Joel* 1:4 *c.* eat. and *c.-w.* left, 2:25
*Nah.* 3:15 like *c.-w.* make thyself many as the *c.-w.*
16 *c.-w.* spoileth and flieth

**CANNOT.**
*Is.* 1:13 calling of assemblies I *c.*
*Jer.* 18:6 *c.* I do with you
*Luke* 16:26 from hence to you *c.*

**CANST.**
*Mat.* 8:2 thou *c.* make me clean
*Mark* 9:22 if thou *c.* do any thing

CAPERNAUM. *Mat.* 4:13; 8:5; 11:23; 17:24; *Luke* 4:23; 10:15; *John* 2:12; 4:46; 6:17, 24, 59
CAPHTOR. *Jer.* 47:4; *Amos* 9:7

**CAPPADOCIA.**
*Acts* 2:9 dwellers in C. we hear
1 *Pet.* 1:1 strangers throughout C.

**CAPTAIN.**
*Gen.* 37:36 sold him to Potiph. *c.*
40:4 *c.* charged Jos. with them
*Num.* 14:4 make a *c.* *Neh.* 9:17
*Jos.* 5:14 as *c.* of host of the L.
15 *c.* of the L. host said to Jos.
*Jud.* 4:2 *c.* of Jabin's host was Sisera, 7; 1 *Sam.* 12:9
11:6 said to Jephthah, be our *c.*
11 made him *c.* over them
1 *Sam.* 9:16 anoint him *c.* 10:1
13:14 Lord com. him to be *c.*
17:18 carry th. ten cheeses to *c.*
22:2 David became *c.* over them
2 *Sam.* 5:2 shalt be *c.* over Israel
8 he shall be *c.* 1 *Chr.* 11:6
19:13 if thou be not *c.* of the
23:19 Abishai was therefore *c.*
1 *K.* 16:16 Isr. made Omri *c.* king
2 *K.* 1:9 king sent a *c.* with fifty
4:13 wouldest be spo. for to *c.*?
5:1 Naaman *c.* of host of Syria
9:5 an errand to thee, O *c.*
15:25 Pekah a *c.* of his conspired
18:24 face of one *c.* *Is.* 36:9
20:5 Hezekiah *c.* of my people
25:8 Nebuzar-adan. *c.* *Jer.* 52:12
1 *Chr.* 11:21 honorable, he was *c.*
27:5 *c.* for 3d month Benaiah
2 *Chr.* 13:12 God himself is our *c.*
*Is.* 3:3 doth take away *c.* of fifty
*Jer.* 37:13 a *c.* Irijah took Jer.
40:5 *c.* gave Jer. victuals
51:27 appoint a *c.* against her
*John* 18:12 band and *c.* took Jes.
*Acts* 5:26 *c.* with officers brought
*Heb.* 2:10 *c.* of their salvation

**CAPTAINS.**
*Ex.* 15:4 chosen *c.* are drowned
*Deut.* 1:15 I made wise men *c.*
20:9 make *c.* to lead the p.
1 *Sam.* 8:12 he will appoint him *c.*
22:7 son of Jesse make you *c.*?
2 *Sam.* 18:5 *c.* charge con. Absal.
23:8 that sat chief among the *c.*
1 *K.* 2:5 what Joab did to the *c.*
20:24 kings away, and put *c.*
22:33 when *c.* perceived he was not the king, 2 *Chr.* 18:32
1 *Chr.* 11:15 three of 30 *c.* went
2 *Chr.* 33:11 brought on them *c.*
*Job* 39:25 the thunder of the *c.*
*Jer.* 13:21 taught them to be *c.*
51:23 I will break in pieces *c.*
57 I will make drunk her *c.*
*Ezek.* 21:22 *c.* to open the mouth
23:6 *c.* all desirable men, 12, 23
*Nah.* 3:17 thy *c.* as great grassh.
*Mark* 6:21 H. made a supper to *c.*
*Luke* 22:4 J. communed with *c.*
*Rev.* 19:18 may eat the flesh of *c.*

**CAPTIVE.**
*Gen.* 14:14 brother was taken *c.*
34:29 their wives took they *c.*
*Ex.* 12:29 unto first-born of *c.*
2 *K.* 5:2 bro. away *c.* a little m.
6:22 those thou hast taken *c.*
*Is.* 49:21 I am desolate, a *c.*
24 shall lawful *c.* be delivered
51:14 *c.* exile hasteneth
52:2 loose thys. O *c.*, dau. of Z.
*Amos* 6:7 *c.* with first that go *c.*
2 *Tim.* 2:26 taken *c.* by him

**Carry** *or* **carried CAPTIVE,** *or* **CAPTIVES.**
*Gen.* 31:26 *car.* my daughters *c.*
*Num.* 24:22 until A. *car.* thee *c.*
1 *K.* 8:46 *car.* them *c.* 2 *Chr.* 6:36
47 they bethink thems. in land whither *carried c.* 2 *Chr.* 6:37
2 *K.* 15:29 T.-pileser *car.* them *c.*
16:9 *c.* peo. of Damas. *c.* to Kir
1 *Chr.* 5:6 king of Assyria *c. c.*
2 *Chr.* 25:12 10,000 did Judah *c. c.*
28:5 *car.* a great multitude *c.*
8 Is. *car. c.* of brethren 200,000
*Ps.* 106:46 pitied of th. *c.* them *c.*
137:3 *c.* us *c.* required a song
*Jer.* 13:17 Lord's flock is *car. c.*
19 J. shall be wholly *c.* away *c.*
20:4 shall *c.* them *c.* to Babylon
24:5 acknowledge them *car. c.*
29:4 saith the Lord to all *car. c.*
14 bring you into place whence I caused you to be *car. c.*
41:10 Ishm. *c. c.* all the residue
43:12 *carry* the Egyptians *c.*
52:29 *c. c.* from Jer. 832 persons
30 *c. c.* of the Jews 745 persons
*Ezek.* 6:9 nations whither be *c. c.*
*Dan.* 11:8 also *c. c.* into Egypt
*Amos* 1:6 bec. they *c. c.* captivity
*Ob.* 11 in day strangers *car. c.*

**Carrying CAPTIVE.**
*Jer.* 1:3 to *car.* of Jerusalem *c.*

**Lead,** *or* **led CAPTIVE.**
*Jud.* 5:12 *lead* thy captivity *c.*
1 *K.* 8:48 return unto thee in land of enemies which *l.* them *c.*
2 *Chr.* 30:9 shall find compassion before them that *lead c.*
*Ps.* 68:18 *led* captiv. *c.* *Eph.* 4:8
*Jer.* 22:12 die whither *led* him *c.*
*Amos* 7:11 Israel shall be *led c.*
*Nah.* 2:7 Huzzab shall be *led c.*
*Luke* 21:24 shall be *led* away *c.*
2 *Tim.* 3:6 *lead c.* silly women

**CAPTIVES.**
*Num.* 31:9 women of Midian *c.*
12 brought *c.*; 19 purify your *c.*
*Deut.* 21:11 am. *c.* a beauti. wo.
32:42 drunk with blood of *c.*
1 *Sam.* 30:5 David's two wives *c.*
2 *K.* 24:14 from Jerus. 10,000 *c.*
2 *Chr.* 28:11 deliver the *c.* again
13 ye shall not bring in *c.*
*Is.* 14:2 take them *c.* whose *c.*
20:4 the Ethiopians *c.*
45:13 let go my *c.* not for price
49:25 *c.* of mighty be taken
61:1 liberty to the *c.* *Luke* 4:18
*Jer.* 48:46 thy sons and d. are *c.*
50:33 took them *c.* held them
*Ezek.* 1:1 as I was among *c.*
16:53 captivity of thy *c.*
*Dan.* 2:25 found a man of *c.* of J.

**CAPTIVITY.**
*Num.* 21:29 his daughters into *c.*
*Deut.* 21:13 raiment of *c.* from of
30:3 Lord will turn thy *c.*
2 *K.* 24:15 carried he into *c.* to B.
25:27 37th year of *c.* *Jer.* 52:31
1 *Chr.* 5:22 dwelt in steads until *c.*
6:15 Jehozadak went into *c.*
2 *Chr.* 6:37 pray in land of *c.*
38 if they return to thee in *c.*
29:9 our sons and wives are in *c.*
*Ezr.* 9:7 have been delivered to *c.*
*Neh.* 1:2 Jews wh. were left of *c.*
4:4 for a prey in land of their *c.*
*Est.* 2:6 Mordecai carried with *c.*
*Job* 42:10 L. turned the *c.* of Job
*Ps.* 14:17 Lord bring back *c.* 85:1
78:61 deliv. his strength into *c.*
126:1 when L. turned ag. *c.* of Z.
4 turn again our *c.* O L. as str.
*Is.* 5:13 my peo. are gone into *c.*
22:17 carry thee with mighty *c.*
46:2 themselves are gone into *c.*
*Jer.* 15:2 for the *c.* to the *c.* 43:11
29:14 I will turn away your *c.* 30:3; 32:44; 33:7, 11, 26
20 hear all of *c.*; 28 *c.* is long
22 taken up a curse by all *c.*
31 send to all them of *c.*
30:10 seed from land of *c.* 46:27
48:11 hath Moab gone into *c.*
*Lam.* 1:3 Judah is gone into *c.*
5 her children are gone into *c.*

2:14 discov. to turn away thy *c.*
4:22 no more carry thee into *c.*
*Ezek* 1:2 fifth y. of Jehoiac. *c.*
3:11 get to them of *c.* and speak
11:25 I spake to them of *c.* all
12:7 my stuff, as stuff for *c.*
16:53 bring again their *c.* the *c*
of Sodom and Samaria
25:3 went into *c.* thou saidst
33:21 in 12th year of *c.* one esc.
39:23 house of Isr. went into *c.*
40:1 in the 25th year of our *c.*
*Dan.* 6:13 D. of the *c.* of Judah
11:33 shall fall by *c.* many days
*Hos.* 6:11 returned *c.* of my peo.
*Ob.* 20 *c.* of this host, *c.* of Jer.
*Mic.* 1:16 gone into *c.* from thee
*Nah.* 3:10 No went into *c.* her ch.
*Hab.* 1:9 gather *c.* as the sand
*Zep.* 2:7 shall turn away *c.* 3:20
*Zec.* 6:10 take of them of the *c.*
*Rom.* 7:23 *c.* to the law of sin
2 *Cor.* 10:5 into *c.* every thought
*See* CAPTIVE.

**Bring CAPTIVITY.**

*Ps.* 53:6 when God *b.* back *c.*
*Jer.* 30:18 *b.* ag. *c.* of Jacob's t
31:23 I shall *b.* again their *c.*
48:47 *bring* again *c.* of Moab
49:6 I will *b.* again *c.* of Ammon
39 will *bring* again *c.* of Elam
*Ezek.* 29:14 *b.* again *c.* of Egypt
39:25 now will I *b.* again *c.* of J.
*Joel* 3:1 I *b.* again *c.* of Judah
*Amos* 9:14 *b.* again *c.* of my peo.

**Children of CAPTIVITY.**

*Ezr.* 4:1 *c. c.* builded temple
10:7 proclamation to the *c. c.*
16 *c. of c.* did so, all were sep.
*Dan.* 5:13 which art *c. c.* of Ju.

**Go into CAPTIVITY.**

*Deut.* 28:41 sons and daugh. *g. c.*
*Jer.* 20:6 and house shall *go c.*
22:22 thy lovers shall *go into c.*
30:16 adver. every one shall *go c.*
46:19 O daugh. furnish to *go c.*
48:7 Chem. shall *c.*; 49:3 king
*Ezek.* 12:4 go as they that *go c.*
30:17 these cities shall *go into c.*
18 Egypt, her dau. shall *go c.*
*Amos.* 1:5 people of S. shall *go c.*
15 their king shall *go into c.*
5:5 Gilgal shall surely *go into c.*
27 I cause you to *go into c.*
7:17 Is. shall surely *go into c.*
9:4 they *go c.* before enemies
*Zec.* 14:2 city shall *go into c.*
*Rev.* 13:10 lead. into *c.* shall *go c*

**Out of CAPTIVITY.**

*Ezr.* 2:1 went up *o. c. Neh.* 7:6
6:21 come *out c.* kept the feast
8:35 come *out of c.* offered

**CARBUNCLE, S.**

*Ex.* 28:17 first row a *c.* 39:10
*Is.* 54:12 make thy gates of *c.*
*Ezek.* 28:13 and *c.* thy covering

**CARCASS.**

*Lev.* 5:2 touch *c.* unclean thing
11:8 *c.* not touch, *Deut.* 14:8
*Deut.* 28:26 *c.* be meat to fowls
*Jos.* 8:29 should take his *c.* down
*Jud.* 14:8 to see *c.* of lion honey
1 *K.* 13:22 thy *c.* not come
24 a lion stood by the *c.*
2 *K.* 9:37 *c.* of Jez. be as dung
*Is.* 14:19 cast out as *c.* trodden
*Mat.* 24:28 *c.* is there will eagles

**CARCASSES.**

*Gen.* 15:11 fowls came on *c.*
*Lev.* 11:11 *c.* in abomination, 26
26:30 cast your *c.* on *c.* of idols
*Num.* 14:29 *c.* shall fall in wilder.
1 *Sam.* 17:46 I will give *c.* of Ph.
*Is.* 5:25 their *c.* torn in streets
34:3 stink come up out of *c.*
66:24 *c.* of them transgressed
*Jer.* 7:33 *c.* of this people be
meat for fowls, 16:4; 19:7
16:18 filled mine inh. with the *c.*
*Ezek.* 6:5 lay *c.* of Isr. before id.
43:9 *c.* of their kings far from
*Nah.* 3:3 a great number of *c.*
*Heb.* 3:17 *c.* fell in wilderness

**CARCHEMISH.**

2 *Chr.* 35:20 to fight against C.
*Is.* 10:9 is not Calno as C.?
*Jer.* 46:2 river Euphrates in C.

**CARE.**

1 *Sam.* 10:2 father left *c.* of asses
2 *K.* 4:13 careful with all this *c.*
*Jer.* 49:31 the nation without *c.*
*Ezek.* 4:16 shall eat bread with *c.*
*Luke* 10:34 he took *c.* of him
35 said, Take *c.* of him
1 *Cor.* 9:9 God take *c.* for oxen?
12:25 same *c.* one for another
2 *Cor.* 7:12 *c.* for you might ap.
8:16 same earnest *c.* in Titus
11:28 *c.* of all the churches
1 *Tim.* 3:5 how take *c.* of church
1 *Pet.* 5:7 casting your *c.* on him

**CARE, ED.**

2 *Sam.* 18:3 if we flee, not *c.* for
*Ps.* 142:4 no man *c.* for my soul
*Luke* 10:40 *c.* that my sister left
*John* 12:6 he *c.* for the poor
*Acts* 18:17 G. *c.* for none of those
1 *Cor.* 7:21 a servant? *c.* not
*Phil.* 2:20 natur. *c.* for your state

**CAREFUL.**

2 *K.* 4:13 thou hast been *c.* for us
*Jer.* 17:8 *c.* in year of drought
*Dan.* 3:16 we are not *c.* to answer
*Luke* 10:41 *c.* about many things
*Phil.* 4:6 be *c.* for nothing, but
10 *c.* but lacked opportunity
*Tit.* 3:8 *c.* to maintain good w.

**CAREFULLY.**

*Deut.* 15:5 thou *c.* hearken to L.
*Mic.* 1:12 inha. of M. waited *c.*
*Phil.* 2:28 I sent him the more *c.*
*Heb.* 12:17 sought it *c.* with tears

**CAREFULNESS.**

*Ezek.* 12:18 drink water with *c.*
19 shall eat their bread with *c.*
1 *Cor.* 7:32 have you without *c.*
2 *Cor.* 7:11 what *c.* it wrought

**CARELESS.**

*Jud.* 18:7 saw how they dwelt *c.*
*Is.* 32:9 hear, ye *c.* daughters
10 ye *c.* women; 11 ye *c.* ones
*Ezek.* 30:9 *c.* Ethiopians afraid

**CARELESSLY.**

*Is.* 47:8 thou that dwellest *c.*
*Ezek.* 39:6 fire am. them dwell *c.*
*Zep.* 2:15 rejoicing city dwelt *c.*

**CARES.**

*Mark* 4:19 *c.* of this world choke
*Luke* 8:14 chok. with *c.* and rich.
21:34 overcharged with *c.* of life

**CAREST, ETH, ING.**

*Deut.* 11:12 a land which L. *c.*
*Mat.* 22:16 *c.* thou for any man
*Mark* 4:38 *c.* thou not we perish
12:14 art true, and *c.* for no man
*John* 10:13 hireling *c.* not for sh.
1 *Cor.* 7:32 is unmarried *c.* 34
33 is married, *c.* for world, 34
1 *Pet.* 5:7 for he *c.* for you

**CARMEL.**

1 *Sam.* 25:2 posses. in C. 7, 40
1 *K.* 18:19 gather all Is. to mt. C.
*Cant.* 7:5 head u. thee is like C.
*Is.* 35:2 excellency of C.
*Jer.* 46:18 as C. by the sea
*Amos* 1:2 C. shall wither, 9:3
*Mic.* 7:14 in the midst of C.

**CARMELITE.**

1 *Sam.* 30:5 N. C. 2 *Sam.* 2:2; 3:3
2 *Sam.* 23:35 Hezrai C. one of D.

CARMI. *Gen.* 46:9; *Jos.* 7:1; 1
*Chr.* 2:7; 4:1

**CARNAL.**

*Rom.* 7:14 I am *c.* sold under sin
8:7 *c.* mind is enmity against G.
15:27 to minister in *c.* things
1 *Cor.* 3:1 unto *c.* even to babes
3 are yet *c.*; 4 are ye not *c.*?
9:11 if we reap your *c.* things
2 *Cor.* 10:4 w. of warfare not *c.*
*Heb.* 7:16 law of a *c.* command.
9:10 stood in *c.* ordinances

**CARNALLY.**

*Lev.* 18:20 not lie *c.* with n. wife
19:20 lieth *c.* with a bondmaid
*Num.* 5:13 man lie with her *c.*
*Rom.* 8:6 *c.* minded is death

**CARPENTER, S.**

2 *Sam.* 5:11 *c.* to D. 1 *Chr.* 14:1
2 *Chr.* 24:12 hired *c. Ezr.* 3:7
*Is.* 41:7 *c.* encouraged goldsmith
44:13 *c.* stretcheth out his rule
*Jer.* 24:1 *c.* he carried away, 29:2
*Zec.* 1:20 Lord showed me four *c.*
*Mat.* 13:55 is not this the *c.* son?
*Mark* 6:3 is not this the *c.*

CARPUS. 2 *Tim.* 4:13

**CARRIAGE, S.**

1 *Sam.* 17:22 David left his *c.*
*Is.* 10:28 Michmash laid up *c.*
46:1 your *c.* were heavy laden
*Acts* 21:15 we took up our *c.*

**CARRY.**

*Gen.* 50:25 *c.* up my b. *Ex.* 13:19
*Ex.* 33:15 pres. go not, *c.* us
*Lev.* 10:4 *c.* your breth. out of c.
*Num.* 11:12 *c.* them in bosom
*Deut.* 14:24 too long to *c.* it
*Jos.* 4:3 *c.* the twelve stones
1 *Sam.* 20:40 *c.* them to the city
2 *Sam.* 19:18 *c.* king's household
1 *K.* 18:12 spirit of L. sh. *c.* thee
2 *K.* 4:19 *c.* him to his mother
9:2 *c.* Jehu to an inner chamber
17:27 *c.* thith. one of the priests
1 *Chr.* 15:2 none ought to *c.* ark
23:26 L. no more *c.* tabernacle
2 *Chr.* 36:6 *c.* him to B. *Jer.* 39:7
*Ec.* 10:20 a bird shall *c.* the v.
*Is.* 23:7 own feet *c.* her afar off
30:6 *c.* riches on young asses
40:11 *c.* lambs in his bosom
46:4 to hoary hairs will I *c.* you
7 *c.* him, set him in his place
*Jer.* 20:5 and *c.* them to Babylon
39:14 should *c.* Jeremiah home
*Ezek.* 22:9 thee are men *c.* tales
*Mark* 6:55 began to *c.* in beds
11:16 to *c.* a vessel th. temple
*Luke* 10:4 *c.* nei. purse nor scrip
*John* 5:10 not lawful to *c.*
21:18 *c.* thee whit. wouldst not

**CARRY away.**

2 *K.* 18:11 king of A. did *c. a.* Is.
25:11 fugitives did N. *c. away*
2 *Chr.* 20:25 more than could *c. a.*
*Job* 15:12 thy heart *c.* thee *a.*?
*Ps.* 49:17 dieth he sh. *c.* noth. *a.*
*Ec.* 5:15 noth. wh. he may *c. a.*
*Is.* 5:29 shall *c.* prey *away* safe
15:7 shall they *c. away*
22:17 Lord will *c.* thee *away*
41:16 wind *c.* them *a.* 57:13
*Lam.* 4:22 *c.* thee *a.* O Zion
*Ezek.* 38:13 art come to *c. a.*
*Acts* 7:43 *c.* you *a.* bey. Babylon
*See* CAPTIVE.

**CARRY back.**

2 *Sam.* 15:25 *c. back* ark
1 *K.* 22:26 *c.* Mic. *b.* 2 *Chr.* 18:25

**CARRY forth.**
Ex. 12:46 not c. forth aught
14:11 c. us forth out of Egypt
Lev. 4:12 whole bullock c. f. 21
2 Chr. 29:5 c. f. the filthiness
Jer. 17:22 nor c. f. a burden
Ezek. 12:6 c. it f. in the twilight

**CARRY out.**
Gen. 47:30 c. me out of Egypt
Deut. 28:38 c. much seed out
1 K. 22:34 c. me o. 2 Chr. 18:33
Ezek. 12:5 dig wall, c. o. thereby
Acts 5:9 at door, shall c. thee o.
1 Tim. 6:7 we c. nothing out

**CARRIED.**
Gen. 46:5 sons of Is. c. Jac. 50:13
Lev. 10:5 c. them in their coats
Jud. 16:3 Samson c. them up
1 Sam. 5:8 let ark be c. to Gath
2 Sam. 6:10 c. ark, 1 Chr. 13:13
15:29 Abiathar c. ark to Jerusa.
1 K. 17:19 he c. him into a loft
2 K. 20:17 have laid up in store shall be c. to Baby. Is. 39:6
24:13 he c. out all the treasures
25:7 c. Zedekiah to Babylon
2 Chr. 28:15 c. all the feeble
33:11 c. Manasseh to Babylon
36:4 Necho. c. Jehoahaz to Eg.
Job 5:13 the froward is c. headlo.
10:19 I should been c. from w.
Ps. 46:2 mount. be c. into sea
Is. 46:3 remnant c. from the w.
49:22 daugh. be c. on shoulders
53:4 he hath c. our sorrows
63:9 c. them all the days of old
Jer. 27:22 be c. to Babylon, 28:3; 52:11, 17
Ezek. 17:4 he c. twigs into a land
Ezek. 37:1 c. me out in Sp. of L.
Dan. 1:2 c. into land of Shinar
Hos. 10:6 also c. unto Assyria
12:1 and oil is c. into Egypt
Joel 3:5 c. into your temples
Luke 7:12 dead man c. out
16:22 was c. by the angels
24:51 was c. up into heaven
Acts 3:2 one lame from womb c.
5:6 young men c. Ananias out
7:16 fathers were c. to Sychem
8:2 c. Stephen to his burial
21:34 com. to be c. into castle
Eph. 4:14 c. with every wind
Heb. 13:9 c. with divers doctrines
2 Pet. 2:17 c. with a tempest
Jude 12 clouds without water c.
See CAPTIVE.

**CARRIED away.**
Gen. 31:18 J. c. a. all his cattle
26 c. a. my daughters
1 Sam. 30:2 c. them a. 18.
2 K. 17:6 c. Is. into Assyria, 23
11 heathen whom the L. c. a.
28 one of priests they had c. a.
24:14 c. a. all Jerusalem
15 c. a. Jehoiachin to Babylon
25:21 so Judah was c. a. out of
1 Chr 5:26 c. a. the Reubenites
6:15 when L. c. a. J. and Jerus.
9:1 c. a. for their transgression
2 Chr. 14:13 Asa c. away, 21:17
Ezr. 2:1 been c. a. Neh. 7:6
9:4 transg. of those c. a. 10:6
Jer. 29:4 caused to be c. a.
Dan. 2:35 wind c. them away
Nah. 3:10 No was c. a. into cap.
Mat. 1:11 about time c. a. to B.
Mark 15:1 c. Jesus a. to Pilate
1 Cor. 12:2 G. c. a. dumb idols
Gal. 2:13 Barnabas c. a.
Rev. 12:15 be c. a. of flood
17:3 c. me a. in spirit, 21:10

**CARRIEST, ETH, ING.**
Job 21:18 as chaff storm c. away
27:21 cast wind c. rich away
Ps. 78:9 Ephraim c. bows turned
90:5 c. them away with flood
Mat. 1:17 till the c. into Babylon
Rev. 17:7 mystery of beast th. c.

**CART.**
1 Sam. 6:7 makes a new c. and
2 Sam. 6:3 set ark on a new c.
1 Chr. 13:7 Uzziah drave the c.
Is. 28:28 corn with wheel of c.
Amos 2:13 as a c. is pressed

**CART-ROPE.**
Is. 5:18 draw sin as with a c.-r.

**CART-WHEEL.**
Is. 28:27 nor is c.-w. turned

**CARVED, ING, INGS.**
Ex. 31:5 Bezaleel in c. 35:33
Jud. 18:18 fetched the c. image
1 K. 6:18 cedar within was c.
2 Chr. 33:7 c. image in house G.
34:4 Josiah cut down c. images
Ps. 74:6 they break c. work
Prov. 7:16 my bed with c. work

**CASE, S.**
Ex. 5:19 did see were in evil c.
Ps. 144:15 happy p. in such a c.
Mat. 5:20 in no c. enter kingdom
19:10 c. of man be so with wife
John 5:6 long time in that c.
1 Cor. 7:15 bondage in such c.

**CASEMENT**
Prov. 7:6 looked through my c.

CASIPHIA Ezr. 8.17

**CASSIA.**
Ex. 30:24 of c. 500 shekels
Ps. 45:8 garments smell of c.
Ezek. 27:19 c. in thy market

**CAST, passive.**
Job 18:8 he is c. into a net
Ps. 22:10 I was c. on thee
76:6 are c. into a dead sleep
140:10 let them be c. into fire
Prov. 16:33 the lot is c. into lap
Is. 25:7 covering c. over all
Jer. 22.28 c. into a land know not
38.11 old c. clouts and rags
Dan. 3:6 c. into fiery furnace
6:7 be c. into den of lions, 16
Jon. 2:4 am c. out of thy sight
Mat. 4:12 John was c. into prison
5:25 and thou be c. into prison
29 body be c. into hell, 30
6:30 c. into the oven, Lu. 12:28
21:21 mountain, Be c. into sea
Mark 9:42 c. into sea, Luke 17:2
45 to be c. into hell, 47
Luke 3:9 c. it into, Mat. 3:10; 7:19
23:19 c. into prison, 25
John 3:24 not yet c. into prison
Acts 27:26 c. on a certain island
Rev. 8:7 hail and fire c. on earth
8 mountain burning c. into sea
12:13 dragon was c. unto earth
19:20 both c. alive into the lake
20:10 the devil was c. into lake
14 death and hell c. into lake
15 not found in book of life, c.

**CAST, active.**
Gen. 31:38 she-goats have not c.
37:20 c. him into some pit
39:7 c. eyes on Joseph
Ex. 1:22 every son c. into river
4:3 he c. rod on the ground
15:4 Ph. chariots he c. into sea
25 had c. tree into the waters
22:31 flesh torn, c. it to the dogs
23:26 nothing c. their young
25:12 c. 4 rings, 37:3, 13; 38:5
32:19 Moses c. tables out
Num. 35:23 c. it on him
Deut. 29:28 L. c. into an. land
Jos. 8:29 c. king of Ai at gate
10:27 c. them into cave
Jud. 9:53 a woman c. a piece of millstone, 2 Sam. 11:21
1 Sam. 18:11 S. c. javelin, 20:33
2 Sam. 16:6 S. c. stones at Dav.
18:17 c. Absalom into a pit
1 K. 7:46 c. them, 2 Chr. 4:17
14:9 c. me behind thy back
19:19 E. c. his mantle on him
2 K. 2:16 c. him on some mount.
21 spring, and c. salt in there
3:25 c. each his stone
4:41 meal he c. into the pot
6:6 he c. in stick, iron swam
9:25 c. into portion of N. 26
13:21 c. into sepulchre of Elisha
23 c. from his presence as yet
19:18 c. gods into fire, Is. 37:19
32 c. a bank ag. it, Is. 37:33
Neh. 9:26 c. law behind
Est. 3:7 c. Pur, 9:24
Job 20:23 shall c. fury of wrath
27:22 God shall c. upon him
30:19 hath c. me into mire
40:11 c. abroad rage of wrath
Ps. 55:3 they c. iniquity on me
22 c. thy burden on the Lord
74:7 c. fire into thy sanctuary
78:49 c. on them his wrath
Prov. 1:14 c. in thy lot among us
Ec. 11:1 c. thy bread on waters
Is. 2:20 shall c. his idols to bats
38:17 has c. all my sins behind
Jer. 26:23 c. Urijah's body into
36:23 c. it into fire on hearth
38:6 c. Jerem. into dungeon, 9
41:7 Ishmael c. them into pit
Lam. 3:53 c. a stone upon me
Ezek. 11:16 I have c. them far off
23:35 c. me behind thy back
28:17 I will c. thee to ground
Dan. 3:20 c. them into furnace
24 did not we c. three into fire
6:24 c. them into den of lions
Jon. 2:3 c. me into the deep
Mic. 4:7 I will make her c. off
7:19 c. all their sins into sea
Nah. 3:6 I will c. filth on thee
Zec. 5:8 c. it into the ephah, c.
11:13 c. it unto potter, c. them
Mal. 3:11 nor vine c. fruit before
Mat. 3:10 is c. into fire, 7:19
5:29 c. it from thee, 30; 18:8, 9
7:6 nor c. pearls before swine
15:26 c. it to dogs, Mark 7:27
17:27 c. a hook and take up fish
18:30 c. into prison till he pay
22:13 c. into outer dark. 25:30
27:44 c. same in his teeth
Mark 9:22 c. him into fire
11:7 c. gar. on him, Luke 19:35
12:4 and at him they c. stones
41 c. money into t. Luke 21:4
43 widow hath c. more in, 44
Luke 12:5 to c. into hell
19:43 enemies shall c. a trench
John 8:7 first c. a stone at her
21:7 Peter c. himself into sea
Acts 12:8 c. garment about thee
16:23 c. Paul and S. into prison
27:43 who could swim, c. th.
1 Cor. 7:35 may c. a snare on you
Rev. 2:10 devil c. some into pris.
14 Balak to c. stumbling-block
22 I will c. her into a bed
4:10 elders c. their crowns
18:21 and c. it into sea

**CAST away.**
Lev. 26:44 I will not c. them a.
2 Sam. 1:21 sh. of mighty is c. a.
2 K. 7:15 vessels Syrians c. a.
2 Chr. 29:19 vessels Ahaz c. a.
Job 8:4 c. them a. for transgress
Job 8:20 G. will not c. a. perfect
Ps. 2:3 c. a. their cords
51:11 c. me not a. from presence
Ec. 3:5 a time to c. a. stones, 6
Is. 5:24 because they have c. a.
30:22 c. a. as menstruous cloth
31:7 c. a. his idols of silver

41:9 chosen and not c. thee a.
Jer. 7:29 cut thy hair and c. it a.
33:26 c. a. seed of Jacob
Ezek. 18:31 c. a. all transgress.
20:8 did not c. a. abominations
Hos. 9:17 God will c. them a.
Mat. 13:48 but c. the bad away
Luke 9:25 if a man be c. away
Rom. 11:1 God c. a. his people?
2 not c. away people
Heb. 10:35 c. not a. your confid.

**CASTAWAY.**

1 Cor. 9:27 lest I myself be a c.

**CAST down.**

Ex. 7:10 Aaron c. down his rod
Jos. 10:11 L. c. d. great stones
Jud. 6:28 Baal was c. down
1 K. 18:42 Elijah c. himself d.
2 Chr. 25:8 G. hath power to c. d.
12 c. them d. from top of rock
Neh. 6:16 c. d. in their own eyes
Job 18:7 counsel sh. c. him d.
22:29 when men are c. down
29:24 my count. they c. not d.
41:9 be c. d. at sight of him?
Ps. 17:13 disap. him, c. him d.
36:12 they are c. down
37:14 bent bow to c. d. needy
24 shall not be utterly c. d.
42:5 c. d. O my soul? 11; 43:5
6 my soul is c. d. within me
56:7 in thine anger c. d. people
62:4 consult to c. him down
89:44 c. his throne d. to ground
102:10 lifted me up, and c. d.
Prov. 7:26 c. d. many wounded
Is. 28:2 shall c. d. with his hand
Jer. 6:15 shall be c. down, 8:12
Lam. 2:1 c. d. the beauty of Isr.
Ezek. 6:4 c. d. your slain
19:12 thy mother was c. d.
31:16 when I. c. Assyrian d.
32:18 wail for E. and c. her d.
Dan. 7:9 the thrones were c. d.
8:7 he-goat c. d. ram to the gr.
10 it c. d. some of host
12 c. down truth to ground
11:12 he shall c. d. ten thous.
Mat. 4:6 c. thyself d. Luke 4:9
15:30 c. them d. at Jesus' feet
27:5 he c. d. pieces of silver
Luke 4:29 c. Jesus d. headlong
2 Cor. 4:9 c. d. but not destroyed
7:6 that comforteth those c. d.
2 Pet. 2:4 c. angels down to hell
Rev. 12:10 the accuser is c. d.

**CAST forth.**

Neh. 13:8 I c. forth household
Ps. 144:6 c. f. lightning
Jer. 22:19 Jehoi. c. f. beyond g.
Ezek. 32:4 c. thee f. on op. field
Hos. 14:5 c. f. his roots at Leb.
Jon. 1:15 c. f. Jonah into sea
Mark 7:26 c. f. devil
John 15:6 he is c. f. as a branch

**CAST lots.**

Lev. 16:8 c. lots on the two g.
Jos. 18:10 Joshua c. lots in Sh.
1 Sam. 14:42 c. l. bet. me and Jon.
1 Chr. 26:13 c. l. as well small
Ps. 22:18 c. l. upon my vesture, Mat. 27:35; John 19:24
Is. 34:17 he hath c. lots
Joel 3:3 c. lots for my people
Ob. 11 foreigners c. l. on Jer.
Jon. 1:7 c. lots that we may k.
Nah. 3:10 c. l. for her hon. men

**CAST off.**

2 K. 23:27 I will c. off Jerusa.
1 Chr. 28:9 c. thee off forever
2 Chr. 11:14 J. had c. them off
Job 15:33 c. off his flower
Ps. 43:2 why dost c. me off?
44:9 but thou hast c. off, 60:1, 10; 89:38; 108:11
23 Lord c. us not off for ever
71:9 c. me not off in old age
74:1 why hast c. us off for ever?
77:7 will Lord c. off for ever?
94:14 not c. o. his p. Lam. 3:31
Jer. 28:16 I will c. Hananiah off
31:37 c. off seed of Isr. 33:24
Lam. 2:7 L. hath c. off his altar
Hos. 8:3 Is. hath c. off thing good
5 thy calf, O Sam. c. thee off
Amos 1:11 bec. he c. off all pity
Zec. 10:6 tho' I not c. them off
Acts 22:23 and c. off their clothes
Rom. 13:12 let us c. off works
1 Tim. 5:12 c. off their first faith

**CAST out.**

Gen. 21:10 c. o. this bondwoman
Ex. 34:24 c. out the nations
Lev. 18:24 nations I c. o. 20:23; Deut. 7:1
Deut. 9:17 c. tables out
1 K. 9:7 this house will I c. out of my sight, 2 Chr. 7:20
21:26 Amorites c. out, 2 K. 16:3
2 K. 10:25 captains c. them out
17:20 c. them out, 24:20
2 Chr. 13:9 have ye not c. out
20:11 to c. us out of thy posses.
Neh. 1:9 there were of you c. out
Job 20:15 c. them out of his belly
39:3 they c. out their sorrows
Ps. 5:10 c. them out in trans.
18:42 did c. them out as dirt in
44:2 afflict people, and c. th. o.
60:8 will I c. out my shoe, 108:9
78:55 he c. out the heathen, 80:8
Prov. 22:10 c. out the scorner
Is. 14:19 art c. out of thy grave
16:52 as a wandering bird c. out
26:19 earth shall c. out the dead
34:3 their slain shall be c. out
58:7 that thou bring poor c. out
66:5 c. you out for my name's s.
Jer. 7:15 c. you out of my sight
9:19 our dwellings have c. us o.
15:1 c. out of my s. 23:39; 52:3
16:13 will I c. you out
22:26 I will c. thee out
36:30 dead body shall be c. out
51:34 Nebuch. hath c. me out
Ezek. 16:5 wast c. o. in open field
28:16 c. thee out of mountain
Amos 8:8 c. out and drowned
Mic. 2:9 women have ye c. out
Zep. 3:15 hath c. o. thine enemy
Zec. 1:21 to c. out horns of Gen.
9:4 Lord will c. her out
Mat 5:13 unsav. c. o. Luke 14:35
7:5 first c. out beam, Luke 6:42
22 in thy name c. out devils?
8:12 child. of kingdom be c. out
16 c. out spirits with his word
31 if thou c. us out suffer us
9:33 devil was c. o. dumb spake
10:1 power against spir. to c. o.
8 raise dead, c. out devils
12:24 c. o. but by B. Luke 11:18
26 if Satan c. out Satan
28 by spirit of God c. o. devils
15:17 and is c. out into draught
17:19 we c. him o.? Mark 9:28
21:12 Jesus c. o. all that sold, Mark 11:15; Luke 19:45
39 c. o. v. Mark 12:8; Luke 20:15
Mark 1:34 c. o. m. dev. 39; 6:13
3:15 have power to c. out devils
23 how can Satan c. o. Satan?
16:9 out of whom c. 7 devils
17 shall c. out devils
Luke 6:22 c. out your name
11:20 with finger of G. c. o. dev.
13:32 I c. out devils and do cures
20:12 wounded him c. him out
John 6:37 I will in no wise c. out
9:34 teach us? they c. him out
12:31 pr. of this world be c. out
Acts 7:19 c. out their young
21 when Moses was c. out
58 c. Stephen out and stoned
27:19 we c. out tackling of ship
Gal. 4:30 c. out the bondwoman
Rev. 12:9 great dragon was c. out
15 serpent c. out water, 16

**Lord CAST out.**

1 K. 14:24 L. c. o. bef. ch. of Isr. 2 K. 16:3; 2 Chr. 28:3; 33:2
2 K. 17:8 L. c. o. before Is. 21:2
Zec. 9:4 behold L. will c. her out

**CAST up.**

2 Sam. 20:15 c. up bank ag. city
Is. 57:14 c. ye up, pre. way, 62:10
20 whose waters c. up mire
Jer. 18:15 in way not c. up
50:26 c. her up as heaps
Lam. 2:10 c. up dust, Ezek. 27:30
Dan. 11:15 shall c. up a mount

**CASTEST, ETH.**

Job 15:4 yea thou c. off fear
21:10 cow c. not her calf
Ps. 50:17 c. my words behind
73:18 c. them into destruction
88:14 why c. thou off my soul
147:6 Lord c. the wicked down
17 he c. forth his ice
Prov. 10:3 c. away subst. of w.
19:15 slothful. c. into deep sleep
21:22 c. down strength
26:18 a madman c. firebrands
Jer. 6:7 so she c. out wickedness
Mat. 9:34 he c. out devils, Mark 3:22; Luke 11:15
1 John 4:18 per. love c. out fear
3 John 10 c. them out of church
Rev. 6:13 fig-tree c. untimely figs

**CASTING.**

Ez. 10:1 c. himself down
Job 6:21 ye see my c. down
Ps. 74:7 by c. down dwelling-p.
89:39 profaned crown by c. it
Mic. 6:14 thy c. down be in mid.
Mat. 27:35 c. lots, Mark 15:24
Mark 9:38 c. out dev. Luke 9:49
Luke 21:2 wid. c. in two mites
Rom. 11:15 if c. away be recon.
2 Cor. 10:5 c. down imaginations
1 Pet. 5:7 c. all your care on him

**CASTLE.**

1 Chr. 11:5 David took c. of Zion
7 David dwelt in c. city of D.
Prov. 18:19 like bars of a c.
Acts 21:34 Paul to be carried into the c. 37; 22:24; 23:10
23:16 entered into c. told Paul

**CASTLES.**

Gen. 25:16 names by their c.
Num. 31:10 burnt their goodly c.
2 Chr. 17:12 Jehoshaphat built c.
27:4 in the forest built c.

CASTOR. See SIGN.

**CATCH.**

1 K. 20:33 men did hastily c.
2 K. 7:12 we shall c. them alive
Ps. 10:9 in wait to c. the poor
35:8 let his net c. himself
109:11 extor. c. all he hath
Jer. 5:26 set a trap they c. men
Ezek. 19:3 it learned to c. prey, 6
Hab. 1:15 c. them in their net
Mark 12:13 to c. him in his wo.
Luke 5:10 from hencef. c. men
11:54 to c. something

**CATCHETH,**

Mat. 13:19 c. what was sown
John 10:12 wolf c. the sheep

**CATERPILLAR, S.**

1 K. 8:37 if any c. 2 Chr. 6:28
Ps. 78:46 their increase to c.
105:34 he spake, and c. came
Is. 33:4 like gathering of c.
Jer. 51:14 with men as c.
27 horses come up as rough c.

Joel 1:4 c.-w. left hath c. eaten
2:25 restore years c. hath eaten

**CATTLE.**

Gen. 1:25 God made the c.
3:14 art cursed above all c.
8:1 God remembered c. in ark
9:10 establish covenant with c.
13:2 Abram was rich in c.
31:9 taken away c. of your fath.
43 these c. are my c. and all
34:5 his sons were with his c.
46:32 their trade to feed c.
47:6 make them rulers over c.
17 Joseph gave bread for c.
Ex. 9:4 sever. bet. c. of Is. and c.
20 and c. flee into the houses
12:29 smote first-born of c.
Num. 3:41 take c. of Levi
20:19 c. drink, I will pay for it
32:4 land for c. and thy servants
Jos. 8:2 only c. take for a prey
Job 36:33 c. concerning vapor
Ps. 50:10 c. on a thousand hills
104:14 grass to grow for the c.
148:10 all c. praise the Lord
Ec. 2:7 great and small c.
Is. 7:25 for treading of lesser c.
43:23 not brought me small c.
46:1 their idols were upon c.
Jer. 9:10 nor hear voice of the c.
Ezek. 34:17 judge bet. c. 20:22
Hag. 1:11 for a drought upon c.
Zec. 2:4 for multitude of c.
13:5 man taught me to keep c.
Luke 17:7 servants feeding c.
John 4:12 dr. thereof, and his c.

**Much CATTLE.**

Gen. 30:43 Jacob had much c.
Ex. 12:38 out of Egy. with m. c.
Deut. 3:19 ye have much c.
Jos. 22:8 with very much c.
2 Chr. 26:10 Uzziah had much c.
Jon. 4:11 Nin. wherein is m. c.

**Our CATTLE.**

Ex. 10:26 our c. shall also go
17:3 kill our c. with thirst
Num. 32:16 sheepfolds for o. c.
Jos. 21:2 with suburbs for our c.
Neh. 10:36 bring first-born of o. c.

**Their CATTLE.**

Gen. 34:23 shall not their c.
Num. 35:3 sub. for t. c. Jos. 14:4
Jud. 6:5 Midian. came with t. c.
1 Sam. 23:5 brought away t. c.
Ps. 78:48 he gave up their c.
107:38 suff. not their c. to dec.
Jer. 49:32 a booty, t. c. a spoil

**Thy CATTLE.**

Gen. 30:29 thy c. was with me
31:41 served thee 6 years for t. c.
Ex. 9:19 and gather t. c.
20:10 t. c. do any w. Deut. 5:14.
34:19 firstling among thy c.
Lev. 25:7 sab. be meat for thy c.
Deut. 11:15 send grass for thy c.
28:4 fruit of t. c. 11; 30:9
51 he shall eat fruit of thy c.
Is. 30:23 t. c. feed in large past.

**Your CATTLE.**

Gen. 47:16 bread for your c.
Deut. 3:19 y. c. in c. Jos. 1:14
7:14 be barren among your c.

**CAUGHT.**

Gen. 22:13 behind him a ram c.
Ex. 4:4 and c. the serpent
Num. 31:32 prey men had c.
Jud. 8:14 c. young man of Suc.
21:23 danced, whom they c.
1 Sam. 17:35 I c. him by his bea.
2 Sam. 2:16 c. every one his fellow
18:9 Absalom's head c. hold of
1 K. 1:50 Adon. c. hold on altar
2:28 J. c. hold on horns of altar
11:30 Ahijah c. new garment
2 K. 4:27 she c. Elisha by feet
2 Chr. 22:9 they c. Ahaziah
Prov. 7:13 so she c. him
Jer. 50:24 O Babylon, thou art c.
Mat. 14:31 Jesus c. Peter
21:39 the husbandman c. him
Mark 12:3 they c. the servant
Luke 8:29 oftentimes it c. him
John 21:3 that night c. nothing
Acts 6:12 Stephen and c. him
8:39 the spirit c. away Philip
16:19 they c. Paul and Silas
26:21 the J. c. me in the temple
27:15 when ship was c. we let
2 Cor. 12:2 I knew a man c. up
4 he was c. up into paradise
16 crafty I c. you with guile
1 Thes. 4:17 we shall be c. up to
Rev. 12:5 child was c. up to God

**CAUL, S.**

Ex. 29:13 c. above the liver, 22;
Lev. 3:4, 10, 15; 4:9; 7:4; 8:16, 25; 9:10, 19
Is. 3:18 will take away their c.
Hos. 13:8 rend c. of their heart.

**CAUSE, Substantive.**

Ex. 22:9 c. of both before judges
23:2 nor speak in a c. to decline
3 counten. a poor man in his c.
6 wrest judg. of poor in his c.
Num. 16:11 for which c. thou and all thy company are ga.
27:5 Moses brought c. before L.
Deut. 1:17 the c. too hard for you
1 Sam. 17:29 is there not a c.?
25:39 L. pleaded c. of my rep.
2 Sam. 13:16 there is no c.
15:4 hath any c. might come
1 K. 8:45 maintain their c. 49, 59;
2 Chr. 6:35, 39
11:27 c. that he lift up his hand
12:15 c. was fr. L. 2 Chr. 10:15
1 Chr. 21:3 a c. of tresp. to Is.?
2 Chr. 19:10 what c. shall come
Job 5:8 would I commit my c.
13:18 I have ordered my c.
23:4 order my c. before him
29:16 c. I knew not I searched
31:13 if I did despise c. of serv.
Ps. 9:4 hast maintained my c.
35:23 awake to my c. my God
140:12 Lord will maintain the c.
Prov. 18:17 he first in his own c.
25:9 debate thy c. with neighbor
29:7 considereth c. of poor
31:8 for the dumb in the c.
Ec. 7:10 say not, what is the c.
Is. 1:23 nor c. of widow come
41:21 produce your c. saith Lord
51:22 God that pleadeth the c.
Jer. 5:28 judge not c. of fatherl.
11:20 to thee revealed my c.
20:12 unto thee I opened my c.
22:16 he judged the c. of poor
Lam. 3:36 subv. a man in his c.
59 seen my wrong, jud. my c.
Jon. 1:7 for whose c. 8
Mat. 5:32 saving for c. of forni.
19:3 put aw. his wife for ev c.
Luke 23:22 no c. of death in him
Acts 10:21 c. where. ye are come
13:28 found no c. of death
28:18 was no c. of death in me
2 Cor. 4:16 which c. we faint not
5:13 we be sober, it is for yo. c.
2 Cor. 7:12 his c. that h. done w.
Phil. 2:18 same c. do ye joy
2 Tim. 1:12 for which c. I suffer
Heb. 2:11 c. he is not ashamed to

**Plead CAUSE.**

1 Sam. 24:15 Lord plead my c. Ps. 35:1; 43:1; 119:154
Ps. 74:22 plead thine own c.
Prov. 22:23 will plead their c.
23:11 plead their c. with thee
31:9 p. the c. of poor and needy
Jer. 30:13 none to plead thy c.
50:34 Lord thor. plead their c.
51:36 behold I will plead thy c.
Mic. 7:9 until he plead my c.

**For this CAUSE.**

Ex. 9:16 f. t. c. raised up Ph.
John 12:27 f. t. c. came I
18:37 f. t. c. came I into the w.
Rom. 15:9 f. c. I will confess
1 Cor. 11:30 f. this c. many
Eph. 3:14 f. this c. I bow
1 Thes. 2:13 f. this c. thank we
1 Tim. 1:16 f. t. c. I obtained
Heb. 9:15 f. this c. he is med.
1 Pet. 4:6 f. t. c. was gospel pr.

**Without CAUSE.**

1 Sam. 19:5 slay D. without a c.
Job 2:3 to destroy him without c.
9:17 multipli. my wounds w. c.
Ps. 7:4 that w. c. is my enemy
25:3 that transgress w. c.
35:7 w. c. dig. a pit without c.
19 w. c. 69:4; John 15:25
109:3 fought ag. me with. a c.
119:78 perv. with me with. c.
161 persecuted me with. c.
Prov. 1:11 lurk for innocent w. c.
3:30 st. not with a man with. c.
23:29 hath wounds without c.
24:28 be not witness without c.
Is. 52:4 oppressed them w. c.
Lam. 3:52 chased me sore w. c.
Ezek. 14:23 have not done w. c.
Mat. 5:22 angry with bro. w. c.

**CAUSE.**

Gen. 45:1 c. every man to go out
Num. 16:5 will c. him to come
Deut. 1:38 c. to inh. 3:28; 31:7
12:11 c. his name to dwell there
2 Sam. 13:13 c. my shame to go
Est. 3:13 c. to perish, 8:11
Job 6:24 c. me to understand
34:11 c. every man to find
Ps. 10:17 wilt c. thine ear
67:1 c. his face to sh. 80:3, 7, 19
76:8 c. judgment to be heard
143:8 c. me to hear
Prov. 4:16 unless c. some to fall
Ec. 5:6 to c. thy flesh to sin
Cant. 8:13 voice, c. me to hear it
Ps. 3:12 lead c. thee to err, 9:16
27:6 c. them of Jacob take root
30:30 c. his glor. voice be heard
42:2 nor c. his voice to be heard
58:14 c. thee to ride on high
61:11 c. righteousness to spring
66:9 and not c. to bring forth
Jer. 3:12 not c. mine anger
7:3 c. to dwell in this place, 7
23:27 c. people forget my name
31:2 I went to c. him to rest
9 c. to walk by rivers of waters
Lam. 3:32 but though he c. grief
Ezek. 20:37 c. to pass under rod
34:15 I will c. them to lie down
36:12 c. men to walk upon you
Dan. 9:17 G. c. thy face to shine
Joel 3:11 thither c. mighty ones
Hab. 1:3 why c. me behold
Mat. 10:21 c. par. to be put to d. Mark 13:12; Luke 21:16
Rom. 16:17 mark them c. divi.
Col. 4:16 c. it be read in church

AUSE to cease. See CEASE.

**CAUSED.**

Gen. 2:21 Lord c. a deep sleep
20:13 God c. me wander
Deut. 34:4 the land c. thee
2 Sam 7:11 c. thee to rest
2 Chr. 34:32 c. all to stand to it
Ezr. 6:12 c. his name to dwell
Job 31:16 c. eyes of widow
Ps. 66:12 c. men to ride over
119:49 on which c. me to hope
Is. 19:14 have c. Egypt to err
63:14 Sp. of Lord c. him to rest
Jer. 12:14 c. my people to inher.
13:11 c. to cleave house of Isr.

29:31 c. you to trust in a lie
32:23 thou hast c. all this evil
48:4 little ones have c. a cry
Zec. 3:4 c. thy iniquity to pass
Mal. 2:8 c. many to stumble
John 11:37 c. this man not died
Acts 15:3 c. great joy to brethren
2 Cor. 2:5 if any have c. grief

**CAUSELESS.**
1 Sam. 25:31 hast shed blood c.
Prov. 26:2 curse c. shall not co.

**CAUSES.**
Ex. 18:19 bring c. to God
26 hard c. brought to Moses
Deut. 1:16 c. between brethren
Jer. 3:8 c. whereby backsliding
Lam. 3:58 pleaded c. of my soul
Acts 26:21 c. the Jews caught me

**CAUSEST.**
Job 30:22 c. me to ride on wind
Ps. 65:4 blessed c. approach thee

**CAUSETH.**
Job 20:3 spirit of under. c. me
37:13 c. it come for correction
Ps. 135:7 he c. vapors to ascend, Jer. 10:13; 51:16
Prov. 10:5 son c. sh. 17:2; 19:26
17:2 rule over a son c. shame
19:27 instruction that c. to err
28:10 c. righteous to go ast.
Mat. 5:32 c. her to commit adul.
2 Cor. 2:14 which c. us triumph
9:11 c. through us thanksgiving

**CAUSEWAY.**
1 Chr. 26:16 lot came by the c.

**CAUSING.**
Cant. 7:9 c. lips of those asleep
Jer. 29:10 in c. you to return

**CAVE, S.**
Gen. 19:30 Lot dwelt in a c. he
23:19 buried Sarah in the c.
49:29 bury me in the c.
Jos. 10:16 kings hid in a c. 17
Jud. 6:2 Israel made c.
1 Sam. 13:6 Israel did hide in c.
22:1 David escaped to the c.
24:10 delivered thee in the c.
1 K. 18:4 prophets hid in c. 13
19:9 Elijah came to a c. and
Is. 2:19 go into c. for fear of L.
Ezek. 33:27 die that be in the c.
John 11:38 it was a c. a stone
Heb. 11:38 they wandered in c

**CEASE.**
Gen. 8:22 day and night not c.
Num. 8:25 age of fifty years. c.
11:25 prophesied, did not c.
17:5 to c. the murmurings
Deut. 15:11 poor shall never c.
32:26 rememb. of them to c.
Jos. 22:25 child. c. from fearing
Jud. 15:7 after that I will c.
20:28 ag. go up, or shall I c.?
1 Sam. 7:8 c. not to cry to G.
2 Chr. 16:5 B. let his work c.
Ezr. 4:23 to c. by force
Neh. 6:3 why should the work c.
Job 3:17 c. from troubling
10:20 my days few? c. then
14:7 tender branch will not c.
Ps. 37:8 c. from anger
46:9 he maketh wars to c.
89:44 hast made his glory to c.
Prov. 19:27 c. to hear instruction
20:3 an honor to c. from strife
22:10 and reproach shall c.
23:4 c. from thy wisdom.
Ec. 12:3 grinders c. bec. few
Is. 1:16 c. to do evil
2:22 c. ye from man whose br
10:25 and indignation shall c.
16:10 vintage shouting to c.
17:3 fortress c. from Ephraim
21:2 all the sighing made to c.
33:1 shalt c. to spoil, be spoiled
Jer. 14:17 let tears not c.
17:8 nor c. from yielding fruit
31:36 seed of Israel shall c.
Lam. 2:18 apple of thine eye c.
Ezek. 6:6 that your idols may c.
7:24 pomp of the strong to c.
12:23 will make this proverb c.
23:27 make thy lewdness to c.
30:10 multitude of Egypt to c.
18 pomp of her str. c. 33:28
Amos 7:5 Lord c. I beseech thee
Acts 13:10 not c. to pervert right
1 Cor. 13:8 tongues they shall c.
Eph. 1:16 I c. not to give thanks
Col. 1:9 not c. to pray for you
2 Pet. 2:14 cannot c. from sin

**Cause to CEASE.**
Ezr. 5:5 could not c. them c.
Neh. 4:11 cause the work to c.
Ps. 85:4 cause thine anger to c.
Prov. 18:18 c. contentions to c.
Is. 13:11 c. arrog. of proud to c.
30:11 cause H. O. of Israel to c.
Jer. 7:34 c. mirth to c. Hos. 2:11
36:29 cause to c. man and beast
48:35 c. to c. him that offereth
Ezek. 23.48 cause lewdness to c.
Ezek. 26:13 cause n. of songs to c.
30:13 cause their images to c.
34:10 c. to c. from feeding, 25
Dan. 9:27 shall c. oblation to c.
11:18 cause reproach offered to c.
Hos. 1:4 c. to c. kingdom of Isr.

**CEASED.**
Gen. 18:11 it c. to be with Sarah
Jud. 2:19 c. not from their d.
5:7 inhabitants of villages c.
1 Sam 2:5 that were hungry c.
25:9 in name of David and c.
Ezr. 4:24 then c. work of house
Job 32:1 three men c. to answer
Ps. 35:15 did tear me and c. not
77:2 my sore ran and c. not
Is. 14:4 opp. c. golden city c.
Lam. 5:14 elders have c.
15 the joy of our heart is c.
Jon. 1:15 sea c. from raging
Mat. 14:32 w. c. Mark 4:39; 6:51
Luke 7:45 not c. to kiss my feet
11:1 was praying, when he c.
Acts 5:42 c. not to preach Jesus
20:1 after uproar was c. Paul
31 three years I c. not to warn
21:14 not be persuaded, we c.
Gal. 5:11 offence of cross c.
Heb. 4:10 c. from his own works
10:2 not have c. to be offered
1 Pet. 4:1 hath c. from sin

**CEASETH.**
Ps. 12:1 for the godly man c.
49:8 redemption precious, it c.
Prov. 26:20 talebearer, strife c.
Is. 16:4 the spoiler c.
24:8 tabrets c. joy of the harp c.
33:8 the wayfaring man c.
Lam. 3:49 eye trickleth, c. not
Acts 6:13 c. not to speak blasph.

**CEASING.**
1 Sam. 12:23 sin in c. to pray
Acts 12:5 prayer made without c.
Rom. 1:9 c. make m. 1 Thes. 1:3
1 Thes. 2:13 we think G. w. c.
5:17 pray without c.
2 Tim. 1:3 without c. I have re.

**CEDAR.**
2 Sam. 7:2 I dwell in house of c.
7 wl y build ye not house of c.
1 K. 4:33 he spake from the c.
5:8 I will do thy desire conc. c.
2 K. 14:9 sent to c. 2 Chr. 25:18
Job 40:17 moveth tail like a c.
Ps. 92:12 righteous grow like c.
Cant. 1:17 beams of our house c.
8:9 inclose her with boards of c.
Is. 41:19 in wilderness the c.
Jer. 22:14 it is ceiled with c.
15 because closest thyself in c.
Ezek. 17:3 took highest br. of c.
23 it shall be a goodly c.
27:24 chests made of c. among
31:3 Assyrian was a c.
Zep. 2:14 shall uncover c. work
Zec. 11:2 howl, for c. is fallen

**CEDAR-TREES.**
Num. 24:6 Is. tabernac. as c.-t.
2 Sam. 5:11 H. sent c.-t to Dav.
1 K. 5:6 they hew me c.-t.
10 H. gave Solomon c.-t. 9:11
2 K. 19:23 cut down tall c.-t.
1 Chr. 22:4 David prepared c.-t.
2 Chr. 1:15 c.-t. as sycamo. 9:27
2:8 send me c.-t. out of Lebanon
Ezr. 3:7 gave mon. to bring c.-t.

**CEDAR-WOOD.**
Lev. 14:4 take c.-w. 6, 49, 51, 52
Num. 19:6 priest shall take c.-w.
1 Chr. 22:4 much c.-w. to David

**CEDARS.**
1 K. 10:27 c. as sycamore-trees
1 Chr. 17:1 dwell in a house of c.
2 Chr. 2:3 didst send c. to build
Ps. 29:5 voice of L. breaketh c.
80:10 the boughs like goodly c.
148:9 praise him all c.
Cant. 5:15 his countenance as c.
Is. 9:10 change them into c.
37:24 I will cut down the tall c.
44:14 heweth him down c.
Jer. 22:7 cut down thy choice c.
23 makest thy nest in the c.
Ezek. 31:8 c. in garden
Amos 2:9 Amor. height of the c.
Zec. 11:1 fire may devour thy c.

**CEDARS of Lebanon.**
Jud. 9:15 bramble dev. c. of Leb.
Ps. 104:16 c. of Leb. he planted
Is. 2:13 Lord on all c. of Leb.
14:8 c. of Leb. rejoice at thee
Ezek. 27:5 c. from Leb. to make

CEDRON. John 18:1

**CEILED.**
2 Chr. 3:5 he c. the greater house
Jer. 22:14 it is c. with cedar
Hag. 1:4 to dwell in c. houses?

**CEILING.**
1 K. 6:15 he built walls of the c.

**CELEBRATE.**
Lev. 23:32 even c. sabbath, 41
Is. 38:18 death cannot c. thee

**CELESTIAL.**
1 Cor. 15:40 c. bodies, glory of c.

**CELLARS.**
1 Chr. 27:28 over the c. of oil

**CENCHREA.**
Acts 18:18 shorn his head in C.
Rom. 16:1 serv. of church at C.

**CENSER, S.**
Lev. 10:1 sons of Aaron took c.
16:12 a c. full of burning coals
Num. 16:6 take ye c. 17
39 Eleazar took the brazen c.
1 K. 7:50 c. of gold, 2 Chr. 4:22
2 Chr. 26:19 Uzziah had a c.
Ezek. 8:11 with every man his c.
Heb. 9:4 holiest had the golden c.
Rev. 8:3 angel having a golden c.
5 angel took the c. and filled it

**CENTURION, S.**
Mat. 8:5 came unto him a c.
8 c. said, L. I am not worthy
27:54 when c. saw earthquake
Luke 7:2 c. servant was sick
23:47 c. saw what was done
Acts 10:1 Cornelius was a c.
22 Cornelius the c. a just man
21:32 immediately took c.
22:26 when the c. heard that
23:17 Paul called one of the c.
23 he called to him two c.

24:23 command. a *c.* to keep P.
27:1 J. a *c.* of Augustus' band
11 *c.* believ. m. more than P.
43 *c.* willing to save Paul
28:16 *c.* delivered the prisoners

**CEPHAS.**

*John* 1:42 shalt be called C.
1 *Cor.* 1:12 I am of C. 3:22
9:5 breth. of the L. and C. 15:5
*Gal.* 2:9 James, C. and John

**CEREMONIES.**

*Num.* 9:3 passover accord. to *c.*

**CERTAIN,** *some.*

*Deut.* 13:13 *c.* men children of B.
25:2 beaten by *c.* number
*Jer.* 41:5 came *c.* from Shechem
52:15 carried away *c.* poor
*Dan.* 8:27 D. was sick *c.* days
*Mat.* 20:20 desiring *c.* thing
*Mark* 14:57 *c.* bare false witness
*Luke* 5:12 he was in a *c.* city
11:27 a *c.* woman lift up voice
18:9 parable to *c.* who trusted
24:22 *c.* women made us aston.
24 *c.* with us went to sepulchre
*John* 5:4 went at a *c.* season
*Acts* 9:19 Saul *c.* days with disc.
10:48 Peter to tarry *c.* days
12:1 to vex. *c.* of the church
15:24 *c.* which went from us
17:28 as *c.* of your own poets
*Rom.* 15:26 to make a *c.* contrib.
*Gal.* 2:12 before *c.* came from J.
*Heb.* 2:6 one in a *c.* place testified
4:4 in *c.* place of seventh day
7 he limiteth a *c.* day, saying
10:27 *c.* looking for of judgm.
*Jude* 4 *c.* men crept in unawares

A CERTAIN *man.* *See* MAN.

**CERTAIN,** *sure.*

*Deut.* 13:14 the thing *c.* 17:4
1 *K.* 2:37 kn. for *c.* 42; *Jer.* 26:15
*Dan.* 2:45 the dream is *c.*
*Acts* 25:26 no *c.* thing to write
1 *Cor.* 4:11 no *c.* dwelling-place
1 *Tim.* 6:7 it is *c.* we can carry

**CERTAINLY.**

*Gen.* 18:10 will *c.* return to thee
26:28 saw *c.* L. was with thee
43:7 *c.* know he would say
*Ex.* 3:12 *c.* I will be with thee
*Jos.* 9:24 it was *c.* told thy serv.
1 *Sam.* 20:9 if I knew *c.* evil
25:28 *c.* make my lord a sure
1 *K.* 1:30 so will I *c.* do this day
2 *K.* 8:10 thou mayest *c.* recover
2 *Chr.* 18:27 if *c.* return in peace
*Jer.* 8:8 lo *c.* in vain made he it
42:19 *c.* I have admonished
44:17 *c.* do what goeth out
*Lam.* 2:16 *c.* this is day looked
*Dan.* 11:10 *c.* come and over. 13
*Luke* 23:47 *c.* this was a r. man

**CERTAINTY.**

*Jos.* 23:13 *c.* Lord will no more
1 *Sam.* 23:23 with the *c.*
*Prov.* 22:21 *c.* of words of truth
*Dan.* 2:8 *c.* ye would gain time
*Luke* 1:4 know *c.* of those things
*Acts* 22:30 would have known *c.*

**CERTIFY, IED.**

*Ezr.* 4:14 we have *c.* the king
16 *c.* king that if city be built
*Gal.* 1:11 I *c.* you the gospel

**CESAR.**

*Mat.* 22:17 tribute to C. *Mark* 12:14; *Luke* 20:21, 22
*Luke* 2:1 a decree from C.
*John* 19:12 not C.'s friend; ag. C.
*Acts* 17:7 dec. of C. 25:8, 11, 21
*Phil.* 4:22 they that are of C.

**CESAREA.**

*Mat.* 16:13 into coasts of C.
*Mark* 8:27 into the towns of C.
*Acts* 8:40; 9:30; 10:24; 23:23; 25:4

**CHAFED.**

2 *Sam.* 17:8 they be *c.* as a bear

**CHAFF.**

*Job* 21:18 as *c.* storm carrieth
*Ps.* 1:4 like the *c.* which wind
35:5 be as *c.* before the wind
*Is.* 5:24 as flame consumeth *c.*
17:13 nations be chased as *c.*
29:5 terrible ones shall be as *c.*
33:11 conc. *c.* and bring forth
41:15 shalt make the hills as *c.*
*Jer.* 23:28 what is *c.* to the wheat
*Dan.* 2:35 *c.* of threshing floor
*Hos.* 13:3 as *c.* driven with wh.
*Zep.* 2:2 day pass as the *c.*
*Mat.* 3:12 b. up the *c.* *Luke* 3:17

**CHAIN.**

*Gen.* 41:42 put a gold *c.* about his neck, *Dan.* 5:7, 16, 29.
*Ps.* 73:6 pride compasseth as a *c.*
*Cant.* 4:9 ravished me with one *c.*
*Lam.* 3:7 he made my *c.* heavy
*Ezek.* 7:23 *c.* land is full of crim.
16:11 I put a *c.* on thy neck
*Acts* 28:20 for hope bound with *c.*
2 *Tim.* 1:16 O. not ashamed of *c.*
*Rev.* 20:1 angel *c.* in his hand

**CHAINS.**

*Jud.* 8:26 *c.* about camels' necks
1 *K.* 6:21 *c.* of gold before oracle
*Ps.* 149:8 to bind kings with *c.*
*Prov* 1:9 instruction shall be *c.*
*Cant.* 1:10 neck comely with *c.*
*Is.* 3:19 L. will take away thy *c.*
40:10 goldsmith casteth silver *c.*
45:14 come after thee in *c.*
*Jer.* 40:4 l. thee this day from *c.*
*Ezek.* 19:4 brought him with *c.*
9 they put him in ward in *c.*
*Mark* 5:3 no not with *c.*
*Acts* 12:7 Peter's *c.* fell off
2 *Pet.* 2:4 deliv. into *c.* of dark.
*Jude* 6 reserved in everlasting *c.*

*See* BOUND.

**CHALCEDONY.**

*Rev.* 21:19 foundation was a *c.*

**CHALCOL.**

1 *K.* 4:31 Sol. was wiser than C.
1 *Chr.* 2:6 sons of Z. Heman, C.

**CHALDEA.**

*Jer.* 50:10 C. shall be a spoil
51:24 to inhabitants of C. 35
*Ezek.* 16:29 thy fornication to C.
23:16 messeng. to them into C.

**CHALDEAN.**

*Ezr.* 5:12 them into hand of C.
*Dan.* 2:10 such things at any C.

**CHALDEANS.**

*Job* 1:17 C. made out three bands
*Is.* 23:13 C. the Assyrian foun.
*Dan.* 1:4; 2:2; 3:8; 4:7; 5:7, 11
*Hab.* 1:6 lo, I raise up the C.
*Acts* 7:4 out of the land of the C.

**CHALDEES.**

2 *K.* 24:2 of the C. 25:4, 10, 26
2 *Chr.* 36:17 the king of the C.
*Is.* 13:19 Bab. the beauty of C.

**CHALK-STONES.**

*Is.* 27:9 stones of altar as *c.-s.*

**CHALLENGETH.**

*Ex.* 22:9 another *c.* to be his

**CHAMBER.**

*Gen.* 43:30 J. entered into his *c.*
*Jud.* 15:1 my wife into the *c.*
16:9 in wait abiding in *c.* 12
2 *K.* 4:11 Elisha turned into *c.*
*Neh.* 13:5 prepared for Tobiah *c.*
*Ps.* 19:5 as bridegroom out of *c.*
*Cant.* 3:4 *c.* of her conceived me
*Jer.* 36:10 book in *c.* of Gemariah
20 laid roll in *c.* of Elishama
*Ezek.* 40:45 *c.* prospect to south
*Dan.* 6:10 windows open in his *c.*
*Joel* 2:16 bridegr. go forth of *c.*

**Inner CHAMBER.**

1 *K.* 20:30 Benh. came into *in. c.*
22:25 *inner c.* 2 *Chr.* 18:24
2 *K.* 9:2 carry Jehu into *inner c.*

**Little CHAMBER.**

2 *K.* 4:10 a *little c.* on the wall
*Ezek.* 40:7 *little c.* one reed, 13

**Side CHAMBER.**

*Ezek.* 41:5 every *side c.* four cub.

**Upper CHAMBER.**

2 *K.* 1:2 thro' a lattice in *u. c.*
23:12 altars on top of *upper c.*
*Acts* 9:37 Dorcas in an *upper c.*
39 P. when come into *upper c.*
20:8 many lights in *upper c.*

**CHAMBERS.**

1 *K.* 6:5 against the wall built *c.*
1 *Chr.* 9:26 porters over *c.* 23:28
2 *Chr.* 31:11 com. to prepare *c.*
*Job* 9:9 maketh *c.* of the south
*Ps.* 104:3 beams of *c.* in waters
13 watereth hills from *c.*
105:30 in the *c.* of their kings
*Prov.* 7:27 down to *c.* of death
24:4 by knowledge *c.* be filled
*Cant.* 1:4 brought me into his *c.*
*Is.* 26:20 *c.* and shut thy doors
*Jer.* 22:13 buildeth *c.* by wrong
14 a wide house and large *c.*
35:2 Rechabites into one of *c.*
*Ezek.* 8:12 in *c.* of his imagery
21:14 sword entereth privy *c.*
42:13 holy *c.* where priests eat
*Mat.* 24:26 he is in secret *c.*

**CHAMBERING.**

*Rom.* 13:13 *c.* and wantonness

**CHAMBERLAIN, S.**

2 *K.* 23:11 Nathan-melech the *c.*
*Est.* 1:10 seven *c.* that served
2:21 king's *c.* were wroth
*Acts* 12:20 Blastus the king's *c.*
*Rom.* 16:23 Erastus *c.* saluteth

**CHAMELEON.**

*Lev.* 11:30 be unclean, the *c.*

**CHAMOIS.**

*Deut.* 14:5 ye shall eat, the *c.*

**CHAMPAIGN.**

*Deut.* 11:30 in *c.* over against G.

**CHAMPION.**

1 *Sam.* 17:4 there went out a *c.*
51 saw their *c.* was dead

**CHANCE.**

1 *Sam.* 6:9 *c.* that happened to us
*Ec.* 9:11 time and *c.* happeneth
*Luke* 10:31 by *c.* a priest came
1 *Cor.* 15:37 it may *c.* of wheat

**CHANCELLOR.**

*Ezr.* 4:8 Rehum the *c.* 9, 17

**CHANGE.**

*Gen.* 45:22 each *c.* to Ben. five *c.*
*Jud.* 14:12 *c.* of garments, 13
2 *K.* 5:5 took ten *c.* of raiment
22 two *c.* of garments
23 bound two *c.* of garments
*Job* 10:17 *c.* and war are ag. me
14:14 I wait till my *c.* come
*Ps.* 55:19 no *c.* they fear not
*Prov.* 24:21 them given to *c.*
*Heb.* 7:12 of necessity a *c.* of law

**CHANGE, Verb.**

*Gen.* 35:2 and *c.* your garments
*Lev.* 27:10 he shall not *c.* it
33 nor *c.* it, if he *c.*
*Job* 17:12 *c.* the night into the day
*Ps.* 102:26 as vesture *c.* them
*Is.* 9:10 will *c.* them into cedars
*Jer.* 2:36 so much to *c.* thy way?
13:23 can Ethiopian *c.* his skin
*Dan.* 7:25 think to *c.* times
*Hos.* 4:7 *c.* their glory to shame
*Hab.* 1:11 his mind *c.* and pass

*Mal.* 3:6 I am the Lord I *c.* not
*Acts* 6:14 shall *c.* the customs
*Rom.* 1:26 women did *c.* the use
*Gal.* 4:20 I desire to *c.* my voice
*Phil.* 3:21 C. shall *c.* our vile b.

**CHANGED, ETH.**

*Gen.* 31:7 your father *c.* wages
41:14 Joseph *c.* his raiment
*Lev.* 13:16 flesh turn and be *c.*
55 plague have not *c.* his color
1 *Sam.* 21:13 *c.* behavior before
2 *Sam.* 12:20 Dav. *c.* his apparel
2 *K.* 24:17 *c.* name to Zedekiah
25:29 *c.* prison gar. *Jer.* 52:33
*Job* 30:18 is my garment *c.*
*Ps.* 15:4 sweareth to hurt, *c.* not
102:26 as a vesture *c. Heb.* 1:12
106:20 *c.* their glory to an ox
*Ec.* 8:1 bold. of face shall be *c.*
*Is.* 24:5 *c.* the ordinance
*Jer.* 2:11 *c.* their gods, my people
48:11 and his scent is not *c.*
*Lam.* 4:1 how is the fine gold *c.*
*Ezek.* 5:6 hath *c.* my judgments
*Dan.* 2:9 to speak till time be *c.*
21 he *c.* times and seasons
3:19 form of his visage was *c.*
27 coats *c.* nor smell of fire
4:16 heart be *c.* from man's
6:8 writing that it be not *c.*
15 no decree may be *c.*
*Mic.* 2:4 *c.* portion of my people
*Acts* 28:6 barbarians *c.* their m.
*Rom.* 1:23 *c.* glory of uncor. God
25 *c.* truth of God into a lie
1 *Cor.* 15:51 we shall all be *c.* 52
2 *Cor.* 3:18 *c.* into same image
*Heb.* 7:12 for priesthood being *c.*

**CHANGEST, ED, countenance.**

*Job* 14:20 *c.* his *c.* and sendest
*Dan.* 5:6 king's *c.* was *c.* 9
7:28 my *countenance c.* in me

**CHANGERS.**

*Mat.* 21:12 tables of money *c.* *Mark* 11:15; *John* 2:14, 15

**CHANGING.**

*Ruth* 4:7 manner concerning *c.*

**CHANNEL, S.**

2 *Sam.* 22:16 *c.* of the s. *Ps.* 18:15
*Is.* 8:7 shall come up over his *c.*
27:12 beat off from *c.* of the riv.

**CHANT.**

*Amos* 6:5 *c.* to sound of the viol

**CHAPEL.**

*Amos* 7:13 it is the king's *c.*

**CHAPITER, S.**

*Ex.* 36:38 *c.* with gold, 38:28
38:17 overlaying of *c.* 19
2 *K.* 7:16 *c.* of brass, 2 *K.* 25:17; 2 *Chr.* 4:12, 13; *Jer.* 52:22

**CHAPMEN.**

2 *Chr.* 9:14 what *c.* brought

**CHAPPED.**

*Jer.* 14:4 because the ground is *c.*

**CHARGE, Substantive.**

*Gen.* 26:5 Abraham kept my *c.*
28:6 Isaac gave Jacob a *c.*
*Ex.* 6:13 Moses and Aaron a *c.*
*Num.* 9:19 kept the *c.* of L. 23
27:23 Joshua a *c. Deut.* 31:23
*Jos.* 22:3 Reubenites kept *c.*
2 *Sam.* 18:5 *c.* concerning Abs.
1 *K.* 11:28 Jeroboam ruler over *c.*
2 *K.* 7:17 lord *c.* of the gate
1 *Chr.* 9:27 bec. *c.* was on them
*Neh.* 7:2 Hanani *c.* over Jerus.
*Job* 34:13 *c.* over the earth?
*Ps.* 35:11 *c.* things I knew not
*Jer.* 39:11 *c.* concerning Jeremiah
47:7 seeing L. hath given it *c.*
*Ezek.* 9:1 have *c.* over the city
44:8 not kept *c.* of holy things
15 kept *c.* of my sanctuary
48:11 my *c.* went not astray
*Acts* 7:60 lay not sin to their *c.*
8:27 had *c.* of treasure
16:24 rec. *c.* thrust into prison
23:29 to his *c.* worthy of death
*Rom.* 8:33 to *c.* of God's elect?
1 *Cor.* 9:18 gospel without *c.*
1 *Tim.* 1:18 *c.* I commit to thee
2 *Tim.* 4:16 not be laid to their *c.*
*See* KEEP.

**Give CHARGE.**

*Num.* 27:19 *give* Joshua a *c.*
*Deut.* 31:14 call J. *give* him a *c.*
2 *Sam.* 14:8 I will *g. c.* con. thee
1 *Chr.* 22:12 L. *g.* thee wis. and *c.*
*Ps.* 91:11 *g.* ang. *c. Mat.* 4:6; *Luke* 4:10
1 *Tim.* 5:7 these things *give* in *c.*
6:13 *give* thee *c.* in sight of God

**CHARGE, Verb.**

*Ex.* 19:21 go down *c.* the people
*Deut.* 3:28 *c.* Joshua encourage
*Neh.* 10:32 to *c.* ourselves yearly
*Cant.* 2:7 I *c.* dau. 3:5; 5:8; 8:4
5:9 that thou dost so *c.* us
*Mark* 9:25 I *c.* thee, come out
1 *Tim.* 1:3 *c.* that they teach no
5:21 *c.* thee bef. God, 2 *Tim.* 4:1
6:17 *c.* them that are rich

**CHARGEABLE.**

2 *Sam.* 13:25 not all go, lest be *c.*
*Neh.* 5:15 governors were *c.*
2 *Cor.* 11:9 I was *c.* to no man
1 *Thes.* 2:9 we would not be *c.*
2 *Thes.* 3:8 might not be *c.* to any

**CHARGED.**

*Gen.* 26:11 Abimelech *c.* his peo.
28:1 Isaac called J. and *c.* him
40:4 captain *c.* Jos. with them
49:29 Jacob *c.* his sons, and said
*Ex.* 1:22 Pharaoh *c.* his people
*Deut.* 1:16 I *c.* your judges
24:5 nor be *c.* with business
27:11 Moses *c.* people same day
1 *Sam.* 14:27 heard not when S. *c.*
2 *Sam.* 18:12 hearing, king *c.*
1 *K.* 2:1 David *c.* Solomon
13:9 so *c.* me by word of Lord
2 *Chr.* 36:23 *c.* me to b. *Ezr.* 1:2
*Job* 1:22 nor *c.* God foolishly
4:17 angels he *c.* with folly
*Jer.* 32:13 I *c.* Baruch saying
35:8 obeyed Jonadab in all he *c.*
*Mat.* 9:30 *c.* that no man know it, *Mark* 5:43; *Luke* 9:21
11:16 J. *c.* not to make known
*Mark* 7:36 *c.* not to tell, 8:30; 9:9; *Luke* 5:14; 8:56
10:48 *c.* him should hold peace
1 *Thes.* 2:11 *c.* every one of you
1 *Tim.* 5:16 let not church be *c.*

**CHARGEDST.**

*Ex.* 19:23 *c.* us, saying

**CHARGER, S.**

*Num.* 7:13 offering silver *c.* 19–79
85 each *c.* of silver 130 shekels
*Ezr.* 1:9 one thousand *c.*
*Mat.* 14:8 head in a *c. Mark* 6:25

**CHARGES.**

2 *Chr.* 8:14 Levites to their *c.*
31:17 twenty years in their *c.*
35:2 set priests in their *c.*
*Acts* 21:24 be at *c.* with them
1 *Cor.* 9:7 warfare at his own *c.*?

**CHARGING.**

*Acts* 16:23 *c.* jailer to keep safely
2 *Tim.* 2:14 *c.* strive not about w.

**CHARIOT.**

*Gen.* 41:43 ride in second *c.*
*Ex.* 14:25 Lord took off *c.* wheels
1 *K.* 18:44 prep. ran *c.* get down
20:25 number *c.* for *c.*
22:35 the blood thy into *c.*
2 *K.* 2:11 appeared a *c.* of fire
12 cried, *c.* of Israel, 13:14
5:21 from *c.* to meet Gehazi
9:16 J. rode in *c.*; 27 smite in *c.*
28 carried him in a *c.* 23:30
2 *Chr.* 35:24 took him out of *c.*
*Ps.* 46:9 he burneth the *c.* in fire
76:6 *c.* and horse cast into sleep
*Cant.* 3:9 *c.* of wood of Lebanon
*Is.* 21:7 saw a *c. c.* of asses
*Jer.* 51:21 will I break in pieces *c.*
*Mic.* 1:13 bind *c.* to swift beast
*Zec.* 6:2 first *c.* red horses
9:10 cut off *c.* from Ephraim
*Acts* 8:29 join thyself to this *c.*
38 commanded *c.* to stand still

**His CHARIOT.**

*Gen.* 46:29 J. made ready *his c.*
*Ex.* 14:6 Ph. made ready *his c.*
*Jud.* 4:15 Sisera lighted off *his c.*
5:28 *his c.* so long in coming
1 *K.* 12:18 to *his c.* 2 *Chr.* 10:18
22:34 to driver of *his c.*
2 *K.* 5:9 Naaman came with *h. c.*
9:21 went out each in *his c.*
24 Jehoram sunk down in *h. c.*
10:16 made him ride in *his c.*
*Ps.* 104:3 maketh clouds *his c.*
*Jer.* 4:13 *his c.* like whirlwind
*Acts* 8:28 in *his c.* read Esaias

**CHARIOT-CITIES.**

2 *Chr.* 1:14 placed in *c.-c.*
8:6 Solomon built all *c.-c.*
9:25 bestowed the *c.-c.*

**CHARIOT-HORSES.**

2 *Sam.* 8:4 hou. *c.-h.* 1 *Chr.* 18:4
2 *K.* 7:14 they took two *c.-h.*

**CHARIOT-MAN.**

2 *Chr.* 18:33 to *c.-m.* turn thy h.

**CHARIOTS.**

*Gen.* 50:9 went with Joseph *c.*
*Ex.* 14:7 Pharaoh took 600 *c.*
28 waters covered all the *c.*
15:4 Ph.'s *c.* cast into sea, 19
*Jos.* 17:16 *c.* of iron 18; *Jud.* 1:19
4:3
*Jud.* 5:28 wheels of his *c.*
1 *Sam.* 8:11 king appoint for his *c.*
13:5 to fight Israel 30,000 *c.*
2 *Sam.* 1:6 the *c.* followed Saul
1 *K.* 10:26 Solomon had 1,400 *c.*
22:32 captains of *c.* saw Jeh.
2 *K.* 13:7 left but ten *c.*
18:24 trust on E. for *c. Is.* 36:9
*Ps.* 68:17 *c.* of God are 20,000
*Cant.* 6:12 my soul like *c.* of Am
*Is.* 2:7 nor any end of their *c.*
22:18 *c.* of thy glory be shame
31:1 woe to them that trust in *c.*
37:24 by mul. of *c.* am I come
66:15 with *c.* like whirlwind. *Jer.* 4:13; *Dan.* 11:40
*Jer.* 47:3 at rushing of his *c.*
*Ezek.* 23:24 against thee with *c.*
26:10 walls shake at noise of *c.*
*Joel* 2:5 like noise of *c.* shall leap
*Mic.* 5:10 I will destroy thy *c.*
*Nah.* 2:3 *c.* shall be with torches
4 *c.* shall rage in the streets
13 I will burn her *c.* in smoke
*Hag.* 2:22 I will overthrow the *c.*
*Rev.* 9:9 sound of wings as of *c.*

**CHARIOTS *with* horses.**

*Deut.* 11:4 he did to *h.* and *c.*
20:1 seest *horses* and *c.* fear not
*Jos.* 11:6 hough their *h.* burn *c.*
9 Josh. burnt their *c.* with fire
2 *Sam.* 15:1 Absal. pre. *h.* and *c.*
1 *K.* 20:1 Samaria with *c.* and *h.*
2 *K.* 6:17 mount. full of *c.* and *h.*
7:6 to hear a noise of *h.* and *c.*
10:2 with you *c.* and *horses*
*Ps.* 20:7 trust in *c.* some in *h.*
*Cant.* 1:9 comp. to *h.* in Phar. *c.*
*Is.* 66:20 bring brethren in *c.*
*Jer.* 17:25 princes in *c.* 22:4
46:9 come up, ye *h.* rage ye *c.*
50:37 on their *horses* and *c.*

*Ezek.* 26:7 Tyrus Neb. with *c.*
39:20 at table with *h.* and *c.*
*Nah.* 3:2 *h.* and jumping *c.*
*Hab.* 3:8 thy *c.* of salvation
*Rev.* 18:13 buys their *h.* and *c.*

**CHARITABLY.**

*Rom.* 14:15 now walkest not *c.*

**CHARITY.**

1 *Cor.* 8:1 but *c.* edifieth
13:1 and have not *c*, 2, 3
4 *c.* suffereth long, *c.* env. not
13 faith, hope, *c.* greatest is *c.*
14:1 follow *c.* desire spir. gifts
16:14 let all be done with *c.*
*Col.* 3:14 above all put on *c.*
1 *Thes.* 3:6 good tidings of your *c.*
2 *Thes.* 1:3 *c.* to each other
1 *Tim.* 1:5 end of command. is *c.*
2:15 if continue in faith and *c.*
4:12 example in *c.* in spirit
2 *Tim.* 2:22 follow righteous. *c.*
3:10 known my life, faith, *c.*
*Tit.* 2:2 aged men be sound in *c.*
1 *Pet.* 4:8 fervent *c. c.* cover sins
5:14 greet with a kiss of *c.*
2 *Pet.* 1:7 brotherly kindness *c.*
3 *John* 6 borne witness of thy *c.*
*Jude* 12 spots in your feasts of *c.*
*Rev.* 2:19 I know thy works, *c.*

**CHARMED.**

*Jer.* 8:17 wh. will not be *c.*

**CHARMER, S.**

*Deut.* 18:11 not be found a *c.*
*Ps.* 58:5 not hearken to *c.*

CHARRAN. *Acts* 7:2, 4

**CHASE.**

*Lev.* 26:8 shall *c.* a hundred, 36.
*Deut.* 32:30 *c.* 1,000, *Jos.* 23:10
*Ps.* 35:5 angel of L. *c.* them

**CHASED, ETH, ING.**

*Deut.* 1:44 Amorites *c.* you
*Jud.* 9:40 Abimelech *c.* him
*Neh.* 13:28 I *c.* him from me
*Job* 18:18 be *c.* out of the world
20:8 be *c.* as a vision of night
*Prov.* 19:26 *c.* away his mother
*Is.* 13:14 shall be as the *c.* roe
17:13 they shall be *c.* as chaff
*Lam.* 3:52 *c.* me sore like a bird

**CHASTE.**

2 *Cor.* 11:2 pres. you as *c.* virgin
*Tit.* 2:5 young women be *c.*
1 *Pet.* 3:2 your *c.* conversation

**CHASTEN.**

2 *Sam.* 7:14 *c.* with rod of men
*Ps.* 6:1 *c.* me in hot displ. 38:1
*Prov.* 19:18 *c.* son while hope
*Dan.* 10:12 *c.* thyself before God
*Rev.* 3:19 I rebuke and *c.*

**CHASTENED.**

*Deut.* 21:18 they have *c.* him
*Job* 33:19 is *c.* also with pain
*Ps.* 69:10 *c.* my soul
73:14 and *c.* every morning
118:18 Lord hath *c.* me sore
1 *Cor.* 11:32 *c.* that we be not
2 *Cor.* 6:9 as *c.* and not killed
*Heb.* 12:10 for a few days *c.* us

**CHASTENEST, ETH, ING.**

*Deut.* 8:5 *c.* his son, so L. *c.* thee
*Job* 5:17 *c.* of Almighty, *Prov.* 3:11; *Heb.* 12:5.
*Ps.* 94:12 bless. is whom thou *c.*
*Prov.* 13:24 lov. him, *c.* betimes
*Is.* 26:16 *c.* was on them
*Heb.* 12:6 whom Lord loveth he *c.*
*Heb.* 12:7 if ye end. *c.* what son
11 no *c.* seemeth to be joyous

**CHASTISE, ED, ETH.**

*Lev.* 26:28 I will *c.* seven times
*Deut.* 22:18 elders shall *c.* him
1 *K.* 12:11 I will *c.* you with scorpions, 14; 2 *Chr.* 10:11, 14
*Ps.* 94:10 he that *c.* heathen
*Jer.* 31:18 *c.* me, and I was *c.*
*Hos.* 7:12 I will *c.* them as cong.
10:10 I should *c.* them
*Luke* 23:16 *c.* him and release, 22

**CHASTISEMENT.**

*Deut.* 11:2 have not seen the *c.*
*Job* 34:31 I have borne *c.*
*Is.* 53:5 *c.* of our peace
*Jer.* 30:14 with *c.* of a cruel one
*Heb.* 12:8 with, *c.* then bastards

**CHATTER.**

*Is.* 38:14 so did I *c.*

CHEBAR. *Ezek.* 1:1, 3; 3:15, 23; 10:15, 20

**CHECK.**

*Job* 20:3 heard *c.* of my reproach

**CHECKER-WORK.**

1 *K.* 7:17 Hir. made nets of *c.*

CHEDORLAOMER. *Gen.* 14:4

**CHEEK.**

1 *K.* 22:24 Zed. smote Mic. on *c.*
*Job* 16:10 smitten me on the *c.*
*Lam.* 3:30 *c.* to him that smiteth
*Mic.* 5:1 smite the judge on the *c.*
*Mat.* 5:39 right *c.* turn other
*Luke* 6:29 to him smiteth one *c.*

**CHEEKBONE.**

*Ps.* 3:7 smitten enemies on *c.*

**CHEEKS.**

*Cant.* 1:10 thy *c.* comely
5:13 his *c.* are as a bed of spices
*Is.* 50:6 my *c.* to them
*Lam.* 1:2 her tears are on her *c.*

**CHEEKTEETH.**

*Joel* 1:6 he hath *c.* of a great lion

**CHEER.**

*Deut.* 24:5 shall *c.* up his wife
*Ec.* 11:9 thy heart *c.* thee

**Good CHEER.**

*Mat.* 9:2 son, be of *g. c.*
14:27 be of *g. c. Mark* 6:50
*John* 16:33 be of *g. c.* I have
*Acts* 23:11 be of *good c.* Paul
27:22 to be of *good c.* 25, 36

**CHEERETH.**

*Jud.* 9:13 which *c.* God and man

**CHEERFUL.**

*Prov.* 15:13 a *c.* countenance
*Zec.* 8:19 be to Judah *c.* feasts
9:17 corn make young men *c.*
2 *Cor.* 9:7 God loveth a *c.* giver

**CHEERFULLY.**

*Acts* 24:10 *c.* answer for myself

**CHEERFULNESS.**

*Rom.* 12:8 showeth mercy with *c.*

**CHEESE, S.**

1 *Sam.* 17:18 carry ten *c.* to capt.
2 *Sam.* 17:29 *c.* of kine for David
*Job* 10:10 curdled me like *c.*

CHEMARIM. *Zep.* 1:4

**CHEMOSH.**

*Num.* 21:29 O people of C.
*Jud.* 11:24 what C. giveth?
1 *K.* 11:7, 33; *Jer.* 48:7, 13, 46

CHENAANAH. 1 *K.* 22:24; 2 *Chr.* 18:23.

**CHENANIAH.**

1 *Chr.* 15:22 C. chief of Lev. 27

CHERETHIM. *Ezek.* 25:16

**CHERETHITES.**

1 *Sam.* 30:14 invasion on the C.
2 *Sam.* 8:18 the C. 20:23; 1 *Chr.* 18:17.
*Zep.* 2:5 woe unto nation of C.

**CHERISH, ED, ETH.**

1 *K.* 1:2 let her *c.* him, and lie
4 damsel *c.* the king
*Eph.* 5:29 *c.* flesh, as L. church
1 *Thes.* 2:7 as a nurse *c.* children

CHERITH. 1 *K.* 17:3.

**CHERUB.**

*Ex.* 25:19 *c.* on one end *c.* 37:8
2 *Sam.* 22:11 on a *c. Ps.* 18:10
1 *K.* 6:25 other *c.* was ten cubits
*Ezek.* 9:3 gone up from *c.* 10:4
10:14 first face was face of a *c.*
28:16 destroy thee, O covering *c.*
41:18 every *c.* had two faces

**CHERUBIM.**

*Gen.* 3:24 placed at the east *c.*
*Ex.* 37:7 made two *c.* of gold
1 *K.* 6:25 both the *c.* of one meas.
8:7 *c.* covered ark, 2 *Chr.* 5:8; *Heb.* 9:5
2 *Chr.* 3:10 most holy house two *c.*
*Ezek.* 10:16 *c.* went wheels went
19 the *c.* lifted wings, 11:22

**Between the CHERUBIM.**

*Ex.* 25:22 from *b.* two *c.*
*Num.* 7:89 *betw. the* two *c.*
1 *Sam.* 4:4 wh. dw. *bet. c.* 2 *Sam.* 6:2; 2 *K.* 19:15; *Is.* 37:16
*Ps.* 80:1 dwellest *bet. c.* shine
99:1 he sitteth *bet. t. c.*
*Ezek.* 10:2 fire from *bet. t. c.* 6
7 hand from *betw. the c.*

CHESED. *Gen.* 22:22

**CHESNUT-TREE, S.**

*Gen.* 30:37 Jac. took rods of *c.-t.*
*Ezek.* 31:8 *c.-t.* not like his bran.

**CHEST, S.**

2 *K.* 12:9 a *c.* and bored a hole
2 *Chr.* 24:8 at king's com. made *c.*
*Ezek.* 27:24 thy merchants in *c.*

**CHEW, ED, ETH.**

*Lev.* 11:4 *c.* the cud, *Deut.* 14:7
7 *c.* not the cud, *Deut.* 14:8
*Num.* 11:33 ere flesh *c.* wrath

**CHICKENS.**

*Mat.* 23:37 hen gathereth her *c.*

**CHIDE.**

*Ex.* 17:2 people did *c.* why *c.*
*Jud.* 8:1 Eph. did *c.* with Gid.
*Ps.* 103:9 he will not always *c.*

**CHIDING.**

*Ex.* 17:7 Meribah, because of *c.*

**CHIEF.**

*Gen.* 40:21 restored the *c.* butler
22 but he hanged the *c.* baker
*Num.* 3:32 Eleazar *c.* over the *c.*
2 *Sam.* 23:18 Abishai was *c.*
1 *Chr.* 5:2 of Judah came *c.* ruler
11:6 smit. Jebusites be *c.* Joab
18:17 the sons of David were *c.*
26:10 though not first-born *c.*
*Ezr.* 9:2 rulers *c.* in this trespass
*Job* 12:24 taketh away heart of *c.*
29:25 chose out their way, sat *c.*
40:19 behemoth is *c.* of ways
*Ps.* 78:51 *c.* of strength, 105:36
137:8 Jerusalem above my *c.* joy
*Prov.* 1:21 crieth in *c.* places
16:28 whisperer sep. *c.* friends
*Is.* 14:9 hell stirreth up *c.* ones
*Jer.* 13:21 taught them as *c.* over
31:7 shout among *c.* of nations
*Lam.* 1:5 her adversaries are *c.*
*Dan.* 11:41 *c.* of children of Am.
*Amos* 6:1 *c.* of the nations
*Mat.* 20:27 whosoever will be *c.*
23:6 love *c.* seats, *Mark* 12:39
*Mark* 6:21 supper to his *c.* estates
*Lu.* 11:15 cast. out devils thro' *c.*
14:1 house of one of *c.* Pharisees
7 they chose *c.* rooms, 20:46
22:26 he *c.* as he that serveth
*John* 12:42 *c.* rulers many believ.
*Acts* 14:12 he was the *c.* speaker
17:4 of *c.* women not a few
*Eph.* 2:20 *c.* corner-st. 1 *Pet.* 2:6

1 *Tim.* 1:15 of whom I am *c.*
1 *Pet.* 5:4 *c.* Sheph. shall appear

**CHIEF captain.**

2 *Sam.* 5:8 he shall be *c.* and *cap.*
*Acts* 21:31 came to *c. captain*
32 saw *c. captain* they left
23:17 bring young man to *c. c.*
24:7 *c. captain* L. came upon us
22 *c. c.* shall come, I will know

**CHIEF captains.**

2 *Sam.* 23:8 sat *c.* among the *c.*
2 *Chr.* 8:9 Is. *c.* of Solomon's *cap.*
*Acts* 25:23 Ag. entered with *c. c.*
*Rev.* 6:15 *c. c.* hid themselves

**CHIEF fathers.**

*Num.* 31:26 *c. f.* of the congreg.
1 *Chr.* 9:34 *c. fathers* of Levites
24:31 *c. fathers* of priests
26:32 2,700 *c. f.* D. made rulers
2 *Chr.* 26:12 number of *c. fathers*
*Ezr.* 1:5 rose up *c. fath.* of Jud.
*Neh.* 7:70 *c.* of *f.* gave to work, 71

**CHIEF house.**

*Jos.* 22:14 *c. h.* a prince was sent

**CHIEF man, *or* men.**

*Lev.* 21:4 not defile hims. a *c. m.*
1 *Chr.* 7:3 sons of Uzzi *c. men.*
24:4 more *c. men* of Eleazar
*Ezr.* 7:28 I gath. *c. m.* to go up
*Is.* 41:9 I called thee from *c. m.*
*Acts* 13:50 Jews stirred up *c. m.*
15:22 Judas and Silas *c. men*
*Acts* 28:7 poss. of *c. man* of isl.

**CHIEF priest.**

2 *K.* 25:18 took Ser. the *c. priest*
1 *Chr.* 27:5 Benaiah a *c. priest*
29:22 anointed Z. to be. *c. priest*
2 *Chr.* 19:11 Amariah *c. priest*
26:20 Azariah *c. p.* looked on

**CHIEF priests.**

*Ezr.* 10:5 *c. p.* and all Israel
*Mat.* 16:21 suffer of the *c. priests*
26:47 multitude from *c. priests*
27:12 accu. of *c. p. Mark* 15:3
41 *c. p.* mocking, *Mark* 15:31
*Mark* 14:1 *c. p.* sought. 55; *Mat.* 26:59; *Luke* 9:22; 22:2.
*Luke* 23:23 voices of *c. p.* prev.
*John* 7:32 *c. p.* sent officers, 18:3
*Acts* 9:14 auth. from *c. p.* 26:10
22:30 commanded *c. p.* to appear

**CHIEF prince, *or* princes.**

1 *Chr.* 7:40 children of A. *c.* of *p.*
*Ezek.* 38:2 Gog *c. prince*, 3; 39:1
*Dan.* 10:13 Michael one of *c. p.*

**CHIEF singer, *or* singers.**

*Neh.* 12:46 in days of D. *c.* of *s.*
*Hab.* 3:19 to *c. singer* on instru.

**CHIEFEST.**

1 *Sam.* 2:29 yoursel. fat with *c.*
9:22 Sam. made sit in *c.* place
2 *Chr.* 32:33 in *c.* of sepulchres
*Cant.* 5:10 the *c.* among 10,000
*Mark* 10:44 *c.* shall be servant
2 *Cor.* 11:5 *c.* apostles, 12:11

**CHIEFLY.**

*Rom.* 3:2 *c.* because to them
*Phil.* 4:22 *c.* they of Cesar's h.
2 *Pet.* 2:10 *c.* them walk after fl.

**CHILD.**

*Gen.* 21:16 not see death of *c.*
37:30 *c.* is not, and I whither
42:22 do not sin against the *c.*
*Ex.* 2:8 maid called *c.* mother
22:22 not afflict any fatherless *c.*
*Jud.* 11:34 his daughter, only *c.*
13:8 teach us what we do to *c.*
1 *Sam.* 1:25 brought the *c.* to Eli
3:8 Eli perc. L. had called *c.*
2 *Sam.* 12:14 the *c.* born shall die
15 L. stru. *c.* Uriah's wife bare
16 David besought God for *c.*
1 *K.* 3:25 divide living *c.* in two
14:3 what shall become of *c.*
17:22 soul of the *c.* came
2 *K.* 4:31 told *c.* is not awaked
35 *c.* sneezed, *c.* opened eyes
*Prov.* 23:13 correction from *c.*
*Ec.* 4:8 hath neither *c.* nor bro.
15 second *c.* that shall stand
*Is.* 3:5 *c.* shall behave proudly
7:16 before *c.* know to refuse
8:4 before *c.* know to cry
11:8 *c.* put hand on cockatrice
65:20 *c.* shall die 100 years old
*Jer.* 4:31 bring. forth her first *c.*
31:20 Eph. is he a pleasant *c.?*
44:7 cut off man, woman, and *c.*
*Mat.* 10:21 deliver *c.* to death
17:18 *c.* was cured from that h.
23:15 more the *c.* of hell
*Luke* 1:59 came to circumcise *c.*
1:66 what manner of *c.*
76 *c.* called prophet of Highest
80 *c.* grew, waxed strong, 2:40
2:27 parents brought in *c.* Jesus
9:38 look on my son, only *c.*
*John* 4:49 come down ere *c.* die
16:21 as soon as delivered of *c.*
*Acts* 4:27 against thy holy *c.* J.
30 done by name of thy *c.* J.
13:10 Saul said, Thou *c.* of devil
*Rev.* 12:4 to devour her *c.* as soon
5 her *c.* was caught up to God

**A CHILD.**

*Gen.* 18:13 bear *a c.* who am old?
44:20 and *a c.* of his own age
*Ex.* 2:2 *a* goodly *c. Heb.* 11:23
1 *Sam.* 2:18 *c.* girded with linen
1 *K.* 13:2 *a c.* born to house of D
*Job* 33:25 flesh fresher than *a c.*
*Ps.* 131:2 as *a c.* as *a* weaned *c.*
*Prov.* 20:11 *a c.* is known
22:6 train up *a. c.* in way he
15 foolish. is in heart of *a c.*
29:15 *a c.* left to himself
21 bringing up serv. from *a c.*
*Ec.* 4:13 better is *a* wise *c.* than
10:16 when thy king is *a c.*
*Is.* 9:6 for unto us *a c.* is born
10:19 *a c.* may write
*Jer.* 1:6 for I am *a c.* 7
20:15 *a* man *c.* is born to thee
*Hos.* 11:1 Is. *a c.* I loved him
*Mark* 9:21 he said of *a c.*
36 took *a c.* set it, *Luke* 9:47
1 *Cor.* 13:11 *a c.* I spake as *a. c.*
*Gal.* 4:1 as long as he is *a c.*
2 *Tim.* 3:15 from *a c.* known sc.
*Heb.* 11:11 S. deliv. of *a c.* past a.
*Rev.* 12:5 *a* man *c.* to rule nations

**Little CHILD.**

1 *K.* 3:7 I am but a *l. c.*
11:17 H. fled being yet a *little c.*
2 *K.* 5:14 the flesh of a *little c.*
*Is.* 11:6 *a little c.* shall lead them
*Mat.* 18:2 J. called a *little c.* to him
5 receive one such *l. c.* in my
*Mark* 10:15 whoso not rec. kingdom of G. as *lit. c. Luke* 18:17

**No CHILD.**

*Gen.* 11:30 Sarai had *no c.*
*Lev.* 22:13 priest's dau. have *n. c.*
*Deut.* 25:5 brother die, have *n. c.*
2 *Sam* 6:23 Michal had *no c.*
2 *K.* 4:14 verily she hath *no c.*
*Luke* 1:7 they had *no. c.* bec. E.
*Acts* 7:5 when he had *no c.*

**Sucking CHILD.**

*Num.* 11:12 beareth *sucking c.*
*Is.* 11:8 *suck. c.* play on hole
49:15 woman forget *suck. c.*
*Lam.* 4:4 tongue of *suck. c.*

**This CHILD.**

*Luke* 2:17 told concerning *this c.*
34 *t. c.* is set for fall and rising
9:48 receive *t. c.* in my name

**With CHILD.**

*Gen.* 16:11 Hagar thou art *w. c.*
19:36 daughters of Lot *with c.*
38:24 T. thy daughter is *w. c.*
25 whose these are, am I *w. c.*
*Ex.* 21:22 hurt a woman *w. c.*
1 *Sam.* 4:19 Phin. wife was *w. c.*
2 *Sam.* 11:5 B. said, I am *w. c.*
2 *K.* 8:12 wilt rip up their woman *with c.* 15:16
*Ec.* 11:5 in womb of her *w. c.*
*Is.* 26:17 *with c.* that draweth
18 we have been *with c.*
54:1 that didst not trav. *with c.*
*Jer.* 30:6 whe. a man trav. *w. c.*
31:8 the woman *with c.*
*Hos.* 13:16 *with c.* shall be rip.
*Amos* 1:13 rip. up woman, *w. c.*
*Mat.* 1:18 *with c.* of the H. Ghost
23 a virgin shall be *with c.*
24:19 woe to them that are *w. c.* *Mark* 13:17; *Luke* 21:23
*Luke* 2:5 Mary, great *with c.*
1 *Thes.* 5:3 travail on wom. *w. c.*
*Rev.* 12:2 and she being *with c.*

**Young CHILD.**

1 *Sam.* 1:24 the *c.* was *young*
*Mat.* 2:8 search dilig. for *y. c.*
13 take *young c.* and his moth.

**CHILD-BEARING.**

1 *Tim.* 2:15 shall be saved in *c.-b.*

**CHILDHOOD.**

1 *Sam.* 12:2 before you from *c.*
*Ec.* 11:10 *c.* and youth are vanity

**CHILDISH.**

1 *Cor.* 13:11 I put away *c.* things

**CHILDLESS.**

*Gen.* 15:2 seeing I go *c.*
*Lev.* 20:20 they shall die *c.*
1 *Sam.* 15:33 as thy sword made women *c.* so thy mother be *c.*
*Jer.* 22:30 write ye this man *c.*
*Luke* 20:30 sec. took her, died *c.*

**CHILDREN.**

*Gen.* 3:16 in sorrow bring forth *c.*
16:2 I may obtain *c.* by her
25:22 the *c.* struggled within her
30:1 give me *c.* or I die
33:5 *c.* God hath given
49:8 thy father's *c.* shall bow
*Ex.* 20:5 iniq. of fath. on *c.* 34:7; *Num.* 14:18; *Deut.* 5:9
21:4 *c.* shall be her masters
*Num.* 13:28 saw *c.* of Anak there
26:11 *c.* of Korah died not
*Deut.* 9:2 before *c.* of Anak?
13:13 *c.* of Belial are gone out
14:1 ye are the *c.* of the Lord
23:8 *c.* begotten of them
24:16 fath. not put to death for *c.* nor *c.* for fath. 2 *Chr.* 25:4
32:20 *c.* in whom there is no f.
33:24 Asher be blessed with *c.*
*Jud.* 8:18 resembled *c.* of king
20:13 deliver us the *c.* of Belial
1 *Sam.* 2:5 she that hath many *c.* is waxed feeble
2 *Sam.* 7:10 *c.* of wickedness affl. any more, 1 *Chr.* 17:9
1 *K.* 21:13 came in two *c.* of Bel.
2 *K.* 2:24 she-bears tare 42 *c.*
10:13 *c.* of king *c.* of queen
14:6 *c.* of murderers, 2 *Chr.* 25:4
17:34 as Lord com. *c.* of Jacob
19:3 *c.* are come to b. *Is.* 37:3
1 *Chr.* 2:30 Seled died without *c.*
32 and Jether died without *c.*
4:27 Shimei's bre. not many *c.*
16:13 ye *c.* of Jacob, *Ps.* 105:6
2 *Chr.* 13:7 to Jeroboam *c.* of B.
25:7 L. is not with all *c.* of E.
*Ezra* 10:44 by whom had *c.*
*Neh.* 9:23 *c.* multipliedst as stars
*Job* 19:17 I entreated for *c.* sake
30:8 *c.* of fools, yea *c.* of base

41:34 king over all c. of pride
Ps. 17:14 they are full of c.
34:11 come ye c. hearken to me
69:8 an alien to my mother's c.
72:4 he shall save c. of needy
78:6 c. wh. sh. be born might
82:6 all of you c. of Most High
83:8 holpen c. of Lot, Selah
102:28 c. of thy serv. continue
113:9 barren to be mother of c.
127:3 c. are a heritage of Lord
4 as arrows in hand, so are c.
137:7 remember, c. of Edom
148:12 old men and c. praise L.
149:2 let c. of Zion be joyful
Prov. 4:1 hear, ye c. the instruction, 5:7; 7:24; 8:32
17:6 glory of c. are their fathers
31:28 her c. call her blessed
Ec. 6:3 if a man beget 100 c.
Cant. 1:6 my mother's c. angry
Is. 1:2 brought up c. they reb.
4 c. that are corrupters
2:6 in the c. of strangers
3:4 give c. to be their princes
12 c. are their oppressors
8:18 c. Lord hath giv. Heb. 2:13
13:18 eyes shall not spare c.
21:17 mighty of c. of K. dimin.
23:4 nor bring forth c.
30:1 woe to rebellious c.
9 lying c. c. will not hear law
38:19 father to c. make known
47:8 neither know loss of c.
9 loss of c. widowhood
49:20 c. shalt have, shall say
54:1 are c. of desolate than c. of married wife, Gal. 4:27
57:4 are ye not c. of transg.
5 slaying the c. in the valleys
63:8 c. that will not lie
66:8 Zion brought forth c.
Jer. 3:14 O backsliding c. 22
19 how put thee among the c.
4:22 my people are sottish c.
6:11 pour it out on c. abroad
7:18 c. gather wood, fathers
9:21 death entered to cut off c.
15:7 I will bereave them of c.
31:15 R. weep. for c. Mat. 2:18
Lam. 2:20 shall the women eat c.
5:13 c. fell under the wood
Ezek. 2:4 are imprudent c.
20:21 the c. rebelled against me
33:30 c. talking against thee
47:22 to strangers that beget c.
Dan. 1:4 c. in whom no blemish
17 four c. God gave knowledge
12:1 Michael shall stand for c.
Hos. 1:2 take c. of whoredoms
2:4 not have mercy on her c.
11:10 c. shall tremble
13:13 breaking forth of c.
Joel 2:16 gather c. and those
23 be glad, then, ye c. of Zion
Amos 9:7 c. of the Ethiopians?
Mic. 1:16 poll thee for delicate c.
Zep. 1:8 I will punish king's c.
Mal. 4:6 heart of fathers to c. of c. to fathers, Luke 1:17
Mat. 2:16 Herod slew all the c.
3:9 to raise up c. Luke 3:8
5:45 be the c. of your Father
8:12 but the c. shall be cast out
9:15 c. of bridechamber mourn, Mark 2:19; Luke 5:34
10:21 c. ag. parents, Mark 13:12
11:19 justi. of her c. Luke 7:35
13:38 good seed are c. of kingd.
15:26 c. bread, Mark 7:27
17:26 then are the c. free
19:29 forsaken c. Mark 10:29
20:20 mother of Zebedee's c.
21:15 saw c. crying in temple
Mark 7:27 let the c. first be filled
28 dogs eat of the c. crumbs
9:37 receive one of such c. 41
Luke 6:35 shall be c. of Highest
16:8 c. of this world are wiser
20:29 the first died without c.
34 the c. of this world marry
John 8:39 were Abraham's c.
Acts 3:25 ye are c. of prophets
Rom. 8:17 if c. then heirs, heirs
9:7 seed of Abra. are they all c.
11 the c. being not yet born
1 Cor. 14:20 not c. in understand.
2 Cor. 12:14 c. not lay up
Gal. 3:7 of faith, are c. of Abra.
4:3 when c. were in bondage
25 Jeru. in bondage with her c.
31 we are not c. of bondwoman
Eph. 1:5 to the adoption of c.
2:2 in c. of disobedience
3 were by nature c. of wrath
4:14 we be no more c. tossed
5:1 followers of God as dear c.
6 wrath on c. of dis. Col. 3:6
6:1 c. obey your par. Col. 3:20
1 Tim. 5:4 if any widow have c.
10 if she brought up c.
Heb. 2:14 as c. are partakers
12:5 speaketh to you as c.
1 Pet. 1:14 as obedient c.
2 Pet. 2:14 cursed c.
2 John 1 to elect lady and her c.
13 c. of elect sister greet thee
Rev. 2:23 I will kill her c.

See AMMON, CAPTIVITY.

**CHILDREN of Benjamin.**

Jud. 20:13 c. of B. would not
2 Sam. 2:25 c. of B. gathered
1 Chr. 12:16 c. of B. to hold to D.
Jer. 6:1 O ye c. of B. gather

**Children's CHILDREN.**

Gen. 45:10 thou and thy c. c.
Ex. 34:7 iniq. of fathers on c. c.
Deut. 4:25 beget c. and c. c.
2 K. 17:41 served images child. c.
Ps. 103:17 righteousness to c. c.
128:6 shalt see thy c. c.
Prov. 13:22 inherit. to his c. c.
17:6 child. c. crown of old men
Jer. 2:9 with your c. c. will I pl.
Ezek. 37:25 and c. c. for ever

**Fatherless CHILDREN.**

Ps. 109:12 to favor his f. c.
Jer. 49:11 leave thy f. c.

**CHILDREN of God.**

Mat. 5:9 peacemakers c. of God
Luke 20:36 c. of God being c.
John 11:52 in one the c. of God
Rom. 8:16 we are the c. of God.
21 glor. liberty of the c. of G.
9:8 c. of the flesh, not c. of G.
26 called c. of the living God
Gal. 3:26 c. of God by faith in C.
John 3:10 c. G. manifest, c. of d.
5:2 know we love c. of God

**His CHILDREN.**

Gen. 18:19 Abra. will com. h. c.
Deut. 17:20 pro. days and his c.
32:5 is not spot of his c.
33:9 nor knew his own c.
2 Sam. 12:3 ewe-l. grew with h. c.
2 K. 8:19 give a light, and to h. c.
2 Chr. 28:3 burnt h. c. after h.
33:6 his c. to pass through fire
Job 5:4 his c. are far from safety
17:5 eyes of his c. shall fail
20:10 h. c. shall seek to please
21:19 iniquity for his c.
27:14 if his c. be multiplied
Ps. 89:30 if his c. forsake
103:13 as a father pitieth his c.
109:9 let his c. be fatherless
10 let his c. be vagabonds
Prov. 14:26 his c. shall have ref.
20:7 his c. are blessed after him
Is. 14:21 slaughter for his c.
29:23 seeth his c. in midst
Hos. 9:13 shall bring forth his c.
John 4:12 his c. drank thereof
1 Thes. 2:11 ch. you as fath. h. c.
1 Tim. 3:4 his c. in subjection

**CHILDREN of Israel.**

Ex. 1:7 c. of I. were fruitful
12 grieved bec. of the c. of I.
2:25 God looked on c. of Israel
4:31 heard L. had visited c. of I.
6:13 c. of I. o. of Eg. 26, 27; 12:51
29:43 I will meet with c. of I.
Lev. 25:55 c. of I. are servants
Num. 14:10 gl. of L. ap. bef. c. I.
Jos. 7:12 c. I. not stand bef. ene.
2 Sam. 21:2 Gib. not of c. of I.
2 K. 17:24 instead of the c. of I.
Ps. 103:7 his acts to the c. of I.
148:14 c. of I. a people near
Is. 27:12 gath. one by one, c. I.
Ezek. 44:15 c. I. w. astray, 48:11
Amos 2:11 thus, O c. of I.?
4:5 liketh you, O ye c. of I.
Luke 1:16 c. of Is. shall turn
Acts 7:23 visit breth. the c. of I.
37 Moses which said to c. of I.
9:15 bear my name bef. c. of I.
10:36 word of G. sent to c. I.
Rom. 9:27 c. of I. be as the sand
Heb. 11:22 mention of d. of c. I.
Rev. 7:4 sealed 144,000 of c. of I.
21:12 twelve tribes of c. of I.

**CHILDREN of Judah.**

Num. 1:26 c. of J. by their gen.
Jos. 14:6 c. of J. came to Joshua
2 Sam. 1:18 teach c. of J.
2 Chr. 13:18 c. of J. prevailed
28:10 keep under the c. of Jud.
Jer. 50:4 they and c. of Judah
33 Is. and c. of J. were oppres.
Joel 3:19 for violence ag. c. of J.

**CHILDREN of light.**

Luke 16:8 wiser than c. of light
John 12:36 ye may be the c. of l.
Eph. 5:8 walk as c. of light
1 Thes. 5:5 ye are all the c. of l.

**Little CHILDREN.**

Num. 16:27 l. c. stood in the door
2 K. 2:23 came l. c. and mocked
Est. 3:13 to destroy l. c.
Ezek. 9:6 slay maids, little c.
Mat. 18:3 except bec. as little c.
19:13 brought to him little c.
14 suffer l. c. to come unto me, Mark 10:14; Luke 18:16
John 13:33 l. c. yet a little while
Gal. 4:19 l. c. of whom I travail
1 John 2:1 my little c. 12, 13
4:4 ye are of God little c.
5:21 little c. keep from idols

**CHILDREN of men.**

1 Sam. 26:19 if c. m. cursed be
2 Sam. 7:14 the stripes of c. m.
1 K. 8:39 knowest hearts of c. of men, 2 Chr. 6:30
Ps. 11:4 his eyelids try c. of men
12:1 faith. fail from among c. m.
14:2 heaven upon c. m. 53:2
36:7 c. m. put trust under sha.
45:2 fairer than the c. of men
90:3 return ye c. of men
107:8 works to c. m. 15, 21, 31
115:16 given to c. of men
Prov. 15:11 hearts of c. of men
Lam. 3:33 doth not grieve c. m.
Dan. 2:38 wherever the c. of m.

**Men-CHILDREN.**

Ex. 1:17 midw. saved men-c. 18
34:23 men-c. shall app. bef. L.

**Men, Women, and CHILDREN.**

Deut. 3:6 in B. we dest. m. w. c.
31:12 gather m. w. and c.
Ezra 10:1 great cong. of m. w. c.
Jer. 40:7 to Gedaliah m. w. c.
Mat. 14:21 eaten, were 5,000 m. beside women and c. 15:38

**My CHILDREN.**
Gen. 30:26 give me my c.
31:43 these c. are my c. and
42:36 me ye have ber. of my c.
43:14 if bereaved of my c. I am
Ex. 21:5 I love my master my c.
1 K. 20:7 he sent to me for my c.
Job 29:5 my c. were about me
Is. 49:21 I have lost my c.
Jer. 10:20 my c. gone forth of me
Lam. 1:16 my c. are desolate
Ezek. 16:21 thou hast slain my c.?
Luke 11:7 my c. are with me
2 Cor. 6:13 speak as to my c.
3 John 4 that my c. walk in truth

**No CHILDREN.**
Gen. 16:1 Sarai bare him no c.
30:1 Rachel saw she bare no c.
1 Sam. 1:2 but Hannah had no c.
Mat. 22:24 having no c. Mark 12:19; Luke 20:31 seven left

**Our CHILDREN.**
Gen. 31:16 riches ours and our c.
Num. 14:3 that our c. be a prey
Deut. 29:29 bel. to us and our c.
Jos. 22:24 c. might sp. to our c.
22:25 your c. make o. c. cease
Neh. 5:5 our c. as their children
Mat. 27:25 his blood be on our c.

**CHILDREN of promise.**
Rom. 9:8 c. prom. counted
Gal. 4:28 as Isaac, are c. of prom.

**Strange CHILDREN.**
Ps. 144:7 rid me from str. c. 11
Hos. 5:7 have begotten strange c.

**Their CHILDREN.**
Gen. 31:43 can I do to their c.?
Deut. 4:10 may teach their c.
5:29 might be well with their c.
31:13 their c. may learn
2 K. 8:12 thou wilt dash their c.
17:31 burnt their c. to the gods
41 t. c. served images
2 Chr. 20:13 before L. with th. c.
25:4 he slew not their c.
Neh. 9:23 their c. multi. as stars
13:24 their c. spake
Job 21:11 their c. dance
24:5 yieldeth food for their c.
Ps. 78:4 not hide them from t. c.
6 and declare them to their c.
90:16 let thy glory appear to t. c.
132:12 t. c. sh. sit on thy throne
Is. 13:16 t. c. be dashed to pieces
Jer. 17:2 t. c. remember altars
18:21 deliver their c. to famine
30:20 t. c. shall be as aforetime
32:18 into bosom of their c.
39 good of them and their c.
47:3 not look back to their c.
Lam. 4:10 have sodden their c.
Ezek. 20:18 I said to their c.
23:39 when had slain their c.
37:25 they and their c. sh. dwell
Hos. 9:12 t. c. yet I will bereave
Joel 1:3 your c. tell t. c. and t. c.
Mic. 2:9 from their c. taken
Zec. 10:7 t. c. shall see it
9 live with their c. and turn
Acts 13:33 same to us their c.
1 Tim. 3:12 ruling their c. well
Tit. 2:4 women to love their c.

**Thy CHILDREN.**
Deut. 4:40 w. with thy c. 12:25, 28
6:7 shalt teach them to thy c.
30:2 thou and thy c. obey with
Jos. 14:9 be thine and thy c.
1 Sam. 16:11 are here all thy c.
1 K. 2:4 if thy c. take heed
8:25 thy c. take h. 2 Chr. 6:16
20:3 thy wives and thy c.
2 K. 10:30 thy c. of fourth gen.
2 Chr. 21:14 L. shall smite thy c.
Job 8:4 if thy c. have sinned
Ps. 45:16 inst. of fathers be thy c.
73:15 offend ag. gen. of thy c.
128:3 thy c. like olive-plants
132:12 if thy c. keep covenant
147:13 blessed thy c. within thee
Is. 49:17 thy c. shall make haste
25 and I will save thy c.
54:13 all thy c. be taught of L. and great be peace of thy c.
Jer. 5:7 thy c. have forsaken me
31:17 that thy c. come again
38:23 bring out thy c. to Chald.
Ezek. 16:36 by the blood of thy c.
Hos. 4:6 I will also forget thy c.
Mat. 23:37 how oft. would I have gath. thy c. Luke 13:34
Luke 19:44 lay thy c. within thee
2 John 4 thy c. walking in truth

**Your CHILDREN.**
Ex. 12:26 your c. shall say
22:24 your c. shall be fatherless
Lev. 26:22 beasts rob you of y. c.
Deut. 1:39 your c. shall go in
11:2 I speak not with your c.
19 ye shall teach your c.
21 days of your c. be multiplied
32:46 com. your c. to observe
Jos. 4:22 then let your c. know
1 K. 9:6 if y. c. turn from fol. me
1 Chr. 28:8 inh. to y. c. Ezr. 9:12
2 Chr. 30:9 your c. shall find
Ps. 115:14 you and your c.
Jer. 2:30 have I smitten y. c.
Mat. 7:11 gifts to y. c. Luke 11:13
12:27 by whom do y. c. cast out
Luke 23:28 weep for y. and y. c.
Acts 2:39 is to you and y. c.
1 Cor. 7:14 were your c. unclean
Eph. 6:4 pro. not y. c. Col. 3:21

**Young CHILDREN.**
Job 19:18 young c. despised me
Lam. 4:4 y. c. ask bread
Nah. 3:10 young c. were dashed
Mark 10:13 brought y. c. to him
Acts 7:19 they cast out y. c.

CHILEAB. 2 Sam. 3:3
CHILION. Ruth 1:2, 5
CHILMAD. Ezek. 27:23

**CHIMHAM.**
2 Sam. 19:37 C. let him go, 38, 40
Jer. 41:17 habitation of C.

**CHIMNEY.**
Hos. 13:3 be as smoke out of c.

CHIOS. Acts 20:15
CHISLEU. Neh. 1:1; Zec. 7:1

**CHITTIM.**
Num. 24:24 from coasts of C.
Is. 23:1 from the land of C. 12
Jer. 2:10 pass over the isles of C.
Ezek. 27:6 ivory out of isles of C.
Dan. 11:30 ships of C. shall come

CHIUN. Amos 5:26
CHLOE. 1 Cor. 1:11

**CHODE.**
Gen. 31:36 Jacob c. with Laban
Num. 20:3 people c. with Moses

**CHOICE.**
1 Sam. 9:2 Saul a c. young man
2 Sam. 10:9 c. of Is. 1 Chr. 19:10
2 Chr. 25:5 300,000 c. men
Cant. 6:9 c. one of her that bare
Acts 15:7 God made c. among us

**CHOICEST.**
Is. 5:2 planted with the c. vine
22:7 c. valleys full of chariots

**CHOKE.**
Mat. 13:22 deceitfulness of riches c. the word, Mark 4:19

**CHOKED.**
Mat. 13:7 thorns c. Mar. 4:7; Lu. 8:7
Mark 5:13 c. in sea, Luke 8:33
Luke 8:14 and are c. with cares

**CHOLER.**
Dan. 8:7 he-goat moved with c.
11:11 k. of south moved with c.

**CHOOSE,** *as an act of God.*
Num. 16:7 man L. doth c. be holy
Deut. 7:7 did not c. you because
12:5 place Lord shall c. 11, 14, 18, 26; 14:23, 24, 25; 15:20; 16:2, 6, 7, 15, 16; 17:8, 10; 18:6; 26:2; 31:11; Jos. 9:27
17:15 king, whom Lord shall c.
1 Sam. 2:28 did I c. him of all
2 Sam. 16:18 and this people c.
21:6 hang in G. whom L. did c.
1 K. 14:21 the city the L. did c.
Neh. 9:7 God who didst c. Abram
Ps. 25:12 teach in way he shall c.
47:4 he shall c. our inheritance
Is. 14:1 Lord will yet c. Israel
49:7 Holy One of Israel shall c.
66:4 I will c. their delusions
Zec. 1:17 Lord shall c. Jer. 2:12

**CHOOSE.**
Deut. 23:16 in place he shall c.
30:19 therefore c. life that both
Jos. 24:15 c. this day whom serve
1 Sam. 17:8 c. you a man for you
2 Sam. 17:1 let me c. 12,000 men
24:12 three, c. one, 1 Chr. 21:10
Job 9:14 c. my words to reason
34:4 let us c. to us judgment
33 or whether thou c.
Prov. 1:29 did not c. fear of L.
3:31 and c. none of his ways
Is. 7:15 know to c. good, 16
56:4 eunuchs c. things
65:12 did c. wherein I del. not
Ezek. 21:19 c. a place c. it
Phil. 1:22 what I shall c. I wot n.

**CHOOSEST, ETH, ING.**
Job 7:15 my soul c. strangling
15:5 thou c. tongue of crafty
Ps. 65:4 blessed is man thou c.
Is. 40:20 c. a tree will not rot
41:24 abomination is he c. you
Heb. 11:25 c. to suffer affliction

**CHOP.**
Mic. 3:3 c. bones of my people

CHORAZIN. Mat. 11:21; Lu. 10:13

**CHOSE.**
Ex. 18:25 Moses c. able men
Deut. 4:37 he c. their seed, 10:15
Jos. 8:3 J. c. 30,000 mighty
Jud. 5:8 they c. new gods
2 Sam. 6:21 c. me before thy fath.
1 K. 8:16 I c. no city to build a house, 2 Chr. 6:5
1 Chr. 28:4 Lord c. me before all
Job 29:25 I c. out their way
Ps. 78:67 c. not tribe of Ephr.
68 but c. the tribe of Judah
70 he c. David also his servant
Is. 66:4 c. that I delighted not
Ezek. 20:5 in the day I c. Israel
Luke 6:13 he c. twelve apostles
14:7 how they c. chief rooms
Acts 6:5 c. Stephen, full of faith
13:17 G. of Israel c. our fathers
15:40 Paul c. Silas and departed

**CHOSEN.**
Num. 16:5 him c. cause to come
Jos. 24:22 have c. you the Lord
Jud. 10:14 cry to gods ye have c.
1 Sam. 8:18 king ye have c. 12:13
20:30 hast c. the son of Jesse
1 K. 3:8 hast c. a great people
8:44 city c. 48; 2 Chr. 6:34, 38
1 Chr. 16:13 children of J. c. ones
Job 36:21 c. rather than affliction
Ps. 33:12 c. for his inheritance
89:3 a covenant with my c.
19 exalted one c. out of people
105:6 ye child. of Jacob, his c.
43 forth his c. with gladness
106:5 I may see good of thy c.
23 had not Moses his c. stood

*Prov.* 16:16 underst. rather *c.*
22:1 a good name rather *c.*
*Is.* 43:20 to give drink to my *c.*
65:15 name a curse to my *c.*
66:3 have *c.* their own ways
*Jer.* 8:3 death shall be *c.* rather
49:19 who is a *c.* man, 50:44
*Mat.* 20:16 but few *c.* 22:14
*Mark* 13:20 elect whom hath *c.*
*Luke* 10:42 M. hath *c.* good part
*Acts* 1:24 whether thou hast *c.*
9:15 for he is a *c.* vessel to me
*Rom.* 16:13 Rufus *c.* in Lord
2 *Cor.* 8:19 *c.* of churches to trav.
2 *Tim.* 2:4 *c.* him to be a soldier
1 *Pet.* 2:9 ye are a *c.* generation
*Rev.* 17:14 they are called, and *c.*

**CHOSEN of God.**

*Luke* 23:35 if C. the *c. of God*
*Acts* 10:41 witnesses *c.* bef. *of G.*
1 *Pet.* 2:4 living stone *c. of God*

**God hath CHOSEN.**

*Deut.* 12:21 *G. h. c.* to put, 16:11
21:5 *G. h. c.* to minister
1 *Chr.* 29:1 Sol. whom al. *G. h. c.*
*Acts* 22:14 *G.* of fathers *h. c.*
1 *Cor.* 1:27 *G.h.c.* foolish th. *G.h.c.*
28 things despised *G. h. c.*
2 *Thes.* 2:13 *G.* from begin. *h. c.*
*Jam.* 2:5 *h.* not *G. c.* poor of w.

**I have CHOSEN.**

1 *K.* 11:13 Jer. sake which *I h. c.*
2 *K.* 21:7; 23:27; 2 *Chr.* 6:6
32 *I h. c.* out of all tribes
*Neh.* 1:9 *I h. c.* to set my name
*Ps.* 119:30 *I h. c.* way, 173
*Is.* 41:8 Jacob whom *I have c.*
9 *I have c.* and not cast away
43:10 my serv. *I h. c.* *Mat.* 12:18
44:1 Israel whom *I h. c.* 2 Jesu.
48:10 *I have c.* thee in furnace
58:5 the fast that *I have c.?* 6
*Hag.* 2:23 *I have c.* thee
*John* 13:18 whom *I have c.*
15:16 ye have not *c.* me, *I h. c.*
19 *I have c.* you out of world

**Lord hath CHOSEN.**

*Deut.* 7:6 *L.h.c.* thee a sp. peo. 14:2
18:5 *L. h. c.* him out of all
1 *Sam.* 10:24 see ye him *L. h. c.*
16:10 Samuel said, *L. h.* not *c.*
1 *Chr.* 28:4 *Lord hath c.* Judah
5 *L. h. c.* Sol. to sit on throne, 10
2 *Chr.* 29:11 *L. h. c.* you to serve
*Ps.* 105:26 A. whom he had *c.*
132:13 *L. c.* Zion: 135:4 *L. c.* J.
*Jer.* 33:24 two families *L. h. c.*
*Zec.* 3:2 *L.* that *h. c.* Jeru. reb.
*Eph.* 1:4 acc. as he *hath c.* us

**CHOSEN men.**

*Jud.* 20:16 700 *c. m.* left-handed
2 *Chr.* 13:3 Ab. with 400,000 *c. m.*
Jeroboam with 800,000 *c. m.*
*Ps.* 78:31 smote *c. m.* of Israel
*Acts* 15:22 to send *c. men,* 25

**CHRIST.**

*Mat.* 2:4 where C. sh. be born
16:16 thou art C. the Son
23:8 one is Master, even C. 16
24:5 saying I am C. *Mark* 13:6; *Luke* 21:8
26:68 prophesy to us, thou C.
*Mark* 9:41 bec. ye belong to C.
15:32 let C. descend from cross
*Luke* 2:26 before he had seen C.
4:41 devils knew he was C.
23:35 save himself, if he be C.
39 if C. save thyself and us
24:26 ought not C. to have suff.
46 it behooved C. to suffer
*John* 4:25 Mes. cometh called C.
7:27 C. cometh, 31
41 C. come out of Galilee?
42 C. cometh of seed of David
9:22 did confess he was C.
12:34 heard C. abideth for ever
*Acts* 2:30 would raise up C. to sit
36 Jesus both Lord and C.
3:18 showed C. should suffer
8:5 Philip preached C. to them
9:20 straightway preached C.
17:3 C. must needs have suff.
26:23 C. should suffer
*Rom.* 5:6 in due time C. died
8 yet sinners, C. died for us
6:4 C. was raised from dead
9 C. being raised dieth no m.
7:4 by the body of C.
8:9 have not the spirit of C.
10 if C. be in you, body is d.
11 raised up C. from dead
9:3 accursed from C.
5 of whom C. came
10:4 C. is end of law for right.
6 to bring C. down from above
7 that is, to bring C. up again
14:9 to this end C. both died
15 not him for whom C. died
18 in these things serveth C.
15:3 C. pleased not himself
7 as C. also received us
*Rom.* 15:18 wh. C. not wrought
20 not where C. was named
16:5 Epenetus first-fruits to C.
1 *Cor.* 1:23 we preach C. crucif.
24 C. the power of God, and
3:23 ye are C. and C. is God's
5:7 C. our passover sacrificed
8:11 perish, for whom C. died
9:21 under law to C. that I m.
10:4 and that Rock was C.
9 nor let us tempt C.
15:3 how C. died for our sins
12 if C. be preached
16 rise not, is not C. raised
17 if C. not raised, faith is v.
23 in his order, C. first-fruits
2 *Cor.* 3:4 thro' C. to God-ward
5:16 known C. after flesh
6:15 what concord C. with B.
11:2 as a chaste virgin to C.
*Gal.* 2:20 C. liveth in me
21 then C. is dead in vain
3:13 C. redeemed us from curse
24 schoolmaster to br. us to C.
29 if ye be C. then Abr.'s seed
4:7 heir of God through C.
19 till C. be formed in you
5:1 wherewith C. m. us free
2 if circum. C. profit nothing
4 C. is of none effect unto you
24 that are C. have crucified
*Eph.* 2:12 without C.
3:17 that C. may dwell by faith
4:15 which is the head, even C.
20 ye have not so learned C.
5:2 as C. also loved us
14 C. shall give thee light
23 as C. is head of the church
24 as church is subject to C.
25 love wives as C. loved ch.
32 concerning C. and church
6:5 singlen. of heart as to C.
*Phil.* 1:15 some preach C.
16 preach C. of contention
18 C. is preached, and I rejoice
20 C. be magnified in my body
3:8 dung that I may win C.
4:13 I can do all through C.
*Col.* 2:8 world, and not after C.
3:1 C. sitteth on right hand
4 C. who is our life shall ap.
11 but C. is all and in all
13 as C. forgave you, so do ye
24 for ye serve the Lord C.
*Heb.* 3:6 C. as a son
5:5 so C. glorified not himself
9:11 C. a high-priest of good
24 C. is not entered into holy
28 C. was once offered to bear
1 *Pet.* 2:21 C. also suffered for us
3:18 C. once suffered for sins
4:1 as C. suffered in the flesh
*Rev.* 11:15 kingdom of L. and C.
12:10 is come power of his C.

**Against CHRIST.**

*Acts* 4:26 kings gath. *a.* his C.
1 *Cor.* 8:12 brethren, ye sin *a.* C.
1 *Tim.* 5:11 wax wanton *a.* C.

**By CHRIST.**

2 *Cor.* 1:5 aboundeth *by* C.
*Gal.* 2:17 to be justified *by* C.
*Eph.* 3:21 glory in church *by* C.

**For CHRIST.**

1 *Cor.* 1:17 C. sent me not to b.
4:10 we are fools *for* C. sake
2 *Cor.* 5:20 ambassadors *for* C.
12:10 in distresses *for* C.
*Eph.* 4:32 as God *for* C. sake
*Phil.* 3:7 I counted loss *for* C.
2 *Thes.* 3:5 patient waiting *for* C.

**Jesus, *with* CHRIST.**

*Mat.* 1:16 J. called C. 27:17, 22
*John* 1:17 and truth by J. C.
17:3 may know thee, and J. C.
*Acts* 2:38 in name of J. C.
3:6 in name of J. C. rise up
20 J. C. who was preached
4:10 of J. C. doth this man
5:42 ceased not to preach J. C.
8:12 Philip preach. things concern. the name of J. C.
37 I believe J. C. is Son of God
9:34 J. C. maketh thee whole
10:36 preaching peace by J. C.
16:18 in name of J. C. come out
17:3 *Jesus* I preach to you is C.
18:5 testified that *Jesus* was C.
28 by scripture, *Jesus* was C.
19:4 should believe on C. *Jesus*
*Rom.* 1:1 serv. of J. C. *Phil.* 1:1
3 concerning his son J. C.
6 are ye the called of *Jesus* C.
8 I thank God through J. C.
2:16 secrets of men by J. C.
3:22 by faith of J. C.
24 redemption in *Jesus* C.
*Rom.* 5:15 gr. by one man J. C.
17 reign in life by one J. C.
6:3 baptized into *Jesus* C.
8:1 to them in C. *Jesus*
2 C. J. made me free
16:3 my helpers in C. *Jesus*
1 *Cor.* 1:1 J. C. 2 *Cor.* 1:1; *Eph.* 1:1
2 call on name of J. C.
4 grace given you by J. C.
30 of him are ye in C. *Jesus*
2:2 save J. C. crucified
4:15 in C. J. have I begotten
2 *Cor.* 4:6 in face of J. C.
5:18 reconciled us by J. C.
13:5 that *Jesus* C. is in you
*Gal.* 2:16 justified by faith of J. C.
3:14 blessings on G. through J. C.
28 ye are all one in C. *Jesus*
4:14 me as an angel, as C. J.
*Eph.* 2:6 heav. places in C. J.
20 J. C. chief corner-stone
*Phil.* 1:8 I in bowels of *Jesus* C.
2:5 mind in you, was in C. J.
11 J. C. is Lord to glory of G.
21 seek not th. wh. are J. C.
3:8 for excellency of C. J.
12 I am apprehended of C. J.
4:19 riches in glory by C. J.
*Col.* 2:6 rec. C. J. so walk ye
1 *Tim.* 1:15 C. J. ca. to save sin.
2:5 one mediator, the man C. J.
6:13 C. *Jesus* who witnessed
2 *Tim.* 1:9 grace given us in C. J.
13 faith and love in C. *Jesus*
*Phile.* 1 P. a priso. of J. C. 9, 23
*Heb.* 13:8 *Jesus* C. the same yes.
1 *John* 1:7 blood of *Jesus* C.
2:1 an advocate *Jesus* C.
5:6 by water and blood J. C.
20 even in *Jesus* C.

**Lord Jesus CHRIST.**

*Acts* 11:17 believed on L. J. C.
15:11 through grace of L. J. C.
16:31 believe on L. J. C.
20:21 faith toward L. J. C.
*Rom.* 5:1 p. with G. thro' L. J. C.
11 joy in God through L. J. C.
6:23 eternal life through L. J. C.
8:39 love of G. in C. J. our L
13:14 put ye on the L. J. C.
16:20 grace of L. J. C. be w. you,
24; 2 *Cor.* 13:14; *Gal.* 6:18;
2 *Thes.* 3:18; *Rev.* 22:21
1 *Cor.* 1:7 coming of our L. J. C.
8:6 one L. J. C. by whom are
15:57 victory thro' our L. J. C.
16:22 if any love not L. J. C.
2 *Cor.* 1:2 from G. and L. J. C.
*Gal.* 1:3; *Eph.* 1:2; *Col.* 1:2
8:9 ye know grace of L. J. C.
*Gal.* 6:14 in cross of L. J. C.
*Eph.* 1:3 Father of L. J. C.
17 God of L. J. C.
1 *Thes.* 1:3 hope in L. J. C.
2:19 in presence of L. J. C.
3:13 at coming of L. J. C.
5:23 pres. to coming of L. J. C.
2 *Thes.* 2:1 by coming of L. J. C.
16 our L. J. C. who hath
1 *Tim.* 5:21 I charge thee before
L. J. C. 2 *Tim.* 4:1
2 *Tim.* 4:22 L. J. C. be with thy
2 *Pet.* 1:11 kingdom of L. J. C.
3:18 in knowledge of L. J. C.

**In CHRIST.**

*Acts* 24:24 concerning faith *in* C.
*Rom.* 9:1 I say the truth *in* C.
12:5 many, are one body *in* C.
16:7 were *in* C. before me
9 Urbane our helper *in* C.
10 Apelles approved *in* C.
1 *Cor.* 3:1 as unto babes *in* C.
4:10 but ye are wise *in* C.
15:18 asleep *in* C.
19 in this life hope *in* C.
22 *in* C. all be made alive
2 *Cor.* 1:21 establish us *in* C.
2:14 to triumph *in* C.
17 in sight of God speak *in* C.
3:14 veil is done away *in* C.
5:17 *in* C. he is a new creature
19 *in* C. reconciling the world
20 *in* C. stead, be reconciled
12:2 a man *in* C. 14 years
19 we speak before God *in* C.
*Gal.* 1:22 to churches of J. *in* C.
3:17 confirmed of God *in* C.
27 as many as baptized *in* C.
*Eph.* 1:3 spiritual bless. *in* C.
10 in one all things *in* C.
12 who first trusted *in* C.
20 *in* C. when he raised
3:6 his promise *in* C.
*Phil.* 1:13 my bonds *in* C.
2:1 if any consolation *in* C.
*Col.* 2:5 your faith *in* C.
1 *Thes.* 4:16 dead *in* C. rise first
1 *Tim.* 2:7 I speak the truth *in* C.
1 *Pet.* 3:16 good conversation *in* C.

**Is CHRIST.**

*Mat.* 24:23 h. *is* C. *Mark* 13:21
*Mark* 12:35 C. *is* son. *Luke* 20:41
*Luke* 2:11 a Saviour, wh. *is* C.
23:2 saying, that he *is* C.
*John* 7:41 said this *is* the C.
*Acts* 9:22 Saul proving this *is* C.
17:3 Jesus I preach to you *is* C.
*Rom.* 8:34 it *is* C. that died
1 *Cor.* 1:13 *is* C. divided?
7:22 being free *is* C. servant
11:3 head of every man *is* C.
12:12 are one body, so *is* C.
15:13 if dead rise not, *is* C. 16
20 now *is* C. risen from dead
2 *Cor.* 10:7 if any trust he *is* C.
*Gal.* 2:17 *is* C. minister of sin?
3:16 to thy seed, which *is* C.
*Phil.* 1:21 to live *is* C.
*Col.* 1:27 *is* C. in you hope

**Of CHRIST.**

*Mat.* 11:2 John heard works *of* C.
22:42 what think ye *of* C.?
*Rom.* 8:9 any have not S. *of* C.
35 sep. us from love *of* C.?
14:10 judgment-seat *of* C.
1 *Cor.* 1:17 cross *of* C. be made
2:16 we have the mind *of* C.
6:15 your bodies members *of* C.
10:16 communion of blood *of* C.
11:1 be foll. of me as I *of* C.
3 the head *of* C. is God
12:27 ye are the body *of* C.
2 *Cor.* 1:5 as sufferings *of* C.
2:10 forgave I it in person *of* C.
15 we are a sweet savor *of* C.
3:3 epistle *of* C. ministered
4:4 light of gospel *of* C. shine
5:14 love *of* C. constraineth us
8:23 they are glory *of* C.
10:1 by the meekness *of* C.
5 bringing to obedience *of* C.
11:10 the truth *of* C. is in me
12:9 power *of* C. *Rev.* 12:10
13:3 proof *of* C. speaking
*Gal.* 1:10 be servant *of* C.
2:16 be justified by faith *of* C.
6:12 persecution for cross *of* C.
*Eph.* 2:13 by the blood *of* C.
3:4 in mystery *of* C.
8 the unsearchable riches *of* C.
19 love *of* C. which passeth
4:7 measure of gift *of* C.
5:5 inheritance in king. *of* C.
6:6 as servants *of* C.
*Phil.* 1:10 till the day *of* C.
29 it is given in behalf *of* C.
2:16 rejoice in the day *of* C.
30 work *of* C. nigh to death
3:18 enemies of the cross *of* C.
*Col.* 1:24 afflictions *of* C.
2:2 mystery of God, and *of* C.
17 but the body is *of* C.
3:16 let the word *of* C. dwell
4:3 to speak the mystery *of* C.
2 *Tim.* 2:19 the name *of* C.
*Heb.* 3:14 made partakers *of* C.
9:14 more, blood *of* C. purge
11:26 reproach *of* C. greater
1 *Pet.* 1:11 Spirit *of* C. did signify
19 with precious blood *of* C.
4:13 partakers *of* C. sufferings
14 reproached for name *of* C.
*Rev.* 20:6 priests of G. and *of* C.

**That CHRIST.**

*John* 1:25 if thou be not *that* C
6:69 sure that thou art *that* C.

**The CHRIST.**

*Mat.* 16:20 he was *the* C.
26:63 whether thou be *the* C.
*Mark* 8:29 saith, thou art *the* C.
14:61 *the* C. son of the B.?
*Luke* 3:15 whether he were *t.* C.
9:20 Peter said thou art *the* C.
22:67 saying art thou *the* C.
*John* 1:20 I am not *the* C.
41 found the Messias, *the* C.
3:28 I said I am not *the* C.
4:29 is not this *the* C.?
42 this is indeed *the* C. 7:26
7:41 others said, this is *the* C.
10:24 be *the* C. tell us plainly
11:27 I believe thou art *the* C
20:31 believe Jesus is *the* C.
1 *John* 2:22 Jesus is *the* C.
5:1 believeth Jesus is *the* C.

**With CHRIST**

*Rom.* 6:8 if we be dead *with* C.
8:17 then joint-heirs *with* C.
*Gal.* 2:20 I am crucified *with* C.
*Eph.* 2:5 quickened us tog. *w.* C.
*Phil.* 1:23 a desire to be *with* C.
*Col.* 2:20 if dead *with* C.
3:1 if risen *w.* C. seek things
*Col.* 3:3 your life is hid *with* C.
*Rev.* 20:4 reigned *with* C.

**CHRISTIAN, S.**

*Acts* 11:26 called *c.* at Antioch
26:28 almost pers. me to be a *c.*
1 *Pet.* 4:16 if any suffer as a *c.*

**CHRISTS.**

*Mat.* 24:24 false *c.* *Mark* 13:22

**CHRONICLES.**

1 *Chr.* 27:24 number put in *c.*
*Est.* 6:1 to bring the book of *c.*
*See* BOOK.

**CHRYSOLITE.**

*Rev.* 21:20 seventh found. a *c.*

**CHRYSOPRASUS.**

*Rev.* 21:20 tenth foundation a *c.*

**CHURCH.**

*Mat.* 16:18 on this rock b. my *c.*
18:17 tell it to the *c.*
*Acts* 2:47 added to *c.* daily such
5:11 great fear came on *c.*
8:1 persecution against *c.*
11:26 assembled with the *c.*
14:23 ordained elders in every *c.*
27 had gathered *c.* together
15:3 brought on way by the *c.*
22 it pleased elders with the *c.*
18:22 when he had saluted *c.*
*Rom.* 16:5 greet *c.* in their house
1 *Cor.* 4:17 as I teach in every *c.*
14:4 prophesieth edifieth *c.*
5 that *c.* may receive edifying
23 if *c.* be come into one place
16:19 *c.* in their house
*Eph.* 1:22 head over all to the *c.*
3:10 known by *c.* wisdom of G.
5:24 as *c.* is subject to Christ
25 as Christ loved the *c.*
27 might present a glorious *c.*
29 cherisheth it, as Lord the *c.*
32 speak concern. Christ and *c.*
*Phil.* 3:6 persecuting the *c.*
4:15 no *c.* communicated
*Col.* 1:18 head of the body the *c.*
24 for his body's sake, the *c.*
4:15 salute *c.* in Nymphas' ho.
1 *Tim.* 5:16 let not *c.* be charged
*Phile.* 2 Paul to *c.* in thy house
*Heb.* 12:23 to *c.* of first-born
1 *Pet.* 5:13 *c.* at Babylon saluteth
3 *John* 6 thy charity before *c.*
9 I wrote to the *c.* but Diotre

**In the CHURCH.**

*Acts* 7:38 that was *in the c.*
13:1 proph. *in the c.* at Antioch
1 *Cor.* 6:4 least esteemed *in the c.*
11:18 come together *in the c.*
12:28 hath set some *in the c.*
14:19 yet *in the c.* I had rather
28 keep silence *in the c.*
35 sh. for wo. to speak *in the c.*
*Eph.* 3:21 be glory *in the c.*
*Col.* 4:16 to be read *in the c.*

**Of the CHURCH.**

*Acts* 8:3 S. made havoc *of the c.*
11:22 came to ears *of the c.*
12:1 H. vexed certain *of the c.*
5 prayer was made *of the c.*
15:4 were received *of the c.*
20:16 Paul called elders *of the c.*
*Rom.* 16:1 P. a servant *of the c.*
23 Gaius my host and *of the c.*
1 *Cor.* 14:12 excel to edify. *of c.*
*Eph.* 5:23 as C. is head *of the c.*
*Heb.* 2:12 in midst *of the c.*
3 *John* 10 D. casteth out *of c.*
*Rev.* 2:1 angel *of c.* of Ephesus
8 Smyrna; 12 Perga.; 18 Thya.
3:1 Sardis; 7 Philad.; 14 Laodi.

**CHURCH of God.**

*Acts* 20:28 feed the *c. of God*
1 *Cor.* 1:2 to *c. of God* at Corinth
10:32 none offence to *c. of God*

11:22 despise ye the *c. of God*
15:9 I pers. *c. of God*, *Gal.* 1:13
1 *Tim.* 5:3 take care of *c. of God*

**CHURCHES.**

*Acts* 9:31 then had the *c.* rest
15:41 Paul confirming the *c.*
16:5 *c.* established in the faith
19:37 these neither robbers of *c.*
*Rom.* 16:4 all *c.* gave thanks
16 the *c.* of Christ salute you
1 *Cor.* 7:17 so ordain I in all *c.*
11:16 such custom, nei. the *c.*
14:33 author of peace as in all *c.*
34 women keep silence in *c.*
16:1 order to *c.* of Galatia
19 the *c.* of Asia salute you
2 *Cor.* 8:1 grace bestow. on the *c.*
19 chosen of the *c.* to travel
23 they are messengers of *c.*
11:8 I robbed other *c.*
2 *Cor.* 11:28 the care of all the *c.*
12:13 inferior to other *c.*?
*Gal.* 1:22 unknown by face to *c.*
1 *Thes.* 2:14 fol. of the *c.* of God
2 *Thes.* 1:4 glory in you in *c.*
*Rev.* 1:4 John to the seven *c.*
11 send it to the seven *c.*
20 seven stars are angels of *c.* candlesticks are the seven *c.*
2:7 what the Spirit saith unto the *c.* 11, 17, 29; 3:6, 13, 22
23 *c.* know I am he searcheth
22:16 testify these things in *c.*

**CHURL.**

*Is.* 32:5 *c.* said to be bountiful
7 instruments of *c.* are evil

**CHURLISH.**

1 *Sam.* 25:3 Nab. was *c.* and evil

**CHURNING.**

*Prov.* 30:33 surely *c.* of m. bringeth butter

**CHUSHAN-RISHATHAIM.**

*Jud.* 3:8 sold Is. into hand of C.

CHUZA. *Luke* 8:3

**CILICIA.**

*Acts* 6:9; 15:23, 41; 21:39; 22:3; 23:34; 27:5
*Gal.* 1:21 into regions of C.

**CINNAMON.**

*Ex.* 30:23 sweet *c.*
*Prov.* 7:17 perf. bed with *c.*
*Cant.* 4:14 are an orchard of *c.*
*Rev.* 18:13 buyeth her *c.*

**CIRCLE.**

*Is.* 40:22 sitteth on *c.* of earth

**CIRCUIT, S.**

1 *Sam.* 7:16 year to year in *c.*
*Job* 22:14 in *c.* of heaven
*Ps.* 19:6 his *c.* unto the ends
*Ec.* 1:6 according to his *c.*

**CIRCUMCISE.**

*Gen.* 17:11 ye shall *c.* foreskin
*Deut.* 10:16 *c.* foreskin
30:6 Lord will *c.* thy heart
*Jos.* 5:2 *c.* again children of Isr.
*Jer.* 4:4 *c.* yourselves to the L.
*Luke* 1:59 came to *c.* the child
*John* 7:22 on Sabbath *c.* a man
*Acts* 15:5 needful to *c.* them
21:21 they ought not to *c.*

**CIRCUMCISED.**

*Gen.* 17:10 every man-child be *c.*
14 not *c.* shall be cut off
26 Abraham was *c.* and Ishm.
34:15 every male *c.*
24 every male was *c.* *Ex.* 12:48
*Jos.* 5:3 J. *c.* children of Israel
*Jer.* 9:25 punish all *c.* with uncir.
*Acts* 15:1 except *c.* not saved, 24
16:3 Paul *c.* Timothy
*Rom.* 4:11 though not *c.*
1 *Cor.* 7:18 being *c.*? in uncircumcision? let him not be *c.*
*Gal.* 2:3 Titus compelled to be *c.*
5:2 if *c.* C. shall profit nothing
6:12 they constrain you to be *c.*
13 they *c.* keep not the law
*Phil.* 3:5 *c.* eighth day
*Col.* 2:11 in whom also ye are *c.*

**CIRCUMCISING.**

*Luke* 2:21 days accomp. for *c.*

**CIRCUMCISION.**

*John* 7:22 M. gave unto you *c.*
23 if on the sabbath receive *c.*
*Rom.* 2:25 *c.* profiteth, if thou keep the law; thy *c.* is made
28 nor is that *c.* which is outw.
29 *c.* is that of the heart
3:30 shall justify *c.* by faith
4:9 this blessedness on *c.* only?
10 when he was in *c.*? not in *c.*
1 *Cor.* 7:19 *c.* is keeping of com.
*Gal.* 2:9 they should go unto *c.*
5:6 neither *c.* availeth, 6:15
11 and I, if I yet preach *c.*
*Eph.* 2:11 by that called *c.*
*Phil.* 3:3 *c.* which worship God
*Col.* 2:11 *c.* without hands, by *c.*
3:11 there is nei. *c.* nor uncir.

**Of CIRCUMCISION.**

*Ex.* 4:26 bloody hus. bec. *of c.*
*Acts* 7:8 Abrah. covenant *of c.*
10:45 they *of c.* were astonished
11:2 *of c.* contended with Peter
*Rom.* 3:1 what profit *of c.*?
4:11 he received the sign *of c.*
12 *of c.* to them not *of c.*
15:8 J. C. was a minister *of c.*
*Gal.* 2:7 gospel *of c.* com. to Pe.
8 in Peter to apostleship *of c.*
*Col.* 4:11 who are *of* the *c.* salute
*Tit.* 1:10 unruly, especially *of c.*

**CIRCUMSPECT, LY.**

*Ex.* 23:13 in all things be *c.*
*Eph.* 5:15 see that ye walk *c.*

**CISTERN, S.**

2 *K.* 18:31 drink ev. one of his *c.*
*Prov.* 5:15 drink of thine own *c.*
*Ec.* 12:6 wheel broken at the *c.*
*Is.* 36:16 every one of own *c.*
*Jer.* 2:13 hewed out *c.* of brok. *c.*

**CITY.**

*Gen.* 4:17 Cain builded a *c.*
11:4 build *c.* and a tower
5 Lord came down to see *c.*
8 they left off to build the *c.*
18:26 find fifty righteous in *c.*
34:25 came upon the *c.* boldly
*Num.* 21:28 flame is gone from *c.*
*Deut.* 2:36 not one *c.* too strong
3:4 not a *c.* we took not from
13:15 smite inhabit. of that *c.*
*Jos.* 3:16 very far from *c.* Adam
6:3 compass the *c.* six days, 7
24 burnt *c.* *Deut.* 13:16 *Jos.* 8:8, 19; *Jud.* 1:8; 18:27
8:2 lay ambush for *c.* behind
20 smoke of *c.* ascended to h.
15:13 *c.* of Arba, which *c.* is H.
19:50 gave Joshua *c.* he asked
*Jud.* 6:27 he feared men of *c.*
9:45 *c.* and sowed it with salt
20:40 flame of the *c.* ascended
*Ruth* 1:19 all the *c.* was moved
3:11 for *c.* of my people know
1 *Sam.* 1:3 out of *c.* yearly to w.
4:13 told it, all the *c.* cried out
8:22 every man to his *c.* 1 *K.* 22:36; *Ezr.* 2:1; *Neh.* 7:6
28:3 Israel b. him in his own *c.*
2 *Sam.* 12:1 two men in one *c.*
15:2 of what *c.* art thou?
19:37 I may die in my own *c.*
20:19 seekest to destroy a *c.*
1 *K.* 1:45 so that *c.* rang again
11:32 *c.* I have chosen, 36
2 *K.* 6:19 neither is this the *c.*
11:20 and the *c.* was in quiet
24:10 *c.* Jer. was besieged, 25:2
2 *Chr.* 15:6 *c.* was destroyed of *c.*
19:5 and he set judges *c.* by *c.*
30:10 posts passed from *c.* to *c.*
32:18 that they might take *c.*
*Ezr.* 4:12 building rebellious *c.*
*Neh.* 2:3 why not sad, *c.* waste, 5
11:9 Judah was second over *c.*
*Est.* 8:15 the *c.* Shushan rejoiced
*Ps.* 48:2 *c.* of gr. king, *Mat.* 5:35
59:6 go round about the *c.* 14
72:16 they of *c.* shall flourish
107:4 found no *c.* to dwell in
122:3 Jerusalem as a *c.* compact
127:1 except the Lord keep *c.*
*Prov.* 8:3 crieth at entry of *c.*
10:15 his strong *c.* 18:11
11:10 the *c.* rejoiceth
11 by blessing of upright *c.*
16:32 than he that taketh a *c.*
25:28 like a *c.* broken down
29:8 scornful bring *c.* into snare
*Ec.* 9:14 there was a little *c.*
15 poor wise man delivered *c.*
*Is.* 1:26 *c.* of right. faithful *c.* 21
14:31 howl, O gate, cry O *c.*
17:1 Damascus from being a *c.*
19:2 shall fight, *c.* against *c.*
24:10 *c.* of confusion is broken
25:2 of a *c.* a heap, to be no *c.*
33:20 Zion *c.* of our solemnities
60:14 shall call thee *c.* of Lord
62:12 a *c.* not forsaken
*Jer.* 3:14 take you one of a *c.*
4:29 *c.* shall flee for the noise
19:12 make this *c.* as Tophet
25:29 *c.* called by my name
32:24 come to *c.* and *c.* is given
39:2 the *c.* was broken up, 52:7
46:8 I will destroy the *c.*
49:25 how *c.* of praise not left
*Lam.* 1:1 how doth *c.* sit solitary
2:15 *c.* men call perf. of beauty
*Ezek.* 4:1 portray *c.* Jerusalem
7:23 the *c.* is full of violence
9:1 that have charge over *c.*
4 go thro' midst of *c.* Jerusa.
9 *c.* is full of perverseness
10:2 coals of fire over the *c.*
27:32 what *c.* is like Tyrus
33:21 saying, the *c.* is smitten
48:35 name of *c.* be, L. is there
*Dan.* 9:18 *c.* called by thy na. 19
*Hos.* 6:8 G. *c.* of th. work iniq.
*Amos* 4:7 to rain on one *c.*
5:3 *c.* that went up by thous.
*Mic.* 6:9 Lord's voice crieth to *c.*
*Hab.* 2:12 stablish a *c.* by iniq.
*Zep.* 3:1 woe to the oppressing *c.*
*Zec.* 8:3 Jerusalem a *c.* of truth
5 streets of *c.* be full of boys
*Zec.* 14:2 the *c.* shall be taken
*Mat.* 5:14 a *c.* set on hill cannot
35 Jerusalem is *c.* of great King
8:34 *c.* came out to meet Jesus
10:11 whatsoever *c.* ye enter
15 that *c.* *Mark* 6:11; *Luke* 10:12
21:10 all the *c.* was moved
22:7 king burnt up their *c.*
23:34 persecute from *c.* to *c.*
*Mark* 1:33 *c.* was gathered
5:14 told it in the *c.* *Luke* 8:34
*Luke* 2:3 taxed, ev. one to own *c.*
7:12 much people of *c.* with her
19:41 he beheld the *c.* and wept
23:51 he was of Arimathea a *c.*
*John* 4:39 many of th. *c.* believed
*Acts* 8:8 was great joy in that *c.*
13:44 almost whole *c.* to h.
16:12 in that *c.* certain days
17:5 set all the *c.* in an uproar
19:29 *c.* was filled with confus.
21:30 all the *c.* was moved
*Heb.* 11:10 *c.* that hath found.
16 hath prepared for them a *c.*
12:22 the *c.* of the living God
13:14 we have no continuing *c.*

*Jam.* 4:13 will go into such a *c.*
*Rev.* 20:9 comp. the beloved *c.*
21:14 wall of *c.* had foundations
18 the *c.* was pure gold
23 *c.* had no need of the sun

**Bloody CITY.**

*Ezek.* 22:2 judge the *bloody c.?*
24:6 *bloody c.* 9; *Nah.* 3:1

**Defenced CITY.**

*Is.* 25:2 of a *defenced c.* a ruin
27:10 the *d. c.* shall be desolate
*Jer.* 1:18 thee this day a *d. c.*

**CITY of David.**

2 *Sam.* 5:9 *c. of D.* 1 *Chr.* 11:7
6:10 remove ark into *c. of D.*
12 brought ark into *c of D.* 16
1 *K.* 2:10 D. was buried in *c. D.*
3:1 Sol. brought her to *c. of D.*
8:1 out of *c. of D.* 2 *Chr.* 5:2.
11:43 bur. in *c. D.* 2 *Chr.* 9:31
14:31 R. bur. *c. D.* 2 *Chr.* 12:16
15:8 bur. A. *c. of D.* 2 *Chr.* 14:1
22:50 J. bur. *c. D.* 2 *Chr.* 21:1
2 *K.* 8:24 J. bur. *c. D.* 2 *Chr.* 21:20
9:28 A. was buried in *c. of D.*
12:21 J. bur. *c. D.* 2 *Chr.* 24:25
14:20 Amaziah; 15:7 Azariah
15:38 Jot. 2 *Chr.* 27:9; 28:27 Ahaz
2 *Chr.* 24:16 bur. Jeh. in *c. of D.*
*Is.* 22:9 breaches of *c. of D.*
29:1 woe to A. *c.* where *David*
*Luke* 2:4 Joseph went to *c. of D.*
11 born in *c. of D.* a Saviour

**Elders, *with* CITY.**

*Deut.* 19:12 *elders* of his *c.*
21:6 *elders* of that *c.* next
20 say to *e* of *c.* our son is
22:17 cloth before *elders* of *c.*
25:8 *elders* of his *c.* shall call
*Jos.* 20:4 dec. his cause to *e.* of *c.*
*Jud.* 8:16 Gideon took *elders* of *c.*
*Ruth* 4:2 took ten men of *e.* of *c.*
*Ezr.* 10:14 *elders* of every *c*

**Every CITY.**

2 *K.* 3:19 smite *every* fenced *c.*
2 *Chr.* 31:19 of sons of A. in *e. c.*
*Jer.* 4:29 *every c.* shall be forsak.
48:8 spoiler shall come on *e. c.*
*Mat.* 12:25 *e. c.* divided ag. itself
*Luke* 10:1 two into *every c.*
*Acts* 15:21 in *e. c.* them that p.
36 visit brethren in *every c.*
20:23 H. G. witnesseth in *e. c.*
*Tit.* 1:5 ordain elders in *every c.*

**Fenced CITY.**

2 *K.* 10:2 with you a *fenced c.*
17:9 tower of watchmen to *f. c.*
2 *Chr.* 11:23 he dispersed of chil. unto every *fenced c.*

**CITY of God.**

*Ps.* 46:4 make glad *c. of God*
48:1 to be praised in *c. of God*
8 *c. of God* will establish it
87:3 glorious things spoken of thee, O *c. of God*
*Heb.* 12:22 *c. of* living *God*
*Rev.* 3:12 name of *c. of* my *God*

**Great CITY.**

*Gen.* 10:12 builded R. a *great c.*
*Jos.* 10:2 Gibeon was *great c.*
*Neh.* 7:4 *c.* was large and *great*
*Jer.* 22:8 done thus to *great c.*
*Jon.* 1:2 Nineveh that *g. c.* 3:2
3:3 N. was an exceeding *g. c.*
*Rev.* 11:8 in street of *great c.*
14:8 Bab. *g. c.* 18:10, 16, 19, 21
16:19 *great c.* was divided
17:18 woman is that *great c.*
21:10 he showed me that *g. c.*

**Holy CITY.**

*Neh.* 11:1 Jerusalem the *holy c.*
*Is.* 48:2 call themselves of *holy c.*
52:1 put on beau. garm. O *h. c.*
*Dan.* 9:24 seventy w. on thy *h. c.*
*Mat.* 4:5 devil taketh him to *h. c.*
27:53 went to *h. c.* and appeared
*Rev.* 11:2 *holy c.* shall they tread
21:2 I John saw the *h. c.* coming
22:19 take his part out of *h. c.*

**In, *or* into the CITY.**

*Gen.* 19:12 hast *in the c.* bring
*Deut.* 20:14 all *in the c.* take
28:3 blessed shalt be *in the c.*
16 cursed shalt be *in the c.*
*Jos.* 6:21 destroyed all *in the c.*
8:19 *into c.* and set it on fire
*Jud.* 1:24 entrance *into c.*
2 *Sam.* 15:25 car. back ark *into c.*
27 return *into the c.*
1 *K.* 14:11 dieth of Jerob. *in c.*
12 when thy feet enter *into c.*
16:4 that dieth of Baasha *in c.*
2 *K.* 7:4 we will enter *into c.*
12 catch them, get *into c.*
*Ps.* 31:21 showed me his marvellous kindness *in* a strong *c.*
55:9 seen violence *in the c.*
*Prov.* 1:21 *in c.* wisdom uttereth
*Ec.* 7:19 mighty men *in the c.*
8:10 wicked were forgotten *in c.*
*Is.* 24:12 *in the c.* is left deso.
*Jer.* 14:18 if I enter *into the c.*
38:9 no more bread *in the c.*
52:6 famine was sore *in the c.*
*Lam.* 1:19 gave up ghost *in c.*
*Hos.* 11:9 not enter *into the c.*
*Joel* 2:9 run to and fro *in the c.*
*Amos* 3:6 be blown *in the c.* shall there be evil in a *c.*
7:17 thy wife be harlot *in c.*
*Jon.* 3:4 J. began to enter *into c.*
*Mat.* 9:1 came *into* his own *c.*
10:5 *c.* of the Samaritans
11 *into* whatsoever *c.* ye enter
26:18 go *into c.* to such a man
28:11 some of watch came *into c.*
*Mark* 14:13 *into the c.* *Acts* 9:6
*Luke* 2:3 every one *into* his *c.*
7:37 a woman *in the c.* a sinner
18:2 there was *in* a *c.* a judge
22:10 ye are entered *into c.*
24:49 tarry ye *in c.* of Jerusalem
*John* 4:8 disciples gone *into c.*
*Acts* 11:5 *in the c.* of Joppa
14:20 he came *into the c.*
21:29 with him *in the c.*
24:12 synagogues nor *in the c.*
2 *Cor.* 11:26 in perils *in the c.*
*Rev.* 22:14 through gates *into c.*

**CITY of the Lord.**

*Ps.* 101:8 cut off all wicked doers from *c. of the Lord.*
*Is.* 60:14 call thee *c. of Lord*

**Out of the CITY.**

*Gen.* 44:4 gone *out of the c.*
*Ex.* 9:29 soon as I am *out of c.*
33 Moses went *out of the c.*
*Jos.* 8:22 issued *out of the c.*
*Jud.* 1:24 saw man come *o. of c.*
2 *Sam.* 18:3 succor us *out of c.*
20:16 wise woman *out of the c.*
2 *K.* 7:12 they come *out of c.*
9:15 none escape *out of the c.*
*Job* 24:12 groan from *out of t. c.*
*Jer.* 39:4 Zed. went *o. of c.* 52:7
*Ezek.* 48:30 are goings *o. of the c.*
*Mic.* 4:10 go forth *out of the c.*
*Mat.* 21:17 went *out of the c.*
*Mark* 11:19 he went *out of c.*
*Luke* 4:29 thrust him *out of t. c.*
9:5 go *out of c.* shake off dust
*John* 4:30 they went *out of c.*
*Acts* 7:58 cast Steph. *out of the c.*
14:19 drew him *out of c.*
16:13 we went *out of the c.*
21:5 brought us till *out of the c.*

**CITY of Refuge.**

*Num.* 35:25 rest. him to *c. of ref.*
*Jos.* 21:13 *c. of r.* 1 *Chr.* 6:57
21 Shech.; 27 Golan; 32 Ked.

**This CITY.**

*Gen.* 19:14 L. will destroy *this c.*
20 *this c.* is near to flee unto
21 I will not overthrow *this c.*
*Jos.* 6:26 buildeth *this c.*
*Jud.* 19:11 turn into *this c.*
1 *Sam.* 9:6 in *this c.* a man of G.
2 *K.* 2:19 *this c.* is pleasant
18:30 *t. c.* not be deliv. *Is.* 36:15
19:32 into *this c.* 33; *Is.* 37:34
34 def. *t. c.* 20:6; *Is.* 37:35; 38:6
23:27 cast off *this c.* Jerusalem
2 *Chr.* 6:34 pray toward *this c.*
*Ezr.* 4:13 if *this c.* be builded, 16
*Neh.* 13:18 bring evil on *this c.?*
*Jer.* 6:6 *this* is the *c.* to be visited
17:25 *this c.* shall remain
19:8 will make *this c.* desolate
15 bring on *this c.* all the evil
20:5 deliver strength of *this c.*
21:9 abideth in *this c.* shall die
10 set my face against *this c.*
22:8 why L. done thus unto *t. c.*
26:6 I will make *this c.* a curse
15 innocent blood on *this c.*
27:17 *this c.* be laid waste
32:3 give *t. c.* to Chald. 28; 34:2
31 *this c.* been as a provocation
33:5 hid my face from *this c.*
34:22 cause them return to *t. c.*
38:17 *this c.* shall not be burnt
39:16 words on *this c.* for evil
*Ezek.* 11:3 *this c.* is the caldron, 7
*Mat.* 10:23 persecute in *this c.*
*Acts* 18:10 much people in *this c.*
22:3 brought up in *this c.* at feet

**Without CITY.**

*Gen.* 19:16 men set Lot *with. c.*
*Num.* 35:5 measure from *w. c.*
*Rev.* 14:20 w.-press trodden *w. c.*

**CITIES.**

*Gen.* 19:29 when God destroy. *c.*
35:5 terror of God on *c.* round
47:21 he rem. people to *c.*
*Num.* 13:19 what *c.* they dwell in
35:8 give of his *c.* to Levites
*Deut.* 2:37 nor to *c.* in mountains
3:19 abide in *c.* I have given you
6:10 to give thee goodly *c.*
19:5 flee to one of these *c.*
*Jos.* 10:19 suf. th. not to enter *c.*
11:13 as for *c.* still in strength
18:9 described it by *c.* in a book
*Jud.* 20:48 set on fire *c.*
21:23 they repaired the *c.*
1 *Sam.* 31:7 Israelites forsook *c.*
2 *Sam.* 10:12 *c.* our God, 1 *Chr.* 19:13
1 *K.* 9:12 Hiram came to see *c.*
20:34 *c.* father took I restore
*Job* 15:28 dwell. in desolate *c.*
*Ps.* 9:6 O enemy, destroyed *c.*
*Is.* 6:11 Until *c.* be wasted
14:21 nor fill world with *c.*
19:18 day shall five *c.* in E.
33:8 he hath despised the *c.*
64:10 thy holy *c.* a wilderness
*Jer.* 2:15 his *c.* are burnt
28 number of thy *c.* 11:13
13:19 *c.* of south be shut up
20:16 be as the *c.* L. overthrew
31:21 O virgin, to these thy *c.*
49:13 *c.* be perpetual wastes
50:32 I will kindle fire in his *c.*
*Ezek.* 26:19 like *c.* not inhabited
30:17 these *c.* into captivity
35:9 thy *c.* shall not return
*Hos.* 8:14 send fire upon his *c.*
11:6 sword shall abide on his *c.*
*Amos* 4:8 three *c.* to one for wat.
*Mic.* 5:14 so will I destroy thy *c.*
*Zep.* 3:6 their *c.* are destroyed
*Zec.* 1:17 my *c.* shall yet spread
*Mat.* 10:23 not have gone over *c.*
11:1 to preach in their *c.*
*Acts* 26:11 persec. to strange *c.*

2 Pet. 2:6 c. of S. and G. to ashes
Jude 7 c. about them in like m.
Rev. 16:19 c. of the nations fell

**All CITIES.**
Num. 21:25 Is. took all these c.
Deut. 2:34; 3:4; Jos. 10:39
31:10 burnt their c. Jud. 20:48
Deut. 20:15 thus do to all c. afar
Jos. 11:12 all c. of kings destr.
21:19 all c. of Aaron were 13 c.
41 all c. of Levites were 48 c.
1 Sam. 18:6 came out of all c.
2 Sam. 24:7 came to all c. of Hiv.
Neh. 10:37 tithes in all the c.
Jer. 4:26 all the c. broken down
33:12 in all c. habita. of sheph.
Hos. 13:10 save thee in all thy c.
Acts 8:40 he preached in all c.

**Defenced CITIES.**
Is. 36:1 Sennacherib ag. def. c.
37:26 to lay waste defenced c.
Jer. 4:5 go to defenced c. 8:14
34:7 defenced c. remained of J.

**Fenced CITIES.**
Num. 32:17 ones in fenced c.
Deut. 3:5 c. fenced with high w.
9:1 c. f. to heaven, Jos. 14:12
Jos. 10:20 entered into fen. c.
2 Sam. 20:6 get him fenced c.
2 Chr. 12:4 Shishak took fen. c.
14:6 Asa built fenced c. in Jud.
21:3 Jehosh. gave sons fen. c.
Jer. 5:17 impoverish thy fen. c.
Dan. 11:15 k. of north take f. c.
Hos. 8:14 J. multiplied fenced c.
Zep. 1:16 day of alarm ag. f. c.

**CITIES of Judah.**
2 Sam. 2:1 I go up to c. of J.?
2 K. 23:5 burnt inc. in c. of J.
1 Chr. 6:57 sons of Aaron c. of J.
2 Chr. 17:7 to teach in c. of J. 13
19:5 set judges in the c. of J.
23:2 gather Lev. out of c. of J.
Neh. 11:3 in c. of Judah each
Ps. 69:35 will build c. of Judah
Is. 40:9 c. of Jud. behold your G.
44:26 c. of J. ye shall be built
Jer. 1:15 fam. of north ag. c. of J.
4:16 voice against c. of J.
7:17 what they do in c. of J.
9:11 c. of J. des. 10:22; 34:22
11:12 c. of Judah cry to gods
32:44 witness in the c. of Judah
33:10 man and beast in c. of J.
13 in the c. of Ju. shall flocks
44:6 fury kindled in c. of Jud.
21 incense ye burn in c. of J.
Zec. 1:12 not mercy on c. of J.

**CITIES of Refuge.**
Num. 35:6 six c. for ref. 13,14
11 ap. c. of refuge, Jos. 20:2
1 Chr. 6:67 to sons of K. of c. r.

**Six CITIES.**
Jos. 15:59 mount. of Jud. six c.

**CITIES, with Suburbs.**
Lev. 25:34 sub. of c. not be sold
Num. 35:2 give to L. sub. for c.
Jos. 21:3 to Levites c. with s.

**CITIES, with Villages.**
1 Sam. 6:18 c. and of country v.
Mat. 9:35 J. went about all c. and villages teaching, Luke 13:22
Mark 6:56 into villages or c.

**CITIES, with waste.**
Lev. 26:31 your c. waste, 33
Is. 61:4 shall repair waste c.
Jer. 4:7 c. shall be laid waste
Ezek. 6:6 in dwell. c. shall be w.
19:7 w. their c.; 35:4 thy c. w.
36:35 w. c. are become fenced
38 w. c. be filled with flocks
Amos 9:14 build the waste c.

**Your CITIES.**
Is. 1:7 your c. are burnt
Jer. 40:10 dwell in your c.

**CITIZEN, S.**
Luke 15:15 prodigal joined to c.
19:14 his c. hated him, and
Acts 21:39 a c. of no mean city
Eph. 2:19 fellow-c. with saints

**CLAD.**
1 K. 11:29 Jerob. had c. himself
Is. 59:17 c. with zeal as a cloak

**CLAMOR, OUS.**
Prov. 9:13 a foolish woman is c.
Eph. 4:31 let all c. be put away

**CLAP hands.**
Job 27:23 shall c. their hands
Ps. 47:1 c. your h. all ye people
98:8 let the floods c. their hands
Is. 55:12 trees of field c. their h.
Lam. 2:15 c. their h. at thee
Nah. 3:19 bruit of thee c. hands

**CLAPPED, ETH.**
2 K. 11:12 c. their hands
Ezek. 25:6 hast c. thy hands
Job 34:37 c. his hands among us

**CLAVE, cleft.**
Gen. 22:3 A. c. wood for bur.-off.
Num. 16:31 ground c. asunder
Jud. 15:19 God c. hollow in jaw
1 Sam. 6:14 c. wood of cart
Ps. 78:15 c. rocks, Is. 48:21

**CLAVE, adhered.**
Gen. 34:3 his soul c. to Dinah
Ruth 1:14 R. c. to mother-in-law
2 Sam. 20:2 Jud. c. to their king
23:10 till his hand c. to sword
1 K. 11:2 Sol. c. to these in love
2 K. 18:6 Hezekiah c. to the Lord
Neh. 10:29 c. to their brethren
Acts 17:34 certain men c. to Paul
CLAUDA. Acts 27:16
CLAUDIA. 2 Tim. 4:21

**CLAWS.**
Deut. 14:6 the cleft into two c.
Dan. 4:33 his nails like birds' c.
Zec. 11:16 he shall tear their c.

**CLAY.**
Job 4:19 dwell in houses of c.
10:9 hast made me as the c.
13:12 are like to bodies of c.
27:16 prepare raiment as c.
33:6 I am formed out of c.
38:14 it is turned as c. to seal
Ps. 40:2 up out of the miry c.
Is. 29:16 esteem. as potter's c.
Is. 41:25 as potter treadeth c.
45:9 c. say to him fashioneth it
64:8 we the c. thou our potter
Jer. 18:4 vessel made of c. marred
6 as c. is in the potter's hand
43:9 stones, hide them in c.
Dan. 2:33 his feet, part c. 34, 42
Nah. 3:14 go into c. and tread
Hab. 2:6 ladeth with thick c.
John 9:6 he made c. of spittle
15 he put c. on mine eyes
Rom. 9:21 potter power over c.?

**CLAY-GROUND.**
1 K. 7:46 into c.-g. 2 Chr. 4:17

**CLEAN.**
Lev. 23:22 not make c. riddance
Jos. 3:17 c. over Jordan, 4:1, 11
Ps. 77:8 is his mercy c. gone
Is. 24:19 earth is c. dissolved
Joel 1:7 he hath made it c. bare
2 Pet. 2:18 those c. escaped

**CLEAN, Adjective.**
Gen. 8:20 took of every c. beast
35:2 be c. and change garments
Lev. 7:19 all c. shall eat thereof
10:10 difference betw. c. 11:47; 20:25; Ezek. 22:26; 44:23
16:30 be c. from all your sins
22:4 not eat holy things till c.
Num. 19:18 a c. person take hys.
Deut. 12:15 c. may eat, 15:22
1 Sam. 20:26 surely he is not c.
2 K. 5:10 flesh come ag. be c. 14
12 wash in them and be c.
13 he saith, Wash and be c.
Job 11:4 I am c. in thine eyes
14:4 c. thing out of an unclean?
15:14 what is man he sh. be c.?
15 heavens not c. in his sight
25:4 he be c. born of a woman
33:9 I am c. without transgr.
Prov. 16:2 c. in his own eyes
Ec. 9:2 alike to c. and unclean
Is. 1:16 wash ye, make you c.
28:8 so there is no place c.
52:11 be ye c. that bear vessels
Jer. 13:27 wilt not be made c.?
Ezek. 36:25 sprinkle c. water on
Mat. 8:2 thou canst make me c. Mark 1:40; Luke 5:12
3 thou c. Mark 1:41; Lu. 5:13
23:25 c. the outside, Luke 11:39
Luke 11:41 all things are c.
John 13:11 Ye are not all c.
15:3 ye are c. through the word
Acts 18:6 own heads, I am c.
Rev. 19:8 linen, c. and white, 14

**CLEAN hands.**
Job 9:30 make hands never so c.
17:9 c. hands shall be stronger
Ps. 24:4 he that hath c. hands

**CLEAN heart.**
Ps. 51:10 create in me a c. heart
73:1 God is good to such of c. h.
Prov. 20:9 made my heart c.?

**Is CLEAN.**
Lev. 13:13 he is c. 17, 37, 39
Ps. 19:9 fear of the Lord is c.
Prov. 14:4 no oxen are, crib is c.
John 13:10 but is c. every whit

**Pronounce CLEAN.**
Lev. 13:6 pronounce him c. 14:7

**Shall be CLEAN.**
Lev. 11:36 wh. is water s. be c.
12:8 she s. be c. 15:28; 13:58 it s. be c.
14:20 he s. be c 53; 15:13; 17:15; 22:7; Num. 19:12, 19
Num. 31:24 shall be c. Ezek. 36:25
Ps. 51:7 hyssop and I shall be c.

**CLEANNESS.**
2 Sam. 22:21 c. of my hands recompensed me, Ps. 18:20
25 c. in his eyesight, Ps. 18:24
Amos 4:6 give you c. of teeth

**CLEANSE.**
Ex. 29:36 c. the alt. Lev. 16:19
Num. 8:6 take Lev. and c. them
2 Chr. 29:15 c. house of Lord, 16
Neh. 13:22 Levites should c. th.
Ps. 19:12 c. from secret faults
51:2 and c. me from my sin
119:9 a young man c. his way?
Jer. 4:11 a dry wind not to c.
33:8 c. them, Ezek. 37:23
Ezek. 36:25 from idols will I c.
39:12 that they may c. land, 16
45:18 and c. the sanctuary
Joel 3:21 c. their blood
Mat. 10:8 heal the sick, c. lepers
23:26 c. first within the cup
2 Cor. 7:1 c. ourselves
Eph. 5:26 c. it with washing
Jam. 4:8 c. your hands, ye sinn.
1 John 1:9 c. us from unright.

**CLEANSED.**
Lev. 14:14 to be c. 17, 18, 25, 28
Num. 35:33 land cannot be c.
Jos. 22:17 we are not c.
2 Chr. 29:18 c. all the house of L.
30:19 his heart though not c.
34:5 Josiah c. Judah and Jerus.
Neh. 13:9 they c. the chambers
Job 35:3 what profit if I be c.

*Ps.* 73:13 *c.* my heart in vain
*Ezek.* 22:24 art the land not *c.*
44:26 he is *c.* reck. seven days
*Dan.* 8:14 then sanctuary be *c.*
*Mat.* 8:3 his leprosy was *c.*
11:5 lepers are *c.* *Luke* 7:22
*Mark* 1:42 leprosy dep. he was *c.*
*Luke* 4:27 none *c.* save Naaman
17:17 were not ten *c.* but where
*Acts* 10:15 what God hath *c.* 11:9

**CLEANSETH, ING.**
*Job* 37:21 but the wind *c.* them
*Prov.* 20:30 blueness of a wo. *c.*
1 *John* 1:7 bl. of Jesus Christ *c.*
*Mark* 1:44 offer for *c.* *Luke* 5:14

**CLEAR.**
*Gen.* 44:16 how shall we *c.* ours.
*Exod.* 34:7 by no means *c.* guilty
2 *Sam.* 23:4 *c.* shining after rain
*Ps.* 51:4 *c.* when thou judgest
*Cant.* 6:10 *c.* as the sun
*Is.* 18:4 like a *c.* heat on herbs
*Amos* 8:9 darken earth in *c.* day
*Zec.* 14:6 light shall not be *c.*
2 *Cor.* 7:11 ap. yourselves to be *c.*
*Rev.* 21:11 *c.* as crystal, 22:1
18 pure gold like to *c.* glass

**CLEARER.**
*Job* 11:17 shall be *c.* than noon

**CLEARING.**
*Num.* 14:18 no means *c.* guilty
2 *Cor.* 7:11 what *c.* of yourselves

**CLEARLY.**
*Job* 33:3 utter knowledge *c.*
*Mat.* 7:5 *c.* to pull, *Luke* 6:42
*Mark* 8:25 and saw every man *c.*
*Rom.* 1:20 from creation *c.* seen

**CLEARNESS.**
*Exod.* 24:10 body of heaven in *c.*

**CLEAVE.**
*Lev.* 1:17 *c.* it with the wings
*Ps.* 74:15 didst *c.* the fountain
*Hab.* 3:9 *c.* the earth with rivers
*Zec.* 14:4 mount shall *c.* in midst
*Gen.* 2:24 shall *c.* to his wife, *Mat.* 19:5; *Mark* 10:7
*Deut.* 4:4 ye that did *c.* to the L.
10:20 to him shalt thou *c.* 11:22; 13:4; 30:20; *Jos.* 22:5
*Jos.* 23:8 *c.* to Lord your God
*Job* 38:38 the clods *c.* together
*Ps.* 101:3 hate work, not *c.*
102:5 my bones *c.* to my skin
137:6 let my tongue *c.* to roof
*Is.* 14:1 *c.* to house of Jacob
*Jer.* 13:11 caused to *c.* to me Is.
*Ezek.* 3:26 make thy tongue *c.*
*Dan.* 2:43 not *c.* one to another
11:34 *c.* to them with flatteries
*Acts* 11:23 heart *c.* to Lord
*Rom.* 12:9 *c.* to that wh. is good

**CLEAVED.**
2 *K.* 3:3 J. *c.* to Jeroboam's sins
*Job* 29:10 their tongue *c.* to roof
31:7 blot hath *c.* to my hands

**CLEAVETH.**
*Job* 19:20 my bone *c.* to my skin
*Ps.* 22:15 tongue *c.* to my jaws
41:8 an evil disease *c.* to him
44:25 our belly *c.* to the earth
119:25 my soul *c.* to the dust
*Jer.* 13:11 as girdle *c.* to loins
*Lam.* 4:4 tongue of suck. child *c.*
8 their skin *c.* to their bones
*Luke* 10:11 dust of city which *c.*

**CLEAVETH,** *divideth.*
*Deut.* 14:6 beast that *c.* the cleft
*Job* 16:13 he *c.* my reins asunder
*Ps.* 141:7 as when one *c.* wood
*Ec.* 10:9 *c.* wood be endangered

**CLEFT.**
*Mic.* 1:4 valleys sh. be *c.* as wax

**CLEFTS.**
*Cant.* 2:14 that art in *c.*
*Is.* 2:21 to go into *c.* for fear
*Jer.* 49:16 dw. in the *c.* *Ob.* 3
*Am.* 6:11 smite house with *c.*

**CLEMENCY.**
*Acts* 24:4 hear us of thy *c.*

CLEMENT. *Phil.* 4:3
CLEOPAS. *Lu.* 24:18; *Jo.* 19:25

**CLERK.**
*Acts* 19:35 town *c.* had appeased

**CLIFT, S.**
*Ex.* 33:22 will put thee in a *c.*
2 *Chr.* 20:16 come by *c.* of Ziz
*Job* 30:6 to dwell in *c.* of valleys
*Is.* 57:5 slay. children under *c.*

**CLIMB, ED, ETH.**
1 *Sam.* 14:13 Jonathan *c.* up
*Jer.* 4:29 they shall *c.* up rocks
*Joel* 2:7 *c.* wall like men of war
9 they shall *c.* up on houses
*Amos* 9:2 though *c.* up to heaven
*Luke* 19:4 Zaccheus *c.* up a tree
*John* 10:1 *c.* up some other way

**CLIPPED.**
*Jer.* 48:37 every beard shall be *c.*

**CLOAK.**
*Is.* 59:17 clad with zeal as a *c.*
*Mat.* 5:40 let him have *c.* also
*Luke* 6:29 taketh *c.* forbid not
*John* 15:22 no *c.* for their sin
1 *Thes.* 2:5 nor used *c.* of covet.
2 *Tim.* 4:13 *c.* I left at Troas
1 *Pet.* 2:16 lib. for *c.* of malicious

**CLODS.**
*Job* 7:5 clothed with *c.* of dust
21:33 *c.* of valley be sweet
38:38 *c.* cleave fast together
*Is.* 28:24 ploughm. break the *c.*
*Hos.* 10:11 J. shall break his *c.*
*Joel* 1:17 seed is rotten under *c.*

**CLOSE.**
*Num.* 5:13 kept *c.* from husband
2 *Sam.* 22:46 afraid out of their *c.* places, *Ps.* 18:45
1 *Chr.* 12:1 David kept himself *c.*
*Job* 28:21 kept *c.* from fowls
*Jer.* 42:16 follow *c.* after you
*Amos* 9:11 *c.* up the breaches
*Luke* 9:36 they kept it *c.*

**CLOSED.**
*Num.* 16:33 earth *c.* upon them
*Is.* 1:6 they have not been *c.*
29:10 Lord hath *c.* your eyes
*Dan.* 12:9 the words are *c.* up
*Jon.* 2:5 the depth *c.* me around
*Mat.* 13:15 eyes *c.* *Acts* 28:27
*Luke* 4:20 and he *c.* the book

**CLOSER.**
*Prov.* 18:24 a friend sticketh *c.*

**CLOSEST.**
*Jer.* 22:15 thou *c.* thyself in ced.

**CLOSET, S.**
*Joel* 2:16 bride go out of her *c.*
*Mat.* 6:6 prayest, enter thy *c.*
*Luke* 12:3 spok. in the ear in *c.*

**CLOTH.**
*Num.* 4:8 spread a *c.* of scarlet
*Deut.* 22:17 spread *c.* bef. elders
1 *Sam.* 19:13 M. cov. im. with *c.*
21:9 sword is wrapt in a *c.*
2 *Sam.* 20:12 cast a *c.* on Amasa
2 *K.* 8:15 Hazael took a thick *c*
*Is.* 30:22 as a menstruous *c.*
*Mat.* 9:16 new *c.* *Mark* 2:21
27:59 wrapped it in a linen *c.*
*Mark* 14:51 linen *c.* about body

**CLOTHE.**
*Ex.* 40:14 his sons and *c.* them
*Est.* 4:4 raiment to *c.* Mordecai
*Ps.* 132:16 *c.* priests with salva.
18 his enemies *c.* with shame
*Prov.* 23:21 drowsiness *c.* with
*Is.* 22:21 *c.* him with thy robe
49:18 shalt *c.* thee with them
50:3 *c.* heavens with blackness
*Ezek.* 26:16 *c.* with trembling
34:3 *c.* you with the wool
*Hag.* 1:6 ye *c.* but none warm
*Zec.* 3:4 I will *c.* thee
*Mat.* 6:30 if God so *c.* the grass, much more *c.* you, *Lu.* 12:28

**CLOTHED.**
*Gen.* 3:21 coats of skins, *c.* them
*Lev.* 8:7 Moses *c.* A. with robe
2 *Sam.* 1:24 *c.* with scarlet
1 *Chr.* 21:16 Israel *c.* with sack.
2 *Chr.* 6:41 priests be *c.* with salv.
18:9 king of Israel and Judah *c.*
28:15 *c.* all that were naked
*Est.* 4:2 king's gate *c.* with
*Job* 7:5 my flesh *c.* with worms
10:11 *c.* me with skin and flesh
29:14 righteousness it *c.* me
39:19 *c.* his neck with thunder?
*Ps.* 35:26 be *c.* with sh. 109:29
65:13 pastures *c.* with flocks
93:1 Lord is *c.* with majesty
104:1 thou art *c.* with honor
109:18 *c.* himself with cursing
132:9 priests be *c.* with right.
*Prov.* 31:21 *c.* with scarlet
*Is.* 61:10 *c.* me with garm. of sal.
*Ezek.* 16:10 *c.* thee wi. broidered
*Dan.* 5:29 *c.* Daniel with scarlet
*Zep.* 1:8 *c.* with strange apparel
*Zec.* 3:3 *c.* with filthy garments
*Mat.* 11:8 *c.* in soft, *Luke* 7:25
25:36 and ye *c.* me not, 43
*Mark* 1:6 *c.* with camel's hair
5:15 they see him *c.* *Luke* 8:35
15:17 they *c.* Jesus with purple
*Luke* 16:19 rich man *c.* in purple
2 *Cor.* 5:2 desiring to be *c.* upon
3 if so being *c.* not be naked
1 *Pet.* 5:5 be *c.* with humility
*Rev.* 3:18 that thou mayest be *c.*
10:1 saw angel *c.* with a cloud
11:3 prophesy *c.* in sackcloth
12:1 a woman *c.* with the sun
19:13 was *c.* with vesture

**CLOTHED,** *with* **linen.**
*Ezek.* 9:2 one man was *c.* with *l.*
44:17 shall be *c.* with *l.* garm.
*Dan.* 10:5 certain man *c.* with *l.*
12:6 one said to man *c.* in *linen*
*Rev.* 15:6 *c.* in wh. *l.* 18:16; 19:14

**Shall be CLOTHED.**
*Job* 8:22 *shall be c.* with shame
*Ezek.* 7:27 *s. be c.* with desola.
*Dan.* 5:7 read this writ. *s. be c.*
*Mat.* 6:31 wherewithal *s.* we *b. c.*
*Rev.* 3:5 overcometh *s. be c.* 4:4

**CLOTHES.**
*Gen.* 49:11 his *c.* in blood of gr.
*Ex.* 35:19 *c.* of service, 39:1, 41
*Lev.* 10:6 nor rend your *c.* 21:10
*Deut.* 29:5 *c.* not old, *Neh.* 9:21
1 *Sam.* 19:24 S. stripped off his *c.*
1 *K.* 1:1 covered David with *c.*
2 *K.* 2:12 took own *c.* and rent
2 *Chr.* 34:27 didst rend thy *c.*
*Neh.* 4:23 none of us put off *c.*
*Job* 9:31 my *c.* shall abhor me
*Prov.* 6:27 his *c.* not be burnt
*Ezek.* 16:39 strip thee of *c.* 23:26
*Mat.* 24:18 not return to take *c.*
*Mark* 5:28 If I touch but his *c.* I
15:20 put his own *c.* on him
*Luke* 2:7 in swaddling *c.* 12
8:27 ware no *c.* neither abode
19:36 spread their *c.* in way
24:12 beheld linen *c.* *John* 20:5
*John* 11:44 bound with grave-*c.*
19:40 and wound it in linen *c.*
20:7 napkin not with linen *c.*
*Acts* 7:58 laid their *c.* at S.'s feet
22:23 as they cried, cast off *c.*

**Rent CLOTHES.**
Gen. 37:29 Reuben; 34 Jacob
44:13 Joseph's brethren rent c.
Num. 14:6 Joshua and C. rent c.
Jos. 7:6 Josh.; Jud. 11:35 Jeph.
2 Sam. 3:31 r. c. gird with sack.
1 K. 21:27 Ahab; 2 K. 5:8 king
2 K. 11:14 Atha. 2 Chr. 23:13
19:1 Hezekiah rent c. Is. 37:1
Est. 4:1 Mordecai rent his c.
Mat. 26:65 h.-pr. r. c. Mark 14:63
Acts 14:14 Bar. and Paul rent c.
16:22 magistrates r. off their c.

**CLOTHES rent.**
Lev. 13:45 leper's c. shall be rent
1 Sam. 4:12 came to Shiloh c. r.
2 Sam. 1:2 man from Saul c. r.
13:31 servants stood with c. r.
2 K. 18:37 to Hez. c. r. Is. 36:22
Jer. 41:5 to Mizpah with c. rent

**Wash CLOTHES.**
Ex. 19:10 wash the. c. Num. 8:7
Lev. 11:25 w. his c. 40; 13:6; 14:8, 9, 47; 15:5, 8, 11, 22; 16:26, 28; Num. 19:10, 21; 31:24

**Washed CLOTHES.**
Ex. 19:14 people wash. their c.
Num. 8:21 Levi. washed their c.
2 Sam. 19:24 Mephib. w. not c.

**CLOTHEST.**
Jer. 4:30 though c. with crimson

**CLOTHING.**
Job 22:6 hast stripped nak. of c.
24:7 naked to lodge without c.
31:19 any perish for want of c.
Ps. 35:13 my c. was sackcloth
45:13 king's daughter, her c.
Prov. 27:26 lambs for thy c.
31:22 virtuous wom.'s c. is silk
25 strength and honor her c.
Is. 3:6 thou hast c. be thou ruler
7 for in my house is neither c.
23:18 merchandise be for dur. c.
59:17 garments of veng. for c.
Jer. 10:9 and purple is their c.
Mat. 7:15 sheep's c.; 11:8 soft c.
Mark 12:38 scribes love long c.
Acts 10:30 man stood in bright c.
Jam. 2:3 to him weareth gay c.

**CLOUD.**
Gen. 9:13 set my bow in the c.
Ex. 14:20 it was a c. to them
16:10 glory of L. appeared in c.
19:9 lo, I come in a thick c.
24:15 a c. covered the mount
16 God called to Mos. out of c.
34:5 L. desc. in c. Num. 11:25
40:34 a c. covered tent of cong.
38 c. on tabernacle by day
Lev. 16:2 I will appear in the c.
Num. 9:19 c. tarried long
10:34 c. was upon them by day
1 K. 8:10 c. filled house of Lord, 2 Chr. 5:13; Ezek. 10:4
18:44 a little c. like a man's h.
Job 3:5 that day let c. dwell
22:13 judge through dark c.?
30:15 my welf. passeth as a c.
38:9 I made c. the garment
Ps. 78:14 daytime led with c.
105:39 he spread a c. for a cov.
Prov. 16:15 is as c. of rain
Is. 4:5 create on assemblies a c.
18:4 like a c. of dew in harvest
19:1 Lord rideth upon a swift c.
44:22 as a thick c. thy transgressions, as a c. thy sins
60:8 who are these flee as a c.
Lam. 2:1 dau. of Zion with a c.
3:44 covered thyself with a c.
Ezek 1:4 c. and fire infolding it
28 as appearance of bow in c.
8:11 thick c. of incense went up
10:4 house was filled with the c.
30:18 as for her, a c. cover her
32:7 I will cover sun with a c.
38:9 like c. to cover land, 16
Mat. 17:5 c. ov. Mark 9:7; Luke 9:34 v. out of c. Luke 9:35
Luke 12:54 when ye see a c.
21:27 Son of man coming in c.
Acts 1:9 a c. received him
1 Cor. 10:1 our fathers under c.
2 baptized to Moses in the c.
Heb. 12:1 so great a c. of witn.
Rev. 10:1 angel clothed with a c.
11:12 they ascended in a c.
14:14 white c. on c. 15, 16

**CLOUD abode.**
Ex. 40:35 a c. abode therein
Num. 9:17 c. abode there

**Morning CLOUD.**
Hos. 6:4 goodness as morning c.
13:3 be as m. c. and early dew

**Pillar of CLOUD.**
Ex. 13:21 in a pillar of c.
14:24 on Egyp. through pil. of c.
Num. 12:5 down in pillar of c.
Deut. 31:15 L. app. in p. of c.
Neh. 9:19 the pil. of c. dep. not

**CLOUD taken up.**
Ex. 40:36 c. t. up, Num. 9, 17
37 c. not t. up journeyed not

**CLOUDS.**
Deut. 4:11 c. and thick darkness
Jud. 5:4 c. dropped with water
2 Sam. 22:12 about him thick c.
23:4 as a morning without c.
1 K. 18:45 heaven black with c.
Job 20:6 his head reached to c.
22:14 thick c. covering to him
26:8 bindeth up water in c.
36:29 spreading of c.?
37:16 balancings of the c.?
38:37 number c. in wisdom?
Ps. 36:5 thy faithfulness to c.
57:10 thy truth to the c. 108:4
68:34 his strength is in the c.
77:17 the c. poured out water
78:23 tho' he com. c. from ab.
97:2 c. and darkness about him
104:3 maketh c. his chariot
147:8 covereth heaven with c.
Prov. 3:20 c. drop down
8:28 he established the c.
25:14 c. without rain
Ec. 11:4 reg. c. shall not reap
12:2 nor c. return after rain
Is. 5:6 c. that they rain not
14:14 I will ascend above the c.
Jer. 4:13 he shall come up as c.
Dan. 7:13 S. of man came with c.
Joel 2:2 a day of c. Zep. 1:15
Nah. 1:3 the c. dust of his feet
Zec. 10:1 shall make bright c.
Mat. 24:30 Son of man com. in c. 26:64; Mark 13:26; 14:62
1 Thes. 4:17 caught up in c.
2 Pet. 2:17 they are c. carried
Jude 12 c. they are without wat.
Rev. 1:7 he cometh with c.

**CLOUDY.**
Ex. 33:9 the c. pillar descended
Neh. 9:12 leddest by a c. pillar
Ps. 99:7 he spake in c. pillar
Ezek. 30:3 day of L. near, a c. d.
34:12 been scattered in c. day

**CLOUTED.**
Jos. 9:5 took old shoes and c.

**CLOUTS.**
Jer. 38:11 Ebed. took old cast c.

**CLOVEN.**
Lev. 11:3 c. footed that eat
7 swine c. footed, unclean
Acts 2:3 appeared c. tongues

**CLUSTER.**
Num. 13:23 branch with one c.
Cant. 1:14 as a c. of camphire
Is. 65:8 new wine is found in c.
Mic. 7:1 there is no c. to eat

**CLUSTERS.**
Gen. 40:10 c. bro. forth ripe gr.
Deut. 32:32 their c. are bitter
Cant. 7:7 thy breasts two c. 8
Rev. 14:18 gather c. of vine

**COAL.**
2 Sam. 14:7 quench my c. left
Is. 6:6 ser. hav. live c. in hand
47:14 shall not be c. to warm at
Lam. 4:8 visage blacker than a c.

**COALS.**
Lev. 16:12 take a cen. full of c.
1 K. 19:6 a cake baken on c.
Job 41:21 his breath kindleth c.
Ps. 18:8 c. were kindled by it
12 hailstones and c. of fire
120:4 arrows with c. of juniper
140:10 burning c. fall on them
Prov. 6:28 can one go on hot c.
25:22 c. of fire, Rom. 12:20
26:21 as c. to burning c.
Cant. 8:6 c. thereof are c. of fire
Is. 44:12 smith worketh in c.
19 baked bread on c. thereof
54:16 smith that bloweth the c.
Ezek. 1:13 appearance burning c.
10:2 fill thy hand with c. of fire
24:11 set it empty on the c.
Hab. 3:5 burning c. forth
John 18:18 serv. made fire of c.
21:9 saw fire of c. and fish laid

**COAST.**
Num. 24:24 ships from c. of Chit.
Deut. 11:24 uttermost sea your c.
19:8 if the Lord enlarge thy c.
Jos. 1:4 down of sun be your c.
Jud. 11:20 Is. to pass through c.
1 Sam. 6:9 if it go by his own c.
7:13 no more into c. of Israel
27 1 seek me in any c. of Isr.
30:14 invasion on c. of Judah
2 K. 14:25 Jeroboam restored c.
1 Chr. 4:10 and enlarge my c.
Zep. 2:7 c. for remnant of Judah

**Sea-COAST.**
Ezek. 25:16 dest. remnant of s.-c.
Zep. 2:6 sea-c. dwell. for sheph.
Mat. 4:13 J. dwelt in C. on s.-c.
Luke 6:17 from sea-c. came

**COASTS.**
Deut. 2:4 through c. of your bre.
18:3 divide c. of thy land
1 Sam. 7:14 c. did Israel deliver
11:3 send mess. into all c. 7
2 Sam. 21:5 be destroyed from c.
1 Chr. 21:12 a. destroy. throu. c.
2 Chr. 11:13 to Rehob. out of c.
Ps. 105:31 lice in all their c.
33 he brake trees of their c.
Jer. 25:32 a whirlwind from c.
Ezek. 33:2 take a man of their c.
Joel 3:4 all the c. of Palestine?
Mat. 2:16 H. slew child. in all c.
8:34 out of their c. Mark 5:17
15:21 departed into c. of Tyre
Mark 7:31 dep. from c. of Tyre
Acts 13:50 expelled them out of c.

**COAT.**
Gen. 37:3 c. of many colors, 32
Ex. 28:4 Aaron, a broidered c.
Lev. 8:7 he put on him the c.
16:4 put on the holy linen c.
1 Sam. 2:19 made him a little c.
17:5 Goliah c. of mail, 38
2 Sam. 15:32 Hushai came c. rent
Job 30:18 bindeth as collar of c.
Cant. 5:3 I have put off my c.
Mat. 5:40 take away thy c.
Luke 6:29 forbid not to take c.
John 19:23 c. was without seam
21:7 Peter girt his fisher's c.

**COATS.**
Gen. 3:21 God made c. of skins
Lev. 8:13 put c. upon A.'s sons
10:5 their c. out of camp

*Dan.* 3:21 were bound in their c.
27 nor were their c. changed
*Mat.* 10:10 neither provide two c.
*Mark* 6:9 and put not on two c.
*Luke* 3:11 hath two c. impart
*Acts* 9:39 c. which Dorcas made

### COCK.

*Mat.* 26:34 c. crow, 75; *Mark* 14:30, 72; *Luke* 22:34, 61
74 c. crew, *Lu.* 22:60; *John* 18:27
*Mark* 13:35 cometh at c. crowing
14:68 and the c. crew, 72
*John* 13:38 c. not crow till thou hast denied me thrice

### COCKATRICE, S.

*Is.* 11:8 put his hand on c. den
14:29 of serpent's root come c.
59:5 they hatch c. eggs
*Jer.* 8:17 will send c. among you

### COCKLE.

*Job* 31:40 c. grow inst. of barley

### COFFER.

1 *Sam.* 6:8 put jewels in a c.
11 laid the c. on the cart

### COFFIN.

*Gen.* 50:26 Joseph was put in a c.

### COGITATIONS.

*Dan.* 7:28 c. much troubled me

### COLD.

*Gen.* 8:22 c. and heat not cease
*Job* 24:7 naked no covering in c.
37:9 c. cometh out of north
*Ps.* 147:17 stand before his c.?
*Prov.* 20:4 not plough by re. of c.
25:13 as c. of snow in harvest
20 taketh away garment in c.
25 c. waters to a thirsty soul
*Jer.* 18:14 c. water be forsaken?
*Nah.* 3:17 in hedges in c. day
*Mat.* 10:42 a cup of c. water
24:12 love of many wax c.
*John* 18:18 a fire, for it was c.
*Acts* 28:2 received us, bec. of c.
2 *Cor.* 11:27 in c. and nakedness
*Rev.* 3:15 neither c. nor hot, 16

### COLLAR, S.

*Jud.* 8:26 jewels beside c.
*Job* 30:18 disease bindeth as c.

### COLLECTION.

2 *Chr.* 24:6 to bring in the c. 9
1 *Cor.* 16:1 conc. c. for saints

### COLLEGE.

2 *K.* 22:14 in c. 2 *Chr.* 34:22

### COLLOPS.

*Job* 15:27 c. of fat on his flanks

### COLONY.

*Acts* 16:12 and a c.

### COLOR, S.

*Gen.* 37:3 a coat of many c.
*Num.* 11:7 the c. as bdellium
*Jud.* 5:30 a prey of divers c.
2 *Sam.* 13:18 garm. of divers c.
1 *Chr.* 29:2 stones of divers c.
*Is.* 54:11 lay stones with fair c.
*Prov.* 23:31 giveth his c. in cup
*Ezek.* 1:4 midst as c. of amber
7 like c. of brass, *Dan.* 10:6
16 like c. of beryl, *Dan.* 10:9
22 firmament as c. of crystal
16:16 places with divers c.
17:3 eagle with divers c. to L.

COLOSSE. *Col.* 1:2

### COLT, S.

*Gen.* 32:15 thirty camels with c.
49:11 binding ass's c. to vine
*Jud.* 10:4 thirty s. rode on 30 c.
12:14 Abdon's sons ro. on 70 c.
*Job* 11:12 man be born like c.
*Zec.* 9:9 riding upon a c. *Mat.* 21:5; *John* 12:15
*Mat.* 21:2 find an ass tied, a c. *Mark* 11:2; *Luke* 19:30
7 brought ass and c. *Mark* 11:7
*Mark* 11:5 loos. c.? *Luke* 19:33
*Luke* 19:35 cast their garm. on c.

### COME.

*Gen.* 26:27 wherefore c. ye to me
42:7 whence c. ye? *Jos.* 9:8
49:10 sceptre until Shiloh c.
*Num.* 10:29 c. thou with us
24:19 out of Jacob shall c. he that shall have dominion
*Deut.* 18:6 if a L. c. with desire
1 *Sam.* 2:34 c. on thy two sons
10:8 thou shalt tarry till I c.
17:45 I c. to thee in name of L.
20:21 then c. there is peace
2 *Sam.* 19:33 c. thou over
2 *K.* 5:8 let him c. now to me
18:32 till I c. *Is.* 36:17
1 *Chr.* 29:14 all things c. of thee
*Job* 13:13 let c. on me what will
14:14 wait till my change c.
21 his sons c. to honor
37:13 to c. for correction
38:11 hitherto shalt thou c.
*Ps.* 40:7 lo, I c. *Heb.* 10:7, 9

*Ps.* 42:2 when shall I c. and app.
50:3 our God shall c. and not
65:2 unto thee shall all flesh c.
80:2 and c. and save us
86:9 all nations shall c.
101:2 when wilt thou c. to me
109:17 loved cursing, so let it c.
119:41 let thy mercies c. 77
*Ec.* 9:2 all things c. alike
*Cant.* 2:10 love, c. away, 13
*Is.* 13:5 c. from a far country
6 day of L. c. as destruction
21:12 inquire ye, return, c.
26:20 c. my people, enter
35:4 your G. will c. with veng.
40:10 will c. with strong hand
41:25 raised up one, he shall c.
44:7 things coming, and shall c.
45:20 assem. and c. draw near
24 even to him shall men c.
51:11 redeemed shall c. to Z.
55:1 c. ye to the waters, c. ye
3 c. unto me, hear
59:20 Redeemer shall c. to Z.
60:3 Gentiles c. to thy light, 5
66:15 Lord will c. with fire
*Jer.* 2:31 will c. no more to thee
3:22 we c. to thee
13:22 wherefore c. these things
17:15 word of Lord? let it c.
40:4 seem good to c. if ill to c.
46:18 as Carmel so shall he c.
49:4 who shall c. unto me?
*Lam.* 1:4 none c. to solemn fea.
*Ezek.* 21:27 till he c. whose right
33:31 c. to thee as the people
33 it will c. then shall know
36:8 they are at hand to c.
*Hos.* 6:1 c. let us return to Lord
3 he shall c. to us as the rain
10:12 time to seek L. till he c.
*Joel* 1:15 as destruction sh. it c.
2:31 be. terrible day of Lord c.
*Hab.* 2:3 it will c. and not tarry
*Zec.* 1:21 what c. these to do?
14:5 God shall c. and all saints
*Mal.* 3:1 the Lord ye seek shall c.

*Mat.* 2:6 out of thee c. Governor
6:10 thy kingdom c. *Luke* 11:2
8:9 c. and he cometh, *Luke* 7:8
11 many shall c. from the east
11:3 he that sh. c.? *Luke* 7:19, 20
28 c. all ye that labor
16:24 if any man will c. after me
17:10 Elias must first c.? 11
24:14 then shall the end c.
42 know not hour Lord doth c.
25:34 c. ye blessed of my Father
*Mark* 8:34 if any will c. after me, *Luke* 9:23; 14:27
10:14 child. to c. *Luke* 18:16
*Luke* 10:1 place whither he w. c.
17:20 when kingdom should c.
19:13 occupy till I c.
22:18 till king. of God shall c.
*John* 1:39 he saith, c. and see
3:26 baptizeth, and all men c.
5:14 lest worse thing c. to thee
40 ye will not c. to me that ye
6:37 F. giveth shall c. to me
44 no man can c. except F. 65
7:34 I am, thither ye cannot c.
37 if any man thirst, let him c.
8:14 ye cannot tell whence I c.
13:19 before it c. that when c.
14:18 I will c. unto you
23 and we will c. unto him
17:11 I c. to thee, 13
21:22 I will he tarry till I c. 23
*Acts* 1:11 this Jesus shall so c. as
2:20 before great day of Lord c.
8:24 pray none of these things c.
9:38 he would not delay to c.
13:40 lest that c. upon you
16:9 c. over into Macedonia
19:4 believe on him should c.
26:22 Moses did say should c.
*Rom.* 3:8 do evil th. good may c.
1 *Cor.* 4:5 judg nothing till L. c.
11:26 show L.'s death till he c
34 will I set in order when I c.
2 *Cor.* 1:15 I was minded to c.
12:20 for I fear, lest when I c.
2 *Thes.* 1:10 shall c. to be glori.
2:3 except c. a falling away
1 *Tim.* 4:8 life now is, and to c.
2 *Tim.* 4:3 time will c. they will
*Heb.* 4:16 c. boldly to throne.
7:25 able to save them c. to God
10:37 he that shall c. will c.
*Rev.* 2:5 else I will c. quickly
25 ye have, hold fast till I c.
3:11 I c. quickly, 22:7, 20
6:1 saying, c. and see, 3, 5, 7
22:17 and let him athirst c.

### COME again.

*Gen.* 28:21 so that I c. *ag.*
*Ex.* 14:26 waters c. a. on E.
*Jud.* 8:9 I c. a. in peace
13:8 let man of God c. *again*
1 *K.* 2:41 Shimei was c. *again*
12:5 thr. d. and c. a. 2 *Chr.* 10:5
17:21 let this child's soul c. a.
*Ps.* 126:6 he shall c. *again*
*Prov.* 3:28 say not, Go and c. a
*Luke* 10:35 I c. *ag.* will repay
*John* 14:3 I will c. *aga.* and rec.
28 I go away, and c. a.
2 *Cor.* 2:1 not c. a. in heaviness
12:21 I c. a. God will humble
13:2 if I c. a. I will not spare

### COME down.

*Gen.* 45:9 saith Jos. c. d. to me
*Ex.* 3:8 I am c. d. to deliver
19:11 Lord will c. d. on Sinai
*Num.* 11:17 I will c. d. and talk
*Deut.* 28:24 it shall c. d.
*Jud.* 7:24 c. d. against Midian.
1 *Sam.* 23:11 S. c. d.? will c. d:
20 c. d. according to desire
2 *K.* 1:4 not c. d. from, 6, 16
9 thou man of God c. *down*
*Neh.* 6:3 I cannot c. d.
*Ps.* 7:16 c. d. on his own pate
72:6 shall c. *down* like rain
144:5 bow thy heavens and c. d.
*Is.* 47:1 c. *down* O virgin
64:1 that thou wouldst c. d.
*Jer.* 13:18 principali. shall c. d.
21:13 who shall c. d. ag. us?
48:18 c. *down* from thy glory
*Ezek.* 26:16 prin. of sea shall c. d.
30:6 pride of power shall c. d.
*Joel* 3:11 thy mighty ones to c. d.
*Mat.* 24:17 on house-top not c. d.
27:40 c. d. fr. cr. 42; *Mark* 15:30
*Luke* 19:5 J. said, Zaccheus c. d.

*John* 4:49 *c. down* ere child die

**COME forth.**

*Gen.* 15:4 *c. f.* of thy bowels
1 *Sam.* 14:11 Hebrews *c. f.*
1 *K.* 2:30 saith the king, *c. forth*
2 *K.* 10:25 slay, let none *c. forth*
*Job* 23:10 I shall *c. f.* as gold
*Ps.* 17:2 let my sentence *c. f.*
88:8 I cannot *c. forth*
*Ec.* 7:18 feareth God shall *c. f.*
*Is.* 11:1 *c. f.* rod out stem of J.
48:1 art *c. forth* of waters of J.
*Jer.* 46:9 let mighty men *c. forth*
*Ezek.* 21:19 twain *c. forth*
*Dan.* 3:26 ye serv. of God, *c. f.*
*Joel* 3:18 a fountain shall *c. forth*
*Mic.* 5:2 out of thee *c. forth* ruler
*Mat.* 15:18 *c. f.* from heart
*Mark* 9:29 *c. f.* by prayer
*Luke* 12:37 will *c. f.* and serve
*John* 5:20 *c. f.* they done good
11:43 he cried, Lazarus, *c. forth*
*Acts* 7:7 shall *c. f.* and serve me

**COME hither.**

*Gen* 15:16 the fourth gen. *c. h.*
*Jud.* 16:2 Samson *c. hither*
1 *Sam.* 10:22 man should *c. h.*
16:11 not sit down till he *c. h.*
2 *Sam.* 20:16 say to Joab, *c.h.*
*Prov.* 25:7 bet. be said, *c.* up *h.*
*Dan.* 3:26 servants of G. *c. h.*
*John* 4:16 call husband and *c. h.*
*Acts* 17:6 turned world, are *c. h.*
*Rev.* 4:1 *c.* up *hither* 11:12; 17:1; 21:9

**COME in *or* into.**

*Gen.* 19:31 not a man to *c. in*
24:31 *c. in* thou blessed of Lord
*Num.* 27:21 his word shall *c. in*
*Deut.* 31:2 I can no more *c. in*
*Jos.* 14:11 my strength to *c. in*
1 *K.* 1:14 I will *c. in* after thee
3:7 I know not how to *c. in* or
14:6 *c. in* thou wife of Jeroboam
15:17 any to go out or *c. in*
2 *K.* 4:4 when *c. in*, shut door
11:9 each his men to *c. in* and
2 *Chr.* 1:10 and *c. in* before peo.
16:1 none go out or *c. in* to A.
23:6 *c. into* house, save priests
*Neh.* 2:7 till I *c. into* Judah
*Est.* 6:5 said, let Haman *c. in*
*Ps.* 24:7 king of glory *c. in*, 9
69:1 for the waters are *c. in*
96:8 and *c. into* his courts
*Is.* 19:1 Lord shall *c. into* Egypt
19:23 Assyrian sh. *c. into* E.
24:10 no man *c. in*
*Jer.* 17:19 kings of Judah *c. in*
51:50 Jerus. *c. into* your mind
*Mic.* 5:5 Assyrian shall *c. into*
*Mat.* 16:27 Son of man sh. *c. in*
24:5 many sh. *c. in* my name, *Mark* 13:6; *Luke* 21:8
25:31 Son of man shall *c. in*
*Luke* 11:33 wh. *c. in* may see
*Luke* 12:46 *c. in* a d. ne look. n.
14:23 compel them to *c. in*
*John* 5:43 I am *c. in* my Father's name, if another shall *c.*
6:14 prophet, that sh. *c.* 11:27
*Acts* 16:15 *c. into* my house
*Rom.* 11:25 fulness of G. be *c. in*
1 *Cor.* 14:23 *c. in* those unlearned
24 if *c. in* one believeth not
*Jam.* 2:2 there *c. in* a poor man
*Rev.* 3:20 *c. in* to him, and sup

**COME near.**

*Gen.* 20:4 Abime. had not *c. n.*
*Ex.* 16:9, say *c. n.* bef. the L.
*Num.* 16:5 cause him to *c. near*
1 *Sam.* 10:20 tribes to *c. near*
*Ps.* 32:9 lest they *c. n.* thee
119:169 let my cry *c. near* thee
*Is.* 41:1 *c. near* to judgment
48:16 *c.* ye *near* hear ye this
50:8 mine adversary? *c. near*
*Ezek.* 40:46 *c. near* to L. to min
44:15 *c. near* to me to minister
*Mal.* 3:5 *c. near* to you to judg.
*Luke* 19:41 *c. near* he beheld city
*Acts* 23:15 or ever he *c. near*

**COME nigh.**

*Ex.* 34:30 were afraid to *c. n.*
*Lev.* 10:3 he sanc. in all *c. nigh*
*Luke* 10:9 kingdom of G. *c. n.* 11

**COME not.**

*Ex.* 24:2 they shall *not c.* nigh
*Num.* 16:12 we will *n. c.* up, 14
*Jos.* 3:4 *c. not* near unto ark
23:7 ye *c. not* among nations
2 *Sam.* 14:29 Joab would *not c.*
2 *K.* 19:32 king of Assyria *not c.* into city, 33; *Is.* 37:33, 34
2 *Chr.* 35:21 I *c. not* against thee
*Ezr.* 10:8 *not c.* within
*Job* 13:16 hypocrite *n. c.* before
*Ps.* 32:6 they shall *not c.*
69:27 let them *not c.* into
91:7 it shall *not c.* nigh thee
*Prov.* 5:8 *c. not* nigh door of h.
*Is.* 7:17 L. shall bring days *not c.*
32:10 gathering shall *not c.*
54:14 terror shall *not c.* near
65:5 which say, *c. not* near me
*Ezek.* 16:16 things shall *not c.*
*Hos.* 4:15 *c. not* ye unto Gilgal
9:4 soul shall *n. c.* into house
*Zec.* 14:18 if fam. of E. *c. not*
*Mat.* 22:3 and they would *not c.*
*Mark* 2:4 *not c.* for pr. *Luke* 8:19
*Luke* 14:20 married, I *cannot c.*
*John* 5:24 *not c.* into condemn.
40 *not c.* that ye might
7:34 thither ye *cannot c.* 36
15:22 if I had *not c.* not had sin
16:7 the Comforter will *not c.*
1 *Cor.* 4:18 as tho. I would *not c.*

**COME out.**

*Gen.* 15:14 *c. o.* with substance
17:6 kings *c. out* of thee, 35:11
*Num.* 11:20 it *c. out* at nostrils
12:4 *c. out* ye three to taberna.
22:5 people *c. out* of Egypt, 11
*Deut.* 28:7 *c. out* one way
*Jud.* 9:29 in. army and *c. out*
1 *Sam.* 11:3 to mor. will *c. out*, 10
24:14 after whom is king *c. out?*
2 *Sam.* 16:7 *c. out*, bloody man
1 *K.* 6:1 480th year after Isr. *c. o.*
20:17 men *c. out* of Samaria
2 *K.* 5:11 he will *c. out* to me
18:31 agree. and *c. out*, *Is.* 36:16
*Ps.* 14:7 O that salva. *c. out* of Z.
68:31 princes shall *c. out* of E.
*Nah.* 1:11 one *c. out* imagineth
*Mat.* 5:26 *c. out* till thou hast
26:55 are ye *c. out* as ag. a thief? *Mark* 14:48; *Luke* 22:52
*Mark* 1:25 *c. o.* of him, *Luke* 4:35
5:8 *c. out* unclean, *Luke* 8:29
*John* 1:46 any good *c. out* of N.
7:41 Christ *c. out* of Galilee?
*Acts* 16:18 to *c. out* of her
*Rom.* 11:26 *c. out* of Zion Deliv.
2 *Cor.* 6:17 *c. out* from among
*Heb.* 7:5 *c. out* of loins of Abra.
*Rev.* 16:13 spirits *c. out* of drag.
18:4 *c. out* of her, my people

**COME to pass.**

*Num.* 11:23 my word *c. to p.*
*Deut.* 13:2 wonder *c. to pass*
*Jos.* 23:14 all *c. to pass*
*Jud.* 13:12 M. said, words *c. to p.*
21:3 why is this *c. to pass*
1 *K.* 13:32 saying shall *c. to pass*
*Is.* 7:7 not stand, nor *c. to p.*
14:24 so shall it *c. to p.*
42:9 former things are *c. to p.*
*Jer.* 32:24 has spoken is *c. to p.*
*Ezek.* 12:25 I speak shall *c. to p.*
24:14 spoken, it shall *c. to p.*
*Dan.* 2:29 what shall *c. to p.*
*Zec.* 6:15 this shall *c. to p.*
7:13 *c. to pass* that as he cried
*Mat.* 24:6 these must *c. to pass*
*Mark* 11:23 th. he saith sh. *c. to p*
13:29 see these things *c. to p.*
*Luke* 2:15 see this thing *c. to p.*
21:7 when these *c. to pass?* 28
24:12 wond. at what was *c. to p.*
18 not known things *c. to pass*
*John* 13:19 *c. to p.* may b. 14:29
*Rev.* 1:1 must shortly *c. to pass*

**COME short.**

*Rom.* 3:23 all *c. sh.* of glory of G.
*Heb.* 4:1 seem to *c. short* of it

**COME together**

*Job* 9:32 should *c. t.* in judgment
19:12 troops *c. t.* against me
*Jer.* 3:18 *c. t.* out of land of north
50:4 Israel and Judah shall *c. t.*
*Acts* 1:6 wh. they were *c. t.* 28:17
10:27 he found many *c. together*
19:32 knew not wherefore *c. t.*
21:22 multitude must needs *c. t.*
1 *Cor.* 7:5 *c. together* again,
11:17 you *c. t.* not for the better
18 when ye *c. t.* 20, 33; 14:26
34 ye *c.* not *t.* to condemna.
14:23 if whole church be *c. t.*

**COME up.**

*Ex.* 19:24 *c. up* thou and Aaron
24:12 *c. up* to me into mount
33:5 I will *c. up* in a moment
34:3 no man shall *c. up* with
*Num.* 20:5 why *c. up* out of E.
*Jos.* 10:6 *c. up* to us quickly
*Jud.* 1:3 Jud. said *c. up* with me
15:10 why are ye *c. up* ag. us?
16:18 Del. sent, *c. up* this once
1 *Sam.* 14:10 if they say *c. up*
17:25 seen man that is *c. up?*
1 *K.* 1:35 then *c. up* after him
20:22 will *c. up* against thee
2 *K.* 18:25 am I *c. u. Is.* 36:10
*Job* 7:9 to grave *c. up* no more
*Prov* 25:7 better said, *c. up*
*Is.* 8:7 *c. up* over his channels
14:8 no feller is *c. up* against us
60:7 *c. up* with acceptance
*Jer.* 49:19 he shall *c. up*, 50:44
22 shall *c. up* and fly as eagle
*Ezek.* 38:16 *c. up* aga. my people
*Hos.* 1:11 shall *c. up* out of land
13:15 wind of the L. shall *c. up*
*Ob.* 21 saviors shall *c. up* on Z.
*Zec.* 14:17 whose will not *c. up*
18 if family of Egypt *c.* not *up*
*Acts* 8:31 Philip to *c. up* and sit
10:4 Cornel. the alms are *c. up*
*Rev.* 4:1 *c. up* hither, 11:12

**COME, *passive.***

*Gen.* 6:13 the end of all flesh is *c.*
18:5 are ye *c.* to your servant
21 accord. to cry wh. *c.* to me
*Ex.* 3:9 cry of Israel is *c.* to me
*Num.* 22:11 there is a people *c.*
*Jos.* 5:14 as captain am I *c.*
*Jud* 16:2 Samson is *c.* hither
1 *Sam.* 4:7 G. is *c.* into the camp
9:16 bec. their cry is *c.* to me
2 *K.* 8:7 man of God is *c.* hither
*Ezr.* 9:13 after all that is *c.*
*Job* 3:25 thing I feared is *c.* 4:5
*Ps.* 44:17 all this is *c.* on us, yet
53:6 O that salvation were *c.*
55:5 fear. and trembling are *c.*
69:2 I am *c.* into deep waters
102:13 yea, the set time is *c.*
*Is.* 10:28 he is *c.* to Aiath
56:1 my salvation near to *c.*
60:1 shine, for thy light is *c.*
63:4 year of my redeemed is *c.*
*Jer.* 40:3 theref. this is *c.* on you
50:27 their day is *c.*
31 thy day is *c.* I will visit thee
51:13 on waters, thy end is *c.*

*Lam.* 4:18 our end is *c.*
5:1 rememb. what is *c.* upon us
*Ezek.* 7:2 an end is *c.* on land, 6
7 the morning is *c,* upon thee
10 day. behold it is *c.* 39:8
21:25 whose day is *c.* 29
*Dan.* 9:13 all this evil is *c.* on us
*Amos* 8:2 the end is *c.* on Israel
*Mic.* 1:9 *c.* to gate of my people
*Mat.* 12:28 kingdom of God is *c.*
18:11 Son of man is *c.* to save
*Mark* 14:41 hour is *c.*
*Luke* 19:10 *c.* to seek and to save
*John* 4:25 is *c.* he will tell us all
11:28 Master is *c.* and calleth
12:23 J. answ. the hour is *c.* 17:1
1 *Cor.* 13:10 when that perf. is *c.*
*Col.* 1:6 which gospel is *c.* to y.
1 *John* 4:3 that confesseth n. C. is *c.* in the flesh, 2 *John* 7
1 *John* 5:20 we k. Son of G. is *c.*

**I am COME,** *or* **am I COME**
*Ex.* 18:6 *I* Jethro *am c.* to thee
*Num.* 22:38 Bal. said, lo, *I am c.*
2 *Sam.* 14:32 *am I c.* fr. Gesh.?
*Ps.* 69:2 *I am c.* into deep wat.
*Ec.* 1:16 lo, *I am c.*
*Dan.* 9:23 *I am c.* to show, 10:14
10:12 *I am c.* for thy words
*Mat.* 5:17 *I am c.* to destroy law
9:13 *I am* not *c.* to call right.
10:34 not *I am c.* to send peace
35 *I am c.* to set at variance
*Luke* 12:51 *I am c.* to give peace?
*John* 1:31 therefore *am I c.*
5:43 *I am c.* in my F.'s name
7:28 *I am* not *c.* of myself
9:39 for judgment *I am c.*
10:10 *I am c.* th. might ha. life
12:46 *I am c.* a light into world
16:28 *I am c.* again I leave wor.

**COME,** *joined with* **Time.**
*Gen.* 30:33 answer in *t.* to *c.*
*Ex.* 13:14 asketh in *time* to *c.* *Deut.* 6:20; *Jos.* 4:6, 21
*Ps.* 102:13 the set *time* is *c.*
*Prov.* 31:25 rejoice in *t.* to *c.*
*Cant.* 2:12 *t.* of sing. of birds *c.*
*Is.* 13:22 her *time* is near to *c.*
30:8 be for *time* to *c.*
42:23 will hear for *time* to *c.*?
*Ezek.* 7:7 *t.* is *c.* 12; *Hag.* 1:2 not *c.*
*Luke* 9:51 *t. c.* he sh. be received
*Gal.* 4:4 when fulness of *t.* w. *c.*
1 *Tim.* 6:19 founda. aga. *t.* to *c.*
1 *Pet.* 4:17 *t.* is *c.* judgm. must b.

**Yet COME.**
*Deut.* 12:9 not *yet c.* to the rest
*John* 2:4 my hour is not *yet c.*
7:6 my time is not *yet c.*
30 hour was not *yet c.* 88:20
11:30 J. was not *y. c.* into town
*Rev.* 17:10 the other is not *yet c.*

**COMELINESS.**
*Is.* 53:2 hath no form nor *c.*
*Ezek.* 16:14 perfect through my *c.*
27:10 they of Lud set fo. thy *c.*
*Dan.* 10:8 my *c.* into corruption
1 *Cor.* 12:23 more abundant *c.*

**COMELY.**
1 *Sam.* 16:18 David a *c.* person
*Job* 41:12 con. his *c.* proportion
*Ps.* 33:1 praise is *c.* for, 147:1
*Prov.* 30:29 four are *c.* in going
*Ec.* 5:18 it is *c.* for one to eat
*Cant.* 1:5 I am black, but *c.*
10 cheeks are *c.* with jewels
2:14 thy countenance is *c*
4:3 thy speech is *c.*
6:4 art *c.* O my love, as Jerus.
*Is.* 4:2 the fruit shall be *c.*
*Jer.* 6:2 daugh. of Zion to a *c.* w.
1 *Cor.* 7:35 I speak for that *c.*
12:24 *c.* parts have no need

**COMERS.**
*Heb.* 10:1 *c.* thereunto perfect

**COMEST.**
*Deut.* 28:6 blessed when thou *c.*
19 cursed when thou *c.* in
*Jud.* 17:9 Mic. said, whence *c.*
19:17 old man said, whence *c.*
1 *Sam.* 16:4 *c.* peacea.? 1 *K.* 2:13
17:45 thou *c.* to me w. a sword
2 *K.* 5:25 whence *c.* th. Gehazi?
*Job* 1:7 whence *c.* thou? 2:2
*Jon.* 1:8 whence *c.* thou?
*Mat.* 3:14 and *c.* thou to me?
*Luke* 23:42 wh. *c.* into thy king.

**COMETH.**
*Deut.* 23:13 that *c.* from thee
1 *Sam.* 4:3 when ark *c.*
9:6 all he saith *c.* surely to pass
20:29 he *c.* not to king's table
*Job* 28:20 wh. then *c.* wisdom?
*Ps.* 30:5 but joy *c.* in morning
75:6 promotion *c.* not from east
96:13 for he *c.* to judge
118:26 blessed is he *c.* in name
121:2 my help *c.* from the Lord
*Ec.* 6:4 he *c.* in with vanity
*Cant.* 2:8 he *c.* leaping on mou.
*Is.* 13:9 day of L. *c.* with wrath
30:27 name of L. *c.* from far
62:11 Zion thy salvation *c.*
63:1 who is this *c.* from Edom
*Jer.* 17:6 not see when good *c.*
43:11 *c.* he shall smite Egypt
*Lam.* 3:37 and it *c.* to pass
*Ezek.* 20:32 *c.* in your mind
21:7 because it *c.* behold it *c*
24:24 when this *c.* kn. I am L.
33:31 they come as people *c.*
33 when this *c.* to pass, then
*Dan.* 12:12 *c.* to 1,335 days
*Joel* 2:1 day of L. *c.* *Zec.* 14:1; *Thes.* 5:2
*Mal.* 4:1 day *c.* that shall burn
*Mat.* 3:11 he that *c.* after is mig. *Mark* 1:7; *Luke* 3:16
5:37 more than these *c.* of evil
8:9 come, and he *c.* *Luke* 7:8
21:5 thy king *c.* *John* 12:15
9 ble. is he *c.* in name of Lord, *Mark* 11:9; *Luke* 13:35; 19:38
25:19 after long time Lord *c.*
*Mark* 8:38 when he *c.* in glory
9:12 Elias *c.* first and restoreth
14:43 while he spake *c.* Judas
*Luke* 6:47 whoso *c.* to me, and
12:37 he *c.* shall find watching
40 *c.* at an hour ye think not
43 when he *c.* shall find
55 will be heat, and it *c.*
17:20 *c.* not with observation
18:8 *c.* shall he find faith
*John* 3:8 canst not tell wh. it *c.*
20 nor *c.* to the light
4:21 woman, hour *c.* 23; 16:32
6:35 *c.* to me never hunger, 37
45 learned of Father, *c.* to me
7:27 C. *c.* no man knoweth, 31
42 Christ *c.* of seed of David
9:4 night *c.* no man can work
14:6 no man *c.* to Father but
16:32 hour *c.* ye shall be scat.
*Acts* 10:32 when he *c.* shall speak
1 *Cor.* 15:24 then *c.* the end
2 *Cor.* 11:28 beside wh. *c.* on me
1 *Thes.* 5:2 day of L. *c.* as a thief
*Heb.* 11:6 *c.* to G. must believe
*Jude* 14 L. *c.* with 10,000 saints
*Rev.* 1:7 he *c.* with clouds
17:10 *c.* continue a short space

**COMETH down.**
*Is.* 55:10 rain *c. d.* from heaven
*John* 6:33 he *c. down,* 50
*Jam.* 1:17 every good gift *c. d.*
*Rev.* 3:12 new Jeru. which *c. d.*

**COMETH forth.**
*Ex.* 4:14 *c. forth* to meet thee
*Jud.* 11:31 *c. forth* of doors
1 *Sam.* 11:7 *c.* not *f.* after S.
*Job* 5:6 affliction *c.* not *forth*
14:2 he *c. forth* like a flower
*Is.* 28:29 this also *c. forth*
*Ezek.* 33:30 what word *c. forth*
*Mic.* 1:3 L. *c. f.* out of his place

**COMETH nigh.**
*Num.* 1:51 stranger that *c. n.* be put to death, 3:10, 38; 18:7

**COMETH out.**
*Deut.* 28:57 young one *c. out*
*Is.* 26:21 Lord *c. out* of his place
42:5 earth, and what *c. out*
*Mat.* 15:11 *c. out* of mouth, this defileth a man, *Mark* 7:20

**COMETH up.**
1 *Sam.* 28:14 an old man *c. up*
*Cant.* 8:5 *c.* up. from wilderness?
*Jer.* 46:7 that *c. up* as a flood?
50:3 out of north *c. up* a nation

**COMFORT.**
*Job* 6:10 then should I yet have *c.*
10:20 alone that I may take *c.*
*Ps.* 119:50 my *c.* in affliction
76 let kindness be for my *c.*
*Is.* 57:6 sh. I receive *c.* in these?
*Ezek.* 16:54 thou art a *c.* to them
*Mat.* 9:22 be of good *c.* *Luke* 8:48
*Mark* 10:49 be of g. *c.* he calleth
*Acts* 9:31 walking in *c.* of H. G.
*Rom.* 15:4 *c.* of the scriptures
1 *Cor.* 14:3 speaketh to ex. and *c.*
2 *Cor.* 1:3 blessed be God of all *c.*
4 *c.* wherewith we are comfort.
7:4 I am filled with *c.*
13 were comforted in your *c.*
13:11 brethren, be of good *c.*
*Phil.* 2:1 if any *c.* of love
19 of good *c.* when I know
*Col.* 4:11 been *c.* to me

**COMFORT, Verb.**
*Gen.* 5:29 *c.* us concerning work
18:5 *c.* ye your hearts
27:42 Esau doth *c.* himself
37:35 sons rose to *c.* him
*Jud.* 19:5 *c.* heart with bread. 8
2 *Sam.* 10:2 David sent to *c.* him
1 *Chr.* 7:22 came to *c.* him
*Job* 2:11 friends came to *c.* him
7:13 say, My bed shall *c.* me
9:27 if I say, I will *c.* myself
21:34 how then *c.* ye me in vain
*Ps.* 23:4 thy staff, they *c.* me
71:21 shalt *c.* me on every side
119:82 when wilt thou *c.* me?
*Cant.* 2:5 *c.* me with apples
*Is.* 22:4 labor not to *c.* me
40:1 *c.* ye, *c.* ye my people
*Is.* 51:3 L. shall *c.* Zion, *c.* was.
19 by whom shall I *c.* thee?
61:2 to *c.* all that mourn
66:13 so will I *c.* you in Jeru.
*Jer.* 8:18 when I would *c.* myself
16:7 nor men tear to *c.* them
31:13 I will *c.* and make rejoice
*Lam.* 1:2 hath none to *c.* her, 17
21 there is none to *c.* me
2:13 equal, that I may *c.* thee?
*Ezek.* 14:23 *c.* when ye see ways
*Zec.* 1:17 Lord shall yet *c.* Zion
10:2 they *c.* in vain
*John* 11:19 to *c.* them concerning
2 *Cor.* 1:4 may be able to *c.* them
2:7 ye ought rather to comfort
*Eph.* 6:22 might *c.* your hearts
*Col.* 4:8 and *c.* your hearts
1 *Thes.* 3:2 to *c.* you conc. faith
4:18 *c.* one another
5:11 wherefore *c.* yourselves
14 *c.* the feeble-minded
2 *Thes.* 2:17 L. J. *c.* your hearts

**COMFORTABLE.**
2 *Sam.* 14:17 w. of L. now be *c.*
*Zec.* 1:13 L. answ. with *c.* words

**COMFORTABLY.**
2 *Sam.* 19:7 speak *c.* to thy serv.
2 *Chr.* 30:22 spake *c.* to Levites
32:6 set captains, and spake *c.*
*Is.* 40:2 speak ye *c.* to Jerusalem
*Hos.* 2:14 I will speak *c.* to her

**COMFORTED.**
*Gen.* 24:67 Isaac was *c.*
37:35 Jacob refused to be *c.*
38:12 Judah was *c.*
50:21 Joseph *c.* his brethren
*Ruth* 2:13 for hast *c.* me
2 *Sam.* 12:24 David *c.* Bath-sheba
13:39 he was *c.* concerning A.
*Job* 42:11 brethren *c.* him.
*Ps.* 77:2 my soul refused to be *c.*
86:17 bec. thou L. hast *c.* me
119:52 and have *c.* myself
*Is.* 49:13 God *c.* his people, 52:9
54:11 Oh thou afflicted, not *c.*
66:13 shall be *c.* in Jerusalem
*Jer.* 31:15 Rachel refused to be *c.*
*Ezek.* 5:13 fury to rest, I w. be *c.*
14:22 be *c.* concerning
31:16 all that drink water be *c.*
32:31 Pharaoh shall be *c.*
*Mat.* 2:18 not be *c.* bec. were not
5:4 mourn, for they shall be *c.*
*Luke* 16:25 he is *c.* thou torm.
*John* 11:31 the Jews which *c.* her
*Acts* 16:40 seen brethren, *c.* them
20:12 brought man alive, were *c.*
*Rom.* 1:12 I may be *c.* with you
1 *Cor.* 14:31 and all be *c.*
2 *Cor.* 1:4 we are *c.* of God
7:6 God *c.* us by coming of Titus
7 consola. wh. he was *c.* in you
13 we are *c.* in your comfort
*Col.* 2:2 hearts be *c.* being knit
1 *Thes.* 2:11 know how he *c.* you
3:7 we were *c.* in our affliction

**COMFORTEDST.**
*Is.* 12:1 and thou *c.* me.

**COMFORTER, S.**
2 *Sam.* 10:3 sent *c.* 1 *Chr.* 19:3
*Job* 16:2 miserable *c.* are ye all
*Ps.* 69:20 I looked for *c.* but
*Ec.* 4:1 oppressed, had no *c.*
*Lam.* 1:9 she had no *c.*
16 *c.* that should relieve is far
*Nah.* 3:7 whence shall I seek *c.*
*John* 14:16 give you another *C.*
26 *C.* which is the Holy Ghost
15:26 when the *C.* is come
16:7 *C.* will not come

**COMFORTETH.**
*Job* 29:25 as one that *c.* mourners
*Is.* 51:12 I am he that *c.* you
66:13 as one his mother *c.* so
2 *Cor.* 1:4 who *c.* us in tribula.
7:6 God that *c.* those cast down

**COMFORTLESS.**
*John* 14:18 I will not leave you *c.*

**COMFORTS.**
*Ps.* 94:19 thy *c.* delight my soul
*Is.* 57:18 and restore *c.* to him.

**COMING.**
*Gen.* 30:30 since my *c.*
*Num.* 22:16 let noth. hinder *c.*
*Jud.* 5:28 chariot so long in *c.?*
1 *Sam.* 16:4 trembled at his *c.*
29:6 thy *c.* in with me is good
2 *Sam.* 3:25 to know thy *c.* in
2 *K.* 19:27 know thy *c.* *Is.* 37:28
*Ps.* 37:13 seeth his day is *c*
121:8 L. shall preserve thy *c.* in
*Is.* 44:7 things *c.* let them show
*Jer.* 8:7 observe time of their *c.*
*Mic.* 7:15 accord. to days of thy *c.*

*Mal.* 3:2 abide day of his *c.?*
4:5 before *c.* of the great day
*Mat.* 16:28 till see Son of man *c.*
24:3 shall be sign of thy *c.?*
27 *c.* of Son of man be, 37, 39
30 Son of man *c.* 26:64; *Mark* 13:26; 14:62; *Luke* 21:27
48 Lord delayeth *c.* *Luke* 12:45
25:27 at *c.* received my own, *Luke* 19:23
*Mark* 6:31 many *c.* and going
*Luke* 18:5 continual *c.* she w. me
*John* 5:7 I am *c.* another step.
25 hour is *c.* 28; 10:12 wolf *c.*
*Acts* 7:52 before *c.* of Just One
9:28 Saul was with them *c.* in.
13:24 preached before his *c.*
1 *Cor.* 1:7 waiting for *c.* of L. J.
15:23 that are Christ's at his *c.*
16:17 glad of *c.* of Stephanas
2 *Cor.* 7:6 G. comf. us by *c.* of T.
7 not by his *c.* only
*Phil.* 1:26 abundant, by my *c.*
1 *Thes.* 2:19 rejoicing at his *c.?*
3:13 unblameable at *c.* of Lord
4:15 which remain to *c.* of L.
5:23 blameless to *c.* of our Lord
2 *Thes.* 2:1 we beseech by *c.* of L.
8 destroy with brightness of *c.*
9. *c.* is after working of Satan
*Jam.* 5:7 be patient to *c.* of Lord
8 *c.* of Lord draweth nigh
1 *Pet.* 2:4 *c.* as unto a live stone
2 *Pet.* 1:16 power and *c.* of L. J.
3:4 the promise of his *c.?*
12 hasting to *c.* of day of God
1 *John* 2:28 not be ash. at his *c.*
*Rev.* 13:11 another beast *c.* up
21:2 new Jer. *c.* down from G.

**COMINGS.**
*Ezek.* 43:11 show them the *c.* in

**COMMAND, Substantive.**
*Job* 39:27 eagle mount at thy *c.*

**COMMAND, Verb.**
*Gen.* 18:19 Ab. will *c.* children
*Ex.* 18:23 and God *c.* thee so
*Num.* 9:8 I will hear what L. *c.*
36:6 the thing Lord doth *c.*
*Deut.* 28:8 Lord *c.* blessing
32:46 *c.* children to observe
*Jos.* 11:15 so did Moses *c.* Joshua
*Ps.* 42:8 L. *c.* his loving-kindness
44:4 *c.* deliverance for Jacob
*Is.* 45:11 work of my hands, *c.*
*Jer.* 27:4 *c.* to say to masters
*Lam.* 1:10 *c.* should not enter
*Mat.* 19:7 why did Moses *c.*
27:64 *c.* sepulchre be made sure
*Mark* 10:3 what did Moses *c.* you
*Luke* 8:31 not *c.* to go into deep
9:54 wilt thou we *c.* fire
*Acts* 5:28 we straitly *c.* you
15:5 to *c.* to keep law of Moses
2 *Thes.* 3:4 will do things we *c.*
6 we *c.* you in name of Lord
12 such we *c.* and exhort
1 *Tim.* 4:11 these things *c.*

**I COMMAND.**
*Ex.* 7:2 all *I c.* *Jer.* 1:7, 17
34:11 obs. what *I c.* *Deut.* 12:28
*Lev.* 25:21 *I* will *c.* my blessing
*Deut.* 4:2 not add to word *I c.* you
7:11 wh. *I c.* 8:11; 10:13; 11:8, 27; 13:18; 30:8
24:18 *I c.* thee to do this, 22
30:16 *I c.* thee this day love L.
*Jer.* 11:4 do all which *I c.* you
*Amos* 9:9 *I* will *c.* and sift house
*John* 15:14 if ye do what *I c.* you
17 *I c.* you, that ye love
*Acts* 16:18 *I c.* thee in na. of J.

**COMMANDED.**
*Gen.* 50:12 J.'s sons did as he *c.*
*Ex.* 1:17 did not as k. *c.*
*Deut.* 1:18 I *c.* you, 3:18
*Jos.* 4:8 child. of I. did as J. *c.*
22:2 obeyed my voice in all I *c.*
*Jud.* 13:14 all I *c.* let her observe
1 *Sam.* 20:29 *c.* me to be there
21:2 the king *c.* me a business
2 *Sam.* 21:14 perform all king *c.*
2 *K.* 11:9 accor. to all Jehoiada *c.*
16:16 according to all Ahaz *c.*
2 *Chr.* 8:14 so had David *c.*
14:4 Asa *c.* Judah to seek Lord
32:12 Hezekiah; 33:16 Manas.
*Est.* 4:17 Mord. did as Esther *c.*
8:9 writ. accor. to all Mord. *c.*
*Job* 38:12 hast thou *c.* morning
*Jer.* 35:6 Jon. *c.* us, 10,14, 16, 18
*Ezek.* 12:7 I did as I was *c.* 37:7
*Dan.* 3:4 to you it is *c.* O people
*Mat.* 14:19 *c.* multitude to sit, 15:35; *Mark* 6:39
18:25 his lord *c.* him to be sold
21:6 disciples did as Jesus *c.*
*Mat.* 28:20 teac. to observe all I *c.*
*Luke* 9:21 *c.* them to tell no man
*Acts* 25:6 Festus *c.* Paul to be b.
1 *Cor.* 14:34 *c.* to be under obed.
1 *Thes.* 4:11 work as we *c.*
*Heb.* 12:20 not endure that *c.*

**God COMMANDED.**
*Gen.* 6:22 according to al. *G. c.*
7:9 as *God* had *c.* 16; 21:4; *Deut.* 20:17; *Jos.* 10:40
*Deut.* 5:32 observe to do as *God c.*
6:1 *God c.* to teach 20; 13:5
26:16 day *God c.* thee to keep
1 *Chr.* 14:16 David did as *God c.*
*Ezr.* 7:23 whatsoever is *c.* by *G.*
*Ps.* 68:28 *God* hath *c.* thy str.
*Acts* 10:33 all *c.* thee of *God*
2 *Cor.* 4:6 *God* who *c.* light shine

**Lord COMMANDED.**
2 *Sam.* 24:19 D. went up as *L. c.*
*Ps.* 106:34 whom *L. c.* them
133:3 for there *L. c.* blessing
*Lam.* 1:17 *L.* hath *c.* concern. J.
*Acts* 13:47 turn to Gent. so *L. c.*

**Lord *or* God COMMANDED,** *implicitly*
*Ex.* 23:15 as I *c.* in time ap.
*Deut.* 17:3 I have not *c.* 18:20; *Jer.* 19:5; 23:32; 29:23
*Jos.* 1:9 have not I *c.* thee? be
1 *K.* 11:10 *c.* Sol. concerning this
1 *Chr.* 16:15 word he *c.* to 1000 generations, *Ps.* 105:8
*Ps.* 7:6 awake to judgm. hast *c.*
33:9 he *c.* and it stood fast
111:9 he hath *c.* his covenant
119:4 *c.* us to keep thy precepts
138 testimonies hast *c.* are r.
148:5 he *c.* they were created
*Is.* 13:3 *c.* my sanctified ones
34:16 for my mouth it hath *c.*
45:12 heavens and host have I *c.*
*Jer.* 7:31 I *c.* not, 19:5; 32:35
*Lam.* 2:17 he *c.* in days of old
*Ezek.* 9:11 I have done as thou *c.*
24:18 I did in morn. as *c.* 37:10
*Zec.* 1:6 words I *c.* did they not
*Mal.* 4:4 rem. law I *c.* in Horeb
*Luke* 14:22 Lord, it is done as *c.*
*Acts* 10:42 he *c.* us to preach

**Moses COMMANDED.**
*Deut.* 31:29 turn from way I *c.*
33:4 *Moses c.* us a law, even
*Jos.* 1:7 observe to do all *Moses c.*
22:2 ye have kept all *Moses c.*
*Mat.* 8:4 offer the gift *Moses c.*
*Mark* 1:44 of. for thy cleansing things *Moses c.* *Luke* 5:14
*John* 8:5 *Moses c.* such be stoned

**COMMANDEDST.**
*Neh.* 9:14 thou *c.* them precepts
*Jer.* 32:23 done nothing thou *c.*

**COMMANDER.**
*Is.* 55:4 and *c.* to the people

**COMMANDEST.**
*Jos.* 1:16 all thou *c.* us we will do
18 not hearken in all thou *c.*
*Jer.* 32:23 done nothing of all *c.*
*Acts* 23:3 *c.* me to be smitten

**COMMANDETH.**
Num. 32:25 will do as my lord c.
Job 9:7 c. sun, and it riseth not
37:12 may do whatever he c.
Lam. 3:37 when L. c. not?
Mark 1:27 c. spirits, Luke 4:36
Acts 17:30 c. all men to repent

**COMMANDING.**
Gen. 49:33 Jacob an end of c.
Mat. 11:1 Jesus made end of c.

**COMMANDMENT.**
Ex. 34:32 c. all L. had spoken
Num. 15:31 broken c. be cut off
23:20 have received c. to bless
27:14 rebelled against my c.
Deut. 30:11 this c. I command
1 K. 2:43 why hast not kept c.
1 Chr. 12:32 were at their c.
28:21 people will be at thy c.
2 Chr. 19:10 between law and c.
30:12 one heart to do c. of king
31:5 as soon as c. came abroad
Ezr. 8:17 I sent with c. to Iddo
10:3 of those tremble at c.
Neh. 11:23 king's c. conc. them
Est. 1:12 refused to come at c.
3:3 why transgressest king's c.?
9:1 when king's c. drew nigh
Job 23:12 nor gone back from c.
Ps. 119:96 c. exceeding broad
147:15 forth his c. upon earth
Prov. 6:23 the c. is a lamp
8:29 waters not pass his c.
13:13 feareth c. be rewarded
19:16 keepeth c. keepeth soul
Ec. 8:5 keepeth c. feel no evil
Jer. 35:14 obey their father's c.
Dan. 3:22 king's c. was urgent
9:23 the c. came forth, and I am
Hos. 5:11 he walked after c.
Mal. 2:1 O priests, c. is for you
4 I have sent this c. to you
Mat. 15:3 transgress c. of God?
6 the c. of God of no effect
22:36 which is the great c.
38 this is great c. Mark 12:30
Mark 7:8 laying aside c. of God
9 full well ye reject c. of God
12:31 no c. greater than these
Luke 15:29 nor transgressed I c.
23:56 rested sab. accord. to c.
John 10:18 this c. I received of
12:49 a c. what I should say
50 his c. is life everlasting
14:31 Father gave me c. so I do
15:12 c. that ye l. 1 John 3:23
Acts 15:24 we gave no such c.
23:30 gave c. to his accusers
Rom. 7:8 occasion by the c. 11
9 c. came, sin revived
10 c. which was ordained to l.
12 c. is holy, just, and good
13:9 if any other c. it is
16:26 accord. to c. of everl. God
1 Cor. 7:6 I speak this, not of c.
2 Cor. 8:8 not by c. but by occa.
Eph. 6:2 first c. with promise
1 Tim. 1:1 by c. of G. Tit. 1:3
5 end of the c. is charity out of
Heb. 7:16 after law of a carnal c.
18 disannulling of the c.
11:23 not afraid of king's c.
2 Pet. 2:21 turn from holy c.
3:2 mindful of c. of us apos.
1 John 2:7 but an old c.
3:23 this is his c.
4:21 this c. have we from him,
2 John 4 received a c. from Fath.
6 this is the c.

**Give or given COMMANDMENT.**
Ex. 25:22 I will give in c.
Deut. 1:3 Lord had g. him in c.
Ezr. 4:21 g. c. till ano. c. be g.
Ps. 71:3 hast given c. to save
Is. 23:11 hath g. c. against city
Nah. 1:14 L. hath g. c. con. thee
John 11:57 g. c. if any knew

**Keep COMMANDMENT.**
See KEEP.

**COMMANDMENT of the Lord**
Num. 24:13 can. go bey. c. of L.
Jos. 22:3 charge of c. of the L.
1 Sam. 12:14 against c. of the L.
15 but rebel ag. c. of the L.
13:13 hast not kept c. of the L.
15:13 S. said, I perf. c. of the L.
24 I have trans. c. of the L.
2 Sam. 12:9 despised c. of the L.
2 K. 24:3 at c. of L. came on J.
2 Chr. 29:25 was c. of the Lord
Ps. 19:8 the c. of the Lord is pure
1 Cor. 7:25 I have no c. of the L.

**New Commandment.**
John 13:34 a new c. I give
1 John 2:7 no new c.; 8 a new c.
2 John 5 not as tho' I wrote n. c.

**Rebelled against the COMMANDMENT.**
Num. 27:14 rebelled against my c.
Deut. 1:26 ye r. a. c. of L. 43
9:23 then ye r. a. the c. of Lord
Lam. 1:18 I have reb. ag. his c.

**COMMANDMENTS.**
Gen. 26:5 Abraham kept my c
Ex. 15:26 if give ear to his c.
34:28 ten c. Deut. 4:13; 10:4
Lev. 4:13 against any c. 27
5:17 commit sin forbidden by c.
27:34 these are c. L. command.
Num. 15:39 rem. all c. of Lord
Deut. 8:11 in not keeping his c.
11:13 if you shall hearken to my c. 28:13; Jud. 3:4
27 if ye will obey the c. of L.
28 if ye will not obey the c.
1 Sam. 15:11 Saul not perf. my c.
1 K. 11:34 b. he hath kept my c.
14:8 David who kept my c.
18:18 ye have forsaken c.
2 K. 17:16 they left all the c.
19 Judah kept not c. of the L.
18:6 kept his c. which he com.
2 Chr. 7:19 if ye forsake my c.
24:20 why transgress ye the c.
Ezr. 9:10 have forsaken thy c.
14 sh. we again break thy c.
Ps. 89:31 if they keep not my c.
111:7 all his c. are sure
112:1 blessed he delighteth in c.
119:10 not wander from c.
Ps. 119:19 hide not thy c. from me
35 to go in path of thy c.
47 I will delight in thy c.
66 for I have believed thy c.
73 that I may learn thy c.
86 c. are faithful; 151 truth
98 through c. made me wiser
127 I love thy c.; 131 I longed
143 c. my delights; 172 right.
166 done thy c.; 176 not forget
Prov. 2:1 wilt hide my c.
7:1 lay up my c. with thee
10:8 wise in heart will rec. c.
Is. 48:18 hadst hearkened to c.
Mat. 5:19 whoso. break least c.
15:9 teach. c. of men, Mark 7:7
22:40 on these two c. hang law
Mark 10:19 thou knowest c. Luke 18:20
12:29 first of c. is, Hear, O Is.
Luke 1:6 walking in c. blameless
John 14:21 he that hath my c.
15:10 if keep my c. as I kept
1 Cor. 7:19 nothing, but keep. c.
14:37 things I write you are c.
Col. 2:22 c. and doctr. of men
1 Thes. 4:2 ye know c. we gave
1 John 2:4 keepeth not c. is a liar
3:24 that keepeth c. dwelleth
2 John 6 this is love, walk after c.

**Do COMMANDMENTS**
Num. 15:40 do all my c.
Deut. 6:25 to do all c. 15:5
1 Chr. 28:7 to do my c.
Ps. 103:18 that rem. his c. to do
111:10 understanding that do c.
Rev. 22:14 blessed are they do c.

**Not do COMMANDMENTS.**
Lev. 26:14 if ye will not do c.
See KEEP.

**COMMEND.**
Luke 23:46 into thy hands I c.
Acts 20:32 breth. I c. you to God
Rom. 3:5 unrigh. c. right. of G.
16:1 I c. unto you Phebe
2 Cor. 3:1 we begin again to c
5:12 for we c. not ourselves
10:12 compare with some that c.

**COMMENDATION.**
2 Cor. 3:1 need we epistles of c.

**COMMENDED.**
Gen. 12:15 princes c. Sarai
Prov. 12:8 man c. accor. to wisd.
Ec. 8:15 then I c. mirth
Luke 16:8 Lord c. unjust steward
Acts 14:23 c. them to Lord
2 Cor. 12:11 have been c. of you

**COMMENDETH.**
Rom. 5:8 God c. his love tow. us
1 Cor. 8:8 meat c. us not to God
2 Cor. 10:18 c. himself is approv.

**COMMENDING.**
2 Cor. 4:2 c. ourselves

**COMMISSION, S.**
Ezra 8:36 delivered the king's c.
Acts 26:12 as I went with c.

**COMMIT.**
Ex. 20:14 not c. adult. Deut. 5:18; Mat. 5:27; 19:18; Rom. 13:9
Lev. 5:17 c. things forbidden
18:29 c. any of these abomina.
Num. 5:6 c. any sin that men c.
Deut. 19:20 c. no more such evil
2 Chr. 21:11 J. to c. fornication
Job 5:8 would I c. my cause
Ps. 31:5 thy hand I c. my spirit
37:5 c. thy way to the Lord
Prov. 16:3 c. thy works unto Lord
12 to kings to c. wickedness
Is. 22:21 I will c. thy government
Jer. 44:7 why c. ye this evil?
Ezek. 8:17 c. abomina. they c. h.
16:43 shalt not c. this lewdness
22:9 in midst of thee c. lewdness
Hos. 6:9 priests c. lewdness
7:1 for they c. falsehood
Luke 12:48 c. worthy of stripes
16:11 c. the true riches?
John 2:24 Jes. did not c. himself
Rom. 1:32 c. such worthy of d.
2:2 is ag. them c. such things
22 dost thou c. sacrilege?
1 Cor. 10:8 nei. let us c. fornica.
1 Tim. 1:18 charge I c. to thee
2 Tim. 2:2 c. to faithful men
Jam. 2:9 respect to persons ye c.
1 Pet. 4:19 c. keeping of souls
1 John 3:9 born of God, not c. sin
Rev. 2:14 taught Is. to c. fornica.
20 my servants to c. fornica.
See ADULTERY.

**COMMIT iniquity.**
2 Sam. 7:14 c. i. I will chasten
Job 34:10 Almighty he sh. c. i.
Jer. 9:5 weary th. to c. iniquity
Ezek. 3:20 right. and c. i. 33:13

**COMMIT trespass.**
Lev. 5:15 if a soul c. t. thro' ig.
Num. 5:12 if a man's wife c. tres.
31:16 caused Israel to c. trespass
Jos. 22:20 Achan c. a trespass

**COMMIT whoredom, *or* whoredoms.**
*Lev.* 20:5 that *c. w.* with Molech
*Num.* 25:1 to *c. w.* with dau. of M.
*Ezek.* 16:17 *c. w.* with images
34 followeth to *c. whoredom*
20:30 *c.* ye *w.* after their abo.?
23:43 will they *c. w.* with her
*Hos.* 4:10 *c. w.* and not increase
13 your daugh. shall *c. w.* 14

**COMMITTED**
*Gen.* 39:8 *c.* all he hath to my h.
22 *c.* to Joseph the prisoners
*Lev.* 20:23 *c.* these and I abhorr.
*Jud.* 20:6 *c.* lewdness in Israel
1 *K.* 8:47 we have *c.* wickedness
14:22 with sins they *c.*
*Jer.* 2:13 my people *c.* two evils
5:30 a horrible thing is *c.*
16:10 what is our sin we *c.*
44:3 *c.* to provoke me, 9
*Ezek.* 16:26 hast also *c.* fornica.
51 nor Sam. *c.* half of thy sins
18:21 from sins he *c.* 22, 28
23:3 *c.* whored. in Eg. in youth
7 *c.* her whoredoms with them
33:16 none of sins he *c.*
*Hos.* 1:2 land hath *c.* great who.
4:18 they have *c.* whoredom
*Mark* 15:7 who had *c.* murder
*Luke* 12:48 have *c.* much, of him
*John* 5:22 *c.* all judgment to Son
*Acts* 8:3 *c.* them to prison
25:11 if I have *c.* any th. worthy
25 found he *c.* nothing worthy
27:40 *c.* themselves to the sea
28:17 *c.* nothing against people
*Rom.* 3:2 were *c.* oracles of God
2 *Cor.* 5:19 *c.* to us word of rec.
12:21 lasciviousness they *c.*
*Gal.* 2:7 gospel of the uncircum. was *c.* to me, 1 *Tim.* 1:11
1 *Tim.* 6:20 what is *c.* to thee
2 *Tim.* 1:12 to keep what I *c.*
*Jam.* 5:15 if he *c.* sins be forgiv.
1 *Pet.* 2:23 *c.* himself to him jud.
*Jude* 15 ungodly deeds they *c.*
*Rev.* 17:2 have *c.* forni. 18:3, 9
*See* ABOMINATIONS.

**COMMITTED iniquity.**
*Ps.* 106:6 we have *c. iniquity*
*Ezek.* 33:13 *iniqui. c.* he shall die
*Dan.* 9:5 *c. i.* and done wickedly

**COMMITTED trespass.**
*Jos.* 7:1 Is. *c. t.* in accurs. thing
22:16 what *t.* is this ye have *c.*
31 because not *c.* this *t.* aga. L.
*Ezek.* 15:8 have *c. t.* I will make
20:27 in that they *c.* a *t.* ag. me

**COMMITTEST, ETH, ING.**
*Ps.* 10:14 *c.* himself to thee
*Ezek.* 8:6 abomination Is. *c.*
33:15 without *c.* iniquity, 18
*Hos.* 4:2 by lying, *c.* adultery
5:3 O Ephraim, *c.* whoredom
*John* 8:34 *c.* sin, is servant of sin
1 *Cor.* 6:18 *c.* fornication sinneth
1 *John* 3:4 *c.* sin transgresseth l.
8 he that *c.* sin is of the devil

**COMMODIOUS.**
*Acts* 27:12 the haven was not *c.*

**COMMON.**
1 *Sam.* 21:4 there is no *c.* bread
*Ec.* 6:1 there is an evil, it is *c.*
*Jer.* 31:5 eat them as *c.* things
*Ezek.* 23:42 with men of *c.* sort
*Acts* 2:44 had all things *c.* 4:32
10:14 eaten any thing *c.* 11:8
15 cleansed, call not *c.* 11:9
28 should not call any man *c.*
1 *Cor.* 10:13 no temptation but *c.*
*Tit.* 1:4 my son after *c.* faith
*Jude* 3 to write of *c.* salvation

**COMMON people.**
*Jer.* 26:23 the graves of *c. people*
*Mark* 12:37 *c. peo.* heard him

COMMONLY. *See* REPORTED.

**COMMONWEALTH.**
*Eph.* 2:12 aliens from the *c.* of Is.

**COMMOTION, S.**
*Jer.* 10:22 a great *c.* out of north
*Luke* 21:9 when ye hear of *c.* be

**COMMUNE.**
*Ex.* 25:22 there *c.* with thee
1 *Sam.* 18:22 *c.* with D. secretly
1 *Sam.* 19:3 I will *c.* with my fa.
*Job* 4:2 if assay to *c.* with thee
*Ps.* 4:4 *c.* with your own heart
64:5 *c.* of laying snares privily
77:6 night I *c.* with my heart

**COMMUNED.**
*Gen.* 23:8 Abra.; 34:6 Hamor, 8
42:24 Joseph; *Jud.* 9:1 Abim.
1 *Sam.* 9:25 Samuel; 25:39 David
1 *K.* 10:2 the queen of Sheba *c.* with Solomon, 2 *Chr.* 9:1
2 *K.* 22:14 *c.* with Huldah
*Ec.* 1:16 I *c.* with my own heart
*Dan.* 1:19 king *c.* with them
*Luke* 6:11 *c.* what do to Jesus
24:15 while *c.* Jesus drew nigh
*Acts* 24:26 Felix *c.* the oftener

**COMMUNICATE.**
*Gal.* 6:6 *c.* to him that teacheth
*Phil.* 4:14 *c.* with my affliction
1 *Tim.* 6:18 be willing to *c.*
*Heb.* 13:16 and to *c.* forget not

**COMMUNICATED.**
*Gal.* 2:2 *c.* to them that gospel
*Phil.* 4:15 no church *c.* with me.

**COMMUNICATION, S.**
2 *Sam.* 3:17 A. had *c.* with elders
2 *K.* 9:11 ye know his *c.*
*Mat.* 5:37 let your *c.* be yea, yea
*Luke* 24:17 what manner of *c.*
1 *Cor.* 15:33 evil *c.* corrupt good
*Eph.* 4:29 no corrupt *c.* *Col.* 3:8
*Phile.* 6. *c.* of thy faith effectual

**COMMUNING.**
*Gen.* 18:33 left *c.* with Abraham
*Ex.* 31:18 an end of *c.* on Sinai

**COMMUNION.**
1 *Cor.* 10:16 *c.* of blood, *c.* of body
2 *Cor.* 6:14 wh. *c.* light with dark.
13:14 *c.* H. G. be with you all

**COMPACT.**
*Ps.* 122:3 Jerusalem is a city *c.*

**COMPACTED,**
*Eph.* 4:16 the whole body *c.*

**COMPANY, Substantive.**
*Gen.* 32:8 E. come to the one *c.*
35:11 *c.* of nations be of thee
*Num.* 16:16 thou and all thy *c.*
40 be not as Korah and his *c.*
22:4 this *c.* lick up all round
26:9 strove in *c.* of Korah, 27:3
*Jud.* 9:37 another *c.* by plain
18:23 comest with such a *c.*?
1 *Sam.* 30:15 bring me to this *c.*?
2 *K.* 5:15 his *c.* came to Elisha
9:17 he spied the *c.* of Jehu
2 *Chr.* 24:24 Syrians with small *c.*
*Job* 16:7 made desolate all my *c.*
34:8 in *c.* with workers of iniq.
*Ps.* 55:14 to house of God in *c.*
68:30 rebuke the *c.* of spearmen
106:17 covered *c.* of Abiram
18 fire was kindled in their *c.*
*Prov.* 29:3 keepeth *c.* with harl.
*Cant.* 1:9 to a *c.* of horses in Ph.
6:13 as it were *c.* of two armies
*Ezek.* 16:40 bring a *c.* against thee
23:46 I will bring a *c.* on them
32:22 Ashur is there and her *c.*
38:7 prepare, thou and thy *c.*
*Hos.* 6:9 so *c.* of priests murder
*Luke* 2:44 suppos. him in the *c.*
6:17 and *c.* of his disciples
22 separate you from their *c.*
9:14 sit by fifties in a *c.*
38 a man of the *c.* cried out
24:22 a woman of our *c.* made
*Acts* 4:23 went to their own *c.*
10:28 unl. for a Jew to keep *c.*
15:22 to send chosen men of *c.*
17:5 gathered a *c.* and set city
21:8 we of Paul's *c.* departed
*Rom.* 15:24 filled with your *c.*
1 *Cor.* 5:11 not to keep *c.* with
2 *Thes.* 3:14 have no *c.* with him
*Heb.* 12:22 an innum. *c.* of angels
*Rev.* 18:17 *c.* in ships afar off

**Great COMPANY.**
*Gen.* 50:9 with Joseph a *great c.*
2 *Chr.* 9:1 queen of S. with *g. c.*
20:12 no might ag. this *great c.*
*Ps.* 68:11 *g.* was *c.* of those pub.
*Jer.* 31:8 a *great c.* return thither
*Ezek.* 17:17 Pharaoh with *great c.*
*John* 6:5 saw a *great c.* come
*Acts* 6:7 *g. c.* of priests obedient

**COMPANY, Verb.**
1 *Cor.* 5:9 not to *c.* with fornica.

**COMPANIED.**
*Acts* 1:21 which have *c.* with us

**COMPANIES.**
*Jud.* 7:16 300 into three *c.*
1 *Sam.* 11:11 Saul put in three *c.*
13:17 spoilers in three *c.*
2 *K.* 5:2 Syrians gone by *c.*
*Neh.* 12:31 *c.* gave thanks, 40
*Job* 6:19 the *c.* of Sheba waited
*Is.* 21:13 O ye travelling *c.*
57:13 let thy *c.* deliver thee
*Mark* 6:39 to make all sit by *c.*

**COMPANION.**
*Ex.* 32:27 slay every man his *c.*
*Jud.* 14:20 S.'s wife to *c.* 15:6
1 *Chr.* 27:33 Hushai king's *c.*
*Job* 30:29 I am a *c.* to owls
*Ps.* 119:63 *c.* to all that fear thee
*Prov.* 13:20 *c.* of fools be destroy.
28:7 *c.* of riotous shameth fath.
24 same is *c.* of a destroyer
*Mal.* 2:14 she is thy *c.* wife of
*Phil.* 2:25 Epaph. my *c.* in labor
*Rev.* 1:9 I John your *c.* in tribu.

**COMPANIONS.**
*Jud.* 11:38 went with *c.*
14:11 thirty *c.* to be with him
*Job* 35:4 will answer thee and *c.*
41:6 *c.* make a banquet of him?
*Ps.* 45:14 her *c.* shall be brought
122:8 for my *c.* sake I will say
*Cant.* 1:7 aside by flocks of thy *c.*
8:13 *c.* hearken to thy voice
*Is.* 1:23 princes *c.* of thieves
*Ezek.* 37:16 Judah and Isr. his *c.*
*Dan.* 2:17 thing known to his *c.*
*Acts* 19:29 caught Paul's *c.*
*Heb.* 10:33 *c.* of them so used

**COMPARABLE.**
*Lam.* 4:2 sons of Zion *c.* to gold

**COMPARE, ED, ING.**
*Ps.* 89:6 who in heaven *c.* to L.?
*Prov.* 3:15 not be *c.* 8:11
*Cant.* 1:9 I have *c.* thee
*Is.* 40:18 wh. likeness *c.* to him?
46:5 to whom will ye *c.* me
*Rom.* 8:18 to be *c.* with the glory
1 *Cor.* 2:13 *c.* spiritual things
2 *Cor.* 10:12 *c.* ours. with some that com. *c.* thems. amongst

**COMPARISON.**
*Jud.* 8:2 I done in *c.* of you? 3
*Hag.* 2:3 in your eyes in *c.* of it
*Mark* 4:30 with what *c.* shall we

**COMPASS.**
2 *Sam.* 5:23 but fetch a *c.* behind
2 *K.* 3:9 fetched a *c.* of 7 days
*Prov.* 8:27 *c.* on face of the deep
*Is.* 44:13 marketh it with *c.*
*Acts* 28:13 fetched a *c.* to Rheg.

**COMPASS, Verb.**
Num. 21:4 c. the land of Edom
Jos. 6:3 ye shall c. the city
2 K. 11:8 c. the king. 2 Chr. 23:7
Job 16:13 his archers c. me about
40:22 willows of brook c. him
Ps. 5:12 with favor c. as a shield
7:7 congregation c. thee about
17:9 deadly enemies who c. me
26:6 so will I c. thine altar
32:7 c. me with songs of deliv.
10 trust. in Lord mercy c. him
49:5 iniquity of my heels c. me
140:9 as for head of those c. me
142:7 the righteous shall c. me
Is. 50:11 c. yoursel. with sparks
Jer. 31:22 a wom. shall c. a man
Hab. 1:4 wicked c. righteous
Mat. 23:15 for ye c. sea and land
Luke 19:43 thine enemies shall c.

**COMPASSED.**
Deut. 2:1 we c. Seir many days
Jos. 6:11 so the ark c. the city
Jud. 11:18 c. the land of Edom
16:2 they c. Samson in
1 Sam. 23:26 Saul c. David and
2 Sam. 22:5 when waves of death c. me, Ps. 18:4; 116:3
2 K. 6:15 behold a host c. city
2 Chr. 21:9 Edomites which c.
Job 19:6 God c. me with his net
26:10 c. waters with bounds
Ps. 17:11 now c. us in our steps
22:12 bulls c. me; 16 dogs
Lam. 3:5 c. me with gall and
Luke 21:20 when ye see Jer. c.
Heb. 5:2 himself c. with infirmity

**COMPASSED about.**
2 Sam. 18:15 c. Absalom about
22:6 c. me ab. Ps. 18:5
2 K. 6:14 Syrians c. city about
2 Chr. 18:31 c. about Jehoshaph.
Ps. 40:12 innum. evils c. me a.
88:17 c. me ab. 109:3; 118:11, 12
118:10 all nations c. me about
Jon. 2:3 floods c. me about
Heb. 11:30 after c. a. seven days
12:1 c. a. with such cloud of w.
Rev. 20:9 c. camp of saints about

**COMPASSEST, ETH.**
Gen. 2:11 c. Havilah; 13 Ethio.
Ps. 73:6 pride c. them as a chain
139:3 thou c. my path, and
Hos. 11:12 Ephraim c. with lies

**COMPASSION.**
1 K. 8:50 give them c. before
2 Chr. 30:9 children shall find c.
Mat. 9:36 Jesus moved with c. 14:14; Mark 1:41; 6:34
18:27 lord was moved with c.
1 Pet. 3:8 hav. c. one of another
1 John 3:17 shut. his bowels of c.

**Full of COMPASSION.**
Ps. 78:38 he being full of c.
86:15 G. f. of c. 111:4; 112:4; 145:8

**Have or had COMPASSION.**
Ex. 2:6 babe wept, she had c.
Deut. 13:17 L. may h. c. on thee
30:3 Lord will have c. on thee
1 Sam. 23:21 for ye have c. on me
1 K. 8:50 they may h. c. on them
2 K. 13:23 Lord had c. on them
2 Chr. 36:15 had c. on his people
17 Chaldees had no c. on man
Is. 49:15 she not have c. on son
Jer. 12:15 I will have c. on them
Lam. 3:32 he have c. Mic. 7:19
Mat. 15:32 c. on mult. Mark 8:2
18:33 c. on thy fellow-servant
20:34 so Jesus had c. on them
Mark 5:19 how L. had c. on thee
9:22 have c. on us and help us
Luke 7:13 L. saw her, he had c.
10:33 Samaritan had c. on him
15:20 father had c. and ran and
Rom. 9:15 will have c. on whom
Heb. 5:2 can have c. on ignorant
10:34 had c. of me in my bonds
Jude 22 of some have c. making

**COMPASSIONS.**
Lam. 3:22 because his c. fail not
Zec. 7:9 show c. ev. man to bro.

**COMPEL.**
Mat. 5:41 c. thee to go a mile go
Mark 15:21 c. one Simon to bear
Luke 14:23 c. them to come in

**COMPELLED, EST.**
2 Chr. 21:11 c. Judah thereto
Mat. 27:32 him c. to bear cross
Acts 26:11 c. them to blaspheme
2 Cor. 12:11 glorying, ye c. me
Gal. 2:3 c. to be circumcised
14 c. Gentiles to live as Jews?

**COMPLAIN, ED, ING**
Num. 11:1 c. it displeased Lord
Jud. 21:22 bre. come to us to c.
Job 7:11 I will c. in bitterness
31:38 the furrows thereof c.
Ps. 77:3 I c. and my spirit was
144:14 be no c. in our streets
Lam. 3:39 doth a living man c.?

**COMPLAINERS.**
Jude 16 these are murmurers, c.

**COMPLAINT, S.**
1 Sam. 1:16 abundance of my c.
Job 7:13 couch shall ease my c.
9:27 if I say, I will forget my c.
10:1 I will leave c. on myself
21:4 is my c. to man?
23:2 even to-day is my c. bitter
Ps. 55:2 I mourn in my c.
142:2 I poured out my c.
Acts 25:7 c. against Paul

**COMPLETE.**
Lev. 23:15 seven sabbaths be c.
Col. 2:10 and ye are c. in him
4:12 that ye may stand c. in all

**COMPOSITION.**
Ex. 30:32 any like it after c. 37

**COMPOUND, ETH.**
Ex. 30:25 an ointment c.
33 whosoever c. any like it

**COMPREHEND.**
Job 37:5 doeth he, we cannot c.
Eph. 3:18 able to c.

**COMPREHENDED.**
Is. 40:12 c. dust of the earth
John 1:5 the darkness c. it not
Rom. 13:9 it is briefly c. in this

**CONCEAL, ED, ETH.**
Gen. 37:26 bro. and c. his blood
Deut. 13:8 spare, neither c. him
Job 6:10 I have not c. the words
27:11 Almighty will I not c.
41:12 I will not c. his parts
Ps. 40:10 not c. thy loving-kind.
Prov. 11:13 of a faithful spirit c.
12:23 prudent c. knowledge
25:2 glory of God to c. a thing
Jer. 50:2 publish and c. not

**CONCEIT, S.**
Prov. 18:11 as high wall in own c.
Prov. 26:5 he be wise in own c.
12 a man wise in his own c.?
16 sluggard wiser in own c.
28:11 rich is wise in own c.
Rom. 11:25 in your own c.
12:16 be not wise in own c.

**CONCEIVE.**
Gen. 30:38 c. when came to drink
Jud. 13:3 shalt c. and bear a son, 5:7; Luke 1:31
Job 15:35 c. mischief, Is. 59:4
Ps. 51:5 in sin did mother c. me
Is. 7:14 a virgin shall c. and
33:11 c. chaff; 59:13 c. falsehood
Heb. 11:11 Sarah rec. str. to c.

**CONCEIVED.**
Gen. 4:1 Eve c.; 17 Cain's wife c.
16:4 Hagar c.; 21:2 Sarah c.
25:21 Reb. c.; 29:32 Leah, 33
30:5 Bilhah c.; 23 Rachel c.
39 flocks c.; 38:3 Shuah c.
38:18 Tamar c.; Ex. 2:2 Joch. c.
Lev. 12:2 have c. seed, and borne
Num. 11:12 have I c. all this?
1 Sam. 1:20 Hannah c. 2:21
2 Sam. 11:5 Bath-sheba c.
2 K. 4:17 Shun.; Is. 8:3 proph.
Job 3:3 there is a man-child c.
Ps. 7:14 c. mischief, brought
Cant. 3:4 chamber of her c. me
Jer. 49:30 c. a purpose ag. you
Hos. 1:3 Gomer c.
2:5 c. hath done shamefully
Mat. 1:20 c. in her is of Holy G.
Luke 1:36 Elizabeth hath c. a son
2:21 so named before he was c.
Acts 5:4 c. this in thy heart?
Rom. 9:10 Rebecca had c.
Jam. 1:15 when lust hath c.

**CONCEPTION.**
Gen. 3:16 multiply thy c.
Ruth 4:13 the Lord gave her c.
Hos. 9:11 glory flee from the c.

**CONCERN, ETH.**
Ps. 138:8 L. perfect that c. me
Acts 28:31 things which c. Christ
2 Cor. 11:30 c. mine infirmities

**CONCERNING.**
Gen. 19:21 accepted thee c. this
Num. 10:29 spoken good c. Isr.
1 K. 11:10 command him c. this
Ec. 7:10 inquire wisely c. this
Is. 30:7 therefore I cried c. this
Ezek. 21:28 saith L. c. Ammon.
47:14 c. which lifted my hand
Luke 24:27 exp. things c. hims.
44 written in Psalms c. me
Acts 13:34 as c. he raised him
Rom. 9:5 as c. flesh Christ came
11:28 as c. gospel enemies for
2 Cor. 11:21 I sp. as c. reproach
Eph. 5:32 but I speak c. Christ
Phil. 4:15 as c. giving and receiv.
1 Thes. 5:18 will of God in C. c.

**CONCISION.**
Phil. 3:2 beware of the c.

**CONCLUDE.**
Rom. 3:28 c. a man is justified

**CONCLUDED.**
Acts 21:25 touching Gent. we c.
Rom. 11:32 c. them all in unbel.
Gal. 3:22 hath c. all under sin

**CONCLUSION.**
Ec. 12:13 hear c. of matter

**CONCORD.**
2 Cor. 6:15 what c. Ch. with B.

**CONCOURSE.**
Prov. 1:21 crieth in place of c.
Acts 19:40 give acc. of this c.

**CONCUBINE.**
Jud. 19:2 c. played the whore
29 c. and divided her, 20:6
20:4 I and my c. to lodge
2 Sam. 3:7 unto my father's c.?
21:11 what Rizpah c. of Saul

**CONCUBINES.**
Gen. 25:6 to sons of c. gave gifts
2 Sam. 5:13 David took more c.
16:22 Abs. went in to father's c.
19:5 and the lives of thy c.
20:3 king put his c. in ward
1 K. 11:3 Solomon had 300 c.
2 Chr. 11:21 took threescore c.
Est. 2:14 Shaashgaz kept c.
Cant. 6:8 there are eighty c.
9 and c. they praised her
Dan. 5:3 c. drank in them, 23

**CONCUPISCENCE.**
Rom. 7:8 sin wr. all manner of c.
Col. 3:5 mortify evil c.
1 Thes. 4:5 not in the lust of c.

**CONDEMN.**
Ex. 22:9 whom judges shall c
Deut. 25:1 judges shall c. wicked
Job 9:20 my mouth shall c. me
10:2 I will say, Do not c. me
34:18 wilt th. c. him most just?
40:8 wilt thou c. me, that
Ps. 37 33 nor c. him
94.21 they c. innocent blood
109:31 those that c. his soul
Prov. 12:2 wick. devices will he c.
Is. 50:9 who is he shall c. me?
54:17 that rise against thee c.
Mat. 12:41 shall c. it, Luke 11:32
42 queen of south shall c. it
20:18 c. him to d. Mark 10:33
Luke 6:37 c. not, sh. not be con.
John 3:17 his Son to c. the world
8:11 neither do I c. thee, go
2 Cor. 7:3 I speak not this to c.
1 John 3:20 if our heart c. us
21 if our heart c. us not, we

**CONDEMNATION.**
Luke 23:40 thou art in same c.
John 3:19 c. that light is come
5:24 believeth, not come into c.
Rom. 5:16 judgment by one to c.
18 judgment came to c.
8:1 there is no c. to them in C.
1 Cor. 11:34 come not togeth. to c.
2 Cor. 3:9 minist. of c. be glory
1 Tim. 3:6 lest he fall into c. of
Jam. 3:1 receive the greater c.
5:12 be nay, lest ye fall into c.
Jude 4 of old ordained to this c.

**CONDEMNED.**
Job 32:3 yet had c. Job
Ps. 109:7 judged, let him be c.
Amos 2:8 they drink wine of c.
Mat. 12:7 not have c. guiltless
37 by thy words shalt be c.
27:3 J. when he saw he was c.
Mark 14:64 c. him to be guilty
Luke 24:20 delivered him to be c.
John 3:18 believ. on him, is not
c. believ. not, is c. already
8:10 hath no man c. thee?
Rom. 8:3 for sin c. sin in flesh
1 Cor. 11:32 not be c. with world
Tit. 2:8 speech that cannot be c.
3:11 sinneth, being c. of hims.
Heb. 11:7 by which he c. world
Jam. 5:6 c. and killed the just
9 grudge not, lest ye be c.
2 Pet. 2:6 c. with overthrow

**CONDEMNEST, ETH, ING.**
1 K. 8:32 c. wicked
Job 15:6 own mouth c. thee
Prov. 17:15 he that c. the just
Acts 13:27 fulfilled them in c. him
Rom. 2:1 judgest thou c. thyself
8:34 who is he that c.?
14:22 c. not himself in thing

**CONDESCEND.**
Rom. 12:16 c. to men of low est.

**CONDITION, S.**
1 Sam. 11:2 on this c. make cov.
Luke 14:32 desireth c. of peace

**CONDUCT, ED.**
2 Sam. 19:15 c. king over Jor. 31
40 people of Judah c. king
Acts 17:5 that c. Paul brought
1 Cor. 16:11 but c. him in peace

**CONDUIT.**
2 K. 18:7 stood by c. Is. 36:2
20:20 how he made a pool and c.
Is. 7:3 to meet Ahaz at end of c.

**CONFECTION.**
Ex. 30:35 make a c. after art

**CONFECTIONARIES.**
1 Sam. 8:13 your dau. to be c.

**CONFEDERACY.**
Is. 8:12 c. to whom people say c.
Ob. 7 men of thy c. brought

**CONFEDERATE.**
Gen. 14:13 these c. with Abram
Ps. 83:5 they are c. against thee
Is. 7:2 Syria is c. with Ephraim

**CONFERENCE.**
Gal. 2:6 they in c. added nothing

**CONFERRED.**
1 K. 1:7 Adonijah c. with Joab
Acts 4:15 c. among themselves
25:12 Festus, when he had c.
Gal. 1:16 I c. not with flesh and

**CONFESS.**
Lev. 5:5 c. that he hath sinned
16:21 c. over him all the iniq.
26:40 if they c. their iniquity
Num. 5:7 they shall c. their sin
1 K. 8:33 c. thy name, 35; 2 Chr. 6:24, 26
Neh. 1:6 c. sins of children of Is.
Job 40:14 c. thy hand can save
Ps. 32:5 I said, I will c. my tr.
Mat. 10:32 c. me before, Lu. 12:8
John 9:22 if c. that he was Christ
12:42 did not c. him, lest they
Acts 23.8 but Pharisees c. both
24:14 I c. after the way
Rom. 10:9 c. with thy mouth
14:11 every tongue shall c.
15:9 c. to thee among Gentiles
Phil. 2:11 every tongue should c.
Jam. 5:16 c. your faults
1 John 1:9 if we c. our sins
4:15 c. Jesus is the Son of God
2 John 7 c. not Jesus Christ
Rev. 3:5 c. his name bef. my Fa.

**CONFESSED, ETH, ING.**
Ezr. 10:1 Ezra had c. weeping
Neh. 9:2 stood and c. their sins
Prov. 28:13 whoso c. and forsak.
Dan. 9:20 c. my sin and the sin
Mat. 3:6 baptized c. their sins
John 1:20 c. I am not the Christ
Acts 19:18 many c. and showed
Heb. 11:13 c. they were strangers
1 John 4:2 spirit that c. Christ
3 c. not Jesus Christ is come

**CONFESSION.**
Jos. 7:19 and make c. to God
2 Chr. 30:22 offer. and making c.
Ezr. 10:11 make c. to the Lord
Dan. 9:4 I prayed and made c.
Rom. 10:10 with mouth c. is m.
1 Tim. 6:13 witnessed a good c.

**CONFIDENCE.**
Jud. 9:26 Shech. put c. in Gaal
2 K. 18:19 what c. is this? Is. 36:4
Job 4:6 is not this thy fear, thy c.
31:24 fine gold thou art my c.
Ps. 65:5 art c. of all the earth
118:8 than put c. in man
9 than to put c. in princes
Prov. 3:26 Lord shall be thy c.
14:26 fear of Lord is strong c.
21:22 strength of c.
25:19 c. in unfaithful
Is. 30:15 in c. be your strength
Jer. 48:13 ashamed of B. their c.
Ezek. 28:26 shall dwell with c.
29:16 E. be no more c. of Israel
Mic. 7:5 put ye not c. in a guide
Acts 28:31 preaching with all c
2 Cor. 1:15 in this c. minded
2:3 c. that my joy is the joy
7:16 that I have c. in you
8:22 great c. I have in you
10:2 the c. I think to be bold
11:17 as foolishly in this c.
Gal. 5:10 I have c. in you
Eph. 3:12 access with c. by faith
Phil. 1:25 having this c.
3:3 we have no c. in the flesh
4 I might have c. in flesh
2 Thes. 3:4 c. in L. touching you
Phile. 21 c. in thy obedience
Heb. 3:6 if we hold fast c.
14 beginning of our c. steadf.
10:35 cast not away your c.
1 John 2:28 we may have c.
3:21 then have we c. toward G.
5:14 the c. we have in him

**CONFIDENCES.**
Jer. 2:37 Lord rejected thy c.

**CONFIDENT.**
Ps. 27:3 in this I be c.
Prov. 14:16 fool rageth and is c.
Rom. 2:19 art c. thou art a guide
2 Cor. 5:6 we are always c.
8 c. and willing to be absent
9:4 ashamed in same c. boasting
Phil. 1:6 c. of this very thing
14 waxing c. by my bonds

**CONFIDENTLY.**
Luke 22:59 c. affirmed, This fel.

**CONFIRM.**
Ruth 4:7 manner to c. all things
1 K. 1:14 I will c. thy words
2 K. 15:19 to c. the kingdom in
Est. 9:31 to c. these days of P.
Ps. 68:9 c. thine inheritance
Is. 35:3 and c. the feeble knees
Ezek. 13:6 they would c. the w.
Dan. 9:27 c. cov. for one week
11:1 I stood to c. him
Rom. 15:8 to c. promises made
1 Cor. 1:8 also c. you to the end
2 Cor. 2:8 ye would c. your love

**CONFIRMATION.**
Phil. 1:7 in the c. of the gospel
Heb. 6:16 an oath for c. is an end

**CONFIRMED.**
2 Sam. 7:24 c. to thyself Israel
2 K. 14:5 as soon as king was c.
1 Chr. 14:2 Lord had c. him k.
16:17 c. same to J. Ps. 105:10
Est. 9:32 Esther c. mat. of Pur.
Dan. 9:12 c. words he spake
Acts 15:32 exhorted and c. them
1 Cor. 1:6 testim. of C. c. in you
Gal. 3:15 if c. no man disannul.
17 the covenant that was c.
Heb. 2:3 was c. to us by them
6:17 he c. it by an oath

**CONFIRMETH, ING.**
Num. 30:14 bonds on her, he c.
Deut. 27:26 cursed be he c. not
Is. 44:26 c. word of his servant
Mark 16:20 c. the word
Acts 14:22 c. souls of disciples
15:41 Syria c. the churches

**CONFISCATION.**
Ezr. 7:26 judgm. be exec. to c.

**CONFLICT.**
Phil. 1:30 same c. ye saw in me
Col. 2:1 knew what c. I have

**CONFORMABLE.**
Phil. 3:10 made c. to his death

**CONFORMED.**
Rom. 8:29 c. to image of his Son
12:2 be not c. to this world

**CONFOUND.**
Gen. 11:7 c. their language, 9
Jer. 1:17 lest I c. thee before
1 Cor. 1:57 to c. the wise, to c.

**CONFOUNDED.**
2 K. 19:26 inhab. were c. Is. 37:27
Job 6:20 c. bec. they had hoped
Ps. 35:4 be c. that seek my soul
69:6 let not those seek L. be c.
71:13 be c. that are adversaries
24 are c. that seek my hurt
83:17 let them be c. for ever
97:7 c. be all that serve images
129:5 let all be c. that hate Zion

Is. 1:29 c. for the gardens
19:9 that weave net-work be c.
37:27 inhabitants were c.
Jer. 9:19 c. bec. we have forsaken
10:14 founder c. by image, 51:17
17:18 be c. that persecute me
46:24 dau. of E. c.; 48:20 Moab
49:23 Hamath is c.; 50:2 Bel.
50:12 your mother be sore c.
51:47 Babylon whole land be c.
51 c. bec. we heard reproach
Ezek. 16:52 be thou c. 54, 63
Mic. 7:16 nations c. at their m.
Zec. 10:5 riders and horses be c.
Acts 2:6 multitude were c.
9:22 Saul c. Jews at Damascus

**Ashamed and CONFOUNDED.**

Ps. 40:14 ash. c. seek soul, 70:2
Is. 24:23 moon be c. sun be ash.
41:11 inc. ag. thee be a. and c.
45:16 idol mak. be ash. and c.
54:4 not be asham. neither c.
Jer. 14:3 nob. and lit. ones a. c.
15:9 borne seven been a. and c.
22:22 shalt be ashamed and c.
31:19 ash. yea c. bec. I did bear
Ezek. 36:32 be a. a. c. for your w.
Mic. 3:7 seers be a. diviners c.

**Not CONFOUNDED.**

Ps. 22:5 were not c.
Is. 45:17 nor c. world with. end
50:7 God will help, I not be c.
1 Pet. 2:6 believeth shall not be c.

**CONFUSED.**

Is. 9:5 battle is with c. noise
Acts 19:32 the assembly was c.

**CONFUSION.**

Lev. 18:23 a beast to lie, it is c.
20:12 they have wrought c.
1 Sam. 20:30 chosen D. to thy c.
Ezr. 9:7 delivered to c. of face
Job 10:15 I am full of c.
Ps. 35:4 to c. that devise
44:15 my c. is cont. before me
70:2 to c. that desire my hurt
71:1 let me never be put to c.
109:29 cover with their own c.
Is. 24:10 the city of c. is broken
30:3 trust in shadow of Egypt c.
34:11 stretch on it line of c.
41:29 their molten images are c.
45:16 makers of idols go to c.
61:7 for c. they shall rejoice in
Jer. 3:25 and our c. covereth us
7:19 provoke to the c.
20:11 everl. c. never be forgot
Dan. 9:7 belongeth c. of faces, 8
Acts 19:29 city was filled with c.
1 Cor. 14:33 God not author of c.
Jam. 3:16 where strife is, is c.

**CONGEALED.**

Ex. 15:8 depths were c. in sea

**CONGRATULATE.**

1 Chr. 18:10 his welfare, and c.

**CONGREGATION.**

Lev. 10:17 to bear iniquity of c.
16:33 atonement for all the c.
Num. 1:16 the renowned of c.
14:27 bear with this evil c.?
15:15 one ordinance be for c.
16:21 sep. yours. from this c.
45 get you up from am. this c.
47 Aaron ran into midst of c.
27:16 Lord set a man over c.
35:12 bef. c. for judg. Jos. 20:6
Jud. 20:1 c. gath. as one man
21:5 came not up with c. to L.
1 K. 12:20 called Jeroboam to c.
Ezr. 10:8 himself sep. from c.
Neh. 13:1 Moab. not come into c.
Job 15:34 c. of hypoc. desolate
30:28 and I cried in the c.
Ps. 1:5 nor sinners in c. of right.
22:22 midst of c. will I praise
26:5 hated the c. of evil-doers
58:1 speak righteousness, O c.?
74:2 rem. c. thou hast purch.
19 forget not the c. of thy poor
75:2 when I receive the c.
82:1 G. standeth in c. of mighty
89:5 thy faithfulness in c.
107:32 exalt him also in c.
111:1 praise the Lord in c.
Prov. 5:14 in midst of c.
21:16 remain in c. of the dead
Is. 14:13 will sit on mount of c.
Jer. 6:18 O c. what is among
30:20 c. be established before
Lam. 1:10 not enter into c.
Hos. 7:12 chas. them as their c.
Joel 2:16 sanctify the c.
Acts 13:43 when c. was broken

**All the CONGREGATION.**

Lev. 8:3 gather all the c.
16:17 atonement for all the c.
Num. 16:3 all the c. are holy
22 be wroth with all the c.?
20:27 sight of all the c. 25:6
Jos. 22:20 wrath fell on all the c.
1 K. 8:14 king blessed all the c. 55
1 Chr. 29:20 all the c. blessed L.
2 Chr. 23:3 a. t. c. made covenant
29:8 all the c. worshipped
Neh. 5:13 all the c. said, Amen
8:17 all the c. come again

**Elders of the CONGREGATION.**

Lev. 4:15 e. of c. shall lay hands

**Great CONGREGATION.**

1 K. 8:65 Sol. held feast, and all Is. a gr. c. 2 Chr. 7:8; 30:13
Ezr. 10:1 assem. to him a gr. c.
Ps. 22:25 pr. be of thee in g. c.
35:18 give thee thanks in g. c.
40:9 preached right. in g. c.
10 not conc. truth from great c.

**CONGREGATION of Israel.**

Lev. 4:13 if c. of Is. sin
2 Chr. 24:6 accord. to com. of c. I.

**CONGREGATION of the Lord.**

Num. 16:3 you above c. L.
27:17 c. of t. Lord. not as sheep
Deut. 23:1 not en. c. of t. L. 2, 3
1 Chr. 28:8 in sight of c. L.

**Tabernacle of the CONGREGATION.**

Ex. 29:44 sanctify t. of t. c.
33:7 called it the tab. of the c.
Lev. 16:33 atone. for t. of the c.
Num. 4:3 ta. of the c. 23, 25
8:9 Levites before t. of the c.
12:4 come out to t. of t. c.
14:10 glory of L. ap. in t. of c.
18:4 charge of taber. of the c.
Deut. 31:14 pres. yours. in t. of c.
Jos. 18:1 set up t. of t. c. at Shil.
1 K. 8:4 bro. up the t. 2 Chr. 5:5
2 Chr. 1:3 there was t. of the c.

See DOOR.

**Tent of the CONGREGATION.**

Ex. 39:32 tent of the c. finished
40:34 a cloud cov. tent of the c.
35 M. not able to enter t. of c.

**Whole CONGREGATION.**

Ex. 16:2 w. c. of Isa. murmured
Num. 3:7 keep charge of whole c.
Jos. 22:18 wroth with w. c.
Jud. 21:13 wh. c. sent to Benj.
2 Chr. 6:3 king blessed whole c.
Ezr. 2:64 whole c. 42,360, Neh. 7:66
Prov. 26:26 be showed bef. w. c.

**CONGREGATIONS.**

Ps. 26:12 in c. will I bless L.
68:26 bless ye God in the c.
74:4 enemies roar in thy c.

CONIAH. Jer. 22:24, 28; 37:1

**CONQUER.**

Rev. 6:2 conquering and to c.

**CONQUERORS.**

Rom. 8:37 we are more than c.

**CONSCIENCE.**

John 8:9 convicted by own c.
Acts 23:1 I have lived in good c.
24:16 a c. void of offence
Rom. 2:15 c. bearing witness
9:1 my c. bearing witness
13:5 be subject for c. sake
1 Cor. 8:7 with c. of idol eat it
10 weak c. be emboldened
12 wound weak c. ye sin
10:25 no question for c. sake, 27
28 eat not, for his and c. sake
29 c. I say, not thine own, but
2 Cor. 1:12 testimony of our c.
4:2 com. to every man's c.
1 Tim. 1:5 and of a good c.
19 holding faith and a good c.
3:9 mystery of faith in pure c.
4:2 c. seared with a hot iron
2 Tim. 1:3 whom I serve with c.
Tit. 1:15 but their c. is defiled
Heb. 9:9 as pertaining to c.
14 purge c. from dead works
10:2 worshippers no more c.
22 sprinkled from an evil c.
13:18 trust we have good c.
1 Pet. 2:19 for c. endure grief
3:16 having a good c.
21 but the answer of a good c.

**CONSCIENCES.**

2 Cor. 5:11 manifest in your c.

**CONSECRATE.**

Ex. 29:9 c. A. and sons, 30:30
32:29 c. yourselves this day to L.
1 Chr. 29:5 c. his service to Lord
Ezek. 43:26 shall c. themselves
Mic. 4:13 I will c. their gain

**CONSECRATED.**

Jud. 17:5 M. c. one of sons, 12
1 K. 13:33 whosoever would, he c.
2 Chr. 29:31 c. yourselves to Lord
33 c. things six hundred oxen
31:6 tithe of holy things c.
Heb. 7:28 Son, who is c. evermore
10:20 by a living way c. for us

**CONSECRATION, S.**

Ex. 29:22 for it is a ram of c.
Lev. 7:37 this is law of the c.
8:28 c. for sweet savor to Lord
31 with bread in basket of c.
33 days of your c. be at end
Num. 6:9 defiled head of his c.

**CONSENT, ED, ING.**

Gen. 34:23 only let us c. to them
Deut. 13:8 shalt not c. to him
1 K. 20:8 hearken not, nor c.
Ps. 50:18 sawest thief, thou c.
Prov. 1:10 entice thee, c. th. not
Dan. 1:14 so he c. in this matter
Luke 23:51 same had not c.
Acts 8:1 c. to his death, 22:20
18:20 to tarry longer, he c. not
Rom. 7:16 I c. to law
1 Tim. 6:3 c. not to whole. words

**CONSENT, Substantive.**

1 Sam. 11:7 came out with one c.
Ps. 83:5 consulted with one c.
Hos. 6:9 of priests murder by c.
Zep. 3:9 serve him with one c.
Luke 14:18 one c. to make excuse
1 Cor. 7:5 ex. with c. for a time

**CONSIDER.**

Deut. 4:39 c. it in thy heart
32:29 wise to c. latter end
Jud. 18:14 c. what ye have to do
1 Sam. 12:24 c. how great things
25:17 c. what thou wilt do
Job 11:11 will he not then c. it?
23:15 I c. I am afraid of him

34:27 would not c. his ways
37:14 c. wondrous works of God
Ps. 5:1 c. my meditation
9:13 c. my trouble
8:3 when I c. thy heavens
13:3 c. and hear, 45:10
25:19 c. my enemies
37:10 diligently c. his place
48:13 c. her palaces, that ye
50:22 c. this, ye that forget God
64:9 wisely c. of his doing
119:95 I will c. thy testimonies
153 c. mine affliction, deliver
159 c. how I love thy precepts
Prov. 6:6 go to ant, c. her ways
23:1 c. what is before thee
24:12 that pondereth heart c. it?
Ec. 5:1 c. not that they do evil
7:13 c. work of God, who can
14 but in day of adversity c.
Is. 1:3 my people doth not c.
5:12 c. operation of his hands
Is. 14:16 shall narrowly c. thee
18:4 c. in my dwelling-place
41:20 that they may see, and c.
43:18 nor c. the things of old
52:15 not heard shall they c.
Jer. 2:10 c. if there be such thing
23:20 in the latter days ye sh. c.
it perfectly, 30:24
Lam. 2:20 c. to whom done this
5:1 O Lord, c. our reproach
Ezek. 12:3 it may be they will c.
Dan. 9:23 and c. the vision
Hos. 7:2 c. not that I remember
Hag. 1:5 c. your ways, 7
2:15 I pray c. from this day, 18
Mat. 6:28 c. the lilies, Lu. 12:27
Luke 12:24 c. the ravens
John 11:50 nor c. it is expedient
Acts 15:6 elders came to c. of this
2 Tim. 2:7 c. and L. give thee
Heb. 3:1 brethren c. the Apostle
7:4 c. how great this man was
10:24 let us c. one another
12:3 c. him endured such con.

**CONSIDERED, EST.**

1 K. 5:8 I have c. things
Job 1:8 hast thou c. Job? 2:3
Ps. 31:7 hast c. my trouble
Prov. 24:32 then I c. it well
Ec. 4:1 I c. all the oppressions
4 again I c. all travel, and
9:1 all this I c. to declare this
Jer. 33:24 c. not people have spo.
Acts 12:12 when Peter had c.
Rom. 4:19 c. not his body dead

**CONSIDERETH, ING.**

Ps. 33:15 he c. all their works
41:1 blessed is he c. the poor
Prov. 21:12 c. house of wicked
28:22 c. not poverty shall come
29:7 righteous c. cause of poor
31:16 she c. a field, buyeth it
Is. 44:19 none c. to say, I burnt
57:1 none c. right. is tak. away
Ezek. 18:14 c. and doeth not, 28
Gal. 6:1 c. lest also be tempted
Heb. 13:7 c. end of their conver.

**CONSIST, ETH.**

Luke 12:15 life c. not in abund.
Col. 1:17 by him all things c.

**CONSOLATION.**

Jer. 16:7 nor give them cup of c.
Luke 2:25 Simeon waiting for c.
6:24 woe to you rich, rec. yo. c.
Acts 4:36 interpreted, son of c.
15:31 they rejoiced for the c.
Rom. 15:5 God of c. grant you
2 Cor. 1:5 our c. aboundeth by C.
6 afflicted for your c. comforted
7 so ye be partakers of the c.
7:7 c. wherewith he was comf.
Phil. 2:1 if any c. in Christ
2 Thes. 2:16 given us everlast. c.
Phile. 7 joy and c. in thy love

Heb. 6:18 might have strong c.

**CONSOLATIONS.**

Job 15:11 are c. of God small
21:2 and let this be your c.
Is. 66:11 with breasts of her c.

**CONSORTED.**

Acts 17:4 c. with Paul and Silas

**CONSPIRACY.**

2 Sam. 15:12 Absalom's c. strong
2 K. 12:20 a c. and slew Joash
14:19 c. ag. A. 2 Chr. 25:27
15:15 acts of Shallum and c.
17:4 found c. in Hoshea
Jer. 11:9 c. among men of Judah
Ezek. 22:25 a c. of her prophets
Acts 23:13 forty which made c.

**CONSPIRATORS.**

2 Sam. 15:31 Ahith. is among c.

**CONSPIRED.**

Gen. 37:18 c. ag. Jos. to slay him
1 Sam. 22:13 c. thou and son of J.
1 K. 15:27 Baasha c. aga. Nadab
16:9 Zimri c. against Elah, 16
2 K. 9:14 Jehu c. against Joram
10:9 I c. against my master
15:10 Shallum c. ag. Zechariah
25 Pekah c. against Pekahiah
21:23 serv. of Amon c. ag. him
24 c. against him, 2 Chr. 33:25
2 Chr. 24:21 c. against Jehoiada
25 serv. of Joash c. ag. him, 26
Neh. 4:8 c. all to come and fight
Amos 7:10 Amos hath c. ag. thee

**CONSTANT, LY.**

1 Chr. 28:7 if he be c. to do com.
Prov. 21:28 heareth, speaketh c.
Acts 12:15 she c. affirmed it was
Tit. 3:8 I will thou affirm c.

**CONSTELLATIONS.**

Is. 13:10 c. thereof

**CONSTRAIN, ED, ETH.**

2 K. 4:8 women c. him to eat
Job 32:18 the spirit in me c. me
Mat. 14:22 J. c. disc. Mark 6:45
Luke 24:29 c. him, saying, Abide
Acts 16:15 Lydia c. us to come
28:19 I was c. to appeal to
2 Cor. 5:14 love of Christ c. us
Gal. 6:12 c. you to be circum.

**CONSTRAINT.**

1 Pet. 5:2 oversight, not by c.

**CONSULTATION.**

Mark 15:1 chief priests held a c.

**CONSULT, ED, ETH.**

1 K. 12:6 Rehoboam c. 8
1 Chr. 13:1 D. c. with captains
2 Chr. 20:21 Jeh. c. with people
Neh. 5:7 then I c. with myself
Ps. 62:4 c. to cast him down
83:3 c. against hidden ones
5 have c. with one consent
Ezek. 21:21 king of B. c. images
Dan. 6:7 presidents and capt. c.
Mic. 6:5 rem. what Balak c.
Hab. 2:10 c. shame to thy house
Mat. 26:4 c. might take Jesus
Lu. 14:31 c. w. able with 10,000
John 12:10 c. to put L. to death

**CONSULTER.**

Deut. 18:11 a c. with spirits

**CONSUME.**

Ex. 33:3 lest I c. thee in way, 5
Deut. 5:25 this fire will c. us
7:16 shalt c. all the people
28:38 locust shall c. it, 42
32:22 fire kindled in anger c.
Jos. 24:20 c. after done you good
1 Sam. 2:33 to c. thine eyes
2 K. 1:10 let fire c. thy fifty, 12
Job 15:34 fire c. tabern. of brib.
20:26 a fire not blown c. him
24:19 and heat c. snow waters
Ps. 37:20 c. into smoke shall c.

39:11 his beauty to c. away
49:14 their beauty c. in grave
78:33 their days did he c.
Is. 7:20 it shall c. the beard
10:18 c. glory of his forest
27:10 shall calf c. branches
Jer. 49:27 fire c. pal. of Ben-ha
Ezek. 4:17 c. away for iniquity
13:13 great hailstones to c. it
21:28 sword is furbished to c.
22:15 I will c. thy filthiness
24:10 kindle fire, c. the flesh
35:12 they are giv. us to c.
Dan. 2:44 it shall c. these kingd.
Hos. 11:6 sword c. his branches
Zep. 1:2 I will c. all off land
3 I will c. man and beast
Zec. 5:4 in house and c. it
14:12 tongue shall c. away
2 Thes. 2:8 whom L. shall c.
Jam. 4:3 may c. it on your lusts

**CONSUME them.**

Ex. 32:10 that I may c. t. 12
Num. 16:21 c. t. in a moment, 45
Deut. 7:22 mayest not c. t.
Neh. 9:31 not utterly c. them
Est. 9:24 H. cast lot to c. them
Ps. 59:13 c. t. in wrath, c. them
Jer. 8:13 I will utterly c. t.
14:12 I will c. them by sword
Ezek. 20:13 fury on them to c. t.
Luke 9:54 fire to c. them

**CONSUMED.**

Gen. 19:15 be c. in the iniquity
17 escape to mount, lest be c.
31:40 in day drought c. me
Ex. 3:2 behold, bush was not c.
15:7 wrath c. them as stubble
22:6 if corn be c. therewith
Num. 11:1 c. them were in utter.
12:12 of whom flesh is half c.
16:26 lest ye be c. in their sins
35 fire c. the 250 men
21:28 fire hath c. Ar of Moab
25:11 that I c. not child. of Isr.
32:13 gener. done evil was c.
Deut. 2:16 men of war were c.
Jud. 6:21 fire out of rock c. flesh
2 Sam. 21:5 the man that c. us
1 K. 18:38 fell and c. 2 Chr. 7:1
2 K. 1:10 fire c. his fifty, 12
2 Chr. 8:8 children of Isr. c. not
Neh. 2:3 gates thereof are c. 13
Job 1:16 fire of God c. sheep
4:9 by breath of his nostrils c.
6:17 snow and ice are c.
7:9 as cloud is c. and vanisheth
19:27 reins c.; 33:21 flesh is c.
Ps. 6:7 mine eye c. 31:9
10 my bones c. 102:3
39:10 c. by blow of thy hand
71:13 let them be c. that are
Ps. 73:19 utterly c. with terrors
78:63 fire c. their young men
90:7 we are c. by thine anger
104:35 let sinners be c. out of
119:87 almost c. me upon earth
139 my zeal hath c. me, becau.
Prov. 5:11 flesh and body are c.
Is. 16:4 oppressors c. out of land
29:20 the scorner is c. and all
64:7 c. us because of iniquities
Jer. 5:3 c. refused correction
6:29 lead is c.; 12:4 beasts
20:18 should be c. with shame
36:23 till all the roll was c.
44:18 we have been c. by sword
Lam. 2:22 those I swad. enemy c.
3:22 of Lord's mercies not c.
Ezek. 19:12 rods fire c. 22:31
24:11 scum of it may be c.
43:8 wherefore I have c. them
Mal. 3:6 sons of Jacob are not c.
Gal. 5:15 ye be not c.

**Shall be CONSUMED.**

Num. 14:35 wilder. sh. they be c.

17:13 *shall* we *be c.* with dying?
1 *Sam.* 12:25 ye *s. be c.*
*Is.* 1:28 that forsake L. *sh. be c.*
66:17 eat swine's flesh, *s. be c.*
*Jer.* 16:4 *s. be c.* by sw. 44:12, 27
*Ezek.* 5:12 with famine *shall be c.*
13:14 and ye *shall be c.*
34:29 *sh. be* no more *c.*
47:12 nor *shall* fruit thereof *be c.*
*Dan.* 11:16 land which *shall be c.*

**CONSUMED, *with* till *or* until.**
*Deut.* 2:15 *until c. Jos.* 5:6
28:21 *until* he have *c.* thee
*Jos.* 10:20 slaying them *till c.*
1 *Sam.* 15:18 *until* they be *c.*
2 *Sam.* 22:38 I turned not *until* I had *c.* them, *Ps.* 18:37
1 *K.* 22:11 push Syr. *u. c.* them, 2 *K.* 13:17, 19; 2 *Chr.* 18:10
*Ezr.* 9:14 angry *till* hadst *c.* us
*Jer.* 9:16 send a sword *till* I have *c.* them, 24:10; 27:8; 49:37

**CONSUMETH, ING.**
*Deut.* 4:24 a *c.* fire, *Heb.* 12:29
9:3 L. goeth bef. thee as *c.* fire
*Job* 13:28 he *c.* as a garment that
22:20 remnant of them fire *c.*
31:12 fire that *c.* to destruction
*Is.* 5:24 as the flame *c.* chaff

**CONSUMMATION.**
*Dan.* 9:27 desolate until *c.*

**CONSUMPTION.**
*Lev.* 26:16 appoint over you *c.*
*Deut.* 28:22 smite thee with *c.*
*Is.* 10:22 *c.* dec. shall overflow
23 the Lord shall make a *c.*
28:22 I have heard from L. a *c.*

**CONTAIN.**
1 *K.* 8:27 heaven of heav. cannot *c.* thee, 2 *Chr.* 2:6; 6:18
*John* 21:25 world not *c.* the books
1 *Cor.* 7:9 if cannot *c.* marry

**CONTAINED, ETH, ING.**
*Ezek.* 23:32 thy sister's cup *c.*
*Rom.* 2:14 by nat. thi. *c.* in law
*Eph.* 2:15 abol. law *c.* in ordin.
1 *Pet.* 2:6 it is *c.* in scripture

**CONTEMN, ED, ETH.**
*Ps.* 10:13 wicked *c.* God?
15:4 eyes a vile person is *c.*
107:11 *c.* counsel of Most High
*Cant.* 8:7 substance would be *c.*
*Is.* 16:14 glory of Moab be *c.*
*Ezek.* 21:10 it *c.* rod of my son

**CONTEMPT.**
*Est.* 1:18 thus arise too much *c.*
*Job* 12:21 *c.* on princes, *Ps.* 107:40
31:34 *c.* of families terrify me
*Ps.* 119:22 remove from me *c.*
123:3 we are ex. filled with *c.*
4 soul filled with *c.* of proud
*Prov.* 18:3 wicked com. then *c.*
*Is.* 23:9 into *c.* the honorable
*Dan.* 12:2 awake to everlast. *c.*

**CONTEMPTIBLE.**
*Mal.* 1:7 say, table of Lord is *c.*
12 meat *c.*; 2:9 I made you *c.*
2 *Cor.* 10:10 his speech *c.*

**CONTEMPTUOUSLY.**
*Ps.* 31:18 speak *c.* against right.

**CONTEND.**
*Deut.* 2:9 neither *c.* in battle, 24
*Job* 9:3 if *c.* he cannot answer
13:8 will ye *c.* for God?
*Prov.* 28:4 such as keep law *c.*
*Ec.* 6:10 may he *c.* with him
*Is.* 49:25 I will *c.* with him
50:8 who will *c.* with me?
*Is.* 57:16 I will not *c.* for ever, nor
*Jer.* 12:5 how *c.* with horses?
18:19 to voice of them that *c.*
*Amos* 7:4 Lord called to *c.* by fire
*Mic.* 6:1 *c.* thou bef. the mount.
*Jude* 3 earnestly *c.* for the faith

**CONTENDED.**
*Neh.* 13:11 *c.* I with rulers, 17
*Job* 31:13 servants when they *c.*
*Is.* 41:12 not find them that *c.*
*Acts* 11:2 they of circum. *c.* with

**CONTENDEST.**
*Job* 10:2 show me wherefore *c.*

**CONTENDETH.**
*Job* 40:2 that *c.* with Almighty
*Prov.* 29:9 if wise *c.* with foolish

**CONTENDING.**
*Jude* 9 when *c.* with the devil

**CONTENT.**
*Gen.* 37:27 sell him, brethren *c.*
*Lev.* 10:20 heard that, he was *c.*
*Jos.* 7:7 would we had been *c.*
2 *K.* 6:3 one said, Be *c.* and go
*Job* 6:28 now therefore be *c.*
*Prov.* 6:35 nor will he rest *c.*
*Mark* 15:15 Pilate willing to *c.*
*Luke* 3:14 be *c.* with your wages
*Phil.* 4:11 in every state to be *c.*
1 *Tim.* 6:8 raiment, let us be *c.*
*Heb.* 13:5 be *c.* with such things
3 *John* 10 not *c.* with prating

**CONTENTION.**
*Prov.* 13:10 by pride cometh *c.*
17:14 leave off *c.* before it be
18:6 a fool's lips enter into *c.*
22:10 cast out scorner, *c.* sh. go
*Jer.* 15:10 borne me a man of *c.*
*Hab.* 1:3 that raise up *c.*
*Acts* 15:39 the *c.* was so sharp
*Phil.* 1:16 preach Christ of *c.*
1 *Thes.* 2:2 speak gospel with *c.*

**CONTENTIONS.**
*Prov.* 18:18 causeth *c.* to cease
19 *c.* like bars of a castle
19:13 *c.* of a wife, 27:15
23:29 who hath *c.*?
1 *Cor.* 1:11 there are *c.* am. you
*Tit.* 3:9 avoid *c.* and strivings

**CONTENTIOUS.**
*Prov.* 21:19 with *c.* woman
26:21 a *c.* man to kindle strife
27:15 dropping and *c.* woman
*Rom.* 2:8 to them that are *c.*
1 *Cor.* 11:16 if any seem to be *c.*

**CONTENTMENT.**
1 *Tim.* 6:6 godli. with *c.* is gain

**CONTINUAL.**
*Ex.* 29:42 be a *c.* burnt-offering
2 *Chr.* 2:4 for *c.* show-bread
*Prov.* 15:15 merry heart a *c.* feast
*Is.* 14:6 smote with a *c.* stroke
*Jer.* 48:5 *c.* weeping shall go up
*Ezek.* 39:14 men of *c.* employm.
*Luke* 18:5 lest by her *c.* coming
*Rom.* 9:2 *c.* sorrow in my heart
*See* BURNT-OFFERING.

**CONTINUALLY.**
*Gen.* 6:5 imagination was evil *c.*
*Ex.* 28:30 on heart before L. *c.*
1 *Chr.* 16:11 seek his face *c.*
*Job* 1:5 thus did Job *c.*
*Ps.* 34:1 his praise be *c.* 71:6
35:27 *c.* L. be mag. 40:16; 70:4
38:17 sorrow *c.* before me
40:11 truth *c.* preserve me
42:3 *c.* say, Where is thy God?
44:15 confusion *c.* before me
50:8 burnt-offer. *c.* before me
52:1 goodness of G. endureth *c.*
71:3 whereunto I may *c.* resort
6 my praise be *c.* of thee
14 but I will hope *c.* and yet
73:23 I am *c.* with thee, thou
74:23 the tumult increaseth *c.*
109:15 let them be before L. *c.*
119:44 shall I keep thy law *c.*
109 my soul is *c.* in my hand
117 respect to thy statutes *c.*
140:2 *c.* are gathered for war
*Prov.* 6:14 deviseth mischief *c.*
21 bind them *c.* on thy heart
*Is.* 21:8 *c.* upon the watch-tower
49:16 thy walls are *c.* before me
51:13 hast feared *c.* because
52:5 my name *c.* is blasph.
58:11 L. shall guide thee *c.*
60:11 gates shall be open *c.*
65:3 provoketh me to anger *c.*
*Jer.* 6:7 before me *c.* is grief
*Dan.* 6:16 G. whom servest *c.* 20
*Hos.* 12:6 wait on thy God *c.*
*Ob.* 16 heathen drink *c.*
*Nah.* 3:19 thy wick. passed *c.*?
*Luke* 24:53 *c.* in temple
*Acts* 6:4 ourselves *c.* to prayer
*Rom.* 13:6 *c.* on this very thing
*Heb.* 7:3 abideth a priest *c.*
10:1 sacrifices year by year *c.*
13:15 the sacrifice of praise *c.*

**CONTINUANCE.**
*Deut.* 28:59 plag. and of long *c.*
*Ps.* 139:16 in *c.* were fashioned
*Is.* 64:5 in those is *c.*
*Rom.* 2:7 patient *c.* in well-doing

**CONTINUE.**
*Ex.* 21:21 if he *c.* a day or two
1 *Sam.* 12:14 *c.* following the L.
13:14 thy kingdom not *c.*
2 *Sam.* 7:29 it may *c.* for ever
1 *K.* 2:4 L. may *c.* word he spake
*Job* 15:29 neither substance *c.*
17:2 eye *c.* in their provocation?
*Ps.* 36:10 O *c.* thy loving-kind.
49:11 that their houses shall *c.*
102:28 children of thy serv. *c.*
119:91 *c.* according to thy ordin.
*Is.* 5:11 *c.* till night, till wine
*Jer.* 32:14 may *c.* many days
*Dan.* 11:8 *c.* more years than k.
*Mat.* 15:32 *c.* now three days
*John* 8:31 if ye *c.* in my word
15:9 *c.* ye in my love
*Acts* 13:43 to *c.* in grace of God
14:22 exhorting to *c.* in faith
26:22 I *c.* unto this day
*Rom.* 6:1 shall we *c.* in sin
11:22 if thou *c.* in his goodness
*Gal.* 2:5 truth of gospel might *c.*
*Phil.* 1:25 I shall *c.* with you all
*Col.* 1:23 if ye *c.* in the faith
4:2 *c.* in prayer, and watch
1 *Tim.* 2:15 if they *c.* in faith
4:16 doctrine, *c.* in them
2 *Tim.* 3:14 *c.* in things hast
*Heb.* 7:23 not suffer to *c.*
13:1 let brotherly love *c.*
*Jam.* 4:13 *c.* there a year
2 *Pet.* 3:4 things *c.* as they were
1 *John* 2:24 ye shall *c.* in the Son
*Rev.* 13:5 power to *c.*
17:10 he must *c.* a short space

**CONTINUED.**
*Ps.* 72:17 his name be *c.* as sun
*Dan.* 1:21 Daniel *c.* to year of C.
*Luke* 6:12 *c.* all night in prayer
22:28 ye *c.* with me in tempt.
*Acts* 1:14 these *c.* in prayer
2:42 *c.* stead. in apostles' doc.
8:13 Simon *c.* with Philip
20:7 P. *c.* speech until midnight
*Heb.* 8:9 *c.* not in my covenant
1 *John* 2:19 no doubt *c.* with us

**CONTINUETH, ING.**
*Job* 14:2 as shadow, and *c.* not
*Jer.* 30:23 a *c.* whirlwind, it
*Acts* 2:46 *c.* daily with one ac.
*Rom.* 12:12 *c.* instant in prayer
*Gal.* 3:10 cursed *c.* not in all th.
1 *Tim.* 5:5 *c.* in supplications
*Heb.* 7:24 because he *c.* ever
13:14 we have no *c.* city, but
*Jam.* 1:25 perfect law, *c.* in it

**CONTRADICTING.**
*Acts* 13:45 with envy *c.* blasph.

**CONTRADICTION.**
*Heb.* 7:7 without *c.* less is blessed
12:3 endured such *c.* of sinners

**CONTRARIWISE.**
2 *Cor.* 2:7 *c.* rather to forgive him
*Gal.* 2:7 *c.* when saw gospel was
1 *Pet.* 3:9 railing, but *c.* blessing

**CONTRARY.**
*Lev.* 26:24 will I walk *c.* 28, 41
*Est.* 9:1 though turned to *c.*
*Ezek.* 16:34 *c.* is in thee, art *c.*
*Mat.* 14:24 for the wind was *c.*
*Acts* 17:7 these do *c.* to decrees
18:13 to worship God *c.* to law
23:3 to be smitten *c.* to the law
26:9 *c.* to the name of Jesus
*Rom.* 11:24 graffed *c.* to nature
16:17 *c.* to doctrine ye learned
*Gal.* 5:17 *c.* one to the other
*Col.* 2:14 handwriting *c.* to us
1 *Thes.* 2:15 and are *c.* to all men
1 *Tim.* 1:10 *c.* to sound doctrine
*Tit.* 2:8 he of a *c.* part be asham.

**CONTRIBUTION.**
*Rom.* 15:26 *c.* for the poor saints

**CONTRITE.**
*Ps.* 34:18 such as of *c.* spirit
51:17 *c.* heart, wilt not despise
*Is.* 57:15 of a *c.* spirit, to revive
heart of the *c.* ones
66:2 of *c.* spirit and trembleth

**CONTROVERSY.**
*Deut.* 17:8 being matters of *c.*
*Deut.* 19:17 between whom *c.* is
21:5 by their word *c.* be tried
25:1 if there be a *c.* betw. men
2 *Sam.* 15:2 that had a *c.* came
2 *Chr.* 19:8 set the Levites for *c.*
*Is.* 34:8 year of recom. for *c.*
*Jer.* 25:31 hath *c.* with nations
*Ezek.* 44:24 in *c.* they shall stand
*Hos.* 4:1 L. hath a *c.* with inhab.
12:2 Lord hath a *c.* with Judah
*Mic.* 6:2 L. hath *c.* with people
1 *Tim.* 3:16 with. *c.* great is mys.

**CONVENIENT, LY.**
*Prov.* 30:8 with food *c.* for me
*Jer.* 40:4 it seemeth *c.* to go, 5
*Mark* 6:21 a *c.* day was come
14:11 might *c.* betray him
*Acts* 24:25 a *c.* season, I will call
*Rom.* 1:28 to do things not *c.*
1 *Cor.* 16:12 when have *c.* time
*Eph.* 5:4 talking, nor jesting, *c.*
*Phile.* 8 to enjoin thee that *c.*

**CONVERSANT.**
*Jos.* 8:35 strangers *c.* am. them
1 *Sam.* 25:15 long as we were *c.*

**CONVERSATION.**
*Ps.* 37:14 as be of upright *c.*
50:23 ordereth his *c.* aright
2 *Cor.* 1:12 in godly sinc. had *c.*
*Gal.* 1:13 ye have heard of my *c.*
*Eph.* 2:3 had our *c.* in times past
4:22 concerning the former *c.*
*Phil.* 1:27 *c.* as becometh gospel
3:20 for our *c.* is in heaven
1 *Tim.* 4:12 be an example in *c.*
*Heb.* 13:5 *c.* be without covet.
7 considering end of their *c.*
*Jam.* 3:13 show out of a good *c.*
1 *Pet.* 1:15 in all manner of *c.*
18 not redeemed from vain *c.*
2:12 *c.* honest among Gentiles
3:1 may be won by *c.* of wives
2 while they behold chaste *c.*
16 falsely accuse your good *c.*
2 *Pet.* 2:7 vexed with the filthy *c.*
3:11 to be in all holy *c.*

**CONVERSION.**
*Acts* 15:3 declaring *c.* of Gentiles

**CONVERT, ED.**
*Ps.* 51:13 sinners be *c.* unto thee
*Is.* 6:10 lest *c.* and be healed
60:5 abundance of sea be *c.*
*Mat.* 13:15 be *c.* *Mark* 4:12
18:3 *c.* and become as children
*Luke* 22:32 when *c.* strengthen
*John* 12:40 be *c.* *Acts* 28:27
*Acts* 3:19 repent ye and be *c.*
*Jam.* 5:19 do err, and one *c.* him

**CONVERTETH, ING.**
*Ps.* 19:7 law is perfect, *c.* soul
*Jam.* 5:20 he which *c.* a sinner

**CONVERTS.**
*Is.* 1:27 her *c.* be redeemed with

**CONVEY, ED.**
1 *K.* 5:9 I will *c.* them by sea
*Neh.* 2:7 *c.* me over till I come
*John* 5:13 Jesus *c.* himself away

**CONVICTED.**
*John* 8:9 *c.* by their cons cience

**CONVINCE, ED, ETH.**
*Job* 32:12 none of you *c.* Job
*John* 8:46 which of you *c.* me
*Acts* 18:28 mightily *c.* the Jews
1 *Cor.* 14:24 he is *c.* of all, he is
*Tit.* 1:9 be able to *c.* gainsayers
*Jam.* 2:9 *c.* of law as transgres.
*Jude* 15 to *c.* all that are ungodly

**CONVOCATION.**
*Ex.* 12:16 a holy *c.* *Lev.* 23:7, 24,
35; *Num.* 28:18; 29:1
*Num.* 28:26 first-fruit a holy *c.*

**CONY, IES.**
*Lev.* 11:5 *c.* chew. cud, *Deut.* 14:7
*Ps.* 104:18 a refuge for the *c.*
*Prov.* 30:26 the *c.* a feeble folk

**COOK, S.**
1 *Sam.* 8:13 daughters to be *c.*
9:23 Sam. said to the *c.* Bring

**COOL.**
*Gen.* 3:8 walking in *c.* of day
*Luke* 16:24 and *c.* my tongue

**COPIED.**
*Prov.* 25:1 men of Hezekiah *c.*

**COPING.**
1 *K.* 7:9 from foundation to *c.*

**COPPER.**
*Ezr.* 8:27 two vessels of fine *c.*

**COPPERSMITH.**
2 *Tim.* 4:14 Alexander the *c.* did

**COPULATION.**
*Lev.* 15:16 seed of *c.* 17, 18

**COPY.**
*Deut.* 17:18 write a *c.* of law
*Jos.* 8:32 *c.* of law of Moses
*Ezr.* 4:11 *c.* of letter sent, 5:6
*Est.* 3:14 *c.* of writing, 8:13

**COR.**
*Ezek.* 45:14 a bath out of the *c.*

**CORAL.**
*Job* 28:18 no mention made of *c*
*Ezek.* 27:16 Syria merchant in *c.*

**CORBAN.**
*Mark* 7:11 it is *c.* that is, a gift

**CORD.**
*Jos.* 2:15 let spies down by a *c.*
*Job* 30:11 he hath loosed my *c.*
41:1 dr. out tongue with a *c.*?
*Ec.* 4:12 threefold *c.* not quickly
12:6 or ever silver *c.* be loosed
*Is.* 54:2 lengthen thy *c.*
*Mic.* 2:5 a *c.* by lot in the congr.

**CORDS.**
*Jud.* 15:13 Samson with new *c.*
*Job* 36:8 in *c.* of affliction
*Ps.* 2:3 let us cast away their *c.*
118:27 bind the sacrifice with *c*
129:4 hath cut *c.* of the wicked
140:5 proud have hid *c.* for me
*Prov.* 5:22 with *c.* of his sins

*Is.* 5:18 draw iniquity with *c.*
33:20 any of the *c.* be broken
*Jer.* 10:20 spoiled, and all my *c.*
38:13 drew up Jeremiah with *c.*
*Ezek.* 27:24 apparel bound with *c.*
*Hos.* 11:4 drew with *c.* of a man
*John* 2:15 a scourge of small *c.*

**CORIANDER.**
*Ex.* 16:31 *c.* seed, *Num.* 11:7

**CORINTH.**
*Acts* 18:1 after, Paul came to C.
19:1 while Apollos was at C.
1 *Cor.* 1:2; 2 *Cor.* 1:1, 23
2 *Tim.* 4:20 Erastus abode at C.

**CORINTHIANS.**
*Acts* 18:8 of the C. 2 *Cor.* 6:11

**CORMORANT.**
*Lev.* 11:17 owl and *c.* *Deut.* 14:17
*Is.* 34:11 *c.* possess it, *Zep.* 2:14

**CORN.**
*Gen.* 41:57 all came to buy *c.*
42:2 *c.* in Egypt, *Acts* 7:12
*Ex.* 22:6 stacks of *c.* be consum
*Lev.* 2:16 burn part of beaten *c.*
23:14 eat bread nor parched *c.*
*Num.* 18:27 *c.* of threshing-floor
*Deut.* 16:9 put sickle to *c.*
25:4 not muzzle ox treadeth *c.*
1 *Cor.* 9:9; 1 *Tim.* 5:18
*Jos.* 5:11 did eat of old *c.* 12
*Ruth* 3:7 lie down at heap of *c.*
1 *Sam.* 17:17 for breth. parched *c.*
25:18 Abigail took of parched *c.*
2 *Sam.* 17:28 brought parched *c.*
2 *K.* 19:26 blasted *c.* *Is.* 37:27
*Neh.* 5:2 we take up *c.* for them
*Job* 5:26 as a shock of *c.* cometh
24:6 reap every one *c.* in field
39:4 young grow up with *c.*
*Ps.* 65:9 thou preparest them *c.*
13 the valleys covered with *c.*
72:16 handful of *c.* in the earth
78:24 given of the *c.* of heaven
*Prov.* 11:26 with. *c.* people curse
*Is.* 17:5 harvestman gather. *c.*
21:10 and *c.* of my floor
62:8 no more give *c.* to enemies
*Ezek.* 36:29 I will call for *c.* and
*Hos.* 2:9 I will take away my *c.*
10:11 Ephraim loveth to tread *c.*
14:7 shall revive as the *c.* and
*Joel* 1:10 for the *c.* is wasted
17 the *c.* is withered
*Amos* 8:5 that we may sell *c.*
9:9 like as *c.* sifted in sieve
*Mark* 4:28 after that the full *c.*
*John* 12:24 except *c.* of wheat

**Ears of CORN.**
*Gen.* 41:5 seven *ears of c.* came
*Lev.* 2:14 offer green *ears of c.*
*Ruth* 2:2 glean *ears of c.*
2 *K.* 4:42 brought full *ears of c.*
*Job* 24:24 cut off as *ears of c.*
*Mat.* 12:1 to pluck *ears of c.* *Mark*
2:23; *Luke* 6:1

**CORN-FLOOR.**
*Hos.* 9:1 reward on every *c.-fl.*

**Standing CORN.**
*Ex.* 22:6 so that *s. c.* be consum.
*Deut.* 23:25 *stand. c.* of neighbor
*Jud.* 15:5 foxes go into *s. c.*

**CORN and wine.**
*Gen.* 27:28 G. gave plenty of *c. w.*
37 with *c. and w.* I sust. him
*Deut.* 7:13 bless thy *c. and wine*
*Deut.* 11:14 gather in thy *c. w.*
12:17 tithe of thy *c. w.* 14:23
18:4 first fruit of *c. and wine*
28:51 leave thee *c. and wine*
33:28 J. shall be on land of *c. w.*
2 *K.* 18:32 land of *c. w.* *Is.* 36:17
2 *Chr.* 31:5 first-fruits of *c. w.*
32:28 storehouses for *c. and w.*
*Neh.* 5:11 part of *c. and wine*
10:39 offer. of *c. and w.* 13:5, 12

*Ps.* 4:7 in time *c. w.* increased
*Lam.* 2:12 Where is *c. and w.?*
*Hos.* 2:8 I gave her *c. and wine*
22 the earth shall hear *c. w.*
7:14 assemble for *c. and wine*
*Joel* 2:19 I will send you *c. a. w.*
*Hag.* 1:11 drought on *c. and w.*
*Zec.* 9:17 *c.* make men cheer. *w.*

CORNELIUS. *Acts* 10:1, 7, 25, 31

**CORNER.**

*Lev.* 21:5 nor shave off *c* of beard
2 *Chr.* 28:24 altars in every *c.*
*Ps.* 118:22 is head stone of *c.*
*Prov.* 7:8 passing near her *c.*
12 she lieth in wait at every *c.*
21:9 better to dwell in *c.* 25:24
*Is.* 30:20 thy teachers into a *c.*
*Jer.* 31:38 city built to gate of *c.*
48:45 devour *c.* of Moab
51:26 nor take a stone for a *c.*
*Ezek.* 46:21 in every *c.* of court
*Amos* 3:12 in S. in *c.* of a bed
*Zec.* 10:4 out of him came *c.*
*Mat.* 21:42 same is bec. head of *c.* *Ps.* 118:22; *Mark* 12:10; *Luke* 20:17; *Acts* 4:11; 1 *Pet.* 2:7
*Acts* 26:26 was not done in a *c.*

**CORNER-GATE.**

*Zec.* 14:10 be inhabited to *c.-g.*

**CORNER-STONE, S.**

*Job* 38:6 who laid *c.-s.* thereof?
*Ps.* 144:12 daughters as *c.-stone*
*Is.* 28:16 in Zion a *c.-s.* 1 *Pet.* 2:6
*Eph.* 2:20 Christ being chief *c.-s.*

**CORNERS.**

*Lev.* 19:9 not reap the *c.* 23:22
27 not round *c.* of your heads
*Num.* 24:17 smite *c.* of Moab
*Deut.* 32:26 I will scatter into *c.*
*Neh.* 9:22 divide them into *c.*
*Job* 1:19 smote four *c.* of house
*Is.* 11:12 gather disp. from four *c.*
*Jer.* 9:26 I will punish all in uttermost *c.* 25:23; 49:32
*Ezek.* 7:2 end is come upon four *c.*
45:19 put blood upon four *c.*
*Mat.* 6:5 they love to pray in *c.*
*Acts* 10:11 knit at four *c.* 11:5
*Rev.* 7:1 four angels on four *c.*

**CORNET.**

1 *Chr.* 15:28 ark with sound of *c.*
*Ps.* 98:6 of *c.* make a joyful noise
*Dan.* 3:5 time ye hear *c.* 15
*Hos.* 5:8 blow ye the *c.* in Gibeah

**CORNETS.**

2 *Sam.* 6:5 David played on *c.*
2 *Chr.* 15:14 shouting with *c.*

**CORPSE, S.**

2 *K.* 19:35 all dead *c. Is.* 37:36
*Nah.* 3:3 no end of their *c.* they
*Mark* 6:29 took up John's *c.* and

**CORRECT.**

*Ps.* 39:11 *c.* man for iniquity
94:10 shall not he *c.?*
*Prov.* 29:17 *c.* thy son
*Jer.* 2:19 own wickedness *c.* thee
10:24 O Lord, *c.* me, but with
30:11 *c.* thee in measure 46:28

**CORRECTED, ETH.**

*Job* 5:17 happy is man God *c.*
*Prov.* 3:12 whom L. loveth he *c.*
29:19 servant not be *c.* by words
*Heb.* 12:9 fathers which *c.* us

**CORRECTION.**

*Job* 37:13 rain whether for *c.*
*Prov.* 3:11 nei. be weary of his *c.*
7:22 goeth as a fool to the *c.*
15:10 *c.* grievous to him
22:15 rod of *c.* drive it from him
23:13 withhold not *c.* from child
*Jer.* 2:30 children received no *c.*
5:3 have refused to receive *c.*
7:28 nation receiveth not *c.*
*Hab.* 1:12 establish them for *c.*

*Zep.* 3:2 she received not *c.*
2 *Tim.* 3:16 scrip. profitable for *c.*

**CORRUPT, Adjective.**

*Gen.* 6:11 the earth also was *c.* 12
*Job* 17:1 my breath is *c.*
*Ps.* 14:1 they are *c.* 53:1; 73:8
38:5 my wounds are *c.* because
*Prov.* 25:26 as a *c.* spring
*Ezek.* 20:44 not accor. to *c.* doings
23:11 *c.* in her inordinate love
*Dan.* 2:9 ye have prep. *c.* words
*Mal.* 1:14 sacrificeth a *c.* thing
*Mat.* 7:17 a *c.* tree evil fruit
18 *c.* tree good fruit, *Luke* 6:43
12:33 or else make tree *c.* and
*Eph.* 4:22 put off the old man *c.*
29 let no *c.* communication
1 *Tim.* 6:5 disputings of men of *c.*
2 *Tim.* 3:8 men of *c.* minds

**CORRUPT, Verb.**

*Deut.* 4:16 lest ye *c.* yours. 25
31:29 after my death ye will *c.*
*Dan.* 11:32 sh. he *c.* by flatteries
*Mal.* 2:3 I will *c.* your seed
*Mat.* 6:19 moth and rust doth *c.*
20 moth nor rust doth *c.*
1 *Cor.* 15:33 evil communica. *c.*
2 *Cor.* 2:17 that *c.* the word
*Jude* 10 in those things they *c.*
*Rev.* 19:2 *c.* earth with her forn.

**CORRUPTED, ETH.**

*Gen.* 6:12 all flesh had *c.* his way
*Ex.* 32:7 people have *c.* themselves, *Deut.* 9:12; 32:5
*Jud.* 2:19 *c.* more than fathers
*Ezek.* 16:47 *c.* more than they
28:17 hast *c.* thy wisdom
*Hos.* 9:9 deeply *c.* themselves
*Zep.* 3:7 and *c.* their doings
*Mal.* 2:8 *c.* covenant of Levi
*Luke* 12:33 nor moth *c.*
2 *Cor.* 7:2 wronged *c.* no man
11:3 your minds be *c.*
*Jam.* 5:2 your riches are *c.*

**CORRUPTERS.**

*Is.* 1:4 children that are *c.*
*Jer.* 6:28 they are all *c.*

**CORRUPTIBLE.**

*Rom.* 1:23 image like to *c.* man
1 *Cor.* 9:25 to obtain a *c.* crown
15:53 *c.* must put on incorrup.
1 *Pet.* 1:18 not redeemed with *c.*
23 born again, not of *c.* seed
3:4 be in that which is not *c.*

**CORRUPTING.**

*Dan.* 11:17 dau. of women *c.* her

**CORRUPTION.**

*Lev.* 22:25 their *c.* is in them
2 *K.* 23:13 right of mount of *c.*
*Job* 17:14 I said to *c.* my father.
*Ps.* 16:10 nei. suffer thy H. One to see *c. Acts* 2:27; 13:35
49:9 live and not see *c.*
*Is.* 38:17 deliv. it from pit of *c.*
*Dan.* 10:8 comeliness into *c.*
*Jon.* 2:6 br. up my life from *c.*
*Acts* 2:31 nei. his flesh did see *c.*
13:34 no more to return to *c.*
36 David saw *c.*
37 whom God raised saw no *c.*
*Rom.* 8:21 from bondage of *c.*
1 *Cor.* 15:42 is sown in *c.* raised
50 *c.* inherit incorruption
*Gal.* 6:8 of the flesh reap *c.*
2 *Pet.* 1:4 escaped the *c.* that is
2:12 perish in their own *c.*
19 they are servants of *c.*

**CORRUPTLY.**

2 *Chr.* 27:2 people did yet *c.*
*Neh.* 1:7 we have dealt *c.* ag. thee

**COST.**

2 *Sam.* 19:42 eaten of king's *c.?*
24:24 offer of that *c.* nothing
1 *Chr.* 21:24 b.-offering without *c.*

*Luke* 14:28 and counteth the *c.*

**COSTLINESS.**

*Rev.* 18:19 made rich by her *c.*

**COSTLY.**

1 *K.* 7:9 all these were of *c.* stones
*John* 12:3 took spikenard, *c.*
1 *Tim.* 2:9 not with *c.* array

**COTES.**

2 *Chr.* 32:28 Hezekiah made *c.*

**COTTAGE, S.**

*Is.* 1:8 dau. of Zion is left as a *c.*
24:20 earth be removed like a *c.*
*Zep.* 2:6 coasts be *c.* for sheph.

**COUCH, ES.**

*Gen.* 49:4 Reuben went to my *c.*
*Job* 7:13 I say my *c.* shall ease
*Ps.* 6:6 I water *c.* with tears
*Amos* 3:12 in Damascus in a *c.*
6:4 that stretch upon their *c.*
*Luke* 5:19 tiling with his *c.*
24 arise take up thy *c.* and go
*Acts* 5:15 laid sick folks on *c.*

**COUCH, ED.**

*Job* 38:40 when they *c.* in dens
*Gen.* 49:9 Judah *c.* as a lion
*Num.* 24:9 he *c.* he lay as a lion

**COUCHETH, ING.**

*Gen.* 49:14 a strong ass *c.* down
*Deut.* 33:13 deep that *c.* beneath
*Ezek.* 25:5 a *c.* place for flocks

**COULD.**

*Ps.* 37:36 but he *c.* not be found
*Jer.* 15:1 *c.* not be toward this p.
*Mark* 9:18 they *c.* not, *Lu.* 9:40
14:8 she hath done what she *c.*

**COULTER.**

1 *Sam.* 13:20 sharpen each his *c.*

**COUNCIL.**

*Ps.* 68:27 princes of J. and *c.*
*Mat.* 5:22 Raca, in danger of *c.*
12:14 Pharisees held a *c.*
26:59 *c.* so. false wit. *Mark* 14:55
*Mark* 15:1 *c.* bound Jesus
*Luke* 22:66 led Jesus into their *c.*
*John* 11:47 gather *c. Acts* 5:21
*Acts* 4:15 com. to go out of *c.*
5:27 and set them before *c.*
34 stood up in *c.* a Pharisee
41 departed from *c.* rejoicing
6:12 brought Stephen to *c.*
22:30 he com. their *c.* to appear
23:15 ye with *c.* sig. to captain
24:20 evil in me, while before *c.*

**COUNCILS.**

*Mat.* 10:17 del. to *c. Mark* 13:9

**COUNSEL.**

*Ex.* 18:19 I will give thee *c.*
*Num.* 27:21 Eleazar ask *c.*
31:16 *c.* of Balaam to trespass
*Deut.* 32:28 a nation void of *c.*
*Jos.* 9:14 asked not *c.* at the L.
*Jud.* 20:7 give here your *c.*
2 *Sam.* 15:31 *c.* of A. foolishness
16:23 all *c.* of Ahith. with D.
17:14 defeated good *c.* of Ah.
20:18 surely ask *c.* at Abel
1 *K.* 1:12 let me give thee *c.*
12:8 forsook *c.* 2 *Chr.* 10:8
2 *K.* 6:8 took *c.* with his servants
18:20 I have *c.* for war, *Is.* 36:5
1 *Chr.* 10:13 died for asking *c.*
2 *Chr.* 22:5 Ahaziah after their *c.*
25:16 art thou made of king's *c.*
*Ezr.* 10:8 accord. to *c.* of princes
*Neh.* 4:15 brought *c.* to naught
*Job* 5:13 *c.* of froward headlong
10:3 shine on *c.* of the wicked
12:13 hath *c.* and understand.
21:16 *c.* of wicked is far, 22:18
38:2 darkeneth *c.* by words?
42:3 hideth *c.* without knowl.?

*Ps.* 1:1 not in *c.* of ungodly
14:6 shamed the *c.* of poor
16:7 who hath given me *c.*
20:4 the Lord fulfil all thy *c.*
31:13 they took *c.* against me
33:10 *c.* of heathen to naught
55:14 we took sweet *c.* together
64:2 from secret *c.* of wicked
73:24 guide me with thy *c.*
83:3 crafty *c.* against thy people
106:13 waited not for his *c.* but
43 provoked him with their *c.*
107:11 contemned *c.* of M. High
*Prov.* 8:14 *c.* is mine, and wisd.
11:14 where no *c.* is, people fall
12:15 hearkeneth to *c.* is wise
15:22 without *c.* purposes disap.
19:20 hear *c.* receive instruction
20:5 *c.* in man like deep water
18 purpose established by *c.*
21:30 no wisdom nor *c.* ag. L.
24:6 by wise *c.* shalt make war
27:9 friend, by hearty *c.*
*Is.* 5:19 *c.* of Holy One
7:5 taken evil *c.* against thee
11:2 spirit of *c.* rest upon him
19:3 I will destroy *c.* of Egypt
11 *c.* of counsellors brutish
23:8 hath taken this *c.* ag. T.?
28:29 which is wonderful in *c.*
29:15 to hide *c.* from Lord
40:14 with whom took he *c.*
44:26 performeth *c.* of his mes.
*Jer.* 18:18 nor *c.* perish from w.
23 knowest all their *c.* ag. me
19:7 make void the *c.* of Judah
32:19 mighty God, great in *c.*
38:15 if I give *c.* wilt not thou
49:7 is *c.* perished from prudent
30 king of Babylon taken *c.*
*Ezek.* 7:26 *c.* perish from ancients
11:2 give wicked *c.* in this city
*Dan.* 2:14 D. answered with *c.*
*Hos.* 4:12 my people ask *c.*
*Mic.* 4:12 understand his *c.*
*Zec.* 6:13 *c.* of peace between
*Mark* 3:6 *c.* ag. Jes. *John* 11:53
*Luke* 23:51 not consented to *c.* of
*John* 18:14 now Caiaphas gave *c.*
*Acts* 4:28 thy *c.* determined bef.
5:33 they took *c.* to slay them
38 if this *c.* be of men
9:23 Jews took *c.* to kill him
*Acts* 27:42 soldiers *c.* to kill pris.
*Eph.* 1:11 after *c.* of his own will
*Heb.* 6:17 immutability of his *c.*

**COUNSEL of God, *or* Lord.**

*Jud.* 18:5 said, Ask *c. of God*
20:18 chil. of Is. asked *c. of G.* 23
1 *Sam.* 14:37 Saul asked *c. of G*
*Ps.* 33:11 *c. of L. Prov.* 19:21
*Is.* 19:17 bec. of the *c. of Lord*
*Jer.* 23:18 stood in *c. of Lord*
49:20 hear *c. of Lord*, 50:45
*Luke* 7:30 rejected *c. of God*
*Acts* 2:23 determinate *c. of God*
20:27 to declare all *c. of God*

**My COUNSEL.**

2 *Chr.* 25:16 not heark. to *my c.*
*Job* 29:21 kept silence at *my c.*
*Prov.* 1:25 set at naught *my c.*
30 they would none of *my c.*
*Is.* 46:10 *my c.* shall stand
11 executeth *my c.*
*Jer.* 23:22 had stood in *my c.*
*Dan.* 4:27 O king, let *my c.* be

**Own COUNSEL.**

*Job* 18:7 his *own c.* cast down
*Hos.* 10:6 ashamed of his *own c.*

**Take COUNSEL.**

*Neh.* 6:7 come now, let us *take c.*
*Ps.* 2:2 rulers *t. c.* against Lord
13:2 how long *t. c.* in my soul
71:10 wait for my soul, *take c.*
*Is.* 8:10 *t. c.* it come to naught
16:3 *take c.* execute judgment
30:1 that *take c.* but not of me
45:21 yea, let them *take c.*

**COUNSEL, LED.**

2 *Sam.* 16:23 which Ahith. *c.*
17:15 Ahithophel *c.* thus I *c.* 21
*Job* 26:3 how *c.* him hath no wis.
*Ec.* 8:2 I *c.* thee to keep
*Rev.* 3:18 I *c.* to buy of me gold

**COUNSELLOR.**

2 *Sam.* 15:12 D.'s *c.* 1 *Chr.* 27:33
1 *Chr.* 26:14 Zechariah a wise *c.*
27:32 Jonathan was a *c.*
2 *Chr.* 22:3 Athaliah was his *c.*
*Is.* 3:3 Lord taketh away *c.*
9:6 be called Wonderful, *C.*
40:13 or who being his *c.* hath
41:28 for I beheld, was no *c.*
*Mic.* 4:9 is thy *c.* perished?
*Nah.* 1:11 out of thee a wicked *c.*
*Mark* 15:43 J. a *c. Luke* 23:50
*Rom.* 11:34 hath been his *c.*

**COUNSELLORS.**

2 *Chr.* 22:4 *c.* after father's death
*Ezr.* 4:5 hired *c.* against them
7:14 sent of king and his sev. *c.*
28 ext. mercy to me before *c.*
*Job* 3:14 at rest with *c.* of earth
12:17 leadeth *c.* away spoiled
*Ps.* 119:24 thy testimonies my *c.*
*Prov.* 11:14 multitude of *c.* 24:6
12:20 to *c.* of peace is joy
15:22 in multitude of *c.* estab.
*Is.* 1:26 restore thy *c.* as at begin.
19:11 wise *c.* of Pharaoh brutish
*Dan.* 3:27 the king's *c.* saw these
4:36 my *c.* sought unto me
6:7 all the *c.* have consulted

**COUNSELS.**

*Job* 37:12 turned about by his *c.*
*Ps.* 5:10 fall by their own *c.*
81:12 walked in their own *c.*
*Prov.* 1:5 shall attain to wise *c.*
12:5 *c.* of wicked are deceit
22:20 excellent things in *c.*?
*Is.* 25:1 *c.* of old are faithful
47:13 wearied in mul. of thy *c.*
*Jer.* 7:24 in *c.* of their evil heart
*Hos.* 11:6 because of their own *c.*
*Mic.* 6:16 in *c.* of house of Ahab
1 *Cor.* 4:5 manifest *c.* of heart

**COUNT.**

*Lev.* 23:15 *c.* from morrow after
25:27 let *c.* years of sale, 52
*Num.* 23:10 can *c.* dust of Jacob
1 *Sam.* 1:16 *c* not. me dau. of B.
*Job* 19:15 maids *c.* me a stranger
31:4 doth not he *c.* all my steps
*Ps.* 87:6 L. *c.* when he writeth
139:18 if I *c.* them, more than s.
22 I *c.* them mine enemies
*Mic.* 6:11 shall I *c.* them pure
*Acts* 20:24 neither *c.* I my life
*Phil.* 3:8 I *c.* all loss, *c.* but dung
13 I *c.* not to have apprehend.
2 *Thes.* 1:11 *c.* you worthy
3:15 *c.* him not as an enemy
1 *Tim.* 6:1 *c.* masters worthy of
*Phile.* 17 if thou *c.* me a partner
*Jam.* 1:2 *c.* it joy when ye fall
5:11 we *c.* happy which endure
2 *Pet.* 2:13 *c.* it pleasure to riot
2 *Pet.* 3:9 as some men *c.* slackn.
*Rev.* 13:18 *c.* number of beast

**COUNTED.**

*Gen.* 15:6 *c.* it to him *Ps.* 106:31; *Rom.* 4:3; *Gal.* 3:6
30:33 be *c.* stolen with me
31:15 are we not *c.* strangers
1 *K.* 3:8 cannot be *c.* for multi.
1 *Chr.* 21:6 Benjamin *c.* he not
*Neh.* 13:13 were *c.* faithful
*Job* 18:3 where. are we *c.* as beas.
41:29 darts are *c.* as stubble
*Ps.* 44:22 we are *c.* as sheep for
88:4 *c.* with them go to the pit
*Prov.* 17:28 hold. peace is *c.* wise
27:14 be *c.* a curse to him
*Is.* 5:28 hoofs be *c.* like flint
32:15 field be *c.* for a forest
33:18 where is he *c.* towers
40:15 nations *c.* as small dust
17 nations *c.* less than nothing
*Hos.* 8:12 were *c.* as strange
*Mat.* 14:5 *c.* him, *Mark* 11:32
*Luke* 21:36 *c.* worthy to escape
*Acts* 5:41 rejoic. were *c.* worthy
19:19 burn books, and *c.* price
*Rom.* 2:26 uncir. be *c.* for circ.
4:5 his faith is *c.* for right.
9:8 child. of promise *c.* for seed
*Phil.* 3:7 those I *c.* lost for Christ
2 *Thes.* 1:5 *c.* worthy of kingdom
1 *Tim.* 1:12 he *c.* me faithful
5:17 elders *c.* worthy
*Heb.* 3:3 *c.* worthy of more glory
7:6 he whose descent is not *c.*
10:29 *c.* blood of cov. unholy
*See* ACCOUNTED.

**COUNTETH, ING.**

*Job* 19:11 *c.* me of enem. 33:10
*Ec.* 7:27 *c.* one by one, to find
*Luke* 14:28 and *c.* the cost

**COUNTENANCE, Verb.**

*Ex.* 23:3 neither *c.* a poor man

**COUNTENANCE.**

*Gen.* 4:5 Cain was wroth, *c.* fell
31:2 Jacob beheld *c.* of Laban
5 father's *c.* not toward me
*Num.* 6:26 lift up his *c.* on thee
*Deut.* 28:50 a nation of fierce *c.*
*Jud.* 13:6 his *c.* like *c.* of angel
1 *Sam.* 1:18 her *c.* no more sad
16:7 look not on his *c.* or height
12 David was of beau. *c.* 17:42
25:3 Abigail; 2 *Sam.* 14:27 Tam.
2 *K.* 8:11 he settled his *c.* on H.
*Neh.* 2:2 why is thy *c.* sad
3 why not *c.* sad, when city
*Job* 14:20 thou changest his *c.*
29:24 light of *c.* cast not down
*Ps.* 4:6 lift light of thy *c.* on us
10:4 pride of *c.* not seek God
11:7 *c.* doth behold upright
21:6 made him glad with thy *c.*
42:5 praise him for help of his *c.*
11 who is health of my *c.* 43:5
44:3 light of thy *c.* did save
80:16 perish at rebuke of thy *c.*
89:15 walk in light of thy *c.*
90:8 secret sins in light of thy *c.*
*Prov.* 15:13 maketh a cheerful *c.*
16:15 in light of king's *c.* is life
25:23 so angry *c.* a backbiting
27:17 so man sharpeneth *c.* of
*Ec.* 7:3 by sadness of *c.*
*Cant.* 2:14 see *c.* thy *c.* is comely
5:15 his *c.* is as Lebanon
*Is.* 3:9 *c.* doth witness ag. them
*Ezek.* 27:35 be troubled in their *c.*
*Dan.* 5:6 king's *c.* was changed
8:23 king of fierce *c.* stand up
*Mat.* 6:16 as hypocrites, of sad *c.*
28:3 *c.* like lightning, *Luke* 9:29
*Acts* 2:28 full of joy with thy *c.*
2 *Cor.* 3:7 not behold Mos. for *c.*
*Rev.* 1:16 *c.* was as sun shineth
*See* CHANGED.

**COUNTENANCES.**

*Dan.* 1:13 let our *c.* be looked on
15 their *c.* appeared fairer and

**COUNTERVAIL.**

*Est.* 7:4 not *c.* the k.'s damage

**COUNTRY.**

*Gen.* 24:4 thou shalt go to my *c.*
29:26 not be so done in our *c.*
30:25 that I may go to my *c.*
42:33 lord of *c.* said unto us
*Num.* 15:13 born in *c.* shall do
32:4 *c.* Lord smote before Israel
*Deut.* 26:3 come into *c.* L. sware

*Jos.* 2:2 to search out the *c.* 3
7:2 go up and view the *c.*
*Jud.* 11:21 Isr. possessed that *c.*
16:24 the destroyer of our *c.*
*Ruth* 1:2 came into *c.* of Moab
2 *Sam.* 15:23 all the *c.* wept
1 *K.* 20:27 Syrians filled the *c.*
2 *K.* 3:20 *c.* filled with water
*Is.* 1:7 *c.* is desolate, cities burnt
22:18 like a ball in a large *c.*
*Jer.* 22:10 not see his native *c.*
31:8 bring them from north *c.*
48:21 judgment upon plain *c.*
50:9 an assembly from north *c.*
*Ezek.* 20:38 bring them forth of *c.*
25:9 glory of *c.* Beth-jeshimoth
47:22 be to you as born in the *c.*
*Jon.* 4:2 when yet in my *c.*
*Mat.* 9:31 his fame in all that *c.*
*Mark* 5:10 not send th. out of *c.*
14 told it in the *c.* *Luke* 8:34
*Luke* 15:15 joined to cit. of th. *c.*
*Acts* 12:20 their *c.* was nourished
27:27 they drew near to some *c.*
*Heb.* 11:9 as in a strange *c.*
14 plainly that they seek a *c.*
15 been mindful of that *c.*
16 desire better *c.* a heavenly

**Far COUNTRY.**

*Jos.* 9:6 we be come from *f. c.* 9
1 *K.* 8:41 out of a *far c.* for thy sake, 2 *Chr.* 6:32
2 *K.* 20:14 fr. *f. c.* fr. Bab. *Is.* 39:3
*Prov.* 25:25 good news from *f. c.*
*Is.* 13:5 from *f. c.* to destroy
46:11 exec. counsel from *far c.*
*Jer.* 4:16 watchers come fr. *far c.*
8:19 because of them in a *far c.*
*Mat.* 21:33 householder went into *far c.* *Mark* 12:1
25:14 a man trav. into a *far c.*
*Luke* 15:13 journey into a *far c.*

**Own COUNTRY.**

*Lev.* 16:29 one of *own c.* 24:22
1 *K.* 10:13 went to her *o. c.*
11:21 I may go to my *own c.*
22:36 every man to *own c.*
*Jer.* 51:9 every one into his *o. c.*
*Mat.* 2:12 dep. into their *own c.*
13:57 without honor save in his *o. c.* *Mark* 6:4; *Luke* 4:24
*Mark* 6:1 came into his *own c.*
*John* 4:44 proph. no honor in *o. c.*

**Thy COUNTRY.**

*Gen.* 12:1 out of *thy c.* *Acts* 7:3
32:9 return to *t. c.* and kindred
*Num.* 20:17 let us pass thro' *t. c.*
*Jon.* 1:8 what is *thy c.?*
*Luke* 4:23 do here in *thy c.*

**COUNTRY Villages.**

1 *Sam.* 6:18 both of *c. villages*

**COUNTRYMEN.**

2 *Cor.* 11:26 in perils by own *c.*
1 *Thes.* 2:14 like things of your *c.*

**COUNTRIES.**

*Gen.* 26:3 to thy seed these *c.* 4
41:57 all *c.* came to buy corn
1 *Chr.* 22:5 glory through *c.*
2 *Chr.* 20:29 fear of G. on all *c.*
*Ezr.* 3:3 because of people of *c.*
4:20 which ruled over all *c.*
*Ps.* 110:6 wound over many *c.*
*Is.* 8:9 give ear ye of far *c.*
*Jer.* 23:3 I will gather my flock out of all *c.* 8; 32:37
28:8 prophesied against many *c.*
*Ezek.* 5:5 Jerusalem in midst of *c.*
6 changed statutes more th. *c.*
6:8 when scattered through *c.*
11:16 I scattered them among *c.* little sanctuary in *c.*
17 out of *c.* 20:34, 41
22:4 a mocking to all *c.*
25:7 to perish out of *c.*
29:12 disperse through *c.* 36:19
35:10 these two *c.* shall be mine
*Dan.* 11:40 he shall enter into *c.*
42 forth his hand upon the *c.*
*Zec.* 10:9 remember me in far *c.*
*Luke* 21:21 that are in *c.* enter

**COUPLED.**

1 *Pet.* 3:2 conversation *c.* with f.

**COURAGE.**

*Jos.* 2:11 nor any more *c.* in any
2 *Chr.* 15:8 took *c.* put away idols
*Dan.* 11:25 stir up *c.* ag. king
*Acts* 28:15 thanked God took *c.*

**Good COURAGE.**

*Num.* 13:20 *good c.* bring fruit
*Deut.* 31:6 strong and of *good c.* 7, 23; *Jos.* 1:6, 9, 18; 10:25; 1 *Chr.* 22:13; 28:20
2 *Sam.* 10:12 be of *g. c.* 1 *Chr.* 19:13; *Ezr.* 10:4; *Is.* 41:6
*Ps.* 27:14 be of *g. c.* he shall stre. thy heart, 31:24

**COURAGEOUS, LY.**

*Jos.* 1:7 be *c.* 23:6; 2 *Chr.* 32:7
2 *Sam.* 13:28 be *c.* valiant
2 *Chr.* 19:11 deal *c.*
*Amos* 2:16 he *c.* shall flee naked

**COURSE.**

1 *Chr.* 27:1 of every *c.* 24,000
2 *Chr.* 5:11 did not wait by *c.*
*Ezr.* 3:11 sang together by *c.*
*Ps.* 82:5 foundations out of *c.*
*Jer.* 8:6 every one turned to his *c.*
23:10 their *c.* is evil, their force
*Luke* 1:5 Zacharias *c.* of Abia
8 in the order of his *c.*
*Acts* 13:25 John fulfilled his *c.*
16:11 with straight *c.* 21:1
20:24 finish my *c.* with joy
21:7 finished *c.* from Tyre
1 *Cor.* 14:27 by three, by *c.*
2 *Thes.* 3:1 may have free *c.*
2 *Tim.* 4:7 I have finished my *c.*
*Jam.* 3:6 on fire the *c.* of nature
*See* WATERCOURSE.

**COURSES.**

*Jud.* 5:20 the stars in their *c.*
1 *Chr.* 23:6 the Levites into *c.*
2 *Chr.* 23:8 Jeh. dismissed not *c.*
31:2 Hezekiah appointed *c.*
35:10 Levites stood in their *c.*

**COURT.**

*Ex.* 27:9 shalt make the *c.*
40:8 thou shalt set up the *c.*
2 *K.* 20:4 afore Isaiah was into *c.*
2 *Chr.* 20:5 Jehosh. bef. new *c.*
24:21 stoned Zechariah in *c.*
29:16 brought unclean. into *c.*
*Est.* 6:5 beh. H. standeth in *c.*
*Is.* 34:13 shall be a *c.* for owls
*Jer.* 19:14 Jeremiah stood in *c.*
26:2 stand in *c.* of Lord's house
32:2 Jeremiah was shut up in *c.* of prison, 33:1; 39:15
*Ezek.* 8:7 brou. me to door of *c.* 16
10:3 the cloud filled inner *c.*
40:17 to outward *c.* 42:1; 46:21
28 he brought me to inner *c.*
43:5 brought me to inner *c.*
46:21 in every cor. of *c.* was a *c.*
*Amos* 7:13 and it is the king's *c.*
*Rev.* 11:2 *c.* without the temple

**COURTS.**

2 *K.* 21:5 built altars for hosts of heav. in two *c.* 2 *Chr.* 33:5
1 *Chr.* 23:28 office to wait in *c.*
28:6 Solomon shall build my *c.*
2 *Chr.* 23:5 all the people be in *c.*
*Ps.* 65:4 he may dwell in thy *c.*
84:2 soul fainteth for *c.* of Lord
92:13 flourish in *c.* of our God
96:8 bring offering come into *c.*
100:4 enter his *c.* with praise
116:19 pay vows in the *c.* of
135:2 ye that stand in the *c.* of
*Is.* 1:12 to tread my *c.?*
62:9 drink it in *c.* of holiness
*Ezek.* 9:7 fill *c.* with the slain
*Zec.* 3:7 shalt also keep my *c.*
*Luke* 7:25 delicately in king's *c.*

**COURTEOUS, LY.**

*Acts* 27:3 Julius *c.* entreated P.
28:7 and Publius lodged us *c.*
1 *Pet.* 3:8 love as brethren, be *c.*

**COUSIN, S.**

*Luke* 1:36 thy *c.* Elisabeth
1:58 her *c.* heard how

**COVENANT.**

*Gen.* 9:12 tok. of *c.* 13, 17; 17:11
17:4 my *c.* is with thee
13 my *c.* be in your flesh
14 hath broken my *c.*
*Ex.* 31:16 sab. a perpetual *c.*
34:28 wrote upon tables the *c.*
*Lev.* 26:15 that ye break my *c.*
*Num.* 25:12 my *c.* of peace
13 *c.* of everlasting priesthood
*Deut.* 4:13 dec. unto you his *c.*
23 lest ye forget *c.* of Lord
31 Lord not forget *c.*
9:11 Lord gave me tables of *c.*
29:1 these are the words of *c.*
12 thou shouldest enter into *c.*
21 ac. to all curses of *c.*
25 because ye have forsaken *c.*
31:20 they will break my *c.*
*Jud.* 2:1 I will never break *c.*
1 *Sam.* 20:8 thy serv. in *c.* of L.
1 *K.* 19:10 Israel forsaken *c.* 14
20:34 send thee aw. with this *c.*
2 *K.* 13:23 bec. of *c.* with Abrah.
23:3 to perform *c.* all the people stood to *c.* 2 *Chr.* 34:31
1 *Chr.* 16:15 be mindful of his *c.*
2 *Chr.* 15:12 into *c.* to seek Lord
*Neh.* 13:29 defiled *c.* of priestho.
*Ps.* 25:14 will show them his *c.*
44:17 neither dealt fal. in thy *c.*
50:16 take my *c.* in thy mouth
55:20 he hath broken his *c.*
74:20 respect to *c.* for dark pla.
*Ps.* 78:37 neit. were stead. in his *c.*
89:28 my *c.* st. fast with him
34 my *c.* will I not break, nor
39 made void *c.* of thy servant
111:5 ever be mindful of his *c.*
9 commanded his *c.* for ever
*Prov.* 2:17 forgetteth *c.* of her G.
*Is.* 28:18 *c.* with death be disan.
33:8 broken *c.* he hath despised
42:6 for *c.* of people, 49:8
54:10 nor *c.* of my peace be rem.
56:4 eunuchs hold of my *c.* 6
59:21 as for me this is my *c.*
*Jer.* 11:2 hear ye words of *c.* 6
3 cursed obeyeth not w. of *c.*
14:21 break not thy *c.* with us
22:9 bec. they have forsaken *c.*
31:32 which my *c.* they break
33:20 if you can break *c.* of day
21 may *c.* be broken with Da.
25 if my *c.* be not with day
34:18 not performed words of *c.*
50:5 join to L. in perpetual *c.*
*Ezek.* 16:8 into a *c.* with thee
59 in breaking *c.* 17:18
61 give th. for daugh. not by *c.*
17:15 or break *c.* and be deliv.?
16 whose *c.* he brake
19 my *c.* he hath broken, it
20:37 bring you into bond of *c.*
44:7 they have broken my *c.*
*Dan.* 9:27 confirm *c.* for one week
11:22 also the prince of *c.*
28 his heart be against holy *c.*
30 indignation against holy *c.*
32 do wickedly against *c.*
*Hos.* 10:4 falsely in making a *c.*
*Zec.* 11:10 I might break my *c.*
*Mal.* 2:4 my *c.* be with Levi, 5
8 ye have corrupted *c.* of Levi

10 by profaning *c.* of fathers
14 she is the wife of thy *c.*
3:1 messenger of *c.* ye delight in
*Acts* 3:25 children of *c.* G. made
7:8 gave him *c.* of circumcision
*Rom.* 1:31 *c.* breakers
11:27 this is my *c.* when I take
*Gal.* 3:15 tho' it be but a m.'s *c.*
17 the *c.* confirmed bef. of God
*Heb.* 8:6 mediator of a better *c.*
7 if first *c.* had been faultless
9 they continued not in my *c.*
9:1 first *c.* had also ordinances
4 and the tables of the *c.*

*See* ARK, BLOOD, BREAK.

**Book of the COVENANT.**
*Ex.* 24:7 Moses took *book of c.*
2 *K.* 23:2 Josiah read all the w. of *book of c.* 2 *Chr.* 34:30

**Establish COVENANT.**
*Gen.* 6:18 *establish* my *c.* 9:9
17:7 *est. c.* bet. me and Abra.
19 *esta. c* with I. and seed, 21
*Ezek.* 16:60 *e.* to thee an everl. *c.*

**Everlasting COVENANT.**
*Gen.* 9:16 I may remember *e. c.*
17:13 your flesh for *everlast. c.*
19 *c.* with Isaac for an *ever. c.*
2 *Sam.* 23:5 an *ever. c.* ordered
1 *Chr.* 16:17 confirmed to Israel for an *everlast. c. Ps.* 105:10
*Is.* 24:5 have broken *everlast. c.*
55:3 *e. c.* w. you, 61:8; *Jer.* 32:40
*Ezek.* 37:26 *everlast. c.* with them
*Heb.* 13:20 thro' blood of *ever. c.*

**Keep, keepeth, *or* kept COVENANT.**
*Gen.* 17:9 thou shalt *keep* my *c.*
*Ex.* 19:5 if ye will *keep* my *c.*
*Deut.* 7:9 God wh. *k. c.* 12; 1 *K.* 8:23; 2 *Ch.* 6:14; *Neh.* 1:5; 9:32
29:9 *keep* words of this *c.* and do
33:9 they have *kept* thy *c.*
1 *K.* 11:11 hast not *k. c. Ps.* 78:10
*Ps.* 25:10 to such as *k. c.* 103:18
132:12 if thy child. *keep* my *c.*
*Ezek.* 17:14 by *k.* of *c.* it might
*Dan.* 9:4 *keep c.* and mercy

**Made COVENANT.**
*Gen.* 15:18 same day L. *m. c.*
21:27 Abra. and Abim. *m. c.* 32
*Deut.* 5:2 L. *m.* a *c.* with us in H.
3 *m.* not *c.* with fa. *Heb.* 8:9
29:1 besides *c.* he *made* in Ho
31:16 will break my *c.* I *made*
*Jos.* 24:25 Joshua *m.* a *c.*
1 *Sam.* 18:3 J. and D. *m. c.* 23:18
20:16 J. *m. c.* with house of D.
1 *K.* 8:21 ark w. is *c.* of L. he *m.*
20:34 Ahab *made c.* with Benj.
2 *K.* 11:4 Jehoiada *m. c.*
17 *made c.* bet. Lord and king
17:15 *c. made* with fathers
38 *c. made* with you not forget
23:3 Josiah *m. c.* 2 *Chr.* 34:31
1 *Chr.* 11:3 David *m. c.* with eld.
1 *Chr.* 16:16 mind. of *c.* he *made* with A. *Neh.* 9:8; *Ps.* 105:9
2 *Chr.* 21:7 *c.* he had *m.* with D.
23:3 *m.* a *c.* with king Joash
*Job* 31:1 *m.* a *c.* with mine eyes
*Ps.* 50:5 *m.* a *c.* with me
89:3 *made* a *c.* with my chosen
*Is.* 28:15 *m.* a *c.* with death
57:8 enlarg. thy bed and *m.* a *c.*
*Jer.* 11:10 broke *c.* I *m.*
31:32 not ac. to *c.* I *m.* with fa.
34:8 Zed. *m. c.* with people, 15
13 I *made* a *c.* with your fath.
15 ye had *made c.* before me
*Ezek.* 17:13 *made* a *c.* with him

**Make COVENANT.**
*Gen.* 17:2 *m. c.* bet. me and thee
26:28 *m. c.* with thee, 31:44
*Ex.* 23:32 *m.* no *c. Deut.* 7:2
34:10 I *m. c.* before thy people
12 *m. c.* with inhabitants, 15
*Deut.* 29:14 nor with you *m. c.*
1 *Sam.* 11:2 on this cond. I *m. c.*
2 *Chr.* 29:10 in my he. to *m.* a *c.*
*Neh.* 9:38 we *make* a sure *c.*
*Job* 41:4 will he *m.* a *c.*
*Jer.* 31:33 this is the *c.* I will *m. Heb.* 8:10; 10:16
*Ezek.* 34:25 *m. c.* of peace, 37:26
*Hos.* 2:18 *m. c.* for them.
12:1 do *m. c.* with Assyrians

**New COVENANT.**
*Jer.* 31:31 *n. c.* with Is. *Heb.* 8:8
*Heb.* 8:13 a *new c.* the first old
12:24 mediator of the *new c.*

**Remember COVENANT.**
*Gen.* 9:15 I will *r.* my *c. Lev.* 26:42; *Ezek.* 16:60
*Lev.* 26:45 for their sakes *r. c.*
*Ps.* 105:8 he hath *r.* his *c.* 106:45
*Amos* 1:9 *rem.* not the broth. *c.*
*Luke* 1:72 and to *rem.* his holy *c.*

**COVENANT of Salt.**
*Lev.* 2:13 *salt of c.* to be lacking
*Num.* 18:19 it is a *c. of s.*
2 *Chr.* 13:5 to David by *c. of salt*

**Transgressed, ing COVENANT.**
*Deut.* 17:2 wickedness in *t.* his *c.*
*Jos.* 7:11 *trangressed* my *c.*
15 because he *t. c.* of the Lord, *Jud.* 2:20; 2 *K.* 18:12
23:16 ye have *trans. c.* of Lord
*Jer.* 34:18 men that *trans.* my *c.*
*Hos.* 6:7 like men *trans.* the *c.*
8:1 they have *trans.* my *c.*

**COVENANTED.**
2 *Chr.* 7:18 as I have *c.* with D.
*Hag.* 2:5 word I *c.* with you
*Mat.* 26:15 *c.* for thirty pieces.
*Luke* 22:5 *c.* to give him money

**COVENANTS.**
*Rom.* 9:4 to whom pertaineth *c.*
*Gal.* 4:24 two *c.* one from Sinai
*Eph.* 2:12 strangers from *c.*

**COVER.**
*Ex.* 33:22 *c.* thee while I pass
*Num.* 22:5 they *c.* face of earth
*Deut.* 23:13 *c.* wh. com. from thee
33:12 shall *c.* him all the day
1 *Sam.* 24:3 S. went to *c.* his feet
*Neh.* 4:5 *c.* not their iniquity
*Job* 16:18 earth, *c.* not thy blood
21:26 worms shall *c.* them
22:11 waters *c.* thee, 38:34
40:22 the shady trees *c.* him
*Ps.* 91:4 *c.* thee with his feath.
104:9 they turn not to *c.* earth
109:29 *c.* with own confusion
139:11 darkness shall *c.* me
140:9 mischief of lips *c.* them
*Is.* 11:9 waters *c.* sea, *Hab.* 2:14
14:11 worms *c.* thee
22:17 L. will surely *c.* thee
26:21 earth no more *c.* her slain
30:1 *c.* with a covering, but
58:7 naked, that thou *c.* him
59:6 nor *c.* themsel. with works
60:2 darkness shall *c.* the earth
6 multi. of camels shall *c.* thee
*Jer.* 46:8 I will *c.* the earth
*Ezek.* 7:18 horror shall *c.* them
12:6 thou shalt *c.* thy face
12 he shall *c.* his face, that
24:7 pour. it not on the gr. to *c.*
17 *c.* not thy lips,
22 ye shall not *c.* your lips
26:10 horses, their dust *c.* thee
19 when waters shall *c.* thee
30:18 as for her a cloud *c.* her
32:7 I will *c.* the heaven, sun
37:6 *c.* you with skin and
38:9 be like cloud to *c.* land, 16
*Hos.* 2:9 flax given to *c.* her
10:8 mount. *c.* us, *Luke* 23:30
*Ob.* 10 shame shall *c.* thee
*Mic.* 3:7 shall all *c.* their lips
7:10 shame *c.* her said to me
*Hab.* 2:17 violence of L. *c.* thee
*Mark* 14:65 and *c.* his face
1 *Cor.* 11:7 man not to *c.* head
1 *Pet.* 4:8 charity *c.* mult. of sins

**COVERED.**
*Gen* 7:19 mountains were *c.* 20
9:23 *c.* naked. of their father
24:65 Rebekah *c.* herself
38:14 Tam. *c.* her with a veil
*Ex.* 14:28 waters *c.* chariots
15:5 the depths *c.* them
10 the sea *c.* them, *Jos.* 24:7
24:15 a cloud *c.* the mount. 16
37:9 *c.* with wings mercy-seat
40:21 veil *c.* ark of testimony
*Num.* 4:20 when holy things *c.*
*Deut.* 32:15 art *c.* with fatness
*Jud.* 4:18 Jael *c.* Sisera, 19
1 *Sam.* 19:13 Mich. *c.* the image
28:14 old man cometh up *c.*
1 *K.* 1:1 *c.* David with clothes
8:7 cher. *c.* the ark, 2 *Chr.* 5:8
2 *K.* 19:1 Hezekiah *c.* himself with sackcloth, *Is.* 37:1
*Job* 23:17 *c.* dark. from my face
31:33 if I *c.* my transgressions
*Ps.* 44:15 shame of face *c.* me
19 *c.* us with shadow of death
65:13 valleys *c.* over with corn
68:13 w. of dove *c.* with silver
71:13 *c.* with reproach that seek
89:45 hast *c.* him with shame
106:17 *c.* company of Abiram
139:13 *c.* me in mother's womb
*Prov.* 26:23 a potsherd *c.* with
26 whose hatred is *c.* by deceit
*Ec.* 6:4 his name *c.* with dark.
*Is.* 6:2 with twain he *c.* his face
29:10 the seers hath he *c.*
51:16 I have *c.* thee in shadow
61:10 *c.* me with robe
*Jer.* 51:42 she is *c.* with waves
*Lam.* 2:1 *c.* dau. of Z. with clo.
3:16 he hath *c.* me with ashes
43 hast *c.* with anger
44 *c.* thyself with a cloud
*Ezek.* 1:11 two wings *c.* bod. 23
16:8 and *c.* thy nakedness
10 I *c.* thee with silk
18:7 and hath *c.* the naked, 16
24:8 her blood should not be *c.*
27:7 blue and purple *c.* thee
31:15 I *c.* the deep for him
37:8 and skin *c.* them above
*Jon.* 3:8 and beast he *c.* with sa.
*Hab.* 3:3 his glory *c.* heavens
*Mat.* 8:24 was *c.* with waves
10:26 nothing *c.* that shall not be revealed, *Luke* 12:2
1 *Cor.* 11:6 the woman be not *c.*

**COVERED face.**
*Gen.* 38:15 Tamar had *c.* her *face*
2 *Sam.* 19:4 but David *c.* his *face*
*Est.* 7:8 they *c.* Haman's *face*
*Ps.* 69:7 shame hath *c.* my *face*
*Prov.* 24:31 nettles *c. face* there.
*Is.* 6:2 with twain he *c.* his *face*
*Jer.* 51:51 shame hath *c.* our *fac.*

**Head COVERED.**
2 *Sam.* 15:30 David had his *h. c.*
*Est.* 6:12 Haman, his *head c.*
*Ps.* 140:7 *c.* my *head* in battle
*Jer.* 14:3 and *c.* their *heads*, 4
1 *Cor.* 11:4 ev. man praying, *h. c.*

**COVERED sin**
*Ps.* 32:1 *sin* is *c. Rom.* 4:7
85:2 thou hast *c.* all their *sin*

**COVEREDST.**
*Ps.* 104:6 *c.* it with deep
*Ezek.* 16:18 br. garm. and *c.* them

**COVEREST.**
*Deut.* 22:12 vesture wherewith *c.*
*Ps.* 104:2 *c.* thyself with light

**COVERETH.**
*Num.* 22:11 *c.* face of the earth
*Jud.* 3:24 surely he *c.* his feet
*Job* 9:24 he *c.* faces of judges
15:27 *c.* his face with fatness
36:30 he *c.* bottom of the sea
32 with clouds he *c.* the light
*Ps.* 73:6 violence *c.* as garment
109:19 garment which *c.* him
147:8 *c.* heaven with clouds
*Prov.* 10:6 vio. *c.* the mouth, 11
12 love *c.* all sins
12:16 prudent man *c.* shame
17:9 *c.* transgression seek. love
28:13 *c.* his sins, shall not pros.
*Jer.* 3:25 our confusion *c.* us
*Ezek.* 28:14 art cherub that *c.*
*Mal.* 2:16 for one *c.* violence
*Luke* 8:16 candle *c.* it with ves.

**COVERING, Participle.**
*Ex.* 25:20 *c.* mercy-seat with
*Num.* 4:5 shall take down *c.* veil
*Ezek.* 28:16 O *c.* cherub
*Mal.* 2:13 *c.* the altar with tears

**COVERING, Substantive.**
*Gen.* 20:16 thee a *c.* of the eyes
*Ex.* 22:27 it is his *c.* for his skin
*Lev.* 13:45 put *c.* on upper lip
2 *Sam.* 17:19 *c.* over well's mou.
*Job* 22:14 thick clouds *c.* to him
24:7 naked have no *c.* in cold
26:6 destruction hath no *c.*
31:19 any poor without *c.*
*Ps.* 105:39 he spread cloud for *c.*
*Cant.* 3:10 he made *c.* of purple
*Is.* 22:8 discovered *c.* of Judah
25:7 *c.* cast over all people
28:20 *c.* narrower, than can wr.
30:1 with *c.* not of my Spirit
22 ye shall defile *c.* of images
50:3 I make sackcloth their *c.*
*Ezek.* 28:13 precious stone thy *c.*
1 *Cor.* 11:15 hair is given for *c.*
*See* BADGER.

**COVERINGS.**
*Prov.* 7:16 deck. my bed with *c.*
31:22 maketh herself *c.* of tap.

**COVERS.**
*Ex.* 25:29 make *c.* 37:16
*Num.* 4:7 put *c.* to cover withal

**COVERT.**
2 *K.* 16:18 *c.* for the sabbath, Ahaz took down
*Job* 38:40 when lions abide in *c.*
40:21 behemoth lieth in *c.* of
*Ps.* 61:4 trust in *c.* of thy wings
*Is.* 4:6 a tabernacle for a *c.*
16:4 be thou a *c.* from spoiler
32:2 a man be *c.* from tempest
*Jer.* 25:38 forsaken his *c.*

**COVET.**
*Ex.* 20:17 thou shalt not *c.* *Deut.* 5:21; *Rom.* 7:7; 13:9
*Mic.* 2:2 they *c.* fields and take
1 *Cor.* 12:31 but *c.* the best gifts
14:39 *c.* to prophesy

**COVETED.**
*Jos.* 7:21 then I *c.* them, and
*Acts* 20:33 I *c.* no man's silver
1 *Tim.* 6:10 while some *c.* after

**COVETETH.**
*Prov.* 21:26 *c.* all the day long
*Hab.* 2:9 woe to him *c.* evil cov.

**COVETOUS.**
*Ps.* 10:3 wicked blesseth *c.*
*Luke* 16:14 Pharis. who were *c.*
1 *Cor.* 5:10 yet not altog. with *c.*
11 *c.* with such not to eat
6:10 nor *c.* inherit, *Eph.* 5:5
1 *Tim.* 3:3 bishop must not be *c.*
2 *Tim.* 3:2 in last times m. be *c.*
2 *Pet* 2:14 exer. with *c.* practices

**COVETOUSNESS.**
*Ex.* 18:21 men hating *c.*
*Ps.* 119:36 incline not heart to *c.*
*Prov.* 28:16 hateth *c.* sh. prolong
*Is.* 57:17 for iniquity of his *c.*
*Jer.* 6:13 given to *c.* 8:10
22:17 eyes are not but for thy *c.*
51:13 and measure of thy *c.*
*Ezek.* 33:31 heart goeth after *c.*
*Hab.* 2:9 that coveteth an evil *c.*
*Mark* 7:22 out heart proceed. *c.*
*Luke* 12:15 he said, beware of *c.*
*Rom.* 1:29 filled with all *c.*
2 *Cor.* 9:5 as a matter not of *c.*
*Eph.* 5:3 *c.* let it not be named
*Col.* 3:5 mortify *c.* wh. is idola.
1 *Thes.* 2:5 nor used cloak of *c.*
*Heb.* 13:5 conver. be without *c.*
2 *Pet.* 2:3 through *c.* make mer.

**COW.**
*Lev.* 22:28 *c.* or ewe, sh. not kill
*Num.* 18:17 firstling of *c.*
*Job* 21:10 their *c.* casteth not
*Is.* 7:21 nourish a young *c.*
11:7 *c.* and the bear shall feed
*Ezek.* 4:15 given thee *c.* dung for
*Amos* 4:3 every *c.* at that before

COZBI. *Num.* 25:15, 18

**CRACKLING.**
*Ec.* 7:6 *c.* of thorns under pot

**CRACKNELS.**
1 *K.* 14:3 take with thee *c.*

**CRAFT.**
*Dan.* 8:25 cause *c.* to prosper
*Mark* 14:1 take him by *c.*
*Acts* 18:3 he was of same *c.*
19:27 not only our *c.* is in dan.
*Rev.* 18:22 whatsoever *c.* he be

**CRAFTINESS.**
*Job* 5:13 in their *c.* 1 *Cor.* 3:19
*Luke* 20:23 he perceived their *c.*
2 *Cor.* 4:2 not walking in *c.* nor
*Eph.* 4:14 carried by cunning *c.*

**CRAFTY.**
*Job* 5:12 he disap. devices of *c.*
15:5 thou chooseth tongue of *c.*
*Ps.* 83:3 *c.* counsel against
2 *Cor.* 12:16 being *c.* I caught

**CRAFTSMAN.**
*Deut.* 27:15 the work of the *c*
*Rev.* 18:22 no *c.* be found.

**CRAFTSMEN.**
2 *K.* 24:14 carried away *c.* 16
1 *Chr.* 4:14 for they were *c.*
*Neh.* 11:35 the valley of *c.*
*Hos.* 13:2 the work of *c.*
*Acts* 19:24 no small gain to *c.*
38 *c.* have matter against any

**CRAG.**
*Job* 39:28 eagle abideth on *c.*

**CRANE.**
*Is.* 38:14 like *c.* so did I chatter
*Jer.* 8:7 *c.* obs. time of coming

**CRASHING.**
*Zep.* 1:10 great *c.* from hills

**CRAVED, ETH.**
*Prov.* 16:26 for his mouth *c.* it
*Mark* 15:43 Joseph *c.* body of J.

**CREATE.**
*Ps.* 51:10 *c.* in me a clean heart
*Is.* 4:5 *c.* on every d.-p. a cloud
45:7 *c.* darkness, I *c.* evil
57:19 I *c.* the fruits of the lips
65:17 I *c.* new heavens
18 rejoice in that which I *c.*

**CREATED.**
*Gen.* 1:1 in the begin. God *c.* he
21 God *c.* great whales
27 God *c.* man in his own image, male and female, 5:2
2:3 in it rested from all he *c.*
6:7 will destroy man I have *c.*
*Deut.* 4:32 day God *c.* man
*Ps.* 89:12 north and south h. *c.*
102:18 people to be *c.*
104:30 forth spirit they are *c.*
148:5 com. and they were *c.*
*Is.* 40:26 hath *c.* these things
41:20 Holy One of Is. hath *c.* it
42:5 he that *c.* the heavens
43:1 Lord that *c.* thee, O Jacob
7 I have *c.* him for my glory
45:8 I the Lord have *c.* it
12 I have *c.* man upon it
18 he *c.* it not in vain
48:7 *c.* now, not from begin.
54:16 have *c.* smith, *c.* waster
*Jer.* 31:22 L. hath *c.* a new thing
*Ezek.* 21:30 judge where wast *c.*
28:13 in day thou wast *c.*
15 from day thou wast *c.*
*Mal.* 2:10 hath not one God *c.*
*Mark* 13:19 creation G. *c.*
1 *Cor.* 11:9 man *c.* for the wom.
*Eph.* 1:10 workmanship *c.* in C.
3:9 who *c.* all things by Jes. C.
4:24 God is *c.* in righteousness
*Col.* 1:16 were all things *c.*
3:10 after image of him *c.* him
1 *Tim.* 4:3 G. *c.* to be received
*Rev.* 4:11 hast *c.* all things, for thy pleasure are and were *c.*
10:6 who *c.* heaven and the

**CREATETH.**
*Amos* 4:13 *c.* w. L. is his name

**CREATION.**
*Mark* 10:6 from *c.* male and fe.
13:19 as was not from the *c.*
*Rom.* 1:20 from *c.* are clearly
8:22 that whole *c.* groaneth
2 *Pet.* 3:4 continue as from the *c.*
*Rev.* 3:14 beginning of *c.* of God

**CREATOR.**
*Ec.* 12:1 remember *c.* in youth
*Is.* 40:28 *c.* of ends of the earth
43:15 I am the Lord, *c.* of Israel
*Rom.* 1:25 creature more than *c.*
1 *Pet.* 4:19 as to a faithful *c.*

**CREATURE.**
*Gen.* 1:20 bring forth moving *c.*
*Lev.* 11:46 this is law of every *c.*
*Mark* 16:15 gospel to every *c.* *Col.* 1:23
*Rom.* 8:19 expectation of *c.*
20 *c.* made subject to vanity
21 *c.* be delivered from bond.
39 any *c.* able to separate us
2 *Cor.* 5:17 he is a new *c.*
*Gal.* 6:15 nor uncir. but new *c.*
*Col.* 1:15 first-born of every *c.*
1 *Tim.* 4:4 every *c.* of G. is good
*Heb.* 4:13 any *c.* not manifest
*Rev.* 5:13 every *c.* in heaven

**Living CREATURE.**
*Gen.* 1:21 God created every *l. c.*
24 let earth bring forth *liv. c.*
2:19 Adam called every *liv. c.*
9:10 cov. with every *living c.*
12 between me and ev. *l. c.* 15
*Lev.* 11:46 law of every *living c.*
*Ezek.* 1:20 spirit of *l. c.* 21; 10:17
10:15 *l. c.* I saw by Chebar, 20

**CREATURES.**
*Is.* 13:21 houses full of doleful *c.*
*Jam.* 1:18 of first-fruits of his *c.*
*Rev.* 8:9 third of *c.* in sea died

**Living CREATURES.**
*Ezek.* 1:5 likeness of four *liv. c.*
14 *l. c.* ran, returned as light.
19 *l. c.* went the wheels went
3:13 noise of wings of *living c.*

**CREDITOR, S.**
*Deut.* 15:2 *c.* that lendeth shall
2 *K.* 4:1 *c.* to take my two sons
*Is.* 50:1 to which of my *c.*

*Luke* 7:41 *c.* had two debtors

**CREEK.**
*Acts* 27:39 discovered a certain *c*

**CREEP.**
*Lev.* 11:31 unclean all that *c.*
*Ps.* 104:20 beasts of forest *c.*
2 *Tim.* 3:6 of this sort *c.* into

**CREEPETH.**
*Gen.* 1:25 every thing that *c.* 26
30 given to every thing *c.* herb
7:8 *c.* went in two and two, 14
21 of thing that *c.*
8:17 bring forth every thing *c.*
19 whatsoever *c.* went forth
*Lev.* 11:41 that *c.* shall be an abomination, 43, 44; 20:25
*Deut.* 4:18 of any thing that *c.*

**CREEPING thing, s.**
*Gen.* 1:26 dominion over ev. *c. t.*
*Lev.* 5:2 unclean *c. thing*
11:21 ye eat, of every *c. thing*
22:5 or whoso. toucheth any *c. t.*
*Deut.* 14:19 *c. thing* that flieth
1 *K.* 4:33 he spake of *c. t.* fishes
*Ps.* 104:25 *c. things* innumerable
148:10 all *c. things* praise the L.
*Ezek.* 8:10 form of *c. t.* portrayed
38:20 all *c. t.* shake at my pres.
*Hos.* 2:18 covenant with *c. things*
*Hab.* 1:14 men as *c. things*
*Acts* 10:12 P. saw *c. things*, 11:6
*Rom.* 1:23 like to *c. things*

**CREPT.**
*Jude* 4 certain *c.* in unawares

CRESCENS. 2 *Tim.* 4:10
CRETE. *Acts* 27:7, 12, 21; *Tit.* 1:5
CRETES. *Acts* 2:11
CRETIANS. *Tit.* 1:12

**CREW.**
*Mat.* 26:74 the cock *c. Mar.* 14:68; *Luke* 22:60; *John* 18:27

**CRIB.**
*Job* 39:9 unicorn abide by thy *c.?*
*Prov.* 14:4 no oxen are *c.* is clean
*Is.* 1:3 ass know. his master's *c.*

CRIED. *See* after CRY.

**CRIME, S.**
*Job* 31:11 his is a heinous *c.*
*Ezek.* 7:23 land is full of bloody *c.*
*Acts* 25:16 conc. *c.* laid ag. him
27 not to signify the *c.* laid

**CRIMSON.**
2 *Chr.* 2:7 cun. to work in *c.* 14
3:14 he made the veil of *c.*
*Is.* 1:18 your sins be like *c.*
*Jer.* 4:30 thou clothest with *c.*

**CRIPPLE.**
*Acts* 14:8 being a *c.* from womb

**CRISPING-PINS.**
*Is.* 3:22 L. will take away *c.-p.*

CRISPUS. *Acts* 18:8; 1 *Cor.* 1:14

**CROOK-BACKED.**
*Lev.* 21.20 *c.-b.* not approach

**CROOKED.**
*Deut.* 32:5 are a *c.* generation
*Job* 26:13 formed the *c.* serpent
*Ps.* 125:5 aside to their *c.* ways
*Prov.* 2:15 whose ways are *c.*
*Ec.* 1:15 *c.* not be m. stra. 7:13
*Is.* 27:1 pun. lev. that *c.* serpent
40:4 *c.* be made, 42:16; *Luke* 3:5
45:2 make the *c.* places straight
59:8 have made them *c.* paths
*Lam.* 3:9 hath made my paths *c.*
*Phil.* 2:15 midst of a *c.* nation

**CROP.**
*Lev.* 1:16 he shall pluck away *c.*

**CROPPED.**
*Ezek.* 17:4 *c.* off top of y. twigs, 22

**CROSS.**
*Mat.* 10:38 taketh not his *c.* is not worthy of me, *Luke* 14:27
16:24 *c.* and follow me, *Mark* 8:34; 10:21; *Luke* 9:23
27:32 compelled to bear *c. Mark* 15:21; *Luke* 23:26
40 if S. of God come down from the *c.* 42; *Mark* 15:30, 32
*John* 19:17 bearing *c.* went forth
19 wrote title, and put it on *c.*
25 stood by the *c.* his mother
31 not remain on *c.* on sabbath
1 *Cor.* 1:17 lest *c.* be of none ef.
18 preaching of *c.* foolishness
*Gal.* 5:11 offence of the *c.* ceased
6:12 suf. persecution for *c.* of C.
14 should glory, save in the *c.*
*Eph.* 2:16 reconcile both by *c.*
*Phil.* 2:8 obedient to death of *c.*
3:18 are enemies of *c.* of Christ
*Col.* 1:20 through blood of *c.*
2:14 nailing it to his *c.*
*Heb.* 12:2 endured the *c.*

**CROSS-WAY.**
*Ob.* 14 nor have stood in *c.-w.*

**CROUCH, ETH.**
1 *Sam.* 2:36 *c.* for piece of silver
*Ps.* 10:10 he *c.* and humbleth

CROW, CROWING. *See* COCK.

**CROWN.**
*Ex.* 25:25 a golden *c.* to border
29:6 holy *c.* upon the mitre
*Lev.* 8:9 on his forefront holy *c.*
21:12 *c.* of anointing oil
2 *K.* 11:12 *c.* on J. 2 *Chr.* 23:11
*Est.* 1:11 Vashti with *c.* royal
*Job* 31:36 bind it as a *c.* to me
*Ps.* 89:39 hast profaned his *c.*
132:18 upon himself *c.* flourish
*Prov.* 4:9 *c.* of glory deliver
12:4 a virtuous woman is a *c.*
14:24 *c.* of wise is their riches
16:31 hoary head is *c.* of glory
17:6 children's child. *c.* of old
27:24 *c.* endure to every genera.
*Cant.* 3:11 behold S. with the *c.*
*Is.* 28:1 woe to the *c.* of pride
5 shall be for a *c.* of glory
62:3 shalt also be a *c.* of glory
*Jer.* 13:18 *c.* of glory come down
*Ezek.* 21:26 take off the *c.*
*Zec.* 9:16 as the stones of a *c.*
*John* 19:5 J. wearing *c.* of thorns
1 *Cor.* 9:25 a corruptible *c.*
*Phil.* 4:1 beloved, my joy and *c.*
1 *Thes.* 2:19 our *c.* of rejoicing
2 *Tim.* 4:8 *c.* of righteousness
*Jam.* 1:12 he shall rec. *c.* of life
1 *Pet.* 5:4 shall receive *c.* of glory
*Rev.* 2:10 give thee a *c.* of life
3:11 that no man take thy *c.*
6:2 a *c.* was given to him

**CROWN of gold.**
*Ex.* 25:11 *c. of g.* round about, 24; 30:3; 37:2; 11, 12, 26
*Est.* 8:15 Mordecai with *c. of g.*
*Ps.* 21:3 *c. of g.* on his head

**CROWN, *with* Head.**
*Gen.* 49:26 on *c.* of Joseph's *h.*
*Deut.* 33:20 teareth arm with *c.*
2 *Sam.* 1:10 the *c.* on his *head*
12:30 *c.* from *h.* 1 *Chr.* 20:2
14:25 sole to *c.* of *h. Job* 2:7
*Est.* 2:17 king set *c.* on her *h.*
6:8 *c.* royal set upon his *head*
*Job* 19:9 taken *c.* from my *head*
*Is.* 3:17 smite with a scab *c.* of *h.*
*Jer.* 2:16 broken *c.* of thy *head*
48:45 *c.* of *h.* of tumultuous ones
*Lam.* 5:16 *c.* fallen from our *head*
*Ezek.* 16:12 beautiful *c.* on thy *h.*
*Mat.* 27:29 put a *c.* of thorns, *Mark* 15:17; *John* 19:2
*Rev.* 12:1 a *c.* of twelve stars
14:14 on his *head* a golden *c.*

**CROWNED.**
*Ps.* 8:5 hast *c.* him with glory
*Prov.* 14:18 *c.* with knowledge
*Cant.* 3:11 his mother *c.* him
*Nah.* 3:17 thy *c.* are as locusts
2 *Tim.* 2:5 not *c.* except he strive
*Heb.* 2:9 Jesus *c.* with glory

**CROWNEDST.**
*Heb.* 2:7 *c.* him with glory and

**CROWNEST, ETH.**
*Ps.* 65:11 *c.* year with thy goodn.
103:4 *c.* thee with loving-kind.

**CROWNING.**
*Is.* 23:8 against Tyre the *c.* city

**CROWNS.**
*Ezek.* 23:42 beau. *c.* on their h.
*Zec.* 6:11 make *c.*; 14 *c.* to Helem.
*Rev.* 4:4 elders had *c.* of gold
10 cast their *c.* before throne
9:7 on locusts' heads were *c.*
12:3 dragon having seven *c.*
13:1 upon his horns ten *c.*
19:12 on his head many *c.*

**CRUCIFY.**
*Mat.* 20:19 to Gentiles, to *c.* him
23:34 some of them ye shall *c.*
27:31 to *c.* him, *Mark* 15:20
*Mark* 15:13 cried again *c.* him, 14
*Luke* 23:21 *c.* him, *c. John* 19:6, 15
*Heb.* 6:6 *c.* Son of God afresh

**CRUCIFIED.**
*Mat.* 26:2 bet. to be *c. Luke* 24:7
27:22 said, Let him be *c.* 23
26 del. him to be *c. John* 19:16
35 *c.* him, *John* 19:23
38 thieves *c.* 44; *Mark* 15:32; *Luke* 23:33; *John* 19:18
28:5 Jesus w. was *c. Mark* 16:6
*John* 19:20 where Jesus was *c.* 41
*Acts* 2:23 by wicked hands *c.*
36 made J. whom ye *c.* L. 4:10
*Rom.* 6:6 old man is *c.* with him
1 *Cor.* 1:13 was Paul *c.* for you?
23 preach Christ *c.* unto Jews
2:2 Jesus Christ and him *c.*
8 not have *c.* Lord of glory
2 *Cor.* 13:4 tho' *c.* through weak.
*Gal.* 2:20 I am *c.* with Christ
3:1 Chr. set forth, *c.* among you
5:24 are Christ's have *c.* flesh
6:14 by whom the world is *c.*
*Rev.* 11:8 where Lord was *c.*

**CRUEL.**
*Gen.* 49:7 wrath, for it was *c.*
*Ex.* 6:9 for *c.* bondage
*Deut.* 32:33 *c.* venom of asps
*Job* 30:21 art become *c.* to me
*Ps.* 25:19 hate me with *c.* hatred
71:4 deliver out of hand of *c.*
*Prov.* 5:9 thou give years to *c.*
11:17 he *c.* troubleth own flesh
12:10 mercies of wicked are *c.*
17:11 *c.* messenger be sent
27:4 wrath is *c.*
*Cant.* 8:6 jealousy is *c.*
*Is.* 13:9 day of Lord cometh *c.*
19:4 Egyptians give to *c.* lord
*Jer.* 6:23 they are *c.* 50:42
30:14 chastisement of *c.* one
*Lam.* 4:3 daughter of my peo. *c.*
*Heb.* 11:36 trial of *c.* mockings

**CRUELLY.**
*Ezek.* 18:18 bec. he *c.* oppressed

**CRUELTY.**
*Gen.* 49:5 instruments of *c.*
*Jud.* 9:24 *c.* to sons of Jerubbaal
*Ps.* 27:12 such as breathe out *c.*
74:20 are full of habitations of *c.*
*Ezek.* 34:4 with *c.* ye ruled them

**CRUMBS.**
*Mat.* 15:27 eat of *c. Mark* 7:28
*Luke* 16:21 to be fed with the *c.*

**CRUSE.**
1 *Sam.* 26:11 take the *c.* of water
12 so David took the *c.* 16

1 *K.* 14:3 take a *c.* of honey
17:12 I have a little oil in *c.*
14 nor *c.* of oil fail till, 16
19:6 Elijah had *c.* of water
2 *K.* 2:20 bring me a new *c.*

**CRUSH.**

*Job* 39:15 forgetteth foot may *c.*
*Lam.* 1:15 to *c.* my young
3:34 to *c.* all the prisoners
*Amos* 4:1 which *c.* the needy

**CRUSHED.**

*Lev.* 22:24 not offer what is *c.*
*Num.* 22:25 ass *c.* Balaam's foot
*Deut.* 28:33 and *c.* alway
*Job* 4:19 are *c.* before the moth
5:4 his children *c.* in the gate
*Is.* 59:5 *c.* breaketh into a viper
*Jer.* 51:34 Nebuch. hath *c.* me

**CRY, Substantive.**

*Gen.* 18:21 accord. to *c.* come up
*Ex.* 2:23 their *c.* came up, 3:9
3:7 I have heard their *c.* I
*Num.* 16:34 Is. fled at *c.* of them
1 *Sam.* 5:12 *c.* of city went up
9:16 because their *c.* is come up
2 *Sam.* 22:7 my *c.* did enter
1 *K.* 8:28 hearken to *c.* and prayer, 2 *Chr.* 6:19
*Neh.* 5:6 angry when I heard *c.*
9:9 heardest *c.* by Red sea
*Est.* 4:1 cried with bitter *c.*
9:31 of fastings and their *c.*
*Job* 16:18 let my *c.* have no place
34:28 *c.* of poor to come to him, he heareth *c.* of afflicted
*Ps.* 5:2 hearken to my *c.* my K.
*Ps.* 9:12 forget. not *c.* of humble
17:1 O Lord attend unto my *c.*
18:6 my *c.* came before him
34:15 his ears open to their *c.*
39:12 O Lord, give ear to my *c.*
40:1 inclined and heard my *c.*
88:2 incline thine ear to my *c.*
102:1 let my *c.* come unto thee
106:44 when he heard their *c.*
119:169 let my *c.* come near
142:6 attend to my *c.* I am
*Prov.* 21:13 at *c.* of poor
*Ec.* 9:17 more than *c.* of him
*Is.* 5:7 for right. behold a *c.*
15:5 raise up *c.* of destruction
8 *c.* gone about borders of Mo.
30:19 will be gracious at thy *c.*
43:14 whose *c.* is in the ships
*Jer.* 7:16 neither lift up *c.* 11:14
8:19 voice of *c.* of my people
14:2 *c.* of Jerusalem is gone up
18:22 *c.* be heard from houses
25:36 *c.* of shepherds be heard
46:12 thy *c.* hath filled land
48:4 little ones caused a *c.*
5 enem. heard *c.* of destruction
49:21 moved at *c.* of Edom
50:46 *c.* heard at taking of Bab.
51:54 sound of *c.* from Babylon
*Lam.* 3:56 hide not ear at my *c.*
*Ezek.* 27:28 shake at *c.* of pilots
*Zep.* 1:10 be a *c.* from fish-gate
*Mat.* 25:6 midnight was *c.* made

**Great CRY.**

*Gen.* 18:20 *c.* of S. is *great*, 19:13
27:34 Esau cried with a *great c.*
*Ex.* 11:6 be a *great c.* thro' Egy.
12:30 there was *great c.* in Eg.
*Neh.* 5:1 a *g. c.* of the people
*Acts* 23:9 so said, arose a *great c.*

**Hear CRY.**

*Ex.* 22:23 I will *hear* their *c.*
*Job* 27:9 *hear c.* when trouble
*Ps.* 61:1 *hear* my *c.* O God
145:19 he also will *hear* their *c.*
*Jer.* 14:12 I will not *h.* their *c.*
20:16 *hear c.* in the morning

**CRIES.**

*Jam.* 5:4 *c.* of them that reaped

**CRY, Verb.**

*Ex.* 5:8 idle therefore they *c.*
22:23 if thou afflict and they *c.*
32:18 voice of them that *c.*
*Lev.* 13:45 and *c.* Unclean
*Jud.* 10:14 go *c.* to the gods
2 *Sam.* 19:28 right have I to *c.*
2 *K.* 8:3 to *c.* for her house
2 *Chr.* 20:9 *c.* in afflict. wilt hear
*Job* 30:20 I *c.* thou dost not hear
24 they *c.* in his destruction
35:9 oppressed to *c.* they *c.* out
12 they *c.* none giveth answer
36:13 *c.* not when he bindeth
38:41 his young ones *c.* to God
*Ps.* 22:2 I *c.* in the daytime
27:7 O Lord, when I *c.* 28:2
28:1 to thee will I *c.* 2
34:17 righteous *c.* Lord heareth
56:9 when I *c.* mine enem. turn
57:2 I will *c.* to God most high
61:2 from end of earth will I *c.*
86:3 be merciful, for I *c.* daily
89:26 shall *c.* thou art my father
141:1 Lord I *c.* make haste
147:9 to young ravens which *c.*
*Prov.* 8:1 doth not wisdom *c.* and
21:13 shall *c.* but not be heard
*Is.* 8:4 before child *c.* My father
13:22 beasts of islands shall *c.*
14:31 *c.* O city, thou Palestina
15:4 and Heshbon shall *c.* and
33:7 their valiant ones shall *c.*
34:14 satyr shall *c.* to fellow
40:2 *c.* to Jerus. warfare accom.
6 voice said, *c.* what shall I *c.*?
42:2 he shall not *c.* nor lift voice
13 he shall *c.* yea, prevail
14 I *c.* like travailing woman
46:7 one shall *c.* to him, yet can
58:9 *c.* he shall say, Here I am
65:14 shall *c.* for sorrow of heart
*Jer.* 2:2 go and *c.* in ears of Jer.
3:4 wilt not from this time *c.*
4:5 blow trumpet, *c.* gather
11:11 though they *c.* to me
12 *c.* to gods
14 not hear when *c.* *Ezek.* 8:18
22:20 go up to Lebanon, and *c.*
25:34 and *c.* 48:20; *Ezek.* 21:12
31:6 watchmen on Ephraim *c.*
*Lam.* 3:8 when I *c.* he shutteth
*Ezek.* 9:4 *c.* for abominations
24:17 forbear to *c.* make no
26:15 shake, when wounded *c.*
27:30 *c.* bitterly for Tyrus
*Hos.* 8:2 Israel *c.* we know thee
*Joel* 1:19 Lord, to thee will I *c.*
20 the beasts *c.* unto thee
*Jon.* 3:8 man and beast *c.* to G.
*Mic.* 3:5 bite with teeth, *c.* peace
*Nah.* 2:8 *c.* but none look back
*Zep.* 1:14 mighty sh. *c.* bitterly
*Zec.* 1:14 angel said, *c.* thou
*Mat.* 12:19 not strive nor *c.*
*Luke* 18:7 avenge elect, which *c.*
*Rom.* 8:15 whereby we *c.* Abba
*Gal.* 4:27 *c.* that travailest not

**CRY against.**

*Deut.* 15:9 *c.* to L. *a.* thee, 24:15
2 *Chr.* 13:12 to *c.* alarm *ag.* you
*Job* 31:38 if my land *c. ag.* me
*Jon.* 1:2 go to Nineveh, *c. ag.* it

**CRY aloud.**

1 *K.* 18:27 Elijah said, *c. aloud*
*Job* 19:7 I *c. aloud* but no judgm.
*Ps.* 55:17 at noon will I *c. aloud*
*Is.* 24:14 *c. aloud* from the sea
54:1 break forth into sing. *c. a.*
58:1 *c. aloud* spare not
*Hos.* 5:8 *c. a.* at Beth-a. after
*Mic.* 4:9 why *c. a.*? is there no

**CRY to the Lord.**

1 *Sam.* 7:8 cease not to *c.* for us
*Ps.* 107:19 *c. to the Lord*, 28
*Is.* 19:20 *c. to L.* bec. of oppres.
*Joel* 1:14 sanctify fast, *c. to the L.*
*Mic.* 3:4 *c. to the L.* he will not

**CRY out.**

1 *Sam.* 8:18 ye shall *c. out*
*Job* 19:7 I *c. out* of wrong,
35:9 *c. o.* by r. of arm of mighty
*Is.* 12:6 *c. out* and shout
15:4 soldiers of M. shall *c. out*
5 my heart shall *c. out* for M.
29:9 wonder, *c. out*, and cry
*Jer.* 48:31 I will *c. out* for Moab
*Lam.* 2:19 *c. out* in the night
*Amos* 3:4 y. lion *c. out* of den?
*Hab.* 1:2 I *c. out* to thee
2:11 stone shall *c. out* of wall
*Mark* 10:47 *c. out*, Have mercy
*Luke* 19:40 stones would *c. out*

**CRIED.**

*Gen.* 27:34 E. *c.* with bitter cry
39:15 he heard that I *c.*
41:55 *c.* to Pharaoh for bread
*Num.* 11:2 *c.* to Moses
*Deut.* 22:24 dam. bec. she *c.* not
27 damsel *c.* and none to save
*Jud.* 5:28 mother *c.* through lat.
7:21 all the host ran, and *c.*
10:12 ye *c.* and I delivered you
1 *Sam.* 17:8 G. *c.* to armies of Isr.
20:37 Jonathan *c.* after lad, 38
2 *Sam.* 20:16 then *c.* a wise w.
22:7 I *c.* to my G. he did hear
1 *K.* 13:2 *c.* against altar, 4, 32
18:28 *c.* aloud and cut them.
2 *K.* 2:12 Elisha *c.* My father
6:5 he *c.* Alas, it was borrowed
8:5 woman *c.* to king for house
11:14 Athaliah *c.* Treason
1 *Chr.* 5:20 *c.* to God in the battle
2 *Chr.* 32:20 Isaiah *c.* to heaven
*Neh.* 9:27 they *c.* thou heard. 28
*Job* 29:12 I delivered poor that *c.*
30:5 they *c.* as after a thief
*Ps.* 18:6 in my distress I *c.* to G.
41 *c.* but none to save them
22:5 they *c.* and were delivered
24 *c.* unto him, he heard
30:2 O Lord I *c.* to thee
8 I *c.* to thee O Lord and made
31:22 heardest sup. when I *c.*
34:6 this poor man *c.* and the L.
66:17 I *c.* with my mouth, 77:1
88:1 I *c.* day and night
13 I *c.* O Lord, in the morning
119:145 I *c.* with whole heart
130:1 out of the depths have I *c.*
138:3 I *c.* thou answeredst
*Is.* 6:4 moved at voice of him *c.*
30:7 have I *c.* concerning this
*Jer.* 4:20 destru. on destru. is *c.*
*Ezek.* 9:8 I fell on my face, and *c.*
10:13 it was *c.* to them
*Dan.* 6:20 he *c.* O Daniel
*Hos.* 7:14 not *c.* to me with heart
*Jon.* 1:5 mariners *c.* ev. man to
2:2 I *c.* by reason of affliction to L. out of belly of hell *c.* I
*Zec.* 7:13 as he *c.* and they would not hear, so they *c.*
*Mat.* 14:30 Peter *c.* Lord save me
20:31 *c.* the more, Have mercy, *Mark* 10:48; *Luke* 18:39
*Mark* 9:26 spirit *c.* and rent him
*John* 7:37 Jesus *c.* If any thirst
*Acts* 19:32 some *c.* one th. 21:34
22:24 wheref. they *c.* so ag. him
*Rev.* 10:3 he *c.* seven thunders
12:2 and she *c.* travailing
*Rev.* 14:18 *c.* to him that had sic.
18:2 he *c.* mightily, 18
19 they *c.* weeping and wailing

**CRIED to the Lord.**

*Ex.* 8:12 Moses *c. to the L.* 15:25; 17:4; *Num.* 12:13
14:10 Israel *c. to the Lord*, *Jud.* 3:9, 15; 4:3; 6:7; 10:1
*Num.* 20:16 we *c. to the Lord* he heard, *Deut.* 26:7

Jos. 24:7 c. to the L. he put dark.
1 Sam. 7:9 S. c. to the L. 15:11
2 Chr. 13:14 they c. to the L. Ps. 107:6, 13; Jon. 1:14
14:11 Asa c. to the Lord
Ps. 3:4 I c. to the L. 120:1; 142:1
Lam. 2:18 c. to L. O dau. of Z.

**CRIED with a loud voice.**

1 Sam. 28:12 En-dor c. w. l. v.
2 Sam. 19:4 D. c. w. l. v. O Absa.
Neh. 9:4 Levites; Ezek. 11:13 Ez.
Mat. 27:46 ninth hour J. c. w. l. v. 50; Mark 15:34, 37; Luke 23:46; John 11:43
Mark 1:26 evil spirit c. w. a l. v.
Acts 7:60 S. c. w. a loud voice
16:28 Paul c. with a loud voice
Rev. 6:10 c. w. a l. v. How long
7:2 angel c. w. l. v. 10:3: 19:17
10 stood bef. Lamb c. w. l. v.

**CRIED out.**

1 Sam 4:13 city c. out; 5:10 Ek.
1 K. 22:32 Jehosh. 2 Chr. 18:31
Jer. 20:8 I c. out I cried violence
Mat. 8:29 spirits c. out, Luke 4:33
14:26 c. o. for fear, Mark 6:49
20:30 blind men c. out
Mark 1:23 unclean spirit c. out
9:24 father c. out, Luke 9:38
15:13 c. o. again, Mat. 27:23; Luke 23:18; John 19:6
Acts 19:28 c. out Great is D. 34
22:23 c. out and threw dust
23:6 Paul c. out I am a Pharisee

**CRIEST, ETH.**

Gen. 4:10 brother's blood c.
Ex. 14:15 where. c. thou to me?
22:27 when he c. I will hear
1 Sam. 26:14 that c. to the king?
Job 24:12 soul of wounded c.
Ps. 72:12 del. needy when he c.
84:2 c. out for living God
Prov. 1:20 wisdom c. 8:3; 9:3
2:3 if thou c. after knowledge
Is. 26:17 as a woman c. out
40:3 that c. in the wilderness
57:13 c. let companies deliver
Jer. 12:8 my heritage c. ag. me
30:15 why c. thou
Mic. 6:9 Lord's voice c. to city
Mat. 15:23 for she c. after us
Luke 9:39 he c. out
Rom. 9:27 Esa.as also c.
Jam. 5:4 hire of laborers c

**CRYING.**

1 Sam. 4:14 Eli heard noise of c.
2 Sam. 13:19 Tamar went on c.
Job 39:7 nor reg. he c. of driver
Prov. 19:18 soul spare for his c.
30:15 horseleech dau. c. Give
Is. 22:5 day of c. to mountains
24:11 a c. for wine in streets
65:19 of c. no more heard in her
Jer. 48:3 of c. be from Horonaim
Zec. 4:7 the headstone with c.
Mal. 2:13 covering altar with c.
Mat. 3:3 c. in wilderness, Mark 1:3; Luke 3:4; John 1:23
21:15 children c. in the temple
Acts 8:7 c. spirits came out
14:14 ran among people c. out
21:28 c. out, Men of Israel, help
36 multitude c. away with him
Gal. 4:6 c. Abba, Father
Heb. 5:7 prayers with strong c.
Rev. 21:4 no more death, nor c.

**CRYSTAL.**

Job 28:17 and c. cannot equal it
Ezek. 1:22 as color of terrible c.
Rev. 4:6 a sea of glass, like c.
21:11 light of city clear as c.
22:1 a pure river, clear as c.

**CUBIT.**

Deut. 3:11 after the c. of a man
Ezek. 43:13 the c. is a c.
Mat. 6:27 one c. to stat. Lu. 12:25

**CUBITS.**

Gen. 6:15 length of the ark 300 c.
1 Sam. 17:4 Gol.'s height, six c.
1 K. 6:2 length of the house 60 c.
2 K. 14:13 brake wall of Jerusalem, 400 c. 2 Chr. 25:23
Est. 5:14 gallows 50 c. high, 7:9
Ezek. 40:23 gate to gate 100 c.
43:17 the settle fourteen c.
Dan. 3:1 height of image 60 c.
John 21:8 were from land, 200 c.
Rev. 21:17 wall of city 144 c.

**CUCKOO.**

Lev. 11:16 c. ab. Deut. 14:15

**CUCUMBERS.**

Num. 11:5 we remember the c.
Is. 1:8 as lodge in garden of c.

CUD. *See* CHEW *and* CHEWETH.

**CUMBERED, ETH.**

Luke 10:40 c. about much serv.
13:7 why c. it the ground?

**CUMBRANCE.**

Deut. 1:12 I alone bear your c.?

**CUMMIN.**

Is. 28:25 doth he not scatter c.
27 on c. but c. is beaten
Mat. 23:23 ye pay tithe of c.

**CUNNING.**

Gen. 25:27 Esau was a c. hunter
Ex. 31:4 to devise c. works
1 Sam. 16:18 son of J. c. in play.
1 Chr. 25:7 c. in songs, were 288
2 Chr. 2:13 I sent a c. man of H.
Ps. 137:5 right hand forget her c.
Cant. 7:1 work of a c. workman
Is. 3:3 take away c. artificer
40:20 he seeketh a c. workman
Jer. 9:17 send for c. women
10:9 all the work of c. men
Dan. 1:4 children c. in knowl.
Eph. 4:14 car. by c. craftiness

**CUNNINGLY.**

2 Pet. 1:16 c. devised fables

**CUP.**

Gen. 40:11 Phar.'s c. in my hand
44:2 silver c. in sack's mouth
2 Sam. 12:3 drank of his own c.
Ps. 11:6 be portion of their c.
16:5 L. is the portion of my c.
23:5 my c. runneth over
73:10 waters of a full c. wrung
75:8 in hand of Lord is a c.
116:13 I will take c. of salvation
Prov. 23:31 giveth its color in c.
Is. 51:17 hast drunk the c. the dregs of the c. of trembling
22 taken out of thy hand c. of
Jer. 16:7 give c. of consolation
25:15 take wine c. of this fury
17 took I c. at Lord's hand
28 they refuse c. at thy hand
49:12 judgment not to drink c.
51:7 Babylon been a golden c.
Lam. 4:21 c. also pass through
Ezek. 23:31 her c. into thy hand
32 drink of thy sister's c. deep
Hab. 2:16 c. of L. right hand
Zec. 12:2 Jerus. c. of trembling
Mat. 10:42 c. of c. wat. Mark 9:41
20:22 to drink c. Mark 10:38
23 indeed of my c. Mark 10:39
23:25 make clean outside of c.
26 cleanse first that within c.
26:27 he took the c. gave thanks, Mark 14:23; Luke 22:17, 20; 1 Cor. 11:25.
39 let this c. pass from me, Mark 14:36; Luke 22:42
42 if c. may not pass from me
Luke 22:20 this c. is new testament in my bl. 1 Cor. 11:25
John 18:11 c. Father hath given
1 Cor. 10:16 c. of blessing
21 cannot drink c. of L. and c.
11:26 as often as ye drink of c.
27 drink c. of Lord unworthily
Rev. 14:10 without mixt. into c
16:19 to her c. of his wrath
17:4 woman having golden c.
18:6 in c. fill to her double

**CUP-BEARER.**

Neh. 1:11 I was the king's c.-b.

**CUP-BEARERS.**

1 K. 10:5 saw c.-b. 2 Chr. 9:4

**CUPS.**

1 Chr. 28:17 pure gold for the c.
Is. 22:24 hang the vessels of c.
Jer. 52:19 Chaldeans took aw. c.
Mark 7:4 as washing of c. 8

**CURDLED.**

Job 10:10 c. me like cheese?

**CURE, Substantive.**

Jer. 33:6 I will bring it c.

**CURE, ED.**

Jer. 33:6 I will c. them, and
46:11 O Egypt, shalt not be c.
Hos. 5:13 could he not c. you
Mat. 17:16 disciples, not c. him
18 child c. that very hour
Luke 7:21 same hour he c. many
9:1 gave power to c. diseases
John 5:10 Jews said to him c.

**CURES.**

Luke 13:32 I do c. to-day

**CURIOUS, LY.**

Ex. 28:8 c. girdle, 27, 28; 29:5; 39:5; Lev. 8:7
35:32 and to devise c. works
Ps. 139:15 c. wrought in lowest
Acts 19:19 that used c. arts

**CURRENT.**

Gen. 23:16 c. money with mer.

**CURSE, Substantive.**

Gen. 27:12 bring c. on me
13 mother said, Upon me be c.
Num. 5:18 bitter water that causeth the c. 19, 22, 24, 27
27 woman be c. am. her peo.
Deut. 11:26 a bless. and c. 30:1
28 a c. if ye will not obey
29 and put the c. upon Ebal
23:5 c. into blessing, Neh. 13:2
29:19 heareth words of this c.
Jos. 6:18 camp of Israel a c.
Jud. 9:57 came c. of Jotham
1 K. 2:8 with a grievous c.
2 K. 22:19 should become a c.
Neh. 10:29 they entered into a c.
Job 31:30 wishing c. to his soul
Prov. 3:33 c. of L. in ho. of wic.
26:2 so c. causeless not come
27:14 be counted a c. to him
28:27 hid. eyes have many a c.
Is. 24:6 therefore c. dev. earth
34:5 down on people of my c.
43:28 given Jacob to the c.
65:15 leave your name for a c.
Jer. 24:9 deliv. them to be a c. 25:18; 29:18; 42:18; 44:8
26:6 this city a c. to all nations
44:22 therefore is your land a c.
49:13 Bozrah shall become a c.
Lam. 3:65 give thy c. unto them
Dan. 9:11 the c. is poured upon
Zec. 5:3 this is c. that goeth
8:13 ye were c. among heathen
Mal. 2:2 I will send c.
3:9 ye are cursed with a c. ye
4:6 lest I smite earth with a c.
Acts 23:12 bound under a c. 14
Gal. 3:10 of law are under c.
13 redeemed us from c. of law
Rev. 22:3 shall be no more c.

**CURSE, Verb.**

Gen. 8:21 I will not c. ground
12:3 will c. him curseth thee
Ex. 22:28 not c. ruler of thy peo.
Lev. 19:14 shalt not c. the deaf

*Num.* 22:6 *c.* me this people, 17
11 now *c.* me them, 23:7, 13
12 God said, Thou shalt not *c.*
23:8 how I *c.* whom God hath
11 I took thee to *c.* enem. 24:10
25 neither *c.* at all, nor bless
*Deut.* 23:4 Bal. to *c.* *Neh.* 13:2
27:13 shall stand on Ebal to *c.*
*Jos.* 24:9 B. called Bal. to *c.* you
*Jud.* 5:23 *c.* Meroz, said angel, *c.*
2 *Sam.* 16:9 dead dog *c.* king?
10 let him *c.* L. hath said, *c.* D.
*Job* 1:11 *c.* thee to thy face, 2:5
2:9 said his wife, *c.* God and die
3:8 let them *c.* it that *c.* day
*Ps.* 62:4 but they *c.* inwardly
109:28 let them *c.* but bless thou
*Prov.* 11:26 people shall *c.* him
24:24 him shall the people *c.*
30:10 accuse not serv. lest he *c.*
*Ec.* 7:21 hear servant *c.* thee
10:20 *c.* not king, *c.* not the rich
*Is.* 8:21 *c.* their king, and God
*Jer.* 15:10 every one doth *c.* me
*Mal.* 2:2 I will *c.* your blessings
*Mat.* 5:44 bl. th. that *c.* *Lu.* 6:28
26:74 began to *c.* *Mark* 14:71
*Rom.* 12:14 bless, and *c.* not
*Jam.* 3:9 therewith *c.* we men

**CURSED.**

*Gen.* 3:14 serpent *c.*; 17 ground
4:11 Cain *c.*; 9:25 *c.* be Canaan
5:29 bec. of ground Lord hath *c.*
27:29 *c.* that curseth, *Num.* 24:9
49:7 *c.* be their anger, for
*Lev.* 20:9 hath *c.* his father or
24:11 Israelitish woman's son *c.*
14 bring forth him hath *c.* 23
*Num.* 22:6 wh. thou cursest is *c.*
*Deut.* 27:15 *c.* be he, 16–26
28:16 *c.* be in city, *c.* in field
17 *c.* shalt be thy basket and
18 *c.* be fruit of thy body
19 *c.* when comest in and goest
*Jos.* 6:26 *c.* be man bu. Jericho
9:23 ye Gibeonites are *c.*
*Jud.* 9:27 and *c.* Abimelech
21:18 *c.* giveth a wife to Benj.
1 *Sam.* 14:24 *c.* that eateth
17:43 Goliath *c.* David
1 *Sam.* 26:19 if men, *c.* be they
2 *Sam.* 16:5 Shimei *c.* still, 7, 13
19:21 he *c.* Lord's anointed
1 *K.* 2:8 *c.* me with grievous *c.*
2 *K.* 2:24 *c.* them in name of Lord
9:34 go see now this *c.* woman
*Neh.* 13:25 I *c.* them
*Job* 1:5 it may be my sons *c.* G.
3:1 then Job *c.* his day
5:3 suddenly I *c.* his habitation
24:18 portion is *c.* in the earth
*Ps.* 37:22 *c.* of him shall be cut
119:21 rebuked proud that are *c.*
*Ec.* 7:22 likewise hast *c.* others
*Jer.* 11:3 *c.* obeyeth not covenant
17:5 *c.* man that trust. in man
20:14 *c.* be the day I was born
15 *c.* man brought tid. to father
48:10 *c.* doeth Lord's work dec.
*c.* keepeth back sword
*Mal.* 1:14 but *c.* be the deceiver
2:2 *c.* your blessings already
3:9 ye are *c.* with a curse for
*Mat.* 25:41 depart from me ye *c.*
*John* 7:49 know not law are *c.*
*Gal.* 3:10 *c.* that continueth not
13 *c.* every one hang. on a tree
2 *Pet.* 2:14 *c.* children, who have

**CURSED thing.**

*Deut.* 7:26 lest thou be a *c. thing*, for it is a *c. thing*.
13:17 cleave naught of *c. thing*

**CURSEDST.**

*Jud.* 17:2 silver about which *c.*
*Mark* 11:21 fig-tree thou *c.* is

**CURSES.**

*Num.* 5:23 priest write these *c.*
*Deut.* 28:15 th. *c.* shall come, 45
29:20 all the *c.* written in this book, 27; 2 *Chr.* 34:24
21 accord. to all the *c.* of cov.
30:7 put these *c.* on enemies

**CURSETH.**

*Ex.* 21:17 he that *c.* his father, *Lev.* 20:9; *Prov.* 20:20
*Lev.* 24:15 whose *c.* his God
*Prov.* 30:11 genera. *c.* their father
*Mat.* 15:4 *c.* his father or mother, let him die, *Mark* 7:10

**CURSING.**

*Num.* 5:21 charge with oath of *c.*
*Deut.* 28:20 shall send on thee *c.*
30:19 before you blessing and *c.*
2 *Sam.* 16:12 good for his *c.*
*Ps.* 10:7 full of *c.* *Rom.* 3:14
59:12 *c.* and lying they speak
109:17 loved *c.* so let it come
18 he clothed himself with *c.*
*Prov.* 29:24 hear *c.* bewrayeth not
*Heb.* 6:8 thorns, is nigh to *c.*
*Jam.* 3:10 out of same mouth *c.*

**CURSINGS.**

*Jos.* 8:34 read blessings and *c.*

**CURTAIN.**

*Ps.* 104:2 stretchest out the heavens like a *c.* *Is.* 40:22

**CURTAINS.**

*Ex.* 26:1 with ten *c.* 2; 36:9
*Num.* 4:25 Gershonites bear *c.*
2 *Sam.* 7:2 within *c.* 1 *Chr.* 17:1
*Cant.* 1:5 comely as *c.* of Solom.
*Is.* 54:2 stretch forth the *c.*
*Jer.* 4:20 my *c.* spoiled in a mom.
10:20 none to set up my *c.*
49:29 shall take their *c.*
*Hab.* 3:7 *c.* of Midian did tremble

**CUSH.**

*Gen.* 10:6 Ham, C. 7; 1 *Ch.* 1:8, 9
*Is.* 11:11 remnant left from C.

CUSHAN. *Hab.* 3:7

**CUSHI.**

2 *Sam.* 18:21 C. tell the king, 23
*Jer.* 36:14 princes sent son of C.
*Zep.* 1:1 Zephaniah, son of C.

**CUSTODY.**

*Num.* 3:36 *c.* of sons of Merari
*Est.* 2:3 virgins to *c.* of Hege, 8
14 to *c.* of Shaashgaz

**CUSTOM.**

*Gen.* 31:35 *c.* of women is on me
*Jud.* 11:39 was a *c.* in Israel
1 *Sam.* 2:13 the priest's *c.* was
*Ezr.* 3:4 accord. to *c.* *Jer.* 32:11
4:13 then will they not pay *c.*
20 and *c.* was paid to them
7:24 not impose *c.* on priests
*Mat.* 9:9 saw Matthew at receipt of *c.* *Mark* 2:14; *Luke* 5:27
17:25 whom do kings take *c.*?
*Luke* 1:9 ac. to *c.* of priest's office
2:27 do for him after *c.* of law
42 Jerusalem after *c.* of feast
*Luke* 4:16 as J. *c.* was, he went
*John* 18:39 *c.* I should release one
*Rom.* 13:7 *c.* to whom *c.* is due
1 *Cor.* 11:16 we have no such *c.*

**CUSTOMS.**

*Lev.* 18:30 these abominable *c.*
*Jer.* 10:3 *c.* of this people
*Acts* 6:14 shall change *c.* of M.
16:21 *c.* not lawful to receive
21:21 ought not to walk after *c.*
26:3 thee to be expert in all *c.*
28:17 I com. nothing against *c.*

**CUT, Participle.**

*Lev.* 22:24 not offer what is *c.*
*Ezek.* 16:4 thy navel was not *c.*
*Acts* 5:33 *c.* to the heart, 7:54

**CUT, Verb.**

*Deut.* 14:1 shall not *c.* yourselves
*Jud.* 20:6 concubine, and *c.* her
1 *K.* 18:28 *c.* thems. after manner
2 *K.* 24:13 he *c.* all the vessels of gold, 2 *Chr.* 28:24
1 *Chr.* 20:3 he *c.* peop. with saws
*Ps.* 58:7 let them be as *c.*
107:16 *c.* bars of iron *Is.* 45:2
*Is.* 51:9 art thou not it *c.* Rahab
*Jer.* 16:6 nor *c.* themselves
36:23 he *c.* roll with penknife
41:5 having *c.* themselves
47:5 how long wilt *c.* thyself
*Dan.* 2:5 ye will not shall be *c.*
3:29 speak ag. God shall be *c.*
*Amos* 9:1 *c.* them in the head
*Zec.* 12:3 bur. them with it be *c.*

**CUT asunder.**

*Ps.* 129:4 *c. a.* cords of wicked
*Jer.* 50:23 hammer of earth *c. a.*
*Zec.* 11:10 Beauty and *c.* it *a.*
14 I *c. asun.* mine other staff
*Mat.* 24:51 *c.* him *a.* *Luke* 12:46

**CUT down.**

*Ex.* 34:13 *c. down* their groves, *Deut.* 7:5; 2 *K.* 18:4; 23:14
*Num.* 13:23 *c. down* a branch, 24
*Deut.* 20:19 tr. for meat not *c. d.*
*Job* 8:12 in greenness not *c. d.*
14:2 like a flower, and is *c. d.*
7 hope of a tree if it be *c. d.*
22:16 wicked *c. d.* out of time
20 our substance is not *c. d.*
*Ps.* 37:2 shall soon be *c. down*
80:16 branch is burnt, it is *c. d.*
90:6 in the even. it is *c. down*
*Is.* 9:10 sycamores are *c. down*
14:12 how art thou *c. d.* to gr.
22:25 the nail shall be *c. down*
*Jer.* 22:7 *c. d.* thy choice cedars
25:37 habitations *c. down*
48:2 shalt be *c. d.* O Madmen
*Nah.* 1:12 thus shall be *c. down*
*Zep.* 1:11 merch. people *c. down*
*Mat.* 21:8 *c. d.* bra. *Mark* 11:8
*Luke* 13:7 *c.* it *down*
9 thou shalt *c.* it *down*

**CUT off.**

*Gen.* 9:11 nor all flesh be *c. off*
*Ex.* 12:15 that soul be *c. off*, 19; 31:14; *Num.* 15:30; 19:13
23:23 and I will *c.* them *off*
30:33 be *c. off* from his people, 38; *Lev.* 7:20, 27; 17:4, 9; 19:8; 23:29; *Num.* 9:13
*Lev.* 17:10 will *c.* him *off*, 18:29; 20:3, 6, 18; *Num.* 19:20
14 eateth blood shall be *c. off*
20:17 *c. off* in sight of people
*Num.* 4:18 *c.* not *off* tribe of K.
15:31 that soul utterly be *c. off*
*Deut.* 12:29 G. shall *c. off* nations
19:1 God hath *c. off* nations
23:1 hath privy member *c. off*
25:12 *c. off* her hand pity not
*Jos.* 3:13 the waters of Jordan shall be *c. off*, 16; 4:7
7:9 and shall *c. off* our name
11:21 Joshua *c. off* Anakim
*Jud.* 21:6 one tribe *c. off*
*Ruth* 4:10 dead be not *c. off*
1 *Sam.* 2:31 I will *c. off* thy arm
33 man whom I shall not *c. off*
17:51 David *c. off* Goliath's head
20:15 not *c. off* thy kind.; 24:21 when L. *c. off* enemies of D.
24:4 David *c. off* the skirt of, 5
28:9 how Saul *c. off* wizards
31:9 and they *c. off* Saul's head
2 *Sam.* 4:12 and *c. off* their hands
10:4 H. *c. off* their garments in the middle, 1 *Chr.* 19:4
20:22 *c. off* the head of Sheba

1 *K.* 9:7 will I *c. off* Is. out of
11:16 *c. off* every male in Edom
13:34 to *c. off* Jer. house, 14:14
14:10 *c. off* from Jeroboam him
18:4 Jezebel *c. off* prophets
1 *K.* 21:21 *c. off* from Ahab him that pisseth, 2 *K.* 9:8
1 *Chr.* 17:8 *c. off* all thine enem.
2 *Chr.* 22:7 *c. off* house of Ahab
32:21 angel *c. off* mighty men
*Job* 4:7 where were right. *c. off?*
6:9 loose his hand, and *c.* me *off*
8:14 whose hope shall be *c. off*
11:10 if he *c. off* who can hinder
18:16 above, his branch be *c. off*
23:17 I was not *c. off* before
24:24 *c. off* as tops of ears of c.
36:20 people *c. off* in their place
*Ps.* 12:3 *c. off* flattering lips
31:22 *c. off* from bef. thine eyes
34:16 to *c. off* remem. of them
37:9 evil-doers shall be *c. off*
22 they cursed of him be *c. off*
28 seed of wicked sh. be *c. off*
34 wicked are *c. off* shalt see it
38 end of wicked shall be *c. off*
54:5 *c.* them *off* in thy truth
75:10 horns of wick. will I *c. off*
76:12 *c. off* spirit of princes
83:4 said, let us *c.* them *off*
88:5 are *c. off* from thy hand
16 terrors have *c.* me *off*
94:23 *c.* them *off* in their wick.
101:5 slandereth will I *c. off*
8 *c. off* wicked doers from city
109:13 let his posterity be *c. off*
15 Lord may *c. off* memory
143:12 *c. off* enemies
*Prov.* 2:22 wicked shall be *c. off*
23:18 expect. not be *c. off*, 24:14
*Is.* 9:14 will *c. off* head and tail
10:7 to *c. off* nations not a few
11:13 adversary of Jud. be *c. off*
14:22 *c. off* from Babylon
15:2 every beard *c. off*
29:20 watch for iniquity *c. off*
38:12 *c.* me *off* with pining
48:9 that I *c.* thee not *off*
19 should not been *c. off*
53:8 he was *c. off* out of land
55:13 that shall not be *c. off*
66:3 as if he *c. off* a dog's neck
*Jer.* 7:28 truth is *c. off* fr. mouth
29 *c. off* thy hair, O Jerusalem
9:21 to *c. off* children fr. without
11:19 let us *c.* him *off* from land
44:7 *c. off* man and woman
11 to *c. off* all Judah
47:4 to *c. off* from Tyrus
5 Ashkelon is *c. off*
48:2 *c.* it *off* from being a nation
25 the horn of Moab is *c. off*
49:26 men of war shall be *c. off*
50:16 *c. off* sower from Babylon
51:6 be not *c. off* in her iniquity
62 this place, to *c.* it *off*
*Lam.* 2:3 *c. off* in anger
3:53 *c. off* my life
*Ezek.* 14:8 *c.* him *off* from people
13 *c. off* man and beast, 17, 19, 21; 25:13; 29:8
17:9 not *c. off* fruit thereof
17 forts to *c. off* many persons
21:3 *c.* off right. and wicked, 4
25:7 I will *c.* thee *off* from peo.
16 I will *c. off* Cherethim
30:15 *c. off* multitude of No
31:12 ter. of nations *c.* him *off*
35:7 I will *c. off* from Seir him
37:11 we are *c. off* for our parts
*Dan.* 4:14 *c. off* his branches
9:26 Messiah shall be *c. off*
*Hos.* 8:4 that they may be *c. off*
10:7 king is *c. off* as foam, 15
*Joel* 1:5 the new wine is *c. off*, 9
16 meat *c. off* before our eyes?
*Amos* 1:5 *c. off* inhabitant, 8
2:3 I will *c. off* judge from midst
3:14 horns of altar shall be *c. off*
*Ob.* 5 how art thou *c. off?*
9 every one of E. may be *c. off*
10 shalt be *c. off* for ever
14 to *c. off* those did escape
*Mic.* 5:9 thine enemies be *c. off*
10 horses; 12 witchcrafts
13 will I *c. off*, *Nah.* 1:14
*Nah.* 1:15 wicked is utterly *c. off*
2:13 *c. off* thy prey from earth
3:15 the sword shall *c.* thee *off*
*Hab.* 3:17 tho' the flock be *c. off*
*Zep.* 1:3 *c. off* man from land
4 *c. off* a remnant of Baal
11 that bear silver *c. off*
3:6 I have *c. off* the nations
7 so dwellings sh. not be *c. off*
*Zec.* 5:3 sweareth, shall be *c. off*
9:6 *c. off* pride of Philistines
10 *c. off* chariot from Ephraim
11:8 three shepherds also I *c. off*
9 to be *c. off*, let it be *c. off*
13:2 I will *c. off* names of idols
8 two parts shall be *c. off*
14:2 residue shall not be *c. off*
*Mal.* 2:12 Lord will *c. off* man
*Mat.* 5:30 if right hand offend *c.* it *off*, 18:8; *Mark* 9:43, 45
*Mark* 14:47 *c. off* his ear, *Luke* 22:50; *John* 18:10, 26
*Rom.* 11:22 shalt also be *c. off*
2 *Cor.* 11:12 I may *c. off* occasion
*Gal.* 5:12 I would they were *c. off*

**CUT out.**

*Prov.* 10:31 fro. tongue be *c. out*
*Dan.* 2:34 a stone was *c. out*, 45
*Rom.* 11:24 *c. out* of olive tree

**CUT short.**

2 *K.* 10:32 began to *c.* Israel *sh.*
*Rom.* 9:28 *c.* it *short* in right.

**CUT up.**

*Job* 30:4 who *c. up* mallows
*Is.* 33:12 as thorns *c. up* shall

**CUTTEST, ETH.**

*Deut.* 24:19 when thou *c.* harvest
*Job* 28:10 he *c.* out rivers
*Ps.* 46:9 he *c.* the spear in sunder
141:7 as when one *c.* wood
*Prov.* 26:6 mess. by fool, *c.* off
*Jer.* 10:3 for one *c.* a tree out of
22:14 and *c.* him out windows

**CUTTING.**

*Ex.* 31:5 in *c.* of stones, 35:33
*Is.* 38:10 I said in *c.* off of days
*Hab.* 2:10 by *c.* off many people
*Mark* 5:5 *c.* himself with stones

**CUTTINGS.**

*Lev.* 19:28 not make any *c.* 21:5
*Jer.* 48:37 upon all hands be *c.*

**CYMBAL.**

1 *Cor.* 13:1 I am as tinkling *c.*

**CYMBALS.**

2 *Sam.* 6:5 play. on *c.* 1 *Chr.* 13:8
1 *Chr.* 15:16 harps and *c.* 16:42
16:5 Asaph made sound with *c.*
25:6 these were for song with *c.*
2 *Chr.* 5:13 lift up voice with *c.*
29:25 Levites in house with *c.*
*Ezr.* 3:10 sons of Asaph with *c.*
*Ps.* 150:5 upon high sounding *c.*

**CYPRESS.**

*Is.* 44:14 he taketh the *c.*

**CYPRUS.**

*Acts* 4:36 country of C. 11:20
13:4 from Seleucia sailed to C.
15:39 Mark, and sailed to C.
27:4 we sailed under C.

**CYRENE.**

*Mat.* 27:32 found a man of C.
*Acts* 2:10 parts of Libya about C.
11:20 men of Cyprus and C.
13:1 Lucius of C. was in church

CYRENIAN. *Mark* 15:21
CYRENIANS. *Acts* 6:9
CYRENIUS. *Luke* 2:2

**CYRUS.**

2 *Chr.* 36:22 the first year of C.
*Ezr.* 1:7; 3:7; 4:3; 5:13
*Is.* 44:28 that saith of C. 45:1
*Dan.* 1:21 to the first year of C.
6:28 Dan. prosp. in reign of C
10:1 in the third year of C.

# D

DABBASHETH. *Jos.* 19:11
DABERATH. *Jos.* 19:12; 1 *Ch.* 6:72

**DAGGER.**

*Jud.* 3:16 Ehud made him a *d.*
21 took *d.* from right thigh, 22

DAGON. *Jud.* 16:23; 1 *Sam.* 5:2, 3, 7; 1 *Chr.* 10:10

DAILY. *See* after DAYS.

**DAINTY, IES.**

*Gen.* 49:20 Asher yield royal *d.*
*Job* 33:20 abhorreth *d.* meat
*Ps.* 141:4 let me not eat of *d.*
*Prov.* 23:3 be not desirous of *d.*
6 neither desire his *d.* meats
*Rev.* 18:14 *d.* are departed

**DALE.**

*Gen.* 14:17 valley of S. king's *d.*
2 *Sam.* 18:18 a pillar in king's *d.*

DALMATIA. 2 *Tim.* 4:10
DALMANUTHA. *Mark* 8:10

**DAM.**

*Ex.* 22:30 seven days with *d.* *Lev.* 22:27
*Deut.* 22:6 not take *d.* with you.

**DAMAGE.**

*Ezr.* 4:22 why should *d.* grow
*Est.* 7:4 not count. king's *d*
*Prov.* 26:6 and drinketh *d.*
*Dan.* 6:2 should have no *d.*
*Acts* 27:10 voy. will be with *d.*
2 *Cor.* 7:9 *d.* by us in nothing

DAMARIS. *Acts* 17:34

**DAMASCUS.**

*Gen.* 15:2 Eliezer of D.
2 *Sam.* 8:6 put garrisons in D.
2 *K.* 5:12 Pharpar rivers of D.
8:7 E. came to D. 14:28; 16:9
*Is.* 7:8; 8:4; 10:9; 17:1, 3
*Ezek.* 27:18; *Amos* 1:3; 3:12; 5:27
*Acts* 9:2 desired letters to D. 10, 19, 22, 27; 22:6, 10; 26:12
2 *Cor.* 11:32 in D. the gov. desir.
*Gal.* 1:17 I returned again to D.

**DAMNABLE.**

2 *Pet.* 2:1 who bring in *d.* heres.

**DAMNATION.**

*Mat.* 23:14 shall receive greater *d.* *Mark* 12:40; *Luke* 20:47
33 can ye escape *d.* of hell
*Mark* 3:29 in danger of eternal *d.*
*John* 5:29 to the resurrection of *d.*
*Rom.* 3:8 whose *d.* is just
13:2 receive to themselves *d.*
1 *Cor.* 11:29 eateth and drink. *d.*

29:3 by his *light* I walk. thro' *d.*
30:26 I waited for *light* came *d.*
*Ps.* 112:4 ariseth *light* in *d.*
139:12 *d.* and *l.* are both alike
*Ec.* 2:13 as *light* excelleth *d.*
*Is.* 5:20 that put *d.* for *l. l.* for *d.*
9:2 peo. that walk. in *d.* have seen a great *l. Mat.* 4:16
42:16 make *d. light* before them
45:7 I form *light* and create *d.*
50:10 walketh in *d.* hath no *l.*
*Jer.* 13:16 look for *l.* he make it *d.*
*Lam.* 3:2 bro't me into *d.* not *l.*
*Amos* 5:18 is *d.* and not *light*
*Mic.* 7:8 I sit in *d.* L. be a *light*
*Mat.* 6:23 *l.* be *d.* how gr. that *d.*
10:27 what I tell in *d.* speak in *l.* *Luke* 12:3
*Luke* 1:79 *l.* that sit *d. Rom.* 2:19
11:35 that *light* in thee be not *d.*
*John* 1:5 *l.* shineth in *d. d.* com.
3:19 loved *d.* rather than *light*
12:35 while ye have *l.* lest *d.*
*Acts* 26:18 from *d.* to *light*
*Rom.* 13:12 works of *d.* put on *l.*
1 *Cor.* 4:5 to *l.* hid. things of *d.*
2 *Cor* 4:6 *l.* to shine out of *d.*
6:14 communion *light* with *d.*
1 *Pet.* 2:9 out of *d.* into marv. *l.*
1 *John* 1:5 in Him is no *d.* at all
2:8 *d.* is passed true *l.* shineth

**Out of DARKNESS.**

*Deut.* 5:23 voice *out of* the *d.*
*Job* 12:22 deep things *out of d.*
*Job* 15:22 he shall return *out of d.*
30 shall not depart *out of d.*
*Ps.* 107:14 brought them *out of d.*
*Is.* 29:18 blind see *out of d.*

**DARLING.**

*Ps.* 22:20 *d.* from power of dog
35:17 rescue my *d.* from lions

**DART, S.**

2 *Sam.* 18:14 Joab took three *d.*
2 *Chr.* 32:5 Hezekiah made *d.*
*Job* 41:26 nor the *d.* cannot hold
29 *d.* are counted as stubble
*Prov.* 7:23 till *d.* strike thro' liver
*Eph.* 6:16 to quench fiery *d.* of
*Heb.* 12:20 thrust thro' with a *d.*

**DASH.**

2 *K.* 8:12 wilt *d.* their children
*Ps.* 2:9 *d.* in pieces like a pot.
91:12 lest thou *d.* foot against a stone, *Mat.* 4:6; *Luke* 4:11
*Is.* 13:18 shall *d.* young men
*Jer.* 13:14 will *d.* one ag. another

**DASHED.**

*Ex.* 15:6 thy right hand, O L. *d.*
*Is.* 13:16 child. be *d.* to pieces, *Hos.* 13:16; *Nah.* 3:10
*Hos.* 10:14 mo. was *d.* on child.

**DASHETH.**

*Ps.* 137:9 *d.* little ones ag. stones

DATHAN. *See* ABIRAM.

**DAUB, ED, ING.**

*Ex.* 2:3 she *d.* ark with slime
*Ezek.* 13:10 *d.* it with untempered
22:28 her prophets *d.* them

**DAUGHTER.**

*Gen.* 20:12 *d.* of my father, not *d.*
24:23 whose *d.* art thou, 47
48 master's brother's *d.* to son
34:7 in lying with Jacob's *d.*
8 my son longeth for your *d.*
*Ex.* 1:16 if a *d.* she shall live
21:31 have gored a son or a *d.*
*Lev.* 12:6 days fulfilled for a *d.*
18:17 nor take her daughter's *d.*
21:9 if *d.* of priest profane
*Num.* 27:9 if no *d.* give his inh.
36:8 *d.* that possess. an inher.
*Deut.* 27:22 lieth with *d.* of father
28:56 eye be evil toward her *d.*
*Jud.* 11:40 lament Jephthah's *d.*
1 *Sam.* 1:16 handmaid a *d.* of B.
18:19 Saul's *d.* should been giv.
2 *Sam.* 12:3 lamb unto him as a *d.*
1 *K.* 3:1 Solo. took Pharaoh's *d.*
11:1 many with *d.* of Pharaoh
2 *K.* 8:18 *d.* Jehoram's wife
9:34 bury her, she is a king's *d.*
1 *Chr.* 2:49 *d.* of Caleb Achsa
*Est.* 2:7 uncle's *d.* for his own
*Ps.* 45:10 O *d.* and consider, and
13 king's *d.* glorious within
*Cant.* 7:1 shoes, O prince's *d.*
*Jer.* 31:22 backsliding *d.* 49:4
46:19 O *d.* in Egypt, furnish
48:18 *d.* dost inhabit Dibon
*Ezek.* 14:16 deliv. son nor *d.* 18, 20
16:44 as mother, so is her *d.*
45 art mother's *d.* that loatheth
*Dan.* 11:6 king's *d.* of south come
17 shall give him *d.* of women
*Hos.* 1:6 conce. ag. and bare a *d.*
*Mic.* 5:1 O *d.* of troops
7:6 *d.* riseth up ag. mother, *Mat.* 10:35; *Luke* 12:53
*Zep.* 3:10 *d.* of my dispersed
*Mal.* 2:11 mar. *d.* of strange god
*Mat.* 9:22 *d*, be of good comfort, *Mark* 5:34; *Luke* 8:48
10:37 loveth *d.* more than me
14:6 *d.* of Herodias danced
15:28 her *d.* was made whole
*Mark* 7:26 cast devil out of her *d.*
*Luke* 8:42 he had one only *d.*
13:16 this woman being a *d.*
*Acts* 7:21 Pharaoh's *d.* nourished
*Heb.* 11:24 son of Pharaoh's *d.*

**DAUGHTER of Babylon.**

*Ps.* 137:8 O *d. of B.* to be destr
*Is.* 47:1 O *d. of B.* sit on ground
*Jer.* 50:42 battle ag. thee *d. of B.*
51:33 *d. of B.* like a thr.-floor
*Zec.* 2:7 dwellest with *d. of B.*

**DAUGHTER of the Chaldeans.**

*Is.* 47:1 throne, O *d. of Chal.*
5 into darkness, *d. of Chal.*

**DAUGHTER of Edom.**

*Lam.* 4:21 be glad, *d. of E.*
22 thine iniquity, O *d. of E.*

**DAUGHTER of Egypt.**

*Jer.* 46:11 go into G. *d. of Eg.*
24 *d. of Egypt* be confounded

**DAUGHTER of Gallim.**

*Is.* 10:30 thy voice *d. of Gallim*

**His DAUGHTER.**

*Ex.* 21:7 sell *his d.* to be servant
*Num.* 27:8 to pass to *his d.*
30:16 statutes bet. fa. and *his d.*
*Deut.* 7:3 nor *his d.* take
18:10 *his d.* pass, 2 *K.* 23:10
*Jud.* 21:1 not give *his d.* to B.
1 *Sam.* 17:25 king give him *his d.*

**DAUGHTER of Jerusalem.**

2 *K.* 19:21 *d. of J.* hath shaken her head at thee, *Is.* 37:22
*Lam.* 2:13 liken to thee, *d. of J.*
15 wag their head at *d. of J.*
*Mic.* 4:8 shall come to *d. of J.*
*Zep.* 3:14 rej. with heart, *d. of J.*
*Zec.* 9:9 *d. of J.* thy king cometh

**DAUGHTER of Judah.**

*Lam.* 1:15 hath trodden *d. of J.*
2:2 strong-holds of *d. of J.*
5 inc. in *d. of J.* mourning

**DAUGHTER-IN-LAW.**

*Gen.* 38:16 she was *d.-in-law*
24 Tamar thy *d.-in-law* played
*Lev.* 18:15 naked. of thy *d.-in-law*
20:12 man lie with his *d.-in-l.*
*Ruth* 4:15 *d.-in-l.* which lov. thee
1 *Sam.* 4:19 *d.-in-law* with child
*Ezek.* 22:11 defileth his *d.-in-l.*
*Mic.* 7:6 *d.* aga. mother-in-law, *Mat.* 10:35; *Luke* 12:53

**My DAUGHTER.**

*Deut.* 22:17 tokens of *my d.* virg.
*Jos.* 15:16 him will I give *my d.*
*Jud.* 11:35 *my d.* hast brou. me
19:24 here is *my d.* a maiden
*Ruth* 2:2 she said, Go *my d.*
3:10 blessed be thou *my d.*
*Mat.* 9:18 *my d.* is even now d.
15:22 *my d.* is vexed
*Mark* 5:23 *my d.* at point of d.

**DAUGHTER of my people.**

*Is.* 22:4 spoiling of *d. of p.*
*Jer.* 4:11 wind toward *d. of p.*
6:14 healed *d. of p.* 8:11
26 O *d. of my p.* gird with sack.
8:19 the cry of *d. of my p.*
21 for hurt of *d. of my p.*
22 health of *d. of p.* recovered
9:1 weep for slain of *d. of p.*
7 shall I do for *d. of my p.*
14:17 virgin *d. of p.* is broken
*Lam.* 2:11 destr. of *d. of p.* 3:48
4:3 the *d. of my p.* is bec. cruel
6 iniquity of *d. of my p.*
10 in destruction of *d. of p.*

**DAUGHTER of Tarshish.**

*Is.* 23:10 as river, *d. of T.*

**Thy DAUGHTER.**

*Gen.* 29:18 serve 7 y. for *thy d.*
*Ex.* 20:10 nor *thy d. Deut.* 5:14
*Lev.* 18:10 nakedness of *thy d. d.*
19:29 do not prostitute *thy d.*
*Deut.* 7:3 *thy d.* not give
13:6 if *thy d.* entice thee
22:17 found not *thy d.* a maid
2 *K.* 14:9 give *thy d.* to my son
*Mark* 5:35 *t. d.* is dead, *Luke* 8:49
7:29 devil is gone out of *thy d.*

**DAUGHTER of Tyre.**

*Ps.* 45:12 *d. of T.* be there

**DAUGHTER of Zidon.**

*Is.* 23:12 O oppressed *d. of Z.*

**DAUGHTER of Zion.**

2 *K.* 19:21 *d. of Z.* desp. *Is.* 37:22
*Ps.* 9:14 in gates of *d. of Zion*
*Is.* 1:8 *d. of Z.* left as a cottage
4:4 washed away filth of *d. of Z.*
10:32 mount of *d. of Z.* 16:1
52:2 thyself captive *d. of Zion*
62:11 *d. of Zion* thy sal. cometh
*Jer.* 4:31 voice of *d. of Zion*
6:2 *d. of Z.* to a comely woman
23 men of war ag. thee, *d. of Z.*
*Lam.* 1:6 *d. of Zion* beauty dep.
2:1 L. cover *d. of Z.* with cloud
4 tabernacle of *d. of Zion*
8 destroy wall of *d. of Z.*
10 elders of *d. of Zion*
13 equal to thee, *d. of Zion*
18 O wall of *d. of Zion*
4:22 accomplished *d. of Zion*
*Mic.* 1:13 sin to *d. of Zion*
4:8 strong-hold of *d. of Zion*
10 to bring forth, *d. of Zion*
13 arise and thresh, O *d. of Z.*
*Zep.* 3:14 sing, O *d. of Zion*
*Zec.* 2:10 rejoice, *d. of Zion*, 9:9
*Mat.* 21:5 *d. of Zion* king cometh
*John* 12:15 fear not *d. of Zion*

**DAUGHTERS.**

*Gen.* 6:2 sons of God saw *d.*
*Gen.* 19:36 both *d.* of Lot with c.
24:3 *d.* of Can. 37; 28:1, 6
13 *d.* came out to draw water
27:46 weary of life bec. of *d.*
30:13 *d.* will call me blessed
31:26 hast carried away my *d.*
43 *d.* my *d.*; 50 if afflict my *d.*
34:1 Dinah went out to see *d.*
9 give your *d.* take our *d.*

*Ex.* 2:16 priest of Midan had 7 *d.*
21:9 deal after the manner of *d.*
34:16 *d.* go a whoring after gods
*Lev.* 26:29 flesh of *d.* shall ye eat
*Num.* 26:33 *d.* of Zeloph. *Jos.* 17:3
27:7 *d.* of Zeloph. speak right
36:10 so did *d.* of Zelophehad
*Deut.* 23:17 no whore of *d.* of Is.
*Jud.* 3:6 took *d.* to be wives
21:7 not give them of our *d.* 18
*Ruth* 1:11 turn again my *d.* 12
1 *Sam.* 8:13 *d.* confectionaries
*Neh.* 5:5 our *d.* into bondage
7:63 one of *d.* of B. *Ezr.* 2:61
10:30 not give *d.* to peo. of land
*Job* 42:15 none so fair as *d.* of J.
*Ps.* 45:9 king's *d.* am. hon. wom.
144:12 *d.* be as corner-stones
*Prov.* 31:29 *d.* done virtuously
*Cant.* 2:2 so is my love among *d.*
6:9 the *d.* saw and blessed her
*Is.* 32:9 ye careless *d.* give ear
60:4 *d.* be nursed at thy side
*Jer.* 9:20 teach your *d.* wailing
29:6 give your *d.* to husbands
49:2 her *d.* be burnt with fire
3 cry, ye *d.* of Rabbah, gird ye
*Lam.* 3:51 bec. of *d.* of my city
*Ezek.* 13:17 set face ag. *d.* of peo.
16:46 Samaria and her *d.* Sod.
49 idlen. was in her, and in *d.*
55 sister Sodom and *d.* return
61 give them unto thee for *d.*
23:2 two wom. *d.* of one mother
26:6 her *d.* be slain in field, 8
30:18 her *d.* go into captivity
32:16 *d.* of nations lament her
*Hos.* 4:13 *d.* shall commit whor.
14 I will not punish your *d.*
*Luke* 1:5 his wife of *d.* of Aaron
*Acts* 21:9 had four *d.* virgins
1 *Pet.* 3:6 whose *d.* ye are as long

**DAUGHTERS of Israel.**
*Deut.* 23:17 no whore of *d. of I.*
*Jud.* 11:40 *d. of I.* yearly to lam.
2 *Sam.* 1:24 *d. of I.* weep over S.

**DAUGHTERS of Jerusalem.**
*Cant.* 1:5 comely, O *d. of J.*
2:7 you *d. of J.* 3:5; 5:8; 8:4
3:10 paved with love for *d. of J.*
5:16 my beloved, O *d. of J.*
*Luke* 23:28 *d. of J.* weep not

**DAUGHTERS of Judah.**
*Ps.* 48:11 let *d. of Judah* be glad
97:8 the *d. of Judah* rejoiced

**DAUGHTERS-IN-LAW.**
*Ruth* 1:8 Naomi said *d.-in-law*

**DAUGHTERS of Moab.**
*Num.* 25:1 whore. with *d. of M.*
*Is.* 16:2 *d.* be at fords of Arnon

**DAUGHTERS of music.**
*Ec.* 12:4 *d. of m.* be bro. low

**DAUGHTERS of the Philistines.**
2 *Sam.* 1:20 lest the *d. of P.* rej.
*Ezek.* 16:27 deliver thee to *d. of P.*
57 the *d. of P.* which despise

**DAUGHTERS of Shiloh.**
*Jud.* 21:21 if *d. of Shiloh* come

**DAUGHTERS,** *joined with* **sons.**
*Gen.* 5:4 begat *s. d.* 7, 10; 11:11
19:12 thy *sons* and *d.* bring out
31:28 not suff. to kiss *s.* and *d.*
55 kissed his *sons* and *d.*
37:35 *sons d.* rose to comfort
*Ex.* 10:9 with *s.* and *d.* will we
21:4 have borne him *sons* or *d.*
34:16 take of their *d.* to thy *s.*
*Num.* 21:29 *sons d.* into captiv.
26:33 no *sons* but *d. Jos.* 17:3
*Deut.* 12:12 and *s.* and *d.* rejoice
31 *sons* and *d.* they have burnt,
2 *K* 17:17; *Jer.* 7:31; 32:35
28:32 *s. d.* given to another peo.
41 begat *sons d.* but not enjoy
53 eat flesh of *sons* and *d.*
32:19 provoking of his *s.* and *d.*
*Jos.* 7:24 brought Ach. *s.* and *d.*
17:6 *d.* of Manasseh inh. am. *s.*
*Jud.* 3:6 gave their *d.* to their *s.*
12:9 Ibzan 30 *d.* for his *sons*
1 *Sam.* 30:19 noth. lack. *s.* nor *d.*
1 *Chr.* 23:22 Ele. had no *s.* but *d.*
25:5 God gave Heman 14 *s.* 3 *d.*
2 *Chr.* 11:21 Rehob. had 28 *s.* 60 *d.*
13:21 Abijah begat 22 *sons* 16 *d.*
*Ezr.* 9:12 *d.* to their *s. Neh.* 13:25
*Neh.* 4:14 fight for your *s.* and *d.*
5:2 our *sons* and *d.* are many
10:28 *s.* and *d.* clave to brethren
*Job* 1:2 born to Job 7 *s.* 3 *d.* 42:13
*Ps.* 106:37 sacrificed *sons* and *d.*
38 shed blood of their *s.* and *d.*
*Is.* 43:6 bring my *s.* from far. *d.*
49:22 bring thy *sons* in arms, *d.*
56:5 better than *sons* and *d.*
*Jer.* 3:24 shame dev. *sons* and *d.*
16:2 nor shalt have *sons* nor *d.*
19:9 cause eat flesh of *s.* and *d.*
29:6 wives, beget *sons* and *d.*
48:46 *s.* and *d.* taken captive
*Ezek.* 14:16 deliver *sons* nor *d.*
16:20 *s.* and *d.* and sacrificed
23:4 mine, bare *sons* and *d.*
46 shall slay their *sons* and *d.*
24:21 *s. d.* fall by sw. *Amos* 7:17
25 when I take their *s.* and *d.*
*Joel* 2:28 *s.* and *d.* prop. *Acts* 2:17
3:8 sell *sons* and *d.* to Judah
2 *Cor.* 6:18 be my *s.* and *d.* saith L.

**Two DAUGHTERS.**
*Gen.* 19:8 I have *two d.* let me
15 take thy wife and *two d.*
29:16 Laban had *two d* Leah
31:41 I served for thy *two d.*
*Ruth* 1:7 N. went out with *t. d.*
1 *Sam.* 2:21 Hannah bare *two d.*
14:49 Saul's *two d.* were Merab
*Prov.* 30:15 horseleech hath *t. d.*

**DAUGHTERS of the uncircumcised.**
2 *Sam.* 1:20 lest *d. of u.* triumph

**DAUGHTERS of Zion.**
*Cant.* 3:11 go forth, O ye *d. of Z.*
*Is.* 3:16 *d. of Zion* are haughty
4:4 filth of *d. of Zion*

**DAVID.**
*Ruth* 4:22 Jesse begat *D. Mat.* 1:6; *Luke* 3:31
1 *Sam.* 16:13 came upon *D.*
2 *Sam.* 5:1 all tribes of Is. to *D.*
1 *K.* 2:10 *D.* slept, 1 *Chr.* 29:28
*Ps.* 72:20 prayers of *D.* son of J.
*Mat.* 9:27 son of *D.* 15:22; 20:30; *Mark* 10:47; *Luke* 18:38
12:3 *D.* did when hungered, *Mark* 2:25; *Luke* 20:41
21:9 S. of *D.* 15; 22:42; *Mark* 12:35
*Rom.* 1:3 C. seed of *D.* 2 *Tim.* 2:8
*Heb.* 4:7 saying in *D.* to-day
*Rev.* 3:7 key of *D.*; 5:5 root, 22:16

**Hand of DAVID.**
1 *Sam.* 20:16 Lord req. at *h. of D.*
2 *Sam.* 3:8 not into *hand of D.* 18
21:22 fell by *h. of D.* 1 *Chr.* 20:8

**House of DAVID.**
1 *K.* 12:19 fol. *D.* but J. 2 *Chr.* 10:19
*Ps.* 122:5 thrones of the *h. of D.*
*Is.* 7:2 it was told *house of D.* 13
22:22 key of *h. of D.* I wil lay
*Zec.* 12:7 gl. of *h. of D.* 8, 10, 12
13:1 fountain opened to *h. of D.*
*Luke* 1:27 Joseph, of *h. of D.* 69
2:4 the *house* and lineage of *D.*

**DAVID,** *joined with* **king.**
1 *Sam.* 21:11 this *D. k.* of land?
2 *Sam.* 2:4 anointed *D. k.* over J.
*Jer.* 30:9 Lord and *D.* the *king*
*Hos.* 3:5 seek L. and *D.* their *k.*
*Mat.* 1:6 *D.* the *k.* and *D.* the *k.*
*Acts* 13:22 raised *D.* to be the *k.*

**Servant DAVID.**
2 *Sam.* 7:5 my *servant D.* 8, 26
1 *K.* 8:25 thy *s. D.* 2 *Chr.* 6:16
11:13 for *D. s.* sake, *Ps.* 132:10; *Is.* 37:35
*Ps.* 78:70 *D.* his *servant*, 89:20
*Jer.* 33:21 brok. with *D.* my *s.* 22
*Ezek.* 34:23 even my *servant D.*
37:24 *D.* my *ser.* shall be king
*Luke* 1:69 salva. in house of *s. D.*
*Acts* 4:25 mouth of thy *serv. D.*

**DAWN, ING.**
*Jos.* 6:15 rose about *d.* of day
*Jud.* 19:26 came woman in *d.*
*Job* 3:9 nor let it see *d.* of day
7:4 I am full of tossings to *d.*
*Ps.* 119:147 I prevented the *d.*
*Mat.* 28:1 as it began to *d.*
2 *Pet.* 1:19 till the day *d.* and the

**DAY.**
*Gen.* 1:5 God called the light *d.*
32:26 let me go, *d.* breaketh
*Lev.* 23:37 every thing on his *d.*
*Num.* 14:34 each *d.* for a year
*Deut.* 4:10 *d.* thou stoodest be. L.
9:24 rebellious from *d.* I knew
24:15 at his *d.* give him his hire
*Jos.* 10:13 sun not down ab. a *d.*
14 was no *d.* like that
*Jud.* 16:2 when it is *d.* kill Sam.
1 *Sam.* 9:15 told S. a *d.* before
24:4 *d.* of which Lord said
26:10 or his *d.* shall come to die
2 *Sam.* 3:35 while yet *d. Jer.* 15:9
1 *K.* 2:37 on *d.* thou goest out
2 *K.* 4:8 fell on a *d.* Elisha, 11, 18
*Neh.* 4:2 make an end in a *d.*?
*Job* 1:4 feasted, every one his *d.*
6 was a *d.* when sons, 13; 2:1
3:3 *d.* per. wherein I was born
14:6 till he accomplish his *d.*
18:20 be astonished at his *d.*
19:25 stand at latter *d.* on earth
21:30 reserved to *d.* of destruction
*Ps.* 19:2 *d.* unto *d.* uttereth
37:13 he seeth his *d.* is coming
78:42 nor rem. *d.* he delivered
84:10 a *d.* in thy courts better
119:164 7 times a *d.* I praise
*Prov.* 4:18 and more to perfect *d.*
7:20 home at the *d.* appointed
27:1 what a *d.* may bring forth
*Cant.* 2:17 till the *d.* break, 4:6
*Is.* 7:17 from *d.* Ephraim dep.
43:13 before *d.* was, I am he
58:5 a *d.* to afflict soul? call this an acceptable *d.* to Lord?
61:2 *d.* of vengeance of G. 63:4
*Jer.* 12:3 prep. for *d.* of slaughter
27:22 there be till *d.* I visit
32:31 from the *d.* they built it
36:2 from the *d.* I spake to thee
38:28 *d.* Jerusalem was taken
47:4 of *d.* that cometh to spoil
50:27 woe, for their *d.* is come
*Ezek.* 4:6 each *d.* for a year
7:10 behold the *d.* it is come
21:25 prince, whose *d.* is come
28:15 from *d.* thou wast created
30:2 woe worth the *d.*; 3 near
18 at Tehaphne. *d.* be darken.
*Dan.* 6:10 petition 3 times a *d.*
*Hos.* 9:5 what do in solemn *d.*?
*Joel* 2:2 a *d.* of darkness and
*Amos* 5:8 maketh *d.* dark
8:10 end thereof as a bitter *d.*
*Mic.* 3:6 *d.* be dark over them
7:4 the *d.* of thy watchmen
*Zep.* 2:2 before *d.* pass as chaff
3:8 till *d.* I rise up to the prey
*Zec.* 4:10 desp. *d.* of small things
*Mal.* 3:2 abide *d.* of his coming?
4:1 *d.* cometh that shall burn

Mat. 24:38 d. Noe ent. Luke 17:27
50 L. shall come in a d. when he looketh not, Luke 12:46
25:13 know the d. nor the hour
Mark 1:35 great while before d.
Luke 1:20 d. these be performed
80 d. of his showing to Israel
17:4 trespass seven times in a d.
24 so Son of man be in his d.
John 6:39 raise it ag. at last d.
40 raise him at last d. 44, 54
8:56 Abra. rejoiced to see my d.
9:4 work while it is d.
Acts 1:2 until d. he was tak. up
12:21 on a set d. Herod sat
16:35 it was d. 28:12; 27:39
17:31 he hath appointed a d.
27:29 they wished for d.
Rom. 2:5 wrath ag. d. of wrath
13:12 d. is at hand, let us
14:6 regardeth d. to the Lord
1 Cor. 3:13 the d. shall declare it
2 Cor. 6:2 now is the d. of salv.
Eph. 4:30 sealed to d. of redem.
Phil. 1:6 perf. it un. the d. of C.
1 Thes. 5:5 children of the d.
8 who are of the d. be sober
Heb. 4:7 he limiteth a certain d.
8 have not spoken of anoth. d.
10:25 see the d. approaching
2 Pet. 1:19 till the d. dawn, and
3:12 to coming of d. of God
Rev. 9:15 were prepared for a d.
See ATONEMENT, BATTLE, CALAMITY, DARKNESS, EVIL, HOLY, LAST.

**All the DAY.**

Ps. 25:5 do I wait all the d.
71:15 thy salvation all the d.
89:16 rejoice all the d.
102:8 reproach me all the d.
119:97 meditation all the d.
Is. 28:24 ploughman plo. a. d.
65:2 spread out hands all the d.
5 a fire burneth all the d.
Lam. 1:13 desolate all the d.
3:3 his hand ag. me all t. d.
14 derision to people all the d.
62 their devices ag. me a. t. d.
Mat. 20:6 stand all the d. idle

**All the DAY long.**

Deut. 28:32 longings a. t. d. l.
33:12 cover him all the d. l.
Ps. 32:3 my roaring all the d. l.
35:28 thy praise all the d. l.
38:6 mourning all the d. long
12 imagine deceits all the d. l.
44:8 we boast all the d. long
22 are killed all t. d. l.
71:24 thy righteousness a. t. d. l.
73:14 a. t. d. l. have I been pla.
Prov. 21:26 coveteth all the d. l.
23:17 in fear of Lord all the d. l.
Rom. 10:21 a. t. d. l. stret. my h.

**By DAY.**

Gen. 39:10 spake to Jos. d. by d.
Ex. 13:21 L. went be. them by d.
40:38 cloud was upon the tabernacle by d. Num. 9:16
Num. 10:34 cloud on them by d. 14:14; Deut. 1:33; Neh. 9:19
Jud. 6:27 could not do it by d.
2 Chr. 30:21 praised L. d. by d.
Ezr. 6:9 let it be given d. by d.
Neh. 8:18 d. by d. he read in law
Ps. 91:5 nor arrow flieth by d.
121:6 sun not smite thee by d.
136:8 sun to rule by d. for
Is. 60:19 no more thy light by d.
Jer. 31:35 sun for a light by d.
Ezek. 12:3 remove by d. in sight
Luke 11:3 give us d. by d. bread
2 Cor. 4:16 is renewed d. by d.
Rev. 21:25 g. not to be shut by d.

**Day of DEATH.**

Gen. 27:2 I know not d. of my d.
Jud. 13:7 Nazarite to d. of d.
1 Sam. 15:35 Saul till d. of d.
2 Sam. 20:3 shut up to d. of d.
2 K. 15:5 Uzziah lep. to d. of d.
Ec. 7:1 d. of d. better than birth
8:8 nor ha. he power in d. of d.
Jer. 52:11 in prison, till d. of d.
34 a portion till d. of d.

**Every DAY.**

Ps. 7:11 angry with wicked e. d.
56:5 e. d. they wrest my words
145:2 every d. will I bless thee
Is. 51:13 hast feared every d.
52:5 my name e. d. blasphemed
Luke 16:19 sumptuously every d.
Rom. 14:5 esteem. every d. alike

**Feast DAY.**

Ps. 81:3 blow trumpet on feast-d.
Mat. 26:5 Not on f.-d. Mark 14:2
John 2:23 in feast-d. many bel.

**First DAY.**

Gen. 1:5 evening and morn. f. d.
Neh. 8:18 from f. unto last d.
Dan. 10:12 from f. d. thou didst
Mat. 26:17 f. d. of unl. b. Mark 14:12
Acts 20:18 f. d. I came into A.
Phil. 1:5 fellowship from f. d.
See WEEK.

**Third DAY.**

Hos. 6:2 third d. he will raise us
Mat. 16:21 be raised again the third d. 17:23; Luke 9:22
20:19 and the third d. he shall rise again, Mark 9:31; 10:34; Luke 18:33; 24:7, 46
Luke 13:32 t. d. I shall be perf.
24:21 to-day is the third d.
1 Cor. 15:4 he rose again third d.

**Seventh DAY.**

Gen 2:3 G. bless. s. d. Ex. 20:11
Ex. 12:15 fr. first d. to s. d. 13:6
16:26 s. d. is the sabbath, 20:10; Lev. 23:3; Deut. 5:14
27 there went out some on s. d.
31:17 on seventh d. God rested
Heb. 4:4 spake of s. d.

**Eighth DAY.**

Lev. 12:3 on eighth d. be circum.
Luke 1:59 e. d. came to circumcise ch. Acts 7:8; Phil. 3:5

**Good DAY.**

1 Sam. 25:8 we co. in a good d.
Est. 8:17 J. had a good d. 9:19
9:22 mourning into a good d.

**Great DAY.**

Jer. 30:7 alas, that d. is great
Hos. 1:11 great shall be d. of J.
Joel 2:11 d. of L. is great and te.
31 bef. the great and terrible d. of the Lord come, Acts 2:20
Zep. 1:14 g. d. of the L. is near
Mal. 4:5 before coming of g. d.
John 7:37 great d. of feast
Rev. 6:17 g. d. of his wrath
16:14 to gather to battle of g. d.

**In the DAY.**

Gen. 2:4 i. t. d. L. made the ear.
Gen. 2:17 in the d. thou eatest
3:5 in the d. ye eat
31:40 in d. drought consumed
35:3 in the d. of my distress
Ex. 32:34 in the d. when I. visit
Job 20:28 away in d. of wrath
Ps. 95:8 in d. of temp. Heb. 3:8
102:2 hide not face in d. of tro. in the d. when I call
110:3 in the d. of thy power
5 kings in the d. of his wrath
137:7 Edom, in the d. of Jerus.
138:3 in d. I cried, thou answ.
Prov. 6:34 not spare in d. of ven.
11:4 riches profit not in d. of w.
24:10 in the d. of adversity
Ec. 7:14 in the d. of prosperi. be joyful, in d. of adversity
8:8 nor hath power in d. of d.
12:3 in the d. keepers sh. trem.
Cant. 3:11 in d. of his espousals
8:8 in the d. she shall be spok.
Is. 9:4 as in the d. of Midian
10:3 what do in the d. of visit.
11:16 d. come out Eg. Hos. 2:15
13:13 remove, in d. of his anger
17:11 in the d. shalt make thy plant grow, in the d. of grief
30:25 in the d. of great slaught.
26 in the d. Lord bindeth up
58:3 in d. of your fast
Jer. 16:19 in t. d. of affliction
17:17 my hope in the d. of evil
18:17 in the d. of calamity
36:30 body be cast out in t. d.
Lam. 1:12 in d. of anger
2:1 footstool in d. of anger
3:57 drewest near in the d.
Ezek. 7:19 gold not deliver i. t. d.
16:4 in the d. thou wast born, 5
56 Sod. not men. in d. of pride
27:27 fall in the d. of thy ruin
30:9 as in d. of Egypt
32:10 in the d. of thy fall
33:12 in t. d. he turneth from wick. not able to live in d.
Hos. 2:3 in the d. she was born
4:5 therefore shalt fall in the d.
Amos 1:14 in the d. of whirlwind
8:9 the earth in the clear d.
Ob. 11 in d. stoodest
12 nor rejoiced in d. of destr.
Mal. 4:3 in t. d. that I shall do
Luke 17:30 in the d. Son is rev.
John 11:9 if any walk in the d.
Rom. 2:16 in d. G. shall judge
13:13 walk honestly as in the d.
1 Cor. 1:8 blameless in t. d. of L.
2 Cor. 6:2 in d. of salvat. I suc.
Phil. 2:16 rejoice in d. of Chr.
Heb. 8:9 in d. I took them
1 Pet. 2:12 glorify G. in d. of vis.

**DAY of Judgment.**

Mat. 10:15 more tolerable for S. in d. of j. 11:24; Mark 6:11
11:22 Tyre and Sidon at d. of j.
12:36 account in the d. of ju.
2 Pet. 2:9 res. unjust to d. of ju.
3:7 res. unto fire aga. d. of ju.
1 John 4:17 boldness in d. of ju.

**DAY of the Lord.**

Is. 2:12 d. of L. be on every one
13:6 is at ha. Joel 1:15; Zep. 1:7
9 cometh, Joel 2:1; Zec. 14:1
34:8 d. of Lord's vengeance
Jer. 46:10 d. of L. G. of hosts
Lam. 2:22 d. of L. anger
Ezek. 13:5 battle d. of the Lord
30:3 d. is near, Joel 3:14; Ob. 15
Amos 5:18 desired d. of L.
Zep. 1:8 d. of Lord's sacrifice
18 deliver them in d. of L.
2:2 before d. of the L. anger
3 in d. of the Lord's anger
Mal. 4:5 coming of d. of Lord
1 Cor. 5:5 saved in d. of Lord
2 Cor. 1:14 ye are ou. in d. of L.
1 Thes. 5:2 as a thief, 2 Pet. 3:10
Rev. 1:10 the Spirit on Lord's d.
See Great DAY.

**DAY, joined with Night.**

Gen. 1:14 to divide d. from n.
18 rule over the d. and night
8:22 d. and night shall not cea.
31:39 whether stolen by d. or n.
Ex. 13:21 to go by d. and n.
Num. 11:32 that d. and all n.
Deut. 28:66 shalt fear d. and n.
Jos. 1:8 shalt meditate therein d. and night, Ps. 1:2
1 Sam. 19:24 naked all d. and n.

1 K. 8:29 eyes be opened towards
house n. and d. 2 Chr. 6:20
Neh. 1:6 I pray d. and night
Job 17:12 change night into d.
26:10 d. and n. come to an end
Ps. 32:4 d. and n. thy hand
42:3 tears my meat d. and night
55:10 d. and night they go abo.
74:16 d. is thine, n. also is thi.
88:1 I have cried d. and n.
139:12 night shineth as the d.
Ec. 8:16 d. nor night seeth
Is. 4:5 sm. by d. fla. fire by n.
27:3 L. will keep it d. and n.
34:10 not be quenched d. nor n.
38:12 sickness from d. to n.
13 d. to n. wilt make an end
60:11 gates not be sh. d. nor n.
62:6 hold their peace d. nor n.
Jer. 9:1 weep d. and night
14:17 tears d. and n. Lam. 2:18
16:13 serve other gods d. and n.
33:20 should not be d. nor n.
Zec. 14:7 d. kn. to L. not d. n. n.
Mark 4:27 and rise, n. and d.
5:5 d. and n. he was in mount.
Luke 2:37 prayers night and d.
18:7 which cry d. and night
Acts 9:24 watched gates n. and d.
20:31 cease not to warn n. a. d.
26:7 instantly serv. G. d. and n.
1 Thes. 2:9 laboring d. and n.
3:10 n. and d. pray. 1 Tim. 5:5
2 Thes. 3:8 labor night and d.
2 Tim. 1:3 in prayers n. and d.
Rev. 4:8 rest not d. and night
7:15 serve him d. and n.
8:12 d. shone not for a third p.
12:10 accused bef. G. d. and n.
14:11 have no rest d. nor night
20:10 torment. d. and n. for ev.

**One DAY.**

Gen. 27:45 dep. of both in o. d.?
1 Sam. 2:34 in one d. shall die
27:1 one d. perish by hand of S.
Is. 9:14 bra. and rush in one d.
10:17 dev. thorns and br. in o. d.
47:9 two things sh. co. in o. d.
66:8 earth bring forth in one d.?
Zec. 3:9 remove iniquity in o. d.
14:7 o. d. which shall be known
Acts 21:7 abode with breth. o. d.
Rom. 14:5 esteemeth o. d.
1 Cor. 10:8 fell in one d. 23,000
2 Pet. 3:8 o. d. with L. as 1,000 y.
Rev. 18:8 plagues come in one d.

**Sabbath DAY.**

Ex. 16:26 seventh d. is sa. 20:10
20:8 s.-d to keep it h. Deut. 5:12
11 Lord blessed the s.-d.
31:15 doeth any work on s.-d.
35:3 shall kindle no fire on s.-d.
Num. 15:32 gath. sticks on s.-d.
Deut. 5:15 God com. to keep s.-d.
Neh. 13:15 burdens to J. on s.-d.
17 and profane the s.-d.
22 keep gates, to sanctify s.-d.
Jer. 17:21 bear no burd. on s.-d.
Ezek. 46:4 prince sh. offer in s.-d.
Mat. 12:1 Jesus went on s.-d th.
corn-fields, Mark 2:23
8 for Son of man is Lo. of s.-d.
11 into a pit on s.-d. Luke 14:5
24:20 pray flight be not on s.-d.
Mark 2:24 s.-d. that not lawful
3:2 heal on s.-d. Luke 6:7
6:2 went into the synagogue on
s.-d. Luke 4:17; Acts 13:4
Luke 13:16 this bond on s.-d.
14:1 went to eat bread on s.-d.
23:56 and rested the s.-d.
John 5:10 s.-d not lawful
16 because done these on s.-d.
7:22 on s.-d. circumcise a man
9:14 it was s.-d. J. made clay
19:31 not rem. on cross on s.-d.
Acts 13:27 read every s.-d. 15:21
44 next s.-d. came the wh. city

**Same DAY.**

Ezek. 24:2 the name of this s. d.
Zep. 1:9 s. d. will I punish those
Luke 23:12 s. d. P. and H. frien.
John 5:9 on s. d. was the sabbath
20:19 same d. J. stood in midst
Acts 1:22 sa. d. he was taken up
2:41 s. d. were added 3,000 souls

**Since the DAY.**

Deut. 4:32 s. the d. God created
1 Sam. 8:8 s. t. d. I bro. them o.
of E. 1 K. 8:16; 1 Chr. 17:5
Jer. 7:25 s. the d. fathers came
Col. 1:6 since the d. ye hea. of it
9 s. the d. we heard it

**That DAY.**

Ex. 10:28 t. d. seest my face
14:30 Lord saved Israel th. d.
Deut. 21:23 bury him t. d.
31:18 hide my face in that d.
1 Sam. 8:18 shall cry out in t. d.
and Lord will not hear you
14:23 Lord saved Israel that d.
1 Sam. 14:37 S. ask. he a. not t. d.
16:13 Spirit of L. on D. fro. t. d.
18:9 Saul eyed David from t. d.
2 Sam. 6:9 D. afraid of L. that d.
11:12 Uriah abode in Jeru. t. d.
Job 3:4 let that d. be darkness
Ps. 146:4 in t. d. his thoughts
Is. 2:11 L. alone exalted in t. d.
19:21 E. shall know L. in t. d.
24:21 in t. d. L. shall punish
26:1 in t. d. this be sung in Ju.
29:18 in t. d. shall deaf hear
52:6 shall know in that d.
Jer. 39:16 accomplished in t. d.
17 I will deliver thee in t. d.
Ezek. 29:21 in t. d. Is. be exalted
38:19 in t. d. be a great shaking
39:22 know I am L. from t. d.
Hos. 2:18 in t. d. make a cov.
Joel 3:18 t. d. mount. drop wine
Amos 2:16 flee away nak. in t. d.
8:3 songs be howlings in t. d.
Zep. 1:15 that d. is a day of wra.
Zec. 2:11 joined to L. in t. d.
9:16 G. shall save them in t. d.
11:11 covenant, broken in t. d.
12:8 feeble at t. d. sh. be as D.
11 in that d. be a great mour.
13:1 in t. d. be a foun. opened
14:4 his feet t. d. on the mount.
9 t. d. be one L. his name one
Mal. 3:17 t. d. I make up jewels
Mat. 7:22 will say in that d. Lo.
24:36 t. d. kn. no m. Mark 13:32
26:29 t. d. I drink, Mark 14:25
Luke 6:23 rejoice in th. d.
10:12 more tol. in t. d. for Sod.
21:34 so that d. come unawares
23:54 t. d. was the preparation
John 1:39 abode with him that d.
11:53 from t. d. they took coun.
14:20 t. d. know I am in the F.
16:23 in th. d. shall ask me no.
26 t. d. shall ask in my name
1 Thes. 5:4 t. d. overtake as thi.
2 Thes. 1:10 believed in t. d.
2:3 that d. shall not come
2 Tim. 1:12 com. to h. ag. t. d.
18 find mercy of L. in that d
4:8 L. shall give me at t. d.

**This DAY.**

Gen. 48:15 who fed me to t. a.
Ex. 12:14 t. d. for a memorial
17 observe t. d. in your gener.
13:3 remem. t. d. ye came out, 4
Deut. 4:4 alive every one t. d. 5:3
5:24 t. d. God talk with man
6:24 at t. d. 8:18; Ezr. 9:7
11:8 I com. you t. d. 13:27, 28;
13:18; 15:5; 19:9; 27:1, 4
26:17 avou. t. d. L. to be thy G.
27:9 t. d. art bec. people of Lord
29:4 not ears to hear, to this d.
10 ye stand this d. before L.
30:15 this d. life and death, 19
16 I command thee t. d.
31:27 I am yet alive this d.
Jos. 14:11 I am as strong t. d.
22:17 are not cleansed till t. d.
22 save us not this d.
23:8 as done unto t. d.
24:15 choose this d. whom serv.
Jud. 10:15 deliver us only this d.
19:30 since Isr. came out of E.
to th. d. 1 Sam. 8:8; 2 Sam.
7:6; 2 K. 21:15; 1 Chr. 17:5;
Jer. 7:25
1 Sam. 10:19 t. d. rejected y. G.
14:45 J. wrought with God t. d.
17:10 I defy armies of Is. this d.
18:21 this d. be my son-in-law
22:8 lie in wait as at t. d.? 13
25:33 t. d. from com. to shed bl.
26:21 my soul precious this d.
2 Sam. 3:39 I this d. weak
1 K. 8:61 to keep com. as at t. d.
2 K. 7:9 t. d. day of good tidings
17:34 to t. d. do after former
2 Chr. 5:9 there it is unto t. d.
35:21 I come not ag. thee t. d.
Neh. 9:36 we are servants this d.
Ps. 2:7 my S. t. d have I begot.
thee, Acts 13:33; Heb. 1:5
118:24 t. is the d. L. hath made
119:91 continue t. d. accord. to
Prov. 7:14 this d. I paid my vo.
22:19 known to thee this d.
Is. 38:19 praise thee this d.
56:12 to-mor. shall be as this d.
Jer. 25:18 hiss. as at t. d. 44:22
36:2 from Josiah even to this d.
44:10 are not humbled to this d
Lam. 2:16 this is d. we looked f.
Ezek. 39:8 t. the d. I have spok.
Dan. 9:7 conf. of faces as at t. d.
Hag. 2:15 consider from t. d. 18
19 from this d. will I bless you
Mat. 6:11 give us this d. daily b.
11:23 Sodom remain. to this d.
28:15 among Jews to t. d.
Luke 2:11 is born t. d. a Saviour
4:21 this d. scripture fulfilled
19:9 t. d. salvation to this house
42 at least in this thy d.
Acts 22:3 as ye are all t. d.
23:1 good conscience till t. d.
24:21 called in question this d.
26:22 continue to t. d. witness.
29 all that hear me t. d.
Rom. 11:8 sh. not hear to t. d.

**To-DAY.**

Gen. 21:26 heard I of it but to-d.
Ex. 2:18 come so soon to-d.?
14:13 salvation show you to-d.
Lev. 9:4 to-d. Lord will appear
1 Sam. 11:13 to-d. Lord wrought
24:10 how Lord delivered thee
to-d. into my hand, 26:23
2 Sam. 13:4 lean from d. to-d.?
16:3 to-d. house of Is. resto. me
1 K. 18:15 will show myself to-d.
22:5 inq. at L. to-d. 2 Chr. 18:4
2 K. 4:23 why go to him to-d.?
1 Chr. 16:23 show from day to-d.
his salvation, Ps. 96:2
Job 23:2 to-d. my complaint
Ps. 95:7 to-d. if ye will hear his
voice, Heb. 3:7, 15; 4:7
Zec. 9:12 to-d. do I declare
Mat. 6:30 to-d. is, and to-mor.
is cast into oven, Luke 12:28
21:28 work to-d. in vineyard
Luke 5:26 strange things to-d.
13:32 I do cures to-d. and to-mo.
33 must walk to-d. and d. fol.
19:5 to-d. I abide at thy house
23:43 to-d. be with me in para.
24:21 to-d. is the third day

*Heb.* 3:13 while it is called *to-d.*
5:5 *to-d.* have I begotten thee
13:8 the same yesterday, *to-d.*
*Jam.* 4:13 ye that say *to-d.* or
2 *Pet.* 2:8 vexed his soul d. *to-d.*

**DAY of trouble.**

2 *K.* 19:3 this is *d. of t. Is.* 37:3
*Ps.* 20:1 L. hear thee in *d. of t.*
50:15 call upon me in *d. of t.*
59:16 my refuge in *d. of trou.*
77:2 in *d. of t.* I sought the L.
86:7 in *d. of t.* I will call
*Is.* 22:5 it is a *d. of trouble*
*Jer.* 51:2 *d. of t.* shall be ag. her
*Ezek.* 7:7 time is come, *d. of tr.*
*Nah.* 1:7 strong-hold in *d. of t.*
*Hab.* 3:16 I might rest in *d. of t.*
*Zep.* 1:15 that day is a *d. of t.*

**DAYTIME.**

*Job* 5:14 meet with dark. in *d.*
24:16 houses they marked in *d.*
*Ps.* 22:2 I cry in *d.* hearest not
42:8 his loving kindness in *d.*
78:14 in *d.* led with a cloud
*Is.* 4:6 a taber. for shadow in *d.*
21:8 on watch-tower in the *d.*
*Luke* 21:37 in *d.* he was teaching
2 *Pet.* 2:13 pleasure to riot in *d.*

**DAYS.**

*Gen.* 8:3 after 150 *d.* waters ab.
27:41 *d.* of mourning for my f.
47:9 *d.* of my pilgrimage
50:4 *d.* of his mourning past
*Deut.* 4:32 ask now of the *d.* past
10:10 I stayed in mount forty *d.*
1 *Sam* 13:11 came not within *d.*
18:26 the *d.* were not expired
29:3 been with me these *d.*
1 *Chr.* 23:1 David was full of *d.*
29:15 *d.* as a shadow, *Job* 8:9
28 he died full of *d.* riches, and
2 *Chr.* 24:15 Jehoiada full of *d.*
*Ezr.* 9:7 since *d.* of fathers
*Neh.* 1:4 I mourned certain *d.*
*Est.* 9:26 they called these *d.*
*Job* 3:6 not joined to *d.* of year
7:1 his *d.* like *d.* of a hireling?
12:12 length of *d.* understand.
21:13 spend their *d.* in wealth
30:16 *d.* of afflict. taken hold
27 *d.* of affliction prevent. me
32:7 I said, *d.* should speak
33:25 return to *d.* of his youth
36:11 spend their *d.* in prosper.
42:17 so Job died, full of *d.*
*Ps.* 21:4 gavest him length of *d.*
37:18 L. knoweth *d.* of upright
44:1 work thou didst in their *d.*
55:23 not live half their *d.*
77:5 considered the *d.* of old
78:33 their *d.* did he consume
89:29 his throne as *d.* of heaven
45 *d.* of his youth shortened
90:9 all our *d.* are passed away
10 *d.* of our years threescore
*Ps.* 90:12 so tea. us to nu. our *d.*
14 we may be glad all our *d.*
94:13 rest from *d.* of adversity
119:84 many are *d.* of thy ser.
143:5 I remember the *d.* of old
*Prov.* 3:2 leng. of *d.* add to thee
16 length of *d.* is in right hand
*Ec.* 5:20 not much remember *d.*
7:10 that former *d.* were better
8:15 abide with him *d.* of his li.
11:8 remember *d.* of darkness
12:1 while the evil *d.* come not
*Is.* 23:7 antiquity of ancient *d.*
15 according to *d.* of one king
60:20 *d.* of mourn. shall be end.
65:20 be no more infant of *d.*
22 as *d.* of a tree *d.* of my peo.
*Jer.* 2:32 *d.* without number
6:11 aged with him full of *d.*
31:33 after those *d.* put my law
36:2 *d.* of Josiah to this day

*Lam.* 4:18 our *d.* are fulfilled,
*Ezek.* 12:23 *d.* at hand, effect of
16:22 rem. *d.* of thy youth, 43
*Dan.* 8:14 unto 2,300 *d.* sanctuary
12:11 set up shall be 1,290 *d.*
12 blessed waiteth to 1,335 *d.*
*Hos.* 2:13 visit on her *d.* of Baal.
9:7 *d.* of visitation, recompense
10:9 sinned from *d.* of Gibeah
*Mic.* 7:15 acc. to *d.* of thy com.
*Zec.* 8:9 ye that hear in these *d.*
11 I will not be as in former *d.*
15 thought in these *d.*
*Mal.* 3:7 *d.* of fat. ye are gone
*Mat.* 11:12 *d.* of John Baptist
24:22 those *d.* be shortened, no flesh be saved, *Mark* 13:20
37 as *d.* of Noe, so com. of S.
*Luke* 21:22 these be *d.* of veng.
*Acts* 3:24 foretold of these *d.*
5:36 bef. these *d.* rose up Theu.
12:3 *d.* of unleav. bread, 20:6
*Gal.* 4:10 ye observe *d.* months
*Eph.* 5:16 because the *d.* are evil
*Heb.* 7:3 beg. of *d.* nor end of life
10:32 call to remem. former *d.*
1 *Pet.* 3:10 see good *d.* let refrain
*Rev.* 11:3 shall prophesy 1,260 *d.*
12:6 feed her there 1,260 *d.*

*See* DAVID, LAST, OLD, JOURNEY.

**All the DAYS.**

*Gen.* 5:5 *all t. d.* A. lived 930 ye.
8 *d.* of Seth; 11 of Enos
14 of Cainan; 23 Enoch
27 Methuselah; 9:29 Noah
*Deut.* 4:9 they depart *all the d.*
10 to fear me *all t. d.* 1 *K.* 8:40
12:1 to possess it *all the d.*
*Jos.* 24:31 served L. *all t. d.* of J.
1 *Sam.* 1:11 give him to L. *a. t. d.*
1 *K.* 4:25 safely *all t. d.* of Sol.
*Job* 14:14 *all d.* of my ap. time
*Ps.* 23:6 mercy fol. me *all t. d.*
27:4 house of L. *all d.* of my life
*Prov.* 15:15 *all t. d.* of afflicted
31:12 good *all the d.* of her life
*Luke* 1:75 holi. *all t. d.* of our life

*See His* LIFE, *Thy* LIFE.

**DAYS come.**

*Is.* 7:17 *d.* that have not *come*
*Jer.* 23:5 behold *d. c.* 7; 31:31
*Amos* 4:2 *d. c.* he will take you
*Mat.* 9:15 *d. c.* brideg. shall be taken, *Mark* 2:20; *Luke* 5:35
*Luke* 17:22 *d. c.* ye sh. des. to see
21:6 *d. c.* there shall not be left
*Heb.* 8:8 *d. c.* I will make new c.

**Few DAYS.**

*Gen.* 29:20 seemed but a *few d.*
47:9 *f.* and evil *d.* of my pilgr.
*Job* 14:1 man b. of wo. is of *f. d.*
*Ps.* 109:8 let his *d.* be *few*
*Dan.* 11:20 *f. d.* he be destroyed
*Heb.* 12:10 for a *f. d.* chasten. us

**His DAYS.**

*Gen.* 6:3 *his d.* shall be 120 years
10:25 in *h. d.* was earth divided
*Deut.* 22:19 put her away all *h. d.*
1 *K.* 15:14 A. was perf. all *h. d.*
21:29 not bring the evil in *h. d.*
2 *K.* 8:20 in *his d.* Edom revolted
12:2 Jehoash did right all *h. d.*
1 *Chr.* 22:9 and quietness in *h. d.*
*Job* 14:5 seeing *h. d.* determined
15:20 travail with pain all *h. d.*
24:1 know him, not see *his d.*?
*Ps.* 72:7 in *his d.* right. flourish
103:15 man, *his d.* are as grass
144:4 *his d.* are as a shadow
*Ec.* 2:23 all *his d.* are sorrows
5:17 all *h. d.* eateth in darkness
*Is.* 65:20 hath not filled *his d.*
*Jer.* 17:11 in the midst of *his d.*
22:30 a man not prosper in *h. d.*
23:6 in *his d.* J. shall be saved

**In the DAYS.**

1 *K.* 10:21 silver noth. accounted of *in d.* of Sol. 2 *Chr.* 9:20
1 *Chr.* 13:3 inq. not *in d.* of Saul
2 *Chr.* 26:5 sought G. *in d.* of Z.
32:26 came not *in d.* of Hezek.
*Job* 29:2 *in d.* God preserved me
4 as I was *in the d.* of my you.
*Ps.* 37:19 *in d.* of famine satis.
49:5 whefore fear *in d.* of evil
*Ec.* 2:16 *in d.* to come be forgot.
11:9 heart cheer thee *in the d.*
12:1 remember thy Creator *in d.*
*Lam.* 1:7 Jer. remembered *in d.*
*Ezek.* 16:60 remem. my cov. in *d.*
22:14 hands be strong *in the d.*
*Dan.* 2:44 *in the d.* of these kings
5:11 *in the d.* of thy father
*Hos.* 2:15 as *in d.* of her youth
9:9 corrupted as *in d.* of Gibeah
12:9 *in the d.* of solemn feasts
*Joel* 1:2 *in d.* of your fathers
*Mat.* 2:1 J. was born *in d.* of H.
23:30 been *in d.* of our fathers
24:38 for as *in the d.* bef. flood
*Mark* 2:26 *in the d.* of Abiathar
*Luke* 1:25 L. dealt with me *in d.*
4:25 widows *in d.* of Elias
17:26 *in the d.* of Noe; 28 Lot
*Acts* 5:37 Judas *in d.* of taxing
11:28 *in t. d.* of Claudius Cesar
*Heb.* 5:7 who *in t. d.* of his flesh
1 *Pet.* 3:20 waited *in the d.* of N.
*Rev.* 10:7 *in d.* of seventh angel

**In those DAYS.**

1 *Sam.* 3:1 precious *in those d.*
*Jer.* 33:16 *in those d.* J. be saved
50:4 *in th. d.* Isr. shall seek God
20 *in th. d.* iniquity be sought
*Joel* 2:29 *in th. d.* will I pour out my Spirit, *Acts* 2:18
*Luke* 1:39 Mary arose *in those d.*
20:1 one of *th. d.* as he taught

**Latter DAYS.**

*Num.* 24:14 peo. do to pe. in *l. d.*
*Deut.* 4:30 *l. d.* if thou turn to L.
31:29 evil befall you in *latter d.*
*Jer.* 23:20 in *lat. d.* con. it, 30:24
48:47 captivity of Moab in *l. d.*
49:39 captivity of Elam in *l. d.*
*Ezek.* 38:16 ag. my people in *l. d.*
*Dan.* 2:28 what shall be in *l. d.*
10:14 befall thy people in *l. d.*
*Hos.* 3:5 shall fear Lord in *l. d.*

**Many DAYS.**

*Gen.* 37:34 J. mourned *many d.*
1 *K.* 17:15 she and he d. eat *m. d.*
*Ps.* 34:12 he that loveth *m. d.*?
119:84 *m.* are *d.* of thy serv.?
*Ec.* 6:3 *d.* of his years be *many*
11:1 shalt find it after *many d.*
*Is.* 24:22 after *many d.* shall they be visited, *Ezek.* 38:8
32:10 *m. d.* shall ye be troubled
*Jer.* 32:14 continue *many d.* 35:7
37:16 Jer. had remained *m. d.*
*Ezek.* 12:27 vision that he seeth is for *m. d. Dan.* 8:26; 10:14
*Dan.* 11:33 fall by captivity *m. d.*
*Hos.* 3:3 abide for me *many d.*
4 Is. abide *m. d.* witho. a king
*Luke* 15:13 *m. d.* after younger
*John* 2:12 continued not *many d.*
*Acts* 1:5 baptized not *many d.*
13:31 he was seen *many d.*
16:18 this did she *many d.*
27:20 nor stars in *m. d.* appear.

**My DAYS.**

2 *K.* 20:19 if truth be in *my d.*?
*Job* 7:6 *my d.* swifter th. shuttle
16 let alone, *my d.* are vanity
9:25 *my d.* swifter than a post
10:20 are not *my d.* few?
17:1 *my d.* are extinct
11 *my d.* are past, my purposes
29:18 multiply *my d.* as sand

Ps. 39:4 the measure of my d.
5 my d. as a handbreadth
102:3 m. d. consum. like smoke
11 my d. are like a shadow
23 he shortened my d.
24 not away in midst of my d.
Is. 38:10 in cutting off my d.
39:8 be peace and truth in m. d.
Jer. 20:18 my d. consu. with sh.

**Prolong, ed, eth DAYS.**

Deut. 4:26 not p. your d. 30:18
40 mayest prolong thy d. 22:7
5:16 thy d. may be prolong. 6:2
33 that ye may prolong d. 11:9
17:20 he may prolong his d.
32:47 ye shall prolong your d.
Prov. 10:27 fear of the L. prol. d.
28:16 hateth covetous. p. his d.
Ec. 8:12 tho' sinner's d. be pro.
13 nei. shall wicked pro. his d.
Is. 13:22 her d. shall not be p.
53:10 his seed, he shall pro. d.
Ezek. 12:22 d. are p. vision fail.

**Sabbath DAYS.**

Mat. 12:15 on sab. d. priests prof.
10 lawful to heal on sab. d.?
12 lawful to do well on s. d.?
Mark 3:4 good on s. d.? Lu. 6:9
Luke 4:31 taught them on sab. d.
6:2 not lawful to do on sab. d.
Acts 17:2 three sabbath d. reason.
Col. 2:16 judge in respect of s. d.

**Thy DAYS.**

Ex. 20:12 hon. thy father that t. d. may be long, Deut. 25:15
23:26 the number of t. d.
Deut. 23:6 seek peace all thy d.
30:20 thy life, length of thy d.
31:14 thy d. ap. thou must die
33:25 as thy d. so thy strength
1 Sam. 25:28 not found all thy d.
2 Sam. 7:12 when thy d. be ful.
1 K. 3:13 any like thee all thy d.
14 then will I lengthen thy d.
11:12 in thy d. I will not do it
2 K. 20:6 add to thy d. Is. 38:5
1 Chr. 17:11 when thy d. be exp.
Job 10:5 thy d. as the d. of man
38:12 morning since thy d.
21 number of thy d. is great
Prov. 9:11 thy d. be multiplied
Ezek. 22:4 caused t. d. draw near

**Two DAYS.**

Num. 9:22 whe. two d. or mon.
11:19 not eat one, nor two d.
Hos. 6:2 after two d. will revive
Mat. 26:2 t. d. is feast, Mark 14:1
John 4:40 he abode there two d.
11:6 he abode two d. still

**Three DAYS.**

Gen. 40:12 branches are three d.
18 three baskets three d.
42:17 put all into ward three d.
Ex. 3:18 three d. journey into wilderness, 5:3; 8:27; 15:22
10:23 nor rose any for three d.
Jos. 1:11 within t. d. ye sh. pass
2:16 hide here three d. 22
Jud. 19:4 abode with him th. d.
1 Sam. 21:5 kept fr. us these t. d.
30:12 eaten no bread three d.
13 three d. agone I fell sick
2 Sam. 20:4 assemble J. in t. d.
24:13 th. d. pestil. 1 Chr. 21:12
1 K. 12:5 dep. for t. d. 2 Chr. 10:5
2 K. 2:17 sought him three d.
Ezr. 10:8 not come in three d. 9
Jon. 1:17 in fish th. d. Mat. 12:40
Mat. 15:32 they continue with me three d. Mark 8:2
26:61 destroy the temple, and to build it in t. d. 27:40; Mark 14:58; 15:29; John 2:19
27:63 after t. d. I will, Mark 8:31
Luke 2:46 after t. d. found in t.
Acts 9:9 S. th. d. without sight
28:7 Publius lodged us t. d.
Rev. 11:9 three d. and a half
11 after t. d. spirit of life ent.

**Four DAYS.**

John 11:39 he ha. been dead f. d.
Acts 10:30 f. d. ago I was fasting

**Five DAYS.**

Num. 11:19 nor five d. nor ten d.

**Six DAYS.**

Ex. 20:9 six d. shalt thou labor, 23:12; 34:21; Deut. 5:13
11 in s. d. made heaven, 31:17
31:15 six d. may work be done, 35:2; Lev. 23:3
Jos. 6:3 thus shalt do six d.
Ezek. 46:1 shut six working d.
Luke 13:14 six d. ought to work
John 12:1 J. six d. bef. passover

**Seven DAYS.**

Is. 30:26 light of sun as of s. d.
Ezek. 3:15 I remained aston. s. d.
Heb. 11:30 compassed seven d.

**Eight DAYS.**

Gen. 17:12 e. d. old, be cir. 21:4
Luke 2:21 when e. d. were ac.
John 20:26 after eight d. J. came

**Ten DAYS.**

Dan. 1:12 prove thy servant t. d.
Rev. 2:10 have tribulation ten d.

**Forty DAYS.**

Ex. 24:18 Moses in mount forty d. 34:28; Deut. 9:9; 10:10
Num. 13:25 after forty d. 14:34
Deut. 9:25 I fell before L. f. d.
Ezek. 4:6 bear iniquity of J. f. d.
Jon. 3:4 yet f. d. Ninev. be over.
Mat. 4:2 he had fasted forty d.
Mark 1:13 f. d. tempted, Lu. 4:2
Acts 1:3 seen of them forty d.

**Your DAYS.**

Deut. 11:21 y. d. may be multi.
Jer. 16:9 cease in your d. mirth
35:7 y. d. ye sh. dwell in tents
Ezek. 12:25 in your d. will I say
Joel 1:2 hath this been in your d.
Hab. 1:5 in your d. Acts 13:41

**DAILY.**

Jud. 16:16 she pressed him d.
Est. 3:4 spake d. he heark. not
Ps. 13:2 sorrow in my heart d.
42:10 d. to me, Wh. is thy God?
56:1 fighting d. oppresseth me
2 would d. swallow me up
61:8 I may d. perform my vows
68:19 Lord, who d. loadeth us
72:15 and d. shall he be praised
74:22 foolish reproach thee d.
86:3 I cry d.; 88:9 I called d.
88:17 about me d. like water
Prov. 8:30 I was d. his delight
34 watching d. at my gates
Is. 58:2 yet they seek me d.
Jer. 7:25 d. rising up early
20:7 I am in derision d. 8
Ezek. 30:16 N. have distresses d.
Dan. 8:11 by him the d. sacrifice was tak. away, 11:31; 12:11
Hos. 12:1 Eph. d. increaseth
Mat. 6:11 d. bread, Luke 11:3
26:55 I sat d. with you, Mark 14:49; Luke 19:47; 22:53
Luke 9:23 take up his cross d.
Acts 2:46 continuing d. with one
47 Lord added to church d.
6:1 neglected in d. ministration
16:5 the churches increased d.
17:11 searched the scriptures d.
1 Cor. 15:31 I die d.
Heb. 3:13 but exhort d.
7:27 needeth not d. to offer
Jam. 2:15 sister desti. of d. food

**DAYSMAN.**

Job 9:33 nor any d. betwixt us

**DAYSPRING.**

Job 38:12 d. to know his place
Luke 1:78 d. from on high visited

**DAYSTAR.**

2 Pet. 1:19 d. arise in your hearts

**DEACON, S.**

Phil. 1:1 the saints with the d.
1 Tim. 3:8 d. must be grave
10 then use office of a d. 13
12 d. the husband of one wife

**DEAD.**

Gen. 20:3 thou art but a d. man
23:3 A. stood up from before d.
Ex. 4:19 d. which sought thy li.
9:7 not one of Israel. cattle d.
12:30 where was not one d.
33 Eg. said, We be all d. men
14:30 Egyptians d. on the shore
21:34 d. beast shall be his, 36
35 d. ox they shall divide
Lev. 22:4 unclean by the d.
Num. 5:2 whoso. is defiled by d.
12:12 let her not be as one d.
16:48 he stood bet. d. and living
Jud. 3:25 their lord was d.
4:22 behold, Sisera lay d.
16:30 d. he slew at death more
Ruth 4:5 raise up name of the d.
1 Sam. 4:17 Hophni and P. are d.
24:14 pursue after a d. dog
2 Sam. 9:8 look on such d. dog
13:33 think all king's sons d.
16:9 this d. dog curse my lord?
19:28 father's house but d. men
1 K. 3:22 the d. is thy son, 23
13:31 when I am d. bury me
21:15 arise, for Naboth is d.
Job 26:5 d. formed from under
Ps. 31:12 forgotten as a d. man
76:6 chariot and horses in d. sl.
88:5 among the d. like slain
10 show wonders to the d.?
106:28 ate sacrifices of the d.
115:17 d. praise not the Lord
143:3 as those been long d.
Prov. 2:18 her paths unto the d.
9:18 knoweth not d. are there
21:16 remain in cong. of the d.
Ec. 4:2 I praised d. already d.
9:3 after that they go to d.
4 liv. dog better than d. lion
5 the d. know not any thing
Is. 8:10 for living to the d.?
14:9 it stirreth up d. for thee
22:2 not slain nor d. in battle
26:14 are d. they shall not live
19 thy d. men shall live, with
59:10 desolate places as d. men
Lam. 3:6 they that be d. of old
Ezek. 44:25 come at no d. person
Mat. 2:20 are d. sou. child's life
8:22 let the d. bury their d.
9:24 maid is not d. but sleepeth, Mark 5:39; Luke 8:52
10:8 heal the sick, raise the d.
11:5 d. are raised, Luke 7:22
22:31 touch. res. of d. Mar. 12:26
32 God is not the God of the d. Mark 12:27; Luke 20:38
23:27 full of d. men's bones
28:4 keepers became as d. men
Mark 9:26 was as one d. he is d.
15:44 Pilate marv. if he were d.
Luke 7:12 a d. man carried out
10:30 leaving him half d.
24:5 why seek living am. d.?
John 5:21 Father raiseth up d.
25 d. shall hear voi. of S. of G.
6:49 eat manna, and are d. 58
11:25 though d. yet shall live
Acts 2:29 patriarch David is d.
10:42 ordained to be judge of quick and d. 2 Tim. 4:1

14:19 supposing he had been d.
20:9 Eutychus was taken up d.
26:8 God should raise the d.
28:6 have swollen, or fallen d.
Rom. 4:17 quickeneth the d.
19 considered not his body d.
5:15 offence of one, many be d.
6:2 we that are d. to sin, live
8 if we be d. with Christ, we
11 reckon ye to be d. to sin
7:2 if husb. be d. 3; 1 Cor. 7:39
4 ye also d. to law, Gal. 2:19
14:9 Lord of the d. and living
1 Cor. 15:15 if so be d. rise not
35 will say, How are d. raised
52 d. be raised incorruptible
2 Cor. 1:9 God who raiseth d.
5:14 for all, then were all d.
Eph. 2:1 d. in tres. 5; Col. 2:13
Col. 2:20 if d. with C. 2 Tim. 2:11
3:3 ye are d. and your life hid
1 Thes. 4:16 d. in Chr. shall rise
Heb. 6:1 repent. from d. works
9:14 purge consc. from d. works
17 is of force after men are d.
11:4 he being d. yet speaketh
12 and him as good as d.
35 women received d. raised
1 Pet. 2:24 we being d. to sin
4:5 ready to judge quick and d.
6 gospel preached to them d.
Jude 12 twice d. plucked by
Rev. 1:5 J. first-begotten of d.
17 I fell at his feet as d.
3:1 thou livest, and art d.
14:13 blessed are d. die in Lord
16:3 sea, as blood of a d. man
20:5 rest of d. lived not again
12 I saw the d. stand bef. God; the d. were judged
13 sea gave up d.

See BODY, BURY, CARCASS, CORPSE, RESURRECTION.

**For the DEAD.**

Lev. 19:28 not make cut. f. t. d.
Deut. 14:1 any baldness f. d.
26:14 not give aught for the d.
2 Sam. 14:2 had mourned for d.
Jer. 16:7 to comfort for t. d.
22:10 weep ye not for the d.
Ezek. 24:17 no mourning f. t. d.
1 Cor. 15:29 are baptized for the d. why baptized for d.?

**From the DEAD.**

Mat. 14:2 J. is risen from the d.
Mark 9:10 rising from the d.
Luke 16:31 though one rose f. d.
24:46 fr. t. d. day, John 20:9
Acts 10:41 after he rose f. t. d.
26:23 that should rise from t. d.
Rom. 6:13 those alive from the d.
10:7 to bring up Christ f. t. d.
11:15 rec. of them be life f. t. d.
1 Cor. 15:12 he rose from the d.
Eph. 5:14 arise f. d. C. give light
Col. 1:18 first-born from t. d.
Heb. 11:19 to raise him from t. d.
13:20 brought again f. t. d.

See RAISED, RISEN.

**Is DEAD.**

Gen. 42:38 his brother is d. 44:20
Jos. 1:2 Moses my servant is d.
Jud. 20:5 forced that she is d.
2 Sam. 2:7 S. 4:10; 11:21 Uriah
12:18 child; 13:32 Amnon only
14:5 my husband is d. 2 K. 4:1
18:20 because king's son is d.
19:10 Absa.; 1 K. 21:14 Naboth
Ezek. 44:31 that is d. of itself
Mat. 9:18 my daugh. is d. Mark 5:35; Luke 8:49
Mark 9:26 many said, He is d.
John 8:52 Abraham is d. 53
11:14 said Jesus, Lazarus is d.
Rom. 6:7 he is d. is freed fr. sin
8:10 if C. be in you, body is d.
Gal. 2:21 if right. by law C. is d.
1 Tim. 5:6 is d. while she liveth.
Jam. 2:17 without works is d. 20
26 as body without spirit is d.

**Was DEAD.**

Jud. 2:19 when the judge was d.
9:55 Israel saw Abimelech w. d.
1 Sam. 17:51 saw champion w. d.
31:5 Saul was d. 1 Chr. 10:5
2 Sam. 4:1 heard Abner was d.
11:26 Bath. heard her h. was d.
12:19 D. perceived child was d.
13:39 Amnon, seeing he was d.
1 K. 3:21 give child suck, it w. d.
2 K. 4:32 behold the child was d.
11:1 Athaliah saw her son w. d.
Mat. 2:19 when Herod was d.
Luke 7:15 he that was d. sat up
8:53 knowing that she was d.
15:24 this my son was d.
32 thy bro. was d. and is alive
John 11:44 he that was d. came
19:33 Jesus was d. brake not
Acts 25:19 Jesus which was d.
Rom. 7:8 without law sin was d.
Rev. 1:18 liveth and was d.

**DEADLY.**

1 Sam. 5:11 d. destruction
Ps. 17:9 from my d. enemies
Ezek. 30:24 of a d. wounded man
Mark 16:18 drink d. thing
Jam. 3:8 tongue full of d. poison
Rev. 13:3 d. wound healed, 12

**DEADNESS.**

Rom. 4:19 nor d. of Sar.'s womb

**DEAF.**

Ex. 4:11 who maketh the d.
Lev. 19:14 shalt not curse the d.
Ps. 38:13 as a d. man, heard not
58:4 they are like the d. adder
Is. 29:18 d. hear words
35:5 ears of the d. be unstopped
42:18 hear, ye d. look, ye blind
19 who is d. as my messenger
43:8 bring d. that have ears
Mic. 7:16 their ears shall be d.
Mat. 11:5 the d. hear, Luke 7:22
Mark 7:32 brought to him one d.
37 he maketh the d. to hear
9:25 thou d. spirit come out

**DEAL.**

Gen. 19:9 d. worse with thee
24:49 if ye d. truly with master
32:9 I will d. well with thee
34:31 d. with sister as harlot?
Ex 1:10 d. wisely with them
21:9 d. with her after manner
23:11 like manner d. with vine
Lev. 19:11 not steal nor d. falsely
Num. 11:15 if d. thus, kill me
Deut. 7:5 shall ye d. with them
2 Chr. 2:3 as thou didst d. with David, so d. with me
Job 42:8 lest I d. after your folly
Ps. 75:4 to fools, d. not foolishly
119:17 d. bountifully with, 142:7
124 d. with me acco. to thy m.
Prov. 12:22 they that d. truly
Is. 26:10 land of uprightness d.
52:13 my servant d. prudently
58:7 to d. thy bread to hungry
Jer. 18:23 d. thus in thine anger
21:2 Lord will d. with us
Ezek. 8:18 will I also d. in fury
16:59 d. with thee as hast done
22:14 in days I d. with thee?
23:25 d. furiously with thee
31:11 shall surely d. with him
Dan. 1:13 d. with thy servants
11:7 and shall d. against them

See TREACHEROUSLY.

**DEAL, Substantive.**

Ex. 29:40 d. of flour, Lev. 14:21; Num. 15:4; 28:13; 29:4
Mark 10:48 cried more a great d.

**DEALER, S.**

Is. 21:2 treacherous d. dealeth
24:16 d. dealt treacherously

**DEALEST, ETH, ING, S.**

Jud. 18:4 thus d. Micah with me
1 Sam. 2:23 I hear of your evil d.
23:22 that he d. subtilely
Ps. 7:16 violent d. on his pate
Prov. 10:4 poor that d. w. slack
13:16 prudent d. with knowl.
14:17 he soon angry d. foolishly
21:24 who d. in proud wrath
Is. 21:2 treacherous dealer d.
33:1 woe to thee d. treacher.
Jer. 6:13 from prophet to priest, every one d. falsely, 8:10
John 4:9 no d. with Samaritans
Heb. 12:7 God d. as with sons

**DEALT.**

Gen. 16:6 Sar. d. hardly with her
33:11 God hath d. graciously
43:6 d. ye so ill with me
Ex. 1:20 God d. well with midw.
14:11 wherefore d. so ill with us
18:11 in thing they d. proudly
Jud. 9:16 if d. well with Jerub.
Ruth 1:8 ye have d. with dead
20 Almig. d. bitterly with me
1 Sam. 24:18 d. well with me
25:31 L. have d. well with thee
2 Sam. 6:19 he d. am. the people
2 K. 12:15 they d. faithfu. 22:7
21:6 d. with fam. sp. 2 Chr. 33:6
2 Chr. 6:37 we have d. wickedly
11:23 Rehoboam d. wisely
Neh. 1:7 d. corrupt. against thee
9:10 knewest d. proudly, 16, 29
Job 6:15 brethren d. deceitfully
Ps. 13:6 d. bountifully with me
44:17 nor d. falsely in thy cov.
78:57 d. unfaithfully like fathers
103:10 d. with us after our sins
116:7 L. d. bountifully with thee
119:65 d. well with thy servant
78 d. perversely without cause
147:20 not d. so with any nation
Is. 24:16 d. very treach. Jer. 3:20; 5:11; 12:6; Lam. 1:2
Ezek. 22:7 in thee d. by oppres.
25:12 Edom hath d. ag. Judah
15 Philis. have d. by revenge
Hos. 5:7 they have d. treach.
6:7 d. treacherously against me
Joel 2:26 God that d. wondrously
Zec. 1:6 thought, so d. with us
Mal. 2:11 Judah d. treacherously
14 whom hast d. treacherously
Luke 1:25 hath L. d. with me
2:48 son, why thus d. with us
Acts 7:19 d. subtil. with kindred
25:24 mult. of Jews have d.
Rom. 12:3 G. hath d. to ev. man

**DEAR.**

Jer. 31:20 is Ephraim my d. son
Luke 7:2 servant who was d.
Acts 20:24 neither count I life d.
Eph. 5:1 foll. of God, as d. child.
Col. 1:7 Epaphras our d. fel.-ser.
13 into kingdom of his d. Son
1 Thes. 2:8 bec. ye were d. to us

**DEARLY beloved.**

Jer. 12:7 given d. belov. to enem.
Rom. 12:19 d. beloved avenge not
1 Cor. 10:14 my d. b. Phil. 4:1; 2 Tim. 1:2
2 Cor. 7:1 d. belov. 12:19; Phil. 4:1; 1 Pet. 2:11
Phile. 1 unto Philemon our d. b.

**DEARTH.**

Gen. 41:54 d. was in all lands
2 K. 4:38 was a d. in the land
2 Chr. 6:28 if there be d. mildew
Neh. 5:3 buy corn because of d.
Jer. 14:1 word came to J. conc. d.
Acts 7:11 came a d. over all land
11:28 there should be a great d.

**DEATH.**

*Gen.* 21:16 let not see *d.* of child
24:67 after his mother's *d.*
27:7 bless thee before my *d.*
10 bless thee before his *d.*
*Ex.* 10:17 take me from this *d.*
*Num.* 16:29 common *d.* of all
23:10 let me die *d.* of righteous
35:31 of a murderer guilty of *d.*
*Deut.* 30:15 I have set before you life and *d.* 19; *Jer.* 21:8
31:27 more rebel after my *d.*
29 after my *d.* ye will corrupt
33:1 Moses blessed Isr. before *d.*
*Jud.* 5:18 their lives to the *d.*
16:16 his soul vexed unto *d.*
30 dead he slew at his *d.* more
*Ruth* 1:17 if aught but *d.* part
1 *Sam.* 4:20 about time of her *d.*
15:32 bitterness of *d.* is past
20:3 a step between me and *d.*
22:22 *d.* of father's house
2 *Sam.* 1:23 in *d.* were not divid.
15:21 in *d.* or life, there
22:5 when waves of *d.* compassed me. *Ps.* 18:4; 116:3
6 snares of *d.* *Ps.* 18:5
2 *K.* 2:21 sh. not be any more *d.*
4:40 *d.* is in the pot
1 *Chr.* 22:5 D. prepared before *d.*
2 *Chr.* 22:4 after *d.* of father
32:33 did him honor at his *d.*
*Ezr.* 7:26 *d.* or banishment
*Job* 3:21 long for *d.* it com. not
7:15 my soul chooseth *d.*
18:13 first-born of *d.* devour
*Job* 27:15 remain be buried in *d.*
28:22 destruction and *d.* say
30:23 thou wilt bring me to *d.*
*Ps.* 6:5 in *d.* no remem. of thee
7:13 prepared instruments of *d.*
13:3 lest I sleep the sleep of *d.*
22:15 brought me into dust of *d.*
48:14 God be our guide unto *d.*
49:14 *d.* shall feed on them
55:4 terrors of *d.* fallen on me
15 let *d.* seize on them
73:4 no bands in their *d.*
89:48 and shall not see *d.*?
102:20 to loose those ap. to *d.*
116:15 precious is *d.* of saints
118:18 not given me over to *d.*
*Prov.* 2:18 house inclineth to *d.*
5:5 her feet go down to *d.*
7:27 down to chambers of *d.*
8:36 they that hate me, love *d.*
11:19 pursueth it to his own *d.*
12:28 in pathways there is no *d.*
13:14 from snares of *d.* 14:27
14:12 end, ways of *d.* 16:25
32 right. hath hope in his *d.*
16:14 wrath of king as m. of *d.*
18:21 *d.* life in power of tongue
21:6 van. tossed of them seek *d.*
24:11 deliver them drawn to *d.*
26:18 madman who casteth *d.*
*Ec.* 7:26 bitter than *d.*
*Cant.* 8:6 for love is strong as *d.*
*Is.* 25:8 swallow up *d.* in victory
38:18 *d.* cannot celebrate thee
53:9 with the rich in his *d.*
12 poured out his soul unto *d.*
*Jer.* 8:3 *d.* chosen rather than life
9:21 *d.* come up to windows
15:2 as are for *d.* to *d.* 43:11
*Lam.* 1:20 at home there is as *d.*
*Ezek.* 18:32 I have no pleasure in *d.* of the wicked, 33:11
31:14 are all delivered unto *d.*
*Hos.* 13:14 O *d.* I be thy plagues
*Jon.* 4:9 to be angry unto *d.*
*Hab.* 2:5 is as *d.* not satisfied
*Mat.* 2:15 there till *d.* of Herod
10:21 del. bro. to *d.* *Mark* 13:12
15:4 curseth fath. or moth. let him die the *d.* *Mark* 7:10
16:28 some here shall not taste of *d.* *Mark* 9:1; *Luke* 9:27
20:18 con. him to *d.* *Mark* 10:33
26:38 sorrowf. to *d.* *Mark* 14:34
66 guilty of *d.* *Mark* 14:64
*Mark* 5:23 daugh. at point of *d.*
*Luke* 2:26 not see *d.* bef. seen C.
22:33 to prison and *d.*
23:22 I found no cause of *d.*
*John* 4:47 he was at point of *d.*
8:51 he shall never see *d.* 52
11:4 this sickness not unto *d.*
13 Jesus spake of his *d.*
12:33 signifying what *d.* 18:32
21:19 by what *d.* glorify God
*Acts* 2:24 loosed the pains of *d.*
8:1 consenting to his *d.* 22:20
13:28 no cause of *d.* in him
22:4 I pers. this way to the *d.*
*Rom.* 5:10 reconciled to God by the *d.* of his Son, *Col.* 1:22
12 and *d.* by sin, so *d.* passed
14 *d.* reigned from Adam to M.
21 as sin hath reigned unto *d.*
6:3 were baptized into his *d.*
4 buried by baptism into *d.*
5 planted in likeness of his *d.*
9 *d.* no more domin. over him
16 whether of sin unto *d.*
21 end of those things is *d.*
23 for the wages of sin is *d.* but
7:5 to bring forth fruit unto *d.*
10 com. to life I found unto *d.*
13 that good made *d.* unto me?
24 from body of this *d.*?
8:2 free from law of sin and *d.*
6 to be carnally minded is *d.*
38 *d.* nor life separ. from love
1 *Cor.* 3:22 life or *d.* all are yours
4:9 were appointed to *d.*
11:26 ye do show the Lord's *d.*
15:21 for since by man came *d.*
26 last enemy be destroy. is *d.*
54 *d.* is swallowed up in vict.
55 O *d.* where is thy sting?
56 the sting of *d.* is sin
2 *Cor.* 1:9 sentence of *d.*
10 del. us from so great a *d.*
2:16 the savor of *d.* unto *d.*
3:7 if ministration of *d.* glorious
4:11 del. to *d.* for Jesus' sake
12 so then *d.* worketh in us
7:10 sorrow of world worketh *d.*
*Phil.* 1:20 whether by life or *d.*
2:8 obedient to *d.* the *d.* of cross
27 Epaph. sick nigh unto *d.*
30 work of C. he was nigh *d.*
3:10 made conformable to his *d.*
2 *Tim.* 1:10 hath abolished *d.*
*Heb.* 2:9 suffering of *d.* crowned, that he taste *d.* for ev. man
14 through *d.* destroy him that had power of *d.*
15 who through fear of *d.*
7:23 to continue, by reason of *d.*
9:15 by means of *d.* for redem.
16 of necessity *d.* of testator
11:5 that he should not see *d.*
*Jam.* 1:15 sin, bringeth forth *d.*
1 *John* 3:14 not abideth in *d.*
5:16 sin unto *d.*; 17 not unto *d.*
*Rev.* 1:18 keys of hell and of *d.*
2:10 be faithful unto *d.*
11 not be hurt of second *d.*
6:8 his name sat on him was *d.*
9:6 shall seek *d.* *d.* shall flee
12:11 loved not lives to the *d.*
13:3 as it were wounded to *d.*
18:8 her plagues in one day, *d.*
20:6 second *d.* hath no power
13 *d.* and hell deliver. up dead
14 *d.* cast into lake, second *d.*
21:4 there shall be no more *d.*

*See* DAY.

**From DEATH.**

*Jos.* 2:13 deliver our lives *f. d.*
*Job* 5:20 redeem thee *f. d.*
*Ps.* 33:19 to del. their soul *f. d.*
56:13 del. my soul *f. d.* 116:8
68:20 to L. belong issues *f. d.*
78:50 spared not their soul *f. d.*
*Prov.* 10:2 delivereth *f. d.* 11:4
*Hos.* 13:14 redeem them *f. d.*
*John* 5:24 *fr. d.* 1 *John* 3:14
*Heb.* 5:7 able to save *from d.*
*Jam.* 5:20 shall save a soul *f. d.*

**Gates of DEATH.**

*Job* 38:17 *g. of d.* been opened
*Ps.* 9:13 liftest me from *g. of d.*
107:18 draw near to *gates of d.*

**Put to DEATH.**

*Gen.* 26:11 this man *p. to d.*
*Ex.* 35:2 who. doth work, *p. to d.*
*Lev.* 19:20 not be *p. to d.*
24:21 be *p. to d.* *Num.* 35:30
*Num.* 1:51 stranger that cometh nigh *p. to d.* 3:10, 38; 18:7
*Deut.* 13:5 dreamer be *put to d.*
17:6 one witness not be *p. to d.*
24:16 the fathers not be *put to d.* for children, 2 *K.* 14:6
*Jos.* 1:18 ag. thy com. *p. to d.*
*Jud.* 6:31 plead. for B. *p. to d.*
20:13 may *p. to d.* 1 *Sam.* 11:12
1 *Sam.* 11:13 be *put to d.*
2 *Sam.* 8:2 two lines to *p. to d.*
19:21 shall no Shi. be *put to d.*
1 *K.* 2:8 I will not *put* thee *to d.*
24 Adonijah shall be *put to d.*
26 at this time *put* thee *to d.*
2 *Chr.* 15:13 seek L. be *put to d.*
23:7 cometh into house, *p. to d.*
*Est.* 4:11 law to *put* him *to d.*
*Jer.* 18:21 their men be *put to d.*
26:15 know, if ye *put* me *to d.*
19 did J. *put* him at all *to d.*?
38:4 this man be *put to d.*
16 not *put* thee *to d.*
52:27 *put* them *to d.* in Riblah
*Mat.* 10:21 cause them to be *p. to d.* *Mark* 13:12; *Luke* 21:16
14:5 have *put* him *to d.*
26:59 sou. false wit. ag. J. to *p.* him *to d.* 27:1; *Mark* 14:55
*Mark* 14:1 and *put* him *to d.*
*Luke* 18:33 shall *put* him *to d.*
23:32 malefact. to be *put to d.*
*John* 11:53 to *put* him *to d.*
12:10 might *put* Lazarus *to d.*
18:31 not lawful to *p.* any *to d.*
*Acts* 12:19 keepers to be *put to d.*
26:10 *put to d.* I gave my voice
1 *Pet.* 3:18 *put to d.* in the flesh

*See* SURELY.

**Shadow of DEATH.**

*Job* 3:5 the *shadow of d.* stain it
10:21 land of dark. and *s. of d.*
12:22 bringeth to light *s. of d.*
16:16 on eyelids is *shadow of d.*
24:17 is as the *shad. of d.*
28:3 searcheth out *shad. of d.*
34:22 no *s. of d.* sinners
38:17 doors of the *shad. of d.*?
*Ps.* 23:4 valley of *shad. of d.*
44:19 covered us with *s. of d.*
107:10 darkness and in *s. of d.*
14 darkness and *shad. of d.*
*Is.* 9:2 in land of *shad. of d.*
*Jer.* 2:6 land of the *shad. of d.*
13:16 he turn it to *shad. of d.*
*Amos* 5:8 *s. of d.* into the morn.
*Mat.* 4:16 that sat in *s. of d.*
*Luke* 1:79 light to them in *s. of d.*

**With DEATH.**

*Is.* 28:15 have made cov. *w. d.*
18 cov. *w. d.* be disannulled
*Rev.* 2:23 kill her children *w. d.*
6:8 power given to kill *with d.*

**Worthy of DEATH.**

*Deut.* 17:6 is *w. of d.*
19:6 he was not *w. of d.*
21:22 have com. sin *w. of d.*
1 *K.* 2:26 Abiathar, art *w. of d.*
*Luke* 23:15 nothing *w. of d.*

*Acts* 23:29 to his charge *w. of d.*
25:11 any thing *wor. of d.*
25 committed nothing *w. of d.*
26:31 doth nothing *w. of d.*
*Rom.* 1:32 com. such *wor. of d.*

### DEATHS.

*Jer.* 16:4 shall die of grievous *d.*
*Ezek.* 28:8 die *d.* of them slain
10 die *d.* of uncircumcised
2 *Cor.* 11:23 in *d.* oft

### DEBASE.

*Is.* 57:9 *d.* thyself unto hell

### DEBATE, Verb.

*Prov.* 25:9 *d.* cause with neigh.
*Is.* 27:8 in measure wilt *d.*

### DEBATE, S.

*Is.* 58:4 fast for strife and *d.*
*Rom.* 1:29 full of envy, *d.*
2 *Cor.* 12:20 lest there be *d.*

### DEBORAH.

*Gen.* 35:8 D. died, was buried
*Jud.* 4:4 and D. judged Israel
5:7 D. a mother in Isr. 12, 15

### DEBT, S.

1 *Sam.* 22:2 ev. one in *d.* w. to D.
2 *K.* 4:7 sell oil, pay thy *d.*
*Neh.* 10:31 exaction of every *d.*
*Prov.* 22:26 are sureties for *d.*
*Mat.* 6:12 forgive us our *d.* as
18:27 forgave him the *d.*
30 into prison till he pay *d.*
32 I forgave all that *d.*
*Rom.* 4:4 reward reckoned of *d.*

### DEBTOR.

*Ezek.* 18:7 restored to *d.* pledge
*Mat.* 23:16 swear by gold, is a *d.*
*Rom.* 1:14 I am *d.* to the Greeks
*Gal.* 5:3 a *d.* to do the whole law

### DEBTORS.

*Mat.* 6:12 as we forgive our *d.*
*Luke* 7:41 a creditor had two *d.*
16:5 he called his lord's *d.*
*Rom.* 8:12 therefore, we are *d.*
15:27 and their *d.* they are

### DECAPOLIS.

*Mat.* 4:25 followed him from D.
*Mark* 5:20 to publish in D. 7:31

### DECAY, ED, ETH.

*Lev.* 25:35 if brother fallen in *d.*
*Neh.* 4:10 strength of bearers *d.*
*Job* 14:11 and as the flood *d.*
*Ec.* 10:18 by sloth. building *d.*
*Is.* 44:26 I will raise up *d.* places
*Heb.* 8:13 *d.* is ready to vanish

### DECEASE.

*Luke* 9:31 and spake of his *d.*
2 *Pet.* 1:15 after my *d.* in rem.

### DECEASED.

*Is.* 26:14 *d.* they shall not rise
*Mat.* 22:25 when he married, *d.*

### DECEIT, S.

*Job* 15:35 belly prepareth *d.*
27:4 nor my tongue utter *d.*
31:5 or if my foot hasted to *d.*
*Ps.* 10:7 his mouth is full of *d.*
36:3 words of his mouth are *d.*
38:12 imagine *d.* all the day
50:19 thy tongue frameth *d.*
55:11 *d.* and guile depart not
72:14 redeem their soul from *d.*
101:7 worketh *d.* not dwell
119:118 their *d.* is falsehood
*Prov.* 12:5 coun. of wicked are *d.*
17 false witness showeth *d.*
20 *d.* is in them that imag. ev.
14:8 the folly of fools is *d.*
20:17 bread of *d.* is sweet
26:24 hateth layeth up *d.*
26 hatred i covered by *d.*
*Is.* 30:10 speak smooth, proph. *d.*
53:9 nor any *d.* in his mouth
*Jer.* 5:27 their houses full of *d.*
8:5 they hold fast *d.* they refuse
9:6 through *d.* refuse to know
8 their tongue, it speaketh *d.*
14:14 prophesy *d.* of their heart
23:26 are prophets of the *d.* of
*Hos.* 11:12 compasseth me w. *d.*
12:7 balances of *d.* in his hand
*Amos* 8:5 falsify. balances by *d.*
*Zep.* 1:9 masters' houses with *d.*
*Mark* 7:22 out of he. proceed *d.*
*Rom.* 1:29 full of debate, *d.*
3:13 with tongues have used *d.*
*Col.* 2:8 spoil you thro. vain *d.*
1 *Thes.* 2:3 exhortation not of *d.*

### DECEITFUL.

*Ps.* 5:6 Lord will abhor *d.* man
35:20 devise *d.* matters ag. th.
43:1 deliver me from *d.* man.
52:4 O thou *d.* tongue
55:23 *d.* not live half their days
78:57 turned aside like *d.* bow
109:2 mouth of *d.* opened ag. me
120:2 del. my soul fr. *d.* tongue
*Prov.* 11:18 worketh a *d.* work
14:25 *d.* witness speaketh lies
23:3 his dainties are *d.* meat
27:6 kisses of enemy are *d.*
29:13 poor and *d.* meet together
31:30 favor is *d.* beauty vain
*Jer.* 17:9 heart is *d.* above all
*Hos.* 7:16 they are like a *d.* bow
*Mic.* 6:11 with bag of *d.* weights
12 tongue is *d.* in their mouth
*Zep.* 3:13 nor *d.* tongue be found
2 *Cor.* 11:13 such are *d.* workers
*Eph.* 4:22 according to *d.* lusts

### DECEITFULLY.

*Gen.* 34:13 answered Hamor *d.*
*Ex.* 8:29 let not Pharaoh deal *d.*
*Lev.* 6:4 or the thing *d.* gotten
*Job* 6:15 brethren dealt *d.*
13:7 will you talk *d.* for God
*Ps.* 24:4 nor sworn *d.*
52:2 like a razor, working *d.*
*Jer.* 48:10 doeth work of Lord *d.*
*Dan.* 11:23 after league work *d.*
2 *Cor.* 4:2 handling word of G. *d.*

### DECEITFULNESS.

*Mat.* 13:22 the *d.* of rich. choke the word, *Mark* 4:19
*Heb.* 3:13 hardened thro' *d.* of sin

### DECEIVABLENESS.

2 *Thes.* 2:10 all *d.* of unrighte.

### DECEIVE.

2 *Sam.* 3:25 Abner came to *d.* th.
2 *K.* 4:28 say, do not *d.* me
18:29 let not Hezekiah *d.* you, 2 *Chr.* 32:15; *Is.* 36:14
19:10 let not God *d.* *Is.* 37:10
*Prov.* 24:28 *d.* not with thy lips
*Jer.* 9:5 *d.* every one his neigh.
29:8 diviners in midst *d.* you
37:9 saith L. *d.* not yourselves
*Zec.* 13:4 rough garment to *d.*
*Mat.* 24:4 no m. *d.* *Mark* 13:5
5 *d.* many, 11; *Mark* 13:6
24 they shall *d.* the very elect
*Rom.* 16:18 f. speeches *d.* simple
1 *Cor.* 3:18 let no man *d.* himself
*Eph.* 4:14 they lie in wait to *d.*
5:6 let no man *d.* you, 2 *Thes.* 2:3; 1 *John* 3:7
1 *John* 1:8 have no sin, we *d.*
*Rev.* 20:3 *d.* the nations no more
8 go to *d.* nations

### DECEIVED.

*Gen.* 31:7 your father hath *d.* me
*Lev.* 6:2 or if *d.* his neighbor
*Deut.* 11:16 your heart be not *d.*
1 *Sam.* 19:17 why *d.* me? 28:12
2 *Sam.* 19:26 my servant *d.* me
*Job* 12:16 *d.* and deceiver are his
15:31 let not *d.* trust in vanity
31:9 if been *d.* by a woman
*Is.* 19:13 princes of Noph are *d.*
44:20 a *d.* heart turned him
*Jer.* 4:10 greatly *d.* this people
20:7 O Lord thou hast *d.* me
49:16 thy terribleness *d.* thee
*Lam.* 1:19 my lovers, they *d.* me
*Ezek.* 14:9 if proph. be *d.* I. *d.* h.
*Ob.* 3 pride of heart *d.* thee
7 men at peace with thee *d.*
*Luke* 21:8 take heed ye be not *d.*
*John* 7:47 answ. Are ye also *d.*
*Rom.* 7:11 for sin *d.* me
1 *Cor.* 6:9 not *d.* 15:33; *Gal.* 6:7
1 *Tim.* 2:14 Adam was not *d.* but
2 *Tim.* 3:13 deceiv. and being *d.*
*Tit.* 3:3 were foolish. *d.*
*Rev.* 18:23 all nations were *d.*
19:20 *d.* them received the mark
20:10 devil that *d.* was cast

### DECEIVER.

*Gen.* 27:12 to my father as a *d.*
*Job* 12:16 deceived and *d.* are his
*Mal.* 1:14 cursed *d.* hath a male
*Mat.* 27:63 we rem. that *d.* said
2 *John* 7 this is a *d.* and antich.

### DECEIVERS.

2 *Cor.* 6:8 as *d.* and yet true
*Tit.* 1:10 many *d.* especially
2 *John* 7 for many *d.* are entered

### DECEIVETH.

*Prov.* 26:19 so is man *d.* neighbor
*John* 7:12 said, he *d.* the people
*Gal.* 6:3 nothing, he *d.* himself
*Jam.* 1:26 but *d.* his own heart
*Rev.* 12:9 serpent which *d.*
13:14 and *d.* them that dwell

### DECEIVING, S.

1 *Tim.* 3:13 *d.* and being deceiv.
*Jam.* 1:22 not hearers only, *d.*
2 *Pet.* 2:13 sporting with their *d.*

### DECENTLY.

1 *Cor.* 14:40 done *d.* and in order

### DECIDED.

1 *K.* 20:40 thyself hast *d.* it

### DECISION.

*Joel* 3:14 multi. in valley of *d.*

### DECK, ED.

*Job* 40:10 *d.* thyself with majesty
*Prov.* 7:16 I have *d.* my bed
*Jer.* 10:4 they *d.* it with silver
*Ezek.* 16:11 I *d.* thee with orna.
13 thus wast thou *d.* with gold
*Hos.* 2:13 she *d.* with ear-rings
*Rev.* 17:4 wom. was *d.* with gold
18:16 alas, city that was *d.*

### DECKEDST.

*Ezek.* 16:16 *d.* thy high places
23:40 and *d.* with ornaments

### DECKEST, ETH.

*Is.* 61:10 as a bridegroom *d.*
*Jer.* 4:30 though thou *d.* with g.

### DECLARATION.

*Job* 13:17 hear my *d.* with ears
*Luke* 1:1 set forth in order a *d.*
2 *Cor.* 8:19 to *d.* of ready mind

### DECLARE.

*Jos.* 20:4 *d.* cause in ears
*Jud.* 14:12 ye *d.* it in 7 days
1 *K.* 22:13 proph. *d.* good to k.
1 *Chr.* 16:24 *d.* his glory among the heathen, *Ps.* 96:3
*Job* 12:8 fishes shall *d.* unto thee
21:31 *d.* his way to his face
28:27 did he see it and *d.* it
31:37 *d.* to him numb. of steps
38:4 *d.* if hast understanding
40:7 *d.* thou to me, 42:4
*Ps.* 9:11 *d.* among people
19:1 the heavens *d.* glory of G.
22:31 *d.* his right. 50:6; 97:6
30:9 shall dust *d.* thy truth?
40:5 I wo. *d.* and speak of them
50:16 to do to *d.* my statutes?
64:9 all shall *d.* work of God

73:28 I may d. all thy works
75:1 thy wondrous works d.
78:6 d. them to their children
102:21 to d. name of Lord in Z.
107:22 d. works with rejoicing
118:17 live and d. works of L.
145:4 shall d. thy mighty acts
Ec. 9:1 considered to d. all this
Is. 3:9 d. thy sins as Sodom
12:4 d. his doings am. people
21:6 let him d. what he seeth
41:22 d. to us things to come
42:9 new things do I d. before
12 d. his praise in the islands
43:9 who among them can d.
26 d. thou mayest be justified
44:7 and who, as I, shall d. it
45:19 I the Lord d. things right
48:6 and will not ye d. it?
53:8 d. his generat.? Acts 8:33
66:19 d. my glory among Gent.
Jer. 5:20 d. this in house of Jac.
9:12 spoken that he may d.
31:10 d. it in the isles afar off
38:15 if I d. it to thee wilt thou
42:20 what God say d. to us
50:28 d. in Z. vengeance of L.
51:10 d. in Zion work of Lord
Ezek. 12:16 d. their abom. 23:36
40:4 d. all thou seest to Israel
Mic. 3:8 d. to Jacob his transg.
Zec. 9:12 I d. that I will render
Mat. 13:36 d. parable of tares
15:15 said Peter, d. this parable
Acts 13:32 we d. glad tidings
41 though a man d. it to you
17:23 worship, him d. I to you
20:27 d. to you counsel of God
Rom. 3:25 to d. his righteous. 26
1 Cor. 3:13 the day shall d. it
11:17 that I d. I praise you not
15:1 I d. unto you the gospel
Col. 4:7 my state shall Tych. d.
Heb. 11:14 d. plainly they seek
1 John 1:3 have seen d. we to y.
5 message we d. unto you.

**I will DECLARE.**

Job 15:17 I have seen I will d.
Ps. 2:7 I will d. the decree
22:22 I w. d. name, Heb. 2:12
Ps. 38:18 I will d. mine iniquity
66:16 I will d. what done
75:9 but I will d. forever, I will
145:6 I will d. thy greatness
Is. 57:12 I will d. thy right.
Jer. 42:4 I will d. it
John 17:26 and will d. it

**DECLARE ye.**

Is. 48:20 voice of singing d. ye
Jer. 4:5 d. ye in Judah, publish
46:14 d. ye in Egypt, publish
50:2 d. ye among the nations
Mic. 1:10 d. ye it not at Gath

**DECLARED.**

Ex. 9:16 my name may be d.
Deut. 4:13 d. to you his covenant
Job 26:3 plentifully d. the thing
Ps. 40:10 d. thy faithfulness
71:17 I d. thy wondrous works
77:14 d. thy strength am. peop.
88:11 thy loving-kindness be d.
119:13 have I d. all judgments
26 I have d. my ways, and th.
Is. 21:2 grievous vision is d.
10 what I heard of G. have I d.
41:26 d. from beginning, 45:21
43:12 I have d. 44:8; 48:5
48:3 I have d. former things
14 which d. these things?
Jer. 36:13 Michaiah d. words
42:21 I this day d. it to you
Luke 8:47 she d. to him before all
John 1:18 seen God; Son d. him
17:26 d. to them thy name
Acts 9:27 he d. how he had seen
10:8 he had d. these things
12:17 d. how Lord brought him
15:4 d. all God hath done
14 Simeon d. how God at first
25:14 Festus d. Paul's cause to
Rom. 1:4 d. to be the Son
9:17 my name might be d.
1 Cor. 1:11 been d. to me of you
2 Cor. 3:3 ye are d. to be the ep.
Col. 1:8 who d. to us your love
Rev. 10:7 mys. finished, as he d.

**DECLARETH, ING.**

Is. 41:26 there is none that d.
46:10 d. the end from beginning
Jer. 4:15 a voice d. from Dan
Hos. 4:12 their staff d. unto them
Amos 4:13 d. to man his thought
Acts 15:3 d. conversion of Gent.
12 d. what miracles God wro.
1 Cor. 2:1 d. to you testimony

**DECLINE.**

Ex. 23:2 to d. after many
Deut. 17:11 nor d. from sentence
Ps. 119:157 d. from thy testi.
Prov. 4:5 not d. from words of my
7:25 let not heart d. to her ways

**DECLINED, ETH.**

2 Chr. 34:2 d. neither to right
Job 23:11 his way I kept, not d.
Ps. 44:18 nor have our steps d.
102:11 days as shadow that d.
109:23 like shadow when it d.
119:51 yet not d. from thy law

**DECREASE, ED.**

Gen. 8:5 waters d. continually
Ps. 107:38 not their cattle to d.
John 3:30 he must increase, I d.

**DECREE, S.**

Ezr. 5:13 Cyrus made a d. 17
6:1 Darius, 12; 7:21 Artaxerxes
Est. 3:15 d. in Shushan, 9:14
9:32 the d. of Esther confirmed
Job 28:26 made a d. for the rain
Ps. 2:7 declare d. Lord hath said
148:6 hath made a d. not pass
Prov. 8:29 gave to the sea his d.
Is. 10:1 decree unrighteous d.
Jer. 5:22 bound of sea by per. d.
Dan. 2:9 but one d. for you
4:17 this is by d. of watchers
24 this is d. of the Most High
6:8 now, O king, establish d.
13 Daniel regardeth not the d.
26 I make d. that in every do.
Jon. 3:7 d. of king and nobles
Mic. 7:11 in that day d. far rem.
Zep. 2:2 before the d. bring forth
Luke 2:1 a d. from C. Augustus
Acts 16:4 delivered d. to keep
17:7 do contrary to d. of Cesar

**DECREE, ED.**

Est. 2:1 rememb. what was d.
Job 22:28 shalt d. and it shall be
38:10 break up for it d. place
Prov. 8:15 princes d. justice
Is. 10:22 consumption d.
1 Cor. 7:37 hath so d. he will k.

**DEDAN.**

Gen. 10:7 sons of Raamah, D.
1 Chr. 1:9 Sheba, D. 32
Jer. 25:23 I made D. drink, 49:8
Ezek. 25:13 D. fall by sw. 27:20

DEDANIM. Is. 21:13

**DEDICATE.**

1 Chr. 26:27 spoils did they d.
2 Chr. 2:4 I build to d. it to God

**DEDICATED.**

Deut. 20:5 a new house, not d. it
1 K. 7:51 which D. his father had
d. 1 Chr. 18:11; 2 Chr. 5:1
8:63 d. the house, 2 Chr. 7:5
15:15 Asa bro. in the things his
father had d. 2 Chr. 15:18
2 Chr. 24:7 d. things did bestow
31:12 brought d. things faith.
Ezek. 44:29 ev. d. thing be theirs
Heb. 9:18 nor d. without blood

**DEDICATION.**

Ezr. 6:17 at d. of this house
John 10:22 at Jerus. feast. of d.

**DEED.**

Gen. 44:15 what d. is this
Ex. 9:16 very d. for this cause
Jud. 19:30 no such d. done
1 Sam. 26:4 was come in very d.
2 Sam. 12:14 by this d. given
Est. 1:17 d. of queen come
Luke 23:51 not consented to d.
24:19 J. who was mighty in d.
Acts 4:9 examined of good d.
Rom. 15:18 Gentiles obe. by d.
1 Cor. 5:2 hath done this d.
3 hath so done this d.
Col. 3:17 ye do in word or d.
Jam. 1:25 be blessed in his d.
1 John 3:18 in word, but in d.

**DEEDS.**

Gen. 20:9 done d. ought not to
1 Chr. 16:8 make known his d.
among the people, Ps. 105:1
Ezr. 9:13 all is come for evil d.
Neh. 6:19 reported his good d.
13:14 wipe not out my good d.
Ps. 28:4 give them ac. to their d.
Is. 59:18 ac. to d. he will repay
Jer. 5:28 overpass d. of wicked
25:14 recompense accord. to d.
Luke 11:48 ye allow d. of fathers
23:41 receive reward of our d.
John 3:19 their d. were evil
20 his d. should be reproved
21 d. may be made manifest
8:41 ye do d. of your father
Acts 7:22 Moses was mighty in d.
9:36 Dorcas was full of alms-d.
19:18 many showed their d.
24:2 worthy d. are done
Rom. 2:6 to every man acc. to d.
3:20 by d. of law no flesh justi.
28 justified by faith without d.
8:13 mortify d. of body
2 Cor. 12:12 signs and mighty d.
Col. 3:9 off old man with his d.
2 Pet. 2:8 vexed with unlawful d.
2 John 11 partaker of his evil d.
3 John 10 I will remember his d.
Jude 15 conv. of their ungod. d.
Rev. 2:6 hatest d. of Nicolaitans
22 except repent of d.
16:11 repented not of their d.

**DEEMED.**

Acts 27:27 the shipmen d. drew

**DEEP, Substantive.**

Gen. 1:2 darkness on face of d.
7:11 fountains of d. were brok.
8:2 fountains of d. were stop.
49:25 with blessings of the d.
Deut. 33:13 d. that coucheth ben.
Job 38:30 face of d. is frozen
41:31 the d. to boil like a pot
32 think the d. to be hoary
Ps. 36:6 judgments a great d.
42:7 d. calleth to d. at noise of
69:15 nor let d. swallow me up
104:6 coveredst it with the d. as
107:24 see his wonders in the d.
Prov. 8:28 strength. fount. of d.
Is. 44:27 saith to the d. Be dry
51:10 which dried waters of d.
63:13 led them through the d.
Ezek. 26:19 bring up d. on thee
31:4 d. set him on high
15 I covered the d. for him
Amos 7:4 devoured the great d.
Jon. 2:3 hadst cast me into d.
Hab. 3:10 d. uttered his voice
Luke 5:4 launch out into the d.
8:31 command to go into d.
Rom. 10:7 who descend into d.
2 Cor. 11:25 night and day in d.

**DEEP, Adjective.**
*Job* 12:22 discovereth *d.* things
*Ps.* 64:6 and the heart is *d.*
*Ps.* 69:2 I sink in *d.* mire, *d.* wat.
14 be delivered out of *d.* wat.
80:9 didst cause it take *d.* root
92:5 thy thoughts are very *d.*
95:4 in his hands are *d.* places
135:6 in seas, and all *d.* places
140:10 be cast into *d.* pits
*Prov.* 18:4 words are as *d.* waters
20:5 counsel like *d.* water
22:14 of strange wom. is a *d.* pit
23:27 for a whore is a *d.* ditch
*Ec.* 7:24 exceeding *d.* who can
*Is.* 29:15 seek *d.* to hide counsel
30:33 he hath made Tophet *d.*
*Jer.* 49:8 dwell *d.* O inhab. of D.
*Ezek.* 23:32 drink sister's cup *d.*
32:14 make their waters *d.*
34:18 drunk of *d.* waters
*Dan.* 2:22 revealeth *d.* things
*Luke* 6:48 and digged *d.*
*John* 4:11 and the well is *d.*
1 *Cor.* 2:10 search. *d.* things
2 *Cor.* 8:2 *d.* poverty abounded

**DEEP sleep.**
*Gen.* 2:21 a *d. sleep* to fall on A.
15:12 a *d. sleep* fell on Abram
1 *Sam.* 26:12 *d. s.* was on them
*Job* 4:13 *d. sleep* falleth 33:15
*Prov.* 19:15 sloth. casteth in *d. s.*
*Is.* 29:10 spirit of *d. sleep*
*Dan.* 8:18 I was in a *d. s.* 10:9
*Acts* 20:9 Eutychus into *d. sleep*

**DEEPER.**
*Job* 11:8 it is *d.* than hell, what
*Is.* 33:19 a people of *d.* speech

**DEEPLY.**
*Is.* 31:6 Israel have *d.* revolted
*Hos.* 9:9 they have *d.* corrupted
*Mark* 8:12 Jesus sighed *d.*

**DEEPNESS.**
*Mat.* 13:5 had no *d.* of earth

**DEEPS.**
*Neh.* 9:11 persecutors into *d.*
*Ps.* 88:6 hast laid me in the *d.*
148:7 praise the Lord, all *d.*
*Zec.* 10:11 *d.* of river shall dry

**DEER.**
*Deut.* 14:5 ye shall eat fallow *d.*
1 *K.* 4:23 Solomon had *d.*

**DEFAMED, ING.**
1 *Cor.* 4:13 being *d.* we entreat
*Jer.* 20:10 I heard *d.* of many

**DEFEAT.**
2 *Sam.* 15:34 *d.* coun. of A. 17:14

**DEFENCE.**
*Num.* 14:9 their *d.* is departed
*Job* 22:25 Almighty be thy *d.*
*Ps.* 7:10 my *d.* is of God, who
31:2 be thou for house of *d.*
59:9 God is my *d.* 17; 62:2, 6
16 hast been my *d.* in trouble
89:18 L. is our *d.*; 94:22 my *d.*
*Ec.* 7:12 wisdom is a *d.* money
*Is.* 4:5 on glory shall be a *d.*
19:6 brooks of *d.* be emptied
33:16 his *d.* munitions of rocks
*Nah.* 2:5 *d.* shall be prepared
*Acts* 19:33 made his *d.*
22:1 hear ye my *d.* I make now
*Phil.* 1:7 and in *d.* of the gospel
17 I am set for *d.* of gospel

DEFENCED. *See* CITY, CITIES.

**DEFEND.**
*Jud.* 10:1 Tola son of Puah arose to *d.* Israel
2 *K.* 19:34 I will *d.* this city, 20:6; *Is.* 37:35; 38:6
*Ps.* 20:1 name of G. of Jacob *d.*
59:1 *d.* me from them rise up
82:3 *d.* the poor and fatherless
*Is.* 31:5 so will Lord *d.* Jerusal.
*Zec.* 9:15 Lord sl all *d.* them
12:8 in that day L. *d.* inhabit.

**DEFENDED, EST, ING.**
2 *Sam.* 23:12 Shammah *d.* ground
*Ps.* 5:11 because thou *d.* them
*Is.* 31:5 *d.* Jerus. will deliver it
*Acts* 7:24 he *d.* him, and aveng.

**DEFER, RED, ETH.**
*Prov.* 13:12 hope *d.* maketh sick
19:11 discretion *d.* anger
*Ec.* 5:4 vowest *d.* not to pay it
*Is.* 48:9 will I defer mine anger
*Dan.* 9:19 *d.* not, for own sake
*Acts* 24:22 Felix *d.* them

**DEFY, IED.**
*Num.* 23:7 curse me Jacob, *d.* Is.
8 how I *d.* whom L. not *defied?*
1 *Sam.* 17:10 I *d.* armies of Israel
25 to *d.* Israel is he come up
26 that he should *d.* the armies
36 *d.* armies of living God
45 God of Israel whom hast *d.*
2 *Sam.* 21:21 when he *d.* Is. Jonathan slew him, 1 *Chr.* 20:7
23:9 when they *d.* Philistines

**DEFILE.**
*Lev.* 11:44 nor *d.* yours. 18:24
18:28 spue not out when ye *d.*
*Num.* 35:34 *d.* not land ye sh. in.
*Cant.* 5:3 how shall I *d.* them?
*Is.* 30:22 *d.* covering of images
*Ezek.* 7:22 robbers shall *d.* it
9:7 *d.* the house
20:7 *d.* not with the idols, 18
28:7 shall *d.* thy brightness
33:26 *d.* every man neigh. wife
37:23 *d.* themselves any more
43:7 my name Israel no more *d.*
*Dan.* 1:8 not *d.* with king's meat
*Mat.* 15:18 *d.* the man, *Mark* 7:15
1 *Cor.* 3:17 if any *d.* temple
1 *Tim.* 1:10 law is for them *d.*
*Jude* 8 filthy dreamers *d.* flesh

**DEFILED.**
*Gen.* 34:2 Shechem *d.* Dinah
*Lev.* 18:24 in all these, nations *d.*
1 *Chr.* 5:1 as he *d.* his father's b.
*Job* 16:15 *d.* my horn in the dust
*Ps.* 74:7 *d.* the dwelling-pl. 79:1
106:39 *d.* with their own works
*Is.* 24:5 earth is *d.* under inhab.
59:3 your hands *d.* with blood
*Jer.* 2:7 entered ye *d.* my land
16:18 because they *d.* my land
*Ezek.* 4:13 shall Isr. eat *d.* bread
5:11 because *d.* my sanctuary
7:24 their holy places shall be *d.*
18:6 nor *d.* neighbor's wife, 15
20:43 doings wherein been *d.*
22:4 *d.* thyself in idols, 23:7
11 another *d.* daughter-in-law
23:38 *d.* my sanctuary same day
28:18 hast *d.* thy sanctuaries
43:8 *d.* my holy name
*Hos.* 5:3 and Israel is *d.* 6:10
*Mic.* 4:11 say, let her be *d.*
*Mark* 7:2 disc. eat with *d.* hands
*John* 18:28 went not in, lest be *d.*
1 *Cor.* 8:7 conscience weak, is *d.*
*Tit.* 1:15 them that are *d.* their mind and conscience is *d.*
*Heb.* 12:15 thereby many be *d.*
*Rev.* 3:4 not *d.* their garments
14:4 were not *d.* with women

**DEFILEDST, ETH.**
*Gen.* 49:4 father's bed, *d.* it
*Ex.* 31:14 *d.* sab. put to death
*Mat.* 15:11 goeth into mouth *d.*
20 with unwashen hand *d.* not
*Mark* 7:20 that cometh out *d.*
*Jam.* 3:6 tongue, it *d.* whole bo.
*Rev.* 21:27 enter anything *d.*

**DEFRAUD, ED.**
*Lev.* 19:13 shalt not *d.* neighbor
1 *Sam.* 12:3 whom have I *d.?*
*Mark* 10:19 *d.* not
1 *Cor.* 6:7 rather suffer to be *d.*
8 you *d.* your brethren
7:5 *d.* not, except with consent
2 *Cor.* 7:2 we have *d.* no man
1 *Thes.* 4:6 no man *d.* his brother

**DEGENERATE.**
*Jer.* 2:21 turned into *d.* plant

**DEGREE, S.**
2 *K.* 20:9 back. ten *d. Is.* 38:8
1 *Chr.* 17:17 a man of high *d.*
*Ps.* 62:9 low *d.* vanity, high *d.*
*Luke* 1:52 exalted them of low *d.*
1 *Tim.* 3:13 purchase a good *d.*
*Jam.* 1:9 brother of low *d.* rej.

**DELAY, ED, ETH.**
*Ex.* 22:29 not *d.* to offer fi.-fruits
32:1 Moses *d.* to come down
*Ps.* 119:60 *d.* not to keep com.
*Mat.* 24:48 Lord *d. Luke* 12:45
*Acts* 9:38 not *d.* to come to them
25:17 without *d.* morrow I sat

**DELECTABLE.**
*Is.* 44:9 their *d.* things not profit

**DELICACIES.**
*Rev.* 18:3 merc. rich thro' her *d.*

**DELICATE.**
*Deut.* 28:54 the *d.* man or w. 56
*Is.* 47:1 no more be called *d.*
*Jer.* 6:2 likened Zion to *d.* wom.
*Mic.* 1:16 bald for thy *d.* child.

**DELICATES.**
*Jer.* 51:34 filled belly with my *d.*

**DELICATELY.**
1 *Sam.* 15:32 Agag came *d.*
*Prov.* 29:21 that *d.* bringeth up
*Lam.* 4:5 did feed *d.* are desolate
*Luke* 7:25 live *d.* are in kings'

**DELICATENESS.**
*Deut.* 28:56 foot on ground for *d.*

**DELICIOUSLY.**
*Rev.* 18:7 she lived *d.* 9

**DELIGHT, Substantive.**
*Deut.* 10:15 L. had *d.* in thy fath.
1 *Sam.* 15:22 great *d.* in offering
18:22 the king hath *d.*
2 *Sam.* 15:26 I have no *d.* in thee
*Job* 22:26 have *d.* in Almighty
*Ps.* 1:2 his *d.* is in law of the L.
16:3 in whom is all my *d.*
119:24 testimonies are my *d.*
77 for thy law is my *d.* 174
*Prov.* 8:30 I was daily his *d.*
11:1 just weight is Lord's *d.*
20 such as upright, are his *d.*
12:22 deal truly are his *d.*
15:8 prayer of upright is his *d.*
16:13 righteous lips *d.* of kings
18:2 a fool no *d.* in unders.
19:10 *d.* not seemly for a fool
24:25 to them that reb. sh. be *d.*
29:17 he give *d.* to thy soul
*Cant.* 2:3 under sha. wi. great *d.*
*Is.* 58:2 take *d.* in app. to God
13 if thou call sabbath a *d.*
*Jer.* 6:10 no *d.* in word of Lord

**DELIGHT, Verb.**
*Num.* 14:8 if Lord *d.* in us
2 *Sam.* 24:3 why should king *d.*
*Job* 27:10 he *d.* in Almighty?
34:9 should *d.* himself with G.
*Ps.* 37:4 *d.* thyself also in Lord
11 *d.* in abundance of peace
40:8 I *d.* to do thy will, O God
62:4 *d.* in lies; 68:30 *d.* in war
94:19 thy comforts *d.* my soul
119:16 *d.* in thy statutes, 35
47 *d.* in thy com.; 70 *d.* in law
*Prov.* 1:22 long will scorners *d.*
2:14 *d.* in frowardness
*Is.* 1:11 I *d.* not in blood of bul.
13:17 as for gold, not *d.* in it
55:2 let your soul *d.* in fatness

58:2 they *d.* to know my ways
14 shalt *d.* thyself in the Lord
*Jer.* 9:24 in these things I *d.*
*Mal.* 3:1 messenger of cov. ye *d.*
*Rom.* 7:22 I *d.* an law after in. m.

**DELIGHTED.**

1 *Sam.* 19:2 Jonath. *d.* in David
2 *Sam.* 22:20 *d.* in me, *Ps.* 18:19
1 *K.* 10:9 L. *d.* in thee, 2 *Chr.* 9:8
*Neh.* 9:25 *d.* in thy great goodn.
*Est.* 2:14 except king *d.* in her
*Ps.* 22:8 seeing he *d.* in him
109:17 as he *d.* not in blessing
*Is.* 65:12 did choose that wherein
I *d.* not, 66:4
66:11 be *d.* with her glory

**DELIGHTEST, ETH.**

*Est.* 6:6 *d.* to honor, 7, 9, 11
*Ps.* 37:23 and he *d.* in his way
51:16 *d.* not in burnt-offering
112:1 *d.* greatly in his command
147:10 *d.* not in str. of horse
*Prov.* 3:12 son in whom he *d.*
*Is.* 42:1 in whom my soul *d.*
62:4 for the Lord *d.* in thee
66:3 soul *d.* in abominations
*Mic.* 7:18 because he *d.* in mercy
*Mal.* 2:17 G. *d.* in them do evil

**DELIGHTS.**

2 *Sam.* 1:24 clothed you with *d.*
*Ps.* 119:92 law been my *d.*
143 yet thy comman. are my *d.*
*Prov.* 8:31 my *d.* with sons of m.
*Ec.* 2:8 I gat me the *d.* of men
*Cant.* 7:6 how pleasant for *d.*

**DELIGHTSOME.**

*Mal.* 3:12 ye shall be a *d.* land

DELILAH. *Jud.* 16:4, 12

**DELIVER.**

*Ex.* 23:31 I will *d.* the inhabit.
*Num.* 21:2 indeed *d.* this people
*Deut.* 7:24 *d.* kings into thy h.
32:39 neither any that can *d.* out
of my hand, *Is.* 43:13
*Jos.* 2:13 *d.* our lives from death
*Jud.* 7:7 by the 300 will I *d.* M.
1 *Sam.* 12:21 cannot profit nor *d.*
24:4 *d.* enemy into thy hand
28:19 L. will *d.* Is. to Phil.
1 *K.* 20:13 I will *d.* this multi.
22:6 *d.* into king's hand, 12, 15;
2 *Chr.* 18:5, 11
2 *K.* 3:18 he will *d.* Moabites
18:35 should *d.* Jer. *Is.* 36:20
2 *Chr.* 25:15 could not *d.* own p.
32:13 able to *d.* their lands?
14 that your God should *d.* you
*Job* 10:7 none can *d.* out
22:30 shall *d.* island of innocent
33:28 *d.* soul from going into pit
*Ps.* 6:4 *d.* my soul, 17:13; 22:20;
116:4; 120:2
*Ps.* 7:2 none to *d.* 50:22
33:17 *d.* any by his great str.
19 to *d.* their soul from death
56:13 *d.* my feet from falling?
72:12 *d.* needy when he
74:19 *d.* not soul of turtle-dove
82:4 *d.* needy out of the hand
89:48 *d.* his soul from grave
*Prov.* 4:9 a crown shall she *d.* to
6:3 do this now *d.* thyself
23:14 shalt *d.* his soul from hell
*Ec.* 8:8 wick. *d.* those given
*Is.* 5:29 none shall *d.* prey
29:11 men *d.* to one learned
31:5 defending also he will *d.* it
44:20 that he cannot *d.* his soul
46:2 they could not *d.* burden
47:14 not *d.* thems. from flame
50:2 have I no power to *d.*?
*Jer.* 15:9 residue will I *d.*
18:21 *d.* their children to famine
20:5 *d.* strength of this city
21:7 *d.* Zedekiah from sword
22:3 *d.* spoiled out of hand of
43:11 *d.* such as are for death
51:6 *d.* every man his soul, 45
*Ezek.* 13:21 I will *d.* my peo. 23
14:14 *d.* but their own souls
16 shall *d.* sons nor dau. 18:20
33:5 taketh warning *d.* his soul
34:10 *d.* flock from their mouth
*Dan.* 3:29 no god *d.* after this
8:4 nor any could *d.* from ram
*Hos.* 2:10 none *d.* her out of hand
*Amos* 2:14 nor mighty *d.* himself
6:8 *d.* city with a therein
*Mic.* 5:8 teareth, and none can *d.*
6:14 shalt take hold, but not *d.*
*Zec.* 2:7 *d.* thyself, O Zion
11:6 *d.* every one into n. hand
*Mat.* 10:21 bro. *d.* bro. to death
*Acts* 25:16 to *d.* any man to die
1 *Cor.* 5:5 *d.* such a one to Satan
2 *Cor.* 1:10 death, and doth *d.*
2 *Pet.* 2:9 Lord know. how to *d.*

**DELIVER him.**

*Gen.* 37:22 *d. him* to his father
1 *Sam.* 23:20 part be to *d. him*
2 *Sam.* 14:7 *d. him* smote his bro.
20:21 *d. him*, and I will depart
*Job* 33:24 *d. h.* from going to pit
*Ps.* 22:8 *d. him*, let him *d. him*
41:1 L. *d. him* in time of troub.
2 not *d. h.* to will of enemies
71:11 for there is none to *d. h.*
91:14 his love on me, I *d. him*
15 be with him, I will *d. him*
*Prov.* 19:19 if *d. him* must do it
*Jer.* 21:12 *d. him* spoiled
*Ezek.* 33:12 shall not *d. him*
*Mat.* 20:19 *d. him* to G. *Mark*
10:33; *Luke* 20:20; *Acts* 21:11
26:15 and I will *d. him*
27:43 let him *d. him* now

**DELIVER me.**

*Gen.* 32:11 *d. me* from Esau
1 *Sam.* 17:37 *d. me* from Goliath
23:11 men of Keilah *d. me* up?
24:15 Lord be judge and *d. me*
26:24 *d. me* out of all tribulat.
*Job* 6:23 *d. me* from enemies, *Ps.*
31:15; 59:1
*Ps.* 7:1 save me from them, *d. m.*
25:20 keep my soul, and *d. me*
27:12 *d. me* not to will of enem.
31:2 *d. me* speedily
39:8 *d. me* from all my transg.
40:13 be pleased to *d. me*
43:1 O *d. me* from the deceitful
51:14 *d. me* from blood-guilti.
59:2 *d. me* from workers of iniq.
69:14 *d. me* out of the mire
18 draw nigh to my soul, *d. me*
70:1 make haste to *d. me*
71:2 *d. me* in thy righteous. 31:1
4 *d. me* out of hand of wicked
109:21 mercy is good, *d.* thou *me*
119:134 *d. me* from op. of man
153 consider affliction, *d. me*
154 plead my cause, and *d. me*
170 *d. me* according to thy w.
140:1 *d. me* from the evil man
142:6 *d. me* from my persecutors
143:9 *d. me* from mine enemies
144:7 *d. me* out of great waters
11 *d. me* from strange children
*Is.* 44:17 *d. me*, thou art my God
*Jer.* 38:19 afraid lest Jews *d. me*
*Acts* 25:11 no man may *d. me*
*Rom.* 7:24 *d. me* from body of d.?
2 *Tim.* 4:18 *d. me* from evil work

**DELIVER thee.**

*Deut.* 23:14 in camp to *d. thee*
1 *Sam.* 17:46 *d. thee* into
2 *K.* 20:6 *d. t.* and city, *Is.* 38:6
*Job* 5:19 *d. t.* in six troubles
*Job* 36:18 ransom cannot *d. thee*
*Ps.* 50:15 *d. t.* thou shalt glorify
91:3 *d. thee* from snare of fowler
*Prov.* 2:12 *d. t.* from way of evil
16 *d. t.* from strange woman
*Is.* 57:13 thy companies *d. thee*
*Jer.* 1:8 with thee to *d. t.* 15:20
38:20 J. said they shall not *d. t.*
39:17 I will *d. thee* in that day
*Ezek.* 21:31 *d. thee* to brutish
23:28 *d. t.* to them thou hatest
25:4 I will *d. t.* to men of east
7 I will *d. thee* for spoil
*Dan.* 6:16 thy G. will *d. thee*
*Hos.* 11:8 how shall I *d. thee*, Is.
*Mat.* 5:25 judge *d. t.* *Luke* 12:58

**DELIVER them.**

*Ex.* 3:8 down to *d. t.* *Acts* 7:34
*Deut.* 7:2 Lord shall *d. them*, 23
*Jos.* 11:6 *d. them* up all slain
*Jud.* 20:28 to-morrow I will *d. t.*
1 *Sam.* 14:37 wilt thou *d. them*,
2 *Sam.* 5:19; 1 *Chr.* 14:10
1 *K.* 8:46 *d. t.* to ene. 2 *K.* 21:14
2 *Chr.* 25:20 came to G. to *d. t.*
*Neh.* 9:28 didst *d. them*
*Job* 5:4 neither any to *d. them*
*Ps.* 22:4 didst *d. them*
37:40 the L. shall *d. them*
106:43 many times did he *d. t.*
*Prov.* 11:6 right. of upr. sha. *d. t.*
12:6 the mouth of upright *d. t.*
24:11 forbear to *d. them*
*Is.* 19:20 a Saviour and *d. them*
*Ezek.* 7:19 not *d. them*, *Zep.* 1:18
34:12 my sheep and *d. them*
*Acts* 7:25 God by his hand *d. t.*
*Heb.* 2:15 *d. t.* who through fear

**DELIVER us.**

*Jud.* 10:15 *d. us* only, this day
20:13 *d. us* children of Belial
1 *Sam.* 4:8 who shall *d. us*
12:10 now *d. us* from enemies
2 *K.* 18:30 will *d. us*, *Is.* 36:15
1 *Chr.* 16:35 *d. us* from heathen
2 *Chr.* 32:11 Lord shall *d. us*
*Ps.* 79:9 *d. us*, purge away sins
*Jer.* 43:3 to *d. us* to Chaldeans
*Lam.* 5:8 none that doth *d. us*
*Dan.* 3:17 able and will *d. us*
*Mat.* 6:13 *d. us* fr. evil, *Luke* 11:4
2 *Cor.* 1:10 he will yet *d. us*
*Gal.* 1:4 *d. us* from evil world

**DELIVER you.**

*Jud.* 10:13 I will *d. you* no more
14 *d. you* in tribulation
2 *Chr.* 32:14 *d. you* out of hand
*Is.* 36:14 H. not be able to *d. you*
46:4 I will carry and *d. you*
*Ezek.* 11:9 *d. you* to strangers
*Dan.* 3:15 that God sh. *d. you*
*Mat.* 10:17 *d. you* up, *Mark* 13:9

**DELIVERANCE, S.**

*Gen.* 45:7 to save by a great *d.*
*Jud.* 15:18 given this great *d.*
2 *K.* 5:1 had given *d.* to Syria
13:17 arrow of Lord's *d.* of *d.*
1 *Chr.* 11:14 saved by a great *d.*
2 *Chr.* 12:7 I will grant some *d.*
*Ezr.* 9:13 given such *d.* as this
*Est.* 4:14 then *d.* arise to Jews
*Ps.* 18:50 great *d.* giveth to king
32:7 compass with songs of *d.*
44:4 command *d.* for Jacob
*Is.* 26:18 not wrought any *d.*
*Joel* 2:32 in Z. and in Jeru. be *d.*
*Ob.* 17 upon Zion shall be *d.*
*Luke* 4:18 to preach *d.* to capt.
*Heb.* 11:35 not accepting *d.*

**DELIVERED.**

*Gen.* 9:2 into your h. are they *d.*
14:20 blessed be God who *d.*
25:24 her days to be *d.* fulfilled
*Ex.* 1:19 *d.* ere midwives come
5:23 nor hast *d.* thy people
12:27 and *d.* our houses
*Deut.* 2:36 Lord *d.* all unto us
1 *Sam.* 4:19 P. wife near to be *d.*
17:35 *d.* it of his mouth
30:23 *d.* company came ag. us
1 *K.* 3:17 *d.* of a child with her

*2 K.* 19:11 and shalt thou be *d.?*
*Job* 22:30 *d.* by puren. of hands
23:7 be *d.* for ever from judge
29:12 I *d.* the poor that cried
*Ps.* 22:5 they cried and were *d.*
33:16 not *d.* by much strength
55:18 *d.* my soul in peace
56:13 *d.* soul, 86:13; 116:8
60:5 beloved may be *d.* 108:6
69:14 *d.* from them that hate me
78:61 *d.* his strength into capt.
*Prov.* 11:8 is *d.* out of trouble
9 through knowledge just be *d.*
21 seed of righteous shall be *d.*
28:26 walk. wisely, shall be *d.*
*Ec.* 9:15 by wisdom he *d.* city
*Is.* 36:19 *d.* Samaria out
38:17 *d.* it from pit of corrupt.
49:24 or lawful captive be *d.?*
25 prey of terrible shall be *d.*
66:7 was *d.* of a man-child
*Jer.* 20:13 *d.* soul of the poor
*Ezek.* 3:19 *d.* thy soul, 33:9
14:16 they only shall be *d.*
17:15 break cov. and be *d.?*
31:14 all *d.* unto death
32:20 she is *d.* to the sword
*Dan.* 3:28 *d.* serv. that trusted
6:27 who *d.* Daniel from lions
12:1 thy people be *d.*
*Joel* 2:32 call on L. shall be *d.*
*Amos* 9:1 shall not be *d.*
*Mic.* 4:10 go to Bab. there be *d.*
*Hab.* 2:9 *d.* from power of evil
*Mal.* 3:15 tempt God are even *d.*
*Mat.* 11:27 all things are *d.* to me of my Father, *Luke* 10:22
27:58 Pilate com. body to be *d.*
*Mark* 10:33 be *d.* to chief priests
15:15 and *d.* Jesus, *Luke* 23:25
*Luke* 1:57 she should be *d.* 2:6
4:6 that is *d.* to me
17 *d.* to book of Esaias
9:44 Son be *d.* into hands of m.
12:58 give dilig. mayest be *d.*
18:32 he shall be *d.* to Gentiles
*John* 16:21 as soon as she is *d.*
18:36 should not be *d.* to Jews
*Acts* 2:23 *d.* by counsel of God
15:30 Judas and Silas *d.*
27:1 they *d.* Paul to one Julius
28:17 *d.* prisoner from Jerusal.
*Rom.* 4:25 was *d.* for our offenc.
7:6 now we are *d.* from the law
8:21 creature itself shall be *d.*
15:31 *d.* from them not believe
*2 Cor.* 4:11 are always *d.* to dea.
*2 Thes.* 3:2 *d.* from unreas. men
*1 Tim.* 1:20 whom I ha. *d.* to S.
*2 Tim.* 4:17 I was *d.* out of the mouth of the lion
*Heb.* 11:11 by faith Sarah was *d.*
*2 Pet.* 2:7 and *d.* just Lot, vexed
21 turned from the com. *d.*
*Jude* 3 faith once *d.* to the sain.
*Rev.* 12:2 and pained to be *d.*
*See* HAND, HANDS.

**DELIVERED him.**
*Gen.* 37:21 Reuben *d. him*
*Deut.* 2:33 God *d. him* before us
*1 K.* 13:26 Lord *d. h.* to the lion
17:23 Elijah *d. h.* to his mother
*Ps.* 7:4 *d. h.* that is mine enemy
*Mat.* 18:34 *d. him* to tormentors
27:2 *d. him* to P. Pilate, *Mark* 15:1
18 for envy *d. him*, *Mark* 15:10
26 *d. h.* to be cruc. *John* 19:16
*Luke* 7:15 Jesus *d. h.* to his mot.
24:20 how our rulers *d. him*
*John* 18:30 wo. not *d. h.* to thee
*Acts* 7:10 *d. h.* out of afflictions
12:4 *d. h.* to four quarternions

**DELIVERED me.**
*Ex.* 18:4 *d. me* fr. swo. of Pha.
*Jud.* 12:3 I saw ye *d. me* not
*2 Sam.* 22:18 he *d. me* from my strong enemy, *Ps.* 18:17
20 he *d. me* because he delighted in me, *Ps.* 18:19
49 *d. me* from vio. *Ps.* 18:48
*Job* 16:11 *d. me* to the ungodly
*Ps.* 18:43 *d. me* from striv. of pe.
34:4 L. *d. me* from all my fears
54:7 *d. me* out of all my trouble
*John* 19:11 *d. me* hath great. sin
*2 Tim.* 3:11 of them all L. *d. me*

**DELIVERED thee.**
*1 Sam.* 24:10 *d. t.* to-d. into m. h.
*2 Sam.* 12:7 I *d. thee* out of the h.
*Ps.* 81:7 calledst and I *d. thee*
*Ezek.* 16:27 I *d. t.* to them th. h.
*John* 18:35 ch. priests *d. t.* to me

**DELIVERED them.**
*Ex.* 18:8 Mos. told how L. *d. t.*
*Jud.* 3:9 r. up. deliv. who *d. th.*
*2 K.* 19:12 gods *d. th. Is.* 37:12
*2 Chr.* 29:8 *d. them* to trouble
*Ps.* 78:42 he *d. th.* from enemy
107:6 he *d. th.* out of distresses
20 he *d. th.* from destructions
*Is.* 34:2 hath *d. th.* to slaughter
*Mat.* 25:14 *d.* to *them* his goods
*Luke* 1:2 as they *d. them* un. us
*Acts* 16:4 *d. t.* decrees for to ke.
*1 Cor.* 11:2 keep ordin. as I *d. t.*
*2 Pet.* 2:4 *d. t.* into chains of d.

**DELIVERED up.**
*Num.* 21:3 Lord *d. up* the Can.
*2 Sam.* 18:28 *d. up* men that lift
*Ob.* 14 nor *d. up* those that rem.
*Acts* 3:13 glorified Son ye *d. up*
*Rom.* 8:32 but *d.* him *up* for us
*1 Cor.* 15:24 have *d. up* kingdom
*Rev.* 20:13 and hell *d. up* dead

**DELIVERED us.**
*Ex.* 2:19 Egyp. *d. us* fr. shep.
*Acts* 6:14 ch. customs Mos. *d. us*
*2 Cor.* 1:10 *d. us* from so gr. dea.
*Col.* 1:13 *d. us.* fr. pow. of dark.
*1 Thes.* 1:10 who *d. us* fr. wrath

**DELIVERED you.**
*Rom.* 6:17 obeyed doctrine *d. y.*
*1 Cor.* 11:23 that I *d. y.* 15:3

**DELIVEREDST, EST.**
*Ps.* 35:10 *d.* poor fr. him spoil.
*Mic.* 6:14 what *d.* I give to swo.

**DELIVERER.**
*Jud.* 3:9 L. raised up *d.* to Is. 15
18:28 there was no *d.*
*2 Sam.* 22:2 L. is my *d. Ps.* 18:2
*Ps.* 40:17 thou art my *d.* 70:5
144:2 my fortress and my *d.*
*Acts* 7:35 did God send to be a *d.*
*Rom.* 11:26 come out of Sion *d.*

**DELIVERETH.**
*Job* 36:15 *d.* poor in his affliction
*Ps.* 18:48 *d.* me from enemies
34:7 that fear him, and *d.* them
17 *d.* them out of troubles, 19
97:10 *d.* out of hand of wicked
144:10 who *d.* David from swo.
*Prov.* 10:2 right. *d.* fr. d. 11:4
14:25 a true witness *d.* souls
*Is.* 42:22 are for a prey, none *d.*
*Dan.* 6:27 God *d.* and rescueth

**DELIVERING.**
*Luke* 21:12 *d.* you up to synag.
*Acts* 22:4 *d.* men and women
26:17 *d.* thee from the Gentiles

**DELIVERY.**
*Is.* 26:17 near the time of her *d.*

**DELUSION, S.**
*Is.* 66:4 I will choose their *d.*
*2 Thes.* 2:11 send them strong *d.*

**DEMAND.**
*Dan.* 4:17 *d.* by word of h. ones.

**DEMAND, ED.**
*Job* 38:3 *d.* of thee, 40:7; 42:4
*Mat.* 2:4 *d.* wh. C. sh. be born
*Luke* 3:14 Soldi. *d.* what shall
17:20 when he was *d.* of Phar.
*Acts* 21:33 cap. *d.* who he was

**DEMAS.**
*Col.* 4:14; *Phile.* 24
*2 Tim.* 4:10 D. hath forsaken me

**DEMETRIUS.**
*Acts* 19:24 D. a silver. *3 John* 12

**DEMONSTRATION.**
*1 Cor.* 2:4 but in *d.* of the Spirit

**DEN, S.**
*Jud.* 6:2 Israel made them *d.*
*Job* 37:8 th. the beasts go into *d.*
38:40 when they couch in *d.*
*Ps.* 10:9 lieth as a lion in his *d.*
104:22 lay them. down in *d.*
*Cant.* 4:8 look from the lions' *d.*
*Is.* 11:8 hand on cockatrice *d.*
32:14 towers be for *d.* forever
*Jer.* 7:11 house a *d.* of robbers
9:11 Jerusalem a *d.* of dragons
10:22 cit. of Judah a *d.* of drag.
*Dan.* 6:16 cast him into *d.* of li.
24 cast them into *d.* of lions
*Amos* 3:4 y. lion cry out of *d.?*
*Nah.* 2:12 filled *d.* with ravin
*Mat.* 21:13 a *d.* of th. *Mark* 11:17
*Heb.* 11:38 they wandered in *d.*
*Rev.* 6:15 bond and free hid in *d.*

**DENY.**
*Jos.* 24:27 lest ye *d.* your God
*1 K* 2:16 *d.* me not, *Prov.* 30:7
*Job* 8:18 then it shall *d.* him
*Prov.* 30:9 lest I be full and *d.*
*Mat.* 10:33 *d.* me, him will I *d.*
16:24 let him *d.* himself, *Mark* 8:34; *Luke* 9:23
26:34 *d.* me thrice, 75; *Mark* 14:30, 72
*Luke* 20:27 *d.* th. is any resur.
*2 Tim.* 2:12 *d.* him, he will *d.* us
13 he cannot *d.* himself
*Tit.* 1:16 in works they *d.* him

**DENIED.**
*1 K.* 20:7 sent and I *d.* him not
*Job* 31:28 I sh. have *d.* God above
*Mat.* 26:70 Peter *d.* before all, 72; *Mark* 14:70; *Luke* 22:57; *John* 18:25, 27
*Luke* 8:45 all *d.* th. touched him
12:9 be *d.* bef. angels of God
*John* 1:20 John *d.* not
*Acts* 3:13 wh. *d.* in pres. of Pi.
14 but ye *d.* the Holy One
*1 Tim.* 5:8 he hath *d.* the faith
*Rev.* 2:13 hast not *d.* my faith
3:8 and hast not *d.* my name

**DENIETH, ING.**
*Luke* 12:9 that *d.* me before men
*2 Tim.* 3:5 *d.* the power thereof
*Tit.* 2:12 that *d.* ungodliness
*2 Pet* 2:1 *d.* L. that bought them
*1 John* 2:22 a liar *d.* esus is C.
23 who *d.* Son, hath not Fath.
*Jude* 4 and *d.* the only Lord God

**DENOUNCE.**
*Deut.* 30:18 I *d.* this day

**DEPART.**
*Ex.* 33:1 *d.* thou and the peo.
*1 Sam.* 22:5 abide not in hold, *d.*
29:10 as soon as ye be up, *d.*
*2 Sam.* 15:14 speed to *d.* lest he
*1 K.* 12:5 *d.* for three days
*Job* 20:28 incr. of his house *d.*
*Is.* 11:13 envy of Ephr. shall *d.*
52:11 *d.* ye, *d.* ye, *Lam.* 4:15
54:10 the mountains shall *d.*
*Jer.* 50:3 *d.* both man and beast
*Mic.* 2:10 *d.* this is not your rest
*Zec.* 10:11 sceptre of Eg. shall *d.*
*Mat.* 8:34 *d.* out of c. *Mark* 5:17
10:14 when ye *d.* out of that ho. *Mark* 6:11; *Luke* 9:4

Luke 2:29 thy serv. d. in peace
13:31 d. Herod will kill thee
21:21 let them in midst d. out
John 7:3 said d. go into Judea
13:1 Jesus knew he should d.
16:7 but if I d. I will send him
Acts 16:36 d. and go in peace
39 desired them to d. out of ci.
20:7 Paul preached ready to d.
22:21 d. I will send thee to Gen.
25:4 would d. shortly thither
27:12 more part advised to d.
1 Cor. 7:15 if unb. d. let him d.
Phil. 1:23 d. and to be with Chr.
Jam. 2:16 d. in peace, be clothed

**DEPART from.**

Num. 16:26 d. f. tents of these
Deut. 4:9 they d. fr. thy heart
Jud. 7:3 fearful d. from Gilead
2 Sam. 12:10 sw. never d. f. ho.
20:21 del. Sheba, and I will d. f.
2 Chr. 18:31 G. moved to d. f. h.
Job 21:14 say to G. d. f. us, 22:17
28:28 to d. f. evil is unders.
Ps. 6:8 d. from me, wo. of iniq.
Mat. 7:23; Luke 13:27
34:14 d. f. evil, do good, 37:27
101:4 a froward heart d. f. me
119:115 d. f. me, ye evil-doers
139:19 d. f. me ye bloody men
Prov. 3:7 fear Lord, d. from evil
13:14 d. fr. sna. of death, 14:27
19 abom. to fools to d. f. evil
15:24 he may d. from hell ben.
16:6 by fear of L. men. d. f. ev.
17 highway, is to d. from evil
Is. 14:25 burden d. f. shoulders
Jer. 6:8 lest my soul d. f. thee
17:13 d. fr. me be wri. in earth
31:36 if ordin d. f. before me
Ezek. 16:42 my jeal. d. fr. thee
Hos. 9:12 woe to th. wh. I d. f.
Mat. 25:41 d. f. me, ye cursed
Mark 6:10 abide, till ye d. f.
Luke 5:8 d. f. me, I am sinful
8:37 Gadar. bes. him to d. fr.
Acts 1:4 should not d. f. Jerus.
18:2 com. Jews to d. f. Rome
2 Cor. 12:8 that it might d. f. me
1 Tim. 4:1 some shall d. f. faith
2 Tim. 2:19 nameth C. d. f. iniq.

**Not DEPART.**

Gen. 49:10 sceptre not d. from J.
Jos. 1:8 book of law shall not d.
Jud. 6:18 d. n. hence till I come
2 Sam. 7:15 mercy n. d. from hi.
22:23 sta. I did n. d. from them
Job 7:19 long not d. from me
15:30 he shall not d. out
Ps. 55:11 guile d. not from str.
Prov. 3:21 not d. from eyes, 4:21
5:7 d. not from words of my m.
17:13 evil not d. from his house
22:6 when old, he will not d.
27:22 will not his foolishness d.
Is. 54:10 kindness shall not d.
59:21 my Spirit and wo. not d.
Jer. 32:40 shall not d. from me
37:9 the Chalde shall not d.
Mat. 14:16 they need not d. give
Luke 4:42 that he should not d.
12:59 not d. till thou hast paid

**DEPARTED.**

Gen. 12:4 so Abraham d.
Num. 12:9 kindled, and he d.
Ps. 105:38 E. glad when they d.
Is. 38:12 mine age is d.
Lam. 1:6 all her beauty is d.
Mat. 2:9 the wise men d. 12
14 Joseph and Mary d. in. E.
4:12 Jesus d. 9:27; 11:1; 12:9;
13:53; 14:13; 15:21, 29; 16:4;
19:15; Mark 1:35; 6:46; 8:13;
Luke 4:42; John 4:3, 43;
6:15; 12:36
Luke 5:25 he d. to his own house
7:24 mesengers of John were d.
10:30 thieves wounded him, d.
Acts 15:39 Paul and Barna. d.
Phile. 15 perhaps he therefore d.
Rev. 6:14 heaven d. as a scroll

**DEPARTED from.**

Gen. 31:40 sleep d. f. mine eyes
Num. 14:9 defence is d. f. them
33:3 they d. f. Rameses, 3-49
Deut. 1:19 when we d. f. Horeb
Jud. 16:20 wist not L. was d. f.
1 Sam. 4:21 glory is d. f. Isr. 22
16:14 Spirit d. f. Saul. 18:12
23 the evil spirit d. from him
28:15 God is d. from me
Ps. 18:21 not wicked d. f. my G.
Is. 7:17 Ephraim d. fr. Judah
Dan. 4:31 kingdom is d. f. thee
Hos. 10:5 glory of Sam. d. fr. it
Mat. 28:8 d. quickly f. sepulc.
Luke 4:13 d. f. him for a season
Rev. 18:14 fruits thy soul lusted
after are d. from thee

**DEPARTED not from.**

2 Sam. 22:22 not d. f. my G. Ps.
18:21
2 K. 3:3 he d. not therefrom, 13:2
10:29 d. n. f. sins of Jer. 31:13,
6:11; 14:24; 15:9, 18; 17:22
18:6 H. d. n. f. following Lord
2 Chr. 34:33 they d. n. f. fol. L.
Ps. 119:102 n. d. f. thy judgm.
Luke 2:37 Anna d. not f. temple

**DEPARTED out.**

Jud. 6:21 an. d. o. of his sight
Mal. 2:8 ye are d. o. of the way
Mat. 17:18 rebuked d. and he
d. out

**DEPARTETH.**

Job 27:21 w. car. away and he d.
Prov. 14:16 wise man d. fr. evil
Ec. 6:4 d. in darkness
Is. 59:15 that d. fr. evil, a prey
Jer. 3:20 as a wife treach. d.
17:5 whose heart d. from Lord
Nah. 3:1 the prey d. not
Luke 9:39 bruis. him hardly d.

**DEPARTING.**

Is. 59:13 in d. away from God
Dan. 9:5 d. from thy precepts
Hos. 1:2 whoredom, d. from Lo.
Mark 6:33 people saw them d.
Acts 20:29 aft. my d. sh. wolves
Heb. 3:12 in d. from living God
11:22 mention of the d. of Isra.

**DEPARTURE.**

Ezek. 26:18 be troubled at thy d.
2 Tim. 4:6 time of my d. is at h.

**DEPOSED.**

Dan. 5:20 he was d. from throne

**DEPRIVED.**

Gen. 27:45 d. of both in one day
Job 39:17 God d. her of wisdom
Is. 38:10 d. of residue of years

**DEPTH.**

Job 28:14 d. saith, It is not in me
38:16 or walked in search of d.?
Ps. 33:7 the d. in storehouses
Prov. 8:27 compass on face of d.
25:3 and the earth for d.
Is. 7:11 ask it either in the d.
Jon. 2:5 d. closed me round ab.
Mat. 18:6 drowned in d. of sea
Mark 4:5 no d. of earth wither.
Rom. 8:39 nor d. sep. us fr. love
11:33 O the d. of the riches bot.
Eph. 3:18 d. of the love of Christ

**DEPTHS.**

Ex. 15:5 d. have covered them
8 d. congealed in heart of sea
Deut. 8:7 d. spring out of valleys
Ps. 68:22 br. peo. from d. of sea
71:20 br. me up fr. d. of earth
77:16 the d. were troubled
78:15 drink, as out of great d.
106:9 led them through the d
107:26 they go down again to d.
130:1 out of the d. have I cried
Prov. 3:20 by his knowl. d. bro.
8:24 when no d. I was br. forth
9:18 her guests are in d. of hell
Is. 51:10 made d. of sea a way
Ezek. 27:34 shalt be broken in d
Mic. 7:19 cast sins into d. of sea
Rev. 2:24 not known d. of Satan

**DEPUTED.**

2 Sam. 15:3 no man d. of the ki.

**DEPUTY.**

1 K. 22:47 a d. was king
Acts 13:8 to turn d. fr. the faith
18:12 Gallio was d. of Achaia

**DEPUTIES.**

Acts 19:38 are d. let th. implead

DERBE. Acts 14:6

**DERIDE, ED.**

Hab. 1:10 sh. d. ev. strong-hold
Luke 16:14 the Pharisees d. him
23:35 rulers also with peo. d.

**DERISION.**

Job 30:1 younger, have me in d.
Ps. 2:4 L. shall have them in d.
44:13 a d. to them ab. us, 79:4
59:8 shalt have heathen in d.
119:51 proud have had me in d.
Jer. 20:7 in d. daily; 8 a d. daily
48:26 Moab shall be in d. 39
27 was not Israel a d. to thee
Lam. 3:14 a d. to all my people
Ezek. 23:32 shalt be had in d.
36:4 to cities which bec. a d.
Hos. 7:16 be their d. in Egypt

**DESCEND.**

Ps. 49:17 glory not d. after him
Ezek. 26:20 that d. into pit, 31:16
Mark 15:32 let C. d. from cross
Acts 11:5 I saw a vision, ves. d.
Rom. 10:7 who d. into the deep?
1 Thes. 4:16 L. sh. d. fr. heaven

**DESCENDED.**

Ex. 19:18 L. d. on Sinai in fire
34:5 L. d. in the cloud
Ps. 133:3 as dew that d. on Zion
Prov. 30:4 as. to heaven or d.?
Mat. 7:25 rain d. floods came, 27
28:2 angel of L. d. from heaven
Luke 3:22 H. G. d. in bod. shape
Acts 24:1 Ananias high-priest d.
Eph. 4:10 he that d. is the same

**DESCENDETH, ING.**

Gen. 28:12 the angels of God ascending and d. John 1:51
Mat. 3:16 saw Sp. d. Mark 1:10
John 1:32 Spirit d. like a dove
33 on whom shalt see spirit d.
Acts 10:11 a vessel d. as a sheet
Jam. 3:15 this wisdom d. not
Rev. 21:10 city d. out of heaven

**DESCENT.**

Luke 19:37 d. of mount of Olives
Heb. 7:3 Melchizedek without d.
6 d. is not counted from them

**DESCRIBE, ED, ETH.**

Jos. 18:4 go th. land and d. it
Jud. 8:14 d. to him the princes
Rom. 4:6 as D. d. the blessedn.
10:5 Mos. d. righteousn. of law

**DESERT,** *Wilderness.*

Ex. 5:3 three days jour. into d.
Num. 27:14 rebelled in d. of Zin
Job 24:5 as wild asses in d. go
Ps. 78:40 grieve him in d.
102:6 I am like an owl of d.
106:14 tempted God in the d.
Is. 13:21 wild beasts of d. shall
lie there, 34:14; Jer. 50:39
21:1 so it cometh from the d.

35:1 the *d.* shall rejoice
6 streams in the *d.*
40:3 straight in *d.* a highway
41:19 I will set in *d.* the fir-tree
43:19 make rivers in the *d.* 20
51:3 her *d.* like garden of Lord
*Jer.* 17:6 sh. be like heath in *d.*
25:24 peo. dwell in *d.* sh. drink
50:12 Chaldea shall be a *d.*
*Ezek.* 47:8 these waters go in. *d.*
*Mat.* 24:26 behold, he is in the *d.*
*John* 6:31 did e. manna in the *d.*

**DESERT land.**

*Deut.* 32:10 found him in a *d. l.*

**DESERT place.**

*Mark* 6:31 come ye into a *d. p.*
32 departed into a *d. place*, *Mat.* 14:13; *Luke* 4:42
*Luke* 9:10 aside priv. into a *d. p.*

**DESERTS.**

*Is.* 48:21 he led them through *d.*
*Jer.* 2:6 led us thro. a land of *d.*
*Ezek.* 13:4 proph. like foxes in *d.*
*Luke* 1:80 J. was in the *d.* till
*Heb.* 11:38 they wandered in *d.*

**DESERT, S.**

*Ps.* 28:4 render to them their *d.*
*Ezek.* 7:27 ac. to *d.* will I judge

**DESERVE, ETH, ING.**

*Jud.* 9:16 ac. to *d.* of his hands
*Ezr.* 9:13 less than our iniq. *d.*
*Job* 11:6 less than thy iniq. *d.*

**DESIRABLE.**

*Ezek.* 23:6 *d.* young men, 12, 23

**DESIRE, Substantive.**

*Gen.* 3:16 *d.* shall be to thy hus.
4:7 to thee shall be his *d.*
*Deut.* 18:6 all *d.* of his mind
1 *Sam.* 9:20 on whom *d.* of Isra.
2 *Sam.* 23:5 salva. and all my *d.*
1 *K.* 10:13 queen of S. all her *d.*
2 *Chr.* 15:15 with their whole *d.*
*Job* 14:15 *d.* to work of thy han.
31:16 if withheld poor from *d.*
35 *d.* is Almigh. would answer
34:36 *d.* is Job be tried to end
*Ps.* 10:3 boast. of his heart's *d.*
17 hast heard *d.* of humble
21:2 given him his heart's *d.*
38:9 all my *d.* is before thee
54:7 seen *d.* on enemies, 92:11
59:10 let me see *d.* on enemies
78:29 gave them their own *d.*
92:11 sh. hear my *d.* of wicked
112:8 till he see *d.* on enemies
10 *d.* of wicked shall perish
118:7 shall I see my *d.* on them
145:16 satisfiest *d.* of ev. living
19 fulfil *d.* of them fear him
*Prov.* 10:24 *d.* of righte. be gr.
11:23 *d.* of righte. is only good
13:12 *d.* cometh, a tree of life
19 *d.* accomplished is sweet
19:22 *d.* of a man is his kindn.
21:25 *d.* of slothful killeth him
*Ec.* 6:9 than wandering of *d.*
12:5 and *d.* shall fail, because
*Cant.* 7:10 his *d.* is towards me
*Is.* 26:8 *d.* of soul to thy name
*Jer.* 44:14 ye have a *d.* to return
*Ezek.* 24:16 take *d.* of thine eyes
21 profane *d.* of your eyes, 25
*Dan.* 11:37 nor reg. *d.* of women
*Hos.* 10:10 my *d.* I should chas.
*Mic.* 7:3 uttereth mischievous *d.*
*Hab.* 2:5 enlargeth his *d.* as hell
*Hag.* 2:7 *d.* of all nations shall
*Luke* 22:15 with *d.* I des. to eat
*Rom.* 10:1 my heart's *d.* for Isr.
15:23 having great *d.* to come
2 *Cor.* 7:7 told us your earnest *d.*
11 what vehement *d.* yea, what
*Phil.* 1:23 having a *d.* to depart
1 *Thes.* 2:17 see yo. face with *d.*

**DESIRE, Verb.**

*Ex.* 10:11 for that ye did *d.*
34:24 nor shall any *d.* thy land
*Deut.* 5:21 nor *d.* neighbor's wife
7:25 not *d.* the silver or gold
1 *K.* 2:20 I *d.* one small petition
2 *K.* 4:28 *d.* a son of my lord?
*Neh.* 1:11 *d.* to fear thy name
*Job* 13:3 I *d.* to reason with God
21:14 *d.* not knowl. of thy ways
33:32 for I *d.* to justify thee
36:20 *d.* not the night, when
*Ps.* 40:6 offer. thou didst not *d.*
45:11 greatly *d.* thy beauty
70:2 to confusion *d.* my hurt
73:25 none I *d.* beside thee
*Prov.* 3:15 canst *d.* not to be co.
23:6 neither *d.* his dainty meats
24:1 nor *d.* to be with them
*Is.* 53:2 no beauty we sh. *d.* him
*Jer.* 22:27 land they *d.* to return
*Dan.* 2:18 *d.* mercies of G. of h.
*Amos* 5:18 woe to you *d.* day of
*Mark* 9:35 any *d.* to be first
10:35 for us whatev. we sh. *d.*
11:24 what ye *d.* when ye pray
15:8 *d.* to do as he had done
*Acts* 28:22 *d.* to hear what think.
1 *Cor.* 14:1 *d.* spiritual gifts
2 *Cor.* 11:12 from them *d.* occas.
*Gal.* 4:9 *d.* ag. to be in bondage
20 I *d.* to be present with you
21 ye that *d.* to be under law
6:12 as *d.* to make a fair show
*Eph.* 3:13 I *d.* that ye faint not
*Phil.* 4:17 not because *d.* a gift
1 *Tim.* 3:1 *d.* office of a bishop
*Heb.* 6:11 *d.* ev. one of you do
11:16 they *d.* a better country
*Jam.* 4:2 ye *d.* to have, not obt.
1 *Pet.* 1:12 angels *d.* to look into
2:2 as babes, *d.* the sincere milk
*Rev.* 9:6 men shall *d.* to die, and

**DESIRED.**

*Gen.* 3:6 tree to be *d.* to m. wise
1 *Sam.* 12:13 behold king ye *d.*
1 *K.* 9:19 Solom. *d.* 2 *Chr.* 8:6
*Est.* 2:13 what. she *d.* was giv.
*Job* 20:20 not save of that he *d.*
*Ps.* 19:10 more to be *d.* th. gold
27:4 one thing I *d.* of the Lord
107:30 bringeth to th. *d.* haven
*Ps.* 132:13 *d.* it for his habitation
14 here dwell for I have *d.* it
*Prov.* 8:11 *d.* not to be compared
21:20 there is a treasure to be *d.*
*Ec.* 2:10 what my eyes *d.* I kept
*Is.* 26:9 with my soul I *d.* thee
*Jer.* 17:16 neither *d.* woful day
*Hos.* 6:6 I *d.* mercy, not sacrifice
*Zep.* 2:1 O nation not *d.*
*Mat.* 13:17 righte. have *d.* to see
*Mark* 15:6 one pris. whom th. *d.*
*Luke* 9:9 and he *d.* to see him
10:24 kings have *d.* to see those
22:31 Satan hath *d.* to sift you
*Acts* 12:20 they *d.* peace
13:7 Sergius Paulus *d.* to hear
21 afterward they *d.* a king
28 *d.* Pilate he should be slain
16:39 *d.* to depart out of city
25:3 *d.* favor against Paul
1 *Cor.* 16:12 *d.* him to come
1 *John* 5:15 have petitions we *d.*

**DESIREDST, EST.**

*Deut.* 18:16 acc. to all thou *d.*
*Ps.* 51:6 *d.* truth in inw. parts
16 thou *d.* not sacrifice, else
*Mat.* 18:32 forgave bec. thou *d.*

**DESIRES.**

*Ps.* 37:4 give thee *d.* of thy h.
140:8 grant not *d.* of wicked
*Eph.* 2:3 fulfilling *d.* of the flesh

**DESIRETH.**

1 *Sam.* 20:4 wh. thy soul *d.* will
2 *Sam.* 3:21 reign over all h. *d.*
*Job* 7:2 as a serv. *d.* the shadow
23:13 his soul *d.* that he doeth
*Ps.* 34:12 wh. man is he that *d.*
68:16 hill God *d.* to dwell in
*Prov.* 12:12 wicked *d.* net of evil
13:4 sluggard *d.* and hath not
21:10 soul of wicked *d.* evil
*Ec.* 6:2 nothing of all that he *d.*
*Luke* 5:39 drunk old w. *d.* new
14:32 he *d.* conditions of peace
1 *Tim.* 3:1 bishop, *d.* a good w.

**DESIRING.**

*Mat.* 12:46 *d.* to speak with him
20:20 *d.* a certain thing of him
*Luke* 8:20 breth. *d.* to see thee
2 *Cor.* 5:2 *d.* to be clothed upon
1 *Thes.* 3:6 *d.* greatly to see us
2 *Tim.* 1:4 greatly *d.* to see thee

**DESIROUS.**

*Prov.* 23:3 not *d.* of his dainties
*Luke* 23:8 H. was *d.* to see him
2 *Cor.* 11:32 *d.* to apprehend me
*Gal.* 5:26 not be *d.* of vain-glory
1 *Thes.* 2:8 affectiona. *d.* of you

**DESOLATE.**

2 *Sam.* 13:20 Tamar remained *d.*
*Job* 15:28 dwelleth in *d.* cities
16:7 made *d.* all my company
30:3 wildern. in former times *d.*
38:27 to satisfy the *d.* ground
*Ps.* 25:16 mercy, for I am *d.*
40:15 be *d.* for a reward
69:25 let their habitation be *d.*
143:4 my heart within me is *d.*
*Is.* 1:7 your country is *d.*
3:26 she *d.* shall sit on ground
7:19 shall rest all in *d.* valleys
13:22 beasts sh. cry in *d.* houses
24:6 that dwell therein are *d.*
49:8 to inherit *d.* heritages
21 lost my children, and am *d.*
54:1 chil. of *d.* *Gal.* 4:27
3 *d.* cities to be inhabited
*Jer.* 2:12 be ye very *d.* saith L.
6:8 lest I make thee *d.* a land
9:11 I will make the cities of J. *d.* 10:20; 33:10; 44:6
10:25 made his habitation *d.*
12:11 and being *d.* it mourneth
19:8 this city *d.* and a hissing
32:43 is *d.* without man, 33:12
49:20 their habitations *d.* 50:45
*Lam.* 1:13 *d.* all day, 3:11
16 my children are *d.*
4:5 did feed delicately are *d.*
5:18 mount. of Zion which is *d.*
*Ezek.* 6:6 altars may be made *d.*
19:7 he knew their *d.* palaces
20:26 make them *d.* to the end
35:3 Seir, I will make thee *d.*
15 didst rejoice, bec. it was *d.*
36:3 made you *d.* and swal.
35 *d.* cities are fenced and inh.
36 I the L. plant that was *d.*
*Dan.* 9:17 to shine on sanct. *d.*
11:31 abomi. th. maketh *d.* 12:11
*Hos.* 13:16 Sam. shall become *d.*
*Joel* 1:17 the garners are laid *d.*
18 flocks of sheep are made *d.*
*Mic.* 1:7 id. thereof will I lay *d.*
6:13 making thee *d.* bec. of sins
*Zep.* 3:6 their towers are *d.*
*Mat.* 23:38 is left *d.* *Luke* 13:35
*Acts* 1:20 let his habitation be *d.*
1 *Tim.* 5:5 a wid. indeed, and *d.*
*Rev.* 17:16 and make her *d.*
18:19 in one hour is she made *d.*

**Land DESOLATE.**

*Lev.* 26:34 enjoy sab. as long as it lieth *d.* 35:43; 2 *Chr.* 36:21
*Is.* 6:11 until the *land* be ut. *d.*
13:9 of L. cometh to lay *land d.*
62:4 nor thy *l.* more be term. *d.*
*Jer.* 4:7 gone to make thy *l. d.*
27 Lord said, whole *l.* sh. be *d.*

*Prov.* 1:32 prosp. of fools *d.* th.
11:3 perverseness of transgr. *d.*
15:25 L. will *d.* house of proud
21:7 robberies shall *d.* them
*Ec.* 5:6 *d.* work of thy hands?
7:16 why shouldest *d.* thyself?
*Is.* 3:12 *d.* way of thy paths
11:9 nor *d.* in holy mount. 65:25
13:9 shall *d.* sinners thereof
25:7 *d.* in this mount. the face
*Jer.* 5:10 go upon walls, and *d.*
6:5 by night *d.* her palaces.
12:17 I will *d.* that nation
13:14 I will not spare, but *d.*
15:6 stretch my hand, and *d.*
17:18 *d.* with double destruct.
23:1 pastors that *d.* the sheep
49:9 if thieves, they will *d.*
*Lam.* 3:66 persecute and *d.* them
*Ezek.* 9:8 *d.* all residue of Israel?
*Dan.* 8:25 by peace shall he *d.*
9:26 shall *d.* city and sanctuary
11:26 feed on his meat, *d.* him
*Ob.* 8 *d.* wise men out of Edom?
*Mic.* 2:10 polluted, it shall *d.* you
*Mat.* 12:14 how they might *d.* him, *Mark* 3:6; 11:18
21:41 *d.* those wicked men
27:20 ask Barab. and *d.* Jesus
*Mark* 12:9 *d.* husband. *Lu.* 20:16
*John* 2:19 J. said, *d.* this temple
*Acts* 6:14 this Jesus *d.* this place
1 *Cor.* 6:13 *d.* both it and them
2 *Thes.* 2:8 shall *d.* with brightn.
*Heb.* 2:14 *d.* him had power
1 *John* 3:8 might *d.* works of d.
*Rev.* 11:18 *d.* th. wh. *d.* the earth

**I will, *or* will I DESTROY.**

*Gen.* 6:7 *I will d.* man whom I
*Ex.* 23:27 *I will d.* the people
*Ps.* 101:8 *I will* early *d.* wicked
118:10 in n. of L. *d.* them, 11, 12
*Is.* 19:3 *I will d.* counsel thereof
42:14 *I will d.* and dev. at once
*Jer.* 15:7 *I will d.* my people
*Ezek.* 25:7 *I will d.* thee, 28:16; *Zep.* 2:5
30:13 saith Lord *I will d.* idols
*Amos* 9:8 *I will d.* sinf. kingdom
*Mark* 14:58 *I will d.* this temple
1 *Cor.* 1:19 *I will d.* wisd. of wise

**Not DESTROY.**

*Gen.* 18:31 *not d.* it for 20's sake
*Deut.* 4:31 not fors. thee, *nor d.*
9:26 *d. not* thy people
10:10 Lord would *not d.* thee
1 *Sam.* 24:21 *not d.* my name
2 *K.* 8:19 *n. d.* Jud. for Dav. sake
13:23 would *not d.* them, nor
2 *Chr.* 12:12 *not d.* him. altog.
21:7 *not d.* the house of David
35:21 forbear fr. G. he *d. not*
*Ps.* 106:34 did *not d.* nations
*Is.* 65:8 *d.* it *not*, bless. is in it
*Dan.* 2:24 *d. n.* wise men of Ba.
*Rom.* 14:20 *d. n.* work of God

**To DESTROY.**

*Gen.* 19:13 hath sent us *to d.* it
*Deut.* 9:19 was wroth *to d.* you
28:63 L. will rejoice *to d.* you
1 *Sam.* 26:15 came one *to d.* ki.
2 *Sam.* 1:14 not af. *to d.* anoint.
20:19 *to d.* city and a mother
24:16 hand on Jerusa. *to d.* it
1 *Chr.* 21:15 angel to Jeru. *to d.*
2 *Chr.* 25:16 determin. *to d.* thee
*Est.* 3:6 *to d.* all the Jews, 13; 4:7, 8; 9:24
*Job* 2:3 *to d.* him without cause
6:9 it would p. God *to d.* me
*Ps.* 40:14 seek soul *to d.* it, 63:9
119:95 wicked waited *to d.* me
*Is.* 10:7 it is in his heart *to d.*
13:5 they come from far *to d.*
23:11 Lord given a com. *to d.*
32:7 wicked devices *to d.* poor
51:13 as if oppressor ready *to d.*
54:16 created the waster *to d.*
*Jer.* 1:10 set *to d.* 18:7; 31:28
51:11 device ag. Baby. *to d.* it
*Ezek.* 22:27 *to d.* souls, to get
25:15 despiteful heart *to d.* it
*Dan.* 2:12 *to d.* wise of Bab. 24
7:26 *to d.* his domin. unto end
11:44 go forth with fury *to d.*
*Hos.* 11:9 not return *to d.* Eph
*Zec.* 12:9 seek *to d.* all nations
*Mat.* 2:13 Herod seek child *to d.*
5:17 not come *to d.* but to fulfil
10:28 fear him, able *to d.* both
26:61 I am able *to d.* temple
*Mark* 1:24 art thou come *to d*
*Luke* 6:9 to save life or *d.* it?
9:56 not come *to d.* men's lives
19:47 chief sought *to d.* him
*John* 10:10 thief cometh *to d.*
*Jam.* 4:12 one lawgiver able *to d.*

**DESTROYED.**

*Gen.* 19:29 *d.* cities of plain
*Ex.* 10:7 knowest not E. is *a.*?
*Deut.* 2:21 *d.* them bef. them, 4:3; 11:4; 2 *K.* 21:9; 2 *Chr.* 33:9
9:8 Lord angry to have *d.* you
28:20 until thou be *d.* 24, 45
*Jud.* 20:21 Ben. *d.* that day, 25
2 *Sam.* 21:5 devised we sh. be *d.*
24:16 angel that *d.* 1 *Chr.* 21:15
2 *K.* 10:28 thus Jehu *d.* Baal
2 *Chr.* 14:13 were *d.* before Lord
15:6 nation was *d.* of nation
*Ezr.* 4:15 which cause city *d.*
*Job* 19:10 *d.* me on every side
*Ps.* 9:5 thou hast *d.* the wicked
73:27 *d.* all that go a whoring
137:8 O daugh. Bab. to be *d.*
*Prov.* 13:23 *d.* for want of judg.
*Is.* 14:20 because *d.* thy land
26:14 theref. hast thou *d.* them
*Jer.* 12:10 many pastors have *d.*
48:4 Moab; 51:8 Babylon is *d.*
51:55 hath *d.* out of Babylon the
*Lam.* 2:5 *d.* his strong-holds
*Ezek.* 27:32 like *d.* in the sea
*Hos.* 13:9 O Israel, *d.* thyself
*Amos* 2:9 yet *d.* I the Am. I *d.*
*Mat.* 22:7 he *d.* those murderers
*Luke* 17:27 flood came, and *d.*
*Acts* 9:21 *d.* them that called
13:19 *d.* seven nations in Can.
19:27 her magnificence be *d.*
*Rom.* 6:6 body of sin might be *d.*
1 *Cor.* 10:9 *d.* of serpents
*Gal.* 1:23 preacheth faith he *a.*
2:18 if I build again things I *d.*
*Heb.* 11:28 lest he *d.* first-born
2 *Pet.* 2:12 beasts made to be *d.*
*Jude* 5 *d.* them that believed not

**Are DESTROYED.**

*Job* 4:20 *are d.* from morn. to n
34:25 so that they *are d.*
*Is.* 9:16 they led of them *are d.*
*Jer.* 22:20 for thy lovers *are d.*
*Hos.* 4:6 *a. d.* for lack of knowl.
*Zep.* 3:6 their cities *are d.*

**Not DESTROYED.**

2 *Chr.* 26:10 *d.* th. *n. Ps.* 78:38
*Dan.* 7:14 his kingdom *not* bed.
2 *Cor.* 4:9 cast down, but *not d.*

**Shall be DESTROYED.**

*Gen.* 34:30 I *shall be d.* I and
*Est.* 4:14 father's house *s. be d.*
*Ps.* 37:38 transgressors *sh. be d.*
92:7 they *s. be d.* forever
*Prov.* 13:13 des. word *s. be d.*
20 companion of fools *s. be d.*
29:1 hardeneth his neck *s. be d.*
*Is.* 10:27 yoke *shall be d.* bec.
*Jer.* 48:8 the plain *shall be d.*
*Ezek.* 30:8 her helpers *s. be d.*
*Dan.* 2:44 *sh.* never *be d.* 6:26
11:20 within few days *s. be d.*
*Hos.* 10:8 the sin of Is. *sh. be d.*
*Acts* 3:23 will not hear *s. be d.*
1 *Cor.* 15:26 last ene. that *s. be d.*

**Utterly DESTROYED.**

*Deut.* 4:26 shall be *u. d.*
*Is.* 34:2 L. hath *ut. d.* all nations

**DESTROYER.**

*Ex.* 12:23 *d.* come into houses
*Jud.* 16:24 the *d.* of our country
*Job* 15:21 in prosperity *d.* come
*Ps.* 17:4 kept from paths of *d.*
*Prov.* 28:24 is companion of a *d.*
*Jer.* 4:7 *d.* of Gentiles is
1 *Cor.* 10:10 were destroyed of *d.*

**DESTROYERS.**

*Job* 33:22 life draweth near to *d.*
*Is.* 47:19 thy *d.* go forth of thee
*Jer.* 22:7 prepare *d.* against thee
50:11 O *d.* of my heritage

**DESTROYEST, ETH.**

*Deut.* 8:20 as nat. which L. *d.*
*Job* 9:22 he *d.* perfect and wick.
12:23 incr. nat. and *d.* them
14:19 thou *d.* hope of man
*Prov.* 6:32 doeth it, *d.* own soul
11:9 with mouth *d.* neighbor
31:3 thy ways to that *d.* kings
*Ec.* 7:7 and a gift *d.* the heart
9:18 one sinner *d.* much good
*Jer.* 51:25 O mountain, *d.* earth
*Mat.* 27:40 *d.* temple, *Mark* 15:29

**DESTROYING.**

1 *Chr.* 21:15 as he was *d.* L. rep.
*Is.* 28:2 strong one, as *d.* storm
*Jer.* 2:30 sword like a *d.* lion
51:1 a *d.* wind; 25 O *d.* mount.
*Lam.* 2:8. not withd. hand fr. *d.*
*Ezek.* 9:1 *d.* weapon in his hand
20:17 eye spared from *d.* them

*See* UTTERLY.

**DESTRUCTION.**

*Deut.* 7:23 with a mighty *d.*
32:24 devoured with bitter *d.*
1 *Sam.* 5:9 ag. city with great *d.*
11 was a deadly *d.* thro. city
1 *K.* 20:42 appointed to utter *d.*
2 *Chr.* 22:4 counsellors to his *d*
7 *d.* of Ahaziah was of God
26:16 heart lifted up to his *d.*
*Est.* 8:6 to see *d.* of my kindred
*Job* 5:21 neither be afraid of *d.*
22 *d.* and famine shalt laugh
18:12 *d.* sh. be ready at his side
21:17 how oft cometh *d.*
20 his eyes shall see his *d.*
30 wicked reserved to day of *d.*
26:6 *d.* hath no covering
28:22 *d.* and death say, We
30:12 ag. me ways of their *d.*
24 though they cry in his *d.*
31:3 is not *d.* to the wicked?
12 a fire that consumeth to *d.*
23 *d.* from God terror to me
29 if I rejoiced at the *d.* of him
*Ps.* 35:8 let *d.* come unawares, into that very *d.* let him fall
55:23 shalt bring to pit of *d.*
73:18 castedst th. down into *d.*
88:11 faithfuln. declared in *d.*
90:3 thou turnest man to *d.*
91:6 *d.* that wasteth at noon-d.
103:4 redeemeth thy life fr. *d.*
*Prov.* 1:27 your *d.* as a whirlw.
10:14 mouth of foolish near *d.*
15 *d.* of the poor is poverty
29 *d.* to workers of iniq. 21:15
13:3 wide his lips shall have *d.*
14:28 want of people is *d.* of
15:11 hell and *d.* are bef. Lord
16:18 pride goeth before *d.*
17:19 exalteth gate seeketh *d.*
18:7 a fool's mouth is his *d.*
12 before *d.* heart is haughty

*Prov.* 24:2 for their heart stu. *d.*
27:20 hell and *d.* are never full
31:8 such as are appointed to *d.*
*Is.* 1:28 *d.* of transgr. together
10:25 anger cease in their *d.*
13:6 as *d.* from the Almighty
14:23 Bab. with bosom of *d.*
15:5 shall raise up a cry of *d.*
19:18 shall be called city of *d.*
24:12 gate is smitten with *d.*
49:19 land of thy *d.* too narrow
51:19 desol. and *d.* are come
59:7 wast. and *d.* are in th. paths
60:18 *d.* no more be heard in
*Jer.* 4:6 from north a gr. *d.* 6:1
20 *d.* upon *d.* is cried, for
17:18 dest. th. with double *d.*
46:20 *d.* cometh out of north
48:3 a voice, spoiling and *d.* 5
50:22 sound of gr. *d.* in land
*Lam.* 2:11 *d.* of dau. of my p. 3:48
3:47 and *d.* is come upon us
4:10 in *d.* of daugh of my peo.
*Ezek.* 7:25 *d.* cometh, seek peace
*Hos.* 7:13 *d.* to them, transgr.
9:6 are gone, because of *d.*
13:14 O grave, I will be thy *d.*
*Joel* 1:15 as *d.* from Almighty
*Ob.* 12 neither rej. in their *d.*
*Mic.* 2:10 dest. you with sore *d.*
*Zec.* 14:11 be no more utter *d.*
*Mat.* 7:13 br. is way lead. to *d.*
*Rom.* 3:16 *d.* and mis. in ways
9:22 ves. of wrath fitted to *d.*
1 *Cor.* 5:5 Satan for *d.* of flesh
2 *Cor.* 10:8 not for your *d.* 13:10
*Phil.* 3:19 walk, whose end is *d.*
1 *Thes.* 5:3 then sud. *d.* cometh
2 *Thes.* 1:9 pun. with everlas. *d.*
1 *Tim.* 6:9 drown men in *d.*
2 *Pet.* 2:1 and bring swift *d.*
3:16 unstable wrest to own *d.*

**DESTRUCTIONS.**

*Ps.* 9:6 *d.* come to perp. end
35:17 rescue my soul from *d.*
107:20 delivereth from their *d.*

**DETAIN, ED.**

*Jud.* 13:16 *d.* me I will not eat
1 *Sam.* 21:7 D. was that day *d.*

**DETERMINATE.**

*Acts* 2:23 *d.* counsel of God

**DETERMINATION.**

*Zep.* 3:8 *d.* is to gather nations

**DETERMINED.**

1 *Sam.* 20:7 be sure evil is *d.*
25:17 evil is *d.* ag. our master
2 *Sam.* 13:32 by Absal. been *d.*
2 *Chr.* 25:16 *d.* to destroy thee
*Est.* 7:7 evil *d.* against him
*Job* 14:5 seeing his days are *d.*
*Is.* 19:17 counsel he hath *d.*
*Dan.* 9:24 seventy weeks are *d.*
11:36 that is *d.* shall be done
*Luke* 22:22 goeth, as it was *d.*
*Acts* 3:13 Pil. *d.* to let him go
4:28 what thy counsel *d.* bef.
11:29 ev. man *d.* to send relief
15:2 *d.* Paul and B. to go to Je.
37 Barn. *d.* to take John
17:26 *d.* times to be appointed
19:39 be *d.* in a lawful assembly
25:25 *d.* to send him to August.
1 *Cor.* 2:2 I *d.* not to know sa. J.
2 *Cor.* 2:1 I *d.* this with myself

**DETEST.**

*Deut.* 7:26 thou shalt utterly *d.* it

**DETESTABLE things.**

*Ezek.* 11:18 shall take away *d. t.*
21 heart walk. after their *d. th.*
37:23 no more defile with *d. t.*

**DEVICE.**

2 *Chr.* 2:14 to find out every *d.*
*Est.* 9:25 *d.* return on his head
*Ps.* 21:11 imag. mischievous *d.*
140:8 further not his wicked *d.*
*Ec.* 9:10 no work nor *d.*
*Jer.* 18:11 I devise a *d.* ag. you
51:11 his *d.* is ag. Bab. to dest.
*Lam.* 3:62 their *d.* ag. me all d.
*Acts* 17:29 graven by man's *d.*

**DEVICES.**

*Job* 5:12 disappoint. *d.* of crafty
21:27 *d.* ye wrongfully imagine
*Ps.* 10:2 let them be taken in *d.*
33:10 *d.* of people of none effect
37:7 bringeth wicked *d.* to pass
*Prov.* 1:31 be filled with own *d.*
12:2 of wicked *d.* will he cond.
19:21 many *d.* in a man's heart
*Is.* 32:7 wicked *d.* to dest. poor
*Jer.* 11:19 had devised *d.* ag. me
18:12 walk after our own *d.*
18 let us devise *d.* ag. Jeremi.
*Dan.* 11:24 shall forecast his *d.*
2 *Cor.* 2:11 not ignorant of his *d.*

**DEVIL.**

*Mat.* 4:1 to be tempted of the *d.*
9:32 man poss. with *d.* 12:22
11:18 he hath a *d.* *Luke* 7:33
13:39 that sowed them is the *d.*
15:22 is vexed with a *d.*
17:18 Jesus rebuked the *d.*
25:41 fire, prepared for the *d.*
*Mark* 5:15 poss. with *d.* 16, 18
7:29 *d.* is gone out of thy dau.
*Luke* 4:2 forty days tempt. of *d.*
13 when *d.* had ended tempt.
33 a spirit of an unclean *d.*
35 *d.* had thrown him
8:12 *d.* taketh away the word
29 driven of *d.* into wilderness
9:42 the *d.* threw him down
11:14 when the *d.* was gone out
*John* 6:70 and one of you is a *d.*
7:20 said, Thou hast a *d.* 8:48
8:44 ye are of your father the *d.*
49 I have not a *d.*; 52 hast a *d.*
10:20 many said, He hath a *d.*
21 words of him that hath a *d.*
13:2 *d.* having put into Judas
*Acts* 10:38 heal. all oppr. with *d.*
13:10 thou child of the *d.*
*Eph.* 4:27 neither give pla. to *d.*
6:11 to stand aga. wiles of *d.*
1 *Tim.* 3:6 fall into cond. of *d.*
7 lest he fall into snare of *d.*
2 *Tim.* 2:26 rec. out of sna. of *d.*
*Heb.* 2:14 p. of death, that is *d.*
*Jam.* 4:7 resist *d.* and he will fl.
1 *Pet.* 5:8 your adversary the *d.*
1 *John* 3:8 commit. sin is of *d.*
might destroy works of *d.*
10 children of *d.* are manifest
*Jude* 9 Mich. contend. with *d.*
*Rev.* 2:10 *d.* cast some into pris.
12:9 old serpent called the *d.*
12 *d.* is come down
20:2 old serpent which is the *d.*
10 *d.* that deceived, was c. out

**DEVILISH.**

*Jam.* 3:15 this wisd. earthly, *d.*

**DEVILS.**

*Lev.* 17:7 no more of. sac. to *d.*
*Deut.* 32:17 they sacrified to *d.*
2 *Chr.* 11:15 ordained prie. f. *d.*
*Ps.* 106:37 sacrificed sons to *d.*
*Mat.* 4:24 poss. with *d.* 8:16, 28, 33; *Mark* 1:32; *Luke* 8:36
8:31 the *d.* besought, *Mark* 5:12
*Mark* 9:38 saw one casting out *d.* in thy name, *Luke* 9:49
16:17 in my name cast out *d.*
*Luke* 4:41 *d.* came out of many
8:2 out of whom went seven *d.*
36 by what means he pos. of *d.*
9:1 authority over all *d.*
10:17 even *d.* are subject to us
13:32 tell that fox, I cast out *d.*
1 *Cor.* 10:20 Gent. sacrifice to *d.* I wo. not ye have fel. with *d.*
21 the cup of *d.* of the Lord's table, and of the table of *d.*
1 *Tim.* 4:1 heed to doctr. of *d.*
*Jam.* 2:19 *d.* believe and tremble
*Rev.* 9:20 should not worship *d.*
16:14 the spirits of *d.* working
18:2 become habitation of *d.*

*See* CAST.

**DEVISE.**

2 *Sam.* 14:14 *d.* means that ban.
*Ps.* 35:4 confusion, *d.* my hurt
20 *d.* deceitful matters ag. th.
41:7 ag. me do they *d.* my hurt
*Prov.* 3:29 *d.* not evil ag. neigh.
14:22 that *d.* evil? but mercy and truth be to them *d.* good
16:30 shutteth eyes to *d.* frow.
*Jer.* 18:11 *d.* a device against you
18 let us *d.* devices ag. Jerem.
*Ezek.* 11:2 men that *d.* mischief
*Mic.* 2:1 woe to them *d.* iniquity
3 ag. this fam. do I *d.* an evil

**DEVISED.**

2 *Sam.* 21:5 that *d.* against us
1 *K.* 12:33 month which he *d.*
*Est.* 8:3 device he had *d.* ag. J.
*Ps.* 31:13 *d.* to take my life
*Jer.* 11:19 *d.* devices against me
51:12 *d.* and done, *Lam.* 2:17
2 *Pet.* 1:16 cunningly *d.* fables

**DEVISETH.**

*Ps.* 36:4 *d.* mischief on his bed
52:2 thy tongue *d.* mischiefs
*Prov.* 6:14 *d.* mischief contin.
18 *d.* wicked imaginations
16:9 a man's heart *d.* his way
24:8 *d.* evil be called mischievous
*Is.* 32:7 he *d.* wicked devices to
8 the liberal *d.* liberal things

**DEVOTED.**

*Lev.* 27:28 *d.* thing is most holy
*Num.* 18:14 every thing *d.*
*Ps.* 119:38 whose is *d.* to thy fear

**DEVOTIONS.**

*Acts* 17:23 as I beheld your *d.*

**DEVOUR.**

*Gen.* 49:27 in morning *d.* prey
*Deut.* 32:42 sword shall *d.* flesh
2 *Sam.* 2:26 sh. sw. *d.* for ever?
*Job* 18:13 first-born of death *d.*
*Ps.* 80:13 wild beast doth *d.* it
*Is.* 1:7 land, strangers *d.* it
9:12 *d.* Israel with open mouth
18 wickedness sh. *d.* briers
31:8 sword, not of mean man *d.*
42:14 destroy and *d.* at once
56:9 ye beasts of the field, come to *d.* *Jer.* 12:9; 15:3
*Jer.* 2:3 all *d.* Israel shall offend
12:12 sw. of L. shall *d.* 46:10, 14
30:16 all that *d.* thee be dev.
*Ezek.* 36:14 shalt *d.* men no mo.
*Dan.* 7:5 *d.* much flesh
23 *d.* the whole earth
*Hos.* 5:7 month *d.* with portions
13:8 will I *d.* them like a lion
*Amos* 1:4 fire *d.* palaces, 7, 10, 12
*Ob.* 18 kindle in them, and *d.*
*Nah.* 2:13 sw. *d.* the young lions
*Hab.* 3:14 rejoic. to *d.* the poor
*Zec.* 12:6 *d.* all people
*Mat.* 23:14 ye *d.* widows' houses, *Mark* 12:40; *Luke* 20:47
2 *Cor.* 11:20 if a man *d.* you
*Gal.* 5:15 if bite and *d.* one ano.
*Heb.* 10:27 shall *d.* adversaries
1 *Pet.* 5:8 seeking wh. he may *d.*
*Rev.* 12:4 to *d.* her child as soon

**Fire DEVOUR.**

*Jud.* 9:15 let *fire d.* the cedars
20 let *fire d.* the men of Shec.

Ps. 21:9 the fire shall d. them
50:8 a fire shall d. before him
Is. 26:11 f. of enemies d. them
33:11 your breath as fire d. you
Ezek. 15:7 another fire d. them
23:37 through the fire to d.
Amos 5:6 break out like f. d. it
Nah. 3:13 fire shall d. thy bars
Zec. 11:1 fire may d. thy cedars

**It shall DEVOUR.**

Job 18:13 i. s. d. strength of skin
Is. 10:17 it shall d. his thorns
Jer. 5:14 fire, it s. d. them
17:27 and it shall d. the palaces of Jerusalem, Amos 2:5
Hos. 8:14 it s. d. Amos 1:14; 2:2

**DEVOURED.**

Gen. 37:20 some evil beast d. h.
Lev. 10:2 fire from Lord d. them
Num. 26:10 fire d. 250 men
Deut. 31:17 hide face shall be d.
32:24 be d. with burning heat
2 Sam. 18:8 wood d. more than
22:9 his mouth d. Ps. 18:8
Ps. 79:7 for they have d. Jacob
Is. 1:20 be d. with the sword
24:6 therefore curse d. earth
Jer. 2:30 your sword d. prophets
3:24 shame hath d. the labor
8:16 and have d. the land
10:25 eaten up Jacob, d. him
30:16 devour thee shall be d.
50:7 all that found d. them
17 the king of Assyr. hath d.
51:34 Nebuchadrezzar d. me
Lam. 4:11 hath d. found. thereof
Ezek. 15:5 when fire hath d. it
16:20 sacrificed sons to be d.
19:3 to catch prey, it d. men, 6
14 fire hath d. her fruit
22:25 a roaring lion, d. souls
23:25 the residue be d. by fire
33:27 I will give to be d. 39:4
Dan. 7:7 it d. and brake, 19
Hos. 7:7 have d. their judges
9 strangers have d. his streng.
Joel 1:19 fire d. pastures, 20
Amos 4:9 palmer worm d. trees
7:4 and it d. the great deep
Nah. 1:10 shall be d. as stubble
Zep. 1:18 be d. by jealousy
3:8 earth shall be d. with fire
Zec. 9:4 shall be d. with fire
Mat. 13:4 fowls came d. them, Mark 4:4; Luke 8:5
Luke 15:30 thy son d. living
Rev. 20:9 fire came and d. them

**DEVOURER.**

Mal. 3:11 I will rebuke the d.

**DEVOUREST, ETH.**

Ezek. 36:13 thou land d. up men
2 Sam. 11:25 sword d. one
Prov. 19:28 wicked d. iniquity
Prov. 20:25 a snare to man d.
Is. 5:24 fire d. stubble, Joel 2:5
Lam. 2:3 flaming fire, which d.
Ezek. 15:4 fire d. both ends of it
Joel 2:3 a fire d. before them
Hab. 1:13 wicked d. more right
Rev. 11:5 fire d. their enemies

**DEVOURING.**

Ex. 24:17 appearance d. fire
Ps. 52:4 lovest all d. words
Is. 29:6 visit. with d. fire, 30:30
30:27 his tongue as a d. fire
33:14 who dwell with d. fire?

**DEVOUT.**

Luke 2:25 Sim. was just and d.
Acts 2:5 at Jerusal. Jews d. men
8:2 d. men car. Steph, to burial
10:2 Cornelius; 7 d. soldier
13:50 Jews stirred up d. women
17:4 of d. Greeks a great mult.
17 P. disputed with d. persons
22:12 Ananias a d. man

**DEW.**

Gen. 27:28 G. give thee of the d.
Ex. 16:13 morning the d. lay
Num. 11:9 when d. fell on camp
Deut. 32:2 my speech distil as d.
33:13 blessed is J.'s land for d.
28 his heavens shall drop d.
Jud. 6:37 if d. on fleece only
39 on ground let there be d.
2 Sam. 1:21 be no d. upon you
17:12 light on him as d. falleth
1 K. 17:1 there shall not be d.
Job 29:19 d. lay on my branch
38:28 hath begot drops of d.?
Ps. 110:3 hast d. of thy youth
133:3 as the d. of Hermon
Prov. 3:20 clouds drop down d.
19:12 but his favor is as d.
Cant. 5:2 head is filled with d.
Is. 18:4 cloud of d. in harvest
26:19 thy d. as d. of herbs
Dan. 4:33 body wet with d. 5:21
Hos. 6:4 early d. it goeth, 13:3
14:5 I will be as the d. to Israel
Mic. 5:7 Jacob shall be as the d.
Hag. 1:10 heaven stayed from d.
Zec. 8:12 heavens give their d.

**DIADEM.**

Job 29:14 my judgment as a d.
Is. 28:5 and for a d. of beauty
62:3 a royal d. in hand of God
Ezek. 21:26 remove the d.

**DIAL.**

2 K. 20:11 down in the d. Is. 38:8

**DIAMOND.**

Ex. 28:18 second row a d. 39:11
Jer. 17:1 sin is written with a d.

DIANA. Acts 19:24, 35

DIBON. Num. 21:30; Jos. 13:17; Neh. 11:25; Is. 15:2; Jer. 48:18, 22

DIBON-GAD. Num. 33:45, 46

**DID.**

Neh. 2:16 knew not what I d.
Mat. 12:3 read what David d.?
21:15 wond. things that he d.
Mark 3:8 great things he d.
John 4:29 told me all ever I d. 39
9:26 said, What d. he to thee?
15:24 works none other man d.
Acts 3:17 ye d. it as d. rulers
26:10 which thing I d. in Jerus.
2 Cor. 8:5 d. not as we hoped
1 Pet. 2:22 who d. no sin, nor

**DID, joined with as.**

Ex. 7:6 d. as L. com. 10, 20; 12:28, 50; 39:32; Lev. 8:4; 16:34; 24:23; Num. 1:54; 2:34; 20:27; 27:22; 31:31
Jud. 15:11 as they d. to me
2 Sam. 3:36 as what king d.
5:25 David d. as L. commanded
2 K. 17:41 as d. fathers, so do
1 Chr. 14:16 David d. as G. com.
Mat. 21:6 d. as Jesus com. 26:19
28:15 so watch d. as taught
Luke 9:54 con. them as Elias d.
Acts 3:17 ignor. as d. your rulers
7:51 as your fathers d. so do ye
Heb. 4:10 ceased, as God d.

**DID, joined with evil.**

Gen. 50:15 he req. us evil we d.
Jud. 2:11 d. evil in sight of L. 3:7, 12; 4:1; 6:1; 10:6; 13:1; 1 K. 14:22; 15:26, 34; 16:7, 30; 2 K. 8:27; 13:2, 11; 14:24; 15:9, 18, 24, 28; 17:2; 2 Chr. 22:4
1 K. 11:6 Solomon d. evil
2 K. 21:2 Manasseh, 2 Chr. 33:2
23:32 Jehoahaz; 37 Jehoiakim
24:9 Jehoiachin; 19 Zedekiah
2 Chr. 12:14 Rehob.; 33:22 Amon
Neh. 9:28 had rest, they d. evil
Is. 65:12 d. evil bef. m. eyes, 66:4
2 Tim. 4:14 Alex. d. me much e.

**DID not.**

2 K. 16:2 Ahaz d. not right
Jer. 11:8 but they d. them not
Mat. 13:58 he d. not many works
25:45 d. it not to one of these
John 8:40 this d. not Abraham
2 Cor. 7:12 I d. it not for his cau.

**Thus DID.**

Job 1:5 thus d. Job continually

**DIDST.**

2 Sam. 12:12 thou d. it secretly
Ps. 39:9 dumb, because thou d.
44:1 work thou d. in their days
Is. 64:3 d. terrible things

**DIDYMUS.**

John 11:16 T. cal. D. 20:24; 21:2

**DIE.**

See on DEAD and DEATH.
Gen. 6:17 every thing shall d.
44:22 his father would d.
46:30 now let me d.
47:29 that Israel must d.
Ex. 9:4 nothing d. of Israel's
10:28 seest my face, shalt d.
11:5 first-born in Egypt shall d.
Num. 14:35 in wilder. they sh. d.
16:29 if these d. common death
20:26 and Aaron shall d. there
23:10 let me d. death of right.
Deut. 25:5 if one d. and have no children, Mark 12:19
31:14 days approach th. must d.
32:50 and d. in the mount
Jud. 16:30 let me d. with Phil.
1 Sam. 2:33 increase of house d.
34 sons in one day shall d.
14:45 said, Shall Jonathan d.
2 Sam. 18:3 nor if half of us d.
1 K. 14:12 feet enter child sha. d.
2 K. 20:1 shalt d. and not live
2 Chr. 25:4 every man shall d. for his own sin, Jer. 31:30
Job 2:9 said, Curse God and d.
4:21 they d. without wisdom
12:2 wisdom shall d. with you
14:8 and the stock thereof d.
14 if man d. shall he live ag.
34:20 in a moment shall they d.
36:12 shall d. without knowl.
14 they d. in youth, their life
Ps. 49:10 seeth that wise men d.
104:29 aw. their breath, they d.
Prov. 10:21 fools d. for want of
Ec. 7:17 d. before thy time
9:5 living know they shall d.
Is. 22:18 large country, there d.
51:6 that dwell therein shall d.
12 afraid of a man that shall d.
65:20 child shall d. 100 years old
Jer. 11:22 you. man shall d. by sw. sons and dau. by famine
16:4 shall d. of grievous deaths
6 great and the small shall d.
28:16 this year thou shalt d.
34:5 but thou shalt d. in peace
Ezek. 18:4 soul sin. shall d. 20
28:8 d. deaths of them slain
33:8 that wicked man shall d.
27 in caves d. of the pestilence
Amos 2:2 Moab shall d.
6:9 they shall d.
7:17 shalt d. in a polluted land
9:10 sinners of my people d.
Zec. 11:9 that dieth, let it d.
13:8 two parts be cut off and d.
Mat. 15:4 curs. father or mother let him d. Mark 7:10
22:24 d. hav. no s. Luke 20:28
Luke 20:36 nei. can d. any more
John 4:49 come ere my child d.
11:50 one d. for the peo. 18:14
51 J. should d. for that nation
12:24 except a corn of wheat d.
Rom. 5:7 for a r. man will one d.
1 Cor. 15:22 as in Adam all d.
36 not quickened except it d.

*Heb.* 7:8 that *d.* receive tithes
*Rev.* 14:13 blessed that *d.* in L.

**He DIE.**

*Gen.* 38:11 lest *he d.* as bre. did
*Num.* 35:16 if he smite him that *he d.* 20, 21, 23; *Deut.* 13:10; 19:5, 11; 21:21
*Deut.* 20:5 lest *he d.* in battle
*Jud.* 6:30 bring son, that *he d.*
2 *Sam.* 11:15 that Uriah may *d.*
1 *K.* 1:52 if wick. in him *he* sh. *d.*
2:1 David, that *he* should *d.*
19:4 E. requested he might *d.*
*Ps.* 41:5 when shall *he d.* and
*Prov.* 5:23 *he d.* without instruc.
15:10 *he* that hateth rep. shall *d.*
*Prov.* 19:16 *he* de. his ways sh. *d.*
*Jer.* 22:12 *he d.* whither led cap.
38:10 take up Jer. before *he d.*
*Ezek.* 3:19 *he* shall *d.* in his iniq. 18:18; 33:9, 13, 18
12:13 not see it, though *he d.*
17:16 in Babylon *he* shall *d.*
*John* 12:33 death *he* sh. *d.* 18:32

**I DIE.**

*Gen.* 26:9 Lest *I d.* for her
27:4 may bless thee before *I d.*
30:1 give me children or *I d.*
45:28 see him before *I d.*
48:21 Israel said to Joseph, *I d.*
50:5 lo, *I d.*; 24 Jos. said, *I d.*
*Deut.* 4:22 *I* must *d.* in this land
*Jud.* 15:18 shall *I d.* for thirst
*Ruth* 1:17 where diest will *I d.*
1 *Sam.* 14:43 and lo, *I* must *d.*
2 *Sam.* 19:37 *I d.* in m. own city
1 *K.* 2:30 nay, *I* will *d.* here
*Job* 27:5 justify you; till *I d.*
29:18 *I* shall *d.* in my nest
*Prov.* 30:7 deny me not bef. *I d.*
*Jer.* 37:20 not return, lest *I d.*
*Mat.* 26:35 *I* sh. *d.* *Mark* 14:31
1 *Cor.* 15:31 *I d.* daily

**Not DIE.**

*Gen.* 42:20 be verified *not d.*
*Deut.* 18:16 see fire, that I *d. not*
33:6 let Reuben live and *not d.*
*Jud.* 6:23 shalt *not d.* 1 *Sam.* 20:2; 2 *Sa.* 12:13; 19:23; *Jer.* 38:24
1 *Sam* 12:19 pray that we *d. not*
20:14 kind. of Lord that I *d. not*
2 *K.* 18:32 ye may live and *not d.*
2 *Chr.* 25:4 fath. *n. d.* for child.
*Ps.* 118:17 I shall *n. d.* but live
*Prov.* 23:13 shall *n. d.* *Ezek.* 18:17, 21, 28; 33:15; *John* 21:23
*Is.* 51:14 he should *not d.*
66:24 their worm shall *not d.*
*Jer.* 11:21 *d. not* by our hand
34:4 shalt *not d.* by the sword
*Ezek.* 13:19 souls should *not d.*
*Hab.* 1:12 we shall *not d.* Lord
*John* 6:50 eat thereof and *not d.*
21:23 that disciple should *not d.*

**Surely DIE.**

*Gen.* 2:17 *s. d.* 20:7; 1 *Sam.* 14:44; 22:16; 1 *K.* 2:37, 42; *Jer.* 26:8; *Ezek.* 3:18; 33:8, 14
3:4 ye shall not *surely d.*
*Num.* 26:65 they shall *surely d.*
*Jud.* 13:22 *s. d.* bec. we ha. seen
1 *Sam.* 14:39 he shall *s. d.* 20:31; 2 *Sam.* 12:5; 2 *K.* 8:10; *Ezek.* 18:13
2 *Sam.* 12:14 child born shall *s. d.*
2 *K.* 1:4 but shalt *surely d.* 6, 16

**To DIE.**

*Gen.* 25:32 I am at point *to d.*
*Ex.* 14:11 *to d.* in wil. *Num.* 21:5
*Num.* 35:30 test. to cau. him *to d.*
1 *Sam.* 26:10 or his day co. *to d.*
28:9 a snare to cause me *to d.*
2 *Chr.* 32:11 give yoursel. *to d.*
*Ps.* 79:11 that are appointed *to d.*
88:15 and ready *to d.* from youth
*Ec.* 3:2 born, and a time *to d.*
*Jer.* 26:11 worthy *to d.*; 16 not
38:9 he is like *to d.* for hunger
26 to Jonathan's house *to d*
*Jon.* 4:3 better for me *to d.*
8 Jonah wished in himself *to d.*
*Luke* 7:2 centu. serv. ready *to d.*
*John* 19:7 by law he ought *to d.*
*Acts* 21:13 I am ready also *to d.*
25:11 I refuse not *to d.*
16 of Romans to del. any *to d.*
*Rom.* 5:7 some would dare *to d.*
1 *Cor.* 9:15 better for me *to d.*
2 *Cor.* 7:3 in our hearts *to d.*
*Phil.* 1:21 to live is C *to d.* is
*Heb.* 9:27 app. to men once *to d.*
*Rev.* 3:2 that are ready *to d.*
9:6 desire *to d.* and death flee

**We DIE.**

*Gen.* 47:15 *we d.* in thy pres. 19
*Ex.* 14:12 than *we* sh. *d.* in wil.
20:19 speak lest *we d.* *Deut.* 5:25
*Num.* 17:12 *we d.* we all perish
20:4 that *we* and cattle *d.* there
1 *Sam.* 12:19 pray that *we d.* not
2 *Sam.* 14:14 for *we* must needs *d.*
1 *K.* 17:12 *we* may eat it and *d.*
2 *K.* 7:3 why sit here till *we d.?*
4 if kill us, *we* shall but *d.*
*Is.* 22:13 for to-morrow *we* sh. *d.* 1 *Cor.* 15:32
*John* 11:16 *we* may *d.* with him
*Rom.* 14:8 *we d.* *we d.* unto the L.

**Ye DIE.**

*Gen.* 3:3 nor touch it lest *ye d.*
*Ps.* 82:7 *ye* shall *d.* like men
*Is.* 22:14 not be purged till *ye d.*
*Jer.* 22:26 there shall *ye d.* 42:16
27:13 why will *ye d.* *Ezek.* 18:31; 33:11
42:22 *ye* shall *d.* by the sword
*John* 8:21 *ye* sh. *d.* in yo. sins, 24
*Rom.* 8:13 if live after flesh *ye d.*

**DIED.**

*Gen.* 7:21 all flesh *d.* 22
23:2 Sarah *d.*; 25:8 Abraham
25:17 Ishmael; 35:8 Deborah
35:18 Rachel, 48:7; 35:29 Isaac
50:16 Jacob; 26 Jos. *Ex.* 1:6
*Ex.* 2:23 the king of Egypt *d.*
16:3 would to God we had *d.* in Eg. *Num.* 14:2; 20:3; 26:10
*Lev.* 10:2 Nad. and Ab. *d.* 16:1; *Num.* 3:4; 26:61; 1 *Chr.* 24:2
*Num.* 14:37 searchers of land *d.*
20:28 Aaron *d.* 33:38, 39
16:49 now they that *d.* besides
20:1 Miriam; 21:6 much peo.
25:9 *d.* in the plague were 24,000
26:11 children of Korah *d.* not
27:3 our father *d.* in the wilderness but *d.* in his own sin
*Deut.* 34:5 Moses *d.*
*Jos.* 5:4 all the men of war *d.*
24:29 Joshua *d.* *Jud.* 2:8
1 *Sam.* 25:1 Sam.; 37 Nab. heart
31:5 Saul and his armor-bearer *d.* 6; 1 *Chr.* 10:5, 13
2 *Sam.* 3:33 *d.* Abner as a fool
6:7 there Uzzah *d.* 1 *Chr.* 13:10
11:17 Uriah the Hittite *d.*
12:18 on seventh day child *d.*
18:33 I had *d.* for thee, O Ab.
19:6 and all we had *d.* this day
24:15 *d.* of peo. even from Dan
1 *K.* 3:19 this woman's child *d.*
14:17 came to threshold, child *d.*
2 *K.* 4:20 sat on her knees, *d.*
13:14 Elisha. 20; 24 Haz el
2 *Chr.* 24:22 he *d.* said, L. look
*Job* 3:11 why *d.* I not fr. womb?
42:17 so Job *d.* being old
*Is.* 6:1 Uzziah *d.*; 14:28 Ahaz *d.*
*Ezek.* 24:18 at even my wife *d.*
*Hos.* 13:1 offended in Baal, he *d.*
*Mat.* 22:27 last of all woman *d.* *Mark* 12:22; *Luke* 20:32
*Luke* 16:22 beggar *d.* rich man *d.*
*John* 11:21 my bro. had not *d.* 32
37 even this man sh. not ha. *d.*
*Acts* 9:37 Dorcas was sick and *d.*
*Rom.* 5:6 in due time Christ *d.* 8
7:9 sin revived and I *d.*
8:34 it is Christ that *d.*
14:9 to this end Christ both *d.*
15 for whom C. *d.* 1 *Cor.* 8:11
1 *Cor.* 15:3 how C. *d.* for our sins
2 *Cor.* 5:14 if one *d.* for all, then
15 live to him who *d.* for them
1 *Thes.* 4:14 if we believe Jesus *d.*
5:10 *d.* for us, that we sho. live
*Heb.* 10:28 desp. Moses' law *d.*
11:13 these all *d.* in faith, not
22 by faith Joseph when he *d.*
*Rev.* 8:9 the third part *d.*
11 many men *d.* of wa. bitter
16:3 every living soul *d.* in sea

**And he, So he, That he DIED.**

*Gen.* 5:5 *and* Adam *d.*
*Jud.* 4:21 nail into tem. *so he d.*
1 *Sam.* 4:18 E. neck bra. *a. he d.*
14:45 rescued Jon. *th. he d.* not
2 *Sam.* 11:21 sm. Abim. *th. he d.*
2 *K.* 1:17 Ahaziah *d.* according
8:15 cl. on his face, *so th. he d.*
2 *Chr.* 13:20 struck him, *a. he d.*
*Luke* 20:29 *a. he d.* without chil.
*Acts* 7:15 *he d.* in Egypt, he and
*Rom.* 6:10 in *th. he d.* *he d.* to
2 *Cor.* 5:15 *t. he d.* for all, th. they

**DIEST.**

*Ruth* 1:17 wh. thou *d.* I will die

**DIET.**

*Jer.* 52:34 for his *d.* continual *d.*

**DIETH.**

*Lev.* 22:8 wh. *d.* of itself, not eat
2 *Sam.* 3:33 died A. as a fool *d.*
1 *K.* 14:11 him *d.* in city dogs eat
16:4 *d.* in field fowls eat, 21:24
*Job* 14:10 man *d.* wasteth away
21:23 one *d.* in his full strength
25 *d.* in bitterness of soul
*Ps.* 49:17 when he *d.* carry noth.
*Prov.* 11:7 wicked *d.* his expect.
*Ec.* 2:16 how *d.* the wise man?
3:19 as one *d.* so *d.* the other
*Is.* 50:2 their fish *d.* for thirst
59:5 that eateth of their eggs *d.*
*Ezek.* 18:26 iniquity, *d.* in them
32 no pleas. in death of him *d.*
*Zec.* 11:9 that that *d.* let it die
*Mark* 9:44 worm *d.* not, 46, 48
*Rom.* 6:9 Christ *d.* no more
14:7 no man *d.* to himself

**DYING.**

*Num.* 17:13 be consumed wi. *d.?*
*Mark* 12:20 first *d.* left no seed
*Luke* 8:42 Jairus' dau. lay a *d.*
2 *Cor.* 4:10 in body the *d.* of Jesus
6:9 as *d.* and behold we live
*Heb.* 11:21 by faith Jac. when *d.*

**DIFFER.**

1 *Cor.* 4:7 who maketh thee to *d.*

**DIFFERENCE, S.**

*Ex.* 11:7 L. put *d.* b. Eg. and Is.
*Lev.* 10:10 *d.* bet. holy and unh.
*Ezek.* 22:26 they have put no *d.*
44:23 teach my people the *d.*
*Acts* 15:9 no *d.* bet. us and them
*Rom.* 3:22 that believe, for no *d.*
10:12 no *d.* bet. Jew and Greek
1 *Cor.* 12:5 *d.* of administrations
*Jude* 22 compassion, making a *d.*

**DIFFERETH, ING.**

*Rom.* 12:6 gifts *d.* acc. to grace
1 *Cor.* 15:41 one star *d.* from ano.
*Gal.* 4:1 the heir when a child *d.*

**DIG.**
Job 3:21 d. for it more than for
6:27 ye d. a pit for your friend
11:18 thou shalt d. about thee
24:16 in dark d. thro' houses
Ezek. 8:8 d. now in the wall
12:5 d. thro' wall in their sight
Amos 9:2 tho' they d. into hell
Luke 13:8 let it alone till I d.
16:3 I cannot d.

**DIGGED.**
Gen. 49:6 in self-will d. down
50:5 my grave I have d. for me
Num. 21:18 princes d. the well
Deut. 6:11 wells d. diggedst not
2 K. 19:24 I have d. and drunk strange waters, Is. 37:25
Ps. 7:15 a pit and d. it, 57:6
35:7 they d. a pit for my soul
94:13 till pit be d. for wicked
119:85 proud d. pits for me
Is. 5:6 not be pruned nor d.
7:25 on hills d. with mattock
51:1 hole of pit whence ye are d
Jer. 18:20 d. pit for my soul, 22
Mat. 21:33 d. a wine-press in it
25:18 d. and hid lord's money
Luke 6:48 d. and laid foundation
Rom. 11:3 d. down thine altars

**DIGGETH.**
Prov. 16:27 ungodly d. up evil
26:27 d. pit shall fall, Ec. 10:8

**DIGNITY, IES.**
Gen. 49:3 Reu. excellency of d.
Est. 6:3 what d. to Mordecai
Ec. 10:6 folly is set in great d.
Hab. 1:7 d. proceed of themsel.
2 Pet. 2:10 sp. evil of d. Jude 8

**DILIGENCE.**
Prov. 4:23 keep heart with all d.
Luke 12:58 art in way, give d.
Rom. 12:8 that ruleth, with d.
2 Cor. 8:7 as ye abound in all d.
2 Tim. 4:9 do thy d. to come, 21
Heb. 6:11 ev. one do sh. same d.
2 Pet. 1:5 giv. all d. add to faith
10 d. to make calling sure
Jude 3 I gave all d. to write

**DILIGENT.**
Deut. 19:18 make d. inquisition
Jos. 22:5 take d. heed to do com.
Ps. 64:6 accomplish a d. search
77:6 my spirit made d. search
Prov. 10:4 hand of d. mak. rich
12:24 hand of d. shall bear rule
27 substance of d. is precious
13:4 soul of d. sh. be made fat
21:5 thoughts of d. tend to pl.
22:29 seest a man d. in busi.
27:23 be d. to know state of fl.
2 Cor. 8:22 whom we have often proved d. how much more d.
2 Pet. 3:14 d. ye be fou. in peace

**DILIGENTLY.**
Ex. 15:26 if wilt d. heark. Deut. 11:13; 28:1; Jer. 17:24
Deut. 4:9 and keep thy soul d.
6:7 teach them d. to thy child.
17 d. keep commandm. 11:22
13:14 ask d. and if it be truth
Ezr. 7:23 d. done for house of G.
Job 13:17 hear d. my sp. 21:2
Ps. 37:10 d. consider his place
119:4 to keep thy precepts d.
Prov. 7:15 d. to seek thy face
11:27 he that d. seeketh good
23:1 consider d. what is before
Is. 21:7 he hearkened d.
55:2 hearken d. to me, and eat
Jer. 2:10 consider d. see if
12:16 d. learn ways of my peo.
Zec. 6:15 if d. obey voice of L.
Mat. 2:8 search d. for yo. child
16 d. inquired of the wise men
Luke 15:8 seek d. till she find it
Acts 18:25 taught d. things of L.
1 Tim. 5:10 she followed d. every
2 Tim. 1:17 in Ro. sought me d.
Heb. 11:6 rew. of them d. seek
12:15 looking d. lest any fail
1 Pet. 1:10 prophets searched d.

**DIM.**
Gen. 27:1 Is. was old, his eyes d.
48:10 the eyes of Israel were d.
Deut. 34:7 Moses' eye was not d.
1 Sam. 3:2 Eli's eyes wax d. 4:15
Job 17:7 mine eye is d. by sorrow
Is. 32:3 that see, shall not be d.
Lam. 4:1 how is gold become d.
5:17 these things our eyes d.

**DIMINISH, ED, ING.**
Ex. 5:8 you shall not d. aught
Lev. 25:16 acc. to years shalt d.
Deut. 4:2 nor d. aught, 12:32
Prov. 13:11 w. got. by vanity d.
Is. 21:17 men of Kedar sh. be d.
Jer. 26:2 I com. d. not a word
29:6 may be inc. and not d.
Ezek. 5:11 therefore also d. thee
16:27 I have d. thine ordi. food
29:15 I will d. them
Rom. 11:12 d. of them the riches

**DIMNESS.**
Is. 8:22 behold, d. of anguish
9:1 d. not be such as in her

DIMON. Is. 15:9
DINAH. Gen. 30:21; 34:5

**DINE, D.**
Gen. 43:16 d. with me at noon
Luke 11:37 Pha. bes. him to d.
John 21:12 J. saith, Come and d.
15 had d. Jesus saith to Simon

**DINNER.**
Prov. 15:17 better is a d. of herbs
Mat. 22:4 I have prepared my d.
Luke 11:38 not washed before d.
14:12 when thou makest a d.

DIONYSIUS. Acts 17:34
DIOTREPHES. 3 John 9

**DIP.**
Deut. 33:24 Asher d. foot in oil
Ruth 2:14 d. morsel in vinegar
Luke 16:24 that he may d. finger

**DIPPED, ETH.**
Gen. 37:31 d. coat in the blood
Lev. 9:9 and he d. finger in bl.
Jos. 3:15 priest's feet d. in brim
1 Sam. 14:27 d. rod in honey-co.
2 K. 5:14 Naaman d. in Jordan
Ps. 68:23 thy foot be d. in blood
Mat. 26:23 d. wi. me, Mark 14:20
John 13:26 have d. it, when he d.
Rev. 19:13 with vesture d. in bl.

**DIRECT.**
Gen. 46:28 d. his face to Goshen
Ps. 5:3 morning d. my prayer
Prov. 3:6 he shall d. thy paths
11:5 righte. of the perf. shall d.
Ec. 10:10 wisd. is profitable to d.
Is. 45:13 I will d. all his ways
61:8 d. their work in truth
Jer. 10:23 to d. his steps
1 Thes. 3:11 J. C. d. our way to
2 Thes. 3:5 L. d. hearts into love

**DIRECTED, ETH.**
Job 32:14 not d. his words aga.
37:3 d. it under whole heaven
Ps. 119:5 ways were d. to keep
Prov. 16:9 the Lord d. his steps
21:29 upright, he d. his way
Is. 40:13 who hath d. the Spirit

**DIRT.**
Jud. 3:22 and the d. came out
Ps. 18:42 I cast them out as d.
Is. 57:20 whose waters cast up d.

**DISALLOW, ED.**
Num. 30:5 father d. her not, 8, 11
1 Pet. 2:4 d. indeed of men, but
7 stone builders d. is made h.

**DISANNUL.**
Job 40:8 wilt thou d. my judg.?
Is. 14:27 L. purposed, who d. it?
Gal. 3:17 coven. law cannot d.

**DISANNULLED, ETH, ING.**
Is. 28:18 coven. with death be d.
Gal. 3:15 no man d. or addeth
Heb. 7:18 there is a d. of com.

**DISAPPOINT, ED, ETH.**
Job 5:12 d. devices of crafty
Ps. 17:13 arise, O Lord, d. him
Prov. 15:22 purposes are d.

**DISCERN.**
Gen. 31:32 d. thou what is thine
2 Sam. 14:17 so is my Lord to d.
19:35 can I d. bet. good and ev.?
1 K. 3:9 I may d. betw. good
11 asked unders. to d. judg.
Ezr. 3:13 not d. noise of joy
Job 4:16 not d. form thereof
6:30 taste d. perverse things?
Ezek. 44:23 cause d. bet. uncl.
Jon. 4:11 d. bet. right and left
Mal. 3:18 d. bet. right. and wick.
Mat. 16:3 can d. sky, Luke 12:56
Heb. 5:14 senses exer. to d. good

**DISCERNED, ETH.**
1 K. 20:41 king of Israel d. him
Prov. 7:7 I d. among the youths
Ec. 8:5 wise d. time and judg.
1 Cor. 2:14 because spiritually d.

**DISCERNER.**
Heb. 4:12 is a d. of the thoughts

**DISCERNING.**
1 Cor. 11:29 not d. the L. body
12:10 to another, d. of spirits

**DISCHARGE, D.**
1 K. 5:9 will cause be d. there
Ec. 8:8 there is no d. in that war

**DISCIPLE.**
Mat. 10:24 d. is not above his master, Luke 6:40
42 give cup of cold water to d.
27:57 Joseph also was Jesus' d.
John 9:28 art his d. we are Mo.
18:16 went out that other d.
19:26 d. standing by, Je. loved
27 to that d. Behold thy mo.
38 being a d. but secretly
20:2 d. Jesus loved, 21:7, 20
4 the other d. did outrun Pet.
8 went in also that other d.
21:23 that that d. should not die
24 this is the d. which testifi.
Acts 9:10 a certain d. at Damas.
26 believed not that he was d.
36 Joppa a d. named Tabitha
21:16 old d. with whom lodge

**My DISCIPLE.**
Luke 14:26 not be my d.
27 bear cross cannot be my d.
33 fors. not all, not be my d.

**DISCIPLES.**
Mat. 9:14 then came d. of John
11:1 end of commanding his d.
14:26 when d. saw him on sea
17:6 d. heard it, fell on th. face
19:13 d. reb. them, Mark 10:13
20:17 twelve d. apart in way
22:16 Pharisees sent their d.
26:26 J. took bread, gave to d.
35 likewise also said all the d.
56 d. forsook him and fled
Mark 2:18 why d. of John and of Pharisees fast, Luke 5:33
8:14 d. forgotten to take bread
Luke 19:37 d. began to rejoice
John 3:25 betw. John's d. and
4:1 Je. bap. more d. that John
9:28 but we are Moses' d.
13:5 began to wash the d. feet

18:17 art one of this man's d.?
20:18 told d. she had seen Lord
Acts 9:1 breath. slaughter ag. d.
26 Saul assayed to join the d.
11:26 d. called Christians first
19:1 Ephesus, finding certain d.
30 the d. suffered him not
20:7 d. came to break bread
30 to draw away d. after them

**His DISCIPLES.**

Mat. 8:25 his d. awoke him
9:19 Jes. followed, so did his d.
28:7 tell his d. he is risen
13 say ye, h. d. came by night
Luke 5:30 murmur against h. d.
6:20 lifted up his eyes on his d.
11:1 as John taught his d.
John 2:11 his d. believed on him
4:2 Jes. baptized not but his d.
27 came his d. and marvelled
6:22 his d. were gone away
9:27 will ye also be his d.?
18:1 with his d. over Cedron
2 resorted thither with his d.
20:26 again his d. were within

**Of his DISCIPLES.**

Mat. 11:2 sent two of his d. Mark 11:1; 14:13; Luke 19:29
Mark 7:2 d. eat with unw. hands
John 6:66 many of his d. went
18:19 high-p. asked J. of his d.
25 art not th. also one of h. d.
21:12 none of his d. durst ask

**To his DISCIPLES.**

Mat. 14:19 gave loaves to his d.
Mark 4:34 expounded all to h. d.
Luke 10:23 he turned to his d.
John 21.14 showed hims. to h. d.

**My DISCIPLES.**

Is. 8:16 seal law among my d.
Mat. 26:18 keep passover with my d. Mark 14:14; Luke 22:11
John 8:31 my d. indeed, 13:35
15:8 so shall ye be my d.

**Thy DISCIPLES.**

Mat. 9:14 t. d. fast not, Mark 2:18
12:2 thy d. do what is not lawf.
15:2 t. d. transgress tradition?
17:16 d. they could not cure
Mark 7:5 walk not t. d. accor. to
9:18 t. d. to cast him, Luke 9:40
Luke 19:39 Master rebuke thy d.
John 7:3 t. d. see works thou

**DISCIPLINE.**

Job 36:10 openeth their ears to d.

**DISCLOSE.**

Is. 26:21 earth shall d. her blood

**DISCOMFITED.**

Jos. 10:10 L. d. them before Is.
Jud. 4:15 the Lord d. Sisera
8:12 Gideon d. all the host
1 Sam. 7:10 thundered on Ph. d.
2 Sam. 22:15 d. them. Ps. 18:14
Is. 31:8 young men shall be d.

**DISCOMFITURE.**

1 Sam. 14:20 was a very great d.

**DISCONTENTED.**

2 Sam. 22:2 d. gathered to David

**DISCONTINUE.**

Jer. 17:4 d. from thy heritage

**DISCORD.**

Prov. 6:14 he soweth d.
19 soweth d. among brethren

**DISCOVER.**

1 Sam. 14:8 d. ourselves to them
Job 41:13 d. face of his garment?
Prov. 18:2 his heart may d. itself
25:9 d. not a secret to another
Is. 3:17 L. will d. th. secret parts
Jer. 13:26 d. thy skirts, Nah. 3:5
Lam. 4:22 he will d. thy sins
Ezek. 16:37 I will d. thy nakedn.
Hos. 2:10 will I d. her lewdness
Mic. 1:6 I will d. the foundations

**DISCOVERED.**

1 Sam. 14:11 d. thems. to garri.
22:6 Saul heard David was d.
2 Sam. 22:16 foundations of the world were d. Ps. 18:15
Is. 22:8 he d. covering of Judah
57:8 hast d. thyself to another
Jer. 13:22 thy skirts d.
Lam. 2:14 not d. thine iniquity
Ezek. 13:14 foundat. shall be d.
16:36 nakedness d. thro' whor.
57 before thy wickedn. was d.
21:24 that your transgr. are d.
22:10 d. their father's nakedn.
23:10 these d. her nakedness
Hos. 7:1 iniq. of Ephraim was d.

**DISCOVERETH, ING.**

Job 12:22 he d. deep things out
Ps. 29:9 voice of Lord d. forests
Hab. 3:13 d. foundation to neck

**DISCOURAGE, D.**

Num. 21:4 soul of people was d.
32:7 why d. heart of people? 9
Deut. 1:21 fear not, nor be d.
28 brethren have d. our heart
Is. 42:4 shall not fail nor be d.
Col. 3:21 children, lest they be d.

**DISCREET.**

Gen. 41:39 none so d. and wise
Tit. 2:5 teach yo. women to be d.

**DISCREETLY.**

Mark 12:34 Jesus saw he ans. d.

**DISCRETION.**

Ps. 112:5 guide affairs with d.
Prov. 1:4 to the young man d.
2:11 d. shall preserve thee
3:21 keep wisdom and d.
5:2 thou mayest regard d.
11:22 a fair woman without d.
19:11 d. deferreth his anger
Is. 28:26 God instruct him to d.
Jer. 10:12 stretched heav. by d.

**DISDAINED.**

1 Sam. 17:42 Goliah d. David
Job 30:1 fathers I would have d.

**DISEASE.**

2 K. 1:2 if I sh. recov. of this d.
8:8 shall I recover of this d.? 9
2 Chr. 16:12 in his d. he sought
21:15 have d. of thy bowels
18 L. smote him with incur. d.
Job 30:18 by d. garment changed
Ps. 38:7 filled with loathsome d.
41:8 an evil d. say they, cleav.
Ec. 6:2 this is vanity, an evil d.
Mat. 4:23 healing d. 9:35; 10:1
John 5:4 whole of whatsoever d.

**DISEASES.**

Ex. 15:26 none of these d.
Deut. 28:60 bring on thee d.
2 Chr. 21:19 he died of sore d.
24:25 they left him in great d.
Ps. 103:3 who healeth all thy d.
Mat. 4:24 were taken with divers d. Mark 1:34; Luke 4:40
Luke 9:1 gave power to cure d.
Acts 19:12 d. departed from them
28:9 had d. in island, came

**DISEASED.**

1 K. 15:23 Asa was d. in his feet
Ezek. 34:4 d. not strengthened
21 because ye have pushed d.
Mat. 9:20 woman d. with issue
14:35 brought all d. Mark 1:32
John 6:2 miracles he did on d.

**DISFIGURE.**

Mat. 6:16 hypocrites d. faces

**DISGRACE.**

Jer. 14:21 do not d. the throne

**DISGUISE, ED, ETH.**

1 Sam. 28:8 and Saul d. himself
1 K. 14:2 Jerob. said, d. thyself
20:38 one of prophets d. himself
22:30 d. myself, 2 Chr. 18:29
2 Chr. 35:22 Josiah d. to fight
Job 24:15 adulterer d. his face

**DISH, ES.**

Jud. 5:25 butter in a lordly d.
2 K. 21:13 as a man wipeth a d.
Mat. 26:23 dip. in d. Mark 14:20

DISHONEST. See GAIN.

**DISHONESTY.**

2 Cor. 4:2 renounced things of d.

**DISHONOR.**

Ezr. 4:14 to see king's d.
Ps. 35:26 clothed with d. 71:13
69:19 thou hast known my d.
Prov. 6:33 and d. shall he get
Rom. 9:21 another vessel to d.
1 Cor. 15:43 sown in d. raised in
2 Cor. 6:8 by honor and d.
2 Tim. 2:20 are vess. some to d.

**DISHONOR, EST, ETH.**

Mic. 7:6 the son d. the father
John 8:49 Father, and ye d. me
Rom. 1:24 to d. their own bodies
2:23 breaking law, d. God
1 Cor. 11:4 man d. head; 5 wom.

**DISINHERIT.**

Num. 14:12 I will d. them

**DISMAYED.**

Deut. 31:8 nor be d. Jos. 1:9; 8:1; 10:25; 1 Chr. 22:13; 28:20; 2 Chr. 20:15, 17; 32:7
1 Sam. 17:11 they were d. 2 K. 19:26; Is. 37:27
Is. 21:3 I was d. at seeing of it
41:10 not d. Jer. 1:17; 10:2; 23:4; 30:10; 46:27; Ezek. 2:6; 3:9
23 that we may be d.
Jer. 8:9 the wise men are d. 10:2
17:18 let them be d. let not me
46:5 have I seen them d. and
48:1 M. is d.; 49:37 Elam be d.
50:36 mighty of Babylon be d.
Ob. 9 mighty men shall be d.

**DISMAYING.**

Jer. 48:39 Moab shall be a d.

**DISMISSED.**

Acts 15:30 d. they came to Anti
19:41 spoken, he d. assembly

**DISOBEDIENCE.**

Rom. 5:19 by one man's d.
2 Cor. 10:6 readiness to rev. d.
Eph. 2:2 worketh in child. of d.
5:6 on children of d. Col. 3:6
Heb. 2:2 d. received just recom.

**DISOBEDIENT.**

1 K. 13:26 man of G. who was d.
Neh. 9:26 they were d. rebelled
Luke 1:17 turn d. to wis. of just
Acts 26:19 not d. to heav. vision
Rom. 1:30 d. to par. 2 Tim. 3:2
10:21 forth my hands to d. peo.
1 Tim. 1:9 law was made for d.
Tit. 1:16 deny him, being d.
3:3 we also were sometimes d.
1 Pet. 2:7 to them d. the stone
8 stumble at word, being d.
3:20 which sometime were d.

**DISOBEYED.**

1 K. 13:21 as hast d. mouth of L.

**DISORDERLY.**

2 Thes. 3:6 withd. from broth. d.
2 Thes. 3:7 behaved not ours. d.
11 some walk among you d.

**DISPATCH.**

Ezek. 23:47 d. them with swords

**DISPENSATION.**

1 Cor. 9:17 a d. of gospel
Eph. 1:10 d. of fulness of times
3:2 heard of d. of grace of God
Col. 1:25 minister acc. to d. of G.

**DISPERSE, ED.**
2 Chr. 11:23 Rehob. d. of child.
Est. 3:8 certain people d. among
Ps. 112:9 he hath d. 2 Cor. 9:9
Prov. 5:16 let thy fountains be d.
15:7 lips of wise d. knowledge
Is. 11:12 gather d. of Judah
Ezek. 12:15 d. them in the coun.
20:23; 29:12; 30:23, 26
22:15 d. thee in the countries
36:19 were d. through countries
Zep. 3:10 my d. shall bring
John 7:35 will he go to the d.
Acts 5:37 obeyed him, were d.

**DISPERSIONS.**
Jer. 25:34 days of d. accomp.

**DISPLAYED.**
Ps. 60:4 ban. that it may be d.

**DISPLEASE.**
Num. 22:34 if it d. thee
1 Sam. 29:7 d. not the lords
2 Sam. 11:25 Joab, let not this d.
Prov. 24:18 L. see it, it d. him

**DISPLEASED.**
Gen. 48:17 hand on Ephr. it d.
Num. 11:1 complained, it d. L.
10 Moses also was d.
1 Sam. 8:6 the thing d. Samuel
18:8 saying d. Saul, and he said
2 Sam. 11:27 th. D. had done, d.
1 K. 1:6 father had not d. him
20:43 went to his house d. 21:4
1 Chr. 21:7 God was d. with this
Ps. 60:1 thou has been d.
Is. 59:15 it d. him
Dan. 6:14 king d. with himself
Jon. 4:1 it d. Jonah exceedingly
Hab. 3:8 Lord d. against rivers
Zec. 1:2 L. been d. with fathers
15 sore d. with heathen at ease,
for I was but a little d.
Mat. 21:15 scribes saw, were d.
Mark 10:14 Jesus saw it, was d.
41 d. with James and John
Acts 12:20 Herod highly d. with

**DISPLEASURE.**
Deut. 9:19 I was afraid of hot d.
Jud. 15:3 though I do them a d.
Ps. 2:5 vex them in his sore d.
6:1 chasten me in hot d. 38:1

**DISPOSED, ING.**
Job 34:13 who d. whole world?
37:15 know when God d. them
Prov. 16:33 d. thereof is of L.
1 Cor. 10:27 feast, ye be d. to go

**DISPOSITION.**
Acts 7:53 law by d. of angels

**DISPOSSESS, ED.**
Num. 33:53 shall d. the inhabi.
Deut. 7:17 How can I d. them?
Jud. 11:23 God hath d. the A.

**DISPUTATION, S.**
Acts 15:2 had no small d.
Rom. 14:1 but not to doubtful d.

**DISPUTE, ED.**
Job 23:7 righteous might d.
Mark 9:34 d. who sh. be greatest
Acts 9:29 S. d. ag. the Grecians
17:17 Paul d. in the synagogue
Jude 9 Mich. d. about body of M.

**DISPUTER.**
1 Cor. 1:20 where is d. of world?

**DISPUTING, S.**
Acts 6:9 d. with Stephen
15:7 been much d. Peter rose
19:8 d. and persuading, 9
24:12 they neither found me d.
Phil. 2:14 all things without d.
1 Tim. 6:5 perverse d.

**DISQUIET, ED, NESS.**
1 Sam. 28:15 why hast thou d.
Ps. 38:8 roared by reason of d.
39:6 surely are d. in vain
42:5 O my soul, why art thou d.
within me? 11; 43:5
Prov. 30:21 earth is d.
Jer. 50:34 d. inhabitants of Bab.

**DISSEMBLED, ETH.**
Jos. 7:11 stolen, and d. also
Prov. 26:24 he that hateth d.
Jer. 42:20 for ye d. when ye sent
Gal. 2:13 other Jews d. likewise

**DISSEMBLERS.**
Ps. 26:4 nor will I go in with d.

**DISSENSION.**
Acts 15:2 had no small d.
23:7 arose a d. between Phari.

**DISSIMULATION.**
Rom. 12:9 let love be without d.
Gal. 2:13 carried away with d.

**DISSOLVE, ED, EST.**
Job 30:22 thou d. my substance
Ps. 75:3 inhab. thereof are d.
Is. 14:31 thou Palestina art d.
24:19 the earth is clean d.
34:4 the host of heaven be d.
Dan. 5:16 thou canst d. doubts
Nah. 2:6 palace shall be d.
2 Cor. 5:1 house of this taber. d.
2 Pet. 3:11 all these things be d.
12 heavens on fire shall be d.

**DISTAFF.**
Prov. 31:19 her hands hold d.

**DISTIL.**
Deut. 32:2 my speech d. as dew
Job 36:28 the clouds d. on man

**DISTINCTION.**
1 Cor. 14:7 exc. d. in the sounds

**DISTINCTLY.**
Neh. 8:8 in book of the law d.

**DISTRACTED, ION.**
Ps. 88:15 I suff. thy ter. I am d.
1 Cor. 7:35 attend without d.

**DISTRESS, Substantive.**
Gen. 35:3 answered me in my d.
42:21 therefore is this d. come
Jud. 11:7 ye come when in d.
1 Sam. 22:2 in d. came to David
2 Sam. 22:7 in my d. I called on
L. Ps. 18:6; 118:5; 120:1
1 K. 1:29 redeemed soul out of d.
2 Chr. 28:22 in d. Ahaz trespass.
Neh. 2:17 ye see the d. we are in
9:37 and we are in great d.
Ps. 4:1 enlarged me when in d.
Prov. 1:27 mock when d. cometh
Is. 25:4 stre. to the needy in d.
Lam. 1:20 O Lord, for I am in d.
Ob. 12 nor spoken proudly in d.
14 nor deliv. those in day of d.
Zep. 1:15 that day is a day of d.
17 I will bring d. upon men
Luke 21:23 great d. in land
25 on the earth d. of nations
Rom. 8:35 love of C.? shall d.
1 Cor. 7:26 good for the present d.
1 Thes. 3:7 comforted in your d.

**DISTRESS, ED.**
Gen. 32:7 Jacob was greatly d.
Deut. 2:9 d. not the Moabites
19 d. not the Ammonites
28:53 wherewith d. thee, 55, 57
Jud. 2:15 Israel d. 10:9
1 Sam. 13:6 the people were d.
14:24 men of Is. d.; 28:15 Saul
30:6 David d. for people spake
2 Sam. 1:26 d. for thee, Jonathan
2 Chr. 28:20 king of Assy. d. A.
Is. 29:2 yet I will d. Ariel
7 that d. her be as a dream
Jer. 10:18 will d. the inhabitants
2 Cor. 4:8 troubled yet not d.

**DISTRESSES.**
Ps. 25:17 O bring me out of d.
107:6 he deliv. them out of d.
13 he saved them out of d. 19
28 bringeth them out of d.
Ezek. 30:16 Noph have d. daily
2 Cor. 6:4 approv. ourselves in d.
12:10 I take pleasure in d. for

**DISTRIBUTE.**
Neh. 13:13 their office was to d.
Luke 18:22 sell all and d. to poor
1 Tim. 6:18 rich to be ready to d.

**DISTRIBUTED, ETH, ING.**
Job 21:17 God d. sorrows
John 6:11 Je. d. to the disciples
Rom. 12:13 d. to neces. of saints
1 Cor. 7:17 God hath d. to every
2 Cor. 10:13 ac. to rule G. hath d.

**DISTRIBUTION.**
Acts 4:35 d. made to every one
2 Cor. 9:13 for your liberal d.

**DITCH, ES.**
2 K. 3:16 make valley full of d.
Job 9:31 plunge me in the d.
Ps. 7:15 fallen into d. he made
Prov. 23:27 a whore is a deep d.
Is. 22:11 a d. between two walls
Mat. 15:14 fall into d. Luke 6:39

**DIVERS, E.**
Deut. 22:9 not sow with d. seed
11 not wear garment of d. sorts
25:13 shalt not have d. weights
Deut. 25:11 in house d. measures
Jud. 5:30 to S. a prey of d. colors
2 Sam. 13:18 gar. of d. colors, 19
1 Chr. 29:2 stones of d. colors
2 Chr. 30:11 d. of Asher humbled
Est. 3:8 their laws d. from all
Ps. 78:45 sent d. sort of flies
105:31 came d. sorts of flies
Prov. 20:10 d. weights, d. meas.
23 d. weights are abomination
Ec. 5:7 there are also d. vanities
Ezek. 17:3 a great eagle d. colors
Dan. 7:3 beasts d. one from ano.
23 d. from all kingdoms
Mat. 4:24 sick with d. diseases,
Mark 1:34; Luke 4:40
24:7 earthquakes in d. places,
Mark 13:8; Luke 21:11
Mark 8:3 for d. came from far
Acts 19:9 when d. were hardened
1 Cor. 12:10 d. kinds of tongues
2 Tim. 3:6 led away with d. lusts
Tit. 3:3 serving d. lusts and ple.
Heb. 1:1 in d. manners spake
2:4 witness with d. miracles
9:10 d. washings; 13:9 d. doct.
Jam. 1:2 fall into d. temptations

**DIVERSITIES.**
1 Cor. 12:4 d. of gifts; 6 opera.
28 set in church d. of tongues

**DIVIDE.**
Gen. 1:6 let firmament d. waters
14 be lights to d. the day, 18
49:27 at night he shall d. spoil
Ex. 14:16 over the sea and d. it
26:33 veil shall d. between holy
Num. 31:27 d. the prey into two
Jos. 1:6 d. for inheritance, 18:5
22:8 d. the spoil with brethren
2 Sam. 19:29 thou and Z. d. land
1 K. 3:25 d. living child, 26
Neh. 9:11 didst d. sea, Ps. 74:13
22 didst d. them into corners
Job 27:17 innocent shall d. silver
Ps. 55:9 and d. their tongues
Prov. 16:19 to d. spoil with proud
Is. 9:3 rejoice when d. the spoil
53:12 shall d. spoil with strong
Ezek. 5:1 take balances, and d.
45:1 d. land by lot, 47:21, 22
48:29 this is land ye shall d.
Dan. 11:39 he shall d. land
Luke 12:13 that he d. the inheri.
22:17 d. it among yourselves

**I will DIVIDE.**
Gen. 49:7 I will d. them in Jacob

*Ex.* 15:9 said, *I will d.* spoil
*Ps.* 60:6 *I will d.* Shech. 108:7
*Is.* 53:12 *will I d.* him a portion

**DIVIDED.**

*Gen.* 1:4 *d.* light; 7 *d.* waters
10:5 were isles of Gentiles *d.*
25 in his days was the earth *d.*
32 nations *d.* after the flood
14:15 Abram *d.* himself ag. them
15:10 *d.* Abram *d.* them in midst
32:7 Jacob *d.* people
*Ex.* 14:21 the waters were *d.*
*Deut.* 4:19 which God hath *d.*
32:8 Most High *d.* to nations
*Jos.* 14:5 they *d.* land, 18:10
*Jud.* 5:30 *d.* the prey to every
19:29 the Levite *d.* her
2 *Sam.* 1:23 in death were not *d.*
1 *K.* 16:21 were people of Isr. *d.*
18:6 Ahab and Ob. *d.* the land
2 *K.* 2:8 waters were *d.* hither
*Job* 38:25 hath *d.* a watercourse
*Ps.* 68:12 she that tar. *d.* spoil
78:13 he *d.* the sea, and caused
55 *d.* them an inheritance by line, *Acts* 13:19
136:13 to him which *d.* Red sea
*Is.* 33:23 prey of great spoil *d.*
34:17 his hand *d.* it by line
51:15 I am the Lord that *d.* sea
*Lam.* 4:16 anger of Lord *d.* them
*Ezek.* 37:22 nor be *d.* into two k.
*Dan.* 2:41 kingdom shall be *d.*
5:28 kingdom *d.* given to M.
11:4 kingdom *d.* toward four w.
*Hos.* 10:2 their heart is *d.*
*Amos* 7:17 thy land shall be *d.*
*Mic.* 2:4 he hath *d.* our fields
*Zec.* 14:1 spoil be *d.* in midst
*Mat.* 12:25 house *d.* not stand, *Mark* 3:24; *Luke* 11:17
*Luke* 12:52 five in one house *d.*
53 father be divided aga. son
15:12 *d.* unto them his living
*Acts* 14:4 multi. was *d.* 23:7
1 *Cor.* 1:13 is Christ *d.*? was P.
*Rev.* 16:19 city was *d.*

**DIVIDER.**

*Luke* 12:14 made me *d.* over you

**DIVIDETH.**

*Job* 26:12 *d.* sea with his power
*Ps.* 29:7 voice of L. *d.* flames
*Jer.* 31:35 *d.* sea when waves roar.
*Mat.* 25:32 *d.* his sheep fr. goats
*Luke* 11:22 and *d.* his spoils

**DIVIDING.**

*Is.* 63:12 *d.* water before them
*Dan.* 7:25 and a *d.* of time
1 *Cor.* 12:11 *d.* to every man
2 *Tim.* 2:15 rightly *d.* the word
*Heb.* 4:12 to *d.* asunder of joints

**DIVINATION, S.**

*Num.* 22:7 rewards of *d*
23:23 nor any *d.* against Israel
*Deut.* 18:10 useth *d.* 2 *K.* 17:17
*Jer.* 14:14 they prophesy *d.*
*Ezek.* 12:24 nor flattering *d.* in Is.
13:7 not spoken a lying *d*
23 see no more divine *d.*
21:21 the king of Babylon stood to use *d.*
*Acts* 16:16 pos. with spirit of *d*

**DIVINE, Verb.**

*Gen.* 44:15 a man as I can *d.*?
1 *Sam.* 28:8 *d.* to me by fam. sp.
*Ezek.* 13:9 prophets that *d.* lies
21:29 while they *d.* a lie
*Mic.* 3:6 that ye shall not *d.*
11 prophets *d.* for money

**DIVINE, Adjective.**

*Prov.* 16:10 *d.* sentence in lips
*Heb.* 9:1 ordinances of *d.* service
2 *Pet.* 1:3 *d.* power hath given
4 be partakers of *d.* nature

**DIVINER, S.**

*Deut.* 18:14 hearkened to *d.*
1 *Sam.* 6:2 Philis. called for *d.*
*Is.* 44:25 that maketh *d.* mad
*Jer.* 27:9 hearken not to your *d.*
29:8 let not your *d.* deceive you
*Mic.* 3:7 and the *d.* confounded
*Zec.* 10:2 the *d.* have seen a lie

**DIVINETH, ING.**

*Gen.* 44:5 this it whereby he *d.*?
*Ezek.* 22:28 and *d.* lies to them

**DIVISION, S.**

*Ex.* 8:23 put a *d.* between
*Jud.* 5:15 for *d.* of Reuben, 16
*Luke* 12:51 nay but rather *d.*
*John* 7:43 there was a *d.* among the people, 9:16; 10:19
*Rom.* 16:17 mark them wh. ca. *d.*
1 *Cor.* 1:10 be no *d.* among you
3:3 whereas there is am. you *d.*
11:18 I hear there be *d.* am. you

**DIVORCE, ED.**

*Jer.* 3:8 given her a bill of *d.*
*Mat.* 5:32 shall marry her *d.*

**DIVORCEMENT.**

*Deut.* 24:1 write her bill of *d.* 3
*Is.* 50:1 your mother's *d.*?
*Mark* 10:4 M. suffered bill of *d.*
*See* WRITING.

**DO.**

*Gen.* 18:25 Judge of all *d.* right?
31:16 what God hath said, *d.*
41:25 what he is to *d.* 28
*Ex.* 4:15 teach you what ye sh. *d.*
19:8 all L. hath spok. we will *d.*
*Lev.* 18:5 if man *d.* he shall live, *Neh.* 9:29; *Ezek.* 20:11, 13, 21
*Num.* 22:20 word I say shalt *d.*
24:14 this peo. *d.* to thy people
*Deut.* 7:11 command. to *d.* them
19:19 *d.* to him as he thought to
27:26 words of law, to *d.* them
30:12 may hear it and *d.* it? 13
*Jos.* 7:9 *d.* to thy great name?
22:24 what have ye to *d.* with L.
23:6 *d.* all written in the law, 1 *Chr.* 16:40; 2 *Chr.* 34:21
*Jud.* 7:17 as I *d.* so shall ye *d.*
8:3 to *d.* in comparison of you?
10:15 *d.* to us what seem. good
18:18 the priest, What *d.* ye?
1 *Sam.* 16:3 show thee what *d.*
22:3 what God will *d.* for me
26:25 thou shalt *d.* great things
2 *Sam.* 3:18 now then *d.* it
15:26 *d.* to me as seemeth good
1 *K.* 2:6 *d.* acc. to thy wisdom
8:32 *d.* and judge thy servants.
39 forgive, and *d.* 2 *Chr.* 6:23
11:33 to *d.* right, 38; 14:8
2 *K.* 9:18 to *d.* with peace? 19
17:34 *d.* after former manners
20:9 L. will *d.* as he hath spok.
1 *Chr.* 17:2 *d.* all in thy heart
23 and *d.* as thou hast said
21:8 *d.* away iniq. of thy serv.
2 *Chr.* 19:6 take heed what ye *d.*
20:12 nor know we what to *d.*
25:8 if thou wilt go, *d.* it
*Ezr.* 4:2 we seek God as ye *d.*
7:10 to seek law and to *d.* it
*Neh.* 2:12 put in my heart to *d.*
9:24 *d.* with them as they
*Job* 7:20 *d.* to thee? O Preserver
11:8 high as heav. what *d.*?
13:20 *d.* not two things to me
*Ps.* 40:8 I delight to *d.* thy will
50:16 to *d.* to dec. my statutes?
109:21 but *d.* thou for me
119:132 to *d.* to those
143:10 teach me to *d.* thy will
*Prov.* 3:27 power of hand to *d.*
*Ec.* 9:10 *d.* it with thy might
*Is.* 10:3 *d.* in day of visitation?
45:7 Lord *d.* all these things
*Jer.* 5:31 *d.* in the end thereof?
11:4 obey my voice and *d.* them
14:7 *d.* it for thy name's sake
39:12 *d.* to him as he shall say
42:3 show thing we may *d.*
50:15 hath done, *d.* to her, 29
*Lam.* 1:22 *d.* to them as done
*Ezek.* 8:6 seest thou what they *d.*
24:22 ye shall *d.* as I have done
36:37 be inquired of, to *d.* it for
*Dan.* 9:19 Lord, hearken and *d.*
11:3 *d.* accord. to his will, 16, 36
*Hos.* 10:3 should king *d.* to us?
*Amos* 3:7 Lord *d.* nothing
*Jon.* 4:9 I *d.* well to be angry
*Mic.* 6:8 but to *d.* justly
*Zec.* 1:21 what come these to *d.*?
8:16 these are things ye shall *d.*
*Mat.* 5:19 shall *d.* and teach
47 what *d.* ye more than oth.?
8:29 wh. have we to *d.* wi. thee? *Mark* 1:24; *Luke* 4:34
12:50 whosoever sh. *d.* the will of my Father, *Mark* 3:35
20:15 *d.* what I will with own
32 wh. will ye I *d.* *Mark* 10:36
21:27 author. I *d.* these things, *Mark* 11:33; *Luke* 20:8
23:5 works they *d.*
27:19 to *d.* with that just man
*Mark* 7:8 such like ye *d.* 13
*Luke* 4:23 *d.* also in thy country
6:2 why *d.* that not lawful
11 what they might *d.* to Jes.
31 as ye would that men sh. *d.*
8:21 hear word of God and *d.* it
16:4 I am resolved what to *d.*
17:10 done what was duty to *d.*
23:34 know not what they *d.*
*John* 2:5 whatsoever he saith *d.*
4:34 my meat is to *d.* will
5:30 I can of myself *d.* nothing
6:6 he knew what he would *d.*
28 what shall we *d.*? *Acts* 2:37
7:17 if any man will *d.* his will
8:29 I *d.* those things please
9:33 of G. he could *d.* nothing
11:47 Pharisees said, What *d.*?
13:7 what I *d.* knowest not
15 ye shall *d.* as I have done
17 happy are ye if ye *d.* them
14:12 works I *d.* shall he *d.* also
14 ask in my name, I will *d.* it
15:14 if ye *d.* what I command
21 will they *d.* unto you, 16:3
17:4 work thou gavest me to *d.*
21:21 what shall this man *d.*?
*Acts* 1:1 of all Jesus began to *d.*
4:28 *d.* whatsoever thy counsel
9:6 what wilt thou have me *d.*?
10:6 what thou oughtest to *d.*
14:15 why *d.* ye these things?
*Rom.* 1:32 not only *d.* the same
2:14 *d.* by nature things in law
7:15 for what I *d.* I allow not, but what I hate, that *d.* I
1 *Cor.* 7:36 let him *d.* what he
10:31 ye *d.* all to glory of God
2 *Cor.* 8:10 not only to *d.* but
*Gal.* 3:10 writ. in law to *d.* them
5:21 *d.* such shall not inherit
*Eph.* 6:21 know and how I *d.*
*Phil.* 2:13 G. worketh both to *d.*
4:9 heard and seen in me, *d.*
*Col.* 3:17 whatsoe. ye *d.* in word or deed, *d.* all in na. of L. J.
23 whats. ye *d.* *d.* it heartily
1 *Thes.* 4:10 ye *d.* it tow. breth.
5:11 edify, even as also ye *d.*
24 faithful who also will *d.* it
2 *Thes.* 3:4 ye both *d.* and will *d.*
*Phile.* 21 wilt *d.* more than I say
*Heb.* 4:13 whom we have to *d.*
10:7 lo, I come to *d.* thy will, 9
13:6 not fear what man shall *d.*
21 perfect to *d.* his will
2 *Pet.* 1:10 if ye *d.* these, never

1 John 3:22 and d. those things
Rev. 2:5 and d. the first works

**Can, *or* canst DO.**
Job 22:17 what can Almighty d.
Job 42:2 thou c. d. every thing
Ps. 11:3 can the righteous d.?
56:4 fear what flesh can d. 11
118:6 not fear what man can d.
Mark 9:22 if canst d. anything
Luke 12:4 no more they can d.
John 5:19 Son can d. nothing, 30
15:5 without me ye can d. noth.
Phil. 4:13 I can d. all through C.
See DO COMMANDMENTS.

**DO, *with* evil.**
Ex. 23:2 not fol. a mult. to d. e.
Lev. 5:4 soul swear to d. evil
Deut. 31:29 bec. ye will d. evil
2 Sam. 12:9 despised L. to d. e.
2 K. 8:12 evil thou wilt d.
17:17 sold themselves to d. evil
21:9 Man. seduced to d. more e.
Ps. 34:16 face ag. them d. evil
37:8 fret not thyself to d. evil
Prov. 2:14 who rejoice to d. evil
24:8 he that deviseth to d. evil
Ec. 5:1 consider not they d. evil
8:11 fully set in them to d. evil
12 a sinner d. evil 100 times
Is. 1:16 wash ye, cease to d. evil
41:23 d. good or evil that we
Jer. 4:22 people are wise to d. e.
10:5 for they cannot d. evil
13:23 accustomed to d. evil
18:10 if it d. evil in my sight
Ezek. 6:10 I would d. this evil
Mic. 7:3 d. evil with both hands
Zep. 1:12 nor will he d. evil
Mark 3:4 to d. evil? Luke 6:9
Rom. 3:8 d. evil that good come
13:4 if thou d. evil be afraid
2 Cor. 13:7 I pray that ye d. no e.
1 Pet. 3:12 against them that d. e.

**DO, *joined with* good.**
Gen. 27:46 g. shall my life d.
Num. 24:13 to d. g. or bad
Deut. 8:16 to d. thee good
28:63 Lord rejoice to d. you g.
30:5 and he will d. thee good
Jud. 17:13 Lord will d. me good
1 Sam. 1:23 d. what seemeth g.
14:36, 40; 2 Sam. 19:27, 37
3:18 the Lord d. what seemeth him good, 2 Sam. 10:12
2 K. 10:5 d. that g. in thine eyes
1 Chr. 19:13 Lord d. what is g.
Neh. 5:9 it is not g. that ye d.
Ps. 34:14 d. g. 37:3, 27; 51:18; 125:4; Mat. 5:44; Luke 6:9, 35
36:3 he hath left off to d. g.
Prov. 31:12 she will d. him g.
Ec. 3:12 for a man to d. good
Is. 41:23 yea, d. good, or d. evil
Jer. 4:22 to d. good no knowl.
10:5 nei. is it in them to d. g.
13:23 then may ye d. good
26:14 d. with me as seemeth g.
29:32 nor behold the g. I will d.
32:40 turn away to d. them g.
41 rejoice over them to d. g.
33:9 hear all the good I d.
Mic. 2:7 words d. g. to upright
Zep. 1:12 the L. will not d. good
Mark 3:4 is it lawful to d. g. on the sabbath days? Luke 6:9
14:7 poor, ye may d. them g.
Luke 6:33 if ye d. g. to them that d. good to you
Rom. 7:19 g. that I would, I d.
21 when I would d. g. evil is
13:3 d. good thou shalt have
Gal. 6:10 d. good unto all men
1 Tim. 6:18 that they d. good
Heb. 13:16 to d. g. and commun.
Jam. 4:17 knoweth to d. good
1 Pet. 3:11 eschew evil, and d. g.

**What have I to DO.**
2 Sam. 16:10 w. d. with? 19:22
1 K. 17:18 w. h. I to d. with thee? 2 K. 3:13; 2 Chr. 35:21; Mark 5:7; Luke 8:28; John 2:4
Hos. 14:8 w. d. any more
1 Cor. 5:12 what d. to judge

**I shall, I will, will I, *or* shall I DO.**
Gen. 27:37 what s. I d. now
Num. 22:17 I will d. what sayest
33:56 I s. d. to you, as I th. to d.
1 Sam. 3:11 I w. d. a thing in Isr.
20:4 thy soul desireth, I will d.
28:15 known wh. I s. d.
2 Sam. 18:4 best I will d. 19:38
Job 31:14 what d. when G. riseth
34:32 I will d. no more
Prov. 24:29 I will d. so to him
Is. 5:5 I w. d. to my vineyard
43:19 I will d. a new thing
46:10 I will d. all my pleasure
11 have purposed, I will al. d.
48:11 for own sake will I d. it
Jer. 29:32 good I will d. for my
Ezek. 5:9 I will d. in thee what I
7:27 d. to them after their way
22:14 spoken, and will d. it
24:14; 36:36
Hos. 6:4 what shall I d. to thee?
Amos 4:12 thus will I d. to thee
Mat. 19:16 good thing shall I d.
27:22 what shall I d. with J.?
Luke 16:3 what shall I d.? 20:13; Acts 22:10
John 14:13 ask, that will I d.
14 ask in my name, I will d. it
2 Cor. 11:12 what I do, I will d.
See JUDGMENT.

**Must DO.**
Num. 23:26 that I must d.
Acts 16:30 wh. m. I d. to be sav.?

**DO, *joined with* no *or* not.**
Ex. 20:10 in it thou shalt not d. any work, Lev. 23:31
23:24 not d. after their works
Lev. 16:29 d. no work, 23:3, 28; Deut. 15:19; Jer. 17:24
18:3 after their doings, not d.
Num. 23:19 and shall he n. d. it?
Deut. 12:8 n. d. after all we d.
1 K. 11:12 not d. it for D.'s sake
2 K. 7:9 said, We d. not well
17:15 should not d. like them
18:12 not hear nor d. them
Ezr. 7:26 whoso will not d. law
Job 13:20 only d. not two things
34:12 God will not d. wickedly
41:8 remem. battle, d. no more
Ps. 119:3 also d. no iniquity
Jer. 18:6 d. with you
Ezek. 5:9 not d. any more
33:31 hear thy words, but not d.
Mat. 5:46 d. n. publ. the same?
6:1 d. not your alms before men
12:2 d. that not lawful to d.
20:13 I d. thee no wrong
23:3 they say and d. not
Mark 6:5 d. no mighty work
Luke 6:46 d. not the things I say
John 6:38 not to d. mine own
10:37 if I d. not works of my F.
Rom. 7:15 that d. I not, 19
8:3 what the law could not d.
Gal. 5:17 ye cannot d. the things
Rev. 19:10 see thou d. it not, 22:9

**Observe, *with* DO.**
Deut 5:32 ob. to d. 8:1; 11:32; 12:1; 24:8; 2 K. 17:37
6:3 ob. to d. it, 12:32; 28:13, 15, 58; 31:12; 32:46
25 if we obs. to d. these com.
15:5 to ob. to d. all these com.
Jos. 1:7 ob. to d. all the law
Ezek. 37:24 observe and d. them
Mat. 23:3 you, that obser. and d.

**Will we, *or* we will DO.**
Ex. 19:8 said, we w. d. 24:3, 7
Deut. 5:27 w. w. hear it, and d.
Jos. 1:16 command. us, w. w. d.
2 K. 10:5 d. all thou shalt bid
Jer. 42:20 and w. w. d. it
44:17 we will certainly d.

**Shall we, *or* we shall DO.**
Jud. 13:8 what we shall d.
2 Sam. 16:20 what we shall d.
17:6 sh. we d. after his saying?
2 K. 6:15 alas, how shall we d.?
Est. 1:15 what sh. we d. to V.?
Ps. 60:12 through God w. sh. d. valiantly, 108:13
Cant. 8:8 what sh. we. d.
Jon. 1:11 what shall we d.?
Luke 3:10 what s. we d.? 12, 14
John 6:28 d. th. we might work?
Acts 2:37 what shall we d.?
4:16 what sh. we d. to these m.?

**DO, *joined with* so.**
Num. 22:30 wont to d. so to th.?
32:23 not d. so, ye have sinned
Deut. 12:30 so will I d.
1 Sam 8:8 served oth. gods, so d.
1 K. 17:41 as fathers, so d. they
Prov. 24:29 I will d. so to him
Is. 10:11 so d. to Jerusalem
Jer. 28:6 L. d. so, L. perform
Mat. 7:12 sh. d. to you, so d. ye
18:35 so shall Father d. to you
John 14:31 Fa. gave com. so I d.
Acts 7:51 fathers did, so d. ye
Col. 3:13 forgave you, so d. ye
Jam. 2:12 so d. ye, as they that

**DO, *joined with* this.**
Gen. 42:18 this d. and live
2 K. 19:31 zeal of the Lord shall d. this, Is. 37:32
Mat. 8:9 d. this, Luke 7:8
9:28 I am able to d. this?
Mark 11:3 Why d. this?
Luke 10:28 th. d. and thou sh. l.
22:19 this d. in remembrance of me, 1 Cor. 11:24, 25
1 Cor. 9:17 for if I d. this
Heb. 6:3 this will we d.
13:19 rather to d. this.
Jam. 4:15 we will d. this
See THING.

**DO well.**
Is. 1:17 cease d. evil, lea. d. well
Jon. 4:9 I d. well to be angry
Zec. 8:15 to d. well to Jerusalem
Mat. 12:12 to d. well on sabbath
John 11:12 he shall d. well
1 Pet. 2:14 them that d. w.
20 if ye d. well and suffer for it
2 Pet. 1:19 ye d. w. that ye take
3 John 6 if bring shalt d. well

**DOER.**
Gen. 39:22 Joseph was d. of it
2 Sam. 3:39 reward d. of evil
Ps. 31:23 rewardeth the proud d.
Prov. 17:4 wicked d. giveth heed
Jam. 1:23 be not d. of word
25 not a forgetful hearer, but d.
4:11 thou art not a d. of the law

**DOERS.**
2 K. 22:5 give it to d. of work
Ps. 101:8 cut off all wicked d.
Rom. 2:13 d. of law be justified
Jam. 1:22 be ye d. of the word
See EVIL-DOER, S.

**DOEST.**
Gen. 4:7 if d. well; if not well
21:22 with thee in all thou d.
Deut. 12:28 when thou d. good
1 K. 2:3 prosper in all thou d.
19:9 what d. here, Elijah? 13
20:22 mark and see what d.
Job 9:12 say, What d. thou?
35:6 what d. against him?

Ps. 49:18 d. well to thyself
77: 14 the God that d. wonders
86:10 and d. wondrous things
119:68 art good, and d. good
Ec. 8:4 what d. thou? Dan. 4:35
Jer. 11:15 d. evil, then rejoicest
15:5 to ask how thou d.?
Ezek. 12:9 house said, What d.?
16:30 seeing, d. all these things
John 2:18 thou d. these things?
13:27 that thou d. do quickly
Acts 22:26 take heed what th. d.
Rom. 2:1 judg. d. same things, 3
Jam. 2:19 believest, thou d. well
3 John 5 d. faithfully what th. d.

**DOETH.**

Ex. 31:14 for whosoever d. any work therein, 15; Lev. 23:30
Job 5:9 d. great things, 9:10; 37:5; Ps. 72:18; 136:4
23:13 soul desireth, that he d.
Ps. 1:3 what. he d. shall prosper
14:1 none d. 3; 53:1, 3; Ro. 3:12
15:5 d. these never be moved
118:15 hand d. valiantly, 16
Ec. 2:2 said of mirth, What d. it
3:14 whatsoever God d. it shall be for ever, and God d. it
7:20 not a man that d. good
8:3 he d. whatso. pleaseth him
Is 56:2 blessed is man d. this
Dan. 4:35 d. accord. to his will
9:14 L. is righteous in all he d.
Mal. 2:12 L. cut off man d. this
Mat. 6:3 left know what right d.
7:24 sayings and d. them
26 and d. not, Luke 6:49
8:9 and he d. it, Luke 7:8
John 5:19 he d. these d. the Son
7:51 before it know what he d.
9:31 d. his will, him he heareth
15:15 knoweth not what lord d.
Rom. 10:5 that d. these things shall live by them, Gal. 3:12
Eph. 6:8 good thing any man d.

**DOCTOR, S.**

Luke 2:46 J. in midst of the d.
5:17 d. of the law sitting by
Acts 5:34 Gamaliel a d. of law

**DOCTRINE.**

Is. 28:9 make to understand d.
29:24 murmured, shall learn d.
Jer. 10:8 stock is d. of vanities
Mat. 7:28 aston. at his d. 22:33; Mark 1:22; 11:18; Luke 4:32
16:12 beware of d. of Pharisees
Mark 1:27 what new d. is this?
4:2 in his d. 12:38
John 7:17 shall know of the d.
18:19 asked Jesus of his d.
Acts 2:42 conti. in apostles' d.
5:28 filled Jerus. with your d.
13:12 being astonished at the d.
17:19 what this new d. is?
Rom. 6:17 that form of d.
16:17 contrary to the d.
1 Cor. 14:6 except I speak by d.
26 every one of you hath a d.
Eph. 4:14 with every wind of d.
1 Tim. 1:3 teach no other d.
4:13 give attendance to d.
16 heed to thyself to thy d.
5:17 who labor in word and d.
6:1 his d. be not blasphemed
3 the d. according to godliness
2 Tim. 3:16 is profitable for d.
4:2 exhort with long suf. and d.
Tit. 2:7 in d. showing incorrupt.
10 adorn d. of God our Saviour
Heb. 6:1 principles of the d.
2 of the d. of baptisms, and
2 John 9 abideth not in the d. of Christ; abideth in d.
Rev. 2:14 that hold d. of Balaam
15 that hold d. of Nicolaitans

**Good DOCTRINE.**

Prov. 4:2 I give you good d.
1 Tim. 4:6 in words of good d.

**My DOCTRINE.**

Deut. 32:2 my d. drop as rain
Job 11:4 my d. is pure
John 7:16 my d. is not mine
2 Tim. 3:10 fully known my d.

**Sound DOCTRINE.**

1 Tim. 1:10 contrary to sound d.
2 Tim. 4:3 not endure sound d.
Tit. 1:9 by sound d. to exhort
2:1 speak things become s. d.

**This DOCTRINE.**

2 John 10 and bring not this d.
Rev. 2:24 as have not this d.

**DOCTRINES.**

Mat. 15:9 for d. com. Mark 7:7
Col. 2:22 comm. and d. of men
1 Tim. 4:1 heed to d. of devils
Heb. 13:9 not carried with str. d.

DOEG. 1 Sam. 21:7; 22:18, 22

**DOG.**

Ex. 11:7 ag. Is. not a d. move
Deut. 23:18 a d. into house
Jud. 7:5 as a d. lappeth
1 Sam. 17:43 am I a d.? 2 K. 8:13
24:14 wh. dost purs.? after a d.?
2 Sam. 3:8 am I a d. head?
9:8 upon such a dead d. as I am
16:9 this dead d. curse my lord?
Ps. 22:20 from power of d.
59:6 make a noise like a d. 14
Prov. 26:11 as a d. returneth to his vomit, 2 Pet. 2:22
17 taketh a d. by the ears
Ec. 9:4 a living d. is better than
Is. 66:3 as if he cut off d. neck

**DOGS.**

Ex. 22:31 cast it to the d. Mat. 15:26; Mark 7:27
1 K. 14:11 d. eat, 16:4; 21:24
21:19 the place where d. licked
23 d. shall eat J. 2 K. 9:10, 36
22:38 d. licked up his blood
Job 30:1 I disd. to set with d.
Ps. 22:16 d. have compassed me
68:23 and the tongue of thy d.
Is. 56:10 dumb d.; 11 greedy d.
Jer. 15:3 and the d. to tear
Mat. 7:6 which is holy unto d.
15:27 d. eat of cru. Mark 7:28
Luke 16:21 the d. licked his sores
Phil. 3:2 beware of d.
Rev. 22:15 for without are d.

**DOING.**

Ex. 15:11 d. wonders
1 K. 22:43 d. right, 2 Chr. 20:32
1 Chr. 22:16 arise and be d.
Job 32:22 in so d. my Maker
Ps. 64:9 wisely consider of his d.
66:5 he is terrible in his d.
118:23 the L.'s d. it is marvellous, Mat. 21:42; Mark 12:11
Is. 56:2 keepeth hand from d. ev.
Mat. 24:46 find so d. Luke 12:43
Acts 10:38 went about d. good
24:20 found any evil d. in me
Rom. 12:20 in so d. shalt heap
2 Cor. 8:11 perform the d. of it
Eph. 6:6 d. the will of God
1 Tim. 4:16 in d. this,

**Well-DOING.**

Rom. 2:7 continuance in w.-d.
Gal. 6:9 w. in w.-d. 2 Thes. 3:13
1 Pet. 2:15 with w.-d. ye silence
3:17 better suffer for w.-d.
4:19 com. souls to him in w.-d.

**DOINGS.**

Lev. 18:3 after d. of Egypt and Canaan, shall ye not do
Deut. 28:20 wickedness of thy d.
Jud. 2:19 ceased not from own d.
2 Chr. 17:4 not after d. of Israel
Ps. 9:11 declare his d. Is. 12:4
77:12 I will also talk of thy d.
Prov. 20:11 known by his d.
Is. 1:16 put away evil of your d.
3:8 their d. are against the L.
10 shall eat the fruit of their d.
Jer. 4:4 because of evil of your d. 21:12; 26:3; 44:22
18 thy d. have procured these
7:3 am. your d. 5; 26:13; 35:15
11:18 showedst me their d.
17:10 fruit of his d. 21:14
18:11 and make your d. good
23:2 visit on you evil of your d.
22 evil of d. 25:5; Zec. 1:4
32:19 give accord. to fruit of d.
Ezek. 14:22 ye shall see their d.
20:43 shall ye remember d.
44 nor according to corrupt d.
21:24 in all your d. sins do ap.
24:14 thy d. shall judge
36:17 defiled it by their own d.
19 according to d. I judged th.
31 shall remember d. not good
Hos. 4:9 reward them their d.
5:4 not frame d. to turn to God
7:2 their own d. have beset th.
9:15 for wicked. of d. I will dr.
12:2 acc. to d. will he recomp.
Mic. 2:7 are these his d.?
3:4 have behaved ill in their d.
7:13 be desolate, for fruit of d.
Zep. 3:7 corrupted all their d.
11 not be ashamed for thy d.?
Zec. 1:6 accord. to our d. so d.

**DOLEFUL.**

Is. 13:21 full of d. creatures
Mic. 2:4 with a d. lamentation

**DOMINION.**

Gen. 1:26 d. over the fish, 28
27:40 thou shalt have the d.
37:8 shalt thou have d. over us?
Num. 24:19 he that shall have d.
Jud. 5:13 have d. over nobles
1 K. 4:24 Solomon had d.
1 Chr. 18:3 to establish his d.
Neh. 9:37 have d. over our bod.
Job 25:2 d. and fear are with him
38:33 thou set the d. thereof
Ps. 8:6 to have d. over the works
19:13 sins, let them not have d.
49:14 the upright shall have d.
72:8 have d. from sea to sea
103:22 in all places of his d.
114:2 and Israel his d.
119:133 let not any iniq. have d.
145:13 thy d. endureth
Is. 26:13 other lords have had d.
Dan. 4:3 his d. from generation
22 d. reacheth to end of earth
34 d. is an everlasting d. 7:14
6:26 his d. be even unto the end
7:6 d. was given to the beast
12 beasts had d. taken away
14 was given him d. and glory
26 they shall take away his d.
27 d. sh. be given to the saints
11:3 shall rule with great d. 5
Mic. 4:8 to thee, even the first d.
Zec. 9:10 his d. be from sea
Mat. 20:25 princes exercise d
Rom. 6:9 death hath no more d.
14 sin not have d. over you
7:1 law hath d. over a man
2 Cor. 1:24 d. over your faith
Eph. 1:21 above might and d.
1 Pet. 4:11 to whom be praise and d. for ever, 5:11; Rev. 1:6
Jude 8 despise d.
25 to the only wise God be d.

**DOMINIONS.**

Dan. 7:27 all d. shall serve him
Col. 1:16 whether thrones or d.

**DONE.**

Ex. 18:9 goodness L. had d. to I.
31:15 six days may work be d. 35:2; Lev. 23:3
Lev. 5:17 things forbid. to be d.

*Num.* 22:2 saw all Israel had *d.*
27:4 name of our father *d.* aw.?
32:13 all had *d.* evil were cons.
*Deut.* 10:21 thy God that hath *d.*
29:24 wherefore hath the L. *d.* thus, 1 *K.* 9:8; 2 *Chr.* 7:21
2 *Sam.* 13:12 to be *d.* in Israel
24:17 they *d.*? 1 *Chr.* 21:17
*Neh.* 9:33 we have *d.* wickedly, *Ps.* 106:6; *Dan.* 95, 15
*Est.* 6:6 shall be *d.* to the man
*Job* 21:31 repay what he hath *d.*?
*Ps.* 33:9 he spake, and it was *d.*
71:19 hast *d.* gr. things, 106:21; 126:2, 3
120:3 *d.* to thee, false tongue?
*Ec.* 1:9 is *d.* is what shall be *d.*
2:12 hath been already *d.*
*Is.* 41:4 who hath *d.* it?
44:23 for the Lord hath *d.* it
*Jer.* 48:19 him fleeth, what is *d.*
*Ezek* 39:8 it is *d.* saith the Lord
*Dan.* 11:36 determined sh. be *d.*
*Mat.* 6:10 thy will be *d.* 26:42; *Luke* 11:2; 22:42
8:13 so be it *d.* to thee
11:21 works *d.* in you, had been *d.* in Tyre, *Luke* 10:13
18:19 it shall be *d.* for them
23:23 these ought ye to have *d.* *Luke* 11:42
25:21 well *d.* good servant, 23
40 as ye have *d.* it to one of these, ye have *d.* it to me
27:54 things that were *d.* 28:11
*Mark* 5:19 things the L. hath *d.* for thee, 20; *Luke* 8:39
6:30 told him what they had *d.*
9:13 *d.* to him what. they listed
13:30 not pass till these be *d.*
15:8 to do, as he had ever *d.*
*Luke* 1:49 hath *d.* great things
3:19 evils Herod had *d.*
8:56 tell no man what was *d.*
9:10 told him all they had *d*
14:22 it is *d.* as thou hast com.
17:10 we have *d.* that which was our duty to do
*John* 5:29 they that have *d.* good to life; they that have *d.* ev.
15:7 what ye will, it shall be *d.*
*Acts* 4:28 determ. before to be *d.*
14:27 reh. all G. had *d.* 15:4
21:14 the will of the Lord be *d.*
*Rom.* 9:11 *d.* any good or evil
1 *Cor.* 9:15 nor be so *d.* unto me
13:10 in part shall be *d.* away
14:26 let all be *d.* to edifying
40 be *d.* decently
16:14 be *d.* with charity
2 *Cor.* 5:10 things *d.* in body
*Eph.* 6:13 having *d.* all to stand
*Phil.* 2:3 nothing be *d.* through strife
*Col.* 4:9 known all things *d.*
*Rev.* 16:17 saying, It is *d.* 21:6
22:6 which must shortly be *d.*

**Have I DONE.**

*Num.* 22:28 what *h. I d.* to thee, 1 *K.* 19:20; *Mic.* 6:3
*Jud.* 8:2 what *have I* now *d.*? 1 *Sam.* 17:29
1 *Sam.* 20:1 what *have I d.*? 26:18; 29:8; *Jer.* 8:6

**He hath, *or* hath he DONE.**

*Lev.* 24:19 as *h. d.* so be done
*Jud.* 15:10 as *he hath d.* to us
1 *Sam.* 6:9 *h. h. d.* us this gr. ev.
12:24 great things *he hath d.*
20:32 what *hath he d.*?
1 *Chr.* 16:12 rem. his works *he hath d. Ps.* 78:4; 98:1; 105:5
*Ps.* 66:16 declare wha. *he hath d.*
115:3 *he h. d.* what he pleased
*Prov.* 24:29 as *he hath d.* to me
*Is.* 12:5 *he hath d.* excel. things
*Ezek.* 24:24 that *he hath d.* shall ye do
33:16 *he hath d.* that is lawful
*Joel* 2:20 *he hath d.* great things
*Mark* 7:37 *he hath d.* all things
2 *Cor.* 5:10 receive accor. *h. h. d.*

**I have DONE.**

*Gen.* 28:15 till *I have d.* that I h.
*Jos.* 24:7 seen what *I have d.*
*Jud.* 1:7 as *I h. d.* so G. req. me
15:11 as th. did to me, so *h. I d.*
2 *Sam.* 14:21 *I have d.* this thing
24:10 *I h. d.* foolishly, 1 *Ch.* 21:8
2 *K.* 19:25 how *I have d.* it?
*Job* 34:32 if *I have d.* iniquity
*Ps.* 7:3 O L. if *I have d.* this
119:121 *I h. d.* judgment
*Is.* 10:13 by st. of hand *I h. d.* it
33:13 what *I have d.*
37:26 heard how *I have d.* it?
*Ezek.* 12:11 as *I h. d.* so be done
14:23 *I have* not *d.* without ca. all *I have d.* in it
*John* 13:12 what *I have d.* to you?
15 do as *I have d.* to you

**Hast thou DONE.**

*Gen.* 4:10 what *h. t. d.*? 31:26; *Num.* 23:11; 1 *Sam.* 13:11; 2 *Sam.* 3:24; *John* 18:35
20:9 what *h. th. d.*? *Jud.* 15:11
2 *Sam.* 7:21 to thy heart *h. t. d.*
16:10 wherefore *hast thou d.* so?
1 *K.* 1:6 saying, Why *h. t. d.* so?
1 *Chr.* 17:19 *h. t. d.* all this
*Ps.* 60:21 these things *h. thou d.*
*Jon.* 1:10 why *hast thou d.* this?

**Thou hast DONE.**

*Gen.* 3:13 what is this *thou h. d.*? 12:18; 26:10; 29:25; *Jud.* 15:11; 2 *Sam.* 12:21
14 because *thou hast d.* this, 22:16; 2 *Chr.* 25.16
20:9 *t. h. d.* deeds ou. n. to be *d.*
27:45 he forget what *t. h. d.*
31:28 *thou h. d.* foolish. 1 *Sam.* 13:13; 2 *Chr.* 16:9
*Jos.* 7:19 tell me what *thou hast d.* 1 *Sam.* 14:43
*Ps.* 40:5 wonderful works *t. h. d.*
52:9 praise thee bec. *t. h. d.* it
109:27 know that *thou h. d.* it
*Jer.* 2:23 know what *thou hast d.*
*Lam.* 1:21 are glad *thou h. d.* it
22 as *thou hast d.* unto me
2:20 consider to whom *t. h. d.*
*Ezek.* 16:48 Sod. not *d.* as *t. h. d.*
59 deal with these as *thou h. d.*
*Ob.* 15 as *t. h. d.* be done to thee
*Jon.* 1:14 *t. h. d.* as it pleaseth

**Not DONE.**

*Gen.* 20:9 deeds ought *not* be *d.*
*Num.* 16:28 *not d.* of mine own
*Deut.* 32:27 Lord hath *not d.* all
*Is.* 5:4 done that I have *not d.*?
46:10 declaring things *not* yet *d.*
*Jer.* 3:16 neither shall that be *d.*
*Ezek.* 5:9 that I have *not d.*
*Dan.* 9:12 *not* been *d.* as on Jer.
11:24 do what his fat. *not d.*
*Amos* 3:6 in city, L. *not d.* it?
*Acts* 26:26 was *not d.* in a corner

**DONE, *with* this.**

*Gen.* 21:26 wot n. who hath *d. t.*
42:28 what is *this* God hath *d.*
*Jud.* 2:2 not obeyed, why *d. t.*?
6:29 Who hath *d. this*? 15:6
1 *Sam.* 28:18 hath Lord *d. this*
*Ps.* 7:3 O Lord, if I have *d. this*
22:31 declare that he hath *d. th.*
51:4 and *d. this* evil in my sight
*Is.* 41:20 hand of Lord hath *d. this*
*Ezek.* 23:38 moreover *this* they have *d.* unto me
*Mark* 5:32 her that had *d. this*
*Luke* 23:41 *t.* man *d.* nothing amiss
*Acts* 4:7 by what p. ha. ye *d. t.*?

**DOOR.**

*Gen.* 4:7 sin lieth at the *d.*
19:9 came near to break the *d.*
*Ex.* 12:23 will pass over the *d.*
*Deut.* 15:17 thrust it through ear to *d.*
2 *Sam.* 13:17 bolt the *d.* after h.
2 *K.* 4:15 she stood in the *d.*
9:3 then open the *d.* and flee
*Est.* 2:21 which kept the *d.* 6:2
*Job* 31:9 laid wait at neighb. *d.*
34 I went not out of the *d.*?
*Ps.* 141:3 keep the *d.* of my lips
*Prov.* 26:14 as *d.* turneth
*Cant.* 5:4 in hand by hole of *d.*
8:9 if she be a *d.* we will inclose
*Ezek.* 8:8 in wall, behold a *d.*
10:19 stood at *d.* of the east gate
11:1 at *d.* of the gate 25 men
41:2 breadth of *d.* ten cubits
46:3 peo. shall worship at the *d.*
*Hos.* 2:15 valley of A. *d.* of hope
*Amos* 9:1 smite the lint. of the *d.*
*Mat.* 27:60 rolled great stone to *d.* of sepulchre, *Mark* 15:46
28:2 rolled stone from the *d.*
*Mark* 1:33 city was gather. at *d.*
2:2 no room, no not about the *d.*
16:3 who roll us stone from *d.*?
*John* 10:1 entereth not by the *d.*
2 that entereth in by the *d.*
7 I am the *d.* 9.
18:16 but Peter stood at the *d.*
*Acts* 5:9 feet at *d.* to carry thee
12:13 as Peter knocked at the *d.*
14:27 opened *d.* of faith to Gen.
1 *Cor.* 16:9 great *d.* and effectual
2 *Cor.* 2:12 a *d.* was opened to me
*Col.* 4:3 open a *d.* of utterance
*Jam.* 5:9 judge standeth bef. *d.*
*Rev.* 3:8 before thee an open *d.*
20 stand at *d.* if any man open
4:1 a *d.* was open in heaven

**DOOR, *with* house.**

*Gen.* 19:11 that were at *d.* of *h.*
43:19 communed at *d.* of *house*
*Ex.* 12:22 no. of you go out at *d.*
*Jud.* 19:26 fell down at *d.* 27
2 *Sam.* 11:9 slept at *d.* of *house*
2 *K.* 5:9 Naam. stood at *d.* of *h.*
*Neh.* 3:21 Meremoth rep. from *d.*
*Prov.* 5:8 not nigh *d.* of her *h.*
9:14 she sitteth at *d.* of her *h.*
*Ezek.* 8:14 to *d.* of Lord's *h.* 47:1

**DOOR, *with* keeper, s.**

2 *K.* 25:18 captain of the guard took the three *k.* of *d. Jer.* 52:24
1 *Chr.* 15:24 Obed. and Jeh. *d.-k.*
*Est.* 6:2 *k.* of *d.* sought to lay
*Ps.* 84:10 I had rather be a *d.-k.*
*Jer.* 35:4 Maaseiah *keep.* of the *d.*

**DOOR, *with* posts.**

*Ex.* 12:7 blood on upper *d.-p.*
21:6 master bring him to *d.-p.*
*Deut.* 11:20 write them on *d.-p.*
*Is.* 6:4 *p.* of *d.* moved at the vo.
*Ezek.* 41:3 he measured *p.* of *d.*
16 measured the *d.-p.*

**DOOR, *with* shut.**

*Gen.* 19:6 L. *s. d.*; 10 ang. *s. d.*
2 *K.* 4:4 shalt *shut d.* upon thee
6:32 *shut d.* hold him fast at *d.*
*Mat.* 6:6 hast *shut* thy *d.* pray
25:10 *d.* was *s.*; *Luke* 11:7 *d.* is now *s.*
*Luke* 13:25 hath *s.* to the *d.*
*Rev.* 3:8 open *d.* no man can *s.*

**DOOR, *with* tabernacle.**

*Ex.* 29:4 bring to *d.* of *tab.* 40:12; *Lev.* 4:4; 8:3, 4; 12:6; *Num.* 6:10

11 by *d.* of *t.* 32; 40:29; *Lev.* 1:5; *Num.* 27:2
42 burnt-offering at *d.* of *t.* 33:9, 10; 38:8; 40:28; *Lev.* 1:3; 3:2; 4:7, 18
40:6 *d.* of *taber. Num.* 25:6
*Lev.* 8:31 at *d.* of *t.* 35; 14:11; 16:7; 17:6; *Num.* 6:18; 10:3; *Jos.* 19:51
33 shall not go out of *d.* of *t.*
10:7 not go out from *d.* of *t.*
14:23 *d.* of *t.* 15:14, 29; 19:21; *Num.* 6:13; 16:19, 50; 20:6
17:4 bring. it not to *d.* of *tab.* 9
*Num.* 12:5 in *d.* of *tab.* 16:18
*Deut.* 31:15 pillar of cloud ov. *d.*

**DOOR, *joined with* tent.**

*Gen.* 18:1 Abra. sat in the *tent d.*
10 Sarah heard it in the *tent d.*
*Ex.* 33:8 ev. man at his *t. d.* 10
*Num.* 11:10 weep. ev. man in *d.*
16:27 Abiram stood in *t. d.*
*Jud.* 4:20 Stand in *d.* of *tent*

**DOORS.**

*Jos.* 2:19 whosoever go out of *d.*
*Jud.* 3:25 opened not *d.* of parlor
11:31 cometh forth of *d.*
16:3 Samson took *d.* of the city
1 *Sam.* 3:15 Samuel opened t. *d.*
21:13 D. scrabbled on *d.* of gate
*Job* 31:32 opened *d.* to traveller
38:10 set bars and *d.* to the sea
17 seen *d.* of shadow of death?
41:14 who open. *d.* of his face?
*Ps.* 24:7 up, ye everlasting *d.* 9
78:23 though opened *d.* of heav.
*Prov.* 8:3 wisdom crieth at the *d.*
34 waiting at posts of my *d.*
*Is.* 57:8 behind *d.* set up
*Ezek.* 33:30 talking in the *d.*
*Mic.* 7:5 *d.* of mouth from her
*Zec.* 11:1 open thy *d.* O Lebanon
*Mat.* 24:33 at the *d. Mark* 13:29
*Acts* 5:19 angel opened prison *d.*
23 keepers standing before *d.*
16:26 all the *d.* were opened
27 keeper seeing prison *d.* op.

**Shut DOORS.**

*Jud.* 3:23 Ehud *shut d.* of parlor
2 *Chr.* 28:24 *s.* up *d.* of L.'s ho.
29:7 have *shut d.* of the porch
*Neh.* 6:10 let us *shut d.* of temple
7:3 *shut* the *d.* and bar them
*Job* 3:10 *shut* not up *d.* of womb
38:8 shut up the sea with *d.*?
*Ec.* 12:4 *d.* be *s.* in the streets
*Is.* 26:20 enter. and shut thy *d.*
*Mal.* 1:10 *shut d.* for naught
*John* 20:19 *d. sh.* Jesus came, 26
*Acts* 21:30 the *d.* were *shut*

DOR. *Jud.* 1:27; 1 *K.* 4:11
DORCAS. *Acts* 9:36, 39

**DOTE, ED, ING.**

*Jer.* 50:36 and they shall *d.*
*Ezek.* 23:5 Aholah *d.* on Assyri.
1 *Tim.* 6:4 *d.* about questions

DOTHAN. *Gen.* 37:17; 2 *K.* 6:13

**DOUBLE.**

*Gen.* 43:12 and take *d.* money
*Ex.* 22:4 theft be found, rest. *d.*
7 if found, let him pay *d.*
*Deut.* 15:18 worth a *d.* hired ser.
21:17 giving him a *d.* portion
2 *K.* 2:9 *d.* portion of thy spirit
1 *Chr.* 12:33 were not of *d.* heart
*Job* 11:6 *d.* to that which is
*Job* 41:13 to him with *d.* bridle?
*Ps.* 12:2 with a *d.* heart do speak
*Is.* 40:2 rec. *d.* for all her sins
61:7 your shame have *d.* in their land they shall possess *d.*
*Jer.* 16:18 recomp. their sin *d.*
17:18 with *d.* destruction
*Zec.* 9:12 I will render *d.* to thee
1 *Tim.* 3:8 deacons not *d.*-tong.
5:17 worthy of *d.* honor
*Rev.* 18:6 *d.* unto her *d.* in cup she hath filled, fill to her *d.*

**DOUBLE-MINDED.**

*Jam.* 1:8 a *d.-m.* man is unstable
4:8 purify your hearts, ye *d.-m.*

**DOUBLED.**

*Gen.* 41:32 dream was *d.* twice
*Ex.* 28:16 four-square, being *d.*
39:9 span was breadth, being *d.*
*Ezek.* 21:14 sword be *d.* third ti.

**DOUBT, S.**

*Deut.* 28:66 thy life hang in *d.*
*Dan.* 5:16 thou canst dissolve *d.*
*Acts* 28:4 no *d.* this man is a mur.
*Gal.* 4:20 for I stand in *d.* of you
1 *John* 2:19 wo. no *d.* have con.

**DOUBT.**

*Mat.* 14:31 wheref. didst thou *d.*?
21:21 if ye have faith and *d.* not
*Mark* 11:23 not *d.* in his heart
*John* 10:24 how long make us *d.*?

**DOUBTED, ETH.**

*Mat.* 28:17 but some *d.*
*Acts* 5:24 *d.* where. would grow
10:17 Peter *d.* in himself
25:20 I *d.* of such questions
*Rom.* 14:23 *d.* is damned

**DOUBTFUL.**

*Luke* 12:29 nei. be ye of *d.* mind
*Rom.* 14:1 not to *d.* disputations

**DOUBTING.**

*John* 13:22 *d.* of whom he spake
*Acts* 10:20 go, nothing *d.* 11:12
1 *Tim.* 2:8 men pray without *d.*

**DOUBTLESS.**

*Ps.* 126:6 *d.* come again rejoicing
*Is.* 63:16 *d.* thou art our father
1 *Cor.* 9:2 yet *d.* I am to you
*Phil.* 3:8 *d.* I count all but loss

**DOUGH.**

*Ex.* 12:39 unleavened cakes of *d.*
*Num.* 15:20 offer a cake of *d.* 21
*Neh.* 10:37 first-fruits of our *d.*
*Jer.* 7:18 women knead their *d.*
*Ezek.* 44:30 give priest first of *d.*
*Hos.* 7:4 after he hath kneaded *d.*

**DOVE.**

*Gen.* 8:8 N. sent forth a *d.* 10, 12
9 the *d.* found no rest
*Ps.* 55:6 that I had w. like a *d.*
68:13 ye shall be as w. of a *d.*
*Cant.* 1:15 thou hast *d.* eyes, 4:1
2:14 my *d.* let me see thy coun.
5:2 my sister, my *d.*
6:9 my *d.* my undefiled
*Is.* 38:14 I did mourn as a *d.*
*Jer.* 48:28 and be like the *d.*
*Hos.* 7:11 Eph. is like a silly *d.*
11:11 they shall tremble as a *d.*
*Mat.* 3:16 like a *d. Mark* 1:10; *Luke* 3:22; *John* 1:32

**DOVES.**

2 *K.* 6:25 of a cab of *d.* dung
*Cant.* 5:12 eyes are as eyes of *d.*
*Is.* 59:11 we mourn sore like *d.*
60:8 flee as *d.* to their windows.
*Ezek.* 7:16 like *d.* of the valleys
*Nah.* 2:7 lead as with voice of *d.*
*Mat.* 10:16 harmless as *d.*
21:12 that sold *d. Mark* 11:15
*John* 2:14 those that sold *d.*

**Up and DOWN.**

*Job* 1:7 walking *up and d.* 2:2
*Ps.* 59:15 wander *up and d.*
109:23 I am tossed *up and d.*
*Ezek.* 28:14 *up a. d.* in midst
*Zec.* 10:12 shall walk *up a. d.*
*Acts* 27:27 were driven *up and d.*

**DOWNSITTING.**

*Ps.* 139:2 thou knowest my *d.*

**DOWNWARD.**

2 *K.* 19:30 take root *d. Is.* 37:31
*Ec.* 3:21 spirit of beast goeth *d.*
*Ezek.* 1:27 appear. of loins *d.* 8:2

**DOWRY.**

*Gen.* 30:20 end. me with good *d.*
34:12 ask me never so much *d.*
*Ex.* 22:17 according to the *d.*
1 *Sam.* 18:25 king desireth not *d.*

**DRAG.**

*Hab.* 1:15 gather them in their *d.*
16 burn incense to their *d.*

**DRAGGING.**

*John* 21:8 *d.* the net with fishes

**DRAGON.**

*Ps.* 91:13 *d.* shalt thou trample
*Is.* 27:1 slay *d.* that is in sea
51:9 cut Rahab and wounded *d.*
*Jer.* 51:34 swallow. me up like *d.*
*Ezek.* 29:3 Pharaoh, the great *d.*
*Rev.* 12:3 behold, a great red *d.*
9 *d.* was cast out, 13
17 *d.* was wroth with the wom.
13:2 the *d.* gave him his power
4 they worshipped the *d.*
11 he spake as a *d.*
16:13 come out of mouth of *d.*
20:2 he laid hold on the *d.*

**DRAGON-WELL.**

*Neh.* 2:13 I went out before *d.-w.*

**DRAGONS.**

*Deut.* 32:33 wine is poison of *d.*
*Job* 30:29 I am a brother to *d.*
*Ps.* 44:19 brok. us in place of *d.*
74:13 breakest the heads of t. *d.*
148:7 praise the Lord, ye *d.*
*Is.* 13:22 *d.* in pleasant palaces
34:13 be habitation for *d.* 35:7
43:20 *d.* and owls shall hon. me
*Jer.* 9:11 Jerusalem a den of *d.*
10:22 cities of Judah a den of *d.*
14:6 snuffed up wind like *d.*
51:37 Babylon a dwelling for *d.*
*Mic.* 1:8 make wailing like *d.*
*Mal.* 1:3 heritage waste for the *d.*

**DRAMS.**

1 *Chr.* 29:7 gave of gold 10,000 *d.*
*Ezr.* 2:69 gave 61,000 *d.* of gold
8:27 20 basins of gold, of 1,000 *d.*
*Neh.* 7:70 gave to treas. 1,000 *d.*
71 gave 20,000 *d.* of gold, 72

**DRANK.**

*Gen.* 9:21 Noah *d.* of the wine
24:46 I *d.* made camels drink
27:25 brought wine and he *d.*
*Num.* 20:11 the congregation *d.*
*Deut.* 32:38 *d.* wine of drink-of.
1 *Sam.* 30:12 nor *d.* water
2 *Sam.* 12:3 *d.* of his own cup
1 *K.* 13:19 eat bread in h. *d.* wa.
17:6 and he *d.* of brook
*Dan.* 1:5 king ap. of wine he *d.*
5:1 *d.* before the thousand
3 his concubines *d.* in them
*Mark* 14:23 and they all *d.* of it
*Luke* 17:27 they eat, they *d.* 28
*John* 4:12 Jacob *d.* thereof
1 *Cor.* 10:4 *d.* of that spirit. rock

**DRAUGHT.**

*Mat.* 15:17 out in *d. Mark* 7:19
*Luke* 5:4 let down nets for a *d.*
9 astonished at *d.* of fishes

**DRAUGHT-HOUSE.**

2 *K.* 10:27 made Baal's house a *d.*

**DRAVE.**

*Ex.* 14:25 they *d.* them heavily
*Jos.* 16:10 *d.* not out Canaanites
24:12 and *d.* them out from before you, *Jud.* 6:9
18 Lord *d.* out before us
*Jud.* 1:19 J. *d.* out inhabitants
2 *Sam.* 6:3 *d.* the cart, 1 *Chr.* 13:7
2 *K.* 17:21 Jeroboam *d.* Israel from following the Lord

*Acts* 7:45 whom God *d.* out
18:16 *d.* them from judgm.-seat
*See* DROVE.

**DRAW.**

*Gen.* 24:44 will *d.* for thy camels
*Ex.* 15:9 I will *d.* my sword
*Jud.* 4:7 I will *d.* to thee Sisera
9:54 *d.* thy sword, and slay me,
1 *Sam.* 31:4; 1 *Chr.* 10:4
20:32 *d.* from city to highways
2 *Sam.* 17:13 *d.* city into t. river
*Job* 21:33 every man *d.* after him
*Ps.* 28:3 *d.* me not with the w.
*Cant.* 1:4 *d.* me, we will run aft.
*Is.* 5:18 *d.* iniquity with cords
66:19 nations that *d.* the bow
*Ezek.* 21:3 will *d.* forth my sw.
28:7 strangers *d.* their swords
30:11 *d.* their swords ag. Egypt
32:20 *d.* her and all her multi.
*John* 4:11 hast nothing to *d.* w.
15 nor come hither to *d.*
6:44 except the Father *d.* him
12:32 I will *d.* all men unto me
21:6 were not able to *d.* it
*Acts* 20:30 to *d.* away disciples
*Jam.* 2:6 *d.* you before judg.-seat

**DRAW back.**

*Heb.* 10:38 but if any *d. back*
39 not of them who *d. back*

**DRAW near.**

1 *Sam.* 14:36 let us *d. near* to G.
1 *Sam.* 14:38 *d.* ye *n.* h. all t. ch.
*Ps.* 73:28 good to *d. n.* to God
107:18 *d. near* to gates of death
*Is.* 29:13 *d. near* with their lips
45:20 *d. n.* ye that are escaped
57:3 *d. near* ye sons of sorceress
*Jer.* 30:21 cause him to *d. near*
46:3 and *d. near* to battle
*Ezek.* 9:1 charge ov. city, to *d. n*
22:4 caused thy days to *d. near*
*Joel* 3:9 let all men of war *d. n.*
*Heb.* 10:22 *d. n.* with true heart

**DRAW nigh.**

*Ex.* 3:5 said *d.* not *nigh* hither
*Ps.* 69:18 *d. nigh* to my soul
119:150 *d. nigh* that fol. misch.
*Ec.* 12:1 nor years *d. nigh*
*Is.* 5:19 coun. of Holy One *d. n.*
*Heb.* 7:19 by the which we *d. n.*
*Jam.* 4:8 *d. n.* to G. he will *d. n.*

**DRAW out.**

*Ex.* 12:21 *d. out* and take a lamb
*Lev.* 26:33 *d. out* a sword after
*Jud* 3:22 not *d.* dagger *out* of
*Job* 41:1 canst *d. out* leviathan?
*Ps.* 35:3 *d. out* also the spear
85:5 wilt thou *d. o.* thine anger
*Prov.* 20:5 m. of und. will *d.* it *o.*
*Is.* 57:4 do ye *d. o.* tongue
58:10 *d. out* soul to the hungry
*Jer.* 49:20 *d.* them *out*, 50:45
*Lam.* 4:3 sea-monster *d. out*
*Ezek.* 5:2 I will *d. out* a sword
after them, 12; 12:14
*Hag.* 2:16 to *d. out* fifty vessels
*John* 2:8 *d. out* now, and bear

**DRAW up.**

*Job* 40:23 he can *d. up* Jordan

**DRAW,** *joined with* **water.**

*Gen.* 24:13 dau. come to *d. wa.*
1 *Sam.* 9:11 maid going to *d. wa.*
*Is.* 12:3 with joy shall ye *d. wa.*
*Nah.* 3:14 *d. waters* for the siege
*John* 4:7 woman of S. to *d. wa.*

**DRAWN.**

*Num.* 22:23 his sword *d.* 31; *Jos.*
5:13; 1 *Chr.* 21:16
*Deut.* 30:17 *d.* away, and w. gods
*Jos.* 8:6 till *d.* them from city
*Job* 20:5 it is *d.* and cometh out
*Ps.* 37:14 wicked *d.* out sword
55:21 than oil, yet *d.* swords
*Prov.* 24:11 that are *d.* to death
*Is.* 21:15 fled from *d.* swords
28:9 that are *d.* from breasts
*Jer.* 31:3 with loving-kindness *d.*
*Lam.* 2:3 *d.* back his right hand
*Ezek.* 21:5 Lord *d.* my sword, 28
*Acts* 11:10 *d.* up again to heaven
*Jam.* 1:14 *d.* away of his own

**DRAWER, S.**

*Deut.* 29:11 to *d.* of water
*Jos.* 9:21 be *d.* of water, 23, 27

**DRAWETH.**

*Deut.* 25:11 the one *d.* near
*Jud.* 19:9 day *d.* towards even.
*Job* 24:22 he *d.* the mighty
33:22 his soul *d.* near to grave
*Ps.* 10:9 *d.* him into his net
88:3 life *d.* nigh to the grave
*Is.* 26:17 *d.* near delivery
*Ezek.* 7:12 the day *d.* near
*Mat.* 15:8 *d.* nigh with their lips
*Luke* 21:8 the time *d.* near
28 your redemption *d.* nigh
*Jam.* 5:8 coming of L. *d.* nigh

**DRAWING.**

*Jud.* 5:11 in places of *d.* water
*John* 6:19 Jesus *d.* nigh to ship

**DREAD, Substantive.**

*Gen.* 9:2 *d.* of you be on ev. beast
*Ex.* 15:16 *d.* shall fall upon them
*Deut.* 2:25 to put *d.* of thee upon
the nations, 11:25
*Job* 13:11 his *d.* fall upon you?
21 let not thy *d.* make me afr.
*Is.* 8:13 and let him be your *d.*

**DREAD, Verb.**

*Deut.* 1:29 I said to you, *d.* not
1 *Chr.* 22:13 be strong, *d.* not

**DREADFUL.**

*Gen.* 28:17 how *d.* is this place
*Job* 15:21 a *d.* sound is in his ears
*Ezek.* 1:18 rings, they were *d.*
*Dan.* 7:7 a fourth beast *d.* 19
9:4 O Lord the great and *d.* God
*Hab.* 1:7 the Chaldeans are *d.*
*Mal.* 1:14 name *d.* among heath.
4:5 great and *d.* day of the Lord

**DREAM, Substantive.**

*Gen.* 20:3 to Abimelech in a *d.*
31:10 Jacob saw in a *d* the rams
24 God came to Laban in a *d.*
37:5 Joseph dreamed a *d.* 9, 10
*Gen.* 40:5 but. and ba. a *d.* both
41:7 it was a *d.* 1 *K.* 3:15
25 *d.* of Pharaoh is one, 26
*Num.* 12:6 L. will speak in a *d.*
*Jud.* 7:13 told a *d.* to his fellow
1 *K.* 3:5 to Solomon in a *d.*
*Job* 20:8 he shall fly away as a *d.*
33:15 in a *d.* openeth ears
*Ps.* 73:20 as a *d.* when one awak.
*Ec.* 5:3 a *d.* com. through busin.
*Is.* 29:7 fight ag. Ariel be as a *d.*
*Jer.* 23:28 hath *d.* let him tell *d.*
*Dan.* 2:4 tell thy servants the *d.*
36 this is the *d.*
4:19 *d.* be to th. that hate thee
7:1 Daniel had a *d.* wrote *d.*
*Mat.* 1:20 angel of Lord app. to
Joseph in a *d.* 2:13, 19
2:12 warned of God in a *d.* 22
27:19 I have suffered in a *d.*

**DREAM, Verb.**

*Ps.* 126:1 were like them that *d.*
*Joel* 2:28 old men *d.* *Acts* 2:17

**DREAMED.**

*Gen.* 28:12 Jac. *d.*; 37:5 Jos. *d.*
40:5 officers *d.*; 41:1 Phar. 15
*Jer.* 23:25 proph. said, I have *d.*
29:8 dreams you cause to be *d.*
*Dan.* 2:1 Nebuchadnezzar *d.*

**DREAMER, S.**

*Gen.* 37:19 said, This *d.* cometh
*Deut.* 13:3 not hearken to *d.*
5 *d.* shall be put to death
*Jer.* 27:9 hearken not to your *d.*
*Jude* 8 filthy *d.* defile the flesh

**DREAMS.**

*Gen.* 37:8 hated him for his *d.*
20 what will become of his *d.*
41:12 and he interpreted our *d.*
42:9 Joseph remembered the *d.*
1 *Sam.* 28:6 answer. not by *d.* 15
*Job* 7:14 thou scarest me with *d.*
*Ec.* 5:7 in multitude of *d.* are
*Jer.* 23:27 forget my name by *d.*
32 that prophesy false *d.*
*Dan.* 1:17 understand. in *d.* 5:12
*Zec.* 10:2 diviners told false *d.*

**DREAMETH.**

*Is.* 29:8 hungry man *d.* a thirsty

**DREGS.**

*Ps.* 75:8 *d.* wicked shall drink
*Is.* 51:17 drunken *d.* of cup, 22

**DRESS.**

*Gen.* 2:15 into garden to *d.* it
18:7 young man hasted to *d.* it
*Deut.* 28:39 plant viney. *d.* them
2 *Sam.* 12:4 to *d.* for wayfaring
13:5 Tamar *d.* meat in my sight
1 *K.* 18:25 Elijah said, *d.* it first

**DRESSED.**

2 *Sam.* 12:4 *d.* poor man's lamb
19:24 Mephib. not *d.* his feet
*Heb.* 6:7 for them by wh. it is *d.*

**DRESSER.**

*Luke* 13:7 said to *d.* of vineyard

**DREW.**

*Gen.* 24:20 Rebekah *d.* water, 45
37:28 they *d.* up Joseph
38:29 as Zarah *d.* back his hand
*Ex.* 2:10 I *d.* him out of water
16 Jethro's daughters *d.* water
*Jos.* 8:26 Jos. *d.* not hand back
*Jud.* 8:10 fell 120,000 *d.* sword
20 the youth *d.* not his sword
20:2 400,000 that *d.* sword
*Ruth* 4:8 so he *d.* off his shoe
2 *Sam.* 22:17 he *d.* me out of
many waters, *Ps.* 18:16
23:16 mighty men *d.* water out
well Beth. 1 *Chr.* 11:18
24:9 in Israel 800,000 *d.* sword
1 *K.* 22:34 *d.* a bow, 2 *Chr.* 18:33
2 *K.* 9:24 Jehu *d.* bow
1 *Chr.* 19:16 *d.* forth the Syrians
21:5 Israel were 1,100,000 that *d.*
sword, Judah 470,000
*Jer.* 38:13 *d.* up Jeremiah
*Hos.* 11:4 *d.* with cords of a man
*Mat.* 13:48 *d.* to shore, *Mark* 6:53
26:51 Peter *d.* his sword, *Mark*
14:47; *John* 18:10
*Luke* 23:54 and the sabbath *d.* on
*John* 2:9 servants *d.* the water
21:11 *d.* the net full of fishes
*Acts* 5:37 *d.* away much people
14:19 *d.* Paul out of the city
16:19 *d.* P. and S. into mark.-pl.
27 jailer *d.* his sword
17:6 *d.* Jason and certain breth.
19:33 they *d.* Alexander out
21:30 *d.* Paul out of temple
*Rev.* 12:4 *d.* third part of stars

**DREW near, *or* nigh.**

*Gen.* 47:29 time *d. n.* Is. m. die
1 *Sam.* 17:40 David *d. n.* to Goli.
2 *Sam.* 18:25 Ahimaaz *d. near*
*Zep.* 3:2 *d.* not *near* to her God
*Mat.* 21:1 when they *d. n.* to Jer.
34 time of fruit *d. near*, he sent
*Luke* 15:25 elder son *d. n.* to ho.
22:47 Judas *d. n.* to J. to kiss
24:15 Jesus himself *d. near*
28 they *d. nigh* to the village
*Acts* 7:17 time of promise *d. n.*
31 as Mos. *d. near* to behold it
27:27 *d. near* some country

**DREWEST.**

*Lam.* 3:57 *d.* near in day I called

DRIED. *See* after DRY.

**DRINK, Substantive.**
Gen. 21:19 and gave the lad d.
24:14 thy camels d. also, 46
Lev. 11:34 d. drunk in such ves.
Num. 20:8 give congregation d.
Jud. 4:19 she gave Sisera d.
Est. 1:7 d. in vessels of gold
Ps. 78:15 d. as out of gr. depths
102:9 mingled my d. with weep.
104:11 gave d. to every beast
Is. 32:6 cause d. of thirsty
43:20 to give d. to my people
Hos. 2:5 lovers that give me d.
4:18 their d. is sour
Hab. 2:15 giveth his neighbor d.
Hag. 1:6 ye are not filled with d.
Mat. 25:35 and ye gave me d.
37 g. thee d.; 42 gave me no d.
John 4:9 a Jew, askest d. of me
6:55 my blood is d. indeed
Rom. 12:20 enemy thirst, give d.
14:17 kingdom not meat and d.
1 Cor. 10:4 drink same spirit. d.
Col. 2:16 judge in meat or in d.

**Strong DRINK.**
Lev. 10:9 do not drink strong d.
Num. 6:3 Nazarite sep. fr. s. d.
Deut. 14:26 money for str. d.
29:6 nor drunk s. d. forty years
Jud. 13:4 wife not drink s. d.
1 Sam. 1:15 wine nor str. d.
Prov. 20:1 strong d. is raging
31:4 princes to drink str. d.
6 s. d. to him ready to perish
Is. 5:11 may follow strong d.
22 men of strength min. s. d.
24:9 str. d. bitter to them
28:7 erred through st. d. they are out of the way thro' s. d.
29:9 stag. but not with strong d.
56:12 fill ourselves with str. d.
Mic. 2:11 prophesy of strong d.
Luke 1:15 shall not drink s. d.

**DRINK-OFFERING.**
Ex. 29:40 for a d.-o. Num. 15:5
Lev. 23:13 d.-o. shall be of wine
Is. 57:6 hast poured d.-o.
65:11 furnish d.-o.
Joel 1:9 d.-o. cut off
13 the d.-o. is withholden
2:14 return, and leave a d.-o.

**DRINK-OFFERINGS.**
Lev. 23:18 with d.-o. 37; Num. 6:15; 28:31; 29:11, 18, 19, 21, 24, 30, 33, 37, 39
Num. 28:14 d.-o. half a hin of w.
Deut. 32:38 drank wine of d.-o.
Ezr. 7:17 buy speedily d.-o.
Ps. 16:4 their d.-o. of blood
Jer. 7:18 d.-o. to oth. gods, 19:13; 32:29
44:17 d.-o. to qu. of heaven, 18
Ezek. 20:28 there poured out d.-o.
45:17 princes part to give d.-o.

**DRINK, Verb.**
Gen. 24:18 d. my lord, 46
30:38 when flocks came to d.
Ex. 15:24 what shall we d.?
32:20 made children of Israel d.
Lev. 10:9 do not d. wine nor
Num. 6:3 nor d. liquor of grapes
Jud. 7:5 boweth down to d.
Ruth 2:9 go to the vessels, and d.
2 Sam. 23:16 would not d. thereof, 17; 1 Chr. 11:18, 19
1 K. 17:4 shalt d. of the brook
Est. 3:15 king and Haman to d.
Job 21:20 d. wrath of Almighty
Ps. 36:8 d. of river of thy pleas.
60:3 d. wine of astonishment
69:21 gave me vinegar to d.
75:8 wicked of earth shall d.
78:44 into blood that not d.
80:5 givest them tears to d.
110:7 d. of the brook
Prov. 4:17 they d. wine
31:5 lest they d. and forget law
7 d. and forget his poverty
Cant. 5:1 d. yea, d. abundantly
Is. 24:9 drink bit. to them d. it
Is. 51:22 no more d. it again
62:9 d. it in courts of holiness
65:13 my servant shall d.
Jer. 16:7 cup of consolation to d.
23:15 make d. water of gall
25:15 cause nations to d. it
16 they shall d. and be moved
27 d. ye, be drunken, and spue
28 Ye shall certainly d.
35:14 to this day they d. none
49:12 whose judgm. was not to d. of cup, but thou shalt d.
Ezek. 4:11 time to time shalt d.
23:32 d. of thy sister's cup
34:19 d. that ye have fouled
Dan. 5:2 concubines might d.
Amos 4:1 masters, Let us a.
Ob. 16 the heathen d. continually, yea, they shall d.
Hab. 2:16 d. and let thy foreskin
Hag. 1:6 ye d. but are not filled
Zec. 9:15 d. and make a noise
Mat. 10:42 whoso giveth to d to
20:22 are ye able to d. of the cup I shall d. of? Mark 10:38
23 shall d. indeed, Mark 10:39
26:27 saying, d. ye all of it
29 not d. till that day I d. it, Mark 14:25; Luke 22:18
42 may not pass, except I d. it
27:34 gave him vinegar to d.
48 put it on a reed, and gave him to d. Mark 15:36
Mark 16:18 if d. any deadly th.
John 4:10 saith, Give me to d.
7:37 let him come to me and d.
18:11 shall I not d.?
1 Cor. 10:4 did all d. the same
21 d. cup of L. and of devils
11:25 this do, as oft as ye d. it
12:13 all to d. into one Spirit

**DRINK water, or waters.**
Gen. 24:43 w. of thy pitcher to d.
Ex. 7:24 for w. to d.
15:23 could not d. waters of M.
17:1 no water for the peo. to d.
Num. 5:24 d. bitter water, 26, 27
20:5 neither any w. to d. 33:14
17 nor d. water of wells, 21:22
Deut. 2:6 wa. for money, d. 28
Jud. 4:19 w. to d. for I am thir.
7:6 rest bowed to d. water
1 Sam. 30:11 Egyptian d. w.
2 Sam. 23:15 give me to d. of w. of Bethlehem, 1 Chr. 11:17
1 K. 13:8 nor will I d. water, 9
17:10 a little w. that I may d.
2 K. 3:17 val. fill. with w. may d.
18:31 d. ev. one wa. cis. Is. 36:16
Job 22:7 given w. to weary to d.
Prov. 5:15 d. wa. out of thy cist.
25:21 give w. to d.
Jer. 2:18 d. water of Sihor
8:14 w. of gall to d. 9:15
Ezek. 4:11 d. water by meas. 16
12:18 d. thy water with tremb.
19 d. their wa. with astonish.
31:14 their trees that d. w. 16
Dan. 1:12 pulse to eat, wat. to d.
Amos 4:8 wandered to d. water
Jon. 3:7 let not feed nor d. w.
Mark 9:41 cup of w. to d.
John 4:7 Give me w. to d.
1 Tim. 5:23 d. no longer water

**DRINK, with wine.**
Gen. 19:32 our father d. wine
Lev. 10:9 not d. wine when go
Num. 6:3 d. no vinegar of w.
20 Nazarite may d. w.
Deut. 28:39 plant vineyards, but not d. of wine, Amos 5:11
Jud. 13:4 M. wife d. no w. 7, 14
2 Sam. 16:2 w. such as faint m. d.
Ps. 60:3 d. wine of astonishment
Prov. 4:17 d. wine of violence
9:5 d. of wine I have mingled
31:4 it is not for kings to d. w.
Ec. 9:7 d. thy w. with a merry
Cant. 8:2 d. of spiced w.
Is. 5:22 are mighty to d. wine
24:9 shall not d. w. with a song
62:8 sons of stranger not d. w.
Jer. 35:2 give Rechabites w. to d.
6 d. no w. ye shall d. no w.
Ezek. 44:21 nor any priest d. w.
Dan. 1:16 wine they should d.
Joel 3:3 sold a girl for w. to d.
Amos 2:8 d. w. of condemned
12 ye gave Nazarites wine to d.
6:6 that d. wine in bowls
9:14 plant vineyards and d. w.
Mic. 6:15 not d. wine, Zep. 1:13
Mark 15:23 gave to d. w. mingled
Luke 1:15 J. shall d. neither w.
Rom. 14:21 not good to d. wine
Rev. 14:8 all nations d. of w.
10 d. of wine of wrath of G.

**DRINKERS.**
Joel 1:5 howl, all ye d. of wine

**DRINKS.**
Heb. 9:10 only in meats and d.

**DRINKETH.**
Gen. 44:5 in which my lord d.?
Deut. 11:11 land d. water of rain
Job 6:4 poison d. up my spirit
15:16 d. iniquity like water
34:7 like Job who d. scorning
40:23 behold, he d. up a river
Prov. 26:6 d. damage
Is. 29:8 he d. but he awaketh
44:12 the smith, he d. no water
Mark 2:16 d. with publicans?
John 4:13 d. this wa. shall thirst
14 d. of water I shall give him
6:54 d. my blood hath eter. life
56 d. my blood, dwelleth in me
1 Cor. 11:29 d. unworth. d. dam.
Heb. 6:7 which d. in the rain

**DRINKING.**
Gen. 24:22 camels had done d.
Ruth 3:3 till Boaz have done d.
1 Sam. 30:16 were eating and d.
1 K. 4:20 Judah and Israel d.
10:21 Solomon's d. vessels
16:9 E. was d.; 20:12 Benhad.
1 Chr. 12:39 with D. three days d.
Est. 1:8 d. was according to law
Job 1:13 sons and daughters d.
Is. 22:13 eating flesh, and d. w.
Mat. 11:18 John came neither eating nor d. Luke 7:33
19 eating and d. Luke 7:34
24:38 and d. till the flood came
Luke 10:7 d. such as they give

**DRIVE.**
Ex. 6:1 with a strong hand d. out
23:28 hornets, which shall d.
29 I will not d. out in one year
30 by little and little I will d.
33:2 I will d. out the Canaanite
34:11 behold, I d. out Amorite
Num. 22:6 I may d. them out
11 able to overcome, and d.
33:55 if ye will not d. out the
Deut. 4:38 d. out nations from bef. thee, 9:4, 5; Jos. 3:10
9:3 so shalt thou d. them out
11:23 then will the Lord d. out
18:12 Lord doth d. them out
Jos. 13:6 them will I d. out
14:12 then I shall be able to d.
15:63 Judah could not d. out
17:12 Manasseh could not d. out
13 not utterly d. out, Jud. 1:28
18 shalt d. out the Canaanites
23:5 d. them out of your sight
13 no more d. out, Jud. 2:3, 21

*Jud.* 1:19 Judah could not *d.* out
21 Benjamin not *d.* out Jebus.
27 Manasseh; 29 Ephraim
31 Asher; 33 Naphtali
11:24 whom Lord shall *d.* out
2 *K.* 4:24 *d.* slack not thy riding
2 *Chr.* 20:7 *d.* out inhabitants
*Job* 18:11 ter. *d.* him to his feet
24:3 *d.* away ass of fatherless
*Ps.* 44:2 didst *d.* out heathen
68:2 as smoke, so *d.* them away
*Prov.* 22:15 rod of correction *d.* it
*Is.* 22:19 *d.* thee from thy station
*Jer.* 24:9 be a curse whether I *d.*
27:10 I should *d.* you out, 15
46:15 Lord did *d.* them
*Ezek.* 4:13 whether I will *d.* them
*Dan.* 4:25 *d.* thee from men, 32
*Hos.* 9:15 *d.* th. out of my house
*Joel* 2:20 *d.* the northern army
*Zep.* 2:4 *d.* out Ashd. at noonday
*Acts* 27:15 ship, we let her *d.*

**DRIVEN.**

*Gen.* 4:14 hast *d.* me out this day
*Ex.* 10:11 *d.* from Pharaoh's pre.
22:10 the beast be *d.* away
*Num.* 32:21 *d.* out his enemies
*Deut.* 4:19 be *d.* to worship them
30:1 whither Lord hath *d.* thee
4 if any of thine be *d.* out
*Jos.* 23:9 L. *d.* out great nations
1 *Sam.* 26:19 *d.* me out this day
*Job* 6:13 wisdom *d.* from me?
13:25 break leaf *d.* to and fro?
18:18 *d.* from light to darkness
30:5 *d.* forth from among men
*Ps.* 40:14 let be *d.* backward
68:2 as smoke is *d.* away, so
114:3 Jordan was *d.* back, 5
*Prov.* 14:32 wicked is *d.* away
*Is.* 8:22 shall be *d.* to darkness
19:7 sown by brooks *d.* away
41:2 as *d.* stubble to his bow
*Jer.* 8:3 in places whither *d.*
23:3, 8; 29:14, 18; 32:37
16:15 from all lands whither *d.*
*Jer.* 23:2 *d.* them away not visit.
12 be *d.* on, and fall therein
40:12 places whither *d.* 43:5
46:28 end of nations, whither *d.*
49:5 shall be *d.* out every man
50:17 lions have *d.* him away
*Ezek.* 31:11 I have *d.* him out for
34:4 brought that *d.* away, 16
*Dan.* 4:33 *d.* from men, 5:21
9:7 through all countries *d.*
*Hos.* 13:3 as chaff *d.* with whirl.
*Mic.* 4:6 gather her *d.* *Zep.* 3:19
*Luke* 8:29 *d.* of devil into wilder.
*Acts* 27:17 and so were *d.*
27 *d.* up and down in Adria
*Jam.* 1:6 like wave *d.* with wind
3:4 though *d.* of fierce winds

**DRIVER.**

*Job* 39:7 nor regard. crying of *d.*

**DRIVETH.**

2 *K.* 9:20 for he *d.* furiously
*Ps.* 1:4 like chaff wind *d.*
*Prov.* 25:23 wind *d.* away rain
*Mark* 1:12 *d.* him to wilderness

**DRIVING.**

*Jud.* 2:23 *d.* them out hastily
2 *K.* 9:20 *d.* is like *d.* of Jehu
1 *Chr.* 17:21 by *d.* out nations

**DROMEDARY, IES.**

1 *K.* 4:28 brought barley for *d.*
*Est.* 8:10 sent letters on young *d.*
*Is.* 60:6 *d.* of Midian cover thee
*Jer.* 2:23 thou art a swift *d.*

**DROP, S.**

*Job* 36:27 maketh small the *d.*
38:28 who begotten *d.* of dew?
*Cant.* 5:2 locks with *d.* of night
*Is.* 40:15 nat. are as *d.* of bucket
*Luke* 22:44 as great *d.* of blood

**DROP.**

*Deut.* 32:2 doctrine *d.* as rain
33:28 heav. *d.* dew, *Prov.* 3:20
*Job* 36:28 which the clouds do *d.*
*Ps.* 65:11 thy paths *d.* fatness
12 *d.* on pastures of wilderness
*Prov.* 5:3 lips of a str. woman *d.*
*Cant.* 4:11 lips *d.* as honey-comb
*Is.* 45:8 *d.* down, ye heavens
*Ezek.* 20:46 *d.* thy word
21:2 *d.* thy word to. holy places
*Joel* 3:18 mountains shall *drop* down new wine, *Amos* 9:13
*Amos* 7:16 *d.* not thy word ag. Is.

**DROPPED, ETH.**

*Jud.* 5:4 heavens *d.* clouds *d.*
1 *Sam.* 14:26 the honey *d.*
2 *Sam.* 21:10 water *d.* on them
*Job* 29:22 my speech *d.* on them
*Ps.* 68:8 heavens *d.* at pres. of G.
*Ec.* 10:18 thr. idleness house *d.*
*Cant.* 5:5 hands *d.* with myrrh

**DROPPING.**

*Prov.* 19:13 a continual *d.* 27:15
*Cant.* 5:13 his lips *d.* myrrh

**DROPSY.**

*Luke* 14:2 a man wh. had the *d.*

**DROSS.**

*Ps.* 119:119 the wicked like *d.*
*Prov.* 25:4 take *d.* from silver
26:23 covered with silver *d.*
*Is.* 1:22 thy silver is become *d.*
25 purely purge away thy *d.*
*Ezek.* 22:18 house of Israel *d.* 19

**DROUGHT.**

*Gen.* 31:40 in day *d.* consumed
*Deut.* 8:15 fiery serpents and *d.*
*Job* 24:19 *d.* consu. snow-waters
*Ps.* 32:4 my moisture into the *d.*
*Is.* 58:11 L. satisfy thy soul in *d.*
*Jer.* 2:6 through a land of *d.*
17:8 not be careful in year of *d.*
50:38 a *d.* is upon her waters
*Hos.* 13:5 know thee in land of *d.*
*Hag.* 1:11 and I called for a *d.*

**DROVE.**

*Gen.* 32:16 ev. *d.* by themselves
33:8 what meanest by all this *d.*

**DROVE, Verb.**

*Gen.* 3:24 so God *d.* out the man
15:11 Abram *d.* fowls away
*Ex.* 2:17 shepherds *d.* them
*Num.* 21:32 *d.* out the Amorites
*Hab.* 3:6 *d.* asunder the nations
*John* 2:15 *d.* them out of temple

**DROWN.**

*Cant.* 8:7 neither can floods *d.* it
1 *Tim.* 6:9 *d.* men in perdition

**DROWNED.**

*Ex.* 15:4 are *d.* in Red sea
*Amos* 8:8 *d.* as by flood of E. 9:5
*Mat.* 18:6 better *d.* in the sea
*Heb.* 11:29 Egyptians were *d.*

**DROWSINESS.**

*Prov.* 23:21 *d.* shall clo. with rags

**DRUNK.**

*Deut.* 29:6 nor have you *d.* wine
32:42 my arrows *d.* with blood
*Jud.* 15:19 *d.* his spirit came ag.
1 *Sam.* 1:15 I have *d.* nei. wine
2 *Sam.* 11:13 Dav. made Uriah *d.*
1 *K.* 13:22 hast eaten and *d.*
16:9 Elah drinking himself *d.*
20:16 Benha. drinking hims. *d.*
2 *K.* 6:23 eat. and *d.* he sent aw.
19:24 *d.* strange wat. *Is.* 37:25
*Cant.* 5:1 *d.* my wine
*Is.* 51:17 hast *d.* cup of his fury
63:6 make them *d.* in my fury
*Jer.* 46:10 be *d.* with their blood
51:57 I will make *d.* her princes
*Ezek.* 34:18 *d.* of the deep waters
*Dan.* 5:4 *d.* praised gods of gold
23 thou and concubines have *d.*
*Ob.* 16 *d.* on my holy mountain
*Luke* 5:39 having *d.* old wine
13:26 eaten and *d.* in thy pres.
*John* 2:10 well *d.* then worse
*Eph.* 5:18 *d.* wherein is excess
*Rev.* 17:2 *d.* with wine of fornic.
18:3 all nations *d.* of wine

**DRUNKARD.**

*Deut.* 21:20 this our son is a *d.*
*Prov.* 23:21 *d.* sh. come to pov.
26:9 as a thorn into hand of *d.*
*Is.* 24:20 the earth reel like a *d.*
1 *Cor.* 5:11 with bro. a *d.* eat not

**DRUNKARDS.**

*Ps.* 69:12 I was song of the *d.*
*Is.* 28:1 woe to *d.* of Ephraim, 3
*Joel* 1:5 awake, ye *d.* and weep
*Nah.* 1:10 while drunken as *d.*
1 *Cor.* 6:10 nor *d.* inherit kingd.

**DRUNKEN.**

*Gen.* 9:21 Noah was *d.*
1 *Sam.* 1:14 How long be *d.*?
25:36 Nabal was very *d.*
*Job* 12:25 stag. like *d.* *Ps.* 107:27
*Is.* 19:14 as a *d.* man staggereth
29:9 *d.* but not with wine, 51:21
49:26 be *d.* with their own blood
51:17 *d.* dregs of cup of tremb.
*Jer.* 23:9 I am like a *d.* man
25:27 be *d.* and spue, and fall
48:26 *d.* for he magnified hims.
49:12 they have assuredly *d.*
51:7 golden cup made earth *d.*
39 make *d.* that they may sleep
*Lam.* 3:15 *d.* with wormwood
4:21 thou shalt be *d.* *Nah.* 3:11
5:4 *d.* our water for money
*Ezek.* 39:19 dri. blood till ye be *d.*
*Nah.* 1:10 while *d.* as drunkards
*Hab.* 2:15 and makest him *d.* also
*Mat.* 24:49 begin to eat and drink with the *d.* *Luke* 12:45
*Luke* 17:8 serve me till I have *d.*
*Acts* 2:15 not *d.* as ye suppose
1 *Cor.* 11:21 and another is *d.*
1 *Thes.* 5:7 be *d.* are *d.* in night
*Rev.* 17:6 woman *d.* with blood

**DRUNKENNESS.**

*Deut.* 29:19 to add *d.* to thirst
*Ec.* 10:17 eat for strength not *d.*
*Jer.* 13:13 fill inhabitants with *d.*
*Ezek.* 23:33 shalt be filled with *d.*
*Luke* 21:34 overcharged with *d.*
*Rom.* 13:13 not in rioting and *d.*
*Gal.* 5:21 works of flesh are *d.*

DRUSILLA. *Acts* 24:24

**DRY.**

*Lev.* 13:30 it is a *d.* scall
*Jos.* 9:5 bread was *d.* 12
*Jud.* 6:37 it be *d.* on all the earth
39 let it be *d.* only on fleece
*Job* 13:25 pursue the *d.* stubble?
*Ps.* 105:41 they ran in *d.* places
*Prov.* 17:1 better is a *d.* morsel
*Is.* 25:5 as the heat in a *d.* place
32:2 be as rivers in a *d.* place
44:27 saith to the deep, Be *d.*
56:3 say, I am a *d.* tree
*Jer.* 4:11 a *d.* wind, not to fan
51:36 I will make her springs *d.*
*Ezek.* 17:24 made *d.* tree flourish
20:47 devour every *d.* tree
30:12 I will make the rivers *d.*
37:2 bones *d.*; 4 O ye *d.* bones
*Hos.* 9:14 give them *d.* breasts
13:15 his spring shall become *d.*
*Nah.* 1:4 rebuk. sea, maketh it *d.*
10 be dev. as stubble fully *d.*
*Zep.* 2:13 make Nineveh *d.* like
*Mat.* 12:43 *d.* places, *Luke* 11:24
*Luke* 23:31 be done in the *d.*?

**DRY ground.**

*Gen.* 8:13 face of *ground* was *d.*
*Ex.* 14:16 on *d. g.* in sea, 22

*Jos.* 3:17 the priests stood firm on *d. ground* in Jordan
2 *K.* 2:8 Elisha went over on *d. g.*
*Ps.* 107:33 water-spr. into *d. g.*
35 turneth *d. g.* into water-sp.
*Is.* 44:3 will pour floods on *d. g.*
53:2 as a root out of a *d. g.*
*Ezek.* 19:13 planted in a *d. g.*

*See* LAND.

**DRY, Verb.**
*Job* 12:15 waters, they *d.* up
15:30 flame *d.* up his branches
*Is.* 42:15 will *d.* up herbs, pools
44:27 *d.* up thy rivers; 50:2 sea
*Jer.* 51:36 I will *d.* up her sea
*Zec.* 10:11 deeps of river shall *d.*

**DRIED.**
*Gen.* 8:7 until waters were *d.* up
*Lev.* 2:14 green ears of corn *d.* by
*Num.* 6:3 moist grapes or *d.*
11:6 our soul is *d.* away
*Jos.* 2:10 Lord *d.* up Red sea
4:23 *d.* up waters of Jordan
5:1 heard Lord had *d.* up Jord.
*Jud.* 16:7 with withs never *d.*
1 *K.* 13:4 Jeroboam's hand *d.*
17:7 brook *d.* because no rain
2 *K.* 19:24 with sole of feet have I *d.* the rivers, *Is.* 37:25
*Job* 18:16 his roots be *d.* beneath
28:4 they are *d.* up
*Ps.* 22:15 my strength is *d.*
69:3 my throat is *d.* eyes fail
106:9 Red sea, it was *d.* up
*Is.* 5:13 multi. *d.* up with thirst
19:5 river be wasted and *d.* up
6 brooks of defence be *d.* up
51:10 it which hath *d.* the sea?
*Jer.* 23:10 places of wilder. *d.* up
50:38 her waters shall be *d.* up
*Ezek.* 17:24 *d.* up the green tree
19:12 east wind *d.* up her fruit
37:11 they say, Our bones are *d.*
*Hos.* 9:16 their root is *d.* up
13:15 his fountain be *d.* up
*Joel* 1:10 the new wine is *d.* up
12 vine is *d.*; 20 rivers are *d.*
*Zec.* 11:17 arm be clean *d.* up
*Mark* 5:29 fount. of her blood *d.*
11:20 saw the fig-tree *d.* up
*Rev.* 16:12 Euphrates was *d.* up

**DRIEDST, ETH.**
*Job* 14:11 and as the flood *d.* up
*Ps.* 74:15 *d.* up mighty rivers
*Prov.* 17:22 broken spirit *d.* bon.
*Nah.* 1:4 Lord *d.* up all the riv.

**DRY-SHOD.**
*Is.* 11:15 make men go over *d.-s.*

**DUE.**
*Lev.* 10:13 thy *d.* thy sons' *d.* 14
*Deut.* 18:3 shall be the priest's *d.*
1 *Chr.* 15:13 sought not after *d.*
16:29 the glory *d.* to his name, *Ps.* 29:2; 96:8
*Prov.* 3:27 with. not to whom *d.*
*Mat.* 18:34 pay all that was *d.*
*Luke* 23:41 we receive *d.* reward
*Rom.* 13:7 to whom tribute is *d.*
1 *Cor.* 7:3 to the wife *d.* benevol.

**DUE season.**
*Lev.* 26:4 in *d. s. Deut.* 11:14
*Num.* 28:2 to offer to me in *d. s.*
*Ps.* 104:27 meat in *d. s.* 145:15
*Prov.* 15:23 a word spoken in *d. s.*
*Ec.* 10:17 princes eat in *d. s.*
*Mat.* 24:45 in *d. s. Luke* 12:42
*Gal.* 6:9 in *d. s.* we shall reap

**DUE time.**
*Deut.* 32:35 foot slide in *d. time*
*Rom.* 5:6 in *d. time* Christ died
1 *Cor.* 15:8 one born out of *d. t.*
1 *Tim.* 2:6 be testified in *d. t.*
*Tit.* 1:3 in *d. time* manifested
1 *Pet.* 5:6 he may exalt you in *d. t.*

**DUES.**
*Rom.* 13:7 render to all their *d.*

**DUKE, S.**
*Gen.* 36:15 *d.* of sons of Esau, 19
21 *d.* of the Horites, 29
40 *d.* Alvah, *d.* Jetheth
*Ex.* 15:15 *d.* of Edom amazed
*Jos.* 13:21 Hur and Reba, *d.*

**DULCIMER.**
*Dan.* 3:5 *d.* and music, 10, 15

**DULL.**
*Mat.* 13:15 ears are *d. Acts* 28:27
*Heb.* 5:11 ye are *d.* of hearing

**DUMAH.**
*Gen.* 25:14; *Jos.* 15:52; *Is.* 21:11

**DUMB.**
*Ex.* 4:11 or who maketh the *d.*
*Ps.* 38:13 I was as a *d.* man
39:2 I was *d.* with silence, 9
*Prov.* 31:8 open thy mouth for *d.*
*Is.* 35:6 tongue of *d.* shall sing
53:7 sheep before shearers is *d.*
56:10 his watchmen all *d.* dogs
*Ezek.* 3:26 *d.* and not be reprover
24:27 speak, and be no more *d.*
33:22 and I was no more *d.*
*Dan.* 10:15 to the grou. I bec. *d.*
*Hab.* 2:18 to make him *d.* idols
19 saith to *d.* stone, Arise
*Mat.* 9:32 bro. to him a *d.* man
33 the *d.* spake, *Luke* 11:14
12:22 and *d.* and he healed
15:30 having with them those *d.*
31 saw the *d.* speak, *Mark* 7:37
*Mark* 9:25 thou *d.* spirit, come
*Luke* 1:20 shalt be *d.* until the
*Acts* 8:32 lamb *d.* before shearer
1 *Cor.* 12:2 carried away to *d.*
2 *Pet.* 2:16 the *d.* ass speaking

**DUNG, Substantive.**
*Ex.* 29:14 and *d.* burn, *Lev.* 4:11; 8:17; 16:27; *Num.* 19:5
1 *K.* 14:10 as taketh away *d.*
2 *K.* 6:25 cab of doves' *d.*
9:37 carcass of Jezebel be as *d.*
18:27 eat their own *d. Is.* 36:12
*Job* 20:7 perish like his own *d.*
*Ps.* 83:10 they became as *d.*
*Jer.* 8:2 be for *d.* on the earth
9:22 carcasses fall as *d.*
16:4 shall be as *d.*; 25:33 be *d.*
*Ezek.* 4:12 shalt bake it with *d.*
15 given cow's *d.* for man's *d.*
*Zep.* 1:17 their flesh be as the *d.*
*Mal.* 2:3 spread *d.* on your faces, even *d.* of solemn feasts
*Phil.* 3:8 I count all things but *d.*

**DUNG, Verb.**
*Luke* 13:8 dig about, and *d.* it

**DUNG-GATE.**
*Neh.* 3:13 Ha. rep. to *d.-g.* 12:31

**DUNGHILL, S.**
1 *Sam.* 2:8 beg. from *d. Ps.* 113:7
*Ezr.* 6:11 let his house be a *d.*
*Is.* 25:10 as straw trodden for *d.*
*Lam.* 4:5 embrace *d.*
*Dan.* 2:5 houses be made a *d.*
3:29 their houses be made a *d.*
*Luke* 14:35 salt not fit for the *d.*

**DUNGEON.**
*Gen.* 40:15 should put me into *d.*
41:14 Joseph hastily out of *d.*
*Ex.* 12:29 to first-born in the *d.*
*Jer.* 37:16 Jeremiah entered *d.*
38:6 cast him into the *d.*
10 take up Jere. out of the *d.*
11 let them into *d.* to Jerem.
*Lam.* 3:53 cut off my life in *d.*
55 called on thy name out of *d.*

DURA. *Dan.* 3:1

**DURABLE.**
*Prov.* 8:18 *d.* riches are with me
*Is.* 23:18 be for *d.* clothing

**DURETH.**
*Mat.* 13:21 but *d.* for a while

**DURST.**
*Est.* 7:5 that *d.* presume to do so
*Job* 32:6 *d.* not show my opinion
*Mat.* 22:46 *d.* not ask more ques. *Mark* 12:34; *Luke* 20:40
*John* 21:12 none *d.* ask him
*Acts* 5:13 *d.* no man join to them
7:32 then Moses *d.* not behold
*Jude* 9 *d.* not bring a railing ac.

**DUST.**
*Gen.* 3:14 *d.* shalt eat all the d.
19 *d.* thou art, to *d.* shalt ret.
13:16 if number the *d.* of earth
18:27 who am but *d.* and ashes
*Ex.* 8:16 say to Aaron, smite *d.*
9:9 it shall become small *d.*
*Lev.* 14:41 pour out *d.*
17:13 blood, and cover it with *d.*
*Num.* 23:10 who can count *d.*
*Deut.* 9:21 I cast *d.* into brook, 2 *K.* 23:12
28:24 make rain of thy land *d.*
*Jos.* 7:6 elders put *d.* on heads
2 *Sam.* 16:13 Shimei cast *d.*
1 *K.* 18:38 fire of L. consumed *d.*
20:10 if the *d.* of Samaria suffice
2 *Chr.* 34:4 made *d.* of images
*Job* 2:12 sprinkled *d.* upon heads
7:5 flesh clothed with clods of *d.*
10:9 bring me into *d.* again?
28:6 earth, it hath *d.* of gold
34:15 shall turn again to *d.*
38:38 *d.* groweth into hardness
42:6 and repent in *d.* and ashes
*Ps.* 22:15 brought me into the *d.*
30:9 shall *d.* praise thee, shall
72:9 enemies shall lick the *d.*
78:27 rained flesh on them as *d*
*Ps.* 102:14 serva. favor *d.* thereof
103:14 remembereth we are *d.*
*Ec.* 12:7 shall *d.* return to earth
*Is.* 34:7 their *d.* shall be made fat
9 *d.* be turned into brimstone
40:12 comprehended *d.* of earth
49:23 lick up the *d.* of thy feet
52:2 shake thyself from the *d.*
65:25 *d.* be the serpent's meat
*Lam.* 2:10 cast *d.* on their heads, *Ezek.* 27:30
*Ezek.* 24:7 to cover it with *d.*
26:4 I will scrape her *d.* from
10 their *d.* shall cover thee
*Amos* 2:7 pant after *d.* of earth
*Mic.* 7:17 they shall lick the *d.*
*Nah.* 1:3 clouds are *d.* of his feet
*Hab.* 1:10 for they shall heap *d.*
*Mat.* 10:14 sha. off the *d.* of your feet, *Mark* 6:11; *Luke* 9:5
*Luke* 10:11 the *d.* we do wipe off
*Acts* 13:51 they shook off the *d.*
22:23 as threw *d.* into the air
*Rev.* 18:19 cast *d.* on their heads

**As the DUST.**
*Gen.* 13:16 thy seed *as the d.* of the earth, 28:14; 2 *Chr.* 1:9
*Deut.* 9:21 calf small *as the d.*
2 *Sam.* 22:43 I beat them as small *as the d. Ps.* 18:42
*Job* 22:24 lay up gold *as the d.*
27:16 heap up silver *as d.*
*Is.* 5:24 their blossom go up *as d.*
40:15 nations *as* small *d.* of bal.
41:2 he gave *as d.* to his sword
*Zep.* 1:17 blood be pour. out *as d.*
*Zec.* 9:3 heaped up silver *as d.*

**In the DUST.**
*Job* 4:19 foundation is *in the d.*
7:21 now shall I sleep *in the d.*
16:15 defiled my horn *in the d.*
17:16 rest together is *in the d.*
20:11 lie down with him *in t. d.*
21:26 lie down alike *in the d.*
39:14 warmeth eggs *in the d.*
40:13 hide them *in the d.* toget.

*Ps.* 7:5 lay my honor *in the d.*
*Is.* 2:10 hide thee *in the d.*
26:19 and sing, ye *in the d.*
47:1 and sit *in the d.* O virgin
*Lam.* 3:29 putteth mouth *in t. d.*
*Dan.* 12:2 sleep *in d.* shall awake
*Mic.* 1:10 roll thyself *in the d.*
*Nah.* 3:18 nobles shall dwell *in d.*

**Like the DUST.**

2 *K.* 13:7 *like the d.* by thresh.
*Is.* 29:5 thy strangers be *like d.*

**Of the DUST.**

*Gen.* 2:7 L. formed man *of the d.*
*Num.* 5:17 take *of d.* in the tab.
*Deut.* 32:24 serpents *of d.*
1 *Sam.* 2:8 out *of d.* *Ps.* 113:7
*Job* 5:6 cometh not *of the d.*
*Prov.* 8:26 highest part *of d.*
*Ec.* 3:20 all are *of the d.*
*Is.* 29:4 be low out *of d.*

**To the DUST.**

*Ps.* 22:29 that go down *to the d.*
44:25 soul is bowed down *to d.*
104:29 they die and return *to d.*
119:25 soul cleaveth *to the d.*
*Ec.* 3:20 all are *d.* and turn *to d.*
*Is.* 25:12 bring fortress *to d.*
26:5 bringeth city even *to the d.*

**DUTY.**

*Ex.* 21:10 *d.* of mar. not dimin.
*Deut.* 25:5 *d.* of a husband's bro.
*Ec.* 12:13 whole *d.* of man
*Luke* 17:10 that which was *d.*
*Rom.* 15:27 their *d.* to minister

**DWARF.**

*Lev.* 21:20 a *d.* shall not come

**DWELL.**

*Gen.* 9:27 Japhet *d.* in tents of
*Ex.* 2:21 content to *d.* with man
29:45 I will *d.* amongst Israel
*Lev.* 13:46 unclean shall *d.* alone
*Num.* 23:9 the people sh. *d.* alone
35:34 L. *d.* am. child. of Israel
*Deut.* 12:11 cause his name *d.*
33:12 *d.* between his shoulders
*Jud.* 9:41 Gaal not *d.* in Shech.
17:10 M. said Levite *d.* with me
1 *Sam.* 27:5 that I may *d.* there
1 *K.* 6:13 I will *d.* among Israel
8:12 he would *d.* in thick dark.
17:9 get to Zareph. and *d.* there
2 *K.* 4:13 *d.* among mine own p.
*Job* 3:5 let a cloud *d.* upon it
11:14 not wickedness *d.* in tab.
18:15 shall *d.* in his tabernacle
30:6 *d.* in clefts of the valleys
*Ps.* 5:4 nei. sh. evil *d.* with thee
15:1 who sh. *d.* in thy holy hill
25:13 his soul shall *d.* at ease
*Ps.* 37:27 depart from evil, and *d.*
65:4 that he may *d.* in thy cou.
8 that *d.* in the uttermost pa.
68:16 hill God desireth to *d.* in
18 Lord might *d.* among them
72:9 that *d.* in wilderness
84:10 than *d.* in tents of wicked.
101:6 faithful, that they may *d.*
120:5 that I *d.* in tents of Kedar
132:14 my rest, here will I *d.*
139:9 I *d.* in uttermost parts
143:3 made me to *d.* in darkness
*Prov.* 1:33 whoso hearken. sh. *d.*
8:12 I wisdom *d.* with prudence
21:19 better to *d.* in wilderness
*Is.* 6:5 I *d.* in midst of a people
11:6 wolf shall *d.* with lamb
13:21 owls shall *d.* there
26:5 bringeth down them th. *d.*
19 awake ye that *d.* in the dust
30:19 the people shall *d.* in Z.
32:16 judgment shall *d.* in wil.
18 people *d.* in a habitation
33:14 *d.* with devouring fire?
16 he shall *d.* on high
24 the people that *d.* therein
34:11 the owl and raven sh. *d.*
40:22 spread. out as tent to *d.* in
49:20 place to me that I may *d.*
58:12 restorer of paths to *d.* in
65:9 my servants shall *d.* there
*Jer.* 49:8 *d.* deep, O inhabitants
*Ezek.* 2:6 dost *d.* among scorp.
43:7 *d.* in midst, 9; *Zec.* 2:10, 11
*Hos.* 12:9 I make to *d.* in taber.
14:7 that *d.* under his shadow
*Joel* 3:20 Judah shall *d.* for ever
*Mic.* 4:10 shalt *d.* in the field
7:14 flock which *d.* solitarily
*Nah.* 3:18 O Assy. nobles sh. *d.*
*Hag.* 1:4 to *d.* in ceiled houses?
*Zec.* 9:6 a bastard sh. *d.* in Ash.
*Mat.* 12:45 *d.* there, *Luke* 11:26
*Luke* 21:35 that *d.* on the face of the earth, *Acts* 17:26
*Acts* 7:4 land wherein ye now *d.*
28:16 P. suff. to *d.* by himself
*Rom.* 8:9 Sp. of G. *d.* in you, 11
1 *Cor.* 7:12 she pleased to *d.* with
2 *Cor.* 6:16 G. hath said I will *d.*
*Eph.* 3:17 C. *d.* in hearts by faith
*Col.* 1:19 in him sh. all fulness *d.*
3:16 let word of C. *d.* in you
1 *Pet.* 3:7 husbands *d.* with them
1 *John* 4:13 we *d.* in him
*Rev.* 7:15 he on throne shall *d.*
12:12 ye heavens, and ye that *d.*
13:6 against them that *d.*
21:3 and he will *d.* with them

**DWELL, *with* earth.**

1 *K.* 8:27 will God *d.* on *earth?* 2 *Chr.* 6:18
*Dan.* 4:1 languages that *d.* in all the *earth*, 6:25
*Rev.* 3:10 try them that *d.* in *e.*
6:10 blood on them that *d.* on *e.*
13:8 all that *d.* on *e.* shall wors.
14 deceiveth them that *d.* on *e.*
14:6 preach to them th. *d.* on *e.*
17:8 they that *d.* on *earth*

**DWELL, *with* house.**

*Deut.* 28:30 build *house* and not *d.* *Amos* 5:11
2 *Sam.* 7:2 I *d.* in a *house* of cedar, 1 *Chr.* 17:1
5 build *ho.* to *d.* 1 *Chr.* 17:1
1 *K.* 2:36 build *h.* in Jer. and *d.*
3:17 I and th. wom. *d.* in one *h.*
8:13 surely built *h.* to *d.* in
*Job* 4:19 that *d.* in *h.* of cl.
19:15 *d.* in *h.* count stranger
*Ps.* 23:6 *d.* in *h.* of the Lord
27:4 that I may *d.* in *h.* of Lord
84:4 they that *d.* in thy *house*
101:7 work deceit not *d.* my *h.*
*Prov.* 21:9 better *d.* in the corner of a *house*, 25:24
*Jer.* 29:5 build *h.* *d.* in them, 28

**DWELL, *with* Jerusalem.**

1 *Chr.* 23:25 that ye may *d.* in *J.*
*Neh.* 11:2 offered them. to *d.* at *J.*
*Jer.* 33:16 *J.* shall *d.* safely
*Zec.* 8:3 I will *d.* in midst of *J.*
*Acts* 2:14 all ye that *d.* at *Jerus.*
4:16 manifest to all that *d.* in *J.*

**DWELL, *with* land.**

*Gen.* 24:37 Canaan. in wh. *l.* I *d.*
26:2 *d.* in *l.* which I shall tell
34:21 let them *d.* in the *land*
45:10 shalt *d.* in *l.* of Goshen
46:34 may *d.* in *l.* of Goshen
47:6 in *l.* of Goshen let them *d.*
*Ec.* 8:22 *l.* in wh. my people *d.*
*Lev.* 25:18 shall *d.* in *l.* in safety
26:5 and *d.* in your *l.* safely
*Num.* 35:34 defile not *l.* wh. I *d.*
*Deut.* 30:20 thou mayest *d.* in *l.*
*Jos.* 17:12 the Canaanites would *d.* in that *land*, *Jud.* 1:27
2 *K.* 25:24 fear not to *d.* in *land*, *Jer.* 25:5; 40:9
*Ps.* 37:3 so thou shalt *d.* in *l.*
68:6 rebellious *d.* in a dry *land*
85:9 that glory may *d.* in our *l.*
*Is.* 9:2 *d.* in *l.* of shadow of death
*Jer.* 50:3 *l.* desol. none shall *d.*
*Ezek.* 28:25 they *d.* in their *land*
38:12 the people that *d.* in *land*
*Hos.* 9:3 shall not *d.* in Lord's *l.*

**DWELL, *with* place.**

*Ex.* 15:17 in *p.* th. hast ma. to *d.*
1 *Sam.* 12:8 *d.* in this *place*
2 *K.* 6:1 the *p.* we *d.* is strait
2 a *place* where we may *d.*
1 *Chr.* 17:9 shall *d.* in their *pla.*
*Is.* 57:15 *d.* in high and holy *p.*

**DWELL safely.**

*Prov.* 1:33 to me shall *d.* *safely*
*Jer.* 23:6 Israel shall *d.* *safely*, *Ezek.* 28:26; 34:25, 28; 38:8
32:37 cause them to *d.* *safely*
*Ezek.* 38:11 them that *d.* *safely*

**DWELL in safety.**

*Lev.* 25:18 ye shall *d.* in the land *in safety*, 19; *Deut.* 12:10
*Deut.* 33:12 beloved of the Lord shall *d.* *in safety*
28 Israel shall *d.* *in safety*
*Ps.* 4:8 L. makest me to *d.* *in s.*

**DWELL therein.**

*Num.* 14:30 to make you *d. t.*
33:53 shall *d. t.* *Deut.* 11:31
*Ps.* 24:1 and they that *d.* *therein*
37:29 the righteous shall *d. th.*
69:36 love his name shall *d. t.*
*Is.* 33:24 people that *d.* *therein*
51:6 that *d.* *therein* shall die
*Jer.* 4:29 and not a man *d. th.*
12:4 wick. of them. that *d. t.*
48:9 cities without any to *d. t.*
50:39 the owls shall *d.* *therein*
*Acts* 1:20 let no man *d.* *therein*

**DWELL together.**

*Ps.* 133:1 brethren to *d.* *together*

**DWELLERS.**

*Is.* 18:3 ye *d.* on earth, see ye
*Acts* 1:19 was known to *d.* at Jer.
2:9 *d.* in Mesopotamia we do

**DWELLEST.**

2 *K.* 19:15 which *d.* betw. cherubim, *Ps.* 80:1; *Is.* 37:16
*Ps.* 123:1 thou that *d.* in heaven
*Jer.* 49:16 *d.* in the clefts, *Ob.* 3
51:13 thou that *d.* upon waters
*Ezek* 12:2 thou *d.* in midst
*John* 1:38 Master, where *d.* th.?
*Rev.* 2:13 works where thou *d.*

**DWELLETH.**

*Lev.* 19:34 stranger that *d.*
25:39 brother that *d.* poor, 47
*Deut.* 33:20 God *d.* as a lion
*Jos.* 6:25 Rahab *d.* in Israel
22:19 the Lord's tabernacle *d.*
1 *Sam.* 4:4 who *d.* bet. cherubim, 2 *Sam.* 6:2; 1 *Chr.* 13:6
2 *Sam.* 7:2 the ark *d.* within
*Job* 15:28 he *d.* in desolate cities
38:19 way where light *d.*?
*Ps.* 9:11 sing to the Lord who *d.*
26:8 place where thine honor *d.*
91:1 he that *d.* in secret places
113:5 L. our G. who *d.* on high
135:21 blessed L. who *d.* at Jer.
*Is.* 8:18 L. who *d.* in mount Z.
33:5 the Lord, for he *d.* on high
*Jer.* 44:2 desolation, no man *d.*
49:31 that *d.* without care
*Lam.* 1:3 J. *d.* among heathen
*Ezek.* 16:46 sister *d.* at right ha.
*Dan.* 2:22 and light *d.* with him
*Hos.* 4:3 every one that *d.* there. shall mourn, *Amos* 8:8
*Joel* 3:21 I cleanse, for L. *d.* in Z.
*Mat.* 23:21 sweareth by him *d.*
*John* 6:56 my blood *d.* in me
14:10 Father that *d.* in me
17 the Spirit, for he *d.* in you
*Acts* 7:48 *d.* not in temples made with hands, 17:24

*Rom.* 7:17 I, sin th. *d.* in me, 20
18 in my flesh *d.* no good th.
8:11 quicken by Spirit that *d.*
1 *Cor.* 3:16 Spirit of G. *d.* in you
*Col.* 2:9 *d.* the fulness of God
2 *Tim.* 1:14 H. G. *d.* in us
*Jam.* 4:5 spirit that *d.* in us
2 *Pet.* 3:13 earth where. *d.* right.
1 *John* 3:17 how *d.* love of G.?
24 that keepeth com. *d.* in him
4:12 if we love, God *d.* in us
15 J. is S. of G. God *d.* in him
1 *John* 4:16 he that *d.* in love, *d*
2 *John* 2 which *d.* in us
*Rev.* 2:13 slain am. you, Satan *d.*

**DWELLING, Substantive.**

*Gen.* 27:39 thy *d.* shall be fatness
2 *Chr.* 6:2 built place for thy *d.*
*Ps.* 49:14 cons. in grave from *d.*
91:10 no plague come nigh *d.*
*Prov.* 21:20 in the *d.* of the wise
24:15 against *d.* of the righteous
*Dan.* 2:11 gods *d.* not with flesh
4:25 thy *d.* with beasts, 32; 5:21
*Zep.* 3:7 *d.* should not be cut off
*Nah.* 2:11 wh. is *d.* of the lions?
*Mark* 5:3 his *d.* among tombs

**DWELLING.**

*Gen.* 25:27 plain man, *d.* in tents
*Lev.* 25:29 if a man sell a *d.* hou.
*Num.* 24:21 strong is thy *d.* place
1 *K.* 8:30 in heaven thy *d.* place
39, 43, 49; 2 *Chr.* 6:21, 30, 39
2 *Chr.* 30:27 prayer up to holy *d.*
36:15 compassion on *d.* place
*Job* 8:22 *d.* place of the wicked
21:28 *d.* places of the wicked?
*Ps.* 49:11 *d.* places to all genera.
52:5 shall pluck thee out of *d.*
74:7 cast. *d.* place of thy name
76:2 his *d.* place in Zion
79:7 laid waste his *d.* place
90:1 hast been our *d.* place
*Is.* 4:5 create on every *d.* place
18:4 will consider in my *d.* pla.
*Jer.* 46:19 daughter *d.* in Egypt
51:30 have burnt their *d.* places
37 Babylon shall become a *d.*
*Ezek.* 38:11 all them *d.* without
*Joel* 3:17 Lord your God *d.* in Z.

*Hab.* 1:6 possess *d.* places
*Acts* 2:5 were *d.* at Jerusalem
19:17 known to Greeks *d.* at E.
1 *Cor.* 4:11 no certain *d.* place
1 *Tim.* 6:16 *d.* in light
*Heb.* 11:9 *d.* in taberna. with I.
2 *Pet.* 2:8 Lot, righteous man *d.*

**DWELLINGS.**

*Ex.* 10:23 child, of Isr. li. in *d.*
*Lev.* 3:17 a perpet. statute thro' all *d.* 23:14: *Num.* 35:29
7:26 eat no blood in any of *d.*
23:3 do no work in all your *d.* 31
*Job* 18:21 the *d.* of wicked
39:6 made barren land his *d.*
*Ps.* 55:15 wicked. is in their *d.*
87:2 gates of Z. than all *d.* of J.
*Is.* 32:18 people dwell in sure *d.*
*Ezek.* 25:4 men of east make *d.*
*Zep.* 2:6 coast shall be *d.*

**DWELT.**

*Gen.* 11:2 and they *d.* there, 31; 26:17; 2 *K.* 16:6; 1 *Chr.* 4:43; 2 *Chr.* 28:18
*Num.* 31:10 they *d.* 2 *K.* 17:29
1 *K.* 13:11 *d.* old proph. in B. 25
*Job* 29:25 and I *d.* as a king
*Ps.* 74:2 Z. wherein thou hast *d.*
*Is.* 29:1 the city where David *d.*
*Jer.* 2:6 a land where no man *d.*
39:14 J. *d.* among the people
*Ezek.* 3:15 that *d.* by river Cheb.
31:6 und. shadow *d.* nations, 17
*Dan.* 4:21 beasts of field *d.*
*Zep.* 2:15 rejoicing city that *d.*
*Luke* 1:65 fear ca. on all that *d.*
*John* 1:14 W. made flesh and *d.*
39 and saw where he *d.*
*Acts* 13:17 they *d.* as strangers
28:30 Paul *d.* in hired house
*Rev.* 11:10 torm. them that *d.*

**DWELT at.**

*Gen.* 22:19 and Abraham *d. at* B.
*Jud.* 9:41 Abimelech *d. at* A.
1 *K.* 15:18 Benhad. *d.* at Damas. 2 *Chr.* 16:2
2 *K.* 19:36 Sen. *d. at* N. *Is.* 37:37
1 *Chr.* 2:55 scribes which *d. at* J.
9:34 Levites *d. at* Jerusalem
*Acts* 9:22 S. conv. Jews that *d. at*
32 saints who *d. at* Lydda

**DWELT in.**

*Num.* 20:15 we have *d. in* Egypt
21:31 Is. *d. in* land of Amorites
*Deut.* 2:12 *d. in* their stead, 21, 22, 23; 1 *Chr.* 5:22
13:16 of him that *d. in* bush
*Jud.* 8:11 of them *d. in* tents
2 *Sam.* 7:6 not *d. in* any house since I b. Is. out, 1 *Chr.* 17:5
9:12 all that *d. in* house of Ziba
14:28 Absalom *d.* 2 years *in* J.
1 *K.* 2:38 Shimei *d. in* Jerusalem
12:2 J. fled from Sol. *d. in* E.
2 *K.* 13:5 Israel *d. in* their tents
15:5 A. *d. in* house, 2 *Chr.* 26:21
22:14 H. the prophetess *d. in* Jer. in college, 2 *Chr.* 34:22
*Ezr.* 2:70 Levites, Nethinim, *d. in* cities, *Neh.* 3:26; 11:21
*Neh.* 7:73 Israel *d. in* their cities
*Ps.* 94:17 almost *d. in* silence
*Is.* 13:20 shall it be *d. in* from generation, *Jer.* 50:39
*Jer.* 35:10 we have *d. in* tents
*Ezek.* 36:17 Israel *d. in* own land
39:26 *d.* safely *in* their land
*Dan.* 4:12 the fowls *d. in* boughs
*Mat.* 2:23 Joseph *d. in* city Naz.
4:13 Jesus *d. in* Capernaum
*Luke* 13:4 above all that *d. in* J.
*Acst* 7:2 Abraham *d. in* Charr. 4
19:10 they who *d. in* Asia heard
2 *Tim.* 1:5 *d. in* grandmother

**DWELT therein.**

*Deut.* 2:10 E. *d. t.*; 20 giants *d. t.*
1 *K.* 11:24 went to Dam. and *d. t.*
12:25 Jerob. built S. and *d. th.*
*Neh.* 13:16 *d.* men of Tyre *th.*
*Ps.* 68:10 congregation hath *d. t.*

**DWELT with.**

*Ruth* 2:23 and Ruth *d. with* her
1 *Sam.* 22:4 moth. *d. w.* k. of M.
1 *Chr* 4:23 they *d. with* king
*Ps.* 120:6 my soul hath long *d. w.*
*Jer.* 40:6 J. *d. w.* him among peo.

**DYED.**

*Is.* 63:1 with *d.* garm. from Boz.
*Ezek.* 23:15 *d.* attire upon heads

DYING. *See* after DIE.

# E

**EACH.**

*Gen.* 15:10 Abraham laid *e.* piece
34:25 Sim. and Levi took *e.* man
40:5 *e.* his dr. 45:22 *e.* changes
*Ex.* 18:7 asked *e.* other of welf.
*Num.* 1:44 *e.* one was for house
7:3 they brought for *e.* one an ox
16:17 Aaron *e.* of you his censer
*Jos.* 22:14 of *e.* chief house *e.* one
*Jud.* 21:22 reserved not to *e.* man
*Ruth* 1:9 may find rest *e.* of you
1 *K.* 4:7 *e.* man his month
22:10 kings *e.* sat on his throne
2 *K.* 15:20 of *e.* man fifty shekels
*Ps.* 85:10 right. and pe. kissed *e.*
*Is.* 2:20 they made *e.* one
6:2 seraphim, *e.* had six wings
35:7 where *e.* lay, shall be grass
57:2 *e.* one walking in his upr.
*Ezek.* 4:6 thee *e.* day for a year
*Luke* 13:15 doth not *e.* on sabbath
*Acts* 2:3 tongues sat upon *e.* of
*Phil.* 2:3 let esteem other better
2 *Thes.* 1:3 charity toward *e.* oth.
*Rev.* 4:8 beasts had *e.* six wings

**EAGLE.**

*Lev.* 11:13 *e.* have, *Deut.* 14:12
*Deut.* 28:49 swift as the *e.* flieth
32:11 as an *e.* stirreth her nest
*Job* 9:26 *e.* that hasteth to prey

39:27 doth the *e.* mount up?
*Prov.* 23:5 riches fly away as an *e.*
30:19 way of an *e.* in the air
*Jer.* 48:40 shall fly as an *e.*
14:16 make thy nest high as *e.*
*Ezek.* 1:10 had face of an *e.* 10:14
17:3 a great *e.* with gr. wings, 7
*Dan.* 4:33 hairs gro. like *e.* feath.
7:4 a lion, and had *e.* wings
*Hos.* 8:1 as an *e.* aga. the house
*Mic.* 1:16 thy baldness as the *e.*
*Hab.* 1:8 Chaldeans shall fly as *e.*
*Rev.* 4:7 fourth beast like fly. *e.*
12:14 to woman wings of gr. *e.*

**EAGLES.**

*Ex.* 19:4 I bare you on *e.* wings
2 *Sam.* 1:23 were swifter than *e.*
*Ps.* 103:5 thy youth is ren. like *e.*
*Prov.* 30:17 young *e.* shall eat it
*Is.* 40:31 mount with wings as *e.*
*Jer.* 4:13 his horses swifter th. *e.*
*Lam.* 4:19 pers. swifter than *e.*
*Mat.* 24:28 *e.* be gath. *Luke* 17:37

**EAR.**

*Ex.* 21:6 bore *e.* *Deut.* 15:17
1 *Sam.* 9:15 L. hath told S. in *e.*
2 *K.* 19:16 bow down *e.* *Ps.* 31:2; 86:1
*Neh.* 1:6 let thine *e.* be attent. 11

*Job* 4:12 and mine *e.* received
12:11 *e.* try words? 34:3
13:1 mine *e.* hath heard
29:11 when the *e.* heard me
21 to me men gave *e.* waited
36:10 he openeth also their *e.*
42:5 I heard by hearing of *e.*

*Ps.* 10:17 wilt cause thine *e.*
31:2 bow down thine *e.* to me
58:4 like adder that stoppeth *e.*
77:1 and he gave *e.* unto me
94:9 he that planted the *e.*

*Ps.* 116:2 he hath inclined his *e.*

*Prov.* 5:1 and bow thine *e.* to
5:13 incline mine *e.* to them
15:31 the *e.* that heareth
17:4 and a liar giveth *e.* to
18:15 the *e.* of the wise seeketh
20:12 hearing *e.* seeing eye
22:17 thine *e.* hear the words
25:12 reprover on obedient *e.*
28:9 turneth away *e.* from hear.

*Ec.* 1:8 nor is the *e.* filled with

*Is.* 48:8 time thine *e.* was not
50:4 he wakeneth my *e.* to hear
5 Lord hath opened mine *e.*
59:1 *e.* heavy that it cannot h.
64:4 nor perceived by the *e.*

*Jer.* 6:10 their *e.* is uncircumc.
7:24 inclined their *e.* 26; 11:8; 17:23; 25:4; 34:14; 44:5
9:20 let your *e.* receive the word
35:15 ye have not inclined *e.*
*Lam.* 3:56 hide not *e.*
*Amos* 3:12 fr. the lion piece of *e.*
*Mat.* 10:27 what ye hear in the *e.*
26:51 smote off his *e.* *Mark* 14:47
*Luke* 12:3 ye have spoken in *e.*
22:51 touched his *e.* and healed
*John* 18:26 servant whose *e.* Pet
1 *Cor.* 2:9 not seen, nor *e.* heard
12:16 if the *e.* shall say
*Rev.* 2:7 he that hath *e.* let hear, 11, 17, 29; 3:6, 13, 22; 13:9

**Incline EAR.**

*Ps.* 17:6 *in.* thine *e.* to me, 71:2; 88:2; *Is.* 37:17; *Dan.* 9:18
45:10 O daughter, *incline* th. *e.*
49:4 I will *incline* mine *e.* to
*Prov.* 2:2 that thou *in.* thine *e.*
4:20 *in.* thine *e.* to my saying
*Is.* 55:3 *in.* your *e.* and come

**Give EAR.**

*Ex.* 15:26 if thou wilt *give e.*
*Deut.* 1:45 not *g. e.* to your voice, 2 *Chr.* 24:19; *Neh.* 9:30
32:1 *give e.* O heavens
*Jud.* 5:3 *give e.* O ye princes
*Job* 34:2 *give e.* to me
*Ps.* 5:1 *g. e.* to my words, 54:2
17:1 *g. e.* to my pra. 55:1; 86:6
39:12 *give e.* to my cry, 141:1
49:1 *give. e.* all ye inhabitants
78:1 *g. e.* O. p.; 80:1 *g. e.* sheph.
84:8 *give e.* O God of Jacob
143:1 *g. e.* to my supplications
*Is.* 1:2 *give e.* O earth
10 *g. e.* to the law of our God
8:9 *give e.* all of far countries
28:23 *give* ye *e.* and hear
42:23 who among you will *g. e.*?
51:4 hearken and *g. e.* to me
*Jer.* 13:15 *give e.* be not proud
*Hos.* 5:1 and *give* ye *e.* O house
*Joel* 1:2 *g. e.* all ye inhabitants

**Right EAR.**

*Ex.* 29:20 tip of *right e.* *Lev.* 8:23, 24; 14:14, 17, 25, 28
*Luke* 22:50 c. off *ri. e.* *John* 18:10

**EAR, *of corn.***

*Ex.* 9:31 for barley was in the *e.*
*Mark* 4:28 the *e.* full corn in *e.*

**EAR, Verb.**

1 *Sam.* 8:12 set them to *e.* ground
*Is.* 30:24 oxen that *e.* the ground

**EARED, ING.**

*Gen.* 45:6 neither *e.* nor harvest
*Ex.* 34:21 in *e.* time and harvest
*Deut.* 21:4 valley neither *e.* sown

**EARLY.**

*Gen.* 19:2 ye shall rise *e.* and go
*Jud.* 7:3 let him depart *e.*
*Ps.* 46:5 God shall help right *e.*
57:8 I will awake *e.* 108:2
63:1 my God, *e.* will I seek thee
78:34 they inquired *e.* after God
90:14 satisfy us *e.* with mercy
101:8 *e.* destroy the wicked
*Prov.* 1:28 they shall seek me *e.*
8:17 seek me *e.* shall find me
*Is.* 26:9 will I seek thee *e.*
*Hos.* 5:15 they will seek me *e.*
6:4 as *e.* dew it goeth, 13:3
*Luke* 24:22 woman *e.* at sepulch.
*John* 18:28 led J. and it was *e.*
20:1 com. Mary Magdalene *e.*
*Jam.* 5:7 till he receive *e.* rain

*See* AROSE, RISE, RISEN, RISING, ROSE, MORNING.

**EAR-RING.**

*Gen.* 24:22 took a golden *e.-r.*
30 when Laban saw *e.-r.*
47 I put *e.-r.* upon her face
*Job* 42:11 ev. one gave J. an *e.-r.*
*Prov.* 25:12 *e.-r.* of gold

**EAR-RINGS.**

*Gen.* 35:4 gave J. all their *e.-r.*
*Ex.* 32:2 break off the gold. *e.-r.*
35:22 brought *e.-r.* for offering
*Num.* 31:50 we have broug. *e.-r.*
*Jud.* 8:24 give ev. man the *e.-r.*
*Is.* 3:20 L. will take away *e.-r.*
*Ezek.* 16:12 I put *e.-r.* in th. ears
*Hos.* 2:13 decked hers. with *e.-r.*

**EARS.**

*Gen.* 44:18 speak in my lord's *e.*
50:4 speak in the *e.* of Pharaoh
*Ex.* 10:2 mayest tell in *e.* of son
17:14 rehearse in *e.* of Joshua
*Jud.* 9:2 in *e.* of men of Shech. 3
1 *Sam.* 3:11 the *e.* shall tingle, 2 *K.* 21:12; *Jer.* 19:3
2 *Sam.* 7:22 we heard with our *e.* 1 *Chr.* 17:20
22:7 my cry did enter into his *e.*
*Job* 15:21 dreadful sound in his *e.*
28:22 heard fame with our *e.*
33:16 he openeth the *e.* of men
*Ps.* 18:6 cry came into his *e.*
34:15 his *e.* are open
44:1 we heard with our *e.*
115:6 have *e.* hear not, 135:17
*Prov.* 21:13 whoso stop. his *e.*
23:9 speak not in the *e.* of a fool
26:17 taketh a dog by the *e.*
*Is.* 11:3 the hearing of his *e.*
32:3 the *e.* of them that hear
33:15 stoppeth *e.* from hearing
35:5 *e.* of deaf shall be unstop.
43:8 and deaf that have *e.*
*Jer.* 2:2 and cry in the *e.* of Jer.
5:21 O people, which have *e.*
29:29 Zep. read in the *e.* of Jer.
*Mat.* 28:14 come to governor's *e.*
*Mark* 7:33 put fingers into his *e.*
35 his *e.* were opened
8:18 having *e.* hear ye not?
*Acts* 7:51 uncirc. in heart and *e.*
17:20 bring. strange things to *e.*
*Rom.* 11:8 hath given *e.*
2 *Tim.* 4:3 having itching *e.*
*Jam.* 5:4 *e.* of Lord of sabaoth
1 *Pet.* 3:12 and his *e.* are open to

**EARS to hear.**

*Deut.* 29:4 L. hath not g. *e. to h.*
*Ezek.* 12:2 they have *e. to hear*
*Mat.* 11:15 *e. to h.* 13:9, 43; *Mark* 4:9, 23; 7:16; *Luke* 8:8; 14:35

**Mine EARS.**

*Num.* 14:28 have spoken in *m. e.*
*Jud.* 17:2 spakest of in *m. e.*
1 *Sam.* 15:14 bleat. of sh. in *m. e.*
2 *K.* 19:28 tumult come into *mine e.* *Is.* 37:29
*Ps.* 40:6 *m. e.* hast thou opened
92:11 *mine e.* shall hear
*Is.* 5:9 in *mine e.* said the Lord
22:14 revealed in *mine e.*
*Ezek.* 8:18 tho' they cry in *m. e.*
9:1 he cried also in *mine e.*
*Luke* 1:44 salut. sounded in *m. e.*

**EARS of the People.**

*Ex.* 11:2 speak in *e. of the peo.*
*Deut.* 32:44 M. spake in *e. of pe.*
*Jud.* 7:3 proclaim in *e. of pe.*
1 *Sam.* 11:4 told tid. in *e. of p.*
2 *K.* 18:26 not in *e.* *Is.* 36:11
*Neh.* 8:3 *e. of p.* were attentive

**Their EARS.**

*Gen.* 35:4 ear-rings were in *t. e.*
*Ex.* 32:3 ear-rings in *their e.*
2 *K.* 23:2 read in *their e.* 2 *Chr.* 34:30; *Jer.* 36:15
*Is.* 6:10 *t. e.* heavy, lest hear with *t. e.* *Mat.* 13:15; *Acts* 28:27
*Mic.* 7:16 *their e.* shall be deaf
*Zec.* 7:11 stopped *t. e.* *Acts* 7:57
2 *Tim.* 4:4 turn *th. e.* from truth

**Thine EARS.**

*Ps.* 10:17 cause *thine e.* to hear
*Prov.* 23:12 apply *thine e.*
*Is.* 30:21 *thine e.* shall hear
49:20 children say in *thine e.*
*Ezek.* 3:10 hear w. *th. e.* 40:4; 44:5
16:12 I put ear-rings in *thine e.*
23:25 shall take away *thine e.*
24:26 to hear with *thine e.*

**Your EARS.**

*Job* 13:17 declaration with *y. e.*
*Ps.* 78:1 incline *your e.* to words
*Jer.* 26:11 as heard with *your e.*
15 Lord sent to speak in *your e.*
*Mat.* 13:16 but blessed are *your e.*
*Luke* 4:21 scripture fulfil. in *y. e.*
9:44 let sayings sink in *your e.*

**EARS of Corn.**

*Gen.* 41:5 seven *e. of corn*, 22
*Lev.* 2:14 meat-offering, green *e.*
23:14 not eat green *e. of corn*
*Deut.* 23:25 mayest pluck the *e.*
*Ruth* 2:2 go and glean *e. of*
2 *K.* 4:42 brought full *e. of corn*
*Mat.* 12:1 discip. began to pluck *e. of c.* *Mark* 2:23; *Luke* 6:1

*See* SEVEN.

**EARNEST, Substantive.**

2 *Cor.* 1:22 *e.* of the Spirit, 5:5
*Eph.* 1:14 *e.* of our inheritance

**EARNEST, Adjective.**

*Rom.* 8:19 *e.* expecta. of creature
2 *Cor.* 7:7 when he told *e.* desire
8:16 put same *e.* care into Titus
*Phil.* 1:20 accord. to my *e.* expec.
*Heb.* 2:1 to give more *e.* heed

**EARNESTLY.**

*Num.* 22:37 did I not *e.* send
1 *Sam.* 20:6 D. *e.* asked leave, 28
*Job* 7:2 serv. *e.* desireth shadow
*Jer.* 11:7 I *e.* protested to fathers
31:20 I do *e.* remember him still
*Mic.* 7:3 evil with both hands *e.*
*Luke* 22:44 he prayed *e.*
56 a certain maid *e.* looked
*Acts* 3:12 why look ye so *e.*
23:1 Paul *e.* beholding council
1 *Cor.* 12:31 covet *e.* the best gifts
2 *Cor.* 5:2 we groan *e.* desiring
*Jam.* 5:17 pray. *e.* that it not rain
*Jude* 3 should *e.* con. for faith

**EARNETH.**

*Hag.* 1:6 *e.* wages *e.* to put in bag

**EARTH.**

*Gen.* 1:2 the *e.* was without form
10 God called the dry land *e.*
11 let *e.* bring forth, 24
12 *e.* brought forth grass
28 replenish the *e.* 9:1
6:11 *e.* was corrupt before God
7:17 the ark was lifted above *e.*
8:14 in second mo. was *e.* dried
22 *e.* rem. seed-time not cease
10:25 the *e.* divided, 1 *Chr.* 1:19
18:18 all nations of *e.* blessed in him, 22:18; 26:4; 28:14
27:28 God give thee fatness of *e.*
41:47 *e.* brought forth by hand.
*Ex.* 9:29 *e.* is the Lord's, *Deut* 10:14; *Ps.* 24:1; 1 *Cor.* 10:26
15:12 the *e.* swallowed them
20:24 altar of *e.* thou shalt make
*Num.* 16:30 *e.* open her mouth
32 *e.* opened mouth and swallowed, 26:10; *Ps.* 106:17
34 lest *e.* swallow us up

Deut. 28:23 e. under thee be iron
32:1 hear, O e. the words
13 ride on high places of e.
22 a fire shall consume the e.
1 Sam. 2:8 pil. of the e. are L.'s
4:5 so that the e. rang again
14:15 and the e. quaked
2 Sam. 1:2 with e. on head, 15:32
22:8 then the e. shook, Ps. 18:7
1 K. 1:40 so that the e. rent
2 K. 5:17 two mules' burden of e.
1 Chr. 16:31 let e. rej. Ps. 96:11
33 cometh to judge the e. Ps. 96:13; 98:9
Neh. 9:6 thou made e. Is. 45:12
Job. 5:25 offspring as grass of e.
9:6 shaketh e. out of her place
24 e. given into hand of wicked
11:9 measure longer than e.
15:19 to whom e. was given
16:18 O e. cover not my blood
24:4 the poor of the e. hide
26:7 hangeth e. upon nothing
30:6 to dwell in caves of the e.
8 were viler than the e.
37:17 when he quieteth the e.
38:4 I laid foundations of the e.
18 the breadth of the e.?
Ps. 2:8 uttermost parts of the e.
10 be instr. ye judges of the e.
12:6 silver tried in furnace of e.
25:13 his seed shall inherit the e.
33:5 e. is full of goodness of L.
37:9 wait on L. inherit e. 11, 22
46:2 though the e. be removed
6 uttered voice, the e. melted
47:9 the shields of the e.
48:2 joy of whole e. is mount Z.
60:2 made the e. to tremble
63:9 the lower parts of the e.
65:9 thou visitest the e.
67:6 e. yield incr. Ezek. 34:27
68:8 e. shook, heavens dropped
32 sing, kingdoms of e.
71:20 from the depths of the e.
72:6 showers that water the e.
75:3 e. and inhabit. Is. 24:19
8 wicked of the e. shall wring
76:8 e. feared; 77:18 e. tre. 97:4
82:8 O God, judge the e.
90:2 or ever thou hadst form. e
Ps. 97:1 let the e. rejoice
99:1 let the e. be moved
102:25 laid the founda. of the e. 104:5; Prov. 8:29; Is. 48:13
148:13 his glory is above the e.
Prov. 3:19 L. founded e. Is. 24:1
8:23 or ever e. was
26 not made the e. nor fields
25:3 e. for depth unsearchable
30:16 the e. not filled with wat.
21 for three things e. disquiet.
Ec. 1:4 the e. abideth for ever
5:9 the profit of the e. for all
Is. 4:2 fruit of e. excellent
11:4 smite the e. with rod
9 e. full of knowledge of Lord
24:4 the e. mourneth, 33:9
19 e. broken, e. is dissolved
20 e. shall reel; 26:19 cast out
26:21 e. shall disclose blood
40:22 sit. on the circle of the e.
28 the Creator of ends of the e.
45:8 let e. open; 12 I m. the e.
22 be saved, all ends of the e.
51:6 look on e. e. shall wax old
66:1 the e. is my footstool
Jer. 4:23 I beheld e. with. form
28 for this shall the e. mourn
6:19 hear, O e. I will bring evil
22:29 O e. e. e. hear the word of the Lord, Mic. 1:2
46:8 saith, I will cover the e.
49:21 the e. is moved, 50:46
Ezek. 7:21 give to wick. of the e.
9:9 Lord hath forsaken the e.
43:2 e. shined with his glory
Hos. 2:22 the e. shall hear corn
Amos 8:9 I will darken the e.
Jon. 2:6 the e. with her bars
Mic. 7:17 like worms of the e.
Nah. 1:5 the e. is burnt up
Hab. 2:14 e. filled with knowl.
3:3 e. was full of his praise
9 didst clea. the e. with rivers
Zec. 1:10 to and fro thro. e. 6:7
4:10 eyes wh. run through the e.
Mal. 4:6 I smite e. with curse
Mat. 5:5 meek shall inherit e.
35 sw. not by e. it is footstool
13:5 had not much e. Mark 4:5
Mark 4:28 e. bringeth forth fruit
John 3:31 of the e. is earthly
1 Cor. 15:47 first man of e.
2 Tim. 2:20 ves. of wood and e.
Heb. 12:26 whose voice shook e.
Jam. 5:7 precious fruit of the e.
2 Pet. 3:10 e. and works therein
Rev. 7:3 hurt not the e. nor sea
11:6 have power to smite the e.
12:16 the e. opened her mouth
13:12 caus. e. to worship beast
18:1 and the e. was lightened
19:2 whore which did corrupt e.
20:11 from whose face the e. fled
See BEASTS, DUST, ENDS, FACE, KINGS, HEAVEN, PEOPLE, WHOLE.

**All the EARTH.**

Gen. 1:26 dominion over all the e.
7:3 seed on the face of all t. e.
11:9 confound lang. of all t. e.
18:25 Judge of all t. e do right?
19:31 after manner of all the e.
Ex. 19:5 for all the e. is mine
34:10 not been done in all the e.
Num. 14:21 all t. e. filled with gl.
Jos. 3:11 all t. e. 13; Zec. 6:5
23:14 way of all the e. 1 K. 2:2
1 Chr. 16:14 judgments in all the e. Ps. 105:7
30 fear a. t. e. Ps. 33:8; 96:9
Ps. 8:1 excellent in all the e. 9
47:2 k. over all e. 7; Zec. 14:9
57:5 be above all e. 11; 108:5
66:4 all the e. shall worship
83:18 high over all the e. 97:9
Is. 10:14 I gathered all t. e.
12:5 this is known in all the e.
Jer. 26:6 city a curse to all the e.
51:7 made all the e. drunken
Dan. 2:39 kingd. rule over a. t. e.
Hab. 2:20 let all the e. keep sil.
Zec. 1:11 all the e. sitteth still
Luke 23:44 darkn. over all the e.
Rom. 10:18 sou. went into a. t. e.
Rev. 5:6 sp of G. sent into all e.

**From the EARTH.**

Gen. 2:6 went up a mist f. the e.
7:23 destroyed from the e.
8:11 waters abated from the e.
Ex. 9:15 from the e. Jos. 7:9; Ps. 199:15; Prov. 2:22; Nah. 2:13
2 Sam. 12:20 D. arose from the e.
Job 18:17 rememb. perish f. t. e.
Ps. 148:7 praise Lord from the e.
Amos 3:5 a snare from the e.
John 12:32 if lifted up f. the e.
Acts 8:33 his life is taken f. the e.
Acts 9:8 Saul arose from the e.
22:22 away with fellow f. the e.
Rev. 6:4 to take peace f. the e.
14:3 144,000 redeemed f. the e.

**In the EARTH.**

Gen. 1:22 let fowl mult. in the e.
4:12 a vagabond in the e. 14
6:5 wickedness great in the e.
10:8 Nim. mighty one in the e.
19:31 not a man in t. e.
45:7 pres. a posterity in the e.
Ex. 20:4 in the e. beneath
2 Sam. 7:9 name like great men in the e. 1 Chr. 17:8
23 what nat. in t. e. like Israel? 1 Chr. 17:21
14:20 know all things in the e.
1 Chr. 29:11 all in the e. is thine
2 Chr. 6:14 no G. like thee in t. e.
Job 1:7 to and fro in the e. 2:2
8 none like Job in the e. 2:3
14:8 root wax old in the e.
24:18 portion cursed in the e.
39:14 ostrich leav. eggs in the e.
Ps. 16:3 saints that are in the e.
46:8 desolations made in the e.
10 I will be exalted in the e.
58:11 God that judgeth in the e.
72:16 a handful of corn in the e.
119:19 I am a stranger in the e.
Is. 26:9 thy judgm. are in the e.
18 not wrought deliver. in t. e.
40:24 stock not take root in t. e.
42:4 he set judgment in the e.
62:7 Jerusalem a praise in the e.
65:16 blesseth himself in the e. sweareth in the e.
Jer. 31:22 a new thing in the e.
Joel 2:30 show wonders in the e.
Mat. 25:18 digged in the e.
25 hid thy talent in the e.
Mark 4:31 mustard seed sown in t. e. less than all seeds in t. e.
1 John 5:8 three that witn. i. t. e.

**On, or upon the EARTH.**

Gen. 6:12 God looked upon the e.
7:4 I will cause rain upon the e.
8:17 multiply upon the e. and
19:23 sun was risen upon the e.
28:12 ladder set upon the e.
Ex. 10:6 since they were u. the e.
Deut. 4:10 live up. e. 12:1, 19
36 upon the e. showed great fire
12:16 pour it upon the e. 24
2 Sam. 12:16 David lay u. the e.
1 K. 8:27 will God dwell on the e.? 2 Chr. 6:18
17:14 L. sends rain upon the e
1 Chr. 29:15 days on e. Job 8:9
Job 7:1 time to man on e.?
19:25 stand at latter day u. t. e.
20:4 man was placed on the e.
37:6 snow, be thou on the e.
41:33 on e. there is not his like
Ps. 7:5 enemy tread life on the e.
67:2 thy way known upon the e.
73:25 none upon e. I desire bes.
Prov. 30:24 four th. little u. the e.
Ec. 7:20 not a just man u. the e.
10:7 princes as serv. upon the e.
11:3 clouds empty th. upon t. e.
Cant. 2:12 flowers appear on t. e.
Is. 28:22 consumption upon the e.
Jer. 9:3 not valiant for truth u. e.
Lam. 2:11 liver poured u. the e.
Amos 3:5 fall in snare u. the e.
Mat. 6:19 lay not up treas. on e.
9:6 Son hath power on e. to forgive, Mark 2:10; Luke 5:24
10:34 come to send peace on e.
16:19 thou shalt bind on e. 18:18
23:9 call no man father u. the e.
Mark 9:3 no fuller on e. can wh.
Luke 2:14 glory to God, on e.
12:49 come to send fire o. t. e.
51 come to give peace on e.?
18:8 shall he find faith on e.?
John 17:4 glorified thee on the e.
Rom. 9:28 a short work on the e.
Col. 3:2 affec. not on things on e.
5 mortify your members o. t. e.
Heb. 8:4 on e. not be a priest
11:13 strangers on the e.
12:25 ref. him that spake on e.
Jam. 5:5 lived in pleas. on the e.
17 it rained not on the e.
Rev. 3:10 that dwell upon the e.
5:10 we shall reign on e.
8:7 hail and fire cast upon the e.
11:10 dw. on e. 13:8; 14:6; 17:8
16:2 poured vial upon the e.

**Out of the EARTH.**

1 Sam. 28:13 ascend. out of the e.
2 Sam. 23:4 grass out of the e.

*Job* 28:2 iron is taken *out of the e.*
5 *e. out of* it cometh bread
*Ps.* 85:11 truth sh. spr. *o. of t. e.*
104:35 sinners be cons. *o. of t. e.*
*Dan.* 7:17 four kings *out of the e.*
*Hos.* 2:18 battle *out of the e.*
*Mic.* 7:2 good perish *out of the e.*
*Rev.* 13:11 beast up *out of the e.*

**To, *or* unto the EARTH.**
*Gen.* 24:52 bow. himself *to the e.*
42:6 they bowed *to the e.* 43:26
*Jos.* 5:14 Josh. fell *to the e.* 7:6
1 *Sam.* 5:3 D. on his face *to the e.*
17:49 Goliath his face *to the e.*
25:41 bow. herself *to e.* 1 *K.* 1:31
26:8 smite him *to the e.*
20 let not my blood fall *to t. e.*
2 *Sam.* 14:11 not one hair shall fall *to the e.* 1 *K.* 1:52
2 *K.* 10:10 fall *to t. e.* no word
*Job* 12:8 or speak *to the e.*
*Ps.* 17:11 bowing down *to the e.*
44:25 belly cleaveth *unto the e.*
50:4 he shall call *to the e.*
146:4 he returneth *to* his *e.*
*Ec.* 3:21 sp. of beast goeth *to e.*
12:7 dust ret. *to t. e.* spirit to G.
*Jer.* 15:10 conten. *to the* whole *e.*
*Hos.* 6:3 and former rain *to the e.*
*Acts* 9:4 and Saul fell *to the e.*
10:11 great sheet down *to the e.*
*Rev.* 6:13 stars of heav. fell *t. t. e.*
12:13 dragon cast *unto the e.*

**EARTHEN.**
*Lev.* 6:28 *e.* ves. wherein sodden
11:33 *e.* vessel wherein falleth
14:5 birds killed in *e.* vessel, 50
*Num.* 5:17 water in *e.* vessel
*Jer.* 19:1 a potter's *e.* bottle
32:14 evidences in an *e.* vessel
*Lam.* 4:2 esteemed as *e.* pitchers
2 *Cor.* 4:7 treasure in *e.* vessels

**EARTHLY.**
*John* 3:12 if I told you *e.* things
31 he that is of the earth is *e.*
2 *Cor.* 5:1 our *e.* house of tabern.
*Phil.* 3:19 who mind *e.* things
*Jam.* 3:15 this wisd. is *e.* sensual

**EARTHQUAKE.**
1 *K.* 19:11 an *e.* L. was not in *e.*
12 after the *e.* a fire
*Is.* 29:6 visited of Lord with *e.*
*Amos* 1:1 two years before the *e.*
*Zec.* 14:5 ye fled before the *e.*
*Mat.* 27:54 centurion saw the *e.*
28:2 a great *e.* *Acts* 16:26; *Rev.* 6:12; 11:13
*Rev.* 8:5 thunder. and *e.* 11:19
16:18 great *e.* so mighty an *e.*

**EARTHQUAKES.**
*Mat.* 24:7 famines and *e.* *Mark* 13:8; *Luke* 21:11

**EARTHY.**
1 *Cor.* 15:47 first man of earth, *e.*
49 have borne image of *e.*

**EASE, Substantive.**
*Deut.* 28:65 shalt thou find no *e.*
*Jud.* 20:43 trod down with *e.*
*Job* 12:5 of him that is at *e.*
16:12 at *e.*; 21:23 being at *e.*
*Ps.* 25:13 soul shall dwell at *e.*
123:4 scorning of those at *e.*
*Is.* 32:9 rise up, ye women at *e.*
11 tremble, ye women at *e.*
*Jer.* 48:11 Moab hath been at *e.*
*Ezek.* 23:42 voice of multi. at *e.*
*Amos* 6:1 woe to them at *e.* in Z.
*Luke* 12:19 take thine *e.* eat

**EASE, Verb.**
*Deut.* 23:13 thou wilt *e.* thyself
2 *Chr.* 10:4 *e.* thou somewhat, 9
*Is.* 1:24 *e.* me of adversaries

**EASED.**
*Job* 16:6 forbear, what am I *e.*?
2 *Cor.* 8:13 that other men be *e.*

**EASIER.**
*Ex.* 18:22 be *e.* for thyself
*Mat.* 9:5 whether is *e.* to say, *Mark* 2:9; *Luke* 5:23
19:24 *e.* for camel to go thro' eye, *Mark* 10:25; *Luke* 18:25
*Luke* 16:17 *e.* for heaven to pass

**EASILY.**
1 *Cor.* 13:5 is not *e.* provoked
*Heb.* 12:1 sin which doth *e.* beset

**EAST.**
*Gen.* 3:24 *e.* of garden of Eden
13:11 Lot journeyed *e.*
28:14 abroad to the west and *e.*
29:1 land of the people of the *e.*
*Num.* 23:7 brought me out of *e.*
*Jud.* 6:3 children of the *e.* 33; 7:12; 8:10; 1 *K.* 4:30
1 *K.* 7:25 three tow. *e.* 2 *Chr.* 4:4
1 *Chr.* 9:24 the porters toward *e.*
1 *Chr.* 12:15 to flight them to. *e.*
*Job* 1:3 of all the men of the *e.*
*Ps.* 75:6 promotion not from *e.*
103:12 far as the *e.* is from west
107:3 gathered them from *e.*
*Is.* 11:14 sp. them of *e.* *Jer.* 49:28
41:2 righteous man from the *e.*
43:5 seed from *e.* *Zec.* 8:7
46:11 bird from the *e.* the man
*Ezek.* 8:16 faces toward the *e.*
40:6 gate toward the *e.* 22; 43:1; 44:1; 46:1, 12
47:8 waters issue toward the *e.*
48:10 toward the *e.* ten thousa.
*Dan.* 8:9 horn great toward *e.*
11:44 tidings out of the *e.*
*Zec.* 14:4 mo. sh. cleave tow. *e.*
*Mat.* 2:1 wise men from the *e.*
2 seen his star in the *e.* 9
8:11 come from *e.* *Luke* 13:29
24:27 as lightning out of the *e.*
*Rev.* 7:2 angel ascending from *e.*
16:12 the way of kings of *e.*
21:13 on the *e.* three gates

**EAST border.**
*Num.* 34:10 point out your *e. bor.*
*Jos.* 4:19 encamped in the *e. bor.*
15:5 the *e. border* was salt sea

**EASTER.**
*Acts* 12:4 after *e.* to bring him

**EAST gate.**
*Neh.* 3:29 Shem. keeper of *e. gate*
*Jer.* 19:2 entry of the *e. gate*
*Ezek.* 10:19 stood at door of *e. g.*
11:1 Spirit brought to the *e. g.*

**EAST side.**
*Num.* 2:3 on *e. side* shall J. pitch
*Jos.* 7:2 Ai, on *e. side* of Bethel
*Jud.* 11:18 came by *e. side* of M.
*Ezek.* 48:2 fr. the *e. s.* even unto, 3, 4, 5, 6, 7, 8, 23, 24, 25, 26, 27
*Jon.* 4:5 Jonah sat on *e. s.* of city

**EASTWARD.**
*Gen.* 13:14 th. eyes *e.* *Deut.* 3:27
2 *K.* 13:17 open the window *e.*
1 *Chr.* 26:17 *e.* were six Levites
*Ezek.* 47:3 man with line went *e.*

**EAST wind.**
*Gen.* 41:6 blasted with *e. w.* 23, 27
*Ex.* 10:13 brought an *e. w.* 14:21
*Job* 15:2 fill his belly with *e. w.*
38:24 scattereth the *e. wind*
*Ps.* 48:7 breakest ship with *e. w.*
78:26 caused *e. wind* to blow
*Is.* 27:8 rough in day of *e. w.*
*Ezek.* 17:10 the *e. wind* touch. it
19:12 and the *e. wind* drieth up
27:26 the *e. wind* hath broken
*Hos.* 12:1 Ephra. follow. *e. w.*
13:15 an *e. wind* shall come
*Jon.* 4:8 God prepared *e. wind*
*Hab.* 1:9 faces sup. up as *e. wind*

**EASY.**
*Prov.* 14:6 knowledge is *e.* to h.
*Mat.* 11:30 my yoke is *e.*
1 *Cor.* 14:9 *e.* to be understood
*Jam.* 3:17 wisdom from ab. is *e.*

**EAT.**
*Gen.* 2:16 of ev. tree thou may. *e.*
3:5 day ye *e.* eyes sh. be opened
6 Eve did *e.*; 12 I did *e.* 13
14 and dust shalt thou *e.*
16 in sorrow shalt thou *e.*
27:4 savory meat that I may *e.*
31:46 and they did *e.* there
40:17 the birds did *e.* them
43:32 Egyptians *e.* by themsel.
*Ex.* 10:5 the locusts shall *e.*
12 locusts may *e.* every herb
12:8 bitter herbs they shall *e.*
43 no str. sh. *e.* 48; *Lev.* 22:13
44 then shall he *e.* thereof
16:25 *e.* that to-day
35 *e.* manna, *John* 6:31, 49, 58
29:32 Aaron and sons shall *e.*
*Lev.* 6:16; 8:31
*Lev.* 6:18 all males shall *e.* 29; 7:6; *Num.* 18:10
7:19 clean shall *e.* *Num.* 18:11
24 but in no wise *e.* of it
10:12 *e.* it without leaven
11:21 ye may *e.* 22; *Deut.* 14:20
24:9 Aaron and his sons shall *e.*
25:20 what shall we *e.* sev. year
26:16 your enemies shall *e.*
*Num.* 11:5 fish we did *e.* freely
13 flesh that we may *e.*
23:24 till he *e.* of the prey
25:2 the peo. did *e.* of sacrifices
*Deut.* 12:15 *e.* in gates, 21; 15:22
15 unc. and clean *e.* 22; 26:12
18 must *e.* bef. L. 14:26; 15:20
20 I will *e.* flesh
14:21 give to stra. th. he may *e.*
23:24 thou mayest *e.* grapes
*Deut.* 28:29 for worms shall *e.* th.
53 *e.* fruit of body, *Lam.* 2:20
32:38 *e.* fat of sacrifices
*Jos.* 5:11 they *e.* of old corn
*Jud.* 19:8 they tarried, and did *e.*
1 *Sam.* 1:18 Hannah did *e.*
9:13 they *e.* that be bidden
14:34 and *e.* and sin not
20:34 Jonathan did *e.* no meat
2 *Sam.* 9:11 *e.* at table, 1 *K.* 2:7
1 *K.* 14:11 him that dieth of J. dogs *e.* 16:4; 21:23; 2 *K.* 9:10, 36
17:12 that we may *e.* and die
19:5 arise *e.* *Acts* 10:13; 11:7
2 *K.* 4:43 they shall *e.* and
44 they did *e.* and left thereof
6:28 give son that we may *e.*
29 we boiled my son, and did *e.*
18:31 *e.* eve. m. of vine, *Is.* 36:16
2 *Chr.* 30:18 yet did *e.* passover
*Neh.* 5:2 that we may *e.*
9:25 so they did *e.* *Ps.* 78:29
*Job* 3:24 sighing cometh before I *e.*
31:8 and let another *e.*
*Ps.* 22:26 the meek shall *e.*
29 fat on earth shall *e.*
50:13 will I *e.* the flesh of bulls
78:25 man did *e.* angels' food
128:2 thou shalt *e.* the labor
*Prov.* 1:31 *e.* fruit, *Is.* 3:10
18:21 they that love shall *e.* fruit
24:13 my son, *e.* thou honey
30:17 young eagles shall *e.* it
*Ec.* 2:25 for who can *e.*?
5:11 are increased that *e.* them
12 whether he *e.* little or much
10:16 princes *e.* in the morning
17 princes *e.* in due season
*Cant.* 4:16 come into gar. and *e.*
*Is.* 4:1 we will *e.* our own bread
7:15 butter and honey sh. he *e.*
22 butter and honey sh. one *e.*

9:20 e. on left hand, e. flesh
11:7 lion shall e. straw, 65:25
30:24 oxen and asses shall e.
37:30 plant vineyards, and e. the fruit, 65:21; Jer. 29:5, 28
51:8 worms shall e. them
55:1 come ye, buy and e.
2 hearken to me, and e. good
65:4 peo. which e. swine's flesh
13 my servants shall e.
22 not plant and another e.
Jer. 15:16 found, and I did e.
19:9 shall e. the flesh of friend
Ezek. 2:8 open thy mouth and e.
3:1 e. that thou findest, e. roll
4:10 e. by wei.; 5:10 fath. e. so.
16:13 thou didst e. fine flour
34:3 ye e. the fat
Dan. 4:33 Nebuch. did e. grass
Hos. 4:10 shall e. and not have enough, Mic. 6:14; Hag. 1:6.
9:3 shall e. unclean things
4 e. thereof shall be polluted
Amos 6:4 that e. the lambs
Mic. 3:3 who also e. the flesh
Zec. 11:9 let the rest e.
Mat. 12:4 David did e. shew-bre.
14:20 did all e. 15:37; Mark 6:42; 8:8; Luke 9:17
15:27 dogs e. of cru. Mark 7:28
38 they that did e. were 4,000
26:21 as they did e. he said. Mark 14:18, 22
26 take e. this my body, Mark 14:22; 1 Cor. 11:24
Mark 2:16 e. with publicans
6:44 that did e. were above 5,000
11:14 no man e. fruit of thee
14:12 mayest e. the passover. 14; Luke 22:8, 11; John 18:28
Luke 6:1 did e. rubbing them
10:8 e. such things as are set
15:23 let us e. and be merry
24:43 he took it, and did e.
John 4:31 saying, Master, e.
6:26 because ye did e. of loaves
53 exc. ye e. fle. of Son of m.
Acts 2:46 they did e. their meat
11:3 and didst e. with them
23:14 e. nothing till slain Paul
Rom. 14:2 believeth he may e. all
23 doubteth is damned if he e.
1 Cor. 8:8 e. are better, if we e. n.
13 I will e. no flesh while
10:18 who e. of the sacrifices
25 what. sold in shamb. that e.
27 e. asking no question
2 Thes. 3:10 work not, neither e.
2 Tim. 2:17 word will e. as cank.
Jam. 5:3 and shall e. your flesh
Rev. 17:16 shall e. her flesh
19:18 that e. flesh of kings

See BLOOD BREAD, FAT.

**EAT, *with* drink.**

Gen. 24:54 e. and drink, 26:30; Ex. 24:11; Jud. 9:27; 19:4
Ex. 32:6 to e. and d. 1 Cor. 10:7
34:28 e. br. nor d. Deut. 9:9, 18
2 Sam. 11:11 to e. and d.?
12:3 e. of his meat and drink
19:35 taste what I e. or drink?
1 K. 13:8 not e. bread nor drink water, 9, 17, 22
18:41 E. said, e. and drink
2 K. 6:22 th. they may. e. and d.
18:27 e. du. and d. piss, Is. 36:12
Ezr. 10:6 E. e. no bread nor dr.
Neh. 8:10 e. the fat and d. the s.
Est. 4:16 nor e. nor d. three days
Job 1:4 called sisters to e. and d.
Ec. 2:24 nothing better than e. and drink, 3:13; 5:18; 8:15
Cant. 5:1 e. O friends, yea, dri.
Is. 21:5 e. drink, ye princes
22:13 e. and drink, 1 Cor. 15:32
Ezek. 25:4 e. fruit and dr. milk
39:17 e. flesh and drink blood
Dan. 1:12 pulse to e. water to d.
Mat. 6:25 e. or d. 31; Luke 12:29
24:49 e. and d. w. d. Luke 12:45
Luke 5:30 e. and d. with publi.?
33 thy disciples e. and drink
12:19 take thine ease, e. drink
17:27 they did e. they drank. 28
Acts 9:9 did neither e. nor drink
23:12 e. nor d. till killed P. 21
Rom. 14:21 e. flesh nor d. wine
1 Cor. 9:4 power to e. and to d.
10:31 whether ye e. or drink
11:22 houses to e. and drink in?
26 ye e. bread and drink cup
27 e. and drink unworthily
28 so let him e. and drink

**He did EAT.**

Gen. 25:28 he did e. of his ven.
27:25 to Isaac, and he did e.
39:6 save the bread he did e.
Mark 1:6 John did e. locusts
Luke 4:2 days he did e. nothing
Gal. 2:12 he did e. with Gentiles

**EAT not.**

Gen. 2:17 shall not e. 3:1, 3
3:11 I commanded not to e. 17
9:4 blood not e. Lev. 19:26; Deut. 12:16, 23-25; 15:23
32:32 child. of Is. e. not of sinew
43:32 Egyptians might not e.
Ex. 12:9 e. n. of raw nor sodden
45 foreigner shall not e. thereof
Lev. 22:4 leper n. e. 6:10, 12
Deut. 14:21 not e. of thing that dieth, Ezek. 44:31
Jud. 13:4 e. not unc. thing, 7, 14
1 Sam. 9:13 the people will not e.
28:23 Saul refused, I will not e.
2 K. 7:2 but not e. thereof, 19
Ezr. 2:63 not e. Neh. 7:65
Ps. 141:4 let me not e.
Prov. 23:6 e. not bread of him
Mark 7:3 exc. they wash e. not, 4
Luke 22:16 I will not e. thereof
1 Cor. 5:11 with such no not to e.
10:28 e. not for his sake

**Shall ye EAT.**

Ex. 12:11 s. ye e. with loins gird.
15 seven days shall ye e. 20
22:31 shall ye e. any flesh torn
Lev. 10:14 wave-breast shall ye e.
11:3 cheweth the cud, that shall ye e. Deut. 14:4, 6
19:25 in the fifth year shall ye e.

**Ye shall EAT.**

Ex. 12:11 ye shall e. it with haste
18 ye shall e. unleavened bread
16:12 at even ye shall e. flesh
Lev. 7:23 ye shall e. no fat, 24
26 ye shall e. no blood, 17:14
23:14 ye shall e. neither bread
25:12 ye shall e. the increase
19 ye shall e. your fill
22 ye sh. e. of old store, 26:10
Deut. 14:11 clean birds ye sh. e.
2 K. 19:29 e. this year, Is. 37:30
Is. 1:19 if obedient ye shall e.
61:6 ye sh. e. riches of Gentiles
Joel 2:26 ye shall e. in plenty
Luke 12:22 what ye s. e.

**To EAT.**

Ex. 16:8 L. shall give flesh to e.
Deut. 12:20 longeth to e. flesh
2 K. 4:40 poured out for m. to e.
2 Chr. 31:10 had enough to e.
Neh. 9:36 land thou gavest to e.
Ps. 78:24 manna on them to e.
Prov. 23:1 sit. to e. with a ruler
25:27 not good to e. much honey
Ec. 5:19 given power to e.
Is. 23:18 shall be for them to e.
Jer. 19:9 cause th. to e. the flesh
Ezek. 3:2 caused me to e. th. roll
3 cause thy belly to e.
Dan. 4:25 to e. grass, 32
Mic. 7:1 there is no cluster to e.
Hab. 1:8 eagle that hasteth to e.
Mat. 12:1 to pluck ears and to e.
4 not lawful to e. Mark 2:26; Luke 6:4
14:16 give them to e. Mark 6:37; Luke 9:13
15:20 to e. with unwash. hands
32 nothing to e. Mark 8:1, 2
26:17 prepare to e. passover?
Mark 5:43 given her to e.
6:31 no leisure to e.
Luke 22:15 to e. this passover
John 4:32 meat to e. ye know not
33 brought him aught to e.?
6:52 man give us his flesh to e.?
1 Cor. 8:10 embolden to e. things
11:20 not to e. Lord's supper
Heb. 13:10 an altar no right to e.
Rev. 2:7 to e. of the tree of life
14 to e. things sacrificed, 20
17 to e. of hidden manna

**EAT up.**

Gen. 41:4 did e. up seven fat, 20
Num. 24:8 he shall e. up nations
Ps. 27:2 enemies came to e. up
105:35 did e. up all the herbs
Is. 50:9 moth shall e. up, 51:8
Jer. 5:17 e. up thy harvest, e. up flocks, e. up vines
22:22 wind e. up all pastures
Hos. 4:8 they e. up the sin of
Nah. 3:15 shall e. up like canker
Rev. 10:9 take it, and e. it up

**EATEN.**

Gen. 3:11 hast thou e. of tree
14:24 which young men have e.
41:21 when they had e. them
Ex. 12:46 in one ho. sh. it be e.
13:3 no leavened br. be e. 7
21:28 his flesh shall not be e.
29:34 not be e. because it is ho.
Lev. 6:16 shall be e. in the holy place, 26; 7:6
23 wholly burnt not be e. 7:19
30 no sin-offering shall be e.
7:15 shall be e. the same day, 16
10:17 why not e. sin offering?
11:13 not be e. 41; Deut. 14:19
19:6 shall be e. same day, 22:30
Num. 28:17 br. be e. Ezek. 45:21
Deut. 6:11 shalt have e. 8:10, 12
26:14 I have not e. in mourning
29:6 ye have not e. bread
31:20 when they shall have e.
Jos. 5:12 had e. of old corn.
Ruth 3:7 when Boaz had e. and
1 Sam. 28:20 e. no bread all day
30:12 had e. his spirit came
1 K. 13:28 lion not e. the carcass
Neh. 5:14 have not e. the bread
Job 6:6 unsavory e. without salt
31:17 or have e. my morsel
39 if I have e. the fruits
Ps. 69:9 zeal of thy house hath e. me up, John 2:17
102:9 I have e. ashes like bread
Prov. 9:17 bread e. in secret
23:8 morsel e. shalt thou vomit
Cant. 5:1 I have e. my honey-co.
Is. 3:14 ye have e. up vineyard
Jer. 10:25 they have e. up Jacob
24:2 could not be e. 3:8; 29:17
31:29 e. sour grapes, Ezek. 18:2
Hos. 10:13 ye have e. the fruit
Joel 1:4 locust left c.-w. e. 25
Mat. 14:21 and they that had e. Mark 8:9
Luke 13:26 we have e. and drunk
17:8 I have e. afterward thou e.
Acts 10:10 would have e.
14 I have nev. e. anyth. com.
12:23 he was e. of worms
27:38 when they had e. enough
Rev. 10:10 had e. it, belly bitter

**EATER, S.**

Jud. 14:14 out of e. came forth
Prov. 23:20 riotous e. of flesh

*Is.* 55:10 give bread to the *e.*
*Nah.* 3:12 fall into mouth of *e.*

**EATEST.**

*Gen.* 2:17 day thou *e.* thou shalt
1 *Sam.* 1:8 why *e.* thou not?

**EATETH.**

*Ex.* 12:15 who *e.* leav. bread, 19
*Lev.* 7:18 that *e.* 20, 25; 17:10
*Num.* 13:2 land *e.* up inhabit.
1 *Sam.* 14:24 cursed m. that *e.* 28
*Job* 5:5 harvest the hungry *e.* up
21:25 never *e.* with pleasure
40:15 behemoth *e.* grass as an ox
*Ps.* 106:20 an ox that *e.* grass
*Prov.* 13:25 righteous *e.* to satisfy
*Prov.* 30:20 she *e.* and wipeth m.
31:27 she *e.* not bread of idlen.
*Ec.* 4:5 fool *e.* his own flesh
*Is.* 29:8 he *e.* but awaketh
44:16 with part he *e.* flesh
59:5 that *e.* of their eggs
*Mat.* 9:11 why *e.* your master, *Mark* 2:16; *Luke* 15:2
*John* 6:54 whoso *e.* my flesh
56 that *e.* my flesh dwelleth in
57 so he that *e.* me shall live
58 he that *e.* of this bread
*Rom.* 14:2 another weak *e.* herbs
3 let not him that *e.* despise
6 *e.* to L. that *e.* not, to L. *e.* n.
20 evil for who *e.* with offence
23 because *e.* not of faith
1 *Cor.* 9:7 planteth vineyard and *e.* not? and *e.* not of milk
11:29 that *e.* unworth. *e.* damn.

**EATING.**

*Ex.* 12:4 ev. man to his *e.* 16:18
*Jud.* 14:9 Samson went on *e.*
1 *Sam.* 14:34 sin not in *e.* with b.
2 *K.* 4:40 as they were *e.* pottage
*Job* 20:23 upon him while he is *e.*
*Is.* 66:17 *e.* swine's flesh
*Amos* 7:2 made an end of *e.* grass
*Mat.* 26:26 were *e.* Jes. took br.
1 *Cor.* 8:4 *e.* of things sacrificed
11:21 in *e.* ev. one tak. own sup
*See* DRINKING.

**EBAL.**

*Deut.* 11:29 mount E. 27:4, 13
*Jos.* 8:30 an altar in mount E.

EBED. *Jud.* 9:30; *Ezr.* 8:6

**EBED-MELECH.**

*Jer.* 38:8 E. spake to king, 39:16

**EBEN-EZER.**

1 *Sam.* 4:1 and pitched beside E.
5:1 bro. the ark from E. 7:12

EBER. *Gen.* 10:21, 25; *Num.* 24:24

ED. *Jos.* 22:34

**EDEN.**

*Gen.* 2:15 man into garden of E.
*Is.* 51:3 her wilderness like E.
*Ezek.* 28:13; 31:9, 16, 18; 36:35
*Joel* 2:3 is as the garden of E.
*Amos* 1:5 cut off sceptre from E.

**EDGE.**

*Ex.* 13:20 *e.* of wild. *Num.* 33:6
26:10 loops in the *e.* of curtain
*Ec.* 10:10 do not whet the *e.*
*See* TEETH.

**EDGE of the sword.**

*Gen.* 34:26 slew H. with *e. of s.*
*Ex.* 17:13 Amalek with *e. of s.*
*Num.* 21:24 smote S. with *e. of s.*
*Jos.* 8:24 smote Ai. with *e. of s.*
*Jud.* 4:15 Sisera; 21:10 Jabe.-gil.
*Job* 1:15 Job's ser. with *e. of s.* 17
*Ps.* 89:43 turned the *e. of the s.*
*Jer.* 21:7 smite them with *e. of s.*
*Luke* 21:24 Jews fall by *e. of sw.*
*Heb.* 11:34 thro' faith esca. *e. of s.*

**EDGED.**

*Ps.* 149:6 two-*e.* sword in hand
*Prov.* 5:4 sharp as a two-*e.* sword
*Heb.* 4:12 word of God sharper than two-*e.* sword
*Rev.* 1:16 mouth sharp two-*e.* 6

**EDGES.**

*Ex.* 28:7 joined at two *e.* 39:4
*Jud.* 3:16 Eh.'s dag. had two *e.*
*Rev.* 2:12 sharp sw. with two *e.*

**EDIFICATION.**

*Rom.* 15:2 please neighbor to *e.*
1 *Cor.* 14:3 speaketh to men to *e.*
2 *Cor.* 10:8 L. hath given us for *e.*
13:10 Lord hath given me to *e.*

**EDIFIED.**

*Acts* 9:31 churches had rest, *e.*
1 *Cor.* 14:17 the other is not *e.*

**EDIFIETH.**

1 *Cor.* 8:1 knowledge puffeth charity *e.*
14:4 he that speaks *e.* hims. he that prophes. *e.* the church

**EDIFY.**

*Rom.* 14:19 one may *e.* another
1 *Cor.* 10:23 lawful but *e.* not
1 *Thes.* 5:11 *e.* one another.

**EDIFYING.**

1 *Cor.* 14:5 church may receive *e.*
12 that ye may excel to the *e.*
14:26 let all things be done to *e.*
2 *Cor.* 12:19 all thin. for your *e.*
*Eph.* 4:12 *e.* of body of Christ
16 the body to the *e.* of itself
29 good to the use of *e.*
1 *Tim.* 1:4 quest. rather than *e.*

**EDOM.**

*Gen.* 25:30 was called E. 36:1
*Ex.* 15:15 dukes of E. amazed
*Num.* 20:21 E. refused to give Israel passage, 24:18
2 *Sam.* 8:14 gar. in E. 1 *Chr.* 18:13
2 *K.* 8:20 E. revolted, 14:10; 2 *Chr.* 25:20
*Ps.* 60:8 over E. cast shoe, 108:9
*Is.* 63:1 that cometh from E.?
*Jer.* 49:7 concerning E. saith Lord, *Ezek.* 25:12
*Amos* 2:1 king of E. 9:12
*Ob.* 8 dest. wise men out of E.

EDOMITE. *Deut.* 23:7; 2 *K.* 8:21
EDREI. *Deut.* 1:4

**EFFECT, Substantive.**

*Num.* 30:8 make vow of no *e.*
*Ps.* 33:10 devices of peo. of no. *e.*
*Is.* 32:17 the *e.* of righteousness
*Ezek.* 12:23 and *e.* of every vision
*Mat.* 15:6 com. of G. of none *e.*
*Mark* 7:13 word of God of none *e.*
*Rom.* 3:3 unbelief make the faith of God without *e.*
4:14 prom. of none *e.* *Gal.* 3:17
9:6 word hath taken none *e.*
1 *Cor.* 1:17 cr. of C. be of none *e.*
*Gal.* 5:4 Chr. is become of no *e.*

**EFFECT, Verb.**

*Jer.* 48:30 lies shall not so *e.* it

**EFFECTED.**

2 *Chr.* 7:11 Sol. prosperously *e.*

**EFFECTUAL.**

1 *Cor.* 16:9 a great door and *e.*
2 *Cor.* 1:6 is *e.* in enduring suff.
*Eph.* 3:7 by the *e.* working of
4:16 according to *e.* working
*Phile.* 6 faith may become *e.*
*Jam.* 5:16 the *e.* prayer of right.

**EFFECTUALLY.**

*Gal.* 2:8 he that wrought *e.* in P.
1 *Thes.* 2:13 the word *e.* worketh

**EFFEMINATE.**

1 *Cor.* 6:9 nor *e.* shall inherit

**EGG.**

*Job* 6:6 any taste in white of *e.*?
*Luke* 11:12 ask *e.* will offer scor.?

**EGGS.**

*Deut.* 22:6 whet. young ones or *e.*
*Job* 39:14 ostr. leaveth *e.* in earth
*Is.* 10:14 one gathereth *e.*
59:5 hatch cockatrice's *e.*
*Jer.* 17:11 partridge sitteth on *e.*

EGLAH. 2 *Sam.* 3:5
EGLAIM. *Is.* 15:8
EGLON. *Jud.* 3:14, 17

**EGYPT.**

*Gen.* 15:18 from the river of E.
45:19 made me lord of all E.
*Ex.* 3:20 will smite E. 7:4; 10:7
2 *K.* 18:21 thou trustest on E. 24
*Is.* 19:16 E. like unto women, 24
*Jer.* 2:18 in way of E.? 36
*Ezek.* 29:2 ag. E. 30:15; 32:12
*Joel* 3:19 E. a desolat. *Zec.* 10:11
*Nah.* 3:9 Ethiopia and E. were
*Acts* 7:10 governor over E.
*Heb.* 11:27 by faith he forsook E.
*Rev.* 11:8 is called Sodom and E.

**In, *and* into EGYPT.**

*Gen.* 46:4 go down with thee *i.* E.
*Ex.* 10:2 things I wrought *in* E.
12:30 cry *in* E.; 14:11 graves *in* E.
*Num.* 11:18 well with us *in* E.
14:6 for us to return *into* E. 4
20:15 and we have dwelt *in* E.
*Deut.* 1:30 did for you *in* E. 4:34
*Jos.* 9:9 all that he did *in* E.
*Is.* 19:1 Lord shall come *into* E.
*Jer.* 26:21 fled and went *into* E.
41:17 to go *into* E. 42:15
42:19 Go ye not *into* E. 43:2
*Mat.* 2:13 flee *into* E. 14

**Land of EGYPT.**

*Gen.* 13:10; 41:19, 54; 45:18; 47:6
*Ps.* 78:12 marvel. th. in E. 81:5
*Heb.* 8:9 out of the *land of* E.
*Jude* 5 saved peo. out of *l. of* E.

**Out of EGYPT.**

*Gen.* 13:1 Abraham *out of* E.
47:30 carry me *out of* E.
*Ex.* 3:11; 12:39; 13:9, 16
*Num.* 11:20 came forth *out of* E.
22:11 is a people come *out of* E.
*Jud.* 2:1 made you go *out of* E.
*Heb.* 3:16 all that came *out of* E.

**To EGYPT.**

*Is.* 19:21 L. shall be known *to* E.
31:1 woe to them that go *to* E.
*Hos.* 7:11 they call *to* E.

**EGYPTIAN, S.**

*Gen.* 16:1, 3; 21:9; 39:1, 5; 41:55
*Ex.* 2:11 E. smiting Heb. 12, 19
3:22 shall spoil the E. 12:36
14:9 E. pursued after, 10, 13, 25
19:4 seen what I did to the E.
32:12 wherefore should the E.
*Num.* 14:13 M. said, Then the E.
20:15 and E. vexed us and our
1 *Sam.* 30:11 found an E. in field
*Is.* 19:2 I will set the E. 4, 21, 23
*Acts* 21:38 art not thou that E.?
*Heb.* 11:29 E. assaying to do

**EHUD.**

*Jud.* 3:15 raised up E. 16, 23, 26
1 *Chr.* 7:10 sons of Bilham, E. 8:6

**EIGHT.**

*Gen.* 17:12 he that is *e.* days old, 21:4; *Luke* 2:21
22:23 these *e.* Milcah did bear
*Num.* 29:29 *e.* bullocks, two rams
*Jud.* 3:8 Israel served *e.* years
12:14 Abdon judged Is. *e.* y.
1 *K.* 7:10 of stones of *e.* cubits
2 *K.* 8:17 Jehor. reigned *e.* years
22:1 Josi. was *e.* years old, 2 *Chr.* 34:1
2 *Chr.* 29:17 sanct. L. in *e.* days
*Ec.* 11:2 to seven, also to *e.*
*Ezek.* 40:31 had *e.* steps, 34:37
41 *e.* tables slew sacrifices
*Mic.* 5:5 seven shepherds, *e.* men

*Luke* 9:28 about an *e.* days after
*John* 20:26 after *e.* days
*Acts* 9:33 E. kept his bed *e.* years
1 *Pet.* 3:20 *e.* souls were saved

**EIGHTH.**

*Lev.* 25:22 shall sow *e.* year
1 *K.* 6:38 which is *e.* month
1 *Chr.* 24:10 the *e.* lot came forth
*Zec.* 1:1 in *e.* month word came
2 *Pet.* 2:5 saved Noah the *e.* per.
*Rev.* 17:11 beast that was, is the *e.*
21:20 *e.* foundation was a beryl
*See* DAY, DAYS.

**EIGHT hundred.**

*Gen.* 5:4 Adam lived *e. h.* years

**EIGHTEEN.**

1 *K.* 7:15 two pillars of brass *e.* cubits, 2 *K.* 25:17; *Jer.* 52:21
2 *Chr.* 11:21 Reho. took *e.* wives
*Luke* 13:4 *e.* on whom tower fell
16 Satan hath bound *e.* years

**EIGHTEENTH.**

1 *K.* 15:1 *e.* year of Jer. 2 *Chr.* 13:1
1 *Chr.* 24:15 *e.* lot came forth
25:25 the *e.* to Hanani
*Jer.* 32:1 was *e.* year of Nebuch.

**EITHER.**

*John* 19:18 crucifi. on *e.* side one
*Rev.* 22:2 *e.* side river tree of life

**EKRON.**

1 *Sam.* 5:10 as ark came to E.
2 *K.* 1:2 the god of E. 3:6, 16
*Amos* 1:9 my hand against E.
*Zep.* 2:4 E. shall be rooted up
*Zec.* 9:5 E. very sorrowful, 7

**EKRONITES.**

*Jos.* 13:3 the land of the E. not
1 *Sam.* 5:10 ark ca. to Ekron, E.

**ELAH.**

*Gen.* 36:41 duke E. 1 *K.* 4:18
1 *Sam.* 17:2 by the valley of E.
21:9 Goliath in valley of E.
1 *K.* 16:8 E. son of Baasha
2 *K.* 15:30 son of E. 17:1; 18:1, 9
1 *Chr.* 4:15 son of Caleb, E. 9:8

**ELAM.**

*Gen.* 10:22 children of Shem, E.
14:1 Chedorlaomer king of E.
*Is.* 11:11 recover people from E.
21:2 go up, O E.; 22:6 E. bare
*Jer.* 25:25 kings of E. 49:34, 36, 39
*Ezek.* 32:24 there is E. and all
*Dan.* 8:2 in the province of E.

**ELAMITES.**

*Ezr.* 4:9 E. wrote letter, *Acts* 2:9

ELATH. 2 *K.* 14:22; 16:6
EL-BETHEL. *Gen.* 35:7
ELDAD. *Num.* 11:26, 27

**ELDER.**

*Gen.* 10:21 S. brother of Ja. the *e.*
25:23 *e.* serve young. *Rom.* 9:12
1 *K.* 2:22 he is mine *e.* brother
*Job* 15:10 much *e.* than father
*Ezek.* 16:46 thy *e.* sister is Sama.
*Luke* 15:25 his *e.* son was in field
1 *Tim.* 5:2 entreat the *e.* women
1 *Pet.* 5:5 younger, submit to *e.*

**ELDER,** *for ruler.*

1 *Tim.* 5:1 rebuke not an *e.*
19 against *e.* receive not accu.
1 *Pet.* 5:1 who am also an *e.*
2 *John* 1 the *e.* to the elect lady
3 *John* 1 the *e.* unto Gaius

**ELDERS.**

*Gen.* 50:7 *e.* of his house went
*Lev.* 4:15 *e.* of congr. lay hands
*Num.* 11:25 L. gave spirit to 70 *e.*
*Deut.* 29:10 before the L. your *e.*
31:28 gather to me all *e.*
32:7 ask thy father and *e.*
1 *Sam.* 16:4 *e.* of the town
1 *K.* 21:11 *e.* did as Jezebel sent
2 *K.* 6:32 Elisha and *e.* sat
10:1 Jehu sent to *e.* of Jezreel
19:2 Hezekiah sent *e.* *Is.* 37:2
*Ps.* 107:32 in assembly of *e.*
*Prov.* 31:23 known among *e.*
*Lam.* 1:19 *e.* gave up the ghost
2:10 *e.* of Zion sit upon ground
4:16 favored not *e.* 5:12
*Ezek.* 8:1 and the *e.* of Judah sat
*Joel* 1:14 gather the *e.* 2:16
*Mat.* 15:2 tradition of the *e.*?
16:21 suffer things of *e.* 27:12
26:59 *e.* sought false witness
27:20 *e.* persuaded the multit.
41 mocking with the *e.* said
28:12 assembled with the *e.*
*Mark* 7:3 tradition of the *e.*
8:31 rejected of the *e.* *Luke* 9:22
15:1 held a consultation with *e.*
*Acts* 4:5 *e.* were gath. together
23 all that the *e.* had said
6:12 stirred up the peo. and *e.*
11:30 sent it to the *e.* by Barna.
14:23 ordained *e.* in ev. church
15:4 of the church and of the *e.*
6 the apostles and *e.* came
23 apostles, *e.* and brethren
16:4 decrees ordained of the *e.*
20:17 the *e.* of the church
1 *Tim.* 5:17 *e.* rule well
*Tit.* 1:5 ordain *e.* in every city
*Heb.* 11:2 by faith the *e.* obtained
*Jam.* 5:14 call for *e.* of church
1 *Pet.* 5:1 *e.* which are am. you
*Rev.* 4:4 I saw twenty-four *e.*
10:24 *e.* fall, 5:8, 14; 11:16; 19:4
5:5 and one of *e.* saith
6 in midst of *e.* stood a Lamb
7:11 angels stood about the *e.*
13 one of the *e.* answered

**ELDERS,** *with* **city.**

*Deut.* 19:12 *e.* of *city* shall fetch
21:3 *e.* of *city* shall take heifer
6 *e.* of that *city* shall wash
21:19 bring son to *e.* of his *city*
*Jud.* 8:16 he took *e.* of the *city*
*Ruth* 4:2 B. took men of *e.* of *c.*
*Ezr.* 10:14 the *e.* of every *city*

**ELDERS of Israel.**

*Ex.* 3:16 gather the *e. of Israel*
12:21 M. called for *e. of Israel*
18:12 *e. of Israel* came to eat
24:1 seventy of *e.* 9; *Num.* 11:16
*Deut.* 27:1 *e. of Isr.* commanded
31:9 delivered law to *e. of Isr.*
*Jos.* 7:6 *e. of Isr.* put dust on
2 *Sam.* 5:3 *e. of I.* came to king at Hebron, 1 *K.* 8:3; 2 *Chr.* 5:4
17:4 pleased all *e. of Israel*
15 Ahithophel counsel *e. of Is.*
*Ezek.* 20:1 *e. of I.* came to inqu.
*Acts* 4:8 rulers of peo. and *e. of I.*

**ELDERS,** *with* **people.**

*Num.* 11:24 M. gathered seventy men of the *e.* of the *people*
1 *Sam.* 15:30 honor before *e.* of *p.*
*Mat.* 21:23 the *e.* of *people* came, *Luke* 22:66
27:1 *e.* of the *peo.* took counsel

**ELDEST.**

*Gen.* 24:2 Ab. said to his *e.* serv.
27:1 Isaac called Es. his *e.* son
44:12 began at the *e.*
*Num.* 1:20 Reuben *e.* son, 26:5
1 *Sam.* 17:13 *e.* sons of Jesse, 14
28 Eliab his *e.* brother
2 *K.* 3:27 he took his *e.* son
*Job* 1:13 in *e.* brother's house, 18
*John* 8:9 one by one, begin. at *e.*

ELEALEH. *Num.* 32:37; *Is.* 15:4; 16:9; *Jer.* 48:34

**ELEAZAR.**

*Ex.* 6:25; 28:1; *Num.* 3:2; 26:60; 1 *Chr.* 6:3; 24:1; *Ezr.* 8:33
*Lev.* 10:16 M. was angry with E.
*Num.* 3:4 E. minister. in priests'
34:17 E. and Joshua shall divide
*Jos.* 17:4 ca. near bef. E. 24:33
1 *Sam.* 7:1 they sanctified E. to
*Neh.* 12:42 Shemaiah and E.
*Mat.* 1:15 Eliud begat E. and E.

**ELECT.**

*Is.* 42:1 mine *e.* in whom my
45:4 Israel mine *e.* I have called
65:9 mine *e.* shall inherit it
22 mine *e.* shall long enjoy
*Mat.* 24:22 for the *e.* those days shall be short. *Mark* 13:20
24 dec. the very *e.* *Mark* 13:22
31 angels gather *e.* *Mark* 13:27
*Luke* 18:7 G. avenge his own *e.*?
*Rom.* 8:33 to charge of God's *e.*?
*Col.* 3:12 put on as *e.* of G. bow.,
1 *Tim.* 5:21 before the *e.* angels
2 *Tim.* 2:10 endure for the *e.* sak
*Tit.* 1:1 to the faith of God's *e.*
1 *Pet.* 1:2 *e.* according to foreknow.
2:6 chief corner-stone, *e.* prec.
2 *John* 1 the elder to the *e.* lady
13 the children of thy *e.* sister

**ELECTED.**

1 *Pet.* 5:13 church at Bab. *e.* with

**ELECTION.**

*Rom.* 9:11 purpose accord. to *e.*
11:5 remn. according to the *e.*
7 the *e.* hath obtained it
28 the *e.* they are beloved
1 *Thes.* 1:4 knowing your *e.* of G
2 *Pet.* 1:10 your calling and *e.*

EL-ELOHE-*Israel.* *Gen.* 33:20

**ELEMENTS.**

*Gal.* 4:3 under *e.* of the world
9 the weak and beggarly *e.*
2 *Pet.* 3:10 *e.* melt with heat, 12

**ELEVEN.**

*Gen.* 32:22 Jacob took his *e.* sons
37:9 sun, moon, and *e.* stars
*Ex.* 26:7 *e.* curtains shalt make
36:14 *e.* curt.; 15 *e.* of one size
*Num.* 29:20 *e.* bullocks, two rams
*Deut.* 1:2 *e.* days' journey fr. H.
*Jos.* 15:51 *e.* cities with villages
*Jud.* 16:5 *e.* hun. pieces of silver
17:2 *e.* hundred shekels of silv.
2 *K.* 23:36 Jehoiakim reigned *e.* years in Jeru. 2 *Chr.* 36:5
24:18 Zedekiah reigned *e.* years, 2 *Chr.* 36:11; *Jer.* 52:1
*Mat.* 28:16 *e.* disciples went to G.
*Mark* 16:14 he appeared to the *e.*
*Luke* 24:9 told to the *e.* and rest
33 found the *e.* gath. together
*Acts* 1:26 numb. with *e.* apostles
2:14 P. with the *e.* said to them

**ELEVENTH.**

1 *K.* 6:38 *e.* year was ho. finished
1 *Chr.* 24:12 the *e.* lot came forth
25:18 the *e.* to Azareel
27:14 *e.* capt. for the *e.* month
*Jer.* 1:3 Jer. proph. *e.* year of Z.
39:2 in *e.* year city was bro. up
*Ezek.* 26:1 word of L. came to E. in *e.* year, 30:20; 31:1
*Mat.* 20:6 about *e.* hour he went
9 were hired about the *e.* hour
*Rev.* 21:20 *e.* foundat. of the city

ELHANAN. 2 *Sam.* 21:19; 23:24; 1 *Chr.* 11:26; 20:5

**ELI.**

1 *Sam.* 1:25 brou. the child to E. 2:12, 27; 3:5, 6, 8, 12, 14; 4:14
1 *K.* 2:27 spake concerning E.
*Mat.* 27:46 cried, E. E. lama, *Mark* 15:34

**ELIAB.**

*Num.* 1:9; 2:7; 7:24, 29; 10:16
16:1 sons of E. 12; 26:8, 9
*Deut.* 11:6 he did to sons of E.
1 *Sam.* 17:28 E. heard, 1 *Chr.* 2:13
1 *Chr.* 6:27 E. the son of Nahath
15:18 E. port. 20; 16:5 E. with

*2 Chr.* 11:18 took daughter of E.

**ELIADA.**
*2 Sam.* 5:16; *1 Chr.* 3:8; *2 Chr.* 17:17

**ELIAKIM.**
*2 K.* 18:18 out to Rab-shakeh E.
23:34 made E. son, *2 Chr.* 36:4
*Is.* 22:20; 36:3; 37:2
*Mat.* 1:13 Abiud begat E. and E.

ELIAM. *2 Sam.* 11:3; 23:34

**ELIASHIB.**
*Ezr.* 10:6 the son of E. 24, 27, 36
*Neh.* 3:1; 12:10, 23; 13:4, 7, 28

**ELIEZER.**
*Gen.* 15:2 steward of house is E.
*Ex.* 18:4 name of Moses' son E.
*1 Chr.* 7:8; 15:24; 23:15, 17; 27:16
*2 Chr.* 20:37 E. prophesied aga.
*Ezr.* 10:18 E. had taken, 23, 31
*Luke* 3:29 Jose was the son of E.

ELIHOREPH. *1 K.* 4:3

**ELIHU.**
*1 Chr.* 12:20; 26:7; 27:18; *Job* 32:2

**ELIJAH, *or* ELIAS.**
*1 K.* 17:1 E. the Tishbite, 15, 22
23 E. took the child down
18:2 E. went to A. 7, 16, 40, 46
19:1 E. had done, 9:20; 21:20
*2 K.* 1:8 is E. the Tishbite, 13, 17
2:1 E. into heaven, 8, 11, 14, 15
3:11 poured wa. on hands of E.
*2 Chr.* 21:12 came a writing fr. E.
*Mal.* 4:5 behold I will send you E.
*Mat.* 11:14 E. which was to come
16:14 say E. *Mark* 6:15; *Lu.* 9:8
17:3 app. E. *Mark* 9:4; *Lu.* 9:30
11 E. shall come, *Mark* 9:12
12 E. come already, *Mark* 9:13
27:47 calleth for E. *Mark* 15:35
49 E. will come, *Mark* 15:36
*Luke* 1:17 before in power of E.
9:54 fire to consume as E. did
*John* 1:21 art thou E.? art th. 25
*Rom.* 11:2 scripture saith of E.
*Jam.* 5:17 E. was a man subject

**ELIM.**
*Ex.* 15:27; 16:1; *Num.* 33:9, 10

**ELIMELECH.**
*Ruth* 1:2 name E. 3; 2:1; 4:9

**ELIPHALET.**
*2 Sam.* 5:16 E. D. son, *1 Chr.* 3:6, 8

**ELIPHAZ.**
*Gen.* 36:4, 10, 11, 12, 15; *1 Chr.* 1:35
*Job* 2:11; 4:1; 15:1; 22:1; 42:9

ELISABETH. *Luke* 1:5, 24, 40, 57

**ELISHA, ELISEUS.**
*1 K.* 19:16 E. to be proph. 17, 19
*2 K.* 2:5 proph. came to E. 12, 15
3:11 Here is E. 4:1, 8, 17
5:9 Naaman stood at door of E.
6:20 E. said, open the eyes, 31
8:4 that E. hath done 5, 14
13:14 E. fallen sick, 16, 17, 21
*Luke* 4:27 lepers in days of E.

ELISHAH. *Ezek.* 27:7

**ELISHAMA.**
*Num.* 1:10; 2:18; 7:48, 53; 10:22
*2 Sam.* 5:16 E. David's son
*1 Chr.* 2:41; 3:6, 8; 7:26; 14:7
*2 Chr.* 17:8 he sent with them E.
*Jer.* 36:12 E. the scribe, 41:1

ELISHEBA. *Ex.* 6:23

**ELISHUA.**
*2 Sam.* 5:15 E. D. sons, *1 Chr.* 14:5

ELIUD. *Mat.* 1:14, 15

**ELKANAH.**
*Ex.* 6:24 Korah, Assir, and E.
*1 Sam.* 1:1 name was E. 21; 2:11
*1 Chr.* 6:23 son of E. 26, 34, 35
12:6 E. the Korhite, 9:16
15:23 E. was door-keeper for ark
*2 Chr.* 28:7 E. was next to king

ELMODAM. *Luke* 3:28

**ELNATHAN.**
*2 K.* 24:8 the daughter of E.
*Ezr.* 8:16 I sent for E. and Jarib
*Jer.* 26:22 sent E. into, 36:12, 25

**ELON.**
*Gen.* 26:34 daughter of E. 36:2
46:14 the sons of Zebulun, E.
*Jud.* 12:11 E. judged Israel, 12

**ELOQUENT.**
*Ex.* 4:10 O my lord, I am not *e.*
*Is.* 3:3 doth take away *e.* orator
*Acts* 18:24 Apollos, an *e.* man

**ELSE.**
*Deut.* 4:35 God, there is none *e.*
39; *1 K.* 8:60; *Is.* 45:5, 6, 14,
18, 21, 22; 46:9; *Joel* 2:27
*Jud.* 7:14 noth. *e.* save sw. of Gid.
*1 Chr.* 21:12 or *e.* three days
*Ps.* 51:16 not sacrifice *e.* give it
*Is.* 47:8 none *e.* beside me, 10
*John* 14:11 or *e.* believe me
*Rom.* 2:15 accusing or *e.* excus.
*Rev.* 2:5 repent, or *e.* I come, 16

ELUL. *Neh.* 6:15
ELYMAS. *Acts* 13:8

**EMBALM, ED.**
*Gen.* 50:2 Jos. commanded physician to *e.* his father; physicians *e.* Israel
26 they *e.* Joseph in Egypt

**EMBOLDENED, ETH.**
*Job* 16:3 *e.* thee that answerest?
*1 Cor.* 8:10 the conscience be *e.*

**EMBRACE.**
*2 K.* 4:16 thou shalt *e.* a son
*Prov.* 4:8 when thou dost *e.* her
5:20 why wilt thou *e.* bosom?
*Ec.* 3:5 to *e.* and to refrain
*Cant.* 2:6 hand doth *e.* me, 8:3
*Lam.* 4:5 in scarlet, *e.* dunghills

**EMBRACED,**
*Gen.* 29:13 Laban *e.* Jacob
33:4 Esau ran and *e.* Jacob
48:10 Jacob *e.* Joseph's sons
*Acts* 20:1 Paul *e.* disciples
*Heb.* 11:13 and *e.* the promises

**EMBRACING.**
*Ec.* 3:5 time to refrain from *e.*
*Acts* 20:10 Paul *e.* Eutychus

**EMBROIDER.**
*Ex.* 28:39 thou shalt *e.* the coat

**EMBROIDERER.**
*Ex.* 35:35 work of the *e.*
38:23 Aholiab, an *e.* in blue

**EMERALD, S.**
*Ex.* 28:18 second row *e.* 39:11
*Ezek.* 27:16 Syria in fairs with *e.*
28:13 precious stone, the *e.*
*Rev.* 4:3 rainbow like unto an *e.*
21:19 fourth found. was an *e.*

**EMERODS.**
*Deut.* 28:27 smite thee with *e.*
*1 Sam.* 5:6 smote Ashdod with *e.*
9 *e.* in their secret parts
12 were smitten with *e.*
6:4 answered, Five golden *e.* 17
5 make images of your *e.* 11

**EMIM.**
*Gen.* 14:5 sm. the E. *Deut.* 2:10

**EMINENT.**
*Ezek.* 16:24 built an *e.* place, 31
39 throw down thine *e.* place
17:22 a high and *e.* mountain

**EMMANUEL.**
*Is.* 7:14 his name E. *Mat.* 1:23
8:8 breadth of thy land, O E.

EMMAUS. *Luke* 24:13
EMMOR. *Acts* 7:16

**EMPIRE.**
*Est.* 1:20 publish. throughout *e.*

**EMPLOY, ED.**
*Deut.* 20:19 tree, to *e.* in siege
*1 Chr.* 9:33 sing. *e.* day and night

**EMPLOYMENT.**
*Ezek.* 39:14 sever out men of *e.*

**EMPTY, Adjective.**
*Gen.* 31:42 hadst sent me away *e.*
37:24 pit was *e.* no water in it
41:27 the seven *e.* ears blasted
*Ex.* 23:15 none shall appear before me *e.* 34:20; *Deut.* 16:16
*Jud.* 7:16 in hand *e.* pitchers
*Ruth* 1:21 brought me home *e.*
3:17 go not *e.* to mother-in-law
*1 Sam.* 6:3 send not ark away *e.*
20:18 thy seat will be *e.* 25:27
*2 Sam.* 1:22 sword return. not *e.*
*2 K.* 4:3 borrow thee *e.* vessels
*Job* 22:9 sent widows away *e.*
26:7 the north over the *e.* place
*Is.* 24:1 Lord maketh earth *e.*
29:8 hungry man awak. soul *e.*
32:6 to *e.* the soul of the hung.
*Hos.* 10:1 Israel is an *e.* vine
*Nah.* 2:10 Nineveh is *e.* and void
*Mat.* 12:44 he findeth it *e.*
*Mark* 12:3 away *e.* *Luke* 20:10
*Luke* 1:53 rich he sent *e.* away

**EMPTY, Verb.**
*Lev.* 14:36 that they *e.* the house
*Ec.* 11:3 clouds *e.* themselves
*Jer.* 51:2 fanners shall *e.* her land
*Hab.* 1:17 shall they *e.* their net
*Zec.* 4:12 which *e.* the golden oil

**EMPTIED.**
*Gen.* 42:35 they *e.* their sacks
*2 Chr.* 24:11 officer *e.* the chest
*Is.* 24:3 land shall be utterly *e.*
*Jer.* 48:11 Moab not been *e.*
*Nah.* 2:2 emptiers have *e.* them

**EMPTIERS.**
*Nah.* 2:2 have emptied them

**EMPTINESS.**
*Is.* 34:11 out upon it stones of *e.*

**EMULATION, S.**
*Rom.* 11:14 prov. to *e.* my breth.
*Gal.* 5:20 works of the flesh are *e.*

**ENABLED.**
*1 Tim.* 1:12 Ch. Jesus hath *e.* me

**ENCAMP.**
*Ex.* 14:2 *e.* before Pi-hahiroth
*Num.* 2:17 as they *e.* so shall th.
3:38 *e.* before the tabernacle
10:31 how we are to *e.* in wild.
*2 Sam.* 12:28 *e.* against Rabbah
*Job* 19:12 his troops *e.* about tab.
*Ps.* 27:3 a host *e.* against me
*Zec.* 9:8 I will *e.* about my house

**ENCAMPED.**
*Ex* 13:20 *e.* in Etham
15:27 *e.* by the waters
18:5 Moses *e.* at mount of G.
*Num.* 33:10 from E. *e.* by Red sea
11 from Red sea, and *e.* in Sin
*Jos.* 4:19 peo. *e.* in Gilgal, 5:10
*Jud.* 6:4 Midianites *e.* ag. Israel
9:50 Abimelech *e.* ag. Thebez

**ENCAMPETH.**
*Ps.* 34:7 angel of Lord *e.* round
53:5 bones of him that *e.* ag. th.

**ENCHANTER, S.**
*Deut.* 18:10 not be found an *e.*
*Jer.* 27:9 heark. not to dr. or *e.*

**ENCHANTMENT, S.**
*Ex.* 7:11 magicians did so with their *e.* 22; 8:7, 18
*Lev.* 19:26 nor shall ye use *e.*
*Num.* 23:23 there is no *e.* aga. J.
24:1 B. went not to seek for *e.*

2 *K.* 17:17 used *e.* and did evil
21:6 Manas. used *e.* 2 *Chr.* 33:6
*Ec.* 10:11 serpent will bite w. *e.*
*Is.* 47:9 great abund. of thine *e.*
12 stand now with thine *e.*

**ENCLOSE, ED.**

*Ex.* 39:6 onyx-sto. *e.* in gold, 13
*Ps.* 17:10 they are *e.* in their fat.
22:16 assem. of wicked have *e.*
*Cant.* 4:12 a garden *e.* is my sis.
8:9 we will *e.* her with cedar
*Lam.* 3:9 he hath *e.* my ways
*Luke* 5:6 *e.* great multi. of fishes

**ENCLOSINGS.**

*Ex.* 28:20 stones in gold *e.* 39:13

**ENCOUNTERED.**

*Acts* 17:18 philosophers *e.* him.

**ENCOURAGE.**

*Deut.* 1:38 *e.* him, sh. cause, 3:28
2 *Sam.* 11:25 and *e.* thou him
*Ps.* 64:5 they *e.* themselves

**ENCOURAGED.**

1 *Sam.* 30:6 David *e.* himself
2 *Chr.* 31:4 Levites might be *e.*
35:2 Josiah *e.* th. to serv. of L.
*Is.* 41:7 carpenter *e.* goldsmith

**END.**

*Gen.* 6:13 *e.* of all flesh is come
47:21 one *e.* of Egypt to other *e.*
*Ex.* 25:19 on one *e.* other *e.*
*Deut.* 28:64 L. scatter from one *e.*
*Jud.* 6:21 angel put *e.* of his staff
19:9 day groweth to an *e.*
1 *Sam.* 14:27 Jonath. put *e.* of rod
2 *K.* 10:21 Baal full from *e.*
2 *Chr.* 21:19 after *e.* of two years
*Job* 6:11 what is my *e.* that I
16:3 shall vain words have *e.?*
26:10 until night come to an *e.*
28:3 he setteth an *e.* to darkness
*Ps.* 7:9 wickedness come to an *e.*
9:6 are come to a perpetual *e.*
19:6 going forth from *e.* of heav.
37:37 *e.* of that man is peace
38 *e.* of wicked shall be cut off
39:4 make me know mine *e.*
73:17 I understood their *e.*
102:27 thy years have no *e.*
119:96 seen an *e.* of perfection
*Prov.* 5:4 *e.* bitter; 23:18 the. is *e.*
14:12 *e.* thereof are ways of d.
*Ec.* 4:8 no *e.* of all his labor
16 there is no *e.* of all the peo.
7:2 *e.* of men; 8 better *e.*
10:13 *e.* of his talk is madness
12:12 of mak. books th. is no *e.*
*Is.* 2:7 any *e.* of their treasures, any *e.* of their chariots
9:7 of his governm. sh. be no *e.*
13:5 come from the *e.* of heaven
16:4 the extortioner is at an *e.*
23:15 after *e.* of seventy y. 17
42:10 his praise from *e.* of earth
45:17 world without *e.*
46:10 the *e.* from the beginning
*Jer.* 12:12 one *e.* to other *e.* 25:33
17:11 at his *e.* he shall be a fool
29:11 to give you an expected *e.*
31:17 there is hope in thine *e.*
51:13 dwellest, thine *e.* is come
31 his city is taken at one *e.*
*Lam.* 4:18 our *e.* near, *e.* come
*Ezek.* 7:2 an *e.* the *e.* is come, 3, 6
21:25 iniquity have *e.* 29; 35:5
*Dan.* 7:28 is the *e.* of the matter
8:17 time of *e.* shall be the vis.
19 at the time *e.* shall be, 11:27
9:26 the *e.* thereof be with flood
11:6 and in the *e.* of years
35 even to the time of the *e.*
40 time of *e.* king of sou.
45 yet he shall come to his *e.*
12:4 seal the book even to the *e.*
8 O Lord, what shall be the *e.*
9 words are clos. up, till the *e.*
13 go thy way till the *e.* be
*Amos* 3:15 houses sha. have an *e.*
5:18 to what *e.* is it for you
8:2 *e.* is come upon people of Is.
*Nah.* 2:9 there is none *e.* of store
3:3 there is none *e.* of corpses
*Mat.* 13:39 harvest is *e.* of world
24:3 sign of *e.* of the world?
14 then shall the *e.* come
31 gath. from one *e.* of heaven
26:58 Peter sat to see the *e.*
28:1 in the *e.* of the sabbath
*Luke* 1:33 his kingdom be no *e.*
18:1 a para. to them, to this *e.*
22:37 concern. me have an *e.*
*John* 18:37 to this *e.* was I born
*Rom.* 6:21 *e.* of those th. is death
22 the *e.* everlasting life
10:4 Christ is the *e.* of the law
14:9 to this *e.* Christ hath died
2 *Cor.* 11:15 *e.* according to works
*Eph.* 3:21 glory, world without *e.*
*Phil.* 3:19 whose *e.* is destruction
1 *Tim.* 1:5 *e.* of com. is charity
*Heb.* 6:8 whose *e.* is to be burned
16 an oath is an *e.* of all strife
7:3 neither begin. nor *e.* of life
9:26 in the *e.* hath appeared
13:7 the *e.* of their conversation
*Jam.* 5:11 ye have seen *e.* of Lord
1 *Pet.* 1:9 receiv. *e.* of your faith
4:17 *e.* of them that obey not
*Rev.* 21:6 Alpha and Omega, the beginning and the *e.* 22:13

**At the END.**

*Deut.* 15:1 *at e.* of sev. ye. rel.
*Ps.* 107:27 are *at* their wit's *e.*
*Dan.* 12:13 stand in lot *at the e.*
*Hab.* 2:3 *at the e.* it shall speak
*Mat.* 13:40 so be in *e.* of world

**But the END.**

*Prov.* 14:12 *but the e.* thereof are the ways of death, 16:25
20:21 *the e.* thereof not be bles.
*Mat.* 24:6 *but the e.* is not yet, *Mark* 13:7; *Luke* 21:9
1 *Pet.* 4:7 *but e.* of all things

**Last END.**

*Num.* 23:10 let my *l. e.* be like h.
*Jer.* 12:4 shall not see our *last e.*
*Lam.* 1:9 remembereth not *l. e.*
*Dan.* 8:19 known what be in *l. e.*

**Latter END.**

*Num.* 24:20 *l. e.* be that he per.
*Deut.* 8:16 to do thee good at *l. e.*
32:29 consider their *l. e.*
*Ruth* 3:10 kindness in *latter e.*
2 *Sam.* 2:26 bitterness in *lat. e.*
*Job* 8:7 thy *latter e.* greatly incr.
42:12 L. blessed *latter e.* of Job
*Prov.* 19:20 mayest be wise in *l. e.*
*Is.* 41:22 consid. them, know *l. e.*
47:7 nor didst remember *lat. e.*
2 *Pet.* 2:20 *l. e.* worse than begin.

**Made an END.**

*Gen.* 27:30 Isaac *m. e.* of blessing
*Deut.* 32:45 *m. e.* of speaking, *Jud.* 15:17; 1 *Sam.* 18:1; 24:16; 2 *Sam.* 13:36; 1 *K.* 1:41; 3:1; *Jer.* 26:8; 43:1; 51:63
*Mat.* 11:1 *m. a. e.* of com. discip.

**Make an END.**

1 *Sam.* 3:12 I will also *m. an e.*
*Neh.* 4:2 will they *m. an e.?*
*Job* 18:2 ere you *m. an e.?*
*Is.* 38:12 *make e.* of me, 13
*Ezek.* 20:17 nor did I *make e.*
*Dan.* 9:24 70 weeks to *m. e.*
*Nah.* 1:8 *make* utter *e.* 9

**Make a full END.**

*Jer.* 4:27 yet will I not *make a full e.* 5:18; 30:11; 46:28
5:10 but make not *a. f. e.*
*Ezek.* 11:13 ah L. wilt *m. a. f. e.?*

**To the END.**

*Ex.* 8:22 *to the e.* thou mayest kno. I am the L. *Ezek.* 20:26
*Deut.* 17:20 *to the e.* that he may prolong his days
*Ps.* 19:4 words *to e.* of world
30:12 *to the e.* my glo. may sing
119:112 perf. statutes *to the e.*
*Ec.* 3:11 find out from beg. *to e.*
7:14 *to the e.* man shou. find no.
*Is.* 48.20 *to the e.* of earth
49:6 my salvation *to e.* of earth
*Jer.* 3:5 keep anger *to the e.?*
*Dan.* 4:22 dominion *to the e.*
*Mat.* 10:22 endur. *to the e.* shall be saved, 24:13; *Mark* 13:13
*Acts* 7:19 *to the e.* might not live
*Rom.* 1:11 *to the e.* you be estab.
4:16 *to the e.* promise be sure
2 *Cor.* 1:13 acknowledge *to the e.*
3:13 look *to e.* of that abolished
1 *Thes.* 3:13 *to the e.* he may est.
1 *Pet.* 1:13 and hope *to the e.*

**Unto the END.**

*Job* 34:36 Job be tried *unto e.*
*Ps.* 46:9 wars cease *unto e.*
119:33 I shall keep it *unto the e.*
*Is.* 62:11 proclaimed *u. e.* of earth
*Dan.* 6:26 his dominion be *u. e.*
*Mat.* 28:20 I am with you *u. e.*
*John* 13:1 loved them *u. the e.*
1 *Cor.* 1:8 confirm you *unto the e.*
*Heb.* 3:6 hold fast confidence *u. e.*
14 if hold begin. steadfast *u. e.*
6:11 assurance of hope *unto e.*
*Rev.* 2:26 keepeth my works *u. e.*

**ENDAMAGE.**

*Ezr.* 4:13 *e.* the revenue of kings

**ENDANGER, ED.**

*Ec.* 10:9 cleav. wood shall be *e.*
*Dan.* 1:10 *e.* my head to the king

**ENDED, ETH, ING.**

*Gen.* 2:2 seventh day G. *e.* work
2 *Sam.* 20:18 so they *e.* the mat.
*Job* 31:40 the words of Job are *e.*
*Ps.* 72:20 prayers of David are *e.*
*Is.* 24:8 noise of them rejoice *e.*
60:20 days of mourn. shall be *e.*
*Jer.* 8:20 the summer is *e.*
*Mat.* 7:28 when Jesus *e.* sayings
*Luke* 4:2 forty days *e.* he hunger.
13 devil had *e.* all temptation
*John* 13:2 supper being *e.*
*Rev.* 1:8 the beginning and *e.*

**ENDLESS.**

1 *Tim.* 1:4 heed to *e.* genealogies
*Heb.* 7:16 after power of an *e.* life

**ENDEAVOR, ED, ING.**

*Acts* 16:10 *e.* to go into Macedo.
*Eph.* 4:3 *e.* to keep unity of spir.
1 *Thes.* 2:17 we *e.* to see your f.
2 *Pet.* 1:15 will *e.* ye may be able

**ENDEAVORS.**

*Ps.* 28:4 accord. to wicked. of *e.*

**EN-DOR.**

*Jos.* 17:11 E. and her t. *Ps.* 83:10
1 *Sam.* 28:7 woman at E. hath s.

**ENDOW.**

*Ex.* 22:16 *e.* her to be his wife

**ENDS.**

*Deut.* 33:17 push peo. to *e.* of e.
1 *Sam.* 2:10 shall judge *e.* of e.
*Job* 28:24 looketh to *e.* of the e.
37:3 lightning unto *e.* of earth
38:13 take hold of *e.* of earth
*Ps.* 19:6 his circuit to the *e.* of it
22:27 *e.* of world shall remember
48:10 so is thy praise to the *e.* of
59:13 G. ruleth in Jacob to the *e.*
65:5 confidence of *e.* of the e.
67:7 *e.* of the earth sh. fear him
98:3 *e.* of earth seen salvation
135:7 vapors to ascend from the *e.* of earth, *Jer.* 10:13; 51:16

Prov. 17:24 eyes of fool are in e.
30:4 established e. of the earth?
Is. 40:28 Creator of e. of the earth
41:5 e. of the earth were afraid
9 taken from e. of the earth
43:6 daughters from e. of earth
45:22 be saved, all the e.
52:10 all e. see salvation of God
Jer. 16:19 shall come from the e.
25:31 a noise to e. of the earth
Ezek. 15:4 fire devoureth both e.
Mic.. 5:4 shall he be great to e.
Zec. 9:10 his dominion to e. of
Acts 13:47 be for salvation to e.
Rom. 10:18 words to e. of world
1 Cor. 10:11 e. of world are come

**ENDUED.**

Gen. 30:20 e. me with good dow.
2 Chr. 2:12 son e. with prudence
13 cunning man e. with under.
Luke 24:49 ye be e. with power
Jam. 3:13 e. with knowledge

**ENDURE.**

Gen. 33:14 children be able to e.
Ex. 18:23 thou shalt be able to e.
Est. 8:6 can I e. to see the evil
Job 8:15 fast, but it shall not e.
31:23 I could not e.
Ps. 9:7 the Lord shall e. for ever,
102:12, 26; 104:31
30:5 weeping may e. for a night
72:5 fear thee as long as sun e.
17 his name shall e. as the sun
89:29 his seed to e. for ever, 36
Prov. 27:24 crown e. to every g.
Ezek. 22:14 can thy heart e.
Mat. 24:13 he that shall e. to the
end, Mark 13:13
Mark 4:17 so e. but for a time
2 Thes. 1:4 tribulations that ye e.
2 Tim. 2:3 therefore e. hardness
10 e. all things for elect's sake
4:3 will not e. sound doctrine
5 in all things, e. afflictions
Heb. 12:7 if ye e. chastening, God
Heb. 12:20 not e. what was com.
Jam. 5:11 count them hap. w. e.
1 Pet. 2:19 for conscience e. grief

**ENDURED.**

Ps. 81:15 should have e. for ever
Rom. 9:22 God e. with long-suff.
2 Tim. 3:11 what persecut. I e.
Heb. 6:15 after he had patient. e.
10:32 e. great fight of afflictions
11:27 e. as seeing him invisible
12:2 e. cross; 3 e. such contrad.

**ENDURETH.**

Ps. 30:5 anger e. but a moment
52:1 goodness of G. e. continu.
72:7 peace, so long as moon e.
100:5 truth e. to all generations
145:13 dominion e. through all
Mat. 10:22 e. to the end be saved
John 6:27 meat which e. unto life
1 Cor. 13:7 charity e. all things
Jam. 1:12 bless. that e. tempta.

**ENDURETH for ever.**

1 Chr. 16:34 his mercy e. for ever,
41; 2 Chr. 5:13; 7:3, 6; 20:21;
Ezr. 3:11; Ps. 106:1; 107:1;
118:1-4; 136:1-3, etc.; 138:8;
Jer. 33:11
Ps. 111:3 righte. e. f. e. 112:3, 9
10 his praise e. for ever
117:2 his truth e. for ever
119:160 thy judgments e. for e.
135:13 thy name. O L. e. for e.
1 Pet. 1:25 word of the L. e. f. e.

**ENDURING.**

Ps. 19:9 fear of Lord clean, e.
2 Cor. 1:6 effectual in e. same
Heb. 10:34 in heaven e. substance

ENEAS. Acts 9:34
EN-EGLAIM. Ezek. 47:10

**ENEMY.**

Ex. 15:6 right hand dashed the e.
9 the e. said, I will pursue
23:22 I will be e. to thine en.
Num. 10:9 if go to war against e.
35:23 and was not his e.
Deut. 32:27 feared wrath of the e.
42 beginning of revenges on e.
33:27 he shall thrust out the e.
Jud. 16:23 God delivered our e.
1 Sam. 2:32 e. in my habitation
18:29 Saul became David's e.
24:19 his e. will he let him go?
1 K. 8:33 when thy people be
smitten before e. 2 Chr. 6:24
46 if sin, and thou deliver to e.
2 Chr. 25:8 make thee fall bef. e.
Est. 7:4 e. not counterv. damage
6 the e. is this wicked Haman
Job 33:10 counteth me for his e.
Ps. 7:5 let the e. persecute
8:2 mightest still e. and avenger
9:6 O thou e. destructions are
42:9 mourning bec. of e.? 43:2
44:10 makest us to turn from e.
55:3 I mourn bec. of voice of e.
12 not an e. that reproached
61:3 a strong tower from the e.
64:1 preserve life from fear of e.
74:3 all that e. hath done
10 e. blaspheme thy name?
18 remember e. hath reproach.
78:42 he delivered from e. 61
89:22 the e. not exact upon him
143:3 e. hath persecuted
Prov. 27:6 kisses of e. are deceit.
Is. 59:19 e. come in like a flood
63:10 was turned to be their e.
Jer. 6:25 sword of e. is on ev. side
15:11 cause e. to entreat thee
18:17 scatter them before e.
30:14 with wound of an e.
Lam. 1:9 e. hath magnified
16 because e. prevailed
2:3 drawn back hand bef. the e.
4 hath bent his bow like an e.
5 the Lord was as an e.
4:12 e. should have entered
Ezek. 36:2 the e. had said, Aha
Hos. 8:3 Is. e. shall pursue him
Mic. 2:8 my people risen up as e.
Nah. 3:11 seek strength bec. of e.
Mat. 13:25 his e. sowed tares
28 said, An e. hath done this
39 e. that sowed is the devil
Luke 10:19 all power of the e.
Acts 13:10 thou e. of all righte.
1 Cor. 15:26 the last e. is death
Gal. 4:16 am I become your e.
2 Thes. 3:15 not as an e.
Jam. 4:4 friend of world e. of G.

**Hand of the ENEMY.**

Lev. 26:25 shall be delivered into
the hand of the e. Neh. 9:27
Ps. 31:8 me up into h. of e.
78:61 he deliv. his glory in. e. h.
Ps. 106:10 red. from h. of e. 107:2
Lam. 1:7 people fell into h. of e.

**Mine ENEMY.**

1 Sam. 19:17 sent away mine e.?
2 Sam. 22:18 mine e. Ps. 18:17
1 K. 21:20 found me, O mine e.?
Job 16:9 mine e. sharpe. his eyes
27:7 let mine e. be as wicked
Ps. 7:4 I deliv. him th. is mine e.
13:2 how long mine e. be exalt.
4 lest mine e. say, I have prev.
41:11 mine e. not triumph
Lam. 2:22 I swaddled, mine e.
Mic. 7:8 rej. not aga. me, O m. e.
10 she that is m. e. shall see it

**Thine ENEMY.**

Deut. 28:57 thine e. shall distress
1 Sam. 24:4 deliver thine e. 26:8
28:16 Lord is become thine e.
2 Sam. 4:8 the head of thine e.
Job 13:24 holdest me for thine e.
Prov. 24:17 rej. not when t. e. fall
25:21 if t. e. hunger, Rom. 12:20
Lam. 2:17 thine e. to rejoice
Zep. 3:15 the L. cast out thine e.
Mat. 5:43 Thou shalt hate th. e.
Rom. 12:20 if th. e. hung. feed h.

**ENEMIES.**

1 Sam. 18:25 avenged of king's e.
20:15 when Lord cut off e. of D.
16 req. it at hand of David's e.
2 Sam. 12:14 occasion to e. to bl.
18:32 e. be as that young man
2 Chr. 20:29 Lord fought aga. e.
Ps. 17:9 hide me from deadly e.
37:20 e. of L. be as fat of lambs
45:5 arrows sharp in king's e.
127:5 shall speak with e. in gate
Jer. 12:7 belov. into hand of h. e.
48:5 e. heard cry of destruction
Lam. 1:2 friends are become e.
5 her e. prosper
Mic. 7:6 e. are of own house
Rom. 5:10 when e. we were rec.
11:28 as con. gospel, they are e.
1 Cor. 15:25 put all e. under feet
Phil. 3:18 e. of the cross of Chr.
Col. 1:21 e. in your mind

**His ENEMIES.**

Gen. 22:16 possess gate of his e.
Num. 24:8 the nations his e.
32:21 he hath driven out his e.
Deut. 33:7 be a help from his e.
2 Sam. 7:1 rest from his e.
18:19 Lord avenged of his e.
22:1 out of the hand of all his e.
1 Chr. 22:9 give rest fr. all h. e.
Job 19:11 count. me one of his e.
Ps. 10:5 his e. he puffeth at them
41:2 not deliv. h. to will of h. e.
68:1 let his e. be scattered
21 G. shall wound head of h. e.
72:9 and his e. shall lick the d.
78:66 smote his e. in hinder pa.
89:42 hast made his e. to rejoice
97:3 a fire burneth up his e.
112:8 till he see des. upon h. e.
132:18 his e. clothe with shame
Prov. 16:7 his e. be at peace
Is. 9:11 shall join his e. together
42:13 he shall prevail ag. his e.
59:18 recompense to his e.
66:6 rendereth recomp. to his e.
14 indig. be known tow. h. e.
Jer. 44:30 Phar. into hand of h. e.
Nah. 1:2 reserveth wrath of h. e.
8 darkness shall pursue his e.
Heb. 10:13 h. e. made footstool

**Mine ENEMIES.**

Num. 23:11 curse mine e. 24:10
Deut. 32:41 vengeance to mine e.
1 Sam. 2:1 enlarged over m. e.
14:24 be avenged on mine e.
2 Sam. 5:20 L. hath broken forth
upon mine. e. 1 Chr. 14:11
22:4 saved from m. e. Ps. 18:3
38 pursued mine e. Ps. 18:37
41 necks of m. e. Ps. 18:40
49 bringeth me forth fr. m. e.
1 Chr. 12:17 betray me to mine e.
Ps. 3:7 hast smitten all mine e.
5:8 lead me, O L. bec. of m. e.
6:7 eye waxeth old bec. of m. e.
10 let all mine e. be ashamed
7:6 because of rage of mine. e.
9:3 m. e. are turned
18:48 he deliv. me from mine. e
23:5 in presence of mine e.
25:2 let not m. e. triumph, 35:19
19 consider m. e. they are ma.
27:2 m. e. came to eat my flesh
6 he lifted up above mine e.
11 because of mine e.
12 deliv. me n. to will of m. e.
31:11 I was a reproach am. m. e.
15 from hand of mine e.

*Ps.* 38:19 but *mine e.* are lively
41:5 *mine e.* speak evil of me
42:10 *m. e.* reproach me, 102:8
54:5 shall reward evil to *m. e.*
7 desire upon *mine e.* 59:10
56:2 *m. e.* would swal. me up
9 *m. e.* shall turn back
59:1 deliver me from *m. e.* 143:9
69:4 they being *mine e.*
18 deliver me, bec. of *mine e.*
71:10 *mine e.* speak against me
92:11 see desire on *mine e.*
119:98 wiser than *mine e.*
139 *m. e.* have forgotten
157 many are *mine e.*
138:7 forth thy hand ag. *m. e.*
139:22 I count them *mine e.*
143:12 cut off *mine e.*
*Is.* 1:24 avenge me of *mine e.*
*Lam.* 1:21 *m. e.* heard of my tro.
3:52 *m. e.* chased me like a bird
*Luke* 19:27 *m. e.* bring and slay

**Our ENEMIES.**

*Ex.* 1:10 they join also to *our e.*
*Deut.* 32:31 *our e.* being judges
1 *Sam.* 4:3 save us from *our e.*
12:10 but deliver us from *our e.*
2 *Sam.* 19:9 saved us fr. *o. e.* *Ps.* 44:7
*Ps.* 44:5 push down *our e.*
60:12 tread *our e.* 108:13
80:6 *our e.* laugh am. themselves
136:24 redeemed us from *our e.*
*Lam.* 3:46 *o. e.* op. their mouths
*Luke* 1:71 be saved from *our e.*
74 being delivered from *our e.*

**Their ENEMIES.**

*Lev.* 26:36 in land of *their e.*
*Jos.* 7:8 turn. backs before *t. e.* 12
21:44 stood not a man of *th. e.*
23:1 rest from *t. e.* *Est.* 9:16
*Jud.* 2:14 into the hand of *t. e.*
18 deliv. them from *t. e.* 8:34
2 *K.* 21:14 into the hand of *th. e.* 2 *Chr.* 6:36; 25:20; *Neh.* 9:27
*Ps.* 78:53 sea overwhelmed *t. e.*
81:14 should soon subdue *th. e.*
105:24 stronger than *their e.*
106:11 waters covered *their e.*
42 *their e.* oppressed them
*Jer.* 15:9 deliver to sw. bef. *t. e.*
19:7 fall before *their e.* 20:4
9 *their e.* shall straiten them
20:5 into the hands of *t. e.* 21:7; 34:20, 21; *Ezek.* 39:23
*Ezek.* 39:27 out of *their e.* hands
*Amos* 9:4 captivity before *th. e.*
*Zec.* 10:5 tread down *their e.*
*Rev.* 11:5 fire devoureth *their e.*
12 *their e.* beheld them

**Thine ENEMIES.**

*Gen.* 14:20 del. *t. e.* into thy hand
49:8 thy hand be in neck of *t. e.*
*Ex.* 23:22 an enemy to *thine e.*
27 make *thine e.* to turn
*Num.* 10:35 let *thine e.* be scat.
*Deut.* 6:19 cast out all *thine e.*
28:53 *t. e.* shall distress, 55:57
33:29 *thine e.* be found liars
*Jos.* 7:13 not stand bef. *t. e.*
*Jud.* 5:31 so let *t. e.* perish
11:36 veng. for thee of *thine e.*
1 *Sam.* 25:29 souls of *th. e.* sling
2 *Sam.* 7:9 cut off *t. e.* 1 *Chr.* 17:8
19:6 lov. *th. e.* hat. thy friends
24:13 three months before *t. e.*
1 *K.* 3:11 nor asked the life of *thine e.* 2 *Chr.* 1:11
*Ps.* 8:2 because of *thine e.*
21:8 thy hand find out all *th. e.*
66:3 thy power *thine e.* submit
68:23 dipped in blood of *thine e.*
74:4 *t. e.* roar; 83:2 *t. e.* make t.
23 forget not the voice of *th. e.*
89:10 scat. *th. e.* with thy arm
51 wherewith *th. e.* reproached
92:9 *thine e.* O Lord, shall per.
110:1 *thine e.* thy footstool, *Mat* 22:44; *Mark* 12:36; *Luke* 20:43; *Heb.* 1:13
2 in the midst of *thine e.*
139:20 *th. e.* take thy name in v.
*Is.* 26:11 fire of *t. e.* devour them
62:8 no m. give corn to *th. e.*
*Jer.* 15:14 to pass with *thine e.*
*Lam.* 2:16 *th. e.* have opened m.
*Dan.* 4:19 interpreta. be to *th. e.*
*Mic.* 4:10 red. thee from *thine e.*
5:9 all *thine e.* shall be cut off
*Nah.* 3:13 gate be opened to *t. e.*
*Luke* 19:43 *t. e.* shall cast trench

**Your ENEMIES.**

*Lev.* 26:7 ye shall chase *your e.*
8 *your e.* fall bef. you by sword
15 sow in vain, *y. e.* shall eat it
17 shall be slain bef. *your e.*
*Lev.* 26:37 to stand before *your e.*
*Num.* 10:9 be saved from *your e.*
14:42 before *y. e.* *Deut.* 1:42
*Deut.* 20:4 L. goeth to fight *y. e.*
28:68 ye shall be sold to *y. e.*
*Jos.* 10:25 shall Lord do to *y. e.*
1 *Sam.* 12:11 L. delivered you out of hand of *y. e.* 2 *K.* 17:39
*Mat.* 5:44 love *y. e.* *Luke* 6:27, 35

**ENGAGED.**

*Jer.* 30:21 who is this *e.* his heart

**EN-GEDI.**

*Jos.* 15:62 wilder. of Judah E.
1 *Sam.* 23:29 D. dwelt at E. 24:1
2 *Chr.* 20:2 Jehoshap. are in E.

**ENGINES.**

2 *Chr.* 26:15 Uzziah made *e.*
*Ezek.* 26:9 set *e.* of war ag. walls

**ENGRAFTED.**

*Jam.* 1:21 with meekness *e.* wo.

**ENGRAVE, EN.**

*Zec.* 3:9 I will *e.* graving thereof
2 *Cor.* 3:7 ministration of dea. *e.*

**ENGRAVER.**

*Ex.* 28:11 work of an *e.* in stone
38:23 Aholiab, an *e.*

**ENJOIN, ED.**

*Job* 36:23 hath *e.* him his way
*Phile.* 8 to *e.* what is convenient
*Heb.* 9:20 blood which G. hath *e.*

**ENJOY, ED.**

*Lev.* 26:34 land *e.* her sab. 43
*Num.* 36:8 Is. may *e.* inheritance
*Deut.* 28:41 beget sons, not *e.* th.
*Jos.* 1:15 ret. to land, and *e.* it
2 *Chr.* 36:21 till land *e.* sabbaths
*Ec.* 2:1 *e.* pleasure, this is vanity
24 his soul *e.* good, 3:13; 5:18
*Is.* 65:22 elect long *e.* the work
*Acts* 24:2 we *e.* great quietness
1 *Tim.* 6:17 giv. all things to *e.*
*Heb.* 11:25 th. *e.* pleasures of sin

**ENLARGE.**

*Gen.* 9:27 God shall *e.* Japheth
*Ex.* 34:24 I will *e.* thy borders
1 *Chr.* 4:10 wouldst *e.* my coast
*Ps.* 119:32 shalt *e.* my heart
*Is.* 54:2 *e.* the place of thy tent
*Amos* 1:13 might *e.* their border
*Mic.* 1:16 *e.* thy baldness as eagle
*Mat.* 23:5 *e.* borders of garments

**ENLARGED.**

1 *Sam.* 2:1 mouth is *e.* over ene.
2 *Sam.* 22:37 *e.* steps, *Ps.* 18:36
*Ps.* 4:1 *e.* me when in distress
25:17 troubles of my heart are *e.*
*Is.* 5:14 hell hath *e.* herself
57:8 thou hast *e.* thy bed
60:5 heart shall fear and be *e.*
2 *Cor.* 6:11 O Cor. our heart is *e.*
13 for recompense, be ye also *e.*
10:15 that we shall be *e.* by you

**ENLARGETH, ING.**

*Deut.* 33:20 blessed be he *e.* Gad
*Job* 12:23 he *e.* the nations, and
*Ezek.* 41:7 and there was an *e.*
*Hab.* 2:5 who *e.* his desire as hell

**ENLARGEMENT.**

*Est.* 4:14 *e.* from another place

**ENLIGHTEN, ED.**

*Ps.* 18:28 L. will *e.* my darkness
1 *Sam.* 14:27 Jon.'s eyes were *e.*
*Job* 33:30 *e.* with light of living
*Ps.* 97:4 his lightnings *e.* world
*Eph.* 1:18 eyes of understand. *e.*
*Heb.* 6:4 impos. for those once *e.*

**ENLIGHTENING.**

*Ps.* 19:8 is pure, *e.* the eyes.

EN-MISHPAT. *Gen.* 14:7

**ENMITY.**

*Gen.* 3:15 I will put *e.* betw. thee
*Num.* 35:22 he thrust without *e.*
*Luke* 23:12 before they were at *e.*
*Rom.* 8:7 carnal mind is *e.* ag. G.
*Eph.* 2:15 abolished in his flesh *e.*
16 having slain the *e.* thereby
*Jam.* 4:4 friendship of world is *e.*

**ENOCH.**

*Gen.* 4:17 bare E.; 5:18 begat E.
5:22 E. walked with God.
*Luke* 3:37 Mathus. was son of E.
*Heb.* 11:5 E. was translated
*Jude* 14 E. also prophesied

ENON. *John* 3:23

**ENOS.**

*Gen.* 4:26 call. his son's name E.
*Luke* 3:38 Cainan was son of E.

**ENOUGH.**

*Gen.* 33:9 Esau said, I have *e.*
11 take my blessing, I have *e.*
34:21 land is large *e.* for them
*Gen.* 45:28 it is *e.* Jos. is yet alive
*Ex.* 9:28 entreat Lord, for it is *e.*
36:5 bring much more than *e.*
*Jos.* 17:16 hill is not *e.* for us
2 *Sam.* 24:16 it is *e.* 1 *K.* 19:4; 1 *Chr.* 21:15; *Mark* 14:41; *Luke* 22:38
2 *Chr.* 31:10 we have had *e.* to e.
*Prov.* 30:15 things say not, It is *e.*
16 fire that saith not, It is *e.*
*Is.* 56:11 can never have *e.*
*Jer.* 49:9 will destroy till have *e.*
*Hos.* 4:10 eat, and not have *e.*
*Hag.* 1:6 ye eat, but have not *e.*
*Mal.* 3:10 not room *e.* to rec. it
*Mat.* 10:25 *e.* for disciple to be
25:9 be not *e.* for us and you
*Luke* 15:17 servants have bread *e.*

ENQUIRE. *See* INQUIRE.

**ENRICH, ED, EST.**

1 *Sam.* 17:25 king will *e.* him
*Ezek.* 27:33 didst *e.* kings of earth
*Ps.* 65:9 *e.* it with river of God
1 *Cor.* 1:5 in everything ye are *e.*
2 *Cor.* 9:11 being *e.* in every th.

**EN-ROGEL.**

2 *Sam.* 17:17 Ahim. stayed by E.
1 *K.* 1:9 sheep and oxen by E.

**ENSAMPLE.**

*Phil.* 3:17 as ye have us for an *e.*
2 *Thes.* 3:9 to make oursel. an *e.*
2 *Pet.* 2:6 Sodom and Gomor. *e.*

**ENSAMPLES.**

1 *Cor.* 10:11 hap. to them for *e.*
1 *Thes.* 1:7 so that ye w. *e.* to all
1 *Pet.* 5:3 but being *e.* to the flo.

**ENSIGN, S.**

*Ps.* 74:4 set up their *e.* for signs
*Is.* 5:26 he will lift up an *e.*
11:10 stand for an *e.* to people
12 set up an *e.* for the nations
18:3 when he lifteth up an *e.*
30:17 till ye be left as *e.* on hill
31:9 his princes be afraid of *e.*

*Zec.* 9:16 lifted as an *e.*

**ENSNARED.**
*Job* 34:30 lest people be *e.*

**ENSUE.**
1 *Pet.* 3:11 seek peace, and *e.* it

**ENTANGLE, ED, ETH.**
*Ex.* 14:3 they are *e.* in the land
*Mat.* 22:15 how they might *e.* him
*Gal.* 5:1 be not *e.* with yoke
2 *Tim.* 2:4 *e.* him affairs of life
2 *Pet.* 2:20 they are again *e.*

**ENTER.**
*Deut.* 23:8 children shall *e.* cong.
29:12 shouldest *e.* into covenant
2 *Sam.* 22:7 my cry did *e.* his e.
2 *K.* 7:4 if *e.* city, then famine
19:23 I will *e.* into the lodgings of his borders, *Is.* 37:24
2 *Chr.* 30:8 *e.* into his sanctuary
*Job* 22:4 will he *e.* into judgm. ?
34:23 *e.* into judgment with God
*Ps.* 37:15 sword *e.* their heart
45:15 shall *e.* into king's palace
100:4 *e.* into gates with thanks.
118:20 gate into which right. *e.*
*Prov.* 18:6 fool's lips *e.* content.
*Is.* 2:10 *e.* into the rock
3:14 *e.* into judg. with ancients
26:2 righteous nation may *e.* in
20 *e.* thou into thy chambers
57:2 he shall *e.* into peace
*Jer.* 7:2 that *e.* gates, 17:20; 22:2
14:18 if I *e.* into the city, famine
17:25 shall *e.* gates, kings, 22:4
21:13 shall *e.* our habitations ?
42:15 if ye set faces to *e.* Egypt
*Ezek.* 7:22 robbers shall *e.* in. it
13:9 nor *e.* into land of Israel
26:10 as men *e.* into a city
37:5 cause breath to *e.* into you
44:2 gate shut, no man *e.* by it
16 shall *e.* into my sanctuary
*Dan.* 11:7 shall *e.* into fortress
24 he shall *e.* peaceably
40 he shall *e.* into the countries
41 he shall *e.* into glorious land
*Joel* 2:9 *e.* in at the windows
*Amos* 5:5 nor *e.* into Gilgal
*Mat.* 5:20 in no case *e.* into king.
6:6 prayest *e.* into thy closet
7:13 *e.* in at str. gate, *Luke* 13:24
21 that saith, Lord, shall *e.* in
10:11 city ye *e.* *Luke* 10:8, 10
12:29 *e.* str. man's h. *Mark* 3:27
45 *e.* in dwell there, *Luke* 11:26
18:8 it is better to *e.* into life halt, 9; *Mark* 9:43, 45, 47
19:17 if thou wilt *e.* into life
24 rich man to *e.* into kingdom, *Mark* 10:25; *Luke* 18:25
*Mat.* 25:21 *e.* into joy of thy Lord
*Mark* 1:45 no more openly *e.* city
5:12 *e.* into swine, *Luke* 8:32
6:10 house ye *e.* *Luke* 9:4; 10:5
9:25 and *e.* no more into him
14:38 *e.* into tempt. *Luke* 22:46
*Luke* 8:16 which *e.* in may see
13:24 many will seek to *e.* in
24:26 and to *e.* into his glory ?
*John* 3:4 can he *e.* into womb
5 he cannot *e.* into king. of G.
10:9 by me if any man *e.* in
*Acts* 14:22 through tribulation *e.*
20:29 grievous wolves shall *e.* in
*Heb.* 4:3 *e.* into rest, if *e.* rest, 5
6 remaineth, some must *e.*
11 let us labor to *e.* that rest
10:19 *e.* holiest by blood of Jes.
*Rev.* 15:8 no man able to *e.* tem.
21:27 in no wise *e.* that defileth
22:14 *e.* in thro. gates into city

**ENTER not.**
*Ps.* 143:2 *e. not* into judgment
*Prov.* 4:14 *e. not* path of wicked
23:10 *e. not* fields of fatherless
*Jer.* 16:5 *e. not* house of mourn.
*Mat.* 10:5 any city of Samar. *e. n.*
26:41 *e. n.* into temp. *Luke* 22:40

**Not ENTER.**
*Num.* 20:24 Aaron *not e.* into la.
2 *Chr.* 7:2 priests could *n. e.* ho.
*Ps.* 95:11 should *not e.* my rest
*Is.* 59:14 and equity *cannot e.*
*Lam.* 1:10 should *not e.* congreg.
*Ezek.* 20:38 they shall *not e.* land
44:9 nor uncircumcised *e.* sanct.
*Hos.* 11:9 *not e.* into the city
*Mat.* 18:3 *not e.* king. of heaven
*Mark* 10:15 *n. e.* ther. *Luke* 18:17
*Heb.* 3:11 *not e.* into my rest, 18
19 *not e.* because of unbelief

*See* KINGDOM.

**ENTERED.**
2 *Chr.* 15:12 *e.* into co. to seek L.
27:2 Jotham *e.* not temple of L.
*Job* 38:16 *e.* into springs of sea ?
22 *e.* into treas. of the snow ?
*Jer.* 2:7 but when ye *e.* ye defiled
9:21 death is *e.* into our palaces
34:10 which had *e.* into coven.
*Lam.* 1:10 heath. *e.* her sanctuary
4:12 enemy should have *e.* gates
*Ezek.* 2:2 spirit *e.* into me, 3:24
16:8 I *e.* into a cove. with thee
36:20 they *e.* unto heathen
44:2 God of Isr. hath *e.* in by it
*Ob.* 11 foreigners *e.* his gates
13 shouldest not have *e.* gate
*Hab.* 3:16 rottenness *e.* my bones
*Mat.* 12:4 he *e.* the house of God
24:38 Noah *e.* ark, *Luke* 17:27
*Mark* 6:56 whith. he *e.* laid sick
*Luke* 1:40 Mary *e.* ho. of Zachar.
7:44 I *e.* thy house, thou gavest
9:34 they feared as they *e.* cloud
11:52 lawyers, ye *e.* not in your.
22:3 *e.* Satan into J. *John* 13:27
10 are *e.* city, there shall meet
*John* 4:38 are *e.* into their labors
18:1 a garden, into which he *e.*
33 then Pilate *e.* judgment-hall
*Acts* 11:8 nothing uncl. *e.* mouth
28:8 to whom Paul *e.* in
*Rom.* 5:12 sin *e.*; 20 the law *e.*
1 *Cor.* 2:9 nor have *e.* heart of m.
*Heb.* 4:6 *e.* not bec. of unbelief
10 for he that is *e.* into his rest
6:20 forerunner is for us *e.*
9:12 he *e.* once holy place, 24
*Jam* 5:4 *e.* ears of L. of Sabaoth
2 *John* 7 many deceivers are *e.*
*Rev.* 11:11 S. of life *e.* into them

**ENTERETH.**
*Prov.* 2:10 when wisdom *e.* heart
17:10 a reproof *e.* more into wise
*Mat.* 15:17 whatsoever *e.* in at the mouth, *Mark* 7:18
*Mark* 5:40 *e.* where damsel was
*Luke* 22:10 fol. into house he *e.*
*John* 10:1 *e.* not by door into fold
2 *e.* in by door, is the sheph.
*Heb.* 6:19 *e.* into that within veil
9:25 as high-priest *e.* every year

**ENTERING.**
*Is.* 23:1 there is no house, no *e.* in
*Ezek.* 44:5 mark *e.* in of the ho.
*Mat.* 23:13 neither suffer ye them *e.* to go in, *Luke* 11:52
*Mark* 4:19 the lusts *e.* in choke
7:15 noth. without *e.* can defile
16:5 and *e.* into the sepulchre
*Luke* 19:30 at your *e.* find colt
*Acts* 8:3 Saul *e.* into every house
1 *Thes.* 1:9 what manner of *e.* in
*Heb.* 4:1 promise of *e.* into his rest

**ENTERPRISE.**
*Job* 5:12 hands cannot perform *e.*

**ENTERTAIN.**
*Heb* 13:2 not forgetful to *e.* stran.

**ENTICE.**
*Ex.* 22:16 if a man *e.* a maid
*Deut.* 13:6 wife *e.* thee secretly
*Jud.* 14:15 *e.* thy husband
16:5 said to Delilah, *e.* him
2 *Chr.* 18:19 who shall *e.* Ahab ?
20 I will *e.* him; 21 sh. *e.* him
*Prov.* 1:10 if sinners *e.* cons. not

**ENTICED, ETH.**
*Job* 31:27 if heart been secretly *e.*
*Prov.* 16:29 a viol. man *e.* neigh.
*Jer.* 20:10 peradvent. he will be *e.*
*Jam.* 1:14 is tempted when *e.*

**ENTICING words.**
1 *Cor.* 2:4 preaching not w. *e. w.*
*Col.* 2:4 any beguile with *e. w.*

**ENTIRE.**
*Jam.* 1:4 that ye be per. and *e.*

**ENTRANCE.**
*Jud.* 1:24 show us *e.* into city
*Ps.* 119:130 *e.* of word giv. light
1 *Thes.* 2:1 yoursel. know our *e.*
2 *Pet.* 1:11 so an *e.* be ministered

**ENTREAT.**
*Ex.* 8:8 P. called for Moses, and said *e.* L. 28; 9:28; 10:17
9 when shall I *e.* for thee
29 I will *e.* Lord that swarms
*Ruth* 1:16 *e.* me not to leave thee
1 *Sam.* 2:25 man sin, who sh. *e.* ?
1 *K.* 13:6 *e.* the face of L. thy G.
*Ps.* 45:12 among people, *e.* favor
*Prov.* 19:6 many will *e.* favor of
*Jer.* 15:11 cause enemy *e.* thee
*Acts* 7:6 should *e.* them evil
1 *Cor.* 4:13 being defamed, we *e.*
*Phil.* 4:3 I *e.* thee also, y.-fellow
1 *Tim.* 5:1 but *e.* him as a father

**ENTREATED.**
*Gen.* 12:16 he *e.* Abraham well
25:21 I. *e.* for his wife, L. was *e.*
*Ex.* 5:22 why hast evil *e.* peo. ?
8:30 Moses went and *e.* L. 10:18
*Deut.* 26:6 Egyptians evil *e.* us
2 *Sam.* 24:25 L. was *e.* for the la.
*Ezr.* 8:23 sought G. and was *e.*
*Job* 19:16 *e.* him with my mouth
17 I *e.* for children's sake
*Ps.* 119:58 *e.* thy favor
*Is.* 19:22 he shall be *e.* of them
*Mat.* 22:6 *e.* spiteful. *Luke* 18:32
*Luke* 15:28 his father, *e.* him
20:11 *e.* him shamefully
*Acts* 7:19 same evil *e.* our fathers
1 *Thes.* 2:2 we were shameful. *e.*
*Heb.* 12:19 *e.* word not be spoken
*Jam.* 3:17 wisd. is easy to be *e.*

**ENTREATETH.**
*Job* 24:21 he evil *e.* the barren

**ENTREATIES.**
*Prov.* 18:23 poor useth *e.* but rich
2 *Cor.* 8:4 pray. us with much *e.*

**ENTRY.**
*Prov.* 8:3 wis. crieth at *e.* of city

**ENVY, Substantive.**
*Job* 5:2 *e.* slayeth the silly one
*Prov.* 14:30 *e.* is rotten. of bones
27:4 who able to stand bef. *e.* ?
*Ec.* 9:6 hatred and *e.* is perished
*Is.* 11:13 *e.* of Ephraim shall dep.
26:11 be ashamed for their *e.*
*Ezek.* 35:11 according to thine *e.*
*Mat.* 27:18 for *e.* *Mark* 15:10
*Acts* 7:9 patriarchs mov. with *e.*
13:45 Jews filled with *e.* spake
17:5 the Jews moved with *e.*
*Rom.* 1:19 full of *e.* murder
*Phil.* 1:15 prea. Christ even of *e.*
1 *Tim.* 6:4 whereof cometh *e.*
*Tit.* 3:3 living in malice and *e.*
*Jam.* 4:5 spirit in us lusteth to *e.*

**ENVY, Verb.**
Prov. 3:31 e. not the oppressor
23:17 let not heart e. sinners
Is. 11:13 Ephraim sh. not e. Jud.

**ENVIED.**
Gen. 26:14 Philistines e. Isaac
30:1 Rachel e. her sister
37:11 Joseph's brethren e. him
Ps. 106:16 they e. Moses also
Ec. 4:4 a man is e. of neighbor
Ezek. 31:9 trees in garden e. him

**ENVIES.**
1 Pet. 2:1 laying aside malice, e.

**ENVIEST, ETH.**
Num. 11:29 e. thou for my sake?
1 Cor. 13:4 charity e. not

**ENVYING.**
Rom. 13:13 let us walk, not in e.
1 Cor. 3:3 for whereas there is e.
Gal. 5:26 e. one another
Jam. 3:14 but if ye have bitter e.
16 where e. is, is confusion

**ENVYINGS.**
2 Cor. 12:20 I fear lest there be e.
Gal. 5:21 wor. of the flesh are e.

**ENVIOUS.**
Ps. 37:1 e. aga. workers of iniq.
73:3 for I was e. at the foolish
Prov. 24:1 be not e. ag. evil men
19 neither be e. at the wicked

**ENVIRON.**
Jos. 7:9 Canaanites e. us round

**EPAPHRAS.**
Col. 1:7 as ye learned of E. our
4:12 E. saluteth you, Phile. 23

**EPAPHRODITUS.**
Phil. 2:25 send to you E. 4:18

EPENETUS. Rom. 16:5

**EPHAH.**
Lev. 19:36 a just e. Ezek. 45:10
Is. 5:10 seed of homer yield an e.
Amos 8:5 making the e. small
Zec. 5:8 and he cast it into the e.

EPHAH. Gen. 25:4; 1 Chr. 1:33; 2:46, 47; Is. 60:6
EPHES-DAMMIM. 1 Sam. 17:1
EPHESIANS. Acts 19:28, 34, 35

**EPHESUS.**
Acts 18:19 P. came to E. 21; 19:17
1 Cor. 15:32 fought with be. at E.
2 Tim. 1:18 minis. to me at E.
Rev. 1:11 to E.; 2:1 angel at E.

**EPHOD.**
Ex. 28:4 they shall make an e. 6
Lev. 8:7 he put the e. upon him
Jud. 8:27 Gideon made an e.
17:5 the man Micah made an e.
1 Sam. 2:18 Samuel gird. with e.
23:9 David said, Bring e. 30:7
2 Sam. 6:14 D. was girded with linen e. 1 Chr. 15:27
Hos. 3:4 many days without e.
EPHPHATHA. Mark 7:34

**EPHRAIM, *a place.***
2 Sam. 13:23 sheep-sh. beside E.
2 Chr. 13:19 A. took E. and tow.
John 11:54 into city called E.

**Mount EPHRAIM.**
Jos. 17:15 if mo. E. be too narrow
Jud. 2:9 buried Joshua in m. E.
7:24 through mount E. 17:1, 8
1 Sam. 1:1 of m. E. 2 Sam. 20:21
9:4 Saul passed through mo. E.
2 K. 5:22 two men co. fr. m. E.
Jer. 31:6 upon m. E. 50:19

**EPHRAIM, *a person or people.***
Gen. 41:52 Jos.'s s. son was E.
48:14 right hand on E. head, 20
Num. 1:10 the prince of E. 7:48
2:18 shall be the standard of E.
Deut. 33:17 ten thousands of E.
Jud. 5:14 out of E. was a root
12:4 Jephthah fought with E.
1 Chr. 7:22 E. their fath. mourn.
2 Chr. 17:2 garrisons in E. 25:10
30:18 E. not clea.; 31:1 images
Ps. 80:2 before E. stir up stren.
Is. 7:5, 8, 9, 17; 9:9, 21; 11:13; 28:1
Jer. 7:15 cast out wh. seed of E.
Ezek. 37:16 stick of E. 19; 48:5
Hos. 5:3, 5, 9, 13, 14; 6:10; 7:1, 8
8:9 E. hired lov.; 11 E. to sin, 9:3, 8; 10:6, 11; 11:3, 9, 12
14:8 E. say. Wh. to do with id.?
Zec. 9:10 chariot from E. 13

**EPHRAIM is.**
Ps. 60:7; Jer. 31:9, 20; Hos. 4:17
Hos. 7:11 E. silly d.; 10:11 heifer

**EPHRAIM, *with* tribe.**
Num. 1:33 nu. of E. 13:8; 33:24
Jos. 16:8 inheritance of E. 21:5
Ps. 78:67 chose not tribe of E.

EPHRAIMITE, S. Jud. 12:5, 6

**EPHRATAH.**
Ruth 4:11 worthily in E.
1 Chr. 2:50 first-born of E. 4:4
Ps. 132:6 we heard of it at E.
Mic. 5:2 Beth-lehem E. tho' little

EPHRATH. Gen. 35:16, 19; 48:7; 1 Chr. 2:19
EPHRATHITE, S. Ruth 1:2; 1 Sam. 1:1; 17:12; 1 K. 11:26
EPHRON. Gen. 23:8, 16; 25:9; 49:30; 50:13
EPICUREANS. Acts 17:18

**EPISTLE.**
Acts 15:30 they deliv. e. 23:33
Rom. 16:22 I Tert. who wrote e.
1 Cor. 5:9 I wrote to you in an e.
2 Cor. 3:2 ye are our e. written
3 declared to be e. of Christ
7:8 the same e. made you sorry
Col. 4:16 wh. this e. is read, likewise read e. from Laodicea
1 Thes. 5:27 this e. be read to all
2 Thes. 2:15 taught by word or e.
3:14 if obey not word by this e.
17 which is the tok. in every e.
2 Pet. 3:1 this sec. e. I now write

**EPISTLES.**
2 Cor. 3:1 or need e. of commen.
2 Pet. 3:16 as in all his e. speak.

**EQUAL.**
Ps. 17:2 eyes behold things e.
55:13 but it was thou, mine e.
Prov. 26:7 legs of lame are not e.
Is. 40:25 to wh. sh. I be e.? 46:5
Lam. 2:13 e. to thee. O virgin
Ezek. 18:25 The way of the Lord is not e. 29; 33:17, 20
29 O Isr. are not my ways e.?
33:17 their way is not e.
Mat. 20:12 hast made them e.
Luke 20:36 are e. unto angels
John 5:18 himself e. with God
Phil. 2:6 not rob. to be e. with G.
Col. 4:1 gave servants what is e.
Rev. 21:16 breadth and height e.

**EQUAL, Verb.**
Job 28:17 gold and crystal not e.
19 topaz of Ethi. shall not e. it

**EQUALITY.**
2 Cor. 8:14 by an e. may be an e.

**EQUALS.**
Gal. 1:14 I profited above my e.

**EQUITY.**
Ps. 98:9 he shall judge with e.
99:4 thou dost establish e.
Prov. 1:3 to rec. instruction of e.
2:9 shalt thou understand e.
17:26 to strike princes for e.
Ec. 2:21 whose labor is in e.
Is. 11:4 repr. with e. for meek
59:14 and e. cannot enter
Mic. 3:9 ye that pervert all e.
Mal. 2:6 walked with me in e.

ER. Gen. 38:3, 7; 1 Chr. 2:3; 4:21; Luke 3:28

**ERASTUS.**
Acts 19:22 sent Timoth. and E.
2 Tim. 4:20 E. abode at Corinth

**ERRAND.**
Gen. 24:33 I have told mine e.
Jud. 3:19 I have a secret e.
2 K. 9:5 an e. to thee, O captain

**ERR.**
2 Chr. 33:9 M. made Judah to e.
Ps. 95:10 do e. in their heart
119:21 which do e. from thy
118 hast trodden them that e.
Prov. 14:22 not e. that dev. evil?
19:27 instruc. that causeth to e.
Is. 3:12 they wh. lead thee cause thee to e. 9:16
19:14 have caused Egypt to e.
28:7 they e. in vision
30:28 a bridle caus. them to e.
35:8 wayfaring men shall not e.
63:17 hast thou made us to e.
Jer. 23:13 the prophets caused Israel to e. 32; Mic. 3:5
Hos. 4:12 whoredoms caused to e.
Amos 2:4 their lies caused to e.
Mat. 22:29 ye do e. not know. the scriptures, Mark. 12:24, 27
Heb. 3:10 e. in their hearts
Jam. 1:16 do not e. my beloved
5:10 if any e. from the truth

**ERRED.**
Lev. 5:18 ignor. wherein he e.
1 Sam. 26:21 have e. exceedingly
Job 6:24 wherein I have e.
19:4 indeed that I have e.
Ps. 119:110 I e. not from thy pre.
Is. 28:7 have e. thro' wine, priest and prophet have e.
27:24 that e. in spirit shall come
1 Tim. 6:10 have e. from the faith
21 some have e. concern. faith
2 Tim. 2:18 concern. tru. have e.

**ERRETH.**
Prov. 10:17 refuseth reproof e.
Ezek. 45:20 for every one that e.

**ERROR.**
2 Sam. 6:7 smote Uzzah for his e.
Job 19:4 e. remain. with myself
Ec. 5:6 neither say it was an e.
10:5 an evil I have seen as an e.
Is. 32:6 to utter e. against the L.
Dan. 6:4 nor was e. found in him
Mat. 27:64 last e. worse than first
Rom. 1:27 recompense of their e.
Jam. 5:20 from the e. of his way
2 Pet. 2:18 them who live in e.
3:17 led away with e. of wicked
1 John 4:6 know we spirit of e.
Jude 11 after the e. of Baalam

**ERRORS.**
Ps. 19:12 can understand his e.?
Jer. 10:15 the work of e. 51:18
Heb. 9:7 he offer. for e. of people

ESAIAS. See ISAIAH.
ESAR-HADDON. 2 K. 19:37; Ezr. 4:2; Is. 37:38

**ESAU.**
Gen. 25:25 his name E. 27, 29
27:11 E. is a hairy m. 21, 24, 42
32:3 sent messengers to E. 11, 18
33:4 E. ran to meet him, 9; 35:1
36:1 genera. of E.; 43 fa. of E.
Deut. 2:5 mt. S. to E. Jos. 24:4
Jer. 49:10 I have made E. bare
Ob. 6 E. searched out, 18:21
Mal. 1:2 E. J.'s br.? 3; Rom. 9:13
Heb. 11:20 Isaac blessed E.
12:16 profane person as E.

**ESCAPE, Substantive.**
Ps. 55:8 hasten my e. from storm

**ESCAPE, Verb.**

Gen. 19:17 e. to the mountain
20 Oh let me e.; 22 e. thither
32:8 the other company shall e.
Jos. 8:22 they let none of them e.
1 Sam. 27:1 e. to land of Philist.
2 Sam. 15:14 let us flee, not else e.
1 K. 18:40 let none e. 2 K. 9:15
2 K. 10:24 if any of the men e.
19:31 e. out of Zion, Is. 37:32
Ezr. 9:8 to leave a remnant to e.
Est. 4:13 think not thou shalt e.
Job 11:20 the wicked shall not e.
Ps. 56:7 shall they e. by iniq.?
71:2 and cause me to e.
141:10 wicked fall, whilst I e.
Prov. 19:5 speak. lies, shall not e.
Ec. 7:26 pleaseth God shall e.
Is. 20:6 and how shall we e.
66:19 those that e. to the nati.
Jer. 11:11 evil not be able to e.
25:35 nor princip. of the flock e.
32:4 Zed. not e. 34:3; 38:18, 23
42:17 go into Egypt e. 44:14
44:14 none return but such as e.
28 yet a small number that e.
46:6 let not mighty man e.
48:8 spoiler come, no city sh. e.
50:28 the voice of them that e.
29 let none e. recompense her
Ezek. 6:8 may have some shall e.
9 they that e. shall remem. me
7:16 shall e. and be like doves
17:15 e. that doeth such things?
18 done these things, sh. not e.
Dan. 11:41 e. out of his hand
42 the land of Egypt sh. not e.
Joel 2:3 nothing shall e. them
Ob. 14 cut of those that did e.
Mat. 23:33 e. damnati. of hell?
Luke 21:36 account. worthy to e.
Acts 27:42 kill prison. lest any e.
Rom. 2:3 shalt e. judg. of God?
1 Cor. 10:13 will make a way to e.
1 Thes. 5:3 and they shall not e.
Heb. 2:3 how sh. e. if we neglect
12:25 much more shall not we e.

**ESCAPED.**

Gen. 14:13 there came one had e.
Num. 21:29 sons that e. into cap.
Deut. 23:15 not deliver servant e.
Jud. 3:29 e. not, 1 Sam. 30:17
21:17 inherit. for them that e.
1 Sam. 14:41 J. taken, but peo. e.
19:10 D. fled and e. that night
2 Sam. 1:3 out of the ca. am I e.
4:6 and Rachab and Baanah e.
1 K. 20:20 Ben-hadad the king e.
2 K. 19:30 remnant e. of Judah shall take root, Is. 37:31
2 Chr. 16:7 is host of Syria e.
30:6 he will return to you that e.
Ezr. 9:15 for we remain yet e. as
Job 1:15 I only am e. 16, 17, 19
19:20 e. with the sk. of my teeth
Ps. 124:7 our soul is e. as a bird
Is. 4:2 be comely for them e.
10:20 and such as are e. of Jacob
45:20 draw near, ye that are e.
Jer. 51:50 have e. rem. L. afar off
Lam. 2:22 none e. nor remain
Ezek. 24:27 opened to him e.
33:21 one that had e. came
John 10:39 e. out of their hands
Acts 27:44 so they e. all safe
28:4 tho' he e. the sea, yet ven.
2 Cor. 11:33 I was let down and e.
Heb. 11:34 through faith e.
12:25 if e. not who refused him
2 Pet. 1:4 e. corruption in world
2:18 those that were clean e.
20 e. the pollutions of world

**ESCAPETH.**

1 K. 19:17 that e. swo. of Hazael shall Jehu slay; that e. Jehu
Is. 15:9 bring lions upon him e.
Jer. 48:19 ask her e. Wh. is done?
Ezek. 24:26 e. sh. come unto thee
Amos 9:1 he that e. not be deliv.

**ESCAPING.**

Ezr. 9:14 there should be no e.

**ESCHEW.**

1 Pet. 3:11 let him e. evil, do good

**ESCHEWED, ETH.**

Job 1:1 feared God, e. evil, 8; 2:3

ESEK. Gen. 26:20

**ESHCOL.**

Gen. 14:13 M. brother of E. 24
Num. 13:24 place called brook E.
32:9 went up unto valley of E.

ESLI. Luke 3:25

**ESPECIALLY.**

Ps. 31:11 e. am. my neighbors
Acts 25:26 e. before thee, O king
Gal. 6:10 e. the househ. of faith
1 Tim. 4:10 e. of tho. that believe
5:8 prov. s. for them of his own
17 e. they who labor in word
2 Tim. 4:13 but e. the parchments
Phile. 16 a brother beloved s.

**ESPOUSALS.**

Cant. 3:11 crowned in day of e.
Jer. 2:2 I remem. love of thine e.

**ESPOUSED.**

2 Sam. 3:14 deliv. me Michal I e.
Mat. 1:18 when Mary was e. to J.
Luke 1:27 to a virgin e. to a man
2 Cor. 11:2 e. you to one husband

**ESPY.**

Jos. 14:7 Moses sent me to e.

See SPY, SPIED.

ESROM. Mat. 1:3; Luke 3:33

**ESTABLISH.**

Gen. 6:18 will I e. cov. 9:9; 17:7; Lev. 26:9; Ezek. 16:62
17:19 I will e. my covenant, 21
Deut. 8:18 that he may e. his cov.
28:9 L. shall e. thee a holy peo.
29:13 he may e. thee for a peo.
1 Sam. 1:23 L. e. 2 Sam. 7:25
2 Sam. 7:12 e. his kingdom, 13; 1 Chr. 17:11; 22:10; 28:7
1 K. 9:5 e. throne of thy kingdom
15:4 and to e. Jerusalem
1 Chr. 17:12 e. his throne for ever
2 Chr. 7:18 will I s. throne
9:8 God loved Israel to e. them.
Job 36:7 doth e. them for ever
Ps. 7:9 e. just; 48:8 G. will e. it
87:5 the Highest shall e. her
89:2 faithfulness shalt e.
4 thy seed will I e. for ever
90:17 e. work of our hands, e. it
99:4 thou dost e. equity, thou
119:38 s. thy word to thy serv.
Prov. 15:25 e. border of the wid.
Is. 9:7 to e. it with judgment
49:8 for a cov. to e. the earth
62:7 till he e. and make Jerus.
Jer. 33:2 that formed it, to e. it
Ezek. 16:60 will e. an everla. cov.
Dan. 6:7 consult. to e. royal stat.
11:14 exalt thems. to e. vision
Amos 5:15 e. judgm. in the gate
Rom. 3:31 yea, we e. the law
10:3 going about to e. own
16:25 power to e. you
1 Thes. 3:2 sent Tim. to e. you
13 s. your hearts unblameable
2 Thes. 2:17 s. you in ev. g. word
3:3 Lord shall s. you, and keep
Heb. 10:9 that he may e. second
Jam. 5:8 patient, s. your hearts
1 Pet. 5:10 the God of all grace s.

**ESTABLISHED.**

Gen. 9:17 token of covenant I e.
41:32 because thin. is e. by God
Ex. 6:4 I have also e. my cov.
Deut. 32:6 made and e. thee?
1 Sam. 3:20 S. was e. a prophet
13:13 would L. e. thy kingdom
20:31 thou shalt not be e. nor
2 Sam. 5:12 perc. L. had e. him
7:25 let the house of thy servant David be e. 1 Chr. 17:24
1 K. 2:12 king. was e. greatly
1 Chr. 17:23 let thing be e.
2 Chr. 1:9 L. let thy promise be e.
Job 21:8 seed is e. in their sight
Ps. 24:2 hath e. it on the floods
40:2 feet on rock, e. my goings
78:5 e. a testimony in Jacob
69 earth he e. for ever, 119:90
93:1 world e.; 2 throne e. of old
112:8 his heart is e.
140:11 let not evil speaker be e.
148:6 e. the waters for ever and
Prov. 3:19 L. hath e. the heavens
4:26 let all thy ways be e.
8:28 he e. the clouds above
12:3 shall not be e. by wicked.
15:22 in multi. of counsell. e.
16:12 throne is e. by righteous.
20:18 ev. purp. is e. by counsel
24:3 by understand. is a house e.
30:4 hath e. ends of the earth
Is. 7:9 if not believe, not be e.
16:5 in mercy shall throne be e.
45:18 made earth, he hath e. it
Jer. 10:12 e. world, 51:15
Dan. 4:36 was e. in my kingdom
Hab. 1:12 e. them for correction
Mat. 18:16 of two witn. ev. w. e.
Acts 16:5 churches e. in the faith
Rom. 1:11 to the end you m. be e.
Col. 2:7 and s. in the faith
Heb. 8:6 e. upon better promises
13:9 that heart be e. with grace
2 Pet. 1:12 tho. e. in present tru.

**Shall be ESTABLISHED.**

Lev. 25:30 h. s. be e. 2 Sam. 7:16
Deut. 19:15 at mouth of two or t. wit. s. matter be e. 2 Cor. 13:1
1 Sam. 24:20 kingd. s. be e. in h.
2 Sam. 7:16 thy house, kingdom, throne shall be e. 1 K. 2:45
1 Chr. 17:14 his throne shall be e. for evermore, Ps. 89:37
2 Chr. 20:20 believe in G. s. be e.
Job 22:28 shalt decree, it s. be e.
Ps. 89:21 my hand shall be e.
96:10 the world shall be e.
102:28 their seed shall be e.
Prov. 12:19 lip of truth sh. be e.
16:3 and thy thoughts s. be e.
25:5 throne s. be e. for e. 29:14
Is. 2:2 mount. of L. house s. be e.
16:5 in mercy shall throne be e.
54:14 in righteousn. s. thou be e.
Jer. 30:20 their congrega. s. be e.
Mic. 4:1 mount. of ho. of L. s. be e.
Zec. 5:11 a house, and it s. be e.

**ESTABLISHETH.**

Prov. 29:4 by judgment e. land
Dan. 6:15 no decree e. be chang.
Hab. 2:12 that e. a city by iniq.
2 Cor. 1:21 e. us with you in Ch.

**ESTATE.**

Gen. 43:7 man asked us of our s.
1 Chr. 17:17 e. of man of high d.
2 Chr. 24:13 house of G. in his s.
Est. 1:19 give her royal e. to an.
2:18 gifts according to s. of king
Ps. 39:5 man at best s. is vanity
136:23 remembered us in low e.
Prov. 27:23 to know s. of flocks
28:2 man of knowl. s. prolonged
Ec. 1:16 I am come to great e.
3:18 concern. e. of sons of men
Is. 22:19 thy s. pull thee down
Ezek. 16:55 S. return to former e.
Dan. 11:7 stand up in his e. 21
38 in his e. honor God of forces
Mat. 12:45 last s. of that man w. than first, Luke 11:26
Luke 1:48 low e. of his handm.

*Acts* 22:5 *e.* of elders bear witn.
*Rom.* 12:16 con. to men of low *e.*
*Phil.* 2:19 when I know your *e.*
20 naturally care for your *e.*
4:11 whatso. *e.* I am to be cont.
*Col.* 4:7 all my *e.* shall Tychicus
8 that he might know your *e.*
*Jude* 6 ang. who kept not first *e.*

**ESTATES.**
*Ezek.* 36:11 settle you after old *e.*
*Mark* 6:21 a supper to his chief *e.*

**ESTEEM.**
*Job* 36:19 will he *e.* thy riches?
*Ps.* 119:128 I *e.* all thy precepts
*Is.* 53:4 *e.* him smitten of God
*Phil.* 2:3 *e.* other better than th.
1 *Thes.* 5:13 *e.* highly for work's

**ESTEEMED.**
*Deut.* 32:15 lightly *e.* rock of sal.
1 *Sam.* 2:30 desp. me, be lightly *e.*
18:23 seeing I am lightly *e.*
*Job* 23:12 I *e.* words of his mouth
*Prov.* 17:28 *e.* a man of underst.
*Is.* 29:16 be *e.* as potter's clay
17 fruitful field be *e.* as a forest
53:3 and we *e.* him not
*Lam.* 4:2 *e.* as earthen pitchers
*Luke* 16:15 *e.* among men is abo.
1 *Cor.* 6:4 to judge who least *e.*

**ESTEEMETH.**
*Job* 41:26 he *e.* iron as straw
*Rom.* 14:5 *e.* one day ab. another
14 that *e.* any thing unclean

**ESTEEMING.**
*Heb.* 11:26 *e.* reproach of Christ

**ESTIMATION.**
*Lev.* 5:15 bring a ram with thy *e.*
27:2 thy *e.* 3, 5, 25; *Num.* 18:16

**ESTRANGED.**
*Job* 19:13 acquaintance are *e.*
*Ps.* 58:3 wicked *e.* from womb
78:30 they were not *e.* from lust
*Jer.* 19:4 they have *e.* this place
*Ezek.* 14:5 they are all *e.* from me

ETAM. *Jud.* 15:8, 11

**ETERNAL.**
*Deut.* 33:27 *e.* God is thy refuge
*Is.* 60:15 make thee *e.* excellency
*Mark* 3:29 in danger of *e.* damn.
*Rom.* 1:20 *e.* power and Godhead
2 *Cor.* 4:17 an *e.* weight of glory
18 which are not seen, are *e.*
5:1 a house *e.* in the heavens
*Eph.* 3:11 ac. to *e.* purpose in C.
1 *Tim.* 1:17 to king *e.* be honor
2 *Tim.* 2:10 obt. salv. with *e.* glo.
*Heb.* 5:9 author of *e.* salvation
6:2 the doctrine of *e.* judgment
9:12 obt. *e.* redemption for us
14 *e.* Spirit offered himself
15 promise of *e.* inheritance
1 *Pet.* 5:10 called us to his *e.* glo.
*Jude* 7 suff. vengeance of *e.* fire

**ETERNAL life.**
*Mat.* 19:16 that I may have *e. l.*?
25:46 right. shall go into *life e.*
*Mark* 10:17 that I may inherit *e. life*? *Luke* 10:25; 18:18
30 rec. in world to come *e. life*
*John* 3:15 believe sh. have *e. l.*
4:36 gathereth fruit unto *life e.*
5:39 in them think ye have *e. l.*
6:54 drink. my blood, hath *e. l.*
68 thou hast the words of *e. l.*
10:28 give unto my sheep *e. life*
12:25 hateth life, keep it to *e. l.*
17:2 give *e. life* to as many
3 this is *l. e.* might know thee
*Acts* 13:48 were ordained to *e. l.*
*Rom.* 2:7 seek for glory, *e. life*
5:21 grace reign to *e. life*
6:23 but the gift of God is *e. l.*
1 *Tim.* 6:12 lay hold on *e. life*, 19
*Tit.* 1:2 in hope of *e. l.* which G.
3:7 accord. to hope of *e. life*
1 *John* 1:2 *e. l.* which was with F.
2:25 promise he promised, *e. l.*
3:15 no murderer hath *e. life*
5:11 that God given to us *e. life*
13 may know ye have *e. life*
20 the true God, and *e. life*
*Jude* 21 for mercy of L. to *e. life*

**ETERNITY.**
*Is.* 57:15 lofty One that inhab. *e.*

**ETHAM.**
*Ex.* 13:20 encamped in E. *Num.* 33:6, 8

**ETHAN.**
1 *K.* 4:31 Sol. was wiser than E.
1 *Chr.* 2:6 sons of Ze. Zim. and E.

ETHANIM. 1 *K.* 8:2
ETHBAAL. 1 *K.* 16:31

**ETHIOPIA.**
2 *K.* 19:9 king of E. *Is.* 37:9
*Est.* 1:1 from India to E. 8:9
*Job* 28:19 E. shall not equal it
*Ps.* 68:31 E. shall stretch hands
87:4 Philistia and Tyre with E.
*Is.* 20:5 ashamed of E.
43:3 for thy ransom E. for thee
45:14 merch. of E. *Nah* 3:9
*Acts* 8:27 a man of E. an eunuch

**ETHIOPIAN.**
*Num.* 12:1 because of E. woman
2 *Chr.* 14:9 E. came out ag. Asa
*Jer.* 13:23 can E. change his skin?
38:6 Ebed-mel. E. 10, 12; 39:16

**ETHIOPIANS.**
2 *Chr.* 14:12; 16:8; 21:16; *Is.* 20:4
*Dan.* 11:43 E. sh. be at his steps
*Amos* 9:7 are ye not chil. of E.?
*Zep.* 2:12 ye E. shall be slain by
*Acts* 8:27 under queen of E.

EUBULUS. 2 *Tim.* 4:21
EUNICE. 2 *Tim.* 1:5

**EUNUCH, S.**
2 *K.* 9:32 there looked out *e.*
20:18 thy sons be *e.* in palace of king of Babylon, *Is.* 39:7
*Is.* 56:3 *e.* say I am a dry tree
4 thus saith L. unto the *e.*
*Jer.* 29:2 after *e.* were departed
38:7 Ebed-melech one of the *e.*
*Dan.* 1:9 favor with prince of *e.*
*Mat.* 19:12 some *e.* so born, some are made *e.* made themsel. *e.*
*Acts* 8:27 *e.* had come to worship
39 the *e.* saw Philip no more

EUODIAS. *Phil.* 4:2

**EUPHRATES.**
*Gen.* 2:14 the fourth river is E.
15:18 great river, the river E.
*Deut.* 1:7 go to river E. *Jos.* 1:4
2 *K.* 23:29 up to E. 2 *Chr.* 35:20
24:7 from Eg. to E. 1 *Chr.* 5:9
*Jer.* 13:4 go to E. 5, 7; 46:10
51:63 m. of E. *Rev.* 9:14; 16:12

**EUROCLYDON.**
*Acts* 27:14 arose a wind called *e.*

EUTYCHUS. *Acts* 20:9

**EVANGELIST, S.**
*Acts* 21:8 house of Philip the *e.*
*Eph.* 4:11 he gave some *e.*
2 *Tim.* 4:5 do the work of an *e.*

**EVE.**
*Gen.* 3:20; 4:1
2 *Cor.* 11:3 as serpent beguiled E.
1 *Tim.* 2:13 A. first form. then E.

**EVEN, Substantive.**
*Ex.* 18:14 people stand by thee from morning to *e.*
*Lev.* 23:5 at *e.* is the L. passover, *Num.* 9:3; *Deut.* 16:6
*Deut.* 28:67 would God it were *e.*
*Jud.* 20:23 they wept till *e.*
26 fasted till *e.* 2 *Sam.* 1:12
21:2 peo. abode till *e.* before G.
1 *Chr.* 23:30 praise the L. every *e.*
*Ezek.* 12:7 in *e.* I digged thro. w.
*Mat.* 8:16 when *e.* was come, 20:8; 26:20; 27:57; *Mark* 4:35; 6:47; 11:19; 15:42
*Mark* 1:32 at *e.* brought disease
13:35 at *e.* at midnight, or at
*John* 6:16 when *e.* was now come

**EVEN, Adverb.**
1 *K.* 1:48 mine eyes *e.* seeing it
*Prov.* 22:19 known *e.* to thee

**EVEN, Adjective.**
*Job* 31:6 be weighed in *e.* balance
*Ps.* 26:12 standeth in an *e.* place
*Cant.* 4:2 a flock of sheep *e.* shorn
*Luke* 19:44 lay thee *e.* with gro.

**EVENING.**
*Ex.* 12:6 Israel shall kill it in *e.*
*Jud.* 19:9 day draweth towards *e.*
1 *Sam.* 14:24 cursed eateth till *e.*
*Ps.* 59:6 they return at *e.* they
14 at *e.* let them return
90:6 in the *e.* it is cut down
104:23 goeth to labor until *e.*
*Prov.* 7:9 went to her house in *e.*
*Ec.* 11:6 in *e.* withhold not hand
*Jer.* 6:4 shadows of *e.* stretched
*Ezek.* 33:22 hand of L. on me in *e.*
*Zep.* 2:7 they lie down in *e.*
*Mat.* 14:23 *e.* he was there alone
16:2 when it is *e.* ye say, It will
*Luke* 24:29 for it is toward *e.*
*John* 20:19 same day at *e.* ca. J.

**EVENING, *with* morning.**
*Gen.* 1:5 *e.* and *m.* were first day
*Ex.* 18:13 stood by M. fr. *m.* to *e.*
1 *Sam.* 17:16 drew near *m.* and *e.*
*Job* 4:20 destroyed from *m.* to *e.*
*Ps.* 55:17 *e. m.* at noon w. I pray
65:8 outgoings of *m. e.* to rej.
*Dan.* 8:26 vision of *e.* and *m.*
*Acts* 28:23 persuad. from *m.* to *e.*

**EVENING, Adjective.**
*Ezr.* 9:4 astonished till *e.* sacri.
*Ps.* 141:2 prayer be as *e.* sacrifice
*Dan.* 9:21 touched me about *e.*
*Hab.* 1:8 mo. fierce than *e.* wolv.
*Zep.* 3:3 her judges are *e.* wolves
*Zec.* 14:7 at *e.* time it sh. be light

**EVENINGS.**
*Jer.* 5:6 wolf of the *e.* spoil them

**EVENT.**
*Ec.* 2:14 one *e.* to them all, 9:3
9:2 one *e.* to right. and wicked

**EVEN- *or* EVENING-TIDE**
*Gen.* 24:63 to meditate at *e.-tide*
*Is.* 17:14 behold, at *e. t.* trouble
*Mark* 11:11 *e.-t.* Jesus went out
*Acts* 4:3 in hold, now *e.-t.*

**EVER.**
*Num.* 22:30 *e.* since I was thine
*Deut.* 4:33 did *e.* peo. hear voice
19:9 to walk *e.* in his ways
*Job* 4:7 who *e.* perished inno.?
*Ps.* 5:11 let them *e.* shout for joy
25:6 tender mercies *e.* of old
*Ps.* 25:15 mine eyes are *e.* tow. L.
37:26 *e.* merciful, and lendeth
51:3 my sin is *e.* before me
90:2 *e.* formed earth, *Prov.* 8:23
111:5 *e.* be mindful of covenant
119:98 command. are *e.* with me
*Cant.* 6:12 or *e.* I was aware, my
*Joel* 2:2 hath not been *e.* the like
*Mat.* 24:21 no, nor *e.* shall be
*Mark* 15:8 to do as he had *e.*
*Luke* 15:31 thou art *e.* with me
*John* 4:29 told me all *e.* I did
8:35 but the Son abideth *e.*
1 *Thes.* 4:17 so *e.* be with the L.
5:15 *e.* follow that wh. is good
2 *Tim.* 3:7 *e.* learning, never able
*Heb.* 7:24 this man continueth *e.*
25 *e.* liveth to make interces.

*Jude* 25 be glory, now and *e.*
*See* ENDURETH.

**For EVER.**

*Gen.* 13:15 give it and to seed *f. e.*
43:9 bear blame *for e.* 44:32
*Ex.* 3:15 this is my name *for e.*
14:13 see them no more *for e.*
19:9 peo. may believe thee *f. e.*
21:6 he shall serve him *for e.*
*Lev.* 25:30 house established *f. e.*
46 be your bondmen *for e.*
*Num.* 18:19 a coven. of salt *f. e.*
*Deut.* 5:29 with them *for e.* 12:28
15:17 shall be thy servant *for e.*
23:6 not seek their peace *for e.*
29:29 revealed belong to us *f. e.*
*Jos.* 4:24 ye might fear L. *for e.*
1 *Sam.* 2:30 walk before me *f. e.*
20:15 not cut off kindness *for e.*
2 *Sam.* 7:24 confi. Is. to thee *f. e.*
26 thy name be magnified *f. e.*
29 that it may continue *for e.*
1 *K.* 10:9 the L. loved Israel *f. e.*
11:39 afflict D. seed, not *for e.*
1 *Chr.* 17:22 make thine *for e.*
28:9 he will cast thee off *for e.*
29:18 O Lord, keep this *for e.*
2 *Chr.* 7:16 name be there *for e.*
33:4 Jerusalem name be *for e.*
*Job* 4:20 they perish *for e.*
14:20 prevailest *for e.* ag. him
20:7 perish *for e.* like his dung
23:7 deliv. *f. e.* from my judge
36:7 doth establish them *for e.*
*Ps.* 9:7 Lord shall endure *for e.*
18 exp. of poor not perish *f. e.*
12:7 shall preserve them *for e.*
13:1 forget me, O Lord, *for e.?*
19:9 fear clean, enduring *for e.*
21:6 made him most blessed *f. e.*
23:6 dwell in house of Lord *f. e.*
28:9 and lift them up *for e.*
29:10 Lord sitteth King *for e.*
30:12 give thanks *for e.* 79:13
33:11 counsel of L. standeth *f. e.*
37:18 their inheritance be *for e.*
28 his saints preserved *for e.*
29 righteous dwell in land *f. e.*
41:12 settest me before face *f. e.*
44:8 we praise thy name *for e.*
23 arise, cast us not off *for e.*
45:2 God hath blessed thee *f. e.*
49:8 red. of soul ceaseth *for e.*
11 houses shall continue *for e.*
52:5 likewise destroy thee *f. e.*
9 I will praise thee *for e.*
61:4 abide in tabernacle *for e.*
7 shall abide before God *for e.*
8 I will sing praise *for e.*
66:7 ruleth by his power *for e.*
68:16 Lord will dwell in it *for e.*
72:17 name shall endure *for e.*
19 bless. be glorious name *f. e*
73:26 God is my portion *for e.*
74:1 why cast us off *for e.?*
10 blaspheme thy name *for e.?*
19 forget not con. of poor *f. e.*
75:9 I will declare *for e.* I will
77:7 will the Lord cast off *for e.?*
8 his mercy clean gone *for e.?*
79:5 wilt thou be angry *for e.?*
81:15 their time sh. endure *f. e.*
83:17 them be confounded *f. e.*
85:5 wilt be angry with us *f. e.?*
89:1 sing of mercies of L. *for e.*
2 mercy shall be built up *for e.*
29 his seed to endure *for e.* 36
46 wilt thou hide thyself *f. e.?*
92:7 it is that be destroyed *f. e.*
93:5 holiness becom. house *f. e.*
103:9 neither keep anger *for e.*
105:8 remembered covenant *f. e.*
110:4 a priest *for e.* after order
*Heb.* 5:6; 6:20; 7:17, 21
111:9 commanded covenant *f. e.*
112:6 shall not be moved *for e.*
125:2 from henceforth even *f. e.*
131:3; *Is.* 9:7
132:14 this is my rest *for e.*
*Ps.* 146:6 L. keepeth truth *f. e.*
10 the Lord shall reign *for e.*
*Prov.* 27:24 riches are not *for e.*
*Ec.* 2:16 no rem. of wise *for e.*
3:14 God doeth, shall be *for e.*
9:6 nor any more a portion *f. e.*
*Is.* 26:4 trust ye in Lord *for e.*
32:17 quietness and assu. *for e.*
34:10 smoke thereof go up *f. e.*
17 they shall possess it *for e.*
40:8 word of G. shall stand *f. e.*
51:6 my salvation shall be *for e.*
8 my righteousness be *for e.*
57:16 I will not contend *for e.*
59:21 my words not depart *f. e.*
60:21 thy peo. inherit land *f. e.*
64:9 nor remember iniquity *f. e.*
65:18 be glad and rejoice *for e.*
*Jer.* 3:5 he reserve anger *for e.*
12 I will not keep anger *for e.*
17:4 fire which shall burn *for e.*
25 J. and this city remain *f. e.*
31:40 plucked up any more *f. e.*
32:39 they may fear me *for e.*
*Lam.* 3:31 will not cast off *for e.*
5:19 thou, O L. remainest *for e.*
20 wherefore forget us *for e.?*
*Ezek.* 37:25 be their prince *for e.*
43:7 in midst of Israel *for e.* 9
*Dan.* 2:44 his kingdom stand *f. e.*
4:34 praised him that liveth *f. e.*
6:26 G. of Daniel, steadfast *f. e.*
7:18 saints possess kingdom *f. e.*
12:7 sw. by him that liveth *f. e.*
*Joel* 3:20 Judah shall dwell *for e.*
*Ob.* 10 shalt be cut off *for e.*
*Mic.* 2:9 tak. away my glory *f. e.*
4:7 Lord reign over them *for e.*
7:18 retaineth not anger *for e.*
*Mal.* 1:4 L. hath indignation *f. e.*
*Mat.* 6:13 power and glory *for e.*
*Luke* 1:33 reign over Jacob *for e.*
55 spake to Ab. and seed *f. e.*
*John* 8:35 serv. abideth not *f. e.*
12:34 that Christ abideth *for e.*
*Rom.* 1:25 Creator, blessed *for e.*
9:5 over all, God blessed *for e.*
11:36 be glory *for e.* 16:27
2 *Cor.* 9:9 righte. remaineth *f. e.*
*Phile.* 15 shouldst rec. him *for e.*
*Heb.* 10:12 *for e.* sat down
14 perfected *f. e.* them sancti.
13:8 J. C. same to-day and *f. e.*
1 *Pet.* 1:23 which liveth *for e.*
25 word of Lord endureth *f. e.*
2 *John* 2 be with us *for e.*

**Live for EVER.**

*Gen.* 3:22 tree of life and *l. for e.*
*Deut.* 32:40 and say, I *live for e.*
1 *K.* 1:31 let king David *l. for e.*
*Ps.* 22:26 heart shall *live for e.*
49:9 should still *live for e.*
*Dan.* 2:4 O king *live for e.* 3:9; 5:10; 6:6, 21
*Zec.* 1:5 prophets, do they *l. for e.*
*John* 6:51 if any man eat of this bread, he shall *l. for e.* 58

**For EVER and EVER.**

*Ex.* 15:18 reign *for e. and e.*
1 *Chr.* 16:36 blessed be God *for e. and e.* 29:10; *Dan.* 2:20
*Neh.* 9:5 bless your G. *for e. a. e.*
*Ps.* 9:5 their name *for e. and e.*
10:16 Lord is king *for e. and e.*
21:4 length of days *for e. and e.*
45:6 thy throne, O G. is *for e. a.*
17 praise thee *for e. and e.*
48:14 this G. is our God *for e. a.*
52:8 I trust in mercy of G. *f. e. a.*
111:8 stand fast *for e. and e.*
119:44 I keep thy law *for e. a. e.*
145:1 bless thy name *for e. a. e.*
2 thy name *for e. and e.* 21
148:6 stablish. them *for e. and e.*
*Is.* 30:8 be for time to come *for e.*
34:10 none pass thro' it *for e. a.*
*Jer.* 7:7 land I gave *for e. and e.*
25:5 to you and fathers *for e. a.*
*Dan.* 7:18 pos. kingdom *f. e. a. e.*
12:3 as the stars *for e. and e.*
*Mic.* 4:5 in name of God *f. e. a. e.*
*Gal.* 1:5 glory *for e. and e. Phil.* 4:20; 1 *Tim.* 1:17; 2 *Tim.* 4:18; *Heb.* 13:21
*Heb.* 1:8 throne O G. is *for e. a. e.*
*Rev.* 4:9 who liveth *for e. a. e.* 10; 5:14; 10:6; 15:7
5:13 honor be to L. *for e. and e.*
7:12 power be to our G. *f. e. a. e.*
11:15 C. shall reign *for e. and e.*
20:10 be tormented *for e. and e.*
22:5 shall reign *for e. and e.*

**EVERLASTING.**

*Gen.* 17:8 an *e.* possession, 48:4
21:33 the *e.* God, *Is.* 40:28; *Rom.* 16:26
*Gen.* 49:26 bound of the *e.* hills
*Ex.* 40:15 *e.* priesth. *Num.* 25:13
*Deut.* 33:27 undern. are *e.* arms
*Ps.* 24:7 *e.* doors, 9; 100:5 mercy *e.*
112:6 righte. in *e.* remembrance
119:142 thy righteousn. is *e.* 144
139:24 lead me in the way *e.*
145:13 kingd. is an *e.* kingdom, *Dan.* 4:3; 7:27; 2 *Pet.* 1:11
*Prov.* 10:25 an *e.* foundation
*Is.* 9:6 be called, the *e.* Father
26:4 in L. Jehov. is *e.* strength
33:14 dwell with *e.* burnings?
35:10 with *e.* joy, 51:11; 61:7
45:17 *e.* salva.; 54:8 *e.* kindness
55:13 *e.* sign; 56:5 *e.* na. 63:12
60:19 L. be to thee an *e.* lig. 20
*Jer.* 10:10 *e.* king; 20:11 *e.* confu.
23:40 bring an *e.* reproach on y.
31:3 loved thee with an *e.* love
*Dan.* 4:34 is an *e.* dominion, 7:14
*Hab.* 3:6 *e.* mountains scattered
*Mat.* 18:8 cast into *e.* fire, 25:41
25:46 go into *e.* punishment
*Luke* 16:9 into *e.* habitations
2 *Thes.* 1:9 pun. with *e.* destruc.
2:16 hath given us *e.* consolation
1 *Tim.* 6:16 be honor and pow. *e.*
*Jude* 6 the angels res. in *e.* cha.
*Rev.* 14:6 the *e.* gospel to preach
*See* COVENANT.

**From EVERLASTING.**

*Ps.* 14:31 bles. be G. *f. e.* 106:48
90:2 *from e.* to *e.* thou art God
93:2 throne of old, thou art *f. e.*
103:17 mercy of the L. is *f. e.*
*Prov.* 8:23 I was set up *from e.*
*Is.* 63:16 O. L. thy name is *f. e.*
*Mic.* 5:2 whose goings forth *f. e.*
*Hab.* 1:12 art thou not *f. e.* O L.

**EVERLASTING life.**

*Dan.* 12:2 awake, some to *e. life*
*Mat.* 19:29 shall inherit *e. life*
*Luke* 18:30 world to come *e. life*
*John* 3:16 believeth, have *e. l.* 36
4:14 water springing up to *e. l.*
5:24 heareth my words hath *e. l.*
6:27 which endureth to *e. life*
40 the Son, may have *e. life*
47 believeth on me hath *e. life*
12:50 commandment is *life e.*
*Acts* 13:46 unworthy of *e. life*
*Rom.* 6:22 ye have the end, *e. l.*
*Gal.* 6:8 shall of the Sp. reap *l. e.*
1 *Tim.* 1:16 hereafter bel. to *l. e.*

**EVERMORE.**

2 *Sam.* 22:51 mercy unto Dav. *e.*
1 *Chr.* 17:14 throne be estab. *e.*
*Ps.* 16:11 are pleasures for *e.*
18:50 mercy to his seed for *e.*
37:27 do good, and dwell for *e.*
77:8 doth his promise fail for *e.?*
86:12 will glorify thy na. for *e.*

89:28 mercy keep for him for e.
52 blessed be the L. for e. am.
92:8 Lord, art most high for e.
105:4 seek Lord, seek his face e.
106:31 counted for righte. for e.
113:2 blessed be na. of L. for e.
115:18 will bless the Lord for e.
121:8 L. preser. thy going out e.
132:12 sit upon thy throne for e.
133:3 Lord command. life for e.
*John* 6:34 e. give us this bread
2 *Cor.* 11:31 Father blessed for e.
1 *Thes.* 5:16 rejoice e.
*Heb.* 7:28 who is consecra. for e.
*Rev.* 1:18 behold, I am alive for e.

**EVERY.**

*Gen.* 6:5 e. imagination was evil
*Ps.* 119:101 refrained fr. e. evil
104 I hate e. false way, 128
*Prov.* 15:3 eyes of L. are in e. pl.
30:5 e. word of God is pure
*Is.* 45:23 e. knee, *Rom* 14:11
*Mat.* 4:4 by e. word that proc.
1 *Cor.* 4:17 as I teach e. wh. in e.
2 *Cor.* 10:5 into captiv. e. thoug.
*Eph.* 1:21 abo. e. name, *Phil.* 2:9
2 *Tim.* 2:21 prep. to e. good work
*Heb.* 12:1 lay aside e. weight
*Jam.* 1:17 e. good and perf. gift
1 *John* 4:1 believe not e. spirit
*See* BEAST, CITY, DAY, MAN, MORNING, WAY, SIDE, THING.

**EVERY one.**

*Num.* 16:3 cong. are holy e. *one*
*Deut.* 4:4 ye are alive e. *one* of y.
1 *K.* 22:28 hearken e. *one* of you
2 *Chr.* 30:18 Lord pardon e. *one*
*Ps.* 71:18 thy power to e. *one*
115:8 e. o. that trusteth, 135:18
*Is.* 43:7 e. o. called by my name
55:1 ho, e. o. that thirsteth
*Jer.* 25:5 turn e. o. from evil way
*Dan.* 12:1 e. o. found writ. in b.
*Mat.* 7:8 e. o. that ask. *Lu.* 11:10
*Mark* 7:14 hearken to me e. *one*
*Luke* 19:26 to e. *one* which hath
*John* 3:8 so is e. *one* born of Sp.
18:37 e. o. that is of truth,
*Acts* 17:27 not far from e. o.
*Rom.* 14:12 e. o. sh. give account
2 *Tim.* 2:19 e. o. that nameth

**EVERY where.**

1 *Chr.* 13:2 abroad to breth. e. w.
*Mark* 16:20 and preached e. w.
*Luke* 9:6 pre. gos. e. w. *Acts* 8:4
*Acts* 17:30 com. all e. w. to rep.
28:22 e. w. spoken against
1 *Cor.* 4:17 as I teach e. *where* in
*Phil.* 4:12 e. w. in all things
1 *Tim.* 2:8 that men pray e. w.

**EVIDENCE.**

*Jer.* 32:10 I subscribed the e. and
*Heb.* 11:1 e. of things not seen

**EVIDENCES.**

*Jer.* 32:44 buy fields, subscribe e.

**EVIDENT.**

*Job* 6:28 for it is e. to you if I lie
*Gal.* 3:11 justified by the law is e.
*Phil.* 1:28 e. token of perdition
*Heb.* 7:14 e. L. sprang out of J.
15 it is yet far more e. for that

**EVIDENTLY.**

*Gal.* 3:1 Jesus C. been e. set forth

**EVIL.**

*Gen.* 19:19 some e. take me, I die
44:5 ye have done e. in so doing
34 e. that shall come on my fa.
50:20 ye thought e. against me
*Ex.* 5:23 done e. to this people
10:10 look to it, e. is before you
32:14 the L. repented of the e.
2 *Sam.* 24:16; 1 *Chr.* 21:15
*Deut.* 19:20 com. no more such e.
29:21 Lord sh. sep. him unto e.
30:15 set bef. thee death and e.
31:29 e. befall you in latter days
*Jos.* 24:15 seem e. to serve Lord
*Jud.* 2:15 hand of L. ag. th. for e.
9:57 e. of Shechem did G. rend.
20:34 they knew not e. was near
1 *Sam.* 20:7 e. is determined
24:11 e. nor transg. in my hand
17 whereas I rewarded thee e.
25:17 e. is determ. aga. master
28 e. hath not been found
26:18 what e. is in my hand?
29:6 I have not found e. in thee
2 *Sam.* 3:39 Lord rew. doer of e.
12:11 I will raise up e. ag. thee
19:7 worse than all e. that befell
1 *K.* 14:9 e. above all before thee
16:25 Omri wrought e. in eyes of
22:23 the L. hath spoken e. concerning thee, 2 *Chr.* 18:22
2 *K.* 21:12 bringing such e. on J.
22:20 eyes not see all the e.
1 *Chr.* 21:17 that have done e.
2 *Chr.* 20:9 if when e. cometh
*Est.* 7:7 he saw e. determined
*Job.* 1:1 and eschewed e. 8; 2:3
5:19 in seven no e. touch thee
31:29 lift up when e. found him
42:11 comforted him over all e.
*Ps.* 5:4 nor sh. e. dwell with thee
7:4 if I rewarded e. to him
15:3 nor doeth e. to his neighbor
21:11 intended e. against thee
23:4 I will fear no e. for thou art
34:21 e. shall slay the wicked
36:4 he abhorreth not e.
40:14 put to shame wish me e.
41:5 mine enemies speak e.
49:5 in days of e.?
50:19 givest thy mouth to e.
54:5 reward e. to my enemies
56:5 thoughts aga. me for e.
90:15 years wherein we seen e.
91:10 e. befall thee, *Jer.* 23:17
97:10 that love the Lord, hate e.
109:20 that speak e. ag. my soul
140:11 e. shall hunt the viol. m.
*Prov.* 1:16 feet run to e. *Is.* 59:7
33 shall be quiet from fear of e.
3:29 devise not e. ag. neighbor
5:14 almost in all e. in midst
11:19 pursueth e. pur. it to dea.
12:20 in them that imagine e.
21 no e. happen to the just
13:21 e. pursueth sinners
14:22 they err that devise e.?
16:4 wicked for the day of e.
27 ungodly man diggeth up. e
30 moving lips bringeth e.
19:23 shall not be visited with e.
20:8 scat. away e. with his eyes
22 say not, I will recompen. e.
21:10 soul of the wicked des. e.
22:3 pru. man foreseeth e. 27:12
*Prov.* 30:32 if thought e. lay thy
*Ec.* 2:21 is vanity, and a great e.
5:13 there is a sore e. which I, 16
6:1 e. which I have seen, 10:5
9:3 an e. am. things done, heart of the sons of m. is full of e.
11:2 know. not what e. on earth
*Is.* 3:9 rewarded e. to themselves
13:11 punish the world for e.
33:15 shut. eyes from seeing e.
45:7 I make peace and create e.
47:11 theref. sh. e. come on thee
56:2 keepeth hand from doing e.
57:1 the righte. is taken from e.
*Jer.* 1:14 out of north an e. 6:1
2:3 e. shall come upon them,
4:4 because of e. of your doings, 23:2; 26:3; 44:22
5:12 neit. shall e. come upon us
7:30 chil. of Judah have done e
11:15 doest e. th. thou rejoicest
17 pronounced e. for e. of Isr.
15:11 entreat well in time of e.
17:17 my hope in the day of e.
18 bring on them the day of e.
18:8 turn from e. I will repent of the e. 26:3: 13, 19; 42:10
11 I frame e. against you
19:15 bring e. I have pronounced
21:10 my face ag. this city for e.
25:32 e. go from nation
28:8 prophets prophesied of e.
29:11 thoughts of peace not of e.
32:30 chil. of Jud. only done e.
35:17 the e. that I have pronounced against them, 36:31
38:9 these men have done e.
44:11 set my face ag. you for e.
17 had plenty, and saw no e.
27 watch over them for e.
29 words stand aga. you for e.
51:24 render to Bab. all the e.
60 wrote e. sho. come on Bab.
*Ezek.* 7:5 an e. an only e. is come
14:22 be comforted conc. the e.
*Dan.* 9:14 L. watched upon the e.
*Joel* 2:13 Lord repenteth of the e.
*Amos* 3:6 e. in city?
9:10 e. shall not overtake us
*Jon.* 3:10 God repented of e. 4:2
*Mic.* 1:12 e. came down from L.
2:1 work e. upon their beds
3 do I devise an e.
3:11 Lord amo. us? none e. can
*Nah.* 1:11 imagineth e. ag. L.
*Hab.* 1:13 eyes that behold e.
2:9 delivered from power of e.
*Zep.* 3:15 not see e. any more
*Zec.* 7:10 none imagine e. 8:17
*Mal.* 1:8 ye of. sick, is it not e.?
2:17 every one that doeth e.
*Mat.* 5:11 all manner of e.
37 more than these, com. of e.
39 I say, that ye resist not e.
6:34 sufficient to the d. is the e.
9:4 why th. ye e. in your hearts?
27:23 What e. hath he done? *Mark* 15:14; *Luke* 23:22
*Mark* 9:39 lightly speak e. of
*Luke* 6:45 bring. forth what is e.
*John* 3:20 doeth e. hateth light
5:29 that have done e. to resur.
18:23 if spoken e. bear witness
*Acts* 9:13 much e. he hath done
23:9 we find no e. in this man
*Rom.* 2:9 every soul that doeth e.
7:19 e. I would not, that I do
12:9 abhor that which is e.
17 recomp. to no man e. for e.
21 be not overcome of e. but
13:4 exec. wrath on him doeth e.
14:20 e. for him who eateth wit.
16:19 simple concerning e.
1 *Cor.* 13:5 charity thinketh no e.
1 *Thes.* 5:15 none render e. for e.
22 abstain from appear. of e.
1 *Tim.* 6:10 money root of all e.
*Tit.* 3:2 to speak e. of no man
*Jam.* 3:8 tongue is an unruly e.
1 *Pet.* 3:9 not rendering e. for e.
3 *John* 11 doeth e. not seen God

**Bring, brought EVIL.**

*Jos.* 23:15 b. on you all e.
2 *Sam.* 15:14 lest A. b. e. on us
17:14 L. might b. e. upon Absa.
1 *K.* 14:10 b. e. on house of Jero.
17:20 also b. e. on the widow?
21:29 not b. the e. in his days
2 *K.* 22:16 I will b. e. upon this place, 2 *Chr.* 34:24
2 *Chr.* 34:28 eyes see e. I will b.
*Is.* 31:2 b. e. not call back word
*Jer.* 4:6 I will b. e. from the north
6:19 I will b. e. upon this people
11:11 I will b. e. upon them.
19:3 b. e. upon this place, 15
23:12 b. e. the year of visitation
*Jer.* 25:29 I begin to b. e. on the
35:17 b. on Judah all the e. 36:31
39:16 b. words on this city for e.
45:5 I will b. e. upon all flesh
*See* DID, DO.

**EVIL, *joined with* good.**
Gen. 2:9 tree of kno. g. and e. 17
3:5 as gods know. g. and e. 22
44:4 wheref. rewarded e. for g.?
Deut. 1:39 no kno. bet. g. and e.
1 Sam. 25:21 requit. me e. for g.
2 Sam. 19:35 disc. bet. g. and e.?
1 K. 22:8 prophesy g. but e. 18
2 Chr. 18:7 nev. prophe. g. but e.
17 not prophesy good but e.
Job 2:10 receive g. and not e.?
30:26 I looked for good, e. came
Ps. 35:12 rew me e. for g. 109:5
38:20 render e. for g.
52:3 thou lovest e. more than g.
Prov. 15:3 behold. e. and the g.
17:13 rewardeth e. for good
31:12 will do him good, not e.
Is. 5:20 woe to th. call e. g. g. e.
7:15 refuse e. and choose g. 16
Jer. 18:20 e. be recomp. for g.?
42:6 whe. g. or e. we will obey
Lam. 3:38 proceed. not e. and g.
Amos 5:14 seek g. and not e. that
9:4 eyes on them for e. not g.
Mic. 3:2 hate good and love e.
Rom. 7:21 do g. e. is present
9:11 having done good or e.
Heb. 5:14 exerc. to disc. g. and e.
3 John 11 follow not e. but good
See GREAT.

**From EVIL.**
Gen. 48:16 redeemed me f. all e.
1 Sam. 25:39 kept his serv. f. e.
1 Chr. 4:10 keep me from e.
Job 28:28 to depart f. e.
Ps. 34:13 keep thy tongue f. e.
14 dep. f. e. 37:27; Prov. 3:7
121:7 preserve thee f. all e.
Prov. 4:27 remove thy foot f. e.
13:19 abomination to depart f. e.
14:16 a wise man departeth f. e.
16:6 men depart from e.
17 to depart from e.
Is. 59:15 f. e. makes himself
Jer. 9:3 they proceed f. e. to e.
23:22 should have turned f. e. way, and e. of their doings
51:64 Bab. not rise from the e.
Mat. 6:13 del. us f. e. Luke 11:4
John 17:15 keep them f. e.
2 Thes. 3:3 and keep you f. e.
1 Pet. 3:10 refrain his tong. f. e.

**Put away EVIL.**
Deut. 13:5 p. the e. a. from m.
17:7 put the e. a. from am. 19:19; 21:21; 22:21, 24; 24:7
12 put e. away from Israel, 21:22; Jud. 20:13
Ec. 11:10 put a. e. from thy flesh
Is. 1:16 wash you p. away e.

**EVIL in the sight of the Lord.**
Num. 32:13 e. in s. Jud. 3:12
Jud. 2:11 Isr. did e. in s. of the Lord, 3:7, 12; 4:1; 6:1; 10:6; 13:1; 1 K. 11:6; 14:22; 15:26, 34; 16:7, 30; 22:52; 2 K. 8:18, 27; 13:2, 11; 14:24; 15:9, 18, 24, 28; 17:2; 21:2, 20; 2 Chr. 22:4; 33:2, 22; 36:5, 9, 12
1 Sam. 15:19 didst e. in s. of L.
1 K. 16:19 in doing e. in s. of L.
21:20 sold to work e. in s. of L.
2 K. 3:2 wrought e. in s. of L.
17:17 to do e. in s. of Lord
21:16 in doing what was e. in s. of Lord, 23:32, 37; 24:9, 19
1 Chr. 2:3 Er was e. in s. of L.
2 Chr. 33:6 Man. wro. e. in s. of L.

**This EVIL.**
Ex. 32:12 repent of t. e.
1 Sam. 6:9 hath done us t. gr. e.
12:19 added t. e. to ask a k.
2 Sam. 13:16 t. e. in send. away
1 K. 9:9 L. brought on th. t. e.
2 K. 6:33 behold t. e. is of Lord
2 Chr. 7:22 theref. brought t. e.
Neh. 13:18 our G. bring this e.
Job 2:11 J.'s friends heard of t. e.
Ps. 51:4 done t. e. in thy sight
Jer. 16:10 pronounced t. e. ag. us
32:23 thou hast caused all t. e.
42 as I brought t. e. on people
40:2 pronoun. t. e. on th. place
44:7 wheref. commit t. great e.
23 theref. t. e. is happen. to y.
Dan. 9:13 all t. e. is come on us
Jon. 1:7 for whose cause t. e. 8

**EVIL, Adjective.**
Gen. 6:5 thoughts only e. 8:21
Gen. 37:20 e. beast dev. him. 33
Ex. 5:19 did see were in. e. case
33:4 when heard these e. tidings
Num. 14:27 how long bear e. con.
20:5 bring us unto this e. place
Deut. 1:35 not one of this e. gen.
22:14 an e. name upon her, 19
28:54 his e. toward brother
56 her eye be e. toward husb.
1 Sam. 2:23 your e. dealings
1 K. 5:4 nor e. occurrent
Ezr. 9:13 come for our e. deeds
Ps. 41:8 e. disease cleav. to him
64:5 encourage in an e. matter
78:49 by sending e. angels
112:7 not be afraid of e. tidings
140:11 let not e. speaker be est.
Prov. 6:24 to keep from e. woman
14:19 the e. bow before the good
Ec. 5:14 perish by e. travel
6:2 end it is an e. disease
9:12 fishes taken in e. net
Is. 7:5 taken e. counsel aga. thee
32:7 instruments of churl are e.
Jer. 8:3 that remain of e. family
12:14 against mine e. neighbors
13:10 e. people refuse to hear
23:10 their course is e.
24:3 e. figs, very e. 8; 29:17
49:23 they have heard e. tidings
Ezek. 5:16 e. arrows of famine
17 will I send on you e. beasts
6:11 for all the e. abominations
34:25 cause e. beasts to cease
38:10 shalt think an e. thought
Hab. 2:9 coveteth an e. covetous.
Mat. 5:45 sun to rise on the e.
7:11 if being e. Luke 11:13
18 cannot bring forth e. fruit
12:34 how can ye being e. speak
39 an e. generation, Luke 11:29
15:19 out of the heart proceed e. thoughts, Mark 7:21
24:48 if e. servant say in heart
Luke 6:22 cast out name as e.
35 kind to unthankful and e.
John 3:19 because deeds were e.
Acts 24:20 found e. doing in me
1 Cor. 15:33 e. communications
Gal. 1:4 deliver us from e. world
Eph. 4:31 e. speaking be put aw.
Phil. 3:2 beware of evil workers
Col. 3:5 mortify e. concupiscence
1 Tim. 6:4 cometh e. surmisings
Tit. 1:12 Cretians are e. beasts
Heb. 10:22 sprinkled from e.
Jam. 2:4 judges of e. thoughts
4:16 all such rejoicing is e.
1 Pet. 2:1 laying aside e. speak.
Rev. 2:2 canst not bear them e.

**EVIL day *or* days.**
Gen. 47:9 few and e. d. of life
Prov. 15:15 d. of afflicted are e.
Ec. 12:1 e. days come not
Amos 6:3 put far away e. d.
Eph. 5:16 because days are e.
6:13 able to withstand in e. day
Day of EVIL. See EVIL, Subst.

**EVIL doer *or* doers.**
Job 8:20 neither will he help e. d.
Ps. 26:5 hated congrega. of e. d.
37:1 fret not because of e. d.
9 e. d. shall be cut off, but
94:16 will rise up aga. e. do.?
119:115 depart from me ye e. d.
Is. 1:4 sinful nation seed of e. d.
9:17 every one is an e. d.
14:20 seed of e. d.
31:2 will arise ag. house of e. d.
Jer. 20:13 deliv. poor from e. d.
23:14 strengtnen hands of e. d.
2 Tim. 2:9 I suffer troub. as e. d.
1 Pet. 2:12 speak ag. you as e. d.
14 sent for punishment of e. d.
3:16 speak e. of you as of e. d.
4:15 let none suffer as an e. d.
See DOINGS, EYE.

**EVIL heart.**
Gen. 8:21 imagination of h. is e.
Jer. 3:17 after imagina. of e. h.
7:24 walked in imagina. of e. h.
11:8 every one in imagi. of e. h.
16:12 after imagination of e. h.
18:12 do imagination of e. h.
Heb. 3:12 be an e. h. of unbelief

**EVIL man *or* men.**
Job 35:12 bec. of pride of e. men
Ps. 10:15 break arm of e. man
140:1 deliver me from e. man
Prov. 2:12 deli. from way of e. m.
4:14 go not in way of e. men
12:12 wicked desir. net of e. m.
17:11 e. man seeketh only rebel.
24:1 be not envious aga. e. men
19 fret not because of e. men
20 shall be no reward to e. m.
Prov. 28:5 e. m. unders. not judg.
29:6 in transg. of e. m. is snare
Mat. 12:35 e. m. out of e. treasure, bring. e. th. Luke 6:45
2 Tim. 3:13 e. m. shall wax wor.
See REPORT.

**EVIL spirit *or* spirits.**
Jud. 9:23 e. s. betw. Abimelech
1 Sam. 16:14 e. s. troub. him, 15
16 when e. spirit is upon thee
23 e. spirit departed from him
18:10 e. spirit came on S. 19:9
Luke 7:21 cured many of e. s.
8:2 a woman healed of e. spirits
Acts 19:12 e. s. went out of them
15 e. s. said, Jesus, I know, Pa.

**EVIL thing.**
Neh. 13:17 what e. t. is th. ye do?
Ps. 141:4 incline not heart to e. t.
Ec. 8:3 stand not in an e. thing
5 keepeth com. sh. feel no e. t.
12:14 secret t. wheth. good or e.
Jer. 2:19 it is an e. th. and bitter
Tit. 2:8 no e. t. to say of you

**EVIL things.**
Jos. 23:15 bring on you all e. t.
Prov. 15:28 poureth out e. t.
Jer. 3:5 hast done e. t.
Mat. 12:35 e. man br. forth e. t.
Mark 7:23 e. t. come from within
Luke 16:25 likewise Lazarus e. t.
Rom. 1:30 inventors of e. things
1 Cor. 10:6 not lust after e. t.

**EVIL time.**
Ps. 37:19 not be ashamed in e. t.
Ec. 9:12 are snared in an e. t.
Amos 5:13 it is an e. t.
Mic. 2:3 nor go haughtily, t. is e.

**EVIL way.**
1 K. 13:33 J. ret. not from e. w.
Ps. 119:101 refrained fr. ev. e. w.
Prov. 8:13 fear of L. to hate e. w.
28:10 to go astray in e. way
Jer. 18:11 return ye from e. w. 25:5; 26:3; 35:15; 36:3, 7
23:22 turned them from e. way
Jon. 3:8 turn ev. one from e. w.
10 saw they turned from e. w.

**EVIL ways.**
2 K. 17:13 turn from your e. ways, Ezek. 33:11

Ezek. 36:31 remember your e. w.
Zec. 1:4 turn ye now from e. w.

**EVIL work or works.**

Ec. 4:3 hath not seen e. work
8:11 sentence against an e. work
John 7:7 works thereof are e.
Rom. 13:3 terror to good but e. w.
2 Tim. 4:18 deliver me from e. w.
Jam. 3:16 and every e. w.
1 John 3:12 his own w. were e

**EVIL, Adverb.**

Ex. 5:22 e. entreated this peo.?
Deut. 26:6 Egypt e. entreated us
1 Chr. 7:23 went e. with his ho.
Job 24:21 e. entreated the barren
John 18:23 spoken e. bear witn.
Acts 7:6 entreat e. 400 years
19 same e. entreated our fath.
14:2 e. affected against brethren
19:9 spake of e. that way before
23:5 not speak e. of ruler of peo.
Rom. 14:16 not good be e. spoken
1 Cor. 10:30 am I e. spoken of
Jam. 4:11 sp. not e. he that spe.
e. of brother, speaks e. of law
1 Pet. 3:16 whereas they speak e.
17 than suffer for e. doing
4:4 speaking e. of you
14 on their part e. spoken of
2 Pet. 2:2 way of truth e. spok. of
10 speak e. of dignities, Jude 8
12 speak e. of things they understand not, Jude 10

EVIL-MERODACH. 2 K. 25:27; Jer. 52:31

**EVILS.**

Deut. 31:17 e. shall befall them, will say, Are not these e.
Ps. 40:12 innumer. e. comp. me
Jer. 2:13 have committed two e.
Ezek. 6:9 loathe themselves for e.
20:43 loathe yourselves for all e.
Luke 3:19 for all e. H. had done

**EWE or EWES.**

Gen. 21:28 Abraham set seven e.
31:38 thy e. not cast their young
Lev. 14:10 take one e. lamb
2 Sam. 12:3 nothing save e. lamb
Ps. 78:71 from following the e.

**EXACT.**

Deut 15:3 of foreigner may e. ag.
Neh. 5:10 I likewise might e.
Neh. 5:11 hundredth of mo. ye e.
Ps. 89:22 enemy not e. upon him
Is. 58:3 in fasts you e. all labors
Luke 3:13 e. no more than is app

**EXACTED, ETH.**

2 K. 15:20 Menahem e. of Israel
23:35 Jehoakim e. the gold
Job 11:6 G. e. less than iniquity

**EXACTION, S.**

Neh. 10:31 would leave e. of debt
Ezek. 45:9 take away your e.

**EXACTORS.**

Is. 60:17 make e. righteousness

**EXALT.**

Ex. 15:2 father's G. I will e.
1 Sam. 2:10 e. horn of anointed
Job 17:4 shalt thou not e. them
Ps. 34:3 let us e. his name
37:34 e. thee to inherit the land
66:7 let not rebellious e. thems.
92:10 my horn e. like the horn
99:5 e. ye the Lord our God, 9
107:32 let e. him in congregation
118:28 art my God, I will e. thee
140:8 lest wicked e. themselves
Prov. 4:8 e. her, she shall prom.
Is. 13:2 e. the voice unto them
14:13 I will e. throne above sta.
25:1 art my God, I will e. thee
Ezek. 21:26 e. him that is low
29:15 nor e. itself above nations
31:14 to the end none of trees e.
Dan. 11:14 robbers of thy peo. e.
36 e. himself above every god
Hos. 11:7 none would e. him
Ob. 4 tho' e. thyself as the eagle
Mat. 23:12 whoso shall e. himself
2 Cor. 11:20 if a man e. himself
1 Pet. 5:6 may e. you in time

**EXALTED.**

Num. 24:7 kingdom shall be e.
1 Sam. 2:1 said, My horn is e.
2 Sam. 5:12 he had e. kingdom
22:47 e. be the God of the rock of my salvation, Ps. 18:46
1 K. 1:5 Adonijah e. himself
14:7 I e. thee from people, 16:2
2 K. 19:22 against whom hast thou e. thy voice? Is. 37:23
1 Chr. 29:11 thou art e. as head
Neh. 9:5 is e. above all blessing
Job 5:11 mourn be e. to safety
24:24 are e. for a little while
36:7 establish, and they are e.
Ps. 12:8 when the vilest are e.
13:2 how long ene. e. over me?
21:13 be e. in thine own streng.
46:10 I will be e. am. heathen, I will be e. in the earth
47:9 to God, he is greatly e
57:5 be e. above heavens, 11
75:10 horns of right. shall be e.
89:16 thy right. sh. they be e.
17 in thy favor our horn be e.
19 e. one chosen out of people
24 in my name his horn be e.
97:9 art e. far above all gods
108:5 e. above the heavens
112:9 his horn be e. with honor
118:16 right hand of Lord is e.
Prov. 11:11 by blessing city is e.
Is. 2:2 mount. of Lord's house be e. above the hills, Mic. 4:1
11 L. be e. 17; 5:16
12:4 mention that his name is e.
30:18 be e. that he have mercy
33:5 L. is e.; 10 now will I be e.
40:4 every valley shall be e.
49:11 my highways shall be e.
52:13 my servant shall be e.
Ezek. 17:24 I the Lord e. low tr.
19:11 her stature was e. 31:5
Hos. 13:1 Ephraim e. himself
6 and their heart was e.
Mat. 11:23 e. to heav. Luke 10:15
23:12 humble himself shall be e. Luke 14:11; 18:14
Luke 1:52 e. them of low degree
Acts 2:33 by right hand of God e.
5:31 him hath God e.
13:17 God of Israel e. the people
2 Cor. 11:7 that you might be e.
12:7 be e. above measure, 7
Phile. 2:9 God hath high. e. him
Jam. 1:8 bro. rejoice that he is e.

**EXALTEST, ETH.**

Ex. 9:17 e. thyself against my people
Job 36:22 God e. by his power
Ps. 148:14 e. horn of his people
Prov. 14:29 hasty of sp. e. folly
34 righteousness e. a nation
17:19 e. gate, seek. destruction
Luke 14:11 e. him, 18:14
2 Cor. 10:5 every thing that e.
2 Thes. 2:4 e him above all

**EXAMINATION.**

Acts 25:26 after e. had, I might

**EXAMINE.**

Ezr. 10:16 sat down to e. matter
Ps. 26:2 e. me O Lord
1 Cor. 9:3 answer to them that e.
11:28 let a man e. himself
2 Cor. 13:5 e. yourselves, prove

**EXAMINED, ING.**

Luke 23:14 I have e. him
Acts 4:9 if we be e. of good deed
12:19 Herod e. the keepers
22:24 should be e. by scourging
29 departed who should e. him
24:8 by e. of whom thou mayest
28:18 e. me, would ha. let me go

**EXAMPLE, S.**

Mat. 1:19 make her a public e.
John 13:15 have given you an e.
1 Cor. 10:6 were our e.
1 Tim. 4:12 e. of believers
Heb. 4:11 fall after same e.
8:5 serve unto e. of heavenly
Jam. 5:10 prophets for e. suffer.
1 Pet. 2:21 C. suff. leav. us an e.
Jude 7 for an e. suffering

See ENSAMPLE, S.

**EXCEED.**

Deut. 25:3 forty stripes and not e. lest if he e. brother
Mat. 5:20 right. e. the scribes
2 Cor. 3:9 ministration e.

**EXCEEDED.**

1 Sam. 20:41 wept, till David e.
1 K. 10:23 Sol. e. all for riches

**EXCEEDEST, ETH.**

1 K. 10:7 wisdom e. the fame
2 Chr. 9:6 e. fame that I heard

**EXCEEDING.**

Gen. 15:1 thy e. great reward
17:6 make thee e. fruitful
27:34 E. cried with e. bitter cry
Ex. 1:7 Israel waxed e. mighty
19:16 the trumpet e. loud
Num. 14:7 land we passed is e.
1 Sam. 2:3 no more e. proudly
2 Sam. 8:8 D. took e. much brass
12:2 man had e. many flocks
1 K. 4:29 G. gave Sol. wisdom e.
1 Chr. 20:2 brought e. much spoil
22:5 must be e. magnifical
2 Chr. 11:12 cities e. strong
14:14 was e. much spoil in them
16:12 Asa, disease was e. great
32:27 Hez. had e. much riches
Ps. 21:6 hast made him e. glad
43:4 I go unto God, my e. joy
119:96 thy command. is e. broad
Prov. 30:24 four things are e. w.
Ec. 7:24 which is e. deep
Ezek. 9:9 iniq. of Is. is e. great
16:13 and wast e. beautiful
37:10 e. great army
47:10 fish of great sea e. many
Dan. 3:22 the furnace was e. hot
7:19 fourth beast was e. dreadful
8:9 horn, which waxed e. great
Jon. 3:3 was an e. great city
4:6 Jonah was e. glad
Mat. 2:10 rej. with e. great joy
16 Herod mocked, was e. wro.
4:8 taketh up into e. high moun.
5:12 rejoice and be e. glad
8:28 possess. with devils e. fier.
26:22 they were e. sorrowful
38 e. sorrowful, Mark 14:34
Mark 6:26 the king was e. sorry
9:3 his raiment e. white as snow
Acts 7:20 M. born, and was e. fa.
Rom. 7:13 sin become e. sinful
2 Cor. 4:17 work. e. weight glory
9:14 for e. grace of God in you
Eph. 1:19 e. greatness
2:7 might show e. riches of gra.
3:20 is able to do e. abundantly
1 Tim. 1:14 grace of L. e. abund.
1 Pet. 4:13 be glad al. with e. joy
2 Pet. 1:4 e. great promises
Jude 24 you faultless with e. joy
Rev. 16:21 the pla. was e. great

**EXCEEDINGLY.**

Gen. 7:19 the waters prevailed e.
13:13 men of S. were sinners e.
16:10 I will multiply thy seed e.
17:2 I will multiply thee e.
20 I will multiply Ishmael e. a
27:33 and Isaac trembled very e.
30:43 Jacob increased e. 47:27

2 *Sam.* 13:15 Amnon hated her *e.*
2 *K.* 10:4 elders Samaria *e.* afraid
1 *Chr.* 29:25 L. magnified Solomon *e.* 2 *Chr.* 1:1
2 *Chr.* 17:12 Jeh. waxed great *e.*
26:8 Uzziah strength. himself *e.*
*Neh.* 2:10 it grieved them *e.*
*Est.* 4:4 queen was *e.* grieved
*Job* 3:22 rejoice *e.* when they find
*Ps.* 68:3 the righteous *e.* rejoice
106:14 lusted *e.* in the wildern.
119:167 testim. I love them *e.*
123:3 *e.* filled with contempt, 4
*Is.* 24:19 the earth is moved *e.*
*Dan.* 7:7 a fourth beast strong *e.*
*Jon.* 1:10 men were *e.* afraid
16 the men feared the Lord *e.*
4:1 it displeased Jonah *e.*
*Mat.* 19:25 they were *e.* afraid
*Mark* 4:41 they feared *e.* and said
15:14 cried out the more *e.*
*Acts* 16:20 these men do *e.* trou.
26:11 being *e.* mad against them
27:18 *e.* tossed with a tempest
2 *Cor.* 7:13 and *e.* the more joyed
*Gal.* 1:14 *e.* zealous of the tradit.
1 *Thes.* 3:10 praying *e.*
2 *Thes.* 1:3 your faith groweth *e.*
*Heb.* 12:21 Moses said, I *e.* fear

**EXCEL.**

*Gen.* 49:4 unsta. as wa. sh. not *e.*
1 *Chr.* 15:21 with harps on Sh. *e.*
*Ps.* 103:20 that *e.* in strength
*Is.* 10:10 images did *e.* them
1 *Cor.* 14:12 seek that ye may *e.*

**EXCELLED, EST.**

1 *K.* 4:30 Sol's wisdom *e.* Egypt
*Prov.* 31:29 but thou *e.* them all

**EXCELLETH.**

*Ec.* 2:13 wis. *e.* folly, light *e.* da.
2 *Cor.* 3:10 reason of glory that *e.*

**EXCELLENCY.**

*Gen.* 49:3 *e.* of dignity, *e.* of pow.
*Ex.* 15:7 greatness of thine *e.*
*Deut.* 33:26 who rideth in his *e.*
29 who is the sword of thy *e.*
*Job* 4:21 their *e.* go away?
13:11 his *e.* make afraid?
20:6 *e.* mount up to the heavens
37:4 thunder, with voice of h. *e.*
40:10 deck with majesty and *e.*
*Ps.* 47:4 the *e.* of Jacob
62:4 cast him down from his *e.*
68:34 his *e.* is over Israel
*Ec.* 7:12 the *e.* of knowledge is
*Is.* 13:19 beauty of the Chald. *e.*
35:2 *e.* of Carmel, *e.* of our God
60:15 I make thee an eternal *e.*
*Ezek.* 24:21 the *e.* of your streng.
*Amos* 6:8 I abhor the *e.* of Jacob
8:7 L. hath sworn by *e.* of Jacob
*Nah.* 2:2 *e.* of Jacob, the *e.* of Is.
1 *Cor.* 2:1 not with *e.* speech
2 *Cor.* 4:7 that *e.* of pow. may be
*Phile.* 3:8 all things lost for *e.*

**EXCELLENT.**

*Est.* 1:4 showed *e.* majesty
*Job* 37:23 Almighty is *e.* in power
*Ps.* 8:1 how *e.* thy name! 9
16:3 *e.* in wh. is all my delight
36:7 how *e.* is thy loving-kind.
76:4 more *e.* than the mountains
141:5 it shall be an *e.* oil
148:13 Lord, his name alone is *e.*
150:2 accord. to his *e.* greatness
*Prov.* 8:6 will speak of *e.* things
12:26 righte. more *e.* th. neigh.
17:7 *e.* speech become. n. a fool
*Cant.* 5:15 countenance *e.*
*Is.* 4:2 fruit of earth shall be *e.*
12:5 L. hath done *e.* things
28:29 L. of hosts *e.* in working
*Ezek.* 16:7 come to *e.* ornaments
*Dan* 2:31 whose brightn. was *e.*
4:36 *e.* majesty was added unto
5:12 *e.* spirit found in D. 6:3
14 *e.* wisdom is found in thee
*Luke* 1:3 most *e.* Theophilus
*Acts* 23:26 the *e.* governor Felix
*Rom.* 2:18 approvest things more *e.* *Phile.* 1:10
1 *Cor.* 12:31 show I a more *e.* way
*Heb.* 1:4 obtained a more *e.* name
8:6 obtained a more *e.* ministry
11:4 A. offered more *e.* sacrifice
2 *Pet.* 1:17 voice from the *e.* glo.

**EXCEPT.**

*Gen.* 32:26 not go *e.* thou bless
42:15 *e.* young. bro. come. 43:3, 5
*Num.* 16:13 *e.* make thyself a pr.
*Deut.* 32:30 *e.* their Rock had sold
*Jos.* 7:12 *e.* you destroy accursed
1 *Sam.* 25:34 *e.* thou hadst hasted
2 *Sam.* 3:13 *e.* thou first bring M.
5:6 *e.* thou take away the blind
2 *K.* 4:24 slack not riding, *e.*
*Est.* 2:14 *e.* king delighted.
4:11 *e.* king hold golden sceptre
*Ps.* 127:1 *e.* L. build, *e.* L. keep
*Prov.* 4:16 sleep not *e.* done mis.
*Is.* 1:9 *e.* L. left remn. *Rom.* 9:29
*Dan.* 3:28 nor wors. god, *e.* o. G.
*Dan.* 6:5 *e.* find it con. law of
*Amos* 3:3 two walk *e.* agreed?
*Mat.* 5:20 *e.* righteousness exc.
12:29 *e.* bind str. m. *Mark* 3:27
18:3 I say to you *e.* ye be conv.
19:9 put away wife *e.* for forni.
24:22 *e.* day be short, *Mark* 13:20
26:42 may not pass *e.* I drink
*Mark* 7:3 Phar. *e.* wash oft
*Luke* 9:13 *e.* we go and buy meat
13:2 *e.* ye repent, ye shall per. 5
*John* 3:2 *e.* G. be with him
3 *e.* a man be born again
3:5 *e.* a man be born of water
27 nothing *e.* it be given
4:48 *e.* ye see signs and wonders
6:44 *e.* the Father draw him
53 *e.* ye eat fle. of the S. of m.
65 *e.* it were given him
12:24 *e.* a corn of wheat fall into
15:4 ye cannot bear fruit *e.* ye
19:11 no power *e.* it were given
20:25 *e.* I see print of the nails
*Acts* 8:1 all scat. *e.* the apostles
31 *e.* some man guide me?
15:1 *e.* ye be circumcised
24:21 *e.* it be for this one voice
26:29 all as I am, *e.* these bonds
27:31 *e.* these abide in ship
*Rom.* 7:7 not known lust *e.* law
10:15 how preach *e.* they be sent
1 *Cor.* 14:5 with tongues *e.* he in.
6 *e.* I shall speak by revelation
7 *e.* they gave distinction
9 *e.* ye utter words easy under.
15:36 not quickened *e.* it die
2 *Cor.* 12:13 *e.* I was not burden.
13:5 *e.* ye be reprobates?
2 *Thes.* 2:3 *e.* come a falling aw.
2 *Tim.* 2:5 not crowned, *e.* he st.
*Rev.* 2:5 remove candle *e.* th. rep.
22 tribulation *e.* they repent

**EXCEPTED.**

1 *Cor.* 15:27 is *e.* who put things

**EXCESS.**

*Mat.* 23:25 within are full of *e.*
*Eph.* 5:18 wine, wherein is *e.*
1 *Pet.* 4:3 lusts, and *e.* of wine
4 ye run not to the same *e.*

**EXCHANGE.**

*Gen.* 47:17 Jos. gave bread in *e.*
*Lev.* 27:10 *e.* thereof shall be
*Job* 28:17 *e.* sh. not be for jewels
*Mat.* 16:26 wh. sh. a man give in *e.* for his soul? *Mark* 8:37

**EXCHANGE, Verb.**

*Ezek.* 48:14 nor *e.* first-fruits

**EXCHANGERS.**

*Mat.* 25:27 to put money to *e.*

**EXCLUDE, D.**

*Rom.* 3:27 boasting? it is *e.*
*Gal.* 4:17 they would *e.* you

**EXCUSE.**

*Luke* 14:18 began to make *e.*
*Rom.* 1:20 so they are without *e.*

**EXCUSE, Verb.**

2 *Cor.* 12:19 think you we *e.* our.

**EXCUSED, ING.**

*Luke* 14:18 have me *e.* 19
*Rom.* 2:15 thoughts accus. or *e.*

**EXECRATION.**

*Jer.* 42:18 and ye shall be an *e.*
44:12 an *e.* and reproach

**EXECUTE.**

*Ex.* 12:12 will *e.* judgment
*Num.* 5:30 priest shall *e.* upon
8:11 that they may *e.* service
*Deut.* 10:18 doth *e.* judg. of wid.
*Ps.* 119:84 when wilt thou *e.*
149:7 to *e.* venge. upon heathen
9 to *e.* the judgment written
*Jer.* 7:5 *e.* judg. between man and
21:12 *e.* judgm. in the morning
22:3 *e.* judgm. and righteousn.
23:5 branch shall *e.* judg. 33:15
*Ezek.* 5:8 will *e.* judg. in thee, 10
15 when I shall *e.* judg. in thee
11:9 I will *e.* judg. among you
25:11 I will *e.* judg. upon Moab
17 I will *e.* venge. upon them
30:14 and *e.* judgments in No
19 thus I will *e.* judg. in Egypt
45:9 *e.* judgment and justice
*Hos.* 11:9 not *e.* the fierceness
*Mic.* 5:15 and I will *e.* vengeance
7:9 and *e.* judgment for me
*Zec.* 7:9 *e.* true judgment
8:16 *e.* the judgment of truth
*John* 5:27 given authority to *e.*
*Rom.* 13:4 minister of G. *e.* wrath
*Jude* 15 to *e.* judgment on all

**EXECUTED.**

*Num.* 33:4 on gods the L. *e.* judg.
*Deut.* 33:21 he *e.* justice of the L.
2 *Sam.* 8:15 D. *e.* ju. 1 *Chr.* 18:14
1 *Chr.* 6:10 *e.* the priest's office
24:2 E. and Ith. *e.* priest's office
*Ezr.* 7:26 let judg. be *e.* speedily
*Ps.* 106:30 Phinehas, and *e.* judg.
*Ec.* 8:11 sentence not *e.* speedily
*Jer.* 23:20 anger of the L. have *e.*
*Ezek.* 11:12 nei. *e.* my judg. 20:24
18:8 *e.* true judg. bet. man, 17
23:10 they had *e.* judg. upon her
28:22 I shall have *e.* judg. 26
39:21 shall see judg. I have *e.*
*Luke* 1:8 wh. Z. *e.* priest's office

**EXECUTEDST.**

1 *Sam.* 28:18 nor *e.* wrath on A.

**EXECUTEST, ETH.**

*Ps.* 9:16 is known by judg. he *e.*
99:4 thou *e.* judgment in Jacob
103:6 Lord *e.* right. and judgm.
146:7 L. *e.* judgm. for the oppr.
*Is.* 46:11 that *e.* my counsel
*Jer.* 5:1 if any *e.* judgment
*Joel* 2:11 he is str. that *e.* word

**EXECUTING.**

2 *Chr.* 11:14 Jero. cast off from *e.*
22:8 J. *e.* judg. on Ahab's house

**EXECUTION, ER.**

*Est.* 9:1 decree to be put in *e.*
*Mark* 6:27 king sent an *e.*

**EXEMPTED.**

1 *K.* 15:22 a procla. none was *e.*

**EXERCISE.**

1 *Tim.* 4:8 bodily *e.* profit. little

**EXERCISE, Verb.**

*Ps.* 131:1 nor do I *e.* things
*Jer.* 9:24 L. which *e.* loving-kind.

*Mat.* 20:25 princes of the Gen. *e.* dominion, that are great *e.* autho. *Mark* 10:42; *Lu.* 22:25
*Acts* 24:16 I *e.* mys. to have cons.
1 *Tim.* 4:7 *e.* thyself to godliness

**EXERCISED, ETH.**

*Ec.* 1:13 sore trav. to be *e.* 3:10
*Ezek.* 22:29 peo. of land *e.* robb.
*Heb.* 5:14 senses *e.* to disc. good
12:11 fruit of right. to them *e.*
2 *Pet.* 2:14 heart *e.* with covetous
*Rev.* 13:12 *e.* power of first beast

**EXHORT.**

*Acts* 2:40 many words did he *e.*
27:22 I *e.* you to be of good ch.
1 *Thes.* 4:1 brethren, and *e.* you
5:14 now we *e.* you, warn unru.
2 *Thes.* 3:12 comm. and *e.* by C.
1 *Tim.* 2:1 I *e.* that first of all
6:2 these things teach and *e.*
2 *Tim.* 4:2 *e.* with long-suffering
*Tit.* 1:9 may be able to *e.* and co.
2:6 young men *e.* to be sober
9 *e.* servants to be obedient
15 speak, *e.* and rebuke
*Heb.* 3:13 *e.* one another daily
1 *Pet.* 5:1 the elders am. you I *e.*
*Jude* 3 for me to write and *e.*

**EXHORTATION.**

*Luke* 3:18 many things in *e.*
*Acts* 13:15 ye have word of *e.* say
20:2 when P. had given much *e.*
*Rom.* 12:8 exhort. let wait on *e.*
1 *Cor.* 14:3 speak. unto men to *e.*
2 *Cor.* 8:17 he accepted the *e.*
1 *Thes.* 2:3 *e.* was not of deceit
1 *Tim.* 4:13 give attendance to *e.*
*Heb.* 12:5 ye have forgot. the *e.*
13:22 suffer the word of *e.*

**EXHORTED, ING.**

*Acts* 11:23 B. *e.* to cleave to Lord
14:22 *e.* them to con. in fai.
15:32 *e.* brethren with m. words
18:27 breth. wrote *e.* disciples
*Heb.* 10:25 but *e.* one anoth. and
1 *Pet.* 5:12 by S. I have written *e.*
1 *Thes.* 2:11 you know how we *e.*

**EXILE.**

2 *Sam.* 15:19 a stranger and an *e.*
*Is.* 51:14 captive *e.* hasteneth

**EXORCISTS.**

*Acts* 19:13 vagabond Jews, *e.*

**EXPECTATION.**

*Ps.* 9:18 *e.* of poor shall not per.
62:5 wait on G. my *e.* from him
*Prov.* 10:28 *e.* of wicked, 11:7
11:23 *e.* of the wicked is wrath
23:18 *e.* sh. not be cut off, 24:14
*Is.* 20:5 be ashamed of their *e.*
6 behold, such is our *e.*
*Zec.* 9:5 her *e.* shall be ashamed
*Luke* 3:15 as peo. were in *e.* J.
*Acts* 12:11 delivered fr. *e.* of Jews
*Rom.* 8:19 *e.* of creature waiteth
*Phil.* 1:20 my earnest *e.*

**EXPECTED, ING.**

*Jer.* 29:11 to give an *e.* end
*Acts* 3:5 *e.* to receive something
*Heb.* 10:13 *e.* enemies be made

**EXPEDIENT.**

*John* 11:50 *e.* for us one man die
16:7 *e.* for you that I go away
18:14 *e.* that one man die for pe.
1 *Cor.* 6:12 all things not *e.* 10:23
2 *Cor.* 8:10 *e.* for you who begun
12:1 it is not *e.* for me to glory

**EXPEL, LED.**

*Jos.* 13:13 Is. *e.* not Geshurites
23:5 G. shall *e.* them before you
*Jud.* 1:20 he *e.* three sons of A.
11:7 ye *e.* me out of house?
2 *Sam.* 14:14 his banish. be not *e.*
*Acts* 13:50 *e.* them out of coasts

**EXPENSES.**

*Ezr.* 6:4 *e.* be given out
8 I decree that *e.* be given to

**EXPERIENCE.**

*Gen.* 30:27 by *e.* the Lord blessed
*Ec.* 1:16 my heart had *e.* of wis.
*Rom.* 5:4 worketh *e.* and *e.*

**EXPERIMENT.**

2 *Cor.* 9:13 by *e.* of this minist.

**EXPERT.**

1 *Chr.* 12:33 Zeb. 50,000 *e.* in war
35 Danites *e.* in war: 36 Asher
*Cant.* 3:8 hold swords, *e.* in war
*Jer.* 50:9 shall be as *e.* man
*Acts* 26:3 know thee *e.* in custo.

**EXPIRED.**

1 *Sam.* 18:26 the days were not *e.*
2 *Sam.* 11:1 y. was *e.* 1 *Chr.* 20:1
1 *Chr.* 17:11 come wh. days be *e.*
2 *Chr.* 36:10 when year *e.* Neb.
*Est.* 1:5 when days were *e.*
*Ezek.* 43:27 when days are *e.*
*Acts* 7:30 forty years were *e.*
*Rev.* 20:7 1000 years *e.* S. loosed

**EXPLOITS.**

*Dan.* 11:28 he shall do *e.*
32 shall be strong and do *e.*

**EXPOUND, ED.**

*Jud.* 14:14 could not *e.* riddle
14:19 garments to them who *e.*
*Mark* 4:34 when alone *e.* all th.
*Luke* 24:27 *e.* to them all script.,
*Acts* 11:4 but Peter *e.* it by order
18:26 Aq. and Pris. *e.* to him
28:23 Paul *e.* the kingdom of G.

**EXPRESS.**

*Heb.* 1:3 being *e.* image of person

**EXPRESS, ED.**

*Num.* 1:17 took men *e.* by names
1 *Chr.* 12:31 M. 18,000 *e.* by name
16:41 who were *e.* by name
2 *Chr.* 28:15 men *e.* took captives
31:19 *e.* to give portions
*Ezr.* 8:20 Nethinim *e.* by name

**EXPRESSLY.**

1 *Sam.* 20:21 if I *e.* say to the lad
*Ezek.* 1:3 word came *e.* to Ezek.
1 *Tim.* 4:1 Spirit speak. *e.* some

**EXTEND, ED.**

*Ezr.* 7:28 *e.* mercy; 9:9 to us
*Ps.* 109:12 be none to *e.* mercy
*Is.* 66:12 will *e.* peace like river

**EXTENDETH.**

*Ps.* 16:2 goodness *e.* not to thee

**EXTINCT.**

*Job* 17:1 my days are *e.*
*Is.* 43:17 are *e.* they quenched

**EXTOL, LED.**

*Ps.* 30:1 I will *e.* thee, O Lord
66:17 he was *e.* with my tongue
68:4 *e.* him that rideth on heav.
145:1 I will *e.* thee, my God
*Is.* 52:13 my servant shall be *e.*
*Dan.* 4:37 I Nebuchad. *e.* King

**EXTORTION, ER, ERS.**

*Ps.* 109:11 *e.* catch all he hath
*Is.* 16:4 *e.* at an end, the spoiler
*Ezek.* 22:12 has gained by *e.*
*Mat.* 23:25 they are full of *e.*
*Luke* 18:11 not as other men, *e.*
1 *Cor.* 5:10 not altogether with *e.*
11 if any be drunkard, an *e.*
6:10 nor *e.* inherit kingd. of G.

**EXTREME.**

*Deut.* 28:22 L. smite with *e.* burn.

**EXTREMITY.**

*Job* 35:15 knoweth not in great *e.*

**EYE.**

*Ex.* 21:24 *e.* for *e.* *Lev.* 24:20; *Deut.* 19:21; *Mat.* 5:38
26 if man smite *e.* of servant
*Lev.* 21:20 hath blemish in *e.*
*Deut.* 28:54 his *e.* shall be evil
56 *e.* shall be evil to. husband
32:10 as apple of his *e.*
34:7 his *e.* was not dim
*Ezr.* 5:5 *e.* of God was on elders
*Job* 7:8 *e.* that hath seen me
10:18 and no *e.* had seen me
20:9 *e.* wh. saw sh. see no more
24:15 *e.* of adulterer waiteth for twil. saying, No *e.* shall see
29:11 wh. *e.* saw me, it gave wi.
*Ps.* 33:18 *e.* of Lord on them
35:19 nei. let them with *e.*
21 aha, aha, our *e.* hath seen it
94:9 formed *e.* sh. he not see?
*Prov.* 10:10 winketh with the *e.*
20:12 the seeing *e.* L. hath made
22:9 bountif. *e.* shall be blessed
30:17 *e.* that mocketh at father
*Ec.* 1:8 *e.* not satisfied
4:8 neither *e.* satis. with riches
*Is.* 13:18 *e.* shall not spare child.
52:8 for they shall see *e.* to *e.*
64:4 nei. hath *e.* seen, 1 *Cor.* 2:9
*Lam.* 2:4 slew all pleasant to *e.*
*Ezek.* 9:5 let not your *e.* spare
*Mic.* 4:11 let our *e.* look on Zion
*Mat.* 6:22 light of the body is the *e.* *Luke* 11:34
7:3 mote in brother's *e.* beam in thine own *e.* *Luke* 6:41, 42
18:9 if *e.* offend thee pluck out
19:24 camel go thro' *e.* of needle, *Mark* 10:25; *Luke* 18:25
1 *Cor.* 12:16 bec. I am not the *e.*
17 the whole body were an *e.*
21 *e.* cannot say
15:52 in twinkling of an *e.*
*Rev.* 1:7 every *e.* shall see him

**Evil EYE.**

*Prov.* 23:6 bread of him hath *e. e.*
28:22 hast. to be rich hath *e. e.*
*Mat.* 6:23 if *e.* be *e.* *Luke* 11:34
20:15 is thine *e. e.*
*Mark* 7:22 of heart proceed. *e. e.*

**Mine EYE.**

1 *Sam.* 24:10 *mine e.* spared thee
*Job* 7:7 *m. e.* shall no more see
13:1 *mine e.* hath seen all this
16:20 *mine e.* pour. tears to God
17:7 *mine e.* is dim by sorrow
42:5 but *mine e.* seeth thee
*Ps.* 6:7 *m. e.* con. with grief, 31:9
32:8 guide thee with *mine e.*
54:7 *mine e.* hath seen his desire
88:9 *mine e.* mourn. by reason
92:11 *mine e.* sh. see my desire
*Lam.* 1:16 *m. e. m. e.* run. 3:48
3:49 *mine e.* trickleth down
51 *mine e.* affecteth my heart
*Ezek.* 5:11 neith. sh. *m. e.* spare, 7:4, 9; 8:18; 9:10; 20:17

**Thine EYE.**

*Deut.* 7:16 *thine e.* sh. not pity, 13:8; 19:13, 21; 25:12
15:9 *thine e.* be evil ag. brother
*Mat.* 6:22 *t. e.* be sing. *Lu.* 11:34
7:3 beam in *th.* own *e.* *Luke* 6:41
18:9 *t. e.* offend, *Mark* 9:47

*See* APPLE.

**EYEBROWS.**

*Lev.* 14:9 shall shave hair off *e.*

**EYELIDS.**

*Job* 16:16 on mine *e.* is shadow
41:18 eyes like *e.* of the morning
*Ps.* 11:4 his *e.* try child. of men
132:4 or slumber to mine *e.*
*Prov.* 4:25 let thine *e.* look
6:4 or slumber to thine *e.*
25 neither let her take with *e.*
30:13 their *e.* are lifted up
*Jer.* 9:18 *e.* may gush with wat.

**Right EYE.**

*Zec.* 11:17 on his *r. e.* his *r. e.* shall be utterly darkened
*Mat.* 5:29 if *r. e.* off. pluck it out

**EYE-SALVE.**
Rev. 3:18 anoint eyes with e.-s.
**EYE-SERVICE.**
Eph. 6:6 not with e.-s. Col. 3:22
**EYESIGHT.**
2 Sam. 22:25 accor. to my cleanness in his e. Ps. 18:24
**EYE-WITNESSES.**
Luke 1:2 from beginning e.-w.
2 Pet. 1:16 were e.-w. of majesty
**EYED.**
1 Sam. 18:9 Saul e. David
**Tender EYED.**
Gen. 29:17 Leah was tender e.
**EYES.**
Gen. 3:6 and pleasant to the e.
7 e. of them both were opened
16:4 mistress was despised in e.
5 I was despised in her e.
20:16 is to thee a covering of e.
21:19 God opened Hagar's e.
39:7 wife cast her e. on Joseph
Gen. 48:10 e. of Israel were dim
Ex. 5:21 abhorred in e. of Phar.
24:17 like fire in e. of Israel
Lev. 4:13 hid from e. of assembly
26:16 burning ague sh. cons. e.
Num. 10:31 instead of e.
20:12 to sanctify me in e. of Is.
22:31 Lord opened e. of Balaam
24:3 man whose e. are open, 15
Deut. 16:19 doth blind e. of wise
28:65 L. shall give failing of e.
Jud. 16:28 avenged for two e.
2 Sam. 6:20 uncov. in e. of hand.
24:3 that e. of king may see it
1 K. 1:20 e. of all Isr. upon thee
2 K. 6:17 L. open. e. of young m.
20 Lord, open e. of these men
25:7 out e. of Z. Jer. 39:7; 52:11
1 Chr. 13:4 right in e. of people
Job 10:4 hast thou e. of flesh?
11:20 e. of the wicked shall fail
17:5 e. of his children shall fail
28:21 hid from the e. of all liv.
29:15 I was e. to the blind
31:16 caused e. of widow to fail
39:29 and her e. behold afar off
Ps. 15:4 in whose e. vile person
19:8 commandment enlighten e.
115:5 e. have they, 135:16
123:2 e. of servant, e. of maiden
145:15 e. of all wait upon thee
146:8 L. openeth e. of the blind
Prov. 10:26 as smo. to e. so slug.
15:30 light of e. rejoiceth heart
17:8 precious stone in e. of him
24 e. of fool in ends of earth
23:29 who hath redness of e.?
27:20 e. of man are never satis.
Ec. 2:14 wise man's e. in head
6:9 better the sight of e. than
11:7 pleasant for e. to behold
Cant. 1:15 thou hast doves' e. 4:1
Is. 3:8 to provoke e. of his glory
16 daugh. of Z. with wanton e.
5:15 e. of lofty shall be humbled
29:18 e. of the blind shall see
32:3 e. of them that see
35:5 then e. of blind sh. be ope.
42:7 open the blind e. to bring
43:8 blind that have e.
52:10 made bare his arm in e. of
59:10 grope as if we had no e.
Jer. 5:21 ha. e. see not, Ezek. 12:2
Ezek. 1:18 rings were full of e.
10:12 the wheels were full of e.
38:23 be known in e. of nations
Dan. 7:8 in horn e. like e. of man
20 that had e. and a mouth
Hab. 1:13 purer e. than beh. evil
Zec. 3:9 upon one stone seven e.
8:6 marvellous in e. of remnant
Mat. 18:9 rather than hav. two e. cast into hell fire, Mark 9:47
Mark 8:18 having e. see ye not?
Luke 4:20 e. of all fast. on him
10:23 blessed are e. which see
John 9:6 anoint. e. of blind man
32 opened e. of one born blind
10:21 can devil open e. of blind
Acts 9:40 Dorcas opened her e.
Rom. 11:8 given e. should not see
Gal. 3:1 before e. Christ been set
Eph. 1:18 e. of your understand.
Heb. 4:13 all things naked to e.
2 Pet. 2:14 e. full of adultery
1 John 2:16 lust of the e. and pri.
Rev. 4:6 four beasts full of e.
8 and were full of e. within
5:6 a Lamb having seven e.

**His EYES.**
Gen. 27:1 Isaac, his e. were dim
49:12 h. e. sh. be red with wine
Num. 24:4 having his e. open, 16
Jud. 16:21 Philist. put out his e.
1 Sam. 3:2 Eli, his e. dim, 4:15
14:27 his e. were enlightened
1 K. 14:4 Ahijah, his e. were set
2 K. 4:34 child, put his e. on h. e.
35 child sneezed, opened his e.
6:17 open his e. that he may see
25:7 slew sons of Zedekiah bef. his e. Jer. 39:6; 52:10
1 Chr. 21:23 k. do good in his e.
Est. 8:5 and I pleasing in his e.
Job 16:9 enemy sharpeneth his e.
21:20 his e. shall see his destruc.
24:23 his e. are on their ways
27:19 the rich man open. his e.
34:21 h. e. are on the ways of m.
36:7 he withdraweth not his e.
40:24 he taketh it with his e.
41:18 his e. are like eyelids of m.
Ps. 10:8 his e. set against poor
11:4 h. e. behold child. of men
36:1 no fear of God before his e.
66:7 his e. behold the nations
Prov. 6:13 he winketh with his e.
Prov. 16:30 he shut. his e. to dev.
20:8 scattereth evil with his e.
21:10 find no favor in h. e.
28:27 hid. his e. sh. have curse
Ec. 8:16 sleep with his e.
Cant. 5:12 his e. are as eyes of d
8:10 in h. e. as one that found
Is. 11:3 after sight of his e.
17:7 his e. have res. to holy One
33:15 shutteth his e. from seeing
Jer. 32:4 his e. shall behold his e.
Ezek. 12:12 see not gr. with his e.
20:7 cast away abomin. of his e.
Dan. 8:5 horn between his e. 21
10:6 his e. were as lamps of fire
Mark 8:23 he had spit on his e.
25 after he put hands on his e.
John 9:14 and opened his e.
21 or who hath opened his e.
Acts 3:4 P. fastening his e. upon
9:8 when his e. were opened
18 there fell from his e. scales
13:9 then Saul set his e. on him
1 John 2:11 dark. hath blind. h. e.
Rev. 1:14 his e. as a flame of fire, 2:18; 19:12
**Lift or lifted up EYES.**
Gen. 13:10 Lot lifted up his e.
14 lift up th. e. and look, 31:12; Deut. 3:27; 2 K. 19:22; Is. 49:18; 60:4; Jer. 3:2; Ezek. 8:5; Zec. 5:5
18:2 Abra. lift up his e. 22:4, 13
24:63 Isaac; 64 Reb. l. up her e.
31:10 Ja. 33:1; 43:29 Jo. l. u. e.
Ex. 14:10 lift up their e. Egypt.
Num. 24:2 Balaam lift up his e.
Deut. 4:19 l. u. e. to heaven
Jos. 5:13 Joshua lifted up his e.
Jud. 19:17 old man lift up his e.
1 Sam. 6:13 lift up e. and saw ark
2 Sam. 13:34 watch. l. u. e. 18:24
1 Chr. 21:16 D. l. up e. saw angel
Job 2:12 they lift up e.
Ps. 121:1 I will lift up mine e.
123:1 to thee lift I up mine e.
Is. 51:6 lift up your e. Ezek. 33:25; John 4:35
Ezek. 18:6 nor l. up e. to idols, 15
12 hath lift up his e. to idols
Dan. 4:34 I Neb. l. up mine e.
8:3 lifted up mine e. 10:5; Zec. 1:18; 2:1; 5:1, 5, 9; 6:1
Mat. 17:8 l. up e. saw no man
Luke 6:20 Jesus lifted up his e. John 6:5; 11:41; 17:1
16:23 in hell he lift up his e.
18:13 not l. up so much as e.
**EYES of the Lord.**
Gen. 6:8 N. found gr. in e. of L.
Deut. 11:12 e. of the L. alw. on it
13:18 do what is right in e. of L.
1 Sam. 26:24 life set by in e. of L.
1 K. 15:5 D. did right in e. of the Lord, 11; 22:43; 2 Chr. 14:2
2 Chr. 16:9 the e. of the Lord run to and fro. Zec. 4:10
Ps. 34:15 e. of the Lord are on the righteous, 1 Pet. 3:12
Prov. 15:3 e. of L. in every place
22:12 e. of the L. preserve kno.
Is. 49:5 glorious in e. of the L.
Amos 9:8 e. of L. are on sin. kin.
**Mine EYES.**
Gen. 31:40 sleep depart. fr. m. e.
44:21 I may set mine e. on him
1 Sam. 12:3 bribe to blind m. e.
14:29 how mine e. enlightened
26:24 life much set by in m. e.
1 K. 1:48 one to sit, m. e. see. it
9:3 mine e. shall be there perpetually, 2 Chr. 7:16
10:7 until m. e. seen it, 2 Chr. 9:6
11:33 to do that which is right in m. e. 14:8; 2 K. 10:30
2 Chr. 7:15 now m. e. sh. be open
Job 4:16 an image was bef. m. e.
19:27 mine e. shall behold
31:1 a covenant with mine e.
31:7 heart walked after m. e.
Ps. 13:3 lighten mine e.
25:15 m. e. are ever toward the
26:3 lov.-kindness is before m. e.
38:10 light of m. e. it is gone
69:3 m. e. fail, whilst I wait for
77:4 thou holdest mine e. wak.
101:3 no evil thing before m. e.
6 mine e. shall be on faithful
116:8 hast deliv. m. e. from tears
119:18 open m. e.; 37 turn m. e.
82 mine e. fail for thy word
123 m. e. fail for thy salvation
136 rivers of wa. run down m. e.
148 m. e. prev. night-watches
131:1 nor mine e. lofty
132:4 not give sleep to mine e.
Ps. 141:8 m. e. are unto thee, O G.
Ec. 2:10 whatso. m. e. desired
Is. 1:15 hide mine e. from you
16 away evil doings from m. e.
6:5 mine e. have seen the King
38:14 mine e. fail with looking
65:12 did evil before mine e. 66:4
Jer. 9:1 m. e. were foun. of tears
13:17 mine e. shall weep sore
14:17 m. e. run down with tears
16:17 m. e. are on their ways, nor their iniq. hid from mine e.
24:6 I will set mine e. on them
Lam. 2:11 m. e. do fail with tears
Hos. 13:14 repent. hid from m. e.
Amos 9:4 set mine e. on them
Mic. 7:10 mine e. shall behold
Zec. 8:6 marvellous in mine e.
12:4 open mine e. on house of J.
Luke 2:30 mine e. have seen
John 9:11 J. anointed mine e. 15
30 yet he hath opened mine e.
Acts 11:6 when I had fast. m. e.

**Our EYES.**
Num. 11:6 manna before our e.

*Deut.* 6:22 signs before *our e.*
21:7 nor have *our e.* seen it
2 *Chr.* 20:12 *our e.* are upon thee
*Ezr.* 9:8 our God lighten *our e.*
*Ps.* 118:23 marvellous in *our e.* *Mat.* 21:42; *Mark* 12:11
123:2 *our e.* wait upon Lord
*Jer.* 9:18 *our e.* run with tears
*Lam.* 4:17 *our e.* as yet failed
5:17 for these things *o. e.* are dim
*Joel* 1:16 meat cut before *our e.?*
*Mat.* 20:33 that *our e.* be opened
1 *John* 1:1 have seen with *our e.*

**Own EYES.**

*Num.* 15:39 seek not after *own e.*
*Deut.* 12:8 what is right in his *own e. Jud.* 17:6; 21:25
*Neh.* 6:16 ene. cast down in *o. e.*
*Job* 32:1 because righteous in *o. e.*
*Ps.* 36:2 he flattereth him. in *o. e.*
*Prov.* 3:7 be not wise in *own e.*
12:15 way of fools is right in *o. e.*
16:2 ways of man clean in *o. e.*
21:2 way of man is right in *o. e.*
30:12 generat. pure in their *o. e.*
*Is.* 5:21 woe to them wise in *o. e.*
*Gal.* 4:15 would have plucked *o. e.*

**Their EYES.**

*Gen.* 42:24 bound S. before *t. e.*
*Ex.* 8:26 abom. of E. before *t. e.*
*Lev.* 20:4 any ways hide *their e.*
*Num.* 20:8 speak to rock bef. *t. e.*
27:14 sanctify at water bef. *t. e.*
*Ezr.* 3:12 founda. laid before *t. e.*
*Job* 21:8 offspring before *their e.*
*Ps.* 17:11 they have set *their e.*
69:23 let *their e.* be darkened
73:7 *their e.* stand out
*Prov.* 29:13 L. lighten. both *t. e.*
30:13 O how lofty are *their e.*
*Ec.* 5:11 behold. them with *t. e.*
*Is.* 6:10 shut *t. e.* lest see with *t. e. Mat.* 13:15; *Acts* 28:27
44:18 for he hath shut *their e.*
*Jer.* 14:6 *their e.* did fail because
*Ezek.* 6:9 with *t. e.* wh. go whor.
21:6 bitterness sigh before *t. e.*
22:26 hid *t. e.* from my sabbaths
24:25 desire of *their e.*
36:23 be sanctified before *t. e.*
37:20 sticks in thy hand be. *t. e.*
38:16 sanctified, O Gog, bef. *t. e.*
*Zec.* 14:12 and *t. e.* shall consume
*Mat.* 9:29 touched he *their e.*
30 *their e.* were opened
13:15 *their e.* they have closed
20:34 Jesus touched *their e. th. e.* received sight
26:43 *t. e.* were heavy, *Mk.* 14:40
*Luke* 24:16 *their e.* were holden
31 *their e.* were opened
*John* 12:40 he hath blinded *t. e.*
*Acts* 26:18 to open *t. e.* and to
*Rom.* 3:18 no fear of G. bef. *t. e.*
11:10 let *their e.* be darkened
*Rev.* 7:17 all tears from *t. e.* 21:4

**Thine EYES.**

*Gen.* 30:27 found favor in *thine e.*
46:4 J. put his hand on *thine e.*
47:19 shall we die before *thine e.*
*Ex.* 13:9 memorial between *t. e.*
16 frontlets betw. *t. e. Deut.* 6:8
*Deut.* 3:21 *thine e.* have seen all
27 lift up *t. e.* behold it with *t. e.*
4:9 forget things wh. *t. e.* have
7:19 temptations *t. e.* saw, 29:3
10:21 things which *thine e.* seen
28:31 shall be slain before *t. e.*
32 *thine e.* shall look, and fail
34 for the sight of *thine e.* 67
34:4 to see with *thine e.*
*Ruth* 2:9 let *t. e.* be on the field
10 have I found grace in *t. e.?*
1 *Sam.* 2:33 to consume *thine e.*
24:10 *t. e.* seen how L. delivered
25:8 men find favor in *thine e.*
26:21 soul precious in *thine e.*
27:5 found grace in *thine e.*
2 *Sam.* 12:11 thy wives be. *t. e.*
22:28 *t. e.* are on the haughty
1 *K.* 8:29 *t. e.* open toward this house, 52; 2 *Chr.* 6:20, 40
20:6 is pleasant in *thine e.*
2 *K.* 7:2 thou shalt see it with *t. e.*
10:5 what is good in *thine e.*
19:16 open Lord *t. e. Is.* 37:17
22:20 *t. e.* shall not see all evil
1 *Chr.* 17:17 small thing in *t. e.*
2 *Chr.* 34:28 nor shall *thine e.* see
*Neh.* 1:6 let *thine e.* open
*Job* 7:8 *thine e.* are upon me
11:4 I am clean in *thine e.*
14:3 dost thou open *t. e.* on such?
15:12 what do *t. e.* wink at?
*Ps.* 31:22 cut off from be. *t. e.*
50:21 set in order before *t. e.*
91:8 with *t. e.* shalt thou behold
139:16 *t. e.* did see my substance
*Prov.* 4:25 let *thine e.* look right
6:4 give not sleep to *thine e.*
20:13 open *thine e.* and thou
23:5 set *t. e.* on that wh. is not?
26 let *thine e.* observe my ways
33 *t. e.* shall beh. strange wom.
25:7 prince whom *t. e.* have seen
*Ec.* 11:9 walk in sight of *thine e.*
*Cant.* 4:9 ravished heart with *t. e.*
6:5 turn away *thine e.* from me
7:4 *thine e.* like the fish-pools
*Is.* 30:20 *t. e.* shall see teachers
33:17 *thine e.* shall see king
20 *t. e.* see Jeru. quiet habitat.
*Jer.* 5:3 are not *t. e.* on truth?
20:4 fall by sword *t. e.* behold it
22:17 *t. e.* are not but for covet.
31:16 refrain *thine e.* from tears
32:19 *t. e.* open on ways of men
34:3 *t. e.* behold king of Bab.
42:2 as *thine e.* do behold us
*Lam.* 2:18 let not apple of *t. e.*
*Ezek.* 23:40 for wh. paintedst *t. e.*
24:16 take fr. thee desire of *t. e.*
40:4 behold with *thine e.* 44:5
*Dan.* 9:18 open *t. e.* and behold
*Luke* 19:42 now hid from *thine e.*
*John* 9:10 were *t. e.* opened? 26
17 he hath opened *thine e.?*
*Rev.* 3:18 anoint *thine e.*

**Your EYES.**

*Gen.* 3:5 day eat *y. e.* be opened
19:8 them as is good in *your e.*
34:11 Let me find grace in *y. e.*
12 *y. e.* and eyes of brother
50:4 found grace in *your e.*
*Num.* 33:55 ye let remain shall be pricks in *y. e. Jos.* 23:13
*Deut.* 1:30 that he did before *y. e.* 4:34; 29:2
4:3 *your e.* have seen what Lord did, 11:7; *Jos.* 24:7
9:17 I brake two tables bef. *y. e.*
11:18 as frontlets between *y. e.*
14:1 not make boldness bet. *y. e.*
1 *Sam.* 11:2 thrust out *y.* right *e.*
12:16 what Lord do before *y. e.*
2 *Chr.* 29:8 as see with *your e.*
*Is.* 29:10 Lord hath closed *y. e.*
40:26 lift up *y. e. Jer.* 13:20
*Jer.* 7:11 den of robbers in *y. e.*
29:21 slay them before *your e.*
*Ezek.* 24:21 the desire of *your e.*
*Hag.* 2:3 in *your e.* in comparison
*Mal.* 1:5 *your e.* shall see, the L.
*Mat.* 13:16 blessed are *your e.*

EZEKIEL. *Ezek.* 24:24
EZEL. 1 *Sam.* 20:19
EZRA. *Ezr.* 7:12, 25; 10:1; *Neh.* 8:2, 6; 12:13, 26, 36

# F

**FABLES.**

1 *Tim.* 1:4 nor give heed to *f.*
4:7 but refuse old wives' *f.*
2 *Tim* 4:4 shall be turned unto *f.*
*Tit.* 1:14 not giving heed to *f.*
2 *Pet.* 1:16 cunningly devised *f.*

**FACE.**

*Gen.* 3:19 in sweat of *f.* shall eat
16:8 I flee from *f.* of mistress
24:47 I put ear-rings upon her *f.*
35:1 fleddest from *f.* of Esau, 7
36:6 E. went from *f.* of brot. J.
46:28 to direct his *f.* to Goshen
48:12 J. bowed with *f.* to earth
*Ex.* 2:15 Moses fled *f.* of Pharaoh
14:25 let us flee from *f.* of Israel
34:29 skin of his *f.* shone, 30, 35
*Ex.* 34:33 he put a veil on his *f.*
*Lev.* 13:41 hair fallen tow. his *f.*
19:32 shalt honor *f.* of old man
*Num.* 12:14 father had spit in *f.*
19:3 slay red heifer before *f.*
*Deut.* 1:17 not be af. of *f.* of man
8:20 nations L. destroyed bef. *f.*
25:2 wicked be beaten bef. his *f.*
9 and spit in his *f.* and say
28:31 ass sh. be taken bef. thy *f.*
*Jos.* 7:10 wheref. liest upon *f.?*
1 *Sam.* 5:3 D. falleth on his *f.* 4
24:8 D. stooped with *f.* to earth
25:41 Abigail bowed on *f.*
28:14 stooped with *f.* to ground
2 *Sam.* 2:22 hold up my *f.* to J.?
14:33 A. bowed on *f.* to ground
24:20 Araunah bowed himself bef. king on *f.* 1 *Chr.* 21:21
1 *K.* 1:23 Nathan bowed with *f.*
31 B.-sheba bowed with her *f.*
8:14 turned his *f.* 2 *Chr.* 6:3
18:42 E. put *f.* between knees
19:13 wrapped his *f.* in mantle
20:38 prophet disg. ashes on *f.*
21:4 Ahab turned away his *f.*
2 *K.* 4:29 lay staff on *f.* of child
31 G. laid his staff on *f.* of child
8:15 Hazael spread it on his *f.*
9:30 Jezebel painted her *f.*
32 J. lifted up his *f.* to window
13:14 Joash wept over his *f.*
20:2 H. turn. *f.* to wall, *Is.* 38:2
2 *Chr.* 6:42 turn not away the *f.* of thine anointed, *Ps.* 132:10
30:9 L. will not turn *f.* from you
32:21 returned with shame of *f.*
35:22 Jos. would not turn his *f.*
*Ezr.* 9:6 I blush to lift up my *f.*
7 confusion of *f. Dan.* 9:8
*Job* 1:11 will curse thee to *f.* 2:5
4:15 a spirit passed before my *f.*
11:15 lift up *f.* without spot
16:8 leanness beareth wit. to *f.*
16 my *f.* is foul with weeping
21:31 who declare his way to *f.?*
22:26 lift up thy *f.* unto God
24:15 and disguiseth his *f.*
26:9 he holdeth back *f.* of throne
30:10 spare not to spit in my *f.*
41:13 who discover *f.* of garm.?
14 can open doors of his *f.?*
*Ps.* 5:8 way straight before my *f.*
17:15 I will beh. thy *f.* in right.
21:12 make ready arrows ag. *f.*
41:12 set. me before thy *f.*
84:9 look upon *f.* of th. anoint.

89:14 mercy and truth go bef. *f.*
*Prov.* 7:13 with an impudent *f.*
21:29 wicked man hard. his *f.*
*Ec.* 8:1 boldness of *f.* be chang.
*Is.* 16:4 the *f.* of the spoiler
25:7 will destroy *f.* of covering
28:25 made plain the *f.* thereof
29:22 nei. shall his *f.* wax pale
49:23 shall bow to thee with *f.*
65:3 that provoketh me to my *f.*
*Jer.* 2:27 turn. back, not *f.* 32:33
4:30 thou rentest *f.* with paint
13:26 thy skirts upon thy *f.* that shame may appear. *Nah.* 3:5
18:17 the back, and not the *f.*
22:25 whose *f.* thou fearest
*Lam.* 3:35 right of man before *f.*
*Ezek.* 1:10 *f.* of man, *f.* of lion, *f.* of an ox, the *f.* of an eagle
3:8 made thy *f.* strong ag. faces
7:22 my *f.* will I turn fr. them
10:14 *f.* of man, lion, eag. 41:19
14:3 stumbling-block before *f.*
38:18 fury shall come in my *f.*
*Dan.* 8:18 in a sleep on *f.* 10:9
10:6 *f.* as appear. of lightning
11:18 turn *f.* unto the isles
*Hos.* 5:5 Is. testifieth to *f.* 7:10
*Joel* 2:6 before *f.* people be pain.
20 will drive him with his *f.*
*Nah.* 2:1 dasheth come before *f.*
*Mat.* 6:17 anoint head, wash *f.*
11:10 I send my messenger bef. thy *f.* *Mark* 1:2; *Luke* 7:27
18:10 angels behold *f.* of my F.
26:67 did they spit in his face
*Luke* 2:31 hast prepared bef. *f.*
9:52 messengers before *f.* 10:1
53 *f.* as tho' he would go to J.
22:64 they struck him on the *f.*
*John* 11:44 *f.* bound with napkin
*Acts* 2:25 I foresaw L. bef. my *f.*
7:45 G. drave before *f.* of fath.
1 *Cor.* 14:25 falling down on *f.*
2 *Cor.* 3:7 could not behold *f.*
13 M. who put a veil over *f.*
18 with open *f.* beholding
4:6 glory of God in *f.* of Jesus
11:20 if man smite you on *f.*
*Gal.* 1:22 unkn. by *f.* to churches
2:11 I withstood him to the *f.*
*Jam.* 1:23 natural *f.* in glass
*Rev.* 4:7 beast had *f.* as a man
10:1 *f.* was as it were the sun
12:14 nourished from *f.* of serp.
20:11 from whose *f.* heaven fled

*See* SEEK, SET, SHINE, SKY, WATERS, WILDERNESS, WORLD.

**FACE, *with* cover, *or* covered.**
*Gen.* 38:15 harlot bec. she *c. f.*
*Ex.* 10:5 locusts *c. f.* of earth, 15
*Num.* 22:5 *cover f.* of the earth
2 *Sam.* 19:4 *c.* his *f.* and cried
*Est.* 7:8 *covered* Haman's *f.*
*Job* 15:27 *c.* his *f.* with fatness
23:17 *c.* darkness from my *f.*
*Ps.* 44:15 shame of my *f.* hath *c.*
69:7 shame *cov.* my *f.*
*Prov.* 24:31 nettles had *c. f.*
*Is.* 6:2 with twain he *c. f.*
*Ezek.* 12:6 thou shalt *c.* thy *f.*
12 the prince shall *c.* his *f.*
*Mark* 14:65 to spit and *c.* his *f.*

**FACE of the country.**
2 *Sam.* 18:8 scattered over *f. of c.*

**FACE of the deep.**
*Gen.* 1:2 darkness upon *f. of t. d.*
*Job* 38:30 *f. of the deep* is frozen
*Prov.* 8:27 compass on *f. of the d.*

**FACE of the earth.**
*Gen.* 1:29 herb on *f. of the earth*
4:14 driven me from *f. of the e.*
6:1 multiply on *f. of the earth*
7:3 seed alive on *f. of* all *the e.*
4 destroy from *f. of the e. Deut.* 6:15; 1 *K.* 13:34; *Amos* 9:8
8:9 on the *f. of the* whole *earth*
11:4 we be scat. on *f. of the e.*
41:56 famine over the *f. of the e.*
*Num.* 12:3 abo. all on *f. of the e.*
*Deut.* 7:6 peo. on the *f. of the e.*
1 *Sam.* 20:15 off from *f. of the e.*
*Ps.* 104:30 renewest *f. of the e.*
*Is.* 23:17 kingd. on *f. of the earth*
*Jer.* 8:2 on the *f. of the e.* 16:4
*Ezek.* 38:20 all on *f. of the earth*
*Dan.* 8:5 came on *f. of the earth*
*Amos* 5:8 pour. on *f. of the e.* 9:6
*Zec.* 5:3 curse over *f. of the earth*
*Luke* 12:56 can discern *f. of the e.*
21:35 on the *f. of the* whole *e.*
*Acts* 17:26 to dwell on *f. of the e.*

**FACE to FACE.**
*Gen.* 32:30 I have seen G. *f. to f.*
*Ex.* 33:11 L. spake to M. *f. to f.*
*Num.* 14:14 Lord art seen *f. to f.*
*Deut.* 5:4 talked with you *f. to f*
34:10 M. whom L. knew *f. to f*
*Jud.* 6:22 seen angel *f. to f.*
*Prov.* 27:19 *f.* answereth *to f.*
*Ezek.* 20:35 I will plead *f. to f.*
*Acts* 25:16 have accusers *f. to f.*
1 *Cor.* 13:12 a glass, but *f. to f.*
2 *John* 12 and speak *f. to f.*
3 *John* 14 and speak *f. to f.*

**Fell on FACE, *or* FACES.**
*Gen.* 50:1 J. *f. on* his father's *f.*
18 brethren *fell* d. before his *f.*
*Lev.* 9:24 they *fell on* their *f.*
*Num.* 14:5 A. *f. on f.* 16:22, 45
16:4 Moses; 22:31 B. *f.* flat *on f.*
*Jos.* 5:14 Joshua *f. on* his *f.* 7:6
*Jud.* 13:20 M. and wife *fell on f*
1 *Sam.* 17:49 Gol.; 20:41 D. *f. on f.*
25:23 Abig.; 2 *Sam.* 9:6 Mephib.
2 *Sam.* 14:4 wo. of T. *f. on* her *f.*
22 Joab; 18:28 Ahimaaz *f. on f.*
1 *K.* 18:7 Obad.; 39 peo. *f. on f.*
*Ezek.* 1:28 *f. on* my *f.* 3:23; 9:8; 11:13; 43:3; 44:4; *Dan.* 8:17
*Dan.* 2:46 Nebuch. *f. upon* his *f.*
*Mat.* 17:6 disci.; 26:39 J. *f. on f.*
*Luke* 5:12 leper; 17:16 S. *f. on f.*
*Rev.* 11:16 24 elders *f. on* their *f.*

**FACE of the field.**
2 *K.* 9:37 Jez. dung on *f. of the f.*

**FACE of the gate.**
*Ezek.* 40:15 *f. of the g.* of entrance

**FACE of the ground.**
*Gen.* 2:6 mist watered *f. of the g.*
7:23 destr. that was on *f. of the g.*
8:8 abated from off *f. of the g.*
13 *f. of the ground* was dry

**Hide, hideth, *or* hid FACE.**
*Gen.* 4:14 from thy *f.* sh. I be *h.*
*Ex.* 3:6 and Moses *hid* his *f.*
*Deut.* 31:17 *hid* my *f.* 18; 32:20
*Job* 13:24 wherefore *hidest* thou thy *f. Ps.* 44:24; 88:14
*Ps.* 10:11 he *hideth* his *f.*
13:1 how long wilt *hide* thy *f.*
27:9 *h.* not *f.* 69:17; 102:2; 143:7
30:7 didst *hide* thy *f.* 104:29
51:9 *hide* thy *f.* from my sins
*Is.* 8:17 *h.* his *f.* from house of J.
*Is.* 50:6 I *hid* not my *f.* from sh.
54:8 in wrath I *hid* my *f.*
59:2 sins have *h.* his *f.* from you
64:7 thou hast *hid* thy *f.*
*Jer.* 16:17 not *hid* from my *f.*
33:5 *hid* my *f.* from city
*Ezek.* 39:23 *h.* I my *f.* fr. them, 24
29 nor will I *hide* my *f.*
*Mic.* 3:4 he will *h. f.* at that time
*Rev.* 6:16 *hide* us from *f.* of him

**FACE of the house.**
*Ezek.* 41:14 breadth of *f. of house*

**FACE of the Lord.**
*Gen.* 19:13 cry before *f. of the L.*
1 *Sam.* 26:20 blood before *f. of L.*
1 *K.* 13:6 entreat *f. of the Lord*
*Ps.* 34:16 *f. of the Lord* against them that do evil, 1 *Pet.* 3:12
*Lam.* 2:19 heart before *f. of L.*
*Luke* 1:76 go before *f. of Lord*

**FACE of the porch.**
*Ezek.* 40:15 *f. of the p.* 50 cubits
41:25 thick planks on *f. of the p.*

**FACE, *with* look, looked, see, saw, seen.**
*Gen.* 32:20 afterw. I will *s.* his *f.*
33:10 therefore have I *s.* thy *f.*
43:3 shall not *s.* my *f.* 5; 44:23
46:30 let me die since I have *s. f.*
48:11 not thought to *see* thy *f.*
*Ex.* 10:28 *see* my *f.* no more
29 Moses said, I will *see* thy *f.*
33:20 thou canst not *see* my *f.*
23 but my *f.* shall not be *seen*
34:35 children of Is. *s. f.* of M.
2 *Sam.* 14:28 two y. *s.* not king's *f.*
2 *K.* 14:8 let us *look* one another in the *f.* 2 *Chr.* 25:17
11 *looked* one another in the *f.*
*Est.* 1:14 7 princes w. *s.* king's *f.*
*Acts* 6:15 *saw* his *f.* as *f.* of angel
20:25 sh. *see* my *f.* no more, 38
*Col.* 2:1 as have not *seen* my *f.*
*Rev.* 22:4 they shall *see* his *f.*

**Seek FACE.**
1 *Chr.* 16:11 *seek* his *f. Ps.* 105:4
2 *Chr.* 7:14 if my people *s.* my *f.*
*Ps.* 24:6 that *seek* thy *f.* O Jacob
27:8 *s.* ye my *f.* thy *f.* L. will I *s.*
*Prov.* 7:15 I came to *seek* thy *f.*
*Hos.* 5:15 till they *seek* my *f*

**Set FACE.**
*Gen.* 31:21 J. *set f.* to mount Gil.
*Lev.* 17:10 *set f.* against soul, 20:6
20:3 *set f.* ag. that m. 5; *Eze.* 14:8
26:17 *set* my *f.* aga. *Jer.* 44:11
*Is.* 50:7 have *set* my *f.* like flint
*Jer.* 21:10 *set* my *f.* ag. this city
*Ezek.* 4:3 *set* my *f.* against it
6:2 *set* thy *f.* tow. mountains
13:17 *set* thy *f.* ag. daughters
15:7 *set* my *f.* against them
20:46 *set* thy *f.* toward the south
21:2 *set* thy *f.* toward Jerusalem
16 whithersoever thy *f.* is *set*
28:21 *f.* ag. Zidon; 29:2 *f.* ag. P.
35:2 *f.* ag. mount S.; 38:2 *f.* a. G.
*Dan.* 9:3 I *set* my *f.* to Lord God
10:15 *set* my *f.* toward ground
11:17 he shall *set* his *f.* to enter
*Luke* 9:51 *set f.* to go to Jerusa.

**FACE shine.**
*Num.* 6:25 L. make *f.* to *s.* on thee
*Ps.* 31:16 make thy *f.* to *shine* on thy servant, 119:135
67:1 cause his *f. to shine* on us
80:3 cause thy *f.* to *shine*, 7, 19
104:15 to make his *f.* to *shine*
*Ec.* 8:1 maketh his *f.* to *shine*
*Dan.* 9:17 cause thy *f.* to *shine*
*Mat.* 17:2 his *f.* did *shine* as sun

**FACE of the sky.**
*Mat.* 16:3 disc. the *f. Luke* 12:56

**FACE of the waters.**
*Gen.* 1:2 S. of G. mov. *f. of w.*
7:18 ark went upon *f. of the w.*

**FACE of the wilderness.**
*Ex.* 16:14 on *f. of the w.* lay

**FACE of the world.**
*Job* 37:12 command. on *f. of w.*
*Is.* 14:21 nor fill *f. of w.*
27:6 Israel fill *f. of w.* with fruit

**FACES.**
*Gen.* 9:23 their *f.* were backward
*Ex.* 19:7 Moses laid before th. *f.*
20:20 his fear be before your *f.*
25:20 *f.* shall look one to anoth.
37:9 mercy-seat-ward *f.* of cher.
2 *Sam.* 19:5 shamed *f.* of serv.
1 *K.* 2:15 all Israel set *f.* on me
1 *Chr.* 12:8 *f.* were like *f.* of lions

2 Chr. 3:13 their f. were inward
Job 9:24 he covereth f. of judges
40:13 and bind their f. in secret
Ps. 34:5 f. were not ashamed
Is. 3:15 that ye grind f. of poor
13:8 their f. shall be as flames
25:8 will wipe tears from all f.
53:3 hid as it were our f. from
Jer. 1:8 be not afraid of their f.
5:3 their f. harder than a rock
30:6 all f. turned into paleness
42:15 set f. to enter, 17; 44:12
50:5 Zion, with f. thitherward
Lam. 5:12 f. of elders not hon.
Ezek. 1:6 ev. one four f. 10, 11, 15
7:18 shame shall be on their f.
8:16 with f. toward the east
14:6 turn f. from abominations
20:47 all f. shall be burnt
41:18 every cherub had two f.
Dan. 9:7 unto us confusion of f.
Joel 2:6 f. shall gather blackness
Hab. 1:9 f. shall sup up as east w.
Mal. 2:3 I will spread dung on f.
Mat. 6:16 hypocrites disfigure f.
Luke 24:5 have bowed f. to earth
Rev. 7:11 fell before throne on f.
9:7 f. of locusts as f. of men
See Fell on FACE, or FACES.

**FADE.**
2 Sam. 22:46 strangers shall f. away, Ps. 18:45
Is. 64:6 and we all f. as a leaf
Jer. 8:13 and the leaf shall f.
Ezek. 47:12 who. leaf shall not f.
Jam. 1:11 rich man shall f. away

**FADETH.**
Is. 1:30 as an oak, whose leaf f.
24:4 and f. the world f.
40:7 grass withereth, flower f. 8
1 Pet. 1:4 inheritance f. not away
5:4 cro. of glory that f. not aw.

**FADING.**
Is. 28:1 glorious beauty f. flow.
4 beauty shall be f. flower

**FAIL, Substantive.**
Jos. 3:10 without f. drive Can.
Jud. 11:30 without f. deliver A.
Ezr. 6:9 day by day without f.

**FAIL, Verb.**
Gen. 47:16 cattle, if money f.
Deut. 28:32 eyes f. with longing
31:6 he will not f. thee, 8; Jos. 1:5; 1 Chr. 28:20
1 Sam. 17:32 no man's heart f.
20:5 sho. not f. to sit with king
1 K. 2:4 shall not f. man on thro. of Isr. 8:25; 9:5; 2 Chr. 6:16
17:14 neith. sh. cruse of oil f. 16
Est. 6:10 let nothing f. of all
9:27 not f. keep days of P. 28
Job 11:20 eyes of wicked shall f.
14:11 as waters f. from the sea
17:5 eyes of his children sh. f.
31:16 caused eyes of wid. to f.
Ps. 12:1 faithful f. fr. am. men
69:3 mine eyes f. while I wait
77:8 doth his promise f. for ever
119:82 mine eyes f. for thy word
123 mine eyes f. for thy salva.
Prov. 22:8 rod of his anger sh. f.
Ec. 12:5 desire f. man goeth
Is. 19:5 wat. f.; 21:16 gl. of K. f.
31:3 they all shall f. together
32:6 cause drink of thirsty to f.
10 for the vintage shall f.
34:16 no one of these shall f.
38:14 mine eyes f. with looking
42:4 not f. nor be discouraged
57:16 spirit should f. before me
58:11 spring whose waters f. not
Jer. 14:6 eyes did f. bec. no gra.
15:18 as waters that f.?
48:33 wine to f. Hos. 9:2
Lam. 2:31 mine eyes f. with tea.
3:22 because compassions f. not
Hab. 3:17 labor of olive shall f.
Luke 16:9 ye f. they may receive
17 one tittle of the law to f.
22:32 that thy faith f. not
1 Cor. 13:8 prophecies they sh. f.
Heb. 1:12 thy years shall not f.
11:32 time would f. me to tell
12:15 any man f. of grace of G.

**FAILED.**
Gen. 42:28 their heart f. them
47:15 money f. in land of Egypt
Jos. 3:16 waters f. were cut off
21:45 f. not any good which L. promised, 23:14; 1 K. 8:56
Job 19:14 my kinsfolk have f.
Ps. 142:4 refuge f. no man cared
Cant. 5:6 soul f. when he spake
Lam. 4:17 our eyes as yet f.

**FAILETH.**
Gen. 47:15 sho. we die? money f.
Job 21:10 gendereth and f. not
Ps. 31:10 strength f. me, 38:10
Ps. 40:12 my heart f. me, 73:26
71:9 forsake not when strength
109:24 my flesh f. of fatness
143:7 O Lord, my spirit f.
Ec. 10:3 wisdom f. him
Is. 15:6 grass f. no green thing
41:17 their tongue f. for thirst
44:12 hungry and his strength f.
Ezek. 12:22 and every vision f.
Luke 12:23 treas. in heaven f. not
1 Cor. 13:8 charity never f. but

**FAILING.**
Deut. 28:65 L. shall give f. of ey.
Luke 21:26 men's heart f. for fe.

**FAIN.**
Job 27:22 f. flee out of his hand
Luke 15:16 f. filled belly

**FAINT, Adjective.**
Gen. 25:29 E. and he was f. 30
Deut. 25:18 when thou wast f.
Jud. 8:4 f. yet pursuing them
1 Sam. 14:28 peo. were very f. 31
30:10 so f. could not go over, 21
2 Sam. 16:2 such as be f.
Is. 1:5 the whole heart is f.
13:7 shall all hands be f.
29:8 awaketh, behold he is f.
40:29 he giveth power to the f.
Jer. 8:18 my heart is f.
Lam. 5:17 for this our heart is f

**FAINT, Verb.**
Deut. 20:3 let not your hearts f.
8 lest his brethren's heart f.
Jos. 2:9 inhabitants of land f.
Prov. 24:10 f. in day of adversity
Is. 40:30 shall f. Amos 8:13
31 walk and not f.
Jer. 51:46 and lest your hearts f.
Lam. 2:19 young children f.
Ezek. 21:7 every spirit shall f.
15 their heart may f.
Mat. 15:32 fasting, lest they f.
Mark 8:3 away fasting, will f.
Luke 18:1 to pray, not to f.
2 Cor. 4:1 rec. mercy we f. not
16 for which cause we f. not
Gal. 6:9 shall reap, if we f. not
Eph. 3:13 f. not at my tribula.
Heb. 12:3 and f. in your minds
5 nor f. when rebuked of him

**FAINTED.**
Gen. 45:26 Jacob's heart f.
Ps. 27:13 f. unl. I had believed
107:5 their soul f. in them
Is. 51:20 thy sons f. they lie
Jer. 45:3 I f. in my sighing
Ezek. 31:15 trees of field f.
Dan. 8:27 I Daniel f.
Jon. 2:7 soul f. I rememb. Lord
4:8 f. and wished in him. to die
Mat. 9:36 comp. on them bec. f.
Rev. 2:3 labored, and hast not f.

**FAINTEST, ETH.**
Job 4:5 upon thee, and thou
Ps. 84:2 soul f. for courts of L.
119:81 my soul f. for salvation
Is. 10:18 a standard-bearer f.
40:28 ends of earth f. not

**FAINT-HEARTED.**
Deut. 20:8 and f. let him return
Is. 7:4 nor be f. for the two tails
Jer. 49:23 H. and Arpad are f

**FAINTNESS.**
Lev. 26:36 send f. into hearts

**FAIR.**
Gen. 6:2 daugh. of men were f.
12:11 Sar. f. 14; 24:16 R. 26:7
2 Sam. 13:1 Tamar was f. 14:27
1 K. 1:4 Abishag a f. damsel
Est. 1:11 Vashti f.; 2:7 Est. f.
2:2 f. young virgins be sought
Job 37:22 f. weather cometh out
42:15 so f. as Job's daughters
Prov. 7:21 with f. speech
11:22 f. woman with. discretion
26:25 when he speaketh f.
Cant. 1:15 thou art f. 16; 4:1, 7
2:10 my love, my f. one, 13
4:10 f. is thy love, my sister
6:10 f. as moon; 7:6 f. art thou
Is. 5:9 many houses great and f.
54:11 lay stones with f. colors
Jer. 11:16 and olive-tree f.
12:6 though they speak f. words
46:20 Egypt like a very f. heifer
Ezek. 16:17 hast taken f. jewels
39 shall take f. jewels, 23:26
31:3 cedar in L. with f. branches
7 f. in his greatness
9 made him f. by multitude
Dan. 4:12 leaves were f. 21
Amos 8:13 f. virgins shall faint
Zec. 3:5 let them set a f. mitre
Mat. 16:2 it will be f. weather
Acts 7:20 Moses was exceeding f.
Rom. 16:18 f. speeches deceive
Gal. 6:12 make f. show in flesh

**FAIRER, EST.**
Jud. 15:2 younger sist. f. than
Ps. 45:2 f. than child. of men
Cant. 1:8 O f. am. wo. 5:9; 6:1
Dan. 1:15 countenances app. f.

**FAIR-HAVENS.**
Acts 27:8 place called the f.-h.

**FAIRS.**
Ezek. 27:12 tra. in f. 14, 16, 19, 22
27 thy f. shall fall into the seas

**FAITH.**
Deut. 32:20 in whom is no f.
Mat. 6:30 O ye of little f. 8:26; 14:31; 16:8; Luke 12:28
8:10 great f. no not, Luke 7:9
17:20 f. as grain of mustard seed
23:23 judgment, mercy, and f.
Mark 4:40 ye have no f.?
11:22 Jesus saith, Have f. in G.
Luke 17:5 Lord increase our f.
6 if ye had f. ye might say
18:8 wh. S. of man com. fi. f.?
Acts 6:5 Ste. a man full of f. 8
7 priests were obedie. to the f.
11:24 Barnabas good, full of f.
13:8 seek. to turn deputy fr. f.
14:9 that he had f. to be healed
22 exhorting to continue in f.
27 opened door of f. to Genti.
16:5 churches established in f.
20:21 f. toward our L. Jesus C.
24:24 Felix heard P. concern. f.
Rom. 1:5 obedience to f.
17 righte. of G. rev. fr. f. to f.
3:3 make f. of God without ef.
27 excluded by law of f.
4:5 f. counted for righteous. 9
11 circum. seal of righte. of f.
12 steps of that f. of Abraham
13 through righteous. of f.

14 they of law be heirs *f.* is v.
16 of *f.* of the *f.* of Abraham
9:30 righte. which is of *f.* 10:6
10:8 word of *f.* which we prea.
17 so then *f.* cometh by hear.
12:3 God dealt measure of *f.*
6 according to proportion of *f.*
14:22 hast thou *f.*?
23 eat. not of *f.* not of *f.* is sin
16:26 for the obedience of *f.*
1 *Cor.* 12:9 another *f.* by same S.
13:2 though I have all *f.*
13 now abideth *f.* hope, chari.
*Gal.* 1:23 *f.* which once destroy.
3:2 or by the hearing of *f.* 5
7 they which are of *f.* 9
12 law is not of *f.* but man
23 before *f.* came; 25 *f.* is co.
5:6 *f.* which worketh by love
22 fruit of Sp. is love, joy, *f.*
6:10 are of the household of *f.*
*Eph.* 4:5 one L. one *f.* one bapt.
13 come in the unity of the *f.*
6:16 taking the shield of *f.*
*Phil.* 1:25 further. and joy of *f.*
27 striving tog. for *f.* of gospel
1 *Thes.* 1:3 rememb. work of *f.*
5:8 the breastplate of *f.*
2 *Thes.* 1:11 work of *f.* with pow.
3:2 for all men have not *f.*
1 *Tim.* 1:5 *f.* unfeigned
19 holding *f.* concerning *f.*
3:9 holding the mystery of *f.*
4:1 some shall depart fr. the *f.*
5:8 he hath denied the *f.* and is
12 have cast off their first *f.*
6:10 have erred from the *f.* 21
11 follow *f.*; 12 fight fight of *f.*
2 *Tim.* 1:5 unfeigned *f.* in thee
2:18 overthrow the *f.* of some
22 follow *f.*; 3:8 reprobate *f.*
3:10 thou hast fully known *f.*
4:7 have kept the *f.* henceforth
*Tit.* 1:1 the *f.* of God's elect
4 T. mine own son aft. com. *f.*
*Phile.* 5 hearing of thy *f.*
*Heb.* 4:2 not mixed with *f.*
6:1 not laying the foundat. of *f.*
10:22 in full assurance of *f.*
23 hold fast profession of *f.*
11:1 *f.* is substance of things
6 without *f.* impossi. to pl. G.
12:2 and finisher of our *f.*
13:7 whose *f.* follow, consider.
*Jam.* 2:1 *f.* with respect of pers.
14 he hath *f.* can *f.* save him?
17 *f.* with. works is dead, 20, 26
18 hast *f.* and I have works
22 *f.* wrought with works, and by works was *f.* made perf.
5:15 prayer of *f.* shall save sick
2 *Pet.* 1:1 obtained like prec. *f.*
1 *John* 5:4 overcome. wor. our *f.*
*Jude* 3 earnestly contend for *f.*
*Jude* 20 building yours. on h. *f.*
*Rev.* 2:13 hast not denied my *f.*
19 I know thy works and *f.*
13:10 patience and *f.* of saints
14:12 that keep the *f.* of Jesus

**By FAITH.**

*Hab.* 2:4 shall live *by f.* *Rom.* 1:17; *Gal.* 3:11; *Heb.* 10:38
*Acts* 15:9 purifying hearts *by f.*
26:18 sanctified *by f.*
*Rom.* 3:22 righteous. of G. *by f.*
28 justi. *b. f.* 5:1; *Gal.* 2:16; 3:24
30 justify circumcision *by f.*
5:2 we have access *by f.*
11:20 standest *by f.* 2 *Cor.* 1:24
2 *Cor* 5:7 walk *by f.* not by sight
*Gal.* 2:20 I live *by f.* of S. of God
3:22 promise *by f.* might be giv.
26 child. of G. *by f.* in Chr. J.
5:5 hope of righteousness *by f.*
*Eph.* 3:12 we have access *by f.*
17 C. may dwell in hearts *by f.*
*Phil.* 3:9 righteousn of G. *by f.*
*Heb.* 11:4 *by f.* Abel; 5 *by f.* En.
7 *by f.* Noah; 8 *by f.* Ara. 9, 17
20 *by f.* Isaac; 21 Jac.; 22 Jos.
23 *by f.* Moses, 24:27; 31 Rah.
29 *by f.* passed through Red s.
30 *by f.* walls of Jer. fell down
*Jam.* 2:24 works justi. not *by f.*

**In FAITH.**

*Rom.* 4:19 being not weak *in f.*
20 but was strong *in f.*
14:1 him weak in *f.* receive you
1 *Cor.* 16:13 stand fast *in f.*
2 *Cor.* 13:5 exam. wh. ye be *in f.*
*Col.* 1:23 if ye continue *in* the *f.*
2:7 and stablished *in* the *f.*
1 *Tim.* 1:2 Tim. my own son *i. f.*
4 godly edifying which is *in f.*
2:7 teacher of the Gentiles *in f.*
15 saved, if they continue *in f.*
3:13 they purchase boldn. *in f.*
4:12 example of believers *in f.*
2 *Tim.* 1:13 hold fast form *in f.*
*Heb.* 11:13 these all died *in f.*
*Jam.* 1:6 but let them ask *in f.*
2:5 poor of this world, rich *in f.*
1 *Pet.* 5:9 resist, steadfast *in f.*

**Their FAITH.**

*Mat.* 9:2 Jesus seeing *their f.* *Mark* 2:5; *Luke* 5:20

**Through FAITH.**

*Acts* 3:16 *through f.* in his name
*Rom.* 3:25 propitiation *t. f.*
30 justify uncircumcision *t. f.*
31 do we make void law *t. f.*?
*Gal.* 3:8 God justify heathen *t. f.*
14 promise of the Spirit *t. f.*
*Eph.* 2:8 are ye saved *t. f.*
*Phil.* 3:9 righteousn. wh. is *t. f.*
*Col.* 2:12 risen *t. f.* of ope. of G.
2 *Tim.* 3:15 wise to salvation *t. f.*
*Heb.* 6:12 *t. f.* inherit promises
11:3 *t. f.* we und. worlds framed
11 *t. f.* S. received strength
28 *thro' f.* he kept the passover
33 *thro' f.* subdued kingdoms
39 obtained a good report *t. f.*
1 *Pet.* 1:5 kept *t. f.* to salvation

**Thy FAITH.**

*Mat.* 9:22 *t. f.* hath made thee whole, *Mark* 5:34; 10:52; *Luke* 8:48; 17:19
15:28 O woman, great is *thy f.*
*Luke* 7:50 *t. f.* h. saved th. 18:42
22:32 prayed that *thy f.* fail not
*Phile.* 6 communication of *thy f.*
*Jam.* 2:18 show *t. f.* without w.

**Your FAITH.**

*Mat.* 9:29 according to *y. f.* be it
*Luke* 8:25 where is *your f.*?
*Rom.* 1:8 *y. f.* is spoken
1 *Cor.* 2:5 *y. f.* not stand in wis.
15:14 *your f.* is also vain, 17
2 *Cor.* 1:24 dominion over *y. f.*
10:15 when *your f.* is increased
*Eph.* 1:15 after I heard of *y. f.*
*Phil.* 2:17 offer. on service of *y. f.*
*Col.* 1:4 since we heard of *y. f.*
2:5 steadfastness of *y. f.* in Ch.
1 *Thes.* 1:8 *your f.* to God-ward
3:5 I sent to know *your f.*
7 we were comforted by *y. f.*
10 what is lacking in *your f.*
2 *Thes.* 1:3 *y. f.* groweth exceed.
*Jam.* 1:3 trying of *y. f.* worketh
1 *Pet.* 1:7 trial of *y. f.* precious
9 end of *y. f.* even salvation
21 that *y. f.* might be in God
2 *Pet.* 1:5 add to *your f.* virtue

**FAITHFUL.**

*Num.* 12:7 Mo. *f.* *Heb.* 3:2, 5
*Deut.* 7:9 *f.* G. who keepeth cov.
1 *Sam.* 2:35 will raise up *f.* prie.
2 *Sam.* 20:19 *f.* in Israel
*Neh.* 13:13 *f.* to distribute
*Ps.* 12:1 the *f.* fail from am. men
31:23 the Lord preserveth the *f.*
89:37 as a *f.* witness in heaven
101:6 mine eyes shall be on *f.*
119:86 commandments are *f.*
138 thy testimonies very *f.*
*Prov.* 11:13 *f.* spirit conc. matter
13:17 a *f.* ambassador is health
14:5 a *f.* witness will not lie
20:6 a *f.* man who can find?
27:6 *f.* the wounds of a friend
*Is.* 1:21 how is *f.* city become
26 shalt be called the *f.* city
8:2 I took unto me *f.* witness.
*Jer.* 42:5 L. be *f.* witness bet. us
*Dan.* 6:4 forasmuch as he was *f.*
*Hos.* 11:12 Ju. is *f.* with saints
*Mat.* 24:45 who then is *f.*
25:21 well done, good and *f.* se.
23 *f.* in a few th. *Luke* 19:17
*Luke* 12:42 who is *f.* and wise?
16:10 *f.* in least is *f.* in much
12 not *f.* in what is ano. man's
*Acts* 16:15 ye have judged me *f.*
1 *Cor.* 1:9 God is *f.* 10:13
4:2 stewards, that a man be *f.*
17 sent Timothy, *f.* in the L.
7:25 mercy of the Lord to be *f.*
*Gal.* 3:9 blessed with *f.* Abraham
*Eph.* 1:1 to saints and *f.* in C. J.
6:21 Tychicus a *f.* minister
*Col.* 1:2 saints and *f.* breth. in C.
7 Ep. for you *f.* minister, 4:7
4:9 Onesimus, a *f.* brother
1 *Thes.* 5:24 *f.* is he that calleth
2 *Thes.* 3:3 L. is *f.* who stablish
1 *Tim.* 1:12 Christ he counted *f.*
15 a *f.* saying, 4:9: *Tit.* 3:8
2 *Tim.* 2:2 same commit to *f.* m.
11 *f.* saying; 13 he abideth *f.*
*Tit.* 1:6 having *f.* children
9 holding fast the *f.* word
*Heb.* 2:17 he might be *f.*
3:2 *f.* to him that appointed h.
10:23 is *f.* that promised; 11:11
1 *Pet.* 4:19 souls as to a *f.* Crea.
1 *John* 1:9 he is *f.* to forgive us
*Rev.* 1:5 C. the *f.* witness, 3:14
2:10 be *f.* unto death
19:11 was called *f.*
21:5 words are true and *f.* 22:6

**FAITHFULLY.**

2 *K.* 12:15 for they dealt *f.* 22:7
2 *Chr.* 31:12 brought offerings *f.*
34:12 men did the work *f.*
*Prov.* 29:14 *f.* judgeth the poor
*Jer.* 23:28 speak my word *f.*

**FAITHFULNESS.**

1 *Sam.* 26:23 render to man his *f.*
*Ps.* 5:9 no *f.* in their mouth
36:5 thy *f.* reacheth unto clouds
40:10 I have declared thy *f.*
89:1 I will make known thy *f.*
2 thy *f.* shalt thou establish
5 thy *f.* also in the congrega.
8 to thy *f.* round about thee?
24 *f.* and mercy be with him
92:2 good to show *f.* every night
119:75 in *f.* hast afflicted me
90 thy *f.* is unto all genera.
143:1 in thy *f.* answer me
*Is.* 11:5 *f.* shall be girdle
25:1 thy counsels of old are *f.*
*Lam.* 3:23 great thy *f.*
*Hos.* 2:20 I will betroth thee in *f.*

**FAITHLESS.**

*Mat.* 17:17 O *f.* generation, *Mark* 9:19; *Luke* 9:41
*John* 20:27 not *f.* but believing

**FALL, Substantive.**

*Prov.* 16:18 haughty spirit bef. *f.*
29:16 righteous shall see their *f.*
*Jer.* 49:21 moved at noise of *f.*
*Mat.* 7:27 great was the *f.* of it
*Luke* 2:34 child set for *f.*
*Rom.* 11:11 thro' their *f.* salvation is come to the Gentiles
12 if *f.* of them be riches

**FALL, Verb.**

Gen. 2:21 deep sleep to f. on A.
45:24 see that ye f. n. out by w.
49:17 his rider shall f. backwa.
Lev. 19:29 land f. to whoredom
26:36 sh. f. when none pursue
37 shall f. one upon another
Num. 14:29 carc. sh. f. wild. 32
Jud. 15:12 ye will not f. me
18 f. into hand of uncircum.
Ruth 2:16 let f. some handfuls
1 Sam. 3:19 none of words f. gr.
14:45 not hair of head f. ground, 2 Sam. 14:11; 1 K. 1:52; Acts 27:34
22:17 would not f. on the pric.
1 Sam. 22:18 turn th. and f. on pr.
2 Sam. 1:15 f. on h. 1 K. 2:29, 31
24:14 f. in hand of G. not f. into hand of man, 1 Chr. 21:13
2 K. 7:4 let us f. unto host of S.
10:10 f. nothing of word of L.
1 Chr. 12:19 he will f. to master
2 Chr. 21:15 till bowels f. out
25:8 G. f. before enemy
Est. 6:13 thou begun to f.
Job 13:11 his dread f. on you
31:22 arm f. fr. shoulder-blade
Ps. 5:10 f. by own counsels
9:3 enemies sh. f. and perish
10:10 that the poor may f.
35:8 into destruction let him f.
37:24 he f. shall not be utterly
64:8 make their tongue to f. on
82:7 shall f. like one of princes
91:7 a thousand shall f.
118:13 thrust at me I might f.
140:10 burning coals f. on them
141:10 wicked f. into own nets
145:14 Lord upholdeth all th. f.
Prov. 10:8 a prating fool sh. f. 10
11:5 wicked shall f.
14 wh. no counsel is the peo. f.
28 trusteth in his riches sh. f.
22:14 abhor. of L. sh. f. therein
24:16 shall f. into mischief
26:27 whoso diggeth pit shall f.
28:14 that hardeneth heart sh. f.
18 perverse shall f. at once
Ec. 4:10 if they f. one lift fellow
11:3 if the tree f. tow. the south
Is. 10:4 they sh. f. under slain
34 Leb. shall f. by mighty one
22:25 nail fast. sure place sh. f.
24:18 shall f. into the pit.
20 earth shall f. and not rise
30:13 iniq. as breach ready to f.
40:30 young man sh. utterly f.
47:11 mischiefs sh. f. upon thee
Jer. 6:15 f. am. them that f. 8:12
21 fathers and sons shall f.
8:4 shall they f. and not arise?
9:22 carcasses of men shall f.
15:8 I have caused him to f.
19 whirlwind f. on head, 30:23
25:27 drunken, and spue, and f.
37:14 I f. not away to Chaldeans
44:12 shall all f. in land of Eg.
46:6 they shall stumble and f.
48:44 that fleeth shall f. into pit
49:26 young men f. 50:30
50:32 most proud stumble and f.
51:4 slain f. in land of C. 47, 49
44 wall of Babylon shall f.
Lam. 1:14 made strength to f.
Ezek. 6:7 shall f. in the midst
13:11 it shall f. and ye, O great hailstones, shall f.
24:6 piece by piece, let no lot f.
29:5 shalt f. on open fields, 39:5
30:6 they that uphold E. sh. f.
22 I will cause the sword to f.
32:12 will I cause multit. to f.
33:12 not f. thereby in the day
35:8 in all thy rivers shall th. f.
38:20 steep places f. ev. wall f.
39:3 arrows to f.; 4 sh. f. mo.
44:12 caused Is. to f. into iniq.
Dan. 11:14 robbers of peo. sh. f.
19 but he shall stumble and f.
34 they shall f.; 35 some f.
Hos. 4:5 shalt thou f. in the day, the prophet also shall f.
5:5 Eph. shall f. Judah shall f.
10:8 shall say to hills f. on us
14:9 transgressors shall f.
Amos 3:5 can a bird f. in snare?
14 horns of altar sh. f. to gro.
9:9 shall not least grain f.
Mic. 7:8 mine enemy, when I f.
Nah. 3:12 sh. f. into the mouth
Mat. 10:29 not one sparrow f.
12:11 if it f. into a pit on sab.
15:14 f. into ditch, Luke 6:39
27 crumbs wh. f. masters' tab.
21:44 whoso f. on this stone be broken, Luke 20:18
24:29 stars shall f. from heaven, Mark 13:25
Luke 10:18 I beheld S. as light. f.
23:30 say to mountains f. on us
John 12:24 except a corn f.
Acts 27:17 lest they f. into quic.
32 cut ropes and let her f. off
34 shall not a hair f. from he.
Rom. 11:11 stumbled that th. f.
14:13 to f. in brother's way
1 Cor. 10:12 take heed lest he f.
1 Tim. 3:6 f. into condemnation
7 lest f. into reproach
6:9 will be rich f. into tempt.
Heb. 4:11 lest any f. after same
10:31 fearful to f. into hands
Jam. 1:2 ye f. into temptations
Jam. 5:12 swear not, lest ye f.
2 Pet. 1:10 do th. things, ye n. f.
3:17 lest ye f. from steadfastn.
Rev. 6:16 mount. and ro. f. on us
9:1 I saw a star f. from heaven

**FALL away.**

Luke 8:13 in time of tempt. f. a.
Heb. 6:6 if they f. a. to renew

**FALL down.**

Deut. 22:4 thy brother's ass f. d.
Jos. 6:5 wall of city shall f. d.
1 Sam. 21:13 David let spit. f. d.
Ps. 72:11 all kings shall f. down
Is. 31:3 that is holp. shall f. d.
34:4 their host shall f. d.
44:19 sh. I f. d. to sto. of tree?
45:14 the Sabeans shall f. d.
46:6 they f. d. yea, they worsh.
Ezek. 30:25 arms of Pha. sh. f. d.
Dan. 3:5 f. d. and wor. image, 10
15 if ye f. d. and worship im.
11:26 and many shall f. down
Mat. 4:9 f. d. and wors. Luke 4:7
Rev. 4:10 twenty-four elders f. d.

**FALL, joined with sword.**

Ex. 5:3 he f. with pest. or s.
Num. 14:3 to this land to f. by s.
43 and ye shall f. by the sword
2 K. 19:7 Senacherib f. by swo.
Ps. 63:10 sh. f. by s. Ezek. 6:11
Is. 3:25 thy men shall f. by s.
13:15 every one shall f. by the s.
37:7 I will cause him to f. by the s. in h. own la. Jer. 19:7
Jer. 20:4 P.'s friends sh. f. by s.
Ezek. 5:12 third part sh. f. by s.
6:12 that is near shall f. by s.
11:10 ye shall f. by the s.
17:21 fugitives shall f. by the s.
23:25 remnant shall f. by the s.
25:13 they of D. sh. f. by the s.
30:5 men in league sh. f. by t. s.
22 I will cause the sword to f.
Dan. 11:33 underst. f. by the s.
Hos. 7:16 princes sh. f. by the s
13:16 Samaria shall f. by the s.
Joel 2:8 they f. on the sword
Luke 21:24 shall f. by edge of s.

**FALLEN.**

Gen. 4:6 why is thy counte. f.?
Lev. 13:41 hair f. off from head
25:35 thy brother be f. in decay
Jud. 3:25 their lord was f. dead
19:27 the woman was f. at door
1 Sam. 5:3 D. was f. upon his fa.
26:12 a deep sleep f. upon them
31:8 S. and h. sons f. 1 Chr. 10:8
2 Sam. 3:38 a great man f. this d.
2 K. 13:14 Elisha was f. sick
2 Chr. 20:24 dead bodies f.
29:9 our fathers have f.
Est. 7:8 Ham. was f. on the bed
Ps. 20:8 brought down and f.
36:12 the workers of iniquity f.
Is. 14:12 thou f. fr. heaven, O L.
Ezek. 32:22 all of them f. 23:24
Hos. 14:1 hast f. by iniquity
Luke 14:5 an ox f. into a pit?
Acts 8:16 H. G. was f. on none
20:9 Eutychus f. into deep sl.
26:14 when we were all f.
27:29 lest they have f. on rock
28:6 looked when P. sh. f. dead
Phile. 1:12 f. out to fur. of gospel
Rev. 2:5 rem. whence thou art f.

**Are FALLEN.**

2 Sam. 1:4 ma. of the peo. are f.
19 how are mighty f.! 25:27
22:39 a. f. under feet, Ps. 18:38
Ps. 16:6 lines are f. to me
55:4 ter. of death are f. on me
69:9 reproaches of them are f.
Is. 9:10 the bricks are f. down
Jer. 38:19 Jews that are f. to C.
46:12 they are f. both togeth.
50:15 Bab.'s foundations are f.
Lam. 2:21 my virgins are f.
Ezek. 31:12 his branches are f.
Hos. 7:7 all their kings are f.
1 Cor. 15:6 some are f. asleep. 18
Gal. 5:4 law, ye are f. from grace
Rev. 17:10 seven kings, five a. f.

**Is FALLEN.**

Num. 32:19 lot is f. on th. side J.
Jos. 2:9 I know your terror is f.
Job 1:16 fire of G. is f. fr. heaven
Ps. 7:15 and is f. into the ditch
Is. 3:8 Jer. ruined, and Jud. is f.
21:9 B. is f. is f. Rev. 14:8; 18:2
59:14 truth is f. in the streets
Jer. 48:32 spoil. is f. on sum. fr.
51:8 Babylon is suddenly f.
Lam. 5:16 crown is f. from our heads
Ezek. 13:12 when the wall is f.
Amos 5:2 virgin of Israel is f.
Amos 9:11 raise up tab. th. is f.
Acts 15:16 taber. of D. wh. is f.

**FALLEST, ETH.**

Ex. 1:10 when f. out any war
2 Sam. 3:29 not fail one that f.
34 as a man f. bef. wick. men
17:12 as dew f. on ground
Job 4:13 deep sleep f. 33:15
Prov. 13:17 mess. f. into misch.
17:20 perv. tongue f. into mis.
24:16 just man f. seven times
17 rejoice not when enemy f.
Ec. 4:10 him alone when f.
11:3 wh. tree f. there shall it be
Is. 34:4 the leaf f. off the vine
44:15 image and f. down, 17
Jer. 37:13 thou f. away to Chald.
Dan. 3:6 whoso f. not down, 11
Mat. 17:15 ofttimes f. into fire
Luke 11:17 house div. ag. ho. f.
15:12 goods that f. to me
Rom. 14:4 master he stand. or f.
Jam. 1:11 flower th. f. 1 Pet. 1:24

**FALLING.**

Num. 24:4 f. into trance, 16
Job 4:4 upholden him that f.
14:18 mount f. cometh to nau.
Ps. 56:13 del. feet from f. 116:8
Prov. 25:26 righte. f. bef. wick.
Is. 34:4 as a f. fig from fig-tree

Luke 8:47 trembling f. down
22:44 drops of blood f. down
Acts 1:18 and Judas f. headlong
1 Cor. 14:25 f. he will worsh. G.
2 Thes. 2:3 except come a f. aw.
Jude 24 is able to keep from f.

### FALLOW.

Jer. 4:3 f. ground, Hos. 10:12

### FALSE.

Ex. 23:1 shalt not raise f. report
7 keep thee far from a f. mat.
2 K. 9:12 it is f. tell us now
Job 36:4 my words shall n. be f.
Ps. 119:104 I hate ev. f. way, 128
120:3 done thee, f. tongue
Prov. 11:1 f. balance is abomination
17:4 giveth heed to f. lips
20:23 a f. balance is not good
25:14 whoso boasteth of a f. gift
Jer. 14:14 prophesy a f. vision
23:32 prophesy f. dreams
37:14 it is f. I fall not away
Lam. 2:14 seen for thee f. burdens
Ezek. 21:23 shall be as a f. divin.
Zec. 8:17 evil, love no f. oath
10:2 divin. have told f. dreams
Mal. 3:5 witness ag. f. swearers
Mat. 24:24 shall arise f. Christs and f. prophets, Mark 13:22
Luke 19:8 any thing by f. accusa.
2 Cor. 11:13 such are f. apostles
26 in perils among f. brethren
Gal. 2:4 because of f. brethren
Tit. 2:3 they be not f. accusers
2 Pet. 2:1 there sh. be f. teachers
See PROPHET.

### FALSE prophets.

Mat. 7:15 f. p. in sheep's cloth.
24:11 many f. p. shall rise, 24
Mark 13:22 f. p. rise show signs
Luke 6:26 did fathers to the f. p.
2 Pet. 2:1 there were f. p. am. p.
1 John 4:1 f. p. gone out

### FALSE witness, es.

Ex. 20:16 thou shalt not bear f. wit. Deut. 5:20; Mat. 19:18
Deut. 19:16 if a f. witness rise up
18 if the witness be a f. witness
Ps. 27:12 f. witnesses are risen
35:11 f. w. did rise
Prov. 6:19 a f. w. speaketh lies
12:17 a f. w. show. deceit, 14:5
19:5 f. w. not be unpunished, 9
21:28 f. witness shall perish
25:18 that beareth f. w.
Mat. 15:19 out of heart pro. f. w.
26:59 elders sought f. w. ag. Je.
60 many f. witnesses came, at last came two f. witnesses
Mark 14:56 bear f. w. ag. him, 57
Acts 6:13 and set up f. w.
1 Cor. 15:15 we are found f. w.

### FALSEHOOD.

2 Sam. 18:13 sh. have wroug. f.
Job 21:34 in answers remaineth f.
Ps. 7:14 he hath brought forth f.
119:118 for deceit is f.
144:8 a right hand of f. 11
Is. 28:15 under f. have we hid
57:4 seed of f.? 59:13 words of f.
Jer. 10:14 image is f. 51:17
Hos. 7:1 for they commit f.
Mic. 2:11 walking in spirit and f.

### FALSELY.

Gen. 21:23 thou wilt not deal f.
Lev. 6:3 lost, and sweareth f.
19:11 neither deal f. nor lie
12 not swear by my name f.
Deut. 19:18 witn. have testifi. f.
Ps. 44:17 nor have we dealt f.
Jer. 5:2 L. liveth, they swear f.
31 prophets prophesy f. 29:9
6:13 every one dealeth f. 8:10
7:9 ye steal, mur. and swear f.?
40:16 for thou speakest f. of Is.
43:2 speakest f. L. hath not sent
Hos. 10:4 swe. f. in making cov.
Zec. 5:4 enter house swear f.
Mat. 5:11 say evil against you f.
Luke 3:14 nor accuse any f.
1 Tim. 6:20 opp. of science f.
1 Pet. 3:16 f. accuse good conv.

### FALSIFYING.

Amos 8:5 f. balances by deceit

### FAME.

Gen. 45:16 f. was heard in Phar.
Num. 14:15 have heard f. of thee
Jos. 6:27 Joshua's f. was noised
9:9 we heard the f. of God
1 K. 4:31 f. was in all nations
10:1 heard f. of Sol. 2 Chr. 9:1
7 wish. exceedeth f. 2 Chr. 9:6
1 Chr. 14:17 f. of D. was to all
Est. 9:4 Mordecai's f. thro' prov.
Job 28:22 we have heard f.
Is. 66:19 that have not heard f.
Jer. 6:24 we have heard the f.
Zep. 3:19 and I will get them f.
Mat. 4:24 f. of J. abroad, Mark 1:28; Luke 4:14, 37; 5:15
9:26 the f. thereof went abroad
31 they spread abroad his f.
14:1 Herod heard of f. of Jesus

### FAMILIAR.

Job 19:14 my f. friends have for.
Ps. 41:9 my f. friend lift up heel

### FAMILIAR spirit.

Lev. 20:27 man or wom. of a f. s.
1 Sam. 28:7 wo. that hath f. s. 8
2 Chr. 33:6 Man. dealt with f. s.
Is. 29:4 as one that hath a f. s.

### FAMILIAR spirits.

Lev. 19:31 reg. not th. have f. s.
20:6 soul that turneth after f. s.
Deut. 18:11 nor consulter w. f. s.
1 Sam. 28:3 S. put away th. f. s. 9
2 K. 21:6 with f. s.; 23:24 f. s.
Is. 8:19 seek f. s.; 19:3 hath f. s.

### FAMILIARS.

Jer. 20:10 f. watched for halting

### FAMILY.

Lev. 20:5 I will set face ag. his f.
25:10 return ev. man to his f. 41
47 the stock of the strang. f.
Num. 36:6 f. of father's tribe, 12
Deut. 29:18 lest a f. turn from L.
Jos. 7:14 f. which Lord taketh
Jud. 1:25 go man and all his f.
6:15 my f. is poor in Manasseh
Jer. 3:14 one of a cit. two of a f.
Zec. 12:12 f. sh. mourn, 13, 14
Eph. 3:15 f. in heav. and earth

### FAMILIES.

Gen. 10:5 Gentiles divided aft. f.
12:3 all f. of earth, 28:14
Ex. 12:21 take lamb ac. to yo. f.
Neh. 4:13 people after their f.
Job 31:34 did cont. of f. ter. me?
Ps. 68:6 G. setteth solitary in f.
107:41 mak. him f. like a flock
Jer. 1:15 will call all f. of north
10:25 fury on f. call not name
25:9 will take all the f. of north
31:1 God of all the f. of Israel
33:24 f. which L. hath chosen
Ezek. 20:32 as f. of countries
Amos 3:2 you have I kn. of all f.
Nah. 3:4 selleth f. thro' witchr.
Zec. 12:14 f. that remain
14:17 will not come of all f.

### FAMINE.

Gen. 12:10 f. was grievous in la.
26:1 f. in land, besides first f.
41:27 7 empty ears 7 years f.
30 f. shall consume the land
31 plenty not kn. by rea. of f.
56 f. was over all face of earth
47:13 fainted by reason of f.
Ruth 1:1 ruled there was f.
2 Sam. 21:1 f. in the days of D.
24:13 shall years of f. come?
1 K. 8:37 in land f. 2 Chr. 20:9
18:2 f. in Samaria, 2 K. 6:25
2 K. 7:4 then the f. is in the city
8:1 the Lord hath call. for a f.
25:3 f. prevailed in J. no bread
2 Chr. 32:11 H. per. you to die f.
Job 5:20 in f. he shall red. thee f.
Job 5:22 at destruc. f. thou sh. la.
30:3 want and f. were solitary
Ps. 33:19 keep them alive in f.
37:19 in days of f.
105:16 he called for a f.
Is. 14:30 I will kill root with f.
51:19 destruction, f. and sword
Jer 14:15 by f. sh. proph. be con.
18 them that are sick with f.
15:2 such for the f. to the f.
18:21 deliver up children to f.
21:7 deliver from the f. to Neb.
24:10 send f. am. them, 29:17
27:8 nation will I pun. with f.
34:17 liberty for you to the f.
42:16 the f. shall follow
52:6 the f. was sore in the city
Lam. 5:10 skin black, bec. of f.
Ezek. 5:12 part consumed with f.
16 evil arrows of f.
17 I send on you f. 14:13
7:15 f. within f. and pestilence
12:16 leave a few men from f.
36:29 will lay no f. upon you
Amos 8:11 I will send f.
Luke 4:25 great f. through land
15:14 a mighty f. in that land
Rom. 8:35 f. sep. fr. love of C.?
Rev. 18:8 in one day, death, f.

### By the FAMINE.

Jer. 11:22 sons and d. die by t. f.
14:12 I will consume by t. f. 15
16:4 be con. by t. f. 44:12, 18, 27
21:9 abideth in city die by t. f.
38:2 shall die by f. Ezek. 6:12
42:17 they shall die by the f.
22 that ye shall die by the f.
44:13 I have punish. J. by t. f.
Ezek. 6:11 they shall fall by the f.

### FAMINES.

Mat. 24:7 shall be f. pestilences, Mark 13:8; Luke 21:11

### FAMISH, ED.

Gen. 41:55 all land of Egypt f.
Prov. 10:3 not suffer right. to f.
Is. 5:13 their honor. men are f.
Zep. 2:11 will f. gods of earth

### FAMOUS.

Num. 16:2 f. in congrega. 26:9
Ruth 4:11 be thou f. in Bethleh.
14 his name may be f. in Israel
1 Chr. 5:24 were f. men, 12:30
Ps. 74:5 was f. as he lifted axes
136:18 to him who slew f. kings
Ezek. 23:10 became f. am. wom.
32:18 daughters of f. nations

### FAN, Substantive.

Is. 30:24 winnowed with f.
Jer. 15:7 I will fan with f.
Mat. 3:12 wh. f. is in h. Luke 3:17

### FAN, Verb.

Is. 41:16 sh. f. them, winds sh.
Jer. 4:11 a dry wind not to f.
15:7 I will f. them with a fan
51:2 fanners that shall f. her

### FAR.

Gen. 18:25 f. from thee to slay
Ex. 8:28 ye shall not go very f.
23:7 keep f. from false matter
Deut. 12:21 f. from thee, 14:24
29:22 stranger from a f. land
Jos. 9:22 f. from you
Jud. 9:17 adventured life f.
19:11 day was f. spent
1 Sam. 20:9 J. said, f. be it from

2 Chr. 26:15 name spr. f. abroad
Neh. 4:19 separ. one f. from an.
Est. 9:20 Jews both nigh and f.
Job 5:4 his child. f. from safety
11:14 iniquity f. away, 22:23
34:10 f. be it from God
Ps. 10:5 judg. are f. out of sight
22:1 why so f. from help. me?
73:27 that are f. from thee
97:9 L. exalted f. above all gods
103:12 as f. as east fr. west, so f.
109:17 blessing be f. from him
119:155 salva. is f. from wicked
Prov. 4:24 and perver. lips put f.
15:29 Lord is f. from the wicked
22:15 rod of cor. sh. drive it f.
31:10 her price is f. above rub.
Ec. 2:13 f. as light excel. dark.
Is. 19:6 shall turn rivers f. away
46:12 hear ye that f. from right.
54:14 thou shalt be f. from opp.
59:9 is judgment f. from us
Jer. 51:64 thus f. are words of J.
Lam. 3:17 my soul f. from peace
Ezek. 11:15 get ye f. from the L.
Dan. 11:2 fourth king f. richer
Amos 6:3 put f. away evil day
Mat. 16:22 be it f. from thee, L.
Mark 6:35 day was now f. spent
12:34 not f. from kingd. of God
Mark 13:34 man taking a f. jour.
Luke 7:6 was not f. from house
22:51 Jesus said, Suf. ye thus f.
24:29 for the day is f. spent
50 out as f. as to Bethany
John 21:8 were not f. from land
Acts 17:27 not f. from every one
22:21 send thee f. hence to Gen.
28:15 meet us as f. as Ap.-forum
Rom. 13:12 the night is f. spent
2 Cor. 4:17 f. more ex. weight
Eph. 1:21 f. abo. all principality
4:10 ascended up f. above all
Phil. 1:23 with C. wh. is f. bet.
Heb. 7:15 it is yet f. more evid.
See COUNTRY, COUNTRIES.

**FAR from me.**

1 Sam. 2:30 Be it f. from me,
22:15; 2 Sam. 20:20; 23:17
Job 13:21 thy hand f. from me
19:13 hath put my bre. f. f. me
21:16 wicked is f. f. m. 22:18
30:10 they flee f. from me
Ps. 22:11 O Lord be not f. f. me,
19; 35:22; 38:21; 71:12
27:9 hide not thy face f. fr. me
88:8 mine acquaintance f. f. me
18 lover and friend f. from me
Prov. 30:8 remove f. f. me vanity
Ec. 7:23 but was f. from me
Is. 29:13 their heart f. from me
Jer. 2:5 they are gone f. from me
Lam. 1:16 comfort. is f. from me
Ezek. 44:10 Lev. are gone f. f. me
Mat. 15:8 is f. f. me, Mark. 7:6

**From FAR.**

Deut. 28:49 na. ag. f. f. Jer. 5:15
Job 36:3 fetch my know. f. f.
Is. 5:26 lift up ensign f. f.
10:3 desol. which sh. come f. f.
22:3 which are fled from f.
30:27 the name of L. com. f. f.
43:6 bring my sons from f. 60:9
49:1 hearken, ye people from f.
12 these shall come from f.
60:4 thy sons shall come from f.
Jer. 30:10 I will save thee from f.
Ezek. 23:40 for men to come f. f.
Mark 8:3 div. of them came f. f.
See AFAR.

**FAR off.**

Deut. 13:7 serve the gods f. off
20:15 thus do to cities very f. off
30:11 nor is com. f. off
2 Sam. 15:17 king tarried f. off
2 Chr. 6:36 captives to land f. off
Ps. 55:7 would I wander f. off
Prov. 27:10 than a brother f. off
Ec. 7:24 f. off who find out?
Is. 17:13 they shall flee f. off
33:13 ye f. off, what I done
17 behold land that is f. off
46:13 my right. not be f. off
57:19 peace to him f. off
59:11 salvation, but it is f. off
Ezek. 6:12 f. off die of pestilence
8:6 f. off from my sanctuary?
11:16 I have cast them f. off
12:27 prophesieth of times f. off
22:5 those that be f. off sh. mock
Dan. 9:7 confus. to Israel f. off
Joel 2:20 rem. f. off north. army
3:8 sell them to Sabeans f. off
Mic. 4:7 her cast f. off, a nation
Zec. 6:15 f. off come and build
Eph. 2:13 f. off are made nigh

**FARE, ED.**

1 Sam. 17:18 look how thy br. f.
Jon. 1:3 paid the f. thereof
Luke 16:19 rich man f. sumptu.

**FAREWELL.**

Luke 9:61 bid them f. at home
Acts 15:29 well, f. 18:21; 23:30
2 Cor. 13:11 finally brethren, f.

FARTHER. See FURTHER.

**FARTHING, S.**

Mat. 5:26 paid the uttermost f.
10:29 two sparrows sold for f.?
Mark 12:42 threw two mites, a f.
Luke 12:6 five sparr. for two f.

**FASHION.**

Mark 2:12 never saw it on this f.
Luke 9:29 f. of his countenance
Acts 7:44 make tabernacle to f.
1 Cor. 7:31 f. world pass. away
Phil. 2:8 found in f. as a man
Jam. 1:11 the grace of f. perish.

**FASHION, ED, ETH, ING.**

Job 10:8 hands f. me, Ps. 119:73
31:15 not one f. us in the wo.?
Ps. 33:15 he f. their hearts alike
139:16 in continuance were f.
Is. 22:11 nei. respect to him f. it
44:12 the smith f. it with ham.
Is. 45:9 clay say to him that f.
Ezek. 16:7 thy breasts are f.
Phil. 3:21 f. like to his glo. body
1 Pet. 1:14 not f. to former lusts

**FAST, Adverb.**

Jud. 15:13 we will bind thee f.
Ps. 65:6 strength set f. moun.
Prov. 4:13 f. hold of instruction
Jer. 48:16 afflic. of M. hasteth f.
50:33 took captiv. held them f.
Jon. 1:5 lay in ship, f. asleep

**FAST, Substantive.**

1 K. 21:9 pro. a f. 2 Chr. 20:3;
Ezr. 8:21; Jer. 36:9; Jon. 3:5
Is. 58:3 in f. you find pleasure
5 a f. wilt thou call this a f.?
6 this the f. I have chosen?
Joel 1:14 sanc. f. call assem. 2:15
Zec. 8:19 f. of 4th, 5th, 7th, 10th month
Acts 27:9 f. was now already past

**FAST, Verb.**

2 Sam. 12:23 child dead, why f.?
Is. 58:4 ye f. for strife, sh. not f.
Jer. 14:12 when f. I will not hear
Zec. 7:5 did ye at all f. unto me?
Mat. 6:16 ye f. be not of sad counten. that may ap. to f.
9:14 disc. f. not? Mark 2:18
15 then f. Mark 2:20; Lu. 5:35
Mark 2:18 disc. of J. used to f.
19 children of bridechamber f.
Luke 5:33 discip. of J. f. often?
18:12 I f. twice in the week

**FASTED, EST.**

Jud. 20:26 f. th. day, 1 Sam. 7:6
1 Sam. 31:13 f. 7 d. 1 Chr. 10:12
2 Sam. 1:12 f. for S.; 1 K. 21:27 A.
Neh. 1:4 Neh. f. and pra. Ez. 8:23
Is. 58:3 why have we f.?
Mat. 4:2 Jesus f. forty days
6:17 when thou f. anoint head
Acts 13:3 f. laid hands on them

**FASTING, S.**

Neh. 9:1 were assembled with f.
Est. 4:3 dec. came there was f.
Ps. 35:13 humbled soul with f.
69:10 chast. my soul with f.
109:24 knees weak through f.
Jer. 36:6 the words on f. day
Dan. 6:18 passed the night f.
9:3 D. set him. to seek by f.
Joel 2:12 turn ye with f.
Mat. 15:32 send them away f.
17:21 but by f. Mark 9:29
Mark 8:3 if I send them away f.
Luke 2:37 Anna served G. with f.
Acts 10:30 four days ago I was f.
14:23 and had prayed with f.
27:33 fourteenth day ye cont. f.
1 Cor. 7:5 give yourselves to f.
2 Cor. 6:5 approv. ourselves in f.
11:27 f. often, in cold and nak.

**FASTEN, ED, ING.**

Judg. 4:21 J. f. nail into ground
1 Chr. 10:10 f. head in temple
Job 38:6 wher. are foundations f.
Ec. 12:11 as nails f. by masters
Is. 22:23 I will f. him as a nail
25 nail f. in the sure place
41:7 he f. it, it sh. not be moved
Jer. 10:4 they f. it with nails
Luke 4:20 eyes of all f. on him
Acts 3:4 Peter f. his eyes on him
11:6 when I had f. my eyes
28:3 a viper f. on his hand

**FAT.**

Gen. 4:4 Abel brought f. of flock
Ex. 29:13 take the f. 22; Lev. 3:3, 4, 9, 10; 4:8; 7:3, 4
Lev. 3:16 all the f. is the Lord's
4:26 burn his f. 6:12; 17:6
7:24 f. of beast that dieth
9:24 fire from Lord consumed f.
Deut. 32:14 f. of lambs, f. of kid
Jud. 3:22 f. closed on the blade
1 Sam. 2:15 before they burnt f.
15:22 hearken is better than f.
2 Sam. 1:22 from f. of mighty
2 Chr. 35:14 offer. f. until night
Job 15:27 collops of f. on flanks
Ps. 17:10 inclosed in th. own f.
Is. 1:11 full of f. of fed beasts
34:6 f. with the f. of kidneys
43:24 nor filled me with f.
Ezek. 44:7 ye offer f. and blood

**Eat FAT.**

Gen. 45:18 shall eat f. of land
Lev. 3:17 eat no f. 7:23
7:25 whoso eateth f. be cut off
Deut. 32:38 eat f. of sacrifices
Neh. 8:10 eat f. drink the sweet
Ezek. 34:3 ye eat f. and clothe
39:19 ye shall eat f. till full
Zec. 11:16 shall eat flesh of f.

**FAT, Adjective.**

Gen. 41:2 came up seven kine f.
49:20 out of A. his bread be f.
Num. 13:20 land is f. or lean
Deut. 31:20 when waxen f. then
32:15 Jeshurun waxed f. kicked
Jud. 3:17 Egl. was very f. man
1 Sam. 2:29 to make f. with off.
28:24 the woman had a f. calf
1 Chr. 4:40 they found f. pasture
Neh. 9:25 took a f. land bec. f.
Ps. 22:29 they f. on earth
37:20 enemies as f. of lambs
92:14 shall be f. and flourish.
119:70 heart is as f. as grease
Prov. 11:25 lib. soul be made f.
13:4 soul of diligent be made f.

15:30 good report mak. bones f.
28:25 trusteth in L. be made f.
Is. 5:17 of f. ones strangers eat
6:10 make the hea. of th. peo. f.
10:16 send am. f. ones leanness
25:6 feast of f. th. full of mar.
28:1 on head of the f. valleys, 4
30:23 bread be f. and plenteous
34:6 sword of the L. is made f.
7 dust shall be f. with fatness
58:11 L. shall make f. thy bones
Jer. 5:28 waxen f. they shine
50:11 ye are grown f. as heifer
Ezek. 34:14 in f. pasture sh. feed
16 I will destroy f. and strong
20 judge bet. f. cattle and lean
45:15 lamb out of f. pastures
Amos 5:22 nor reg. off. of f. bea.
Hab. 1:16 by them portion is f.

**FATHER.**

Gen. 17:4 be f. of many nations, 5; Rom. 4:17, 18
44:19 have ye a f.? 20 we have
45:8 made me a f. to Pharaoh
Lev. 24:10 f. was an Egyptian
Num. 11:12 as nursing f.
30:16 statutes betw. f. and dau.
Jud. 17:10 be to me a f.
18:19 be to us a f. and a priest
Est. 2:7 Esther had nei. f. nor
Job 29:16 I was a f. to the poor
31:18 with me as with a f.
38:28 hath the rain a f.?
Ps. 68:5 a f. of fatherless is God
103:13 as a f. pitieth children
Prov. 3:12 correcteth, as f. son
4:1 hear the instruction of a f.
10:1 maketh a glad f. 15:20
17:21 f. of a fool hath no joy
23:24 f. of righteous sh. rejoice
Is. 9:6 called everlasting F.
22:21 Eliakim be f. to inhabit.
38:19 f. to child. make kn. truth
Jer. 31:9 for I am a f. to Israel
Ezek. 18:4 as soul of f. so of son
20 son shall not bear iniq. of f.
22:7 in thee they set light by f.
Mic. 7:6 son dishonoreth the f.
Mal. 1:6 a f. where mine honor?
2:10 have we not all one f.?
Mat. 10:20 f. del. ch. Mark 13:12
37 that loveth f. more than me
11:25 Jesus said, I th. thee, F.
26 so F. Lu. 10:21; John 11:41
27 knoweth the Son but the F.
15:4 that curseth f. Mark 7:10
19:5 leave f. and cleave to wife
29 that hath forsaken f. for my name's sake, Mark 10:29
28:19 baptizing in name of F.
Mark 9:24 f. of child cried
13:32 knoweth no man but F.
14:36 Abba, F. all th. possible
Luke 10:22 who the F. is, but S.
11:11 if a son ask bread of a f.
12:53 f. be divided against the son and son against the f.
15:21 f. I have sinned aga. hea.
16:27 I pray thee f. send him
22:42 F. if willing, remove cup
23:34 F. forgive them, they
46 F. into thy hands I com.
John 1:14 only begotten of F.
18 Son who is in bosom of F.
3:35 F. loveth the Son, 5:20
4:11 nor at Jerusal. worship F.
23 shall worship F. in spirit
5:19 do noth. but what F. do
21 as F. rais. up dead, so Son
22 the F. judgeth no man, but
23 honor the Son even as F.
26 the F. hath life in himself
36 works F. hath giv. me bear witness F. hath sent me
37 F. which hath sent, 8:16; 12:49; 14:24; 1 John 4:14
5:45 will ac. you to the F.
6:37 all the F. giveth me, shall
39 F. will that I lose nothing
42 Jesus whose f. we know?
John 6:44 exc. the F. draw him
45 learned of F. cometh to me
46 not any hath seen the F. he
57 se. me, and I live by the F.
8:16 am not alone, but I and F.
18 F. beareth witness of me
27 unders. not he spake of F.
29 F. hath not left me alone
41 we have one F. even God
44 devil is liar, and the f. of it
10:15 F. know. me, so I the F.
36 whom the F. hath sanctified
38 F. is in me, and I in him
12:27 F. save me from this hour
28 F. glorify thy name, then
50 as F. said to me, so I speak
13:1 should depart unto the F.
3 that F. had given all things
14:6 com. to the F. but by me
8 Lord, show us the F.
9 seen me, hath seen the F.
11 I in F. and F. in me, 17:21
13 F. may be glorified in Son
16 pray the F. for you, 16:26
31 I love the F. as F. gave co.
15:9 as the F. hath loved me, so
16 whatsoever ye ask F. 16:26
26 I will send Comfor. from F.
16:3 not known the F. nor me
15 all things F. hath, are mine
16 because I go to the F. 17
25 show you plainly of the F.
27 the F. loveth you, because
28 I came from F. and go to F.
32 am not alone, F. is with me
17:1 F. hour is come, glorify S.
5 O F. glorify thou me with
11 holy F. keep th. given me
24 F. I will they be where I am
25 O right. F. world hath not
Acts 1:4 wait for promise of F.
7 F. put in his own power
2:33 received of F. the promise
Rom. 4:11 be f. of them believe
12 f. of circumcision to them
16 Abraham, who is f. of us all
6:4 as Christ was raised by F.
8:15 whereby we cry, Abba, F.
11:28 are belov. for the F. sake
15:6 F. of our L. J. C. 2 Cor. 1:3; 11:31; Eph. 1:3; 1 Pet. 1:3
1 Cor. 8:6 is but one God, the F.
15:24 deliv. up kingdom to F.
2 Cor. 1:3 F. of mercies
6:18 I will be a F. unto you
Gal. 1:3 peace from F. 2 Tim. 1:2; Tit. 1:4
4 ac. to will of God and our F.
4:2 until time appointed of F.
6 Spirit crying, Abba, F.
Eph. 1:17 G. of Jesus F. of glory
2:18 access by one Spirit to F.
3:14 bow my knees unto the F.
4:6 one God and F. all
5:20 giving thanks to F. Col. 1:3, 12; 3:17
6:23 love with faith from F.
Phil. 2:11 is Lord, to glory of F.
22 as a son with the f. he hath
Col. 1:19 it plea. F. that all fuln.
2:2 acknowl. of mystery of F.
1 Thes. 1:1 church in God the F.
2:11 charged you, as a f. doth
1 Tim. 5:1 entreat him as a f.
Heb. 1:5 I will be to him a F. he
7:3 Melchizedek without f.
12:7 what son f. chasten. not?
9 in subjection to F. of spirits
Jam. 1:17 com. from F. of lights
3:9 bless we God, even the F.
1 Pet. 1:2 foreknowl. of the F.
17 call on F. who judgeth
2 Pet. 1:17 receiv. from F. honor
1 John 1:2 life wh. was with F.
3 our fellow. is with F.
2:1 an advocate with the F. J.
13 because ye have known F.
15 love of the F. is not in him
16 pride of life is not of the F.
22 antichrist deni. F. and Son
23 whoso deni. S. hath not F.
24 continue in the S. and in F.
3:1 what manner of love the F.
5:7 three bear record, the F.
2 John 3 mercy and peace fr. F.
4 we received a com. from F.
9 abideth in Christ hath F.
Jude 1 sanctified by God the F.
See ABRAHAM.

**Her FATHER.**

Gen. 19:33 fi.-born lay with her f.
29:12 he was her f. brother
Lev. 21:9 she profaneth her f.
Num. 12:14 if h. f. had but spit
Deut. 21:13 bewail h. f. a month
Jud. 15:6 Philistines burnt h. f.
Est. 2:7 h. f. and mother dead

**His FATHER.**

Gen. 2:24 shall a man leave his f. Mark 10:7; Eph. 5:31
28:7 Jacob obeyed his f. and his
31:53 J. sware by fear of his f.
37:1 his f. was a stranger
22 to deliver him to his f.
44:22 the lad cannot leave his f.
46:1 sacrifices to God of his f.
29 Joseph went to meet his f.
47:12 Joseph nourished his f.
Ex. 21:15 smit. f. be put to dea.
17 curseth his f. Lev. 20:9
Lev. 19:3 fear every man his f.
Deut. 21:18 will not obey his f.
27:16 setteth light by his f.
33:9 his f. I have not seen him
1 Sam. 14:1 Jona. told not his f.
19:4 spake good of D. to his f.
20:34 h. f. had done him shame
2 Sam. 7:14 will be his f. he son
10:2 as his f. showed kindness to me, 1 Chr. 19:2
1 K. 11:4 not perf. as David h. f.
6 as did Dav. his f. 15:11; 2 K. 18:3; 2 Chr. 28:1; 29:2
33 not as f. 2 K. 14:3; 16:2
15:3 walked in all sins of his f.
26 way of f. 22:43; 2 K. 21:21
2 K. 3:2 did evil, but not like f.
1 Chr. 17:13 I will be his f. 28:6
2 Chr. 3:1 L. appeared to D. his f.
17:4 Jehos. sought God of his f.
34:2 in ways of David his f. 3
Prov. 13:1 hear. instruction of f.
15:5 despiseth h. f. instruction
17:25 foolish son a grief to h. f.
19:13 is the calamity of his f.
26 wasteth his f. caus. shame
20:20 curseth h. f. lamp put out
28:7 com. of riot, shameth his f.
24 whoso robbeth his f.
29:3 lov. wisdom rejoiceth h. f.
30:17 mocketh f. ravens pick
Is. 45:10 woe to him saith to h. f.
Ezek. 18:14 son seeth h. f. sins
17 not die for iniquity of his f.
Amos 2:7 his f. go in to maid
Zec. 13:3 his f. thrust him thro'
Mal. 1:6 a son honors his f.
Mat. 10:35 at variance ag. his f.
15:5 to h. f. it is gift, Mark 7:11
6 and honor not his f. be free
16:27 Son come in glory of h. F. Mark 8:38; Luke 9:26
21:31 whether did will of h. f.?
Luke 1:32 give him thr. of his f.
59 called after name of his f.
62 they made signs unto his f.
9:42 J. delivered him to his f.
14:26 and hate not his f.
15:12 younger said to his f.
20 arose and came to his f.

**His FATHERS.**

2 *K.* 15:9 did evil as *his f.* had
21:22 fors. G. of *h. f.* 2 *Chr.* 21:10
2 *Chr.* 21:19 like burning of *h. f.*
28:25 A. provoked L. G. of *h. f.*
30:19 to seek God of *his f.*
33:12 humbled before G. of *h. f.*
*Ps.* 49:19 generation of *his f.*
109:14 iniquity of *his f.*
*Dan.* 11:24 what *his f.* not done
37 nor regard the God of *his f.*
38 a god whom *his f.* knew not
*Acts* 13:36 Dav. was laid to *h. f.*

**My FATHERS.**

*Gen.* 47:9 not at. years of *my f.*
30 I will lie with *my f.*
48:16 name of *my f.* be named
49:29 bury me with *my f.*
*Ex.* 15:2 he is *my f.* God
1 *K.* 19:4 no better than *my f.*
21:3 inheritance of *my f.* 4.
2 *K.* 19:12 which *my f.* destroyed,
2 *Chr.* 32:14; *Is.* 37:12
2 *Chr.* 32:13 I and *my f.* done
*Ps.* 39:12 soj. as *my f.* were
*Dan.* 2:23 O God of *my f.*
*Acts* 24:14 worship God of *my f.*
*Gal.* 1:14 traditions of *my f.*

**Our FATHERS.**

*Gen.* 46:34 we and also *o. f.* 47:3
*Num.* 20:15 *our f.* went down
*Deut.* 5:3 not covenant with *o. f.*
6:23 he sware to *our f.* 26:3, 15
26:7 cried to the God of *our f.*
*Jos.* 24:17 brought *o. f.* out of E.
*Jud.* 6:13 mirac. *o. f.* told us of?
1 *K.* 8:57 as he was with *our f.*
58 statutes he commanded *o. f.*
2 *K.* 22:13 *our f.* not hearkened
1 *Chr.* 12:17 G. of *o. f.* rebuke it
29:15 are sojourners, as *our f.*
18 O L. God of *our f.* keep for
ever in the heart, 2 *Chr.* 20:6
2 *Chr.* 6:31 gavest *o. f.* *Neh.* 9:36
29:6 for *our f.* have trespassed
9 *o. f.* have fallen by the sword
34:21 *our f.* have not kept word
*Ezr.* 5:12 after *o. f.* provoked G.
7:27 blessed be the God of *o. f.*
9:7 since *o. f.* in great trespass
*Neh.* 9:9 see affliction of *our f.*
16 *our f.* dealt proudly
*Ps.* 22:4 *our f.* trusted in thee
44:1 *o. f.* told what didst, 78:3
106:6 we have sinned with *o. f.*
7 *o. f.* understood not wonders
*Is.* 64:11 *our f.* praised thee
*Jer.* 3:24 devoured labor of *o. f.*
25 and *our f.* not obeyed voice
16:19 *our f.* have inherited lies
44:17 as we have done, *our f.*
*Lam.* 5:7 *our f.* sinned
*Dan.* 9:8 confus. of face to *our f.*
16 our sins and iniq. of *our f.*
*Mic.* 7:20 sworn to *o. f.* from old
*Mal.* 2:10 profaning cov. of *our f.*
*Mat.* 23:30 in days of *our f.*
*Luke* 1:55 as he spake to *our f.*
72 mercy promised to *our f.*
*John* 4:20 *our f.* wors. in mount.
6:31 *our f.* eat manna in desert
*Acts* 3:13 God of *o. f.* hath glori.
25 cove. God made with *our f.*
5:30 G. of *o. f.* raised up Jesus
7:11 *our f.* found no sustenance
15 Jacob died, he and *our f.*
19 and evil entreated *our f.*
38 he which spake with *our f.*
39 whom *o. f.* would not obey
13:17 God of Israel chose *our f.*
15:10 yoke *o. f.* not able to bear
26:6 promise made to *our f.*
28:25 well spake by E. to *our f.*
1 *Cor.* 10:1 *o. f.* were under cloud

**Slept with FATHERS.**

1 *K.* 2:10 David *slept w. f.* 11:21
43 Sol. *slept w. f.* 2 *Chr.* 9:31
2 *K.* 20:21 H. *s. w. f.* 2 *Chr.* 32:33
2 *Chr.* 26:23 Uzziah *slept with f.*

**Their FATHERS.**

*Ex.* 4:5 G. of *t. f.* hath appeared
*Lev.* 26:39 in iniquity of *their f.*
26:40 confess iniq. of *their f.*
*Num.* 11:12 swarest to *t. f.* 14:23;
*Deut.* 10:11; 31:20; *Jos.* 1:6;
5:6; 21:43, 44; *Jer.* 32:22
*Deut.* 29:25 forsaken cov. of *t. f.*
*Jos.* 4:6 children ask *their f.* 21
22:14 head of house of *their f.*
*Jud.* 2:10 gathered to *their f.*
12 forsook the God of *their f.*
17 out of way *t. f.* walked in
19 corrupted more than *t. f.*
20 covenant I commanded *t. f.*
*Jud.* 2:22 keep way of L. as *t. f.*
1 *K.* 8:34 land thou gavest to *t. f.* 48; 2 *Chr.* 6:25, 38
9:9 brought *t. f.* out of Egypt
14:15 he gave to *their f.* 2 *K.* 21:8; *Jer.* 16:15; 24:10
22 provok. above all *t. f.* done
1 *Chr.* 5:25 transgr. ag. God of *f.*
29:20 blessed God of *their f.*
2 *Chr.* 7:22 for. G. of *f.* 24:24; 28:6
11:16 sacrifice to God of *their f.*
13:18 relied on God of *their f.*
14:4 to seek God of *t. f.* 15:12
19:4 back to the God of *their f.*
20:33 prepa. hearts to G. of *t. f.*
30:7 trespassed ag. God of *t. f.*
22 confession to God of *their f.*
34:33 following the God of *t. f.*
36:15 G. of *t. f.* sent messengers
*Neh.* 9:2 confessed iniq. of *t. f.*
*Job* 8:8 prepare to search of *t. f.*
15:18 wise men told from *t. f.*
*Ps.* 78:8 might not be as *their f.*
12 marv. things in sight of *t. f.*
57 dealt unfaithfully like *t. f.*
*Prov.* 17:6 glory of child. are *t. f.*
*Is.* 14:21 slaughter for iniq. of *f.*
*Jer.* 7:26 did worse than *their f.*
9:14 Baalim, which *t. f.* taught
16 nor *t. f.* have known, 19:4
23:27 as *t. f.* forgotten my name
31:32 not accord. to covenant I made with *t. f.* 11:10; *Heb.* 8:9
50:7 sinned ag. L. hope of *t. f.*
*Ezek.* 2:3 *t. f.* have transgressed
5:10 and sons shall eat *their f.*
20:4 cause know abom. of *t. f.*
*Amos* 2:4 after which *t. f.* walked
*Mal.* 4:6 heart of children to *t. f.*
*Luke* 6:23 like manner did *t. f.*
26 so did *t. f.* to false prophets

**Thy FATHERS.**

*Gen.* 15:15 shalt go to *thy f.*
*Ex.* 13:5 sware to *thy f.* 11; *Deut.* 6:10, 18; 7:12, 13; 8:18; 9:5; 13:17; 19:8; 28:11; 29:13; 30:20
*Deut.* 4:31 not forget cov. of *t. f.*
37 because he loved *thy f.* 10:15
10:22 *thy f.* went with 70 persons
12:1 land the G. of *thy f.* giveth
19:8 land he prom. *thy f.* 27:3
30:5 multipl. thee above *thy f.*
9 as he rejoiced over *thy f.*
31:16 with *thy f.* 2 *Sam.* 7:12
1 *K.* 13:22 not to sepulchre of *t. f.*
2 *K.* 20:17 *thy f.* laid up
22:20 to *thy f.* 2 *Chr.* 34:28
1 *Chr.* 17:11 go to be with *thy f.*
*Ps.* 45:16 instead of *thy f.*
*Jer.* 34:5 the burnings of *thy f.*
*Acts* 7:32 I am the God of *thy f.*

**Your FATHERS.**

*Gen.* 48:21 bring to land of *y. f.*
*Ex.* 3:13 God of *your f.* sent me
*Deut.* 1:11; 4:1; *Jos.* 18:3
2 *Chr.* 28:9; 29:5
*Num.* 32:14 risen up in *y. f.* stead
*Jos.* 24:2 *your f.* dwell other side
6 I brought *y. f.* out of Egypt
1 *Sam.* 12:7 acts L. did to *y. f.*
8 *y. f.* cried, L. bro. forth *y. f.*
15 hand of L. ag. you as *y. f.*
2 *Chr.* 13:12 not ag. God of *y. f.*
30:7 not like *y. f.* 8; *Zec.* 1:4
*Ezr.* 10:11 confes. to G. of *y. f.*
*Ps.* 95:9 *your f.* tempted, *Heb.* 3:9
*Is.* 65:7 and iniquities of *your f.*
*Jer.* 2:5 iniq. *y. f.* found in me?
11:7 I earnestly protested to *y. f.*
16:11 *your f.* have forsaken me
12 done worse than *your f.*
34:14 *y. f.* heark. not unto me
44:3 knew not, they nor *your f.*
8 forgotten wickedn. of *y. f.*?
*Ezek.* 20:18 not in statutes of *y. f.*
27 in this *your f.* blasphemed
30 after manner of *your f.*?
36 as I pleaded with *your f.*?
37:25 dwell in land *y. f.* dwelt
*Hos.* 9:10 I saw *y. f.* as first ripe
*Joel* 1:2 been in days of *your f.*?
*Zec.* 1:2 L. displeased with *y. f.*
4 be not as *your f.*
5 *your f.* where are they?
6 words take hold of *your f.*?
8:14 when *your f.* provoked me
*Mal.* 3:7 days of *y. f.* ye are gone.
*Mat.* 23:32 fill up measure of *y. f.*
*Luke* 11:47 *your f.* killed them
48 ye allow deeds of *your f.*
*John* 6:49 *your f.* did eat manna
58 *your f.* eat, and are dead
*Acts* 7:51 resist Holy G. as *y. f.*
52 have not *y. f.* persecuted?
1 *Pet.* 1:18 by tradition from *y. f.*

**FATHERLESS.**

*Ex.* 22:22 not afflict *f.* child
*Ex.* 22:24 your children sh. be *f.*
*Deut.* 10:18 execute judgment of *f.* *Ps.* 82:3; *Is.* 1:17
*Job* 6:27 ye overwhelm the *f.*
22:9 arms of *f.* been broken
24:3 drive away ass of the *f.*
9 pluck *f.* from the breast
29:12 because I delivered the *f.*
31:17 the *f.* not eaten thereof
21 if I lifted up my hand ag. *f.*
*Ps.* 10:14 thou art helper of *f.*
18 judge the *f.* and oppressed
68:5 a father of the *f.*
109:9 let his children be *f.*
12 nor any favor his *f.* children
*Prov.* 23:10 enter not fields of *f.*
*Is.* 1:23 judge not *f.* *Jer.* 5:28
9:17 not have mercy on their *f.*
10:2 that they may rob the *f.*
*Jer.* 49:11 leave thy *f.* children
*Lam.* 5:3 we are orphans and *f.*
*Ezek.* 22:7 in thee have vexed *f.*
*Hos.* 14:3 in thee *f.* findeth mercy
*Mal.* 3:5 witness ag. those op. *f.*
*Jam.* 1:27 pure religion to visit *f.*

**FATHERLESS, *with* stranger.**

*Deut.* 14:29 *stra.* and *f.* shall eat, 24:19, 20, 21; 26:12, 13
16:11 *s.* and *f.* rejoice with thee
24:17 not perv. jud. of *s.* nor *f.*
27:19 perv. judg. of *s.* and *f.*
*Ps.* 94:6 slay *s.* and murder *f.*
146:9 Lord preserveth *s.* and *f.*
*Jer.* 7:6 if ye oppress not the *st.* and *f.* 22:3; *Zec.* 7:10

**FATHOMS.**

*Acts* 27:28 found it twenty *f.*

**FATLING, S.**

1 *Sam.* 15:9 Saul spared best of *f.*
*Ps.* 66:15 burnt sacrifices of *f.*
*Is.* 11:6 lion, and the *f.* together
*Ezek.* 39:18 all of them *f.* of B.
*Mat.* 22:4 oxen and *f.* are killed

**FATNESS.**

*Gen.* 27:28 G. give thee of the *f.*
39 dwelling be *f.* of the earth
*Deut.* 32:15 art covered with *f.*

Jud. 9:9 should I leave my f.
Job 15:27 cover. face with his f.
36:16 thy table sh. be full of f.
Ps. 36:8 satisfied with f.
63:5 my soul satisfied as with f.
65:11 all thy paths drop f.
73:7 eyes stand out with f.
109:24 my flesh faileth of f.
Is. 17:4 f. of his flesh wax lean
34:6 sword of Lord is fat with f.
7 their dust be made fat wi. f.
55:2 let soul delight itself in f.
Jer. 31:14 soul of priests with f.
Rom. 11:17 partak. of f. of olive

**FATS.**

Joel 2:24 f. shall overflow, 3:13

**FATTED.**

Jer. 46:21 men like f. bullocks
See CALF.

**FATTEST.**

Ps. 78:31 wrath of God slew f.
Dan. 11:24 enter on the f. places

**FAULT, S.**

Gen. 41:9 I remember f. this day
Ex. 5:16 f. is in thine own peo.
Deut. 25:2 beaten accord. to h. f.
1 Sam. 29:3 I found no f. in him
2 Sam. 3:8 chargest me with a f.
Ps. 19:12 cleanse from secret f.
59:4 they prepare without my f.
Dan. 6:4 could find no f. in him
Mat. 18:15 tresp. tell him his f.
Mark 7:2 unw. hands they f. f.
Luke 23:4 I find no f. in th. man,
14; John 18:38; 19:4, 6
Rom. 9:19 doth he yet find f.?
1 Cor. 6:7 utterly a f. among you
Gal. 6:1 man be overtaken in f.
Heb. 8:8 finding f. with them
Jam. 5:16 conf. f. one to another
1 Pet. 2:20 if when buffeted for f.
Rev. 14:5 without f. bef. throne

**FAULTLESS.**

Heb. 8:7 if first cov. had been f.
Jude 24 is able to present you f.

**FAULTY.**

2 Sam. 14:13 king speak as one f.
Hos. 10:2 shall they be found f.

**FAVOR, Substantive.**

Gen. 39:21 gave Jos. f. in sight
Ex. 3:21 give peop. f. in sight of
Egyptians, 11:3; 12:36
Deut. 28:50 not show f. to young
33:23 O Naph. satisfied with f.
Jos. 11:20 they might have no f.
Sam. 2:26 Samuel in f. with L.
Job 10:12 granted me life and f.
Ps. 5:12 with f. compass him
30:5 in his f. is life,
7 by f. made mountain to sta.
44:3 because hadst a f. to them
45:12 rich shall entreat thy f.
89:17 in thy f. our horn exalted
106:4 remember me with f. thou
112:5 a good man showeth f.
119:58 I entreated thy f.
Prov. 11:27 seek. good procur. f.
13:15 good understand. giv. f.
14:9 among righteous there is f.
35 king's f. toward wise serv.
16:15 his f. is as a cloud of rain
19:6 many entreat f. of prince
12 king's f. is as dew up. grass
21:10 his neighbor findeth no f.
22:1 lov. f. rather to be chosen
29:26 many seek the ruler's f.
31:30 f. is deceitful
Ec. 9:11 nor f. to men of skill
Is. 26:10 f. be showed to wicked
27:11 formed show them no f.
60:10 but in my f. I had mercy
Jer. 16:13 I will not show f.
Dan. 1:9 brought Daniel into f.
Luke 2:52 Jesus increased in f.
Acts 2:47 f. with all the people
7:10 God gave Moses f. in sight
25:3 high-priest desired f.

**Find or found FAVOR.**

Gen. 18:3 if I have f. f. 30:27;
Num. 11:15; 1 Sam. 20:29;
Neh. 2:5; Est. 5:8; 7:3; 8:5
Num. 11:11 why h. I not f. f.?
Deut. 24:1 that she find no f.
1 Sam. 16:22 David hath f. f.
25:8 let the young men find f.
2 Sam. 15:25 if I f. f. in ey. of L.
Prov. 3:4 so f. f. in sight of God
28:23 find more f. than he flat.
Cant. 8:10 I was as one found f.
Luke 1:30 hast f. f. with God
Acts 7:46 who f. f. before God

**Obtain, ed, eth FAVOR.**

Est. 2:15 Esther ob. f. 17; 5:2
Prov. 8:35 findeth me shall ob. f.
12:2 good man ob. f. of Lord
18:22 findeth a wife, obtaineth f.

**FAVOR, Verb.**

1 Sam. 29:6 the lords f. thee not
Ps. 35:27 f. my righteous cause
102:13 set time to f. her is come
14 thy servants f. dust thereof
109:12 to f. fatherless children

**FAVORABLE.**

Jud. 21:22 be f. for our sakes
Job 33:26 God will be f. unto him
Ps. 77:7 will L. be f. no more?
85:1 hast been f. to thy land

**FAVORED, EST, ETH.**

Gen. 29:17 Rachel was well-f.
39:6 Jos. well-f.; 41:2 kine, 18
41:3 il-f. kine, 4, 19, 21, 27
2 Sam. 20:11 f. Joab, go after J.
Ps. 41:11 by this I know thou f.
Lam. 4:16 they f. not the elders
Dan. 1:4 children well-f. skilful
Nah. 3:4 whored. of well-f. har.
Luke 1:28 hail, thou highly f.

**FEAR, Substantive.**

Gen. 9:2 f. of you be on ev. beast
31:42 f. of Is. had been with me
53 Jacob sware by f. of Isaac
Ex. 15:16 f. sh. fall upon them
23:27 send my f. before thee
Deut. 2:25 f. of thee on nations
11:25 lay f. of you on land
1 Chr. 14:17 f. of him on nations
Ezr. 3:3 f. was on them because
Neh. 6:14 that put me in f. 19
Est. 8:17 f. of Jews fell on them
9:3 f. of Mordecai fell on them
Job 4:6 is not this thy f.
14 f. came on me and tremb.
6:14 forsaketh f. of Almighty
9:34 let not his f. terrify me
15:4 yea, thou castest off f. and
21:9 their houses are safe from f.
22:10 sudden f. troubleth thee
25:2 dominion and f. with him
39:22 he mocketh at f.
Ps. 5:7, in thy f. will I worship
9:20 put them in f. O Lord
14:5 there were they in great f.
31:11 I was a f. to acquaintance
13 f. was on every side
48:6 f. took hold upon them
53:5 were in f. where no f. was
64:1 pres. my life fr. f. of enemy
90:11 to thy f. so is thy wrath
105:38 f. of them fell upon them
119:38 thy serv. devot. to thy f.
Prov. 1:26 mock when f. cometh
27 when your f. cometh as d.
Prov. 1:33 be quiet from f. of evil
3:25 be not afraid of sudden f.
10:24 f. of wicked come on him
20:2 f. of king as roaring of lion
29:25 f. of man bringeth a snare
Cant. 3:8 sw. bec. of f. in night
Is. 7:25 not come the f. of briers
8:12 neither fear ye their f.
13 the Lord, let him be your f.
14:3 shall give thee rest from f.
21:4 night of pleasure into f.
24:17 f. and the pit upon thee
18 fleeth from f. Jer. 48:44
29:13 their f. is taught by men
63:17 hardened heart from thy f.
Jer. 2:19 that my f. is not in thee
6:25 f. is on ev. side, 20:10
30:5 we have heard a voice of f.
32:40 put my f. in their hearts
48:43 f. shall be on thee, O M.
49:5 I will bring a f. upon thee
24 f. hath seized on Damascus
29 shall cry. f. is on every side
Lam. 3:47 f. and snare is come
Ezek. 30:13 put a f. in land of E.
Mal. 1:6 where is my f.?
Luke 1:12 Z. saw him, f. fell on
65 f. ca. on all, 7:16; Acts 2:43;
5:5, 11; 19:17; Rev. 11:11
Rom. 13:7 f. to whom f. is due
1 Cor. 2:3 in weakness and f.
2 Cor. 7:11 what f. what vehem.
2 Tim. 1:7 not giv. us spirit of f.
Heb. 2:15 through f. of death
12:28 reverence and godly f.
1 Pet. 1:17 pass time of soj. in f.
3:15 with meekness and f.
1 John 4:18 no f. in l. cast out f.

**For FEAR.**

Deut. 28:67 f. the f. thou sh. fear
Jos. 22:24 done it f. f. of thing
1 Sam. 21:10 fled f. f. of S. 23:26
Job 22:4 reprove f. f. of thee?
Is. 31:9 to his strong-hold f. f.
Jer. 46:5 f. f. was round about
50:16 f. f. of oppressing sword
Mal. 2:5 f. f. wherew. he feared
Mat. 14:26 discip. cried out f. f.
28:4 f. f. of him keepers shake
Luke 21:26 hearts failing for f.
John 7:13 spake openly f. f.
19:38 but secretly f. f. of Jews
20:19 assembled f. f. of the J.
Rev. 18:10 f. f. of torment, 15

**Fear of GOD.**

Gen. 20:11 f. of G. not in place
2 Sam. 23:3 ruling in f. of God
2 Chr. 20:29 f. of G. on all king.
Neh. 5:9 to walk in the f. f. G.?
15 so did not I, bec. of f. of G.
Ps. 36:1 no f. of G. bef. his eyes
Rom. 3:18 no f. of G. bef. th. ey.
2 Cor. 7:1 holiness in f. of God
Eph. 5:21 submitting in f. of G.

**Fear of the LORD.**

1 Sam. 11:7 f. of L. 2 Chr. 17:10
2 Chr. 14:14 f. of L. ca. on them
19:7 f. of the L. be upon you
9 thus do in f. of the Lord
Job 28:28 f. of the L. is wisdom
Ps. 19:9 f. of the Lord is clean
34:11 I will teach you f. of t. L.
111:10 f. of L. begin. of wisdom
Prov. 1:7 f. of L. beg. of kn. 9:10
29 did not choose the f. of t. L.
2:5 shalt understand f. of the L.
8:3 f. of t. L. is to hate evil
10:27 f. of the L. prolong. days
14:26 in f. of Lord is str. confid.
27 f. of L. is a fountain of life
15:16 better is lit. with f. of L.
33 f. of L. is instruction
16:6 by f. of L. men dep. fr. evil
19:23 f. of the L. tendeth to life
22:4 by f. of L. are riches and h.
23:17 be in f. of Lord all day
Is. 2:10 hide in dust, for f. of L.
19 go into caves for f. of L.
21 go into clefts, for f. of Lord
11:2 spirit of know. and f. of L.
3 quick understand. in f. of L.
33:6 f. of L. is his treasure
Acts 9:31 walking in f. of the L.

**With FEAR.**

Ps. 2:11 serve the Lord with f.
Mat. 28:8 with f. and great joy
Luke 5:26 were all filled with f.
8:37 Gadarenes tak. w. great f.
2 Cor. 7:15 with f. received him
Eph. 6:5 obedience w. f. and tr.
Phil. 2:12 work out salva. w. f.
Heb. 11:7 N. w. f. prepared ark
1 Pet. 2:18 be subj. to mast. w. f.
3:2 chaste conv. coup. w. f.
Jude 23 and others save with f.

**Without FEAR.**

Job 39:16 her labor in vain w. f.
41:33 not his like, made w. f.
Luke 1:74 serve him with f.
1 Cor. 16:10 may be with y. w. f.
Phil. 1:14 bold to sp. word w. f.
Jude 12 feeding themselv. w. f.

**FEARS.**

Ps. 34:4 delivered me fr. all my f.
Ec. 12:5 when f. be in the way
Is. 66:4 bring their f. upon them
2 Cor. 7:5 within were f.

**FEAR, Verb.**

Lev. 19:3 f. every man his moth.
Num. 14:9 nei. f. people of land
Deut. 4:10 may learn to f. me
5:29 O that they would f. me
28:58 f. glori. name, the Lord
66 thou shalt f. day and night
67 fear wherewith thou sha. f.
Jud. 7:10 if thou f. to go down
1 K. 8:40 f. thee, 2 Chr. 6:31
43 name to f. thee, 2 Chr. 6:33
2 K. 17:38 neither f. other gods
39 the Lord your G. ye shall f.
1 Chr. 16:30 f. before him all the earth, Ps. 96:9
Neh. 1:11 desire to f. thy name
Job 31:34 did I f. a great multi
Ps. 23:4 I will f. no evil,
27:1 whom shall I f.?
31:19 goodness for them f. thee
40:3 many shall see it, and f.
49:5 I f. in days of evil?
52:6 righte. also shall see and f.
60:4 a banner to them that f.
61:5 herit. of those f. thy name
64:9 shall f. and declare work
72:5 f. thee as long as sun end.
86:11 unite my heart to f. name
102:15 so heath. shall f. thy n.
119:39 my reproach which I f.
63 compan. of them that f. th.
74 they that f. thee will be gl.
79 let those f. thee turn to me
Ec. 3:14 that men f. before him
Is. 8:12 neither f. ye their fear
19:16 Eg. shall be afraid and f.
25:3 city of ter. nations f. thee
44:11 the workmen shall f.
59:19 so shall they f. name of L.
60:5 thy heart f. and be enlarg.
Jer. 10:7 who would not f. th. O
23:4 and they shall f. no more
32:39 one heart that they f. me
33:9 shall f. for the goodness
51:46 and lest ye f. for rumor
Dan. 6:26 f. before G. of Daniel
Hos. 10:5 inhab. of Samaria sh. f.
Mic. 7:17 and f. because of thee
Zep. 3:7 said, Surely wilt f. me
Hag. 1:12 people did f. before L.
Zec. 9:5 Ashk. shall see it, and f.
Mal 4:2 to you f. my name
Mat. 21:26 we say, Of men, we f.
Luke 12:5 whom ye shall f.
Rom. 8:15 spirit of bondage to f.
11:20 be not high-minded, but f.
2 Cor. 12:20 I f. lest not find you
1 Tim. 5:20 others also may f.
Heb. 4:1 let us f. lest a promise
12:21 M. said, I exceedingly f.
Rev. 2:10 f. none of those things
11:18 rew. to them f. thy name

**FEAR God.**

Gen. 42:18 and live, for I f. G.
Ex. 18:21 provide such as f. God
Lev. 19:14 shalt f. thy God, 32
25:17 thou sh. f. thy G. 36, 43
Job 1:9 doth J. f. G. for naught?
Ps. 66:16 all ye that f. God
Ec. 5:7 vanities, but f. thou God
8:12 well with them that f. G.
12:13 f. G. and keep his com.
Is. 29:23 they sh. f. G. of Israel
Luke 23:40 dost not thou f. G.?
Acts 13:16 f. God, give audience
1 Pet. 2:17 f. God, honor the k.
Rev. 14:7 f. God, and give glory

**Hear and FEAR.**

Deut. 13:11 Is. shall h. a. f. 21:21
17:13 all the peo. shall h. a. f.
19:20 who remain sh. hear a. f.

**FEAR him.**

Deut. 13:4 walk after G. and f. h.
2 K. 17:36 him shall ye f.
Job 37:24 men therefore f. him
Ps. 22:23 f. him, seed of Israel
25 before them that f. him.
25:14 secret of L. with th. f. h.
33:18 eye of L. on them f. him
34:7 encamp. about them f. h.
9 no want to them that f. him
67:7 ends of the earth shall f. h.
85:9 salva. is nigh them f. him
103:11 his mercy to them f. h.
Ps. 103:13 L. pit. th. that f. him
17 mercy of L. is on them f. h.
111:5 meat to them that f. him
145:19 desire of them f. him
147:11 pleas. in them that f. h.
Mat. 10:28 f. h. able Luke 12:5
Luke 1:50 mercy on them f. him
Rev. 19:5 praise G. ye that f. h.

**Fear the LORD.**

Deut. 6:2 mightest f. t. L. thy G.
13 shalt f. L. 10:20; 2 K. 17:39
24 to f. L. for our good always
10:12 f. the L. walk in his ways
14:23 to f. L. 17:19; 31:12, 13
Jos. 4:24 might f. Lord your G.
24:14 now therefore f. the Lord
1 Sam. 12:14 if ye will f. the L.
24 f. L. serve him in truth
1 K. 18:12 but I f. L. 2 K. 4:1
2 K. 17:28 taught them how f. L.
Ps. 15:4 honoreth them f. Lord
22:23 ye that f. L. praise him
33:8 let all the earth f. the Lord
34:9 O f. the L. ye his saints
115:11 ye that f. L. trust in L.
13 he will bless them that f. L.
118:4 f. L. say, his mercy end.
135:20 ye that f. L. bless the L.
Prov. 3:7 f. L. depart from evil
24:21 f. the Lord, and the king
Jer. 5:24 nor say th. Let us f. L.
26:19 did he not f. the Lord
Hos. 3:5 afterwards sh. Is. f. L.
Jon. 1:9 I f. L. the G. of heaven

**FEAR not.**

Gen. 15:1 f. not Ab. I am shield
26:24 f. not, I am with thee
35:17 midwife said to R. f. n.
43:23 Peace be to you, f. not
46:3 f. not to go down to Egypt
50:19 f. not, am I in place of G.?
Ex. 14:13 f. n. stand, see salva.
20:20 f. not, G. is come to prove
Num. 14:9 L. with us, f. them n.
21:34 L. saith to Mo. f. him not
Deut. 20:3 f. not your enemies
31:8 L. doth go before thee, f. not, Jos. 8:1; 1 Chr. 28:20
Jud. 6:10 f. not gods of Amorites
23 peace, f. not, thou sh. not d.
1 Sam. 4:20 said to her, f. not
12:20 Sam. said to people, f. not
22:23 abide thou with me, f. n.
23:17 Jonathan said to D. f. not
2 Sam. 13:28 kill Amnon, f. not
1 K. 17:13 said to widow, f. not
2 K. 6:16 f. not, more with us
17:34 to this day they f. not L.
25:24 f. not to serve Chaldees
2 Chr. 20:17 be with you, f. n.
Ps. 55:19 therefore they f. not G.
64:4 shoot at him, and f. not
Is. 7:4 f. not tails of firebrands
35:4 to them of fear. heart, f. n.
41:10 f. n. I am with thee, 43:5
13 hold thy hand, saying, f. n.
41:14 f. not, thou worm Jacob
43:1 f. n. I have redeemed thee
44:2 f. not, O Jacob my servant, Jer. 30:10; 46:27, 28
8 f. ye not, ha. not I told th.?
51:7 f. not the reproach of men
54:4 f. n. thou shalt not be ash.
Jer. 5:22 f. ye not me?
Lam. 3:57 thou saidst, f. not
Dan. 10:12 f. not, Daniel, 19
Joel 2:21 f. not, O land, be glad
Zep. 3:16 be said to Jer. f. not
Hag. 2:5 Sp. rem. am. you, f. not
Zec. 8:13 sh. be a blessing, f. not
15 do well to Judah, f. ye not
Mal. 3:5 witness ag. them f. not
Mat. 1:20 f. n. to take to thee M.
10:26 f. them not, nothing cov.
28 f. not them who kill body
28:5 angel said to women, f. not
Luke 1:13 f. not Zach.; 30 Mary
2:10 shepherds, f. n.; 5:10 Sim.
8:50 Jairus f. not, believe only
12:32 f. not, little flock
18:4 though I f. not God,
John 12:15 f. not daughter of S.
Acts 27:24 f. not, Paul,
Rev. 1:17 f. not. I am the first

**Not FEAR.**

Ex. 9:30 ye will n. yet f. the L.
2 K. 17:35 not f. other gods, 37
Job 9:35 I speak, and not f. him
11:15 steadfast, thou shalt n. f.
Ps. 27:3 tho. host encamp, not f.
46:2 not f. though earth be rem.
56:4 n. f. wh. flesh can do, 118:6
Is. 54:14 from oppression, n. f.
Jer. 10:7 who would not f. thee
Amos 3:8 who will not f.?
Luke 23:40 dost not thou f. God?
Heb. 13:6 not f. what man do
Rev. 15:4 who shall n. f. thee,

**FEARED.**

Gen. 26:7 f. to say, She is my w.
Ex. 9:20 he that f. word of Lord
Deut. 25:18 Amalek f. not God
32:17 to new gods fathers f. not
27 were it not I f. the wrath of
Jos. 4:14 f. Josh. as they did M.
1 Sam. 14:26 people f. the oath
15:24 because I f. the people
1 K. 3:28 and all Israel f. king
2 K. 17:25 they f. not the Lord
1 Chr. 16:25 to be f. above all gods, Ps. 96:4
Ps. 76:7 art to be f.; 8 earth f.
11 pres. to him ought to be f.
78:53 led them safely, so f. not
130:4 forgiveness, mayest be f.
Is. 41:5 the isles saw it, and f.
51:13 hast f. continually
57:11 whom hast thou f.
Jer. 3:8 treach. sister Jud. f. not
42:16 sword ye f. overtake you
44:10 nor have they f.
Ezek. 11:8 ye have f. the sword
Dan. 5:19 nations f. before him
Mal. 2:5 wherewith he f. me
Mat. 14:5 Herod f. multi. 21:46
Mark 4:41 they f. exceedingly
6:20 Herod f. John, knowing
11:18 and chief priests f. Jesus
32 f. the people, 12:12; Luke 20:19; 22:2; Acts 5:26

*Ps.* 28:9 *f.* them, and lift them
49:14 death shall *f.* on them
78:71 he brought David to *f.* J.
*Prov.* 10:21 lips of right. *f.* many
*Cant.* 4:5 roses which *f.* am. lil.
6:2 belov. gone to *f.* in gardens
*Is.* 5:17 *f.* after their manner
11:7 the cow and the bear sh. *f.*
14:30 first-b. of the poor sh. *f.*
27:10 their calf *f.* and lie down
30:23 thy cattle *f.* in large past.
40:11 *f.* his flock as a shepherd
49:9 they shall *f.* in the ways
61:5 strangers sh. *f.* your flocks
65:25 wolf and lamb shall *f.* tog.
*Jer.* 3:15 sh. *f.* you with knowl.
6:3 sh. *f.* every one in his place
23:2 ag. pastors that *f.* my peo.
4 shepherds shall *f.* them
50:19 Israel shall *f.* on Carmel
*Lam.* 4:5 *f.* delicately are desol.
*Ezek.* 34:2 shepherds that *f.* th.
3 but ye *f.* not the flock
10 neither shepherds *f.* thems.
23 servant David shall *f.* them
*Dan.* 11:26 *f.* of his meat destroy
*Hos.* 4:16 Lord will *f.* them
*Hos.* 9:2 wine-press not *f.* them
*Jon.* 3:7 let them not *f.*
*Mic.* 5:4 *f.* in strength of Lord
*Zep.* 2:7 they shall *f.* thereupon
3:13 shall *f.* none make afraid
*Zec.* 11:9 I will not *f.* you
16 not *f.* that that standeth
*Luke* 15:15 sent him to *f.* swine
*Acts* 20:28 take heed to *f.* church
*1 Cor.* 13:3 I give all to *f.* poor
*Rev.* 7:17 L. sh. *f.* and lead them
12:6 sho. *f.* her there 1,260 days

**FEED,** *imperatively.*

*Gen.* 25:30 *f.* me with red pottage
29:7 water ye the sheep, *f.* them
*1 K.* 22:27 *f.* him with bread and water of afflict. *2 Chr.* 18:26
*Prov.* 30:8 *f.* me with food conv.
*Cant.* 1:8 *f.* thy kids beside tents
*Mic.* 7:14 *f.* thy people
*Zec.* 11:4 *f.* flock of the slaughter
*John* 21:15 *f.* my lambs
16 *f.* my sheep, 17
*Rom.* 12:20 if ene. hunger *f.* him
*1 Pet.* 5:2 *f.* flock of God

**I will FEED.**

*Gen.* 30:31 *I will* ag. *f.* thy flock
*2 Sam.* 19:33 *I will f.* thee
*Is.* 49:26 *I w. f.* them oppr. thee
58:14 *I w. f.* thee with heritage
*Jer.* 9:15 *f.* with wormw. 23:15
*Ezek.* 34:14 *I w. f.* them
16 *I will f.* the fat with judgm.
*Zec.* 11:7 *I w. f.* flock of slaught.

**FEED, EST, ETH.**

*Ps.* 80:5 *f.* with bread of tears
*Prov.* 15:14 the mouth of fools *f.*
*Cant.* 1:7 tell me where thou *f.*
2:16 *f.* among the lilies, 6:3
*Is.* 44:20 he *f.* on ashes
*Hos.* 12:1 Ephraim *f.* on wind
*Mat.* 6:26 heav. Father *f.* them
*Luke* 12:24 sow not, God *f.* them
*1 Cor.* 9:7 who *f.* a flock

**FEEDING.**

*Gen.* 37:2 Joseph was *f.* the flock
*Job* 1:14 ploughing, the asses *f.*
*Ezek.* 34:10 cause to cease *f.* flock
*Nah.* 2:11 where *f.* pl. of lions?
*Mat.* 8:30 swi. *f. Mark* 5:11; *Luke* 8:32
*Luke* 17:7 a servant *f.* cattle
*Jude* 12 *f.* themsel. without fear

**FEEL, ING.**

*Gen.* 27:21 that I may *f.* thee
*Jud.* 16:26 I may *f.* the pillars
*Job* 20:20 shall not *f.* quietness
*Ps.* 58:9 bef. pots can *f.* thorns
*Ec.* 8:5 keep. comman. *f.* no evil
*Acts* 17:27 if haply might *f.* after
*Eph.* 4:19 who being past *f.*
*Heb.* 4:15 *f.* of our infirmities

**FEET.**

*Gen.* 49:10 from between his *f.*
33 J. gathered up his *f.* in bed
*Ex.* 3:5 shoes off thy *f. Acts* 7:33
*Deut.* 2:28 pass thro' on my *f.*
28:57 young one from bet. *f.*
33:3 and they sat down at thy *f.*
*Jos.* 3:15 *f.* of priests in Jordan
10:24 *f.* on necks of these kings
14:9 land thy *f.* have trodden
*Jud.* 3:24 he covereth his *f.*
4:15 Sisera fled on his *f.* 17
5:27 at her *f.* he fell down dead
*Ruth* 3:8 a woman lay at his *f.*
*1 Sam.* 2:9 keep *f.* of his saints
24:3 Saul went in to cover his *f.*
*2 Sam.* 3:34 nor thy *f.* put in. fet.
4:4 lame of his *f.* 9:3, 13
12 cut off th. hands and th. *f.*
19:24 Mephib. not dressed his *f.*
22:34 maketh my *f.* like hinds' *f. Ps.* 18:33; *Hab.* 3:19
37 *f.* did not slip. *Ps.* 18:36
*1 K.* 2:5 blo. of war in shoes on *f.*
14:6 A. heard the sound of h. *f.*
12 *f.* enter the city
15:23 A. diseased *f.* *2 Chr.* 16:12
*2 K.* 4:27 she caught by the *f.*
6:32 sound of master's *f.* beh.?
9:35 found no more than the *f.*
13:21 dead man stood on his *f.*
21:8 *f.* of Israel move any more
*Neh.* 9:21 their *f.* swelled not
*Job* 12:5 to slip with his *f.*
13:27 my *f.* in the stocks; 33:11 a print on heels of my *f.*
18:8 cast into a net by own *f.*
11 terrors shall drive him to *f.*
29:15 *f.* was I to the lame
30:12 youth push away my *f.*
*Ps.* 22:16 pierced hands and *f.*
25:15 pluck my *f.* out of the net
31:8 set my *f.* in a large room
40:2 he set my *f.* on a rock, and
*Ps.* 56:13 del. my *f.* fr. falling?
66:9 suff. not our *f.* to be moved
73:2 my *f.* were almost gone
74:3 lift up thy *f.* to desolations
105:18 whose *f.* hurt with fet.
115:7 *f.* have they but walk not
116:8 deliv. my *f.* from falling
119:59 turned my *f.* to testim.
101 refr. my *f.* from evil way
105 thy wo. is a lamp to my *f.*
122:2 *f.* stand within thy gates
*Prov.* 1:16 *f.* run to evil, 6:18; *Is.* 59:7
4:26 ponder the path of thy *f.*
5:5 her *f.* go down to death, her
6:13 wicked man speak. with *f.*
28 go on coals, *f.* n. be burnt?
7:11 her *f.* abide not in house
19:2 hasteth with his *f.* sinneth
26:6 cutteth off *f.* and drinketh
29:5 spreadeth a net for his *f.*
*Cant.* 7:1 beautiful are thy *f.*
*Is.* 3:16 a tinkling with their *f.*
18 ornaments about their *f.*
6:2 with twain he covered his *f.*
7:20 lord shall shave hair off *f.*
23:7 own *f.* shall carry her afar
26:6 *f.* of poor sh. tread it down
32:20 send forth the *f.* of ox
41:3 he had not gone with *f.*
49:23 sh. lick up dust of thy *f.*
52:7 *f.* of him bring. good tid.
60:13 place of my *f.* glorious
*Jer.* 13:16 before *f.* stumble on mountain
14:10 have not refrained their *f.*
18:22 they hid snares for my *f.*
38:22 thy *f.* are sunk in mire
*Lam.* 1:13 spread a net for my *f.*
*Ezek.* 1:7 their *f.* were straight *f.*
2:2 Spirit set me on my *f.* 3:24
16:25 opened thy *f.* to every one
24:17 put thy shoes upon thy *f.*
25:6 beca. stamped with the *f.*
32:2 troubledst wat. with thy *f.*
34:18 foul residue with your *f.*?
19 what ye have fouled with *f.*
37:10 and stood upon their *f.*
*Dan.* 2:33 his *f.* part of iron, 42
34 smote image upon his *f.*
7:7 stamped residue with *f.* 19
10:6 *f.* like br. *Rev.* 1:15; 2:18
*Nah.* 1:3 clouds are dust of his *f.*
15 *f.* of him bringeth good tid.
*Zec.* 14:4 *f.* stand on mount of O.
*Mat.* 10:14 shake off the dust of your *f. Mark* 6:11; *Luke* 9:5
15:30 cast the lame at Jesus' *f.*
18:8 rather than having two *f.*
28:9 held by *f.* worshipped him
*Luke* 1:79 *f.* into way of peace
7:38 kissed his *f.* and anointed
8:35 found man at *f.* of Jesus
41 Jai. fell down at Jesus' *f.*
10:39 M. which sat at Jesus' *f.*
15:22 put shoes on his *f.*
24:39 beh. my hands and my *f.*
*John* 11:2 and wiped his *f.* 12:3
20:12 the other angel at the *f.*
*Acts* 3:7 his *f.* received strength
4:35 laid at apostles' *f.* 37; 5:2
5:9 the *f.* of them which buried
7:58 clothes at young man's *f.*
13:25 shoes of his *f.* not worthy
51 shook off dust of their *f.*
14:10 Stand upright on *f.*
16:24 their *f.* fast in the stocks
21:11 Agabus bound his own *f.*
22:3 brought up at *f.* of Gamal.
26:16 rise and stand upon thy *f.*
*Rom.* 3:15 *f.* swift to shed blood
10:15 *f.* of them preach gospel
*1 Cor.* 12:21 to *f.* I have no need
*Eph.* 6:15 *f.* shod with prepara.
*Heb.* 12:13 stra. paths for your *f.*
*Rev.* 3:9 worship before thy *f.*
10:1 his *f.* as pillars of fire
11:11 witnesses stood on th. *f.*
13:2 his *f.* as the *f.* of a bear
22:8 I fell to worship bef. his *f.*

**At his FEET.**

*Jud.* 4:10 with 10,000 *at his f.*
*Hab.* 3:5 burning coals *at his f.*
*Mat.* 18:29 fel. serv. fell *at his f.*
*Mark* 7:25 Syroph. fell *at his f.*
*Luke* 7:38 she stood *at his f.*
*Acts* 5:10 Sapphira fell *at his f.*
*Rev.* 1:17 I fell *at his f.* as dead
19:10 I fell *at his f.* to worship

**FEET,** *joined with* **sole, s.**

*Deut.* 11:24 *s.* of *f.* tread be yours
*1 K.* 5:3 wars, under *s.* of his *f.*
*2 K.* 19:24 *s.* of *f.* dried. *Is.* 37:25
*Is.* 60:14 bow down at *s.* of *f.*
*Ezek.* 1:7 *s.* of *f.* was like a calf's
43:7 *s.* of my *f.* no more defiled
*Mal.* 4:3 ashes under *s.* of your *f.*

**Under FEET.**

*Ex.* 24:10 *under* his *f.* sapphire
*2 Sam.* 22:10 dark. *u. f. Ps.* 18:9
39 they are fallen *under* my *f.*
*Ps.* 8:6 put all things *under* his *f.* *1 Cor.* 15:27; *Eph.* 1:22
47:3 subdue nations *u.* our *f.*
91:13 dragon shalt trample *u. f.*
*Is.* 14:19 a carcass trodden *u. f.*
28:3 drunkards be trodden *u. f.*
*Lam.* 3:34 *u.* his *f.* all prisoners
*Mat.* 7:6 trample *u.* their *f.*
*Rom.* 16:20 bruise Sat. *u.* your *f.*
*1 Cor.* 15:25 all enemies *u.* his *f.*
*Heb.* 2:8 in subjection *u.* his *f.*
*Rev.* 12:1 moon *under* her *f.*

**FEET,** *with* **wash, ed.**

*Ex.* 30:19 A. and his sons shall *wash* their *f.* 21; 40:31

2 *Sam.* 11:8 Uriah, go *w.* thy *f.*
*Ps.* 58:10 *w. f.* in blood of wick.
*Cant.* 5:3 I have *washed* my *f.*
*Luke* 7:38 *wash* his *f.* with tears
*John* 13:5 *wash* the disciples' *f.*
6 Lord, dost thou *wash* my *f.*?
10 needeth not save to *w.* h. *f.*
14 if I your L. have *w.* your *f.*
1 *Tim.* 5:10 she ha. *w.* saints' *f.*

**FEIGN, ED, EST.**

1 *Sam.* 21:13 D. *f.* himself mad
2 *Sam.* 14:2 *f.* thyself a mourner
1 *K.* 14:5 *f.* herself another wom.
*Neh.* 6:8 thou *f.* them
*Ps.* 17:1 prayer not out *f.* lips
*Luke* 20:20 *f.* them. just men
*Pet.* 2:3 with *f.* words

**FEIGNEDLY.**

3:10 turn to me *f.* saith L.

FELIX. *Acts* 23:24; 24:3, 25; 25:14

**FELL.**

*Gen.* 4:5 Cain's countenance *f.*
44:14 Joseph's breth. *f.* bef. him
*Jos.* 22:20 wrath *f.* on congrega.
*Jud.* 7:13 smote tent that it *f.*
8:10 there *f.* 120,000 men
16:30 the house *f.* on the lords
1 *Sam.* 4:18 Eli *f.* from seat
11:7 fear of Lord *f.* on people
14:13 Philistines *f.* before Jon.
22:18 Doeg *f.* upon the priests
28:20 Saul *f.* straightway along
29:3 no fault since he *f.* to me
31:4 Saul took sw. and *f.* on it
2 *Sam.* 4:4 Mephibosheth *f.*
20:8 Joab's sword *f.* out, as he
21:9 they *f.* all seven together
1 *K.* 2:25 Benaiah *f.* on Adonijah
32 *f.* on two men more right.
34 Benaiah *f.* on J.; 46 Shimei
20:30 a wall *f.* on 27,000 men
2 *K.* 1:13 captain *f.* on his knees
2:13 mantle that *f.* from Elijah
4:8 it *f.* on a day, Elisha, 11,18
6:5 axe head *f.* into the water
1 *Chr.* 21:14 *f.* of Isr. 70,000 men
27:24 *f.* wrath for it against Isr.
2 *Chr.* 17:10 fear of L. *f.* on all
20:18 inhabitants *f.* before Lord
21:19 his bowels *f.* out by reas.
*Ezr.* 9:5 I *f.* on my knees, and
*Est.* 9:3 fear of Mor. *f.* on them
*Job* 1:15 Sabe. *f.* on the asses, 17
19 house *f.* on the young men
*Ps.* 27:2 eat up my flesh, they *f.*
78:64 their priests *f.* by sword
105:38 fear of Israel *f.* on Egypt
*Jer.* 39:9 *f.* away, *f.* to him, 52:15
46:16 one *f.* upon another
*Lam.* 1:7 her people *f.* into hand
5:13 children *f.* under the wood
*Ezek.* 8:1 ha. of L. *f.* on me, 11:5
39:23 so *f.* they all by the sw.
*Dan.* 4:31 *f.* a voice from heaven
7:20 before whom three *f.*
10:7 great quaking *f.* on them
*Mat.* 7:25 the house *f.* not
27 house *f.* *Luke* 6:49
13:4 seed *f.* by the wayside, *Mark* 4:4; *Luke* 8:5
*Mark* 9:20 he *f.* and wallowed
14:35 Jesus *f.* on the ground
*Luke* 1:12 fear *f.* upon Zacharias
10:30 *f.* among thieves, 36
13:4 on whom tower in Silo. *f.*
15:20 his father *f.* on his neck
16:21 crumbs wh. *f.* from table
*John* 18:6 went backward, and *f.*
*Acts* 1:25 Jud. by transgress. *f.*
26 the lot *f.* upon Matthias
7:60 had said this, he *f.* asleep
9:4 Saul *f.* and heard a voice
10:10 Peter *f.* into a trance
44 Holy Ghost *f.* on all, 11:15
12:7 chains *f.* off Peter's hands
13:11 there *f.* on him a mist
*Acts* 13:36 D. *f.* on sleep, saw cor.
19:17 fear *f.* on Jews at Ephesus
20:10 Paul *f.* on Eutychus
37 they all *f.* on Paul's neck
22:7 I *f.* unto the ground, and
*Rom.* 11:22 on them wh. *f.* sever.
15:3 reproached thee, *f.* on me
1 *Cor.* 10:8 *f.* in one day 23,000
*Heb.* 3:17 whose carcasses *f.*
2 *Pet.* 3:4 the fathers *f.* asleep
*Rev.* 1:17 I *f.* at his feet as dead
6:13 and the stars of heaven *f.*
8:10 *f.* great star from heaven
11:11 fear *f.* on them which saw
13 tenth of city *f.* by earthqua.
16:2 there *f.* a grievous sore
19 and the cities of nations *f.*
21 there *f.* on men a great hail
19:10 I *f.* at his feet to worship

*See* FACE, FACES.

**FELL down.**

*Deut.* 9:18 I *f. down* before L. 25
*Jos.* 6:20 shouted, the wall *f. d.*
*Jud.* 5:27 he bowed, he *f. d.*
19:26 concubine *f. d.* at door
1 *Sam.* 31:1 *f. d.* in Gil. 1 *Chr.* 10:1
2 *Sam.* 2:16 so they *f. d.* together
23 Asahel *f. d.* there and died
19:18 Shimei *f. down*
2 *K.* 1:2 Ahaziah *f. d.* thro' latt.
2 *Chr.* 13:17 *f. d.* of Is. 500,000 m.
*Job* 1:20 Job *f. d.* on the ground
*Ps.* 107:12 *f. down* none to help
*Dan.* 3:7 all nations *f. d.* and w.
23 these three *f. d.* in furnace
*Mat.* 2:11 wise men *f. d.* and wo.
18:26 servant *f. d.* saying, 29
*Mark* 3:11 unclean spirits *f. d.*
*Luke* 5:8 P. *f. d.* at Jesus' knees
8:28 man which had devils *f. d.*
41 Jairus *f. d.*; 17:16 Samar.
*Acts* 5:5 Ananias *f. d.*; 10 Sapp.
10:25 Cornelius; 16:29 jailer
19:35 the image which *f. down*
20:9 Eutychus *f. d.*
*Heb.* 11:30 by faith the walls *f. d.*
*Rev.* 5:8 elders *f. d.* 14; 19:4
22:8 John *f. d.* before the angel

**FELL, EST, ING.**

2 *Sam.* 3:34 bef. wick. so *f.* thou
2 *K* 3:19 shall *f.* every good tree
6:5 as one was *f.* a beam

**FELLER.**

*Is.* 14:8 no *f.* is come up. ag. us

**FELLOW.**

*Gen.* 19:9 this *f.* came in to soj.
*Ex.* 2:13 why smit. thou thy *f.*?
*Jud.* 7:22 the L. set every man's sword ag. his *f.* 1 *Sam.* 14:20
1 *Sam.* 21:15 brought this *f.* to play the madman, sh. this *f.*
25:21 kept all this *f.* hath
29:4 make this *f.* return
2 *Sam.* 2:16 caught ev. one his *f.*
1 *K.* 22:27 *f.* in pris. 2 *Chr.* 18:26
2 *K.* 9:11 why came this mad *f.*
*Ec.* 4:10 fall, one will lift his *f.*
*Is.* 34:14 satyr shall cry to his *f.*
*Zec.* 13:7 awake, O sword, agai. my Sh. and man th. is my *f.*
*Mat.* 26:71 *f.* also w. J. *Lu.* 22:59
*Luke* 23:2 this *f.* pervert. nation
*John* 9:29 for this *f.* we know not
11:16 Didymus said to *f.* dis.
*Acts* 18:13 *f.* pers. to worship G.
22:22 away with such a *f.* from
24:5 found this man a pestil. *f.*

**FELLOW-CITIZENS.**

*Eph.* 2:19 *f.-citizens* with saints

**FELLOW-HEIRS.**

*Eph.* 3:6 Gentiles sh. be *f.-heirs*

**FELLOW-HELPER, S.**

2 *Cor.* 8:23 Titus, my *f.-helper*
3 *John* 8 be *f.-h.* to the truth

**FELLOW-LABORER, S.**

1 *Thes.* 3:2 sent Tim. our *f.-lab.*
*Phil.* 4:3 with other *f.-laborers*
*Phile.* 1 Paul to Phile. our *f.-l.*
24 Marcus, Demas, Lucas, *f.-l.*

**FELLOW-PRISONER, S.**

*Rom.* 16:7 And. and Junia *f.-p.*
*Col.* 4:10 Aristarch. *f.-p.* saluteth
*Phile.* 23 Epaphras my *f.-p.* in C.

**FELLOW-SERVANT, S.**

*Mat.* 18:28 *f.-ser.* who owed him
29 *f.-s.* fell down at his feet
24:49 begin to smite his *f.-s.*
*Col.* 1:7 Epaphras our dear *f.-ser.*
4:7 Tychicus, who is a *f.-serv.*
*Rev.* 6:11 *f.-s.* should be fulfilled
19:10 I am thy *f.-servant*, 22:9

**FELLOW-SOLDIER.**

*Phil.* 2:25 Epaphroditus my *f.-s.*
*Phile.* 2 Paul to Archippus, *f.-s.*

**FELLOW-WORKERS.**

*Col.* 4:11 these only are my *f.-w.*

**FELLOWS.**

*Jud.* 18:25 angry *f.* run on thee
2 *Sam.* 6:20 as one of vain *f.*
*Ps.* 45:7 with the oil of gladness above thy *f.* *Heb.* 1:9
*Is.* 44:11 his *f.* shall be ashamed
*Ezek.* 37:19 tribes of Israel his *f.*
*Dan.* 2:13 D. and his *f.* to be sla.
7:20 look more stout than his *f.*
*Zec.* 3:8 thou and thy *f.* that sit
*Mat.* 11:16 calling to their *f.*
*Acts* 17:5 lewd *f.* of baser sort

**FELLOWSHIP.**

*Lev.* 6:2 deliv. to keep, or in *f.*
*Ps.* 94:20 iniq. have *f.* wi. thee?
*Acts* 2:42 contin. in apostles' *f.*
1 *Cor.* 1:9 called to *f.* of his Son
10:20 sh. have *f.* with devils
2 *Cor.* 6:14 what *f.* hath righte.
8:4 *f.* of ministering to saints
*Gal.* 2:9 the right hand of *f.*
*Eph.* 3:9 is *f.* of the mystery
5:11 no *f.* with works of darkn.
*Phil.* 1:5 your *f.* in the gospel
2:1 if there be any *f.* of the Sp.
3:10 know *f.* of his sufferings
1 *John* 1:3 have *f.* with us, our *f.* is with the Father
6 if we say we have *f.* with h.
7 walk in light, we have *f.*

**FELT.**

*Gen.* 27:22 and Isaac *f.* Jacob
*Ex.* 10:21 darkn. that may be *f.*
*Prov.* 23:35 beaten me, I *f.* it not
*Mark* 5:29 she *f.* she was healed
*Acts* 28:5 off beast and *f.* no harm

**FEMALE.**

*Gen.* 1:27 male and *f.* created, 5:2
6:19 two of ev. sort, male and *f.*
7:16 went in male and *f.*
*Lev.* 4:28 offering, a *f.* 32; 5:6
*Num.* 5:3 male and *f.* sh. ye put
*Deut.* 4:16 likeness of male or *f.*
7:14 not be male nor *f.* barren
*Mat.* 19:4 m. and *f.* *Mark* 10:6
*Gal.* 3:28 in Christ male nor *f.*

**FENCE.**

*Ps.* 62:3 ye sh. be as a tottering *f.*

**FENCED, Verb.**

*Job* 10:11 *f.* me with bones
19:8 he hath *f.* up my way
*Is.* 5:2 a vineyard, and he *f.* it

**FENCED, Adjective.**

*Deut.* 28:52 *f.* walls come down
2 *Sam.* 23:7 touch th. must be *f.*
2 *K.* 3:19 shall smite every *f.* city
17:9 from tower to *f.* city, 18:8
*Is.* 2:15 day of L. on ev. *f.* wall
*Jer.* 15:20 make thee a *f.* wall
*Ezek.* 36:35 ruined cities bec. *f.*

**FENCED cities.**
Num. 32:17 dwell in f. c.
Deut. 9:1 pos. c. f. up to heaven
Jos. 10:20 rest entered into f. c.
14:12 that the cities were f.
2 Sam. 20:6 lest he get f. c.
2 K. 19:25 should. lay waste f. c.
2 Chr. 8:5 Solomon built f. cities
12:4 Shishak took f. c. of Judah
Jer. 5:17 sh. impoverish thy f. c.
Dan. 11:15 shall take most f. c.
Hos. 8:14 Judah hath multi. f. c.
Zep. 1:16 day of alarm ag. f. c.

**FENS.**
Job 40:21 Behemoth in cov. of f.

**FERRET.**
Lev. 11:30 the f. unclean

**FERRY-BOAT.**
2 Sam. 19:18 f.-b. for king's hou.

**FERVENT, LY.**
Acts 18:25 Apollos, f. in spirit
Rom. 12:11 f. in spirit, serv. L.
2 Cor. 7:7 your f. mind tow. me.
Col. 4:12 laboring f. in prayers
Jam. 5:16 f. pray. of a righteous
1 Pet. 1:22 ye love one another f.
4:8 above all th. have f. charity
2 Pet. 3:10 melt with f. heat, 12

FESTUS. Acts 24:27; 25:9,14,23; 26:25

**FETCH.**
Gen. 18:5 will f. morsel of bread
27:45 I will f. thee from thence
Num. 20:10 f. water out of rock?
Deut. 30:4 thence will L. f. thee
Jud. 11:5 went to f. Jephthah
1 Sam. 4:3 f. ark of covenant
6:21 come and f. ark up to you
16:11 send and f. Saul, 20:31
2 Sam. 5:23 f. a compass behind
14:13 king doth not f. banished
2 Sam. 14:20 f. ab. this form of
1 K. 17:10 f. me a little water
2 K. 6:13 wh. that I may f. him
2 Chr. 18:8 f. quick. Micaiah son
Job 36:3 f. my knowl. from far
Is. 56:12 I will f. wine
Acts 16:37 come, and f. us out

**FETCHED.**
1 Sam. 7:1 f. up ark of the Lord
10:23 they f. Saul thence
2 Sam. 9:5 and f. Mephibosheth
11:27 f. Bath-sheba to his house
1 K. 9:28 they f. from Ophir gold
2 K. 11:4 Jehoiada f. rulers
Jer. 26:23 f. Urijah out of Egypt
Acts 28:13 thence we f. compass

**FETTERS.**
Jud. 16:21 bound Samson with f.
2 Sam. 3:34 nor thy feet put in f.
2 K. 25:7 bound Zedeki. with f.
2 Chr. 33:11 Mana. bound with f.
36:6 Jehoiakim bound with f.
Ps. 105:18 feet they hurt with f.
149:8 to bind nobles with f.
Mark 5:4 often with f. Lu. 8:29

**FEVER.**
Deut. 28:22 smite thee with a f.
Mat. 8:14 P. wife's mother sick of f. Mark 1:30; Luke 4:38
John 4:52 at 7th hour f. left him
Acts 28:8 father of Pub. sick of f.

**FEW.**
Gen. 34:30 I being f. th. will slay
47:9 f. and evil have the days
Lev. 26:22 you f. Deut. 4:27; 28:62
Num. 13:18 the people wheth. f.
26:54 to f. give less inher. 35:8
56 divided betw. many and f.
Deut. 26:5 sojourned with a f.
33:6 let not Reuben's men be f.
1 Sam. 14:6 to save by many or f.
2 Chr. 29:34 the prie. were too f.
Neh. 7:4 city large, but people f.
Job 10:20 are not my days f.?
14:1 man is of f. days
16:22 when a f. years are come
Ps. 109:8 let his days be f.
Ec. 5:2 let thy words be f.
9:14 a little city, and f. men
12:3 grinders cease, because f.
Is. 10:19 rest of trees shall be f.
24:6 are burned, and f. men left
Ezek. 5:3 also take a f. in numb.
12:16 leave a f. men from sword
Dan. 11:20 f. days be destroyed
Mat. 7:14 f. there be that find it
9:37 laborers are f. Luke 10:2
20:16 call. but f. chosen, 22:14
25:21 faithful in f. things, 23
Mark 6:5 hands on a f. sick folk
Luke 12:48 beaten with f. stripes
13:23 f. that be saved?
Acts 24:4 wouldest hear f. words
Eph. 3:3 wrote afore in f. words
Heb. 12:10 for f. days chastened
13:22 I have written in f. words
1 Pet. 3:20 where. f. that is eight
Rev. 2:14 a f. things ag. thee, 20
3:4 a f. names even in Sardis

**But a FEW.**
Gen. 29:20 seemed but a f. days
Lev. 25:52 if remain b. a f. years
Jos. 7:3 men of Ai are but a f.
1 Chr. 16:19 but f. Ps. 105:12
Jer. 42:2 for we are left but a f.

**Not a FEW.**
Is. 10:7 cut off nations not a f.
Jer. 30:19 multi. them, not be a f.
Acts 17:4 chief women not a f.

**FEWER, EST.**
Num. 33:54 to f. give less inher.
Deut. 7:7 ye were f. of all people

**FEWNESS.**
Lev. 25:16 accord. to f. of years

**FIDELITY.**
Tit. 2:10 serv. showing good f.

**FIELD.**
Gen. 23:20 f. and cave made sure
27:27 smell of son is as of a f.
31:4 Rachel and Leah to the f.
49:30 in f. Abra. bought, 50:13
Ex. 22:5 cause a f. to be eaten
6 so that the f. be consumed
Lev. 25:3 six years sh. sow thy f.
27:17 if he sanctify his f. 18
20 if he will not redeem the f.
Deut 5:21 neith. sh. covet his f.
Jos. 15:18 ask a f. Jud. 1:14
Ruth 2:8 go not to gl. in ano. f.
4:5 day thou buyest f. of Naomi
2 Sam. 14:30 Joab's f. is near
31 why serv. set my f. on fire?
2 K. 18:17 in highway of fuller's f. Is. 7:3; 36:2
Neh. 13:10 every one to his f.
Ps. 96:12 let the f. be joyful
Prov. 24:30 went by f. of slothful
27:26 goats are the price of f.
31:16 considereth a f. and buy.
Ec. 5:9 king is served by the f.
Is. 5:8 woe to them lay f. to f.
16:10 taken out of plentiful f.
Jer. 12:4 herbs of ev. f. wither?
26:18 plou. like a f. Mic. 3:12
32:7 buy thee my f. 8:25
35:9 nei. have we vineyard, f.
48:33 gladn. is taken from the f.
Joel 1:10 the f. is wasted
Mat. 13:24 good seed in his f. 31
38 the f. is the world, the good
44 is like unto treas. hid in a f.
27:7 bought the potter's f. 10
8 the f. of blood, Acts 1:19
Luke 17:7 when come from the f.
Acts 1:18 this man purchas. a f.

**Fruitful FIELD.**
Is. 10:18 consume glory of f. f.
29:17 Leban. turned into a f. f.
32:15 wilderness be a fruitful f.
fruit. f. be counted a forest
16 righteous. in the fruit. f.
Ezek. 17:5 planted seed in a f. f.

**In the FIELD.**
Gen. 4:8 when they were in t. f.
24:63 out to meditate in the f.
37:15 Joseph wander. in the f.
Ex. 9:19 all thou hast in f.
25 the hail smote all in the f.
16:25 to-day not find it in the f.
Deut. 21:1 slain, lying in the f.
28:3 bless. sh. thou be in the f.
16 cursed sh. thou be in the f.
Jud. 13:9 angel came to w. in f.
1 Sam. 19:3 beside fath. in the f.
30:11 found an Egypt. in the f.
2 Sam. 14:6 two strove in the f.
1 K. 11:29 two alone in the f.
14:11 dieth of Jerob. in the f.
21:24 that die. of Ahab in the f.
1 Chr. 19:9 kings were in the f.
Job 24:6 reap ev. one corn in t. f.
Ps. 78:12 marv. things in t. f. 43
Prov. 24:27 fit for thyself in t. f.
Jer. 14:5 hind also calved in t. f.
17:3 O my mountain in the f.
41:8 treasures in the f. of wheat
Ezek. 7:15 in the f. shall die
26:6 slay thy daughters in f. 8
Mic. 4:10 shalt dwell in the f.
Zec. 10:1 to ev. one grass in t. f.
Mal. 3:11 vine cast fruit in the f.
Mat. 24:18 nor let him in f. ret. Mark 13:16; Luke 17:31
40 two be in the f. Luke 17:36
Luke 2:8 sheph. abiding in the f.
12:28 clothe grass to-day in t. f.
15:25 his elder son was in the f.

**Into the FIELD.**
Num. 22:23 ass went into the f.
Jud. 9:42 people went into the f.
1 Sam. 6:14 cart came into the f.
20:11 J. said, Let us go into f.
2 Sam. 20:12 removed Am. into f.
Cant. 7:11 let us go forth in. t. f.
Jer. 6:25 go not forth into the f.
14:18 if I go into the f.

**Of the FIELD.**
Gen. 2:5 every plant of the f.
34:7 sons of J. came out of t. f.
47:24 four parts for seed of t. f.
Lev. 26:4 trees of f. sh. yield fru.
27:28 no devoted thing of the f.
Deut. 20:19 tree of the f.
Jud. 5:4 marchedst out of the f.
19:16 man from work out of f.
2 K. 9:25 cast in portion of the f.
37 carc. as dung on face of t. f.
Job 5:23 in league with sto. of f.
Ps. 103:15 as flower of f. he flou.
Cant. 2:7 the roes of the f. 3:5
Is. 37:27 inhabit. as grass of f.
40:6 and as the flower of the f.
43:20 beast of the f. shall honor
55:12 trees of the f. sh. clap han.
Jer. 4:17 as keepers of the f.
18:14 snow from rock of the f.
Lam. 4:9 want of fruits of the f.
Ezek. 16:7 multiply as bud of t. f.
17:24 trees of the f. shall know
34:27 tree of f. shall fruit
36:30 multiply increase of the f.
39:10 take no wood out of f.
Dan. 4:15 tender grass of the f.
Hos. 10:4 as hemlock in the f.
12:11 heaps in furrows of the f.
Joel 1:11 harv. of the f. is perish.
Mic. 1:6 Sama. as a heap of t. f.
Mat. 6:28 consider lilies of the f.
30 if G. so clothe grass of t. f.

See BEAST, BEASTS.

**Open FIELD.**
Lev. 14:7 liv. bird loose into o. f.
17:5 sacrifices in the open f.

*Ezek.* 16:5 cast out in the *o. f.*
32:4 cast thee on the *open f.*
33:27 that is in *o. f.* give to
39:5 shalt fall upon the *open f.*

**FIELDS.**

*Lev.* 25:31 counted as the *f.*
*Num.* 16:14 hast not given us *f.*
20:17 not pass through *f.* 21:22
*Deut.* 11:15 send grass into thy *f*
32:13 eat increase of the *f.*
32 as vine of the *f.* of Gomor.
*Jos.* 21:12 *f.* gave they to Caleb
1 *Sam.* 8:14 he will take your *f.*
22:7 will son of J. give you *f.?*
25:15 a wall to us when in *f.*
1 *K.* 2:26 get thee to thi. own *f.*
1 *Chr.* 16:32 let *f.* rejoice and all
27:25 storehouses in *f.* cities
*Job* 5:10 sendeth waters on *f.*
*Ps.* 107:37 sow the *f.* and plant
132:6 found it in *f.* of the wood
*Prov.* 8:26 had not made the *f.*
23:10 enter not to *f.* of fatherl.
*Is.* 16:8 *f.* of Heshbon languish
*Jer.* 32:15 *f.* shall be possessed
43 *f.* bought; 44 men sh. buy *f.*
*Ob.* 19 sh. possess *f.* of Ephraim
*Mic.* 2:2 they covet *f.* and take
4 he hath divided our *f.*
*Hab.* 3:17 altho. *f.* yield no meat
*Mark* 2:23 through *f.* *Luke* 6:1
*John* 4:35 up eyes, and look on *f.*
*Jam.* 5:4 which reaped your *f.*

**Open FIELDS.**

*Lev.* 14:53 let go liv. bird in *o. f.*
*Num.* 19:16 slain with sw. in *o. f.*
2 *Sam.* 11:11 encamped in *o. f.*
*Ezek.* 29:5 shalt fall upon the *o. f.*

**FIERCE.**

*Gen.* 49:7 anger, for it was *f.*
*Deut.* 28:50 nation of a *f.* count.
*Job* 4:10 voice of *f.* lion
10:16 huntest me as *f.* lion
28:8 nor hath *f.* lion passed by
41:10 none so *f.* dare stir him
*Is.* 19:4 a *f.* king shall rule over
33:19 thou shalt not see a *f.* peo.
*Dan.* 8:23 a king of *f.* counten.
*Hab.* 1:8 horses more *f.* than wol.
*Mat.* 8:28 devils, exceeding *f.*
*Luke* 23:5 they were more *f.*
2 *Tim.* 3:3 inconti. *f.* despisers
*Jam.* 3:4 ships driven of *f.* winds

**FIERCENESS.**

*Job* 39:24 swallo. ground with *f.*
*Jer.* 25:38 land desolate *f.* of opp.

*See* ANGER, WRATH.

**FIERCER.**

2 *Sam.* 19:43 words of J. were *f.*

**FIERY.**

*Num.* 21:6 the L. sent *f.* serpents
8 make thee a *f.* serpent
*Deut.* 8:15 wherein were *f.* serp.
33:2 from right hand went *f.* law
*Ps.* 21:9 make them as a *f.* oven
*Is.* 14:29 fruit be *f.* flying serp.
*Dan.* 3:6 into midst of *f.* furnace
7:9 his throne was like *f.* flame
10 a *f.* stream issued and came
*Eph.* 6:16 able to quench *f.* darts
*Heb.* 10:27 judgment and *f.* indi.
1 *Pet.* 4:12 not stran. con. *f.* trial

**FIFTH.**

2 *Sam.* 2:23 smote A. under *f.* rib
3:27 Ab. under *f.*; 4:6 Ish-bosh.
20:10 J. smote Ama. under *f.* rib
*Rev.* 6:9 when he opened *f.* seal
9:1 the *f.* angel sounded
16:10 *f.* angel poured out vial

**FIFTEEN.**

*John* 11:18 Bethany *f.* furl. off J.
*Acts* 27:28 found it *f.* fathoms
*Gal.* 1:18 I abode with P. *f.* days

**FIFTY.**

*Num.* 4:3 from 30 y. old and upw. even to *f.* 23, 30, 35, 39
8:25 fr. age of *f.* serve no more
1 *K.* 18:4 hid them by *f.* in cave
2 *K.* 1:9 cap. of *f.* with his *f.* 11,13
10 fire consume thee and *f.* 12
*Est.* 5:14 gal. *f.* cubits high, 7:9
*Luke* 7:41 one 500 pence, other *f.*
16:6 sit down quickly, write *f.*
*John* 8:57 art not yet *f.* years old

**FIFTY, *with* six.**

*Ezr.* 2:22 men of Netop. *f.* and *s.*

**FIFTY thousand.**

*Acts* 19:19 price books burnt *f. t.*

**FIFTIES.**

*Mark* 6:40 sat d. by *f.* *Luke* 9:14

**FIFTIETH.**

*Lev.* 25:10 shall hallow *f.* year
11 a jubilee shall that *f.* year be

**FIG, S.**

*Gen.* 3:7 *f.* leaves for aprons
1 *Sam.* 25:18 A. took 200 cakes *f.*
30:12 gave Egyptian cake of *f.*
2 *K.* 20:7 take lump *f.* *Is.* 38:21
*Neh.* 13:15 sab. some brought *f.*
*Cant.* 2:13 fig-t. put. for. green *f.*
*Is.* 34:4 fall *f.* from fig-tree
*Jer.* 8:13 shall be no *f.* on fig-tree
24:1 two baskets *f.* one good, 2,3
8 evil *f.* that cannot be eaten
29:17 make them like vile *f.*
*Nah.* 3:12 fig-t. with first ripe *f.*
*Mat.* 7:16 do men gather *f.* of thistles? *Luke* 6:44
*Jam.* 3:12 fig bear ber. or vine *f.?*
*Rev.* 6:13 fig-tree casteth unt. *f.*

**FIG-TREE.**

*Jud.* 9:10 trees said to *f.-t.* 11
1 *K.* 4:25 dw. under *f.-t.* *Mic.* 4:4
2 *K.* 18:31 eat ev. one *f.-t.* *Is.*36:16
*Prov.* 27:18 keepeth *f.-t.*
*Hos.* 9:10 first ripe in *f.-t.* thereof
*Joel* 1:7 he hath barked my *f.-t.*
12 the *f.-t.* languisheth
*Hab.* 3:17 altho' *f.-t.* sh. not blo.
*Zec.* 3:10 call ev. man under *f.-t.*
*Mat.* 21:19 he saw *f.-t.* in way, *Mark* 11:13
20 *f.-t.* withered, *Mark* 11:20,21
24:32 parable of *f.-t.* *Mark* 13:28
*Luke* 13:6 man had *f.-t.* planted
7 seeking fruit on this *f.-t.*
21:29 behold the *f.-t.*
*John* 1:48 und. *f.-t.* I saw thee, 50

**FIG-TREES.**

*Deut.* 7:8 land of vines, and *f.-t.*
*Ps.* 105:33 smote vines and *f.-t.*
*Jer.* 5:17 eat thy vines and *f.-t.*
*Hos.* 2:12 I will destroy her *f.-t.*
*Amos* 4:9 when g. and *f.-t.* incr.
*Nah.* 3:12 strong-ho. be like *f.-t.*

**FIGHT, Substantive.**

1 *Sam.* 17:20 host was going to *f.*
1 *Tim.* 6:12 fight the good *f.*
2 *Tim.* 4:7 I have fought a good *f.*
*Heb.* 10:32 endured great *f.*
11:34 waxed valiant in *f.*

**FIGHT, Verb.**

*Deut.* 1:41 we will go up and *f.*
42 go not up, nor *f.* for I am
1 *Sam.* 4:9 quit like men, and *f.*
17:10 give man that we may *f.*
2 *Sam.* 11:20 nigh when ye did *f.?*
1 *K.* 22:31 *f.* not gr. 2 *Chr.* 18:30
2 *Chr.* 20:17 shall not need to *f.*
*Ps.* 144:1 teach. my fingers to *f.*
*Jer.* 51:30 men forborne to *f.*
*Zec.* 10:5 *f.* bec. L. is with them
14:14 Judah shall *f.* at Jerusa.
*John* 18:36 then would my ser. *f.*
1 *Cor.* 9:26 *f.* I not as beateth air
*Jam.* 4:2 ye kill, ye *f.* and war

**FIGHT against.**

*Ex.* 1:10 join enemies and *f. a.*
*Deut.* 20:10 nigh to a city to *f. a.*
*Jos.* 19:47 Danites went *f. a.* Le.
*Jud.* 1:1 shall go up first *f. a.?*
11:8 Jephth. to *f. a.* Ammon, 9
25 against Israel, or *f. a.* them?
1 *Sam.* 15:18 *f. a.* A. consumed
23:1 Philistines *f. a.* Keilah
29:8 I may not *f. a.* enemies
1 *K.* 12:24 not *f. a.* 2 *Chr.* 11:4
20:23 let us *f. a.* them, 25
22:32 turned to *f. a.* Jehosh.
2 *K.* 3:21 kings were come to *f. a.*
2 *Chr.* 13:12 *f.* ye not *a.* the Lord
32:2 Sen. purposed to *f. a.* Jer.
35:20 Necho come to *f. a.* Car.
*Neh.* 4:8 come and *f. a.* Jerusa.
*Ps.* 35:1 *f. a.* them that *f. a.* me
56:2 they be many that *f. a.* me
*Is.* 19:2 sh. *f.* every one *a.* brot.
29:7 all nations that *f. a.* Ariel
8 nations that *f. a.* mount Z.
*Jer.* 1:19 shall *f. a.* thee, 15:20
21:5 I myself will *f. against* you
32:24 Ch. *f. a.* 29; 34:22; 37:8
*Zec.* 14:3 L. *f. a.* those nations
*Acts* 5:39 ye be found *f. a.* God
23:9 let us not *f. against* God
*Rev.* 2:16 *f. a.* them with sword

**FIGHT for.**

*Ex.* 14:14 L. *f. for*, *Deut.* 1:30; 3:22; 20:4
2 *K.* 10:3 *f. for* master's house
*Neh.* 4:14 *f. for* your brethren
20 our God shall *f. for* us
*Is.* 31:4 L. shall come to *f. for* Z.

**FIGHT with.**

*Jud.* 9:38 go out and *f. with* Ab.
*Jud.* 11:6 may *f. w.* chil. of Am.
1 *Sam.* 13:5 Phi. *f. w.* Israel, 28:1
17:9 if he be able to *f. with* me
32 thy ser. will go and *f. w.* P.
2 *Chr.* 35:22 Jo. disguised to *f. w.*
*Is.* 30:32 shaking will he *f. w.* us
*Jer.* 32:5 though ye *f. w.* Chald.
*Dan.* 10:20 return to *f. w.* prince
11:11 king of south came *f. w.*

**FIGHTETH, ING.**

*Ex.* 14:25 L. *f.* for them ag. Eg.
*Jos.* 23:10 L. God that *f.* for you
1 *Sam.* 25:28 my lord *f.* battles
*Ps.* 56:1 O God, he *f.* oppresseth

**FIGHTINGS.**

2 *Cor.* 7:5 without *f.* within fears
*Jam.* 4:1 wh. come wars and *f.?*

**FIGURE.**

*Deut.* 4:16 similitude of any *f.*
*Is.* 44:13 maketh after *f.* of man
*Rom.* 5:14 *f.* of him that was
1 *Cor.* 4:6 these I have in *f.* tra.
*Heb.* 9:9 which was a *f.* of time
11:19 whence he rec. him in a *f.*
1 *Pet.* 3:21 like *f.* even baptism

**FIGURES.**

1 *K.* 6:29 with carved *f.* of cher.
*Acts* 7:43 *f.* wh. ye made to wor.
*Heb.* 9:24 are the *f.* of the true

**FILE.**

1 *Sam.* 13:21 a *f.* for mattocks

**FILL, Substantive.**

*Lev.* 25:19 ye shall eat your *f.*
*Deut.* 23:24 may. eat grapes thy *f.*
*Prov.* 7:18 take our *f.* of love

**FILL, Verb.**

*Gen.* 1:22 *f.* waters in the seas
42:25 Jos. com. to *f.* sacks, 44:1
*Ex.* 10:6 locusts shall *f.* houses
16:32 Mo. said, *f.* a homer of it
1 *Sam.* 16:1 *f.* thy horn with oil
18:33 *f.* four barrels with water
*Job* 18:21 *f.* mouth with laughing
15:2 sh. wise man *f.* his belly?
20:23 when about to *f.* his belly

23:4 would *f.* mouth with argu.
38:39 or *f.* appe. of young lions
41:7 *f.* skin with barbed irons?
*Ps.* 81:10 mouth wide I will *f.*
83:16 *f.* their faces with shame
110:6 *f.* places with dead bodies
*Prov.* 1:13 we shall *f.* our houses
8:21 I will *f.* their treasures
*Is.* 8:8 sh. *f.* breadth of thy land
14:21 nor *f.* the face of world
27:6 Isr. shall *f.* face of world
56:12 will *f.* with strong drink
*Jer.* 13:13 I will *f.* inh. wi. drun.
23:24 I *f.* heaven and earth?
51:14 I will *f.* thee with men
*Ezek.* 3:3 *f.* thy bowels
9:7 *f.* the courts with the slain
10:2 *f.* hands with coals of fire
24:4 *f.* it with the choice bones
30:11 shall *f.* land with slain
32:4 will *f.* beasts of whole earth
5 I will *f.* val. with thy height
35:8 I will *f.* mount. with slain
*Zep.* 1:9 who *f.* master's house
*Hag.* 2:7 will *f.* house with glory
*Mat.* 9:16 which is put in to *f.* it
15:33 wh. bread to *f.* multitude?
23:32 *f.* ye up then the measure
*John* 2:7 *f.* water-pots with water
*Rom.* 15:13 God of hope *f.* you
*Eph.* 4:10 he might *f.* all things
*Col.* 1:24 *f.* up what is behind
1 *Thes.* 2:16 to *f.* up their sins
*Rev.* 18:6 cup filled, *f.* double

**FILLED.**

*Gen.* 6:13 earth is *f.* with viol.
21:19 and *f.* bottle with water
24:16 Rebekah *f.* her pitcher
26:15 P. had *f.* wells with earth
*Ex.* 2:16 they *f.* troughs to water
28:3 I have *f.* with wisd. 35:35
31:3 I have *f.* with S. of G. 35:31
40:34 glory of L. *f.* tabern. 35
*Jos.* 9:13 bottles we *f.* were new
1 *K.* 8:10 cloud *f.* house of Lord
11 gl. *f.* house, 2 *Chr.* 5:14; 7:1,2
18:35 *f.* trench also with water
20:27 the Syrians *f.* the country
2 *K.* 21:16 *f.* Je. with blood, 24:4
23:14 J. *f.* their places wi. bones
*Job* 3:15 princes *f.* houses with
16:8 hast *f.* me with wrinkles
22:18 yet he *f.* houses with good
*Ps.* 38:7 loins *f.* with loath. dis.
71:8 my mouth be *f.* with praise
72:19 let earth be *f.* with glory
80:9 deep root, it *f.* the land
104:28 hand, are *f.* with good
123:3 we are *f.* with contempt
4 soul is exceedingly *f.* with
*Prov.* 5:10 strang. *f.* with wealth
25:16 lest thou be *f.* with honey
30:16 the earth not *f.* with water
22 a fool when *f.* with meat
*Ec.* 1:8 nor is ear *f.* with hearing
6:3 his soul be not *f.* with good
7 and yet the appetite in not *f.*
*Cant.* 5:2 my head is *f.* with dew
*Is.* 6:1 his train *f.* the temple
21:3 are my loins *f.* with pain
33:5 L. hath *f.* Zion with judg.
34:6 sword of L. is *f.* with blood
43:24 *f.* me with fat of sacrifices
*Jer.* 15:17 hast *f.* me with indig.
46:12 thy cry hath *f.* the land
51:34 he hath *f.* belly
*Lam.* 3:15 he hath *f.* with bitter.
30 he is *f.* full with reproach
*Ezek.* 8:17 *f.* land with violence
10:3 and cloud *f.* the inner court
11:6 ye have *f.* streets with slain
28:16 they *f.* midst with viol.
36:38 waste cities *f.* flocks of
43:5 glory of Lord *f.* house, 44:4
*Dan.* 2:35 stone cut *f.* whole earth
*Nah.* 2:12 lion *f.* holes with prey
*Hab.* 2:16 thou art *f.* with shame
*Hag.* 1:6 ye are not *f.* with drink
*Zec.* 9:13 I have *f.* bow with E.
*Mat.* 27:48 *f.* sponge with vinegar. *Mark* 15:36; *John* 19:29
*Mark* 2:21 new piece that *f.* it up
7:27 let the children first be *f.*
*Luke* 1:53 he hath *f.* the hungry
2:40 Jesus *f.* with wisdom
5:7 came and *f.* both the ships
14:23 compel that house be *f.*
15:16 would fain have *f.* belly
*John* 2:7 they *f.* them up to brim
6:13 *f.* twelve baskets with fra.
16:6 sorrow hath *f.* your heart
*Acts* 2:2 mighty wind *f.* house
4:8 Peter *f.* with the Holy Ghost
5:3 why hath Satan *f.* thy heart
28 have *f.* Jerus. with doctr.
9:17 be *f.* with the Holy Ghost
13:9 Paul *f.* with Holy Ghost
*Rom.* 1:29 *f.* with all unright.
15:14 *f.* with all knowledge
24 I be somewhat *f.* with
2 *Cor.* 7:4 I am *f.* with comfort
*Eph.* 3:19 be *f.* with all fulness
5:18 with wine, but *f.* with Sp.
*Phil.* 1:11 *f.* with fruits of right.
*Col.* 1:9 be *f.* with knowledge
2 *Tim.* 1:4 I may be *f.* with joy
*Jam.* 2:16 be ye warmed and *f.*
*Rev.* 8:5 angel *f.* censer with fire
15:1 is *f.* up the wrath of God
18:6 cup which she *f.* fill double

**Shall be FILLED.**

*Ex.* 16:12 in morning ye *s. be f.*
*Num.* 14:21 earth *s. be f.* with gl.
2 *K.* 3:17 val. *s. be f.* with water
*Prov.* 1:31 *s. be f.* with own dev.
3:10 so *shall* thy barns *be f.*
12:21 wicked *s. be f.* with misc.
14:14 backslider *shall be f.* with
20:17 mouth *s. be f.* with gravel
24:4 by knowl. *s.* chambers *be f.*
*Jer.* 13:12 bottle *s. be f.* with wine
*Ezek.* 23:33 *s. be f.* with drunk.
39:20 ye *shall be f.* at my table
*Hab.* 2:14 earth *s. be f.* with kn.
*Zec.* 9:15 *shall be f.* like bowls
*Mat.* 5:6 that hunger, they *s. be f.*
*Luke* 1:15 J. *s. be f.* with Holy G.
3:5 every valley *shall be f.*
6:21 blessed hunger, ye *sh. be f.*

**Was FILLED.**

*Gen.* 6:11 earth *was f.* with viol.
1 *K.* 7:14 Hiram *was f.* with wis.
2 *K.* 3:20 country *was f.* with wa.
2 *Chr.* 5:13 house *w. f.* with cloud
16:14 bed *w. f.* with sweet odors
*Ps.* 126:2 mouth *w. f.* with laug.
*Is.* 6:4 house *was f.* with smoke
*Jer.* 51:5 land *w. f.* with sin ag.
*Ezek.* 10:4 house *f.* with the cloud
*Luke* 1:41 Elis. *w. f.* with H. G.
67 Zacharias *was f.* with H. G.
*John* 12:3 house *was f.* with odor
*Acts* 19:29 city *w. f.* with confu.
*Rev.* 15:8 temple *w. f.* with smoke

**Were FILLED.**

*Hos.* 13:6 *were f.* and their heart
*Luke* 4:28 they *w. f.* with wrath
5:26 *were f.* with fear, saying
6:11 they *were f.* with madness
8:23 they *were f.* with water
*John* 6:12 when they *were f.*
26 eat of the loaves, and *were f.*
*Acts* 2:4 *w.* all *f.* with H. G. 4:31
3:10 they *were f.* with wonder
5:17 *were f.* with indignation
13:45 Jews *were f.* with envy
*Acts* 13:52 disciples *were f.* joy
*Rev.* 19:21 fowls *w. f.* with flesh
*See* EAT.

**FILLEDST.**

*Deut.* 6:11 houses full, thou *f.*

**FILLEST.**

*Ps.* 17:14 whose belly thou *f.*

**FILLETH.**

*Job* 9:18 he *f.* me with bitterness
*Ps.* 84:6 rain also *f.* the pools
107:9 he *f.* the hungry soul
129:7 where. mower *f.* not hand
147:14 *f.* thee with finest wheat
*Eph.* 1:23 fulness of him that *f.*

**FILLET, S.**

*Ex.* 27:10 their *f.* shall be of silver, 11; 38:10, 11, 12, 17, 19
36:38 overlaid chapiters and *f.*
*Jer.* 52:21 a *f.* of twelve cubits

**FILLETED.**

*Ex.* 27:17 be *f.* with silver, 38:17
38:28 overlaid chapiters and *f.*

**FILLING.**

*Acts* 14:17 *f.* our hearts with food

**FILTH.**

*Is.* 4:4 when L. washed *f.* of Z.
*Nah.* 3:6 will cast abominable *f.*
1 *Cor.* 4:13 as the *f.* of the world
1 *Pet.* 3:21 not put away *f.* of flesh

**FILTHINESS.**

2 *Chr.* 29:5 carry *f.* out of holy
*Ezr.* 6:21 sep. from *f.* of heathen
9:11 unclean with *f.* of people
*Prov.* 30:12 not washed from *f.*
*Is.* 28:8 full of vomit and *f.*
*Lam.* 1:9 her *f.* is in her skirts
*Ezek.* 22:15 I will consume thy *f.*
24:11 *f.* of it may be molten
13 in thy *f.* is lewdness
36:25 from all *f.* will I cleanse
2 *Cor.* 7:1 cleanse ours. from all *f.*
*Eph.* 5:4 nor let *f.* be once named
*Jam.* 1:21 wheref. lay apart all *f.*
*Rev.* 17:4 full of abomin. and *f.*

**FILTHY.**

*Job* 15:16 much more *f.* is man?
*Ps.* 14:3 altogether become *f.* 53:3
*Is.* 64:6 all our right. as *f.* rags
*Zep.* 3:1 woe to her that is *f.*
*Zec.* 3:3 J. clothed with *f.* garm.
4 take away the *f.* garments
*Col.* 3:8 you put off *f.* communi.
1 *Tim.* 3:3 not greedy of *f.* lucre, 8
*Tit.* 1:7 not given to *f.* lucre
11 teaching for *f.* lu. 1 *Pet.* 5:2
2 *Pet.* 2:7 Lot vexed with *f.* con.
*Jude* 8 *f.* dreamers defile the flesh
*Rev.* 22:11 *f.* let him be *f.* still

**FINALLY.**

2 *Cor.* 13:11 *f.* farewell, *Eph.* 6:10 *Phil.* 3:1; 4:8; 2 *Thes.* 3:1; 1 *Pet.* 3:8

**FIND.**

*Gen.* 19:11 wearied to *f.* the door
*Num.* 32:23 sin shall *f.* you out
*Deut.* 22:25 man *f.* damsel, 28
*Ruth* 1:9 L. grant ye may *f.* rest
1 *Sam.* 20:21 go, *f.* out arrows, 36
24:19 *f.* enemy let him go?
1 *K.* 18:5 perad. we may *f.* grass
2 *Chr.* 2:14 to *f.* out every device
*Job* 23:3 O where I might *f.* him
*Ps.* 10:15 seek wicked till *f.* none
*Prov.* 2:5 shalt *f.* knowl. of God
4:22 words life to those that *f.*
8:12 *f.* out know. of witty inv.
*Ec.* 7:27 one by one *f.* out acc.
12:10 to *f.* out acceptable words
*Cant.* 5:8 if *f.* my beloved
*Is.* 34:14 screechowl shall *f.* place
58:3 in day of fast you *f.* pleas.
*Lam.* 1:6 like harts that *f.* no
2:9 prophets also *f.* no vision
*Dan.* 6:4 sought to *f.* occasion ag. Daniel but could *f.* none
5 except we *f.* it con. law of G.
*Mat.* 7:14 few there be that *f.* it
18:13 and if so be that he *f.* it

Mark 11:13 if haply he might f.
13:36 he f. you sleeping
Luke 6:7 might f. accusation
12:38 f. them so, blessed serv.
13:7 seeking fruit and f. none
15:4 that wh. is lost till he f. it
8 seek diligently till she f. it?
John 10:9 in and out, f. pasture
Acts 7:46 desired to f. tabernacle
17:27 feel after him and f. him
23:9 we f. no evil in this man
Rom. 9:19 doth he yet f. fault?
2 Cor. 9:4 and f. you unprepared
2 Tim. 1:18 f. mercy of Lord
See FAVOR.

**Can, or canst FIND.**

Gen. 41:38 can f. such one
Ex. 5:11 get straw where c. f. it
Ezr. 7:16 silver and gold can f.
Job 3:22 glad when they can f.
11:7 c. thou by searching f. out G. c. thou f. out Almighty?
Prov. 20:6 faith. man who c. f.?
31:10 who c. f. a virtuous wom.?
Ec. 3:11 c. f. out work G. maketh
7:24 exceed. deep, who c. f. it?
Jer. 5:1 if ye c. f. man seek. tru.

**Cannot FIND.**

1 K. 18:12 c. f. thee, will slay
Job 17:10 I c. f. one wise man
37:23 Almighty, we c. f. him
Ec. 8:17 a man c. f. out work

**FIND grace.**

Gen. 32:5 I may f. grace in thy sight, Ex. 33:13
33:8 to f. g. in sight of my lord
15 let me f. g.; 34:11 l. me f. g.
47:25 let us f. grace in sight of
Ruth 2:2 in wh. sight I shall f. g.
1 Sam. 1:18 let thy handm. f. g.
2 Sam. 16:4 f. grace in thy sight
Heb. 4:16 we may f. g. to help

**I FIND.**

Gen. 18:26 I f. in Sod. 50 righte.
28 if I f. 45; 30 if I f. 30 there
Ps. 132:5 I f. out place for L.
Ec. 7:26 I f. more bit. th. death
Cant. 8:1 when I sh. f. thee
Luke 23:4 I f. no fault in this man, John 18:38; 19:4, 6
Rom. 7:18 th. wh. is good I f. not
21 I f. law, that wh. I do good

**Not FIND, or FIND not.**

Ex. 16:25 to-day ye shall not f.
2 Sam. 17:20 could not f. them
Prov. 1:28 but shall not f. me, Hos. 5:6; John 7:34, 36
Ec. 7:28 soul seeketh, but I f. n.
Cant. 5:6 but I could not f. him
Is. 41:12 sh. not f. them, Hos. 2:7
Hos. 2:6 she shall not f. paths
Luke 5:19 not f. what way they
19:48 not f. what might do to J.
John 7:35 we shall not f. him
Rom. 7:18 how to do good, I f. n.
2 Cor. 12:20 I shall not f. you
Rev. 9:6 death, and shall not f. it

**Shall, or shalt FIND.**

Deut. 4:29 seek L. thou s. f. him
28:65 s. f. no ease am. nations
Jud. 9:33 as thou s. f. occasion
2 Chr. 20:16 s. f. at end of brook
30:9 children s. f. compassion
Ezr. 4:15 thou s. f. in book
Ps. 17:3 and s. f. nothing
21:8 thy hand s. f. out enemies
Prov. 8:17 they that seek me early s. f. me, Jer. 29:13
Ec. 11:1 s. f. it after many days
Jer. 6:16 s. f. rest Mat. 11:29
Mat. 7:7 and ye s. f. Luke 11:9
10:39 los. life for my sake s. f. it
17:27 thou s. f. a piece of money
21:2 s. f. an ass tied, Mark 11:2
22:9 as many as ye shall f. bid
24:46 when cometh, s. f. so doing, Luke 12:37, 43
Luke 2:12 ye shall f. babe wrapt
18:8 shall he f. faith on earth?
Rev. 18:14 thou s. f. th. no more

**FINDETH.**

Gen. 4:14 that f. me sh. slay me
Job 33:10 he f. occasions aga. me
Ps. 119:162 I rej. as one f. spoil
Prov. 3:13 happy man f. wisdom
8:35 whoso f. me f. life,
14:6 seeketh wisdom f. it not
18:22 whoso f. wife f. good th.
21:10 his neighbor f. no favor
21 that followeth mercy f. life
Ec. 9:10 whats. thy hand f. to do
Lam. 1:3 am. heathen, f. no rest
Hos. 14:3 fatherless f. mercy
Mat. 7:8 seeketh f. Luke 11:10
10:39 that f. his life shall lose it
12:43 seeking rest, f. none
44 f. it empty, Luke 11:25
John 1:41 he first f. own brother
43 Jes. f. Philip; 45 Phi. f. N.

**FINDING.**

Gen. 4:15 lest any f. Cain
Job 9:10 doeth things past f. out
Is. 58:13 f. thine own pleasure
Luke 11:24 seeking rest f. none
Rom. 11:33 and his ways past f.
Heb. 8:8 for f. fault with them

**FINE, Verb.**

Job 28:1 place for gold where f.

**FINE, Adjective.**

Ezr. 8:27 ves. of f. cop. as gold
Is. 19:9 that work in f. flax
Rev. 1:15 feet like f. brass, 2:18

**FINE flour or meal.**

Gen. 18:6 three measures of f. m.
Lev. 2:1 offering be of f. fl. 24:5
4 cakes of f. fl. mingled wi. oil 5:7; 7:12; 14:10, 21; 23:13; Num. 6:15; 7:13, 19, 25, 31, 37, 43, 49, 55, 61; 8:8
1 K. 4:22 30 measures of f. flour
2 K. 7:1 mea. f. f for she. 16, 18
Ezek. 16:13 thou didst eat f. fl.
19 I gave thee f. flour, and oil
Rev. 18:13 merchandise of f. fl.

**FINE gold.**

2 Chr. 3:5 overlaid with f. gold
8 most holy overlaid with f. g.
Job 31:24 to f. g. Thou art confi.
Ps. 19:10 desired th. much f. g.
119:127 I love com. above f. g.
Prov. 3:14 gain of wisd. th. f. g.
8:19 better than gold, than f. g.
25:12 as ornament of f. g.
Cant. 5:11 head is as most f. g.
15 as pill. set on sock. of f. g.
Is. 13:12 more preci. than f. g.
Lam. 4:1 most f. g. changed
2 sons of Z. comparab. to f. g.
Dan. 2:32 image's head f. gold
10:5 girded with f. g. of Uphaz
Zec. 9:3 T. heaped f. g. as mire

**FINE linen.**

Ex. 25:4 ye shall take f. linen
26:1 curtains of f. twined linen
31 v. of f. l. 36:35; 2 Chr. 3:14
36 f. twined linen 27:9, 16, 18; 36:37; 38:9, 16, 18
28:5 they sh. take gold and f. l.
6 the ephod of f. linen, 39:2
8 girdle f. l. 39:5, 29; 39:8
35:35 all manner of work and f. linen, 38:23; 2 Chr. 2:14
36:8 curtains of f. linen
39:27 coats of f. l. for Aaron
28 mitre of f. l. bonnets of f. l.
1 Chr. 15:27 clothed wi. robe f. l.
Est. 8:15 M. wi. garment of f. l.
Prov. 7:16 decked bed with f. l.
31:24 maketh f. l. and selleth
Ezek. 27:7 f. linen from Egypt
Mark 15:46 Jose. bought f. linen
Luke 16:19 man in pur. and f. l.
Rev. 18:12 merchandise of f. lin.
19:8 granted to be arrayed f. l.
14 armies in heav. clot. in f. l.

**FINER.**

Prov. 25:4 come forth ves. for f.

**FINEST.**

Ps. 81:16 fed with f. of wheat
147:14 filleth thee with f. of wh.

**FINING.**

Prov. 17:3 f. pot is for sil. 27:21

**FINGER.**

Ex. 8:19 mag. said, This f. of G.
29:12 blood on altar with thy f.
31:18 tables written with the f. of God, Deut. 9:10
Lev. 4:6 sh. dip f. in blood, 17, 25, 30, 34; 8:15; 9:9; 16:14, 19
14:16 priest dip right f. in oil, 27
1 K. 12:10 my little f. thicker, 2 Chr. 10:10
Is. 58:9 putting forth of the f.
Luke 11:20 with f. of G. cast out
16:24 may dip tip of f. in water
John 8:6 with f. wrote on g.
20:25 put my f. into the print
27 reach hither thy f. and beh.

**FINGERS.**

2 Sam. 21:20 on every hand six f. 1 Chr. 20:6
Ps. 8:3 thy heav. work of thy f.
144:1 teacheth my f. to fight
Prov. 6:13 wicked teach. with f.
7:3 bind them on f. write them
Cant. 5:5 my f. wi. sweet myrrh
Is. 2:8 which own f. made, 17:8
Jer. 52:21 thickn. of pillar four f.
Dan. 5:5 came forth f. of man's
Mat. 23:4 will not move with one of their f. Luke 11:46
Mark 7:33 he put his f. into ears

**FINISH.**

Gen. 6:16 in cubit sh. f. it above
Dan. 9:24 f. transgression, make
Luke 14:28 whe. sufficient to f.
29 and is not able to f. it
John 4:34 to do his will, f. work
5:36 works F. given me to f.
Acts 20:24 I might f. my course
Rom. 9:28 he will f. the work
2 Cor. 8:6 would also f. in you

**FINISHED.**

Gen. 2:1 heav. and earth were f.
Ex. 39:32 all work f. 40:33
1 K. 6:9 Sol. built house and f. it, 14, 22, 38; 2 Chr. 5:1; 7:11
7:1 Solomon f. all his house, 9:1, 25; 2 Chr. 8:16
1 Chr. 28:20 till thou hast f.
Ezr. 5:16 build. and yet not f.
6:14 eld. of J. built and f. it, 15
Neh. 6:15 wall f. in 52 days
Dan. 5:26 numbe. kingd. and f.
Mat. 13:53 when Jes. f. parables
19:1 Jesus had f. sayings, 26:1
John 17:4 f. work thou gavest
19:30 said, It is f. bowed head
2 Tim. 4:7 I have f. my course
Heb. 4:3 works f. from foundat.
Jam. 1:15 sin, wh. f. bring death
Rev. 10:7 mystery of G. sho. be f.
11:7 witnesses ha. f. testimony
20:5 till thousand years were f.

**FINISHER.**

Heb. 12:2 J. author and f. of faith

**FINS.**

Lev. 11:9 hath f. eat. Deut. 14:9
10 hath not f. be abomina. 12

**FIRE.**

Gen. 22:6 Abra. took f. in hand
7 father, behold f. and wood

*Ex.* 3:2 the bush burned with *f.*
9:23 Lord sent hail and *f.* ran
12:8 that night roast with *f.* 9
19:18 Lord on mount Sinai in *f.*
22:6 if *f.* break out, and catch
40:38 *f.* was on tabernacle by night, *Num.* 9:16; *Deut.* 1:33
*Lev.* 1:7 s. of priest put *f.* on al.
8 upon wood in *f.* 12, 17; 3:5
2:14 ears of corn dried by *f.*
9:24 came *f.* out from before L.
10:1 sons of A. put *f.* in censers
2 out *f.* from L. and devoured
18:21 any seed pass th. *f.* *Deut.* 18:10; 2 *K.* 17:17; 23:10
*Num.* 6:18 and put it in the *f.*
11:2 M. prayed, *f.* was quenched
16:46 censer, and put *f.* therein
21:28 *f.* gone out from Heshbon
31:23 ev. thing th. may abide *f.*
*Deut.* 4:11 mount. burnt with *f.*
36 he showed thee his great *f.*
5:5 were afraid by reason of *f.*
*Jos.* 7:25 Isr. burned A. with *f.*
*Jud.* 6:21 rose up *f.* out of rock
9:15 let *f.* come out of bramble
16:9 th. of tow when touch. *f.*
1 *K.* 18:23 lay wood, put no *f.* 25
24 God that answereth by *f.*
38 *f.* of L. fell, 2 *Chr.* 7:1, 3
19:12 after earthquake *f.* but L. not in *f.* after *f.* still small
2 *K.* 1:10 then let *f.* come down
2:11 a chariot and horses of *f*
6:17: mount. full of char. of *f.*
16:3 A. made son pass thro' *f*
19:18 have cast gods into *f.*
21:6 Manasseh made son pass thro' *f.* 2 *Chr.* 33:6
1 *Chr* 21:26 ans. fr. heaven by *f.*
*Job* 1:16 the *f.* of God is fallen
18:5 spark of his *f.* shall not
41:19 and sparks of *f.* leap out
*Ps.* 39:3 I was musing *f.* burned
46:9 burneth chariot in the *f.*
66:12 went thro' *f.* and water
68:2 as wax melteth bef. *f.* so
74:7 have cast *f.* into sanctu.
78:14 with light of *f.* 105:39
83:14 as the *f.* burneth the wood
97:3 *f.* goeth before him,
118:12 quenched as *f.* of thorns
140:10 let them be cast into *f.*
148:8 *f.* and hail, stormy wind
*Prov.* 6:27 take *f.* in bosom?
16:27 in his lips is as burning *f.*
26:20 no wood is, *f.* goeth out
30:16 and *f.* saith not enough
*Is.* 9:5 burning and fuel of *f.*
18 wickedness burneth as *f.*
19 people shall be as fuel of *f.*
10:16 burning like burn. of a *f.*
30:14 to take *f.* from hearth
33 the pile is *f.* and much wo.
31:9 saith Lord, whose *f.* is in Z.
37:19 kings of A. cast gods to *f.*
43:2 walk. thro' *f.* not be burnt
44:16 burneth part in the *f.* and saith, Aha, I have seen *f.*
50:11 walk in the light of your *f.*
64:2 when melti. *f.* burneth, *f.* causeth waters to boil
65:5 *f.* that burneth all the day
66:24 nei. their *f.* be quenched
*Jer.* 4:4 fury come forth like *f.*
5:14 my words in thy mouth *f.*
20:9 word as *f.* shut up in bones
21:12 lest my fury go out like *f.*
*Jer.* 22:7 choice cedars in the *f.*
29:22 king of Baby. roasted in *f.*
32:35 sons to pass through *f.* unto Mol. *Ezek.* 16:21; 20:26, 31
36:22 there was *f.* on hearth
23 roll, and cast it into the *f.*
*Lam.* 2:3 burned like flaming *f.*
4 he poured out his fury like *f.*
*Ezek.* 1:4 a *f.* infolding itself
13 *f.* bright, out of *f.* lightning
10:6 *f.* from between wheels
21:31 will blow thee in *f.* 22:21
22:20 blow *f.* upon it, to melt
24:9 even make pile for *f.* 12
36:5 in the *f.* of my jeal. 38:19
*Dan.* 3:27 upon bod. *f.* had no p.
7:9 wheels like burning *f.*
10:6 and his eyes as lamps of *f.*
*Hos.* 7:6 burneth as a flaming *f.*
*Joel* 2:30 *f.* pillars, *Acts* 2:19
*Amos* 5:6 lest he break like *f.*
7:4 God called to contend by *f.*
*Ob.* 18 house of J. shall be a *f.*
*Mic.* 1:4 molten as wax before *f.*
*Nah.* 1:6 fury poured out like *f.*
*Hab.* 2:13 sh. labor in very *f.*
*Zec.* 2:5 unto her a wall of *f.*
3:2 brand plucked out of the *f.*?
12:6 hearth of *f.* like torch of *f.*
13:9 bring third part thro' *f.*
*Mal.* 3:2 he is like a refiner's *f.*
*Mat.* 3:10 ev. tree that bringeth not good fruit is cast into *f.* 7:19; *Luke* 3:9; *John* 15:6
11 baptize with Holy Ghost and *f.* *Luke* 3:16
13:42 cast into furnace of *f.* 50
17:15 he falleth into *f.* *Mar.* 9:22
18:8 be cast into everlasting *f.* *Mark* 9:43, 46
25:41 cursed, into everlasting *f.*
*Mark* 9:14 wh. *f.* is not quen. 45
14:54 P. warmed himself at *f.*
*Luke* 9:54 wilt thou that we c. *f.*?
17:29 the same day it rained *f.*
22:56 beh. him as he sat by *f.*
*Acts* 3:3 cloven tong. like as of *f.*
28:3 when Paul laid sticks on *f.*
5 he shook off the beast into *f.*
1 *Cor.* 3:13 sh. be reveal. by *f.* 15
2 *Thes.* 1:8 in flamin. *f.* taking
*Heb.* 1:7 ministers a flame of *f.*
11:34 faith quench. violence *f.*
12:18 mount that burned with *f.*
*Jam.* 3:5 great mat. little *f.* kin.
6 tongue is a *f.* a world of ini.
5:3 eat your flesh as it were *f.*
1 *Pet.* 1:7 though tried with *f.*
2 *Pet.* 3:7 reserved unto *f.* ag. day
12 heav. being on *f.* sh. be dis.
*Jude* 7 the venge. of eternal *f.*
23 pulling them out of the *f.*
*Rev.* 3:18 buy gold tried in *f.*
4:5 seven lamps of *f.* burning
8:5 angel filled censer with *f.*
7 there followed hail and *f.*
8 great mount. burning with *f.*
9:17 out of mouths issued *f.* 11:5
13:13 maketh *f.* come down
14:18 angel had power over *f.*
15:2 sea of glass mingled w. *f.*
16:8 power to scorch men w. *f.*
20:9 *f.* came down from God
10 dev. was cast into lake of *f.*
14 dea. and hell cast lake of *f.*
21:8 in lake wh. burneth with *f.*

*See* BRIMSTONE, BURN *or* BURNT, COALS, CONSUME, CONSUMING, DEVOUR, DEVOURED, DEVOURING, FLAME, HELL, MIDST.

**Kindle, *or* kindled FIRE.**

*Ex.* 22:6 that *k. f.* make restitu.
35:3 ye sh. *k.* no *f.* on the sab.
*Deut.* 32:22 for a *f.* is *k.* in my anger, *Jer.* 15:14; 17:4
2 *Sam.* 22:13 coals of *f.* *kindled*
*Ps.* 78:21 *f.* was *k.* against Jacob
*Is.* 50:11 beh. all ye that *k.* a *f.*
*Jer.* 7:18 gather. wood, fath. *k. f.*
11:16 hath *k. f.* on green olive, 21:14; 43:12; 49:27; 50:32
*Lam.* 4:11 L. hath *k.* a *f.* in Z.
*Ezek.* 20:47 I will *k. f.* in forest
24:10 *k. f.* consume the flesh
*Mal.* 1:10 nor do ye *k. f.* on altar
*Luke* 12:49 *f.* what if already *k.*?
22:55 when had *k.* a *f.* in hall
*Acts* 28:2 barbarians *kindled f.*

**Made by FIRE.**

*Ex.* 29:18 an offering *made by f.* 25, 41; *Lev.* 1:9, 13, 17; 2:2, 9, 16; 3:3, 5, 9, 11, 14, 16; 7:5, 25; 8:21, 28; 21:6; 22:27; 23:8, 13, 18, 25, 27, 36, 37; 24:7; *Num.* 15:3, 10, 13, 14; 18:17; 28:3
*Lev.* 2:3 offerings of Lord *m.* by *f.* 10; 3:3; 4:35; 5:12; 6:17, 18; 7:30, 35; 10:12, 15; 21:21; 24:9; *Deut.* 18:1; 1 *Sam.* 2:28

**Pillar of FIRE.**

*Ex.* 14:24 L. looked thro' *p. of f.*
*Rev.* 10:1 and his feet as *p. of f.*

**Send, *or* sent FIRE.**

*Lam.* 1:13 from above be *sent f.*
*Ezek.* 39:6 I will *s. f.* on Magog
*Amos* 1:4 I will *s. f.* into h. of H.
7 I will *s. f.* on the wall of G.
10 I will *s. f.* on wall of Ty. 12
2:2 I will *s.* a *f.* on M.; 5 Judah
*Luke* 12:49 come to *s. f.* on earth

**Set FIRE.**

*Deut.* 32:22 *s.* on *f.* foundations
*Jos.* 8:8 *s.* city of Ai on *f.* 19
*Jud.* 1:8 Judah had *s.* Jer. on *f.*
9:49 the people *s.* the hold on *f.*
15:5 had *s.* the brands on *f.*
2 *Sam.* 14:30 *s.* J.'s field on *f.* 31
2 *K.* 8:12 H. will *s.* holds on *f.*
*Ps.* 57:4 am. th. that are *s.* on *f.*
*Is.* 27:11 women *set* them on *f.*
42:25 he hath *set* him on *f.*
*Jer.* 6:1 *s.* up a sign of *f.* in Bet.
32:29 C. shall *s.* on *f.* this city
*Ezek.* 30:8 *s.* a *f.* in Egypt, 14, 16
39:9 *s.* on *f.* burn weapons of G.
*Jam.* 3:6 tongue *s.* on *f.* course of nature, is *set* on *f.* of hell

**Strange FIRE.**

*Lev.* 10:1 N. and Abi. offered *s. f.*
*Num.* 3:4 died wh. off. *s. f.* 26:61

## FIREBRAND, S.

*Jud.* 15:4 S. took *f.* put *f.* midst
*Prov.* 26:18 madman casteth *f.*
*Is.* 7:4 two tails of these smok. *f.*
*Amos* 4:11 *f.* plucked out of bur

## FIRE-PANS.

*Ex.* 27:3 make basons and *f.-p.*
38:3 he made the *f.-p.* of brass
2 *K.* 25:15 *f.-p.* car. *Jer.* 52:19

## FIRES.

*Is.* 24:15 glorify ye Lord in *f.*

## FIRKINS.

*John* 2:6 containing two or th. *f.*

## FIRM.

*Jos.* 3:17 pri. stood *f.* on gr. 4:3
*Job* 41:23 are *f.* in themselves
24 his heart is as *f.* as a stone
*Ps.* 73:4 no bands, but stre. is *f.*
*Dan.* 6:7 consulted to make *f.*
*Heb.* 3:6 rejoic. of hope *f.* to end

## FIRMAMENT.

*Gen.* 1:6 *f.* in midst of waters
7 G. *f.* waters under and ab. *f.*
8 and God called the *f.* Heaven
14 let th. be lights in *f.* 15, 17
20 fowl that fly in open *f.*
*Ps.* 19:1 *f.* showeth handiwork
150:1 praise him in *f.* power
*Ezek.* 1:22 likeness of *f.* as cryst.
25 a voice from *f.* over heads
26 above *f.* likeness of throne
*Dan.* 12:3 shine as bright. of *f.*

## FIR.

1 *K.* 5:8 concerning timber of *f.*
6:15 cov. floor with planks of *f.*
*Cant.* 1:17 cedar, our rafters of *f.*

**FIR-TREE, S.**

1 K. 5:10 H. gave Solo. f.-t. 9:11
6:34 the two doors were of f.-t.
2 K. 19:23 cut tall f.-t. Is. 37:24
2 Chr. 2:8 send f.-t.; Is. 14:8 f.-t.
3:5 house he ceiled with f.-t.
Ps. 104:17 for stork f.-t. are house
Is. 41:19 I set in the desert f.-t.
55:13 inst. of th. sh. come f.-t.
60:13 the f.-t. the pine-tree
Ezek. 27:5 ship-boards, f.-t.
Hos. 14:8 like g. f. t.; Zec. 11:2
Nah. 2:3 f.-t. sh. be terribly sha.

**FIR-WOOD.**

2 Sam. 6:5 instru. made of f.-w.

**FIRST.**

Gen. 25:25 f. came out red
38:28 said, This came out f.
Ex. 23:19 f. of fruits bring to L.
28:17 f. row sh. be sardius, 39:10
34:1 like to f. 4; Deut. 10:1, 3
Num. 2:9 J. these sh. f. set forth
24:20 Amalek was f. of nations
Deut. 11:14 give f. rain and lat.
17:7 hands of witn. shall be f.
1 Sam. 14:35 f. altar S. built L.
2 Sam. 23:19 attained not to f. three, 23; 1 Chr. 11:21, 25
Ezr. 3:12 glory of the f. house
Job 15:7 art th. the f. man born?
Prov. 18:17 is f. in own cause
Is. 43:27 f. father hath sinned
Dan. 6:2 Daniel was f. president
7:4 the f. beast was like a lion
Hag. 2:3 saw house in f. glory
Zec. 12:7 save tents of Judah f.
Mat. 5:24 f. be reconciled to bro.
6:33 seek ye f. kingdom of God
7:5 f. cast beam out of own eye, Luke 6:42
8:21 f. to go and bury, Luke 9:59
12:45 worse than f. Luke 11:26
17:10 must f. come, Mark 9:12
27 take up fish that f. cometh
21:31 of twain? They say, the f.
36 other servants more than f.
22:38 this f. com. Mark 12:28, 30
Mark 4:28 f. the blade, then ear
7:27 let the children f. be filled
9:35 desire to be f. shall be
13:10 gospel must f. be publish.
16:9 appeared f. to Mary Magd.
Luke 6:1 on second sab. after f.
11:38 that he had not f. washed
14:28 sit. not down f. and coun.
John 5:4 f. step. in made whole
8:7 with. sin, let him f. cast st.
Acts 3:26 to you f. God sent him
11:26 called Christ. f. in Antio.
12:10 passed f. and second ward
26:23 C. f. that sho. rise fr. dead
Rom. 2:9 of Jew f. also of G. 10
11:35 who hath f. given to him?
1 Cor. 12:28 f. apostles, sec. pro.
14:30 let the f. hold his peace
15:45 f. man A. made liv. soul
47 f. man is of the earth, eart.
2 Cor. 8:5 f. gave selves to Lord
12 if there be f. a willing mind
Eph. 1:12 f. trusted in Christ
6:2 f. command. with promise
1 Thes. 4:16 dead in C. sh. rise f.
2 Thes. 2:3 exc. a falling away f.
1 Tim. 1:16 in me f. C. J. might
2:13 Ad. was f. formed, then E.
3:10 let these also f. be proved
5:12 have cast off their f. faith
2 Tim. 1:5 faith dwelt f. in gran.
2:6 husbandman must f. part.
4:16 at my f. ans. no man stood
Tit. 3:10 after f. and sec. admo.
Heb. 5:12 which be f. principles
7:27 offer f. for his own sins
8:7 f. covenant, 13; 9:1, 15, 18
9:2 f. tab. where. show-bre. 6, 8
10:9 taketh away f. that he may
Jam. 3:17 wisd. from above is f.
1 John 4:19 love him bec. he f.
Jude 6 angels who kept not f. es.
Rev. 2:4 thou hast left thy f. love
5 do f. works, else I will come
13:12 the power of the f. beast
20:5 this is the f. resurrection
21:1 f. heaven and f. earth

**At the FIRST.**

Gen. 13:4 A. made altar at t. f.
43:20 came at t. f. to buy food
Deut. 9:18 I fell bef. L. as at f. 25
Is. 1:26 restore judges as at the f.
9:1 at the f. he lightly afflicted
Jer. 7:12 wh. I set my name at f.
John 19:39 at the f. came to Jes.
Acts 15:14 G. at t. f. did visit G.
Heb. 2:3 at t. f. beg. to be spoken

**FIRST-BORN.**

Gen. 19:31 f.-b. said to youn. 34
33 f.-b. went in lay with f. 37
27:19 said, I am Es. thy f.-b. 32
29:26 give younger bef. the f.-b.
43:33 f.-b. accord. to birthright
Ex. 4:22 Is. is my son, my f.-b.
23 will slay thy son, thy f.-b.
11:5 all f.-b. in land of E. shall
12:12 I will smite all f.-b.
29 smote all f.-b. in Egypt. 13:15
13:2 sanctify unto me all f.-b.
22:29 f.-b. of thy sons shalt thou give
34:20 f.-b. sons red. Num. 18:15
Num. 3:12 instead of f.-b. 41, 45
13 bec. all f.-b of Is. are mine
Deut. 21:17 for the right of f.-b.
Jos. 6:26 lay foundation in f.-b.
1 K. 16:34 laid found. in Ab. f.-b.
Job 18:13 f.-b. of death shall dev.
Ps. 78:51 he smote all f.-b. in E. 105:36; 135:8; 136:10
89:27 my f.-b. higher th. kings
Is. 14:30 the f.-b. of poor sh. feed
Jer. 31:9 and Ephraim is my f.-b.
Mic. 6:7 give f.-b. for transgr.?
Zec. 12:10 in bitterness for f.-b.
Ma. 1:25 bro. forth f.-b. Luke 2:7
Rom. 8:29 f.-b. am. many breth.
Col. 1:15 f.-b. of every creature
18 beginning, f.-b. from dead
Heb. 11:28 he that destroyed f.-b.
12:23 are come to church of f.-b.

**FIRST-FRUIT, S.**

Ex. 22:29 to offer the f. ripe fr.
23:16 f.-f of thy labor thou hast
19 f.-f. of la. 34:26; Deut. 26:2
Lev. 2:12 oblat. of f.-f. ye shall
14 meat-offer. of f.-f. green ears
23:10 a sheaf of f.-f. 17:20
Num. 18:12 f.-f. of oil, wine
Deut. 18:4 the f.-fruit of thy corn
26:10 brought f.-f of land
2 K. 4:42 brought man of G. f.-f.
2 Chr. 31:5 in abundance the f.-f.
Neh. 10:35 f.-fruits of our ground
37 the f.-fruits of our dough
12:44 chambers for f.-f. 13:31
Prov. 3:9 honor L. with f.-fruits
Jer. 2:3 Israel f.-f. of his increase
Mic. 7:1 my soul desired f. fruit
Rom. 8:23 have f.-f. of Spirit
11:16 if f.-f. be holy
16:5 f.-f. of Achaia, 1 Cor. 16:15
1 Cor. 15:20 C. f.-f. of them th. 23
Jam. 1:18 kind of f.-fr. of creat.
Rev. 14:4 being the f.-f unto God

**FIRSTLING, S.**

Gen. 4:4 Abel brought f. of flock
Ex. 13:12 set apart eve. f. 34:19
13 f. of ass thou shalt red. 34:20
Lev. 27:26 L.'s f. no man sancti.
Num. 18:15 f. of uncl. beasts, 17
Deut. 12:6 ye sh. bring f. of her.
15:19 f. males sanctify to the L.
33:17 J.'s glory like f. of bullock

**FISH.**

Gen. 1:26 dom. over f. of sea, 28
Ex. 7:18 f. in river shall die, 21
Num. 11:22 all f. of sea be gath.
Deut. 4:18 liken. of any f. in wa.
Ps. 8:8 put the f. under his feet
105:29 waters into blood, slew f.
Is. 19:10 sluices and ponds for f.
50:2 their f. stinketh
Ezek. 29:4 f. to stick to thy scal.
5 and all the f. of thy rivers
47:10 f. sh. be as f. of great sea
Jon. 1:17 Lord prepared great f.
2:1 prayed to L. out of f.'s belly
10 L. spoke to f. it vomited J.
Mat. 7:10 if he ask f. will he give
17:27 take up f. that first com.
Luke 24:42 gave him piece br. f.
John 21:9 they saw f. laid, 10, 13

**FISH, ING.**

Jer. 16:16 fishers, and they sh. f.
John 21:3 S. Peter saith, I go a f.

**FISH-GATE.**

2 Chr. 33:14 M. built to ent. f.-g.
Neh. 3:5 f.-g. did sons of H. bui.
12:39 from above the f.-gate
Zep. 1:10 noise of cry from f.-g.

**FISH-HOOKS.**

Amos 4:2 will take poster. w. f.

**FISH-POOLS.**

Cant. 7:4 th. eyes like f.-p. of H.

**FISH-SPEARS.**

Job 41:7 fill head with f.-s.

**FISHERMEN.**

Luke 5:2 f. were gone out of th.

**FISHER, S.**

Is. 19:8 f. also shall mourn and
Jer. 16:16 send for many f. sa. L.
Ezek. 47:10 f. shall stand upon it
Mat. 4:18 they were f. Mark 1:16
19 f. of men, Mark 1:17
John 21:7 Peter girt f. coat to h.

**FISHES.**

Gen. 9:2 fear of you be on all f.
1 K. 4:33 of creeping thi. and f.
Job 12:8 f. of sea shall declare
Ec. 9:12 f. that are taken in evil
Hab. 1:14 mak. men as f. of sea
Mat. 14:17 five loaves and two f. Mar. 6:38; Lu. 9:13; John 6:9
15:34 sev. loaves lit. f. Mark 8:7
Luke 5:6 multit. of f. John 21:6
5:9 astonished at draught of f.
John 21:11 P. drew net full gr. f.
1 Cor. 15:39 flesh of be. and of f.

**FIST, S.**

Ex. 21:18 one smite ano. with f.
Prov. 30:4 hath gath. wind in f.?
Is. 58:4 smite with f. of wicked.

**FIT.**

Lev. 16:21 by hand of a f. man
1 Chr. 7:11 f. to go to war, 12:8
Job 34:18 f. to say king, Th. wic.?
Ezek. 15:5 made f. for no work
Luke 9:62 is f. for kingdom of G.
14:35 not f. for the land
Acts 22:22 not f. that he sh. live
Col. 3:18 wives, submit as f. in L.

**FITCHES.**

Is. 28:25 doth he not cast f.?
Is. 28:27 f. not thresh. f. are bea.
Ezek. 4:9 wheat, barley, millet, f.

**FITLY.**

Prov. 25:11 word f. spok. appl. of
Eph. 2:21 the building f. framed
4:16 form wh. whole body f. jo.

**FITTED, ETH.**

1 K. 6:35 gold f. up. carved work
Is. 44:13 carpent. f. it with plan.
Rom. 9:22 ves. of wrath f. to des.

**FIVE.**

Gen. 14:9 of S. four kings with f.
18:28 destroy all for lack of f.?

Jos. 13:3 f. lords of Ph. Jud. 3:3
Is. 19:18 f. cities speak lang. of C.
30:17 at rebuke of f. shall ye flee
Mat. 14:17 we have here but f. loaves, Mark 6:38; Luke 9:13
25:2 f. of them wise, f. foolish
Luke 12:6 are not f. spar. sold?
16:28 father's house I have f. b.
John 4:18 hast had f. husbands
5:2 a pool having f. porches
1 Cor. 14:19 I rath. speak f. wor.
2 Cor. 11:24 f. times rec. 40 strip.
Rev. 17:10 sev. kings f. are fallen

**FIXED.**

Ps. 57:7 heart is f. I w. sing, 108:1
112:7 heart f. trusting in Lord
Luke 16:26 betw. us is a gulf f.

**FLAG, S.**

Ex. 2:3 she laid the ark in the f.
5 when she saw ark am. the f.
Job 8:11 can f. grow with. water?
Is. 19:6 reeds and f. shall wither

**FLAGON, S.**

2 Sam. 6:19 f. of wine, 1 Chr. 16:3
Cant. 2:5 stay me wi. f. com. me
Is. 22:24 even to all vessels of f.
Hos. 3:1 love f. of wine

**FLAKES.**

Job 41:23 f. of his flesh are join.

**FLAME, S.**

Ex. 3:2 in f. of fire, Acts 7:30
Num. 21:28 f. fr. city, Jer. 48:45
Jud. 13:20 f. w. up, angel in f.
Job 15:30 f. sh. dry up branches
41:21 f. goeth out of his mouth
Ps. 29:7 voice of L. div. f. of fire
106:18 f. burnt up the wicked
Cant. 8:6 coals wh. hath a veh. f.
Is. 5:24 f. consumeth the chaff
10:17 Holy One shall be for a f.
13:8 their faces shall be as f.
29:6 visited with f. of devo. fire
43:2 nei. sh. f. kindle upon thee
66:15 rebuke with f. of fire
Ezek. 20:47 f. sh. not be quench.
Dan. 7:9 throne was like fiery f.
11 till body given to burning f.
Joel 1:19 f. hath burnt trees
2:3 behind them a f. burneth
Ob. 18 house of Jos. shall be a f.
Luke 16:24 tormented in this f.
Heb. 1:7 mak. ministers f. of fire
Rev. 1:14 as f. of fire, 2:18; 19:12

**FLAMING.**

Gen. 3:24 at gard. of Eden f. sw.
Ezek. 20:47 f. flame not be quen.
Nah. 2:3 chariots be wi. f. torch.

**FLANKS.**

Lev. 3:4 the fat which is by the f. 10, 15; 4:9; 7:4
Job 15:27 mak. collops of fat on f.

**FLASH.**

Ezek. 1:14 appear. of f. of lightn.

**FLAT**

Lev. 21:18 that hath f. nose
Num. 22:31 Balaam fell f. on face
Jos. 6:5 wall of city sh. fall f. 20

**FLATTER, ETH.**

Ps. 5:9 they f. with their tongue
36:2 he f. him. in his own eyes
78:36 did f. him with mouth
Prov. 2:16 stranger who f. 7:5
20:19 med. not with him that f.
28:23 more favor than he that f.
29:5 man that f. spreadeth a net

**FLATTERING.**

Job 32:21 nei. let me gi. f. tit. 22
Ps. 12:2 with f. lips
Prov. 7:21 with the f. of her lips
26:28 a f. mouth worketh ruin
Ezek. 12:24 shall be no more f.
1 Thes. 2:5 neither used f. words

**FLATTERY, IES.**

Job 17:5 speaketh f. to friends
Prov. 6:24 f. of strange woman
Dan. 11:21 he sh. obt. king. by f.
32 shall he corrupt by f.?
34 many shall cleave with f.

**FLAX.**

Ex. 9:31 f. was smitten f. bolled
Jos. 2:6 she hid with stalks of f.
Jud. 15:14 cords became as f.
Prov. 31:13 she seeks wool and f.
Is. 19:9 work in fine f. confound.
42:3 the smoking f. he shall not quench. Mat. 12:20
Hos. 2:5 lovers that give me f.

**FLAY, ED.**

Mic. 3:3 f. their skins
2 Chr. 35:11 blood, the Levites f.

**FLEA.**

1 Sam. 24:14 come after f.? 26:20

**FLED.**

Gen. 14:10 kings of So. and G. f.
16:6 H. f.; 31:22; J. f. Hos. 12:12
Ex. 2:15 M. f. fr. P. 4:3; Acts 7:29
14:5 told king of Egypt peop. f.
Ps. 31:11 did see me f. from me
114:3 the sea saw it and f. Jord.
Is. 22:3 thy rulers are f. tog.
Jer. 4:25 birds of the heavens f.
9:10 the fowl and beast are f.
Jon. 4:2 theref. I f. to Tarshish
Zec. 14:5 as ye f. before earthqu.
Mat. 8:33 they that kept them f.
26:56 forsook and f. Mark 14:50
Mark 16:8 f. from the sepulchre
Acts 16:27 supposing prisoners f.
Heb. 6:18 f. for ref. to lay hold
Rev. 12:6 wom. f.; 16:20 ev. isl. f.
20:11 face earth and heaven f.

**He FLED.**

Gen. 35:7 wh. he f. from brother
39:12 he left ga. and f. 13, 15, 18
Jos. 20:6 fr. whence he f. Num. 35:25
Jon. 1:10 he f. from pres. of L.
Mark 14:52 he left lin. clo. and f.

**Is FLED.**

Num. 35:32 no sat. for him th. f.
Is. 10:29 Gibeah of Saul is f.

**They FLED.**

Gen. 14:10 t. th. remained f. to
Jos. 10:11 as t. f. L. cast gr. ston.
1 Sam. 4:10 f. every man to tent, 2 K. 14:12
Ps. 104:7 at thy rebuke they f.
Is. 21:15 they f. from the swords
Lam. 4:15 when t. f. away
Dan. 10:7 they f. to save themse.
Hos. 7:13 woe for they have f.
Luke 8:34 saw what done t. f.
Acts 19:16 they f. out of house

**FLEDDEST.**

Gen. 35:1 when f. from face of E.
Ps. 114:5 wh. ailed O sea, th. f.?

**FLEECE.**

Deut. 18:4 first of f. give Levites
Jud. 6:37 f. of wool in flo. 38, 39
Job 31:20 warm. with f. of sheep

**FLEE.**

Gen. 16:8 f. fr. face of mistress
19:20 this city is near to f. unto
Ex. 21:13 place whither he sh. f.
Lev. 26:17 f. when none purs. 36
Num. 10:35 hate thee f. Ps. 68:1
35:6 cities, that man-slayer may f. 11, 15; Deut. 4:42; 19:3, 4, 5; Jos. 20:3, 4, 9
Deut. 28:7 and f. seven ways, 25
Jos. 8:5 as at first we will f. 6
20 had no power to f. this way
Jud. 20:32 let us f. and draw th.
2 Sam. 4:4 nurse haste to f. fell
24:13 wilt thou f. three months?
2 K. 9:3 open door and f. tar. not
Neh. 6:11 should such a man f.?
Job 20:24 he sh. f. from weapon
27:22 fain f. out of his hand
41:28 arrow cannot make him f.
Ps. 11:1 how say ye to my soul f.
68:12 kings of armies f. apace
139:7 whither sh. I f. fr. pres.?
143:9 O Lord, I f. to thee
Prov. 28:1 wick. f. no man purs.
Is. 10:3 will ye f. for help?
15:5 fugitives shall f. unto Zoar
30:16 for we will f. on horses
17 at rebuke of five shall ye f.
Jer. 4:29 city f. for noi. of horse.
48:6 f. save lives, be like heath
Amos 5:19 man did f. from lion
Jon. 1:3 Jon. rose up to f. to T.
Mat. 2:13 take young child and f.
3:7 to f. from wrath? Luke 3:7
10:23 when perse. in this city f.
24:16 let them in J. f. to mountains, Mark 13:14; Luke 21:21
John 10:5 stranger not follow but f.
1 Cor. 6:18 f. forni.; 10:14 f. idol.
1 Tim. 6:11 man of G. f. th. thin.
2 Tim. 2:22 f. also youthful lusts
Jam. 4:7 res. the devil, he will f.
Rev. 9:6 death shall f. from them

**FLEE away.**

Gen. 31:27 didst f. a. secretly?
Job 9:25 days f. a. th. see no good
20:8 he shall f. away as a dream
Ps. 64:8 all that see them sh. f. a.
Cant. 2:17 shadows f. away, 4:6
Is. 35:10 sighing sh. f. a. 51:11
Jer. 46:6 let not the swift f. away
Amos 7:12 seer, go f. a. into land
9:1 that fleeth shall not f. away
Nah. 2:8 Nineveh shall f. away
3:17 as grasshoppers they f. a.

**FLEEING, ETH.**

Lev. 26:36 sh. flee as f. from sw.
Deut. 4:42 f. to one of th. cities
19:11 f. into one of cities
Job 14:2 he f. also as a shadow
30:3 want and famine f. to wil.
Jer. 48:19 ask him that f.
Amos 9:1 that f. of them
John 10:12 a hireling f. 13

**FLESH.**

Gen. 2:21 G. closed up f. instead
24 and they shall be one f.
6:3 man, for he is f.
17:11 circum. f. of foresk. 14, 23
Ex. 4:7 hand turned as other f.
29:14 f. burn with fire, Lev. 9:11; 16:27; Num. 19:5
Lev. 6:27 wh. touch f. sh. be holy
8:31 boil f. at door of tabernacle
13:10 quick raw f. 14, 15, 16, 24
38 if in skin of f. 39
15:19 if issue in her f. be blood
21:5 nor sh. make cuttings in f.
Num. 11:33 f. was betw. teeth
Deut. 32:42 sword shall devour f.
Jud. 6:20 take f. and unl. cakes
21 fire out of rock consumed f.
1 Sam. 2:13 f. was in seething
15 give f. to roast for the prie.
1 K. 17:6 ravens brought bread f.
2 K. 4:34 f. of child waxed warm
2 Chr. 32:8 with him is arm of f.
Neh. 5:5 our f. is as f. of breth.
Job 10:4 hast thou eyes of f.?
11 clothed me with skin and f.
Ps. 56:4 not fear what f. can do
78:20 can he provide f. for peo.?
27 he rained f. upon them
39 remembered th. were but f.
79:2 f. of saints given to beasts
Prov. 4:22 sayings health to f.
23:20 not am. riot. eaters of f.
Is. 31:3 horses are f. not spirit
49:26 feed them with own f.
Jer. 11:15 f. is passed from thee
17:5 cursed be man that mak. f.

*Ezek.* 4:14 nor came abomina. *f.*
11:3 city is caldron, and we *f.*
19 I will give heart of *f.* 36:26
23:20 whose *f.* is as *f.* of asses
24:10 consume the *f.* spice it
*Dan.* 2:11 gods, who. dw. not *f.*
7:5 Arise, devour much *f.*
10:3 neither *f.* nor wine
*Hos.* 8:13 sacrif. *f.* for sacrifices
*Mic.* 3:2 pluck *f.* from off bones
*Zep.* 1:17 *f.* shall be poured
*Hag.* 2:12 bear holy *f.* in skirt
*Zec.* 14:12 their *f.* shall consume
*Mat.* 16:17 *f.* and blood not rev.
19:5 sh. be one *f.* 6; *Mark* 10:8;
1 *Cor.* 6:16; *Eph.* 5:31
24:22 no *f.* be saved, *Mark* 13:20
26:41 sp. will. *f.* we. *Mark* 14:38
*Luke* 24:39 hath not *f.* and bones
*John* 1:14 the WORD was made *f.*
6:63 the *f.* profiteth nothing
*Acts* 2:30 seed of David according to *f.* *Rom.* 1:3
*Rom.* 3:20 shall no *f.* be justified
4:1 Abraham as pertaining to *f.*
7:25 with *f.* I serve law of sin
8:3 law was weak through *f.*
G. sent Son in like. of sin. *f.*
9:3 and kinsmen according to *f.*
5 concerning *f.* Christ came
13:14 not provision for the *f.*
1 *Cor.* 1:29 that no *f.* should glo.
15:39 one *f.* of men, ano. of bea.
50 *f.* and blood cannot inherit
2 *Cor.* 4:11 life of J. be manifest *f.*
7:5 *f.* had no rest but troubled
10:2 as if we walked accord. to *f.*
*Gal.* 1:16 confer not with *f.*
2:16 shall no *f.* be justified
3:3 made perfect by the *f.*?
5:13 liberty for an occasion to *f.*
17 *f.* lusteth ag. Sp. Sp. ag. *f.*
24 that are C.'s crucified *f.*
*Eph.* 2:3 conv. in lusts of our *f.*
6:5 masters accord. to *f.* *Col.* 3:22
12 wrestle not ag. *f.* and blood
*Heb.* 2:14 child. are partak. of *f.*
12:9 fathers of *f.* who corrected
*Jude* 7 and going after strange *f.*
*Jude* 8 filthy dream. defile the *f.*
23 even garments spotted by *f.*
*Rev.* 19:18 *f.* of capt. *f.* of might.
21 all fowls were filled with *f.*

*See* EAT, EATETH.

**After the FLESH.**

*John* 8:15 ye judge *after the f.*
*Rom.* 8:1 walk not *after the f.* 4
5 are *a. t. f.* mind things of *f.*
12 not debtors to live *after t. f.*
13 if ye live *aft. t. f.* ye sh. die
1 *Cor.* 1:26 not ma. wise m. *a. t. f.*
10:18 behold Israel *after the f.*
2 *Cor.* 5:16 we know no man *af. the f.* have kn. Ch. *a. t. f.*
10:3 we do not war *after the f.*
11:18 that many glory *af. the f.*
*Gal.* 4:23 Ishm. born *af. t. f.* 29
2 *Pet.* 2:10 th. that walk *af. t. f.*

**All FLESH.**

*Gen.* 6:12 *a. f.* had corrupt. way
13 end of *all f.* is come bef. me
6:19 of *all f.* two of ev. sort, 7:15
7:21 *a. f.* died that moved, 8:17;
9:11, 15, 16, 17
*Lev.* 17:14 life of *a. f.* is the blood
*Num.* 8:7 let them shave *all f.*
16:22 G. of spirits of *all f.* 27:16
*Job* 34:15 *all f.* sh. perish togeth.
*Ps.* 65:2 to thee shall *all f.* come
136:25 who giveth food to *all f.*
145:21 let *all f.* bless holy name
*Is.* 40:5 *all f.* sh. see it together
6 *all f.* 's grass, 1 *Pet.* 1:24
49:26 *a. f.* know I am S. *Ez.* 21:5
66:16 will L. plead with *all f.*
23 *all f.* shall come to worship
24 they sh. be abhorr. to *all f.*

*Jer.* 25:31 will plead with *all f.*
32:27 I am the Lord God of *a. f.*
*Ezek.* 21:4 sword go against *a. f.*
*Dan.* 4:12 and *all f.* was fed of it
*Joel* 2:28 pour S. on *a. f.* *Acts* 2:17
*Zec.* 2:13 silent *all f.* before Lord
*Luke* 3:6 *a. f.* sh. see salv. of G.
*John* 17:2 given power over *a. f.*
1 *Cor.* 15:39 *a. f.* is not same fl.

**His FLESH.**

*Ex.* 29:31 seethe *h. f.* in holy pl.
*Lev.* 4:11 burn all *h. f.* 8:17
6:10 linen breeches on *h. f.* 16:4
13:3 in skin of *his f.* 4, 11, 13
14:9 wash *h. f.* in water, 15:16;
16:24, 28; *Num.* 19:7
1 *K.* 21:27 Ah. put sack. on *h. f.*
2 *K.* 5:14 *his f.* came again as
6:30 Jor. had sackcloth on *his f.*
*Job* 2:5 touch bone and *his f.*
31:31 O that we had of *his f.*
33:25 *f.* sh. be fresh. than child's
41:23 flakes of *his f.* are joined
*Prov.* 11:17 that is cruel troub. *f.*
*Ec.* 4:5 foldeth hands eateth *f.*
*Is.* 17:4 fatness of *f.* sh. wax lean
*John* 6:52 this man give *f.* to eat?
*Acts* 2:31 nei. *his f.* did see cor.
*Gal.* 6:8 that soweth to *his f.*
*Eph.* 2:15 abolished in *his f.*
5:29 no man hated *his* own *f.*
30 memb. of his body, of *h. f.*
*Col.* 1:22 reconc. in body of *his f.*
*Heb.* 5:7 who in the days of *h. f.*
10:20 veil, that is to say, *his f.*

**In the FLESH,** *or* **in FLESH.**

*Gen.* 17:24 A. circum. *in t. f.* 25
*Ezek.* 44:7 uncircum. *in the f.* 9
*Dan.* 1:15 fairer and fatter *in t. f.*
*Rom.* 2:28 circ. outward *in the f.*
7:5 *in the f.* the motions of sin
8:3 sin condemned sin *in the f.*
8 that are *in t. f.* cannot pl. G.
9 are not *in t. f.* but in the Sp.
1 *Cor.* 7:28 sh. have trouble *in f.*
2 *Cor.* 10:3 tho' we walk *in the f.*
12:7 was given a thorn *in the f.*
*Gal.* 2:20 life wh. I now live *in f.*
6:12 to make fair show *in the f.*
*Eph.* 2:11 Gentiles *in the f.*
*Phil.* 1:22 if I live *in the f.* this
24 abide *in t. f.* more needful
3:3 have no confidence *in t. f.* 4
*Col.* 2:1 have not seen face *in f.* 5
1 *Tim.* 3:16 G. was manif. *in t. f.*
1 *Pet.* 3:18 put to death *in the f.*
4:1 Christ hath suffered *in the f.*
2 live rest of his time *in the f.*
6 according to men *in the f.*
1 *John* 4:2 den. C. come *in t. f.* 3
2 *John* 7 that C. come *in the f.*

**My FLESH.**

*Job* 4:15 hair of *my f.* stood up
6:12 or is *my f.* brass?
7:5 *my f.* is clothed with worms
13:14 take *my f.* in my teeth?
19:26 yet in *my f.* shall I see G.

*Ps.* 16:9 *my f.* shall rest in hope, *Acts* 2:26
38:3 no soundness in *my f.* 7
63:1 *my f.* longeth for thee
73:26 *my f.* faileth
84:2 my heart and *my f.* crieth
109:24 *my f.* faileth of fatness
119:120 *my f.* trembleth for fear
*Lam.* 3:4 *my f.* hath he made old
*John* 6:51 bread I give, is *my f.*
54 eat. *my f.* hath eter. life, 56
55 *my f.* is meat indeed
*Rom.* 7:18 in *my f.* dwel. no good
11:14 prov. them wh. are *my f.*
*Gal.* 4:14 tem. wh. was in *my f.*
*Col.* 1:24 afflict. of Ch. in *my f.*

*See* BONE.

**Of the FLESH.**

*Ex.* 29:34 aught *of t. f* remain
*Prov.* 14:30 sound h. is life *of f.*
*Ec.* 12:12 much study is w. *of f.*
*John* 1:13 not of will *of the f.*
3:6 which is born *of t. f.* is flesh
*Rom.* 8:5 mind the things *of t. f.*
9:8 are the children *of t. f.*
1 *Cor.* 5:5 to S. for destruc. *of f.*
2 *Cor.* 7:1 fr. all filthiness *of t. f.*
*Gal.* 4:13 thro' infirmity *of t. f.*
5:16 shall not fulfil lusts *of t. f.*
19 works *of t. f.* are manifest
6:8 soweth to *f.* sh. *of t. f.* reap
*Eph.* 2:3 walked in lusts *of the f.*
*Col.* 2:11 the body of sins *of t. f.*
23 to the satisfying *of the f.*
*Heb.* 9:13 the purifying *of the f.*
1 *Pet.* 3:21 put. away filth *of t. f.*
2 *Pet.* 2:18 thro' the lusts *of t. f.*
1 *John* 2:16 lust *of t. f.*

**Thy FLESH.**

*Gen.* 40:19 birds shall eat *thy f.*
1 *Sam.* 17:44 give *t. f.* unto fowls
2 *Sam.* 5:1 bo. and *t. f.* 1 *Chr.* 11:1
2 *K.* 5:10 and *t. f.* shall come
*Prov.* 5:11 mourn wh. *t. f.* is con.
*Ec.* 5:6 to cause *t. f.* to sin
*Is.* 58:7 hide not from *thy* own *f.*
*Ezek.* 32:5 will lay *t. f.* on moun.

**Your FLESH.**

*Lev.* 19:28 not make cut. in *y. f.*
*Jud.* 8:7 then I will tear *y. f.*
*Ezek.* 36:26 heart out of *y. f.*
*Rom.* 6:19 infirmity of *your f.*
*Gal.* 6:13 they may glory in *y. f.*
*Col.* 2:13 dead in uncir. of *y. f.*
*Jam.* 5:3 rust shall eat *your f.*

FLESHED. *See* FAT, LEAN.

**FLESH-HOOK, S.**

*Ex.* 27:3 shalt make his *f.-h.*
38:3 the vessels and the *f.-h.*
*Num.* 4:14 put on pur. cloth *f.-h.*
1 *Sam.* 2:13 servant with a *f.-h.*
14 all that *f.-h.* brought up
1 *Chr.* 28:17 pure gold for *f.-h.*
2 *Chr.* 4:16 pots and the *f.-h.*

**FLESHLY.**

2 *Cor.* 1:12 not with *f.* wisdom
3:3 but in *f.* tables of the heart
*Col.* 2:18 puff. up by his *f.* mind
1 *Pet.* 2:11 abstain from *f.* lusts

**FLESH-POTS.**

*Ex.* 16:3 when we sat by *f.-p.*

**FLEW.**

1 *Sam.* 14:32 peo. *f.* upon the sp.
*Is.* 6:6 then *f.* one of seraphim

**FLIES.**

*Ex.* 8:21 send swarms of *f.* 31
*Ps.* 78:45 sent divers sorts of *f.*
105:31 divers sorts of *f.*
*Ec.* 10:1 dead *f.* cause ointment

**FLIETH.**

*Deut.* 14:19 creeping thing *f.*
28:49 as swift as the eagle *f.*
*Ps.* 91:5 arrow that *f.* by day
*Nah.* 3:16 cank. spoileth and *f.*

**FLIGHT.**

*Amos* 2:14 *f.* sh. perish from swift
*Mat.* 24:20 pray *f.* be not in winter, *Mark* 13:18
*Heb.* 11:34 turned to *f.* armies

*See* PUT.

**FLINT.**

*Deut.* 8:15 water out of rock of
*Ps.* 114:8 turning *f.* into fount.
*Is.* 5:28 hoofs sh. be counted *f.*
50:7 have I set my face like *f.*
*Ezek.* 3:9 harder than *f.*

**FLINTY.**

*Deut.* 32:13 oil out of *f.* rock

**FLOATS.**

1 *K.* 5:9 I will conv. them by sea in *f.* 2 *Chr.* 2:16

**FLOCK.**

*Gen.* 4:4 Ab. bro. firstlings of *f.*
37:2 J. was feeding *f.* with bre.
12 brethren went to feed *f.* 13
*Ex.* 2:16 troughs to wat. fath. *f.*
17 Moses helped, watered *f.* 19
3:1 Moses led *f.* back of desert
*Lev.* 5:18 a ram without blemish out of *f.* 6:6; *Ezr.* 10:19; *Ezek.* 43:23, 25
27:32 tithe of the herd or of *f.*
*Deut.* 15:19 first males of *f.*
1 *Sam.* 17:34 took lamb out of *f.*
*Job* 30:1 set with dogs of my *f.*
*Cant.* 1:7 makest *f.* to rest
8 by the footsteps of the *f.*
4:1 hair as a *f.* of goats, 6:5
2 teeth like a *f.* of sheep, 6:6
*Is.* 40:11 he sh. feed *f.* like shep.
*Jer.* 13:17 L. *f.* is carried captive
20 wh. is *f.* given thee beauti. ?
23:2 ye have scattered my *f.*
3 gather remnant of my *f.*
25:34 principal of the *f.* 35, 36
31:12 the young of the *f.*
49:20 least of *f.* sh. draw, 50:45
51:23 break shepherd and his *f.*
*Ezek.* 24:5 take the choice of *f.*
34:3 but ye feed not *f.*
6 *f.* scattered on face of earth
8 because my *f.* became a prey
10 I will require my *f.* I will
12 as a sheph. seek. out his *f.*
15 feed my *f.*; 17 O my *f.*
22 therefore will I save my *f.*
31 *f.* of my pasture are men
*Amos* 7:15 as I followed *f.*
*Jon.* 3:7 let not herd nor *f.* taste
*Mic.* 4:8 thou, O tower of the *f.*
7:14 feed thy people, the *f.* of
*Hab.* 3:17 the *f.* shall be cut off
*Zec.* 9:16 save them as *f.* of peo.
11:4 will feed *f.* of slaughter, 7
7 poor of the *f.* that waited, 11
17 idle sheph. that leaveth *f.*
*Mal.* 1:14 deceiver wh. hath in *f.*
*Mat.* 26:31 sheep of *f.* sh. be scat.
*Luke* 2:8 keeping watch over *f.*
12:32 fear not, little *f.*
*Acts* 20:28 take heed to all the *f.*
29 griev. wolves not sparing *f.*
1 *Cor.* 9:7 who feedeth a *f.*
1 *Pet.* 5:2 feed *f.* of God am. you
3 being ensamples to the *f.*

**Like a FLOCK.**

*Job* 21:11 send little ones *l. a. f.*
*Ps.* 77:20 leddest people *l. a. f.*
80:1 thou th. leddest Jos. *l. a. f.*
107:41 mak. him families *l. a f.*
*Ezek.* 36:37 increase them *l. a. f.*

**FLOCKS.**

*Gen.* 29:2 three *f.* of sheep, 3, 8
30:38 J. set rod he pill. bef. *f.* 39
37:14 whether it be well with *f.*
47:4 have no pasture for *f.*
*Lev.* 1:10 if his offering be of *f.*
*Num.* 31:9 took spoil of their *f.*
*Deut.* 7:13 will also bless the *f.*
28:4 blessed be *f.* of thy sheep
18 cursed sh. be *f.* of thy sheep
*Jud.* 5:16 to hear bleating of *f.*
1 *K.* 20:27 two little *f.* of kids
*Job* 24:2 violently take away *f.*
*Ps.* 65:13 past. are clothed wi. *f.*
78:48 he gave *f.* to hot thunder.
*Cant.* 1:7 turn aside by *f.*
*Is.* 32:14 palaces sh. be pasture *f.*
60:7 *f.* of Kedar sh. be gathered
61:5 stand and feed *f.*
65:10 Sh. shall be a fold for *f.*
*Jer.* 33:12 sheph. causing *f.* to lie
13 *f.* sh. pass ag. under the rod
50:8 be as he-goats before the *f.*
*Ezek.* 34:2 sh. not sheph. feed *f.* ?
*Joel* 1:18 *f.* of sheep desolate
*Mic.* 5:8 lion among *f.* of sheep
*Zep.* 2:6 sea-coast folds for *f.* 14

**FLOCKS, *with* herds.**

*Gen.* 13:5 Lot also had *f.* and *h.*
24:35 L. hath given A. *f.* and *h.*
26:14 Isa. had poss. of *f.* and *h.*
50:8 *f.* and *h.* left in land of G.
*Ex.* 10:9 will go with *f.* and *h.*
12:32 your *f.* and *h.* and be gone
34:3 let *f.* nor *h.* feed bef. mount
*Num.* 11:22 sh. *f.* and *h.* be slain
*Deut.* 12:6 firstlings of *h.* and *f.* 17; 14:23; *Neh.* 10:36
1 *Sam.* 30:20 David *f.* and *h.*
2 *Sam.* 12:2 had many *f.* and *h.*
*Prov.* 27:23 know *f.* look to *h.*
*Jer.* 3:24 shame devour. *f.* and *h.*
*Hos.* 5:6 shall go with *f.* and *h.*

**FLOOD.**

*Gen.* 6:17 bring a *f.* of water
7:6 *f.* of waters on earth, 7, 10
*Gen.* 7:17 *f.* was forty d. on earth
9:11 any more a *f.* to destroy
28 Noah lived after *f.* 350 years
10:1 were sons born after *f.* 32
*Jos.* 24:2 other side of *f.* 3, 14, 15
*Job* 14:11 *f.* decayeth and drieth
22:16 foun. overthrown with *f.*
28:4 *f.* breaketh from inhabitant
*Ps.* 29:10 Lord sitteth upon *f.*
66:6 went through *f.* on foot
69:15 let not water-*f.* overflow
90:5 carriest away as with *f.*
*Is.* 59:19 enemy come in like *f.*
*Jer.* 46:7 who that cometh as *f.* ?
8 Egypt riseth up like a *f.*
*Dan.* 9:26 end shall be with a *f.*
11:22 arms of *f.* sh. be overflo.
*Amos* 8:8 rise up wholly as *f.* 9:5
9:5 drowned as by *f.* of Egypt
*Nah.* 1:8 an overrunning *f.*
*Mat.* 24:38 in days before *f.*
39 till *f.* came, *Luke* 17:27
*Luke* 6:48 *f.* arose stream beat
2 *Pet.* 2:5 bring. in *f.* on world
*Rev.* 12:15 poured water as *f.* 16

**FLOODS.**

*Ex.* 15:8 *f.* stood upright
2 *Sam.* 22:5 *f.* of ungodly made me afraid, *Ps.* 18:4
*Job* 28:11 bindeth *f.* from overfl.
*Ps.* 24:2 hath estabI. it upon *f.*
32:6 surely in *f.* of great waters
69:2 waters where *f.* overfl. me
78:44 turned their *f.* into blood
93:3 *f.* have lifted up, O Lord
98:8 let the *f.* clap their hands
*Cant.* 8:7 neither can *f.* drown
*Is.* 44:3 pour *f.* on dry ground
*Jon.* 2:3 *f.* compassed me about
*Mat.* 7:25 *f.* came, winds bl. 27

**FLOOR, Verb.**

2 *Chr.* 34:11 timber to *f.* houses

**FLOOR, S, Substantive.**

*Gen.* 50:10 to thresh. *f.* of A. 11
*Num.* 5:17 pri. sh. take dust in *f.*
15:20 thresh. *f.* 18:27, 30
*Deut.* 15:14 furnish out of *f.*
*Jud.* 6:37 a fleece of wool in *f.*
*Ruth* 3:2 he win. in threshing *f.*
2 *Sam.* 6:6 Nach. th. *f.* 1 *Chr.* 13:9
24:18 rear alt. in thresh. *f.* of A.
21 D. said, to buy threshing *f.*
1 *K.* 6:30 overlaid *f.* of house
2 *K.* 6:27 out of barn *f.*
2 *Chr.* 3:1 threshing *f.* of Ornan
*Is.* 21:10 and the corn of my *f.*
*Jer.* 51:33 dau. of B. like thre. *f.*
*Dan.* 2:35 chaff of sum. thres. *f.*
*Hos.* 9:1 reward on every corn *f.*
2 *f.* and wine-pr. not feed them
13:3 as chaff driven out of *f.*
*Joel* 2:24 *f.* shall be full of wheat
*Mic.* 4:12 gather as sheaves to *f.*
*Mat.* 3:12 thor. purge *f.* *Lu.* 3:17

**FLOUR.**

*Ex.* 29:2 wheat. *f.* sh. thou make
*Lev.* 2:2 handful of the *f.* 6:15
*Num.* 28:5 part of ephah of *f.* for meat-off. 20, 28; 29:3, 9, 14
*Jud.* 6:19 ephah of *f.*; 1 *Sam.* 1:24
1 *Sam.* 28:24 took *f.* and kneaded it, 2 *Sam.* 13:8
2 *Sam.* 17:28 bro. *f.* parched corn
*See* DEAL, FINE.

**FLOURISH.**

*Ps.* 72:7 in his days sh. right. *f.*
16 they of city sh. *f.* like grass
92:7 when all workers of iniq. *f.*
12 righteous shall *f.*
13 shall *f.* in courts of our G.
132:18 upon himself sh. crown *f.*
*Prov.* 11:28 right. sh. *f.* as bran.
14:11 tabern. of upright shall *f.*
*Ec.* 12:5 almond-tree shall *f.*
*Is.* 17:11 thou sh. make seed *f.*
66:14 your bones shall *f.*
*Ezek.* 17:24 have made dry tree *f.*

**FLOURISHED.**

*Cant.* 6:11 went to see vine *f.*
*Phil.* 4:10 your care of me hath *f.*

**FLOURISHETH, ING.**

*Ps.* 90:6 in the morning it *f.*
92:14 they shall be fat and *f.*
103:15 as flower of field, he *f.*
*Dan.* 4:4 I was at rest, and *f.*

**FLOW.**

*Job* 20:28 his goods shall *f.* away
*Ps.* 147:18 wind blow, waters *f.*
*Cant.* 4:16 the spices may *f.* out
*Is.* 2:2 nations shall *f.* unto it
48:21 waters to *f.* out of rock
60:5 shalt see and *f.* together
64:1 mountains might *f.* down
*Jer.* 31:12 *f.* to goodness of L.
*Jer.* 51:44 nations sh. not *f.* tog.
*Joel* 3:18 hills shall *f.* with milk, rivers of Jud. *f.* with waters
*Mic.* 4:1 peo. sh. *f.* to mou. of L.
*John* 7:38 out of belly sh. *f.* l. w.

**FLOWED.**

*Jos.* 4:18 Jordan *f.* over banks
*Is.* 64:3 mount. *f.* down at pres.
*Lam.* 3:54 waters *f.* over my head

**FLOWETH.**

*Lev.* 20:24 *f.* with milk and hon. *Num.* 13:27; 14:8; 16:13, 14; *Deut.* 6:3; 11:9; 26:15; 27:3; 31:20; *Jos.* 5:6

**FLOWING.**

*Ex.* 3:8 *f.* with milk and honey, 17; 13:5; 33:3; *Jer.* 11:5; 32:22; *Ezek.* 20:6, 15
*Prov.* 18:4 well-sp. of wis. as *f.*
*Is.* 66:12 glo. of G. like *f.* stream
*Jer.* 18:14 cold *f.* waters be fors. ?
49:4 gloriest thou in *f.* valley ?

**FLOWER.**

*Ex.* 25:33 *f.* in one branch, 37:19
1 *Sam.* 2:33 incr. die in *f.* of age
*Job* 14:2 forth as *f.* is cut down
15:33 he shall cast *f.* as olive
*Ps.* 103:15 as *f.* of field
*Is.* 18:5 sour grape is rip. in *f.*
28:1 glorious beauty is fad. *f.* 4
40:6 goodliness is as *f.* of field
7 *f.* fadeth, 8; *Neh.* 1:4; *Jam.* 1:10, 11; 1 *Pet.* 1:24
1 *Cor.* 7:36 she pass *f.* of her age

**FLOWERS.**

*Ex.* 25:31 *f.* of the same, 37:17
37:20 almonds, knops, and his *f.*
*Lev.* 15:24 her *f.* be upon him, 33
1 *K.* 6:18 carved with knops and open *f.* 29, 32, 35; 7:26, 49
2 *Chr.* 4:5 cup with *f.* of lilies, 21
*Cant.* 2:12 *f.* appear on earth
5:13 bed of spices, as sweet *f.*

**FLUTE, S.**

*Dan.* 3:5 hear sound of *f.* 7, 10, 15

**FLUTTERETH.**

*Deut.* 32:11 as eagle *f.* ov. young

**FLUX.**

*Acts* 28:8 lay sick of a *f.*

**FLY.**

*Is.* 7:18 sh. hiss for the *f.* in E.

**FLY, Verb.**

*Gen.* 1:20 fowl th. may *f.* earth
1 *Sam.* 15:19 didst *f.* on the spoil
2 *Sam.* 22:11 did *f.* on wings of wind, *Ps.* 18:10
*Job* 5:7 as sparks *f.* upward
39:26 doth hawk *f.* by thy wis.
*Ps.* 55:6 then would I *f.* away
90:10 cut off, and we *f.* away
*Prov.* 23:5 riches *f.* away
*Is.* 6:2 with two he did *f.*
11:14 *f.* on shoulders of Philist.
60:8 who are these that *f.*
*Jer.* 48:40 he shall *f.* as an eagle
*Ezek.* 13:20 hunt souls to make *f.*
*Dan.* 9:21 G. caused to *f.* swiftly
*Hos.* 9:11 sh. *f.* away like a bird
*Hab.* 1:8 they shall *f.* as eagle
*Rev.* 14:6 saw another angel *f.*
19:17 that *f.* midst of heaven

**FLYING.**

*Lev.* 11:21 eat of every *f.* thing
*Ps.* 148:10 all cattle and *f.* fowl
*Prov.* 26:2 as swallow by *f.*
*Is.* 14:29 shall be fiery *f.* serpent
31:5 birds *f.* so will L. defend J.
*Zec.* 5:1 and behold a *f.* roll, 2
*Rev.* 4:7 beast like a *f.* eagle
8:13 angel *f.* thro' midst of hea.

**FOAL, S.**

*Gen.* 32:15 J. took 20 asses, 10 *f.*
49:11 binding his *f.* to the vine
*Zec.* 9:9 colt *f.* of ass, *Mat.* 21:5

**FOAM.**

*Hos.* 10:7 king of S. cut off as *f.*

**FOAMETH, ING.**

*Mark* 9:18 *f.* and gnasheth with his teeth, *Luke* 9:39
20 on ground and wallowed, *f.*
*Jude* 13 waves *f.* out own shame

**FODDER.**

*Job* 6:5 or loweth ox over his *f.*?

**FOES.**

1 *Chr.* 21:12 destroyed before *f.*
*Est.* 9:16 Jews slew of *f.* 75,000
*Ps.* 27:2 mine enemies and *f.*
30:1 not made my *f.* to rejoice
89:23 I will beat down his *f.*
*Mat.* 10:36 man's *f.* be of house
*Acts* 2:35 I make *f.* footstool

**FOLD**

*Heb.* 1:12 as a vesture sh. thou *f.*

**FOLD, Substantive.**

*Is.* 13:20 sheph. make their *f.*
65:10 Sharon shall be *f.*
*Ezek.* 34:14 on mount. shall *f.*
*Hab.* 3:17 flock sh. be cut from *f.*
*Mat.* 13:8 bro. forth fruit, some thirty *f.* 23; *Mark* 4:8, 20
19:29 forsaken ho. receive 100 *f.*
*John* 10:16 sheep wh. not of this *f.* one *f.* and one shepherd

**FOLDS.**

*Num.* 32:24 build *f.* for sheep, 36
*Ps.* 50:9 take no he-goats of *f.*
*Zep.* 2:6 sea-coast be *f.* for flocks

**FOLDEN.**

*Nah.* 1:10 wh. they be *f.* together

**FOLDETH, ING.**

*Prov.* 6:10 *f.* of hands, 24:33
*Ec.* 4:5 *f.* his hands together

**FOLK.**

*Prov.* 30:26 conies but feeble *f.*
*Jer.* 51:58 *f.* shall labor in fire
*Mark* 6:5 hands on few sick *f.*
*John* 5:3 multitude of impotent *f.*
*Acts* 5:16 about, bringing sick *f.*

**FOLLOW.**

*Gen.* 24:8 not willing to *f.*
44:4 Jos. said, Up, *f.* after men
*Ex.* 14:4 harden P. he shall *f.*
21:22 no mischief *f.* 23
23:2 not *f.* multitude to do evil
*Deut.* 16:20 what just sh. thou *f.*
*Jud.* 9:3 hearts inclined to *f.* A.
1 *K.* 19:20 I will *f.* thee
*Ps.* 45:14 companions *f.* her
119:150 that *f.* after mischief
*Is.* 5:11 may *f.* strong drink
51:1 that *f.* after righteousness
*Jer.* 17:16 being pastor to *f.* thee
*Ezek.* 13:3 prophets *f.* own spirit
*Hos.* 6:3 we *f.* on to know the L.
*Mat.* 8:19 Master, I will *f.* thee, *Luke* 9:57, 61
*Mark* 16:17 signs *f.* them th. be.
*John* 10:5 stran. will they not *f.*
13:37 L. why cannot I *f.* thee?
*Acts* 3:24 prophets from S. that *f.*
*Rom.* 14:19 *f.* thi. th. make peace
1 *Cor.* 14:1 *f.* after charity, desire
*Phil.* 3:12 I *f.* after, if that I may
1 *Thes.* 5:15 *f.* that which is good
2 *Thes.* 3:9 ensample to you to *f.*
1 *Tim.* 5:24 men they *f.* after
6:11 man of God *f.* 2 *Tim.* 2:22
*Heb.* 12:14 *f.* peace with all men
13:7 whose faith *f.* considering
1 *Pet.* 1:11 testified glory sh. *f.*
2:21 example, that ye should *f.*
2 *Pet.* 2:2 shall *f.* pernicious ways
3 *John* 11 *f.* not that which is evil
*Rev.* 14:4 they that *f.* the Lamb
13 and their works do *f.* them

**FOLLOW him.**

1 *K.* 18:21 if Lord be God, *f. him*
*Mark* 5:37 suff. no man to *f. him*
*Lu.* 22:10 *f. h.* into ho. *Mark* 14:13
*John* 10:4 and the sheep *f. him*

**FOLLOW me.**

*Gen.* 24:5 woman not *f. me*, 39
2 *K.* 6:19 *f. me*, I will bring you
*Ps.* 23:6 goodn. and mercy *f. me*
*Mat.* 4:19 Jes. saith, *f. me*, 8:22; 9:9; *Mark* 2:14; *Luke* 5:27
16:24 take up cross *f. me*, *Mark* 8:34; 10:21; *Luke* 9:23
19:21 sell that thou hast, *f. me*, *Luke* 18:22
*Luke* 9:59 *f. me*, *John* 1:43; 21:22
*John* 10:27 sheep hear voi. *f. me*
12:26 if man serve, let him *f. me*
13:36 thou canst not *f. me* now
*Acts* 12:8 garm. about thee, *f. me*

**FOLLOWED.**

*Gen.* 24:61 R. and damsels *f.* m.
*Num.* 32:12 *f.* Lord, *Deut.* 1:36
*Jos.* 6:8 ark of covenant *f.* them
14:8 I wholly *f.* L. my God, 9, 14
*Jud.* 2:12 forsook L. *f.* oth. gods
1 *Sam.* 14:22 they *f.* hard after P.
31:2 Philistines *f.* Saul, 2 *Sam.* 1:6; 1 *Chr.* 10:2
2 *Sam.* 2:10 house of Judah *f.* D.
3:31 king David himself *f.* bier
17:23 Ahith. saw counsel not *f.*
1 *K.* 16:21 half of people *f.* Tibni, half *f.* Omri, 22
2 *K.* 17:15 *f.* vanity, became vain
*Ps.* 68:25 play. on instruments *f.*
*Ezek.* 10:11 head looked they *f.*
*Amos* 7:15 L. took me as I *f.* flock
*Mat.* 27:55 many wom. wh. *f.* J.
*Mark* 10:28 we left all and *f.* thee, *Luke* 18:28
*Luke* 22:54 and Peter *f.* afar off
*Acts* 13:43 relig. proselytes *f.* P.
16:17 the same *f.* Paul and us
*Rom.* 9:30 Gent. who *f.* not righ.
31 who *f.* after law of righteo.
1 *Cor.* 10:4 drank of rock that *f.*
1 *Tim.* 5:10 *f.* every good work
2 *Pet.* 1:16 not *f.* cun. dev. fables
*Rev.* 6:8 Death, hell *f.* with him
14:8 *f.* another angel, saying
9 third angel *f.* them saying

**FOLLOWED him.**

*Num.* 16:25 M. elders of Is. *f. h.*
*Jud.* 9:4 light persons who *f. h.*
2 *Sam.* 11:8 *f. h.* a mess of meat
*Mat.* 4:20 they left their nets and *f. him*, *Mark* 1:18
22 left the ship and *f. him*
25 *f. him* great multitude, 8:1; 12:15; 19:2; 20:29; *Mark* 2:15; 5:24; *Luke* 23:27; *John* 6:2
8:23 disciples *f.* him, *Luke* 22:39
9:27 two blind men *f. him*
26:58 Peter *f. him*, *Mark* 14:54
*Luke* 5:11 forsook all, *f. him*, 28
*Acts* 12:9 P. went out and *f. him*
*Rev.* 19:14 armies *f. him*

**FOLLOWED me.**

*Num.* 14:24 servant C. hath *f. me*
1 *K.* 14:8 D. *f. me* with all heart
*Mat.* 19:28 *f. me* in regeneration

**FOLLOWEDST.**

*Ruth* 3:10 thou *f.* not young men

**FOLLOWERS.**

1 *Cor.* 4:16 *f.* of me, 11:1; *Phil.* 3:17
*Eph.* 5:1 be ye *f.* of God
1 *Thes.* 1:6 *f.* of us and of the L.
2:14 ye became *f.* of churches
*Heb.* 6:12 *f.* of them who thro' fa.
1 *Pet.* 3:13 be *f.* of that is good

**FOLLOWETH.**

*Ps.* 63:8 soul *f.* hard after thee
*Prov.* 12:11 *f.* vain persons, 28:19
15:9 loveth him *f.* righte. 21:21
*Hos.* 12:1 Eph. *f.* after east wind
*Mat.* 10:38 tak. not up cro. and *f.*
*Mark* 9:38 *f.* not us, *Luke* 9:49
*John* 8:12 *f.* me not walk in dar.

**FOLLOWING.**

*Deut.* 12:30 not snared by *f.* them
*Jos.* 22:16 from *f.* Lord, 18, 23, 29; 1 *Sam.* 12:20; 2 *K.* 17:21; 2 *Chr.* 25:27; 34:33
*Jud.* 2:19 in *f.* other gods
2 *Sam.* 2:19 Asahel turned not from *f.* Abner, 26, 30
7:8 I took thee from *f.* sheep, 1 *Chr.* 17:7; *Ps.* 78:71
1 *K.* 21:26 abominably in *f.* idols
*Ps.* 48:13 may tell to generat. *f.*
109:13 gen. *f.* let name be blot.
*Mark* 16:20 word with signs *f.*
*Luke* 13:33 to-morrow and day *f.*
*John* 1:43 day *f.*; 6:22 the day
*Acts* 23:11 night *f.* Lord stood by
2 *Pet.* 2:15 *f.* way of Balaam

**FOLLY.**

*Gen.* 34:7 Sh. wrought *f.* in Isr.
*Deut.* 22:21 *f.* by playing whore
*Jos.* 7:15 Ach. wrought *f.* in Is.
*Jud.* 19:23 do not this *f.*
20:6 have committed *f.* in Israel
1 *Sam.* 25:25 Nab. *f.* is with him
2 *Sam.* 13:12 do not thou this *f.*
*Job* 4:18 angels he charg. with *f.*
24:12 God layeth not *f.* to them
42:8 lest I deal with you after *f.*
*Ps.* 49:13 their way is their *f.*
85:8 not turn again to *f.*
*Prov.* 5:23 in his *f.* he sh. go ast.
13:16 a fool layeth open his *f.*
14:8 the *f.* of fools is deceitful
18 the simple inherit *f.*
24 the foolishness of fools is *f.*
29 hasty of spirit exalteth *f.*
15:21 *f.* joy to him dest. of wis.
16:22 instruction of fools is *f.*
17:12 a fool in his *f.*
18:13 it is *f.* and shame
26:4 answer not fool accord. to *f.*
5 answer fool according to *f.*
11 so a fool returneth to his *f.*

*Ec.* 1:17 to know wisdom and *f.*
2:3 I sought to lay hold on *f.*
12 to behold *f.*; 13 excelleth *f.*
7:25 to know wickedness of *f.*
10:1 so a little *f.* him in reput.
6 *f.* is set in dignity
*Is.* 9:17 every mouth speaketh *f.*
*Jer.* 23:13 seen *f.* in the prophets
2 *Cor.* 11:1 bear with me in my *f.*
2 *Tim.* 3:9 *f.* be made manifest

### FOOD.

*Gen.* 2:9 every tree good for *f.*
3:6 saw the tree was good for *f.*
*Gen.* 6:21 take unto thee of all *f.*
41:35 gather *f.* of th. good years
42:7 came to buy *f.* 43:2; 44:25
33 take *f.* for famine
44:1 commanded fill sacks wi. *f.*
47:24 for *f.* for your little ones
*Ex.* 21:10 her *f.* not diminished
*Lev.* 3:11 the *f.* of the offering, 16
19:23 have planted trees for *f.*
22:7 holy things, it is his *f.*
*Deut.* 10:18 in giving stranger *f.*
1 *Sam.* 14:24 eateth *f.* till even
2 *Sam.* 9:10 master's son have *f.*
1 *K.* 5:9 in giving *f.* for my hous.
*Job* 23:12 words more than *f.*
24:5 wilderness yieldeth *f.*
38:41 provideth for raven *f.*?
40:20 mount. bring him forth *f.*
*Ps.* 78:25 man did eat angels' *f.*
104:14 forth *f.* out of the earth
136:25 who giveth *f.* to all flesh
146:7 who giveth *f.* to hungry
147:9 giveth to the beast his *f.*
*Prov.* 6:8 ant gathereth *f.* in har.
13:23 much *f.* in tillage of poor
27:27 goats' milk eno. for thy *f.*
28:3 rain which leaveth no *f.*
30:8 feed me with *f.* convenient
31:14 bringeth her *f.* from afar
*Ezek.* 16:27 I dimin. ordinary *f.*
48:18 increase thereof be for *f.*
*Acts* 14:17 fill. our hearts with *f.*
2 *Cor.* 9:10 minister bread for *f.*
1 *Tim.* 6:8 hav. *f.* and raiment
*Jam.* 2:15 be destitute of daily *f.*

### FOOL.

1 *Sam.* 26:21 have played the *f.*
*Ps.* 14:1 *f.* said in heart, 53:1
49:10 *f.* and brutish person
92:6 neither doth *f.* understand
*Prov.* 10:8 prating *f.* sh. fall, 10
23 sport to a *f.* to do mischief
11:29 *f.* be servant to the wise
12:15 way of *f.* right in own eyes
16 *f.* wrath is presently known
13:16 a *f.* layeth open his folly
14:16 *f.* rageth and is confident
15:5 *f.* despiseth father's instr.
17:7 excel. speech becom. not *f.*
10 than 100 stripes into a *f.*
12 a bear meet rather than *f.*
16 a price in hand of *f.*
21 he that begetteth a *f.*
28 *f.* when he hold. his peace
18:2 a *f.* no delight in underst.
6 *f.* lips enter into contention
7 *f.* mouth is his destruction
20:3 every *f.* will be meddling
26:4 answer not *f.*; 5 answer *f.*
8 so is he giveth honor to a *f.*
26:10 God rewardeth *f.*
11 so a *f.* returneth to his folly
27:3 *f.* wrath heavier than both
22 tho' bray a *f.* in a mortar
29:11 a *f.* uttereth all his mind
*Ec.* 2:14 *f.* walketh in darkness
15 happeneth to *f.* even to me
16 no rem. of wise more than *f.*
19 whether he be wise or a *f.*?
4:5 *f.* foldeth his hands together
5:3 *f.* voice known by multitude
6:8 what ha. wise more than *f.*?
10:2 a *f.* heart is at his left hand
14 a *f.* also is full of words
*Jer.* 17:11 and at his end be a *f.*
*Mat.* 5:22 wh. shall say, Thou *f.*
*Luke* 12:20 *f.* this night thy soul
1 *Cor.* 3:18 *f.* that he may be wise
15:36 thou *f.* that thou sowest
2 *Cor.* 11:16 no man think me a *f.*
12:6 to glory, I shall not be a *f.*
11 am become a *f.* in glorying

### As a FOOL.

2 *Sam.* 3:33 died Abner *as a f.*?
*Prov.* 7:22 *as a f.* to correction
*Ec.* 2:16 dieth wise man? *as f.*
2 *Cor.* 11:16 *as a f.* receive me
23 ministers? I speak *as a f.*

### For a FOOL.

*Prov.* 19:10 not seemly *for a f.*
24:7 wisdom is too high *for a f.*
26:1 honor not seemly *for a f.*
3 and a rod *for* the *f.* back
30:22 *for a f.* when he is filled

### Is a FOOL.

*Prov.* 10:18 utter. slander *is a f.*
19:1 perverse in lips, and *is a f.*
28:26 trust. in own heart *is a f.*
*Ec.* 10:3 that *is a f.* walketh, he
saith to ev. one that he *is a f.*
*Hos.* 9:7 the prophet *is a f.*

### Of a FOOL.

*Prov.* 12:15 way *of a f.* is right
17:21 father *of a f.* hath no joy
24 eyes *of a f.* are in ends of
23:9 speak not in the ears *of a f.*
*Prov.* 26:6 a me. by hand *of a f.*
12 more hope *of a f.* 29:20
*Ec.* 7:6 so is laughter *of* the *f.*
10:12 lips *of a f.* will swallow

### FOOLS.

2 *Sam.* 13:13 be as one of the *f.*
*Job* 12:17 maketh the judges *f.*
30:8 they were children of *f.*
*Ps.* 75:4 to *f.* deal not foolishly
94:8 *f.* when will ye be wise?
107:17 *f.* bec. of transgression
*Prov.* 1:7 *f.* despise wisdom
22 how long, ye *f.* will ye hate
32 prosperity of *f.* destr. them
3:35 shame sh. be promot. of *f.*
8:5 *f.* be ye of underst. heart
10:21 *f.* die for want of wisdom
12:23 heart of *f.* proclaim. fool.
13:19 to *f.* to depart from evil
20 companion of *f.* be destr.
14:8 folly of *f.* is deceit
9 *f.* make a mock at sin
24 the foolishness of *f.* is folly
33 midst of *f.* is made known
15:2 mouth of *f.* poureth foolis.
14 mouth of *f.* feedeth on fool.
16:22 instruction of *f.* is folly
19:29 stripes prep. for back of *f.*
26:7 parable in mouth of *f.* 9
*Ec.* 5:1 than give sacrifice of *f.*
4 he hath no pleasure in *f.*
7:4 heart of *f.* in house of mirth
5 than to hear the song of *f.*
9 anger resteth in bosom of *f.*
9:17 cry of him ruleth among *f.*
*Is.* 19:11 princes of Zoan *f.* 13
35:8 *f.* shall not err therein
*Mat.* 23:17 *f.* and bl. 19; *Luke* 11:40
*Luke* 24:25 O *f.* slow to believe
*Rom.* 1:22 to be wise, became *f.*
1 *Cor.* 4:10 are *f.* for Christ's sake
2 *Cor.* 11:19 for ye suffer *f.* gladly
*Eph.* 5:15 see ye walk not as *f.*

### FOOLISH.

*Deut.* 32:6 requite L. *f.* people?
21 provoke them to anger with
a *f.* nation, *Rom.* 10:19
*Job* 2:10 as one of *f.* women
5:2 for wrath killeth the *f.* man
3 I have seen the *f.* taking root
*Ps.* 5:5 *f.* not stand in thy sight
39:8 make me not reproach of *f.*
73:3 for I was envious at the *f.*
22 so *f.* was I and ignorant
74:18 *f.* people have blasphemed
22 *f.* reproacheth thee daily
*Prov.* 9:6 forsake the *f.* and live
13 a *f.* woman is clamorous
10:1 *f.* son heaviness of mother
14 mouth of *f.* near destruct.
14:1 the *f.* plucketh house down
3 mouth of *f.* is a rod of pride
7 go from presence of a *f.* man
15:7 heart of the *f.* doeth not so
20 *f.* man despiseth his mother
17:25 *f.* son is grief to his father
19:13 *f.* son calamity of father
21:20 a *f.* man spendeth a treas.
29:9 if wise contendeth with *f.*
*Ec.* 4:13 wise child than *f.* king
7:17 be not wicked, neither *f.*
10:15 labor of the *f.* wearieth
*Is.* 44:25 maketh knowledge *f.*
*Jer.* 4:22 for my people is *f.*
5:4 these are poor, they are *f.*
21 hear now this, O *f.* people
10:8 they are brutish and *f.*
*Lam.* 2:14 proph. seen *f.* things
*Ezek.* 13:3 woe to the *f.* prophets
*Zec.* 11:15 instru. of *f.* shepherds
*Mat.* 7:26 be likened to a *f.* man
25:2 five were wise and five *f.*
*Rom.* 1:21 *f.* heart was darkened
2:20 an instructor of the *f.*
1 *Cor.* 1:20 *f.* wis. of this world
*Gal.* 3:1 O *f.* Galatians
3 are ye so *f.*? having begun
*Eph.* 5:4 filthiness, nor *f.* talking
1 *Tim.* 6:9 rich, fall into *f.* lusts
2 *Tim.* 2:23 *f.* questions, *Tit.* 3:9
*Tit.* 3:3 we were sometimes *f.*
1 *Pet.* 2:15 silence ignorance of *f.*

### FOOLISHLY.

*Gen.* 31:28 thou hast now done
*f.* 1 *Sam.* 13:13; 2 *Chr.* 16:9
*Num.* 12:11 sin wherein done *f.*
2 *Sam.* 24:10 I have done very *f.*
*Job* 1:22 nor charged God *f.*
*Ps.* 75:4 to the fools, deal not *f.*
*Prov.* 14:17 soon angry dealeth *f.*
30:32 if *f.* in lifting up thyself
2 *Cor.* 11:17 I speak as it were *f.*
21 I speak *f.* I am bold also

### FOOLISHNESS.

2 *Sam.* 15:31 counsel of A. into *f.*
*Ps.* 38:5 stink, because of my *f.*
*Ps.* 69:5 O G. thou knowest my *f.*
*Prov.* 12:23 heart of fools pro. *f.*
14:24 but the *f.* of fools is folly
15:2 mouth of fools pour. out *f.*
14 mouth of fools feedeth on *f.*
19:3 *f.* of man pervert. his way
22:15 *f.* bound in heart of child
24:9 the thought of *f.* is sin
27:22 yet will not his *f.* depart
*Ec.* 7:25 know wickedness of *f.*
10:13 beginning of words is *f.*
*Mark* 7:22 *f.* come from within
1 *Cor.* 1:18 to them that perish *f.*
21 by *f.* of preaching to save
23 preach Christ to Greeks *f.*
25 *f.* of God is wiser than men
2:14 things of Spirit *f.* unto him
3:19 wisdom of this world is *f.*

### FOOT.

*Gen.* 41:44 without thee no man
shall lift up his *f.*
*Ex.* 21:24 *f.* for *f.* *Deut.* 19:21
*Num.* 22:25 crushed Balaam's *f.*
*Deut.* 8:4 nor did thy *f.* swell
11:10 wateredst it with thy *f.*
29:5 shoe is not waxen old on *f.*
32:35 *f.* shall slide in due time
33:24 let Asher dip his *f.* in oil
*Jos.* 1:3 every place *f.* sh. tread
5:15 loose shoe from off thy *f.*
*Jud.* 5:15 Barak was sent on *f.*
2 *Sam.* 2:18 Asa. was as light of *f.*
21:20 on *f.* six toes, 1 *Chr.* 20:6

2 *K.* 9:33 trod Jezebel under *f.*
2 *Chr.* 33:8 nor remove *f.* of Isr.
*Job* 23:11 *f.* hath held his steps
28:4 even waters forgotten of *f.*
31:5 if my *f.* hasted to deceit
39:15 forgetteth *f.* may crush
*Ps.* 9:15 they hid *f.* taken
26:12 *f.* standeth in even place
36:11 let not the *f.* of pride
38:16 *f.* slippeth, they magnify
66:6 went thro' the flood on *f.*
68:23 *f.* may be dipped in blood
91:12 lest thou dash *f.* against a stone, *Mat.* 4:6; *Luke* 4:11
94:18 I said, My *f.* slippeth
121:3 not suffer *f.* to be moved
*Prov.* 1:15 thy *f.* from their path
3:23 thy *f.* shall not stumble
26 keep thy *f.* fr. being taken
4:27 remove thy *f.* from evil
25:17 *f.* from neighbor's house
19 like a *f.* out of joint
*Ec.* 5:1 keep thy *f.* when goest
*Is.* 14:25 on mount. tread under *f.*
18:7 a nation trodden under *f.*
20:2 put off shoe from off thy *f.*
26:6 the *f.* shall tread it down
41:2 called righteous to his *f.*
58:13 turn *f.* from my sabbath
*Jer.* 2:25 thy *f.* fr. being unshod
12:10 my portion under *f.*
*Lam.* 1:15 Lord trodden under *f.*
*Ezek.* 6:11 stamp with thy *f.*
29:11 no *f.* of man, of beast
32:13 *f.* of man trouble them
*Dan.* 8:13 to be trodden under *f.*
*Amos* 2:15 swift of *f.* not deliver
*Mat.* 5:13 salt trodden under *f.*
14:13 people followed him on *f.*
18:8 if thy *f.* offend, *Mark* 9:45
22:13 bind him hand and *f.* and
*Mark* 6:33 many ran a *f.* thither
*John* 11:44 bound hand and *f.*
*Acts* 7:5 so much as to set his *f.*
20:13 minding himself to go a *f.*
1 *Cor.* 12:15 if the *f.* say, Bec. I
*Heb.* 10:29 trodden under *f.* the S.
*Rev.* 1:13 clothed with garm. to *f.*
11:2 city shall tread under *f.*

**Sole of FOOT.**

*Gen.* 8:9 no rest for *sole of f.*
*Deut.* 28:56 not set *s. of f.* on gr.
65 nor shall *sole of* thy *f.* rest
*Jos.* 1:3 ev. place *s. of f.* tread on
2 *Sam.* 14:25 like Abs. fr. *s. of f.*
*Is.* 1:6 *s. of f.* to head
*Ezek.* 1:7 *sole of f.* like calf's

**FOOT-BREADTH.**

*Deut.* 2:5 not so much as *f.-br.*

**Right FOOT, left FOOT.**

*Rev.* 10:2 he set his *r. f.* upon the sea, and his *l. f.* on the earth

*See* TOE.

**FOOTED.**

*Lev.* 11:3 cloven *f.* that ye sh. eat
7 though cloven *f.* unclean
21:19 broken *f.* not approach
*Acts* 10:12 of four *f.* beasts, 11:6
*Rom.* 1:23 like four *f.* beasts

**FOOTMEN.**

1 *Sam.* 22:17 to the *f.* Slay priests
*Jer.* 12:5 if thou hast run with *f.*

**FOOTSTEPS.**

*Ps.* 17:5 that my *f.* slip not
77:19 thy *f.* are not known
89:51 reproa. *f.* of anointed
*Cant.* 1:8 go by *f.* of the flock

**FOOTSTOOL.**

1 *Chr.* 28:2 house for *f.* of God
*Ps.* 99:5 worship at his *f.* 132:7
110:1 enem. thy *f.* *Mat.* 22:44; *Mark* 12:36; *Luke* 20:43; *Acts* 2:35; *Heb.* 1:13
*Is.* 66:1 earth is my *f.* *Acts* 7:49
*Lam.* 2:1 remembered not his *f.*
*Mat.* 5:35 by the earth it is his *f.*
*Heb.* 10:13 till enemies be *f.*
*Jam.* 2:3 sit here under my *f.*

**FORBADE.**

*Deut.* 2:37 nor to whatso. L. *f.*
*Mat.* 3:14 John *f.* him, saying, I
*Mark* 9:38 we *f.* him, *Luke* 9:49
2 *Pet.* 2:16 ass *f.* madn. of proph.

**FORBARE.**

1 *Sam.* 23:13 Saul *f.* to go forth
*Jer.* 41:8 Ishmael *f.* and slew not

**FORBEARANCE.**

*Rom.* 2:4 or despis. riches of *f.* ?
3:25 remission of sins thro' *f.*

**FORBEAR, ING.**

*Deut.* 23:22 *f.* to vow it
1 *K.* 22:6 go or *f.* ? 2 *Chr.* 18:5
2 *Chr.* 25:16 *f.* why be smitten ?
35:21 *f.* thee from meddling
*Neh.* 9:30 many years didst *f.*
*Job* 16:6 I *f.* what am I eased ?
*Prov.* 24:11 if *f.* to deliver them
25:15 by long *f.* prince persuad.
*Jer.* 20:9 I was weary with *f.*
40:4 if it seem ill unto thee *f.*
*Ezek.* 2:5 will hear, or *f.* 7; 3:11
3:27 that forbeareth, let him *f.*
24:17 *f.* to cry, make no mourn.
*Zec.* 11:12 give price, if not *f.*
1 *Cor.* 9:6 power to *f.* working ?
2 *Cor.* 12:6 I *f.* lest any think
*Eph.* 4:2 *f.* in love, *Col.* 3:13
6:9 masters *f.* threatening
1 *Thes.* 3:1 could no longer *f.* 5

**FORBID.**

*Num.* 11:28 my lord M. *f.* them
*Mark* 9:39 *f.* him not, *Luke* 9:50
10:14 suffer little child. and *f.* them not, *Luke* 18:16
*Luke* 6:29 *f.* not to take coat also
*Acts* 10:47 can any man *f.* water
24:23 *f.* none of his acquaint.
1 *Cor.* 14:39 *f.* not sp. with tong.

**God FORBID.**

*Gen.* 44:7 *God f.* 17; *Jos.* 22:29; 24:16; 1 *Sam.* 12:23; 14:45; 20:2; *Job* 27:5; *Luke* 20:16; *Rom.* 3:4, 6, 31; 6:2, 15; 7:7, 13; 9:14; 11:1, 11; 1 *Cor.* 6:15; *Gal.* 2:17; 3:21; 6:14

**FORBIDDEN, ETH, ING.**

*Lev.* 5:17 commit any of things *f.*
*Deut.* 4:23 the likeness of what *f.*
*Luke* 23:2 *f.* to give tribute to C.
*Acts* 16:6 were *f.* to preach in A.
28:31 preaching no man *f.* him
1 *Thes.* 2:16 *f.* us to speak to G.
1 *Tim.* 4:3 *f.* to marry and com.
3 *John* 10 *f.* them that would re.

**FORBORNE.**

*Jer.* 51:30 mighty men *f.* to fight

**FORCE, Substantive.**

*Deut.* 34:7 his natural *f.* abated
1 *Sam.* 2:16 I will take it by *f.*
*Ezr.* 4:23 made them cease by *f.*
*Job* 30:18 great *f.* of my disease
40:16 his *f.* in navel of his belly
*Jer.* 18:21 out blood by *f.* of swo.
23:10 is evil, their *f.* is not right
48:45 shadow because of *f.*
*Ezek.* 34:4 with *f.* ye ruled them
35:5 shed blood by *f.* of the sw.
*Amos* 2:14 stro. not strengthen *f.*
*Mat.* 11:12 violent take it by *f.*
*John* 6:15 would take him by *f.*
*Acts* 23:10 to take Paul by *f.*
*Heb.* 9:17 testament is of *f.* after

**FORCE, ED.**

*Deut.* 22:25 if the man *f.* her
*Jud.* 20:5 concubine have they *f.*
1 *Sam.* 13:12 I *f.* myself
2 *Sam.* 13:12 brother do not *f.*
14 Amnon *f.* Tamar, 22, 32
*Est.* 7:8 will he *f.* the queen ?
*Prov.* 7:21 with flat. she *f.* him

**FORCES.**

*Job* 36:19 will not esteem the *f.*
*Is.* 60:5 *f.* of Gentiles shall come
11 may bring *f.* of the Gentiles.
*Jer.* 40:7 captains of *f.* 13; 41:11, 13, 16; 42:1, 8; 43:4, 5
*Dan.* 11:10 assemble multi. of *f.*
38 shall he honor the God of *f.*
*Ob.* 11 strangers carried away *f.*

**FORCIBLE.**

*Job* 6:25 how *f.* are right words

**FORCING.**

*Deut.* 20:19 *f.* an axe aga. them
*Prov.* 30:33 *f.* of wrath bringeth

**FORDS.**

*Is.* 16:2 daughters at *f.* of Arnon

**FORECAST.**

*Dan.* 11:24 sh. *f.* his devices, 25

**FOREFATHERS.**

*Jer.* 11:10 turn. to iniquities of *f.*
2 *Tim.* 1:3 whom I served from *f.*

**FOREFRONT.**

2 *Sam.* 11:15 Uriah in *f.* of battle
2 *Chr.* 20:27 Jehoshaphat in *f.*

**FOREHEAD.**

1 *Sam.* 17:49 stone sunk in his *f.*
2 *Chr.* 26:20 Uzziah leprous in *f.*
*Jer.* 3:3 thou hast a whore's *f.*
*Ezek.* 3:9 as adamant I made *f.*
16:12 and I put jewel on thy *f.*
*Rev.* 14:9 mark of beast in his *f.*
17:5 on her *f.* a name written

**FOREHEADS.**

*Ezek.* 3:8 strong against their *f.*
9:4 on the *f.* of them that sigh
*Rev.* 7:3 sealed serv. of God in *f.*
9:4 not seal of God in their *f.*
13:16 all to receive a mark in *f.*
14:1 Father's name in their *f.*
20:4 nor received his mark on *f.*
22:4 his name sh. be in their *f.*

**FOREIGNER, S.**

*Ex.* 12:45 a *f.* not eat thereof
*Deut.* 15:3 of a *f.* exact it again
*Ob.* 11 in the day *f.* entered gat.
*Eph.* 2:19 ye are no more *f.*

**FOREKNEW, KNOW.**

*Rom.* 8:29 whom he did *f.*
11:2 not cast away people he *f*

**FOREKNOWLEDGE.**

*Acts* 2:23 delivered by *f.* of God
1 *Pet.* 1:2 according to *f.* of God

**FOREORDAINED.**

1 *Pet.* 1:20 who verily was *f.*

**FOREPART.**

*Acts* 27:41 *f.* of ship stuck fast

**FORERUNNER.**

*Heb.* 6:20 whither *f.* is for us

**FORESAW.**

*Acts* 2:25 *f.* Lord always before

**FORESEETH, ING.**

*Prov.* 22:3 man *f.* the evil, 27:12
*Gal.* 3:8 the scripture *f.* that God

**FORESKIN, S.**

*Gen.* 17:11 circumc. flesh of *f.* 23
*Ex.* 4:25 Zip. cut off *f.* of son
*Lev.* 12:3 flesh of his *f.* sh. be cir.
*Deut.* 10:16 circumcise *f.* of heart
*Jos.* 5:3 circumcised at hill of *f.*
1 *Sam.* 18:25 100 *f.* of Philistines
27 D. brought *f.* and gave th.
2 *Sam.* 3:14 I espoused for 100 *f.*
*Jer.* 4:4 take away the *f.* of heart
*Hab.* 2:16 let thy *f.* be uncovered

**FOREST, S.**

1 *Sam.* 22:5 D. came to *f.* of H.
1 *K.* 7:2 Solomon built hou. of *f.*
2 *K.* 19:23 will enter into *f.* of his Carmel, *Is.* 37:24
2 *Chr.* 27:4 J. built castles in *f.*

*Ps.* 29:9 voice of L. discover. *f.*
50:10 ev. beast of the *f.* is mine
104:20 beasts of *f.* do creep forth
*Is.* 9:18 kindle in thickets of *f.*
10:18 consume glory of his *f.*
19 rest of trees of his *f.* be few
34 cut down the thickets of *f.*
21:13 in *f.* of Ara. shall ye lodge
22:8 didst look to armor of *f.*
29:17 esteemed as a *f.* 32:15
32:19 hail coming down on *f.*
44:14 cypress from am. trees *f.*
23 break forth into sing. O *f.*
56:9 yea, all ye beasts in the *f.*
*Jer.* 5:6 lion out of *f.* shall slay
10:3 one cutteth a tree out of *f.*
12:8 heritage, as a lion in *f.*
21:14 will kindle a fire in the *f.*
26:18 high places of *f.* *Mic.* 3:12
46:23 they shall cut down her *f.*
*Ezek.* 15:6 vine-tree am. trees *f.*
20:46 prophesy aga. *f.* of south
39:10 neither cut any out of *f.*
*Hos.* 2:12 I will make them a *f.*
*Amos* 3:4 will lion roar in the *f.*
*Mic.* 5:8 as a lion am. beasts of *f.*
*Zec.* 11:2 *f.* of vintage is come

**FORETELL.**

2 *Cor.* 13:2 I *f.* you as if present

**FORETOLD.**

*Mark* 13:23 I have *f.* you all
*Acts* 3:24 proph. *f.* of these days

**FOREWARN, ED.**

*Luke* 12:5 *f.* whom ye shall fear
1 *Thes.* 4:6 we also have *f.* you

**FORFEITED.**

*Ezr.* 10:8 substance should be *f.*

**FORGAT.**

*Gen.* 40:23 Joseph, but *f.* him
*Jud.* 3:7 children of Israel *f.* L.
1 *Sam.* 12:9 when they *f.* the L.
*Ps.* 78:11 and they *f.* his works
106:13 soon *f.*; 21 *f.* God th. S.
*Lam.* 3:17 peace, I *f.* prosperity
*Hos.* 2:13 after lovers and *f.* me

**FORGAVE, EST.**

*Ps.* 32:5 *f.* iniquity of my sin
78:38 he *f.* their iniquity, and
99:8 wast a God that *f.* them
*Mat.* 18:27 and *f.* him the debt
32 O wicked servant, I *f.* all
*Luke* 7:42 he frankly *f.* them
42 that he to whom he *f.* most
2 *Cor.* 2:10 if I *f.* any thing, for
your sakes *f.* I it
*Col.* 3:13 as Christ *f.* you

**FORGED.**

*Ps.* 119:69 proud have *f.* a lie

**FORGERS.**

*Job* 13:4 ye are *f.* of lies

**FORGET.**

*Gen.* 27:45 till thy brother *f.*
41:51 God made me *f.* my toil
*Deut.* 4:9 *f.* things eyes ha. seen
23 lest ye *f.* covenant of Lord
31 Lord will not *f.* the coven.
6:12 beware lest *f.* L. 8:11, 14, 19
9:7 *f.* not how provokedst Lord
25:19 blot out Amalek, not *f.*
1 *Sam.* 1:11 if not *f.* handmaid
2 *K.* 17:38 covenant shall not *f.*
*Job* 8:13 so paths of all that *f.* G.
9:27 I will *f.* my complaint
11:16 thou shalt *f.* thy misery
24:20 the womb shall *f.* him
*Ps.* 9:17 all nations that *f.* God
10:12 O Lord *f.* not the humble
13:1 how long wilt thou *f.* me?
45:10 *f.* thine own people, and
50:22 consider this ye that *f.* G.
59:11 lest my people *f.*
74:19 *f.* not congrega. of poor
23 *f.* not voice of thine enem.
78:7 might not *f.* works of God
102:4 that I *f.* to eat my bread
103:2 *f.* not all his benefits
119:16 I will not *f.* thy word
83 do I not *f.* statutes, 109, 141
93 I will never *f.* thy precepts
153 for I do not *f.* thy law
176 for I not *f.* thy command.
137:5 if I *f.* thee, O Jerusalem,
let right hand *f.* cunning
*Prov.* 3:1 my son *f.* not my law
4:5 get wisdom, *f.* it not
31:5 lest they drink and *f.* law
7 drink and *f.* his poverty
*Is.* 49:15 can a woman *f.* child?
54:4 shalt *f.* shame of thy youth
65:11 that *f.* my holy mountain
*Jer.* 2:32 maid *f.* her ornaments?
23:27 my people to *f.* my name
39 even I, will utterly *f.* you
*Lam.* 5:20 dost *f.* us for ever?
*Hos.* 4:6 also *f.* thy children
*Amos* 8:7 never *f.* any of works
*Heb.* 6:10 G. not unrighte. to *f.*
13:16 to communicate *f.* not

**FORGETFUL, NESS.**

*Ps.* 88:12 known in land of *f.*?
*Heb.* 13:2 not *f.* to entertain str.
*Jam.* 1:25 a *f.* hearer, but a doer

**FORGETTEST, ETH, ING.**

*Job* 39:15 *f.* foot may crush them
*Ps.* 9:12 *f.* not cry of humble
44:24 why *f.* thou our affliction?
*Prov.* 2:17 *f.* covenant of her God
*Is.* 51:13 and *f.* Lord thy Maker
*Phil.* 3:13 *f.* those things behind
*Jam.* 1:24 he *f.* what manner of

**FORGIVE.**

*Gen.* 50:17 *f.* trespass of brethren
*Ex.* 10:17 *f.* my sin this once
32:32 yet now if wilt *f.* their sin
*Num.* 30:5 Lord shall *f.* her, 8, 12
*Jos.* 24:19 will not *f.* your sins
1 *Sam.* 25:28 pray *f.* the trespass
1 *K.* 8:30 hear. *f.* 39; 2 *Chr.* 6:21
34 hear and *f.* the sin of Israel
36 *f.* sin of servant. 2 *Chr.* 6:25
50 *f.* thy peo. that have sinned
2 *Chr.* 7:14 then will I hear and *f*
*Ps.* 25:18 and *f.* all my sins
86:5 L. art good and ready to *f.*
*Is.* 2:9 therefore *f.* them not
*Jer.* 18:23 *f.* not their iniquity
31:34 for I will *f.* their iniquity
36:3 I may *f.* their iniquity and
*Dan.* 9:19 O Lord, hear, O L. *f.*
*Amos* 7:2 I said, *f.* I beseech th.
*Mat.* 6:12 *f.* us as we *f.* *Luke* 11:4
14 if ye *f.* men their trespasses
15 ye *f.* not, neither will your
9:6 hath power on earth to *f.*
sins, *Mark* 2:10; *Luke* 5:24
18:21 how oft sin, and I *f.* him?
35 if ye from your hearts *f.* not
*Mark* 2:7 can *f.* sins, *Luke* 5:21
11:25 praying, *f.* that your
26 if not *f.* your F. will not *f.*
*Luke* 6:37 *f.* ye shall be forgiven
17:3 brother repent, *f.* him, 4
23:34 Father *f.* them
2 *Cor.* 2:7 ye ought rather to *f.*
10 to whom ye *f.* any, I *f.* also
12:13 to you, *f.* me this wrong
1 *John* 1:9 to *f.* us our sins

**FORGIVEN.**

*Lev.* 4:20 it sh. be *f.* 26, 31, 35;
5:10, 13, 16, 18; 6:7; 19:22;
*Num.* 15:25, 26, 28; *Deut.* 21:8
*Num.* 14:19 pardon, as *f.* from E.
*Ps.* 32:1 wh. trans. is *f.* *Rom.* 4:7
85:2 hast *f.* iniquity of thy peo.
*Is.* 33:24 people be *f.* their iniq.
*Mat.* 9:2 sins *f.* thee, 5; *Mark*
2:5, 9; *Luke* 5:20, 23; 7:48
12:31 all sin be *f.* but ag. Holy
G. 32; *Mark* 3:28; *Luke* 12:10
*Mark* 4:12 sin should be *f.* them
*Luke* 6:37 forgive and ye sh. be *f.*
7:47 her sins which are many
are *f.* to whom little is *f.*
*Acts* 8:22 thought of heart be *f.*
*Eph.* 4:32 for Christ's sake *f.* you
*Col.* 2:13 having *f.* all trespasses
*Jam.* 5:15 com. sins they sh. be *f.*
1 *John* 2:12 bec. your sins are *f.*

**FORGIVETH, ING.**

*Ex.* 34:7 *f.* iniq. *Num.* 14:18
*Ps.* 103:3 *f.* all thine iniquities
*Luke* 7:49 who is this *f.* sins?
*Eph.* 4:32 *f.* one ano. *Col.* 3:13

**FORGIVENESS, ES.**

*Ps.* 130:4 there is *f.* with thee
*Dan.* 9:9 the L. our G. belong *f.*
*Mark* 3:29 nev. *f.* but in danger
*Acts* 5:31 him G. exalt. to give *f*
13:38 through him is preached *f.*
26:18 they may receive *f.* of sins
*Eph.* 1:7 have *f.* of sins, *Col.* 1:14

**FORGOTTEN.**

*Gen.* 41:30 the plenty shall be *f.*
*Deut.* 24:19 and hast *f.* a sheaf
26:13 neither have I *f.* them
31:21 this song shall not be *f.*
32:18 *f.* God that formed thee
*Job* 19:14 familiar friends *f.* me
28:4 even waters *f.* of the foot
*Ps.* 9:18 needy not always be *f.*
10:11 said in heart, God hath *f.*
31:12 I am *f.* as dead man
42:9 My rock, why hast *f.* me?
44:17 yet have we not *f.* thee
20 if we have *f.* name of our G.
77:9 hath G. *f.* to be gracious?
119:61 but I have not *f.* thy law
139 mine enemies *f.* thy words
*Ec.* 2:16 days to come all be *f.*
8:10 wicked were *f.* in the city
9:5 the memory of them is *f.*
*Is.* 17:10 *f.* God of thy salvation
23:15 Tyre shall be *f.* 70 years
16 take a harp, thou harlot *f.*
44:21 O Isr. thou shalt not be *f.*
49:14 Zion said, Lord hath *f.* me
65:16 the former troubles are *f.*
*Jer.* 2:32 peo. *f.* me, 13:25; 18:15
3:21 have *f.* the Lord their God
20:11 never be *f.* 23:40
23:27 forget as fathers have *f.*
30:14 all thy lovers have *f.* thee
44:9 *f.* wickedness of your fath.
50:5 join in cov. shall not be *f.*
6 have *f.* their resting-place
*Lam.* 2:6 sabbaths to be *f.* in Z.
*Ezek.* 22:12 hast *f.* me, saith L.
23:35 because thou hast *f.* me
*Hos.* 4:6 seeing thou hast *f.* law
8:14 Israel hath *f.* his Maker
13:6 therefore have they *f.* me
*Mat.* 16:5 *f.* bread, *Mark* 8:14
*Luke* 12:6 not one of them is *f.*
*Heb.* 12:5 ye have *f.* exhortation
2 *Pet.* 1:9 *f.* that he was purged

**FORKS.**

1 *Sam.* 13:21 they had a file for *f.*

**FORM, Substantive.**

*Gen.* 1:2 the earth was without *f.*
1 *Sam.* 28:14 what *f.* is he of?
2 *Sam.* 14:20 this *f.* of speech
*Job* 4:16 could not discern the *f.*
*Is.* 52:14 his *f.* more than sons
53:2 hath no *f.* nor comeliness
*Jer.* 4:23 lo, it was without *f.*
*Ezek.* 10:8 appeared *f.* of a hand
43:11 show them *f.* of the house
*Dan.* 3:19 *f.* of visage changed
25 *f.* of fourth like Son of God
*Mark* 16:12 he app. in another *f.*
*Rom.* 2:20 hast *f.* of knowledge
6:17 obeyed that *f.* of doctrine
*Phil.* 2:6 who being in *f.* of God
7 took upon him *f.* of a servant
2 *Tim.* 1:13 *f.* of sound words
3:5 having a *f.* of godliness

**FORM, Verb.**
Is. 45:7 I f. the light

**FORMED.**
Gen. 2:7 God f. man of the dust
19 out of ground G. f. ev. beast
Deut. 32:18 forgot. G. that f. thee
2 K. 19:25 that I f. it? Is. 37:26
Job 26:5 things f. under water
13 his hand f. crooked serpent
33:6 am f. out of the clay
Ps. 90:2 or ever hadst f. earth
94:9 f. the eye, sh. he not see?
95:5 his hands f. the dry land
Prov. 26:10 great God that f. all
Is. 27:11 f. them show no favor
43:1 he that f. thee, O Israel
7 I have f. him, yea, made him
10 before me was no god f.
21 this peo. have I f. for mys.
44:2 and f. thee from the womb
10 who hath f. a god or image
21 my servant, I have f. thee
24 thus saith he that f. thee
45:18 G. hath f. earth, he f. it
49:5 f. me to be his servant
54:17 no weapon f. against thee
Jer. 1:5 before I f. thee in belly
33:2 the L. that f. it to establish
Amos 7:1 he f. grasshoppers
Rom. 9:20 th. f. say to him f. it
Gal. 4:19 till Christ be f. in you
1 Tim. 2:13 Adam first f. then E.

**FORMER.**
1 Sam. 17:30 answer. after f. ma.
2 K. 17:34 do after f. manner, 40
Job 8:8 inquire, I pray, of f. age
30:3 wilderness in f. time waste
Ps. 79:8 O rem. not f. iniquities
89:49 f. loving-kindnesses?
Ec. 1:11 no rem. of f. things
7:10 that f. days were better
Is. 41:22 show f. things, 43:9
42:9 f. things are come to pass
43:18 remember ye not f. things
46:9 remember f. things of old
48:3 I have declared f. things
61:4 shall raise up f. desolations
65:7 measure f. work into bos.
16 because f. troubles are forg.
17 the f. shall not be rememb.
Jer. 5:24 giveth f. and latter rain
Hos. 6:3; Joel 2:23
10:16 is f. of all things, 51:19
34:5 the f. kings before thee
36:28 write in it all f. words
Ezek. 16:55 return to f. estate
Dan. 11:29 shall not be as the f.
Hag. 2:9 great. than of f. house
Zec. 1:4 the f. prophets, 7:7, 12
8:11 I will not be as in f. days
14:8 waters, half toward f. sea
Mal. 3:4 pleasant as in f. years
Acts 1:1 f. treatise have I made
Eph. 4:22 concern. f. conversa.
1 Pet. 1:14 according to f. lusts
Rev. 21:4 f. things passed away

**FORMETH.**
Amos 4:13 that f. the mountains
Zec. 12:1 and f. spirit of man

**FORNICATION.**
Ezek. 16:29 multi. f. in Canaan
Mat. 5:32 saving for f. 19:9
John 8:41 we be not born of f.
Acts 15:20 abstain fr. f. 29; 21:25
Rom. 1:29 being filled with all f.
1 Cor. 5:1 f. among you, such f.
6:13 the body is not for f. but
18 flee f.; 7:2 to avoid f.
2 Cor. 12:21 not repented of f.
Gal. 5:19 works of the flesh, f.
Eph. 5:3 f. let it not be named
Col. 3:5 mortify therefore f.
1 Thes. 4:3 should abstain fr f.
Jude 7 giving themsel. over to f.
Rev. 2:21 to repent of her f.
9:21 nor repent of their f.
14:8 wine of wrath of f. 18:3
17:2 dr. with wine of her f.
4 cup full of filthiness of her f.
19:2 corrupt earth with her f.

**FORNICATIONS.**
Ezek. 16:15 poured out thy f.
Mat. 15:19 proceed f. Mark 7:21

See COMMIT, COMMITTED.

**FORNICATOR, S.**
1 Cor. 5:9 not to comp. with f.
10 altogether with f. of world
11 called a brother be a f.
6:9 nor shall f. inherit kingdom
Heb. 12:16 lest there be any f. or

**FORSAKE.**
Deut. 31:16 this people will f. me
17 in that day I will f. them
Jos. 24:16 G. forbid we sh. f. L.
20 if ye f. the Lord, and serve
Jud. 9:11 sho. I f. my sweetness
2 K. 21:14 I will f. remnant
1 Chr. 28:9 if thou f. him, he wi.
2 Chr. 7:19 if ye f. my statutes
15:2 if ye f. him he will f. you
Ezr. 8:22 wrath ag. them f. him
Ps. 27:10 father and mother f.
37:8 cease from anger, f. wrath
89:30 if his children f. my law
94:14 will he f. his inheritance
119:53 bec. wicked f. thy law
Prov. 3:3 not mercy and truth f.
9:6 f. the foolish, and live
28:4 that f. law, praise wicked
Is. 1:28 that f. L. be consumed
55:7 let the wicked f. his way
65:11 ye are they that f. the L.
Jer. 17:13 f. L. shall be ashamed
23:33 I will even f. you, 39
51:9 f. Babylon, and let us go
Lam. 5:20 why dost f. us so long
Dan. 11:30 that f. holy covenant
Jon. 2:8 f. their own mercy
Acts 21:21 teachest to f. Moses

**FORSAKE not.**
Deut. 12:19 take heed f. n. Levite
Job 20:13 spare it and f. it not
Ps. 38:21 f. me not, 71:9, 18
119:8 O f. me not utterly
138:8 f. not works of thy hands
Prov. 1:8 f. n. law of moth. 6:20
4:2 doctrine, f. ye not my law
6 f. her n. she sh. preserve thee
27:10 and father's friend f. not

**Not FORSAKE.**
Deut. 4:31 he will not f. thee, 31:6, 8; 1 Chr. 28:20
14:27 thou shalt not f. Levite
Jos. 1:5 nor f. thee, Heb. 13:5
1 Sam. 12:22 not f. his people, 1 K. 6:13
1 K. 8:57 let him not f. us
Neh. 9:31 thou didst not f. them
10:39 not f. the ho. of our God
Ps. 27:9 neither f. me, O God
Is. 41:17 I will not f. them
42:16 will I do, and not f. them
Ezek. 20:8 nor did f. idols of Eg.

**FORSAKEN.**
2 Chr. 21:10 had f. L. 24:24; 28:6
Neh. 13:11 why is house of G. f.?
Job 18:4 sh. earth be f. for thee?
Ps. 37:25 not seen righteous f.
Is. 7:16 land be f. of both kings
17:2 the cities of Aroer are f.
9 shall be as a f. bough
27:10 the habitation sh be f.
32:14 because palaces s . be f.
54:6 called thee as a wo an f.
62:4 shalt no more be t ned f.
Jer. 4:29 every city shall be f.
18:14 wat. from ano. pl. be f.?
Ezek. 36:4 saith Lord to cities f.
Amos 5:2 virgin of Israel is f.
Zep. 2:4 G. be f. and Ash elon

**Have, hast, hath FORSAKEN.**
Deut. 28:20 whereby f. me
29:25 bec. f. Lord, Jud. 10:10
Jud. 6:13 now Lord hath f. us
10:13 yet ye have f. me and
1 Sam. 8:8 works wherewith f.
12:10 because we h. f. Lord
1 K. 11:33 because they h. f. me
18:18 ye h. f. commandm. of L.
19:10 Israel h. f. covenant, 14
2 K. 22:17 because they h. f. me, 2 Chr. 34:25; Jer. 16:11; 19:4
2 Chr. 12:5 he have f. me, and I
13:11 but ye have f. him
24:20 ye have f. L. he ha. f. you
29:6 our fathers have f. him
Ezr. 9:10 h. f. thy commandm.
Job 20:19 because he hath f. poor
Ps. 22:1 why hast thou f. me? Mat. 27:46; Mark 15:34
71:11 saying, God hath f. him
Is. 1:4 they have f. the Lord
49:14 Zion said, Lord hath f. me
54:7 for a moment have I f. thee
Jer. 1:16 who have f. me
2:13 h. f. me, fountain of waters
17 in that thou hast f. Lord, 19
5:7 thy children have f. me, 19
9:13 because they h. f. my law
19 confound. bec. we h. f. land
12:7 I have f. my house, I have
15:6 thou hast f. me, saith Lord
17:13 h. f. fount. of living wat.
22:9 they h. f. covenant of God
25:38 hath f. his covert
Ezek. 8:12 Lord hath f. earth, 9:9
Mat. 19:27 we have f. all
29 every one that h. f. houses
2 Tim. 4:10 Demas hath f. me
2 Pet. 2:15 which h. f. right way

**Not FORSAKEN.**
2 Chr. 13:10 the Lord is our God, we have not f. him
Ezr. 9:9 n. f. us in our bondage
Ps. 9:10 not f. them seek thee
Is. 62:12 be called a city not f.
Jer. 51:5 Israel hath not been f.
2 Cor. 4:9 persecuted, but not f.

**FORSAKETH, ING.**
Job 6:14 he f. fear of Almighty
Ps. 37:28 Lord f. not his saints
Prov. 2:17 f. guide of her youth
15:10 griev. to him that f. way
28:13 whoso confesseth and f.
Is. 6:12 until there be a great f.
Luke 14:33 whoso f. not all hath
Heb. 10:25 not f. the assembling

**FORSOOK, EST.**
Deut. 32:15 f. G. that made him
Jud. 2:12 they f. Lord, 13; 10:6
1 Sam. 31:7 f. cities, 1 Chr. 10:7
1 K. 9:9 because f. Lord their G.
12:8 Rehoboam f. counsel of old men, 13; 2 Chr. 10:8, 13
2 K. 21:22 Amon f. G. of fathers
2 Chr. 7:22 they f. God of fathers
12:1 Rehoboam f. law of Lord
Neh. 9:17 slow to anger, f. not
19 f. them not in wilderness
Ps. 78:60 f. tabernacle of Shiloh
119:87 but I f. not thy precepts
Is. 58:2 f. not ordinance of God
Jer. 14:5 hind calved, and f. it
Mat. 26:56 f. him, Mark 14:50
Mark 1:18 they f. their nets
Luke 5:11 f. all, followed him
2 Tim. 4:16 all men f. me
Heb. 11:27 by faith Moses f. E.

**FORSWEAR.**
Mat. 5:33 thou sh. not f. thyself

**FORT, S.**
2 Sam. 5:9 David dwelt in the f.
2 K. 25:1 build f. ag. J. Jer. 52:4

*Is.* 25:12 *f.* of walls bring down
29:3 I will raise *f.* against thee
32:14 the *f.* be for dens forever
*Ezek.* 4:2 a *f.* ag. it, 21:22; 26:8
17:17 building *f.* cut off many
21:22 divination to build a *f.*
26:8 shall make a *f.* against thee
33:27 they in the *f.* shall die
*Dan.* 11:19 tow. *f.* of own land

**FORTH.**

*Ps.* 113:2 blessed be Lord, from this time *f.* 115:18; 121:8
*Jer.* 49:5 be driven out right *f.*
*Mat.* 16:21 that time *f.* began J.
22:46 that day *f.* ask questions
*John* 11:53 that day *f.*

**FORTHWITH.**

*Mat.* 13:5 and *f.* they sprung up
*Mark* 1:43 and *f.* sent him away
*John* 19:34 *f.* came out blood and
*Acts* 12:10 *f.* the angel departed

FORTUNATUS. 1 *Cor.* 16:17

**FORTY.**

*Acts* 23:13 more than *f.* consp. 21

**FORTY stripes.**

*Deut.* 25:3 *f. str.* he may give
2 *Cor.* 11:24 of the Jews rec. *f. s.*

**FORTY years.**

*Ex.* 16:35 man. *f. y. Neh.* 9:21
*Num.* 14:33 wander *f. y.* 32:13
34 bear your iniquities *f. y.*
*Deut.* 2:7 thy walking these *f. y.*
8:2 God led thee *f. years,* 29:5
*Jos.* 5:6 walked *f. y.* in wildern.
14:7 *f. years* old was I when M.
*Jud.* 3:11 rest *f. y.* 5:31; 8:28
13:1 Isr. into the hand of P. *f. y.*
2 *Sam.* 15:7 after *f. y.* Absa. said
*Ps.* 95:10 *f. y.* long was I grieved
*Ezek.* 29:11 nor be inhabited *f. y.*
13 end of *f. y.* will gather Eg.
*Amos* 2:10 I led you *f. y.*
*Amos* 5:25 sacrifi. *f. y. Acts* 7:42
*Acts* 4:22 was above *f. y.* old
7:23 M. *f. y.* old visited breth.
36 wonders in wilderness *f. y.*
13:18 *f. y.* suffered he
21 gave Saul by space of *f. y.*
*Heb.* 3:9 fathers saw works *f. y.*
17 with whom grieved *f. y.* ?

**FORTY-TWO**

2 *K.* 2:24 bears tear *f.-t.* children
*Rev.* 11:2 tread *f.-t.* months
13:5 to continue *f.-t.* months

**FORTY-FIVE years.**

*Jos.* 14:10 kept me alive *f.-f. y.*

**FORTY-SIX years.**

*John* 2:20 *f.-s. y.* temple build.

**FORTY-NINE years.**

*Lev.* 25:8 space be *f.-n. years*

**FORTIFY, IED.**

*Jud.* 9:31 *f.* city against thee
*Neh.* 4:2 Jews *f.* themselves ?
*Is.* 22:10 broken to *f.* wall
*Jer.* 51:53 she *f.* her strength
*Mic.* 7:12 come from *f.* cities
*Nah.* 2:1 *f.* thy power mightily
3:14 *f.* thy strong-holds

**FORTRESS, ES.**

2 *Sam.* 22:2 my *f. Ps.* 18:2; 31:3; 71:3; 91:2; 144:2
*Is.* 17:3 *f.* sh. cease from Ephra.
25:12 *f.* shall he bring down
34:13 nettles come up in the *f.*
*Jer.* 6:27 I have set thee for a *f.*
10:17 O inhabitant of the *f.*
16:19 O Lord, my *f.* in affliction
*Dan.* 11:7 *f.* of king of the north
10 be stirred up even to his *f.*
*Hos.* 10:14 thy *f.* shall be spoiled
*Amos* 5:9 spoiled sh. come ag. *f.*
*Mic.* 7:12 sh. come to thee fr. *f.*

**FORWARD, NESS.**

*Jer.* 7:24 and they went not *f.*
*Zec.* 1:15 helped *f.* the affliction
2 *Cor.* 8:8 occasion of *f.* of others
8:10 to be *f.* a year ago
17 more *f.* of his own accord
9:2 I know the *f.* of your mind
*Gal.* 2:10 same I also was *f.* to do
3 *John* 6 if bring *f.* on journey

*See That* DAY, GO, SET, WENT.

**FOUGHT.**

*Jos.* 10:14 L. *f.* for Isr. 42; 23:3
*Jud.* 1:5 *f.* against Adoni-bezek
8 Judah had *f.* ag. Jerusalem
5:19 kings *f.* kings of Canaan
20 they *f.* from heaven, stars *f.*
9:17 my father *f.* for you, and
39 Gaal *f.* with Abimelech
12:4 Gilead *f.* with Ephraim
1 *Sam.* 4:10 Philist. *f.* 1 *Chr.* 10:1
14:47 Saul *f.* ag. all his enemies
19:8 David *f.* Philistines, 23:5
2 *Sam.* 2:28 nor *f.* they any more
10:17 Syr. *f.* ag. D. 1 *Chr.* 19:17
2 *Chr.* 20:29 L. *f.* ag. enemies
*Ps.* 109:3 *f.* ag. me with. cause
*Is.* 20:1 Tartan *f.* ag. Ashdod
63:10 turned enemy *f.* ag. them
*Jer.* 34:1 peo. *f.* ag. Jerusalem, 7
*Zec.* 14:3 *f.* in the day of battle
12 L. smite them *f.* ag. Jerus.
1 *Cor.* 15:32 I have *f.* with beasts
2 *Tim.* 4:7 I have *f.* a good fight
*Rev.* 12:7 Michael *f.* ag. dragon

**FOUL.**

*Job* 16:16 my face is *f.* wi. weep.
*Mat.* 16:3 it will be *f.* weather
*Mark* 9:25 rebuked the *f.* spirit
*Rev.* 18:2 Bab. hold of ev. *f.* spi.

**FOUL, ED, EDST.**

*Ezek.* 32:2 and *f.* their rivers
34:18 ye must *f.* the residue
19 they drink what ye have *f.*

**FOUND.**

*Gen.* 8:9 the dove *f.* no rest for
26:19 Isaac's servants *f.* a well
27:20 how hast *f.* it so quickly !
31:33 Laban *f.* not images
37:32 said, This coat have we *f.*
38:23 I sent kid, hast not *f.* her
44:16 G. hath *f.* out the iniquity
*Lev.* 6:3 have *f.* that was lost
*Num.* 15:32 *f.* man gather. sticks
*Deut.* 22:3 with what *f.* do likew.
14 I *f.* her not a maid, 17
27 *f.* her in field, damsel cried
24:1 *f.* some uncleanness in her
32:10 he *f.* him in a desert land
*Jos.* 2:22 pursuers *f.* them not
*Jud.* 14:8 had not *f.* out riddle
21:12 *f.* four hundred virgins
1 *Sam.* 9:4 they *f.* not the asses
11 *f.* maidens going to draw
12:5 not *f.* aught in my hand
1 *Sam.* 13:22 no sword *f.* in hand
25:28 evil not been *f.* with thee
29:3 I have *f.* no fault in him
30:11 *f.* an Egyptian in the field
31:8 *f.* S. and three sons fallen
2 *Sam.* 7:27 *f.* in his heart to pray this prayer, 1 *Chr.* 17:25
1 *K.* 7:47 nor weight of brass *f.*
11:29 Ahijah *f.* Jerobo. in way
13:28 *f.* his carcass cast in way
18:10 took an oath *f.* thee not
20:36 lion *f.* him and slew him
21:20 *f.* me mine enemy ?
2 *K.* 2:17 Elijah, but *f.* him not
9:35 *f.* no more of her than skull
22:8 I *f.* law in house of the L.
25:19 took sixty men *f.* in city
1 *Chr.* 4:40 th. *f.* fat pasture and
2 *Chr.* 19:3 good th. *f.* in thee
*Neh.* 5:8 *f.* nothing to answer

*Job* 28:13 nor wisdom *f.* in land
31:29 when evil *f.* mine enemy
32:3 bec. they had *f.* to answer
13 We have *f.* wisdom
33:24 the pit, I have *f.* a ransom
42:15 *f.* so fair as daught. of Job
*Ps.* 69:20 comforters, but *f.* none
76:5 none have *f.* their hands
84:3 sparrow hath *f.* a house
89:20 I have *f.* Dav. my servant
107:4 and *f.* no city to dwell in
116:3 I *f.* trouble and sorrow
132:6 we *f.* it in the fields
*Prov.* 7:15 and I have *f.* thee
24:14 so wisdom be when *f.* it
25:16 hast *f.* honey ?
*Ec.* 7:28 I *f.* a woman not *f.*
29 I *f.* God made man upright
*Cant.* 3:1 but I *f.* him not, 2
3 the watchman *f.* me, 5:7
4 but I *f.* him my soul loveth
*Is.* 10:10 *f.* kingdoms of idols
14 my hand *f.* riches of people
22:3 all *f.* in thee are bound
57:10 hast *f.* the life of thy hand
65:1 *f.* of them sought me not
*Jer.* 2:5 iniquity fath. *f.* in me ?
34 in thy skirts is *f.* the blood
5:26 my people are *f.* wicked
15:16 words *f.* I did eat them
23:11 in my house *f.* wickedn.
41:8 *f.* that said, Slay us not
50:7 all that *f.* them dev. them
*Lam.* 2:16 this is day we have *f.*
*Ezek.* 22:30 for a man, I *f.* none
*Dan.* 5:12 ex. spirit *f.* in Daniel
27 art weighed and *f.* wanting
6:4 nor any fault *f.* in Daniel
11 these men *f.* Daniel praying
*Hos.* 9:10 I *f.* Israel like grapes
12:4 he *f.* him in Beth-el, and
8 I have *f.* me out substance
14:8 from me is thy fruit *f.*
*Mic.* 1:13 transg. of Is. *f.* in thee
*Mat.* 2:8 have *f.* him bring word
8:10 not *f.* so gr. faith, *Luke* 7:9
13:44 when a man *f.* he hideth
46 *f.* one pearl of great price
18:28 *f.* one of his fellow serv.
20:6 *f.* others standing idle
21:19 he *f.* nothing thereon, *Mark* 11:13; *Luke* 13:6
22:10 gath. as many as they *f.*
26:43 he *f.* them asleep, *Mark* 14:40; *Luke* 22:45
60 sou. wit. *f.* none, *Mar.* 14:55
27:32 they *f.* a man of Cyrene
*Mark* 1:37 when they had *f.* him
7:2 eat with def. hands *f.* fault
30 she *f.* the devil gone out
11:4 *f.* colt tied by door without
*Luke* 2:16 *f.* babe ly. in a manger
46 after three days *f.* him
4:17 *f.* place where it was writ.
7:10 they *f.* the servant whole
8:35 *f.* the man clothed
15:6 for I have *f.* my sheep
9 when she hath *f.* the piece
17:18 none *f.* that ret. to give gl.
19:32 *f.* even as he said, 22:13
23:2 we *f.* perverting the nation
14 I have *f.* no fault
24:2 *f.* the stone rolled away
3 *f.* not body of the Lord Jesus
23 when they *f.* not his body
33 *f.* the eleven gath. together
*John* 1:41 we have *f.* Messias, 45
2:14 Jesus *f.* in the temp. those
*Acts* 5:10 came in, and *f.* her de.
22 officers *f.* them not in pris.
7:11 our fathers *f.* no sustena.
9:2 that if he *f.* any of this way
10:27 P. *f.* many come together
12:19 when Herod *f.* not Peter
13:6 they *f.* a certain sorcerer
22 I have *f.* David a man after
17:23 I *f.* altar with inscription
24:5 *f.* this man a pestilent

Acts 24:20 if they f. any evil do.
25:25 I f. noth. worthy of death
28:14 Puteoli, wh. we f. breth.
Rom. 4:1 what Abraham f.
7:10 to life I f. to be unto death
1 Cor. 15:15 we are f. false witn.
2 Cor. 2:13 bec. I f. not Titus
Gal. 2:17 we also are f. sinners
Phil. 2:8 f. in fashion as a man
1 Tim. 3:10 being f. blameless
2 Tim. 1:17 Onesiphorus f. me
Heb. 12:17 f. no place of repent.
1 Pet. 1:7 faith be f. to praise
2 John 4 f. of thy children
Rev. 2:2 and hast f. them liars
3:2 not f. thy works perfect
12:8 nor their place f. in heaven
16:20 mountains were not f.

**Be FOUND.**

Gen. 18:29 peradvent. be forty f.
Ex. 21:16 a man if he be f.
22:2 if that be f. breaking up, 7
4 if the theft be certainly f.
1 Sam. 10:21 Saul could not be f.
2 Sam. 17:12 come on him where he shall be f.
1 K. 1:52 if wickedness be f.
1 Chr. 28:9 seek him he will be f. of thee, 2 Chr. 15:2
Job 20:8 fly away and not be f.
28:12 where shall wisdom be f.?
Ps. 32:6 pray when may be f.
36:2 till his iniq. be f. hateful
37:36 but he could not be f.
Prov. 6:31 if he be f. he sh. rest.
16:31 if it be f. in way of right.
30:6 and thou be f. a liar
10 and thou be f. guilty
Is. 30:14 shall not be f. a sherd
35:9 nor any beast be f. there
51:3 joy and gladness be f.
55:6 seek L. while he may be f.
Jer. 29:14 I will be f. of you
50:20 sins of J. shall not be f.
Ezek. 26:21 shalt never be f.
Dan. 11:19 he sh. fall and n. be f.
12:1 ev. one that be f. written
Hos. 10:2 sh. they be f. faulty
Zep. 3:13 nor deceit. tongue be f.
Zec. 10:10 place not be f.
Acts 5:39 lest be f. to fight ag. G.
1 Cor. 4:2 a steward be f. faithful
2 Cor 5:3 shall not be f. naked
11:12 may be f. even as we
12:20 be f. such as would not
Phil. 3:9 be f. in him
2 Pet. 3:14 be f. of him in peace
Rev. 18:21 Baby. be f. no more
22 no craftsman be f. in thee

See FAVOR.

**FOUND grace.**

Gen. 6:8 Noah f. g. in eyes of L.
19:19 servant f. g. in thy sight
33:10 if I have f. g. 47:29; 50:4
39:4 Joseph f. grace in his sight
Ex. 33:12 thou hast also f. g. 17
13 if I have f. g. 34:9; Jud. 6:17; 1 Sam. 27:5
16 known that I have f. g.?
Num. 32:5 if we have f. grace
1 Sam. 20:3 father know I f. g.
Jer. 31:2 people f. g. in wildern.

**Is FOUND.**

Gen. 44:10 with whom cup is f.
1 K. 14:13 is f. some good thing
2 K. 22:13 this book that is f.
Ezr. 4:19 it is f. city been reb.
Job 19:28 root of the matter is f.
Prov. 10:13 in lips wisdom is f.
Is. 13:15 that is f. be thrust
65:8 new wine is f. in cluster
Jer. 2:26 the thief when he is f.
34 is f. the blood of innocents
11:9 a conspiracy is f. am. Jud.
Dan. 5:14 excel. wisdom is f. 12
Hos. 14:8 from me is thy fruit f.
Luke 15:24 was lost and is f. 32
2 Cor. 7:14 boasting is f. a truth

**Was FOUND.**

Gen. 44:12 cup w. f. in B. sack
1 Sam. 13:22 with S. and J. w. f.
2 Chr. 15:4 he was f. of them, 15
Ezr. 6:2 there w. f. at A. a roll
Ec. 9:15 w. f. in it poor wise m.
Jer. 48:27 w. he f. among thiev.?
Ezek. 28:15 iniqui. was f. in thee
Dan. 1:19 none w. f. like Daniel
2:35 no place was f. for them
5:11 wisd. of gods was f. in him
6:22 innocency was f. in me
Mat. 1:18 w. f. wi. child of H. G.
Luke 9:36 Jesus was f. alone
Acts 8:40 Philip was f. at Azotus
Rom. 10:20 I was f. of them that
1 Pet. 2:22 nor w. guile f. in mou.
Rev. 5:4 was f. worthy to open
Rev. 14:5 in th. mo. w. f. no guile
18:24 in her was f. blood of pro.
20:11 was f. no place for them

**Was not FOUND.**

Mal. 2:6 iniq. w. n. f. in his lips
Heb. 11:5 Enoch was not f.
Rev. 20:15 was not f. written.

**FOUNDATION.**

Ex. 9:18 not been in Eg. since f.
Jos. 6:26 lay f. in his first-born
1 K. 5:17 hewn stones to lay f.
6:37 in fourth year was f. laid
7:9 of costly stones from the f.
16:34 laid f. of Jericho
2 Chr. 8:16 prepared to day of f.
31:7 began to lay f. of the heaps
Ezr. 3:10 when build. laid f. 12
5:16 Sheshbazzar laid the f.
Job 4:19 whose f. is in the dust
22:16 f. overflown with a flood
Ps. 87:1 f. is in holy mountains
102:25 of old thou hast laid f.
137:7 rase it, rase it, even to f.
Prov. 10:25 righteous is everl. f.
Is. 28:16 I lay in Zion for a f. a
44:28 thy f. shall be laid
48:13 my hand laid f. of earth
Ezek. 13:14 f. thereof be discov.
Hab. 3:13 discovering f. to neck
Hag. 2:18 day the f. was laid
Zec. 4:9 Zerubbabel hath laid f.
8:9 prophets when the f. was laid
12:1 which lay. f. of the earth
Luke 6:48 laid the f. on a rock
49 without a f. built a house
14:29 after he hath laid the f.
Rom. 15:20 bui. on ano. man's f.
1 Cor. 3:10 master-build. laid f.
11 for other f. can no man lay
12 if any build on this f. gold
Eph. 2:20 on f. of the prophets
1 Tim. 6:19 laying up a good f.
2 Tim. 2:19 f. of G. standeth sure
Heb. 1:10 laid f. of the earth
6:1 not laying f. of repentance
Rev. 21:19 the first f. jasper

**FOUNDATION of the world.**

Mat. 13:35 secret from f. of w.
25:34 kingdom prep. fr. f. of w.
Luke 11:50 bl. shed from f. of w.
John 17:24 before f. of w.
Eph. 1:4 chosen us bef. f. of w.
Heb. 4:3 works finish. fr. f. of w.
9:26 suffered since f. of w.
1 Pet. 1:20 foreord. bef. f. of w.
Rev. 13:8 L. slain from f. of w.
17:8 names not writ. fr. f. of w.

**FOUNDATIONS.**

Deut. 32:22 set on fire f. of moun.
2 Sam. 22:8 f. of heaven moved
16 f. were discov. Ps. 18:7, 15
Ezr. 4:12 and joined the f.
6:3 let the f. be strongly laid
Job 38:4 when I laid f. of earth?
6 whereupon are the f. fasten.
Ps. 11:3 if f. be destroyed, what
82:5 all the f. are out of course
104:5 who laid f. of the earth
Prov. 8:29 appointed f. of earth
Is. 16:7 for f. of Kir-hareseth
24:18 f. of the earth do shake
40:21 not unders. from the f.
51:13 Lord that laid f. of earth
16 I may lay f. of the earth
54:11 lay f. with sapphires
58:12 raise up f. of many gener.
Jer. 31:37 if f. can be searched
50:15 her f. are fallen
51:26 not take of thee sto. for f.
Lam. 4:11 it hath devour. the f.
Ezek. 30:4 Egypt's f. brok. down
41:8 the f. of the side chambers
Mic. 1:6 will discover f. thereof
6:2 ye strong f. of the earth
Acts 16:26 f. of prison were shak.
Heb. 11:10 for a city that hath f.
Rev. 21:14 walls of city had 12 f.
19 f. garnished with precious stones

**FOUNDED.**

Ps. 24:2 he hath f. it on the seas
89:11 fuln. thereof thou f. them
104:8 to place thou f. for them
119:152 testimonies, hast f. th.
Prov. 3:19 by wisdom hath f.
Is. 14:32 the Lord hath f. Zion
23:13 was not till Assyrian f. it
Amos 9:6 f. his troop in earth
Mat. 7:25 it fell not, f. on a rock
Luke 6:48 it was f. on a rock

**FOUNDER.**

Jud. 17:4 gave them to the f.
Jer. 6:29 the f. melteth in vain
10:9 work of the hands of the f.
14 f. conf. by graven im. 51:17

**FOUNTAIN.**

Gen. 16:7 found Hagar by a f.
Lev. 11:36 a f. wherein is water
20:18 he discovered her f. the f
Deut. 33:28 f. of J. be on a land
Ps. 36:9 with thee is the f.
68:26 bless Lord from f. of Isr.
74:15 thou didst cleave the f.
114:8 flint into a f. of water
Prov. 5:18 let thy f. be blessed
13:14 law of wise is a f. of life
14:27 fear of Lord is a f. of life
25:26 is as a troubled f.
Ec. 12:6 pitcher be broken at f.
Cant. 4:12 f. sealed; 15 f. of gar.
Jer. 2:13 f. of living wat. 17:13
6:7 as f. casteth out waters
9:1 Oh that mine eyes were a f.
Joel 3:18 a f. come forth
Zec. 13:1 that day a f. be opened
Mark 5:29 f. of her blo. dried up
Jam. 3:11 f. send forth sw. wat.
12 no f. can yield salt water
Rev. 21:6 I will give of f. of life

**FOUNTAINS.**

Gen. 7:11 f. of deep broken up
8:2 f. of the deep were stopped
Deut. 8:7 bringeth into land of f.
1 K. 18:5 go to all f. of water
2 Chr. 32:4 much pe. who stop. f.
Prov. 5:16 let thy f. be dispersed
8:24 no f. abounding with wat.
28 he strengthened f. of deep
Is. 41:18 will open f. in valleys
Hos. 13:15 f. shall be dried up
Rev. 7:17 lead them to living f.
8:10 star fell on the f. of waters
14:7 worship him made the f.
16:4 angel poured his vial on f

**FOUR.**

Gen. 2:10 river became f. heads
14:9 f. kings joined battle
47:24 f. parts be own, for seed

*Ex.* 22:1 shall restore *f.* sheep
*Lev.* 11:20 fowls going on all *f.*
27 go on all *f.* unclean. 42
*Job* 42:16 son's sons, even *f.*
*Prov.* 30:15 *f.* say not, It is eno.
18 be *f.* things wh. I know not
24 be *f.* things little on earth
29 *f.* things are comely
*Is.* 17:6 *f.* or five in out. branch.
*Jer.* 15:3 app. over them *f.* kinds
*Ezek.* 1:5 *f.* living creatures
14:21 *f.* sore judgments on Jer.
37:9 from *f.* winds, O breath
*Dan.* 3:25 lo, I see *f.* men loose
7:2 *f.* winds strove on sea
17 these *f.* beasts are *f.* kings
8:8 came *f.* notable horns
22 *f.* kingdoms shall stand
11:4 kingdom towards *f.* winds
*Amos* 1:3 for *f.* w. not turn away punish. 6, 9, 11, 13; 2:1, 4, 6
*Zec.* 1:18 and behold *f.* horns
*Mat.* 24:31 gather his elect from the *f.* winds, *Mark* 13:27
*John* 4:35 yet *f.* months, harvest
11:17 Lazarus in grave *f.* days
19:23 made *f.* parts of his garm.
*Acts* 10:30 *f.* days ago was fast.
21:9 Philip had *f.* daughters
23 we have *f.* men have a vow
*Rev.* 4:6 round throne *f.* beasts
5:14 *f.* beasts said, Amen. 6:6
9:14 *f.* angels who are bound
14:3 a new song before *f.* beasts
19:4 and the *f.* beasts fell down
*See* CORNERS, DAYS.

**FOUR times.**
*Neh.* 6:4 sent *f. t.* after this sort

**FOURFOLD.**
2 *Sam.* 12:6 restore the lamb *f.*
*Luke* 19:8 any thing, I restore *f.*
*See* FOOTED, TWENTY, HUNDRED, THOUSAND.

**FOURSCORE.**
*Ex.* 7:7 Moses was *f.* years old, when spake to Pharaoh
*Jud.* 3:30 land had rest *f.* years
2 *Sam.* 19:32 Barzillai was *f.* yea.
2 *K.* 6:25 ass's head for *f.* pieces
*Ps.* 90:10 and if they be *f.* years
*Cant.* 6:18 and *f.* concubines
*Luke* 2:37 wid. *f.* and four years
16:7 take thy bill and write *f.*

**FOURSCORE and five.**
*Jos.* 14:10 I am this day *f. and fi.*

**FOURSQUARE.**
*Rev.* 21:16 the city lieth *f.*

**FOURTEEN.**
*Gen.* 31:41 serv. *f.* years for dau.
*Mat.* 1:17 from Dav. to carrying away *f.* to Ch. *f.* generations
2 *Cor.* 12:2 man above *f.* years
*Gal.* 2:1 *f.* years after I went up

**FOURTEENTH.**
*Acts* 27:27 *f.* night was come
*See* DAY.

**FOURTH.**
*Gen.* 15:16 in *f.* gen. come hither
*Ex.* 20:5 iniq. to *f.* generation, 34:7; *Num.* 14:18; *Deut.* 5:9
*Lev.* 19:24 in *f.* year fruit holy
2 *K.* 10:30 child. of *f.* gen. 15:12
*Dan.* 2:40 *f.* kingdom str. as iron
3:25 *f.* is like the Son of God
7:23 *f.* beast be the *f.* kingdom
11:2 the *f.* shall be far richer
*Mat.* 14:25 J. came in *f.* watch
*Rev.* 4:7 *f.* beast like flying eagle
6:7 when opened the *f.* seal
8:12 the *f.* angel sounded
16:8 *f.* angel poured vial
*See* DAY, MONTH, PART.

**FOWL.**
*Gen.* 1:26 dominion over *f.* 28
2:19 God formed every *f.* of air
7:23 *f.* of heaven was destroyed
8:17 bring forth of *f.* of cattle
9:2 fear of you be on every *f.*
10 establish covenant with *f.*
*Deut.* 4:17 likeness of winged *f.*
*Job* 28:7 a path no *f.* knoweth
*Ps.* 8:8 have dominion over *f.*
148:10 flying *f.* praise the L.
*Jer.* 9:10 *f.* of heavens are fled
*Ezek.* 17:23 under it sh. dw. all *f.*
39:17 speak to ev. feathered *f.*
44:31 not eat torn *f.* or beast
*Dan.* 7:6 four wings of a *f.*

**FOWLS.**
*Gen.* 7:3 take of *f.* also by sevens
15:11 when *f.* came on carcasses
*Lev.* 1:14 burnt sacrifice be of *f.*
11:13 *f.* have in abomination
*Deut.* 14:20 of clean *f.* may eat
28:26 carcass be meat to all *f.*
1 *Sam.* 17:44 thy flesh to the *f.* 46
1 *K.* 4:33 Solomon spake of *f.*
14:11 dieth, *f.* eat, 16:4; 21:24
*Neh.* 5:18 *f.* were prepar. for me
*Job* 12:7 ask *f.* and they sh. tell
*Ps.* 50:11 I know all the *f.*
78:27 rained *f.* as sand of sea
*Is.* 18:6 be left to *f.* of mountains, *f.* shall summer upon them
*Dan.* 4:14 *f.* get from his branch.
*Mat.* 6:26 the *f.* they sow not
13:4 *f.* dev. *Mark* 4:4; *Lu.* 8:5
*Mark* 4:32 *f.* m. lodge, *Lu.* 13:19
*Luke* 12:24 are ye better than *f.*?
*Acts* 10:12 wherein were *f.* 11:6
*Rev.* 19:17 an angel cried to all *f.*
21 *f.* were filled with th. flesh

**FOWLS of heaven.**
*Job* 35:11 wiser than *f. of heaven*
*Ps.* 79:2 thy servants meat to *f.*
104:12 *f. of h.* have their habit.
*Jer.* 7:33 carcasses of peo. meat for *f. of h.* 16:4; 19:7; 34:20
15:3 appoint *f. of hea.* to destr.
*Ezek.* 29:5 Ph. for meat to *f. of h.*
31:6 *f. of h.* made nests in Assy.
13 on his ruin sh. *f. of h.* rem.
32:4 *f. of heaven* to remain
38:20 *f. of h.* shake at my pres.
*Dan.* 2:38 *f. of h.* to Nebuchad.
*Hos.* 2:18 covenant with *f. of h.*
4:3 shall languish with *f. of hea.*
7:12 bring them down as *f. of h.*
*Zep.* 1:31 will consume *f. of hea.*
*Luke* 13:19 *f. of h.* lodged in bra.

**FOWLER, S.**
*Ps.* 91:3 from the snare of the *f.*
124:7 soul out of the snare of *f.*
*Prov.* 6:5 as a bird from the *f.*
*Hos.* 9:8 prophet is a snare of *f.*

**FOX, ES.**
*Jud.* 15:4 Samson caught 300 *f.*
*Neh.* 4:3 *f.* shall break stone-wa.
*Ps.* 63:10 shall be portion for *f.*
*Cant.* 2:15 take the *f.* the little *f.*
*Lam.* 5:18 the *f.* walk upon Zion
*Ezek.* 13:4 thy proph. are like *f.*
*Mat.* 8:20 *f.* ha. holes, *Luke* 9:58
*Luke* 13:32 go tell *f.* I cast out

**FRAGMENTS.**
*Mat.* 14:20 took up the *f. Mark* 6:43; *Luke* 9:17; *John* 6:13
*Mark* 8:19 many baskets of *f.*?
*John* 6:12 gather up the *f.*

**FRAIL.**
*Ps.* 39:4 may know how *f.* I am

**FRAME.**
*Ps.* 103:14 he knoweth our *f.* he
*Ezek.* 40:2 was as the *f.* of a city

**FRAME, ED, ETH.**
*Jud.* 12:6 not *f.* to pronounce it
*Ps.* 50:19 thy tongue *f.* deceit
94:20 which *f.* mischi. by a law
*Is.* 29:16 *f.* say to him that *f.* it?
*Jer.* 18:11 I *f.* evil against you
*Hos.* 5:4 will not *f.* to turn to G.
*Eph.* 2:21 in whom the build. *f.*
*Heb.* 11:3 worlds *f.* by word of G.

**FRANKINCENSE.**
*Ex.* 30:34 spices with pure *f.*
*Lev.* 2:1 put *f.* 5:11; 24:7; *Num.* 5:15
16 priest burn oil with *f.* 6:15
1 *Chr.* 9:29 appoint. to oversee *f.*
*Neh.* 13:5 where they laid the *f.*
*Cant.* 3:6 who this perf. with *f.*?
4:6 I will get me to the hill of *f.*
14 cinnam. with all trees of *f.*
*Mat.* 2:11 they present. to him *f.*
*Rev.* 18:13 no man buy. their *f.*

**FRANKLY.**
*Luke* 7:42 *f.* forgave them both

**FRAUD.**
*Ps.* 10:7 his mouth is full of *f.*
*Jam.* 5:4 hire kept back by *f.*

**FRAY.**
*Deut.* 28:26 *f.* them, *Jer.* 7:33
*Zec.* 1:21 these are come to *f.*

**FRECKLED.**
*Lev.* 13:39 it is a *f.* spot groweth

**FREE.**
*Ex.* 21:2 in sev. year go out *f.* *Deut.* 15:12; *Jer.* 34:9, 14
5 if servant say, I will not go out *f.*
11 she go out *f.* with. money
26 let him go *f.* for eye's sake
*Lev.* 19:20 not put to dea. not *f.*
*Num.* 5:19 be *f.* from bitter wat.
28 if woman not defiled, be *f.*
*Deut.* 15:18 not hard wh. sen. *f.*
24:5 sh. be *f.* at home one year
1 *Sam.* 17:25 father's house *f.*
2 *Chr.* 29:31 were of *f.* heart off.
*Job* 3:19 servant *f.* from master
39:5 who sent out wild ass *f.*?
*Ps.* 51:12 uphold me with *f.* Sp.
88:5 *f.* am. the dead, like slain
105:20 the king let him go *f.*
*Is.* 58:6 to let the oppressed go *f.*
*Jer.* 34:9 each let servant go *f.*
11 whom they let go *f.* to ret.
*Mat.* 15:6 honor not father, be *f.*
17:26 then are the children *f.*
*Mark* 7:11 it is Corb. he sh. be *f.*
*John* 8:32 truth sh. make you *f.*
33 sayest, Ye shall be made *f.*
36 if Son make you *f. f.* indeed
*Acts* 22:28 but I was *f.* born
*Rom.* 5:15 not as offence, so *f.*
16 *f.* gift is of many offences
18 *f.* gift came upon all men
6:18 being made *f.* from sin, 22
20 were *f.* from righteousness
7:3 husband be dead, she is *f.*
8:2 life made me *f.* from death
1 *Cor.* 7:21 if mayest be made *f.*
9:1 not an apostle, am I not *f.*?
19 though I be *f.* from all men
12:13 by one Spirit, bond or *f.*
*Gal.* 3:28 bond nor *f.* *Col.* 3:11
4:26 Jerus. which is above is *f.*
31 but children of the *f.*
5:1 liberty where. C. made us *f.*
*Eph.* 6:8 receive of L. bond or *f.*
2 *Thes.* 3:1 word have *f.* course
1 *Pet.* 2:16 as *f.* not using liberty
*Rev.* 13:16 *f.* and bond to receive
19:18 flesh of both bond and *f.*

**FREED.**
*Jos.* 9:23 shall none of you be *f.*
*Rom.* 6:7 he dead, is *f.* from sin

**FREEDOM.**
*Lev.* 19:20 wom. not *f.* given her
*Acts* 22:28 with great sum this *f.*

**FREELY.**
*Gen.* 2:16 of every tree f. eat
*Num.* 11:5 the fish we did eat f.
1 *Sam.* 14:30 if people eaten f.
*Ezr.* 2:68 chief fathers offered f.
7:15 king hath offered f. to God
*Ps.* 54:6 will f. sacrifice to thee
*Hos.* 14:4 I will love them f.
*Mat.* 10:8 f. received, f. give
*Acts* 2:29 breth. let me f. speak
26:26 before whom I speak f.
*Rom.* 3:24 justified f. by grace
8:32 also f. give us all things
1 *Cor.* 2:12 the things f. given us
2 *Cor.* 11:7 preach. gospel of G. f.
*Rev.* 21:6 of fountain of life f.
22:17 whosoever will, let him take f.

**FREEMAN.**
1 *Cor.* 7:22 called, is the Lord's f.
*Rev.* 6:15 bond and f. hid them.

**FREE offerings.**
*Ex.* 36:3 f. *offerings* every morn
*Amos* 4:5 publish the f. *offerings*

**FREQUENT.**
2 *Cor.* 11:23 in prisons more f.

**FREEWILL-OFFERING.**
*Lev.* 22:21 a f.-*off.* sh. be perfect
*Deut.* 23:23 f.-*off.* shalt thou keep
*Ezr.* 3:5 willingly offered a f.-*off.*
7:16 silver canst find with f.-*off.*
8:28 silver and gold f.-*offering*

**FREEWILL-OFFERINGS.**
*Deut.* 12:6 thither bring f.-*offer.*
*Ps.* 119:108 accept f.-*offerings*

**FREE-WOMAN.**
*Gal.* 4:22 had two sons by f.-*w.*
23 but he of f. was by promise
31 not child. of bondw. of f.-*w.*

**FRESH, ER.**
*Num.* 11:8 taste of manna as f.
*Job* 29:20 my glory was f. in me
33:25 flesh be f. than a child's
*Ps.* 92:10 anointed with f. oil
*Jam.* 3:12 yield salt water and f.

**FRET.**
*Lev.* 13:55 burn it in fire, it is f.

**FRET, TED, ETH, ING.**
*Lev.* 13:51 is a f. leprosy, 14:44
1 *Sam.* 1:6 to make her f.
*Ps.* 37:1 f. not, 7, 8; *Prov.* 24:19
*Prov.* 19:3 his heart f. against L.
*Is.* 8:21 when hungry they sh. f.
*Ezek.* 16:43 f. me in these things

**FRIEND.**
*Ex.* 33:11 G. spake as man to f.
*Deut.* 13:6 if thy f. entice thee
*Jud.* 14:20 he used as his f.
2 *Sam.* 13:3 Amnon had a f. Jon.
15:37 Hushai, David's f. 16:16
16:17 is this thy kindness to f.?
2 *Chr.* 20:7 to seed of Abr. thy f.
*Job* 6:14 pity be showed from f.
27 and you dig a pit for your f.
*Ps.* 35:14 as though been my f.
41:9 familiar f. lift up his heel
88:18 lover and f. far from me
*Prov.* 6:1 if be surety for thy f.
3 hand of f. make sure thy f.
17:17 a f. loveth at all times
18 surety in presence of his f.
18:24 a f. closer than a brother
19:6 is a f. to him giveth gifts
22:11 the king shall be his f.
27:6 faithful are wounds of a f.
9 man's f. by hearty counsel
10 own f. father's f. forsa. not
14 bless. his f. with loud voice
17 sharpeneth counten. of f.
*Cant.* 5:16 beloved, this is my f.
*Is.* 41:8 art seed of Abra. my f.
*Jer.* 6:21 the neighbor and his f.
19:9 eat every one flesh of his f.
*Hos.* 3:1 belo. of her f. adulteress
*Mic.* 7:5 trust ye not in a f.
*Mat.* 11:19 f. of public. *Luke* 7:34
20:13 f. I do thee no wrong
22:12 f. how camest in hither?
26:50 f. why art thou come?
*Luke* 11:5 shall have a f. and say, f. lend me three loaves
14:10 may say, f. go up higher
*John* 3:29 f. of bridegr. rejoiceth
11:11 our f. Lazarus sleepeth
19:12 thou art not Cesar's f.
*Acts* 12:20 made Blastus their f.
*Jam.* 2:23 Abraham call. f. of G.
4:4 f. of world, is enemy of G.

**FRIENDLY.**
*Jud.* 19:3 to speak f. to her
*Ruth* 2:13 spoken f. to handm.
*Prov.* 18:24 show himself f.

**FRIENDS.**
1 *Sam.* 30:26 D. sent spoil to f.
2 *Sam.* 3:8 kindness to Saul's f.
19:6 lovest enemies hatest f.
1 *K.* 16:11 left not one of his f.
*Est.* 5:10 Haman called for his f.
14 then said wife and f. to him
6:13 Haman told f. every thing
*Job* 2:11 when Job's three f. he.
16:20 my f. scorn me
17:5 speaketh flattery to his f.
19:14 my f. have forgotten me
19 my inward f. abhorred me
21 have pity on me, O ye f.
32:3 Elihu's wrath kind. ag. f.
42:7 kindled ag. Eliphaz and f.
10 when he prayed for his f.
*Ps.* 38:11 f. aloof from my sore
*Prov.* 14:20 the rich hath many f.
16:28 whisperer separat. chief f.
*Prov.* 17:9 repeat. matter, sep. f.
18:24 hath f. show him. friendly
19:4 wealth maketh many f.
7 more do f. go far from him
*Cant.* 5:1 eat, O f. drink, yea
*Jer.* 20:4 thee a terror to thy f.
6 buried there, thou and thy f.
38:22 thy f. have set thee on
*Lam.* 1:2 her f. have dealt treac.
*Zec.* 13:6 wounded in house of f.
*Mark* 3:21 when his f. heard of it
5:19 J. saith, Go home to thy f.
*Luke* 7:6 centurion sent f. to him
12:4 my f. be not afraid of them
14:12 a dinner, call not thy f.
15:6 he calleth together his f.
9 she calleth her f. saying
29 make merry with my f.
16:9 make f. of the mammon
21:16 ye shall be betrayed by f.
23:12 Pilate and Herod made f.
*John* 15:13 down his life for his f.
14 ye are my f. if ye do what I
15 but I have called you f.
*Acts* 10:24 Cornelius called his f.
19:31 who were f. sent to him
27:3 liberty to go to his f.
3 *John* 14 f. salute thee, greet f.

**FRIENDSHIP.**
*Prov.* 22:24 no f. with angry man
*Jam.* 4:4 f. of world is enmity

**FRINGE, S.**
*Num.* 15:38 make f. put on f. 39
*Deut.* 22:12 make thee f.

**To and FRO.**
*Gen.* 8:7 a raven, went *to and f.*
2 *K.* 4:35 Elisha walked *to and f.*
*Job* 1:7 said, Fr. going *to a. f.* 2:2
7:4 I am full of tossings *to and f.*
13:25 a leaf driven *to and f.*?
*Ps.* 107:27 they reel *to and f.*
*Prov.* 21:6 vanity tossed *to and f.*
*Is.* 24:20 earth shall reel *to a. f.*
33:4 running *to and f.* of locusts
49:21 and removing *to and f.*
*Ezek.* 27:19 Dan going *to and f.*
*Zec.* 1:10 L. sent to walk *to a. f.*
11 we have walked *to and f.*
6:7 walk *to a. f.* so they walked *to and f.* through earth
*Eph.* 4:14 no more tossed *to a. f.*
*See* RUN.

**FROGS.**
*Ex.* 8:2 all thy borders with f.
7 the magicians brought up f.
*Ps.* 78:45 he sent f. which destr.
105:30 the land brought forth f.
*Rev.* 16:13 unclean spirits like f.

**FRONT.**
2 *Sam.* 10:9 f. of battle ag. him

**FRONTLETS.**
*Ex.* 13:16 be for f. between eyes
*Deut.* 6:8 shall be as f. 11:18

**FROST.**
*Gen.* 31:40 f. consumed by night
*Ex.* 16:14 as small as the hoar f.
*Job* 37:10 by breath of G. f. given
38:29 f. of heaven, who hath
*Ps.* 78:47 dest. syca. trees with f.
147:16 he scattereth the hoar f.
*Jer.* 36:30 Jeh. body cast out to f.

**FROWARD.**
*Deut.* 32:20 a very f. generation
2 *Sam.* 22:27 with f. wilt show thyself f. *Ps.* 18:26
*Job* 5:13 counsel of f. carried he.
*Ps.* 101:4 a f. heart shall depart
*Prov.* 2:12 man speaketh f. thin.
15 ways crooked, f. in paths
3:32 f. is abomination to Lord
4:24 put away fr. thee f. mouth
6:12 walketh with a f. mouth
8:8 there is nothing f. in them
13 and the f. mouth do I hate
10:31 f. tongue shall be cut out
11:20 of a f. heart, are abomin.
16:28 a f. man soweth strife
30 shut. eyes to devise f. things
17:20 f. heart, findeth no good
21:8 the way of a man is f.
22:5 thorns are in way of the f.
1 *Pet.* 2:18 serv. be subject to f.

**FROWARDLY.**
*Is.* 57:17 he went on f. in way

**FROWARDNESS.**
*Prov.* 2:14 delight in f. of wicked
6:14 f. is in his heart
10:32 mouth of wicked speak. f.

**FROZEN.**
*Job* 38:30 face of the deep is f.

**FRUIT.**
*Gen.* 1:29 every tree wherein is f.
4:3 Cain brought of the f.
*Gen.* 30:2 hath with. f. of womb
*Ex.* 21:22 so that her f. depart
*Lev.* 19:23 count f. uncircumc.
24 fourth year f. shall be holy
25:3 six years shalt gather in f.
27:30 the tithe of f. is the Lord's
*Num.* 13:26 showed th. f. of land
*Deut.* 1:25 the f. in their hands
7:13 he will bless f. of thy land
22:9 lest f. of viney. be defiled
26:2 take of first of all the f.
28:4 blessed be f. of thy body
11 plent. in f. of thy body, 30:9
18 cursed be the f. of thy body
40 thine olive shall cast his f.
42 thy f. shall locust consume
*Jud.* 9:11 sho. I forsake my f.?
2 *Sam.* 16:2 summer f. for young
*Ps.* 21:10 their f. shalt destroy
72:16 f. thereof shake like Leb.
104:13 earth is satisfied with f.
105:35 locusts devoured the f.
127:3 f. of womb is his reward
132:11 of f. of thy body
*Prov.* 8:19 my f. is bet. than gold
10:16 f. of wicked tendeth to sin
11:30 f. of righteous tree of life
12:14 satisfied by f. of mouth
18:20 satisfied with f. of mouth

31:16 with *f.* of her hand she
31 give her of *f.* of her hands
*Cant.* 2:3 his *f.* sweet to my taste
8:11 for the *f.* bring silver
12 that keep *f.* two hundred
*Is.* 3:10 sh. eat *f.* of their doings
4:2 *f.* of earth shall be excellent
10:12 punish *f.* of stout heart
13:18 no pity on *f.* of the womb
14:29 his *f.* be a fiery serpent
27:6 fill face of the world with *f.*
9 the *f.* to take away his sin
28:4 hasty *f.* before the summer
57:19 I create *f.* of lips, peace
65:21 and eat the *f.* of them
*Jer.* 6:19 will bring *f.* of thoug.
7:20 my fury be on *f.* of ground
11.16 olive-tree of goodly *f.*
19 let us destroy tree with *f.*
17:10 *f.* of doings, 21:14; 32:19
*Ezek.* 17:9 cut off the *f.* thereof
19:12 east wind dried up her *f.*
14 fire is gone, hath devour. *f.*
25:4 they shall eat thy *f.* and
36:30 I will multiply *f.* of tree
47:12 nor *f.* thereof be consum.
*Dan.* 4:12 *f.* thereof much, 21
14 and said thus, Scatter his *f.*
*Hos.* 10:13 have eaten *f.* of lies
14:8 from me is thy *f.* come
*Amos* 2:9 destroyed *f.* from ab.
6:12 *f.* of right. into hemlock
7:14 a gatherer of sycamore *f.*
8:1 a basket of summer *f.* 2
*Mic.* 6:7 *f.* of bo. for sin of soul?
7:13 land deso. for *f.* of doings
*Hab.* 3:17 neither *f.* be in vines
*Hag.* 1:10 earth stayed fr. her *f.*
*Zec.* 8:12 vine shall give her *f.*
*Mal.* 1:12 table is pollut. and *f.*
3:11 nor your vine cast her *f.*
*Mat.* 12:33 and his *f.* good, for the tree is known by his *f.*
21:19 let no *f.* grow on thee
34 when time of *f.* drew near
26:29 I will not drink of *f.* of the vine, *Mark* 14:25
*Mark* 12:2 might rec. *f.* of vine.
*Luke* 1:42 bles. is *f.* of thy womb
13:6 sought *f.* and found none
7 I come seeking *f.* on fig-tree
20:10 should give him of the *f.*
*John* 4:36 gather. *f.* to life eter.
*Acts* 2:30 of *f.* of his loins raise
*Rom.* 1:13 I might have some *f.*
6:21 what *f.* had ye in th. thin.
22 have your *f.* unto holiness
15:28 sealed to them this *f.*
*Gal.* 5:22 *f.* of Spirit is love
*Eph.* 5:9 *f.* of Sp. is in all good.
*Phil.* 1:22 this is *f.* of my labor
4:17 desire *f.* that may abound
*Heb.* 13:15 offer *f.* of our lips
*Jam.* 3:18 *f.* of right. so. in peace
5:7 waiteth for the precious *f.*
*Jude* 12 *f.* withereth, without *f.*

*See* EAT.

**Bear, *or* beareth FRUIT.**

2 *K.* 19:30 *b. f.* upward, *Is.* 37:31
*Ezek.* 17:8 that it might *bear f.*
23 in height of Is. it shall *b. f.*
*Hos.* 9:16 they shall *bear* no *f.*
*Joel* 2:22 the tree *beareth* her *f.*
*Mat.* 13:23 is he who *beareth f.*
*Luke* 8:8 good ground, and *b. f.*
13:9 if it *bear f.* well
*John* 15:2 ev. branch in me that *beareth* not *f.* that *beareth f.*
*John* 15:4 branch cannot *b. f.*
8 *b.* much *f.* so be my disciples

**Bring, bringeth, *or* brought forth FRUIT.**

*Lev.* 25:21 *b. forth f.* three years
*Num.* 13:20 and *bring* of the *f.*
*Neh.* 10:35 *b. f.* of all trees, 37
*Ps.* 1:3 *bring. forth f.* in season
92:14 *bring forth f.* in old age
*Jer.* 12:2 wicked *bring forth f.*
*Ezek.* 36:11 they shall *bring f. f.*
47:12 sh. *b. f.* new *f.* for meat
*Hos.* 10:1 Is. *b. f. f.* to himself
*Mat.* 3:10 *bringeth* not *forth* good *f.* 7:19; *Luke* 3:9
7:17 every good tree *b. f.* good *f.*
18 good tree cannot *b. f.* evil *f.*
13:26 when blade *brought f. f.*
*Mark* 4:20 hear word and *b. f. f.*
28 earth *b. forth f.* of herself
*Luke* 8:14 *b.* no *f.* to perfection
15 *bring forth f.* with patience
*John* 12:24 if it die, it *b. f.* much *f.*
15:2 it may *bring forth* more *f.*
6 abideth in me, *b. f.* much *f.*
16 I ordained that you sh. *b. f. f.*
*Rom.* 7:4 we should *b. f. f.* to G.
5 work to *b. f. f.* unto death
*Col.* 1:6 gospel *b. forth f.* in you
*Jam.* 5:18 E. prayed earth *b. f. f.*

*See* FIRST-FRUITS.

**FRUIT-TREES.**

*Neh.* 9:25 possessed *f.-t.* in abun.

**Yield, yieldeth, yielding FRUIT.**

*Gen.* 1:11 fruit-tree *yielding f.*
*Lev.* 25:19 land shall *yield* her *f.*
26:4 trees of field shall *y.* their *f.*
*Deut.* 11:17 land *yield* not her *f.*
*Prov.* 12:12 root of righteous *y. f.*
*Jer.* 17:8 nor shall cease fr. *y. f.*
*Ezek.* 34:27 tree of field shall *y. f.*
36:8 *yield* your *f.* to my people
*Mark* 4:7 thorns chok. it, *y.* no *f.*
8 on good ground, and did *y. f.*
*Heb.* 12:11 *y.* peace. *f.* of righte.
*Rev.* 22:2 *y.* her *f.* every month

**FRUITFUL.**

*Gen.* 1:22 be *f.* 28; 8:17; 9:7; 35:11
17:6 I will make thee exceed. *f.*
20 Ishmael *f.*; 48:4 Jacob *f.*
26:22 made room, we shall be *f.*
28:3 God Almighty make thee *f.*
41:52 for God caused me to be *f.*
49:22 Joseph is a *f.* bough, even
*Ex.* 1:7 children of Israel were *f.*
*Lev.* 26:9 I will make you *f.*
*Ps.* 107:34 *f.* land into barrenness
128:3 thy wife shall be a *f.* vine
148:9 *f.* trees, praise the Lord
*Is.* 5:1 hath vineyard in a *f.* hill
17:6 in the outmost *f.* branches
32:12 shall lament for *f.* vine
*Jer.* 4:26 *f.* place was a wildern.
23:3 they sh. be *f.* and increase
*Ezek.* 19:10 she was *f.*
*Hos.* 13:15 though he be *f.*
*Acts* 14:17 gave rain and *f.*
*Col.* 1:10 *f.* in every good work

*See* FIELD.

**FRUITS.**

*Gen.* 43:11 take of the best *f.*
*Ex.* 22:29 to offer first of ripe *f.*
23:10 six years gather in the *f.*
*Lev.* 25:15 accor. to years of *f.* 10
22 till her *f.* come in, eat old
26:20 nor sh. trees yield their *f.*
*Deut.* 33:14 precious *f.* by sun
2 *Sam.* 9:10 thy sons bring in *f.*
2 *K.* 8:6 restore to her all the *f.*
19:29 plant vineyards, and eat *f.*
*Job* 31:39 if eaten *f.* with. money
*Ps.* 107:37 which may yield *f.*
*Ec.* 2:5 trees of all kind of *f.*
*Cant.* 4:13 orchard with pleas. *f.*
16 my beloved eat pleasant *f.*
6:11 I went to see *f.* of valley
7:13 at gates all manner of *f.*
*Is.* 33:9 B. and Car. shake off *f.*
*Lam.* 4:9 pine aw. for want of *f.*
*Mal.* 3:11 he shall not destroy *f.*
*Mat.* 3:8 *f.* meet for rep. *Luke* 3:8
7:16 ye sh. know them by *f.* 20
21:34 they might receive the *f.*
41 render him *f.* in th. season
43 given to nation bringing *f.*
*Luke* 12:17 where to bestow *f.*
2 *Cor.* 9:10 increase *f.* of righte.
*Phil.* 1:11 filled with *f.* of right.
2 *Tim.* 2:6 first partaker of the *f.*
*Jam.* 3:17 wisdom full of good *f.*
*Rev.* 18:14 *f.* thy soul lusted after
22:2 bare twelve manner of *f.*

*See* FIRST.

**Summer FRUITS.**

2 *Sam.* 16:1 Ziba with 100 of *s. f.*
*Is.* 16:9 thy *summer f.* are fallen
*Jer.* 40:10 gather wine and *s. f.*
48:32 spoiler is fallen on *s. f.*
*Mic.* 7:1 as when gathered *s. f.*

**FRUSTRATE, ETH.**

*Ezr.* 4:5 hired to *f.* their purpose
*Is.* 44:25 *f.* tokens of the liars
*Gal.* 2:21 I do not *f.* grace of G.

**FRYING-PAN.**

*Lev.* 2:7 meat-off. baken in *f.-p.*
7:9 dress. in *f.-p.* be the priest's

**FUEL.**

*Is.* 9:5 with burn. and *f.* of fire
19 people be as *f.* of the fire
*Ezek.* 15:4 vine-t. into fire for *f.* 6
21:32 shalt be for *f.* to fire

**FUGITIVE.**

*Gen.* 4:12 a *f.* shalt thou be
14 I sh. be a *f.* and a vagabond

**FUGITIVES.**

*Jud.* 12:4 ye Gileadites are *f.*
2 *K.* 25:11 *f.* that fell to king
*Is.* 15:5 Moab, his *f.* flee to Zoar
*Ezek.* 17:21 all his *f.* fall by swo.

**FULFIL.**

*Gen.* 29:27 *f.* her week, and we
*Ex.* 5:13 *f.* your daily tasks
23:26 num. of thy days I will *f.*
1 *K.* 2:27 he might *f.* word of L.
1 *Chr.* 22:13 takest heed to *f.*
2 *Chr.* 36:21 *f.* threescore and ten
*Job* 39:2 number months they *f.*?
*Ps.* 20:4 Lord *f.* all thy counsel
5 the Lord *f.* all thy petitions
145:19 *f.* desire of them fear him
*Mat.* 3:15 to *f.* all righteousness
5:17 not come to destr. but to *f.*
*Acts* 13:22 shall *f.* all my will
*Rom.* 2:27 uncircum. if it *f.* law
13:14 to *f.* the lusts thereof
*Gal.* 5:16 sh. not *f.* lusts of flesh
6:2 and so *f.* the law of Christ
*Phil.* 2:2 *f.* ye my joy, that ye be
*Col.* 1:25 to *f.* the word of God
4:17 take heed thou *f.* ministry
2 *Thes.* 1:11 *f.* good pl. of his will
*Jam.* 2:8 if ye *f.* the royal law
*Rev.* 17:17 in hearts to *f.* his will

**FULFILLED.**

*Gen.* 25:24 when her days were *f.*
29:21 give me wife, days are *f.*
50:3 forty days were *f.* for so
*Ex.* 5:14 why not *f.* your task?
*Lev.* 12:4 till days of puri. be *f.* 6
*Num.* 6:13 days of separation *f.*
2 *Sam.* 7:12 when thy days be *f.*
1 *K.* 8:15 with his hand *f.* it
24 *f.* it with hand, 2 *Chr.* 6:15
2 *Chr.* 6:4 hath *f.* that he spake
*Ezr.* 1:1 word of L. might be *f.*
*Job* 36:17 hast *f.* judgment
*Lam.* 2:17 *f.* his word
4:18 our days are *f.* end come
*Ezek.* 5:2 when days of siege *f.*
*Dan.* 4:33 same hour was thi. *f.*
10:3 till three whole weeks *f.*
*Mat.* 1:22 that it might be *f.* 2:15 23; 8:17; 12:17; 13:35; 21:4; 27:35; *John* 12:38; 15:25; 17:12; 18:9, 32; 19:24, 28
2:17 was *f.* that spoken, 27:9
5:18 in no wise pass till all be *f.*
13:14 is *f.* prophecy of Esaias
24:34 shall not pass till all be *f.*

Mark 1:5 the time is f.
13:4 wh. sign when all sh. be f.?
Luke 1:20 words wh. shall be f.
2:43 when they had f. the days
21:22 that all written may be f.
24 until times of Gentiles be f.
22:16 not eat till f. in kin. of G.
24:44 all must be f. spoken by M.
John 3:29 my joy therefore is f.
17:13 my joy f. in themselves
Acts 3:18 showed, he hath so f.
9:23 many days f. the Jews took
12:25 Paul and Bar. f. ministry
13:25 and as John f. his course
27 f. them in condemning him
29 when had f. all written
33 God hath f. the same to us
14:26 to grace for work they f.
Rom. 8:4 right. of law be f. in us
13:8 loveth another hath f. law
2 Cor. 10:6 when obedience is f.
Gal. 5:14 law is f. in one word
Rev. 6:11 killing of breth. be f.
15:8 till seven plagues were f.
17:17 till the words of God be f.
20:3 no more till 1,000 yrs. be f.

See SCRIPTURE.

### FULFILLING.

Ps. 148:8 stormy wi. f. his word

Rom. 13:10 love is the f. of law
Eph. 2:3 f. desires of flesh

### FULL.

Gen. 15:16 iniq. of A. not yet f.
25:8 Abra. old, and f. of years
35:29 Isa. being old, and f. days
41:7 thin ears dev. seven f. ears
Ex. 22:3 sh. make f. restitution
Num. 22:18 house f. of sil. 24:13
Jud. 6:38 bowl f. of water
Ruth 1:21 I went out f. and Lord
2:12 a f. reward be given thee
1 Sam. 18:27 in f. tale to king
2 K. 3:16 make val. f. of ditches
6:17 the mountain f. of horses
7:15 all the way f. of garments
10:21 house of Baal f.
1 Chr. 21:22 grant for f. price, 24
Job 5:26 come to grave in f. age
7:4 f. of tossings to and fro
10:15 I am f. of confusion, see
11:2 man f. of talk be justified?
14:1 few days f. of trouble
20:11 bones f. of sins of youth
21:23 dieth in his f. strength
24 his breasts f. of milk
32:18 I am f. of matter
Ps. 17:14 f. of child. leave rest
69:20 I am f. of heaviness
73:10 waters of a f. cup wrung
74:20 f. of habitations of cruelty
78:25 sent them meat to the f.
104:16 trees of Lord are f. of sap
127:5 hath quiver f. of them
144:13 our garners may be f.
Prov. 17:1 house f. of sacrifices
27:7 f. soul loatheth honey-co.
20 hell and destruction never f.
30:9 lest I be f. and deny thee
Ec. 1:7 into sea, yet sea not f.
11:3 clouds f. of rain
Is. 1:11 f. of burnt offerings
15 your hands are f. of blood
11:9 earth sh. be f. of kno. of L.
25:6 a feast f. of marrow
28:8 for all table are f. of vomit
Jer. 6:11 I am f. of fury of the L.
Lam. 1:1 city that was f. of peo
Ezek. 1:18 rings were f. of eyes
10:12 wheels were f. of eyes
37:1 valley wh. was f. of bones
Joel 2:24 floors sh. be f. of wheat
Mic. 3:8 f. of power by spirit
Hab. 3:3 earth f. of his praise
Zec. 8:5 st. f. of boys and girls
Mat. 6:22 f. of light, Luke 11:36
14:20 of fragments twelve bask. f. Mark 6:43
15:37 left seven baskets f.
23:25 within are f. of extortion
27 f. of dead men's bones, 28
Luke 1:57 now Eliz. f. time came
4:1 Jesus being f. of Holy Gh.
6:25 woe unto you f.
16:20 L. laid at gate f. of sores
John 1:14 among us f. of grace
7:8 my time is not yet f. come
15:11 your joy might be f. 16:24
Acts 2:13 men f. of new wine
6:3 look out men f. of Holy G. 5
9:36 Dorcas f. of good works
13:10 said, O f. of all subtilty
Rom. 1:29 f. of envy, murder
1 Cor. 4:8 now ye are f. now rich
Phil. 4:12 instructed to be f.
18 and abound, I am f.
2 Tim. 4:5 f. proof of ministry
Heb. 5:14 meat to them of f. age
Jam. 3:8 tongue f. of deadly poi.
1 Pet. 1:8 joy unspeak. f. of glo.
2 Pet. 2:14 eyes f. of adultery
1 John 1:4 your joy may be f.
Rev. 4:6 four beasts f. of eyes, 8
5:8 golden vials f. of odors
15:7 gold. vials f. of wrath of G.
17:3 f. of names of blasphemy
4 golden cup f. of abominat.
21:9 sev. vials f. of seven plag.

See ASSURANCE, COMPASSION.

### Is FULL.

Ps. 10:7 mouth is f. Rom. 3:14
26:10 right hand is f. of bribes
29:4 voice of L is f. of majesty
33:5 earth is f. of goodness of L.
65:9 river of G. wh. is f. of wat.
75:8 wine red, it is f. of mixture
104:24 earth is f. of thy riches
119:64 earth, O L. is f. of mercy
Ec. 10:14 a fool is f. of words
Is. 2:7 land is f. of silver, is f.
8 their land also is f. of idols
6:3 whole earth is f. of his glo.
Jer. 5:27 cage is f. of birds,
Ezek. 7:23 land is f. of crimes
9:9 land is f. of blood, city is f.
Nah. 3:1 is all f. of lies and rob.

Luke 11:34 body is f. of light, is f.
39 inward part is f. of ravening

### To the FULL.

Ex. 16:3 did eat bread to the f. 8
Lev. 26:5 shall eat bread to the f.

### FULLER, S.

2 K. 18:17 in highway of the f. field, Is. 7:3; 36:2
Mal. 3:2 like refiner's fire, f. soap
Mark 9:3 no f. on earth can wh.

### FULLY.

Num. 14:24 C. that followed me f.
Ec. 8:11 heart of sons of m. is f.
Nah. 1:10 dev. as stubble f. dry
Acts 2:1 day of Pentec. was f. c.
Rom. 4:21 being f. persuaded,
14:5 let ev. man be f. persuaded
2 Tim. 3:10 hast f. kno. my doc.
Rev. 14:18 thrust sickle, grapes f.

### FULLNESS.

1 Chr. 16:32 let sea roar and the f. thereof, Ps. 96:11; 98:7
Ps. 16:11 in thy pres. is f. of joy
24:1 L.'s and f. 1 Cor. 10:26, 28
50:12 world mine, and f. 89:11
John 1:16 his f. have we received
Rom. 11:12 much more their f.?
25 f. of the Gentiles be come
15:29 shall come in f. of gospel
Gal. 4:4 wh. f. of time was come
Eph. 1:10 in f. of times
23 f. of him that filleth
3:19 be filled with all f. of God
4:13 come to stature of f. of C.
Col. 1:19 in him sho. all f. dwell
2:9 in him dwelleth f. of God.

### FURBISH, ED.

Jer. 46:4 f. spears, put on briga.
Ezek. 21:9 sword sharpened. f. 10
11 given to be f.; 28 sword f.

### FURIOUS.

Prov. 22:24 with f. man not go
29:22 f. man aboundeth in tran.
Ezek. 5:15 exec. judg. in f. 25:17
Dan. 2:12 Nebuchad. was very f.
Nah. 1:2 Lord revengeth and is f.

### FURIOUSLY.

2 K. 9:20 like Jehu, he driveth f.

### FURLONGS.

Luke 24:13 Emmaus from J. 60 f.
John 6:19 had rowed about 25 f.
11:18 Bethany nigh J. abo. 15 f.
Rev. 14:20 by space of 1,600 f.
21:16 he measured city, 12,000 f.

### FURNACE, S.

Gen. 15:17 smoking f. burning
19:28 smoke went as smo. of f.
Ex. 9:8 handf. of ashes of f. 10
19:18 ascended as smoke of f.
Deut. 4:20 L. hath taken out of f.
1 K. 8:51 fr. midst of f. Jer. 11:4
Neh. 3:11 rep. tower of f. 12:38
Ps. 12:6 silver tried in f. of earth
Prov. 17:3 f. for gold, 27:21
Is. 31:9 fire in Zion, f. in Jerusa.
48:10 chosen in f. of affliction
Ezek. 22:18 Is. dross in mid. of f.
20 as tin in the midst of f. 22
Dan. 3:6 into midst of fiery f. 11
Mat. 13:42 cast into f. of fire, 50
Rev. 1:15 feet as if burned in a f.
9:2 as the smoke of a great f.

### FURNISH.

Deut. 15:14 thou shalt f. him
Ps. 78:19 G. f. table in wilder.?
Is. 65:11 f. the drink-offering
Jer. 46:19 f. to go into captivity

### FURNISHED.

1 K. 9:11 Hiram f. Sol. with ced.
Prov. 9:2 hath also f. her table
Mat. 22:10 wed. f. with guests
Mark 14:15 a room f. Luke 22:12
2 Tim. 3:17 f. unto all good wor.

### FURNITURE.

Gen. 31:34 Rachel put in cam. f.
Ex. 31:7 and his f. 39:33
35:14 the candlestick and his f.
Nah. 2:9 end of all pleasant f.

### FURROW, S.

Job 31:38 or f. thereof complain
39:10 canst bind unicorn in f.?
Ps. 65:10 thou settlest f. thereof
129:3 plough. made long their f.
Ezek. 17:7 might water it by f.
10 it shall wither in the f.
Hos. 10:4 hemlock in f. of field
12:11 their altars as heaps in f.

### FURTHER.

Job 38:11 hither. come, but no f.
40:5 but I will proceed no f.
Ec. 12:12 f. my son, be admon.
Mat. 26:65 what f. need of wit.? Mark 14:63; Luke 22:71

Luke 24:28 tho' he would gone f.
Acts 4:17 spread no f. am. people
24:4 be not f. tedious unto thee
27:28 gone a little f. th. sounded
2 Tim. 3:9 shall proceed no f.
Heb. 7:11 what f. need an. priest

**FURTHER, ED, Verb.**
Ezr. 8:36 f. peo. and house of G.
Ps. 140:8 O L. f. not wicked dev.
**FURTHERANCE.**
Phil. 1:12 rather to f. of gospel
25 sh. abide with you for yo. f.
**FURTHERMORE.**
Ex. 4:6 Lord said f. to Moses
Ezek. 8:6 Lord said f. to Ezekiel
**FURY.**
Gen. 27:44 thy brother's f. turn
Job 20:23 God cast f. of wrath
Is. 27:4 f. is not in me
34:2 his f. is upon their armies
51:13 bec. of f. of oppressor; and where is f. of oppressor?
17 Jer. wh. has drunk cup of f.
20 are full of f. of the Lord
22 even dregs of cup of my f.
59:18 repay f. to adversaries
63:3 trample them in my f.
5 my f. it upheld me, 6
Jer. 4:4 lest my f. come like fire
6:11 I am full of f. of the Lord
21:5 will fight against you in f.
12 lest my f. go out like fire
23:19 gone forth in f. 30:23
25:15 the wine-cup of this f.
36:7 great f. L. hath pronounced
Lam. 4:11 L. hath accomplish. f.
Ezek. 5:13 cause my f. to rest
6:12 will I accomplish my f.
8:18 therefore will I deal in f.
13:13 stormy wind in my f.
16:38 I will give thee blood in f.
19:12 she was plucked up in f.
20:33 with f. pou. out will I rule
21:17 I will cause my f. to rest
24:8 it might cause f. to come
13 till I have caused f. to rest
38:18 that my f. shall come up
Dan. 3:13 Nebuchadnez. in f. 19
8:6 ran unto him in the f.
9:16 let thy f. be turned away
11:44 shall go forth with great f.
Mic. 5:15 execute f. on heathen
Zec. 8:2 jealous with great f.
See POUR, POURED.

# G

GAAL. Jud. 9:41
GABRATHA. John 19:13
GABRIEL. Dan. 8:16; 9:21; Luke 1:19, 26
**GAD.**
Gen. 30:11 she called his name G.
35:26 sons of Zilp. G. and Asher
46:16 the sons of G. Num. 1:24; 26:15, 18
49:19 G. a troop shall overcome
Num. 1:14 prin. of G. 2:14; 7:42
32:1 ch. of G. had cat. 2, 29, 33
Deut. 27:13 mount E. to curse G.
Jos. 4:12 children of G. passed over
22:9 chil. of G. returned fr. Shi.
2 Sam. 24:11 G. D.'s seer, 1 Chr. 29:9
1 Chr. 29:29 in book of G. 12:14
Ezek. 48:27 a portion for G. 34
**Tribe of GAD.**
Num. 1:25 of t. of G. 45,650, 2:14
Jos. 20:8 out of the tribe of G.
Rev. 7:5 tribe of G. sealed 12,000
GADARENES. Mark 5:1; Luke 8:26, 37
**GADDEST.**
Jer. 2:36 why g. thou to change?
**GADITE, S.**
Deut. 3:12 land gave I unto G. 16
1 Chr. 12:8 G. separated, 26:32
**GAIN, Substantive.**
Jud. 5:19 kings of C. took no g.
Job 22:3 it g. to make way per.?
Prov. 1:19 every one greedy of g.
3:14 g. is better than fine gold
15:27 is greedy of g. troubleth
28:8 by unjust g. increaseth
Is. 33:15 despis. g. of oppression
56:11 for his g. from quarter
Ezek. 22:13 smit. hand at dish. g.
27 princes wolves to get dis. g.
Dan. 11:39 divide land for g.
Mic. 4:13 I will consec. g. to L.
Acts 16:16 bro. masters much g.
19:24 no small g. to craftsmen
2 Cor. 12:17 did I make g. of y.?
18 Titus make a g. of you?
Phil. 1:21 live is Christ, die is g.
3:7 what things were g. to me
1 Tim. 6:5 supposing g. is godli.
6 godliness with content. is g.
Jam. 4:13 buy, sell, and get g.
**GAIN, Verb.**
Dan. 2:8 that ye would g. time
Mat. 16:26 g. who. wor. and lose soul, Mark 8:36; Luke 9:25
1 Cor. 9:19 I might g. the more
20 might g. Jews; 22 g. weak
21 might g. them without law
**GAINED.**
Job 27:8 wh. hope tho' hath g.?
Ezek. 22:12 thou hast greedily g.
Mat. 18:15 hast g. thy brother
25:17 that received two g. 22
20 have g. besides five talents
Luke 19:15 how much ev. man g.
16 Lord, thy pound hath g. ten
18 Lord, thy pound hath g. five
Acts 27:21 to have g. this harm
**GAINS.**
Acts 16:19 hope of g. was gone
**GAINSAY, ERS.**
Luke 21:15 advers. not able to g.
Tit. 1:9 might be able to conv. g.
**GAINSAYING.**
Acts 10:29 came I to you with. g.
Rom. 10:21 hands to a g. people
Jude 11 perished in g. of Korah
**GAIUS.**
Acts 19:29 G. man of Macedonia
20:4 G. of Derbe accompan. P.
Rom. 16:23 G. host saluteth you
1 Cor. 1:14 I baptiz. none but G.
3 John 1 un. the well-beloved G.
**GALATIA.**
Acts 16:6; 1 Cor. 16:1; 2 Tim. 4:10
1 Pet. 1:1 scat. through Pont. G.
GALATIANS. Gal. 3:1
GALBANUM. Ex. 30:34
GALEED. Gen. 31:47, 48
**GALILEE.**
Jos. 20:7 G. for a city of refuge
1 K. 9:11 gave H. 20 cities in G.
Is. 9:1 did more afflict her in G.
Mat. 2:22 J. in the parts of G.
3:13 cometh J. fr. G. Mark 1:9
4:15 G. of Gent 21:11 Js. of G.
15:29 sea of G. 26:32; 27:55
Mark 1:39 throughout G. 15:41
Luke 4:14, 44; 23:5, 55; John 7:41, 52
Acts 1:11 men of G.; 5:37 G. rose
9:31 churches rest through. G.
10:37 word began from G.
13:31 seen of them from G.
**GALILEAN, S.**
Mark 14:70 art a G. Luke 22:59
Luke 13:1 told him of the G.
23:6 asked whe. man were a G.
John 4:45 was come, G. rec. him
Acts 2:7 all these that speak, G.?
**GALL.**
Deut. 29:18 a root that beareth g.
32:32 grapes are grapes of g.
Job 16:13 he poureth out my g.
20:14 his meat is the g. of asps
25 sword cometh out of his g.
Ps. 69:21 gave me g. for meat
Jer. 8:14 G. hath given water g.
9:15 will give water of g. 23:15
Lam. 3:5 compassed me with g.
19 remembering worm. and g.
Amos 6:12 turned judg. into g.
Mat. 27:34 vine. mingled with g.
Acts 8:23 art in g. of bitterness
**GALLANT.**
Is. 33:21 nor shall g. ship pass
**GALLERY, IES.**
Cant. 7:5 king is held in the g.
Ezek. 41:15 measured g. thereof
42:3 against pave. g. against g.
**GALLEY.**
Is. 33:21 wherein shall go no g.
**GALLIM.**
1 Sam. 25:44 Phal. of G. Is. 10:30
GALLIO. Acts 18:12, 17
**GALLOWS.**
Est. 6:4 to hang Mordecai on g.
7:10 hanged Haman on g. 8:7
9:13 ten sons be hanged on g. 25
**GAMALIEL.**
Num. 1:10; 2:20; 7:54, 59; 10:23
Acts 5:34 P. named G.; 23:3 feet
GAMMADIM. Ezek. 27:11
**GAP, S.**
Ezek. 13:5 have not gone up to g.
22:30 that should stand in g.
**GAPED.**
Job 16:10 ha. g. on me. Ps. 22:13
**GARDEN.**
Gen. 2:15 and put him in the g.
3:23 Lord sent him forth from g.
13:10 as g. of Lord, Is. 51:3
Deut. 11:10 waterest it as g.
1 K. 21:2 may have it for g.
Job 8:16 branch shoot. in his g.
Cant. 4:12 g. enclosed is my sis.
16 blow on g. let him come g.
5:1 I am come into my g.
6:2 my beloved gone to his g. 11
Is. 1:8 daugh. of Z. as lodge in g.
30 as a g. which hath no water
58:11 shalt be like a watered g.
61:11 g. causeth things sown
Jer. 31:12 souls be as a watered g.
Lam. 2:6 taberna. as it were of g.
Ezek. 28:13 in Eden the g. of G.
31:8 cedars in g. of G. not hide
9 trees in g. of God envied him
36:35 desolate land like g. of E.
Joel 2:3 land as g. of Eden before
Luke 13:19 took and cast into g.
John 18:1 over Ced. where was g.
26 did not I see thee in the g.?
19:41 a g. and in g. a sepulchre
**GARDENS.**
Num. 24:6 as g. by river side
Ec. 2:5 I made me g. and orch.
Cant. 4:15 a fountain of g.
6:2 feed in g. and gather lilies
8:13 thou that dwellest in the g.
Is. 1:29 sh. be confounded for g.
65:3 a peo. that sacrificeth in g.
66:17 purify themselves in g.
Jer. 29:5 plant g. eat fruit, 28
Amos 4:9 blasting, when g. incr.
9:14 they shall also make g.

**GARDENER.**

*John* 20:15 supposing he been *g.*

**GARLANDS.**

*Acts* 14:13 priest bro. oxen and *g.*

**GARLICK.**

*Num.* 11:5 we rem. *g.* eat in Eg.

**GARMENT.**

*Gen.* 9:23 Sh. and Japhet took *g*
25:25 first red, like a hairy *g.*
39:12 caught Joseph by his *g.*
15 he left his *g.* with me, 18
16 laid up his *g.* till lord came
*Lev.* 13:47 *g.* wh. plag. of lep. 49
51 if plague be spread in the *g*
59 plague of lep. in *g.* 14:55
15:17 *g.* whereon seed of copula.
19:19 *g.* mingled, *Deut.* 22:11
*Deut.* 22:5 man not put on w. *g.*
*Jos.* 7:21 a goodly Babylonish *g.*
*Jud.* 8:25 spread *g.* and cast
1 *K.* 11:29 Jero. clad with new *g.*
*Ezr.* 9:5 rent *g.* and mantle
*Est.* 8:15 Mor. went *g.* of purple
*Job* 13:28 a *g.* that is moth-eaten
30:18 by force of dis. *g.* changed
38:9 I made the cloud the *g.*
41:13 can discover face of *g.*?
*Ps.* 69:11 I made sackcloth my *g.*
73:6 violence cover. them as *g.*
102:26 wax old like *g.* *Is.* 50:9; 51:6; *Heb.* 1:11
104:2 cov. with lights as with *g.*
6 cov. with the deep as with *g.*
109:18 clothed with cursing as *g.*
*Prov.* 20:16 *g.* is surety, 27:13
25:20 taketh *g.* in cold weather
30:4 hath bound waters in a *g.*?
*Is.* 51:8 moth sh. eat them like *g.*
61:3 *g.* of praise for spirit
*Ezek.* 18:7 cov. naked with *g.* 16
*Dan.* 7:9 *g.* was white as snow
*Mic.* 2:8 pull off robe with the *g.*
*Hag.* 2:12 holy flesh in skirt of *g.*
*Zec.* 13:4 nei. shall wear rough *g.*
*Mal.* 2:16 cover. violence with *g.*
*Mat.* 9:16 new cloth to old *g.* *Mark* 2:21; *Luke* 5:36
20 touched hem of *g.* 21; 14:36; *Mark* 5:27; *Luke* 8:44
22:11 had not wedding *g.* 12
*Mark* 13:16 not turn back take *g.*
*Luke* 22:36 let him sell *g.*
*Acts* 12:8 cast thy *g.* about thee
*Jude* 23 hating *g.* spotted by fle.
*Rev.* 1:13 clothed with *g.*

**GARMENTS.**

*Gen.* 35:2 clean. change your *g.*
38:14 Tamar put widow's *g.* off
49:11 washed his *g.* in wine
*Ex.* 28:3 Aaron's *g.* 20 consecrate
29:21 blood on A.'s *g.* *Lev.* 8:30
*Lev.* 6:11 *g.* on other *g.* 16:23, 24
*Num.* 15:38 fringes in bord. of *g.*
20:26 strip A. of *g.* put on E. 28
*Jos.* 9:5 Gibeonites brou. old *g.*
1 *Sam.* 18:4 J. gave David his *g.*
2 *Sam.* 10:4 cut off their *g.* in the middle, 1 *Chr.* 19:4
2 *K.* 5:26 is it time to receive *g.*
7:15 all the way was full of *g.*
*Ezr.* 2:69 gave 100 priests' *g.*
*Neh.* 7:70 Tirsh. 530 priests' *g.*
72 the peo. gave 67 priests' *g.*
*Job* 37:17 *g.* warm, when quieteth
*Ps.* 2:18 part my *g.* among them
45:8 all thy *g.* smell of myrrh
133:2 ointm. went to skirt of *g.*
*Ec.* 9:8 let thy *g.* be alw. white
*Cant.* 4:11 smell of *g.* smell of L.
*Is.* 9:5 battle is *g.* rolled in blood
52:1 put on beautiful *g.* O Jer.
59:6 their webs sh. not beco. *g.*
17 put on the *g.* of vengeance.
61:10 clothed me with *g.* of sal.
63:1 cometh with dyed *g.* 3
*Ezek.* 16:18 took. thy broidered *g.*
42:14 there shall lay their *g.*
*Dan.* 3:21 in coats and other *g.*
*Joel* 2:13 rend heart, and not *g.*
*Zec.* 3:3 J. clothed wi. filthy *g.* 4
*Mat.* 21:8 spread *g.* *Mark* 11:8
23:5 they enlarge borders of *g.*
27:35 parted his *g.* *Mark* 15:24
*Mark* 10:50 Bartim. casting his *g.*
11:7 cast *g.* on colt, *Luke* 19:35
*Luke* 24:4 two men in shining *g.*
*John* 13:4 laid aside *g.* and took
*Acts* 9:39 coats and *g.* Dor. made
*Jam.* 5:2 your *g.* are moth-eaten
*Rev.* 3:4 few names not defiled *g.*
16:15 blessed that keepeth his *g.*

**Holy GARMENTS.**

*Ex.* 28:2 make *h. g.* for Aaron, 4
31:10 wisdom to make *holy g.*
*Lev.* 16:4 *h. g.* he sh. wash, 32

**GARNER, S.**

*Ps.* 144:13 our *g.* may be full
*Joel* 1:17 the *g.* are laid desolate
*Mat.* 3:12 wheat into *g.* *Lu.* 3:17

**GARNISH, ED.**

2 *Chr.* 3:6 he *g.* the house with
*Job* 26:13 by S. he *g.* heavens
*Mat.* 12:44 sw. and *g.* *Luke* 11:25
23:29 *g.* sepulchres of righteous
*Rev.* 21:19 foundations of wall *g.*

**GARRISON, S.**

1 *Sam.* 10:5 hill where *g.* of Phil.
13:3 Jonathan smote *g.* of Phil.
14:1 to the Philistines' *g.* 6
15 the *g.* and spoilers trembled
2 *Sam.* 8:6 David put *g.* in Syria, 1 *Chr.* 18:6
14 put *g.* in Ed. 1 *Chr.* 18:13
23:14 *g.* of Philistines was then in Bethlehem, 1 *Chr.* 11:16
2 *Chr.* 17:2 Jehosh. set *g.* in Ju.
*Ezek.* 26:11 strong *g.* go down
2 *Cor.* 11:32 gov. kept city wi. *g.*

**GAT.**

2 *Sam.* 8:13 David *g.* him a name
1 *K.* 1:1 cov. him, but *g.* no heat
*Ps.* 116:3 pains of hell *g.* hold
*Ec.* 2:8 I *g.* men-singers
*Lam.* 5:9 *g.* our bread with peril

**GATE.**

*Gen.* 22.17 poss. *g.* of enem. 24:60
28:17 this is the *g.* of heaven
*Ex.* 32:27 go in and out *g.* to *g.*
*Deut.* 21:19 bring him to *g.*
*Jud.* 16:3 Sams. took doors of *g.*
*Ruth* 4:1 then went Boaz to *g.*
2 *Sam.* 23:15 water of Bethlehem by *g.* 16; 1 *Chr.* 11:18
2 *K.* 7:17 lord have charge of *g.*
1 *Chr.* 26:13 cast lots for every *g.*
*Neh.* 13:19 commanded *g.* be shut
*Est.* 4:2 M. before king's *g.* 6:12
*Ps.* 118:20 his *g.* of the Lord
*Is.* 14:31 howl, O *g.* cry, O city
24:12 *g.* smit. with destruction
28:6 turn battle to the *g.*
*Lam.* 5:14 elders have ceased from *g.*
*Ezek.* 11:1 at door of *g.* 25 men
43:4 glory of Lord by way of *g.*
44:2 this *g.* shall be shut, none
45:19 put blood on posts of *g.*
46:1 *g.* of inner court be shut, 2
48:31 one *g.* of R. one *g.* of Ju.
*Mic.* 1:9 come into *g.* of my peo.
*Mat.* 7:13 enter in at straight *g.* wide is *g.* broad is way, 14; *Luke* 13:24
*Luke* 7:12 came nigh *g.* of city
16:20 beggar Lazarus laid at *g.*
*Acts* 10:17 men fr. C. stood be. *g.*
12:10 the iron *g.* wh. opened.
14 Rhoda opened not *g.*
*Heb.* 13:12 J. suffered without *g.*
*Rev.* 21:21 several *g.* of one pearl
*See* ENTERING, ENTERETH.

**His GATE.**

*Prov.* 17:19 exalteth *h. g.*

**At the GATE.**

2 *K.* 11:6 *at the g.* of Sur. third *at the g.* 2 *Chr.* 23:5
2 *Chr.* 24:8 *at g.* of house of L.
*Est.* 5:13 M. sitting *at* king's *g.*
*Acts* 3:2 daily *at g.* of temple
10 sat for alms *at* beautiful *g.*

**High GATE.**

2 *Chr.* 23:20 came thro. *high g.*
27:3 Joth. built *high g.* of house
*Jer.* 20:2 Jerem. in stocks in *h. g.*

**In the GATE.**

*Gen.* 19:1 Lot sat *in the g.* of So.
*Ex.* 32:26 M. stood *in g.* of camp
*Jud.* 16:2 laid wait for S. *in t. g.*
*Ruth* 4:11 peo. *in g.* said
2 *Sam.* 3:27 J. took Abner *in t. g.*
2 *K.* 7:20 peo. trod on him *in t. g.*
*Est.* 2:19 sat *in t.* king's *g.* 21
5:9 Ha. saw him *in t.* king's *g.*
*Job* 5:4 children crushed *in t. g.*
31:21 I saw my help *in the g.*
*Ps.* 69:12 sit *in t. g.*
127:5 speak with enemies *in g.*
*Prov.* 22:22 oppress affic. *in t. g.*
*Is.* 29:21 snare for him rep. *in g.*
*Jer.* 7:2 *in t. g.* of Lord's house
38:7 king sitting *in t. g.* of B.
*Dan.* 2:49 Daniel sat *in t. g.*
*Amos* 5:10 him that rebuk. *in g.*
12 they turn aside poor *in t. g.*
15 establish judgment *in the g.*

**Old GATE.**

*Neh.* 3:6 *old g.* repaired Jehoiada
12:39 priests went above *old g.*

**Prison GATE.**

*Neh.* 12:39 th. stood still in *p. g.*

**Sheep GATE.**

*Neh.* 12:39 went even unto *s. g.*

**Valley GATE.**

2 *Chr.* 26:9 U. built tow. at *v. g.*
*Neh.* 2:13 went out by *g.* of *v.* 15
3:13 *valley g.* repaired Hanun

**Water GATE.**

*Neh.* 3:26 Nethin. dwelt ag. *w. g*
8:1 street before *water g.* 3, 16
12:37 priests went even to *w. g.*

**GATES.**

*Deut.* 12:12 rejoice with. your *g.*
*Jos.* 6:26 in youngest son set up *g.* 1 *K.* 16:34
*Jud.* 5:8 new gods, war in *g.*
11 people of Lord shall go to *g.*
2 *Chr.* 31:2 A. app. to prai. in *g.*
*Neh.* 1:3 *g.* burnt, 2:3 13, 17
12:30 priests and Lev. purifi. *g.* 9
*Ps.* 9:14 thy praise in the *g.*
24:7 lift up your heads, O ye *g.*
87:2 Lord loveth the *g.* of Zion
100:4 enter into *g.* with thanks.
107:16 he hath broken *g.* of br.
118:19 open *g.* of righteousness
*Prov.* 1:21 in opening of *g.* 8:3
8:34 watching daily at my *g.*
14:19 wicked at *g.* of righteous
31:23 husband is known in *g.*
31 let own works praise in *g.*
*Is.* 3:26 and her *g.* shall lament
26:2 open *g.* righteous may ent.
38:10 I shall go to *g.* of grave
45:1 open bef. him two-leaved *g.*
2 I will break the *g.* of brass
62:10 go through, go through *g.*
*Jer.* 14:2 Jud. mourn. *g.* languish
15:7 fan them with fan in *g.*
17:21 no burden on sab. by *g.* 24
25 then shall enter into *g.* 22:4
22:19 cast forth beyond the *g.*
*Lam.* 1:4 Zion's *g.* are desolate
2:9 her *g.* are sunk into ground

Ezek. 21:15 point of sw. ag. th. g.
22 battering rams aga. the g.
26:2 broken that was g. of peo.
Ob. 11 foreigners entered g.
Nah. 2:6 g. of rivers sh. be open.
Zec. 8:16 truth and peace in g.
Mat. 16:18 g. of hell not prevail
Acts 9:24 they watched g.
Rev. 21:12 city had twelve g. at
g. twelve angels
13 east thr. g. on north thr. g.
21 twelve g. were twel. pearls
25 g. of it shall not be shut
See BARS, DEATH.

**Thy GATES.**

Ex. 20:10 str. wi. t. g. Deut. 5:14
Deut. 6:9 write them t. g. 11:20
12:15 eat flesh in t. g. 17, 18, 21
14:21 str. in t. g.; 27 Le. in t. g.
28 tithe in t. g.; 29 wid. in t. g.
16:5 passover in thy g.; Levite
in thy g. 14; 26:12
31:12 gather peo. within t. g.
Ps. 122:2 feet stand wi. t. g. O J.
Is. 54:12 I will make t. g. of car.
60:11 thy g. sh. be open contin.
18 walls salvation, thy g. praise

**GATH.**

1 Sam. 5:8 ark be car. to G. 6:17
2 Sam. 1:20 tell it not in G.
21:22 to giant in G. 1 Chr. 20:8
2 K. 12:17 Hazael fought ag. G.
1 Chr. 18:1
Amos 6:2 to G. of Philistines
Mic. 1:10 declare ye it not at G.

**GATHER.**

Gen. 31:46 g. stones, th. took st.
41:35 g. all food of those years
Ex. 5:7 g. straw; 12 g. stubble
9:19 g. cattle; 16:4 g. cer. rate
16:5 g. twice as m.; 26 six da. g.
23:10 six y. sow and g. Lev. 25:3
Lev. 19:9 sh. not g. glean. 23:22
10 thou sh. not g. every grape
Num. 10:4 trumpet, princes g.
11:16 g. seventy men of elders
19:9 man clean g. ashes
Deut. 28:30 vine. and not g. 39
38 much seed out, g. little in
30:3 g. from all nations, Ezek.
36:34
2 K. 4:39 went to field to g. her.
22:20 g. to fathers, 2 Chr. 34:28
2 Chr. 24:5 g. money to rep. ho.
Job 24:6 g. vintage of wicked
34:14 g. to himself his spirit
39:12 seed, and g. it into barn?
Ps. 26:9 g. not soul wi. sinners
104:28 that givest them they g.
106:47 g. us from am. heathen
Prov. 28:8 g. for him pity poor
Ec. 2:26 travail to g. and heap
Is. 34:15 owl g. under shadow
40:11 shall g. lambs with arms
43:5 will g. thee from the west
54:7 with great mercies will I g.
62:10 highway, g. out the stones
66:18 will g. all nations
Jer. 6:1 g. to flee; 7:18 chil. g. w.
9:22 none sh. g.; 10:17 g. up w.
29:14 g. you from all nations
31:8 g. from coasts of earth,
32:37; Ezek. 20:34, 41; 34:13
31:10 scatter Israel will g. him
Ezek. 11:17 will g. you fr. people
16:37 I will g. all thy lovers
22:19 will g. you to midst of J.
20 as g. silver so I g. you, 21
24:4 g. pieces; 29:13 will g. Eg.
Hos. 8:10 hired am. nat. I will g.
9:6 Egypt shall g. them up.
Joel 2:6 faces shall g. blackness
16 g. people, g. children
3:2 I will g. all nations
Mic. 2:12 I will g. remnant of Is.
4:6 g. her driven, Zep. 3:19
12 he shall g. them as sheaves
5:1 g. in troops, O da. of troops
Nah. 2:10 faces of all g. blackn.
Hab. 1:9 they shall g. captivity
15 and g. them in their drag.
Zep. 3:18 will g. th. are sorrowf.
Zec. 10:8 I will hiss and g. 10
Mat. 3:12 g. wheat, Luke 3:17
6:26 nor do they g. into barns
7:16 g. grapes of th.? Luke 6:44
13:28 wilt thou that we g. them
29 while ye g. up the tares
30 burn tares but g. the wheat
41 shall g. out of his kingdom
25:26 I g. wh. I have not strewed
Luke 13:34 as hen doth g. brood
John 6:12 g. fragments that rem.
15:6 men g. them and cast them
Rev. 14:8 g. clusters of vine
16:14 g. them to battle of that
day

**GATHER together.**

Gen. 34:30 few they shall g. tog.
49:1 g. selves to. ye sons of J. 2
Lev. 8:3 g. congregation of Israel
together, Num. 8:9
Num. 21:16 g. people together,
Deut. 4:10; 31:12
2 Sam. 12:28 g. the rest together
1 Chr. 16:35 O God, and g. us to.
22:2 com. to g. tog. strangers
Est. 2:3 g. together fair virgins
4:16 g. tog. Jews in Shushan
Job 11:10 if he g. t. who hinder
Ps. 50:5 g. saints tog. unto me
104:22 they g. themselves tog.
Ec. 3:5 a time to g. stones tog.
Is. 11:12 g. to. dispersed of Jud.
49:18 g. to. come to me, 60:4
Jer. 4:5 blow trumpet, cry g. to.
Zep. 2:1 g. to. yea, g. to. O nat.
Mat. 13:30 g. together first tares
24:31 g. t. his elect, Mark 13:27
John 11:52 g. t. in one, Eph. 1:10
Rev. 19:17 g. to. to supper of G.
20:8 to g. Gog and Magog tog.

**GATHERED.**

Gen. 25:8 Abr. was g. to his peo.
17 Ishmael g.; 35:29 Isaac g.
49:29 J. was g. to his people, 33
Ex. 16:18 he that g. much, he
that g. little 2 Cor. 8:15
Lev. 23:39 when ye have g.
Num. 11:32 g. qu.? 15:32 g. stic.
20:24 Aaron be g. to people, 26
27:13 Moses g. to his people,
31:2; Deut. 32:50
Jud. 1:7 g. meat under table
6:34 Abiezer was g. after him
1 Sam. 5:8 th. g. lords of Philist.
22:2 ev. one in distress g. to D.
2 Sam. 14:14 wat. spilt can. be g.
2 K. 22:20 Josiah be g. to grave
in peace, 2 Chr. 34:28
Job 27:19 rich lie, but not be g.
Ps. 107:3 g. them out of lands
Prov. 27:25 herbs of mount. are g.
30:4 hath g. wind in fists?
Is. 5:2 and g. out the stones
10:14 gathereth eggs, have I g.
27:12 g. one by one, O Israel
34:15 vultures g.; 16 Sp. g. th.
49:5 Is. not g. yet I be glorious
Jer. 3:17 all nations be g.
Ezek. 28:25 wh. I have g. hou. of
38:13 hast thou g. thy company
39:28 have g. them to own land
Mic. 7:1 when g. sum. of fruits
Mat. 13:40 as tares are g.
47 net cast and g. of every kind
25:32 bef. him be g. all nations
27:27 g. to him the whole band
John 11:47 g. chief priests and
Acts 28:3 Paul g. bundle of sticks
Rev. 14:19 angel g. vine of earth

**GATHERED together.**

Ex. 8:14 g. them to. on heaps
Num. 11:22 fish of sea be g. tog.
Jud. 20:1 congreg. g. tog. as one
man, 11; Ezr. 3:1; Neh. 8:1
Job 30:7 under nettles were g. t.
Ps. 47:9 princes of peo. are g. t.
102:22 people g. tog. to serve L.
Hos. 1:11 chil. of Judah be g. t.
Zec. 12:3 tho. all people be g. t.
Mat. 18:20 two or three are g. t.
23:37 how often would I have g.
children to. Luke 13:34
24:28 be g. tog. Luke 17:37
Mark 1:33 all the city was g. t.
Luke 15:13 younger son g. all t.
Acts 4:26 rulers g. to. against L.
12:12 many g. together praying
1 Cor. 5:4 g. t. and my spirit
Rev. 16:16 g. t. into pl. Armaged.
19:19 beast and army g. t.

**GATHERER, S.**

Jer. 6:9 hand as grape g. into
49:9 if grape g. come, Ob. 5
Amos 7:14 I was g. of sycamore

**GATHERETH.**

Num. 19:10 that g. ashes shall
Ps. 33:7 g. waters of sea together
41:6 heart g. iniquity to itself
147:2 g. outcasts of Is. Is. 56:8
Prov. 6:8 ant g. food in harvest
10:5 that g. in summer is wise
Is. 10:14 one g. eggs th. are left
17:5 when the harvest-man g.
Hab. 2:5 g. to him all nations
Mat. 12:30 g. not scat. Luke 11:23
23:37 as a hen g. her chickens
John 4:36 he that reapeth g. fruit

**GATHERING, S.**

Gen. 49:10 to him shall g. of peo.
Num. 15:33 found him g. sticks
1 K. 17:10 widow was g. sticks
Is. 33:4 spoil like g. of caterpil.
Mat. 25:24 g. where not strewed
Acts 16:10 assuredly g. L. called
1 Cor. 16:2 be no g. wh. I come

**GAVE.**

Gen. 2:20 Ad. g. names to cattle
3:12 woman g. me of the tree
14:20 g. tithes of all, Heb. 7:2, 4
Jos. 21:44 L. g. them rest, 2 Chr.
15:15; 20:30
1 Sam. 10:9 G. g. Saul ano. heart
Job 1:21 L. g. Lord hath taken
Ps. 18:13 Highest g. his voice
69:21 g. me gall, g. vinegar
Ec. 12:7 spir. return to G. th. g.
Is. 43:3 I g. Egypt for ransom
50:6 I g. my back to the smiters
Ezek. 20:12 I g. them my sab. 25
Hos. 13:11 I g. thee a king in
anger
Mat. 14:19 g. loaves to disciples,
15:36; 26:26; Mark 6:41; 8:6;
14:22; Luke 9:16; 22:19
Mat. 21:23 who g. thee author-
ity? Mark 11:28; Luke 20:2
25:35 ye g. me meat, g. drink
John 1:12 g. he power to bec. so.
3:16 G. so loved w. he g. Son
10:29 Fa. who g. them me is
14:31 as Father g. me command.
Acts 2:4 to speak as Sp. g. utter
1 Cor. 3:6 watered, but G. g. inc.
2 Cor. 8:5 but first g. selves to L.
Gal. 1:4 g. him. for sins, Tit. 2:14
2:20 loved me, g. himself for me
Eph. 1:22 g. him to be head over
4:8 captive and g. gifts
11 he g. some apostles, some
5:25 loved church g. hims. for
1 Tim. 2:6 g. himself ransom
Rev. 13:2 dragon g. him power

**GAVE up.**

Gen. 25:8 Abraham g. up ghost
17 Ishmael; 35:29 Isaac g. up

*Lam.* 1:19 my elders *g. up* ghost
*Mark* 15:37 J *g. up* ghost, 39; *Luke* 23:46; *John* 19:30
*Acts* 5:5 An. *g. up* gh.; 12:23 He.
*Rev.* 20:13 the sea *g. up* the dead

**GAVEST.**

*Gen.* 3:12 wom. whom thou *g.*
1 *K.* 8:34 land which thou *g.* to fathers, 40, 48; 2 *Cor.* 6:25, 31, 38; *Neh.* 9:35
*Neh.* 9:20 *g.* Spirit, *g.* water for
22 *g.* kingdoms; 27 *g.* saviours
*Ps.* 21:4 he asked life, th. *g.* it
*Luke* 7:44 *g.* me no water, 45
*John* 17:4 I finis. work thou *g.*
12 those thou *g.* I have kept
22 the glory thou *g.* I have g.
18:9 thou *g.* me ha. I lost none

**GAY.**

*Jam.* 2:3 that weareth *g.* cloth.

**GAZA.**

*Jud.* 16:1 Samson went to G.
*Jer.* 47:1 Pharaoh smote G. 5
*Amos* 1:7 send fire on wall of G.
*Zec.* 9:5 king sh. perish from G.
*Acts* 8:26 goeth from Jeru. to G.

**GAZE.**

*Ex.* 19:21 break thro' to L. to *g.*

**GAZING.**

*Nah.* 3:6 I will set thee *g.* stock
*Acts* 1:11 why stand ye *g.* to h.?
*Heb.* 10:33 were made *g.* stock

**GEBA.**

*Jos.* 21:17 G. with, 1 *Chr.* 6:60
1 *K.* 15:22 Asa b. G. 2 *Chr.* 16:6
*Is.* 10:29 taken lodging at G.
*Zec.* 14:10 be as plain from G.

GEBAL. *Ps.* 83:7; *Ezek.* 27:9
GEBIM. *Is.* 10:31

**GEDALIAH.**

2 *K.* 25:24 G. sware, *Jer.* 40:9
1 *Chr.* 25:3 G. and Z. *Ezr.* 10:18
*Jer.* 38:1 G. son of Pashur heard
41:2 Ishmael smote G. 43:6
*Zep.* 1:1 son of Cushi, son of G.

GEHAZI. 2 *K.* 4:12, 27; 5:21, 25; 8:4
GEMARIAH. *Jer.* 29:3; 36:25

**GENDER.**

*Lev.* 19:19 sh. not let cat. *g.* wi.
2 *Tim.* 2:23 knowing th. *g.* str.

**GENDERED, ETH.**

*Job* 21:10 bull *g.* and faileth not
38:29 hoary frost, who *g.* it?
*Gal.* 4:24 mount Sin. wh. *g.* to

**GENEALOGY.**

1 *Chr.* 5:1 *g.* not to be reckoned
*Ezr.* 2:62 sought *g.* *Neh.* 7:64
8:1 *g.* of them that went up
*Neh.* 7:5 I found register of *g.*

**GENEALOGIES.**

1 *Chr.* 9:1 Israel reckoned by *g.*
2 *Chr.* 12:15 book of She. con. *g.*
31:19 portions to all reck. by *g.*
1 *Tim.* 1:4 no heed to endless *g.*
*Tit.* 3:9 avoid fool. questions *g.*

**GENERAL.**

1 *Chr.* 27:34 *g.* king's army Joab
*Heb.* 12:23 *g.* assembly and chu.

**GENERALLY.**

2 *Sam.* 17:11 Is. be *g.* gathered
*Jer.* 48:38 lamenta. *g.* on house-t.

**GENERATION.**

*Gen.* 7:1 ha. I seen right. in *g.*
*Ex.* 17:16 war with Amal. fr. *g.*
*Deut.* 23:2 not enter to tenth *g.*
3 Am. to tenth *g.* not enter
8 Ed. and Eg. in third *g.* shall
32:5 perverse and crooked *g.* 20
*Jud.* 2:10 that *g.* gath. to father
*Ps.* 12:7 preserve them from *g.*
*Ps.* 14:5 God is in *g.* of righte.
22:30 accounted to Lord for a *g.*
24:6 this *g.* of them that seek
49:19 he shall go to *g.* of fathers
73:15 I should offend ag. the *g.*
78:4 show. to *g.* praise of Lord
6 that *g.* to come might know
8 a stubborn and rebellious *g.*
95:10 grieved with *g.* *Heb.* 3:10
109:13 *g.* fol. name be blotted
112:2 *g.* of upright be blessed
145:4 one *g.* praise thy works
*Prov.* 27:24 crown end. eve. *g.*?
30:11 a *g.* that curseth father
12 there is *g.* pure in own eyes
13 *g.* lofty; 14 *g.* whose teeth
*Ec.* 1:4 one *g.* passeth, another *g.*
*Is.* 13:20 not dwelt in from *g.* to *g.* *Jer.* 50:39
34:10 from *g.* to *g.* it shall lie, 17
51:8 my salvat. be from *g.* to *g.*
53:8 who decl. his *g.* *Acts* 8:33
*Lam.* 5:19 throne rem. fr. *g.* to *g.*
*Dan.* 4:3 his. dom. f. *g.* to *g.* 34
*Mat.* 1:1 book of *g.* of Jesus Ch.
3:7 O *g.* of vipers, 12:34; 23:33; *Luke* 3:7
11:16 shall liken *g.* *Luke* 7:31
12:39 adulterous *g.* seeketh sign, 16:4; *Mark* 8:12; *Luke* 11:29
41 in jugdm. with *g.* *Luke* 11:32
42 queen of S. wi. *g.* *Luke* 11:31
17:17 O perverse *g.* *Mark* 9:19; *Luke* 9:41
23:36 things come on this *g.*
24:34 this *g.* not pass, *Mark* 13:30; *Luke* 21:32
*Mark* 8:38 asha. of me in sin. *g.*
*Luke* 1:50 mercy on them *g.* to *g.*
11:30 so sh. S. of man be to *g.*
50 blood of proph. req. of *g.* 51
16:8 child. of world in *g.* wiser
*Acts* 2:40 save from untoward *g.*
13:36 David, after served own *g.*
1 *Pet.* 2:9 ye are a chosen *g.*

*See* FOURTH.

**GENERATIONS.**

*Gen.* 2:4 these are *g.* of heavens
5:1 *g.* of Ad.; 6:9 *g.* of N. 10:1
6:9 Noah was perfect in his *g.*
9:12 covenant for perpetual *g.*
11:10 *g.* of Shem; 27 *g.* of Te.
17:12 every man-ch. in *g.* circ.
25:12 *g.* of Ish. 13; 1 *Chr.* 1:29
19 *g.* of Isaac; 36:1 *g.* of E. 9
37:2 these are the *g.* of Jacob
*Ex.* 3:15 memorial to all *g.*
12:14 feast to Lord through. *g.*
42 a night to be observed in *g.*
16:32 homer to be kept for *g.* 33
27:21 a statute forever to their *g.* 30:21; *Lev.* 3:17; 6:18; 7:36; 10:9; 17:7; 23:14, 21, 31, 41
30:8 incense; 31 oil through. *g.*
31:13 sab. a sign through *g.* 16
40:15 everlasting priest. thro' *g.*
*Deut.* 7:9 L. keepeth cov. 1,000 *g*
32:7 consider years of many *g.*
*Jud.* 3:2 *g.* of Israel might teach
*Ruth* 4:18 these are *g.* of Pharez
1 *Chr.* 16:15 word which he commanded to a 1,000 *g.* *Ps.* 105:8
*Job* 42:16 J. saw son's s. four *g.*
*Ps.* 33:11 thoughts of h. to all *g.*
45:17 name remember. in all *g.*
61:6 the king's years as many *g.*
72:5 shall fear thee thro' all *g.*
79:13 will show praise to all *g.*
85:5 th. draw anger to all *g.*?
89:4 will build throne to all *g.*
90:1 our dwelling-pla. in all *g.*
100:5 his truth end. to all *g.*
102:12 thy remem. to all *g.*
24 thy years through all *g.*
106:31 counted righte. to all *g.*
119:90 thy faith. is to all *g.*
135:13 thy mem. through. all *g.*
145:13 thy dom. through. all *g.*
146:10 thy G. O Zion to all *g.*
*Is.* 41:4 calling *g.* from begin.
51:9 awake, O arm of L. as in *g.*
60:15 make thee joy of *g.*
61:4 repair desolations of *g.*
*Mat.* 1:17 *g.* fr. Abr. to Dav. 14 *g.*
*Luke* 1:48 *g.* sh. call me blessed
*Col.* 1:26 mys. hid fr. ages and *g.*

GENNESARET. *Mat.* 14:34; *Mark* 6:53; *Luke* 5:1

**GENTILE.**

*Rom.* 2:9 Jew first, also of *g.* 10

**GENTILES.**

*Gen.* 10:5 isles of *g.* were divided
*Is.* 11:10 root of Jes. to it sh. *g.*
42:1 judgm. to *g.* *Mat.* 12:18
*Is.* 42:6 light to *g.* 49:6; *Luke* 2:32; *Acts* 13:47
49:22 I will lift my hand to *g.*
54:3 thy seed shall inherit the *g.*
60:3 *g.* shall come to thy light
5 forces of *g.* shall come, 11
16 shalt suck the milk of *g.*
61:6 ye shall eat the riches of *g.*
9 seed sh. be known am. the *g.*
62:2 *g.* sh. see thy righteousness
66:12 glory of *g.* like flow. stre.
19 declare my glory among *g.*
*Jer.* 4:7 destroyer of *g.* is on way
14:22 vanities of *g.* cause rain?
*Lam.* 2:9 king and princes am. *g.*
*Ezek.* 4:13 eat defil. bread am. *g.*
*Joel* 3:9 proclaim ye this am. *g.*
*Mic.* 5:8 remnant of Jacob am. *g.*
*Zec.* 1:21 to cast out horns of *g.*
*Mal.* 1:11 name sh. be gr. am. *g.*
*Mat.* 4:15 Galilee of the *g.*
6:32 after all th. things *g.* seek
10:5 go not into way of the *g.*
18 testimony ag. them and *g.*
12:21 in his name sh. the *g.* tru.
20:19 shall deliver him to the *g.* *Mark* 10:33; *Luke* 18:32
25 prin. of *g.* exer. *Luke* 22:25
*Luke* 21:24 Jerusal. trodden of *g.* till times of *g.* be fulfilled
*John* 7:35 to disp. am *g.* teach *g.*
*Acts* 7:45 with Je. into pos. of *g.*
9:15 to bear my name before *g.*
10:45 on the *g.* was poured gift
11:1 *g.* received word of God
18 hath G. to *g.* granted rep.?
13:42 *g.* besought words preach.
46 P. and B. said, We turn to *g.*
14:27 opened door of faith to *g.*
15:3 declare the conversion of *g.*
7 *g.* by my mou. sh. hear word
12 wonders G. wrought am. *g.*
14 God at first did visit *g.* 17
19 them which from am. the *g.*
23 greeting to breth. of the *g.*
18:6 henceforth I will go to *g.*
21:19 God wrought am. the *g.*
21 teach. J. am. *g.* to forsake
25 touch. the *g.* which believe
22:21 I will send thee far to *g.*
26:20 *g.* that they should repent
23 Ch. sh. show light to the *g.*
28:28 salvation of God sent to *g.*
*Rom.* 1:13 fruit, as am. other *g.*
2:14 *g.* which have not the law
24 God blasphemed am. the *g.*
3:9 proved Jews and *g.* und. sin
29 is he not of *g.*? yes of *g.*
9:24 not of Jews, but also of *g.*
30 *g.* wh. follo. not after right.
11:11 salvation come to the *g.*
12 dimin. of them riches of *g.*
13 to you *g.* as the apos. of *g.*
25 till the fulness of *g.* be come
15:9 that *g.* might glorify God; I will confess among *g.*
10 rejoice, ye *g.* with his peo.
11 praise L. all *g.* and laud

12 over *g.* in him shall *g.* trust
16 minist. of Jesus Christ to *g.*
that offering up of the *g.* 18
27 if *g.* have been made parta.
16:4 all the churches of the *g.*
1 *Cor.* 5:1 not named among *g.*
10:20 thing *g.* sacrifice to devils
32 offence neither to J. nor *g.*
12:2 ye know ye were *g.* carried
13 whether we be Jews or *g.*
*Gal.* 2:12 he did eat with *g.*
14 man. of *g.* why compel. *g.*?
15 Jews, and not sinners of *g.*
3:14 blessing of Abraham on *g.*
*Eph.* 2:11 in time past *g.* in flesh
3:1 prisoner of Jesus Ch. for *g.*
6 that *g.* should be fellow-heirs
8 preach am. *g.* unsea. riches
4:17 ye walk not as other *g.*
*Col.* 1:27 glory of mystery am. *g.*
1 *Thes.* 2:16 forbid. to spe. to *g.*
4:5 in lust of concupis. as the *g.*
1 *Tim.* 2:7 ordained teacher of *g.*
3:16 preached to the *g.*
2 *Tim.* 1:11 teacher of *g.*
1 *Pet.* 2:12 convers. honest am. *g.*
4:3 to have wrought will of *g.*
3 *John* 7 taking nothing of the *g.*
*Rev.* 11:2 the court is given to *g.*

**GENTLE.**

1 *Thes.* 2:7 were *g.* among you
2 *Tim.* 2:24 ser. of L. must be *g.*
*Tit.* 3:2 *g.* showing all meekness
*Jam.* 3:17 wisd. from ab. pure *g.*
1 *Pet.* 2:18 subject not only to *g.*

**GENTLENESS.**

2 *Sam.* 22:36 thy *g.* made me great, *Ps.* 18:35
2 *Cor.* 10:1 I bes. you by *g.* of C.
*Gal.* 5:22 fruit of the Spirit is *g.*

**GENTLY.**

2 *Sam.* 18:5 deal *g.* with Absalom
*Is.* 40:11 *g.* lead those wi. young

GERA. *Jud.* 3:15; 2 *Sam.* 16:5
GERAHS. *Ex.* 30:13; *Lev.* 27:25; *Num.* 3:47; 18:16; *Eze.* 45:12
GERAR. *Gen.* 20:1, 2; 26:6, 20
GERGESENES. *Mat.* 8:28

**GERIZIM.**

*Deut.* 11:29 bles. on mt. G. 27:12
*Jos.* 8:33 aga. mount G. *Jud.* 9:7

**GERSHOM, GERSHON.**

*Gen.* 46:11 G. Kohath and Merari
*Ex.* 6:16; *Num.* 3:17; 1 *Chr.* 6:1; 23:6
*Ex.* 2:22 name of Moses' son G.
*Num.* 3:21 G. family of Libnites
4:28 sons of G. 7:7; 10:17
*Jos.* 21:6 children of G. had, 27
*Ezr.* 8:2 sons of Phinehas, G.

**GESHUR.**

2 *Sam.* 13:37 and went to G. 38
14:23 Joab went to G. 32
15:8 servant vowed a vow at G.

**GESHURITES.**

*Jos.* 13:13 G. dw. among, 1 *Sam.* 27:8

**GET.**

*Gen.* 34:4 *g.* me damsel to wife
*Ex.* 14:17 will *g.* honor up. Pha.
*Lev.* 14:21 poor and cannot *g.* 22
*Deut.* 8:18 power to *g.* wealth
*Jud.* 14:2 *g.* her me to wife, 3
1 *K.* 1:2 that king may *g.* heat
*Ps.* 119:104 precepts I *g.* under.
*Prov.* 4:5 *g.* wisdom, *g.* underst.
16:16 better *g.* wisd. than gold
17:16 in hand of fool to *g.* wis.
*Ec.* 3:6 there is a time to *g.*
*Lam.* 3:7 I cannot *g.* out
*Ezek.* 22:27 to *g.* dishonest gain
*Dan.* 4:14 beasts *g.* from under
*Zep.* 3:19 I will *g.* them praise
*Luke* 9:12 lodge and *g.* victuals
2 *Cor.* 2:11 lest Sat. *g.* advantage
*Jam.* 4:13 buy, sell, and *g.* gain

**GET thee.**

*Gen.* 12:1 *g. t.* out of co. *Acts* 7:3
*Ex.* 10:28 *g. thee* from me
11:8 *g. thee* out, and all people
19:24 Lord said to Moses, *g. th.* down, 32:7; *Deut.* 9:12
1 *K.* 17:3 *g. t.* hence; 9 to Zarep.
18:41 Elijah said, *g. thee* up
2 *K.* 3:13 *g. t.* to prophets of fath.
*Is.* 40:9 O Z. *g. t.* to high mount.
47:5 and *g. thee* into darkness
*Jer.* 13:1 *g. thee* a linen girdle
*Mat.* 4:10 J. saith, *g. t.* hence, S.
16:23 said to Peter, *g. t.* behind me, S. *Mark* 8:33; *Luke* 4:8
*Acts* 10:20 arise, *g. thee* down
22:18 *g. t.* quickly out of Jerus.

**GET ye.**

*Gen.* 19:14 said, Up, *g. ye* out
*Is.* 30:11 *g. ye* out of way
*Jer.* 49:31 *g. ye* to wealthy nat.
*Joel* 3:13 *g. ye* down
*Zec.* 6:7 *g. ye* hence, walk to

**GET you.**

*Gen.* 34:10 *g. you* possessions
42:2 *g. you* down thither
*Ex.* 5:4 *g. you* to your burdens
11 *g. you* str. wh. you can find
*Num.* 16:24 *g. y.* up fr. tab. of K.
*Jos.* 2:16 *g. you* to the mountain
1 *Sam.* 25:5 *g. you* up to Carmel
*Jer.* 49:30 flee, *g. you* far off

**GETHSEMANE.**

*Mat.* 26:36 called G. *Mark* 14:32

**GETTETH.**

2 *Sam.* 5:8 whoso *g.* to gutter
*Prov.* 3:13 man that *g.* underst.
9:7 reproveth scorner *g.* shame, rebuketh wicked man *g.* blot
15:32 hear. reproof *g.* underst.
18:15 prudent *g.* knowledge
19:8 that *g.* wisdom loveth soul
*Jer.* 17:11 *g.* riches not by right
48:44 that *g.* out of pit

**GETTING.**

*Gen.* 31:18 J. carried cattle of *g.*
*Prov.* 4:7 with all thy *g.* get und.
21:6 *g.* of treas. by lying tongue

**GHOST.**

*Gen.* 49:33 J. yielded up the *g.*
*Job* 10:18 I had given up *g.*
11:20 hope as giving up of *g.*
14:10 man giveth up *g.*
*Jer.* 15:9 she hath given up *g.*
*Mat.* 27:50 J. cried, yielded up *g.*
*Acts* 5:10 Sapphira yielded up *g.*
*See* GAVE, GIVE, HOLY.

GIAH. 2 *Sam.* 2:24

**GIANT.**

2 *Sam.* 21:16 of *g.* 18; 1 *Chr.* 20:4
1 *Chr.* 20:6 son of *g.*; 8 born to *g.*
*Job* 16:14 runneth on me like *g.*

**GIANTS.**

*Gen.* 6:4 there were *g.* in earth
*Num.* 13:33 we saw *g.* sons of A.
*Deut.* 2:11 Em. were counted *g.*
3:11 Og. of B. remained of remnant of *g.* *Jos.* 12:4; 13:12
13 Bash. called the land of *g.*
*Jos.* 15:8 lot of J. at valley of *g.*
17:15 get thee up to land of *g.*
18:16 Benj. came to valley of *g.*

**GIBEAH.**

*Jud.* 19:14 by G. 16; 20:9, 13
1 *Sam.* 10:26 home to G. 15:34
2 *Sam.* 21:6 sev. sons to L. in G.
*Is.* 10:29 afraid, G. of Saul is fled
*Hos.* 5:8 blow cornet in G. 9:9
10:9 sinned from days of G.

**GIBEON.**

*Jos.* 10:12 stand still upon G.
2 *Sam.* 3:30 slain Asahel at G.
1 *K.* 3:5 in G. L. app. to Sol. 9:2
1 *Chr.* 8:29 at G. dw. father, 9:35
21:29 altar of b.-offering at G.
*Is.* 28:21 as in the valley of G.

GIBEONITES. 2 *Sam.* 21:1, 9

**GIDEON.**

*Jud.* 6:11, 24, 34; 7:1, 14, 18; 8:21
*Heb.* 11:32 wou. fail to tell of G.

GIDEONI. *Nu.* 1:11; 2:22; 7:60, 65

**GIEREAGLE.**

*Lev.* 11:18 abom. *g.* *Deut.* 14:17

**GIFT.**

*Gen.* 34:12 so much dowry and *g.*
*Ex.* 23:8 take no *g.* for *g.* blindeth the wise, *Deut.* 16:19
*Num.* 8:19 given Lev. as *g.* 18:6
*Ps.* 45:12 daughter of T. with *g.*
*Prov.* 17:8 *g.* as precious stone
23 wicked tak. *g.* out of bosom
18:16 a man's *g.* maketh room
21:14 *g.* in secret pacifieth ang.
25:14 whoso boasteth of false *g.*
*Ec.* 3:13 it is the *g.* of G. 5:19
7:7 *g.* destroyeth the heart
*Mat.* 5:23 bring *g.* to the altar
24 leave *g.* before altar and go
8:4 offer *g.* that M. commanded
15:5 a *g.* by whatso. thou mightest be profited, *Mark* 7:11
23:18 whoso sweareth by *g.* 19
*John* 4:10 thou knewest *g.* of G.
*Acts* 2:38 sh. receive *g.* of H. G.
8:20 thought *g.* of G. be purch.
10:45 on Gentiles poured out *g.*
11:17 God gave them like *g.*
*Rom.* 1:11 impart spiritual *g.*
5:15 not as offence, so is free *g.*
16 *g.* free *g.* of many offences
17 which receive *g.* of righte.
18 the free *g.* came on all men
6:23 the *g.* of God is eternal life
1 *Cor.* 1:7 ye come behi. in no *g.*
7:7 ev. man hath pro. *g.* of God
13:2 tho' I have *g.* of prophecy
2 *Cor.* 8:4 that we would rec. *g.*
9:15 thanks to God for unsp. *g.*
*Eph.* 2:8 faith is the *g.* of God
4:7 accord. to meas. of *g.* of Ch.
*Phil.* 4:17 not bec. I desire a *g.*
1 *Tim.* 4:14 neglect not *g.* in thee
2 *Tim.* 1:6 stir up the *g.* in thee
*Heb.* 6:4 tasted of heavenly *g.*
*Jam.* 1:17 every good *g.* and perfect *g.* is from above

**GIFTS.**

*Gen.* 25:6 Abra. gave *g.* to sons
*Lev.* 23:38 feasts, besides your *g.*
*Num.* 18:29 of all your *g.* offer
2 *Chr.* 19:7 with L. is no tak. *g.*
*Est.* 2:18 Ahasuerus gave *g.*
9:22 sending *g.* to the poor
*Ps.* 68:18 received *g.* for men
72:10 kings of Sheba offer *g.*
*Prov.* 6:35 though thou givest *g.*
15:27 that hateth *g.* shall live
19:6 man friend to him giv. *g.*
29:4 *g.* overthroweth judgment
*Is.* 1:23 every one loveth *g.*
*Ezek.* 16:33 *g.* to whor. *g.* to lov.
20:26 I polluted them in own *g.*
31 when ye offer *g.* ye pollute
39 pollute name no more wi. *g.*
22:12 in thee have they taken *g.*
*Dan.* 2:48 king gave Daniel *g.*
5:17 let thy *g.* be to thyself
*Mal.* 2:11 presented to him *g.*

*Mat.* 7:11 to gi. good *g.* *Lu.* 11:13
*Luke* 21:1 rich casting their *g.*
5 temple was adorned with *g.*
*Rom.* 11:29 *g.* of G. without rep.
12:6 *g.* differing accor. to grace
1 *Cor.* 12:1 concerning spirit. *g.*
4 there are diversities of *g.*
9 another *g.* of healing, 28, 30

31 covet earnestly the best g.
14:1 and desire spiritual g.
Eph. 4:8 and gave g. to men
Heb. 2:4 God witness with g.
5:1 may offer g. and sacrifices
8:3 high-priest ord. to offer g.
4 there are priests that offer g.
9:9 offered, both g. and sacrif.
11:4 God testifying of Abel's g.
Rev. 11:10 dwell on earth send g.

**GIHON.**

Gen. 2:13 name of river is G.
1 K. 1:33 bring Sol. to G. 38, 45

**GILBOA.**

1 Sam. 31:1, 8; 2 Sam. 21:12; 1 Chr. 10:1, 8
2 Sam. 1:21 G. let th. be no dew

**GILEAD.**

Num. 32:1 G. place for cattle, 40
Ps. 60:7 G. mine, Man. 108:8
Cant. 4:1 hair as goats fr. G. 6:5
Jer. 8:22 there no balm in G.?
22:6 art G.; 46:11 go into G.
Hos. 6:8 G. is the city of them
12:11 is there iniquity in G.?

GILEADITE, S. Jud. 10:3; 11:1; 12:4, 5; 2 Sam. 17:27

**GILGAL.**

Jos. 4:19 enc. in G. 9:6; 10:6
Jud. 2:1 angel came from G.
1 Sam. 7:16 S. went to G. 11:14
13:7 Saul in G.; 8 Sam. 15:33
Amos 4:4 at G. multiply trans.
Mic. 6:5 him from Shittim to G.

GILONITE. 2 Sam. 15:12; 23:34

**GIN, S.**

Job 18:9 g. sh. take him by heel
Ps. 140:5; 141:9; Is. 8:14; Am. 3:5

**GIRD.**

Ex. 29:5 g. him with girdle, 9
Jud. 3:16 Ehud did g. dagger
1 Sam. 25:13 g. on ev. man sword
Ps. 45:3 g. sword on thy thigh
Is. 8:9 g. yours. ye shall be br.
Ezek. 44:18 g. what caus. sweat
Joel 1:13 g. yours. and lament
Luke 12:37 sh. g. himself and
17:8 g. thyself and serve me
John 21:18 old, another g. thee
Acts 12:8 g. and bind on sandals

See LOINS, SACKCLOTH.

**GIRDED.**

Lev. 8:7 he g. him with girdle
1 Sam. 2:18 Sam. g. wi. linen ep.
2 Sam. 6:14 David g. with ephod
20:8 Joab's garment g. to him
22:40 g. with strength Ps. 18:39
1 K. 20:32 g. sackcloth on loins
Ps. 30:11 g. me with gladness
65:6 being g. with power
93:1 strength wherewith he g.
109:19 girdle wherewith he is g.
Is. 45:5 I g. thee, though thou
Lam. 2:10 elders of Zion g. with
Ezek. 16:10 I g. thee with fine li.
23:15 images g. with girdles
Joel 1:8 lament like a virgin g.
John 13:4 took towel and g. him.
5 towel wherewith he was g.
Rev. 15:6 breasts g. with girdle

See LOINS, SWORD.

**GIRDEDST.**

John 21:18 when young g. thys.

**GIRDETH.**

1 K. 20:11 him that g. his harn.
Job 12:18 and he g. their loins
Ps. 18:32 it is God that g. me
Prov. 31:17 she g. her loins

**GIRDING.**

Is. 3:24 inst. of stom. g. of sack.
22:12 L. did call to g. with sack.

**GIRDLE.**

Ex. 28:4 they shall make a g.
8 curious g. of ephod, 27, 28; 29:5; 39:5, 20; Lev. 8:7
39 thou make g. of needlework
39:29 g. of fine twined linen
1 Sam. 18:4 gave Da. bow and g.
1 K. 2:5 blood of war on his g.
2 K. 1:8 Elij. girt with g. of lea.
Job 12:18 loins of kings with g.
Ps. 109:19 g. wherewith he is
Is. 3:24 instead of a g. a rent
5:27 nor shall g. of loins be
Is. 11:5 righteous. be g. of loins faithfulness g. of reins
22:21 strengthen Eliakim wi. g.
Jer. 13:1 get thee a linen g.
10 as this g. good for nothing
Mat. 3:4 J. had a l. g. Mark 1:6
Acts 21:11 took P.'s g. owneth g.
Rev. 1:13 gi. about paps gold. g.

**GIRDLES.**

Ex. 28:40 for Aaron's sons g.
29:9 Aaron and sons with g.
Prov. 31:24 deliver. g. to merch.
Ezek. 23:15 images of C. with g.
Rev. 15:6 angels g. wi. golden g.

**GIRGASHITE, S.**

Gen. 10:16 beg. the G. 1 Chr. 1:14
15:21 the land G. Neh. 9:8
Jos. 3:10 will drive out the G.

**GIRL, S.**

Joel 3:3 have sold g. for wine
Zec. 8:5 full of boys and g.

**GIRT.**

1 Sam. 2:4 that stumbled are g.
2 K. 1:8 g. with girdle of leather
John 21:7 S. Pet. g. fisher's coat
Eph. 6:14 loins g. with truth
Rev. 1:13 g. about paps golden g.

GITTITE. 2 Sam. 6:10; 15:19; 21:19

**GIVE.**

Gen. 15:2 what wilt g. me?
23:11 the field I g. thee and
28:22 all thou g. me I will g.
Ex. 10:25 must g. us sacrifices
30:12 shall g. ev. man ransom
13 g. every one half a shekel
Num. 11:4 sh. g. flesh to eat? 18
22:18 if B. g. me house, 24:13
35:2 shall g. to Levites suburbs
Deut. 16:17 every man g. as he is able, Ezek. 46:5, 11
25:3 forty stripes he may g.
1 Sam. 22:7 son of Jesse g. fields?
2 Sam. 23:15 oh th. one g. me dr. of well of Beth. 1 Chr. 11:17
1 K. 13:8 if thou wilt g. me
2 Chr. 30:12 hand of G. to g. one
Ezr. 9:8 and to g. us a nail
9 to g. us a reviving in Judah
Job 2:4 man hath he g. for life
Ps. 2:8 I shall g. thee heathen
37:4 he shall g. thee desires
49:7 none can g. to God a rans.
51:16 not sac. else wo. I g. it
78:20 can he g. bread also?
91:11 g. angels charge, Mat. 4:6
109:4 I g. myself unto prayer
Prov. 29:15 rod and reproof g.
17 he shall g. rest, g. delight
Ec. 2:26 he may g. to him good
Cant. 8:7 if man g. substance
Is. 30:23 then he shall g. rain
55:10 that it g. seed to sower
61:3 g. them beauty for ashes
Jer. 3:19 shall I g. pleas. land?
17:10 g. man ac. to ways, 32:19
29:11 g. you an expected end
Ezek. 2:8 eat that I g. thee
3:3 fill bowels with roll I g.
46:16 prince g. gift to sons, 17
Dan. 9:22 come to g. thee skill
Mic. 6:7 I g. first-born for tran.?

Zec. 8:12 vine shall g. fruit, gro. shall g. incre. heav. g. dew
Mat. 7:9 ask bread, will g. sto.?
10 will he g. serp.? Luke 11:11
11 how to g. gifts to child. so F. to g. that ask, Luke 11:13
14:7 to g. what she would ask
16:26 g. in exchange for soul? Mark 8:37
19:7 g. writing of divorcement?
26:15 what will ye g. me
Mark 6:25 g. me head of John
12:9 he will g. vineyard to oth.
Luke 4:6 to whom. I will, I g. it
6:38 good measure shall men g.
11:8 g. as many as he needeth
John 4:14 water I shall g. him
6:27 meat Son of man shall g.
52 can this man g. his flesh?
10:28 I g. to them eternal life
12:22 what thou ask G. will g.
13:29 that he should g. to poor
14:16 he shall g. you Comforter
27 my peace I g. to you: not as world giveth, g. I unto you
15:16 what. ye ask he may g.
16:23 what. ye ask he will g.
17:2 he should g. eternal life
Acts 3:6 such as I have g. I thee
6:4 will g. ourselves to prayer
20:35 more blessed to g. than r.
Rom. 8:32 him also freely g.
Eph. 1:17 God may g. you spirit
4:28 have to g. to him needeth
2 Tim. 4:8 righte. Judge shall g.
Heb. 2:1 to g. more earnest heed
1 John 5:16 g. life for them that
Rev. 13:15 power to g. life to im.
16:19 to g. her cup of wine
22:12 g. every man ac. to work

See ACCOUNT, GLORY, SWARE.

**GIVE,** *imperatively.*

Gen. 14:21 g. me the persons
27:28 G. g. thee dew of heaven
29:21 g. me wife; 30:1 g. child.
Num. 6:26 Lord g. thee peace
Jos. 2:12 and g. me true token
15:19 g. bless. g. spr. Jud. 1:15
1 Sam. 8:6 g. us a king to judge
17:10 g. me man that we may
1 K. 3:9 g. servant understand.
26 g. her the living child, 27
2 K. 6:29 I said; g. thy son that
1 Chr. 16:28 g. to Lord glory and strength, 29; Ps. 29:1; 96:7, 8
22:12 the Lord g. thee wisdom
2 Chr. 1:10 g. me now wisdom
Job 32:21 nor let me g. flat. titles
Ps. 28:4 g. according to deeds
60:11 g. help fr. trouble, 108:12
86:16 g. strength to thy servant
119:34 g. me understanding, 73, 125, 144, 169
Prov. 9:9 g. instru. to wise man
23:26 my son, g. me thy heart
25:21 if enemy hunger, g. him bread, Rom. 12:20
30:8 g. me neither poverty nor
15 two daughters, crying g. g.
Ec. 11:2 g. a portion to seven
Is. 62:7 g. no rest till establish J.
Jer. 18:19 g. heed to me, O Lord
Lam. 2:18 g. thyself no rest
3:65 g. them sorrow of heart
Ezek. 3:17 g. warning from me
Dan. 5:17 g. rewards to another
Hos. 4:18 rulers do love, g. ye
9:14 g. O Lord, what wilt g.?
13:10 g. me a king and princes
Zec. 11:12 g. me my price
Mat. 5:42 g. to him that asketh
6:11 g. us our daily b. Luke 11:3
9:24 g. place; 10:8 freely g.
14:16 g. them to eat, Mark 6:37; Luke 9:13
17:27 and g. to them for me
19:21 g. to poor, Mark 10:21

20:8 and g. them their hire
25:8 g. us of your oil, lamps out
Luke 6:38 g. and it shall be giv.
11:41 g. alms of such, 12:33
14:9 say, g. this man place
15:12 give me portion of goods
John 4:7 J. saith, g. me drink, 10
6:34 L. everm. g. us this bread
9:24 g. God praise, man is sin.
Acts 8:19 S. said, g. me power
Rom. 12:19 g. place to wrath
1 Cor. 10:32 g. none offence
2 Cor. 9:7 let him g. not grudg.
Col. 4:1 g. servants that is just
1 Tim. 4:13 g. attend. to reading
15 g. thyself to them
Rev. 10:9 g. me the little book
18:7 torment and sorrow g. her
See CHARGE, EAR, GLORY, LIGHT.

**I will GIVE.**

Gen. 17:8 I will g. to thee land wherein thou art a stranger, 48:4; Deut. 34:4
16 I will g. son; 28:22 tenth to
Ex. 3:31 I will g. favor; 33:14
Lev. 26:4 I w. g. rain, Deut. 11:14
6 I will g. peace in the land
1 Sam. 1:11 I will g. him to L.
2 Sam. 12:11 I will g. wives to
1 K. 11:13 I will g. one tribe
31 I will g. ten tribes to thee
13:7 I will g. reward; 21:2
21:7 I will g. vineyard of Nab.
1 Chr. 22:9 I will g. rest, I w. g.
2 Chr. 1:12 I will g. thee riches
Ps. 30:12 O L. I will g. thanks
57:7 I will sing g. praise, 108:1
Prov. 3:28 to-morrow I will g.
Is. 3:4 I w. g. child. to be princ.
41:27 I will g. to Jerusalem one that bringeth good tidings
42:6 I will g. thee for cove. 49:8
45:3 I will g. treas.; 49:6 light
Jer. 3:15 I will g. you pastors
9:15 I will g. waters of gall to
14:13 I will g. peace in land
17:3 I will g. substance to spoil
24:7 I will g. heart to know me
32:39 I w. g. heart, Ezek. 11:19
Ezek. 7:21 I will g. to strangers
11:17 I will g. you land of Isr.
16:38 I w. g. thee blood in fury
39 I w. g. thee into their hand
Ezek. 16:61 I will g. them for dau.
21:27 whose right it is, I will g.
29:21 I will g. opening of mouth
36:26 I will g. you heart of flesh
Mat. 11:28 and I will g. you rest
16:19 I will g. to thee the keys
20:4 what. is right I will g. you
14 I will g. to last even as to
Mark 6:22 ask, I will g. it thee
Luke 21:15 I w. g. you a mouth
John 6:51 bread I will g. is my
Acts 13:34 I will g. mercies of D.
Rev. 2:10 I will g. thee a crown
17 I will g. him a white stone
23 I w. g. ev. one ac. to works
28 I will g. him the morn. star
11:3 I will g. power to my two
21:6 I w. g. him athirst w. of l.

**Will I GIVE.**

Gen. 12:7 to thy seed w. I g. this land, 13:15; 24:7; 28:13; 35:12; Ex. 32:13; 33:1
Deut. 1:36 to him will I g. land
1 Sam. 18:17 M. her w. I g. thee
Ps. 18:49 will I g. thanks to
Cant. 7:12 will I g. thee my
Is. 43:4 will I g. men for thee
Ezek. 36:26 new heart w. I g. you
Hag. 2:9 this place will I g. peace
Mat. 4:9 Th. things will I g.
Luke 4:6 this power will I g. thee
Rev. 2:7 over. will I g. 17, 26

**Lord GIVE.**

Ex. 12:25 to land which L. will g. you, Lev. 14:34; 23:10; 25:2 Num. 15:2
16:8 Lord shall g. flesh to eat
Num. 22:13 Lord refuseth to g.
36:2 L. com. to g. land by lot
Deut. 1:25 land the Lord doth g.
28:65 L. shall g. tremb. heart
Jos. 17:4 L. com. to g. inherit.
1 K. 15:4 L. his God did g. lamp
2 Chr. 25:9 L. is able to g. much
Ps. 29:11 L. g. strength to peo.
84:11 L. will g. grace and glory
85:12 L. shall g. which is good
Is. 7:14 L. hims. shall g. a sign
14:3 the Lord shall g. thee rest
30:20 Lord g. you bread of adv.
Zec. 10:1 L. g. showers of rain
Luke 1:32 L. shall g. him throne
2 Tim. 1:16 L. g. mercy to house

**Not GIVE, or GIVE not.**

Ex. 5:10 I will not g. straw
30:15 rich n. g. more, poor n. l.
Lev. 25:37 shall not g. money on
Deut. 7:3 dau. shall not g. to son
Jud. 21:7 we will not g. wives
Ezr. 9:12 g. not your daughters, Neh. 10:30; 13:25
Ps. 132:4 will n. g. sleep to eyes
Prov. 6:4 g. not sleep to eyes
31:3 g. not thy strength to wo.
Is. 13:10 constel. not g. light
42:8 glory not g. to anot. 48:11
62:8 I will no more g. thy corn
Ezek. 32:7 moon sh. n. g. her lig. Mat. 24:29; Mark 13:24
Joel 2:17 g. not heritage to rep.
Mat. 7:6 g. n. that is holy to the
Mark 12:15 sh. we g. or not g.?
Eph. 4:27 neither g. place to de.
Jam. 2:16 g. n. things they need

**GIVE thanks.**

2 Sam. 22:50 I will g. t. to thee, Ps. 18:49
1 Chr. 16:8 g. t. to the L. Ps. 105:1; 106:1; 107:1, 118:1, 29; 136:1, 3
35 save us, that we may g. th. to thy holy name, Ps. 106:47
25:3 with a harp to g. thanks
Ps. 6:5 in grave who shall g. t.
30:4 g. th. at the remembrance of his holiness, 97:12
12 O Lord, I will g. t. for ever
35:18 I will g. t. in congregation
75:1 to thee, O God, do we g. t.
79:13 so we thy people will g. t.
92:1 good thing to g. t. to Lord
106:47 to g. t. to holy name
119:62 at midnight I will g. t.
122:4 tribes go up to g. thanks
136:2 g. t. to God of gods, 26
140:13 right. g. t. to thy name
Rom. 16:4 to whom I g. thanks
1 Cor. 10:30 that for which I g. t.
Eph. 1:16 I cease not to g. t. for
Col. 1:3 we g. t. to G. and Father
1 Thes. 1:2 we g. thanks to God
5:18 in everything g. thanks
2 Thes. 2:13 we are bound to g. t.
Rev. 11:17 we g. thee t. L. G. A.

**GIVE up.**

Deut. 23:14 Lord walketh to g. up thine enemies, 31:5
1 K. 14:16 he shall g. Israel up
Job 3:11 why did not I g. up gh.?
13:19 I shall g. up the ghost
Is. 43:6 I say to north, g. up
Hos. 11:8 how sh. I g. up Eph.?

**GIVEN.**

Lev. 20:3 he hath g. seed to Mo.
Num. 18:6 g. as a gift for the L.
Ruth 2:12 reward g. thee of L.
2 Sam. 12:8 have g. such things
18:11 would have g. ten shekels
19:42 or hath king g. us gift?

1 K. 13:5 sign man of G. had g.
1 Chr. 29:14 thine have we g.
Est. 3:11 silver is g. to thee
7:3 my life be g. at my petition
Job 3:20 light g. him in misery?
Ps. 79:2 dead bodies g. to be m.
112:9 hath g. to poor, 2 Cor. 9:9
115:16 earth hath he g. of men
Prov. 19:17 hath g. will he pay
Ec. 8:8 wicked deliv. those g. it
12:11 which are g. fr. one shep.
Is. 9:6 Child born, Son is g.
Jer. 6:13 ev. one g. to cov. 8:10
Ezek. 11:15 to us is land g. 33:24
35:12 they are g. to consume
Dan. 2:38 fowls hath he g. into
7:4 lion, man's heart was g.
Mat. 13:11 g. you to know mys. of king. Mark 4:11; Lu. 8:10
19:11 save they to whom it is g.
21:43 g. to nation bring. fruits
22:30 are g. in marriage, Mark 12:25; Luke 20:35
26:9 and g. to poor, Mark 14:5
28:18 power g. to me in heaven
Mark 4:24 that hear more be g.
Luke 12:48 much g. much req.
John 3:27 nothing, except it be g.
5:26 g. to the Son to have life
6:39 of all he hath g. me
65 no man come except g. him
19:11 except it were g. from
Acts 4:12 none other name g.
Rom. 5:5 H. Ghost which is g.
11:35 who hath first g. to him
15:15 grace that is g. me of God
1 Cor. 2:12 things freely g. of G.
Gal. 3:21 law g. could have g.
Eph. 3:2 is g. me to you-ward
8 me who am least is grace g.
5:2 C. loved and g. hims. for us
Phil. 1:29 you g. in behalf of C.
2:9 g. him a name above ev. n.
Heb. 4:8 if Jes. had g. them rest
1 John 3:24 Sp. wh. he hath g. us
4:13 bec. he hath g. us of Spirit
Rev. 6:11 white robes g. to every
13:5 power g. to con. 42 months
7 it was g. him to make war

**God, or Lord hath, had GIVEN.**

Gen. 24:35 L. h. g. Abrah. flocks
30:6 said, God hath g. me a son
18 God hath g. me my hire
43:23 God hath g. you treasure
Ex. 16:15 bread which Lord h. g.
29 Lord h. g. you the sabbath
Num. 32:7 going over to land wh. Lord hath g. them, 9; Deut. 3:18; 28:52; Jos. 2:9, 14; 23:13, 15; Jer. 25:5
Jos. 6:16 shout, Lord h. g. city
1 Sam. 1:27 L. h. g. me my peti.
15:28 L. h. g. it to neigh. 28:17
2 Chr. 36:23 all kingd. of earth. hath God g. me. Ezr. 1:2
Ec. 5:19 to who. G. h. g. riches
Is. 8:18 I and the children Lord hath g. Heb. 2:13
50:4 Lord h. g. me tongue
Jer. 11:18 L. hath g. me knowl.
47:7 Lord hath g. it a charge
John 6:23 Lord hath g. thanks
Acts 27:24 G. h. g. thee all that
Rom. 11:8 G. h. g. spirit of slum.
2 Cor. 10:8 the Lord h. g. us for edification, 13:10
1 Thes. 4:8 G. who h. g. Holy S.
1 John 5:11 record G. hath g. us
See REST.

**I have, or have I GIVEN.**

Gen. 27:37 bret. h. I g. for serv.
1 K. 3:13 I h. g. th. hast not asked
Is. 55:4 I h. g. him for witness
Ezek. 4:15 I h. g. thee cow's du.
Amos 4:6 I h. g. clean. of teeth.
9:15 no more out of land I h. g.

John 13:15 I h. g. an example
17:8 I h. g. words thou gave, 14
22 glory gavest me, I h. g. th.
1 Cor. 16:1 I h. g. order to chur.

**Not GIVEN.**

Deut. 26:14 I have not g. thereof
29:4 L. hath not g. you a heart
1 Chr. 22:18 hath he n. g. you rest
Job 22:7 hast not g. water
Ps. 78:63 maid. n. g. to marriage
Ezek. 3:20 hast not g. warning
Mat. 13:11 to them it is not g.
John 7:39 Holy G. was not yet g.
1 Tim. 3:3 bishop not g. to wine, no striker, Tit. 1:7
8 deacons not g. to much wine
2 Tim. 1:7 G. n. g. us sp. of fear
Tit. 2:3 aged wom. n. g. to wine

**Shall be GIVEN.**

Est. 5:3 s. be g. to half of kingd.
Ps. 72:15 s. be g. of gold of Sheba
120:3 what shall be g. thee
Is. 3:11 reward of hands s. be g.
33:16 bread shall be g. him
35:2 glory of Lebanon s. be g.
Ezek. 47:11 marshes, shall be g.
Dan. 7:25 saints s. be g. to hand
27 kingdom s. be g. to saints
Mat. 7:7 it shall be g. Luke 11:9
10:19 s. be g. sa. hour, Mark 13:11
12:39 no sign s. be g. Mark 8:12; Luke 11:29
13:12 to him shall be g. 25:29; Mark 4:25; Luke 8:18
20:23 it s. be g. for whom prep.
21:43 kin. of G. s. be g. to nation
Luke 6:38 give, and it shall be g.
Phile. 22 thro' prayers I s. be g.
Jam. 1:5 ask of G. and it s. be g.

**Thou hast, or hast thou GIVEN.**

Gen. 15:3 to me t. hast g. no seed
Jos. 15:19 thou hast g. south land, Jud. 1:15
1 Sam. 22:13 t. hast g. him bread
2 Sam. 12:14 thou hast g. occasion
22:36 thou hast also g. Ps. 18:35
41 t. h. g. me necks of e. Ps. 18:40
Ezr. 9:13 thou hast g. us deliver.
Ps. 21:2 thou h. g. heart's desire
44:11 thou hast g. us like sheep
60:4 thou h. g. a banner to them
61:5 thou h. g. me the heritage
71:3 thou hast g. com. to save
John 17:2 thou hast g. him power
7 all things thou hast g. me
9 I pray for them thou h. g. me
11 keep those thou hast g. me
Rev. 16:6 t. h. g. blood to drink

**GIVER.**

Is. 24:2 taker of usury, so with g.
2 Cor. 9:7 G. loveth a cheerful g.

**GIVEST.**

Deut. 15:9 g. him naught, 10
Job 35:7 if righteous, what g.?
Ps. 50:19 g. thy mouth to evil
80:5 thou g. them tears to drink
104:28 that g. them, they gather
145:15 thou g. them their meat
Prov. 6:35 tho' thou g. many gifts
Ezek. 16:33 thou g. to thy lovers
34 g. reward, none is given
1 Cor. 14:17 thou g. thanks well

**GIVETH.**

Ex. 16:29 g. on sixth day bread
20:12 days long in land which L. g. Deut. 4:40; 5:16; 25:15
25:2 ev. man that g. it willingly
Deut. 2:29 into land which L. G. g. thee, 4:1, 21; 11:17, 31; 12:1, 10; 15:4, 7; 16:20; 17:14; 18:9; 19:1, 2, 10, 14; 21:1, 23; 24:4; 26:1, 2; 27:2, 3; 28:8; Jos. 1:11, 15
8:18 he g. power to get wealth
9:6 g. not land for thy righteo.
13:1 if a prophet g. thee a sign
16:5 which L. g. thee, 18; 17:2
Job 5:10 who g. rain upon earth
33:13 he g. no account of ways
34:29 g. quiet; 35:10 g. songs
36:6 g. right; 31 g. meat
Ps. 18:50 deliv. g. he to king
68:35 God of Is. that g. strength
119:130 entr of words g. light
127:2 so he g. his beloved sleep
Prov. 2:6 L g. wisdom out of m.
3:34 g. grace to lowly, Jam. 4:6; 1 Pet. 5:5
13:15 good understand. g. favor
21:26 right. g spareth not, 22:9
28:27 that g. to poor sh. not lack
Ec. 2:26 God g. to good man wisdom, to sinner g. travail
6:2 God g. him not power to eat
Is. 40:29 he g. power to the faint
42:5 he that g. breath to people
Jer. 5:24 g. rain; 31:55 g. sun
Lam. 3:30 g. cheek to him smit.
Hab. 2:15 woe to him. g. neigh.
Mat. 5:15 it g. light to all in ho.
John 3:34 God g. not Spirit
6:32 Father g. you true bread
John 6:33 who g. life to the world
37 all the Father g. me
10:11 good shepherd g. his life
14:27 not as the world g. give I
Acts 17:25 he g. to all life
Rom. 12:8 g. with simplicity
1 Cor. 3:7 G. that g. the increase
7:38 that g. in marriage
15:38 G. g. body as pleased him
57 thanks to G. who g. victory
2 Cor. 3:6 letter killeth, sp. g. life
1 Tim. 6:17 g. richly all things
Jam. 1:5 ask of God that g. to all
4:6 g. more grace, God g. grace
1 Pet. 4:11 of ability that God g.
Rev. 22:5 L. God g. them light

**GIVING.**

Deut. 10:18 stranger in g. food
21:17 g. him a double portion
Ruth 1:6 visited peo. in g. bread
Job 11:20 hope as g. up of ghost
Mat. 24:38 and g. in marriage
Acts 8:9 g. out himself
15:8 g. them the Holy Ghost
Rom. 4:20 st. in faith, g. G. glory
9:4 g. of law, service of God
1 Cor. 14:7 g. sou.; 16 g. thanks
2 Cor. 6:3 g. no offence
Phil. 4:15 conc. g. and receiving
1 Tim. 4:1 g. heed to seducing sp.
1 Pet. 3:7 g. honor to the wife
2 Pet. 1:5 g. all diligence
Jude 7 g. thems. to fornication
See THANKS.

**GLAD.**

Ex. 4:14 he will be g. in heart
1 K. 8:66 w. to tents g. 2 Chr. 7:10
Est. 5:9 Haman g.; 8:15 Sh. g.
Job 3:22 g. when find the grave
22:19 righte. see, g. Ps. 64:10
Ps. 16:9 my heart g. glory rejoi.
21:6 made him g. with count.
34:2 hear and be g. 69:32
45:8 have made thee g.
46:4 make g. city of God
67:4 the nations be g. and sing
90:15 make us g.; 92:4 made g.
97:1 let isles be g.; 8 Z. was g.
104:15 wine that maketh g.
34 be g. in Lord; 105:38 Eg. g.
107:30 are they g. bec. quiet
122:1 g. when said, Let us go
126:3 things, whereof are g.
Prov. 10:1 a g. father, 15:20
12:25 a good word maketh it g.
17:5 that is g. at calamities
23:25 father and mother be g.
24:17 heart not be g.
27:11 make my heart g.
Is. 35:1 wilderness be g.
Jer. 20:15 child born, ma. him g.
Dan. 6:23 king exceeding g.
Jon. 4:6 Jonah g. bec. of gourd
Zec. 10:7 chil. see it and be g.
Mark 14:11 g. and prom. Lu. 22:5
Luke 1:19 to show these g. tid.
8:1 g tidings of the kingdom
15:32 we make merry, be g.
John 8:56 saw my day, was g.
Acts 11:23 seen grace of G. was g.
13:48 Gentiles heard, were g.
Rom. 16:19 am g. on your behalf
1 Cor. 16:17 g. of coming of Step.
2 Cor. 2:2 that maketh me g.?
13:9 are g. when we are weak
1 Pet. 4:13 ye may be g. also

**GLAD, joined with rejoice.**

1 Chr. 16:31 let heav. be g. earth rej. Lord reigneth, Ps. 96:11
Ps. 9:2 I will be g. and rejoice
14:7 Jacob rejoice Is. be g. 53:6
31:7 be g. and rejoice in mercy
32:11 be g. and re. ye ri. 68:3
40:16 thee, be g. and rej. 70:4
48:11 Z. re. daugh. of J. be g.
90:14 we may be g. and rejoice
118:24 we will r. and be g. in it
Cant. 1:4 we will be g. and rej.
Is. 25:9 we will rej. and be g.
65:18 be you g. and rej. for ever
66:10 rej. ye with Jer. and be g.
Lam. 4:21 re. and be g. O dau.
Joel 2:21 O land, be g. and rej.
23 be g. ye child. of Zion, rej.
Hab. 1:15 they rejoice and are g.
Zep. 3:14 be g. and rej. O dau.
Mat. 5:12 r. and be g. great re.
Acts 2:26 heart r. tongue was g.
Rev. 19:7 be g. and r. marriage

**GLADLY.**

Mark 12:37 people heard Ch. g.
Acts 2:41 g. re. words were bapt.
21:17 the breth. received us g.
2 Cor. 11:19 ye suffer fools g.
12:9 most g. will I rather glory
15 I will g. spend and be spent

**GLADNESS.**

Num. 10:10 in day of g. ye shall
2 Sam. 6:12 Da. br. ark with g.
1 Chr. 16:27 strength and g. in
2 Chr. 29:30 sang praises with g.
30:21 Israel kept feast with g.
23 kept other seven days w. g.
Neh. 8:17 there was great g.
Est. 8:16 had light, and g. 17
9:17 day of feast, and g. 18, 19
Ps. 4:7 thou put g. in my heart
30:11 thou girded me with g.
45:7 anoi. with oil of g. Heb. 1:9
15 with g. shall they be brou.
51:8 make me to hear joy and g.
97:11 g. is sown for the upright
100:2 serve the Lord with g.
105:43 brought chosen with g.
106:5 that I may rejoice in g.
Cant. 3:11 day of g. of his heart
Is. 22:13 joy and g. slay. oxen
30:29 have song and g. of heart
35:10 obtain joy and g. 51:11
51:3 joy and g. found therein
Jer. 7:34 voice of mirth and g. 16:9; 25:10
31:7 sing with g. for Jacob
33:11 heard voice of joy and g.
48:33 joy and g. taken fr. field
Joel 1:16 joy and g. from h. of G.
Zec. 8:19 h. of Jud. joy and g.
Mark 4:16 who receive it with g.
Luke 1:14 shalt have joy and g.
Acts 2:46 eat meat w. g. of heart
12:14 she opened not gate for g.
14:17 fill. hea. with food and g.
Phil. 2:29 receive him with all g.

**GLASS, ES.**

Is. 3:23 Lord will take away g.

*1 Cor.* 13:12 we see through a *g.*
*2 Cor.* 3:18 beholding as in a *g.*
*Jam.* 1:23 man behold. face in *g.*
*Rev.* 4:6 sea of *g.* like unto crys.
15:2 sea of *g.* mingled with fire
21:18 city pure gold, like c. *g.* 21

*See* LOOKING.

**GLEAN, ED.**

*Lev.* 19:10 not *g.* v. *Deut.* 24:21
*Ruth* 2:2 let me go to field and *g.*
3 she came and *g.* after reapers
*Jer.* 6:9 they shall *g.* the remnant

**GLEANING, S.**

*Lev.* 19:9 not gath. *g.* of h. 23:22
*Jud.* 8:2 is not *g.* of gr. of Eph.
*Is.* 17:6 *g.* grapes shall be left
24:13 as *g.* grapes when vint.
*Jer.* 49:9 they not leave some *g.*?
*Mic.* 7:1 as grape *g.* of the vint.

**GLEDE.**

*Deut.* 14:13 shall not eat the *g.*

**GLISTERING.**

*1 Chr.* 29:2 I have pre. *g.* stones
*Job* 20:25 the *g.* sword cometh
*Luke* 9:29 his raim. white and *g.*

**GLITTER, ING.**

*Deut.* 32:41 if I whet. *g.* sword
*Job* 39:23 the *g.* spear rattleth
*Ezek.* 21:10 furb. that it may *g.*
28 furbished to cons. bec. of *g.*
*Nah.* 3:3 horseman lifteth *g.* sp.
*Hab.* 3:11 shining of thy *g.* spear

**GLOOMINESS.**

*Joel* 2:2 darkn. *g.* *Zep.* 1:15

**GLORIFY.**

*Ps.* 22:23 seed of Jacob *g.* him
50:15 and thou shalt *g.* me
86:9 nations shall come and *g.*
12 and I will *g.* thy name
*Is.* 24:15 *g.* ye Lord in the fires
25:3 the strong people *g.* thee
60:7 I will *g.* house of my glory
*Jer.* 30:19 I will also *g.* them
*Mat.* 5:16 *g.* Father in heaven
*John* 12:28 F. *g.* thy name
13:32 God sh. *g.* him in himself
16:14 he shall *g.* me
17:1 *g.* thy son, that thy Son *g.*
5 *g.* me with thine own self
21:19 what death he sho. *g.* G.
*Rom.* 15:6 mind and mouth *g.* G.
9 that Gentiles might *g.* God
*1 Cor.* 6:20 *g.* God in body and s.
*2 Cor.* 9:13 *g.* God for your subj.
*1 Pet.* 2:12 *g.* God in day of visi.
4:16 *g.* God on this behalf
*Rev.* 15:4 and *g.* thy name

**GLORIFIED.**

*Lev.* 10:3 bef. all peo. I will be *g.*
*Is.* 26:15 increased nation, art *g.*
44:23 L. hath *g.* himself in Is.
49:3 O Is. in whom I will be *g.*
55:5 Holy One of Is. hath *g.* 60:9
60:21 that I may be *g.*
61:3 planting of L. that he be *g.*
*Is.* 66:5 said, Let the Lord be *g.*
*Ezek.* 28:22 I will be *g.* in midst
39:13 the day that I shall be *g.*
*Dan.* 5:23 God hast thou not *g.*
*Mat.* 9:8 marvelled, and *g.* God, *Mark* 2:12; *Luke* 5:26
15:31 they *g.* the God of Israel
*Luke* 4:15 synagogues, being *g.*
7:16 and they *g.* God
13:13 made straight, and *g.* G.
17:15 leper *g.* G.; 23:47 centur.
*John* 7:39 because Jes. not yet *g.*
11:4 Son of God might be *g.*
12:16 but when Jesus was *g.*
23 the Son of men should be *g.*
28 I have *g.* it, will glorify it
13:31 Son of man *g.* God is *g.*
32 if G. be *g.* in him G. sh. gl.
14:13 Father may be *g.* in Son
15:8 my Father *g.* ye bear fruit
17:4 I have *g.* thee on earth
10 and I am *g.* in them
*Acts* 3:13 G. of fathers hath *g.* S.
4:21 men *g.* God
11:18 held peace, and *g.* God
13:48 Gentiles *g.* word of Lord
21:20 they of Jerusalem *g.* Lord
*Rom.* 1:21 they *g.* him not as G.
8:17 that we may be also *g.*
30 wh. he justified, them he *g.*
*Gal.* 1:24 and they *g.* God in me
*2 Thes.* 1:10 wh. he come to be *g.*
12 name of Jesus may be *g.*
3:1 that word of Lord may be *g.*
*Heb.* 5:5 so Christ *g.* not himself
*1 Pet.* 4:11 G. in all things be *g.*
14 but on your part he is *g.*
*Rev.* 18:7 how much *g.* herself

**GLORIFIETH, ING.**

*Ps.* 50:23 whoso. offer. praise *g.*
*Luke* 2:20 sheph. returned, *g.* G.
5:25 departed to own ho. *g.* God
18:43 blind man followed, *g.* G.

**GLORY, Substantive.**

*Gen.* 31:1 father's gotten this *g.*
*Ex.* 28:2 garm. for A. for *g.* 40
*1 Sam.* 2:8 inherit throne of *g.*
4:21 *g.* is departed from Isr. 22
*1 Chr.* 22:5 ho. for L. must be *g.*
29:11 thine is greatness, power and *g.* *Mat.* 6:13
*Est.* 5:11 H. told *g.* of riches
*Job* 39:20 *g.* of nostrils terrible
40:10 and array thyself with *g.*
*Ps.* 24:7 King of *g.* sh. come in, 9
10 who is this King of *g.*?
29:3 the God of *g.* thundereth
49:16 *g.* of house is increased
73:24 afterward receive me to *g.*
79:9 O God, for *g.* of name
85:9 that *g.* may dwell in land
89:17 art *g.* of their strength
106:20 changed *g.* into similit.
145:11 *g.* of thy kingdom
149:5 the saints be joyful in *g.*
*Prov.* 3:35 wise shall inherit *g.*
17:6 *g.* of children are fathers
20:29 *g.* of young men is stren.
25:27 to search own *g.* is not *g.*
28:12 righteous rej. there is *g.*
*Is.* 2:10 hide for *g.* of maj. 19:21
4:5 the *g.* shall be a defence
5:14 *g.* and pomp desc. unto it
10:3 where will ye leave *g.*?
12 punish *g.* of high looks
18 consume *g.* of his forest
13:19 Babylon *g.* of kingdoms
14:18 all lie in *g.* each in house
16:14 *g.* of M. sh. be contemned
17:3 as *g.* of children of Israel
4 *g.* of Jacob sh. be made th.
20:5 ashamed of Egypt their *g.*
21:16 the *g.* of Kedar shall fail
22:24 on him *g.* of father's ho.
23:9 to stain pride of *g.*
24:16 songs, even *g.* to righte.
35:2 *g.* of Lebanon be given
61:6 their *g.* ye boast yourselv.
66:11 delighted wi. abund. of *g.*
12 *g.* of Gentiles as flowing st.
*Jer.* 2:11 people have changed *g.*
13:11 might be to me for a *g.*
18 crown of your *g.*
*Ezek.* 20:6 the *g.* of all lands, 15
24:25 from them joy of their *g.*
25:9 open *g.* of the country
26:20 *g.* in land of the living
31:18 art thou thus like in *g.*?
*Dan.* 2:37 power and *g.* 7:14
4:36 *g.* of kingdom returned
11:39 increase with *g.*
*Hos.* 4:7 change *g.* into shame
9:11 Ephraim, their *g.* fly away
10:5 priests rejoi. for *g.* thereof
*Mic.* 1:15 Adullam the *g.* of Isr.
*Nah.* 2:9 none end of store and *g.*
*Hab.* 2:16 filled wi. shame for *g.*
*Hag.* 2:3 saw house in first *g.*?
7 fill house with *g.* saith Lord
9 *g.* of latter house greater
*Zec.* 2:5 I will be *g.* in midst
8 after *g.* sent me to nations
6:13 build temple, he bear *g.*
11:3 their *g.* is spoiled
12:7 *g.* of house of Dav. *g.* of J.
*Mat.* 4:8 kingd. and *g.* of them
6:2 sound trumpet, have *g.*
16:27 in *g.* of Fa. *Mark* 8:38
24:30 S. coming with power and *g.* *Mark* 13:26; *Luke* 21:27
*Luke* 2:14 *g.* to G. in high. 19:38
32 the *g.* of thy people Israel
4:6 power will I give th. and *g.*
9:31 in *g.* spake of his decease
*John* 17:5 *g.* wh. I had with thee
22 *g.* thou gavest me
*Acts* 7:2 G. of *g.* appeared
12:23 because he gave not G. *g.*
22:11 I could not see *g.* of light
*Rom.* 4:20 strong, giving *g.* to G.
6:4 raised by *g.* of the Father
8:18 not wor. be com. with *g.*
9:4 pertaineth *g.* and covenants
23 had afore prepared unto *g.*
11:36 *g.* for ev. *Gal.* 1:5; *2 Tim.* 4:18; *Heb.* 13:21; *1 Pet.* 5:11
16:27 to God be *g.* *1 Tim.* 1:17
*1 Cor.* 2:7 God ordained to our *g.*
8 not crucified the Lord of *g.*
11:7 woman is the *g.* of the man
15 wo. ha. long hair, is *g.* to h.
15:40 *g.* of celestial, *g.* of terres.
41 one *g.* of sun, ano. *g.* of m.
43 sown in dishon. raised in *g.*
*2 Cor.* 3:7 *g.* of his countenance
9 if condemnation be *g.* righteousness exceed in *g.*
10 no *g.* by reason of *g.* th. ex.
18 all are changed from *g.* to *g.*
4:17 work. eternal weight of *g.*
8:19 administered, to *g.* of Lord
23 messengers, and *g.* of Christ
*Eph.* 1:6 praise of *g.* of his grace
17 Father of *g.* give you Spirit
18 know what is riches of *g.*
3:13 tribulations, wh. is your *g.*
21 *g.* in the church by Chr. J.
*Phil.* 1:11 fruits, by Christ to *g.*
3:19 whose *g.* is in their shame
4:19 according to his rich. in *g.*
20 God and our F. be *g.* for ev.
*Col.* 1:27 Christ the hope of *g.*
3:4 ye sh. appear with him in *g.*
*1 Thes.* 2:6 nor of men sought *g.*
12 called you to king. and *g.*
20 for ye are our *g.* and joy
*2 Thes.* 1:9 pun. from *g.* of power
2:14 obtaining of *g.* of our Lord
*1 Tim.* 3:16 received up unto *g.*
*2 Tim.* 2:10 Christ, with eter. *g.*
*Heb.* 2:10 bringing sons unto *g.*
3:3 man counted worthy mo. *g.*
9:5 cherubim of *g.* shadowing
*Jam.* 2:1 faith of Jesus, L. of *g.*
*1 Pet.* 1:8 rej. with joy full of *g.*
11 testified *g.* that sho. follow
21 God raised him, gave him *g.*
24 *g.* of man as flower of grass
2:20 what *g.* is it, when buffet.?
4:14 spirit of *g.* resteth on you
5:1 the *g.* that shall be revealed
10 called us to eternal *g.* by C.
*2 Pet.* 1:3 that hath called us to *g.*
17 voice to him from excel. *g.*
3:18 to him be *g.* ever. *Rev.* 1:6
*Jude* 25 only G. our Savio. be *g.*
*Rev.* 4:11 worthy to rec. *g.* 5:12
7:12 blessing and *g.* to our God
11:13 rem. affrighted, gave *g.*

*See* CROWN, HONOR, VAIN.

**Give GLORY.**

*Jos.* 7:19 my son, *give g.* to God

1 Sam. 6:5 shall give g. to God
1 Chr. 16:28 g. to L. g. 29; Ps. 29:1, 2; 96:7, 8; Jer. 13:16
Ps. 84:11 L. will g. grace and g.
115:1 to thy name give g.
Is. 42:12 let them g. g. unto L.
Mal. 2:2 to heart, to give g.
Luke 17:18 returned to give g.
Rev. 4:9 those beasts give g.
14:7 fear God, give g. to him
16:9 repented not to give g.

### GLORY of God.

Ps. 19:1 heavens declare g. of G.
Prov. 25:2 g. of God to conceal
Ezek. 8:4 the g. of G. of Israel
9:3 g. of G. gone up fr. cherub
10:19 g. of God over th. 11:22
43:2 g. of God came from east
John 11:4 sickness is for g. of G.
40 shouldst see g. of God
Acts 7:55 S. looked, saw g. of G.
Rom. 3:23 short of g. of God
5:2 rej. in hope of the g. of God
15:7 as C. receiv. us, to g. of G.
1 Cor. 10:31 all to g. of G.
11:7 man is image and g. of God
2 Cor. 4:6 lig. of kno. of g. of G.
15 thanks. redound to g. of G.
Phil. 1:11 by Ch. to the g. of God
2:11 J. is Lord to the g. of God
Rev. 15:8 filled w. sm. f. g. of G.
21:11 Jerusa. having g. of God
23 the g. of God did lighten it

### His GLORY.

Deut. 5:24 L. hath showed his g.
33:17 his g. firstling of bullock
1 Chr. 16:24 declare his g. among the heathen, Ps. 96:3
Ps. 21:5 his g. is great in salva.
29:9 every one speak of his g.
49:17 his g. shall not descend
72:19 earth be filled with his g.
78:61 deliv. his g. to enemy's h.
89:44 hast made h. g. to cease
97:6 and all the people see h. g.
102:16 build J. appear in his g.
113:4 h. g. above heav. 148:13
Is. 3:8 to provoke eyes of his g.
6:3 whole earth full of his g.
10:16 his g. kindle a burning
59:19 his g. from rising of sun
60:2 his g. shall be seen
Jer. 22:18 Ah L. or Ah his g
Ezek. 43:2 earth shin. with h. g.
Dan. 5:20 took h. g. from him
Hab. 3:3 his g. covered heavens
Mat. 6:29 Sol. in h. g. Luke 12:27
19:28 S. of m. sit in h. g. Lu. 9:26
Luke 9:32 wh. awake, saw his g.
24:26 to enter into his g.
John 1:14 beheld h. g. g. of only
2:11 J. manifested forth his g.
12:41 said E. when saw his g.
Rom. 3:7 thro. my lie unto h. g.
9:23 known riches of his g.
Eph. 1:12 the praise of his g. 14
3:16 according to riches of his g.
Heb. 1:3 the brightness of his g.
1 Pet. 4:13 when h. g. be revealed
Jude 24 before presence of h. g.
Rev. 18:1 earth light. with h. g.

### My GLORY.

Gen. 45:13 of all my g.
Ex. 29:43 sanctified by my g.
33:22 while m. g. passeth by
Num. 14:22 wh. have seen m. g.
Job 19:9 hath stript me of my g.
29:20 my g. was fresh in me
Ps. 3:3 thou art m. g. and lifter
4:2 long turn m. g. to shame?
16:9 m. g. rej.; 30:12 m. g. sing
57:8 awake, m. g.; 62:7 m. g.
108:1 give praise with m. g.
Is. 42:8 m. g. not give, 48:11
43:7 created him for my g.
46:13 salvation for Israel my g.
60:7 will glorify house of my g.
66:18 shall come and see my g.
19 seen m. g. declare m. g.
Ezek. 39:31 set my g. am. heath.
Mic. 2:9 from chil. taken my g.
John 8:50 I seek not mi. own g.
17:24 they may behold my g.

### GLORY of the Lord.

Ex. 16:7 ye shall see g. of t. L.
10 g. of t. L. appear. Lev. 9:23; Num. 14:10; 16:19, 42; 20:6
24:16 g. of the Lord abode on S.
17 g. of the L. like devour. fire
40:34 g. of the L. filled taber. 35
Lev. 9:6 g. of the L. shall appear
Num. 14:21 filled with g. of L.
1 K. 8:11 the g. of the L. filled the house, 2 Chr. 5:14; 7:1, 2, 3; Ezek. 43:5; 44:4
Ps. 104:31 g. of the L. sh. endure
138:5 for great is the g. of t. L.
Is. 35:2 they shall see g. of t. L.
40:5 g. of the L. shall be reveal.
58:8 g. of the L. sh. be rearward
60:1 g. of the L. is risen
Ezek. 1:28 likeness of g. of t. L.
3:12 blessed be g. of the Lord
23 g. of the L. stood there
10:4 g. of the L. went fr. cherub
18 g. of L. departed from thre.
11:23 g. of the L. went from city
43:4 g. of t. L. came into house
Hab. 2:14 filled wi. kn. of g. of L.
Luke 2:9 g. of t. L. shone round
2 Cor. 3:18 g. of the Lord

### Thy GLORY.

Ex. 33:18 said, Show me thy g.
Ps. 8:1 thy g. above the heavens
45:3 sword on thigh, with thy g.
57:5 thy g. ab. earth, 11; 108:5
63:2 see thy power and g.
Ps. 90:16 let t. g. app. unto chil.
102:15 all kings of earth thy g.
Is. 22:18 chariots of t. g.
60:19 God thy g.; 62:2 see thy g.
63:15 behold from habit. of t. g.
Jer. 14:21 not dis. throne of t. g.
48:18 come down from thy g.
Hab. 2:16 spewing sh. be on t. g.

### GLORIOUS.

Ex. 15:6 right hand, O Lord, g.
11 like Lord, g. in holiness
Deut. 28:58 fear this g. name
2 Sam. 6:20 g. was the k. of Isr.
1 Chr. 29:13 praise thy g. name
Neh. 9:5 blessed be thy g. name
Ps. 45:13 king's dau. g. within
66:2 make his praise g.
72:19 blessed be g. name
76:4 more g. than mountains
87:3 g. things spoken of thee
111:3 work honorable and g.
145:5 speak of g. honor of maj.
12 make known g. majesty
Is. 4:2 branch of the Lord be g.
11:10 root of Jesse, his rest g.
22:23 for a g. throne to house
28:1 g. beauty is fading flower
4 g. beauty on head of valley
33:21 g. L. be a place of streams
49:5 I shall be g. in eyes of L.
60:13 the place of my feet g.
63:1 who is this, g. in apparel?
12 led them with his g. arm
14 people to make g. name
Jer. 17:12 a g. high throne from
Ezek. 27:25 g. in midst of seas
Dan. 11:16 he sh. stand in g. land
41 he shall enter into g. land
45 between seas, in g. holy m.
Luke 13:17 rejoiced for g. things
Rom. 8:21 into g. liberty of chil.
2 Cor. 3:7 ministration engra. g.
3:8 ministration of Sp. rather g.
4:4 lest light of g. gospel shine
Eph. 5:27 present it a g. church
Phil. 3:21 fashioned like g. body
Col. 1:11 accord. to his g. power
1 Tim. 1:11 accord. to g. gospel
Tit. 2:13 looking for g. appearing

### GLORIOUSLY.

Ex. 15:1 he hath triumphed g.
Is. 24:23 reign before ancients g.

### GLORY, Verb.

Ex. 8:9 Moses said, g. over me
2 K. 14:10 g. of this, and tarry
1 Chr. 16:10 g. ye in his holy name, Ps. 105:3
35 we may g. in thy praise
Ps. 63:11 swear. by him shall g.
64:10 the upright in heart sh. g.
106:5 I may g. with thy inheri.
Is. 41:16 shalt g. in Holy One
45:25 in L. shall seed of Isr. g.
Jer. 4:2 and in him shall they g.
9:23 let not wise, rich man g.
24 g. in this, that he knoweth
Rom. 4:2 he hath whereof to g.
5:3 we g. in tribulations also
15:17 I have whereof I may g.
1 Cor. 1:29 no flesh g. in his pre.
31 glor. g. in L. 2 Cor. 10:17
3:21 let no man g. in men
4:7 g. as if hadst not received?
9:16 nothing to g. of
2 Cor. 5:12 to g. on our behalf, who g. in apppearance
11:12 wherein g. be found
18 g. after the flesh, I will g.
30 if g. I will g. of my infirmi.
12:1 not expedient for me to g.
5 I g. of myself I will not g.
6 I desire to g. not be a fool
9 rather g. in my infirmities
Gal. 6:13 may g. in your flesh
14 I should g. save in the cross
2 Thes. 1:4 so that we g. in you
Jam. 3:14 if ye have envy. g. not

### GLORIEST, ETH.

Jer. 9:24 let him that g. 1 Cor. 1:31; 2 Cor. 10:17
49:4 why g. thou in valleys?

### GLORYING.

1 Cor. 5:6 your g. is not good
9:15 than any sh. make g. void
2 Cor. 7:4 great is my g. of you
12:11 I am become a fool in g.

### GLUTTON.

Deut. 21:20 this our son is a g.
Prov. 23:21 g. sh. come to pover.

### GLUTTONOUS.

Mat. 11:19 a man g. Luke 7:34

### GNASH, ED, ED, ETH, ING.

Job 16:9 he g. on me, Ps. 37:12
Ps. 35:16 g. on me with teeth
Ps. 112:10 he shall g. w. his teeth
Lam. 2:16 hiss and g. the teeth
Mat. 8:12 g. of t. 13:42, 50; 23:13; 24:51; 25:30; Luke 13:28
Mark 9:18 he foameth and g.
Acts 7:54 g. on him with teeth

### GNAT.

Mat. 23:24 strain at g. sw. camel

### GNAW, ED.

Zep. 3:3 they g. not the bones
Rev. 16:10 g. tongues for pain

### GO.

Gen. 3:14 on thy belly shalt g.
16:8 whither wilt thou g.?
24:42 prosper my way wh. I g.
58 wilt thou g. with this man?
26:16 Abi. said to Is. g. from us
28:20 if G. keep me in way I g.
32:26 let me g.; I will not let thee g. except thou bless me
37:30 whither shall I g.?
43:8 send the lad, we will g.

*Ex.* 3:19 will not let you *g.* 4:21
21 when ye *g.* sh. not *g.* empty
4:23 let my son *g.* if thou refuse,
8:2, 21; 9:2; 10:4
5:1 let my people *g.* 7:16; 8:1,
20; 9:1, 13; 10:3
2 nor will I let Israel *g.*
8:8 I will let people *g.* 28; 9:28
32 nor would he let people *g.*
7:14; 9:35; 10:26, 27
10:9 *g.* with our young and old
13:21 light to *g.* *Neh.* 9:12, 19
14:5 that we have let Israel *g.*
17:5 *g.* on before the people
23:23 angel *g.* bef. thee, 32:34
32:23 to *g.* before us, *Acts* 7:40
33:14 my pres. sh. *g.* with thee
34:9 if found grace, *g.* am. us
*Num.* 22:13 L. refuse. leave to *g.*
20 if the men called thee, *g.*
24:14 now I *g.* unto my people
31:23 make it *g.* through fire
32:6 *g.* to war, and ye sit here?
17 but we will *g.* ready armed
*Deut.* 1:33 way ye should *g.*
4:5 ye *g.* 6:1; 11:8, 11; 30:18
40 that it *g.* well, 5:16; 19:13
11:28 if ye *g.* after gods, 28:14
31:6 he it is that doth *g.*
7 must *g.* with this people
8 he it is that doth *g.* bef. thee
16 whither they *g.* amongst
21 know imagina. they *g.* abo.
*Jos.* 1:16 whither sendest will *g.*
3:4 may know way ye must *g.*
*Jud.* 1:25 let *g.* man and family
4:8 if thou wilt *g.* then I will *g.*
6:14 said, *g.* in this thy might
7:4 this shall *g.* the same sh. *g.*
18:6 is way wherein ye *g.*
9 not slothful to *g.* to possess
19:25 day began, they let her *g.*
*Ruth* 1:18 steadf. minded to *g.*
1 *Sam.* 5:11 let it *g.* th. its place
6:6 did they not let people *g.*?
12:21 ye *g.* after vain things
16:2 how can I *g.*? if Saul hear
17:33 not able to *g.* aga. Philist.
18:2 let him *g.* no more home
23:13 D. went whither could *g.*
2 *Sam.* 12:23 I shall *g.* to him
13:13 whither cause shame to *g.*
15:20 seeing I *g.* whither I may
17:11 *g.* to battle in thy person
20:11 David, let him *g.* after J.
1 *K.* 2:2 I *g.* way of all the earth
11:22 let me *g.* in any wise
13:17 nor *g.* by way thou camest
20:42 let *g.* a man appointed
22:4 *g.* with me, 2 *Chr.* 18:3
2 *K.* 3:7 *g.* with me ag. Moab?
4:23 wilt thou *g.* to him to-day?
6:22 set bread that he may *g.*
10:24 he that letteth him *g.*
18:21 *g.* into hand, *Is.* 36:6
2 *Chr.* 14:11 in thy name we *g.*
25:7 let not army of Israel *g.*
8 if thou wilt *g.* do it, be stro.
*Job* 6:18 they *g.* to nothing
10:21 before I *g.* whence I shall
not return, 16:22
20:26 it *g.* ill with him
21:29 not asked th. *g.* by way?
27:6 righteous. I will not let *g.*
*Ps.* 32:8 teach in way shalt *g.*?
39:13 before I *g.* hence, and be
42:9 why *g.* I mourning, 43:2
49:19 *g.* to generation of fathers
84:7 *g.* fr. strength to strength
85:13 right. shall *g.* before him
89:14 mercy and truth *g.* before
107:7 might *g.* to a city of habi.
132:7 we will *g.* into his taber.
139:7 whither *g.* from thy pres.
*Prov.* 2:19 none that *g.* return
3:28 *g.* and come ag. to-morrow
6:28 can one *g.* on hot coals
9:15 passengers who *g.* right on
14:7 *g.* from presence of foolish
15:12 neither scorner *g.* to wise
19:7 more do his friends *g.* far
22:6 train child in way he sh. *g.*
30:29 three things which *g.* well
*Ec.* 3:20 all *g.* unto one place
5:15 naked to *g.* as he came, 16
6:6 do not all *g.* to one place?
7:2 to *g.* to house of mourning
9:3 they *g.* to the dead
10:15 kn. not how to *g.* to city
12:5 mourners *g.* about streets
*Cant.* 3:4 I would not let him *g.*
*Is.* 3:16 and mincing as they *g.*
6:8 and who will *g.* for us?
9 *g.* tell his people, *Acts* 28:26
27:4 I would *g.* through them
28:13 they might *g.* and fall
45:13 shall let *g.* my captives
48:17 by way shouldest *g.*
58:8 righteousn. *g.* before thee
62:10 *g.* thro' *g.* thro' the gates
*Jer.* 1:7 shalt *g.* to all I send th.
9:2 I might *g.* from my people
31:22 how long *g.* about, O dau.
34:3 *g.* to Babylon, *Mic.* 4:10
40:4 good to *g.* there *g.* 5
42:22 die, whither ye des. to *g.*
46:22 voice shall *g.* like serpent
50:33 refused to let them *g.*
*Ezek.* 8:6 sho. *g.* far fr. sanctu.?
14:17 sword *g.* through the land
21:16 *g.* thee one way or other
*Hos.* 5:6 *g.* with floc. to seek L.
7:11 they *g.* to Assyria
12 when they *g.* I will spread
11:3 I taught Ephr. also to *g.*
*Mic.* 5:8 if he *g.* through tread.
*Zec.* 6:7 the bay sought to *g.*
8 these *g.* towards the north
8:21 inhab. of one city *g.* to an.
23 *g.* with you, we have heard
9:4 *g.* with whirlwinds of south
*Mat.* 2:22 Joseph was afraid to *g.*
5:41 *g.* mile, *g.* twain, *Luke* 7:8
8:7 and I say *g.* and he goeth
10:6 *g.* rath. to lost sheep of Is.
21:30 I *g.* sir, and went not
25:9 *g.* rather to them that sell
28:19 *g.* ye and teach all nations
*Mark* 6:38 *g.* see; 11:6 let th. *g.*
*Luke* 1:17 shall *g.* before him
9:51 set face to *g.* to Jerusalem
60 *g.* and preach kingd. of God
10:37 *g.* thou and do likewise
22:33 I am ready to *g.* to prison
68 not ans. me, nor let me *g.*
23:22 chastise him, let him *g.*
*John* 6:68 L. to whom sh. we *g.*
7:33 I *g.* unto him sent me
8:14 but I know whither I *g.*
21 I *g.* my way, whither I *g.*
13:36 whither I *g.* not follow
14:2 I *g.* to pre. place for you
4 whither I *g.* ye know
12 bec. I go to Father, 16:10
28 I *g.* to Father, 16:17, 28
19:12 if thou let this man *g.*
*Acts* 1:25 *g.* to his own place
3:13 when deter. to let him *g.*
4:21 threatened, let them *g.*
23 being let *g.* went to comp.
5:40 sh. not speak, let them *g.*
16:35 saying, Let those men, *g.*
20:22 *g.* bound in spirit to Jer.
25:12 to Cesar shalt thou *g.*
28:18 examined me, let me *g.*
*Rom.* 15:25 now I *g.* to Jerusal.
1 *Cor* 6:1 *g.* to law before unjust
10:27 and ye be disposed to *g.*
16:4 if meet I *g.* also, they sh. *g.*
2 *Cor.* 9:5 exhort breth. *g.* before
*Phil.* 2:23 how it will *g.* with me
*Jam.* 4:13 will *g.* un. such a city

*See* FREE.

**GO aside,**
*Num.* 5:12 if any man's wi. *g. a.*
*Deut.* 28:14 shalt not *g. a.* from
*Jer.* 15:5 *g. a.* to ask how doest
*Acts* 4:15 commanded th. to *g. a.*

**GO astray.**
*Deut.* 22:1 not see br.'s ox *g. a.*
*Ps.* 58:3 *g. a.* as soon as born
*Prov.* 5:23 in great. of folly *g. a.*
7:25 *g.* not *a.* into her paths
28:10 causeth righteous to *g. a.*
*Jer.* 50:6 shepherds caused *g. a.*
*Ezek.* 14:11 Israel *g.* no more *a.*

**GO away.**
*Ex.* 8:28 not *g.* very far *away*
*Deut.* 15:16 say, I will not *g. a.*
1 *Sam.* 24:19 he let ene. *g. a.*?
*Job* 4:21 doth not excel. *g. a.*?
15:30 by breath of mouth *g. a.*
*Jer.* 51:40 escaped sword *g. a.*
*Hos.* 5:14 I will tear and *g. a.*
*Mat.* 25:46 *g. a.* to ever. punish.
*John* 6:67 will ye also *g. a.*?
14:28 how I said, I *g. a.* 16:7

**GO their way**
*John* 18:8 let these *g. their way*

**GO thy way.**
*Dan.* 12:13 *g. t. way* till the end
*Acts* 24:25 *g. thy w.* for this time

**GO your way.**
*Mark* 11:2 *g. your w.* into village
*Luke* 10:10 rec. you not, *g. y. w.*

**GO back**
*Ex.* 14:21 caused sea to *g. back*
*Jos.* 23:12 ye in any wise *g. back*
*Jud.* 11:35 mouth, I cannot *g. b.*
2 *K.* 20:9 shall the shadow *g. b.*
*Ps.* 80:18 not *g. back* from thee
*Jer.* 40:5 *g. back* to Gedaliah, son
*Ezek.* 24:14 I will not *g. back*

**GO down.**
*Gen.* 46:3 fear not to *g. d.* to Eg.
*Num.* 16:30 *g. d.* into the pit
*Deut.* 24:15 nor sun *g. d.* on hire
*Jos.* 10:13 sun hasted not to *g. d.*
*Jud.* 7:10 fear to *g. d.* *g.* with P.
2 *Sam.* 11:8 *g. d.* to thy house.
15:20 make thee *g.* up and *d.*
2 *K.* 1:15 *g. down* with him
20:10 shadow to *g. d.* ten deg.
*Job* 21:13 in moment *g. d.* to gr.
*Ps.* 22:29 all that *g. d.* to dust
28:1 like th. *g. d.* to pit, 143:7
55:15 let *g. d.* quick into hell
107:23 that *g. d.* to sea in ships
115:17 any that *g. d.* into silence
*Prov.* 5:4 her feet *g. d.* to death
*Is.* 14:19 cast out, as those *g. d.*
30:2 woe to th. *g. d.* to Eg. 31:1
38:18 *g. d.* into pit cannot hope
60:20 sun sh. not *g. d.* nor moon
*Jer.* 50:27 let *g. d.* to slaughter
*Ezek.* 26:20 them that *g. d.* to
the pit, 31:14; 32:18, 24, 25,
29, 30
47:8 th. waters *g. d.* into desert
*Amos* 8:9 sun to *g. d.* at noon
*Mic.* 3:6 sun *g. d.* over prophets
*Mark* 13:15 him on ho. not *g. d.*
*Acts* 25:5 able to *g. d.* with me
*Eph.* 4:26 not sun *g. d.* on wrath

**GO forth.**
*Gen.* 8:16 *g. f.* of the ark, thou
42:15 not *g. f.* hence, except
2 *Sam.* 11:1 at time kings *g. f.*
18:2 I will *g. f.* with you myself
19:7 if thou *g.* not *f.* not tarry
1 *K.* 2:36 *g.* not *f.* any whither
22:22 he said, I will *g. forth*
2 *K.* 9:15 let none *g. forth*
19:31 out of Jerusalem shall *g.*
*forth* a remnant, *Is.* 37:32
*Job* 24:5 as wild asses *g.* they *f.*
*Ps.* 78:52 made his people to *g. f.*
108:11 wilt not *g. f.* with hosts?
*Prov.* 25:8 *g.* not *f.* hastily to st.
30:29 no king, *g. f.* by bands

Cant. 3:11 g. f. O dau. of Zion
7:11 let us g. f. into villages
Is. 2:3 out of Z. shall g. f. law, Mic. 4:2
42:13 L. sh. g. f. mighty man
48:20 g. f. Babylon, Jer. 50:8
49:9 say to prisoners, g. f.
17 made thee waste shall g. f.
62:1 till righteous. thereof g. f.
Jer. 6:25 g. not forth into field
14:18 if I g. f. into the field
15:2 whither shall we g. forth?
25:32 evil g. f. from nation to
31:4 thou shalt g. f. in dances
39 the measur. line shall g. f.
38:17 wilt g. f. to king of Baby.
43:12 he shall g. f. in peace
Ezek. 12:4 they that g. f. to capt.
30:9 in that day messen. sh. g. f.
Dan. 11:44 he sh. g. f. with fury
Joel 2:16 let brideg. g. f. cham.
Hab. 1:4 judgment never g. f.
Zec. 6:5 four spirits wh. g. f.
6 black horses g. f. to north
14:3 then sh. L. g. f. and fight
Mal. 4:2 ye sh. g. f. and grow
Mat. 24:26 is in desert, g. not f.
Acts 16:3 would Paul have g. f.
Heb. 13:13 let us g. forth to him
Rev. 16:14 sp. of devils wh. g. f.

**GO forward.**

Ex. 14:15 speak to Is. they g. f.
2 K. 20:9 shadow g. f. ten deg.
Job 23:8 I g. forw. but he is not there

**GO in, into, *or* not GO in.**

Num. 4:19 A. and sons sh. g. in
8:15 after that sh. Levites g. in
27:17 g. out and g. in before
32:9 should not g. into the land
Deut. 1:38 Josh. sh. g. in thither
4:1 and g. in and possess, 8:1
Ps. 26:4 not g. in with dissem.
118:19 open gates, I will g. in
119:35 g. in path of thy com.
132:7 we will g. into his tabern.
Prov. 27:10 nor g. i. brother's h.
Is. 2:19 g. into holes of rocks
Jer. 4:5 let us g. into def. cities
36:5 I cannot g. into house of L.
42:14 we will g. into land of E.
19 L. said, g. ye not i. Egypt
Ezek. 46:10 when they g. into
Nah. 3:14 g. into clay, and tread
Zec. 6:10 g. into house of Josiah
Mat. 2:20 take child, g. into Isr.
7:13 many there be that g. in
20:4 g. into the vineyard, 7
21:2 g. into village, Luke 19:30
31 harlots g. into king. of God
22:9 g. into highways, bid to
23:13 neither g. in, nor suffer
26:18 g. into city, Mark 14:13
Mark 6:36 may g. into country
8:26 nor g. into town, nor tell
16:15 g. into all the world
Luke 15:28 and would not g. i.
John 10:9 he shall g. in and out
Acts 1:11 ye see him g. i. heaven
Rev. 17:8 beast shall g. i. perdi.

*See* CAPTIVITY.

**GO in.**

Gen. 16:2 g. in unto my maid
19:34 make drink wine, g. in
30:3 my maid Bilhah, g. in to
38:8 g. in unto brother's wife
Deut. 21:13 thou g. in to her
22:13 take a wife, g. in to her
25:5 husb. brother g. in to her
Jos. 23:12 make marriages, g. in
Jud. 15:1 will g. in to my wife
2 Sam. 16:21 g. in to fath. concu.
1 K. 11:2 ye sh. not g. in to them
Ezek. 23:44 as they g. in to wom.
Amos 2:7 man and father g. in

**GO in peace.**

Gen. 15:15 g. to thy fathers in p.
Ex. 4:18 J. said to Mos. g. in p.
18:23 people g. to place in p.
Jud. 18:6 said to Danites, g. in p.
1 Sam. 1:17 E. said to H. g. in p.
20:42 Jona. said to Dav. g. in p.
25:35 David said to Ab. g. in p.
29:7 Achish said to Da. g. in p.
2 Sam. 15:9 said to Abs. g. in g.
1 K. 2:6 let not head g. do. in p.
2 K. 5:19 Elisha said, g. in peace
Mark 5:34 g. in p. and be whole
Luke 7:50 saved thee, g. in p. 8:48
Acts 15:33 they were let g. in p.

**Let us GO.**

Gen. 37:17 let us g. to Dothan
Ex. 3:18 now let us g. three days' journey, 5:3
5:8 they say, let us g. sac. 17
13:15 Ph. would hardly l. us g.
Deut. 13:2 l. us g. aft. gods, 6:13
1 Sam. 9:9 let us g. to seer, 10
11:14 let us g. to Gilgal, and
14:1 let us g. to Philistines, 6
2 K. 6:2 let us g. to Jordan
Ps. 122:1 let us g. into h. of Lord
Is. 2:3 let us g. to mount. of L.
Jer. 4:5 let us g. into def. cities
6:5 let us g. destroy her palaces
35:11 let us g. to Jeru. for fear
46:16 let us g. to our people
51:9 let us g. ev. one to country
Mark 1:38 let us g. to next towns
14:42 let us g. he that betrayeth
Luke 2:15 let us g. to Bethlehem
John 11:7 let us g. to Judea
15 let us g. to him; 16 that we
14:31 arise, let us g. hence
Acts 15:36 let us g. visit brethren
Heb. 6:1 let us g. to perfection

**I will GO.**

Gen. 13:9 I w. g. right, I w. g. l.
24:58 wilt g. with man? I. w. g.
33:12 I will g. bef. thee, Is. 45:2
45:28 I w. g. see him bef. I die
Num. 20:19 I will g. on feet
23:3 stand by burnt-off. I w. g.
Deut. 2:27 I will g. along high.
Jud. 1:3 I w. g. with thee
4:8 if thou g. with me, I w. g.
9 I will surely g. with thee
16:20 I w. g. as at other times
Ruth 1:16 wh. thou goest, I w. g.
2 K. 6:3 he answered, I will g.
2 Chr. 18:29 said, I w. g. to battle
Ps. 43:4 then w. I g. to altar of
66:13 I will g. into thy house
71:16 I will g. in strength of L.
118:19 open gates, I will g. in
Jer. 2:25 strangers, after I will g.
Ezek. 38:11 I will g. to them.
Hos. 2:5 said, I w. g. after lovers
7 I will g. to my first husband
5:15 I will g. to my place, till
Mic. 1:8 I w. g. stript and naked
Zec. 8:21 seek the Lord, I will g.
Mat. 26:32 I w. g. before into Galilee, Mark 14:28
Luke 15:18 I w. arise and g. to
Acts 18:6 hence I w. g. to Gent.

**GO near.**

Deut. 5:27 g. n. hear all L. says
2 Sam. 1:15 g. n. fall upon him
Job 31:37 as a prince wou. I g. n.
Acts 8:29 g. n. join to chariot

**GO not, *or* not GO.**

Ex. 33:15 if thy presence g. not
Num. 10:30 Hob. said, I will n. g.
20:20 he said, Thou shalt n. g.
22:12 said to Bal. shalt not g.
18 n. g. bey. word of L. 24:13
Deut. 3:27 shalt n. g. over Jordan
6:14 ye shall n. g. after other gods, 1 K. 11:10
24:19 thou sh. n. g. to fetch it
32:52 thou shalt not g. thither
Jos. 8:4 g. n. far from the city
Jud. 20:8 we will n. g. to tent
Ruth 3:17 g. n. empty to mother
1 Sam. 17:39 D. said, I cannot g.
29:8 I may not g. to fight enc.
2 Sam. 13:25 n. all g. would n. g.
2 K. 2:18 did I not say, g. n.?
1 Chr. 21:30 David could n. g.
2 Chr. 25:13 soldiers should n. g.
Prov. 4:13 take instruc. let n. g.
14 g. n. into way of evil men
22:24 with furious man sh. n. g.
Is. 52:12 shall n. g. with haste
Jer. 10:5 be borne, they cann. g.
16:8 sh. n. g. to house of feast.
25:6 g. n. after other gods, 35:15
27:18 vessels left g. not to Baby.
42:19 g. not into Egypt, 43:2
49:12 thou shalt not g. unpun.
Lam. 4:18 cannot g. in streets
Ezek. 42:14 priests sh. not g.
Mat. 10:5 g. n. into way of Gent.
Luke 10:7 g. n. fr. house to house
17:23 there, g. n. after, 21:8

**GO over.**

Deut. 3:25 let me g. o. see land
28 Joshua sh. g. o. before, 31:3
4:14 land whither ye g. over, 26; 31:13; 32:47
22 I must not g. o. Jordan
24:20 shalt not g. o. the boughs
30:13 who shall g. o. sea for us
31:3 the Lord will g. o. before
34:4 thou shalt not g. o. thither
Jos. 1:2 arise, g. over this Jordan
Jud. 12:5 Eph. said, Let me g. o.
1 Sam. 13:1 let us g. o. to Ph. 6
30:10 so faint, could not g. o.
2 Sam. 16:9 let me g. o. and take
19:37 Chimham, let him g. o.
Is. 8:7 come and g. over banks
11:15 make men g. o. dry-shod
51:23 bow down, we may g. o.
54:9 waters of N. no more g. o.
Jer. 41:10 Ishm. departed to g. o.

**GO out.**

Gen. 9:10 all that g. out of ark
24:11 women g. o. to draw wat.
45:1 every man g. o. from me
Ex. 6:11 let child. of Isr. g. out
8:29 behold, I g. out from thee
11:8 after that I will g. out
10 not let chil. of Israel g. out
12:22 none shall g. out at door
16:4 people g. o. and gather
29 no man g. o. on sev. day
21:2 in sev. year he sh. g. o. free
3 came by hims. g. o. by him.; if marr. wife g. o. with him
4 he shall g. out by himself
5 if serv. say, I will not g. o.
7 maid-serv. not g. o. as men
11 then shall she g. o. free
Lev. 6:13 fire on altar never g. o.
8:33 not g. o. of tab. in sev. days
10:7 not g. out at door, lest die
14:38 priest shall g. o. of house
15:16 if man's seed of cop. g. o.
16:18 sh. g. o. to altar before L.
21:12 nor g. out of sanctuary
25:28 in jubilee it sh. g. o. 31, 33
30 not g. o. in jub.; 54 sh. g. o.
Deut. 24:5 taken wife, not g. o.
28:25 thou shalt g. out one way
Jos. 2:19 who g. o. blood on head
Jud. 9:38 g. o. and fight them
16:20 will g. o. as at oth. times
20:28 sh. I again g. out to battle
1 Sam. 19:3 g. o. stand bes. fath.
20:11 let us g. out into the field
28:1 Achish said, g. o. with me
2 Sam. 5:24 the L. sh. g. o. befo.
21:17 thou sh. g. no more o.
1 K. 15:17 not suf. any to g. o. or come in to Asa, 2 Chr. 16:1
20:31 ropes on our heads, g. o.

1 Chr. 20:1 kings g. o. to battle
2 Chr. 18:21 g. o. be a lying spirit
20:17 to-morrow g. out against
26:18 g. o. of sanctuary, hast. tr.
20 yea, himself hasted to g. o.
Job 15:13 words g. o. of mouth
Ps. 60:10 not g. o. with armies
Prov. 22:10 scorner, conten. g. o.
Ec. 8:3 not hasty to g. o. of sight
Is. 52:11 depart, g. o. fr. thence
12 ye sh. not g. o. with haste
55:12 ye shall g. out with joy
Jer. 21:12 lest fury g. o. like fire
51:45 g. ye o. of midst of her
Ezek. 15:7 shall g. out from fire
44:3 prince sh. g. o. same way
46:9 enter. by north, g. o. by s.
Amos 4:3 sh. g. out at breaches
Zec. 14:8 liv. waters g. o. fr. J.
Mat. 25:6 bridegr. cometh, g. o.
Luke 9:5 when ye g. o. of city
14:21 g. o. into streets and lanes
23 g. o. into high. and hedges
1 Cor. 5:10 must g. o. of world
Heb. 11:8 A. when he call. to g. o.
Rev. 3:12 over. g. no more out
20:8 sh. g. o. to deceive nations

**GO to.**

Gen. 11:3 g. to, let us make brick
4 g. to, let us build; 7
Ec. 2:1 g. to no now, I will prove
Is. 5:5 g. to, I tell what I will
Jam. 4:13 g. to, ye that say
5:1 g. to now, ye rich men

**GO up.**

Gen. 35:1 arise, g. up to Bethel, 3
44:33 let lad g. up with breth.
34 sh. I g. up to father? 45:9
50:6 Phar. said, g. up, bury fa.
Ex. 8:3 frogs g. up into house
19:12 g. not up into mount
20:26 nor sh. g. up by steps
24:2 neither sh. peo. g. up with
32:30 sinned a sin, I will g. up
33:1 g. up, thou and the people
3 I will not g. up in midst
34:24 not desire land, g. up
Lev. 19:16 thou shalt not g. up and down as a tale-bearer
Num. 13:30 let g. up and pos. it
31 not able to g. up ag. people
14:42 g. not up; 44 pres. to g.
Deut. 25:7 let bro.'s wife g. up
30:12 who sh. g. up to heaven
Jos. 7:3 g. up, 3000 g. up
22:33 not intend to g. up again.
Jud. 1:1 who g. up for us to fight
2 L. said, Judah sh. g. up, 20:18
2:1 I made you g. up out of Eg.
11:37 g. up and down on moun.
18:9 we may g. up against them
20:9 g. up by lot against Gibeah
18 which sh. g. up first to bat.
23 shall I g. up? 28 g. up aga.
1 Sam. 1:22 not g. up till child
6:20 to whom sh. he g. up fr. us?
9:13 find him before he g. up
14 Samuel to g. up to place, 19
14:9 say, Tarry, will not g. up
10 come unto us, we will g. up
2 Sam. 2:1 I g. up to any cities of Ju.? L. said, g. up to Hebr.
5:19 shall I g. up aga. Philis.?
15:20 I make thee g. up with us
19:34 how long have I to live, that I should g. up?
24:18 g. up, rear alt. 1 Chr. 21:18
1 K. 12:24 not g. up, 2 Chr. 11:4
27 people g. up to do sacrifice
28 too much to g. up to Jerus.
18:43 g. up look towards sea
22:6 g. up, for the Lord shall deliver it, 12; 2 Chr. 18:11, 14
20 g. up fall at Ram. 2 Ch. 18:19
2 K. 1:3 g. up meet messengers
2:23 g. up, thou bald head
3:7 wilt thou g. up ag. Moab?
8 Which way sh. we g. up.?
12:17 Haz. set face to g. up to J.
18:25 g. up ag. land, Is. 36:10
20:5 on third day sh. g. up
8 sign that I g. up? Is. 38:22
22:4 g. up to Hilkiah, high-pr.
1 Chr. 14:10 sh. I g. up? 14 g. not
2 Chr. 18:5 sh. we g. up to Ram.?
36:23 let him g. up, Ezr. 1:3
Ezr. 7:9 to g. up from Babylon
13 minded to g. up, go with me
Neh. 4:3 fox g. up he break down
Ps. 104:8 g. up by mountains
132:3 I will not g. up into bed
Cant. 6:6 sheep g. up from wash.
7:8 I will g. up to palm-tree
Is. 2:3 let us g. up to mountain of Lord, Mic. 4:2
7:6 let us g. up against Judah
15:5 with weep. sh. they g. up
21:2 g. up, E.; 34:10 smoke g. up
35:9 nor ravenous beast g. up
36:10 g. up against this land
Jer. 5:10 g. ye up upon her walls
6:4 and let us g. up at noon
21:2 Nebuchadnezzar may g. up
22:20 g. up to Lebanon, and cry
31:6 let us g. up to Z. to the L.
46:8 I will g. up and cov. earth
11 g. up into Gilead, take balm
48:5 continual weep. sh. g. up
49:28 g. up to Kedar, spoil
50:21 g. up aga. land of Merath.
Ezek. 38:11 g. up to unwalled v.
40:26 seven steps to g. up to it
Hos. 4:15 nei. g. up to Bethaven
Hag. 1:8 g. up to mount. bring
Zec. 14:16 g. up fr. year to year
Mat. 20:18 we g. up to Jerusal. Mark 10:33; Luke 18:31
Luke 14:10 Friend, g. up higher
John 7:8 g. up to feast, I g. not
Acts 15:2 g. up to Jer. about qu.
21:4 Paul not g. up to Jerus. 12
25:9 wilt thou g. up to Jeru.?

**GO a whoring.**

Ex. 34:15 g. a whor. after gods
16 sons, daughters g. a whor.
Lev. 20:5 cut off all that g. a w.
Num. 15:39 ye use to g. a whor.
Deut. 31:16 people will g. a who.
2 Chr. 21:13 Je. made Ju. g. a w.
Ps. 73:27 destroyed all g. a who.
Ezek. 6:9 g. a whor. after idols

**GOEST.**

Gen. 28:15 keep thee wh. thou g.
32:17 whi. g. thou? Jud. 19:17; Zec. 2:2; John 13:36; 16:5
Ex. 33:16 that thou g. with us
34:12 no cove. whither thou g.
Num. 14:14 g. bef. them by day
Deut. 11:10 thou g. is not as E.
12:29 cut off nations wh. thou g.
20:1 g. to battle, seest, 21:10
23:20 God bless thee whither thou g. Jos. 1:7
28:6 blessed when thou g. out
19 cursed when thou g. out
21 pestilence whither thou g.
63 plucked land whi. thou g.
32:50 die in mount whither g.
Jos. 1:9 L. with thee whi. th. g.
Jud. 14:3 g. take a wife of Phil.
Ruth 1:16 whi. thou g. I will go
2 Sam. 15:19 where. g. with us?
1 K. 2:37 day g. over brook, 42
Ps. 44:9 g. not forth with armies
Prov. 4:12 when g. steps not str.
6:22 when thou g. it shall lead
Ec. 5:1 keep thy foot, g. to hou.
9:10 wisdom in grave whith. g.
Jer. 45:5 for prey whith. thou g.
Mat. 8:19 I will follow whithersoever thou g. Luke 9:57
Luke 12:58 thou g. with adver.
John 11:8 g. thou thither again?
14:5 we know not whi. thou g.

**GOETH.**

Ex. 7:15 he g. out into water
22:26 del. by that sun g. down
28:29 Aaron bear when he g.
30 Aaron's heart when he g. in
35 sound heard when he g. in
Lev. 11:21 eat that g. on all four
14:46 that g into house unclean
15:32 seed g. from him, 22:4
16:17 none in taber. when he g
22:3 who g. to holy things unc
27:21 when it g. in jubilee
Num. 5:29 when wife g. aside
Deut. 1:30 L. which g. before
9:3 God is he that g. before you
20:4 Lord your G. g. with you
23:9 when host g. ag. enemies
24:13 deli. pledge when sun g
Jud. 5:31 when g. in might
1 Sam. 22:14 Dav. who g. at bid.
30:24 his part is that g. to bat.
2 K. 5:18 g. to house of Rimmon
11:8 king as he g. 2 Chr. 23:7
Job 7:9 g. to grave, no more
9:11 he g. by me, I see him not
34:8 g. with workers of iniquity
37:2 sound g. out of mouth
39:21 he g to meet armed men
Ps. 17:1 g. not out of feigned lips
41:6 when he g. abroad, he tell.
68:21 such as g. on in trespass.
88:16 fierce wrath g. over me
97:3 a fire g. before him, burn.
104:23 man g. forth to work
126:6 he g. forth and weepeth
146:4 breath g. forth, he return.
Prov. 6:29 g. in to neigh. wife
11:10 when g. well with right.
16:18 pride g. befo. destruction
20:19 g. about as tale-bearer
26:9 thorn g. into hand
20 wh. no wood is, fire g. out
31:18 candle g. not out by night
Ec. 1:5 sun g. down, and hasteth
3:21 the spirit of man g. up, the spirit of beast g. down
12:5 bec. man g. to long home
Is. 28:19 from time it g. forth
30:29 when one g. with a pipe
55:11 my word be that g. forth
59:8 g. therein sh. not know pe.
63:14 a beast g. down into val.
Jer. 5:6 g. out thence be torn
6:4 woe unto us, for day g.
21:9 g. out to Chal. sh. live, 38:2
22:10 weep for him that g.
30:23 whirlwind of Lord g. forth
44:17 do what g. out of mouth
49:17 g. by it be aston. 50:13
Ezek. 7:14 but none g. to battle
33:31 heart g. after covetousn.
44:27 in day he g. into sanct.
Hos. 6:4 good. as dew g. away
5 judgments as light that g.
Zec. 5:3 this the curse that g.
6 this is an ephah that g. forth
Mat. 8:9 Go. and he g. Luke 7:8
13:44 for joy g. and selleth all
15:11 what g. into mouth defil.
17:21 g. not out but by prayer
26:24 Son of man g. as it is wri. Mark 14:21; Luke 22:22
28:7 g. bef. to Gali. Mark 16:7
John 3:8 canst not tell whi. it g.
7:20 g. about to kill thee?
10:4 he g. before, sheep follow
11:31 she g. unto the grave
12:35 knoweth not whither he g. 1 John 2:11
1 Cor. 6:6 bro. g. to law wi. bro.
9:7 g. a warf. at own charges?
Jam. 1:24 beholdeth him. and g.

*Rev.* 14:4 follow Lamb whi. he *g.*
17:11 of the seven, *g.* into perd.
19:15 out of mouth *g.* sharp sw.

**GOING.**

*Ex.* 17:12 to *g.* down of sun
23:4 if thine ene.'s ox *g.* astray
*Num.* 34:4 *g.* forth be from south
*Deut.* 16:6 pass. at *g.* down of sun
33:18 rejoice, Zebulun, in *g.* out
*Jos.* 7:5 smote them in *g.* down
10:11 in *g.* down to Bethoron
27 *g.* down of sun car. taken
23:14 *g.* the way of all the earth
*Jud.* 19:18 I am *g.* to house of L.
1 *Sam.* 10:3 3 men *g.* up to God
2 *Sam.* 2:19 in *g.* he turned not
5:24 sound of *g.* in, 1 *Chr.* 14:15
1 *K.* 17:11 she was *g.* to fetch it
22:36 proc. at *g.* down of sun
2 *K.* 2:23 *g.* by way, child. mock.
9:27 smote Ahaziah at *g.* to Gur
2 *Chr.* 18:34 sun *g.* down, he died
*Job* 1:7 from *g.* to and fro, 2:2
33:24 deliv. from *g.* down to pit
28 deliver soul from *g.* into pit
*Ps.* 19:6 *g.* from end of heaven
50:1 from rising of sun to *g.* down, 113:3; *Mal.* 1:11
104:19 sun knoweth his *g.* down
*Prov.* 7:27 *g.* to chamb. of death
14:15 prudent looketh well to *g.*
30:29 yea, four are comely in *g.*
*Is.* 13:10 sun darkened in *g.*
*Jer.* 50:4 *g.* and weeping seek L.
*Ezek.* 40:31 *g.* up 8 steps, 34, 37
44:5 every *g.* forth of sanctuary
46:12 after *g.* forth, shut gate
*Dan.* 6:14 till *g.* down of sun
9:25 *g.* forth of commandment
*Hos.* 6:3 his *g.* forth is prepared
*Mat.* 26:46 let us be *g.* he is at h.
*Luke* 14:31 what king *g.* to war?
*John* 8:59 *g.* thro. midst of them
*Acts* 20:5 *g.* before, tar. at Troas
*Rom.* 10:3 *g.* to estab. own right.
1 *Tim.* 5:24 sins *g.* bef. to judg.
*Heb.* 7:18 a disannul. of com. *g.*
*Jude* 7 *g.* after strange flesh, are

*See* COMING.

**GOINGS.**

*Num.* 33:2 Mos. wrote th. *g.* out
*Num.* 34:5 the *g.* out of their bor. 8, 9, 12; *Jos.* 15:4, 7, 11; 16:3, 8; 18:12, 14
*Job* 34:21 he seeth all his *g.*
*Ps.* 17:5 hold my *g.* in thy paths
40:2 and established my *g.*
68:24 seen thy *g.* even *g.* of God
140:4 purposed to overthrow *g.*
*Prov.* 5:21 he pondereth all his *g.*
20:24 man's *g.* are of the Lord
*Is.* 59:8 no judgment in their *g.*
*Ezek.* 42:11 *g.* out accord. to fas.
43:11 show them *g.* out thereof
*Mic.* 5:2 whose *g.* forth from

**GOAD, S.**

*Jud.* 3:31 slew 600 with ox *g.*
1 *Sam.* 13:21 had file to sharp. *g.*
*Ec.* 12:11 words of wise as *g.*

**GOAT.**

*Lev.* 3:12 if his offering be a *g.*
4:24 lay his hand on head of *g.*
7:23 eat no fat of ox, sheep, or *g.*
9:15 the *g.* which was sin-offer.
10:16 Moses sought *g.* sin-offer.
16:9 Aaron shall bring the *g.*
22 let go the *g.* in wilderness
17:3 whosoever killeth a *g.*
22:27 *g.* is brought forth 7 days
*Num.* 15:27 thro. ignor. bring *g.*
18:17 first. of *g.* sh. not redeem
28:22 one *g.* for a sin-offering, 29:22, 28, 31, 34, 38
*Deut.* 14:4 eat ox, sheep, and *g.*
*Ezek.* 43:25 prepa. every day a *g.*
*Dan.* 8:5 the *g.* had a nota. horn
21 rough *g.* is king of Grecia

**He-GOAT, S.**

*Num.* 7:17 five rams, five *he-g.* 23, 29, 35, 41, 47, 53, 59, 65, 71, 77, 83
88 *he-g.* sixty, the lambs sixty
*Deut.* 32:14 *he-g.* of breed of Bas.
2 *Chr.* 17:11 Arab. br. 7,700 *he-g.*
29:21 seven *he-g.* for sin-offering
*Ezr.* 6:17 at dedication 12 *he-g.*
8:35 children offered 12 *he-g.*
*Ps.* 50:9 I will take no *he-g.* out
*Prov.* 30:31 com. in going, a *he-g.*
*Is.* 1:11 not in the blood of *he-g.*
*Jer.* 50:8 as the *he-g.* before flocks
51:40 bring like rams with *he-g.*
*Ezek.* 34:17 betw. rams and *he-g.*
*Dan.* 8:5 behold, a *he-g.* fr. west
8 the *he-g.* waxed very great

**Live GOAT.**

*Lev.* 16:20 bring *l. g.*; 21 lay ha.

**Scape-GOAT.**

*Lev.* 16:8 the other lot for *sca.-g.*
10 let him go for *sca.-g.* to wil.
26 that let go *scape-g.* shall

**She-GOAT, S.**

*Gen.* 15:9 heifer, a *she-g.* of 3 ye.
31:38 *she-g.* not cast th. young
32:14 200 *she-g.* and 20 he-goats

**Wild GOAT.**

*Deut.* 14:5 ye sh. eat the *wild g.*

**GOATS.**

*Gen.* 27:9 fetch two kids of *g.*
16 put skins of *g.* on his hands
30:32 spotted and speck. am. *g.*
33 speckled *g.*; 35 removed *g.*
37:31 killed a kid of the *g.*
*Ex.* 12:5 take it fr. sheep or *g.*
*Lev.* 1:10 offering be sheep or *g.*
4:23 if sin come to knowl. shall bring a kid of the *g.* 28; 5:6
9:3 kid of *g.* for a sin-offering
16:5 two kids of *g.*; 7 two *g.* pr.
22:19 a male of the sheep or *g.*
23:19 kid of *g.* for a sin-offering, *Num.* 7:16; 15:24
*Num.* 7:87 kids of *g.* for a sin-of.
1 *Sam.* 25:2 Nabal had a thou. *g.*
*Ps.* 50:13 or will I drink bl. of *g.*
66:15 I will offer bullo. with *g.*
*Prov.* 27:26 *g.* are price of field
27 thou sh. have *g.* milk enou.
*Cant.* 4:1 hair as flock of *g.* 6:5
*Is.* 34:6 sw. fat with blood of *g.*
*Ezek.* 27:21 Arabia occup. in *g.*
39:18 drink blood of la. and *g.*
43:22 second day offer kid of *g.*
45:23 kid of *g.* daily for sin-off.
*Zec.* 10:3 I punished the *g.*
*Mat.* 25:32 divid. sheep from *g.*
33 set the *g.* on his left hand
*Heb.* 9:12 entered by blood of *g.*
13 if the blood of *g.* sanctifieth
19 took blood of *g.* and sprink.
10:4 pos. blood of *g.* take sins

**GOAT'S hair.**

*Ex.* 25:4 offer. ye sh. take, *g. h.*
26:7 make curtains of *g. hair*
35:6 let him bring *g. hair*
*Ex.* 35:23 with wh. was fo. *g. h.*
26 all the women spun *g. hair*
36:14 curtains of *g. h.* for tent
*Num.* 31:20 purify work of *g. h.*
1 *Sam.* 19:13 pillow of *g. hair*, 16

**GOAT-SKINS.**

*Heb.* 11:37 wandered in *g.-skins*

**Wild GOATS.**

1 *Sam.* 24:2 Da. on rocks of *w. g.*
*Job* 39:1 when *wild g.* br. forth
*Ps.* 104:18 high hills ref. for *w. g.*

GOB. 2 *Sam.* 21:18

**GOBLET.**

*Cant.* 7:2 thy navel like round *g.*

**GOD,** *referred to man.*

*Ex.* 4:16 be to Aaron inst. of G.
7:1 made thee a G. to Pharaoh

**GOD,** *for idol.*

*Jud.* 6:31 if a *g.* let him plead
8:33 made Baal-berith their *g.*
9:27 went into house of their *g.*
11:24 which Chemo. thy *g.* giv.
16:23 Philis. *g.* was Dagon, 24
1 *Sam.* 5:7 hand is sore on our *g.*
1 *K.* 11:33 worshipp. *g.* of Moab
18:27 he is a *g.* either talking or
2 *K.* 1:2 B. the *g.* of Ekron, 16
19:37 wors. in house of Nisroch, his *g.* 2 *Chr.* 32:21; *Is.* 37:38
*Ps.* 16:4 hasten after another *g.*
*Is.* 44:10 formed *g.* or molt. im.?
15 maketh *g.* worship. it, 17
45:20 pray to a *g.* cannot save
46:6 maketh it a *g.* they wors.
*Dan.* 1:2 ves. to house of his *g.*
4:8 according to name of my *g.*
11:36 magnify him. above ev. *g.*
*Amos* 5:26 star of y. *g.* *Acts* 7:43
8:14 say, Thy *g.* O Dan, liveth
*Jon.* 1:5 cried ev. man to his *g.*
*Mic.* 4:5 walk in name of his *g.*
*Hab.* 1:11 imput. power to his *g.*
*Acts* 12:22 voice of a *g.* not a man

**Any GOD.**

*Ex.* 22:20 sac. to *a. g.* save L.
2 *Sam.* 7:22 is there *any g.* besides, 1 *Chr.* 17:20
*Dan.* 3:28 not worship *a. g.* exc.
6:7 petition of *a. g.* or man, 12
11:37 neither sh. he regard *a. g.*

**Other GOD.**

*Ex.* 34:14 shalt worship no *o. g.*
*Dan.* 3:29 no *other g.* can deliver
1 *Cor.* 8:4 is none *o. g.* but one

**Strange GOD.**

*Deut.* 32:12 no *s. g.* with them
*Ps.* 44:20 out hands to *strange g.*
81:9 no *strange g.* be in thee
*Is.* 43:12 no *s. g.* among them
*Dan.* 11:39 thus sh. do with *s. g.*

**GOD.**

*Gen.* 16:13 Lord, thou G. seest
17:7 a G. to thee and thy seed
31:13 I am the G. of Bethel
42:28 what is this G. done us?
45:8 you sent me hither, but G.
48:21 I die, but G. be with you
*Ex.* 6:7 you to me, to you G.
18:19 and G. shall be with thee
*Num.* 23:23 what G. hath wro.?
24:23 who live when G. do. this?
*Deut.* 4:7 wh. nat. hath G. so ni.?
29:13 he may be to thee a G.
1 *Sam.* 3:17 G. do so and more al. 14:44; 25:22; 2 *Sam.* 3:9, 35; 19:13; 1 *K.* 2:23; 2 *K.* 6:31
17:46 know there is a G. in Is.
22:3 know what G. will do
2 *Sam.* 22:32 who is G. save the Lord? *Ps.* 18:31
1 *K.* 18:21 if the L. be G. follow
39 the Lord, he is G. the Lord
2 *K.* 19:15 thou art G. even thou
2 *Chr.* 20:6 O Lord G. art thou not G. in heaven?
*Ezr.* 1:3 his G. be with him
*Neh.* 9:17 a G. ready to pardon
*Job* 22:13 doth G. kn.? *Ps.* 73:11
*Ps.* 5:4 not a G. hast pleasure in
52:7 made not G. his strength
86:10 th. art G. alone, *Is.* 37:16
*Is.* 12:2 behold, G. is my salvat.
44:8 is there a G. besides me?
45:22 I am G. there is none else
46:9 I am G. th. is none like me
*Jer.* 31:33 I will be their G. 32:38

*Ezek.* 28:2 said, I sit in seat of G.
9 thou sh. be a man, and no G.
*Hos.* 8:6 workm. made it, no G.
11:9 I am G. not man, Holy One
*Mic.* 7:18 who is a G. like thee?
*Mat.* 1:23 Immanuel, which is G.
6:24 ye cannot serve G. and mammon, *Luke* 16:13
*Mat.* 19:17 there is none good but one, that is G. *Mark* 10:18; *Luke* 18:19
*Mark* 12:32 there is one G.
*John* 1:1 the Word was with G.
3:2 do miracles, ex. G. with him
8:41 have one Father, even G.
42 I proceeded, came from G.
17:3 know thee, only true G.
*Acts* 2:22 wonders which G. did
5:29 obey G. rather than men
7:9 sold Joseph, but G. wi. him
10:34 G. no respecter of persons
*Rom.* 3:4 G. be true, man a liar
8:31 if G. for us, who ag. us?
15:5 G. of patience and consol.
1 *Cor.* 8:6 but one G. the Father
15:28 that G. may be all in all
2 *Cor.* 1:21 he wh. an. us is G.
4:4 *g.* of this world blinded
13:11 G. of love and peace with
2 *Thes.* 2:4 above all called G.
1 *Tim.* 3:16 G. mani. in the flesh
*Tit.* 1:16 profess they know G.
*Heb.* 3:4 he that built all thi. is G.
4:10 ceased from works, as G.
8:10 to them a G. they a people
1 *John* 1:5 G. light, him no dark.
4:12 no man seen G. any time
*Rev.* 21:3 G. hims. be with them
4 G. shall wipe away all tears
7 I will be his G. he be my son

**Against GOD.**

*Gen.* 39:9 wickedn. and sin *a.* G.
*Num.* 21:5 peo. sp. *a.* G. *Ps.* 78:19
1 *Chr.* 5:25 they transgr. *ag.* G.
2 *Chr.* 32:19 spake *ag.* G. of Jer.
*Job* 15:13 turn. thy spirit *ag.* G.
25 stretch. out his hand *a.* G.
34:37 multip. his words *a.* G.
*Dan.* 3:29 speak amiss *a.* G. of S.
11:36 marv. things *a.* G. of gods
*Hos.* 13:16 hath rebelled *a.* G.
*Acts* 5:39 be found to fight *a.* G.
6:11 spoken blas. words *a.* G.
23:9 let us not fight *against* G.
*Rom.* 8:7 carnal mind en. *a.* G.
9:20 who art thou repliest *a.* G.?
*Rev.* 13:6 opened his mouth *a.* G.

*See* ALMIGHTY.

**Before GOD.**

*Gen.* 6:11 earth was corrupt *b.* G.
*Ex.* 18:12 eat wi. M. father *b.* G.
*Jos.* 24:1 presented thems. *b.* G.
*Jud.* 21:2 people abode *before* G.
1 *Chr.* 13:8 D. and Is. played *b.* G.
10 and there Uzzah died *b.* G.
16:1 offered burnt sacri. *bef.* G.
2 *Chr.* 33:12 Manasseh hum. *b.* G.
34:27 Josiah's heart hum. *b.* G.
*Ezr.* 7:19 deliver *b.* G. of Jerus.
*Job* 15:4 restrainest prayer *b.* G.
*Ps.* 42:2 shall I appear *b.* G.?
56:13 *b.* G. in light of living
61:7 he shall abide *b.* G. for ever
68:3 let righteous rejoice *b.* G.
84:7 ev. one in Zion appear *b.* G.
*Ec.* 2:26 give to him good *b.* G.
5:2 heart hasty to utter *bef.* G.
8:13 because he feareth not *b.* G.
*Dan.* 6:10 gave thanks *before* G.
11 found making supplic. *b.* G.
26 men tremble *b.* G. of Daniel
*Luke* 1:6 were both right. *b.* G.
12:6 not one is forgotten *b.* G.
24:19 a prophet mighty *bef.* G.
*Acts* 7:46 who found favor *b.* G.
10:4 come for a memorial *b.* G.
33 all here present *before* G.
23:1 lived in good consci. *b.* G.
*Rom.* 2:13 not hearers just *b.* G.
3:19 world may bec. guilty *b.* G.
4:2 whereof to glory, not *b.* G.
14:22 have faith to thyself *b.* G.
2 *Cor.* 12:19 speak *b.* G. in Chr.
*Gal.* 1:20 behold, *b.* G. I lie not
1 *Thes.* 3:13 estab. hearts *b.* G.
1 *Tim.* 5:4 good and accept. *b.* G.
21 charge thee *b.* G. 2 *Tim.* 4:1
*Jam.* 1:27 pure religion *before* G.
*Rev.* 3:2 works not perfect *b.* G.
9:13 voice from horns of al. *b.* G.
12:10 accus. *b.* G. day and night
16:19 Babylon in rememb. *b.* G.
20:12 I saw dead stand *b.* G.

*See* CALLED, CHOSEN, COMMANDED.

**Eternal GOD.**

*Deut.* 33:27 the *e.* G. is thy refuge

**Everlasting GOD.**

*Gen.* 21:33 A. called name *e.* G.
*Is.* 40:28 the *e.* G. fainteth not
*Rom.* 16:26 command. of *e.* G.

*See* FATHER, FEAR, FORBID, GAVE, GLORIFY.

**High GOD.**

*Gen.* 14:18 priest of the most *h.* G. *Heb.* 7:1
19 blessed be Ab. of most *h.* G.
20 blessed be the most *h.* G.
22 lift up my hand to most *h.* G.
*Ps.* 57:2 cry unto G. most *high*
78:35 the *h.* G. their Redeemer
56 tempted the most *high* G.
*Dan.* 3:26 servants of most *h.* G.
4:2 wonders *high* G. wrought
5:18 *h.* G. gave Nebuch. king.
21 he knew most *h.* G. ruled
*Mic.* 6:6 bow my. bef. most *h.* G.
*Mark* 5:7 Son of m. *h.* G. *Lu.* 8:28
*Acts* 16:17 serv. of most *high* G.

**Holy GOD.**

*Jos.* 24:19 he is a *holy* G. jealous
1 *Sam.* 6:20 who stand bef. *h.* G.?
*Ps.* 99:9 the Lord our G. is *holy*
*Is.* 5:16 G. that is *h.* be sancti.

**GOD of heaven.**

2 *Chr.* 36:23 all kingdoms of earth hath G. *of h.* giv. me, *Ezr.* 1:2
*Ezr.* 5:11 servants of G. *of h.*
12 our fath. provoked G. *of h.*
6:9 burnt-offerings of G. *of h.* 10
7:12 scribe of law of G. *of h.* 21
23 commanded by G. *of h.*
*Neh.* 1:4 prayed bef. G. *of h.* 2:4
*Ps.* 136:26 give thanks to G. *of h.*
*Dan.* 2:18 desire mer. of G. *of h.*
19 Daniel blessed the G. *of h.*
44 G. *of h.* sh. set up kingdom
*Jon.* 1:9 I fear the L. G. *of h.*
*Rev.* 11:13 gave glory to G. *of h.*
16:11 they blasphemed G. *of h.*

**GOD of hosts.**

*Ps.* 80:7 turn us, O G. *of h.* 19
14 return, we beseech, G. *of h.*
*Amos* 5:27 wh. name is G. *of h.*

*See* LORD GOD.

**GOD is.**

*Gen.* 21:22 G. *is* with thee in all
31:50 G. *is* witness betwixt
*Ex.* 20:30 fear not, G. *is* come
*Num.* 23:19 G. *is* not a man, that
*Deut.* 3:24 what G. *is* in heaven
33:27 eternal G. *is* thy refuge
*Jos.* 24:19 G. *is* a j. G. *Nah.* 1:2
1 *Sam.* 4:7 G. *is* come into camp
10:7 G. *is* with thee, 1 *Chr.* 17:2
28:15 G. *is* departed from me
2 *Sam.* 22:33 G. *is* my strength
1 *Chr.* 14:15 G. *is* gone forth bef.
2 *Chr.* 13:12 G. himself *is* wi. us
*Job* 33:12 G. *is* greater than man
36:5 G. *is* mighty, despis. not
26 G. *is* great, we know him
*Ps.* 7:11 G. *is* angry with wicked
10:4 G. *is* not in his thoughts
14:5 G. *is* in generation of righ.
33:12 whose G. *is* Lord, 144:15
46:1 G. *is* refuge and str. 62:8
5 G. *is* in midst of her
47:5 G. *is* gone up; 7 G. *is* king
48:3 G. *is* known in her palaces
50:6 G. *is* judge, Selah, 75:7
54:4 Behold, G. *is* my helper
56:9 I know, for G. *is* for me
59:9 I wait, G. *is* my def. 17
62:7 in G. *is* my salvat. *Is.* 12:2
68:5 father of fatherless *is* G.
73:1 truly G. *is* good to Israel
26 G. *is* the str. of my heart
74:12 G. *is* my king of old
89:7 G *is* greatly to be feared
116:5 Lord our G. *is* merciful
118:27 G. *is* L. that showed light
*Ec.* 5:2 G. *is* in hea. thou on ear.
*Is.* 5:16 G. that *is* holy be sancti.
8:10 G. *is* with us; 45:14 G. in
*Zec.* 8:23 heard G. *is* with you
*Mat.* 3:9 G. *is* able of these stones to raise, *Luke* 3:8
22:32 G. *is* not of dead, but liv.
*John* 3:33 to seal that G. *is* true
4:24 G. *is* a Spirit; 13:31
*Acts* 10:34 G. *is* no resp. of per.
*Rom.* 1:9 G. *is* wit. wh. I serve
11:23 G. *is* able to graff them
14:4 G. *is* able to make him
1 *Cor.* 1:9 G. *is* faith. by wh. call.
10:13 G. *is* faith. will not suffer
14:25 report that G. *is* in you
33 G. *is* not author of confusion
2 *Cor.* 1:18 G. *is* true, our word
9:8 G. *is* able make grace
*Gal.* 3:20 G. one; 6:7 not mocked
*Eph.* 2:4 G. who *is* rich in mercy
*Phil.* 1:8 G. *is* record, I long
3:19 many walk, G. *is* th. belly
1 *Thes.* 2:5 nor cloak, G. *is* wit.
*Heb.* 6:10 G. *is* not unrighteous
11:16 G. *is* not ash. to be called
12:29 G. *is* a consuming fire
*Heb.* 13:16 with such sac. G. *is* pl.
1 *John* 1:5 G. *is* light; 4:8 *is* love, 16
3:20 G. *is* greater th. our heart

**GOD of Israel.**

*Ex.* 24:10 went, saw G. *of Israel*
*Num.* 16:9 G. *of Is.* separated you
*Jos.* 7:19 gl. to G. *of I.* 1 *Sam.* 6:5
12:33 G. *of Is.* their inheritance
22:16 what trespass ag. G. *of Is.*?
24 what ye do with G. *of Is.*?
24:23 incline heart to G. *of Is.*
*Jud.* 11:23 G. *of Is.* dispossessed
*Ruth* 2:12 reward of G. *of Is.*
1 *Sam.* 1:17 G. *of Is.* grant petit.
5:11 send away ark of G. *of Is.*
1 *K.* 8:23 Lord G. *of Israel*, no god is like thee, 2 *Chr.* 6:14
14:13 good thing tow. G. *of Is.*
1 *Chr.* 4:10 Ja. called on G. *of I.*
17:24 Lord of hosts is G. *of Is.*
2 *Chr.* 15:13 not seek G. *of Is.*?
*Ezr.* 7:15 freely offered G. *of Is.*
9:4 tremb. at words of G. *of Is.*
*Ps.* 41:13 blessed be the L. G. *of Is.* from everlasting to ever. 72:18; 106:48; *Luke* 1:68
*Is.* 41:17 G. *of Is.* will not fors.
45:3 I which call am G. *of Is.*
48:2 stay themselves on G. *of I.*
*Ezek.* 8:4 the glory of G. *of Is.*
*Mat.* 15:31 multitude glo. G. *of I.*

**Living GOD.**

*Deut.* 5:26 heard voice of *liv.* G.
*Jos.* 3:10 hereby know the *l.* G.
1 *Sam.* 17:26 defy arm. of *l.* G. 36
2 *K.* 19:4 king of Assyria sent to reproach *l.* G. 16; *Is.* 37:4,17

Ps. 42:2 my soul thirst. for l. G.
84:2 my heart crieth for l. G.
Jer. 10:10 the l. G. everlas. King
23:36 perverted words of l. G.
Dan. 6:26 l. G. steadfast for ever
Hos. 1:10 ye are sons of living G.
Mat. 16:16 art Christ, Son of living G. John 6:69
26:63 I adjure thee by l. G. tell
Acts 14:15 turn from van. to l. G.
Rom. 9:26 be called chil. of l. G.
2 Cor. 3:3 with the Spirit of l. G.
6:16 ye are the temple of l. G.
1 Thes. 1:9 fr. idols to serve l. G.
1 Tim. 3:15 church of the l. G.
4:10 we trust in the l. G. 6:17
Heb. 3:12 evil heart dep. fr. l. G.
9:14 purge cons. to serve l. G.
10:31 to fall into hands of l. G.
12:22 come to Zion, city of l. G.
Rev. 7:2 angel hav. seal of l. G.

Lord GOD, Lord his GOD, Lord our, their, your GOD. See these in the divisions of the word LORD.

**Merciful GOD.**

Ex. 34:6 the Lord G. m. gracious
Deut. 4:31 L. thy G. is a m. G.
2 Chr. 30:9 L. your G. is merciful
Neh. 9:31 art a gracious, m. G.
Ps. 116:5 gracious is L. G. is m.
Jon. 4:2 I knew thou art a G. m.

**Mighty GOD.**

Gen. 49:24 hands of m. G. of Ja.
Deut. 7:21 Lord is among you, a mighty G. 10:17
Neh. 9:32 therefore our G. the m.
Job 36:5 G. is m. and despiseth
Ps. 50:1 the m. G. hath spoken
132:2 vowed to m. G. of Jacob
5 till I find a habitat. for m. G.
Is. 9:6 name sh. be called m. G.
10:21 remnant sh. ret. to m. G.
Jer. 32:18 m. G. the L. of hosts
Hab. 1:12 O m. G. thou hast stab.

**My GOD.**

Gen. 28:21 then sh. L. be my G.
Ex. 15:2 he is my G. my father's
Ruth 1:16 people, thy G. my G.
2 Sam. 22:7 cried to my G. Ps. 18:6
22 not dep. fr. my G. Ps. 18:21
30 my G. I leaped, Ps. 18:29
1 Chr. 28:20 my G. be with thee
2 Chr. 18:13 what my G. saith
Neh. 5:19 on me, my G. 13:31
13:14 remember me, my G. 22
Ps. 22:1 my G. my G. why hast thou forsaken me? Mat. 27:46
10 my G. fr. my mother's belly
31:14 I said, Thou art my G.
38:21 O my G. be not far, 71:12
89:26 thou art my Fath. my G.
104:33 praise to my G. 146:2
118:28 my G. I will praise thee
145:1 I will extol thee, my G.
Prov. 30:9 name of my G. in vain
Is. 7:13 ye weary my G. also?
40:27 judg. passed from my G.
44:17 deliver me, thou art my G.
Is. 61:10 soul be joyful in my G.
Dan. 6:22 my G. sent his angel
Hos. 2:23 they shall say, Thou art my G. Zec. 13:9
8:2 Is. cry, my G. we know thee
9:17 my G. will cast them away
Mic. 7:7 wait, my G. will hear
John 20:17 say, I ascend to my G.
28 Th. said, my Lord and my G.
Rom. 1:8 I thank my G. through J. Christ, for you all, 1 Cor. 1:4; 14:18; Phil. 1:3; Phile. 4
2 Cor. 12:21 my G. will humble
Phil. 4:19 my G. supply need
Rev. 3:12 write name of my G.

See LORD my God.

**No GOD.**

Deut. 32:39 th. is no G. with me
1 K. 8:23 no G. like thee, 2 Ch. 6:14
2 K. 1:16 is it bec. no G. in Is.
5:15 I know th. is no G. in earth
2 Chr. 32:15 no G. of any nation
Ps. 14:1 said, There is no G. 53:1
Is. 43:10 bef. me no G. formed
44:6 besides me there is no G. 8; 45, 5, 14, 21
Ezek. 28:9 shalt be a man, no G.
Hos. 13:4 sh. know no G. but me

**O GOD.**

Num. 12:13 heal her now, O G.
Jud. 16:28 strengthen me, O G.
Ps. 4:1 hear me, O G. of right.
25:22 redeem Is. O G. out of tr.
51:14 deliver from guilti. O G.
56:12 thy vows upon me, O G.
Is. 64:4 nor hath eye seen, O G.
Heb. 10:7 come to do will, O G. 9

**Of GOD.**

2 Chr. 10:15 the cause of G.
Ps. 7:10 my defence is of G.
Is. 53:4 esteem him smit. of G.
Mat. 16:23 savorest not things of G. Mark 8:33
John 1:13 not will of man, of G.
6:46 he of G. seen the Father
7:17 know doc. whether of G.
8:47 he that is of G. heareth
9:16 this man not of G.; 33
12:43 praise of men than of G.
Acts 5:39 if of G. ye cannot over.
Rom. 2:29 pr. not of men, of G.
9:16 but of G. that show. mercy
13:1 powers that be ord. of G.
1 Cor. 1:30 who of G. is made
6:19 have of G. not your own
11:12 things of G. 2 Cor. 5:18
2 Cor. 2:17 in sight of G. speak
3:5 our sufficiency is of G.
Phil. 1:28 salvation, that of G.
3:9 the right. which is of G.
Heb. 5:4 he called of G. as Aaron
1 John 3:10 doeth not righteousness, is not of G.
4:1 try the spirits whether of G.
3 con. not Chr. come, not of G.
6 we are of G.; 5:19 we know
3 John 11 that doeth good is of G

See ANGEL, ARK, BORN, CHILDREN, CHOSEN, CHURCH, COUNSEL, FEAR, GLORY, GRACE, HAND, HOUSE, KINGDOM, KNOWLEDGE, LOVE, MAN, PEOPLE, POWER, SERVANT, SIGHT, SON, SONS, SPIRIT, WILL, WORDS, WORK, WORKS, WORLD, WRATH.

**Our GOD.**

Ex. 5:8 let us sacri. to our G.
Deut. 31:17 o. G. not amongst us
32:3 ascribe great. unto our G.
Jos. 24:18 serve L. he is our G.
Jud. 10:10 have forsaken our G.
1 Sam. 2:2 nei. rock like our G.
2 Sam. 10:12 let us play the men for cities of o. G. 1 Chr. 19:3
22:32 a rock save o. G.? Ps. 18:31
1 Chr. 29:13 o. G. we thank thee
2 Chr. 2:5 great is o. G. above all
14:11 O Lord, thou art our G.
20:7 o. G. who didst drive out
Ezr. 9:10 O o. G. what shall we
Neh. 4:4 our G.; 20 our G. fight
6:16 work wrought of our G.
9:32 o. G. the great, mighty G.
13:2 o. G. turned curse to bless.
Ps. 40:3 a new song, pr. to o. G.
48:14 God is our G. for ever
50:3 our G. sh. not keep silence
67:6 G. our G. shall bless us
68:20 our G. is the G. of salvat.
77:13 so great a G. as our G.?
95:7 is o. G.; 115:3 o. G. in hea.
116:5 gracious is L. G. is merc.
Is. 25:9 this is o. G. we have wai.
55:7 o. G. will abund. pardon
59:13 departing from our G.
Is. 61:2 day of veng. of our G.
Dan. 3:17 our G. able to deliver
Zec. 9:7 remaineth be for our G.
1 Cor. 6:11 sancti. by Sp. of o. G.
Heb. 12:29 o. G. is a consum. fire
Rev. 5:10 made us to o. G. kings
7:10 salv. to our G. who sitteth
12 blessing and honor to o. G.

See PEACE, SAID, SAITH, SERVE, SENT, SPEED, SPEAK, SPOKEN.

**Their GOD.**

Gen. 17:8 I will be t. G. Ex. 29:45; Jer. 24:7; 31:33; 32:38; Ezek. 11:20; 34:24; 37:23, 27; Zec. 8:8; 2 Cor. 6:16; Rev. 21:3
Lev. 21:6 shall be holy to t. G.
26:45 might be t. G. Ezek. 14:11
2 Sam. 7:24 thou art become their G. 1 Chr. 17:22
Ezr. 5:5 eye of t. G. on elders
Ps. 79:10 where their G.? 115:2; Joel 2:17
Is. 8:19 sh. not peo. seek t. G.?
21 curse their king and their G.
58:2 forsook not ordin. of t. G.
Jer. 5:4 know not judg. of t. G.
Dan. 11:32 people that know t. G.
Hos. 4:12 gone a who. from t. G.
5:4 frame doings to turn to t. G.
Zec. 12:5 strength in Lord t. G.
Heb. 11:16 not ashamed to be t. G.

See LORD their God.

**Thy GOD.**

Lev. 19:14 fear thy G. 25:17, 43
Deut. 10:21 he is thy praise, t. G.
26:17 this day the L. to be t. G.
Ruth 1:16 peo. my pe. t. G. my G.
2 K. 19:10 let not thy G. deceive thee, Is. 37:10
1 Chr. 12:18 thy G. helpeth thee
2 Chr. 9:8 because t. G. loved Is.
Ezr. 7:14 accord. to law of thy G.
25 after the wisdom of thy G.
Neh. 9:18 t. G. that brought thee
Ps. 42:3 say, Wh. is thy G.? 10
45:7 thy G. anointed, Heb. 1:9
50:7 O Is. I am G. even thy G.
68:28 t. G. com. thy strength
147:12 praise thy G. O Zion
Is. 41:10 be not dism. I am t. G.
51:20 full of rebuke of thy G.
52:7 saith to Zion, thy G. reign.
60:19 thy G. shall be thy glory
62:5 so shall t. G. rej. over thee
Dan. 6:16 thy G. whom thou ser.
20 is thy G. able to deliver?
10:12 chasten thyself bef. t. G.
Hos. 4:6 hast forgot. law of t. G.
9:1 gone a whoring from thy G.
12:6 turn to t. G. wait on t. G.
Amos 4:12 prepare to meet thy G.
Jon. 1:6 arise, call upon t. G.
Mic. 6:8 walk humbly with t. G.

See LORD thy GOD.

**To, or unto GOD.**

Gen. 40:8 interpreta. be. to G.?
Ex. 2:23 their cry came to G.
Lev. 21:7 he is holy unto his G.
Deut. 32:17 sac. not to G. 1 Cor. 10:20
33:26 none like to G. of Jeshu.
Jud. 13:5 a Naz. u. G. 7; 16:17
1 Sam. 10:3 3 men go. up to G.
1 Chr. 26:32 matter perta. to G.
Job 22:2 can man be pr. to G.?
34:31 is meet to be said un. G.
Ps. 62:11 power belongeth to G.
68:20 to G. be. issues fr. death
31 Ethio. stretch hands to G.
73:28 good to draw near to G.
77:1 I cried un. G. even unto G.
Ec. 12:7 spirit sh. return unto G.
Is. 58:2 delight in appr. to G.

Lam. 3:41 hearts wi. hands *to* G.
Mat. 22:21 render *u.* G. things which are G.'s, Mark 12:17; Luke 20:25
John 13:3 come from G. w. *to* G.
Acts 4:19 hearken than *unto* G.
5:4 not lied unto men, *unto* G.
26:18 fr. power of Satan *unto* G.
20 turn *to* G. and do works
Rom. 6:10 liveth *unto* G.; 11
13 yield yourselves *u.* G. alive
7:4 bring forth fruit *unto* G.
12:1 your bodies a liv. sac. *u.* G.
14:12 account of himself *to* G.
1 Cor. 14:2 speaketh *unto* G.
15:24 deliv. up kingdom *to* G.
Phil. 4:20 now *u.* G. our Father
Heb. 7:25 to save th. come *un.* G.
11:6 that cometh *to* G. must be.
12:23 are come *to* G. the Judge
Jam. 4:7 submit yourselves *to* G.
1 Pet. 3:18 Ch. suf. bring us *to* G.
4:6 live according *to* G. in spirit
Rev. 5:9 redeemed us *to* G. by b.
12:5 child caught up *unto* G.
14:4 first-fr. *unto* G. and Lamb

*See* TRUE.

**With GOD.**

Gen. 5:22 En. walked *w.* G. 24.
6:9 N. walked *w.* G.; 32:28 Jac.
Ex. 19:17 br. peo. to meet *w.* G.
1 Sam. 14:45 wrought *w.* G.
2 Sam. 23:5 ho. be not so *w.* G.
2 Chr. 35:21 forbear med. *w.* G.
Job 9:2 sh. man be just *with* G.
13:3 I desire to reason *with* G.
16:21 plead for a man *with* G.
25:4 can a man be just *w.* G.?
27:13 por. of wicked man *w.* G.
34:9 sh. delight himself *w.* G.
23 he enter into judg. *w.* G.
37:22 *with* G. is ter. majesty
Ps. 78:8 spirit not stead. *w.* G.
Hos. 11:12 Judah yet ruleth *w.* G.
12:3 Jacob had power *with* G.
Mat. 19:26 *w.* G. all things possi. Mark 10:27; Lu. 1:37; 18:27
Luke 1:30 hast found favor *w.* G.
2:25 increased in favor *with* G.
John 1:1 the Word was *with* G.
5:18 him. equal *w.* G. Phil. 2:6
Rom. 2:11 no resp. of pers. *w.* G
5:1 by faith, we have pe. *w.* G.
9:14 is there unright. *with* G.?
1 Cor. 3:9 we are laborers *w.* G.
19 wisdom of world fool. *w.* G.
7:24 ev. man therein abide *w.* G.
2 Thes. 1:16 a right. thing *with* G.
Jam. 4:4 friendsh. enmity *w.* G.
1 Pet. 2:20 is acceptable *w.* G.

*Would* GOD. *See* WOULD.

**Your GOD.**

Gen. 43:23 *y.* G. hath given trea.
Ex. 8:25 go ye, sacrifice to *y.* G.
Lev. 11:45 bringeth you out of Egypt be *your* G. 22:33; 25:38; Num. 15:41
26:12 I will be *your* God, ye my people, Jer. 7:23; 11:4; 30:22; Ezek. 36:28
Num. 10:10 a memorial bef. *y.* G.
15:40 my com. be holy to *y.* G.
Jos. 24:27 lest ye deny *your* G.
1 Sam. 10:19 have rejected *y.* G.
2 Chr. 32:14 that *y.* G. deliver y.
15 much less sh. *y.* G. deliver?
Is. 35:4 *y* G. come with veng.
40:1 com. my people, saith *y.* G.
9 cities of Judah, behold *y.* G.
59:2 separ. bet. you and *y.* G.
Ezek. 34:1 I am *y.* G. saith Lord
Dan. 2:47 of a truth it is, *y.* G. is
Hos. 1:9 I will not be *your* G.
John 8:54 ye say that he is *y.* G.
20:17 ascend to my God, *y.* G.

*See* LORD *your God.*

**GODDESS.**

1 K. 11:5 Sol. went after the *g.*
33 worshipped Ashtor. the *g.*
Acts 19:27 temple of gr. *g.* Diana
35 Ephesians worshippers of *g.*
37 nor yet blasph. of your *g.*

**GODHEAD.**

Acts 17:29 nor think *g.* like gold
Rom. 1:20 his eter. power and *g.*
Col. 2:9 in him fulness of the *g.*

**GODLY.**

Ps. 4:3 L. set apart him that is *g.*
12:1 help, for the *g.* man ceas.
32:6 for this every one *g.* pray
Mal. 2:15 he might seek *g.* seed
2 Cor. 1:12 in *g.* sincer. our con.
7:9 sorry after a *g.* manner, 11
10 for *g.* sorrow worketh rep.
11:2 jeal. over you with *g.* jeal.
2 Tim. 3:12 all that live *g.* in C.
Tit. 2:12 that ye should live *g.*
Heb. 12:28 serve G. with *g.* fear
2 Pet. 2:9 how to deliver the *g.*
3 John 6 bring for after *g.* sort

**GODLINESS.**

1 Tim. 2:2 may lead a life in *g.*
10 becometh women profes. *g.*
3:16 great is the mystery of *g.*
4:7 exer. thyself rather unto *g.*
8 *g.* is profit. unto all things
6:3 the doctrine according to *g.*
5 supposing that gain is *g.*
6 *g.* with contentment is gain
11 follow righteousness, *g.* fai.
Tim. 3:5 having a form of *g.*
Tit. 1:1 truth which is after *g.*
2 Pet. 1:3 things pertain to *g.*
6 add to *g.* brotherly kind. 7.
3:11 persons ought to be in *g.*

**GOD-WARD.**

Ex. 18:19 be thou for peo. to G.
2 Cor. 3:4 have we thro. C. to G.
1 Thes. 1:8 faith to G. is spread.

**GODS.**

Gen. 3:5 ye shall be as *g.*
31:30 where. hast stolen my *g.*?
Ex. 12:12 ag. all *g.* of Egypt
20:23 sh. not make *g.* of silver
22:28 thou sh. not revile the *g.*
23:24 shalt not bow to their *g.*
32 make no cove. with their *g.*
32:4 these be thy *g.* O Israel, 8
31 they have made *g.* of gold
34:15 go a whoring after their *g.*
17 make no molt. *g.* Lev. 19:4
Num. 25:2 people to sac. of *g.*
33:4 the Egyptians' *g.* L. exec. judgme. Jer. 43:12, 13; 46:25
Deut. 7:25 im. of their *g.* burn
10:17 Lord your G. is God of *g.*
12:3 hew down im. of their *g.*
30 inquire not after their *g.*
31 have done abomina. to their *g.* sons and dau. in fire to *g.*
13:7 entice thee to *g.* of people
20:18 not do as they to their *g.*
32:37 sh. say, Where are th. *g.*?
Jos. 22:22 Lord God of *g.* know.
23:7 nor mention of their *g.*
Jud. 5:8 they chose new *g.*
6:10 fear not *g.* of Amorites
10:14 cry to *g.* ye have chosen
17:5 Micah had a house of *g.*
18:24 ye have taken my *g.*
Ruth 1:15 sister-in-law ba. to *g.*
1 Sam. 4:8 the *g.* smote Egypt.
6:5 his hand from off your *g.*
17:43 Phil. cursed Da. by his *g.*
28:13 I saw *g.* as. out of earth
2 Sam. 7:23 redeem. from th. *g.*
1 K. 11:2 turn your heart after *g.*
8 Solomon sacrificed to their *g.*
12:28 behold thy *g.* O Israel
18:24 call name of your *g.* 25
19:2 let *g.* do so to me, 20:10
20:23 their *g.* are *g.* of hills

2 K. 17:29 every nation made *g.*
33 feared the L. served own *g.*
18:33 hath *g.* delivered his land? 19:12; 2 Chr. 32:13, 14; Is. 36:18; 37:12
34 wh. are *g.* of H.? Is. 36:19
19:18 cast *g.* in. fire, were no *g.*
1 Chr. 5:25 went a whoring af. *g.*
10:10 armor in house of their *g.*
14:12 left their *g.* David burnt
2 Chr. 13:8 calv. Jero. ma. for *g.*
9 a priest to th. that are no *g.*
25:14 br. *g.* of Seir to be his *g.*
28:23 Ahaz sacrificed to the *g.*
32:17 *g.* of nations have not de.
Ezr. 1:7 vessels in house of *g.*
Ps. 82:1 he judg. among the *g.*
6 said, Ye are *g.* John 10:34
136:2 give thanks unto God of *g.*
138:1 bef. the *g.* will I praise
Is. 21:9 Bab. fall. her *g.* broken
41:23 we may know ye are *g.*
42:17 images, Ye are our *g.*
Jer. 2:11 changes *g.* are no *g.*?
28 where are thy *g.* thou made? to number of cit. are thy *g.* 11:13
5:7 sworn by th. that are no *g.*
10:11 *g.* have not made heaven
11:12 to *g.* they offer incense
16:20 man make *g.* are no *g.*?
48:35 that burn. incense to *g.*
Dan. 2:11 can show it, except *g.*
47 your God is a God of *g.*
4:8 in whom is spirit of holy *g.*
9 sp. of *g.* is in thee. 18; 5:14
5:4 *g.* of gold and silver, 23
11 like the wisdom of the *g.*
11:8 carry into E. *g.* w. princes
36 speak things ag. God of *g.*
Hos. 14:3 ne. say, Ye are our *g.*
Nah. 1:14 out of house of thy *g.*
John. 10:35 if he called them *g.*
Acts 14:11 the *g.* are come down
19:26 be no *g.* made with hands
1 Cor. 8:5 called *g.* there be *g.*
Gal. 4:8 ser. to th. wh. are no *g.*

*See* SERVE.

**All GODS.**

Ex. 18:11 L. greater than *all g.*
1 Chr. 16:25 ab. *all g.* Ps. 96:4
26 *all g.* of peo. idols, Ps. 96:5
2 Chr. 2:5 G. ab. *all g.* Ps. 135:5
Ps. 95:3 L. is a K. above *all g.*
97:7 worship *all g.*; 9 ab. *all g.*
Zep. 2:11 famish *all g.* of earth

**Among the GODS.**

Ex. 15:11 *am. t. g.* who like th.?
2 K. 18:35 who *a. t. g.* could del. cou.? 2 Chr. 32:14; Is. 36:20
Ps. 86:8 *a. t. g.* none like thee

**Other GODS.**

Ex. 20:3 no *other g.* before me, Deut. 5:7
23:13 make no mention of *o. g.*
Deut. 6:14 ye shall not go after *o. g.* 11:28; 28:14; 1 K. 11:10; Jer. 25:6; 35:15
7:4 turn thy son to serve *o. g.*
8:19 if thou walk after *o. g.*
13:2 let us go after *o. g.* 6:13
17:3 hath gone and served *o. g.* 29:26; Jos. 23:16; Jud. 10:13; 1 Sam. 8:8; Jer. 11:10
18:20 speak in name of *o. g.*
30:17 *o. g.* and serve, Jer. 22:9
31:18 that day turned to *o. g.*
20 will they turn to *other g.*
Jud. 2:12 forsook L. fol. *other g.*
17 went a whoring after *o. g.*
19 follow. *other g.* to serve th.
1 Sam. 26:19 say, Go serve *o. g.*
1 K. 9:9 have taken hold upon *other g.* 2 Chr. 7:22
11:4 wives turned heart af. *o. g.*
14:9 hast gone and made *o. g.*

2 *K.* 5:17 not offer sacri. to *o. g.*
17:7 Is. sinned and feared *o. g.*
35 ye shall not fear *o. g.* 37, 38
22:17 and burnt incense to *oth. g.* 2 *Chr.* 34:25; *Jer.* 1:16; 19:4
2 *Chr.* 28:25 Ahaz bur. in. to *o. g.*
*Jer.* 7:6 nor walk after *other g.*
9 *o. g.* wh. ye know not, 13:10
16:11 for. me, walked after *o. g.*
44:5 burn no incense to *other g.*
8 burning incense to *o. g.* 15
*Hos.* 3:1 look to *o. g.* love wine

*See* SERVE.

**Strange GODS.**

*Gen.* 35:2 put a. *s. g.* 1 *Sam.* 7:3
4 gave Jacob *s. g. Jos.* 24:23
*Deut.* 32:16 provoked with *s. g.*
*Jos.* 24:20 forsake L. serve *s. g.*
*Jud.* 10:16 put away their *s. g.*
2 *Chr.* 14:3 Asa took altar of *s. g.*
33:15 Josiah took away *s. g.*
*Jer.* 5:19 as ye served *strange g.*
*Acts* 17:18 a setter forth of *s. g.*

**GOG**

1 *Chr.* 5:4; *Ezek.* 38:2, 3, 16, 18; 39:11
*Rev.* 20:8 G. and Magog, to gath.

**GOLD.**

*Gen.* 2:11 land of Havilah, is *g*
12 the *g.* of that land is good
41:42 put chain of *g.* on Jos.
*Ex.* 20:23 sh. make gods of *g.*
25:12 shalt cast four rings of *g.* for ark, 26; 26:29; 28:23, 26, 27; 37:3, 13
13 stav. of shittim-wood, overlay with *g.* 28; 26:29, 37; 30:5; 37:4, 15, 28
18 two cherubim of *g.* 37:7
26:8 fifty taches of *g.* 36:13
32 hooks sh. be of *g.* 37; 36:38
28:6 ephod *g.*; 8 girdle; 15 b. p.
11 ouches of *g.* 13; 39:6, 13, 16
24 chains of *g.*; 33 bells of *g.*
32:24 who hath *g.* let him br. it
31 have made them gods of *g.*
35:22 they brought jewels of *g.*
36:34 over. the boards with *g.*
38 over. chapiters, fillets w. *g.*
38:34 all the *g.* was occupied
39:3 beat *g.* into thin plates
40:5 set altar of *g.* before ark
*Num.* 7:14 ten shekels of *g.* 20
84 at dedication 11 spoons of *g.*
86 *g.* of spoons 120 shekels
31:50 captains' obla. *g.* chains
*Jos.* 7:21 a wedge of *g.* fifty shek.
24 took Ach. and wedge of *g.*
*Jud.* 8:26 ear-r. 1,700 shek. of *g.*
1 *Sam.* 6:8 jewels of *g.* in coffer
11 laid mice of *g.* on the cart
15 coffer with jewels of *g.*
2 *Sam.* 8:7 Dav. took shiel. of *g.*
1 *K.* 6:22 house he overlaid w. *g.*
28 overlaid cherub. with *g.* 2 *Chr.* 3:10
7:48 S. made altar and table *g.*
49 lamps and tongs *g.*; 50 hin.
9:11 Hiram king of Tyre furnished *g.* and cedar, 10:11; 2 *Chr.* 9:10
10:2 queen of Sh. came with *g.*
14 wt. of *g.* in year, 2 *Chr.* 9:13
16 made 200 targ. of beaten *g.*
17 made 300 shields of *g.*
18 overlaid throne with best *g.*
12:28 Jerob. made calves of *g.*
22:48 Jehos. made sh. go for *g.*
2 *K.* 18:16 Hezek. cut *g.* fr. doors
1 *Chr.* 28:14 David gave *g.* for *g.*
2 *Chr.* 3:6 the *g.* was *g.* of Parv.
2 *Chr.* 4:7 cand'sticks of *g.*; 8 ba.
22 snuffers, censers, spoons, *g.*
9:18 steps to throne, foots. *g.*
12:9 Shishak carried shield of *g.*
*Ezr.* 8:27 copper precious as *g.*

*Neh.* 7:70 Tirsh. gave 1,000 dr. *g.*
71 chief of fath. gave *g.*; 72
*Job* 22:24 lay up as dust *g.* of O.
23:10 I shall come forth like *g.*
28:6 earth hath the dust of *g.*
15 cannot be gotten for *g.*
16 it cannot be valued with *g.*
17 *g.* and crys. cannot equal it
31:24 if I made *g.* my hope
36:19 he esteem riches? not *g.*
42:11 gave Job an ear-ring of *g.*
*Ps.* 19:10 more to be des. than *g.*
45:9 stand queen in *g.* of Ophir
72:15 him be given *g.* of Sheba
*Prov.* 11:22 je. of *g.* in swine's s.
16:16 better to get wis. than *g.*
20:15 *g.* and a multi. of rubies
*Cant.* 1:10 comely *g.* chains *g.*
5:14 as *g.* rings set with beryl
*Is.* 30:22 ornament of im. of *g.*
40:19 spreadeth it over with *g.*
60:17 for brass I will bring *g.*
*Jer.* 4:30 deckest with orna. of *g.*
*Lam.* 4:1 how is *g.* become dim
*Ezek.* 27:22 merchants oc. wi. *g.*
*Dan.* 2:38 head of *g.*; 3:1 im. *g.*
5:23 hast praised the gods of *g.*
29 chain of *g.* about Dan. neck
*Zec.* 4:2 a candlestick all of *g.*
13:9 I will try th. as *g.* is tried
*Mat.* 2:11 they pres. to him *g.*
23:16 swear by *g.* of the temple
17 whe. greater, *g.* or temple?
1 *Tim.* 2:9 not adorned with *g.* or pearls, 1 *Pet.* 3:3
*Heb.* 9:4 ark over. round with *g.*
*Jam.* 2:2 come man with *g.* ring
1 *Pet.* 1:7 faith more pre. than *g.*
*Rev.* 3:18 to buy of me *g.* tried
4:4 elders on heads crowns of *g.*
9:7 locusts on heads crowns *g.*
17:4 woman was decked with *g.*
18:16 great city decked with *g.*

*See* BEATEN, CROWN, FINE.

**Pure GOLD**

*Ex.* 25:11 overlay ark with *pure g.* 24; 30:3; 37:2, 11, 26
17 a mercy-seat of *p. g.* 37:6
29 dishes, of *pure g.* 37:16, 23
31 candl. *p. g.* 37:17; 1 *K.* 7:49
38 snuff dishes *p. g.* 2 *Chr.* 4:22
28:14 chains of *p. g.* 22; 39:15
1 *K.* 6:20 oracle overlaid w. *p. g.*
10:21 ve. of Le. *p. g.* 2 *Chr.* 9:20
1 *Chr.* 28:17 *p. g.* for flesh-hooks
2 *Chr.* 3:4 over. porch with *p. g.*
9:17 over. throne with *pure g.*
*Job* 28:19 wisd. not val. wi. *p. g.*
*Ps.* 21:3 a crown of *p. g.* on head
*Rev.* 21:18 city *p. g.*; 21 street

**GOLD, *with* silver.**

*Gen.* 13:2 Ab. rich in *s.* and *g.* 24
44:8 steal of lord's hou. *s.* or *g.*
*Ex.* 3:22 jewels of *silver* and *g.* 11:2; 12:35
25:3 this offering, take *s.* and *g.*
31:4 in *g. s.* and brass, 35:32
*Num.* 22:18 ho. fu. *s.* and *g.* 24:13
31:22 only *g.* and *s.* abide fire
*Deut.* 7:25 shall not des. *s.* and *g.*
8:13 *s.* and *g.* is multiplied
17:17 sh. he multiply *s.* and *g.*
29:17 seen their idols, *s.* and *g.*
*Jos.* 6:19 *s.* and *g.* con. to L. 24
22:8 ret. to tents with *s.* and *g.*
2 *Sam.* 8:11 *silver* and *g.* David dedicated, 1 *K.* 7:51
21:4 will have no *s.* or *g.* of Sa.
1 *K.* 15:15 Asa brought into hou of L. *s.* and *g.* 2 *Chr.* 15:18
18 Asa took *s.* and *g.* 2. *Chr.* 16:2
19 a pr. of *s.* and *g.* 2 *Chr.* 16:3
20:3. *s.* and *g.* mine; 5 *s.* and *g.*
1 *Chr.* 29:3 my o. good, *g.* and *s.*
2 *Chr.* 1:15 *s.* and *g.* plenteous

*Ezr.* 1:4 help with *silver* and *g.*
2:69 gave *s.* and *g.*; 7:15
8:25 weighed *silver* and *g.* 33
*Est.* 1:6 beds were of *g.* and *s.*
*Job* 28:1 vein for *s.* a place for *g.*
*Ps.* 68:13 with *s.* feathers w. *g.*
105:37 br. forth with *s.* and *g.*
115:4 idols are *s.* and *g.* 135:15
119:72 law better than *g.* and *s.*
*Prov.* 8:10 not *silver* receive knowledge rather than *g.*
17:3 fining-pot for *s.* fur. for *g.* 27:21
22:1 favor rather than *s.* or *g.*
25:11 apples of *g.* in pict. of *s.*
*Ec.* 2:8 I gathered also *s.* and *g.*
*Cant.* 1:11 bord. of *g.* studs of *s.*
3:10 pillars of *s.* bottom of *g.*
*Is.* 2:7 the land full of *s.* and *g.*
20 cast idols of *s.* and *g.* 31:7
13:17 shall not regard *s.* or *g.*
46:6 lavish *g.* and weigh *silver*
60:9 bring th. *s.* and *g.* w. them
*Jer.* 10:4 deck it with *s.* and *g.*
*Ezek.* 7:19 cast away *s.* and *g.* *s.* and *g.* not able del. *Zep.* 1:18
16:13 decked with *g.* and *silver*
*Dan.* 2:35 *s.* and *g.* broken, 45
5:4 praised gods of *s.* and *g.* 23
11:38 a god honor w. *g.* and *s.*
43 power over treas. of *g.* and *s.*
*Hos.* 2:8 I multi. her *s.* and *g.*
8:4 of *s.* and *g.* they made idols
*Joel* 3:5 have taken my *s.* and *g.*
*Nah.* 2:9 take spoil of *s.* and *g.*
*Hab.* 2:19 laid over with *s.* and *g.*
*Hag.* 2:8 the *s.* is mine, *g.* mine
*Zec.* 6:11 *s.* and *g.* make crowns
*Mal.* 3:3 purge them as *g.* and *s.*
*Mat.* 10:9 provide nei. *g.* nor *s.*
*Acts* 3:6 *s.* and *g.* have I none
17:29 think Godh. like *s.* and *g.*
20:33 I cov. no man's *s.* or *g.*
1 *Cor.* 3:12 build on found. *g. s.*
2 *Tim.* 2:20 essels of *s.* and *g.*
*Jam.* 5:3 your *g.* and *s.* cankered
1 *Pet.* 1:18 not red. w. *s.* and *g.*
*Rev.* 9:20 rep. not of idols of *s. g.*

**Talent *and* talents of GOLD.**

*Ex.* 25:39 a *t. of g.* sh. he make
37:24 of a *tal. of* pure *g.* made
2 *Sam.* 12:30 weight of crown a *talent of g.* 1 *Chr.* 20:2
1 *K.* 9:14 Hir. sent Sol. 120 *t. of g.*
28 sent from Ophir 420 *t. of g.*
10:10 she gave Solomon 120 *talents of g.* 2 *Chr.* 9:9
14 in 1 yr. came to S. 666 *t. of g.*
2 *K.* 23:33 put the land to a *talent of g.* 2 *Chr.* 36:3
1 *Chr.* 22:14 D. pre. 100,000 *t. of g.*
29:4 my own good 3,000 *t. of g.*
7 chief of fa. gave 5,000 *t. of g.*
2 *Chr.* 8:18 took fr. O. 450 *t. of g.*
*Ezr.* 8:26 weigh. *of g.* ves. 100 *t.*

**Vessels of GOLD.**

2 *Sam.* 8:10 Toi sent to David *vessels of g.* 1 *Chr.* 18:10
1 *K.* 10:21 Solomon's drinking *v.* were *of g.* 2 *Chr.* 9:20
25 broke *v. of g.* 2 *Chr.* 9:24
2 *K.* 12:13 for house of L. *v. of g.*
24:13 Neb. cut in pieces *v. of g.*
2 *Chr.* 24:14 money made *v. of g.*
*Ezr.* 1:11 *v. of g.* and silver 5,400
5:14 the *v. of g.* Cyrus delivered
8:26 weighed of *v. of g.* 100 tal.
*Est.* 1:7 gave drink in *v. of g.*
*Dan.* 11:8 carry into E. *v. of g.*
2 *Tim.* 2:20 not only *v. of g.*

**GOLDEN.**

*Ex.* 25:25 a *g.* crown to border
28:34 a *g.* bell; 30:4 rings, 39:20
32:2 Aar. said, Break *g.* ear-r.
*Lev.* 8:9 on forefront put *g.* plate
*Num.* 7:26 *g.* spoon of 10 shekels

Jud. 8:24 had g. ear-rings
26 the weight of g. ear-rings
1 Sam. 6:4 emer. g. mice, 17, 18
2 K. 10:29 departed not fr. g. ca.
1 Chr. 28:17 for g. basins gave
2 Chr. 13:8 are with you g. calv.
Ezr. 6:5 let g. ves. be restored
Est. 4:11 the king shall hold out a g. sceptre, 5:2; 8:4
Ec. 12:6 the g. bowl be broken
Is. 13:12 more prec. than g. w.
14:4 hath the g. city ceased
Jer. 51:7 Baby. hath been g. cup
Dan. 3:5 worship g. image, 12
5:2 Bel. commanded bring. g. vessels
3 they brought the g. vessels
Zec. 4:12 g. pipes empty g. oil
Heb. 9:4 g. censer and ark. g. pot
Rev. 1:12 I saw 7 g. candlesticks
13 girt ab. paps with g. girdle
20 mystery of 7 g. candlesticks
2:1 in midst of g. candlesticks
5:8 g. vials, 15:7; 8:3 g. censer
14:14 on head g. cr.; 17:4 g. cup
21:15 a g. reed to measure city
See ALTAR.

**GOLDSMITH, S.**

Neh. 3:8 Uzziel of the g. repaired
31 the g. son; 32 g. and mer.
Is. 40:19 g. spread. it with gold
41:7 carpenter encourag. the g.
46:6 hire a g. and mak. it a god

GOLGOTHA. Mat. 27:33; Mark 15:22; John 19:17

**GOLIATH.**

1 Sam. 17:4 G. of G. went out, 23
21:9 sword of G. is here, 22:10
2 Sam. 21:19 brother of G. 1 Chr. 20:5

**GOMER.**

Gen. 10:2 Japheth, G. 1 Chr. 1:5
Ezek. 38:6 G. and all his bands
Hos. 1:3 he took G. the daughter

**GOMORRAH.**

Gen. 13:10; 14:11; 18:20; 19:24, 28
Deut. 29:23; Is. 1:9; 13:19; Jer. 23:14; 49:18; 50:40; Amos 4:11; Rom. 9:29; 2 Pet. 2:6; Jude 7
32:32 vine is of the fields of G.
Is. 1:10 ye peo. of G. Zep. 2:9
Mat. 10:15 toler. for G. Mark 6:11

**GONE.**

Gen. 34:17 take daugh. we be g.
42:33 take food, and be g.
Ex. 12:32 take flocks, and be g.
Deut. 32:36 seeth their pow. is g.
1 Sam. 14:3 knew not Jo. was g.
17 see who is g. from us
15:20 g. the way the Lord sent
20:41 as soon as the lad was g.
2 Sam. 3:7 g. into fath. concub.
24 quite g.; 13:15 arise, be g.
1 K. 2:41 Shimei g. from Jerusa.
13:24 when g. a lion met him
18:12 soon as g. Spirit sh. carry
20:40 as I was busy, he was g.
1 Chr. 17:5 g. from tent to tent
Job 7:4 sh. I rise, and night be g.
19:10 destroyed me, and I am g.
24:24 exalted for a while, but g.
28:4 they are dried up and g.
Ps. 38:10 light of mine eyes is g.
42:4 I had g. with multitude
73:2 my feet were almost g.
77:8 is his mercy g. for ever?
103:16 wind pass. over it, is g.
109:23 I am g. like the shadow
Prov. 20:14 g. his way, boasting
Ec. 8:10 who had come and g.
Cant. 2:11 the rain is over and g.
5:6 beloved had withd. and g.
6:1 whither is thy beloved g.?
Is. 5:13 my people g. into capti.
24:11 the mirth of the land is g.
41:3 by the way he had not g.
Jer. 2:5 iniquity that th. are g.?
23 say, I have not g. after B.?
5:23 people are revolted and g.
9:10 beasts g.; 15:6 thou art g.
44:14 none g. into E. sh. escape
28 remnant that are g. sh. kn.
50:6 g. from mountain to hill
Lam. 1:3 Ju. g.; 5 Zion's ch. g.
6 g. with. strength; 18 virg. g.
Ezek. 37:21 from heathen whi. g.
Dan. 2:5 the thing is g. fr. me, 8
Hos. 9:6 g. bec. of destruction
Amos 8:5 when will moon be g.?
Luke 2:15 angels g. from them
24:28 made as would g. further
John 4:8 disciples were g. to buy
12:19 the world is g. after him
Acts 16:19 saw hope of gains g.
20:25 g. preaching kingd. of G.
1 Pet. 3:22 who is g. into heaven
Jude 11 have g. in way of Cain

**GONE about.**

1 Sam. 15:12 Saul is g. a. and
Job 1:5 days of feast. were g. a.
Is. 15:8 g. a. borders of Moab
Acts 24:6 g. a. to profane temple

**GONE aside.**

Num. 5:19 not g. a. to unclean.
20 if thou hast g. a. to another
Ps. 14:3 they are all g. a. filthy
Acts 26:31 when they were g. a.

**GONE astray.**

Ps. 119:176 have g. a. like sheep
Is. 53:6 we like sheep have g. a.
Mat. 18:12 if a man have 100 sheep, one be g. a. he seeketh that g. a.
2 Pet. 2:15 forsak. way, and g. a.

**GONE away.**

2 Sam. 3:22 Ab. g. a. in peace, 23
23:9 the men of Israel were g. a.
Job 28:4 wat. were g. a. from m.
Is. 1:4 they are g. a. backward
Ezek. 44:10 Levites g. a. from me
Mal. 3:7 g. a. fr. my ordinances
John 6:22 his disciples g. a. alo.

**GONE back.**

Ruth 1:15 thy sister-in-law g. b.
Job 23:12 nor have I g. back
Ps. 53:3 every one is g. b. none
Jer. 40:5 while he was not g. b.

**GONE down.**

1 Sam. 15:12 Saul is g. d. to Gil.
1 K. 1:25 Adonijah is g. down
21:18 Ahab g. d. to possess vin.
2 K. 20:11 the shadow had g. d. in dial of Ahaz, Is. 38:8
Cant. 6:2 my beloved is g. down
Jer. 15:9 sun is g. d. while day
48:15 his young men are g. d.
Ezek. 31:12 peo. g. d. from shad.
32:21 strong g. d. slain by swo.
24 Elam g. d.; 27 Tubal; 30 Z.
Jon. 1:5 Jonah g. d. sides of ship

**GONE forth.**

Ex. 19:1 when Israel was g. f.
2 K. 6:15 when servant was g. f.
1 Chr. 14:15 God is g. f. before
Is. 51:5 my salvation is g. f.
Jer. 4:7 g. f. to make land desol.
10:20 my children are g. f.
23:15 profaneness g. f. into land
19 whirlwind of Lord is g. f.
29:16 brethren that are not g. f.
Ezek. 7:10 day come, morn. g. f.
36:20 people of Lord are g. f.
Dan. 2:14 g. f. to slay wise men
10:20 when I am g. f. pr. come
Mark 10:17 when he g. f. one

**GONE out.**

Ex. 9:29 as soon as I am g. o.
Num. 16:46 wrath g. o. from L.
Deut. 13:13 certain men g. out
23:23 which is g. o. of thy lips
Jud. 4:14 is not the Lord g. out
Ruth 1:13 hand of the L. is g. o.
1 Sam. 25:37 wine g. o. of Nabal
2 K. 5:2 Syrians g. o. by comp.
7:12 we hungry, there. they g. o.
20:4 Isaiah was g. o. to court
Ps. 19:4 g. o. through the earth
89:34 the thing that is g. out
Is. 45:23 word g. o. of my mouth
Ezek. 24:6 whose scum not g. out
Mat. 12:43 when unclean spirit is g. out, Luke 11:24
25:8 give us oil, our lamps g. o.
Mark 5:30 virtue g. o. Luke 8:46
7:29 devil is g. out of daughter, 30; Luke 11:14
John 13:31 when g. o. Jesus said
Rom. 3:12 they are all g. o.
1 John 4:1 many false prop. g. o.

**GONE over.**

2 Sam. 17:20 they be g. o. brook
Ps. 38:4 mine iniquities g. o.
42:7 waves and billows are g. o.
124:4 stream g. over our soul
5 waters had g. over our soul
Is. 10:29 they are g. o. passage
16:8 are g. o. the sea, Jer. 48:32
Mat. 10:23 g. o. cities of Israel

**GONE up.**

Gen. 49:9 my son, thou art g. up
2 K. 1:4 not come off bed on which g. up, 6, 16
Ps. 47:5 G. is g. up with a shout
Is. 15:2 he is g. up to Bajith
57:8 discov. to another, art g. up
Jer. 3:6 she is g. up on mount.
14:2 the cry of Jerusa. is g. up
34:21 king's army wh. are g. up
48:15 Moab is g. up out of cities
Ezek. 9:3 glory of G. of Isr. g. up
13:5 have not g. up into gaps
Hos. 8:9 they are g. up to Assy.
John 7:10 his breth. were g. up
Acts 18:22 g. up and saluted chu.

**GONE a whoring.**

Lev. 17:7 whom th. have g. a w.
Ezek. 23:30 bec. thou hast g. a w.
Hos. 4:12 g. a w. fr. under th. G.
9:1 thou hast g. a w. from God

**GOOD, Substantive**

Gen. 32:12 I will do thee g.
45:18 g. of the land of Egypt
20 g. of land of Egypt is yours
50:20 God meant it unto g.
Num. 10:29 Lord hath spoken g.
Jos. 24:20 consume you, after he hath done you g.
1 Sam. 20:12 there be g. tow. D.
24:17 rewarded me g. for evil
19 wheref. Lord rew. thee g.
25:30 according to g. spoken
2 Sam. 14:32 g. for me to been
16:12 L. will requite g. for curs.
1 K. 22:13 words of prophets declare g. to king, 2 Chr. 18:12
1 Chr. 29:3 I prepared of my g.
2 Chr. 24:16 had done g. in Isr.
Ezr. 9:12 eat the g. of the land
Est. 7:9 spoken g. for the king
Job 2:10 rec. g. at hand of God?
5:27 know thou it for thy g.
7:7 mine eye sh. no more see g.
9:25 days flee, they see no g.
15:3 with speeches can do no g.
21:16 their g. is not in th. hand
Job 22:21 peace, g. sh. co. to th.
24:21 he doeth not g. to widow
Ps. 4:6 who will show us g.?
14:1 do g. 3; 53:1; Rom. 3:12
34:12 loveth days, he may see g.
39:2 I h. my peace, even from g.
104:28 they are filled with g.
106:5 see the g. of thy choice
122:9 Lord, I will seek thy g.
128:5 shall see g. of Jerusalem

Prov. 3:27 with. not g. from th.
11:17 doeth g. to his own soul
27 he that diligently seek. g.
12:14 a man satisfied with g.
13:2 eat g. by fruit of his mouth
21 to righteous g. sh. be repaid
14:22 truth to them that dev. g.
16:20 hand. matter wisely fi. g.
17:20 froward heart find. no g.
22 a merry heart doeth g.
19:8 keep understand. find g.
Ec. 2:24 soul en. g. 3:13; 5:18
3:12 there is no g. in them
4:8 I labor. bereave soul of g.?
5:11 what g. there to owners?
6:3 his soul be not filled with g.
6 seen no g. all g. to one place
7:20 doeth g. and sinneth not
9:18 one sinner destro. much g
Is. 1:19 ye sh. eat the g. of land
52:7 bringeth good tidings of g.
Jer. 8:15 no g. came, 14:19
17:6 sh. not see when g. cometh
18:10 if do evil, I will rep. of g
20 I stood bef. thee to speak g.
29:32 neither sh. behold g. I do
32:42 I will bring thee g. I pro.
33:9 hear all the g. I do them
Ezek. 16:50 I took them I saw g.
Zec. 11:12 if g. give my price
Mat. 26:24 been g. not been born
John 5:29 done g. to resurrection
Acts 10:38 went about doing g.
14:17 he did g. and gave rain
Rom. 2:10 hon. ev. man. work. g.
1 Thes. 3:1 g. be left Athens
1 John 3:17 hath this world's g.

**For GOOD.**

Deut. 6:24 fear the L. for our g.
10:13 com. thee this day for g.
30:9 L. will rej. over thee for g.
Ezr. 8:22 God on them for g.
Neh. 5:19 O my G. for g. 13:31
Job 5:27 know thou it for thy g.
Ps. 86:17 show a token for g.
119:122 be surety for ser. for g.
Jer. 14:11 pray not for their g.
24:5 sent out of place f. their g.
6 set mine eyes on them f. g.
32:39 for fear, for the g. of them
Mic. 1:12 Maroth waited for g.
Rom. 8:28 all things work for g.
13:4 he is minister of God for g.
15:2 ev. one please neighb. f. g.

See BAD, EVIL.

**GOOD, Adjective.**

Gen. 24:12 send me g. speed
26:29 we have done noth. but g
27:46 what g. sh. my life do me?
41:5 g. ears; 26 g. kine; 35 g. y.
43:28 our father is in g. health
46:29 Joseph wept a g. while
Deut. 33:16 for g. will of him
1 Sam. 2:24 it is no g. report
12:23 I will teach the g. way
25:15 men were very g. to us.
29:9 thou art g. in my sight
2 Sam. 15:3 see thy mat. are g.
19:18 what the king thought g.
1 K. 8:36 teach them the g. way
56 no word of g. promise fail.
12:7 speak g. words, 2 Chr. 10:7
2 K. 20:19 g. is word of L. Is. 39:8
2 Chr. 19:11 Lord sh. be with g.
30:18 the g. Lord pardon every
Ezr. 8:18 the g. hand of our God
Neh. 9:13 gave them g. statutes
20 thou gav. g. Spirit to them
Job 10:3 is it g. thou oppress?
13:9 is it g. he search you out?
39:4 their young in g. liking
Ps. 25:8 g. and upright is the L.
37:23 steps of g. man ord. by L.
45:1 my heart is inditing g.
86:5 thou, Lord, art g. 119:68
112:5 a g. man showeth favor
119:39 thy judgments are g.
66 teach g. judg. and knowl.
Prov. 2:9 shalt unders. ev. g. pa.
20 walk in way of g. men
12:25 g. word mak. heart glad
14:19 the evil bow before the g.
15:23 word in season, how g.
30 g. report maketh bones fat
20:18 with g. advice make war
22:1 g. name rather than riches
Ec. 4:9 g. reward for their labor
5:11 what g. to owners thereof?
9:2 one event to g. and clean
11:6 whet. they both alike be g.
Jer. 6:16 the g. way and walk
24:2 g. figs; 3 very g.; 5 g. figs
29:10 I will perform my g. word
Ezek. 17:8 planted in g. soil by
24:4 gather every g. piece, thigh
Dan. 4:2 I thought g. to show
Zec. 1:13 L. ans. with g. words
Mal. 2:13 receiv. it with g. will
Mat. 7:11 g. gifts, Luke 11:13
17 g. tree bringeth g. fruit, 18
9:22 be of g. comfort, Luke 8:48
13:8 in g. ground, 23; Mark 4:8, 20; Luke 8:8, 15
24 g. seed; 19:16 g. Mas. g. th.
19:17 call. me g.? none g. but
20:15 th. eye evil bec. I am g.?
25:21 well done, thou g. servant
Luke 2:14 g. will toward men
6:38 g. measure, pressed down
10:42 Mary hath chosen g. part
12:32 your Fa.'s g. pleasure
John 2:10 thou hast kept g. wine
10:11 I g. shep. the g. shepherd
Acts 15:7 ye know that a g. whi.
Rom. 7:12 com. is holy, just, g.
12:2 g. and perfect will of God
1 Cor. 15:33 corrupt g. manners
1 Thes. 3:6 have g. remem. of us
2 Tim. 3:3 despis. of those are g.
Tit. 1:8 must be lover of g. men
Heb. 6:5 tasted the g. word of G.
Jam. 1:17 g. gift; 2:3 sit in a g.
1 Pet. 2:18 only to g. and gentle
3:10 love life, and see g. days

See BAD, CHEER, CONSCIENCE, COURAGE, DO, DAY, OLD AGE.

**GOOD heed.**

Deut. 2:4 take g. heed, Jos. 23:11
Ec. 12:9 preacher gave g. heed

**Is GOOD.**

Gen. 2:12 gold of that land is g.
Deut. 1:14 thing thou spok. is g.
6:18 that which is g. in sight L.
1 Sam. 29:6 co. in with ho. is g.
1 K. 2:38 Shi. said, The say. is g.
42 the word I have heard is g.
22:13 speak that which is g.
2 K. 20:3 done wh. is g. Is. 38:3
1 Chr. 16:34 L. is g. 2 Chr. 5:13; 7:3; Ezr. 3:11; Ps. 100:5; 106:1; 107:1; 118:1, 29; 135:3; 136:1; 145:9; Jer. 33:11; Lam. 3:25; Nah. 1:7
19:13 which is g. in his sight
Job 34:4 am. ourselves wh. is g.
Ps. 34:8 and see the Lord is g.
69:16 thy loving kindness is g.
73:1 truly, God is g. to Israel
85:12 L. sh. give that wh. is g.
109:21 because thy mercy is g.
143:10 Spirit is g. lead into land
Prov. 11:23 desire of right. is g.
25:25 so is g. news from far co.
31:18 perce. her merchand. is g.
Ec. 2:26 giveth to a man that is g. to him that is g. bef. God
6:12 know. what is g. for man?
7:11 wisd. is g. with an inherit.
9:2 as is the g. so is the sinner
Is. 55:2 eat ye that which is g.
Jer. 13:10 this girdle is g. for no.
Hos. 4:13 shadow thereof is g.
Mic. 6:8 showed thee, what is g.
Mal. 2:17 ev. one doeth evil is g.
Mark 9:50 salt is g. Luke 14:34
Luke 6:45 bringeth that wh. is g.
18:19 none is g. save one
Rom. 7:13 wh. is g. made death
18 that is g. I find not
12:9 cleave to that which is g.
16:19 wise to what is g.
1 Cor. 7:26 this is g. for the pre.
Eph. 4:29 no com. but that is g.
1 Thes. 5:15 what is g. 3 John 11
21 hold fast that which is g.
1 Tim. 1:8 we know the law is g.
2:3 this is g. in the sight of G.
4:4 every creature of God is g.
5:4 for that is g. before God
1 Pet. 3:13 fol. of that which is g.

**It is GOOD.**

Ps. 52:9 name, for it is g. 54:6
73:28 it is g. to draw near to G.
92:1 it is a g. thing to give than.
119:71 it is g. I have been afflic.
147:1 it is g. to sing praises
Prov. 24:13 eat honey, be. it is g.
Ec. 5:18 it is g. to eat and drink
7:18 it is g. that thou take hold
Lam. 3:26 it is g. bear yoke in
Mat. 5:13 it is g. for nothing.
Mat. 17:4 it is g. for us to be here, Mark 9:5; Luke 9:33
Rom. 7:16 I con. to law, it is g.
14:21 it is g. nei. to eat flesh nor
1 Cor. 7:1 it is g. for a man not to touch a woman, 8
26 I say it is g. for a man
Gal. 4:18 it is g. zeal. affected

**GOOD land.**

Ex. 3:8 come to g. l. Deut. 8:7
Num. 14:7 the land is a g. land
Deut. 1:25 a g. l. the L. doth give
35 none of that gener. see g. l.
3:25 let me go and see the g. l.
4:21 should not go unto g. land
22 ye shall possess that g. land
6:18 go in and possess g. land
8:7 bringeth thee into a g. land
10 bless the L. for the g. land
9:6 giveth not g. l. for thy righ.
11:17 lest ye perish from off g. l.
Jos. 23:13 perish from g. l. 15
16 perish quickly from off g. l.
Jud. 18:9 seen the land very g.
1 K. 14:15 root Israel out of g. l.
2 K. 3:19 mar ev. g. piece of l. 25
1 Chr. 28:8 possess this g. land

**GOOD, with make.**

Ex. 21:34 shall make it g. 22:14
22:11 sh. not make it g. 13, 15
Lev. 24:18 killeth a beast m. g.
Num. 23:19 sh. he not m. it g.?
Jer. 18:11 m. ways and doings g.

**GOOD man.**

2 Sam. 18:27 Ahimaaz is a g. m.
Ps. 37:23 steps of a g. man
112:5 a g. man showeth favor
Prov. 7:19 g. man is not at home
12:2 a g. man obtaineth favor
13:22 g. m. leaveth an inherit.
14:14 a g. m. is satisfied, 12:14
Mic. 7:2 the g. man is perished
Mat. 12:35 a g. man out of good treasure, Luke 6:45
20:11 murmured ag. the g. m.
24:43 g. man had kn. Luke 12:39
Luke 23:50 Joseph was a g. man
John 7:12 said, He is a g. man
Acts 11:24 Barnabas was a g. m.
Rom. 5:7 for a g. m. some w. die

**Not GOOD.**

Gen. 2:18 not g. man be alone
2 Sam. 17:7 counsel not g.
Ps. 36:4 in way that is not g.

*Prov.* 16:29 lead into way *not g.*
17:26 to punish just is *not g.*
18:5 is *not g.* to accept wicked
19:2 soul with. know. *n. g.*
20:23 a false balance is *not g.*
24:23 *n. g.* respect of per. 28:21
25:27 *not g.* to eat much honey
*Is.* 65:2 walketh in way *n. g.*
*Ezek.* 18:18 did that wh. is *n. g.*
20:25 I gave them statutes *n. g.*
36:31 your doings were *n. g.*
*Mat.* 19:10 it is *not g.* to marry
*Acts* 15:38 Paul thought *not g.*
1 *Cor.* 5:6 your glorying is *not g.*

**Seem, seemed, seemeth GOOD.**

*Jos.* 9:25 as it *seemeth g.* to do unto us, *Jud.* 10:15; 1 *Sam.* 14:36, 40; *Ezr.* 7:18; *Est.* 3:11; *Jer.* 26:14; 40:4
*Jud.* 19:24 do what *s. g.*
1 *Sam.* 1:23 what *seemeth g.* 3:18; 11:10; 24:4
2 *Sam.* 3:19 all that *seem g.* to Is.
10:12 do that *s.* him *g.* 15:26
19:37 do to C. what *seem g.* 38
24:22 and offer up what *s. g.*
1 *K.* 21:2 if it *seem g.* to thee, *Jer.* 40:4
1 *Chr.* 13:2 if it *seem g.* to you
*Ezr.* 5:17 *s. g.* to king, *Est.* 5:4
*Jer.* 18:4 as *seemed g.* to potter
*Mat.* 11:26 *s. g.* in sig. *Luke* 10:21
*Luke* 1:3 it *seemed g.* to me
*Acts* 15:25 it *seemed g.* unto us
28 it *seemed g.* to the H. Ghost

**GOOD, *with* thing.**

*Ex.* 18:17 *thing* doest is not *g.*
*Deut.* 26:11 rejoice in every *g. t.*
*Jos.* 21:45 failed not any *g. t.*
1 *Sam.* 26:16 this *thing* is not *g.*
1 *K.* 14:13 him is fou. some *g. t.*
2 *K.* 8:9 took of ev. *g. t.* of Da.
*Ps.* 34:10 seek L. not want *g. t.*
38:20 I follow *thing* that *g.* is
84:11 no *g. th.* will he withhold
92:1 it is *g. t.* to give thanks
*Prov.* 18:22 a wife, findeth *g. th.*
*Jer.* 33:14 will perform *g. t.*
*Hos.* 8:3 cast off *thing* that is *g.*
*Mat.* 19:16 what *g. thing* sh. I do
*John* 1:46 any *g. t.* out of Naz.?
*Rom.* 7:18 in my flesh dw. no *g. t.*
*Gal.* 4:18 zeal. affected in *g. t.*
*Eph.* 4:28 working *th.* which is *g.*
6:8 knowing *g. t.* man doeth
2 *Tim.* 1:14 *g. t.* commit to thee
*Phile.* 6 ack. every *g. th.* in you
*Heb.* 13:9 a *g. t.* heart be establ.

**GOOD things.**

*Deut.* 6:11 houses full of *g. t.*
*Jos.* 23:14 not one failed of *g. t.*
15 that all *g. things* are come
*Job* 22:18 filled th. hous. wi. *g. t.*
*Ps.* 103:5 sat. thy mouth w. *g. t.*
*Prov.* 28:10 upright sh. have *g. t.*
*Jer.* 5:25 sins have withh. *g. t.*
*Mat.* 7:11 give *g. things* to them
12:34 being evil, speak *g. t.*
35 a good man bringeth *g. th.*
*Luke* 1:53 filled hungry with *g. t.*
16:25 in lifetime receivedst *g. t.*
*Rom.* 10:15 glad tidings of *g. th.*
*Gal.* 6:6 communicate in all *g. t.*
*Tit.* 2:3 women teachers of *g. t.*
3:8 these *t.* are *g.* and profitable
*Heb.* 9:11 Christ high-pr. of *g. t.*
10:1 a shadow of *g. th.* to come

**GOOD tidings.**

2 *Sam.* 4:10 have brought *g. tid.*
18:27 cometh with *g. tidings*
1 *K.* 1:42 and bringest *g. tidings*
2 *K.* 7:9 a day of *g. tidings*
*Is.* 40:9 O Zion that bringest *g. t.*
41:27 give J. one bringeth *g. t.*
52:7 him that bringeth *g. t.*
61:1 anointed to preach *g. tid.*
*Nah.* 1:15 beh. him bringeth *g. t.*
*Luke* 2:10 I bring you *g. t.*
1 *Thes.* 3:6 *g. t.* of your faith

**GOOD understanding.**

1 *Sam.* 25:3 Abi. was wo. of *g. u.*
*Ps.* 111:10 *g. u.* have all that do
*Prov.* 3:4 find favor and *g. und.*
13:15 *g. understan.* giveth favor

**Was GOOD.**

*Gen.* 1:4 saw that it *w. g.* 10, 25
31 G. saw ev. th. it *w.* very *g.*
3:6 the woman saw tree *was g.*
40:16 baker saw interpre. *w. g.*
41:37 thing *w. g.* in eyes of Phar.
49:15 Issachar saw rest *w. g.*
1 *Sam.* 15:9 S. spar. all that *w. g.*
2 *Chr.* 14:2 Asa did that wh. *w. g.*
31:20 Hezekiah wro. what *w. g.*
*Ec.* 2:3 see what *w.* that *g.*

**GOOD work.**

*Neh.* 2:18 strengthen for *g. w.*
*Mat.* 26:10 wro. *g. w.* *Mark* 14:6
*John* 10:33 for *g. w.* we stone not
2 *Cor.* 9:8 abound to every *g. w.*
*Phil.* 1:6 which hath begun *g. w.*
*Col.* 1:10 fruitful in every *g. w.*
2 *Thes.* 2:17 in every *g. w.*
1 *Tim.* 3:1 a bishop, desir. *g. w.*
5:10 diligently followed *g. w.*.
2 *Tim.* 2:21 prepared to ev. *g. w.*
*Tit.* 1:16 to every *g. w.* reprobate
3:1 to be ready to every *g. w.*
*Heb.* 13:21 make perf. in ev. *g. w.*

**GOOD works.**

1 *Sam.* 19:4 *w.* to thee been *g.*
*Mat.* 5:16 may see your *g. w.*
*John* 10:32 *g. w.* have I showed
*Acts* 9:36 Dorcas full of *g. works*
*Rom.* 13:3 not a terror to *g. w.*
*Eph.* 2:10 created in Ch. to *g. w.*
1 *Tim.* 2:10 be adorned w. *g. w.*
5:10 well reported for *g. works*
25 *g. w.* of some are manifest
6:18 that they be rich in *g. w.*
2 *Tim.* 3:17 furnished to all *g. w.*
*Tit.* 2:7 thyself a pattern in *g. w.*
14 zealous of *g. works*
3:8 careful to maintain *g. w.* 14
*Heb.* 10:24 prov. to love and *g. w.*
1 *Pet.* 2:12 by *g. w.* glorify God

**GOODLY.**

*Gen.* 39:6 Joseph was a *g.* person
49:21 Nap. a hind, giv. *g.* words
*Ex.* 2:2 saw he was a *g.* child
39:28 made *g.* bonnets
*Num.* 24:5 *g.* are thy tents, O J.
*Deut.* 3:25 that *g.* mountain
6:10 *g.* cities which build. not
8:12 thou hast built *g.* houses
*Jos.* 7:21 a *g.* Babylon. garment
1 *Sam.* 9:2 S. a young man, and *g.*
16:12 David was *g.* to look to
2 *Sam.* 23:21 Ben. slew a *g.* man
1 *K.* 1:6 Adonijah was a *g.* man
*Job* 39:13 *g.* wings to peacocks
*Ps.* 16:6 I have a *g.* heritage
80:10 boughs were like *g.* cedars
*Jer.* 3:19 sh. I give thee *g.* heri.?
11:16 olive-tree of *g.* fruit
*Ezek.* 17:8 it might be a *g.* vine
23 bear fruit, and be a *g.* cedar
*Hos.* 10:1 have made *g.* images
*Joel* 3:5 your tem. my *g.* things
*Zec.* 10:3 made them as *g.* horse
11:13 a *g.* price I was prized at
*Mat.* 13:45 merch. seek. *g.* pearls
*Luke* 21:5 adorned with *g.* stones
*Jam.* 2:2 a man in *g.* apparel
*Rev.* 18:14 things dainty and *g.*

**GOODLIER, EST.**

1 *Sam.* 8:16 your *g.* young men
9:2 not in Israel a *g.* person
1 *K.* 20:3 child. even *g.* are mine

**GOODNESS.**

*Ex.* 18:9 rejo. for *g.* L. had done
33:19 make *g.* pass before thee
34:6 Lord God abundant in *g.*
*Num.* 10:32 wh. *g.* L. sh. do to us
2 *Sam.* 7:28 prom. *g.* 1 *Chr.* 17:26
1 *K.* 8:66 joyful for *g.* 2 *Chr.* 7:10
2 *Chr.* 6:41 saints rejoice in *g.*
32:32 Hezek. *g.*; 35:26 Josiah *g.*
*Neh.* 9:25 delighted thems. in *g.*
35 have not served thee in *g.*
*Ps.* 16:2 my *g.* ext. not to thee
21:3 prev. with blessings of *g.*
23:6 surely *g.* shall follow me
25:7 remem. me, for thy *g.* sake
27:13 I believed to see *g.* of L.
31:19 O how great is thy *g.*
33:5 earth is full of *g.* of Lord
52:1 *g.* of God endureth contin.
65:4 satis. with *g.* of thy house
11 crownest the year with *g.*
68:10 prep. of thy *g.* for poor
107:8 pr. L. for his *g.* 15, 21, 31
9 filleth hungry soul with *g.*
144:2 my *g.* and my fortress
145:7 utter memory of thy *g.*
*Prov.* 20:6 procla. ev. one his *g.*
*Is.* 63:7 *g.* toward the house of Israel
*Jer.* 2:7 bro. you to eat *g.* thereof
31:12 flow together to *g.* of L.
14 people satisfied with my *g.*
33:9 shall tremble for all the *g.*
*Hos.* 3:5 fear the Lord and his *g.*
6:4 your *g.* is as a morn. cloud
10:1 according to *g.* of his land
*Zec.* 9:17 great is his *g.*
*Rom.* 2:4 *g.* of G. lead. to repent.
11:22 behold, the *g.* of G. towa. thee *g.* if thou continue in *g.*
15:14 that you are full of *g.*
*Gal.* 5:22 fru. of Sp. is *g.* *Eph.* 5:9
2 *Thes.* 1:11 fulfil *g.* ple. of his *g.*

**GOODS.**

*Gen.* 14:16 Abr. brought back *g.*
21 take the *g.* to thyself
24:10 *g.* of master in his hand
31:18 J. carried away his *g.* 46:6
*Ex.* 22:8 hand to neighbor's *g.* 11
*Num.* 16:32 earth swall. their *g.*
31:9 spoil of Midian and their *g.*
35:3 for Levites' cattle and *g.*
*Deut.* 28:11 make plenteous in *g.*
2 *Chr.* 21:14 smite wives, thy *g.*
*Ezr.* 1:4 the men help him wi. *g.*
6 strength. their hands with *g.*
6:8 king's *g.* expenses be given
7:26 banishm. or to confis. of *g.*
*Neh.* 9:25 poss. houses full of *g.*
*Job* 20:10 his hands sh. restore *g.*
21 therefore no man look for *g.*
28 his *g.* shall flow away
*Ec.* 5:11 when *g.* increase
*Ezek.* 38:12 have cattle and *g.*
13 come to take cattle and *g.*?
*Zep.* 1:13 *g.* shall bec. a booty
*Mat.* 12:29 enter str. man's hou. and take *g.*? *Mark* 3:27
24:47 make him ruler over *g.*
25:14 deliver. unto them his *g.*
*Luke* 6:30 taketh away thy *g.*
11:21 his *g.* are in peace
12:18 there will I bestow my *g.*
19 thou hast much *g.* laid up
15:12 give me the portion of *g.*
16:1 accused that he wasted *g.*
19:8 half of my *g.* give to poor
*Acts* 2:45 sold *g.* and parted th.
1 *Cor.* 13:3 I bestow all my *g.*
*Heb.* 10:34 spoiling of your *g.*
*Rev.* 3:17 and increased with *g.*

**GOPHER wood.**

*Gen.* 6:14 an ark of *g. w.*

**GORE, ED.**

*Ex.* 21:28 if ox *g.* man or woman
31 whe. *g.* a son or daughter

**GORGEOUS, LY.**
*Ezek.* 23:12 Assyrians clothed *g.*
*Luke* 7:25 *g.* apparel, in king's
23:11 H. arrayed Jesus in *g.* robe

**GOSHEN.**
*Gen.* 45:10 dwell in land of G. 46:34; 47:4, 6, 27
*Ex.* 8:22; 9:26; *Jos.* 10:41; 11:16; 15:51

**GOSPEL.**
*Mark* 1:1 beginning of *g.* of J. C.
15 said, Repent and believe *g.*
8:35 lose life for my sake and *g.*
10:29 for my sake and *g.*
13:10 the *g.* must be published
*Acts* 15:7 by my mouth hear *g.*
20:24 the *g.* of the grace of God
*Rom.* 1:1 separat. to the *g.* of G.
9 I serve with my spirit in *g.*
16 not ashamed of *g.* of Christ
2:16 judge secrets ac. to my *g.*
10:16 have not all obeyed the *g.*
11:28 concerning *g.* are enemies
15:16 ministering the *g.* of God
29 blessing of the *g.* of Christ
16:25 estab. you according to *g.*
1 *Cor.* 4:15 begotten you thro' *g.*
9:12 lest we hinder *g.* of Christ
17 a dispensation of *g.* is com.
18 I preach *g.* I may make *g.* of Christ with. charge; that I abuse not my po. in the *g.*
23 this I do for the *g.* sake
2 *Cor.* 4:3 if *g.* hid, hid to them
4 light of glor. *g.* should shine
8:18 whose praise is in *g.*
9:13 prof. subjection to the *g.*
11:4 receive another *g.* *Gal.* 1:6
*Gal.* 1:7 would pervert *g.* of Chr.
2:2 communicated *g.* I preach
5 truth of *g.* might continue
7 *g.* of uncir. committed to me
14 according to truth of the *g.*
*Eph.* 1:13 *g.* of your salvation
3:6 partake prom. in Chr. by *g.*
6:15 preparation of *g.* of peace
19 make known mystery of *g.*
*Phil.* 1:5 fellowship in the *g.*
7 def. and confirmation of *g.* 17
12 fallen out to furthera. of *g.*
27 let your conversation be as beco. *g.* striv. for faith of *g.*
2:22 hath served with me in *g.*
4:3 help-women with me in *g.*
15 in the beginning of the *g.*
*Col.* 1:5 heard bef. of truth of *g.*
23 not moved from hope of *g.*
1 *Thes.* 1:5 *g.* came not in word
2:2 bold to speak the *g.* of God
4 to be put in trust with *g.*
8 willing to impart not *g.* only
3:2 Ti. our fellow-laborer in *g.*
2 *Thes.* 1:8 on them that obey not the *g.* 1 *Pet.* 4:17
2:14 whereunto called you by *g.*
1 *Tim.* 1:11 according to *g.* of G.
2 *Tim.* 1:8 partaker of affl. of *g.*
10 immortality to light thro' *g.*
2:8 J. C. raised according to *g.*
*Phile.* 13 minist. in bonds of *g.*

**GOSPEL, *with* preach, ed, ing.**
*Mat.* 4:23 Jesus went *preaching* the *g.* 9:35; *Mark* 1:14
11:5 poor have *g. p.* *Luke* 7:22
24:14 *g.* be *p.* 26:13; *Mark* 14:9
*Mark* 16:15 *p. g.* to ev. creature
*Luke* 4:18 anointed me to *p. g.*
9:6 *p.* the *g.* and healing
20:1 he taught and *preached g.*
*Acts* 8:25 *pre. g.* to Samaritans
16:10 L. had called us to *p. g.*
*Rom.* 1:15 I am ready to *p. g.*
10:15 beautiful feet that *p. g.*
15:19 I have fully *pre. g.* of Ch.
20 so have I strived to *prea. g.*
1 *Cor.* 1:17 not to bapt. but *pr. g.*
9:14 that *p. g.* should live of *g.*
16 tho' I *p. g.* nothing to glory of, woe to me if I *pr.* not *g.*
18 when I *p. g.* I may make *g.*
15:1 I declare the *g.* which I *pr.*
2 *Cor.* 2:12 I came to T. to *pr. g.*
10:14 as far as to you in *p. g.*
11:7 I *pr.* to you freely the *g.*
*Gal.* 1:8 tho' we *pr.* any other *g.*
11 *g. p.* of me not after man
3:8 *prea.* before the *g.* to Abra.
4:13 infirmity of flesh I *p. g.*
1 *Thes.* 2:9 we *p.* to you *g.* of G.
*Heb.* 4:2 to us was *g* *preached*
1 *Pet.* 1:12 them that *pre.* the *g.*
25 which by *g.* is *pr.* to you
4:6 for this cause was the *g. pr.*
*Rev.* 14:6 having everl. *g.* to *p.*

**GOT.**
*Gen.* 39:12 Jos. *g.* him out, 15
*Ps.* 44:3 *g.* not land by sword
*Ec.* 2:7 I *g.* servan. and maidens

**GOTTEN.**
*Gen.* 4:1 I have *g.* a man

*Ex.* 14:18 when I have *g.* honor
*Lev.* 6:4 thing he hath deceit. *g.*
*Deut.* 8:17 hand hath *g.* wealth
2 *Sam.* 17:13 be *g.* into a city
*Job* 28:15 wisdom not *g.* for gold
31:25 rejoic. bec. hand *g.* much
*Ps.* 98:1 arm hath *g.* victory
*Prov.* 13:11 wealth *g.* by vanity
20:21 inheritance *g.* hastily
*Ec.* 1:16 *g.* more wisdom than all
*Is.* 15:7 abundance *g.* they carry
*Ezek.* 28:4 wisdom hast *g.* riches
*Dan.* 9:15 thou hast *g.* renown
*Rev.* 15:2 them that *g.* victory

**GOVERN.**
1 *K.* 21:7 dost *g.* kingdom of Is.?
*Job* 34:17 shall he that hateth *g.*?
*Ps.* 67:4 thou sh. *g.* the nations

**GOVERNMENT, S.**
*Is.* 9:6 *g.* shall be upon shoulder
7 of inc. of his *g.* sh. be no end
22:21 I commit *g.* to his hand
1 *Cor.* 12:28 *g.* divers. of tongues
2 *Pet.* 2:10 them that despise *g.*

**GOVERNOR.**
*Gen.* 42:6 Jos. *g.* over land, 45:26
1 *K.* 18:3 Ob. *g.* over Ahab's ho.
1 *Chr.* 29:22 anointed S. chief *g.*
*Ezr.* 5:14 C. deliv. vessels to *g.*
*Neh.* 5:14 not eaten bread of *g.*
18 required not the bread of *g.*
*Ps.* 22:28 he is *g.* am. the nation.
*Jer.* 30:21 *g.* sh. proceed fr. them
40:5 go back to Gedaliah the *g.*
41:2 Ish. smote Gedaliah the *g.*
*Hag.* 1:14 L. stirred up Zerub. *g.*
2:2 speak to Zerub. the *g.* 21
*Zec.* 9:7 sh. be as a *g.* in Judah
*Mal.* 1:8 offer it now to thy *g.*
*Mat.* 2:6 out of thee sh. come *g.*
28:14 if this come to *g.*'s ears
*John* 2:8 bear to *g.* of the feast
*Acts* 24:1 informed *g.* against P.
2 *Cor.* 11:32 the *g.* under Aretas
*Jam.* 3:4 ships turned wh. *g.* lis.

**GOVERNORS.**
*Jud.* 5:9 my heart tow. *g.* of Isr.
14 out of Machir came down *g.*
*Ezr.* 8:36 delivered com. to *g.*
*Neh.* 2:7 let letters be given to *g.*
5:15 the *g.* chargeable to people
*Dan.* 2:48 made Dan. chief of *g.*
*Zec.* 12:5 *g.* of Judah shall say
6 will make *g.* of J. like hearth
*Mat.* 10:18 sh. be brought bef. *g.*
*Gal.* 4:2 under tutors and *g.*
1 *Pet.* 2:14 submit yoursel. to *g.*

**GOURD, S.**
2 *K.* 4:39 one gathered wild *g.*
*Jon.* 4:6 God prepared *g.* J. glad
7 a worm smote *g.* it withered
10 thou hast had pity on the *g.*

GOZAN. 2 *K.* 17:6; 18:11; 19:12; 1 *Chr.* 5:26; *Is.* 37:12

**GRACE.**
*Ezr.* 9:8 little space *g.* showed
*Est.* 2:17 E. obtained *g.* in sight
*Ps.* 45:2 *g.* poured into lips
84:11 Lord is a sun, will give *g.*
*Prov.* 1:9 an ornament of *g.*
3:22 so shall they be life and *g.*
34 giveth *g.* to lowly, *Jam.* 4:6
4:9 to head ornament of *g.*
22:11 for *g.* of lips king his fri.
*Zec.* 4:7 shoutings, crying, *g. g.*
12:10 will pour the Sprit of *g.*
*John* 1:14 begotten of F. full of *g.*
16 have all received *g.* for *g.*
17 *g.* and truth came by J. C.
*Acts* 4:33 great *g.* was on them
14:3 testimony to word of his *g.*
18:27 which believed thro' *g.*
20:32 com. you to word of *g.*
*Rom.* 1:5 by wh. we received *g.*
7 *g.* and peace from G. our F. 1 *Cor.* 1:3; 2 *Cor.* 1:2; *Gal.* 1:3; *Eph.* 1:2; *Phil.* 1:2; *Col.* 1:2; 1 *Thes.* 1:1; 2 *Thes.* 1:2; *Phile.* 3
3:24 justified freely by his *g.*
4:4 reward is not reckoned of *g.*
16 that it might be by *g.*
5:2 we have access into this *g.*
17 receive abundance of *g.*
20 sin abounded, *g.* more
21 *g.* reign thro' righteousness
6:1 con. in sin, that *g.* abound?
14 under *g.*, 15 bec. under *g.*?
11:5 according to election of *g.*
6 if by *g.* no more of works
12:3 through *g.* given unto me
6 gifts differing according to *g.*
15:15 the *g.* given to me of God
1 *Cor.* 10:30 if I by *g.* be partak.
15:10 *g.* bestowed not in vain
2 *Cor.* 4:15 *g.* red. to glory of G.
8:6 finish in you the same *g.*
7 see that ye abound in this *g.*
19 travel with us with this *g.*
9:8 G. is able to make *g.* abound
12:9 my *g.* is sufficient for thee
*Gal.* 1:6 who called you to *g.*
15 G. who called me by his *g.*
2:9 when James perceived *g.*
5:4 justi. by law, fallen from *g.*
*Eph.* 1:6 praise of the glory of *g.*
7 according to riches of *g.*
2:5 by *g.* saved through faith, 8
7 might show the riches of *g.*
3:8 to me is this *g.* given
4:7 to ev. one of us is given *g.*
29 may minister *g.* to hearers
6:24 *g.* with all that love L. J.
*Phil.* 1:7 are all partakers of *g.*
*Col.* 3:16 sing. with *g.* in hearts
4:6 let speech be alway with *g.*
18 *g.* be with you, 2 *Tim.* 4:22; *Tit.* 3:15; *Heb.* 13:25
2 *Thes.* 2:16 hope through *g.*
1 *Tim.* 1:2 *g.* mercy, and peace from G. our Father, 2 *Tim.* 1:2; *Tit.* 1:4; 2 *John* 3
1:14 *g.* of Lord abundant
6:21 *g.* be with thee. Amen
2 *Tim.* 1:9 called us accord. to *g.*
2:1 be strong in the *g.* in Christ
*Tit.* 3:7 justified by *g.*
*Heb.* 4:16 boldly to throne of *g.*
10:29 despite to the Spirit of *g.*
12:28 let us have *g.* to serve G.
13:9 the heart be estab. with *g.*
*Jam.* 1:11 *g.* of fashion perisheth
4:6 giveth more *g.* *g.* to humble
1 *Pet.* 1:2 *g.* be multi. 2 *Pet.* 1:2
10 prophesied of *g.* to come

13 hope for *g.* 3:7 heirs of *g.*
5:5 God giveth *g.* to humble
10 G. of *g.* called us to glory
2 *Pet.* 3:18 grow in *g.* and in Ch.
*Jude* 4 turning *g.* of G. to lasciv.
*Rev.* 1:4 *g.* from him

*See* FIND, or FOUND.

**GRACE of God.**

*Luke* 2:40 *g. of God* upon him
*Acts* 11:23 he had seen *g. of God*
13:43 persua. to con. in *g. of G.*
14:26 recom. to *g. of G.* 15:40
20:24 the gospel of *g. of God*
*Rom.* 5:15 *g. of G.* hath abound.
1 *Cor.* 1:4 *g. of G.* given by J. C.
3:10 ac. to *g. of G.* given to me
15:10 by *g. of God* I am what I am, yet not I, but *g. of God*
2 *Cor.* 1:12 by *g. of G.* we had
6:1 rec. not the *g. of G.* in vain
8:1 *g of G.* bestow. on churches
9:14 the exceeding *g. of G.*
*Gal.* 2:21 not frustrate *g. of G.*
*Eph.* 3:2 dispensation of *g. of G.*
7 accor. to the gift of *g. of G.*
*Col.* 1:6 ye knew the *g. of G.*
2 *Thes.* 1:12 according to *g. of G.*
*Tit.* 2:11 *g. of G.* bringeth salv.
*Heb.* 2:9 by *g. of G.* taste death
12:15 any man fail of *g. of G.*
1 *Pet.* 4:10 stewards of *g. of G.*
5:12 this is the true *g. of God*

**GRACE of our Lord Jesus.**

*Acts* 15:11 *g. of L. J.* sh. be saved
*Rom.* 16:20 *g. of our Lord J.* be with you, 24; 1 *Cor.* 16:23; *Phil.* 4:23; 1 *Thes.* 5:28; 2 *Thes.* 3:18
2 *Cor.* 8:9 the *g. of our L. J. C.*
13:14 the *g. of our L. J. Christ*
*Gal.* 6:18 *g. of L. J.* wi. s. *Phi.* 25
*Rev.* 22:21 *g. of L. J.* be with you

**GRACIOUS.**

*Gen.* 43:29 God be *g.* to thee
*Ex.* 22:27 I will hear, I am *g.*
33:19 be *g.* to whom I be *g.*
34:6 the Lord God, *g.* 2 *Chr.* 30:9; *Ps.* 103:8; 116:5; 145:8; *Joel* 2:13
*Num.* 6:25 make face shine *g.*
2 *Sam.* 12:22 tell wh. G. will be *g.*
*Neh.* 9:17 a God *g.* merciful, 31
*Job* 33:24 then he is *g.* to him
*Ps.* 77:9 God forgotten to be *g.*?
86:15 art God *g.* 111:4; 112:4
*Prov.* 11:16 *g.* wo. retain. honor
*Ec.* 10:12 words of wise man *g.*
*Is.* 30:18 L. wilt wait that he be *g.*
19 be *g.* to thee; 33:2 *g.* to us
*Jer.* 22:23 *g.* when pangs come
*Amos* 5:15 the Lord will be *g.*
*Jon.* 4:2 thou art a *g.* God
*Mal.* 1:9 beseech G. he will be *g.*
*Luke* 4:22 wondered at *g.* words
1 *Pet.* 2:3 if ye tasted the L. is *g.*

**GRACIOUSLY.**

*Gen.* 33:5 child. God *g.* given me
*Gen.* 33:11 G. hath dealt *g.* with
*Ps.* 119:29 grant me thy law *g.*
*Hos.* 14:2 receive us *g.*

**GRAFT, ED.**

*Rom.* 11:17 wild olive-t. wert *g.*
19 that I might be *g.* in
23 they sh. be *g.* G. is able to *g.*
24 cut out and *g.* these be *g.*

**GRAIN, S.**

*Amos* 9:9 not least *g.* fall on ear.
*Mat.* 13:31 kingdom of heaven is like a *g.* of mustard-seed, *Mark* 4:31; *Luke* 13:19
17:20 faith as a *g.* of mustard-s. ye shall say to this mount. remove, *Luke* 17:6
1 *Cor.* 15:37 *g.* wheat, or other *g.*

**GRANDMOTHER.**

2 *Tim.* 1:5 faith dwelt in thy *g.*

**GRANT, Substantive.**

*Ezr.* 3:7 accord. to *g.* of Cyrus

**GRANT, Verb.**

*Lev.* 25:24 *g.* a redemption
1 *Sam.* 1:17 God *g.* thee petition
1 *Chr.* 21:22 *g.* this threshing-fl.; thou shall *g.* it me
2 *Chr.* 12:7 I will *g.* them deliv.
*Neh.* 1:11 *g.* mercy in sight of
*Est.* 5:8 the king *g.* my petition
*Job* 6:8 G. *g.* the thing I long for
*Ps.* 20:4 *g.* thee to thine heart
85:7 O Lord, *g.* us salvation
119:29 *g.* me thy law graciously
140:8 *g.* not, O L. de. of wicked
*Mat.* 20:21 *g.* my two sons may sit, *Mark* 10:37
*Luke* 1:74 *g.* to us that we being
*Acts* 4:29 *g.* with boldness
*Rom.* 15:5 G. *g.* you to be like-m.
*Eph.* 3:16 *g.* you to be strength.
2 *Tim.* 1:18 L. *g.* he find mercy
*Rev.* 3:21 *g.* to sit in my throne

**GRANTED.**

1 *Chr.* 4:10 God *g.* what he requ.
2 *Chr.* 1:12 and knowl. is *g.* thee
*Ezr.* 7:6 king *g.* all his requests
*Neh.* 2:8 *g.* accord. to hand of G.
*Est.* 5:6 petit. sh. be *g.* 7:2; 9:12
9:13 let it be *g.* to Jews in Shu.
*Job* 10:12 hast *g.* life and favor
*Prov.* 10:24 desire of right. be *g.*
*Acts* 11:18 G. *g.* Gen. repentance
14:3 *g.* signs to be done by han.
*Rev.* 19:8 *g.* she sh. be arrayed

**GRAPE.**

*Lev.* 19:10 not gather *g.* of wine
*Deut.* 32:14 drink blood of *g.*
*Job* 15:33 shake off unripe *g.*
*Cant.* 2:13 *g.* give good smell
7:12 the tender *g.* appear
*Is.* 18:5 sour *g.* is ripening
*Jer.* 31:29 have eaten a sour *g.*
30 ev. man that eateth sour *g.*
*Mic.* 7:1 as *g.* gleanings of vint.

**GRAPE-GATHERER.**

*Jer.* 6:9 turn back hand as *g.-g.*
49:9 if *g.-g.* come, *Ob.* 5

**GRAPES.**

*Gen.* 40:10 clusters bro. ripe *g.*
49:11 washed clothes in bl. of *g.*
*Lev.* 25:5 nor gather *g.* undressed
11 in jubilee, nor ga. *g.* of vine
*Num.* 6:3 nor shall eat moist *g.*
13:20 time of the first ripe *g.*
23 cut a branch with clus. of *g.*
*Deut.* 23:24 mayest eat *g.* thy fill
24:21 wh. thou gatherest the *g.*
28:30 plant vine. not ga. *g.* 39
32:32 their *g.* are *g.* of gall
*Jud.* 8:2 gleaning of *g.* of Ephr.
*Neh.* 13:15 wine and *g.* on sab.
*Cant.* 2:15 vines have tender *g.*
7:7 breasts are like clust. of *g.*
*Is.* 5:2 it should bring forth *g.*
4 bring forth *g.* bro. wild *g.*?
17:6 gleaning *g.* shall be left
24:13 *g.* when vintage is done
*Jer.* 8:13 there sh. be no *g.* on vi.
25:30 as they that tread *g.*
49:9 gleaning *g.* *Ob.* 5
*Ezek.* 18:2 have eaten sour *g.*
*Hos.* 9:10 like *g.* in wilderness
*Amos* 9:13 treader of *g.* ov. sower
*Mat.* 7:16 man ga. *g.* of thorns?
*Luke* 6:44 nor of brambles ga. *g.*
*Rev.* 14:18 her *g.* are fully ripe

**GRASS.**

*Gen.* 1:11 earth bring forth *g.*
12 the earth brought forth *g.*
*Num.* 22:4 licketh up *g.* of field
*Deut.* 11:15 send *g.* for thy cattle
29:23 any *g.* groweth therein
32:2 distil as showers upon *g.*
2 *Sam.* 23:4 the *g.* springing out
1 *K.* 18:5 find *g.* to save horses
2 *K.* 19:26 as *g.* of the field, as *g.* on the house-tops, *Is.* 37:27
*Job* 5:25 offspring as *g.* of earth
6:5 ass bray when he hath *g.*
40:15 behem. eateth *g.* as an ox
*Ps.* 37:2 sh. be cut down like *g.*
72:6 like rain upon mown *g.*
16 they shall flourish like *g.*
90:5 they are like *g.* wh. grow.
92:7 the wicked spring as *g.*
102:4 heart is withered like *g.*
11 a shadow, withered like *g.*
103:15 man, his days are as *g.*
104:14 causeth *g.* to grow
106:20 an ox that eateth *g.*
129:6 as *g.* upon the house-tops
147:8 *g.* to grow upon mount.
*Prov.* 19:12 as dew on *g.*
27:25 tender *g.* showeth itself
*Is.* 15:6 the *g.* faileth
35:7 in hab. of dragons sh. be *g.*
40:6 All flesh is *g.* 1 *Pet.* 1:24
7 *g.* wither. surely peo. is *g.* 8
44:4 sh. spring up as am. the *g.*
*Jer.* 14:5 forsook it because no *g.*
50:11 grown fat as heifer at *g.*
*Dan.* 4:15 leave stump in *g.* 23
25 eat *g.* as oxen, 32, 33; 5:21
*Mic.* 5:7 as showers upon the *g.*
*Zec.* 10:1 L. shall give ev. one *g.*
*Mat.* 6:30 clothe *g.* *Luke* 12:28
14:19 sit down on *g.* *Mark* 6:39
*John* 6:10 there was much *g.*
*Jam.* 1:10 as *g.* he sh. pass away
11 sun risen, withereth the *g.*
*Rev.* 8:7 all green *g.* burnt up
9:4 should not hurt *g.* of earth

**GRASSHOPPER, S.**

*Lev.* 11:22 the *g.* after his kind
*Num.* 13:33 in our sight as *g.*
*Jud.* 6:5 as *g.* for multitude, 7:12
*Job* 39:20 afraid as a *g.*?
*Ec.* 12:5 *g.* shall be a burden
*Is.* 40:22 inhabitants are as *g.*
*Jer.* 46:23 they are more than *g.*
*Amos* 7:1 formed *g.* in the begin.
*Nah.* 3:17 thy captains are as *g.*

GRATE. *See* BRAZEN.

**GRAVE, Substantive.**

*Gen.* 35:20 J. set a pillar on her *g.*
37:35 will go down to *g.*
42:38 with sorrow to *g.* 44:31
50:5 bury me in my *g.*
*Num.* 19:16 who touch. *g.* is unc.
1 *Sam.* 2:6 L. bring down to *g.*
2 *Sam.* 3:32 and peo. wept at *g.*
19:37 by the *g.* of my father
1 *K.* 2:6 not his head go to *g.*
9 bring to the *g.* with blood
14:13 Jeroboam shall come to *g.*
2 *K.* 22:20 to thy *g.* 2 *Chr.* 34:28
*Job* 3:22 when they find the *g.*
5:26 come to *g.* in full age
7:9 goeth to *g.* come up no more
10:19 carried from womb to *g.*
14:13 O that thou hide me in *g.*
17:13 the *g.* is my house
21:13 they go down to the *g.*
32 yet shall he be brought to *g.*
30:24 not stretch hand to the *g.*
33:22 soul draweth near to *g.*
*Ps.* 6:5 in *g.* who give thanks?
30:3 brought my soul from *g.*
31:17 wicked be silent in the *g.*
49:14 laid in *g.* consume in *g.*
15 red. soul from power of *g.*
88:3 my life draweth nigh to *g.*
11 loving-kindness decl. in *g.*
89:48 del. soul from hand of *g.*
141:7 bones scat. at *g.*'s mouth
*Prov.* 1:12 swallow them as *g.*
30:13 *g.* and barren womb
*Ec.* 9:10 no wisdom in *g.*
*Cant.* 8:6 jealousy is cruel as *g.*

*Is.* 14:11 pomp is brought to *g.*
19 cast out of thy *g.* like a br.
38:10 shall go to the gates of *g.*
18 the *g.* cannot praise thee
53:9 made his *g.* with wicked
*Jer.* 20:17 mother might been *g.*
*Ezek.* 32:23 company round *g.*
*Hos.* 13:14 ransom from power of *g.* O *g.* I will be destruction
*Nah.* 1:14 make thy *g.*
*John* 11:17 had lain in *g.* 4 days
31 goeth to *g.* to weep there
12:17 called Lazarus out of *g.*
1 *Cor.* 15:55 *g.* wh. is thy victory?

**GRAVE-CLOTHES.**

*John* 11:44 Laz. bound with *g.-c.*

**GRAVE, Adjective.**

1 *Tim.* 3:8 deac. be *g.*; 11 wives *g.*
*Tit.* 2:2 aged men be sober, *g.*

**GRAVE, Verb.**

*Ex.* 28:9 sh. *g.* on onyx-stones
*Ex.* 29:36 pl. of pure gold, *g.* on
2 *Chr.* 2:7 send a man that can *g.*
14 sent a cunning man to *g.*

**GRAVED.**

1 *K.* 7:36 on borders *g.* cherubim
2 *Chr.* 3:7 *g.* cherubim on walls

**GRAVEL.**

*Prov.* 20:17 shall be filled with *g.*
*Is.* 48:19 offsp. of bowels like *g.*
*Lam.* 3:16 broken teeth with *g.*

**GRAVEN, Verb.**

*Is.* 49:16 *g.* thee on pa. of hands
*Hab.* 2:18 the maker hath *g.* it

**GRAVEN.**

*Ex.* 32:16 writing of God *g.*
39:6 signets *g.* with names of Is.
*Job* 19:24 were *g.* with iron pen
*Jer.* 17:1 is *g.* upon table of heart
*Acts* 17:29 Godhead is like gold *g.*

**GRAVEN image.**

*Ex.* 20:4 sh. not make unto thee any *g. i. Lev.* 26:1; *Deut.* 5:8
*Deut.* 4:16 lest make a *g. im.* 25
27:15 cursed man maketh *g. i.*
*Jud.* 17:3 for son to make *g. im.*
18:30 Dan set up *g. image*, 31
2 *K.* 21:7 Manasseh set *g. image*
*Is.* 40:19 workmen melteth *g. i.*
20 workman to prepare *g. in* .
44:9 they that make *g. image*
10 who hath molten a *g. im.*
17 with residue he maketh *g. i.*
45:20 set up wood of their *g. i.*
48:5 my *g. i.* hath commanded
*Jer.* 10:14 conf. by *g. im.* 51:17
*Nah.* 1:14 I will cut off the *g. i.*
*Hab.* 2:18 what profit. the *g. i.?*

**GRAVEN images.**

*Deut.* 7:5 shall burn their *g. im.*
12:3 ye shall hew down *g. im.*
2 *K.* 17:41 feared L. served *g. i.*
2 *Chr.* 34:7 he had beaten *g. im.*
*Ps.* 78:58 moved to jeal. with *g. i.*
97:7 conf. all that serve *g. im.*
*Is.* 21:9 Bab. fallen, and *g. im.*
30:22 defile the cover. of *g. im.*
42:8 nei. give my praise to *g. i.*
17 ashamed that trust in *g. i.*
*Jer.* 8:19 prov. to anger with *g. i.*
50:38 it is the land of *g. images*
51:47 do judgment on *g. im.* 52
*Hos.* 11:2 burnt incense to *g. i.*
*Mic.* 1:7 *g. i.* be beaten to pieces
5:13 thy *g. images* will I cut off

**GRAVES.**

*Ex.* 14:11 were no *g.* in Egypt
2 *K.* 23:6 cast the powder on *g.*
2 *Chr.* 34:4 strewed it on the *g.*
*Job* 17:1 the *g.* are ready for me
*Is.* 65:4 which remain among *g.*
*Jer.* 8:1 bri. priests' bones out *g*
*Ezek.* 32:22 *g.* about him, 23,25,26
37:12 open *g.* cause to come up
13 I have brought out of *g.*
39:11 give Gog place of *g.* in Is.
*Mat.* 27:52 the *g.* were opened
53 bod. of saints came out of *g.*
*Luke* 11:44 as *g.* wh. appear not
*John* 5:28 all in *g.* sh. hear voice
*Rev.* 11:9 not suffer bod. put in *g.*

**GRAVETH.**

*Is.* 22:16 he that *g.* a habitation

**GRAVING.**

*Ex.* 32:4 fash. *g.* calf with *g.* tool

**GRAVING, S.**

1 *K.* 7:31 upon mouth of laver *g.*
2 *Chr.* 2:14 any manner of *g.*
*Zec.* 3:9 engrave *g.* thereof

**GRAVITY.**

1 *Tim.* 3:4 chil. in subject. wi. *g.*
*Tit.* 2:7 in doctrine showing *g.*

GRAY. *See* HAIRS *and* HEAD.

**GRAY-HEADED.**

1 *Sam.* 12:2 I am old and *g.-h.*
*Job* 15:10 with us are the *g.-h.*
*Ps.* 71:18 wh. I am old and *g.-h.*

**GREASE.**

*Ps.* 119:70 heart is as fat as *g.*

**GREAT.**

*Gen.* 12:2 make name *g.*
39:9 how can I do this *g* sin?
48:19 my son, he also shall be *g.*
*Deut.* 10:17 the Lord your God is a *g* God, 2 *Chr.* 2:5
11:7 have seen *g.* acts of the L.
18:16 nei. let me see this *g.* fire
29:24 what mean. this *g.* anger?
*Jos.* 7:9 what do unto *g.* name?
*Jud.* 5:15 *g.* thoughts of heart
2 *Sam.* 7:9 made thee *g.* name
22 thou art *g.* O Lord God
22:36 thy gentleness hath made me *g. Ps.* 18:35
1 *K.* 8:42 h. of *g.* name, 2 *Chr.* 6:32
2 *K.* 4:8 Shunem, was *g.* woman
1 *Chr.* 16:25 *g.* is Lord, *Ps.* 48:1; 96:4; 135:5; 145:3
21:13 very *g.* are his mercies
29:12 in thy hand is to make *g.*
2 *Chr.* 2:5 house is *g. g.* is our G.
28:13 tresp. *g.*; 34:21 *g.* wrath
*Neh.* 4:14 remember L. who is *g.*
9:32 our God the *g.* the mighty
*Est.* 1:20 published, for it is *g.*
*Job* 22:5 is not thy wickedn. *g.?*
36:18 a *g.* ransom; 26 God is *g.*
39:11 wilt trust bec. strength *g.*
*Ps.* 14:5 they in *g.* fear, 53:5
19:11 keeping them *g.* reward
21:5 glory *g.* in thy salvation
25:11 pardon iniquity, it is *g.*
31:19 O how *g.* is thy goodness
86:10 art *g.* and doest wondrous
92:5 how *g.* are thy works
139:17 God, how *g.* is the sum
*Ec.* 9:13 wisdom seemed *g.* to me
*Is.* 5:9 houses even *g.* and fair
9:2 seen *g.* light, *Mat.* 4:46
12:6 *g.* is the Holy One of Israel
19:20 send a Saviour a *g.* one
53:12 a portion with *g.*
54:13 *g.* shall be peace of child.
*Jer.* 5:27 are become *g.* and rich
10:6 thy name is *g.* in might
32:18 *g.* the mighty G. is name
19 *g.* in counsel
*Lam.* 3:23 *g.* is thy faithfulness
*Ezek.* 17:3 *g.* eagle *g.* wings, 7
36:23 sanctify my *g.* name
*Dan.* 4:3 how *g.* his signs
*Joel* 3:13 their wickedness is *g.*
*Zec.* 9:17 how *g.* his goodness
*Mal.* 1:11 name *g.* among Gen. 11
*Mat.* 5:12 be glad, *g.* is reward in heaven, *Luke* 6:23, 35
19 be called great in kingd. of
6:23 how *g.* is that darkness
13:46 *g.* price; 15:28 *g.* faith
19:22 *g.* posses. *Mark* 10:42
20:25 they *g.* exercise authority
26 who *g.* am. you, *Mark* 10:43
22:36 which is *g.* commandm.?
38 first and *g.* commandment
*Luke* 1;15 *g.* in sight of the Lord
9:48 least among you shall be *g.*
10:2 harvest *g.* the laborers few
16:26 bet. us and you *g.* gulf
*Acts* 8:9 that he was some *g.* one
19:28 *g.* is D. of Ephesians! 34
2 *Cor.* 7:4 *g.* my boldn. *g.* glory
*Col.* 4:13 hath a *g.* zeal for you
1 *Tim.* 3:16 *g.* is mys. of godlin.
2 *Tim.* 2:20 in *g.* house
*Tit.* 2:13 appearing of the *g.* God
*Jam.* 3:5 *g.* matter little fire kin.
*Rev.* 16:19 *g.* Babylon came in
17:5 Babylon the *g.* 18:2

*See* CITY, COMPANY, CONGREGATION, CRY, DAY, DESTRUCTION.

**GREAT evil.**

1 *Sam.* 6:9 hath done us this *g. e.*
*Ec.* 2:21 is vanity and a *g. evil*
*Jer.* 16:10 L. pronounced this *g.e.*
32:42 brought *g. e.* upon people
44:7 why commit this *g. evil?*

*See* EXCEEDING, JOY.

**GREAT King *or* kings.**

*Ps.* 47:2 the Lord is a *g. King*
48:2 Zion, the city of the *g. K.*
95:3 L. is a *g. K.* above all gods
136:17 to him that smote *g. k.*
*Ec.* 9:14 there came *g. k.* against
*Jer.* 25:14 *g. k.* sh. serve th. 27:7
*Mal.* 1:14 I am a *g. K.* saith the L.
*Mat.* 5:35 Jerus. is city of *g. K.*

**GREAT men.**

2 *Sam.* 7:9 like name of *g. men* in earth, 1 *Chr.* 17:8
*Job* 32:9 *g. men* not always wise
*Prov.* 25:6 stand not in pl. of *g. m.*
*Jer.* 5:5 I will get me unto *g. m.*
*Ezek.* 21:14 it is the sw. of *g. m.*
*Nah.* 3:10 all her *g. m.* in chains
*Rev.* 6:15 *g. men* hid themselves
18:23 thy merchants were *g. m.*

**GREAT multitude, s.**

2 *Chr.* 13:8 ye be a *g. multitude*
20:15 not dis. by reason of *g. m.*
28:5 carried *g. m.* captive to D.
*Job* 31:34 did I fear *g. m.* or con.
*Is.* 16:14 *g. m.* sh. be contemned
*Jer.* 44:15 wo. stood by, a *g. m.*
*Ezek.* 47:9 a very *g. mul.* of fish
*Dan.* 11:11 k. of south set *g. m.*
*Mat.* 4:25 *g. mult.* followed him, 8:1; 12:15; 19:2; 20:29; *Mark* 3:7; *John* 6:2
*Mat.* 8:18 when J. saw *g. multitudes*, 14:14; *Mark* 9:14
15:30 *g. multitudes* came
33 bread as fill so *g.* a *multit.*
21:8 a *g. m.* spread their garm.
26:47 *g. m.* with sw. *Mark* 14:43
*Luke* 5:6 inclus. a *g. m.* of fishes
*Acts* 14:1 a *g. m.* of J. believed
17:4 of devout Greeks a *g. m.*
*Rev.* 7:9 *g. m.* no man could nu.
19:6 the voice of a *g. multitude*

**GREAT nation, s.**

*Gen.* 12:2 I will make of thee a *g. n.* 18:18; 46:3; *Ex.* 32:10
17:20 make Ishm. a *g. n.* 21:18
*Deut.* 26:5 he bec. there a *n. g.*
*Ps.* 135:10 smote *g. n.* slew kings
*Jer.* 6:22 a *g. n.* shall be raised
*Ezek.* 31:6 under shad. dwelt *g. n.*

**GREAT people.**

*Deut.* 2:10 Em. dwelt a *p. g.* 21
21 Zamzummim, a *people g.*
*Jos.* 7:14 seeing I am a *g. people*
15 be a *g. p.*; 17 art a *g. people*

1 *K.* 3:9 this *g. p.*? 2 *Chr.* 1:10
5:7 given wise son over *g. p.*
*Is.* 13:4 noise in moun. as of *g. p.*

**GREAT power.**

*Ex.* 32:11 out of Egypt with *g. p.*
2 *K.* 17:36; *Neh.* 1:10
*Num.* 14:17 *p.* of my lord be *g.*
*Job* 23:6 plead ag. me with *g. p.*
*Ps.* 147:5 great Lord and of *g. p.*
*Jer.* 27:5 made the earth, man, and beast by my *g. p.* 32:17
*Nah.* 1:3 slow to anger, *g.* in *p.*
*Mark* 13:26 in clouds with *g. p.*
*Acts* 4:33 with *g. p.* gave apostles
8:10 this man is the *g. p.* of God
*Rev.* 11:17 hast taken thy *g. p.*

**GREAT sea.**

*Num.* 34:6 have *g. s.* for a border
*Jos.* 1:4 from wilder. to the *g. s.*
15:12 west border to *g. sea*
*Ezek.* 47:10 as a fish of the *g. sea*
15 border of land from the *g. s.*
*Dan.* 7:2 four winds upon *g. sea*
*See* SIN.

**GREAT slaughter.**

*Jos.* 10:10 slew them with *g. s.*
*Jud.* 11:33 Jeph. smote with *g. s.*
15:8 Samson smote with *g. s.*
1 *Sam.* 4:10 Ph. smote w. *g. s.* 17
6:19 smitten people with *g. s*
19:8 D. slew with a *g. s.* 23:5
2 *Sam.* 18:7 a *g. s.* of 20,000
1 *K.* 20:21 Israel slew A. w. *g. s.*
2 *Chr.* 28:5 Is. smote Ah. w. *g. s.*
*Is.* 30:25 day of *g. slaughter*
34:6 L. hath *g. s.* in land of Id.

**Small and GREAT.**

*Gen.* 19:11 sm. w. blind. *s. and g.*
*Deut.* 1:17 hear *s.* as well as *g.*
25:13 divers weights, *g. and sm.*
1 *Sam.* 5:9 smote men *s. and g.*
20:2 will do noth. *g.* or *s.*
30:2 slew not any either *g.* or *s.*
2 *K.* 23:2 *s. and g.* went to house, 2 *Chr.* 34:30
25:26 peo. *s. and g.* came to Eg.
1 *Chr.* 26:13 lots as well *s.* as *g.*
2 *Chr.* 15:13 put to death, *s.* or *g.*
31:15 give to brethren, *g. and s.*
*Est.* 1:5 A. made a feast to *g. a. s.*
20 to husbands honor *g. and s.*
*Job* 3:19 *small and g.* are there
37:6 the *s.* rain *and g.* rain
*Ps.* 104:25 th. creeping, *s. and g.*
115:13 fear the L. *small and g.*
*Ec.* 2:7 pos. of *g. and s.* cattle
*Jer.* 16:6 *g. and s.* sh. die in land
*Amos* 8:5 ephah *s.* the shekel *g.*
*Acts* 26:22 witnessing to *s. and g.*
*Rev.* 11:18 that fear him, *s. a. g.*
13:16 *s. and g.* to receive mark
19:5 praise our G. *small and g.*
20:12 *s. and g.* stand before G.

**So GREAT.**

*Ex.* 32:21 bro. *so g.* sin on them
*Deut.* 4:7 nat. *so g.* hath G.? 8
1 *K.* 3:9 *so g.* people, 2 *Chr.* 1:10
*Ps.* 77:13 *so g.* a God as our G.?
103:11 *so g.* is his mercy
*Mat.* 8:10 not *so g.* faith, *Luke* 7:9
2 *Cor.* 1:10 deliv. from *so g.* death
*Heb.* 2:3 if we neglect *so g.* salv.
12:1 *so g.* a cloud of witnesses
*Jam.* 3:4 *so g.* turned with helm

**GREAT stone, s.**

*Gen.* 29:2 *g. s.* on well's mouth
*Deut.* 27:2 set up *g. s.*
*Jos.* 10:11 cast *g. s.* from heaven
24:26 Joshua took *g. s.*
1 *Sam.* 6:18 the *g. stone* of Abel
14:33 roll a *g. stone* unto me
2 *Sam.* 20:8 were at *g. s.* in Gib.
1 *K.* 5:17 brought *g. s.* to lay
7:10 founda. of *g. s.* *Ezr.* 5:8
2 *Chr.* 26:15 engines to shoot *g. s.*
*Ezr.* 6:4 three rows of *g. s.*
*Jer.* 43:9 take *g. s.* and hide them
*Mat.* 27:60 rolled a *g. s.* to door

**GREAT thing, s.**

*Deut.* 10:21 God hath done *g. t.*
1 *Sam.* 12:16 this *g. t.* L. will do
2 *Sam.* 7:21 word's sa. done *g. t.*
23 and to do for you *g. things*
2 *K.* 5:13 if prophet bid thee *g. t.*
8:4 the *g. t.* Elisha hath done
1 *Chr.* 17:19 making kn. th. *g. t.*
*Job* 5:9 doeth *g. t.* 9:10; 37:5
*Ps.* 71:19 done *g. things*
106:21 God who had done *g. t.*
126:2 L. had done *g. things*, 3
*Jer.* 33:3 show *g.* and mighty *t.*
45:5 seek. thou *g. t.* for thyself?
*Dan.* 7:8 speak *g. t.* 20; *Rev.* 13:5
*Hos.* 8:12 have written the *g. t.*
*Joel* 2:20 bec. he hath done *g. t.*
*Mark* 3:8 heard what *g. t.* he did
5:19 tell *g. t.* L. done, *Luke* 8:39
*Luke* 1:49 mighty hath done *g. t.*
8:39 published *g. t.* J. had done
*Acts* 9:16 *g. t.* he must suffer
1 *Cor.* 9:11 *g. t.* if we reap carnal?
2 *Cor.* 11:15 no *g. t.* if min. be tr.
*Jam.* 3:5 tongue boasteth *g. t.*

**Very GREAT.**

*Ex.* 11:3 Mos. was *v. g.* in land
*Num.* 13:28 walled and *v. g.*
2 *Sam.* 19:32 Barz. was a *v. g.* m.
1 *K.* 10:2 S. came w. *v. g.* train
1 *Chr.* 21:13 *v. g.* are his mercies
2 *Chr.* 16:14 a *v. g.* burning for A.
*Job* 2:13 saw his grief was *v. g.*
*Ps.* 104:1 my God, thou art *v. g.*
*Mark* 8:1 the multitude *v. g.*
16:4 sto. was away, it was *v. g.*

**Was GREAT.**

*Gen.* 6:5 wickedn. of man *w. g.*
13:6 their substance *w. g.*
*Job* 31:25 I rej. my wealth *w. g.*
*Ec.* 2:9 I *w. g.* and increased
*Lam.* 1:1 she *w. g.* am. nations
*Dan.* 4:10 the tree's height *w. g.*
*Mat.* 7:27 *g. w.* the fall, *Luke* 6:49

**GREAT waters.**

*Ps.* 32:6 in floods of *g. w.*
77:19 thy path in *g. waters*
107:23 that do business in *g. w.*
144:7 deliver me out of *g. w.*
*Jer.* 51:55 waves roar like *g. w.*
*Ezek.* 1:24 noi. of wings like *g. w.*
17:5 placed the seed by *g. w.*
8 planted in good soil by *g. w.*
26:19 *g. w.* shall cover thee
27:26 brought thee to *g. w.*
31:7 for his root was by *g. w.*
15 the *g. waters* were stayed
*Heb.* 3:15 walk through *g. w.*

**GREAT while.**

2 *Sam.* 7:19 spoken of servant's house for *g. w.* 1 *Chr.* 17:17
*Mark* 1:35 rising a *g. w.* bef. day
*Luke* 10:13 a *g. w.* ago repented
*Acts* 28:6 barbar. looked a *g. w.*

**GREAT work, s.**

*Ex.* 14:31 saw *g. w.* the L. did
*Jud.* 2:7 seen the *g. w.* of the L.
1 *Chr.* 29:1 and *w.* is *g.*
*Neh.* 4:19 *w.* is *g.* and we separ.
6:3 doing a *g. w.* I cannot come
*Ps.* 111:2 *w.* of L. *g.* *Rev.* 15:3

**GREATER.**

*Gen.* 1:16 *g.* light to rule the day
4:13 punish. *g.* than I can bear
41:40 only in throne will I be *g.*
*Ex.* 18:11 L. is *g.* than all gods
*Num.* 14:12 *g.* nation, *Deut.* 9:14
*Deut.* 1:28 *g.* and taller than we
4:38 drive nations *g.* than thou, 7:1; 9:1; 11:23
1 *K.* 1:37 throne *g.* than Dav. 47
1 *Chr.* 11:9 Dav. waxed *g.* and *g.*
2 *Chr.* 3:5 *g.* house ceiled
*Job* 33:12 God is *g.* than man
*Hag.* 2:9 latter house *g.* than for.
*Mat.* 11:11 not risen a *g.* than J. Bapt. least *g.* *Luke* 7:28
12:6 is one *g.* than the temple
41 a *g.* than J. here, *Luke* 11:32
42 a *g.* than S. here, *Luke* 11:31
23:14 receive *g.* damnat. *Mark* 12:40; *Luke* 20:47
17 *g.* the gold, or the temple?
19 is *g.* the gift, or the altar?
*Luke* 22:27 *g.* he that sit. or ser.?
*John* 1:50 thou shalt see *g.* things, 5:20; 14:12
4:12 art *g.* than our father J.?
*John* 5:36 *g.* witn. than that of J.
8:53 art *g.* than father Abrah.?
10:29 Father *g.* than all, 14:28
13:16 ser. not *g.* th. lord, 15:20
15:13 *g.* love hath no man
19:11 that del. me hath *g.* sin
*Acts* 15:28 no *g.* burden
*Heb.* 6:13 could swear by no *g.*
16 men verily swear by the *g.*
9:11 *g.* and more perfect tabern.
11:26 reproach of Ch. *g.* riches
*Jam.* 3:1 receive *g.* condemnat.
2 *Pet.* 2:11 angels are *g.* in power
1 *John* 3:20 G. is *g.* th. our heart
4:4 *g.* is he that is in you,
5:9 witness of G. is *g.*
3 *John* 4 no *g.* joy than to hear

**GREATEST.**

*Job* 1:3 this man was *g.* of all
*Jer.* 31:34 all know me from least to the *g.* *Heb.* 8:11
42:1 from least to *g.* came near
44:12 shall die, from least to *g.*
*Jon.* 3:5 sack. from *g.* to least
*Mat.* 13:32 it is the *g.* am. herbs
18:1 who is *g.* in king. of heav.?
4 humble as child, same is *g.*
23:11 he that is *g.* be your serv.
*Mark* 9:34 should be *g.* *Luke* 9:46
*Luke* 22:24 a strife who sho. be *g.*
26 he that is *g.* be as younger
1 *Cor.* 13:13 *g.* of these is charity

**GREATLY.**

*Gen.* 3:16 I will *g.* multiply sor.
*Ex.* 19:18 wh. mount quaked *g.*
*Deut.* 15:4 the Lord sh. *g.* bless
1 *Sam.* 12:18 peo. *g.* feared the L.
1 *K.* 18:3 Obadiah feared L. *g.*
1 *Chr.* 4:38 house of fath. inc. *g.*
16:25 the L. is *g.* to be praised, *Ps.* 48:1; 96:4; 145:3
2 *Chr.* 25:10 anger *g.* kindled
33:12 Manas. humbled hims. *g.*
*Job* 8:7 latter end should *g.* inc.
*Ps.* 21:1 in thy salva. *g.* rejoice
28:7 heart *g.* rejoiceth
45:11 shall *g.* desire thy beauty
47:9 he is *g.* exalted
62:2 I shall not be *g.* moved
65:9 thou *g.* enrichest it
71:23 *g.* rejoice when I sing
78:59 wroth, and *g.* abhorred Is.
105:24 increased peo. *g.* 107:38
109:30 I will *g.* praise the Lord
112:1 delighteth *g.* in his com.
116:10 I was *g.* afflicted, I said
*Prov.* 23:24 father of righteous *g.* rejoice
*Is.* 42:17 *g.* ashamed th. trust
61:10 I will *g.* rejoice in the L.
*Jer.* 4:10 hast *g.* deceived people
*Ezek.* 20:13 sabbath *g.* polluted
*Dan.* 5:9 Belshazzar *g.* troubled
9:23 art *g.* beloved, 10:11, 19
*Ob.* 2 thou art *g.* despised
*Zep.* 1:14 day of L. hasteth *g.*
*Zec.* 9:9 rejoice *g.* daugh. of Z.
*Mat.* 27:14 governor marvelled *g.*
*Mark* 5:38 wept and wailed *g.*
9:15 they were amazed *g.*
12:27 ye therefore do *g.* err

John 3:29 rejoiceth g. because
Acts 6:7 disciples mult. in J. g.
1 Cor. 16:12 I g. desired Apollos
Phil. 1:8 g. I long after you all
1 Thes. 3:6 desiring g. to see us
2 Tim. 1:4 g. desiring to see thee
4:15 g. withstood our words
1 Pet. 1:16 g. rejoiced tho. in he.
2 John 4 I rejoiced g. that I fou.
3 John 3 I rejoiced g. when bre.
See FEARED.

**GREATNESS.**

Ex. 15:7 g. of thy excellency
Num. 14:19 according to g.
Deut. 3:24 to show servant g.
5:24 Lord hath showed his g.
9:26 redeemed through thy g.
11:2 chil. who have not seen g.
32:3 ascribe ye g. unto our God
1 Chr. 17:21 make a name of g.
29:11 thine, O Lord, is the g.
2 Chr. 9:6 half of g. not showed
Neh. 13:22 according to g.
Ps. 66:3 by g. of thy power
71:21 thou shalt increase my g.
79:11 accord. to g. power
145:3 g. unsearch.; 6 declare g.
150:2 accord. to his excellent g.
Prov. 5:23 in g. of folly go astray
Is. 40:26 by g. of his might
57:10 wearied in g. of thy way
63:1 travelling in g. of strength
Jer. 13:22 g. of iniquity discove.
Ezek. 31:2 whom art like in g.?
Dan. 4:22 g. reacheth heaven
Dan. 7:27 g. of king. given saints
Eph. 1:19 exceed. g. of his power

**GREAVES.**

1 Sam. 17:6 Gol. had g. of brass

GRECIA. Dan. 8:21; 10:20; 11:2

**GRECIANS.**

Joel 3:6 Judah have ye sold to G.
Acts 6:1 arose murmuring of G.
9:29 Paul disputed ag. G. 11:20

**GREECE.**

Zec. 9:13 against thy sons, O G.
Acts 20:2 Paul came to G. and

**GREEDY.**

Ps. 17:12 a lion g. of prey
Prov. 1:19 every one g. of gain
15:27 he that is g. troub. house
Is. 56:11 g. dogs never have en.
1 Tim. 3:3 not g. of filthy luc. 8

**GREEDILY.**

Prov. 21:26 coveteth g. all day
Ezek. 22:12 hast g. gained
Jude 11 ran g. after error of B.

**GREEDINESS.**

Eph. 4:19 uncleanness with g.

**GREEK**—*language.*

Luke 23:38 sup. in G. John 19:20
Acts 21:37 canst thou speak G.?
Rev. 9:11 in G. tongue name A.

**GREEK.**

Rom. 1:16 to Jew first, also to G.
10:12 no diff. betw. Jew and G.
Gal. 2:3 a G. 3:28; Col. 3:11

**GREEKS.**

John 12:20 cert. G. came to wor.
Acts 14:1; 17:4, 12; 18:4, 17
19:10 the Jews and G. heard, 17
20:21 testifying to Jews and G.
21:28 brought G. into temple
Rom. 1:14 a debtor both to G.
1 Cor. 1:22 G. seek after, 23, 24

**GREEN.**

Gen. 1:30 g. herb for meat
9:3 g. herb I have given you
Lev. 2:14 for first-fruits g. ears
23:14 eat no g. ears, till ye have
Jud. 16:7 bind me with g. withs
8 brought to her sev. g. withs
2 K. 19:26 inhabitants were as g. herbs, Is. 37:27
Job 8:16 he is g. before the sun
15:32 his branch shall not be g.
39:8 wild ass searcheth after g.
Ps. 23:2 lie down in g. pastures
37:2 shall wither as the g. herb
35 wicked spr. like g. bay-tree
Cant. 1:16 art fair, our bed g.
2:13 fig-tr. putteth forth g. figs
Is. 15:6 there is no g. thing
Jer. 11:16 L. called name g. olive
17:8 tree spreadeth, leaf be g.
Hos. 14:8 I am like a g. fir-tree
Mark 6:39 companies on g. grass
Rev. 8:7 all g. grass burnt up
9:4 com. not to hurt any g.

**GREEN tree.**

Deut. 12:2 served gods under g. t.
1 K. 14:23 images under every g. tree, 2 K. 17:10
2 K. 16:4 Asa sacrificed under every g. tree, 2 Chr. 28:4
Ps. 52:8 g. olive t. in house of G.
Is. 57:5 infla. yours. under g. t.
Jer. 2:20 under g. t. thou wande.
3:6 under g. tree played harlot
Ezek. 17:24 dried up the g. tree
20:47 it shall devour every g. t.
Luke 23:31 do these things in g. t.

**GREEN trees.**

Jer. 17:2 remem. groves by g. t.

**GREENISH.**

Lev. 13:49 if plague g. on garm.
14:37 plague be with strakes g.

**GREENNESS.**

Job 8:12 whilst it is yet in his g.

**GREET.**

1 Sam. 25:5 go to Na. and g. him
Rom. 16:3 g. Priscilla and Aquil.
5 g. the church; 6 g. Mary
8 g. Amplias; 11 g. household
1 Cor. 16:20 br. g. you, Phil. 4:21
20 g. one another, 2 Cor. 13:12; 1 Pet. 5:14
Col. 4:14 Luke and Demas g. you
1 Thes. 5:26 g. brethren
Tit. 3:15 g. them that love us
2 John 13 children of sister g. th.
3 John 14 g. the friends by name

**GREETETH.**

2 Tim. 4:21 Eubulus g. thee, P.

**GREETING, S.**

Mat. 23:7 g. in the markets, Luke 11:43; 20:46
Acts 15:23 apostles, elders send g.
23:26 Lysias to Felix sendeth g.
Jam. 1:1 to the 12 tribes abr. g.

**GREW.**

Gen. 2:5 L. made herb bef. it g.
21:8 Is. g. 26:13; 21:20 Ishmael
25:27 boys g.; 47:27 Israel g.
Ex. 1:12 more afflicted, more g
2:10 M. g.; Jud. 11:2 wife's so.
1 Sam. 2:21 child Samuel g. 26
2 Sam. 5:10 D. went on, g. great
12:3 it g. up together with him
Ezek. 17:6 g. and bec. spreading
Dan. 4:11 tree g. and was strong
Mark 4:7 and the thorns g. up
Luke 1:80 g. and waxed, 2:40
13:19 g. and waxed great tree
Acts 7:17 peo. g. and multiplied
12:24 the word of God g. and
19:20 mightily g. the word of

**GREYHOUND.**

Prov. 30:31 comely in going, a g.

**GRIEF, S.**

Gen. 26:35 a g. unto Isaac and R.
1 Sam. 1:16 abundance of g.
2 Chr. 6:29 ev. one know own g.
Job 6:2 O that g. were weighed
16:5 moving of lips assuage g.
6 tho. I speak, g. not assuaged
Ps. 6:7 my eye is consumed because of g. 31:9
31:10 my life is spent with g.
69:26 to g. of those wounded
Prov. 17:25 fool. son g. to father
Ec. 1:18 in much wisd. much g.
2:23 days are sorrows, travail g.
Is. 17:11 harv. a heap in day of g.
53:3 a man acquainted with g.
4 borne our g. carried sorrows
10 pleased Lord put him to g.
Jer. 10:19 Truly this is a g.
45:3 L. hath added g. to sorrow
Lam. 3:32 tho. he cause g.
Jon. 4:6 a gourd to del. from g.
2 Cor. 2:5 if caused g.
Heb. 13:17 do it with joy, not g.
1 Pet. 2:19 consc. to. G. endure g.

**GRIEVANCE.**

Hab. 1:3 why cause me to b. g.?

**GRIEVE.**

1 Sam. 2:23 man to g. thy heart
1 Chr. 4:10 keep from evil, not g.
Ps. 78:40 oft did they g. him
Lam. 3:33 not willingly g. men
Eph. 4:30 g. not H. Spirit of God

**GRIEVED.**

Gen. 6:6 it repented L. that he had made man, it g. him
45:5 be not g. that ye sold me
49:23 archers have sorely g. him
Deut. 15:10 not g. wh. thou giv.
Jud. 10:16 g. for misery of Israel
1 Sam. 1:8 why is thy heart g.?
20:34 Jonathan was g. for David
30:6 soul of all the peo. was g.
2 Sam. 19:2 king g. for his son
Neh. 13:8 it g. me sore,
Est. 4:4 queen exceedingly g.
Job 4:2 commune, wilt be g.?
30:25 my soul g. for the poor?
Ps. 73:21 heart g. I was pricked
95:10 forty years was I g.
112:10 wicked see it, and be g.
119:158 I beh. transgressors, g.
139:21 am not I g. with those
Is. 54:6 L. called as a woman g.
Jer. 5:3 stricken, they not g.
Dan. 7:15 I Daniel was g.
11:30 he shall be g. and return
Amos 6:6 not g. for affliction
Mark 3:5 g. for hardn. of hearts
10:22 he went away g.
John 21:17 Peter was g.
Acts 4:2 g. that they taught peo.
16:18 P. being g. said to spirit
Rom. 14:15 if brother g.
2 Cor. 2:4 not that ye be g.
5 he hath not g. me.
Heb. 3:10 I was g. with generati.
17 with whom g. forty years?

**GRIEVETH.**

Ruth 1:13 g. me for your sakes
Prov. 26:15 g. him to bring

**GRIEVING.**

Ezek. 28:24 no more a g. thorn

**GRIEVOUS.**

Gen. 12:10 famine was g.
18:20 their sin is very g.
41:31 famine shall be very g.
50:11 g. mourning to the Egypt.
Ex. 8:24 a g. swarm of flies
9:3 very g. murrain in Egypt
8 to rain very g. hail, 24
10:14 locusts were very g.
1 K. 2:8 Shim. cursed w. g. curse
12:4 g. service, 2 Chr. 10:4
Ps. 10:5 his ways always g.
31:18 speak g. things ag. right.
Prov. 15:1 g. words stir up anger
10 correct. g. to him that fors.
Ec. 2:17 work wro. under sun g.
Is. 15:4 life shall be g. unto him
21:2 g. vision is declared to me

Jer. 6:28 are all g. revolters
10:19 my wound is g.
14:17 broken with very g. blow
16:4 they shall die of g. deaths
23:19 g. whirlwind shall fall
30:12 wound is g. Nah. 3:19
Mat. 23:4 burdens g. Luke 11:46
Acts 20:29 g. wolves enter am. y.
25:7 g. complaints against Paul
Phil. 3:1 to me indeed is not g.
Heb. 12:11 no chast. joyous but g.
1 John 5:3 commandments not g.
Rev. 16:2 a g. sore on men

**GRIEVOUSLY.**

Is. 9:1 afterward did g. afflict
Lam. 1:8 Jerusa. hath g. sinned
20 heart is turned, I g. rebelled
Ezek. 14:13 sin. by trespassing g.
Mat. 8:6 servant g. tormented
15:22 my daughter is g. vexed

**GRIEVOUSNESS.**

Is. 10:1 that write g. they presc.
21:15 fled from the g. of war

**GRIND.**

Jud. 16:21 Sam. did g. in prison
Job 31:10 let my wife g. to anot.
Is. 3:15 mean ye to g. faces ?
47:2 millstones and g. meal
Lam. 5:13 took young men to g.
Mat. 21:44 g. him to p. Lu. 20:18

**GRINDERS, ING.**

Ec. 12:3 g. cease, bec. are few
4 when sound of g. is low
Mat. 24:41 two wom. g. Lu. 17:35

**GRIZZLED.**

Gen. 31:10 speckled and g. 12
Zec. 6:3 in chariot we. g. horses
6 the g. go forth to. the south

**GROAN.**

Job 24:12 men g. from out of city
Jer. 51:52 thro' land wounded g.
Joel 1:18 how do the beasts g.
Rom. 8:23 we ourselves g. within
2 Cor. 5:2 we g. des. to be cloth.
4 we in this tabernacle do g.

**GROANED, ETH.**

John 11:33 he g. in spirit
Rom. 8:22 the whole creation g.

**GROANING, S.**

Ex. 2:24 God heard their g.
6:5 heard g. of Israel, Acts 7:34
Job 23:2 stroke is heavier than g.
Ps. 6:6 I am weary with g.
38:9 my g. is not hid from thee
102:5 g. bones cleave to skin
20 to hear the g. of prisoner
Ezek. 30:24 g. of wounded man
John 11:38 Jesus g. in himself
Rom. 8:26 g. that cannot be ut.

**GROPE, ETH.**

Deut. 28:29 g. at noon as blind g.
Job 5:14 g. in noonday
12:25 g. in dark without light
Is. 59:10 g. for wall like blind

**GROSS.**

Is. 60:2 g. darkness cover people
Jer. 13:16 make it g. darkness
Mat. 13:15 waxed g. Acts 28:27

**GROVE.**

Gen. 21:33 planted g. in Beer-sh.
Deut. 16:21 not plant g. near alt.
Jud. 6:25 cut down g. by it, 28
1 K. 15:13 made idol in g. 2 Chr. 15:16
16:33 A. made g. to provoke G.
2 K. 13:6 remained g. in Samar.
17:16 Israel made g. served Baal
21:3 reared up altars, made a g.
23:6 brought g. from ho. of L.
15 Josiah burnt high place and g.

**GROVES.**

Ex. 34:13 cut down g. Deut. 7:5
Deut 12:3 burn their g. with fire
Jud. 3:7 served g. 2 Chr. 24:18
1 K. 14:23 built g. on every high hill, 2 K. 17:10
18:19 prophets of the g. 400
2 K. 18:4 Hezekiah cut down g.
23:14 Jos. cut g. 2 Chr. 34:3, 4
2 Chr. 14:3 brake images, cut g.
17:6 Jehos. took away the g.
33:3 M. made g., 19 set up g.
34:3 purge Judah from the g.
Is. 17:8 neither sh. he respect g.
Jer. 17:2 remember altars and g.
Mic. 5:14 I will pluck up thy g.

**GROUND, Verb.**

Ex. 32:20 g. to powder, Deut. 9:21
Num. 11:8 the people g. manna

**GROUND corn.**

2 Sam. 17:19 g. c. on well's mou.

**GROUND.**

Gen. 2:5 not a man to till g.
7 God formed man of dust of g.
19 of g. the Lord formed every
3:17 cursed is g. for thy sake
4:2 Cain was a tiller of the g.
10 blood crieth to me from g.
5:29 the g. the L. hath cursed
8:21 not again curse the g.
Ex. 3:5 stan. is holy g. Acts 7:33
Num. 16:31 g. clave asunder
Jud. 4:21 fastened nail into g.
1 Sam. 8:12 set them to ear his g.
2 Sam. 23:11 g. full of lentiles
2 K. 2:19 water naught. g. barren
9:26 cast him into the plat of g.
1 Chr. 11:13 g. full of barley
2 Chr. 4:17 cast them in clay g.
Neh. 10:35 first-fruits of our g.
Job 5:6 trouble spring out of g.
14:8 tho. stock thereof die in g.
18:10 snare is laid for him in g.
38:27 desolate and waste g.
39:24 swal. the g. with fiercen.
Ps. 105:35 dev. fruit of their g.
107:33 turn. springs into dry g.
35 turneth dry g. to water-spr.
Is. 28:24 break clods of his g.
29:4 shalt break out of the g.
30:23 thou shalt not sow the g.
24 asses that ear the g. sh. eat
35:7 parched g. shall bec. a pool
51:23 hast laid thy body as g.
Jer. 4:3 br. your fal. g. Hos. 10:12
14:4 because g. is chapt
Lam. 2:9 gates are sunk into g.
Ezek. 12:6 thou see not the g. 12
Dan. 8:5 came, touched not g.
Hos. 2:18 coven. for things of g.
Zec. 8:12 g. shall give increase
Mal. 3:11 not destroy fruit of g.
Mat. 13:8 into good g. Luke 8:8
23 send into good g. Luke 8:15
Mark 4:26 sho. cast seed into g.
Luke 12:16 g. of a certain man
13:7 why cumbereth it the g.?
14:18 have bought a piece of g.
19:44 sh. lay thee with the g.
John 4:5 the parcel of g. J. gave
12:24 corn of wheat fall into g.

See DRY, FACE.

**On, or upon the GROUND.**

Gen. 38:9 On. spilled it on the g.
Ex. 4:3 cast rod o. g. cast o. g.
9:23 fire ran along upon the g.
14:16 go on dry g. thro' sea, 22
Deut. 22:6 bird's nest be on t. g.
Jud. 6:39 u. t. g. let there be dew
40 dew upon all the g.
1 Sam. 14:25 honey u. the g.
2 Sam. 14:14 water spilt on t. g.
17:12 as dew falleth on t. g.
2 K. 13:18 smite u. t. g. he smote
Job 1:20 Job fell u. the g.
2:13 sat down with him u. t. g.
16:13 pour. out my gall u. g.
Is. 3:26 desolate shall sit on g.
47:1 O daughter, sit on the g.
Jer. 25:33 shall be dung u. the g.
27:5 man and beast u. the g.
Lam. 2:10 dau. of Z. sit on the g.
21 young and old lie on the g.
Ezek. 24:7 poured it not u. the g.
26:16 princes shall sit u. the g.
Mat. 15:35 sit on t. g. Mark 8:6
Mark 4:5 so. fell on stony g. 16
8 on good g. 20; Luke 8:8, 15
9:20 fell on the g. and foaming
14:35 and fell on g. and prayed
John 8:6 he wrote on the g. 8
9:6 spat on t. g. and made clay

**To, or unto the GROUND.**

Gen. 3:19 till thou return u. t. g.
33:3 J. bowed himself to the g.
Jud. 20:21 dest. to the g. 22,000
25 dest. to the g. 18,000 men
Ruth 2:10 Ruth bowed to the g.
1 Sam. 3:19 his words to the g.
5:4 Dagon fallen on face to g.
25:23 Abigail bowed to the g.
28:14 S. stooped wi. face to t. g.
2 Sam. 14:4 fell on face to the g.
22 Joab fell to the g. on his fa.
33 Absalom bowed to the g.
20:10 Amasa's bowels to t. g.
1 K. 1:23 Nathan bowed to the g.
2 K. 2:15 sons of prophets, to t. g.
1 Chr. 21:21 Ornan bowed to t. g.
2 Chr. 7:3 Is. bow. with fa. to g.
Neh. 8:6 worship. Lo. faces to g.
Ps. 74:7 dwe. of thy name to t. g.
89:39 prof. crown, casting to g.
44 cast his throne down to t. g.
147:6 casteth the wicked to t. g.
Is. 14:12 cut down to the g.!
21:9 im. he hath brok. to the g.
25:12 bring to the g.
26:5 lofty city he layeth to t. g.
Jer. 14:2 languish, black to t. g.
Lam. 2:2 stron. of Judah, to t. g.
10 virgins hang heads to t. g.
Ezek. 19:12 mother cast to the g.
26:11 thy garrison sh. go to t. g.
Dan. 8:7 cast ram down to t. g.
10 hosts and stars to the g.
12 cast down the truth to t. g.
Amos 3:14 h. of altar fall to t. g.
Ob. 3 shall bring me to the g.
Mat. 10:29 shall not fall to the g.
Luke 22:44 dr. of blood fall. to g.
John 18:6 and fell to the g.
Acts 22:7 fell to the g.

**GROUND.**

1 Tim. 3:15 pillar and g. of truth

**GROUNDED.**

Is. 30:32 g. staff shall pass
Eph. 3:17 rooted and g. in love
Col. 1:23 in faith, g. and settled

**GROW.**

Gen. 2:9 L. G. ma. ev. tree to g.
Num. 6:5 the locks of his hair g.
Jud. 16:22 hair of head be. to g.
2 Sam. 23:5 th. he make it not g.
2 K. 19:29 eat such things as g.
Job 8:11 can rush g. with. mire?
14:19 things that g. out of dust
31:40 thistles g. inst. of wheat
39:4 they g. up with the corn
Ps. 92:12 g. like cedar in Leba.
104:14 grass to g. 147:8
Ec. 11:5 how the bones g.
Is. 11:1 br. sh. g. out of his roots
53:2 sh. g. up as a tender plant
Jer. 12:2 they g. yea, bring forth
33:15 branch of right. to g. to D.
Ezek. 44:20 nor suffer locks g. lo.
Hos. 14:5 he shall g. as the lily
7 shall revive, and g. as vine
Jon. 4:10 madest g. which came
Zec. 6:12 the BRANCH, he shall g.
Mal. 4:2 ye shall g. up as calves
Mat. 6:28 how they g. Luke 12:27
13:30 let both g. together
21:19 no fruit g. on thee hence.

*Mark* 4:27 seed *g.* kno. not how
*Acts* 5:24 doubted whereunto this *g.*
*Eph.* 4:15 may *g.* into him
1 *Pet.* 2:2 milk of word, th. ye *g.*
2 *Pet.* 3:18 *g.* in grace and kno.

**GROWETH.**

*Ex.* 10:5 locusts eat ev. tree *g.*
*Lev.* 13:39 spot that *g.* in skin
25:5 *g.* of its own accord, 11
*Deut.* 29:23 nor any grass *g.*
*Jud.* 19:9 the day *g.* to an end
*Job* 38:38 dust *g.* into hardness
*Ps.* 90:5 grass which *g.* up, 6
129:6 withereth afore it *g.* up
*Is.* 37:30 such as *g.* of itself
*Mark* 4:32 when it is sown it *g.*
*Eph.* 2:21 *g.* unto holy temple
2 *Thes.* 1:3 faith *g.* exceedingly

**GROWN.**

*Gen.* 38:11 Sh. be *g.*; 14 was *g.*
*Ex.* 2:11 when Moses was *g.*
*Deut.* 32:15 thou art *g.* thick
*Ruth* 1:13 till they were *g.*?
2 *Sam.* 10:5 tarry at Je. till your beards be *g.* 1 *Chr.* 19:5
2 *K.* 19:26 as corn blasted before it be *g.* *Is.* 37:27
*Ezr.* 9:6 tresp. *g.* up to heavens
*Ps.* 144:12 sons as plants *g.* up
*Prov.* 24:31 *g.* over with thorns
*Jer.* 50:11 ye are *g.* fat as heifer
*Ezek.* 16:7 bre. fashioned, hair *g.*
*Dan.* 4:22 *g.* strong, greatness *g.*
33 *g.* like eagles' feathers
*Mat.* 13:32 when *g.* greatest

**GROWTH.**

*Amos* 7:1 shooting up of lat. *g.*

**GRUDGE.**

*Lev.* 19:18 nor bear *g.* against pe.

**GRUDGE, Verb.**

*Ps.* 59:15 let them *g.* if not satis.
*Jam.* 5:9 *g.* not one ag. another

**GRUDGING, LY.**

2 *Cor.* 9:7 let him give, not *g.*
1 *Pet.* 4:9 hospitality without *g.*

**GUARD.**

*Gen.* 37:36 sold to capt. of *g.* 39:1
41:12 servant to captain of *g.*
1 *K.* 14:27 committed shields to chief of *g.* 2 *Chr.* 12:10
28 *g.* bro. them, 2 *Chr.* 12:11
2 *K.* 25:8 capt. of *g.* *Jer.* 52:12
10 cap. of *g.* b. walls, *Jer.* 52:14
11 captain of *g.* carried away
12 captain of *g.* left of poor
*Neh.* 4:22 in night may be a *g.*
23 nor men of *g.* put off clothes
*Jer.* 40:5 cap. of *g.* gave him vic.
52:30 cap. of *g.* took capt. 4,600
*Ezek.* 38:7 be thou a *g.* to them
*Dan.* 2:14 Dan. ans. capt. of *g.*
*Acts* 28:16 deli. pris. to cap. of *g.*

**GUARD-CHAMBER.**

1 *K.* 14:28 guard bare them to *g.-c.* 2 *Chr.* 12:11

**GUEST.**

*Luke* 19:7 to be *g.* with sinner

**GUEST-CHAMBER.**

*Mark* 14:14 whe. *g.-c.*? *Lu.* 22:11

**GUESTS.**

1 *K.* 1:41 Adonijah and *g.* heard
*Prov.* 9:18 *g.* in depths of hell
*Zep.* 1:7 L. hath prep. and bid *g.*
*Mat.* 22:10 wed. furnished wi. *g.*
11 the king came in to see *g*

**GUIDE, S.**

*Ps.* 48:14 our *g.* even to death
55:13 it was thou, a man, my *g.*
*Prov.* 2:17 forsak. *g.* of her youth
6:7 having no *g.* overseer, ruler
*Jer.* 3:4 thou art *g.* of my youth
*Mic.* 7:5 put not confidence in *g.*
*Mat.* 23:16 ye blind *g.* 24
*Acts* 1:16 *g.* to them that took J.
*Rom.* 2:19 thou art *g.* of blind

**GUIDE.**

*Job* 38:32 canst th. *g.* Arcturus?
*Ps.* 25:9 meek will *g.* in judgm.
31:3 for thy name's sake *g.* me
32:8 I will teach and *g.* thee
73:24 shalt *g.* me with counsel
112:5 *g.* his affairs with discre.
*Prov.* 11:3 integrity of upright *g.*
*Is.* 49:10 by springs he sh. *g.* th.
51:18 there is none to *g.* her
58:11 L. shall *g.* thee continual.
*Luke* 1:79 *g.* feet into way of pe.
*John* 16:13 he will *g.* you
*Acts* 8:31 can I, ex. some *g.* me?
1 *Tim.* 5:14 you. women *g.* house

**GUIDED, ING.**

*Gen.* 48:14 *g.* hands wittingly
*Ex.* 15:13 *g.* them in strength
2 *Chr.* 32:22 Lord *g.* on ev. side
*Job* 31:18 *g.* her from mother's
*Ps.* 78:52 *g.* them in wilderness
72 *g.* them by skilful. of hands

**GUILE.**

*Ex.* 21:14 if a man slay with *g.*
*Ps.* 32:2 in whose spirit is no *g.*
34:13 lips from *g.* 1 *Pet.* 3:10
55:11 deceit and *g.* depart not
*John* 1:47 Israelite in wh. no *g.*
2 *Cor.* 12:16 I caught you with *g.*
1 *Thes.* 2:3 exhortation not in *g.*
1 *Pet.* 2:1 lay aside malice and *g.*
22 nor was *g.* found in his mo.
*Rev.* 14:5 in mo. was found no *g.*

**GUILT.**

*Deut.* 19:13 *g.* of inno. blood, 21:9

**GUILTY.**

*Gen.* 42:21 we are verily *g.*
*Ex.* 34:7 not clear *g.* *Num.* 14:18
*Lev.* 5:2 he shall be uncl. and *g.*
3 wh. he knoweth not, be *g.* 4
5 when *g.* he shall con. his sin
17 he wist it not, yet is he *g.*
6:4 he sinned and is *g.*
*Num.* 35:27 kill slayer not be *g.*
31 for a murderer *g.* of death
*Jud.* 21:22 not g. that sh. be *g.*
*Prov.* 30:10 lest curse, thou be *g.*
*Ezek.* 22:4 art become *g.* in blo.
*Mat.* 23:18 by gift on it, he *g.*
26:66 he is *g.* of death, *Mark* 14:64
*Rom.* 3:19 the world may bec. *g.*
1 *Cor.* 11:27 *g.* of body and blood
*Jam.* 2:10 offend in one, *g.* of all

**GUILTINESS.**

*Gen.* 26:10 shouldest have bro. *g.*
*Ps.* 51:14 del. me from blood-*g.*

**GUILTLESS.**

*Ex.* 20:7 hold him *g.* *Deut.* 25:11
*Num.* 32:22 and be *g.* before L.
*Jos.* 2:19 blood on him, we be *g.*
1 *Sam.* 26:9 ag. L.'s anointed *g.*
2 *Sam.* 3:28 I and kingdom *g.* of blood
14:9 king and his throne be *g.*
1 *K.* 2:9 hold him not *g.* for thou
*Mat.* 12:7 not have condemned *g.*

**GULF.**

*Luke* 16:26 bet. us and you a *g.*

GUR. 2 *K.* 9:27

**GUSH, ED.**

1 *K.* 18:28 till the blood *g.* out
*Ps.* 78:20 sm rock, waters *g.* out
105:41 open. rock, waters *g.* out
*Is.* 48:21 cl. rock, waters *g.* out
*Jer.* 9:18 eyelids *g.* out with wat.
*Acts* 1:18 burst as. bowels *g.* out

**GUTTER, S.**

*Gen.* 30:38 Jacob set rods in *g.*
41 laid rods bef. cat. in the *g.*
2 *Sam.* 5:8 getteth up to the *g.*

# H

**HA.**

*Job* 39:25 saith am. trump. *a, ha*

**HABERGEON.**

*Ex.* 28:32 hole of a *h.* 39:23
*Job* 41:26 dart, *h.* cannot hold

**HABERGEONS.**

2 *Chr.* 26:14 *h.* Uzziah prepared
*Neh.* 4:16 half of servants held *h.*

**HABITABLE.**

*Prov.* 8:31 in the *h.* part of earth

**HABITATION.**

*Ex.* 15:2 I will prepare him a *h.*
*Lev.* 13:46 with. the camp his *h.*
1 *Sam.* 2:29 offering com. in *h.*
32 shalt see an enemy in my *h.*
2 *Sam.* 15:25 show me it and *h.*
2 *Chr.* 6:2 a house of *h.* for thee
29:6 turned from the *h.* of Lord
*Ezr.* 7:15 G. of Is. whose *h.* in J.
*Job* 5:3 but suddenly I cursed *h.*
24 shalt visit *h.* and sh. not sin
8:6 *h.* of righteousness prosper.
18:15 brimstone scat. upon *h.*
*Ps.* 26:8 loved *h.* of thy house
33:14 from place of *h.* looketh
69:25 let their *h.* be desolate
71:3 be thou my strong *h.*
89:14 the *h.* of thy throne, 97:2
91:9 made the Most High thy *h.*
104:12 fowls of heaven have *h.*
107:7 might go to a city of *h.* 36
132:5 find a *h.* for God of Jacob
13 L. hath desired it for his *h.*
*Prov.* 3:33 blesseth the *h.* of just
*Is.* 22:16 graveth *h.* for himself
32:18 peo. dwell in peaceable *h.*
33:20 shall see Jerus. a quiet *h.*
34:13 it shall be a *h.* of dragons
35:7 *h.* of dragons sh. be grass
63:15 from the *h.* of thy holiness
*Jer.* 9:6 thy *h.* in midst of deceit
10:25 have made his *h.* desolate
25:30 L. sh. mightily roar on *h.*
31:23 L. bless, O *h.* of just, 50:7
41:17 dwelt in the *h.* of Chim.
49:19 not c. ag. *h.* of stro. 50:44
50:19 bri. Israel again to his *h.*
45 he sh. make their *h.* desol.
*Ezek.* 29:14 cause E. return to *h.*
*Ob.* 3 wh. *h.* high, saith in heart
*Hab.* 3:11 sun and moon st. in *h.*
*Acts* 1:20 let his *h.* be desolate
17:26 determined bounds of *h.*
*Eph.* 2:22 *h.* of God thro' Spirit
*Jude* 6 angels wh. left their *h.*
*Rev.* 18:2 Baby. become *h.* of de.

**Holy HABITATION.**

*Ex.* 15:13 guided them to *h. h.*
*Deut.* 26:15 look down from *h. h.*
*Ps.* 68:5 Ju. of wid. is G. in *h. h.*
*Jer.* 25:30 utter voice from *h. h.*
*Zec.* 2:13 raised out of *holy h.*

**HABITATIONS.**

*Gen.* 49:5 instru. of cruelty in *h.*
*Ex.* 12:20 in *h.* eat unl. bread
35:3 kindle no fire thro' your *h.*

Ps. 74:20 dark places full of h.
Is 54:2 stretch forth curt. of h.
Jer. 9:10 h. of wild. lamentation
21:13 who sh. enter into our h.?
25:37 peaceable h. are cut down
49:20 sh. make their h. desolate
Lam. 2:2 L. swallowed h. of J.
Ezek. 6:14 h. make land desolate
Amos 1:2 h. of shepherds mourn
Luke 16:9 receive into everl. h.

**HACHILAH.**

1 Sam. 23:19 D. hid in H. 26:1

**HAD.**

Job 31:31 O that we h. of his fl.!
42:10 twice as much as he h.
Ps. 84:10 I h. rather be a door-k.
89:7 to be h. in reverence of all
Mat. 13:46 he sold all that he h.
22:28 of sev. for they all h. her
Mark 12:44 did cast in all she h.
John 4:18 hast h. five husbands
John 12:6 Judas h. the bag. and
15:22 h. not come they h. not h.
17:5 the glory I h. with thee
Acts 2:44 believed h. all common
Heb. 7:6 blessed him h. promises
1 John 2:7 com. h. fr. beginning
2 John 5 we h. from beginning.
See ALL, COMPASSION.

**HADST.**

Gen. 30:30 little h. bef. I came
Heb. 10:8 offer. for sin h. no plc.

**HADADEZER, HADAREZER.**

2 Sam. 8:3, 5, 7, 8, 9, 10, 12; 10:16;
1 K. 11:23; 1 Chr. 18:3

HADADRIMMON. Zec. 12:11
HADASSAH. Est. 2:7

**HADORAM.**

Gen. 10:27; 1 Chr. 1:21 ; 18:10
2 Chr. 10:18 Rehoboam sent H.

HADRACH. Zec. 9:1

**HAFT.**

Jud. 3:22 the h. also went in

HAGAR. Gen. 16:1, 3, 8, 16;
21:9, 14, 17; 25:12
HAGARENES. Ps. 83:6
HAGARITES. 1 Chr. 5:10, 19, 20

**HAGGAI.**

Ezr. 5:1 H. prophesied to J. 6:14
Hag. 1:1 L. by H. 3; 2:1, 10, 20

HAGGITH. 2 Sam. 3:4; 1 K.
1:5; 2:13; 1 Chr. 3:2

**HAIL.**

Ex. 9:18 cau. to rain grievous h.
23 Lord sent thunder and h.
26 children of Is. were, no h.
29 any more h.; 33 h. ceased
Job 38:22 seen treasures of h.?
Ps. 78:47 destroyed vines wi. h.
48 gave cattle also to h.
105:32 he gave them h. for rain
148:8 fire, h. snow, and vapor
Is. 28:17 h. shall sweep away
Hag. 2:17 I smote you with h.
Rev. 8:7 there follow. h. and fire
11:19 temple opened, great h.
16:21 th. fell on men a great h.

**HAIL, Verb.**

Is. 32:19 people dwell, it shall h.

**HAIL.**

Mat. 26:49 Judas said, h. Master
27:29 h. king of the Jews, Mark
15:18; John 19:3
Luke 1:28 ang. came to M. said h.

**HAILSTONES.**

Jos. 10:11 which died with h.
Ps. 18:12 h. and coals of fire, 13
Is. 30:30 L. show indig. with h.
Ezek. 13:11 O great h. shall fall
13 shall be great h. in my fury
38:22 great h. fire, brimstone

**HAIR.**

Lev. 13:3 h. in plague tur. white
30 plague yellow h.; 31 bl. h.
37 there is black h. grown
14:8 and shave off all his h. 9
Num. 6:19 h. of separa. shaven
Jud. 20:16 sling stones at h.
2 Sam. 14:26 bec. h. was heavy
1 K. 1:52 not a h. fall to earth
Neh. 13:25 I plucked off their h.
Job 4:15 h. of my flesh stood up
Cant. 4:1 h. as flock of goats, 6:5
Is. 3:4 instead of well-set h.
7:20 L. shave head, and h.
50:6 plucked off h.
Jer. 7:29 cut off thy h. O Jerus.
Ezek. 5:1 div. h.; 16:7 h. grown
Mat. 3:4 camel's h. Mark 1:6
5:36 not make one h. wh. or bl.
John 11:2 wiped feet with h. 12:3
1 Cor. 11:14 if a man have long h.
15 woman have long h. glory
1 Tim. 2:9 not with broidered h.
1 Pet. 3:3 plaiting h. wear. gold
Rev. 6:12 black as sackcl. of h.
9:8 had h. as the h. of women
See GOATS, HEAD.

**HAIRS.**

Gen. 42:38 br. down h. 44:29, 31
Deut. 32:25 man of gray h.
Ps. 40:12 more than h. of h. 69:4
Is. 46:4 to hoar h. will I carry
Dan. 4:33 h. like eagles' feathers
Hos. 7:9 gray h. here and there
Mat. 10:30 the h. of your head
are numbered, Luke 12:7
Luke 7:38 wipe with h. of h. 44
Rev. 1:14 h. were white like wool

**HAIRY.**

Gen. 25:25 all over like h garm.
27:11 Esau h. man; 23 hands h.
2 K. 1:8 Elijah was a h. man
Ps. 68:21 h. scalp of such a one

**HALE, ING.**

Luke 12:58 advers. h. thee to ju.
Acts 8:3 Saul h. men and women

**HALF.**

Ex. 24:6 h. blood, h. sprinkled
Lev. 6:20 h. in morn. h. at night
1 Sam. 14:14 with h. acre of land
2 Sam. 10:4 shave off h. of beards
19:40 h. of Israel conducted D.
1 K. 3:25 h. child to one, h. oth.
10:7 h. was not told, 2 Chr. 9:6
13:8 wilt give me h. thy house
16:21 h. followed Tibni, h. Omri
Neh. 13:24 h. in speech of Ashd.
Est. 5:3 to the h. of the kingdom, 7:2; Mark 6:23
Ps. 55:23 bl. men not live h. days
Dan. 12:7 and a h. Rev. 12:14
Zec. 14:2 h. of city into captivity
4 h. tow. south; 8 h. tow. sea
Luke 10:30 leaving him h. dead
19:8 h. of goods I give to poor
Rev. 8:1 silence about h. an hour
11:9 bodies three days and h. 11
See SHEKEL, HIN, TRIBE.

**HALL.**

Mat. 27:27 sold. took Jes. into h.
Mark 15:16 soldiers led him to h.
Luke 22:55 kindled fire in the h.
See JUDGMENT.

**HALLOW.**

Ex. 29:1 h. them to minister
Lev. 22:32 I am the L. who h.
25:10 shall h. the fiftieth year
Num. 6:11 shall h. his head
1 K. 8:64 king h. court, 2 Chr. 7:7
Jer. 17:22 h. ye sabbath-d. 24, 27
Ezek. 20:20 and h. my sabbaths
44:24 keep laws h. my sabbaths

**HALLOWED.**

Ex. 20:11 bless. sabbath and h. it
29:21 Aaron be h. and his garm.
Lev. 12:4 shall touch no h. thing
22:32 be h. am. children of Isr.
Num. 3:13 h. to me first-b. in Is.
5:10 every man's h. things
16:37 censers, they are h. 38
Deut. 26:13 bro. away h. things
1 Sam. 21:4 there is h. bread, 6
1 K. 9:3 I have h. this house, 7
2 Chr. 36:14 pollu. hou. L. had h.
Mat. 6:9 h. be thy na. Luke 11:2

**HALT.**

Mat. 18:8 into life h. Mark 9:45
Luke 14:21 bring hither h.
John 5:3 h. wait. moving of wa.

**HALT, ING.**

1 K. 18:21 how long h. ye?
Ps. 38:17 for I am ready to h.
Jer. 20:10 familiars watch. my h.

**HALTED, ETH.**

Gen. 32:31 J. passed, h. on thigh
Mic. 4:6 assemble her that h.
7 make her that h. a remnant
Zep. 3:19 I will save her that h.

**HAM.**

Gen. 5:32; 6:10; 9:18; 10:1; 1 Chr.
1:4
1 Chr. 4:40 they of H. dwelt
Ps. 105:23 la. of H. 27; 106:22

**HAMAN.**

See Book of Esther.

**HAMATH.**

Num. 34:8 Hor to entr. of H. Jos.
13:5; Jud. 3:3; 1 K. 8:65;
2 K. 14:25; 2 Chr. 7:8
2 K. 14:28; 18:34; 19:13; Is. 36:19
1 Chr. 18:3 D. sm. to H. 2 Chr. 8:4
Is. 10:9 H. as A.? 11:11; Jer. 39:5;
49:23; 52:9; Ezek. 47:17

HAMMEDATHA. Est. 8:5; 9:10

**HAMMER, S.**

Jud. 4:21 J. took h. in her hand
5:26 with h. she smote Sisera
1 K. 6:7 neither h. nor axe heard
Ps. 74:6 br. carved work with h.
Is. 41:7 smootheth with the h.
44:12 smith fashioneth it wi. h.
Jer. 10:4 fast. it wi. nails and h.
23:29 like h. that breaketh rock
50:23 h. of wh. earth cut asund.

HAMON-GOG. Ezek. 39:11 15

**HAMOR.**

Gen. 33:19 H. Shechem's father,
Jos. 24:32
34:6 H. went out to Ja. 8, 24, 26
Jud. 9:28 serve the men of H.

HANAMEEL. Jer. 32:7, 8, 9, 12
HANANEEL. Neh. 3:1; 12:39;
Jer. 31:38; Zec. 14:10

**HANANI.**

1 K. 16:1 to Jehu son of H. 7
1 Chr. 25:4 H. son of Heman, 25
2 Chr. 16:7 H. seer, Neh. 1:2; 7:2
19:2 Jehu son of H. 20:34
Neh. 12:36 H. with musical inst.

**HANANIAH.**

1 Chr. 3:19 sons of Zerub. H.
Ezr. 10:28 H. Zab. stra. wives
Neh. 3:8 H. repaired, 7:2; 10:23;
12:12
Jer. 28:12 H. had broken J.'s, 17
37:13 son of H. took Jeremiah
Dan. 1:7 to H. name of S. 2:17

**HAND.**

Gen. 9:2 into h. are they deliv.
44:17 in whose h. cup found
Ex. 6:1 strong h. drive them out
13:3 strength of h. L. brought
14:8 Israel went out with a high
h. Num. 33:3
16 stretch out h. over the sea
19:13 there sh. not a h. touch it
21:24 h. for h. Deut. 19:21

34:29 tables of testi. in Mos. h.
38:15 on this h. and that h.
Deut. 13:9 h. of all the people
25:12 cut off her h.
Jos. 2:19 blo. on head h. on him
Jud. 1:35 h. of house of Joseph
4:9 sell Sisera into h. of a wom.
15:18 fall into h. of uncircum.
1 Sam. 12:3 who. h. rec. bribe?
13:22 nor spear fou. in h. of Is.
17:50 no sword in h. of David
20:19 when business was in h.
22:17 their h. also is with Dav.
2 Sam. 13:5 eat it at her h. 6
14:19 the h. of Joab in all this
21:20 had on every h. six fing. 1 Chr. 20:6
24:14 into h. of men, 1 Chr. 21:13
1 K. 2:46 established in h. of Sol.
13:6 king's h. was restored aga.
18:44 ariseth cloud like man's h.
22:6 L. sh. deliver it into king's h. 12, 15; 2 Chr. 18:5; 28:5
2 K. 7:2 who. h. king leaned, 17
Ezr. 7:9 good h. of God on him
9:2 h. of princes chief in tresp.
Job 9:24 given into h. of wicked
12:6 into whose h. G. bringeth
10 in h. is soul of ev. liv. thing
20:22 h. of wicked come on him
21:16 good is not in their h.
34:20 mighty take. away wit. h.
37:7 sealeth up h. of ev. man
Ps. 31:8 not shut into h. of ene.
36:11 let not h. of wicked rem.
71:4 deliver me out of h. of wicked, 82:4; 97:10
123:2 serv. look to h. of masters
127:4 in h. of mighty man
149:6 two-edged sword be in h.
Prov. 6:3 come into h. of friend
10:4 poor, dealeth slack h. but h. of diligent maketh rich
11:21 h. join h. not unpun. 16:5
12:24 h. of diligent bear rule
17:16 in h. of fool get wisdom?
26:9 thorn goeth into h. of dru.
Is. 10:5 staff in h. my indigna.
13:2 shake h. may go into gates
19:4 into h. of cruel lord
28:2 cast down to earth wi. h.
Jer. 12:7 belo. into h. of enemies
18:4 vessel marred in h. of pot.
6 as clay in the potter's h.
21:5 outstretch. h. against you
26:24 h. of Ahikam with Jere. not to give him into h. of pe.
Lam. 5:6 given h. to Egyptians
12 princes are hanged by th. h.

Ezek. 2:9 a h. was sent me
8:3 put forth form of h. 10:8
16:49 nor. strength. h. of needy
28:9 no god in h. that slayeth
34:10 require flock at their h.
37:19 stick in h. of Ephraim
40:5 in man's h. a measur. reed

Dan. 5:5 came fing. of man's h.
23 G. in whose h. thy breath is
8:25 he shall be broken with. h.
10:10 behold, a h. touched me

Joel 3:8 sons and dau. to h. Jud
Mat. 8:15 tou. h.; 22:13 bind h.
Mark 3:1 withered h. 3; Lu. 6:8
14:41 is betrayed into h. of sin.
Luke 1:1 taken in h. to set forth
74 delivered out of h. of enem.
22:21 h. that betray. is with me
John 10:39 escaped out of th. h.
11:44 bound h. and foot
Acts 12:17 becko. to them wi. h.
1 Cor. 12:15 bec. I am not the h.
21 eye cannot say to h. no need
Gal. 3:19 by angels in h. of med.

Rev. 10:8 book in h. of angel
17:4 a golden cup in her h.
19:2 avenged blood of serv. at h.

**At, or at the HAND.**

Gen. 9:5 at h. of ev. beast, at h. of man, at h. of man's brot.
33:19 J. bought at h. of children
Deut. 15:9 year of release is at h.
1 Sam. 20:16 at h. of D.'s enem.
2 K. 9:7 blood at h. of Jezebel
Is. 13:6 day of Lord at h. Joel 1:15; Zep. 1:7
Jer. 23:23 am I a God at h.?
Ezek. 12:23 the days are at h.
33:6 blood req. at watchm.'s h.
Joel 2:1 day of Lord is nigh at h.
Mat. 3:2 heaven at h. 4:17; 10:7
26:18 ti. is at h.; 45 hour at h.
46 at h. that bet. me, Mar. 14:42
Mark 1:15 kingdom of God is at h. Luke 21:31
Luke 21:30 summer is nigh at h.
John 2:13 pass. was at h. 11:55
7:2 feast of tabernac. was at h.
19:42 sepulchre was nigh at h.
Rom. 13:12 night far sp. day at h.
Phil. 4:5 the Lord is at h.
2 Thes. 2:2 the day of Ch. is at h.
2 Tim. 4:6 time of depart. is at h.
1 Pet. 4:7 end of all things at h.
Rev. 1:3 the time is at h. 22:10

**By the HAND.**

Ex. 4:13 send by the h. of him
Lev. 8:36 Lord command. by t. h. of Moses, 10:11; 26:46; Num. 4:37, 45, 49; 9:23; 10:13; 15:23; 16:40; 27:23; 36:13; Jos. 14:2; 20:2; 21:2, 8; 22:9; Jud. 3:4; 1 K. 8:53, 56; 2 Chr. 33:8; 35:6; Neh. 9:14; Ps. 77:20
16:21 by t. h. of a fit man
Jos. 20:9 not die by t. h. of aven.
Jud. 16:26 to lad held by t. h.
1 Sam. 18:25 fall by h. of Philis.
27:1 one day perish by t. h. of S.
2 Sam. 3:18 by h. of my serv. D.
11:14 a letter, sent by t. h. of U.
12:25 sent by h. of Nathan
21:22 fell by h. of D. 1 Chr. 20:8
1 K. 2:25 sent by h. of Benaiah
14:18 he spake by h. of his serv.
2 K. 14:25 spake by h. of Jonah
27 saved them by t. h. of Jero.
2 Chr. 10:15 by t. h. of Ahijah
12:7 wrath by t. h. of Shishak
Prov. 26:6 message by h. of fool
Is. 51:18 that taketh by the h.
Jer. 27:3 yokes by h. of messeng.
31:32 took th. by t. h. Heb. 8:9
Ezek. 25:14 vengeance by h. of Is.
30:12 land waste by h. of strang.
Mat. 9:25 took her by t. h. Mark 1:31; 5:41; Luke 8:54
Mark 8:23 took blind man by h.
9:27 Jesus took him by the h.
Acts 7:35 a deliv. by t. h. of angel
9:8 but they led him by the h.
13:11 seek. some lead him by h.
Col. 4:18 salutation by the h.
See CHALDEANS, ENEMY.

**HAND, joined with enemies.**

1 Sam. 4:3 ark of coven. save out h. of e. 12:10; 2 Sam. 3:18
12:11 deli. out of h. e. 2 K. 17:39
2 Sam. 19:9 out of h. of enemies
2 K. 21:14 will deliver them to h. of e. 2 Chr. 25:20; Neh. 9:27
Neh. 9:28 left them in h. of th. e.
Ps. 31:15 del. from h. of mine e.
Jer. 20:5 give this city into h. of e. 21:7; 34:20, 21; Ezek. 39:23
44:30 give Phar. to h. of his e.
Mic. 4:10 red. thee from h. of e.
Luke 1:74 del. out of h. of our e.

**From the HAND.**

Gen. 32:11 del. f. t. h. of brother
Deut. 7:8 redeemed f. h. of Pha.
Jud. 8:22 deliv. f. h. of Midian
1 Sam. 25:39 pleaded f. h. of N.
Job 5:15 saveth poor f. h. of mi.
6:23 redeem me f. h. of mighty
Ps. 89:48 del. soul f. h. of grave
106:10 sav. f. h. of him that hat. redeemed f. h. of the enemy
144:7 del. f. t. h. of children, 11
Prov. 6:5 del. as roe f. h. of hun.
Jer. 20:13 deliv. poor f. h. of evil
31:11 f. h. of him stronger
Luke 1:71 f. h. of all that hate

**HAND of God.**

1 Sam. 5:11 h. of G. heavy
2 Chr. 30:12 h. of G. give heart
Ezr. 7:9 ac. to h. of G. Neh. 2:8
8:18 by good h. of God upon us
22 h. of G. is upon them

Neh. 2:18 told them of h. of G.
Job 2:10 re. good at the h. of G.?
19:21 h. of God touched me
27:11 teach you by h. of G.
Ec. 2:24 from the h. of God
9:1 wise are in the h. of God
Is. 62:3 diadem in h. of God
Mark 16:19 and sat on right h. of G. Rom. 8:34; Col. 3:1; Heb. 10:12; 1 Pet. 3:22
Acts 2:33 by right h. of God
7:55 stand. on right h. of G. 56
1 Pet. 5:6 under the h. of God

**His HAND.**

Gen. 3:22 forth h. h. take t. of life
16:12 his h. be agai. every man
41:42 Pharaoh took ring off h. h.
Ex. 4:4 h. h. became rod in h. h.
6 his h. was as leprous as snow
20 M. took rod of God in his h.
8:6 stretched h. h. over wat. 17
10:22 stretched his h. to heaven
17:11 held up his h. down his h.
21:16 fou. in h. h.; 20 und. h. h.
22:4 if theft be found in his h.
8 hath put his h. to goods, 11
24:11 on nobles laid not his h.
32:15 tab. of testi. in his h. 34:4
Lev. 1:4 h. h. on head of burnt-o.
Num. 5:18 in his h. bitter water
22:23 sw. in h. h. 31; 1 Ch. 21:16
25:7 Phin. took a javelin in h. h.
Deut. 19:5 his h. fetch. a stroke
Jos. 5:13 with sword in his h.
8:26 drew not his h. till destroy.
Jud. 6:21 end of staff in his h.
7:14 to h. h. G. delivered Midian
1 Sam. 6:3 his h. not removed
9 it is not his h. that smote us
14:26 put his h. to his mouth
27 Jon. put his h. to his mouth
16:16 he shall play with his h.
23 played with his h. 18:10
17:40 his staff and sling in h. h.
57 head of Philistine in his h.
19:5 life in h. h. and slew Phil.
23:16 strenthened his h. in God
2 Sam. 6:6 h. h. to ark, 1 Ch. 13:10
1 K. 11:34 kingdom out of his h.
13:4 his h. he put forth ag. him
2 K. 5:11 call on L. strike his h.
10:15 and he gave him his h.
11:8 man with his weapon in his h. 11; 2 Chr. 23:7
14:5 kingdom confirmed in h. h.
15:19 his h. might be with him
18:21 a man lean go into his h.
1 Chr. 28:19 understand by his h.
2 Chr. 26:19 a censer in his h.
Neh. 6:5 serv. with letter in h. h.
Job 6:9 let loose h. h. cut me off
15:23 day of dark. ready at h. h.
25 stretcheth out h. h. ag. God
26:13 his h. formed crooked ser.
27:22 fain flee out of his h.
28:9 putteth forth his h.
Ps. 37:24 L. uphold. him wi. h. h.
33 will not leave him in his h.
78:42 remembered not his h.
89:25 set his h. also in the sea

95:4 in *his h.* are deep places
7 sheep of *his h.* to-day
106:26 lifted up *h. h.* ag. them
129:7 mower filleth not *his h.*
*Prov.* 19:24 a slothful man hideth *his h.* 26:15
*Ec.* 5:14 a son, nothing in *his h.*
15 he may carry in *his h.*
*Cant.* 5:4 put in *his h.* by hole
*Is.* 5:25 *h. h.* is stretch. out still, 9:12, 17, 21; 10:4; 14:27
10:32 shake *h. h.* aga. mount Z.
11:11 set *h. h.* again the sec. ti.
15 shake *his h.* over the river
22:21 thy government into *h. h.*
28:4 while yet in *his h.*
31:3 L. shall stretch out *his h.*
37:20 O L. save us from *his h.*
40:12 waters in hollow of *his h.*
44:5 subscribe with *his h.*
49:2 in shad. of *his h.* he hid me
53:10 ple. of L. prosper in *h. h.*
56:2 keepeth *his h.* fr. doing ev.
*Jer.* 27:8 consumed th. by *his h.*
*Lam.* 1:14 transgression by *h. h.*
2:8 hath not withdrawn *his h.*
3:3 turneth *his h.* against me
*Ezek.* 8:11 with censer in *his h.*
9:1 destroying weapon *his h.*
17:18 lo, he had given *his h.*
30:24 put my sword in *his h.*
46:7 according as *h. h.* shall at.
*Dan.* 4:35 none can stay *his h.*
8:4 could deliver out of *his h.* 7
25 cause craft prosper in *his h.*
11:41 shall escape out *his h.*
*Hos.* 7:5 he stretched out *his h.*
*Hos.* 12:7 bal. of dec. are in *his h.*
*Hab.* 3:4 horns com. out of *his h.*
*Zep.* 2:15 hiss and wag *his h.*
*Zec.* 8:4 man with staff in *his h.*
14:13 *h. h.* rise ag. hand of nei.
*Mat.* 3:12 fan is in *h. h.* *Lu.* 3:17
26:23 he that dippeth *h. h.*
*Mark* 3:5 *h. h.* resto. *Luke* 6:10
7:32 bes. to put *h. h.* upon him
*John* 3:35 given all th. into *h. h.*
18:22 struck with palm of *his h.*
*Acts* 7:25 God by *his h.* del. them
28:3 a viper fastened on *his h.*
4 saw the beast hang on *his h.*
*Rev.* 6:5 pair of balances in *h. h.*
10:2 had in *his h.* a little book
14:9 in his forehead, or in *his h.*
14 in *his h.* sharp sickle
20:1 angel with chain in *his h.*

**HAND of the Lord,** *or* **Lord's HAND.**

*Ex.* 9:3 *h. of the L.* upon cattle
16:3 wo. had died by *h. of t. L.*
*Num.* 11:23 *L.'s h.* waxed short?
*Jos.* 4:24 know *h. of L.* mighty
*Jud.* 2:15 *h. of Lord* ag. them
*Ruth* 1:13 *h. of the L.* is gone out
1 *Sam.* 5:6 *h. of Lord* heavy
7:13 *h. of the L.* ag. Philistines
12:15 then sh. *h. of L.* be ag. you
2 *Sam.* 24:14 *h. of L.* 1 *Chr.* 21:13
1 *K.* 18:46 *h. of L.* was on Elijah
2 *K.* 3:15 *h. of L.* came on Elisha
*Ezr.* 7:6 granted acc. to *h. of L.*
*Job* 12:9 *h. of L.* wro. this, *Is.* 41:20
*Ps.* 75:8 in *h. of the L.* is a cup
*Prov.* 21:1 king's he. in *h. of L.*
*Is.* 19:16 shaking off *h. of the L.*
25:10 in moun. sh. *h. of L.* rest
40:2 rec. of the *L.'s h.* double
51:17 hast drunk at *h. of the L.*
59:1 *Lord's h.* is not shortened
62:3 crown of gl. in *h. of the L.*
66:14 *h. of L.* known tow. serv.
*Jer.* 25:17 took cup at the *L.'s h.*
51:7 Bab. golden cup in *L.'s h.*
*Ezek.* 1:3 *h. of the L.* upon him
3:14 *h. of L.* u. me, 22; 8:1; 37:1
33:22 *h. of L.* on me in evening
40:1 *h. of the L.* was with him
*Luke* 1:66 *h. of the L.* with him
*Acts* 11:21 *h. of the L.* with them
13:11 *h. of the L.* is upon thee

*See* LAY, or LAID.

**Left HAND.**

*Gen.* 13:9 if thou wilt take *left h.*
24:49 turn to the right *h.* or *left*
48:13 Joseph took Ephr. in his right *h.* and Man. in his *left*
14 Is. laid *l. h.* on Manasseh's
*Ex.* 14:22 wall on right *h.* and *l.*
*Lev.* 14:15 pour oil into *left h.* 27
*Num.* 20:17 not turn to right *h.* nor to *left*, *Deut.* 2:27; 5:32; 17:11, 20; 28:14
22:26 no way to turn, r. *h.* or *l.*
*Jos.* 1:7 to right *h.* or *left*, 23:6; 1 *Sam.* 6:12; *Prov.* 4:27
*Jud.* 3:21 E. put forth his *left h.*
7:20 held lamps in their *left h.*
2 *Sam.* 2:19 he turned not to *l. h.*
14:19 none turn to right *h.* or *l.*
1 *K.* 22:19 host of heaven on his *left h.* 2 *Chr.* 18:18
2 *K.* 22:2 J. turn. not to r. *h.* or *l.*
1 *Chr.* 12:2 use both r. *h.* and *l.*
2 *Chr.* 3:17 name of that on *l. h.*
4:7 five candlest. on r. *h.* 5 on *l.*
*Neh.* 8:4 on his *l. h.* stood Ped.
*Job* 23:9 on *left h.* he doth work
*Prov.* 3:16 in her *left h.* riches
*Ec.* 10:2 fool's heart at his *l. h.*
*Cant.* 2:6 *l. h.* is under my head
8:3 his *left h.* under my head
*Is.* 9:20 he shall eat on *left h.*
30:21 when ye turn to *left h.*
54:3 break forth on r. *h.* and *l.*
*Ezek.* 16:46 dau. dwell at *left h.*
39:3 smite bow out of *left h.*
*Dan.* 12:7 he held up his *left h.*
*Jon.* 4:11 betw. right *h.* and *left*
*Zec.* 12:6 people on r. *h.* and *left*
*Mat.* 6:3 let not *l. h.* know what
20:21 one r. *h.* other *l.* *Mar.* 10:37
23 sit on r. *h.* and *l.* *Mark* 10:40
25:33 sheep on r. *h.* goats on *l.*
41 say to them on *l. h.* Depart
27:38 one on right *h.* other on *left*, *Mark* 15:27; *Luke* 23:33
*Acts* 21:3 left Cyprus on the *l. h.*
2 *Cor.* 6:7 armor on right *h.* and *l.*

*See* LIFT *hand*, or *hands*.

**Mighty HAND.**

*Ex.* 3:19 let go, not with *m. h.*
*Deut.* 3:24 show serv. thy *m. h.*
4:34 take him a nation by *m. h.*
*Deut.* 5:15 God bro. out of Eg. by a *mighty h.* 6:21; 7:8, 19; 9:26; 11:2; 26:8; 34:12
2 *Chr.* 6:32 is come for thy *m. h.*
*Ezek.* 20:33 with a *m. h.* I rule
*Dan.* 9:15 out of Eg. with *m. h.*
1 *Pet.* 5:6 hum. under *m. h.* of G.

**My HAND.**

*Gen.* 14:22 lifted *my h.* to Lord
31:39 of *my h.* didst thou req. it
33:10 rec. my present at *my h.*
42:37 deliver him into *my h.*
43:9 of *my h.* shalt thou require
*Ex.* 7:17 smite with rod in *my h.*
15:9 *my h.* destroy; 17:9 in *my h.*
33:22 cover thee with *my h.*
*Num.* 22:29 a sword in *my h.*
*Deut.* 8:17 might of *my h.*
10:3 the two tables in *my h.*
32:39 del. out of *my h.* *Is.* 43:13
40 I lift up *my h.* to heaven
41 if *my h.* take hold on judg.
*Jud.* 6:36 save Is. by *my h.* 37
7:2 *My* own *h.* saved me
9:29 wo. peo. were under *my h.*
17:3 dedi. silv. to L. from *my h.*
1 *Sam.* 12:5 not fo. aught in *my h.*
17:46 L. will deliver into *my h.*
21:4 no com. bread under *my h.*
24:6 stretch *my h.* ag. L.'s ano.
11 no transgression in *my h.*
12 *my h.* shall not be upon, 13
26:18 what evil is in *my h.*?
23 Lord deliv. into *my h.* 24:10
28:21 put my life in *my h.*
2 *Sam.* 5:19 wilt deliver Philistines into *my h.*? 1 *Chr.* 14:10
1 *K.* 13:6 that *my h.* may be rest.
2 *K.* 5:18 he leaneth on *my h.* in
2 *Chr.* 32:15 del. out of *my h.*? 17
*Job* 13:14 wher. put life in *my h.*?
29:20 bow was renewed in *my h.*
31:25 bec. *my h.* had gotten
27 mouth had kissed *my h.*
33:7 nei. shall *my h.* be heavy
*Ps.* 81:14 turned *my h.* ag. ene.
89:21 *my h.* shall be established
119:109 soul is contin. in *my h.*
*Prov.* 1:24 I have stretched *my h.*
*Is.* 1:25 turn *my h.* upon me
10:10 *my h.* hath found kingd.
13 by strength of *my h.*
14 *my h.* found riches of peo.
48:13 *my h.* laid foundation
50:2 *my h.* short. 11 this of *my h.*
51:16 cov. in shadow of *my h.*
66:2 *my h.* made, *Acts* 7:50
*Jer.* 6:12 I will stretch out *my h.* 15:6; 51:25
16:21 cause them to know *my h.*
25:15 wine-cup of fury at *my h.*
*Ezek.* 6:14 I stretch out *my h.*
12:7 dig. thro' wall with *my h.*
13:9 *my h.* shall be upon proph.
20:5 I lifted up *my h.* saying, I am the Lord your God, 6:23, 28, 42; 36:7; 44:12; 47:14
22 I withdrew *my h.*
22:13 smitten *my h.* at thy dish.
*Hos.* 2:10 none del. out of *my h.*
*Amos* 9:2 shall *my h.* take them
*Zec.* 2:9 shake *my h.* on them
13:7 turn *my h.* upon little ones
*John* 10:28 nor pluck out of *my h.*
29 none pluck out of *my F. h.*
20:25 thrust *my h.* into his side
1 *Cor.* 16:21 salutation of me, P. with *my* own *h.* 2 *Thes.* 3:17
*Gal.* 6:11 writ. wi. *my h.* *Phile.* 19

**Our HAND.**

*Gen.* 37:27 let not *our h.* be
*Deut.* 32:27 lest adv. say, *our h.*
*Jud.* 16:23 del. Samuel into *o. h.*
1 *Sam.* 14:10 into *our h.* 30:23
*Jer.* 11:21 thou die not by *our h.*
2 *Cor.* 10:16 made ready to *our h.*

**Out of,** *or* **out of the HAND.**

*Gen.* 48:22 took *o. of the h.* of A.
*Num.* 5:25 offering *o. of* wom. *h.*
11:15 kill me, I pray, *out of h.*
35:25 del. *out of h.* of avenger
1 *Sam.* 4:8 shall del. us *out of h.*
2 *Sam.* 12:7 *out of h.* of S. 22:1
23:21 spear *out of* Egyptian's h.
1 *K.* 11:12 rend kingdom *out of h.*
*Ps.* 71:4 del. *out of h.* of wicked
82:4 rid them *out of h.* of wick.
97:10 del. *out of h.* of wicked
*Jer.* 15:21 deliver thee *out of h.*
21:12 *out of the h.* of oppr. 22:3
32:4 *out of h.* of Chal. 38:18, 23
*Lam.* 5:8 none del. *out of* their *h.*
*Zec.* 11:6 *out of* their *h.* not del.
*John* 10:39 escaped *out of* their *h.*
*Acts* 12:11 deliver *out of h.* of H.
*Rev.* 8:4 *out of* angel's *h.* 10:10

**Right HAND.**

*Gen.* 48:14 *r. h.* on Ephraim's
*Ex.* 15:6 thy *r. h.* O L. is glori.
29:20 blood on thumb of *r. h.* *Lev.* 8:23, 24; 14:14, 17, 25, 28
*Deut.* 33:2 fr. *r. h.* went fiery law
*Jud.* 5:26 *right h.* to workman's
2 *Sam.* 20:9 J. took Am. w. *r. h.*
2 *K.* 23:13 on *right h.* of mount.

Job 23:9 hideth himself on r. h.
30:12 upon my r. h. rise youth
40:14 thine own r. h. can save
Ps. 16:8 he is at my right h.
11 at thy r. h. are pleasures
17:7 sav. by r. h. them that tru.
18:35 r. h. hath holden me up
20:6 saving strength of right h.
21:8 r. h. find those that hate
26:10 their r. h. is full of bribes
44:3 r. h. and arm saved them
45:4 thy r. h. shall teach ter. t.
9 on thy right h. the queen
48:10 thy r. h. full of righteous.
60:5 save with thy right h.
63:8 thy right h. upholdeth
73:23 holden me by my r. h.
74:11 why withdra. thy r. h.?
77:10 remember years of r. h.
78:54 mount. which r. h. purc.
80:15 vineyard wh. r. h. planted
17 hand be upon man of r. h.
89:25 I will set his r. h. in riv.
42 set up r. h. of adversaries
91:7 ten thousand fall at r. h.
98:1 his r. h. hath gotten victory
108:6 save me with thy right h.
109:6 let Satan stand at his r. h.
31 he shall stand at r. h. of poor
110:1 sit thou at my r. h. Luke 20:42; Acts 2:34; Heb. 1:13
5 L. at right h. shall strike
118:15 r. h. of L. doeth valiantly
16 r. h. of Lord is exalted
121:5 Lord is shade on thy r. h.
137:5 let r. h. forget cunning
138:7 thy r. h. shall save me
139:10 thy r. h. shall hold me
142:4 looked on my r. h. none
144:8 r. h. is r. h. of falseh. 11
Prov. 3:16 length of days in r. h.
27:16 ointm. of r. h. bewrayeth
Ec. 10:2 wi. man's heart at r. h.
Cant. 2:6 r. h. doth embrace me
8:3 r. h. should embrace me
Is. 41:10 uphold thee with r. h.
13 thy God will hold thy r. h.
44:20 is there not a lie in r. h.?
45:1 whose r. h. I have holden
48:13 r. h. hath spanned heav.
62:8 hath sworn by his right h.
63:12 led them by r. h. of Mos.
Jer. 22:24 signet on my right h.
Lam. 2:3 drawn back his r. h.
Ezek. 21:22 r. h. divinat. for Jer.
Hab. 2:16 cup of Lord's right h.
Zec. 3:1 Satan standing at r. h.
Mat. 5:30 if thy r. h. offend thee
6:3 let not left know r. h. doeth
Mark 14:62 see Son of man sit. on r. h. of power, Luke 22:69
16:19 on r. h. of God, Heb. 1:3; 8:1; 10:12; 12:2; 1 Pet. 3:22
Luke 6:6 man whose r. h. with.
Acts 2:25 he is on my right h.
33 by r. h. of God exalted, 5:31
3:7 he took him by the right h.
7:55 Jesus standing on r. h. 56
Rom. 8:34 is even at r. h. of God
Eph. 1:20 set him at his right h.
Col. 3:1 Ch. sitteth on r. h. of G.
Rev. 1:16 in r. h. 7 stars, 20; 2:1
5:1 I saw in his r. h. a book, 7
13:16 receive mark in their r. h.
See Left HAND.

**Right HANDS.**

Gal. 2:9 gave Bar. r. h. of fellow.

**Stretch forth, or out HAND.**

Gen. 22:10 Abra. s. f. h. to slay
Ex. 3:20 I will stretch out my h. on Egypt, 7:5; 9:15
14:16 s. out h. over sea, 26:7, 19
21 M. stretch o. h. over sea, 27
1 Sam. 26:9 s. forth h. ag. Lord's
Prov. 31:20 s. out h. to the poor
Ezek. 14:9 s. o. h. on that prophet
25:13 s. o. my h. upon Edom, 16
Dan. 11:42 s. f. h. on countries
Zep. 1:4 on Judah; 2:13 ag. Assy.
See STRONG.

**Thy HAND.**

Gen. 4:11 brother's blood fr. t. h.
16:6 thy maid is in thy h.
22:12 lay not thy h. upon the lad
24:2 thy h. under my thigh, 47:29
49:8 thy h. be in neck of enem.
Ex. 4:2 what is that in thy h.?
Ex. 4:17 take rod in t. h. 7:15; 17:5
8:5 stretch forth thy h. 9:22; 10:12,21; Mat. 12:13; Mark 3:5
Deut. 2:7 in works of thy h. 14:29; 15:10; 23:20; 28:8, 12, 20
24 have given into thy h. Sihon
3:2 del. Og and people into t. h.
13:9 thy h. shall be first on him
17 cleave nau. cursed th. to t. h.
14:25 bind up money in thy h.
15:7 shut thy h. fr. poor brother
8 open thy h. wide to brother
23:25 pluck the ears with thy h.
33:3 all his saints are in thy h.
Jos. 6:2 given into thy h. Jericho
9:25 we are in thy h. to do to us
10:6 slack not thy h. from serv.
Jud. 4:7 deliver Sisera into t. h.
8:15 Zeba and Zalmunna in t. h.
18:19 lay thy h. on thy mouth
1 Sam. 14:19 withdraw thy h.
2 Sam. 13:10 I may eat of thy h.
24:16 stay thy h. 1 Chr. 21:15
17 thy h. be ag. me, 1 Chr. 21:17
1 K. 17:11 morsel of bread in t. h.
20:42 let out of thy h. a man
2 K. 4:29 take my staff in thy h.
8:8 take a present in thy h.
9:1 take this box of oil in thy h.
13:16 put thy h. upon the bow
1 Chr. 4:10 t. h. might be with me
29:12 in thy h. power
16 cometh of thy h.
2 Chr. 20:6 in t. h. is th. not p.?
Ezr. 7:14 law of God is in thy h.
25 wisdom of G. that is in t. h.
Job 1:11 but put forth thy h. 2:5
12 put not forth thy h.
2:6 he is in thy h. save his life
10:7 none can del. out of thy h.
11:14 iniq. in thy h. put away
13:21 with. thy h. far from me
35:7 what receiv. he of thy h.?
Ps. 10:12 O God, lift up thy h.
14 to requite it with thy h.
17:14 from men which are thy h.
21:8 thy h. sh. find out all ene.
31:5 into thy h. I com. my spirit
15 my times are in thy h.
32:4 day and night thy h. heavy
38:2 thy h. press.; 39:10 blow of
74:11 why withd. thou thy h.?
80:17 t. h. on man of t. right h.
104:28 openest thy h. 145:16
119:173 t. h. help; 139:5 t. h. on
139:10 there shall t. h. lead me
144:7 send thy h. from above
Prov. 3:27 in power of thy h.
6:1 stricken thy h. with a stra.
30:32 lay t. h. upon thy mouth
Ec. 7:18 withdraw not thy h.
9:10 whats. thy h. findeth to do
11:6 in evening with. not thy h.
Is. 26:11 when thy h. is lifted up
42:6 I the Lord will hold thy h.
47:6 given my inheritance into thy h.
51:22 out of thy h. cup of trem.
57:10 th. hast found life of t. h.
64:8 we are the work of thy h.
Jer. 6:9 back t. h. as grape-gath.
15:17 I sat alone bec. of thy h.
25:28 refuse to take cup at t. h.
36:14 take in thy h. the roll
40:4 chains wh. were upon t. h.
Ezek. 3:18 his blood will I require at thy h. 20; 33:8
6:11 smite with thy h.
10:2 fill thy h. with coals of fire
23:31 give her cup into thy h.
37:17 shall become one in thy h.
38:12 turn thy h. on des. places
Dan. 2:38 fowls given into thy h.
Mic. 5:9 thy h. shall be lift up on
12 cut off witchc. out of thy h.
Mat. 18:8 if thy h. off. Mark 9:43
John 20:27 reach t. h. and thrust
Acts 4:28 to do whatever thy h.
30 stretch. forth thy h. to heal

**Your HAND.**

Gen. 43:12 double money in y. h.
Ex. 12:11 your staff in your h.
23:31 inhab. of land into y. h.
Deut. 12:7 rej. in all put y. h. to
Jos. 8:7 deliver it into your h. 20
24:8 gave Amorites into y. h.
Jud. 3:28 Moabites; 7:15 Midi.
2 Sam. 4:11 not req. blood of y. h.
2 Chr. 28:9 G. deliv. them to y. h.
Is. 1:12 require this at your h.?
Jer. 26:14 I am in your h.
44:25 and fulfilled with your h.
Mal. 1:10 nor accept offering at your h.
13 sho. I accept this of y. h.?
2:13 rec. with good will at y. h.
HANDED. See LEFT, WEAK.

**HANDBREADTH.**

Ex. 25:25 a h. round about, 37:12
1 K. 7:26 sea a h. thick, 2 Chr. 4:5
Ps. 39:5 made my days as a h.
Ezek. 40:5 six cubits long and a h.

**HAND broad.**

Ezek. 40:43 hooks a h. b. fastened

**HANDFUL.**

Lev. 2:2 take thereout h. flour, 5:12; 6:15; 9:17; Num. 5:26
1 K. 17:12 h. of meal in a barrel
Ps. 72:16 a h. of corn in earth
Ec. 4:6 better is h. with quietn.
Jer. 9:22 as h. after harvest-man

**HANDFULS.**

Gen. 41:47 brought forth by h.
Ex. 9:8 h. of ashes of furnace
Ruth 2:16 let fall also some h.
1 K. 20:10 dust of S. suffice for h.
Ezek. 13:19 pol. for h. of barley?

**HANDIWORK.**

Ps. 19:1 firmament show. his h.

**HANDKERCHIEFS.**

Acts 19:12 from body to sick h.

**HANDLE, S.**

Gen. 4:21 J. father such as h. harp
Jud. 5:14 that h. pen of writer
1 Chr. 12:8 h. spear, 2 Chr. 25:5
Ps. 115:7 hands, but they h. not
Cant. 5:5 myrrh on h. of lock
Jer. 2:8 that h. law knew me not
46:9 Libyans that h. the shield
Ezek 27:29 all that h. the oar
Luke 24:39 h. me; Col. 2:21 h. not

**HANDLED.**

Ezek. 21:11 furbished, may be h.
Mark 12:4 away shamefully h.
1 John 1:1 have h. of word of life

**HANDLETH, ING.**

Prov. 16:20 that h. matter wisely
Jer. 50:16 him that h. sickle
Ezek. 38:4 all of them h. swords
Amos 2:15 stand that h. bow
2 Cor. 4:2 not h. word of God

**HANDMAID.**

Gen. 16:1 Sarai had a h. Hagar
29:24 Zilpah to be L.'s h. 35:26
29 Bil. Rachel's h. 30:4; 35:25
Ex. 23:12 son of h. be refreshed
Jud. 19:19 bread and wine for h.
Ruth 2:13 spoken friendly to h.
3:9 answer. I am Ruth, thy h.

1 Sam. 1:11 affliction of h.
16 count not thy h. dau. of Bel.
18 let h. find grace in thy sight
25:24 let h. speak; 31 rem. h.
41 let thy h. wash feet of serv.
2 Sam. 14:6 thy h. had two sons
1 K. 1:13 didst swear to thy h.?
3:20 while thy h. slept
2 K. 4:2 thy h. hath not anything
16 do not lie to thy h.
Ps. 86:16 save the son of thy h.
116:6 servant, and son of h.
Prov. 30:23 a h. heir to mistress
Luke 1:38 behold the h. of the L.

**HANDMAIDEN.**

Luke 1:48 reg. low estate of h.

**HANDMAIDS.**

Gen. 33:1 divided children to h.
2 put h. and children foremost
Ruth 2:13 not like to one of h.
2 Sam. 6:20 uncov. in eyes of h.
Joel 2:29 on h. I pour S. Acts 2:18

**HANDS.**

Gen. 27:22 the h. are the h. of E.
49:24 h. made strong by h. of G.
Ex. 17:12 but Moses' h. heavy
Lev. 8:27 A. h. on his son's h.
Num. 6:19 put on h. of Nazarite
Deut. 4:28 gods, work of men's h.
27:15; 2 K. 19:18; 2 Chr. 32:19
9:15 tables of cov. in two h.
17 I cast th. out of my two h.
17:7 h. of witnesses first on him
Jud. 8:6 h. of Zeba and Zalm. 15
34 delivered them out of h. of enemies, 1 Sam. 14:48
19:27 h. were upon threshold
2 Sam. 2:7 h. be str. Zec. 8:9, 13
16:21 h. of all shall be strong
2 K. 3:11 water on h. of Elijah
9:35 fou. skull and palms of h.
1 Chr. 25:2 under the h. of Asaph
3 h. of Jedu. 6 h. of father
2 Chr. 15:7 let not h. be weak
Ezr. 4:4 weakened h. of people
Job 4:3 strengthened weak h.
16:11 turned me into h. of wick.
17:3 will strike h. with me?
9 clean h. shall be stronger
Ps. 24:4 he that hath clean h.
26:10 h. is mis. 47:1 clap h.
58:2 weigh the viol. of your h.
Ps. 68:31 Ethiopia stretch out h.
115:4 their idols the work of men's h. 135:15; Is. 37:19
7 they have h. but handle not
134:2 lift up h. in the sanctuary
140:4 keep me fr. h. of wicked
Prov. 6:10 folding of h. 24:33
17 hate the h. shed inno. blo.
12:14 recompense of man's h.
14:1 foolish plucketh it with h.
17:18 striketh h. becom. surety
22:26 be not one that strike h.
30:28 spider taketh hold wi. h.
31:13 work. willing. with her h.
19 layeth her h. to the spindle
31 give her of the fruit of h.
Ec. 4:6 both h. full with travel
7:26 h. as ba. 10:18 idlen. of h.
Cant. 7:1 work of h. of workm.
Is. 1:15 spread your h. hide my eyes, your h. full of blood
2:8 worship work of th. own h.
13:7 theref. shall all h. be faint
35:3 strengthen ye weak h.
45:9 he hath no h.
59:3 h. are defiled with blood
Jer. 4:31 spr. h. say. Woe is me
10:3 work of h. of workmen
9 and of the h. of the founder
23:14 they strengthen also h. of evil-doers, Ezek. 13:22
33:13 under h. of him that tell.
38:4 weaken h. of men of war
48:37 upon all h. sh. be cuttings

Lam. 1:17 Zion spreadeth her h.
4:2 the work of h. of the potter
10 h. of pitiful women have s.
Ezek. 7:17 h. sh. be feeble, 21:7
Dan. 2:34 stone cut without h. 45
Mic. 7:3 may do evil wi. both h.
Nah. 3:19 shall clap h. over thee
Hag. 2:17 lab. of h. I smote you
Zec. 4:9 h. of Zer. laid founda.
Mat. 15:20 unwa. h. Mark 7:2, 5
17:22 betra. into h. of men, 26:45; Mark 9:31; Luke 9:44
18:8 two h. c. into fire, Mark 9:43
Mark 14:58 temple made with h.
Luke 22:53 stretched forth no h.
24:7 delivered to h. of sinful m.
Acts 2:23 wicked h. have crucifi.
5:12 h. of apostles wonders wr.
7:48 not in te. made w. h. 17:24
8:18 laying on of the apostles' h.
11:30 by h. of Barnabas and S.
17:25 nei. worship. wi. men's h.
19:26 no gods are made with h.
20:34 h. minis. to my necessities
2 Cor. 5:1 house not made with h.
Eph. 2:11 circum. in flesh by h.
Col. 2:11 circumcision without h.
1 Thes. 4:11 study to work w. h.
1 Tim. 2:8 lifting up holy h.
4:14 h. of the presby. Heb. 6:2
Heb. 9:11 taberna. not made w. h.
24 not ent. place made with h.
10:31 fall in h. of the living G.
12:12 wherefore lift up the h.
Jam. 4:8 cleanse your h. sinners

See CLAP.

**His HANDS.**

Gen. 27:23 his h. hairy as brother
48:14 guiding his h. wittingly
Ex. 17:12 A. and H. stayed h. h.
32:19 M. cast tables out of h. h.
Lev. 15:11 not rinsed h. h. in w.
16:21 lay both h. h. upon head
Num. 24:10 Balak smote h. h. to.
Deut. 33:11 accept work of h. h.
34:9 M. laid his h. upon Joshua
Jud. 9:16 accord. to des. of h. h.
1 Sam. 5:4 palms of h. h. cut off
14:13 Jona. climbed up on h. h.
1 K. 8:22 S. spread h. h. tow. heaven, 38:54; 2 Chr. 6:12, 13, 29
16:7 pro. him with work of h. h.
2 K. 4:34 and put h. h. upon h. h.
13:16 put h. h. up. king's hands
Job 1:10 blessed work of his h.
5:18 and his h. make whole
20:10 h. h. restore their goods
34:37 clappeth h. h. among us
Ps. 9:16 wicked snared in h. h.
28:5 regard not opera. of h. h.
78:72 guided by skilful. of h. h.
81:6 h. h. were deliv. from pots
95:5 his h. formed dry land
111:7 works of h. h. are verity
Prov. 21:25 his h. refuse to labor
Ec. 4:5 fool fold. his h. together
Cant. 5:14 h. h. are as gold rings
Is. 3:11 reward of h. h. be given
5:12 nor consider opera. of h. h.
17:8 altars, work of h. h.
25:11 L. shall spread forth his h.
33:15 shaketh his h.
Jer. 30:6 man w. h. h. on loins?
Hab. 3:10 lifted his h. on high
Mat. 19:13 h. h. on th. Mark 10:16
27:24 washed h. h. be. multitude
Mark 8:23 his h. on his eyes, 25
Luke 24:40 show. h. h. John 20:20
50 lifted up h. h. blessed them
John 13:3 given all th. into his h.
20:25 see in h. h. print of nails
Acts 9:17 putting his h. on him
12:1 Herod stretched forth his h.
7 his chains fell off from h. h.
2 Cor. 11:33 by wall, escap. h. h.
Eph. 4:28 working with h. h.

See LAY, LAID.

**My HANDS.**

Gen. 20:5 in innocency of my h.
Jud. 12:3 I put my life in my h.
2 Sam. 22:21 according to cleanness of my h. Ps. 18:20, 24
35 he teacheth my h. to war, Ps. 18:34; 144:1
Neh. 6:9 O God, strengthen my h.
Job 9:30 make my h. ne. so clean
16:17 any injustice in my h.
31:7 any blot cleaved to my h.
Ps. 7:3 if there be iniq. in my h.
22:16 pierced my h. and my feet
26:6 wash my h. in innocency
28:2 lift my h. tow. thy oracle
63:4 lift my h. in thy name
73:13 I have washed my h.
119:48 my h. will I lift
141:2 lifting up my h. as even.
143:6 stretch forth my h.
Is. 19:25 bless. be work of my h.
45:11 concerning work of my h.
12 my h. stretched out heavens
49:16 on palms of my h.
60:21 people the work of my h.
65:2 I have spread out my h.
Dan. 3:15 del. you out of my h.
10:10 on the palms of my h.
Luke 24:39 be. my h. John 20:27
John 13:9 also my h. and head
Rom. 10:21 I stretched my h.
2 Tim. 1:6 by putting on of m. h.

**Our HANDS.**

Gen. 5:29 concerning toil of o. h.
Deut. 21:7 o. h. have not shed b.
Jos. 2:24 delivered into our h.
Jud. 13:23 a meat-off. at our h.
1 Sam. 17:47 give you into o. h.
Ps. 44:20 stretched out our h.
90:17 establish work of our h.
Jer. 6:24 our h. wax feeble
Lam. 3:41 our heart with our h.
Hos. 14:3 work of our h.
1 Cor. 4:12 work. with our own h.
1 John 1:1 our h. hand. word of

**Their HANDS.**

Ex. 29:10 put t. h. on head
15 put t. h. on head of ram, 19
Num. 8:10 put their h. on Levit.
12 lay their h. on the bullock
Deut. 1:25 brought fruit in t. h.
21:6 wash t. h. over the heifer
2 Sam. 4:12 they cut off their h.
2 K. 11:12 they clapped their h.
22:17 prov. me to anger with works of their h. 2 Chr. 34:25
Ezr. 1:6 strengthened their h.
5:8 work prospereth in their h.
6:22 strengthen t. h. in work
Neh. 2:18 streng. t. h. for work
6:9 their h. shall be weakened
Job 5:12 t. h. cannot perf. enter.
30:2 whereto stre. t. h. profit?
Ps. 76:5 m. of mi. not found t. h.
91:12 angels bear thee in t. h.
125:3 lest right. put t. h. to in.
Is. 25:11 tog. with spoils of t. h.
59:6 act of violence is in t. h.
65:22 elect enjoy work of t. h.
Jer. 1:16 worshipped works t. h.
32:30 prov. with works of t. h.
Ezek. 10:12 t. h. and wings full
23:37 blood is in their h. 45
Jon. 3:8 turn from viol. in t. h.
Hag. 2:14 ev. work of t. h. uncl.
Mat. 4:6 in their h. they shall bear thee up, Luke 4:11
15:2 wash not t. h. wh. they eat
26:67 others smote him with the palms of t. h. Mark 14:65
Mark 7:3 exc. wash t. h. eat not
Luke 6:1 rubbing them in t. h.
John 19:3 smote him with their h.
Acts 14:3 won. to be done by t. h.

Rev. 7:9 wh. robes, palms in t. h.
9:20 repented not of wor. of t. h.
20:4 nor had rec. mark in t. h.

**Thy HANDS.**

Deut. 16:15 Lord shall bless thee in all works of thy h. 24:19
Jud. 7:11 afterw. thy h. be stren.
2 Sam. 3:34 t. h. were not bound
Job 10:3 to despise work of h.?
8 thy h. made and fashion. me
14:15 desire to work of thy h.
22:30 deliv. by pureness of t. h.
Ps. 8:6 domin. over works of t. h.
102:25 heavens work of thy h.
119:73 thy h. have made me
128:2 shalt eat labor of thy h.
138:8 forsake not works of t. h.
143:5 I muse on work of thy h.
Jer. 2:37 thy h. on thy head
Lam. 2:19 lift thy h. for thy chil.
Mic. 5:13 no more worship t. h.
Zec. 13:6 wh. are these in t. h.?
Luke 23:46 to thy h. I com. my
John 21:18 shalt stretch thy h.
Heb. 1:10 heavens works of t. h.
2:7 set him over works of thy h.

**HANDSTAVES.**

Ezek. 39:9 shall burn the h.

**HANDWEAPON.**

Num. 35:18 smite him with h.

**HANDWRITING.**

Col. 2:14 blotting out the h.

**HANG.**

Gen. 40:19 Pharaoh shall h. thee
Num. 25:4 h. them bef. the Lord
Deut. 21:22 if thou h. him
28:66 thy life shall h. in doubt
Est. 6:4 speak to h. Mordecai
7:9 king said, h. him thereon
Is. 22:24 they sh. h. on him glory
Lam. 2:10 virgins h. their heads
Ezek. 15:3 take pin to h. any ves.
Mat. 22:40 on th. two h. all law
Acts 28:4 ven. beast h. on hand
Heb. 12:12 up hands wh. h. down

**HANGED.**

Gen. 40:22 h. chief baker, 41:13
Deut. 21:23 that is h. is accursed
2 Sam. 17:23 Ahitho. h.; 18:10 A.
21:9 seven sons of Saul h. they
Est. 2:23 chamberlains were h.
7:10 h. Ham.; 9:14 h. ten sons
Ps. 137:2 h. harps on willows
Lam. 5:12 princes h. by hands
Ezek. 27:10 h. the shield, 11
Mat. 18:6 bet. millst. were h. ab. his neck, Mark 9:42; Lu. 17:2
27:5 Judas went and h. himself
Luke 23:39 thieves who were h.
Acts 5:30 and h. on tree, 10:39

**HANGETH.**

Job 26:7 h. earth upon nothing
Gal. 3:13 cursed ev. one h. on tr.

**HANGING.**

Jos. 10:26 h. on trees till evening

**HANGING, Substantive.**

Ex. 26:36 make h. for door of tent
37 make for the h. five pillars
27:16 h. for court-gate, 38:18; 39:40; 40:8, 33
35:15 h. for door enter. tabernacle, 36:37; 39:38; 40:5, 28

**HANGINGS.**

Ex. 27:9 h. 100 cub. 11; 38:9, 11
12 shall be h. of 50 cubits, 38:12
35:17 h. of court, 38:9, 16, 18; 39:40; Num. 3:26; 4:26
2 K. 23:7 women wove h. for gr.

HANNAH. 1 Sam. 1:2; 2:21
HANOCH. Gen. 25:4; 46:9; Num. 26:5; 1 Chr. 1:33; 5:3

**HANUN.**

2 Sam. 10:1 H. reig. 1 Chr. 19:4
Neh. 3:13 H. repaired val. gate, 30

**HAPLY.**

Mark 11:13 if h. he mi. find fruit
Luke 14:29 lest h. after laid fou.
Acts 5:39 lest h. found fight a. G.
17:27 if h. they might feel

**HAPPEN.**

Prov. 12:21 no evil h. to the just
Is. 41:22 show us what shall h.

**HAPPENED.**

2 Sam. 1:6 as I h. by chance on
Jer. 44:23 therefore evil is h.
Rom. 11:25 blindness is h. to Is.
1 Cor. 10:11 th. h. for ensamples
Phil. 1:12 things h. me fallen
1 Pet. 4:12 strange thing h. to y.
2 Pet. 2:22 h. according to prov.

**HAPPENETH.**

Ec. 2:14 one ev. h. to them all
15 as it h. to fool, so it h. to me
9:11 time and chance h. to all

**HAPPY.**

Deut. 33:29 h. art thou, O Israel
1 K. 10:8 h. thy men, h. thy servants, 2 Chr. 9:7
Job 5:17 h. is man. wh. G. correc.
Ps. 127:5 h. man hath quiver full
137:8 h. he who reward. thee, 9
144:15 h. people in such a case, h. peo. whose God is the L.
146:5 h. is he that hath G. of J.
Prov. 3:13 h. man find. wisdom
14:21 h. he hath mercy on poor
16:20 whoso trust. in L. h. is he
28:14 h. is man that fear. alway
29:18 that keepeth law, h. is he
Jer. 12:1 why h. deal treacher.?
Mal. 3:15 we call the proud h.
Jon. 13:17 kn. things, h. if do th.
Rom. 14:22 h. is he that condemn.
Jam. 5:11 them h. who endure
1 Pet. 3.14 suffer for righte. h. ye
4:14 reproached for Ch. h. ye

**HAPPIER.**

1 Cor. 7:40 she is h. if she abide

**HARAN, a man.**

Gen. 11:26 T. begat H. 27, 28, 31

**HARAN, a place.**

Gen. 11;31 Terah came to H. 32
12:4 Abram departed out of H.
27:43 flee to H. 28:10; 29:4
2 K. 19:12 fath. destr. H. Is. 37:12

HARBONAH. Est. 1:10; 7:9

**HARD.**

Gen. 18:14 any th. too h. for L.?
35:16 Rachel had h. labor, 17
Ex. 1:14 lives bit. with h. bond.
Deut. 1:17 cause too h. bring me
17:8 matter too h. in judgment
26:6 Egypt laid on h. bondage
2 Sam. 3:39 sons of Zeruiah too h.
1 K. 10:1 to prove with h. questions, 2 Chr. 9:1
2 K. 2:10 thou hast asked h. th.
Job 41:24 as h. as piece of millst.
Ps. 60:3 showed peo. h. things
94:4 how long wick. spe. h. th.
Prov. 13:15 way of transgr. is h.
Jer. 32:17 nothing too h. 27
Ezek. 3:5 to people of h. lang. 6
Mat. 25:24 I knew thou art h.
Mark 10:24 h. for th. tru. in rich.
John 6:60 this is a h. saying
Acts 9:5 h. to kick ag. pri. 26:14
Heb. 5.11 and h. to be uttered
2 Pet. 3:16 thi. h. to be underst.
Jude 15 convince of h. speeches

**HARD, Adjective.**

Lev. 3:9 rump off h. backbone
1 Chr. 19:4 cut garm. h. by but.
Ps. 63:8 followeth h. after thee
Jon. 1:13 rowed h. to br. to land
Acts 18:7 joined h. to synagogue

**HARDEN.**

Ex. 4:21 I will h. Pharaoh's heart, 7:3; 14:4
14:17 h. hearts of Egyptians
Deut. 15:7 shalt not h. thy heart
Jos. 11:20 L. to h. their hearts
Job 6:10 h. myself in sorrow
Ps. 95:8 h. not your hearts, Heb. 3:8, 15; 4:7

**HARDENED.**

Ex. 7:13 L. h. Phar.'s heart, 9:12; 10:1, 20, 27; 11:10; 14:8
14 he. h.; 22 was h. 8:19; 9:7, 35
8:15 he h. his heart, 32; 9:34
Deut. 2:30 G. h. his spirit
2 K. 17:14 they h. their necks
Neh. 9:16 h. th. necks, 17, 29
Job 9:4 who hath h. himself.
39:16 h. against her young ones
Is. 63:17 why hast thou h. heart?
Jer. 7:26 but h. their neck
Dan. 5:20 his mind h. in pride
Mark 6:52 for their heart was h.
8:17 have ye your heart yet h.?
John 12:40 blinded eyes, h. heart
Acts 19:9 when divers were h.
Heb. 3:13 lest any of you be h.

**HARDENETH.**

Prov. 21:29 wicked man h. face
28:14 h. heart fall into mischief
29:1 being reproved h. his neck
Rom. 9:18 whom he will he h.

**HARD-HEARTED.**

Ezek. 3:7 house of Israel are h.-h.

**HARDER.**

Prov. 18:19 h. to be won th. city
Jer. 5:3 made faces h. than rock
Ezek. 3:9 h. than flint made fore.

**HARDLY.**

Is. 8:21 shall pass through it h.
Mat. 19:23 rich m. h. ent. kingd. of G. Mark 10:23; Luke 18:24
Luke 9:39 h. departeth from him

**HARDNESS.**

Job 38:38 dust groweth into h.
Mat 19:8 h. of hearts, Mark 10:5
Mark 3:5 grieved for h. of heart
Mark 16:14 upb. with h. of heart
Rom. 2:5 h. and impenitent heart
2 Tim. 2:3 h. as soldier of J. C.

**HARE.**

Lev. 11:6 h. is uncl. Deut. 14:7

**HARLOT.**

Gen. 34:31 d. wi. sister as wi. h.
38:15 he thought her to be a h.
Lev. 21:14 high-priest not take h.
Jos. 2:1 spies came to h.'s house
6:17 only Rahab the h. sh. live
Jud. 16:1 Sam. saw there a h.
Prov. 7:10 woman wi. attire of h.
Is. 1:21 faithful city become h.
23:15 after 70 years T. sing as h.
Jer. 2:20 wanderest, playing h.
3:1 thou hast played the h. 6, 8
Ezek. 16:15 playedst the h.
16 playedst h.; 28 played h.
41 cause to cease from play. h.
23:5 Aholah played the h.
Hos. 2:5 mother hath played h.
4:15 though Israel play the h.
Joel 3:3 given a boy for a h.
Mic. 1:7 return to the hire of h.
Nah. 3:4 whored. of well fav. h.
1 Cor. 6:15 make th. mem. of h.
16 is joined to a h. is one body
Heb. 11:31 h. Rahab perished not
Jam. 2:25 R. the h. just. by wor.

**HARLOTS.**

Prov. 29:3 keepeth comp. with h.
Jer. 5:7 assemble troops in h. h.
Hos. 4:14 sacrifice with h.
Mat. 21:31 h. go into king. of G.
32 publicans and h. believed h.
Luke 15:30 devoured liv. with h.

Rev. 17:5 Babylon, mother of h.

**HARM.**

Lev. 5:16 amends for h. done
2 K. 4:41 was no h. in the pot
1 Chr. 16:22 pro. no h. Ps. 105:15
Prov. 3:30 if he have done no h.
Jer. 39:12 do him no h.
Acts 16:28 no h.; 27:21 gained h.
28:5 felt no h.; 6 saw no h.; 21 spake any h.

**HARM, Verb.**

1 Pet. 3:13 h. you, if fol. of good.

**HARMLESS.**

Mat. 10:16 serp. and h. as doves
Phil. 2:15 may be h. sons of G.
Heb. 7:26 holy, h. and undefiled

**HARNESS, Substantive.**

2 K. 20:11 girdeth on h. boast
22:34 joints of h. 2 Chr. 18:33
2 Chr. 9:24 brought every man h.

**HARNESS, ED, Verb.**

Ex. 13:18 Israel went up h.
Jer. 46:4 h. horses, up horsemen

HAROD. Jud. 7:1
HAROSHETH. Jud. 4:2

**HARP.**

Gen. 4:21 fa. of th. th. handle h.
1 Sam. 10:5 meet proph. with h.
16:16 cunning player on h.
1 Chr. 25:3 prophesied with h.
Job 21:12 the timbrel and h.
30:31 h. is turned to mourning
Ps. 33:2 praise L. with h. 150:3
43:4 on the h. will I praise thee
49:4 open dark saying upon h.
57:8 psaltery and h. 108:2
71:22 I will sing with h. 92:3; 98:5; 147:7; 149:3
81:2 bring hither the pleasant h.
Is. 5:12 h. and viol in their feasts
16:11 bowels sound like a h.
Dan. 3:5 sound of h. 7, 10, 15
1 Cor. 14:7 whether pipe or h.

**HARPS.**

2 Sam. 6:5 D. and Is. played h.
1 K. 10:12 made of almug-trees h.
Ps. 137:2 hanged h. upon willows
Rev. 5:8 every one of them h.
14:2 harp. with h.; 15:2 h. of G.

See CYMBAL.

**HARPED.**

1 Cor. 14:7 kn. what piped or h.?

**HARPERS.**

Rev. 14:2 I heard the voice of h.
18:22 voice of h. heard no more

**HARROW.**

Job 39:10 will he h. valleys.

**HARROWS.**

2 Sam. 12:31 under h. of iron
1 Chr. 20:3 cut with saws and h.

**HART, S.**

Deut. 12:15 may eat flesh of the h. 14:5; 15:22
Ps. 42:1 as h. panteth after water
Is. 35:6 lame man leap as a h.
Lam. 1:6 princes become like h.

See YOUNG.

**HARVEST.**

Gen. 8:22 earth rem. h. not cease
45:6 shall nei. be earing nor h.
Ex. 23:16 the feast of h. 34:22
Lev. 25:5 accord of h. not reap
1 Sam. 6:13 men reaping their h.
12:17 is it not wheat-h. to-day?
Job 5:5 whose h. hungry eateth
Prov. 6:8 ant gather food in h.
10:5 sleepeth in h. caus. shame
26:1 snow in sum. as rain in h.
Is. 9:3 according to joy in h.
16:9 shouting for h. is fallen
17:11 h. be heap in day of grief
18:4 cloud of dew in heat of h.
5 afore h. when bud is perfect
23:3 h. of the river is her reven.
Jer. 5:17 they shall eat up thy h.
24 reserveth to us weeks of h.
8:20 h. is past, sum. is ended
Joel 1:11 the h. of field perished
3:13 in sickle, for the h. is ripe
Amos 4:7 yet three months to h.
Mat. 9:37 the h. is plenteous
38 pray L. h. to send, Luke 10:2
13:30 grow together until h.
39 the h. is end of the world
Mark 4:29 put in sickle, h. come
Luke 10:2 said, The h. is great
John 4:35 fields are white to h.
Rev. 14:15 the h. of earth is ripe

**HARVEST-MAN.**

Is. 17:5 when h. m. gather. corn
Jer. 9:22 the handful after h.-m.

**Time of HARVEST.**

Jos. 3:15 Jord. overfloweth t. h.
Prov. 25:13 cold of snow t. of h.
Jer. 50:16 handleth sickle in h.-t.
51:33 the t. of her h. shall come
Mat. 13:30 t. of h. say to reapers

**HAST.**

Mat. 19:21 sell all thou h. Mark 10:21; Luke 18:22
25:25 there thou h. that is thine
John 6:68 h. words of eternal life
7:20 thou h. a devil, 8:48, 52
Rom. 14:22 h. thou faith?
1 Cor. 4:7 what h. thou that did.
Jam. 2:18 thou h. faith
Rev. 2:6 but this thou h.
8 h. a little strength, 3:1, 4
11 hold that fast which thou h.

**HASTE, Substantive.**

Ex. 12:11 ye shall eat in h.
33 out of land in h. Deut. 16:3
1 Sam. 21:8 king's business required h.
Ps. 31:22 said in h. I am cut off
116:11 I said in h. All men liars
Is. 52:12 shall not go out with h.
Dan. 3:24 king rose in h.
6:19 went in h. to den of lions
Mark 6:25 came in h. to the king
Luke 1:39 went to hill-cou. w. h.

**HASTE.**

Gen. 19:22 h. thee, escape thither
1 Sam. 23:27 h. thee, for Philis.
Ps. 22:19 strength, h. to help me

See MAKE HASTE.

**HASTED.**

Gen. 18:7 and he h. to dress it
Jos. 4:10 people h. over Jordan
10:13 the sun h. not to go down
1 Sam. 17:48 David h. and ran to
25:23 Abigail saw Da. she h. 42
28:24 the witch at Endor h.
1 K. 20:41 prophet h. and took
2 Chr. 26:20 himself h. to go out
Est. 6:12 Haman h. to his house
14 they h. to bring Haman
Job 31:5 foot hath h. to deceit
Ps. 48:5 and h. away, 104:7
Acts 20:16 Paul h. to Jerusalem

**HASTEN.**

Ps. 16:4 h. after another god
55:8 I would h. my escape
Ec. 2:25 who can h. more than I?
Is. 60:22 L. will h. in his time
Jer. 1:12 I will h. my word

**HASTENED, ETH.**

Est. 3:15 being h. by king, 8:14
Is. 51:14 the exile h. to be loosed
Jer. 17:16 not h. fr. being pastor

**HASTETH.**

Job 9:26 as eagle that h. to prey
Prov. 7:23 as a bird h. to snare
19:2 he that h. wi. his feet sin.
28:22 h. to be rich, hath evil eye
Ec. 1:5 sun h. to where he arose
Hab. 1:8 fly as eagle that h.
Zep. 1:14 day of Lord h. greatly

**HASTILY.**

Jud. 2:23 without driving th. h.
Prov. 20:21 inheritance gotten h.
25:8 go not forth h. to strive
John 11:31 saw Mary she rose h.

**HASTING.**

Is. 16:5 and h. righteousness
2 Pet. 3:12 h. to day of the Lord

**HASTY.**

Prov. 14:29 h. of spirit exal. folly.
29:20 a man h. in words?
Ec. 5:2 let not thy heart be h.
7:9 be not h. in thy spirit
8:3 not too h. to go out of sight
Is. 28:4 as h. fruit before summer
Dan. 2:15 why is decree so h.?
Hab. 1:6 bitter and h. nation

**HATCH, ETH.**

Is. 34:15 owl shall h. and gather
59:5 they h. cockatrice's eggs
Jer. 17:11 as partridge on eggs h.

**HATE.**

Gen. 24:60 possess of those th. h.
Lev. 19:17 shalt not h. brother
26:17 th. h. you sh. reign over
Num. 10:35 let them that h. thee
Deut. 22:13 go unto her and h.
24:3 if the latter husband h. her
2 Chr. 19:2 love them that h. L.?
Job 8:22 h. thee clothed with sh.
Ps. 21:8 find those that h. thee
34:21 th. h. righteous sh. be des.
68:1 that h. him flee before him
83:2 h. thee have lifted up head
89:23 plague them that h. him
97:10 ye that love Lord h. evil
105:25 turned their heart to h.
129:5 let th. be turned that h. Z.
Prov. 1:22 fools, will ye h. know.
6:16 these six doth the Lord h.
8:13 fear of the Lord is to h. evil
9:8 rep. not scorner, lest h. thee
19:7 all brethren of poor h. him
29:10 bloodthirsty h. the uprig.
Ec. 3:8 time to l. and time to h.
Amos 5:10 they h. him that reb.
15 h. the evil, love the good
Mic. 3:2 h. good, and love evil
Mat. 5:43 love neigh. h. enemy
44 good to th. h. y. Luke 6:27
6:24 he will h. one, Luke 16:13
24:10 betray and h. one another
Luke 1:71 saved from hand th. h.
6:22 blessed are ye when men h.
14:26 h. not his father
John 7:7 the world cannot h. you
15:18 world h. you, 1 John 3:13
Rev. 17:16 these shall h. whore

**I HATE.**

1 K. 22:8 I h. him, 2 Chr. 18:7
Ps. 101:3 I h. work of them
119:104 I h. every false way, 128
113 I h. vain th. thy law I love
163 I h. and abhor lying
139:21 I h. them that hate thee?
22 I h. them with perfect hatr.
Prov. 8:13 froward mouth do I h.
Is. 61:8 I h. robbery for burnt-off.
Jer. 44:4 do not this thing I h.
Amos 5:21 I h. your feast-days
Zec. 8:17 these are things I h.
Rom. 7:15 what I h. that do I
Rev. 2:6 deeds of Nicolait. I h. 15

**HATE me.**

Gen. 26:27 come, seeing h. me?
Ex. 20:5 to third and fourth gen. of them that h. me, Deut. 5:9
Deut. 32:41 rew. them that h. me
2 Sam. 22:41 destroy them that h. me, Ps. 18:40
Ps. 9:13 suff. of them that h. me
25:19 h. me with cruel hatred
35:19 let them wink that h. me
38:19 h. me wrong. many, 69:4

41:7 all that h. me whisper tog.
69:14 deliv. fr. them that h. me
118:7 see desire on th. that h. me
Prov. 8:36 they that h. me

**HATED.**

Gen. 27:41 Esau h. Jacob
37:4 h. Joseph yet the more, 5, 8
49:23 shot at him and h. him
Deut. 1:27 bec. Lord h. us, 9:28
4:42 h. him n. 19:4, 6; Jos. 20:5
21:17 sh. acknowledge son of h.
Jud. 15:2 I thought thou h. her
2 Sam. 5:8 lame and blind are h.
Est. 9:1 rule them that h. them
Ps. 26:5 h. congreg. of evil-doers
31:6 I h. them that regard lying
44:7 put them to shame that h.
106:41 they that h. them ruled
Prov. 1:29 they h. knowledge
5:12 how have I h. instruction!
14:17 man of wicked dev. is h.
Prov. 14:20 poor is h. even of nei.
Ec. 2:17 h. life; I h. labor
Is. 60:15 been forsaken and h.
Jer. 12:8 have I h. my heritage
Ezek. 16:37 gather them thou h.
35:6 since thou hast not h. blood
Hos. 9:15 h. them for wicked.
Mal. 1:3 I h. Esau, Rom. 9:13
Mat. 10:22 ye shall be h. Mark 13:13; Luke 21:17
24:9 ye shall be h. of all nations
Luke 19:14 his citizens h. him
John 15:18 it h. me bef. it h. you
24 seen and h. both me and F.
25 they h. me without a cause
17:14 the world hath h. them
Eph. 5:29 no man h. own flesh
Heb. 1:9 thou hast h. iniquity

**HATEFUL, LY.**

Ps. 36:2 iniq. be found to be h.
Ezek. 23:29 sh. deal with thee h.
Tit. 3:3 h. hating one another
Rev. 18:2 cage uncl. and h. bird

**HATERS.**

Ps. 81:15 h. of L. should submit
Rom. 1:30 backbiters, h. of God

**HATEST.**

2 Sam. 19:6 and h. thy friends
Ps. 5:5 h. workers of iniquity
45:7 lov. righte. h. wickedness
50:17 thou h. instruction
Rev. 2:6 h. deeds of Nicolaitans

**HATETH.**

Deut. 7:10 not slack to him h.
16:22 nor set up image Lord h.
Job 34:17 sh. he who h. right go.?
Ps. 11:5 loveth viol. his soul h.
120:6 dwelt him that h. peace
Prov. 11:15 h. suretyship is sure
12:1 he that h. reproof is brutish
13:5 a righteous man h. lying
24 he that spareth rod h. son
15:10 that h. reproof shall die
27 he that h. gifts shall live
26:24 that h. dissemb. with lips
28 lying tongue h. those afflic.
28:16 h. cove. sh. prolong days
29:24 partner with thief h. soul
Is. 1:14 appo. feasts my soul h.
Mal. 2:16 he h. putting away
John 3:20 ev. one doeth evil h. l.
7:7 me world h. bec. I testify
12:25 h. life in world sh. keep it
15:19 not of world, world h. you
23 h. me h. my Father also
1 John 2:9 h. bro. is in darkn. 11
3:15 h. his brother is murderer
4:20 I love G. h. brother, is liar

**HATING.**

Ex. 18:21 h. coveteousness
Tit. 3:3 and h. one another
Jude 23 h. garm. spotted by flesh

**HATH.**

Prov. 23:29 who h. woe? who h. sorrow? who h. wounds?
Is. 45:9 h. no ha. 50:10 no light
55:1 h. no money, buy and eat
Jer. 49:1 h. I. no sons? h. no heir?
Mat. 8:20 h. not where to lay his head, Luke 9:58
11:15 he that h. ears to hear. 13:9, 43; Mark 4:9; Luke 8:8; 14:35; Rev. 2:7'
13:12 whoso. h. to him shall be giv. who h. not, sh. be taken that he h. 25:29; Mark 4:25; Luke 8:18; 19:26
44 selleth all he h. buyeth field
1 John 5:12 he that h. the Son h. life, h. not Son, h. not life
2 John 9 abideth not in Ch. h. not G. abideth h. Father and S.

**HATRED.**

Num. 35:20 he thrust him of h.
Ps. 25:19 hate me with cruel h.
109:3 comp. me about with h.
5 rewarded me h. for my love
139:22 hate them with perf. h.
Prov. 10:12 h. stirreth up strifes
18 hideth h. with lying lips
15:17 than stalled ox and h.
Ec. 9:1 know. either love or h.
6 their h. and envy perished
Ezek. 25:15 destroy it for old h.
35:5 thou hast had perpetual h.
Hos. 9:8 proph. is h. in ho. of G.
Gal. 5:20 witchcraft, h. variance

**HATS.**

Dan. 3:21 bound in hosen and h.

**HAUGHTY.**

2 Sam. 22:28 th. eyes are upon h.
Ps. 131:1 L. my heart is not h.
Prov. 16:18 h. spirit before a fall
18:12 before destruction heart h.
21:24 h. scorner is his name
Is. 3:16 daughters of Zion are h.
24:4 the h. people of the earth
Zep. 3:11 no more h.

**HAUGHTINESS.**

Is. 2:11 h. of men bowed down
17 h. of men shall be made low
13:11 lay low the h. of terrible
16:6 heard h. of Moab, Jer. 48:29

**HAUNT, Substantive.**

1 Sam. 23:22 see where his h. is

**HAUNT.**

1 Sam. 30:31 where D. wont to h.
Ezek. 26:17 ter. be on all that h.

HAVE. See COMPASSION, DOMINION, etc.

**HAVEN.**

Gen. 49:13 Zebulun dwell at h.
Ps. 107:30 bringeth to desired h.
Acts 27:12 h. not commodious

**HAVOC.**

Acts 8:3 S. made h. of the church

**HAWK.**

Lev. 11:16 h. abom. Deut. 14:15
Job 39:26 doth h. fly by wisdom?

**HAY.**

Prov. 27:25 h. appear. and grass
Is. 15:6 the h. is withered away
1 Cor. 3:12 buildeth on found. h.

**HAZAEL.**

1 K. 19:15 ano. H. to be king, 17
2 K. 8:9 H. went to meet Elisha
10:32 H. smote them, Amos 1:4
12:17 H. set face to go to Jeru.
13:3 Israel into the hand of H.

**HAZEL.**

Gen. 30:37 Jacob took rods of h.

HAZELELPONI. 1 Chr. 4:3
HAZEROTH. Num. 11:35; 12:16; 33:17

**HAZOR.**

Jos. 11:10 Joshua took H.
Jud. 4:2; 1 K. 9:15; 2 K. 15:29
Jer. 49:30 dwell deep, inh. of H.

**HE.**

Gen. 3:16 h. shall rule over thee
49:8 h. whom bret. shall praise
Deut. 32:39 I am h. and there is no God with me, Is. 41:4; 43:10, 13; 46:4; 48:12
Mat. 24:26 h. is in desert
Mark 12:32 is none other but h.
Luke 24:6 said, h. is not here
John 1:15 h. of whom I spake, 30
7:11 wh. is h.? 25 is not this h.?
8:28 then shall ye kn. th. I am h.
9:9 is h. but h. said, I am h.
36 and said, Who is h. L.? 37
1 Cor. 10:22 we stronger than h.?

See BLESSED, DID, SAITH.

**HEAD.**

Gen. 3:15 it shall bruise thy h.
40:13 Ph. sh. lift up thy h. 19
49:26 blessings on head of Jos. and on top of h. Deut. 33:16
Ex. 29:10 A. and sons put hands on h. of bul. Lev. 4:4; 8:14
15 Aar. and sons put hands on h. of ram, 19; Lev. 8:18, 22
Lev. 1:4 hand on h. of b.-offering
3:2 lay hand on h. of offering
4:29 hand on h. of s.-offering, 33
13:45 clothes rent, and his h. b.
19:32 shalt rise before hoary h.
21:5 not make bald. on their h.
Num. 5:18 priest uncov. wo. h.
6:5 no razor come on Nazar. h.
7 consecration of God on his h.
9 sh. shave h. 18; Deut. 21:12
Jud. 13:5 no razor come on h.
1 Sam. 17:57 Goliath's h. in hand
31:9 and they cut off Saul's h.
28:2 make the keeper of my h.
2 Sam. 1:2 earth upon h. 15:32
3:8 and said, Am a dog's h.?
16:9 take off his h.
2 K. 2:3 master from h. to-day, 5
4:19 said to his fa. My h. my h.
6:31 h. of E. shall stand on him
19:21 dau. of Jeru. hath shaken her h. at thee, Is. 37:22
2 Chr. 6:23 recompens. way on h.
Ezr. 9:6 iniq. increased over h.
Neh. 4:4 turn reproach on own h.
Est. 9:25 device ret. on own h.
Job 1:20 shaved h. and fell down
10:15 yet will I not lift up my h.
16:4 I could shake my h. at you
Ps. 3:3 the lifter up of my h.
7:16 mischief return on own h.
22:7 shoot out lip, shake the h.
23:5 anointest my h. with oil
27:6 now sh. my h. be lifted up
Ps. 38:4 iniq. gone over my h.
60:7 Ephr. strength of h. 108:8
68:21 G. shall wound h. of ene.
110:7 therefore sh. he lift up h.
140:9 h. of those that comp. me
141:5 which shall not break h.
Prov. 10:6 blessings on h. of just
11:26 blessing on h. selleth corn
25:22 of fire on h. Rom. 12:20
Ec. 2:14 wise man's eyes in h.
Cant. 2:6 hand under my h. 8:3
5:2 my h. is filled with dew
11 h. as fine gold; 7:5 h. as C.
Is. 1:5 the whole h. is sick
51:11 everlasting joy on their h.
58:5 bow down h. as a bulrush?
59:17 helmet of salvation on h.
Jer. 2:37 and thy hands on thy h.
9:1 O that my h. were waters
Ezek. 9:10 recompense way on h.
29:18 every h. was made bald
Dan. 2:38 thou art this h. of gold
Joel 3:4 recompense on your h. 7

Amos 2:7 dust on h. of the poor
8:10 bring baldness on every h.
9:1 he said, Cut them in the h.
Zec. 1:21 no man did lift up h.
6:11 set crowns on h. of Joshua
Mat. 5:36 neither swear by thy h.
27:30 sm. him on h. Mark 15:19
Mark 6:24 h. of John the Baptist
Luke 7:46 h. wi. oil didst not an.
John 13:9 also my hands and h.
1 Cor. 11:4 h. cov. dishonoreth
10 ought to ha. power on her h.
12:21 the h. to the feet
Eph. 1:22 gave him h. to church,
4:15; Col. 1:8
Col. 2:19 holding h. from body
Rev. 19:12 on h. many crowns
See BEARD, BALD, BOW, BOWED, COVER, COVERED, CROWN.

**Bed's HEAD.**
Gen. 47:31 bowed hims. on b. h.

**HEAD of the corner.**
Mat. 21:42 beco. h. Mark 12:10; Lu. 20:17; Acts 4:11; 1 Pet. 2:7

**HEAD, *for ruler, governor.***
Num. 17:3 one rod h. of house
Deut. 28:13 L. will make thee h.
44 sh. be h. and thou the tail
Jud. 11:9 I your h.? 11 him h.
2 Sam. 22:44 thou hast kept me to be h. Ps. 18:43
Is. 7:8 h. of Damascus is Rezin, 9
9:14 cut off from Is. h. and tail
15 ancient and honorable is h.
Jer. 22:6 Gilead to me, h. of Leb.
Hos. 1:11 ap. themselves one h.
Hab. 3:13 h. out of ho. of wicked
14 strike through h. of villages
1 Cor. 11:3 h. of man is Ch. h. of woman man, h. of Ch. is G.
Eph. 5:23 husband is h. of wife, even as Christ is h. of church
Col. 2:10 who h. of principality

**HEAD, *for top, chief.***
Is. 28:1 on h. of fat valleys, 4
51:20 lie at the h. of all streets
Ezek. 16:25 built places at h.
21:21 king stood at h. of 2 ways

**HEAD, *with* hair, s.**
Lev. 13:40 h. is fallen off h. 41
14:9 leper shave hair off his h.
Num. 6:5 locks of h. of h. grow
18 take h. of h. of his separat.
Jud. 16:22 h. of h. began to grow
1 Sam. 14:45 not h. of h. fall gr.
2 Sam. 14:26 h. of h. at 200 shek.
Ezr. 9:3 plucked off h. of my h.
Ps. 40:12 more than h. of h. 69:4
Cant. 7:5 h. of thy h. like purple
Dan. 3:27 nor hair of h. singed
7:9 h. of his h. like pure wool
Mat. 10:30 h. of your h. number. Luke 12:7
Luke 7:38 wipe with h. of h. 44
21;18 shall not a h. of h. perish
Acts 27:34 nor a hair fall from h.
Rev. 1:14 his h. and h. were white

**HEADBANDS.**
Is. 3:20 take away h.

**HEADLONG.**
Job 5:13 counsel of frow. car. h.
Luke 4:29 cast him down h.
Acts 1:18 falling h. he burst asu.

**Spear's HEAD.**
1 Sam. 17:7 spear's h. weighed 600 shekels, 2 Sam. 21:16

**HEADSTONE.**
Ps. 118:22 be h. of corner
Zec. 4:7 bring h. with shoutings

**HEADS.**
Gen. 43:28 bowed th. h. Ex. 4:31
Lev. 10:6 uncover not your h.
1 K. 20:31 let us put ropes on h.
32 put ropes on their h.
2 K. 10:6 h. of your master's sons
8 brought the h. of king's sons
Ps. 24:7 lift your h. O ye gates, 9
66:12 men to ride over our h.
74:13 breakest the h. of dragon
14 brakest the h. of leviathan
109:25 shaked their h.
Is. 15:2 on their h. be baldness
35:10 everlasting joy on their h.
Jer. 14:3 they covered their h.
Ezek. 7:18 bald. sh. be on their h.
11:21 recomp. way on h. 22:31
32:27 laid swords under h.
44:18 linen bonnets on their h.
20 they shall poll their h.
Mat. 27:39 wag. h. Mark 15:29
Luke 21:28 and lift up your h.
Acts 18:6 yo. blood be on your h.
Rev. 9:7 their h. as it were cro.
13:1 a beast having seven h.
3 I saw one of his h. wounded
17:9 seven h. seven mountains
18:19 they cast dust on their h.

**HEADS, *for governors.***
Ex. 18:25 made th. h. over peo.
Num. 25:4 take all the h. of peo.
Ps. 110:6 wound h. over countr.
Mic. 3:1 hear, O h. of Jacob, 9
11 h. thereof judge for reward
See FATHERS.

**HEADY.**
2 Tim. 3:4 men be h. high-mind.

**HEAL.**
Deut. 32:29 I kill, I wound, I h.
2 K. 20:5 h. thee, add to thy da.
2 Chr. 7:14 forgive sin, h. land
Ps. 6:2 h. me, for bones are vex.
41:4 h. my soul, I have sinned
60:2 h. the breaches thereof
Ec. 3:3 time to kill, time to h.
Is. 57:18 seen ways, and h. 19
Jer. 3:22 I will h. your backslid.
17:14 h. me, O Lord
30:17 I will h. thee of wounds
Lam. 2:13 br. great, who can h.?
Hos. 6:1 ha. torn, and will h. us
14:4 I will h. their backslidings
Mat. 8:7 I will come and h. him
10:8 h. the sick, Luke 9:2; 10:9
12:10 h. on sab.-day Luke 14:3
13:15 be converted and I sho. h. them, John 12:40; Acts 28:27
Mark 3:2 h. on sabbath, Luke 6:7
Luke 4:18 to h. broken-hearted
23 Physician, h. thyself
John 4:47 come down and h.
Acts 4:30 stretching hand to h.

**HEALED.**
Ex. 21:19 sh. cause him to be h.
Lev. 13:18 boil h.; 37 scall is h.
14:3 plague of leprosy be h. 48
2 K. 2:21 h. waters; 22 waters h.
2 Chr. 30:20 L. heark. and h. pe.
Ps. 30:2 cried to thee, thou h.
107:20 sent his word and h. th.
Is. 6:10 and convert, and be h.
53:5 with his stripes we are h.
Jer. 6:14 have h. the hurt, 8:11
17:14 and I shall be h.
51:9 we would have h. Babylon
Ezek. 34:4 neither have h. sick
47:8 the waters shall be h. 9
11 the marshes shall not be h.
Hos. 7:1 when I would have h.
11:3 knew not that I h. them
Mat. 4:24 palsy, and he h. them
8:8 my serv. shall be h. Lu. 7:7
12:15 follow. he h. them, 14:14
Luke 8:43 nor could be h. of any
13:14 therefore come and be h.
17:15 saw he was h. turned ba.
22:51 touch. his ear and h. him
John 5:13 h. wist not who it was
Acts 4:14 beh. man who was h.
14:9 that he had faith to be h.
Heb. 12:13 but let it rather be h.
Jam. 5:16 pray that ye may be h.
1 Pet. 2:24 wh. stri. ye were h.
Rev. 13:3 deadly wo. was h. 12

**HEALER.**
Is. 3:7 saying, I will not be a h.

**HEALETH.**
Ex. 15:26 the L. that h. thee
Ps. 103:3 bless Lord who h. dis.
147:3 he h. the broken in heart
Is. 30:26 h. stroke of th. wound

**HEALING, Substantive.**
Jer. 14:19 there is no h. for us
Nah. 3:19 th. is no h. thy bruise
Mal. 4:2 with h. in his wings
Luke 9:11 healed them need h.
Acts 4:22 miracle of h. showed
1 Cor. 12:9 another gift of h. 28
30 have all the gifts of h.?
Rev. 22:2 leaves for h. of nations

**HEALING.**
Jer. 30:13 thou hast no h. medic.
Mat. 4:23 h. all man. of sickness
Luke 9:6 preach. gos. h. everyw.
Acts 10:38 h. all oppressed

**HEALTH.**
Gen. 43:28 our father in good h.
2 Sam. 20:9 in h. my brother?
Ps. 42:11 h. of my count. 43:5
67:2 saving h. may be known
Prov. 3:8 it sh. be h. to thy nav.
4:22 they are h. to their flesh
12:18 tongue of the wise is h.
13:17 a faithful ambassador is h.
16:24 sweet to soul, h. to bones
Is. 58:8 thy h. shall spring forth
Jer. 8:15 looked for a time of h.
22 not h. of my peo. recover.?
30:17 I will restore h. unto thee
Acts 27:34 take meat, this is h.
3 John 2 mayest be in h.

**HEAP, Substantive.**
Gen. 31:46 a h. eat on the h.
52 this h. be witness
Ex. 15:8 floods stood as h. Jos. 3:13, 16; Ps. 33:7; 78:13
Deut. 13:16 shall be a h. for ever
Jos. 7:26 over him h. of stones
Ruth 3:7 lie down at h. of corn
2 Sam. 18:17 great h. on Absal.
Cant. 7:2 belly like h. of wheat
Is. 17:11 harvest shall be a h.
25:2 hast made of a city a h.
Jer. 30:18 city builded on own h.
Mic. 1:6 Samaria a h. of the field
Hab. 3:15 walk thro' h. of waters
Hag. 2:16 came to h. of 20 meas.

**HEAP, Verb.**
Deut 32:23 h. misch. upon them
Job 16:4 h. up words against you
27:16 he h. up silver as the dust
36:13 hypocrites in heart h. wr.
Prov. 25:22 h. coals, Rom. 12:20
Ec. 2:26 to gather and to h. up
Ezek. 24:10 h. on wood, kindle
Hab. 1:10 sh. h. dust and take it
2 Tim. 4:3 h. to themsel. teach.

**HEAPED, ETH.**
Ps. 39:6 he h. up riches
Hab. 2:5 h. unto him all people
Jam. 5:3 have h. treasure toget.

**HEAPS.**
Jud. 15:16 jaw of ass, h. on h.
2 K. 10:8 lay ye them in two h.
2 Chr. 31:6 and laid them by h.
Job 15:28 houses ready to bec. h.
Ps. 79:1 laid Jerusalem on h.
Jer. 9:11 make Jerusal. h. 26:18
31:21 set thee up, make high h.
Hos. 12:11 their altars are as h.
Mic. 3:12 Jerus. shall become h.

**HEAR.**
Gen. 21:6 all that h. laugh
Ex. 32:18 them that sing do I h.

Num. 23:18 ri. up, Balak, and h.
30:4 h. her vow and her bond
Deut. 1:16 h. causes betw. breth.
4:10 make them h. my words
5:1 h. Is. the statutes, 6:3; 9:1; 20:3; Is. 48:1; Mark 12:29
27 h. all the L. our G. doth say
12:28 h. these words, I com.
13:12 shall h. say in one of cit.
30:12 bring it that we may h.
31:12 h. and fear L. 13; Jer. 6:10
Jos. 3:9 h. the words of the L.
Jud. 5:3 h. O ye kings, give ear
1 Sam. 2:23 h. your evil dealings
15:14 low. of oxen which I h.
16:2 if Saul h. it, he will kill me
2 Sam. 20:16 cr. out of city, h. h.
22:45 soon as h. Ps. 18:44
1 K. 4:34 h. wisdom of Solomon, 10:8, 24; 2 Chr. 9:7, 23; Mat. 12:42; Luke 11:31
8:30 h. in heaven and forg. 32, 34, 36, 39, 43, 45, 49; 2 Chr. 6:21
18:26 saying, O Baal, h. us
2 K. 7:6 h. a noise of chariots
18:28 h. the word of the great King, Is. 36:13; 37:17
1 Chr. 14:15 wh. thou h. sound
Neh. 1:6 h. the prayer of servant
4:4 h. O God, we are despised
8:2 could h. with understand
Job 5:27, h. it, and know thou it
13:17 h. dilig. my speech, 21:2
27:9 h. his cry? 34:2 h. words
42:4 h. I beseech thee
Ps. 4:1 h. my prayer, O G. 39:12; 54:2; 84:8; 102:1; 143:1
20:1 L. h. thee in day of troub.
Ps. 20:9 let the king h. us
27:7 h. O Lord, when I cry
30:10 h. O L. and have mercy
49:1 h. this all ye people
50:7 h. peo. I will speak, 81:8
51:8 make me h. joy and gladn
59:7 who, say they, doth h.?
61:1 h. my cry, O God
66:16 h. all ye that fear God
102:20 h. groaning of prisoner
138:4 h. words of thy mouth
143:8 to h. thy loving-kindness
Prov. 1:8 h. instruction of father
4:1 h. ye children, instruction
10 h. and rec. sayings, 19:20
8:6 h. I speak of excel. things
33 h. instruction, and be wise
19:27 cease to h. instruction
22:17 h. the words of the wise
23:19 h. thou, my son, be wise
Ec. 5:1 more ready to h. than
7:5 better to h. rebuke of wise
12:13 h. conclusion of matter
Cant. 8:13 cause me to h.
Is. 1:2 h. O heavens, give ear
6:9 h. ye indeed, Mark 4:12
18:3 bloweth a trumpet, h. ye
33:13 h. ye that are afar off
34:1 earth h, all that is therein
42:18 h. ye deaf; 23 will h.
43:9 let them h. and say truth
48:14 assemble yoursel. and h.
55:3 h. soul sh. live, John 5:25
Jer. 6:18 h. ye nat. 19 O earth
11:2 h. words of covenant, 6
10 forefathers ref. to h. 13:10
13:15 h. ye, give ear, L. spoken
18:2 cause thee to h. my words
23:22 cause my peo. to h. words
38:25 princes h. that I have tal.
49:20 h. counsel of Lord, 50:45
Lam. 1:18 h. I pray you, all peo.
Ezek. 2:8 h. wh. I say unto thee
3:17 h. wo. at my mouth, 33:7
27 he that heareth, let him h.
33:31 h. words, not do them, 32
Dan. 9:17 h. prayer of thy serv.
19 h. O Lord, forgive, hearken
Hos. 5:1 h. ye this, O priests
Joel 1:2 h. this, old men

Amos 3:1 h. this word L. hath spoken, 4:1; 5:1; 8:4
Mic. 1:2 h. all ye people
3:1 h. I pray you, heads of J. 9
6:2 h. O mountains; h. ye rod
Nah. 3:19 all that h. bruit sh.
Mat. 11:4 show John thin. ye h.
5 deaf h. Mark 7:37; Luke 7:22
13:17 h. things ye h. Luke 10:24
15:10 he said to multitude, h.
17:5 bel. Son, h. him, Mark 9:7
18:17 if he neglect to h. them
Mark 4:18 are such as h. the word, 20; Luke 8:12, 13
24 heed wh. ye h. you that h.
Luke 5:1 pressed on him to h.
15 multit. came together to h.
6:17 came to h. him
8:18 take heed there. how ye h.
21 wh. h. word and do it, 11:28
9:9 who is this of whom I h.?
16:2 how is it I h. this of thee?
29 Moses and prophets h. them
19:48 peop. very attentive to h.
21:38 come to temple to h. him
John 5:30 I h. I ju. 6:60 who h.?
7:1 judge man before it h. him
9:27 wheref. wo. ye h. it aga.?
10:3 sheep h. voice
12:47 if man h. words, bel. not
14:24 word wh. ye h. is not mi.
Acts 2:8 h. ev. man in own tong.
33 which ye now see and h.
10:22 and to h. words of thee
33 h. all things command. thee
13:7 desired to h. word of God
44 whole city came to h. word
15:7 Gen. by my mouth h. word
17:21 h. some new thing
22:1 h. ye my defence
24:4 h. us of thy clemency
25:22 I would h. man myself
28:22 to h. what thou thinkest
1 Cor. 11:18 I h. th. be divisions
Phil. 1:27 may h. of your affairs
2 Thes. 3:11 we h. that some wa.
1 Tim. 4:16 and them that h. th.
2 Tim. 4:17 all Gentiles mig. h.
Jam. 1:19 eve. one be swift to h.
1 John 5:15 know that he h. us
3 John 4 h. children walk in tru.
Rev. 1:3 bless. h. words of prop.
9:20 neither see, nor h. nor wa.

See EAR, EARS, VOICE.

**HEAR me.**

Ex. 6:12 then shall Phar. h. me?
1 K. 18:37 h. me, O Lord h. me
1 Chr. 28:2 h. me, my brethren
2 Chr. 13:4 h. me, thou Jeroboam
15:2 h. me, Asa: 20:20 h. me, J.
29:5 h. me, ye Levites, sanctify
Job 31:35 O that one wo. h. me
Ps. 4:1 h. me when I call, O God
13:3 consider and h. me, O Lord
17:6 thou wilt h. me
38:16 for I said, h. me, lest they
55:2 attend unto me, and h. me
60:5 save with right hand, h. me
69:13 in multi. of mercy, h. me
17 h. me speedily, 143:7
Mic. 7:7 God will h. me
Acts 26:3 I beseech thee to h. me
29 all h. me, were such as I am
1 Cor. 14:21 will they not h. me?

**HEAR not, or not HEAR.**

1 Sam. 8:18 Lord will not h. you
Job 30:20 dost not h. me
35:13 God will not h. vanity.
Ps. 66:18 regard iniq. L. not h.
94:9 planted ear, sh. he not h.?
Is. 1:15 many prayers I will not h. Jer. 7:16; 11:14; 14:12; Ezek. 8:18; Amos 5:23
30:9 will not h. the law of Lord
59:1 ear heavy that it can not h.
2 will n. h.; 65:12 ye did n. h.
66:4 they did not h. Zec. 1:4

Jer. 5:21 have ears, and h. not, Ezek. 12:2; Mark 8:18
13:17 will n. h. 22:5; Mal. 2:2
17:23 mi. not h. 19:15; Zec. 7:11
22:21 thou saidst, I will not h.
Dan. 5:23 praised gods of silver, wh. see not nor h. Rev. 9:20
Mic. 3:4 cry to L. he will not h.
Hab. 1:2 long cry, wilt not h.?
Mat. 10:14 rec. you, nor h. wor.
13:16 if he will not h. thee
Luke 16:31 if he h. n. M. and pr.
John 8:43 bec. ye can not h. wo.
47 ye therefore h. them not
9:27 I told you, and ye did n. h.
10:8 the sheep did not h. them
Acts 3:23 soul will n. h. destroy.
1 Cor. 14:21 will they not h. me
Gal. 4:21 do ye not h. the law?

**Would not HEAR.**

Ex. 7:16 hitherto thou w. not h.
Deut. 1:43 Is. 3:26; 2 K. 17:14
2 K. 14:11 Amaziah, 2 Chr. 25:20
18:12 Is. Neh. 9:29; Zec. 7:13
Jer. 13:11 they w. n. h. 29:19
36:25 he w. n. h.; Zec. 7:13 I w. not h.

**HEAR now, or now HEAR.**

Num. 12:6 h. now my wor., 20:10
1 Sam. 22:7 said h. now, Benjam.
Job 13:6 h. now my reasoning
Prov. 5:7 h. me now, therefore
Is. 7:13 h. n. O house of David
44:1 n. h. O Jacob, my servant
47:8 h. now, thou given to pleas.
51:21 h. now this, thou afflicted
Jer. 5:21 h. now, O foolish peop.
28:15 h. now, Hananiah
37:20 h. now, I pray thee
Mic. 6:1 h. ye now what L. saith
Zec. 3:8 h. n. Josh. high-priest
Acts 2:33 which ye n. see and h.
Phil. 1:30 saw in me, and now h.

**Shall HEAR.**

Ex. 15:14 shall h. be afraid, Deut. 13:11; 17:13; 19:20; 21:21
Num. 14:13 Egyptians shall h. it
Deut. 4:6 s. h. all these statutes
1 K. 8:42 s. h. of thy great name
2 K. 19:7 shall h. rumor, Is. 37:7
Job 22:27 prayer to him, he s. h.
Ps. 34:2 humble shall h. thereof
55:17 cry, and he s. h. my voice
19 God s. h. and afflict them
92:11 ears s. h. desire of wicked
141:6 they shall h. my words
Is. 29:18 in that day s. deaf h.
30:19 shall h. he will answer
21 thine ears shall h. a word
Jer. 33:9 s. h. all good that I do
Hos. 2:21 heaven shall h. earth
22 earth shall h. corn and wine
Mat. 13:14 ye shall h. Acts 28:26
18:15 shall h. thee
24:6 ye shall h. of wars and rumors, Mark 13:7; Luke 21:9
John 5:25 the dead shall h. voice
16:13 whatsoever he shall h.
Acts 3:22 him shall ye h. 7:37
25:22 to-morrow thou s. h. him
Rom. 10:14 how s. they h. with.

**Will HEAR.**

Ex. 20:19 will h. Deut. 5:27
22:23 cry, I will surely h. 27
Num. 9:8 will h. what L. com.
2 K. 19:4 God will h. the words
2 Chr. 7:14 w. h. fr. hea. Ps. 20:6
20:9 thou w. h. Ps. 38:15
Ps. 4:3 L. will h.; 17:6 w. h. me
85:8 will h. what God will speak
145:19 he also will h. their cry
Prov. 1:5 w. h. and increase
Is. 41:17 the Lord will h. them
65:24 are yet speaking, I will h.
Jer. 36:3 may be hou. of J. w. h.
Ezek. 2:5 whether will h. 7; 3:11
Hos. 2:21 I will h. the heavens

*Mic.* 7:7 wait for G. God *will h.*
*Zec.* 10:6 God *will h.* them, 13:9
*Acts* 17:32 we *will h.* thee again
21:22 *will h.* that thou art come
23:35 *will h.* thee wh. accusers
28:28 sal. sent Gentile, *will h.*

**HEAR the word of the Lord.**

1 *K.* 22:19 *h. the word of the Lo.*
2 *Ch.* 18:18; *Jer.* 29:20; 42:15; *Amos* 7:16
2 *K.* 7:1 Elisha said, *h. word of the Lord*, *Jer.* 17:20; 21:11
20:16 Isa. said to Hezekiah, *h. the word of the Lo. Is.* 39:5
*Is.* 1:10 *h. w. of L.* rulers of So.
28:14 *h. w. of L.* scornful men
66:5 *h. w. of L.* ye that tremble
*Jer.* 2:4 *h. w. of L.* ho. of J. 10:1
7:2 *h. w. of Lord* all ye of *h.*
9:20 yet *h. w. of Lord*, O ye wo.
19:3 *h. w. of L.* kings of J. 22:2
22:29 O earth, *h. the w. of t. L.*
31:10 *h. w. of L.* O ye nations
34:4 *h. word of Lord*, O Zedek.
44:24 *h. word of Lord*, all J. 26
*Ezek.* 6:3 mountains of Is. *h.* 36:1
13:2 say to prophets, *h. w. of L.*
16:35 O harlot, *h. w. of the L.*
20:47 forest of south, *h. w. of L.*
34:7 shepherds, *h. w. of the L.* 9
*Hos.* 4:1 *h. w. of L.* child. of Isr.
*Amos* 7:16 Amaziah, *h. w. of L.*

**HEARD.**

*Gen.* 16:11 Lord *h.* thy affliction
21:26 neither yet *h.* I of it
*Ex.* 2:24 God *h.* their groaning
28:35 sound *h.* when goeth in
*Lev.* 24:14 that *h.* him
*Num.* 11:1 complained, L. *h.* it
12:2 spoke ag. Moses, L. *h.* it
14:15 nations have *h.* fame
1 *Sam.* 7:9 cried, the L. *h.* him
1 *K.* 1:11 *h.* Adonijah doth reign
6:7 any tool of iron *h.* in house
2 *K.* 19:25 *h.* long ago, *Is.* 37:26
2 *Chr.* 5:13 one *h.* in praising
33:13 and *h.* his supplications
*Ezr.* 3:13 the noise was *h.* afar
*Neh.* 12:43 joy of Jerusa. *h.* afar
*Job* 15:8 hast *h.* secret of God?
19:7 out of wrong, but not *h.*
26:14 how little a portion is *h.*?
29:11 when the ear *h.* me
*Ps.* 6:9 L. hath *h.* my supplica.
10:17 *h.* desire of the humble
22:21 for thou hast *h.* me
24 but when he cried he *h.* 34:6; 40:1; 120:1
34:4 I sought the L. he *h.* me
38:13 I as a deaf man *h.* not
61:5 O God, hast *h.* my vows
66:19 verily God hath *h.* me
76:8 cause judgment to be *h.*
78:21 therefore the Lord *h.* this
59 when God *h.* this
81:5 where I *h.* a language
97:8 Zion *h.* and was glad
118:21 for thou hast *h.* me
132:6 we *h.* of it at Ephratah
*Prov.* 21:13 cry hims. but not *h.*
*Is.* 10:30 cause it to be *h.* to L.
40:21 have ye not *h.*?
28 not *h.* everl. G. fainteth not
48:6 thou hast *h.* see all this
52:15 had not *h.* sh. they consi.
60:18 viol. no more *h.* in land
64:4 not *h.* what he prepared
65:19 weeping be no more *h.*
66:8 who hath *h.* such thing?
*Jer.* 4:19 *h.* sound of trumpet
6:7 wickedn. spoil, is *h.* in her
7:13 rising early, but ye *h.* not
8:6 I hearkened and *h.*
18:13 who hath *h.* such
22 let cry be *h.* from houses
25:36 howling of flock sh. be *h.*

26:11 prophesied as ye have *h.*
34:10 *h.* man-servant sh. go free
35:17 but they have not *h.*
46:12 nations have *h.* of shame
50:46 cry is *h.* among nations
51:46 rumor shall be *h.* in land
*Lam.* 3:61 hast *h.* their reproach
*Ezek.* 26:13 shall be no more *h.*
*Dan.* 12:8 I *h.* but underst. not
*Jon.* 2:2 I cried to L. and he *h.*
*Mic.* 5:15 such as have not *h.*
*Mal.* 3:16 hearkened and *h.*
*Mat.* 5:21 ye *h.* it, 27, 33, 38, 43
6:7 shall be *h.* for much speak.
13:17 have not *h. Luke* 10:24
22:7 when the king *h.* thereof
26:65 have *h.* blas. *Mark* 14:64
*Mark* 4:15 they have *h.* Satan
14:11 they *h.* it they were glad
*Luke* 1:13 prayer is *h. Acts* 10:31
12:3 spoken, shall be *h.*
20:16 when they *h.* it, they said
*John* 3:32 he hath *h.* he testifieth
6:45 ev. man that hath *h.* of F.
8:6 wrote on ground as *h.* not
11:41 I thank thee thou hast *h.*
18:21 ask them which *h.* me
21:7 Simon P. *h.* it was the Lord
*Acts* 1:4 the promise ye *h.* of me
2:37 when *h.* this they were
4:4 many which *h.* the word be.
5:5 fear came on all that *h.*
13:48 when G. *h.* this were glad
14:9 the same *h.* Paul speak
16:14 woman worship. G. *h.* us
25 and the prisoners *h.* them
22:15 sh. wit. what seen and *h.*
24:24 *h.* concerning faith in C.
*Rom.* 10:14 they have not *h.*
18 have they not *h.*? yes, veri.
15:21 they that have not *h.*
1 *Cor.* 2:9 eye not seen, nor ear *h.*
*Gal.* 1:13 ye have *h.* of my conv.
*Eph.* 1:13 ye *h.* word of truth
15 after I *h.* of your faith
4:21 if so be ye have *h.* him
*Phil.* 4:9 ye have *h.* and seen
*Col.* 1:4 we *h.* of your faith in C.
6 ye *h.* of it, knew grace of G.
9 we *h.* it, do not cease to pray
2 *Tim.* 2:2 things thou hast *h.*
*Heb.* 2:3 confirmed by them th. *h.*
3:16 when they had *h.*
4:2 with faith in them that *h.*
5:7 offered up prayers, was *h.*
*Jam.* 5:11 have *h.* of pati. of Job
1 *John* 2:18 ye *h.* antichrist, 4:3
24 *h.* from begin. 3:11; 2 *John* 6
*Rev.* 3:3 remem. how th. hast *h.*
7:4 I *h.* number of them sealed
9:16 I *h.* number of horsemen
16:5 I *h.* the angel of waters
18:22 shall be *h.* no more
23 voice of bride be *h.* no more
22:8 saw these things, *h.* them

**I have HEARD.**

*Gen.* 17:20 for Ishmael *I h. h.*
42:2 *I h. h.* there is corn Egypt
*Ex.* 3:7 *I h. h.* cry; 6:5 *I h. h.* g.
16:12 *I h. h.* mur. *Num.* 14:27
1 *K.* 9:3 *I h. h.* thy prayer, 2 *K.* 20:5; 2 *Chr.* 7:12; *Is.* 38:5
2 *K.* 19:20 hast prayed *I have h.*
22:19 *I h. h.* sa. L. 2 *Chr.* 34:27
*Job* 16:2 *I h. h.* many su. things
20:3 *I have h.* check of reproach
42:5 *I h. h.* by hearing of ear
*Ps.* 31:13 *I have h.* the slander
62:11 twice *I have h.* this
*Is.* 49:8 time *h. I h.* 2 *Cor.* 6:2
*Jer.* 23:25 *I h. h.* what prophets
31:18 *I h. h.* Ephraim bemoan.
49:14 *I h. h.* a rumor from Lord
*Ezek.* 35:12 *I h. h.* thy blasphe.
*Hos.* 14:8 *I have h.* and observed
*Hab.* 3:2 *I have h.* thy speech
*John* 8:26 those things *I have h.*

40 truth, which *I h. h.* of God
15:15 *I have h.* of my Father
*Acts* 7:34 *I have h.* their groaning
9:13 *I h. h.* by many of th. man

**HEARD, *with* voice.**

*Gen.* 3:8 they *h. voice* of the Lord
10 I *h.* thy *voice*, and was afraid
21:17 God *h.* the *voice* of the lad
30:6 G. hath *h.* my *v.* and given
39:15 when he *h.* I lifted up *v.*
*Num.* 7:89 he *h.* the *v.* of one
20:16 we cried, he *h.* our *voice*
*Deut.* 1:34 L. *h.* the *v.* of words
4:12 similitude, only he *h.* a *v.*
33 *v.* of God thou hast *h.* 5:26
5:23 ye *h.* the *v.* out of darkness
24 *h.* his *voice* out of the fire
28 L. *h.* the *v.* of your words
26:7 the L. *h.* our *v.* and looked
*Jud.* 18:25 let not *voice* be *h.*
1 *Sam.* 1:13 lips moved, *v.* not *h.*
1 *K.* 17:22 L. *h.* the *v.* of Elijah
2 *Chr.* 30:27 *v. h.* prayer came
*Job* 4:16 th. was silence, I *h.* a *v.*
33:8 *h.* the *v.* of thy words
37:4 not stay them when *v.* is *h.*
*Ps.* 3:4 L. with my *v.* he *h.* me
6:8 L. hath *h. v.* of my weeping
18:6 *h.* my *v.* out of his temple
*Ps.* 19:3 no speech where *v.* not *h.*
28:6 *h. v.* of my supplication
66:8 make *v.* of praise to be *h.*
116:1 I love L. he hath *h.* my *v.*
*Cant.* 2:12 *v.* of the turtle is *h.*
*Is.* 6:8 also I *h. v.* of the Lord
30:30 L. cause his gl. *v.* to be *h.*
42:2 *v.* to be *h.* in street
58:4 make your *voice* to be *h.*
65:19 *v.* of weeping no more *h.*
*Jer.* 3:21 a *v.* was *h.* upon high
4:31 have *h.* a *v.* as of a woman
9:19 *v.* of wailing is *h.* out of Z.
30:5 have *h.* a *v.* of trembling
31:15 *v.* was *h.* in R. *Mat.* 2:18
*Lam.* 3:56 thou hast *h.* my *voice*
*Ezek.* 1:28 I *h.* a *v.* of one that s.
3:12 I *h.* behind me *v.*
27:30 cause their *v.* to be *h.*
*Dan.* 8:16 *h.* a man's *v.* between
10:9 yet *h.* I the *v.* of his words
*Nah.* 2:13 *v.* of mes. no more *h.*
*John* 5:37 neither *h.* his *v.* at any
*Acts* 9:4 and *h.* a *voice* saying, Saul, Saul, 22:7; 26:14
11:7 *h.* a *v.* saying to me, Arise
22:9 *h.* not the *voice* of him
*Heb.* 12:19 wh. *voice* they that *h.*
2 *Pet.* 1:18 *v.* came fr. heav. we *h.*
*Rev.* 1:10 I *h.* a *v.* 16:1; 19:1; 21:3
4:1 first *v.* I *h.* was as a trumpet
5:11 I *h.* the *v.* of many angels
6:6 I *h.* a *v.* in the midst
7 I *h.* a *v.* of the fourth beast
9:13 *h.* a *v.* fr. the four horns
10:4 *h.* a *v.* from heaven 8; 14:2, 13; 18:4
12:10 and I *h.* a loud *voice*
14:2 I *h.* the *v.* of harpers
19:6 I *h. v.* of multitude

**We have HEARD.**

*Jos.* 9:9 *we have h.* fame of him
2 *Sam.* 7:22 none like thee accor. to all *we h. h.* 1 *Chr.* 17:20
*Ps.* 44:1 *we h. h.* with our ears
48:8 as *we h. h.* so have we seen
78:3 sayings which *we have h.*
*Is.* 16:6 *we h. h.* of M. *Jer.* 48:29
24:16 *we have h.* songs, glory to
*Jer.* 30:5 *we h. h.* voice of tremb.
51:51 confou. *we h. h.* reproach
*Ob.* 1 *we h. h.* rumor from Lord
*Zec.* 8:23 for *we have h.* that God
*Mark* 14:58 *we have h.* him say
*Luke* 4:23 whatever *we have h.*
22:71 *we* ourselves *have h.*

*John* 4:42 believe, *we have h.*
12:34 *we have h.* out of the law
*Acts* 4:20 cannot but sp. *we h. h.*
6:11 *we have h.* him speak
14 *we have h.* him say, This J.
15:24 *we have h.* that certain
*Heb.* 2:1 heed to things *we h. h.*
1 *John* 1:1 which *we have h.* 3
5 message which *we have h.*

**HEARD,** *with* **word, s.**
*Num.* 24:4 wh. *h. w.* of God, 16
*Jos.* 24:27 *h.* all the *w.* of Lord
1 *Sam.* 17:23 same *w.* D. *h.* them
31 wh. *w.* were *h.* David spake
1 *K.* 2:42 the *w.* that I *h.* is good
2 *K.* 6:30 king *h. w.* of woman
19:6 afraid of *w.* hast *h. Is.* 37:6
*Job* 33:8 I have *h.* voice of *words*
*Ec.* 9:16 poor man's *w.* not *h.*
17 *w.* of wise men are *h.*
*Is.* 37:4 the *w.* wh. God hath *h.*
*Jer.* 23:18 and *h.* his *words*
25:8 bec. ye have not *h.* my *w.*
26:21 princes *h.* his *word*
36:13 decl. all the *w.* he had *h.*
24 not afraid that *h.* these *w.*
38:1 Pashur *h.* the *w.* of Jerem.
*Mat.* 22:22 wh. they *h.* these *w.*
*Mark* 5:36 as Jesus *h.* the *word*
*Luke* 10:39 at Jes. feet, *h.* his *w.*
*Acts* 10:44 fell on them *h. word.*
2 *Cor.* 12:4 *h.* unspeakable *word*
*Eph.* 1:13 ye *h.* the *w.* of truth
*Col.* 1:5 ye *h. w.* of the gospel
1 *Thes.* 2:13 *w.* which ye *h.* of us
2 *Tim.* 1:13 sound *w.* hast *h.*
*Heb.* 12:19 that *h.* entre. that *w.*
1 *John* 2:7 *w.* ye ha. *h.* from beg.

**HEARDEST.**
*Deut.* 4:36 thou *h.* his words
2 *K.* 22:19 thou *h.* what I spake ag. this place, 2 *Chr.* 34:27
*Neh.* 9:9 thou *h.* their cry
27 they cried, thou *h.* them, 28
*Ps.* 31:22 thou *h.* voice of sup.
119:26 I dec. my ways, thou *h.*
*Is.* 48:7 day when thou *h.* not
8 thou *h.* not, thou knew. **not**
*Jon.* 2:2 I cried, thou *h.*

**HEARER, S.**
*Rom.* 2:13 not *h.* of law are just.
*Eph.* 4:29 minister grace unto *h.*
2 *Tim.* 2:14 subverting of the *h.*
*Jam.* 1:22 doers of word, not *h.*
23 if any be a *h.* of the word
25 he being not a forgetful *h.*

**HEAREST.**
1 *Sam.* 24:9 *h.* thou m.'s words?
2 *Sam.* 5:24 *h.* sound in mulb.-t.
1 *K.* 8:30 *h.* forgive. 2 *Chr.* 6:21
*Ps.* 22:2 cry in daytime, *h.* not
65:2 thou that *h.* prayer
*Mat.* 21:16 *h.* thou what th. say?
27:13 *h.* thou not how many th.
*John* 3:8 and thou *h.* the sound
11:42 that thou *h.* me always

**HEARETH.**
*Deut.* 29:19 *h.* words of curse
1 *Sam.* 3:9 L. thy servant *h.* 10
*Job* 34:28 *h.* cry of the afflicted
*Ps.* 34:17 righte. cry, the Lord *h.*
38:14 as a man that *h.* not
69:33 L. *h.* poor, desp. not pris.
*Prov.* 8:34 blessed is man *h.* me
13:1 *h.* his father's instruction
8 but poor *h.* not rebuke
15:29 he *h.* prayer of righteous
31 that *h.* reproof of life, 32
18:13 answ. matter before *h.* it
21:28 the man that *h.* speaketh
25:10 that *h.* it put thee to sha.
29:24 *h.* cursing, bewrayeth not
*Is.* 42:20 open ears, but *h.* not
*Ezek.* 3:27 he that *h.* let him hear

*Mat.* 7:24 *h.* say. 26; *Luke* 6:47, 49
13:19 *h.* word of the kingdom
20 that *h.* the word, 22, 23
*Luke* 10:16 he that *h.* you *h.* me
*John* 3:29 standeth and *h.* him
5:24 *h.* my word, and believeth
8:47 that is of G. *h.* G.'s words
9:31 God *h.* not sinners
18:37 that is of truth, *h.* voice
2 *Cor.* 12:6 above th. he *h.* of me
1 *John* 4:5 the world *h.* them
6 he that knoweth God *h.* us
5:14 ask accord. to will, he *h.* us
*Rev.* 22:17 him that *h.* say, Come
18 to ev. man that *h.* the words

**HEARING.**
*Deut.* 31:11 read this law in th. *h.*
2 *Sam.* 18:12 our *h.* king charged
2 *K.* 4:31 neither voice nor *h.*
*Job* 33:8 hast spoken in my *h.*
42:5 I have heard of thee by *h.*
*Is.* 11:3 nor reprove af. *h.* of ears
21:3 bowed down at the *h.* of it
33:15 stoppeth ears fr. *h.* blood
*Ezek.* 9:5 said in my *h.* Go
10:13 cried unto them in my *h.*
*Amos* 8:11 *h.* word of the Lord
*Acts* 25:21 reserved to *h.* of Aug.
23 entered into the place of *h.*
*Rom.* 10:17 faith cometh by *h.*
1 *Cor.* 12:17 where were the *h.*?
*Gal.* 3:2 or by the *h.* of faith, 5
*Heb.* 5:11 seeing ye are dull of *h.*

**HEARING, Verb.**
*Prov.* 20:12 *h.* ear, L. hath made
28:9 away ear from *h.* the law
*Ec.* 1:8 nor is ear filled with *h.*
*Mat.* 13:13 and *h.* they hear not
14 by *h.* ye shall hear
15 dull of *h. Acts* 28:27; *Heb.* 5:11
*Mark* 6:2 many *h.* were aston.
*Luke* 2:46 *h.* them and asking
*Acts* 5:5 Ananias *h.* these words
8:6 *h.* and seeing miracles
9:7 *h.* a voice, but seeing no m.
18:8 Corinthians *h.* believed
*Phile.* 5 *h.* of thy love and faith
2 *Pet.* 2:8 Lot in seeing and *h.*

**HEARKEN.**
*Ex.* 6:30 sh. Pharaoh *h.* to me?
*Deut.* 7:12 *h.* to these judgments
11:13 *h.* dilig. to my commands
15:5 *h.* to voice of L. *Jer.* 17:24
18:15 to him ye shall *h.*
28:13 if thou *h.* to commandments, 1 *K.* 11:38
*Jos.* 1:17 so will we *h.* unto thee
1 *Sam.* 15:22 to *h.* th. fat of rams
30:24 who will *h.* to you in this?
1 *K.* 8:28 have thou respect to *h.*
29 *h.* to prayer, 52; 2 *Chr.* 6:19, 20
*Neh.* 13:27 *h.* then to you?
*Ps.* 81:8 if thou wilt *h.* unto me
*Prov.* 29:12 if a ruler *h.* to lies
*Is.* 32:3 ears of th. that hear *h.*
42:23 will *h.* for time to come?
*Jer.* 26:3 will *h.* and turn fr. evil
5 *h.* to prophets whom I sent
29:12 pray to me, and I will *h.*
35:13 not rec. instruction to *h.*
*Zec.* 7:11 but they refused to *h.*
*Acts* 4:19 *h.* to you
12:13 a damsel came to *h.*

**HEARKEN,** *imperatively.*
*Gen.* 23:15 *h.* to me; 49:2 *h.* to Is.
*Num.* 23:18 *h.* to me, son of Zip.
*Deut.* 4:1 *h.* O Israel, to statutes
27:9 take heed, and *h.* O Israel
*Jud.* 9:7 *h.* to me, men of Shech.
1 *K.* 8:30 *h.* to the supplications, 2 *Chr.* 6:21
22:28 *h.* O peo. every one of you
2 *Chr.* 18:27 he said, *h.* all peop.
20:15 *h.* ye, all Judah, and Jer.

*Job* 13:6 *h.* to pleadings
32:10 I said *h.* to me, 33:31
33:1 I pray, *h.* to my words
34:10 *h.* unto me, men of under.
34 w. man *h.* 37:14 *h.* to this
*Ps.* 34:11 *h.* I will teach you
45:10 *h.* O daughter, and consid.
*Prov.* 7:24 *h.* to me, O chil. 8:32
*Is.* 28:23 *h.* and hear my speech
34:1 ye nations, *h.* ye peo. 49:1
46:3 *h.* unto me, O house of Jacob, 48:12; *Hos.* 5:1
12 *h.* to me, stout-hearted
51:1 *h.* to me, th. fol. righteous.
4 *h.* unto me, my people
7 *h.* to me, ye th. know right.
55:2 *h.* diligently unto me
*Dan.* 9:19 O Lord, *h.* and do
*Mic.* 1:2 *h.* O earth, and all ther.
*Mark* 7:14 *h.* to me every one
*Acts* 2:14 *h.* to my words
7:2 brethren, and fathers, *h.*
15:13 men and brethren, *h.*
*Jam.* 2:5 my beloved brethren

*See* VOICE.

**HEARKEN,** *with* **not.**
*Gen.* 34:17 *not h.* to be circum.
*Ex.* 7:4 *not h.* to you, 22; 11:9
*Deut.* 13:3 *n. h.* to that dreamer
17:12 will *not h.* to the priest
18:19 will *not h.* to my words
21:18 he will *not h.* to them
23:5 *n. h.* to Bal. *Jos.* 24:10
*Jos.* 1:18 will *n. h.* to thy words
*Jud.* 2:17 would *not h.* to judges
1 *K.* 20:8 elders said, *h. n.* to him
2 *K.* 17:40 *n. h.* but after manner
18:31 *h. n.* to Hezek. *Is.* 36:16
2 *Chr.* 10:16 Rehob. would *not h.*
33:10 L. spake, they would *n. h.*
*Job* 33:33 if *n. h.* hold thy peace
*Ps.* 58:5 *n. h.* to voice of charm.
81:11 would *not h.* to my voice
*Jer.* 6:10 uncircumcised *cannot h.*
17 said, We will *not h.* 44:16
7:27 they will *not h.* unto thee
11:11 tho. they cry, I will *not h.*
16:12 they may not *h.* to me
17:27 if ye will *not h.* to me, 26:4; *Ezek.* 20:39
23:16 *h. not* to prophets, 27:9, 14, 16, 17; 29:8
38:15 wilt thou *not h.* to me?
*Ezek.* 3:7 *n. h.* to thee, *n. h.* to me
20:8 and would *not h.* unto me
*Hos.* 9:17 did *n. h. Zec.* 1:4

**HEARKENED.**
*Gen.* 30:17 God *h.* unto Leah
22 God *h.* to Rachel and open.
34:24 to Hamor *h.* all that went
39:10 that Joseph *h.* not to her
*Ex.* 6:12 chil. of Is. not *h.* to me
7:13 Phar. *h.* not, 8:15, 19; 9:12
*Deut.* 9:19 Lord *h.* to me, 10:10
18:14 nations *h.* to obs. of times
34:9 Is. *h.* to Joshua, *Jos.* 1:17
1 *Sam.* 28:21 wom. of En. *h.* to S.
1 *K.* 12:15 king *h.* not to people, 16; 2 *Chr.* 10:15
24 they *h.* to word of the Lord
15:20 *h.* to king Asa, 2 *Chr.* 16:4
2 *K.* 13:4 the Lord *h.* to Jehoahaz
16:9 king of Assyria *h.* to Asa
20:13 Hezekiah *h.* to messengers
21:9 Judah *h.* not to the law
22:13 our fathers *h.* not to words
2 *Chr.* 24:17 J. *h.* to the princes
25:16 Amaz. *h.* not to the prop.
35:22 Josiah *h.* not to Pharaoh
*Neh.* 9:16 *h.* not to thy commandments, 29, 34; *Jer.* 34:14
*Est.* 3:4 Mordecai *h.* not to them
*Ps.* 81:13 O that my peo. had *h.*
*Is.* 21:7 and he *h.* diligently
48:18 O that thou hadst *h.*

*Jer.* 6:19 have not *h.* to my word,
7:24, 26; 25:3, 4, 7; 26:5;
29:19; 32:33; 34:17; 35:14, 15,
16; 36:31; 44:5
37:14 Irijah *h.* not to Jeremiah
*Ezek.* 3:6 would have *h.* not thee
*Dan.* 9:6 neither *h.* to thy serv
*Mal.* 3:16 the Lord *h. Jer.* 8.
*Acts* 27:21 should have *h.* to me
*See* VOICE.

**HEARKENEDST.**

*Deut.* 28:45 thou *h.* not to the L.

**HEARKENETH, ING.**

*Ps.* 103:20 angels *h.* to the voice
*Prov.* 1:33 *h.* to me sh. dw. safely
12:15 he that *h.* to coun. is wise

**HEART, Noun.**

*Gen.* 45:26 and Jacob's *h.* fainted
*Ex.* 23:9 know *h.* of a stranger
28:30 they shall be on Aaron's *h.*
35:35 hath filled with wisd. of *h.*
*Lev.* 26:16 and cause sorrow of *h.*
*Num.* 32:7 discourage *h.* of Is.?
9 they discouraged the *h.* of Is.
*Deut.* 5:29 such a *h.* in them
28:28 smite wi. astonish. of *h.*
47 serv. not L. with glad. of *h.*
65 L. sh. give thee trembling *h.*
29:4 L. hath not given *h.* to per.
*Jos.* 14:8 made *h.* of people melt
*Jud.* 5:15 great thoughts of *h.*
16 were great searchings of *h.*
18:20 the priest's *h.* was glad.
1 *Sam.* 1:13 Han. spake in her *h.*
10:9 God gave him another *h.*
16:7 the Lord looketh on the *h.*
17:32 Let no man's *h.* fail
24:5 and David's *h.* smote him
25:31 offence of *h.* to my lord
36 and Nabal's *h.* was merry
2 *Sam.* 6:16 she despised him in
*h.* 1 *Chr.* 15:29
14:1 king's *h.* was tow. Absalom
18:14 darts thro. *h.* of Absalom
14 bowed *h.* of men of Judah
1 *K.* 3:9 an understanding *h.*
12 given thee understanding *h.*
8:66 glad of *h.* 2 *Chr.* 7:10
10:2 com. of all in *h.* 2 *Chr.* 9:1
11:4 perfect, as the *h.* of David
12:27 then sh. the *h.* of this peo.
2 *K.* 6:11 *h.* of king of As. troub.
12:4 into man's *h.* 2 *Chr.* 29:31
1 *Chr.* 12:33 not of double *h.*
16:10 let the *h.* rej. *Ps.* 105:3
29:17 triest *h.* 18; *Jer.* 11:20
2 *Chr.* 7:11 came into Solom.'s *h.*
*Ezr.* 6:22 turned *h.* of king
7:27 such as this in the king's *h.*
*Neh.* 2:2 noth. else but sor. of *h.*
*Est.* 1:10 *h.* of king merry
5:9 H. went forth with glad *h.*
*Job* 9:4 wise in *h.* and mighty
12:24 he taketh away *h.* of chief
29:13 caused widow's *h.* to sing
37:24 respecteth not wise of *h.*
38:36 given understanding to *h.*
*Ps.* 12:2 double *h.* they speak
19:8 sta. of L. right, rejoicing *h.*
34:18 nigh them of broken *h.*
44:21 knoweth secrets of the *h.*
45:5 arrows sharp in *h.* of ene.
58:2 *h.* ye work; 64:6 *h.* deep
73:7 more than *h.* could wish
101:4 froward *h.* shall depart
5 a proud *h.* will not I suffer
104:15 wine mak. glad the *h.*
bread strengthene. man's *h.*
*Prov.* 6:18 a *h.* that devis. wicked
7:10 a woman subtle of *h.*
8:5 be of an understanding *h.*
10:8 wise in *h.* will rec. comma.
12:8 he of perverse *h.*
20 deceit is in the *h.* of them
25 heaviness in *h.* of man
13:12 hope defer. maketh *h.* sick
14:10 *h.* knoweth own bittern.
13 in laughter *h.* is sorrowful
14 backslider in *h.* be filled
30 a sound *h.* is life of the flesh
33 wisdom resteth in *h.* of him
15:7 *h.* of foolish doeth not so
13 merry *h.* mak. cheer. coun.
by sorrow of *h.* sp. is broken
14 *h.* of him th. understandeth
15 a merry *h.* hath contin. feast
28 *h.* of righte. studieth to an.
30 light of eyes rejoiceth the *h.*
16:1 preparation of *h.* from L.
5 proud *h.* abomination to L.
9 a man's *h.* deviseth his way
23 *h.* of wise teach. his mouth
17:16 price in hand, hath no *h.*
20 a froward *h.* find. no good
22 merry *h.* doeth good
18:12 bef. destruc. *h.* is haughty
15 *h.* of prudent getteth kno.
19:21 devices in a man's *h.*
20:5 counsel in *h.* like deep wa.
21:1 king's *h.* is in hand of L.
4 a high look and a proud *h.*
22:11 pureness of *h.* king his fr.
15 foolish. bound in *h.* of child
*Prov.* 24:12 pon. the *h.* cons. it?
25:3 *h.* of k. is unsearchable
20 he that singeth to heavy *h.*
26:23 wicked *h.* is like potsherd
27:9 ointment and perf. rej. *h.*
19 *h.* of man answereth man
28:25 proud *h.* stirreth up strife
31:11 *h.* of her husb. doth trust
*Ec.* 7:3 sadn. of count. *h.* is bet.
4 *h.* of wise in house of mourn.
*h.* of fools in house of mirth
8:5 a wise man's *h.* discerneth
11 *h.* of men is set to do evil
9:3 the *h.* of men is full of evil
7 drink thy wine wi. merry *h.*
10:2 a wise man's *h.* at ri. hand,
but a fool's *h.* is at his left
*Is.* 6:10 make their *h.* fat, *Mat.*
13:15; *Acts* 28:27
10:12 I will punish the stout *h.*
13:7 every man's *h.* shall melt
30:29 shall have gladness of *h.*
32:4 *h.* of rash shall understand
35:4 say to them of fearful *h.*
44:20 dec. *h.* turned him aside
57:1 man layeth to *h. Jer.* 12:11
15 revive the *h.* of contrite on.
59:13 uttering from *h.* words
65:14 my serv. sing for joy of *h.*
but ye cry for sorrow of *h.*
*Jer.* 4:9 the *h.* of king sh. perish
5:23 people hath a rebellious *h.*
9:26 Is. are uncircumcised in *h.*
11:20 that triest reins and *h.*
17:9 *h.* is deceitful ab. all things
10 I the Lord search *h.*
20:12 L. that seest reins and *h.*
24:7 I will give a *h.* to know me
*Lam.* 3:65 give them sorrow of *h.*
*Ezek.* 11:19 stony *h.* out of flesh
13:22 ye made *h.* of righte. sad
18:31 make a new *h.* and new s.
21:7 ev. *h.* sh. melt, all be feeble
25:15 veng. with despiteful *h.*
36:26 give you a *h.* of flesh
44:7 uncir. in *h.* 9; *Acts* 7:51
*Dan.* 4:16 a beast's *h.* be giv. him
7:4 and a man's *h.* was given it
*Hos.* 4:11 new wine take away *h.*
7:11 E. is like dove without *h.*
*Nah.* 2:10 *h.* melt. knees smite
*Zep.* 2:15 this city said in her *h.*
*Mal.* 2:2 ye do not lay it to *h.*
4:6 the *h.* of fathers, *h.* of child.
*Mat.* 11:29 meek and lowly in *h.*
12:34 of abund. of *h. Luke* 6:45
35 treasure of *h. Luke* 6:45
15:18 from the *h.* and defile man
19 out of *h.* evil th. *Mark* 7:21
*Mark* 16:14 upbra. with hard *h.*
*Luke* 2:19 M. pondered in her *h.*
51 moth. kept sayings in her *h.*
24:25 fools, slow of *h.* to believe
*John* 13:2 devil put into *h.* of J.
*Acts* 2:46 eat meat wi. singl. of *h.*
5:33 were cut to *h.* 7:54
11:23 purpose of *h.* they cl. to L.
*Rom.* 2:5 thy impeni. *h.* treas. up
29 circumcision of *h.* in the sp.
6:17 ye obeyed from *h.* that doc.
10:10 with the *h.* man believeth
1 *Cor.* 2:9 nei. enter. in *h.* of man
7:37 hath so decreed in his *h.*
2 *Cor.* 2:4 anguish of *h.* I wrote
3:3 written in fleshly tables of *h.*
8:16 earnest care into *h.* of Tit.
*Eph.* 6:6 doing will of G. from *h.*
*Col.* 3:22 in singl. of *h.* fear. God
1 *Thes.* 2:17 in presence, not in *h.*
*Heb.* 4:12 is a discerner of the *h.*
10:22 draw near with a true *h.*
13:9 good the *h.* be established
1 *Pet.* 3:4 let be hidden man of *h.*
2 *Pet.* 2:14 a *h.* ex. with covetous
*Rev.* 18:7 she saith in her *h.* I sit

**HEART.**

*Ex.* 15:8 congealed in *h.* of sea
*Is.* 19:1 *h.* of Egypt shall melt
*Mat.* 12:40 Son of man in *h.*

**HEART, *with* all.**

*Deut.* 11:13 with *all* your *h. Jos.*
22:5; 1 *Sam.* 12:20, 24
13:3 love the Lord with *all*
your *h.* 30:6; *Mat.* 22:37;
*Mark* 12:30, 33; *Luke* 10:27
26:16; do them with *all* thy *h.*
30:2 to L. *all h.* 10; *Joel* 2:12
*Jud.* 16:17 S. told *all* his *h.* 18
1 *K.* 2:4 walk before me with *all*
*h.* 8:23
8:48 return to thee with *all* th.
*h.* 2 *K.* 23:25; 2 *Chr.* 6:38
14:8 David fol. me wi. *all* his *h.*
2 *K.* 23:3 a covenant to walk with
*all* their *h.* 2 *Chr.* 34:31
2 *Chr.* 15:12 G. of fa. with *all h.*
15 had sworn with *all* their *h.*
2 *Chr.* 22:9 J. so. L. w. *all* his *h.*
31:21 did it with *all* his *h.*
*Ps.* 86:12 praise, O L. with *all h.*
*Prov.* 3:5 trust L. with *all* thy *h.*
*Jer.* 29:13 search me with *all h.*
*Ezek.* 36:5 joy of *all* their *h.*
*Zep.* 3:14 rejoice with *all* the *h.*
*Acts* 8:37 if thou beli. with *all h.*
*See* APPLY, BROKEN, CLEAN,
EVIL, HARDEN, HARDENED.

**His HEART.**

*Gen.* 6:5 imag. of *his h.* only evil
6 it grieved him at *his h.*
8:21 L. said in *h. h.*; 17:17 Abr.
27:41 E. said in *his h.* the days
*Ex.* 4:14 will be glad in *his h.*
7:23 neither did he set *his h.*
28:29 breastpl. of judg. on *h. h.*
35:34 he hath put in *his h.*
*Deut.* 2:30 L. made *his h.* obstin.
17:17 *his h.* turn not away
20 *his h.* be not lifted up above
19:6 aveng. pursue, *his h.* is hot
20:8 brethren's *h.* faint as *his h.*
24:15 poor, setteth *his h.* on it
29:19 blesseth himself in *his h.*
*Ruth* 3:7 *his h.* was merry
1 *Sam.* 4:13 *his h.* trem. for ark
25:37 it came that *his h.* died
27:1 D. in *his h.*; 28:5 *his h.* tre.
2 *Sam.* 7:27 thy servant found in
*his h.* 1 *Chr.* 17:25
13:33 let not lord take to *his h.*
1 *K.* 10:24 which God had put in
*his h.* 2 *Chr.* 9:23
11:3 turned away *his h.* 4, 9
12:26 Jeroboam said in *his h.*
2 *K.* 9:24 arrow went out at *his h.*

2 Chr. 12:14 prepared not his h.
17:6 his h. was lift. up in ways
26:16 his h. was lifted up to des.
30:19 prepareth his h. to seek G.
32:25 for his h. was lifted up
26 hum. him. for pride of his h.
31 he might know all in his h.
Ezr. 7:10 Ezra prepared his h.
Neh. 9:8 foundest his h. faithful
Est. 6:6 H. thought in his h.
7:5 durst presume in his h.
Job 34:14 set his h. upon man
41:24 his h. is as firm as a stone
Ps. 10:3 boasteth of his h. desire
6 said in his h. 11, 13; 14:1; 53:1
15:2 speaketh truth in his h.
21:2 given him his h. desire
33:11 thoughts of his h.
37:31 law of his God in his h.
41:6 his h. gathereth iniquity
55:21 smooth, war in his h.
78:72 accor. to integrity of h. h.
112:7 his h. is fixed
8 his h. is established
Prov. 6:14 frowardn. is in his h.
18:2 his h. may discover itself
19:3 his h. fretteth ag. the Lord
23:7 as think. in his h. so is he: but his h. is not with thee
28:14 that hardeneth his h. sh. f.
Ec. 2:23 his h. taketh no rest
5:20 God answer. in joy of h. h.
Cant. 3:11 day of gladn. of h. h.
Is. 7:2 his h. moved, h. of people
10:7 neither doth his h. think so
32:6 his h. will work iniquity
44:19 none considereth in his h.
57:17 frowardly in way of h. h.
Jer. 9:8 in his h. he layeth
30:21 his h. to approach to me
24 performed intents of his h.
48:29 heard haughtine. of his h.
Ezek. 14:4 set. up idols in h. h. 7
31:10 his h. lifted up, Dan. 5:20
Dan. 4:16 h. h. be changed, 5:21
11:12 his h. shall be lifted up
28 his h. be ag. the covenant
Mat. 5:28 com. adultery in his h.
13:19 was sown in his h.
24:48 say in his h. Luke 12:45
Mark 7:19 enter. not into his h.
11:23 not doubt in h. h. but bel.
Luke 6:45 good treasure of h. h.
Acts 7:23 came into h. h. to visit
1 Cor. 7:37 stand. stead. in h. h.
14:25 secrets of h. h. made man.
2 Cor. 9:7 purposeth in his h.

**My HEART.**

Deut. 29:19 in imagina. of my h.
Jos. 14:7 as it was in my h.
Jud. 5:9 my h. tow. governors
1 Sam. 2:1 my h. rejoiceth in L.
1 K. 9:3 my h. there, 2 Chr. 7:16
2 K. 5:26 went not my h. wi. th.
10:15 thy heart right as my h.?
1 Chr. 12:17 my h. shall be knit
28:2 in my h. to build a house
2 Chr. 29:10 my h. to make a co.
Neh. 2:12 God put in my h. 7:5
Job 17:11 thoughts of my h.
23:16 God maketh my h. soft
27:6 my h. sh. not reproach me
31:7 my h. walk. af. mine eyes
9 my h. been dec. by a woman
27 my h. hath been se. enticed
33:3 words of uprightn. of my h.
37:1 my h. trembleth
Ps. 4:7 put gladness in my h.
13:2 sorrow in my h. daily
5 my h. sh. rejoice in thy salv.
16:9 my h. glad; 17:3 pro. my h.
19:14 medita. of my h. be accep.
22:14 my h. is like wax
26:2 try my reins, and my h.
25:17 troubles of my h. enlarged
27:3 my h. shall not fear
8 my h. said to thee, Thy face
28:7 my h. trust. my h. greatly
38:8 by reason of disq. of my h.
10 my h. panteth, Is. 21:4
39:3 my h. was hot within me
40:8 thy law is within my h.
10 not hid righteous. in my h.
12 therefore my h. faileth me
45:1 my h. is indi. good matter
Ps. 49:3 meditation of my h.
55:4 my h. is sore pained
57:7 my h. is fixed, 108:1
61:2 my h. is overwhelmed
66:18 if I regard iniq. in my h.
69:20 repro. hath broken my h.
73:13 cleansed my h. in vain
21 thus my h. was grieved
26 my h. faileth
84:2 my h. crieth out for liv. G.
86:11 unite my h. to fear
102:4 my h. is smitten and with.
109:22 my h. is wounded within
119:11 word have I hid in my h.
32 thou shalt enlarge my h.
36 incline my h. to thy testim.
80 my h. be sound in thy stat.
111 testim. the rejoic. of my h.
112 inclined my h. to thy stat.
131:1 L. my h. is not haughty
139:23 search me, know my h.
141:4 incline not my h. to evil
143:4 my h. within me is deso.
Prov. 5:12 my h. desp. reproof
20:9 say, I made my h. clean?
23:15 be wise, my h. sh. rejoice
Ec. 1:13 I gave my h. to seek
16 my h. had great experience
17 gave my h. to know wisdom
2:1 my h. I will pro. 15; 3:17, 18
3 in my h. to give to wine
10 withheld not my h. from joy
20 to cause my h. to despair
7:25 ap. my h. to know, 8:9, 16
Cant. 4:9 thou ravished my h. 9
5:2 I sleep, but my h. waketh
Is. 63:4 day of veng. in my h.
Jer. 3:15 pastors accord. to my h.
4:19 pain. my h. my h. m. noise
7:31 neither came it into my h.
8:18 comf. myself, my h. is faint
12:3 seen me and tried my h.
15:16 joy and rejoicing of my h.
20:9 his word was in my h.
23:9 my h. broken; 48:31 sh. m.
48:36 my h. shall sound for M.
Lam. 1:20 my h. is turned
22 my h. is faint
3:51 mine eye affecteth my h.
Hos. 11:8 my h. turned with. me
Acts 2:26 therefore did my h. rej.
21:13 to weep, and break my h.?
Rom. 9:2 contin. sorrow in my h.
10:1 my h. desire to G. for Is. is
Phil. 1:7 bec. I have you in my h.
See APPLIED.

**One HEART.**

2 Chr. 30:12 to give one h.
Jer. 32:39 give one h. Ezek. 11:19
Acts 4:32 multitude were of o. h.

**Our HEART.**

Deut. 1:28 breth. have disc. o. h.
Ps. 33:21 for our h. shall rejoice
44:18 our h. is not turned back
Lam. 3:41 let us lift up our h.
5:15 joy of o. h.; 17 our h. faint
Luke 24:32 did not our h. burn
2 Cor. 6:11 our h. is enlarged
1 John 3:20 if our h. cond. us, 21

**Own HEART.**

Num. 15:39 seek not after own h.
1 Sam. 13:14 m. after o. h. Acts 13:22
2 Sam. 7:21 accord. to thine o. h. hast thou done, 1 Chr. 17:19
1 K. 8:38 the plague of his o. h.
Neh. 6:8 feignest th. out of o. h.
Ps. 4:4 commune with own h.
20:4 grant according to own h.
Ps. 37:15 sword sh. ent. th. o. h.
77:6 commune with mine o. h.
Prov. 28:26 trusteth his own h.
Ec. 1:16 I com. with own h.
7:22 own h. hast cursed others
Jer. 9:14 imagin. of own h. 23:17
23:16 a vision of their own h.
26 deceit of o. h. Ezek. 13:17
Jam. 1:26 deceiveth his own h.

**Perfect HEART.**

1 K. 8:61 h. be p. with the Lord
11:4 h. not p. with Lord, 15:3
15:14 nevertheless Asa's h. was p. with Lord, 2 Chr. 15:17
2 K. 20:3 walked before thee with a perfect h. Is. 38:3
1 Chr. 12:38 p. h. to make D. ki.
28:9 serve God with a p. h.
29:9 with p. h. they off. willing.
19 give to Sol. my son a p. h.
2 Chr. 16:9 them whose h. is p.
25:2 right, but not with a p. h.
Ps. 101:2 in my house with p. h.

**Pure HEART.**

Ps. 24:4 ascend? that hath p. h.
Mat. 5:8 blessed are pure in h.
1 Tim. 1:5 charity out of p. h.
2 Tim. 2:22 call on L. out of p. h.
1 Pet. 1:22 love one an. with p. h.

**Their HEART.**

Gen. 42:28 their h. failed them
1 Chr. 29:18 prep. t. h. unto thee
Job 8:10 words out of t. h.?
17:4 hid t. h. from understand.
Ps. 10:17 Lord wilt prepare t. h.
78:8 gen. that set not t. h. arig.
18 they tempted God in t. h.
37 t. h. was not right with him
95:10 peo. that do err in t. h.
105:25 turned t. h. to hate
107:12 he brought down t. h.
119:70 t. h. is as fat as grease
140:2 imagine mischiefs in t. h.
Prov. 24:2 t. h. stud. destruction
Ec. 3:11 hath set world in t. h.
9:3 madness is in t. h. while
Is. 6:10 understand with t. h. Mat. 13:15; Acts 28:27
29:13 t. h. is far from me, Mat. 15:8; Mark 7:6
Jer. 13:10 walk in imag. of t. h.
14:14 proph. the deceit of t. h.
17:1 sin of Judah graven on t. h.
Lam. 2:18 t. h. cried to the Lord
Ezek. 14:3 set up idols in t. h.
20:16 t. h. went after idols
21:15 that t. h. may faint, ruins
33:31 t. h. goeth after covetous.
Hos. 4:8 they set t. h. on iniquity
7:6 made ready t. h. like an ov.
10:2 t. h. divided; 13:6 t. h. exa.
13:8 will rend the caul of t. h.
Zec. 10:7 t. h. rejoice in the Lord
Mark 6:52 t. h. hard. Rom. 1:21
Luke 9:47 perce. thought of t. h.
John 12:40 he hath harden. t. h.
Acts 2:37 were pricked in t. h.
2 Cor. 3:15 M. read, vail on t. h.
Eph. 4:18 of the blindness of t. h.

**Thy HEART.**

Gen. 20:6 the integrity of t. h.
Lev. 19:17 not hate brot. in t. h.
Deut. 4:29 if seek him with t. h.
6:5 love the Lord with all t. h.
7:17 if thou shalt say in t. h. these nations are more than I, 8:17; 18:21; Jer. 13:22
8:14 t. h. be lifted, forget Lord
9:5 not for uprightness of t. h.
10:12 serve L. t. G. with all t. h.
15:9 not a thou. in t. wicked h.
10 t. h. shall not be grieved
28:67 for the fear of thy h.

30:6 circumc. t. h. and heart of
14 word is very nigh to thy h.
17 if t. h. turn, so that th. not
Jud. 19:6 let t. h. be merry, 9; 1 K. 21:7
1 Sam. 2:33 man be to grieve t. h.
14:7 do all that is in t. h. 2 Sam. 7:3; 1 Chr. 17:2
17:28 pride and naught. of t. h.
2 Sam. 3:21 over all t. h. desire.
1 K. 2:44 wicked. t. h. is privy
8:18 in t. h. to build, 2 Chr. 1:11; 6:8
2 K. 10:15 Jehu said, Is t. h. rig.
14:10 t. h. lifted, 2 Chr. 25:19
22:19 t. h. tender, 2 Chr. 34:27
2 Chr. 19:3 prep. t. h. to seek G.
Job 10:13 things hid in t. h.
11:13 prep. t. h. and stretch out
22:22 lay up his words in t. h
Ps. 27:14 shall strengthen t. h.
37:4 give thee desires of t. h.
Prov. 2:2 apply t. h. to underst.
Prov. 2:10 when wisd. ent. t. h.
3:1 let t. h. keep my command.
3 write them on ta. of t. h. 7:3
4:4 let t. h. ret. my words, 21
23 keep t. h. with all diligence
6:21 bind continually upon t. h.
7:25 let not t. h. decline to ways
23:15 my son, if t. h. be wise
17 let not t. h. envy sinners
19 hear, my son, guide t. h. in
26 give me t. h. let eyes obser.
33 t. h. shall utter perverse th.
Ec. 5:2 not t. h. be hasty to utter
11:9 t. h. cheer, in ways of t. h.
10 remove sorrow from t. h.
Is. 14:13 thou hast said in t. h.
33:18 t. h. shall meditate terror
47:7 not lay things to t. h. 57:11
8 that sayest in t. h. I am, 10
Jer. 4:14 O Jerusalem wash t. h.
18 bitter, bec. it reach. to t. h.
31:21 set t. h. toward high.
49:16 pride of t. h. decei. Ob. 3
Lam. 2:19 pour out t. h. bef. L.
Ezek. 3:10 my words received in thy h.
16:30 weak is t. h. saith L. G.
22:14 can t. h. endure in days
28:2 because t. h. is lifted up
6 hast set t. h. as heart of G.
17 t. h. was lifted up because
Dan. 2:30 know the thou. of t. h.
5:22 thou hast not humb. t. h.
Acts 5:3 why hath Satan fi. t. h.?
4 why conceived this in t. h.?
8:21 t. h. not right in sight of G.
22 thought of t. h. forgiven
Rom. 10:6 say not in t. h. who
9 believe in t. h. that G. raised

**Upright in HEART.**

2 Chr. 29:34 Levites were u. in h.
Ps. 7:10 which saveth u. in h.
11:2 that they shoot at u. in h.
32:11 shout for joy ye u. in h.
36:10 contin. righte. to u. in h.
64:10 all uprig. in h. shall glory
94:15 upri. in h. shall follow it
97:11 gladness sown for u. in h.

**Uprightness of HEART.**

1 K. 3:6 walketh in u. of h. 9:4
Ps. 119:7 praise thee with h.

**Whole HEART.**

Ps. 9:1 I praise thee, O Lord, w. my w. h. 111:1; 138:1
119:2 seek him with the w. h.
10 with my w. h. I sought
34 I shall observe it with w. h.
58 entreated favor with w. h.
69 thy precepts with w. h.
145 I cried with my w. h. O L.
Is. 1:5 head is sick, w. h. faint
Jer. 3:10 not turned with w. h.
24:7 return to me with w. h.
32:41 plant in land with w. h.

**Whose HEART.**

Ex. 35:26 women w. h. stirred
Deut. 29:18 w. h. turneth from L.
2 Sam. 17:10 w. h. is as h. of lion
1 K. 8:39 w. h. kn. 2 Chr. 6:30
2 Chr. 16:9 them w. h. is perfect
Ps. 84:5 in w. h. are ways of
Ec. 7:26 woman w. h. is snares
Is. 51:7 in w. h. is my law
Ezek. 11:21 w. h. walketh after
Acts 16:14 w. h. the L. opened

**Your HEART.**

Deut. 10:16 foresk. of your h. Jer. 4:4
11:16 that y. h. be not deceived
18 lay up my words in y. h.
1 K. 11:2 will turn away your h.
1 Chr. 22:19 set y. h. to seek L.
Ps. 22:26 y. h. shall live for ever
31:24 he shall strengthen y. h.
62:8 pour out y. h. before him
10 riches, set not y. h. on them
69:32 y. h. live that seek God
Is. 66:14 see this, y. h. shall rej.
Jer. 51:46 and lest your h. faint
Joel 2:13 rend y. h. not garments
Zec. 7:10 none imag. evil in y. h.
Mat. 6:21 y. h. be also, Luke 12:34
Mark 8:17 have ye y. h. hard.?
10:5 for hard. of y. h. he wrote
John 14:1 not y. h. be troubl. 27
16:6 said this, sorrow filled y. h.
22 I will see you, y. h. shall
Eph. 6:5 single. of y. h. as to C.

**HEARTED.**

Ex. 35:22 as were willing-h.
Deut. 20:8 what man is faint-h.?
Ps. 76:5 the stout-h. are spoiled
Is. 24:7 all the merry-h. do sigh
61:1 sent me to bind up brok.-h.
Ezek. 3:7 house of Israel hard-h.

**Tender-HEARTED.**

2 Chr. 13:7 Reho. young and t.-h.
Eph. 4:32 kind one to ano. t.-h.

**Wise-HEARTED.**

Ex. 28:3 spe. to all th. are w.-h.
31:6 hearts of all that are w.-h.
35:10 w.-h. among you sh. come
25 women that were w.-h.
36:1 wro. every w.-h. man, 2, 8

**HEARTH.**

Gen. 18:6 make cakes upon h.
Ps. 102:3 bones are burnt as h.
Is. 30:14 sherd to take fire fr. h.
Jer. 36:22 a fire on the h. burni.
23 roll into fire that was on h.
Zec. 12:6 governors of J. like h.

**HEARTY, ILY.**

Prov. 27:9 friend by h. counsel
Col. 3:23 do it h. as to the Lord

**HEARTS.**

Jos. 7:5 h. of the people melted
1 Sam. 10:26 h. G. had touched
2 Sam. 15:6 Absal. stole h. of Is.
1 K. 8:39 thou only knowest the h. 2 Chr. 6:30
1 Chr. 28:9 Lord searcheth all h.
Ps. 7:9 God trieth h. Prov. 17:3
Prov. 15:11 more then h. men
21:2 the Lord pondereth the h.
31:6 wine to those of heavy h.
Ezek. 32:9 also vex h. of people
Dan. 11:27 kings' h. to do misc.
Luke 1:17 turn h. of the fathers
2:35 thoughts of h. be revealed
21:26 men's h. failing them
Acts 1:24 know. h. of men, 15:8
Rom. 8:27 he that searcheth h.
16:18 deceive h. of the simple
1 Cor. 4:5 manifest counsels of h.
Rev. 2:23 I am he searcheth h.

**Our HEARTS.**

Jos. 2:11 heard, our h. did melt
1 K. 8:58 incline our h. to him
Acts 14:17 filling o. h. with food
Rom. 5:5 love of G. abr. in our h.
2 Cor. 1:22 earnest of S. in our h.
3:2 our epistle written in o. h.
4:6 God hath shined in our h.
7:3 in our h. to die and live
1 Thes. 2:4 God, who trieth o. h.
Heb. 10:22 our h. fr. evil consci.
1 John 3:19 assure o. h. bef. him

**Their HEARTS.**

Lev. 26:36 a faintness into t. h.
Jud. 9:3 t. h. inclined to fol. A.
19:22 making their h. merry
2 Chr. 6:14 be. thee with all t. h.
11:16 set their h. to seek the L.
20:33 not prep. their h. to God
Job 1:5 sons cursed G. in their h.
Ps. 28:3 mischief is in their h.
33:15 fashioneth their h. alike
35:25 let them not say in t. h.
81:12 gave up to t. own h. lust
125:4 that are upright in t. h.
Is. 44:18 hath shut their h. they
Jer. 31:33 law in t. h. Heb. 8:10
32:40 I will put my fear in t. h.
Ezek. 13:2 prop. out of t. own h.
Zec. 7:12 t. h. as an adamant
Mark 2:6 reasoning in their h.
3:5 grieved for hardness of t. h.
4:15 word sown in t. h. Lu. 8:12
Luke 1:51 imaginations of t. h.
66 heard laid them up in t. h.
3:15 all men mused in their h.
Acts 7:39 t. h. turned back to E.
Rom. 1:24 through lust of th. h.
2:15 work of law written in t. h.
Col. 2:2 t. h. might be comforted
Heb. 3:10 always err in their h.
Rev. 17:17 G. hath put it in t. h.

**Your HEARTS.**

Gen. 18:5 comfort ye your h.
Deut. 20:3 O Is. let not y. h. faint
32:46 set y. h. to all the words
Jos. 24:23 incline y. h. to the L.
1 Sam. 6:6 do ye harden your h.?
7:3 return to L. with all your h. and prepa. your h. to the L.
Jer. 42:20 dissembled in your h.
Zec. 8:17 none imag. evil in y. h.
Mat. 9:4 think evil in your h.?
18:35 if from y. h. forgive not
19:8 bec. of hardness of y. h.
Mark 2:8 why reas. th. in y. h.?
Luke 5:22 reason ye in your h.?
16:15 God knoweth your h.
21:14 settle in y. h. not to me.
34 time y. h. be overcharged
24:38 do thoughts arise in y. h.?
Gal. 4:6 sent S. of Son into y. h.
Eph. 3:17 Ch. may dwell in y. h.
5:19 mel. in y. h. to L. Col. 3:16
6:22 that he might comfort y. h.
Phil. 4:7 keep y. h. and minds
Col. 3:15 peace of G. rule in y. h.
4:8 estate and comfort y. h.
1 Thes. 3:13 may stablish y. h.
2 Thes. 2:17 comfort your h.
3:5 Lord direct your h. into love
Jam. 3:14 if ye ha. strife in y. h.
4:8 pur. y. h. ye double-minded
5:5 ye have nourished y. h.
8 be ye patient, stablish y. h.
1 Pet. 3:15 sanctify Lord in y. h.
2 Pet. 1:19 day-star arise in y. h.

**HEAT.**

Gen. 8:22 cold and h. summer
18:1 tent-door in h. of the day
Deut. 29:24 what meaneth the h.
1 Sam. 11:11 slew till h. of day
1 K. 1:1 gat no h.; 2 Lord get h.
Job 24:19 drought and h. consu.
30:30 bones are burnt with h.
Ps. 19:6 is nothing hid from h.
Ec 4:11 toge. then they have h.

Is. 4:6 shad. in day from h. 25:4
18:4 clear h. on herbs, and like cloud of dew in h. of harvest
25:5 as h. in a dry place, even h.
49:10 neither h. nor sun smite
Jer. 17:8 not see when h. cometh
36:30 dead body cast out to h.
51:39 in h. I will make feasts
Ezek. 3:14 I went in h. of spirit
Mat. 20:12 borne burden and h.
Luke 12:55 so. wind blow, be h.
Acts 28:3 came viper out of the h.
Jam. 1:11 sun risen with bur. h.
2 Pet. 3:10 elements melt with h.

### HEATED.

Dan. 3:19 more th. wont to be h.
Hos. 7:4 as an oven h. by baker

### HEATH.

Jer. 17:6 like h. in desert, 48:6

### HEATHEN.

2 Sam. 22:44 kept me to be head of h. Ps. 18:43
2 K. 16:3 abominat. of h. 17:15; 21:2; 2 Chr. 28:3; 36:14
17:8 Is. walked in statutes of h.
1 Chr. 16:35 deliver us from h.
2 Chr. 20:6 rulest over king. of h.
33:9 Judah do worse than the h.
Ezr. 6:21 fr. filthiness of the h.
Neh. 5:8 redeem. Jews sold to h.
Ps. 2:1 do h. rage? Acts 4:25
8 I give the h. for inheritance
9:5 thou hast rebuked the h.
15 the h. are sunk in the pit
19 let h. be judged in thy sight
10:16 the h. perish. out his land
33:10 counsel of h. to naught
44:2 how th. didst drive out h.
46:6 the h. raged, the kingdoms
47:8 God reigneth over the h.
59:5 theref. awake to visit all h.
8 have all the h. in derision
78:55 cast out the h. also, 80:8
79:1 h. are come into thine inh.
6 pour wrath on h. Jer. 10:25
10 h. say, Wh. their G.? 115:2
94:10 he that chastiseth the h.
98:2 openly show. in sight of h.
102:15 h. shall fear name of L.
106:41 gave them to hand of h.
111:6 give them heritage of h.
149:7 exe. vengeance upon h.
Is. 16:8 lords of h. broken down
Jer. 10:2 learn not way of h.
Lam. 1:10 seen that h. entered
Ezek. 11:12 after manners of h.
20:9 not be polluted be. h. 14:22
32 say, we will be as the h.
41 sanctified before h. 28:25
22:4 made thee a repr. to the h.
16 thine inheri. in sight of h.
23:30 gone a whoring after h.
25:7 deliver. thee for spoil to h.
8 house of Jud. is like to all h.
31:11 hand of mighty one of h.
34:29 neither bear shame of h.
36:3 possession to residue of h.
4 derision to the residue of h.
6 ye have borne shame of h.
23 h. know that I am the Lord, 36; 37:28; 38:16; 39:7
39:21 the h. shall see my judg.
Joel 2:17 h. sho. rule over them
3:11 come, all ye h. gather
12 let the h. be wakened
Amos 9:12 possess rem. of all h.
Ob. 15 day of L. is near on h.
16 so sh. h. drink continually
Mic. 5:15 exe. fury upon the h.
Hab. 3:12 didst thr. h. in anger
Zep. 2:11 isles of h. sh. worship
Hag. 2:22 destroy strength of h.
Zec. 1:15 displeased with h.
9:10 he sh. speak pea. to the h.
14:14 wealth of h. shall be
Mat. 6:7 use not repeti. as h. do
18:17 let him be to thee as a h.
2 Cor. 11:26 in perils by the h.
Gal. 2:9 should go unto the h.
3:8 God would justify the h.

### Among the HEATHEN.

Lev. 26:33 I will scat. you a. t. h. Jer. 9:16; Ezek. 20:23; 22:15
38 ye shall perish am. the h.
2 Sam. 22:50 I will gi. thanks to thee, O L. a. t. h. Ps. 18:49
1 Chr. 16:24 declare his glory am. the h. Ps. 96:3
Ps. 44:11 thou scatter us a. t. h.
14 mak. us a by-word a. the h.
46:10 I will be exalted a. t. h.
96:10 say a. t. h. Lord reigneth
106:35 were mingled a. the h.
47 O L. gather us from a. t. h.
110:6 he shall judge am. the h.
126:2 a. h. L. ha. done great
Jer. 49:15 ma. thee small a. t. h.
Lam. 4:15 a. h. shall no more so.
20 under his shad. live a. t. h.
Ezek. 11:16 cast th. far off a. t. h.
12:16 declare abomina. a. t. h.
16:14 renown went forth a. t. h.
36:19 scatter them am. the h.
21 Isr. profaned a. the h. 22, 23
24 will take you fr. a. h. 37:21
39:21 will set my glory a. t. h.
Joel 2:19 no more a repro. a. t. h.
Ob. 1 an ambas. is sent a. t. h.
2 made thee small a. the h.
Hab. 1:5 behold ye a. the h.
Zec. 8:13 were a curse a. t. h.
Mal. 1:11 name be great a. h. 14
Gal. 1:16 preach him a. t. h.

### HEAVE, D.

Ex. 29:27 h. of ram of consecra.
Num. 15:20 offering so sh. ye h.
18:30 ye h. the best thereof, 32

See OFFERING, SHOULDER.

### HEAVEN.

Gen. 1:1 G. created h. and earth
8 God called the firmament h.
14 lights in firmam. of h. 15
20 fowl that fly in firma. of h.
7:11 windows of h. were open.
8:2 windows of h. were stopped
14:19 pos. h. and earth, 22
19:24 rained fire from Lord of h.
27:28 G. give thee of d. of h. 39
28:17 This is the gate of h.
49:25 bless thee wi. bless. of h.
Ex. 20:11 Lord made h. 31:17
24:10 as it were the body of h.
Lev. 26:19 make your h. as iron
Deut. 4:11 burned to midst h.
26 I call h. and earth to witness, 30:19; 31:28
32 ask from side of h. to other
36 out of h. made th. hear voi.
10:14 h. and h. of h. Ps. 115:16
11:17 he shut up h. 1 K. 8:35; 2 Chr. 6:26; 7:13
28:12 open h. to give thee rain
23 h. over thy head shall be
30:4 utmost part of h. Neh. 1:9
33:13 the precious things of h.
26 God of J. rid. upon the h.
1 Sam. 2:10 out of h. sh. he thun.
2 Sam. 18:9 up bet. h. and earth
21:10 water dropped out of h.
22:8 the foundations of h. mov.
1 K. 8:27 h. and h. of heav. not contain thee, 2 Chr. 2:6; 6:18
35 when h. is shut up no rain
2 K. 19:15 th. hast made h. and earth, 2 Chr. 2:12; Neh. 9:6
1 Chr. 21:16 angel betw. h. and
Job 11:8 it is as high as h.?
20:27 h. shall reveal his iniquity
22:12 is not G. in height of h.?
14 walketh in the circuit of h.
26:11 the pillars of h. tremble
38:29 frost of h. who ha. ge. it?
33 knowest thou ordin. of h.?
37 who can stay bottles of h.?
Ps. 19:6 going is from end of h.
69:34 h. and earth praise him
78:23 he opened the doors of h.
24 given them of corn of h.
89:29 th. to endure as days of h.
103:11 h. is high above earth
105:40 sat. them wi. bread of h.
115:15 L. who ma. h. and earth, 121:2; 124:8; 134:3; 146:6; Is. 37:16; Jer. 32:17; Acts 4:24; 14:15; Rev. 14:7
147:8 covereth h. with clouds
148:13 gl. is above earth and h.
Prov. 25:3 h. for height, earth
Is. 40:12 hath meted out h.?
66:1 h. is my throne, Acts 7:49
Jer. 7:18 cakes to queen of h.
10:2 be not dism. at signs of h.
23:24 do not I fill h. and earth?
31:37 if h. above can be meas.
33:25 not appointed ordin. of h
44:17 inc. to qu. of h. 18, 19, 25
51:15 hath stretched out the h.
Lam. 4:19 swifter th. eagles of h.
Ezek. 8:3 lift. me be. earth and h.
32:7 I will cover the h.
8 lights of h. will I make dark
Dan. 4:15 be wet with dew of h. 23, 25, 33; 5:21
35 doeth will in army of h.
5:23 lifted thyself ag. L. of h.
7:2 four winds of h. strove
13 man came with clouds of h.
8:8 toward four winds of h. 11:4
Amos 9:6 build his stories in h.
Hag. 1:10 h. is stayed from dew
Zec. 2:6 spr. you as winds of h.
Mal. 3:10 not open wind. of h.
Mat. 5:18 till h. and earth pass
34 nor swear by h. Jam. 5:12
11:25 thee, L. of h. Luke 10:21
23:22 swear by h. swear by G.
24:30 S. of man com. in clouds of h. 26:64; Mark 14:62
31 elect from one end of h.
35 h. and earth sh. pass away, Mark 13:31; Luke 21:33
36 not angels of h. but my F.
Mark 13:27 elect fr. ut. part of h.
Luke 3:21 J. praying, h. opened
4:25 when the h. was shut up
15:18 have sinned against h. 21
16:17 easier for h. and earth
21:26 powers of h. sh. be shaken
John 1:51 ye shall see h. open
Acts 3:21 wh. the h. must receive
10:11 saw h. opened, Rev. 19:11
Jam. 5:18 and the h. gave rain
Rev. 3:12 cometh down out of h.
6:14 h. departed as a scroll
8:13 angel flying thro' h. 14:6
10:6 created h. and the things
11:6 these have power to shut h.
16:17 a great voice out of h.
21 a great hail out of h.
18:20 rejoice over her, thou h.
19:17 to the fowls that fly in h.
20:9 fire came from G. out of h.
11 earth and h. fled away
21:1 I saw a new h. and earth
10 Jerus. descending out of h.

See FOWL, FOWLS.

### From HEAVEN.

Ex. 16:4 rain bread from h.
20:22 talked with you from h. Neh. 9:13
Deut. 26:15 look down from h. Is. 63:15; Lam. 3:50
28:24 as dust f. h. shall it come
Jos. 10:11 L. cast great sto. f. h.
Jud. 5:20 fought f. h. the stars
2 Sam. 22:14 L. thundered fr. h.

2 K. 1:10 let fire come down f. h.
th. came down fi. f. h. 12, 14
1 Chr. 21:26 answ. f. h. by fire
2 Chr. 6:21 hear f. h. 23, 27, 30
7:1 fire came down from h.
14 will I hear f. h. and forgive
Neh. 9:15 gav. them bread f. h.
Job 1:16 fire of G. fallen from h.
Ps. 14:2 L. look. down f. h. 53:2
33:13 the Lord looketh from h.
76:8 judment to be heard f. h.
80:14 O God, look down f. h.
85:11 right. shall look from h.
102:19 f. h. did the L. behold
Is. 14:12 how art thou fal. f. h.
55:10 as snow falleth from h.
Lam. 2:1 Lord cast down f. h.
Dan. 4:31 a voice f. h. Mat. 3:17; Luke 3:22; John 12:28
Mat. 16:1 show them sign f. h.
21:25 wh. was it? f. h. or of men? Mark 11:30; Lu. 20:4
28:2 for the angel descended f. h. Rev. 10:1; 18:1; 20:1
Mark 8:11 sign f. h. Luke 11:16
Luke 9:54 com. fire to come f. h.
10:18 behe. S. as lightning f. h.
17:29 fire and brimstone f. h.
21:11 great signs sh. th. be f. h.
22:43 angel f. h. strengthening
John 1:32 I saw S. descend. f. h.
3:13 came down from h. 6:33
27 exc. it be given him fro. h.
31 he that com. f. h. is above
6:31 he gave bread from h.
32 M. gave you not bread f. h.
38 I came f. h. not to do, 42
41 bread came f. h. 50, 51, 58
Acts 2:2 there came a sound f. h.
9:3 a light f. h. sh. 22:6; 26:13
11:5 a great sheet let down f. h.
Acts 14:17 and gave us rain f. h.
Rom. 1:18 wra. of G. is rev. f. h.
1 Cor. 15:47 se. man is Lord f. h.
2 Cor. 5:2 clothed with ho. f. h.
Gal. 1:8 angel f. h. preach
1 Thes. 1:10 wait for Son from h.
4:16 the L. shall descend fr. h.
2 Thes. 1:7 L. J. be revealed f. h.
Heb. 12:25 him that speak. f. h.
1 Pet. 1:12 with H. G. sent f. h.
Rev. 8:10 fell a great star f. h.
9:1 I saw a star fall from h.
10:4 I heard a voice f. h. saying, Seal things and write them not, 8; 11:12; 14:2, 13; 18:4
13:13 fire come down from h.

See GOD of Heaven.

**Host, s of HEAVEN.**

Deut. 4:19 h. of h. worship him
17:3 hath worship. the h. of h.
1 K. 22:19 saw L. sit on thr. and h. of h. sta. by, 2 Chr. 18:18
2 K. 17:16 Israel worshi. h. of h.
21:3 Manasseh worshipped all the host of h. 2 Chr. 33:3
5 alt. for host of h. 2 Chr. 33:5
23:4 bro. vessels for host of h. 5
Neh. 9:6 made h. of h. with their h. and host of h. worsh. thee
Is. 34:4 h. of h. sh. be dissolved
Jer. 8:2 spread them bef. h. of h.
19:13 burnt incense to host of h.
33:22 as h. of h. cannot be num.
Dan. 8:10 great, even to h. of h.
Zep. 1:5 off them worship h. of h.
Acts 7:42 to worship host of h.

**In HEAVEN.**

Ex. 20:4 nor likeness of anything in h. Deut. 5:8
Deut. 3:24 what God in h. can
4:39 the Lord is G. in h. above
Jos. 2:11 he is God in h. above
1 K. 8:23 is no God like thee in h. 2 Chr. 6:14
30 hear thou in h. 32–49
2 K. 7:2 L. make wind. in h. 19
1 Chr. 29:11 all in h. and earth
Job 16:19 my witness is in h.
Ps. 11:4 Lord's throne is in h.
73:25 wh. have I in h. but thee
77:18 voice of thunder in h.
78:26 east wind to blow in h.
89:6 who in h. can be co. to L.?
37 as faithful witnesses in h.
113:6 hum. him. to things in h.
119:89 thy word is settled in h.
Ec. 5:2 God in h. thou up. earth
Is. 34:5 sw. shall be bathed in h.
Dan. 2:28 G. in h. reveal. secrets
Amos 9:6 buildeth stories in h.
Mat. 5:12 great is your rew. in h.
16 glorify your Father in h.
45 chil. of your F. who is in h.
48 be perfect as your F. in h.
6:9 Our Father in h. Luke 11:2
10 on earth as in h. Luke 11:2
20 but lay up treasures in h.
7:11 F. in h. give good things
21 will of my F. in h. 12:50
10:32 confess bef. my F. in h.
33 him will I deny bef. F. in h.
16:17 F. wh. is in h. revealed it
19 shall be bound in h. 18:18
18:10 desp. not little ones in h.
19:21 treasure in h. Luke 18:22
22:30 angels in h. Mark 12:25
23:9 one is your F. who is in h.
24:30 sign of Son of man in h.
28:18 all power given me in h.
Mark 11:26 nor F. in h. forgive
13:25 powers in h. sh. be shak.
32 not angels which are in h.
Luke 6:23 your re. is great in h.
10:20 your names are writ. in h.
15:7 joy in h. over one sinner
19:38 peace in h. glory in high
John 3:13 even Son of man in h.
Acts 2:19 wonders in h. above
1 Cor. 8:5 whe. in h. or in earth
Eph. 1:10 gath. in one, thi. in h.
3:15 family in h. is named
6:9 your Master in h. Col. 4:1
Phil. 2:10 of things in h.
3:20 our conversation is in h.
Col. 1:5 hope wh. is laid up in h.
16 things created that are in h.
20 to reconcile all things in h.
Heb. 10:34 have in h. better sub.
12:23 first-born written in h.
1 Pet. 1:4 inherit. reserved in h.
1 John 5:7 three bear rec. in h.
Rev. 4:1 a door was opened in h.
2 a throne was set in h.
5:13 every creature in h. saying
8:1 sil. in h.; 11:15 voices in h.
11:19 temple of G. opened in h.
Rev. 12:1 ap. great wonder in h. 3
7 there was war in h.
8 nor place fou. any more in h.
13:6 to blaspheme them in h.
14:17 came out of temple in h.
15:1 I saw another sign in h.
5 tabernacle of testimony in h.
19:14 the armies in h. followed

**Into HEAVEN.**

2 K. 2:1 L. wo. take Elijah i. h.
11 Eli. went by a whirlw. i. h.
Ps. 139:8 ascend into h. art there
Prov. 30:4 ascend. i. h. Rom. 10:6
Is. 14:13 I will ascend into h.
Mark 16:19 L. was received i. h.
Luke 2:15 angels gone away i. h.
24:51 he was parted, carried i. h.
Acts 1:11 gazing i. h. taken i. h.
7:55 Stephen looked up into h.
10:16 vessel received i. h. 11:10
Heb. 9:24 but into h. itself
1 Pet. 3:22 gone i. h. on right h.

See KINGDOM.

**HEAVEN, with stars.**

Gen. 1:17 G. set stars in fir. of h.
22:17 will multiply thy seed as stars of h. 26:4; Ex. 32:13; 1 Chr. 27:23; Neh. 9:23
Deut. 1:10 are as stars of h. 10:22
28:62 were as s. of h. for multi.
Is. 13:10 s. of h. sh. not give light
Ezek. 32:7 cover h. make s. dark
Nah. 3:16 multiplied as s. of h.
Mat. 24:29 s. fall fr. h. Mark 13:25
Rev. 6:13 stars of h. fell on earth
12:4 his tail drew third of s. of h.

**To, or unto HEAVEN.**

Gen. 11:4 tower may reach u. h.
28:12 top of it may reach to h.
Deut. 1:28 cities walled to h. 9:1
30:12 who sh. go up for us to h.
32:40 for I lift up my hand to h.
1 Sam. 5:12 cry of city w. up to h.
1 K. 8:54 with hands spread to h.
2 Chr. 28:9 a rage th. reach. u. h.
Ps. 107:26 they mount up to h.
Jer. 51:9 her judg. reacheth u. h.
Dan. 4:11 tree reached to h. 20
Amos 9:2 tho' they climb up t. h.
Mat. 11:23 Cap. art exalted to h.
14:19 look. up to h. he blessed, Mark 6:41; Luke 9:16
Mark 7:34 looking to h. he sighed
Luke 18:13 not lift his eyes u. h.
John 3:13 no man ascen. up to h.
17:1 Je. lifted up his eyes to h.
2 Cor. 12:2 caught up to third h.
Rev. 10:5 angel lifted hand to h.
11:12 ascend. up to h. in cloud
18:5 her sins have reached u. h.

**Toward HEAVEN.**

Gen. 15:5 look now toward h.
Ex. 10:22 stretch. his hand t. h.
Jud. 13:20 flame went up t. h.
1 K. 8:22 Solomon spread forth his hands tow. h. 2 Chr. 6:13
Job 2:12 dust on their heads t. h.
Prov. 23:5 fly aw. as eagle t. h.
Acts 1:10 looked steadfastly t. h.

**Under HEAVEN.**

Gen. 1:9 waters under h. be gat.
6:17 to destroy all flesh fr. u. h.
7:19 high hills u. the whole h.
Deut. 4:19 to all nations u. h.
7:24 dest. th. name fr. u. h. 9:14
29:20 L. blot out name fr. u. h.
2 K. 14:27 blot na. of Is. fr. u. h.
Job 28:24 G. seeth u. the whole h.
37:3 directeth it u. the whole h.
41:11 whatsoever is u. h. is mine
Ec. 1:13 search out all th. u. h.
2:3 that good they sho. do u. h.
3:1 a time to ev. purpose u. h.
Luke 17:24 lighte. one part u. h.
Acts 2:5 devout of ev. nation u. h.
4:12 none oth. name u. h. given
Col. 1:23 gospel to ev. creat. u. h.

**HEAVENLY.**

Mat. 6:14 h. Father will forgive
26 your h. Father feedeth them
32 h. F. knoweth ye have need
15:13 ev. plant h. F. hath not
18:35 so shall my h. Father do
Luke 2:13 the h. host praising G.
11:13 your h. F. sh. give the Sp.
John 3:12 I tell you of h. things
Acts 26:19 not disob. to h. vision
1 Cor. 15:48 as is the h. such are
49 shall bear the image of the h.
Eph. 1:3 blessings in h. places
20 right hand in h. places, 2:6
3:10 the powers in h. places
2 Tim. 4:18 Lord pres. to h. king.
Heb. 3:1 partakers of h. calling
6:4 have tasted of the h. gift
Heb. 8:5 exa. and sh. of h. things
9:23 h. things with better sacri.
11:16 h. country; 12:22 h. Jeru.

**HEAVENS.**
Gen. 2:1 h. and earth finished
4 generat. of the h. and earth
Deut. 32:1 O h. I will sp. Is. 1:2
33:28 his h. sh. drop down dew
Jud. 5:4 trembled, h. dropped
2 Sam. 22:10 bow. the h. Ps. 18:9
1 K. 8:27 h. cannot contain thee
1 Chr. 16:26 Lord made h. Neh. 9:6; Ps. 96:5; 102:25; 136:5
31 let the h. be glad, earth rej.
2 Chr. 6:25 hear fr. the h. 33,35,39
Job 14:12 till h. be no more
15:15 h. not clean in his sight
20:6 excellency mount up to h.
26:13 by Sp. he garnished the h.
35:5 look to the h. and see
Ps. 8:1 thy glory above h. 113:4
3 when I consider thy h.
19:1 h. declare the glory of God
33:6 by word of L. were h. made
50:4 sh. call to the h. from above
6 h. shall declare his righteou.
57:5 be thou exalted, O God, above the h. 11; 108:5
10 mercy is great to h. 108:5
68:4 that rideth upon the h. 33
8 h. dropped at presence of G.
73:9 set their mouth ag. the h.
89:5 h shall praise thy wonders
11 the h. are thine, earth also
96:11 the h. rejoice, Rev. 12:12
97:6 h. declare his righteousness
104:2 stretchest out h. Is. 40:22
108:4 mercy is great above h.
115:16 the h. are the Lord's
144:5 bow thy h. O L. and come
148:1 praise ye the Lord from h.
4 praise him hea. of h. and wa.
Prov. 3:19 he established the h.
8:27 when he prepared the h.
Is. 13:13 shake the h. Hag. 2:6,21
34:4 the h. shall be rolled toget.
44:23 sing, O ye h. for L. done it
24 stretch. forth the h. 45:12; 51:13; Jer. 10:12; Zec. 12:1
45:8 drop down, ye h. fr. above
48:13 my right hand spanned h.
49:13 sing, O h. be joy, O earth
50:3 I clothe h. with blackness
51:6 lift your eyes to h.
16 that I may plant the h.
55:9 as h. are higher than earth
64:1 rend the h. and come down
65:17 behold, I create new h.
66:22 new h. which I will make
Jer. 2:12 be astonished, O ye h.
4:23 I beh. h. they had no light
25 birds of h. were fled, 9:10
28 earth mourn, h. above black
10:11 gods not made h. sh. peri.
14:22 can the h. give showers?
Ezek. 1:1 h. were open. Mat. 3:16
Dan. 4:26 known that h. do rule
Hos. 2:21 I will hear the h.
Joel 2:10 the h. shall tremble
Hab. 3:3 his glory covered the h.
Zec. 6:5 four spirits of the h.
8:12 the h. shall give their dew
Mat. 24:29 powers of h. shaken
Mark 1:10 he saw the h. opened
Acts 2:34 D. is not ascended to h.
7:56 behold, I see the h. opened
Heb. 1:10 h. work of thy hands
4:14 High-p. is passed into h.
7:26 H.-p. made higher than h.
2 Pet. 3:5 word of G. h. we. of old
7 h. wh. are now are kept in st.
10 h. sh. pass away with gr. no.
12 h. being on fire shall be dis.

**In the HEAVENS.**
Ps. 2:4 he that sitteth in the h.
18:13 L. also thundered in the h.
36:5 thy mercy, O L. is in the h.
89:2 faithfulness estab. in the h.
103:19 L. prep. his throne in h.
115:3 God is in the h.
123:1 O thou that dwell. in t. h.
Jer. 10:13 waters in the h. 51:16
Lam. 3:41 lift hearts to G. in h.
Joel 2:30 show wonders in the h.
Luke 12:33 a treasure in the h.
2 Cor. 5:1 not made w. hands, in h.
Heb. 8:1 thr. of Majesty in t. h.
9:23 patterns of things in the h.

**HEAVY.**
Ex. 17:12 Moses' hands were h.
18:18 this thing is too h.
Num. 11:14 not able, bec. too h.
1 Sam. 4:18 Eli was old man h.
2 Sam. 14:26 hair was h. on him
1 K. 12:4 father's h. yoke, 10, 11, 14; 2 Chr. 10:4, 10, 11, 14
1 K. 14:6 sent to thee with h. tid.
Neh. 5:18 bondage h. on people
Job 33:7 neither shall hand be h.
Ps. 32:4 thy hand was h. on me
38:4 h. burden, they are too h.
Prov. 25:20 songs to a h. heart
27:3 stone is h. sand weighty
31:6 wine to those of h. hearts
Is. 6:10 and make their ears h.
24:20 transgression shall be h.
30:27 the burden thereof is h.
46:1 carriages were h. loaden
58:6 to undo the h. burdens?
59:1 nei. his ear h. that it cannot
Lam. 3:7 made chain h.
Mat. 11:28 ye that are h. laden
23:4 for they bind h. burdens
26:37 be sorrowful, and very h.
43 eyes were h. Mark 14:33, 40
Luke 9:32 were h. with sleep

**HEAVIER.**
Job 6:3 h. than sand of the sea
23:2 my stroke is h. than groan.
Prov. 27:3 a fool's wrath is h.

**HEAVILY.**
Ex. 14:25 that drave them h.
Ps. 35:14 bowed h. as one mour.
Is. 47:6 on ancient h. laid yoke?

**HEAVINESS.**
Ezr. 9:5 I rose from h.
Job 9:27 I will leave off my h.
Ps. 69:20 broken heart full of h.
119:28 my soul melteth for h.
Prov. 10:1 fool. son h. of mother
12:25 h. in heart mak. it stoop
14:13 end of that mirth is h.
Is. 61:3 garm. of praise for h.
Rom. 9:2 great h. and sorrow
2 Cor. 2:1 wou. not come ag. in h.
Phil. 2:26 brother was full of h.
Jam. 4:9 your joy be turned to h.
1 Pet. 1:6 if need be ye are in h.

**HEBER.**
Gen. 46:17 Beriah, H. 1 Chr. 7:31
Jud. 4:11 H. the Kenite, 17; 5:24
Luke 3:35 Phalec, was son of H.

**HEBREW.**
Gen. 14:13 Abra. the H. 39:14
41:12 a young man, a H.
Ex. 2:11 Egyptian smiting a H.
Jer. 34:9 should let a H. go free
Jon. 1:9 unto them I am a H.

**HEBREWS.**
Gen. 40:15 sto. out of land of H.
Ex. 2:6 this one of H. chil. 13; 3:18; 5:3; 7:16; 9:1; 10:3
1 Sam. 4:6 shout in camp of H. 9
13:3 let H. hear, 19; 14:11, 21
29:3 what do these H. hear?
Acts 6:1 murmuring ag. the H.
2 Cor. 11:22 H. or Israelites?
Phil. 3:5 of Benja. a Heb. of H.

**HEBREW, language.**
Luke 23:38 writ. in H. John 19:20
John 5:2 called in H. 19:13, 17
Acts 21:40 spake in H. 22:2; 26:14
Rev. 9:11 in H. Abaddon, 16:16

**HEBREW man.**
Deut. 15:12 if brother, a H. man

**HEBREW servant.**
Gen. 39:17 H. s. came, Ex. 21:2

**HEBREW woman, women.**
Ex. 1:16 midwife to H. w. 19
2:7 a nurse of the H. women?
Deut. 15:12 if any H. w. be sold

HEBREWESS. Jer. 34:9

**HEBRON, place.**
Gen. 23:2 Sarah died in H. 35:27; Jos. 14:15; 20:7; Jud. 1:10
37:14 Jacob sent Jos. out of H.
Num. 13:22 H. built before Zoan
2 Sam. 2:11 Dav. was king in H. 5:5; 1 K. 2:11; 1 Chr. 29:27
3:32 buried Abner in H. 4:12
5:3 in H. 1 Chr. 11:3; 12:38
15:7 Absalom vowed in H. 10
1 Chr. 12:38 perfect heart to H.

**HEBRON, person.**
Ex. 6:18 Kohath, H. Num. 3:19
1 Chr. 2:42, 43; 6:2, 18; 15:9; 23:12, 19; 24:23

**HEDGE, S.**
Job 1:10 not made a h. ab. him?
Ps. 80:12 broken her h.? 89:40
Prov. 15:19 way of sloth h. of th.
Ec. 10:8 breaketh h. serpent bite
Is. 5:5 take away the h. thereof
Jer. 49:3 run to and fro by the h.
Ezek. 13:5 nor made up h. 22:30
Mic. 7:4 sharper than a thorn h.
Nah. 3:17 as grasshoppers in h.
Mark 12:1 he set a h. about it
Luke 14:23 go to highways and h.

**HEDGE, D.**
Job 3:23 way is hid, whom G. h.
Lam. 3:7 he hath h. me about
Hos. 2:6 h. up thy way with tho.
Mat. 21:33 vineyard, h. it round

**HEED.**
2 K. 10:31 Jehu took no h.
Ps. 119:9 tak. h. ac. to thy word
Prov. 17:4 giveth h. to false lips
Ec. 12:9 preacher gave good h.
Jer. 18:18 not gi. h. to any words
19 give h. to me, O Lord
Acts 3:5 he gave h. unto them
8:6 people of Sam. gave h. to P.
10 gave h. to Simon least to
1 Tim. 1:4 h. to fables, Tit. 1:14
4:1 giving h. to seducing spirits
Heb. 2:1 we ought to give more h.
See TAKE.

**HEEL, S.**
Gen. 3:15 thou sh. bruise his h.
25:26 hold on E. h. Hos. 12:3
49:17 an adder biteth horse h.
Job 13:27 print on h. of my feet
18:9 gin shall take him by h.
Ps. 41:9 h. ag. me, John 13:18
49:5 iniq. of my h. compass me
Jer. 13:22 iniq. thy h. made bare

HEGE. Est. 2:3

**HEIFER.**
Num. 19:2 red h.; 5 burn the h.
Deut. 21:3 the elders sh. take a h.
4 strike off the h. neck
6 shall wash hands over the h.
Jud. 14:18 not plou. with my h.
Is. 15:5 cry out for Moab as h.
Jer. 46:20 Egypt is like a fair h.
48:34 uttered their voice as a h.
50:11 grown fat as h. at grass
Hos. 4:16 Is. as a backsliding h.
10:11 Ephraim is as h. taught
Heb. 9:13 ashes of h. sp. unclean

**HEIGHT, S.**
Gen. 6:15 h. of ark sh. be 30 cu.
Ex. 25:10 ark of Shittim-wood, a cu. and half h. 23; 37:1, 10

27:1 h. of altar, three cu. 38:1
18 h. of court, five cubits, 38:18
30:2 h. of altar of incense, 37:25
1 Sam. 16:7 look not on h. of sta.
17:4 Goliath's h. 6 cu. and a sp.
1 K. 6:2 h. of house of G. 30 cu.
20 oracle twenty cubits in h.
26 h. of cherub was ten cubits
7:2 h. of house of Leb. 30 cubits
16 h. of one chapiter 5 cubits
23 h. of molten sea five cubits
27 h. of one base three cubits
Ezr. 6:3 h. of God's house 60 cu.
Job 22:12 God in h. of heaven?
Ps. 102:19 looked fr. h. of sanct.
148:1 praise the Lord in the h.
Prov. 25:3 the heaven for h.
Is. 7:11 ask it in the h. above
14:14 I will ascend above the h.
Jer. 49:16 O thou that holdest h.
51:53 fortify h. of her strength
Ezek. 17:23 in h. of Israel, 20:40
19:11 she appeared in her h.
31:5 therefore his h. was exalted
14 none of the trees exalt for h.
32:5 fill the valleys with thy h.
Dan. 3:1 image wh. h. was 60 cu.
4:11 h. reached unto heaven, 20
Amos 2:9 h. was like h. of cedars
Rom. 8:39 nor h. nor depth
Eph. 3:18 the h. of love of Ch.?
Rev. 21:16 breadth and h. equal

**HEINOUS.**

Job 31:11 for this is a h. crime

**HEIR, S.**

Gen. 15:3 born in my house is h.
4 This shall not be thine h.
21:10 Ishmael shall not be h.
2 Sam. 14:7 we will destroy h.
Prov. 30:23 handmaid h. to mis.
Jer. 49:1 hath Is. no sons? no h.?
2 Is. h. to them that were his h.
Mic. 1:15 I will bring h. to thee
Mat. 21:38 this is the h. Mark 12:7; Luke 20:14
Rom. 4:13 should be h. of world
14 if they wh. are of law be h.
8:17 h. of G. joint h. with Ch.
Gal. 3:29 h. according to promise
4:1 h. as long as he is a child
7 an h. of God through Christ
30 son of bond-w. sh. not be h.
Eph. 3:6 Gent. sh. be fellow-h.
Tit. 3:7 h. according to the hope
Heb. 1:2 whom he appointed h.
14 who shall be h. of salvation
6:17 God willing to show to h.
11:7 became h. of righteousness
Jam. 2:5 h. of the kingdom
1 Pet. 3:7 as h. together of grace

HELAM. 2 Sam. 10:16
HELBON. Ezek. 27:18

**HELD.**

Ex. 17:11 wh. Moses h. up hand
Jud. 7:20 h. lamps in left hands
2 Chr. 4:5 sea h. 3,000 baths
Neh. 4:16 half h. both spears
17 other hand he h. a weapon
Est. 5:2 king h. out golden scep.
Job 23:11 my foot h. his steps
Ps. 32:9 wh. mouth must be h.
94:18 thy mercy, O L. h. me up
Cant. 3:4 I h. him, and wo. not
7:5 king is h. in the galleries
Jer. 50:33 took captives, h. them
Dan. 12:7 h. up his right hand
Mat. 12:14 h. a coun. Mark 15:1
Luke 22:63 men that h. Jesus
Acts 3:11 man was healed, h. P.
14:4 part h. with J. part apostles
Rom. 7:6 wherein we were h.
Rev. 6:9 slain for testim. they h.

**HELD peace.**

Gen. 24:21 wondering h. his p.
Lev. 10:3 Aaron h. his peace
Num. 30:7 husband h. p. 11, 14
Neh. 5:8 h. th. p. found nothing
Job 29:10 nobles h. their peace
Ps. 39:2 I h. my p. from good
Is. 36:21 h. their p. Mark 3:4; 9:34
57:11 have not I h. my peace?
Mat. 26:63 Jesus h. his peace
Luke 14:4 h. p. 20:26; Acts 11:18
Acts 15:13 h. their p. Ja. answer

HELDAI. Zec. 6:10
HELI. Luke 3:23
HELKATH-HAZZURIM. 2 Sam. 2:16

**HELL.**

Deut. 32:22 fire burn unto low. h.
2 Sam. 22:6 sorrows of h. compassed me, Ps. 18:5; 86:13
Job 11:8 deeper than h.
26:6 h. is naked before him
Ps. 9:17 wicked turned into h.
16:10 not le. soul in h. Acts 2:27
55:15 go down quick to h.
116:3 pains of h. gat hold on me
139:8 bed in h. thou art there
Prov. 5:5 steps take hold on h.
7:27 house way to h. going do.
9:18 guests are in depths of h.
15:11 h. and destruction bef. L.
24 he may depart from h.
23:14 deliver his soul from h.
27:20 h. and destruction ne. full
Is. 5:14 h. hath enlarged herself
14:9 h. from beneath is moved
15 shalt be brought down to h.
28:15 with h. are we at agreem.
18 agreem. with h. not stand
57:9 debase thyself even to h.
Ezek. 31:16 I cast him down to h.
17 went down to h. with him
32:21 speak to him out of h.
27 down to h. with weapons
Amos 9:2 tho' they dig into h.
Jon. 2:2 out of belly of h.
Hab. 2:5 enlargeth desire as h.
Mat. 5:22 in danger of h. fire
29 body be cast in h. 30
10:28 body in h. Luke 12:5
11:23 Capernaum brought down to h. Luke 10:15
16:18 gates of h. sh. not prevail
18:9 having two eyes to be cast into h. Mark 9:47
23:15 twofold more child of h.
33 can ye escape damna. of h.?
Luke 16:23 in h. lifted up his eyes
Acts 2:31 soul was not left in h.
Jam. 3:6 tong. is set on fire of h.
2 Pet. 2:4 cast angels down to h.
Rev. 1:18 keys of h. and death
6:8 name Death, h. followed
20:13 death and h. del. up dead
14 death and h. cast in lake

**HELM.**

Jam. 3:4 turn. about wi. small h.

**HELMET, S.**

2 Chr. 26:14 Uzziah prepared h.
Is. 59:17 h. of salvation on head
Jer. 46:4 stand forth with your h.
Ezek. 23:24 ag. the shield and h.
27:10 shield and h. in thee
38:5 with shield and h.
Eph. 6:17 the h. of salvation
1 Thes. 5:8 h. hope of salvation

**HELP, Substantive.**

Gen. 2:18 a h. meet for him
20 not found a h. meet for him
Ex. 18:4 G. said he, was my h.
Deut. 33:7 h. to him fr. enemies
26 rideth on heaven in thy h.
Deut. 33:29 sa. by L. shi. of thy h.
Jud. 5:23 came not to h. of Lord
Job 6:13 is not my h. in me?
31:21 when I saw h. in the gate
Ps. 3:2 say of soul no h. for him
20:2 L. send h. from sanctuary
27:9 been my h. leave not, O God
33:20 waits for L. he is our h.
35:2 stand up for my h. 44:26
40:17 my h. and my deliv. 70:5
42:5 praise for h. of countenance
46:1 God very present h.
60:11 h. vain h. of man, 108:12
63:7 bec. thou hast been my h.
71:12 God, make haste for my h.
89:19 h. on one that is mighty
94:17 unless L. had been my h.
115:9 their h. and shield, 10, 11
121:1 fr. whence cometh my h.
2 my h. cometh from the Lord
124:8 our h. is in name of Lord
146:3 tr. not man, in whom no h.
5 happy hath God of J. for h.
Is. 10:3 to wh. will ye flee for h.?
30:5 nor be a h. nor profit
34:1 them that go to Eg. for h.
2 ag. h. of them that work ini.
Lam. 4:17 eyes failed for vain h.
Dan. 11:34 holpen with little h.
Hos. 13:9 in me is thy h.
Acts 26:22 obtained h. of God

**HELP, Verb.**

Gen. 49:25 God of fa. who sh. h.
Deut. 32:38 let them rise and h.
2 Sam. 10:11 then h. me, I will h. thee, 1 Chr. 19:12
14:4 said, h. O king, 2 K. 6:26
2 Chr. 14:11 it is nothing with thee to h. h. us, O Lord
19:2 should. thou h. the ungodly
20:9 thou wilt hear and h.
25:8 for God hath power to h.
26:13 power to h. the king
28:23 h. them that they may h.
32:8 with us is the L. to h. us
Job 8:20 nei. will he h. evil-doers
Ps. 12:1 h. L.; 22:11 none to h.
22:19 haste thee to h. 38:22; 40:13; 70:1
37:40 L. h. them; 46:5 G. h. her
59:4 awake to h.; 79:9 h. us
107:12 was none to h. Is. 63:5
109:26 h. me, O Lord my God
118:7 my part with th. that h.
119:86 h. me; 173 thy hand h.
175 let thy judgments h. me
Ec. 4:10 hath not another to h.
Is. 30:7 Egypt. shall h. in vain
41:10 will h. thee, 13, 14: 44:2
50:7 the Lord God will h. me, 9
Lam. 1:7 people fell, none did h.
Ezek. 32:21 speak out of hell with them that h. him
Dan. 11:45 come to end, none h.
Mat. 15:25 saying, Lord, h. me
Mark 9:22 have compass. h. us
24 L. I believe, h. mine unbel.
Luke 5:7 they sh. come and h.
10:40 bid her therefore h. me
Acts 16:9 co. to Macedonia, h. us
21:28 crying out, M. of Israel, h.
Phil. 4:3 h. women wh. labored
Heb. 4:16 to h. in time of need

**HELPED.**

Ex. 2:17 Moses stood up and h.
1 Sam. 7:12 hitherto the L. h. us
1 K. 1:7 follow. Adonijah h. him
1 Chr. 15:26 God h. the Levites
2 Chr. 20:23 ev. one h. to destroy
26:15 was marvellously h.
Job 26:2 how hast thou h. him
Ps. 28:7 I am h.; 118:13 L. h. me
116:6 brought low, he h. me
Is. 41:6 h. ev. one his neighbor
49:8 in day of salvation h. thee
Zec. 1:15 h. forw. the affliction
Acts 18:27 he h. them much
Rev. 12:16 earth h. the woman

**HELPER.**

2 K. 14:26 nor any h. for Israel
Job 30:13 mar my path, no h.

Ps. 10:14 art h. of fatherless
30:10 L. my h.; 54:4 G. my h.
72:12 deliver him hath no h.
Jer. 47:4 Tyrus and Zidon ev. h.
Rom. 16:9 Urbane our h. in Ch.
Heb. 13:6 Lord is my h.

**HELPERS.**

1 Chr. 12:18 peace be to thy h.
Job 9:13 proud h. do stoop under
Ezek. 30:8 her h. sh. be destroyed
Nah. 3:9 Put and Lubim were h.
Rom. 16:3 Prisc. and Aq. my h.
2 Cor. 1:24 but are h. of your joy
3 John 8 be fellow-h. to the truth

**HELPETH.**

1 Chr. 12:18 for thy God h. thee
Is. 31:3 both he that h. shall fall
Rom. 8:26 Sp. also h. infirmities
1 Cor. 16:16 sub. to ev. one h. us

**HELPING.**

Ezr. 5:2 were prophets of G. h.
Ps. 22:1 why art so far from h.
2 Cor. 1:11 h. together by prayer

**HELPS.**

Acts 27:17 used h. undergi. ship
1 Cor. 12:28 healings, h. govern.

**HELVE.**

Deut. 19:5 head slippeth from h.

**HEM, S.**

Ex. 28:33 on h. thou shalt make
pomegran. 34; 39:24, 25, 26
Mat. 9:20 touch. h. of gar. 14:36

**HEMAN.**

1 K. 4:31 Sol. was wiser than H.
1 Chr. 2:6; 6:33; 15:17, 19; 16:42;
2 Chr. 5:12; 29:14; 35:15

**HEMLOCK.**

Hos. 10:4 judgment spr. up as h.
Amos 6:12 fruit of righte. to h.

HEN. Zec. 6:14

**HEN.**

Mat. 23:37 h. gath. ch. Lu. 13:34

**HENCE.**

Ex. 33:15 carry us not up h.
Ps. 39:13 bef. I go h. be no more
Mat. 17:20 remove h. to yon. pla.
Luke 4:9 cast thyself down fr. h.
16:26 pass from h. to you cannot
John 2:16 take these things h.
14:31 let us go h.; 18:36 not h.
Acts 22:21 send thee h. to Gen.

**HENCEFORTH.**

Ps. 125:2 L. about people from h.
131:3 hope in the Lord from h.
Is. 9:7 estab. with justice fr. h.
52:1 h. there sh. no more come
59:21 thy seed's seed h.
Mic. 4:7 L. reign in Zion from h.
Mat. 23:39 ye shall not see me h.
Luke 5:10 fear not, from h. thou
12:52 h. sh. be five in one house
Acts 18:6 h. I will go to Gentiles
2 Cor. 5:15 not h. live to themsel.
Eph. 4:17 h. walk not as other
2 Tim. 4:8 h. laid up a crown
Rev. 14:13 blessed die in L. fr. h.

**HENCEFORWARD.**

Num. 15:23 h. am. generations
Mat. 21:19 no fruit gr. on thee h.

**HEPHZI-BAH.**

2 K. 21:1 Manasseh's mother, H.
Is. 62:4 thou shalt be called H.

**HERALD.**

Dan. 3:4 then a h. cried aloud

**HERB.**

Gen. 1:11 bring forth the h. 12
29 every h. bearing seed
2:5 made every h.; 3:18 eat h.
9:3 h. I have given all things
Ex. 9:22 hail smote ev. h. 25
10:12 locusts eat every h. 15
Deut. 32:2 rain on tender h.
2 K. 19:26 as green h. Is. 37:27
Job 8:12 withereth bef. other h.
38:27 bud of tender h. to spring
Ps. 37:2 shall wither as green h.
104:14 causeth h. to grow
Is. 66:14 bones flourish like h.

**HERBS.**

Ex. 12:8 with bitter h. Num. 9:11
Deut. 11:10 as a garden of h.
1 K. 21:2 have it for gard. of h.
Ps. 105:35 did eat up all the h.
Prov. 15:17 better a dinner of h.
27:25 h. of mountains gathered
Is. 18:4 like a heat on h.
26:19 thy dew is as dew of h.
42:15 I will dry up all their h.
Jer. 12:4 h. of every field wither
Mat. 13:32 is greatest among all
h. Mark 4:32
Luke 11:42 all manner of h.
Rom. 14:2 who is weak, eat. h.
Heb. 6:7 and bringeth forth h.

**HERD, S.**

Ex. 10:9 with flocks and h.
Lev. 27:32 concerning tithe of h.
Deut. 12:21 shalt kill of thy h.
2 Sam. 12:4 spared to take of h.
1 Chr. 27:29 over the h. in Shar.
Is. 65:10 a place for h. to lie
Jer. 31:12 toge. for young of h.
Joel 1:18 h. of cattle perplexed
Jon. 3:7 let not h. taste any
thing
Hab. 3:17 shall be no h. in stalls

**Mat. 8:30 a h. of swine feeding**
**Mark 5:11; Luke 8:32**

See FLOCKS.

**HERDMAN, MEN.**

Gen. 13:7 strife betw. h. 26:20
1 Sam. 21:7 Doeg chiefest of h.
Amos 1:1 who was am. h. of Te.
7:14 I was no prophet, but a h.

**HERE.**

Deut. 5:3 who are all of us h.
Ps. 132:14 my rest, h. I dwell
Is. 28:10 h. a little, th. a little, 13
Hos. 7:9 gray hairs h. and there
Mat. 12:41 a greater than Jonas
is h. 42; Luke 11:31, 32
16:28 standing h. Luke 9:27
17:4 L. it is good for us to be h.
24:23 lo, h. is Ch. Mark 13:21
28:6 he is not h. he is risen,
Mark 16:6; Luke 24:6
Mark 13:1 what buildings are h.
John 11:21 if th. hadst been h. 32
Acts 9:10 behold, I am h. Lord
10:33 we are all h. before God
Heb. 13:14 h. have we no city

See STAND.

**HEREAFTER.**

Is. 41:23 things that come h.
Dan. 2:29 come to pass h. 45
Mat. 26:64 h. sh. ye see S. of m.
Mark 11:14 no man eat of thee h.
Luke 22:69 h. sh. Son of man sit
John 1:51 h. ye sh. see heaven
13:7 thou shalt know h.
14:30 h. I will not talk with you
1 Tim. 1:16 to them wh. h. beli.
Rev. 1:19 things which sh. be h.
4:1 show things wh. must be h.
9:12 come two woes more h.

**HEREBY.**

Jos. 3:10 h. know G. is am. you
1 John 2:3 h. we do know him
5 h. know that we are in him
3:16 h. perceive we love of God
19 h. know we are of the truth
24 h. we know he abideth in us
4:2 h. know ye Spirit of God
6 h. know we the Sp. of truth
13 h. know that we dw. in him

**HEREIN.**

1 John 4:10 h. is love, not that

**HERESY, IES.**

Acts 24:14 the way they call h.
1 Cor. 11:19 there be h. am. you
Gal. 5:20 works of flesh wrath, h.
2 Pet. 2:1 bring in damnable h.

**HERETIC.**

Tit. 3:10 h. after sec. admonition

**HERETOFORE.**

1 Sam. 4:7 been such a thing h.
2 Cor. 13:2 them which h. sinned

**HEREUNTO.**

1 Pet. 2:21 even h. were ye called

**HEREWITH.**

Mal. 3:10 and prove me now h.

**HERITAGE, S.**

Ex. 6:8 I will give it you for h.
Job 20:29 h. appointed by God
27:13 h. of oppressors they rec.
Ps. 16:6 yea, I have a goodly h.
61:5 h. of those fear thy name
94:5 break thy peo. afflict thy h.
111:6 give them h. of heathen
119:111 testimonies taken as h.
127:3 children are a h. of the L.
135:12 gave their land for a h.
136:21, 22
Is. 49:8 inherit the desolate h.
54:17 h. of servants of the Lord
58:14 feed thee with h. of Jacob
Jer. 2:7 my h. an abomination
3:19 sh. I give thee goodly h.?
12:7 left h.; 8 my h. is as lion
9 my h. is as speckled bird
15 bring ag. every man to his h.
17:4 thou shalt discont. from h.
50:11 O destroyers of my h.
Joel 2:17 give not h. to reproach
3:2 I will plead wi. them for h.
Mic. 2:2 oppress a man and h.
7:14 feed the flock of thy h.
18 passeth transgression of h.
Mal. 1:3 I laid Esau's h. waste
1 Pet. 5:3 being lords over G.'s h.

HERMAS, HERMES. Ro. 16:14
HERMOGENES. 2 Tim. 1:15

**HERMON.**

Jos. 13:11 all mt. H. Reuben had
Ps. 89:12 H. shall rejoice in thy
133:3 dew of H. that descended
Cant. 4:8 look from the top of H.

HERMONITES. Ps. 42:6

**HEROD.**

Mat. 2:12 not return to H. 15, 16
14:3 for H. had laid hold, 6
Mark 8:15 leaven of H. 6:17, 21
Luke 3:1 H. tetrarch of Galil. 19
9:7 H. heard of Jesus, 13:31
23:7 sent J. to H. 8, 11, 12, 15
Acts 4:27 H. and Pontius Pilate
12:1 H. vexed the chu. 6, 11, 21

**HERODIANS.**

Mat. 22:16 they sent th. disciples
with the H. Mark 12:13
Mark 3:6 P. took coun. with H.

**HERODIAS.**

Mat. 14:3 John in prison for H. 6
Mark 6:19 H. had quarrel, 17, 22
Luke 3:19 H. reprov. by J. for H.

HERODION. Rom. 16:11

**HERON.**

Lev. 11:19 h. uncl. Deut. 14:18

HERSELF. See SELF.

**HESHBON.**

Num. 21:28 fire go. out of H. 30
Jud. 11:26 Is. dw. in H. Neh. 9:22
Cant. 7:4 like fish-pools of H.
Is. 15:4 H. shall cry, Jer. 49:3
16:8 for field of H. languish, 9
Jer. 48:2 in H. they dev. evil, 45

HETH. *Gen.* 10:15; 23:7; 25:10; 27:46; 49:32; 1 *Chr.* 1:13

**HEW, ED.**

*Ex.* 34:1 *h.* 2 tables, *Deut.* 10:1
4 *h.* two tables, *Deut.* 10:3
*Deut.* 12:3 *h.* down grav. images
19:5 goeth with his neigh. to *h.*
1 *Sam.* 11:7 S. *h.* oxen in pieces
15:33 Samuel *h.* Agag in pieces
2 *Chr.* 2:2 Solo. told 80,000 to *h.*
*Jer.* 2:13 my peo. *h.* them cist.
*Dan.* 4:14 *h.* down the tree, 23
*Hos.* 6:5 I *h.* them by the proph.

**HEWER, S.**

*Deut.* 29:11 from *h.* of wood
*Jos.* 9:21 be *h.* of wood, 23
27 Jos. made them *h.* of wood
1 *K.* 5:15 80,000 *h.* in mountains, 2 *Chr.* 2:18
*Jer.* 46:22 ag. Eg. as *h.* of wood

**HEWETH.**

*Is.* 10:15 boast aga. him that *h.*
22:16 *h.* him out a sepulchre

**HEWN.**

*Prov.* 9:1 *h.* out seven pillars
*Is.* 10:33 high ones shall be *h.*
33:9 Leb. is asha. and *h.* down
51:1 rock whence ye are *h.*
*Mat.* 3:10 *h.* down and cast into fire, 7:19; *Luke* 3:9
27:60 *h.* out of a rock, *Mark* 15:46; *Luke* 23:53
*See* STONE.

**HEZEKIAH,** *called* **EZEKIAS.**

2 *K.* 16:20 H. reign. in his stead.
18:15 H. gave all silver, 22, 31
19:1 H. hea. it, 15; 20:1, 3, 12, 21
2 *Chr.* 29:27 H. com. burnt-offerings, 30:18; 32:15, 33; 33:3
30:20 the Lord hearkened to H.
31:2 H. appoin. 32:8, 17, 22, 30
*Is.* 36:7, 14, 16; 37:1, 15; 38:1, 3; 39:1, 2, 8

**HEZRON.**

*Gen.* 46:9 Reuben, H. *Ex.* 6:14
*Ruth* 4:19 H. begat Ram
1 *Chr.* 2:9 sons of H. 18, 21, 25

**HID.**

*Gen.* 3:8 Adam and his wife *h.*
10 I was naked, and I *h.* myself
*Ex.* 2:2 *h.* Moses three months
12 M. *h.* the Egyptian in sand
3:6 and Moses *h.* his face
*Jos.* 2:4 Rahab *h.* the spies, 6
6:17 she *h.* the messengers, 25
1 *K.* 18:4 Obadiah *h.* prophets, 13
2 *K.* 4:27 the Lord *h.* it from me
11:2 they *h.* him and his nurse, 2 *Chr.* 22:11
*Job* 17:4 *h.* heart fr. understand.
29:8 saw me, and *h.* themselves
*Ps.* 9:15 in net which they *h.*
22:24 nei. *h.* his face from him
35:7 they *h.* for me their net
8 net he hath *h.* catch himself
119:11 word I *h.* in my heart
140:5 proud *h.* a snare for me
*Is.* 49:2 in quiver he *h.* me
50:6 I *h.* not my face fr. shame
53:3 we *h.* our faces from him
54:8 in little wrath I *h.* my face
57:17 I *h.* me and was wroth
59:2 *h.* his face from you
64:7 hast *h.* thy face from us
*Jer.* 13:5 and *h.* it by Euphrates
18:22 they *h.* snares for my feet
33:5 I *h.* my face from this city
36:26 but the Lord *h.* them
*Ezek.* 22:26 *h.* their eyes fr. sab.
39:23 therefore *h.* I my face, 24
*Mat.* 11:25 *h.* fr. wise, *Lu.* 10:21
13:33 *h.* in three meas. *Lu.* 13:21
25:18 and *h.* his lord's money
25 and *h.* thy talent in earth
*Luke* 1:24 Elizabeth *h.* herself
*John* 8:59 but Jesus *h.* himself
*Rev.* 6:15 bondm. and freem. *h.*

**HID, Participle.**

2 *Sam.* 18:13 no mat. *h.* fr. king, 1 *K.* 10:3; 2 *Chr.* 9:2
*Job* 3:21 more than for *h.* treas.
28:11 thing *h.* bringeth forth
21 *h.* from eyes of all living
38:30 wat. are *h.* as with a stone
*Ps.* 17:14 belly filled wi. *h.* treas.
19:6 nothing *h.* from the heat
*Prov.* 2:4 as for *h.* treasure
*Is.* 40:27 my way is *h.* from L.
42:22 are *h.* in prison-houses
*Jer.* 16:17 iniq. *h.* fr. mine eyes
*Hos.* 13:12 sin of Ephraim is *h.*
*Mat.* 10:26 noth. *h.* th. sh. not be kn. *Mark* 4:22; *Lu.* 8:17; 12:2
*Luke* 9:45 saying was *h.* 18:34
19:42 are *h.* from thine eyes
*Eph.* 3:9 fr. begin. been *h.* in G.
*Col.* 1:26 been *h.* from ages
2:3 *h.* all the treas. of wisdom
3:3 your life is *h.* with Ch. in G.
*Heb.* 11:23 by faith Moses was *h.*

**Be HID.**

*Gen.* 4:14 from thy face sh. I *be h.*
*Lev.* 4:13 *be h.* fr. assembly, 5:3, 4
*Job* 20:26 sh. *be h.* in secret plac.
*Is.* 29:14 under. of pru. men *be h.*
*Hos.* 13:14 repentance shall *be h.*
*Amos* 9:3 they *be h.* fr. my sight
*Nah.* 3:11 thou shalt *be h.*
*Zep.* 2:3 ye shall *be h.*
2 *Cor.* 4:3 if our gospel *be h.*

**Not be HID.**

*Mat.* 5:14 city on hill *not be h.*
*Mark* 7:24 but he could *not be h.*
1 *Tim.* 5:25 otherwise *not be h.*

**Not HID.**

*Ps.* 32:5 mine iniq. have I *not h.*
38:9 my groaning is *not h.*
40:10 I have *n. h.* thy righteous.
69:5 my sins are *not h.* fr. thee
139:15 my substance was *not h.*
*Jer.* 16:17 are *not h.* fr. my face, nor their ini. *h.* fr. mine eyes

**HIDDEKEL.**

*Gen.* 2:14 river is H. *Dan.* 10:4

**HIDDEN.**

*Lev.* 5:2 *h.* from him
*Deut.* 30:11 it is not *h.* from thee
*Job* 24:1 are not *h.* from thee
*Ps.* 51:6 in *h.* part make know
83:3 consulted ag. thy *h.* ones
*Prov.* 28:12 wicked rise, man *h.*
*Is.* 45:3 give thee *h.* riches
48:6 showed thee things, *h.* th.
*Ob.* 6 *h.* things sought up
*Acts* 26:26 none of these *h.*
1 *Cor.* 2:7 *h.* wisdom G. ordained
4:5 bring to light *h.* things
2 *Cor.* 4:2 renounced *h.* things
1 *Pet.* 3:4 the *h.* man of heart
*Rev.* 2:17 give to eat of *h.* manna

**HIDE, Substantive.**

*Lev.* 8:17 *h.* flesh be burnt, 9:11

**HIDE, Verb.**

*Gen.* 18:17 shall I *h.* from Abra.?
1 *Sam.* 3:17 *h.* it not from me, if thou *h.* 2 *Sam.* 14:18
*Job* 13:20 not *h.* myself from thee
14:13 wouldest *h.* me in grave
20:12 he *h.* it under his tongue
33:17 and *h.* pride from man
40:13 *h.* them in dust together
*Ps.* 17:8 *h.* me under thy wings
27:5 in time of tro. he sh. *h.* me, in his tabern. sh. he *h.* me
31:20 sh. *h.* them in thy pres.
55:1 *h.* not thyself fr. my sup.
64:2 *h.* me fr. counsel of wick.
78:4 not *h.* them from their chi.
89:46 O L. wilt thou *h.* thyself
119:19 *h.* not thy commandm.
143:9 I flee to thee to *h.* me
*Prov.* 2:1 *h.* my com. with thee
*Is.* 1:15 I will *h.* mine eyes
2:10 and *h.* thee in the dust
3:9 *h.* not sin; 16:3 *h.* outcasts
26:20 *h.* thyself a little moment
58:7 *h.* not fr. thine own flesh
*Jer.* 36:19 *h.* thee and Jeremiah
*Lam.* 3:56 *h.* not ear at my brea.
*Ezek.* 28:3 no secret they can *h.*
31:8 cedars could not *h.* him
39:29 neither will I *h.* my face
*Jam.* 5:20 *h.* a multitude of sins
*Rev.* 6:16 *h.* us from him that
*See* FACE.

**HIDE himself.**

*Jer.* 23:24 *h. h.* in secret places
*John* 12:36 J. did *h. h.* fr. them

**HIDE themselves.**

2 *K.* 7:12 gone out to *h. t.* in fie.
*Job* 24:4 poor of the earth *h. t.*
34:22 where work. of iniq. *h. t.*
*Ps.* 56:6 *h. t.* mark my steps
*Prov.* 28:28 wick. rise, men *h. t.*
*Amos* 9:3 *h. t.* in top of Carmel

**HIDEST.**

*Job* 13:24 why *h.* thy face? *Ps.* 44:24; 88:14
*Ps.* 10:1 why *h.* thy. in trouble?
104:29 thou *h.* thy face
*Is.* 45:15 thou art G. th. *h.* thys.

**HIDETH.**

*Job* 23:9 *h.* himself on right hand
34:29 when he *h.* his face
42:3 who is he that *h.* counsel?
*Ps.* 10:11 he *h.* face will nev. see
139:12 darkn. *h.* not from thee
*Prov.* 10:18 *h.* hated with lying
19:24 sloth. *h.* his hand, 26:15
22:3 pru. man *h.* himself, 27:12
27:16 whosoever *h.* her, *h.* wind
28:27 that *h.* eyes sh. ha. curse
*Is.* 8:17 *h.* face from house of J.
*Mat.* 13:44 man hath found, he *h.*

**HIDING.**

*Job* 31:33 *h.* iniq. in my bosom
*Ps.* 32:7 art my *h.* place, 119:114
*Is.* 28:17 waters overflow *h.* pla.
32:2 as a *h.* place from the wind
*Hab.* 3:4 was *h.* of his power

HIEL. 1 *K.* 16:34
HIGGAION. *Ps.* 9:16

**HIGH.**

*Gen.* 29:7 Lo, it is yet *h.* day
*Deut.* 12:2 served gods on *h.* mo.
28:43 get up above the very *h.*
1 *Chr.* 17:17 state of man *h.* deg.
*Job* 11:8 *h.* as heaven
22:12 stars, how *h.* they are!
38:15 the *h.* arm sh. be broken
41:34 he beholdeth all *h.* things
*Ps.* 18:27 bring down *h.* looks
49:2 give ear, both low and *h.*
62:9 men of *h.* degree are a lie
71:19 thy righteous. O G. is *h.*
80:13 and *h.* is thy right hand
97:9 thou L. art *h.* above earth, 99:2; 113:4
101:5 him that hath a *h.* look
103:11 heaven is *h.* above earth
131:1 things too *h.* for me
138:6 L. be *h.* he hath respect
139:6 it is *h.* I cannot attain
149:6 let *h.* praises of God be
150:5 praise him on *h.* sounding
*Prov.* 18:11 as *h.* wall in conceit
21:4 *h.* look, and proud heart
24:7 wisdom is too *h.* for a fool
*Ec.* 12:5 afraid of that wh. is *h.*

Is. 2:13 L. on cedars that h.
6:1 Lord on a throne, h. and
10:12 I will punish his h. looks
24:21 pun. h. ones that are on h.
30:13 as a breach in a h. wall
52:13 my servant sh. be very h.
57:15 the h. and lofty One
Jer. 17:12 a glorious h. throne
49:16 tho. thou make thy ne. h.
Ezek. 21:26 abase him is h.
Ob. 3 habitation is h. that saith
John 19:31 sabbath was a h. day
Acts 18:17 with a h. arm bro. he
Rom. 12:16 mind not h. things
13:11 it is h. time to awake
2 Cor. 10:5 cast. down ev. h. th.
Phil. 3:14 prize of the h. calling
Rev. 21:12 Jerusal. had a wall h.

See GATE, GOD, HILL, HILLS.

**Most HIGH.**

Num. 24:16 knowledge of M. H.
2 Sam. 22:14 M. H. ut. his voice
Ps. 7:17 sing praise to name of the Lord the M. H. 9:2; 92:1
46:4 tabernacles of the M. H.
47:2 the Lord M. H. is terrible
50:14 pay thy vows to the M. H.
56:2 fight aga. thee, O M. H.
57:2 I will cry unto God M. H.
73:11 is there knowl. in M. H.
77:10 right hand of M. H.
78:17 provoking the M. H. 56
82:6 are the children of M. H.
83:18 art M. H. over all earth
Ps. 91:1 dwelleth in pl. of M. H.
9 made M. H. thy habitation
92:8 but thou, Lord, art m. h.
107:11 contem. counsel of M. H.
Is. 14:14 will be like the M. H.
Lam. 3:35 before face of M. H.
38 out of M. H. proc. not evil
Dan. 4:17 M. H. ruleth in kingd.
24 the decree of the M. H.
25 M. H. rules kingdom, 32
34 and I blessed the M. H.
7:18 saints of M. H. take king.
22 judg. given saints of M. H.
25 speak words against M. H.
27 saints of the M. H.
Hos. 7:16 return not to M. H.
11:7 called them to the M. H.
Acts 7:48 M. H. dwelleth not

See MOUNTAIN.

**On HIGH.**

Deut. 28:1 G. will set thee on h.
Job 5:11 set on h. th. that be low
16:19 and my record is on h.
39:18 she lifteth up herself on h.
27 eagle make her nest on h.
Ps. 7:7 for th. sakes return on h.
68:18 thou hast ascended on h.
69:29 O God, set me up on h.
91:14 I will set him on h.
93:4 L. on h. is mightier than
107:41 setteth he the poor on h.
Is. 26:5 bring. down them on h.
32:15 Sp. poured on us fr. on h.
40:26 lift up your eyes on h.
58:4 your voice heard on h.
Luke 1:78 day-spring from on h.
Eph. 4:8 he ascended up on h.

See PLACE, PLACES, PRIEST, TOWER.

**HIGHER.**

1 Sam. 9:2 S. h. than any of pe.
Job 35:5 clouds, which are h.
Ps. 61:2 lead to Rock that is h.
89:27 make him h. than kings
Ec. 5:8 there be h. than they
Is. 55:9 as hea. are h. than earth, so my ways h. th. your ways
Jer. 36:10 Bar. read in h. court
Dan. 8:3 one horn h. than other
Luke 14:10 may say, Go up h.
Rom. 13:1 subject to h. powers
Heb. 7:26 high-p. made h. than

**HIGHEST.**

Ps. 18:13 the H. gave his voice
87:5 H. himself shall establish
Prov. 8:26 nor h. part of dust
9:3 crieth on h. places of city
Ec. 5:8 higher than h. regard.
Ezek. 17:3 h. branch of cedar
Mat. 21:9 hosan. in h. Mark 11:10
Luke 1:32 called Son of the H.
35 power of H. overshad. thee
76 be called prophet of the H.
2:14 glory to G. in H. 19:38
6:35 ye shall be chil. of the H.
14:8 sit not down in h. room
20:46 love h. seats in synagog.

**HIGHLY.**

Luke 1:28 Thou art h. favored
16:15 h. esteemed among men
Rom. 12:3 think of him. more h.
Phil. 2:9 G. hath h. exalted him
1 Thes. 5:13 to est. them very h.

**HIGH-MINDED.**

Rom. 11:20 not h.-m. 1 Tim. 6:1
2 Tim. 3:4 traitors, heady, h.-m.

**HIGHNESS.**

Job 31:23 his h. I could not en.
Is. 13:3 that rejoice in my h.

**HIGHWAY, S.**

Jud. 5:6 days Jael h. unoccupied
Prov. 16:17 h. of upright
Is. 11:16 a h. for his people
19:23 a h. out of Eg. to Assyria
33:8 h. lie waste, way-faring
35:8 and a h. shall be there
40:3 make in desert a h. for G.
49:11 my h. shall be exalted
62:10 cast up h. gather stones
Jer. 31:21 thy heart towards h.
Amos 5:16 shall say in all h.
Mat. 22:9 go into h. Luke 14:23
Mark 10:46 Bartimeus sat by h.

**HILKIAH.**

2 K. 18:18 Eliak. son of H. 22:12
Neh. 8:4 H. on E.'s right, 12:7
Is. 22:20 s. of H. 2 Chr. 34:20, 22

**HILL.**

Jos. 24:33 Eleazar buried in h.
1 Sam. 10:5 come to h. of G. 10
Ps. 24:3 shall ascend to h. of L.
42:6 remember thee from h. M.
68:15 h. of G. is as h. of Bashan
16 h. G. desireth to dwell in
Cant. 4:6 get to h. of frankinc.
Is. 5:1 viney. in very fruitful h.
10:32 shake hand ag. h. of Jeru.
30:17 as an ensign on a h.
31:4 Lord shall fight for h.
40:4 mount. and h. be made low
Jer. 16:16 hunt them from ev. h.
31:39 measuring line on h. G.
49:16 holdest height of the h.
50:6 gone from mountain to h.
Mat. 5:14 city that is set on a h.
Luke 3:5 ev. h. be brought low
4:29 led him to brow of the h.
9:37 were come down from h.
Acts 17:22 Paul stood in Mars h.

**Hill-COUNTRY.**

Jos. 13:6 inh. of h.-c. drive out
Luke 1:39 Mary went to h.-c.
65 nois. through all h.-c. of J.

**High HILL, S.**

Gen. 7:19 h. h. under heaven
1 K. 14:23 groves on every high h. 2 K. 17:10
Ps. 68:15 high h. as hill of B.
16 ye high h.? this is the h.
Is. 30:25 on high h. rivers of wa.
Jer. 2:20 on h. h. thou wand. 23
17:2 remember groves on h. h.
Ezek. 6:13 sla. am. idols on h. h.
34:6 sheep wand. on every h. h.

**Holy HILL.**

Ps. 2:6 set my king on h. h. of
3:4 Lord heard me out of h. h.
15:1 who sh. dwell in thy h. h.
43:3 bring me to thy h. h.?
99:9 worship at his h. h.

**HILL, with top.**

Ex. 17:9 will stand on top of h.
Num. 14:44 pres. to go to h. t.
Jud. 16:3 S. carried to top of h.
2 K. 1:9 Elijah sat on top of a h.

**HILLS.**

Gen. 49:26 ut. bound of everl. h.
Num. 23:9 fr. the h. I behold him
Deut. 8:7 spring out val. and h
11:11 a land of h. and valleys
33:15 precious things of last. h.
1 K. 20:23 gods are gods of h. 28
22:17 saw all Is. scattered on h.
2 K. 16:4 burnt incense on the h. 2 Chr. 28:4
Job 15:7 wast thou made bc. h.?
Ps. 18:7 foundations of h. moved
50:10 cattle on thousand h.
65:12 little h. rejoice on ev. side
72:3 the little h. by righteousn.
80:10 h. covered with shadow
95:4 strength of the h. is his
97:5 h. melted like wax
98:8 the h. be joyful together
104:10 springs, which run am. h.
13 watereth h. from chambers
32 he touch. h. and they smo.
114:4 little h. skip. like lam. 6
121:1 will lift mine eyes to h.
148:9 mount. and h. praise Lord
Prov. 8:25 h. I brought forth
Cant. 2:8 he cometh skip. on h.
Is. 2:2 shall be exalted above h.
14 day of L. shall be on all h.
7:25 on all h. sh. not come fear
40:12 weighed h. in balance?
41:15 shalt make h. as chaff
42:15 make waste moun. and h.
54:10 mount. depart, h. remov.
55:12 h. break forth into singi.
65:7 blasphemed me up. the h.
Jer. 3:23 salva. hoped for from h.
13:27 thy abominations on h.
Ezek. 6:3 thus saith L. to h. 36:4
36:6 to h. to rivers and valleys
Hos. 10:8 say to h. Fall on us
Joel 3:18 h. shall flow with milk
Mic. 4:1 be exalted above h.
6:1 let the h. hear thy voice
Nah. 1:5 h. melt, earth is burnt
Hab. 3:6 perpetual h. did bow
Luke 23:30 say to h. Cover us

**HIM.**

Rom. 11:36 of h. through h. and to h. are all things

**HIN.**

Ex. 29:40 fourth part of h. of oil
30:24 of oil-olive a h.
Lev. 19:36 a just h. shall ye have
23:13 the fourth part of a h. of oil, Num. 15:4; 28:14
Num. 15:5 fo. part of h. of wine
6 the third part of a h. of oil
9 mingled with half a h. of oil
Ezek. 4:11 sixth part of h. of wa.
45:24 h. of oil for ep. 46:5, 7, 11
46:14 a h. of oil to temper with

**HIND, S.**

Gen. 49:21 Naph. is a h. let loose
2 Sam. 22:34 my feet like h. feet, Ps. 18:33; Hab. 3:19
Job 39:1 mark when h. calve?
Ps. 29:9 voice of L. mak. h. calve
Prov. 5:19 as loving h. and roe
Cant. 2:7 by h. of field, 3:5
Jer. 14:5 h. calved in the field

**HINDER, Verb.**

Gen. 24:56 h. me not, seeing L.
Neh. 4:8 and h. the building

Job 9:12 taketh away, who h. ?
11:10 shut up, who h. him?
Acts 8:36 what h. me to be bap.?
1 Cor. 9:12 lest we sho. h. gospel
Gal. 5:7 who did h. you?

**HINDERED, ETH.**

Ezr. 6:8 exp. given, be not h.
Is. 14:6 is persecuted, none h.
Luke 11:52 entering in, ye h.
1 Thes. 2:18 wo. ha. come, S. h.
1 Pet. 3:7 your prayers be not h.

**HINDER end, sea.**

2 Sam. 2:23 smote with h. e. of
Zec. 14:8 half toward the h. sea

**HINDERMOST, or HINDMOST.**

Gen. 33:2 put Rachel and Jos. h.
Num. 2:31 go h. with standards
Deut. 25:18 and smote h. of thee
Jos. 10:19 and smite h. of them
Jer. 50:12 h. of nations wildern.

**HINDER part, s.**

1 K. 7:25 their h. parts were inward, 2 Chr. 4:4
Ps. 78:66 smote enemies in h. p.
Joel 2:20 h. part tow. utmost sea
Mark 4:38 J. was in h. p. of ship
Acts 27:41 h. p. broken with wa.

**HINGES.**

1 K. 7:50 the h. of gold for doors
Prov. 26:14 door turneth upon h.

**HINNOM.**

Jos. 15:8 border by valley of H.
2 K. 23:10 Tophet, in val. of H.
2 Chr. 28:3 incense in val. of H.
33:6 to pass through fire in H.
Jer. 19:2 valley of the son of H.
32:35 high places in valley of H.

**HIP.**

Jud. 15:8 sm. them h. and thigh

**HIRAM.**

2 Sam. 5:11 H. king, 1 Chr. 14:1
1 K. 5:1 H. sent his servants, 8
7:13 Sol. sent and fetched H.
9:12 H. came to see, 27; 10:11

**HIRE, Substantive.**

Gen. 31:8 ring-stra. sh. be thy h.
Ex. 22:15 hired thing ca. for h.
Deut. 23:18 not br. h. of a whore
1 K. 5:6 to thee will I give h.
Is. 23:17 she shall turn to her h.
18 her h. be holiness to Lord
Ezek. 16:31 not as harlot scor. h.
Mic. 1:7 the hires shall be burnt; gathered of h. of harlot, return to the h. of a harlot
3:11 priests thereof teach for h.
Zec. 8:10 th. was no h. for man
Mat. 20:8 give them their h.
Luke 10:7 labor. worthy of his h.
Jam. 5:4 h. of laborers kept back

**HIRE, EST.**

Is. 46:6 h. goldsmith maketh god
Ezek. 16:33 h. them may come
Mat. 20:1 went out to h. labore.

**HIRED.**

Gen. 30:16 h. with son's mandr.
Lev. 19:13 wages of him h.
Deut. 23:4 they h. ag. thee Balaam, Neh. 13:2
Jud. 18:4 Micah h. me
2 K. 7:6 king of Israel h. ag. us
2 Chr. 24:12 h. masons and carp.
Ezr. 4:5 h. counsellors ag. them
Neh. 6:12 Sanballat had h. him
Is. 7:20 sh. with razor that is h.
Jer. 46:21 h. men like fatted bul.
Hos. 8:9 Ephraim hath h. lovers
10 they have h. am. nations
Mat. 20:7 bec. no man hath h. us
9 were h. about eleventh hour
Acts 28:30 P. two years in h. ho.

**HIRED servant, s.**

Ex. 12:45 a h. servant shall not eat thereof, Lev. 22:10
Lev. 25:6 sab. be meat for h. s.
40 as a h. s. sh. he be with th.
53 yearly h. s. shall he be with him
Deut. 15:18 worth double h. ser.
24:14 thou sh. not oppress h. s.
Mark 1:20 Zeb. in ship with h. s.
Luke 15:17 h. s. have bread, 19

**HIRELING.**

Job 7:1 days are like days of h.?
2 a h. looketh for rew. of work
14:6 accomplish as a h.
Is. 16:14 years of h. 21:16
Mal. 3:5 against those oppress h.
John 10:12 a h. not the shepherd
13 h. fleeth, because he is a h.

**HIS.**

Cant. 2:16 bel. is mine, I am h.
Acts 16:33 baptized, he and all h.
2 Tim. 2:19 L. kno. them are h.

**HISS.**

1 K. 9:8 at house every one sh. h.
Job 27:23 h. him out of place
Is. 5:26 h. to them fr. end of ear.
7:18 Lord shall h. for fly in Eg.
Jer. 19:8 passeth thereby sh. h. 49:17; 50:13
Lam. 2:15 h. at daughter of Jer.
16 enemies h. and gnash teeth
Ezek. 27:36 merchants h. at thee
Zep. 2:15 ev. one passeth shall h.
Zec. 10:8 I will h. for them

**HISSING.**

2 Chr. 29:8 delivered them to h.
Jer. 18:16 make land perpet. h.
19:8 make our city des. and a h.
25:9 and I will make them a h. 18; 29:18
51:37 Babylon shall be a h.
Mic. 6:16 make inhabitants a h.

**HIT.**

1 Sam. 31:3 archers h. 1 Chr. 10:3

**HITHER.**

Gen. 45:8 not you sent me h.
Ex. 3:5 draw not nigh h.
2 K. 2:8 Jordan divided h. 14
Prov. 9:4 let turn in h. 16
Mat. 14:18 bring them h. to me
17:17 bring h. to me, Luke 9:41
22:12 friend, how camest th. h.
Luke 14:21 bring in h. the poor
15:23 bring h. the fatted calf
19:27 bring h. and slay them
John 20:27 reach h. thy finger

See COME.

**HITHERTO.**

Ex. 7:16 h. thou would. not hear
Jos. 17:14 L. hath blessed me h
Jud. 16:13 h. thou hast mocked
1 Sam. 7:12 h. hath L. helped us
1 Chr. 9:18 h. waited in king's
12:29 h. greatest part kept war
Job 38:11 h. shalt thou come
John 5:17 my Father worketh h.
16:24 h. have ye asked nothing
1 Cor. 3:2 h. ye were not able

**HITTITE.**

Gen. 25:9 in field of Eph. the H.
49:30 bought of Eph. H. 50:13
Ex. 23:28 out H. 33:2; 34:11
2 Sam. 11:6 Send Uriah the H
Ezek. 16:3 thy mother a H. 45

**HITTITES.**

Gen. 15:20 hand of H. Jos. 1:4
Ex. 3:8, 17; 13:5; 23:23; Deut. 7:1; 20:17; Jos. 3:10; 12:8; Jud. 3:5; 1 K. 9:20; Neh. 9:8

HIVITES, much in HITTITES.

**HO.**

Ruth 4:1 h. such a one, sit down
Is. 55:1 h. ev. one that thirsteth
Zec. 2:6 h. h. come forth

HOAR, HOARY. See FROST, HAIRS, HEAD.

**HOARY.**

Job 41:32 would think deep h.

**HOBAB.**

Num. 10:29 sa. to H. Jud. 4:11

**HOISED.**

Acts 27:40 they h. up mainsail

**HOLD, S, Substantive.**

Jud. 9:46 entered h. of god Ber.
49 put them to h. set h. on fire
1 Sam. 22:4 David in h. 24:22; 2 Sam. 5:17; 23:14
Jer. 51:30 remained in their h.
Ezek. 19:9 brought him into h.
Acts 4:3 in h. to next day
Rev. 18:2 the h. of ev. foul spirit

See STRONG.

**HOLD.**

Gen. 21:18 h. him in thy hand
Ex. 5:1 that they may h. feast
9:2 and wilt h. them still?
10:9 we must h. a feast unto L.
20:7 L. not h. guiltl. Deut. 5:11
2 Sam. 2:22 h. up my face to Joab
6:6 Uzziah put ha. to ark of G. and took h. of it, 1 Chr. 13:9
1 K. 2:9 now h. him not guiltless
Est. 4:11 h. out golden sceptre
Job 6:24 and I will h. my tongue
9:28 wilt not h. me innocent
13:19 if I h. my tongue
17:9 right. shall h. on his way
Ps. 17:5 h. my goings in thy pa.
119:53 hor. hath taken h. on me
117 h. thou me up, I sh. be safe
139:10 thy right hand sh. h. me
Prov. 31:19 her hands h. distaff
Cant. 3:8 they all h. swords
Is. 41:13 L. h. thy right hand
42:6 and I will h. thy hand
Jer. 2:13 broken cist. h. no wat.
50:43 anguish took h. of him
Amos 6:10 he say, h. thy tongue
Zec. 11:5 h. themsel. not guilty
Mat. 6:24 h. to one, Luke 16:13
21:26 for all h. J. as a prophet
Mark 7:4 they received to h.
Rom. 1:18 h. truth in unrighte.
Phil. 2:29 h. such in reputation
2 Thes. 2:15 h. traditions ye have
Heb. 3:14 if we h. our confidence
Rev. 2:14 h. doctrine of Balaam
15 h. doctrine of Nicolaitans

See CAUGHT.

**HOLD fast.**

Job 8:15 he sh. h. it f. but not en.
27:6 my righteousness I h. fast.
Jer. 8:5 they h. f. deceit
1 Thes. 5:21 h. fast that is good
2 Tim. 1:13 h. f. form of so. wor.
Heb. 3:6 we h. f. the confidence
4:14 h. f. our profession, 10:23
Rev. 2:25 h. f. till I come
3:3 and h. fast and repent
11 h. that f. which thou hast

**HOLD peace.**

Ex. 14:14 ye shall h. your peace
Num. 30:4 if her father h. his p.
14 if her husband h. his p.
Jud. 18:19 h. p. lay hand on m.
2 Sam. 13:20 h. thy p. my sister
2 K. 2:3 h. you your peace, 5
Neh. 8:11 h. your p. day is holy
Job 11:3 lies make men h. p.?
13:13 h. your p. let me alone
33:31 h. thy p. and I will speak
33 h. thy p. I will teach thee
Ps. 83:1 O. G. h. not thy p. 109:1
Is. 62:1 for Z's sake not h. my p.
6 h. their p. day nor night
64:12 h. peace and afflict us?

*Jer.* 4:19 cannot *h.* *peace*
*Zep.* 1:7 *h.* thy *p.* at pres. of L.
*Mat.* 20:31 reb. them bec. they sh. *h.* *p.* *Mark* 10:48; *Luke* 18:39
*Mark* 1:25 *h.* thy *p.* *Luke* 4:35
*Luke* 19:40 if they *h.* *p.* the sto.
*Acts* 12:17 beckoning to *h.* th. *p.*
18:9 be not afraid, *h.* not thy *p.*
1 *Cor.* 14:30 let the first *h.* his *p.*
*See* TAKE.

**HOLDEN.**

2 *K.* 23:22 not *h.* such a pass. 23
*Job* 36:8 *h.* in cords of affliction
*Ps.* 18:35 right hand hath *h.* me
71:6 by thee have I been *h.* up
73:23 *h.* me up by right hand
*Prov.* 5:22 *h.* with cords
*Is.* 45:1 wh. right hand I have *h.*
*Luke* 24:16 their eyes were *h.*
*Acts* 2:24 not possi. he sho. be *h.*
*Rom.* 14:4 yea, he shall be *h.* up

**HOLDEST.**

*Est.* 4:14 *h.* thy peace this time
*Job* 13:24 wherefore *h.* thou me
*Ps.* 77:4 thou *h.* my eyes waking
*Jer.* 49:16 O thou that *h.* height
*Rev.* 2:13 thou *h.* fast my name

**HOLDETH.**

*Job* 2:3 he *h.* fast his integrity
26:9 *h.* back face of his throne
*Ps.* 66:9 bless God who *h.* soul
*Prov.* 11:12 man of und. *h.* peace
17:28 a fool when he *h.* peace
*Dan.* 10:21 none *h.* w. me but M.
*Rev.* 2:1 *h.* stars in right hand

**HOLDING.**

*Is.* 33:15 shak. hands fr. *h.* bribes
*Jer.* 6:11 I am weary with *h.* in
*Mark* 7:3 *h.* tradition of elders
*Phil.* 2:16 *h.* forth word of life
*Col.* 2:19 and not *h.* the head
1 *Tim.* 1:19 *h.* faith
3:9 *h.* the mystery of faith
*Tit.* 1:9 *h.* fast faithful word
*Rev.* 7:1 four angels *h.* four win.

**HOLE, S.**

*Ex.* 28:32 a *h.* in the top of it
1 *Sam.* 14:11 Heb. come out of *h.*
2 *K.* 12:9 Jehoiada bored a *h.*
*Cant.* 5:4 in hand by *h.* of door
*Is.* 2:19 go into *h.* of rocks, 7:19
11:8 child sh. play on *h.* of asp.
42:22 they are all snared in *h.*
51:1 look to the *h.* of the pit
*Jer.* 16:16 hunt them out of *h.*
*Ezek.* 8:7 behold a *h.* in the wall
*Nah.* 2:12 filled his *h.* with prey
*Hag.* 1:6 put it in a bag with *h.*
*Zec.* 14:12 eyes consume in th. *h.*
*Mat.* 8:20 foxes ha. *h.* *Luke* 9:58

**HOLIER, EST.**

*Is.* 65:5 for I am *h.* than thou
*Heb.* 9:3 tabern. is called the *h.*
8 way to *h.* not yet manifest
10:19 to enter *h.* by blood of J.

**HOLILY.**

1 *Thes.* 2:10 how *h.* we behaved

**HOLINESS.**

*Ex.* 15:11 who like thee, in *h.?*
28:36 *h.* to Lord, 39:30; *Zec.* 14:20, 21
1 *Chr.* 16:29 worship L. in beauty of *h.* *Ps.* 29:2; 96:9
2 *Chr.* 20:21 praise beauty of *h.*
31:18 sanctified themselv. in *h.*
*Ps.* 30:4 rememb. of his *h.* 97:12
47:8 God sitteth on throne of *h.*
48:1 praised in mount. of his *h.*
60:6 G. hath spoken in *h.* 108:7
89:35 sw. by my *h.* I will not lie
93:5 *h.* becom. thy house, O L.
110:3 willing, in beauties of *h.*
*Is.* 23:18 her hire sh. be *h.* to
35:8 sh. be called the way of *h.*
62:9 drink it in courts of my *h.*
63:15 from habitation of thy *h.*
18 peo. of thy *h.* have posse. it
*Jer.* 2:3 Israel was *h.* to the Lord
31:23 O mountain of *h.*
*Amos* 4:2 hath sworn by his *h.*
*Ob.* 17 on mount Z. shall be *h.*
*Mal.* 2:11 Ju. hath prof. *h.* of L.
*Luke* 1:75 might serve him in *h.*
*Acts* 3:12 by *h.* made man walk
*Rom.* 1:4 according to spirit of *h.*
6:19 servants to righte. unto *h.*
22 ye have your fruit unto *h.*
2 *Cor.* 7:1 perfect. *h.* in fear of G.
*Eph.* 4:24 new man created in *h.*
1 *Thes.* 3:13 stablish hearts in *h.*
4:7 not to uncleanness, but to *h.*
1 *Tim.* 2:15 conti. in faith and *h.*
*Tit.* 2:3 in behavior as becom. *h.*
*Heb* 12:10 be partakers of his *h.*
14 peace with men, and *h.*

**HOLLOW.**

*Gen.* 32:25 *h.* of thigh, 32
*Ex.* 27:8 altar *h.* boards, 38:7
*Jud.* 15:19 God clave a *h.* place
*Is.* 40:12 waters in *h.* of hand

**HOLPEN.**

*Ps.* 83:8 have *h.* the chil. of Lot
86:17 bec. thou, L. hast *h.* me
*Is.* 31:3 he that is *h.* shall fall
*Dan.* 11:34 *h.* with a little help
*Luke* 1:54 hath *h.* his servant Is.

**HOLY.**

*Ex.* 3:5 pl. th. standest *h.* ground
16:23 to-morrow is *h.* sabbath
19:6 a *h.* nation, 1 *Pet.* 2:9
20:8 remember sabbath keep *h.*
28:38 hallow in all th. *h.* gifts
29:33 they are *h.*; 34 bec. it is *h.*
30:25 an oil of *h.* ointment
32 it is *h.* and sh. be *h.* unto y.
31:14 keep sabbath, it is *h.* 15
*Lev.* 8:9 put on A. the *h.* crown
10:10 difference bet. *h.* and unh.
16:4 put on the *h.* linen coat
33 atonement for *h.* sanctua.
19:2 I the L. your G. am *h.* 21:8
20:7 be ye *h.*; 21:7 he is *h.*
27:14 house to be *h.* to the Lord
30 tithe of the land is *h.* to L.
*Num.* 5:17 priest take *h.* water
15:40 remember and be *h.* to G.
16:3 all the congregation are *h.*
5 show who are his, who is *h.*
18:17 not red. them, they are *h.*
1 *Sam.* 2:2 none *h.* as the Lord
21:5 ves. of young men are *h.*
2 *K.* 4:9 this is a *h.* man of God
1 *Chr.* 22:19 *h.* ves. to hon. of G.
2 *Chr.* 23:6 for they are *h.*
35:3 Levites which were *h.*
13 *h.* offerings sod they in pots
*Ezr.* 8:28 ye are *h.* to the Lord
9:2 *h.* seed mingled themselves
*Neh.* 9:14 madest known *h.* sab.
*Ps.* 20:6 hear from his *h.* heaven
22:3 but thou art *h.* O thou that
28:2 lift hands tow. thy *h.* orac.
86:2 pres. my soul, for I am *h.*
98:1 his *h.* arm hath gotten vic.
99:5 worship at footst. he is *h.*
9 exalt L. worship at his *h.* hill
*Ps.* 105:42 remembered *h.* prom.
145:17 L. is *h.* in all his works
*Prov.* 9:10 knowl. of *h.* is under
30:3 nor have I knowl. of the *h.*
*Is.* 4:3 Jerus. shall be called *h.*
6:3 *h.* *h.* *h.* is the Lord of Hosts
13 *h.* seed substance thereof
27:13 worship in *h.* mountain
52:10 L. made bare his *h.* arm
58:13 call sabbath, *h.* of the L.
64:10 *h.* cities are a wilderness
11 *h.* and beaut. house is burnt
*Jer.* 11:15 *h.* flesh passed fr. thee
*Ezek.* 22:26 no difference betwe. *h.* and profane
36:38 incr. them as the *h.* flock
42:13 *h.* chambers where priests
14 their garments, they are *h.*
44:19 lay them in *h* chambers
23 differ. betw. *h.* and profane
45:1 offer *h.* portion of land, 4
46:19 *h.* chambers of priests
48:10 for priests be *h.* oblation
20 shall offer *h.* oblation, 21
*Dan.* 4:8 D. before me, in whom is spirit of *h.* gods, 9, 18; 5:11
11:28 heart against *h.* covenant
30 indignation ag. *h.* covenant intel. with forsakers of *h.* c.
*Hag.* 2:12 if one bear *h.* flesh, skirt touch br. sh. it be *h.?*
*Zec.* 2:13 L. raised up *h.* habita.
*Mat.* 7:6 gi. not th. is *h.* to dogs
25:31 and *h.* angels with him
*Mark* 6:20 he was just and *h.*
8:38 with *h.* angels, *Luke* 9:26
*Luke* 1:70 by the mouth of *h.* prophets, *Acts* 3:21
72 remember his *h.* covenant
2:23 every male called *h.* to L.
*John* 17:11 *h.* Father keep those
*Acts* 4:27 against thy *h.* child J.
30 won. done by name of *h.* ch.
7:32 place thou standest is *h.*
10:22 warned from G. by *h.* ang.
*Rom.* 1:2 prom. in *h.* scriptures
7:12 commandment is *h.* just
11:16 fir. fruit be *h.* if root be *h.*
12:1 bodies *h.* sacrifice to G.
16:16 salute with *h.* kiss, 1 *Cor.* 16:20; 2 *Cor.* 13:12; 1 *Thes.* 5:26; 1 *Pet.* 5:14
1 *Cor.* 3:17 temple of God is *h.*
7:14 are *h.*; 34 she may be *h.*
*Eph.* 1:4 be *h.* with. blame, 5:27
*Col.* 1:22 present *h.* and unblam.
3:12 elect of G. *h.* and beloved
1 *Thes.* 5:27 to all *h.* brethren
1 *Tim.* 2:8 up *h.* hands
2 *Tim.* 1:9 called us with *h.* call.
3:15 hast known *h.* scriptures
*Tit.* 1:8 bishop be sober, *h.* tem.
*Heb.* 3:1 *h.* brethren, partakers
7:26 high-pr. beca. us who is *h.*
1 *Pet.* 1:15 *h.* in conversation, 16
2:5 *h.* priesth. offer up sacrifices
3:5 *h.* women who trusted in G.
2 *Pet.* 1:18 with him in *h.* mount
21 *h.* men spake mov. by H. G.
2:21 turn fr. *h.* commandment
3:2 spoken before by *h.* prophe.
11 persons to be in all *h.* conv.
*Rev.* 3:7 saith he that is *h.*
4:8 *h.* *h.* *h.* L. God Almighty
6:10 how long, O L. *h.* and true
14:10 in presence of *h.* angels
15:4 not fear thee? thou art *h.*
18:20 *h.* apostles and prophets
20:6 *h.* who ha. part in first res.
21:10 showed me *h.* Jerusalem
22:6 Lord G. of the *h.* prophets
11 he th. is *h.* let him be *h.* st.
*See* CONVOCATION.

**HOLY day.**

*Ex.* 35:2 seventh shall be *h.* *day*
*Neh.* 8:9 *d.* is *h.* unto L. 10, 11
10:31 not buy it on sab. or *h.* *d.*
*Ps.* 42:4 multi. that kept *h.* *d.*
*Is.* 58:13 doing plea. on my *h.* *d.*
*Col.* 2:16 no man judge of a *h.* *d.*
*See* GARMENTS.

**HOLY Ghost.**

*Mat.* 1:18 with child of H. G. 20
3:11 with H. G. *Mark* 1:8; *Luke* 3:16; *John* 1:33; *Acts* 1:5
12:31 blasph. ag. H. G. not forgiven, *Mark* 3:29; *Luke* 12:10
32 whoso. speak. against H. G.
28:19 baptize in name of H. G.

*Mark* 12:36 David said by the H. Ghost, *Acts* 1:16
13:11 not ye speak, but H. G.
*Luke* 1:15 John filled with H. G.
35 H. G. shall come upon thee
41 Elizabeth filled with H. G.
67 Zacharias filled with H. G.
*Luke* 2:25 Sim. H. G. upon him
26 revealed unto him by H. G.
3:22 H. G. desc. in bodily shape
4:1 Jesus being full of H. G.
12:12 H. G. shall teach you
*John* 7:39 H. G. not yet given
14:26 Comforter, who is H. G.
20:22 receive ye H. G. *Acts* 2:38
*Acts* 1:2 he thro. H. G. had given
8 the H. G. is come on you
2:4 all filled with H. G. 4:31
33 promise of the H. G.
4:8 filled with the H. Ghost
5:3 S. filled he. to lie to H. G.?
32 are witnesses, so is H. G.
6:3 men full of the H. Ghost
5 Stephen, man full of H. G.
7:51 stiff-n. alw. resist H. G.
55 Stephen full of H. Ghost
8:15 prayed th. might re. H. G.
17 hands on th. received H. G.
18 when S. saw H. G. was giv.
19 hands, they receive H. G.
9:17 might. be filled with H. G.
31 walking in comfort of H. G.
10:38 G. anoint. J. with H. G.
44 H. G. fell on all who heard
45 on Gentiles was pou. H. G.
47 received H. G. as well as we
11:15 H. G. fell on them
16 shall be baptized with H. G.
24 Barnabas, full of H. G.
13:4 being sent forth by H. G.
9 filled with H. Ghost
52 disciples filled with H. G.
15:8 giving H. G. as he did
28 it seemed good to the H. G.
16:6 forbidden of H. G. to prea.
19:2 received H. G.? we have not heard there be H. G.
6 hands on them, H. G. came
20:23 save that the H. G. witn.
28 H. G. made you overseers
21:11 thus saith the H. Ghost
28:25 spake H. G. by Esaias
*Rom.* 5:5 shed in hearts by H. G.
9:1 consci. bear. wit. in H. G.
14:17 kingd. of G. joy in H. G.
15:13 through power of H. G.
16 being sancti. by the H. G.
1 *Cor.* 2:13 words wh. H. G. tea.
6:19 body is temple of H. G.
12:3 Jesus is Lord, but by H. G.
2 *Cor.* 6:6 by the H. G. by love
13:14 communion of H. G.
1 *Thes.* 1:5 gospel came in H. G.
6 rec. word with joy of H. G.
2 *Tim.* 1:14 good th. k. by H. G.
*Tit.* 3:5 by renewing of H. G.
*Heb.* 2:4 with gifts of H. G.
3:7 H. G. saith, To-day if ye h.
6:4 made partakers of H. G.
9:8 H. Ghost this signifying
10:15 whereof H. G. is a witness
1 *Pet.* 1:12 H. G. sent fr. heaven
2 *Pet.* 1:21 as moved by H. G.
1 *John* 5:7 Fat. Word, and H. G.
*Jude* 20 beloved, pray. in H. G.
*See* GOD, HABITATION, HILL.

**Most HOLY.**

*Ex.* 26:33 betw. holy and *m. h.*
29:37 an altar *most h.* 40:10
*Lev.* 2:3 remnant be Aaron's, it is *m. h.* 10; 6:17; 10:12
6:25 sin-offering *m. h.* 29; 10:17
7:1 tresp.-offering *m. h.* 6; 14:13
21:22 both of *m. h.* and holy
24:9 cakes of flour *m. h.* to him
*Num.* 4:4 about *m. h.* things
19 approach *m. h.* things
18:9 offering to me shall be *m. h.*
10 in *m. h.* place sh. thou eat it
1 *K.* 6:16 built th. for *m. h.* plac.
7:50 made ves. for *m. h.* place
8:6 brought the ark unto *most h.* place, 2 *Chr.* 5:7
1 *Chr.* 23:13 A. to sanctify *m. h.*
2 *Chr.* 3:8 Sol. *m. h.* house
10 in *m. h.* house made cheru.
4:22 inner doors for *m. h.* place
*Ezr.* 2:63 not eat of *most h.* things, *Neh.* 7:65
*Ezek.* 43:12 whole limit be *m. h.*
44:13 not come near *m. h.* place
45:3 sanctuary and *m. h.* place
*Dan.* 9:24 to anoint *most h.*
*Jude* 20 building on *m. h.* faith

**HOLY mountain.**

*Ps.* 87:1 foundation is in *h. m.*
*Is.* 11:9 nor dest. in *h. m.* 65:25
56:7 will I bring to my *h. m.*
57:13 he shall inherit my *h. m.*
65:11 ye are th. forget my *h. m.*
*Ezek.* 20:40 in *h. m.* th. serve me
28:14 wast upon *h. m.* of G.
*Dan.* 9:16 anger turned fr. *h. m.*
*Dan.* 9:20 pres. suppli. for *h. m.*
11:45 plant tabernacles in *h. m.*
*Joel* 2:1 so. an alarm in my *h. m.*
3:17 L. dwelling in Z. my *h. m.*
*Ob.* 16 drunk on my *h. m.*
*Zec.* 8:3 mount. of L. called *h. m.*

**HOLY name.**

*Lev.* 20:3 Molech, prof. my *h. n.*
22:2 profane not my *h. n.* 32
1 *Chr.* 16:10 glory ye in his *h. name*, *Ps.* 105:3
35 thanks to *h. n.* *Ps.* 106:47
29:16 build a house for thy *h. h.*
*Ps.* 33:21 trusted in his *h. name*
99:3 praise terrible *n.* it is *h.*
103:1 L. bless his *h. n.* 145:21
111:9 *h.* and rev. his *n.* *Lu.* 1:49
*Is.* 57:15 lofty One, wh. *n.* is *h.*
*Ezek.* 20:39 pollute you my *h. n.*
36:20 profaned my *h. n.*
22 your sakes, for *h. n.'s* sake
39:7 make known *h. n.* in Isr.
25 be jealous for my *h. n.*
43:7 my *h. n.* Is. no more defile
8 defiled my *h. n.* by abomi.
*Amos* 2:7 to profane my *h. n.*

**HOLY oil.**

*Ex.* 30:25 *h.* anoint. *o.* 31; 37:29
*Ps.* 89:20 with *h. oil* I anoi. him

**HOLY One.**

*Deut.* 33:8 Thummim and Urim be with thy H. One.
*Job* 6:10 not con. words of H. O.
*Ps.* 16:10 nor suffer H. O. to see corruption, *Acts* 2:27; 13:35
89:19 in vision to thy H. O.
*Is.* 10:17 H. O. sh. be for a flame
29:23 sanctify H. O. of Jacob
40:25 sh. I be equal? saith H. O.
43:15 I am the Lord, your H. O.
49:7 Redeemer of Is. his H. O.
*Dan.* 4:13 H. O. down fr. heaven
*Hos.* 11:9 H. O. in midst of thee
*Hab.* 1:12 from everl. my H. O.
3:3 H. O. came from mount P.
*Mark* 1:24 I know th. who th. a. the H. O. of G. *Luke* 4:34
*Acts* 3:14 ye denied the H. One
1 *John* 2:20 unction from H. One

**HOLY One of Israel.**

2 *K.* 19:22 lifted thy eyes against the H. O. *of Israel*, *Is.* 37:23
*Ps.* 71:22 O thou H. O. *of Israel*
78:41 limited the H. O. *of Israel*
89:18 the H. O. *of Is.* is our ki.
*Is.* 1:4 provoked the H. O. *of Is.*
5:19 coun of H. O. *of Israel*
24 despised word of H. O. *of I.*
12:6 great is H. O. *of Is.* in mid.
17:7 have respect to H. O. *of I.*
29:19 rejoice in H. O. *of Israel*
30:11 cause H. O. *of Is.* to cease
12 saith the H. O. *of Is.* 15
31:1 look not to the H. O. *of Is.*
41:14 saith thy Red. H. O. *of I.*
16 shalt glory in H. O. *of Is.*
20 H. O. *of Is.* hath created it
43:3 I am the L. the H. O. *of Is.*
45:11 the L. the H. O. *of Israel*
47:4 L. is his name, H. O. *of Is.*
48:17 Red. H. O. *of Israel*, 54:5
49:7 Red. of *I.* and his H. O.
55:5 nat. run to thee, H. O. *of I.*
60:9 bring th. gold to H. O. *of I.*
14 the Z. of the H. O. *of Is.*
*Jer.* 50:29 proud aga. H. O. *of I.*
51:5 filled w. sin ag. H. O. *of I.*
*Ezek.* 39:7 I am the L. H. O. *in I.*

**HOLY ones.**

*Dan.* 4:17 dem. by word of *h. o.*

**HOLY people.**

*Deut.* 7:6 *h. p.* to the L. 14:2, 21
26:19 thou may be *h. p.* to Lord
28:9 L. shall establ. thee a *h. p.*
*Is.* 62:12 shall call them *h. p.*
*Dan.* 8:24 and destroy *h. p.*

**HOLY place.**

*Ex.* 28:29 goeth in unto *h. p.* 35
43 to minister in *h. place*, 29:30
29:31 seethe his flesh in the *h. p.*
31:11 sweet incense for *h. p.*
35:19 do service in *h. p.* 39:1, 41
38:24 gold in all work of *h. p.*
*Lev.* 6:16 unlea. bread sh. be eat. in *h. p.* 26; 7:6; 10:13; 24:9
27 shalt wash that in the *h. p.*
10:17 eaten sin-offer. in *h. p.*?
18 blood not bro. within *h. p.*
14:13 slay burnt-offering in *h. p.*
16:2 come not at all tim. to *h. p.*
16 atonement for *h. p.* 17, 27
20 end of reconciling the *h. p.*
24 shall wash his flesh in *h. p.*
*Jos.* 5:15 *p.* wh. thou stand is *h.*
1 *K.* 8:8 staves were seen in *h. p.*
2 *Chr.* 29:5 carry filth. out of *h. p.*
30:27 prayer came to his *h. p.*
*Ezr.* 9:8 to give us a nail in *h. p.*
*Ps.* 24:3 sh. stand in his *h. p.*?
46:4 streams make glad the *h. p.*
68:17 Lord is am. them in *h. p.*
*Ec.* 8:10 had gone from *p.* of *h.*
*Is.* 57:15 I dw. in high and *h. p.*
*Ezek.* 41:4 this is the most *h. p.*
42:13 *p.* is *h.*; 14 out of *h. p.*
*Mat.* 24:15 abomination in *h. p.*
*Acts* 6:13 blasph. words ag. *h. p.*
21:28 this man polluted *h. p.*
*Heb.* 9:12 Christ entered *h. p.*
25 priest entered ev. year *h. p.*

**HOLY places.**

2 *Chr.* 8:11 bec. the *places* are *h.*
*Ps.* 68:35 terrible out of thy *h. p.*
*Ezek.* 21:2 drop thy word to. *h. p.*
*Heb.* 9:24 Ch. is not entered *h. p.*

**Shall be HOLY.**

*Ex.* 22:31 *s. be h.* men unto me
29:37 what. touch. altar *s. be h.*
30:32 it *shall be h.* unto you, 37
40:9 anoint. tab. and it *s. be h.*
*Lev.* 11:44 ye *shall be h.* for I am holy, 45; 19:2; 20:26
19:24 fruit *sh. be h.* to praise L.
21:6 priests *s. be h.* unto th. G.
23:20 they *shall be h.* to the L.
25:12 jubilee, it *sh. be h.* to you
27:9 man giveth to L. *s. be h.*
10 exchange thereof *s. be h.* 33
21 the jubilee, it *s. be h.* to L.
32 the tenth *s. be h.* unto the L.
*Num.* 6:5 Nazarite *s. be h.* to L.
*Deut.* 23:14 theref. *s.* camp *be h.*
*Ezek.* 45:1 portion *s. be h.*
*Joel* 3:17 then *s.* Jerusalem *be h.*

**HOLY Spirit.**
Ps. 51:11 take not H. S. fr. me
Is. 63:10 rebel. and vexed H. S.
11 put his H. S. within him?
Luke 11:13 heav. Fa. give H. S.
Eph. 1:13 sealed wi. H. S. of pro.
4:30 grieve not the H. S. of God
1 Thes. 4:8 given us his H. S.

**HOLY temple.**
Ps. 5:7 worship tow. h. t. 138:2
11:4 the Lord is in his h. temple
65:4 satis. with goodness of h. t.
79:1 h. temple have they defiled
Jon. 2:4 look again tow. thy h. t.
7 my prayer came to thy h. t.
Mic. 1:2 L. from h. t. be witness
Hab. 2:20 the Lord is in his h. t.
Eph. 2:21 groweth to h. t.

**HOLY thing.**
Lev. 22:10 no stranger eat of h. t.
Num. 4:15 sh. not touch any h. t.
Ezek. 48:12 obla. to them. a t. h.
Luke 1:35 that h. th. born of thee

**HOLY things.**
Ex. 28:38 bear iniq. of h. t.
Lev. 5:15 thro. ignorance in h. t.
22:2 sep. from the h. t. of Is.
4 not eat of h. t. till clean, 6, 12
7 shall afterward eat of h. t.
15 shall not profane h. t. of Is.
16 to bear iniq. when eat h. t.
Num. 4:20 not see, h. t. are cov.
18:32 neither sh. ye pollute h. t.
Deut. 12:26 thy h. t. take and go
1 Chr. 23:28 office purifying h. t.
2 Chr. 31:6 bro. in tithe of h. t.
Neh. 10:33 ordinances for h. t.
12:47 sanctified h. t. to Levites
Ezek. 22:8 thou despised my h. t.
26 priests have profaned h. t.
44:8 not kept charge of my h. t.
1 Cor. 9:13 minister about h. t.

**HOME.**
Gen. 43:16 bring these men h.
Ex. 9:19 not brought h. sh. die
Deut. 21:12 br. her h. to thy hou.
24:5 shall be free at h. one year
Ruth 1:21 L. hath brought me h.
1 Sam. 6:7 bring their calves h.
10 men shut up th. calves at h.
18:2 go no more h. to fath.'s ho.
2 Sam. 14:13 not fetch h. banish.
17:23 Ahithophel gat him h.
1 K. 5:14 a month in L. two at h.
13:7 come h. with me, 15
1 Chr. 13:12 bring ark of G. h. 13
2 Chr. 25:10 go h. they return h.
Est. 5:10 when Haman came h.
Job 39:12 will bring h. thy seed
Ps. 68:12 she that tarried at h.
Prov. 7:19 good man is not at h.
20 come h. at day appointed
Ec. 12:5 man goeth to his long h.
Lam. 1:20 at h. there is as death
Hab. 2:5 neither keepeth at h.
Hag. 1:9 when ye brought it h.
Mat. 8:6 my serv. lieth at h. sick
Mark 5:19 go h. to thy friends
Luke 9:61 bid th. farewell at h.
John 19:27 took her to his own h.
20:10 disc. went to their own h.
1 Cor. 11:34 hunger, eat at h.
14:35 ask husbands at h.
2 Cor. 5:6 we are at h. in body
1 Tim. 5:4 to show piety at h.
Tit. 2:5 be discreet, keepers at h.

**HOME-BORN.**
Ex. 12:49 to him that is h.-b.
Lev. 18:9 whe. b. at h. or abroad
Jer. 2:14 is Israel a h.-b. slave?

**HOMER.**
Lev. 27:16 a h. of barley-seed
Is. 5:10 seed of a h. yield ephah
Ezek. 45:14 for ten baths are a h.
Hos. 3:2 bou. for h. and half h.

**HONEST.**
Luke 8:15 an h. and good heart
Acts 6:3 seven of h. report
Rom. 12:17 h. in sight of all
2 Cor. 8:21 h. th. in sight of L.
13:7 do that which is h.
Phil. 4:8 whatso. things are h.
1 Pet. 2:12 having conversat. h.

**HONESTLY.**
Rom. 13:13 walk h. as in the day
1 Thes. 4:12 walk h. toward them
Heb. 13:18 in all things to live h.

**HONESTY.**
1 Tim. 2:2 lead life god. and h.

**HONEY.**
Gen. 43:11 carry a little h. spices
Ex. 16:31 wafers made with h.
Lev. 2:11 burn no leaven, nor h.
Deut. 8:8 a land of oil-olive and h. 2 K. 18:32
32:13 he made him to suck h.
Jud. 14:8 h. in carcass of lion, 9
18 what is sweeter than h.?
1 Sam. 14:25 was h. upon ground
26 h. dropped; 29 I tasted h. 43
2 Sam. 17:29 bro. h. and butter
1 K. 14:3 take a cruse of h.
Job 20:17 sh. not see brooks of h.
Ps. 19:10 judgment sweeter than h. 119:103
Ps. 81:16 h. out of rock sati. thee
Prov. 24:13 eat h. is good, 25:16
25:27 not good to eat much h.
Cant. 4:11 h. and milk and. ton.
5:1 honey-comb with my h.
Is. 7:15 butter and h. sh. he eat
22 butter and h. sh. ev. one eat
Jer. 41:8 treasures of h. in field
Ezek. 3:3 in my mouth as h.
27:17 Ju: traded in h. and balm
Mat. 3:4 J. Baptist's meat locus. and wild h. Mark 1:6
Rev. 10:9 thy mouth sweet as h.
10 in my mouth sweet as h.
See FLOWETH, FLOWING.

**HONEY-COMB.**
1 Sam. 14:27 and dip. it in h.-c.
Ps. 19:10 sweeter than h.-c.
Prov. 5:3 lips of str. wo. as h.-c.
16:24 pleasant words are as h.-c.
24:13 eat h.-c. sweet to thy taste
27:7 full soul loatheth a h.-c.
Cant. 4:11 thy lips drop as a h.-c.
5:1 eaten my h.-c. with honey
Luke 24:42 gave piece of h.-c.

**HONOR, S.**
Gen. 49:6 h. be not thou united
Ex. 14:17 get me h. on Phar. 18
Num. 22:17 promote thee to h. 37
24:11 L. hath kept thee from h.
Deut. 26:19 above nations in h.
Jud. 4:9 journey not be for th. h.
13:17 pass, we may do thee h.
2 Sam. 6:22 shall I be had in h.
1 K. 3:13 given thee rich. and h.
1 Chr. 16:27 glory and h. are in
29:12 riches and h. come of thee
28 D. died, full of riches and h.
2 Chr. 1:11 not asked riches or h.
12 riches, wealth, and h.
26:18 nor shall it be for thy h.
32:33 inhabit. of Jer. did him h.
Est. 1:4 h. of his excel. majesty
20 wives shall give to husb. h.
6:3 wh. h. ha. been done for th.?
8:16 the Jews had joy and h.
Job 14:21 his sons come to h.
Ps. 7:5 ene. lay mine h. in dust
8:5 crowned with h. Heb. 2:7, 9
21:5 h. and maj. thou laid on him
26:8 where thine h. dwelleth
49:12 man being in h. abid. not
20 in h. and understandeth
66:2 sing forth h. of his name
71:8 mouth filled with thy h.
96:6 h. and majesty are bef. him
104:1 thou art clothed with h.
112:9 horn sh. be exalt. with h.
145:5 speak of h. of thy majesty
149:9 this h. have all his saints
Prov. 3:16 left hand riches and h.
4:8 she shall bring thee to h.
5:9 lest thou give th. h. to oth.
8:18 riches and h. are with me
11:16 gracious woman retain. h.
14:28 the people is the king's h.
15:33 bef. h. is humility, 18:12
20:3 an h. to cease from strife
21:21 follow. mercy, findeth h.
22:4 fear of L. are riches and h.
25:2 h. of kings to search
26:1 h. is not seemly for a fool
8 so is he that giv. h. to a fool
29:23 h. shall uphold humble
31:25 and h. are her clothing
Ec. 6:2 to wh. G. hath given h.
10:1 that is in reputation for h.
Jer. 33:9 an h. before all nations
Dan. 2:6 receive rewards and h.
4:30 built for h. of my majesty
36 h. and brightness returned
5:18 G. gave father glory and h.
11:21 shall not give h. of king.
Mal. 1:6 where is mine h.?
Mat. 13:57 prophet not without h. Mark 6:4: John 4:44
John 5:41 I rec. not h. from men
44 receive h. one of another
8:54 honor myself, h. is nothing
Acts 28:10 hon. us with many h.
Rom. 2:7 seek glory and h.
10 h. to ev. man worketh good
9:21 of same lump ma. ves. to h.
12:10 in h. prefer. one another
13:7 render h. to wh. h. is due
1 Cor. 12:23 bestow abund. h. 24
2 Cor. 6:8 by h. and dishonor
Col. 2:23 not in h. to satis. flesh
1 Thes. 4:4 to possess vessel in h.
1 Tim. 1:17 to G. be h. and glory
5:17 elders worthy of double h.
6:1 count masters worthy of h.
16 to whom be h. and power
2 Tim. 2:20 some to h. 21
Heb. 3:3 more h. than house
5:4 no man taketh h. to himself
1 Pet. 1:7 to praise, h. glory
3:7 h. to wife as weaker vessel
2 Pet. 1:17 from G. the Father h.
Rev. 4:9 beasts give glory and h.
11 to receive glory and h. 5:12
5:13 h. power, and might, be to him, 7:12; 19:1
19:7 let us rejoice, give h.
21:24 glory and h. to it, 26

**HONOR, Verb.**
Ex. 20:12 h. thy father and thy mother, Deut. 5:16; Mat. 15:4; 19:19; Mark 7:10; 10:19; Luke 18:20; Eph. 6:2
Lev. 19:15 not h. per. of mighty
32 shalt h. the face of old man
Jud. 9:9 by me they h. God
1 Sam. 2:30 th. th. h. me I will h.
15:30 yet h. me now bef. elders
Est. 6:6 delighteth to h. 7, 9, 11
Ps. 91:15 deliver him and h. him
Prov. 3:9 h. L. with thy substa.
Is. 29:13 with lips do h. me
43:20 beast of field shall h. me
58:13 h. him, not doing own
Dan. 4:37 and h. King of heaven
11:38 h. God of forces, a god whom fa. knew not sh. he h.
Mat. 15:6 h. not fath. or mother
John 5:23 all men h. Son as h. F.
8:49 I h. Father, ye dishonor me
54 if I h. myself, my h. is noth.
12:26 him will Father h.
1 Tim. 5:3 h. wid. that are wid.
1 Pet. 2:17 h. all men, h. the king

**HONORABLE.**
Num. 22:15 sent princes more h.

1 Sam. 9:6 th. is in the city a man of God, and he is an h. man
2 Sam. 23:19 was he not most h. of three? 1 Chr. 11:21
23 was more h. than the thirty
2 K. 5:1 Naaman h. with master
1 Chr. 4:9 more h. than brethren
Job 22:8 the h. man dwelt in it
Ps. 45:9 daughters am. h. women
111:3 his work is h. and glori.
Is. 3:3 doth take away h. man
5 base behave proudly ag. h.
5:13 their h. men are famished
9:15 ancient and h. he is head
23:8 traffickers are h. of earth
9 into contempt all h. of earth
42:21 magnify law, make it h.
43:4 been h., 58:13 holy of L. h.
Nah. 3:10 cast lots for her h. men
Mark 15:43 Jos. an h. counsellor
Luke 14:8 lest more h. man be
Acts 13:50 J. stirred up h. wom.
17:12 h. women not few believ.
1 Cor. 4:10 ye are stro. ye are h.
12:23 members we think less h.
Heb. 13:4 marriage h. bed unde.

**HONORED.**

Ex. 14:4 I will be h. on Pharaoh
Prov. 13:18 regard. reproof be h.
27:18 wait. on master sh. be h.
Is. 43:23 nor h. me wi. sacrifices
Lam. 1:8 all that h. her despise
5:12 faces of elders were not h.
Dan. 4:34 I praised and h. him
1 Cor. 12:26 or one member be h.

**HONOREST, ETH.**

1 Sam. 2:29 h. thy sons above me
Ps. 15:4 h. them that fear Lord
Prov. 12:9 he that h. himself.
14:31 that h. him hath mercy
Mal. 1:6 son h. father
Mat. 15:8 h. me w. lips, Mar. 7:6
John 5:23 h. not Son, h. not Fa.
8:54 it is my Father that h. me

**HOODS.**

Is. 3:23 I will take away the h.

**HOOF, S.**

Ex. 10:26 shall not a h. be left
Lev. 11:3 whatever parteth h.
4 of them that divide the h.
5 divideth not h. 6; Deut. 14:7
7 swine, tho' div. h. Deut. 14:8
Jud. 5:22 were horse h. broken
Ps. 69:31 better than ox with h.
Is. 5:28 horses' h. shall be coun.
Jer. 47:3 noise of stamping of h.
Mic. 4:13 will make thy h. brass

**HOOK, S.**

Ex. 26:32 h. of gold, 37; 38:36
2 K. 19:28 h. in nose, Is. 37:29
Job 41:1 dr. leviathan wi. h.? 2
Is. 2:4 sp. into prun. h. Mic. 4:3
18:5 cut off sprigs with prun. h.
Ezek. 29:4 put h. in thy jaw, 38:4
40:43 with. were h. hand broad
Joel 3:10 pruning h. into spears
Mat. 17:27 cast a h. take up fish

**HOPE.**

Ezr. 10:2 there is h. in Israel
Job 4:6 this thy fear, thy h.?
5:16 poor hath h. iniq. stoppeth
7:6 my days spent without h.
8:13 hypocrite's h. sh. peri. 14
11:18 because there is h.
20 h. be as giving up of ghost
14:7 h. of tree if it be cut down
19 thou destroyest h. of man
27:8 what is h. of hypocrite?
Ps. 78:7 might set their h. in G.
146:5 happy he whose h. is in L.
Prov. 10:28 h. of right. gladness
11:7 h. of unjust men perisheth
13:12 h. defer. mak. heart sick
14:32 the right. hath h. in death
19:18 chast. son wh. there is h.
26:12 h. of fool than him, 29:20
Ec. 9:4 joined to liv. there is h.
Is. 57:10 no h. Jer. 2:25; 18:12
Jer. 14:8 O the h. of Israel, 17:13
17:7 blessed man whose h. L. is
31:17 there is h. in end, saith L.
50:7 the Lord, h. of their fath.
Lam. 3:21 therefore have I h.
Ezek. 37:11 our bones dri. h. lost
Hos. 2:15 val. of Achor door of h.
Joel 3:16 L. will be h. of his peo.
Zec. 9:12 turn, ye prisoners of h.
Acts 16:19 h. of gains was gone
23:6 h. and resurrection of dead
24:15 h. tow. G. which th. allow
26:6 judged for h. of the prom.
27:20 all h. we should be saved
28:20 for h. of Israel I am bound
Rom. 5:4 patience, experien. h.
5 h. maketh not ashamed
8:24 sa. by h. but h. seen is not h.
15:4 thro' patien. might have h.
13 that ye may abound in h.
1 Cor. 9:10 be partaker of his h.
13:13 faith, h. charity, th. three
15:19 in this life only we ha. h.
2 Cor. 1:7 our h. of you is stead.
3:12 seeing that we have such h.
10:15 h. when faith is increased
Gal. 5:5 the Spirit wait for h.
Eph. 1:18 h. of his calling
2:12 no h. with. G. in world
4:4 as ye are called in one h.
Col. 1:5 h. laid up for you in hea.
23 not moved from h. of gospel
27 Christ in you, h. of glory
1 Thes. 1:3 patience of h. in Jes.
2:19 for what is our h. or joy?
4:13 as others who have no h.
5:8 helmet the h. of salvation
2 Thes. 2:16 given us good h.
1 Tim. 1:1 Lord Jesus, is our h.
Tit. 2:13 for that blessed h.
3:7 accord. to h. of eternal life
Heb. 3:6 rejoic. of h. firm to end
6:11 full assurance of h. to end
18 to lay hold on h. before us
19 wh. h. we have as an anch.
7:19 bringing in of a better h.
1 Pet. 1:3 begot. us to a lively h.
21 faith and h. might be in G.
3:15 reason of h. that is in you
1 John 3:3 man that hath this h.

**In HOPE.**

Ps. 16:9 rest in h. Acts 2:26
Rom. 4:18 ag. hope believ. in h.
5:2 rejoice in h. of glory of God
8:20 subjected the same in h.
12:12 rejoicing in h. patient
15:13 that ye may abound in h.
1 Cor. 9:10 plougheth in h. thres.
Tit. 1:2 in h. of eternal life

**My HOPE.**

Job 17:15 where is now my h.?
19:10 my h. hath he removed
31:24 if I have made gold my h.
Ps. 39:7 my h. is in thee
71:5 thou art my h. Jer. 17:17
119:116 asha. of my h. Phil. 1:20
Lam. 3:18 my h. perished

**HOPE, Verb.**

Job 6:11 stren. that I should h.
Ps. 22:9 didst make me h.
31:24 all that h. in the L.
33:18 h. in his mercy, 147:11
22 as we h. in thee
38:15 L. do I h. thou wilt hear
42:5 h. thou in God, 11; 43:5
71:14 but I will h. continually
119:49 hast caused me to h.
81 h. in thy word, 114; 130:5
130:7 let Israel h. in L. 131:3
Lam. 3:24 there. will I h. in him
26 that man both h. and wait
Luke 6:34 them of whom ye h.
Acts 26:7 our tribes h. to come
Rom. 8:24 why doth he h. for?
25 if we h. for that we see not
Phil. 2:23 him I h. to send pres.
1 Pet. 1:13 be sober, and h. to end

**HOPED.**

Job 6:20 con. bec. they had h.
Ps. 119:43 have h. in thy judgm.
74 I have h. in thy word, 147
166 L. I have h. for thy salva.
Jer. 3:23 vain is salvation h. for
Luke 23:8 h. to have seen mirac.
Acts 24:26 h. money sho. be giv.
Heb. 11:1 substance of th. h. for

**HOPING, ETH.**

Luke 6:35 lend, h. for nothing ag.
1 Cor. 13:7 charity h. all things

**HOPHNI.** 1 Sa. 1:3; 2:34; 4:11, 17

**HOREB.**

Ex. 3:1 came to H. 1 K. 19:8
Deut. 1:6 spake to us in H. 4:15
Ps. 106:19 made a calf in H.
Mal. 4:4 commanded M. in H.

**HOR-HAGIDGAD.** Num. 33:32

**HORMAH.**

Num. 14:45 discomfi. to H. 21:3
1 Sam. 30:30 pre. to H. 1 Chr. 4:30

**HORN.**

Ex. 21:29 if ox push with h.
1 Sam. 2:1 my h. is exalted in L.
10 sh. exalt h. of his anointed
16:1 fill thy h. with oil, 13
2 Sam. 22:3 h. of my sal. Ps. 18:2
1 K. 1:39 Zadok took a h. of oil
Job 16:15 defiled my h. in dust
Ps. 75:4 wicked, lift not up h. 5
89:17 our h. shall be exalted
24 in my name sh. h. be exalted
92:10 my h. shalt thou exalt
112:9 his h. shall be exalted
132:17 make h. of David to bud
Lam. 2:3 cut off all the h. of Is.
17 set up h. of thine adversaries
Ezek. 29:21 cause h. of Is. to bud
Dan. 7:8 am. them a little h. 20
11 great words which h. spake
21 h. made war with saints
8:5 the goat had a notable h.
8 great h. was broken
9 came forth little h.
21 great h. that is betw. eyes
Mic. 4:13 I will make thy h. iron
Zec. 1:21 lift up h. over the land
Luke 1:69 raised up h. of salvat.

**HORNS.**

Gen. 22:13 caught in thic. by h.
Ex. 27:2 make h. of it on four corners, his h. be of the same, 30:2; 37:25; 38:2
Ex. 29:12 put off the bl. on h. of the altar, Lev. 4:7, 18, 25, 30, 34; 8:15; 9:9; 16:18
30:3 pure gold overlay h. 37:26
Deut. 33:17 h. like h. of unicorns
1 K. 22:11 Zedekiah made h. of iron, 2 Chr. 18:10
Ps. 22:21 from h. of unicorns
69:31 bullock that hath h.
75:10 h. of wicked will I cut off, but h. of righ. sh. be exalted
118:27 bind sacrifice to h. of alt.
Ezek. 27:15 a present h. of ivory
34:21 pushed all diseased wi. h.
Dan. 7:7 fou. beast had ten h. 20
8 I consid. h. three h. pluc. up
24 ten h. ten kings
8:3 ram two h. two h. were high
6 he-goat ca. to ram had two h.
7 smote ram, brake his two h.
20 two h. kings of Me. and P.
Amos 6:13 not taken h. by stre.?
Hab. 3:4 h. coming out of hand
Zec. 1:18 and behold, four h.
19 h. have scattered Judah, 21

Rev. 5:6 in midst L. having 7 h.
12:3 a red dragon, having ten h.
13:1 beast ten h. on h. ten cro.
11 beast had two h. like a lamb
17:3 scarlet-colored beast, ten h.
7 beast seven heads and ten h.
12 ten h. thou saw. ten kin. 16
See RAMS.

**HORNET, S.**
Ex. 23:28 will send h. bef. thee
Deut. 7:20 L. send h. am. them
Jos. 24:12 I sent the h. bef. you

HORONAIM. Jer. 48:3, 5, 34

**HORRIBLE.**
Ps. 11:6 on wicked rain h. temp.
40:2 brought me out of h. pit
Jer. 5:30 h. thing committed
18:13 virgin of Is. done h. thing
23:14 seen in proph. a h. thing
Hos. 6:10 seen h. thing in Israel

**HORRIBLY.**
Jer. 2:12 be h. afraid, O ye heav.
Ezek. 32:10 kings sh. be h. afraid

**HORROR.**
Gen. 15:12 a h. of great darkness
Ps. 55:5 h. hath overwhelmed
119:53 h. hath taken hold on me

**HORSE.**
Gen. 49:17 adder biteth h. heels
Ex. 15:21 h. and rider thr. in sea
Jud. 5:22 were h. hoofs broken
1 K. 10:29 a h. for 150 shekels, 2 Chr. 1:17
Est. 6:8 h. king rideth on, 9, 10
Job 39:18 scorneth h. and rider
19 hast thou giv. h. strength?
Ps. 32:9 be not as the h. or mule
33:17 a h. vain thing for safety
76:6 char. and h. cast into sleep
147:10 del. not in strength of h.
Prov. 21:31 h. prep. ag. battle
26:3 a whip for h. a rod for fool
Is. 63:13 led thro' deep, as a h.
Jer. 8:6 h. rusheth into the battle
Amos 2:15 he th. rideth h. deliv.
Zec. 1:8 riding upon a red h.
9:10 cut off the h. from Jerus.
10:3 made them as goodly h.
12:4 smite every h. with blind.
14:15 shall be plague of the h.
Rev. 6:2 behold white h. 19:11
4 red h.; 5 black h.; 8 a pale h.
14:20 blood came to h. bridles
19:19 war ag. him that sat on h.
21 slain wi. sw. of him sat on h.

**HORSEBACK.**
2 K. 9:18 on h. to meet Jehu, 19
Est. 6:9 on h. through city, 11
8:10 sent letters by posts on h.

**HORSE-GATE.**
2 Chr. 23:15 entering of h.-g.
Neh. 3:28 from above the h.-g.
Jer. 31:40 to corner of the h.-g.

**HORSES.**
Gen. 47:17 bread in exch. for h.
Ex. 9:3 hand of Lord is upon h.
Deut. 17:16 not multi. h. to himself, to end he sho. multi. h.
1 K. 10:28 Solomon had h. out of Egypt, 2 Chr. 1:16, 17; 9:28
18:5 grass to save h. and mules
22:4 my h. are as thy h. 2 K. 3:7
2 K. 2:11 there appeared h. of fire
5:9 Naaman came wi. h. and ch.
7:10 h. tied; 13 take five of h.
9:33 Jez. blood sprinkled on h.
18:23 del. thee 2,000 h. Is. 36:8
23:11 took away h. given to son
Ec. 10:7 I have seen serv. on h.
Is. 2:7 th. land is also full of h.
5:28 their h. hoofs sh. be coun.
30:16 for we will flee upon h.
31:1 stay on h. trust in chariots
3 th. h. are flesh and not spirit
Jer. 4:13 h. are swifter than eag.
5:8 were as fed h. in the morn.
8:16 snorting of his h. was heard
12:5 canst thou contend wi. h.?
46:4 harness the h. and get up
47:3 stamping of hoof of his h.
51:27 cause h. come up as cater.
Ezek. 17:15 give him h. and peo.
23:6 horsemen riding on h. 12
20 whose issue is like iss. of h.
23 all of th. riding on h. 38:15
27:14 traded in thy fairs with h.
Hos. 1:7 save th. by battle nor h.
14:3 we will not ride on h.
Joel 2:4 app. of h. and horsemen
Amos 6:12 sh. h. run upon rock?
Hab. 1:8 their h. also are swifter
3:8 thou didst ride on thy h.
15 didst walk thro' sea with h.
Hag. 2:22 overthrow h. and rid.
Zec. 1:8 behind him were red h.
6:2 first chariot red h. sec. black
3 third white h. in fou. bay h.
10:5 riders on h. be confounded
14:20 that day upon bells of the h. Holiness to the Lord
Jam. 3:3 we put bits in h. mou.
Rev. 9:7 the locusts were like h.
17 I saw the h. the heads of h.
18:13 buyeth merchandise of h.
19:14 armies follow. on white h.
18 eat flesh of kings and h.
See CHARIOTS.

**HORSELEECH.**
Prov. 30:15 h. had two daugh.

**HORSEMAN, MEN.**
Gen. 50:9 with Jos. chariots, h.
Ex. 14:9 h. of Pharaoh pursued
17 honor on Pharaoh and his h.
15:19 Pharaoh and h. went into sea, Jos. 24:6
1 Sam. 8:11 your sons to be h.
2 Sam. 1:6 h. followed after him
1 K. 4:26 Sol. had 12,000 h. 10:26
9:19 Solomon had cities for h. 22; 2 Chr. 8:6, 9
2 K. 2:12 chariot of Is. h. thereof
13:14 O my father, the h. of Is.
18:24 put thy trust in Eg. for h.
2 Chr. 16:8 host with many h.
Ezr. 8:22 ashamed to ask h.
Neh. 2:9 sent captains and h.
Is. 21:7 saw a chariot with h. 9
22:7 h. shall set themselves
31:1 trust in h. bec. they strong
36:9 put thy trust on Eg. for h.
Jer. 4:29 shall flee for noise of h.
46:4 get up ye h. and stand
Ezek. 23:6 h. riding on horses, 12
26:10 walls shake at noise of h.
38:4 bring forth horses and h.
Dan. 11:40 the king of the north shall come with h.
Hos. 1:7 not save by horses nor h.
Joel 2:4 as h. so shall they run
Nah. 3:3 h. lifteth up bright sw.
Hab. 1:8 h. shall spread thems. and th. h. sh. come from far
Acts 23:23 ready h. threescore
Rev. 9:16 number of army of h.

**HOSANNA.**
Mat. 21:9 h. to the Son of D. 15
Mark 11:9 h. bles. is he that com. h. in highest, 10; John 12:13

**HOSEN.**
Dan. 3:21 men bound in their h.

**HOSHEA.**
Deut. 32:44 H. spake to people
2 K. 15:30 H. made, 17:1, 3; 18:10
1 Chr. 27:20 ruler of Ephraim, H.
Neh. 10:23 H. and Han. seal. co.

**HOSPITALITY.**
Rom. 12:13 giv. to h. 1 Tim. 3:2
Tit. 1:8 but a lover of h.
1 Pet. 4:9 use h. one to another

**HOST.**
Luke 10:35 and gave them to h.
Rom. 16:23 Gaius my h.

**HOST.**
Gen. 2:1 earth finish. all h. of th.
32:2 he said, This is God's h.
Ex. 14:4 I honored on his h. 17
24 L. looked to h. of Egyptians
28 waters covered h. of Phar.
16:13 dew lay round about h.
Num. 31:14 wroth with offi. of h.
48 officers of h. came to Moses
Deut. 2:14 men of war wa. fr. h.
23:9 when the h. goeth forth ag.
Jos. 1:11 pass thro' h. and com.
Jos. 3:2 officers went thro' the h.
5:14 as capt. of the h. of the L.
Jud. 4:2 captain of h. was Sisera
7:8 h. of Midian was beneath
9 get thee down unto the h. 10
13 cake of bre. tumbled into h.
8:11 Gideon smote the h. 12
1 Sam. 11:11 S. came into the h.
14:15 there was trembling in h.
19 the noise of the h. went on
17:20 D. came as h. was going
28:5 S. saw the h. of Philistines
29:6 coming with me in h.
2 Sam. 20:23 Joab was over all h. 1 Chr. 18:15
23:16 brake thro' h. 1 Chr. 11:18
1 K. 2:32 Abner captain of the h.
22:34 carry me out of the h.
2 K. 3:9 no water for the h.
4:13 be spoken to capt. of h.?
6:14 horses and h. to Dothan
7:4 let us fall to h. of the Syri.
6 L. made h. to he. noise of h.
9:5 captains of h. were sitting
25:19 prin. scribe of h. Jer. 52:25
1 Chr. 9:19 fathers over h. of L.
12:22 a great h. like the h. of G.
2 Chr. 18:33 carry me out of h.
24:24 the L. delivered a great h.
Ps. 27:3 tho' a h. should encamp
33:6 all h. made by thy mouth
16 no king saved by mul. of h.
Is. 13:4 L. muster. h. of battle
24:21 L. sh. pun. h. of high ones
40:26 bring. out h. by number
Jer. 51:3 destroy utterly all her h.
Ezek. 1:24 speech, as noise of h.
Dan. 8:10 cast down some of h.
11 magni. hims. to prince of h.
12 h. given him ag. daily sacr.
13 h. to be trodden under foot
Ob. 20 the captivity of this h.
Luke 2:13 heavenly h. prais. G.
See HEAVEN.

**HOSTAGES.**
2 K. 14:14 Jehoash took h. and returned to Sam. 2 Chr. 25:24

**HOSTS.**
Ex. 12:41 h. of L. went out of E.
Ps. 103:21 bless L. all ye his h.
108:11 O G. go forth with our h.?
148:2 praise ye him, all his h.
Jer. 3:19 heritage of h. of nations
See GOD, LORD.

**HOT.**
Ex. 16:21 when the sun waxed h.
Lev. 13:24 there is a h. burning
Deut. 19:6 anger and h. displeas.
19:6 while his heart is h.
Jos. 9:12 our bread we took h.
Jud. 2:14 L. was h. against Isr. 20; 3:8; 10:7
6:39 let not thine anger be h.
1 Sam. 11:9 by the time sun be h.
21:6 put h. bread when taken
Neh. 7:3 not open. till sun be h.
Job 6:17 when h. they are cons.
Ps. 6:1 neither chasten in thy h. displeasure, 38:1
39:3 my h. was h. within me
78:48 flocks to h. thunderbolts

*Prov.* 6:28 one go upon *h.* coals?
*Ezek.* 24:11 brass of it may be *h.*
*Dan.* 3:22 furnace was exceed. *h.*
*Hos.* 7:7 they are all *h.* as oven
1 *Tim.* 4:2 seared with *h.* iron
*Rev.* 3:15 neither cold nor *h.* I would thou wert cold or *h.* 16
*See* WAX, *Verb.*

**HOTLY.**

*Gen.* 31:36 th. hast so *h.* pursued

**HOTTEST.**

2 *Sam.* 11:15 front of the *h.* bat.

**HOUGH, ED.**

*Jos.* 11:6 shall *h.* their horses
9 *h.* horses, burnt chariots
2 *Sam.* 8:4 Da. *h.* chariot horses

**HOUR.**

*Dan.* 4:19 D. astonish. for one *h.*
*Mat.* 9:22 whole from that *h.*
15:28 dau. whole from that *h.*
17:18 ch. was cured from that *h.*
20:3 went out about the third *h.*
5 sixth and ninth *h.*; 6 elev. *h.*
12 these have wro. but one *h.*
24:36 that *h.* knoweth no man, 42; *Mark* 13:32
44 such an *h.* as ye think not, 50; *Luke* 12:40, 46
25:13 know neither day nor *h.*
26:40 wa. one *h.*? *Mark* 14:37
45 the *h.* is at hand, S. of man
27:45 from sixth *h.* was darkness over the land to ninth *h.* *Mark* 15:33; *Luke* 23:44
*Mat.* 27:46 ninth *h.* Jesus cried, *Mark* 15:34
*Mark* 13:11 given you in that *h.*
14:35 if pos. the *h.* might pass
15:25 third *h.* they cruci. him
*Luke* 10:21 in that *h.* J. rejoiced
12:39 what *h.* thief would come
22:53 your *h.* and power of dar.
59 about the space of one *h.*
*John* 2:4 mine *h.* is not yet come
4:6 it was about sixth *h.* 19:14
21 believe me, *h.* cometh, 23
52 then inq. he the *h.* he began to amend, at sev. *h.* fev. left
5:25 the *h.* is coming, 28; 16:32
7:30 *h.* was not yet come, 8:20
12:23 *h.* is come, Son be gl. 17:1
27 Fa. save me from this *h.* for this cause came I to this *h.*
13:1 Jes. knew his *h.* was come
16:21 because her *h.* is come
19:27 from that *h.* disciple took
*Acts* 2:15 it is third *h.* of day
3:1 *h.* of prayer being ninth *h.*
10:3 about ninth *h.* angel com.
9 P. went to pray about 6th *h.*
23:23 make ready at the third *h.*
1 *Cor.* 4:11 to this present *h.*
15:30 in jeopardy every *h.*?
*Gal.* 2:5 gave place, not for an *h.*
*Rev.* 3:3 not know what *h.* I will
10 from *h.* of temptation
8:1 was silence about half an *h.*
9:15 prepar. for an *h.* and a day
14:7 *h.* of his judgment is come
17:12 rec. power as kings one *h.*
18:10 in one *h.* is thy jud. come
17 in one *h.* great riches is co.
19 city in one *h.* made desolate

**Same HOUR.**

*Dan.* 3:6 *s. h.* cast into furn. 15
4:33 *same h.* was thing fulfilled
5:5 in *s. h.* came forth fingers
*Mat.* 8:13 serv. was healed *s. h.*
10:19 given you *s. h.* *Luke* 12:12
*Luke* 7:21 *same h.* cured many
20:19 *s. h.* sou. to lay ha. on him
*John* 4:53 knew it was at *s. h.*
*Acts* 16:18 he came out *same h.*
33 took them *s. h.* of the night
*Rev.* 11:13 *s. h.* was earthquake

**HOURS.**

*John* 11:9 twelve *h.* in day?
*Acts* 5:7 about three *h.* after
19:34 all cried about two *h.*

**HOUSE.**

*Gen.* 19:4 men compassed the *h.*
24:31 I have prepared *h.* room
39:5 L. blessed Egyptian's *h.*
45:2 the *h.* of Pharaoh heard
*Ex.* 8:3 frogs shall come into *h.*
12:3 a lamb according to the *h.*
30 not *h.* wh. was not one dead
46 not carry flesh out of the *h.*
13:3 out of the *h.* of bond. 14; *Deut.* 5:6; 6:12
20:17 shalt not covet neighbor's *h.* *Deut.* 5:21
*Lev.* 14:36 priest sh. empty the *h.*
38 priest shall go out of the *h.* and shut up *h.* 45, 46, 49
25:30 *h.* sold in walled city
*Deut.* 7:8 red. out of *h.* of bond.
8:14 brought you out of land of E. from *h.* of bondage, 13:5, 10; *Jos.* 24:17; *Jud.* 6:8; *Jer.* 34:13; *Mic.* 6:4
25:10 *h.* of him hath shoe loosed
*Jos.* 2:15 *h.* was on town wall
*Jud.* 16:26 pillars wher. *h.* stand.
27 *h.* full of men and women
30 the *h.* fell upon the lords
17:5 Micah had a *h.* of gods
19:18 no man receiveth me to *h.*
22 sons of Belial beset *h.* 20:5
1 *Sam.* 3:14 I have sw. to *h.* of E.
5:2 brought ark into *h.* of Dag.
7:1 bro. ark to *h.* of Abinadab
9:18 tell me where seer's *h.* is
25:28 L. make my lord sure *h.*
2 *Sam.* 3:1 war betw. *h.* of Saul
8 show kindness to *h.* of Saul
5:8 lame and blind not co. to *h.*
6:11 L. blessed *h.* of Obed-edom, David brought ark from his *h.* 12; 1 *Cor.* 13:14
7:6 not dw. in any *h.* 1 *Chr.* 17:5
11 he will make thee a *h.*
29 bless *h.* of serv. 1 *Chr.* 17:27
12:8 I gave thee thy master's *h.*
1 *K.* 2:24 who made me a *h.*
6:22 whole *h.* overlaid with gold
9:25 so Solomon finished the *h.*
12:31 and Jeroboam made a *h.*
17:15 her *h.* did eat many days
21:22 thy *h.* like *h.* of Jeroboam
2 *K.* 8:3 cry to the king for her *h.*
2 *K.* 8:18 as did the *h.* of Ahab, 27; 2 *Chr.* 21:6; 22:4
9:8 *h.* of Ahab shall perish
10:3 fight for your master's *h.*
21 and the *h.* of Baal was full
27 the *h.* of Baal a draught *h.*
20:13 Hez. showed *h.* of precio. things, *h.* of arm. *Is.* 39:2
23:27 *h.* of wh. my name sh. be
25:9 ev. great man's *h.* he burnt
2 *Chr.* 7:1 glory of the Lord filled the *h.* *Ezek.* 43:4, 5
12 chosen this place for *h.*
*Ezr.* 5:8 went to *h.* of great God
6:3 at Jer. let the *h.* be builded
*Est.* 2:3 gather all virgins to *h.*
8:1 give *h.* of Ha. to Esther, 7
*Job* 1:13 drink. in brother's *h.* 18
19 wind came smote cor. of *h.*
20:19 *h.* which he builded not
21:28 where is *h.* of the prince?
30:23 to *h.* appointed for all liv.
38:20 know paths to the *h.*
39:6 whose *h.* I made wildern.
*Ps.* 31:2 rock be *h.* of defence
84:3 sparrow hath found a *h.*
104:17 stork, fir-trees are her *h.*
*Prov.* 2:18 *h.* inclineth to death
7:8 yo. man went way to her *h.*
11 her feet abide not in her *h.*
27 her *h.* is the way to hell

9:1 wisdom hath builded her *h.*
12:7 *h.* of righteous shall stand
14:11 *h.* of wicked overthrown
15:25 L. will destroy *h.* of proud
17:1 *h.* full of sacrifices
19:14 *h.* and riches are inherit.
21:9 dwell in *h.*-top, 25:24
12 right. consider. *h.* of wicked
24:3 through wisdom is *h.* built
25:17 withdraw fr. neighbor's *h.*
27:10 brot. *h.* day of calamity
*Ec.* 7:2 to go to *h.* of mourning, than *h.* of feasting
10:18 thro' idleness *h.* droppeth
12:3 keepers of *h.* shall tremble
*Cant.* 1:17 beams of our *h.* cedar
2:4 brought me to banquet. *h.*
3:4 bro. him to my mother's *h.*
8:2 br. thee into my mother's *h.*
*Is.* 5:8 woe to them join *h.* to *h.*
6:4 *h.* was filled with smoke
14:17 open. not *h.* of prisoners
23:1 th. is no *h.*; 24:10 *h.* shut
31:2 against *h.* of evil-doers
60:7 I will glo. *h.* of my glory
64:11 holy and beaut. *h.* burnt
*Jer.* 16:5 enter not *h.* of mourn.
8 sh. not go into *h.* of feasting
37:20 not return to *h.* of J. 38:26
*Ezek.* 2:5 they are a rebellious *h.* 3:9, 26, 27; 12:3
8 be not rebellious like that *h.*
12:2 dwellest in midst of reb. *h.*
17:12 say now to rebellious *h.*
24:3 utter parable to rebel. *h.*
43:11 show them the form of *h.*
12 law of *h.* on top of mount.
*Amos* 1:5 sceptre from *h.* of E.
3:15 winter *h.* with summer *h.*
5:19 or went into *h.*
6:11 smite great *h.* and little *h.*
7:16 not word ag. *h.* of Isaac
*Ob.* 18 *h.* of Es. be for stubble
*Mic.* 3:12 mountain of the shall be as high places
4:2 let us go up to *h.* of God
*Nah.* 1:14 out of *h.* of thy gods
*Zec.* 5:4 enter into *h.* of thief, into *h.* of him that sweareth falsely
*Mat.* 7:25 and beat upon that *h.* 27; *Luke* 6:48
10:12 come into *h.* salute it
13 if *h.* be worthy, let your peace come, *Luke* 10:5
12:25 every *h.* divided ag. itself
29 strong man's *h.* *Mark* 3:27
20:11 murmured ag. man of *h.*
23:38 your *h.* is left to you desolate, *Luke* 13:25
24:43 man of *h.* kn. what watch thief wou. come, *Luke* 12:39
*Mark* 3:25 *h.* divided ag. itself
10:29 hath left *h.* or brethren
14:14 good man of *h.* *Lu.* 22:11
*Luke* 10:7 in that *h.* remain
15:8 light candle and sweep *h.*
*John* 12:3 *h.* was filled with odor
*Acts* 2:2 sound fr. heaven fill. *h.*
46 breaking bread from *h.* to *h.*
10:6 Simon, tanner, *h.* by seasi.
17:5 Jews assaulted *h.* of Jason
18:7 *h.* joined hard to synagog.
19:16 fled out of that *h.* naked
20:20 tau. publicly, from *h.* to *h.*
*Rom.* 16:5 greet church in th. *h.*
1 *Cor.* 1:11 are of the *h.* of Chloe
1 *Cor.* 16:15 the *h.* of Stephan. 19
2 *Cor.* 5:1 earthly *h.* be dissolved
2 clothed with *h.* from heaven
1 *Tim.* 5:13 wander. from *h.* to *h.*
14 younger women guide *h.*
2 *Tim.* 1:16 mercy to *h.* of Ones.
2:20 in a great *h.* vessels of gold
*Heb.* 3:3 built *h.* more h. than *h.*
4 every *h.* is built by some m.
6 wh. *h.* are we, if we hold fast
2 *John* 10 receive him not into *h.*

See AARON, BORN, BUILD or BUILT, CHIEF, DAVID, DOOR, DWELL.

**HOUSE, with father.**

Gen. 12:1 get thee fr. father's h.
24:7 G. took me from father's h.
38 thou sh. go to my fa.'s h.
40 wife for my son of f.'s h.
31:14 portion for us in f.'s h.
38:11 remain widow at f.'s h.
41:51 God made me forget f.'s h.
46:31 breth. and f.'s h. are come
50:22 in Egypt, he and f.'s h.
Ex. 12:3 accord. to h. of fathers
Num. 1:2 sum of Israel by h. of their f. 18, 22, 24, 28
4 every one head of h. of his f. 44; Jos. 22:14
2:2 pitch with ensign of f.'s h.
3:15 children of Levi after h. of their fathers, 20; 4:46
17:2 accord. to h. of their f.'s, 3
18:1 thou and f.'s h. bear. iniq.
30:3 being in her father's h. 16
Deut. 22:21 play whore in f.'s h.
Jos. 2:12 show kindn. to f.'s h.
Jud. 6:15 least in my f.'s h.
9:18 risen against my f.'s h.
11:2 shalt not inherit in f.'s h.
14:15 we burn thee and f.'s h.
16:31 the h. of his f. buried him
1 Sam. 2:27 appear to h. of thy f.
30 h. of thy f. should walk
17:25 will make his f.'s h. free
18:2 go no more home to f.'s h.
22:16 thou and all f.'s h. sh. die
24:21 not destr. name out f.'s h.
2 Sam. 3:29 rest on Joab and his father's h.
14:9 iniq. be on me, and f.'s h.
19:28 all of f.'s h. dead men
1 K. 2:31 innoc. blood fr. f.'s h.
18:18 thou and f.'s h. trou.
1 Chr. 28:4 God chose me bef. h. of f.
Ezr. 2:59 their f.'s h. Neh. 1:6
10:16 chief of the h. of f.
Neh. 1:6 I and f.'s h. have sinned
Est. 4:14 and f.'s h. be destroyed
Ps. 45:10 forget peo. and f.'s h.
Is. 3:6 hold of brother of h. of f.
7:17 bring on thy f.'s h. days
22:23 glorious throne to f.'s h.
24 hang on him glory of f.'s h.
Jer. 12:6 h. of f. dealt treacher.
Luke 16:27 send him to f.'s h.
John 2:16 make not my F.'s h. a house of merchandise
14:2 in F.'s h. are many mans.
Acts 7:20 M. nourished in f.'s h.

**HOUSE of God.**

Gen. 28:17 none oth. but h. of G.
22 this sto. I set sh. be G.'s h.
Jos. 9:23 draw. water for h. of G.
Jud. 18:31 h. of G. was in Shiloh
20:26 came unto h. of G. 21:2
31 high. goeth up to h. of G.
2 Chr. 5:14 gl. of L. fill. h. of G.
22:12 he was hid in h. of G.
24:13 set h. of G. in his state
33:7 Man. set image in h. of G.
36:19 they burnt the h. of G.
Ezr. 5:8 went to h. of great G.
15 let h. of G. be builded, 6:7
7:23 let it be done for h. of G.
Neh. 6:10 let us meet in h. of G.
13:11 why is h. of G. forsaken?
Ps. 42:4 went to h. of G. 55:14
52:8 an olive-tree in h. of G.
84:10 door-keeper in h. of G.
Ec. 5:1 when goest to h. of G.
Is. 2:3 come, let us go up to the h. of G. Mic. 4:2
Hos. 9:8 proph. hated in h. of G.
Joel 1:13 drink-offering with-holden from h. of G.
16 gladness cut off fr. h. of G.

Zec. 7:2 sent to h. of G. men
Mat. 12:4 entered h. of G. did eat shewbread, Mark 2:26; Luke 6:4
1 Tim. 3:15 beh. thy. in h. of G.
Heb. 10:21 High-p. over. h. of G.
1 Pet. 4:17 judg. begin at h. of G.

**His HOUSE.**

Gen. 12:17 L. plagu. P. and h. h.
Gen. 17:27 men of h. h. circumc.
39:4 overseer over h. h. 5
45:8 Lord of h. h. Acts 7:10
Lev. 16:6 atonement for h. h. 11
27:14 a man shall sanctify h. h.
Num. 22:18 if B. give h. h. full of silver and gold, 24:13
Deut. 20:5 return to h. h. 6, 7, 8
24:10 shalt not go into his h.
Jud. 8:27 bec. a snare to his h.
1 Sam. 3:12 spoken concer. h. h.
13 I will judge h. h. for ever
7:17 to Ramah, there was h. h.
25:1 Is. buried Samuel in h. h.
2 Sam. 6:21 bef. thy fa. and h. h.
11:9 U. went not to h. h. 10, 13
27 David fetched her to h. h.
19:11 bring king back to h. h.
21:1 for Saul and h. bloody h.
1 K. 2:33 on h. h. th. sh. be pea.
7:1 S. building, and finish. h. h.
12:24 return every man to h. h. 22:17; 1 Chr. 16:43; 2 Chr. 11:4; 18:16
13:19 did eat bread in h. h.
20:43 went to h. h. heavy, 21:4
2 K. 6:32 Elisha sat in his h.
20:13 nothing in h. h. Hezekiah
1 Chr. 10:6 all h. h. died togeth.
13:14 the ark remained in h. h.
2 Chr. 24:16 good toward God and h. h.
Ezr. 6:11 h. h. be made dunghill
Neh. 3:28 repaired over ag. h. h.
5:13 God shake ev. man fr. h. h.
Job 1:10 a hedge about his h.?
8:15 he shall lean on his h.
20:28 increase of his h.
21:21 what plea. ha. he in h. h.?
27:18 he buildeth his h.
Ps. 49:16 gl. of h. h. is increased
105:21 made him Lord of h. h.
112:3 wealth and riches in h. h.
Prov. 6:31 give the substance of his h. Cant. 8:7
17:13 evil shall not dep. fr. h. h.
Mic. 2:2 oppress a man and h. h.
Hab. 2:9 an evil covet. to h. h.
Mat. 12:29 then he will spoil h. h. Mark 3:27
24:17 an. out of h. h. Mark 13:15
43 not suffered h. h. to be bro.
Luke 8:41 he wo. come to h. h.
18:14 man went down to h. h.
John 4:53 himself beli. and h. h.
Acts 10:2 feared G. with all h. h.
22 to send for thee to his h.
11:13 had seen an angel in h. h.
16:34 jailer brou. into his h. be-lievi. in G. with all h. h. 18:8
Col. 4:15 salute church in h. h.
Heb. 3:2 M. faithful in h. h. 5
11:7 prep. ark for saving h. h.

**HOUSE of Jacob.**

Gen. 46:27 souls of h. of Jacob
Ps. 114:1 h. of J. from people
Is. 2:5 h. of Jacob walk in light
6 forsaken thy people, h. of J.
8:17 hideth face from h. of J.
14:1 shall cleave to h. of Jacob
58:1 show h. of Jacob their sins
Jer. 2:4 hear word of L. h. of J.
5:20 declare this in h. of Jacob
Ezek. 20:5 lifted hand to h. of J.
Amos 9:8 not ut. destroy h. of J.
Ob. 17 h. of J. pos. possessions
18 h. of J. shall be a fire

Mic. 2:7 art named the h. of J.
3:9 ye heads of the h. of Jacob
Luke 1:33 reign over h. of Jacob

**HOUSE of Joseph.**

Gen. 43:17 bro. men into J.'s h.
Jos. 18:5 h. of J. abide in coast
Jud. 1:22 h. of J. went aga. B.
35 hand of h. of Jos. prevailed
Amos 5:6 like fire in h. of Jos.
Ob. 18 h. of J. shall be a flame
Zec. 10:6 I will save the h. of J.

**HOUSE of Israel.**

Lev. 10:6 let h. of Israel bewail
17:3 what man th. be of h. of Is. kill. ox or lamb, 8:10; 22:18
1 Sam. 7:2 the h. of I. lamented
2 Sam. 6:5 h. of I. played bef. L.
15 h. of I. brought up ark
12:8 I gave thee the h. of Israel
1 K. 20:31 kings of h. of I. merc.
Ps. 98:3 truth toward h. of I.
115:12 he will bless h. of Israel
135:19 O h. of Israel, bless Lord
Is. 5:7 vineyard of L. is h. of I.
14:2 h. of Israel possesses them
46:3 remn. of h. of I. hearken
63:7 goodness tow. the h. of I.
Jer. 2:26 so is h. of I. ashamed
3:18 h. of J. walk with h. of Is.
Jer. 3:20 dealt tr. O. h. of I. 5:11
79:26 all h. of I. uncircumcised
11:10 h. of I. broken covenant
17 evil for evil, of h. of Israel
13:11 cleave to me, h. of Israel
31:27 sow h. of I. wi. seed of m.
31 make cov. with h. of I. 33
33:14 that I promised to h. of I.
48:13 h. of I. ashamed of Bethel
Ezek. 3:1 sp. to h. of Israel, 17:2, 20:27, 30; 24:21; 33:10; 36:22
7 h. of I. not hearken unto me, h. of I. impud. and hard-he.
17 watchman to h. of I. 33:7.
4:4 lay iniq. of h. of I. upon it
5 bear iniquity of h. of Israel
5:4 fire come forth into h. of I.
8:10 idols of h. of I. portrayed
9:9 iniq. of h. of I. is great
12:24 nor more divi. in h. of I.
13:5 nor made hedge for h. of I.
9 in the writing of h. of Israel
14:11 h. of I. go no more astray
18:6 eyes to idols of h. of I. 15
25 h. of I. is not my way eq.?
31 O h. of Israel? 33:11
20:13 h. of I. rebelled ag. me
39 for you, O h. of I. go ye
40 there shall h. of I. serve me
22:18 h. of I. is to me bec. dross
28:24 no more prick. br. h. of I.
29:6 a staff of reed to h. of I.
16 no more confid. of h. of I.
21 cause horn of h. of I. to bud
36:10 multiply all the h. of I.
17 h. of I. dwelt in own land
21 my name wh. h. of I. prof.
32 be ashamed, O h. of Israel
37 I will be inq. of by h. of I.
37:11 bones are whole h. of I.
16 for the h. of I. his compan.
39:12 7 mo. h. of I. be burying
22 h. of I. sh. know I am the L.
23 h. of I. went into captivity
29 pour. out my Sp. on h. of I.
44:12 caused h. of Israel fall
22 maidens of seed of h. of I.
45:6 possession for who. h. of I.
8 rest of land give to h. of I.
17 reconciliation for h. of I.
Hos. 1:4 cease kingd. of h. of I.
6 no more ha. mer. on h. of I.
6:10 a horrible thing in h. of I.
11:12 h. of I. compasseth me
Amos 5:3 sh. leave ten to h. of I.
25 offered sacrifices, O. h. of I.
7:10 consp. ag. thee in h. of I.
9:9 sift h. of I. am. all nations

*Mic.* 1:5 for sins of *h. of I.* is this
*Zec.* 8:13 were a curse, O *h. of I.*
*Mat.* 10:6 sheep of *h. of I.* 15:24
*Acts* 2:36 let all *h. of I.* know
7:42 O *h. of I.* have off. beasts?
*Heb.* 8:8 new cov. with *h. of I.* 10

**HOUSE of Judah.**

2 *Sam.* 2:4 anointed D. king ov. *h. of J.* 7, 11; 1 *Chr.* 28:4
12:8 I gave thee the *h. of Jud.*
2 *K.* 19:30 remnant escaped of the *h. of Judah*, *Is.* 37:31
*Is.* 22:21 be a father to *h. of J.*
*Jer.* 3:18 *h. of J.* walk with h. I.
5:11 *h. of J.* dealt treacherously
11:10 *h. of J.* broken covenant
12:14 pluck *h. of J.* fr. am. them
13:11 caused cle. to me *h. of J.*
31:27 sow *h. of J.* with seed
31 make new cov. with *h. of J.*
33:14 good I promised to *h. of J.*
36:3 *h. of J.* hear all the evil
*Ezek.* 4:6 bear iniq. of *h. of J.* 9:9
8:17 a light thing to *h. of J.?*
25:3 Am. said, Aha, ag. *h. of J.*
8 *h. of J.* like to all heathen
12 Edom hath dealt ag. *h. of J.*
*Hos.* 1:7 mercy upon *h. of J.*
5:12 be to *h. of J.* as rottenness
14 as a young lion to *h. of J.*
*Zep.* 2:7 for remnant of *h. of J.*
*Zec.* 8:13 a curse, O *h. of Judah*
15 to do well to *h. of Judah*
19 be to *h. of J.* joy and glad.
10:3 Lord hath visited *h. of J.*
6 I will strengthen the *h. of J.*
12:4 open m. eyes unto *h. of J.*
*Heb.* 8:8 a new cov. with *h. of J.*

**King's HOUSE.**

2 *Sam.* 11:2 wal. on roof of *k.'s h.*
1 *K.* 9:1 Sol. had finished *k.'s h.*
14:26 took away the treasure of *king's h.* 15:18; 2 *K.* 16:8; 2 *Chr.* 12:9; 25:4
2 *K.* 7:11 told it to the *k.'s h.*
2 *Chr.* 23:5 third part be at *k.'s h.*
28:21 took a port. out of *h. of k.*
*Ezr.* 6:4 expe. given out *k.'s h.*
*Est.* 2:9 seven maid. out *k.'s h.*
*Est.* 4:13 think not esc. in *k.'s h.*
9:4 Mordecai was great in *k.'s h.*
*Hos.* 5:1 give ye ear, O *h.* of *k.*

**HOUSE of Levi.**

*Num.* 17:8 rod of A. for *h. of L.*
*Ps.* 135:20 bless the L. O *h. of L.*
*Zec.* 12:13 family of *h. of L.*

**In the HOUSE.**

*Gen.* 34:29 spoiled all *in the h.*
39:5 bless. of L. on all *in the h.*
8 wot. not what is with me *in the h.*
46:16 fame was heard *in* P.'s *h.*
*Ex.* 12:46 *in* one *h.* passover
*Lev.* 14:34 put plague of leprosy *in a h.* 35, 43, 44, 47, 48
*Jos.* 2:19 with thee *in the h.*
*Ruth* 1:9 each *in h.* of husband
2:7 she tarried a little *in the h.*
1 *Sam.* 28:24 a fat calf *in the h.*
31:9 publ. it *in the h.* of their id.
10 put armor *in the h.* of Asht.
1 *K.* 3:17 I and this wom. dw. *in one h.* deli. of a child *in t. h.*
6:7 not any tool heard *in the h.*
14:13 found good *in the h.* if J.
2 *K.* 4:2 wh. hast thou *in t. h.?*
35 walked *in the h.* to and fro
5:18 I bow *in the h.* of Rimmon
19:37 as he was worshipping *in h.* of Nisroch, *Is.* 37:38
2 *Chr.* 36:17 slew yo. men *in t. h.*
*Ezr.* 1:7 *in the h.* of his gods
6:1 search made *in t. h.* of rolls
*Est.* 7:8 force queen *in the h.?*
9 gallows standeth *in h.* of Ha.
*Ps.* 119:54 *in the h.* of my pilg.
*Prov.* 3:33 curse of Lord *in h.*
5:10 be *in t. h.* of a stranger
7:11 her feet abide not *in h. h.*
15:6 *in the h.* of the righteous
*Ec.* 7:4 heart of wise is *in h.* of mourn. he. of fools *in h.* mi.
*Is.* 44:13 mak. idol remain *in h.*
*Jer.* 7:30 abominations *in h.* 32:34
34:15 a covenant bef. me *in t. h.*
*Amos* 6:9 ten men *in one h.*
*Mic.* 6:10 wicked. *in h.* of wicked
*Zec.* 13:6 wounded *in h.* of frien.
*Mat.* 5:15 light to all are *in t. h.*
*Mark* 9:33 being *in the h.*
14:3 being *in t. h.* S. the leper
*Luke* 8:27 *in any h.* but tombs
*John* 8:35 abideth not *in the h.*
11:20 Mary sat still *in the h.*
*Acts* 9:11 inq. *in t. h.* of Judas
10:32 P. is lodged *in h.* of Sim.

**HOUSE, *with* Lord.**

*Ex.* 23:19 first fruits bring into *h.* of *L.* 34:26; *Neh.* 10:35
*Deut.* 23:18 pr. of dog to *h.* of *L.*
*Jos.* 6:24 put in treas. of *h.* of *L.*
1 *Sam.* 1:7 she went to *h.* of *L.*
24 Hannah bro. him unto the *h.* of the *L.* 2 *K.* 12:4, 9, 13; 22:4; 2 *Chr.* 34:14
1 *K.* 3:1 end of building *h.* of *L.*
6:37 the foundation of the *h.* of the *Lord* laid, 2 *Chr.* 8:16; *Ezr.* 3:11; *Zec.* 8:9
7:40 work made for *h.* of *Lord*, 45:51; 2 *Chr.* 4:16; 5:1; 24:14
8:10 cloud filled *h.* of *L.* 11; 2 *Chr.* 5:13; 7:2; *Ezek.* 44:4
63 so Israel dedicated *h.* of *L.*
2 *K.* 11:3 hid in *h.* of *L.* six yea.
4 took an oath in *h.* of the *L.*
15 let her not be slain in *h.* of *Lord*, 2 *Chr.* 23:14
12:10 money found in *h.* of the *Lord*, 14:14; 16:8; 18:15
11 oversight of the *h.* of the *L.*
16 press.-money not in *h.* of *L.*
20:5 third day sh. go to *h.* of *L.*
8 L. will heal me, that I shall go up to the *h.* of *L.* *Is.* 38:22
23:2 words found in *h.* of *Lord*, 24; 2 *Chr.* 34:17, 30
7 Sodomites were by *h.* of *L.*
25:9 he burnt *h.* of *L.* *Jer.* 52:13
1 *Chr.* 6:31 service in the *h.* of *L.*
22:1 D. said, This is the *h.* of *L.*
11 build the *h.* of *L.* thy God
14 I have prepared for *h.* of *L.*
23:4 set forw. work of *h.* of *L.*
26:12 to minister in *h.* of the *L.*
2 *Chr.* 8:16 *h.* of *L.* was perfected
29:5 sanctify *h.* of the *Lord*
15 came to cleanse *h.* of *Lord*
33:15 M. took idol out *h.* of *L.*
34:15 book of law in *h.* of *L.*
36:14 priests polluted *h.* of *L.*
*Ezr.* 7:27 beautify *h.* of the *L.*
*Ps.* 23:6 dw. in *h.* of *L.* for ever
27:4 dwell in *h.* of *L.* all my life
92:13 be planted in *h.* of *Lord*
*Ps.* 116:19 pay my vows in *L.'s h.*
118:26 bless. you out of *h.* of *L.*
122:1 let us go into the *h.* of *L.*
9 bec. of *h.* of *L.* seek thy good
134:1 th. stand in *h.* of *L.* 135:2
*Is.* 2:2 *L.'s h.* be established in the top of mount. *Mic.* 4:1
*Jer.* 17:26 praise to *h.* of the *L.*
26:2 come to worship in *L.'s h.*
36:5 I cannot go into *h.* of *L.*
6 in *L.'s h.* upon fasting day
51:51 come to sanctua. of *L.'s h.*
*Lam.* 2:7 made a noise in *h.* of *L.*
*Hag.* 1:2 time *L.'s h.* be built
*See* COURT, DOOR, GATE, TREASURES, VESSELS.

**My HOUSE.**

*Gen.* 15:2 stew. of *my h.* is Eliez.
3 one born in *my h.* is mi. heir
*Num.* 12:7 is faithful in all *m. h.*
*Jos.* 24:15 me and *m. h.* serve *L.*
*Jud.* 11:31 fo. of doors of *m. h.*
1 *Sam.* 21:15 fel. come to *m. h.?*
2 *Sam.* 7:18 O L. G. what is *my h.?* 1 *Chr.* 17:16
11:11 shall I then go into *m. h.?*
23:5 tho' *my h.* be not so wi. G.
1 *K.* 21:2 bec. it is near to *my h.*
1 *K.* 20:15 all things that are in *my h.* *Is.* 39:4
1 *Chr.* 17:14 settle him in *my h.*
*Job* 17:13 the grave is *my h.*
*Ps.* 101:2 in *my h.* wi. perf. heart
132:3 not come to tab. of *my h.*
*Prov.* 7:6 at window of *my h.*
*Is.* 3:7 in *my h.* is neither bread
56:5 I give in *my h.* a name
7 make them joyful in *my h.* of prayer, *my h.* sh. be called a *h.* of prayer. *Mat.* 21.13; *Mark* 11:17; *Luke* 19:46
*Jer.* 11:15 wh. bel. do in *my h.?*
12:7 I have forsaken *my h.*
23:11 in *my h.* I found wickedn.
*Ezek.* 8:1 as I sat in *my h.*
44:7 to pollute it, even *my h.*
*Dan.* 4:4 N. was at rest in *my h.*
*Hag* 1:9 *my h.* that is waste
*Zec.* 3:7 shalt also judge *my h.*
9:8 I will encamp about *my h.*
*Mal.* 3:10 meat in *my h.*
*Mat.* 12:44 I will return into *my h.* *Luke* 11:24
*Luke* 9:61 bid farewell at *my h.*
14:23 that *my h.* may be filled
*Acts* 10:30 I pray. in *my h.*
16:15 come into *my h.*

**Own HOUSE.**

*Gen.* 14:14 serv. born in his *o. h.*
2 *Sam.* 4:11 person in his *o. h.*
12:11 ev. ag. thee out of th. *o. h.*
19:30 come in peace to *own h.*
1 *K.* 2:34 Joab buried in his *o. h.*
3:1 an end of building *own h.*
7:1 S. building his *o. h.* 13 years
12:16 now see to thine *own h.* David, 2 *Chr.* 10:16
1 *K.* 14:12 get thee into th. *o. h.*
2 *K.* 21:18 Man. was buried in garden of *o. h.* 2 *Chr.* 33:20
23 slew the king in his *own h.* 2 *Chr.* 33:24
2 *Chr.* 7:11 in his heart in *o. h.*
*Est.* 1:22 man rule in his *o. h.*
*Prov.* 11:29 that troubleth *o. h.*
15:27 greedy troubleth *own h.*
*Is.* 14:18 in glory, ev. one *o. h.*
*Mic.* 7:6 enemies are of *o. h.*
*Hag.* 1:9 run ev. man to *own h.*
*Mat.* 13:57 proph. is not without honor, save in *o. h.* *Mark* 6:4
*Luke* 1:23 departed to *o. h.* 5:25
56 Mary returned to her *o. h.*
5:29 Levi made a feast in *o. h.*
8:39 return to thy *own h.*
*John* 7:53 ev. man went to *o. h.*
*Acts* 28:30 P. dw. 2 years in *o. h.*
1 *Tim.* 3:4 ruleth well his *o. h.*
5 know not how to rule *o. h.*
5:8 especially for those of *o. h.*
*Heb.* 3:6 Ch. as a Son over *o. h.*

**This HOUSE.**

*Gen.* 39:9 none gre. in *t. h.* th. I
1 *K.* 6:12 *t. h.* thou art building
8:27 how much less *t. h.* I bu.?
29 eyes be opened toward *t. h.*
31 before thine altar in *this h.*
33 supplica. to thee in *t. h.* 42
38 spread his hands tow. *t. h.*
9:3 I have hallowed *this h.*
8 at *this h.* every one sh. hiss
2 *Chr.* 6:20 eyes be open on *t. h.*
22 oath come bef. altar in *t. h.*
24 make supplication in *t. h.*
32 if th. come and pray in *t. h.*
7:16 now have I sancti. *t. h.* 20

2 Chr. 7:21 and t. h. which is hi.
Ezr. 3:12 foundation of this h.
Jer. 7:10 stand before me in t. h.
11 is t. h. bec. a den of rob.?
22:5 t. h. shall bec. a desolation
26:6 will I make t. h. like Shil.
9 t. h. shall be like Shiloh
Hag. 1:4 this h. lie waste?
2:3 who is left saw t. h. first?
7 I will fill t. h. with glory
9 glory of t. h. greater than
Luke 10:5 Peace be to this h.
19:9 this day salv. come to t. h.

**Thy HOUSE.**

Gen. 7:1 come thou and t. h.
Num. 18:11 is clean in t. h. 13
Deut. 6:7 talk of th. in t. h. 11:19
9 write on posts of t. h. 11:20
7:26 an abomination to t. h.
21:12 bring her home to t. h.
22:8 bring not blood upon t. h.
25:14 in t. h. divers measures
26:11 G. given to thee and t. h.
Jos. 2:3 men entered into thy h.
Jud. 12:1 will burn thy h.
Ruth 4:11 woman come into t. h.
12 let t. h. be like house of P.
1 Sam. 2:30 t. h. sh. walk before
31 not be an old man in t. h.
33 t. h. sh. die in flower of age
36 every one in thy h. crouch
25:6 peace to thy h.
2 Sam. 7:16 t. h. estab. for ever
11:8 go to thy h. wash thy feet
12:10 sw. never depart fr. t. h.
1 K. 13:8 if thou give half thy h.
2 K. 20:1 thy h. in order, Is. 38:1
15 wh. seen in thy h.? Is. 39:4
17 thy h. sh. be carri. Is. 39:6
Ps. 5:7 I will come into thy h.
26:8 loved habitation of t. h.
36:8 satisf. with fatness of t. h.
50:9 will take no bullock of t. h.
65:4 sati. with goodness of t. h.
66:13 go to t. h. with b.-offerin.
69:9 zeal of t. h. hath eaten me up, John 2:17
93:5 holiness becometh thy h.
128:3 as fruitful vine by thy h.
Is. 58:7 that are cast to thy h.
Jer. 38:17 thou sh. live, and t. h.
Ezek. 3:24 shut thyself wit. t. h.
44:30 blessing to rest in thy h.
Hab. 2:10 consulted sh. to t. h.
Mat. 9:6 arise, go to t. h. Mark 2:11; Luke 5:24
26:18 keep passover at thy h.
Luke 7:44 entered thy h.
19:5 to-day I must abide at t. h.
Acts 11:44 all t. h. saved, 16:31
Phile. 2 to the church in thy h.

See TOPS.

**HOUSES.**

Ex. 1:21 he made midwives' h.
12:7 upper door-posts of the h.
13 blood be for token on the h.
15 put away leaven out of y. h.
Lev. 25:31 h. of vill. be counted
Num. 16:32 swallowed their h.
32:18 will not return to our h.
Deut. 6:11 h. of good things
8:12 built goodly h. dw. therein
19:1 dw. in their h. Neh. 9:25
Jos. 9:12 hot provision out of h.
Jud. 18:14 know th. is in th. h.
1 K. 13:32 he cried against the h.
20:6 search h. of thy servants
2 K. 17:29 in the h. of high pla.
23:7 brake down h. of Sodomit.
19 h. of high pla. Josiah took
25:9 burnt h. of Jeru. Jer. 52:13
1 Chr. 15:1 David made h. in ci.
28:11 gave to Sol. pattern of h.
2 Chr. 34:11 buy timber to fl. h.
35:4 prepare yourselves by h.

Neh. 4:14 fight for wives and h.
5:3 we mortg. our lands and h.
7:4 peo. few and h. not builded
Job 1:4 feasted in their h.
3:15 filled their h. with silver.
4:19 that dwell in h. of clay
15:28 dw. in h. no man inhabit.
21:9 their h. are safe from fear
22:18 filled their h. with good
24:16 they dig through h.
Ps. 49:11 h. sh. continue for ever
83:12 let us take the h. of God
Prov. 1:13 fill our h. with spoil
30:26 make they th. h. in rocks
Ec. 2:4 I builded me h.
Is. 3:14 spoil of poor in your h.
5:9 h. shall be desolate, 6:11
8:14 rock of offence to both h.
13:16 h. spoiled, wives ravished
21 h. full of doleful creatures
15:3 on tops of h. ev. one howl
Is. 22:10 h. ha. ye broken to for.
32:13 upon all the h. of joy
Jer. 5:7 by troops in harlot's h.
27 so are their h. full of deceit
29:5 build h. dwell in them, 28
32:15 h. and fields be possessed
29 h. on wh. roofs the, offered
33:4 h. of this city, h. of kings
43:12 fire in h. of gods of Eg. 13
Lam. 5:2 our h. turned to aliens
Ezek. 7:24 heathen possess th. h.
16:41 they sh. burn thy h. 23:47
26:12 destroy thy pleasant h.
28:26 build h. plant vineyards
33:30 ag. thee in doors of the h.
Dan. 2:5 h. made a dunghill
3:29 h. sh. be made a dunghill
Joel 2:9 shall climb up upon h.
Amos 3:15 h. of ivory sh. perish
Mic. 1:14 h. of A. be lie to kings
2:2 covet h. take them away
9 women ye cast from their h.
Zep. 1:9 fill master's h. with vio.
13 their h. become a desolation
Hag. 1:4 dwell in your ceiled h.?
Zec. 14:2 the h. shall be rifled
Mat. 11:8 soft cloth. kings' h.
19:29 hath forsaken h. or wife
23:14 for ye devour widows' h. Mark 12:40; Luke 20:47
Mark 8:3 if send them fast. to h.
Luke 16:4 receive me into th. h.
Acts 4:34 possess. of h. sold th.
1 Cor. 11:22 ye not h. to eat in?
1 Tim. 3:12 deacons rul. h. well
2 Tim. 3:6 which creep into h.
Tit. 1:11 subvert whole h.

**HOUSEHOLD, S.**

Gen. 18:19 will command his h.
35:2 J. said to his h. put away
45:11 th. and h. come to poverty
47:12 Jos. nourished his fa.'s h.
24 four par. be food for your h.
Ex. 1:1 ev. man and h. came
12:4 if h. be little for the lamb
Lev. 16:17 an atonement for h.
Num. 18:31 eat it, and your h.
Deut. 6:22 showed wonders on h.
11:6 swallowed them and h.
15:20 eat it bef. L. thou and h.
Jos. 2:18 bring thy father's h.
6:25 saved R. her father's h.
Jud. 18:25 with lives of thy h.
1 Sam. 25:17 evil determi. ag. h.
27:3 ev. man with his h. even Da. with wives, 2 Sam. 2:3
2 Sam. 6:11 blessed him and h.
20 D. returned to bless his h.
16:2 asses be for king's h. to ri.
17:23 and put his h. in order
19:18 a boat to carry king's h.
1 K. 4:7 victuals for king and h.
5:11 S. gave Hiram wheat to h.
2 K. 8:1 go and thy h. sojourn
Job 1:3 3,000 camels great h.

Prov. 27:27 goat's milk for h.
31:15 riseth and giv. meat to h.
21 not afraid of snow for her h. for all her h. are clothed
27 look. well to ways of her h.
Mat. 10:25 call them of his h.
36 man's foes sh. be of own h.
24:45 ruler over h. Luke 12:42
Acts 16:15 baptized and her h.
1 Cor. 1:16 baptized h. of Steph.
Gal. 6:10 are of the h. of faith
Eph. 2:19 but of the h. of God
Phil. 4:22 that are of Cæsar's h.
2 Tim. 4:19 salute h. of Onesiph.

**HOUSEHOLDER.**

Mat. 13:27 servants of h. came
52 like a man that is a h. 20:1
21:33 a certain h. planted viney.

**HOUSEHOLD-SERVANTS.**

Acts 10:7 Cornel. called two h.-s.

**HOUSEHOLD-STUFF.**

Gen. 31:37 hast found of h.-s.?
Neh. 13:8 cast out all h.-s. of T.

**HOW long.**

Num. 14:11 h. l. ere th. believe?
2 Sam. 19:34 h. l. have I to live?
1 K. 18:21 h. l. halt ye between?
Job 8:2 h. l. wilt thou speak? h. l. sh. words be like st. wind?
18:2. h. l. ere ma. end of words?
Ps. 4:2 h. l. will ye turn my glo. to shame? h. l. love vanity?
6:3 but thou, O Lord, h. long?
13:1 h. l. wilt forget me, O L.?
2 h. l. take coun. in my soul? h. l. enemy be ex. over me?
74:9 nor any am. us know h. l.
10 O G. h. l. advers. reproach?
79:5 h. l. wilt be angry? 80:4
82:2 h. l. wilt judge unjustly?
89:46 h. l. L. wilt hide thyself?
Ps. 90:13 return, O Lord, h. lo.?
94:3 h. l. shall wick triumph?
4 h. l. sh. th. utter ha. things?
Prov. 1:22 h. l. will love simplic.
Is. 6:11 then said I, Lord h. l.?
Jer. 4:21 h. l. sh. I see standard?
12:4 h. l. sh. the land mourn?
23:26 h. l. be in heart of prop.?
47:6 O sw. of L. h l. ere be qu.?
Dan. 8:13 h. l. be vision of sac.?
12:6 h. l. to end of wonders?
Hab. 1:2 h. long shall I cry?
Mat. 17:17 h. l. shall I be with you? h. l. suf.? Mark 9:19; Luke 9:41
Mark 9:21 h. l. since this came?
John 10:24 h. l. make to doubt?
Rev. 6:10 h. l. O L. holy and tr.

**HOW many times.**

1 K. 22:16 h. many times shall I adjure thee? 2 Chr. 18:15

**HOW much.**

2 K. 5:13 h. much rather he saith
Cant. 4:10 h. m. better thy love
Mat. 12:12 h. m. is man better
Luke 16:5 h. m. owest thou? 7
Heb. 8:6 by h. m. he is Mediator
10:29 of h. m. sorer punishment
Rev. 18:7 h. m. she hath glorified

**HOW much less.**

1 K. 8:27 h. much less this house wh. I have built, 2 Chr. 6:18
2 Chr. 32:15 h. m. l. sh. G. deliv.
Job 4:19 h. m. l. in houses of cl.

**HOW much more.**

Luke 12:24 h. m. m. are ye better
28 h. m. m. will he clothe you?
Rom. 11:12 h. m. m. th. fullness?
Phile. 16 bro. h. m. m. to thee?

**HOWL.**
*Is.* 13:6 *h.* day of L. is at hand
14:31 *h.* O gate, cry O city
15:2 Moab sh. *h.* 3; 16:7
23:1 *h.* ye ships of Tarshish
6 over to Tarsh. *h.* inhabitants
52:5 rule over make them *h.*
65:14 *h.* for vexation of spirit
*Jer.* 4:8 lament and *h.* 4:20
25:34 *h.* ye shepherds and cry
47:2 inhabitants of land shall *h.*
48:31 *h.* for M.; 39 they shall *h.*
49:3 *h.* O Heshb.: 51:8 *h.* for B.
*Ezek.* 21:12 cry and *h.* son of m.
30:2 prophesy and say, *h.* ye
*Joel* 1:5 *h.* drinkers; 11 *h.* v.-dre.
13 *h.* ye ministers of the altar
*Mic.* 1:8 theref. I will wail and *h.*
*Zep.* 1:11 *h.* inhabit. of Maktesh
*Zec.* 11:2 *h.* fir-tree, *h.* O ye oaks
*Jam.* 5:1 ye rich m. weep and *h.*

**HOWLED, ING.**
*Deut.* 32:10 found him in was. *h.*
*Hos.* 7:14 they *h.* on their beds

**HOWLING, S.**
*Is.* 15:8 *h.* is gone to Eglaim
*Jer.* 25:36 *h.* of principal of flock
*Amos* 8:3 songs of tem. sh. be *h.*
*Zep.* 1:10 a *h.* from second gate
*Zec.* 11:3 voice of *h.* of shepher.

**HUGE.**
2 *Chr.* 16:8 Eth. and Lub. *h.* ho.

**HUMBLE.**
*Job* 22:29 he shall save *h.* person
*Ps.* 9:12 forgetteth not cry of *h.*
10:12 O Lord, forget not the *h.*
17 L. hast heard desire of *h.*
34:2 the *h.* shall hear thereof
69:32 *h.* shall hear this and be
*Prov.* 16:19 better be of *h.* spirit
29:23 honor shall uphold the *h.*
*Is.* 57:15 with him of *h.* spirit, to revive spirit of *h.*
*Jam.* 4:6 giv. gra. to *h.* 1 *Pet.* 5:5

**HUMBLE, Verb.**
*Ex.* 10:3 wilt ref. to *h.* thyself
*Deut.* 8:2 *h.* thee and pr. thee, 16
*Jud.* 19:24 bring out, and *h.* th.
2 *Chr.* 7:14 shall *h.* themselves
34:27 didst *h.* thyself bef. God
*Prov.* 6:3 *h.* thyself, make sure
*Jer.* 13:18 *h.* yourselves, sit do.
*Mat.* 18:4 *h.* himself, 23:12
2 *Cor.* 12:21 my God will *h.* me
*Jam.* 4:10 *h.* your. in sight of L.
1 *Pet.* 5:6 *h.* yourselves under G.

**HUMBLED.**
*Lev.* 26:41 uncircum. hearts *h.*
*Deut.* 8:3 *h.* thee and suffered
21:14 hast *h.* her, 22:29
22:24 hath *h.* his neighbor's wi.
2 *K.* 22:19 *h.* thyself before L.
2 *Chr.* 12:6 princes and king *h.*
7 L. saw they *h.* themselves
12 he *h.* himself, wrath turned
2 *Chr.* 32:26 Heze. *h.* himself be
33:12 Manas. *h.* himself greatly
19 set up images be. he was *h*
23 A. *h.* not himself before L. as Manas. his father *h.* him.
36:12 Zedekiah *h.* not himself
*Ps.* 35:13 I *h.* my soul with fast.
*Is.* 2:11 lofty looks of man be *h.*
5:15 man be *h.* eyes of lof. be *h.*
10:33 the haughty shall be *h.*
*Jer.* 44:10 not *h.* even to this day
*Lam.* 3:20 soul in rem. and is *h.*
*Ezek.* 22:10 in thee have they *h.*
11 another hath *h.* his sister
*Dan.* 5:22 his son not *h.* heart
*Phil.* 2:8 *h.* himself and became

**HUMBLEDST, ETH.**
1 *K.* 21:29 Ahab *h.* because he *h.*
2 *Chr.* 34:27 bec. thou *h.* thyself
*Ps.* 10:10 crouch. and *h.* himself
113:6 *h.* himself to behold thin.
*Is.* 2:9 the great man *h.* himself
*Luke* 14:11 *h.* hims. be ex. 18:14

**HUMBLENESS.**
*Col.* 3:12 put on *h.* of mind

**HUMBLY.**
2 *Sam.* 16:4 I *h.* beseech thee
*Mic.* 6:8 and to walk *h.* with G.

**HUMILIATION.**
*Acts* 8:33 in his *h.* his judgment

**HUMILITY.**
*Prov.* 15:33 bef. honor is *h.* 18:12
22:4 by *h.* are riches and honor
*Acts* 20:19 serving L. with *h.*
*Col.* 2:18 no man begu. you in *h.*
23 in will-worship and *h.*
1 *Pet.* 5:5 and be clothed with *h.*

HUNDRED-FOLD. *See* FOLD.

**HUNDRED.**
*Gen.* 17:17 child be born to him *h.* ye. old? 21:5; *Rom.* 4:19
*Lev.* 26:8 chase *h.* a *h.* to flight
*Deut.* 22:19 amerce in *h.* shekels
*Jud.* 20:10 ten of *h.* a *h.* of 1,000
1 *Sam.* 18:25 but a *h.* foreski. 2 *Sam.* 3:14
25:18 a *h.* clusters, 2 *Sam.* 16:1
1 *K.* 4:23 Provision for *h.* sheep
18:4 Obad. took a *h.* proph. 13
2 *K.* 4:43 I set this bef. *h.* men?
1 *Chr.* 12:14 least was over a *h.*
21:3 L. make his people *h.* tim
*Ezr.* 2:69 gave *h.* priests' garm.
6:17 at dedication a *h.* bullocks
7:22 done to a *h.* talents of sil *h.* measures of wheat and wine, and a *h.* baths of oil
*Neh.* 5:11 *h.* part of the money
*Prov.* 17:10 than *h.* strip. to fool
*Ec.* 6:3 if a man beget a *h.* child.
8:12 sinner do evil a *h.* times
*Is.* 65:20 the child shall die a *h.* ye. old, but the sinner being a *h.* years old sh. be accurs.
*Ezek.* 40:19 measured a *h.* cubits, 23, 47; 41:13, 14, 15; 42:8
*Amos* 5:3 went out by a 1,000, sh. leave a *h.* that wh. went forth by a *h.* shall leave ten
*Mat.* 18:12 if a man have a *h.* sheep, *Luke* 15:4
28 who owed him a *h.* pence
*Luke* 16:6 a *h.* measures of oil
7 how much ow. thou? *h.* me.
*John* 19:39 myrrh and aloes *h.*

**One HUNDRED and twenty.**
*Gen.* 6:3 his days be *h. and t.* y.
*Deut.* 31:2 a *h. and t.* years old
34:7 M. *h. t.* years when he died

**One HUNDRED and twenty-seven.**
*Est.* 1:1 Ahasu. reigned over *h. twenty-s.* prov. 8:9; 9:30

**One HUNDRED and thirty.**
*Gen.* 47:9 years of my pilgrimage are a *h. and thirty*

**One HUNDRED and fifty.**
*Gen.* 7:24 wa. prev. *h. f.* da. 8:3

**One HUNDRED and fifty-three.**
*John* 21:11 full of fishes a *h. f. t.*

**One HUNDRED and eighty.**
*Est.* 1:4 A. feast for *h. e.* days

**A HUNDRED and forty-four thousand.**
*Rev.* 7:4 *h. f.-f. t.* tribes of Israel
14:1 *h. f.-f. t.* having F.'s name
3 no man le. song but *h. f.-f. t.*

**A HUNDRED and eighty-five thousand.**
2 *K.* 19:35 that night the angel of the L. smote of the Assy. *h. eighty-five th. Is.* 37:36

**Two HUNDRED.**
*John* 6:7 *t. h.* penny. not suffi.

**Three HUNDRED.**
*Jud.* 7:6 number lap. *t. h.* men
15:4 Samson caught *t. h.* foxes
2 *Sam.* 21:16 sp. weigh. *t. h.* sh.
1 *K.* 11:3 S. had *t. h.* concubines
*John* 12:5 ointm. for *t. h.* pence

**Four HUNDRED.**
*Gen.* 15:13 afflict *f. h.* ye. *Acts* 7:6
1 *Sam.* 30:17 *f. h.* young men
1 *K.* 18:19 prop. of groves, *f. h.*
*Acts* 5:36 *f. h.* joined themselves

**Four HUNDRED and thirty.**
*Ex.* 12:40 in E. *f. h. t.* years
*Gal.* 3:17 law. wh. was *f. h. t.* y.

**Four HUNDRED and fifty.**
1 *K.* 18:19 pro. of Baal *f. h. f.* 22
*Acts* 13:20 judges about *f. h. f.*

**Four HUNDRED and eighty.**
1 *K.* 6:1 in *f. h. e.* years Solom.

**Four HUNDRED thousand.**
*Jud.* 20:2 Benjamin *f. h. t.* 17
2 *Chr.* 13:3 array wi. *f. h. t.* men

**Four HUNDRED and seventy thousand.**
1 *Chr.* 21:5 *f. h. s. t.* drew sword

**Five HUNDRED.**
*Num.* 31:28 one soul *f. h.* for L.
*Luke* 7:41 one owned *f. h.* pence
1 *Cor.* 15:6 *f. h.* brethren at once

**Six HUNDRED.**
*Gen.* 7:6 N. *s. h.* ye. flood ca. 11
*Jud.* 3:31 Shamgar slew *six h.*
1 *Sam.* 17:7 spear weigh. *s. h.* sh.
1 *K.* 10:16 *six h.* shekels of gold to one target, 2 *Chr.* 9:15

**Six HUNDRED and sixty-six.**
*Rev.* 13:18 num. be *six h. a. s.-s.*

**Six HUNDRED thousand.**
*Num.* 1:46 all numb. were *s. h. t.*

**Seven HUNDRED.**
1 *K.* 11:3 Sol. had *seven h.* wives

**Nine HUNDRED and thirty.**
*Gen.* 5:5 Adam lived *nine h. t.* y.

**Nine HUNDRED sixty-nine.**
*Gen.* 5:27 Methus. *n. h. s.-n.* ye.

**HUNDREDS.**
*Ex.* 18:21 rul. of *h.* 25; *Deut.* 1:15
*Num.* 31:14 wr. with capt. ov. *h.*
1 *Sam.* 22:7 J. make capta. of *h.*
2 *Sam.* 18:1 D. set captains of *h.*
4 all the people came out by *h.*
2 *K.* 11:4 Jehoi. set rul. over *h.*
10 to captains over *h.* did pri. give spears, 2 *Chr.* 23:9
1 *Chr.* 13:1 consu. wi. capt. of *h.*
28:1 D. assembled capt. over *h.*
29:6 captains of *h.* off. willingly
2 *Chr.* 23:1 Jeh. took capt. of *h.*
*Mark* 6:40 sat do. in ranks by *h.*

**HUNGER, Substantive.**
*Ex.* 16:3 kill this assembly wi. *h.*
*Deut.* 28:48 serve thine ene. in *h.*
32:24 shall be burnt with *h.*
*Neh.* 9:15 bread fr. heaven for *h.*
*Ps.* 34:10 do lack and suffer *h.*
*Prov.* 19:15 idle soul sh. suffer *h.*
*Jer.* 38:9 he is like to die for *h.*
42:14 see no war nor have *h.*
*Lam.* 2:19 faint for *h.*
4:9 they that be slain with *h.*
*Ezek.* 34:29 no more con. with *h.*
*Luke* 15:17 and I perish with *h.*
2 *Cor.* 11:27 I have been in *h.*
*Rev.* 6:8 to kill with *h.*

**HUNGER, Verb.**
*Deut.* 8:3 he suffered thee to *h.*
*Is.* 49:10 shall not *h.* nor thirst
*Mat.* 5:6 blessed are they that *h.* after righteous. *Luke* 6:21

Luke 6:25 woe to full, ye shall h.
John 6:35 com. to me sh. never h.
Rom. 12:20 if enemy h. feed him
1 Cor. 4:11 we both h. and thirst
11:34 if any man h. let him eat
Rev. 7:16 they shall h. no more

**HUNGER-BITTEN.**
Job 18:12 his stren. sh. be h.-b.

**HUNGERED.**
Mat. 4:2 afterwards a h. Luke 4:2
12:1 his disciples were a h.
3 what David did when he was a h. Mark 2:25; Luke 6:3
21:18 as he returned to city he h.
25:35 I h. and ye gave me meat
37 when saw we thee a h.? 44
42 I h. and ye gave me no meat

**HUNGRY.**
2 Sam. 17:29 the people is h.
2 K. 7:12 they kn. that we be h.
Job 5:5 whose harv. the h. eateth
22:7 withholden bread from h.
24:10 take the sheaf fr. the h.
Ps. 50:12 if h. I would not tell
107:5 h. and thirsty
9 filleth h. soul with goodness
36 there he maketh h. to dwell
146:7 Lord giveth food to the h.
Prov. 6:30 to satis. soul when h.
25:21 if enemy be h. give bread
27:7 to h. soul bitter th. is sw.
Is. 8:21 hardly bestead and h. when h. shall fret themselv.
9:20 snatch on right hand, be h.
29:8 when a h. man dreameth
32:6 to make empty soul of h.
44:12 is h. and strength faileth
58:7 not deal thy bread to h.?
10 draw out thy soul to the h.
65:13 serv. eat, but ye sh. be h.
Ezek. 18:7 giv. his bread to h. 16
Mark 11:12 from Beth. he was h.
Luke 1:53 filled h. with good th.
Acts 10:10 Peter became very h.
1 Cor. 11:21 one h. another drun.
Phil. 4:12 to be full and be h.

**HUNT.**
Gen. 27:5 Es. went to h. venison
1 Sam. 26:20 as wh. one doth h.
Job 38:39 wilt h. prey for lion?
Ps. 140:11 evil sh. h. violent man
Prov. 6:26 adulteress will h.
Jer. 16:16 h. them from ev. mou.
Lam. 4:18 they h. our steps
Ezek. 13:18 will ye h. souls?
20 wherewith ye there h. souls
Mic. 7:2 h. every man his broth.

**HUNTED.**
Ezek. 13:21 no more in y. hand h.

**HUNTER, S.**
Gen. 10:9 he was a mighty h. be. L. even as N. the mighty h.
25:27 Esau was a cunning h.
Prov. 6:5 as a roe fro. hand of h.
Jer. 16:16 and after I send for h.

**HUNTEST, ETH.**
Lev. 17:13 h. and catcheth beast
1 Sam. 24:11 yet thou h. my soul
Job 10:16 h. me as a fierce lion

**HUNTING.**
Gen. 27:30 E. brother came fr. h.
Prov. 12:27 roast. not took in h.

**HUR.**
Ex. 17:10 H. we. up, 12; 24:14
1 Chr. 2:19 which bare H. 20, 50

**HURL, ETH, ING.**
Num. 35:20 h. at him by lying
1 Chr. 12:2 ri. hand and left in h.
Job 27:21 as a stone h. him out

**HURT, Substantive.**
Gen. 4:23 slain yo. man to my h.
26:29 that thou wilt do us no h.
31:29 in power of hand to do h.
1 Sam. 20:21 peace to thee, no h.
24:9 behold, David seek. thy h.
2 Sam. 18:32 all that rise to do h.
2 K. 14:10 why shouldest thou med. to thy h.? 2 Chr. 25:19
Ezr. 4:22 damage to h. of kings?
Ps. 15:4 that sweareth to his h.
35:4 that devise my h. 70:2
26 ashamed that rej. at my h.
38:12 seek my h. speak misch.
41:7 aga. me do they devise h.
71:13 cov. with reproach seek h.
24 brought to sha. seek my h.
Ec. 5:13 riches for owners to h.
8:9 ruleth over another to his h.
Jer. 6:14 healed h. of peo. 8:11
7:6 neith. walk after gods to h.
8:21 for h. of my people am I h.
10:19 woe is me for my h.
25:6 and I will do you no h.
7 ye provo. me to your own h.
38:4 not welfare of peo. but h.
Dan. 3:25 ha. no h.; 6:22 do. no h.
6:23 no manner of h. found
Acts 27:10 this voyage be with h.

**HURT, Participle.**
Ex. 22:10 if a beast be h. 14
1 Sam. 25:15 and we not h.
Ec. 10:9 remov. stones sh. be h.
Jer. 8:21 for h. of my peo. am I h.
Rev. 2:11 not be h. of sec. death

**HURT, Verb.**
Gen. 31:7 G. suf. hi. not to h. me
Ex. 21:22 h. woman with child
35 if one man's ox h. another's
1 Sam. 25:7 shepherds we h. not
Job 35:8 wickedn. may h. a man
Ps. 105:18 wh. feet h. with fett.
Is. 11:9 shall not h. nor destroy in my holy mountain, 65:25
27:3 lest any h. it, I will keep it
Dan. 6:22 lions have not h. me
Mark 16:18 it shall not h. them
Luke 4:35 out of him, h. him not
Acts 18:10 set on thee to h.
Rev. 6:6 see thou h. not the oil
7:2 given to h. earth and sea
3 h. not earth, neither sea
9:4 should not h. grass of earth
10 their power was to h. men
19 heads, with them they h.
11:5 if any h. them, fire proceed.

**HURTFUL.**
Ps. 144:10 deli. David fr. h. swo.
1 Tim. 6:9 rich fall into h. lusts

**HURTING.**
1 Sam. 25:34 Lord kept me fr. h.

**HUSBAND.**
Ex. 4:25 bloody h. art thou, 26
Lev. 19:20 lieth with woman betrothed to a h. Deut. 22:23
21:3 may be defiled for sister who had no h. Ezek. 44:25
Num. 30:6 if she had at all a h.
Deut. 22:22 woman married to h.
24:3 if the latter h. hate her
4 former h. may not take her
25:5 duty of a h. brother to her
28:56 eye sh. be evil to. h.
Ruth 1:12 I am too old to have h.
Jer. 6:11 h. with wife sh. be tak.
31:32 altho' I was a h. to them
Joel 1:8 girded with sackcl. for h.
Luke 2:36 lived wi. h. sev. years
John 4:17 have no h.
Rom. 7:2 h. dead she is loosed, 3
1 Cor. 7:3 h. render to wife due benevolence, like. wife to h.
4 h. hath not power of own
11 let not h. put away his wife
14 unbeliev. h. is sanctified by wife, and wife sancti. by h.
2 Cor. 11:2 espoused to one h.
Gal. 4:27 more chil. than hath h.
Eph. 5:23 the h. is head of wife
1 Tim. 3:2 h. of one wi. Tit. 1:6

**Her HUSBAND.**
Gen. 3:6 eat fruit, gave to h. h.
Lev. 21:7 wo. put away fr. h. h.
Num. 5:29 to anoth. inst. of h. h.
30:7 h. h. heard it, and held peace, 8, 10, 11, 12, 13, 14
Deut. 25:5 h. h. brot. go in unto
Ruth 1:9 in house of h. h.
2:1 Nao. had kinsman of her h.
1 Sam. 1:22 sa. to h. h. I will not
2:19 she came up with her h.
2 Sam. 11:26 wife of U. heard h. h. was dead, she mo. for h. h.
2 K. 4:14 hath no child, h. h. old
Prov. 12:4 virt. wife cro. to h. h.
31:11 heart of h. h. trust in her
23 her h. is known in the gates
28 h. h. riseth up and prai. her
Jer. 3:20 as wife depa. from h. h.
Ezek. 16:32 strangers inst. of h. h.
45 loatheth her h. and children
Hos. 2:2 neither I h. h.
Mat. 1:19 Jos. her h. being just
Luke 16:18 mar. her aw. fr. h. h.
Acts 5:10 buried her by her h.
Rom. 7:2 bound by law to h. h.
3 her h. dead she is free
1 Cor. 7:2 woman have h. own h.
10 let not wife depart fr. her h.
11 be reconciled to her h.
34 how she may please her h.
39 bound as long as her h.
Eph. 5:33 wife reverence her h.
Rev. 21:2 bride adorned for her h.

**My HUSBAND.**
Gen. 29:32 my h. will love me
34 will my h. be joined to me
30:18 given maiden to my h.
20 now will my h. dw. wi. me
Deut. 25:7 my h. brother refuseth
2 Sam. 14:5 I am a widow, my h. dead, 2 K. 4:1
Hos. 2:7 and return to my first h.

**Thy HUSBAND.**
Gen. 3:16 desire shall be to t. h.
Num. 5:19 anoth. inst. of t. h. 20
Jud. 14:15 to wife, Entice t. h.
2 K. 4:26 is it well with thy h.
Is. 54:5 thy Maker is thy h.
Acts 5:9 that have buried t. h.
1 Cor. 7:16 thou shalt save thy h.

**HUSBANDMAN.**
Gen. 9:20 Noah began to be a h.
Jer. 51:23 break in pieces the h.
Amos 5:16 call h. to mourning
Zec. 13:5 no prophet, am a h.
John 15:1 I true vine, Fath. is h.
2 Tim. 2:6 the h. that laboreth
Jam. 5:7 h. waiteth for fruit of earth

**HUSBANDMEN.**
2 K. 25:12 he left of the poor to be h. Jer. 52:16
Jer. 31:24 shall dwell in Judah h.
Joel 1:11 be ashamed ye h. howl
Mat. 21:33 he let it out to h. Mark 12:2; Luke 20:9
34 sent his servants to h. Mark 12:2; Luke 20:10
38 when h. saw the son, Mark 12:7; Luke 20:14
40 what will he do to those h.?
41 let out vineyard to other h.
Mark 12:2 might receive fr. h. 9

**HUSBANDRY.**
2 Chr. 26:10 Uzziah loved h.
1 Cor. 3:9 ye are God's h. ye are

**HUSBANDS.**
Ruth 1:11 they may be your h.?
13 stay for them fr. having h.?
Est. 1:17 despise h. in their eyes
20 wives give to their h. honor
Ezek. 16:45 loathed h. and child.
John 4:18 thou hast had five h.
1 Cor. 14:35 ask their h. at home

*Eph.* 5:22 wives submit to *h.* 24
25 *h.* love your wives, *Col.* 3:19
*Col.* 3:18 wives, submit to own *h.*
1 *Tim.* 3:12 deac. *h.* of one wife
*Tit.* 2:4 teach women to love *h.*
5 be obedient to their own *h.*
1 *Pet.* 3:1 in subjection to own *h.*
7 ye *h.* dwell with them accor.

**HUSHAI.**
2 *Sam.* 15:32 H. to meet D. 17:5
1 *Chr.* 27:33 H. king's compani.

**HUSK, S.**
*Num.* 6:4 kernel even to the *h.*
2 *K.* 4:42 full ears of corn in *h.*
*Luke* 15:16 filled belly with *h.*

HUZZAB. *Nah.* 2:7

**HYMENEUS.**
1 *Tim.* 1:20 wh. is H. 2 *Tim.* 2:17

**HYMN, S.**
*Mat.* 26:30 when they had sung a *h.* *Mark* 14:26
*Eph.* 5:19 spea. in psalms and *h.*
*Col.* 3:16 admo. in psalms and *h.*

**HYPOCRISY, IES.**
*Is.* 32:6 iniquity, to practise *h.*
*Mat.* 23:28 within are full of *h.*
*Mark* 12:15 he knowing their *h.*
*Luke* 12:1 leaven of Pharisees *h.*
1 *Tim.* 4:2 speaking lies in *h.*
1 *Pet.* 2:1 aside all malice and *h.*
*Jam.* 3:17 wisdom pure witho. *h.*

**HYPOCRITE.**
*Job* 8:13 the *h.* hope shall perish
13:16 *h.* shall not come bef. him
17:8 innocent stir up against *h.*
20:5 joy of *h.* but for a moment
27:8 what is the hope of the *h.*?
34:30 that the *h.* reign not, lest
*Prov.* 11:9 *h.* with mouth destroy
*Is.* 9:17 for every one is a *h.*
*Mat.* 7:5 *h.* first cast out beam
*Luke* 6:42 thou *h.* cast beam out
13:15 *h.* doth not each loose ox?

**HYPOCRITES.**
*Job* 15:34 congrega. of *h.* desolate
36:13 *h.* in heart heap up wrath
*Is.* 33:14 fearfulness surprised *h.*
*Mat.* 6:2 not sound trump. as *h.*
5 thou shalt not be as *h.*
16 when ye fast, be not as *h.*
15:7 ye *h.* well did Esaias prophesy, *Mark* 7:6
16:3 O *h.* ye discern face of sky, *Luke* 12:56
22:18 Why tempt ye me, ye *h.*
23:13 Phari. *h.* ye shut kingd. ag. men, 14, 15, 23, 25, 27, 29
24:51 ap. him portion with *h.*
*Luke* 11:44 scribes and Phari. *h.*

**HYPOCRITICAL.**
*Ps.* 35:16 *h.* mockers in feasts
*Is.* 10:6 send him ag. *h.* nation

**HYSSOP.**
*Ex.* 12:22 bunch of *h.* and dip it
*Lev.* 14:4 scar. and *h.* 6, 49, 51, 52
*Num.* 19:6 cast *h.* into midst of
18 take *h.* dip it in water
1 *K.* 4:33 cedar-tree, even unto *h.*
*Ps.* 51:7 purge with *h.* be clean
*John* 19:29 sponge put it on *h.*
*Heb.* 9:19 blood with *h.* sprinkl.

# I

*Ex.* 3:14 I AM, THAT I AM.
*Deut.* 32:39 I, even I, am he
*Is.* 41:4 I the Lord, the first, I am he, 43:11, 25
10 I am with thee, I am thy G.
*Mat.* 26:22 be. to say, L. is it I?

IBHAR. 2 *Sa.* 5:15; 1 *Ch.* 3:6; 14:5

**ICE.**
*Job* 6:16 blackish by reason of *i.*
38:29 out of wh. womb came *i.*?
*Ps.* 147:17 he casteth forth his *i.*

ICHABOD. 1 *Sam.* 4:21; 14:3

**ICONIUM.**
*Acts* 13:51 Barnab. came unto I.
14:1 in I. went into synago. 19
2 *Tim.* 3:11 afflictions came at I.

**IDDO.**
2 *Chr.* 9:29 I. seer, 12:15; 13:22
*Ezr.* 5:1 I. prophesied, *Zec.* 1:1, 7
*Neh.* 12:4 I. with priests went up

**IDLE.**
*Ex.* 5:8 be *i.* therefore they cry
17 he said, Ye are *i.* ye are *i.*
*Prov.* 19:15 *i.* soul suffer hunger
*Mat.* 12:36 ev. *i.* word men speak
20:3 standing *i.* in market-pl. 6
*Luke* 24:11 seemed as *i.* tales
1 *Tim.* 5:13 they learn to be *i.*

**IDLENESS.**
*Prov.* 31:27 eateth not bread of *i.*
*Ec.* 10:18 thro' *i.* house droppeth
*Ezek.* 16:49 abundan. of *i.* in her

**IDOLATER, S.**
1 *Cor.* 5:10 with the covet. or *i.*
11 any called a brother be an *i.*
6:9 *i.* not inherit kingdom of G.
10:7 neither be *i.* as some were
*Eph.* 5:5 who is *i.* hath any inh.
*Rev.* 21:8 *i.* have part in the lake
22:15 murderers and *i.* and liars

**IDOLATROUS.**
2 *K.* 23:5 Jos. put down *i.* priests

**IDOLATRY, IES.**
1 *Sam.* 15:23 is as iniquity and *i.*
*Acts* 17:16 city wholly given to *i.*
1 *Cor.* 10:14 beloved, flee from *i.*
*Gal.* 5:20 the works of the flesh *i.*
*Col.* 3:5 covetousness, which is *i.*
1 *Pet.* 4:3 walked in abomina. *i.*

**IDOL, Adjective.**
*Zec.* 11:17 woe to *i.* shepherd

**IDOL.**
1 *K.* 15:13 she made an *i.* in grove, 2 *Chr.* 15:16
2 *Chr.* 33:7 set *i.* in house of God
*Is.* 48:5 lest say, Mine *i.* hath
66:3 inc. as if he blessed an *i.*
*Jer.* 22:28 is this C. a broken *i.*?
*Acts* 7:41 offered sacrifice to *i.*
1 *Cor.* 8:4 *i.* noth. in world, 10:19
7 some with conscience of *i.*

**IDOLS.**
*Lev.* 19:4 turn not to *i.*; 26 no *i.*
26:30 cast your carcasses on *i.*
*Deut.* 29:17 ye have seen their *i.*
1 *Sam.* 31:9 pub. it in house of *i.*
1 *K.* 15:12 Asa removed the *i.*
21:26 A. did abomi. in follow. *i.*
2 *K.* 17:12 th. serv. *i.* 2 *Chr.* 24:18
21:11 made Judah to sin with *i.*
23:24 *i.* that were spied in land
1 *Chr.* 10:9 carry tidin. to their *i.*
16:26 all gods of the peo. are *i.*
2 *Chr.* 15:8 Asa put *i.* out of Jud.
34:7 Josiah cut down all *i.* in Is.
*Ps.* 96:5 all gods of nations are *i.*
97:7 that boast themselves of *i.*
106:36 and they served their *i.*
115:4 *i.* are silv. and g. 135:15
*Is.* 2:8 land is full of *i.* worship
18 *i.* he shall utterly abolish
20 shall cast away his *i.* 31:7
10:11 as I done to Samaria and her *i.* so do to Jer. and her *i.*
19:1 *i.* of Egypt shall be moved
3 seek to *i.* and to charmers
45:16 mak. of *i.* go to confusion
46:1 their *i.* were on the beasts
57:5 inflam. yourselves with *i.*
*Jer.* 50:2 her *i.* are confounded
38 they are mad upon their *i.*
*Ezek.* 6:6 your *i.* may be broken
9 go a whoring after their *i.*
13 did offer savor to their *i.*
8:10 I saw all the *i.* of Israel
14:3 set up their *i.* in heart, 4, 7
6 turn yourselves from your *i.*
16:36 wi. *i.* of thy abomination
18:6 nor lift eyes to *i.* 12, 15
20:7 defile not yourse. with *i.* 18
16 heart after *i.*; 24 eyes af. *i.*
31 ye pollute yourselves with your *i.* 22:4; 23:7, 30, 37
39 pol. my name no more wi. *i.*
22:3 the city maketh *i.*
23:39 slain their chil. to their *i.*
49 bear the sins of your *i.*
30:13 I will destroy *i.*
*Ezek.* 36:25 fr. *i.* clea. you, 37:23
44:10 went astray after *i.*
12 ministered before their *i.*
*Hos.* 4:17 Ephra. is joined to *i.*
8:4 of silver and gold made *i.*
14:8 what have I to do with *i.*
*Mic.* 1:7 the *i.* will I lay desolate
*Hab.* 2:18 trust. to make dumb *i.*
*Zec.* 10:2 *i.* have spoken vanity
13:2 I will cut off names of *i.*
*Acts* 15:20 abst. fr. polluti. of *i.*
29 abst. fr. meats offer. *i.* 21:25
*Rom.* 2:22 thou that abhorrest *i.*
1 *Cor.* 8:1 touching th. offered to *i.* 4, 10; 10:19, 28; *Rev.* 2:14, 20
12:2 Gentiles carried to dumb *i.*
2 *Cor.* 6:16 agree. of G. with *i.*?
1 *Thes.* 1:9 turned to God from *i.*
1 *John* 5:21 keep yoursel. from *i.*
*Rev.* 9:20 not wor. devils and *i.*

**IDUMEA.**
*Is.* 34:5 sword sh. come on I. 6
*Ezek.* 35:15 all I. shall be, 36:5
*Mark* 3:8 multi. followed from I.

**IGNOMINY.**
*Prov.* 18:3 and with *i.* reproach

**IGNORANCE.**
*Lev.* 4:2 if a soul sh. sin thro' *i.* 5:15; *Num.* 15:24, 27, 28, 29
13 congre. sin thro' *i.*; 22 ruler
27 if the people sin through *i.*
*Num.* 15:25 forgiv. them, it is *i.*
*Acts* 3:17 through *i.* ye did it
17:30 times of *i.* God winked at
*Eph.* 4:18 alienated through *i.*
1 *Pet.* 1:14 according to lusts in *i.*
2:15 put to silen. *i.* of fool. men

**IGNORANT.**
*Ps.* 73:22 and *i.* I was as a beast
*Is.* 56:10 all *i.* they are all dumb
63:16 though Abram be *i.* of us
*Acts* 4:13 perceived they were *i.*
*Rom.* 1:13 I would not have you *i.* brethren, 1 *Cor.* 10:1; 12:1; 2 *Cor.* 1:8; 1 *Thes.* 4:13
10:3 being *i.* of God's righteous.
11:25 sh. be *i.* of this mystery
1 *Cor.* 14:38 man *i.* let him be *i.*
2 *Cor.* 2:11 not *i.* of Satan's devi.
*Heb.* 5:2 have compassion on *i.*
2 *Pet.* 3:5 they willingly are *i.*
8 be not *i.* of this one thing

**IGNORANTLY.**
*Num.* 15:28 soul sinneth *i.*
*Deut.* 19:4 wh. killeth neighbor *i.*

Acts 17:23 ye i. worship I declare
1 Tim. 1:13 because I did it i.

**ILL.**

Gen. 41:3 kine i.-fav. 4, 19, 20, 21
43:6 why dealt so i. with me?
Deut. 15:21 hath any i. blemish
Ps. 106:32 it went i. with Moses
Is. 3:11 woe to wicked, sh. be i.
Joel 2:20 i. savor shall come up
Rom. 13:10 love worketh no i.

**ILL, or evil-favoredness.**

Deut. 17:1 not sac. sheep wherein is blemish or e.-f.

**ILLUMINATED.**

Heb. 10:32 after ye i. endur. fight

**ILLYRICUM.**

Rom. 15:19 round about unto I.

**IMAGE.**

Gen. 1:26 let us make man in our i. 27; 9:6
5:3 in his own i. after his i.
Lev. 26:1 nor rear up a standing i. Deut. 16:22
1 Sam. 19:13 Michal took an i.
2 Chr. 33:7 set car. i. in ho. of G.
Job 4:16 i. was before mine eyes
Ps. 73:20 shalt despise their i.
Ezek. 8:3 there was seat of i. 5
Dan. 2:31 great i. stood bef. thee
35 stone smote i. bec. mount.
3:1 Nebuchad. made i. of gold
6 worship the golden i. 10, 15
Hos. 3:4 sh. abide without an i.
Mat. 22:20 said, Whose is this i.? Mark 12:16; Luke 20:24
Acts 19:35 i. which fell from Ju.
Rom. 1:23 changed gl. of G. to i.
8:29 be conformed to i. of Son
11:4 bowed the knee to i. of B.
1 Cor. 11:7 he is i. and gl. of G.
15:49 we have borne i. of earthy
2 Cor. 3:18 changed into same i.
4:4 Christ is i. of God, Col. 1:15
Col. 3:10 i. of him that created
Heb. 1:3 express i. of his person
10:1 not the very i. of things
Rev. 13:14 make i. to the beast
15 give life to the i. of beast
14:9 if any man worship i.
11 have no rest, who worsh. i.
Rev. 15:2 vic. ov. beast and his i.
16:2 sore fell on them wors. i.
19:20 he deceived them wors. i.
20:4 not worshipped bea. nor i.
See GRAVEN.

**IMAGE-WORK.**

2 Chr. 3:10 two cherubim i.-w.

**Molten IMAGE.**

Deut. 9:12 made them a m. i.
Ps. 106:19 worshipped molten i.
Jer. 10:14 his m. i. falseh. 51:17
Hab. 2:18 what profit. the m. i.

**IMAGES.**

Gen. 31:19 stolen fath.'s i. 34, 35
Ex. 23:24 sh. break their i. 34:13; Deut. 7:5; Num. 33:52
Lev. 26:30 will cut down your i.
1 Sam. 6:5 i. of emerods, 11
1 K. 14:9 hast made i. to pro. me
23 high places, i. and groves
2 K. 10:26 they brought i. out
11:18 i. brake, 18:4; 23:14
17:10 set up i.; 16 they made i.
23:24 Josiah put away i. in land
Is. 17:8 not look to groves or i.
27:9 groves and i. not stand up
30:22 ye shall defile orna. of i.
41:29 their molten i. are wind
Jer. 43:13 break i. of B.-shemesh
50:2 her i. are broken in pieces
Ezek. 6:4 your i. shall be broken
6 that your i. may be cut down
7:20 made i. of abominations
16:17 mad. to thyself i. of men
21:21 king of Bab. consulted i.
23:14 i. of Chaldeans portrayed
30:13 will cause their i. to cease
Hos. 10:1 have made goodly i.
2 break their alt. spoil their i.
13:2 they have made i. of silver
Amos 5:26 borne tab. of your i.
Mic. 5:13 standing i. will I cut off

**IMAGERY.**

Ezek. 8:12 in chamber of i.

**IMAGINATION, S.**

Gen. 6:5 i. of his heart was evil
8:21 i. of man's heart is evil
Deut. 29:19 though I walk in i.
31:21 for I know their i.
1 Chr. 28:9 understands all the i.
29:18 keep this in i. of heart
Prov. 6:18 heart th. devis. wic. i.
Jer. 23:17 ev. one walketh after i.
Lam. 3:60 hast seen i. ag. me
61 hast heard their i. ag. me
Luke 1:51 scattered proud in i.
Rom. 1:21 became vain in th. i.
2 Cor. 10:5 casting down i.
See HEART.

**IMAGINE.**

Job 6:26 ye i. to reprove words?
21:27 devices wrong. i. ag. me
Ps. 2:1 do peo. i. vain thing?
38:12 and i. deceits all day long
62:3 how long will ye i. mischief
140:2 i. mischiefs in their heart
Prov. 12:20 deceit in them i. evil
Hos. 7:15 yet do they i. mischief
Nah. 1:9 what do ye i. ag. L.?
Zec. 7:10 let none i. evil, 8:17
Acts 4:25 do peo. i. vain things?

**IMAGINED, ETH.**

Gen. 11:6 nothing rest. they i.
Ps. 10:2 taken in devices they i.
21:11 they i. mischievous device
Nah. 1:11 one i. evil ag. the L.

**IMMEDIATELY.**

Mat. 26:74 i. the cock crew, Luke 22:60; John 18:27
Mark 1:31 i. the fever left her
4:15 Satan cometh i. and taketh
Lu. 6:49 i. fell; 8:44 i. stanched
19:11 kingdom of God i. appear
John 5:9 and i. man was whole
Acts 12:23 i. angel of L. smote
16:26 i. all doors were opened
Gal. 1:16 i. conferred not
Rev. 4:2 and i. was in the Spirit

**IMMORTAL.**

1 Tim. 1:17 K. eternal, i. invis.

**IMMORTALITY.**

Rom. 2:7 to them who seek for i.
1 Cor. 15:53 mortal must put on i.
54 mortal shall have put on i.
1 Tim. 6:16 i. dwelling in light
2 Tim. 1:10 brought i. to light

**IMMUTABLE.**

Heb. 6:18 that by two i. things

**IMMUTABILITY.**

Heb. 6:17 the i. of his counsel

**IMPART, ED.**

Job 39:17 nor i. to her underst.
Luke 3:11 him i. to him ha. none
Rom. 1:11 i. some spiritual gift
1 Thes. 2:8 willing to ha. i. souls

**IMPEDIMENT.**

Mark 7:32 had i. in his speech

**IMPENITENT.**

Rom. 2:5 thou, after thy i. heart

**IMPERIOUS.**

Ezek. 16:30 work of an i. woman

**IMPLACABLE.**

Rom. 1:31 without affection, i.

**IMPLEAD.**

Acts 19:38 let them i. one anoth.

**IMPORTUNITY.**

Luke 11:8 because of his i.

**IMPOSE, ED.**

Ezr. 7:24 not be lawful to i. toll
Heb. 9:10 carnal ordinances i. on

**IMPOSSIBLE.**

Mat. 17:20 nothing i. unto you
19:26 with men is i. Mark 10:27; Luke 18:27
Luke 1:37 with G. noth. i. 18:27
17:1 i. but offences will come
Heb. 6:4 i. for those enlightened
18 it was i. for G. to lie
11:6 without faith i. to please G.

**IMPOTENT.**

John 5:3 a multitude of i. folk
Acts 4:9 good deed done i. man
14:8 man at Lystra, i. in feet

**IMPOVERISH, ED.**

Jud. 6:6 Israel was greatly
Is. 40:20 he that is so i.
Jer. 5:17 shall i. fenced cities
Mal. 1:4 Edom saith, We are i.

**IMPRISONED.**

Acts 22:19 I i. and beat them

**IMPRISONMENT, S.**

Ezr. 7:26 banishment or i.
2 Cor. 6:5 approv. in stripes, in i.
Heb. 11:36 mockings, bonds, i.

**IMPUDENT.**

Prov. 7:13 with i. face she said
Ezek. 2:4 for they are i. children
3:7 house of Is. i. hard-hearted

**IMPUTE, ED.**

Lev. 7:18 nor sh. it be i. to him
17:4 blood sh. be i. to that man
1 Sam. 22:15 let not king i. any t.
2 Sam. 19:19 not my lord i. iniq.
Rom. 4:8 Lord will not i. sin
11 righteous. mi. be i. to them
22 therefore it was i. to him for righteousness, 23; Jam. 2:23
24 to whom it shall be i.
5:13 sin not i. wh. th. is no law

**IMPUTETH, ING.**

Ps. 32:2 whom Lord i. not iniq.
Hab. 1:11 i. his power to his god
Rom. 4:6 to whom G. i. righte.
2 Cor. 5:19 not i. tresp. to them

**INASMUCH.**

Mat. 25:40 i. as ye have done it
45 i. as ye did it not to one

**INCENSE.**

Ex. 30:8 shall burn perpetual i.
9 ye shall offer no strange i.
37:29 pure i. of sweet spices
40:5 altar of gold for i. bef. ark
Lev. 10:1 took censer, put i.
16:13 put i. on fire before Lord
Num. 7:14 spoon full of i. 86
16:35 fire cons. 250 men offer. i.
46 Mo. said to Aar. Put on i.
47 put on i. and made atonem.
Deut. 33:10 shall put i. bef. thee
2 Chr. 30:14 altars of i.
34:25 burned i. to other gods
Ps. 66:15 offer to thee i.
141:2 prayer set bef. thee as i.
Is. 1:13 i. is an abomination
43:23 not wearied thee with i.
60:6 shall bring gold and i.
65:3 burn. i. on altars of brick
66:3 burneth i. as if he blessed
Jer. 6:20 why cometh i. from S.?
11:17 prov. to anger, offering i.
41:5 offerings and i. in th. hand
48:35 him that burneth i. to g.
Ezek. 8:11 thick cloud of i. went
16:18 mine oil and i. before them
Mal. 1:11 ev. place i. be offered
Luke 1:10 without at time of i.
Rev. 8:3 given to him much i.
4 smoke of i. ascended bef. G.
See ALTAR, BURN, BURNT.

**Sweet INCENSE.**

Ex. 25:6 spices for sweet i. 35:8, 28; Num. 4:16
31:11 oil and s. i. for holy place
39:38 brought oil and s. i. to M.
Lev. 16:12 hands full of sweet i.

**INCENSED.**

Is. 41:11 i. ag. thee be ashamed
45:24 i. against him be ashamed

**INCLINE.**

Jos. 24:23 i. your heart to the L.
1 K. 8:58 he may i. our hearts
Ps. 78:1 i. your ears to words
119:36 i. my heart to thy testi.
141:4 i. not my heart to evil
See EAR.

**INCLINED, ETH.**

Jud. 9:3 hearts i. to follow A.
Ps. 40:1 Lord i. unto me, 116:2
119:112 i. my heart to thy stat.
Prov. 2:18 her house i. to death
5:13 nor i. mine ear to them
Jer. 7:24 nor i. ear, 26; 11:8; 17:23; 34:14
25:4 not i. y. ear, 35:15; 44:5

**INCONTINENCY.**

1 Cor. 7:5 tempt you not for y. i.

**INCONTINENT.**

2 Tim. 3:3 without affection, i.

**INCORRUPTIBLE.**

Rom. 1:23 changed glory of i. G.
1 Cor. 9:25 to obtain an i. crown
15:52 the dead shall be raised i.
1 Pet. 1:4 an inheri. i. undefiled
23 born of i. seed by word of G.

**INCORRUPTION.**

1 Cor. 15:42 cor. it is raised in i.
50 nei. doth corruption inh. i.
53 corruptible must put on i.
54 corrup. shall have put on i.

**INCREASE, Substantive.**

Lev. 25:36 no usury of him or i.
37 lend him victuals for i.
26:4 the land shall yield her i.
20 land shall not yield her i.
Num. 18:30 i. of threshing-floor
32:14 an i. of sinful men
Deut. 14:22 tithe all i. of seed
28 bring forth tithe of i.
28:18 cursed be i. of kine, 51
1 Sam. 2:33 i. of thy house sh. die
Job 20:28 i. of house shall depart
31:12 root out all mine i.
Ps. 67:6 earth shall yield her i.
78:46 gave their i. to caterpillar
85:12 our land shall yield her i.
Prov. 14:4 much i. by stre. of ox
18:20 with i. of lips sh. be filled
Ec. 5:10 not be satisfied with i.
Is. 9:7 i. of his gov. be no end
Jer. 2:3 i. was holiness to Lord
Ezek. 18:8 nor hath taken i. 17
13 on usury, taken i. 22:12
34:27 earth shall yield her i.
Zec. 8:12 ground sh. give her i.
1 Cor. 3:6 I planted, G. gave i. 7
Eph. 4:16 maketh i. of the body
Col. 2:19 body incr. wi. i. of G.

**INCREASE, Verb.**

Lev. 25:16 by years thou i. price
Deut. 6:3 ye may i. mightily
7:22 beasts of field i. on thee
1 Chr. 27:23 would i. Is. like stars
Job 8:7 thy latter end greatly i.
Ps. 44:12 dost not i. thy wealth
62:10 riches i. set not heart
73:12 in world, i. in riches
115:14 the L. shall i. you more
Prov. 1:5 wise man i. learn. 9:9
22:16 oppresseth poor to i. rich.
28:28 they perish, righteous i.
Ec. 5:11 goods i. increased eat
6:11 be many things that i.
Is. 29:19 meek i. their joy in L.
Ezek. 5:16 I will i. famine on you
36:29 i. it, lay no famine on you
37 i. them with men like a flock
Dan. 11:39 he shall i. with glory
Hos. 4:10 commit whored. not i.
Zec. 10:8 i. as they have increa.
Luke 17:5 said, Lord, i. our faith
John 3:30 must i. I must decrea.
2 Cor. 9:10 i. fruits of righteous.
1 Thes. 3:12 L. make y. i. in love
4:10 that ye i. more and more
2 Tim. 2:16 i. to more ungodli.

**INCREASED.**

Gen. 7:17 wat. i. bare up ark, 18
30:30 little hadst, it is now i.
43 Jacob i.; Ex. 1:7 Israel i.
1 Sam. 14:19 noise went on and i.
1 Chr. 4:38 house of fa. i. greatly
Ezr. 9:6 iniq. i. over our head
Ps. 3:1 they i. that trouble me
4:7 their corn and wine i.
49:16 glory of his house is i.
Prov. 9:11 years of life sh. be i.
Ec. 2:9 I i. more than all bef. me
5:11 they are i. that eat them
Is. 9:3 multip. nation, not i. joy
26:15 thou hast i. nation, O L.
Jer. 5:6 their backslidings are i.
15:8 widows i. ab. sands of sea
30:14 bec. thy sins were i. 15
Ezek. 16:26 i. thy whored. 23:14
28:5 by wisdom hast thou i.
Dan. 12:4 knowledge shall be i.
Hos. 4:7 as they i. so th. sinned
10:1 accord. to fruit, he i. altars
Zec. 10:8 incr. as they have i.
Mark 4:8 that sprang up and i.
Luke 2:52 Jesus i. in wisdom
Acts 6:7 and the word of God i.
16:5 churches i. in number daily
2 Cor. 10:15 hope when faith is i.
Rev. 3:17 rich, and i. with goods

**INCREASEST, ETH.**

Job 10:16 afflic. i.; 12:23 i. nati.
17 i. thine indig. upon me
Ps. 74:23 the tumult of those i.
Prov. 11:24 scattereth and yet i.
23:28 i. transgressors am. men
24:5 man of know. i. strength
28:8 unjust gain, i. substance
29:16 wicked multip. transg. i.
Ec. 1:18 i. knowledge, i. sorrow
Is. 40:29 he i. strength
Hos. 12:1 i. lies and desolation
Hab. 2:6 woe to him that i. that
Col. 2:19 body i. with inc. of G.

**INCREASING.**

Col. 1:10 i. in knowledge of God

**INCREDIBLE.**

Acts 26:8 i. G. should raise dead?

**INCURABLE.**

2 Chr. 21:18 smote him wi. i. di.
Job 34:6 my wound is i. without
Jer. 15:18 why is my wound i.?
30:12 bruise is i.; sorrow is i.
Mic. 1:9 wound i. it is come to J.

**INDEBTED.**

Luke 11:4 forgive every one i.

**INDEED.**

Gen. 37:8 sh. thou i. reign ov. us?
10 mother and breth. i. come?
1 K. 8:27 but will God i. dwell on earth? 2 Chr. 6:18
1 Chr. 4:10 wouldest bless me i.
Job 19:4 be it i. that I have erred
Is. 6:9 hear ye i. see ye i. but
Mat. 3:11 I i. baptize, Mark 1:8; Luke 3:16
Mark 11:32 he was a prophet i.
Luke 23:41 i. just.; 24:34 risen i.
John 1:47 behold an Israelite i.
4:42 that this is i. the Christ
6:55 flesh meat i. blood drink i.
7:26 do rulers know i. this is C.?
8:36 Son make free, ye be free i.
Rom. 8:7 law, neither i. can be
1 Tim. 5:3 hon. widows are wi. i.
5 that is widow i. desolate, 16
See ENDEAVOR.

**INDIGNATION.**

2 K. 3:27 great i. against Israel
Job 10:17 increasest i. upon me
Ps. 69:24 pour out thy i. on them
78:49 cast on them wrath, i.
102:10 bec. of thine i. and wrath
Is. 10:5 staff in hand is mine i.
25 yet a little, the i. sh. cease
13:5 weapons of i. Jer. 50:25
26:20 till i. be overpast
30:27 his lips are full of i.
34:2 i. of Lord is on all nations
66:14 i. kno. towards enemies
Jer. 10:10 not able to abide i.
15:17 thou hast filled me with i.
Lam. 2:6 despised in i. of anger
Ezek. 21:31 pour mi. i. upon thee
22:24 not rained on day of his i.
31 poured out mine i. on them
Dan. 11:30 i. against holy cove.
Mic. 7:9 I will bear i. of Lord
Nah. 1:6 who can stand bef. i.?
Hab. 3:12 march thro' land in i.
Zec. 1:12 had i. seventy years
Mal. 1:4 against whom L. hath i.
Mat. 20:24 moved wi. i. ag. two
26:8 had i. saying, To what
Luke 13:14 ruler answer. with i.
Acts 5:17 they were filled with i.
Rom. 2:8 obey unright. i. wrath
2 Cor. 7:11 yea, what i.!
Heb. 10:27 looking for of fiery i.
Rev. 14:10 poured out cup of i.

**INDITING.**

Ps. 45:1 heart is i. good matter

**INDUSTRIOUS.**

1 K. 11:28 young man was i.

**INEXCUSABLE.**

Rom. 2:1 therefore thou art i.

**INFALLIBLE.**

Acts 1:3 showed hims. by i. proo.

**INFAMOUS.**

Ezek. 22:5 mock thee wh. art i.

**INFAMY.**

Prov. 25:10 th. i. turn not away
Ezek. 36:3 are an i. of the people

**INFANT, S.**

1 Sam. 15:3 slay man, wo. and i.
Job 3:16 as i. wh. never saw light
Is. 65:20 no more an i. of days
Hos. 13:16 i. be dashed in pieces
Luke 18:15 they bro. i. to him

**INFERIOR.**

Job 12:3 understand. not i. 13:2
Dan. 2:39 another kingdom i.
2 Cor. 12:13 i. to other churches

**INFIDEL.**

2 Cor. 6:15 that believ. with i.?
1 Tim. 5:8 is worse than an i.

**INFINITE.**

Job 22:5 are not th. iniquities i.?
Ps. 147:5 his understanding is i.
Nah. 3:9 her strength, it was i.

**INFIRMITY.**

Lev. 12:2 days of separation for i.
Ps. 77:10 this is mine i.
Prov. 18:14 sp. of man sustain i.
Luke 13:11 woman which had i.
12 thou art loosed fr. thine i.
John 5:5 an i. thirty-eight years
Rom. 6:19 bec. of i. of your flesh
Gal. 4:13 through i. I preached
Heb. 5:2 himself comp. with i.
7:28 high-priests which have i.

**INFIRMITIES.**

Mat. 8:17 himself took our i.

*Luke* 5:15 to be healed of *i.*
7:21 cured many of their *i.* 8:2
*Rom.* 8:26 Sp. also helpeth our *i.*
15:1 strong bear *i.* of the weak
2 *Cor.* 11:30 things conc. mine *i.*
12:5 I gl. not, but in mine *i.* 9
10 I take pleasure in mine *i.*
1 *Tim.* 5:23 use wine for thine *i.*
*Heb.* 4:15 touched with feel. of *i.*

**INFLAME, ING.**

*Is.* 5:11 conti. till wine *i.* them
57:5 *i.* yourselves with idols

**INFLAMMATION.**

*Lev.* 13:28 an *i.* of the burning
*Deut.* 28:22 L. smite thee with *i.*

**INFLICTED.**

2 *Cor.* 2:6 punishm. which was *i.*

**INFLUENCES.**

*Job* 38:31 bind *i.* of Pleiades?

**INFOLDING.**

*Ezek.* 1:4 *i.* itself, and a brightn.

**INFORM, ED.**

*Deut.* 17:10 accord. to all they *i.*
*Dan.* 9:22 *i.* me, talked with me
*Acts* 21:21 are *i.* thou teachest, 24
24:1 *i.* against Paul, 25:2, 15

**INGATHERING.**

*Ex.* 23:16 feast of *i.* end of year

**INGRAFTED.**

*Jam.* 1:21 rec. with meek *i.* word

**INHABIT.**

*Num.* 35:34 defile not land sh. *i.*
*Prov.* 10:30 wicked not *i.* earth
*Is.* 42:11 villages Kedar doth *i.*
65:21 sh. build houses and *i.* th.
22 sh. not build, and anoth. *i.*
*Jer.* 17:6 shall *i.* parched places
*Ezek.* 33:24 that *i.* wastes of Isr.
*Amos* 9:14 waste cities *i.* them
*Zep.* 1:13 build houses, not *i.*

**INHABITANT.**

*Is.* 5:9 houses great without *i.*
6:11 cities be wasted without *i.*
12:6 cry out and shout, *i.* of Zi.
20:6 the *i.* of this isle shall say
24:17 snare on thee, O *i.* of earth
33:24 *i.* shall not say, I am sick
*Jer.* 2:15 cities burned without *i.*
4:7 cities laid waste without *i.*
9:11; 26:9; 33:10; 34:22
44:22 land a curse without an *i.*
46:19 desolate, with. *i.* 51:29, 37
*Amos* 1:5 will cut off *i.* from A.
8 I will cut off *i.* from Ashdod
*Mic.* 1:12 the *i.* of Maroth waited
13 *i.* of Lachish, bind chariot
15 to thee, O *i.* of Mareshah
*Zep.* 2:5 destroy, th. sh. be no *i.*
3:6 cities destroyed, is none *i.*

**INHABITANTS.**

*Gen.* 19:25 overthrew *i.* of cities
*Ex.* 15:15 *i.* of Canaan melt away
*Lev.* 18:25 land vomiteth out *i.*
25:10 procl. liberty to *i.* thereof
*Num.* 13:22 land eateth up *i.*
*Deut.* 13:15 surely smite *i.* of city
*Jos.* 2:24 *i.* of country do faint
11:19 peace, save *i.* of Gibeon
17:12 could not drive out the *i.*
*Jud.* 1:19, 27
*Jud.* 5:7 *i.* of the villages ceased
23 curse ye bitterly *i.* thereof
*Ruth* 4:4 buy it before the *i.*
2 *K.* 19:26 *i.* were of small power
2 *Chr.* 20:23 aga. *i.* of mount Seir
*Job* 26:5 are formed from und. *i.*
*Ps.* 33:8 *i.* of world stand in awe
14 he looketh on all *i.* of earth
49:1 give ear, all ye *i.* of world
75:3 earth and *i.* thereof dissolv.
*Is.* 10:13 put down *i.* like a man
18:3 ye *i.* of the world, see ye
23:2 be still, ye *i.* of the isle, 6
24:1 and scattere. abroad the *i.*
5 earth defiled under *i.* thereof
6 the *i.* of the earth are burned
26:9 *i.* of world learn righteous.
18 nor have *i.* of the world fal.
38:11 no more with *i.* of world
40:22 *i.* thereof as grasshoppers
42:10 *i.* sing to Lord a new song
11 let *i.* of rock sing
49:19 land nar. by reason of *i.*
*Jer.* 13:13 fill *i.* wi. drunkenness
21:6 I will smite *i.* of this city
23:14 as Sodom, and *i.* thereof
25:29 sw. upon *i.* thereof, 50:35
26:15 bring innocent blood on *i.*
49:8 dwell deep, O *i.* of D. 30
50:34 L. disquiet *i.* of Babylon
51:35 blood upon *i.* of Chaldea
*Lam.* 4:12 *i.* of world not believ.
*Dan.* 4:35 *i.* of earth as nothing
*Mic.* 6:12 *i.* thereof spoken lies
16 I should make *i.* a hissing
*Zec.* 8:20 come *i.* of many cities
21 *i.* of one city go to another
*Rev.* 17:2 *i.* of earth made drunk
*See* JERUSALEM.

**INHABITANTS of the land.**

*Gen.* 34:30 stink among *i. of l.*
*Ex.* 34:12 lest ma. cov. *i. of l.* 15
*Num.* 32:17 because of *i. of l.*
*Jos.* 2:9 all the *i. of the l.* faint
7:9 *i. of t. land* shall hear of it
9:24 to destroy all *i. of the land*
*Jer.* 1:14 evil sh. break on *i. of l.*
10:18 I will fling out *i. of land*
47:2 all the *i. of l.* shall howl
*Hos.* 4:1 hath controv. wi. *i. of l*
*Joel* 2:1 let the *i. of the l.* tremble
*Zec.* 11:6 no more pity *i. of land*

**INHABITED.**

*Ex.* 16:35 till th. came to land *i.*
*Lev.* 16:22 iniqu. to a land not *i.*
*Is.* 13:20 it shall never be *i.*
44:26 saith to J. Thou shalt be *i.*
45:18 he formed earth to be *i.*
54:3 make desola. cities to be *i.*
*Jer.* 6:8 lest I make land not *i.*
17:6 in a salt land and not *i.*
22:6 make thee cities not *i.*
46:26 sh. be *i.* as in days of old
50:13 not be *i.*; 39 no more *i.*
*Ezek.* 12:10 cities *i.* be laid waste
29:11 nor sh. it be *i.* forty years
36:10 cities *i.* and wastes build.
38:12 desolate places now *i.*
*Zec.* 2:4 Jerusal. be *i.* as towns
12:6 Jerusalem shall be *i.* again
14:10 lifted up, *i.* in her place
11 Jerusalem shall be safely *i.*

**INHABITERS.**

*Rev.* 8:13 woe, woe, to *i.* of earth
12:12 woe to *i.* of earth and sea

**INHABITEST, ETH.**

*Job* 15:28 in houses no man *i.*
*Ps.* 22:3 thou that *i.* prais. of Is.
*Is.* 57:15 lofty One that *i.* eterni.

**INHABITING.**

*Ps.* 74:14 meat to peo. *i.* wilder.

**INHERIT.**

*Gen.* 15:8 sh. I kn. th. I sh. *i.* it?
*Ex.* 32:13 they sh. *i.* it for ever
*Num.* 18:24 given it to Lev. to *i.*
32:19 not *i.* on yonder side Jor
*Deut.* 1:38 shall cause Is. to *i.* it
21:16 maketh his sons to *i.* wh
*Jud.* 11:2 not *i.* in fa.'s house
1 *Sam.* 2:8 *i.* the throne of glory
*Ps.* 25:13 his seed sh. *i.* the earth
37:9 wait on L. sh. *i.* the earth
11 meek sh. *i.* earth, *Mat.* 5:5
22 blessed of him shall *i.* earth
69:36 seed of his serv. shall *i.* it
82:8 O G. thou sh. *i.* all nations
*Prov.* 3:35 the wise shall *i.* glory
8:21 those who love me, *i.* sub.
11:29 troubl. own house, *i.* wi.
14:18 the simple *i.* folly
*Is.* 49:8 to *i.* desolate heritages
*Is.* 54:3 thy seed shall *i.* Gentiles
65:9 and mine elect shall *i.* it
*Jer.* 49:1 why doth th. ki. *i.* Gad?
*Zec.* 2:12 the L. shall *i.* Judah
*Mat.* 19:29 sh. *i.* everlasting life
25:34 come *i.* the kingdom pre.
*Mark* 10:17 that I may *i.* eternal
life, *Luke* 10:25; 18:18
1 *Cor.* 6:9 unrigh. not *i.* king. G.
10 nei. extortion. *i.* *Gal.* 5:21
15:50 flesh and blood cannot *i.*
kingd. of G. nor cor. *i.* inc.
*Heb.* 6:12 thro' faith *i.* promises
1 *Pet.* 3:9 ye should *i.* blessing
*Rev.* 21:7 he overcom. *i.* things

**INHERIT land.**

*Gen.* 28:4 thou mayest *i. land*
*Num.* 34:13 this is *land* ye sh. *i.*
*Deut.* 2:31 thou mayest *i.* his *l.*
16:20 *i. l.* L. giveth thee, 19:3
*Ps.* 37:29 righteous shall *i.* the *l.*
34 he sh. exalt thee to *i.* the *l.*
*Is.* 60:21 shall *i.* the *l.* for ever

**INHERITANCE.**

*Gen.* 31:14 is there any *i.*?
*Ex.* 15:17 plant th. in thine *i.*
*Lev.* 25:46 take them as *i.*
*Num.* 18:20 have no *i.* thine *i.*
27:8 cause his *i.* to pass
9 *i.* breth. 10 father's brethren
32:19 our *i.* is fallen on this
side, 32; 34:15
34:18 to divide the land by *i.*
36:3 put to the *i.* of the tribe, 4
9 nor *i.* remove from one tribe
*Deut.* 4:20 people of *i.* as ye are
9:26 destroy not *i.* 29 thy *i.*
32:9 Jacob is the lot of his *i.*
*Jos.* 13:14 sac. of L. their *i.* 18:7
33 the L. G. of Is. was their *i.*
24:28 people depart, every man
to his *i.* *Jud.* 2:6; 21:24
*Ruth* 4:6 not red. *i.* mar mine *i.*
1 *Sam.* 10:1 anointed thee over *i.*
26:19 from abiding in *i.* of Lord
2 *Sam.* 20:1 neither have we *i.*
in son of Jesse, 1 *K.* 12:16
21:3 ye may bless *i.* of the Lord
1 *K.* 8:51 be thy peo. and t. *i.* 53
*Neh.* 11:20 every one in his *i.*
*Job* 31:2 what *i.* of Almighty?
*Ps.* 16:5 the portion of mine *i.*
28:9 thine *i.* 33:12 cho. for *i.*
37:18 their *i.* shall be for ever
47:4 shall choose our *i.* for us
68:9 thou didst confirm thine *i.*
74:2 thine *i.* th. hast redeemed
78:62 was wroth with his *i.*
71 broug. him to feed Is. his *i.*
79:1 heathen come into thine *i.*
94:14 neither will he forsake *i.*
105:11 Canaan, lot of your *i.*
106:5 may glory with thine *i.*
40 that he abhorred his own *i.*
*Prov.* 13:22 good man leaveth *i.*
17:2 part of *i.* among brethren
19:14 hou. and riches *i.* of fath.
20:21 *i.* may be gotten hastily
*Ec.* 7:11 wisdom good with an *i.*
*Is.* 19:25 blessed be Is. mine *i.*
47:6 I have polluted mine *i.*
63:17 for serv. sake, tribes of *i.*
*Jer.* 10:16 Is. rod of his *i.* 51:19
32:8 for right of *i.* is thine
*Lam.* 5:2 *i.* turned to strangers
*Ezek.* 44:28 to them for *i.* I am *i.*
46:16 *i.* shall be his son's, 17
18 not take people's *i.*
*Mat.* 21:38 let us seize on his *i.*
*Mark* 12:7 *i.* be ours, *Luke* 20:14
*Luke* 12:13 he divide *i.* with me

*Acts* 20:32 *i.* among sanctified
26:18 *i.* am. them sancti. by fa.
*Gal.* 3:18 if the *i.* be of the law
*Eph.* 1:11 in whom obtained *i.*
14 the earnest of our *i.*
18 riches of the glory of his *i.*
5:5 hath any *i.* in kingd. of Ch.
*Col.* 1:12 partakers of *i.* of saints
3:24 ye shall rec. the rew. of *i.*
*Heb.* 1:4 he hath by *i.* obtained
9:15 promise of eternal *i.*
*Pet.* 1:4 begot. *i.* incorruptible

**For INHERITANCE.**
*Ex.* 34:9 take us *for* thine *i.*
*Num.* 18:21 tenth in Isr. *f. i.* 26
26:53 land sh. be divided *f.* an *i.* 33:54; 34:2; 36:2; *Deut.* 4:21, 38; 15:4; 19:10; *Jos.* 13:6, 7, 32; 14:1; 19:49, 51; *Ezek.* 45:1; 47:22; 48:29
*Deut.* 20:16 the Lord doth give thee *for* an *i.* 21:23; 24:4; 25:19; 26:1; *Jos.* 11:23; 13:6; 14:13; 1 *K.* 8:36; 2 *Chr.* 6:27; *Jer.* 3:18
*Ps.* 2:8 give thee heathen *f. i.*
*Ezek.* 33:24 land is given us *f. i.*
47:14 land sh. fall to you *f.* an *i.*
*Heb.* 11:8 a place he sho. rec. *f. i.*

**No, *or* None INHERITANCE.**
*Num.* 18:20 sh. have *no i.* 23, 24; 26:62; *Deut.* 10:9; 14:27, 29; 18:1, 2; *Jos.* 13:14, 33; 14:3
2 *Chr.* 10:16 we have *no i.* in son
*Acts* 7:5 he gave him *none i.*

**INHERITANCES.**
*Jos.* 19:51 the *i.* Joshua divided

**INHERITED, ETH.**
*Num.* 32:18 not return till Is. *i.*
35:8 his inheriting which he *i.*
*Ps.* 105:44 *i.* labor of the people
*Jer.* 16:19 our fathers *i.* lies
*Ezek.* 33:24 Abraham *i.* the land
*Heb.* 12:17 would have *i.* blessing

**INHERITOR.**
*Is.* 65:9 out of Jud. *i.* of mount
*See* ENJOY, ENJOIN.

**INIQUITY.**
*Gen.* 15:16 *i.* of the Amorites
19:15 lest be consumed in *i.*
44:16 G. ha. found out *i.* of ser.
*Ex.* 20:5 visiting the *i.* of fathers upon the children, 34:7; *Num.* 14:18; *Deut.* 5:9
34:7 forgiving *i.* *Num.* 14:18
*Lev.* 18:25 therefore do I visit *i.*
*Num.* 5:15 bringing *i.* to rem.
31 the man be guiltless from *i.*
23:21 not beheld *i.* in Jacob
*Deut.* 32:4 God of truth with. *i.*
*Jos.* 22:17 is *i.* of P. too little?
1 *Sam.* 3:14 *i.* of Eli's not purged
15:23 and stubbornness is as *i.*
20:8 if th. be in me *i.* slay me
25:24 let *i.* be, 2 *Sam.* 14:9
2 *Sam.* 14:32 if there be *i.* in me
19:19 let not L. impute *i.* to me
24:10 to take away *i.* of thy servant, 1 *Chr.* 21:8
2 *Chr.* 19:7 there is no *i.* with L.
*Job* 4:8 they that plough *i.*
5:16 and *i.* stoppeth her mouth
6:29 I pray you, let it not be *i.*
30 is there *i.* in my tongue?
11:6 G. exact. less th. *i.* deserv.
14 if *i.* be in thy hand
15:5 thy mouth uttereth thine *i.*
16 filthy is man wh. drink. *i.*
22:23 put away *i.* from thy tab.
31:11 *i.* to be punished, 28
33:9 nor is there *i.* in me
34:32 if I have done *i.*
36:21 take heed, regard not *i.*
23 who can say, Thou wro. *i.*?

*Ps.* 7:3 if be *i.* in my hands
14 behold, he travaileth with *i.*
32:2 to whom L. imputeth not *i.*
5 thou forgavest *i.* of my sin
36:3 words of his mouth are *i.*
39:11 dost correct man for *i.*
41:6 his heart gather. *i.* to itse.
49:5 *i.* of my heels compass
51:5 behold, I was shapen in *i.*
53:1 have done abominable *i.*
55:3 for they cast *i.* upon me
56:7 shall they escape by *i.*?
66:18 if I regard *i.* in my heart
85:2 forgiven *i.* of thy people
94:20 throne of *i.* have fellowsh.
107:42 *i.* shall stop her mouth
109:14 let *i.* of his fa.'s be rem.
119:3 do no *i.* walk in his ways
133 let not *i.* have dominion
125:3 let put forth hands to *i.*
*Prov.* 16:6 by truth *i.* is purged
19:28 mouth of wicked devou. *i.*
22:8 soweth *i.* shall reap vanity
*Ec.* 3:16 place of right. *i.* there
*Is.* 1:4 a people laden with *i.*
13 *i.* even the solemn meeting
5:18 woe to them that draw *i.*
6:7 thine *i.* is taken away
14:21 prepare for *i.* of fathers
22:14 *i.* not be purged from you
29:20 watch for *i.* are cut off
30:13 *i.* shall be as a breach
40:2 her *i.* is pardoned
53:6 L. laid on him *i.* of us all
57:17 for *i.* of covetousness
59:3 your fingers defiled with *i.*
4 bring forth *i.* 6 works of *i.* 7
64:9 nor remember *i.* for ever
*Jer.* 2:5 what *i.* have fa. fo. in me
22 thine *i.* is marked before me
3:13 only acknowledge thine *i.*
13:22 greatn. of *i.* are thy skirts
14:20 acknowledge *i.* of fathers
16:10 our *i.* 17 *i.* hid from eyes
30:14 multi. of *i.* 15; *Hos.* 9:7
32:18 recompensest *i.* of fathers
*Lam.* 2:14 not discovered thine *i.*
*Lam.* 4:22 punishm. of *i.* accom. will visit *i.* O daug. of Edom
*Ezek.* 4:4 lay *i.* of house of Is. on
7:13 nor strength. himself in *i.*
18:17 not die for *i.* of his father
30 so *i.* shall not be your ruin
21:23 call to remembrance *i.* 24
25 *i.* sh. have an end, 29; 35:5
28:15 till *i.* found in thee
18 defiled sanctu. by *i.* of traf.
44:12 houses of Israel fall into *i.*
*Dan.* 9:24 reconciliation for *i.*
*Hos.* 7:1 *i.* of Ephraim discovered
10:9 children of *i.* 13 reaped *i.*
12:8 they shall find no *i.* in me
11 is there *i.* in Gilead?
13:12 *i.* of Ephraim bound up
14:1 thou hast fallen by thine *i.*
2 take away *i.* rec. graciously
*Mic.* 2:1 woe to them devise *i.*
3:10 build up Jerusalem with *i.*
7:18 G. like thee, pardoneth *i.*?
*Hab.* 1:13 canst not look on *i.*
2:12 woe to him estab. city by *i.*
*Zep.* 3:5 just Lord, will not do *i.*
13 remnant of Israel not do *i.*
*Zec.* 3:4 caused *i.* pass from thee
9 remove *i.* of land in one day
*Mal.* 2:6 *i.* not found in his lips
*Mat.* 13:41 gather them wh. do *i.*
23:28 are full of hypocrisy and *i.*
24:12 because *i.* shall abound
*Acts* 1:18 field with reward of *i.*
8:23 thou art in bond of *i.*
*Rom.* 6:19 servants to *i.* unto *i.*
1 *Cor.* 13:6 rejoiceth not in *i.* but
2 *Thes.* 2:7 mystery of *i.* doth w.
2 *Tim.* 2:19 nameth C. dep. fr. *i.*
*Tit.* 2:14 might redeem us fr. *i.*
*Heb.* 1:9 and thou hast hated *i.*

*Jam.* 3:6 tong. is fire, world of *i.*
*See* BEAR, COMMIT, COMMITTED.

**His INIQUITY.**
*Num.* 15:31 *his i.* be upon him
*Job* 20:27 heavens revealed *his i.*
21:19 G. layeth up *h. i.* for chil.
*Ps.* 36:2 *h. i.* be found hateful
*Jer.* 31:30 die for *his i.* *Ezek.* 3:18, 19; 7:16; 18:26
*Ezek.* 14:7 stum.-block of *h. i.* 14
18:18 sh. die in *h. i.* 33:8, 9
33:6 he is taken away in *his i.*
2 *Pet.* 2:16 Bal. rebuked for *h. i.*

**Mine INIQUITY.**
1 *Sam.* 20:1 what is *mine i.*?
2 *Sam.* 22:24 I kept myself from *mine i.* *Ps.* 18:23
*Job* 7:21 not take away *m. i.*?
10:6 thou inquirest after *m. i.*
14 not acquit me from *mine i.*
14:17 thou sewest up *m. i.*
31:33 hiding *m. i.* in my bosom
*Ps.* 25:11 pardon *m. i.* it is great
31:10 stre. faileth beca. of *m. i.*
32:5 *mine i.* have I not hid
38:18 for I will declare *mine i.*
51:2 wash me thoro. fr. *m. i.*

**Their INIQUITY.**
*Lev.* 26:39 pine away in *their i.*
40 if they confess *th. i.* 41, 43
*Neh.* 4:5 and cover not *their i.*
*Ps.* 69:27 add iniquity unto *t. i.*
78:38 forg. *t. i.* 89:32 visit *t. i.*
94:23 bring upon them *their i.*
106:43 were bro. low for *their i.*
*Is.* 13:11 punish wicked for *t. i.*
26:12 punish inhabitants for *t. i.*
33:24 peo. shall be forgiven *t. i.*
*Jer.* 14:10 will now remem. *th. i.*
16:18 he will recompense *th. i.*
18:23 forgive not *their i.*
25:12 punish nation for *their i.*
31:34 for I will forgive *their i.*
33:8 cleanse them from all *th. i.*
36:3 that I may forgive *their i.*
31 punish his servants for *t. i.*
*Ezek.* 4:5 laid on th. years of *t. i.*
17 may consume away for *t. i*
7:19 stumbling-bl. of *t. i.* 14:3
14:10 bear punishment of *th. i.*
29:16 bringeth *t. i.* to remem.
39:23 Is. into captivity for *t. i.*
*Hos.* 4:8 set their heart on *th. i.*
5:5 shall Is. and Eph. fall in *t. i.*
9:9 he will remember *their i.*

**Work INIQUITY.**
*Ps.* 141:4 with men that *w. i.*
*Is.* 31:2 ag. help of them *w. i.*
32:6 *w. i.* to practise hypocrisy
*Mat.* 7:23 depart fr. me, ye *w. i.*

**Workers of INIQUITY.**
*Job* 31:3 punishment to *w. of i.*
34:8 go in comp. with *w. of i.*
22 *w. of i.* hide themselves
*Ps.* 5:5 hatest all *workers of i.*
6:8 all ye *w. of i.* *Luke* 13:27
*Ps.* 14:4 *w. of i.* no knowl.? 53:4
28:3 draw not away wi. *w. of i.*
36:12 the *w. of i.* fallen
37:1 nor be envious ag. *w. of i.*
59:2 deliver me from *w. of i.*
64:2 insurrection of the *w. of i.*
92:7 all the *w. of i.* do flourish
9 the *w. of i.* shall be scattered
94:4 *w. of i.* boast themselves
16 stand up for me aga. *w. of i.*
125:5 lead th. forth with *w. of i.*
141:9 keep me fr. gins of *w. of i.*
*Prov.* 10:29 dest. to *w. of i.* 21:15

**INIQUITIES.**
*Lev.* 16:21 confess over goat all *i.*
26:39 in *i.* of fa. sh. they pine
*Ezr.* 9:6 *i.* increased over head
13 punished less *i.* deserved
*Neh.* 9:2 Is. confessed *i.* of fath.

Job 13:23 how many are mine i.
26 makest me to poss. i. of yo
22:5 wicked. great, i. infinite
Ps. 38:4 i. gone over my head
40:12 i. have taken hold on me
51:9 hide fa. fr. sins, blot out i.
64:6 search out i. 65:3 i. preva.
79:8 remember not ag. us i.
90:8 hast set our i. before
103:3 L. who forgiveth all i.
10 nor rewarded us accord. to i.
130:3 shou. mark i. who stand?
8 redeem Israel from all his i.
Prov. 5:22 own i. take wicked
Is. 43:24 wearied me with th. i.
53:5 he was bruised for our i.
59:12 our i. we know them
64:6 i. like wind taken us away
7 consum. us because of our i.
Jer. 11:10 to i. of forefathers
14:7 though our i. testify ag. us
Lam. 4:13 for i. of her priests
Ezek. 28:18 by multi. of thine i.
Dan. 4:27 break off thine i.
9:13 we might turn from our i.
Mic. 7:19 he will subdue our i.
Acts 3:26 turn. ev. one fr. his i.
Rom. 4:7 blessed they wh. i. for.
Rev. 18:5 God hath rememb. i.

**Their INIQUITIES.**

Lev. 16:22 goat bear on him t. i.
Ps. 107:17 fools bec. of their i.
Is. 53:11 he shall bear their i.
Jer. 33:8 I will pardon all their i.
Lam. 5:7 we have borne t. i.
Ezek. 32:27 t. i. be on their bones
Heb. 8:12 t. i. rem. no more, 10:17

**Your INIQUITIES.**

Num. 14:34 forty ye. ye bear y. i.
Is. 50:1 for y. i. ye sold yourself
59:2 y. i. separated you and G.
65:7 your i. I will recompense
Jer. 5:25 y. i. turned away thin.
Ezek. 24:23 ye pine away for y. i.
36:31 loathe yourselves for y. i.
Amos 3:2 punish you for y. i.

**INJURED.**

Gal. 4:12 ye have not i. me at all

**INJURIOUS.**

1 Tim. 1:13 a persecutor and i.

**INJUSTICE.**

Job 16:17 not for i. in my hands

**INK.**

Jer. 36:18 wrote them with i.
2 Cor. 3:3 not with i. but the S.
2 John 12 not wr. wi. i. 3 John 13

**INKHORN.**

Ezek. 9:2 writer's i. by side, 3, 11

**INN.**

Gen. 42:27 ass proven. in the i.
43:21 came to i. opened sacks
Ex. 4:24 in the i. L. met him
Luke 2:7 no room for them in i.
10:34 brought him to an i.

**INNER.**

1 K. 6:27 cherubim in i. house
1 Chr. 28:11 patterns of i. parlors
Est. 4:11 to king into i. court
5:1 Esther stood in the i. court
Ezek. 10:3 cloud filled the i. cou.
42:15 end of measuring i. house
46:1 gate of i. court sh. six da.
Acts 16:24 thrust th. into i. pris.
Eph. 3:16 strengthened in i. man

See CHAMBER.

**INNERMOST.**

Prov. 18:8 i. parts of belly, 26:22

**INNOCENCY.**

Gen. 20:5 in the i. of my hands
Ps. 26:6 wash my hands in i.
73:13 I washed hands in i.
Dan. 6:22 i. was found in me
Hos. 8:5 how long ere attain to i.?

**INNOCENT, S.**

Ex. 23:7 i. and right. slay not
Deut. 27:25 tak. reward to slay i.
Job 4:7 who ever perished be. i.?
9:23 laugh at the trial of the i.
28 thou wilt not hold me i.
17:8 i. stir up against hypocrite
22:19 the i. laugh them to scorn
30 shall deliver island of the i.
27:17 i. shall divide the silver
33:9 I am i. nor is iniq. in me
Ps. 10:8 in sec. places murder i.
15:5 taketh reward against i.
19:13 i. fr. great transgression
Prov. 1:11 lurk privily for i.
28:20 haste to be rich not be i.
Jer. 2:34 found blood of poor i.
35 thou sayest, Because I am i.
19:4 filled place with blood of i.
Mat. 27:24 I am i. of the blood of

See BLOOD.

**INNUMERABLE.**

Job 21:33 there are i. before him
Ps. 40:12 i. evils comp. about
104:25 wherein things creep. i.
Jer. 46:23 grasshoppers, are i.
Luke 12:1 an i. mult. gathered
Heb. 11:12 sand by sea-shore i.
12:22 to i. company of angels

**INORDINATE.**

Ezek. 23:11 corrupt in i. love
Col. 3:5 fornication, i. affection

**INQUIRE.**

Gen. 24:57 we will i. at damsel
25:22 Rebekah went to i. of L.
Ex. 18:15 people come to i. of G.
Deut. 12:30 i. not after their gods
13:14 shalt i. and make search
Jud. 4:20 when any man doth i.
1 Sam. 22:15 th. begin to i. of G.
28:7 seek me a woman, that I i.
1 K. 22:5 i. at the word of the Lord to-day, 2 Chr. 18:4
2 K. go, i. of Baal-zebub
16:15 bra. altar for me to i. by
22:13 i. of L. for me, 2 Chr. 34:21
1 Chr. 10:13 familiar spirit to i.
21:30 David not go bef. it to i.
Ezr. 7:14 sent to i. concerning J.
Job 8:8 for i. of the former age
Ps. 27:4 and to i. in his temple
Ec. 7:10 thou dost not i. wisely
Is. 21:12 if ye will i. ye
Jer. 21:2 i. of the Lord for us
37:7 that sent you to i. of me
Ezek. 14:7 cometh to proph. to i.
20:1 elders came to i. of Lord
Mat. 10:11 i. who is worthy
Luke 22:23 to i. among themselves, John 16:19
Acts 9:11 i. for Saul
19:39 if i. concerning other mat.
23:15 as tho' i. something, 20
2 Cor 8:23 any do i. of Titus

**INQUIRED.**

Jud. 20:27 children of Is. i. of L.
1 Sam. 22:10 Abimelech i. of L.
23:2 David i. of the Lord, 4; 30:8; 2 Sam. 2:1; 5:19, 23; 21:1; 1 Chr. 14:10, 14
28:6 Saul i. Lord answered not
2 Sam. 16:23 as if i. at oracle of
1 Chr. 10:14 Saul i. not of Lord
13:3 i. not at ark in days of S.
Ps. 78:34 and i. early after God
Ezek. 14:3 should I be i. of at all
20:3 as I live I will not be i. of
31 shall I be i. of by you, O Israel? I will not be i. of by
36:37 I will yet for this be i. of
Dan. 1:20 in all king i. of them
Zep. 1:6 have not i. for the Lord
Mat. 2:7 Herod i. of wise men, 16
John 4:52 i. hour began to ame.
2 Cor. 8:23 or our brethren be i.
1 Pet. 1:10 of wh. sal. prophets i.

**INQUIREST.**

Job 10:6 i. after mine iniquity

**INQUIRY.**

Prov. 20:25 after vows to make i.

**INQUISITION.**

Deut. 19:18 jud. sh. make dili. i.
Est. 2:23 i. was made of matter
Ps. 9:12 when mak. i. for blood

**INSCRIPTION.**

Acts 17:23 an altar with this i.

**INSIDE.**

1 K. 6:15 cov. walls i. with wood

**INSPIRATION.**

Job 32:8 i. Alm. giv. understan.
2 Tim. 3:16 scripture is by i. of

**INSTANT, LY.**

Is. 29:5 it sh. be at an i. sudden.
30:13 whose breaking com. at i.
Jer. 18:7 at what i. I speak, 9
Luke 2:38 com. th. i. gave than.
7:4 they besought him i.
Acts 26:7 twelve tribes i. serve
Rom. 12:12 continu. i. in prayer
2 Tim. 4:2 be i. in season, out of

**INSTRUCT.**

Deut. 4:36 hear, th. he mi. i. thee
Neh. 9:20 gavest thy S. to i. th.
Job 40:2 shall he that contend i.
Ps. 16:7 my reins also i. me
32:8 I will i. thee and teach th.
Cant. 8:2 who will i. me
Is. 28:26 God doth i. him
Dan. 11:33 underst. sh. i. many
1 Cor. 2:16 that he may i. him

**INSTRUCTED.**

Deut. 32:10 L. led him ab. i. him
Job 4:3 behold thou hast i. many
Ps. 2:10 be i. ye judges of earth
Prov. 5:13 mine ear to th. i. me
21:11 the wise is i. he receiveth
Is. 8:11 L. spake thus and i. me
40:14 i. him and taught him
Jer. 6:8 be i. O J. lest soul dep.
31:19 after i. I smote on thigh
Mat. 13:52 every scribe who is i.
14:8 being bef. i. of her mother
Luke 1:4 things th. hast been i.
Acts 18:25 was i. in way of Lord
Rom. 2:18 being i. out of law
Phil. 4:12 in all things, I am i.

**INSTRUCTING.**

2 Tim. 2:25 i. those that oppose

**INSTRUCTION.**

Job 33:16 open. ears, sealeth i.
Ps. 50:17 seeing thou hatest i.
Prov. 1:2 to know wisdom and i.
3 to receive the i. of wisdom
7 fools des. wisdom and i. 15:5
8 son, hear i. of thy father, 4:1
4:13 take hold of i.
5:12 say, How have I hated i.
23 die without i. go astray
6:23 reproofs of i. way of life
8:10 receive my i.; 33 hear i.
9:9 give i. to a wise man
10:17 in way of life that keep. i.
12:1 loveth i. loveth knowledge
13:1 wise son heareth father's i.
18 shame to him that refus. i.
15:32 refus. i. despiseth his soul
33 fear of L. is the i. of wisd.
16:22 but the i. of fools is folly
19:20 hear counsel and rec. i.
27 cease to hear i.
23:12 apply thy heart to i.
23 buy also i. and understand.
Jer. 17:23 not hear nor rec. i.
32:33 not hearkened to rec. i.
Ezek. 5:15 a repro. a taunt, an i.
Zep. 3:7 surely thou wilt rec. i.
2 Tim. 3:16 scrip. is profitable i.

**INSTRUCTOR, S.**

Gen. 4:22 Tubal Cain an i.
Rom. 2:20 an i. of the foolish

1 *Cor.* 4:15 ye have 10,000 *i.*

**INSTRUMENT.**

*Num.* 35:16 smite him with *i.*
*Ps.* 33:2 wi. *i.* of ten strings, 92:3
144:9 sing new song, O G. on *i.*
*Is.* 28:27 not thr. with thresh. *i.*
41:15 make th. sharp thresh. *i.*
54:16 bringeth forth *i.* for work
*Ezek.* 33:2 song of one play on *i.*

**INSTRUMENTS.**

*Gen.* 49:5 *i.* of cruelty in habita.
*Ex.* 25:9 pattern of all the *i.*
*Num.* 3:8 all *i.* of tabernacle
7:1 sancti. all *i.* thereof, 31:6
1 *Sam.* 8:12 *i.* of war, *i.* of char.
18:6 meet S. with *i.* of music
1 *K.* 19:21 boiled th. flesh with *i.*
1 *Chr.* 9:29 oversee *i.* of sanctu.
16:42 make sou. with musical *i.*
*Ps.* 7:13 prepared *i.* of death
68:25 players on *i.* followed
87:7 players on *i.* be there
150:4 with stringed *i.*
*Ec.* 2:8 musical *i.* of all sorts
*Is.* 32:7 *i.* also of the churl
38:20 sing song to stringed *i.*
*Dan.* 6:18 nor *i.* of music brou.
*Amos* 1:3 threshed G. with *i.* of
6:5 invent to themsel. *i.* of mu.
*Hab.* 3:19 singing on stringed *i.*
*Zec.* 11:15 *i.* of foolish shepherd
*Rom.* 6:13 nor y. mem. *i.* of unright. members as *i.* of righ.

**INSURRECTION.**

*Ezr.* 4:19 this city hath made *i.*
*Ps.* 64:2 *i.* of workers of iniquity
*Mark* 15:7 bound th. th. made *i.* who had commit. mur. in *i.*
*Acts* 18:12 J. made *i.* one accord

**INTEGRITY.**

*Gen.* 20:5 *i.* of my heart, 6
*Job* 2:3 still he holdeth fast his *i.*
9 dost thou still retain th. *i.* ?
27:5 I will not remove my *i.*
31:6 that God may know my *i.*
*Ps.* 7:8 according to my *i.* in me
25:21 *i.* and uprightn. preserve
26:1 I have walked in mine *i.*
11 as for me, I will walk in *i.*
41:12 thou uphold. me in my *i.*
78:72 fed accord. to *i.* of heart
*Prov.* 11:3 *i.* of upright guide th.
19:1 poor that walketh in *i.*
20:7 just man walketh in his *i.*

**INTELLIGENCE.**

*Dan.* 11:30 *i.* with them forsake

**INTEND.**

2 *Chr.* 28:13 *i.* to add more to si.
*Acts* 5:28 *i.* to bring man's blood
35 what ye *i.* to do these men

**INTENDED, EST.**

*Ex.* 2:14 *i.* thou to kill me
*Ps.* 21:11 *i.* evil against thee

**INTENDING.**

*Luke* 14:28 wh. of you *i.* to build
*Acts* 12:4 *i.* after Easter to bring

**INTENT, S.**

2 *Chr.* 16:1 *i.* might let none go
*Jer* 30:24 performed *i.* of heart
*John* 11:15 not there to the *i.*
13:28 for what *i.* he spake
*Acts* 9:21 came hither for that *i.*
10:29 what *i.* ye ha. sent for me
1 *Cor.* 10:6 *i.* we should not lust
*Eph.* 3:10 *i.* that now to princi.
*Heb.* 4:12 discerner of *i.* of heart

**INTERCESSION, S.**

*Is.* 53:12 *i.* for transgressors
*Jer.* 7:16 ne. lift cry, nor make *i.*
27:18 let th. now make *i.* to L.
*Rom.* 8:26 Sp. maketh *i.* 27, 34
11:2 maketh *i.* to G. ag. Israel
*Heb.* 7:25 liveth to make *i.*
1 *Tim.* 2:1 prayers and *i.* be ma.

**INTERCESSOR.**

*Is.* 59:16 wondered th. was no *i.*

**INTERMEDDLE, ETH.**

*Prov.* 14:10 stranger not *i.*
18:1 seeketh and *i.* with wisd.

**INTERMISSION.**

*Lam.* 3:49 ceaseth not without *i.*

**INTERPRET.**

*Gen.* 41:8 none could *i.* to Phar.
12 accord. to dream he did *i.*
1 *Cor.* 12:30 do all *i.* ; 14:5 exc. *i.*
14:13 he may *i.* ; 27 let one *i.*

**INTERPRETATION.**

*Gen.* 40:5 *i.* of dream, 41:11
12 Joseph said, This is the *i.* of it, 18 ; *Dan.* 4:24 ; 5:26
*Prov.* 1:6 unders. proverb and *i.*
*Dan.* 2:4 we shall show *i.* 7, 36
45 dream is certain, and *i.* sure
4:19 *i.* thereof be to thine ene.
*John* 1:42 Cephas, is by *i.* a stone
9:7 pool of Siloam, is by *i.* sent
*Acts* 9:36 Tab. by *i.* called Dorc.
13:8 Elymas sorcerer, na. by *i.*
1 *Cor.* 12:10 another *i.* of tongues
14:26 every one of you ha. an *i.*
*Heb.* 7:2 by *i.* king of righteous.
2 *Pet.* 1:20 no prophecy of pri. *i.*

**INTERPRETATIONS.**

*Gen.* 40:8 do not *i.* belong to G. ?
*Dan.* 5:16 thou canst make *i.*

**INTERPRETED.**

*Ezr.* 4:7 and *i.* in Syrian tongue
*Mat.* 1:23 being *i.* is, G. with us
*Mark* 5:41 wh. is, being *i.* damsel
15:22 being *i.* place of a skull
34 *i.* my God, my God
*John* 1:38 *i.* master ; 41 *i.* Christ
*Acts* 4:36 *i.* son of consolation

**INTERPRETER, S.**

*Gen.* 40:8 and there is no *i.* of it
42:23 Joseph spake to th. by *i.*
*Job* 33:23 and *i.* one am. thous.
1 *Cor.* 14:28 if there be no *i.* keep

**INTERPRETING.**

*Dan.* 5:12 *i.* of dreams found in

INTREAT, ED, etc. *See* ENTREAT.

**INTRUDING.**

*Col.* 2:18 *i.* into things not seen

**INVADE, ED.**

1 *Sam.* 23:27 Philistines *i.* land
2 *K.* 13:20 Moabites *i.* land
2 *Chr.* 20:10 would. not let Is. *i.*
28:18 Philistines had *i.* cities
*Hab.* 3:16 will *i.* them with troops

**INVASION.**

1 *Sam.* 30:14 made *i.* on the south

**INVENT, ED.**

2 *Chr.* 26:15 engines *i.* by cunni.
*Amos* 6:5 *i.* instruments of music

**INVENTIONS.**

*Ps.* 99:8 tookest veng. of their *i.*
106:29 prov. him to anger wi. *i.*
39 whoring with their own *i.*
*Prov.* 8:12 knowledge of witty *i.*
*Ec.* 7:29 sought out many *i.*

**INVENTORS.**

*Rom.* 1:30 *i.* of evil things

**INVISIBLE.**

*Rom.* 1:20 *i.* things clearly seen
*Col.* 1:15 image of the *i.* God
16 heaven and earth, vi. and *i.*
1 *Tim.* 1:17 to King immortal, *i.*
*Heb.* 11:27 seeing him who is *i.*

**INVITED.**

1 *Sam.* 9:24 I have *i.* the people
2 *Sam.* 13:23 Absa. *i.* king's son
*Est.* 5:12 to-morrow am I *i.*

**INWARD.**

*Lev.* 13:55 in fire, it is fret *i.*
1 *K.* 7:25 all hinder parts were *i.*
2 *Chr.* 3:13 and th. faces were *i.*
*Job* 19:19 my *i.* friends abhor. me
38:36 put wisdom in *i.* parts
*Ps.* 5:9 *i.* part is very wickedn.
49:11 *i.* thought is, that houses
51:6 desirest truth in the *i.* par.
64:6 *i.* thought of them is deep
*Prov.* 20:27 all *i.* parts of belly
30 stripes the *i.* parts of belly
*Is.* 16:11 *i.* parts sound for Ker-h.
*Jer.* 31:33 put my law in *i.* parts
*Luke* 11:39 *i.* part full of raven.
*Rom.* 7:22 law of G. after *i.* man
2 *Cor.* 4:16 the *i.* man is renew.
7:15 *i.* affection more abundant

**INWARDLY.**

*Ps.* 62:4 with mouths, curse *i.*
*Mat.* 7:15 but *i.* they are wolves
*Rom.* 2:29 a Jew who is one *i.*

**INWARDS.**

*Ex.* 29:13 covereth *i.* 22 ; *Lev.* 3:3, 9, 14 ; 4:8 ; 7:3 ; 9:19
17 thou shalt wash the *i.* *Lev.* 1:9, 13 ; 9:14
*Lev.* 4:11 *i.* and dung burn
8:16 fat on *i.* M. burnt on altar
21 he washed *i.* and legs

**IRON, Substantive.**

*Num.* 35:16 with instrument of *i.*
*Deut.* 3:11 Og's bedstead was *i.*
4:20 L. brought you out of the *i.* furnace, 1 *K.* 8:51 ; *Jer.* 11:4
8:9 a land whose stones are *i.*
28:23 earth under thee sh. be *i.*
48 yo. of *i.* on neck, *Jer.* 28:14
*Jos.* 8:31 over wh. no man lift *i.*
17:16 chariots of *i.* *Jud.* 1:19
*Jud.* 4:3 900 chariots of *i.* 13
1 *Sam.* 17:7 spear's head weighed 600 shekels of *i.*
2 *Sam.* 12:31 under harrows of *i.* axes of *i.* 1 *Chr.* 20:3
23:7 must be fenced with *i.*
1 *K.* 6:7 nor any tool of *i.* heard
22:11 horns of *i.* 2 *Chr.* 18:10
2 *K.* 6:6 and the *i.* did swim
1 *Chr.* 22:3 prep. *i.* in abundance
29:2 prep. *i.* for things of *i.* 7
*Job* 28:2 *i.* is taken out of earth
40:18 behemoth's bones like *i.*
41:27 he esteemeth *i.* as straw
*Ps.* 2:9 break them with rod of *i.*
105:18 hurt, he was laid in *i.*
107:10 bound in *i.* ; 16 bars of *i.*
149:8 bind nobles with fet. of *i.*
*Prov.* 27:17 *i.* sharpeneth *i.*
*Ec.* 10:10 if the *i.* be blunt
*Is.* 10:34 cut thic. of forest wi. *i.*
45:2 I will cut asunder bars of *i.*
60:17 for *i.* I will bring silver
*Jer.* 15:12 shall *i.* break north. *i.*
17:1 written with pen of *i.*
28:13 make for them yokes of *i.*
*Ezek.* 4:3 *i.* pan, set for wall of *i.*
27:12 Tarshish merchant with *i.*
*Dan.* 2:33 legs of *i.* feet part *i.*
35 the *i.* and clay broken
40 fourth kingdom strong as *i.*
7:19 whose teeth were of *i.*
*Amos* 1:3 Gil. with instru. of *i.*
*Mic.* 4:13 I will make thy horn *i.*
1 *Tim.* 4:2 consc. seared with *i.*
*Rev.* 2:27 rule th. with a rod of *i.* 12:5 ; 19:15
9:9 as it were breastplates of *i.*
*See* BRASS.

**IRON.**

*Deut.* 27:5 not lift up any *i.* tool
*Jos.* 17:18 they have *i.* chariots
*Job* 19:24 graven with *i.* pen
20:24 shall flee from *i.* weapon
*Is.* 48:4 thy neck is an *i.* sinew
*Jer.* 1:18 thee this day *i.* pillar
*Ezek.* 4:3 take unto thee *i.* pan
*Dan.* 7:7 it had great *i.* teeth

*Acts* 12:10 came to the *i.* gate

**IRONS.**

*Job* 41:7 fill skin with barbed *i.* ?

**IS.**

*Rev.* 1:4 which *i.* was, and *i.* to come, 8; 4:8
17:8 that was, *i.* not, yet *i.*
10 one *i.* the other *i.* not come

**IS not.**

*Gen.* 37:30 said, The child *i. not*
42:13 youn. with fa. one *i. n.* 32
42:36 Joseph *i. not*, Simeon *i. n.*
*Rev.* 17:8 beast was, and *i. n.* 11

**ISAAC.**

*Gen.* 17:19 his name I. 21:3, 12
21:10 heir with my son, even I.
22:2 take thine only son I. 9
24:4 take a wife for I. 14
25:5 had unto I. 9, 11, 20, 26
26:1 I. went to Abimelech
28:1 I. called Jacob, blessed h.
31:42 fear of I. had been with
35:27 Jacob came to I. 29
48:15 God before wh. I. walked
*Ex.* 3:6 the God of I. 15, 16; 4:5; *Gen.* 32:9; 1 *K.* 18:36; 1 *Chr.* 29:18; 2 *Chr.* 30:6; *Mat.* 22:32; *Mark* 12:26; *Luke* 20:37; *Acts* 3:13
*Jos.* 24:3 and gave him I.
1 *Chr.* 16:16 unto I. *Ps.* 105:9
*Amos* 7:9 high places of I.
*Mat.* 1:2 Abraham begat I. and I. begat J. *Luke* 3:34; *Acts* 7:8
8:11 many shall sit down with I.
*Luke* 13:28 see I. in kingd. of G.
*Rom.* 9:10 conceived by father I.
*Gal.* 4:28 we, as I. was, are of pro.
*Heb.* 11:9 in tabernacles with I.
17 Abraham offered up I.
20 I. blessed Jacob, *Jam.* 2:21

**ISAIAH, *or* ESAIAS.**

2 *K.* 19:2 Eliakim to I. *Is.* 37:2
20:1 I. came to him, *Is.* 38:1
2 *Chr.* 26:22 acts did I. wr. 32:32
*Is.* 20:3 my serv. I. hath walked
*Mat.* 3:3 pro. E. 4:14; 8:17; 12:17; 13:14; *Luke* 3:4; *John* 1:23
15:7 E. proph. of you, *Mark* 7:6
*Luke* 4:17 book of prophet E.
*John* 12:39 bec. that E. said, 41
*Acts* 8:28 the eunuch read E. 30
28:25 spake the H. Ghost by E.
*Rom.* 9:27 E. crieth conc. Israel
10:16 E. saith, L. who hath? 20
15:12 E. saith, There shall be

ISCARIOT. *See* JUDAS.

ISH-BOSHETH. 2 *Sam.* 2:8; 3:8, 14; 4:8, 12

**ISHMAEL.**

*Gen.* 16:11 call name I. 15, 16
17:18 O that I. mi. live, 20, 25
25:17 these are the years of I.
28:9 then went Esau unto I.
2 *K.* 25:23 I. came to, *Jer.* 40:8
*Jer.* 40:14 Ammon. sent I. 15, 16
41:6 I. went to meet th. 10, 15

**ISHMAELITES.**

*Gen.* 37:27 let us sell him to I.
39:1 Potiphar bought him of I.
*Jud.* 8:24 because they were I.
*Ps.* 83:6 I. confederate ag. thee

**ISLAND.**

*Job* 22:30 deliver *i.* of innocent
*Is.* 34:14 meet wild beasts of *i.*
*Acts* 27:16 running under cert. *i.*
26 must be cast on certain *i.*
28:1 knew *i.* was called Melita
7 possess. of chief man of *i.*
28:9 who had diseases in *i.*
*Rev.* 6:14 every *i.* was moved out
16:20 every *i.* fled away

**ISLANDS.**

*Is.* 11:11 receive people from *i.*
13:22 wild beasts of *i.* shall cry
41:1 keep silence bef. me, O *i.*
42:12 declare Lord's praise in *i.*
15 make rivers *i.* dry up pools
59:18 the *i.* he will pay recomp.
*Jer.* 50:39 wild beasts of *i.* dwell

**ISLE.**

*Is.* 20:6 the inhabitants of the *i.*
23:2 be still, inhabitants of *i.*
6 howl, ye inhabitants of the *i.*
*Acts* 13:6 through *i.* to Paphos
28:11 ship which wintered in *i.*
*Rev.* 1:9 was in *i.* called Patmos

**ISLES.**

*Gen.* 10:5 th. were *i.* of Gentiles
*Est.* 10:1 A. laid a tribute on *i.*
*Ps.* 72:10 kings of *i.* bring pres.
97:1 let multitudes of *i.* be glad
*Is.* 24:15 glorify Lord in the *i.*
40:15 tak. up *i.* as a little thing
41:5 the *i.* saw it and feared
42:4 the *i.* shall wait for his law
49:1 listen, O *i.* unto me
51:5 *i.* shall wait upon me and trust, 60:9
66:19 *i.* afar off not heard fame
*Jer.* 2:10 pass over *i.* of Chittim
25:22 kings of *i.* drink after th.
*Ezek.* 26:15 sh. not *i.* sh. at sou.?
18 *i.* tremble, *i.* shall be troub.
27:3 merch. of peo. for many *i.*
6 brought out of *i.* of Chittim
7 blue and purple from *i.* of E.
15 many *i.* were merchandise
35 inhabit. of *i.* be astonished
39:6 dwell carelessly in the *i.*
*Dan.* 11:18 sh. turn his face to *i.*
*Zep.* 2:11 *i.* of heathen worship

**ISRAEL.**

*Gen.* 32:28 na. no more J. but I.
35:10 I. sh. be name, 1 *K.* 18:31
47:31 I. bowed him. on bed's h.
48:20 in thee sh. I. bless, 49:24
*Ex.* 5:2 voice to let I. go, 14:5, 30
*Num.* 10:29 good concerning I.
36 return to I. 20:14; 21:2, 17
23:7 defy I.; 24:17 out of I.
*Deut.* 33:28 I. dwell, 1 *K.* 4:25
1 *Chr.* 29:18 G. of I. 1 *K.* 18:36; 2 *Chr.* 6:16; 30:6; *Jer.* 31:1
*Ps.* 14:7 I. shall be glad, 53:6
25:22 redeem I. out of all troub.
121:4 that keepeth I. nei. slum.
125:5 peace sh. be upon I. 128:6
*Jer.* 14:8 O Lord, hope of I. 17:13
50:20 iniquity of I. sought, 51:5
*Hos.* 11:1 I. a child, I loved him
8 how deliver thee, I.? 12:12
*Acts* 28:20 for hope of I. bought
*Rom.* 9:6 not all I. of I. 27, 31
10:1 prayer for I. they be saved
19 did not I. know?
11:2 intercession ag. I. 7, 26
1 *Cor.* 10:18 behold I. after flesh
*Gal.* 6:16 peace upon the I. of G.

**O ISRAEL.**

*Ex.* 32:4 these be thy gods, *O* I.
*Num.* 24:5 thy tabernacles, *O* I.
*Deut.* 4:1 hearken, *O* I. 27:9
5:1 *O* I. 6:3, 4; 9:1; 20:3; *Ps.* 50:7; *Is.* 44:1; 48:12
33:29 happy th. *O* I. *Mark* 12:29
2 *Sam.* 20:1 ev. man to his tents, *O* I. 1 *K.* 12:16; 2 *Chr.* 10:16
1 *K.* 12:28 behold thy gods, *O* I.
*Ps.* 115:9 *O* I. trust thou in Lord
*Is.* 40:27 why speak. thou, *O* I.?
43:1 *O* I. fear not, 22; *Jer.* 30:10
44:21 remember these, *O* I. 49:3
*Jer.* 4:1 return, *O* I. *Hos.* 14:1
*Ezek.* 13:4 *O* I. thy prophets
*Hos.* 9:1 rejoice not, *O* I. for joy
10:9 *O* I. thou hast sinned from
13:9 *O* I. thou hast destr. thys.
*Amos* 4:12 to meet thy God, *O* I.
*Zep.* 3:14 shout *O* I. be glad

**ISRAELITE.**

*Num.* 25:14 the I. that was slain
2 *Sam.* 17:25 son of Ithra, an I.
*John* 1:47 behold an I. indeed
*Rom.* 11:1 I also am an I.

**ISRAELITES.**

*Ex.* 9:7 not one of cattle of I.
*Lev.* 23:42 I. shall dwell in booths
*Jos.* 3:17 I. passed on dry ground
1 *Chr.* 9:2 first inhabit. were I.
*Rom.* 9:4 I. to whom pertaineth
2 *Cor.* 11:22 are they I.? so am I.

ISRAELITISH. *Lev.* 24:10, 11

**ISSACHAR.**

*Gen.* 30:18 L. called his name I.
35:23 L. son, I. 46:13; 1 *Chr.* 7:1
49:14 I. is a strong ass
*Deut.* 27:12 I. st. to bless, 33:18
1 *K.* 4:17 Jehosh. an officer in I.
1 *Chr.* 12:40 that were nigh to I.
26:5 I. seventh son of O.-edom
2 *Chr.* 30:18 I. had not cleansed
*Ezek.* 48:25 border of Simeon, I.

**Tribe of ISSACHAR.**

*Num.* 1:29 numbered of *t. of* I.
2:5 next Judah shall be *t. of* I.
34:26 prince of *t. of* I. Paltiel
*Jos.* 19:23 inheritance of *t. of* I.
21:6 families of *tribe of* I. and Asher, 28: 1 *Chr* 6:62, 72
*Rev.* 7:7 *t. of* I. were seal. 12,000

**ISSUE, Substantive.**

*Gen.* 48:6 *i.* which th. begettest
*Lev.* 12:7 *i.* of blood, 15:25; *Mat.* 9:20; *Mark* 5:25; *Luke* 8:43, 44
15:2 hath running *i.* 3; 22:4
8 he that hath *i.* spit upon, 28
*Is.* 22:24 the offspring and *i.*
*Ezek.* 23:20 *i.* like the *i.* of horses
*Mat.* 22:25 having no *i.* left wife

**ISSUE.**

2 *K.* 20:18 sons that *i.* *Is.* 39:7
*Ezek.* 47:8 waters *i.* toward east

**ISSUED.**

*Job* 38:8 break forth as if it *i.*
*Ezek.* 47:1 waters *i.* from under
12 waters *i.* out of sanctuary
*Dan.* 7:10 fiery str. *i.* came forth
*Rev.* 9:17 out of mouth *i.* fire 18

**ISSUES.**

*Ps.* 68:20 to God belong the *i.*
*Prov.* 4:23 out of heart are *i.*

ITALIAN. *Acts* 10:1

**ITALY.**

*Acts* 18:2 cert. Jew come from I.
27:1 that we should sail into I.
*Heb.* 13:24 they of I. salute you

**ITCH, ING.**

*Deut.* 28:27 L. smite thee with *i.*
*2 Tim.* 4:3 teachers having *i.* ears

**ITHAMAR.**

*Ex.* 6:23 Abihu and I. 1 *Chr.* 6:3
*Num.* 4:28 under hand of I.
1 *Chr.* 24:3 Abimel. of sons of I.
*Ezr.* 8:2 of sons of I. Daniel

**ITHIEL.**

*Neh.* 11:7 I. son of Jes. *Prov.* 30:1

ITUREA. *Luke* 3:1

**IVAH.**

2 *K.* 18:34 gods of Hena and I.?
19:13 wh. king of I.? *Is.* 37:13

**IVORY.**

1 *K.* 10:18 throne of *i.* 2 *Chr.* 9:17
22 silver and *i.* 2 *Chr.* 9:21
22:39 *i.* house wh. Ahab made
*Ps.* 45:8 out of the *i.* palaces
*Cant.* 5:14 his belly as bright *i.*
7:4 thy neck is as a tower of *i.*
*Ezek.* 27:6 thy benches of *i.*
15 bro. for present horns of *i.*
*Amos* 3:15 houses of *i.* sh. perish
6:4 that lie upon beds of *i.*
*Rev.* 18:12 no man buy. ves. of *i.*

# J

**JAAZANIAH.**

2 *K.* 25:23 J. came to Gedaliah
*Jer.* 35:3 J. of Rechab. *Ezek.* 8:11

JABAL. *Gen.* 4:20
JABBOK. *Gen.* 32:22; *Deut.* 2:37; 3:16; *Jos.* 12:2

**JABESH.**

1 *Sam.* 11:5 S. of men of J. 31:12
2 *K.* 15:10 the son of J. conspired

**JABESH-GILEAD.**

*Jud.* 21:8 none fr. J.-G. 10, 12, 14
1 *Sam.* 11:1 Naha. enc. ag. J.-G.
31:11 J.-G. heard Phi. had done, 1 *Chr.* 10:12
2 *Sam.* 2:4 men of J.-G. 21:12

JABEZ. 1 *Chr.* 2:55; 4:9, 10

**JABIN.**

*Jos.* 11:1 when J. king of Hazor
*Jud.* 4:2 sold into hand of J. 24
*Ps.* 83:9 do to them as unto J.

**JACHIN.**

1 *K.* 7:21 right h. J. 2 *Chr.* 3:17

**JACINTH.**

*Rev.* 9:17 breastplates of fire, *j.*
21:20 eleventh found. was a *j.*

**JACOB.**

*Gen.* 25:26 he was called J. 27
*Num.* 23:7 curse me, J. and defy
24:17 sh. come a Star out of J.
*Deut.* 33:28 of J. on land of corn
*Ps.* 20:1 God of J. 46:7; 75:9; 76:6; 81:1; 84:8; 94:7; 114:7; 132:2; 146:5
87:2 Z. more than dwell. of J.
105:23 J. sojourned in land of H.
135:4 L. chos. J. *Is.* 10:21; 14:1
*Is.* 2:3 of J. 41:21; *Mic.* 4:2; *Mat.* 22:32; *Mark* 12:26; *Luke* 20:37; *Acts* 3:13; 7:32, 46
27:9 iniq. of J. purged, 48:20
41:14 thou worm J. *Jer.* 30:10
44:5 call himself by name J. 23
58:14 feed with heritage of J.
*Amos* 7:2 by whom sh. J. arise? 5
*Mal.* 1:2 J. yet I loved J. *Ro.* 9:13
3:6 sons of J. not consumed
*Mat.* 1:2 I. begat J.; 15 Matthan
8:11 J. in king. of G. *Luke* 13:28
*John* 4:6 J.'s well was there
*Rom.* 11:26 turn ungodl. from J.
*Heb.* 11:20 by faith Is. bles. J. 21

**JAEL.**

*Jud.* 4:17 fled to tent of J. 5:6

JAH. *Ps.* 68:4

**JAHAZ.**

*Num.* 21:23 fou. at J. *Deut.* 2:32
*Is.* 15:4 heard to J. *Jud.* 11:20

**JAHAZAH.**

*Jos.* 21:36 J. to Lev. *Jer.* 48:21

**JAILER.**

*Acts* 16:23 chargin. *j.* to keep

**JAIR.**

*Num.* 32:41 J. took to. *Deut.* 3:14
*Jud.* 10:3 J. judged Is. 22 years
5 J. died; 1 *Chr.* 2:22 begat J.

**JAIRUS.**

*Mark* 5:22 J. a ruler, *Luke* 8:41

JAMBRES. 2 *Tim.* 3:8

**JAMES.**

*Mat.* 4:21 J. and John, *Mark* 1:19
10:2 J. son of Zeb. *Mark* 3:17
3 J. son, *Mark* 3:18; *Acts* 1:13
13:55 J. and Joses, *Mark* 6:3; 15:40; 16:1; *Luke* 24:10
17:1 Peter, J. and John, *Mark* 5:37; 9:2; 13:3; 14:33; *Luke* 8:51; *Acts* 1:13
*Mark* 10:41 displ. wi. J. *Lu.* 5:10
*Acts* 12:2 Herod killed J. wi. sw.
17 show to J. 15:13; 21:18
1 *Cor.* 15:7 after that seen of J.
*Gal.* 1:19 save J. Lord's brother
2:12 certain came from J. 9

**JANGLING.**

1 *Tim.* 1:6 turned aside to vain *j.*

JANNA. *Luke* 3:24
JANNES. 2 *Tim.* 3:8

**JAPHETH.**

*Gen.* 5:32 J. son of N. 6:10; 7:13
9:23 Shem and J. took garm. 18
27 God sh. enlarge J. 1 *Chr.* 1:4
10:1 unto J. sons born, 21

JAREB. *Hos.* 5:13; 10:6
JARED. *Gen.* 5:15; *Luke* 3:37
JASHER. *Jos.* 10:13; 2 *Sam.* 1:18

**JASON.**

*Acts* 17:5 house of J. *Rom.* 16:21

**JASPER.**

*Ex.* 28:20 onyx and *j.* 39:13
*Ezek.* 28:13 diamond and *j.* cov.
*Rev.* 4:3 to look upon like a *j.*
21:11 light was like to *j.* stone
18 build. of wall of city was *j.*
19 the first foundation was *j.*

**JAVAN.**

*Gen.* 10:2 sons of Jap. J. 1 *Chr.* 1:5
*Is.* 66:19 those that escape to J.
*Ezek.* 27:13 J. and Tubal thy, 19

**JAVELIN.**

*Num.* 25:7 took a *j.* in his hand
1 *Sam.* 18:10 *j.* in S. hand, 19:9
19:10 he smote the *j.* into wall

**JAW, S.**

*Jud.* 15:19 God clave place in *j.*
*Job* 29:17 I break *j.* of the wicked
41:2 bore *j.* thro' with a thorn?
*Ps.* 22:15 tongue cleaveth to *j.*
*Is.* 30:28 a bridle in *j.* of people
*Hos.* 11:4 take off yoke on their *j.*

**JAWBONE.**

*Jud.* 15:15 Samson found *j.* of ass
16 with *j.* of ass have I slain
17 cast away *j.* out of his hand

**JAW-TEETH.**

*Prov.* 30:14 their *j.-t.* as knives

**JAZER.**

*Num.* 32:1 land of J. 3; *Is.* 16:9

**JEALOUS.**

*Ex.* 20:5 I the Lord thy G. am a *j.* God, 34:14; *Deut.* 4:24; 5:9; 6:15; *Jos.* 24:19
*Num.* 5:14 he be *j.* of his wife
1 *K.* 19:10 have been *j.* for L. 14
*Ezek.* 39:25 *j.* for my holy name
*Joel* 2:18 then will the L. be *j.*
*Nah.* 1:2 God is *j.* and L. reven.
*Zec.* 1:14 *j.* for Jer.; 8:2 *j.* for Z.
2 *Cor.* 11:2 for I am *j.* over you

**JEALOUSY.**

*Num.* 5:14 sp. of *j.* come on him
15 it is an offering of *j.* 18, 25
29 this is the law of *j.*
25:11 consumed not Is. in my *j.*
*Deut.* 29:20 *j.* smoke ag. man
32:16 prov. him to *j.* 1 *K.* 14:22
21 moved me to *j.* them to *j.*
*Ps.* 78:58 mov. to *j.* with images
79:5 how long, L. sh. thy *j.* bu.?
*Prov.* 6:34 *j.* is the rage of man
*Cant.* 8:6 *j.* is cruel as the grave
*Is.* 42:13 stir up *j.* like man of w.
*Ezek.* 8:3 wh. seat image of *j.*? 5
16:38 give blood in fury and *j.*
42 my *j.* shall depart from thee
23:25 I will set my *j.* ag. thee
36:5 in *j.* have I spok. 6; 38:19
*Zep.* 1:18 land dev. by *j.* 3:8
*Zec.* 1:14 jealous for Z. wi. *j.* 8:2
*Rom.* 10:19 will provoke you to *j.*
11:11 Gen. to provoke them to *j.*
1 *Cor.* 10:22 do we prov. L. to *j.*?
2 *Cor.* 11:2 jealous with godly *j.*

**JEBUSITE.**

*Gen.* 10:16 Canaan begat the J.
*Ex.* 33:2 will drive out J. 34:11
2 *Sam.* 24:16, 18; 1 *Chr.* 1:14; 21:15

**JEBUSITES.**

*Num.* 13:29 J. dw. in mountains
*Jos.* 15:63 J. dw. with children
*Jud.* 1:21 driveth J. 19:11; 2 *Sam.* 5:8

JECONIAH. 1 *Chr.* 3:16, 17; *Jer.* 24:1; 27:20; 28:4
JEDIDIAH. 2 *Sam.* 12:25
JEDUTHUN. 1 *Chr.* 16:41, 42; 25:6; 2 *Chr.* 29:14

**JEGAR-SAHADUTHA.**

*Gen.* 31:47 La. called heap J.-S.

**JEHOAHAZ,** *called Ahaziah.*

2 *K.* 10:35 J. son of Jehu reigned
13:1 J. son of J. began to reign
23:30 peo. took J. 2 *Chr.* 21:17

**JEHOASH,** *or* **JOASH.**

2 *K.* 11:21 J. seven years old
12:20 slew J. in house M. 13:10
14:8 messengers to J.; J. slept

**JEHOIACHIN.**
2 *K.* 24:8 J. 18 years old when he
25:27 lift head of J. *Jer.* 52:31
2 *Chr.* 36:9 J. eight years old

**JEHOIADA.**
2 *Sam.* 8:18 son of J. 20:23; 1 *Chr.* 11:22, 24; 1 *K.* 1:44; 4:4
2 *K.* 11:17 J. ma. cov. 2 *Chr.* 23:16
2 *Chr.* 24:2 all days of J. 17; 22
*Jer.* 29:26 thee pri. instead of J.

**JEHOIAKIM.**
2 *K.* 23:34 name to J. 2 *Chr.* 36:4
*Jer.* 22:18 concerning J. 26:22
36:28 J. burnt, 30; *Dan.* 1:2
52:2 did wh. was evil as J. had

JEHONADAB. 2 *K.* 10:15, 23

**JEHORAM.**
1 *K.* 22:50 J. son of Jeh. 2 *K.* 8:16
2 *K.* 1:17 J. reigned, 2 *Chr.* 17:8
2 *Chr.* 21:9 J. smote Edom. 16
22:5 went with J. ag. Hazael, 7

**JEHOSHAPHAT.**
2 *Sam.* 8:16 J. recorder, 20:24
1 *K.* 4:3, 17; 15:24; 1 *Chr.* 18:15
22:2 J. came to Ahab, 2 *K.* 3:14
1 *Chr.* 15:24 J. blew with trump.
2 *Chr.* 17:3 L. was with J. 18:9, 28
20:3 J. feared Lord, 21:12; 22:9
*Joel* 3:2 down to valley of J. 12

**JEHOSHUA.**
*Num.* 13:16 Oshea J. 1 *Chr.* 7:27

**JEHOVAH.**
*Ex.* 6:3 by J. was I not known
*Ps.* 83:18 wh. name alone is J.
*Is.* 12:2 Lord J. is my strength
26:4 the Lord J. is everlasting

JEHOVAH-JIREH. *Gen.* 22:14
JEHOVAH-NISSI. *Ex.* 17:15
JEHOVAH-SHALOM. *Jud.* 6:24

**JEHU.**
1 *K.* 16:1 J. son of H. 2 *Chr.* 20:34
19:16 J. son of Nimshi shalt
2 *K.* 9:2 look there J. 13, 14, 24
10:11 J. slew all remain. 18, 31
2 *Chr.* 19:2 J. to meet Jeh. 22:8
*Hos.* 1:4 blood of Jezreel on J.

**JEOPARDED.**
*Jud* 5:18 peo. that *j.* their lives

**JEOPARDY.**
2 *Sam.* 23:17 men that went in *j.* of their lives, 1 *Chr.* 11:19
1 *Chr.* 12:19 to *j.* of our heads
*Luke* 8:23 water, they were in *j.*
1 *Cor.* 15:30 why stand we in *j.*?

**JEPHTHAH.**
*Jud.* 11:1 J. mighty, 3, 11, 40
12:7 J. judged Israel six years
1 *Sam.* 12:11 L. sent J. and del.
*Heb.* 11:32 would fail to tell of J.

JEPHUNNEH. *Num.* 13:6; 1 *Chr.* 7:38
JERAHMEEL. 1 *Chr.* 2:9, 33; 24:29; *Jer.* 36:26

**JEREMIAH.**
2 *K.* 23:31; 24:18; *Jer.* 52:1
2 *Chr.* 35:25 J. lamented for Jos.
36:12 humb. bef. J. 22; *Ezr.* 1:1
*Neh.* 10:2 J. sealed, 12:1, 12, 34
*Jer.* 1:1 words of J. son of Hilk.
51:64 thus far are words of J.
*Mat.* 2:17 was spoken by J. 27:9
16:14 others say thou art J.

**JERICHO.**
*Jos.* 2:1 view J. 3:16; 6:1; 24:11
6:26 cursed man that buildeth J.
1 *K.* 16:34 days did Hiel build J.
*Luke* 10:30 went down to J.
*Heb.* 11:30 walls of J. fell

**JEROBOAM.**
1 *K.* 11:28 J. mighty man of valor
40 Solomon sought to kill J.
13:1 J. st. by altar, 14:1, 6, 30
2 *K.* 10:31; 13:6, 13; 14:24
2 *Chr.* 11:14 J. cast off L. 13:8, 20
*Amos* 7:11 Am. saith, J. shall die

**JEROBOAM,** *with* **Nebat.**
1 *K.* 11:26; 12:15; 16:3, 26, 31; 21:22; 22:52; 2 *K.* 3:3; 9:9; 10:29; 13:2, 11; 14:24; 15:9, 18, 24, 28; 2 *Chr.* 10:15

JERUBBAAL. *Jud.* 6:32; 7:1; 8:29,35; 9:2,5,16,28; 1 *Sam.* 12:11
JERUBBESHETH. 2 *Sam.* 11:21

**JERUSALEM.**
*Jos.* 18:28 wh. is J. *Jud.* 19:10
2 *Sam.* 24:16 on J. 1 *Chr.* 21:15
1 *K.* 3:1 end of build. wall of J.
11:13 J. I have chosen, 2 *K.* 23:27; 2 *Chr.* 6:6
*Ps.* 51:18 build walls of J. 79:1, 3; 147:2
122:3 J. is builded as a city
6 pray for peace of J. 128:5
125:2 as mount. round about J.
137:6 pref. not J. abo. ch. joy, 7
*Is.* 31:5 defend J. 33:20
40:2 sp. comfortably to J. 52:9
62:1 for J.'s sake not rest till, 7
64:10 J. a desola. *Jer.* 2:2; 9:11
*Jer.* 39:8 walls of J. 44:2, 6
*Joel* 3:1 bring captivi. of J. 20; *Zec.* 14:11
*Zec.* 1:17 choose J. 2:12; 8:3
*Mal.* 3:4 offering of J. sh. be ple.
*Mat.* 3:5 out to him J. *Mark* 1:5
16:21 how he must go to J.
*Luke* 2:22 parents bro. him to J.
13:4 above all dwelt in J.?
33 prophet perish out of J.
21:20 J. comp. with armies, 24
24:49 tarry in J.; 47 begin. at J.
*John* 4:20 in J. men ou. to wors.
12:12 heard Jesus coming to J.
*Acts* 9:2 bound unto J. 20:22
21:31 all J. in uproar, 22:18
*Rom.* 15:31 service for J. accept, 1 *Cor.* 16:3
*Gal.* 4:25 J. wh. now is; 26 J. ab.
*Rev.* 3:12 the new J. 21:2, 10

**O JERUSALEM.**
*Ps.* 116:19 midst of thee, *O* J.
122:2 within thy gates, *O* J.
137:5 if I forget, *O* J. 147:12
*Is.* 40:9 *O* J. that bringest good
51:17 up, *O* J.; 52:2 arise, *O* J.
52:1 put on thy garments, *O* J.
*Jer.* 4:14 *O* J. wash thy heart fr.
6:8 be thou instructed, *O* J.
7:29 cut off thy hair, *O* J. and
13:27 *O* J. wilt not be made cl.
15:5 pity upon thee, *O* J.?
*Mat.* 23:37 *O* J. J. *Luke* 13:34

JESHUA. *Ezr.* 2:2; 3:2

**JESHURUN.**
*Deut.* 32:15 J. wax. fat, 33:5, 26
*Is.* 44:2 fear not, thou J.

**JESSE.**
*Ruth* 4:17 O. fath. of J. *Mat.* 1:5
1 *Sam.* 16:1 J. the Beth-lehemite
9 sanctified J. and sons, 18, 19
20:31 as long as son of J. liveth
22:7 son of J. give fields? 8, 9
25:10 who is David? son of J.?
2 *Sam.* 20:1 son of J. 1 *K.* 12:16
1 *Chr.* 12:18 son of J. 2 *Chr.* 10:16
*Is.* 11:1 rod out of the stem of J.
10 a root of J. *Rom.* 15:12
*Acts* 13:22 found David son of J.

**JESTING.**
*Eph.* 5:4 nor *j.* not convenient

JESUITES. *Num.* 26:44

**JESUS.**
*Mat.* 1:21 shalt call his name J.

**JESUS,** *for Joshua.*
*Acts* 7:45 brought in with J. into
*Heb.* 4:8 if J. had given th. rest

JESUS, called *Justus.* *Col.* 4:11

**JETHRO,** *called Reuel.*
*Ex.* 3:1 kept flock of J. his fath.
4:18 Moses returned to J. his
18:1 when J. heard, 5, 6, 9, 12

**JEW.**
*Est.* 3:4 told them he was a J.
*Rom.* 1:16 to J. first, 2:9, 10
2:17 a J. and restest in law
28 he is not a J. 29
3:1 what advantage J.? 10:12; *Gal.* 3:28; *Col.* 3:11
1 *Cor.* 9:20 to J. a J. to gain J.
*Gal.* 2:14 a J. livest as Gentiles

**JEWEL.**
*Prov.* 11:22 *j.* of gold swine's sn.
20:15 lips of knowl. precious *j.*
*Ezek.* 16:12 I put a *j.* on forehead

**JEWELS.**
*Gen.* 24:53 bro. forth *j.* of silver
*Ex.* 3:22 shall borrow *j.* of gold, 11:2; 12:35
35:22 they brought all *j.* of gold
*Num.* 31:51 took gold, even the *j.*
1 *Sam.* 6:8 *j.* of gold in coffer, 15
2 *Chr.* 20:25 riches and preci. *j.*
32:27 treasuries for all pleas. *j.*
*Job* 28:17 excha. of it not be for *j.*
*Cant.* 1:10 cheeks comely with *j.*
7:1 joints of thy thighs like *j.*
*Is.* 61:10 adorneth herself with *j.*
*Ezek.* 16:17 thy *j.* of my gold
39 shall take thy fair *j.* 23:26
*Hos.* 2:13 decked wi. ear.-r. and *j.*
*Mal.* 3:17 when I make up my *j.*

**King of the JEWS.**
*Mat.* 2:2 born *K. of the J.*?
27:11 art thou *K. of t. J.*? *Mar.* 15:2; *Luke* 23:3; *John* 18:33
29 hail, *K. of the J. Mar.* 15:18; *John* 19:3
37 this is *K. of the J. Mark* 15:26; *Luke* 23:38; *Jo.* 19:19
*Mark* 15:9 *K. of the J. John* 18:39
12 whom ye call *K. of the J.*
*Luke* 23:37 if thou be *K. of the J.*
*John* 19:21 I am *K. of the J.*

JEWESS. *Acts* 16:1; 24:24
JEWISH. *Tit.* 1:14
JEWRY. *Dan.* 5:13

**JEZEBEL.**
1 *K.* 16:31 took to wife J. 18:4
21:11 as J. had sent, 15, 23, 25
2 *K.* 9:7 at the hand of J. 10, 36
*Rev.* 2:20 sufferest that wom. J.

**JEZREEL,** *place and person.*
2 *Sam.* 2:9 Ish-bosh. king over J.
1 *K.* 18:45 Ahab went to J. 21:1
21:23 eat Jez. by J. 2 *K.* 9:10
2 *K.* 8:29 went to J. 2 *Chr.* 22:6
10:6 come to me to J. to-morrow
*Hos.* 1:4 avenge blood of J.
5 break bow in valley of J. 11
2:22 wine, and oil shall hear J.

**JOAB.**
2 *Sam.* 2:18 of Zeruiah, J. 22, 24
3:29 Ab. rest on J. 8:16; 20:23
11:7 demand. how J. did, 11, 14
14:3 J. put words in mo. 19, 30
20:9 J. killed Amasa, 17
1 *K.* 1:7 Adonijah confer. with J.
2:28 J. fled to tabernacle of L.
1 *Chr.* 4:14; 11:6; 18:15; 27:34
*Ezr.* 2:6 of chil. of J. *Neh.* 7:11

**JOAH.**
2 *K.* 18:18 J. son of As. *Is.* 36:3
1 *Chr.* 6:21 J. son of Zim. 26:4

JOANNA. *Luke* 3:27; 8:3

**JOASH.**
*Jud.* 6:11 to J. Abi-ezrite, 7:14

1 *K.* 22:26 back to J. king's son
2 *K.* 11:2 st. J. 2 *Chr.* 18:25; 24:22

**JOB.**

*Gen.* 46:13 sons of Issachar, J.
*Job* 1:1 man whose name was J.
42:17 J. died, being old
*Ezek.* 14:14 though D. and J. 20
*Jam.* 5:11 heard of patience of J.

**JOEL.**

1 *Sam.* 8:2 Samuel's first-born, J.
1 *Chr.* 15:11 David called J. 27:20
*Joel* 1:1 the word came to J.
*Acts* 2:16 spok. by the proph. J.

**JOHANAN.**

2 *K.* 25:23 J. ca. to G. *Jer.* 40:8
1 *Chr.* 3:15 sons of J. J. *Ezr.* 10:6
*Jer.* 41:11 wh. J. heard of all evil

**JOHN,** *son of Zacharias.*

*Mat.* 3:4 J. had raim *Mark* 1:6
*Mat.* 3:14 J. came, but J. for. him
14:10 behe. J. *Mark* 6:16; *Lu.* 9:9
21:26 hol. J. *Mar.* 11:32; *Lu.* 20:6
*Luke* 1:13 call his name J. 60
9:7 J. was risen from the dead
*John* 1:6 a man sent from God, J.
*Acts* 13:24 when J. first preached

**JOHN,** *the Apostle.*

*Mat.* 4:21 James and J. he called
th. 10:2; *Mark* 1:19; 3:17
*Luke* 22:8 Pet. and J. to prepare
*Acts* 3:1 Peter and J. went
12:2 Herod killed brother of J.
*Rev.* 1:1 signifi. it to serv. J. 4, 9
21:2 J. saw the new Jerusalem

JOHN. *Acts* 4:6
JOHN, surnamed *Mark. Acts* 12:12, 25; 13:5, 13; 15:37

**JOIN.**

*Ex.* 1:10 lest they *j.* enemies
*Ezr.* 9:14 *j.* in affinity with peo.
*Prov.* 11:21 hand *j.* in ha. 16:5
*Is.* 5:8 woe to them *j.* house
9:11 L. *j.* his enemies together
56:6 sons of stranger *j.* thems.
*Jer.* 50:5 let us *j.* ourselves to L.
*Ezek.* 37:17 *j.* th. one to another
*Acts* 5:13 no man *j.* himself
8:29 *j.* thyself to this chariot
9:26 Saul assayed to *j.* himself

**JOINED.**

*Gen.* 14:3 all these kings were *j.*
29:34 this time husb. be *j.* to me
2 *Chr.* 20:36 *j.* with Ahaziah, 37
*Ezr.* 4:12 up walls, *j.* foundatio.
*Job* 3:6 not be *j.* to days of year
41:17 leviathan's scales are *j.*
23 flakes of his flesh *j.* togeth.
*Ps.* 83:8 A. also is *j.* with them
*Ec.* 9:4 *j.* to all living is hope
*Is.* 13:15 every one *j.* them
14:1 strangers be *j.* with them
20 not *j.* with them in burial
56:3 nor him hath *j.* to L. speak
*Ezek.* 1:9 wings *j.* one to another
*Hos.* 4:17 Ephraim is *j.* to idols
*Zec.* 2:11 many nations *j.* to L.
*Mat.* 19:6 what G. *j.* *Mark* 10:9
*Luke* 15:15 *j.* himself to citizen
*Acts* 5:36 four hund. *j.* themsel.
18:7 house *j.* hard to synagogue
1 *Cor.* 1:10 perfect. *j.* in sa. mind
6:16 *j.* to a harlot is one body
17 *j.* to the Lord is one spirit
*Eph.* 4:16 whole body fitly *j.*
5:31 and shall be *j.* to his wife

*See* BAAL-PEOR.

**JOINING, S.**

1 *Chr.* 22:3 prepared iron for *j.*
2 *Chr.* 3:12 *j.* to wing of cherub

**JOINT.**

*Gen.* 32:25 Jac.'s thigh out of *j.*
*Ps.* 22:14 my bones are out of *j*
*Prov.* 25:19 like foot out of *j.*
*Eph.* 4:16 wh. every *j.* supplieth

**JOINTS.**

1 *K.* 22:34 smote king of I. betw. *j.* of harness, 2 *Chr.* 18:33
*Cant.* 7:1 *j.* of thighs like jewels
*Dan.* 5:6 *j.* of loins were loosed
*Col.* 2:19 body by *j.* knit togeth.
*Heb.* 4:12 divid. of *j.* and marrow

**JOINT-HEIRS.**

*Rom.* 8:17 and *j.-h.* with Christ

**JONADAB,** *or* **JEHONADAB.**

2 *Sam.* 13:3 J. Amnon's friend
2 *K.* 10:15 J. came to meet Jehu
*Jer.* 35:6 J. commanded us, 18

**JONAH,** *or* **JONAS.**

2 *K.* 14:25 spake by his servant J.
*Jon.* 1:3 J. rose up, 7, 15, 17
4:6 the gourd to come over J.
*Mat.* 12:39, 41; 16:4; *Lu.* 11:29, 30
*John* 21:15 Simon son of J. 16, 17

**JONATHAN.**

*Jud.* 18:30 J. and his sons were
1 *Sam.* 13:2 men were with J. 22
14:13 J. climbed on hands
20:13 the Lord do so to J. 16. 37
2 *Sam.* 1:4 S. and J. are dead, 26
4:4 J. had a son was lame, 9:3
*Jer.* 40:8 J. came to Gedal. to M.

**JOPPA.**

2 *Chr.* 2:16 by sea to J. *Ezr.* 3:7
*Jon.* 1:3 Jonah went down to J.
*Acts* 9:36 at J. a disciple, 43
10:5 send to J. call for Sim. 32
11:5 in the city of J. praying

**JORAM,** *called* **JEHORAM.**

2 *Sam.* 8:10 sent J. his son, to David
2 *K.* 8:16 J. of A.; 28 wound. J.
9:14 Jehu conspired ag. J. 24
1 *Chr.* 26:25 Levites J. over tre.
2 *Chr.* 22:7 destr. by com. to J.

**JORDAN.**

*Gen.* 13:11 Lot chose plain of J.
*Jos.* 3:15 J. overfloweth banks
4:3 stones out of midst of J.
22:25 made J. a border betw. us
*Jud.* 3:28 fords of J. 7:24; 12:5
2 *Sam.* 19:15 king returned to J.
2 *K.* 2:13 Elisha stood by J.
5:10 saying, Wash in J. seven
*Job* 40:23 trust. can draw up J.
*Ps.* 42:6 remember fr. land of J.
114:3 J. was driven back, 5
*Jer.* 12:5 do in swelling of J.?
49:19 from swelling of J. 50:44
*Zec.* 11:3 pride of J. is spoiled
*Mat.* 3:6 in J. *Mark* 1:5, 9

**Beyond JORDAN.**

*Gen.* 50:10 floor of Atad *bey.* J. 11
*Deut.* 3:25 good land *beyond* J.
*Jos.* 13:8 inherit. *beyond* J. 18:7
*Is.* 9:1 *bey.* J. in Galil. *Mat.* 4:15
*John* 1:28 Bethabara *bey.* J. 3:26

**Over JORDAN.**

*Gen.* 32:10 I passed *over* J.
*Num.* 32:5 br. us not *o.* J. 33:51
*Deut.* 3:27 not go *o.* J. 4:21; 31:2
9:1 to pass *o.* J. this day, 11:31
*Jos.* 1:2 go *over* J. 11
4:22 Israel came *over* J. 24:11
2 *Sam.* 2:29 passed *o.* J. 17:22; 19:15; 1 *Chr.* 12:15; 19:17

JORIM, JOSE. *Luke* 3:29

**JOSEPH.**

*Gen.* 30:24 she called his name J.
37:5 J. dreamed a dream
39:5 Egypt.'s house for J.'s sake
40:9 butler told his dream to J.
49:22 J. is a fruitful bough, 26
50:7 J. went up to bury father
*Deut.* 33:13 J. blessed be his land
1 *Chr.* 5:2 the birthright was J.
*Ps.* 80:1 leadest J. like a flock
105:17 J. who was sold for a ser.
*Ezek.* 37:16 for J. stick of Ephr.
47:13 J. shall have two portions
48:32 one gate of J. gate of B.
*Amos* 6:6 grieved for afflict. of J.
*Acts* 7:9 patriarchs sold J. 13, 14
*Heb.* 11:21 J. blessed sons of J. 22

**JOSEPH,** *husband of Mary.*

*Mat.* 1:16; 2:13; *Luke* 2:4; 3:23; 4:22; *John* 1:45; 6:42

**JOSEPH,** *name of divers men.*

*Num.* 13:7 of Igal, son of J.
*Mat.* 27:57 J. of Arim. 59; *Mark* 15:43, 45; *Lu.* 23:50; *Jo.* 19:38
*Luke* 3:24 was son of J. 26, 30
*Acts* 1:23 two, J. called Barsabas

**JOSES.**

*Mat.* 13:55 Ja. and J. *Mark* 6:3
27:56 moth. of J. *Mark* 15:40, 47
*Acts* 4:36 J. surnamed Barnabas

**JOSHUA, JEHOSHUA, OSHEA.**

*Ex.* 17:13 J. discomfited Amalek
24:13 Moses and his minister J.
*Jos.* 1:10 J. commanded officers, 2:1 to 24:31
1 *Sam.* 6:14 into field of J. 18
1 *K.* 16:34 wh. he spake by J.
*Hag.* 1:1 J. son of Josed. 12, 14
*Zec.* 3:1 showed me J. h.-priest
6:11 set crowns on head of J.

**JOSIAH.**

1 *K.* 13:2 child born, J. by name
2 *K.* 21:24 J. king, 2 *Chr.* 33:25
22:1 J. was eight years old
23:29 J. ag. Phar. 2 *Chr.* 35:22
2 *Chr.* 35:1 J. kept passo. 18–25
*Jer.* 1:2 in days of J. 3:6
*Zep.* 1:1 word came in days of J.
*Mat.* 1:10 Amon begat J. 11

**JOT.**

*Mat.* 5:18 one *j.* or tittle

**JOTHAM.**

*Jud.* 9:5 J. son of Jerubbaal, 21
2 *K.* 15:5 J. judged, 2 *Chr.* 26:21
1 *Chr.* 2:47 sons of Jahdai, J. 5:17
2 *Chr.* 27:6 J. became mighty
*Is.* 1:1; *Ho.* 1:1; *Mic.* 1:1; *Mat.* 1:9

**JOURNEY.**

*Gen.* 24:21 L. made *j.* prosperous
31:23 La. pursued him 7 days' *j.*
*Ex.* 13:20 took *j.* from Succoth
16:1 Israelites took *j.* from Elim
*Num.* 9:10 be in *j.* yet keep pass.
13 not in *j.* forbear. keep pass.
*Deut.* 1:2 eleven days *j.* from H.
10:11 take thy *j.* before people
*Jos.* 9:11 take victuals for your *j.*
*Jud.* 4:9 *j.* thou takest not
1 *Sam.* 15:18 L. sent thee on a *j.*
1 *K.* 18:27 or he is in a *j.*
19:7 the *j.* is too great for thee
2 *K.* 3:9 compa. of seven days' *j.*
*Neh.* 2:6 how long sh. thy *j.* be?
*Prov.* 7:19 man gone a long *j.*
*Mat.* 10:10 nor scrip for your *j.*
*Mark* 6:8 nothing for *j.* *Luke* 9:3
*Luke* 11:6 a friend of mine in *j.*
15:13 took *j.* into a far country
*John* 4:6 Jesus wearied with *j.*
*Rom.* 1:10 have prosperous *j.*
15:24 I trust to see you in my *j.*
1 *Cor.* 16:6 bring me on my *j.*
*Tit.* 3:13 Zenas and Apollos on *j.*
3 *John* 6 whom bring forw. on *j.*

**Day's JOURNEY.**

*Num.* 11:31 quails fall a *day's j.*
1 *K.* 19:4 went *day's j.* to wild.
*Jon.* 3:4 to enter city *d.'s j.*
*Luke* 2:44 a *d.'s j.* am. acquaint.
*Acts* 1:12 from Jerusal. a *day's j.*

*See Three* DAYS.

**JOURNEYED.**

*Gen.* 12:9 Ab. *j.* going south, 20:1
13:11 Lot *j.* east; 33:17 Jacob *j.*
35:5 Israel *j.* toward Beth-el
*Ex.* 40:37 th. *j.* not, *Num.* 9:21
*Num.* 9:17 children of Israel *j.* 18
19 kept charge of L. and *j.* not
*Acts* 9:3 as S. *j.* he came near Da.
7 men *j.* with him stood, 26:13

**JOURNEYING, S.**

*Num.* 10:28 *j.* of Israel's armies
29 we are *j.* to the place
*Luke* 13:22 as he was *j.* toward J.
2 *Cor.* 11:26 in *j.* often, in perils

**JOURNEYS.**

*Gen.* 13:3 Abram went on his *j.*
*Ex.* 17:1 *j.* according to comma.
40:36 went on in *j.* *Num.* 10:12
38 cloud on taber. thro' their *j.*
*Num.* 10:6 an alarm for their *j.*
33:1 these are the *j.* of Israel, 2

**JOY, Substantive.**

1 *Chr.* 12:40 there was *j.* in Israel
15:16 lift. up the voice with *j.*
25 went to bring the ark wi. *j.*
29:17 seen with *j.* the peo. offer
*Ezr.* 3:13 not discern shout of *j.*
6:16 ded. of hou. of God with *j.*
*Neh.* 8:10 *j.* of L. is your strength
12:43 *j.* of Jeru. heard afar off
*Est.* 8:16 light, *j.* and honor
9:22 turned from sorrow to *j.*
make days of feasting and *j.*
*Job* 8:19 this is the *j.* of his way
20:5 *j.* of hypocrite but for mo.
29:13 caus. widow's hea. sing *j.*
33:26 will see his face with *j.*
41:22 sorrow turned to *j.*
*Ps.* 16:11 presence fulness of *j.*
27:6 offer in tabern. sacrifi. of *j.*
30:5 *j.* cometh in the morning
42:4 I went with the voice of *j.*
43:4 I go to G. my exceeding *j.*
48:2 *j.* of the earth is mount Z.
51:12 restore to me *j.* of salva.
67:4 be glad and sing for *j.*
105:43 bro. forth people with *j.*
126:5 sow in tears sh. reap in *j.*
137:6 prefer not Jer. to chief *j.*
*Prov.* 12:20 counsel. of peace is *j.*
14:10 stranger not intermed. *j.*
15:21 folly is *j.* desti. of wisdom
23 man hath *j.* by ans. of mou.
17:21 father of a fool hath no *j.*
21:15 *j.* to the just to do judg.
23:24 beget. wise child have *j.*
*Ec.* 2:10 with. not heart from *j.*
26 God giveth knowled. and *j.*
5:20 God ans. him in *j.* of heart
9:7 go thy way, eat bread wi. *j.*
*Is.* 9:3 increased *j.* accord. to *j.*
17 L. sh. have no *j.* in yo. men
12:3 with *j.* shall ye draw water
16:10 *j.* taken out plentiful field
24:8 *j.* harp ceas.; 11 *j.* is dark.
29:19 meek sh. incre. th. *j.* in L.
32:13 houses of *j.*; 14 *j.* w. asses
35:2 rej. even with *j.* and sing.
10 everl. *j.* on their heads, 51:11
52:9 br. into *j.*; 55:12 go with *j.*
60:15 a *j.* of many generations
61:3 give them oil of *j.*
7 everlasting *j.* sh. be to them
65:14 servants shall sing for *j.*
18 beho. I create her peo. a *j.*
66:5 he shall appear to your *j.*
10 rejoice for *j.* with her
*Jer.* 15:16 word was *j.* of my hea.
31:13 turn th. mourning into *j.*
33:9 it sh. be to me a name of *j.*
11 there sh. be heard voice of *j.*
48:27 thou skippedst for *j.*
*Jer.* 48:33 *j.* is tak. fr. plen. field
49:25 city of my *j.*
*Lam.* 2:15 the *j.* of whole earth
5:15 the *j.* of our heart is ceased
*Ezek.* 24:25 take fr. them *j.* of gl.
36:5 with the *j.* of all th. heart
*Hos.* 9:1 rejoice not, O Is. for *j.*
*Joel* 1:12 *j.* is withered from men
*Zep.* 3:17 rejo. over thee with *j.*
*Mat.* 13:20 anon with *j.* receiveth it, *Luke* 8:13
44 for *j.* thereof goeth and sell.
25:21 enter into *j.* of thy L. 23
*Lu.* 1:44 babe leaped in wo. for *j.*
6:23 rej. in that day, leap for *j.*
10:17 seventy returned with *j.*
15:7 *j.* in heav. over one sinner
10 there is *j.* in pres. of angels
24:41 they yet believed not for *j.*
*John* 3:29 my *j.* therefo. is fulfil.
15:11 that my *j.* might remain in you, th. your *j.* might be full
16:20 sorrow be turned to *j.*
21 for *j.* that a man is born
22 your *j.* no man tak. fr. you
24 that your *j.* be full
17:13 *j.* fulfilled in themselves
*Acts* 2:28 make me full of *j.*
13:52 discip. were filled with *j.*
20:24 finish my course with *j.*
*Rom.* 14:17 kingdom of God is *j.*
15:13 God filled you with *j.*
32 co. to you wi. *j.* by will of G.
2 *Cor.* 1:24 are helpers of your *j.*
2:3 that my *j.* is *j.* of you all
7:13 more joyed we for *j.* of T.
8:2 their *j.* abounded to riches
*Gal.* 5:22 Spirit is love, *j.* peace
*Phil.* 1:4 making request with *j.*
25 furtherance and *j.* of faith
2:2 my *j.* 4:1 *j.* and crown
1 *Thes.* 1:6 received word with *j.*
2:19 what is our hope or *j.*?
20 for ye are our glory and *j.*
3:9 *j.* wherewith we *j.* before G.
2 *Tim.* 1:4 I may be filled with *j.*
*Phile.* 20 let me have *j.* of thee
*Heb.* 12:2 for *j.* that was bef. him
13:17 do it with *j.* not with grief
*Jam.* 1:2 count it *j.* when ye fall
4:9 *j.* be turned into heaviness
1 *Pet.* 1:8 rej. with *j.* unspeakab.
4:13 glad also with exceeding *j.*
1 *John* 1:4 *j.* be full, 2 *John* 12
3 *John* 4 no greater *j.* than to h.
*Jude* 24 faultless with exceed. *j.*
*See* GLADNESS.

**Great JOY.**

1 *K.* 1:40 peo. rejoiced with *g. j.*
2 *Chr.* 30:26 *g. j.* in Jerusalem
*Neh.* 12:43 rejoice with *great j.*
*Mat.* 2:10 rejoiced with *great j.*
28:8 from sep. wi. fear and *g. j.*
*Luke* 2:10 br. tidings of *great j.*
24:52 returned to Jer. with *g. j.*
*Acts* 8:8 there was *g. j.* in th. city
15:3 caused *g. j* to the brethren
*Phile.* 7 we have *g. j.* in thy love

**Shout, *or* Shouted for JOY.**

*Ezr.* 3:12 *shouted* aloud *for j.*
*Job* 38:7 sons of God *shouted f. j.*
*Ps.* 5:11 let them *sh. f. j.* 35:27
32:11 *s. f. j.* all th. are upright
65:13 the valleys *shout for j.*
132:9 let thy saints *s. for j.* 16

**JOY, Verb.**

*Ps.* 21:1 shall *j.* in thy strength
*Is.* 9:3 *j.* bef. thee accord. to joy
65:19 I rejoice and *j.* in my peo.
*Hab.* 3:18 I will *j.* in G. of salva.
*Zep.* 3:17 *j.* over thee with sing.
*Rom.* 5:11 but we also *j.* in God
*Phil.* 2:17 *j.* and rejoice wi. you
1 *Thes.* 3:9 joy wherewith ye *j.*

**JOYED.**

2 *Cor.* 7:13 more joy for joy of T.

**JOYFUL.**

1 *K.* 8:66 went to their tents *j.*
*Ezr.* 6:22 L. hath made them *j.*
*Job* 3:7 no *j.* voice come therein
*Ps.* 5:11 th. love thy name be *j.*
35:9 my soul be *j.* in the Lord
63:5 praise thee with *j.* lips
66:1 make a *j.* noise to God
81:1 make *j.* noise to G. of Jac.
89:15 blessed peo. know *j.* sound
95:1 make *j.* noise to rock of sa.
2 *j.* noise with psa. 98:4; 100:1
98:6 make a *j.* noise before L.
8 hills be *j.* together before L.
113:9 barren be *j.* mother of ch.
149:2 children of Zion *j.* in king
5 let the saints be *j.* in glory
*Ec.* 7:14 in day of prosper. be *j.*
*Is.* 49:13 sing heav. be *j.* earth
56:7 make *j.* in house of prayer
*Is.* 61:10 soul shall be *j.* in my G.
2 *Cor.* 7:4 *j.* in all our tribulat.

**JOYFULLY.**

*Ec.* 9:9 live *j.* wi. wife th. lovest
*Luke* 19:6 Zacch. received him *j.*
*Heb.* 10:34 took *j.* spoil. of goods

**JOYFULNESS.**

*Deut.* 28:47 servedst not L. w. *j.*
*Col.* 1:11 to long-suffering with *j.*

**JOYING,**

*Col.* 2:5 with you in the spirit, *j.*

**JOYOUS.**

*Is.* 22:2 art full of stirs, a *j.* city
23:7 is this your *j.* city, whose
32:13 all houses of joy in *j.* city
*Heb.* 12:11 no chastening seem. *j.*

JUBAL. *Gen.* 4:21

**JUBILEE.**

*Lev.* 25:9 trumpet of the *j.* 10:54
27:17 his field from year of *j.* 18
*Num.* 36:4 *j.* then th. inheritance

**JUDAH.**

*Gen.* 29:35 she called his name J.
35:23 the sons of Leah, J.
38:15 J. thought Tamar a harlot
46:12 sons of J. 28; *Num.* 26:19
49:8 J. he whom thy brethren
9 J. is a lion's whelp
10 sceptre not depart from J.
*Ex.* 1:2 sons of Israel, Levi, J.
*Num.* 2:3 camp of J. shall pitch
*Deut.* 33:7 blessing of J. 27:12
*Jos.* 7:17 bro. family of J. 18:5
*Jud.* 1:2 J. go first, 19; 10:9
1 *Sam.* 18:16 all J. loved David
2 *Sam.* 5:5 David reigned, 19:15
1 *K.* 14:22 J. did evil, 2 *K.* 17:19
2 *K.* 8:19 L. not destroy J. 14:10
21:11 ma. J. sin, 16; 2 *Chr.* 33:9
23:27 remove J. out of my sight
2 *Chr.* 12:12 in J. things w. well
*Ps.* 60:7 J. my lawgiver, 108:8
76:1 in J. God known, 114:2
*Is.* 1:1 vision conc. J. 3:1; 7:6
11:12 together dispersed of J. 13
22:8 discovered covering of J.
*Jer.* 17:1 sin of J. writ. with iron
33:7 captiv. of J. return, 42:15
50:20 sins of J. not found, 51:5
*Joel* 3:20 J. dw. for ever, Am. 2:4
*Mic.* 5:2 among thousands of J.
*Zec.* 2:12 L. inh. J. 12:7; 14:14
*Mal.* 2:11 J. dealt treacherously
3:4 offering of J. pleasant
*Mat.* 1:2 Ja. begat J. 3 J. begat
*Luke* 3:33 Phares was son of J.
*Heb.* 7:14 our L. sprang of J.

**Land of JUDAH.**

*Deut.* 34:2 showed him *land of* J.
*Ruth* 1:7 to return in *land of* J.
*Is.* 19:17 *l. of* J. a terror, 26:1
*Mat.* 2:6 Bethlehem, in *l. of* J.

**Men of JUDAH.**

*Jud.* 15:10 *m. of* J. why come
2 *Sam.* 2:4 *m. of* J. anointed D.
19:14 heart of J. 43; 20:2
24:9 *men of* J. 500,000
*Ezr.* 10:9 *m. of* J. gathered toget.

Is. 5:7 *m. of* J. his pleas. plant
Jer. 36:31 upon the *men of* J. all
43:9 in sight of *men of* J.
44:27 all *m. of* J. be consumed
Dan. 9:7 confusion to *men of* J.

**Tribe of JUDAH.**

Num. 1:27 numb. of *tribe of* J.
7:12 Nashon, prince of *t. of* J.
1 K. 12:20 *t. of* J. followed Dav.
2 K. 17:18 none left but *t. of* J.
Ps. 78:68 but he chose *t. of* J.
Rev. 5:5 L. of *t. of* J. prevailed
7:5 of *tribe of* J. sealed 12,000

**JUDAS.**

Mat. 13:55 brethren Sim. and J.
26:47 J. one of twelve. Mark 14:43; Lu. 22:47; John 18:3, 5
27:3 J. repented, bro. 30 pieces
John 13:29 because J. had bag
14:22 J. saith, How is it
Acts 1:16 D. spake concern. J. 25
5:37 after this man rose up J.
9:11 inquire in the house of J.
15:22 J. surnamed Barsabas, 27

**JUDAS Iscariot.**

Mat. 10:4 J. I. who betra. Mark 3:19; Luke 6:16; John 6:71; 13:2
26:14 J. I. to chief p. Mark 14:10
Luke 22:3 enter. Satan into J. I.
John 13:26 he gave sop to J. I.

**JUDEA.**

Ezr. 5:8 went into prov. of J.
Mat. 24:16 them wh. be in J. flee, Mark 13:14; Luke 21:21
John 4:3 left J. dep. to Galilee
7:3 and go into J. again, 11:7
Acts 1:8 in all J. ye sh. be witn.
2:14 men of J. be this known
9:31 church. rest thro. J. 10:37
Rom. 15:31 do not believe in J.
1 Thes. 2:14 churches which in J.

**JUDGE, Substantive.**

Gen. 18:25 J. of all the earth
19:9 this fel. ca. needs be a *j.*
Ex. 2:14 *j.* over us, Acts 7:27, 35
Deut. 17:9 come to the *j.* shall be
12 man will not hearken to *j.*
25:2 *j.* sh. cause him to lie down
Jud. 2:18 the Lord was with *j.*
11:27 L. the J. be *j.* this day
2 Sam. 15:4 O that I were ma. *j.*
Job 9:15 make supplica. to my *j.*
23:7 delivered for ever fr. my *j.*
31:28 iniq. be punished by *j.*
Ps. 50:6 for God is *j.* himself
68:5 *j.* of widows; 75:7 G. is *j.*
94:2 thou J. of the earth
Is. 3:2 take away fr. Jer. the *j.*
Amos 2:3 cut off *j.* from midst
Mic. 5:1 shall smite *j.* of Israel
7:3 the *j.* asketh for a reward
Mat. 5:25 adv. deliver thee to *j.* the *j.* to officer, Luke 12:58
Luke 12:14 who made me *j.*?
18:2 in city, a *j.* feared not G.
6 hear what unjust *j.* saith
Acts 10:42 *j.* of quick and dead
18:15 *j.* of no such matters
24:10 many years a *j.* of nation
2 Tim. 4:8 Lord the righteous *j.*
Heb. 12:23 G. the J. of all
Jam. 4:11 not do. of law, but a *j.*
5:9 J. standeth before the door

**JUDGE, Verb,** *applied to* GOD *and* CHRIST.

Gen. 16:5 *j.* between me and thee, 1 Sam. 24:12, 15
Ex. 5:21 L. look on you and *j.*
Deut. 32:36 L. sh. *j.* his people, Ps. 50:4; 135:14; Heb. 10:30
1 Sam. 2:10 L. *j.* ends of earth
1 K. 8:32 *j.* servants, 2 Chr. 6:23
1 Chr. 16:33 cometh to *j.* the earth, Ps. 96:13; 98:9
2 Chr. 20:12 wilt thou not *j.*?
Job 22:13 *j.* through dark cloud?
Ps. 7:8 the L. sh. *j.* the people righteously, 9:8; 50:4; 96:10
10:18 *j.* fatherless and oppressed
26:1 *j.* me, O Lord, 7:8; 35:24; 43:1; 54:1; Lam. 3:59
82:8 arise, O God, *j.* the earth
96:13 *j.* the world with righteousness, 98:9; Acts 17:31
110:6 shall *j.* among the heathen
Ec. 3:17 God shall *j.* righteous
Is. 2:4 shall *j.* among nations
3:13 Lord standeth to *j.* people
11:3 not *j.* after sight of eyes, 4
51:5 mine arm shall *j.* people
Ezek. 7:3 will *j.* accord. to ways
34:17 I *j.* betw. cattle and cattle
Joel 3:12 will I sit to *j.* heathen
Mic. 4:3 shall *j.* among people
John 5:30 I *j.* my judg. is just
8:15 I *j.* no man; 16 yet if I *j.*
26 things to say and to *j.*
12:47 I came not to *j.* world
Rom. 2:16 G. *j.* secrets of men
3:6 how sh. G. *j.* the world?
2 Tim. 4:1 *j.* quick and dead, 1 Pet. 4:5
Heb. 13:4 adulterers God will *j.*
Rev. 6:10 dost thou not *j.*
19:11 in righteousness he doth *j.*

*See*, further, *I will* JUDGE.

**JUDGE,** *applied to* MAN, *or other things.*

Gen. 31:37 *j.* betwixt us both
49:16 Dan shall *j.* his people
Ex. 18:13 Moses sat to *j.* people
16 I *j.* one and another
Lev. 19:15 in right. thou *j.* thy neighbor, Deut. 1:16; 16:18
1 Sam. 2:25 man sin, judge *j.* hi.
8:5 make us a king to *j.* us, 6, 20
1 K. 3:9 underst. heart to *j.* who is to *j.* this peo. 2 Chr. 1:10
2 Chr. 1:11 mayest *j.* my people
19:6 for ye *j.* not for man
Ezr. 7:25 which may *j.* people
Ps. 58:1 *j.* uprightly, sons of m.
72:2 *j.* people with righteousn.
4 *j.* poor of people, Prov. 31:9
82:2 how lo. will ye *j.* unjustly
Is. 1:17 *j.* fath. plead for widow
23 *j.* not fatherless, Jer. 5:28
5:3 *j.* betwixt me and my viney.
Ezek. 23:24 sh. *j.* thee, 45; 24:14
44:24 *j.* according to my judgm.
Ob. 21 saviors come to *j.*
Mic. 3:11 heads thereof *j.* for re.
Zec. 3:7 shalt also *j.* my house
Mat. 7:1 *j.* not that ye be not ju.
2 for with what judgment ye *j.* Luke 6:37
Luke 12:57 why *j.* not what is r.?
John 7:24 *j.* not accord. to appearance, but *j.* right. judg.
51 law *j.* man before it hear
8:15 *j.* after flesh; 12:48 same *j.*
18:31 *j.* him accord. to your law
Acts 4:19 *j.* ye; 13:46 *j.* yoursel.
23:3 sittest thou to *j.* me?
Rom. 2:27 fulfil the law, *j.* thee
14:3 *j.* him eateth; 10 *j.* brother
13 let us not *j.* one another
1 Cor. 4:3 *j.* not myself; 5 *j.* not
5:12 what have I to do to *j.* wi. do ye not *j.* them within?
6:2 do not know saints *j.* world?
3 know ye not we sh. *j.* angels?
4 set to *j.* who are least estee.
5 able to *j.* between his breth.
10:15 *j.* wh. I say; 11:13 *j.* your.
11:31 if we should *j.* ourselves
14:29 proph. speak, the oth. *j.*
2 Cor. 5:14 because we thus *j.*
Col. 2:16 let no man therefore *j.*
Jam. 4:11 but if thou *j.* the law

**I will JUDGE.**

1 Sam. 3:13 *I will j.* house
Ps. 75:2 *I will j.* uprightly
Ezek. 7:3 *I will j.* according to thy ways, 8:27; 33:20
11:10 *I will j.* you in Israel, 11
16:38 *I will j.* thee as women
21:30 *I will j.* thee wh. th. wast
34:20 I, even *I w. j.* fat cattle, 22

**Will I JUDGE.**

Gen. 15:14 the nation they shall serve *will I j.* Acts 7:7
Luke 19:22 out of mouth *w. I j.*

**JUDGED.**

Gen. 30:6 God hath *j.* me
Jud. 3:10 Oth. *j.* 4:4 Deborah
10:2 Tola *j.* 3 Jair; 12:7 Jeph.
12:8 Ibzan *j.* 11 Elon; 14 Abdon
15:20 Samson *j.* I. 20 y'rs, 16:31
1 Sam. 4:18 Eli *j.* 7:6 Sam. 15, 16, 17
Ps. 9:19 let heathen be *j.*
37:33 condemn him wh. he is *j.*
109:7 wh. *j.* let him be condem.
Jer. 22:16 he *j.* cause of the poor
Ezek. 16:38 women shed blood *j.*
28:23 wounded shall be *j.* in her
35:11 known, wh. I have *j.* thee
36:19 accord. to doings I *j.* them
Dan. 9:12 ag. judges that *j.* us
Mat. 7:1 jud. not, th. ye be not *j.*
2 ye shall be *j.* Luke 6:37
Luke 7:43 Thou hast rightly *j.*
John 16:11 pri. of this world is *j.*
Acts 16:15 *j.* me to be faithful
24:6 *j.* according to law
25:9 be *j.* of these things, 20
10 I stand, wh. I ought to be *j.*
26:6 am *j.* for hope of promise
Rom. 2:12 *j.* by law, Jam. 2:12
3:4 overcome when thou art *j.*
7 am I also *j.* as a sinner?
1 Cor. 2:15 he himself *j.* no man
4:3 that I should be *j.* of you
5:3 I have *j.* already, as though
6:2 if the world sh. be *j.* by you
10:29 for why is my liberty *j.* of
11:31 judge we should not be *j.*
32 we are *j.* we are chastened
14:24 convinced, he is *j.* of all
Heb. 11:11 she *j.* him faithful
1 Pet. 4:6 be *j.* according to men
Rev. 11:18 that they should be *j.*
16:5 righteous bec. thou *j.* thus
19:2 he hath *j.* the great whore
20:12 dead *j.* out of those things
13 *j.* ev. man accord. to works

**JUDGES.**

Ex. 21:22 pay as *j.* determine
22:8 master sh. be brought to *j.*
9 cause of both sh. come bef. *j.*
Deut. 1:16 I charged your *j.*
16:18 *j.* sh. thou make in gates
19:18 *j.* sh. make diligent inqu.
21:2 elders and *j.* shall come fo.
32:31 even our enemies bring *j.*
Jos. 23:2 J. called for the. *j.* 24:1
Jud. 2:16 Lord raised up *j.* 18
Ruth. 1:1 wh. *j.* ruled famine was
1 Sam. 8:1 made sons *j.* over I. 2
2 Sam. 7:11 com. *j.* over my peo.
1 Chr. 17:6 sp. a word to any *j.* 10
23:4 6,000 were officers and *j.*
2 Chr. 1:2 Solom. spake to the *j.*
19:5 set *j.* in land; 6 said to *j.*
Ezr. 7:25 set *j.* may judge people
Job 9:24 he cover. the face of *j.*
12:17 he maketh the *j.* fools
31:11 iniq. to be punished by *j.*
Ps. 2:10 be instructed *j.* of earth
141:6 when *j.* are overthrown
148:11 princes, and *j.* of earth
Prov. 8:16 princes rule, and *j.*
Is. 1:26 I will restore thy *j.*
40:23 mak. *j.* of earth as vanity

Dan. 9:12 words against our j.
Hos. 7:7 have devoured their j.
13:10 where are thy j. of whom
Zep. 3:3 j. are evening wolves
Mal. 12:27 be your j. Luke 11:19
Acts 13:20 he gave them j.
Jam. 2:4 become j. of evil thou.

**JUDGEST.**

Ps. 51:4 be clear when thou j.
Jer. 11:20 L. of hosts, j. righte.
Rom. 2:1 whoso. thou art that j.
3 O man, that j. them
14:4 that j. another man's ser.?
Jam. 4:12 who art thou j. ano.?

**JUDGETH.**

Job 21:22 j. those that were high
Ps. 7:11 God j. the righteous
58:11 a God that j. in earth
82:1 of mighty, he j. am. gods
Prov. 29:14 that faithfully j.
John 5:22 the Father j. no man
8:50 one that seeketh and j.
12:48 hath one that j. him
1 Cor. 2:15 he that is spirit. j. all
4:4 he that j. me is the Lord
5:13 th. that are without, G. j.
Jam. 4:11 that j. his brot. j. law
1 Pet. 1:17 with. respect of pe. j.
2:23 com. himself to him that j.
Rev. 18:8 strong is the L. that j.

**JUDGING.**

2 K. 15:5 j. the people of the land, 2 Chr. 26:21
Ps. 9:4 sattest in the thr. j. right
Is. 16:5 sit j. and seeking judgm.
Mat. 19:28 j. 12 tribes, Luke 22:30

**JUDGMENT.**

Ex. 12:12 ag. the gods execute j.
21:31 accord. to this j. be it do.
23:2 after many, to wrest j. 6
28:15 make the breastplate of j.
Num. 27:11 Is. a stat. of j. 35:29
21 after j. of Urim before Lord
Deut. 1:17 not afraid of man, j.
10:18 execute j. of fatherless
16:10 judge people with just j.
19 not wrest j. 17:11 accord. j.
24:17 not pervert j. of stranger
27:19 cursed be that pervert. j.
32:4 for all his ways are j.
41 if my hand take hold on j.
1 Sam. 8:3 took bribes pervert. j.
2 Sam. 8:15 David executed j. and justice, 1 Chr. 18:14
15:2 came to king for j. 6
1 K. 3:11 understan. to discer. j.
28 Israel heard of the j.
7:7 porch of j. 20:40 so thy j.
2 K. 25:6 took king and gave j.
2 Chr. 19:8 chief of fathers for j
20:9 cometh on us as sword, j.
Ezr. 7:26 let j. be executed
Est. 1:13 that knew law and j.
Job 8:3 doth God pervert j.?
9:19 speak of j. 19:7 th. is no j.
19:29 ye may know there is a j.
32:9 neither do aged underst. j.
34:4 let us choose to us j.
12 nei. will Almighty pervert j.
35:14 yet j. is before him
36:17 thou fulfilled j. of wicked j. and just. take hold on th.
Ps. 7:6 awake for me to the j.
9:7 prepared his throne for j.
8 minister j. to people in righ.
16 L. known by j. he execut.
33:5 loveth right. and j. 37:28
37:6 bring forth thy j.
30 his tongue talketh of j.
72:2 shall judge thy poor with j.
76:8 j. to be heard from heaven
9 G. arose to j. save the meek
89:14 justice and j. are hab. 97:2
94:15 j. sh. return to righteous.
99:4 the king's strength loveth j. thou executest j. and rig.
101:1 sing of mercy and j.
103:6 L. execut. j. for op. 146:7
106:3 bless. are they th. keep j.
30 Phine. stood and execut. j.
111:7 works of his hands are j.
119:66 teach me j. and knowle.
121 I have done j. and justice
149 quicken me accord. to j.
122:5 there are set thrones of j.
149:9 exec. on them j. written
Prov. 1:3 instr. of wisdom and j.
Prov. 2:8 he keep. the paths of j.
9 then shalt thou understand j.
8:20 in the midst of paths of j.
13:23 destroyed for want of j.
17:23 tak. gift to perv. ways j.
19:28 ungodly witness scorn. j.
20:8 that sitteth in throne j.
28:5 evil men understand not j.
29:4 king by j. establish. land
26 ev. man's j. cometh from L.
31:5 nor perv. j. of the afflicted
Ec. 3:16 under sun place of j.
5:8 seest violent perverting of j.
8:5 wise man disce. time and j.
6 to ev. purp. th. is time and j.
Is. 1:17 seek j. 21 full of j.
27 Z. shall be redeemed wi. j.
4:4 purged Jeru. by spirit of j.
5:7 looked for j. 16:5 seeking j.
9:7 and to establish it with j.
10:2 turn aside needy from j.
16:3 execute j. Jer. 21:12; 22:3; Ezek. 18:8; 45:9; Zec. 7:9; 8:16
28:6 and for a spirit of j. to him
17 I will also lay j. to the line
30:18 mercy, for L. is God of j.
32:16 j. sh. dwell in wilderness
33:5 L. hath filled Zion with j.
34:5 on people of my curse to j.
40:14 taught him in path of j.
41:1 come near together to j.
42:1 bring forth j. to Gentiles
3 sh. bring forth j. unto truth
4 not fail, till he set j. in earth
53:8 taken from prison and fr. j.
56:1 j. and justice, Hos. 12:6
59:8 there is no j. in their goin.
9 therefore is j. far from us
11 we look for j. there is none
14 j. is turned away backwards
15 displeas. him th. was no j.
61:8 I the L. love j. hate robbe.
Jer. 5:1 if th. be any execute. j.
4 know not the j. of th. G. 8:7
5 they have known the j. of G.
7:5 if ye thoroughly execute j.
9:24 exer. j. and righteousness
10:24 correct me, but with j.
21:12 execute j. in the morning
23:5 execute j. in earth, 33:15
48:21 j. is come upon pl. count.
49:12 whose j. was not to drink
51:9 her j. reacheth to heaven
Ezek. 23:24 I will set j. be. them
Dan. 4:37 all whose ways are j.
7:10 j. was set; 26 j. shalt sit
22 j. was given to the saints
Hos. 5:1 give ear, j. is tow. you
10:4 j. springeth as hemlock
Amos 5:7 turn j. to wormwood
15 and establish j. in the gate
24 let j. run down as waters
6:12 ye have turned j. into gall
Mic. 3:1 not to kn. j.; 8 full of j.
9 that abhor j.; 7:9 execute j.
Hab. 1:4 j. doth never go forth
7 j. sh. proceed of themselves
12 O L. thou ordain. th. for j.
Zep. 2:3 which wrought his j.
3:5 ev. morning bring j. to light
Mal. 2:17 say, Where is G. of j.
Mat. 5:21 in danger of the j. 22
7:2 with what j. ye judged
12:18 show j. to the Gentiles
20 he send forth j. unto victo.
23:23 have omitted j. mercy
Luke 11:42 pass over j. love of G.
John 5:22 committed all j. to S.
27 given him authori. to ex. j.
7:24 but judge righteous j.
9:39 for j. I am come into world
12:31 now is the j. of this world
16:8 reprove the world of j. 11
Acts 8:33 his j. was taken away
24:25 as he reasoned of j. Felix
Rom. 1:32 knowing the j. of God
2:2 j. of G. is according to truth
3 think, thou sh. escape j. of
5 revelation of righteous j. of
5:16 j. by one to condemnation
18 j. came to all to condemna.
1 Cor. 1:10 joined together in j.
4:3 I sh. be judged of man's j.
2 Thes. 1:5 token of the j. of G.
1 Tim. 5:24 open, going before to j.
Heb. 6:2 eternal j.; 9:27 after this the j.
10:27 certain fearful look. for j.
Jam. 2:13 have j. without mercy, rejoiceth against j.
1 Pet. 4:17 j. begin at ho. of G.
2 Pet. 2:3 whose j. lingereth not
4 chains of darkness, reser. j.
Jude 6 to j. of the great day
15 to execute j. upon all
Rev. 14:7 hour of his j. is come
17:1 show j. of the great whore
Rev. 18:10 in one hour thy j. co.
20:4 and j. was given to them

See BEAR, DAY.

**Do JUDGMENT.**

Gen. 18:19 do justice and j. 1 K. 10:9; Prov. 21:3; Jer. 22:15
1 K. 3:28 wisdom of G. to do j.
2 Chr. 9:8 set over them to do j.
Prov. 21:7 they refuse to do j.
15 it is joy to the just to do j.
Jer. 51:47 do j. on gr. images, 52

**JUDGMENT-HALL.**

John 18:28 led Jesus to h. of j. themselves we. not into j.-h.
33 Pilate entered j.-h. again
19:9 went into the j.-h.
Acts 23:35 kept in Herod's j.-h.

**In JUDGMENT.**

Lev. 19:15 no unright. in j. 35
Num. 35:12 bef. congrega. in j.
Deut. 1:17 not respect per. in j.
Jud. 5:10 ye that sit in j.
Job 9:32 come together in j.
37:23 excel. in power and in j.
Ps. 1:5 shall not stand in j.
25:9 meek will he guide in j.
Prov. 16:10 transgress. not in j.
18:5 overthrow righteous in j.
24:23 not good res. persons in j.
Is. 5:16 L. of hosts exalted in j.
28:6 sitteth in j. 7 stumble in j.
32:1 princes shall rule in j.
54:17 tongue rise ag. thee in j.
Jer. 4:2 in righteousn. and in j.
Ezek. 44:24 in contro. stand in j.
Hos. 2:19 betroth thee to me in j.
Mal. 3:5 come near to you in j.
Mat. 12:41 men of Nin. rise in j.
42 queen of south shall rise in j. Luke 11:31, 32
Phil. 1:9 love may abound in j.

**Into JUDGMENT.**

Job 14:3 and bringest me into j.
22:4 enter with thee into j.
34:23 enter into j. with God
Ps. 143:2 enter not i. j. wi. serv.
Ec. 11:9 will bring thee into j.
12:14 God bring ev. work into j.
Is. 3:14 Lord will enter into j.

**My JUDGMENT.**

Job 27:2 taken away my j. 34:5
29:14 my j. was as a robe
40:8 wilt thou disannul my j.?

Ps. 35:23 awake to my j.
Is. 40:27 my j. is passed over
49:4 my j. is with the Lord
51:4 make my j. to rest
Ezek. 39:21 heathen sh. see my j.
John 5:30 my j. just; 8:16 my j.
1 Cor. 7:25 yet I give my j.
40 happier if she abi. in my j.

**JUDGMENT-SEAT.**

Mat. 27:19 set on j.-s. John 19:13
Acts 18:12 J. brought him to j.-s.
16 he drave them from the j.-s.
17 beat Sosthenes before j.-s.
25:10 I stand at Cesar's j.-s.
17 on morrow I sat on j.-s.
Rom. 14:10 sh. all stand before j.-s of Christ, 2 Cor. 5:10
Jam. 2:6 draw you before j.-s.

**JUDGMENTS.**

Ex. 6:6 redeem you with j 7:4
21:1 j. thou sh. set before them
Num. 33:4 on gods L. executed j.
35:24 judge according to th. j.
Deut. 33:10 sh. teach Jac. thy j.
2 Sam. 22:23 his j. were before me, Ps. 18:22
1 Chr. 16:12 j. of mou. Ps. 105:5
14 his j. in all earth, Ps. 105:7
Neh. 9:29 sinned against thy j.
Ps. 10:5 thy j. are out of sight
19:9 the j. of the Lord are true
36:6 thy j. are a great deep
48:11 let Judah be glad of thy j.
72:1 give the king thy j. O God
97:8 because of thy j. O Lord
119:7 I learned thy righteous j.
13 lips declared j. of thy mo.
20 longing it hath unto thy j.
30 thy j. have I laid before me
39 reproach, for thy j. are good
43 for I have hoped in thy j.
52 I remember thy j. of old
62 because of thy right. j. 164
75 I know that thy j. are right
102 have not departed from j.
106 I will keep righteous j.
108 teach me j. 120 afraid of j.
137 right. upright are thy j.
156 quicken me accor. to thy j.
160 ev. one of thy righteou.
175 and let thy j. help me
147:20 his j. they have not kno.
Prov. 19:29 j. prep. for scorners
Is. 26:8 in way of thy j.
9 when thy j. are in the earth
Jer. 12:1 talk with thee of thy j.
Ezek. 5:7 accord. to j. of nations
8 execute j. in midst of thee, 10, 15; 11:9
16:41 exe. j. in sight of women
23:24 judge thee accord. to j.
28:26 executed j. on all those
34:16 I will feed them with j.
Dan. 9:5 departing from thy j.
Hos. 6:5 thy j. are as the light
Zep. 3:15 L. taken away thy j.
Rom. 11:33 unsearch. are his j.
1 Cor. 6:4 have j. of things of life
Rev. 15:4 j. are made manifest
16:7 righteous are thy j. 19:2

**My JUDGMENTS.**

Lev. 18:4 ye shall do my j.
5 ye shall keep my j. 25:18
26:15 if your soul abhor my j.
43 because they despised my j.
1 Chr. 28:7 constant to do my j.
Ps. 89:30 chil. walk not in my j.
Jer. 1:16 utter my j. ag. them
Ezek. 5:6 changed my j. to wick.
7 neither have kept my j.
14:21 send my four sore j. on J.
44:24 judge it accord to my j.

**Statutes and JUDGMENTS.**

Lev. 18:5 keep my stat. and my j. 26; 20:22; Deut. 7:11; 11:1; 26:16, 17; 30:16; 1 K. 2:3; 8:58; 9:4; 11:33
19:37 ye sh. observe all my statutes a. my j. Deut. 11:32; 12:1; 2 Chr. 7:17
Deut. 4:1 I hearken to s. a. j. 5:1
5 I have taught you sta. and j.
8 hath sta. and j. so righteous
14 te. st. and j. 6:1; Ezr. 7:10
5:31 st. and j. thou shalt teach
6:20 what mean statutes and j.
8:11 keeping s. and j. Neh. 1:7
1 K. 6:12 walk in s. execute j.
2 Chr. 19:10 between s. and j.
Neh. 9:13 gav. them right s. a. j.
10:29 to do all his sta. and j.
Ps. 147:19 showeth his s. and j.
Ezek. 5:6 ref. my j. and my sta.
11:12 not walked in my s. nor executed my j. 20:13, 16, 21
18:9 walked in my statutes and j. 17; 20:19; 37:24
20:11 gave them s. and sho. j.
18 not in s. of fath. nor th. j.
25 gave th. sta. not good, a. j.
Mal. 4:4 law of M. with s. and j.

**JUICE.**

Cant. 8:2 wine of j. of pomegra.

JULIA. Rom. 16:15
JULIUS. Acts 27:1

**JUMPING.**

Nah. 3:2 noise of the j. chariots

JUNIA. Rom. 16:7

**JUNIPER.**

1 K. 19:4 Elijah sat under j. 5
Job 30:4 cut j. roots for meat
Ps. 120:4 arrows, coals of j.

**JUPITER.**

Acts 14:12 called Barnabas J.
19:35 which fell down from J

**JURISDICTION.**

Luke 23:7 belong to Herod's j.

**JUST.**

Gen. 6:9 Noah was j. man
Lev. 19:36 j. balance, j. weights, a j. ephah, and a j. hin, Deut. 25:15; Ezek. 45:10
Deut. 16:18 judge with j. judgm.
32:4 a God, j. and right is he
2 Sam. 23:3 rul. men must be j.
Neh. 9:33 j. in all brought on us
Job 4:17 man be more j. than G.
9:2 should man be j. with God
12:4 j. man is laughed to scorn
27:17 but the j. shall put it on
Ps. 7:9 wicked. end, establish j.
37:12 wicked plotteth against j.
Prov. 3:33 bless. habitation of j.
4:18 path of j. as shining light
9:9 teach a j. man, he will incr.
10:6 blessing upon he. of the j.
7 memory of the j. is blessed
20 tongue of j. is as choice sil.
31 mouth of j. bringeth wisd.
11:1 a j. weight is his delight
9 thro' knowledge j. delivered
12:13 j. sh. come out of trouble
21 sh. no evil happen to the j.
13:22 weal. of sin. laid up for j.
16:11 j. we. and balance Lord's
17:15 condemneth j. is abomin.
Prov. 17:26 to punish the j. is
18:17 first in own cause seem. j.
20:7 j. man walketh in integrity
21:15 joy to j. to do judgment
24:16 j. man falleth seven times
29:10 hate upright, j. seek soul
Ec. 7:15 a j. man that perisheth
20 not a j. man on earth
8:14 j. men to wh. it happeneth
Is. 26:7 way of j. is uprightness, dost weigh path of j.
29:21 j. for thing of naught
45:21 a j. God, and a Saviour
Lam. 4:13 shed blood of j. in her
Ezek. 18:5 man be j. and do right
9 he is j. he shall surely live
Hos. 14:9 j. shall walk in them
Amos 5:12 they afflict the j.
Hab. 2:4 j. sh. live by faith, Rom. 1:17; Gal. 3:11; Heb. 10:38
Zep. 3:5 the j. Lord is in midst
Zec. 9:9 he is j. and hav. salva.
Mat. 1:19 Joseph, being a j. man
5:45 send. rain on j. and unjust
13:49 sever wicked from am. j.
27:19 nothing to do with j. man
24 innocent of blood of j. per.
Mark 6:20 know. he was j. man
Luke 1:17 disobed. to wisd. of j.
2:25 Simeon was j. and devout
14:14 at the resurrec. of the j.
15:7 ninety and nine j. persons
20:20 spies feign themselves j.
23:50 Jos. was good man and j.
John 5:30 and my judgment is j.
Acts 10:22 Cornelius, a j. man
24:15 resurrection of j. and unj.
Rom. 2:13 not hear. of law are j.
3:8 damnation j. 26 might be j.
7:12 the commandment holy, j.
Phil. 4:8 whatsoev. things are j.
Col. 4:1 give servants which is j.
Tit. 1:8 bishop must be j. holy
Heb. 2:2 received j. recompense
12:23 sp. of j. men made perfect
Jam. 5:6 condemned and kill. j.
1 Pet. 3:18 the j. for the unjust
2 Pet. 2:7 delivered j. Lot
1 John 1:9 he is j. to forgive sins
Rev. 15:3 j. and tr. are thy ways

**Most JUST.**

Job 34:17 condemn him is m. j.?

**JUST One.**

Acts 3:14 ye denied the J. O.
7:52 show. bef. coming of J. O.
22:14 his will, and see that J. O.

**JUSTICE.**

Gen. 18:19 keep w. of L. to do j.
Deut. 33:21 execute. the j. of L.
2 Sam. 8:15 David executed j. 1 Chr. 18:14
15:4 made judge I would do j.
Job 8:3 doth Almigh. pervert j.?
36:17 and j. take hold on thee
37:23 excellent in plenty of j.
Ps. 82:3 do j. to afflicted
89:14 j. and judgm. are habita.
119:121 have done judg. and j.
Prov. 1:3 to rec. instruction of j.
8:15 kings reign, princes dec. j.
Ec. 5:8 seest perverting of j.
Is. 9:7 to estab. his thro. with j.
56:1 and do j. for my salvation
58:2 ask of me ordinances of j.
59:4 none calleth for j. nor ple.
9 nor doth j. overtake us
14 j. standeth afar of
Jer. 23:5 execute judgm. and j.
31:23 L. bless thee, habita. of j.
Ezek. 45:9 O princes, execute j.

See Do JUDGMENT, before.

**JUSTIFICATION.**

Rom. 4:25 raised again for our j.
5:16 gift of many offences to j.
18 free gift ca. on all men to j.

**JUSTIFY.**

Ex. 23:7 I will not j. the wicked
Deut. 25:1 they sh. j. righteous
Job 9:20 if I j. myself
27:5 God forbid I should j. you
33:32 for I desire to j. thee
Is. 5:23 j. the wicked for reward
53:11 my right. servant j. many
Luke 10:29 willing to j. himself
16:15 j. yourselves before men
Rom. 3:30 God sh. j. circumcis.
Gal. 3:8 foreseeing God j. heath.

**JUSTIFIED.**
*Job* 11:2 man full of talk be *j.*?
13:18 behold, I know I sh. be *j.*?
25:4 can man be *j.* with God?
32:2 *j.* himself rather than God
*Ps.* 51:4 that thou mightest be *j.*
143:2 no man living be *j.*
*Is.* 43:9 may be *j.* 26 thou be
*Is.* 45:25 L. all seed of Isr. be *j.*
*Jer.* 3:11 backsliding Is. *j.* hers.
*Ezek.* 16:51 *j.* sisters in abom. 52
*Mat.* 11:19 wisdom is *j.* of her children, *Luke* 7:35
12:37 by thy words th. sh. be *j*
*Luke* 7:29 and publicans *j.* G.
18:14 this man went down *j.*
*Acts* 13:39 all that believe are *j.* from wh. ye could not be *j.*
*Rom.* 2:13 doers of law sh. be *j.*
3:4 might be *j.* in thy sayings
20 no flesh be *j.* in his sight
24 *j.* freely by his gra. *Tit.* 3:7
28 a man is *j.* by faith, 5:1; *Gal.* 2:16; 3:24
4:2 if Abraham we. *j.* by works
5:1 *j.* by faith we have peace
9 *j.* by his blood, we shall be
8:30 whom he *j.* he also glorifi.
1 *Cor.* 4:4 yet am I not hereby *j.*
6:11 ye are *j.* in name of L. J.
*Gal.* 2:16 not *j.* by law, 3:11
5:4 whosoever are *j.* by law
1 *Tim.* 3:16 *j.* in spirit
*Jam.* 2:21 was not Abraham *j.*?
24 see how by works man is *j.*
25 was not Rahab *j.* by works?

**JUSTIFIER.**
*Rom.* 3:26 *j.* of him who believ.

**JUSTIFYING, ETH.**
1 *K.* 8:32 and *j.* the righteous, 2 *Chr.* 6:23
*Prov.* 17:15 he that *j.* the wicked
*Is.* 50:8 he is near that *j.*
*Rom.* 5:5 him that *j.* ungodly
8:33 God's elect? is G. that *j.*

**JUSTLE.**
*Nah.* 2:4 the chariots shall *j.*

**JUSTLY.**
*Mic.* 6:8 L. require but to do *j.*
*Luke* 23:41 indeed *j.* we receive
1 *Thes.* 2:10 holily and *j.* behav.

**JUSTUS.**
*Acts* 1:23 who was surnamed J.
18:7 ent. man's house named J.
*Col.* 4:11 Jesus who is called J.

# K

**KAB.**
2 *K.* 6:25 *k.* of doves' dung sold

KABZEEL. *Jos.* 15:21

**KADESH.**
*Gen.* 14:8 to Emish. which is K.
*Num.* 13:26 wilder. of Par. to K.
*Deut.* 1:46 ye abode in K. many
*Ps.* 29:8 shak. wilderness of K.

**KADESH-BARNEA.**
*Num.* 32:8 I sent them from K. *Deut.* 9:23; *Jos.* 14:7
*Jos.* 10:41 smote from K. to Gaza

KAREAH, or CAREAH. 2 *K.* 25:23; *Jer.* 40:8, 13; 41:11; 43:4
KEDEMAH. *Gen.* 25:15
KEDEMOTH. *Deut.* 2:26

**KEDAR.**
*Gen.* 25:13 of Ish. K. 1 *Chr.* 1:29
*Ps.* 120:5 I dwell in tents of K.
*Cant.* 1:5 comely as tents of K.
*Is.* 21:16 glory of K. sh. fail, 17
42:11 vil. that K. doth inhabit
60:7 flocks of K. sh. be gather.
*Jer.* 2:10 see and send to K.
49:28 concerning K. thus saith
*Ezek.* 27:21 princes of K. occu.

**KEEP.**
*Gen.* 2:15 L. put him in E. to *k.*
18:19 shall *k.* the way of Lord
28:15 am with thee to *k.* thee, 20
41:35 let them *k.* food in cities
*Ex.* 12:6 *k.* it till fourteenth day
14 ye sh. *k.* it a feast to L. 25; 23:15; 34:18; *Lev.* 23:31
47 congregation of Is. sh. *k.* it
20:8 remember sab.-day to *k.* it, 31:13, 14, 16; *Deut.* 5:12, 15
22:7 man deliver money to *k.* 10
23:7 *k.* thee from false matter
14 three times *k.* a feast
20 I send an angel to *k.* thee
*Lev.* 18:14 ye sh. *k.* my ordinances, 30; 22:9; *Ezek.* 11:20
19:3 ye sh. *k.* my sabbaths, 30; 26:2; *Is.* 56:4
23:39 *k.* a feast sev. 2 *Chr.* 30:13
25:18 *k.* my judg. and do them
*Num.* 6:24 L. bless thee and *k.*
9:3 in fourteenth day ye shall *k.*
29:12 *k.* feast to the L. sev. days
36:7 *k.* himself to inheritance, 9
*Deut.* 7:8 *k.* the oath
12 the L. sh. *k.* the covenant
*Deut.* 16:10 *k.* feast of weeks to
17:19 learn to *k.* words of law
29:9 *k.* words of this covenant
*Jos.* 6:18 *k.* from accursed thing
*Jud.* 2:22 whether *k.* way of L.
1 *Sam.* 2:9 *k.* feet of his saints
2 *Sam.* 18:18 no son to *k.* name
1 *K.* 8:25 *k.* with thy servant David, 2 *Chr.* 6:16
1 *Chr.* 4:10 *k.* me from evil
12:33 50,000 could *k.* rank, 38
29:18 *k.* this forever in heart
2 *Chr.* 22:9 no power to *k.* still
30:23 counsel to *k.* other 7 days
*Ezr.* 8:29 watch and *k.* them
*Neh.* 12:27 *k.* ded. with gladness
*Est.* 3:8 nor *k.* they king's laws
*Job* 14:13 thou wouldest *k.* me
20:13 tho' he *k.* it still within
*Ps.* 12:7 sh. *k.* them, O L. 31:20
17:8 *k.* me as apple of eye
19:13 *k.* from presumptuous sins
25:20 O *k.* my soul, and deliver
34:13 *k.* thy tongue from evil
37:34 *k.* his way; 39:1 *k.* mouth
89:28 my mercy wi. I *k.* for him
91:11 angels charge, to *k.* thee
103:9 nor will *k.* anger for ever
106:3 blessed are they *k.* judg.
113:9 barren women to *k.* house
119:2 blessed they th. *k.* his tes.
4 com. us to *k.* thy precepts
17 live and *k.* thy word, 101
33 teach me, I sh. *k.* it to end
63 compan. of them *k.* thy pr.
69 *k.* thy prec. with heart, 134
88 *k.* testimony of thy mouth
100 because I *k.* thy precepts
106 will *k.* thy righteous judg.
146 I shall *k.* thy testimonies
127:1 except Lord *k.* city
140:4 *k.* me fr. hands of wicked
141:3 O L. *k.* the door of my lips
*Prov.* 2:11 underst. shall *k.* thee
20 mayest *k.* paths of righteous
3:21 my son, *k.* sound wisdom
26 L. shall *k.* thy foot fr. being
4:6 love wisdom, she sh. *k.* thee
13 *k.* instructi. let her not go
21 *k.* my sayings in thy heart
23 *k.* thy heart wi. all diligen.
5:2 thy lips may *k.* knowledge
6:22 when sleepest it sh. *k.* thee
7:1 my son, *k.* my words
5 *k.* thee from strange woman
8:32 blessed they th. *k.* my ways
22:5 he that doth *k.* his soul, 18
28:4 such as *k.* the law contend
*Ec.* 3:6 time to *k.* and cast away
5:1 *k.* foot when goest to house
*Is.* 26:3 *k.* him in perfect peace
27:3 the L. do *k.* it, *k.* it night
42:6 I will *k.* thee
43:6 *k.* not back; 56:1 *k.* judg.
*Jer.* 3:5 will *k.* anger to end? 12
31:10 *k.* him as shep. doth flock
42:4 I will *k.* nothing back
*Ezek.* 20:19 *k.* my judgm. 36:27
43:11 they may *k.* the wh. form
*Hos.* 12:6 *k.* mercy and judgment
*Mic.* 7:5 *k.* the doors of thy mou.
*Nah.* 1:15 *k.* feasts; 2:1 *k.* muni.
*Zec.* 13:5 taught me to *k.* cattle
*Mal.* 2:7 priests' lips sho. *k.* kno.
*Mark* 7:9 *k.* your own tradition
*Luke* 4:10 angels charge to *k.* th.
11:28 blessed th. hear word, *k.* it
19:43 thy enemies shall *k.* thee
*John* 8:51 *k.* my say. never see
55 know him, *k.* his saying
12:25 hateth life in world *k.* it
14:23 man love me *k.* my words
15:20 saying, they will *k.* yours
17:11 *k.* thy name; 15 *k.* fr. evil
*Acts* 5:3 to *k.* back part of price
10:28 that is a Jew to *k.* comp.
15:5 com. them to *k.* law of M.
29 from wh. if ye *k.* yourselves
16:4 deliver. them decrees to *k.*
*Rom.* 2:25 profiteth, if th. *k.* law
26 *k.* the righteousness of law
1 *Cor.* 5:8 therefore let us *k.* feast
11 writ. to you not *k.* company
7:37 decreed he will *k.* his virg.
9:27 I *k.* under my body
15:2 *k.* in mem. wh. I preached
2 *Cor.* 11:9 and so will I *k.* my.
*Gal.* 6:13 nei. do circum. *k.* law
*Eph.* 4:3 to *k.* the unity of Spirit
*Phil.* 4:7 peace of G. *k.* y. hearts
2 *Thes.* 3:3 estab. and *k.* from ev.
1 *Tim.* 5:22 *k.* thyself pure
6:20 *k.* that commit. to thy tru.
2 *Tim.* 1:12 *k.* that I com. to him
14 commit. to thee *k.* by H. G.
*Jam.* 1:27 to *k.* himself unspot.
1 *John* 5:21 *k.* yourselves fr. idols
*Jude* 21 *k.* yoursel. in love of G.
*Jude* 24 him that is ab. to *k.* you
*Rev.* 1:3 blessed th. that *k.* thin.
3:10 *k.* thee from hour of temp.
22:9 who *k.* sayings of this book

**KEEP alive.**
*Gen.* 6:19 into ark to *k.* th. *a.* 20
*Num.* 31:18 chil. *k. a.* for yours.
2 *Sam.* 8:2 one full line to *k. a.*
*Ps.* 22:29 no. can *k. a.* own soul
33:19 *k.* them *alive* in famine
41:2 Lord preser. and *k.* him *a.*

**KEEP charge.**
*Num.* 1:53 Levites *k. c.* of taber. 18:4; 31:30; 1 *Chr.* 23:32
3:8 *k. c.* of the children of Israel
32 *k. c.* of the sanctuary. 18:5
*Ezek.* 44:16 mini. to me, *k.* my *c.*
*Zec.* 3:7 if thou wilt *k.* my *c.*

**KEEP commandments.**
*Ex.* 16:28 refuse ye to *k.* my *c.*
20:6 mercy to th. that *k.* my *c.* *Deut.* 5:10; 7:9; *Dan.* 9:4

Lev. 22:31 sh. ye k. my c. and do
them, Deut. 4:40; 6:17; 7:11
26:3 k. my com. Deut. 11:22;
19:9; 28:9; 30:10; 1 K. 3:14
Deut. 5:29 fear me and k. my c.
8:2 know whet. th. would. k. c.
26:17 avouched Lord to k. his c.
18 that thou shouldest k. c.
Jos. 22:5 take heed to k. com.
1 K. 2:3 charge of Lord to k. c.
6:12 k. my comman. 2 K. 17:13;
Prov. 4:4; 7:2
8:58 incline hearts to k. his c.
61 heart be perfect to k. his c.
9:6 not k. com. I will cut off Is.
1 Chr. 29:19 Sol. perf. hea. to k. c.
Ps. 78:7 works of G. but k. his c.
119:60 delayed not to k. thy c.
115 dep. evil-doers, I will k. c.
Prov. 3:1 let thy heart k. my c.
6:20 my son, k. thy father's c.
Ec. 8:2 coun. thee to k. king's c.
12:13 fear God and k. his com.
Mat. 19:17 enter life, k. the c.
John 14:15 if ye love me, k. my c.
1 Tim. 6:14 k. this c. witho. spot
1 John 2:3 we kn. him if we k. c.
3:22 ask we receive, bec. we k. c.
5:2 we love God and k. his com.
3 love of God that we k. his c.
Rev. 12:17 war with seed wh. k. c.
14:12 they which k. the c. of G.
See COVENANT.

**KEEP passover.**

Ex. 12:48 stranger k. p. to Lord
Num. 9:2 chil. of Is. k. p. in its
seas. 4; Deut. 16:1; 2 K. 23:21
2 Chr. 30:1 co. to k. the p. to G.
35:18 nor did kings k. such a p.
Mat. 26:18 k. p. at thy house

**KEEP silence.**

Jud. 3:19 said, k. s. all went out
Ps. 35:22 k. not silence, 83:1
50:3 shall come, and sh. not k. s.
Ec. 3:7 time to k. s. time to spe.
Is. 41:1 k. s. bef. me, O islands
Lam. 2:10 elders of da. of Z. k. s.
Amos 5:13 the prudent shall k. s.
Hab. 2:20 L. in temp. earth k. s.
1 Cor. 14:28 let him k. s. in chur.
34 let women k. sil. in church.

**KEEP statutes.**

Ex. 15:26 if th. wilt k. all his s.
Deut. 30:10; 1 K. 9:4; 11:38
Lev. 18:5 k. my s. and judg. 26;
19:19; 20:8, 22; Ezek. 44:24
Deut. 6:2 fear Lord to k. his stat.
26:17 avouched Lord to k. his s.
1 K. 11:33 in my ways to k. s.
Ps. 119:5 ways directed to k. s.
8 I will k. thy s. 145
Ezek. 18:21 wicked turn and k. s.

**KEEPER.**

Gen. 4:2 Abel was a k. of sheep
9 am I my brother's k.?
39:22 k. committed to Joseph
33 k. looked not to any thing
1 Sam. 17:20 D. left sheep wi. k.
28:2 make thee k. of my head
2 K. 22:14 k. of the wardrobe,
2 Chr. 34:22
Est. 2:3 Hege k. of women, 8, 15
Job 27:18 booth that k. maketh
Ps. 121:5 Lord thy k.
Cant. 1:6 made me k. of viney.
Acts 16:27 k. of prison awaking

**KEEPERS.**

Ec. 12:3 k. of house tremble
Cant. 5:7 k. took away my veil
8:11 Sol. let out vineyard to k.
Jer. 4:17 as k. of the field
Mat. 28:4 fear of him k. did sha.
Acts 5:23 k. standing bef. doors
Acts 12:6 k. kept pris.; 19 exa. k.
Tit. 2:5 chaste, k. at home
See DOOR.

**KEEPEST.**

1 K. 8:23 who k. covenant with
serv. 2 Chr. 6:14; Neh. 9:32
Acts 21:24 orderly and k. the law

**KEEPETH.**

Ex. 21:18 die not, but k. his bed
Deut. 7:9 faithful God which k.
covenant, Neh. 1:5
1 Sam. 16:11 behold, he k. sheep
Job 33:18 k. back soul from pit
Ps. 34:20 he k. all his bones
121:3 that k. th. not slumber, 4
146:6 L. which k. truth for ever
Prov. 2:8 k. paths of judgment
10:17 in way of life k. instruct.
13:3 k. his mouth k. life, 21:23
6 righteousness k. him upright
16:17 k. way preserv. soul, 19:16
19:8 k. understanding find good
24:12 k. soul, do. not he know?
27:18 k. fig-tree shall eat fruit
28:7 whoso k. law is a wise son
29:11 wise man k. it till afterw.
18 that k. the law, happy is he
Ec. 8:5 k. command. feel no evil
Is. 26:2 nation k. truth
56:2 k. sab. from polluting it, 6
Jer. 48:10 cursed be he k. back
Lam. 3:28 sitteth alone k. silen.
Hab. 2:5 proud, nei. k. at home
Luke 11:21 strong man k. palace
John 7:19 none of you k. law
9:16 bec. he k. not sabbath
14:21 hath com. and k. them
24 k. not my sayings
1 John 2:4 know him, and k. not
5 k. word, in him is love, 3:24
5:18 is begot. of God k. himself
Rev. 2:26 overcom. and k. works
16:15 blessed he that k. garm.
22:7 blessed he that k. sayings

**KEEPING.**

Ex. 34:7 L. k. mercy for thous.
Deut. 8:11 not k. his commands
1 Sam. 25:16 with them k. sheep
Ps. 19:11 k. of them great rew.
Ezek. 17:14 by k. of his covenant
Dan. 9:4 great God k. covenant
Luke 2:8 shepherds k. watch
1 Cor. 7:19 k. commandm. of G.
1 Pet. 4:19 com. k. of souls to him

**KEILAH.**

Jos. 15:44 K. and Achzib
1 Sam. 23:1 Philist. fight aga. K.
Neh. 3:17 ruler of h. part of K. 18

KEMUEL Gen 22:21
KENEZ. Jos. 15:17

**KENITES.**

Gen. 15:19 thy seed have I gi. K.
Num. 24:21 Balaam look. on K.
1 Sam. 15:6 S. said to K. Depart
27:10 road against south of K.

**KEPT.**

Gen. 26:5 Abrah. k. my charge
29:9 came wi. sheep, she k. th.
Ex. 3:1 Moses k. flock of Jethro
16:23 to be k. till the morning
32 manna k. for genera. 33, 34
21:29 owner not k. him in, 36
Num. 17:10 A.'s rod k. for token
19:9 water k. for congregation
24:11 Lord hath k. thee back
Deut. 32:10 k. them as ap. of eye
33:9 observed word, k. covenant
Jos. 14:10 k. me alive 45 years
Ruth 2:23 k. by maidens of Boaz
1 Sam. 17:34 ser. k. fath.'s sheep
21:4 k. themselves from women
25:33 blessed thou who k. me
26:15 why not k. lord the king?
16 ye have not k. your master
2 Sam. 13:34 young man k. watch
22:22 I have kept the ways of
the Lord, Ps. 18:21, 23
24 have kept myself from iniq.
44 k. me to be head of heathen
1 K. 2:43 not k. the oath of Lord
8:24 hast k. with D. what thou
promisedst him, 2 Chr. 6:15
11:11 hast not k. my covenant
13:21 man of G. not k. comman.
1 Chr. 10:13 word of L. S. k. not
12:1 David k. himself close
2 Chr. 7:8 S. k. feast 7 days, 9
30:21 k. feast of unleavened br.
Ezr. 6:22
35:18 no pass. like that k. in Is.
Ezr. 3:4 k. feast of tabernacles
6:19 chil. of captiv. k. passover
Neh. 1:7 have not k. command.
8:18 they k. the feast seven days
Job 23:11 his ways have I k.
Job 28:21 k. clo. from fowls of air
Ps. 17:4 k. fr. paths of destroyer
30:3 k. me alive; 42:4 k. h. day
78:10 k. not the covenant of G.
99:7 they k. his testimonies
119:22 for I k. thy testim. 167
55 k. thy law; 56 k. prec. 168
67 k. thy word; 158 k. not wo.
Ec. 2:10 eyes desired k. not from
5:13 riches k. for owners thereof
Cant. 1:6 vineyard have I not k.
Is. 30:29 when solemnity is k.
Jer. 16:11 k. laws; 35:18 k. prec.
Ezek. 5:7 nor k. my judgm. 20:21
44:8 not k. charge of holy things
15 k. charge of sanctuary, 48:11
Dan. 5:19 he k. alive, he set up
7:28 I k. the matter in my heart
Hos. 12:12 serv. for wife, k. sheep
Amos 1:11 Ed. k. wrath for ever
Mal. 2:9 not k. my ways, 3:7
3:14 profit have k. his ordinan.
Mat. 13:35 things been k. secret
19:20 these have I k. from my
youth, Luke 18:21
Mark 4:22 nor any thing k. secr.
9:10 k. that saying, Luke 9:36
Luke 2:19 k. things in heart, 51
8:29 was k. bound with chains
John 2:10 thou hast k. good wine
15:10 I k. Father's commandm.
20 if they have k. my saying
17:6 and have k. thy word
12 those thou gav. me I have k.
Acts 5:2 k. back part of the price
7:53 received law, and not k. it
12:5 P. k. in prison; 6 k. prison
20:20 k. back nothing profitable
22:20 k. the raiment of them
28:16 with soldier that k. him
Rom. 16:25 mystery k. secret
2 Cor. 11:9 I k. from being burd.
Gal. 3:23 we were k. under law
2 Tim. 4:7 course, I k. the faith
Heb. 11:28 Moses k. the passover
Jam. 5:4 hire is k. back by fraud
1 Pet. 1:5 are k. by power of God
2 Pet. 3:7 same word k. in store
Jude 6 angels k. not first estate
Rev. 3:8 k. word, not deni. name
10 hast k. word of my patience

**KEPT silence.**

Job 29:21 men give ear, and k. s.
31:34 fear multi. that I k. s.?
Ps. 32:3 I k. s. bones waxed old
50:21 things th. done, and I k. s.
Acts 15:12 all the multitude k. s.
22:2 spake Heb. k. the more s.

**KERCHIEFS.**

Ezek. 13:18 k. on head of stature
21 your k. also will I tear

KEREN-HAPPUCH. Job 42:14
KERIOTH. Jer. 48:24,41; Am. 2:2

**KERNELS.**

Num. 6:4 eat noth. from the k.

**KETTLE.**

1 Sam. 2:14 struck into k. or pot

KETURAH. Gen. 25:1, 4; 1 Chr.
1:32, 33

**KEY, S.**

*Jud.* 3:25 took a *k.* and opened
*Is.* 22:22 *k.* of house of David
*Mat.* 16:19 *k.* of kingd. of heaven
*Luke* 11:52 tak. *k.* of knowledge
*Rev.* 1:18 *k.* of hell and of death
3:7 he that hath the *k.* of David
9:1 *k.* of bottomless pit, 20:1

KEZIA. *Job* 42:14
KEZIZ. *Jos.* 18:21
KIBROTH-HATTAAVAH. *Nu.* 11:34, 35

**KICK, ED.**

*Deut.* 32:15 J. waxed fat and *k.*
1 *Sam.* 2:29 *k.* ye at my sacrifice?
*Acts* 9:5 ha. to *k.* ag. pri. 26:14

**KID.**

*Gen.* 37:31 J.'s breth. killed a *k.*
*Ex.* 23:19 sh. not seethe the *k.* 34:26; *Deut.* 14:21
*Lev.* 4:23 offering, a *k.* of goats, 28; 9:3; *Ezek.* 43:22; 45:23
23:19 sacrifice one *k.* of goats, *Num.* 7:16, 22, 28; 15:24; 28:15, 30; 29:5, 11, 16, 19, 25
*Jud.* 6:19 Gid. made ready a *k.*
14:6 Samson rent lion as a *k.*
*Is.* 11:6 leopard lie down with *k.*
*Luke* 15:29 thou never gavest a *k.*

**KIDNEYS.**

*Ex.* 29:13 thou shalt take two *k.* and burn, 22; *Lev.* 3:4, 10, 15; 4:9; 7:4; 8:16, 25
*Lev.* 9:10 *k.* burnt on altar, 19
*Deut.* 32:14 fat of *k.* of wheat
*Is.* 34:6 with fat of *k.* of rams

KIDRON. 2 *Sam.* 15:23

**KIDS.**

*Gen.* 27:9 fetch me from th. 2 *k.*
16 put skins of *k.* on his hands
*Lev.* 16:5 two *k.* of the goats
1 *K.* 20:27 like two lit. floc. of *k.*
*Cant.* 1:8 feed thy *k.* bes. shep.'s

**KILL.**

*Gen.* 4:15 lest any find. C. *k.* him
12:12 th. wi. *k.* me, but save th.
27:42 purposing to *k.* thee
37:21 said, Let us not *k.* him
*Ex.* 1:16 if it be son, ye *k.* him
2:14 intend. to *k.* me? *Acts* 7:28
16:3 *k.* this assembly
17:3 *k.* us and chil. with thirst
20:13 thou shalt not *k.* *Deut.* 5:17; *Mat.* 5:21; *Rom.* 13:9
22:1 if man steal ox, and *k.* it
29:11 *k.* bullock before the L. *Lev.* 1:5; 4:4
*Lev.* 1:11 *k.* it on side altar, 16:15
3:2 *k.* it at door of tabernacle
4:24 *k.* it in place where they *k.*
14:50 he shall *k.* one of the birds
20:4 seed to Moloch, *k.* him not
16 shalt *k.* woman and beast
*Num.* 11:15 if deal thus, *k.* me
14:15 if thou *k.* all this people
16:13 bro. us to *k.* us in wilder.
22:29 for now would I *k.* thee
31:17 *k.* ev. woman known man
*Deut.* 4:42 who *k.* his neighbor
12:15 mayest *k.* and eat flesh
13:9 thou shalt surely *k.* him
32:39 I *k.* and I make alive
*Jud.* 13:23 L. were plea. to *k.* us
16:2 wh. it is day, we sh. *k.* him
20:31 began to *k.* 39
1 *Sam.* 17:9 be able to *k.* me
19:2 Saul seeketh to *k.* thee, 17
30:15 swear thou wilt nei. *k.* me
2 *Sam.* 14:7 that we may *k.* him
32 let him *k.* me
21:4 nor for us sh. th. *k.* any m.
2 *K.* 5:7 am I God, to *k.*?
7:4 if they *k.* us, we sh. but die
11:15 follow. her *k.* with sword
2 *Chr.* 35:6 *k.* the passover
*Est.* 3:13 let. by posts to *k.* Jews
*Ec.* 3:3 time to *k.* time to heal
*Is.* 14:30 *k.* thy root with famine
29:1 let them *k.* sacrifices
*Ezek.* 34:3 *k.* them that are fed
*Mat.* 5:21 who *k.* sh. be in dang.
10:28 fear not them which *k.* the body, *Luke* 12:4
21:38 heir, come let us *k.* him, *Mark* 12:7; *Luke* 20:14
23:34 some of them ye shall *k.*
26:4 take J. by subtl. to *k.* him
*Mark* 3:4 to save life, or to *k.*?
10:19 do not *k.* *Lu.* 18:20; *Ja.* 2:11
*Luke* 13:31 Herod will *k.* thee
15:23 bring fatted calf and *k.* it
*John* 5:18 J. sought to *k.* him, 7:1
7:19 why go ye about to *k.* me?
20 who goeth about to *k.* thee?
25 is this he wh. th. seek to *k.*?
8:22 *k.* himself; 37 to *k.* 40
10:10 thief com. to steal and *k.*
*Acts* 9:23 counsel to *k.* P. 26:21
10:13 rise, Peter, *k.* and eat
23:15 are ready to *k.* him
25:3 lay. wait in way to *k.* him
27:42 counsel to *k.* prisoner
*Jam.* 2:11 yet if thou *k.*
4:2 ye *k.* and desire to have
*Rev.* 2:23 I will *k.* her children
6:4 that they sho. *k.* one anoth.
8 power was given them to *k.*
9:5 that they should not *k.* th.
11:7 beast overco. and *k.* them

**KILLED.**

*Gen.* 37:31 Joseph's coat, *k.* kid
*Ex.* 21:29 the ox hath *k.* a man
*Lev.* 6:25 place wh. burnt-offer. is *k.* sin-off. be *k.* bef. the L.
8:19 ram he *k.* 14:5 bird be *k.*
14:6 dip them in blo. of bird *k.*
*Num.* 16:41 ye *k.* peo. of the L.
31:19 whoso. hath *k.* any person
1 *Sam.* 24:11 cut skirt, *k.* th. not
25:11 take my flesh I have *k.*
2 *Sam.* 12:9 thou hast *k.* Uriah
1 *K.* 21:19 *k.* and tak. possession?
2 *Chr.* 25:3 slew th. that *k.* king
30:15 *k.* the passover, 35:1, 11; *Ezr.* 6:20
*Ps.* 44:22 for thy sake are we *k.*
*Prov.* 9:2 she hath *k.* her beasts
*Lam.* 2:21 thou ha. *k.* not pitied
*Mat.* 16:21 *k.* and raised again, *Mark* 8:31; 9:31
21:35 be. one, and *k.* *Mark* 12:5
*Mat.* 22:4 oxen and fatlin. are *k.*
23:31 chil. of them *k.* prophets
*Mark* 12:8 *k.* him cast him out
14:12 wh. they *k.* the passover
*Luke* 11:47 fathers *k.* them, 48
12:5 after he hath *k.* ha. power
15:27 fa. hath *k.* fatted calf, 30
22:7 day when pass. must be *k.*
*Acts* 3:15 *k.* the Prince of life
12:2 *k.* James, brother of John
16:27 would have *k.* himself
23:12 nor drink till they *k.* Paul
*Rom.* 8:36 for thy sake we are *k.*
11:3 L. they have *k.* thy proph.
2 *Cor.* 6:9 chastened and not *k.*
*Thes.* 2:15 *k.* the Lord Jesus
*Jam.* 5:6 condemned and *k.* just
*Rev.* 6:11 sh. be *k.* as they were
9:18 the third part of man *k.*
20 the rest which were not *k.*
11:5 if hurt him he must be *k.*
13:10 must be *k.* with sword
15 image of beast, should be *k.*

**KILLEDST, EST.**

*Ex.* 2:14 as thou *k.* Egyptian
*Mat.* 23:37 *k.* prophets, *Luke* 13:34

**KILLETH.**

*Lev.* 24:17 he that *k.* any man sh. be put to dea. *Num.* 35:30
18 that *k.* a beast, 21
*Num.* 35:11 *k.* any unawares, 15; *Deut.* 19:4; *Jos.* 20:3, 9
1 *Sam.* 2:6 L. *k.* and maketh alive
*Job* 5:2 wrath *k.* the foolish man
24:14 the murderer *k.* the poor
*Prov.* 21:25 des. of slothful *k.* him
*Is.* 66:3 he that *k.* an ox
*John* 16:2 who *k.* you do. G. ser.
2 *Cor.* 3:6 letter *k.* Sp. giveth life
*Rev.* 13:10 he that *k.* with sword must be killed

**KILLING.**

2 *Chr.* 30:17 charge of *k.* passover
*Is.* 22:13 slaying oxen, *k.* sheep
*Hos.* 4:2 swearing, lying, and *k.*
*Mark* 12:5 beating some, *k.* some

**KIN.**

*Lev.* 18:6 none appro. to near *k.*
20:19 he uncovereth his near *k.*
25:25 *k.* come to redeem it, 49
*Ruth* 2:20 man is near *k.* to us
2 *Sam.* 19:42 king near *k.* to us

**KIND.**

2 *Chr.* 10:7 if thou be *k.* to people
*Luke* 6:35 G. is *k.* to unthankful
1 *Cor.* 13:4 charity suff. and is *k.*
*Eph.* 4:32 be *k.* one to another

**KIND, Substantive.**

*Gen.* 1:11 yield. fruit after *k.* 12
21 waters brought forth after *k.*
25 God made beast after his *k.*
6:20 fowls after th. *k.* cattle aft. *k.* ev. creeping thing after *k.*
*Lev.* 11:14 hawk after his *k.* 15, 16, 19; *Deut.* 14:14
19:19 not let cattle with div. *k.*
*Neh.* 13:20 sellers of all *k.* ware
*Ec.* 2:5 I planted trees of all *k.*
*Mat.* 13:47 gathered of every *k.*
17:21 *k.* go. not out, *Mark* 9:29
1 *Cor.* 15:39 th. is one *k.* of flesh
*Jam.* 1:18 be a *k.* of first-fruits
3:7 every *k.* of beast and birds

**KINDS.**

*Gen.* 8:19 creepeth after their *k.*
2 *Chr.* 16:14 with divers *k.* spices
*Jer.* 15:3 appoint over th. four *k.*
1 *Cor.* 12:10 divers *k.* of tongues
14:10 are so many *k.* of voices

**KINDLE.**

*Prov.* 26:21 con. man to *k.* strife
*Is.* 9:18 shall *k.* in the thickets
10:16 *k.* a burning like a fire
30:33 breath of Lord doth *k.* it
43:2 nor sh. flame *k.* upon thee
*Jer.* 33:18 want man to *k.* m.-off.
*Ob.* 18 fire and flame *k.* in them

**KINDLED.**

*Lev.* 10:6 bewail burn. L. hath *k.*
*Num.* 11:33 wrath of the Lord was *k.* *Deut.* 11:17; 2 *K.* 22:13, 17; *Ps.* 106:40
2 *Sam.* 22:9 coals *k.* *Ps.* 18:8
*Job* 19:11 he hath *k.* his wrath
32:2 then was *k.* wrath of Elihu
42:7 wrath is *k.* against thee
*Ps.* 2:12 wrath is *k.* but a little
124:3 their wrath *k.* against us
*Is.* 50:11 sparks that ye have *k.*
*Jer.* 44:6 wrath *k.* in cities of J.
*Ezek.* 20:48 I the Lord have *k.* it
*Hos.* 11:8 my repentings are *k.*
*Luke* 12:49 will I, if it be *k.*?
*See* ANGER, FIRE.

**KINDLETH.**

*Job* 41:21 his breath *k.* coals
*Is.* 44:15 *k.* it, and baketh bread
*Jam.* 3:5 how great, a little fire *k.*

**KINDLY.**

*Gen.* 24:49 if you deal *k.* 47:29
34:3 Shech. spake *k.* to damsel
50:21 Joseph spake *k.* to breth.
*Jos.* 2:14 deal *k.* and truly
*Ruth* 1:8 the L. deal *k.* with you
1 *Sam.* 20:8 deal *k.* with thy ser.

*Rom.* 12:10 be *k.* one to another

**KINDNESS.**

*Gen.* 20:13 *k.* thou shalt show
21:23 the *k.* I have done to thee
24:12 O L. show *k.* to my master
40:14 and show *k.* I pray thee
*Jos.* 2:12 *k.* to my fa.'s house
*Jud.* 8:35 nor showed *k.* to Jer.
*Ruth* 2:20 not left off *k.* to living
3:10 show. more *k.* in latter end
1 *Sam.* 15:6 ye showed *k.* to Isr.
20:14 show me the *k.* of the L.
2 *Sam.* 2:5 showed *k.* to your lord
6 I also will requite you this *k.*
9:3 that I may show *k.* to him
16:17 is this thy *k.* to friend?
1 *K.* 2:7 *k.* to sons of Barzillai
3:6 kept for David this great *k.*
2 *Chr.* 24:22 J. remember. not *k.*
*Neh.* 9:17 G. gracious, of great *k.*
*Est.* 2:9 maiden obt. *k.* of him
*Ps.* 31:21 showed me marvel. *k.*
117:2 for his merciful *k.* is great
119:76 merciful *k.* be my comf.
141:5 right. smite, it sh. be a *k.*
*Prov.* 19:22 desire of man is his *k.*
31:26 in her tongue is law of *k.*
*Is.* 54:8 with *k.* will I have mercy
10 *k.* shall not depart from thee
*Jer.* 2:2 I remem *k.* of thy youth
*Joel* 2:13 he is of gr. *k.* *Jon.* 4:2
*Acts* 28:2 showed us no little *k.*
2 *Cor.* 6:6 by long-suffering by *k.*
*Eph.* 2:7 in his *k.* toward us
*Col.* 3:12 on *k.* humblen. of mind
*Tit.* 3:4 after the *k.* of G. our
2 *Pet.* 1:7 brotherly-*k.* to *k.* char.

**Loving-KINDNESS.**

*Ps.* 17:7 show thy *l.-k.* 92:2
26:3 thy *l.-k.* is before mine eyes
36:7 how excellent is thy *l.-k.*
10 O continue thy *l.-k.* to them
40:10 not concealed thy *l.-k.*
11 let thy *l.-k.* preserve me
42:8 Lord will command *l.-k.*
48:9 we thought of thy *l.-k.* O G.
51:1 have mercy accord. to *l.-k.*
63:3 thy *l.-k.* is better than life
69:16 for thy *l.-k.* is good
88:11 sh. *l.-k.* be dec. in grave?
89:33 *l.-k.* will I not take fr. him
92:2 to show forth *l.-k.* in morn.
103:4 crowneth thee with *l.-k.*
107:43 understand *l.-k.* of the L.
119:88 quicken me after *l.-k.* 159
138:2 praise thy name for *l.-k.*
143:8 cause me to hear thy *l.-k.*
*Jer.* 9:24 L. which exercise *l.-k.*
16:5 tak. away peace, even *l.-k.*
31:3 with *l.-k.* have I dr. thee
32:18 show. *l.-k.* unto thousands
*Hos.* 2:19 betro. th. to me in *l.-k.*

**Loving-KINDNESSES.**

*Ps.* 25:6 remem. mercies and *l.-k.*
89:49 where are thy former *l.-k.*
*Is.* 63:7 mention *l.-k.* of the Lord

**KINDRED.**

*Gen.* 12:1 get thee fr. *k.* *Acts* 7:3
24:4 go to *k.* and take wife, 38:40
31:3 return to thy *k.* 13; 32:9
43:7 asked us straitly of our *k.*
*Num.* 10:30 dep. to own la. and *k.*
*Jos.* 6:23 brought out all her *k.*
*Ruth* 2:3 of *k.* of Elimelech, 3:2
*Est.* 2:10 show. not peo. or *k.* 20
8:6 end. to see destruction of *k.*
*Ezek.* 11:15 men of thy *k.* said
*Luke* 1:61 none of *k.* called
*Acts* 4:6 were of *k.* of high-priest
7:13 Joseph's *k.* known to Pha.
19 dealt subtilely with our *k.*
*Rev.* 5:9 redeemed us out of ev. *k.*
14:6 gospel to preach to ev. *k.*

**KINDREDS.**

1 *Chr.* 16:28 give to the Lord, ye *k.* *Ps.* 96:7
*Ps.* 22:27 *k.* of nations worship
*Acts* 3:25 all *k.* of earth blessed
*Rev.* 1:7 all *k.* of earth shall wail
7:9 multitude of *k.* bef. throne
11:9 *k.* see dead bodies thr. days
13:7 pow. given him over all *k.*

**KINE.**

*Gen.* 32:15 forty *k.* ten bulls to E.
*Gen.* 41:2 seven well-favored *k.* 18
3 seven *k.* out of river, 4, 19, 20
26 seven good *k.* are sev. years
27 sev. ill-favored *k.* sev. years
*Deut.* 7:13 bless increa. of thy *k.*
28:4 blessed be incr. of thy *k.*
18 cursed be incr. of thy *k.*
32:14 butter of *k.* milk of sheep
1 *Sam.* 6:7 ta. two milch *k.* tie *k.*
10 took two *k.* 12 *k.* took way
2 *Sam.* 17:29 and cheese of *k.*
*Amos* 4:1 hear this, ye *k.* of Bas.

**KING.**

*Gen.* 14:18 M. *k.* of Sal. *Heb.* 7:1
*Ex.* 1:8 arose new *k.* over Egypt
*Num.* 23:21 shout of a *k.* am. th.
24:7 his *k.* be higher than Agag
*Deut.* 17:14 I will set *k.* over me
33:5 and he was *k.* in Jeshurun
*Jud.* 8:18 resem. child. of a *k.*
9:8 trees went to anoint a *k.*
17:6 in those days no *k.* in Isr. 18:1; 19:1; 21:25
1 *Sam.* 2:10 L. give strength to *k.*
8:5 go make us a *k.* to judge us
6 gi. a *k.* 9 show man. of *k.* 11
10 have a *k.* 22 make th. a *k.*
20 that our *k.* may judge us
10:19 nay, but set a *k.* over us
24 said, G. save the *k.* 2 *Sam.* 16:16; 2 *K.* 11:12; 2 *Chr.* 23:11
12:1 I have made a *k.* over you
2 the *k.* walketh before you
12 said, Nay, a *k.* sh. reign ov. us, when God was your *k.*
17 wicked. great in asking a *k.*
19 this evil, to ask a *k.*
25 cons. both you and your *k.*
15:1 to anoint thee to be *k.*
23 rej. thee from being *k.* 26
16:1 I have provided me a *k.*
20:5 not fail to sit with *k.*
22:15 let not *k.* imp. any thing
24:20 I know that thou sh. be *k.*
25:36 Nabal held feast like a *k.*
2 *Sam.* 5:12 estab. him *k.* over I.
11:8 a mess of meat from *k.*
12:7 I anointed thee *k.* over Is.
14:9 *k.* and his throne be guiltl.
17 as an angel of God, so is my lord the *k.* 19:27
15:2 had controversy, ca. to *k.*
3 none deputed of *k.* to hear
16:9 sh. this dead dog curse *k.*?
17:2 I will smite the *k.* only
18:13 is no matter hid from *k.*
19:9 *k.* saved us out of hand of
11 speech of Israel come to *k.*
22 I know that I am *k.* over Is.
28 wh. right to cry more to *k.*?
43 we have ten parts in the *k.*
22:51 tower of salv. for his *k.*
1 *K.* 1:35 Solomon *k.* in my stead
3:7 servant *k.* instead of David
28 heard judg. the *k.* judged
8:62 *k.* and all Is. offer. sacrifice
10:3 not any thing hid from *k.*
11:37 thou shalt be *k.* over Isr.
14:2 who told me I should be *k.*
14 L. raise up a king over Is.
21:10 didst blaspheme G. and *k.*
12:13 prophets declare good to the *k.* 2 *Chr.* 18:12
47 no *k.* in E. a deputy was *k.*
2 *K.* 1:11 *k.* said, Come down, 9
4:13 wouldest be spok. for to *k.*
7:2 lord on whose hand *k.* lean.
8:3 to cry to the *k.* for her hou.
13 L. showed thou shalt be *k.*
20 E. made *k.* over themselves
11:8 be with *k.* as he goeth out
1 *Chr.* 4:23 they dwelt wi. the *k.*
29:20 worshipped Lord and *k.*
2 *Chr.* 2:11 he made thee *k.* 9:8
10:15 *k.* hearkened not to peop.
11:22 he thought to make him *k.*
24:21 stoned him at com. of *k.*
25:16 thou made of *k.* counsel?
*Ezr.* 4:12 be it kn. to *k.* 13; 5:8
6:10 pray for life of *k.* and sons
7:27 put in *k.* heart to beautify
8:22 req. of *k.* band of soldiers
*Neh.* 1:11 I was the *k.* cup-bearer
6:7 saying, There is a *k.* in Ju.
*Est.* 4:16 will go in unto the *k.*
6:6 the *k.* delighteth to honor, 9
7:8 word went out of *k.* mouth
*Job* 15:24 as a *k.* ready to battle
18:14 bring him to *k.* of terrors
29:25 dwelt as a *k.* in the army
34:18 say to *k.* thou art wick.?
41:34 a *k.* over children of pride
*Ps.* 2:6 set my *k.* upon holy hill
5:2 my *k.* and my God, 84:3
10:16 Lord is *k.* for ever, 29:10
18:50 deliverance giveth he to *k.*
20:9 let *k.* hear us when we call
*Ps.* 21:1 *k.* shall joy in thy stren.
7 the *k.* trusted in the Lord
24:7 *k.* of glory shall come in, 9
8 who is *k.* of glory? the Lord
10 L. of hosts, he is *k.* of glory
33:16 no *k.* saved by multitude
45:1 things I made touc. the *k.*
11 so shall the *k.* greatly desi.
14 brought to the *k.* in raim.
47:6 praises to *k.* 7 God is *k.*
61:6 prolong *k.* life and years
63:11 the *k.* shall rejoice in God
72:1 give the *k.* thy judgments
74:12 God is my *k.* of old
89:18 H. One of Israel is our *k.*
98:6 make a noise bef. L. the *k.*
99:4 *k.* also loveth judgment
149:2 children of Z. joyful in *k.*
*Prov.* 14:28 people is the *k.* hon.
35 *k.* favor toward wise serv.
20:28 mercy and truth pres. *k.*
22:11 the *k.* shall be his friend
24:21 fear the Lord and the *k.*
25:5 take wicked from bef. *k.*
30:27 the locusts have no *k.*
31 *k.* against wh. no rising up
*Ec.* 2:12 man do cometh after *k.*
5:9 *k.* hims. served by the field
8:4 where word of a *k.* is power
10:16 woe to thee, wh. *k.* is ch.
17 bles. wh. *k.* is son of nobles
20 curse not the *k.* in thought
*Cant.* 1:4 *k.* bro. me to chamber
12 while the *k.* sitteth at table
3:11 *k.* Solomon with the crown
*Is.* 6:5 mine eyes ha. seen the *k.*
8:21 curse their *k.* and their G.
23:15 according to days of one *k.*
30:33 for the *k.* it is prepared
32:1 *k.* shall reign in righteous.
33:17 thine eyes shall see the *k.*
22 L. is our *k.* he will save us
43:15 Creator of Israel your *k.*
57:9 wentest to *k.* with ointm.
*Jer.* 4:9 heart of *k.* shall perish
8:19 is not her *k.* in her?
10:10 true God, everlasting *k.*
23:5 a *k.* shall reign and prosper
38:25 wh. said to *k.* the *k.* to th.
46:18 *k.* whose name is the Lord of hosts, 48:15; 51:57
49:38 I will des. *k.* and princes
*Lam.* 2:6 L. despised *k.* and pri.
*Ezek.* 17:13 hath tak. of *k.* seed
16 *k.* dwell. that made him *k.*
26:7 I will bring a *k.* of kings
37:22 one *k.* be *k.* to them all, 24

Dan. 2:24 bring me in before the
k. and I will show the k.
4:31 while word was in k. mou.
37 I honor k. of heaven
5:5 k. saw part of hand th. wro.
8:23 a k. of fierce countenance
11:3 a mighty k. shall stand up
36 k. sh. do accord. to his will
Hos. 3:4 Is. sh. abide without k.
5 Is. seek L. and Dav. their k.
7:3 make k. glad with wicked.
5 in day of our k. princes made
10:3 what then should a k. do?
7 her k. is cut off, as the foam
13:10 will be thy k. give me k.
11 gave thee k. in mine anger
Amos 7:13 k. chapel, the k. court
Mic. 4:9 why cry, is there no k.?
Zec. 9:9 k. cometh, Mat. 21:5
14:9 L. shall be k. over all earth
16 go up to worship k. 17
Mat. 18:23 likened to cert. k. 22:2
22:11 when the k. came in
Mark 6:25 came with haste to k.
Luke 14:31 what k. goeth to war
19:38 blessed be k. that cometh
23:2 that he himself is Ch. a k.
John 6:15 to make him k.
12:15 behold thy k. com. on ass
18:37 Pil. said, Art thou a k.?
19:12 whoso. maketh himself k.
14 Pilate saith, Behold your k.
15 shall I crucify your k.?
Acts 7:18 till another k. arose
13:21 afterward they desir. a k.
17:7 th. is another k. one Jesus
1 Tim. 1:17 now to the k. etern.
6:15 K. of kings, and L. of lords
Heb. 11:23 not afraid of k. com.
1 Pet. 2:13 whe. to k. as supreme
17 fear God, honor the k.
Rev. 9:11 they had a k. over th.
15:3 just are thy ways, K. of sai.
17:14 L. of lords, K. of ki. 19:16

KING *of the Amorites.* See SIHON.

**KING of Assyria.**

2 K. 15:19 Pul k. of A. ag. land
20 exac. money to give k. of A.
17:6 Hosea k. of A. took Sama.
2 K. 18:11 k. of A. did car. I. to A.
33 deliv. out of hand of k. of A.
Ezr. 6:22 turned heart of k. of A.
Is. 7:17 L. bring upon k. of Ass.
20 shave by k. of Assyr. head
Jer. 50:17 k. of A. devoured him
Nah. 3:18 slumber, O k. of Assy.

See BASHAN, BABYLON, DAVID.

**KING of Egypt.**

Ex. 3:19 k. of Egypt not let you
2 K. 24:7 k. of Egypt came not
2 Chr. 12:2 k. of E. came ag. Jer.
33:6 k. of E. put him down at J.
4 k. of E. made Eliakim king
Is. 36:6 so is k. of Egypt to all

See PHARAOH, GREAT, HOUSE, JEWS.

**KING of Israel.**

1 Sam. 26:20 k. of Israel is come
2 Sam. 6:20 glorious was k. of Is.
1 K. 22:31 fight only wi. k. of Is.
32 it is k. of Is. 2 Chr. 18:31
2 K. 6:11 which of us for k. of Is.
16:7 out of hand of k. of Israel
2 Chr. 18:30 fight not, sa. wi. k. I.
Hos. 10:15 k. of Israel be cut off
Zep. 3:15 k. of Israel in midst
Mat. 27:42 if he be k. of Israel let
him descend, Mark 15:32
John 1:49 thou art k. of Israel
12:13 blessed is the k. of Israel

**KING of Judah.**

2 K. 22:18 k. of J. wh. sent you
2 Chr. 35:21 what have I to do
with thee, thou k. of Judah
Jer. 37:7 k. of J. who sent you?

**KING of Moab.**

Num. 23:7 k. of M. brought fr. A.
Jos. 24:9 k. of M. warred ag. Is.
Jud. 3:14 Is. ser. k. of M. 18 yrs.
11:25 art thou bet. th. k. of M.?
1 Sam. 12:9 sold them to k. of M.
22:4 Da. bro. father to k. of M.
2 K. 3:4 k. of M. a sheep-master
26 k. of Moab saw battle
Jer. 27:3 send yokes to k. of M.

**O KING.**

1 Sam. 17:55 O k. I cannot tell
26:17 lord, O k. 2 Sam. 14:9, 22;
16:4; 19:26; 1 K. 1:13, 20, 24;
20:4; 2 K. 6:12, 26; 8:5
2 Sam. 14:4 wo. said, Help, O k.
2 Chr. 25:7 O k. let not ar. of Is.
Ps. 145:1 I will extol thee, O k.
Jer. 10:7 thee, O k. of nations?
Dan. 2:4 O k. live for ever, 3:9;
5:10; 6:21
29 O k. thy thoughts came into
31 thou, O k. sawest an image
37 thou, O k. art a k. of kings
3:10 thou, O k. hast ma. a decr.
17 del. us out of thy hand, O k.
18 be it known to thee, O k.
24 they answered, True, O k.
4:22 it is thou, O k. that art gr.
27 O k. let counsel be accept.
6:7 ask peti. save of thee, O k.
8 now, O k. establish decree
22 O k. I have done no hurt
Acts 26:13 O k. I saw in way
19 O k. I was not disobedient

**KING of Persia.**

Ezr. 4:3 k. of Persia commanded
5 reign of Darius k. of P. 9:9
7 Bish. wrote unto k. of P. 6:14

See CYRUS.

**KING of Syria.**

1 K. 20:20 k. of S. esc. on horse
2 K. 5:1 capt. of host of k. of S.
8:7 k. of S. sick; 9 k. of S. sent
13:4 bec. k. of S. oppress. them
16:7 out of hand of k. of Syria
2 Chr. 16:7 relied on k. of Syria

See BENHADAD, HAZAEL, REZIN.

**KING of Tyre.**

2 Sam. 5:11 H. k. of T. 1 Chr. 14:1
1 K. 5:1 k. of T. sent S. servants
2 Chr. 2:11 k. of T. ans. in writ.

**KINGS.**

Gen. 17:6 k. shall come out of
thee, 16; 35:11
36:31 k. that reigned in Edom
Jos. 10:5 five k. of Amorites tog.
24 put feet on necks of those k.
12:24 all these k. thirty and one
Jud. 1:7 seventy k. thu. cu off
2 Sam. 11:1 when k. go to battle
1 K. 3:13 not any am. k. like thee,
10:23; 2 Chr. 1:12; 9:22
4:24 Solomon over all the k.
2 K. 3:10 called three k. together
23 the k. are surely slain
10:4 two k. stood not bef. him
1 Chr. 16:21 reprov. k. Ps. 105:14
2 Chr. 9:23 k. sought presence S.
21:20 the sepulchres of k. 24:25
26:23 field of burial belong. to k.
Ezr. 4:15 city being hurtful to k.
6:12 G. dest. k. alter this house
7:12 Artaxerxes king of k. to E.
Neh. 9:32 trou. little to us and k.
34 nor have our k. kept thy law
Job 3:14 had I been at rest wi. k.
12:18 he looseth the bond of k.
36:7 k. are they on the throne
Ps. 2:2 the k. of the ear. Acts 4:26
10 therefore, O k. be instruct.
45:9 k. daughters among women
48:4 lo, the k. were assembled
68:12 k. of armies did flee apace
14 the Almighty scat. k. in it
29 sh. k. bring presents to thee
72:11 k. shall fall down be. him
76:12 terrible to k. of the earth
89:27 higher than k. of the ear.
102:15 k. of earth sh. fear thy g.
110:5 strike k. in day of wrath
119:46 speak of testim. befo. k.
135:10 smote nations, and sl. k.
136:17 which smote great k. 18
138:4 k. of earth praise th. 148:11
144:10 he that giveth salva. to k.
149:8 bind their k. with chains
Prov. 8:15 by me k. reign
16:12 abom. for k. commit wick.
13 right. lips are delight of k.
22:29 dilig. shall stand before k.
25:2 honor of k. to search mat.
3 heart of k. is unsearchable
30:28 the spider is in k. palaces
31:3 ways to that wh. destroy k.
4 it is not for k. to drink
Ec. 2:8 peculiar treasure of k.
Is. 7:16 land forsaken of both k.
10:8 are not princes altoge. k.?
14:18 k. of nations lie in glory
19:11 I am the son of ancient k.
24:21 L. punish k. of the earth
41:2 who made him ruler over k.
45:1 I will loose the loins of k.
49:7 k. shall see and arise
23 k. sh. be thy nursing fathers
52:15 k. sh. shut mouths at him
60:3 k. to brightn. of thy rising
10 k. shall minister to thee
11 that their k. may be broug.
16 thou shalt suck breast of k.
62:2 all k. shall see thy glory
Jer. 2:26 k. and princes ashamed
13:13 k. that sit on David's thr.
22:4 k. sitting upon throne of D.
25:18 made Judah and k. drink
34:5 with burnings of former k.
44:17 k. and princes bu. incense
46:25 punish their k. and gods
49:3 their k. shall go to captivi.
50:41 many k. shall be raised up
Lam. 4:12 k. of earth not believ.
Ezek. 27:35 k. be sore afra. 32:10
28:17 I will lay thee before k.
43:7 k. no more defile my name
Dan. 2:21 removeth k. set. up k.
44 in the days of these k.
47 that your G. is a Lord of k.
7:17 four great beasts are four k.
24 the ten horns are ten k.
9:6 spake in thy name to our k.
8 to k. and princes belong con.
11:2 three k. 27 these k. hearts
Hos. 7:7 all their k. are fallen
8:4 they set up k. but not by me
Hab. 1:10 they shall scoff at k.
Mat. 10:18 brou. before k. for my
sake, Mark 13:9; Luke 21:12
11:8 wear soft cloth. in k. hous.
17:25 of wh. do k. of earth take?
Luke 10:24 k. have desired to see
22:25 k. of Gentiles exercise
1 Cor. 4:8 ye have reigned as k.
1 Tim. 2:2 pray. be made for k.
6:15 King of k. and Lord of
lords, Rev. 17:14; 19:16
Heb. 7:1 returned from slaug. k.
Rev. 1:5 J. Christ prince of k.
6 k. and priest unto God, 5:10
6:15 k. of earth hid themselves
10:11 must prophesy before k.
16:12 way of k. of east prepared
14 spirits which go forth to k.
Rev. 17:2 k. of earth commit. for.
10 seven k. five are fallen
12 ten k. w. receive pow. as k.
18 wh. reign. over k. of earth
18:3 k. of earth have committed
9 k. of earth who shall bewail
19:18 eat the flesh of k. and cap.
21:24 k. of the earth bring glory

**KINGS of the Amorites.**

*Deut.* 4:47 two *k. of the A.* 31:4; *Jos.* 2:10; 9:10; 24:12
*Jos.* 10:5 five *k. of A.* together. 6
*See* BOOK, GREAT.

**KINGS of Israel.**

1 *K.* 14:19 book of the Chronicles of the *k. of Is.* 15:31; 16:5, 14, 20, 27; 22:39; 2 *K.* 1:18; 10:34; 13:8, 12; 14:15, 28; 15:11, 15, 21, 26, 31
16:33 prov. more th. all *k. of I.*
20:31 *k. of I.* are merciful kings
2 *K.* 17:2 evil but not as *k. of I.*
23:19 away houses *k. of I.* made
22 a passo. in days of *k. of I.*
1 *Chr.* 9:1 written in book of *k. of I.* 2 *Chr.* 16:11; 25:26; 27:7; 28:26; 32:32; 33:18
2 *Chr.* 20:34 in book of Jehu who is mentioned in book of the *k. of I.* 35:27; 36:8
28:27 not into sepul. of *k. of I.*
*Mic.* 1:14 shall be a lie to *k. of I.*

**KINGS of Judah.**

1 *K.* 14:29 the book of the Chronicles of the *k. of Jud.* 15:7, 23; 22:45; 2 *K.* 8:23; 15:6, 36; 16:19; 20:20; 21:17, 25; 23:28; 24:5
2 *K.* 12:19 written in the book of the Chronicles of the *k. of J.* 14:18; 2 *Chr.* 25:26; 28:26; 32:32; 35:27; 36:8
23:11 horses *k. of J.* had given
12 down altars *k. of J.* made
22 not pass. in days of *k. of J.*
2 *Chr.* 34:11 houses *k. of J.* des.
*Jer.* 1:18 made pillar ag. *k. of J.*
8:1 bring out bones of *k. of J.*
19:4 gods *k. of J.* ha. not known
20:5 treas. of *k. of J.* to enemies
44:9 forgot. wickedn. of *k. of J.*
*See* KINGS *of Israel.*

**KINGDOM.**

*Ex.* 19:6 ye sh. be a *k.* of priests
*Deut.* 3:4 took *k.* of Og in Bash.
1 *Sam.* 10:16 mat. of *k.* he told
25 Sam. told manner of the *k.*
11:14 renew *k.* th. 14:47 took *k.*
15:28 Lord rent *k.* of Is. 28:17
18:8 w. can he ha. more but *k.?*
2 *Sam.* 3:10 translate *k.* from S.
16:3 restore me *k.* of my father
1 *K.* 2:22 ask *k.* he is elder brot.
11:11 will rend *k.* from th. 31:35
13 will not rend away all *k.* 34
12:21 to bring *k.* again to Rehoboam, 2 *Chr.* 11:1
14:8 rent *k.* from house of Dav.
18:10 no *k.* my lord ha. not sent
2 *K.* 14:5 soon as *k.* confirmed
1 *Chr.* 16:20 fr. one *k.* to another people, *Ps.* 105:13
29:11 thine is the *k.* O Lord, *Ps.* 22:28; *Mat.* 6:13
2 *Chr.* 13:8 withstand *k.* of Lord
22:9 no power to keep still *k.*
*Neh.* 9:35 not serv. thee in th. *k.*
*Est.* 1:14 pri. wh. sat first in *k.*
4:14 come to *k.* for such a time
5:3 be given to half of *k.* 6; 7:2
*Is.* 19:2 shall fight *k.* ag. *k. Mat.* 24:7; *Mark* 13:8; *Luke* 21:10
60:12 *k.* not serve thee, *Jer.* 27:8
*Jer.* 18:7 I speak concerning a *k.*
*Lam.* 2:2 he hath polluted the *k.*
*Ezek.* 16:13 didst prosper into *k.*
17:14 the *k.* might be base
29:14 shall be there a base *k.*
*Dan.* 2:37 G. hath given thee *k.*
44 sh. G. of heaven set up a *k.*
4:17 ruleth in *k.* of men, 25, 32
31 the *k.* is departed from thee
6:4 against Dan. concerning *k.*
7:18 saints take *k.* and pos. *k.*
22 time came saints posses. *k.*
27 whose *k.* is an everlasting *k.*
11:21 not give the honor of *k.*
*Hos.* 1:4 cause to cease *k.* of Isr.
*Amos* 9:8 eyes of L. upon sinf. *k.*
*Ob.* 21 *k.* shall be the Lord's
*Mat.* 4:23 gosp. of *k.* 9:35; 24:14
8:12 child. of *k.* shall be cast
12:25 *k.* divided is bro. to desolation. *Mark* 3:24; *Lu.* 11:17
13:38 good seed are child. of *k.*
43 shine as sun in *k.* of Father
25:34 inherit *k.* prepared for you
26:29 drink it new in Fath.'s *k.*
*Mark* 11:10 blessed be *k.* of fath.
*Luke* 12:32 F.'s pleas. to give *k.*
19:12 nobleman went to rec. *k.*
22:29 I appoint unto you a *k.*
*Acts* 1:6 restore *k.* again to Isr.?
1 *Cor.* 15:24 have delivered up *k.*
*Col.* 1:13 translated us into the *k.*
*Heb.* 12:28 *k.* th. cannot be mov.
*Jam.* 2:5 heirs of *k.* he promised
2 *Pet.* 1:11 entrance into everl. *k.*
*Rev.* 1:9 companion in *k.*
17:12 which have received no *k.*
17 and give their *k.* to the bea.
*See* THRONE, ESTABLISH, ESTABLISHED.

**KINGDOM of God.**

*Mat.* 6:33 but seek ye first the *k. of God*, *Luke* 12:31
12:28 *k. of God* is come unto you, *Luke* 10:9, 11:20
19:24 than for a rich man to enter into *k. of G. Mark* 10:23; *Luke* 18:24
21:31 harlots go into *k. of God*
43 *k. of G.* be taken from you
*Mark* 1:14 preaching *k. of God*, *Acts* 8:12; 20:25; 28:31
15 the *k. of God* is at hand
4:11 to know the mystery of *k. of God*, *Luke* 8:10
9:1 till they have seen *k. of G.*
47 better to enter into *k. of G.*
10:14 such is *k. of G. Luke* 18:16
15 whoso not receive *k. of G.*
24 hard for th. trust in riches to enter *k. of G.* 25; *Lu.* 18:25
12:34 art not far from *k. of God*
14:25 I drink it new in *k. of G.*
15:43 which waited for the *k. of God*, *Luke* 23:51
*Luke* 4:43 I must preach *k. of G.*
6:20 for yours is the *k. of God*
7:28 least in *k. of G.* greater th.
9:2 sent th. to preach *k. of G.* 60
27 not taste de. till see *k. of G.*
62 lo. back, not fit for *k. of G.*
13:28 see prophets in *k. of God*
14:15 he eat bread in *k. of God*
16:16 time *k. of God* preached
17:20 *k. of God* cometh not
21 *k. of God* is within you
18:29 left child. for *k. of G.* sake
19:11 tho. *k. of G.* sho. appear
21:31 that *k. of G.* is at hand
22:16 be fulfilled in *k. of God*
18 not drink until *k. of G.* co.
*John* 3:3 bo. ag. can see *k. of G.*
5 cannot enter into *k. of God*
*Acts* 1:3 things pertaining to *k. of God*, 8:12; 19:8
14:22 thro' tribul. enter *k. of G.*
28:23 expou. and testi. *k. of G.*
*Rom.* 14:17 *k. of G.* is not meat
1 *Cor.* 4:20 *k. of God* is not in w.
6:9 unright. not inherit *k. of G.*
10 nor extortioners inhe. *k. of God*, *Gal.* 5:21; *Eph.* 5:5
15:50 flesh can. in. *k. of G.*
2 *Thes.* 1:5 worthy *k. of God*
*Rev.* 12:10 is come *k. of* our *God*

**KINGDOM of heaven.**

*Mat.* 3:2 repent, for *k. of heaven* is at hand, 4:17; 10:7
5:3 theirs is *k. of heaven*, 10
19 least in *k. of h.* g. in *k. of h.*
20 in no case ent. *k of h.* 18:3
7:21 saith, Lord, sh. ent. *k. of h.*
8:11 sit with Abrah. in *k. of h.*
11:11 least in *k. of h.* gre. th. he
12 *k. of heaven* suffer. violence
13:11 know mysteries of *k. of h.*
16:19 give thee keys of *k. of h.*
18:1 who is great. in *k. of h.?* 4
23:13 shut up *k. of h.* aga. men

**His KINGDOM.**

*Gen.* 10:10 begin. of *his k.* was B.
*Num.* 24:7 *his k.* shall be exalted
*Deut.* 17:18 sit. on throne of *h. k.*
1 *Chr.* 11:10 strengthened in *h. k.*
2 *Chr.* 1:1 S. strengthen. in *h. k.*
*Ps.* 103:19 *h. k.* ruleth over all
145:12 glorious majesty of *h. k.*
*Is.* 9:7 *h. k.* to order and establi.
*Dan.* 4:3 *his k.* is an everl. king.
34 *h. k.* fr. generat. 6:26; 7:14
11:4 *h. k.* broken and pluck. up
*Mat.* 12:26 *h. k.* stand? *Lu.* 11:18
13:41 gather out of *his k.* all th.
16:28 S. of man coming in *h. k.*
*Luke* 1:33 of *h. k.* sh. be no end
1 *Thes.* 2:12 called you to *h. k.*
2 *Tim.* 4:1 appearing and *his k.*
*Rev.* 16:10 *his k.* full of darkness

**My KINGDOM.**

*Gen.* 20:9 brou. on me and *m. k.*
2 *Sam.* 3:28 I and *m. k.* are guil.
*Dan.* 4:36 glo. of *my k.* in *my k.*
6:26 in every dominion of *my k.*
*Mark* 6:23 to half of *my k.*
*Luke* 22:30 drink at my table in *my k.*
*John* 18:36 *my k.* not of th. world

**Thy KINGDOM.**

1 *Sam.* 13:14 *t. k.* sh. not contin.
*Ps.* 45:6 *t. k.* ri. sceptre, *Heb.* 1:8
145:11 speak of glory of *thy k.*
13 *thy k.* is everlasting kingd.
*Dan.* 4:26 *t. k.* shall be sure
5:11 man in *t. k.* 26 numb. *t. k.*
28 *t. k.* divided to Med. and P.
*Mat.* 6:10 *t. k.* come, *Luke* 11:2
20:21 the other on left in *t. k.*
*Luke* 23:42 thou comest to *t. k.*

**KINGDOMS.**

1 *Sam.* 10:18 out of hand of all *k.*
1 *K.* 4:21 Sol. reigned over all *k.*
2 *K.* 19:15 God of all *k.* of earth
2 *Chr.* 12:8 may know serv. of *k.*
20:6 thou rulest over all the *k.*
36:23 all *k.* hath the Lord given me, *Ezr.* 1:2
*Ps.* 46:6 heath. raged, *k.* moved
79:6 wrath on *k.* have not called
102:22 *k.* gathered to serve Lord
*Is.* 10:10 hand found *k.* of idols
13:4 noise of *k.* of nations gath.
14:16 is this man did shake *k.?*
23:11 shook *k.* 37:16 God of *k.*
*Jer.* 1:10 over *k.* I have set thee
15:4 rem. to all *k.* 24:9; 34:17
25:26 all *k.* of world shall drink
29:18 make th. a terror to all *k.*
34:1 *k.* fought against Jerusal.
*Ezek.* 29:15 be the bas. of the *k.*
37:22 nor be divided into two *k.*
*Dan.* 2:44 shall cons. all these *k.*
7:23 shall be diverse from all *k.*
8:22 four *k.* stand out of nation
*Nah.* 3:5 will show *k.* thy shame
*Zep.* 3:8 assemble the *k.* to pour
*Hag.* 2:22 overthrow throne of *k.*
*Mat.* 4:8 all *k.* of world, *Luke* 4:5
*Heb.* 11:33 thro' faith subdued *k.*
*Rev.* 11:15 *k.* of world are *k.* of L.

**KINGLY.**

*Dan.* 5:20 deposed from *k.* thro.

**KINSFOLK, S.**

1 *K.* 16:11 none of Baasha's *k.*

2 *K.* 10:11 Jehu slew Ahab's *k.*
*Job* 19:14 *k.* failed and forgot. me
*Luke* 2:44 sought Jesus among *k.*
21:16 betrayed by *k.* and friends

**KINSMAN.**

*Num.* 5:8 if the man have no *k.*
27:11 give his inheritance to *k.*
*Ruth* 3:9 near *k.* 12 *k.* nearer
13 perform to thee part of a *k.*
4:1 behold *k.* of whom B. spake
14 not left thee without a *k.*
*John* 18:26 *k.* whose ear P. cut off
*Rom.* 16:11 salute Herodi. my *k.*

**KINSMEN.**

*Ruth* 2:20 is one of our next *k.*
*Ps.* 38:11 lovers and *k.* stood off
*Luke* 14:12 call not breth. nor *k.*
*Acts* 10:24 Cornelius called his *k.*
*Rom.* 9:3 my *k.* according to flesh
16:7 salute *k.* 21 *k.* salute you

**KINSWOMAN, MEN.**

*Lev.* 18:12 is my father's near *k.*
13 she is thy mother's near *k.*
17 for they are her near *k.*
*Prov.* 7:4 call understand. thy *k.*

**KIR.**

2 *K.* 16:9 people captive to K.
*Is.* 15:1 K. of M. is laid waste
*Amos* 9:7 bro. Assyrians from K.

**KIR-HARASETH.**

2 *K.* 3:25 in K. left they stones
*Is.* 16:7 foundations of K. shall

**KIRIATHAIM.**

*Gen.* 14:5 smote E. in Shav. K.
*Jer.* 48:1 K. is confounded, 23

**KIRJATH-ARBA.**

*Gen.* 23:2 Sar. died in K. *Jos.* 14:15; 20:7; *Jud.* 1:10

**KIRJATH-JEARIM.**

*Jos.* 9:17 K. a city of Hivites
1 *Sam.* 7:1 men of K. fetched ark
1 *Chr.* 13:5 the ark of God fr. K.
2 *Chr.* 1:4 broug. the ark fr. K.

KIRJATH-SEPHER. *Jos.* 15:15, 49

**KISH.**

1 *Sam.* 9:1 man wh. na. K. 14:51
10:11 wh. is come to son of K.?
2 *Sam.* 21:14 Sa. in sepulchre K.
*Acts* 13:21 G. gave the son of K.

**KISS, ES.**

*Prov.* 27:6 *k.* of an enemy deceit.
*Cant.* 1:2 *k.* me with *k.* of mouth
*Luke* 7:45 thou gavest me no *k.*
22:48 betra. Son of man wi. *k.*?
*Rom.* 16:16 salute with a holy *k.*
1 *Cor.* 16:20 gr. wi. *k.* 2 *Cor.* 13:12
1 *Thes.* 5:26 greet breth. w. h. *k.*
1 *Pet.* 5:14 greet with *k.* of chari.

**KISS, Verb.**

*Gen.* 27:26 come near and *k.* me
31:28 not suffered to *k.* my sons
2 *Sam.* 20:9 Ama. by beard to *k.*
1 *K.* 19:20 *k.* my father and mot.
*Ps.* 2:12 *k.* Son, lest he be angry
*Prov.* 24:26 every man *k.* his lips
*Cant.* 1:2 *k.* me with kisses of m.
8:1 I would *k.* thee, yet I should
*Hos.* 13:2 men sacrifi. *k.* the calv.
*Mat.* 26:48 whomsoever I *k.* hold him fast, *Mark* 14:44
*Luke* 7:45 not ceased *k.* my feet
22:47 Judas drew near to J. to *k.*

**KISSED.**

*Gen.* 27:27 Ja. came and *k.* him
29:11 Jacob *k.* Rachel and wept
31:55 La. *k.* sons and daughters
45:15 J. *k.* all his brethren
48:10 J. *k.* Joseph's sons
50:1 Jos. fell on fa.'s face *k.* him
*Ex.* 4:27 met Moses and *k.* him
18:7 met father-in-law *k.* him
*Ruth* 1:9 Na. *k.* daughters-in-law
1 *Sam.* 10:1 poured oil and *k.* S.
20:41 Jonathan and David *k.*
2 *Sam.* 14:33 king *k.* Absalom
15:5 Absa. *k.* any man came ni.
1 *K.* 19:18 mouth hath not *k.*
*Job* 31:27 mouth hath *k.* hand
*Ps.* 85:10 and peace *k.* each other
*Prov.* 7:13 caught him *k.* him
*Mat.* 26:49 said, Hail, Master, and *k.* him, *Mark* 14:45
*Luke* 7:38 M. *k.* feet and anointed
15:20 fell on his neck and *k.* him
*Acts* 20:37 fell on P.'s neck *k.* h.

**KITE.**

*Lev.* 11:14 *k.* uncl. *Deut.* 14:13

KITTIM. *Gen.* 10:4; 1 *Chr.* 1:7

**KNEAD, ED**

*Gen.* 18:6 *k.* it and make cakes
1 *Sam.* 28:24 took flour and *k.* it
2 *Sam.* 13:8 Tamar took flour *k.*
*Jer.* 7:18 women *k.* their dough
*Hos.* 7:4 the baker *k.* the dough

**KNEADING.**

*Ex.* 8:3 frogs co. into *k.*-troughs
12:34 *k.*-troughs bound in cloth.

**KNEE.**

*Gen.* 41:43 they cried, Bow the *k.*
*Is.* 45:23 unto me every *k.* sh. bow, *Rom.* 14:11; *Phil.* 2:10
*Mat.* 27:29 bowed the *k.* bef. him
*Rom.* 11:4 bowed the *k.* to Baal

**KNEEL, ED.**

*Gen.* 24:11 ma. his camels *k.* do.
2 *Chr.* 6:13 Solomon *k.* on knees
*Ps.* 95:6 let us *k.* before the L.
*Dan.* 6:10 D. *k.* three times a day
*Luke* 22:41 and Jesus *k.* down
*Acts* 7:60 Stephen *k.* and cried
9:40 Peter *k.* prayed; 20:36 P.
21:5 we *k.* down on the shore

**KNEELING.**

1 *K.* 8:54 Solomon rose from *k.*
*Mat.* 17:14 a man *k.* to him, saying, *Mark* 10:17
*Mark* 1:40 came a leper *k.*

**KNEES.**

*Gen.* 30:3 maid sh. bear on my *k.*
48:12 brou. them fr. between *k.*
50:23 brought up on Joseph's *k.*
*Deut.* 28:35 Lord smite thee in *k.*
*Jud.* 7:5 bowed down *k.* 6
16:19 made Sam. sleep on her *k.*
1 *K.* 8:54 arose fr. kneeling on *k.*
18:42 Elijah put face bet. his *k.*
19:18 *k.* have not bowed to Baal
2 *K.* 1:13 fell on *k.* before Elijah
4:20 sat on mother's *k.* till noon
2 *Chr.* 6:13 Sol. kneeled on his *k.*
*Ezr.* 9:5 I fell on my *k.*
*Job* 3:12 why did *k.* prevent me
4:4 strengthened the feeble *k.*
*Ps.* 109:24 *k.* weak thro' fasting
*Is.* 35:3 confirm the feeble *k.*
66:12 and be dandled on her *k.*
*Ezek.* 7:17 *k.* weak as water, 21:7
47:4 the waters were to the *k.*
*Dan.* 5:6 *k.* smo. one ag. another
6:10 kneeled on *k.* three times
10:10 a hand set me upon my *k.*
*Nah.* 2:10 the *k.* smite together
*Mark* 15:19 bowing *k.* worship.
*Luke* 5:8 Peter fell at Jesus' *k.*
*Eph.* 3:14 bow my *k.* to Father
*Heb.* 12:12 hands hang do. fe. *k.*

**KNEW.**

*Gen.* 4:1 Adam *k.* E. his wife, 25
17 Cain *k.* wife, she conceived
38:26 Jud. *k.* her again no more
*Jud.* 11:39 daughter *k.* no man
19:25 *k.* her and abused her
1 *K.* 1:4 but the king *k.* her not
*Mat.* 1:25 Joseph *k.* her not

**KNEW.**

*Gen.* 3:7 Adam and Eve *k.* that
9:24 Noah *k.* what son had done
38:9 O. *k.* seed should not be h.
42:7 Joseph saw and *k.* breth. 8
*Num.* 24:16 *k.* knowl. of M. H.
*Deut.* 34:10 wh. L. *k.* face to face
1 *Sam.* 3:20 *k.* Sam. was a prop.
18:28 Saul *k.* L. was with David
20:39 D. and Jonathan *k.* mat.
22:17 bec. they *k.* when he fled
26:17 Saul *k.* David's voice
2 *Sam.* 11:16 *k.* that valiant men
2 *Chr.* 33:13 Manas. *k.* L. was G.
*Est.* 1:13 that *k.* law and judgm.
*Job* 23:3 *k.* where I might find
*Is.* 48:4 I *k.* thou art obstinate
7 should. say, Behold, I *k.* th.
*Jer.* 1:5 formed thee, I *k.* thee
32:8 I *k.* this was word of Lord
41:4 slain Gedaliah, no man *k.*
44:15 *k.* wives burnt incense
*Dan.* 5:21 he *k.* Most High ruled
6:10 Daniel *k.* wri. was signed
*Jon.* 4:2 *k.* thou art a graci. God
*Zec.* 11:11 *k.* it was word of L.
*Mat.* 7:23 profess I never *k.* you
12:25 J. *k.* thoughts, *Luke* 6:8
25:24 I *k.* thee, thou art hard m.
*Mark* 1:34 because they *k.* him
*Luke* 4:41 they *k.* he was Christ
12:47 servant *k.* his lord's will
24:31 eyes opened, they *k.* him
*John* 2:24 because he *k.* all men
25 for he *k.* what was in man
6:6 himself *k.* what he would do
64 Jesus *k.* from the beginning
11:42 I *k.* that thou hearest me
57 if any man *k.* where he we.
13:1 Jesus *k.* his hour was co.
11 he *k.* who should betray h.
28 no man at the table *k.* for
18:2 Judas *k.* the place
*Acts* 12:14 Rhoda *k.* Peter's voi.
22:29 *k.* that he was a Roman
*Rom.* 1:21 bec. when they *k.* G.
1 *Cor.* 2:8 no. of princes of wo. *k.*
2 *Cor.* 5:21 sin, who *k.* no sin
12:2 I *k.* a man in Christ, 3
*Col.* 1:6 since ye *k.* grace of God
2:1 *k.* what great conflict I have
*Jude* 5 though ye once *k.* this
*Rev.* 19:12 name writ. no man *k.*

**KNEW not.**

*Gen.* 28:16 place, and *k.* it *not*
38:16 Judah *k.* *not* she was his
*Ex.* 1:8 king which *k.* *n.* Joseph
*Num.* 22:34 I *k.* *not* thou stood.
*Deut.* 8:16 thy fathers *k.* *not*
29:26 gods thy fath. *k.* *not*, 32:17
*Jud.* 2:10 generation *k.* *not* L.
14:4 *k.* *not* that it was of the L.
1 *Sam.* 2:12 sons of Eli *k.* *n.* L.
20:39 the lad *k.* *not* any thing
2 *Sam.* 11:20 *k.* ye *n.* th. would
18:29 but I *k.* *not* what it was
22:44 peop. I *k.* *n.* sh. serve me
*Job* 2:12 Job's friends *k.* him *not*
29:16 cause I *k.* *n.* I search. out
42:3 th. I *k.* *n.* wonder. for me
*Ps.* 35:11 charge things I *k.* *not*
*Prov.* 24:12 behold, we *k.* it *not*
*Is.* 42:16 blind by way they *k.* *n.*
25 set him on fire, yet he *k.* *n.*
55:5 nations that *k.* *not* thee
*Jer.* 2:8 that handle law, *k.* me *n.*
11:19 I *k.* *not* they had devised
44:3 serve gods whom they *k.* *n.*
*Dan.* 11:38 whom fathers *k.* *not*
*Hos.* 8:4 made prin. and I *k.* it *n.*
11:3 they *k.* *not* that I healed
*Mat.* 17:12 E. co. they *k.* him *n.*
24:39 *k.* *not* till the flood came
*Luke* 2:43 Jos. and mother *k.* *n.*
12:48 *k.* *not* and did commit th.
*John* 1:10 the world *k.* him *not*
31 and I *k.* him *not*, 33
20:9 they *k.* *not* the scriptures
14 *k.* *not* that it was J. 21:4

Acts 13:27 because they k. him n.
19:32 k. n. wherefore they came
27:39 when day, they k. n. land
1 Cor. 1:21 by wisdom k. not G.
Gal. 4:8 then when ye k. n. God
1 John 3:1 because it k. him not

**KNEWEST.**

Deut. 8:3 fed with manna, k. not
Ruth 2:11 to people thou k. not
Ps. 142:3 then thou k. my path
Is. 48:8 heardest not, thou k. not
Mat. 25:26 thou k. I reaped where I sowed not, Luke 19:22
Luke 19:44 k. not time of visit.
John 4:10 if thou k. gift of God

**KNIFE.**

Gen. 22:6 Abraham took k. 10
Jud. 19:29 took k. and laid hold
Prov. 23:2 put a k. to thy throat
Ezek. 5:1 take thee a sharp k. 2

**KNIVES.**

Jos. 5:2 make sharp k.
3 Joshua made him sharp k.
1 K. 18:28 cut themselves with k.
Ezr. 1:9 nine and twenty k.
Prov. 30:14 teeth as k. dev. poor

**KNIT.**

Jud. 20:11 Is. were k. together
1 Sam. 18:1 Jonathan k. to Da.
1 Chr. 12:17 my heart be k. to y.
Acts 10:11 sheet k. at four corne.
Col. 2:2 hearts k. together in lo.
19 body k. together increaseth

**KNOCK, ED.**

Mat. 7:7 k. it sh. be op. Lu. 11:9
Luke 13:25 begin to k. at door
Acts 12:13 as Peter k. at the door
Rev. 3:20 I stand at door and k.

**KNOCKETH, ING.**

Cant. 5:2 voice of beloved that k.
Mat. 7:8 him that k. shall be opened, Luke 11:10
Luke 12:36 when he k. they may
Acts 12:16 Peter continued k.

**KNOP, S.**

Ex. 25:31 his k. and his flowers, 33, 34, 36; 37:17, 19, 20, 22
1 K. 6:18 cedar carved with k.
7:24 k. compass. it, k. cast into

**KNOW.**

Gen. 3:5 God doth k. your eyes
22 one of us, to k. good and e.
18:21 I will go and see, I will k.
Ex. 18:16 k. the statutes of God
Num. 14:31 they shall k. the la.
Deut. 4:39 k. this day, 11:2
8:2 k. what was in thy heart
13:3 k. whether ye love the Lo.
Jos. 4:22 let your children k.
22:22 and Israel he shall k.
Ruth 3:11 city of my peo. doth k.
14 before one could k. another
1 Sam. 17:47 assembly shall k. L.
21:2 let no man k. any thing
24:11 k. there is no evil in me
28:2 k. what thy servant can do
2 Sam. 3:25 thy going out, k. all
19:20 serv. k. that I have sinned
1 K. 8:38 k. every man the plague, 2 Chr. 6:29
2 K. 5:8 sh. k. there is a prophet
10:10 k. there shall fall nothing
1 Chr. 28:9 k. thou G. of thy fat.
2 Chr. 13:5 to k. that the L. gave
Est. 4:5 k. what it was, and why
Job 5:24 k. thy tabernacle
25 k. that thy seed sh. be great
27 and k. thou it for thy good
7:10 nor shall his place k. him
8:9 but of yesterday, k. nothing
11:6 k. that God exacteth less
8 what canst thou k.?
13:23 make me k. my transgres.
19:6 k. that G. hath overthrown
21:19 G. reward. him, he sh. k.
22:13 sayest, How doth God k.?
24:1 they that k. him not see?
17 if one k. them, they are in
34:4 k. am. oursel. what is good
37:15 dost k. when God dispos.
38:20 k. the paths to the house
Ps. 4:3 k. L. hath set apart godly
9:10 that k. thy na. trust in thee
39:4 L. make me to k. mine end
46:10 still, and k. that I am G.
51:6 in hid. part make me to k.
59:13 let them k. that G. ruleth
73:11 doth G. k. 16 thought to k.
89:15 blessed are they that k.
103:16 place shall k. it no more
139:23 k. my heart, k. my thou.
142:4 no man would k. me
143:8 k. way wherein I should
Prov. 1:2 k. wisd. and instruct
4:1 attend to k. understanding
10:32 righteous k. wh. is accept.
27:23 dilig. to k. state of flocks
Ec. 1:17 gave heart to k. wisd.
7:25 applied heart to k. wisdom
8:17 tho. a wise man think to k.
9:5 the living k. they shall die
11:9 k. that G. will bring to ju.
Is. 7:16 before the child shall k.
19:21 Egyptians shall k. the L.
41:20 that they may see and k.
49:26 all flesh shall k. I am
50:4 k. how to speak in season
52:6 my people sh. k. my name
58:2 and delight to k. my ways
60:16 k. that I the L. am thy S.
Jer. 2:19 k. it is evil to forsake
Jer. 9:6 thro' deceit refuse to k.
15:15 k. that for thy sake I suf.
16:21 cause them to k. my hand, and they sh. k. my name is
17:9 heart deceit. who can k. it?
24:7 give them a heart to k. me
31:34 k. the Lord, for they shall all k. me, Heb. 8:11
36:19 let no man k. where ye be
Ezek. 2:5 k. ha. been a pro. 33:33
5:13 k. I the Lord have spoken
25:14 they sh. k. my vengeance
28:19 all that k. thee be aston.
34:30 they k. I am with them
37:28 heathen shall k. 39:23
Dan. 2:21 know. to them who k.
4:25 k. that M. High ruleth, 32
7:16 made me k. interpretation
11:32 peo. that k. God be strong
Hos. 2:20 thou shalt k. the Lord
9:7 Israel shall k. it
13:4 thou sh. k. no God but me
14:9 prudent, and he sh. k. th.
Mic. 3:1 for you to k. judgment
Zec. 2:11 k. the L. sent me, 4:9
Mal. 2:4 ye sh. k. I have sent th.
Mat. 6:3 let not thy left hand k.
7:11 k. how to give, Luke 11:13
9:30 see no man k. it: Mark 5:43; 7:24; 9:30
13:11 it is given to you to k. Mark 4:11; Luke 8:10
24:33 k. desolation is near, Mark 13:29; Luke 21:20
John 4:42 we k. that this is Chr.
7:17 he shall k. of the doctrine
10:4 sheep fol. they k. his voice
14 am good Shep. k. my sheep
13:7 thou shalt k. hereafter
35 men k. ye are my disciples
18:21 behold, they k. what I sa.
Acts 1:7 not for you to k. times
22:14 k. his will and see J. One
26:4 from my youth k. all Jews
Rom. 7:1 speak to them that k.
10:19 I say, Did not Israel k.?
1 Cor. 2:14 neither can he k. th.
8:2 know. noth. as ought to k.
Eph. 3:19 k. the love of Christ
1 Thes. 3:5 I sent to k. your faith
4:4 ev. one sho. k. how to pos.
5:12 k. them who labor among
1 Tim. 4:3 believe and k. truth
2 Tim. 3:1 k. also that in last da.
Tit. 1:16 profess that they k. G.
Jam. 2:20 wilt thou k. O vain
Jude 10 what they k. naturally
Rev. 2:23 churches sh. k. I am he
3:9 make them k. I have loved

See CERTAIN, CERTAINLY, CERTAINTY.

**I KNOW.**

Gen. 12:11 I k. thou art fair wo.
15:8 I k. that I shall inherit?
18:19 I k. he will com. his chil.
22:12 I k. that thou fearest God
48:19 I k. it, my son, I k. it
Ex. 3:7 said, I k. their sorrows
4:14 brother? I k. he can speak
18:11 I k. L. grea. than all gods
33:12 I k. thee by thy name, 17
Deut. 31:21 I k. th. imagination
29 I k. that after my death
Jos. 2:9 I k. L. hath given you
Jud. 17:13 k. I L. will do good
1 Sam. 20:30 I k. cho. son of J.?
24:20 I k. thou shalt surely be
29:9 I k. thou art good
2 K. 2:3 I k. it, hold peace, 5
5:15 I k. there is no G. in earth
19:27 I k. thy abode, Is. 37:28
1 Chr. 29:17 I k. thou triest heart
2 Chr. 25:16 I k. G. hath determ.
Job 9:28 I k. not hold me innoc.
13:2 ye know, the same do I k.
18 I k. that I shall be justified
19:25 I k. my Redeemer liveth
21:27 I k. your thoughts
30:23 I k. th. bring me to death
42:2 I k. thou canst do every th.
Ps. 20:6 I k. L. sav. his anointed
41:11 I k. thou favorest me
50:11 I k. all fowls of mountain
119:75 I k. O L. thy judg. right.
135:5 I k. L. is greater above all
140:12 I k. L. will maint. cause
Ec. 3:12 I k. th. no good in them
8:12 I k. it shall be well with
Is. 47:8 nor shall I k. loss of chi.
66:18 I k. works and thoughts
Jer. 10:23 I k. the way of man
11:18 L. given me knowl. I k. it
29:11 I k. the thoughts I think
23 I k. and am witness, sai. L.
48:30 I k. his wrath, saith L.
Ezek. 11:5 I k. things that come
Hos. 13:5 I did k. thee in wilder
Jon. 1:12 I k. for my sake temp.
Mat. 28:5 I k. that ye seek Jesus
Mark 1:24 I k. who thou art, Luke 4:34
Luke 1:18 whereby sh. I k. this
John 4:25 I k. that Messias com.
8:37 I k. ye are Abraham's seed
55 I k. him; 9:25 one thi. I k.
10:15 knoweth me, I k. Father
27 I k. my sheep, they fol. me
11:22 I k. that what thou ask G.
24 I k. that he shall rise again
13:18 I k. whom I have chosen
Acts 12:11 I k. for a surety Lord
19:15 Jesus I k. and Paul I k.
10:25 I k. ye see my fa. no more
Rom. 7:18 I k. in me dw. no good
1 Cor. 4:4 I k. nothing by myself
13:12 I k. in part, then shall I k.
Phil. 1:19 I k. this shall turn
25 I k. I shall abide with you
4:12 I k. how to be abased, I k.
2 Tim. 1:12 I k. whom I believed
1 John 2:4 he that saith, I k. him
Rev. 2:2 I k. thy works, 13; 3:8

**KNOW not, or not KNOW.**

Gen. 4:9 where is Abel? I k. not
27:2 I k. not day of my death
Ex. 5:2 I k. n. L. nor will I let I.
1 Sam. 3:7 Sam. did not yet k. L.
1 K. 18:12 Sp. carry thee I k. not
2 K. 17:26 k. n. manner of God

*Ezr.* 7:25 teach ye th. that *k. not*
*Job* 9:21 would I *not k.* my soul
15:9 know. thou that we *k. n.?*
21:29 do ye *not k.* their tokens?
24:13 *k. not* the ways thereof
16 dig in dark. they *k. n.* light
32:22 *k. not* to give flatter. titles
36:26 God great, we *k.* him *not*
*Ps.* 71:15 *k. n.* numbers thereof
82:5 *k. not* neither understand
94:10 teach man, shall *not* he *k.?*
101:4 I will *n. k.* wicked person
*Prov.* 4:19 *k. n.* at what stumble
24:12 doth *not* he *k.* it, and sh.
30:18 four things which I *k. not*
*Ec.* 9:5 dead *k. not* anything
*Is.* 1:3 but Israel doth *not k.*
43:19 ye *n. k.* it? 44:8 I *k. not*
47:11 *not k.* from wh. it ariseth
59:8 way of peace they *k. not*
*Jer.* 5:4 they *k. not* way of Lord
7:9 after gods, whom ye *k. n.?*
8:7 my people *k.* not judgments
9:3 they *k. not* me, saith Lord
10:25 fury on heathen *k.* thee *n.*
*Ezek.* 38:14 shalt thou *not k.* it
*Hos.* 2:8 did *n. k.* I gave her corn
*Amos* 3:10 th. *k. not* to do right
*Mic.* 4:12 *k. not* thoughts of Lo.
*Mat.* 25:12 I say, I *k.* you *not*
26:70 I *k. not* what thou sayest
72 saying, I *k. not* the man, 74; *Mark* 14:68, 71

*Mark* 10:38 ye *k. not* what ye ask
12:24 because ye *k. n.* scriptures
*Luke* 1:34 seeing I *k. not* a man
13:25 I *k. n.* whence you are, 27
22:57 say. Woman, I *k.* him *not*
60 I *k. not* what thou sayest
23:34 they *k. not* what they do
24:16 that they should *n. k.* him
*John* 1:26 one am. you ye *k. not*
8:55 say, I *k.* him *n.* should lie
9:21 hath opened eyes, we *k. n.*
29 we *k. not* from whence he is
10:5 *k. not* voice of strangers
14:5 we *k. not* whith. thou goest
15:21 *k. not* him that sent me
*Acts* 21:34 could not *k.* certainty
*Rom.* 8:26 *k. n.* what should pray
1 *Cor.* 2:2 determined *not* to *k.* any thing
14:11 *k. not* meaning of voice
1 *Thes.* 4:5 Gentiles wh. *k. n.* G.
2 *Thes.* 1:8 vengeance on them *k. not* God
1 *Tim.* 3:5 man *k. n.* how to rule
*Jude* 10 evil of things they *k. n.*
*Rev.* 3:3 *not k.* what hour I come

*See Ye* KNOW.

**KNOW that I am the Lord.**

*Ex.* 6:7 ye shall *k. that I am the L.* 16:12; 1 *K.* 20:28; *Ezek.* 6:7, 13; 7:4, 9; 11:10, 12; 12:20; 13:9, 14, 21, 23; 14:8; 15:7; 20:38, 42, 44; 23:49; 24:24; 25:5; 35:9; 36:11; 37:6, 13; *Joel* 3:17
7:5 Egyptians *k. that I am the L.* 14:4, 18
17 shalt *k. that I am the L.* 1 *K.* 20:13; *Is.* 49:23; *Ezek.* 16:62; 22:16; 25:7; 35:4, 12

*Ex.* 29:46 they shall *k. that I am the L. Ezek.* 6:10, 14; 7:27; 12:15, 16; 24:27; 25:11, 17; 26:6; 28:22, 23, 24, 26; 29:9, 16:21; 30:8, 19, 25, 26; 32:15; 33:29; 34:27; 35:15; 36:38; 38:23; 39:6, 28
*Jer.* 24:7 heart to *k. t. I am t. L.*
*Ezek.* 20:12 might *k. t. I am L.*
36:23 heath. sh. *k. I am L.* 39:7
39:22 Is. shall *k. t. I am the L.*

**May, mayest, *or* might KNOW.**

*Ex.* 8:10 thou *mayest k.* there is none like God, 9:14
9:29 *m. k.* earth is the Lord's
11:7 *may k.* L. put a difference
33:13 show me way, th. I *m. k.*
*Num.* 22:19 *m. k.* wh. L. will say
*Deut.* 4:35 *m. k.* that L. he is G.
*Jos.* 3:4 *m. k.* way ye should go
4:24 people *m. k.* hand of the L.
1 *Sam.* 17:46 *m. k.* th. is a G. in Is. 1 *K.* 8:43, 60; 2 *K.* 19:19
2 *Sam.* 24:2 *m. k.* num. of peop.
1 *K.* 18:37 people *m. k.* th. art G.
2 *Chr.* 6:33 people *may k.* thy na.
*Job* 19:29 *m. k.* there is a judg.
31:6 that God *may k.* my integ.
37:7 all men *may k.* his work
*Ps.* 9:20 *m. k.* th. to be but men
39:4 that *may k.* how frail I am
83:18 *m. k.* thou art M. High
109:27 *m. k.* th. this is thy hand
119:125 that I *m. k.* thy testim.
*Is.* 5:19 draw nigh that we *m. k.*
7:15 he *may k.* to refuse the ev.
37:20 all *may k.* that thou art L.
41:23 ye *may k.* we are gods
43:10 ye *may k.* and believe me
45:3 thou *m. k.* I am G. of Isr.
6 *may k.* from rising of sun
*Ezek.* 21:5 all flesh *may k.* I have
38:16 that heathen *may k.* me
*Dan.* 2:30 *m. k.* though. of heart
4:17 to intent that living *m. k.*
*Mic.* 6:5 *m. k.* righteousn. of L.
*John* 10:38 ye *may k.* and believe
14:31 the world *may k.* 17:23
17:3 *m. k.* thee the only true G.
*Acts* 17:19 *m. k.* wh. th. doctrine
1 *Cor.* 2:12 *m. k.* things given
2 *Cor.* 2:4 *m. k.* love I ha. to you
9 that I *m. k.* the proof of you
*Eph.* 1:18 ye *m. k.* hope of call.
6:22 ye *might k.* our affairs
*Phil.* 3:10 that I *may k.* him
*Col.* 4:6 ye *m. k.* how to answer
1 *Tim.* 3:15 *m. k.* how thou oug.
1 *John* 5:13 *m. k.* ye ha. eternal
20 we *m. k.* him that is true

**We KNOW, *or* KNOW we.**

*Gen.* 29:5 they said, *we k.* him
*Deut.* 18:21 how shall *we k.* wo.
2 *Chr.* 20:12 nor *k. we* what to do
*Job* 36:26 G. is gr. *we k.* him not
*Is.* 59:12 our iniqui. *we k.* them
*Hos.* 6:3 then sh. *we k.* if we fol.
8:2 cry to me, My G. *we k.* thee
*Mat.* 22:16 *we k.* thou art true, *Mark* 12:14; *Luke* 20:21
*John* 3:11 we speak th. *we* do *k.*
4:22 *we k.* what we worship
6:42 wh. father and moth. *we k.*
7:27 *we k.* whence this man is
8:52 *we k.* that th. hast a devil
9:20 *we k.* that this is our son
29 *we k.* that God spake to Moses
31 *we k.* God heareth not sin.
14:5 L. *we k.* not whi. th. goest
21:24 *we k.* his testimo. is true
*Acts* 17:20 *we* would *k.* wh. these
*Rom.* 7:14 *we k.* law is spiritual
8:28 *we k.* things work for good
1 *Cor.* 8:1 *we k.* we all ha. knowl.
4 *we k.* an idol is noth. in wor.
13:9 for *we k.* in part, and prop.
2 *Cor.* 5:1 *we k.* if our earthly h.
16 *k. we* no man after the flesh
1 *Tim.* 1:8 *we k.* that law is good
*Heb.* 10:30 *we k.* him hath said
1 *John* 2:3 *we k.* that *we k.* him
5 *k.* that *we* are in him
18 *we k.* that it is the last time
3:2 *we k.* that wh. he sh. appear
14 *we k.* we ha. passed fr. dea.
19 *we k.* we are of the truth
24 *we k.* that he abideth in us
4:6 *k. we* sp. of truth and error
13 *k. we* that we dwell in him
5:2 *we k.* we love child. of God
15 *we k.* that he heareth us, *we k.* we have petitions
19 *we k.* that we are of God
20 that *we* may *k.* him that is true

**Ye KNOW, *or* KNOW ye.**

*Gen.* 29:5 he said, *k. ye* Laban?
*Ex.* 16:6 at even *ye* shall *k.*
23:9 *ye k.* the heart of stranger
*Num.* 14:34 *ye k.* breach of prom.
*Jos.* 3:10 *ye* shall *k.* the living G.
2 *K.* 9:11 *ye k.* man and his com.
*Job* 13:2 what *ye k.* same do I kn.
*Ps.* 100:3 *k. ye* that Lord he is G.
*Is.* 51:7 *ye* that *k.* righteousness
*Jer.* 48:17 all *ye* that *k.* his name
*Ezek.* 17:21 *ye k.* I have spo. 37:14
*Joel* 2:27 *ye* sh. *k.* I am in midst
*Zec.* 2:9 *ye* sh. *k.* L. sent me, 6:15
*Mat.* 7:16 *ye* shall *k.* by fruits, 20
20:25 *ye k.* princes of the Gentiles, *Mark* 10:42
24:32 *ye k.* summer is nigh, *Mark* 13:28; *Luke* 21:30
25:13 *ye k.* neither day nor hour
*Mark* 4:13 *k. ye* not this parab.?
*Luke* 21:31 *k. ye* king. of G. is ni.
*John* 7:28 *ye* both *k.* me, and kn.
8:28 then sh. *ye. k.* that I am he
32 and *ye* shall *k.* the truth
11:49 C. said, *k. ye* nothing at all
13:12 *k. ye* what I have done?
17 if *ye k.* these things, happy
14:4 wh. I go *ye k.* and way *ye k.*
7 from henceforth *ye k.* him, 17
20 *ye* shall *k.* I am in my Fath.
15:18 *ye k.* that it hated me
*Acts* 2:22 as *ye* yourselves also *k.*
19:25 *ye k.* that by this craft we
1 *Cor.* 15:58 *ye k.* lab. not in vain
2 *Cor.* 8:9 *ye k.* grace of our Lord
*Gal.* 3:7 *k. ye* they wh. are of fa.
*Phil.* 2:22 *ye k.* the proof of him
1 *Thes.* 1:5 *ye k.* wh. man. of men
2:2 shamefully entreat. as *ye k.*
11 *ye k.* how we exhorted
2 *Thes.* 2:6 *ye k.* what witholdeth
*Heb.* 12:17 *ye k.* he wo. ha. inher.
1 *Pet.* 1:18 *ye k.* ye not redeemed
2 *Pet.* 3:17 *ye k.* these things bef.
1 *John* 2:20 and *ye k.* all things
21 truth, but because *ye k.* it
29 *ye k.* he is rig. *ye k.* ev. one
3:5 *ye k.* he manifested, 15
4:2 hereby *k. ye* Spirit of God
3 *John* 12 *ye k.* our record is true

**Ye KNOW not, *or* KNOW ye not.**

2 *Sam.* 3:38 *k. ye not* th. is a pri.
*Job* 21:29 do *ye not k.* th. tokens
*Mat.* 20:22 *ye k. not* what ye ask
24:42 *ye k. not* wh. hour L. come
*Mark* 4:13 *k. ye not* this parab.?
12:24 bec. *ye k. not* scriptures
13:33 *ye k. not* when time is, 35
*Luke* 9:55 *ye k. not* what manner
*John* 1:26 whom *ye k. not.*
4:22 ye worship *ye k. not* what
32 meat to me *ye k. not* of
7:28 sent me is true, wh. *ye k. n.*
8:19 *ye* neither *k.* me nor Father
9:30 *ye k. not* from whence he is
2 *Cor.* 13:5 *k. ye not* yourselves
*Jam.* 4:14 *ye k. not* wh. be on m.
1 *John* 2:21 *ye k. not* the truth

**KNOWEST.**

*Gen.* 30:26 thou *k.* service I done
47:6 *k.* any man of activ. among
*Ex.* 32:22 *k.* peo. set on mischief
*Num.* 20:14 *k.* travel hath befal.
*Deut.* 28:33 a nation thou *k.* not
*Jos.* 14:6 *k.* thing the Lord said

2 Sam. 2:26 k. thou not th. it w.
7:20 L. k. thy serv. 1 Chr. 17:18
17:8 said Hushai, thou k. father
1 K. 2:5 k. also what Joab did
9 k. what thou oughtest to do
44 k. all thou didst to David
8:39 whose heart thou k. thou only k. 2 Chr. 6:30
2 K. 2:3 k. thou L. will take, 5
4:1 k. thy serv. did fear the L.
Job 10:7 thou k. I am not wicked
15:9 wh. k. th. th. we kn. not?
20:4 k. thou not this of old
34:33 theref. speak what thou k.
38:5 who laid meas. if thou k.?
21 k. thou it, because
39:1 k. when goats bri. forth, 2
Ps. 40:9 O L. thou k. Jer. 15:15
69:5 O God, thou k. my foolish.
139:2 thou k. my down-sitting
4 O Lord, thou k. it altogether
Prov. 27:1 k. not what a day br.
Ec. 11:2 k. not what evil
5 k. not what is way of Spirit
6 thou k. not whe. sh. prosper
Is. 55:5 call a nation thou k. not
Jer. 5:15 nation wh. lang. k. not
12:3 but thou, O Lord, k. me
17:16 nor des. woful day, th. k.
18:23 thou k. their counsel
Jer. 33:3 show things thou k. not
Dan. 10:20 k. thou wheref. I co.
Zec. 4:5 k. not wh. these be, 13
Mark 10:19 k. com. Luke 18:20
Luke 22:34 thrice deny th. k. me
John 1:48 N. said, When. k. me?
3:10 a master, k. not th. things?
13:7 what I do, thou k. not now
16:30 thou k. all things, 21:17
21:15 L. thou k. I love thee, 16
Acts 1:24 k. the hearts of all men
Rom. 2:18 k. his will, and appr.
1 Cor. 7:16 what k. thou, O wife
2 Tim. 1:15 k. all they in Asia
Rev. 3:17 k. not th. art wretched
7:14 said unto him, Sir, thou k.

**KNOWETH.**

Gen. 33:13 k. children are tender
Deut. 2:7 k. thy walk. thro' wild.
34:6 no man k. Mos. sepulchre
Jos. 22:22 God of gods, he k. Is.
1 Sam. 20:3 father certainly k.
2 Sam. 14:22 serv. k. I found gr.
17:10 Is. k. thy father is mighty
Job 11:11 he k. vain men
15:23 k. day of darkness is ready
23:10 but he k. the way I take
28:7 there is a path no fowl k.
23 God understandeth and k.
34:25 therefore he k. their works
Ps. 1:6 Lord k. way of righteous
37:18 the L. k. days of the upri.
44:21 he k. the secrets of heart
74:9 nor is there any am. us k.
94:11 L. k. thou. of man vanity
103:14 he k. our frame
104:19 sun k. his going down
138:6 the proud he k. afar off
139:14 thy works, my soul k.
Ec. 6:8 k. to walk before living
7:22 thy heart k. th. hast cursed
9:1 no man k. eit. love or hatred
Is. 1:3 the ox k. his owner
Jer. 9:24 understandeth and k.
Dan. 2:22 he k. what is in darkn.
Nah. 1:7 L. k. them trust in him
Zep. 3:5 the unjust k. no shame
Mat. 6:8 Fa. k. what ye need
32 k. ye have need, Luke 12:30
11:27 no man k. Son but the Father, nor any k. Father save the Son, Luke 10:22
24:36 that day k. Mark 13:32
Luke 16:15 God k. your hearts
John 7:15 how k. this man let.?
27 no man k. whence he is
10:15 Fa. k. me; 14:17 nor k.
5 he k. that he saith true

Acts 15:8 God which k. hearts
Rom. 8:27 k. what is mind of S.
1 Cor. 2:11 what man k. th. of a man, even th. of G. k. no m.
8:2 if any man think he k. any.
2 Cor. 11:11 love you not? G. k.
31 God, Fa. of our L. k. a lie
12:2 I cannot tell, God k. 3
2 Tim. 2:19 L. k. th. that are his
Jam. 4:17 him that k. to do good
2 Pet. 2:9 L. k. how to de. godly
1 John 3:20 God is greater and k.
4:6 he that k. God heareth us
7 that lov. is born of God, k. G.
Rev. 2:17 name writ. no man k.
12:12 k. he hath but short time

**Who KNOWETH, or not KNOWETH.**

Est. 4:14 w. k. whe. th. art come
Job 12:9 who k. not in all these
14:21 come to honor, he k. it n.
18:21 place of him that k. n. G.
28:13 man k. not the price
Ps. 39:6 k. not who shall gather
90:11 who k. power of anger?
92:6 a brutish man k. not
Prov. 7:23 k. not it is for his life
9:18 he k. not dead are there
24:22 who k. the ruin of them
Ec. 2:19 w. k. whe. he be wise
3:21 who k. the spirit of man
6:12 who k. what is good for m.
8:7 he k. not that wh. shall be
9:12 man also k. not his time
10:15 he k. not how to go to city
Is. 29:15 seeth us, who k. us?
Hos. 7:9 gray hairs, yet k. not
Joel 2:14 who k. if he will return
Mark 4:27 gr. up, he k. not how
John 7:49 peo. w. k. n. the law
12:35 darkness, k. n. whither
15:15 serv. k. n. what lord doeth
1 John 2:11 walk. in dark. k. n.
3:1 therefore the world k. us n.
4:8 k. not God, for God is love

**KNOWING.**

Gen. 3:5 as gods k. good and evil
1 K. 2:32 my father David not k.
Mat. 9:4 k. their thoughts, Luke 11:17
22:29 ye err, not k. scriptures
Mark 5:30 Jesus k. in himself
33 woman k. what was done
6:20 k. that he was a just man
Luke 9:33 E. not k. what he said
John 13:3 Jesus k. Fa. had given
18:4 Jesus k. all that sho. come
19:28 J. k. all things were acco.
21:12 none ask him, k. it was L.
Acts 2:30 k. that God had sworn
5:7 wife not k. what was done
20:22 not k. things shall befall
Rom. 1:32 k. the judgment of G.
2:4 not k. goodness of God
13:11 k. time, now it is high ti.
2 Cor. 4:14 k. he wh. raised L. J.
5:6 k. that wh. we are at home
Eph. 6:8 k. what good any man
Col. 3:24 k. of L. ye rec. reward
1 Tim. 1:9 k. this, law is for la.
2 Tim. 3:14 k. of wh. thou learn.
Heb. 10:34 k. ye have in heaven
11:8 not k. whither he went
Jam. 1:3 k. this, trying of y. fai.
1 Pet. 3:9 k. ye are thereu. called
2 Pet. 1:14 k. shortly I must put

**KNOWLEDGE.**

Gen. 2:9 tree of k. good and ev. 17
Ex. 31:3 filled Bez. in k. 35:31
Lev. 4:23 if sin come to k. 28
Num. 24:16 k. of the Most High
Ruth 2:10 should. take k. of me
1 Sam. 2:3 the L. is a God of k.
1 K. 9:27 k. of sea; 2 Chr. 8:18
2 Chr. 1:11 thou hast asked k.
12 wisdom and k. is granted

Neh. 10:28 every one having k.
Job 15:2 wise man ut. vain k.?
21:14 desire not k. of thy ways
22 shall any teach God k.?
33:3 my lips sh. utter k. clearly
36:3 I will fetch my k. from afar
4 per. in k. is with thee, 37:16
Ps. 19:2 night to night show. k.
73:11 is there k. in Most High?
94:10 he that teacheth man k.
119:66 teach me judgm. and k.
139:6 such k. too wonder. for me
144:3 what is man thou takest k. of?

Prov. 1:7 fear of Lord begi. of k.
22 fools hate k. 2:3 cri. after k.
29 they hated k. did not choose
2:6 out of his mouth cometh k.
10 k. is pleasant to thy soul
3:20 by k. depths are broken up
5:2 that thy lips may keep k.
8:10 k. rather than choice gold
12 and find out k. of inventions
9:10 k. of Holy is understanding
10:14 wise men lay up k.
11:9 thro' k. sh. just be deliver.
12:23 a prud. man concealeth k.
13:16 ev. prud. man deal. wi. k.
14:6 k. easy to him that unders.
7 perceiv. not in him lips of k.
18 prudent are crowned with k.
15:2 tongue of wise useth k.
7 lips of the wise disperse k.
14 hath understanding seek. k.
17:27 hath k. spareth his words
18:15 heart of prudent getteth k. and ear of wise seeketh k.
19:25 and he will understand k.
27 cease to err from words of k.
20:15 lips of k. precious jewel
21:11 wise instructed, he rec. k.
22:12 eyes of the L. preserve k.
23:12 apply th. ear to words of k.
24:4 by k. sh. chambers be filled
5 a man of k. increas. strength
28:2 by man of k. state be pro.
30:3 nor have the k. of Holy

Ec. 1:16 had experience of k.
18 increaseth k. increaseth sor.
2:21 a man whose labor is in k.
26 God giveth a man k. and joy
7:12 excellency of k. is wisdom
9:10 nor k. in grave, whi. goest
Is. 11;2 k. and fear of the Lord
28:9 whom shall he teach k.?
32:4 heart of rash sh. underst. k.
33:6 wisd. and k. shall be stabi.
40:14 judgment, and taught k.
44:19 neither is th. k. nor unde.
25 and maketh their k. foolish
47:10 thy k. hath perverted thee
53:11 by k. right. serv. justify

Jer. 3:15 shall feed you with k.
10:14 ev. man brutish in his k.
Dan. 12:4 k. shall be increased
Hos. 4:6 peo. destroyed for lack of k. thou reject. k. I rej th.
Hab. 2:14 earth fill. with k. of L.
Mal. 2:7 priest's lips sho. keep k.
Luke 1:77 to give k. of salvation
11:52 taken away key of k.
Acts 4:13 marvelled and took k.
24:22 more perfect k. of th way
Rom. 1:28 not like to re. G. in k.
2:20 which hast the form of k.
3:20 for by law is the k. of sin
10:2 a zeal, not according to k.
15:14 are filled with all k.
1 Cor. 1:5 are enriched in all k.
8:1 we all have k. k. puffeth up
10 which hast k. at meat
11 thro' thy k. sh. brother per.
12:8 word of k. by same Spirit
13:2 underst. mysteries and k.
8 there be k. it sh. vanish away
14:6 speak by revelation or k.

2 Cor. 2:14 manif. savor of his k.
4:6 light of k. of the glory of G.
6:6 by k. by long-suffering
8:7 as ye abound in faith and k.
11:6 rude in speech, not in k.
Eph. 1:17 wisdom in k. of him
3:19 love of C. which passeth k.
4:13 unity of faith, and k. of S.
Phil. 1:9 may abound more in k.
3:8 all things loss for k. of Chr.
Col. 1:9 filled with k. of his will
2:3 hid treas. of wisdom and k.
3:10 new man renewed in k.
1 Tim. 2:4 come to k. of truth
2 Tim. 3:7 to come to k. of truth
Heb. 10:26 if we sin after rec. k.
Jam. 3:13 wise man, end. wi. k.?
1 Pet. 3:7 dwell according to k.
2 Pet. 1:5 virtue k. k. temperance
1:8 nor unfruit. in k. of our L.
3:18 grow in k. of our Lord Jes.

**KNOWLEDGE of God.**

Prov. 2:5 thou shalt find k. of G.
Hos. 4:1 nor k. of G. in the land
6:6 k. of G. more than bu.-offer.
Rom. 11:33 of wisd. and k. of G.
1 Cor. 15:34 have not k. of God
2 Cor. 10:5 exalteth ag. k. of G.
Col. 1:10 increasing in k. of God
2 Pet. 1:2 peace, thro' k. of God

**KNOWLEDGE of the Lord.**

2 Chr. 30:22 taught good k. of L.
Is. 11:9 earth full of k. of the L.
2 Pet. 2:20 escaped thro' k. of L.

**No KNOWLEDGE.**

Deut. 1:39 child. that day no k.
Ps. 14:4 work. of iniq. no k. 53:4
Is. 5:13 because they have no k.
45:20 have no k. set up images
58:3 afflicted soul, takest no k.
Jer. 4:22 do good, th. have no k.

**Without KNOWLEDGE.**

Num. 15:24 with. k. of congrega.
Job 35:16 multipli. words w. k.
36:12 perish, and die with. k.
38:2 counsel by wor. w. k. 42:3
Prov. 19:2 not good soul be w. k.

**KNOWN.**

Gen. 24:16 nor had any man k.
Ex. 2:14 surely this thing is k.
Lev. 4:14 they have sinned is k.
Num. 31:17 kill ev. wo. k. man
Deut. 1:13 k. among tribes, 15
Jos. 24:31 k. works of the Lord
1 K. 18:36 let it be k. thou art G.
Ps. 9:16 Lord is k. by judgment
31:7 k. my soul in adversities
48:3 God is k. in her palaces
67:2 thy way may be k. on earth
76:1 in Judah is God k. his na.
77:19 thy footsteps are not k.
79:10 let him be k. among heat.
88:12 shall wond. be k. in dark?
91:14 bec. he hath k. my name
139:1 searched me, and k. me

Prov. 12:16 fool's wrath pres. k.
20:11 a child is k. by his doings
31:23 her husband is k. in gates
Ec. 5:3 fool's voice k. by multit.
Is. 61:9 seed k. among Gentiles
66:14 Lord be k. to his servants
Jer. 5:5 have k. the way of the L.
Ezek. 36:32 saith L. G. be it k. to you, Acts 4:10; 13:38; 28:28
38:23 k. in eyes of many nations
Dan. 4:26 sh. have k. heav. rule
Amos 3:2 you only have I k.
Zec. 14:7 a day shall be k. L.
Mat. 12:33 tree k. by fr. Luke 6:44
24:43 if g. man had k. Luke 12:39
Luke 19:42 k. in this thy day
24:35 k. in breaking of bread
John 7:4 himself seeketh to be k.
8:19 if ye had k. me ye should have k. my Father also, 14:7
10:14 I know sheep, am k.
17:25 these have k. thou sent me
Acts 2:14 be this k. unto you
15:18 k. unto G. are all his wor.
Acts 22:30 k. the certainty, 23:28
Rom. 1:19 wh. may be k. of God
11:34 who hath k. the mind of Lord, 1 Cor. 2:16
1 Cor. 13:12 even as I also am k.
14:7 k. what is piped or harped
2 Cor. 3:2 epistle known and read
5:16 have k. Christ after flesh
6:9 unknown, and yet well k.
Gal. 4:9 k. God or are k. of God
Eph. 3:10 might be k. by church
Phil. 4:5 moderation k. to all m.
2 Tim. 3:10 fully k. my doctrine
15 fr. a child k. holy scriptures
1 John 2:13 bec. ye ha. k. him, 14
2 John 1 them that have k. truth

**Made, or madest KNOWN.**

Gen. 45:1 Joseph m. himself k.
Neh. 9:14 m. k. thy holy sabbath
Ps. 98:2 Lord m. k. his salvation
103:7 m. k. his ways to Moses
Dan. 2:23 m. k. to us king's m.
Hos. 5:9 m. k. that which sh. be
Luke 2:17 m. k. abroad saying
John 15:15 all I heard, I m. k.
Acts 2:28 m. k. to me ways of life
7:13 Joseph m. k. to brethren
Rom. 16:26 m. k. to all nations
Eph. 1:9 m. k. to us mystery
3:3 he m. k. to me mystery
Phil. 4:6 requests be m. k. to G.
2 Pet. 1:16 m. k. coming of our L.

**Make KNOWN.**

Num. 12:6 I will m. myself k.
1 Chr. 16:8 m. k. his deeds amo. people, Ps. 105:1
Ps. 89:1 m. k. thy faithfulness
106:8 m. k. his mighty power
145:12 to m. k. to sons of men
Prov. 1:23 make k. my words

Is. 38:19 father sh. m. k. truth
64:2 m. thy name k. to adversa.
Ezek. 35:11 ma. myself k. among them
39:7 m. my holy name k. in Isr.
Dan. 2:25 man will m. k. to king
28 Lord m. k. to the king, 29
Hab. 3:2 in midst of years m. k.
Rom. 9:22 God will. to m. po. k.
23 m. k. riches of his glory
Eph. 6:19 m. k. mystery of gosp.
Col. 1:27 to whom G. will m. k.

**Not KNOWN.**

Gen. 19:8 two dau. have not k. man, Num. 31:18, 35; Jud. 21:12
41:21 n. be k. they had eaten
31 plenty shall n. be k. in land
Ex. 6:3 by name Jehovah I n. k.
Deut 11:2 chil. have n. k. 31:13
28 after gods ye k. n. 13:6, 13
Jud. 3:1 had not k. wars of Can.
16:9 so his strength was not k.
Ruth 3:14 not be k. wo. came in
1 K. 14:2 n. k. to be wife of Jer.
Ps. 18:43 peo. whom I have n. k.
77:19 thy footsteps are not k.
79:6 wra. on heathen ha. n. k.
95:10 n. k. my ways, Heb. 3:10
147:20 judgm. they have n. k.
Ec. 6:5 not seen sun n. k. any th.
Is. 42:16 paths they have not k.
44:18 have n. k. nor understood
45:4 tho' thou hast n. k. me, 5
Jer. 4:22 they have not k. me
Ezek. 32:9 count. thou hast n. k.
Dan. 2:5 will n. make k. drea 9
4:7 n. make k. interpreta. 5:8
Hos. 5:4 they have not k. the L.
Nah. 3:17 place n. k. w. they are
Mat. 10:26 is nothing hid that shall n. be k. Luke 8:17; 12:2
John 8:55 ye have not k. him
14:9 yet hast thou not k. me
16:3 have not k. the Father nor
17:25 Fa. world hath n. k. thee
Rom. 3:17 way of pe. they not k.
7:7 I had not k. sin but by law
2 Pet. 2:21 not k. way of righte.
1 John 3:6 sinner not seen not k.
Rev. 2:24 not k. the depths of S.

**KOHATH.**

Gen. 46:11; Ex. 6:16; Num. 3:17, 30; 16:1; 1 Chr. 6:2, 22, 61
1 Chr. 15:5 of sons of K. Uriel

KOHATHITES. Num. 4:34; Jos. 21:4; 2 Chr. 34:12

**KORAH.**

Gen. 36:5 Aholibamah bare K. 16
Ex. 6:21 sons of Iz. K. Num. 16:1
Num. 16:6 censers, K. 19, 40
26:9 Dathan str. in comp. of K.
27:3 father not in comp. of K.
1 Chr. 1:35 the sons of Esau, K.
Jude 11 perished in gains. of K.

# L

**LABAN.**

Gen. 24:29 Reb. had a brother L.
30:36 Jac. fed rest of L.'s flocks
31:2 countenance of L. 12, 55
32:4 I have sojourned with L.

**LABOR, Substantive.**

Gen. 31:42 G. seen l. of my hands
35:16 Rachel had hard l. 17
Deut. 26:7 L. heard, looked on l.
Neh. 5:13 God sha. ev. man fr. l.
Job 39:11 wilt th. leave l. to him
Ps. 90:10 their strength l. sorrow
104:23 man goeth to l. till even.
105:44 inherited l. of the people

107:12 bro. down heart with l.
109:11 let stranger spoil his l.
128:2 sh. eat the l. of thy hands
Prov. 10:16 l. tendeth to life
13:11 gathereth by l. shall incr.
14:23 in all l. there is profit

Ec. 1:3 wh. profit hath man of l.
8 all things are full of l. man
2:10 rejoiced in my portion of l.
18 I hated all l. wh. I had tak.
19 shall he rule over all my l.
21 man whose l. is in wisdom
22 what hath man of all his l.?
24 enjoy good in l. 3:13; 5:18

4:8 yet is th. no end of all his l.
9 they have a good rewa. for l.
5:15 nothing of l. he may carry
19 rejoice in l. this is gift of G.
6:7 l. of man is for his mouth
9:9 portion in thy l. under sun
10:15 l. of foolish wearieth
Is. 45:14 l. of Egypt come to thee
55:2 why spend your l. for that
Jer. 3:24 devoured l. of fathers
20:18 came I out of wo. to see l.?
Ezek. 29:20 giv. land of Eg. for l.
Hab. 3:17 though l. of olive fail
Hag. 1:11 drought on l. of hands
John 4:38 reap wh. bestow. no l.

Rom. 16:6 bestow. much *l.* on us
1 Cor. 3:8 man rec. accord. to *l.*
15:58 know your *l.* is not in vain
Gal. 4:11 lest I bestow. *l.* in vain
Phil. 1:22 this is fruit of my *l.*
1 Thes. 1:3 remember. *l.* of love
2:9 remember our *l.* and travail
3:5 and our *l.* be in vain
2 Thes. 3:8 but wrought with *l.*
Heb. 6:10 not forget your *l.* of lo.
Rev. 2:2 I kn. thy *l.* and patience

**LABOR, Verb.**

Ex. 20:9 six days *l.* Deut. 5:13
Jos. 24:13 for wh. he did not *l.*
Neh. 4:22 guard us, and *l.* on day
Job 9:29 why then *l.* I in vain?
Ps. 127:1 exc. L. build *l.* in vain
144:14 oxen may be strong to *l.*
Prov. 21:25 his hands refuse to *l.*
23:4 *l.* not to be rich, cease from
Ec. 4:8 saith, For whom do I *l.*?
8:17 tho' a man *l.* to seek it out
Is. 22:4 weep, *l.* not to comfort
65:23 they shall not *l.* in vain
Jer. 51:58 the peop. sh. *l.* in vain
Lam. 5:5 under persecution we *l.*
Mic. 4:10 *l.* to bring forth, O Zi.
Hab. 2:13 people should *l.* in fire
Mat. 11:28 co. to me all ye th. *l.*
John 6:27 *l.* not for meat th. per.
Rom. 16:12 Tryphosa, who *l.*
1 Cor. 4:12 *l.* with our own hands
2 Cor. 5:9 we *l.* to be accepted
Eph. 4:28 rather *l.* wi. his hands
Col. 1:29 whereunto I *l.* striving
1 Thes. 5:12 know them which *l.*
1 Tim. 4:10 *l.* and suffer reproach
5:17 that *l.* in word and doctrine
Heb. 4:11 *l.* to enter into that rest

**LABORED.**

Neh. 4:21 so we *l.* in the work
Job 20:18 he *l.* for, sh. he restore
Ec. 2:11 looked on labor I *l.* to do
19 rule over my labor I have *l.*
5:16 wh. prof. ha. he th. *l.* wind?
Is. 47:15 with whom thou hast *l.*
49:4 I said, I have *l.* in vain
62:8 not drink, for which thou *l.*
Dan. 6:14 king *l.* to deliv. Daniel
John 4:38 *l.* and ye are entered
Rom. 16:12 salute P. who *l.* in L.
1 Cor. 15:10 I *l.* more abundantly
Phil. 2:16 I have not *l.* in vain
4:3 help those that *l.* with me
Rev. 2:3 for my name's sake *l.*

**LABORER, S.**

Mat. 9:37 harvest plenteous, but *l.* few, 38; Luke 10:2
20:1 went out early to hire *l.*
Luke 10:7 *l.* is worthy of his hire
1 Cor. 3:9 *l.* together with God
1 Tim. 5:18 *l.* is worthy of rewa.
Jam. 5:4 behold the hire of the *l.*

**LABORETH.**

Prov. 16:26 he that *l.* *l.* for hims.
Ec. 3:9 wh. profit in that he *l.*?
1 Cor. 16:16 sub. to ev. one that *l.*
2 Tim. 2:6 the husbandm. that *l.*

**LABORING.**

Ec. 5:12 sleep of *l.* man sweet
Acts 20:35 *l.* ye ou. to sup. weak
Col. 4:12 *l.* for you in prayer
1 Thes. 2:9 *l.* night and day

**LABORS.**

Ex. 23:16 first-fruits of thy *l.*
Deut. 28:33 thy *l.* sh. a nation eat
Prov. 5:10 *l.* be in ho. of stranger
Is. 58:3 in day of fast ye ex. all *l.*
Jer. 20:5 I will deliver all their *l.*
Hos. 12:8 in my *l.* sh. find no ini.
Hag. 2:17 smote you in all the *l.*
John 4:38 are entered in their *l.*
2 Cor. 6:5 in *l.* in watchings
10:15 boasting of other men's *l.*
11:23 *l.* more abund. in stripes
Rev. 14:13 may rest from their *l.*

**LACE.**

Ex. 28:28 sh. bind the breastpla. with *l.* 37; 39:31

**LACHISH.**

Jos. 10:32 the Lord delivered L.
2 K. 14:19 and he fled to L.
18:14 Hezek. sent to king to L.
2 Chr. 11:9 Rehoboam built L.
25:27 they sent to L. after him
Mic. 1:13 O inhabitant of L. bind

**LACK, Substantive.**

Gen. 18:28 wilt des. all for *l.* five?
Ex. 16:18 that gathered little had no *l.* 2 Cor. 8:15
Job 4:11 lion perish. for *l.* of prey
38:41 young wand. for *l.* of meat
Hos. 4:6 peo. destroyed for *l.* kn.
Phil. 2:30 life to supply *l.* of ser.
1 Thes. 4:12 that ye *l.* of nothing

**LACK, Verb.**

Gen. 18:28 if there shall *l.* five
Deut. 8:9 shall not *l.* anything
Ps. 34:10 the young lions do *l.*
Prov. 28:27 giv. to poor sh. not *l.*
Ec. 9:8 let thy head *l.* no ointm.
Mat. 19:20 I kept, wh. *l.* I yet?
Jam. 1:5 any *l.* wisd. ask of God

**LACKED.**

Deut. 2:7 thou hast *l.* nothing
1 K. 4:27 provid. victual, *l.* noth.
Neh. 9:21 sustain th. th. *l.* noth.
Luke 22:35 *l.* ye any thing?
Acts 4:34 any amo. them that *l.*
1 Cor. 12:24 honor to which *l.*
Phil. 4:10 careful, *l.* opportunity

**LACKEST.**

Mark 10:21 but one thing thou *l.* Luke 18:22

**LACKETH.**

Num. 31:49 there *l.* not one man
2 Sam. 3:29 not fail one *l.* bread
Prov. 6:32 adult. *l.* understand.
12:9 honor. himself and *l.* bread
2 Pet. 1:9 th. *l.* th. things is blind

**LACKING.**

Lev. 22:23 th. hath any thing *l.*
Jud. 21:3 th. sho. be one tribe *l.*
Jer. 23:4 no more, nor sh. be *l.*
1 Cor. 16:17 wh. was *l.* they sup.
2 Cor. 11:9 *l.* to me breth. sup.
1 Thes. 3:10 might perf. what is *l.*

**LAD, S.**

Gen. 21:17 God heard voice of *l.*
18 lift up *l.* 19 gave *l.* drink
20 G. was with *l.* and he grew
22:5 I and the *l.* will go yonder
12 lay not thy hand upon *l.*
44:22 *l.* cannot leave father, 30
33 abide inst. of *l.* let the *l.* go
34 his life is bound up in the *l.*
48:16 A. redeemed me, bless *l.*
1 Sam. 20:36 Jona. said to *l.* Run
John 6:9 *l.* ha. five barley loaves

**LADDER.**

Gen. 28:12 behold a *l.* set up

**LADE, ED.**

Gen. 42:26 *l.* asses wi. corn, 44:13
45:17 *l.* beasts, go to Canaan
1 K. 12:11 father did *l.* with yoke
Neh. 4:17 th. *l.* wrought in work
Luke 11:46 *l.* men with burdens
Acts 28:10 *l.* us wi. thi. necessary

**LADEN.**

Gen. 45:23 *l.* with good things
Is. 1:4 a people *l.* with iniquity
Mat. 11:28 all that are heavy *l.*
2 Tim. 3:6 women, *l.* with sins

**LADETH, ING.**

Neh. 13:15 some on sab. *l.* asses
Hab. 2:6 woe to him that *l.* him.
Acts 27:10 damage not only of *l.*

**LADY.**

Is. 47:5 no more be called a *l.*
7 saidst, I shall be a *l.* for ever
2 John 1 the elder to the elect *l.*
5 *l.* that we love one another

**LADIES.**

Jud. 5:29 wise *l.* answered her
Est. 1:18 likew. shall *l.* of Persia

LAID. See after LAY.
LAISH. Jud. 18:14; 1 Sam. 25:44; 2 Sam. 3:15; Is. 10:30

**LAKE.**

Luke 5:1 Jesus stood by *l.* of G.
2 two ships standing by the *l.*
8:23 a storm of wind on the *l.*
33 herd ran violently into *l.*
Rev. 19:20 both cast in *l.* fire
20:10 devil cast into *l.* of fire
14 death and hell cast in *l.*
15 not in bo. of life, cast into *l.*
21:8 murderers have part in *l.*

**LAMB.**

Gen. 22:7 *l.* for a burnt offering?
8 God will provide himself a *l.*
Ex. 12:3 they shall take a *l.* 21
5 *l.* shall be without blemish
13:13 sh. redeem with a *l.* 34:20
29:39 one *l.* th. sh. offer in morn. other *l.* at even. 41; Nu. 28:4
40 a *l.* a tenth deal of flour, Num. 28:21, 29; 29:4, 10, 15
Lev. 9:3 take a *l.* of first year, 14:10; Num. 6:12; 7:15, 21
14:12 the priest shall take *l.*
23:12 sh. offer a *l.* with. blemish
Num. 6:14 ewe-*l.* of first year
15:5 with the sacrifice for one *l.*
1 Sam. 7:9 Samuel off. sucking *l.*
2 Sam. 12:4 took poor man's *l.*
Is. 11:6 wolf shall dwell with *l.*
16:1 send ye *l.* to ruler of land
53:7 he was brought as a *l.* to the slaughter, Jer. 11:19
65:25 wolf and *l.* sh. feed toget.
66:3 sacrificeth a *l.* as if he cut
Ezek. 45:15 one *l.* out of a flock
Hos. 4:16 L. will feed them as *l.*
John 1:29 behold the L. of G. 36
Acts 8:32 a *l.* dumb bef. shearer
1 Pet. 1:19 as a *l.* without blem.
Rev. 5:6 midst of eld. stood a L.
8 four beasts fell down bef. L.
12 worthy the L. that was slain
6:16 hide us from wrath of L.
7:10 salvation to our G. and L.
14 made white in blood of L.
17 L. shall feed and lead
12:11 overc. him by blood of L.
13:8 L. sl. from found. of world
11 he had two horns like a *l.*
14:1 L. stood on the mount Si.
4 these are they that follow L.
10 tormented in presence of L.
15:3 song of M. and song of L.
17:14 war with L. and L. overc.
19:7 for marriage of L. is come
21:9 show thee bride, L. wife
14 twelve apostles of L.
22 God Alm. and L. are temple
23 the L. is the light thereof
27 writ. in the L. book of life
22:1 out of thr. of God and L. 3

**LAMBS.**

Gen. 30:40 J. did separate the *l.*
Num. 7:87 *l.* of first year twelve
Deut. 32:14 with fat of *l.*
1 Sam. 15:9 S. spared the best *l.*
2 K. 3:4 Moab rendered 100,000 *l.*
1 Chr. 29:21 offered to L. 1,000 *l.*
2 Chr. 29:22 priests killed *l.* 32
Ezr. 7:17 thou mayest buy *l.*
Ps. 37:20 wick. sh. be as fat of *l.*
114:4 little hills skip. like *l.* 6
Prov. 27:26 *l.* for thy clothing

Is. 1:11 I deli. not in blood of l.
5:17 l. feed after their manner
34:6 sword of L. with blood of l.
40:11 gather the l. with his arm
Jer. 51:40 like l. to slaughter
Ezek. 39:18 shall drink blo. of l.
46:4 in sab. l. 6 new moons l.
Amos 6:4 and eat l. out of flock
Luke 10:3 as l. among wolves
John 21:15 Jes. saith, Feed my l.

**Seven LAMBS.**

Gen. 21:28 Abrah. set sev. ewe-l.
Lev. 23:18 offer with bread sev. l.
Num. 28:11 ye shall offer s. l. of first year, 19, 27; 29:2, 8, 36
2 Chr. 29:21 brought s. l. for offering

**Two LAMBS.**

Ex. 29:38 two l. of the first year offer, Num. 28:3
Lev. 14:10 on 8th day take two l.
Num. 28:9 and on sabbath two l.

**LAME.**

Lev. 21:18 l. man sh. not appro.
Deut. 15:21 if l. shalt not sacrifi.
2 Sam. 4:4 Jon. had son, l. 9:3, 13
5:6 exc. take away blind and l.
19:26 because thy servant is l.
Job 29:15 eyes to blind, feet to l.
Prov. 26:7 legs of l. are not equal
Is. 33:23 the l. take the prey
35:6 l. man leap as a hart
Jer. 31:8 bring with them the l.
Mal. 1:8 ye offer l. for sacrifice?
Mat. 11:5 the l. walk, 15:31; 21:14; Luke 7:22
Luke 14:13 call poor, l. and blind
Acts 3:2 a man, l. fr. womb, car.
8:7 many th. were l. we. healed
Heb. 12:13 l. be turn. out of way

LAMECH. Gen. 4:18, 19; 5:25; 1 Chr. 1:3; Luke 3:36

**LAMENT.**

Jud. 11:40 dau. of Is. went to l.
Is. 19:8 fishers also mourn and l.
32:12 they shall l. for the teats
Jer. 16:5 neither go to l. them, 6
22:18 they shall not l. for him
34:5 l. thee, saying, Ah, L.
Ezek. 32:16 daugh. of nations l.
Joel 1:8 l. like virgin with sackc.
13 gird yourselves, l. ye priests
Mic. 2:4 l. with doleful lamenta.
John 16:20 Ye shall weep and l.
Rev. 18:9 kings of earth shall l.

**LAMENTED.**

1 Sam. 6:19 people l. because L.
25:1 Israelites l. Samuel, 28:3
2 Sam. 1:17 David l. over Saul
3:33 the king l. over Abner
2 Chr. 35:25 Jeremiah l. for Josi.
Jer. 16:4 die and not be l. 25:33
Mat. 11:17 but ye have not l.
Luke 23:27 a great company l.

**LAMENTABLE.**

Dan. 6:20 king cried wi. l. voice

**LAMENTATION.**

Gen. 50:10 mourned with sore l.
2 Sam. 1:17 D. lamented with l.
Ps. 78:64 widows made no l.
Jer. 7:29 l. on high places
9:10 habitations of wildern. a l.
31:15 in Ramah l. Mat. 2:18
48:38 there shall be l. generally
Lam. 2:5 Lord hath increased l.
Ezek. 19:1 take up a l. for princ.
14 this is a l. and sh. be for a l.
28:12 take up l. on king of Tyr.
32:2 take up a l. for Pharaoh, 16
Amos 5:16 such as are skilf. of l.
8:10 turn all your songs into l.
Acts 8:2 great l. over Stephen

**LAMENTATIONS.**

2 Chr. 35:25 of Josiah in their l.
Ezek. 2:10 was written therein l.

**LAMP.**

Gen. 15:17 burning l. that passed
Ex. 27:20 cause the l. to burn
1 Sam. 3:3 ere l. went out
2 Sam. 22:29 thou art my l. O L.
1 K. 15:4 G. gave him a l. in Je.
Job 12:5 as a l. despised in him
Ps. 119:105 thy word is l. to feet
132:17 ordained l. for mine ano.
Prov. 6:23 commandment is a l.
13:9 l. of wicked sh. be put out
20:20 curs. father, l. be put out
Is. 62:1 salva. as l. that burneth
Rev. 8:10 burning as it were l.

**LAMPS.**

Ex. 25:37 light l. thereof, 40:4
30:7 dress. l. burn incense on it
35:14 his l. with oil for the light
40:25 lighted the l. before the Lord, Num. 8:2, 3
Lev. 24:2 l. to burn 2 Chr. 13:11
Jud. 7:16 put l. within pitchers
20 held the l. in their left hand
1 K. 7:49 l. of gold, 2 Chr. 4:21
Job 41:19 out of mou. go burn. l.
Ezek. 1:13 like appearance of l.
Dan. 10:6 his eyes as l. of fire
Mat. 25:1 ten virgins took l. 3, 4
7 virgins arose, trimmed th. l.
8 give us oil, our l. are go. out

**Seven LAMPS.**

Ex. 37:23 s. l. of pure gold
Zec. 4:2 candlestick and seven l.
Rev. 4:5 seven l. of fire burning

**LANCE.**

Jer. 50:42 they that hold l. cruel

**LANCETS.**

1 K. 18:28 cut themselves with l.

**LAND.**

Gen. 2:12 gold of that l. is good
10:11 out of that l. went Ashur
12:1 into l. I show thee, Acts 7:3
13:6 l. not able to bear them
17:8 I will give unto thee and thy seed the l. 28:13; 35:12
20:15 behold, my l. is before th.
24:37 Canaanite, in wh. l. I dw.
47:20 brought l. so l. beca. Ph.
22 l. of priests he bought not
Ex. 10:15 the l. was darkened
20:12 days may be long upon l.
Lev. 16:22 goat bear iniquit. to l.
18:28 l. spue not you out, 20:22
25:2 l. keep a sabbath, 26:34
23 l. not be sold, the l. is mine
26:4 l. sh. yield increase, 25:19
38 l. of your enem. eat you up
Num. 13:32 l. is a l. eateth inha.
14:24 serv. Cal. I will bring to l.
15:2 wh. come into l. of habita. 18; Deut. 17:14; 18:9; 26:1
32:4 country L. sm. l. for cattle
35:33 for blood defileth the l.
Deut. 2:20 counted l. of gia. 3:13
8:9 l. whose stones are iron
11:12 a l. which L. careth for
29:23 wh. l. brimstone and salt
32:10 found him in a desert l.
43 he will be merciful to his l.
33:13 blessed of the L. be his l.
34:1 Lord showed him all the l.
Jos. 2:1 sent men, say. View l.
11:16 Joshua took all that l. 23
14:15 the l. had rest from war
24:13 a l. for wh. ye did not lab.
Jud. 3:11 l. rest forty years, 5:31
30 l. had rest fourscore years
18:10 ye shall come to a large l.
1 Sam. 14:29 father troubled l.
2 Sam. 3:12 say. Whose is the l.?
9:7 I restore thee all the l. of S.
21:14 God entreated for l. 24:25
2 K. 8:3 to cry to king for her l.
17:26 manner of G. of the l. 27
18:33 delivered his l. Is. 36:18
21:8 move any more out of the l. 2 Chr. 33:8
25:12 left poor of l. Jer. 52:16
1 Chr. 4:40 and the l. was wide
2 Chr. 7:20 pluck them out of l.
34:8 when he had purged the l.
Ezr. 9:12 eat good of l. Is. 1:19
Neh. 5:16 nor bought we any l.
Job 31:38 my l. cry against me
37:13 correct. or his l. or mercy
39:6 the barren l. his dwellings

Ps. 10:16 heathen peri. out of l.
42:6 remember thee fr. l. of Jor.
44:3 got not l. in possession
52:5 root thee out of l. of living
80:9 deep root, and it filled l.
101:6 mine eyes on faithful of l.
8 I will destroy wick. of the l.
105:16 he called for famine on l.
106:24 they despised pleasant l.
38 l. was polluted with blood
107:34 turn. fruitful l. into bar.
143:6 thi. after thee as thirsty l.
10 lead me into l. of uprightn.
Prov. 12:11 tilleth l. 28:19
28:2 for transgression of l.
Ec. 10:16 O l. wh. king is child
17 blessed, O l. wh. king is son

Is. 5:30 look unto l. behold sor.
7:16 l. thou abhorrest be forsa.
9:19 wrath of Lord l. darkened
18:1 woe to the l. shadowing
19:24 a blessing in midst of l.
21:1 com. from desert, terrible l.
24:3 l. shall be utterly emptied
11 the mirth of the l. is gone
30:6 l. of trouble and anguish
32:2 shadow of rock in weary l.
13 on l. of peo. sh. come thor.
33:17 l. that is very far off
35:7 thirsty l. springs of water
49:19 l. of destruction too nar.
53:8 cut off out of l. of living
Jer. 2:2 a l. that was not sown
6 led us through a l. of deserts
7 entered, ye defiled my l. 3:9
15 young lions made l. waste
3:19 shall I give thee plea. l.?
4:20 the whole l. is spoiled
5:19 in a l. that is not yours
6:8 make thee l. not inhabited
8:16 whole l. trembled
9:12 l. perisheth and is burnt
11:19 cut him off from l. of liv.
12:4 how long shall l. mourn?
15 I will bring ev. man to his l.
16:15 bro. fr. l. of north, 31:16
18 bec. they have defiled my l.

Jer. 22:27 l. whereu. they desire
23:15 profanen. gone forth to l.
46:12 thy cry hath filled the l.
50:18 punish king of Bab. and l.
38 it is the l. of graven images
51:43 l. wherein no man dwell.
Ezek. 7:23 l. full of bloody crimes
8:17 have filled l. with violence
9:9 and the land is full of blood
14:17 sword on l. 19 pestilence
17:5 he took also of seed of the l.
13 hath taken mighty of the l.
22:24 the l. is not cleansed
30 stand in gap before me for l.
32:4 then I leave thee up. the l.
33:2 when I bring sw. upon l.
24 l. given us for inheritance
36:5 appointed l. into possess.
13 thou l. devourest up men
38:9 a cloud to cover the l. 16
11 to l. of unwalled villages
39:12 they may cleanse the l.
Dan. 11:16 stand in glorious l. 41
Hos. 4:3 therefore shall l. mourn
Joel 1:6 a nation come up upon l.
2:3 the l. is as garden of Eden
18 then will L. be jealous for l.
21 O l. be glad; 3:2 parted l.

Amos 5:2 forsaken upon her l.
7:10 l. not able to bear words
8:4 make poor of the l. to fail
8 shall not l. tremble for this?
Zep. 3:19 and fame in every l.
Zec. 3:9 remove iniq. of that l.
12:12 l. shall mourn, ev. family
13:2 unclean spirit pass out of l.
Mal. 3:12 shall be delightsome l.
Mat. 9:26 fame went abr. into l.
10:15 tolerable for l. of S. 11:24
27:45 was darkn. over all the l.
Mark 15:33
Mark 6:47 and he alone on the l.
Luke 14:35 neither fit for the l.
John 6:21 immed. ship was at l.
Acts 4:37 Barn. having l. sold it
5:8 tell me whether ye sold l.
27:39 was day, they knew not l.
43 into the sea, and get to l. 44

See BENJAMIN, CHALDEANS, CANAAN, DARKNESS, DESOLATE, DIVIDE, DIVIDED.

**Dry LAND.**

Gen. 1:9 and let the d. l. appear
10 God called the dry l. earth
7:22 all that was in dry l. died
Ex. 4:9 pour water on dry l.
14:21 Lord made the sea dry l.
29 Israel walked on dry l.
15:19 on d. l. mi. of sea, Neh. 9:11
Jos. 4:18 priests' lifted on d. l.
22 Is. came over Jord. on d. l.
Ps. 63:1 long. for thee in a d. l.
66:6 turned the sea into dry l.
68:6 rebellious dwell in dry l.
95:5 his hands formed the d. l.
Is. 41:18 make dry l. springs
Jer. 50:12 hindermost shall be a dry l.
51:43 cities are d. l. and wilder.
Hos. 2:3 lest I set her as a d. l.
Jon. 1:9 who made sea and d. l.
Hag. 2:6 shake sea and dry l.
Heb. 11:29 pass. R. sea as by d. l.

See DWELL, EGYPT, GOOD.

**In the LAND.**

Gen. 13:7 Canaanite dw. in the l.
41:31 plenty not be kn. in the l.
47:4 to sojourn in the l. come
Ex. 8:27 sacrifice to G. in the l.
9:5 L. sh. do this thing in the l.
Lev. 26:6 I will give peace in the l.
Deut. 5:16 go well wi. thee in l.
11:9 that you may prolong your days in the l. 21; 25:15
25:19 given thee rest in the l.
31:13 as long as live in the l.
Jud. 18:7 no magistr. in the l.
2 Sam. 15:4 that I we. judge in l.
2 Chr. 6:31 fear th. so long as in l.
32:31 that was done in the l.
Job 28:13 nor is it found in the l.
Ps. 27:13 good. of the L. in the l.
116:9 walk before L. in the l.
142:5 thou art my port. in the l.
Is. 7:22 sh. every one eat in the l.
26:10 in the l. of uprightness
38:11 not see Lord in the l.
Ezek. 26:20 set glory in the l.
32:23 terror in the l. 24:32
37:22 make them one nat. in l.
45:8 in the l. sh. be his posses.
Hos. 4:1 there is no truth in the l.
Luke 21:23 great distress in the l.
Heb. 11:9 by faith he soj. in the l.

See INHABITANTS, INHERIT, ISRAEL, JUDAH.

**Our LAND.**

Gen. 47:19 buy us and our l.
Ps. 85:12 and o. l. sh. yield incr.
Mic. 5:5 Assyrian sh. come to o. l.

**Own LAND.**

Ex. 18:27 Jethro went into his o. l. Num. 10:30
1 K. 10:6 he. in my o. l. 2 Chr. 9:5
2 K. 18:32 take you to a land like your own l. Is. 36:17
2 Chr. 32:21 retur. wi. sha. to o. l.
Is. 13:14 flee ev. one to his o. l.
14:1 set them in their own l.
37:7 fall by sword in his own l.
Jer. 23:8 dw. in their o. l. 27:11
37:7 Eg. into their own l. 42:12
Ezek. 34:13 bring them to their o. l. 36:24; 37:14, 21; 39:28
Amos 7:11 led capt. out their o. l.

See PEOPLE, POSSESS, POSSESSION, STRANGE.

**Their LAND, S.**

Gen. 47:22 priests sold not t. l.
Num. 18:20 A. had no inh. in t. l.
Deut. 2:5 not give you of t. l. 9
29:28 L. rooted them out of t. l.
1 K. 8:48 pray to thee tow. t. l.
2 Chr. 7:14 forg. sin and heal t. l.
Ps. 105:32 flaming fire in t. l.
135:12 gave t. l. for inher. 136:21
Is. 2:7 their l. is full of silver
8 their l. also is full of idols
Jer. 12:14 pluck them out their l.
16:15 I will bri. them ag. to t. l.
51:5 their l. was filled with sin
Ezek. 34:27 they sh. be safe in t. l.
39:26 dwelt safely in their l.
Amos 9:15 plant them on t. l.

**This LAND.**

Gen. 12:7 L. said, Unto thy seed will I give this l. 15:18; 24:7; 48:4; Ex. 32:13
31:13 get thee out from this l.
50:24 G. will bri. you out of t. l.
Num. 14:3 L. bro. us unto this l.
32:5 let t. l. be given to thy ser.
22 this l. sh. be your possess.
Deut. 4:22 I must die in this l.
29:24 the Lord done thus to this l.? 27; 1 K. 9:8; 2 Chr. 7:21
Jud. 2:2 no league wi. inh. of t. l.
2 Chr. 30:9 shall come into t. l.
Jer. 14:15 sw. sh. not be in t. l.
16:3 fathers that begot in this l.
6 great and small sh. die in t. l.
22:12 he shall see t. l. no more
24:6 I will bring them ag. to t. l.
25:9 bring them against this l.
11 t. whole l. sh. be a desolat.
32:41 I will plant them in t. l.
36:29 king of Bab. destroy t. l.
42:10 ye will abide in this l. 13
45:4 I will pluck up t. whole l.
Ezek. 11:15 to us is this l. given
47:14 t. l. sh. fall to you for inh.
Acts 7:4 removed him into t. l.

**Thy LAND.**

Ex. 23:10 six years sh. sow t. l.
26 noth. sh. cast young in t. l.
34:24 nor sh. any man desire t. l.
Deut. 7:13 will bless fruit of t. l.
21:23 that thy l. be not defiled
28:12 to give the rain to thy l.
18 cursed be fruit of thy l. 42
2 Sam. 24:13 sh. fam. come to t. l.
Ps. 85:1 been favorable to thy l.
Is. 8:8 wings fill breadth of t. l.
60:18 viol. no more heard in t. l.
62:4 nor sh. t. l. be termed des. L. delight. in thee, and t. l.
Ezek. 32:8 set darkness on thy l.
Amos 7:17 thy l. shall be divided
Nah. 3:13 gates of t. l. sh. be wi.

**Your LAND.**

Gen. 47:23 I bought you and y. l.
Lev. 9:9 harvest of y. l. 23:22
26:25 and dwell in y. l. safely
6 nor shall sw. go through y. l.
20 y. l. sh. not yield her inc.
Deut. 11:14 give you rain of y. l.
1 Sam. 6:5 light. hand fr. off y. l.
Jer. 5:19 serv. stran. gods in y. l.
27:10 remove you far from y. l.
44:22 theref. is y. l. a desolation

**LANDED, ING.**

Acts 18:22 when we l. at Cesarea
21:3 sailed to Syria and l. at T.
28:12 l. at Syracuse three days

**LANDMARK, S.**

Deut. 19:14 not remo. thy neighbor's l. Prov. 22:28; 23:10
27:17 cursed that removeth l.
Job 24:2 some remove the l.

**LANDS.**

Gen. 41:54 dearth in all l. 57
47:18 not left but bodies and l.
Jud. 11:13 restore those l. again
1 Chr. 14:17 fame of D. went all l.
2 Chr. 17:10 fear fell on all the l.
32:17 gods of other l. have not
Ezr. 9:1 not separ. fr. peo. of l.
Neh. 5:3 have mortgaged our l.
5 for other men have our l.
11 restore, I pray you, their l.
Ps. 49:11 th. l. after own names
66:1 make noise all ye l. 100:1
105:44 give them l. of heathen
106:27 to scatter them in l.
107:3 gathered them out of l.
Jer. 27:6 these l. to Nebuchadn.
Ezek. 20:6 wh. is glory of all l. 15
39:27 gather out of enemies' l.
Mat. 19:29 hath forsaken houses, l. Mark 10:29
Mark 10:30 rec. hundred-fold, l.
Acts 4:34 were possessors of l.

**LANES.**

Luke 14:21 go quickly into the l.

**LANGUAGE, S.**

Gen. 11:1 wh. earth was of one l.
6 people is one, have all one l.
7 and there confound their l. 9
2 K. 18:26 speak in the Syrian l. Is. 36:11, 13
Neh. 13:24 chil. not speak Jews' l. but accord. to l. of people
Ps. 19:3 no l. wh. voice is heard
81:5 heard a l. I understood not
114:1 from a people of strange l.
Is. 19:18 five cities speak l. Can.
Jer. 5:15 wh. l. thou know. not
Ezek. 3:5 to a people of hard l. 6
Dan. 3:4 people, nations and l.
7 all l. fell down and worship.
29 every l. that speaketh amiss
4:1 Neb. all l. 6:25 D. to all l.
5:19 all l. trembled and feared
7:14 nations, and l. sho. serve
Zep. 3:9 turn to people a pure l.
Zec. 8:23 ten men out of all l.
Acts 2:6 heard th. speak in all l.

**LANGUISH.**

Is. 16:8 the fields of Heshbon l.
19:8 spread nets on wat. sh. l.
24:4 haughty people of earth l.
Jer. 14:2 the gates of Judah l.
Hos. 4:3 every one therein sh. l.

**LANGUISHED, ETH.**

Is. 24:4 world l. and fad. away
7 the vine l. 33:9 the earth l.
Jer. 15:9 that hath borne seven l.
Lam. 2:8 wall lament, l. together
Joel 1:10 the oil l. 12 fig-tree l.
Nah. 1:4 Bashan l. and Carmel l.

**LANGUISHING.**

Ps. 41:3 L. strength. on bed of l.

**LANTERNS.**

John 18:3 Judas cometh with l.

**LAODICEA.**

Col. 2:1 for them at L. 4:13,15,16

**LAODICEANS.**

Col. 4:16 in church of L. Rev. 3:14

**LAP.**

2 K. 4:39 gathered gourds, l. full
Neh. 5:13 I shook my l. and said
Prov. 16:33 lot is cast into the l.

**LAPPED, ETH.**
*Jud.* 7:5 that *l.* water as a dog
6 number *l.* were three hund.
7 by them th. *l.* I will save you

LAPWING. *See* BAT.

**LARGE.**
*Ex.* 3:8 into a good and *l.* land
2 *Sam.* 22:20 he brought me into
a *l.* place, *Ps.* 18:19
*Neh.* 4:19 the work is gre. and *l.*
9:35 not served thee in *l.* land
*Ps.* 31:8 set my feet in a *l.* room
118:5 Lord set me in a *l.* place
*Is.* 22:18 toss thee in a *l.* country
30:23 cattle feed in *l.* past. 33
*Jer.* 22:14 I will build *l.* chamb.
*Ezek.* 23:32 sist. cup deep and *l.*
*Hos.* 4:16 L. feed them in a *l.* pl.
*Mat.* 28:12 gave *l.* money to sol.
*Mark* 14:15 and he will show you
a *l.* upper room, *Luke* 22:12
*Gal.* 6:11 *l.* letter I have written
*Rev.* 21:16 length as *l.* as breadth

**LARGENESS.**
1 *K.* 4:29 God gave S. *l.* of heart

**LASCIVIOUSNESS.**
*Mark* 7:22 out of heart proceed *l.*
2 *Cor.* 12:21 not repented of the *l.*
*Gal.* 5:19 works of flesh manif. *l.*
*Eph.* 4:19 given themselves to *l.*
1 *Pet.* 4:3 when we walked in *l.*
*Jude* 4 turning grace of G. into *l.*

**LAST.**
*Gen.* 49:19 Gad sh. overcome at *l.*
*Num.* 23:10 my *l.* end be like his
2 *Sam.* 23:1 *l.* words of David
1 *Chr.* 23:27 by *l.* words of David
*Neh.* 8:18 from first day to the *l.*
*Prov.* 5:11 thou mourn at the *l.*
*Is.* 41:4 I Lord, first and *l.* 44:6;
48:12; *Rev.* 1:11, 17; 2:8;
22:13
*Lam.* 1:9 remembereth not *l.* end
*Dan.* 8:3 the higher came up *l.*
*Amos* 9:1 will slay the *l.* of them
*Mat.* 12:45 *l.* state of that man is
worse than first, *Luke* 11:26
19:30 first shall be *l.* and *l.* first.
20:16; *Mark* 10:31; *Luke* 13:30
20:12 *l.* have wrought one hour
14 give to *l.* even as unto thee
27:64 *l.* error worse than the fi.
*Mark* 9:35 first, same sh. be *l.*
*Luke* 12:59 till th. hast paid *l.* m.
1 *Cor.* 4:9 set forth us apostles *l.*
15:8 *l.* of all he was seen of me
26 *l.* enemy is death; 45 *l.* Ad.
*Rev.* 2:19 *l.* works be more th. fi.

**LAST day, s.**
*Gen.* 49:1 befall you in *l. days*
*John* 6:39 should raise it up ag.
at the *l. d.* 40, 44, 54
7:37 in *l. d.* great day of feast
11:24 he shall rise again at *l. d.*
2 *Tim.* 3:1 *l. day* perilous times
*Heb.* 1:2 spoken in *l. d.* by his S.
*Jam.* 5:3 heaped treasure for *l. d.*
2 *Pet.* 3:3 come in *l. d.* scoffers

**LAST time, s.**
1 *Pet.* 1:5 to be revealed in *l. t.*
20 manifest in these *l. times*
1 *John* 2:18 children, it is the *l. t.*
*Jude* 18 should be mockers in *l. t.*

**LASTED, ING.**
*Deut.* 33:15 precious th. of *l.* hills
*Jud.* 14:17 wept whilst feast *l.*

**LATCHET.**
*Is.* 5:27 *l.* of their shoes broken
*Mark* 1:7 *l.* of wh. shoes, *Lu.* 3:16

**LATE, LY.**
*Ps.* 127:2 vain for you to sit up *l.*
*Mic.* 2:8 of *l.* my people risen up
*Acts* 18:2 Aquila *l.* come from I.

**LATIN.**
*Luke* 23:38 writ. in L. *John* 19:20

**LATTER.**
*Deut.* 11:14 give first and *l.* rain
*Job* 19:25 Redeemer, st. at *l.* day
29:23 open. mouth, as for *l.* rain
*Prov.* 16:15 as cloud of *l.* rain
19:20 mayest be wise in *l.* end
*Jer.* 3:3 there ha. been no *l.* rain
5:24 form. and *l.* rain in season
*Dan.* 8:23 *l.* time of their kingd.
*Hos.* 6:3 as *l.* and former rain
*Joel* 2:23 *l.* rain in first month
*Amos* 7:1 in beginning of *l.* grow.
*Hag.* 2:9 glory of *l.* house greater
*Zec.* 10:1 rain in time of *l.* rain
1 *Tim.* 4:1 in *l.* times some dep.
*See* DAYS, END.

**LATTICE.**
*Jud.* 5:28 cried through the *l.*
2 *K.* 1:2 Ahaziah fell through *l.*
*Cant.* 2:9 show. himself thro' *l.*

**LAUD.**
*Rom.* 15:11 praise L. and *l.* him

**LAUGH.**
*Gen.* 18:13 wheref. did Sarah *l.*?
21:6 G. made me to *l.* all will *l.*
*Job* 5:22 at famine thou shalt *l.*
9:23 will *l.* at trial of innocent
22:19 innocent *l.* them to scorn
*Ps.* 2:4 sitteth in heavens sh. *l.*
22:7 that see me *l.* me to scorn
37:13 the Lord shall *l.* at him
52:6 righteous also sh. *l.* at him
59:8 thou, O L. shall *l.* at them
80:6 enemies *l.* am. themselves
*Prov.* 1:26 *l.* at your calamity
29:9 rage or *l.* there is no rest
*Ec.* 3:4 time to weep, time to *l.*
*Luke* 6:21 ye that weep, ye sh. *l.*
25 woe unto you that *l.* now

**LAUGHED.**
*Gen.* 17:17 Abra. *l.* 18:12 Sarah
18:15 S. denied, saying, I *l.* not
2 *K.* 19:21 daughter of Zion hath
*l. Is.* 37:22
2 *Chr.* 30:10 they *l.* them to sco.
*Neh.* 2:19 they *l.* us to scorn
*Job* 12:4 upright man *l.* to scorn
29:24 *l.* on them, they beli. not
*Ezek.* 23:32 shalt be *l.* to scorn
*Mat.* 9:24 they *l.* him to scorn,
*Mark* 5:40; *Luke* 8:53

**LAUGHETH, ING.**
*Job* 8:21 he fill thy mouth with *l.*
41:29 he *l.* at shaking of a spear

**LAUGHTER.**
*Ps.* 126:2 mouth filled with *l.*
*Prov.* 14:13 in *l.* heart sorrowful
*Ec.* 2:2 I said of *l.* It is mad
7:3 sorrow is better than *l.*
6 thorns, so is the *l.* of fool
*Jam.* 4:9 *l.* turned to mourning

**LAUNCH, ED.**
*Luke* 5:4 Sim. *l.* out into deep
8:22 go over, and they *l.* forth
*Acts* 21:1 after had *l.* 27:2, 4

**LAVER, S.**
*Ex.* 30:18 make a *l.* of brass
28 *l.* and fo. 31:9; 35:16; 39:39
38:8 he made the *l.* of brass
40:7 thou shalt set the *l.* 30
*Lev.* 8:11 anoint. both *l.* and foot
1 *K.* 7:30 under *l.* were unders.
38 made ten *l.* of brass; one *l.*
40 baths; and ev. *l.* 4 cubits
40 and H. made the *l.*
43 and the ten *l.* on the bases,
2 *Chr.* 4:6, 14
2 *K.* 16:17 king A. removed *l.*

**LAVISH.**
*Is.* 46:6 they *l.* gold out of bag

**LAW.**
*Gen.* 47:26 made it a *l.* over land
*Ex.* 12:49 *l.* to him home-born
*Lev.* 24:22; *Num.* 15:16, 29
*Deut.* 17:11 to sentence of the *l.*
33:2 fr. right hand went fiery *l.*
4 Moses commanded us a *l.*
*Jos.* 8:32 wrote copy of *l.* to M.
22:5 take heed to the *l.* 2 *K.*
17:13, 37; 21:8
2 *K.* 17:34 nor do after the *l.*
1 *Chr.* 22:12 mayest keep *l.* of G.
2 *Chr.* 19:10 between *l.* and com.
30:16 place according to *l.* of M.
*Ezr.* 7:6 scribe in *l.* 12, 21
14 according to *l.* of thy God
26 not do *l.* of G. and *l.* of king
*Neh.* 8:7 cause people underst. *l.*
9 wh. they heard the wo. of *l.*
10:29 made oath to walk in G. *l.*
12:44 gather them portions of *l.*
*Est.* 1:8 drinking according to *l.*
4:11 *l.* of his to put him to dea.
16 which is not according to *l.*
*Job* 22:22 rec. *l.* from his mouth
*Ps.* 1:2 in his *l.* he meditates
37:31 *l.* of his G. is in his heart
78:5 for he appointed a *l.* in Is.
10 refused to walk in his *l.*
81:4 was a *l.* of the G. of Jacob
105:10 confirm. same to J. for *l.*
119:72 *l.* of mouth bet. than gold
*Prov.* 1:8 forsake not the *l.* of thy
mother, 6:20
6:23 command. lamp, *l.* is light
13:14 *l.* of wise is fount. of life
28:4 forsake *l.* praise wick. such
as keep *l.* contend with them
7 keepeth the *l.* is a wise son
29:18 that keep. *l.* happy is he
31:5 lest drink and forget the *l.*
26 in her tongue is *l.* of kindn.
*Is.* 2:3 out of Zion shall go forth
the *l. Mic.* 4:2
8:16 seal *l.* 20 to *l.* and testim.
42:4 the isles sh. wait for his *l.*
21 Lord will magnify the *l.*
51:4 a *l.* shall proceed from me
*Jer.* 2:8 they that handle the *l.*
18:18 *l.* not perish from priest
44:23 not obey, nor walk. in *l.*
*Lam.* 2:9 the *l.* is no more
*Ezek.* 7:26 *l.* perish from priests
*Dan.* 6:5 concerning *l.* of his G.
12 according to *l.* of Medes, 15
*Hos.* 4:6 has forgotten *l.* of God
*Hab.* 1:4 theref. the *l.* is slacked
*Zep.* 3:4 priests done viol. to *l.*
*Mal.* 2:6 *l.* of truth was in mouth
7 sh. seek the *l.* at his mouth
9 have been partial in the *l.*
*Mat.* 5:17 not to come to dest. *l.*
18 sh. in no wise pass fr. the *l.*
40 if any man sue th. at the *l.*
11:13 *l.* pro. till Jo. *Luke* 16:16
22:36 great commandment in *l.*
40 on two command. hang *l.*
23:23 omitted weigh. mat. of *l.*
*Luke* 2:27 do after custom of *l.*
5:17 were doctors of *l.* sitting
16:17 one tittle of the *l.* to fail
*John* 1:17 *l.* was given by Moses
7:19 did not Moses give you *l.*?
23 *l.* of Moses should not be
*John* 7:49 who know. not the *l.*
51 doth *l.* judge before it he.?
10:34 written in *l.* Ye are gods?
12:34 heard out of *l.* that Christ
18:31 judge him according to *l.*
19:7 by our *l.* he ought to die
*Acts* 6:13 blasphe. words aga. *l.*
7:53 have received *l.* by angels
13:15 reading of *l.* and prophets
39 not justified by *l.* of Moses
15:5 command to keep *l.* of Mo.
24 circumcised and keep the *l.*
18:15 a question of *l.* look to it
19:38 *l.* is open; 21:20 zeal. of *l.*

21:28 this man teach. against *l.*
22:12 devout man accord. to *l.*
23:3 sittest thou to jud. after *l.*
25:8 nor against *l.* of the Jews
28:23 persua. them out of the *l.*

*Rom.* 2:12 sin. in *l.* judged by *l.*
13 not hearers of the *l.* are just
14 Gentiles have not *l.* to do things contained in *l.* these hav. not *l.* are a *l.* unto the.
17 called a Jew, and rest. in *l.*
20 the form of truth in the *l.*
23 that makest thy boast of the *l.* through break. the *l.*
3:20 by deeds of *l.* no flesh be justified, for by the *l.* is knowl. of sin, 28; *Gal.* 2:16
21 righ. of God witnessed by *l.*
27 by what *l.* excluded? by *l.*
31 do we make void the *l.*?
4:14 they which are of *l.* be hei.
15 *l.* worketh wrath wh. no *l.*
5:13 until *l.* sin was in world, but sin not im. wh. is no *l.*
20 *l.* entered, offence might
7:1 speak to them wh. know *l.*
2 wo. bound by *l.* to husband
4 ye also become dead to the *l.*
7 is *l.* sin, I had not kno. sin, but by *l.* nor lust, ex. *l.* said
8 without *l.* sin was dead
12 the *l.* is holy, and comman.
14 know th. the *l.* is spiritual
16 *l.* that is good 1 *Tim.* 1:8
22 I delight in the *l.* of God
23 I see another *l.* warring ag. the *l.* of my mind, to *l.* of
25 with mind I serve *l.* of God
8:2 the *l.* of life made me free
3 for what the *l.* could not do
4 righteousness of the *l.* fulfil.
7 carnal mind not subject to *l.*
9:31 Israel followed *l.* of righte.
10:4 Christ is the end of the *l.*
13:8 loveth another, fulfilled *l.*
10 love is the fulfilli. of the *l.*

1 *Cor.* 6:1 dare any of you to *l.*?
6 brother goeth to *l.* with bro.
7:39 wife is bound by the *l.*
15:56 strength of sin is the *l.*

*Gal.* 2:16 not just. by works of *l.*
19 I thro' the *l.* am de. to the *l.*
21 if righteousness come by *l.*
3:2 received ye Spirit by the *l.*?
5 miracles, doeth he it by *l.*?
11 no man is justified by the *l.*
12 and the *l.* is not of faith
13 C. redeem. us fr. curse of *l.*
19 wheref. then serveth the *l.*?
21 is the *l.* aga. the promises? righteous. had been by the *l.*
24 *l.* was our schoolmaster
5:3 is a debtor to do the who. *l.*
4 whosoever are just. by the *l.*
14 all the *l.* is fulfil. in one w.
23 tempera. ag. such is no *l.*
6:2 so fulfil the *l.* of Christ, 13

*Eph.* 2:15 abolished in his fle. *l.*
*Phil.* 3:6 touching righ. in the *l.*
9 mine own righteou. of the *l.*
1 *Tim.* 1:7 to be teache. of the *l.*
9 *l.* is not made for right. man
*Tit.* 3:9 avoid content. about *l.*
*Heb.* 7:5 take tithes accord. to *l.*
12 made of nece. a change of *l.*
16 not after the *l.* of a carnal
19 for the *l.* made noth. perfect
28 *l.* make. men high-priests
8:4 offer gifts accord. to the *l.*
9:22 all things are by the *l.*
10:1 *l.* hav. shadow of good th.
28 he that desp. Moses' *l.* died
*Jam.* 1:25 looketh into perfect *l.*
2:8 fulfil the royal *l.* ye do well
9 convinced of *l.* as transgres.
12 they th. be judged by the *l.*
4:11 that speaketh evil of the *l.*

1 *John* 3:4 whosoever committeth sin transgres. also the *l.*

*See* BOOK.

**LAW of the Lord.**

*Ex.* 13:9 *L's l.* be in thy mouth
2 *K.* 10:31 no heed to wa. in *l. L.*
2 *Chr.* 12:1 R. forsook *l. of t. L.*
31:4 encouraged in *l. of the L.*
*Ezr.* 7:10 heart to seek *l. of L.*
*Ps.* 1:2 delight is in *l. of the L.*
19:7 the *l. of the L.* is perfect
119:1 blessed th. walk in *l. of L.*
*Is.* 5:24 cast away the *l. of L.*
30:9 children not hear *l. of L.*
*Jer.* 8:8 say, *l. of L.* is with us
*Amos* 2:4 they have des. *l. of L.*

**My LAW.**

*Ex.* 16:4 whether walk in *my l.*
2 *Chr.* 6:16 childr. walk in *my l.*
*Ps.* 78:1 my peo. to *my l.* incline
*Prov.* 3:1 my son, forg. not *my l.*
4:2 fors. not *my l.* 7:2 keep *my l.*
*Is.* 51:7 peo. in wh. heart is *my l.*
*Jer.* 6:19 not hearken. unto *my l.*
16:11 forsa. me, not kept *my l.*
31:33 put *my l.* in their parts
44:10 nor walked in *my l.*
*Ezek.* 22:26 priests ha. vio. *my l.*
*Hos.* 8:1 they trespass ag. *my l.*
12 writ. to him things of *my l.*

**This LAW.**

*Num.* 5:30 priests shall exe. *t. l.*
*Deut.* 1:5 Moses to declare *this l*
17:18 write him a copy of *t. l.*
28:58 if th. wilt not observe *t. l.*
31:9 M. wrote *t. l.* 11 read *t. l.*
24 wri. words of *t. l.* in a book

**This is the LAW.**

*Ezek.* 43:12 *this is the l.* of house
*Mat.* 7:12 *this is the l.* and prop.

**Thy LAW.**

*Deut.* 33:10 shall teach Isr. *thy l.*
*Neh.* 9:26 cast *t. l.* behind backs
34 nor our princes kept *thy l.*
*Ps.* 40:8 *t. l.* is within my heart
94:12 teachest him out of *thy l.*
119:18 wondr. things art of *t. l.*
29 and grant *t. l.* graciously
34 and I shall keep *thy l.*
44 so shall keep *t. l.* continu.
51 have I not declined fr. *t. l.*
55 I rememb. and kept *thy l.*
61 I have not forgotten *thy l.*
70 but I delight in *thy l.*
77 for *t. l.* is my delight, 92, 174
85 pits, wh. are not after *t. l.*
97 love *t. l.* 109 not forget *t. l.*
113 *t. l.* I love, 163; 126 ma. vo.
136 because they keep not *t. l.*
142 *t. l.* is truth; 150 far fr. *t. l.*
165 peace have they love *t. l.*
*Jer.* 32:23 nor walk in *t. l.*
*Dan.* 9:11 have transgressed *t. l.*

**Under the LAW.**

*Rom.* 6:14 ye are not *under t. l.*
15 sho. we sin bec. not *u. l.*?
1 *Cor.* 9:20 as *u. t. l.* that I might gain them th. that are *u. t. l.*
21 not without law to G. *u. l.*
*Gal.* 3:23 kept *u. l.* 4:4 made *u. l.*
4:5 sent Son to red. them *un. l.*
5:18 led by Sp. are not *u. t. l.*

**Without LAW.**

2 *Chr.* 15:3 Is. hath been *with. l.*
*Rom.* 2:12 many as sinned *w. l.*
3:21 righteousness of God *w. l.*
7:8 *w. l.* sin dead; 9 I was alive
1 *Cor.* 9:21 *w. l.* not *w. l.* to God

**Written in the LAW.**

1 *K.* 2:3 as it is *written in the l.* of Moses, 2 *Chr.* 23:18; 25:4; 31:3; *Ezr.* 3:2; *Neh.* 10:34, 36; *Dan.* 9:13; *Luke* 2:23
*Dan.* 9:11 oath is *w. in t. l.* of Moses

*Luke* 10:26 what is *wri. in t. l.*?
24:44 all must be ful. *w. in t. l.*
*Acts* 24:14 belie. things *w. in t. l.*

**LAWS.**

*Gen.* 26:5 Abraham kept my *l.*
*Ex.* 16:28 how long ref. my *l.*?
18:16 make them know *l.* of G.
20 teach th. ordinances and *l.*
*Neh.* 9:13 thou gavest th. true *l.*
*Est.* 1:19 among *l.* of Persians
3:8 their *l.* are div. from all peo. nei. keep they the king's *l.*
*Is.* 24:5 th. have transgressed *l.*
*Dan.* 7:25 to change times and *l.*
9:10 nor obeyed to walk in *l.*
*Heb.* 8:10 put my *l.* into th. mind
10:16 put my *l.* in their hearts

**LAWFUL.**

*Is.* 49:24 sh. *l.* captive be deliv.?
*Ezek.* 18:5 do that which is *l.* 21, 27; 33:14, 19
19 son ha. done that is *l.* 33:16
*Mat.* 12:2 do what is not *l.* *Mark* 2:24; *Luke* 6:2
4 was not *l.* for him to eat, *Mark* 2:26; *Luke* 6:4

*Mat.* 12:10 is it *l.* to heal on sab.? 12; *Mark* 3:4; 6:9; 14:3
14:4 it is not *l.* for thee to have her, *Mark* 6:18
19:3 *l.* to put aw. wife? *Mar.* 10:2
*John* 5:10 not *l.* to carry thy bed
18:31 not *l.* to put man to death
*Acts* 19:39 determ. in *l.* assembly
22:25 is it *l.* to scourge a Rom.?
1 *Cor.* 6:12 all things *l.* 10:23
2 *Cor.* 12:4 not *l.* for man to utter

**LAWFULLY.**

1 *Tim.* 1:8 go. if a man use it *l.*
2 *Tim.* 2:5 not crown. except *l.*

**LAWGIVER.**

*Gen.* 49:10 *l.* from betw. his feet
*Num.* 21:18 digged by direc. of *l.*
*Deut.* 33:21 in a portion of the *l.*
*Ps.* 60:7 Judah is my *l.* 108:8
*Is.* 33:22 L. is our *l.* and king
*Jam.* 4:12 one *l.* is able to save

**LAWLESS.**

1 *Tim.* 1.9 law for *l.* disobedient

**LAWYER, S.**

*Mat.* 22:35 a *l.* asked, *Luke* 10:25
*Luke* 7:30 *l.* reject. counsel of G.
11:46 woe to you *l.* 52; 14:3 J.

**LAY.**

*Ex.* 5:8 tale of bricks ye shall *l.*
16:13 *l.* round about host, 14
22:25 neither sh. thou *l.* on him
*Lev.* 1:7 *l.* the wood on the fire
8 priests sh. *l.* parts in ord. 12
*Num.* 12:11 L. *l.* not sin upon us
*Deut.* 7:15 *l.* on them that hate
11:25 *l.* fear of you upon land
21:8 *l.* not innoc. blood to peop.
*Jud.* 16:3 Sam. *l.* till midnight
*Ruth* 3:8 a woman *l.* at his feet
1 *Sam.* 3:15 Samuel *l.* till morn.
26:5 Saul *l.* in the trench, 7
2 *Sam.* 4:5 who *l.* on bed at noon
12:3 ewe-lamb *l.* in his bosom
16 D. *l.* all night on earth, 13:31
1 *K.* 13:31 *l.* my bones beside his
18:23 *l.* it on wood put no fire
2 *K.* 4:34 went and *l.* on the chi.
2 *Chr.* 36:21 long as she *l.* desol.
*Est.* 4:3 *l.* in sackcloth and ashes
*Job* 29:19 dew *l.* all ni. on branch
34:23 not *l.* on man more than
*Ps.* 7:5 *l.* mine honor in the dust
38:12 seek life, *l.* snares for me
84:3 a nest, where she *l.* young
*Ec.* 7:2 living will *l.* it to heart

Is. 5:8 woe to them that l. field
13:9 l. land desolate, Ezek. 33:28
11 will l. low hau. of terrible
22:22 house of D. l. on shoulder
25:12 the fortress shall be l. low
28:16 I will l. in Z. a tried stone
17 judgment will I l. to the li.
29:21 l. a snare for him that re.
34:15 there sh. the great owl l.
38:21 and l. it for a plaster
54:11 l. thy stones with colors
Jer. 6:21 will l. stumbling-blocks before this peop. Ezek. 3:20
Ezek. 4:1 take a tile and l. it be.
4 l. iniquity of house of Israel
25:14 l. vengeance on Edom, 17
32:5 will l. thy flesh on mount
36:29 I will l. no famine upon
34 land be tilled, it l. desolate
37:6 I will l. sinews upon you
Jon. 1:14 l. not on us inno. blood
Mic. 1:7 idols will I l. desolate
Mal. 2:2 if ye will not l. it to he.
Mat. 8:20 hath not where to l. his head, Luke 9:58
28:6 see place where the Lord l.
Mark 2:4 bed wh. sick of palsy l.
Luke 19:44 l. thee with ground
Acts 7:60 L. l. not this sin to th.
15:28 l. on you no grea. burden
Rom. 8:33 l. any thing to God's
9:33 I l. in Zion a stumbling-st
1 Cor. 16:2 every one l. by him
Heb. 12:1 let us l. aside ev. weig.
Jam. 1:21 l. apart all filthiness
1 Pet. 2:6 l. in Zion a chief cor.

See FOUNDATION.

**LAY down.**

Gen. 19:33 L. per. not she l. d. 35
28:11 Jacob l. d. in place to sl.
Num. 24:9 he l. d. as a lion
Jud. 5:27 he l. down at her feet
Ruth 3:4 uncov. feet, l. thee d.
1 Sam. 19:24 Saul l. down naked
Job 17:3 l. d. put me in surety
Ps. 4:8 I will l. me d. in peace
104:22 young lions l. d. in dens
Ezek. 19:2 mother l. d. am. lions
Amos 2:8 l. thems. d. on clothes
John 10:15 l. d. life for sheep, 17
John 10:18 l. it down of myself
13:37 l. d. my li. for thy sake, 38
15:13 l. d. his life for his friends
1 John 3:16 l. d. lives for breth.

**LAY hand.**

Gen. 22:12 l. n. thy h. on the lad
37:22 no blood, l. no h. on Jos.
Ex. 7:4 I may l. my h. on Egypt
Lev. 3:2 l. h. on head of offer. 8
4:4 sh. l. h. on bullock's he. 15
29 sh. l. h. on sin-offering, 33
Num. 27:18 L. said, l. h. on Jos.
Jud. 18:19 l. h. on thy mouth
Job 9:33 any days-man to l. h.
21:5 mark me, l. h. on mouth
40:4 will l. my h. on my mouth
41:8 l. h. on him, remem. battle
Prov. 30:32 tho' evil, l. h. mouth
Is. 11:14 sh. l. their h. on Edom
Mic. 7:16 sh. l. h. on their mou.
Mat. 9:18 come, l. thy h. on her

**LAY hands.**

Lev. 16:21 A. sh. l. bo. h. on goat
Num. 8:12 Lev. l. h. on bullocks
Neh. 13:21 again, l. h. on you
Mat. 21:46 they sought to l. h. on him, Luke 20:19
Mark 5:23 come l. thy h. on her
16:18 l. h. on sick, they recover
Luke 21:12 they shall l. h. on you
1 Tim. 5:22 l. h. suddenly on no

**LAY hold.**

Prov. 3:18 tree of life to th. l. h.
Ec. 2:3 I sought to l. h. on folly
Is. 5:29 roar, and l. h. on prey
Jer. 6:23 l. h. on bow and spear
Zec. 14:13 ev. one l. h. on neigh.
Mark 3:21 friends went to l. h.
12:12 sought to l. hold on him
1 Tim. 6:12 l. h. on eter. life, 19
Heb. 6:18 l. h. on hope set be. us

**LAY up.**

Gen. 41:35 l. up corn under Pha.
Ex. 16:23 l. up manna till morn.
33 l. up a pot of manna
Num. 17:4 sh. l. them up in tab.
Deut. 11:18 l. up my words
Job 22:22 l. up his words in heart
24 then shalt l. up gold as dust
Prov. 7:1 l. up my commandm.
10:14 wise men l. up knowledge
Mat. 6:19 l. not up for you treas.
20 l. up treasures in heaven
2 Cor. 12:14 children not to l. up

**LAY wait.**

Ezr. 8:31 del. fr. such as l. in w.
Ps. 71:10 l. wait for my soul
Prov. 1:11 let us l. wait for blood
18 they l. w. for their own bl.
24:15 l. not w. against righte.
Jer. 5:26 l. w. as he that setteth

**LAY waste.**

Is. 5:6 I will l. it w. it shall not
Ezek. 35:4 I will l. thy cities w.

**LAY with.**

Gen. 19:33 l. w. her father 34, 35
30:16 Jacob l. w. L. that night
34:2 Shechem l. with Dinah
35:22 Reuben l. with Bilhah
Deut. 22:22 man that l. w. wom.
25 man that l. w. her shall die
29 that l. w. her give 50 shek.
1 Sam. 2:22 Eli's sons l. w. wom.
2 Sam. 13:14 A. forc. T. and l. w.
Ezek. 23:8 in her youth l. w. her

**LAID.**

Gen. 22:6 wood, and l. it on Isa.
30:41 Jacob l. rods before cattle
48:14 l. it on Ephraim's head
Ex. 2:3 l. it on flags by river
Deut. 26:6 Egy. l. on us bondage
Jos. 7:23 they l. them bef. the L.
Ruth 4:16 and l. it in her bosom
2 Sam. 18:17 l. heap of stones on
1 K. 3:20 l. it in her bosom, and l. her dead child in my bos.
13:29 prophet l. carcass on ass
17:19 and l. him on his own bed
2 K. 9:25 l. this burden on him
20:7 they l. it on the boil
Job 6:2 calamity l. in balances
18:10 snares l. for him in ground
38:6 or who l. the corner-stone
Ps. 21:5 majesty hast l. on him
31:4 out of the net they l. for me
49:14 they are l. in the grave
62:9 to be l. in the balance
79:1 they have l. Jeru. on heaps
88:6 hast l. me in the lowest pit
89:19 l. help on one mighty
105:18 fetters, he was l. in iron
119:30 judg. have I l. before me
110 l. a snare for me, 141:9
142:3 privily l. a snare for me
Is. 42:25 l. it not to heart, 57:11
Is. 47:6 thou has heavily l. yoke
53:6 L. l. on him iniq. of us all
Jer. 50:24 l. a snare for thee
Ezek. 32:19 l. wi. the uncircum.
35:12 saying, They are l. desol.
Hos. 11:4 I l. meat unto them
Ob. 7 l. a wound under thee
Mic. 5:1 hath l. siege against us
Hab. 2:19 it is l. over with gold
Hag. 2:15 before a stone was l.
Zec. 3:9 behold stone I have l.
Mat. 3:10 axe l. to root, Luke 3:9
27:60 l. it in his own new tomb
Mark 7:30 her daughter l. on bed
15:47 M. beheld where he was l.
16:6 behold where they l. him
Luke 2:7 first-born l. in manger
16:20 Lazarus was l. at his gate
23:53 wherein never man before was l. John 19:41
John 11:34 wh. have ye l. him?
20:2 know not wh. th. l. him, 13
Acts 3:2 l. at gate of temple
4:37 l. money at apostles' f. 5:2
9:37 l. her in an upper chamber
13:36 David l. to his fathers
25:7 l. compla. could not prove
1 Cor. 9:16 necessity l. upon me
2 Tim. 4:16 not l. to their charge

See FOUNDATION.

**LAID down.**

Jos. 2:8 bef. they were l. down
1 Sam. 3:2 Eli l. d. in his place
3 and Samuel was l. d. to sleep
2 Sam. 13:8 Amnon was l. down
1 K. 19:6 and l. him down again
21:4 Ahab came and l. him d.
Ps. 3:5 I l. me d. and slept
Luke 19:22 tak. up th. I l. not d.
Acts 4:35 l. th. d. at apostles' fe.
7:58 l. d. their clothes at young
Rom. 16:4 for my life l. d. necks
1 John 3:16 he l. d. his life for us

**LAID hand.**

Ex. 24:11 on the nobles l. not h.
2 Sam. 13:19 Tamar l. h. on head
Est. 9:10 l. not h. on sp. 15, 16
Job 29:9 princes l. h. on th. mo.
Ps. 139:5 hast l. thy h. upon me
Rev. 1:17 l. his right h. upon me

**LAID hands.**

Lev. 8:14 A. a. h. sons l. h. 18, 22
Num. 27:23 and Moses l. his ha. on Joshua, Deut. 34:9
Ob. 13 nor l. h. on th. substance
Mat. 18:28 l. h. took him by thr.
Mark 6:5 l. h. on a few sick folk
Luke 4:40 l. h. on ev. one of th.
13:13 he l. his h. on her
John 7:30 but no man l. hands on him, 44; 8:20
Acts 4:3 l. h. on apostles, 5:18
6:6 they l. h. on the deacons
13:3 l. h. on Paul and Barnabas
19:6 Paul l. his h. on them

**LAID hold.**

Gen. 19:16 l. h. on Lot's hand
1 Sam. 15:27 S. l. h. on Sam. sk.
2 Chr. 7:22 l. hold on other gods
Mat. 14:3 l. h. on J. Mark 6:17
Luke 23:26 l. h. on one Simon
Rev. 20:2 l. hold on the dragon

**LAID up.**

Gen. 41:48 Jos. l. up food in cit.
Ex. 16:34 A. l. up pot of manna
Num. 17:7 M. l. up rods befo. L.
1 Sam. 10:25 S. l. it up before L.
21:12 David l. up. words in he.
Ezr. 6:1 treasures l. up in Baby.
Ps. 31:19 hast l. up for them
Prov. 13:22 wealth of sin. l. up
Cant. 7:13 fruits I have l. up
Is. 15:7 that l. up sh. they carry
23:18 hire not treasured or l. up
39:6 which fathers l. up
Luke 1:66 all l. them up in hearts
12:19 thou hast mu. goods l. up
Col. 1:5 hope wh. is l. up for you
2 Tim. 4:8 is l. up for me a crown

**LAID wait.**

Job 31:9 l. w. at neighbor's door
Lam. 4:19 l. w. for us in wilder.
Acts 20:3 Jews l. w. for hi. 23:30

**LAID waste.**

Ps. 79:7 l. w. his dwelling-place
Is. 15:1 Kir l. w. 23:1 T. is l. w.
23:14 ships, your strength l. w.
37:18 kings of Assy. l. w. nati
64:11 pleasant things are l. w.
Jer. 4:7 thy cities sh. be l. w. without an inhabita. Ezek. 6:6; 12:20; 19:7; 29:12

*Ezek.* 26:2 sh. be repl. now *l. w.*
*Amos* 7:9 sanctuaries of Is. *l. w.*
*Nah.* 3:7 and say, Ninev. is *l. w*

**LAIDEST.**

*Ps.* 66:11 *l.* affliction on loins
*Luke* 19:21 th. takest up th. th. *l.*

**LAIN.**

*Gen.* 26:10 have *l.* with thy wife
*Jud.* 21:11 destroy wom. th. *l.*
*Job* 3:13 now should I have *l.* st.
*Ps.* 68:13 ye have *l.* am. the pots
*John* 20:12 where body of Jes. *l.*

**LAYEST, ETH.**

*Num.* 11:11 *l.* burden of people
1 *Sam.* 28:9 *l.* a snare for my life?
*Job* 21:19 G. *l.* up his iniquity
24:12 God *l.* not folly to them
41:26 sword of him that *l.* at h.
*Ps.* 104:3 *l.* beams of chambers
*Prov.* 2:7 *l.* up wisd. for righte.
26:24 *l.* up deceit within him
*Is.* 26:5 the lofty city he *l.* low
56:2 blessed is man that *l.* hold
57:1 and no man *l.* it to heart
*Jer.* 9:8 *l.* wait; 12:11 *l.* to heart
*Zec.* 12:1 *l.* foundation of earth
*Luke* 12:21 that *l.* up treasure
15:5 he *l.* it on his shoulders

**LAYING.**

*Num.* 35:20 *l.* wait, th. he die, 22
*Ps.* 64:5 commune of *l.* snares
*Mark* 7:8 *l.* aside commandment
*Luke* 11:54 *l.* wait for him
*Acts* 8:18 *l.* on of apostles' hands
9:24 *l.* wait was known of Saul
23:16 kinsmen heard of th. *l.* w.
25:3 *l.* wait in the way to kill
1 *Tim.* 4:14 with *l.* on of hands
6:19 *l.* up in store good founda.
*Heb.* 6:1 not *l.* again foundation
2 and of *l.* on of hands
1 *Pet.* 2:1 *l.* aside all malice

**LAZARUS.**

*Luke* 16:20 beggar named L.
*John* 11:2 Mary whose broth. L.
12:2 L. one that sat at table, 17

**LEAD.**

*Ex.* 15:10 sank as *l.* in waters
*Num.* 31:22 *l.* that may abide fire
*Job* 19:24 graven with iron and *l.*
*Jer.* 6:29 *l.* is consumed of the fi.
*Ezek.* 22:18 *l.* in midst of furnace
20 as th. gather *l.* I gather you
27:12 and *l.* Tarshish traded
*Zec.* 5:7 lifted up a talent of *l.*
8 weight of *l.* on mouth there.

**LEAD.**

*Gen.* 33:14 *l.* on softly as cattle
*Ex.* 13:21 pillar of cloud *l.* them
32:34 *l.* the people to the place
*Deut.* 32:12 Lord alone did *l.* hi.
*Jud.* 5:12 *l.* thy captivity captive
*Neh.* 9:19 pil. of cloud to *l.* them
*Ps.* 5:8 *l.* me in thy righteousne.
25:5 *l.* in truth; 27:11 *l.* in plain
31:3 for thy name's sake *l.* me
43:3 light and truth, let them *l.*
60:9 *l.* me into Edom? 108:10
61:2 *l.* to rock higher than I
125:5 *l.* th. with workers of ini.
139:10 there sh. thy hand *l.* me
24 *l.* me in the way of everlas.
143:10 *l.* me to land of upright.
*Prov.* 8:20 *l.* in way of righteou.
*Cant.* 8:2 *l.* thee to mother's ho.
*Is.* 3:12 that *l.* thee cause to err
11:6 a little child shall *l.* them
40:11 gently *l.* those with young
42:16 *l.* th. in paths not known
49:10 hath mercy on them, *l.* th.
57:18 I will *l.* him and restore
63:14 so didst thou *l.* thy people
*Jer.* 31:9 with supplica. I *l.* them
*Nah.* 2:7 her maids *l.* her

*Mat.* 6:13 *l.* us not into temptat.
*Luke* 11:4
15:14 if blind *l.* blind, *Lu.* 6:39
*Luke* 13:15 and *l.* him to wateri.
*Acts* 13:11 seeking some to *l.* hi.
1 *Cor.* 9:5 not power to *l.* sister?
1 *Tim.* 2:2 we may *l.* a quiet life
*Heb.* 8:9 *l.* them out of Egypt
*Rev.* 7:17 Lamb feed and *l.* them

**LEADER, S.**

1 *Chr.* 12:27 Jehoi. *l.* of Aaronit.
13:1 David consulted with ev. *l.*
2 *Chr.* 32:21 angel whi. cut off *l.*
*Is.* 9:16 *l.* of people cause to err
55:4 given him a *l.* to the peop.
*Mat.* 15:14 be blind *l.* of the blin.

**LEADEST.**

*Ps.* 80:1 *l.* Joseph like a flock

**LEADETH.**

*Job* 12:17 he *l.* counsellors away
19 he *l.* princes away spoiled
*Ps.* 23:2 *l.* me beside still waters
3 *l.* me in paths of righteousn.
*Prov.* 16:29 *l.* him into way
*Is.* 48:17 thy God which *l.* thee
*Mat.* 7:13 wide is way *l.* to destr.
14 narrow is way that *l.* to life
*John* 10:3 calleth sheep and *l.* th.
*Rom.* 2:4 goodn. of God *l.* to rep.
*Rev.* 13:10 *l.* sh. go into captivity

**LEAF.**

*Gen.* 8:11 in her mou. was oli. *l.*
*Lev.* 26:36 sound of a shaken *l.*
*Job* 13:25 break *l.* dr. to and fro?
*Ps.* 1:3 his *l.* shall not wither
*Is.* 1:30 be as oak whose *l.* fadeth
34:4 host fall as *l.* 64:6 fade as *l.*
*Jer.* 17:8 but her *l.* shall be green
*Ezek.* 47:12 the *l.* shall not fade

**LEAVES.**

*Gen.* 3:7 sew. fig *l.* made aprons
*Jer.* 36:23 when Je. read 3 or 4 *l.*
*Ezek.* 17:9 sh. wither in all the *l.*
*Mat.* 21:19 nothing thereon but *l.*
*Mark* 11:13
24:32 put. forth *l.* *Mark* 13:28
*Rev.* 22:2 *l.* for healing of nations

**LEAVES,** *for doors.*

1 *K.* 6:34 two *l.* of the one door
*Ezek.* 41:24 doors had two *l.* api.

**LEAGUE.**

*Jos.* 9:15 made *l.* wi. Gibeon. 16
*Jud.* 2:2 make no *l.* wi. inhabit.
1 *Sam.* 22:8 made *l.* with David
2 *Sam.* 5:3 David made *l.* wi. th.
1 *K.* 5:12 Hiram and Sol. made *l.*
15:19 a *l.* between me and thee
2 *Chr.* 16:3 break *l.* with Baasha
*Job* 5:23 in *l.* with stones of field
*Ezek.* 30:5 men that is in *l.* sh. f.
*Dan.* 11:23 after *l.* he work dece.

**LEAH.**

*Gen.* 29:16 daughter was L. 30:19
*Ruth* 4:11 L. make wom. like L.

**LEAN, ED.**

*Jud.* 16:26 I may *l.* on pillars
2 *K.* 18:21 on which if a man *l.*
go into hand, *Is.* 36:6
*Job* 8:15 *l.* on house, it not stand
*Prov.* 3:5 *l.* not to own underst.
*Amos* 5:19 *l.* his hand on wall
*Mic.* 3:11 yet they *l.* on the Lord
*John* 21:20 *l.* on his breast at su.

**LEANETH, ING.**

2 *Sam.* 3:29 one *l.* on a staff
2 *K.* 5:18 *l.* on my hand in house
*Cant.* 8:5 cometh up *l.* on belov.
*John* 13:23 was *l.* on Jesus' bos.
*Heb.* 11:21 Jacob *l.* on top of sta.

**LEAN, NESS.**

*Gen.* 41:3 out of river *l.*-flesh. 19
4 *l.*-fleshed eat up sev. fat, 20
2 *Sam.* 13:4 being king's son *l.*
*Ps.* 106:15 sent *l.* into their soul

*Is.* 10:16 L. send am. fat ones *l.*
17:4 fatness of flesh sh. wax *l.*
24:16 I said, My *l.* my *l.* woe
*Ezek.* 34:20 judge betw. fat and *l.*

**LEAP.**

*Gen.* 31:12 rams wh. *l.* on cattle
*Lev.* 11:21 have legs to *l.* withal
*Deut.* 33:22 Dan sh. *l.* from Bash.
*Job* 41:19 sparks of fire *l.* out
*Ps.* 68:16 why *l.* ye, ye high hills
*Is.* 35:6 then shall lame man *l.*
*Joel* 2:5 like chariots sh. they *l.*
*Luke* 6:23 rejoice ye, *l.* for joy

**LEAPED.**

*Gen.* 31:10 rams wh. *l.* upon cat.
2 *Sam.* 22:30 *l.* over wa. *Ps.* 18:29
*Luke* 1:41 babe *l.* in womb, 44
*Acts* 14:10 and he *l.* and walked
19:16 evil spirit was, *l.* on them

**LEAPING.**

2 *Sam.* 6:16 Michal saw David *l.*
*Cant.* 2:8 behold, he cometh *l.*
*Acts* 3:8 and he *l.* up and walked

**LEARN.**

*Deut.* 4:10 may *l.* to fear, 14:23
5:1 may *l.* and keep, and do th.
17:19 read that he may *l.* to fear
31:12 hear, and *l.* and fear the L.
13 children may *l.* to fe. the L.
*Ps.* 119:71 might *l.* statutes, 73
*Prov.* 22:25 lest thou *l.* his ways
*Is.* 1:17 *l.* to do well, seek judg.
2:4 *l.* war any more, *Mic.* 4:3
26:9 inhabitants *l.* righteousne.
10 will not wicked *l.* righteou.
29:24 that murmured *l.* doctrine
*Jer.* 10:2 *l.* not way of heathen
12:16 diligently *l.* ways of peop.
*Mat.* 9:13 go *l.* what th. meaneth
11:29 *l.* of me, for I am meek
1 *Cor.* 14:35 *l.* anythi. let th. ask
1 *Tim.* 2:11 let wom. *l.* in silence
5:4 *l.* first to sh. piety at home
*Tit.* 3:14 *l.* to maint. good works
*Rev.* 14:3 no man could *l.* song

**LEARNED.**

*Gen.* 30:27 have *l.* by experience
*Ps.* 106:35 heathen, and *l.* works
119:7 I have *l.* righteous judg.
*Prov.* 30:3 I neith. *l.* wisdom nor
*Is.* 29:11 deliver to one that is *l.*
50:4 God given me tongue of *l.*
he waken. ear to hear as *l.*
*John* 6:45 man that hath *l.* of F.
7:15 man letters, hav. never *l.*
*Acts* 7:22 Moses *l.* wisdom of E.
*Eph.* 4:20 ye have not so *l.* Chr.
*Phil.* 4:11 *l.* in ev. state to be co.
2 *Tim.* 3:14 contin. in thing thou
*l.* knowing of wh. th. *l.* th.
*Heb.* 5:8 yet *l.* he obedience

**LEARNING.**

*Prov.* 1:5 wise man will incre. *l.*
9:9 just man, he will incre. in *l.*
16:21 sweetn. of lips increas. *l.*
23 he. of wise addeth *l.* to lips
*Dan.* 1:17 G. gave them skill in *l.*
*Acts* 26:24 *l.* doth make thee mad
*Rom.* 15:4 things writ. for our *l.*
2 *Tim.* 3:7 ever *l.* and never able

**LEASING.**

*Ps.* 4:2 how long seek after *l.*?
5:6 shalt destroy them speak *l.*

**LEAST.**

*Gen.* 32:10 not worthy *l.* of merc.
*Jud.* 6:15 *l.* in my father's house
*Mat.* 2:6 not *l.* among the princ.
11:11 *l.* in kingdom of heaven
is greater than he, *Luke* 7:28
1 *Cor.* 15:9 I am least of the apo.
*Eph.* 3:8 less than *l.* of all saints
*See* GREATEST.

**At LEAST.**

1 *Sam.* 21:4 kept *at l.* from wom.
*Luke* 19:42 kno. *at l.* in thy day

**LEATHER.**

2 *K.* 1:8 girt with a girdle of *l.*

**LEATHERN.**

*Mat.* 3:4 John had *l.* girdle about

**LEAVE, Substantive.**

*Num.* 22:13 L. refuseth to give *l.*
1 *Sam.* 20:6 Da. asked *l.* of me, 28
*Neh.* 13:6 obtained I *l.* of king
*Mark* 5:13 Jesus gave them *l.*
*John* 19:38 *l.* to take away body
*Acts* 18:18 Paul took *l.* of breth.
21:6 taken our *l.* one of another
2 *Cor.* 2:13 taking . I went to M.

**LEAVE.**

*Gen.* 2:24 *l.* father and mother, *Mat.* 19:5; *Mark* 10:7; *Eph.* 5:31
33:15 *l.* wi. thee some of the fo.
44:22 the lad cannot *l.* his fath.
*Ex.* 16:19 let no man *l.* manna
23:11 *l.* beasts of field shall eat
*Lev.* 7:15 not *l.* peace-offer. 22:30
16:23 off garm. and *l.* them the.
19:10 *l.* them for the poor, 23:22
*Num.* 9:12 *l.* none of the passov.
32:15 again *l.* them in wildern.
*Deut.* 28:51 shall not *l.* thee corn
54 remnant of chil. he shall *l.*
*Jud.* 9:9 should I *l.* my fatness
13 said, Should I *l.* my wine
*Ruth* 1:16 entreat me not to *l.*
1 *Sam.* 9:5 fa. *l.* caring for asses
2 *Sam.* 14:7 not *l.* husb. a name
2 *K.* 4:43 shall eat and *l.* thereof
13:7 nor did he *l.* of the people
*Ezr.* 9:8 *l.* us remnant to escape
12 *l.* it for inheritance to chil.
*Neh.* 6:3 work cease whi. I *l.* it?
10:31 would *l.* the seventh year
*Job* 39:11 wilt *l.* labor to him?
*Ps.* 16:10 thou wilt not *l.* my soul in hell, *Acts* 2:27
17:14 *l.* substance to their babes
27:9 my help, *l.* me not, 119:121
49:10 *l.* their wealth to others
141:8 O God, *l.* not my soul des.
*Prov.* 2:13 *l.* paths of uprightne.
*Ec.* 2:18 *l.* it to man after me
10:4 ruler ag. thee, *l.* not place
*Is.* 10:3 where will ye *l.* glory?
65:15 *l.* your name for a curse
*Jer.* 9:2 I might *l.* my people
14:9 call. by thy name, *l.* us not
17:11 *l.* th. in midst of his days
48:28 *l.* cities and dwell in rocks
49:9 not *l.* some glean. grapes?
11 *l.* chil. I will preserve them
*Ezek.* 16:39 *l.* thee naked, 23:29
*Hos.* 12:14 *l.* his blood upon him
*Joel* 2:14 *l.* blessing behind him
*Amos* 5:3 shall *l.* ten to Israel
7 *l.* off righteousness in earth
*Mal.* 4:1 *l.* neit. root nor branch
*Mat.* 5:24 *l.* thy gift bef. the alt.
18:12 *l.* ninety and nine, *Luke* 15:4
23:23 and not to *l.* other undone
*Luke* 19:44 not *l.* in th. one stone
*John* 14:27 my peace I *l.* wi. you
16:28 I *l.* world and go to Fath.
32 *l.* me alone, yet I am not al.
*Acts* 6:2 we should *l.* the word
1 *Cor.* 7:13 let her not *l.* him.
*Heb.* 13:5 I will never *l.* thee

**I will, or will I LEAVE.**

*Job* 9:27 *I will l.* off my heavine.
10:1 *I will l.* complaint on mys.
*Ezek.* 6:8 *I will l.* a remnant
12:16 but *I will l.* a few men
29:5 *I w. l.* thee into wilderness
*Zep.* 3:12 *I w. l.* in midst of thee

**I will not LEAVE.**

2 *K.* 2:2 *I will not l.* thee, 4:30
*John* 14:18 *I w. n. l.* you comfort.

**LEAVED.**

*Is.* 45:1 open him two-*l.* gates

**LEAVETH.**

*Prov.* 13:22 good man *l.* inherit.
28:3 sweeping rain wh. *l.* no fo.
*Mat.* 4:11 then the devil *l.* him

**LEAVEN.**

*Ex.* 12:15 away *l.* seven days, 19
13:7 nei. *l.* seen in thy quarters
34:25 not offer the blood with *l.*
*Lev.* 2:11 no meat-off. made wi. *l.*
10:12 eat meat-offeri. without *l.*
*Amos* 4:5 offer a sacrifice with *l.*
*Mat.* 13:33 kingdom of heaven is like *l.* *Luke* 13:21
16:6 beware of *l.* Phar. and Sad. 11; *Mark* 8:15; *Luke* 12:1
12 th. not beware of *l.* of bread
1 *Cor.* 5:6 little *l.* leaveneth wh. lump, *Gal.* 5:9
7 purge out therefore the old *l.*
8 keep the feast, not wi. old *l.*

**LEAVENED.**

*Ex.* 12:15 wh. eateth *l.* bread, 19
20 eat nothing *l.* in habitations
*Mat.* 13:33 till whole was *l.* *Luke* 13:21

*See* BREAD.

**LEAVENETH.**

1 *Cor.* 5:6 little leaven *l.* lump, *Gal.* 5.9

**LEAVING.**

*Rom.* 1:27 *l.* natural use of wom.
*Heb.* 6:1 *l.* principles of Christ
1 *Pet.* 2:21 suffered, *l* an examp.

**LEBANON.**

*Deut.* 3:25 goodly mount. and L.
*Jud.* 3:3 Hiv. dwelt in mount L.
1 *K.* 5:14 ten tho. a month to L.
2 *K.* 19:23 sides of L. *Is.* 37:24
*Ps.* 29:6 L. like young unicorn
72:16 fruit shake like L. 92:12
*Cant.* 4:8 L. my spou. 11, 15; 5:15
7:4 thy nose is as tower of L.
*Is.* 10:34 L. shall fall, 33:9
29:17 L. turned into fruitf. field
35:2 glory of L. be given unto it
40:16 L. not sufficient to burn
60:13 glory of L. sh. come to th.
*Jer.* 18:14 leave the snow of L.?
22:6 thou art head of L. to me
*Ezek.* 31:15 I caused L. to mourn
*Hos.* 14:5 forth roots as L. 6, 7
*Nah.* 1:4 flower of L. languisheth
*Hab.* 2:17 violence of L. sh. cov.
*Zec.* 10:10 them into land of L.
11:1 open thy doors, O L.

LEBBEUS. *Mat.* 10:3

**LED.**

*Gen.* 24:27 being in way, L. *l.* me
48 who hath *l.* me in right
*Ex.* 3:1 Moses *l.* flock to back of
13:17 *l.* not thro' land of Philis.
18 God *l.* them through wilde.
15:13 in mercy *l.* forth the peo.
*Deut.* 8:2 L. *l.* thee forty years
29:5 *l.* you forty years in wilde.
1 *K.* 8:48 *l.* them away captive
*Ps.* 78:14 *l.* them with a cloud
53 *l.* them safely, th. fear. not
106:9 *l.* th. thro' depths as thro' wilderness, 136:16; *Is.* 63:13
107:7 *l.* them by the right way
*Prov.* 4:11 *l.* thee in right paths
*Is.* 9:16 *l.* of them are destroyed
48:21 thirsted not wh. th. *l.* th.
55:12 shall be *l.* forth with pea.
63:12 *l.* them by right hand
*Jer.* 2:6 L. *l.* us thro' wilderness
17 when he *l.* thee by the way
22:12 die in place whi. th. *l.* him
23:8 L. which *l.* house of Israel
*Lam.* 3:2 hath *l.* me into darkn.
*Ezek.* 39:28 to be *l.* into captivi.
*Amos* 2:10 *l.* 40 years thro' wild.
*Mat.* 4:1 Jes. *l.* of Spirit, *Lu.* 4:1
*Luke* 4:29 *l.* Jesus to brow of hill
21:24 shall be *l.* away captive
24:50 *l.* them out as far as Beth.
*Acts* 8:32 *l.* as sheep to slaughter
*Rom.* 8:14 are *l.* by Spirit of God
1 *Cor.* 12:2 even as ye were *l.*
*Gal.* 5:18 if ye be *l.* by the Spirit
2 *Tim.* 3:6 *l.* away with div. lus.

**LEDDEST.**

2 *Sam.* 5:2 *l.* out Is. 1 *Chr.* 11:2
*Neh.* 9:12 *l.* th. by a cloudy pillar
*Ps.* 77:20 *l.* thy peo. like a flock

**LEDGES.**

1 *K.* 7:28 borders between the *l.*
35 *l.* and borders were the sa.
36 plates of *l.* graved cherubim

**LEEKS.**

*Num.* 11:5 rememb. *l.* and onio.

**LEES.**

*Is.* 25:6 feast of wine on the *l.*
*Jer.* 48:11 M. hath set. on his *l.*
*Zep.* 1:12 pun. men settled on *l.*

**LEFT.**

*Gen.* 29:35 Judah, *l.* bear. 30:9
39:12 *l.* gar. in hand, 13, 15, 18
41:49 gathe. till he *l.* numberin.
47:18 not aught *l.* but bodies
50:8 little ones *l.* th. in Goshen
*Ex.* 2:20 why have ye *l.* man?
10:12 all that the hail *l.* 15
16:20 some *l.* of it till morning
34:25 nor sacrifice be *l.* till mor.
*Lev.* 2:10 which is *l.* of meat-off.
26:39 are *l.* of you sh. pine away
43 land also shall be *l.* of them
*Num.* 26:65 not *l.* a man, *Jos.* 8:17; *Jud.* 4:16; *Hos.* 9:12
*Deut.* 2:34 *l.* none to remain, *Jos.* 10:33, 37, 39, 40; 11:8, 11, 14
4:27 ye shall be *l.* few in numb. 28:62; *Is.* 24:6; *Jer.* 42:2
32:36 there is none shut up or *l.*
*Jos.* 8:17 they *l.* the city open
11:15 *l.* nothing undone of all
22:3 have not *l.* your brethren
*Jud.* 2:23 L. *l.* those nations, 3:1
*Ruth* 1:3 was *l.* and her 2 sons, 5
18 then she *l.* speaking to her
2:11 *l.* thy father and mother
4:14 L. not *l.* thee this day
1 *Sam.* 2:36 every one *l.* in house
9:24 which is *l.* set it bef. thee
10:2 father *l.* care of the asses
17:20 *l.* the sheep with a keeper
2 *Sam.* 5:21 there they *l.* images
9:1 is any *l.* of house of Saul?
13:30 there is not one of them *l.*
15:16 *l.* ten concubines, 16:21
17:12 not be *l.* so much as one
1 *K.* 9:21 children *l.* 2 *Chr.* 8:8
14:10 cut off him *l.* 2 *K.* 9:8
19:3 *l.* servant there; 10 I on. *l.*
18 have *l.* me 7,000; 20 *l.* ox.
2 *K.* 4:44 did eat and *l.* thereof
7:7 *l.* tents; 13 all that are *l.*
8:6 since day she *l.* the land
10:11 he *l.* him none remaining
14:26 not any *l.* nor any helper
17:16 *l.* commandments of Lord
19:4 remn. that are *l.* *Is.* 37:4
20:17 nothing *l.* saith the Lord
25:12 *l.* of the poor of the land, *Jer.* 39:10; 52:16
2 *Chr.* 11:14 Levites *l.* suburbs
21:17 th. was never a son *l.* him
24:18 they *l.* house of the Lord
31:10 had enough, have *l.* plen.
32:31 God *l.* him to try him
34:21 inq. for them *l.* in Israel
*Neh.* 1:2 concern. Jews wh. had *l.*
3 remnant *l.* in great affliction
*Job* 20:21 none of his meat be *l.*
26 ill with him *l.* in tabernacle
*Ps.* 106:11 not one of them *l.*
*Prov.* 29:15 a child *l.* to himself

*Is.* 1:9 L. *l.* us a rem. *Rom.* 9:29
4:3 *l.* in Zion shall be call. holy
11:16 remnant that shall be *l.*
24:12 in the city is *l.* desolation
39:6 nothing be *l.* saith the L.
*Jer.* 12:7 *l.* heritage; 31:2 *l.* swo.
49:25 city of prai. not *l.* c. of joy
50:26 let nothing of her be *l.*
*Ezek.* 14:22 shall be *l.* a remnant
31:12 cut him off and ha. *l.* him
*Dan.* 2:44 not be *l.* to other peo.
*Hag.* 2:3 who is *l.* saw h. in glo.?
*Zec.* 13:8 third part be *l.* therein
*Mat.* 4:20 *l.* nets; 22 *l.* their ships
15:37 took up of meat that was *l.* *Mark* 8:8
22:25 *l.* wife to bro. *Mark* 12:20
*Mat.* 23:38 your house is *l.* desol.
24:2 sh. not be *l.* one stone upon anoth. *Mark* 13:2; *Luke* 21:6
40 one shall be tak. the oth. *l.* 41; *Luke* 17:34, 35, 36
26:44 Jesus *l.* them and prayed
*Mark* 10:28 *l.* all and followed
29 hath *l.* house, *Luke* 18:28, 29
11:22 seven had her, *l.* no seed
*Luke* 5:28 *l.* all and followed him
10:40 sister *l.* me to serve alone
*John* 4:52 sev. hour fever *l.* him
*Acts* 2:31 soul was not *l.* in hell
14:17 he *l.* not without witness
21:32 they *l.* beating of Paul
2 *Tim.* 4:20 I *l.* sick at Miletum
*Tit.* 1:5 for this cause I *l.* thee
*Heb.* 2:8 he *l.* nothing that is not
*Jude* 6 angels *l.* their own habit.
*Rev.* 2:4 thou hast *l.* thy first lo.
*See* ALONE.

**LEFT off.**
*Gen.* 17:22 *l. off* talking with him
*Ruth* 2:20 hath not *l. off* kindn.
*Job* 32:15 no more, th. *l. off* spe.
*Ps.* 36:3 he hath *l. off* to be wise
*Jer.* 38:27 *l. off* speaking wi. him
44:18 we *l. off* to burn incense
*Hos.* 4:10 they *l. off* to take heed

**LEFT corner.**
2 *K.* 11:11 guard stood to the *l. c.*
*See* HAND.

**LEFT-HANDED.**
*Jud.* 3:15 Benjam. a man *l.-h.*
20:16 were 700 chosen men *l.-h.*

**LEFT pillar.**
1 *K.* 7:21 he set up the *l. pillar*

**LEFT side.**
2 *Chr.* 23:10 weapon fr. ri. to *l. s.*
*Ezek.* 1:10 face of an ox on *l. side*
4:4 lie also on thy *l. s.* lay iniq.
*Zec.* 4:3 olive tree upon *l. s.* 11

**LEG, S.**
*Ex.* 12:9 roast wi. fire head and *l.*
29:17 inwards and *l.* *Lev.* 9:14
*Lev.* 4:11 head, and his *l.* burn
8:21 washed the inwards and *l.*
11:21 wh. have *l.* above th. feet
*Deut.* 28:35 smite thee in the *l.*
1 *Sam.* 17:6 greaves of brass on *l.*
*Ps.* 147:10 taketh no pleas. in *l.*
*Prov.* 26:7 *l.* of lame not equal
*Cant.* 5:15 *l.* are as pil. of marble
*Is.* 3:20 L. take ornaments of *l.*
47:2 make bare *l.* uncov. thigh
*Dan.* 2:33 his *l.* of iron
*Amos* 3:12 mouth of lion two *l.*
*John* 19:31 besought *l.* mi. he br.
32 soldi. came and brake the *l.*
33 they brake not his *l.*

**LEGION.**
*Mark* 5:9 name is L. *Luke* 8:30
LEGIONS. *Mat.* 26:53

**LEISURE.**
*Mark* 6:31 they had no *l.* to eat
LEMUEL. *Prov.* 31:1, 4

**LEND.**
*Ex.* 22:25 if thou *l.* money
*Lev.* 25:37 not *l.* him thy victuals
*Deut.* 15:6 sh. *l.* to many nations
8 thou sh. *l.* him suffi. for need
23:19 sh. not *l.* on usury to bro.
20 to stranger may *l.* on usury
28:12 *l.* to many nations
44 *l.* thou sh. not *l.* to him
*Luke* 6:34 if *l.* them of whom ye hope to rece. sin. also *l.* sin.
35 love enemies, do good and *l.*
11:5 say, Friend, *l.* me 3 loaves.

**LENDER.**
*Prov.* 22:7 borrower servant to *l.*
*Is.* 24:2 as with *l.* so wi. borrow.

**LENDETH.**
*Ps.* 37:26 merciful, *l.* seed bless.
112:5 good man show. fav. and *l.*
*Prov.* 19:17 pity on poor, *l.* to L.

**LENGTH.**
*Deut.* 30:20 and the *l.* of thy days
*Job* 12:12 *l.* of days, understand.
*Ps.* 21:4 even *l.* of days for ever
*Prov.* 3:2 *l.* of days sh. they add
16 *l.* of days is in her right ha.
*Eph.* 3:18 compre. *l.* of love of C.
*Rev.* 21:16 *l.* as large as breadth

**At LENGTH.**
*Prov.* 29:21 become his son *at l.*
*Rom.* 1:10 *at l.* may ha. journey

**LENGTHEN, ED.**
*Deut.* 25:15 thy days may be *l.*
1 *K.* 3:14 then will I *l.* thy days
*Is.* 54:2 *l.* thy cords, strengthen stakes

**LENGTHENING.**
*Dan.* 4:27 a *l.* of thy tranquillity

**LENT.**
*Ex.* 12:36 *l.* them as th. required
1 *Sam.* 1:28 I *l.* him to the Lord
2:20 loan which is *l.* to the L.
*Jer.* 15:10 I have not *l.* on usury

**LENTILES.**
*Gen.* 25:34 Jacob gave Esau of *l.*
2 *Sam.* 23:11 piece ground full *l.*
*See* BEANS.

**LEOPARD, S.**
*Cant.* 4:8 fr. mountains of the *l.*
*Is.* 11:6 *l.* sh. lie down with kid
*Jer.* 5:6 *l.* shall watch over cities
13:23 can *l.* change his spots?
*Dan.* 7:6 and lo, another like a *l.*
*Hos.* 13:7 I will be to them as a *l.*
*Hab.* 1:8 horses swifter than *l.*
*Rev.* 13:2 beast was like to a *l.*

**LEPER.**
*Lev.* 13:45 *l.* in whom the plague
14:3 if leprosy be healed in *l.*
22:4 the seed of Aaron is a *l.*
*Num.* 5:2 put out of camp ev. *l.*
2 *Sam.* 3:29 Joab, one that is a *l.*
2 *K.* 5:1 Naaman was a *l.*
11 strike his hand, and reco. *l.*
27 went from his presence a *l.*
15:5 Azari. was a *l.* to his death
2 *Chr.* 26:21 Uz. the ki. was a *l.*
23 for they said, He is a *l.*
*Mat.* 8:2 th. came a *l.* *Mark* 1:40
26:6 house of Sim. *l.* *Mark* 14:3

**LEPERS.**
2 *K.* 7:8 *l.* came to utterm. part
*Mat.* 10:8 cleanse *l.* raise dead
11:5 *l.* are cleansed, *Luke* 7:22
*Luke* 4:27 many *l.* were in Israel
17:12 ten men that were *l.*

**LEPROSY.**
*Lev.* 13:2 in skin like plague of *l.*
3 it is a plague of *l.* 8:49
12 if a *l.* break out in the skin
13:13 if the *l.* covered his flesh
59 law of plague of *l.* 14:54, 57
14:3 if plague of *l.* be healed
7 him to be cleansed from *l.*
*Deut.* 24:8 heed in plague of *l.*
2 *K.* 5:6 recover him of his *l.*
27 *l.* of Naaman clea. unto thee
2 *Chr.* 26:19 *l.* rose in his foreh.
*Mat.* 8:3 his *l.* was cleansed, *Mark* 1:42; *Luke* 5:13
*Luke* 5:12 man full of *l.* besought
*See* FRETTING.

**LEPROUS.**
*Ex.* 4:6 hand was *l.* as snow
*Lev.* 13:44 is a *l.* man, unclean
*Num.* 12:10 Miriam became *l.*
2 *K.* 7:3 four *l.* men at the gate
2 *Chr.* 26:20 and Uzziah was *l.*

**LESS.**
*Ex.* 30:15 not *l.* than half shekel
*Num.* 22:18 bey. word of L. do *l.*
*Mark* 4:31 when it is sown it is *l.*
15:40 M. mother of James the *l.*
2 *Cor.* 12:15 more I love, *l.* am lo.
*Eph.* 3:8 am *l.* than the least
*Heb.* 7:7 *l.* is blessed of better

**LESSER.**
*Gen.* 1:16 *l.* light to rule night
*Is.* 7:25 for treading of *l.* cattle

**LET.**
*Gen.* 49:21 Napht. a hind *l.* loose
*Ex.* 3:19 king of Eg. will not *l.* you go, 4:21; 7:14; 8:32; 9:7, 17, 35; 10:20, 27; 11:10
5:1 *l.* my people go, 7:16; 8:1, 20; 9:1, 13; 10:3
8:28 I will *l.* you go, 9:28; 13:7
18:27 M. *l.* father-in-law depart
21:26 *l.* him go free for eye, 27
*Deut.* 15:12 thou sh. *l.* him go fr.
13 not *l.* him go away empty
2 *Sam.* 11:12 to-m. *l.* thee depart
1 *K.* 18:40 *l.* none of them escape
*Job* 6:9 would *l.* loose his hand
27:6 righte. I will not *l.* it go
*Ps.* 69:6 *l.* not those be ashamed
109:6 *l.* Sa. stand at right hand
*Cant.* 3:4 would not *l.* him go
8:11 *l.* out vineyard to keepers
*Is.* 43:13 and who shall *l.* it?
*Jer.* 27:11 those will I *l.* remain
*Mat.* 21:33 planted a vineyard and *l.* it out to husbandmen, *Mark* 12:1; *Luke* 20:9
*Luke* 22:68 not answer nor *l.* go
*John* 19:12 if thou *l.* this man go
*Acts* 27:15 not bear up, *l.* her dr.
*Rom.* 1:13 but was *l.* hitherto
2 *Thes.* 2:7 now letteth, will *l.*
*Heb.* 2:1 lest we sh. *l.* them sleep
*See* ALONE.

**LET down.**
*Ex.* 17:11 wh. he *l. d.* his hands
2 *K.* 13:21 wh. the man was *l. d.*
*Jer.* 38:6 *l. d.* Jeremiah wi. cords
*Ezek.* 1:24 th. *l. d.* th. wings, 25
*Mark* 2:4 they *l. d.* bed wherein sick of palsy lay, *Luke* 5:19
*Luke* 5:4 *l. d.* your nets for drau.
*Acts* 9:25 *l.* him *d.* in a basket, 2 *Cor.* 11:33
10:11 four corners, *l. d.* to earth
27:30 *l. down* boat into the sea

**LETTER.**
2 *Sam.* 11:14 Dav. wrote a *l.* to J.
2 *K.* 5:5 send *l.* to king of Israel
10:2 soon as *l.* cometh to thee
19:14 Hez. received *l.* *Is.* 37:14
*Ezr.* 4:7 *l.* was writ. in Syrian
8 wrote a *l.* against Jerusalem
*Neh.* 2:8 *l.* to As. keeper of forest
*Est.* 9:29 wrote to confirm this *l.*
*Jer.* 29:1 words of *l.* Jerem. sent
*Acts* 23:25 Claud. wrote *l.* to Fel.
34 when governor had read *l.*
*Rom.* 2:27 by *l.* transgress law
29 circumcis. of heart, not in *l.*
7:6 not in the oldness of the *l.*

2 Cor. 3:6 not of l. but of Spirit
7:8 sorry with l. I do not repent
Gal. 6:11 large a l. I have written
2 Thes. 2:2 be not shaken by l.
Heb. 13:22 I have written l.

**LETTERS.**

1 K. 21:8 Jezebel wrote l. 9
2 K. 10:1 Jehu wrote l. and sent
20:12 king of Babylon sent l.
2 Chr. 30:1 Hez. wrote l. to Eph.
6 posts went with l. from king
32:17 wrote l. to rail on G. of Is.
Neh. 2:7 l. be given to governors
6:17 sent l. to Tob. and l. came
Est. 1:22 Ahasuerus sent l.
3:13 l. were sent by post, 8:10
9:20 Mordecai sent l. to Jews, 30
Jer. 29:25 hast l. in thy name
Luke 23:38 writ. in l. of Hebrew
John 7:15 how know. this man l.
Acts 9:2 desired l. to Damascus
15:23 the apostles wrote l.
22:5 fr. whom also I received l.
28:21 neither received l. out Ju.
1 Cor. 16:3 sh. approve by your l.
2 Cor. 3:1 nor need we l. of com.
10:9 I would terrify you by l.
10 l. are weighty and powerf.
11 in word, by l. when absent

**LETTEST.**

Job 15:13 l. su. words out mouth
41:1 with a cord thou l. down ?
Luke 2:29 L. l. thou thy ser. dep.

**LETTETH.**

2 K. 10:24 he that l. him go
Prov. 17:14 as when one l. water
2 Thes. 2:7 only he that now l.

**LEVI.**

Gen. 29:34 called L. Ex. 6:16; Num. 3:17
Num. 16:7 you, ye sons of L.
Deut. 10:9 L. hath no part
1 K. 12:31 priests were not of L.
1 Chr. 21:6 but L. count. he not
Ps. 135:20 bless L. O house of L.
Ezek. 40:46 among the sons of L.
Zec. 12:13 the house of L. apart
Mal. 2:4 cov. be with L. 8; 3:3
Mark 2:14 L. the son of Alpheus
Luke 3:24 Matthat son of L. 29
5:27 a publican named L.
Heb. 7:9 L. payed tithes in Abr.

**Tribe of LEVI.**

Num. 1:49 not num. t. of L. 3:6
Deut. 10:8 separat. t. of L. 18:1
1 Chr. 23:14 we. named of t. of L.
Rev. 7:7 t. of L. sealed 12,000

**LEVIATHAN.**

Job 41:1 canst thou draw out l.
Ps. 74:14 breakest the heads of l.
104:26 is that l. thou hast made
Is. 27:1 shall punish l. even l.

**LEVITE.**

Ex. 4:14 Aaron the L. thy brot. ?
Deut. 12:12 rej.bef. the Lord and the L. 18; 16:11, 14; 26:11, 13
Jud. 17:7 a young man a L. 9
10 thy victuals, so the L. went
12 Micah consecrated the L.
13 I have a L. to my priest
18:3 knew the voice of the L.
19:1 a certain L. sojourning
2 Chr. 20:14 Jahaziel the L. came
31:12 Conon. the L. over things
14 Kore the L. over fr.-will off.
Luke 10:32 likewise a L. came
Acts 4:36 Barnabas a L. hav. land

**LEVITES.**

Ex. 38:21 counted for serv. of L.
Lev. 25:32 cit. of L. may L. rede.
Num. 1:50 sh. appoint L. ov. tab.
51 the L. shall take it down
53 the L. shall pitch round abo.
3:9 shall give L. unto Aaron
12 I have taken L. the L. mine
41 take the L. for me, 45; 8:14
7:5 thou sh. give wago. unto L.
8:6 take L. fr. Is. and cleanse
11 Aaron sh. offer L. bef. the L.
18:6 taken L. to do service, 23
24 tithes I have given to the L.
35:2 give unto the L. cities, 8
Jos. 14:3 to L. he gave none inh.
21:3 Is. gave these cities to L. 8
41 cities of L. were forty-eight
1 Sam. 6:15 L. took down ark
1 Chr. 15:15 child. of L. bare ark
26 G. helped L. that bare ark
2 Chr. 5:12 L. were singers, 7:6
19:11 also the L. shall be officers
23:6 L. shall comp. the king, 7
29:5 ye L. sanctify yourselves
34:13 of the L. there were scrib.
35:14 L. prep. for themselves, 15
Ezr. 6:18 set L. in their courses
Neh. 8:7 L. caused peo. to under.
11 the L. stilled the people
12:27 at dedica. th. sought L.
13:10 L. were fled every one
29 defiled priesthood of the L.
Jer. 33:22 I will multiply the L.
Ezek. 44:10 L. are gone bear ini.
48:11 not astray wh. L. went

**Priests and LEVITES.**

Deut. 17:9 come to pries. and L.
Jos. 3:3 see p. a. L. bearing ark
1 K. 8:4 p. a. L. brought ark
2 Chr. 23:4 p. a. L. sh. be porters
29:34 pri. and L. more upright
30:15 pri. and L. were ashamed
21 L. and pries. praised the L.
27 p. and L. blessed the peop.
31:9 Hez. questioned wi. p. a. L.
35:8 princes gave to pr. and L.
Ezr. 6:20 pr. and L. were purifi.
9:1 p. a. L. have not separated
10:5 Ezra made pr. a. L. to sw.
Neh. 9:38 our princes, L. and p.
10:34 we cast lots amo. p. a. L.
12:30 p. a. L. purified themselv.
Is. 66:21 take of th. for p. and L.
Jer. 33:18 p. a. L. not want a man
21 the L. the p. my ministers
John 1:19 Jews sent p. and L.

**LEVITICAL.**

Heb. 7:11 were by l. priesthood

**LEVY, Substantive.**

1 K. 5:13 Sol. raised l. of 300,000
14 Adoniram was over the l.
9:15 reason of l. Solomon raised

**LEVY, Verb.**

Num. 31:28 l. a tribute to the L.
1 K. 9:21 on those did Solom. l.

**LEWD, LY.**

Ezek. 16:27 asham. of thy l. way
22:11 l. defiled his daughter
23:44 went in, unto the l. wom.
Acts 17:5 Jews took l. fellows

**LEWDNESS.**

Jud. 20:6 th. have committed l.
Jer. 11:15 wrought l. with many
13:27 seen l. of thy whoredom
Ezek. 16:43 sh. not commit this l.
58 thou hast borne l. and abo.
22:9 midst of thee th. commit l.
23:21 remembr. l. of thy youth
27 I make thy l. to cease, 48
29 both thy l. and whoredom
35 theref. bear thou also thy l.
49 shall recompense your l.
24:13 in thy filthiness is l.
Hos. 2:10 will I discover her l.
6:9 priests murder. commit l.
Acts 18:14 matter of wrong or l.

**LIAR.**

Job 24:25 who will make me a l.?
Prov. 17:4 l. giv. ear to naughty
19:22 poor man better than a l.
30:6 and thou be found l.
Jer. 15:18 wilt th. be to me as l.?
John 8:44 l. and the father of it
55 say, I know him not, be l.
Rom. 3:4 God true, ev. man a l.
1 John 1:10 sinned, make him l.
2:4 keepeth not com. is l. 4:20
22 is a l. but he that denieth
5:10 believ. not G. made him l.

**LIARS.**

Deut. 33:29 enemies found l.
Ps. 116:11 haste, all men are l.
Is. 44:25 frustrateth tokens of l.
Jer. 50:36 a sword is upon the l.
1 Tim. 1:10 law is made for l.
Tit. 1:12 Cretians are always l.
Rev. 2:2 and hast found them l.
21:8 all l. have th. part in lake

**LIBERAL, LY.**

Deut. 15:14 shalt furnish him l.
Prov. 11:25 l. soul sh. be made fat
Is. 32:5 vile sh. not be called l.
8 the l. deviseth l. things
2 Cor. 9:13 your l. distribution
Jam. 1:5 God giveth all men l.

**LIBERALITY.**

1 Cor. 16:3 bring your l. to Jeru.
2 Cor. 8:2 the riches of their l.

**LIBERTINES.**

Acts 6:9 called synagogue of l.

**LIBERTY.**

Lev. 25:10 proclaim l. thro' land
Ps. 119:45 and I will walk at l.
Is. 61:1 proclaim l. to captives
Jer. 34:8 covenant to proclaim l.
15 done right, in proclaim. l.
17 not heark. to me proclaiming l. I proclaim a l. for you
Ezek. 46:17 his to the year of l.
Luke 4:18 set at l. them bruised
Acts 24:23 keep P. let him have l.
26:32 man might been set at l.
27:3 gave l. to go to his friends
Rom. 8:21 from bondage into l.
1 Cor. 7:39 she is at l. to marry
8:9 take heed lest th. l. of yours
10:29 my l. judged of another
2 Cor. 3:17 Sp. of L. is, there is l.
Gal. 2:4 came priv. to spy our l.
5:1 stand fast in the l. wherew.
13 ye have been called to l.
Heb. 13:23 brother Tim. set at l.
Jam. 1:25 whoso look. to law of l.
2:12 be judged by the law of l.
1 Pet. 2:16 not using l. for a cloak
2 Pet. 2:19 they promise them l.

**LIBNAH.**

Num. 33:20 pitched in L. 21
Jos. 10:29 passed to L. 21:13
2 K. 8:22 L. revolted, 2 Chr. 21:10

LIBYA. Ezek. 30:5; Acts 2:10
LIBYANS. Jer. 46:9; Dan. 11:43

**LICE.**

Ex. 8:16 dust became l. 17, 18
Ps. 105:31 l. in all their coasts

**LICENSE.**

Acts 21:40 when he had giv. P. l.
25:16 accused have l. to answer

**LICK.**

Num. 22:4 this company l. up all
1 K. 21:19 shall dogs l. thy blood
Ps. 72:9 enemies sh. l. the dust
Is. 49:23 l. up dust of thy feet
Mic. 7:17 sh. l. dust like a serp.

**LICKED, ETH.**

Num. 22:4 l. up all, as ox l. grass
1 K. 18:38 l. up water in trench
21:19 dogs l. blood of Naboth
22:38 the dogs l. up his blood
Luke 16:21 dogs ca. and l. sores

**LID.**

2 K. 12:9 bored a hole in the l.

**LIE, falsehood.**

Ps. 62:9 men of hi. degree are a l.
119:69 proud forged a l. ag. me

*Is.* 44:20 is not a *l.* in rig. hand?
*Jer.* 27:10 prophesy a *l.* to you to rem. you fr. land, 14, 15, 16
28:15 mak. peo. to trust in a *l.*
29:31 caused you to trust in a *l.*
*Ezek.* 21:29 divine a *l.* to thee
*Mic.* 1:14 shall be a *l.* to kings
*Zec.* 10:2 diviners have seen a *l.*
*John* 8:44 speaketh *l.* he speak.
*Rom.* 1:25 changed truth unto *l.*
3:7 through my *l.* to his glory
2 *Thes.* 2:11 they sh. believe a *l.*
1 *John* 2:21 no *l.* is of the truth
27 of all things, and is no *l.*
*Rev.* 21:27 whatso. maketh a *l.*
22:15 whoso. lov. and maketh *l.*

**LIES.**

*Jud.* 16:10 th. hast told me *l.* 13
*Job* 11:3 *l.* make men hold peace?
13:4 ye are forgers of *l.*
*Ps.* 40:4 such as turn aside to *l.*
58:3 wicked go astray, speak. *l.*
62:4 delight in *l.* curse inwardly
63:11 mouth speak. *l.* be stopp.
101:7 tell. *l.* not tarry in my si.
*Prov.* 6:19 hates witness speak. *l.*
14:5 a false witness will utter *l.*
25 deceitful witness speak. *l.*
19:5 speaketh *l.* shall not escape
9 he that speaketh *l.* sh. perish
*Prov.* 29:12 if a ruler heark. to *l.*
30:8 remove fr. me vanity and *l.*
*Is.* 9:15 prophet that teacheth *l.*
28:15 have made *l.* our refuge
17 sweep away the refuge of *l.*
59:3 your lips have spoken *l.*
4 trust in vanity, and speak *l.*
*Jer.* 9:3 bend like th. bow for *l.*
5 tau. their tongue to speak *l.*
14:14 proph. prophe. *l.* 23:25, 26
16:19 our fathers have inher. *l.*
20:6 hast prophesied *l.* vanity
23:14 commit adult. walk in *l.*
32 cause peo. to err by their *l.*
48:30 his *l.* shall not so effect it
*Ezek.* 13:8 spoken vanity, seen *l.*
9 upon prophets that divine *l.*
22 with *l.* ye made right. sad
22:28 divining *l.* unto them
24:12 she wearied herself with *l.*
*Dan.* 11:27 speak *l.* at one table
*Hos.* 7:3 princes glad with *l.*
13 have spoken *l.* against me
10:13 ye have eaten fruit of *l.*
11:12 Ephr. comp. about wi. *l.*
12:1 he increaseth *l.* and desol.
*Amos* 2:4 *l.* caused them to err
*Mic.* 6:12 inhabi. have spoken
*Nah.* 3:1 city, it is full of *l.*
*Hab.* 2:18 and a teacher of *l.*
*Zep.* 3:13 Israel sh. not speak *l.*
*Zec.* 13:3 speak. *l.* in name of L.
1 *Tim.* 4:2 speak. *l.* in hypocrisy

**LIE, Verb.**

*Lev.* 6:2 if a soul *l.* to his neigh.
19:11 steal, nor *l.* one to another
*Num.* 23:19 man, that he sho. *l.*
1 *Sam.* 15:29 Str. of Is. will not *l.*
2 *K.* 4:16 do not *l.* to handmaid
*Job* 6:28 it is evident to you if I *l.*
34:6 should I *l.* against my right
*Ps.* 89:35 I will not *l.* to David
*Prov.* 14:5 faith. witn. will not *l.*
*Is.* 63:8 my peo. that will not *l.*
*Mic.* 2:11 walk. in falsehood do *l.*
*Hab.* 2:3 it shall speak and not *l.*
*Acts* 5:3 hath S. filled heart to *l.*?
*Rom.* 9:1 I say truth in Christ, I *l.* not, 1 *Tim.* 2:7
2 *Cor.* 11:31 L. knoweth, I *l.* not
*Gal.* 1:20 I wrote, behold I *l.* not
*Col.* 3:9 *l.* not one to another
*Tit.* 1:2 life, God that cannot *l.* promised, *Heb.* 6:18
*Jam.* 3:14 *l.* not against the truth
1 *John* 1:6 we *l.* and do not truth
*Rev.* 3:9 they are Jews, but do *l.*

**LIED, ETH.**

*Lev.* 6:3 lost, and *l.* concerning
1 *K.* 13:18 but he *l.* unto him
*Ps.* 78:36 *l.* unto him wi. tongues
*Is.* 57:11 been afraid, thou hast *l.*
*Acts* 5:4 th. hast not *l.* unto men

**LIE,** *to recline.*

*Gen.* 47:30 I will *l.* with my fat.
*Ex.* 23:11 let the ground *l.* still
*Deut.* 29:20 curses in book *l.* on h.
*Jud.* 19:20 thy wants *l.* on me
*Ruth* 3:4 mark the place he sh. *l.*
1 *K.* 1:2 let her *l.* in thy bosom
*Ps.* 57:4 I *l.* among them on fire
88:5 like slain that *l.* in grave
*Ec.* 4:11 two *l.* together ha. heat
*Is.* 13:21 wild beasts sh. *l.* there
14:18 kings of nations *l.* in glory
51:20 sons *l.* at head of streets
*Lam.* 2:21 young and old *l.* gro.
*Ezek.* 4:4 *l.* also upon thy left side
6 *l.* again on thy right side
9 thou sh. lie on thy side 390 d.
31:18 *l.* in midst of uncircumc.
32:21 they *l.* uncircumcised, 30
27 they shall not *l.* wi. mighty
34:14 shall they *l.* in a good fold
*John* 5:6 when Jesus saw him *l.*

**LIE, ETH down.**

*Lev.* 18:23 to *l. d.* thereto, 20:16
26:6 *l. d.* and none make afraid
*Num.* 23:24 not *l. d.* till he eat
*Deut.* 25:2 cause him to *l. down*
*Ruth* 3:7 B. went to *l. d.* at heap
1 *Sam.* 3:5 I call. not, *l. d.* ag. 6:9
2 *Sam.* 11:13 went to *l. d.* on bed
*Job* 7:4 wh. I *l. d.* I say, Sh. I ri.
11:19 *l. d.* none make thee afra.
14:12 so man *l. d.* and ris. not
20:11 *l. d.* with him in the dust
21:26 shall *l. d.* alike in the dust
27:19 rich man shall *l. down*
*Ps.* 23:2 *l. d.* in green pastures
*Prov.* 3:24 *l. d.* thy sleep be sweet
23:34 *l. d.* in the midst of sea
*Is.* 14:30 shall *l. d.* in safety
17:2 be for flocks which sh. *l. d.*
27:10 sh. the calf feed and *l. d.*
43:17 army and power sh. *l. d.*
*Is.* 50:11 shall *l. down* in sorrow
65:10 place for the herds to *l. d.*
*Jer.* 3:25 *l. d.* in shame and conf.
33:12 shep. causing flocks *l. d.*
*Ezek.* 34:15 I will cause them *l. d.*
*Hos.* 2:18 make them *l. d.* safely
*Zep.* 2:7 sh. *l. d.* in the evening
14 flocks sh. *l. d.* 15 beasts *l. d.*
3:13 remnant of Israel shall *l. d.*

**LIE, ETH in wait.**

*Ex.* 21:13 if a man *l.* not *in wait*
*Deut.* 19:11 hate neighbor, *l. w.*
*Jos.* 8:4 sh. *l. in w.* against city
*Jud.* 9:32 *l. in wait* in the field
21:20 *l. in w.* in the vineyards
1 *Sam.* 22:8 my ser. to *l. in w.* 13
*Ps.* 10:9 *l. in w.* secretly as a lion
59:3 they *l. in w.* for my soul
*Prov.* 7:12 *l. in w.* at ev. corner
12:6 wicked are to *l. in wait*
23:28 she *l. in w.* as for a prey
*Mic.* 7:2 they all *l. in w.* for bl.
*Acts* 23:21 *l. in wait* for him
*Eph.* 4:14 *l. in w.* to deceive me

**LIE, ETH waste.**

*Neh.* 2:3 fathers' sepulchres *l. w.*
17 see how Jerusalem *l. waste*
*Is.* 33:8 the highways *l. waste*
34:10 it sh. *l. w.* none sh. pass
*Hag.* 1:4 and this house *l. waste*

**LIE, ETH with.**

*Gen.* 19:32 and we will *l. w.* him
30:15 he shall *l. w.* thee to-night
39:7 *l. w.* me, 12; 2 *Sam.* 13:11
*Ex.* 22:16 if a man *l. w.* a maid
19 whoso *l. with* beast
*Lev.* 15:18 *w.* whom man shall *l.*
15:24 if any man *l. with* her at
18:20 not *l.* carnally *w.* neighb.
22 shall not *l. with* mankind
23 neither sh. thou *l. w.* beast
19:20 *l.* carnally *with* bondmaid
20:11 man *l. w.* his father's wife
12 if a man *l. with* daugh.-in-l.
13 mankind as *l. w.* woman
15 if a man *l. with* a beast
18 if man *l. w.* wom. ha. sick.
*Num.* 5:13 if a man *l. with* her
*Deut.* 22:23 find her, and *l. with*
25 man force her, and *l. w.* her
27:20 that *l. with* father's wife
21 *l. w.* beast; 22 sist. 23 mot.
28:30 betroth a wife, ano. *l. w.*
2 *Sam.* 11:11 go to *l. w.* my wife?
*Cant.* 1:13 sh. *l.* all night betwixt
*Mic.* 7:5 mouth from her that *l.*

**LIERS in wait.**

*Jos.* 8:14 wist not th. were *l. i. w.*
*Jud.* 9:25 men of Sh. set *l. in w.*
16:12 *l. in w.* abid. in chamber
20:33 the *l. in wait* came forth
37 *l. in w.* hasted and rushed

**LIEST.**

*Gen.* 28:13 land whereon thou *l.*
*Deut.* 6:7 wh. thou *l.* down, 11:19
*Jos.* 7:10 wheref. *l.* on thy face?
*Prov.* 3:24 *l.* down sh. not be af.

**LIETH.**

*Gen.* 4:7 not well, sin *l.* at door
49:25 blessings of deep *l.* under
*Lev.* 14:47 that *l.* in house
15:4 bed whereon he *l.* is uncl.
20 th. she *l.* on is unclean, 26
24 bed whereon he *l.* be unc. 33
26:34 S. as long as *l.* desolate
*Jud.* 16:5 where his strength *l.*
*Job* 40:21 he *l.* under shady tree
*Ps.* 41:8 he *l.* he sh. rise no more
88:7 thy wrath *l.* hard on me
*Mat.* 8:6 servant *l.* at home sick
*Mark* 5:23 *l.* at point of death
*Rom.* 12:18 as much as *l.* in you
1 *John* 5:19 world *l.* in wickedn

**LIEUTENANTS.**

*Ezr.* 8:36 king's commis. to *l.*
*Est.* 3:12 commanded king's *l.*
8:9 Mord. had commanded to
9:3 rulers and *l.* helped Jews

**LIFE.**

*Gen.* 1:20 mov. creature hath *l.*
2:7 G. breathed the breath of *l.*
9 tree of *l.* in garden, 3:22
3:24 keep the way of tree of *l.*
6:17 dest. all wherein is *l.* 7:22
9:4 flesh with the *l.* shall ye not eat, *Lev.* 17:14
5 of man will I req. *l.* of man
18:10 return accord. to time of *l.*
42:15 by the *l.* of Pharaoh, 16
45:5 G. did send me to preser. *l.*
47:9 not attained to years of *l.*
*Ex.* 21:23 gi. *l.* for *l.* *Deut.* 19:21
*Lev.* 17:11 *l.* of flesh in the blood
18:18 besides the other in *l.* ti.
*Deut.* 12:23 blood is *l.* not eat *l.*
*Deut.* 20:19 tree of fie. is man's *l.*
24:6 taketh man's *l.* to pledge
30:15 I have set before thee, this day, *l.* 19; *Jer.* 21:8
32:47 not vain thi. bec. your *l.*
*Jos.* 2:14 answ. our *l.* for yours
1 *Sam.* 25:29 bo. up in bun. of *l.*
2 *Sam.* 15:21 whet. in death or *l.*
1 *K.* 3:11 not asked for thyself long *l.* 2 *Chr.* 1:11
2 *K.* 4:16 time of *l.* embrace, 17
7:7 left camp, fled for their *l.*
*Ezr.* 6:10 pray for *l.* of king
*Est.* 8:11 Jews to stand for *l.*

Job 3:20 why l. given to bit. soul?
10:12 thou hast granted me l.
24:22 riseth, no man sure of l.
33:4 breath of Al. given me l.
36:6 preserveth not l. of wicked
14 their l. is among the uncl.
Ps. 16:11 wilt show me path of l.
21:4 asked l. of thee, thou gav.
30:5 in his favor is l.
34:12 wh. man is he th. desi. l.?
36:9 with thee is fountain of l.
61:6 wilt prolong the king's l.
63:3 loving-kin. is better th. l.
66:9 bless G. who hold. soul in l.
78:50 gave l. over to pestilence
91:16 with long l. will I satisfy
133:3 blessing, even l. for ever
Prov. 1:19 which taketh away l.
2:19 take they hold of paths of l.
3:2 long l. and peace shall they
18 she is a tree of l. to them
22 so sh. they be l. to thy soul
4:22 l. to those that find them
23 out of heart are issues of l.
5:6 lest thou pon. the path of l.
6:23 reproofs are the way of l.
8:35 whoso findeth me findeth l.
10:11 mou. of right. is well of l.
11:30 fruit of right. is tree of l.
12:10 right. regardeth l. of bea.
28 in way of righteousness is l.
13:8 ran. of man's l. are riches
12 desire com. it is a tree of l.
14 law of wise is a fount. of l.
14:27 fear of L. is a fount. of l.
30 a sound heart is l. of flesh
15:4 wholes. tongue is tree of l.
24 way of l. is above to wise
31 heareth reproof of l. abideth
16:15 in king's countenance is l.
18:21 death l. in power of tong.
21:21 followeth mercy, find. l.
22:4 by humil. are riches and l.
Ec. 7:12 wisdom giveth l.
Is. 38:16 in all th. things is the l.
20 sing songs all days of our l.
57:10 hast found l. of thy hand
Jer. 8:3 death chos. rather th. l.
21:8 set bef. you the way of l.
Lam. 2:19 lift up thy hands for l.
Ezek. 13:22 not return by prom. l.
33:15 wicked walk in stat. of l.
Jon. 1:14 not perish for man's l.
Mal. 2:5 covenant with him of l.
Mat. 2:20 dead wh. sou. child's l.
6:25 take no thought for your l.
Luke 12:22
18:8 enter into l. halt or maim.
Mark 9:43
9 better to enter into l. with
one eye, Mark 9:45
19:17 enter into l. keep com.
Mark 3:4 is it lawful to save l. or
to kill? Luke 6:9
Luke 1:75 holiness all days of l.
12:15 l. consist. not in abund.
23 l. more than meat, the body
John 1:4 in him w. l. and l. w. li.
3:36 believeth not S. not see l.
5:26 as Fat. hath l. in himself,
so hath he given to the S. l.
29 to resurrection of l.
40 will not come to me that
might have l. 10:10
6:33 giveth l. unto the world
35 I am the bread of l. 48
51 which I will give for the l.
53 blood, ye have no l. in you
63 words I speak to you, are l.
8:12 shall have the light of l.
11:25 the resurrec. and l. 14:6
20:31 believing ye might have l.
Acts 2:28 known to me ways of l.
17:25 seeing he giveth to all l.
27:22 no loss of any man's l.
Rom. 5:17 sh. reign in l. by one
18 all men to justification of l.
6:4 sho. walk in newness of l.
8:2 Spirit of l. in Christ Jesus
6 to be spiritually minded is l.
10 Sp. is l. bec. of righteousn.
11:15 but l. from the dead
1 Cor. 3:22 l. or death all yours
14:7 things with. l. giv. sound
2 Cor. 1:8 we despaired even of l.
2:16 to the other the savor of l.
3:6 letter killeth, Sp. giveth l.
4:10 l. of Jesus be manifested
12 death worketh in us, l. in y.
5:4 mortality swallowed up of l.
Gal. 2:20 l. wh. I now live in fle.
3:21 which could have given l.
Eph. 4:18 alienated fr. the l. of G.
Phil. 1:20 wheth. by l. or death
2:16 holding forth word of l.
Col. 3:3 your l. is hid wi. C. in G.
4 when Christ our l. sh. appear
1 Tim. 2:2 may lead a peacea. l.
4:8 having the promise of the l.
2 Tim. 1:1 accord. to prom. of l.
10 brought l. to light by gospel
3:10 known my manner of l.
Heb. 7:3 nei. days, nor end of l.
16 after power of endless l.
Jam. 1:12 sh. receive crown of l.
4:14 for what is your l.? a vap.
1 Pet. 3:7 heirs of the grace of l.
10 will love l. and see good d.
2 Pet. 1:3 things pertaining to l.
1 John 1:1 handled of word of l.
2 for the l. was manifested
2:16 pride of l. is not of the Fa.
5:12 he that hath the S. hath l.
he that hath not S. of G. n. l.
16 he sh. give him l. for them
Rev. 2:7 I give to eat of tree of l.
10 I will give thee a crown of l.
11:11 Sp. of l. from G. entered
13:15 power to give l. to beast
21:6 I will give to the thirsty l.
22:1 a pure river of water of l.
2 tree of l. bare 12 man. of fr.
14 have right to the tree of l.
17 let him take the water of l.
See BOOK, ETERNAL, EVERLASTING.

**His LIFE.**

Gen. 44:30 his l. is bound up
Ex. 21:30 give for ransom of h. l.
Jud. 9:17 father adventur. h. l.
16:30 which he slew in his l.
1 Sam. 19:5 put h. l. in his hand
1 K. 20:39 thy life be for his l. 42
2 K. 10:24 h. l. be for life of him
Job 2:4 hath will he give for h. l.
6 in thy hand, but save his l.
33:18 and his l. from perishing
20 h. l. abhor. 22 h. l. to destr.
28 and his l. shall see the light
Prov. 7:23 kno. not, for it is h. l.
13:3 keepeth mou. keepeth h. l
Ec. 7:15 wicked man prol. his l
Is. 15:4 his l. shall be grievous
Jer. 21:9 h. l. to him for pr. 38:2
Ezek. 3:18 to warn, to save his l.
7:13 nor stren. in iniq. of h. l.
32:10 every man for his l.
Mat. 10:39 he that find. h. l. sh.
lose it; he that loseth his l.
sh. find it, 16:25; Mark 8:35;
Luke 9:24; 17:33; John 12:25
20:28 to give his l. a ransom for
many, Mark 10:45
Luke 14:26 hate not his own l.
John 10:11 good Shep. give. h. l.
15:13 lay down h. l. for friends
Acts 8:33 his l. is taken fr. earth
20:10 yourselves, h. l. is in him
Rom. 5:10 sh. be saved by his l.
Phil. 2:30 not regarding his l.
1 John 3:16 he laid down his l.

See DAYS.

**My LIFE.**

Gen. 19:19 mercy in saving my l.
27:46 I am weary of my l.
32:30 seen G. and my l. is pres.
48:15 G. which fed me all my l.
Jud. 12:3 my l. in my hands
1 Sam. 18:18 what is my l.?
20:1 that he seeketh my l.?
22:23 that seeketh my l. seeketh
28:9 layest a snare for my l.?
21 I put my l. in my hand
2 Sam. 1:9 my l. is yet whole
16:11 my son seeketh my l.
1 K. 19:4 now, take away my l.
2 K. 1:13 let my l. be precious, 14
Est. 7:3 let my l. be given me
Job 6:11 that I sho. prolong m. l.
7:7 remem. my l. is but wind
15 chooseth death than my l.
9:21 yet I would despise my l.
10:1 my soul is weary of my l.
13:14 put my l. in my hand?
Ps. 7:5 tread down my l.
23:6 mercy sh. fol. me all my l.
26:9 not my l. with bloody men
27:1 the L. is strength of my l.
4 in ho. of L. all days of my l.
31:10 my l. is spent with grief
Ps. 38:12 seek after my l.
42:8 prayer to God of my l.
64:1 preserve my l. from enemy
88:3 my l. draw. nigh to grave
143:3 smitten my l. to ground
Lam. 3:53 cut off my l. in dung.
58 L. thou hast redeemed my l.
Jon. 2:6 bro. my l. from corrupt.
4:3 O Lord, take my l. from me
John 10:15 lay down my l.
17 because I lay down my l.
13:37 lay do. my l. for thy sake
Acts 20:24 nor count I my l. dear

**This LIFE.**

Ps. 17:14 have portion in this l.
Ec. 6:12 is good for man in t. l.
Acts 5:20 speak all words of t. l.
1 Cor. 6:3 thi. that pertain to t. l.
4 of things pertaining to t. l.
15:19 if in t. l. only we ha. hope
1 John 5:11 and t. l. is in his Son

**Thy LIFE.**

Gen. 19:17 escape for thy l.
Ex. 4:19 men dead wh. sou. t. l.
Deut. 28:66 thy l. hang in doubt
Jud. 18:25 and thou lose thy l.
Ruth 4:15 be a restorer of thy l.
1 Sam. 19:11 save not thy l.
26:24 as thy l. was much set by
2 Sam. 4:8 enemy sought thy l.
1 K. 1:12 thou mayest save t. l.
20:31 peradv. he will save t. l.
39 thy l. for his life, 42
Ps. 103:4 redeem. t. l. fr. destru.
Prov. 4:10 years of thy l. 9:11
13 keep her, for she is thy l.
9:11 years of thy l. be increased
Is. 43:4 will I give peo. for t. l.
Jer. 4:30 they will seek thy l.
11:21 of the men that seek thy
l. 22:25; 38:16
39:18 thy l. for a prey, 45:5
Luke 16:25 in t. l. rec. good thi.
John 13:38 lay down t. l. for my

**To LIFE.**

2 K. 8:1 son he restored to l. 5
Prov. 10:16 right. tendeth to l.
11:19 righteousn. tendeth to l.
19:23 fear of Lord tendeth to l.
Mat. 7:14 narrow way lead. to l.
John 5:24 but is passed fr. death
to l. 1 John 3:14
Rom. 7:10 com. ordained to l.
Heb. 11:35 their dead raised to l.

**LIFT.**

Gen. 7:17 ark was l. up above
21:18 l. up the lad, hold him
40:13 Pha. sh. l. up thy head, 19
Ex. 7:20 l. rod, smote wat. 14:16
20:25 if thou l. up a tool on it

*Num.* 6:26 L. *l.* up his counten.
23:24 *l.* up hims. as a young lion
*Deut.* 27:5 not *l.* up an iron tool
on them, *Jos.* 8:31
*Jos.* 4:18 soles of priests' feet *l.*
2 *Sam.* 23:8 *l.* up spear agai. 800
18 *l.* up sp. ag. 300, 1 *Chr.* 11:11
2 *K.* 9:32 *l.* up face to window
19:4 *l.* up thy pr. for rem. *Is.* 37:4
*Ezr.* 9:6 I blush to *l.* up my face
*Job* 10:15 will I not *l.* up head
11:15 thou *l.* up thy face, 22:26
*Ps.* 4:6 *l.* up light of countenance
7:6 in thine anger, *l.* up thyself
24:7 *l.* up your heads, ye gate. 9
25:1 to thee I *l.* soul, 86:4; 143:8
28:2 hear voice wh. I *l.* up han.
9 feed them and *l.* th. up for e.
41:9 hath *l.* up his heel ag. me,
*John* 13:18
74:3 *l.* up feet to perpet. desola.
75:4 to wicked, *l.* not up horn, 5
93:3 floods have *l.* up their wav.
94:2 *l.* up thyself, judge of earth
110:7 theref. shall he *l.* up head
*Ec.* 4:10 will *l.* up his fellow
*Is.* 2:4 nation sh. not *l.* up swo.
against nation, *Mic.* 4:3
10:15 if staff should *l.* up itself
24 shall *l.* up staff against thee
13:2 *l.* up banner upon mounta.
33:10 now will I *l.* up myself
59:19 Lord shall *l.* up standard
62:10 *l.* up standard for the peo.
*Jer.* 7:16 nor *l.* prayer, 11:14
51:14 *l.* up a shout against thee
*Lam.* 3:41 let us *l.* up our hearts
*Ezek.* 8:3 Spirit *l.* me up, 11:1
26:8 shall *l.* up buckler ag. thee
*Zec.* 1:21 no man did *l.* up head
*Mat.* 12:11 will he not *l.* out
*Mark* 1:31 took by hand, and *l.*
*Luke* 13:11 no wise *l.* up herself
21:28 *l.* up heads, your redemp.
*Jam.* 4:10 and he shall *l.* you up
*See* EYES.

**LIFT hand, s.**

*Gen.* 14:22 *l.* up my *h.* to Lord
*Deut.* 32:40 I *l.* up my *h.* and say
*Ps.* 10:12 *l.* up thy *h.* forget not
28:2 *l.* up my *h.* toward oracle
63:4 I *l.* up my *h.* in thy name
119:48 *h.* I *l.* up to command.
134:2 *l.* up *hands* in sanctuary
*Is.* 49:22 *l.* up my *h.* to Gentiles
*Lam.* 2:19 *l.* up *h.* towards him
*Heb.* 12:12 *l.* up *h.* that hang

**LIFT voice.**

*Job* 38:34 canst *l.* up *voice* to
clouds?
*Is.* 24:14 shall *l.* up *v.* shall sing
40:9 *l.* up thy *v.* with strength
42:2 he shall not cry nor *l.* up *v.*
11 wilderness and cit. *l.* up *v.*
52:8 thy watchmen shall *l.* up *v.*
58:1 *l.* up thy *v.* like a trumpet
*Ezek.* 21:22 *l.* up *v.* with shout.

**LIFTED.**

*Gen.* 40:20 *l.* up head of butler
*Lev.* 9:22 Aaron *l.* up hand
*Num.* 20:11 *l.* up hand, sm. rock
*Deut.* 8:14 heart *l.* up thou forget
17:20 heart not *l.* above brethr.
1 *Sam.* 24:16 *l.* up voice and we.
30:4 David and peo. *l.* up voice,
2 *Sam.* 3:22
2 *Sam.* 20:21 *l.* up hand aga. ki.
22:49 thou hast *l.* me up on high
1 *K.* 11:26 Jeroboam *l.* up hand
against king, 27
2 *K.* 14:10 heart hath *l.* thee up
1 *Chr.* 14:2 kingd. was *l.* on high
2 *Chr.* 17:6 *l.* up in ways of Lord
26:16 *l.* up to destruction, 32:25
*Job* 31:21 *l.* up hand ag. fatherl.
29 or *l.* up myself when evil

*Ps.* 24:4 not *l.* up soul unto van.
27:6 now shall my head be *l.* up
30:1 thou hast *l.* me up, 102:10
83:2 hate thee have *l.* up head
93:3 floods have *l.* up their voi.
106:26 *l.* up his hand ag. them
*Prov.* 30:13 their eyelids are *l.* up
*Is.* 2:12 on ev. one that is *l.* up
6:1 sit. on throne high and *l.* up
26:11 when thy hand is *l.* up
*Jer.* 51:9 judgment *l.* up to skies
*Ezek.* 1:19 creatures *l.* up fr. ear.
3:14 so the Spirit *l.* me up
10:16 *l.* up th. wings, 19; 11:22
20:5 *l.* up hand to seed of J. 6
28 land for wh. I *l.* up my hand
to give them, 42; 47:14
28:2 thy heart *l.* up, 5:17; 31:10
*Dan.* 5:20 heart *l.* up and hard.
23 *l.* up thyself against the L.
7:4 first beast was *l.* up fr. earth
*Mic.* 5:9 hand *l.* up on adversari.
*Hab.* 2:4 soul *l.* up is not upright
3:10 *l.* up his hands on high
*Zec.* 5:7 *l.* up a talent of lead
9:16 as stones of a crown, *l.* up
14:10 sh. be *l.* up and inhabited
*Mark* 9:27 but Jesus *l.* him up
*Luke* 6:20 *l.* up eyes on his disc.
24:50 *l.* up hands and blessed
*John* 3:14 as Moses *l.* up serpent
8:28 ye have *l.* up Son of man
12:32 I, if I be *l.* up, will draw
34 Son of man must be *l.* up
*Acts* 4:24 *l.* up their voice to G.
14:11 *l.* voice in speech of Lyc.
1 *Tim.* 3:6 *l.* up with pride he f.
*Rev.* 10:5 angel *l.* up hand

**LIFTER.**

*Ps.* 3:3 the *l.* up of my head

**LIFTEST.**

*Job* 30:22 thou *l.* me up
*Ps.* 9:13 me fr. gates of death
18:48 *l.* above those rise ag. me
*Prov.* 2:3 *l.* up voice for unders.

**LIFTETH.**

1 *Sam.* 2:7 bringeth low, *l.* up. 8
2 *Chr.* 25:19 heart *l.* up to boast
*Ps.* 107:25 wind wh. *l.* up wave
113:7 he *l.* needy out of dunghill
147:6 the Lord *l.* up the meek
*Is.* 18:3 see wh. he *l.* up ensign
*Nah.* 3:3 horseman *l.* up sword

**LIFTING.**

1 *Chr.* 15:16 *l.* up voice with joy
*Neh.* 8:6 amen, with *l.* up hands
*Ps.* 141:2 *l.* up of my hands
*Prov.* 30:32 foolishly in *l.* up. th.
*Is.* 9:18 like *l.* up of smoke
33:3 *l.* up of thyself nations are
1 *Tim.* 2:8 pray, *l.* up holy hands

**LIGHT.**

*Gen.* 44:3 soon as morning was *l.*
*Ps.* 139:11 even the night sh. be *l.*
*Mic.* 2:1 morn. *l.* they practice it
*Zec.* 14:7 even. time it shall be *l.*

**LIGHT.**

*Num.* 21:5 soul loatheth *l.* bread
*Deut.* 27:16 cursed set. *l.* by fath.
*Jud.* 9:4 vain and *l.* persons
2 *Sam.* 2:18 Asahel was *l.* of foot
*Ezek.* 22:7 set *l.* by fath. and mo.
*Zep.* 3:4 prophets *l.* and treach.
*Mat.* 11:30 yoke easy, burden *l.*
22:5 *l.* of it and went their ways
2 *Cor.* 4:17 *l.* affliction worketh

**LIGHT thing.**

1 *Sam.* 18:23 seemeth it a *l. th.*?
2 *K.* 20:10 *l. t.* shadow go down
*Is.* 49:6 *l. t.* that should. be serv.

**LIGHT, Substantive.**

*Gen.* 1:3 God said, Let there be *l.*
4 God saw *l.* 5 G. called *l.* day
16 the lesser *l.* to rule the nig.
*Ex.* 10:23 Is. had *l.* in dwellings

14:20 the pillar gave *l.* by night
*Num.* 4:16 pertaineth oil for *l.*
2 *Sam.* 21:17 quench not *l.* of Is.
23:4 shall be as *l.* of morning
1 *K.* 7:4 *l.* was against *l.*
11:36 David my serv. may ha. *l.*
*Neh.* 9:19 pillar of fire to show *l.*
*Est.* 8:16 J. had *l.* and gladness
*Job* 3:4 neit. let *l.* shine upon it
9 let it look for *l.* but have no.
3:20 *l.* given him in misery, 23
10:22 where the *l.* is as darkness
12:22 bring. to *l.* shadow of de.
18:5 *l.* of wicked sh. be put out
6 *l.* shall be dark in his taber.
22:28 *l.* shall shine on thy ways
24:13 those that rebel ag. the *l.*
14 murderer rising with *l.*
16 they know not the *l.*
25:3 upon wh. doth not *l.* arise?
28:11 thing hid bringeth he to *l.*
33:28 his life shall see the *l.*
30 enlightened with *l.* of living
36:30 spreadeth his *l.* upon it
32 with clouds he covereth *l.*
37:15 caused *l.* of cloud to shine
21 see not bright *l.* in clouds
38:15 fr. wicked *l.* is withholden
19 wh. is way where *l.* dwel.?
24 by what way is *l.* parted?
*Ps.* 4:6 lift up *l.* of countenance
27:1 Lord is my *l.* and salvation
37:6 bring forth righteous. as *l.*
38:10 *l.* of mine eyes, it is gone
49:19 they shall never see the *l.*
74:16 prepared the *l.* and sun
78:14 all the night with a *l.*
97:11 *l.* is sown for the righte.
104:2 coverest thyself with *l.*
118:27 L. who hath showed us *l.*
119:105 and a *l.* to my paths
130 entra. of thy words giv. *l.*
139:12 darkn. and *l.* alike to th.
*Prov.* 4:18 path of just as shin. *l.*
6:23 commandm. lamp, law is *l.*
13:9 *l.* of righteous rejoiceth
15:30 *l.* of eyes rejoiceth heart
*Ec.* 11:7 *l.* is sweet and pleasant
12:2 or the *l.* be not darkened
*Is.* 5:20 darkness for *l. l.* darkn.
30 *l.* is darkened in heavens
8:20 because there is no *l.* in th.
9:2 great *l.* on th. hath *l.* shined
10:17 *l.* of Is. shall be for a fire
13:10 moon sh. not cause her *l.*
to shine, *Mat.* 24:29; *Mark*
13:24
30:26 *l.* of moon as *l.* of sun. *l.*
of sun as the *l.* of seven days
51:4 judgment rest for *l.* to peo.
59:9 wait for *l.* but behold obs.
60:19 L. be to thee everlast. *l.*
*Jer.* 4:23 beheld heav. had no *l.*
25:10 take from them *l.* of cand.
31:35 L. giv. sun for *l.* by day,
moon and stars for *l.* by nig.
*Dan.* 2:22 *l.* dwelleth with him
*Hos.* 6:5 judgm. as *l.* goeth forth
*Mic.* 7:9 L. bring me forth to *l.*
*Hab.* 3:4 his brightness was as *l.*
11 at *l.* of thine arrows
*Zep.* 3:5 morn. bring judgm. to *l.*
*Zec.* 14:6 in that day *l.* not be cl.
*Mat.* 4:16 in death, *l.* sprung up
5:14 *l.* of world; 15 it giveth *l.*
16 let your *l.* so shine be. men
6:22 the *l.* of the body is the
eye, *Luke* 11:34, 36
17:2 his raiment white as the *l.*
*Luke* 2:32 *l.* to lighten Gentiles
8:16 enter in may see *l.* 11:33
16:8 wiser than children of *l.*
*John* 1:4 life was the *l.* of men
7 came to bear witness of *l.* 8
9 true *l.* wh. lighteth every m.
3:19 *l.* is come into the world
20 ev. one doeth evil hateth *l.*
21 that doeth truth com. to *l.*

*John* 5:35 was a burn. and shi. *l.*
8:12 I am *l.* of world, he that fol. me sh. have *l.* of life, 9:5
11:9 because he seeth the *l.*
10 because th. is no *l.* in him
12:35 a little wh. is *l.* with you
36 wh. ye have *l.* believe in *l.*
46 am come a *l.* into world
*Acts* 9:3 shined about him a *l.*
12:7 a *l.* shined in the prison
13:47 to be a *l.* to the Gentiles
16:29 called for a *l.* and sprang
22:6 there shone a great *l.* round
9 they with me saw indeed *l.*
26:13 midday I saw in way a *l.*
23 *l.* to people and to Gentiles
*Rom.* 2:19 *l.* of them are in dark.
13;12 put on the armor of *l.*
1 *Cor.* 4:5 bring to *l.* hid. things
2 *Cor.* 4:4 lest *l.* of gospel shine
6 commanded *l.* to shine out
11:14 transf. into an angel of *l.*
*Eph.* 5:8 are *l.* walk as chil. of *l.*
13 all things made mani. by *l.* whatso. doth manifest is *l.*
*Col.* 1:12 inherit. of saints in *l.*
1 *Thes.* 5:5 are all children of *l.*
1 *Tim.* 6:16 dwelling in *l.* no man
2 *Tim.* 1:10 who brought life to *l.*
1 *Pet.* 2:9 called you to marvel. *l.*
2 *Pet* 1:19 a *l.* shin. in dark place
1 *John* 1:5 G. is *l.* in him no da.
*Rev.* 18:23 *l.* of candle sh. no mo.
21:11 *l.* like a stone most preci.
23 the Lamb is the *l.* thereof
22:5 they need no *l.* of the sun
*See* COUNTENANCE, DARKNESS.

**Give LIGHT.**

*Gen.* 1:15 let them be to *g. l.*
*Ex.* 13:21 pillar of fire to *give l.*
2 *K.* 8:19 *give* him a *l.* 2 *Chr.* 21:7
*Neh.* 9:12 *g.* them *l.* in the way
*Ps.* 105:39 fire to *g. l.* in night
*Is.* 13:10 stars of heaven not *g. l.*
42:6 *g.* for a *l.* to Gentiles, 49:6
60:19 moon *g. l. Ezek.* 32:7
*Mat.* 5:15 *g. l.* to all, *Luke* 11:36
2 *Cor.* 4:6 *g. l.* of knowle. of G.
*Eph.* 5:14 Christ shall *g.* thee *l.*

**In the LIGHT.**

*Ps.* 56:13 may walk *in the l.*
*Is.* 2:5 let us walk *in the l.* of L.
50:11 walk *in the l.* of your fire
*John* 12:36 light, believe *in t. l.*
1 *John* 1:7 *in t. l.* as he is *in l.*
2:9 he that saith he is *in the l.*
10 lov. brother, abideth *in t. l.*
*Rev.* 21:24 nations sh. walk *i. t. l.*

**Thy LIGHT.**

*Ps.* 36:9 in *thy l.* sh. we see light
43:3 send out *t. l.* and thy truth
*Is.* 58:8 then sh. *t. l.* break forth
10 then sh. *t. l.* rise in obscuri.
60:1 shine, for *thy l.* is come
3 Gentiles shall come to *thy l.*
19 the sun sh. be no more *t. l.*
20 L. shall be *t.* everlasting *l.*

**LIGHT, ED.**

*Ex.* 25:37 sh. *l.* the lamps, 40:4
*Ps.* 18:28 thou wilt *l.* my candle
*Mat.* 5:15 nor do men *l.* a candle
*Luke* 8:16 hath *l.* candle, 11:33
15:8 doth not *l.* a candle
*Rev.* 7:16 nor sh. sun *l.* on them

**LIGHT on.**

*Ruth* 2:3 to *l. on* part of B.'s fie.
2 *Sam.* 17:12 will *l. on* him

**LIGHTED.**

*Gen.* 24:64 saw I. she *l.* off camel
*Jos.* 15:18 *l.* off ass, *Jud.* 1:14
*Jud.* 4:15 Sisera *l.* off his chariot
1 *Sam.* 25:23 Abigail *l.* off the ass
2 *K.* 5:21 Naaman *l.* from chari.

**LIGHTED, ETH on.**

*Gen.* 28:11 J. *l. on* certain place
*Deut.* 19:5 slip. and *l. on* neigh.
*Is.* 9:8 word to Jacob it *l. on* Isr.

**LIGHTEN,** *to illumine.*

2 *Sam.* 22:29 L. will *l.* my dark.
*Ezr.* 9:8 our God may *l.* our eyes
*Ps.* 13:3 *l.* mine eyes. lest I sleep
*Luke* 2:32 a light to *l.* Gentiles
*Rev.* 21:23 the glory of G. did *l.* it

**LIGHTEN, ETH.**

*Ps.* 34:5 looked to him and we. *l.*
77:18 the lightnings *l.* the world
*Prov.* 29:13 L. *l.* both their eyes
*Luke* 17:24 lightn. *l.* out one part
*Rev.* 18:1 earth *l.* with his glory
*See* ENLIGHTENED.

**LIGHTEN, ED.**

1 *Sam.* 6:5 he will *l.* his hand
*Jon.* 1:5 cast wares into sea to *l.*
*Acts* 27:18 next day th. *l.* sh. 38

**LIGHTER.**

1 *K.* 12:4 make thou our yoke *l.* 9, 10; 2 *Chr.* 10:10
*Ps.* 62:9 altogether *l.* than vanity

**LIGHTEST, ETH.**

*Ex.* 30:8 Aaron *l.* lamps at even
*Num.* 8:2 when thou *l.* lamps
*John* 1:9 true light *l.* every man

**LIGHTING.**

*Is.* 30:30 L. show *l.* down of arm
*Mat.* 3:16 a dove, and *l.* on him

**LIGHTLY.**

*Gen.* 26:10 might *l.* have lain
*Is.* 9:1 he *l.* afflicted the land
*Jer.* 4:24 all the hills moved *l.*
*Mark* 9:39 *l.* speak evil of me
*See* ESTEEMED.

**LIGHTNESS.**

*Jer.* 3:9 thro' *l.* of her whoredo.
23:32 cause peo. to err by the. *l.*
2 *Cor.* 1:17 minded, did I use *l.*?

**LIGHTNING.**

2 *Sam.* 22:15 sent *l.* and discom.
*Job* 28:26 made way for *l.* of thu.
37:3 directeth *l.* to ends of earth
38:25 divided a way for the *l.*
*Ps.* 144:6 cast forth *l.* scatter th.
*Ezek.* 1:14 ran as appearance of *l.*
*Dan.* 10:6 face as appearance *l.*
*Zec.* 9:14 his arrow go forth as *l.*
*Mat.* 24:27 as *l.* cometh out of the east, *Luke* 17:24
28:3 his countenance was as *l.*
*Luke* 10:18 as *l.* fall from heaven

**LIGHTNINGS.**

*Ex.* 19:16 thunders, *l.* and cloud
20:18 all the people saw the *l.*
*Job* 38:35 send *l.* th. th. may go?
*Ps.* 18:14 *l.* and discomfited th.
77:18 *l.* lighted the world, 97:4
135:7 he maketh *l.* for the rain
*Jer.* 10:13 mak. *l.* wi. rain, 51:16
*Nah.* 2:4 chariots shall run like *l.*
*Rev.* 4:5 out of throne proceed. *l.*
8:5 thunderings and *l.* 11:19
16:18 *l.* and a great earthquake

**LIGHTS.**

*Gen.* 1:14 let there be *l.* in firma.
16 God make two great *l.*
1 *K.* 6:4 windows of narrow *l.*
*Ps.* 136:7 made great *l.*
*Ezek.* 32:8 bri. *l.* will I make d.
*Luke* 12:35 loins girded, *l.* burn.
*Acts* 20:8 *l.* in upper chamber
*Phil.* 2:15 ye shine as *l.* in world
*Jam.* 1:17 down from Father of *l.*

**LIGN-ALOES.**

*Num.* 24:6 trees of *l.-a.* L. plant.

**LIGURE.**

*Ex.* 28:19 third row a *l.* 39:12

**LIKE.**

*Ex.* 15:11 who is *l.* unto thee? *Deut.* 33:29; 1 *K.* 8:23; 2 *Chr.* 6:14; *Ps.* 35:10; 71:19
*Is.* 57:20 wicked *l.* troubled sea
64:6 iniquities *l.* wind have tak.
*Jer.* 11:19 *l.* a lamb bro. to slau.
23:29 is not my word *l.* fire?
*Ezek.* 18:10 doeth *l.* any of these
25:8 house of Ju. *l.* to heathen
31:2 whom art th. *l.* in great. 18
*Dan.* 3:25 fourth is *l.* Son of God
7:13 one *l.* the Son of man came
*Hos.* 4:9 sh. be *l.* people, *l.* priest
6:7 *l.* men have transgressed
*Mat.* 13:31 *l.* to a grain of mustard-seed, *Mark* 4:31; *Luke* 13:19
44 *l.* a treasure; 45 *l.* a merch.
47 *l.* a net; 52 *l.* househol. 20:1
22:2 heav. is *l.* to a certain king
*Acts* 14:15 are men of *l.* passions
*Heb.* 2:17 made *l.* his brethren
7:3 made *l.* to the Son of God
*Jam.* 1:6 that waver. is *l.* a wave
23 *l.* a man beholding his face
5:17 E. was subject to *l.* passio.
2 *Pet.* 1:1 obtain. *l.* precious faith
1 *John* 3:2 we shall be *l.* him
*Rev.* 1:13 *l.* the Son of man, 14:14

**LIKE manner.**

*Ex.* 7:11 in *l. m.* with enchantm.
*Luke* 6:23 in *l. m.* did th. fathers
20:31 in *l. m.* did the seventh
*Acts* 1:11 in *l. m.* as have seen

**LIKE-MINDED.**

*Rom.* 15:5 G. gra. you to be *l.-m.*
*Phil.* 2:2 *l.-m.* 20 no man *l. m.*

**None LIKE.**

*Ex.* 8:10 there is *n. l.* the L. our God, 9:14; *Deut.* 33:26; 2 *Sa.* 7:22; 1 *Chr.* 17:20
11:6 *n. l.* cry of land of Egypt
1 *Sam.* 10:24 *n. l.* S. among peo.
1 *K.* 3:12 there was *n. l.* Solomon
21:25 there was *n. l.* to Ahab.
2 *K.* 18:5 there was *n. l.* Hezeki.
*Ps.* 86:8 among the gods *n. l.* to thee, *Jer.* 10:6, 7
*Is.* 46:9 am G. there is *n. l.* me
*Jer.* 30:7 day is great, *n. l.* it
*Dan.* 1:19 among all *n. l.* Daniel

**Such LIKE.**

*Mark* 7:8 *s. l.* things ye do, 13
*Gal.* 5:21 drunkenness, and *s. l.*

**LIKE, ED.**

*Deut.* 25:7 *l.* not to take her, 8
1 *Chr.* 28:4 sons of my fat. *l.* me
*Rom.* 1:28 did not *l.* to retain G.

**LIKEN.**

*Is.* 40:18 to whom *l.* G.? 25; 46:5
*Lam.* 2:13 what sh. I *l.* to thee?
*Mat.* 7:24 I will *l.* him to a man
11:16 whereunto *l.* this generation? *Luke* 7:31
*Mark* 4:30 *l.* kingd.? *Luke* 13:20

**LIKENED.**

*Ps.* 89:6 who am. sons *l.* to L.?
*Jer.* 6:2 I *l.* the daughter of Zion
*Mat.* 7:26 sh. be *l.* to foolish m.
13:24 heaven is *l.* 18:23; 25:1

**LIKENESS.**

*Gen.* 1:26 make man after *l.* 5:1
5:3 A. begat a son in his own *l.*
*Ex.* 20:4 not make *l.* of anything
*Deut.* 4:16 the *l.* of male or female, 17, 18, 23, 25; 5:8
*Ps.* 17:15 wh. awake with thy *l.*
*Is.* 40:18 what *l.* comp. to him?
*Ezek.* 1:5 *l.* of four liv. creatures
28 *l.* of the glory of the Lord
10:21 *l.* of the hands of man
*Acts* 14:11 gods come in *l.* of men
*Rom.* 6:5 in *l.* of his death, we shall be in *l.* of resurrection
8:3 G. sending Son in *l.* of flesh
*Phil.* 2:7 was made in *l.* of men

**LIKETH.**

*Deut.* 23:16 dwell where it *l.* him

*Amos* 4:5 this *l.* you, O child. of

**LIKING.**

*Job* 39:4 young on. are in good *l.*
*Dan.* 1:10 why see faces worse *l.*

**LIKEWISE.**

*Ps.* 49:10 *l.* brut. person perish
52:5 God shall *l.* destroy thee
*Ec.* 7:22 *l.* hast cursed others
*Mat.* 20:5 abo. sixth hour, did *l.*
21:36 and they did unto them *l.*
*Luke* 6:31 do ye also to them *l.*
13:3 ye shall all *l.* perish, 5
16:25 *l.* Laz. received evil thin.
22:20 *l.* also cup after supper
*John* 5:19 these doeth the Son *l.*
1 *Cor.* 7:3 *l.* the wife to husband
*Heb.* 2:14 he himself *l.* took part
1 *Pet.* 4:1 arm yourselves *l.*
*Jude* 8 *l.* these filthy dreamers
*Rev.* 8:12 day shone not, night *l.*

**LILY.**

*Cant.* 2:1 I am the *l.* of the val.
2 as *l.* am. thorns, so my love
*Hos.* 14:5 Is. shall grow as the *l.*

**LILIES.**

*Cant.* 2:16 belov. feed. am. *l.* 6:3
4:5 like two roses among the *l.*
5:13 lips like *l.* dropping myrrh
7:2 belly like wheat set with *l.*
*Mat.* 6:28 consider the *l.* how they grow, *Luke* 12:27

**LILY-WORK.**

1 *K.* 7:19 chapiters were of *l.-w.*
22 on top of pillars was *l.-w.*

**LIME.**

*Is.* 33:12 peo. be as burnings of *l.*
*Amos* 2:1 bon. of king of E. to *l.*

**LIMIT, ED, ETH.**

*Ps.* 78:41 *l.* Holy One of Israel
*Ezek.* 43:12 *l.* thereof shall be ho.
*Heb.* 4:7 he *l.* a certain day

**LINE, S.**

2 *K.* 21:13 over J. *l.* of Samaria
*Job* 38:5 stretched *l.* on earth?
*Ps.* 16:6 *l.* fallen in pleas. places
19:4 their *l.* is gone thro' earth
78:55 divided inheritance by *l.*
*Is.* 28:10 *l.* must be upon *l.* 13
17 judgm. also will I lay to *l.*
34:11 stretch on it *l.* of confus.
*Amos* 7:17 land be divided by *l.*
*Zec.* 1:16 *l.* be stretched on Jeru.
2 *Cor.* 10:16 in another man's *l.*

**LINEAGE.**

*Luke* 2:4 he was of *l.* of David

**LINEN.**

*Ex.* 28:42 make them *l.* breeches
*Lev.* 6:10 put on *l.* garment, 16:4
1 *Sam.* 2:18 minis. with *l.* ephod
22:18 slew 85 that did we. *l.* ep.
2 *Sam.* 6:14 D. girded wi. *l.* eph.
1 *K.* 10:28 Solomon had *l.* yarn brought, 2 *Chr.* 1:16
*Jer.* 13:1 get thee a *l.* girdle
*Mat.* 27:59 he wrapped it in a clean *l.* cloth, *John* 19:40
*Mark* 14:51 *l.* cloth about his bo.
52 left *l.* cloth and fled naked
*Luke* 24:12 P. beheld *l.* clothes la. by themselves, *John* 20:6
*John* 20:5 John saw the *l.* clothes

**LINEN.**

*Lev.* 19:19 nor shall a garment mingled of *l.* and woollen co. upon thee. *Deut.* 22:11
1 *Chr.* 15:27 D. had on eph. of *l.*
*Mark* 15:46 wrap. in *l.* *Luke* 23:53
*Rev.* 15:6 angels clothed in *l.*

*See* FINE.

**LINGERED, ETH.**

*Gen.* 19:16 Lot *l.* men laid hold
43:10 except *l.* we had returned
2 *Pet.* 2:3 judg. of a long time *l.*

**LINTEL, S.**

*Ex.* 12:22 strike *l.* and two posts
1 *K.* 6:31 *l.* and posts a fifth part
*Amos* 9:1 smite *l.* posts shake
*Zep.* 2:14 bittern lodge in upper *l.*

LINUS. 2 *Tim.* 4:21

**LION.**

*Gen.* 49:9 Judah couched as a *l.*
*Num.* 24:9 Israel lay down as a *l.*
*Deut.* 33:20 Gad dwelleth as a *l.*
*Jud.* 14:8 turned to see carc. of *l.* bees and honey in carc. of *l.*
1 *Sam.* 17:34 ca. a *l.* and took la.
2 *Sam.* 17:10 heart as hea. of a *l.*
23:20 slew *l.* in pit, 1 *Chr.* 11:22
1 *K.* 13:24 a *l.* met him by way and slew him, *l.* also stood
20:36 a *l.* sh. slay thee; a *l.* fou.
*Job* 4:10 roaring of *l.* voice of *l.*
10:16 huntest me as a fierce *l.*
28:8 nor the fierce *l.* passed by
38:39 wilt th. hunt prey for *l.*?
*Ps.* 7:2 lest tear my soul like *l.*
10:9 lieth in wait secretly as a *l.*
17:12 like a *l.* greedy of his prey
22:13 they gaped on me as a *l.*
91:13 thou shalt tread on the *l.*
*Prov.* 19:12 king's wra. is as a *l.*
20:2 fear of king is as roar. of *l.*
22:13 saith, There is a *l.* in way.
26:13 *l.* in way, a *l.* in the street
28:1 righteous are bold as a *l.*
30:30 a *l.* strongest am. beasts
*Ec.* 9:4 liv. dog better th. dead *l.*
*Is.* 5:29 th. roaring sh. be like *l.*
11:7 *l.* sh. eat str. like ox, 65:25
21:8 he cried, A *l.* my lord
35:9 no *l.* there, nor ravenous
38:13 as *l.* so will he bre. bones
*Jer.* 2:30 devour. prophets like *l.*
4:7 *l.* is come from his thicket
5:6 a *l.* out of forest sh. slay th.
12:8 my heritage is to me as a *l.*
25:38 forsak. his covert as the *l.*
49:19 shall come up like *l.* 50:44
*Lam.* 3:10 he was to me as a *l.*
*Ezek.* 1:10 face of *l.* on right side
10:14 third was the face of a *l.*
22:25 a conspir. like a roaring *l.*
*Dan.* 7:4 first like a *l.* had wings
*Hos.* 5:14 I will be to Ephr. a *l.*
11:10 he shall roar like a *l.*
13:7 to them as *l.* 8 will devour
*Joel* 1:6 teeth of a *l.* cheek-teeth
*Amos* 3:4 *l.* roar hath no prey?
8 *l.* roared, who will not fear?
12 taketh out of mouth of *l.*
*Mic.* 5:8 rem. of Jac. sh. be as *l.*
*Nah.* 2:12 *l.* tear in pieces
2 *Tim.* 4:17 de. out of mouth of *l.*
1 *Pet.* 5:8 devil as a *l.* walk. abo.
*Rev.* 4:7 first beast was like a *l.*
5:5 the *l.* of the tribe of Judah
10:3 a loud voice as a *l.* roareth
13:2 his mouth was as mo. of *l.*

*See* BEAR.

**LION-LIKE.**

2 *Sam.* 23:20 slew two *l.-l.* men of Moab 1 *Chr.* 11:22

**Old LION.**

*Is.* 30:6 whence come the *old l.*?
*Nah.* 2:11 even the *old l.* walked

**Young LION.**

*Is.* 11:6 calf and *y. l.* lie down
31:4 like as the *young l.* roaring
*Ezek.* 19:3 it became a *young l.* 6
32:2 like a *y. l.* of the nations
41:19 face of *y. l.* towards tree

**LIONESS, ES.**

*Ezek.* 19:2 wh. is thy moth.? a *l.*
*Nah.* 2:12 lion strangled for his *l.*

**LIONS.**

2 *Sam.* 1:23 S. and Jon. strong. *l.*
1 *K.* 10:19 two *l.* stood beside the stays, 2 *Chr.* 9:18
2 *K.* 17:25 L. sent *l.* among them
1 *Chr.* 12:8 faces like faces of *l.*
*Ps.* 22:21 save me from *l.* mouth
35:17 rescue my darling from *l.*
57:4 my soul is among *l.* I lie
*Cant.* 4:8 top of Am. from *l.* dens
*Is.* 15:9 *l.* upon him that escap.
*Jer.* 50:17 *l.* driven Israel away
51:38 shall roar together like *l.*
*Ezek.* 19:2 she lay down amo. *l.*
*Dan.* 6:27 D. from power of *l.*
*Nah.* 2:11 wh. is dwelling of *l.*?
*Zep.* 3:3 princes are roaring *l.*
*Heb.* 11:33 faith sto. mouths of *l.*
*Rev.* 9:8 teeth as the teeth of *l.*
17 heads of horses as hea. of *l.*

*See* DEN.

**LION'S whelp, s.**

*Gen.* 49:9 Judah is *l.'s w.* from
*Deut.* 33:22 Dan is a *l.'s whelp*
*Job* 4:11 *l.'s w.* scattered abroad
28:8 *l.'s w.* have not trodden it
*Jer.* 51:38 sh. yell as *l.'s whelps*

**Young LIONS.**

*Ps.* 34:10 *y. l.* suffer hunger
58:6 break out gr. teeth of *y. l.*
104:21 *y. l.* roar after their prey
*Jer.* 2:15 *y. l.* roared upon him
*Ezek.* 19:2 nourished among *y. l.*
38:13 the *y. l.* shall say to thee
*Zec.* 11:3 voice of roaring of *y. l.*

**LIP.**

*Lev.* 13:45 a covering on his *l.*
*Ps.* 22:7 they shoot out the *l.*
*Prov.* 12:19 *l.* of truth establish.

**LIPS.**

*Ex.* 6:12 of uncircumcised *l.* 30
1 *Sam.* 1:13 only her *l.* moved
*Ps.* 12:2 flat *l.* do they speak
4 *l.* own, who is lord over us?
17:1 goeth not out of feigned *l.*
31:18 lying *l.* be put to silence
59:7 behold, swords are in th. *l.*
12 words of their *l.* be taken
63:5 praise thee with joyful *l.*
120:2 deli. my soul from lying *l.*
140:3 poison is under their *l.*
9 let mischief of own *l.* cover
*Prov.* 4:24 perverse *l.* put fr. th.
5:3 *l.* of a strange woman drop
7:21 flatter. of *l.* she forced him
10:13 in *l.* of him that hath un.
21 *l.* of righteous feed many
32 *l.* of righteous know
12:22 lying *l.* abomination to L.
14:3 *l.* of wise sh. preserve them
7 not in him *l.* of knowledge
23 talk of *l.* tendeth to penury
15:7 *l.* of wise disperse knowl.
16:13 righte. *l.* delight of kings
21 sweet. of *l.* increaseth learn.
17:4 wicked giv. heed to false *l.*
7 less do lying *l.* bec. a prince
18:6 fools *l.* enter into conten.
20:15 *l.* of knowl. are a jewel
24:2 their *l.* talk of mischief
26:23 burning *l.* like a potsherd
*Ec.* 10:12 *l.* of fool swal. himself
*Cant.* 7:9 causing *l.* of th. asleep
*Is.* 6:5 a man of uncle. *l.* I dwell in midst of people of uncl. *l.*
28:11 stammer. *l.* will he speak
29:13 peo. with *l.* do honor me
57:19 I create the fruit of the *l.*
59:3 your *l.* have spoken lies
*Ezek.* 36:3 tak. up in *l.* of talkers
*Hos.* 14:2 render calves of our *l.*
*Mic.* 3:7 they shall cover their *l.*
*Mal.* 2:7 priest's *l.* keep knowl.
*Mat.* 15:8 that honoreth me with their *l.* *Mark* 7:6
*Rom.* 3:13 poison is under th. *l.*
1 *Cor.* 14:21 other *l.* I speak to
*Heb.* 13:15 fruit of *l.* giv. thanks

**His LIPS.**

*Job* 2:10 did not J. sin with *his l.*
11:5 G. open *his l.* against thee
23:12 back fr. comman. of *his l.*
*Ps.* 21:2 withholden req. of *his l.*
106:33 spake unadvis. with *h. l.*
*Prov.* 10:19 refrain *his l.* is wise
12:13 spared by transg. of *his l.*
16:27 *his l.* as a burning fire
30 *his l.* bringeth evil to pass
17:28 shutteth *his l.* as a man of
18:7 *his l.* are snare of his soul
19:1 that is perverse in *his l.*
20:19 that flattereth with *his l.*
*Prov.* 22:11 for grace of *his l.* the
24:26 kiss *his l.* gives ri. answer
*Cant.* 5:13 *his l.* like lilies drop.
*Is.* 11:4 breath of *h. l.* slay wick.
30:27 *his l.* full of indignation
*Mal.* 2:6 iniq. not found in *his l.*
1 *Pet.* 3:10 *his l.* speak no guile

**My LIPS.**

*Ps.* 16:4 their names into *my l.*
40:9 not refrained *my l.* O Lord
51:15 O Lord, open thou *my l.*
63:3 *my l.* shall praise thee
66:14 vows, which *my l.* uttered
89:34 thing gone out of *my l.*
119:13 wi. *my l.* have I declared
171 *my l.* shall utter thy praise
141:3 Lord, keep door of *my l.*
*Prov.* 8:6 the opening of *my l.* 7
*Jer.* 17:16 came out of *my l.* was
*Dan.* 10:16 sons of men tou. *my l.*

**Thy LIPS.**

2 *K.* 19:28 I will put my bridle
in *thy l.* *Is.* 37:29
*Job* 8:21 fill *thy l.* with rejoicing
15:6 *t.* own *l.* testify aga. thee
*Ps.* 17:4 word of *t. l.* I have kept
34:13 keep *t. l.* from spea. guile
45:2 grace is poured into *thy l.*
*Prov.* 5:2 *thy l.* may keep know.
22:18 they shall be fitted in *t. l.*
23:16 when *thy l.* speak right
24:28 deceive not with *thy l.*
27:2 praise thee, not *t.* own *l.*
*Cant.* 4:3 *thy l.* are like scarlet
11 *thy l.* drop as honey-comb
*Is.* 6:7 this hath touched *thy l.*
*Ezek.* 24:17 cover not *thy l.*

**LIQUOR, S.**

*Ex.* 22:29 offer the first of thy *l.*
*Num.* 6:3 nor drink any *l.* of gr.
*Cant.* 7:2 goblet wh. want. not *l.*

**LISTED.**

*Mat.* 17:12 done to him whatso-
ever they *l.* *Mark* 9:13

**LISTEN.**

*Is.* 49:1 *l.* O isles, unto me

**LISTETH.**

*John* 3:8 wind blow. where it *l.*
*Jam.* 3:4 whithersoever gover. *l.*

**LITTERS.**

*Is.* 66:20 bring your breth. in *l.*

**LITTLE.**

*Gen.* 30:30 but *l.* thou hadst
*Ex.* 12:4 househ. too *l.* for lamb
16:18 that gathered *l.* had no
lack, 2 *Cor.* 8:15
23:30 by *l.* and *l.* drive them
out, *Deut.* 7:22
*Deut.* 28:38 and gather but *l.* in
*Jos.* 22:17 is iniq. in Peor too *l.*?
1 *Sam.* 15:17 *l.* in th. own sight
1 *K.* 12:10 my *l.* finger thicker
than, 2 *Chr.* 10:10
17:12 *l.* oil in cruse; 13 *l.* cake
18:44 *l.* cloud like a man's hand
20:27 Is. pitch. like two *l.* flocks
2 *K.* 5:2 brought captive *l.* maid
*Ezr.* 9:8 give us a *l.* reviving
*Neh.* 9:32 let not trouble seem *l.*
*Job* 4:12 ear received a *l.* thereof
26:14 *l.* portion heard of him
*Ps.* 2:12 wrath kindled but a *l.*
8:5 made him a *l.* lower than
the angels, *Heb.* 2:7
37:16 *l.* that a right. man hath
65:12 *l.* hills rejoice on ev. side
68:27 *l.* Benjamin, with th. rul.
72:3 *l.* hills by righteousness
114:4 *l.* hills skip. like lambs, 6
*Prov.* 6:10 a *l.* sleep, *l.* slumber,
a *l.* folding, 24:33
10:20 heart of wicked is *l.* worth
15:16 better is *l.* with fear of L.
16:8 better is *l.* with righteous.
30:24 four things *l.* on earth
*Ec.* 5:12 whether eat *l.* or much
9:14 a *l.* city and few men in it
10:1 *l.* folly him is in reputation
*Cant.* 8:8 we have a *l.* sister
*Is.* 26:20 hide thy. for *l.* moment
28:10 here a *l.* and there a *l.* 13
40:15 tak. up isles as a *l.* thing
54:8 in a *l.* wrath I hid my face
*Ezek.* 11:16 to them a *l.* sanctu.
16:47 as if that were very *l.* th.
*Dan.* 7:8 up another *l.* horn. 8:9
11:34 be holpen with a *l.* help
*Hos.* 8:10 sorrow a *l.* for burden
*Amos* 6:11 smite *l.* house
*Mic.* 5:2 tho' *l.* among thousands
*Hag.* 1:6 sown much, bring in *l.*
9 looked for much, it ca. to *l.*
*Zec.* 1:15 was but a *l.* displeased
*Mat.* 14:31 O thou of *l.* faith
15:34 seven, and a few *l.* fishes
*Mat.* 26:39 he went a *l.* further,
*Mark* 1:19; 14:35
*Mark* 5:23 my *l.* daughter lieth
*Luke* 7:47 to whom *l.* is forgiven
12:32 *l.* flock; 19:3 *l.* of stature
19:17 been fulfilled in a very *l.*
*John* 6:7 every one may take a *l.*
*Acts* 5:34 apostles forth a *l.* space
28:2 showed us *l.* kindness
1 *Cor.* 5:6 *l.* leaven leav. *Gal.* 5:9
2 *Cor.* 11:1 bear with me a *l.*
16 that I may boast myself a *l.*
1 *Tim.* 4:8 bodily ex. profiteth *l.*
5:23 use *l.* wine for stomach's
*Heb.* 2:9 a *l.* lower than angels
*Jam.* 3:5 tongue is a *l.* member
4:14 vapor appeareth for *l.* time
*Rev.* 3:8 thou hast a *l.* strength
6:11 should rest for a *l.* season
20:3 be loosed a *l.* season

*See* BOOK, CHAMBERS, CHILD, CHILDREN.

**LITTLE one, s.**

*Gen.* 19:20 Lot said, It is a *l. one*
44:20 have a *l. one*, broth. dead
*Ex.* 10:10 go and your *l. ones*, 24
*Jos.* 8:35 before women and *l. o.*
2 *Chr.* 20:13 before Lord and *l. o.*
*Ezr.* 8:21 seek right way for *l. o.*
*Ps.* 137:9 dasheth *l. o.* ag. stones
*Is.* 60:22 *l. one* bec. a thousand
*Zec.* 13:7 turn my hand on *l. o.*
*Mat.* 10:42 dri. to one of th. *l. o.*
18:6 offend one of these *l. ones*,
*Mark* 9:42; *Luke* 17:2
10 despise not one of th. *l. o.*
14 one of these *l. o.* sho. perish

**LITTLE while.**

*Job* 24:24 exalted for a *l. while*
*Ps.* 37:10 a *l. w.* and the wicked
*Is.* 10:25 *l. w.* indignation cease
63:18 possessed it but a *l. w.*
*Jer.* 51:33 a *l. w.* harvest sh. co.
*Hos.* 1:4 a *l. while* I will avenge
*Hag.* 2:6 a *l. w.* I will sh. heaven
*John* 7:33 *l. w.* I am with, 13:33
12:35 a *l. w.* is light with you
14:19 *l. w.* world seeth me no
16:16 *l. w.* ye sh. see me, 17, 19
18 a *l. while* we cannot tell
*Heb.* 10:37 *l. w.* he that sh. come

**LIVE.**

*Is.* 6:6 hav. a *l.* coal in his hand
*See* GOAT.

**LIVE.**

*Gen.* 3:22 tree of life *l.* for ever
19:20 and my soul shall *l.*
20:7 pray for thee, thou shalt *l.*
27:40 by the sword shalt thou *l.*
31:32 fin. thy go. let him not *l.*
42:18 this do, and *l.* for I fear G.
*Ex.* 33:20 no man see me and *l.*
*Lev.* 18:5 he shall *l.* in them,
*Neh.* 9:29; *Ezek.* 20:11, 13, 21
*Num.* 21:8 looketh on ser. sh. *l.*
24:23 shall *l.* when G. doeth
*Deut.* 4:10 fear me all days th. *l.*
33 hear, as thou hast, and *l.*?
8:3 by ev. wo. of L. doth man *l.*
19:5 flee to one of th. cit. and *l.*
33:6 let Reuben *l.* and not die
*Job* 14:14 man die, sh. he *l.* ag.?
21:7 do wicked *l.* become old?
*Ps.* 22:26 your heart *l.* for ever
49:9 *l.* and not see corruption
63:4 will I bless thee while I *l.*
69:32 hearts sh. *l.* that seek G.
72:15 shall *l.* 118:17 not die, *l.*
119:144 understand. and I sh. *l.*
175 let soul *l.* it sh. praise thee
146:2 while I *l.* will I praise L.
*Prov.* 4:4 keep my com. *l.* 7:2
9:6 forsake foolish and *l.*
15:27 he that hateth gifts sh. *l.*
*Ec.* 6:3 *l.* many years, 6; 11:8
9:9 *l.* joyfully wi. wife th. lovest
*Is.* 26:19 dead men. sh. *l.* togeth.
38:16 L. by these things men *l.*
55:3 hear, and your soul shall *l.*
*Jer.* 38:20 and thy soul shall *l.*
*Lam.* 4:20 under shad. we sh. *l.*
*Ezek.* 3:21 he shall surely *l.* 18:9,
17; 33:13, 15, 16
16:6 when thou wast in blood *l.*
18:19 kept my statutes shall *l.*
21, 22; 20:11, 25
24 wicked man doeth sh. he *l.*
32 turn yourselves and *l.* 33:11
33:10 sins on us, how sh. we *l.*?
19 do that wh. is law. he sh. *l.*
37:3 can these bones *l.*?
47:9 ev. thing liveth and mov
eth sh. *l.* everything shall *l.*
*Hos.* 6:2 he will rev. us, we sh. *l.*
*Amos* 5:4 seek me, and ye sh. *l.* 6
*Jon.* 4:3 bet. to die than to *l.* 8
*Hab.* 2:4 just sh. *l.* by his faith,
*Rom.* 1:17
*Mat.* 4:4 not *l.* by bread, *Lu.* 4:4
9:18 she shall *l.* *Mark* 5:23
*Luke* 10:28 this do, and th. sh. *l.*
20:38 not G. of dead, all *l.* unto
*John* 5:25 hear voice of S. and *l.*
6:57 I *l.* by F. so he that eateth
me, even he shall *l.* by me
11:25 tho' he were de. yet sh. *l.*
14:19 because I *l.* ye sh. *l.* also
*Acts* 17:28 in him we *l.* and move
22:22 it is not fit that he sho. *l.*
*Rom.* 6:2 *l.* any longer therein?
8 we believe we sh *l.* with him
8:12 debtors not to *l.* after flesh
13 if ye *l.* after flesh, ye sh. die,
if thro' Sp. mortify bo. ye *l.*
10:5 doeth these things shall *l.*
by them, *Gal.* 3:12
12:18 *l.* peaceably with all men
14:8 whether we *l.* we *l.* to Lo.
whe. we *l.* or die we are L.'s
1 *Cor.* 9:13 *l.* of things of temple
14 preach gospel sho. *l.* of gos.
2 *Cor.* 4:11 *l.* are deliv. to death
6:9 behold, we *l.* as chastened
7:3 to die and *l.* with you
13:4 *l.* with him by power of G.
*Gal.* 2:14 Gentiles to *l.* as Jews
19 that I might *l.* unto God

20 I *l.* yet not I, life I now *l.* in flesh, I *l.* by faith of S. of G.
3:11 just *l.* by faith, *Heb.* 10:38
5:25 if we *l.* in the Spirit
*Phil.* 1:21 for me to *l.* is Christ
22 if I *l.* in the flesh
1 *Thes.* 3:8 we *l.* if sta. fast in L.
5:10 died that we sh. *l.* wi. him
2 *Tim.* 2:11 we sh. also *l.* with
3:12 all *l.* godly suf. persecution
*Tit.* 2:12 we should *l.* soberly
*Heb.* 12:9 to F. of spirits and *l.*
13:18 willing to *l.* honestly
*Jam.* 4:15 if Lord will we sh. *l.*
1 *Pet.* 2:24 we *l.* to righteousness
4:2 no longer should I *l.* in flesh
6 *l.* according to God in Spirit
2 *Pet.* 2:6 to those that *l.* ungodly
18 escaped from them *l.* in err.
1 *John* 4:9 we might *l.* thro' him
*Rev.* 13:14 beast had wound did *l.*
*See* FOR EVER.

**As I LIVE.**

*Num.* 14:21 *as I l.* earth be fill. 28
*Job* 27:6 so long *as I l. Ps.* 104:33; 116:2
*Is.* 49:18 *as I l.* saith the Lord; *Jer.* 22:24; *Ezek.* 5:11; 14:16. 18, 20; 16:48; 17:16, 19; 18:3; 20:3, 33; 33:11, 27; 34:8; 35:6, 11; *Zep.* 2:9; *Rom.* 14:11
*Jer.* 46:18 *as I l.* saith the king

**May, might, *or* mayest LIVE.**

*Deut.* 4:1 do to them, ye *m. l.* 5:33; 8:1; 30:6, 16
42 flee, to one of th. citi. *m. l.*
16:20 what is just fol. that *m. l.*
30:19 thou and thy seed *m. l.*
*Ps.* 119:17 bountif. that I *m. l.*
77 mer. come to me, that I *m. l.*
116 uphold me, that I *may l*
*Jer.* 35:7 that ye *m. l.* many days
*Ezek.* 37:9 slain, that they *m. l.*
*Amos* 5:14 seek good, th. ye *m. l.*
*Eph.* 6:3 *mayest l.* long on earth

**Not LIVE.**

*Ex.* 19:13 touch mountain *not l.*
*Deut.* 8:3 man doth *n. l.* by bread only, *Mat.* 4:4; *Luke* 4:4
2 *K.* 10:19 wanting he shall *not l.*
20:1 thou shalt *not l. Is.* 38:1
*Job* 7:16 I would *not l.* always
*Ps.* 55:23 wick. *n. l.* half th. days
*Is.* 26:14 are dead, they sh. *not l.*
*Ezek.* 13:19 souls that should *n. l.*
18:13 he shall *not l.*
*Zec.* 13:3 say, Thou shalt *not l.*
*Acts* 7:19 to the end they mi. *n. l.*
25:24 ought *not* to *l.* any longer
28:4 vengeance suffereth *n.* to *l.*
2 *Cor.* 5:15 sho. *n. l.* to themsel.

**LIVED.**

*Gen.* 25:6 from Isaac, while he *l.*
*Num.* 14:38 Joshua and C. *l.* still
21:9 beheld serp. of brass he *l.*
*Deut.* 5:26 hea. voice of G. and *l.*
2 *Sam.* 19:6 if Absalom had *l.*
*Ps.* 49:18 while he *l.* blessed soul
*Ezek.* 37:10 into them, and th. *l.*
*Acts* 23:1 *l.* in good conscience
*Col.* 3:7 sometime, wh. *l.* in th.
*Jam.* 5:5 *l.* in pleasure on earth
*Rev.* 18:7 hath *l.* deliciously, 9
20:4 *l.* with Christ; 5 *l.* not ag.

**LIVELY.**

*Ex.* 1:19 Hebrew women are *l.*
*Ps.* 38:19 but my enemies are *l.*
*Acts* 7:38 who received *l.* oracles
1 *Pet.* 1:3 begot. us ag. to *l.* hope
2:5 ye, as *l.* stones, are built

**LIVER.**

*Ex.* 29:13 the caul above the *l.* 22; *Lev.* 3:4, 10, 15; 4:9; 7:4; 8:16, 25; 9:10, 19
*Prov.* 7:23 dart strike through *l.*
*Lam.* 2:11 *l.* poured upon earth
*Ezek.* 21:21 he looked in the *l.*
*See* CAUL.

**LIVES.**

*Ex.* 1:14 they made th. *l.* bitter
*Jos.* 2:13 deliver our *l.* fr. death
*Jud.* 5:18 peo. jeoparded their *l.*
2 *Sam.* 1:23 were lovely in th. *l.*
23:17 that went in jeopardy of their *l.* 1 *Chr.* 11:19
*Prov.* 1:18 lurk privily for own *l.*
*Jer.* 19:7 which seek th. *l.* 46:26
9 seek their *l.* sh. strait. them
*Lam.* 5:9 gat bread wi. peril of *l.*
*Dan.* 7:12 *l.* prolon. for a season
*Luke* 9:56 to destroy men's *l.*
*Acts* 15:26 men have hazarded *l.*
27:10 voy. be with damage of *l.*
1 *John* 3:16 lay down *l.* for breth.
*Rev.* 12:11 they loved not their *l.*

**LIVEST.**

*Gal.* 2:14 a Jew *l.* after manner
*Rev.* 3:1 that thou *l.* and art dead

**LIVETH.**

*Gen.* 9:3 every thing *l.* be meat
*Deut.* 5:24 G. talk with man, he *l.*
1 *Sam.* 1:28 to L. as long as he *l.*
20:31 as son of Jesse *l.* on grou.
2 *Sam.* 2:27 as God *l.* unless th.
22:47 the Lord *l.* blessed be my rock, *Ps.* 18:46
1 *K.* 17:23 Elijah said, Thy son *l.*
*Job* 19:25 I know my Redeemer *l.*
27:2 as G. *l.* who ha. taken away
*Ps.* 89:48 what man *l.* not see de.?
*Jer.* 4:2 the Lord *l.* in truth
5:2 Lord *l.* they swear falsely
12:16 my name, the Lord *l.*
16:14 the Lord *l.* 15; 23:7, 8
44:26 Egypt, saying, The L. *l.*
*Ezek.* 47:9 every thing that *l.*
*Hos.* 4:15 nor swear, the Lord *l.*
*Amos* 8:14 say, Thy G. O Dan, *l.* and the manner of Beersh. *l.*
*John* 4:50 thy way, son *l.* 51, 53
11:26 whosoever *l.* and believ.
*Rom.* 6:10 in that he *l.* he *l.* to G.
7:1 over man as long as he *l.* 2
3 while husb. *l.* she be married
14:7 *l.* or dieth to himself
1 *Cor.* 7:39 as long as her husb. *l.*
2 *Cor.* 13:4 *l.* by the power of G.
*Gal.* 2:20 I live, but Ch. *l.* in me
1 *Tim.* 5:6 *l.* in pleasure is dead
*Heb.* 7:8 it is witnessed that he *l.*
25 ever *l.* to make intercession
9:17 no strength while testa. *l.*
*Rev.* 1:18 he that *l.* and was dead
*See* FOR EVER.

**As the Lord LIVETH.**

*Jud.* 8:19 *as the L. l.* if ye have
1 *Sam.* 14:39 *as the L. l.* 45; 19:6; 20:21; 25:26; 26:10, 16; 28:10; 29:6; 2 *Sam.* 4:9; 12:5; 14:11; 1 *K.* 1:29
20:3 *as t. L. l.* there is but a step
25:34 God of Is. *l.* whi. kept me
2 *Sam.* 15:21 *as L. l.* as my lord
1 *K.* 2:24 *as the Lord l.* 2 *K.* 5:20; 2 *Chr.* 18:13; *Jer.* 38:16
17:1 *as Lord* God of Is. *l.* 18:15
12 *as the Lord* thy God *l.* 18:10
2 *K.* 3:14 *as Lord* of hosts *l.* 5:16

**As thy soul LIVETH.**

1 *Sam.* 1:26 *as s. l.* I am the wom.
17:55 Abner said, *As thy soul l.*
25:26 *as soul l.* seeing Lord hath
2 *Sam.* 11:11 *as t. s. l.* will not do

**LIVING.**

*Gen.* 1:28 dominion over *l.* thing
2:7 and man became a *l.* soul
3:20 she was mother of all *l.*
6:19 every *l.* thing of all flesh
7:4 ev. *l.* substance will I destr.
8:1 Noah and every *l.* thing
*Lev.* 11:10 any *l.* thing in water
*Num.* 16:48 stood bet. dead and *l.*
1 *K.* 3:22 the *l.* is my son, 23
25 divide the *l.* child into two
*Job* 12:10 in his hand ev. *l.* thing
28:13 nor found in land of the *l.*
21 it is hid from eyes of all *l.*
30:23 house appointed for all *l.*
*Job* 33:30 enlight. wi. light of *l.*
*Ps.* 27:13 good. of L. in land of *l.*
52:5 root thee out of land of *l.*
56:13 walk in the light of the *l.*
58:9 sh. take th. away, both *l.*
69:28 blotted out of book of *l.*
116:9 walk bef. L. in land of *l.*
142:5 my portion in land of *l.*
143:2 in thy sight no man *l.*
145:16 satisfiest every *l.* thing
*Ec.* 4:2 more than *l.* are alive
15 I considered all *l.* wh. walk
6:8 knoweth to walk before *l.*
7:2 the *l.* will lay it to heart
9:4 that is joined to all the *l.*
5 the *l.* know that they sh. die
*Cant.* 4:15 a well of *l.* water
*Is.* 4:3 written among *l.* in Jer.
8:19 seek to their God for the *l.*
38:11 not see L. in land of the *l.*
19 the *l.* the *l.* he sh. prai. thee
53:8 cut off out of the land of *l.*
*Jer.* 2:13 forsaken *l.* waters, 17:13
11:19 cut him off fr. land of *l.*
*Lam.* 3:39 wheref. doth *l.* comp.
*Ezek.* 26:20 set glory in land of *l.*
32:23 terror in land of *l.* 24-32
*Dan.* 4:17 that the *l.* may know
*Zec.* 14:8 *l.* waters shall go out
*Mat.* 22:32 God is the God of *l.* *Mark* 12:27; *Luke* 20:38
*Mark* 12:44 cast in even all her *l.*
*Luke* 8:43 spent *l.* on physicians
15:12 he divided to them his *l.*
13 wasted subs. with riot. *l.* 30
24:5 why seek ye *l.* among dead
*John* 4:10 given thee *l.* water
11 fr. whence hast thou *l.* wat.
6:51 I am the *l.* bread wh. came
57 the *l.* Father hath sent me
7:38 sh. flow rivers of *l.* water
*Rom.* 12:1 bodies a *l.* sacrifice
14:9 Lord both of dead and *l.*
1 *Cor.* 15:45 A. was made *l.* soul
*Col.* 2:20 *l.* in world are subject
*Heb.* 10:20 by a new and *l.* way
1 *Pet.* 2:4 coming as to a *l.* stone
*Rev.* 7:17 Lamb lead to *l.* fount.
16:3 every *l.* soul died in the sea
*See* BIRD, CREATURE, GOD.

**LIZARD.**

*Lev.* 11:30 *l.* snail, mole, unclean

**LO.**

*Job* 9:19 strength, *l.* he is strong
*Ps.* 37:36 pas. away, *l.* he was not
40:7 *l.* I come; 132:6 *l.* heard
52:7 *l.* the man that made not G.
73:27 *l.* they th. are far sh. peri.
92:9 *l.* thine enemies sh. perish
*Cant.* 2:11 *l.* the winter is past
*Is.* 25:9 *l.* this is our God
*Jer.* 4:23 *l.* it was without form
25 and *l.* there was no man
*Hag.* 1:9 and *l.* it came to little
*Mat.* 24:23 *l.* here is Chr. *l.* there
28:20 *l.* I am with you always
*Acts* 13:46 *l.* we turn to Gentiles
*Heb.* 10:7 *l.* I co. to do thy will, 9

**LOADEN.**

*Is.* 46:1 carriages were heavy *l.*

**LOADETH.**

*Ps.* 68:19 daily *l.* us wi. benefits

**LOAF.**

*Ex.* 29:23 one *l.* of bread
1 *Chr.* 16:3 D. dealt to ev. one a *l.*
*Mark* 8:14 nei. had more th. one *l.*

LO-AMMI. *Hos.* 1:9

**LOAN.**
1 *Sam.* 2:20 *l.* which is lent to L.

**LOATHE.**
*Ex.* 7:18 Egypt. shall *l.* to drink
*Job* 7:16 I *l.* it, I would not live
*Ezek.* 6:9 *l.* themselves for evils
20:43 *l.* yourselves in own sight
36:31 *l.* yourselves for iniquities

**LOATHED.**
*Jer.* 14:19 hath thy soul *l.* Zion?
*Zec.* 11:8 my soul *l.* them

**LOATHETH.**
*Num.* 21:5 soul *l.* this light bread
*Prov.* 27:7 full soul *l.* honey-co.
*Ezek.* 16:45 *l.* husb. and children

**LOATHING.**
*Ezek.* 16:5 cast out to *l.* of person

**LOATHSOME.**
*Num.* 11:20 till it be *l.* to you
*Job* 7:5 my skin is broken and *l.*
*Ps.* 38:7 loins filled with a *l.* dis.
*Prov.* 13:5 a wicked man is *l.*

**LOAVES.**
*Lev.* 23:17 two *l.* of two tent'h
1 *Sam.* 25:18 Abigail took 200 *l.*
1 *K.* 14:3 take with thee ten *l.*
2 *K.* 4:42 brought man of G. 20 *l.*
*Mat.* 14:17 we have here but 5 *l.*
19 and he took five *l.* *Mark* 6:38; *Luke* 9:13
15:34 how many *l.* have ye?
36 took the seven *l.* *Mark* 8:6
16:9 nor remem. five *l.* of 5,000
10 nor the seven *l.* of the 4,000
*Mark* 6:44 eat of *l.* were 5,000
52 consider. not miracles of *l.*
*Luke* 11:5 say, Fri. lend me 3 *l.*
*John* 6:9 lad here hath 5 barley *l.*
11 Jesus took *l.* and distribut.
13 fragments of five barley *l.*
26 because ye did eat of the *l.*

*See* BREAD.

**LOCK, S.**
*Num.* 6:5 let *l.* of the hair grow
*Jud.* 16:13 weavest the seven *l.*
*Neh.* 3:3 set up doors, and *l.* thereof. 6, 13, 14, 15
*Cant.* 4:1 doves' eyes with. thy *l.*
5:2 my *l.* are filled with drops
5 myrrh on handles of the *l.*
11 his *l.* are bushy, and black
6:7 thy temples within thy *l.*
*Is.* 47:2 uncov. thy *l.* make bare
*Ezek.* 8:3 he took me by *l.* of he.
44:20 nor suffer *l.* to grow long

*See* BARS.

**LOCUST.**
*Lev.* 11:22 *l.* aft. his kind, bald *l.*
*Ps.* 78:46 gave th. labor to the *l.*
109:23 tossed up and down as *l.*
*Joel* 1:4 hath *l.* eaten, wh. *l.* left
2:25 restore years *l.* hath eaten

**LOCUSTS.**
*Ex.* 10:4 to-morrow I will bri. *l.*
*Deut.* 28:38 *l.* shall consume it
*Ps.* 105:34 he spake, and *l.* came
*Prov.* 30:27 the *l.* have no king
*Is.* 33:4 running to and fro of *l.*
*Nah.* 3:15 make thyself ma. as *l.*
*Mat.* 3:4 his meat was *l.* and wild honey, *Mark* 1:6
*Rev.* 9:3 th. came out of smoke *l.*
7 shapes of *l.* we. like to hors.

**LODGE.**
*Is.* 1:8 daughter of Z. left as a *l.*

**LODGE, Verb.**
*Gen.* 24:23 is th. room for us to *l.*?
*Num.* 22:8 *l.* here this night
*Jos.* 4:3 place where ye shall *l.*
*Jud.* 19:9 *l.* here, that thy heart
*Neh.* 4:22 let every one *l.* in Jer.
13:21 why *l.* ye about the wall?
*Job* 24:7 naked *l.* without cloth.
31:32 stran. did not *l.* in street
*Cant.* 7:11 let us *l.* in the villages
*Is.* 21:13 forest in Ara. sh. ye *l.*
65:4 and *l.* in monuments
*Jer.* 4:14 how long vain thoug. *l.*
*Zep.* 2:14 beasts sh. *l.* in lintels
*Mat.* 13:32 birds *l.* in branches, *Mark* 4:32; *Luke* 13:19
*Acts* 21:16 with wh. we should *l.*

**LODGED.**
*Gen.* 32:13 J. *l.* there that night
21 *l.* that night in company
*Jos.* 2:1 a harlot's house, and *l.*
4:8 carried them, where they *l.*
*Jud.* 19:4 eat and drink, *l.* there
1 *K.* 19:9 came into a cave and *l.*
1 *Chr.* 9:27 *l.* round house of God
*Neh.* 13:20 *l.* without Jerusalem
*Is.* 1:21 righteousness *l.* in it
*Mat.* 21:17 went to Betha. and *l.*
*Acts* 10:18 whether Simon *l.* th.
28:7 *l.* us three days courteous.
1 *Tim.* 5:10 if she have *l.* strang.

**LODGEST.**
*Ruth* 1:16 wh. th. *l.* I will lodge

**LODGETH.**
*Acts* 10:6 *l.* with one Si. a tanner

**LODGING, S.**
*Jos.* 4:3 leave them in the *l.*
2 *K.* 19:23 enter *l.* of his borders
*Is.* 10:29 taken up their *l.* at G.
*Acts* 28:23 came to him into *l.*
*Phile.* 22 withal prepare me a *l.*

**LOFT, Y.**
1 *K.* 17:19 carried him into a *l.*
*Ps.* 131:1 not haugh. nor eyes *l.*
*Prov.* 30:13 L. how *l.* are th. eyes
*Is.* 2:11 *l.* looks be humbled, 5:15
26:5 the *l.* city he layeth low
57:7 on *l.* mountain hast set bed
15 thus sai. the high and *l.* one
*Acts* 20:9 Euty. fell from third *l.*

**LOFTILY.**
*Ps.* 73:8 corrupt, they speak *l.*

**LOFTINESS.**
*Is.* 2:17 *l.* of man shall be bowed
*Jer.* 48:29 the pride of Moab, his *l.*

**LOG.**
*Lev.* 14:10 priest take a *l.* 12, 24

**LOINS.**
*Gen.* 35:11 kings co. out of thy *l.*
37:34 J. put sackcloth on his *l.*
46:26 souls out of his *l.* *Ex.* 1:5
*Ex.* 12:11 eat it, with *l.* girded
28:42 breeches reach from the *l.*
*Deut.* 33:11 smite thro' *l.* of them
1 *K.* 2:5 blood in girdle about *l.*
8:19 son shall come forth of thy *l.* 2 *Chr.* 6:9
12:10 thicker than my father's *l.* 2 *Chr.* 10:10
20:31 put sackcloth on our *l.*
2 *K.* 1:8 girdle of leather about his *l.* *Mat.* 3:4; *Mark* 1:6
4:29 gird up thy *l.* 9:1; *Job* 38:3; 40:7; *Jer.* 1:17
*Job* 31:20 if his *l.* ha. not blessed
40:16 lo, his strength is in his *l.*
*Ps.* 38:7 my *l.* filled wi. disease
66:11 laid affliction upon our *l.*
69:23 their *l.* continually shake
*Is.* 5:27 neither girdle of *l.* loosed
11:5 righteousn. girdle of his *l.*
20:2 loose sackcloth from thy *l.*
21:3 are my *l.* filled with pain
32:11 gird sackcl. upon your *l.*
*Jer.* 13:1 a linen girdle put on *l.*
30:6 ev. man with hands on *l.*
48:37 upon *l.* shall be sackcloth
*Ezek.* 1:27 fr. appearance of his *l.*
8:2 from his *l.* downward, fire
21:6 with the breaking of thy *l.*
23:15 with girdles upon their *l.*
44:18 have linen breeches on *l.*
47:4 the waters were to the *l.*
*Dan.* 5:6 joints of *l.* were loosed
10:5 *l.* were gird. with fine gold
*Amos* 8:10 bring sack. on your *l.*
*Nah.* 2:1 make thy *l.* strong
10 and much pain is in all *l.*
*Luke* 12:35 let your *l.* be girded
*Acts* 2:30 of his *l.* he wo. raise C.
*Eph.* 6:14 hav. your *l.* girt about
*Heb.* 7:5 came out of *l.* of Abrah.
10 he was yet in *l.* of his father
1 *Pet.* 1:13 wheref. gird *l.* of mind

LOIS. 2 *Tim.* 1:5

**LONG.**
*Ex.* 19:13 trumpet sound. *l.* 19
20:12 that thy days may be *l.*
*Num.* 9:19 the cloud tarried *l.*
*Deut.* 1:6 ye dwelt *l.* enough, 2:3
19:6 overtake him, way is *l.*
*Jos.* 6:5 they make a *l.* blast
1 *K.* 3:11 not asked *l.* 2 *Chr.* 1:11
2 *Chr.* 15:3 for a *l.* season Israel
*Ps.* 91:16 wi. *l.* life will I satisfy
95:10 forty years *l.* was I grieved
120:6 my soul hath *l.* dwelt
129:3 ploughers made *l.* furrows
143:3 that have been *l.* dead
*Prov.* 3:2 *l.* life sh. th. add to thee
7:19 good man is gone a *l.* jour.
23:30 they that tarry *l.* at wine
25:15 *l.* forbearing is a prince
*Ec.* 12:5 man go. to his *l.* home
*Is.* 65:22 elect *l.* enjoy the work
*Jer.* 29:28 this captivity is *l.*
*Lam.* 2:20 wo. eat child span *l.*?
*Ezek.* 17:3 great eagle *l.* winged
44:20 nor suffer locks to grow *l.*
*Dan.* 10:1 time appointed was *l.*
*Hos.* 13:13 not stay *l.* in the place
*Mat.* 11:21 repented *l.* ago
23:14 for pretence make *l.* pray. *Mark* 12:40; *Luke* 20:47
*Mark* 12:38 who go in *l.* clothing, *Luke* 20:46
16:5 clothed in a *l.* white garm.
*Luke* 18:7 tho' he bear *l.* with th.
23:8 to see him of a *l.* season
*Acts* 20:9 Paul was *l.* preaching
1 *Cor.* 11:14 if a man have *l.* hair
15 wom. have *l.* hair, it is glo.
*Eph.* 6:3 mayest live *l.* on earth
1 *Tim.* 3:15 if I tarry *l.* that thou
*Jam.* 5:7 husbandm. ha. *l.* pati.

*See* AGO.

**As LONG as.**
*Lev.* 26:34 *as l. as* it lieth des. 35
*Num.* 9:18 *as l. as* cloud abode
*Deut.* 31:13 *as l. as* you live
1 *Sam.* 1:28 lent to L. *as l. as* liv.
20:31 *as l. as* son of Jesse liveth
2 *Chr.* 26:5 *as l. as* he sought L.
36:21 *as l. as* she lay desolate
*Ps.* 72:5 *l. as* sun and m. endure
17 name continued *as l. as* sun
104:33 sing to L. *as l. as* I live
116:2 call up. him *as l. as* I live
*Ezek.* 42:11 *as l. as* they, as broad
*Mat.* 9:15 *as l. as* bridegroom is with them, *Mark* 2:19
*John* 9:5 *as l. as* I am in world
*Rom.* 7:1 over man *as l. as* he liv.
1 *Cor.* 7:39 bound *as l. as* husba.
*Gal.* 4:1 heir *as l. as* he is a child
1 *Pet.* 3:6 daught. *as l. as* do well
2 *Pet.* 1:13 *as l. as* I am in taber.

*See* CUBITS, DAY, HOUR.

**So LONG.**
*Jud.* 5:28 chariot *so l.* in coming
2 *Chr.* 6:31 fear thee *so l.* as live
*Est.* 5:13 *so l.* as I see Mordecai
*Job* 27:6 not repro. *so l.* as I live
*Ps.* 72:7 *so l.* as moon endureth
*Luke* 1:21 marvel. he tarried *so l.*

*Rom.* 7:2 her husb. *so l.* as liveth
*Heb.* 4:7 after *so l.* a time

**LONG time.**

*Gen.* 26:8 had been there a *l. t.*
*Num.* 20:15 dwell in Egypt *l. t.*
*Deut.* 20:19 besiege a city a *l. t.*
*Jos.* 11:18 Josh. made war a *l. t.*
23:1 a *l. t.* after Josh. wax. old
1 *Sam.* 7:2 wh. ark abode *t.* was *l.*
*Is.* 42:14 have *l. t.* holden peace
*Lam.* 5:20 forsake us so *l. time*
*Mat.* 25:19 after a *l. t.* the lord of those serv. com. *Luke* 20:9
*Luke* 8:27 man had devils a *l. t.*
20:9 went to far country for *l. t.*
*John* 5:6 a *l. time* in that case
14:9 have I been so *l. t.* wi. you
*Acts* 14:3 *l. time* abode with disciples, 28
2 *Pet.* 2:3 judgm. of *l. t.* lingereth

**LONG while.**

*Acts* 20:11 a *l. w.* till bre. of day

**LONG, Verb.**

*Job* 3:21 *l.* for death, but com. not
6:8 grant me thing that I *l.* for
*Rom.* 1:11 for I *l.* to see you
2 *Cor.* 9:14 prayer wh. *l.* after you
*Phil.* 1:8 greatly I *l.* after you all

**LONGED.**

2 *Sam.* 13:39 David *l.* to go forth
23:15 David *l.* and said, O that one, 1 *Chr.* 11:17
*Ps.* 119:40 I *l.* after thy precepts
131 I *l.* for thy commandments
174 I have *l.* for thy salvation
*Phil.* 2:26 for he *l.* after you all
4:1 dearly beloved and *l.* for

**LONGEDST.**

*Gen.* 31:30 *l.* after father's house

**LONGER.**

*Ex.* 9:28 and ye shall stay no *l.*
*Jud.* 2:14 could not any *l.* stand
2 *K.* 6:33 should I wait for L. *l.?*
*Job* 11:9 measure is *l.* than earth
*Jer.* 44:22 the L. could no *l.* bear
*Luke* 16:2 may. be no *l.* steward
*Acts* 18:20 desired him to tarry *l.*
25:24 he ought not to live any *l.*
*Rom.* 6:2 how live any *l.* therein
2 *Thes.* 3:1 we could no *l.* forb. 5
1 *Pet.* 4:2 *l.* live rest of his time.
*Rev.* 10:6 there sho. be time no *l*

**LONGETH.**

*Gen.* 34:8 my son *l.* for your dau.
*Deut.* 12:20 thy soul *l.* to eat flesh
*Ps.* 63:1 flesh *l.* for thee
84:2 my soul *l.* for courts of L.

**LONGING.**

*Deut.* 28:32 eyes sh. fail *l.* for th.
*Ps.* 107:9 he satisfieth the *l.* soul
119:20 soul break. for *l.* it hath

**LONG-SUFFERING.**

*Ex.* 34:6 Lo. G. *l.-s.* *Num.* 14:18; *Ps.* 86:15; 2 *Pet.* 3:9
*Jer.* 15:15 me not aw. in thy *l.-s.*
*Rom.* 2:4 despi. riches of his *l.-s.*
9:22 endured with much *l.-s.*
2 *Cor.* 6:6 by *l.-s.* by kindness
*Gal.* 5:22 fruit of Sp. is love, *l.-s.*
*Eph.* 4:2 with *l.-s.* forbearing
*Col.* 1:11 strengthened to all *l.-s.*
3:12 elect of G. meekness, *l.-s.*
1 *Tim.* 1:16 Ch. might show *l.-s.*
2 *Tim.* 3:10 kno. my faith, *l.-s.*
4:2 with all *l.-s.* and doctrine
1 *Pet.* 3:20 *l.-s.* of God waited
2 *Pet.* 3:15 *l.-s.* of L. is salvation

**LOOK, S.**

*Ps.* 18:27 bring down high *l.*
101:5 a high *l.* I will not suffer
*Prov.* 6:17 Lord hateth a proud *l.*
21:4 high *l.* and proud heart
*Is.* 2:11 lofty *l.* of man humbled
10:12 punish glory of his high *l.*
*Ezek.* 2:6 nor dismayed at *l.* 3:9
*Dan.* 7:20 *l.* more stout than fel.

**LOOK.**

*Gen.* 15:5 *l.* now towards heaven
19:17 for life, *l.* not behind thee
41:33 let Pharaoh *l.* out a man
42:1 why *l.* one upon another?
*Ex.* 25:20 faces *l.* one to another
*Deut.* 9:27 *l.* not to stubbornness
28:32 thine eyes shall *l.* and fail
1 *Sam.* 16:12 Dav. goodly to *l.* to
2 *K.* 14:8 *l.* one another in face
1 *Chr.* 12:17 G. of fat. *l.* thereon
*Job* 3:9 *l.* for light, have none
20:21 sh. no man *l.* for his goods
35:5 *l.* to the heavens and see
*Ps.* 5:3 prayer to thee and *l.* up
40:12 that I am not able to *l.* up
123:2 eyes of serv. *l.* to masters
*Prov.* 27:23 and *l.* well to herds
*Ec.* 12:3 that *l.* out at windows
*Cant.* 4:8 *l.* from top of Amana
*Is.* 5:30 if one *l.* unto the land
8:21 curse king, and *l.* upward
22 they shall *l.* unto the earth
17:7 shall a man *l.* to his maker
22:4 *l.* away fr. me, I will weep
31:1 they *l.* not to H. One of Is.
42:18 *l.* ye blind, th. ye may see
45:22 *l.* unto me, and be saved
51:1 *l.* to rock whence are hewn
56:11 all *l.* to their own way
69:11 *l.* for judgment, but none
66:2 but to this man will I *l.*
*Jer.* 13:16 while ye *l.* for light
39:12 take and *l.* well to him
40:4 and I will *l.* well to thee
46:5 mighty fled, and *l.* not back
47:3 fathers not *l.* back to chil.
*Hos.* 3:1 who *l.* to other gods
*Jon.* 2:4 *l.* toward holy temple
*Mic.* 7:7 therefore I *l.* to the Lord
*Nah.* 2:8 but none shall *l.* back
*Mat.* 11:3 *l.* for ano.? *Luke* 7:19, 20
*Mark* 8:25 and made him *l.* up
*Luke* 21:28 thi. begin, then *l.* up
*John* 7:52 *l.* for out of Galilee
*Acts* 6:3 *l.* ye out seven men
18:15 quest. of words, *l.* ye to it
2 *Cor.* 3:13 steadfastly *l.* to end
4:18 we *l.* at things wh. are seen
*Phil.* 3:20 we *l.* for the Saviour
*Heb.* 9:28 to them th. *l.* sh. he ap.
1 *Pet.* 1:12 angels desire to *l.* in.
2 *Pet.* 3:13 we *l.* for new heav.
14 seeing ye *l.* for such things
2 *John* 8 *l.* to yourselves
*Rev.* 5:3 no man able to *l.* there.
4 to read book nor *l.* thereon

**LOOK down.**

*Deut.* 26:15 *l. d.* from holy habi.
*Ps.* 80:14 *l. d.* and visit this vine
85:11 right. *l. d.* from heaven
*Is.* 63:15 *l. down* from heaven
*Lam.* 3:50 till L. *l. d.* and behold

**LOOK on, *or* upon.**

*Gen.* 12:11 a fair woman to *l. on*
24:16 Rebekah fair to *l. on*, 26:7
*Ex.* 3:6 Moses afraid to *l. on* G.
39:43 Moses did *l. upon* all work
*Lev.* 13:3 priest *l. u.* the plague
*Num.* 15:39 that ye may *l. u.* it
2 *Sam.* 9:8 *l. u.* such a dead dog
16:12 L. will *l. u.* my affliction
2 *Chr.* 24:22 L. *l. u.* and require
*Job* 6:28 be content, *l. upon* me
40:12 *l. u.* ev. one that is proud
*Ps.* 22:17 bones stare and *l. upon*
25:18 *l. upon* mine affliction
35:17 how long wilt thou *l. u.?*
84:9 *l. u.* face of thine anointed
119:132 *l. u.* me, and be merciful
*Prov.* 4:25 let th. eyes *l.* right *on*
23:31 *l.* not *on* wine wh. it is red
*Cant.* 1:6 *l.* not *on* me
6:13 that we may *l. upon* thee
*Is.* 33:20 *l. upon* Zion, the city
51:6 *l. upon* the earth beneath
*Mic.* 4:11 let our eye *l. u.* Zion
*Nah.* 3:7 that *l. u.* thee, shall flee
*Hab.* 1:13 purer eyes *l. u.* iniq.
2:15 mayest *l. u.* their nakedn.
*Zec.* 12:10 *l. u.* me they pierced
*Luke* 9:38 master, *l. u.* my son
*John* 4:35 lift eyes, *l. upon* fields
19:37 *l. u.* him they have pierced
*Acts* 3:4 P. and J. said, *l. u.* us, 12
*Phil.* 2:4 *l.* not *on* his own things
*Rev.* 4:3 was to *l. u.* like a jasper

**LOOKED.**

*Gen.* 6:12 God *l.* on the earth
19:26 his wife *l.* back fr. behind
26:8 *l.* out at a window
*Ex.* 2:12 *l.* this way and th. way
4:31 *l.* on their afflic. *Deut.* 26:7
14:24 the Lord *l.* on the host
33:8 the people *l.* after Moses
*Num.* 24:20 when he *l.* on Amal.
*Jud.* 5:28 *l.* out at window
6:14 the Lord *l.* upon him
1 *Sam.* 6:19 they had *l.* into ark
2 *Sam.* 6:16 Michal *l.* thro' win.
22:42 *l.* but th. was none to save
1 *K.* 18:43 serv. went up and *l.*
2 *K.* 2:24 El. turned back and *l.*
9:30 Jezebel *l.* out at a window
14:11 *l.* one another in the face
*Ps.* 14:2 L. *l.* if any did underst.
34:5 *l.* to him, and were light.
53:2 G. *l.* down on chil. of men
102:19 *l.* down fr. his sanctuary
109:25 when they *l.* they shaked their heads
*Cant.* 1:6 bec. son hath *l.* on me
*Is.* 5:2 *l.* it sho. br. forth grapes
7 *l.* for judg. behold oppress.
22:11 ye have not *l.* to maker
*Jer.* 8:15 we *l.* for peace, 14:19
*Ezek.* 10:11 whither the head *l.*
21:21 consulted, he *l.* in liver
*Hag.* 1:9 *l.* for much, came to lit.
*Mark* 6:41 he *l.* up to heaven
8:24 he *l.* and said, I see men
*Luke* 1:25 *l.* on me to take away
2:38 all that *l.* for redemption
10:32 a Lev. came and *l.* on him
22:61 Lord turn. *l.* upon Peter
*John* 13:22 disc. *l.* one on anoth.
*Acts* 1:10 *l.* steadfastly to heaven
28:6 after they *l.* a great while
*Heb.* 11:10 *l.* for city hath found.
1 *John* 1:1 which we have *l.* upon

**I LOOKED.**

*Job* 30:26 *I l.* for good, evil came
*Ps.* 69:20 *I l.* for some to take
142:4 *I l.* on my right hand
*Prov.* 7:6 *I l.* thro' my casement
24:32 *I l.* on it, received instr.
*Ec.* 2:11 *I l.* on works my hands
*Is.* 5:4 *I l.* it sho. br. forth grapes
63:5 *I l.* there was none to help
*Acts* 22:13 same hour *I l.* upon
*Rev.* 4:1 *I l.* and beh. a door was opened, 6:8; 14:1, 14; 15:5

**LOOKEST.**

*Job* 13:27 *l.* narrowly to paths
*Hab.* 1:13 *l.* on them deal treach.

**LOOKETH.**

*Num.* 21:8 when he *l.* on it
20 *l.* toward Jeshimon, 23:28
1 *Sam.* 16:7 *l.* on outw. appear.
*Job* 7:2 a hireling *l.* for reward
28:24 he *l.* to ends of the earth
33:27 he *l.* on men, and if any
*Ps.* 33:13 Lord *l.* from heaven
14 he *l.* on inhab. of the world
104:32 *l.* on earth, it trembleth
*Prov.* 31:27 *l.* well to household
*Cant.* 6:10 who is she th. *l.* forth
*Is.* 28:4 when he that *l.* upon it

*Mat.* 5:28 who *l.* on wom. to lust
24:50 lord shall come when he *l.*
not for him, *Luke* 12:46
*Jam.* 1:25 whoso *l.* into perf. law

**LOOKING.**

1 *Chr.* 15:29 Michal *l.* out window
*Is.* 38:14 mine eyes fail with *l.*
*Mat.* 14:19 *l.* up to hea. *Luke* 9:16
*Mark* 7:34 and *l.* up to heaven
15:40 there were also women *l.*
*Luke* 6:10 *l.* round about th. all
9:62 *l.* back, fit for kingd. of G.
21:26 hearts failing for *l.* after
*Acts* 6:15 *l.* steadfastly on him
23:21 *l.* for a promise from thee
*Tit.* 2:13 *l.* for that blessed hope
*Heb.* 10:27 fearful *l.* for of judgm.
12:2 *l.* unto Jesus the author
15 *l.* diligently, lest any fail
2 *Pet.* 3:12 *l.* for the coming of G.
*Jude* 21 *l.* for mercy of our L. J.

**LOOKING-GLASS, ES.**

*Ex.* 38:8 laver and foot of *l.-g.*
*Job* 37:18 spre. out sky as *l.-g.*

**LOOPS.**

*Ex.* 26:4 shalt make *l.* of blue, 5
36:11 made *l.* of blue on curtain

**LOOSE.**

*Gen.* 49:21 Naph. is a hind let *l.*
*Lev.* 14:7 let the living bird *l.*
*Job* 6:9 he would let *l.* his hand
30:11 they have let *l.* the bridle
*Dan.* 3:25 lo, I see four men *l.*

**LOOSE, Verb.**

*Jos.* 5:15 *l.* thy shoe fr. off foot
*Job* 38:31 canst thou *l.* the bands
*Ps.* 102:20 *l.* th. appoin. to death
*Is.* 20:2 *l.* sackcloth fr. thy loins
45:1 I will *l.* the loins of kings
52:2 O. J. *l.* thyself from bands
58:6 *l.* the bands of wickedness
*Jer.* 40:4 behold, I *l.* thee this day
*Mat.* 16:19 ye *l.* on earth, 18:18
*Mat.* 21:2 *l.* and bring them to
me, *Mark* 11:2, 4; *Luke* 19:30
*Luke* 19:31 why do ye *l.* him? 33
*John* 11:44 *l.* him and let him go
*Acts* 13:25 I am not worthy to *l.*
24:26 money given, he might *l.*
*Rev.* 5:2 who is worthy to *l.* seals
5 prevailed to *l.* the 7 seals
9:14 *l.* four angels wh. are bou.

**LOOSED.**

*Deut.* 25:10 that hath his shoe *l.*
*Job* 30:11 bec. he hath *l.* my cord
39:5 who ha. *l.* bands of w. ass?
*Ps.* 105:20 king sent and *l.* him
116:16 thou hast *l.* my bands
*Ec.* 12:6 or ever silver cord be *l.*
*Is.* 5:27 nor girdle of loins be *l.*
51:14 hasten. that he may be *l.*
*Dan.* 5:6 joints of his lo. were *l.*
*Mat.* 16:19 be *l.* in heaven, 18:18
18:27 compassion, and *l.* him
*Mark* 7:35 string of his tongue
was *l.* *Luke* 1:64
*Luke* 13:12 woman art *l.* fr. infir.
16 ought not daughter to be *l.*
*Acts* 2:24 having *l.* pains of death
13:13 when Paul and company *l.*
16:26 every one's bands were *l.*
22:30 he *l.* him from his bands
27:21 and have not *l.* from Crete
*Rom.* 7:2 husb. be dead, she is *l.*
1 *Cor.* 7:27 art thou *l.* fr. wife?
*Rev.* 9:15 the four angels were *l.*
20:3 after that he must be *l.* 7

**LOOSETH.**

*Job* 12:18 he *l.* the bond of kings
*Ps.* 146:7 Lord *l.* the prisoners

**LOOSING.**

*Mark* 11:5 what do you *l.* colt?
*Luke* 19:33 they were *l.* the colt
*Acts* 16:11 therefore *l.* from Tro.

**LOP.**

*Is.* 10:33 the L. sh. *l.* the bough

**LORD, 'S.**

*Gen.* 18:14 any th. too har. for L.?
28:21 then sh. the L. be my G.
*Ex.* 5:2 who is L. I sho. obey?
9:29 know that the earth is the
L.'s, *Ps.* 24:1; 1 *Cor.* 10:26
13:12 the males shall be the L.'s
32:26 who is on the L.'s side
*Lev.* 16:8 Aaron shall cast one lot
for the L. 25:4; 27:2
*Num.* 14:14 that th. L. art seen
18:6 given as a gift for the L.
23:26 all the L. speak. must I do
*Deut.* 4:35 know that the L. he
is God, 39; 1 *K.* 18:39
5:5 I stood bet. the L. and you
10:17 and L. of lords a great G.
29:2 have seen all that the L. did
32:6 do ye thus requite the L.
33:29 O people, saved by the L.
*Jos.* 2:12 swear unto me by the
L. 1 *Sam.* 24:21
*Jud.* 1:19 the L. was with Judah
2:10 generat. wh. knew not L.
6:13 if L. with us, why is this?
11:31 shall surely be L.'s
*Ruth* 1:17 L. do so to me, and
more, 1 *Sam.* 20:13
1 *Sam.* 2:2 th. is none holy as L.
3:18 L. do what seemeth good,
2 *Sam.* 10:12; 1 *Chr.* 19:13;
*John* 21:7
19 the L. was with him, 18:12,
14; 2 *K.* 18:7; 1 *Chr.* 9:20
20:23 L. betw. thee and me, 42
2 *Sam.* 7:24 L. art become their
God, 1 *Chr.* 17:22
1 *K.* 18:21 if L. be G. follow him
1 *Chr.* 16:25 for great is the L.
*Ps.* 48:1; 145:3
17:26 and now, L. thou art God
21:24 not take wh. is th. for L.
2 *Chr.* 19:6 ju. not for man, but L.
11 the L. sh. be with the good
33:13 Manasseh knew L. was G.
*Neh.* 9:6 thou art L. alo. *Is.* 37:20
*Ps.* 4:3 L. hath set apart godly
33:12 nation, whose G. is the L.
45:11 thy L. worship thou him
66:18 regard iniq. L. not hear
92:8 L. art most high, 97:9
100:3 know ye that L. he is G.
109:21 for me, O G. the L. 140:7
116:5 gracious is L. and righte.
118:23 this is the L.'s doing
27 God is L. wh. hath showed
124:1 if it had not been the L. 2
130:3 if thou, L. sh. mark iniq.
132:5 find out a place for the L.
*Prov.* 24:18 lest L. see it, disple.
30:9 and say, Who is the L.?
*Is.* 42:24 did not L. be ag. whom
52:12 the L. will go before you
*Jer.* 5:10 for they are not the L.'s
23:6 L. our righteousness, 33:16
31:34 saying, Know L. *Heb.* 8:11
*Ezek.* 35:10 whereas L. was there
*Dan.* 2:47 God is L. of kings
9:17 face to shine, for L.'s sake
*Hos.* 12:14 reproach sh. L. return
*Joel* 2:21 L. will do great things
*Amos* 3:6 evil in city L. not done
*Ob.* 21 kingdom shall be L.'s
*Mic.* 2:13 the L. on head of them
3:11 lean on L. say. Is not L.
6:8 what doth L. req. of thee?
*Zec.* 1:5 swear by L. and Malch.
*Zec.* 14:3 then shall L. go forth
9 in that day sh. th. be one L.
*Mat.* 7:21 not ev. one that saith,
L. L. shall enter the kingd.
22; *Luke* 13:25
15:27 truth L. 25:11 L. L. open
21:3 L. hath need, *Mark* 11:3;
*Luke* 19:31, 34
22:43 how doth D. call him L.?
45; *Mark* 12:37; *Luke* 20:44
24:42 know not wh. hour L. co.
46 whom his L. shall find so
doing, *Luke* 12:43, 46
50 L. of that servant sh. come
25:21 enter into joy of thy L.
37 L. wh. saw we th. hun.? 44
26:22 began to say, L. is it I?
28:6 the place where the L. lay
*Mark* 2:28 L. of Sab. *Luke* 6:5
5:19 great things L. hath done
10:51 L. that I may rece. sight,
*Mat.* 20:33
16:20 L. working with them
*Luke* 1:17 ready a peo. for the L.
6:46 call me L. L. and do not
14:21 show. his L. these things
17:5 said unto L. Incr. our faith
37 wh. L.? 23:42 L. rem. me
24:34 saying, the L. is risen
*John* 6:68 L. to whom sh. we go
9:36 who is he, L. that I might
13:13 ye call me Master and L.
25 L. who is it? 20:25 seen L.
20:2 taken L. out of sepulchre
21:12 knowing it was L.
*Acts* 2:36 cruci. both L. and Ch.
9:5 Who art thou, L. 26:15
10:4 and said, What is it, L.?
14 Peter said, Not so, L. 11:8
36 Jesus Christ, he is L. of all
22:10 What shall I do, L.?
*Rom.* 10:12 the same L. over all
14:9 might be L. of dead and liv.
1 *Cor.* 2:8 not cruci. L. of glory
3:5 as L. gave to every man
4:4 he that judgeth me is the L.
19 if the L. will, *Jam.* 4:15
6:13 for L. 7:10 not I, but L.
15:47 sec. man is L. fr. heaven
2 *Cor.* 5:8 present with the L.
11:17 I speak it not after the L.
*Eph.* 4:5 one L. one faith
5:29 even as the L. the church
*Phil.* 2:11 confess Jesus C. is L.
4:5 be known, L. is at hand
1 *Thes.* 4:17 we ever be with L.
1 *Tim.* 6:15 K. of kings, L. of l.
2 *Tim.* 3:11 out of all L. deliv.
*Heb.* 2:3 began to be spok. by L.
8:11 know L. for all shall know
*Jam.* 5:15 L. shall raise sick up
2 *Pet.* 3:8 day is with L. as thou.
*Jude* 9 M. said, L. rebuke thee
*Rev.* 11:15 bec. kingdoms of L.
17:14 for he is L. of lords, 19:16

**Against the LORD.**

1 *Sam.* 2:25 if a man sin *a. t.* L.
12:23 sin *a.* L. in ceas. to pray
*Prov.* 21:30 nor counsel *a. t.* L.
*Is.* 3:8 their doings are *a. the* L.
32:6 utter error *against the* L.
*Jer.* 48:26 magni. himself *a.* L. 42
*Dan.* 5:23 lift. up thyself *a. t.* L.
*Hos.* 5:7 dealt treacher. *ag.* L.
*Nah.* 1:9 what do ye imag. *a.* L.?

*See* LIVETH, ANOINTED, APPEARED.

**Before the LORD.**

*Gen.* 18:22 Abra. stood *b. the* L.
*Ex.* 16:9 say, Come near *b. t.* L.
33 lay up *b. the* L. 1 *Sam.* 10:25
23:17 three times in ye. ap. *b.* L.
34:24; *Deut.* 16:16; 1 *Sam.* 1:21
27:21 order lamps *b. t.* L. 40:25
28:12 A. bear their names *b.* L.
*Lev.* 4:6 sprinkle seven times *be.*
*the* L. 17; 14:16, 27
9:24 came a fire out fr. *b. the* L.
10:2 they died *b.* L. *Num.* 3:4
*Num.* 5:16 set her *b.* L. 18:30
10:9 he remem. *b.* L. your God
25:4 hang them up *before the* L.
*Num.* 27:5 Moses brought cause
*b. the* L.

*Deut.* 9:18 I fell down *b. the* L.
12:18 must eat them *b. the* L.
18:7 his breth. stand there *b.* L.
19:17 controv. sh. stand *b.* L.
*Jud.* 18:6 *b. the* L. is your way
1 *Sam.* 21:7 day detained *b.* L.
2 *Sam.* 21:9 hang. th. in hill *b.* L.
2 *K.* 19:14 Hezekiah spread it *b. the* L. *Is.* 37:14
*Ps.* 96:13 *b.* L. com. to jud. 98:8
109:15 be *b. the* L. continually
116:9 walk *b.* L. in land of liv.
*Prov.* 15:11 hell and destr. *b.* L.
*Is.* 23:18 them that dwell *b.* L.
*Mic.* 6:6 where. sh. I come *b.* L.?
*Zec.* 2:13 be sil. all flesh *b. t.* L.
*Mal.* 3:14 walked mournf. *b.* L.
2 *Tim.* 2:14 charg. them *b. t.* L.
2 *Pet.* 2:11 no railing accus. *b.* L.
*See* BLESS, BLESSED, CALLED, CAST *out*, CHOSEN, CHOOSE, COMMANDED, FEAR, FEARED, REJOICE.

**From the LORD.**

*Gen.* 4:1 have gotten man *f.* L.
19:24 fire *f. t.* L. out of heaven
24:50 the thing proceed. *f. t.* L.
*Num.* 11:31 we. forth wind *f.* L
16:35 th. came out a fire *f. t.* L.
46 wrath gone out *from the* L.
1 *Sam.* 16:14 ev. sp. *f. t.* L. 19:9
26:12 sleep *f. t.* L. fallen on th.
1 *K.* 2:15 it was his *from the* L.
33 peace for ever *from the* L.
*Ps.* 24:5 sh. rec. blessing *f. t.* L.
109:20 reward mine adver. *f.* L.
121:2 my help cometh *f. the* L.
*Prov.* 16:1 ans. of tongue is *f.* L.
19:14 a prudent wife is *f. t.* L.
29:26 man's judgm. cometh *f.* L.
*Is.* 29:15 to hide counsel *f. t.* L.
40:27 sayest, My way hid *f.* L.
*Jer.* 7:1 word that came to Jere. *from the* L. 11:1; 18:1; 21:1; 26:1; 27:1; 30:1; 32:1; 34:1, 8, 12; 35:1; 36:1; 40:1
17:5 cursed wh. heart dep. *f.* L.
37:17 is there any word *f. t.* L.?
49:14 I have heard a rumor *f.* L.
*Lam.* 2:9 pro. find no vision *f.* L.
3:18 strength is perished *f.* L.
*Ezek.* 11:15 get you far *f. the* L.
33:30 hear what word com. *f.* L.
*Hos.* 1:2 whored. departing *f.* L.
*Ob.* 1 have heard a rumor *f. t.* L.
*Mic.* 1:12 evil came down *f. t.* L.
5:7 remnant sh. be as dew *f.* L.
*Zec.* 14:13 tumult *f.* L. am. them
*Luke* 1:45 things told her *f. t.* L.
2 *Cor.* 5:6 we are absent *f. t.* L.
*See* GIVE, GIVEN.

**LORD God.**

*Gen.* 24:27 blessed be L. G. of A.
*Ex.* 34:6 L. G. merciful and gra.
*Jos.* 22:22 the L. G. of gods
24:2 the L. G. of Isr. *Jud.* 4:6; 1 *Sam.* 2:30; 1 *K.* 1:30; 1 *Chr.* 23:25; 24:19
1 *Sam.* 6:20 to stand before L. G.
2 *Sam.* 7:18 who am I, O L. G.
2 *K.* 2:14 wh. is L. G. of Elijah?
*Ezek.* 36:23 I am the L. sa. L. G.
39:5 I have spoken it, saith the L. G. 23:34; 26:14; 28:10
*Dan.* 9:3 I set my face unto L. G.
*Hos.* 12:5 L. G. is his memorial
*Amos* 3:7 L. G. will do nothing
8 the L. G. hath spoken
*Hab.* 3:19 L. G. is my strength
1 *Pet.* 3:15 sanctify L. G. in hea.
*Rev.* 4:8 holy, holy, L. God Almighty, 11:17; 16:7
18:8 strong is L. G. who judge.
19:6 L. G. omnipotent reigneth
21:22 the L. G. and the Lamb
22:5 the L. G. giveth them light
*See* AH, FATHERS.

**LORD his God.**

*Num.* 23:21 L. *h. G.* is with him
1 *Sam.* 30:6 David encouraged himself in the L. *his God*
1 *K.* 5:3 hou. to name of L. *h. G.*
11:4 not perfect with L. *h. God* 15:3
15:4 did L. *h. G.* give him lamp
2 *K.* 16:2 right in sig. of L. *h.* G.
2 *Chr.* 1:1 L. *h. G.* was with him
14:11 Asa cried unto the L. *h. G.*
31:20 wrou. right before L. *h. G*
*Ezr.* 7:6 acco. to hand of L. *h. G*
*Mic.* 5:4 in the name of L. *h. G.*

**LORD my God.**

1 *K.* 5:4 L. *my G.* given me rest
1 *K.* 5:5 build house unto name of L. *my G.* 1 *Chr.* 22:7; 2 *Chr.* 2:4
*Ezr.* 7:28 hand of L. *my God*
9:5 I spr. out hands to L. *my G.*
*Jer.* 31:18 thou art the L. *my G.*
*Dan.* 9:4 prayed unto L. *m. G.* 20

**LORD our God.**

*Deut.* 4:7 L. *o. G.* is in all things
5:24 L. *o. G.* showed us glory
6:4 O Israel, the L. *our God* is one Lord, *Mark* 12:29
*Jos.* 22:19 altar of L. *o. G.* 29.
24:17 L. *o. G.* bro. us out of E.
1 *Sam.* 7:8 to cry to L. *our God.*
*Ps.* 20:7 remem. name of L. *o. G.*
90:17 beauty of L. *o. G.* be on us
99:5 exalt ye the L. *our God*, 9
8 O L. *our God* thou forg. th
9 for the L. *our God* is holy
105:7 for he is the L. *our God*
122:9 bec. of house of L. *o. G.*
123:2 eyes wait on L. *our God*
*Jer.* 3:22 thou art the L. *our G*
*Dan.* 9:9 to L. *our G.* be. merc.
*Mic.* 4:5 in name of L. *our God*
*Acts* 2:39 as many as L. *o. G.* call
*Rev.* 19:1 hon. and po. to L. *o. G.*

**LORD their God.**

2 *K.* 17:9 not right ag. L. *t. God*
19 kept not com. of L. *t. G*
*Luke* 1:16 shall turn to L. *t. G.*

**LORD thy God.**

*Ex.* 20:2 the L. *t. G. Ps.* 81:10
*Deut.* 4:24 L. *t. G.* is consum. fire
31 L. *t. G.* is a merciful God
7:9 the L. *thy God*, he is God
8:5 so L. *thy G.* chasteneth thee
12:31 not do so to L. *thy God*
28:58 fearful name, the L. *t. G.*
*Jos.* 1:9 L. *t. G.* is with thee
2 *Sam.* 14:17 L. *t. G.* be wi. thee
24:23 the L. *t. G.* accept thee
*Is.* 42:3 I am the L. *thy God*
*Jer.* 42:2 pray for us to L. *t. God*
*Mic.* 7:10 said, Where L. *t. G.*?
*Mat.* 4:7 thou shalt not tempt the L. *thy God*, *Luke* 4:12

**LORD your God.**

*Lev.* 19:2 I the L. *y. G.* am holy
*Deut.* 10:17 L. *y. G.* is God of go.
*Acts* 3:22 pro. L. *y. G.* raise, 7:37

**LORD of hosts.**

2 *Sam.* 6:2 by name of L. *of h.*
7:26 the L. *of h.* is G. over Isr.
*Ps.* 24:10 L. *of h.* king of glory
46:7. L. *of hosts* is with us, 11
48:8 seen in the city of L. *of h.*
*Is.* 6:3 holy, holy, is L. *of h.*
8:13 sanctify the L. *of hosts*
47:4 L. *of h.* his name, 48:2; 51:15; 54:5; *Jer.* 10:16; 31:35; 32:18; 50:34; 51:19
*Jer.* 46:18 name is L. *of h.* 48:15
*Hab.* 2:13 is it not of L. *of hosts*
*Zec.* 2:9 L. *of h.* sent 11; 4:9
*See Saith the* LORD.

**I the LORD.**

*Lev.* 19:2 for *I the* L. your God, am holy, 20:26; 21:8
*Num.* 14:35 *I the* L. have said it, I will do it, *Ezek.* 21:17
*Is.* 27:3 *I the* L. do keep it
45:7 *I the* L. do all these things
8 *I the* L. have created it
19 *I the* L. speak righteousness
60:22 *I the* L. will hasten it
*Jer.* 17:10 *I the* L. search hearts
*Ezek.* 14:9 *I t.* L. have dec. prop.
34:24 *I the* L. will be their God

**I am the LORD.**

*Gen.* 15:7 *I am the* L. th. brong.
*Ex.* 6:2 *I am t.* L. 6, 8, 29; 12:12; *Lev.* 18:5, 6, 21; *Num.* 3:13; *Is.* 43:11, 15
20:2 *I am t.* L. thy G. who bro.
*Lev.* 22:32 *I am the* L. wh. hal.
*Is.* 42:8 *I am t.* L. that is name
44:5 one shall say, *I am the* L.'s
*Jer.* 9:24 knoweth that *I a. t.* L.
32:27 *I am t.* L. the G. of all fl.
*Mal.* 3:6 *I am t.* L. I change not
*See* KNOW.

LORD *Jesus. See* JESUS.

**In the LORD.**

*Gen.* 15:6 he believed *in the* L.
1 *Sam.* 2:1 heart rejoiceth *in t.* L.
*Ps.* 4:5 put your trust *in the* L.
11:1 *in the* L. put I my trust, 26:1; 31:6; 73:28
31:24 all ye that hope *in the* L.
32:11 be glad *in the* L. and rej.
34:2 my soul shall boast *in t.* L.
35:9 my soul be joy. *in the* L.
*Ps.* 37:4 delight thyself *in the* L. *Is.* 58:14
7 rest *in the* L. and wait
56:10 *in t.* L. will I praise his
64:10 the righteous shall be gl. *in the* L. 104:34
*Prov.* 3:5 trust *in the* L. wi. hea.
*Is.* 26:4 *in t.* L. Jehovah is ever.
45:24 *in the* L. have I righteous.
25 *in the* L. seed of Is. justifi.
*Zep.* 3:2 trusted not *in the* L.
*Acts* 9:42 many believed *in t.* L.
14:3 speaking boldly *in the* L.
*Rom.* 16:2 ye receive her *in t.* L.
8 Amplias, my belov. *in t.* L.
12 who labored much *in t.* L.
13 Rufus chosen *in the* L.
22 Tertius, salute you *in t.* L.
1 *Cor.* 1:31 glorieth, let him glo. *in the* L. 2 *Cor.* 10:17
4:17 faith. *in* L. 7:22 call. *in* L.
7:39 be married, only *in the* L.
9:1 my work *in the* L.?
2 apostleship are ye *in t.* L.
11:11 nor woman wi. man *in* L.
15:58 labor not in vain *in t.* L.
*Eph.* 2:21 a holy temple *in t.* L.
4:17 therefore, testify *in the* L.
5:8 now are ye light *in the* L.
6:1 obey your parents *in the* L.
10 brethren, be strong *in t.* L.
21 a faithful minister *in the* L.
*Phil.* 1:14 brethren *in the* L.
2:29 receive him theref. *in t.* L.
4:1 sta. fast *in t.* L. 1 *Thes.* 3:8
2 be of the same mind *in t.* L.
10 I rejoiced *in the* L. greatly
*Col.* 3:18 submit to husb. *in t.* L.
4:7 Tychicus fellow-ser. *in t.* L.
17 minist. th. received *in t.* L.
1 *Thes.* 5:12 th. over you *in t.* L.
2 *Thes.* 3:4 have confidence *in* L.
*Phile.* 16 the flesh and *in t.* L.
20 let me have joy of thee *in t.* L. refr. my bowels *in t.* L.
*Rev.* 14:13 bless. are dead *in t.* L.
*See* REJOICE, TRUST.

**LORD is.**

Gen. 28:16 the L. is in this place
Ex. 9:27 the L. is righteous, I wicked, 2 Chr. 12:6
15:2 the L. is my strength
3 L. is man of war, L. is name
Num. 14:9 the L. is with us
18 the L. is long-suffering, of great, Nah. 1:3
42 for the L. is not among you
1 K. 8:60 know that the L. is G.
2 Chr. 13:10 the L. is our God
15:2 L. is wi. you wh. ye for h.
Ps. 10:16 the L. is king for ever
34:8 O taste and see L. is good
89:18 L. is our defence and king
92:15 show that L. is upright
93:1 L. is clothed with strength
94:22 L. is my defence and rock
95:3 the L. is a great G. 96:4; 99:2; 135:5
100:5 L. is g. 135:3; 145:9; Jer. 33:11; Lam. 3:25; Nah. 1:7
103:8 L. is merciful and gracious, 111:4; 145:8
113:4 L. is high ab. all nations
118:6 the L. is on my side
121:5 L. is keeper, L. is shade
125:2 the L. is round about
129:4 L. is righteous, 145:17; Lam. 1:18; Dan. 9:14
145:18 L. is nigh to all that call
Prov. 15:29 L. is far from wicked
Is. 30:18 L. is God of judgment
Jer. 10:10 the L. is the true God
17:7 trust in L. who. hope L. is
20:11 L. is with me as terri. one
Lam. 3:24 the L. is my portion
Ezek. 48:35 name of city, L. is t.
Amos 5:8 the L. is his name, 9:6
Zep. 3:5 just L. is in midst, 15
Luke 24:34 the L. is risen indeed
2 Cor. 3:17 the L. is that Spirit
Phil. 4:5 the L. is at hand
Heb. 13:6 the L. is my helper
1 Pet. 2:3 tasted the L. is graci.

See MADE.

**My LORD.**

Gen. 19:18 said, not so, my L.
Jud. 6:13 my L. if L. be wi. us
15 O my L. shall I save Israel
Ps. 16:2 said, Thou art my L.
35:23 stir up thyself, my God and my L. John 20:28
110:1 Lord said to my L. Mat. 22:44; Mark 12:36; Luke 20:42; Acts 2:34
Is. 21:8 my L. I stand on tower
Dan. 10:17 serv. of my L. talk?
Zec. 1:9 O my L. wh. are these? 4:4; 6:4; 4:5 no, my L. 13
Mat. 24:48 my L. delayeth his coming, Luke 12:45
Luke 1:43 mother of my L. come
John 20:13 taken away my L.
Phil. 3:8 knowledge of Ch. Jes. my L.

**Name of the LORD.**

Gen. 12:8 A. called on n. of t. L.
26:25 Isaac called on n. of t. L.
Ex. 20:7 shalt not take name of the L. in vain, Deut. 5:11
33:19 proclaim n. of the L.
34:5 L. proclaimed n. of the L.
Lev. 24:11 blasphe. n. of the L. 16
Deut. 18:5 minister in n. of L. 7
22 prophet speak. in n. of t. L.
28:10 called by the n. of the L.
32:3 I will publish n. of the L.
Jos. 9:9 serv. come of n. of t. L.
1 Sam. 17:45 come in n. of t. L.
20:42 sw. both of us in n. of L.
2 Sam. 6:2 called by n. of the L.
1 K. 22:16 that which is true in name of the L. 2 Chr. 18:15
Job 1:21 blessed be the name of the L. Ps. 113:2
Ps. 20:7 will remember n. of t. L.
102:15 heathen fear n. of the L.
21 to declare n of L. in Zion
113:1 praise the name of t. L 135:1; 148:5, 13; Joel 2:26
116:4 then called I on n. of L.
118:26 cometh in n. of the L.
122:4 give thanks to n. of t. L.
124:8 our help is in n. of t. L.
129:8 we bless you in n. of t. L.
Prov. 18:10 n. of L. strong tower
Is. 18:7 to place of n. of the L.
24:15 glorify the n. of the L.
30:27 n. of t. L. cometh fr. far
56:6 and to love the n. of the L.
59:19 so sh. they fear n. of t. L.
Jer. 3:17 nations gath. to n. of L.
Mic. 4:5 walk in name of the L.
5:4 in majesty of n. of the L.
Zep. 3:12 sh. trust in n. of t. L.
Mat. 21:9 cometh in n. of the L. 23:39; Mark 11:9, 10; Luke 13:35; 19:38; John 12:13
Acts 9:29 spake boldly in n. of L
10:48 baptized in n. of the L.
19:13 call over them n. of t. L.
21:13 ready to die for n. of t. L.

**O LORD.**

Ex. 15:11 who like thee, O L.?
2 Sam. 23:17 far from thee, O L.
1 Chr. 17:20 O L. none like thee
Ps. 6:3 but thou, O L. how long
8:1 O L. our Lord, how excel.
22:19 not far fr. me O L. 35:22
115:1 not unto us, O L.
Rev. 6:10 how long, O L. holy

**Of the LORD.**

2 K. 6:33 beh. this evil is of L.
Prov. 20:24 man's goings of t. L.
21:31 battle, safety is of t. L.
Acts 21:14 will of t. L. be done
1 Cor. 11:23 received of the L.
Jam. 5:11 seen the end of the L.

See ANGER, ANGEL, COMMANDMENT, CONGREGATION, COUNSEL, DAY, EYES, FACE, FEAR, FEAST, GLORY, HAND, HOUSE, KNOWLEDGE, LAW, OFFERINGS, PRAISE.

**Saith the LORD.**

Num. 24:13 what the L. s.
1 K. 22:14 L. s. that will I speak

See LIVE, SAVED.

**LORD, with seek.**

1 Chr. 16:10 heart rejoice that s. L. Ps. 105:3, 4
11 seek the L. and his strength
22:19 set your heart to seek the L. 2 Chr. 11:16
2 Chr. 12:14 pr. not heart to s. L.
14:4 commanded Jud. to s. L.
15:13 whoso. would not seek L.
20:3 Jehosh. set himself to s. L.
4 cities of J. they came to s. L.
Ezr. 6:21 were come to seek L.
Ps. 22:26 praise L. that s. him
34:10 that s. L. shall not want
Prov. 28:5 th. s. L. understand
Is. 9:13 neither do they seek the L. 31:1; Hos. 7:10
51:1 ye that seek the L.
55:6 s. L. wh. he may be found
Jer. 50:4 go and s. the L. God
Hos. 3:5 return and seek the L.
5:6 go with herds to s. the L.
10:12 it is time to seek the L.
Amos 5:6 s. L. and ye shall live
Zep. 2:3 s. the L. meek of earth
Zec. 8:21 let us go and s. the L.
22 many people come and s. L.
Mal. 3:1 L. wh. ye s. sud. come
Acts 15:17 residue might s. the L.
17:27 they should s the L.

**LORD, with sent.**

Ex. 7:16 L. of Hebrews s. me
Jer. 28:9 L. hath truly sent him
15 Hananiah, L. hath not s.
Acts 9:17 L. Jesus s. me to thee
12:11 know L. hath sent angel

**Serve the LORD.**

Ex. 10:7 that they may s. t. L.
22:25 ye shall s. t. L. your God
Deut. 10:12 to s. t. L. thy God
Jos. 24:14 fear and s. ye the L.
15 seem evil un. you to s. t. L.
18 therefore will we s. L. 21, 24
1 Sam. 12:20 s. L. with your hea.
2 Sam. 15:8 then I will s. L.
2 Chr. 30:8 s. L. your God, 35:3
33:16 com. Judah to s. L. 34:33
Ps. 2:11 s. L. wi. fear, rejoice
100:2 serve t. L. with gladness
102:22 kingdoms gather. to s. L.
Col. 3:24 ye serve t. L. Christ

**Servant, s of the LORD.**

Deut. 34:5 Moses, the s. of t. L.
Jos. 1:1 death of Moses s. of L.
13 Moses the servant of the L. commanded, 8:31, 33; 11:12; 22:2, 5; 2 K. 18:12
15 Moses, s. of the L. gave you, 12:6; 13:8; 18:7; 22:4
24:29 Joshua, son of Nun, s. of the L. Jud. 2:8
Ps. 113:1 praise the L. praise, O ye servants of the L. 135:1
134:1 O ye servants of the L.
Is. 42:19 blind or deaf as L.'s s.
54:17 heritage of s. of the L.
2 Tim. 2:24 s. of the L. not strive

See SHOWED.

**Sight of the LORD.**

Gen. 38:7 Er wicked in s. of L.
Lev. 10:19 accepted in s. of L.
Deut. 6:18 good in s. of L. 12:28
12:25 do what is right in s. of the L. 21:9; 2 K. 12:2; 14:3; 15:3, 24; 18:3; 22:2; 2 Chr. 20:32; 24:2; 25:2; 26:4; 27:2; 29:2; 34:2
1 Sam. 12:17 wicked. ha. done in s. of L. 1 K. 21:25; 2 K. 21:6
2 K. 3:18 light thing in s. of L.
16:2 did not what was right in s. of the L. 2 Chr. 28:1
Ps. 116:15 precious in s. of t. L.
Mal. 2:17 good in s. of the L.
Luke 1:15 be great in s. of t. L.
2 Cor. 8:21 not only in s. of t. L.
Jam. 4:10 humble in s. of the L.

See EVIL, SMITE.

**Spirit of the LORD.**

Jud. 3:10 S. of the L. came on O.
6:34 S. of the L. came on Gid.
11:29 S. of the L. came on Jep.
13:25 S. of the L. began to move Samson, 14:6, 19; 15:14
1 Sam. 10:6 S. of the L. ca. on S.
16:13 S. of the L. came on Dav.
14 S. of the L. depart. from S.
2 Sam. 23:2 S. of the L. spake
1 K. 18:12 S. of L. sh. carry thee
22:24 which way went S. of the L. 2 Chr. 18:23
2 K. 2:16 lest S. of L. taken him
2 Chr. 20:14 on Ja. came S. of L.
Is. 11:2 S. of L. sh. rest upon him
40:7 bec. S. of L. bloweth on it
13 hath directed S. of the L.
59:19 S. of L. sh. lift up stand.
61:1 S. of L. up. me, Luke 4:18
63:14 S. of L. caused him rest
Ezek. 11:5 S. of L. fell upon me
37:1 carried me in S. of the L.
Mic. 2:7 is the S. of L. straitened
3:8 full of power by S. of t. L.
Acts 5:9 to tempt S. of the L.
8:39 S. of L. caught away Philip
2 Cor. 3:17 wh. S. of t. L. liberty
18 even as by S. of the L.

**LORD, *with* spoken.**
Ex. 19:8 all L. hath s. will we do
34:32 in command. all L. had s.
Num. 10:29 the L. hath s. good
12:2 hath L. indeed s. by Moses
Jos. 21:45 failed not L. had s.
1 Sam. 25:30 L. done good ha. s.
2 Sam. 3:18 do it, the L. hath s.
7:29 continue, thou, L. ha. s. it
1 K. 13:3 sign which L. hath s.
Ps. 50:1 L. hath s. and called
Jer. 23:35 what hath the L. s. 37
48:8 destroyed, as the L. hath s.
Ezek. 22:28 when L. hath not s.
26:5 for I have s. it, saith the L. 28:10; 39:5
Amos 3:8 L. God hath spoken
Mat. 1:22 wh. was s. of L. 2:15
Mark 16:19 after L. had spoken
Acts 9:27 seen L. and he had s.
Heb. 2:3 began to be s. by the L.

**Temple of the LORD.**
2 Chr. 26:16 U. went in. t. of L.
Jer. 7:4 t. of the L. are these
Ezek. 8:16 at door of t. of L. 25 men, with backs to. t. of L.
Hag. 2:15 bef. sto. laid in t. of L.
Zec. 6:12 build t. of L. 13:15
14 for memorial in t. of the L.
Luke 1:9 Z. went into t. of t. L.

**Voice of the LORD.**
Ps. 29:3 v. of L. is upon waters
106:25 heark. not to v. of t. L.
Is. 6:8 I heard v. of the L.
Acts 7:31 v. of the L. came to M.

**Way of the LORD.**
Gen. 18:19 house. keep w. of L.
Jud. 2:22 will keep way of t. L.
Ps. 119:1 blessed walk w. of L.
Prov. 10:29 way of L. is streng.
Is. 40:3 prepare ye w. of the L. Mat. 3:4; Mark 1:3; Lu. 3:4
Jer. 5:4 know not w. of the L.
John 1:23 make stra. w. of the L.
Acts 18:25 Apollos in. in w. of L.

**Ways of the LORD.**
2 Sam. 22:22 for I have kept the w. of the L. Ps. 18:21
2 Chr. 17:6 lifted up in w. of L.
Ps. 138:5 sing in the w. of L.
Hos. 14:9 the w. of L. are right
Acts 13:10 cease perv. w. of t. L.

**Word of the LORD.**
Num. 22:18 can. go bey. w. of L.
Deut. 5:5 show you w. of the L.
2 Sam. 22:31 w. tried, Ps. 18:30
1 K. 13:1 came man by w. of L.
2 cried ag. altar in word of L.
17:24 w. of L. in my mouth
2 K. 10:10 earth noth. of w. of L.
20:19 good is w. of L. Is. 39:8
Ps. 33:4 the word of L. is right
6 by w. of L. heavens made
105:19 w. of L. tried him
Is. 2:3 the word of the L. from Jerusalem, Mic. 4:2
Jer. 2:31 see ye the w. of the L.
Amos 8:12 to seek w. of L.
Zep. 2:5 w. of L. against you
Zec. 4:6 w. of L. to Zerubbabel
1 Thes. 1:8 sounded out w. of L.
4:15 say unto you by w. of L.
2 Thes. 3:1 w. of L. ha. free cou.
1 Pet. 1:25 w. of L. endu. for. ev.

**Words of the LORD.**
Ex. 24:3 M. told people all w. of the L. Num. 11:24
4 Moses wrote all w. of the L.
2 Chr. 29:15 came by w. of the L.
Ps. 12:6 w. of the L. pure words
Jer. 36:4 Bar. wrote all w. of L.
Amos 8:11 fam. of hear. w. of L.

See CAME, HEAR.

**Work of the LORD.**
Ex. 34:10 people see w. of the L.
Is. 5:12 regard not w. of the L.
Jer. 48:10 cursed doth w. of L.
50:25 this is the work of the L.
51:10 declare in Z. the w. of L.
1 Cor. 15:58 abound in w. of L.
16:10 worketh the w. of the L.

**Works of the LORD.**
Jos. 24:31 known all w. of L.
Jud. 2:7 seen all great w. of L.
Ps. 28:5 regard not w. of L.
46:8 behold great w. of the L.
77:11 I will remember w. of L.
107:24 these see the w. of the L.
111:2 works of the L. are great
118:17 declare the w. of the L.

**Wrath of the LORD.**
Num. 11:33 w. of the L. kindled
Deut. 11:17 w. of L. kindle aga.
2 K. 22:13 for great is the wrath of the L. 2 Chr. 34:21
2 Chr. 12:12 wrath of L. turned
29:8 w. of the L. upon Judah
32:26 w. of L. came not on them
36:16 until wrath of L. arose
Ps. 106:40 w. of the L. kindled
Is. 9:19 thro' w. of L. land dark.
13:13 earth rem. in w. of the L.
Jer. 50:13 because of w. of the L.
Ezek. 7:19 gold not deliver them in day of w. of t. L. Zep. 1:18

**LORD, *as applied to man.***
Gen. 18:12 I am old, l. being old
27:29 be l. over thy brethren
37 I have made him thy l.
32:4 thus shall ye speak to my l.
18 it is a pres. sent to my l. E.
42:10 nay, my l. but to buy food
30 man who is l. of the land, 33
45:8 made me l. of all his house
9 God made me l. of all Egypt
Num. 12:11 my l. I beseech thee
36:2 the Lord commanded my l.
Jud. 4:18 turn in, my l. turn in
19:26 woman fell wh. her l. was
Ruth 2:13 fav. in thy sight, my l.
1 Sam. 1:26 my l. as thy soul liv.
26:17 my voice, my l. O king
2 Sam. 14:17 so is my l. the king
19 turn fr. aught l. hath spok.
1 K. 1:37 Lord been with my l.
2 K. 5:3 would God my l. were
6:26 saying, Help, my l. O king
7:2 l. on which hand king le. 17
8:5 my l. O king, this is woman
Ps. 12:4 who is l. over us?
Jer. 22:18 saying, Ah l. 34:5
37:20 now, I pray thee, my l.
38:9 my l. the king, these men
Dan. 2:10 no l. asked such thin.
4:24 come upon my l. the king.
Mat. 10:24 nor is serv. above l.
25 enough that ser. be as his l.
18:26 l. have patience with me
31 told their l. all that was do.
24:48 my l. delayeth, Lu. 12:45
Luke 12:36 men wait for their l.
16:3 l. taketh away stewardship
5 callest l.'s debtors to him, How mu. ow. thou to my l.?
John 15:15 know not what l. do.
20 serv. not greater than his l.
Acts 25:26 noth. to write to my l.
Gal. 4:1 fr. servant, tho' l. of all
1 Pet. 3:6 Abraham, call. him l.

**LORDS.**
Gen. 19:2 behold, now, my l.
Num. 21:28 consumed l. of high
Deut. 10:17 is Lord of l. 1 Tim. 6:15; Rev. 17:14
Jud. 16:5 l. of Philistines ca. up
30 the house fell upon the l.
1 Sam. 5:8 gathered l. of Phil. 11
7:7 l. of Philistines went ag. Is.
Ezr. 8:25 offering which l. offer.
Is. 16:8 l. of heathen bro. plants
26:13 other l. have dominion
Jer. 2:31 say my peop. we are l.
Dan. 5:1 feast to thous. of his l.
23 and thy l. have drunk wine
6:17 sealed with signet of l.
Mark 6:21 H. make supper to l.
1 Cor. 8:5 gods many, and l. ma.
1 Pet. 5:3 ne. being l. over God's

**LORDSHIP.**
Mark 10:42 they rule over Gentiles exercise l. Luke 22:25

LO-RUHAMAH. Hos. 1:6, 8

**LOSE, ETH.**
Job 31:39 the owners l. their life
Prov. 23:8 and l. thy sweet wor.
Ec. 3:6 time to get, time to l.
Mat. 10:39 he that findeth his life shall l. it, 16:25; Mark 8:35; Luke 9:24
39 he that l. his life for my sa.
42 no wise l. reward, Mark 9:41
16:26 and l. his own soul, Mark 8:36; Luke 9:25
Luke 15:4 if he l. one sheep
8 ten pieces of silver, if she l.
17:33 who shall l. his life prese.
John 6:39 I should l. nothing
12:25 that lov. his life shall l. it
2 John 8 look that we l. none

**LOSS.**
Ex. 21:19 sh. pay for l. of time
Acts 27:21 gain. this harm and l.
22 sh. be no l. of any man's li.
1 Cor. 3:15 burned, he sh. suf. l.
Phil. 3:7 those I counted l. for C.
8 I counted all things l. for C. for wh. I suffered the l. of all

**LOST, *passively*.**
Ex. 22:9 any manner of l. thing, Deut. 22:3
Lev. 6:3 found that which was l.
4 restore l. th. wh. he found
Num. 6:12 days th. were sh. be l.
1 Sam. 9:3 asses of Kish were l.
20 asses that were l. are found
Ps. 119:176 astray like l. sheep
Jer. 50:6 peo. hath been l. sheep
Ezek. 19:5 saw that hope was l.
34:4 nor sought that wh. was l.
16 I will seek that which was l.
37:11 they say, Our hope is l.
Mat. 10:6 rather to the l. sheep
15:24 not sent but to l. sheep
18:11 Son is come to save what was l. Luke 19:10
Luke 15:4 go after that wh. is l.
6 I found my sheep which is l.
24 son was l. 32 brother was l.
John 6:12 fragments, noth. be l.
17:12 none is l. but son of perd.
2 Cor. 4:3 gospel hid to th. that l.

**LOST, *actively*.**
Deut. 22:3 thy brother's he ha. l.
1 K. 20:25 army like that thou l.
Is. 49:20 after thou hast l. other
21 seeing I have l. my children
Mat. 5:13 if salt l. savor, Mark 9:50; Luke 14:34
Luke 15:9 I found piece wh. I l.
John 18:9 gav. me, I have l. none

**LOT.**
Gen. 11:27 Haran begat L. 31
13:5 L. had flocks, 7, 11; 14:12
19:1 L. sat in gate of Sod. 10, 36
Ps. 83:8 holpen children of L.
Luke 17:32 remember L. wife
2 Pet. 2:7 deliver just L. vexed

**LOT.**
Lev. 16:8 one l. for the L. 9, 10
Num. 26:55 land shall be divided by l. Ezek. 48:29
33:54 he sh. divide the land by l. 36:2; Jos. 13:6; Ezek. 47:22
34:13 the land ye sh. inhe. by l.
Deut. 32:9 J. is l. of inheritance

Jos. 15:1 the l. of tribe of Judah
16:1 l. of Joseph; 17:1 Manas.
17:14 hast given me but one l.?
18:11 the l. of tribe of Benjamin
19:1 second l. came forth to Si.
10 third l. came for Zebulon
17 fourth l. came out to Issac.
19:24 fifth l. to tribe of Asher
32 and the sixth l. to Napthali
40 sev. l. came for tribe of Dan
21:4 l. for Kohath. 1 Chr. 6:54
Jud. 1:3 come up with me into my l. to fight ag. Canaanites
20:9 we will go up by l. aga. it
1 Sam. 14:41 G. give me perfe. l.
1 Chr. 16:18 Canaan, l. of your inheritance, Ps. 105:11
24:5 they were divided by l.
Ps. 16:5 thou maintainest my l.
125:3 not rest on l. of righteous
Prov. 1:14 cast in l. among us
16:33 the l. is cast into the lap
18:18 l. caus. contentions cease
Is. 17:14 l. of them that rob us
34:17 hast cast the l. for them
57:6 sm. stones of stream thy l.
Jer. 13:25 this is thy l. from me
Ezek. 24:6 let no l. fall upon it
Dan. 12:13 shall stand in thy l.
Mic. 2:5 none th. cast cord by l.
Luke 1:9 his l. was to burn ince.
Acts 1:26 the l. fell on Matthias
8:21 thou hast no l. in matter
13:19 he divided their land by l.

**LOTS.**

1 Sam. 14:42 cast l. bet. me and
1 Chr. 24:31 cast l. ag. brethren
Mat. 27:35 casting l. Mark 15:24
Acts 1:26 they gave forth their l.

See CAST.

LOTHE. See LOATHE.

**LOUD.**

Ps. 33:3 play skillf. wi. l. noise
98:4 make a l. noise and rejoice
150:5 praise him on l. cymbals

**LOUD, *with* voice, s.**

Gen. 39:14 I cried with a l. voice
Ex. 19:16 v. of trump. exceed. l.
Deut. 27:14 Lev. speak with l. v.
2 Sam. 15:23 wept with l. v.
1 K. 8:55 be blessed with a l. v.
Prov. 27:14 bles. friend with l. v.
Ezek. 8:18 they cry with a l. voi.
9:1 he cried with a l. voice
Luke 1:42 spake out with a l. v.
8:28 sp. cried with l. v. Acts 8:7
17:15 with a l. v. glorified God
23:23 were instant with l. voices
Acts 14:10 said with a l. v. Stand
26:24 Festus said with a l. v. P.
Rev. 5:2 angel proclaim. wi. l. v.
12 angels saying with a l. v.
8:13 angel saying with a l. voice, Woe, woe 14:7, 9, 15
12:10 I heard a l. v. in heaven

**LOUDER.**

Ex. 19:19 trumpet wax. l. and l.

**LOVE.**

2 Sam. 1:26 passing l. of women
13:15 hatred greater than l.
Prov. 5:19 be ravish. with her l.
7:18 let us take our fill of l.
10:12 up strifes, l. covereth sins
15:17 a dinner of herbs wh. l. is
17:9 covereth transg. seeketh l.
27:5 rebuke better than secret l.
Ec. 9:1 no man knoweth l.
6 their l. and hatred is perish.
Cant. 2:4 and his banner was l.
5 comf. me, I am sick of l. 5:8
3:10 midst being paved with l.
7:6 how pleas. O l. for delights!
8:6 l. is strong as death, jealou.
7 many waters cannot quen. l.
Jer. 2:2 the l. of thy espousals
33 why trim. way to seek l.?
31:3 loved thee with everlast. l.
Ezek. 16:8 thy time was ti. of l.
23:11 corrupt in her inordin. l.
17 B. came to her to bed of l.
33:31 mouth they show much l.
Dan. 1:9 bro. Daniel to tender l.
Hos. 3:1 according to the l. of L.
11:4 I drew them wi. ban. of l.
Mal. 24:12 l. of many wax cold
John 13:35 have l. one to anoth.
15:13 greater l. hath no man
17:26 l. wherewith th. loved me
Rom. 8:35 separate from l. of C.?
12:9 l. be without dissimulation
10 affectioned with brother. l.
13:10 l. work. no ill, l. is fulfil.
15:30 I beseech you for l. of Sp.
2 Cor. 2:4 that you may know l.
8 confirm your l. toward him
5:14 l. of Christ constraineth us
6:6 Holy Ghost, by l. unfeigned
8:8 prove the sincerity of yo. l.
24 show the proof of your l.
13:11 God of l. shall be with you
Gal. 5:6 faith which work. by l.
13 by l. serve one another
22 the fruit of the Spirit is l.
Eph. 1:15 after I heard of your l.
3:19 to know the l. of Christ
6:23 and l. with faith from God
Phil. 1:9 th. your l. may abound
17 the other of l. doth preach
2:1 if there be any comfort of l.
2 like-minded, hav. the same l.
Col. 1:4 l. wh. ye have to saints
8 declared to us your l. in Spi.
1 Thes. 1:3 rememb. labor of l.
4:9 as touching brotherly l.
5:8 on breastpla. of faith and l.
2 Thes 2:10 receiv. not l. of tru.
1 Tim. 1:14 abun. wi. faith and l.
6:10 l. of money is root of all e.
11 fol. righteousn. l. patience
2 Tim. 1:7 not spi. of fear, but l.
Phile. 9 for l. sake I beseech thee
Heb. 6:10 work and labor of l.
10:24 unto l. and to good works
13:1 let brotherly l. continue
1 Pet. 1:22 unfeigned l. of breth.
1 John 2:15 l. of F. is not in him
3:1 behold what l. Father ha.
4:7 love one another, l. is of G.
8 God is l. 10 herein is l.
15 known the l. God hath to
17 herein is our l. made perfect
18 there is no fear in l. perf. l.
2 John 6 this is l. that we walk
Jude 2 peace and l. be multiplied
Rev. 2:4 thou hast left thy first l.

**LOVE of God.**

Luke 11:42 judgm. and l. of G.
John 5:42 ye have not l. of G.
Rom. 5:5 l. of G. is shed in hea.
8:39 to separa. us fr. the l. of G.
2 Cor. 13:14 l. of G. be with you
2 Thes. 3:5 dir. hearts to l. of G.
Tit. 3:4 kindness and l. of G.
1 John 2:5 in him veri. is l. of G.
3:16 hereby perceive we l. of G.
17 how dwell. l. of G. in him?
4:9 manifest. l. of G. toward us
5:3 the l. of G. that we keep
Jude 21 keep yoursel. in l. of G.

**His LOVE.**

Deut. 7:7 L. did not set h. l. on
Ps. 91:14 hath set h. l. upon me
Is. 63:9 in h. l. and pity he red.
Zep. 3:17 he will rest in his l.
John 15:10 abide in his l.
Rom. 5:8 G. commended h. l.
1 John 4:12 his l. perfected in us

**In LOVE.**

1 K. 11:2 Sol. clave to these in l.
Is. 38:17 in l. to my soul deliver.
1 Cor. 4:21 I co. wi. rod or in l.?
2 Cor. 8:7 as ye abound in l. to
Eph. 1:4 with bla. bef. him in l.
3:17 rooted and grounded in l.
4:2 forbearing one another in l.
15 but speaking the truth in l.
Eph. 4:16 edifying of itself in l.
5:2 walk in l. as C. hath loved
Col. 2:2 being knit together in l.
1 Thes. 3:12 make you incr. in l.
5:13 esteem them in l. for wor.
2 Tim. 1:13 in faith and l. in Ch.
1 John 4:16 dwe. in l. dwel. in G.
18 there is no fear in l.
2 John 3 Son of F. in tru. and l.

**My LOVE.**

Ps. 109:4 for my l. th. are adver.
5 reward. me hatred for my l.
Cant. 1:9 com. O my l. to horses
15 behold, th. art fair, my l. 4:1
2:2 as lily, so is my l. am. daug.
7 not awake my l. 3:5; 8:4
10 rise up, my l. my fair one, 13
4:7 my l. there is no spot in thee
5:2 open to my l. my dove
6:4 beautiful, O my l. as Tirzah
John 15:9 continue ye in my l.
10 ye shall abide in my l.
1 Cor. 16:24 my l. be with you all

**Thy LOVE.**

Cant. 1:2 t. l. bet. th. wine, 4:10
4 remem. t. l. more than wine
4:10 how fair is thy l. my sister
Phile. 5 hearing of t. l. and faith
7 joy and consolation in thy l.
Rev. 2:4 thou hast left thy first l.

**LOVE, Verb.**

Lev. 19:18 thou shalt l. thy neighbor as thyself, 34; Mat. 19:19; 22:39; Mark 12:31
Deut. 6:5 thou shalt l. the L. thy G. with all thy heart, 10:12; 11:1, 13, 22; 19:9; 30:6
7:9 faithful G. keepeth covenant with th. th. l. him, Dan. 9:4
13 he will l. thee, bless
10:15 delight in fathers to l. th.
19 l. therefore the stranger
13:3 to know whether ye l. L.
30:16 I command thee to l. L.
20 that thou mayest l. the L.
Jos. 22:5 take heed to l. L. 23:11
Jud. 5:31 them that l. him
1 Sam. 18:22 king's serv. l. thee
2 Chr. 19:2 shoul. thou l. them?
Neh. 1:5 mercy for th. th. l. him
Ps. 4:2 how l. will ye l. vanity?
5:11 them that l. thy name
18:1 I will l. thee, O Lord
31:23 O l. the Lord, all ye saints
40:16 such as l. thy salvat. 70:4
69:36 they that l. his name shall
97:10 ye that l. the L. hate evil
119:132 to those that l. thy na.
165 peace have they who l. thy
122:6 they prosper that l. thee
145:20 L. pres. them that l. him
Prov. 1:22 simple, will ye l. sim.
4:6 l. wisdom, she sh. keep thee
8:36 they that hate me, l. death
9:8 reb. wise man he will l. thee
16:13 kings l. him speak. right
18:21 they that l. it sh. eat fruit
Ec. 3:8 time to l. time to hate
Cant. 1:3 do the virgins l. thee
4 more th. wine, upright l. th.
Is. 56:6 serve and l. name of L.
61:8 I the Lord l. judgment
66:10 be glad all ye that l. her
Jer. 5:31 my peo. l. to have it so
Hos. 3:1 l. woman belov. flagons
4:18 her rulers with shame do l.
9:15 I will l. them no more
14:4 I will l. them freely
Amos 5:15 hate evil and l. good
Mic. 3:2 who hate good and l. e.
6:8 l. mercy and do walk hum.

*Zec.* 8:17 and *l.* no false oath
19 therefore *l.* truth and peace
*Mat.* 5:43 said, *l.* thy neighbor
44 but I say, *l.* your enemies, *Luke* 6:27, 32, 35
46 if ye *l.* them which *l.* you
6:5 *l.* to pray, in synagogues
24 hate one *l.* other, *Luke* 16:13
22:37 th. shall *l.* L. thy G. *Mark* 12:30, 33; *Luke* 10:27
23:6 *l.* upper rooms at feasts
*Mark* 12:38 *l.* to go in long cloth.
*Luke* 7:42 wh. will *l.* him most?
11:43 *l.* greet. in markets, 20:46
*John* 14:21 I *l.* him mani. myself
23 if a man *l.* me, Fath. *l.* him
15:12 that ye *l.* one another, 17
19 the world would *l.* his own
*Rom.* 8:28 good to them th. *l.* G.
13:8 any thing, but to *l.* one an.
9 thou shalt *l.* thy neighbor as thyself, *Gal.* 5:14; *Jam.* 2:8
1 *Cor.* 2:9 G. for them that *l.* him
8:3 if any man *l.* God, same known
*Eph.* 5:25 husb. *l.* your wives as C. loved ch. 28, 33; *Col.* 3:19
6:24 grace be with th. *l.* our L.
1 *Thes.* 4:9 taught to *l.* one ano.
2 *Tim.* 4:8 them that *l.* his ap.
*Tit.* 2:4 young women to *l.* hus.
3:15 greet them that *l.* us in fa.
*Jam.* 1:12 them that *l.* him, 2:5
1 *Pet.* 1:8 whom not seen, ye *l.*
22 *l.* one ano. with pure heart
2:17 honor men, *l.* brotherhood
3:8 as *l.* brethren; 10 that *l.* life
1 *John* 2:15 *l.* not the world
3:11 fr. begin. that we should *l.* one anoth. 4:7, 11; 2 *John* 5
14 because we *l.* the brethren
23 *l.* one another, as he gave
4:12 if we *l.* one another
19 *l.* him bec. he first loved us
20 can he *l.* G. hath not seen
21 loveth God *l.* his brother al.
5:2 we *l.* the children of God

**I LOVE.**

*Ex.* 21:5 sh. say, *I l.* my master
*Jud.* 16:15 canst thou say, *I l.*
2 *Sam.* 13:4 *I l.* Tamar, my broth.
*Ps.* 116:1 *I l.* L. bec. he heard
119:97 O how *I l.* thy law
113 but thy law do *I l.* 163
119 theref. *I l.* thy testimonies
127 *I l.* thy commands ab. gold
159 consi. how *I l.* thy precepts
167 thy testimonies *I l.* exce.
*Prov.* 8:17 *I l.* them that *l.* me
*John* 14:31 know th. *I l.* the Fa.
21:15 L. knowest *I l.* thee, 16, 17
2 *Cor.* 12:15 tho' the more *I l.* you
1 *John* 4:20 if a man say, *I l.* God
2 *John* 1 *I l.* in the truth, 3 *John* 1
*Rev.* 3:19 as many as *I l.* I rebuke

**LOVE me.**

*Gen.* 29:32 my husb. will *l. me*
*Ex.* 20:6 showing mercy to them that *l. me*, *Deut.* 5:10
*Prov.* 8:17 I love them that *l. me*
21 that *l. me* to inh. substance
*John* 8:42 G. your F. ye wo. *l. me*
10:17 theref. doth Father *l. me*
14:15 if ye *l. me*, keep my com.
23 man *l. me*, keep my words

**LOVE not.**

*Prov.* 20:13 *l. not* sleep
1 *Cor.* 16:22 if any man *l. not* L.
2 *Cor.* 11:11 because I *l.* you *not*?
1 *John* 2:15 *l. not* the world
3:18 *n. l.* in word nor tongue

**LOVED.**

*Gen.* 24:67 took Rebe. and *l.* her
25:28 *l.* Esau, Rebekah *l.* Jacob
27:14 made such as his father *l.*
29:18 Jacob *l.* Rachel more, 30
34:3 Shechem *l.* Dinah
37:3 Israel *l.* Joseph more, 4
*Deut.* 4:37 bec. he *l.* thy fathers
7:8 because L. *l.* you, 23:5; 33:3
*Jud.* 16:4 Samson *l.* a woman
1 *Sam.* 1:5 Elkanah *l.* Hannah
16:21 and Saul *l.* David
18:1 Jonathan *l.* David, 3; 20:17
16 Israel and Judah *l.* David
20 Michal Saul's daught. *l.* D.
2 *Sam.* 12:24 the L. *l.* Solomon
13:1 Amnon son of David *l.* Ta.
15 love wherewith he *l.* her
1 *K.* 3:3 Solomon *l.* the Lord
10:9 the Lord *l.* Israel, 2 *Chr.* 9:8
11:1 Solomon *l.* many women
2 *Chr.* 2:11 and the Lord *l.* his people, *Is.* 48:14
11:21 Rehoboam *l.* Maachah
26:10 Uzziah *l.* husbandry
*Est.* 2:17 king *l.* Esther abo. all
*Job* 19:19 they whom I *l.* turned
*Ps.* 47:4 excellency of Jacob he *l.*
78:68 mount of Zion which he *l.*
109:17 *l.* cursing, so let it come
*Jer.* 8:2 host of heaven they *l.*
14:10 thus ha. they *l.* to wander
*Ezek.* 16:37 gather th. thou ha. *l.*
*Hos.* 9:1 thou hast *l.* a reward
10 abomina. according as th. *l.*
11:1 when Is. was child, I *l.* him
*Mal.* 1:2 wherein hast th. *l.* us?
2:11 profaned holin. of L. he *l.*
*Mark* 10:21 J. beholding *l.* him
*Luke* 7:47 sins forgiven, *l.* much
*John* 3:16 God so *l.* the world
19 *l.* darkness rather th. light
11:5 Jesus *l.* Martha, and sister
36 said Jews, Behold how he *l.*
12:43 they *l.* the praise of men
13:1 hav. *l.* his own, he *l.* them
23 discip. whom Jesus *l.* 19:26; 20:2; 21:7, 20
14:21 he that lov. me shall be *l.*
28 if ye *l.* me, ye would rejoice
*John* 15:9 as F. *l.* me, so I *l.* you
16:27 Father lov. you, ye *l.* me
17:23 hast *l.* them, as thou *l.* me
26 love wh. thou hast *l.*
*Rom.* 8:37 conquer. thro' him *l.*
2 *Cor.* 12:15 love you, less I be *l.*
*Gal.* 2:20 who *l.* me, gave hims.
*Eph.* 2:4 love wherewith he *l.* us
5:2 as Christ also hath *l.* us
25 even as Christ *l.* the church
2 *Thes.* 2:16 God our F. ha. *l.* us
2 *Tim.* 4:10 Demas *l.* this world
*Heb.* 1:9 thou hast *l.* righteousn.
2 *Pet.* 2:15 Balaam *l.* the wages
1 *John* 4:10 not that we *l.* God
11 if God so *l.* us
19 love him, bec. he first *l.* us
*Rev.* 1:5 to him that *l.* us
12:11 *l.* not their lives to death

**I have LOVED.**

*Ps.* 26:8 *I have l.* thy house
119:47 commands wh. *I h.* .. 48
*Is.* 43:4 *I have l.* thee, therefore
*Jer.* 2:25 *I have l.* strangers
31:3 *I h. l.* with everlasting love
*Mal.* 1:2 *I have l.* you, yet ye say
*John* 13:34 as *I ha. l.* you, 15:12
15:9 Father l. me so *I h. l.* you
*Rom.* 9:13 Jacob *I have l.* but E.
*Rev.* 3:9 make them know *I h. l.*

**LOVEDST.**

*Is.* 57:8 thou *l.* their bed where
*John* 17:24 *l.* me bef. foundation

**LOVELY.**

2 *Sam.* 1:23 S. and Jo. *l.* in lives
*Cant.* 5:16 he is altogether *l.*
*Ezek.* 33:32 art to them as *l.* song
*Phil.* 4:8 whatsoev. things are *l.*

**LOVER.**

1 *K.* 5:1 Hiram was *l.* of David
*Ps.* 88:18 *l.* and friend hast put
*Tit.* 1:8 *l.* of hospitali. *l.* of men

**LOVERS.**

*Ps.* 38:11 *l.* and friends stand
*Jer.* 3:1 played harlot with ma. *l.*
4:30 thy *l.* will despise thee
22:20 for all thy *l.* are destroyed
22 thy *l.* shall go into captiv.
30:14 all thy *l.* have forgot. thee
*Lam.* 1:2 all her *l.* none to comf.
19 called for *l.* they deceiv. me
*Ezek.* 16:33 giv. gifts to all thy *l.*
36 nakedn. discover. wi. thy *l.*
23:22 raise up thy *l.* again. thee
*Hos.* 2:5 go after *l.* 7 follow *l.*
10 discover lewd. in sight of *l.*
12 rewards my *l.* ha. given me
8:9 Ephraim hath hired *l.*
2 *Tim.* 3:2 men be *l.* of own selves
4 *l.* of pleas. more than *l.* of G.

**LOVES.**

*Prov.* 7:18 solace ourselves wi. *l.*
*Cant.* 7:12 there I give thee my *l.*

**LOVEST.**

*Jud.* 14:16 hate me, and *l.* not
2 *Sam.* 19:6 thou *l.* thine enemies
*Ps.* 45:7 thou *l.* righteousness
52:3 thou *l.* evil more than good
4 thou *l.* all devouring words
*Ec.* 9:9 live with wife thou *l.*
*John* 11:3 he whom th. *l.* is sick
21:15 son of Jo. *l.* th. me? 16:17

**LOVETH.**

*Gen.* 44:20 and his father *l.* him
*Deut.* 10:18 Lord *l.* the stranger
*Ps.* 11:5 him that *l.* violence
7 Lord *l.* righteousness, 33:5
34:12 man that *l.* many days?
37:28 Lord *l.* judgment, 99:4
87:2 the Lord *l.* gates of Zion
119:140 word is pure, thy ser. *l.*
146:8 the Lord *l.* the righteous
*Prov.* 3:12 whom L. *l.* he correct.
12:1 *l.* instruction, *l.* knowledge
13:24 that *l.* him, chasten. him
15:9 *l.* him followeth aft. right.
12 scorner *l.* not one th. repro.
17:17 a friend *l.* at all times
19 *l.* transgres. that *l.* strife
19:8 getteth wisdom *l.* own soul
21:17 he that *l.* wine and oil
22:11 that *l.* pureness of heart
29:3 *l.* wisdom rejoiceth father
*Ec.* 5:10 th. *l.* silver, th. *l.* abun.
*Cant.* 1:7 O thou wh. my soul *l.*
3:2 seek him my soul *l.* 3, 4
*Is.* 1:23 every one *l.* gifts
*Mat.* 10:37 that *l.* fath. or mother
*Luke* 7:5 for he *l.* our nation
47 little is forgiven, *l.* little
*John* 3:35 Father *l.* Son, 5:20
12:25 that *l.* his life sh. lose it
14:21 hath com. he it is *l.* me, he that *l.* me be loved of Fa.
24 *l.* me not, keep. not sayings
*John* 16:27 the Fath. hims. *l.* you
*Rom.* 13:8 that *l.* another
*Eph.* 5:28 that *l.* wife *l.* himself
*Heb.* 12:6 whom L. *l.* he chasten.
1 *John* 2:10 he that *l.* his brother
3:10 he that *l.* not his brother
14 *l.* not broth. abideth 4:8, 20
4:7 ev. one that *l.* is born of G.
21 he who *l.* God, *l.* his brother
5:1 *l.* him begat, *l.* him begot.
*Rev.* 22:15 *l.* and maketh a lie

**LOVING.**

*Prov.* 5:19 let her be as *l.* hind
22:1 *l.* favor rather than silver
*Is.* 56:10 sleeping, *l.* to slumber

*See* KINDNESS, KINDNESSES.

**LOW.**

*Deut.* 28:43 sh. co. down very *l.*
1 *Sam.* 2:7 the Lord bringeth *l.*
2 *Chr.* 26:10 cattle in *l.* country
28:18 invaded cities of *l.* count.

*Job* 5:11 set on high th. that be *l.*
40:12 look on proud bring him *l.*
*Ps.* 49:2 high and *l.* rich and poor
62:9 men of *l.* degree are vanity
136:23 remember. us in *l.* estate
*Prov.* 29:23 man's pride br. him *l.*
*Ec.* 10:6 the rich sit in *l.* place
*Is.* 25:12 high walls sh. he lay *l.*
26:5 lofty city he layeth it *l.*
29:4 speech *l.* out of the dust
32:19 city sh. be *l.* in a *l.* place
*Lam.* 3:55 name out of *l.* dunge.
*Ezek.* 17:6 vine of *l.* stature
24 know I have exalted *l.* tree
21:26 exalt him that is *l.*
26:20 set th. in *l.* parts of earth
*Luke* 1:48 he regardeth *l.* estate
52 exalted them of *l.* degree
*Rom.* 12:16 to men of *l.* estate
*Jam.* 1:9 brother of *l.* degree
10 rich in that he is made *l.*

*See* BROUGHT.

**LOWER.**

*Lev.* 13:20 ris. be in sight *l.* than
*Neh.* 4:13 set in *l.* places the peo.
*Ps.* 8:5 thou hast made him *l.* than the angels. *Heb.* 2:7, 9
63:9 go into *l.* parts of the earth
*Prov.* 25:7 *l.* in presen. of prince
*Is.* 22:9 gathered wat. of *l.* pool
44:23 shout ye *l.* parts of earth
*Eph.* 4:9 descended into *l.* parts

**LOWERING.**

*Mat.* 16:3 the sky is red and *l.*

**LOWEST.**

*Deut.* 32:22 shall burn to *l.* hell
1 *K.* 12:31 made priests of *l.* of people, 13:33; 2 *K.* 17:32
*Ps.* 86:13 deliv. soul from *l.* hell
88:6 thou hast laid me in *l.* pit
*Luke* 14:9 begin to take *l.* room
10 and sit down in the *l.* room

**LOWETH, ING.**

1 *Sam.* 6:12 kine went along *l.*
15:14 what meaneth *l.* of oxen?
*Job* 6:5 *l.* the ox over his fodder?

**LOWLY.**

*Ps.* 138:6 hath he respect to *l.*
*Prov.* 3:34 he giveth grace to *l.*
11:2 but with *l.* is wisdom
16:19 be of humble spirit wi. *l.*
*Zec.* 9:9 *l.* and riding on an ass
*Mat.* 11:29 for I am meek and *l.*

**LOWLINESS.**

*Eph.* 4:2 walk with *l.* and meek.
*Phil.* 2:3 in *l.* of mind, esteem

LUCAS. *Phile.* 24
LUCIFER. *Is.* 14:12
LUCIUS. *Acts* 13:1; *Rom.* 16:2

**LUCRE.**

1 *Sam.* 8:3 S. sons turned after *l.*
1 *Tim.* 3:3 bishop not greedy of *l.* 8
*Tit.* 1:7 not given to filthy *l.*
11 teach. things not for filthy *l.*
1 *Pet.* 5:2 flock not for filthy *l.*

LUKE. *Col.* 4:14; 2 *Tim.* 4:11

**LUKEWARM.**

*Rev.* 3:16 because thou art *l.*

**LUMP.**

2 *K.* 20:7 take *l.* of figs, *Is.* 38:21
*Rom.* 9:21 of same *l.* one vessel
11:16 first-fruit holy *l.* is holy
1 *Cor.* 5:6 leav. whole *l.* *Gal.* 5:9
7 old leav. that ye be a new *l.*

**LUNATIC.**

*Mat.* 4:24 those were *l.* he healed
17:15 mercy on my son, he *l.*

**LURK.**

*Prov.* 1:11 come, let us *l.* privily
18 they *l.* privily for own lives

**LURKING.**

1 *Sam.* 23:23 knowl. of *l.* places
*Ps.* 10:8 in *l.* places of villages
17:12 yo. lion *l.* in secret places

**LUST.**

*Ex.* 15:9 my *l.* shall be satisfied
*Ps.* 78:18 asking meat for th. *l.*
30 not estranged from their *l.*
81:12 up to their own hearts' *l.*
*Rom.* 1:27 burned in their *l.* one
7:7 had not known *l.* except law
*Gal.* 5:16 not fulfil *l.* of flesh
*Jam.* 1:14 when drawn of his *l.*
15 when *l.* hath conceived
2 *Pet.* 1:4 corrup. in world thro' *l.*
2:10 after flesh in *l.* of unclean.
1 *John* 2:16 *l.* of flesh, *l.* of eye
17 passeth away, and *l.* thereof

**LUST, Verb.**

*Prov.* 6:25 *l.* not after beauty
*Mat.* 5:28 look. on woman to *l.*
1 *Cor.* 10:6 not *l.* after evil things
*Jam.* 4:2 ye *l.* and have not

**LUSTED, ETH.**

*Num.* 11:34 buried people that *l.*
*Deut.* 12:15 what thy soul *l.* after, 20, 21; 14:26
*Ps.* 106:14 they *l.* exceedingly
1 *Cor.* 10:6 not lust as th. also *l.*
*Gal.* 5:17 flesh *l.* against the Sp.
*Jam.* 4:5 spirit in us *l.* to envy
*Rev.* 18:14 fruits thy soul *l.* after

**LUSTING.**

*Num.* 11:4 mixed multit. fell a *l.*

**LUSTS.**

*Mark* 4:19 *l.* of things cho. word
*John* 8:44 *l.* of father ye will do
*Rom.* 6:12 sho. obey in *l.* thereof
13:14 no provision, to fulfil *l.*
*Gal.* 5:24 crucified flesh with *l.*
*Eph.* 2:3 conversa. in *l.* of flesh
4:22 corrupt accord. to deceit. *l.*
1 *Tim.* 6:9 foolish and hurtful *l.*
2 *Tim.* 2:22 flee youthful *l.*
4:3 after own *l.* heap teachers
*Tit.* 2:12 that denying worldly *l.*
3:3 divers *l.* and pleasures
*Jam.* 4:1 hence, even of your *l.*?
3 may consume it on your *l.*
1 *Pet.* 1:14 according to former *l.*
2:11 you abstain fr. fleshly *l.*
4:2 no longer live to *l.* of men
2 *Pet.* 2:18 allure thro' *l.* of flesh
*Jude* 16 complain. walk. after *l.*
18 walk after their ungodly *l.*

**LUSTY.**

*Jud.* 3:29 slew 10,000 men, all *l.*

LUZ. *Gen.* 28:19; 48:3; *Jud.* 1:23
LYCAONIA. *Acts* 14:6, 11
LYDDA. *Acts* 9:32, 35, 38
LYDIA. *Ezek.* 30:5; *Acts* 16:14, 40

**LYING.**

*Ps.* 31:6 I have hated them that regard *l.* vanities.
18 let *l.* lips be put to silence
52:3 lovest *l.* rather than right.
59:12 cursing and *l.* they speak
109:2 spoken with *l.* tongue
119:29 remove fr. me way of *l.*
163 I hate and abhor *l.* but thy
120:2 deliver my soul fr. *l.* lips
*Prov.* 6:17 proud look, a *l.* tong.
10:18 hatred with *l.* lips is fool
12:19 *l.* tongue is for a moment
22 *l.* lips abomination to the L.
13:5 a righteous man hateth *l.*
17:7 do *l.* lips become a prince
21:6 treas. by *l.* tongue vanity
26:28 *l.* tongue hat. those afflict
*Is.* 30:9 rebellious peo. *l.* childr.
32:7 wicked devices, *l.* words
59:13 in *l.* against the Lord
*Jer.* 7:4 trust ye not in *l.* words
8 behold, ye trust in *l.* words
29:23 spo. *l.* words in my name
*Ezek.* 13:6 vanity and *l.* divina.
19 *l.* to my peo. that hear lies
*Dan.* 2:9 ye have prep. *l.* words
*Hos.* 4:2 swearing, *l.* and killing
*Jon.* 2:8 observe *l.* vanities forsa.
*Eph.* 4:25 put. away *l.* sp. truth
2 *Thes.* 2:9 whose coming is wi. *l.*

**LYING.**

*Ex.* 23:5 ass of him hateth th. *l.*
*Ps.* 139:3 my path and *l.* down
*Is.* 56:10 *l.* down, lov. to slumber
*Luke* 2:12 babe *l.* in manger, 16
*John* 13:25 *l.* on Jesus' breast
20:5 he saw the linen clothes *l.*
7 napkin not *l.* wi. lin. clothes

**LYING spirit.**

1 *K.* 22:22 a *l. spi.* in the mouth of prophets, 2 *Chr.* 18:21
23 Lord hath put a *l. spirit* in prophets, 2 *Chr.* 18:22

**LYING in wait.**

*Jud.* 16:9 th. were men *l. in w.*
*Lam.* 3:10 as a bear *l. in wait*
*Acts* 20:19 by *l. in wait* of Jews
23:16 heard of their *l. in wait*

**LYING with.**

*Gen.* 34:7 *l. with* Jacob's daugh.
*Num.* 31:17 known man by *l. w.*
18 not kn. *l.* 35; *Jud.* 21:12
*Deut.* 22:22 man found *l. w.* wom.

LYSANIAS. *Luke* 3:1
LYSIAS. *Acts* 23:26
LYSTRA. *Acts* 14:6, 8; 16:1, 2; 2 *Tim.* 3:11

# M

MAACHAH. *Gen.* 22:24; 2 *Sam.* 3:3; 1 *Chr.* 3:2

**MAASEIAH.**

2 *Chr.* 28:7 Zic. slew M. *Jer.* 21:1

MAATH. *Luke* 3:26

**MACEDONIA.**

*Acts* 16:9 into M. 18:5; 19:21
*Rom.* 15:26 pleased them of M.
2 *Cor.* 7:5 were come into M.
8:1 grace of God churches of M.
9:2 I boast of you to them of M.
11:9 brethren from M. supplied
1 *Thes.* 1:7 that believe in M. 8
4:10 brethren that are in M.

MACHIR. *Gen.* 50:23; *Nu.* 26:29; 27:1; 32:39; 36:1; *Jos.* 17:1; *Jud.* 5:14; 2 *Sam.* 9:4; 17:27
MACHPELAH. *Gen.* 23:9, 17, 19, 25:9; 49:30; 50:13

**MAD.**

*Deut.* 28:34 *m.* for sight of eyes
1 *Sam.* 21:13 feigned himself *m.*
2 *K.* 9:11 this *m.* fellow to thee
*Ps.* 102:8 they th. are *m.* ag. me
*Ec.* 2:2 it is *m.* of mirth
7:7 oppres. maketh wise man *m.*
*Is.* 44:25 maketh diviners *m.*
*Jer.* 25:16 be moved and be *m.*
29:26 man is *m.* put in prison
50:38 they are *m.* upon idols
51:7 theref. the nations are *m.*
*Hos.* 9:7 the spiritual man is *m.*
*John* 10:20 he hath devil, is *m.*
*Acts* 12:15 said to Rh. Th. art *m.*
26:11 being exceed. *m.* ag. th.
24 much learn. make thee *m.*
25 I am not *m.* most noble F.

1 Cor. 14:23 not say ye are m.?

**MADE,** *meant of God, Lord, Christ.*
Gen. 1:31 G. saw ev. thing he m.
5:1 in liken. of G. m. he him, 9:6
6:6 repent. he had m. man, 7

**I have MADE.**
Gen. 7:4 destroy liv. sub. I h. m.

**MADE haste.**
Gen. 24:46 Rebekah m. haste
Jud. 13:10 Manoah's wife m. h.
2 Sam. 4:4 Mephib.'s nurse m. h.
Ps. 119:60 I m. h. delayed not
Luke 19:6 Zaccheus m. h.

See ISRAEL, SIN, KNOWN.

**MADE manifest.**
Luke 8:17 shall not be m. m.
John 1:31 that he sho. be m. m.
3:21 his deeds may be m. m.
9:3 works of God sho. be m. m.
Rom. 10:20 I was m. m. to them
16:26 now is m. m. to nations
1 Cor. 3:13 work shall be m. m.
11:19 approved may be m. m.
14:25 secrets of his heart m. m.
2 Cor. 4:10 J. should be m. m. 11
11:6 we have been thoro. m. m.
Eph. 5:13 approved are m. m.
Col. 1:26 m. m. to his saints
2 Tim. 1:10 now m. m. by Christ
Heb. 9:8 holiest not yet m. m.
1 John 2:19 they might be m. m.
Rev. 15:4 thy judgm. are m. m.

**MADE peace.**
Jos. 9:15 Joshua m. p. 10:1, 4
11:19 not a city m. p. with Isr.
2 Sam. 10:19 when the servants of Hadarezer were smit. th. m. p. with Isr. 1 Chr. 19:19
1 K. 22:44 Jehoshaphat m. peace

**MADE ready.**
Gen. 43:25 they m. r. present
46:29 Joseph m. ready chariot
Ex. 14:6 Pharaoh m. r. chariot
Jud. 6:19 G. went and m. r. kid
1 Chr. 28:2 had m. r. for building
Ps. 7:12 bent his bow and m. r.
Hos. 7:6 have m. ready their heart
Mat. 26:19 discip. m. r. passov. Mark 14:16; Luke 22:13
2 Cor. 10:16 boast of things m. r.
Rev. 19:7 wife hath m. herself r.

**MADE void.**
Num. 30:12 her husb. hath m. v.
Ps. 89:39 hast m. v. covenant
119:126 they have m. v. thy law
Rom. 4:14 law heirs, faith m. v.

**MADE,** *passively.*
John 1:3 all things m. by him, without him not any th. m.
10 the world was m. by him
14 the Word was m. flesh
5:6 be m. whole? 14 m. whole
8:33 be m. free; 9:39 m. blind

**MADEST.**
Jon. 4:10 neither m. it grow
Heb. 2:7 m. him low. th. angels

**MAD man, men.**
1 Sam. 21:15 ha. I need of m. m.
Prov. 26:18 m. m. casteth firebr.
Jer. 48:2 O m. m. sw. sh. pursue

MADMANNAH, MADMENAH, MADMEN, Jos. 15:31; Is. 10:31; Jer. 48:2

**MADNESS.**
Deut. 28:28 smite thee with m.
Ec. 1:17 to know wisd. and m.
2:12 I turned myself to beh. m.
7:25 wickedness of folly and m.
9:3 m. is in heart, wh. they live
10:13 his talk is mischievous m.
Zec. 12:4 sm. horse and rider m.
Luke 6:11 they were filled w. m.
2 Pet. 2:16 dumb as forbade m.

MAGDALA. Mat. 15:39

**MAGICIAN, S.**
Gen. 41:8 Pharaoh called for m.
Ex. 7:11 the m. of Egypt did so in like manner, 22; 8:7, 18
9:11 m. could not stand bef. M.
Dan. 1:20 ten times bet. than m.
2:2 king commanded to call m.
10 asked such things at any m.
4:7 then came in the m.
9 O Belteshazzar, master of m.
5:11 father made master of m.

**MAGISTRATE, S.**
Jud. 18:7 no m. in the land
Ezr. 7:25 Ezra set m. and judges
Luke 12:11 they bring you to m.
58 when thou goest to the m.
Acts 16:20 Paul and Silas to m.
22 m. commanded to beat them
35 the m. sent the serjeants, 36
Tit. 3:1 put th. in mi. to obey m.

**MAGNIFICAL.**
1 Chr. 22:5 the house must be m.

**MAGNIFICENCE.**
Acts 19:27 her m. sh. be destro.

**MAGNIFY.**
Jos. 3:7 will I begin to m.
Job 7:17 what is man that thou shouldest m. him?
19:5 if ye will m. yourselves
36:24 remember thou m. work
Ps. 34:3 O m. the Lord with me
35:26 cloth. with shame that m.
38:16 th. m. themselves ag. me
55:12 did m. himself against me
69:30 did m. him with thanksg.
Is. 10:15 saw m. itself ag. him?
42:21 he will m. the law
Ezek. 38:23 thus will I m. myself
Dan. 8:25 m. himself in his heart
11:36 the king shall m. himself
Zec. 12:7 not m. thems. ag. Jud.
Luke 1:46 my soul doth m. the L.
Acts 10:46 sp. wi. tongues, m. G.
Rom. 11:13 apostle, I m. office

**MAGNIFIED.**
Gen. 19:19 hast m. thy mercy
2 Sam. 7:26 and let thy name be m. 1 Chr. 17:24
1 Chr. 29:25 m. Solo. 2 Chr. 1:1
Ps. 35:27 let the Lord be m.
40:16 say contin. L. be m. 70:4
138:2 thou hast m. thy word
Jer. 48:26 m. hims. 42; Dan. 8:11
Lam. 1:9 enemy hath m. hims.
Zep. 2:8 m. against their border
Mal. 1:5 L. will be m. from Isr.
Acts 5:13 the people m. them
19:17 name of the L. J. was m.
Phil. 1:20 Ch. be m. in my body

**MAGOG.**
Gen. 10:2; 1 Chr. 1:5; Ezek. 38:2
Rev. 20:8 gather G. and M. battle

MAHALATH. 2 Chr. 11:18

**MAHANAIM.**
Gen. 32:2 J. called the place M.
1 K. 2:8 when I went to M.

**MAHER-SHALAL-HASH-BAZ.**
Is. 8:1 write concerning M.

MAHLAH. Num. 26:33
MAHLON. Ruth 1:2, 5; 4:9, 10

**MAID.**
Gen. 16:2 go in to my m.
6 behold, thy m. is in thy hand
30:3 behold, my m. Bilhah
Ex. 2:5 she sent her m.
8 m. went and called mother
21:20 if a man smite his m.
22:16 if man entice m. not betr.
Deut. 22:14 fou. her not a m. 17
2 K. 5:2 bro. captive little m.
Est. 2:7 m. fair and beautiful
Job 31:1 why sho. I think on m.?
Prov. 30:19 way of man with m.
Is. 24:2 be as with m. with mist.
Jer. 2:32 can m. forget ornam.?
51:22 break young man and m.
Amos 2:7 and fa. go to same m.
Mat. 9:24 m. is not dead
26:71 another m. saw him, Mark 14:69; Luke 22:56
Luke 8:54 called, saying, m. arise

**MAID-CHILD.**
Lev. 12:5 if she bear a m.-c. unc.

**MAIDEN.**
Gen. 30:18 given m. to my husb.
Jud. 19:24 my daughter, a m.
2 Chr. 36:17 comp. on young m.
Ps. 123:2 eyes of m. to mistress
Luke 8:51 father and moth. of m.

**MAIDENS.**
Ex. 2:5 m. walk. along by river
Ruth 2:8 abide fast by my m.
22 good thou go out with m.
1 Sam. 9:11 m. going to dr. wat.
Est. 4:16 I and my m. will fast
Job 41:5 bind him for thy m.?
Ps. 78:63 m. not giv. to marri.
148:12 y. men and m. praise L.
Prov. 9:3 hath sent forth her m.
31:15 she giveth a portion to m.
Ec. 2:7 I got me serv. and m.
Ezek. 44:22 take m. of seed of Is.
Luke 12:45 ser. begin to beat m.

**MAIDS.**
Est. 2:9 preferred her and m.
Job 19:15 m. count me stranger
Lam. 5:11 ravished m. in cities
Ezek. 9:6 slay both m. and chil.
Nah. 2:7 her m. shall lead her
Zec. 9:17 cheerful, new wine m.

**MAID-SERVANT.**
Ex. 11:5 first-born of m.-s.
20:10 thy m.-s. sh. do no work
17 not covet neighbor's m.-s.
21:7 sell daughter to be m.-s.
27 if he smite out m.-s.'s tooth
Deut. 5:14 that thy m.-s. rest
21 nei. desire neighbor's m.-s.
15:17 to thy m.-s. do likewise
Jud. 9:18 Abimel. son of m.-s.
Job 31:13 if I did desp. my m.-s.
Jer. 34:9 man-s. and m.-s. go, 10

**MAID-SERVANTS.**
Gen. 20:17 Ab. wife and m.-s.
31:33 L. entered two m.-s. tents
Deut. 12:12 rejoice, ye and m.-s.
1 Sam. 8:16 sh. take your m.-s.
2 Sam. 6:22 of the m.-s. sh. I be
2 K. 5:26 time to receive m.-s.?

**MAIL.**
1 Sam. 17:5 with coat of m. 38

**MAIMED.**
Lev. 22:22 blind or m. shall not
Mat. 15:30 those that were m.
18:8 bet. enter life m. Mark 9:43
Luke 14:13 mak. feast, call m. 21

**MAINSAIL.**
Acts 27:40 hoised up m. to wind

**MAINTAIN.**
1 K. 8:45 then hear and m. their cause, 49, 59; 2 Chr. 6:35, 39
1 Chr. 26:27 to m. house of the L.
Job 13:15 m. mine own ways
Ps. 140:12 L. will m. afflicted
Tit. 3:8 to m. good works, 14

**MAINTAINED, EST.**
Ps. 9:4 thou hast m. my right
16:5 L. is my portion, m. my lot

**MAINTENANCE.**
Ezr. 4:14 we have m. from king
Prov. 27:27 m. for thy maidens

**MAJESTY.**
1 *Chr.* 29:11 thine, O Lord, is *m.*
25 bestowed on him royal *m.*
*Est.* 1:4 showed honor of his *m.*
*Job* 37:22 with G. is terrible *m.*
40:10 deck thyself now with *m.*
*Ps.* 21:5 honor and *m.* hast thou
29:4 voice of the L. is full of *m.*
45:3 glory and *m.* 4 in *m.* ride
93:1 Lord is clothed with *m.*
96:6 honor and *m.* are bef. him
104:1 thou art clothed with *m.*
145:5 speak of honor of thy *m.*
12 glorious *m.* of his kingdom
*Is.* 2:10 glory of his *m.* 19, 21
24:14 shall sing for *m.* of the L.
26:10 not behold the *m.* of Lord
*Ezek.* 7:20 ornament, he set in *m.*
*Dan.* 4:30 built for honor of *m.*
36 excellent *m.* added to me
5:18 G. gave Nebuchadnez. *m.*
*Mic.* 5:4 feed in *m.* of name of L.
*Heb.* 1:3 on right hand of *m.* 8:1
2 *Pet.* 1:16 eye-witnes. of his *m.*
*Jude* 25 to God be glory and *m.*

**MAKE.**
*Gen.* 1:26 *m.* man; 2:18 *m.* him
3:6 tree desired to *m.* one wise
12:2 will *m.* thee a great nation,
21:18; 46:3; *Ex.* 32:10
2 *Sam.* 7:11 will *m.* thee a house
*Ps.* 39:4 L. *m.* me to kn. mi. end
90:15 *m.* us glad accord. to days
*Is.* 46:5 to wh. will ye *m.* equal
*Zec.* 12:2 *m.* Jerusalem a cup
*Mal.* 2:15 did not he *m.* one?
*Mat.* 27:65 *m.* it sure as ye can
*Mark* 5:39 why *m.* ye this ado?
*John* 10:24 long *m.* us to doubt?
*Eph.* 2:15 to *m.* in himself of tw.
*Rev.* 21:5 I *m.* all things new
*See* AFRAID, ATONEMENT, COVENANT, DESOLATE, DESOLATION, END, FIRE, GOOD.

**MAKE haste.**
*Deut.* 32:35 come on them *m. h.*
2 *Chr.* 35:21 G. comman. to *m. h.*
*Est.* 5:5 cause Haman *m. h.* 6:10
*Job* 20:2 for this I *m. haste*
*Ps.* 38:22 *m. haste* to help me, O
Lord, 40:13; 70:1; 71:12
70:5 needy, *m. h.* to me, 141:1
*Prov.* 1:16 *m. h.* shed b. *Is.* 59:7
*Cant.* 8:14 *m. haste*, my beloved
*Is.* 28:16 believeth sh. not *m. h.*
49:17 thy children sh. *m. haste*
*Jer.* 9:18 *m. h.* take up wailing
*Nah.* 2:5 *m. haste* to wall thereof
*Acts* 22:18 *m. h.* out of Jerusalem
*See* KNOWN.

**MAKE manifest.**
1 *Cor.* 4:5 *m. m.* counsels of hea.
*Eph.* 5:13 wh. doth *m. m.* is light
*Col.* 4:4 may *m.* it *m.* as I ought
*See* MENTION, NOISE.

**MAKE ready.**
*Ps.* 11:2 they *m. r.* their arrow
21:12 when shalt *m. r.* thine ar.
*Ezek.* 7:14 blown trump. to *m. r.*
*Mark* 14:15 *m. r.* *Luke* 22:12
*Luke* 1:17 *m. r.* a peo. prepared
17:8 rather say, *m. r.* wherew.

**MAKE speed.**
2 *Sam.* 15:14 *m. speed* to depart
*Is.* 5:19 let him *m. s.* and hasten

**MAKE waste.**
*Lev.* 26:31 I will *m.* your cit. *w.*
*Is.* 42:15 I will *m. w.* mountains
*Ezek.* 5:14 I will *m.* Jerusa. *w.*
29:10 *m.* land of Egypt *w.* 30:12

**MAKER, S.**
*Job* 4:17 more pure than his M.?
32:22 my M. will soon take me
35:10 where is God my M.?
36:3 ascribe righteou. to my M.
*Ps.* 95:6 kneel before L. our M.
*Prov.* 14:31 reproacheth his M.
17:5 mock. poor, reproach. M.
22:2 rich and poor, L. M. of all
*Is.* 1:31 the *m.* of it as a spark
17:7 shall man look to his M.
22:11 have not looked to the *m.*
45:9 woe to him striv. with M.
16 go to confusion *m.* of idols
51:13 forgettest the L. thy M.
54:5 thy M. is thy husband
*Jer.* 33:2 thus saith the L. the M.
*Hos.* 8:14 Is. hath forgot. his M.
*Hab.* 2:18 what profiteth graven
image that *m.* hath graven?
*Heb.* 11:10 builder and *m.* is God

**MAKEST.**
*Is.* 45:9 shall the clay say to him
that fash. it, What *m.* thou?
*John* 8:53 whom *m.* thou thys.?
10:33 being a man *m.* thyself G.

**MAKETH.**
*Deut.* 29:12 oath which the L. *m.*
1 *Sam.* 2:6 L. killeth and *m.* alive
7 the L. *m.* poor and *m.* rich
*Is.* 44:24 I am L. th. *m.* all thin.
*Acts* 9:34 Jesus C. *m.* thee whole
1 *Cor.* 4:7 who *m.* thee to differ?
2 *Cor.* 2:2 who is he th. *m.* glad?
*Rev.* 21:27 what. *m.* a lie, 22:15

**MAKETH haste.**
*Prov.* 28:20 *m. haste* to be rich

**MAKING.**
*Ps.* 19:7 the testimony of the L.
is sure, *m.* wise simple
*Ec.* 12:12 of *m.* books no end
*Mark* 7:13 *m.* word of G. none eff.
*John* 5:18 *m.* hims. equal wi. G.
2 *Cor.* 6:10 yet *m.* many rich
*Eph.* 1:16 *m.* mention of you,
1 *Thes.* 1:2; *Phile.* 4
*Phil.* 1:4 prayer for you, *m.* req.
*Jude* 22 have compassion, *m.* dif.

**MAKING, Noun.**
*Ezek.* 27:16 wares of thy *m.* 18
MAKKEDAH. *Jos.* 10:10, 16, 20, 28
MALCHAM. *Zep.* 1:5
MALCHUS. *John* 18:10

**MALE.**
*Gen.* 17:23 ev. *m.* circ. 34:15, 22, 24
*Ex.* 13:12 the *m.* shall be Lord's,
34:19; *Luke* 2:23
*Lev.* 1:3 a *m.* without blemish,
10; 4:23; 22:19
7:6 every *m.* am. priests sh. eat
*Num.* 1:2 every *m.* by their polls
3:15 every *m.* from a month old
31:17 kill ev. *m.* am. little ones
*Deut.* 20:13 shalt smite every *m.*
*Jud.* 21:11 ye sh. destroy ev. *m.*
1 *K.* 11:15 smitten every *m.* 16
*Mal.* 1:14 wh. hath in flock a *m.*
*See* FEMALE.

**MALE-CHILDREN.**
*Jos.* 17:2 were *m.-c.* of Manas.

**MALEFACTOR, S.**
*Luke* 23:32 two *m.* led with him
33 they crucified him, and *m.*
*John* 18:30 if he were not a *m.*

**MALES.**
*Gen.* 34:25 Si. and Levi slew *m.*
*Ex.* 12:48 *m.* be circumcised
13:15 sacri. to L. all being *m.*
23:17 thy *m.* shall appear before
the Lord God. *Deut.* 16:16
*Num.* 31:7 Midianites, slew *m.*
*Deut.* 15:19 firstling *m.* sanctify
*Jos.* 5:4 *m.* came out of Egypt
2 *Chr.* 31:19 gi. portions to all *m.*

**MALICE.**
1 *Cor.* 5:8 not with leaven of *m.*
14:20 howbeit in *m.* be ye chil.
*Eph.* 4:31 put away fr. you all *m.*
*Col.* 3:8 also put off all these, *m.*
*Tit.* 3:3 sometimes living in *m.*
1 *Pet.* 2:1 laying aside all *m.*

**MALICIOUS.**
3 *John* 10 ag. us with *m.* words

**MALICIOUSNESS.**
*Rom.* 1:29 with unrighteous. *m.*
1 *Pet.* 2:16 for a cloak of *m.*

**MALIGNITY.**
*Rom.* 1:29 full of envy, mur. *m.*

**MALLOWS.**
*Job* 30:4 cut up *m.* by bushes

**MAMMON.**
*Mat.* 6:24 G. and *m.* *Luke* 16:13
*Luke* 16:9 friends of *m.* of unr. 11

**MAMRE.**
*Gen.* 13:18 A. dwelt in M. 14:13
14:24 Eshcol, M. let th. portion
23:17 bef. M. 19; 49:30; 50:13

**MAN.**
*Gen.* 1:26 God said, Let us make
*m.* in our image, 27; 9:6
2:7 L. G. formed *m.* of the dust
18 is not good *m.* sho. be alone
25 both naked, *m.* and his wife
3:22 the *m.* is bec. as one of us
6:3 Sp. shall not strive with *m.*
19:8 I have two daughters wh.
have not kn. *m.* *Num.* 31:35
24:65 what *m.* is this walketh?
*Deut.* 4:32 since day G. creat. *m.*
5:24 God doth talk with *m.*
8:3 *m.* doth not live by bread
only. *Mat.* 4:4; *Luke* 4:4
20:19 tree of the field is *m.* life
*Jos.* 7:14 come *m.* by *m.* 17, 18
*Jud.* 8:21 as *m.* is, so strength
9:13 wine cheereth G. and *m.*
16:7 weak as another *m.* 11, 17
1 *Sam.* 9:6 *m.* of G. honorable *m.*
16:7 Lord seeth not as *m.* seeth
2 *Sam.* 12:7 said, Th. art the *m.*
16:7 come out, thou bloody *m.* 8
2 *K.* 9:11 ye know the *m.*
2 *Chr.* 19:6 ye judge not for *m.*
*Job* 4:17 sh. *m.* be mo. just th. G.
7:17 what is *m.* that thou sho.?
magnify him? 15:14; *Ps.* 8:4;
144:3; *Heb.* 2:6
9:2 how sh. *m.* be just wi. G.?
10:4 or seest thou as *m.* seeth?
5 are thy days as days of *m.*?
11:12 vain *m.* would be wise
15:7 art thou first *m.* born?
14 wh. is *m.* th. he sh. be cle.?
25:6 much less *m.* that is worm
32:13 G. thrusteth down, not *m.*
33:12 God is greater than *m.*
*Ps.* 56:11 not afr. wh. *m.* can do
78:25 *m.* did eat angels' food
80:17 thy hand be on the *m.*
104:23 *m.* goeth forth to work
118:6 not fear wh. *m.* can do
*Prov.* 20:24 *m.*'s goings are of L.
*Ec.* 6:11 what is *m.* the better?
12 kno. what is good for *m.*?
*Hos.* 11:9 I am God, and not *m.*
*Mic.* 6:8 show. O *m.* wh. is good
*Zec.* 13:7 ag. *m.* that is my fellow
*Mat.* 19:6 what G. ha. joined, let
not *m.* put asun. *Mark* 10:9
26:72 I do not know the *m.* 74
*Mark* 2:27 sab. was made for *m.*
*Luke* 5:20 *m.* thy sins forgiven
18:4 fear not G. nor regard *m.*
22:58 Peter said, *m.* I am not
60 *m.* I kn. not what thou say.
23:53 laid in sepulchre wherein
nev. *m.* was laid, *John* 19:41
*John* 2:25 knew what was in *m.*
19:5 Pilate said, Behold the *m.*
1 *Cor.* 2:11 what *m.* knoweth the
things of a *m.*?
10:13 tempta. as is com. to *m.*
11:3 head of the woman is *m.*
8 the *m.* is not of the woman

9 but the woman for the m.
11 nor is the m. with. the wo. nor woman without the m.
12 even so is m. by woman
15:21 by m. came death, by m.
45 first m. Adam was made
47 first m. is of the earth; the second m. is the L. fr. hea.
2 Cor. 4:16 tho' our outward m. perish, inward m. is renew.
Gal. 1:1 not of men, nei. by m.
11 I preached not after m.
Eph. 2:15 ma. of tw. one new m.
3:16 by his Sp. in the inner m.
4:24 ye have put on new m.
Col. 3:10 put on new m. renewed
1 Thes. 4:8 despi. not m. but G.
1 Tim. 2:5 one Mediator bet. G. and men, the m. Chr. Jesus
1 Pet. 3:4 hidden m. of the heart

### A MAN.

Gen. 4:23 for I have slain a m.
19:31 not a m. to come in unto
41:38 a m. in whom Sp. of G. is
49:6 in their anger slew a m.
1 Sam. 13:14 L. sought him a m.
14:36 let us not leave a m.
16:17 provide me a m. can play
17:8 choose you a m. for you
10 give me a m. we may fight
25:17 a m. cannot speak to him
30:17 there escaped not a m.
2 Sam. 3:34 as a m. falleth before
20:1 there happened to be a m.
1 K. 2:2 and show thyself a m.
4 not fail a m. on throne, 8:25
20:39 behold, a m. turned aside
2 K. 10:21 th. was not a m. left
1 Chr. 22:9 shall be a m. of rest
2 Chr. 6:16 not fail th. a m. 7:18
Neh. 6:11 sho. such a m. flee?
Job 2:4 all a m. ha. give for life
3:23 why is light given to a m.
4:17 a m. be more pure th. M.?
9:32 he is not a m. as I am
12:14 behold, he shut. up a m.
14:14 if a m. die, sh. he live ag.?
16:21 O that one mi. plead for a m. with G. as a m. pleadeth
22:2 can a m. be profit. to God?
34:29 whet. ag. nation or a m.
35:8 thy wicked. may hurt a m.
37:20 if a m. speak
38:3 gird loins like a m. 40:7
Ps. 38:14 as a m. heareth not
55:13 it was thou, a m. equal
88:4 a m. th. hath no strength
105:17 he sent a m. before them
147:10 not pleas. in legs of a m.
Prov. 3:30 strive not with a m.
14:12 seem. right to a m. 16:25
16:2 all ways of a m. are clean
7 when a m.'s ways please L.
27:21 so is a m. to his praise
28:12 wicked rise a m. hidden
Prov. 28:23 he that rebuketh a m.
29:20 seest th. a m. th. is hasty?
Ec. 2:26 God giv. to a m. good
4:4 a m. is envied of neighbor
6:2 a m. wh. G. ha. given rich.
12 who tell a m. what sh. be?
10:14 a m. cannot tell wh. sh.
Cant. 8:7 if a m. would give all
Is. 6:5 a m. of unclean lips
13:12 make a m. more prec.
17:7 at that day shall a m. look
28:20 a m. can stretch himself
29:21 make a m. an offender
32:2 a m. shall be a hiding pl.
47:3 I will not meet th. as a m.
53:3 he is a m. of sorrows
58:5 day for a m. to afflict soul?
Jer. 4:29 not a m. dwell therein
5:1 seek if ye can find a m.
15:10 borne me a m. of strife
16:20 shall a m. make gods?
22:30 a m. that shall not prosp.
23:9 a m. wine hath overcome
30:6 whether a m. doth travail?
31:22 woman sh. compass a m.
33:17 D. shall never want a m.
18 nor shall priest want a m.
35:19 Jon. shall not want a m.
50:42 array like a m. to battle
Lam. 3:26 it is good for a m.
27 good for a m. he bear yoke
39 a m. for punishment of sins
Ezek. 22:30 I sought for a m.
28:2 thou art a m. and not G. 9
32:2 if people of land take a m.
Dan. 2:10 not a m. on earth can
7:4 st. as a m. and a m.'s heart
10:11 O Daniel, a m. beloved
Hos. 9:12 shall not be a m. left
11:4 drew th. wi. cords of a m.
Amos 2:7 a m. and fa. go to maid
5:19 as if a m. did flee fr. lion
Mic. 2:2 oppress a m. and house
7:6 a m.'s enemies the men of his own house, Mat. 10:36
Mal. 3:17 as a m. spareth his son
Mat. 8:9 am a m. und. au. Lu. 7:8
10:35 to set a m. at variance
12:12 is a m. better than sheep?
15:11 out of mouth defileth a m.
19:3 is it lawful for a. m. to put away wife? Mark 10:2
22:24 if a m. die, having no ch.
26:18 go into city, to such a m. Mark 14:3; Luke 22:10
Luke 1:34 seeing I kn. not a m.
5:8 for I am a sinful m. O Lord
John 1:6 a m. sent from God
30 a m. who is pref. before me
3:3 exc. a m. be born again, 5
4 can a m. be born when old?
27 a m. can receive nothing
4:29 come, see a m. which told
7:23 because I made a m.
8:40 a m. that hath told you
9:11 a m. called Jes. made clay
16 can a m. do such miracles?
10:33 being a m. mak. thyself G.
14:23 if a m. love me
16:21 for joy that a m. is born
Acts 2:22 J. a m. approved of G.
10:26 I myself am also a m.
13:22 D. a m. after my heart
41 though a m. declare to you
16:9 there stood a m. of Maced.
21:39 I am a m. who am a Jew
Rom. 2:21 a m. sh. not steal
22 a m. sho. not commit adul.
3:5 I sp. as a m. 7:1 dominion
1 Cor. 9:8 say I th. thin. as a m.
11:7 a m. ought not cover head
28 let a m. examine himself
13:11 wh. a m. put away child.
2 Cor. 2:6 sufficient to such a m.
8:12 according to that a m. ha.
12:2 I knew a m. in Christ, 3
4 not lawful for a m. to utter
Gal. 2:16 a m. not justified
6:1 a m. be overtaken in fault
3 if a m. think himself some
Phil. 2:8 found in fash. as a m.
1 Tim. 1:8 if a m. use it lawfully
3:1 if a m. desire office of bish.
5 if a m. know not how to rule
2 Tim. 2:5 if a m. strive
21 if a m. theref. purge himse.
Jam. 1:23 like a m. beholding
2:2 if th. come a m. with ring
14 thou. a m. say, he hath fai.
18 a m. say, Thou hast faith
24 by works a m. is justified
1 Pet. 2:19 if a m. for conscience
2 Pet. 2:19 of wh. a m. is overc.
1 John 4:20 if a m. say, I love G.
Rev. 4:7 beast had a face as a m.

### Any MAN.

Gen. 24:16 nor had a. m. kn. her
Ex. 24:14 if a. m. have matters
34:3 nor let a. m. be seen thro'
24 nor shall any m. desire land
Num. 6:9 if any m. die suddenly
21:9 if serpent had bitten a. m.
Deut. 19:11 if any m. hate neigh.
22:8 if any m. fall from thence
Jos. 1:5 not a. m. be able to sta.
Jud. 4:20 if any m. inquire, Is there any m. here?
16:17 and be like a. other m.
18:7 no business with a. m. 28
1 Sam. 2:16 a. m. said, Fail not
2 Sam. 15:5 wh. a. m. came nigh
19:22 sh. a. m. be put to death
21:4 nor for us sh. th. kill a. m.
1 K. 8:38 if supplication be made by any m. 2 Chr. 6:29
2 K. 4:29 meet a. m. salute h. n.
2 Chr. 6:5 nor chose I any m.
Neh. 2:12 nor told I a. m. wh. G.
Job 32:21 not accept any m.
Prov. 30:2 more brutish th. a. m.
Is. 52:14 more marred th. a. m.
Jer. 44:26 in mouth of any m.
Ezek. 9:6 come not near any m.
Dan. 6:7 ask petition of a. m. 12
Mat. 5:40 if any m. sue thee
11:27 nor know. a. m. the Fat.
12:19 nor sh. a. m. hear voice
16:24 if any m. will come after me, Luke 9:23
21:3 if a. m. say aught to you Mark 11:3; Luke 19:31
22:16 nor carest thou for a. m.
46 nor durst any m. fr. th. day
24:23 if any m. say, Lo here is Christ, Mark 13:21
Mark 1:44 say nothing to a. m.
4:23 if a. m. hath ears to hear, 7:16; Rev. 13:9
5:4 neit. could a. m. tame him
9:30 not that a. m. sho. know it
Luke 14:26 if a. m. come to me
19:8 taken any thing from a. m.
John 4:33 hath a. m. bro. aught
6:46 not th. a. m. hath seen F.
51 if any m. eat of this bread
7:17 if a. m. do his will know
37 a. m. thirst, let him come
10:9 by me if any m. enter in
11:57 if a. m. knew wh. he were
12:26 if any m. serve me
47 if any m. hear my words
16:30 not that a. m. should ask
Acts 19:38 a matter ag. any m.
27:22 be no loss of a. m.'s life
Rom 8:9 if a. m. ha. not S. of C.
1 Cor. 3:12 if a. m. build on fou.
14 a. m. work; 15 work burnt
18 if a. m. am. you seem. wise
8:2 if a. m. among you think
3 a. m. love God, 11:34 hunger
10:28 if a. m. say this is offered
16:22 if a. m. love not the L. J.
2 Cor. 5:17 if any m. be in Chr.
10:7 if any m. trust to himself
12:6 lest a. m. sho. think of me
Gal. 1:9 if a. m. pre. other gosp.
Eph. 2:9 lest any m. should boa.
1 Thes. 5:15 for evil to any m.
2 Thes. 3:8 nor eat a. m.'s bread
Heb. 4:11 a. m. fall after same
10:38 but if any m. draw back
12:15 a. m. fail of grace of God
Jam. 1:13 nor tempteth any m.
1 Pet. 4:11 if any m. speak
1 John 2:1 if a. m. sin, ha. advo.
15 if any m. love the world
27 need not that any m. teach
Rev. 3:20 if a. m. hear my voice
22:18 if a. m. add to these thin.
19 if any m. take away words

See BEAST, BLESSED, CURSED.

### MAN-CHILD.

Gen. 17:10 m.-c. be circumc. 12
14 uncircumc. m.-c. be cut off
Lev. 12:2 if wom. ha. borne m.-c.
1 Sam. 1:11 give to handm. m.-c.

*Job* 3:3 it was said, There is a *m.-c.* conceived, *Jer.* 20:15
*Is.* 66:7 deliv. of *m.-c. Rev.* 12:5
*Rev.* 12:13 wom. bro. forth *m.-c.*
*See* EACH.

**Every MAN.**

*Gen.* 16:12 his hand be ag. *e. m.*
45:1 cause *e. m.* to go out
*Deut.* 16:17 *e. m.* give as able
2 *Sam.* 13:9 they went out *e. m.*
*Phil.* 2:4 look not *e. m.* on his
*See* EVIL, FOOLISH.

**MAN of God.**

*Deut.* 33:1 M. *m. of G. Jos.* 14:6
*Jud.* 13:6 *m. of G.* came to me
1 *Sam.* 2:27 a *m. of G.* to Eli
9:6 there is in city a *m. of G.*
1 *Sam.* 9:7 not a pr. to br. *m. of G.*
1 *K.* 12:22 Shem. the *m. of G.*
13:1 came *m. of G.* out Judah
26 *m. of G.* who was disobed.
17:18 do with thee, O *m. of G.?*
24 that thou art *m. of G.*
20:28 there came a *m. of God*
2 *K.* 1:9 *m. of G.* king said, 11
13 O *m. of G.* let my life be
4:16 thou *m. of God,* do not lie
40 O *m. of G.* death in pot
42 brought *m. of God* bread
5:14 accord. to saying *m. of G.*
6:10 to place *m. of G.* told him
7:2 lord answered *m. of G.* 19
17 people trod on *m. of G.* 18
8:2 after the saying of *m. of G.*
7 *m. of God; m. of God* wept
8 and go meet the *m. of God*
13:19 *m. of G.* wroth with him
23:16 to word which *m. of God*
17 it is sepulchre of *m. of God*
1 *Chr.* 23:14 concern. M. the *m. of G.* 2 *Chr.* 30:16; *Ezr.* 3:2
2 *Chr.* 8:14 D. the *m. of G. Neh.* 12:24, 36
25:7 came a *m. of G.* to Amaz.
9 *m. of G.* answered, the Lord
*Jer.* 35:4 son of Igda. a *m. of G.*
1 *Tim.* 6:11 O *m. of G.* flee these
2 *Tim.* 3:17 *m. of G.* be perfect.
*See* GOOD.

**Mighty MAN.**

*Jud.* 6:12 L. is with thee, *m. m.*
11:1 Jephthah was a *m. m.*
*Ruth* 2:1 N. had kinsman *m. m.*
1 *Sam.* 9:1 Kish a Benj. *m. m.*
16:18 David *m. m.* 2 *Sam.* 17:10
1 *K.* 11:28 Jeroboam was *m. m.*
2 *K.* 5:1 Naaman was a *m. m.*
1 *Chr.* 12:4 Ismaiah a *m. m.* 30
2 *Chr.* 17:17 Eliada *m. m.* of val.
28:7 Zichri, *m. m.* of Ephraim
*Job* 22:8 as *m. m.* he had earth
*Ps.* 33:16 *m. m.* not deliv. by str.
52:1 boast. in mischief, *m. m.*
78:65 L. awaked like a *m. m.*
127:4 arrows in hand of *m. m.*
*Is.* 3:2 L. doth take away *m. m.*
5:15 *m. m.* shall be humbled
31:8 fall wi. sw. not of a *m. m.*
42:13 L. go forth as a *m. m.*
*Jer.* 9:23 nor let the *m. m.* glory
14:9 shouldest be as a *m. m.*
46:6 *m. m.* escape; 12 stumbled
*Zep.* 1:14 *m. m.* shall cry bitterly
*Zec.* 9:13 as sword of a *m. m.*
10:7 Eph. shall be like a *m. m.*

**No MAN.**

*Gen.* 31:50 *no m.* is with us
41:44 with. thee *no m.* lift hand
*Ex.* 16:19 let *no m.* leave of it
29 let *no m.* go out of his place
22:10 driv. away, *no m.* seeing
33:20 *no m.* sh. see me and live
34:3 *no m.* sh. come up wi. thee
*Num.* 5:19 if *no m.* ha. lain with
*Deut.* 7:24 *no m.* able to st. 11:25
34:6 *no m.* know. his sepulchre
*Jos.* 23:9 *no m.* hath been able
*Jud.* 11:39 J. daugh. knew *no m.*
21:12 virgins th. had kno. *no m.*
1 *Sam.* 2:9 by stre. *no m.* prevail
26:12 *no m.* saw nor knew it
1 *K.* 8:46 for there is *no m.* that sinneth not, 2 *Chr.* 6:36
2 *K.* 7:5 was *no m.* in camp, 10
23:18 let *no m.* move his bones
1 *Chr.* 16:21 he suffered *no m.* to do them wrong, *Ps.* 105:14
*Est.* 5:12 queen let *no m.* come
8:8 *no m.* reverse; 9:2 withstand
*Job* 11:3 *no m.* make thee asha.?
20:21 *no m.* look for his goods
24:22 *no m.* is sure of his life
38:26 wh. *no m.* is, wher. *no m.*
*Ps.* 22:6 I am worm, and *no m.*
142:4 there was *no m. Is.* 41:28; 59:16; *Jer.* 4:25
*Prov.* 1:24 and *no m.* regarded
*Ec.* 8:8 *no m.* ha. power over sp.
9:1 *no m.* know. love or hatred
*Is.* 9:19 *no m.* shall spare bro.
24:10 *no m.* come; 33:8 regard.
50:2 when I came, was th. *no m.*
57:1 and *no m.* layeth it to hea. *Jer.* 12:11
60:15 *no m.* went through thee
*Jer.* 2:6 *no m.* dwelt; 8:6 repent
22:30 *no m.* of his seed sh. pros.
30:17 Zion, whom *no m.* seeketh
36:19 let *no m.* know wh. ye be
38:24 *no m.* know these words
40:15 *no m.* know; 41:4 knew it
44:2 *no m.* dwell. therein, 51:43
49:18 *no m.* abide, 33; 50:40
*Lam.* 4:4 *no m.* breaketh it
*Ezek.* 14:15 *no m.* pass through
44:2 *no m.* sh. enter in by gate
*Hos.* 4:4 let *no m.* reprove anoth.
*Zep.* 3:6 so that there is *no m.*
*Zec.* 1:21 *no m.* did lift his head
7:14 that *no m.* passed through
*Mat.* 6:24 *no m.* can serve two masters, *Luke* 16:13
8:4 tell *no m.* 16:20; *Mark* 7:36; *Luke* 5:14; 9:21
9:30 *no m.* know it, *Mark* 5:43; 7:24; 8:30; 9:9
11:27 *no m.* knoweth the Son but the Father, *Luke* 10:22
17:8 they saw *no m.* save Jesus
22:46 *no m.* was able to answer
23:9 call *no m.* father on earth
24:36 that day and hour know. *no m. Mark* 13:32
*Mark* 10:29 *no m.* that hath left house, *Luke* 18:29
11:14 *no m.* eat fruit of thee
12:14 know thou care, for *no m.*
*Luke* 3:14 vio. to *no m.* 10:4 sal.
*John* 1:18 *no m.* hath seen God, 1 *John* 4:12
5:22 the Father judgeth *no m.*
6:44 *no m.* can come to me, 65
7:30 *no m.* laid hands, 44; 8:20
8:11 *no m.* L. 15 I judge *no m.*
9:4 night com. *no m.* can work
10:18 *no m.* taketh it from me
29 *no m.* able to pluck th. out
13:28 *no m.* at table knew why
14:6 *no m.* com. to F. but by me
*Acts* 4:17 that th. speak to *no m.*
5:13 durst *no m.* join himself
23 we found *no m.* within
9:7 hear. voice, seeing *no m.* 8
18:10 *no m.* shall set on thee
*Rom.* 13:8 owe *no m.* any thing
14:7 and *no m.* dieth to himself
1 *Cor.* 2:11 thi. of G. know. *no m.*
15 he himself judged of *no m.*
3:11 other found. can *no m.* lay
18 let *no m.* deceive himself, 21
10:24 let *no m.* seek his own
2 *Cor.* 5:16 know *no m.* after fle.
7:2 wrong. *no m.* corrupt. *no m.*
*Gal.* 3:11 *no m.* justified by law
*Eph.* 5:6 *no m.* decei. 2 *Thes.* 2:3
29 *no m.* ever hated own flesh
2 *Tim.* 4:16 first ans. *no m.* stood
*Tit.* 3:2 to speak evil of *no m.*
*Heb.* 5:4 *no m.* taketh this honor
12:14 without whi. *no m.* see L.
*Jam.* 3:8 tongue can *no m.* tame
*Rev.* 2:17 a name *no m.* knoweth
3:7 shutteth, and *no m.* openeth
8 *no m.* shut it; 11 take crown
5:3 *no m.* able to open book, 4
13:17 *no m.* might buy or sell
14:3 *no m.* could learn that song
15:8 *no m.* able to enter temple
19:12 a name writ. *no m.* knew

**Of MAN.**

2 *Sam.* 7:19 is th. manner *of m.?*
*Prov.* 30:19 way *of m.* wi. maid
*Ec.* 12:13 whole duty *of m.*
*Rev.* 13:18 the number *of a m.*
21:17 according to meas. *of a m.*
*See* OLD.

**One MAN.**

*Gen.* 42:11 are all *o. m.* sons, 13
*Num.* 14:15 tho. kill peo. as *o. m.*
31:49 there lacketh not *one m.*
*Jos.* 23:10 *o. m.* sh. chase thous.
*Jud.* 20:1 cong. gather. as *o. m.*
8 all the people arose as *o. m.*
2 *Sam.* 19:14 as heart of *o. m.*
*Ec.* 7:28 *o. m.* am. a thousand
*Is.* 4:1 sev. wom. take hold *o. m.*
*John* 11:50 *o. m.* die for peo. 18:14
*Rom.* 5:12 by *o. m.* sin ent. wor.
15 which is by *one m.* Jesus
17 by *o. m.* offence death reig.
19 as by *one m.* disobedience
14:5 *one m.* esteemeth one day
1 *Tim.* 5:9 hav. been wi. of *o. m.*
*See* POOR, RICH, RIGHTEOUS.

**MAN-SERVANT.**

*Ex.* 20:10 not do work, thy *m.-s.* *Deut.* 5:14
17 neighbor's *m.-s. Deut.* 5:21
21:27 smite out *m.-s.'s* tooth
32 if the ox shall push a *m.-s.*
*Deut.* 12:18 thou and thy *m.-s.*
16:11 rejoice, thou and *m.-s.* 14
*Job* 31:13 if I did desp. my *m.-s.*
*Jer.* 34:9 let his *m.-s.* go free, 10

**MAN-SLAYER, S.**

*Num.* 35:6 six cities for *m.-s.*
12 that the *m.-s.* die not
1 *Tim.* 1:9 law was ma. for *m.-s.*

**Son of MAN.**

*Num.* 23:19 nor *s. of m.* repent
*Job* 25:6 *s. of m.* which is worm
*Ps.* 8:4 and the *s. of m.* that thou visitest him, *Heb.* 2:6
80:17 *s. of m.* th. madest strong
144:3 *s. of m.* makest account
146:3 put not trust in *s. of m.*
*Is.* 51:12 not afraid of *son of m.*
56:2 blessed is *s. of m.* lay. hold
*Jer.* 49:18 nor shall the *son of m.* dwell in it, 33; 50:40
51:43 nei. doth any *s. of m.* pass
*Ezek.* 8:15 seen, O *s. of m.?* 17
21:6 sigh, *s. of m.* with bittern.
*Dan.* 7:13 one like the *Son of m.* *Rev.* 1:13; 14:14
*Mat.* 8:20 *S. of m.* ha. not where to lay his head, *Luke* 9:58
9:6 *S. of m.* ha. power to forgi. sins, *Mark* 2:10; *Luke* 5:24
10:23 not gone, *S. of m.* come
11:19 *S. of m.* came, *Luke* 7:34
12:8 *S. of m.* is Lord even of sab. *Mark* 2:28; *Luke* 6:5
32 whosoever speaketh against *Son of m. Luke* 12:10
40 *S. of m.* 3 days and nights
13:37 sow. good seed is *S. of m.*
41 *S. of m.* send forth angels

16:18 say that I, *S. of m.* am?
17:9 *S. of m.* be risen, *Mark* 9:9
22 *S. of m.* shall be betrayed, 20:18; 26:2, 45; *Mark* 14:41; *Luke* 9:44
24:27 so shall coming of *S. of m.* be, 37, 39; *Luke* 17:26
30 shall see *Son of m.* coming, *Mark* 13:26; *Luke* 21:27
44 in such hour as ye think not *S. of m.* cometh, *Luke* 12:40
25:31 *S. of m.* come in glory
26:24 the *Son of m.* goeth, *Mark* 14:21; *Luke* 22:22
*Mark* 8:38 of him shall *S. of m.* be ashamed when he come.
9:12 it is written of *Son of m.*
31 the *S. of m.* is delivered, 10:33; *Luke* 24:7
13:34 *S. of m.* as man taking
*Luke* 6:22 repr. you for *S. of m.*
9:22 *Son of m.* must suffer, 26
56 *S. of m.* not come to destr.
11:30 so shall *Son of m.* be, 17:24
12:8 him shall *S. of m.* confess
17:22 to see day of *S. of m.*
18:8 when *Son of m.* cometh
19:10 *S. of m.* come to save lost
21:36 to stand before *S. of m.*
22:48 betray. *S. of m.* wi. kiss?
*John* 1:51 descending on *S. of m.*
3:13 even *Son of m.* in heaven
14 so must *Son of m.* be lifted
5:27 because he is the *S. of m.*
6:27 *S. of m.* sh. give unto you
53 exc. ye eat flesh of *S. of m.*
62 shall see *S. of m.* ascend
8:28 ye have lift up *S. of m.*
12:23 *S. of m.* should be glorifi.
34 the *S. of m.* must be lifted up, who is this *S. of m.*?
13:31 now is *S. of m.* glorified
*Acts* 7:56 *S. of m.* on right hand

*See* SON.

**That MAN.**

*Lev.* 17:9 *t. m.* be cut off from p.
20:3 I will set my face against *that m.* 5; *Ezek.* 14:8
*Num.* 9:13 not offer. *t. m.* bear
*Deut.* 17:5 stone *that m.* 12
22:18 take *t. m.* chastise him
25:9 so sh. it be done to *that m.*
29:20 jealousy smoke aga. *t. m.*
*Jos.* 22:20 *t. m.* perished not al.
*Ps.* 37:37 end of *t. m.* is peace
87:5 this and *t. m.* born in her
*Acts* 17:31 *t. m.* he hath ordained
2 *Thes.* 2:3 *t. m.* be revealed
3:14 note *t. m.* have no comp.
*Jam.* 1:7 let not *that m.* think

**This MAN.**

*Gen.* 24:58 wilt go with *t. m.*?
26:11 he that toucheth *this m.*
*Ex.* 10:7 how lo. *t. m.* be snare?
*Deut.* 22:16 gave my dau. to *t. m.*
*Jud.* 19:23 *t. m.* come to house
24 to *t. m.* do not so vile a th.
1 *Sam.* 1:3 *t. m.* went yearly
10:27 said, How sh. *t. m.* save?
17:25 seen *this m.* come up?
25:25 let not my lord reg. *t. m.*
1 *K.* 20:7 *t. m.* seeketh mischief
39 and said, Keep *this m.*
2 *K.* 5:7 *this m.* sends to recover
*Neh.* 1:11 mercy in sight of *t. m.*
*Est.* 9:4 *t. m.* M. waxed greater
*Job* 1:3 *t. m.* greatest of men
*Ps.* 87:4 *this m.* born there, 5, 6
*Is.* 66:2 to *this m.* will I look
*Jer.* 22:30 write *this m.* childless
26:11 *t. m.* is worthy to die, 16
38:4 *t. m.* seeketh not welfare
*Dan.* 8:16 *t. m.* understand vision
*Jon.* 1:14 nor per. for *t. m.'s* life
*Mic.* 6:5 *this m.* shall be peace
*Mat.* 8:9 I say to *this m.* Go
13:54 whence had *this m.* this wisdom? *Mark* 6:2
27:47 *this m.* calleth for Elias
*Mark* 14:71 I know not *this m.*
15:39 *this m.* was Son of God
*Luke* 14:9 thee, Give *t. m.* place
22:56 *t. m.* was also with him
23:4 I find no fault in *t. m.* 14
18 saying, Away with *this m.*
*John* 7:27 we know *this m.*
46 never man spake like *t. m.*
18:17 one of *this m.'s* disciples?
40 not *this m.* but Barabbas
19:12 if thou let *this m.* go
21:21 and what shall *this m.* do?
*Acts* 3:12 made *t. m.* to walk, 16
4:10 by him doth *t. m.* stand
8:10 *this m.* is great power of G.
13:23 of *t. m.* God raised Jesus
38 *this m.* is preached to you
*Heb.* 7:24 *t. m.* continueth ever
8:3 *t. m.* have somewhat to offer
10:12 *t. m.* offered one sacrifice

*See* UNDERSTANDING.

**MAN of war.**

*Ex.* 15:3 the Lord is a *m. of w.*
*Jos.* 17:1 Machir was a *m. of w.*
1 *Sam.* 16:18 David a *m. of w.* 2 *Sam.* 17:8; 1 *Chr.* 28:3
17:33 Goliath *m. of w.* fr. youth
*Is.* 3:2 L. take away *m. of war*
42:13 stir up jeal. like *m. of w.*

**Wicked MAN.**

*Deut.* 25:2 *w. m.* worthy to be
*Job* 15:20 *w. m.* travail. with pa.
20:29 portion of *w. m.* 27:13
*Ps.* 109:6 set thou a *w. m.* over
*Prov.* 6:12 a *wicked m.* walketh
9:7 rebuketh *w. m.* getteth blot
11:7 when a *wicked m.* dieth
13:5 a *wicked m.* loathsome
17:23 *w. m.* tak. gift out bosom
21:29 *w. m.* hardeneth his face
24:15 lay not wait, O *wicked m.*
*Ec.* 7:15 *w. m.* prolongeth days
*Ezek.* 3:18 *w. m.* shall die in ini.
18:24 doeth that wh. *w. m.* do.
27 *w. m.* turneth from wicked.
33:8 O *w. m.* th. sh. surely die, that *w. m.* shall die in his

**Wise MAN.**

*Gen.* 41:33 look out *m.* discre. *w.*
1 *K.* 2:9 Solomon was a *wise m.*
1 *Chr.* 27:32 D.'s uncle a *w. m.*
*Job* 15:2 *w. m.* utter vain know.?
17:10 I cannot find one *w. m.*
34:34 let *w. m.* hearken to me
*Prov.* 1:5 a *w. m.* hear and incr.
9:8 rebuke *w. m.* he will love
9 give instruction to *wise m.*
14:16 *w. m.* feareth, and depart.
16:14 a *w. m.* pacify wr. of king
17:10 reproof enter. into a *w. m.*
21:22 *wise m.* scaleth the city
26:12 *m. w.* in own conceit?
29:9 if *w. m.* contend. w. foolish
11 but a *wise m.* keepeth it in
*Ec.* 2:14 *w. m.'s* eyes in head
16 how dieth *wise m.*? as fool
19 wheth. he be *wise m.* or fool
7:7 oppression mak. *w. m.* mad
8:1 who is as *wise m.* who kno.
5 a *wise m.'s* heart discerneth
17 tho' a *w. m.* think to know
9:15 found in it a poor *wise m.*
10:2 *w. m.'s* heart at right hand
12 words of a *wise m.* gracious
*Jer.* 9:12 *w. m.* they may unde.?
23 let not *wise m.* gl. in wisd.
*Mat.* 7:24 liken him to a *w. m.*
1 *Cor.* 6:5 not a *w. m.* am. you
*Jam.* 3:13 who is a *w. m.* endued

**MAN, *with* woman.**

*Gen.* 3:12 *m.* said, The *woman*
20:3 dead *m.* for *w.* is m.'s wife
*Ex.* 36:6 let no *m.* nor *w.* work
*Lev.* 15:18 *w.* with wh. *m.* shall
33 an issue of the *m.* and *w.*
20:27 *m.* or *w.* hath familiar sp.
*Num.* 6:2 *m.* or *w.* separate
31:17 kill *woman* that hath kno. *m. Jud.* 21:11
*Deut.* 17:5 bring *m.* or *w.* st. th.
22:5 *m.* not wear that pertain. to *m.* nor *m.* put on *w.'s* garment
*Deut.* 22:22 *m.* found lying with *w.* both *m.* th. lay with the *w.* and *w.*
1 *Sam.* 15:3 slay both *m.* and *w.*
27:9 left neither *m.* nor *w.* alive
1 *Chr.* 16:3 dealt to *m.* and *w.*
2 *Chr.* 15:13 not seek L. *m.* or *w.*
*Jer.* 44:7 cut off *m. w.* and child.
51:22 break in pieces *m.* and *w.*
1 *Cor.* 11:3 head of the *w.* is *m.*
7 *woman* is the glory of the *m.*
8 *m.* is not of *w.* but *w.* of *m.*
11 nor is *m.* without *w.* in L.
12 as *w.* is of *m.* so is *m.* by *w.*
1 *Tim.* 5:16 any *m.* or *w.* ha. wi.

**Young MAN.**

*Gen.* 4:23 slain *y. m.* to my hurt
18:7 Abraham gave it to a *y. m.*
41:12 there was with us a *y. m.*
*Num.* 11:27 ran *y. m.* and to. M.
*Deut.* 32:25 des. *y. m.* and virgin
*Jud.* 17:12 *y. m.* bec. his priest
1 *Sam.* 9:2 S. was a choice *y. m.*
17:58 whose son art thou, *y. m.*
30:13 I am *young m.* of Egypt
2 *Sam.* 1:5 said to *young m.* 13
14:21 bring *y. m.* Absal. again
18:5 deal gently with the *y. m.*
29 is *y. m.* Absalom safe? 32
32 enemies of lord be as *y. m.*
1 *K.* 11:28 Solomon seeing *y. m.*
2 *K.* 6:17 L. opened eyes of *y. m.*
9:4 the *y. m.* went to Ramoth
1 *Chr.* 12:28 Zadok, a *young m.*
2 *Chr.* 36:17 no compas. on *y. m.*
*Ps.* 119:9 sh. *y. m.* cleanse way?
*Prov.* 1:4 to *y. m.* knowledge
7:7 *y. m.* void of understanding
*Ec.* 11:9 rej. O *y. m.* in youth
*Is.* 62:5 as *y. m.* marrieth virgin
*Jer.* 51:22 break *y. m.* and maid
*Mat.* 19:20 *young m.* said
*Mark* 14:51 follow. certain *y. m.*
16:5 *y. m.* sitting on right side
*Luke* 7:14 *y. m.* I say to thee
*Acts* 7:58 clothes at *y. m.'s* feet
20:9 there sat in window a *y. m.*
23:17 bring *y. m.* to captain, 18
22 captain let the *y. m.* depart

MANAEN. *Acts* 13:1

**MANASSEH.**

*Gen.* 41:51 called first-born M.
48:5 two sons M. and Eph. 20
2 *K.* 20:21 M. reign. 2 *Chr.* 32:33
21:9 M. seduced th. to do ev. 16
24:3 sins of M. this came upon
2 *Chr.* 33:11 M. among thorns
13 M. knew that Lord was G.
*Ps.* 60:7 M. mine, 80:2; 108:8
*Is.* 9:21 M. shall eat Ephraim

**Tribe of MANASSEH.**

*Num.* 1:35 of *tribe of* M. 32,200
*Jos.* 4:12 the half *t. of* M. passed
13:7 and half *tribe of* M.
17:1 lot for M. 20:8; 22:10
1 *Chr.* 5:18 half *t.* M. 6:70; 12:31
26:32 G. half *tribe of* M. 27:21
*Rev.* 7:6 *t. of* M. sealed 12,000

**MANDRAKES.**

*Gen.* 30:14 Reuben found *m.*
15 wouldest take my son's *m.*? he sh. lie wi. thee for s.'s *m.*
16 hired thee with my son's *m.*
*Cant.* 7:13 *m* give a smell

MANEH. *Ezek.* 45:12

**MANGER.**

*Luke* 2:7 and laid him in a *m.*
12 shall find him lying in *m.*
16 found the babe lying in *m.*

**MANIFEST.**

*Ec.* 3:18 with that God might *m.* them
*John* 14:21 *m.* myself to him
22 *m.* thyself to us
*Acts* 4:16 miracle *m.* to all at J.
*Rom.* 1:19 kn. of G. is *m.* in th.
1 *Cor.* 4:5 *m.* counsels of hearts
15:27 it is *m.* he is excepted
2 *Cor.* 2:14 makes *m.* the savor
*Gal.* 5:19 works of flesh are *m.*
*Phil.* 1:13 bonds in Christ are *m.*
*Col.* 4:4 that I may make it *m.*
2 *Thes.* 1:5 a *m.* token of righte.
1 *Tim.* 3:16 God was *m.* in flesh
5:25 good works of some are *m.*
2 *Tim.* 3:9 body be *m.* to all m.
*Heb.* 4:13 no creat. that is not *m.*
1 *Pet.* 1:20 was *m.* in these times
1 *John* 3:10 children of G. are *m.*

*See* MADE.

**MANIFESTATION.**

*Rom.* 8:19 for *m.* of sons of God
1 *Cor.* 12:7 *m.* of S. giv. to man
2 *Cor.* 4:2 *m.* of truth commend.

**MANIFESTED.**

*Mark* 4:22 hid wh. sh. not be *m.*
*John* 2:11 and *m.* forth his glory
17:6 *m.* thy name unto men
*Rom.* 3:21 righteous. of G. is *m.*
*Tit.* 1:3 in due time *m.* his word
1 *John* 1:2 life *m.* we have seen
3:5 *m.* to take away our sins
8 for this purp. was S. of G. *m.*
4:9 in this was *m.* love of God

**MANIFESTLY.**

2 *Cor.* 3:3 *m.* declared to be epi.

**MANIFOLD.**

*Neh.* 9:19 in *m.* mercies forsook.
27 *m.* mercies gavest them
*Ps.* 104:24 how *m.* are works
*Amos* 5:12 I kn. your *m.* transg.
*Luke* 18:30 not receive *m.* more
*Eph.* 3:10 known *m.* wisd. of G.
1 *Pet.* 1:6 through *m.* temptatio.
4:10 stewards of *m.* grace of G.

**MANKIND.**

*Lev.* 18:22 shall not lie with *m.*
20:13 man lie with *m.* as wom.
*Job* 12:10 in hand breath of *m.*
1 *Tim.* 1:10 law of them defile *m.*
*Jam.* 3:7 hath been tamed of *m.*

**MANNA.**

*Ex.* 16:15 they said, It is *m.*
35 Israel did eat *m.* 40 years
*Num.* 11:6 noth. besides this *m.*
7 *m.* was as coriander-seed
9 fell on camp, *m.* fell on it
*Deut.* 8:3 fed thee with *m.* 16; *Neh.* 9:20; *Ps.* 78:24
*Jos.* 5:12 *m.* ceased, no more
*John* 6:31 fathers did eat *m.* 49
58 not as fathers did eat *m.*
*Heb.* 9:4 golden pot that had *m.*
*Rev.* 2:17 to eat of hidden *m.*

**MANNER.**

*Gen.* 25:23 two *m.* of peo. sepa.
*Ex.* 1:14 bitter in *m.* of service
12:16 no *m.* of work done in th.
22:9 *m.* of trespass, *m.* of lost
31:3 *m.* of workmansh. 5; 35:31, 33, 35; 36:1; 1 *Chr.* 28:21
*Lev.* 5:10 offer. ac. to *m.* *Nu.* 9:14
23:31 ye shall do no *m.* of work
24:22 one *m.* of law *Num.* 15:16
*Num.* 5:13 she be taken with *m.*
28:18 do no *m.* of servile work
*Deut.* 4:15 no *m.* of similitude
15:2 this is *m.* of the release
27:21 lieth wi. any *m.* of beast
*Ruth* 4:7 this *m.* in former time
1 *Sam.* 8:9 show *m.* of king, 11
10:25 Samuel told *m.* of kingd.
21:5 bread is in a *m.* common
2 *Sam.* 7:19 is this *m.* of man?
2 *K.* 1:7 what *m.* of man?
11:14 stood by pillar, as *m.* was
17:26 know not *m.* of G. of land
1 *Chr.* 23:29 for all *m.* of meas.
*Est.* 1:13 king's *m.* towards all
*Ps.* 107:18 abhor. all *m.* of meat
*Cant.* 7:13 all *m.* of pleas. fruits
*Is.* 5:17 lambs feed after their *m.*
*Jer.* 22:21 this hath been thy *m.*
*Dan.* 6:23 no *m.* of hurt found
*Mat.* 4:23 heal. all *m.* sickn. 10:1
5:11 say all *m.* of evil ag. you
8:27 what *m.* of man is this, *Mark* 4:41; *Luke* 8:25
12:31 all *m.* of sin forg. to men
*Mark* 13:1 see what *m.* of ston.
*Luke* 1:29 what *m.* of salutation
66 what *m.* of child sh. th. be?
7:39 what *m.* of woman this
9:55 know not wh. *m.* of spirit
24:17 what *m.* of communicat.?
*John* 19:40 as *m.* of J. is to bury
*Acts* 17:2 Paul, as his *m.* was
20:18 know wh. *m.* I have been
22:3 according to perfect *m.*
25:16 it is not *m.* of Romans
26:4 my *m.* of life from youth
2 *Cor.* 7:9 sorry after godly *m.*
1 *Thes.* 1:5 ye kn. what *m.* of m.
9 what *m.* of entering in we
2 *Tim.* 3:10 known my *m.* of life
*Heb.* 10:25 as the *m.* of some is
*Jam.* 1:24 forge. what *m.* of man
1 *Pet.* 1:11 wh. *m.* of time the S.
15 holy in all *m.* of conversa.
2 *Pet.* 3:11 what *m.* of persons
1 *John* 3:1 behold what *m.* of love
*Rev.* 11:5 in this *m.* be killed
22:2 which bare 12 *m.* of fruits

**After the MANNER.**

*Gen.* 18:11 with S. *a. m.* of wom.
19:31 come in unto us *a. t. m.*
*Jud.* 18:7 *a. the m.* of Zidonians
*Is.* 10:24 *a. t. m.* of E. 26; *Am.* 4:10
*Ezek.* 20:30 polluted *a. m.* of fat.
23:15 *a. the m.* of Babylonians
*Ezek.* 23:45 *a. the m.* of adulter.
*John* 2:6 *a. the m.* of purifying J.
*Acts* 15:1 circumcised *a. t. m.* M.
*Rom.* 6:19 I speak *a. the m.* of men, 1 *Cor.* 15:32; *Gal.* 3:15
1 *Cor.* 11:25 *a.* same *m.* he took
*Gal.* 2:14 *a. the m.* of Gentiles

**After this MANNER.**

*Mat.* 6:9 *after this m.* pray ye
1 *Cor.* 7:7 one *a. this m.* and an.

*See* LIKE.

**MANNERS.**

*Lev.* 20:23 not walk in *m.* of nat.
2 *K.* 17:34 do after former *m.*
*Ezek.* 11:12 after *m.* of heathens
*Acts* 13:18 40 years suff. their *m.*
1 *Cor.* 15:33 ev. com. co. good *m.*
*Heb.* 1:1 God in divers *m.* spake

MANOAH. *Jud.* 13:8, 21; 16:31

**MANSIONS.**

*John* 14:2 in Fa.'s ho. many *m.*

**MANTLE, S.**

*Jud.* 4:18 Jael cov. Sis. with *m.*
1 *Sam.* 28:14 covered with a *m.*
1 *K.* 19:13 Elijah wrapped in *m.*
19 El. cast his *m.* upon Elisha
2 *K.* 2:8 Elijah took *m.* smote
13 Elisha took Elijah's *m.* 14
*Ezr.* 9:3 I he. th. I rent my *m.* 5
*Job* 1:20 Job arose and rent *m.*
2:12 they rent every one his *m.*
*Ps.* 109:29 confusion, as with *m.*
*Is.* 3:22 I will take away the *m.*

**MANY.**

*Gen.* 17:4 thou sh. be a father of *m.* nations, 5; *Rom.* 4:17, 18
37:3 a coat of *m.* colors, 23, 32
*Ex.* 19:21 gaze, and *m.* perish
*Num.* 13:18 wheth. be few or *m.*
26:56 pos. divided between *m.*
35:8 from them have *m.* cities
*Deut.* 15:6 to *m.* nations, 28:12
31:17 *m.* evils shall befall, 21
1 *Sam.* 14:6 save by *m.* or few
1 *K.* 4:20 Judah and Is. were *m.*
7:47 they were exceeding *m.*
2 *Chr.* 14:11 no. to help with *m.*
*Neh.* 7:2 he feared God above *m.*
13:26 among *m.* nations no king
*Ps.* 3:1 *m.* are they that rise up
2 be *m.* that say of my soul, 4:6
25:19 mine enemies are *m.* 56:2
32:10 *m.* sor. shall be to wicked
34:19 *m.* are afflictions of right.
40:3 *m.* sh. see it and fear
55:18 for there were *m.* with me
*Prov.* 4:10 years of thy life be *m.*
10:21 lips of righteous feed *m.*
14:20 the rich hath *m.* friends
19:4 wealth maketh *m.* friends
*Ec.* 11:8 days of darkness be *m.*
*Is.* 53:12 he bare the sin of *m.*
*Jer.* 42:3 are left but few of *m.*
46:16 he made *m.* to fall
*Lam.* 1:22 for my sighs are *m.*
*Ezek.* 33:24 we are *m.* land given
*Dan.* 12:4 *m.* sh. run to and fro
*Mat.* 7:13 *m.* there be that go
22 *m.* will say in that day, L.
8:11 *m.* sh. come from east and
13:58 did not *m.* mighty works
19:30 *m.* first be last, *Mark* 10:31
20:16 *m.* called, few chos. 22:14
24:5 *m.* sh. co. in my name and sh. dec. *m.* *Mark* 13:6; *Luke* 21:8
12 love of *m.* shall wax cold
26:28 my blood shed for *m.*
*Luke* 1:16 *m.* sh. he turn to Lord
2:34 fall and ris. of *m.* in Israel
4:25 *m.* widows; 27 *m.* lepers
7:47 her sins *m.* are forgiven
*John* 6:9 are they among so *m.*?
60 *m.* of his disciples said, 66
21:11 for all so *m.* net not brok.
*Acts* 9:13 I have heard by *m.*
19:19 *m.* bro. books and burnt
26:10 *m.* of saints did I shut up
*Rom.* 5:15 off. of one *m.* be dead
19 *m.* made sin. *m.* made righ.
12:5 be. *m.* are one body in Ch.
1 *Cor.* 1:26 not *m.* wise, not *m.*
4:15 yet have ye not *m.* fathers
8:5 there be gods *m.* lords *m.*
10:5 with *m.* G. was not pleased
17 we being *m.* are one bread
33 profit of *m.* that they be sa.
11:30 for this cause *m.* weak
12:14 not one member, but *m.*
2 *Cor.* 1:11 thanks be giv. by *m.*
6:10 as poor, yet mak. *m.* rich
*Gal.* 1:14 and profited above *m.*
3:16 and to seeds, as of *m.*
*Phil.* 3:18 *m.* walk of wh. I told
*Heb.* 2:10 bring *m.* sons to glory
*Heb.* 7:23 they truly were *m.* pr.
9:28 Christ once bear sins of *m.*
11:12 sprang of one so *m.* stars
*Jam.* 3:1 my brethren, be not *m.*

**After MANY.**

*Ex.* 23:2 speak in a cause to decline *after m.*

**As MANY as.**

*Jud.* 3:1 *as m. as* had not known
2 *Sam.* 2:23 *as m. as* came to pl.
2 *Chr.* 29:31 *as m. as* of free hea.
*Mat.* 22:9 *as m. as* ye find bid
*Mark* 6:56 *as m. as* touched him
*Luke* 11:8 *as m. as* he needeth
*John* 1:12 *as m. as* received him

*Acts* 2:39 to *as m. as* L. shall call
3:24 *as m. as* ha. spoken foreto.
5:11 fear ca. on *as m. as* heard
36 *as m. as* obeyed him, 37
13:48 *as m. as* ordained to life
*Rom.* 2:12 *as m. as* have sinned
8:14 *as m. as* are led by Sp. of
*Gal.* 3:10 *as m. as* are of works
6:12 *as m. as* desire to make
16 *as m. as* walk to this rule
*Phil.* 3:15 let *as m. as* be perfect
*Col.* 2:1 *as m. as* not seen my fa.
1 *Tim.* 6:1 *as m.* servants *as* are
*Rev.* 2:24 *as m. as* have not this
3:19 *as m. as* I love I rebuke
13:15 *as m. as* wo. not worship
*See* BELIEVED, DAYS, HOW.

**MANY people.**
*Ex.* 5:5 *p.* of the land are *m*
*Deut.* 2:21 *p.* great and *m.*
*Jud.* 7:2 *p.* too *m.* for; 4 too *m.*
2 *Sam.* 1:4 *m.* of the *p.* are fallen
*Ezr.* 10:13 *p.* are *m.* time of rain
*Est.* 8:17 *m. p.* of land bec. Jews
*Is.* 2:3 *m. people* shall go
17:12 woe to multitude of *m. p.*
*Ezek.* 3:6 not to *m. p.* of strange
17:9 wither with. *m. p.* to pluck
32:9 I will vex hearts of *m. p.*
10 I will make *m. p.* amazed
38:9 and *m. p.* with thee, 15
*Mic.* 4:3 he shall judge am. *m. p.*
13 shalt beat in pieces *m. p.*
5:7 remnant of J. amidst *m. p.*
*Zec.* 8:22 *m. p.* come and seek L
*Rev.* 10:11 must prop. bef. *m. p.*

**MANY things.**
*Job* 23:14 *m.* such *t.* are wi. him
*Ec.* 6:11 *m. t.* that incr. vanity
*Is.* 42:20 seeing *m. t.* but observ.
*Mat.* 13:3 spake *m. t.* in parables
16:21 and suffer *m. things*, *Mark* 8:31; 9:12; *Luke* 9:22; 17:25
25:21 ruler over *m. things*
27:19 I have suffered *m. things*
*Mark* 6:20 he did *m. t.* and heard
*Luke* 10:41 troubled about *m. t.*
*John* 8:26 have *m. t.* to say, 16:12
21:25 *m.* other *t.* wh. Jesus did
*Acts* 26:9 that I ought to do *m. t.*
*Gal.* 3:4 suffer. so *m. t.* in vain?
*Heb.* 5:11 we have *m. t.* to say
*Jam.* 3:2 in *m. t.* we offend all
2 *John* 12 having *m. things* to write to you, 3 *John* 13

**MANY a time, s.**
1 *K.* 22:16 how *m. t.* I adj. thee?
*Neh.* 9:28 *m. times* didst thou deliver them, *Ps.* 106:43
*Ps.* 78:38 *m. a t.* turned anger
129:1 *m. a t.* they afflicted me, 2
*See* WATERS.

**MANY years.**
*Lev.* 25:51 if th. be *m. y.* behind
*Ezr.* 5:11 house builded *m. y.*
*Neh.* 9:30 *m. years* didst forbear
*Ec.* 6:3 if a man live *m. years*
11:8 if a man live *m. y.* and rej.
*Is.* 32:10 *m.* days and *y.* troubled
*Ezek.* 38:17 wh. prophesied *m. y.*
*Zec.* 7:3 weep as I done th. *m. y.*
*Luke* 12:19 goods laid up *m. y.*
15:29 these *m. y.* do I serve
*Acts* 24:10 been *m. y.* a judge
17 after *m. y.* I came to bring
*Rom.* 15:23 desire *m. y.* to come

**MAR.**
*Lev.* 19:27 nor *m.* corn. of beard
*Ruth* 4:6 lest I *m.* own inherit.
1 *Sam.* 6:5 mice that *m.* the land
2 *K.* 3:19 *m.* good piece of land
*Job* 30:13 they *m.* my path, they
*Jer.* 13:9 thus I *m.* pride of Jud.

**MARRED.**
*Is.* 52:14 his visage was so *m.*
*Jer.* 13:7 girdle *m.* 18:4 ves. *m.*
*Nah.* 2:2 and *m.* vine branches
*Mark* 2:22 the bottles will be *m.*

MARA. *Ruth* 1:20

**MARAH.**
*Ex.* 15:23 drink of wat. of M.
*Num.* 33:8 3 days, pitched in M.

**MARAN-ATHA.**
1 *Cor.* 16:22 him be anath. *m.*

**MARBLE.**
1 *Chr.* 29:2 prepared *m.* in abun.
*Est.* 1:6 silver rings, pill. of *m.*
*Cant.* 5:15 his legs as pill. of *m.*
*Rev.* 18:12 ves. of *m.* no man buy.

**MARCH.**
*Ps.* 68:7 didst *m.* thro' wildern.
*Jer.* 46:22 shall *m.* with army
*Joel* 2:7 shall *m.* ev. one his ways
*Hab.* 1:6 *m.* thro' breadth of land
3:12 thou didst *m.* through land

**MARCHED, ST.**
*Ex.* 14:10 Egypt. *m.* after them
*Jud.* 5:4 thou *m.* earth trembled

**MARCUS.**
*Col.* 4:10 M. sister's son to Barn.
*Phile.* 24 M. saluteth, 1 *Pet.* 5:13

**MARK.**
*Acts* 12:12 John, surnam. M. 25
15:39 took M. sailed to Cyprus
2 *Tim.* 4:11 take M. bring him

**MARK, Substantive.**
*Gen.* 4:15 L. set a *m.* upon Cain
1 *Sam.* 20:20 as tho' I shot at *m.*
*Job* 7:20 why set me as a *m.* ag. thee? 16:12; *Lam.* 3:12
*Ezek.* 9:4 a *m.* on men that sigh
*Phil.* 3:14 press tow. *m.* for prize
*Rev.* 13:16 caused all to rec. a *m.*
17 none buy, save that had *m.*
14:9 any man rec. *m.* in foreh.
11 whosoever receiveth his *m.*
15:2 over image, and over his *m.*
16:2 on them had *m.* of beast
19:20 deceived them that rec. *m.*
20:4 nor his *m.* they liv. wi. Ch.

**MARK, Verb.**
*Ruth* 3:4 thou shalt *m.* the place
1 *K.* 20:7 *m.* how this man seek.
22 *m.* and see what thou doest
*Job* 18:2 *m.* and we will speak
21:5 *m.* me and be astonished
33:31 *m.* well, O J. heark. to me
*Ps.* 37:37 *m.* the perfect man
48:13 *m.* well her bulwarks
56:6 they *m.* my steps
130:3 if thou shouldest *m.* iniq.
*Ezek.* 44:5 *m.* entering of house
*Rom.* 16:17 *m.* th. who cause div.
*Phil.* 3:17 *m.* them who walk so

**MARKED.**
1 *Sam.* 1:12 Eli *m.* her mouth
*Job* 22:15 hast thou *m.* old way?
24:16 they had *m.* in daytime
*Jer.* 2:22 iniquity is *m.* befo. me
23:18 *m.* his word and heard it
*Luke* 14:7 *m.* how they ch. rooms

**MARKS.**
*Lev.* 19:28 not print any *m.*
*Gal.* 6:17 I bear in body *m.* of L.

**MARKEST, ETH.**
*Job* 10:14 if I sin, then thou *m.*
33:11 stocks, he *m.* all my paths
*Is.* 44:13 *m.* it out with compass

**MARKET, S.**
*Ezek.* 27:13 traded in *m.* 17, 19, 25
*Mat.* 11:16 children sitting in *m.*
20:3 others standing idle in *m.*
23:7 love greetings in the *m.* *Luke* 11:43; 20:46
*Mark* 7:4 when they come fr. *m.*
12:38 love salutations in *m.*
*Luke* 7:32 child. sitting in *m.*-pl.
*John* 5:2 a pool by the sheep-*m.*
*Acts* 16:19 drew them into *m.*-p.
17:17 disputed in the *m.* daily.

**MARRIAGE.**
*Ex.* 21:10 duty of *m.* sh. he not
*Ps.* 78:63 maid, not given to *m.*
*Mat.* 22:2 king made *m.* for son
4 ready, come unto the *m.*
9 all ye find, bid to the *m.*
30 in resurrection not given in *m.* *Mark* 12:25; *Luke* 20:35
24:38 given in *m.* until day N.
25:10 ready went wi. him to *m.*
*Luke* 17:27 given in *m.* 20:34
*John* 2:1 a *m.* in Cana of Galilee
1 *Cor.* 7:38 giveth her in *m.*
*Heb.* 13:4 *m.* is honorable in all
*Rev.* 19:7 *m.* of Lamb is come
9 called to *m.* supper of Lamb

**MARRIAGES.**
*Gen.* 34:9 make ye *m.* with us
*Deut.* 7:3 nei. shalt thou make *m.*
*Jos.* 23:12 if ye make *m.*

**MARRY.**
*Gen.* 38:8 go to bro. wife, *m.* her
*Num.* 36:6 only to family of th. father's tribe shall they *m.*
*Deut.* 25:5 wife of dead sh. not *m.*
*Is.* 62:5 so shall thy sons *m.*
*Mat.* 5:32 *m.* her that is divorced 19:9; *Mark* 10:11
19:10 be so, it is not good to *m.*
22:24 brother shall *m.* his wife
30 nei. *m.* nor given in marri. *Mark* 12:25; *Luke* 20:35
1 *Cor.* 7:9 cannot cont. let them *m.* better to *m.* than to burn
36 he sinneth not, let them *m.*
1 *Tim.* 4:3 forbidding to *m.* and
5:11 wax wanton, they will *m.*
14 younger wom. *m.* bear chil.

**MARRIED.**
*Gen.* 19:14 to them th. *m.* daugh.
*Ex.* 21:3 *m.* wife go out wi. him
*Lev.* 22:12 if *m.* to a stranger
*Num.* 12:1 E. whom he had *m.*
36:3 if *m.* to sons of other tribes
*Deut.* 22:22 lying with wom. *m.*
1 *Chr.* 2:21 *m.* wh. sixty years old
*Neh.* 13:23 *m.* wives of Ashdod
*Prov.* 30:23 odious wh. she is *m.*
*Is.* 54:1 more of desolate than *m.*
62:4 thy land shall be *m.*
*Jer.* 3:14 turn, for I am *m.* to you
*Mal.* 2:11 *m.* dau. of strange god
*Mat.* 22:25 first when he had *m.*
*Mark* 6:17 for he had *m.* her
10:12 *m.* another com. adultery
*Luke* 14:20 *m.* a wife, can. come
17:27 they drank, they *m.* wives
*Rom.* 7:3 husband liv. she be *m.*
1 *Cor.* 7:10 to the *m.* I command
33 but he that is *m.* careth for
34 she that is *m.* car. for thin.
39 to be *m.* to whom she will

**MARRIETH.**
*Is.* 62:5 as young man *m.* virgin
*Mat.* 19:9 *m.* her is put away, doth com. adult. *Luke* 16:18

**MARRYING.**
*Neh.* 13:27 in *m.* strange wives
*Mat.* 24:38 *m.* giving in marriage

**MARINERS.**
*Ezek.* 27:8 inha. of Zidon thy *m.*
9 ships of sea with their *m.*
27 *m.* fall into midst of seas
29 *m.* come down fr. th. ships
*Jon.* 1:5 the *m.* were afraid

**MARROW.**
*Job* 21:24 bones moisten. with *m.*
*Ps.* 63:5 soul satisfied as wi. *m.*
*Prov.* 3:8 health and *m.* to bones
*Is.* 25:6 feast of things full of *m.*
*Heb.* 4:12 divi. asun. of j. and *m.*

**MARSHES.**
*Ezek.* 47:11 miry places and *m.*

MARS-HILL. *Acts* 17:22

**MART.**
*Is.* 23:3 she is a *m.* of nations
**MARTHA.**
*Luke* 10:38 a woman named M.
40 M. was cumbered, 41
*John* 11:1 town of M. 5, 30; 12:2
**MARTYR, S.**
*Acts* 22:20 blood of thy *m.* Step.
*Rev.* 2:13 Anti. was faithful *m.*
17:6 drunken with blood of *m.*
**MARVEL, S.**
*Ex.* 34:10 *m.* as have not been
2 *Cor.* 11:14 no *m.* Satan transf.
**MARVEL.**
*Ec.* 5:8 *m.* not at the matter
*Mark* 5:20 and all men did *m.*
*John* 5:20 that ye may *m.*
28 *m.* not at this, hour is com.
7:21 done one work, and ye *m.*
*Acts* 3:12 Is. why *m.* ye at this?
*Gal.* 1:6 I *m.* that ye are so soon
1 *John* 3:13 *m.* not if world hate
*Rev.* 17:7 wheref. didst thou *m.*?
**MARVELLED.**
*Gen.* 43:33 men *m.* one at anoth.
*Ps.* 48:5 saw it, and so they *m.*
*Mat.* 8:10 Jesus heard it, he *m.*
27 but the men *m.* saying
9:8 *m.* and glorified God, 33
22:22 they *m.* at him, *Mark* 12:17; *Luke* 20:26
27:14 govern. *m.* *Mark* 15:5, 44
*Mark* 6:6 *m.* because of unbelief
*Luke* 1:21 *m.* he tarried so long
63 name is John, they *m.* all
2:33 Joseph and his mother *m.*
7:9 when J. heard, he *m.* at him
*John* 4:27 *m.* he talked wi. wom.
7:15 Jews *m.* how knoweth this
*Acts* 2:7 *m.* are not th. Galileans?
4:13 *m.* took knowled. of them
**MARVELLOUS.**
*Job* 5:9 who doeth *m.* things
10:16 thou showest thyself *m.*
*Ps.* 17:7 show *m.* loving-kindn.
31:21 showed me *m.* kindness
78:12 *m.* things did he in sight
98:1 he hath done *m.* things
118:23 it is *m.* in our eyes, *Mat.* 21:42; *Mark* 12:11
*Dan.* 11:36 speak *m.* things
*Mic.* 7:15 show unto him *m.* thi.
*Zec.* 8:6 be *m.* in mine eyes?
*John* 9:30 herein is a *m.* thing
1 *Pet.* 2:9 called you into *m.* light
*Rev.* 15:1 ano. sign great and *m.*
**MARVELLOUS work, s.**
1 *Chr.* 16:12 reme. his *m. works*, *Ps.* 105:5
24 declare *m. w.* amo. nations
*Ps.* 9:1 show forth thy *m. w.*
139:14 great and *m.* are thy *w.* *Rev.* 15:3
*Is.* 29:14 I proceed to do *m. w.*
**MARVELLOUSLY.**
2 *Chr.* 26:15 he was *m.* helped
*Job* 37:5 thunder. *m.* with voice
*Hab.* 1:5 beh. regard, wonder *m.*
**MARY.**
*Mat.* 1:16 Joseph husband of M.
13:55 called M. *Mark* 6:3; 16:1
*Luke* 1:27 virgin's name was M.
2:5 with M. his wife, 16, 19
10:42 M. hath cho. *John* 11:1, 20
*John* 12:3 M. took pound of oint.
19:25 M. stood by cross, 20:16
*Acts* 1:14 conti. in prayer. wi. M.
12:12 Peter came to house of M.
*Rom.* 16:6 greet M. besto. labor
**MARY Magdalene.**
*Mat.* 27:56 amo. wh. were M. M. 61; *Mark* 15:40; *John* 19:25
28:1 came M. M. *John* 20:1
*Mark* 16:1 M. M. brought spices, *Luke* 24:10
*John* 20:18 M. M. told disciples
**MASONS.**
2 *Sam.* 5:11 Hiram sent to David *m.* 1 *Chr.* 14:1
2 *K.* 12:12 gave money to *m.* and hew. of stone, 22:6; *Ezr.* 3:7
1 *Chr.* 22:2 set *m.* to hew stones
2 *Chr.* 24:12 hired *m.* to rep. hou.
**MASSAH.**
*Ex.* 17:7 place M. *Deut.* 33:8
*Deut.* 6:16 tempted in M. 9:22
**MAST, S.**
*Prov.* 23:34 lieth on top of a *m.*
*Is.* 33:23 could not strength. *m.*
*Ezek.* 27:5 cedars to make *m.*
**MASTER.**
*Gen.* 39:20 *m.* put Jos. in prison
*Ex.* 21:8 she pleased not her *m.*
22:8 *m.* of the house be brought
*Jud.* 19:22 spake to *m.* of house
23 *m.* of house went out to th.
1 *Sam.* 25:17 determined ag. *m.*
26:16 you have not kept your *m.*
2 *Sam.* 2:7 your *m.* Saul is dead
1 *K.* 22:17 the Lord said, These have no *m.* 2 *Chr.* 18:16
2 *K.* 6:5 alas *m.* it was borrowed
22 drink, and go to their *m.*
10:2 seeing your *m.* sons
6 take heads of your *m.* sons
19:6 say to your *m.* *Is.* 37:6
1 *Chr.* 15:27 Chenan. *m.* of song
*Is.* 24:2 as with serv. so with *m.*
*Dan.* 1:3 king spake to the *m.*
4:9 O B. *m.* of magicians, 5:11
*Mal.* 1:6 if I be *m.* wh. fear?
2:12 the Lord will cut off *m.*
*Mat.* 8:19 *m.* I will follow thee
9:11 why eat. your *m.* wi. pub.?
10:25 if they have called *m.* Be.
12:38 *m.* we would see sign
17:24 doth not your *m.* pay tri.?
22:16 *m.* we know that thou art true, *Mark* 12:14
23:8 one is your *m.* even Ch. 10
26:18 *m.* saith, Time is at hand
25 Judas said, *m.* is it I?
49 hail *m.* kissed, *Mark* 14:45
*Mark* 5:35 why troubl. thou *m.*?
9:5 *m.* it is good for us to be here, *Luke* 9:33
10:17 good *m.* what shall I do? *Luke* 10:25
13:35 ye know not wh. *m.* com.
*Luke* 7:40 *m.* say; 8:24 perish
8:49 daugh. dead, troub. not *m.*
13:25 when *m.* of house is risen
*John* 3:10 art thou a *m.* of Isr.?
11:28 *m.* is come and call. for th.
13:13 ye call me *m.* ye say well
14 I your *m.* washed your feet
*Acts* 27:11 centurion believed *m.*
*Eph.* 6:9 *m.* is in heaven, *Col.* 4:1
**His MASTER.**
*Gen.* 24:9 hand un. thigh of *h. m.*
39:2 Jos. was in house of *his m.*
*Ex.* 21:4 if *h. m.* given him wife
*Deut.* 23:15 thou sh. not deliv. to *his m.* serv. escaped fr. *h. m.*
*Jud.* 19:11 servant said to *h. m.*
1 *Sam.* 25:10 serv. break fr. *h. m.*
29:4 reconcile himself to *his m.*
2 *K.* 5:1 Naaman great wi. *h. m.*
6:32 sound of *h. m.* feet behind?
9:31 had Zi. peace, slew *h. m.*?
19:4 *his m.* hath sent to reproach God, *Is.* 37:4
1 *Chr.* 12:19 he will fall to *h. m.*
*Job* 3:19 servant free from *h. m.*
*Prov.* 27:18 that waiteth on *h. m.*
30:10 accuse not a serv. to *h. m.*
*Is.* 1:3 ass knoweth *his m.* crib
*Mal.* 1:6 a serv. honoreth *his m.*
*Mat.* 10:24 disciple is not above *his m.* *Luke* 6:40
25 that disciple be as *h. m.*
*Luke* 6:40 ev. one perf. as *h. m.*
*Rom.* 14:4 to *h. m.* he standeth
**My MASTER.**
*Gen.* 24:12 *my m.* Abrah. 14:65
39:8 *my m.* wotteth not what is
*Ex.* 21:5 ser. say, I love *my m.*
1 *Sam.* 24:6 God forbid I do this to *my m.*
30:13 *my m.* left me bec. I fell
2 *K.* 5:18 *my m.* goeth into house
20 *my m.* hath spared Naaman
6:15 *my m.* how shall we do?
10:9 I conspired against *my m.*
27 hath *my m.* sent me to thy master? *Is.* 36:12
*Is.* 36:8 give pledges to *my m.*
**Thy MASTER.**
*Gen.* 24:51 be *thy m.* son's wife
1 *Sam.* 29:10 rise early wi. *t. m.*
2 *Sam.* 9:9 I give *t. m.* all that S.
12:8 *t. m.* house, *t. m.* wives
16:3 where is *thy m.* son?
2 *K.* 2:3 will take away *t. m.* 5
9:7 shalt smite house of *t. m.*
18:27 master sent me to *thy m.*
**MASTER-BUILDER.**
1 *Cor.* 3:10 as wise *m.-b.* I have
**MASTERS.**
*Ex.* 21:4 children sh. be her *m.*
*Ps.* 123:2 eyes of serv. look to *m.*
*Prov.* 25:13 refresheth soul of *m.*
*Amos* 4:1 say to *m.* let us drink
*Zep.* 1:9 fill *m.* houses with viol.
*Mat.* 6:24 no man can serve two *m.* *Luke* 16:13
23:10 neither be ye called *m.*
*Acts* 16:16 brought *m.* much gain
*Eph.* 6:5 be obedient to *m.* *Col.* 3:22. *Tit.* 2:9; 1 *Pet.* 2:18
9 ye, *m.* do the same things unto them, *Col.* 4:1
1 *Tim.* 6:1 count their *m.* worthy
2 believ. *m.* let th. not despise
*Jam.* 3:1 not many *m.* knowing
**MASTERY, IES.**
*Ex.* 32:18 them that shout for *m.*
*Dan.* 6:24 lions had *m.* of them
1 *Cor.* 9:25 that striv. for the *m.*
2 *Tim.* 2:5 if a man strive for *m.*
**MATE.**
*Is.* 34:15 every vult. with her *m.*
16 none shall want her *m.*
**MATRIX.**
*Ex.* 13:12 all that open *m.* 15
34:19 all that open. *m.* is mine
*Num.* 3:12 inst. of first-b. op. *m.*
18:15 ev. thing th. open *m.* thi.
MATTAN. 2 *K.* 11:18; 2 *Chr.* 23:17
MATTATHIAS. *Luke* 3:25
**MATTER.**
*Gen.* 24:9 sware concerning *m.*
30:15 is it small *m.* th. ha. tak.
*Ex.* 18:16 have *m.* come to me
22 ev. great *m.* they shall bring
26 ev. small *m.* judged thems.
23:7 keep thee far fr. false *m.*
*Num.* 16:49 died about *m.* of K.
25:18 beguiled you in *m.* of P.
31:16 com. trespass in *m.* of P.
*Deut.* 17:8 if th. arise *m.* too hard
*Ruth* 3:18 know how *m.* will fall
1 *Sam.* 10:16 of the *m.* of kingd.
20:23 *m.* thou and I spoken of
2 *Sam.* 1:4 how went the *m.*?
18:13 no *m.* hid from king
20:18 ended *m.* 21 *m.* not so
1 *K.* 8:59 as the *m.* shall require
2 *Chr.* 26:32 every *m.* pert. to G.
1 *Chr.* 27:1 served king in any *m.*
1 *Chr.* 8:15 departed not from any *m.*
24:5 the *m.* they hastened not
*Ezr.* 5:5 till *m.* came to Darius
*Neh.* 6:13 have *m.* for evil report

*Est.* 2:23 inquisition made of *m.*
*Job* 19:28 seeing root of the *m.*
32:18 answer, I am full of *m.*
*Ps.* 45:1 heart inditing good *m.*
64:5 encourage them. in evil *m.*
*Prov.* 11:13 spirit concealeth *m.*
16:20 that handleth a *m.* wisely
17:9 repeat. *m.* separateth frien.
18:13 answereth *m.* bef. heareth
25:2 honor of kings to search *m.*
*Ec.* 10:20 hath wings tell *m.*
12:13 hear conclusion of *m.*
*Jer.* 38:27 *m.* was not perceived
*Dan.* 2:10 not a man can sh. *m.*
7:28 hitherto is the end of *m.*
9:23 understand *m.* and consid.
*Mark* 10:10 disci. asked same *m.*
*Acts* 15:6 elders consider this *m.*
18:14 said, If it were *m.* of wro.
19:38 if Demetrius have a *m.*
24:22 I will know utterm. of *m.*
1 *Cor.* 6:1 dare any having a *m.*
2 *Cor.* 9:5 as a *m.* of bounty
*Gal.* 2:6 maketh no *m.* to me
*Jam.* 3:5 how gr. a *m.* little fire

**This MATTER.**

*Deut.* 3:26 speak no more of *t. m.*
22:26 slay. neighbor so is *th. m.*
1 *Sam.* 30:24 hearken in *this m.*
2 *Sam.* 19:42 angry for *this m.?*
*Ezr.* 5:5 concerning *this m.*
10:4 *this m.* belongeth to thee
9 people trembling bec. of *t. m.*
*Est.* 9:26 concerning *this m.*
*Dan.* 1:14 M. consented in *t. m.*
3:16 not careful to ans. in *t. m.*
*Acts* 8:21 nei. part nor lot in *t. m.*
17:32 hear thee again of *this m.*
2 *Cor.* 7:11 yoursel. clear in *t. m.*

**MATTERS.**

*Ex.* 24:14 if any have *m.*
1 *Sam.* 16:18 prudent in *m.*
2 *Sam.* 11:19 end of telling *m.*
15:3 see *m.* are good and right
19:29 speakest any more of *m.?*
2 *Chr.* 19:11 Ama. over you in *m.*
*Neh.* 11:24 all *m.* concerning peo.
*Est.* 3:4 Mord.'s *m.* would stand
9:31 the *m.* of the fastings, 32
*Job* 33:13 giv. not account of *m.*
*Ps.* 35:20 deceitful *m.* ag. them
131:1 nor exercise myself in *m.*
*Dan.* 1:20 in *m.* of wisd. he found
7:1 and told the sum of the *m.*
*Mat.* 23:23 omitted weightier *m.*
*Acts* 18:15 no judge of such *m.*
19:39 any thing conc. other *m.*
25:20 be judged of these *m.*
1 *Cor.* 6:2 judge the smallest *m.*
1 *Pet.* 4:15 busybody in men's *m.*

MATTHEW. *Mat.* 9:9; 10:3; *Mark* 3:18; *Luke* 6:15; *Acts* 1:13

MATTHIAS. *Acts* 1:23, 26

**MATTOCK, S.**

1 *Sam.* 13:20 sharpen axe and *m.*
21 they had a file for the *m.*
2 *Chr.* 34:6 did Josiah with th. *m.*
*Is.* 7:25 hills be digged with *m.*

**MAUL.**

*Prov.* 25:18 false witness, is a *m.*

**MAW.**

*Deut.* 18:3 to priest 2 ch. and *m.*

MAZZAROTH. *Job* 38:32

**MEADOW, S.**

*Gen.* 41:2 and they fed in a *m.*
*Jud.* 20:33 out of *m.* of Gibeah

**MEAL.**

*Num.* 5:15 ephah of barley *m.*
2 *K.* 4:41 *m.* cast it into pot
1 *Chr.* 12:40 nigh brought *m.*
*Is.* 47:2 millstones, grind *m.*
*Hos.* 8:7 bud shall yield no *m.*
*See* BARREL, MEASURES.

**MEAL-TIME.**

*Ruth* 2:14 at *m.-t.* come hither

**MEAN, Verb.**

*Ex.* 12:26 *m.* ye by this service?
*Deut.* 6:20 what *m.* testimonies?
*Jos.* 4:6 what *m.* th. stones? 21
*Is.* 3:15 what *m.* ye that ye beat
*Ezek.* 17:12 what these thi. *m.?*
18:2 what *m.* ye that use prov.?
*Mark* 9:10 wh. ris. fr. dead *m.?*
*Acts* 10:17 what vision sho. *m.*
17:20 know what th. things *m.*
21:13 what *m.* ye to weep and
2 *Cor.* 8:13 I *m.* not that oth. men

**MEAN, Adjective.**

*Prov.* 22:29 not stand bef. *m.* men
*Is.* 2:9 *m.* man boweth down
5:15 *m.* man shall be bro. down
31:8 sw. not of *m.* man devour

**MEAN time.**

*Luke* 12:1 *m. t.* gath. multitude

**MEAN while.**

1 *K.* 18:45 *m. w.* heaven black
*John* 4:31 *m. w.* disciples prayed
*Rom.* 2:15 thoughts *m. w.* accus.

**MEANEST, ETH.**

*Gen.* 33:8 what *m.* thou by this?
*Deut.* 29:24 what *m.* this anger?
1 *Sam.* 4:6 wh. *m.* this shout? 14
15:14 what *m.* this bleating?
2 *Sam.* 16:2 what *m.* thou by these? *Ezek.* 37:18
*Is.* 10:7 howbeit he *m.* not so
*Jon.* 1:6 wh. *m.* thou, O sleep.?
*Mat.* 9:13 learn what that *m.*
12:7 if ye had kn. what this *m.*
*Acts* 2:12 saying, What *m.* this?

**MEANING, Substantive.**

*Dan.* 8:15 D. had sought for *m.*
1 *Cor.* 14:11 if I know not the *m.*

**MEANING.**

*Acts* 27:2 *m.* to sail by coa. of A.

**MEANS.**

*Ex.* 34:7 will by no means clear the guilty, *Num.* 14:18
*Jud.* 5:22 broken by *m.* of pran.
16:5 by what *m.* may prevail
2 *Sam.* 14:14 doth he devise *m.*
1 *K.* 20:39 if by any *m.* be miss.
*Jer.* 5:31 priests bear rule by *m.*
*Mal.* 1:9 hath been by your *m.*
*Mat.* 5:26 by no *m.* come out
*Luke* 5:18 sought *m.* to bring
10:19 nothing by any *m.* hurt
*John* 9:21 by what *m.* he seeth
*Acts* 4:9 by what *m.* he is whole
18:21 must by all *m.* keep feast
*Rom.* 1:10 any *m.* I mi. journey
1 *Cor.* 8:9 by any *m.* this liberty
9:22 I might by all *m.* save
27 by any *m.* when I preached
2 *Cor.* 1:11 by *m.* of many
11:3 lest by any *m.* as serpent
*Gal.* 2:2 lest by any *m.* I sho. run
1 *Thes.* 3:5 lest by some *m.*
2 *Thes.* 2:3 no man dec. by any *m.*
3:16 peace always by all *m.*
*Heb.* 9:15 by *m.* of death called

**MEANT.**

*Gen.* 50:20 God *m.* it unto good
*Luke* 15:26 asked what these *m.*
18:36 passed, asked what it *m.*

**MEASURE.**

*Ex.* 26:2 curtains sh. ha. one *m.* 8
*Lev.* 19:35 do not unright. in *m.*
*Deut.* 25:15 just *m.* sh. th. have
1 *K.* 6:25 cub. one *m.* 7:37 bases
2 *K.* 7:1 a *m.* of fine flour, 16, 18
*Job* 11:9 the *m.* thereof is longer
28:25 weigheth the waters by *m.*
*Ps.* 39:4 to know *m.* of my days
80:5 tears to drink in great *m.*
*Is.* 5:14 hell opened without *m.*
27:8 in *m.* when it shoot. forth
40:12 com. dust of earth in *m.*
*Jer.* 30:11 cor. thee in *m.* 46:28
51:13 *m.* of thy covetousness
*Ezek.* 4:11 drink water by *m.* 16
*Mic.* 6:10 scant *m.* abominable
*Mat.* 7:2 with what *m.* you mete, *Mark* 4:24; *Luke* 6:38
23:32 fill ye up *m.* of your fath.
*Mark* 6:51 amazed beyond *m.*
*Luke* 6:38 good *m.* pressed down
*John* 3:34 G. giveth not Sp. by *m.*
*Rom.* 12:3 dealt to every man *m.*
2 *Cor.* 1:8 were pressed out of *m.*
10:13 not boast of things with. our *m.* but acco. to *m.* 14, 15
11:23 in stripes above *m.*
12:7 lest I be exalted above *m.*
*Gal.* 1:13 beyond *m.* I persecuted
*Eph.* 4:7 according to *m.* of Ch.
13 to the *m.* of the stature
16 working in *m.* of every part
*Rev.* 6:6 *m.* of wheat for penny
21:17 according to *m.* of a man

**MEASURE, Verb.**

*Num.* 35:5 *m.* from without city
*Deut.* 21:2 they shall *m.* to cities
*Is.* 65:7 I will *m.* their for. work
*Ezek.* 43:10 let them *m.* pattern
*Rev.* 11:1 and *m.* temple of God
21:15 a golden reed to *m.* city

**MEASURED.**

*Ruth* 3:15 *m.* six meas. of barley
2 *Sam.* 8:2 *m.* with a line
*Is.* 40:42 who *m.* wat. in hand?
*Jer.* 31:37 heaven ab. can be *m.*
33:22 sand of sea cannot be *m.*
*Ezek.* 40:5 he *m.* the breadth of building, 6, 8, 9, 11, 13 24
41:5 he *m.* wall; 13 *m.* house
15 *m.* the length of building
42:16 he *m.* east with a measu.
17 *m.* north; 18 south; 19 west
*Hos.* 1:10 sand of sea not be *m.*
*Hab.* 3:6 he stood and *m.* earth
*Rev.* 21:16 *m.* city; 17 *m.* wall

**MEASURES.**

*Gen.* 18:6 three *m.* of fine meal
*Deut.* 25:14 not have divers *m.*
1 *K.* 4:22 Solo.'s provision 30 *m.* of flour, and 60 *m.* of meal
5:11 gave Hir. 20,000 *m.* wheat, 20 *m.* of pure oil, 2 *Chr.* 2:10
18:32 would contain 2 *m.* seed
1 *Chr.* 23:29 for all manner of *m.*
*Ezr.* 7:22 hundred *m.* of wheat
*Job* 38:5 hath laid *m.* thereof?
*Prov.* 20:10 divers *m.* abo. to L.
*Jer.* 13:25 is portion of thy *m.*
*Ezek.* 40:24 accord. to these *m.* 29
28 gate according to th. *m.* 32
*Hag.* 2:16 a heap of twenty *m.*
*Mat.* 13:33 like unto leaven hid in three *m.* meal, *Luke* 13:21
*Luke* 16:6 a hundred *m.* of oil
7 he said, A hundred *m.* wheat
*See* BARLEY.

**MEASURING.**

*Jer.* 31:39 *m.* line shall go forth
*Ezek.* 40:3 man with *m.* reed, 5
42:16 with *m.* reed, 17, 18, 19
*Zec.* 2:1 with *m.* line in hand
2 *Cor.* 10:12 *m.* thems. by them.

**MEAT.**

*Gen.* 1:29 to you it sh. be for *m.*
30 I have given ev. herb for *m.*
9:3 ev. moving thing sh. be *m.*
27:31 E. also made savory *m.*
*Lev.* 22:11 he that is born in his house shall eat of his *m.*
25:6 land shall be *m.* for you, 7
*Deut.* 2:6 ye sh. buy *m.* of them
28 shalt sell me *m.* for money
20:20 destroy trees not for *m.*
*Jud.* 1:7 kings gathered their *m.*
14:14 of eater came forth *m.*
1 *Sam.* 20:5 not fail to sit at *m.*

2 *Sam.* 11:8 follow. a mess of *m.*
12:3 it did eat of his own *m.*
1 *K.* 10.5 she saw the *m.* of his table, 2 *Chr.* 9:4
19:8 he went in strength of *m.*
1 *Chr.* 12:40 were nigh bro. *m.*
*Ezr.* 3:7 gave *m.* and drink
*Job* 6:7 ref. are as sorrowful *m.*
12:11 doth not mouth taste *m.?*
20:14 *m.* in bowels is turned
33:20 soul abhorreth dainty *m.*
34:3 as the mouth tasteth *m.*
36:31 giveth *m.* in abundance
38:41 wander for lack of *m.*
*Ps.* 42:3 tears have been my *m.*
44:11 given us like sheep for *m.*
59:15 wand. up and down for *m.*
69:21 gave me gall for my *m.*
74:14 gavest him to be *m.* to p.
78:18 tempted G. by asking *m.*
25 he sent them *m.* to the full
30 while *m.* was in mouths
104:21 yo. lions seek *m.* fr. God
27 mayest give them their *m.*
107:18 soul abhorreth all *m.*
111:5 given *m.* to them that fear
145:15 givest them *m.* in season
*Prov.* 6:8 ant provideth her *m.*
30:22 a fool when filled with *m.*
25 they prepare th. *m.* in sum.
31:15 giveth *m.* to household
*Is.* 62:8 no more gi. *m.* to enem.
*Lam.* 1:11 pleasant things for *m.*
19 elders died whi. they sou. *m.*
*Ezek.* 4:10 *m.* shall be by weight
16:19 my *m.* which I gave thee
29:5 I have given thee for *m.* to beasts, 34:5, 8
34:10 may not be *m.* for them
47:12 trees for *m.* fruit for *m.*
*Dan.* 1:8 not defile hims. with *m.*
4:12 in it was *m.* for all, 21
11:26 th. feed of *m.* sh. destroy
*Hos.* 11:4 I laid *m.* unto them
*Joel* 1:16 is not the *m.* cut off?
*Hab.* 1:16 portion is fat, *m.* plen.
3:17 the fields shall yield no *m.*
*Hag.* 2:12 if one touch any *m.*
*Mal.* 3:10 that there may be *m.*
*Mat.* 3:4 and his *m.* was locusts
6:25 life more th. *m.? Lu.* 12:23
9:10 as Jesus sat at *m.* in house, 26:7; *Mark* 2:15; 14:3; 16:14; *Luke* 24:30
*Mat.* 10:10 wor. worthy of his *m.*
15:37 the broken *m. Mark* 8:8
24:45 *m.* in due seas. *Luke* 12:42
25:35 hungered, ye gave me *m.*
42 hungered, gave me no *m.*
*Luke* 3:11 he that hath *m.*
8:55 commanded to give her *m.*
14:10 worship in presence of th. that sit at *m.*
17:7 will say, Sit down to *m.*
22:27 greater, he that sit. at *m.*
24:41 here any *m.? John* 21:5
*John* 4:8 disci. gone to buy *m.*
32 I have *m.* to eat ye know
34 my *m.* is to do will of him
6:27 labor not for the *m.* which perisheth, but for that *m.*
55 for my flesh is *m.* indeed
*Acts* 2:46 eat their *m.* with glad.
9:19 when he had received *m.*
27:33 besou. them to take *m.* 34
*Rom.* 14:15 grie. wi. thy *m.* dest. not with *m.* for wh. C. died
17 kingdom of God not *m.*
20 for *m.* dest. not work of G.
1 *Cor.* 3:2 with milk, not wi. *m.*
8:8 *m.* commend. us not to G.
10 if any man see thee sit at *m.*
13 if *m.* make brother offend
10:3 did eat same spiritual *m*
*Col.* 2:16 no man judge you in *m.*
*Heb.* 5:12 milk, not strong *m.*
14 strong *m.* belongeth to th.
12:16 for *m.* sold his birthright
*See* FOWLS.

**MEAT-OFFERING.**

*Ex.* 29:41 according to *m.-o.*
*Lev.* 2:1 offer a *m.-o.* 4, 5, 7, 14
6:14 this is law of *m.-o.* 7:37
*Num.* 4:16 to Eleazar daily *m.-o.*
15:6 for *m.-o.* two tenth deals of flour, 28:9, 12
*Jos.* 22:23 altar to offer *m.-o.*
*Jud.* 13:19 took kid with *m.-o.*
1 *Chr.* 21:23 wheat for the *m.-o.*
*Is.* 57:6 hast thou offered a *m.-o.*
*Ezek.* 42:13 there they lay *m.-o.*
44:29 they shall eat the *m.-o.*
46:5 *m.-o.* be an ephah for ram
7 *m.-o.* an eph. for bullock, 11
*Joel* 1:9 the *m.-o.* is cut off
13 the *m.-o.* is withholden
2:14 even a *m.-o.* to our God

**MEAT-OFFERINGS.**

*Jos.* 22:29 build altar for *m.-o.*
1 *K.* 8:64 Solomon offered *m.-o.*
*Ezr.* 7:17 buy lambs with *m.-o.*
*Neh.* 13:5 where they laid *m.-o.*
*Jer.* 33:18 not want kindle *m.-o.*
*Ezek.* 45:17 prin. part give *m.-o.*
*Amos* 5:22 though ye offer *m.-o.*

**MEATS.**

*Prov.* 23:6 nei. desire dainty *m.*
*Acts* 15:29 abstain fr. *m.* offered
1 *Cor.* 6:13 *m.* for belly, belly *m.*
1 *Tim.* 4:3 to abstain from *m.*
*Heb.* 9:10 which stood only in *m.*
13:9 estab. with grace, not *m.*

MEDAD. *Num.* 11:26
MEDAN. *Gen.* 25:2

**MEDDLE.**

*Deut.* 2:5 *m.* not that of mount S.
19 *m.* not with child. of Am.
2 *K.* 14:10 why *m.* to thy hurt? 2 *Chr.* 25:19
*Prov.* 20:19 *m.* not with him
24:21 *m.* not th. given to change

**MEDDLED, ETH.**

*Prov.* 17:14 contention bef. it *m.*
26:17 *m.* strife not belonging

**MEDDLING.**

2 *Chr.* 35:21 forbear fr. *m.* with G.
*Prov.* 20:3 every fool will be *m.*

**MEDE, S.**

2 *K.* 17:6 in cities of M. 18:11
*Ezr.* 6:2 in province of M.
*Est.* 1:19 among laws of M.
*Is.* 13:17 will stir M. *Jer.* 51:11
*Dan.* 5:28 kingd. is given to M.
6:8 law of M. 12; 9:1; 11:1

**MEDIA.**

*Est.* 1:3 of Persia and M. 14, 18
10:2 book of kings of M.
*Is.* 21:2 O M. all sighing ceaseth
*Dan.* 8:20 two horns kings of M.

**MEDIATOR.**

*Gal.* 3:19 angels in hand of *m.*
20 a *m.* is not a *m.* of one
1 *Tim.* 2:5 is but one *m.* Jesus
*Heb.* 8:6 *m.* of a better covenant
9:15 he is *m.* of New Testament
12:24 J. *m.* of the new covenant

**MEDICINE, S.**

*Prov.* 17:22 doeth good like a *m.*
*Jer.* 30:13 thou hast no heal. *m.*
46:11 in vain thou use many *m.*
*Ezek.* 47:12 the leaf sh. be for *m.*

**MEDITATE.**

*Gen.* 24:63 Isaac went out to *m.*
*Jos.* 1:8 *m.* therein day and nig.
*Ps.* 1:2 doth *m.* day and night
63:6 *m.* on th. in night watches
77:12 I will *m.* of all thy work
119:15 I *m.* in thy precepts, 78
23 serv. *m.* in thy statutes, 48
148 I might *m.* in thy word
143:5 I *m.* on all thy works
*Is.* 33:18 thy heart sh. *m.* terror
*Luke* 21:14 settle it not to *m.*
1 *Tim.* 4:15 *m.* upon these things

**MEDITATION.**

*Ps.* 5:1 give ear, consider my *m.*
19:14 let *m.* of heart be accept.
49:3 *m.* of heart sh. be of under.
104:34 *m.* of him shall be sweet
119:97 love thy law, it is my *m.*
99 thy testimonies are my *m.*

**MEEK.**

*Num.* 12:3 Moses was very *m.*
*Ps.* 22:26 *m.* sh. eat and be satis.
25:9 *m.* will he guide in judgm.
37:11 *m.* shall inherit the earth
76:9 God arose to save all *m.*
147:6 the Lord lifted up the *m.*
149:4 beautify *m.* with salvation
*Is.* 11:4 for the *m.* of earth
29:19 *m.* shall increase their joy
61:1 good tidings to the *m.*
*Amos* 2:7 turn aside way of *m.*
*Zep.* 2:3 seek L. ye *m.* of earth
*Mat.* 5:5 blessed are the *m.*
11:29 for I am *m.* and lowly
21:5 thy king cometh to thee *m.*
1 *Pet.* 3:4 ornament of a *m.* spirit

**MEEKNESS.**

*Ps.* 45:4 because of truth and *m.*
*Zep.* 2:3 seek *m.* ye shall be hid
1 *Cor.* 4:21 sh. I come in sp. of *m.?*
2 *Cor.* 10:1 beseech by *m.* of Chr.
*Gal.* 5:23 fruit of the Spirit is *m.*
6:1 restore in the spirit of *m.*
*Eph.* 4:2 with lowliness and *m,*
*Col.* 3:12 put on *m.* long-suffer.
1 *Tim.* 6:11 love, patience, *m.*
2 *Tim.* 2:25 in *m.* instruct. those
*Tit.* 3:2 showing *m.* to all men
*Jam.* 1:21 receive with *m.* word
3:13 works with *m.* of wisdom
1 *Pet.* 3:15 reason of hope wi. *m.*

**MEET, Adjective.**

*Gen.* 2:18 make a help *m.* for him
20 not found help *m.* for Adam
*Ex.* 8:26 it is not *m.* so to do
*Deut.* 3:18 all that are *m.* for war
*Jud.* 5:30 *m.* for necks of them
*Job* 34:31 it is *m.* to be said to G.
*Prov.* 11:24 withhol. more th. *m.*
*Jer.* 26:14 do wi. me as seem. *m.*
27:5 to whom it seemed *m.*
*Ezek.* 15:4 is it *m.* for any work
5 less shall it be *m.* for work
*Mat.* 3:8 fruits *m.* for repentance
15:26 not *m.* to take children's bread, *Mark* 7:27
*Acts* 26:20 works *m.* for repent.
*Rom.* 1:27 recomp. wh. was *m.*
1 *Cor.* 15:9 not *m.* to be called
16:4 if it be *m.* that I go also
*Col.* 1:12 made us *m.* to be part.
2 *Thes.* 1:3 thank God, as it is *m.*
*Heb.* 6:7 herbs *m.* for them
2 *Pet.* 1:13 think *m.* to stir you

**MEETEST.**

2 *K.* 10:3 look out the *m.* of

**MEET, Verb.**

*Gen.* 24:65 walketh to *m.* us?
32:6 E. cometh to *m.* thee, 33:4
46:29 Joseph went up to *m.* Is.
*Ex.* 4:14 Aaron com. to *m.* thee
27 go into wildern. to *m.* Mos.
18:7 M. went to *m.* fath.-in-law
19:17 bro. people to *m.* with G.
25:22 there I will *m.* with thee, 29:42, 43; 30:6, 36; *Num.* 17:4
*Num.* 23:15 while I *m.* Lord
*Jos.* 2:16 lest pursuers *m.* you
9:11 take victuals, go *m.* them
*Jud.* 11:31 out doors to *m.* me
34 daughter came to *m.* him
1 *Sam.* 10:3 shall *m.* thee 3 men
5 shalt *m.* company of proph.
18:6 women came to *m.* Saul
25:32 Lord sent thee to *m.* me

2 Sam. 6:20 Michal came to m. D.
1 K. 2:8 Shimei came down to m.
18:16 Obadiah went to meet A.
21:18 go down to m. Ahab
2 K. 1:3 go up to m. messengers
7 man came up to m. you?
2 K. 2:15 sons of prop. came to m.
4:26 run, I pray thee, to m. her
29 if m. any man, sal. him not
8:8 and go, m. the man of God
9 so Hazael went to m. him
9:17 take horseman, send to m.
Neh. 6:2 let us m. together, 10
Job 5:14 m. darkness in daytime
39:21 goeth to m. armed men
Prov. 7:15 came I forth to m.
17:12 bear robbed of whelps m.
22:2 rich and poor m. together
29:13 the poor and deceit. man m. together
Is. 7:3 go forth to m. Ahaz
14:9 hell is moved to m. thee
34:14 beasts of desert shall m.
47:3 I will not m. thee
Jer. 51:31 one post run to m. an.
Amos 4:12 prepare to m. thy G.
Zec. 2:3 angel went out to m.
Mat. 8:34 city came to m. Jesus
25:1 went forth to m. bridegro.
6 bridegro. com. go to m. him
Mark 14:13 there shall m. you a man, Luke 22:10
Luke 14:31 ten thou. to m. him
Acts 28:15 came to m. us as far
1 Thes. 4:17 in clouds to m. Lord

**MEETEST, ETH, ING.**

Gen. 32:17 E. my brother m. thee
Num. 35:19 when he m. him, 21
1 Sam. 21:1 afraid at m. of Dav.
Is. 1:13 iniq. even solemn m.
64:5 thou m. him that rejoiceth

**MEGIDDO.**

Jud. 5:19 fought by wat. of M.
1 K. 9:15 raised a levy build M.
2 K. 9:27; 23:30; 2 Chr. 35:22

MEGIDDON. Zec. 12:11
MEHETABEL. Gen. 36:39
MEHUJAEL. Gen. 4:18
MELCHI. Luke 3:24

**MELCHISEDEK.**

Gen. 14:18 M. bro. forth bread
Ps. 110:4 order of M. Heb. 5:10
Heb. 7:1 M. priest of God, 10, 21

MELITA. Acts 28:1

**MELODY.**

Is. 23:16 make sweet m. sing
51:3 found therein, voice of m.
Amos 5:23 not hear m. of viols
Eph. 5:19 making m. to Lord

**MELONS.**

Num. 11:5 we remember the m.

**MELT.**

Ex. 15:15 inhabit. of Canaan m.
Jos. 2:11 our hearts did m.
14:8 bret. made heart of peo. m.
2 Sam. 17:10 heart of lion, ut. m.
Ps. 58:7 let them m. away
Is. 13:7 every man's heart shall m. Ezek. 21:7
19:1 heart of Egypt shall m.
Jer. 9:7 behold, I will m. them
Ezek. 22:20 to m. it I will leave
Amos 9:5 touch. land, it shall m.
13 the hills shall m. Nah. 1:5
2 Pet. 3:10 elem. m. with heat, 12

**MELTED.**

Ex. 16:21 sun waxed hot it m.
Jos. 5:1 heard that th. hearts m.
7:5 the hearts of the people m.
Jud. 5:5 mountains m. bef. Lord
1 Sam. 14:16 multitude m. away
Ps. 22:14 heart m. in midst
46:6 uttered voice, the earth m.
97:5 the hills m. like wax
107:26 soul m. bec. of trouble
Is. 34:3 mountains m. wi. blood
Ezek. 22:21 m. in midst thereof
22 as silver is m. in furnace

**MELTETH.**

Ps. 58:8 as a snail which m. let
68:2 wax m. so let wicked peri.
119:28 my soul m. for heaviness
147:18 sendeth out word m. th.
Jer. 6:29 the founder m. in vain
Nah. 2:10 heart of Nineveh m.

**MELTING.**

Jam. 64:2 as when m. fire burns.

**MEMBER.**

Deut. 23:1 his privy m. cut off
1 Cor. 12:14 body is not one m.
19 all one m. where were bo.?
26 one m. suffer, one m. honor.
Jam. 3:5 the tongue is a little m.

**MEMBERS.**

Job 17:7 my m. are as a shadow
Ps. 139:16 in book all m. written
Mat. 5:29 one of m. sh. perish, 30
Rom. 6:13 nei. your m. instrum.
7:5 sins did work in our m.
Rom. 7:23 see ano. law in m. wa.
12:4 many m. in one body
5 every one m. one of another
1 Cor. 6:15 your bodies m. of C.
12:12 the body hath many m.
18 but now hath G. set the m.
20 but now are they many m.
26 all the m. suffer with it
27 are the body of Ch. and m.
Eph. 4:25 are m. one of another
5:30 we are m. of his body
Col. 3:5 mortify your m. on ear.
Jam. 3:6 tongue one of our m.
4:1 lusts that war in your m.

**MEMORIAL.**

Ex. 3:15 m. unto all generations
17:14 wri. this for a m. in book
28:12 for stones of m. to Israel
29 for a m. before the L. 39:7
30:16 money may be for a m.
Lev. 23:24 a m. of blowing trumpets, Num. 10:10
24:7 frankinc. on bread for m.
Num. 5:15 it is an offering of m.
18 offering of m. in her hands
16:40 brazen censers a m. to Is.
31:54 gold of captains for m.
Jos. 4:7 th. stones sh. be for m.
Neh. 2:20 have no portion nor m.
Est. 9:28 nor m. of them perish
Ps. 9:6 th. m. perished with th.
135:13 m. through. all generat.
Hos. 12:5 L. of hosts; L. is his m.
Zec. 6:14 the crowns be for a m.
Mat. 26:13 this be told for a m. of her, Mark 14:9
Acts 10:4 prayers come up for m.

**MEMORY.**

Ps. 109:15 cut off m. of them
145:7 utter m. of thy goodness
Prov. 10:7 m. of the just blessed
Ec. 9:5 m. of them is forgotten
Is. 26:14 made their m. to perish
1 Cor. 15:2 keep in m. I preach.

MEMUCAN. Est. 1:14, 16, 21
MEMPHIS. Hos. 9:6

**MEN.**

Gen. 4:26 began m. to call on L.
6:1 when m. began to multiply
18:2 lo, three m. stood by him
19:4 m. of the city, m. of Sodom
32:28 power with God and m.
34:21 these m. are peaceable
42:11 true m. 31; 43:16 bring
46:32 m. are shepherds
Ex. 1:17 saved m. children, 18
10:11 ye th. m. serve the Lord
34:23 thrice in year m. children
Num. 13:32 m. of great stature
16:14 put out eyes of these m.
29 these m. die the death of all
Deut. 1:35 not one of these m. shall see good land
33:6 let R. let not his m. be few
Jud. 6:27 he feared m. of city
9:54 m. say not of me, A woman
1 Sam. 2:26 favor with L. and m.
2 Sam. 3:39 these m. sons of Zer.
10:12 play the m. for our people
19:28 dead m. before the king
23:3 ruleth over m. must be just
20 slew two lion-like m. of Moab, 1 Chr. 11:22
2 Chr. 6:18 will God dw. wi. m.?
Ps. 9:20 kn. thems. to be but m.
17:14 from m. wh. are thy hand
82:7 but ye shall die like m.
Is. 7:13 sm. thing to weary m.?
31:3 now the Egyptians are m.
38:16 O L. by th. things m. live
43:4 there. will I gi. m. for thee
46:8 rememb. show yoursel. m.
Mic. 7:6 man's enemies are m.
Hab. 1:14 makest m. as fishes
Zec. 3:8 they are m. wondered at
Mat. 7:12 whatsoe. ye would m. should do to you, Luke 6:31
10:32 conf. me bef. m. Luke 12:8
13:25 m. slept, enemy came
16:13 m. say I am? Mark 8:27
Mark 8:24 m. as trees walking
10:27 Jesus saith, With m. it is impossible, Luke 18:27
Luke 2:14 good will toward m.
5:10 hencef. thou shalt catch m.
12:48 to wh. m. have commit.
18:11 I am not as other m. are
Acts 2:13 these m. full of wine
5:4 thou hast not lied unto m.
29 to obey God rather than m.
10:19 behold three m. seek thee
14:15 we are m. of like passions
24:16 void of off. to God and m.
Rom. 1:27 m. with m. working
1 Cor. 4:9 spe. to angels and m.
14:2 for he speaketh not to m.
1 Cor. 14:21 with m. of other to.
2 Cor. 8:13 not that other m. be
Eph. 6:7 L. not to m. Col. 3:23
1 Thes. 2:4 speak not as plea. m.
Heb. 6:16 for m. verily swear
7:8 m. that die receive tithes
9:27 is appointed to m. once to
12:23 spir. of just m. made perf.
Jam. 3:9 therewith curse we m.
1 Pet. 4:6 judged according to m.
2 Pet. 1:21 holy m. of G. spake
Rev. 9:4 only those m. wh. have
21:3 tabernacle of G. is with m.

**All MEN.**

Ps. 89:47 made all m. in vain
116:11 I sa. in haste, a. m. liars
Ex. 7:2 that is the end of all m.
Zec. 8:10 set a. m. ag. neighbor
Luke 6:26 woe wh. a. m. speak
John 5:23 all m. sh. honor the S.
12:32 will draw all m. unto me
Rom. 5:12 death pas. upon a. m.
18 judgment came on all m. to condemnation, the free gift came on all m. to justificat.
12:17 honest in sight of all m.
18 live peaceably with all m.
1 Cor. 7:7 I would all m. were as
9:19 for tho' I be free fr. all m.
15:19 we are of all m. most mis.
2 Cor. 3:2 kn. and read of all m.
Gal. 6:10 let us do good to all m.
1 Thes. 2:15 contrary to all m.
5:15 follow wh. is good to all m.
2 Thes. 3:2 all m. have not faith
1 Tim. 2:1 giving tha. for a. m.
4 will have all m. to be saved
4:10 trust in God, Sa. of all m.
2 Tim. 2:24 be gentle to all m.
4:16 no man stood, all m. forso.
Tit. 2:11 grace of G. ap. to all m.
Heb. 12:14 fol. peace with all m.
Jam. 1:5 ask of G. th. giv. all m.

1 Pet. 2:17 honor all m. love bro.
3 John 12 D. good rep. of all m.

See BRETHREN, CHIEF, CHILDREN, CHOSEN, EVIL, GREAT.

**In MEN.**

1 Cor. 3:21 no man glory in m.

See ISRAEL, JUDAH.

**Like MEN.**

1 Sam. 4:9 your. l. m. 1 Cor. 16:13
Ps. 82:7 ye shall die like m.
Hos. 6:7 they l. m. transg. cove.
Luke 12:36 l. m. that wait for L.

**Mighty MEN.**

Gen. 6:4 m. m. whi. were of old
Jos. 1:14 m. m. of valor sh. pass
8:3 Joshua ch. out 30,000 m. m.
1 Sam. 2:4 bows of m. m. broken
2 Sam. 16:6 m. m. on his right
17:8 m. that they may be m.
23:8 these be names of m. m.
16 mighty m. brake host, 17
1 K. 1:8 m. m. not with Adonij.
10 m. m. and Sol. he called not
2 K. 15:20 exact. m. m. of wealth
24:14 carri. away m. m. of valor
1 Chr. 5:24 and were m. m. of valor, 7:7. 9, 11, 40
12:1 they were among the m. m.
29:24 m. m. submitted to Solo.
2 Chr. 13:3 J. set battle against Abijah, being mighty m. of valor, 14:8; 17:13, 14, 16
25:6 Amaz. hired 100,000 m. m.
32:3 H. took counsel with m. m.
21 angel cut off all the m. m.
Neh. 11:14 their brethren m. m.
Job 34:24 break in pieces m. m.
Ec. 7:19 wisdom strength. m. m.
Cant. 4:4 shields of mighty m.
Is. 21:17 m. m. sh. be diminish.
Jer. 5:16 they are all mighty m.
46:9 m. m. come; 48:14 we are
48:41 the hearts of m. m. of M.
49:22 heart of mighty m. of Ed.
50:36 a sword is upon her m. m.
51:30 m. m. of Babylon forbor.
56 her m. m. are taken
57 drunk captains and m. m.
Lam. 1:15 L. hath trodden m. m.
Ezek. 39:20 at table with m. m.
Dan. 3:20 commanded m. m.
Hos. 10:13 trust in mighty m
Joel 2:7 they sh. run like m. m.
3:9 prepare war, wake m. m.
Ob. 9 thy m. m. O Teman
Nah. 2:3 shield of his mighty m.
Zec. 10:5 they shall be as m. m.
Rev. 6:15 m. m. hide themselves
19:18 ye may eat flesh of m. m.

**MEN-PLEASERS.**

Eph. 6:6 eye-servants as m.-p. Col. 3:22

**Sons of MEN.**

Ps. 4:2 O ye s. of m. how l. 58:1
31:19 trust in thee bef. s. of m.
33:13 Lord beholdeth s. of m.
57:4 I lie among the sons of m.
145:12 to make kno. to s. of m.
Prov. 8:31 del. were wi. s. of m.
Ec. 1:13 hath given to s. of m.
2:8 delights of the sons of m.
3:10 God hath given to s. of m.
18 concerning estate of s. of m.
8:11 s. of m. set to do evil
9:3 heart of s. of m. full of evil
12 so are s. of m. snared in ev.
Is. 52:14 form more th. s. of m.
Jer. 32:19 eyes are upon s. of m.
Dan. 5:21 driven from s. of m.
10:16 like simil. of s. of m.
Joel 1:12 joy withered fr. s. of m.
Mic. 5:7 nor waiteth for s. of m.
Mark 3:28 sins be forgi. s. of m.
Eph. 3:5 not made kn. to s. of m.

See OLD, RICH, RIGHTEOUS, SINGING.

**MEN-SERVANTS.**

Gen. 12:16 Abram had m.-s.
20:14 Abimelech gave m.-s.
30:43 J. had m.-s. camels, 32:5
Ex. 21:7 not go out as m.-s.
Deut. 12:12 bef. L. ye and m.-s.
1 Sam. 8:16 will take you m.-s.
2 K. 5:26 is time to rec. m.-s.?
Luke 12:45 begin to beat m.-s.

**MEN-STEALERS.**

1 Tim. 1:10 law is made for m.-s.

See TWO.

**MEN of war.**

Num. 31:49 sum of m. of war
Deut. 2:14 till generation of m. of w. came out, 16; Jos. 5:6
1 K. 9:22 they were m. of w. and his captains, 2 Chr. 8:9
2 K. 25:4 m. of w. fled. Jer. 52:7
Jer. 38:4 weak. hands of m. of w.
49:26 m. of w. be cut off, 50:30
51:32 m. of war are affrighted
Ezek. 27:10 P. were thy m. of w.
27 thy m. of war shall fall
Joel 2:7 climb wall like m. of w.
3:9 let all m. of war draw near
Luke 23:11 H. with his m. of w.

**MEN, with wicked.**

Gen. 13:13 m. of Sodom were w.
Num. 16:26 de. fr. tents of w. m.
2 Sam. 3:34 man fall. bef. w. m.
4:11 more wh. w. m. have slain
Job 22:15 old way w. m. ha. tro.
34:8 which walketh with w. m.
26 striketh them as wicked m.
36 because of answers of w. m.
Ec. 8:14 w. m. to wh. it happen.
Jer. 5:26 am. my peo. fou. w. m.
Mat. 21:41 miser. destroy w. m.
2 Thes. 3:2 delivered from w. m.

**Wise MEN.**

Gen. 41:8 Ph. call. w. m. Ex. 7:11
Ex. 36:4 w. m. wrought work
Deut. 1:13 take ye wise m. and
Job 15:18 which w. m. have told
34:2 hear my words, O ye w. m.
Ps. 49:10 seeth that wise m. die
Prov. 10:14 w. m. lay up knowl.
13:20 walketh with w. m.
29:8 w. m. turn away wrath
Ec. 9:17 words of w. m. heard
Is. 19:12 where are thy wise m.
29:14 wisd. of w. m. shall perish
44:25 turneth w. m. backward
Jer. 8:9 the wise m. are ashamed
10:7 the wise m. of the nations
51:57 make drunken her w. m.
Ezek. 27:8 thy wise m. O Tyrus
9 the w. m. were thy calkers
Dan. 2:12 to destroy all wise m.
4:6 decree to bring in all w. m.
Ob. 8 destroy w. m. out of Edom
Mat. 2:1 came w. m. from east
1 Cor. 1:26 not many wise m.
10:15 I speak as to w. m.

**MEN, with women.**

Deut. 2:34 utterly destroyed the m. and women, Jos. 8:25
Jud. 9:49 about 1,000 m. and w.
16:27 house full of m. and w.
2 Sam. 6:19 dealt to the w. as m.
Acts 5:14 added to L. m. and w.
8:3 Saul, haling m. and women
12 baptized, both m. and w.
9:2 m. or w. bring them bound
22:4 into prisons both m. and w.

MEN, women, and children. See CHILDREN.

**Ye MEN.**

Job 34:10 heark. ye m. of under.
Acts 1:11 ye m. of G. 2:14 of Jud.
5:35 ye m. of Is. 17:22 of Athens
13:15 ye m. and brethren, if ye
19:35 ye m. of Ephesus

**Young MEN.**

Gen. 14:24 wh. y. m. have eaten
Ex. 24:5 y. m. which offer. burn.
Jos. 6:23 y. m. that were spies
Jud. 14:10 so used y. m. to do
Ruth 3:10 followedst not y. m.
1 Sam. 2:17 sin of y. m. very gr.
8:16 take your goodliest y. m.
21:4 if y. m. kept from women
25:8 ask y. m. they will show
25 thy handmaid saw not y. m.
30:17 400 y. m. wh. rode on ca.
2 Sam. 2:14 y. m. arise and play
13:32 sup. they slain all y. m.
18:15 ten y. m. bare J.'s armor
1 K. 12:8 Re. consult. with y. m.
14 counsel of y. m. 2 Chr. 10:8
20:14 young m. of the princes
2 K. 5:22 two y. m. of prophets
8:12 their y. m. wilt thou slay
Job 1:19 fell on y. m. are dead
29:8 y. m. saw me, hid themsel.
Ps. 78:63 fire consum. their y. m.
148:12 praise L. y. m. and maid.
Prov. 20:29 gl. of y. m. strength
Is. 9:17 L. no joy in their y. m.
13:18 bows dash y. m. to pieces
23:4 nei. do I nourish up y. m.
31:8 his y. m. shall be discomfi.
40:30 the y. m. shall utterly fall
Jer. 6:11 fury on assem. of y. m.
9:21 cut off y. m. from streets
11:22 y. m. sh. die by the sword
15:8 brought ag. moth. of y. m.
18:21 let y. m. be slain by swo.
31:13 both y. m. and old rejoice
48:15 chosen young m. gone to slaughter
49:26 y. m. shall fall in streets
50:30 theref. y. m. fall in streets
51:3 spare not y. m. des. utterly
Lam. 1:15 assem. to crush y. m.
18 virgins and y. m. into capt.
2:21 y. m. and old lie on ground
5:13 they took y. m. to grind
14 y. m. ceased fr. their music
Ezek. 23:6 desirable y. m. 12, 23
Joel 2:28 y. m. see vis. Acts 2:17
Amos 2:11 y. m. for Nazarites
4:10 y. m. slain with the sword
8:13 your y. m. faint for thirst
Zec. 9:17 make y. m. cheerful
Mark 14:51 y. m. laid hold
Acts 5:6 y. m. arose, wound him
Tit. 2:6 y. m. exhort to be sober
1 John 2:13 I wr. to you, y. m. 14

MENAHEM. 2 K. 15:14, 16

**MEND, ING.**

2 Chr. 24:12 brass to m. ho. of L.
34:10 workmen to m. house
Mat. 4:21 Z. m. nets, Mark 1:19

MENE. Dan. 5:25

**MENSTRUOUS.**

Is. 30:22 cast away as m. cloth
Lam. 1:17 Jeru. is as m. woman
Ezek. 18:6 come near to m. wo.

**MENTION, Substantive**

Gen. 40:14 m. of me unto Phar.
Ex. 23:13 make no m. of other gods, Jos. 23:7
1 Sam. 4:18 made m. of ark of G.
Ps. 71:16 make m. of thy righte.
87:4 I will make m. of Rahab
Is. 12:4 m. th. his name is exalt.
19:17 make m. thereof be afraid
26:13 will make m. of thy name
48:1 make m. of the God of Isr.
49:1 he made m. of my name
62:6 ye that make m. of the L.
Jer. 4:16 make ye m. to nations
20:9 I will not make m. of him
Amos 6:10 not m. name of Lord
Rom. 1:9 m. you alw. in my pra. Eph. 1:16; 1 Thes. 1:2
Phile. 4 m. of thee in my praye.
Heb. 11:22 m. of departing of Is.

**MENTION, Verb.**
Is. 63:7 m. loving-kindn. of Lord
Jer. 23:36 bur. of L. m. no more

**MENTIONED.**
1 Chr. 4:38 th. m. were princes
2 Chr. 20:34 J. m. in b. of kings
Ezek. 16:56 Sodom was not m.
18:22 his transgres. not be m.
24 his righteous. sh. not be m.
33:16 none of his sins sh. be m.

**MEPHIBOSHETH.**
2 Sam. 4:4 name was M. 9:10
21:7 but the king spared M.

MERAB. 1 Sam. 14:49; 18:19

**MERARI.**
Gen. 46:11; Ex. 6:16; Num. 3:17; 1 Chr. 6:1, 16; 23:6
Num. 4:42 numbered of M. 10:17
Jos. 21:7 M. 40; 1 Chr. 6:63, 77

**MERCHANDISE.**
Deut. 21:14 not make m. of her
24:7 broth. maketh m. of him
Prov. 3:14 m. bet. than m. of go.
31:18 perceiveth her m. is good
Is. 23:18 her m. sh. be holiness
45:14 m. of Ethio. come to thee
Ezek. 26:12 a prey of thy m.
27:9 ships in thee to occupy m.
15 isles were m. of hands
28:16 multit. of m. have filled
Mat. 22:5 farm, another to m.
John 2:16 F.'s house hou. of m.
2 Pet. 2:3 words make m. of you
Rev. 18:11 no man buyeth th. m.

**MERCHANT.**
Gen. 23:16 cur. money with m.
37:28 passed by Midian. m.-m.
1 K. 10:15 he had of m.-men
Prov. 31:14 like the m.-ships
24 delivereth girdles to the m.
Cant. 3:6 perfum. powders of m.
Is. 23:11 command. ag. m. city
Ezek. 27:3 art a m. of pe. for isles
12 Tarshish was thy m.
16 Syria; 18 Damas.; 20 Dedan
Hos. 12:7 a m. balances of deceit
Zep. 1:11 m. peo. are cut down
Mat. 13:45 like a m.-man seeking

**MERCHANTS.**
1 K. 10:15 of traffic of spice m.
28 the king's m. receiv. linen yarn, 2 Chr. 1:16
Neh. 3:32 goldsmiths and the m.
13:20 m. lodged without Jerus.
Job 41:6 shall part him am. m.?
Is. 23:2 m. of Zidon replenished
8 city, whose m. are princes
47:15 even thy m. sh. wander
Ezek. 17:4 set it in a city of m.
27:13 Javan; Tubal; Mesh. m.
15 Dedan; 17 Judah and Israel thy m.
21 in these were they thy m.
22 m. of Sheba and Raam. 23
36 the m. shall hiss at thee
38:13 and the m. of Tarshish
Nah. 3:16 multip. m. above stars
Rev. 18:3 m. of earth waxen rich
11 m. of earth weep over her
23 m. were great m. of earth

MERCURIUS. Acts 14:12

**MERCY.**
Gen. 24:27 destitute master of m.
43:14 God give you m. before
Ex. 34:7 keeping m. for thousands, Dan. 9:4
Num. 14:18 the Lord is of great m. Ps. 103:11; 145:8
Deut. 7:9 keep coven. and m. 12
2 Sam. 7:15 m. not depart from him, 1 Chr. 17:13; Ps. 89:24
15:20 m. and truth be with thee
1 K. 8:23 keepest covenant and m. with serv. Neh. 1:5; 9:32
1 Chr. 16:34 his m. endureth for ever, 41; 2 Chr. 5:13; 7:3, 6; 20:21; Ezr. 3:11; Ps. 106:1; 107:1; 118:1; 136:1-26; Jer. 33:11
Ezr. 7:28 extended m. to me
9:9 extend. m. to us in sight of
Neh. 1:11 m. in sight of man
Job 37:13 for correction or for m.
Ps. 21:7 thro' m. of Most High
23:6 goodness and m. follow me
25:10 paths of the Lord are m.
32:10 m. shall comp. him about
33:18 them that hope in his m.
52:8 I trust in the m. of God
57:3 send forth m. and truth
59:10 God of m. sh. prev. me, 17
61:7 O prepare m. and truth
62:12 unto thee belongeth m.
66:20 not turned m. from me
77:8 is his m. cl. gone for ever?
85:10 m. and truth m. together
86:5 plenteous in m. 15; 103:8
89:2 m. sh. be built up for ever
14 m. and truth go be. thy face
28 my m. will I keep for him
98:3 remembered m. toward Is.
100:5 L. is good, his m. is everl.
101:1 will sing m. and judgm.
103:17 m. of Lord is everlasting
109:12 none extend m. to him
130:7 with the Lord there is m.
147:11 pleas. in those hope m.
Prov. 3:3 let not m. forsake thee
14:21 he that hath m. on poor
22 m. and truth sh. be to them
Prov. 14:31 he that hon. G. ha. m.
16:6 by m. iniquity is purged
20:28 m. and truth preserve the king, and his throne is upholden by m: Is. 16:5
21:21 followeth after m. find. life
Is. 49:10 that hath m. on them
54:10 Lord that hath m. on thee
60:10 my favor had m. on thee
Jer. 6:23 cruel, and have no m.
Hos. 4:1 there is no m. in land
6:6 I desired m. and not sacrif.
10:12 reap in m. 12:6 keep m.
14:3 in thee the fatherl. find m.
Jon. 2:8 forsake their own m.
Mic. 6:8 do justly, and love m.
7:18 because he delight. in m.
20 wilt perform m. to Abraham
Hab. 3:2 L. in wrath remem. m.
Mat. 5:7 merciful, sh. obtain m.
23:23 omitted judgment and m.
Luke 1:50 m. on them fear him
54 Is. in remembran. of his m.
72 to perform the m. promised
78 through tender m. of God
Rom. 9:23 glory on vessels of m.
11:30 obtained m. thro' unbelief
31 your m. th. also may ob. m.
15:9 might glorify God for m.
1 Cor. 7:25 obtai. m. to be faith.
2 Cor. 4:1 as we have received m.
Gal. 6:16 peace and m. on Israel
Eph. 2:4 God who is rich in m.
Phil. 2:27 God had m. on him
1 Tim. 1:2 m. and peace fr. G. 2 Tim. 1:2; Tit. 1:4; 2 John 3
13 I obtained m. because, 16
2 Tim. 1:16 Lord give m. to hou.
18 he may find m. of the Lord
Tit. 3:5 according to m. he saved
Heb. 4:16 that we may obtain m.
10:28 desp. law died without m.
Jam. 2:13 judgm. without m. th. showed no m. m. rejoiceth
3:17 wisd. from above full of m.
5:11 pitiful and of tender m.
1 Pet. 1:3 according to abund. m.
2:10 m. now have obtained m.
Jude 2 m. to you, peace, and love
21 looking for m. of Lord Jes.

**Have MERCY.**
Ps. 4:1 have m. upon me, 6:2; 9:13; 25:16; 27:7; 30:10; 31:9; 51:1; 86:16
102:13 h. m. on Z. 123:2 on us, 3
Prov. 28:13 forsak. sins sh. h. m.
Is. 9:17 nei. h. m. on fatherless
14:1 Lord will have m. on Jac.
27:11 th. made th. will not h. m.
30:18 that he may have m.
49:13 God will h. m. on afflicted
54:8 with kindness will I h. m.
55:7 return, and he will have m.
Jer. 13:14 nor have m. 21:7
30:18 I will have m. on dwelling
31:20 I will surely h. m. 33:26; Ezek. 39:25; Hos. 1:7; 2:23
42:12 that he may h. m. on you
Hos. 1:6 no more h. m. on Is. 2:4
Zec. 1:12 long wilt th. not h. m.
10:6 for I have m. upon them
Mat. 9:13 I will have m. 12:7
27 thou son of David, h. m. on me, 15:22; 20:30, 31; Mark 10:47, 48; Luke 18:38, 39
Luke 16:24 Abraham, h. m. on m.
17:13 Jesus, Master, h. m. on us
Rom. 9:15 I will have m. on wh. I will have m. 18
11:32 that he might h. m. on all

**MERCY-SEAT.**
Ex. 25:17 make a m.-s. of gold
22 from above m.-s. bet. cherubim, Lev. 16:2; Num. 7:89
26:34 put m.-s. on ark, 40:20
Lev. 16:13 incense cover m.-s.

**MERCY, with show, ed, eth, ing.**
Gen. 39:21 Lord was with Josep. and showed him m.
Ex. 20:6 showing m. to thousan. Deut. 5:10
33:19 s. m. on wh. I will s. m.
Deut. 7:2 no covenant, nor s. m.
Jud. 1:24 and we will s. thee m.
2 Sam. 22:51 s. m. to his anoint. Ps. 18:50
1 K. 3:6 hast showed to D. my father, great m. 2 Chr. 1:8
2 Chr. 6:14 s. m. to thy servants
Ps. 37:21 the righteous s. m.
85:7 s. us thy m. O Lord
109:16 remembered not to s. m.
Is. 47:6 didst show them no m.
Jer. 50:42 and will not s. m.
Dan. 4:27 break off sins, s. m.
Zec. 7:9 execute judgm. s. m.
Luke 1:58 L. s. great m. on her
10:37 that showed m. on him
Rom. 9:16 but of God that s. m
Jam. 2:13 that hath s. no m.

**Thy MERCY.**
Gen. 19:19 hast magnified t. m.
Ex. 15:13 in t. m. led forth peo.
Num. 14:19 greatness of thy m.
Neh. 13:22 according to thy m.
Ps. 5:7 in multitude of thy m.
6:4 return, O Lord, save me for thy m.'s sake, 31:16
13:5 I have trusted in thy m.
25:7 accor. to thy m. remem. me
31:7 I will rejoice in thy m.
33:22 let thy m. O L. be upon us
36:5 t. m. O L. is in the heavens
44:26 redeem us for t. m.'s sake
57:10 thy m. is great to heavens
59:16 I will sing aloud of thy m.
69:13 in multitude of thy m.
85:7 show us t. m. 86:13 great
90:14 O satisfy us with thy m.
94:18 t. m. O Lord, held me up
108:4 thy m. is great above hea.
109:21 because thy m. is good
26 according to thy m.
115:1 for t. m. and truth's sake
119:64 earth is full of thy m.
124 deal wi. servant ac. to t. m.

138:8 thy m. endureth for ever
143:12 of t. m. cut off mine ene.

**MERCIES.**

Gen. 32:10 not worthy of thy m.
2 Sam. 24:14 for his m. are great,
1 Chr. 21:13
2 Chr. 6:42 remember m. of Dav.
Neh. 9:19 in m. forsook. th. not
27 accord. to thy m. thou gav.
31 m. didst not consume them
Ps. 51:1 thy m. blot out transg.
69:13 in multitude of thy m.
16 according to thy tender m.
89:1 I will sing of the m. of L.
106:7 remembered not thy m.
45 repented accord. to his m.
119:41 let thy m. also come
Is. 54:7 with m. will I gather
55:3 sure m. of D. Acts 13:34
63:15 where is thy m. tow. me?
Jer. 16:5 taken away my m.
42:12 I will show m. unto you
Lam. 3:22 of L.'s m. we are not
32 compassion according to m.
Dan. 2:18 m. concerning this
9:9 to the L. our God belong m.
18 not for righteousn. but m.
Hos. 2:19 I will betr. thee in m.
Zec. 1:16 am returned with m.
Rom. 12:1 I bes. you by m. of G.
2 Cor. 1:3 Father of m. and God
Phil. 2:1 if there be any fellowship, any bowels of m.
Col. 3:12 put on bowels of m.

**Tender MERCIES.**

Ps. 25:6 remem. thy t. m. 51:1
40:11 withhold not thy ten. m.
77:9 in anger shut up his t. m.
79:8 thy tender m. prevent us
103:4 L. crown. thee with t. m.
119:77 thy t. m. come unto me
156 great are thy ten. m. O L.
145:9 t. m. over all his works
Prov. 12:10 t. m. of wicked cruel

**MERCIFUL.**

Gen. 19:16 Lord being m. to Lot
Ex. 34:6 L. G. m. and gracious
Deut. 21:8 be m. O L. to Israel
32:43 and will be m. to his land
2 Sam. 22:26 with m. thou wilt show thyself m. Ps. 18:25
1 K. 20:31 kings of Is. m. kings
2 Chr. 30:9 L. G. gracious and m.
Neh. 9:17 ready to pardon and m.
Ps. 26:11 redeem me, and be m. to me, 41:4, 10; 56:1; 57:1; 86:3; 119:58, 132
37:26 the righteous is ever m.
59:5 be not m. to any wicked
67:1 G. be m. to us, and bl. us
103:8 Lord is m. and gracious
117:2 his m. kindness is great
119:76 m. kindness for my com.
Prov. 11:17 m. man doeth good
Is. 57:1 m. men are taken away
Jer. 3:12 I am m. saith the Lord
Joel 2:13 he is gracious and m.
Jon. 4:2 knew thou art a m. G.
Mat. 5:7 m. shall obtain mercy
Luke 6:36 be m. as your F. is m.
18:13 God be m. to me a sinner
Heb. 2:17 be a m. high-priest
8:12 be m. to their unright.

**MERIBAH.**

Ex. 17:7 called name of place M.
Num. 20:13, 24; Deut. 32:51; 33:8
Ps. 81:7 proved thee at wat. M.

MERODACH. Jer. 50:2
MERODACH-BALADAN. Is. 39:1
MEROM. Jos. 11:5, 7
MEROZ. Jud. 5:23

**MERRY.**

Gen. 43:34 drank and were m.
Jud. 9:27 trode grapes, made m.
16:25 their hearts were m.
19:6 and let thy heart be m.
Ruth 3:7 Boaz's heart was m.
1 Sam. 25:36 Nabal's heart m.
2 Sam. 13:28 when Amnon is m.
1 K. 4:20 Judah and Isr. were m.
21:7 and let thy heart be m.
2 Chr. 7:10 sent people away m.
Est. 1:10 heart of king was m.
Prov. 15:13 m. heart ma. cheerf.
15 m. heart ha. continual feast
17:22 a m. heart doeth good
Ec. 8:15 better to eat and be m.
9:7 drink wine with a m. heart
10:19 laughter, wine maketh m.
Is. 24:7 the m. hearted do sigh
Jer. 30:19 voi. of th. th. make m.
31:4 dances of th. that make m.
Luke 12:19 ease, eat and be m.
15:23 and be m. 24; 29 I might
32 it was meet we should be m.
Jam. 5:13 is any m.? sing psal.
Rev. 11:10 rejoice and make m.

**MERRILY.**

Est. 5:14 go in m. with king

**MESCHECH.**

Gen. 10:2 M. son of Japheth, 1 Chr. 1:5, 17
Ps. 120:5 I sojourn in M.
Ezek. 39:1 ag. chief prince of M.

**MESOPOTAMIA.**

Gen. 24:10 Eliezer went to M.
Deut. 23:4 Bal. of M. Jud. 3:8
1 Chr. 19:6 hire chari. out of M.
Acts 2:9 dwellers in M. we hear
7:2 G. appeared to Abra. in M.

**MESS, ES.**

Gen. 43:34 sent m. to them, Benjamin's m.
2 Sam. 11:8 Uriah a m. from king

**MESSAGE.**

Jud. 3:20 I have m. from God
1 K. 20:12 Benhad. heard this m.
Prov. 26:6 sendeth m. by fool
Hag. 1:13 spake Hag. in L.'s m.
Luke 19:14 citiz. sent m. aft. him
1 John 1:5 m. we ha. heard, 3:11

**MESSENGER.**

Gen. 50:16 sent a m. to Joseph
1 K. 19:2 Jezebel sent m. to Elij.
22:13 the m. went to call Micaiah, 2 Chr. 18:12
2 K. 6:32 ere the m. came to him
9:18 the m. came to them, but
Job 1:11 there came a m. to Job
33:23 if there be m. interpreter
Prov. 13:17 m. fall. into mischief
17:11 cruel m. shall be sent
25:13 faithful m. to them
Is. 42:19 as my m. that I sent?
Jer. 51:31 one m. run to meet
Ezek. 23:40 to wh. a m. was sent
Hag. 1:13 Haggai, the Lord's m.
Mal. 2:7 he is m. of L. of hosts
3:1 send m. of covenant, Mat. 11:10; Mark 1:2; Luke 7:27
2 Cor. 12:7 m. of Satan to buffet
Phil. 2:25 companion, your m.

**MESSENGERS.**

Gen. 32:3 Jacob sent m. to Esau
Num. 22:5 Balak sent m. to Bal.
Jos. 6:17 Rahab hid the m. 25
1 Sam. 19:11 Saul sent m. to David, 14, 15, 20, 21
25:14 David sent m. to salute
2 Sam. 2:5 sent m. to Jabesh-gil.
3:12 sent m. to D. on his behalf
5:11 H. sent m. to D. 1 Chr. 14:1
11:4 Dav. sent m. to Bathsheba
12:27 Joab sent m. to David
2 K. 1:3 meet the m. of Ahaziah
17:4 Hoshea had sent m. to So
19:23 m. th. hast reproached L.
1 Chr. 19:2 m. to comfort Hanun
2 Chr. 36:15 L. sent them by m.
16 they mocked the m. of God
Prov. 16:14 wrath of king as m.
Is. 14:32 answer m. of nation?
18:2 go ye swift m. to a nation
37:14 letter from m. and read it
44:26 performeth counsel of m.
57:9 didst send thy m. afar off
Jer. 27:3 send by hand of the m.
Ezek. 23:16 sent m. into Chaldea
Ezek. 30:9 m. go forth from me
Nah. 2:13 voice of m. no more
Luke 7:24 m. of John were gone
9:52 and sent m. before his face
2 Cor. 8:23 m. of the churches
Jam. 2:25 Rahab had receiv. m.

**MESSIAH.**

Dan. 9:25 from commandment to build Jerus. unto the M. the Prince shall be 7 weeks
26 after 62 weeks M. be cut off
John 1:41 found M. wh. is Christ
4:25 I know that M. cometh

**MET.**

Gen. 32:1 angel of God m. him
33:8 by this drove I m.?
Ex. 3:18 God of the Hebrews m. with us, 5:3
4:24 L. m. him, sought to kill
27 Aaron went and m. Moses
5:20 they m. Moses and Aaron
Num. 23:4 God m. Balaam, 16
1 Sam. 10:10 prophets m. Saul
1 K. 13:24 was gone, lion m. him
Ps. 85:10 mercy and tru. m. tog.
Prov. 7:10 m. him a woman
Amos 5:19 and a bear m. him
Mat. 8:28 m. him two devils
Mark 11:4 place wh. two ways m.
Luke 9:37 much people m. him, John 12:18
17:12 m. him ten men lepers
John 11:20 Martha m. him, 30
Acts 10:25 Cornelius m. him and
27:41 a place where two seas m.
Heb. 7:1 m. Abraham returning

**METE, D.**

Ex. 16:18 m. it with a homer
Ps. 60:6 m. valley of Suc. 108:7
Is. 18:2 go to a nation m. out, 7
40:12 m. out heaven with span
Mat. 7:2 measure ye m. be meas. to you, Mark 4:24; Luke 6:38

**METEYARD.**

Lev. 19:35 no unrighteous. in m.

METHEG-AMMAH. 2 Sam. 8:1

**METHUSELAH.**

Gen. 5:27 days of M. 969 years
1 Chr. 1:3 M. Lamech, Luke 3:27

**MICAH.**

Jud. 17:1 mount Eph. called M.
Jer. 26:18 M. prophes. Mic. 1:1

MICAIAH. 1 K. 22:8, 24; 2 Chr. 18:8, 23, 25

**MICE.**

1 Sam. 6:4 five golden m. accord.
5 sh. make images of your m.

**MICHAEL.**

Dan. 10:13 M. ch. prince, 21; 12:1
Jude 9 M. contending with dev.
Rev. 12:7 M. fought ag. dragon

**MICHAIAH.**

2 Chr. 17:7 Jehoshaphat sent M.
Neh. 12:35 son of M. give thanks
Jer. 36:11 M. heard Baruch, 13

**MICHAL.**

1 Sam. 14:49 S.'s yr. daughter M.
19:13 M. took an image and
2 Sam. 3:13 ex. first bring M. 14
6:16 M. looked thro', 1 Chr. 15:29

MICHMASH. 1 Sam. 13:2; Is. 10:28

**MID-DAY.**

1 K. 18:29 when m.-d. was past

*Neh.* 8:3 from morning to *m.-d.*
*Acts* 26:13 *m.-d.* I saw in way

**MIDDLE.**

*Jud.* 16:29 hold of two *m.* pillars
1 *K.* 8:64 the king did hallow *m.* court, 2 *Chr.* 7:7
2 *K.* 20:4 Isaiah gone to *m.* court
*Jer.* 39:3 princes sat in *m.* gate
*Eph.* 2:14 broken down *m.* wall

**MIDDLEMOST.**

*Ezek.* 42:5 higher than the *m.* 6

**MIDIAN.**

*Ex.* 2:15 dwelt in land of M.
*Num.* 22:4 M. said to elders of M.
25:15 dau. of chief house of M.
31:3 avenge the L. of M. 8, 9
*Jud.* 6:1 delivered them to M. 2
7:14 into hand G. delivered M.
8:22 deliv. from M. 28; 9:17
*Is.* 9:4 bro. yoke, as in day of M.
10:26 accord. to slaughter of M.
60:6 dromedaries of M. cover
*Hab.* 3:7 curtains of M. tremble

**MIDIANITES.**

*Gen.* 37:28 M. merchantmen, 36
*Num.* 25:17 vex the M. 31:2
*Jud.* 6:7 Is. cried because of M.
7:25 two princes of the M. 8:1
*Ps.* 83:9 do to them as to M.

MIDIANITISH. *Num.* 25:6, 16

**MIDNIGHT.**

*Ex.* 11:4 *m.* I will go into Egypt
12:29 at *m.* L. smote first-born
*Jud.* 16:3 Samson lay till *m.*
*Ruth* 3:8 at *m.* man was afraid
1 *K.* 3:20 she arose at *m.* and
*Job* 34:20 peo. be troubled at *m.*
*Ps.* 119:62 at *m.* I will give than.
*Mat.* 25:6 at *m.* there was a cry
*Mark* 13:35 come at even or *m.*
*Luke* 11:5 shall go to him at *m.*
*Acts* 16:25 at *m.* Paul prayed
20:7 P. continued speech till *m.*

**MIDST.**

*Ex.* 14:16 sh. go on dry ground through *m.* of sea, *Num.* 33:8; *Neh.* 9:11; *Ps.* 136:14
*Deut.* 13:5 put evil away from *m.*
3 *Chr.* 32:4 ran thr. *m.* of land
*Cant.* 3:10 *m.* paved with love
*Is.* 58:9 from *m.* of thee the yoke
*Jer.* 30:21 proceed fr. *m.* of them
*Ezek.* 9:4 go through *m.* of city
14:8 cut him off from *m.* of pe. 9
15:4 *m.* burnt, is it meet
28:16 filled *m.* of thee with viol.
18 bring forth fire from *m.*
*Dan.* 3:26 ca. forth of *m.* of fire
*Luke* 4:30 passing thro' *m.* of th.
*John* 7:14 about the *m.* of feast
8:59 going through *m.* of them
*Rev.* 8:13 flying thro' *m.* of heav.

**In the MIDST.**

*Gen.* 2:9 tr. of life *in t. m.* 3:3
15:10 A. divided them *in t. m.*
*Ex.* 8:22 I am L. *in t. m.* of earth
14:29 dry land *in m.* 15:19
33:3 I will not go up *in m.*
*Num.* 2:17 tabern. *in m.* of camp
35:5 shall be *in m. Ezek.* 48:15
*Deut.* 11:3 acts he did *in m.* of E.
23:14 God walketh *in t. m.*
*Jos.* 3:17 *in m.* of Jordan, 4:10
7:21 hid *in the m.* of my tent
2 *Sam.* 18:14 *in the m.* of oak
2 *K.* 6:20 were *in m.* of Samaria
1 *Chr.* 19:4 garments *in the m.*
*Neh.* 4:11 till we come *in the m.*
*Ps.* 22:14 *in the m.* of bowels
22 *in t. m.* of the congregation will I praise thee, *Heb.* 2:12
46:5 God is *in the m.* of her
102:24 take not away *in m.* of d.
110:2 rule *in m.* of enemies
138:7 I walk *in m.* of trouble
*Prov.* 4:21 keep th. *in m.* heart
5:14 all evil *in m.* of congrega.
8:20 *in the m.* of paths of judg.
14:33 is *in m.* of fools is folly
23:34 lieth down *in m.* of sea
*Is.* 6:5 *in the m.* of a people
7:6 set a king *in the m.* of it
12:6 great is the Holy One *in the m.* of thee, *Hos.* 11:9
19:24 blessing *in t. m.* of land
*Jer.* 14:9 Lord, art *in the m.* of us
17:11 *in m.* of his days
*Lam.* 4:13 blood of just *in m.*
*Ezek.* 5:5 set *in m.* of nations
6:7 shall fall *in m.* of you, 11:7
17:16 *in m.* of Babylon shall die
23:39 *in the m.* of my house
43:7 I will dw. *in t. m.* of Is. 9
*Dan.* 3:25 walking *in m.* of fire
*Joel* 2:27 I am *in the m.* of Israel
*Mic.* 6:14 cast. down shall *in m.*
*Nah.* 3:13 *in m.* of thee are wo.
*Hab.* 3:2 *in the m.* of the years
*Zep.* 3:5 L. is *in the m.* thereof
12 leave *in the m.* a poor people
15 Lord is *in the m.* of thee, 17
*Zec.* 2:5 glory *in the m.* of her
10 will dwell *in m.* of thee, 11
8:3 dwell *in the m.* of Jerusa. 8
*Mat.* 10:16 sheep *in m.* of wolves
14:24 ship was *in the m.* of the sea, *Mark* 6:47
18:2 little child *in m. Mark* 9:36
20 there am I *in the m.* of them
*Luke* 23:45 temple was rent *in m.*
24:36 Jesus himself stood *in the m. John* 20:19, 26
*John* 19:18 and Jesus *in the m.*
*Rev.* 4:6 *in m.* of thr. four beasts
5:6 *in m.* of throne Lamb, 7:17

**Into the MIDST.**

*Ex.* 24:18 Moses went *into t. m.*
33:5 I will come *into the m.*
*Ps.* 57:6 *i. m.* whereof they are
*Jer.* 21:4 assemble th. *i. m.* of ci.
51:63 cast it *into the m.* of river
*Ezek.* 5:4 cast them *i. m.* of fire
22:19 I will gather you *into m.* of Jerusalem

**Out of the MIDST.**

*Ex.* 3:4 *o. of m.* of bush, 24:16
*Deut.* 4:12 L. spake *out of the m.* of fire, 15:33, 36; 5:4, 22, 24
34 take nation *out of m.* of an.
*Jos.* 4:3 *out of m.* of Jordan, 8
*Is.* 24:18 cometh *out of m.* of pit
52:11 depart, go *out of the m.* of her, *Jer.* 50:8; 51:6, 45
*Ezek.* 11:7 forth *out of m.* of it
29:4 br. thee *out of m.* of rivers
32:21 sp. to him *o. of m.* of hell
*Zep.* 3:11 away *out of m.* of thee

**MIDWIFE, VES.**

*Gen.* 35:17 *m.* said unto Rachel
38:28 *m.* bound on hand thread
*Ex.* 1:16 when ye do the office of a *m.* 17, 19, 20, 21

**MIGHT, Substantive.**

*Gen.* 49:3 Re. first-born, my *m.*
*Num.* 14:13 this people in thy *m.*
*Deut.* 3:24 do according to thy *m.*
6:5 love thy God with all thy *m.*
8:17 *m.* of my hand gotten weal.
28:32 be no *m.* in thy hand
*Jud.* 5:31 sun goeth forth in *m.*
6:14 go in thy *m.* 16:30 bowed
2 *Sam.* 6:14 D. danced with all *m.*
2 *K.* 23:25 J. turned to L. wi. *m.*
24:16 king bro. cap. men of *m.*
1 *Chr.* 12:8 men of *m.* came to D.
29:2 I prepared house with *m.*
12 in thy hand is power and *m.* 2 *Chr.* 20:6
2 *Chr.* 20:12 have no *m.* ag. this
*Est.* 10:2 Ahasue. power and *m.*
*Ps.* 76:5 none of the men of *m.*
145:6 speak of *m.* of thy acts
*Ec.* 9:10 find. do it with thy *m.*
*Is.* 11:2 *m.* shall rest on him
33:13 ye that acknow. my *m.*
40:26 call. them by great. of *m.*
29 to them that have no *m.*
*Jer.* 9:23 nor let man glory in *m.*
10:6 thy name is great in *m.*
16:21 cause th. to know my *m.*
49:35 break chief of their *m.*
51:30 their *m.* hath failed
*Ezek.* 32:30 ashamed of their *m.*
*Dan.* 2:20 wisdom and *m.* are his
23 O G. who hast given me *m.*
4:30 built by *m.* of my power
*Mic.* 3:8 full of judgment and *m.*
7:16 nations confound. at th. *m.*
*Zec.* 4:6 not by *m.* nor by power
*Eph.* 1:21 far above all *m.* power
3:16 to be strengthened with *m.* *Col.* 1:11
6:10 L. and in power of his *m.*
2 *Pet.* 2:11 angels greater in *m.*
*Rev.* 7:12 glo. and *m.* be unto G.
*See* FULFILLED.

**MIGHTY.**

*Gen.* 10:9 *m.* hunter before L.
18:18 Abraham bec. a *m.* nation
23:6 thou art a *m.* prince
*Ex.* 1:7 children of Israel, *m.* 20
9:28 be no more *m.* thunderings
10:19 L. turned a *m.* west wind
15:10 sank as lead in *m.* water
*Lev.* 19:15 nor honor person of *m.*
*Num.* 22:6 this people are too *m.*
*Deut.* 4:37 he bro. thee out with *m.* power, 9:29
26:5 a nation, *m.* and populous
*Jud.* 5:13 have dominion over *m.*
23 came not to help L. ag. *m.*
1 *Sam.* 4:8 out of hand of *m.* gods
2 *Sam.* 1:19 how are *m.* fallen! 25
21 shield of the *m.* is cast aw.
2 *K.* 24:15 *m.* of the land captive
1 *Chr.* 1:10 Nim. *m.* 12:28 Zadok
2 *Chr.* 26:13 made war with *m.*
27:6 so Jotham became *m.*
*Ezr.* 4:20 been *m.* king over Jer.
7:28 mercy to me bef. *m.* princes
*Neh.* 3:16 N. repaired to the *m.*
9:11 threw. stone in *m.* waters
*Job* 5:15 he saveth poor from *m.*
6:23 redeem me fr. hand of *m.*?
9:4 wise in heart, *m.* in streng.
12:19 he overthroweth the *m.*
21 weakeneth strength of *m.*
21:7 wherefore are wicked *m.*?
24:22 draweth *m.* wi. his power
34:20 *m.* shall be taken away
35:9 by reason of arm of *m.*
41:25 raiseth himself, *m.* afraid
*Ps.* 24:8 strong and *m.* in battle
29:1 give to the L. O ye *m.* glo.
45:3 gird thy sword, O most *m.*
59:3 *m.* are gathered against me
68:33 send out voice, *m.* voice
74:15 thou driedst up *m.* rivers
82:1 God in congrega. of the *m.*
89:6 who am. sons *m.* like to L.?
*Ps.* 89:13 thou hast a *m.* arm
19 I have laid help upon one *m.*
93:4 L. mightier than *m.* waves
106:8 make *m.* power known
112:2 seed shall be *m.* on earth
135:10 smote nat. slew *m.* kings
*Prov.* 16:32 better than the *m.*
18:18 lot parteth betwe. the *m.*
23:11 their Redeemer is *m.*
*Is.* 3:25 thy *m.* sh. fall in war
5:22 woe to them that are *m.*
11:15 wi. *m.* wind sh. his hand
22:17 carry thee aw. wi. *m.* cap.
49:24 shall prey be taken fr. *m.*?
63:1 in righteousn. *m.* to save
*Jer.* 5:15 *m.* and ancient nation
32:19 gr. in counsel, *m.* in work
33:3 I will show thee *m.* things

*Ezek.* 17:13 hath taken *m.* of land
32:12 swords of *m.* make th. fall
21 strong among *m.* sh. speak
27 not lie wi. *m.* that are fallen
38:15 come with a *m.* army
39:18 ye shall eat flesh of *m.*
*Dan.* 4:3 *m.* are his wonders!
8:24 his power shall be *m.*
11:3 a *m.* king shall stand up
*Amos* 2:14 nei. shall *m.* deliver
16 courageous am. *m.* sh. flee
5:12 *m.* sins; 24 *m.* stream
*Jon.* 1:4 there was a *m.* tempest
*Zec.* 11:2 howl, *m.* are spoiled
*Mat.* 11:20 most of *m.* works
21 if *m.* works which were, 23
13:54 hath this man *m.* works?
58 he did not many *m.* works
there, *Mark* 6:5
14:2 John the Bap. therefore *m.*
works do show, *Mark* 6:14
*Mark* 6:2 *m.* works by his hand
*Luke* 1:49 *m.* hath done great th.
52 he hath put down the *m.*
9:43 amazed at *m.* power of G.
19:37 praised God for *m.* works
24:19 was a prophet *m.* in deed
*Acts* 7:22 Moses was *m.* in words
18:24 Apol. was *m.* in script.
*Rom.* 15:19 obed. thro' *m.* signs
1 *Cor.* 1:26 not many *m.*
27 chos. weak, to confound *m.*
2 *Cor.* 10:4 warfare *m.* thro' God
13:3 is not weak, but *m.* in you
*Gal.* 2:8 the same was *m.* in me
*Eph.* 1:19 working of *m.* power
2 *Thes.* 1:7 J. with his *m.* angels
*Rev.* 6:13 when shak. of *m.* wind
10:1 I saw ano. *m.* angel, 18:21
18:10 *m.* city; 19:6 *m.* thunder.
*See* ACTS, GOD, HAND, MAN, MEN.

**MIGHTY one.**

*Gen.* 10:8 N. began to be a *m. o.*
*Is.* 1:24 Lord of hosts, the *m. O.*
of Is. 30:29; 49:26; 60:16
10:34 Leb. shall fall by a *m. o.*
28:2 L. hath a *m.* and strong *o.*
*Jer.* 20:11 L. is wi. me as a *m. o.*
*Ezek.* 31:11 deliver. him to *m. o.*

**MIGHTY ones.**

*Jud.* 5:22 broken by their *m. o.*
*Is.* 13:3 have called my *m. ones*
*Jer.* 46:5 their *m. o.* are beaten
*Joel* 3:11 cause *m. o.* to come

**MIGHTIER.**

*Gen.* 26:16 thou art *m.* than we
*Ex.* 1:9 child. of Is. *m.* than we
*Num.* 14:12 and *m.* than they,
*Deut.* 4:38; 7:1; 9:1, 14; 11:23
*Ps.* 93:4 L. is *m.* than many wa.
*Ec.* 6:10 nei. contend with *m.*
*Mat.* 3:11 that com. aft. me is *m.*
than I, *Mark* 1:7; *Luke* 3:16

**MIGHTIES.**

1 *Chr.* 11:12 Ele. was one of 3 *m.*
19 these thi. did these three *m.*
24 B. had a name am. three *m.*

**MIGHTILY.**

*Deut.* 6:3 ye may increase *m.*
*Jud.* 4:3 Jabin *m.* oppressed Is.
14:6 Sp. of the L. came *m.* 15:14
*Jer.* 25:30 the Lord shall *m.* roar
*Jon.* 3:8 man and beast cry *m.*
*Nah.* 2:1 fortify thy power *m.*
*Acts* 18:28 *m.* convinced Jews
19:20 so *m.* grew word of God
*Col.* 1:29 worketh in me *m.*
*Rev.* 18:2 cried *m.* saying, Bab.

**MILCAH.**

*Gen.* 11:29 M. daught. of Haran,
22:20; 24:15; *Num.* 26:33

**MILCH.**

*Gen.* 32:15 thirty *m.* camels
1 *Sam.* 6:7 take two *m.* kine, 10

MILCOM. 1 *K.* 11:5, 33; 2 *K.*
23:13
MILDEW. *See* BLASTING.

**MILE.**

*Mat.* 5:41 compel thee to go a *m.*

MILETUM. 2 *Tim.* 4:20
MILETUS. *Acts* 20:15, 17

**MILK, Substantive.**

*Gen.* 18:8 A. took butter and *m.*
49:12 his teeth be white wi. *m.*
*Deut.* 32:14 kine, *m.* of sheep
*Jud.* 4:19 J. opened bottle of *m.*
5:25 asked water, she gave *m.*
*Job* 10:10 not pou. me out as *m.*?
21:24 his breasts are full of *m.*
*Prov.* 27:27 shalt have goats' *m.*
30:33 churning *m.* bring. butter
*Cant.* 4:11 *m.* under thy tongue
5:1 drunk wine with my *m.*
12 his eyes washed with *m.*
*Is.* 7:22 abund. of *m.* shall give
28:9 that are weaned from *m.*
55:1 wi. and *m.* without honey
60:16 thou sh. suck *m.* of Gent.
*Lam.* 4:7 Nazar. whiter than *m.*
*Ezek.* 25:4 eat fruit, and drink *m.*
*Joel* 3:18 hills shall flow with *m.*
1 *Cor.* 3:2 I have fed you with *m.*
9:7 who eateth not of the *m.*?
*Heb.* 5:12 as have need of *m.*?
13 ev. one useth *m.* is a babe
1 *Pet.* 2:2 new-born babes des. *m.*
*See* FLOWING.

**MILK.**

*Is.* 66:11 that ye may *m.* out

**MILL, S.**

*Ex.* 11:5 m.-servant behind *m.*
*Num.* 11:8 ground manna in *m.*
*Mat.* 24:41 two wom. grind. at *m.*

**MILLET.**

*Ezek.* 4:9 take *m.* and make bre.

**MILLIONS.**

*Gen.* 24:60 mother of thous. *m.*

**MILLO.**

*Jud.* 9:6 house of M. gather. 20
2 *Sam.* 5:9 round about from M.
1 *K.* 9:24 Solo. build M. 11:27
2 *K.* 12:20 slew Joash in M.

**MILLSTONE, S.**

*Deut.* 24:6 no man take *m.* pled.
*Jud.* 9:53 a woman cast a piece
of *m.* 2 *Sam.* 11:21
*Job* 41:24 heart as hard as a *m.*
*Is.* 47:2 take *m.* and grind meal
*Jer.* 25:10 take away sound of *m.*
*Mat.* 18:6 a *m.* hanged about his
neck, *Mark* 9:42; *Luke* 17:2
*Rev.* 18:21 an angel took up a
stone like a great *m.*

**MINCING.**

*Is.* 3:16 walk. and *m.* as they go

**MIND, Substantive.**

*Gen.* 26:35 a grief of *m.* to Isaac
*Lev.* 24:12 *m.* of L. showed them
*Deut.* 18:6 come wi. desire of *m.*
28:65 L. sh. give thee sor. of *m.*
30:1 call th. to *m.* am. nations
1 *Chr.* 28:9 serve with willing *m.*
*Neh.* 4:6 peo. had a *m.* to work
*Job* 23:13 one *m.* who turn him?
*Ps.* 31:12 a dead man out of *m.*
*Prov.* 21:27 bring. it wi. wic. *m.*
29:11 a fool uttereth all his *m.*
*Is.* 26:3 wh. *m.* is stayed on thee
46:8 again to *m.* O transgress.
65:17 former sh. not come to *m.*
*Jer.* 3:16 ark sh. not come to *m.*
44:21 came it not into his *m.*?
*Dan.* 5:20 *m.* hardened in pride
*Hab.* 1:11 then sh. his *m.* change
*Mark* 5:15 his right *m.* *Luke* 8:35
14:72 P. called to *m.* words of J.
*Luke* 12:29 nei. be of doubtful *m.*
*Acts* 17:11 all readiness of *m.*
20:19 serv. L. with humi. of *m.*
*Rom.* 1:28 ga. up to reprobate *m.*
7:25 with *m.* I serve law of God
8:7 carnal *m.* enmity against G.
27 knoweth what is *m.* of Sp.
11:34 who hath kno. *m.* of L.?
12:16 same *m.* one tow. another
14:5 persuaded in his own *m.*
15:6 may with one *m.* glori. G.
1 *Cor.* 1:10 joined in the same *m.*
2:16 known *m.* of L. to instruct
him? we have *m.* of Christ
2 *Cor.* 7:7 fervent *m.* toward me
8:12 if a willing *m.* it is accept.
13:11 brethr. be of one *m.* *Phil.*
1:27; 2:2
*Eph.* 2:3 desires of flesh and *m.*
4:17 Gent. walk in vanity of *m.*
*Phil.* 2:3 in lowli. of *m.* let each
5 let this *m.* be in you wh. was
4:2 be of the same *m.* in the L.
*Col.* 2:18 puffed up by fleshly *m.*
3:12 humbleness of *m.* meekn.
2 *Thes.* 2:2 not soon shaken in *m.*
2 *Tim.* 1:7 spirit of sound *m.*
*Tit.* 1:15 *m.* and conscience defi.
3:1 put them in *m.* to be subj.
*Heb.* 8:10 my laws into th. *m.*
1 *Pet.* 3:8 be ye all of same *m.*
4:1 arm yours. like. wi. one *m.*
5:2 filthy lucre, but of ready *m.*
*Rev.* 17:9 *m.* which hath wisdom
13 these have one *m.* and shall
*See* ALIENATED.

**Mine, *or* my MIND.**

*Num.* 16:28 done th. of *m.* own *m.*
24:13 good or bad of *m.* own *m.*
1 *Sam.* 2:35 that wh. is in *m. m.*
1 *Chr.* 22:7 in *m. m.* to build ho.
*Jer.* 15:1 *my m.* could not be
19:5 nei. came it to *my m.* 32:35
*Lam.* 3:21 this I recall to *my m.*
*Rom.* 7:23 war. ag. law of *my m.*

**Thy MIND.**

1 *Sam.* 9:20 set not *t. m.* on asses
*Job* 34:33 should it be according
to *thy m.*?
*Ezek.* 38:10 thi. came into *t. m.*
*Dan.* 2:29 thou. came into *t. m.*
*Mat.* 22:37 love L. the G. wi. all
*t. m.* *Mark* 12:30; *Luke* 10:27
*Phile.* 14 without *thy m.*

**Your MIND.**

*Gen.* 23:8 if *y. m.* I should bury
*Jer.* 51:50 Jer. come into *your m.*
*Ezek.* 11:5 things come into *y. m.*
20:32 that wh. cometh into *y. m.*
*Rom.* 12:2 by renewing of *y. m.*
2 *Cor.* 8:19 declar. of *y.* ready *m.*
9:2 I know forwardness of *y. m.*
*Eph.* 4:23 renewed in sp. of *y. m.*
*Col.* 1:21 enemies in *your m.*
1 *Pet.* 1:13 loins of *y. m.* be sober

**MIND, Verb.**

*Rom.* 8:5 *m.* things of the flesh
12:16 *m.* not high things, but
*Phil.* 3:16 let us *m.* same thing
19 who *m.* earthly things

**MINDED.**

*Ruth* 1:18 she was steadfastly *m.*
2 *Chr.* 24:4 *m.* to repair house
*Ezr.* 7:13 *m.* of th. own free will
*Mat.* 1:19 *m.* to put her away
*Rom.* 8:6 to be carn. *m.* is death,
to be spiritually *m.* is life
11:20 be not high-*m.* but fear
15:5 grant you to be like-*m.*
2 *Cor.* 1:15 I was *m.* to come
17 thus *m.* did I use lightness
*Gal.* 5:10 be no otherwise *m.*
*Phil.* 2:2 that ye be like-*m.*
20 no man like-*m.* will care
3:15 as many as be perf. be thus
*m.* if ye be otherwise *m.*
1 *Thes.* 5:14 comf. the feeble-*m.*
1 *Tim.* 6:17 rich be not high-*m.*

2 *Tim.* 3:4 men heady, high-*m.*
*Tit.* 2:6 exhort to be sober-*m.*
*Jam.* 1:8 double-*m.* man unstab.
4:8 purify hearts ye double-*m.*

**MINDFUL.**

1 *Chr.* 16:15 be *m.* of covenant
*Neh.* 9:17 fathers were not *m.*
*Ps.* 8:4 what is man, that thou art *m.* of him? *Heb.* 2:6
111:5 ever be *m.* of covenant
115:12 L. hath been *m.* of us
*Is.* 17:10 not been *m.* of rock
2 *Tim.* 1:4 being *m.* of thy tears
*Heb.* 11:15 been *m.* of that coun.
2 *Pet.* 3:2 be *m.* of words spoken

**MINDING.**

*Acts* 20:13 P. *m.* himself to go

**MINDS.**

*Jud.* 19:30 consider, speak yo. *m.*
2 *Sam.* 17:8 be chafed in their *m.*
2 *K.* 9:15 if it be your *m.*
*Ezek.* 24:25 they set their *m.*
36:5 with despiteful *m.* to cast
*Acts* 14:2 their *m.* evil affected
28:6 they changed their *m.* and said he was a god
2 *Cor.* 3:14 their *m.* were blind
4:4 god of th. world ha. blin. *m.*
11:3 so your *m.* sho. be corrup.
*Phil.* 4:7 peace of G. keep yo. *m.*
1 *Tim.* 6:5 corrupt *m.* 2 *Tim.* 3:8
*Heb.* 10:16 in *m.* will I write
12:3 wear. and faint in your *m.*
2 *Pet.* 3:1 I stir up your pure *m.*

**MINE.**

*Gen.* 31:43 all that thou seest *m.*
48:5 *m.* as Reuben and S. be *m.*
*Ex.* 19:5 for all the earth is *m.* *Ps.* 50:12
*Ps.* 60:7 Gilead *m.* Man. *m.* 108:8
*Ezek.* 23:4 were *m.* 5 she was
29:9 river *m.* 35:10 count. *m.*
*Hag.* 2:8 silver is *m.* gold is *m.*
*Mal.* 3:17 they sh. be *m.* saith L.
*Mat.* 20:23 not *m.* *Mark* 10:40
*John* 17:10 *m.* are thine, thine *m.*

**MINGLE.**

*Is.* 5:22 men *m.* strong drink
*Dan.* 2:43 *m.* with seed of men

**MINGLED.**

*Ex.* 9:24 fire *m.* with the hail
*Lev.* 19:19 not s. field wi. *m.* seed
*Ezr.* 9:2 holy seed *m.* themsel.
*Ps.* 102:9 *m.* drink wi. weeping
106:35 were *m.* among heathen
*Prov.* 9:2 she hath *m.* her wine
5 drink of wine wh. I have *m.*
*Is.* 19:14 L. *m.* a perverse spirit
*Jer.* 25:20 cup to all *m.* peo. 24
50:37 sw. on *m.* peo. *Ezek.* 30:5
*Luke* 13:1 blood Pilat had *m.*
*Rev.* 8:7 hail and fire *m.* with bl.

**MINISH, ED.**

*Ex.* 5:19 not *m.* aught of task
*Ps.* 107:39 again they are *m.*

**MINISTER.**

*Ex.* 24:13 Moses and his *m.* Jos.
*Jos.* 1:1 spake to Joshua, M. *m.*
*Mat.* 20:26 your *m.* *Mark* 10:43
*Luke* 4:20 gave book again to *m.*
*Acts* 13:5 had also J. to their *m.*
26:16 make th. a *m.* and witn.
*Rom.* 13:4 is *m.* of G. to thee, 6
15:8 Ch. was *m.* of circumcision
16 be *m.* of Jesus to Gentiles
*Gal.* 2:17 is Ch. the *m.* of sin?
*Eph.* 3:7 whereof I was made a *m.* *Col.* 1:23, 25
6:21 Ty. a faithful *m.* *Col.* 4:7
*Col.* 1:7 Epaphras, a faithful *m.*
1 *Thes.* 3:2 brother and *m.* of G.
1 *Tim.* 4:6 a good *m.* of Christ
*Heb.* 8:2 a *m.* of the sanctuary

**MINISTER, Verb.**

*Ex.* 28:1 that he may *m.* to me in the priest's office, 3, 4, 41; 29:1, 44; 30:30; 31:10; 35:19; 39:41; 40:13, 15
35 it shall be upon Aar. to *m.*
29:44 sanctify Aar. to *m.* to me
*Lev.* 7:35 presented them to *m.*
*Num.* 8:26 *m.* wi. their brethren
*Deut.* 10:8 tribe of L. to *m.* to h.
21:5 God hath chos. them to *m.*
1 *Sam.* 2:11 child did *m.* to Lord
1 *K.* 8:11 priest could not stand to *m.* 2 *Chr.* 5:14
1 *Chr.* 15:2 chosen to *m.* bef. hi.
23:13 to *m.* to the Lord and to give thanks, 2 *Chr.* 31:2
2 *Chr.* 13:10 pries. *m.* sons of A.
*Ps.* 9:8 *m.* judgment to people
*Is.* 60:7 rams of Nebaioth *m.*
10 their kings shall *m.* to thee
*Jer.* 33:22 multi. Levites that *m.*
*Ezek.* 40:46 near to *m.* 44:15, 16
44:11 stand before them to *m.*
*Mat.* 20:28 to be ministered to, but to *m.* *Mark* 10:45
25:44 and did not *m.* to thee?
*Acts* 24:23 acquaint. to *m.* to him
*Rom.* 15:25 I go to *m.* to saints
27 *m.* to them in carnal things
1 *Cor.* 9:13 *m.* about holy things
2 *Cor.* 9:10 *m.* bread for your fo.
*Eph.* 4:29 *m.* grace to hearers
1 *Tim.* 1:4 which *m.* questions
*Heb.* 1:14 *m.* to heirs of salvation
6:10 minis. to saints, and do *m.*
1 *Pet.* 1:12 but to us they did *m.*
4:10 *m.* the same one to another
11 if any man *m.* let him do it

**MINISTERED.**

*Num.* 3:4 E. and I. *m.* *Deut.* 10:6
1 *Sam.* 2:18 Samuel *m.* bef. L. 3:1
2 *Sam.* 13:17 his servant that *m.*
1 *K.* 1:4 Abishag *m.* to David, 15
19:21 Elijah, and *m.* to him
*Ezek.* 44:12 *m.* before their idols
*Dan.* 7:10 thousands *m.* unto him
*Mat.* 4:11 angels came and *m.* to him, *Mark* 1:13
8:15 she rose and *m.* *Mark* 1:31
*Luke* 8:3 *m.* to him of substance
*Acts* 13:2 as they *m.* and fasted
20:34 have *m.* to my necessities
2 *Cor.* 3:3 epistle of Ch. *m.* by us
*Phil.* 2:25 that *m.* to my wants
*Col.* 2:19 having nourishment *m.*
2 *Tim.* 1:18 many th. *m.* unto me
*Phile.* 13 he might have *m.*
*Heb.* 6:10 have *m.* to the saints
2 *Pet.* 1:11 entrance be *m.* to you

**MINISTERETH.**

2 *Cor.* 9:10 *m.* seed to the sower
*Gal.* 3:5 that *m.* to you the Spi.

**MINISTERING.**

1 *Chr.* 9:28 charge of *m.* vessels
*Ezek.* 44:11 house, *m.* to house
*Mat.* 27:55 followed J. *m.* to him
*Rom.* 12:7 w. on *m.* 15:16 *m.* gos.
2 *Cor.* 8:4 and take on us the *m.*
9:1 for as touching *m.* to saints
*Heb.* 1:14 are they not *m.* spirits
10:11 every priest standeth *m.*

**MINISTERS.**

1 *K.* 10:5 atten. of his *m.* 2 *Chr.* 9:4
*Ezr.* 7:24 not lawful, toll on *m.*
8:17 they sho. bring un. us *m.*
*Ps.* 103:21 *m.* that do his pleas.
104:4 *m.* a flaming fire, *Heb.* 1:7
*Is.* 61:6 shall call you *m.* of God
*Jer.* 33:21 covenant be broken with David and my *m.*
*Ezek.* 45:4 holy port. for the *m.*
*Joel* 1:9 L.'s *m.* mourn; 13 howl
2:17 *m.* weep between the porch
*Luke* 1:2 from beginni. were *m.*
*Rom.* 13:6 *m.* attend. continually
1 *Cor.* 3:5 *m.* by whom ye belie.
4:1 so account of us as of the *m.*
2 *Cor.* 3:6 who made us able *m.*
6:4 approv. ourselv. as *m.* of G.
11:15 his *m.* also be transformed as the *m.* of righteousness
23 are they *m.* of Christ? I am

**MINISTRATION.**

*Luke* 1:23 days of *m.* were ended
*Acts* 6:1 widows neglected in *m.*
2 *Cor.* 3:7 if *m.* of death glorious
8 *m.* of Spirit be glorious? 9
9:13 the experiment of this *m.*

**MINISTRY.**

*Num.* 4:12 instruments of *m.*
2 *Chr.* 7:6 D. praised by their *m.*
*Hos.* 12:10 used similitud. by *m.*
*Acts* 1:17 had obtain. part of *m.*
25 that he may take part of *m.*
6:4 will give ourselves to *m.*
12:25 when they fulfilled th. *m.*
20:24 finish my course, and *m.*
21:19 things G. wro. by his *m.*
*Rom.* 12:7 *m.* let us wait on our
1 *Cor.* 16:15 addicted to *m.* of sa.
2 *Cor.* 4:1 seeing we have this *m.*
5:18 giv. us *m.* of reconciliation
6:3 that the *m.* be not blamed
*Eph.* 4:12 work of *m.* for edifyi.
*Col.* 4:17 take heed to the *m.*
*Tim.* 1:12 putting me into *m.*
2 *Tim.* 4:5 full proof of thy *m.*
11 profitable to me for the *m.*
*Heb.* 8:6 obtained a more ex. *m.*
9:21 sprinkled the vessels of *m.*

MINNI. *Jer.* 51:27
MINNITH. *Jud.* 11:33

**MINSTREL, S.**

2 *K.* 3:15 but now bring me a *m.*
*Mat.* 9:23 when Jesus saw the *m.*

**MINT.**

*Mat.* 23:23 ye pay tithe of *m.*
*Luke* 11:42 ye tithe *m.* all herbs

**MIRACLE.**

*Ex.* 7:9 P. sh. speak, Show a *m.*
*Mark* 6:52 consid. not *m.* of loa.
9:39 no man which shall do *m.*
*Luke* 23:8 hoped to have seen *m.*
*John* 4:54 second *m.* Jesus did
10:41 many said, Jo. did no *m.*
*Acts* 4:16 a notable *m.* been done
22 on wh. this *m.* was wroug.

**MIRACLES.**

*Num.* 14:22 which have seen *m.*
*Deut.* 11:3 have not seen his *m.*
29:3 th. eyes have seen those *m.*
*Jud.* 6:13 where be all his *m.*
*John* 2:11 beginning of *m.* did J.
23 many beli. wh. they saw *m.*
3:2 no man can do th. *m.* ex. G.
6:26 not because ye saw the *m.*
7:31 will he do more *m.* th. this
9:16 can a sinner do such *m.*?
11:47 this man doeth many *m.*
12:37 he had done so many *m.*
*Acts* 2:22 approved of God by *m.*
6:8 Stephen did great *m.*
8:6 hearing and seeing the *m.*
13 wondered, beholding the *m.*
15:12 what *m.* G. had wrought
19:11 G. wrought spec. *m.* by P.
1 *Cor.* 12:10 to the working of *m.*
28 teachers; after that *m.*
29 are all workers of *m.*?
*Gal.* 3:5 he that worketh *m.*
*Heb.* 2:4 G. bearing witn. wi. *m.*
*Rev.* 13:14 decei. by means of *m.*
16:14 spirits of devils work. *m.*
19:20 false prophet th. wro. *m.*

**MIRE.**

2 *Sam.* 22:43 stamp them as *m.* of street, *Is.* 10:6; *Mic.* 7:10
*Job* 8:11 can rush grow wit. *m.*?
30:19 he hath cast me into *m.*
41:30 spread. things on the *m.*

*Ps.* 69:2 I sink in deep *m.* where
14 deliver me out of the *m.*
*Is.* 57:20 whose wat. cast up *m.*
*Jer.* 38:6 in dung. no wat. but *m.*
22 thy feet are sunk in the *m.*
*Zec.* 9:3 gold as *m.* of streets
10:5 tread th. enemies in the *m.*
2 *Pet.* 2:22 sow wallowing in *m.*

**MIRY.**

*Ps.* 40:2 bro. me out of *m.* clay
*Ezek.* 47:11 *m.* pla. not be healed
*Dan.* 2:41 iron mixed with *m.* 43

**MIRIAM.**

*Ex.* 15:20 M. took a timbrel in
*Num.* 12:1 M. and Aaron, 10, 15
*Deut.* 24:9 what God did to M.
*Mic.* 6:4 I sent before thee M.

**MIRTH.**

*Gen.* 31:27 sent th. away wi. *m.*
*Neh.* 8:12 peo. went to make *m.*
*Ps.* 137:3 that wasted us des. *m.*
*Prov.* 14:13 end of *m.* heaviness
*Ec.* 2:1 I will prove th. with *m.*
2 I said of *m.* what doeth it?
7:4 heart of fools is in ho. of *m.*
8:15 then I commended *m.*
*Is.* 24:8 *m.* of tabrets
11 the *m.* of the land is gone
*Jer.* 7:34 I will cause to cease the voice of *m.* from Judah, 16:9; 25:10; *Hos.* 2:11
*Ezek.* 21:10 sh. we th. make *m.*?

**MISCARRYING.**

*Hos.* 9:14 give them a *m.* womb

**MISCHIEF.**

*Gen.* 42:4 lest some *m.* bef. him
38 if *m.* befall him, 44:29
*Ex.* 21:22 and yet no *m.* follow
32:12 for *m.* did he bring them
22 knowest peo. that are on *m.*
1 *Sam.* 23:9 Saul practised *m.*
2 *Sam.* 16:8 art taken in thy *m.*
1 *K.* 11:25 the *m.* that Hadad did
20:7 this man seeketh *m.*
2 *K.* 7:9 some *m.* will befall us
*Neh.* 6:2 thought to do me *m.*
*Est.* 8:3 E. sou. to put away *m.*
*Job* 15:35 conceive *m.* and vanity
*Ps.* 7:14 *m.* bro. forth falsehood
16 his *m.* shall ret. on his head
10:7 under his tongue is *m.*
14 thou beholdest *m.* and spite
26:10 in whose hands is *m.*
28:3 but *m.* is in their hearts
36:4 wicked dev. *m.* on his bed
52:1 why boast. thyself in *m.*?
55:10 *m.* and sorrow in midst
62:3 how long will ye ima. *m.*?
94:20 frameth *m.* by a law
119:150 draw nigh that fol. *m.*
140:9 *m.* of own lips cover them
*Prov.* 4:16 ex. they ha. done *m.*
6:14 he deviseth *m.* continually
18 feet swift in running to *m.*
10:23 is sport to a fool to do *m.*
11:27 that seek. *m.* it shall co.
12:21 wicked be filled with *m.*
13:17 wicked mes. falleth in *m.*
17:20 a perv. tongue fall. in *m.*
24:2 their heart studieth *m.*
16 wicked fall into *m.* 28:14
*Is.* 47:11 *m.* sh. fall upon thee
59:4 trust in vanity, conc. *m.*
*Ezek.* 7:26 *m.* sh. come upon *m.*
11:2 men that devise *m.*
*Dan.* 11:27 king's hearts to do *m.*
*Hos.* 7:15 do they imagine *m.*
*Acts* 13:10 full of all *m.* th. child

**MISCHIEFS.**

*Deut.* 32:23 heap *m.* on them
*Ps.* 52:2 thy tongue deviseth *m.*
140:2 imagine *m.* in their heart

**MISCHIEVOUS.**

*Ps.* 21:11 imagined a *m.* device
38:12 seek my hurt, speak *m.* t.
*Prov.* 24:8 be called *m.* person
*Ec.* 10:13 end of his talk is *m.*
*Mic.* 7:3 man utter. his *m.* desire

**MISERABLE, LY.**

*Job* 16:2 Job said, *m.* comforters
*Mat.* 21:41 *m.* destroy wicked m.
1 *Cor.* 15:19 are of all most *m.*
*Rev.* 3:17 know. not thou art *m.*

**MISERY, IES.**

*Jud.* 10:16 soul grieved for *m.*
*Job* 3:20 given to him in *m.*
11:16 thou shalt forget thy *m.*
*Prov.* 31:7 rem. his *m.* no more
*Ec.* 8:6 the *m.* of a man is great
*Lam.* 1:7 Jerusal. in days of *m.*
3:19 re. mine affliction and *m.*
*Rom.* 3:16 *m.* are in their ways
*Jam.* 5:1 howl for your *m.*

**MISHAEL.**

*Ex.* 6:22; *Lev.* 10:4; *Neh.* 8:4
*Dan.* 1:6 of childr. of Judah, M

**MISS.**

*Jud.* 20:16 sling at, and not *m.*
1 *Sam.* 20:6 if thy fath. at all *m.*

**MISSED, ING.**

1 *Sam.* 20:18 thou shalt be *m.*
25:7 neither was there aught *m.*
15 neith. *m.* any thing as long
21 nothing was *m.* of all
1 *K.* 20:39 any means he be *m.*

**MIST.**

*Gen.* 2:6 th. went a *m.* fr. earth
*Acts* 13:11 there fell on him a *m.*
2 *Pet.* 2:17 *m.* of darkn. reserved

**MISTRESS.**

*Gen.* 16:4 Sarah her *m.* despised
8 flee fr. my *m.* S. 9 return to
1 *K.* 17:17 son of *m.* fell sick
2 *K.* 5:3 said to her *m.* would G.
*Ps.* 123:2 eyes of maiden to *m.*
*Prov.* 30:23 that is heir to her *m.*
*Is.* 24:2 as with maid so with *m.*
*Nah.* 3:4 the *m.* of witchcrafts

**MISUSED.**

2 *Chr.* 36:16 they *m.* his prophe.

**MITE, S.**

*Mark* 12:42 a certain poor widow threw in two *m.* *Luke* 21:2
*Luke* 12:59 thou hast paid last *m.*

**MITRE.**

*Ex.* 28:4 make a *m.* 39; 39:28
29:6 put the *m.* upon his head
*Lev.* 8:9 put holy crown on *m.*
16:4 wi. lin. *m.* sh. he be attired
*Zec.* 3:5 set fair *m.* on his head

**MIXED.**

*Ex.* 12:38 *m.* multitude went up
*Num.* 11:4 *m.* multi. fell a lusti.
*Neh.* 13:3 separated fr. *m.* multi.
*Prov.* 23:30 go to seek *m.* wine
*Is.* 1:22 thy wine *m.* with water
*Dan.* 2:41 thou saw. the iron *m.*
*Hos.* 7:8 Ephraim *m.* am. people
*Heb.* 4:2 not being *m.* with faith

**MIXTURE.**

*Ps.* 75:8 there is a cup full of *m.*
*John* 19:39 Nicodemus, and bro. a *m.* of myrrh and aloes
*Rev.* 14:10 poured out without *m.*

MIZAR. *Ps.* 42:6

**MIZPAH.**

*Gen.* 31:49 na. of heap called M.
1 *K.* 15:22 Ge. and M. 2 *Chr.* 16:6
2 *K.* 25:23 to Ged. to M. *Jer.* 41:1
*Neh.* 3:7 men of Gibeon and M.
*Jer.* 40:10 I will dwell at M.
41:3 slew all J. that were at M.
*Hos.* 5:1 have been a snare on M.

**MIZPEH.**

*Jos.* 15:38 Dilean and M.
*Jud.* 10:17 in M. 11:11; 21:5
20:1 Israel was gathered in M.
1 *Sam.* 7:5 all Isr. to M. 6; 22:3
10:17 Samuel called peo. to M.

MIZRAIM. *Gen.* 10:6
MNASON. *Acts* 21:16

**MOAB.**

*Gen.* 19:37 daugh.'s son was M.
*Ex.* 15:15 tremb. on men of M.
*Num.* 21:29; 22:3; 24:17; 25:1
*Deut.* 2:18 pass thro' coast of M.
34:5 Moses died in land of M.
*Jud.* 3:29 they slew of M. about
10:6 Israel serv. the gods of M.
11:15 took not away land of M.
*Ruth* 1:2 ca. into country of M.
1 *Sam.* 14:47 Saul fought ag. M.
2 *Sam.* 8:2 David smote M. 1 *Chr.* 18:2
1 *K.* 11:7 the abomination of M.
2 *K.* 1:1 then M. rebelled, 3:7, 23
1 *Chr.* 4:22 dominion in M. 18:11
2 *Chr.* 20:1 M. came ag. Jeh. 10
*Neh.* 13:23 J. married wiv. of M.
*Ps.* 60:8 M. my washpot, 108:9
83:6 M. is confederate ag. thee
*Is.* 11:14 lay the hand upon M.
15:1 burden of M. 16:13; *Jer.* 48:1; *Ezek.* 25:8; *Amos* 2:2
16:6 heard of pride of M. 11, 14; *Jer.* 48:29
25:10 M. shall be trodden down
*Jer.* 9:26 Egypt, Judah, and M.
25:21 made M. to drink of cup
48:2 prai. of M. 9, 11, 20, 26, 47
*Amos* 2:2 send a fire upon M.
*Zep.* 2:9 M. shall be as Sodom

**MOABITE.**

*Deut.* 23:3 M. sh. not, *Neh.* 13:1
1 *Chr.* 11:46 Ithma the M. a val.

**MOABITES.**

*Gen.* 19:37 the father of the M.
*Deut.* 2:9 said, Distress not M.
*Jud.* 3:28 L. hath delivered M.
2 *Sam.* 8:2 M. beca. 1 *Chr.* 18:2
1 *K.* 11:1 loved women of the M.
2 *K.* 3:18 he will deli. the M. 24
13:20 bands of M. invaded, 24:2
*Ezr.* 9:1 to abominations of M.

**MOCK, Substantive.**

*Prov.* 14:9 fools make a *m.* at sin

**MOCK.**

*Gen.* 39:14 bro. Heb. to *m.* us, 17
*Job* 13:9 mocketh, do ye *m.* him
21:3 after I have spoken, *m.* on
*Prov.* 1:26 *m.* wh. your fear com.
*Jer.* 38:19 and they *m.* me
*Lam.* 1:7 did *m.* at her sabbaths
*Ezek.* 22:5 shall *m.* thee who art
*Mat.* 20:19 deliver to G. to *m.* h.
*Mark* 10:34 *m.* him and scourge
*Luke* 14:29 begin to *m.* him

**MOCKED.**

*Gen.* 19:14 one that *m.* to sons
*Num.* 22:29 bec. thou hast *m.* me
*Jud.* 16:10 *m.* me, 13, 15
1 *K.* 18:27 at noon, Elijah *m.* th.
2 *K.* 2:23 little child. *m.* Elisha
2 *Chr.* 30:10 lau. to scorn and *m.*
36:16 *m.* the messengers of God
*Neh.* 4:1 Sanballat *m.* the Jews
*Job* 12:4 one *m.* of his neighbor
*Mat.* 2:16 H. saw that he was *m.*
27:29 they bowed the knee and *m.* 31; *Mark* 15:20
*Luke* 18:32 *m.* spitef. entreated
22:63 men that held J. *m.* him
23:11 Herod *m.* 36 soldiers *m.*
*Acts* 17:32 resurrection, some *m.*
*Gal.* 6:7 not deceiv. G. is not *m.*

**MOCKER, S.**

*Job* 17:2 are th. not *m.* with me?
*Ps.* 35:16 hypocrit. *m.* in feasts
*Prov.* 20:1 wine is a *m.* st. drink
*Is.* 28:22 be not *m.* lest bands be
*Jer.* 15:17 sat not in assem. of *m.*
*Jude* 18 sh. be *m.* latter times

**MOCKEST, ETH.**

*Job* 11:3 when thou *m.* sh. no *m.*

13:9 as one m. anoth. do ye so
39:22 m. at fear, not affrighted
Prov. 17:5 m. poor repro. Maker
30:17 that m. at his father
Jer. 20:7 derision, ev. one m. me

**MOCKING.**

Gen. 21:9 saw son of Hagar m.
Mat. 27:41 priests m. Mark 15:31
Acts 2:13 oth. m. said, These m.

**MOCKING, S.**

Ezek. 22:4 made thee a m. to all
Heb. 11:36 had trial of cruel m.

**MODERATION.**

Phil. 4:5 let your m. be known

**MODERATELY.**

Joel 2:23 gi. you former rain m.

**MODEST.**

1 Tim. 2:9 adorn in m. apparel

**MOIST.**

Num. 6:3 nor shall he eat m. gr.

**MOISTENED.**

Job 21:24 bones m. with marrow

**MOISTURE.**

Ps. 32:4 m. turned to drought
Luke 8:6 because it lacked m.

**MOLADAH.** Jos. 15:26

**MOLE.**

Lev. 11:30 snail and m. are uncl.

**MOLES.** See BATS.

**MOLECH.**

Lev. 18:21 pass thro. fire to M.
20:2 of his seed to M. Jer. 32:35
1 K. 11:7 a high place for M.
2 K. 23:10 son pass thro' to M.

**MOLLIFIED.**

Is. 1:6 nor m. with ointment

**MOLOCH.** Amos 5:26; Acts 7:43

**MOLTEN.**

Ex. 32:4 he had made a m. calf, 8; Deut. 9:12, 16; Neh. 9:18
34:17 no m. gods, Lev. 19:4
1 K. 7:16 chapiters of m. brass
23 a m. sea; 30 underset. m.
Job 28:2 brass is m. out of stone
37:18 sky as a m. looking-glass
Ezek. 24:11 filthiness be m. in it
Mic. 1:4 mountains shall be m.
See IMAGE.

**MOMENT.**

Ex. 33:5 midst of thee in a m.
Num. 16:21 consume th. in a m.
Job 7:18 shouldest try him e. m.
20:5 joy of hypoc. but for a m.
21:13 in a m. go down to grave
34:20 in a m. shall they die
Ps. 30:5 his anger end. but a m.
73:19 into desolation as in a m.
Prov. 12:19 ly. tong. but for a m.
Is. 26:20 as it were for a m.
27:3 I will water it every m.
47:9 things shall come in a m.
54:7 for a small m. have I forsa.
8 I hid my face fr. th. for a m.
Jer. 4:20 my curtains in a m.
Lam. 4:6 Sodom overth. in a m.
Ezek. 26:16 tremble ev. m. 32:10
Luke 4:5 king. of world in a m.
1 Cor. 15:52 be changed in a m.
2 Cor. 4:17 which is but for a m.

**MONEY.**

Gen. 23:9 as much m. as worth
13 I will give thee m. for field
31:15 quite devoured our m.
42:25 to restore every man's m.
27 espied m. 28 m. restored
43:12 double m. in hand, 15
44:1 ev. man's m. in sack's mo.
47:14 gathered all m. in Egypt
15 m. faileth; 18 our m. spent
Ex. 21:11 go out free without m.
21 he is his m. 35 divide m.
30 be laid on him a sum of m.
22:7 man deliver m. to neighbor
25 lend m. to any of my people
30:16 take atonement m. of Isr.
Lev. 25:37 not give him m. on usury, Deut. 23:19
Num. 3:49 Mos. took redemp. m.
Deut. 2:6 and water for m. 28
14:25 turn into m. 26 bestow m.
21:14 not sell her at all for m.
Jud. 5:19 took no gain of m.
16:18 lords bro. m. to Delilah
17:4 restored m. to his mother
1 K. 21:2 give worth of it in m.
2 K. 5:26 is it a time to rec. m.?
12:4 the m. of dedicated things
7 now receive no more m. 8
10 m. in chest, 2 Chr. 24:11
16 and sin m. was not brought
15:20 exacted the m. of Israel
23:35 Jehoakim gave m. to Ph.
Ezr. 3:7 gave m. also to masons
7:17 buy speedily with this m.
Neh. 5:4 borrowed m. for king
10 my servants exact of th. m.
Est. 4:7 sum of m. H. promised
Job 31:39 eaten fruits without m.
42:11 ev. man also gave him m.
Ps. 15:5 putteth not m. to usury
Prov. 7:20 taken bag of m.
Ec. 7:12 wisd. and m. a defence
10:19 but m. answers all things
Is. 52:3 be redeemed without m.
55:1 he that hath no m. come
2 wheref. spend ye m. for that
Jer. 32:9 weigh. m. 17 shekels 10
44 men shall buy fields for m.
Lam. 5:4 drunk. our wa. for m.
Mic. 3:11 prophets divine for m.
Mat. 17:24 received trib. m. ca.
27 thou shalt find a place of m.
22:19 show me the tribute m.
25:18 earth, hid his lord's m.
27 m. to exchang. Luke 19:23
28:12 large m. to soldiers, 15
Mark 6:8 they took no m. in their purse, Luke 9:3
12:41 people cast m. into treas.
14:11 and promised to give him m. Luke 22:5
Acts 4:37 brought m. and laid it
8:18 Simon offered them m.
20 P. said, m. perish with thee
24:26 hoped m. sho. been given
1 Tim. 6:10 love of m. root of all
See BOUGHT.

**MONEY-CHANGERS.**

Mat. 21:12 Jesus overthrew tables of m.-c. Mark 11:15
John 2:14 found in temple m.-c.

**MONSTERS.**

Lam. 4:3 sea m. draw out breast

**MONTH.**

Gen. 29:14 wi. La. space of a m.
Ex. 13:4 came ye out in m. Ab.
23:15 keep feast in the m. Abib
34:18 in m. Abib thou ca. fr. E. Deut. 16:1; Jos. 5:10
Lev. 27:6 from a m. old to 5 years
Num. 3:15 ev. male fr. a m. old, 22, 28, 34, 39, 40, 43; 26:62
9:22 m. or year cloud tarried
11:20 eat flesh, even a wh. m. 21
18:16 from a m. old shalt thou
28:14 burnt-offer. every m. 29:6
Deut. 21:13 in house full m.
1 K. 4:7 his m. made provis. 27
5:14 m. they were in Lebanon
Est. 9:22 m. turned fr. sorrow
Jer. 2:24 her m. they shall find
Hos. 5:7 m. devour th. with por.
Zec. 11:8 I cut off in one m.
Rev. 9:15 prep. for a day and m.
22:2 yielded her fruit every m.
See FIRST.

**Second MONTH.**

Gen. 7:11 s. m. fount. broken up
8:14 in s. m. was earth dried
Ex. 16:1 came to sin in sec. m.
Num. 1:1 in s. m. take sum of
9:11 on s. m. shall keep passover, 2 Chr. 30:2
10:11 on s. m. cloud was taken

**Third MONTH.**

Ex. 19:1 in t. m. came into Sin.
2 Chr. 31:7 t. m. began to lay fo.
Ezek. 31:1 in t. m. word of Lord

**Fourth MONTH.**

2 K. 25:3 f. m. famine prevailed
Jer. 39:2 f. m. city broken up
52:6 f. m. famine sore in city
Zec. 8:19 fast of f. m. be joy
See FIFTH.

**Sixth MONTH.**

Hag. 1:1 in s. m. word of L. ca.
15 in s. m. did work in hou. of
Luke 1:26 in s. m. angel sent
36 s. m. with her called barren
See SEVENTH.

**Eighth MONTH.**

Zec. 1:1 e. m. came word to Ze.

**Ninth MONTH.**

Ezr. 10:9 n. m. peo. sat tremb.
Jer. 36:22 sat in house in n. m.
Hag. 2:10 n. m. came word of L.
Zec. 7:1 word came to Z. in n. m.

**Tenth MONTH.**

Gen. 8:5 decreased until tenth m.
Ezr. 10:16 sat down in tenth m.
Est. 2:16 taken to king in t. m.

**Eleventh MONTH.**

Deut. 1:3 e. m. Moses spake to
Zec. 1:7 e. m. came word to Zec.

**Twelfth MONTH.**

Est. 3:7 cast lots to twelfth m.
Ezek. 32:1 t. m. word of L. came

**This MONTH.**

Ex. 12:2 t. m. sh. be beginning
3 t. m. take every man a lamb
Neh. 9:1 t. m. Israel assembled

**MONTHLY.**

Is. 47:13 the m. prognosticators

**MONTHS.**

Num. 10:10 in begin. of your m.
28:11 in beginnings of m. offer
Jud. 11:37 let me alone two m.
1 Sam. 6:1 ark in country 7 m.
2 Sam. 2:11 D. reign. seven years and six m. 5:5; 1 Chr. 3:4
6:11 ark was with O.-edom 3 m.
1 K. 5:14 two m. were at home
1 Chr. 27:1 thro' the m. of year
Est. 2:12 after she had been 12 m. purified, six m. with oil of myrrh, six m. with odors
Job 3:6 not come to numb. of m.
7:3 made to possess m. of vani.
14:5 number of his m. wi. thee
21:21 number of his m. cut off
29:2 O that I were as in m. past
39:2 canst thou number the m.?
Ezek. 39:14 after end of seven m.
47:12 new fruit according to m.
Dan. 4:29 at the end of twel. m.
Luke 1:24 and hid herself five m.
4:25 when heaven was shut up 3 ye. and 6 m. Jam. 5:17
John 4:35 yet four m. then harv.
Acts 18:11 P. abode year and 6 m.
Gal. 4:10 observed days and m.
Rev. 9:5 be tormented five m. 10
11:2 tread under foot 42 m.
13:5 power given to con. 42 m.
See THREE.

**MONUMENTS.**

Is. 65:4 peo. which lodge in m.

**MOON.**

Deut. 33:14 precious thin. by m.
Jos. 10:12 m. in valley of Aijalon
Job 25:5 behold m. it shine. not

*Ps.* 8:3 when I consider the *m.*
72:7 so long as *m.* endureth
89:37 establ. forever at the *m.*
104:19 appointed *m.* for seasons
*Ec.* 12:2 while sun, *m.* or stars
*Cant.* 6:10 fair as *m.* clear as sun
*Is.* 3:18 round tires like the *m.*
*See* SUN.

**New MOON.**

1 *Sam.* 20:5 to-mor. is *new m.* 18
2 *K.* 4:23 neither *new m.* nor sa.
*Ps.* 81:3 blow trumpet in *n. m.*
*Is.* 66:23 fr. one *new m.* to anoth.
*Ezek.* 46:1 in *n. m.* sh. be opened
6 in *n. m.* offer young bullock
*Amos* 8:5 will *n. m.* be gone?
*Col.* 2:16 judge you of the *n. m.*

**New MOONS.**

1 *Chr.* 23:31 offer burnt sacri. in *n. m.* 2 *Chr.* 2:4; 31:3; *Ezr.* 3:5; *Neh.* 10:33; *Ezek.* 46:3
*Is.* 1:13 *new m.* and sabbaths
14 *n. m.* and feasts my soul ha.
*Ezek.* 45:17 drink-off. in *new m.*
*Hos.* 2:11 cause *new m.* to cease

**MORDECAI.**

*Ezr.* 2:2 M. came up, *Neh.* 7:7
*Est.* 2:5 a Jew, name was M.
10:3 M. was next to Ahasuerus

**MORE.**

*Ex.* 1:12 the *m.* they afflicted them, the *m.* they grew.
16:17 gath. some *m.* some less
30:15 the rich shall not give *m.*
1 *Sam.* 3:17 G. do so to th. a. *m.*
*Ps.* 19:10 *m.* to be des. than gold
71:14 I will praise th. *m.* and *m.*
*Mat.* 18:16 take with th. 1 or 2 *m.*
*John* 21:15 lovest thou me *m.*?
*Heb.* 12:26 once *m.* I shake, 27
*See* ABUNDANTLY.

**Any MORE.**

*Gen.* 8:12 dove ret. not *any m.*
21 not curse ground *a. m.* 9:11
17:5 nor name *a. m.* be call. Ab.
35:10 nor *a. m.* be called Jacob
*Ex.* 8:29 not deal deceitful. *a. m.*
11:6 nor a cry be like it *any m.*
*Jos.* 7:12 nei. be with you *a. m.*
*Ezek.* 5:9 I will not do *any m.*
*Hos.* 14:8 what have I *any m.*?
*Luke* 22:16 I will not eat *any m.*

**Much MORE.**

*Ex.* 36:5 the people bring *m. m.*
*Mat.* 6:30 sh. he not *m. m.* clo.?
*Luke* 7:26 *m. m.* than a prophet
*Rom.* 5:9 *m. m.* be. now justified
10 *much m.* being reconciled
17 *m. m.* they that receive
20 when sin abund. gra. *m. m.*
2 *Cor.* 3:11 *m. m.* wh. remaineth

**No MORE.**

*Est.* 2:14 came *no m.* to king
*Job* 7:8 see me *no m.* 9 come up
10 shall return *no m.* to house
*Rev.* 21:1 *no m.* sea; 4 death; 22:3 curse

**MOREOVER.**

*Ps.* 19:11 *m.* by th. serv. warned
*Is.* 39:8 *m.* there shall be peace
*Heb.* 11:36 *m.* of bonds and imp.

**MORIAH.**

*Gen.* 22:2 get th. into land of M.
2 *Chr.* 3:1 Sol. built house in M.

**MORNING.**

*Gen.* 19:15 when the *m.* arose
24:54 Abra. rose up in the *m.*
26:31 rose betimes in the *m.*
29:25 in the *m.* behold it was L.
40:6 Jos. came into them in *m.*
49:27 in *m.* he sh. devour prey
*Ex.* 7:15 get thee to Phar. in *m.*
10:13 *m.* east wind bro. locusts
14:27 sea returned to stre. in *m.*
16:7 in *m.* ye sh. see glory of L
8 give you in the *m.* bread, 12
13 in the *m.* the dew lay round
29:39 one lamb in *m.* *Num.* 28:4
34:2 be ready in the *m.*
25 nor shall pass. be left to *m.*
*Lev.* 6:9 burning all night to *m.*
*Num.* 9:21 cloud taken up in *m.*
*Deut.* 28:67 in *m.* would it were
*Jud.* 6:31 put to death whilst *m.*
16:2 in the *m.* when it is day
19:37 rose in *m.* opened doors
20:19 chil. of Israel rose in *m.*
2 *Sam.* 23:4 and he shall be as the *m.* when the sun riseth, even a *m.* without clouds
24:11 when D. was up in the *m.*
1 *K.* 3:21 when I consid. it in *m.*
18:26 called on B. fr. *m.* to noon
*Neh.* 4:21 some labored from *m.*
8:3 read from *m.* until mid-day
*Job* 7:21 thou shalt seek me in *m.*
11:17 shine forth, be as the *m.*
24:17 *m.* to th. as sha. of death
38:12 hast thou commanded *m.*
41:18 his eyes like eyelids of *m.*
*Ps.* 5:3 my voice shalt thou hear in the *m.* O Lord, in the *m.*
*Ps.* 30:5 but joy cometh in the *m.*
49:14 dominion over them in *m.*
59:16 will sing thy mercy in *m.*
88:13 in the *m.* shall my prayer
90:5 the *m.* they are like grass
6 in the *m.* it flourisheth up
119:147 I prevented dawn. of *m.*
130:6 they that watch for *m.*
139:9 if I take wings of the *m.*
143:8 thy loving-kindness in *m.*
*Ec.* 10:16 princes eat in the *m.*
11:6 in the *m.* sow thy seed
*Cant.* 6:10 she looketh like *m.*
*Is.* 14:12 O Lucifer, son of *m.*
17:14 before the *m.* he is not
21:12 watchman said, *m.* com.
28:19 *m.* by *m.* sh. it pass over
50:4 he wakeneth *m.* by *m.*
58:8 thy light break forth as *m.*
*Jer.* 5:8 were as fed horses in *m.*
20:16 hear the cry in the *m.*
21:12 execute judgm. in the *m.*
*Ezek.* 7:7 the *m.* is come on thee
10 the *m.* is gone forth, the rod
12:8 in the *m.* came word of L.
24:18 I spake to the peo. in the *m.* at even my wife died, I did in the *m.* as commanded
33:22 it came to me in the *m.*
*Hos.* 6:3 his going forth is as *m.*
4 your goodness is as *m.* cloud
7:6 in the *m.* it burneth as fire
10:15 in a *m.* sh. king be cut off
*Joel* 2:2 as *m.* spread on mount.
*Amos* 4:13 maketh the *m.* dark.
5:8 turn shad. of death into *m.*
*Jon.* 4:7 God prepared a worm when the *m.* rose
*Mic.* 2:1 when the *m.* is light
*Mat.* 16:3 in the *m.* it will be fo.
27:1 when the *m.* was come
*Mark* 11:20 in *m.* as they passed
13:35 at cock-crowing, or in *m.*

**Early in the MORNING.**

*Gen.* 19:27 Abraham gat up *e. in the m.* 21:14; 22:3
28:18 Jacob rose up *e. in the m.*
31:55 Laban rose *e. in the m.*
*Ex.* 8:20 said, Rise *e. in m.* 9:13
24:4 Moses rose *early in m.* 34:4
*Jos.* 3:1 Joshua rose *early in the m.* 6:12; 7:16; 8:10
*Jud.* 6:28 men of city r. *e. in m.*
1 *Sam.* 1:19 they rose up *e. in t. m.* 29:11; 2 *K.* 3:22; 19:35; 2 *Chr.* 20:20; *Is.* 37:36
15:12 Sa. rose *e. in m.* 17:20 D
29:10 wherefore rise *e. in the m.*
*Job* 1:5 Job rose up *e. in the m.*
*Prov.* 27:14 rising *early in the m.*
*Is.* 5:11 woe to th. th. rise *e. in m.*
37:36 arose *e. in t. m.* all dead
*Dan.* 6:19 Darius rose *e. in t. m.*
*Mat.* 20:1 went *early in the m.*
*Mark* 16:2 *early in the m.* came to sepulchre, *Luke* 24:1
*Luke* 21:38 came *e. i. m.* *John* 8:2
*Acts* 5:21 entered temple *e. in m.*
*See* EVENING.

**Every MORNING.**

*Ex.* 16:21 gath. manna *every m.*
30:7 burn sweet incense *e. m.*
*Lev.* 6:12 priest burn wood *e. m.*
1 *Chr.* 9:27 *e. m.* pertain. to por.
2 *Chr.* 13:11 burn to Lord *e. m.*
*Job* 7:18 shouldest visit him *e. m.*
*Ps.* 73:14 have been chaste. *e. m.*
*Is.* 33:2 be thou our arm *e. m.*
*Lam.* 3:23 L.'s mercies new *e. m.*
*Ezek.* 46:13 prepare a lamb *e. m.*
*Amos* 4:4 bring sacrifices *e. m.*
*Zep.* 3:5 *e. m.* doth bring judgm.

**MORNING light.**

1 *Sam.* 14:36 spoil th. until *m. l.*
25:22 pertain to him by *m. l.*
36 Abi. told nothing until *m. l.*
2 *Sam.* 17:22 passed J. by *m. l.*
2 *K.* 7:9 if we tarry until *m. li.*
*See* CLOUD.

**MORNING star, s.**

*Job* 38:7 wh. *m. s.* sang together
*Rev.* 2:28 I will give him *m. s.*
22:16 I, Jesus, am bright *m. s.*

**Until the MORNING.**

*Ex.* 12:10 let noth. of it remain *u. the m.* 16:19; 23:18; 29:34; *Lev.* 7:15; *Num.* 9:12
16:20 some of th. left *u. t. m.*
23 lay up for you *until the m.*
*Lev.* 19:13 not abide *u. t. m.*
*Deut.* 16:4 any flesh rem. *u. m.*
*Jud.* 19:25 abused her *u. t. m.*
*Ruth* 3:13 dawn *u. t. m.* 14 lay
1 *Sam.* 3:15 Samuel lay *u. t. m.*
19:2 take heed to thyself *u. t. m.*
2 *K.* 10:8 heads of kings *u. t. m.*
*Prov.* 7:18 our fill of love *u. m.*
*Is.* 38:13 I reckoned *until the m.*

**MORNING watch.**

*Ex.* 14:24 in *m. w.* L. said to M.
1 *Sam.* 11:11 mi. of host in *m. w.*

**MORROW.**

*Ex.* 8:23 to-*m.* shall this sign be
9:5 to-*m.* the L. sh. do this thi.
6 L. did thing, on *m.* cattle di.
16:23 to-*m.* is rest of holy sab.
19:10 sanc. them to-day and *m.*
32:5 to-*m.* is a feast to the Lord
*Lev.* 7:16 on *m.* remain. cat. 19:6
22:30 leave none of it till *m.*
23:15 ye shall count from *m.*
*Num.* 11:18 sanctify yourselves against to-*m.* *Jos.* 7:13
16:16 they and A. to-*m.* bef. L.
41 on *m.* congreg. murmured
*Jos.* 3:5 to-*m.* L. will do wond.
5:12 manna ceased on the *m.*
22:18 to-*m.* wroth wi. congreg.
*Jud.* 19:9 to-*m.* get early on way
20:28 to-*m.* I will deliver them
1 *Sam.* 11:9 to-*m.* by ti. sun hot
20:5 to-*m.* is the new moon, 18
28:19 to-*m.* shalt thou and sons
1 *K.* 20:6 send ser. to thee to-*m.*
2 *K.* 6:28 will eat my son, to-*m.*
8:15 on *m.* he took a thick cloth
2 *Chr.* 20:16 to-*m.* go ye down, 17
*Est.* 5:8 to-*m.* as king hath said
12 to-*m.* am I invited to her
*Prov.* 3:28 to-*m* I will give
27:1 boast not thyself to-*m.*
*Is.* 22:13 let us eat, for to-*m.* we die, 1 *Cor.* 15:32
56:12 to-*m.* shall be as this day

*Zep.* 3:3 gn. not bones till to-*m.*
*Mat.* 6:30 to-*m.* is cast into the oven, *Luke* 12:28
34 take no thought for *m.* for *m.* sh. take thought for itself
*Luke* 13:32 to-day, and to-*m.*
33 walk to-day and to-*m.*
*Acts* 20:7 P. rea. to depart on *m.*
25:22 to-*m.* thou shalt hear him
*Jam.* 4:13 to-day or to-*m.* will go
14 know not what sh. be on *m.*

**MORSEL.**

*Gen.* 18:5 fetch a *m.* of bread
*Jud.* 19:5 comf. heart with *m.*
*Ruth* 2:14 dip thy *m.* in vinegar
*Job* 31:17 eaten my *m.* myself
*Prov.* 17:1 bet. dry *m.* and quiet
23:8 *m.* hast eaten shall vomit
*Heb.* 12:16 E. for *m.* sold birthri.
*See* BREAD.

**MORSELS.**

*Ps.* 147:17 cast. forth ice like *m.*

**MORTAL.**

*Job* 4:17 *m.* man mo. just th. G.?
*Rom.* 6:12 sin reign in *m.* body
8:11 quicken *m.* bodies by Spi.
1 *Cor.* 15:53 *m.* on immortal. 54
2 *Cor.* 4:11 J. manifest, in *m.* fle.

**MORTALITY.**

2 *Cor.* 5:4 *m.* swallow. up of life

**MORTALLY.**

*Deut.* 19:11 smite neighbor *m.*

**MORTAR.**

*Gen.* 11:3 slime had they for *m.*
*Ex.* 1:14 serve in *m.* and brick
*Lev.* 14:42 take *m.* and plast. ho.
45 break down *m.* of the house
*Is.* 41:25 upon princes as up. *m.*
*Ezek.* 13:10 daubed it with untempered *m.* 11, 14, 15; 22:28
*Nah.* 3:14 clay, and tread the *m.*

**MORTAR.**

*Num.* 11:8 or beat it in a *m.*
*Prov.* 27:22 bray fool in *m.*

**MORTGAGED.**

*Neh.* 5:3 we have *m.* our lands

**MORTIFY.**

*Rom.* 8:13 ye *m.* deeds of body
*Col.* 3:5 *m.* your members

MOSEROTH. *Num.* 33:30

**MOSES.**

*Ex.* 2:10 called his name M.
*Jos.* 1:5 as I was with M. 3:7
*Ps.* 103:7 made kn. ways to M.
105:26 he sent M. and Aaron
106:16 envied M. in camp, 32
*Is.* 63:12 by right hand of M.
*Jer.* 15:1 though M. stood be. me
*Mal.* 4:4 remember law of M.
*Mat.* 17:3 there appeared M. and Elias, *Mark* 9:4; *Luke* 9:30
19:7 why did M. command.?
23:2 Pharisees sit in M.'s seat
*Mark* 10:3 what did M. com.?
*Mark* 12:19 M. wrote, *Luke* 20:28
*Luke* 16:29 M. and prophets
20:37 M. showed at the bush
24:27 beginning at M. and pro.
*John* 1:17 law given by M. 45
3:14 as M. lifted serpent
5:45 M. accuseth; 46 believed M.
6:32 M. ga. you not that bread
7:19 M. give you law? 22, 23
9:28 M. disciples; 29 G. spake
*Acts* 3:22 M. said, A prophet
6:11 blas. words against M. 14
7:20 M. born, 32, 35, 37
13:39 not justified by law of M.
15:1 circumcised after M. 5
21 M. hath in every city them
21:21 teachest to forsake M.
26:22 things M. did say, 28:23
2 *Cor.* 3:13 not as M. who, 15
2 *Tim.* 3:8 as Jan. withstood M.
*Heb.* 3:2 M. faithful, 3, 5, 16
9:19 M. spoken every precept
10:28 despised M. law
11:23 by faith M. was hid three
12:21 M. said, I fear and quake
*Jude* 9 disput. about body of M.
*Rev.* 15:3 sing the song of M.

**MOST.**

*Prov.* 20:6 *m.* men proclaim
*Luke* 7:42 wh. will love him *m.*?
43 he to whom he forgave *m.*
*Acts* 20:38 sorrowing *m.* of all for
1 *Cor.* 14:27 two, or at *m.* three

**MOTE.**

*Mat.* 7:3 *m.* in brother's eye, *Luke* 6:41
4 let me pull *m.* out of th. eye
5 then th. see clear. to cast *m.* out of broth.'s eye, *Luke* 6:42

**MOTH.**

*Job* 4:19 crushed before the *m.*
27:18 buildeth his house as a *m.*
*Ps.* 39:11 beauty consu. like *m.*
*Is.* 50:9 *m.* shall eat them, 51:8
*Hos.* 5:12 I be to Ephr. as a *m.*
*Mat.* 6:19 wh. *m.* and rust corru.
20 nei. *m.* nor rust, *Luke* 12:33

**MOTH-EATEN.**

*Job* 13:28 as garm. that is *m.-e.*
*Jam.* 5:2 your garments are *m.-e.*

**MOTHER.**

*Gen.* 3:20 was *m.* of all living
17:16 shall be a *m.* of nations
24:60 *m.* thousands of millions
32:11 lest he smite *m.* with chi.
*Ex.* 2:8 and called child's *m.*
*Lev.* 20:14 her *m.* is wickedness
*Jud.* 5:7 Deb. arose a *m.* in Isr.
28 *m.* of Sisera looked out
*Ruth* 1:8 ret. each to *m.'s* house
2 *Sam.* 17:25 Zeruiah, Joab's *m.*
20:19 to destroy a *m.* in Israel
1 *K.* 2:19 a seat for the king's *m.*
3:27 child, she is the *m.* thereof
2 *K.* 24:15 carried away king's *m.*
*Ps.* 113:9 be a joyful *m.* of child.
*Prov.* 30:11 generat. not bless *m.*
*Cant.* 6:9 only one of her *m.*
*Is.* 50:1 whe. bill of *m.* divorce?
*Jer.* 50:12 *m.* be sore confounded
*Ez.* 16:44 as is *m.* so is daughter
45 your *m.* was a Hittite
23:2 two, daughters of one *m.*
*Hos.* 2:2 plead with your *m.*
5 th. *m.* hath played the harlot
10:14 *m.* was dashed in pieces
*Mic.* 7:6 daughter riseth up ag. her *m.* *Mat.* 10:35; *Lu.* 12:53
*Mat.* 8:14 P.'s wife's *m.* *Lu.* 4:38
14:8 before instructed of her *m.*
19:12 so born from *m.'s* womb
20:20 *m.* of Zebedee's children
*Luke* 1:43 *m.* of L. come to me?
*John* 2:1 *m.* of J. there, *Acts* 1:14
*Acts* 12:12 hou. of Mary, *m.* of J.
*Gal.* 4:26 Jerusalem *m.* of us all
*Rev.* 17:5 the *m.* of harlots and
*See* FATHER.

**His MOTHER.**

*Gen.* 21:21 *h. m.* took him a wife
24:67 comf. after death of *h. m.*
27:14 Jacob bro. them to *his m.*
43:29 brother Benj. *h. m.'s* son
44:20 he alone is left of *his m.*
*Ex.* 23:19 not seethe kid in *his m.'s* milk, 34:26; *Deut.* 14:21
*Lev.* 20:17 man take *h. m.'s* dau.
*Num.* 12:12 out of *his m.'s* womb
*Deut.* 27:22 lieth with *h. m.'s* da.
*Jud.* 9:1 went to *h. m.'s* brethr.
1 *Sam.* 2:19 *h. m.* made a lit. co.
1 *K.* 15:13 *his m.* he removed
17:23 Elijah deliv. him to *h. m.*
22:52 walked in way of *h. m.*
2 *K.* 4:19 lad, Carry him to *h. m.*
1 *Chr.* 4:9 *h. m.* called name Ja.
2 *Chr.* 22:3 *his m.* was his coun.
*Ps.* 35:14 as one mourn. for *h. m.*
109:14 not sin of *his m.* blotted
131:2 child weaned of *his m.*
*Prov.* 10:1 son is heavi. of *h. m.*
15:20 foolish man despis. *h. m.*
29:15 left bringeth *h. m.* to sh.
31:1 prophecy *h. m.* taught him
*Ec.* 5:15 came forth of *h. m.'s* w.
*Cant.* 3:11 *his m.* crowned him
*Is.* 66:13 wh. *h. m.* comforteth
*Mat.* 1:18 *h. m.* was espoused
2:13 young child and *h. m.* 20
12:46 *h. m.* stood with. *Mark* 3:31; *Luke* 8:19
13:55 is not *h. m.* called Mary?
*Luke* 1:15 Holy G. fr. *h. m.'s* wo.
60 *h. m.* said, He sh. be call. J.
2:51 *h. m.* kept these sayings
7:12 only son of *h. m.* a widow
15 he delivered him to *h. m.*
*John* 3:4 sec. time into *h. m.'s* w.
19:25 *h. m.* stood by cross of J.
26 when J. saw *h. m.*
*Acts* 3:2 lame fr. *h. m.* wo. 14:8
*Rom.* 16:13 salute R. and *his m.*

**MOTHER-IN-LAW.**

*Deut.* 27:23 curs. lieth wi. *m.-i.-l.*
*Ruth* 1:14 Or. kissed her *m.-i.-l.*
2:23 R. dwelt with her *m.-i.-l.*
3:17 go not empty to thy *m.-i.-l.*
*Mic.* 7:6 dau.-in-law ag. *m.-i.-l.* *Mat.* 10:35; *Luke* 12:53

**My MOTHER.**

*Gen.* 20:12 not daughter of *m. m.*
*Jud.* 8:19 the sons of *my m.*
16:17 Nazar. from *my m.'s* wo.
1 *K.* 2:20 to her, Ask on, *my m.*
*Job* 1:21 naked out of *my m.'s* w.
3:10 sh. not doors of *my m.'s* w.
17:14 to worm, Thou art *m. m.*
31:18 guid. her fr. *m. m.'s* wo.
*Ps.* 22:9 wh. on *m. m.'s* breasts
10 my God from *m. m.'s* belly
51:5 in sin did *m. m.* conce. me
69:8 alien to *m. m.'s* children
71:6 out of *m. m.'s* bowels
139:13 cov. me in *my m.'s* womb
*Prov.* 4:3 bel. in sight of *my m.*
*Cant.* 1:6 *my m.'s* children ang.
3:4 brou. him to *my m.'s* house
8:1 sucked the breasts of *my m.*
2 bring th. into *my m.'s* house
*Is.* 49:1 from bowels of *my m.*
*Jer.* 15:10 woe is me, *my m.*
20:14 day wherein *my m.* bare
17 *my m.* might been my grave
*Mat.* 12:48 Jesus said, Who is *my m.*? *Mark* 3:33
49 behold *my m.* and brethren, *Mark* 3:34; *Luke* 8:21
*Gal.* 1:15 separat. fr. *my m.'s* w.

**Thy MOTHER.**

*Gen.* 27:29 let *thy m.'s* sons bow
37:10 I and *thy m.* bow to thee?
*Lev.* 18:7 nakedness of *thy m.*
*Deut.* 13:6 son of *thy m.* ent. th.
1 *Sam.* 15:33 *thy m.* be childless
20:30 confus. of *t. m.'s* nakedn.
2 *K.* 9:22 whoredoms of *thy m.*
*Ps.* 50:20 slander. *t.* own *m.'s* son
*Prov.* 1:8 the law of *thy m.* 6:20
23:22 and despise not *thy m.*
*Cant.* 8:5 *thy m.* brou. thee forth
*Jer.* 22:26 *thy m.* that bare thee
*Ezek.* 16:3 fa. Amorite, *t. m.* Hit.
45 thou art *thy m.'s* daughter
19:2 say, What is *thy m.*?
10 *thy m.* is like a vine
*Hos.* 4:5 I will destroy *thy m.*
*Mat.* 12:47 beh. *t. m.* and breth. *Mark* 3:32; *Luke* 8:20; *John* 19:27
2 *Tim.* 1:5 which dwelt in *t. m.*

**MOTHERS.**

*Is.* 49:23 queens be thy nurs. *m.*

*Jer.* 16:3 saith the L. concern. *m.*
*Lam.* 2:12 say to their *m.* where is corn and wine? soul was poured to their *m.* bosom.
5:3 fatherless, our *m.* as widows
*Mark* 10:30 hun.-fold, sisters, *m.*
1 *Tim.* 1:9 law for murder. of *m.*
5:2 entreat elder women as *m.*

**MOTIONS.**

*Rom.* 7:5 the *m.* of sins did work

**MOULDY.**

*Jos.* 9:5 provision dry and *m.* 12

**MOUNT, 'ING.**

*Job* 20:6 excel. *m.* to heavens
39:27 do. eagle *m.* at thy com.?
*Ps.* 107:26 they *m.* up to heaven
*Is.* 9:18 *m.* as lift. up of smoke
15:5 by *m.* up of Luhith they go
*Is.* 40:31 shall *m.* up with wings
*Jer.* 51:53 tho. Babylon sho. *m.*
*Ezek.* 10:16 cherub. lift to *m.* 19

**MOUNT.**

*Gen.* 31:54 J. offered sacri. on *m.*
*Ex.* 18:5 encamped at *m.* of G.
19:12 whoso toucheth the *m.*
14 Moses went down from the *m.* 32:15; 34:29
16 thick cloud upon *m.* 24:15
18 *m.* Si. was altoget. on smo.
23 set bounds about the *m.*
24:16 glory of Lord upon *m.* Si.
17 devouring fire on top of *m.*
31:18 L. gave Mos. on *m.* Sinai
32:19 M. brake them beneath *m.*
34:2 and come up to *m.* Sinai
3 nor let man be seen thro' *m.*
*Num.* 10:33 they departed fr. *m.*
20:28 Aaron died in *m.* Hor
*Deut.* 1:6 dw. long enough in *m.*
7 turn you, go to *m.* of Amor.
9:15 the *m.* burned with fire
27:13 these shall stand on *m.* E.
33:2 L. shined forth from *m.* P.
*Jud.* 4:6 draw towards *m.* Tabor
2 *Sam.* 15:30 D. went by the *m.*
32 *m.* where he worshipped G.
1 *K.* 19:8 Elijah went to *m.* of G.
11 stand on the *m.* bef. the L.
2 *K.* 23:13 the *m.* of corruption
*Neh.* 9:13 thou camest on *m.* Si.
*Cant.* 4:1 flock of goats fr. *m.* G.
*Is.* 10:32 *m.* of dau. of Zion, 16:1
14:13 I will sit on *m.* of congre.
27:13 worship in holy *m.* at J.
29:3 siege ag. thee with a *m.*
*Jer.* 6:6 cast a *m.* against Jerusa. *Ezek.* 4:2; 21:22; 26:8
*Dan.* 11:15 k. of north cast up *m.*
*Ob.* 8 destroy unders. out *m.* E.
21 saviors sh. come to judge *m.*
*Hab.* 3:3 H. One from *m.* Paran
*Acts* 7:30 in wilderness of *m.* S.
*Gal.* 4:24 one from the *m.* Sinai
25 Agar is *m.* Sinai in Arabia
*Heb.* 12:18 not come to the *m.*

*See* CARMEL, GERIZIM.

**Before the MOUNT.**

*Ex.* 19:2 Israel camped *b. t. m.*
34:3 nei. let flocks feed *b. t. m.*

*See* EPHRAIM.

**In, *or* into the MOUNT.**

*Gen.* 22:14 *in t. m.* of L. be seen
31:54 tarried all night *in t. m.*
*Ex.* 4:27 met him *in t. m.* of God
19:12 take heed, go not up *i. m.*
24:12 come *i. t. m. Deut.* 10:1
13 went *in t. m.* of G. 15, 18
18 M. was *in t. m.* 40 days and 40 nights, *Deut.* 9:9; 10:10
25:40 after pat. showed thee *in t. m.* 26:30; 27:8; *Heb.* 8:5
*Num.* 27:12 get thee *into m.* A.
*Deut.* 32:50 die *in m.* as A. died
*Jos.* 8:30 altar to L. *in m.* Ebal
2 *K.* 28:16 spied sepulchres *in m.*
2 *Chr.* 3:1 house of L. *in m.* Mo.
*Is.* 28:21 L. rise up as *in m.* P.
*Acts* 7:38 angel spake *in m.* Sin.
2 *Pet.* 1:18 we were *in* holy *m.*

*See* GILBOA.

**MOUNT of Olives.**

*Zec.* 14:4 his feet shall stand on *m. of O. m. of O.* shall clea.
*Mat.* 21:1 they were come to the *m. of Olives, Luke* 19:29
24:3 upon *m. of O. Mark* 13:3
26:30 they went out into *m. of O. Mark* 14:26; *Luke* 22:39
*Luke* 19:37 at descent of *m. of O.*
21:37 and abode in *m. of O.*
*Acts* 1:12 returned fr. *m. of O.*

*See* SEIR, ZION.

**MOUNTS.**

*Jer.* 32:24 *m.* are come to city
33:4 houses thrown down by *m.*
*Ezek.* 17:17 for him, by cast. *m.*

**MOUNTAIN.**

*Gen.* 14:10 they th. re. fled to *m.*
19:17 escape to *m.* 19 not escape
*Ex.* 3:1 came to the *m.* of G.
12 peo. sh. serve God on th. *m.*
19:3 L. called to him out of *m.*
20:18 people saw *m.* smoking
*Num.* 14:40 gat th. into top of *m.*
*Deut.* 2:3 ye have compassed *m.*
3:25 let me see that goodly *m.*
4:11 *m.* burnt with fire, 5:23
*Jos.* 2:16 get ye to *m.* and hide
11:16 Jos. took the plain and *m.*
14:12 give me *m.* 17:18 *m.* thine
*Jud.* 1:19 drave out inhabitants of *m.*
1 *Sam.* 17:3 Philistines stood on a *m.* on one side, and Israel stood on a *m.* on the oth. si.
23:26 Saul went on this side of the *m.* and David on th. si.
2 *K.* 2:16 S. cast him on some *m.*
6:17 *m.* full of horses and char.
*Job* 14:18 *m.* fall. com. to naught
*Ps.* 11:1 flee as bird to your *m.*?
30:7 hast made my *m.* to stand
78:54 bro. to *m.* his right hand
*Is.* 2:2 *m.* of L.'s house, *Mic.* 4:1
3 let us go to *m.* of L. *Mic.* 4:2
30:17 as a beacon on top of *m.*
29 one goeth with pipe to *m.*
40:4 every *m.* and hill sh. be made low, *Luke* 3:5
*Jer.* 16:16 hunt them fr. every *m.*
17:3 O my *m.* in the field
26:18 *m.* of the house as high places of forest, *Mic.* 3:12
50:6 people gone fr. *m.* to hill
51:25 O destroying *m.* saith L. I will make thee a burnt *m.*
*Lam.* 5:18 because of *m.* of Zion
*Ezek.* 11:23 gl. of L. stood on *m.*
28:16 cast thee out of *m.* of God
43:12 law of house on top of *m.*
*Dan.* 2:35 stone became great *m.*
45 the stone was cut out of *m.*
*Mic.* 7:12 co. to thee fr. *m.* to *m.*
*Hag.* 1:8 go up to *m.* bring wood
*Zec.* 4:7 who art th. O great *m.*
8:3 be called the *m.* of the Lord
14:4 half of the *m.* shall remove
*Mat.* 5:1 he went up into a *m.* 14:23; 15:29; *Mark* 3:13; 6:46; *Luke* 6:12; 9:28; *John* 6:3, 15
17:1 bringeth them into high *m.*
9 and as they came down from the *m. Mark* 9:9
20 have faith, say to this *m.* Remove, 21:21; *Mark* 11:23
28:16 *m.* where Jesus appointed
*Luke* 8:32 swine feeding on *m.*
*Heb.* 12:20 much as beast tou. *m.*
*Rev.* 6:14 every *m.* and isl. rem.
8:8 a great *m.* burning with fire

**High MOUNTAIN.**

*Is.* 13:2 lift up banner up. *h. m.*
30:25 shall be upon every *h. m.*
40:9 get thee up into the *h. m.*
57:7 on *h. m.* hast th. set thy b.
*Jer.* 3:6 gone up upon ev. *h. m.*
*Ezek.* 17:22 plant it on a *high m.*
40:2 set me on a very high *m.*
*Mat.* 4:8 devil taken him up into an exceeding *h. m. Luke* 4:5
17:1 Jesus taketh P., James and John into a *h. m. Mark* 9:2
*Rev.* 21:10 car. me in Sp. to *h. m.*

*See* HOLY.

**In the, *or* in this MOUNTAIN.**

*Gen.* 19:30 went and dwelt *in m.*
*Ex.* 15:17 plant them *in the m.*
*Num.* 13:17 said, Go up *in. t. m.*
*Deut.* 32:49 get thee up *in t. m.*
*Ps.* 48:1 G. praised *in m.* of holi.
*Is.* 25:6 *in this m.* L. make feast
7 destroy *in t. m.* face of cov.
10 *in this m.* hand of L. rest
*Ezek.* 17:23 *in the m.* of Israel
*Amos* 4:1 *in the m.* of Samaria
6:1 woe to th. trust *in m.* of S.
*John* 4:20 fath. worship. *in t. m.*
21 nei. *in this m.* nor Jerusal.

**MOUNTAINS.**

*Gen.* 7:20 the *m.* were covered
8:4 the ark rested upon the *m.*
5 tenth month tops of *m.* seen
*Num.* 33:48 departed from the *m.*
*Deut.* 12:2 destroy pla. on hi. *m.*
*Jos.* 11:21 cut off Anakim fr. *m.*
*Jud.* 5:5 *m.* melted from bef. L.
11:37 go up and down on *m.*
2 *Sam.* 1:21 *m.* of Gilboa
1 *K.* 19:11 a strong wind rent *m.*
1 *Chr.* 12:8 swift as roes on *m.*
2 *Chr.* 18:16 Israel scatter. on *m.*
*Job* 9:5 which removeth the *m.*
28:9 overturneth *m.* by roots
40:20 *m.* bring him forth food
*Ps.* 36:6 thy right. like great *m.*
46:2 though the *m.* be carried
3 tho' *m.* shake with swelling
65:6 his strength setteth fast *m.*
72:3 *m.* bring peace to the peo.
76:4 more glori. than *m.* of prey
83:14 flame setteth *m.* on fire
90:2 before *m.* we. brought for.
104:6 waters stood above *m.*
8 up by the *m.* down by valle.
114:4 *m.* skipped like rams, 6
125:2 as *m.* round about Jerusa.
133:3 dew that descended on *m.*
144:5 touch *m.* they shall smoke
*Ps.* 147:8 mak. gr. to grow on *m.*
148:9 *m.* and hills praise the L.
*Prov.* 8:25 before *m.* were settled
*Cant.* 2:8 cometh leaping on *m.*
17 be like a roe on the *m.* 8:14
4:8 look from *m.* of the leopards
*Is.* 2:14 day of L. be on high *m.*
14:25 *m.* tread him under foot
18:3 lifteth up ensign on the *m.*
34:3 *m.* melted with their blood
40:12 hath weighed *m.* in scales
41:15 thou shalt thresh the *m.*
42:15 make waste *m.* and hills
44:23 into singing, ye *m.* 49:13
49:11 make all my *m.* a way
52:7 how beautiful on the *m.* are the feet, *Nah.* 1:15
54:10 for the *m.* shall depart
55:12 *m.* shall break forth befo.
64:1 *m.* flow down at presen. 3
65:7 have burned incense on *m.*
*Jer.* 4:24 beh. *m.* and th. tremb.
9:10 for *m.* will I take up weep.
13:16 feet stumble on dark *m.*
17:26 from *m.* bringing offerin.
31:5 plant vines on *m.* of Sama.
46:18 as Tabor among the *m.*
50:6 turned them away on *m.*
*Lam.* 4:19 pursued us on the *m.*

Ezek. 6:2 set face toward m. of I.
7:16 sh. be on the m. like doves
18:6 not eaten upon m. 11, 15
19:9 voice no more heard on m.
22:9 they eat upon the m.
31:12 upon m. branches fallen
32:5 I will lay thy flesh on m.
33:28 m. of Is. shall be desolate
34:6 sheep wander. through m.
13 feed them on m. of Israel. 14
35:8 fill his m. with slain men
36:1 prophesy unto m. Is. 4
8 m. of Is. shoot forth branch
37:22 one nation on m. of Israel
38:8 gathered ag. m. of Is.
20 m. shall be thrown down
21 sw. against him thro' all m.
39:2 bring thee on m. of Israel
4 shalt fall on the m. of Israel
17 great sacrifice on m. of Isr.
Joel 2:2 morn. spread upon m.
3:18 m. sh. drop down new wine
Amos 3:9 assemble on m. of Sa.
4:13 formeth m. L. is his name
9:13 m. shall drop sweet wine
Mic. 1:4 the m. shall be molten
6:1 contend thou before the m.
2 O ye m. the L.'s controversy
Nah. 1:5 the m. quake at him
3:18 people scattered on the m.
Hab. 3:6 everlasting m. scattered
10 m. saw thee, and trembled
Hag. 1:11 for a drought on m.
Zec. 6:1 chariots bet. m. of brass
Mal. 1:3 and laid his m. waste
Mat. 18:12 goeth into the m.
24:16 let them in Jud. flee to m.
1 Cor. 13:2 that I could remo. m.
Rev. 16:20 m. were not found
17:9 seven heads are seven m.

**In the MOUNTAINS.**

Ex. 32:12 to slay them in t. m.
Num. 33:47 pitched in t. m. of A.
Deut. 2:37 cam. not to cit. in m.
Jos. 10:6 kings that dw. in t. m.
Jud. 6:2 Is. made dens in t. m.
1 K. 5:15 80,000 hewers in t. m.
2 Chr. 21:11 high places in t. m.
Is. 13:4 noise of multi. in t. m.
Mark 5:5 ni. and day was in m.
Heb. 11:38 wandered in the m.

**Of the MOUNTAINS.**

Gen. 8:5 tops of t. m. were seen
22:2 offer him on one of the m.
Num. 23:7 out of the m. of east
Deut. 32:22 foundations of t. m.
33:15 chief thin. of t. ancient m.
Jud. 9:25 for him in top of t. m.
36 peo. down from top of t. m.
seest shadow of the m.
2 K. 19:23 to hei. of t. m. Is. 37:24
Job 24:8 showers of the m.
39:8 range of t. m. his pasture
Ps. 50:11 all fowls of t. m.
72:16 handful corn on top of m.
Prov. 27:25 herbs of t. m. gath.
Is. 2:2 in top of the m. Mic. 4:1
42:11 shout from top of the m.
Jer. 3:23 fr. multitude of the m.
32:44 witness. in cities of t. m.
33:13 in cities of the m.
Ezek. 6:13 slain in tops of the m.
7:7 the sounding ag. of the m.
Hos. 4:13 sacri. on tops of the m.
Joel 2:5 char. on tops of the m.
Jon. 2:6 down to bot. of the m.
Zec. 14:5 flee to valley of the m.
Rev. 6:15 hid in rocks of the m.

**To the MOUNTAINS.**

Cant. 4:6 to the m. of myrrh
Is. 22:5 trou. and crying to t. m.
Ezek. 6:3 saith L. to the m. 36:4
32:6 water with blood to the m.
36:1 prophesy to the m. of Is. 6
Hos. 10:8 sh. say to the m. Cover
Mark 13:14 that be in Judea flee
to the m. Luke 21:21
Luke 23:30 to m. Fall, Rev. 6:16

**MOURN.**

Gen. 23:2 Ab. came to m. Sarah
1 Sam. 16:1 how long m. for S.?
2 Sam. 3:31 and m. before Abner
1 K. 13:29 old proph. came to m.
14:13 all Israel sh. m. for him
Neh. 8:9 this day is holy, m. not
Job 2:11 appointm. to m. wi. hi.
5:11 those wh. m. may be exal.
14:22 soul within him shall m.
Ps. 55:2 I m. in my complaint
Prov. 5:11 and th. m. at the last
29:2 wicked rule, the people m.
Ec. 3:4 time to m. time to dance
Is. 3:26 gates sh. lament and m.
16:7 for Kir-hareseth shall ye m.
19:8 fishers m. 38:14 I did m.
59:11 we m. sore like doves
61:2 sent me to comf. all that m.
3 to appoint them that m. in Z.
66:10 rejoice all ye that m.
Jer. 4:28 for this earth shall m.
12:4 how long sh. the land m.?
48:31 m. for the men of Kir-her.
Lam. 1:4 the ways of Zion do m.
Ezek. 7:12 let not the seller m.
27 king shall m. and the prin.
24:16 nei. sh. thou m. nor weep
23 shall pine away and m.
31:15 caused Leb. to m. for him
Hos. 4:3 theref. sh. the land m.?
10:5 peo. shall m. over Samaria
Joel 1:9 the Lord's ministers m.
Amos 1:2 habita. of shepher. m.
8:8 every one m. therein, 9:5
Zec. 12:10 and shall m. for him
12 land m. every family apart
Mat. 5:4 blessed are they that m.
9:15 child. of bride-chamb. m.?
24:30 all the tribes of earth m.
Luke 6:25 laugh, for ye sh. m.
Jam. 4:9 afflicted, m. and weep
Rev. 18:11 merch. weep and m.

**MOURNED.**

Gen. 37:34 Jacob m. for his son
50:3 Egyptians m. for Jacob, 10
Ex. 33:4 heard th. evil tidings,
they m. Num. 14:39
Num. 20:29 congrega. m. for A.
1 Sam. 15:35 Samuel m. for Saul
2 Sam. 1:12 m. for Saul and Jon.
11:26 Bath-sheba m. for Uriah
13:27 David m. for his son Abs.
14:2 one that had m. for dead
1 K. 13:30 they m. over man of G.
14:18 Is. m. for Jeroboam's son
1 Chr. 7:22 Ephr. their father m.
2 Chr. 35:24 Judah m. for Josiah
Ezr. 10:6 m. for transgression
Neh. 1:4 sat and m. certain days
Zec. 7:5 when ye m. and fasted
Mat. 11:17 we have m. unto you,
Luke 7:32
Mark 16:10 as they m. and wept
1 Cor. 5:2 and have not rather m.

**MOURNER, S.**

2 Sam. 14:2 feign thyself a m.
Job 29:25 one that comforteth m.
Ec. 12:5 m. go about the streets
Is. 57:18 restore comf. to his m.
Hos. 9:4 sacrifi. be as bread of m.

**MOURNETH.**

2 Sam. 19:1 king m. for Absalom
Ps. 35:14 I bowed as one that m.
88:9 mine eye m. by affliction
Is. 24:4 earth m. and fad. 33:9
7 new wine m. vine languish.
Jer. 12:11 viney. being desol. m.
14:2 Jud. m. and gates languish
23:10 bec. of swearing land m.
Joel 1:10 land m. corn is wasted
Zec. 12:10 one that m. first-born

**MOURNFULLY.**

Mal. 3:14 we have walked m.

**MOURNING.**

Gen. 27:41 days of m. at hand
50:10 made a m. for his father
11 saw m. this is a grievous m.
Deut. 26:14 not eaten in m.
34:8 days of m. for Mo. ended
2 Sam. 11:27 when m. was past
19:2 victory was turned to m.
Est. 4:3 there was m. am. Jews
9:22 was turned to them fr. m.
Job 3:8 ready to raise their m.
Job 30:31 harp also is turn. to m.
Ps. 30:11 turned m. to dancing
Ec. 7:2 better go to house of m.
4 heart of wise in house of m.
Is. 22:12 Lord did call to m.
51:11 sor. and m. shall flee away
60:20 days of m. shall be ended
61:3 give them oil of joy for m.
Jer. 6:26 m. as for an only son
16:5 enter not into house of m.
31:13 turn their m. into joy
Lam. 2:5 daughter of Judah m.
5:15 our dance is turned into m.
Ezek. 2:10 lamentations, m. woe
24:17 no m. for dead; 31:15 I cau.
Joel 2:12 with weeping and m.
Amos 5:16 call husbandm. to m.
8:10 feasts into m. I will make
it as the m. of an only son
Mic. 1:11 came not forth in m.
Zec. 12:11 m. in Jerusalem as m.
of Hadadrimmon
Mat. 2:18 great m. Rachel weep.
2 Cor. 7:7 he told us your m.
Jam. 4:9 laugh. be turned to m.
Rev. 18:8 one day death and m.

**MOURNING.**

Gen. 37:35 go down to grave m.
2 Sam. 14:2 put on m. apparel
Est. 6:12 H. hasted to house m.
Job 30:28 I went m. without sun
Ps. 38:6 I go m. all day long
42:9 why go I m. because of oppression of enemy? 43:2
Jer. 9:17 call for the m. women
16:7 m. to comf. them for dead
Ezek. 7:16 m. for their iniquities
Dan. 10:2 D. was m. three weeks
Mic. 1:8 will make a m. as owls

**MOUSE.**

Lev. 11:29 weasel and m. be unc.
Is. 66:17 eating abomin. and m.

**MOUTH.**

Gen. 8:11 in her m. was olive le.
24:57 damsel, inquire at her m.
29:2 great stone on well's m.
3 rolled stone fr. well's m. 10
42:27 his money was in sack's
m. 43:12, 21
Ex. 4:11 who made man's m.?
16 he shall be to thee in. of m.
Num. 12:8 him speak m. to m.
16:30 earth open her m. and sw.
23:5 L. put a word in Bal.'s m.
35:30 put to death by m. of witnesses, Deut. 17:6; 19:15
Jos. 10:18 sto. to m. of cave, 27
22 open m. of cave, bring out
1 Sam. 1:12 Eli marked her m.
2 Sam. 14:3 J. put words in m. 19
17:19 a covering over well's m.
1 K. 19:18 every m. not kissed
22:13 the prophets declare good
to the king with one m.
22 lying spirit in m. of his
prophets, 23; 2 Chr. 18:21, 22
2 Chr. 35:22 hea. not to m. of G.
36:21 fulfil word of Lord by m.
of Jeremiah, 22; Ezr. 1:1
Est. 7:8 word we. out king's m.
Job 5:16 iniquity stop. her m.
12:11 doth m. taste meat? 34:3
32:5 there was no answer in m.

Ps. 8:2 out of m. of babes
22:21 save me from the lion's m.
32:9 m. must be held with brid.
37:30 m. of right. speak. wisd.
38:14 in wh. m. are no reproofs
63:11 but m. that speaketh lies
69:15 let not the pit shut her m.
107:42 iniquity shall stop her m.
109:2 m. of wick. m. of deceitf.
126:2 m. filled with laughter
141:7 bones scat. at grave's m.
144:8 whose m. speak. vanit. 11
Prov. 4:24 put away froward m.
5:3 her m. is smoother than oil
6:12 walketh wi. frow. m. 10:32
8:13 the froward m. do I hate
10:6 violence cov. m. of wic. 11
14 m. of fool. near destruction
31 m. of just bringeth wisdom
11:11 city over. by m. of wicked
12:6 m. of upright deliver them
14:3 in m. of fool. is rod of pride
15:2 m. of fools poureth foolish.
14 m. of fools feed. on foolish.
28 m. of wicked pour. out evil
18:4 words of a man's m. deep
7 a fool's m. is his destruction
19:28 m. of wicked devour iniq.
22:14 m. of a strange woman
26:7 parable in m. of fools, 9
28 flattering m. worketh ruin
30:20 eateth and wipeth her m.
Ec. 10:12 words of a w. man's m.
Is. 9:12 devour Is. with open m.
17 and every m. speaketh folly
57:4 ag. wh. make ye wide m.?
59:21 Sp. not depart out of m.
Jer. 32:4 speak m. to m. 34:3
36:4 Baruch wrote from m. of Jeremiah, 27, 32; 45:1
44:17 goeth forth out of m.
26 no more named in m.
Lam. 3:38 out of m. of Most H.
Ezek. 21:22 open m. in slaughter
29:21 will give thee open. of m.
Dan. 4:31 word was in king's m.
6:17 stone laid on m. of the den
7:5 it had three ribs in m. of it
8 a m. speaking gr. things, 20
Hos. 2:17 names of B. out her m.
Amos 3:12 as shep. tak. out of m.
Nah. 3:12 fall into m. of eater
Zec. 5:8 weight of lead on m.
Mat. 4:4 proceed. out of m. of G.
12:34 of the heart m. speaketh
15:11 what go. in m. defil. not
18:16 in m. of two or three witness. every word, 2 Cor. 13:1
21:16 out m. of babes ha. praise
Luke 1:70 spake by m. of proph.
21:15 I will give you a m.
Acts 1:16 the Holy Ghost spake by m. of David, 4:25
3:18 showed by m. of propn. 21
15:27 tell you same things by m.
23:2 commanded to smite on m.
Rom. 3:14 wh. m. is full of curs.
19 every m. may be stopped
10:10 with m. confes. is made
15:6 ye may with one m. glo. G.
1 Cor. 9:9 not muzzle m. of ox
2 Tim. 4:17 deliv. out m. of lion
Jam. 3:10 out of m. proceed bles.
Rev. 13:5 a m. speaking blasph.
16:13 spirits out of m. of dragon

**His MOUTH.**

Ex. 4:15 and put words in his m. and I will be with his m.
Num. 23:16 G. put word in h. m.
Deut. 18:18 put words in h. m.
1 Sam. 14:26 put hand to h. m. 27
17:35 delivered it out of his m.
2 Sam. 18:25 there is tid. in h. m.
22:9 fire out of his m. Ps. 18:8
1 K. 8:15 wi. h. m. to D. 2 Chr. 6:4
2 K. 4:34 he put his m. on his m.
1 Chr. 16:12 judgments of his m.
Job 15:30 by breath of his m.
20:12 wicked. be sweet in h. m.
13 keep it still within h. m.
22:22 receive law from his m.
23:12 esteemed words of his m.
37:2 sound goeth out of his m.
40:23 draw up Jord. into his m.
41:19 out of his m. go bu. lamps
21 a flame goeth out of his m.
Ps. 10:7 h. m. is full of cursing
33:6 made by breath of h. m.
36:3 words of his m. are iniq.
38:13 dumb man open. not h. m.
55:21 words of his m. smoother
105:5 rem. judgments of his m.
Prov. 2:6 out of h. m. knowledge
11:9 his m. destroyeth neighb.
12:14 good by fruit of his m.
13:2 eat good by fruit of his m.
3 keepeth his m. keep. his life
15:23 hath joy by ans. of h. m.
16:10 his m. transgres. not judg.
23 heart of wise teacheth h. m.
26 for his m. craveth it of him
18:6 his m. calleth for strokes
20 satisfied with fruit of his m.
19:24 not bring it to h. m. 26:15
20:17 his m. filled with gravel
21:23 keepeth h. m. keep. soul
Ec. 6:7 labor of man is for h. m.
10:13 words of his m. is foolish.
Cant. 1:2 kiss wi. kisses of h. m.
5:16 h. m. is sweet, is my belo.
Is. 11:4 earth with rod of h. m.
53:9 neither any deceit in h. m.
Jer. 9:8 speak. peace. with h. m.
20 receive the word of his m.
36:17 write all th. words at h. m.
51:44 bring out of h. m. that wh.
Lam. 3:29 putteth his m. in dust
4:4 tong. cleav. to roof of h. m.
Zec. 9:7 take blood out of his m.
Mal. 2:6 law of truth in his m.
7 should seek the law at h. m.
Luke 1:64 and his m. was opened
4:22 gracious words out of h. m.
6:45 abund. of heart h. m. speak
11:54 catch somew. out of h. m.
22:71 have heard of his own m.
John 19:29 and put it to his m.
2 Thes. 2:8 consume with sp. of his m.
1 Pet. 2:22 neither guile in h. m.
Rev. 1:16 out of his m. went a sharp sword, 19:15, 21
12:15 cast out of his m. water
13:2 his m. was as mou. of lion

See LORD.

**My MOUTH.**

Gen. 45:12 my m. speak to you
Num. 22:38 put. in my m. 23:12
Deut. 32:1 hear words of my m.
1 Sam. 2:1 my m. is enlarg. over
Job 7:11 I will not refrain my m.
9:20 my own m. shall cond. me
16:5 strengthen you with my m.
19:16 entreated serv. wi. my m.
23:4 fill my m. with arguments
31:27 my m. kissed my hand
30 neither suffer. my m. to sin
33:2 tongue ha. spok. in my m.
40:4 I lay my hand upon my m.
Ps. 17:3 my m. shall not transgr.
19:14 words of my m. be accept.
34:1 praise continual. in my m.
39:1 keep my m. with a bridle
40:3 put a new song in my m.
49:3 my m. shall speak of wisd.
51:15 my m. sh. forth thy praise
54:2 give ear to words of my m.
63:5 my m. shall praise thee
66:14 my m. hath spoken when I
17 I cried to him with my m.
71:8 my m. be filled with praise
15 my m. show forth righteou.
78:1 incl. ears to wor. of my m.
2 I will open my m. in a para.
89:1 with my m. will I make kn.
109:30 praise the L. with my m.
119:43 word of tr. out of my m.
103 sweet. th. honey to my m.
108 freewill-offerings of my m.
137:6 tongue cl. to roof of my m.
141:3 set a watch before my m.
145:21 my m. sh. speak praise
Prov. 4:5 fr. words of my m. 5:7
7:24 attend to words of my m.
8:7 for my m. shall speak truth
8 words of my m. in righteous.
Is. 6:7 he laid the coal on my m.
30:2 have not asked at my m.
34:16 my m. it hath commanded
45:23 word is gone out of my m.
48:3 things forth out of my m.
49:2 made my m. like sharp
55:11 word that go. out my m.
Jer. 1:9 Lord touched my m.
15:19 thou shalt be as my m.
36:6 hast written from my m.
Ezek. 3:3 in my m. like honey
17 hear word at my m. 33:7
4:14 abomin. flesh into my m.
Dan. 10:3 fle. nor wine in my m.
Hos. 6:5 slain by words of my m.
Mat. 13:35 open my m. in parab.
Acts 11:8 any time enter. my m.
15:7 Gentiles by my m. sh. hear
Eph. 6:19 open my m. boldly
Rev. 2:16 fight with sw. of my m.
3:16 spew thee out of my m.
10:10 book in my m. sweet

**MOUTH, *with* opened.**

Gen. 4:11 earth opened her m.
Num. 16:32 earth op. her m. and swal. them, 26:10; Deut. 11:6
22:28 Lord opened m. of the ass
Jud. 11:35 o. my m. to Lord, 36
Job 3:1 op. Job his m. and curs.
29:23 opened their m. Ps. 35:21
33:2 beh. now, I have op. my m.
Ps. 39:9 I o. not my m. because
109:2 m. of deceitful o. ag. me
119:131 I o. my m. and panted
Is. 5:14 hell hath opened her m.
10:14 there was none that o. m.
53:7 yet he opened not his m.
Ezek. 3:2 I o. my m. he caused
24:27 thy m. be opened, 33:22
Dan. 10:16 I o. my m. and spake
Mat. 5:2 he o. his m. and taught
17:27 when thou hast o. his m.
Luke 1:64 m. was o. immediately
Acts 8:32 so he open. not his m.
35 Philip o. m. 10:34 P. o. m.
2 Cor. 6:11 our m. is ope. to you
Rev. 12:16 earth opened her m.
13:6 he o. his m. in blasphemy

**MOUTH, *with* openeth.**

Ps. 38:13 dumb man o. not his m.
Prov. 24:7 fool o. not his m. in g.
31:26 she o. her m. with wisdom

**Their MOUTH.**

Jud. 7:6 put. their hand to t. m.
Neh. 9:20 not thy manna fr. t. m.
Job 5:15 saveth poor from t. m.
16:10 gaped upon me with t. m.
29:9 princes laid hand on t. m.
10 tongue clea. to roof of t. m.
Ps. 5:9 no faithfulness in t. m.
Ps. 17:10 with their m. they spe. proudly
58:6 bre. teeth, O God, in t. m.
59:7 they belch out with t. m.
12 sin of t. m. and words of li.
62:4 bless with t. m. curse inw.
73:9 set t. m. aga. the heavens
78:36 did flatter him with t. m.
149:6 praises of God be in t. m.
Is. 29:13 peo. draw near wi. t. m.
Jer. 7:28 truth cut off from t. m.
12:2 thou art near in their m.
Lam. 2:16 enemies opened t. m.
Ezek. 33:31 with t. m. they show
34:10 deliver my flock from t. m.

*Mic.* 6:12 tongue deceitf. in *t. m.*
7:16 sh. lay their hand on *t. m.*
*Zep.* 3:13 deceit. tongue in *t. m.*
*Zec.* 14:12 tongue cons. in *th. m.*
*Mal.* 15:8 draweth nigh wi. *t. m.*
*Jude* 16 *t. m.* speak. great words
*Rev.* 9:19 power is in *t. m.*
11:5 fire proceedeth out of *t. m.*
14:5 in *t. m.* was found no guile

**Thy MOUTH.**

*Ex.* 4:12 I will be with *thy m.* 15
13:9 Lord's law may be in *t. m.*
23:13 of other gods out of *t. m.*
*Deut.* 23:23 promised with *t. m.*
30:14 word is nigh to thee, in *thy m. Rom.* 10:8
*Jos.* 1:8 not depart out of *t. m.*
*Jud.* 9:38 where is now *thy m.?*
11:36 opened *thy m.* to the Lord
18:19 h. upon *t. m. Prov.* 30:32
2 *Sam.* 1:16 *t. m.* testifi. ag. thee
1 *K.* 8:24 spa. wi. *t. m.* 2 *Ch.* 6:15
17:24 word of L. in *t. m.* truth
*Job* 8:2 words of *t. m.* like wind
21 fill *thy m.* with laughing
15:5 *thy m.* uttereth thine iniq.
6 *th.* own *m.* condemneth thee
13 let. such words go out *t. m.*
*Ps.* 50:16 take my coven. in *t. m.*
19 thou givest *thy m.* to evil
81:10 open *t. m.* wide I will fill
103:5 satisfi. *t. m.* wi. good th.
119:13 the judgments of *thy m.*
72 law of *thy m.* is better to me
88 keep testimony of *thy m.*
138:4 hear the words of *thy m.*
*Prov.* 6:2 with words of *t. m.*
27:2 praise th. not *thine* own *m.*
31:8 open *thy m.* for the dumb
9 open *t. m.* judge righteously
*Ec.* 5:2 be not rash with *thy m.*
6 suff. not *t. m.* cause fle. to sin
*Cant.* 7:9 roof of *t. m.* like wine
*Is.* 51:16 words in *t. m. Jer.* 1:9
59:21 which I put in *thy m.*
*Jer.* 5:14 make words in *t. m.* fire
*Ezek.* 2:8 open *thy m.* and eat
3:26 tongue cle. to roof of *t. m.*
27 I will open *t. m.* and th. sh.
16:56 S. not mentioned by *t. m.*
*Hos.* 8:1 set trumpet to *thy m.*
*Mic.* 7:5 keep doors of *thy m.*
*Luke* 19:22 out of *thine* own *m.*
*Rom.* 10:9 confess with *thy m.*
*Rev.* 10:9 in *t. m.* sweet as honey

**Your MOUTH.**

*Num.* 32:24 proceed. out of *y. m.*
1 *Sam.* 2:3 come out of *your m.*
*Job* 21:5 lay your hand on *y. m.*
*Ezek.* 35:13 with *y. m.* boasted
*Joel* 1:5 wine is cut off from *y. m.*
*Eph.* 4:29 no corrupt communication out of *your m. Col.* 3:8

**MOUTHS.**

*Deut.* 31:19 put it in their *m.*
21 forgotten out of *m.* of seed
*Ps.* 22:13 gap. on me with th. *m.*
78:30 meat was yet in their *m.*
115:5 have *m.* speak not, 135:16
135:17 nei. is any breath in *m.*
*Is.* 52:15 kings shut *m.* at him
*Jer.* 44:25 spoken with your *m.*
*Lam.* 3:46 enemies opened th. *m.*
*Dan.* 6:22 G. hath shut lions' *m.*
*Mic.* 3:5 putteth not into th. *m.*
*Tit.* 1:11 wh. *m.* must be stopped
*Heb.* 11:33 stop. the *m.* of lions
*Jam.* 3:3 put bits in horses' *m.*
*Rev.* 9:17 out of *m.* issued fire

**MOVE.**

*Ex.* 11:7 not a dog *m.* tongue
*Lev.* 11:10 all that *m.* in waters
*Deut.* 23:25 not *m.* a sickle
32:21 will *m.* them to jealousy
*Jud.* 13:25 Sp. of L. began to *m.*
2 *Sam.* 7:10 may dwell and *m.* no more, 2 *K.* 21:8
2 *K.* 23:18 let no man *m.* bones
*Jer.* 10:4 fasten it that it *m.* not
*Mic.* 7:17 sh. *m.* out their holes
*Mat.* 23:4 they will not *m.* them
*Acts* 17:28 live, *m.* ha. our being
20:24 none of th. things *m.* me

**MOVEABLE.**

*Prov.* 5:6 her ways are *m.*

**MOVED.**

*Gen.* 1:2 Sp. of God *m.* on waters
7:21 all flesh died that *m.*
*Deut.* 32:21 *m.* me to jealousy
*Jos.* 10:21 none *m.* his tongue
15:18 that she *m.* him to ask of father a field, *Jud.* 1:14
*Ruth* 1:19 city was *m.* ab. them
1 *Sam.* 1:13 only her lips *m.*
2 *Sam.* 18:33 king was much *m.*
22:8 foundations of heaven *m.*
24:1 he *m.* David against them
1 *Chr.* 16:30 world stable, that it be not *m. Ps.* 93:1; 96:10
17:9 and shall be *m.* no more
2 *Chr.* 18:31 G. *m.* them to depart
*Ezr.* 4:15 they have *m.* sedition
*Est.* 5:9 Mord. *m.* not for him
*Job* 37:1 at this my heart is *m.*
41:23 they cannot be *m.*
*Ps.* 10:6 I shall not be *m.* 16:8; 30:6; 62:2, 6.
13:4 those rejoice when I am *m.*
15:5 doeth these sh. never be *m.*
18:7 foundations of the hills *m.*
21:7 trusteth in L. sh. not be *m.*
46:5 sh. not be *m.* God sh. help
6 heathen raged, kingdoms *m.*
55:22 never suff. right. to be *m.*
66:9 suffer. not our feet to be *m.*
68:8 S. was *m.* at presence of G.
78:58 they *m.* him to jealousy
99:1 L. reigneth, let earth be *m.*
112:6 surely he shall not be *m.*
121:3 not suffer thy foot to be *m.*
*Prov.* 12:3 root of the righteous shall not be *m.*
*Cant.* 5:4 my bowels *m.* for him
*Is.* 6:4 the posts of the door *m.*
7:2 heart was *m.* as trees are *m.*
10:14 there was none *m.*
14:9 hell fr. ben. is *m.* for thee
19:1 idols of Egypt shall be *m.*
24:19 earth brok. down and *m.*
40:20 im. that sh. not be *m.* 41:7
*Jer.* 4:24 all the hills *m.* lightly
25:16 they sh. drink and be *m.*
46:7 whose waters *m.* 8
49:21 the earth is *m.* at noise
50:46 at taking of Bab. earth *m.*
*Dan.* 8:7 he was *m.* with choler
11:11 king of south shall be *m.*
*Mat.* 9:36 he was *m.* with compassion on them, 14:14; 18:27; *Mark* 1:41; 6:34
20:24 were *m.* with indignation
21:10 all the city was *m.* saying
*Mark* 15:11 chief priests *m.* peo.
*Acts* 2:25 that I sho. not be *m.*
17:5 but the Jews *m.* with envy
21:30 city was *m.* and peo. ran
*Col.* 1:23 be not *m.* from gospel
1 *Thes.* 3:3 no man be *m.* by th.
*Heb.* 11:7 Noah, *m.* with fear
11:28 kingd. wh. cannot be *m.*
2 *Pet.* 1:21 as *m.* by the H. Ghost
*Rev.* 6:14 mount. and island *m.*

**MOVEDST, ETH.**

*Gen.* 1:21 created ev. crea. th. *m.*
9:2 fear sh. be upon all that *m.*
*Lev.* 11:46 every creature that *m.*
*Job* 2:3 thou *m.* against him
*Ps.* 69:34 every thing that *m.*
*Prov.* 23:31 not on wi. wh. it *m.*
*Ezek.* 47:9 that *m.* whithersoever

**MOVER.**

*Acts* 24:5 this fel. *m.* of sedition

**MOVING.**

*Gen.* 1:20 wat. bring forth *m.* cre.
9:3 every *m.* thing sh. be meat
*Prov.* 16:30 *m.* his lips

**MOVING, Substantive.**

*Job* 16:5 *m.* of my lips, assu. gri.
*John* 5:3 waiting for *m.* of water

**MOWER.**

*Ps.* 129:7 *m.* filleth not his hand

**MOWINGS.**

*Amos* 7:1 growth after king's *m.*

**MOWN.**

*Ps.* 72:6 like rain upon *m.* grass

**MUCH.**

*Luke* 12:48 to whom *m.* is given, of him shall *m.* be required

**MUFFLERS.**

*Is.* 3:19 I will take away the *m.*

**MULBERRY-TREES.**

2 *Sam.* 5:23 come upon th. over against the *m.-t.* 1 *Chr.* 14:14
24 sound in the tops of *m.-t.*

**MULE.**

2 *Sam.* 13:29 every man upon *m.*
18:9 Absalom rode upon a *m.*
1 *K.* 1:33 to ride on my *m.* 38:44
*Ps.* 32:9 be not as horse or *m.*
*Zec.* 14:15 plague of horse, of *m.*

**MULES.**

*Gen.* 36:24 found *m.* in wildern.
1 *K.* 10:25 brought *m.* a rate year by year, 2 *Chr.* 9:24
18:5 grass to save the *m.* alive
2 *K.* 5:17 given to serv. two *m.*
1 *Chr.* 12:40 on camels and *m.*
*Ezr.* 2:66 their *m.* were 245, *Neh.* 7:68
*Est.* 8:10 sent letters by *m.* 14
*Is.* 66:20 bring your breth. on *m.*

**MULTIPLY.**

*Gen.* 1:22 be fruitful and *m.* 28; 8:17; 9:7; 35:11
6:1 men began to *m.* on earth
16:10 I will *m.* Hag. seed, 17:20
17:2 *m.* thee exceedingly, 48:4
22:17 in multiplying I will *m.* thy seed, 26:4, 24; *Heb.* 6:14
28:3 G. Almighty bless and *m.*
*Ex.* 1:10 deal wisely, lest th. *m.*
7:3 I will *m.* my signs in Egypt
23:29 lest beast of the field *m.*
32:13 thou saidst, I will *m.* your seed, *Lev.* 26:9; *Deut.* 7:13; 13:17; 28:63; 30:5
*Deut.* 17:16 shall not *m.* horses
17 neither shall he *m.* wives
1 *Chr.* 4:27 neither did family *m.*
*Job* 29:18 I shall *m.* my days
*Jer.* 30:19 I will *m.* them
33:22 so will I *m.* seed of David
*Ezek.* 16:7 I have caused th. to *m.*
36:10 will *m.* men; 11 *m.* man
30 I will *m.* fruit of the tree
37:26 I will place and *m.* them
*Amos.* 4:4 at G. *m.* transgression
2 *Cor.* 9:10 *m.* your seed sown

**MULTIPLIED.**

*Gen.* 47:27 Israel *m. Ex.* 1:7, 20
*Ex.* 1:12 afflicted *m.* and grew
11:9 my wonders may be *m.*
*Deut.* 1:10 L. your G. ha. *m.* you
8:13 gold is *m.* all thou hast *m.*
11:21 that your days be *m.*
*Jos.* 24:3 I *m.* his seed
*Job* 27:14 children be *m.* for sw.
35:6 if thy transgres. be *m.?*
*Ps.* 16:4 their sorrows sh. be *m.*
38:19 they that hate me are *m.*
107:38 bless. them, they are *m.*
*Prov.* 9:11 thy days shall be *m.*
29:16 when wicked are *m.*
*Is.* 9:3 thou hast *m.* the nation
59:12 our transgressions are *m.*
*Jer.* 3:16 when ye be *m.*

*Ezek.* 5:7 ye *m.* more than nati.
11:6 *m.* your slain in this city
16:25 hast *m.* whoredoms, 23:19
29 *m.* fornications; 51 *m.* abo.
21:15 heart may faint, ruins *m.*
31:5 boughs *m.* 35:13 *m.* words
*Dan.* 4:1 peace be *m.* 6:25; 1 *Pet.* 1:2; 2 *Pet.* 1:2; *Jude* 2
*Hos.* 2:8 not know I *m.* her silver
12:10 I have *m.* visions
*Nah.* 3:16 hast *m.* merchants
*Acts* 6:1 number of disciples *m.* 7
7:17 people grew and *m.* in Eg.
9:31 walk. in fear of L. were *m.*
12:24 word of G. grew and *m.*

**MULTIPLIEDST.**

*Neh.* 9:23 their children also *m.*

**MULTIPLIETH.**

*Job* 9:17 he *m.* my wounds
34:37 he *m.* his words ag. God
35:16 *m.* words without knowl.

**MULTIPLYING.**

*Gen.* 22:17 in *m. Heb.* 6:14

**MULTITUDE.**

*Gen.* 16:10 it shall not be numb. for *m.* 32:12; 1 *K.* 3:8
28:3 G. Alm. make thee a *m.*
30:30 it is now incre. unto a *m.*
48:4 make of thee a *m.* 16, 19
*Ex.* 12:38 a mixed *m.* went up
23:2 not follow a *m.* to do evil
*Num.* 11:4 mixed *m.* fell lusting
*Deut.* 1:10 are as the stars for *m.* 10:22; 28:62; *Heb.* 11:12
*Jos.* 11:4 as sand on sea-shore for *m. Jud.* 7:12; 1 *Sam.* 13:5; 2 *Sam.* 17:11; 1 *K.* 4:20
1 *Sam.* 14:16 the *m.* melted away
2 *Sam.* 6:19 dealt among *m.* of I.
1 *K.* 8:5 oxen not be told for *m.*
2 *K.* 7:13 they are as all the *m.*
19:23 with *m.* of my chariots to sides of Lebanon, *Is.* 37:24
2 *Chr.* 1:9 a peo. like dust for *m.*
14:11 in thy name go aga. *m.*
20:24 the *m.* were dead bodies
30:18 a *m.* not cleansed thems.
32:7 be not afraid of all the *m.*
*Neh.* 13:3 separated fr. mixed *m.*
*Est.* 5:11 Haman told of the *m.*
10:3 Mordecai accepted of *m.*
*Job* 11:2 sh. *m.* of words be ans.?
32:7 *m.* of years sh. teach wisd.
35:9 by reason of *m.* of oppres.
39:7 he scorneth *m.* of the city
*Ps.* 5:7 come in *m.* of thy mercy
10 cast out in *m.* of transgres.
33:16 th. is no king saved by *m.*
42:4 gone with *m.* to hou. of G.
49:6 boast in *m.* of their riches
51:1 accord. to *m.* of thy merci.
68:30 rebuke the *m.* of bulls
69:13 O God, in *m.* of mercy
16 accor. to *m.* of thy mercies
74:19 deliver me not to the *m.*
94:19 *m.* of my thoughts within
106:7 rem. not *m.* of thy merc.
45 accor. to *m.* of his mercies
109:30 I will praise am. the *m.*
*Prov.* 10:19 in the *m.* of words
11:14 *m.* of counsellors, 24:6
14:28 in *m.* of peo. king's honor
15:22 *m.* of counsellors establ.
20:15 gold, and a *m.* of rubies
*Ec.* 5:3 through *m.* of business, fool's voice by *m.* of words
7 in *m.* of dreams div. vanities
*Is.* 1:11 wh. purpose *m.* of sacri.
5:13 *m.* dried up with thirst
14 *m.* descend into hell
17:12 woe to *m.* of many people
29:8 *m.* of nations that fight Z.
31:4 when *m.* of shepherds
47:12 stand now with the *m.* 9
13 wearied in *m.* of counsels
60:6 *m.* of camels shall cover
63:7 *m.* of his loving-kindness.
*Jer.* 10:13 *m.* of waters, 51:16
12:6 called a *m.* after thee
30:14 wounded for *m.* of iniq.
46:25 I will punish the *m.*
*Lam.* 1:5 for *m.* of transgress.
3:32 accord. to *m.* of mercies
*Ezek.* 7:12 wrath is on the *m.* 14
13 vision touching whole *m.*
14:4 accord. to *m.* of his idols
27:12 by *m.* of riches, 18, 33
16 by the *m.* of the wares, 18
31:18 Phar. and all his *m.* 32:32
32:24 Elam and *m.* 26 Tubal
39:11 bury Gog, and all his *m.*
*Dan.* 10:6 like voice of a *m.*
11:13 k. of north set forth a *m.*
*Hos.* 9:7 recomp. for *m.* of iniq.
10:13 thou didst trust in *m.*
*Nah.* 3:3 there is a *m.* of slain
*Mat.* 14:5 he feared the *m.* 21:46
15:32 compas. on *m. Mark* 8:2
*Mark* 5:31 *m.* throng. *Luke* 8:45
*Luke* 2:13 th. was wi. angel a *m.*
12:1 gath. an innumerable *m.*
22:6 betr. him in absence of *m.*
47 while he yet sp. behold *m.*
23:1 whole *m.* of them arose
*John* 5:13 a *m.* being in that pl.
21:6 not able for *m.* of fishes
*Acts* 4:32 the *m.* that believed
6:5 saying pleased whole *m.*
16:22 *m.* rose up against them
21:22 *m.* must come together
*Jam.* 5:20 sh. save a soul fr. dea. and shall hide a *m.* of sins
1 *Pet.* 4:8 charity cov. *m.* of sins
*See* GREAT.

**MULTITUDES.**

*Ezek.* 32:20 draw her and her *m.*
*Joel* 3:14 *m. m.* in val. of decis.
*Mat.* 9:33 and the *m.* marvelled
36 when he saw *m.* was mov.
21:9 *m.* cried, saying, Hosanna
*Acts* 5:14 *m.* of men and women
13:45 J. saw the *m.* were filled
*Rev.* 17:15 the waters are *m.*
*See* GREAT.

**MUNITION, S.**

*Is.* 29:7 fight ag. her and her *m.*
33:16 defence sh. be *m.* of rocks
*Nah.* 2:1 keep *m.* watch the way

**MURDER.**

*Ps.* 10:8 in secret doth *m.* inno.
94:6 slay widow, *m.* fatherless
*Jer.* 7:9 *m.* and com. adultery?
*Hos.* 6:9 so priests *m.* in the way

**MURDER, S.**

*Mat.* 15:19 out of the heart proceed *m. Mark* 7:21
19:18 said, Thou shalt do no *m.*
*Mark* 15:7 Barab. committed *m.*
*Luke* 23:19 for *m.* cast in pri. 25
*Rom.* 1:29 envy, *m.* debate
*Gal.* 5:21 flesh are envyings, *m.*
*Rev.* 9:21 nor repented of th. *m.*

**MURDERER.**

*Num.* 35:16 *m.* the *m.* sh. surely be put to death, 17, 18, 21, 30
19 revenger of blood slay *m.* 21
31 no satisfac. for life of a *m.*
2 *K.* 6:32 see how th. son a *m.*
*Job* 24:14 *m.* rising with light
*Hos.* 9:13 Eph. bring chil. to *m.*
*John* 8:44 a *m.* from beginning
*Acts* 3:14 *m.* be granted to you
28:4 no doubt this man is a *m.*
1 *Pet.* 4:15 let none suffer as *m.*
1 *John* 3:15 whoso hateth broth. is a *m.* ye know that no *m.*

**MURDERERS.**

2 *K.* 14:6 child. of *m.* he slew
*Is.* 1:21 lodged in it, but now *m.*
*Jer.* 4:31 wearied, because of *m.*
*Mat.* 22:7 sent and destroyed *m.*
*Acts* 7:52 have been now the *m.*
21:38 4,000 men that were *m.*
1 *Tim.* 1:9 law made for *m.*
*Rev.* 21:8 *m.* shall have part
22:15 with. are whore. and *m.*

**MURMUR.**

*Ex.* 16:7 that ye *m.* against us?
8 hear. your *m. Num.* 14:27
*Num.* 14:36 made congrega. *m.*
16:11 what is Aa. that ye *m.*?
17:5 whereby they *m.* ag. you
*John* 6:43 *m.* not am. yourselves
1 *Cor.* 10:10 neither *m.* as some

**MURMURED.**

*Ex.* 15:24 *m.* against Moses, 17:3
16:2 whole congregation of Isr. *m. Num.* 14:2; 16:41
*Num.* 14:29 20 y. old, wh. ha. *m.*
*Deut.* 1:27 ye *m.* in your tents
*Jos.* 9:18 congre. *m.* ag. princes
*Ps.* 106:25 but *m.* in their tents
*Is.* 29:24 that *m.* sh. learn doctr.
*Mark* 14:5 they *m.* against her
*Luke* 5:30 scribes and Phari. *m.*
15:2 they *m.* saying, This man
19:7 *m.* that he was going to be
*John* 6:41 the Jews *m.* at him
61 he knew his disciples *m.*
7:32 Pharisees heard people *m.*
1 *Cor.* 10:10 as some of them *m.*

**MURMURERS.**

*Jude* 16 these are *m.* complainers

**MURMURING, S.**

*Ex.* 16:7 he heareth your *m.* 8, 9, 12; *Num.* 14:27
8 your *m.* are not against us
*Num.* 17:5 make to cease *m.* of I.
10 take away their *m.* fr. me
*John* 7:12 much *m.* among peo.
*Acts* 6:1 a *m.* against Hebrews
*Phil.* 2:14 do all thi. without *m.*

**MURRAIN.**

*Ex.* 9:3 be a very grievous *m.*

**MUSE, ED, ING.**

*Ps.* 39:3 I was *m.* the fire burned
143:5 I *m.* on works of thy han.
*Luke* 3:15 all men *m.* in th. hear.

MUSHI. *Ex.* 6:13

**MUSIC.**

1 *Sam.* 18:6 meet Saul with *m.*
1 *Chr.* 15:16 instruments of *m.* 2 *Chr.* 5:13; 23:13; 34:12
2 *Chr.* 7:6 wi. instruments of *m.*
*Ec.* 12:4 dau. of *m.* bro. low
*Lam.* 3:63 rising; I am their *m.*
*Dan.* 3:5 kinds of *m.* 7:10, 15
6:18 instruments of *m.* brought
*Amos* 6:5 inv. instruments of *m.*
*Luke* 15:25 elder son heard *m.*

**MUSICAL.**

1 *Chr.* 16:42 *m.* instrum. of God
*Neh.* 12:36 *m.* instru. of David
*Ec.* 2:8 as *m.* instruments.

**MUSICIANS.**

*Rev.* 18:22 vo. of *m.* heard no m.

**MUST.**

*Gen.* 29:26 it *m.* not be so done
30:16 thou *m.* come in to me
43:11 if it *m.* be so now, do this
*Num.* 23:12 *m.* I not take heed
26 Lord speaketh that I *m.* do
*Deut.* 4:22 I *m.* die in this land
1 *Sam.* 14:43 and lo I *m.* die
2 *Sam.* 23:3 rul. men *m.* be just
*Ezr.* 10:12 said, so *m.* we do
*Mark* 8:31 S. of man *m.* suff. 9:12
*Luke* 22:37 the things written *m.* be accomplished, 24:44
24:7 Son of man *m.* be delivered
*John* 3:7 ye *m.* be born again
*Acts* 4:12 whereby we *m.* be sav.
*Acts* 9:6 told th. what th. *m.* do
*Rom.* 13:5 *m.* needs be subject
1 *Cor.* 5:10 then *m.* ye needs go

MUSTARD-SEED. *See* GRAIN.

**MUSTERED, ETH.**
2 *K.* 25:19 scribe *m.* *Jer.* 52:25
*Is.* 13:4 Lord *m.* host of battle

**MUTTER, ED.**
*Is.* 8:19 wizards th. peep and *m.*
59:3 tongue hath *m.* perversen.

**MUTUAL.**
*Rom.* 1:12 comforted by *m.* faith

**MUZZLE.**
*Deut.* 25:4 not *m.* ox, 1 *Cor.* 9:9; 1 *Tim.* 5:18

MYRA. *Acts* 27:5

**MYRRH.**
*Gen.* 37:25 bearing balm and *m.*
43:11 carry man a pres. *m.* nuts
*Ex.* 30:23 pure *m.* 500 shekels
*Est.* 2:12 6 months wi. oil of *m.*
*Ps.* 45:8 *m.* aloes and cassia
*Prov.* 7:17 perf. my bed with *m.*
*Cant.* 1:13 bundle of *m.* is belov.
3:6 perf. with *m.* and frankinc.
4:6 get to moun. of *m.* and aloes
14 *m.* and aloes with chief spi.
5:1 gath. my *m.* with my spice
5 my hands dropped with *m.*
13 dropping sweet-smelling *m.*
*Mat.* 2:11 presented gold and *m.*
*Mark* 15:23 mingled with *m.*
*John* 19:39 bro. a mixture of *m.*

**MYRTLE.**
*Neh.* 8:15 go forth and fetch *m.*
*Is.* 41:19 plant in wildern. the *m.*
55:13 inst. of brier come up *m.*

**MYRTLE-TREES.**
*Zec.* 1:8 stood am. *m.-t.* 10, 11

MYSIA. *Acts* 16:7, 8

**MYSTERY.**
*Mark* 4:11 given to know *m.*
*Rom.* 11:25 that ye be ign. of *m.*
16:25 according to revela. of *m.*
1 *Cor.* 2:7 speak wis. of G. in *m.*
15:51 I show you a *m.*
*Eph.* 1:9 made known to us *m.*
3:3 made known to me the *m.*
4 knowledge in the *m.* of Ch.
9 all see fellowship of *m.*
5:32 this is a great *m.*
6:19 to make known *m.* of the gospel, *Col.* 1:26, 27; 4:3
*Col.* 2:2 acknowledgment of *m.*
2 *Thes.* 2:7 *m.* of iniq. doth work
1 *Tim.* 3:9 holding *m.* of faith
16 great is the *m.* of godliness
*Rev.* 1:20 *m.* of the seven stars
10:7 *m.* of God. sho. be finished
17:5 *m.* Babylon; 7 *m.* of wom.

**MYSTERIES.**
*Mat.* 13:11 *m.* of the kingdom, to them not given, *Luke* 8:10
1 *Cor.* 4:1 stewards of *m.* of God
13:2 tho' I understand all *m.*
14:2 in the Sp. he speaketh *m.*

# N

**NAAMAN.**
2 *K.* 5:1 N. was leper, 11, 20, 27
*Luke* 4:27 none cleansed, sav. N.

**NAASHON, *or* NAHSHON.**
*Num.* 1:7 pri. was N. 2:3; 10:14
7:12 he that off. first day was N.
*Ruth* 4:20 Amminadab begat N. 1 *Chr.* 2:10, 11; *Mat.* 1:4
*Luke* 3:32 Salmon was son of N.

**NABAL.**
1 *Sam.* 25:3 was N. 4, 25, 38, 39
27:3 A. N. wife, 30:5; 2 *Sam.* 2:2

**NABOTH.**
1 *K.* 21:1 N. had vineyard, 7:19
2 *K.* 9:21 in portion of N. 25, 26

**NADAB.**
*Ex.* 6:23 Aaron, N. *Lev.* 10:1
24:1 come up, N. and Abihu, 9
*Num.* 3:4 N. died before L. 26:61
1 *K.* 14:20 N. reigned, 15:25

NAGGE. *Luke* 3:25

**NAHASH.**
1 *Sam.* 11:1 N. came up, 12:12
2 *Sam.* 10:2 son of N. 1 *Chr.* 19:2

**NAHOR.**
*Gen.* 11:22 Se. begat N. 24, 26, 29
22:20 brother N. 23; 24:15, 24
24:10 servant went to city of N.
31:53 God of Abraham and N.

**NAIL.**
*Jud.* 4:21 Jael took a *n.* of tent
22 the *n.* was in his temples
*Jud.* 5:26 she put her h. to the *n.*
*Ezr.* 9:8 give us a *n.* in holy pl.
*Is.* 22:23 a *n.* in a sure place, 25
*Zec.* 10:4 out of him came the *n.*

**NAILS.**
*Deut.* 21:12 sh. head, pare her *n.*
1 *Chr.* 22:3 iron in abund. for *n.*
2 *Chr.* 3:9 weight of *n.* fifty she.
*Ec.* 12:11 *n.* fastened by masters
*Is.* 41:7 his idol with *n.* *Jer.* 10:4
*Dan.* 4:33 his *n.* like bird's claws
7:19 beast, wh. *n.* were of brass
*John* 20:25 finger into print of *n.*

**NAILING.**
*Col.* 2:14 he *n.* it to his cross

NAIN. *Luke* 7:11

**NAIOTH.**
1 *Sam.* 19:18 Da. dwelt at N. 20:1

**NAKED.**
*Gen.* 2:25 were *n.* not ashamed
3:7 knew they were *n.* 10, 11
*Ex.* 32:25 Moses saw peo. were *n.* for Aa. had made them *n.*
1 *Sam.* 19:24 Saul lay down *n.*
2 *Chr.* 28:15 with spoil clothed *n.*
19 Ahaz made Judah *n.*
*Job* 1:21 *n.* came I out of womb, and *n.* shall I return thither
22:6 stripped *n.* of their clothi.
24:7 cause *n.* to lodge with. 10
26:6 hell is *n.* before him
*Ec.* 5:15 *n.* shall he return
*Is.* 58:7 when thou seest the *n.*
*Lam.* 4:21 shalt make thyself *n.*
*Ezek.* 18:7 if he covered the *n.* 16
*Hos.* 2:3 lest I strip her *n.*
*Amos* 2:16 flee away *n.*
*Mic.* 1:8 I will go stripped and *n.*
11 having thy shame *n.*
*Hab.* 3:9 bow was made quite *n.*
*Mat.* 25:36 *n.* and ye clothed me
38 when saw we thee *n.*? 44
*Mark* 14:51 cloth ab. his *n.* body
52 and fled from them *n.*
*John* 21:7 Peter was *n.* and cast
*Acts* 19:16 fled out o house *n.*
1 *Cor.* 4:11 to this hour we are *n.*
2 *Cor.* 5:3 shall not be found *n.*
*Heb.* 4:13 but all things are *n.* to
*Jam.* 2:15 if brother or sis. be *n.*
*Rev.* 3:17 poor, and blind, and *n.*
16:15 garments, lest he walk *n.*
17:16 make her desolate and *n.*

*See* BARE.

**NAKEDNESS.**
*Gen.* 9:22 H. saw *n.* of father, 23
42:9 see the *n.* of the land, 12
*Ex.* 20:26 thy *n.* not discovered
*Lev.* 18:6 none sh. uncover th. *n.*
7 the *n.* of father or mother, 8, 11, 15; 20:11
9 *n.* of sister; 10 of son's dau.
11 *n.* of father's wife's daugh.
12 not uncover *n.* of f.'s sister
13 *n.* of mother's sister, 20:19
14 not uncover *n.* of f.'s broth.
15 *n.* of daughter-in-law
16 *n.* of thy brother's wife
17 *n.* of a woman and daught.
19 *n.* of wo. put apart, 20:18
20:17 sister's *n.* she see his *n.*
20 ha. uncovered his uncle's *n.*
21 hath uncovered brother's *n.*
*Deut.* 28:48 serve thine ene. in *n.*
1 *Sam.* 20:30 confu. of moth.'s *n.*
*Is.* 47:3 thy *n.* sh. be uncovered
*Lam.* 1:8 they have seen her *n.*
*Ezek.* 16:8 I covered thy *n.* yea
36 thy *n.* discovered, 23:18
16:37 discover thy *n.* to them
22:10 discovered th. father's *n.*
23:10 discovered her *n*, slew her
*Hos.* 2:9 wool and flax to cov. *n.*
*Nah.* 3:5 show the nations thy *n.*
*Hab.* 2:15 mayest look on th. *n.*
*Rom.* 8:35 shall *n.* separate us?
2 *Cor.* 11:27 in cold and *n.*
*Rev.* 3:18 shame of *n.* not appear

**NAME.**
*Gen.* 2:19 that was *n.* thereof
5:2 and called their *n.* Adam
11:4 us a *n.* lest we be scattered
48:6 called after *n.* of breth.
*Ex.* 34:14 L. whose *n.* is Jealous
*Lev.* 18:21 nei. profane the *n.* of thy G. 19:12; 21:6; 22:2, 32
*Num.* 17:2 write every man's *n.*
27:4 why should *n.* of our father
*Deut.* 7:24 destroy *n.* under hea.
9:14 blot out *n.* fr. under heav.
22:14 bring up an evil *n.* on her
19 he bro. up evil *n.* on virgin
25:6 succeed in *n.* of his broth.
7 raise his brother a *n.* in Isr.
26:19 high in *n.* and honor
*Deut.* 28:58 fear this gl. and fe. *n.*
*Jos.* 23:7 nor make mention of *n.*
*Ruth* 4:5 raise up *n.* of dead, 10
17 her neighbors gave it a *n.*
2 *Sam.* 6:2 *n.* called by *n.* of Lord
7:9 I made th. great *n.* like *n.* of gre. men in earth, 1 *Chr.* 17:8
23 God redeemed to make him a *n.* 1 *Chr.* 17:21
8:13 David gat him a *n.* when
14:7 not leave to my husb. a *n.*
23:18 Abishai had *n.* amo. three
22 the *n.* among three mighty men, 1 *Chr.* 11:20, 24
1 *K.* 1:47 G. make *n.* of Solomon better than thy *n.*
14:21 Lord did choose to put his *n.* there, 2 *Chr.* 12:13
18:24 call on *n.* of your gods, 25
21:8 Jezebel wrote in Ahab's *n.*
2 *K.* 14:27 not blot out *n.* of Isr.
*Ezr.* 2:61 and was called after their *n.* *Neh.* 7:63
5:1 prophesied in *n.* of G. of Is.
*Neh.* 9:10 didst thou get th. a *n.*
*Est.* 8:8 write for J. in king's *n.*
*Job* 18:17 he shall have no *n.*
*Ps.* 9:5 put out their *n.* for ever
20:1 the *n.* of the God of Jacob
5 in *n.* of G. set up our banne.
44:20 if we forgot. *n.* of our G.
69:30 I will praise the *n.* of God
83:4 the *n.* of Israel be no more
18 whose *n.* alone is Jehovah
99:3 let th. praise thy great *n.*
109:13 let th. *n.* be blotted out
113:3 the L.'s *n.* is to be praised

Prov. 10:7 n. of wicked shall rot
18:10 n. of Lord is strong tower
22:1 good n. rather than riches
30:9 lest I take n. of G. in vain
Ec. 7:1 good n. bet. than ointm.
Is. 14:22 cut off fr. Baby. the n.
55:13 it sh. be to the L. for a n.
56:5 give a n. an everlasting n.
57:15 n. is holy; 62:2 by new
63:12 make himself everlast. n.
14 to make thyself a glori. n.
65:15 ye shall leave your n. for a curse to my chosen, and call his servants by anoth. n.
66:22 your seed and n. remain
Jer. 13:11 might be for n. 33:9
32:20 which hast made thee a n.
33:16 the n. she shall be called
46:18 King, whose n. is the Lord of hosts, 48:15; 51:57
Ezek. 20:29 n. is called Bamah
24:2 son of man, write n.
48:35 the n. of the city shall be
Dan. 2:20 blessed be the n. of G.
4:8 according to the n. of my G.
Hos. 2:17 no more remem. by n.
Amos 5:27 whose n. is G. of hos.
Mic. 4:5 in the n. of his god, we will walk in the n. of our G.
Zep. 1:4 I will cut off n. of Ch.
3:20 I will make you a n.
Zec. 6:12 whose n. is Branch
Mat. 10:41 receiv. prophet in the n. of a prophet, a righteous
42 cup of wat. in n. of disciple
28:19 baptizing them in n. of F.
Luke 1:61 none of ki. call. by n.
63 saying, His n. is John
6:22 sh. cast out your n. as evil
John 1:6 fr. God, who. n. was J.
3:18 not believed in n. of only
5:43 am come in my Fath.'s n.
10:25 I do in my Father's n.
Acts 2:38 baptized in n. of L. J.
3:6 in n. of Jesus Christ rise up
4:7 by wh. n. ha. ye done this?
12 none other n. under heaven
17 sp. to no man in this n. 18
30 wonders done by n. of Jes.
5:28 sh. not teach in this n. 40
8:12 concerning the n. of Jesus
9:21 destroy. them called on n.
27 preached boldly in n. of J.
15:26 hazarded lives for n. of J.
16:18 in n. of Jesus come out
19:5 baptized in n. of Jesus
26:9 to do contrary to n. of J.
Rom. 2:24 n. of God blasphemed
1 Cor. 1:13 baptized in n. of P.?
5:4 in the n. of L. J. Eph. 5:20
6:11 justified in the n. of L. J.
Eph. 1:21 above every n. named
Phil. 2:9 giv. him a n. ab. ev. n.
10 at n. of J. ev. knee shall b.
Col. 3:17 do all in the n. of L. J.
1 Tim. 6:1 n. of G. be not blas.
2 Tim. 2:19 the n. of Ch. depart
Heb. 1:4 obtained a more exc. n.
Jam. 2:7 blasp. that worthy n.?
1 Pet. 4:14 reproach. for n. of C.
1 John 3:23 be. on n. of Son, 5:13
Rev. 2:17 a n. no man knoweth
3:1 hast a n. that thou livest
12 I will write on him n. of G.
13:1 on his heads n. of blasph.
14:1 Father's n. in their forehe.
16:9 men blasph. the n. of God
17:5 on her forehead was a n.
19:12 a n. written no man knew
16 on his thigh a n. written
See CALLED.

**By, *or* by the NAME.**

Ex. 6:3 I appeared by t. n. of G.
33:12 I know thee by n. 17
Num. 4:32 by n. ye shall reckon
Jos. 21:9 th. cities menti. by n.
1 Chr. 4:41 these written by n.
12:31 wh. were expressed by n.
16:41; 2 Chr. 28:15; 31:19
Est. 2:14 exc. were called by n.
Is. 44:5 sh. call himself by the n. of Jacob, and surname him self by the n. of Israel, 48:1
45:3 I the Lord call thee by n.
John 10:3 calleth his sheep by n.
Acts 4:10 by the n. of J. this man
1 Cor. 1:10 I bes. you by n. of L.
3 John 14 greet friends by n.
See EXPRESSED.

**His NAME.**

Ex. 3:13 shall say, What is his n.? Prov. 30:4
15:3 the Lord is his n. Jer. 32:2; Amos 5:8; 9:6
20:7 not guiltless that taketh his n. in vain, Deut. 5:11
28:21 wi. h. n. sh. they be, 39:14
Deut. 6:13 shalt swear by h. n.
10:8 bless in his n. 1 Chr. 23:13
12:5 choose to put his n. there, 21; 1 K. 14:21; 2 Chr. 12:13
11 sh. cause his n. to dw. there
14:23 choose to place his n. there, 24; 16:6, 11; 26:2
25:6 his n. be not put out of Isr.
10 his n. sh. be called in Israel
29:20 Lord shall blot out his n.
Jud. 13:6 neit. told he me his n.
Ruth 4:14 his n. be famous in Is.
1 Sam. 12:22 for his n.'s sake, Ps. 23:3; 106:8; 1 John 2:12; 3 John 7
18:30 his n. was much set by
25:25 as his n. is, Nabal is his n.
1 Chr. 16:8 call up h. n. make known his deeds, Ps. 105:1 Is. 12:4
29 gl. due to h. n. Ps. 29:2; 96:8
Ezr. 6:12 G. caused his n. dwell
Ps. 34:3 let us exalt his n. 66:2
41:5 shall he die h. n. perish?
68:4 rideth on heav. by h. n. J.
69:36 that love his n. dw. there.
72:17 his n. shall endure for ever
19 and blessed be his glori. n.
76:1 his n. is great in Israel
96:2 unto L. bless his n. 100:4
99:6 Samuel that call on his n.
111:9 holy and reverend is h. n.
135:3 praises to h. n. it is pleas.
148:13 praise his n. for his n.
149:3 praise his n. in the dance
Prov. 21:24 haug. scorner is h. n.
Ec. 6:4 his n. cov. with darkness
Is. 7:14 his n. Imman. Mat. 1:23
9:6 his n. be called Wonderful
12:4 that his n. is exalted
47:4 the Lord of hosts is his n 48:2; 51:15; 54:5; Jer. 10:16; 31:35; 32:18; 50:34; 51:19
48:19 h. n. should not have been
Jer. 11:19 h. n. no more remem.
20:9 not spea. any more in h. n.
23:6 this is h. n. he shall be ca.
Amos 4:13 L. God of hosts is h. n.
Zec. 10:12 up and down in h. n.
14:9 shall be one L. and h. n. o.
Mal. 3:16 them th. tho. on h. n.
Mat. 1:23 sh. call h. n. Emman.
25 h. n. Jesus, Luke 1:31; 2:21
12:21 in h. n. shall Gent. trust
Mark 6:14 h. n. was spread abr
Luke 1:13 thou sh. call his n. J.
24:47 remission of sins in h. n.
John 1:12 that believe on his n.
2:23 many believed in his n.
5:43 if ano. come in his own n.
20:31 might have life thro' h. n
Acts 3:16 h. n. thro' faith in h. n.
5:41 worthy to suffer for his n.
10:43 thro' his n. remis. of sins
15:14 take out a peo. for his n.
Rom. 1:5 am. all nations for h. n
Heb. 6:10 love ye show. to. h. n.
13:15 giving thanks to h. n.
Rev. 3:5 not blot out his n.
Rev. 6:8 h. n. sat on him was de.
13:6 ag. God to blaspheme h. n.
17 the number of his n. 15:2
14:11 receiveth mark of h. n.
22:4 his n. sh. be in th. forehea.
See HOLY, LORD.

**My NAME.**

Gen. 32:29 why ask after my n.?
48:16 let my n. be named
Ex. 3:15 this is my n. for ever
9:16 that my n. may be declared
20:24 where I record my n.
23:21 prov. not, my n. is in him
Lev. 19:12 not swear by my n.
20:3 M. to profane my holy n.
Num. 6:27 put my n. on Israel
Deut. 18:19 speak in my n. 20
Jud. 13:18 why ask. after my n.?
1 Sam. 24:21 not destroy my n.
2 Sam. 7:13 house for my n. 1 K. 5:5; 8:18, 19; 1 Chr. 22:10
12:28 city be called after my n.
18:18 no son to keep my n.
1 K. 8:16 my n. might be there. 29; 11:36; 2 K. 21:4, 7; 2 Chr. 6:5, 6; 7:16; 33:4, 7
9:7 house I hallowed for my n.
1 Chr. 22:8 house to my n. 28:3
2 Chr. 6:8 build house for my n.
7:20 house I ha. sanct. for my n.
Neh. 1:9 to set my n. Jer. 7:12
Ps. 89:24 in my n. sh. horn be
91:14 bec. he hath known my n.
Is. 29:23 shall sanctify my n.
41:25 ri. of sun call on my n.
42:8 I am the L. that is my n.
48:9 for my n.'s sake I defer
11 how sho. my n. be pollut.?
49:1 he made mention of my n.
52:5 my n. ev. day is blasphem.
6 my people shall know my n.
66:5 cast out for my n.'s sake
Jer. 14:14 in my n. 15; 23:25
16:21 they sh. know my n. is L.
23:27 they th. to cause peo. forget my n. as fa. forgot my n.
27:15 lie in my n. 29:9, 21, 23
34:16 turned and polluted my n.
44:26 sworn by my great n. my n. no more named.
Ezek. 20:9 wro. for my n. 22:44
36:23 will sanctify my great n.
Zec. 13:9 call on my n.
Mal. 1:6 priests th. despise my n.
11 my n. sh. be great am. Gen. in ev. place incen. off. my n.
14 my n. dreadful am. heathen
2:2 to give glory unto my n.
5 and was afraid before my n.
4:2 you that fear my n. the sun
Mat. 10:22 hat. for my n.'s sake, 24:9; Mark 13:13 Luke 21:17
18:5 receive a child in my n. Mark 9:37; Luke 9:48
20 two or three gath. in my n.
19:29 fors. houses for my n.'s sa.
24:5 many shall come in my n. Mark 13:6; Luke 21:8
Mark 5:9 say. My n. is Legion
9:39 no man do miracle in my n.
41 give water to drink in my n.
16:17 in my n. sh. cast out dev.
Luke 21:12 rulers for my n.'s sa.
John 14:13 what. ye ask in my n. 14; 15:16; 16:23, 24, 26
26 Comf. he will send in my n.
15:21 these thi. do for my n.'s
Acts 9:15 cho. ves. to bear my n.
16 must suffer for my n.'s sake
15:17 on whom my n. is called
Rom. 9:17 that my n. be declared
1 Cor. 1:15 I bapt. in mi. own n.
Rev. 2:3 for my n.'s sake labored
13 holdest fast my n.
3:8 and hast not denied my n.
See CALLED.

**Thy NAME.**
*Gen.* 12:2 make *thy n.* great
17:5 *t. n.* Abram, but *t. n.* be A.
32:27 said, What is *thy n.?* 29; *Jud.* 13:17
28 *thy n.* be no more Jacob, but Israel, 35:10; 1 *K.* 18:31
*Ex.* 5:23 to P. to speak in *thy n.*
*Jos.* 7:9 what do to *t.* great *n.?*
2 *Sam.* 7:26 let *t. n.* be magnifi.
22:50 sing praise to *t. n. Ps.* 9:2; 18:49; 61:8; 66:4; 92:1
1 *K.* 1:47 Solom. better than *t. n.*
8:33 turn and confess *thy n.* and pray, 2 *Chr.* 6:24, 26:32
41 but cometh for *thy n.'s* sake
42 they shall hear of *t.* great *n.*
43 that all peo. may know *thy n.* this house is called by *thy n.* 2 *Chr.* 6:33, 34, 48
1 *K.* 8:44 house I built for *thy n.* 48
1 *Chr.* 17:24 *thy n.* may be mag.
29:13 and praise *t. n. Ps.* 44:8
2 *Chr.* 6:20 wouldest put *thy n.*
14:11 in *thy n.* we go ag. multi.
20:8 built thee a sanctu. for *t. n.*
9 for *thy n.* is in this house
*Neh.* 1:11 servants who fear *t. n.*
9:5 blessed be *t.* glorious *n.*
*Ps.* 5:11 th. love *t. n.* be joyful
8:1 how excel. is *t. n.* in earth, 9
9:10 they that know *t. n.* trust
22:22 will declare *t. n. Heb* 2:12
25:11 for *t. n.'s* sake pardon
31:3 for *t. n.'s* sake lead me
44:5 thro' *thy n.* tread them
45:17 I will make *thy n.* be rem.
48:10 accor. to *t. n.* so is praise
52:9 wait on *t. n.* 54:1 save me
61:5 heritage of those fear *t. n.*
63:4 lift my hands in *thy n.*
74:7 defiled dwelling-pl. of *t. n.*
10 sh. enemy bla. *t. n.* for ev.?
18 fool. peo. blasphemed *t. n.*
21 poor and needy praise *t. n.*
75:1 *t. n.* is near works declare
79:6 not call. on *t. n. Jer.* 10:25
9 help us, O God, for g. of *t. n.* purge our sins for *t. n.'s* sa.
80:18 we will call upon *thy n.*
83:16 that they may seek *thy n.* O Lord
86:9 all nations glorify *t. n.* 12
11 unite my heart to fear *t. n.*
89:12 Hermon sh. rej. in *t. n.* 16
109:21 O Lord, for *t. n.'s* sake
115:1 not to us, but to *t. n.*
119:55 I rememb. *t. n.* in night
132 to do to those love *thy n.*
135:13 *t. n.* O Lord, en. for ever
138:2 praise *t. n.* for lov.-kindn. magnified word above *t. n.*
139:20 enemies take *t. n.* in vain
140:13 righ. give thanks to *t. n.*
142:7 out of pris. I praise *t. n.*
143:11 qui. me for *t. n.'s* sake
145:1 I will bless *thy n.* 2
2 I will praise *t. n. Is.* 25:1
*Cant.* 1:3 *t. n.* is as ointment
*Is.* 26:8 des. of our soul to *thy n.*
13 make mention of *thy n.*
63:16 O L. *t. n.* is from everlas.
64:2 make *t. n.* kn. to adversar.
7 there is none calleth on *t. n.*
*Jer.* 10:6 *thy n.* is great in might
11:16 L. called *thy n.* olive-tree
14:7 do thou it for *thy n.'s* sake
21 not abhor us for *t. n.'s* sake
29:25 sent letters in *thy n.* to J.
*Lam.* 3:55 called on *thy n.*
*Dan.* 9:6 proph. spake in *thy n.*
*Mic.* 6:9 man of wisd. see *thy n.*
*Nah.* 1:14 no more of *t. n.* be so.
*Mal.* 1:6 ha. we despised *thy n.?*
*Mat.* 6:9 hal. be *t. n. Luke* 11:2
7:22 in *t. n.* have we cast out
*Mark* 5:9 wh. is *t. n.? Luke* 8:30
9:38 out dev. in *t. n. Luke* 9:49
*Luke* 10:17 devils subj. thro' *t. n.*
*John* 12:28 Father, glorify *t. n.*
17:6 manifested *t. n* to men, 26
11 F. keep thro' *thi.* own *n.* 12
*Acts* 9:14 all that call on *thy n.*
*Rom.* 15:9 conf. and sing to *t. n.*
*Rev.* 11:18 rew. th. that fear *t. n.*
15:4 who not fear and glo. *t. n.?*
*See* CALLED.

**NAME, Verb.**
1 *Sam.* 16:3 anoi. to me him I *n.*
28:8 bring him up wh. I shall *n.*
*Is.* 62:2 mouth of Lord shall *n.*

**NAMED, ETH.**
*Gen.* 23:16 A. weigh. silver he *n.*
27:36 is he not rightly *n.* Jac.?
48:16 let my name be *n.* on th.
2 *K.* 17:34 chil. of Jacob he *n.* I.
*Ec.* 6:10 what hath been, is *n.*
*Is.* 61:6 shall be *n.* priests of L.
*Jer.* 44:26 shall no more be *n.*
*Amos* 6:1 *n.* chief of the nations
*Mic.* 2:7 O thou that art *n.* of J.
*Luke* 2:21 J. was *n.* of the angel
*Rom.* 15:20 not where Ch. was *n.*
1 *Cor.* 5:1 forni. not *n.* am. Gen.
*Eph.* 1:21 ab. ev. name that is *n.*
3:15 fam. in heav. and earth *n.*
5:3 covetousn. let it not be *n.*
2 *Tim.* 2:19 every one that *n.* C.

**NAMELY.**
*Ec.* 5:13 evil, *n.* riches kept
*Is.* 7:20 L. shave, *n.* by Assyria
*Mark* 12:31 *n.* this, shalt love

**NAMES.**
*Gen.* 2:20 Adam gave *n.* to cattle
26:18 called *n.* after *n.* f. called
*Ex.* 23:13 make no mention of *n.* of other gods, *Deut.* 12:3
28:9 grave *n.* of child. of Isr. 21
12 Aaron bear *n.* before L. 29
*Num.* 1:2 numb. of *n.* by th. poll
*Ezr.* 5:4 what *n.* make building
*Ps.* 16:4 nor take th. *n.* in my lips
49:11 call lands after own *n.*
147:4 stars call. by *n. Is.* 40:26
*Hos.* 2:17 take away *n.* of Baalim
*Zec.* 13:2 cut off the *n.* of idols
*Luke* 10:20 *n.* written in heaven
*Acts* 1:15 number of *n.* were 120
18:15 if it be question of *n.*
*Phil.* 4:3 wh. *n.* are in book of li.
*Rev.* 3:4 hast a few *n.* in Sardis
13:8 whose *n.* not written, 17:8
17:3 woman full of *n.* of blasph.
21:12 *n.* written, *n.* of 12 tribes
14 in them the *n.* of 12 apostl.

**NAOMI.**
*Ruth* 1:2 Elimelech's wife, N. 20
2:1 N. had a kinsman of husb.
4:5 buy. field of hand of N. 9, 17

**NAPKIN.**
*Luke* 19:20 I have kept in *n.*
*John* 11:44 face bound with a *n.*
20:7 *n.* that was about his head

**NAPHTALI.**
*Gen.* 30:8 Rachel called name N.
35:25 Rachel's handmaid, N.
46:24 s. of N. *Nu.* 1:42; 1 *Ch.* 7:13
49:21 N. is a hind let loose
*Deut.* 27:13 E. to curse; Dan, N.
33:23 said, O N. satisfied with
*Jos.* 19:32 sixth lot came to N.
*Jud.* 1:33 nor did N. drive out
4:10 Barak called N. to Kedesh
5:18 Zebulun and N. jeoparded
6:35 Gid. sent messengers to N.
7:23 themselves tog. out of N.
1 *K.* 15:20 smote N. 2 *Chr.* 16:4
2 *K.* 15:29 carried N. cap. to As.
*Ps.* 68:27 there the princes of N.
*Is.* 9:1 he afflicted the land of N.
*Ezek.* 48:3 a portion for N. 34
*Mat.* 4:13 dw. in borders of N. 15

**Tribe of NAPHTALI.**
*Num.* 1:43 of *t. of* N. 53,400
*Jos.* 19:39 inheritance of *t. of* N.
1 *K.* 7:14 widow's son of *t. of* N.
*Rev.* 7:6 of *t. of* N. sealed 12,000

**NARROW.**
*Num.* 22:26 angel of L. sto. in *n.*
*Jos.* 17:15 if Ephraim be too *n.*
1 *K.* 6:4 windows of *n.* light
*Prov.* 23:27 stra. woman is *n.* pit
*Is.* 49:19 land of destruct. too *n.*
*Mat.* 7:14 *n.* is way lead. to life

**NARROWED, ER.**
1 *K.* 6:6 in wall made *n.* rests
*Is.* 28:20 *n.* than he can wrap

**NARROWLY.**
*Job* 13:27 lookest *n.* to my paths
*Is.* 14:16 shall *n.* look upon thee

**NATHAN.**
2 *Sam.* 5:14 son of David, N. 7:2
7:17 so did N. speak, 12:1, 25
1 *K.* 1:10 N. called not, 22, 34
4:5 son of N. was over officers
1 *Chr.* 29:29 writ. in book of N.
2 *Chr.* 9:29 Sol. in book of N.
*Ezr.* 8:16 I sent fr. Ahava for N.
*Zec.* 12:12 family of house of N.
*Luke* 3:31 Matthata, son of N.

**NATHANAEL.**
*John* 1:45 Philip findeth N. 21:2

**NATION.**
*Gen.* 15:14 *n.* th. serve will I jud.
20:4 wilt slay a righteous *n.?*
21:13 bondwoman I make *n.*
35:11 a *n.* kings come of thee
*Ex.* 9:24 in E. since it became *n.*
19:6 shall be a holy *n.* 1 *Pet.* 2:9
21:8 to sell her to a strange *n.*
33:13 this *n.* is thy people
*Lev.* 18:26 nor *n.* commit abomi.
20:23 not walk in manners of *n.*
*Num.* 14:12 I will make of thee a great *n. Deut.* 9:14
*Deut.* 4:34 ha. G. assayed to take a *n.* fr. midst of another *n.?*
28:33 fruit of land shall *n.* eat
36 bring thee and king to a *n.*
49 bring *n.* ag. thee from far
50 a *n.* of fierce countenance
32:28 are a *n.* void of counsel
2 *Sam.* 7:23 what *n.* like thy people? 1 *Chr.* 17:21
1 *K.* 18:10 no *n.* my lord ha. not se. to seek th. took oath of *n.*
2 *K.* 17:29 every *n.* made gods
1 *Chr.* 16:20 went from *n.* to *n.*
2 *Chr.* 15:6 *n.* was destroyed of *n.*
2 *Chr.* 32:15 god of any *n.* was able
*Job* 34:29 done ag. a *n.* or man
*Ps.* 33:12 bless. is *n.* wh. G. is L.
43:1 O G. plead ag. ungodly *n.*
83:4 cut off from being a *n.*
105:13 went from one *n.* to ano
106:5 rejoice in gladness of *n.*
147:20 not dealt so with any *n.*
*Prov.* 14:34 righteous. exalt. *n.*
*Is.* 1:4 sinful *n.* laden with iniq.
2:4 *n.* sh. not lift sword against *n. Mic.* 4:3
9:3 thou hast multiplied the *n.*
10:6 send him aga. hypocrit. *n.*
14:32 what ans. messeng. of *n.?*
18:2 messengers to a *n.* scatter. and peeled, a *n.* meted, 7
26:2 open that righ. *n.* many en.
15 thou increas. *n.* O L. the *n.*
49:7 sai. L. to him *n.* abhorreth
55:5 shalt call *n.* thou know. not
58:2 seek me as a *n.* that did ri.
60:12 *n.* not serve thee perish
22 small one beco. a strong *n.*
65:1 a *n.* not called by my name
66:8 or shall *n.* be born at once?

Jer. 2:11 hath a n. chang. gods?
5:9 my soul be avenged on such
a n. 29; 9:9
15 I will bring a n. on you fr.
afar, a mighty n. ancient n
7:28 a n. that obey. not the L.
12:17 I will utt. destroy that n.
18:7 concern. n. pluck it up, 9
8 n. ag. whom I pronounced
25:12 punish n. for iniq. 27:8
32 evil sh. go forth fr. n. to n.
31:36 Israel cease being n. 33:24
49:31 get you up to wealthy n.
36 no n. whith. E. sh. not come
50:3 out of north cometh n. ag.
Lam. 4:17 have watched for a n.
Ezek. 2:3 send thee to Is. rebe. n
37:22 I will make them one n.
Dan. 8:22 four kingd. out of n.
12:1 trou. nev. was since was n.
Joel 1:6 a n. come upon my land
Amos 6:14 will raise ag. you a n.
Mic. 4:7 will make her strong n.
Hab. 1:6 Ch. bitter and hasty n.
Zep. 2:1 gather together, O n.
5 woe to the n. of Cherethites
Hag. 2:14 this peo. and n. before
Mal. 3:9 this n. have robbed me
Mat. 21:43 king. of G. given to n.
24:7 n. sh. rise against n. Mark
13:8; Luke 21:10
Luke 7:5 loveth our n. built us
John 11:48 R. shall take our n.
50 one man die, n. perish not
51 prophesied, Jesus die for n.
52 not for that n. only, but th.
18:35 thine own n. hath deliver.
Acts 2:5 devout men out of ev. n.
7:7 n. to whom they be in bond
10:22 good rep. am. n. of Jews
28 to come to one of anoth. n.
35 in every n. he that feareth
24:2 worthy deeds done to th. n.
10 thou hast been judge to n.
26:4 life was at first am. own n.
28:19 aught to accuse my n.
Gal. 1:14 profit. ab. equals in n.
Phil. 2:15 midst of perverse n.
Rev. 5:9 redee. us out of every n.
14:6 gospel to preach to ev. n

See FOOLISH.

**NATIONS.**

Gen. 10:32 by th. were n. divided
14:1 Ti. king of n. made war, 9
17:4 shalt be a father of many
n. 5; 48:19; Rom. 4:17, 18
6 I will make n. of thee, 35:11
16 Sarah sh. be a mother of n.
25:23 L. said, Two n. in thy wo.
27:29 let n. bow down to thee
Ex. 34:24 I will cast out the n.
before thee, Deut. 4:38; 7:22;
8:20
Lev. 18:24 the n. are defiled
28 as it spued out the n.
Num. 23:9 not be reckon. am. n
24:8 Israel shall eat up the n.
20 Amalek was first of the n.
Deut. 2:25 I will put fear on n.
4:27 L. shall scatter you among
the n. Neh. 1:8
7:1 Lord hath cast out many n.
9:1 n. great. than thyself, 11:23
12:29 God shall cut off n. 19:1
15:6 shalt lend to many n. 28:12
28:1 L. will set thee abo. all n.
32:8 Most High divid. to the n.
43 rejoice, O ye n. with his pe.
Jud. 2:23 the Lord left those n.
1 K. 11:2 of n. which the L. said
2 K. 17:33 ser. gods aft man. of n.
2 K. 18:33 gods of n. deli. 19:12;
2 Chr. 32:13, 14; Is. 36:18
1 Chr. 16:31 say am. n. L. reign.
17:21 driving out n. bef. people
Neh. 13:26 am. many n. no king
Job 12:23 the n. he enlargeth n.

Ps. 9:20 n. know themselves
22:27 kindreds of n. worsh. thee
28 Lord is governor am. the n.
47:3 shall subdue n. under feet
57:9 sing to thee am. n. 108:3
66:7 his eyes behold the n.
67:4 let the n. be glad
96:5 all gods of the n. are idols
106:27 overthrow seed among n.
34 did not destroy n. L. com.
Prov. 24:24 n. shall abhor him
Is. 2:4 he sh. judge amo. the n.
5:26 will lift up an ensign to n.
10:7 in his heart to cut off n.
11:12 shall set up ensign for n.
14:6 ruled the n. in anger
12 wh. didst weak. the n. 23:3
18 kings of the n. lie in glory
33:3 at lifting up n. were scat.
34:1 come near, ye n. Jer. 31:10
40:15 n. are as a drop of bucket
52:15 so sh. he sprinkle many n.
55:5 n. that knew not thee, run
60:12 those n. shall be wasted
64:2 n. tremble at thy presence
66:19 send th. that escape to n.
Jer. 1:5 ordai. thee prophet to n.
10 I have set thee over the n.
4:2 n. shall bless themselves
10:7 not fear thee, King of n.?
10 n. not able to abide his ind.
22:8 many n. sh. pass this city
25:14 n. shall serve, 27:7
31 L. had a controver. with n.
46:12 n. heard of thy shame
50:12 hindermost of n. a wilder.
46 cry is heard among the n.
51:7 n. have drunken, n. mad
20 wi. thee will I break n.
27 prepare the n. against her
41 Bab. an astonishm. am. n.
44 n. shall not flow together
Lam. 1:1 city that was gr. am. n.
Ezek. 5:6 wickedn. more than n.
14 make thee a reproach am. n.
6:8 remnant shall escape am. n.
9 remember me among n.
12:15 I shall scatter th. am. n.
19:4 the n. also heard of him
8 n. set ag. him on every side
26:3 many n. come against thee
5 it shall become a spoil to n.
28:7 bring upon thee the terri-
ble of the n. 30:11; 31:12
29:12 scatter Egypt am. n. 30:23
15 sh. no more rule over the n.
31:16 I made n. shake at sound
32:2 thou art like lion of the n.
16 daughters of n. lament, 18
35:10 these two n. shall be mine
36:13 land hast bereaved thy n.
37:22 shall be no more two n.
38:8 brought forth out of n. 12
23 be known in eyes of n.
39:27 sancti. in sight of many n.
Hos. 8:10 have hired among n.
9:17 shall be wanderers amo. n.
Joel 3:2 they scattered among n.
Amos 6:1 woe to th. chief of n.
Mic. 4:2 n. shall say, Let us go
3 he shall rebuke strong n.
11 many n. gathered ag. thee
7:16 n. shall see, be confounded
Nah. 3:4 selleth n. thro' whored.
5 I will show n. thy nakedness
Hab. 1:17 sh. not spare to slay n.
2:8 thou hast spoiled many n.
3:6 he drove asunder the n.
Zep. 3:6 I have cut off the n.
8 my determin. is to gather n.
Zec. 2:11 many n. joined to Lord
8:22 strong n. come to seek L.
23 out of all languages of n.
Luke 12:30 these do n. seek after
21:25 upon earth distress of n.
Acts 13:19 he dest. seven n. in C.
Rev. 2:26 I give power over n.
10:11 must prophesy before n.

11:9 n. shall see dead bodies
18 n. were angry, thy wrath
13:7 power given him over all n.
16:19 the cities of the n. fell
17:15 waters are n. and tongues
20:3 should deceive n. no more
21:24 n. wh. are saved sh. walk
26 shall bring honor of n. to it
22:2 leaves were for heal. of n.

See GREAT.

**All NATIONS.**

Deut. 4:19 hath divided to all n.
28:37 become byword am. all n.
1 K. 4:31 his fame was in all n.
1 Chr. 16:24 decl. works am. a. n.
2 Chr. 32:23 mag. in sight of a. n.
Ps. 67:2 saving health am. all n.
72:11 all n. shall serve him
17 all n. shall call him blessed
82:8 for thou shalt inherit all n.
86:9 all n. shall worsh. bef. thee
113:4 L. is high above all n.
117:1 praise Lord all ye n.
118:10 all n. compassed me ab.
Is. 2:2 all n. shall flow unto it
25:7 destroy the vail over all n.
34:2 indignation of L. on all n.
40:17 all n. before him as noth.
66:18 gather all n. Joel 3:2
20 br. your breth. out of all n.
Jer. 27:7 all n. serve, Dan. 7:14
Amos 9:9 house of Is. am. all n.
Hab. 2:5 gathereth to him all n.
Hag. 2:7 I will shake all n. and
desire of all n. shall come
Zec. 14:2 I will gather a. n. ag. J.
19 punish. of all n. come not
Mal. 3:12 all n. call you blessed
Mat. 24:9 hat. of a. n. for my sa.
14 gospel of kingd. preached
to all n. Mark 13:10; Luke
24:47; Rom. 16:26
25:32 bef. him sh. be gath. all n.
28:19 go ye, and teach all n.
Mark 11:17 called of all n.
Luke 21:24 led captive into all n.
Acts 14:16 suffered all n. to walk
17:26 made of one blood all n.
Rom. 1:5 obed. to faith am. all n.
16:26 made known to all n.
Gal. 3:8 shall all n. be blessed
Rev. 7:9 a multitude of all n.
12:5 to rule all n. with a rod
14:8 she made all n. drink, 18:3
15:4 all n. sh. come and worsh.
18:23 by thy sor. all n. deceived

**All the NATIONS.**

Gen. 18:18 all the n. of the earth
be blessed, 22:18; 26:4
Deut. 14:2 ab. all the n. on earth
17:14 set a king over me, as all
the n. 1 Sam. 8:5, 20
30:1 call them to mind am. all n.
3 L. gather thee from all t. n.
Ps. 9:17 all t. n. that forget G.
Is. 14:26 hand stretch. on a. t. n.
29:7 multitude of all the n. 8
37:18 laid waste all the n.
43:9 let all the n. be gathered
52:10 bare arm in eyes of all n.
61:11 spring forth bef. all the n.
Jer. 3:17 all the n. shall be gath.
25:15 a. n. drink; 17 made a. n.
26:6 this city a curse to all t. n.
29:14 gather you from all t. n.
18 a reproach am. all t. n. 44:8
33:9 joy and honor bef. all t. n.
46:28 make full end of all the n.
Zec. 7:14 scat. them am. all t. n.
12:9 destroy all the n. that come
14:16 left of all the n. that came

**These NATIONS.**

Deut. 7:17 th. n. are more than I
9:4 for wickedness of these n. 5
11:23 the Lord drive out all t. n.
12:30 did t. n. serve th. gods?
18:14 t. n. heark. to observers

28:65 am. *t. n.* shalt find no ease
29:18 lest any serve gods of *t. n.*
31:3 Lord will destroy *these n.*
*Jos.* 23:3 what L. done *these n.*
4 divided to you by lot *th. n.*
12 if ye cleave to remn. of *t. n.*
13 will no more drive out *t. n.*
*Jud.* 3:1 *t. n.* L. left to prove Is.
2 *K.* 17:41 so *these n.* feared Lord
*Jer.* 25:9 bring them against *t. n.*
28:14 I put yoke of iron on *t. n.*

**NATIVE.**

*Jer.* 22:10 no more see *n.* country

**NATIVITY.**

*Gen.* 11:28 Ha. died in land of *n.*
*Ruth* 2:11 hast left land of *n.*
*Jer.* 46:16 let us go to land of *n.*
*Ezek.* 16:3 thy *n.* is land of Ca.
4 thy *n.* in day th. wast born
21:30 judge thee in land of *n.*
23:15 Chaldea, land of their *n.*

**NATURE**

*Rom.* 1:26 change th. against *n.*
2:14 do by *n.* things in the law
27 uncircu. by *n.* judge thee?
11:24 olive-tr. wh. is wild by *n.*
were grafted contrary to *n.*
1 *Cor.* 11:14 doth not *n.* tea. you?
*Gal.* 2:15 Jews by *n.* not sinners
4:8 which by *n.* are no gods
*Eph.* 2:3 by *n.* children of wrath
*Heb.* 2:16 took not *n.* of angels
*Jam.* 3:6 set. on fire course of *n.*
2 *Pet.* 1:4 partakers of divine *n.*

**NATURAL.**

*Deut.* 34:7 nor his *n.* force abat.
*Rom.* 1:26 women change *n.* use
27 men leaving *n.* use of wom.
31 without *n.* affec. 2 *Tim.* 3:3
11:21 G. spared not *n.* bran. 23
1 *Cor.* 2:14 *n.* man rece. not Sp.
15:44 sown *n.* body, is *n.* body
46 that which is *n.* was first
*Jam.* 1:23 a man behold. *n.* face
2 *Pet.* 2:12 th. as *n.* brute beasts

**NATURALLY.**

*Phil.* 2:20 *n.* care for your state
*Jude* 10 but what they know *n.*

**NAUGHT.**

*Gen.* 29:15 sho. serve me for *n.*?
*Deut.* 13:17 cle. *n.* cursed thing
15:9 brother, thou givest him *n.*
28:63 L. rej. to bring you to *n.*
2 *K.* 2:19 city pleasant, water *n.*
*Neh.* 4:15 God bro. counsel to *n.*
*Job* 1:9 doth Job fear G. for *n.*?
8:22 place of wick. come to *n.*
14:18 mount. fall. cometh to *n.*
22:6 pledge fr. thy broth. for *n.*
*Ps.* 33:10 counsel of heath. to *n.*
44:12 sellest thy people for *n.*
*Prov.* 1:25 set at *n.* all counsel
20:14 it is *n.* it is *n.* saith buyer
*Is.* 8:10 take counsel, come to *n.*
29:20 terrible one is brok. to *n.*
21 turn aside just for thi. of *n.*
41:12 nothing, as a thing of *n.*
24 nothing, and your work *n.*
49:4 spent my strength for *n.*
52:3 sold yourselves for *n.*
5 people is taken away for *n.*
*Jer.* 14:14 vision, a thing of *n.*
*Amos* 5:5 Beth-el sh. come to *n.*
6:13 which rejoice in thing of *n.*
*Mal.* 1:10 shut doors for *n.*? nei.
kindle fire on mi. altar for *n.*
*Mark* 9:12 set at *n.* *Luke* 23:11
*Acts* 4:11 this is stone set at *n.*
5:36 scattered and brought to *n.*
38 if work of men, come to *n.*
19:27 craft in danger set at *n.*
*Rom.* 14:10 set at *n.* thy broth.?
1 *Cor.* 1:28 to bring to *n.* things
2:6 wisd. of th. world com. to *n.*
2 *Thes.* 3:8 man's bread for *n.*
*Rev.* 18:17 riches come to *n.*

**NAUGHTY.**

*Prov.* 6:12 a *n.* person walketh
17:4 liar giveth ear to *n.* tongue
*Jer.* 24:2 basket had very *n.* figs

**NAUGHTINESS.**

1 *Sam.* 17:28 the *n.* of thy heart
*Prov.* 11:6 taken in their own *n.*
*Jam.* 1:21 all superfluity of *n.*

NAUM. *Luke* 3:25

**NAVEL.**

*Job* 40:16 force is in *n.* of belly
*Prov.* 3:8 sh. be health to thy *n.*
*Cant.* 7:2 thy *n.* is like a goblet
*Ezek.* 16:4 thy *n.* was not cut

**NAVES.**

1 *K.* 7:33 *n.* and spokes molten

**NAVY.**

1 *K.* 9:26 Solo. made *n.* of ships
27 Hir. sent in *n.* his servants
10:11 the *n.* of Hiram bro. gold
22 Solomon had at sea a *n.*

**NAY.**

1 *K.* 2:17 he will not say thee *n.*
20 say not *n.* will not say th. *n.*
*Mat.* 5:37 let your communicati.
be yea, yea, *n. n.* *Jam.* 5:12
*Luke* 13:3 *n.* except ye repent, 5
16:30 he said, *n.* fath. Abraham
*Acts* 16:37 *n.* verily, but let th.
*Rom.* 3:27 *n.* but by law of faith
9:20 *n.* but O man
2 *Cor.* 1:17 be yea, yea, *n. n.*
18 word was not yea and *n.*
19 Jesus Christ was not yea
and *n.*

NAZARENE. *Mat.* 2:23
NAZARENES. *Acts* 24:5

**NAZARETH.**

*Mat.* 2:23 dw. in a city called N.
21:11 Jesus of N. *Mark* 1:24;
10:47; *Lu.* 4:34; 18:37; 24:19
*Mark* 14:67 wast wi. Jesus of N.
*Luke* 1:26 Gabriel was sent to N.
2:51 Jesus came to N. 4:16
*John* 1:45 J. of N. 18, 5, 7; 19:19;
*Acts* 2:22; 4:10; 6:14; 22:8
*Acts* 3:6 in name of Jesus of N.
10:38 God anointed Jesus of N.
26:9 contra. to name of Jesus
of N.

**NAZARITE.**

*Num.* 6:2 a vow of a N. to separate themselves, 18, 19, 20
*Jud.* 13:5 shall be a N. 7; 16:17

**NAZARITES.**

*Lam.* 4:7 her N. purer than snow
*Amos* 2:11 raised yo. men for N.
12 ye gave N. wine to drink

NEAPOLIS. *Acts* 16:11

**NEAR.**

*Gen.* 19:20 city is *n.* to flee to
45:10 thou shalt be *n.* to me
48:10 bro. them *n.* and kissed
*Lev.* 18:6 not appr. any *n.* of kin
*Num.* 16:9 br. you *n.* to him. 10
*Deut.* 5:27 go th. *n.* and hear G.
*Jud.* 20:34 knew not evil was *n.*
2 *Sam.* 19:42 the king is *n.* of kin
*Job* 41:16 one is so *n.* another
*Ps.* 22:11 trou. is *n.* 75:1 name is
119:151 thou art *n.* O Lord
*Is.* 45:21 and bring them *n.*
55:6 call upon L. while he is *n.*
57:19 peace be to him that is *n.*
*Ezek.* 22:5 those that be *n.* mock
*Ob.* 15 day of L. is *n.* *Zec.* 1:14
*Mat.* 24:33 it is *n.* even at doors

*See* CAME, COME, DRAW, DREW.

**NEARER.**

*Ruth* 3:12 is a kinsman *n.* than I
*Rom.* 13:11 our salvation *n.* than

**NEBAIOTH.**

*Gen.* 25:13 Ish. N. 1 *Chr.* 1:29
*Is.* 60:7 rams of N. sh. minister

**NEBO.**

*Num.* 32:3 N. is a land for cattle
*Deut.* 32:49 unto mount N. 34:1
1 *Chr.* 5:8 even unto N. *Ezr.*
2:29; 10:43
*Neh.* 7:33 of the other N. fifty-t.
*Is.* 15:2 Moab shall howl over N.
46:1 N. stoopeth, *Jer.* 48:1
*Jer.* 48:22 judgm. come upon N.

**NEBUCHADNEZZAR, NEBUCHADREZZAR.**

2 *K.* 24:11 N. came against Jerus.
25:1; 2 *Chr.* 36:6; *Jer.* 39:1
25:22 peo. N. left, 1 *Chr.* 6:15;
*Jer.* 24:1; 29:1; 52:28
*Ezr.* 1:7 ves. N. taken, 5:14, 6:5
*Jer.* 27:8 not serve N. 28:11, 14
29:21 them into the hand of N.
32:28 this city into hand of N.
*Ezek.* 26:7 I will br. on Tyrus N.
*Dan.* 2:1 N. dreamed 4:37
3:1 N. ma. image of gold, 19, 24
4:28 this came upon king N. 33
5:18 high G. gave N. a kingdom

**NEBUZAR-ADAN.**

2 *K.* 25:8 N. came to Jerusalem
*Jer.* 39:10 N. left of poor of the

**NECESSARY.**

*Job* 23:12 his words more th. *n.*
*Acts* 13:46 *n.* the word be spoken
15:28 no burden than th. *n.* thi.
28:10 laded us with things *n.*
1 *Cor.* 12:22 memb. feeble are *n.*
2 *Cor.* 9:5 thought it *n.* to exhort
*Phil.* 2:25 supposed it *n.* to send
*Tit.* 3:14 good works for *n.* uses
*Heb.* 9:23 *n.* patterns sh. be puri.

**NECESSITY.**

*Luke* 23:17 of *n.* he must release
*Rom.* 12:13 distr. to *n.* of saints
1 *Cor.* 7:37 having no *n.* and ha.
9:16 for *n.* is laid upon me
2 *Cor.* 9:7 give not grud. or of *n.*
*Phil.* 4:16 once and ag. to my *n.*
*Phile.* 14 not be as it were of *n.*
*Heb.* 7:12 there is of *n.* a change
8:3 it is of *n.* this man have
9:16 there must of *n.* be death

**NECESSITIES.**

*Acts* 20:34 hands minis. to my *n.*
2 *Cor.* 6:4 as ministers of G. in *n.*
12:10 I take pleasure in *n.*

NECHO. 2 *K.* 23:29

**NECK.**

*Gen.* 27:16 skins on smooth of *n.*
40 break yoke from off thy *n.*
33:4 E. fell on his *n.* and kissed
41:42 gold chain ab. Joseph's *n.*
*Ezek.* 16:11; *Dan.* 5:7, 16, 29
45:14 Jos. fell on Benjamin's *n.*
46:29 he fell on Jacob's *n.*
49:8 hand be on *n.* of enemies
*Ex.* 13:13 if not, br. his *n.* 34:20
*Lev.* 5:8 wring off his head fr. *n.*
*Deut.* 21:4 strike off heifer's *n.*
28:48 a yoke of iron on thy *n.*
1 *Sam.* 4:18 his *n.* brake, and di.
2 *Chr.* 36:13 Zed. stiffened his *n.*
*Neh.* 9:29 they hardened their *n.*
*Job* 15:26 on him, even on his *n.*
16:12 hath taken me by the *n.*
39:19 clothed *n.* with thunder?
41:22 in his *n.* remain. strength
*Ps.* 75:5 speak not with a stiff *n.*
*Prov.* 1:9 sh. be chains ab. thy *n.*
3:3 bind them about thy *n.* 6:21
22 life and grace to thy *n.*
*Cant.* 1:10 thy *n.* is comely
4:4 thy *n.* is like the tow. of D.
9 ravi. wi. one chain of thy *n.*
7:4 thy *n.* is a tower of ivory

*Is.* 8:8 sh. reach even to the *n.*
10:27 yoke be taken from thy *n.*
30:28 reach to midst of the *n.*
48:4 thy *n.* is an iron sinew
52:2 loose thyself fr. bands of *n.*
66:3 as if he cut off a dog's *n.*
*Jer.* 17:23 they made their *n.* stiff
27:2 yok. and put th. on thy *n.*
8 put *n.* under yoke of king, 11
28:10 took yoke from Jer. *n.* 12
14 put a yoke on *n.* of nations
30:8 break his yoke from off *n.*
*Lam.* 1:14 transgr. are on my *n.*
*Hos.* 10:11 passed over on her *n.*
*Hab.* 3:13 foundation to the *n.*
*Mat.* 18:6 a millstone hanged ab. his *n.* *Mark* 9:42; *Luke* 17:2
*Luke* 15:20 father fell on his *n.*
*Acts* 15:10 yoke on *n.* of disciples
26:37 fell on P.'s *n.* kissed him

*See* HARDEN.

**NECKS.**

*Jos.* 10:24 feet on *n.* of th. kings
*Jud.* 5:30 *n.* of them take spoil
8:21 ornaments on camels' *n.* 26
*2 Sam.* 22:41 given me *n.* of enemies, *Ps.* 18:40
*Neh.* 3:5 put not *n.* to the work
*Is.* 3:16 with stretched-forth *n.*
*Jer.* 27:12 br. your *n.* under yoke
*Lam.* 5:5 *n.* under persecution
*Ezek.* 21:29 br. thee on *n.* of slain
*Mic.* 2:3 shall not remove your *n.*
*Rom.* 16:4 laid down th. own *n.*

**NECROMANCER.**

*Deut.* 18:11 not be am. you a *n.*

**NEED.**

*Deut.* 15:8 sufficient for his *n.*
*1 Sam.* 21:15 ha. I *n.* of madmen
*2 Chr.* 2:16 as much as shalt *n.*
20:17 shall not *n.* to fight in bat.
*Ezr.* 6:9 let wh. they *n.* be given
*Prov.* 31:11 sh. have no *n.* of sp.
*Mat.* 3:14 I have *n.* to be baptiz.
6:8 your F. knoweth what thin. ye have *n.* of, 32; *Lu.* 12:30
9:12 that be whole *n.* not a physician, *Mark* 2:17; *Luke* 5:31
14:16 they *n.* not depart, give
21:3 the L. hath *n.* of th. *Mark* 11:3; *Luke* 19:31, 34
26:65 what further *n.* have we? *Mark* 14:63; *Luke* 22:71
*Mark* 2:25 D. did when he had *n.*
*Luke* 9:11 healed th. that had *n.*
15:7 just persons *n.* no repent.
*John* 13:29 things we have *n.* of
*Acts* 2:45 as ev. man had *n.* 4:35
*Rom.* 16:2 assist in what she *n.*
*1 Cor.* 7:36 *n.* so require, let him
12:21 not say, I have no *n.*
24 our comely parts have no *n.*
*2 Cor.* 3:1 or *n.* we epistles?
*Phil.* 4:12 I kn. how to suffer *n.*
19 God sh. supply all your *n.*
*1 Thes.* 1:8 that we *n.* not speak
4:9 brotherly love, *n.* not write
5:1 of the times ye have no *n.*
*Heb.* 4:16 to help in time of *n.*
5:12 *n.* one teach you; *n.* milk
7:11 what *n.* th. another priest
10:36 ye have *n.* of patience
*1 Pet.* 1:6 *n.* be, ye are in heavi.
*1 John* 2:27 *n.* not any man teach
3:17 see his brother have *n.*
*Rev.* 3:17 I have *n.* of nothing
21:23 city no *n.* of sun or moon
22:5 *n.* no candle, nor light

**NEEDED.**

*John* 2:25 *n.* not any sho. testify
*Acts* 17:25 tho' he *n.* anything

**NEEDEST, ETH.**

*Gen.* 33:15 Jacob said, What *n.*
*Luke* 11:8 as many as he *n.*
*John* 13:10 *n.* not save to wash
16:30 and *n.* not that any man
*Eph.* 4:28 to give him that *n.*
*2 Tim.* 2:15 workm. *n.* not to be
*Heb.* 7:27 who *n.* not offer sacrif.

**NEEDFUL.**

*Ezr.* 7:20 *n.* for house of thy G.
*Luke* 10:42 but one thing is *n.*
*Acts* 15:5 *n.* to circumcise them
*Phil.* 1:24 abide in flesh more *n.*
*Jam.* 2:16 things *n.* for the body
*Jude* 3 it was *n.* for me to write

**NEEDLE.**

*Mat.* 19:24 to go thro' eye of a *n.* *Mark* 10:25; *Luke* 18:25

**NEEDLE-WORK.**

*Ex.* 26:36 hanging wrought with *n.-w.* 27:16; 36:37; 38:18
28:39 ma. girdle of *n.-w.* 39:29
*Jud.* 5:30 divers colors of *n.-w.*
*Ps.* 45:14 bro. raiment of *n.-w.*

**NEEDS.**

*Gen.* 17:13 must *n.* be circumci.
19:9 this fel. will *n.* be a judge
24:5 must I *n.* bri. thy son ag.?
*2 Sam.* 14:14 for we must *n.* die
*Jer.* 10:5 must *n.* be born, beca.
*Mat.* 18:7 *n.* be that offen. come
*Mark* 13:7 such things must *n.*
*Luke* 14:18 I must *n.* go and see
*John* 4:4 must *n.* go thro' Sama.
*Acts* 17:3 Christ must *n.* have
21:22 multitude must *n.* come
*Rom.* 13:5 ye must *n.* be subject
*1 Cor.* 5:10 must ye *n.* go out
*2 Cor.* 11:30 if I must *n.* glory

**NEEDY.**

*Deut.* 15:11 open thy hand to *n.*
24:14 servant that is poor and *n.*
*Job* 24:4 they turn *n.* out of way
14 murderer kill. poor and *n.*
*Ps.* 9:18 *n.* not alway be forgot.
12:5 the sighing of *n.* will arise
35:10 del. poor and *n.* 72:4, 13
37:14 bent bow to cast down *n.*
40:17 I am poor and *n.* 70:5
72:12 he sh. deliver the *n.* 82:4
13 he sh. spare the poor and *n.*
74:21 poor and *n.* praise thy na.
82:3 justice to afflicted and *n.*
4 del. poor and *n.* from wicked
86:1 I am poor and *n.* 109:22
109:16 persecuted poor and *n.*
113:7 lifteth *n.* out of dunghill
*Prov.* 30:14 de. *n.* from am. men
31:9 plead cause of poor and *n.*
20 reacheth forth hands to *n.*
*Is.* 10:2 turn aside *n.* fr. judgm.
14:30 *n.* shall lie down in safety
25:4 been a strength to the *n.*
26:6 steps of *n.* shall tread it do.
32:7 even when the *n.* speaketh
41:17 poor and *n.* seek water
*Jer.* 5:28 right of *n.* do they not
22:16 judg. cause of poor and *n.*
*Ezek.* 16:49 strength. hands of *n.*
18:12 oppressed the poor and *n.*
22:29 people vexed poor and *n.*
*Amos* 4:1 kine of Bash. crush *n.*
8:4 O ye that swallow up the *n.*
6 buy the *n.* for a pair of shoes

**NEESINGS.**

*Job* 41:18 by his *n.* light doth sh.

**NEGLECT.**

*Mat.* 18:17 if he shall *n.* to hear them; *n.* to hear the church
*1 Tim.* 4:14 *n.* not gift in thee
*Heb.* 2:3 how escape, if *n.* salv.?

**NEGLECTED, ING.**

*Acts* 6:1 widows *n.* in ministra.
*Col.* 2:23 *n.* body, not in honor

**NEGLIGENT.**

*2 Chr.* 29:11 be not *n.* for the L.
*2 Pet.* 1:12 not be *n.* to put you

**NEHEMIAH.**

*Ezr.* 2:2 N. came with, *Neh.* 7:7
*Neh.* 1:1 the words of N. son of
3:16 N. son of Azbuk, repaired
8:9 N. wh. is the Tirsha. 10:1
12:47 Israel in days of N. gave

NEHUSHTAN. *2 K.* 18:4

**NEIGHBOR.**

*Ex.* 3:22 wom. borrow of *n.* 11:2
*1 Sam.* 15:28 hath given it to a *n.*
*Prov.* 27:10 better is a *n.* that is
*Jer.* 6:21 *n.* and friends sh. peri.
9:20 and teach every one her *n.*
*Luke* 10:36 *n.* to him am. thieves

**NEIGHBOR, Adjective.**

*Jer.* 49:18 overthrow of Sod. and the *n.* cities thereof, 50:40

**His NEIGHBOR.**

*Ex.* 12:4 him and *h. n.* take lamb
22:8 put ha. to *h. n.'s* goods, 11
14 borrow ought of *his n.*
32:27 go slay every man *his n.*
*Lev.* 20:10 with *his n.'s* wife sh. be put to death, *Deut.* 22:24
24:19 man cause blemish in *h. n.*
*Deut.* 4:42 kill his *n.* unaw. 19:4
15:2 creditor that lend to *his n.*
19:11 if any hate *his n.*
*Deut.* 22:26 a man ris. ag. *his n.*
27:24 curs. he th. smiteth *h. n.*
*Ruth* 4:7 his shoe, gave to *his n.*
*1 K.* 8:31 if man trespa. ag. *h. n.*
*2 Chr.* 6:22 if a man sin ag. *h. n.*
*Job* 12:4 as one mocked of *h. n.*
16:21 a man pleadeth for *h. n.*
*Ps.* 12:2 sp. vanity each wi. *h. n.*
15:3 nor doeth evil to *his n.*
101:5 whoso slandereth *his n.*
*Prov.* 6:29 goeth to *h. n.'s* wife
11:9 a hypocrite destroy. *h. n.*
12 void of wis. desp. *h. n.* 14:21
12:26 right. more ex. than *h. n.*
14:20 poor is hated even of *h. n.*
16:29 a vio. man enticeth *his n.*
18:17 *his n.* cometh and search.
19:4 poor is separated fr. *his n.*
21:10 *his n.* findeth no favor
25:18 bear false witn. ag. *his n.*
26:19 man that deceiveth *his n.*
29:5 flattereth *h. n.* spreadeth
*Ec.* 4:4 a man envied of *his n.*
*Is.* 3:5 oppressed ev. one by *h. n.*
19:2 fight ev. one against *h. n.*
41:6 helped every one *his n.*
*Jer.* 5:8 neighed after *h. n.'s* wife
7:5 judgm. bet. man and *his n.*
9:4 take ye heed ev. one of *h. n.*
5 th. will deceive ev. one *h. n.*
8 speak peaceably to *his n.*
22:8 say ev. man to *his n.* 23:35
13 useth *his n.'s* service
23:27 drea. tell ev. one to *h. n.*
30 steal words, ev. one fr. *h. n.*
31:34 teach no more every man *his n.* *Heb.* 8:11
34:15 proclaiming li. to *h. n.* 17
*Ezek.* 18:6 nei. defi. *h. n.'s* wi. 15
11 defiled *h. n.* 22:11; 33:26
*Hab.* 2:15 giveth *h. n.* drink
*Zec.* 3:10 call every man *his n.*
8:10 I set men ev. one ag. *h. n.*
16 speak ev. man truth to *h. n.*
17 let none imag. evil ag. *h. n.*
*Mark* 12:33 love *h. n.* as himself
*Acts* 7:27 he that did *his n.* wro.
*Rom.* 13:10 work. no evil to *h. n.*
15:2 let every one please *his n.*
*Eph.* 4:25 speak truth with *h. n.*

**My NEIGHBOR.**

*Job* 31:9 I laid wait at *my n.'s* d.
*Luke* 10:29 to Je. Who is *my n.*?

**Thy NEIGHBOR.**

*Ex.* 20:16 thou sh. not bear false witness ag. *thy n.* *Deut.* 5:20
*Lev.* 18:20 not lie wi. *t. n.'s* wife
19:13 thou sh. not defraud *t. n.*
15 in righte. shalt judge *thy n.*
16 nor stand ag. blood of *t. n.*

17 in any wise rebuke *thy n.*
18 thou sh. love *t. n.* as thyself
*Deut.* 5:21 nor desire *t. n.'s* wife
19:14 not rem. *t. n.'s* landmark
1 *Sam.* 28:17 given it to *thy n.*
*Prov.* 3:28 say not to *thy n.* Go
29 devise not evil against *t. n.*
24:28 be not witness ag. *thy n.*
25:9 debate thy cause with *t. n.*
17 with. foot fr. *t. n.'s* house
*Mat.* 5:43 shalt love *thy n.* 19:19; 22:39 *Mark* 12:31; *Luke* 10:27 *Rom.* 13:9; *Gal.* 5:14; *Jam.* 2:8

**NEIGHBORS.**

*Jos.* 9:16 heard th. were their *n.*
*Ruth* 4:17 her *n.* gave it a name
2 *K.* 4:3 borrow vessels of thy *n.*
*Ps.* 28:3 speak peace to their *n.*
31:11 I was reproach am. my *n.*
44:13 makest us repro. to our *n.*
79:4 are become reproach to *n.*
12 render to our *n.* seven-fold
80:6 makest us a strife to our *n.*
89:41 he is a reproach to his *n.*
*Jer.* 12:14 saith L. ag. all evil *n.*
*Ezek.* 22:12 gained of *n.* by exto.
*Luke* 1:58 her *n.* heard how Lord
14:12 make sup. call not rich *n.*
15:6 he called together his *n.*
*John* 9:8 *n.* who had seen him

**NEIGHED.**

*Jer.* 5:8 one *n.* after neigh. wife

**NEIGHING, S.**

*Jer.* 8:16 tremble at *n.* of strong
13:27 I have seen adult. and *n.*

**NEPHEW, S.**

*Jud.* 12:14 A. had 40 sons, 30 *n.*
*Job* 18:19 neither have son nor *n.*
*Is.* 14:22 I will cut off son and *n.*
1 *Tim.* 5:4 if widow have children or *n.*

NER. 1 *Chr.* 8:33; 9:36, 39
NEREUS. *Rom.* 16:15
NERGAL. 2 *K.* 17:30

**NEST.**

*Num.* 24:21 put. thy *n.* in a rock
*Deut.* 22:6 if a *n.* be before thee
32:11 eagle stirreth up her *n.*
*Job* 29:18 I shall die in my *n.*
39:27 eagle make *n.* on high
*Ps.* 84:3 swal. found *n.* for herse
*Prov.* 27:8 bird that wand. fr. *n.*
*Is.* 10:14 ha. found as *n.* riches
16:2 wander. bird cast out of *n.*
34:15 great owl make *n.*
*Jer.* 22:23 make. thy *n.* in cedars
48:28 dove makes *n.* in holes
49:16 make *n.* as high as eagle
*Ob.* 4 set thy *n.* among stars
*Hab.* 2:9 he may set *n.* on high.

**NESTS.**

*Ps.* 104:17 wh. birds make th. *n.*
*Ezek.* 31:6 all fowls made their *n.*
*Mat.* 8:20 birds of air *n.* *Lu.* 9:58

**NET.**

*Job* 18:8 cast into *n.* by own feet
19:6 God comp. me with his *n.*
*Ps.* 9:15 in *n.* they hid
25:15 plu. my feet out of *n.* 31:4
35:7 hid for me their *n.* in a pit
8 his *n.* he hid catch himself
57:6 prepared *n.* for my steps
66:11 thou broughtest us into *n.*
140:5 spread a *n.* by wayside
*Prov.* 1:17 in vain *n.* is spread
12:12 wick. desir. *n.* of evil men
29:5 man that flatter. spread. *n.*
*Ec.* 9:12 fishes taken in evil *n.*
*Is.* 51:20 as a wild bull in a *n.*
*Lam.* 1:13 spr. a *n.* for my feet
*Ezek.* 12:13 *n.* will I spread, 17:20
19:8 nations shall spread *n.*
32:3 spread my *n.* over thee
*Hos.* 5:1 ye have been *n.* on Ta.
7:12 spread my *n.* on them
*Mic.* 7:2 hunt brother with a *n.*
*Hab.* 1:15 catch them in their *n.*
16 they sacrifice to their *n.*
17 shall they empty their *n.*?
*Mat.* 4:18 cast *n.* into, *Mark* 1:16
13:47 kingd. of heaven is like *n*
*Luke* 5:5 I will let down the *n.*
6 multitude of fishes, *n.* brake
*John* 21:6 cast *n.* on right side
11 *n.* to land · not *n.* broken

**NETS.**

1 *K.* 7:17 *n.* of checker work
*Ps.* 140:10 wick. fall into own *n.*
*Ec.* 7:26 wom. whose heart is *n.*
*Is.* 19:8 they that sp. *n.* languish
*Ezek.* 26:5 spreading of *n.* in sea
14 place to spread *n.* on, 47:10
*Mat.* 4:21 James and J. mending their *n.* *Mark* 1:19; *Lu.* 5:2
*Mark* 1:18 forsook *n.* follow. him
*Luke* 5:4 down *n.* for a draught

**NETHANEEL.**

*Num.* 1:8 N. the son of Zuar
2:5 N. the son of Zuar, shall be captain, 7:18, 23; 10:15
1 *Chr.* 2:14 N. fourth son of Jes.
15:24 N. and Amasai blew with
24:6 the son of N. the scribe
26:4 sons of Obed-e. J. and N.
2 *Chr.* 17:7 Jehoshaphat sent N.
*Ezr.* 10:22 N. prie. *Neh.* 12:21, 36

**NETHANIAH.**

2 *K.* 25:23 son of N. 25; *Jer.* 40:8
1 *Chr.* 25:2 son of Asaph, N. 12
2 *Chr.* 17:8 Le to teach, even N.
*Jer.* 36:14 princes sent son of N.
41:2 Ishmael, son of N. 15

**NETHER.**

*Ex.* 19:17 they stood at *n.* part
*Deut.* 24:6 no man take *n.* millst.
*Jos.* 15:19 gave her upper springs and *n.* springs, *Jud.* 1:15
*Job* 41:24 heart hard as *n.* millst.
*Ezek.* 31:14 del. to death *n.* parts
16 comf. in *n.* parts of earth
18 down to *n.* parts of earth
32:18 cast do. to *n.* parts of ear.
24 E. gone down to *n.* pa. of e.

**NETHERMOST.**

1 *K.* 6:6 *n.* chamb. 5 cub. broad

**NETHINIM.**

1 *Chr.* 9:2 first inhabitants N.
*Ezr.* 2:43 N. went with Zerub.
58 the N. were 392, *Neh.* 7:60
7:7 some of N. went to Jer. 24
8:17 Iddo and breth. the N. 20
*Neh.* 3:26 N. dwelt in Op. 11:21
10:28 N. separated from people
11:21 Zi. and Gispa over the N.

**NETTLES.**

*Job* 30:7 under *n.* th. were gath.
*Prov.* 24:31 *n.* had covered face
*Is.* 34:13 *n.* and bram. in fortres
*Hos.* 9:6 *n.* possess pleas. places
*Zep.* 2:9 M. shall be breeding *n.*

**NETWORK, S.**

*Ex.* 27:4 grate of *n.* brass, 38:4
1 *K.* 7:18 two rows round *n.* 42
41 two *n.* upon the chapiters
42 400 pomegranates for two *n.*
*Is.* 19:9 weave *n.* be confounded
*Jer.* 52:22 with *n.* on chapiters
23 pomegranates on *n.* we. 100

**NEVER.**

*Mat.* 9:33 it was *n.* so seen in Is.
27:14 answered him to *n.* a word

**NEW.**

*Ex.* 1:8 arose a *n.* king over Eg.
*Lev.* 26:10 br. forth old, bec. of *n.*
*Num.* 16:30 Lord make *n.* thing
*Deut.* 20:5 built *n.* house, 22:8
24:5 taken a *n.* wife, not go
32:17 sacri. to devils, to *n.* gods
*Jos.* 9:13 bottles of wine were *n.*
*Jud.* 5:8 they chose *n.* gods
1 *Sam.* 6:7 make a *n.* cart
2 *Sam.* 6:3 on *n.* cart, 1 *Chr.* 13:7
21:16 being girded with *n.* sw.
1 *K.* 11:29 J. clad with *n.* gar. 30
*Job* 32:19 to burst like *n.* bottles
*Ps.* 33:3 sing *n.* song, 96:1; 98:1; 144:9; 149:1; *Is.* 42:10
40:3 put *n.* song in my mouth
*Ec.* 1:9 no *n.* thing under sun
10 may be said, This is *n.*?
*Cant.* 7:13 pleas. frui. *n.* and old
*Is.* 42:9 *n.* things I declare, 48:6
43:19 I will do a *n.* thing
62:2 be called by a *n.* name
65:17 *n.* heavens, *n.* earth, 66:22
*Jer.* 26:10 *n.* gate of L.'s ho. 36:10
31:22 Lord hath creat. *n.* thing
*Lam.* 3:23 Lord's mercies are *n.*
*Ezek.* 11:19 a *n.* spirit, 36:26
18:31 make *n.* heart and *n.* spi.
47:12 trees bring forth *n.* fruit
*Mat.* 9:16 *n.* cloth to an old gar. *Mark* 2:21; *Luke* 5:36
17 put *n.* wine into *n.* bottles, *Mark* 2:22; *Luke* 5:38
13:52 bring. out things *n.* and o.
26:28 is my blood of *n.* testament, *Mark* 14:24; *Lu.* 22:20; 1 *Cor.* 11:25
29 drink it *n.* with, *Mark* 14:25
27:60 Jos. laid body in *n.* tomb
*Mark* 1:27 what *n.* doct. is this?
16:17 speak with *n.* tongues
*John* 13:34 *n.* com. I give you
*Acts* 17:19 what this *n.* doct. is?
21 tell or hear some *n.* thing
1 *Cor.* 5:7 ye may be a *n.* lump
2 *Cor.* 3:6 able minist. of *n.* test.
5:17 in Ch. he is a *n.* creature; all things are become *n.*
*Gal.* 6:15 but a *n.* creature
*Eph.* 2:15 of twain, one *n.* man
4:24 ye put on *n.* man, *Col.* 3:10
*Heb.* 9:15 Media. of *n.* testament
10:20 by *n.* and living way
1 *Pet.* 2:2 as *n.* born babes desi.
2 *Pet.* 3:13 *n.* heavens, *n.* earth
1 *John* 2:7 write no *n.* comman.
8 *n.* commandment I write
2 *John* 5 not as though I wrote *n.* commandment
*Rev.* 2:17 *n.* name written
3:12 name is *n.* Jerusalem; I will write my *n.* name, 21:2
5:9 they sung a *n.* song, 14:3
21:1 I saw *n.* heaven and *n.* ear.
5 behold, I make all things *n.*

*See* COVENANT, MOON.

**NEW wine.**

*Neh.* 10:39 bring off. of *n. wine*
13:5 chamber where *n. w.* laid
12 bro. tithe of *n. w.* to treas.
*Prov.* 3:10 presses burst wi. *n. w.*
*Is.* 24:7 the *n. w.* mourneth
65:8 as *n. w.* is found in cluster
*Hos.* 4:11 *n. w.* take away heart
9:2 the *n. wine* shall fail in her
*Joel* 1:5 *n. w.* cut off; 10 dried up
3:18 mountains shall drop *n. w.*
*Hag.* 1:11 call. for drou. on *n. w.*
*Zec.* 9:17 *n. w.* ma. maids cheer.
*Mat.* 9:17 *n. w.* into old bottles, but *n. wine* into new, *Mark* 2:22; *Luke* 5:37
*Acts* 2:13 these men full of *n. w.*

**NEWLY.**

*Deut.* 32:17 to gods *n.* came up
*Jud.* 7:19 they had *n.* set watch

**NEWNESS.**

*Rom.* 6:4 shall walk in *n.* of life
7:6 should serve in *n.* of spirit

**NEWS.**

*Prov.* 25:25 so good *n.* from a far

**NEXT.**
*Gen.* 17:21 bear at set time *n.* ye.
*Ex.* 12:4 let him *n.* take lamb
*Deut.* 21:3 city whi. is *n.* slain
6 elders of city *n.* to slain man
1 *Sam.* 23:17 I shall be *n.* to th.
30:17 Dav. smote to ev. of *n.* day
*Est.* 10:3 Mordecai was *n.* to A.
*Mat.* 27:62 *n.* day that followed
*Mark* 1:38 go into *n.* towns
*John* 1:29 *n.* day John see. Jes.
*Acts* 4:3 put th. in hold to *n.* day
13:42 words preached *n.* sab. 44

NICANOR. *Acts* 6:5

**NICODEMUS.**
*John* 3:1 N. a ruler of the Jews
7:50 N. came to Jesus, 19:39

NICOLAITANS. *Rev.* 2:6, 15
NICOPOLIS. *Tit.* 3:12
NIGER. *Acts* 13:1

**NIGH.**
*Lev.* 21:3 virgin that is *n.* to him
*Num.* 24:17 beh. him, not *n.* star
*Deut.* 4:7 hath G. so *n.* them?
22:2 if bro. be not *n.* unto thee
30:14 is *n.* to thee, *Rom.* 10:8
2 *Sam.* 11:20 wh. appr. so *n.*? 21
1 *K.* 8:59 let my words be *n.*
*Ps.* 34:18 is *n.* them of bro. hea.
85:9 salva. *n.* them that fear him
145:18 L. is *n.* to all that call
*Joel* 2:1 day of L. is *n.* at hand
*Mat.* 24:32 sum. is *n.* *Luke* 21:30
*Mark* 13:29 know that it is *n.*
*Luke* 21:20 kn. that desola. is *n.*
31 know that king. of G. is *n.*
*John* 6:4 and the passover was *n.*
11:55 the Jews' passover was *n.*
*Eph.* 2:13 made *n.* by blood of C.
17 preach. to th. that were *n.*
*Phil.* 2:27 sick, *n.* unto death, 30
*Heb.* 6:8 is rejected, *n.* to cursing
*See* CAME, DRAW.

**NIGHT.**
*Gen.* 1:5 the darkness he call. *n.*
14 lights, to divide day from *n.*
1:16 lesser light to rule *n.*
19:2 tarry all *n.* *Num.* 22:19; *Jud.* 19:6, 9
33 drink wine that *n.* 34, 35
24:54 tarried all *n.* 28:11; 31:54; 32:13, 21
30:15 shall lie with thee to-*n.* 16
46:2 G. spake to Is. in vis. of *n.*
49:27 at *n.* he shall divide spoil
*Ex.* 12:8 eat the flesh in that *n.*
42 is a *n.* to be observed to L.
14:20 not near other all *n.*
*Lev.* 6:9 burning on altar all *n.*
19:13 not abide with thee all *n.*
*Num.* 14:1 people wept that *n.*
22:8 said, Lodge here this *n.* 19
*Deut.* 16:4 l. bread remain all *n.*
21:23 body not remain all *n.*
*Jud.* 6:40 God did so that *n.*
19:25 and abused her all the *n.*
*Ruth* 1:12 if I have a husb. to-*n.*
1 *Sam.* 15:11 S. cried to L. all *n.*
19:11 if thou save not life to-*n.*
28:25 Saul went away that *n.*
2 *Sam.* 2:29 Abner walked all *n.*
32 J. and his men went all *n.*
12:16 David lay all *n.* on earth
17:1 will pursue after D. this *n.*
16 lodge not this *n.* in plain
2 *K.* 19:35 th. *n.* the angel smote
2 *Chr.* 1:7 that *n.* did G. ap. to S.
*Est.* 6:1 that *n.* cou. not king sl.
*Job* 3:3 let *n.* perish in which
7 let that *n.* be solitary
4:13 the visions of the *n.*
7:4 when shall the *n.* be gone?
29:19 dew lay all *n.* on my bra.
36:20 desire not *n.* peo. cut-off
*Ps.* 6:6 all *n.* make I my bed
19:2 *n.* unto *n.* showeth knowl.
30:5 weep. may endure for a *n.*
78:14 led them all *n.* with light
92:2 show forth faithful. ev., *n.*
104:20 maketh darkn. it is *n.*
139:11 even the *n.* sh. be light
*Prov.* 7:9 passing in the dark *n.*
31:15 ariseth while it is yet *n.*
*Cant.* 1:13 lie all *n.* betw. breas.
5:2 my locks with drops of *n.*
*Is.* 5:11 continue until *n.*
16:3 make thy shadow as the *n.*
21:4 *n.* of pleas. turn. into fear
11 watchman, what of the *n.*?
12 morning cometh, also the *n.*
29:7 shall be as a dream of *n.*
*Jer.* 14:8 turneth aside for a *n.*
*Dan.* 2:19 secret revealed in *n.*
5:30 that *n.* was Belshaz. slain
6:18 king passed the *n.* fasting
*Hos.* 7:6 their baker sleep. all *n.*
*Joel.* 1:13 lie all *n.* in sackcloth
*Amos* 5:8 mak. day dark with *n.*
*Jon.* 4:10 ca. up in *n.* perish. in *n.*
*Mic.* 3:6 *n.* shall be to you
*Mat.* 26:31 sh. be offended beca. of me this *n.* *Mark* 14:27
34 this *n.* thou shalt deny me
*Luke* 5:5 toiled all *n.* taking not.
6:12 he continued all *n.* in pray.
12:20 this *n.* thy soul be requi.
17:34 that *n.* two sh. be in one
*John* 9:4 *n.* com. no man work
13:30 he went out, it was *n.*
21:3 that *n.* they caught noth.
*Acts* 12:6 same *n.* Pe. was sleep.
16:33 took them same hour of *n.*
23:11 *n.* follow. Lord stood by
27:23 stood by me this *n.* angel
*Rom.* 13:12 *n.* is spent
1 *Cor.* 11:23 *n.* he was betrayed
1 *Thes.* 5:5 we are not of the *n.*
*Rev.* 21:25 be no *n.* there, 22:5

**By NIGHT.**
*Gen.* 20:3 to Ab. in dream *by n.*
31:24 G. ca. to La. in dre. *by n.*
39 whet. stolen by day or *by n.*
40 drou. consu. me, frost *by n.*
*Ex.* 12:31 called M. and A. *by n.*
13:21 *by n.* in pillar of fire, 22; 14:20; 40:38; *Neh.* 9:12
*Num.* 9:16 appear. of fire *by n.*
21 taken up by day or *by n.*
*Deut.* 1:33 fire *by n.* to show way
23:10 unclean. chanceth *by n.*
1 *Sam.* 14:36 go after Phili. *by n.*
28:8 Saul came to woman *by n.*
2 *Sam.* 21:10 nor the beasts *by n.*
1 *K.* 3:5 Lord appeared to Solomon *by n.* 2 *Chr.* 7:12
2 *K.* 6:14 came *by n.* compassed
25:4 fled *by n.* *Jer.* 52:7
*Ps.* 91:5 sh. not be afraid *by n.*
121:6 nor moon smite thee *by n.*
134:1 *by n.* stand in house of L.
136:9 moon rule by *n.* *Jer.* 31:35
*Prov.* 31:18 goeth not out *by n.*
*Cant.* 3:1 *by n.* I sought him
*Is.* 4:5 shining of a fire *by n.*
*Jer.* 6:5 let us go *by n.* destroy
39:4 went forth out of city *by n.*
49:9 if thieves *by n.* will destr.
*Dan.* 7:2 I saw in my vision *by n.*
*Ob.* 5 if thieves, if robbers *by n.*
*Mat.* 2:14 too chi. and mo. *by n.*
27:64 disciples come *by n.* 28:13
*Luke* 2:8 watch over flock *by n.*
*John* 3:2 Nicod. came *by n.* 19:39
*Acts* 5:19 angel *by n.* open. pris.
9:25 took P. *by n.* let him down
*See* DAY.

**In the NIGHT.**
1 *K.* 3:19 wom. child died *i. t. n.*
*Neh.* 2:12 arose *i. t. n.* 15 I went
4:22 *in t. n.* they may guard us
6:10 *in t. n.* will they slay thee
*Job* 5:14 in noonday as *in the n.*
24:14 *in t. n.* murder. is as thief
27:20 tempest steal. him *in t. n.*
34:25 overturneth them *in the n.*
35:10 who giv. songs *in the n.*?
*Ps.* 16:7 my reins inst. me *i. t. n.*
17:3 hast visited me *in the n.*
22:2 I cry *in the n.* season
42:8 *in t. n.* his song sh. be wi.
77:2 sore ran *in t. n.* ceased not
6 call to rem. my song *in t. n.*
90:4 1,000 years as watch *in t. n.*
105:39 a fire to give light *i. t. n.*
119:55 remem. thy name *in t. n.*
*Ec.* 2:23 taketh not rest *in the n.*
*Cant.* 3:8 sw. bec. of fear *in t. n.*
*Is.* 15:1 *in t. n.* M. is laid waste
26:9 soul desired thee *in the n.*
30:29 have a song as *in the n.*
59:10 at noonday as *in the n.*
*Jer.* 36:30 be cast out *in the n.*
*Lam.* 1:2 weepeth sore *in the n.*
2:19 arise, cry out *in the n.*
*Hos.* 4:5 shall fall *in the n.*
*John* 11:10 man walk *in the n.*
*Acts* 16:9 vision to P. *in t. n.* 18:9
1 *Thes.* 5:2 day cometh as thief *in the n.* 2 *Pet.* 3:10
7 sleep *in t. n.* drunk *in the n.*

**NIGHTS.**
*Gen.* 7:4 rain 40 days, 40 *n.* 12
*Job* 7:3 wearisome *n.* appointed
*Is.* 21:8 set in ward whole *n.*
*See* DAYS.

**NIGHTHAWK.**
*Lev.* 11:16 *n.* not eat, *Deut.* 14:15

**NIGHT-WATCHES.**
*Ps.* 63:6 I medi. on thee in *n.-w.*
119:148 prevent *n.-w.* to medit.

NIMRIM. *Is.* 15:6

**NIMROD.**
*Gen.* 10:8 C. begat N. 1 *Chr.* 1:10
*Mic.* 5:6 land of Assyria and N.

**NINE.**
*Deut.* 3:11 Og's bedst. *n.* cubits
*Neh.* 11:1 *n.* parts dw. in oth. cit.
*Luke* 17:17 where are the *n.*?
*See* HUNDRED.

**NINETEEN.**
2 *Sam.* 2:30 lacked of D. serv. *n.*

**NINETEENTH.**
2 *K.* 25:8 in the *n.* year of Nebuchadnezzar the house of the Lord was burnt, *Jer.* 52:12

**NINETY.**
*Gen.* 5:9 Enos lived *n.* years
17:17 Sa. that is *n.* y. old, bear?

**NINETY-SIX.**
*Ezr.* 8:35 offer. for Is. *n.-s.* rams

**NINETY-EIGHT.**
1 *Sam.* 4:15 Eli was *n.-e.* ye. old

**NINETY-NINE.**
*Gen.* 17:1 Ab. was *n.-n.* years old
24 *n.-n.* years old when circu.
*Mat.* 18:12 do. he not le. the *n.-n.* and seek.? 13; *Luke* 15:4, 7

**NINEVEH.**
*Gen.* 10:11 Asher builded N.
2 *K.* 19:36 Sen. at N. *Is.* 37:37
*Jon.* 1:2 go to N. 3:2, 3; 4:11
*Nah.* 1:1 the burden of N. 2:8
3:7 N. is waste, who will bem.?
*Zep.* 2:13 make N. a desolation
*Mat.* 12:41 men of N. *Luke* 11:32

NINEVITES. *Luke* 11:30

**NINTH.**
*Lev.* 25:22 eat old fruit till *n.* ye.
1 *Chr.* 12:12 Elzabad, *n.* captain
27:12 *n.* captain for *n.* month
*Mat.* 20:5 went out ab. *n.* hour
27:45 darkness over all the land unto *n.* hour, *Mark* 15:33,
46 *n.* hour Jesus gave up ghost

*Acts* 3:1 hour of prayer, being *n.*
10:3 C. saw. vis. ab. *n.* hour, 30
*Rev.* 21:20 *n.* founda. was topaz
*See* DAY, MONTH.

**NISAN.**
*Neh.* 2:1 in the month N.
*Est.* 3:7 first month N.

NISROCH. 2 *K.* 19:37; *Is.* 37:38

**NITRE.**
*Prov.* 25:20 as vinegar upon *n.*
*Jer.* 2:22 tho' thou wash with *n.*

**NO.**
*Jer.* 46:25 pun. N. *Ezek.* 30:14, 16
*Nah.* 3:8 better th. populous N.

**NOADIAH.**
*Ezr.* 8:33 N. the son of Binnui
*Neh.* 6:14 think on prophet. N.

**NOAH, NOE.**
*Gen.* 5:29 called his name N. 30
6:8 N. found grace in eyes of L.
9 gen. of N. 10:1, 32; 1 *Cor.* 1:4
7:23 N. only remained alive
8:1 God remembered N. 6:20
9:24 N. awoke fr. his wine, 29
*Is.* 54:9 this is as waters of N.
*Ezek.* 14:14 N. Daniel, Job, 20
*Mat.* 24:37 days of N. *Luke* 17:26
*Heb.* 11:7 by faith N. be. warned
1 *Pet.* 3:20 waited in days of N.
2 *Pet.* 2:5 old world, but saved N.

NOAH. *Num.* 26:33; 27:1: 36:11; *Jos.* 17:3

**NOB.**
1 *Sam.* 21:1 David came to N. to
22:9 son of J. com. to N. 11, 19
*Neh.* 11:32 chi. of Ben. dw. at N.
*Is.* 10:32 shall he remain at N.

**NOBLE.**
*Ezr.* 4:10 *n.* Asnapper brought
*Est.* 6:9 one of king's *n.* princes.
*Jer.* 2:21 I planted thee a *n.* vine
*Luke* 19:12 *n.* man went to far
*John* 4:46 *n.* man whose son
49 *n.* man saith, Come ere chi.
*Acts* 17:11 Bere. more *n.* than T.
24:3 we accept it, *n.* Felix, 26:25
1 *Cor.* 1:26 not many *n.* are call.

**NOBLES.**
*Ex.* 24:11 on *n.* of Israel laid not
*Num.* 21:18 the *n.* of peo. digged
*Jud.* 5:13 dominion over the *n.*
1 *K.* 21:8 Jez. sent letter to *n.*
2 *Chr.* 23:20 Jehoiada took the *n.*
*Neh.* 2:16 nor had I told it to *n.*
3:5 *n.* not put necks to work
5:7 I rebuked the *n.* and rulers
6:17 *n.* of Judah sent letters
*Neh.* 7:5 G. put in hea. to gath. *n.*
10:29 they clave to brethren, *n.*
13:17 I contended with *n.* of J
*Job* 29:10 the *n.* held their peace
*Ps.* 83:11 make their *n.* like Oreb
149:8 bind *n* with fet. of iron
*Prov.* 8:16 princes rule, *n.* judg
*Ec* 10:17 wh. king is son of *n.*
*Is* 13:2 go into gates of the *n.*
34:12 shall call *n.* to kingdom
43:14 brought down all their *n.*
*Jer.* 14:3 *n.* sent their little ones
27:20 Nebuc. carried captive *n.*
30:21 *n.* shall be of themselves
39:6 king slew all *n.* of Judah
*Jon.* 3:7 decree of king and *n.*
*Nah.* 3:18 thy *n.* dwell in dust

NOD. *Gen.* 4:16

**NOISE.**
*Ex.* 20:18 heard *n.* of trumpet
32:17 th. is a *n.* of war in camp
18 *n.* of them that sing I hear
*Jos.* 6:10 not shout nor make *n.*
*Jud.* 5:11 deliv. fr. *n.* of archers
1 *Sam.* 4:6 what meaneth *n.*? 14
1 *K.* 1:41 wherefore is this *n.*?
45 this is the *n.* ye have heard
2 *K.* 7:6 *n.* of char. *n.* of horses
11:13 Athali. heard *n.* of guard, 2 *Chr.* 23:12
1 *Chr.* 15:28 making *n.* with psal.
*Ezr.* 3:13 *n.* of joy fr. *n.* of weep.
*Job* 36:29 understand *n.* of taber.
33 *n.* thereof showeth concern.
37:2 hear attentive. *n.* of voice
*Ps.* 33:3 play skilf. with loud *n.*
42:7 call. at *n.* of water-spouts
55:2 I mourn and make a *n.*
59:6 make a *n.* like a dog, 14
65:7 stilleth the *n.* of the seas
66:1 make a joyful *n.* to God, all ye lands, 81:1; 95:1, 2; 98:4, 6; 100:1
93:4 L. mightier than *n.* of wat.
*Is.* 9:5 ev. battle is wi. confu. *n.*
13:4 *n.* of a multitude in mountains, a tumult. *n.* of kingd.
14:11 *n.* of thy viols is down
17:12 a *n.* like *n.* of the seas
24:8 *n.* of them that rej. endeth
18 he who fleeth from the *n.*
25:5 shalt bring *n.* of strangers
29:6 visited of L. with great *n.*
31:4 nor abase himself for *n.*
33:3 at *n.* of tumult people fled
66:6 a voice of *n.* from the city
*Jer.* 4:19 my heart maketh *n.*
29 the city shall flee for the *n.*
10:22 the *n.* of the bruit is come
11:16 *n.* of gr. tumult he kindl.
25:31 *n.* sh. co. to ends of earth
46:17 P. king of Egypt is but *n.*
47:3 at *n.* of stamping of horses
49:21 earth is moved at the *n.* of their fall, at the cry the *n.*
50:46 at *n.* of taking of Babylon
51:55 *n.* of th. voice is uttered
*Lam.* 2:7 made *n.* in house of L.
*Ezek.* 1:24 *n.* of their wings, like the *n.* of great waters, 43:2
3:13 *n.* of wheels, *n.* of rushing
19:7 land was desolate by *n.*
26:10 thy walls sh. shake at *n.*
13 cause *n.* of songs to cease
37:7 as I prophesied, th. was *n.*
*Joel* 2:5 like *n.* of char. *n.* of fire
*Amos* 5:23 take fr. me *n.* of songs
*Mic.* 2:12 they sh. make great *n.*
*Nah.* 3:2 *n.* of whip, *n.* of wheels
*Zep.* 1:10 *n.* of cry fr. fish-gate
*Zec.* 9:15 drink and make a *n.*
*Mat.* 9:23 saw peo. making a *n.*
2 *Pet.* 3:10 hea. past away wi. *n.*
*Rev.* 6:1 I heard the *n.* of thund.

**NOISED.**
*Jos.* 6:27 Joshua, fame was *n.*
*Mark* 2:1 *n.* he was in the house
*Luke* 1:65 th. sayings *n.* abroad
*Acts* 2:6 when this was *n.* abroad

**NOISOME.**
*Ps.* 91:3 deli. thee fr. *n.* pestilen.
*Ezek.* 14:21 send sw. and *n.* bea.
*Rev.* 16:2 fell a *n.* grievous sore

**There was NONE.**
*Num.* 21:35 *t. w. n.* left him alive
2 *Sam.* 22:42 they looked, but *th. was n.* to save, *Ps.* 18:41
*Ps.* 139:16 yet *t. w. n.* of them

**NOON.**
*Gen.* 43:16 sh. dine with me at *n.*
25 present ag. Jos. came at *n.*
*Jud.* 19:8 tarried until after *n.*
2 *Sam.* 4:5 who lay on bed at *n.*
1 *K.* 18:26 called on Ba. until *n.*
27 at *n.* Elijah mocked them
20:16 and they went out at *n.*
2 *K.* 4:20 sat on her knees till *n.*
*Ps.* 55:17 at *n.* will I pray
*Cant.* 1:7 mak. flock to rest at *n.*
*Jer.* 6:4 arise, let us go up at *n.*
*Amos* 8:9 cau. sun go down at *n.*
*Acts* 22:6 about *n.* th. shone lig.

**NOONDAY.**
*Deut.* 28:29 thou sh. grope at *n.*
*Job* 5:14 they grope in the *n.*
11:17 th. age be clearer than *n.*
*Ps.* 37:6 bring forth judgm. as *n.*
91:6 destruction that wast. at *n.*
*Is.* 16:3 as night, in midst of *n.*
58:10 thy darkness sh. be as *n.*
59:10 we stumble at *n.* as night
*Jer.* 15:8 I have a spoiler at *n.*
*Zep.* 2:4 drive out Ashdod at *n.*

**NOONTIDE.**
*Jer.* 20:16 hear the shouting at *n.*

**NOPH.**
*Is.* 19:13 princes of N. deceived
*Jer.* 2:16 the children of N. have
46:14 publish in N. 19 N. shall
*Ezek.* 30:13 ima. cease out N. 16

**NORTH.**
*Gen.* 28:14 thou sh. spread to *n.*
1 *K.* 7:25 three oxen looking toward *n.* 2 *Chr.* 4:4
1 *Chr.* 9:24 porters were tow. *n.*
*Job* 26:7 he stretched out the *n.*
37:9 cold cometh out of the *n.*
22 fair weather com. out of *n.*
*Ps.* 48:2 on sides of *n.* the city
89:12 *n.* and south, thou created
*Ec.* 1:6 wind turneth about to *n.*
11:3 if the tree fall toward the *n.*
*Is.* 14:13 I will sit in sides of *n.*
43:6 I will say to the *n.* G. up
*Jer.* 1:13 pot's face toward the *n.*
14 out of the *n.* an evil break forth, 4:6; 46:20
15 families of kingdoms of *n.*
3:11 proclaim th. words tow. *n.*
18 come together out of the *n.*
6:1 evil appeareth out of the *n.*
23:8 which led Is. out of *n.* 31:8
25:9 take all the families of *n.*
26 the kings of *n.* far and near
46:6 they shall fall toward *n.*
10 L. hath a sacrifice in the *n.*
24 delivered to people of the *n.*
47:2 waters rise up out of the *n.*
50:3 out of *n.* cometh a nation
*Ezek.* 1:4 whirlw. came out of *n.*
8:5 I lifted mine eyes toward *n.*
20:47 all faces from south to *n.*
21:4 all flesh from south to *n.*
32:30 princes of *n.* all of
40:44 prospect toward the *n.* 46
41:11 one door toward *n.* 42:4
42:1 and building toward *n.*
4 doors *n.* 11 chambers *n.* 13
46:19 holy chamb. looked to *n.*
48:10 holy oblation toward *n.*
*Dan.* 11:6 come to king of the *n.*
8 more years than king of *n.*
11 fight wi. the king of the *n.*
13 the king of *n.* shall return
15 k. of the *n.* cast up a m. 40
44 tidings of *n.* sh. trouble hi.
*Zep.* 2:13 stretch hand ag. *n.*
*Zec.* 6:6 black horses go into *n.*
8 have quieted my spirit in *n.*
14:4 mount. sh. remove tow. *n.*
*Rev.* 21:13 on *n.* were three gates

**NORTH border.**
*Num.* 34:7 this sh. be your *n. b.* 9

**From the NORTH.**
*Ps.* 107:3 gathered *from the n.* and the south, *Is.* 49:12; *Jer.* 16:15; 23:8
*Is.* 14:31 come *f. t. n.* a smoke
41:25 I raised up one *from t. n.*
*Jer.* 4:6 I will bring evil *f. the n.* 6:22; 10:22; 50:9, 41; 51:48
*Ezek.* 26:7 king of kings *f. t. n.*
39:2 will cause th. to come *f. n.*
*Amos* 8:12 wander *f. t. n.* to east
*Zec.* 2:6 flee *f.* the land of *t. n.*
*Luke* 13:29 come *f. t. n.* sit down

**NORTH quarter.**
*Jos.* 15:5 Judah's border in *n. q.*

**NORTH side.**
Ex. 26:20 tabernacle on n. s.
35 thou shalt put table on n. s.
Num. 2:25 camp of Dan on n. s.
Jud. 21:19 feast n. s. Beth-el
2 K. 16:14 brazen altar on n. s.
Ezek. 42:17 he measured the n. s.
48:30 goings out of city on n. s.

**NORTHERN.**
Jer. 15:12 break n. iron, and ste.
Joel 2:20 I will remove n. army

**NORTHWARD.**
Gen. 13:14 look n. Deut. 3:27
Ex. 40:22 tabernacle n. without
Lev. 1:11 on side of altar n.
Deut. 2:3 ye mount. turn you n.
1 Sam. 14:5 front of one rock n.
1 Chr. 26:14 Zechar.'s lot ca. n.
17 n. were four Levites a day

**NOSE.**
Lev. 21:18 a flat n. sh. not offer
2 K. 19:28 hook in thy n. Is. 37:29
Job 40:24 his n. pierceth through
41:2 canst thou put hook in n.?
Prov. 30:33 wringing of the n.
Cant. 7:4 thy n. is as tower of L.
8 smell of thy n. like apples
Is. 65:5 th. are a smoke in my n.
Ezek. 8:17 put branch to their n.
23:25 take away thy n. and ears

**NOSES.**
Ps. 115:6 n. have they, smell not
Ezek. 39:11 stop n. of passengers

**NOSE-JEWELS.**
Is. 3:21 L. take away their n. j.

**NOSTRILS.**
Gen. 2:7 G. breath. into m.'s n.
7:22 in wh. n. was breath of life
Ex. 15:8 wi. blast of thy n. wat.
Num. 11:20 eat till it come out n.
2 Sam. 22:9 went a smoke out of his n. Ps. 18:8, 15
16 blast of the breath of his n.
Job 4:9 breath of n. consumed
27:3 Spirit of God is in my n.
39:20 glory of his n. is terrible
41:20 out of his n. goeth smoke
Is. 2:22 whose breath is in his n.
Lam. 4:20 brea. of n. was taken
Amos 4:10 sti. of camps unto n.

**NOTABLE.**
Dan. 8:5 the goat had a n. horn
8 for it came up four n. ones
Mat. 27:16 had then n. prisoner
Acts 2:20 before n. day of L. co.
4:16 n. miracle hath been done

**NOTE, ED.**
Is. 30:8 write it, n. it in book
Dan. 10:21 n. in scripture of tru.
2 Thes. 3:14 n. that man

**NOTE.**
Rom. 16:7 are of n. am. apostles

**NOTHING.**
Gen. 11:6 n. will be restrained
19:8 only unto these men do n.
Ex. 12:10 let n. of it remain
16:18 had n. over, 2 Cor. 8:15
22:3 have n. then he sh. be sold
Deut. 22:26 damsel thou sh. do n.
Jud. 14:6 had n. in his hand
2 Sam. 24:24 wh. doth cost me n.
1 K. 8:9 there was n. in the ark
11:22 answered n. Luke 22:35
Job 6:18 they go to n. and perish
21 for now ye are n. ye see
8:9 of yesterday, and know n.
24:25 make speech n. worth
26:7 hangeth the earth upon n.
34:9 it profiteth a man n.
Ps. 17:3 tried me and sh. find n.
39:5 mine age is as n. bef. thee
49:17 he shall carry n. away
119:165 and n. sh. offend them
Prov. 9:13 and knoweth n.
13:4 desir. and hath n. 20:4
7 mak. himself rich, yet ha. n.
22:27 if thou hast n. to pay
Ec. 3:14 n. can be put to it
5:15 he sh. take n. of his labor
6:2 he wanteth n. for his soul
7:14 should find n. after him
Is. 34:12 her princes shall be. n.
40:17 nations bef. him are as n. are to him less than n. 41:29
23 bring. princes to n. 41:11, 12
Jer. 10:24 lest th. bring me to n.
38:14 ask a thing, hide n. fr. me
39:10 left of poor which had n.
50:26 let n. of her be left
Lam. 1:12 is it n. to you?
Ezek. 13:3 prop. that ha. seen n.
Dan. 4:35 inhabit. of earth as n.
Amos 3:4 lion cry if taken n.
5 taken up snare, and taken n.
7 surely Lord God will do n.
Hag. 2:3 in comp. of it as n.?
Mat. 17:20 n. shall be impossible to you, Luke 1:37
26:62 answerest thou n.?
27:12 he answer. n. Mark 14:60, 61; 15:3, 4, 5
19 ha. n. to do with just man
Mark 5:26 and was n. bettered
9:29 forth by n. but by prayer
Luke 5:5 have toiled all night and taken n. John 21:3
7:42 they had n. to pay
10:19 n. sh. by any means hurt
Luke 11:6 I ha. n. to set bef. him
23:41 this man hath done n.
John 3:27 man can receive n.
5:19 S. can do n. of himself, 30
6:12 gather, that n. be lost
39 given me, I should lose n.
63 the flesh profiteth n.
7:26 they say n. 8:28 I do n.
9:33 could do n. 11:49 know n.
12:19 perc. how ye prevail n.?
14:30 prince of world hath n.
15:5 without me ye can do n.
16:23 that day ye sh. ask me n.
24 ye asked n. in my name
18:20 in secret have I said n.
Acts 10:20 doubting n. 11:12
19:36 quiet, and do n. rashly
20:20 kept back n. profitable
23:14 eat n. until we ha. slain P.
27:33 fasting, having taken n.
1 Cor. 1:19 bring to n. understa.
4:4 I know n. by myself
5 judge n. before the time
8:2 knoweth n. yet as he ought
9:16 I have n. to glory of
13:2 charity, am n. 2 Cor. 12:11
3 not charity, it profit. me n.
2 Cor. 6:10 having n. yet posses.
13:8 can do n. against the truth
Gal. 5:2 Ch. shall profit you n.
Phil. 2:3 let n. be done thro' str.
1 Tim. 4:4 good, n. to be refused
5:21 doing n. by partiality
6:4 he is proud, knowing n.
7 we brought n. carry n. out
Tit. 3:13 that n. be wanting
Phile. 14 thy mind wou. I do n.
Heb. 2:8 left n. that is not put
7:19 for the law made n. perfect
Jam. 1:4 and entire, wanting n.
6 him ask in faith, n. wavering
3 John 7 taking n. of the Gentil.

**For NOTHING.**
Ex. 21:2 seventh go free for n.
Luke 6:35 lend, hoping for n. ag.
Phil. 4:6 be careful for n. but

**In NOTHING.**
Acts 17:21 A. spent time in n.
2 Cor. 12:11 in n. am I behind
Phil. 1:20 in n. I shall be asha.
28 in n. terrified by adversari.

**Is NOTHING.**
Num. 11:6 is n. besides manna
Jud. 7:14 is n. else save sword
1 Sam. 27:1 there is n. bet. than
1 K. 18:43 and said, There is n.
2 K. 20:15 there is n. among my treasure, Is. 39:4
2 Chr. 14:11 is n. with th. to help
Neh 2:2 is n. else but sorrow
Est. 6:3 th. is n. done for him
Ps. 19:6 th. is n. fr. heat thereof
Prov. 8:8 there is n. froward or
Ec. 2:24 is n. bet. for man, 3:22
5:14 and there is n. in his hand
Jer. 32:17 is n. too hard for thee
Mat. 10:26 is n. that sh. not be revea. Mark 4:22; Luke 12:2
23:16 swear by temple, it is n.
18 shall swear by altar, it is n.
Mark 7:15 th. is n. from without
John 8:54 my honor n.
Rom. 14:14 there is n. unclean
1 Cor. 7:19 circumcision is n.
8:4 an idol is n. in the world
Gal. 6:3 is n. he deceiv. himself
Tit. 1:15 that are defiled is n.

**Of NOTHING.**
Is. 41:24 behold, ye are of n.
1 Thes. 4:12 may have lack of n.
Rev. 3:17 increa. have need of n.

**NOTWITHSTANDING.**
Luke 10:11 n. be sure of this
20 n. in this rejoice not
1 Tim. 2:15 n. shall be saved

NOUGHT. See NAUGHT.

**NOURISH.**
Gen. 45:11 will I n. thee, 50:21
Is. 7:21 man sh. n. young cow
23:4 nor do I n. up young men
44:14 an ash, the rain doth n. it

**NOURISHED.**
Gen. 47:12 Joseph n. his father
2 Sam. 12:3 lamb he bought n.
Is. 1:2 n. and brought up child.
Ezek. 19:2 she n. her whelps
Acts 7:20 n. in his father's house
21 Pharaoh's daughter n. him
12:20 n. by the king's country
1 Tim. 4:6 n. up in words of fai.
Jam. 5:5 have n. your hearts as
Rev. 12:14 n. for a time, times

**NOURISHER, MENT.**
Ruth 4:15 shall be n. of old age
Col. 2:19 and bands having n.

**NOURISHETH, ING.**
Dan. 1:5 so n. them three years
Eph. 5:29 but n. his flesh.

**NOVICE.**
1 Tim. 3:6 not n. lest lifted

**NOWADAYS.**
1 Sam. 25:10 many servants n.

**NUMBER, Substantive.**
Gen. 34:30 I being few in n.
41:49 for it was without n.
Ex. 12:4 according to n. of souls
16:16 according to n. of pers.
23:26 n. of thy days I will fulfil
Lev. 25:15 n. of years after jubil. n. of years of fruit, 16, 50
26:22 shall make you few in n.
Num. 1:2 n. of names, 18, 22
3:22 n. of males a mo. old, 28-43
48 odd n. to be redeemed
14:29 n. from twenty years old
15:12 according to n. prep. do to ev. one according to their n.
23:10 who can count n. of Isr.?
31:36 half of portion was in n.
Deut. 4:27 n. am. heathen, 28:62
7:7 more in n. than any people
25:2 to be beaten by a certa. n.
32:8 according to the n. of Isra.
Jos. 4:5 a stone according to n. 8
Jud. 6:5 camels without n. 7:12
7:6 n. that lapped were 300 men
1 Sam. 6:4 n. of lords of Philist.
18 n. of cities of the Philistin.

2 *Sam.* 2:15 and went over by *n.*
24:2 may know *n.* of the peo.
9 gave up sum of *n.* of people
1 *K.* 18:31 12 stones accord. to *n.*
1 *Chr.* 7:2 *n.* was in days of Dav.
9 *n.* of th. after genealogy, 40
11:11 *n.* of mighty men D. had
22:16 gold and silver th. is no *n.*
23:3 their *n.* by their polls
25:7 the *n.* that were instruct.
27:23 David took not *n.* of them
2 *Chr.* 12:3 people were with. *n.*
26:12 *n.* of chief of the fathers
30:24 *n.* of priests sanctified th.
*Ezr.* 1:9 this is *n.* of the vessels
2:2 the *n.* of the people of Isra.
3:4 daily burnt-offerings by *n.*
6:17 according to the *n.* of trib.
8:34 by *n.* and by weight ev. o.
*Job* 1:5 according to *n.* of them
3:6 not come into *n.* of months
5:9 things without *n.* 9:10
14:5 *n.* of months are with thee
15:20 *n.* of years hid. to oppres.
25:3 is th. any *n.* of his armies?
31:37 dec. to him *n.* of my steps
34:24 mighty men without *n.*
36:26 *n.* of his years be search.
38:21 the *n.* of thy days is great
*Ps.* 105:12 but a few men in *n.*
34 caterpillars, and without *n.*
139:18 more in *n.* than the sand
147:4 he telleth *n.* of the stars
*Cant.* 6:8 and virgins without *n.*
*Is.* 21:17 residue of *n.* of archers
40:26 bring. out their host by *n.*
65:11 drink-offering to that *n.*
*Jer.* 2:28 *n.* of cities are thy gods
32 forgotten me days with. *n.*
11:13 accord. to *n.* of thy cities
44:28 small *n.* that escape sword
*Ezek.* 5:3 shalt take a few in *n.*
*Dan.* 9:2 I understood *n.* of years
*Hos.* 1:10 *n.* of Israel, *Rom.* 9:27
*Joel* 1:6 nation come up with. *n.*
*Nah.* 3:3 there is great *n.* of car.
*Luke* 22:3 Judas, being of the *n.*
*John* 6:10 sat, *n.* 5,000, *Acts* 4:4
*Acts* 1:15 *n.* of names were 120
5:36 to The. a *n.* of men joined
6:1 *n.* of discip. was multipl. 7
11:21 great *n.* bel. and turned
16:5 churches were incre. in *n.*
2 *Cor.* 10:12 not make ours. of *n.*
1 *Tim.* 5:9 let not wid. be in *n.*
*Rev.* 5:11 *n.* was 10,000 ti. 10,000
7:4 I heard the *n.* of them which
9:16 *n.* the army of horsemen
13:17 *n.* of name; 18 count *n.*
18 *n.* of a man, his *n.* is 666
15:2 had victory over *n.* of bea.
20:8 *n.* of Gog is as sand of sea

**NUMBER, Verb.**

*Gen.* 13:16 if a man can *n.* dust
15:5 stars, if able to *n.* them
*Lev.* 15:13 *n.* 7 days for cleansing
28 shall *n.* to herself 7 days
23:16 after 7th sab. sh. *n.* 50 days
25:8 sh. *n.* 7 sabbaths of years
*Num.* 1:3 Aaron shall *n.* them
49 thou shalt not *n.* tribe of L.
3:40 *n.* all first-born males of I.
4:23 until fifty years old *n.* th. 30
*Deut.* 16:9 seven weeks shalt thou *n.* begin to *n.*
1 *Sam.* 14:17 *n.* see who is gone
2 *Sam.* 24:1 go *n.* Is. and Judah
2 go *n.* people, 4; 1 *Chr.* 21:2
1 *K.* 20:25 *n.* thee an army like
1 *Chr.* 21:1 provok. Dav. to *n.* I.
27:24 J. began to *n.* finished n.
*Job* 38:37 who can *n.* the clouds?
39:2 canst thou *n.* the months?
*Ps.* 90:12 teach us to *n.* our days
*Is.* 65:12 will I *n.* you to the sw.
*Rev.* 7:9 multi. no man could *n.*

**NUMBERED.**

*Gen.* 13:16 shall thy seed be *n.*
16:10 not be *n.* for multi. 32:12
*Ex.* 38:25 *n.* of congregation, 26
*Num.* 1:21 those th. were *n.* of them, 23, 44, 46; 2:4, 13, 15, 19, 21, 23, 26, 28, 30
47 Levites were not *n.* 2:33
2:9 were *n.* in camp of Judah
16 were *n.* in camp of Reuben
24 *n.* of Ephraim; 31 *n.* of Dan
3:16 and Moses *n.* them, 42
39 *n.* of Levites were 22,000
4:34 *n.* sons of Kohathites, 37
38 were *n.* of Gershonites, 41
42 w. *n.* of sons of Merari, 45
7:2 princes over th. that we. *n.*
14:29 wildern. all that were *n.*
26:51 these were *n.* of chil. of I.
*Jos.* 8:10 Joshua *n.* the people
1 *Sam.* 15:4 S. *n.* peo. in Telaim
2 *Sam.* 18:1 David *n.* the people
24:10 heart sm. him after he *n.*
1 *K.* 3:8 people that cannot be *n.*
8:5 sheep and oxen that could not be *n.* 2 *Chr.* 5:6
20:15 *n.* princes of provinces
27 Is. were *n.* like two flocks
2 *K.* 3:6 Jehoram *n.* all Israel
1 *Chr.* 21:17 com. people to be *n.*
23:3 Lev. were *n.* fr. 30 years, 27
2 *Chr.* 2:17 Solo. *n.* all strangers
25:5 *n.* them from 20 years old
*Ezr.* 1:8 Cyrus *n.* the vessels to
*Ps.* 40:5 more than can be *n.*
*Ec.* 1:15 wanting cannot be *n.*
*Is.* 22:10 ye have *n.* the houses
53:12 *n.* with trans. *Mark* 15:28
*Jer.* 33:22 host of hea. can. be *n.*
*Dan.* 5:26 God hath *n.* thy king.
*Hos.* 1:10 sand of sea, can. be *n.*
*Mat.* 10:30 hairs of your head are all *n.* *Luke* 12:7
*Acts* 1:17 for he was *n.* with us
26 Matthias *n.* wi. 11 apostles

**NUMBEREST.**

*Ex.* 30:12 a ransom, wh. thou *n.* that be no plague wh. th. *n.*
*Job* 14:16 now thou *n.* my steps

**NUMBERING.**

*Gen.* 41:49 corn until he left *n.*
2 *Chr.* 2:17 after *n.* wherewith D.

**NUMBERS.**

1 *Chr.* 12:23 these are *n.* of bands
2 *Chr.* 17:14 these are *n.* of them
*Ps.* 71:15 I know not *n.* thereof

**NURSE.**

*Gen.* 24:59 sent away Re. and *n.*
35:8 Deborah, Rebek.'s *n.* died
*Ex.* 2:7 sh. I call to thee a *n.*?
*Ruth* 4:16 Naomi became *n.*
2 *Sam.* 4:4 *n.* took him up
2 *K.* 11:2 they hid him and his *n.* 2 *Chr.* 22:11
1 *Thes.* 2:7 as *n.* cherish. her ch.

**NURSE, ED.**

*Ex.* 2:7 she may *n.* the child
9 take this child and *n.* it, and the wo. took the ch. and *n.*
*Is.* 60:4 dau. sh. be *n.* at thy side

**NURSING.**

*Num.* 11:12 carry th. as *n.* father
*Is.* 49:23 kings be *n.* fathers, and queens thy *n.* mothers

**NURTURE.**

*Eph.* 6:4 bring th. up in *n.* of L.

**NUTS.**

*Gen.* 43:11 pres. *n.* and almonds
*Cant.* 6:11 down into gard. of *n.*

NYMPHAS. *Col.* 4:15

# O

**OAK.**

*Gen.* 35:4 Jacob hid gods und. *o.*
8 nurse was buried und. an *o.*
*Jos.* 24:26 set it up under an *o.*
*Jud.* 6:11 angel of L. sat und. *o.*
2 *Sam.* 18:9 went under an *o.*
10 Absalom hanged in an *o.*
14 was alive in midst of the *o*
1 *K.* 13:14 found man of G. un. *o.*
1 *Chr.* 10:12 buried bones un. *o.*
*Is.* 1:30 be as *o.* whose leaf. fad.
6:13 as teil-tree, or *o.* whose
44:14 cyp. and *o.* to make a god
*Ezek.* 6:13 idols under every *o.*

**OAKS.**

*Is.* 1:29 shall be asham. of the *o.*
2:13 day of Lord on all the *o.*
*Ezek.* 27:6 of *o.* they made oars
*Hos.* 4:13 burn incense under *o.*
*Amos* 2:9 Amorite strong as *o.*
*Zec.* 11:2 O ye *o.* of Bashan

**OAR, S.**

*Is.* 33:21 sh. go no galley with *o.*
*Ezek.* 27:6 of oaks of Ba. made *o.*
29 all that handle *o.* shall cry

**OATH.**

*Gen.* 24:8 be clear from my *o.* 41
26:3 I will perform the *o.* which I sware to Abraham, *Deut.* 7:8; *Ps.* 105:9; *Jer.* 11:5
28 let there be an *o.* betw. us
50:25 J. took *o.* of childr. of Is.
*Ex.* 22:11 *o.* of Lord be betw. us
*Lev.* 5:4 pronounce with an *o.*
*Num.* 5:19 priest char. her by *o.*
21 L. make thee an *o.* am. peo.
30:2 if a man swear an *o.* 10
13 ev. binding *o.* to afflict soul
*Deut.* 29:12 his *o.* wh. L. maketh
14 you only do I make this *o.*
*Jos.* 2:17 blameless of thine *o.*
9:20 wrath be on us beca. of *o.*
*Jud.* 21:5 Israel made a great *o.*
1 *Sam.* 14:26 people feared the *o.*
27 S. charged them with *o.* 28
2 *Sam.* 21:7 spared M. bec. of *o.*
1 *K.* 2:43 why hast not kept *o.*?
8:31 *o.* be laid on him, *o.* come before thine alt. 2 *Chr.* 6:22
18:10 he took an *o.* of kingdom
2 *K.* 11:4 Jehoiada took *o.*
1 *Chr.* 16:16 mindful of *o.* to Isa.
2 *Chr.* 15:15 Judah rejoiced at *o.*
*Neh.* 5:12 Neh. took *o.* of priests
10:29 an *o.* to walk in God's law
*Ec.* 8:2 in regard of *o.* of God
9:2 as he that feareth an *o.*
*Ezek.* 16:59 despised *o.* 17:18, 19
17:13 hath taken an *o.* of him
16 king, whose *o.* he despised
*Dan.* 9:11 and *o.* written in law
*Zec.* 8:17 love no false *o.*
*Mat.* 14:7 promised with *o.*
9 for the *o.*'s sake, *Mark* 6:26
26:72 deni. with *o.* I do not kn.
*Luke* 1:73 the *o.* which he sware
*Acts* 2:30 God hath swo. with *o.*
23:21 bound themselves with *o.*
*Heb.* 6:16 an *o.* for confirmation
17 God confirmed it by an *o.*
7:20 as not without an *o.* 21
28 *o.* which was since the law
*Jam.* 5:12 sw. not by any oth. *o.*

**OATHS.**
Ezek. 21:23 that have sworn o.
Hab. 3:9 naked, according to o.
Mat. 5:33 perform to L. thine o.

**OBADIAH.**
1 K. 18:3 Ahab called O. 4, 7, 16
2 Chr. 17:7 sent to O. 34:12
Ezr. 8:9 O. son of Jeh. went up
Neh. 10:5 O. seal. 12:25 O. was
Ob. 1 vision of O. thus saith

**OBED.**
Ruth 4:17 called his name O.
21 Boaz begat O. 1 Chr. 2:12; Mat. 1:5
1 Chr. 11:47 O. one of D.'s val. m.
2 Chr. 23:1 son of O. into coven.
Luke 3:32 Jes. wh. was son of O.

**OBED-EDOM.**
2 Sam. 6:10 carried the ark into the house of O. 11, 12; 1 Chr. 13:13, 14; 15:25
1 Chr. 15:18 O. a porter, 21, 24

**OBEDIENCE.**
Rom. 1:5 o. to faith among all
5:19 by o. of one many be made
6:16 or of o. unto righteousness
16:19 your o. is come abroad
26 made known for o. to faith
1 Cor. 14:34 women to be und. o.
2 Cor. 7:15 remembereth o. of all
10:5 ev. thought to o. of Christ
6 disobed. when o is fulfilled
Phile. 21 confidence in thy o.
Heb. 5:8 learned o. by things suf.
1 Pet. 1:2 sanctifica. of Sp. to o.

**OBEDIENT.**
Ex. 24:7 Lord hath said, Be o.
Num. 27:20 that Israel may be o.
Deut. 4:30 be o. to his voice
Deut. 8:20 bec. ye wo. not be o.
2 Sam. 22:45 strangers shall be o.
Prov. 25:12 reprover on o. ear
Is. 1:19 if o. ye shall eat good
42:24 nei. were th. o. to his law
Acts 6:7 priests were o. to faith
Rom. 15:18 make Ge. o. by word
2 Cor. 2:9 know whether ye be o.
Eph. 6:5 servants be o. Tit. 2:9
Phil. 2:8 Ch. became o. to death
Tit. 2:5 wives, be o. to husbands
1 Pet. 1:14 be as o. children

**OBEY.**
Gen. 27:8 son, o. my voice, 13, 43
Ex. 5:2 who is Lord that I o.
19:5 now if ye will o. my voice
23:21 o. his voice; 22 indeed o.
Deut. 11:27 a blessing if ye o. L.
13:4 o. his voice, 27:10; 30:2, 8; 1 Sam. 12:14
30:20 thou mayest o. his voice
Jos. 24:24 L.'s voice will we o.
1 Sam. 8:19 peo. refused to o. S.
15:22 to o. is bet. than sacrifice
Neh. 9:17 and refused to o.
Job 36:11 if they o. and serve
Ps. 18:44 as th. hear, they sh. o.
Prov. 30:17 despis. to o. mother
Is. 11:14 childr. of Am. o. them
Jer. 7:23 o. my voice, 11:4, 7
26:13 amend your ways, o. voice of the Lord your God, 38:20; Zec. 6:15
35:14 Rechab. o. their father's
42:6 we will o. the voice of the L. our God, that it may be well with us wh. we o. the L.
Dan. 7:27 shall serve and o. him
Mat. 8:27 winds and sea o. him.? Mark 4:41; Luke 8:25
Mark 1:27 unclean spirits o. him
Luke 17:6 plucked up, it shall o.
Acts 5:29 o. G. rather than men
32 God hath given to them o.
Rom. 2:8 them that o. unright.
6:12 that ye sho. o. it in lusts
16 servants to o. his servants ye are to whom ye o.
Eph. 6:1 o. parents. Col. 3:20
Col. 3:22 servants o. masters
Tit. 3:1 put them in mind to o.
Heb. 5:9 salvation to all that o.
13:17 o. them that have the rule
Jam. 3:3 put bits that th. may o.

**Not OBEY, OBEY not.**
Deut. 11:28 curse, if ye will not o. 28:62; 1 Sam. 12:12; Job 36:12; Jer. 12:17; 18:10
21:18 not o. voice of his father
1 Sam. 15:19 wh. didst thou n. o.?
Jer. 42:13 we will not o. the L.
Dan. 9:11 might n. o. thy voice
Acts 7:39 our fathers would n. o.
Rom. 2:8 and do not o. the truth
Gal. 3:1 who bewitched you, th. you should not o.? 5:7
2 Thes. 1:8 ven. on th. that o. n.
3:14 if any man o. n. our word
1 Pet. 3:1 if any man o. not word
4:17 them that o. not gospel?

**OBEYED.**
Gen. 22:18 bec. thou hast o. 26:5
28:7 Ja. o. his father and moth.
Jos. 22:2 have o. my voice
1 Sam. 15:20 I have o. voice of L.
24 I feared peo. and o. th. voice
28:21 handmaid o. thy voice
1 Chr. 29:23 Israel o. Solomon
2 Chr. 11:4 they o. words of L.
Jer. 34:10 they o. and let th. go
35:8 we o. voice of Jonadab, 10
18 o. the comm. of your father
Dan. 9:10 nei. have we o. the L.
Hag. 1:12 people o. voice of L.
Acts 5:36 many as o. Theud. 37
Rom. 6:17 o. from heart th. doc.
Phil. 2:12 ye o. not in my pres.
Heb. 11:8 by faith Abraham o.
1 Pet. 3:6 Sarah o. Abraham

**Not OBEYED.**
Jos. 5:6 consumed, they o. n.
Jud. 2:2 n. o. my voice, 6:10
1 K. 20:36 hast n. o. voice of L.
2 K. 18:12 they o. not voice of L.
Prov. 5:13 not o. voice of teach.
Jer. 3:13 ye have n. o. my voice, 25; 42:21; 43:4, 7; 44:23
9:13 n. o. my voice, 11:8; 17:23; 32:23; 40:3; Dan. 9:10, 14
Zep. 3:2 she o. not the voice
Rom. 10:16 have n. all o. gospel

**OBEYEDST, ETH.**
1 Sam. 28:18 o. not voice of L.
Is. 50:10 who o voice of serv.?
Jer. 7:28 a nation that o. not the Lord
Jer. 11:3 cur. be man that o. not
22:21 that thou o. not my voice

**OBEYING.**
Jud. 2:17 fa. o. they did not so
1 Sam. 15:22 as in o. voice of L.
1 Pet. 1:22 puri. souls in o. truth

**OBEISANCE.**
Gen. 37:7 your sheaves made o.
9 sun, moon, 11 stars made o.
43:28 they made o. to Joseph
Ex. 18:7 Moses did o. to father
2 Sam. 1:2 Amalek. did o. to D.
14:4 woman of Tekoah did o.
15:5 when any man ca. to do o.
1 K. 1:16 Bath-sheba did o. to D.
2 Chr. 24:17 princes of J. made o.

**OBJECT.**
Acts 24:19 o. if th. had aught ag.

**OBLATION.**
Lev. 2:4 o. of a meat-off. 5, 7, 13
12 as for o. of first-fruits offer
3:1 if his o. be a sacri. of peace
22:18 offer his o. for his vows
Num. 18:9 o. of theirs be holy
31:50 we have bro. an o. for L.
Is. 19:21 Egypt. sh. do o. to L.
40:20 impoverish, he hath no o.
66:3 offereth o. as swine's flesh
Jer. 14:12 when they offer an o.
Ezek. 44:30 ev. o. sh. be priest's
45:1 when ye divide land, off. o.
13 o. ye shall offer, 48:9, 20, 21
16 give this o. for prince in Is.
Dan. 2:46 sho. offer an o. to Da.
9:21 time of o. 27 o. to cease

**OBLATIONS.**
Lev. 7:38 com. Israel to offer o.
2 Chr. 31:14 distribute o. of Lord
Is. 1:13 bring no more vain o
Ezek. 20:40 require first-fru. of o.

**OBSCURE.**
Prov. 20:20 lamp put in o. dark.

**OBSCURITY.**
Is. 29:18 blind see out of o.
58:10 shall thy light rise in o.
59:9 wait for light, but beho. o.

**OBSERVATION.**
Luke 17:20 king. of G. not wi. o.

**OBSERVE.**
Ex. 12:17 ye shall o. feast of unleav. bread, 24; Deut. 16:1
31:16 o. sabbath; 34:22 o. feast
34:11 o. that wh. I comm. thee this day, Deut. 12:28; 24:8
Lev. 19:26 nor enchant. o. times
37 ye sh. o. all my statutes, 2 Chr. 7:17; Neh. 1:5; Ps. 105:45; Ezek. 37:24
Num. 28:2 sacrifice shall ye o.
Deut. 16:13 o. feast of tabernac.
1 K. 20:33 men did diligently o.
Ps. 107:43 will o. these things
119:34 o. with my whole heart
Prov. 23:26 let thine eyes o. ways
Jer. 8:7 the crane and swallow o.
Ezek. 20:18 neither o. judgments
Hos. 13:7 as a leop. will I o. th.
Jon. 2:8 that o. lying vanities
Mat. 28:20 teaching them to o.
Acts 16:21 custo. not lawful to o.
21:25 Gentiles o. no such thing
Gal. 4:10 ye o. days, and months
1 Tim. 5:21 then o. these things

See DO.

**OBSERVED.**
Gen. 37:11 his father o. saying
Ex. 12:42 it is a night to be o.
Num. 15:22 not o. commandm.
Deut. 33:9 for Levi o. thy word
2 Sam. 11:16 when J. o. the city
2 K. 21:6 Manasseh o. the times, 2 Chr. 33:6
Hos. 14:8 I heard him, o. him
Mark 6:20 He. feared and o. him
10:20 these I o. from my youth

**OBSERVER, S.**
Deut. 18:10 th. shall not be an o.
14 these nations hearken. to o.

**OBSERVEST, ETH.**
Ec. 11:4 he that o. the wind
Is. 42:20 seeing things, o. not

**OBSTINATE.**
Deut. 2:30 L. G. made his hea. o.
Is. 48:4 I knew that thou art o.

**OBTAIN.**
Gen. 16:2 may be I may o. chil.
Prov. 8:35 o. favor of the Lord
Is. 35:10 they shall o. joy, 51:11
Dan. 11:21 shall o. the kingdom
Luke 20:35 worthy to o. th. world
Rom. 11:31 thro' mercy o. mercy
1 Cor. 9:24 so run, that ye may o.
1 Cor. 9:25 do it to o. corrupt. cro.
1 Thes. 5:9 to o. salvation by L.
2 Tim. 2:10 o. salvation in C. J.
Heb. 4:16 that we may o. mercy
11:35 might o. bet. resurrection
Jam. 4:2 ye kill and cannot o.

**OBTAINED.**
*Neh.* 13:6 I *o.* leave of the king
*Est.* 2:9 Esth. *o.* kindn. 17 she *o.*
*Hos.* 2:23 that had not *o.* mercy
*Acts* 1:17 had *o.* part of ministry
22:28 great sum *o.* I freedom
26:22 having *o.* the help of God
27:13 suppos. they *o.* th. purpo.
*Rom.* 11:7 Is. not *o.* what he seek. for, but the elect. hath *o.* it
30 *o.* mercy thro' their unbelief
1 *Cor.* 7:25 one that hath *o.* mer.
*Eph.* 1:11 we have *o.* inheritance
1 *Tim.* 1:13 I *o.* mercy, bec. ig. 16
*Heb.* 1:4 *o.* more excellent name
6:15 endured, he *o.* the promis.
8:6 he *o.* a more excel. ministry
9:12 hav. *o.* eternal redemption
11:2 the elders *o.* good report, 39
4 Abel *o.* witness he was righ.
33 *o.* promises, stop. mouths
1 *Pet.* 2:10 *o.* mercy, now have *o.*
2 *Pet.* 1:1 *o.* like precious faith
*See* FAVOR.

**OBTAINING.**
2 *Thes.* 2:14 *o.* the glory of our L.

**OCCASION.**
*Gen.* 43:18 he may seek *o.* ag. us
*Jud.* 9:33 as find *o.* 1 *Sam.* 10:7
14:4 Samson sought *o.* ag. Phil.
2 *Sam.* 12:14 given *o.* to enemies
*Ezr.* 7:20 thou shalt have *o.*
*Jer.* 2:24 in her *o.* who can turn?
*Ezek.* 18:3 not have *o.* any more
*Dan.* 6:4 sought to find *o.* could find none *o.*
*Rom.* 7:8 *o.* by commandment, 11
14:13 put not *o.* to fall in way
2 *Cor.* 5:12 we give you *o.* to glo.
8:8 I speak by *o.* of forwardness
11:12 that I may cut off *o.* them which desire *o.*
*Gal.* 5:13 use not liberty for an *o.*
1 *Tim.* 5:14 younger give none *o.*
1 *John* 2:10 none *o.* of stumbling

**OCCASIONED.**
1 *Sam.* 22:22 have *o.* death of all

**OCCASIONS**
*Deut.* 22:14 *o.* of speech aga. 17
*Job* 33:10 findeth *o.* against me

**OCCUPATION.**
*Gen.* 46:33 wh. *o.*? 47:3; *Jon* 1:8
*Acts* 18:3 by *o.* were tent-makers
19:25 workmen of like *o.*

**OCCUPY.**
*Ezek.* 27:9 marin. *o.* merchandise
*Luke* 19:13 servan. *o.* till I come

**OCCUPIED, ETH.**
*Ex.* 38:24 gold was *o.* for work
*Jud.* 16:11 ropes th. never we. *o.*
*Ezek.* 27:16 Syria *o.* 19 Javan *o.*
21 Arabia *o.* 22 Sh. *o.* in fairs
1 *Cor.* 14:16 *o.* room of unlearned
*Heb.* 13:9 profited th. that ha. *o.*

**OCCUPIERS.**
*Ezek.* 27:27 *o.* of merchandi. fall

**OCCURRENT.**
1 *K.* 5:4 adversary nor evil *o.*

**ODD.**
*Num.* 3:48 *o.* num. to be redeem.

**ODED.**
2 *Chr.* 15:1 on Azariah son of O.
28:9 prophet was th. called O.

**ODIOUS.**
1 *Chr.* 19:6 made themselves *o.*
*Prov.* 30:23 for an *o.* woman

**ODOR, S.**
*Lev.* 26:31 not smell sav. of sw. *o.*
2 *Chr.* 16:14 in bed of sweet *o.*
*Est.* 2:12 oil of myrrh sweet *o.*
*Jer.* 34:5 sh. they burn *o.* for th.
*Dan.* 2:46 offer sweet *o.* to Daniel
*John* 12:3 filled with *o.* of ointm.
*Phil.* 4:18 an *o.* of a sweet smell
*Rev.* 5:8 golden vials full of *o.*
18:13 no man buyeth their *o.*

**OFFENCE.**
1 *Sam.* 25:31 this shall be no *o.*
*Is.* 8:14 *o.* to both houses of Is.
*Hos.* 5:15 they acknowl. their *o.*
*Mat.* 16:23 Sa. thou art *o.* to me
18:7 woe to man by wh. *o.* com.
*Acts* 24:16 a conscience void of *o.*
*Rom.* 5:15 not as *o.* so is free gift, for thro' *o.* of one m. dead. 18
17 by one man's *o.* death reig.
*Rom.* 5:20 that the *o.* might abo.
9:33 stumbling-stone, rock of *o.*
14:20 man who eateth with *o.*
1 *Cor.* 10:32 give no. *o.* 2 *Cor.* 6:3
2 *Cor.* 11:7 have I committed *o.*
*Gal.* 5:11 *o.* of cross ceased
*Phil.* 1:10 with. *o.* till day of Ch.
1 *Pet.* 2:8 *o.* to them wh. stumble

**OFFENCES.**
*Ec.* 10:4 yielding pacifi. great *o.*
*Mat.* 18:7 beca. of *o.* for it must needs be that *o.* *Luke* 17:1
*Rom.* 4:25 was deliver. for our *o.*
5:16 the free gift of many *o.*
16:17 mark them which cause *o.*

**OFFEND.**
*Job* 34:31 I will not *o.* any more
*Ps.* 73:15 I sho. *o.* ag. generation
119:165 nothing shall *o.* them
*Jer.* 2:3 that devour him shall *o.*
50:7 adversaries said, We *o.* not
*Hos.* 4:15 let not Judah *o.*
*Hab.* 1:11 shall pass over and *o.*
*Mat.* 5:29 if thy right eye *o.* thee
30 if thy right hand *o.* thee, 18:8, 9; *Mark* 9:43, 45, 47
13:41 gather all things that *o.*
17:27 lest we should *o.* them
18:6 whoso *o.* one of these, *Mark* 9:42; *Luke* 17:2
*John* 6:61 said, Doth this *o.* you?
1 *Cor.* 8:13 brother *o.* lest he *o.*
*Jam.* 2:10 yet *o.* in one point
3:2 in many things we *o.* all

**OFFENDED.**
*Gen.* 20:9 ha. I *o.* thee? *Jer.* 37:18
40:1 butler and baker had *o.*
2 *K.* 18:14 have *o.* return fr. me
2 *Chr.* 28:13 have *o.* against L.
*Prov.* 18:19 a brother *o.* is harder
*Ezek.* 25:12 Edom hath greatly *o.*
*Hos.* 13:1 when Ephraim *o.* in B.
*Mat.* 11:6 blessed is he who shall not be *o.* *Luke* 7:23
13:21 when persecution aris. by and by he is *o.* *Mark* 4:17
57 were *o.* in him, *Mark* 6:3
15:12 Pharis. *o.* after they heard
24:10 then shall many be *o.*
26:31 *o.* becau. of me this night
33 tho' all men shall be *o.* yet will I never be *o.* *Mark* 14:29
*John* 16:1 ye should not be *o.*
*Acts* 25:8 nor ag. Cesar ha. I *o.*
*Rom.* 14:21 whereby brother is *o.*
2 *Cor.* 11:29 is *o.* and I burn not?

**OFFENDER, S.**
1 *K.* 1:21 I and my son counted *o.*
*Is.* 29:21 man *o.* for a word
*Acts* 25:11 if I be an *o.* or have

**OFFER.**
*Ex.* 22:29 to *o.* the first-fruits
23:18 shalt not *o.* blood, 34:25
29:39 one lamb *o.* in morning, other at even, 41; *Nu.* 28:4, 8
30:9 *o.* no strange inc. thereon
*Lev.* 1:3 *o.* male without blemish, 3:6; 22:19, 20
2:13 with offerings thou shalt *o.*
3:1 if he *o.* peace-offering, *o.* it without blem. 6; 9:2; 19:5
12 goat he shall *o.* before Lord
5:8 *o.* for sin-offering first, 9:7
6:14 sons of A. *o.* before L. 22; 14:19; 15:15, 30; *Num.* 6:11
7:3 *o.* of it all the fat thereof
12 *o.* it for a thanksgiv. 22:29
38 *o.* their oblations to the L.
17:7 no more *o.* sacri. to devils
9 to the door to *o.* it to Lord
19:6 eaten same day ye *o.* it
21:6 bread of their G. they do *o.*
21 hath blemish, not come to *o.*
*Num.* 7:11 they *o.* their offerings
8:11 Aaron *o.* Levites, 13, 15
9:7 that we may not *o.*
15:7 *o.* th. part of a hin of wine
19 shall *o.* a heave-offer. 18:24, 26, 28, 29
16:40 no stranger come to *o.* in.
28:24 ye shall *o.* daily the meat
*Deut.* 12:14 L. sh. choose, there *o.*
18:3 priest's due fr. them th. *o.*
33:19 shall *o.* sacrifices of righteousness, *Ps.* 4:5
*Jud.* 3:18 made an end to *o.* pre.
1 *Sam.* 1:21 went up to *o.* to L.
2:19 with her husb. to *o.* sacri.
28 him my priest, to *o.* on alt.
2 *Sam.* 24:12 *o.* thee three things, 1 *Chr.* 21:10
1 *K.* 13:2 *o.* priests of high places
1 *Chr.* 29:14 to *o.* so willingly, 17
2 *Chr.* 24:14 made vessels to *o.*
*Ezr.* 6:10 *o.* sacrifices to God
*Ps.* 16:4 of blood will I not *o.*
*Ps.* 27:6 therefore I *o.* in tabern.
50:14 *o.* to God thanksgiving
51:19 then sh. they *o.* bullocks
66:15 will *o.* to thee burnt sacr.
72:10 kings of Sheba sh. *o.* gifts
116:17 *o.* sacrifice of thanksgiv.
*Is.* 57:7 wentest up to *o.* sacrifice
*Jer.* 11:12 gods to wh. th. *o.* inc.
*Ezek.* 20:31 when ye *o.* your gifts
44:7 when ye *o.* my bread
15 they shall *o.* to me the fat
45:1 ye shall *o.* an oblation to the Lord, 13; 48:9
*Dan.* 2:46 *o.* an oblation to Dan.
*Hos.* 9:4 not *o.* wine-off. to Lord
*Amos* 4:5 *o.* sacrifice of thanksg.
*Hag.* 2:14 th. *o.* there is unclean
*Mal.* 1:7 ye *o.* polluted bread
8 *o.* it now to thy governor
3:3 *o.* to the Lord an offering in
*Mat.* 5:24 then come and *o.* gift
8:4 *o.* gift Moses commanded, *Mark* 1:44; *Luke* 5:14
*Luke* 6:29 cheek, *o.* also other
11:12 will he *o.* him scorpion?
*Heb.* 5:1 *o.* gifts and sacrifices
3 ought for hims. to *o.* for sins
7:27 needeth not to *o.* sacrifice
8:3 h.-priest ordained to *o.* this man ha. somewhat also to *o.*
9:25 he should *o.* himself often
13:15 by him let us *o.* sacrifice
1 *Pet.* 2:5 by J. C. to *o.* sacrifice
*Rev.* 8:3 should *o.* with prayers
*See* BURNT-OFFERINGS.

**OFFERED.**
*Gen.* 31:54 Ja. *o.* sacrifice, 46:1
*Ex.* 35:22 every man *o.* offering
*Lev.* 9:15 slew goat, *o.* it for sin
10:1 Nadab and Abi. *o.* strange fire, 16:1; *Num.* 3:4; 26:61
*Num.* 7:2 *o.* for the dedicat. 10
8:21 Aaron *o.* them as offering
22:40 Balak *o.* oxen and sheep, 23:2, 4, 14, 30
*Jud.* 5:2 willingly *o.* themselv. 9
13:19 took a kid and *o.* it
1 *Sam.* 1:4 time that Elkanah *o.*
2 *Sam.* 6:17 *o.* peace-offer. 24:25
1 *K.* 8:62 Solomon and Is. *o.* 63
12:32 Jeroboam *o.* in Beth-el, 33
22:43 peo. *o.* yet in high places

2 *K.* 3:20 meat-offering was *o.*
16:12 A. approached altar and *o.*
1 *Chr.* 29:9 that they *o.* willingly
2 *Chr.* 15:11 Asa *o.* to the Lord
17:16 Amaziah willingly *o.*
*Ezr.* 1:6 that was willingly *o.*
2:68 some of fathers *o.* freely
6:17 *o.* at dedic. of house of God
7:15 freely *o.* to the G. of Israel
10:19 they *o.* a ram of the flock
*Neh.* 11:2 willingly *o.* themselves
12:43 that day th. *o.* great sacri.
*Is.* 57:6 hast *o.* a meat-offering
66:3 as if he *o.* swine's blood
*Jer.* 32:29 have *o.* incense to Ba.
*Ezek.* 20:28 *o.* there th. sacrifices
*Dan.* 11:18 reproach *o.* to cease
*Amos* 5:25 have ye *o.* me sacri.?
*Jon.* 1:16 and *o.* sacrifice to Lord
*Mal.* 1:11 inc. be *o.* to my name
*Acts* 8:18 Simon *o.* them money
15:29 meats *o.* to idols, 21:25
21:26 an offering should be *o.*
1 *Cor.* 8:1 things *o.* to idols, 4, 7, 10; 10:19, 28
*Phil.* 2:17 if I be *o.* on the service
2 *Tim.* 4:6 I am ready to be *o.*
*Heb.* 5:7 he had *o.* up prayers
7:27 when he *o.* up himself
9:7 blood, wh. he *o.* for himself
9 *o.* gifts; 14 *o.* himself to G.
28 C. *o.* to bear sins of many
11:4 by faith Abel *o.* to God
17 Ab. when tried, *o.* up Isaac
*Jam.* 2:21 A. justified when he *o.*

**OFFERETH.**

*Lev.* 6:26 priest that *o.* it for sin
7:18 imputed to him that *o.* it
21:8 he *o.* the bread of thy God
*Ps.* 50:23 *o.* praise glorifieth me
*Is.* 66:3 he that *o.* oblation as if

**OFFERING, Substantive.**

*Gen.* 4:3 Cain brought *o.* unto L.
4 L. had respect to Abel and *o.*
*Ex.* 25:2 bring me *o.* of ev. man
30:13 half shekel be *o.* of Lord
15 *o.* to Lord make atonement
*Lev.* 1:2 bring your *o.* of cattle
14 *o.* of fowls; 2:1 fine flour
2:11 no meat-*o.* made with leav.
3:2 lay his hand on head of *o.* 8
6:20 *o.* of Aaron and sons
7:16 if *o.* be vow, or volunt. *o.*
*Num.* 5:15 *o.* of jeal. *o.* of mem.
*Num.* 7:10 princes off. *o.* bef. alt.
8:11 offer Levites for an *o.* 21
9:13 *o.* of L. in appointed seas.
16:15 said, Respect not their *o.*
1 *Sam.* 2:29 wher. kick at mi. *o.*?
3:14 shall not be purged with *o.*
26:19 if Lord have stirred thee up ag. me, let him accept *o.*
1 *K.* 18:29 prophesied till *o.* of evening sacrifice
1 *Chr.* 16:29 *o.* come, *Ps.* 96:8
*Neh.* 10:39 Is. sh. bring *o.* of corn
*Is.* 43:23 nor caus. th. serv. wi. *o.*
53:10 make his soul *o.* for sin
66:20 bring your breth. for an *o.*
*Ezek.* 20:28 provocat. of their *o.*
*Zep.* 3:10 daughter bring my *o.*
*Mal.* 1:10 nor accept *o.* at hand
13 bro. *o.* should I accept this?
2:13 regardeth not *o.* any more
3:3 offer to Lord an *o.* in right.
*Rom.* 15:16 *o.* of Gent. be accept.
*Eph.* 5:2 an *o.* to God for us
*Heb.* 10:5 *o.* thou wouldest not, 8
10 through *o.* of body of Jesus
14 by one *o.* he hath perfected
18 there is no more *o.* for sin

*See* BURNT, DRINK, FREE.

**OFFERING, Participle.**

1 *Sam.* 7:10 as S. was *o.* burnt-o.
2 *Chr.* 8:13 *o.* according to com.
29:29 made end of *o.* the king
30:22 seven days, *o.* peace-off.
35:14 sons of Aa. were busied *o.*
*Ezr.* 7:16 priests *o.* willingly for
*Jer.* 11:17 provoke me *o.* to Baal
*Luke* 23:36 and *o.* him vinegar
*Heb.* 10:11 ev. priest *o.* sacrifices

**Heave-OFFERING.**

*Ex.* 29:27 sanctify the *h.-o.*
*Lev.* 7:14 oblation for a *heave-o.*
*Num.* 15:19 sh. offer up *h.-o.* 20
21 of first dough gi. *h.-o.* to L.
18:24 tithes they offer as a *h.-o.*
28 give the Lord's *h.-o.* to Aa.
31:29 give to Eleazar for *h.-o.*
41 tribute wh. was the L. *h.-o.*

*See* MADE, MAKE, FIRE, BURNT-*offering.*

**Peace-OFFERING.**

*Lev.* 3:1 sacrifice of *p.-o.* 3, 6, 9

**Sin-OFFERING.**

*Ex.* 29:14 the flesh of bullock sh. thou burn, it is a *s.-o. Lev.* 4:21, 24; 5:9, 11, 12
30:10 bl. of *s.-o.* of atonements
*Lev.* 4:3 let him bring a young bullock without blemish, for a *s.-o.* 16:3, 27; *Num.* 8:8
25 priest take blood of *s.-o.* 5:9
29 lay hand on head of *s.-o.* 33
32 bri. lamb for *s.-o. Num.* 6:14
5:6 lamb or kid of goats for *s.-o.* 9:3; 16:5, 15, 27; 23:19
8 priest shall offer the *s.-o.* fir.
6:25 this is the law of *s.-o.* 7:37
7:7 as *s.-o.* so is trespass, 14:13
9:2 take a young calf for a *s.-o.*
10:16 Moses sought goat of *s.-o.*
17 why have ye not eaten *s.-o.*
12:6 bring turtle-dove for a *s.-o.*
16:25 fat of *s.-o.* shall be burnt
*Num.* 7:16 kid of goats for *s.-o.* 22, 28; 15:24; 28:15; 29:5
2 *Chr.* 29:24 *s.-o.* made for Israel
*Ezr.* 8:35 12 he-goats for *s.-o.*
*Ps.* 40:6 *s.-o.* hast not required
*Ezek.* 43:19 priest bull. for *s.-o.*
25 every day a goat for a *s.-o.*
44:27 sanctuary, shall offer *s.-o.*
29 they shall eat the *sin-o.*
46:20 place wh. priests boil *s.-o.*

**Trespass-OFFERING.**

*Lev.* 5:6 he sh. bring *t.-o.* to L.
15 lambs without ble. for *t.-o.*
6:5 shall give it in day of *t.-o.*
14:12 take one he-lamb for *t.-o.* 21, 24, 25; *Num.* 6:12
1 *Sam.* 6:3 any wise return *t.-o.*
4 what shall be the *t.-o.*? 8, 17
*Ezek.* 40:39 to slay *t.-o.* 42:13
44:29 eat *t.-o.* and ev. dedicated
46:20 where priests sh. boil *t.-o.*

**Wave-OFFERING.**

*Ex.* 29:24 for a *w.-o.* 26; *Lev.* 7:30; 8:27, 29; 9:21; 10:15; 14:12, 24; 23:20; *Num.* 6:20
27 sanctify breast of *w.-o.*
*Lev.* 23:15 bro. sheaf of *wave-o.*

**Wood-OFFERING.**

*Neh.* 10:34 cast lots for *wood-o.*
13:31 *w.-o.* at times appointed

**OFFERINGS.**

*Lev.* 1:10 if his *o.* be of the flocks
*Lev.* 2:13 with all thy *o.* shalt offer salt
1 *Sam.* 2:29 fat with chief of *o.*
2 *Sam.* 1:21 let th. be no fie. of *o.*
2 *Chr.* 31:12 people brought in *o.*
35:8 gave priests for passo. *o.* 9
13 holy *o.* sod they in pots
*Neh.* 10:37 first-fruits of *o.* 12:44
*Ps.* 20:3 L. remember all thy *o.*
*Jer.* 41:5 *o.* and incense in hands
*Ezek.* 20:40 there will I requi. *o.*
*Hos.* 8:13 sacrifice flesh for *o.*
*Amos* 5:25 ye off. me *o.* 40 yrs.?
*Mal.* 3:4 *o.* of Judah be pleasant
8 robbed thee? in tithes and *o.*
*Luke* 21:4 of abund. cast in to *o.*
*Acts* 24:17 to bring alms and *o.*

*See* BURNT, DRINK, FREE.

*Made by* FIRE.

**Heave-OFFERINGS.**

*Num.* 18:8 given charge of *h.-o.*
*Deut.* 12:6 ye shall bring *heave-o.*

**OFFERINGS of the Lord.**

1 *Sam.* 2:17 men abhor. *o. of t. L.*

*See* MEAT.

**Peace-OFFERINGS.**

*Ex.* 24:5 sacrifice *p-o.* of oxen
29:28 a heave-offering of *p.-o*
32:6 people brought *peace-o.*
*Lev.* 4:26 shall burn as fat of *p.-o.* 31, 35; 6:12
7:11 law of sacri. of *p.-o.* 13, 37
17:5 offer them for *p.-o.* 23:19
*Num.* 6:14 lamb *p.-o.* 17 a ram
7:17 sacri. of *p.-o.* two oxen, five lambs, 23, 29, 35, 41; 29:39
10:10 blow over sacrifice of *p.-o.*
*Jos.* 8:31 Joshua sacrificed *p.-o.*
22:23 if offer *p.-o.* let L. req. it
*Jud.* 20:26 Is. offered *p.-o.* 21:4
1 *Sam.* 10:8 offer *peace-o.* 11:15
2 *Sam.* 6:17 D. offered *p.-o.* 24:25; 1 *Chr.* 21:26
1 *K.* 3:15 Sol. offered *p.-o.* 8:63
9:25 thrice a year S. offer. *p.-o.*
2 *Chr.* 31:2 appo. priests for *p.-o.*
33:16 Manasseh offered *p.-o.*
*Prov.* 7:14 I have *p.-o.* with me
*Ezek.* 45:15 *p.-o.* to make rec. 17
46:2 priest prepare his *p.-o.* and
12 prince prep. voluntary *p.-o.*
*Amos* 5:22 not regard *p.-o.* of fat

**Sin-OFFERINGS.**

*Neh.* 10:33 *sin-o.* to make atone.

**Thank-OFFERINGS.**

2 *Chr.* 29:31 bring *t.-o.* to house
33:16 altar, and sacrificed *t.-o.*

**Wave-OFFERINGS.**

*Num.* 18:11 *w.-o.* I have given

**Wine-OFFERINGS.**

*Hos.* 9:4 not off. *w.-o.* pleas. to G.

**OFFICE.**

*Gen.* 41:13 me he restored to *o.*
*Ex.* 1:16 wh. ye do *o.* of midwife
1 *Chr.* 6:32 they waited on th. *o.*
9:22 David did ordain in set *o.*
2 *Chr.* 24:11 chest bro. to king's *o.*
31:18 in th. set *o.* they sancti.
*Neh.* 13:13 their *o.* was to distri.
*Ps.* 109:8 let another take his *o.*
*Ezek.* 44:13 sh. not do *o.* of priest
*Rom.* 11:13 I magnify my *o.*
12:4 all mem. have not same *o.*
1 *Tim.* 3:1 if a man desire *o.*
10 let them use *o.* of deacon, 13
*Heb.* 7:5 receive *o.* of priesthood

**Priest's OFFICE.**

*Ex.* 28:1 minister to me in the *p.'s o.* 3, 4, 41; 29:1, 44; 30:30; 35:19; 40:13, 15; *Lev.* 7:35; 16:32; *Num.* 3:3
29:9 *p.'s o.* shall be theirs
31:10 minister in *p.'s o.* 39:41
*Num.* 3:4 Itha. minis. in *p.'s o.*
18:7 thou and sons keep *p.'s o.*
*Deut.* 10:6 Elea. min. in *p.'s o.*
1 *Chr.* 6:10 Aza. executed *p.'s o.*
2 *Chr.* 11:14 cast th. off fr. *p.'s o.*
*Luke* 1:8 Zacharias exec. *p.'s o.*

**OFFICER.**

*Gen.* 37:36 Poti. *o.* of Phar. 39:1
*Jud.* 9:28 is not Zebul his *o.*?
1 *K.* 4:5 Zabud was principal *o.*
19 Geber was only *o.* in land
22:9 Ahab called an *o.* and said
2 *K.* 8:6 king appointed *o.*
25:19 Nebuzaradan took *o.*

*Mat.* 5:25 deliv. thee to *o.* and *o.* cast into prison, 12:58

**OFFICERS.**

*Gen.* 40:2 Pha. wroth with two *o.*
41:34 let P. appoint *o.* over land
*Ex.* 5:15 *o.* of Israel cried to Ph.
*Ex.* 5:19 *o.* did see th. we. in ev.
*Num.* 11:16 gather unto me the *o.* *Deut.* 31:28
*Deut.* 1:15 made th. *o.* am. tribes
16:18 judges and *o.* sh. th. make
20:5 *o.* shall speak to people, 8
1 *Sam.* 8:15 viney. give to his *o.*
1 *K.* 4:5 Azariah over the *o.*
7 Solomon had 12 *o.* over Isr.
2 *K.* 11:15 Jehoiada comman. *o.*
18 appointed *o.* over the house, 2 *Chr.* 23:18
24:12 Jehoia. went out with *o.*
15 *o.* and mighty car. he away
1 *Chr.* 23:4 6,000 were *o.* and jud.
26:29 Chenaniah and sons for *o.*
2 *Chr.* 8:10 Solomon's *o.* 250 bare
19:11 Levites shall be *o.* bef. y.
*Est.* 9:3 *o.* of kings helped Jews
*Is.* 60:17 I will make th. *o.* peace
*Jer.* 29:26 be *o.* in house of Lord
*John* 7:32 priests sent *o.* to take
46 *o.* answ. Never man spake
18:3 Judas having received *o.*
12 *o.* took Je. 22 *o.* struck Jes.
*Acts* 5:22 the *o.* found them not

**OFFICES.**

1 *Sam.* 2:36 put me into prie. *o.*
1 *Chr.* 24:3 dis. priests acc. to *o.*
2 *Chr.* 7:6 priests waited on th. *o.*
*Neh.* 13:14 not good deeds for *o.*

**OFFSCOURING.**

*Lam.* 3:45 hast made us as *o.*
1 *Cor.* 4:13 *o.* of all things

**OFFSPRING.**

*Job* 5:25 thy *o.* as grass of earth
21:8 *o.* is estab. bef. their eyes
27:14 *o.* not satisfied with bread
31:8 let my *o.* be rooted out
*Is.* 22:24 sh. hang on him, the *o.*
44:3 pour blessing on thine *o.*
48:19 *o.* of bowels like gravel
61:9 their *o.* shall be known
65:23 seed of the blessed, and *o.*
*Acts* 17:28 we are also his *o.* 29
*Rev.* 22:16 I am the *o.* of David

**OFT.**

2 *K.* 4:8 as *o.* as he passed by
*Mat.* 9:14 w. do we and P. fast *o.*?
17:15 ofttimes he fall. into fire, and *o.* into water, *Mark* 9:22
18:21 how *o.* sh. my broth. sin?
*Mark* 7:3 exc. th. wash *o.* eat not
1 *Cor.* 11:25 as *o.* as ye drink
2 *Cor.* 11:23 prisons, in deaths *o.*

**OFTEN, ER.**

*Prov.* 29:1 that being *o.* reproved
*Mal.* 3:16 feared the L. spake *o.*
*Mark* 5:4 *o.* bound with fetters
*Luke* 5:33 why do dis. of J. f. *o.*?
*Acts* 24:26 Felix sent for him *o.*
1 *Cor.* 11:26 as *o.* as ye eat bread
2 *Cor.* 11:26 in journeyings *o.*
27 I have been in watchings *o.*
1 *Tim.* 5:23 use wine for *o.* infir.
*Heb.* 9:25 nor yet offer himself *o.*
26 he must *o.* have suffered
*Rev.* 11:6 smite earth as *o.* as wi.

**OFTENTIMES.**

*Job* 33:29 th. things work. G. *o.*
*Ec.* 7:22 *o.* thy heart knoweth
*Luke* 8:29 *o.* it had caught him
*John* 18:2 Je. *o.* resorted thither
*Rom.* 1:13 *o.* I purposed to come
2 *Cor.* 8:22 have *o.* proved dilig.
*Heb.* 10:11 *o.* off. same sacrifices

**OG.**

*Deut.* 31:4 as he did to O.
*Jos.* 2:10 you did to O. 13:31
1 *K.* 4:19 was in the count. of O.

**OIL.**

*Gen.* 28:18 Jacob poured *o.* on the top of it, 35:14
*Ex.* 25:6 take *o.* for the light, 35:14; 39:37
29:2 cakes tempered with *o.* 40
30:25 make it *o.* for holy ointm.
*Lev.* 2:1 shall pour *o.* upon it, 6
4 cakes of fine flour mingled with *o.* 5; 14:10, 21; 23:13; *Num.* 6:15; 7:13, 19, 25, 31, 37, 43, 49, 55, 61, 67, 73, 79; 8:8; 28:13; 29:3, 9, 14
15 thy meat-offering, put *o.* upon it, 6:21
16 priest shall burn part of *o.*
5:11 he shall put no *o.* upon it, *Num.* 5:15
7:10 meat-offering mingled with *o.* 9:4; 14:10
12 mingled with *o.* *Num.* 6:15
14:16 priest dip right finger in *o.*
17 rest of *o.* in his hand, 18, 29
*Num.* 11:8 as the taste of fresh *o.*
28:12 *o.* for bullock, *o.* for ram
*Deut.* 28:40 sh. not anoint thys. wi. *o.* 2 *Sam.* 14:2; *Mic.* 6:15
32:13 suck *o.* out of rock
33:24 let Asher dip his foot in *o.*
1 *Sam.* 10:1 Sa. took a vial of *o.*
16:1 fill thy horn with *o.* 13
1 *K.* 1:39 Z. took horn of *o.*
5:11 gave Hir. 20 measures of *o.*
17:12 *o.* in cr. 14 nor cr. of *o.* 16
2 *K.* 4:2 nothing in house save *o.*
6 *o.* stayed; 7 go sell the *o.*
9:1 take this box of *o.* to Ra. 3
6 he poured the *o.* on his head
1 *Chr.* 27:28 over the cellars of *o.*
*Ezr.* 3:7 *o.* to them of Zidon
*Est.* 2:12 with *o.* of myrrh
*Job* 24:11 *o.* within their walls
29:6 poured me out rivers of *o.*
*Ps.* 23:5 anoint my head with *o.*
55:21 words were softer than *o.*
104:15 *o.* to make face to shine
109:118 come like *o.* into bones
141:5 be a kindness, an excel. *o.*
*Prov.* 5:3 mouth smoother th. *o.*
21:20 *o.* in dwelling of the wise
*Is.* 61:3 give *o.* of joy for mourn.
*Jer.* 41:8 we have treasures of *o.*
*Ezek.* 16:13 thou didst eat *o.* 19
18 set mine *o.* and incense
27:17 Ju. traded in honey and *o.*
32:14 cause rivers to run like *o.*
45:14 ordinance of *o.* bath of *o.*
24 a hin of *o.* for an ephah
*Hos.* 2:5 lovers that give me *o.*
12:1 *o.* is carried into Egypt
*Mic.* 6:7 with 10,000 rivers of *o.*?
*Zec.* 4:12 empty the golden *o.*
*Mat.* 25:3 the foolish took no *o.*
4 wise took *o.* 8 give us yo. *o.*
*Luke* 7:46 with *o.* didst not ano.
16:6 a hundred measures of *o.*
*See* ANOINTED, ANOINTING, BEATEN, LOG.

**OIL, *with* wine.**

*Num.* 18:12 best of *o.* and *w.* off.
*Deut.* 7:13 L. will bless *w.* and *o.*
11:14 mayest gather *w.* and *o.*
12:17 not eat the tithe of thy *w.* and *o.* 14:23
18:4 first-fr. *w.* and *o.* 2 *Chr.* 31:5
28:51 leave th. ei. *w.* or *o.*
1 *Chr.* 9:29 oversee the *w.* and *o.*
12:40 were nigh bro. *w.* and *o.*
2 *Chr.* 2:10 baths *w.* and *o.* 15
11:11 Rehob. put in *o.* and *w.*
32:28 H. storehou. for *w.* and *o.*
*Ezr.* 6:9 give *w.* *o.* according
7:22 100 baths *w.* 100 baths *o.*
*Neh.* 5:11 restore *wine* and *o.*
10:37 first-fruits of *w.* and *o.*
39 offer. of corn, new *w.* and *o.*
13:5 tithes of corn, *w.* and *o.* 12
*Prov.* 21:17 loveth *wine* and *o.*
*Jer.* 31:12 flow to L. for *w.* and *o.*
40:10 gather ye *w.* fruits and *o.*
*Hag.* 1:11 drought on *w.* and *o.*
2:12 *w.* or *o.* shall it be holy?
*Luke* 10:34 pouring in *o.* and *w.*
*Rev.* 6:6 see hurt not *w.* and *o.*
18:13 no man buy. th. *w.* and *o.*

**OILED.**

*Ex.* 29:23 one cake of *o.* bread. *Lev.* 8:26

**OIL-OLIVE.**

*Ex.* 27:20 *o.*-*o.* beaten for light
30:24 take thou of *o.*-*o.* a hin
*Lev.* 24:2 br. unto thee pure *o.*-*o.*
*Deut.* 8:8 land of *o.*-*o.* 2 *K.* 18:32

**OIL-TREE.**

*Is.* 41:19 plant in wild. the *o.*-*t.*

**OINTMENT.**

*Ex.* 30:25 make oil of holy *o.*
2 *K.* 20:13 Hezek. showed them precious *o.* *Is.* 39:2
1 *Chr.* 9:30 the prie. made the *o.*
*Job* 41:31 maketh sea boil like *o.*
*Ps.* 133:2 it is like precious *o.*
*Prov.* 27:9 *o.* and perfu. rej. hea.
16 *o.* of right hand bewrayeth
*Ec.* 7:1 good name bet. than *o.*
9:8 and let thy head lack no *o.*
10:1 dead flies cause *o.* to stink
*Cant.* 1:3 name is as *o.* poured
*Is.* 1:6 nor mollified with *o.*
57:9 wentest to king with *o.*
*Mat.* 26:7 box of precious *o.* *Mark* 14:3; *Luke* 7:37
9 *o.* might been sold, *John* 12:5
12 hath poured *o.* on my body
*Mark* 14:4 why this waste of *o.*?
*Luke* 7:38 anoin. feet with *o.* 46
*John* 11:2 M. anoin. the L. wi. *o.*
12:3 Mary took pound of *o.* house was filled with odor of the *o.*

**OINTMENTS.**

*Cant.* 1:3 because of thy good *o.*
4:10 smell of thine *o.* is better
*Amos* 6:6 anoi. them. wi. chief *o.*
*Luke* 23:56 prepared spices and *o.*
*Rev.* 18:13 no man buyeth th. *o.*

**OLD.**

*Gen.* 17:12 he th. is eight days *o.*
17 a child to him 100 years *o.*
19:4 comp. house, *o.* and young
*Deut.* 8:4 thy raiment waxed not *o.* 29:5; *Neh.* 9:21
28:50 not regard the person of *o.*
*Jos.* 5:11 did eat *o.* corn, 12
9:4 took *o.* sacks; 5 *o.* shoes 13
13:1 Jos. was *o.* in years, 23:1, 2
14:7 forty years *o.* was I
*Ruth* 1:12 too *o.* to have a husb.
1 *Sam.* 2:22 now Eli was very *o.*
1 *K.* 1:1 now king David was *o.* 15; 1 *Chr.* 23:1
11:4 when S. was *o.* wives turn.
13:11 dwelt *o.* proph. in Beth-el
2 *K.* 4:14 and her husband is *o.*
*Est.* 3:13 dest. J. *o.* and young
*Job* 21:7 wicked live, become *o.*?
32:6 I am young, ye are very *o.*
*Ps.* 32:3 my bones waxed *o.*
37:25 have been young, now *o.*
71:18 now when I am *o.* O God
*Prov.* 22:6 wh. *o.* will not depart
23:10 removed not *o.* land-mark
22 desp. not. moth. when *o.*
*Ec.* 4:13 wise child th. *o.* king
*Cant.* 7:13 pleas. frui. new and *o.*
*Is.* 15:5 heifer 3 ye. *o.* *Jer.* 48:34
20:4 captives, young and *o.*
50:9 they shall wax *o.* as garm.
58:12 build *o.* waste places, 61:4
65:20 child sh. die 100 years *o.* but sinner being 100 years *o.*

Jer. 6:16 see and ask for o. paths
38:11 took o. clouts, o. rags, 12
51:22 I will break young and o.
Lam. 2:21 young and o. lie grou.
3:4 flesh and skin he made o.
Ezek. 9:6 slay utterly o. and you.
23:43 that was o. in adulteries
25:15 vengean. to destroy for o.
36:11 will settle your o. estates
Mic. 6:6 with calv. of a year o.?
Mat. 2:16 H. slew chil. two ye. o.
9:16 new cloth to an o. garment
17 new wine in o. bot. Mark 2:21, 22; Luke 5:36, 37
13:52 bringeth treas. new and o.
Luke 2:42 J. 12 years o. went to
5:39 saith, The o. wine is better
9:8 one of o. prophets is risen
John 3:4 man be born when o.?
8:57 art not yet fifty years o.?
21:18 when thou shalt be o.
Acts 4:22 was above 40 years o.
21:16 brou. Mnason o. disciple
1 Cor. 5:7 purge out the o. leaven
8 keep feast, not wi. o. leaven
2 Cor. 3:14 read of o. testament
5:17 o. things are passed away
1 Tim. 4:7 refuse o. wives' fables
5:9 not taken under 60 years o.
Heb. 8:13 he hath made first o. what wax. o. is ready to van.
2 Pet. 1:9 purged from his o. sins
2:5 if God spared not o. world
1 John 2:7 o. commandm. is word
Rev. 12:9 o. serpent the devil
20:2 hold on dragon that o. ser.

**OLD age.**

Gen. 15:15 buried in a good o. a.
21:2 Abra. a son of his o. age, 7
25:8 Abra. died in a good o. age
37:3 Jo. son of his o. age, 44:20
Jud. 8:32 Gid. died in good o. a.
Ruth 4:15 nourisher in th. o. a.
1 K. 15:23 Asa in o. a. diseased
1 Chr. 29:28 D. died in good o. a.
Job 30:2 in whom o. age perish.
Ps. 71:9 cast not off in o. age
92:14 bring forth fruit in o. age
Is. 46:4 even to your o. a. I am
Luke 1:36 conceived son in o. a.

Days of OLD. See of OLD.
OLD gate. See GATE.

**OLD man.**

Gen. 25:8 Abra. died an o. man
43:27 o. man of whom ye spake
44:20 we have a father, an o. m.
Lev. 19:32 honor face of o. man
Jud. 19:16 came an o. m. fr. wor.
1 Sam. 2:31 not o. m. in hou. 32
4:18 Eli o. man; 17:12 J. o. man
28:14 o. m. cometh up, covered
2 Chr. 36:17 no compas. on o. m.
Is. 65:20 o. m. that hath not
Luke 1:18 I am an o. man
Rom. 6:6 our o man is crucified
Eph. 4:22 off o. m. wh. is corrupt
Col. 3:9 put off o. m. with deeds

**OLD men.**

1 K. 12:6 consulted with o. m.
8 forsook counsel of o. men, 13; 2 Chr. 10:6, 8, 13
Ps. 148:12 o. m. praise the Lord
Prov. 17:6 child. crown of o. m.
20:29 beauty of o. m. gray head
Jer. 31:13 rej. young men and o.
Joel 1:2 hear this ye o. men
2:28 o. m. sh. dream, Acts 2:17
Zec. 8:4 o. m. dwell in streets

**Of OLD.**

Gen. 6:4 of o. men of renown
Neh. 12:46 of o. chief of singers
Job 20:4 kno. thou not this of o.
Ps. 25:6 tender me. ha. been of o.
44:1 work didst in times of o.
68:33 heavens which were of o.
74:2 which hast purchased of o.
12 for God is my king of o.
77:5 I considered the days of o.
11 will rem. thy wonders of o.
78:2 utter dark sayings of o.
93:2 throne is established of o.
102:25 of o. hast laid foundation
119:52 remembered judgm. of o.
152 testimonies I have k. of o.
143:5 I rem. days of o. Is. 63:11
Prov. 8:22 before his works of o.
Is. 25:1 thy counsels of o. are
30:33 Tophet is ordained of o.
46:9 remem. former things of o.
51:9 awake as in genera. of o.
57:11 I held peace of o.?
63:9 carried them all days of o.
Jer. 28:8 bef. me and thee of o.
31:3 L. hath appeared of o.
46:26 inhabited as in days of o.
Lam. 1:7 she had in days of o.
2:17 commanded in days of o.
3:6 as they that be dead of o.
5:21 L. renew our days as of o.
Ezek. 26:20 places desolate of o.
Amos 9:11 as in days of o.
Mic. 5:2 goings have been f. of o.
7:14 feed in Ba. as in days of o.
20 sw. to fath. from days of o.
Nah. 2:8 Nineveh is of o. like a
Mal. 3:4 the L. as in days of o.
2 Pet. 3:5 the heavens were of o.
Jude 4 were of o. ordained

**OLD time.**

Deut. 2:20 giants dw. th. in o. t.
Jos. 24:2 dw. on oth. side in o. t.
2 Sam. 20:18 to speak in o. t.
Ezr. 4:15 moved sedition of o. t.
Jer. 2:20 of o. t. I have broken
Ezek. 26:20 down wi. peo. of o. t.
Mat. 5:21 by them of o. t. 27, 33
Acts 15:21 Mo. of o. time hath in
1 Pet. 3:5 in o. t. women adorned
2 Pet. 1:21 came not in o. t.

See WAX.

**OLD way.**

Job 22:15 o. w. wh. wicked men

**OLDNESS.**

Rom. 7:6 not serve in o. of letter

**OLIVE.**

Gen. 8:11 in mouth was o. leaf
Deut. 28:40 thine o. cast fruit
Neh. 8:15 and fetch o. branches
Job 15:33 cast off his flowers as o.
Ps. 128:3 children like o. plants
Hab. 3:17 althou. labor of o. fail
Zec. 4:12 these two o. branches
Jam. 3:12 fig-tree bear o. berries?

See OIL.

**OLIVES.**

Jud. 15:5 bu. vineyards and o.
Mic. 6:15 shalt tread the o. but

See MOUNT.

**OLIVET.**

2 Sam. 15:30 ascent to mount O.
Acts 1:12 from mount called O.

**OLIVE-TREE.**

Deut. 24:20 beatest thine o.-t.
Jud. 9:8 they said to the o.-t.
1 K. 6:23 two cherubim of o.-t.
31 two doors were of o.-t. 32
33 made for door-posts of o.-t.
Ps. 52:8 like a green o.-t.
Is. 17:6 shaking of o.-t. 24:13
Jer. 11:16 name a green o.-t.
Hos. 14:6 beauty be as the o.-t.
Hag. 2:19 o.-t. hath not brought
Rom. 11:17 the fatness of o.-t.
24 graffed in a good o.-t.

**OLIVE-TREES.**

Deut. 6:11 o.-t. thou plantest not
28:40 thou shalt have o.-t. but
1 Chr. 27:28 over o.-t. Baal-hanan
Amos 4:9 o.-t. increa. worm dev.
Zec. 4:3 two o.-t. by it on right
Rev. 11:4 the two o.-t. standing

**Wild OLIVE-TREE.**

Rom. 11:17 thou being wild o.-t.

**OLIVE-YARD, S.**

Ex. 23:11 thus do wi. thy o.-y.
Jos. 24:13 of vineyards and o.-y. ye planted not, Neh. 9:25
1 Sam. 8:14 king take your o.-y.
2 K. 5:26 recei. money and o.-y.
Neh. 5:11 resto. to th. their o.-y.

OLYMPAS. Rom. 16:15
OMEGA. Rev. 1:8, 11; 21:6; 22:13

**OMITTED.**

Mat. 23:23 o. matters of the law

**OMNIPOTENT.**

Rev. 19:6 Lord God o. reigneth

**OMRI.**

1 K. 16:16 ma. O. king, 21, 25, 30
2 K. 8:26 daugh. of O. 2 Chr. 22:2
Mic. 6:16 statutes of O. are kept

ON. Gen. 41:45, 50; 46:10; Num. 16:1

**ONAN.**

Gen. 38:4 called his name O. 9
46:12 of Ju. Er, O. Num. 26:19

**ONCE.**

Gen. 18:32 will speak but this o.
Ex. 10:17 forgive only this o.
30:10 atonement of incense o. a ye. Lev. 16:34; Heb. 9:7, 12
Jos. 6:3 go round city o. 11, 14
Jud. 6:39 I will spe. but this o.
2 K. 6:10 saved himself not o.
Neh. 13:20 lodged without Jer. o.
Job 33:14 God speak. o. yea twi.
40:5 o. have I spoken, but
Ps. 62:11 God hath spoken o.
89:35 o. have I sworn
Prov. 28:18 perv. shall fall at o.
Is. 42:14 destroy and dev. at o.
66:8 or sh. a nati. be born at o.
Jer. 10:18 sling out inhabit. at o.
13:27 clean, wh. shall it o. be?
16:21 I will this o. cause them
Hag. 2:6 o. it is a little while, Heb. 12:26
Luke 23:18 they cried all at o.
Rom. 6:10 he died unto sin o.
7:9 I was alive without law o.
1 Cor. 15:6 seen of 500 bret. at o.
2 Cor. 11:25 thr. beaten, o. ston.
Gal. 1:23 prea. faith ne o. destr.
Eph. 5:3 let it not be o. named
Phil. 4:16 ye sent o. and again
1 Thes. 2:18 would have come o.
Heb. 7:27 for this he did o. when
9:26 but now o. in end of world
27 appointed to men o. to die
28 o. offered to bear sins, 10:10
10:2 the worshippers o. purged
12:27 yet o. more, signifieth
1 Pet. 3:18 Ch. suffered o. for sins
20 o. long-suffering of God
Jude 3 contend for faith o. deliv.
5 though ye o. knew this.

**ONE.**

Gen. 2:24 shall be o. flesh, Mat. 19:5; Mark 10:8; 1 Cor. 6:16
27:38 hast thou but o. blessing?
42:13 with father, o. is not, 32
44:28 the o. went out from me
Ex. 11:1 I will bring o. plague
12:46 in o. sh. it be eaten
49 o. law to him is home-born Lev. 24:22; Num. 15:16, 29
23:29 not drive th. out in o. ye.
Num. 16:15 take o. as from them
36:8 of tribe shall be wife to o.
Deut. 4:42 fleeing to o. of these cities, 19:5, 11
32:20 should o. chase a thousa.
Jud. 9:2 bet. that o. reign over?
21:8 what o. is there of tribes

1 Sam. 18:21 son-in-law in o. of
2 Sam. 7:23 wh. o. nat. like peo. ?
19:7 will not tarry o. with thee
1 K. 1:48 given me o. to sit on
Job 9:3 answer him o. of a thou.
21:23 o. dieth in full strength
23:13 o. mind, who turn him ?
33:23 interpreter o. am. thous.
Ps. 49:16 not afr. when o. is rich
89:19 help on o. that is mighty
Ec. 3:20 all go unto o. place, 6:6
4:9 two are better than o.
11 how can o. be warm alone ?
12 if o. prevail against him
7:27 counting o. by o. to find
Cant. 6:9 my undefiled is but o.
Is. 23:15 acc. to days of o. king
27:12 shall be gathered o. by o.
30:17 o. thou. flee at reb. of o.
Is. 34:16 no o. of these shall fail
41:25 raised up o. from north
44:5 o. shall say, I am Lord's
45:24 o. say, In L. have I right.
Dan. 7:13 o. like Son, 10:16, 18
Amos. 4:8 wandered to o. city
6:9 remain ten men in o. house
Zec. 3:9 on o. stone be seven eyes
14:9 o. Lord, and his name o.
Mal. 2:15 make o. ? wheref. o. ?
Mat. 5:18 o. jot or o. tit. not pass
17:4 thr. tabernacles, o. for thee, o. for Mo. and o. for Elias, Mark 9:5; Luke 9:33
18:16 take with thee o. or two.
19:17 none good but o. Mark 10:18; Luke 18:19
25:45 ye did it not to o. of least
Mark 14:19 say o. by o. is it I ?
Luke 7:8 to o. go, and he goeth
16:30 if o. went from dead, 31
17:22 to see o. of the days of S.
John 10:30 I and my Fa. are o.
17:11 be o. as we are, 21, 22
Acts 17:7 another king, o. Jesus
Eph. 2:14 both o. 15 o. new m.
4:5 o. faith, o. L. o. bapt. 6 o. G.
1 John 5:7 three o. 8 agree in o.
See ACCORD, ANOTHER, MAN, GOD.

**As ONE.**

Gen. 3:22 behold, man is as o.
Ec. 3:19 as o. dieth, so dieth
Cant. 1:7 be as o. turneth aside ?
See DAY, HEART, EVERY.

**Is ONE.**

Gen. 11:6 peo. is o. 41:25 drea. 26
Deut. 6:4 the Lord our God is o. L. Mark 12:29
Gal. 3:20 med. of one, but G. is o.
See LITTLE, MAN.

**Not ONE.**

Gen. 24:41 if they give n. thee o.
Ex. 8:31 remained not o. 10:19
12:30 not house wh. not o. dead
Deut. 2:36 not o. city too strong
2 Sam. 13:30 is n. o. of them left
Rom. 3:10 is none right. not o.
See MIGHTY.

**ONE, with other.**

Gen. 13:11 separated, o. from o.
Ex. 14:20 o. came not near o.
17:12 stayed han. o. side, and o.
Deut. 4:32 o. side of heav. to o.
13:7 o. end of earth to o. 28:64
Jud. 16:29 hold of o. pill. and o.
1 K. 3:23 o. sai. This my son, o.
25 give half to o. and half to o.
Ec. 3:19 as o. dieth, so dieth o.
7:14 God hath set the o. over o.
Mat. 6:24 hate the o. and love the other, or hold to the o. and despise the o. Luke 16:13
24:40 o. taken, the other left, 41; Luke 17:34, 35, 36
Luke 6:29 if sm. on o. che. off. o.
Gal. 5:17 are contrary, o. to oth.
Rev. 17:10 o. is, oth. is not come
See PEOPLE.

**There is ONE.**

Ec. 4:8 th. is one alone, not seco.
Mark 12:32 the truth; th. is o. G. 1 Tim. 2:5; Jam. 2:19

**ONE of them.**

Ex. 14:28 remained not o. of th.
Mat. 26:73 surely thou art o. of t. Mark 14:69, 70
John 6:7 ev. o. of t. take a little

**ONE thing.**

Job 9:22 this is o. t. theref. I said
Mat. 21:24 I will ask you o. thi. Luke 6:9; 20:3
Mark 10:21 o. t. lack. Luke 18:22
Luke 10:42 o. thing is needful
Acts 19:32 some cried o. t. 21:34
Phil. 3:13 but this o. thing I do

**Wicked ONE.**

Mat. 13:19 then cometh w. o.
38 tares are children of w. o.
1 John 2:13 overcome w. o. 14
3:12 not as C. who was of w. o.
5:18 w. o. toucheth him not

**ONESIMUS.**

Col. 4:9 O. a faithful brother
Phile. 10 beseech for my son O.

**ONESIPHORUS.**

2 Tim. 1:16 mercy to house of O.
4:19 salute the household of O.

**ONLY.**

Gen. 19:8 o. to these men do no.
22:2 take now thine o. son, Isa.
12 not withheld thine o. son, 16
2 K. 19:19 L. even thou o. Is. 37:20
Job 34:29 ag. nation, or man o.
Ps. 51:4 ag. thee o. have I sinned
Cant. 6:9 she is o. one of mother
Luke 7:12 dead man, o. son of m.
8:42 one o. dau. 9:38 o. child
Rom. 5:3 and not o. so, 11
8:23 not o. they, but ourselves
16:27 to God o. wise, be glory, 1 Tim. 1:17; Jude 25
1 Cor. 7:39 o. in the Lord
2 Tim. 4:8 not to me o. but to all
See BEGOTTEN.

**ONIONS.**

Num 11:5 remem. o. and garlic

**ONWARD.**

Ex. 40:36 cloud up, Is. went o.

**ONYCHA.**

Ex. 30:34 take the spices, o

**ONYX.**

Ex. 28:20 4th row an o. 39:13
Job 28:16 wisdom not val. wi. o.
Ezek. 28:13 o. was thy covering
See STONES.

**OPEN, Adjective.**

Gen. 1:20 fowl fly in o. firma.
38:14 Tamar sat in o. place
Num. 19:15 ev. o. vessel is uncl.
24:3 man whose eyes are o. 4, 15
1 Sam. 3:1 word of L. no o. visi.
1 K. 6:18 cedar carved with o. flowers, 29:32, 35
8:29 eyes be o. tow. this house, 52; 2 Chr. 6:20, 40; 7:15
Neh. 1:6 let thine eyes be o.
6:5 Sanb. wi. o. letter sent serv.
Job 34:26 wicked men in o. sight
Ps. 5:9 their throat is an o. sepulchre, Rom. 3:13
34:15 his ears are o. to their cry
Prov. 13:16 fool lay. o. his folly
27:5 o. rebuke bet. th. secret lo.
Is. 9:12 devour Is. with o. mouth
24:18 window from on high o.
60:11 thy gates sh. be o. contin.
Jer. 5:16 quiver is an o. sepulch.
32:11 what was sealed and o.
19 th. eyes o. on ways of men
Ezek. 37:2 many bones in o. val.
Dan. 6:10 windows o. in chamb.
Neh. 3:13 gates of land wide o
John 1:51 ye shall see heaven o.
Acts 16:27 prison doors o. drew
19:38 law o. there are deputies
2 Cor. 3:18 we, wi. o. face behol.
6:11 our mouth is o. to you, our
1 Tim. 5:24 some men's sins o.
Heb. 6:6 put him to o. shame
1 Pet. 3:12 ears are o. to prayers
Rev. 3:8 set bef. thee an o. door
10:2 had in his hand a book o. 8
See FIELD, FIELDS.

**OPEN, Verb.**

Ex. 21:33 if a man shall o. a pit
Num. 8:16 inst. of such as o. wo.
16:30 if earth o. mouth and swa.
Deut. 15:8 thou shalt o. hand, 11
20:11 make ans. of peace and o.
28:12 L. sh. o. to thee his treas.
2 K. 9:3 then o. door, and flee
13:17 o. the window eastward
Job 11:5 O that G. wo. o. his lips
32:20 I will o. my lips and ans.
35:16 doth Job o. mouth in vain
41:14 who can o. doors of face ?
Ps. 49:4 o. my dark saying
78:2 I will o. mouth in parable
81:10 o. thy mouth I will fill it
118:19 o. to me gates of righte.
Prov. 31:8 o. thy mouth for du.
9 o. thy mouth, judge righte.
Cant. 5:2 o. to me, my sister
5 I rose up to o. to my beloved
Is. 22:22 o. none shut, sh. none o.
26:2 o. gates, righte. may enter
28:24 do. he o. clods of ground ?
41:18 o. rivers in high places
42:7 o. blind eyes, bring out pr.
45:1 to o. before him the gates
8 let earth o. bring forth salv.
Jer. 13:19 cities shut up, none o.
50:26 o. her storehouses, cast h.
Ezek. 2:8 o. thy mouth and eat
3:27 when I speak I will o. thy
16:63 conf. and never o. mouth
21:22 to o. mouth in slaughter
25:9 I will o. side of M. fr. cities
37:12 I will o. your graves
46:12 one shall o. gate tow. east
Zec. 11:1 o. thy doors, O Leban.
Mal. 3:10 if I will not o. heaven
Mat. 13:35 o. mouth in parables
25:11 Lord, o. to us, Luke 13:25
Luke 12:36 when knock. may o.
Acts 18:14 P. was about to o. mo.
Eph. 6:19 that I may o. mouth
Col. 4:3 G. would o. door of utte.
Rev. 5:2 wort. to o. book ? 3, 5, 9
See EYES.

**OPENED.**

Gen. 7:11 wind. of heav. were o.
29:31 the Lord o. Leah's womb
30:22 God o. Rachel's womb
41:56 Joseph o. all storehouses
42:27 one o. sack, 43:21; 44:11
Ex. 2:6 wh. she o. ark, saw child
Num. 16:32 earth o. mou. swallowed up Korah, Ps. 106:17
Jud. 3:25 he o. not doors, they o.
4:19 she o. a bottle of milk, and
19:27 her lord o. doors, went out
2 K. 9:10 Elisha o. door and fled
15:16 o. not to him, he smote
2 Chr. 29:3 Hezekiah o. doors of
Neh. 7:3 let not gates of J. be o.
8:5 E. o. book, when he o. peop.
13:19 gates not o. till after sab.
Job 31:32 o. my doors to traveller
38:17 gates of death been o. ?
Ps. 40:6 mine ears hast thou o.
78:23 tho' he o. doors of heaven
105:41 he o. rock, waters gushed
Cant. 5:6 I o. to my beloved, but

*Is.* 14:17 *o.* not house of prison.
48:8 time that th. ear was not *o.*
50:5 Lord God hath *o.* mine ear
*Jer.* 20:12 to thee have I *o.* cause
50:25 Lord hath *o.* his armory
*Ezek.* 1:1 hea. *o.* *Mat.* 3:16; *Mar.* 1:10; *Luke* 3:21; *Acts* 7:56
16:25 hast *o.* thy feet to ev. one
37:13 I have *o.* your graves
44:2 gate shall not be *o.*
46:1 on sabbath it shall be *o.*
*Dan.* 7:10 judgment set, books *o.*
*Nah.* 2:6 gates of rivers sh. be *o.*
*Zec.* 13:1 fountain *o.* to David
*Mat.* 2:11 when they *o.* treasures
7:7 it shall be *o.* *Luke* 11:9, 10
27:52 graves were *o.* bodies aro.
*Mark* 7:34 be *o.* 35 ears were *o.*
*Luke* 4:17 *o.* book, found place
24:32 wh. he *o.* to us scriptures
45 *o.* he their understanding
*Acts* 5:19 angel by night *o.* pris.
10:11 Peter saw heaven *o.*
12:10 iron gates *o.* 14 *o.* not gate
14:27 how he *o.* door to Gentiles
16:14 Lydia, whose heart L. *o.*
26 the prison doors were *o.*
1 *Cor.* 16:9 a gr. door and effect. is *o.* unto me, 2 *Cor.* 2:12
*Heb.* 4:13 all things are *o.* to him
*Rev.* 4:1 a door was *o.* in heaven
6:1 when Lamb *o.* one seal
3 *o.* second; 5 third; 7 fourth
9 *o.* fifth; 12 sixth; 8:1 seventh
9:2 *o.* the bottomless pit and heaven *o.* and white horse
20:12 books *o.* book of life *o.*

*See* DAYS, MOUTH.

**OPENEST.**

*Ps.* 104:28 thou *o.* thy hand
145:16 thou *o.* thy hand

**OPENETH.**

*Ex.* 13:2 sanctify to me what *o.*
12 all *o.* matrix, 15; 34:19; *Nu.* 3:12; 18:15; *Luke* 2:23
*Job* 27:19 rich man *o.* his eyes
33:16 he *o.* ears of men
36:10 *o.* their ear to discipline
15 he *o.* their ears in oppressi.
*Ps.* 38:13 dumb man *o.* not mou.
*Prov.* 13:3 that *o.* wide his lips
24:7 *o.* not his mouth in gate
31:26 she *o.* mouth with wisdom
*Is.* 53:7 so he *o.* not his mouth
*Ezek.* 20:26 all that *o.* the womb
*John* 10:3 to him the porter *o.*
*Rev.* 3:7 *o.* and no man shutteth, shutteth and no man *o.*

**OPENING.**

*Is.* 42:20 *o.* ears, but heareth not
*Acts* 17:3 *o.* and alleging Christ

**OPENING, S.**

1 *Chr.* 9:27 *o.* of house of God
*Job* 12:14 shutteth, there be no *o.*
*Prov.* 1:21 in the *o.* of the gates
8:6 *o.* of my lips shall be right
*Is.* 61:1 proclaim *o.* of the prison
*Ezek.* 29:21 give thee *o.* of mouth

**OPENLY.**

*Gal.* 38:21 wh. harlot th. was *o.?*
*Ps.* 98:2 righteous. he *o.* showed
*Mat.* 6:4 F. reward thee *o.* 6, 18
*Mark* 8:32 spake that saying *o.*
*John* 7:4 seeketh to be known *o.*
10 we. he to feast, not *o.* secre.
13 no man spake of him *o.*
11:54 Jesus walked no more *o.*
13:20 J. said, I spake *o.* to wor.
*Acts* 10:40 God showed him *o.*
16:37 they have beaten us *o.*
*Col.* 2:15 made a show of them *o.*

**OPERATION, S.**

*Ps.* 28:5 regard not *o.* of his
*Is.* 5:12 nor consid. *o.* of hands
1 *Cor.* 12:6 th. are diversity of *o.*
*Col.* 2:12 risen thro' *o.* of faith

**OPHEL.**

2 *Chr.* 27:3 on wall of O. 33:14
*Neh.* 3:26 Nethin. in O. 27; 11:21

**OPHIR.**

*Gen.* 10:29 J. be. O. 1 *Chr.* 1:23
1 *K.* 9:28 came to O. 2 *Chr.* 8:18
10:11 bro. from O. great plenty
22:48 made ships go to O.
1 *Chr.* 29:4 3,000 ta. of gold of O.
*Job* 22:24 lay up the gold of O.
28:16 not valued wi. gold of O.
*Ps.* 45:9 the queen in gold of O.
*Is.* 13:12 prec. than wedge of O.

**OPINION, S.**

1 *K.* 18:21 h. long halt bet. 2 *o.?*
*Job* 32:6 durst not show mine *o.*
10 I also will show mine *o.* 17

**OPPORTUNITY.**

*Mat.* 26:16 *o.* to bet. *Luke* 22:6
*Gal.* 6:10 as we have *o.* do good
*Phil.* 4:10 careful, ye lacked *o.*
*Heb.* 11:15 *o.* to have returned

**OPPOSE, ED.**

*Acts* 18:6 *o.* thems. and blasph.
2 *Tim.* 2:25 instructing th. th. *o.*

**OPPOSEST, ETH.**

*Job* 30:21 wi. strong hand *o.* thy.
2 *Thes.* 2.4 *o.* and exalt. himself

**OPPOSITIONS.**

1 *Tim.* 6:20 avoiding *o.* of science

**OPPRESS.**

*Ex.* 3:9 the Egyptians *o.* them
22:21 neither *o.* stranger, 23:9
*Lev.* 25:14 sh. not *o.* one anc. 17
*Deut.* 23:16 shalt not *o.* servant
24:14 shalt not *o.* a hired serv.
*Jud.* 10:12 Moabites did *o.* you
*Job* 10:3 is it good thou shou. *o.?*
*Ps.* 10:18 m. of earth no more *o.*
17:9 hide me fr. wicked that *o.*
119:122 let not the proud *o.* me
*Prov.* 22:22 nor *o.* the afflicted
*Is.* 49:26 feed them that *o.* thee
*Jer.* 7:6 if ye *o.* not the stranger
30:20 punish all that *o.* them
*Ezek.* 45:8 princes sh. no more *o.*
*Hos.* 12:7 merchant loveth to *o.*
*Amos* 4:1 kine of Bashan *o.* poor
*Mic.* 2:2 *o.* a man and his house
*Zec.* 7:10 *o.* not widow nor fath.
*Mal.* 3:5 witness ag. those that *o.*
*Jam.* 2:6 do not ri. men *o.* you?

**OPPRESSED.**

*Deut.* 28:29 shalt be only *o.* 33
*Jud.* 2:18 by reason of th. that *o.*
4:3 Jabin *o.* Israel; 10:8 Phil. *o.*
6:9 out of the hand of all that *o.* you, 1 *Sam.* 10:18
1 *Sam.* 12:3 whom have I *o.?*
4 hast not defrauded nor *o.* us
2 *K.* 13:4 Assyria *o.* 22 king of
2 *Chr.* 16:10 Asa *o.* some of peo.
*Job* 20:19 *o.* and forsaken poor
35:9 they make the *o.* to cry
*Ps.* 9:9 Lord be a refuge for *o.*
10:18 judge the *o.* 103:6; 146:7
74:21 let not *o.* return ashamed
106:42 their enemies *o.* them
*Ec.* 4:1 tears of such as were *o.*
*Is.* 1:17 seek judgm. relieve *o.*
3:5 people shall be *o.* every one
23:12 O thou, *o.* virgin, daught.
38:14 I am *o.* undertake for me
52:4 Assy. *o.* them without cau.
53:7 he was *o.* and afflicted
58:6 fast? to let the *o.* go free
*Jer.* 50:33 Is. and Judah were *o.*
*Ezek.* 18:7 hath not *o.* any, 16
12 he hath *o.* 18 he cruelly *o.*
22:29 *o.* stranger wrongfully
*Hos.* 5:11 Ephr. is *o.* and broken
*Amos* 3:9 behold thee *o.* in midst
*Acts* 7:24 Moses avenged him *o.*
10:38 J. healed all that were *o.*

**OPPRESSETH.**

*Num.* 10:9 go to war ag. him *o.*
*Ps.* 56:1 he fighting daily *o.* me
*Prov.* 14:31 he that *o.* poor, 22:16
28:3 a poor man that *o.* the poor

**OPPRESSING.**

*Jer.* 46:16 let us go from *o.* swo.
50:16 for fear of the *o.* sword
*Zep.* 3:1 woe to the *o.* city

**OPPRESSION.**

*Ex.* 3:9 *o.* wherewith Egyptians
*Deut.* 26:7 L. looked on our *o.*
2 *K.* 13:4 Lord saw *o.* of Israel
*Job* 36:15 openeth their ears in *o.*
*Ps.* 12:5 for *o.* of poor will I arise
42:9 *o.* of the enemy, 43:2; 55:3
44:24 forget. our *o.* 62:10 trust
73:8 speak wickedly concern. *o.*
107:39 are brought low thro' *o.*
119:134 deliver me fr. *o.* of man
*Ec.* 5:8 if thou seest *o.* of poor
7:7 *o.* maketh a wise man mad
*Is.* 5:7 behold *o.* 30:12 trust *o.*
54:14 thou shalt be far from *o.*
59:13 from our G. speaking *o.*
*Jer.* 6:6 wholly *o.* in midst of h.
22:17 th. eyes and heart for *o.*
*Ezek.* 22:7 by *o.* with stranger
29 people of the land used *o.*
46:18 sh. not take inherit. by *o.*

**OPPRESSIONS.**

*Job* 35:9 by the multitude of *o.*
*Ec.* 4:1 I considered the *o.* done
*Is.* 33:15 despiseth the gain of *o.*

**OPPRESSOR.**

*Job* 3:18 they hear not voice of *o.*
15:20 number of years hid. to *o.*
*Ps.* 72:4 shall break in pieces *o.*
*Prov.* 3:31 envy not *o.* cho. none
28:16 want. understanding is *o.*
*Is.* 9:4 hast broken rod of his *o.*
14:4 say, How hath *o.* ceased!
51:13 hast feared fury of the *o.*
*Jer.* 21:12 out of hand of *o.* 22:3
25:38 because of fierceness of *o.*
*Zec.* 9:8 no *o.* shall pass through
10:4 out of him came every *o.*

**OPPRESSORS.**

*Job* 27:13 this is the herita. of *o.*
*Ps.* 54:3 *o.* seek after my soul
119:121 leave me not to mine *o.*
*Ec.* 4:1 side of *o.* th. was power
*Is.* 3:12 children are their *o.*
14:2 they shall rule over their *o.*
16:4 *o.* consumed out of the land
19:20 cry to Lord because of *o.*

**ORACLE.**

2 *Sam.* 16:23 inquired at *o.* of G.
1 *K.* 6:16 be built them for the *o.*
8:6 priests bro. ark of L. into *o.*
2 *Chr.* 4:20 should burn be. the *o.*
*Ps.* 28:2 lift up hands to. holy *o.*

**ORACLES.**

*Acts* 7:38 received the lively *o.*
*Rom.* 3:2 to them were com. *o.*
*Heb.* 5:12 first princip. of *o.* of G.
1 *Pet.* 4:11 speak of the *o.* of God

**ORATION.**

*Acts* 12:21 Herod made *o.* to th.

**ORATOR.**

*Is.* 3:3 from Ju. the eloquent *o.*
*Acts* 24:1 *o.* named Tertullus

**ORCHARD, S.**

*Cant.* 4:13 an *o.* of pomegranates
*Ec.* 2:5 I made me gard. and *o.*

**ORDAIN.**

1 *Chr.* 9:22 S. did *o.* in their offi.
17:9 I will *o.* a place for my pe.
*Is.* 26:12 L. that wilt *o.* peace
1 *Cor.* 7:17 so *o.* I in all churches
*Tit.* 1:5 thou shouldest *o.* elders

**ORDAINED, ETH.**

*Num.* 28:6 offering that was *o.*

1 K. 12:32 Jerobo. o. a feast, 33
2 K. 23:5 put down id. priests o.
2 Chr. 11:15 Jeroboam o. priests
29:27 instruments o. by David
Est. 9:27 Jews o. feast of Purim
Ps. 7:13 o. arrows ag. persecut.
8:2 out of mouth of babes o.
3 moon and stars thou hast o.
81:5 o. in Joseph for testimony
132:17 I have o. a lamp for mine
Is. 30:33 Tophet is o. of old
Jer. 1:5 I o. thee to be a prophet
Dan. 2:24 king o. to destroy men
Hab. 1:12 O L. thou hast o. them
Mark 3:14 Jesus o. 12 to be with
John 15:16 I o. ye sho. bri. fruit
Acts 1:22 o. to be witness with
10:42 o. of God to be judge
13:48 as were o. to eternal life
14:23 when they o. them elders
16:4 decrees were o. of apostles
17:31 judge by man he hath o.
Rom. 7:10 command. o. to life
13:1 powers that be, are o. of G
1 Cor. 2:7 hidden wisdom God o.
9:14 Lord o. that they which pr.
Gal. 3:19 law was o. by angels
Eph. 2:10 wh. God hath before o.
1 Tim. 2:7 I am o. preacher to G
Heb. 5:1 ev. high-priest is o. 8:3
9:6 when these things were o.
Jude 4 o. to this condemnation

**ORDER, Substantive.**

2 K. 23:4 comp. priests of sec. o.
1 Chr. 6:32 waited accord. to o.
15:13 sought him not aft. due o.
23:31 o. commanded them be. L.
25:2 acc. to o. of D. 6; 2 Ch. 8:14
Job 10:22 land of dark. without o.
Ps. 110:4 pri. after o. of M. Heb. 5:6, 10; 6:20; 7:11, 17, 21
1 Cor. 16:1 have gi. o. to church.
Col. 2:5 beholding your o.
Heb. 7:11 not called after o. of A.

**In ORDER.**

Gen. 22:9 Abr. laid wood in o.
Ex. 40:4 thou sh. set in o. thin. that are to be set in o. Lev. 1:7, 8, 12; 6:12; 24:8
23 he set bread in o. upon it
2 Sam. 17:23 put his house in o.
1 K. 18:33 Elijah put wood in o.
2 K. 20:1 set house in o. Is. 38:1
2 Chr. 13:11 show-bread set in o.
29:35 service of house of L. in o.
Job 33:5 set words in o. bef. me
Ps. 50:21 th. in o. bef. thine eyes
Ec. 12:9 the preacher set in o.
Is. 44:7 set it in o. before me?
Ezek. 41:6 chambers were 30 in o.
Luke 1:1 hand to set forth in o. 3
8 served before God in his o.
Acts 18:23 country of Phry. in o.
1 Cor. 11:34 rest will I set in o.
15:23 ev. man shall rise in his o.
Tit. 1:5 I left thee to set in o.

**ORDER, Verb.**

Ex. 27:21 Aa. o. it, Lev. 24:3, 4
Jud. 13:12 how sh. we o. child?
1 K. 20:14 who shall o. battle?
Job 23:4 o. my cause before him
37:19 we cannot o. our speech
Ps. 119:133 o. steps in thy word
Is. 9:7 upon his kingdom to o. it
Jer. 46:3 o. ye buckler and shield

**ORDERED, ETH.**

Jud. 6:26 build altar in o. place
2 Sam. 23:5 covenant o. and sure
Job 13:18 I have o. my cause, I
Ps. 37:23 steps of good man are o.
50:23 who o. conversation arig.

**ORDERINGS.**

1 Chr. 24:19 these were their o.

**ORDERLY.**

Acts 21:21 walkest o. keepest law

**ORDINANCE.**

Ex. 12:14 feast of passover for an o. forever, 24, 43; 13:10
15:25 made a statute and an o.
Num. 9:14 according to o. of passover, 2 Chr. 35:13
10:8 to be to you for an o. for e.
18:8 and to thy sons by an o. for ever, 2 Chr. 2:4
19:2 o. of L. commanded, 31:21
Jos. 24:25 set them o. in Shech.
1 Sam. 30:25 made it o. for ever
2 Chr. 35:25 made them o. in Is.
Ezr. 3:10 after the o. of David
Is. 24:5 the law changed the o.
58:2 forsook not o. of their God
Ezek. 46:14 offering by perpet. o.
Mal. 3:14 what pro. we kept o.?
Rom. 13:2 power resists o. of G.
1 Pet. 2:13 submit to every o. of

**ORDINANCES.**

Ex. 18:20 shalt teach them o.
Lev. 18:3 neither walk in their o.
4 ye sh. keep mine o. 30; 22:9; 2 Chr. 33:8; Ezek. 11:20; 43:11; 1 Cor. 11:2
Num. 9:12 to o. of passover, 14
2 K. 17:37 o. he wrote for you
Neh. 10:32 made o. made for us
Job 38:33 knowest thou the o. of heaven? Jer. 31:35; 33:25
Ps. 99:7 kept o. he gave them
119:91 continue according to o.
Is. 58:2 ask of me o. of justice
Jer. 31:36 if o. depart before me
Ezek. 43:18 these are o. of altar
44:5 o. of the house of the Lord
Mal. 3:7 gone away fr. mine o.
Luke 1:6 commandments and o. of Lord
Eph. 2:15 commandment contained in o.
Col. 2:14 out handwriting of o.
20 are ye subject to o.?
Heb. 9:1 had o. of divine service
10 carnal o. imposed on them

**ORDINARY.**

Ezek. 16:27 diminished o. food

**OREB.**

Jud. 7:25 of Mid. Zeeb, O. 8:3
Ps. 83:11 their nobles like O.
Is. 10:26 of Midian at rock of O.

**ORGAN, S.**

Gen. 4:21 of such as handle o.
Job 21:12 rejoice at sound of o.
30:31 my o. turned into voice
Ps. 150:4 praised him with o.

**ORION.**

Job 9:9 maketh O. Amos 5:8
38:31 loose the bands of O.?

**ORNAMENT.**

Prov. 1:9 o. of grace to thy head
4:9 give to head an o. of grace
25:12 as an o. of fine gold, so is
Is. 30:22 defile o. of molten ima.
49:18 clothe thee as with an o.
Ezek. 7:20 the beauty of his o.
1 Pet. 3:4 o. of meek, quiet spirit

**ORNAMENTS.**

Ex. 33:4 no man put on him o.
5 put off thy o. from thee, 6
Jud. 8:21 o. on camels' neck
2 Sam. 1:24 S. who put o. on you
Is. 3:18 tinkling o. about feet
61:10 decketh himself with o.
Jer. 2:32 can a maid forget her o.
4:30 deckest thee wi. o. of gold
Ezek. 16:7 come to excellent o.
11 decked thee with o. put
23:40 deckedst thyself with o.

**ORNAN.**

1 Chr. 21:15 floor of O. 18, 28
20 O. turned back, saw angel
25 Da. gave to O. 600 shekels

**ORPAH.**

Ruth 1:4 name of one O. other R.
14 O. kissed Naomi, but Ruth

**ORPHANS.**

Lam. 5:3 are o. our mothers wid.

**OSPREY, OSSIFRAGE.**

Lev. 11:13 o. and o. Deut. 14:12

**OSTRICH, ES.**

Job 39:13 wings and feath. to o.?
Lam. 4:3 like o. in the wildern.

**OTHER.**

Gen. 28:17 none o. but ho. of G.
Jud. 13:10 came to me o. day
16:17 and be like any o. man
20 go out, as at o. times before
1 Sam. 3:10 L. called as at o. ti.
20:25 S. sat on seat as at o. tim.
21:9 there is no o. save th. here
Mat. 12:13 restored whole as o. Mark 3:5; Luke 6:10
Mark 7:4 many o. thin. th. be, 8
12:32 and there is none o. but he
Luke 14:32 o. is yet a gr. way off
18:11 that I am not as o. men
John 15:24 works no. o. man did
21:25 there are many o. things
Acts 4:12 nei. is salva. in any o.
8:34 himself, or of some o. man?

See GOD, GODS, ONE, SIDE.

**OTHERS.**

Mat. 5:47 wh. do ye more th. o.?
Mark 15:31 saved o. Luke 23:35
Phil. 2:4 also on the things of o.
1 Thes. 2:6 not yet of o. sought

**OTHERWISE.**

2 Chr. 30:18 they eat passover o.
Ps. 38:16 o. should rej. over me
Rom. 11:6 o. grace no mo. grace; o. work is no more work
Gal. 5:10 will be none o. minded
Phil. 3:15 any thing you be o.
1 Tim. 6:3 if any man teach o.

**OTHNIEL.**

Jos. 15:17 O. took it, Jud. 1:13
Jud. 3:9 raised deliverer, O. 11

**OUCHES.**

Ex. 28:11 o. of gold, 39:6, 13
13 thou shalt make o. of gold
14 fasten chains to the o. 39:18
25 thou shalt fasten in two o.

**OUGHT, or rather AUGHT.**

Gen. 39:6 he knew not o. he had
47:18 there is not o. left
Ex. 12:46 not car. forth o. flesh
Lev. 11:25 whoso beareth o. car.
19:6 if o. remain unto third day
25:14 sellest o. or buyest o.
Num. 15:24 if o. be committed
30:6 or uttered o. out of her lips
Deut. 4:2 not add or diminish o.
26:14 nei. have I taken o. in my mourn. nor given o. for dead
Jos. 21:45 there failed not o.
Ruth 1:17 if o. but death part
1 Sam. 12:4 nor hast th. taken o.
5 have not found o. in my ha.
25:7 neither was th. o. missing
30:22 he will not give them o.
2 Sam. 3:35 if I taste bread or o.
14:10 whoso saith o. to thee
2 Sam. 14:19 can turn fr. o. my lo.
Mat. 5:23 brother hath o. ag. th.
21:3 if any man say o. to you
Mark 7:12 suf. him no more do o.
8:23 and asked him if he saw o.
11:25 forgive, if ye have o. ag.
John 4:33 brought him o. to eat?
Acts 4:32 nei. said o. was his own
24:19 if they had o. against me
28:19 had o. to ac. my nation of
Phile. 18 if he oweth thee o.

**OUGHT.**

Gen. 20:9 o. not be done, 34:7: Lev. 4:2, 27

2 Sam. 13:12 no such th. o. to be
1 Chr. 12:32 kn. what Is. o. to do
Mat. 23:23 o. ha. done, Lu. 11:42
Acts 24:19 who o. to have been
Rom. 8:26 to pray for as we o.
1 Tim. 5:13 speak. th. they o. not
Tit. 1:11 teach. thi. they o. not
Jam. 3:10 these thi. o. not to be
4:15 that ye o. to say, If the L.
2 Pet. 3:11 what pers. o. ye to be
3 John 8 we therefore o. to rece.

**OUGHTEST.**

1 K. 2:9 wh. thou o. to do to him
Mat. 25:27 o. to put my money
Acts 10:6 tell thee what thou o.
1 Tim. 3:15 how th. o. to behave

OUR. See BROTHER, FATHER, LORD.

**OURS.**

Gen. 31:16 hath taken that is o.
34:23 shall not ev. beast be o.?
Mark 12:7 the inheritance shall be o. Luke 20:14
1 Cor. 1:2 Jesus, both th. and o.
2 Cor. 1:14 ye are o. in day of L.

**OUTCAST, S.**

Ps. 147:2 gathereth o. of Israel
Is. 11:12 shall assemble o. 56:8
16:3 hide o. 4 let my o. dwell
27:13 o. in land of Eg. worship
Jer. 30:17 bec. they called thee o.
49:36 o. of Elam shall not come

**OUTER.**

Ezek. 46:21 broug. me to o. court
Mat. 8:12 o. darkn. 22:13; 25:30

**OUTGOINGS.**

Jos. 17:9 o. of it at sea, 19:29
18 and the o. it shall be thine
18:19 o. of the border at north
19:14 o. thereof are in the valley
22 o. of border at the Jord. 33
Ps. 65:8 makest o. of morning

**OUTLANDISH.**

Neh. 13:26 o. women caused Sol.

**OUTLIVED.**

Jud. 2:7 elders that o. Joshua

**OUTRAGEOUS.**

Prov. 27:4 wrath is cruel, ang. o.

**OUTRUN.**

John 20:4 other disciple o. Peter

**OUTSIDE.**

Jud. 7:11 Gideon went to the o.
1 K. 7:9 o. towards great court
Ezek. 40:5 beho. a wall on the o.
Mat. 23:25 o. of cup, Luke 11:39
26 that o. of them be clean also

**OUTSTRETCHED.**

Deut. 26:8 us out with an o. arm
Jer. 21:5 fight you with o. arm
27:5 made earth by my o. arm

**OUTWARD.**

1 Sam. 16:7 looketh on o. appear.
1 Chr. 26:29 for the o. business
Neh. 11:16 Levites for o. business
Est. 6:4 Ham. come to o. court
Ezek. 40:17 brought into o. court
Mat. 23:27 appear beautiful o.
Rom. 2:28 which is o. in flesh
2 Cor. 4:16 tho' our o. man perish
10:7 things after o. appearance?
1 Pet. 3:3 not that o. adorning

**OUTWARDLY.**

Mat. 23:28 o. appear righteous
Rom. 2:28 not a Jew wh. is one o.

**OUTWENT.**

Mark 6:33 ran afoot, and o. them

**OVEN.**

Lev. 2:4 offering baken in o. 7:9
11:35 whether it be o. or ranges
26:26 bake your bread in one o.
Ps. 21:9 make them as a fiery o.
Lam. 5:10 skin was black like o.
Hos. 7:4 as an o. heated by baker
6 made ready heart like an o. 7
Mal. 4:1 that shall burn as an o.
Mat. 6:30 cast into o. Luke 12:28

**OVENS.**

Ex. 8:3 frogs come into thine o.

**OVER.**

Num. 27:16 set man o. congrega.
Cant. 2:11 winter past, rain is o.

**OVER against.**

Num. 8:2 lamps gi. light o. a. 3
2 Sam. 5:23 come on them o. ag. mulberry-trees, 1 Chr. 14:14
1 K. 20:29 pitched one o. a. other
Neh. 7:3 ev. one to be o. a. house
Ec. 7:14 God set one o. a. other
Jer. 31:39 line go forth o. ag. it

See ALL, HIM, JORDAN, ISRAEL, ME, THEE, THEM, US, YOU.

**OVERCAME.**

Acts 19:16 evil spi. was, o. them
Rev. 3:21 even as I also o.
12:11 o. him by blood of Lamb

**OVERCHARGE, D.**

Luke 21:34 lest your hearts be o.
2 Cor. 2:5 that I may not o. you

**OVERCOME.**

Gen. 49:19 troop shall o. him
Ex. 32:18 that cry for being o.
Num. 13:30 are well able to o. it
22:11 peradventure I sh. o. them
2 K. 16:5 Ahaz, could not o. him
Cant. 6:5 eyes, they have o. me
Is. 28:1 head of them that are o.
Jer. 23:9 man whom wine hath o.
Luke 11:22 stronger shall o. him
John 16:33 I have o. the world
Rom. 3:4 o. wh. thou art judged
12:21 be not o. of evil. o. evil
2 Pet. 2:19 of whom man is o.
20 ag. entangled therein and o.
1 John 2:13 o. wicked one, 14
4:4 are of God, have o. them
Rev. 11:7 beast sh. o. witnesses
13:7 war with saints, o. them
17:14 and Lamb shall o. them

**OVERCOMETH.**

1 John 5:4 born of God o. world, victory o. world, 5
Rev. 2:7 o. will I give tree of life
11 he that o. shall not be hurt
17 him that o. will I gi. to eat
26 him that o. will I give pow.
3:5 he that o. shall be clothed
12 him that o. will I make pil.
21 that o. will I grant to sit
21:7 that o. shall inh. all things

**OVERDRIVE.**

Gen. 33:13 if men sho. o. them

**OVERFLOW.**

Deut. 11:4 water of Red sea o.
Ps. 69:2 come where floods o.
15 let not waterfloods o. me
Is. 8:8 thro' Jud. o. and go over
10:22 consumpti. decreed sh. o.
28:17 waters o. the hiding-place
43:2 rivers they sh. not o. thee
Jer. 47:2 waters of north o. land
Dan. 11:10 certai. come, o. 26, 40
Joel 2:24 fats o. with wine, 3:13

**OVERFLOWED, ETH.**

Jos. 3:15 in harvest Jor. o. banks
Ps. 78:20 smote rock, streams o.
2 Pet. 3:6 world o. with water

**OVERFLOWING.**

Job 28:11 bindeth floods from o.
38:25 watercourse for o. of wat.
Is. 28:2 flood of mighty wat. o.
15 when o. scourge pass, 18
30:28 his breath as o. stream
Jer. 47:2 north sh. be an o. flood
Ezek. 13:11 be an o. shower, 13
38:22 rain o. rain and hailstones
Hab. 3:10 the o. of the water

**OVERFLOWN.**

1 Chr. 12:15 Jor. when it had o.
Job 22:16 wh. foundation was o.
Dan. 11:22 with flood they be o.

**OVERLAY.**

Ex. 25:11 o. ark, 24; 30:3
27:2 o. altar with brass, 38:2

**OVERLAID.**

Ex. 26:32 pillars o. with gold
38:6 o. staves of shittim-wood
1 K. 3:19 died, because she o. it
2 Chr. 4:9 he o. doors with brass
Cant. 5:14 belly as bri. ivory o.

See GOLD.

**OVERLAYING.**

Ex. 38:17 the o. of chapiters, 19

**OVERLIVED.**

Jos. 24:31 days of elders th. o. J.

**OVERMUCH.**

Ec. 7:16 righte. o. 17 be not o.
2 Cor. 2:7 swallow. with o. sor.

**OVERPASS.**

Jer. 5:28 they o. deeds of wicked

**OVERPAST.**

Ps. 57:1 refuge until calam. be o.
Is. 26:20 hide until indign. be o.

**OVERPLUS.**

Lev. 25:27 let him restore the o.

**OVERRAN, RUNNING.**

2 Sam. 18:23 Ahimaaz o. Cushi
Nah. 1:8 an o. flood will he make

**OVERSEE.**

1 Chr. 9:29 appointed to o. vess.
2 Chr. 2:2 3,600 to o. them

**OVERSEER.**

Gen. 39:4 made o. over house, 5
Neh. 11:9 Joel th. o. 14 Zabd. o.
22 o. of Levites; 12:42 Jez. o.
Prov. 6:7 the ant having no o.

**OVERSEERS.**

Gen. 41:34 let Pharaoh appoint o.
2 Chr. 2:18 Solomon set 3,600 o.
31:13 o. under hand of Cononiah
34:12 o. of all that wrought, 13
17 deliv. mon. into hand of o.
Acts 20:28 H. Ghost made you o.

**OVERSHADOW, ED.**

Mat. 17:5 bright cloud o. them, Mark 9:7; Luke 9:34
Luke 1:35 power of High. o. thee
Acts 5:15 shadow of P. o. them

**OVERSIGHT.**

Gen. 43:12 peradv. it was an o.
Num. 3:32 o. of them that keep
4:16 the o. of all the tabernacle
2 K. 12:11 that had o. of house of L. 22:5, 9; 2 Chr. 34:10
1 Chr. 9:23 had the o. of the gates
Neh. 11:16 had the o. of business
13:4 the o. of the house of God
1 Pet. 5:2 taking o. not by const.

**OVERSPREAD, ING.**

Gen. 9:19 of th. the earth was o.
Dan. 9:27 the o. of abominations

**OVERTAKE.**

Gen. 44:4 when thou dost o. th.
Ex. 15:9 I will pursue, I will o.
Deut. 19:6 lest avenger o. slayer
28:2 blessings come and o. thee
15 these curses shall o. thee, 45
Jos. 2:5 for ye shall o. them
1 Sam. 30:8 thou sh. surely o. th.
2 Sam. 15:14 lest Absalom o. us
Is. 59:9 nei. doth justice o. us
Jer. 42:16 sw. ye feared sh. o. you
Hos. 2:7 shall not o. her lovers
10:9 the battle did not o. them
Amos 9:10 evil shall not o. us
13 ploughman sh. o. the reaper
1 Thes. 5:4 should o. you as thief

**OVERTAKEN, ETH.**

1 Chr. 21:12 flee till sword o. th.

*Ps.* 18:37 purs. enemies *o.* them
*Gal.* 6:1 if a man be *o.* in a fault

**OVERTHREW.**

*Gen.* 19:25 God *o.* these cities, 29
*Ex.* 14:27 L. *o.* Eg. *Ps.* 136:15
*Deut.* 29:23 which L. *o.* in anger
*Is.* 13:19 when G. *o.* Sodom and Gomo. *Jer.* 50:40; *Amos* 4:11
*Jer.* 20:16 be as cities the Lord *o.*
*Mat.* 21:12 J. *o.* tables of money-chang. *Mark* 11:15; *John* 2:15

**OVERTHROW, Substantive.**

*Gen.* 19:29 G. sent Lot out of *o.*
*Deut.* 29:23 *o.* of Sod. *Jer.* 49:18
2 *Pet.* 2:6 condem. cities with *o.*

**OVERTHROW, Verb.**

*Gen.* 19:21 I will not *o.* this city
*Ex.* 23:24 thou sh. *o.* their gods
*Deut.* 12:3 ye shall *o.* their altars
2 *Sam.* 10:3 D. sent to spy and *o.*
11:25 make battle strong, *o.* it
1 *Chr.* 19:3 David sent to *o.* land
*Ps.* 106:26 to *o.* them in wildern.
27 to *o.* their seed am. nations
140:4 have pur. to *o.* my goings
11 evil hunt vio. man to *o.* him
*Prov.* 18:5 not good to *o.* righte.
*Hag.* 2:22 I will *o.* the throne of kingd. I will *o.* the chariots
*Acts* 5:39 if it be of G. ye can. *o.*
2 *Tim.* 2:18 *o.* the faith of some

**OVERTHROWETH.**

*Job* 12:19 lead. princes, *o.* mighty
*Prov.* 13:6 wickedness *o.* sinner
21:12 G. *o.* wicked for wickedn.
22:12 *o.* words of transgressor
29:4 he that receiv. gifts *o.* land

**OVERTHROWN.**

*Ex.* 15:7 hast *o.* them that rose
*Jud.* 9:40 and many were *o.*
2 *Sam.* 17:9 some of them be *o.*
2 *Chr.* 14:13 Ethiopians were *o.*
*Job* 19:6 know th. G. hath *o.* me
*Ps.* 141:6 their judges are *o.*
*Prov.* 11:11 city is *o.* by wicked
12:7 wicked *o.* 14:11 ho. of wic.
*Is.* 1:7 your land is desolate as *o.*
*Jer.* 18:23 let them be *o.* bef. th.
*Lam.* 4:6 S. was *o.* as in moment
*Dan.* 11:41 many countries be *o.*
*Amos* 4:11 I have *o.* some of you
*Jon.* 3:4 40 days Ninev. sh. be *o.*
1 *Cor.* 10:5 were *o.* in wilderness

**OVERTOOK.**

*Gen.* 31:23 *o.* Jacob in mount
25 Lab. *o.* Jacob; 44:6 steward
*Jud.* 18:22 Micah *o.* chil. of Dan
20:42 battle *o.* men of Benjamin
2 *K.* 25:5 army of Chaldeans *o.* Zedekiah, *Jer.* 39:5; 52:8
*Lam.* 1:3 her persecutors *o.* her

**OVERTURN.**

*Job* 12:15 waters, they *o.* earth
*Ezek.* 21:27 I will *o.* *o.* *o.* it

**OVERTURNED, ETH.**

*Jud.* 7:13 the tent fell and *o.* it
*Job* 9:5 which *o.* the mountains
28:9 *o.* mountains by the roots
34:25 know th. works and *o.* th.

**OVERWHELM, ED.**

*Job* 6:27 yea, ye *o.* fatherless
*Ps.* 55:5 and horror hath *o.* me
61:2 when my heart is *o.*
77:3 my spirit *o.* 142:3; 143:4
78:53 the sea *o.* their enemies
124:4 then the waters had *o.* us

**OVERWISE.**

*Ec.* 7:16 nor make thyself *o.*

**OWE.**

*Rom.* 13:8 *o.* no man any thing

**OWED.**

*Mat.* 18:24 one *o.* him 10,000 tal.
28 one which *o.* him a 100 pen.
*Luke* 7:41 the one *o.* 500 pence

**OWEST, ETH.**

*Mat.* 18:28 pay me that thou *o.*
*Luke* 16:5 how much *o.* thou? 7
*Phile.* 18 thee, or *o.* thee aught
19 *o.* to me even thine own

**OWL.**

*Lev.* 11:16 *o.* and cuckoo, *Deut.* 14:15, 16: *Is.* 34:11, 15
17 the little *o.* and cormorant
*Ps.* 102:6 I am like *o.* of desert

**OWLS.**

*Job* 30:29 I am companion to *o.*
*Is.* 13:21 *o.* shall dwell there, 34:13; *Jer.* 50:39
43:20 dragons and *o.* honor me
*Mic.* 1:8 make a mourning as *o.*

**OWN.**

1 *Chr.* 29:14 *o.* have we giv. thee
16 we prepared, is all thine *o.*
*Mat.* 20:15 do wh. I will wi. *o.*?
*Luke* 16:12 you that which is *o.*?
*John* 1:11 came to his *o.* *o.* rece.
13:1 loved his *o.* that were
15:19 world would love his *o.*
*Acts* 5:4 was it not in th. *o.* pow.?
1 *Cor.* 6:19 ye are not your *o.*
10:24 let no man seek his *o.*
29 cons. not th. *o.* but of oth.
13:5 charity seeketh not her *o.*
*Phil.* 2:21 seek their *o.* things
1 *Tim.* 5:8 provide not for his *o.*

*See* COUNSEL, COUNTRY, EYES, HEART, HOUSE, LAND, PEOPLE, SELF, SELVES, SOUL, WAY, WAYS, WILL.

**OWNER.**

*Ex.* 21:28 *o.* of ox shall be quit
34 *o.* of pit sh. make it good
36 his *o.* hath not kept him in
22:11 *o.* of it sh. accept thereof
12 make restitution to *o.*
15 but if *o.* thereof be with it
1 *K.* 16:24 Shemer, *o.* of the hill
*Is.* 1:3 the ox knoweth his *o.*
*Acts* 27:11 believed *o.* of the ship

**OWNERS.**

*Job* 31:39 caused *o.* to lose lives
*Prov.* 1:19 taketh away life of *o.*
*Ec.* 5:11 what good is there to *o.*
13 riches kept for *o.* to th. hurt
*Luke* 19:33 *o.* said, Why loose ye

**OWNETH.**

*Lev.* 14:35 he that *o.* the house
*Acts* 21:11 bind man *o.* th. girdle

**OX.**

*Ex.* 20:17 not covet. *o.* *Deut.* 5:21
21:28 if *o.* gore, be stoned, 29–36
22:1 if man steal *o.* or sheep
4 whether it be *o.* or ass, he
23:4 if thou meet th. enemy's *o.*
12 thine *o.* and thine ass rest
*Ex.* 34:19 firstl. of *o.* or sheep mi.
*Lev.* 7:23 eat no fat of *o.*
*Num.* 7:3 for each of princes *o.*
22:4 as the *o.* licketh up grass
*Deut.* 5:14 *o.* do no work on sab.
14:4 *o.* sheep, and goat may eat
22:1 not see bro.'s *o.* go astray
10 not plough with *o.* and ass
25:4 not muzzle *o.* treadeth out corn, 1 *Cor.* 9:9; 1 *Tim.* 5:18
*Jos.* 6:21 they destroy *o.* and sheep, 1 *Sam.* 15:15
*Jud.* 3:31 slew 600 with *o.*-goad
6:4 left neither sheep nor *o.*
1 *Sam.* 12:3 wh. *o.* have I taken?
14:34 bring ev. man *o.* and sheep
*Neh.* 5:18 for me daily one *o.*
*Job* 6:5 loweth *o.* over fodder?
24:3 take widow's *o.* for pledge
40:15 Behemoth eat. grass as *o.*
*Ps.* 69:31 please L. better than *o.*
106:20 glory into similitu. of *o.*
*Prov.* 7:22 *o.* goeth to slaughter
14:4 incre. by strength of the *o.*
15:17 better than a stalled *o.*
*Is.* 1:3 the *o.* knoweth his owner
11:7 lion shall eat straw like *o.*
32:20 send for. the feet of the *o.*
66:3 killeth *o.* as if he slew man
*Jer.* 11:19 was like a lamb or an *o.*
*Ezek.* 1:10 four had face of an *o.*
*Luke* 13:15 each loose *o.* on sab.
14:5 an *o.* or ass fallen into a pit

**Wild OX.**

*Deut.* 14:5 *wild o.* ye may eat

**OXEN.**

*Gen.* 12:16 Ab. had *o.* and asses
32:5 J. said, I have *o.* and asses
34:28 sons of J. took Shech. *o.*
*Ex.* 9:3 hand of Lord is upon *o.*
22:1 restore five *o.* for one ox
*Num.* 7:3 princes bro. twelve *o.*
22:40 Balak offered *o.* and sheep
23:1 prepare me here seven *o.*
*Deut.* 14:26 bestow money for *o.*
1 *Sam.* 11:7 hewed yoke of *o.*
14:14 yoke of *o.* might plough
32 took sheep and *o.* and slew
15:9 Agag and the best of the *o.*
14 what meaneth lowing of *o.*?
15 spared best of sheep and *o.*
27:9 David took away the *o.*
2 *Sam.* 6:6 hold of it, *o.* shook it
13 Da. sacrificed *o.* and fatlings
24:24 bought thres.-floor and *o.*
1 *K.* 1:9 Adonijah slew *o.* 19, 25
4:23 daily provision, ten fat *o.*
7:25 one sea, twelve *o.* under it, 44; 2 *Chr.* 4:4, 15
8:63 S. off. sacrifice to L. 22,000 *o.* 120,000 sheep, 2 *Chr.* 7:5
19:19 El. was ploughing with *o.*
20 Elisha left *o.* ran after Elij.
21 took yoke of *o.* slew them
2 *K.* 5:26 is it a time to rec. *o.*?
2 *Chr.* 15:11 offered of spoil 700 *o.*
18:2 Ahab killed sheep and *o.*
29:33 consecrated things 600 *o.*
31:6 they brought in tithes of *o.*
35:8 for passo. three hundred *o.*
*Job* 1:3 his substance was 500 *o.*
14 *o.* ploughing, asses feeding
42:12 gave him 1,000 yoke of *o.*
*Ps.* 8:7 to have dominion over *o.*
144:14 that our *o.* may be strong
*Prov.* 14:4 wh. no *o.* crib is clean
*Is.* 7:25 for sending forth of *o.*
22:13 joy and gladn. slaying *o.*
30:24 *o.* and asses eat cl. prov.
*Jer.* 51:23 I break husb. and *o.*
*Dan.* 4:25 eat gr. as *o.* 33; 5:21
*Amos* 6:12 plough there with *o.*?
*Mat.* 22:4 *o.* and fatlings killed
*Luke* 14:19 bought 5 yoke of *o.*
*John* 2:14 those in temple sold *o.*
*Acts* 14:13 priest of Jup. bro. *o.*
1 *Cor.* 9:9 doth G. ta. care for *o.*?

OZEM. 1 *Chr.* 2:15
OZIAS. *Mat.* 1:8, 9

# P

PAARAI. 2 *Sam.* 23:35

**PACES.**

2 *Sam.* 6:13 when gone six *p.* he

**PACIFY, ED, ETH.**

*Est.* 7:10 then king's wrath *p.*
*Prov.* 16:14 a wise man *p.* wrath
21:14 a gift in secret *p.* anger
*Ec.* 10:4 yielding *p.* gr. offences
*Ezek.* 16:63 when I am *p.* toward

**PADAN-ARAM.**

*Gen.* 25:20 dau. of Bethuel of P.
28:6 Isa. sent Jacob away to P.
7 his father, and was gone to P.
31:18 had gotten in P.
*Gen.* 35:9 J. when he came fr. P.
26 sons born to him in P. 46:15

**PADDLE.**

*Deut.* 23:13 have *p.* on weapon

**PAGIEL.**

*Num.* 1:13 P. son of Ocran, 7:72

PAID. *See after* PAY.

**PAIN.**

*Job* 14:22 flesh on him sh. have *p.*
15:20 wicked travaileth with *p.*
33:19 is chastened also with *p.*
*Ps.* 25:18 mine affliction and *p.*
48:6 *p.* as a woman in travail, *Is.* 13:8; 26:17
*Is.* 21:3 my loins filled with *p.*
26:18 child, we have been in *p.*
66:7 bef. her *p.* came, she was
*Jer.* 6:24 *p.* as wo. in trav. 22:23
12:13 put themselves to *p.* but
15:18 why is my *p.* perpetual
30:23 with *p.* on head of wicked
51:8 Babylon, take balm for *p.*
*Ezek.* 30:4 great *p.* in Ethiopia, 9
16 Sin shall have great *p.*
*Mic.* 4:10 *p.* and labor to bring
*Nah.* 2:10 much *p.* is in all loins
*Rom.* 8:22 creation travail. in *p.*
*Rev.* 16:10 gnawed tongues for *p.*
21:4 nor shall th. be any more *p.*
*See* PANGS.

**PAINED.**

*Ps.* 55:4 my heart is sore *p.*
*Is.* 23:5 they shall be sorely *p.*
*Jer.* 4:19 I am *p.* at very heart
*Joel* 2:6 people shall be much *p.*
*Rev.* 12:2 and *p.* to be delivered

**PAINS.**

1 *Sam.* 4:19 *p.* came upon her
*Ps.* 116:3 *p.* of hell gat hold
*Acts* 2:24 hav. loosed *p.* of death
*Rev.* 16:11 blasphem. bec. of *p.*

**PAINFUL, NESS.**

*Ps.* 73:16 it was too *p.* for me
2 *Cor.* 11:27 and *p.* in watchings

**PAINTED, ST.**

2 *K.* 9:30 Jezebel *p.* her face
*Jer.* 22:14 and *p.* with vermilion
*Ezek.* 23:40 thou *p.* thy eyes

**PAINTING.**

*Jer.* 4:30 thou rentest face wi. *p.*

**PAIR.**

*Luke* 2:24 offer *p.* of turtle-doves
*Rev.* 6:5 a *p.* of balances in hand

**PALACE.**

1 *K.* 16:18 Zimri burnt king's *p.*
21:1 Naboth had viney. by *p.*
2 *K.* 15:25 smote Pekahiah in *p.*
20:18 eunuchs in *p.* of king
1 *Chr.* 29:1 the *p.* is not for man
19 perfect heart to build the *p.*
*Ezr.* 4:14 maintenance fr. the *p.*
*Neh.* 1:1 was in Shushan the *p.*
7:2 ruler of *p.* charge over Jer.
*Est.* 3:15 in Shushan the *p.* 8:14
9:12 destroyed 500 men in the *p.*
*Ps.* 45:15 enter into king's *p.*
144:12 after similitude of a *p.*
*Cant.* 8:9 build a *p.* of silver
*Is.* 25:2 made *p.* of strangers
*Dan.* 4:4 flourishing in my *p.*
6:18 king went to *p.* pas. night
11:45 he shall plant *p.* between seas
*Amos* 4:3 shall cast them into *p.*
*Nah.* 2:6 opened, *p.* dissolved
*Mat.* 26:58 Pe. followed Jesus to high-priest's *p.* *Mark* 14:54
*Luke* 11:21 a strong man keep. *p.*
*Phil.* 1:13 bonds manifest in *p.*

**PALACES.**

2 *Chr.* 36:19 and burnt all the *p.*
*Ps.* 45:8 myrrh, out of ivory *p.*
48:3 G. is known in *p.* for refu.
13 mark bulwarks, consider *p.*
78:69 sanctuary like high *p.*
122:7 prosperity within thy *p.*
*Prov.* 30:28 spider is in king's *p.*
*Is.* 13:22 dragons sh. cry in thy *p.*
32:14 the *p.* shall be forsaken
34:13 thorns come up in her *p.*
*Jer.* 6:5 let us destroy her *p.*
9:21 death is entered into our *p.*
17:27 fire shall devour *p.* of Jer.
49:27 consume *p.* of Benhadad
*Lam.* 2:5 hath swallowed her *p.*
*Ezek.* 19:7 knew their desol. *p.*
25:4 shall set their *p.* in thee
*Amos* 3:9 publish in *p.* at Ashhod, in *p.* of Egypt
10 store up robbery in their *p.*
11 *p.* be spoiled; 6:8 hate *p.*
*Mic.* 5:5 he shall tread in our *p.*
*See* DEVOUR.

**PALE, NESS.**

*Is.* 29:22 nei. shall face wax *p.*
*Jer.* 30:6 all faces turned into *p.*
*Rev.* 6:8 looked, behold *p.* horse

**PALESTINA.**

*Ex.* 15:14 hold on men of P.
*Is.* 14:29 rej. not thou, whole P.
31 cry, O city, thou, whole P.

**PALM.**

*Lev.* 14:15 pour into *p.* 26
*John* 18:22 struck Jesus with *p.*

**PALM branches.**

*Neh.* 8:15 to mount and fet. *p. b.*

**PALMER-WORM.**

*Joel* 1:4 what *p.-w.* left, loc. eat.
2:25 restore years *p.-w.* eaten
*Amos* 4:9 fig-trees, the *p.-w.* dev.

**PALMS.**

1 *Sam.* 5:4 *p.* of hands cut off
2 *K.* 9:35 they found skull and *p.*
*Is.* 49:16 grav. thee on *p.* of han.
*Dan.* 10:10 set me on *p.* of hands
*Mat.* 26:67 others smote him wi. *p.* of their hands, *Mark* 14:65
*Rev.* 7:9 white robes, *p.* in han.

**PALM-TREE.**

*Jud.* 4:5 dwelt under *p.-t.* of D.
*Ps.* 92:12 right. flour like *p.-t.*
*Cant.* 7:7 stature is like to a *p.-t.*
8 I will go up to the *p.-t.*
*Jer.* 10:5 are upright as the *p.-t.*
*Ezek.* 41:19 face of man tow. *p.-t.*
*Joel* 1:12 *p.-t.* and apple-tree

**PALM-TREES.**

*Ex.* 15:27 El. wh. were 70 *p.-t.*
*Lev.* 23:40 take branches of *p.-t.*
*Deut.* 34:3 show. him city of *p.-t.*
*Jud.* 1:16 out of city of *p.-t.*
3:13 M. possessed city of *p.-t.*
1 *K.* 6:29 wi. figures of *p.-t.* 32,35; 7:36; 2 *Chr.* 3:5; *Ezek.* 40:16
2 *Chr.* 28:15 bro. th. to ci. of *p.-t.*
*John* 12:13 took branches of *p.-t.*

**PALSY, IES.**

*Mat.* 4:24 had *p.* he healed them, *Mark* 2:3; *Luke* 5:18
8:6 ser. lieth at home sick of *p.*
9:2 Je. said to sick of *p.* S. thy sins be forgiven, *Mark* 2:5
*Mark* 2:10 sick of *p.* *Luke* 5:24
*Acts* 8:7 many taken with *p.* and
9:33 Eneas, who was sick of *p.*

**PAMPHYLIA.**

*Acts* 13:13 P. came to Perga in P.
15:38 departed from them fr. P.
27:5 had sailed over sea of P.

**PAN.**

*Lev.* 2:5 meat-offer. baken in *p.*
6:21 in a *p.* it shall be made
7:9 dressed in *p.* shall be pries.
1 *Sam.* 2:14 serv. stuck it into *p.*
2 *Sam.* 13:9 Tam. took *p.* poured
*Ezek.* 4:3 take unto thee iron *p.*

**PANS.**

*Ex.* 27:3 make *p.* to rec. ashes
*Num.* 11:8 baked manna in *p.*
1 *Chr.* 9:31 thi. made in *p.* 23:29
2 *Chr.* 35:13 offer. sod they in *p.*

**PANGS.**

*Is.* 13:8 *p.* sh. take hold of them
21:3 *p.* take hold me as *p.* of w.
26:17 wom. crieth out in her *p.*
*Jer.* 22:23 gracious when *p.* come
48:41 heart of wom. in *p.* 49:22
50:43 *p.* as of a wom. *Mic.* 4:9

**PANNAG.**

*Ezek.* 27:17 traded in market, P.

**PANT, ED, ETH.**

*Ps.* 38:10 my heart *p.* stren. fail.
42:1 as hart *p.* so *p.* my soul
119:131 open. my mouth and *p.*
*Is.* 21:4 at the vision my heart *p.*
*Amos* 2:7 that *p.* after the dust

**PAPER.**

*Is.* 19:7 *p.* reeds shall wither
2 *John* 12 would not write wi. *p.*

PAPHOS. *Acts* 13:6

**PAPS.**

*Ezek.* 23:21 for the *p.* of thy you.
*Luke* 11:27 bles. are *p.* th. suck.
23:29 blessed *p.* never gave suck
*Rev.* 1:13 girt *p.* with gold. gird.

**PARABLE.**

*Num.* 23:7 Balaam took up *p.* and said, 24:3, 15, 20, 21, 23
*Job* 27:1 J. continued his *p.* 29:1
*Ps.* 49:4 I will incline ear to a *p.*
78:2 mouth, in a *p.* will I utter
*Prov.* 26:7 *p.* in mouth of fools, 9
*Ezek.* 17:2 speak a *p.* to Israel.
24:3 utter *p.* to rebellious house
*Mic.* 2:4 take up a *p.* against you
*Hab.* 2:6 these take up *p.* ag. you
*Mat.* 13:18 hear *p.* of the sower
24 ano. *p.* put he, 31, 33; 21:33
34 with. *p.* sp. not, *Mark* 4:34
24:32 learn a *p.* of the fig-tree, *Mark* 13:28; *Luke* 21:29
*Mark* 4:10 asked him of *p.* 7:17; *Luke* 8:9
12:12 spoken *p.* ag. th. *Lu.* 20:19
*Luke* 5:36 he spake a *p.* to them, 6:39; 8:4; 12:16; 13:6; 14:7; 15:3; 18:1, 9; 19:11; 20:9; 21:29; *John* 10:6
12:41 L. spak. thou this *p.* to us?

**PARABLES.**
Ezek. 20:49 doth he not speak p.?
Mat. 13:3 spake many things to them in p. 13:34; 22:1; Mark 3:23; 4:2, 13, 33; 12:1
Mark 4:13 how will ye kn. all p.?
Luke 8:10 p. seeing might not see

**PARADISE.**
Luke 23:43 to-day with me in p.
2 Cor. 12:4 was caught up into p.
Rev. 2:7 in the midst of p. of G.

**PARAMOURS.**
Ezek. 23:20 doted upon their p.

**PARAN.**
Gen. 21:21 wil. of P. Num. 10:12; 12:16; 13:3, 26; 1 Sam. 25:1
Deut. 33:2 forth from mount P.
Hab. 3:3 Holy One came from P.

PARBAR. 1 Chr. 26:18

**PARCEL.**
Gen. 33:19 J. bought p. of a field, Jos. 24:32; John 4:5
Ruth 4:3 Na. selleth a p. of land
1 Chr. 11:13 p. of gr. full of bar. 14

**PARCHED.**
Is. 35:7 p. ground become pool
Jer. 17:6 shall inhabit p. places
See CORN.

**PARCHMENTS.**
2 Tim. 4:13 bri. especially the p.

**PARDON.**
Ex. 23:21 not p. your trangres.
34:9 p. our iniq. Num. 14:19
1 Sam. 15:25 p. my sins
2 K. 5:18 Lord, p. thy servant
24:4 which Lord would not p.
2 Chr. 30:18 good L. p. ev. one
Neh. 9:17 G. ready to p. gracious
Job 7:21 why not p. my transg.?
Ps. 25:11 for name's sake p. ini.
Is. 55:7 he will abundantly p.
Jer. 5:1 I will p. it; 7 shall I p.
33:8 I will p. all their iniquities
50:20 I will p. whom I reserve

**PARDONED, ETH.**
Num. 14:20 I have p. ac. to word
Is. 40:2 tell her that iniq. is p.
Lam. 3:42 thou hast not p.
Mic. 7:18 G. like thee, p. iniq.?

**PARE.**
Deut. 21:12 shave head, p. nails

**PARENTS.**
Mat. 10:21 children shall rise up against their p. Mark 13:12
Luke 2:27 p. brought in child Je.
8:56 her p. were astonished, but
18:29 is no man that hath left p.
21:16 ye shall be betrayed by p.
John 9:2 who did sin, man or p.?
22 these words spake p. 23
Rom. 1:30 diso. to p. 2 Tim. 3:2
2 Cor. 12:14 chi. not lay up for p.
Eph. 6:1 chil. obey p. Col. 3:20
1 Tim. 5:4 learn to requite th. p.
Heb. 11:23 Mo. was hid of his p.

**PARLOR, S.**
Jud. 3:20 Eg. was sitting in p.
23 Ehud shut doors of the p.
1 Sam. 9:22 S. bro. them to p.
1 Chr. 28:11 gave S. pattern of p.

PARMENAS. Acts 6:5

**PART.**
Ex. 19:17 at nether p. of mount.
Lev. 2:16 p. of beaten corn, p. oil
Num. 18:20 nei. have p. am. th. Deut. 10:9; 12:12; 14:27, 29; 18:1; Jos. 14:4; 18:7; I am thy p. and inherit. in Israel
22:41 utmost p. of people, 23:13
Jos. 22:25 ye have no p. in L. 27
Ruth 2:3 to light on p. of field
3:13 perf. to thee p. of kinsman
1 Sam. 23:20 our p. sh. be to del.
30:24 his p. is that goeth to bat.
2 Sam. 20:1 we have no p. in D.
2 K. 18:23 if able on thy p. to set riders. Is. 36:8
1 Chr. 12:29 greatest p. kept ho.
2 Chr. 29:16 prie. we. to inner p.
Neh. 1:9 cast out to uttermost p.
5:11 rest. hundredth p. of mon.
Job 32:17 I will answer my p.
Ps. 5:9 inward p. is wickedness
51:6 in hidden p. know wisdom
118:7 L. takes my p. with them
Prov. 8:26 nor highest p. of dust
31 rejoic. in habitable p. of ear.
17:2 p. of inherit. amo. breth.
Is. 7:18 hiss for fly in utmost p.
24:16 fr. utmost p. heard songs
44:16 he burneth p. in fire, 19
Ezek. 45:17 prince's p. to give
Dan. 2:33 p. iron, p. clay, 41, 42
5:5 king saw p. of the hand, 24
11:31 arms shall stand on his p.
Amos. 7:4 it dev. deep, eat up p.
Mark 4:38 in hinder p. of ship
9:40 not against us, is on our p.
Luke 10:42 M. hath chos. good p.
17:24 lightning lighteneth one p. shining to other p.
John 13:8 wash th. not, ha. no p.
19:23 four parts, ev. soldier a p.
Acts 1:17 obtained p. of ministry
25 may take p. of this minist.
5:2 Ananias kept p. of price, 3
8:21 thou hast neith. p. nor lot
14:4 p. wi. Jews. p. wi. apostles
19:32 p. knew not wheref. came
23:6 the one p. were Sadducees
27:12 more p. advised to depart
1 Cor. 12:24 honor to that p.
15:6 greater p. rem. to this day
16:17 was lacking on your p.
2 Cor. 6:15 p. believ. wi. infidel?
Tit. 2:8 that he of the contr. p.
Heb. 2:14 himself took p. of same
1 Pet. 4:14 on th. p. he is evil spo. of, on your p. glorified
Rev. 20:6 p. in first resurrection
21:8 liars sh. have p. in lake
22:19 G. shall take away his p.

**PART, Verb.**
Lev. 2:6 shalt p. meat-offering
Ruth 1:17 if aught but death p.
1 Sam. 30:24 they shall p. alike
2 Sam. 14:6 th. was none to p.
Job 41:6 shall they p. him among the merchants?
Ps. 22:18 they p. my garments

**In PART.**
Rom. 11:25 blindness in p. to Is.
1 Cor. 13:9 we know in p. and we prophecy in p.
10 that in p. sh. be done away
12 I know in p. but then sh. I
2 Cor. 1:14 acknowledged us in p.
2:5 not grieved me but in p.

**Third PART.**
2 K. 11:5 a t. p. enter on Sabba.
2 Chr. 23:4 t. p. of you be port.
Neh. 10:32 charge ours. wi. t. p.
Ezek. 5:2 burn with fire a t. p. a t. p. smite about it, a third p. scatter in the wind, 12
Zec. 13:8 a third p. shall be left
9 I will bring the t. p. thro' fire
Rev. 8:7 t. p. of trees was burnt
8 t. p. of sea became blood
9 t. p. of creat. died, t. p. ships
11 t. p. of wat. bec. wormwood
12 t. p. of sun, moon, and stars
9:15 prep. to slay t. p. of men
12:4 his tail drew t. p. of stars

**Fourth PART.**
1 Sam. 9:8 have f. part of shekel
1 K. 6:33 posts of olive-tree f. p.
2 K. 6:25 f. p. cab of doves' dung
Neh. 9:3 read one f. p. ano. f. p.
Rev 6:8 power given over f. p.

**Fifth PART.**
Gen. 41:34 take up f. p. of land
47:24 give f. p. to Pharaoh, 26
Lev. 5:16 add f. p. thereto, 6:5; 22:14; 27:13,19,27,31; Num. 5:7

**Tenth PART.**
Ex. 16:36 homer is the tenth p.
Lev. 5:11 tenth p. of an ephah of fine flour, 6:20; Num. 28:5
Num. 5:15 t. p. of ephah of meal
18:26 ye shall offer even t. p.
Ezek. 45:11 ephah may cont. t. p.
Heb. 7:2 Abra. gave a t. p. of all
Rev. 11:13 the t. p. of city fell

**PARTS.**
Gen. 47:24 four p. sh. be yo. own
Lev. 22:23 any thing lack. in p.
Num. 31:27 div. prey into two p.
Deut. 19:3 divide land into 3 p.
Jos. 18:5 divide into seven p. 6, 9
1 Sam. 5:9 emer. in th. secret p.
2 Sam. 19:43 have ten p. in king
1 K. 16:21 Is. divided into two p.
2 K. 11:7 two p. watch ab. king
Neh. 11:1 9 p. dw. in other cities
Job 26:14 th. are p. of his ways
41:12 I will not conceal his p.
Ps. 2:8 uttermost p. of earth
63:9 go into lower p. of earth
65:8 dwell in utmost p. afraid
139:9 dwell in utmost p. of sea
Prov. 18:8 go to innerm. p. 26:22
Is. 3:17 Lord will disc. secret p.
44:23 shout, ye lower p. of earth
Jer. 34:18 between p. thereof, 19
Ezek. 26:20 in the low p. of earth
31:14 to nether p. of earth, 18
16 comforted in the nether p. of earth, 32:18, 24
37:11 we are cut off for our p.
38:15 place out of north p. 39:2
Mat. 12:42 she came from uttermost p. Luke 11:31
John 19:23 garments made 4 p.
Rom. 15:23 no more place in p.
1 Cor. 12:24 comely p. no need
Eph. 4:9 descended into low. p.
Rev. 16:19 city divided into 3 p.
See BACK, HINDER, INWARD.

**PARTED.**
Gen. 2:10 river p. into four heads
2 K. 2:11 chariot p. both asunder
14 waters p. hither and thither
Job 38:24 what way is light p.?
Joel 3:2 scatter. and p. my land
Mat. 27:35 p. his garmen. Mark 5:24; Luke 23:34; John 19:24
Luke 24:51 blessed them, was p.
Acts 2:45 p. them to all men

**PARTETH.**
Rev. 11:3 p. hoof, Deut. 14:6
Prov. 18:18 lot p. betw. mighty

**PARTAKER.**
Is. 50:18 been p. with adulterers
Cor. 9:10 sho. be p. of his hope
23 I be p. thereof with you
10:30 p. why am I evil spok. of?
1 Tim. 5:22 p. of oth. men's sins
2 Tim. 1:8 be thou p. of afflicti.
2:6 husbandman be p. of fruits
1 Pet. 5:1 I am also p. of the gl.
2 John 11 biddeth G. speed is p.

**PARTAKERS.**
Mat. 23:30 not been p. in blood
Rom. 15:27 if Gentiles have been p. of their spiritual things
1 Cor. 9:13 are p. with the altar
10:17 we are all p. of that bread
18 are not they which eat p.?
21 cannot be p. of Lord's table
2 Cor. 1:7 you are p. of sufferings
Eph. 3:6 p. of his promise in Ch.
5:7 be not ye there. p. wi. them

*Phil.* 1:7 all are p. of my grace
*Col.* 1:12 to be p. of inheritance
1 *Tim.* 6:2 they are p. of benefit
*Heb.* 2:14 children p. of flesh and blood
3:1 p. of the heavenly calling
14 for we are made p. of Christ
6:4 made p. of the Holy Ghost
12:8 chastise. where. all are p.
10 that we be p. of his holiness
1 *Pet.* 4:13 p. of Christ's suffer.
2 *Pet.* 1:4 p. of the divine nature
*Rev.* 18:4 that ye be not p. of her

**PARTAKEST.**

*Rom.* 11:17 with them p. of root

PARTHIANS. *Acts* 2:9

**PARTIAL, ITY.**

*Mal.* 2:9 but have been p. in law
1 *Tim.* 5:21 doing nothing by p.
*Jam.* 2:4 are ye not p. yoursel.?
3:17 without p. and hypocrisy

**PARTICULAR, LY.**

*Acts* 21:19 P. declared p. things
1 *Cor.* 12:27 of C. members in p.
*Eph.* 5:33 ev. one in p. love wife
*Heb.* 9:5 we cannot now speak p.

**PARTIES.**

*Ex.* 22:9 both p. come bef. judg.

**PARTING.**

*Ezek.* 21:21 king of B. stood at p.

**PARTITION.**

1 *K.* 6:21 he made a p. of gold
*Eph.* 2:14 bro. middle wall of p.

**PARTLY.**

*Dan.* 2:42 be p. strong, p. broken
1 *Cor.* 11:18 divisions, I p. belie.
*Heb.* 10:33 p. gaz.-stock, p. com.

**PARTNER, S.**

*Prov.* 29:24 whoso is p. with a thief
2 *Cor.* 8:23 Titus, he is my p.
*Phile.* 17 if count me a p. receive
*Luke* 5:7 they beckoned to th. p.
10 James and John were p.

**PARTRIDGE.**

1 *Sam.* 26:20 when one hunt a p.
*Jer.* 17:11 as p. sitteth on eggs

**PASHUR.**

*Neh.* 10:3 P. sealed, *Jer.* 20:6
*Jer.* 20:1 P. son of Im. smote, 2
3 L. call. not thy name P.
21:1 Zedekiah sent unto him P.
38:1 Gedal. the son of P. and P.

**PASS.**

*Gen.* 18:5 after that ye shall p.
41:32 will shortly bring it to p.
*Ex.* 33:19 will make my good p.
*Num.* 27:7 inherit. of fa. to p. 8
*Jos.* 1:14 ye shall p. before breth.
1 *Sam.* 16:10 Jesse made 7 sons p.
*Neh.* 2:14 no place for beast to p.
*Job* 6:15 as stream they p. away
11:16 rem. it as waters that p.
34:20 peo. be troubled, p. away
*Prov.* 16:30 he bringeth evil to p.
22:3 and the simple p. on, 27:12
*Is.* 30:32 grounded staff shall p.
33:21 no gallant ship shall p.
37:26 have I brought it to p.
*Jer.* 8:13 th. I have given shall p.
15:14 make th. p. with enemies
33:13 flocks sh. p. under hands
51:43 nor doth son of man p.
*Ezek.* 20:37 I will cause you to p.
32:19 wh. dost th. p. in beauty?
*Amos* 6:2 p. ye unto Calneh
*Mic.* 1:11 p. ye away, inhabit. of
2:13 their king shall p. before
*Zep.* 2:2 decree br. forth, day p.
*Zec.* 3:4 have caused iniqu. to p.
*Mat.* 5:18 heav. and earth sh. p.
26:39 cup p. fr. me, *Mark* 14:35
*Luke* 16:26 wh. would p. fr. hen. nor can they p. fr. us to you
19:4 he was to p. that way
1 *Cor.* 7:36 if she p. flower of age
2 *Pet.* 3:10 heavens sh. p. away

**PASS by.**

*Ex.* 33:22 cover thee whi. I p. by
*Ps.* 80:12 all they that p. by
89:41 all that p. by way spoil
*Jer.* 22:8 many nations sh. p. by
*Lam.* 1:12 ye that p. by behold
2:15 all that p. by clap th. hands
*Ezek.* 5:14 sight of all that p. by
37:2 caused me to p. by them
*Amos* 7:8 I will not p. by th. 8:2
*Mic.* 2:8 garm. of them that p. by
*Mat.* 8:28 no man might p. by
*Luke* 18:36 hearing multit. p. by

*See* CAME, COME.

**Not PASS.**

*Num.* 20:17 will n. p. thro fields
18 Edom said, Thou shalt n. p.
*Job* 14:5 his bounds he cannot p.
19:8 fenced my way, cannot p.
*Ps.* 148:6 a decree wh. shall n. p.
*Prov.* 8:29 waters should not p.
*Jer.* 5:22 decree that it cannot p.
*Mat.* 24:34 this gene. shall not p. away, *Mark* 13:30; *Luke* 21:32
35 heaven and earth shall pass away, but my word sh. n. p. away, *Mark* 13:31; *Lu.* 21:33

**PASS not.**

*Gen.* 18:3 p. not away from serv.
2 *K.* 6:9 thou p. not such a place
*Prov.* 4:15 avoid it, p. not by it
*Amos* 5:5 we p. not to Beer-sheba

**PASS over.**

*Gen.* 8:1 God made wind p. o.
31:52 I will not p. o. this heap
32:16 p. o. bef. me, put a space
33:14 lord p. o. bef. thy servant
*Ex.* 12:13 I will p. over you, 23
15:16 till thy people p. over
*Num.* 32:27 serv. will p. o. 29:32
30 not p. o. with you armed
*Deut.* 2:18 p. o. thro' Ar this day
3:18 shall p. over armed before
9:1 p. o. Jordan, 11:31; 27:2; *Jos.* 1:11; 3:6, 14; 4:5
*Jos.* 22:19 p. o. into the land
*Jud.* 3:28 suff. not a man to p. o.
1 *Sam.* 14:8 will p. o. to th. men
2 *Sam.* 17:16 but speedily p. over
*Ps.* 104:9 that they may not p. o.
*Prov.* 19:11 to p. o. a transgres.
*Is.* 23:6 p. over to Tarshish
31:9 p. over to his stronghold
35:8 unclean shall not p. over
51:10 way for ransomed to p. o.
*Jer.* 5:22 yet can they not p. o.
*Ezek.* 47:5 river I could not p. o.
*Dan.* 4:16 seven times p. o. 25
11:40 king of north shall p. o.
*Hab.* 1:11 change, he shall p. o.
*Luke* 11:42 p. over judgment

**PASS through.**

*Gen.* 30:32 p. t. thy flock to-day
*Ex.* 12:12 p. t. Eg. this night
*Lev.* 18:21 any of thy seed p. t. fire, *Deut.* 18:10; 2 *K.* 17:17
*Num.* 20:17 p. t. thy country
21:23 Sihon would not suffer Is. to p. thro' *Jud.* 11:20
*Deut.* 2:4 p. thr. coasts of Edom
28 I will p. thro' on my feet
*Jos.* 1:11 p. t. host and command
2 *Sam.* 12:31 p. t. brick kiln
1 *K.* 18:6 divided land to p. t. it
2 *K.* 16:3 to p. t. the fire, 21:6; 23:10; 2 *Chr.* 33:6; *Jer.* 32:35; *Ezek.* 20:26, 31
*Ps.* 78:13 caused to p. t. 136:14
*Is.* 8:8 sh. p. through Judah
23:10 p. thro' thy land as a river
34:10 none sh. p. t. it for ever
*Jer.* 9:10 so that none can p. t.
*Lam.* 3:44 prayers sho. not p. t.
4:21 cup shall also p. t. to thee
*Ezek.* 14:15 noi. beasts p. t. land, no man p. t. 29:11; 33:28
39:15 passengers that p. t. land
*Dan.* 11:10 p. t. and overflow
*Joel* 3:17 shall p. t. her any more
*Amos* 5:17 I will p. thro' thee
*Nah.* 1:12 cut down, wh. he p. t.
15 wicked no more p. t. thee
*Zec.* 9:8 no oppressor p. t. them
1 *Cor.* 16:5 shall p. t. Macedonia

**PASSAGE, S.**

*Num.* 20:21 Edom refused Is. p.
*Jos.* 22:11 an altar at p. of Israel
*Jud.* 12:6 and slew him at p.
1 *Sam.* 13:23 Ph. went out to p.
14:4 betw. p. were sharp rocks
*Is.* 10:29 are gone over the p.
*Jer.* 22:20 lift thy voice, cry fr. p.
51:32 show Bab. p. are stopped

**PASSED.**

*Gen.* 15:17 a lamp that p. betw.
*Num.* 26:17 have p. thy border
*Jos.* 3:4 have not p. this way
1 *Sam.* 15:12 gone about and p.
29:2 Philist. p. on by hundreds
2 *Sam.* 15:18 servants p. on
2 *K.* 4:8 Elisha p. to Shunem
2 *Chr.* 9:22 Solomon p. all kings
*Job* 4:15 spirit p. before my face
9:26 my days are p. away
15:19 no stranger p. am. them
*Ps.* 18:12 his thick clouds p.
37:36 yet he p. away, and lo
90:9 all our days are p. away
*Cant.* 3:4 little that I p. fr. them
*Is.* 41:3 pursued, and p. safely
*Jer.* 11:15 holy flesh p. from thee
46:17 hath p. time appointed
*Dan.* 3:27 smell of fire p. on th.
6:18 went and p. night fasting
*Nah.* 3:19 wicked p. continually
*Mark* 6:35 now the time is far p.
*John* 5:24 but is p. from death to life, 1 *John* 3:14
*Rom.* 5:12 death p. on all men
*Heb.* 4:14 High-pri. p. into heav.
*Rev.* 21:1 first earth were p. aw.
4 former things are p. away

**PASSED by.**

*Ex.* 34:6 Lord p. by before him
1 *K.* 13:25 p. by and saw the lion
19:11 Lord p. by; 19 Elijah p. by
2 *K.* 4:8 as he p. by he turned in
6:30 the king p. by on the wall
*Job* 28:8 nor hath fierce lion p. by
*Ps.* 48:4 the kings p. by together
*Ezek.* 16:6 I p. by and saw thee, 8
36:34 in sight of all that p. by
*Hab.* 3:10 overfl. of waters p. by
*Mat.* 20:30 heard that Jesus p. by
*Mark* 6:48 would have p. by them
*Luke* 10:31 p. by on other side, 32
*John* 8:59 midst of them, so p. by
*Acts* 17:23 as I p. by and beheld

**PASSED over.**

*Gen.* 31:21 and p. over the river
32:10 with staff I p. over Jordan
*Ex.* 12:27 p. over houses of Isr.
*Jos.* 3:17 all p. o. on dry ground
4:10 people hasted and p. over
11 the ark of the Lord p. over
1 *Sam.* 14:23 p. o. to Bethaven
2 *Sam.* 15:23 king and peo. p. o.
*Is.* 40:27 judgment p. o. from G.
*Ezek.* 47:5 river could not be p. o.
*Hos.* 10:11 p. o. upon fair neck
*Jon.* 2:3 billows and waves p. o.

**PASSED through.**

*Gen.* 12:6 Abram p. t. the land
*Num.* 14:7 land which we p. t.
2 *Chr.* 30:10 posts p. t. country
*Mic.* 2:13 they p. thro' the gate
*Zec.* 7:14 that no man p. thro'
*Acts* 12:10 and p. thro' one street

1 Cor. 10:1 our fathers p. t. sea
Heb. 11:29 they p. thro' Red sea

**PASSEDST.**

Jud. 12:1 why p. thou over

**PASSENGERS.**

Prov. 9:15 she standeth to call p.
Ezek. 39:11 will give G. val. of p.
14 bury with p. those that re.
15 when p. see a man's bone

**PASSEST.**

Deut. 30:18 on land whi. thou p.
2 Sam. 15:33 if p. on, thou sh. be
1 K. 2:37 day thou p. over brook
Is. 43:2 when p. through waters

**PASSETH.**

Ex. 30:13 every one that p. 14
33:22 while my glory p. by
Jos 3:11 Lord p. over before you
2 K. 4:9 man of G. wh. p. by us
12:4 money of every one that p.
Job 9:11 he p. on also, but I
14:20 against him, and he p.
37:21 wind p. and clean. them
Ps. 8:8 whatever p. thro' the sea
78:39 are a wind that p. away
103:16 for the wind p. over it
144:4 as a shadow that p. away
Prov. 10:25 as whirlwind p. so is
26:17 he th. p. by and meddleth
Ec. 1:4 one generation p. away
Is. 29:5 as chaff that p. away
Jer. 2:6 no man p. through, 9:12
18:16 every one that p. 19:8
Ezek. 35:7 from it him that p.
Hos. 13:3 early dew that p. away
Mic. 7:18 G. that p. by transgr.
Zep. 2:15 ev. one that p. by her
3:6 streets waste, none p. by
Zec. 9:8 bec. of him that p. by
Luke 18:37 told him th. J. p. by
1 Cor. 7:31 fashion of this world
p. away, 1 John 2:17
Eph. 3:19 love of C. p. knowled.
Phil. 4:7 peace of G. p. underst.

**PASSING.**

2 Sam. 1:26 to me p. love of wo.
Ps. 84:6 p. through valley
Prov. 7:8 p. thro' street near co.
Is. 31:5 p. over, preserve Jerus.
Ezek. 39:14 p. thro' land to bury
Luke 4:30 p. through midst
Acts 5:15 shadow of Peter p. by

**PASSION.**

Acts 1:3 sho. hims. alive after p.

**PASSIONS.**

Acts 14:15 we are men of like p.
Jam. 5:17 Elias subject to like p.

**PASSOVER.**

Ex. 12:11 it is L.'s p. ye sh. eat,
27; Lev. 23:5; Num. 28:16
43 this is the ordinance of p.
Num. 9:5 kept p. Jos. 5:10
Deut. 16:2 sacrifice p. to Lord, 6
2 K. 23:22 not holden such a p.
2 Chr. 30:15 kill. p. in se. month,
35:1, 11; Ezr. 6:20; Mark
14:12; Luke 22:7
18 eat p. otherw. than written
35:1 Jo. kept p. 17, 19; Ezr. 6:19
13 they roasted p. with fire
Ezek. 45:21 shall have p. of 7 da.
Mat. 26:17 wh. wilt we eat p.?
Mark 14:12; Luke 22:8, 11
Luke 22:5 have desired to eat p.
John 2:13 Jews' p. at hand, 11:55
23 when he was in Jer. at p.
11:55 many went to J. before p.
12:1 J. came six days before p.
18:28 that they might eat p.
39 sho. release to you one at p.
19:14 it was preparation of p.
1 Cor. 5:7 Ch. our p. is sacrificed
Heb. 11:28 thro' faith he kept p.
See FEAST, KEEP.

**PASSOVERS.**

2 Chr. 30:17 Le. had charge of p.

**PAST.**

Gen. 50:4 mourn. p. 2 Sam. 11:27
Num. 21:22 until we be p. bord.
Deut. 2:10 E. dwelt in times p.
14:32 ask now of days wh. are p.
1 Sam. 15:32 bitter. of death is p.
2 Sam. 3:17 so. David in time p.
16:1 D. was a little p. top of hill
1 K. 18:29 midday p. no voice
1 Chr. 9:20 Phin. ruler in time p.
Job 9:10 doeth things p. finding
14:13 keep me, until wrath p.
17:11 days are p. my purpose
29:2 O th. I we. as in months p.
Ec. 3:15 requireth that wh. is p.
Mat. 14:15 time is now p. send
Mark 16:1 when sab. was p. Ma.
Luke 9:36 voice p. J was alone
Acts 14:16 times p suff. all nati.
Rom. 11:30 in times p. not belie.
33 his ways are p. finding out
2 Cor. 5:17 old things p. away
Gal. 1:13 conversation in time p.
5:21 as I told you in time p.
Eph. 2:2 in time p. ye walked
4:19 being p. feeling have given
Phile. 11 in time p. unprofitable
Heb. 1:1 spake in time p. to fath.
11:11 conceive, when she was p.
1 Pet. 2:10 in time p. were not
4:3 time p. of our life suffice
1 John 2:8 darkness p. light shi.
Rev. 9:12 one woe p. 11:14 woe p.

**PASTOR, S.**

Jer. 2:8 p. transgr. against me
3:15 p. according to my heart
10:21 for p. are become brutish
12:10 p. have destroy. vineyard
17:16 not hastened fr. being a p
22:22 wind shall eat up thy p.
23:1 woe to p. that destr. sheep
2 against p. that feed my sheep
Eph. 4:11 gave p. and teachers

**PASTURE.**

Gen. 47:4 thy servants ha. no p.
1 Chr. 4:39 they went to seek p.
40 they found fat p. and good
41 there was p. for their flocks
Job 39:8 range of moun. in his p.
Ps. 74:1 anger sm. ag. sheep of p.
79:13 sheep of thy p. give than.
95:7 we are peo. of his p. 100:3
Is. 32:14 joy of asses, p. of flocks
Jer. 23:1 scatter sheep of my p.
25:36 Lord hath spoiled their p.
Lam. 1:6 like harts find no p.
Ezek. 34:14 feed in good p. fat p.
18 small th. to ha. eat. good p.
31 flock of my p. are men, I G.
Hos. 13:6 ac. to their p. so filled
Joel 1:18 beasts groan, ha. no p.
John 10:9 go in and out, find p.

**PASTURES.**

1 K. 4:23 S. had 20 ox. out of p.
Ps. 23:2 maketh me lie green p.
65:12 drop upon p. of wildern.
13 p. are clothed with flocks
Is. 30:23 cat. sh. feed in large p.
49:9 p. shall be in high places
Ezek. 34:18 tread down your p.
45:15 lamb out of flock of fat p.
Joel. 1:19 fire hath devour. p. 20
2:22 p. of wilderness do spring

**PATARA.**

Acts 21:1 from thence unto P.

**PATE.**

Ps. 7:16 sh. come do. on own p.

**PATH.**

Gen. 49:17 D. be an adder in p.
Num. 22:24 angel of L. st. in p.
Job 28:7 p. which no fowl know.
30:13 mar my p. set forward
41:32 he maketh a p. to shine
Ps. 16:11 show me the p. of life
27:11 lead me in a plain p.
77:19 way in sea, p. in great wa.
119:35 make me to go in p.
105 thy word a light to my p.
139:3 thou compassest my p.
142:3 then thou knewest my p.
Prov. 1:15 refrain foot fr. their p.
2:9 sh. understand every good p.
4:15 enter not into p. of wicked
18 p. of just is as shining light
26 ponder the p. of thy feet
5:6 lest thou ponder p. of life
Is. 26:7 dost weigh p. of just
30:11 out of way, turn out of p.
40:14 taught him in p. of judgm.
43:16 maketh p. in mighty wat.
Joel 2:8 walk, every one in his p.
PATHROS. Is. 11:11; Ezek.
29:14; 30:14

**PATHWAY.**

Prov. 12:28 in p. thereof no dea.

**PATHS.**

Job 6:18 p. of way turned aside
8:13 p. of all that forget God
13:27 lookest narrowly to my p.
19:8 hath set darkness in my p.
24:13 nei. abide in p. thereof
33:11 feet in stocks, mar. my p.
38:20 thou sh. keep p. of house
Ps. 8:8 passeth thro' p. of seas
17:4 kept me fr. p. of destroyer
5 hold my goings in p. slip not
23:3 leadeth me in p. of righte.
25:4 O Lord, teach me thy p.
10 p. of L. are mercy and truth
65:11 p. drop fatness on pasture
Prov. 2:8 keep. p. of judgment
Prov. 2:13 leave p. of uprightn.
15 and they froward in their p.
18 her p. incline unto the dead
19 nei. take hold of p. of life
20 keep p. of the righteous
3:6 direct p. 17 p. are peace
4:11 I have led thee in right p.
7:25 go not astray in her p.
8:2 standeth in places of p.
20 I lead in p. of judgment
Is. 2:3 walk in his p. Mic. 4:2
3:12 they destroy way of thy p.
42:16 lead th. in p. not known
58:12 called, the restorer of p.
59:7 destruction are in their p.
8 have made them crooked p.
Jer. 6:16 in way, ask for old p.
18:15 ancient p. to walk in p.
Lam. 3:9 he made my p. crooked
Hos. 2:6 she shall not find p.
Mat. 3:3 make his p. straight,
Mark 1:3; Luke 3:4
Heb. 12:13 made strai. p. for feet

**PATIENCE.**

Mat. 18:26 have p. with me, and
I will pay thee all. 29
Luke 8:15 br. forth fruit with p.
21:19 in p. possess ye your souls
Rom. 5:3 tribulation worketh p.
4 p. experience, experi. hope
8:25 do we with p. wait for it
15:4 we thro' p. might ha. hope
5 G. p. grant you be like-min.
2 Cor. 6:4 ministers of God in p.
12:12 signs we. am. you in all p.
Col. 1:11 strengthened to all p.
1 Thes. 1:3 remem. your p. in J.
2 Thes. 1:4 gl. in you for your p.
1 Tim. 6:11 follow after love, p.
2 Tim. 3:10 hast known my p.
Tit. 2:2 be found in faith, p.
Heb. 6:12 thro' p. inh. promises
10:36 ye have need of p.
12:1 run with p. race before us
Jam. 1:3 trying of faith work. p.
4 let p. have her perfect work
5:7 husbandman hath long p.
10 an example of p. 11 p. of J.

2 *Pet.* 1:6 add to temper. *p.* to *p.*
*Rev.* 1:9 compan. in *p.* of Jesus
2:2 I know thy *p.* 19; 3 hast *p.*
3:10 hast kept word of my *p.*
13:10 here is *p.* of saints, 14:12

**PATIENT.**

*Ec.* 7:8 *p.* in sp. better than pro.
*Rom.* 2:7 *p.* continu. in well-do.
12:12 in hope, *p.* in tribulation
1 *Thes.* 5:14 be *p.* toward all men
2 *Thes.* 3:5 *p.* waiting for Christ
1 *Tim.* 3:3 luc. but *p.* 2 *Tim.* 2:24
*Jam.* 5:7 be *p.* breth. 8 ye also *p.*

**PATIENTLY.**

*Ps.* 37:7 rest in L. and wait *p.*
40:1 I waited *p.* for the Lord
*Acts* 26:3 I bes. thee hear me *p.*
*Heb.* 6:15 after he had *p.* endured
1 *Pet.* 2:20 if ye be buff. take it *p.*
if ye do well and su. ta. it *p.*

**PATMOS.**

*Rev.* 1:9 in the isle called P.

**PATRIARCH, S.**

*Acts* 2:29 freely speak of *p.* Dav.
7:8 Jacob begat the twelve *p.*
9 *p.* sold Joseph into Egypt
*Heb.* 7:4 *p.* Abraham paid tithes

**PATRIMONY.**

*Deut.* 18:8 cometh of sale of *p.*

PATROBAS. *Rom.* 16:14

**PATTERN, S.**

*Ex.* 25:9 *p.* of all instruments
40 make them after their *p.*
*Jos.* 22:28 the *p.* of altar of Lord
2 *K.* 16:10 Ahaz sent *p.* of altar
1 *Chr.* 28:11 D. g. S. *p.* 12, 18, 19
*Ezek.* 43:10 let them measure *p.*
1 *Tim.* 1:16 in me C. mig. sh. *p.*
*Tit.* 2:7 show. thyself *p.* of good
*Heb.* 8:5 accord. to *p.* I showed
9:23 necessary that *p.* of things

**PAUL.**

*Acts* 13:9 then Saul, called P.
28:16 but P. was suffered to
(*Vide* Acts *passim.*)
1 *Cor.* 1:12 I am of P. 13; 3:4, 5
3:22 whether P. or Apollos, or
16:21 saluta. of me P. *Col.* 4:18
1 *Thes.* 2:18 ev. I P. 2 *Thes.* 3:17
*Phile.* 9 such a one as P.
2 *Pet.* 3:15 as our belov. P. wrote

**PAULUS.**

*Acts* 13:7 the deputy Sergius P.

**PAVED.**

*Ex.* 24:10 under feet *p.* work
*Cant.* 3:10 being *p.* with love

**PAVEMENT.**

2 *K.* 16:17 put sea on *p.* of stones
2 *Chr.* 7:3 all Isr. bowed upon *p.*
*Est.* 1:6 beds were on *p.* of red
*Ezek.* 40:17 chambers and a *p.*
18 *p.* by side of gates lower *p.*
42:3 over against *p.* was gallery
*John* 19:13 Pil. sat in pla. call. *P.*

**PAVILION, S.**

2 *Sam.* 22:12 ma. dar. *p.* *Ps.* 18:11
1 *K.* 20:12 Ben. drinking in *p.* 16
*Ps.* 27:5 he shall hide me in *p.*
31:20 keep them secretly in a *p.*
*Jer.* 43:10 Nebuch. spread his *p.*

**PAW, S.**

*Lev.* 11:27 goeth on *p.* unclean
1 *Sam.* 17:37 de. me out of *p.* of

**PAWETH.**

*Job* 39:21 horse *p.* in the valley

**PAY.**

*Ex.* 21:19 sh. *p.* for loss of time
36 he shall surely *p.* ox for ox
22:7 thief be found, *p.* double, 9
*Num.* 20:19 if I drink I will *p.*
*Deut.* 23:21 shall not slack to *p.*
2 *Sam.* 15:7 let me go *p.* my vow
1 *K.* 20:39 thou shalt *p.* a talent
2 *K.* 4:7 sell oil, and *p.* thy debt
2 *Chr.* 8:8 them did S. make to *p.*
*Ezr.* 4:13 will they not *p.* toll
*Est.* 3:9 I will *p.* 10,000 tal. 4:7
*Job* 22:27 and shalt pay thy vows
*Ps.* 22:25 *p.* vows, 66:13; 116:14, 18
50:14 *p.* thy vows to Most High
76:11 vow, and *p.* to the Lord
*Prov.* 19:17 giv. will he *p.* again
22:27 if hast nothing to *p.*
*Ec.* 5:4 defer not to *p.* it, *p.* that
5 not vow, than vow and not *p.*
*Jon.* 2:9 I will *p.* that I vowed
*Mat.* 17:24 doth not mas. *p.* tri.?
18:25 had not to *p.* *Luke* 7:42
26 *p.* thee all; 28 *p.* th. owest
30 cast into prison, till he *p.*
34 till he *p.* all that was due
23:23 ye *p.* tithe of mint, anise
*Rom.* 13:6 for this cause *p.* trib.

**PAID, PAYETH.**

*Ezr.* 4:20 toll and custom *p.* th.
*Ps.* 37:21 wicked borrow. *p.* not
*Prov.* 7:14 this day ha. I *p.* vows
*Jon.* 1:3 *p.* fare thereof
*Mat.* 5:26 *p.* utter. far. *Luke* 12:59
*Heb.* 7:9 Levi *p.* tithes in Abrah.

**PAYMENT.**

*Mat.* 18:25 all sold, *p.* to be made

**PEACE.**

*Mark* 4:39 said to sea, *p.* be still

**PEACE.**

*Gen.* 41:16 G. give P. answ. of *p.*
*Lev.* 26:6 I will give *p.* in land
*Num.* 6:26 L. give thee *p.*
25:12 I give him my cov. of *p.*
*Deut.* 2:26 sent to Sihon with *p.*
20:10 come nigh city, procl. *p.*
11 if it make th. answ. of *p.* 12
23:6 thou sh. not seek their *p.*
29:19 I shall have *p.* tho. walk
*Jud.* 4:17 *p.* betw. Jab. and Heb.
1 *Sam.* 7:14 *p.* betw. Is. and A.
20:7 servant shall have *p.*
21 there is *p.* to thee
1 *K.* 2:33 on his thro. sha. be *p.*
4:24 Solom. had *p.* on all sides
5:12 *p.* betw. Hiram and Solo.
20:18 come for *p.* take th. alive
2 *K.* 9:17 say, Is it *p.* Jehu? 18
19 wh. hast th. to do wi. *p.*? 22
22 what *p.* so long as witchc.?
31 had Z. *p.* who slew mast.?
20:19 *p.* in my days? *Is.* 39:8
1 *Chr.* 22:9 I will give *p.* to Isr.
2 *Chr.* 15:5 th. tim. th. was no *p.*
*Ezr.* 4:17 rest bey. the river, *p.*
5:7 unto Darius, *p.* 7:12 unto E.
9:12 not seek their *p.* or wealth
*Est.* 9:30 Mord. sent words of *p.*
10:3 Mord. speaking *p.* to all
*Job* 5:23 beasts of field be at *p.*
22:21 acqu. thyself, and be at *p.*
25:2 maketh *p.* in high places
*Ps.* 7:4 evil to him th. was at *p.*
28:3 which speak *p.* to neigh.
29:11 bless his people with *p.*
34:14 good, seek *p.* 1 *Pet.* 3:11
35:20 speak not *p.* but devise
37:11 delight in abund. of *p.*
37 end of the upright man is *p.*
55:20 put ag. such as be at *p.*
72:3 mountains shall bring *p.*
7 of *p.* so long as moon endur.
85:8 he will speak *p.* to his peo.
10 righteousness and *p.* kissed
119:165 gr. *p.* have they which
120:6 dw. with him th. hateth *p.*
*Ps.* 120:7 I am for *p.* they for war
122:6 pray for *p.* of Jerusalem
125:5 but *p.* sh. be upon Israel
128:6 thou shalt see *p.* upon Is.
147:14 maketh *p.* in thy borders
*Prov.* 3:17 pleasantness, paths *p.*
12:20 to counsellors of *p.* is joy
16:7 maketh enemies to be at *p.*
*Ec.* 3:8 time of war, time of *p.*
*Is.* 9:6 Prince of *p.* 7 increase *p.*
26:12 Lord thou wilt ordain *p.*
27:5 *p.* with me, he shall ma. *p.*
32:17 work of righteo. sh. be *p.*
33:7 ambassadors of *p.* sh. weep
38:17 or *p.* I had great bittern.
45:7 make *p.* and create evil
48:18 had thy *p.* been as river
22 th. is no *p.* to wicked, 57:21
52:7 publisheth *p.* *Nah.* 1:15
53:5 chastisem. of our *p.* on him
54:10 nor coven. of *p.* be remov.
13 great shall be *p.* of thy chil.
55:12 with joy, led forth with *p.*
57:2 enter into *p.* rest in beds
19 fruit of lips, *p.* *p.* to him
59:8 way of *p.* kn. not, *Rom.* 3:17
60:17 make thine officers *p.*
66:12 I will extend *p.* to her
*Jer.* 4:10 ye sh. have *p.* whereas
6:14 *p.* *p.* when th. is no *p.* 8:11
8:15 for *p.* no good came, 14:19
12:5 if in land of *p.* they weari.
12 sw. devour, no flesh have *p.*
14:13 I will give you assured *p.*
16:5 I have taken away my *p.*
28:9 prophet wh. prophesied *p.*
29:7 seek *p.* of city I caused
11 I think tow. you thou. of *p.*
30:5 a voice of fear, not of *p.*
33:6 reveal to them abund. of *p.*
*Lam.* 3:17 rem. my soul from *p.*
*Ezek.* 7:25 seek *p.* th. shall be n.
13:10 *p.* and there was no *p.* 16
34:25 make a covena. of *p.* 37:26
*Dan.* 8:25 by *p.* he shall destroy
*Ob.* 7 men at *p.* deceived thee
*Mic.* 3:5 bite with teeth, cry *p.*
5:5 this man sh. be *p.* when A.
*Hag.* 2:9 this place I will give *p.*
*Zec.* 6:13 counsel of *p.* betw th.
8:10 nor was th. any *p.* to him.
16 execute judgment and *p.*
19 therefore love truth and *p.*
9:10 he sh. speak *p.* to heathen
*Mal.* 2:5 covenant of life and *p.*
*Mat.* 10:13 worthy, let *p.* come
34 th. not I am come to send *p.*
*Mark* 9:50 have *p.* one with ano.
*Luke* 1:79 guide feet to way of *p.*
2:14 on earth *p.* good will tow.
10:6 if son of *p.* th. your *p.* rest
12:51 I am come to give *p.*?
19:38 *p.* in heaven, gl. in highe.
42 things belong to thy *p.*
*John* 14:27 *p.* I lea. you, *p.* I give
16:33 in me you might have *p.*
*Acts* 10:36 preaching *p.* by Jesus
*Rom.* 1:7 *p.* from God the Fath.
1 *Cor.* 1:3; 2 *Cor.* 1:2; *Gal.*
1:3; *Eph.* 1:2; *Phil.* 1:2
2:10 *p.* to every man work. good
5:1 justified, we have *p.* with G.
8:6 to be spiritually mind. is *p.*
10:15 that preach gospel of *p.*
14:17 the kingdom of God is *p.*
19 fol. things that make for *p.*
15:13 fill you with all joy and *p.*
1 *Cor.* 7:15 G. hath call. us to *p.*
14:33 author of *p.* as in church.
*Gal.* 5:22 Spirit is love, joy, *p.*
*Eph.* 2:14 is our *p.* 15 making *p.*
17 Christ came and preach. *p.*
4:3 unity of Spirit in bond of *p.*
6:15 preparation of gospel of *p.*
*Phil.* 4:7 *p.* of God passeth und.
*Col.* 1:2 grace and *p.* from G. our
Father, 1 *Thes.* 1:1; 2 *Thes.*
1:2; 1 *Tim.* 1:2; 2 *Tim.* 1:2;
*Tit.* 1:4; *Phile.* 3; 2 *John* 3
3:15 *p.* of God rule in your hea.
1 *Thes.* 5:3 when they sh. say *p.*
13 be at *p.* among yourselves
2 *Thes.* 3:16 L. of *p.* give you *p.*
2 *Tim.* 2:22 follow *p.* *Heb.* 12:14
*Heb.* 7:2 king of Salem is k. of *p.*
11:31 Rahab received spies in *p.*

*Jam.* 3:18 *p.* of them th. ma. *p.* ?
*Rev.* 1:4 *p.* from him that is, was
6:4 power giv. to him to take *p.*

**PEACE be.**

*Jud.* 6:23 L. said, *p. be* to thee
1 *Sam.* 25:6 *p. be* to thee—house
1 *Chr.* 12:18 *p. be* to thee, *p. be* to
*Ps.* 122:7 *p. be* within thy walls
8 now say, *p. be* within thee
*Dan.* 4:1 *p. be* multiplied, 6:25; 1 *Pet.* 1:2; 2 *Pet.* 1:2; *Jude* 2
*Dan.* 10:19 *p. be* to thee, be stro.
*Luke* 10:5 *p. be* to this house
24:36 he saith unto them, *p. be* to you, *John* 20:19, 21, 26
*Gal.* 6:16 *p. be* on them
*Eph.* 6:23 *p. be* to brethren, love
1 *Pet.* 5:14 *p. be* with all in Chr.
3 *John* 14 *p. be* to thee, our frie.

**God of PEACE.**

*Rom.* 15:33 *God of p.* be wi. you
16:20 *God of p.* sh. bruise Satan
2 *Cor.* 13:11 the *God of p.* shall be with you, *Phil.* 4:9
1 *Thes.* 5:23 *God of p.* sanctify
*Heb.* 13:20 *God of p.* make you perfect

*See* HELD, HOLD.

**In PEACE.**

*Gen.* 26:29 sent thee away *in p.*
28:21 I come to fa.'s house *in p.*
*Jud.* 11:31 when I return *in p.*
2 *Sam.* 15:27 return to city *in p.*
19:30 king is come again *in p.*
1 *K.* 2:5 Joab shed blood *in p.*
22:17 man *in p.* 2 *Chr.* 18:16, 26
27 in prison, until I come *in p.*
2 *Chr.* 19:1 Jehosh. return. *in p.*
*Job* 5:24 thy taber. shall be *in p.*
*Ps.* 4:8 I will lay me down *in p.*
55:18 he delivered my soul *in p.*
*Is.* 26:3 wilt keep him *in* perf. *p.*
*Jer.* 29:7 *in p.* sh. ye have peace
34:5 but thou shalt die *in p.*
*Mal.* 2:6 walked with me *in p.*
*Luke* 2:29 let. serv. depart *in p.*
1 *Cor.* 16:11 cond. him forth *in p.*
2 *Cor.* 13:11 one mind, live *in p.*
*Jam.* 2:16 depart *in p.* be warm.
3:18 righteousness is sown *in p.*
2 *Pet.* 3:14 be found of him *in p.*

*See* GO, MADE, OFFERINGS.

**PEACEABLE.**

*Gen.* 34:21 these men *p.* with us
2 *Sam.* 20:19 one of them th. *p.*
1 *Chr.* 4:40 land was wi. and *p.*
*Is.* 32:18 peo. dwell in *p.* habita.
*Jer.* 25:37 *p.* habitations are cut
1 *Tim.* 2:2 lead a quiet and *p.* li.
*Heb.* 12:11 yieldeth the *p.* fruit
*Jam.* 3:17 wisd. is pure, *p.* gent.

**PEACEABLY.**

*Gen.* 37:4 could not speak *p.*
*Jud.* 11:13 restore those lands *p.*
21:13 send some *p.* to Benjam.
1 *Sam.* 16:4 said, Comest thou *p.*
5 *p.* I am come, 1 *K.* 2:13
1 *Chr.* 12:17 if ye be come *p.*
*Jer.* 9:8 speaketh *p.* to neighbor
*Dan.* 11:21 shall come in *p.* 24
*Rom.* 12:18 live *p.* with all men

**PEACEMAKERS.**

*Mat.* 5:9 blessed are the *p.*

**PEACOCKS.**

1 *K.* 10:22 the navy came, bringing *p.* 2 *Chr.* 9:21
*Job* 39:13 gav. goodly win. to *p.* ?

**PEARL.**

*Mat.* 13:46 found *p.* of great price
*Rev.* 21:21 ev. gate. was of one *p.*

**PEARLS.**

*Job* 28:18 no menti. of coral or *p.*
*Mat.* 7:6 neither cast *p.* bef. sw.
13:45 like merchant seeking *p.*
1 *Tim.* 2:9 not with *p.* or costly
*Rev.* 17:4 woman decked with *p.*
18:12 no man buy. merc. of *p.* 16
21:21 twelve gates were twe. *p.*

**PECULIAR.**

*Ex.* 19:5 sh. be *p.* treasure to me
*Deut.* 14:2 be a *p.* people unto himself, 26:18; 1 *Pet.* 2:9
*Ps.* 135:4 chosen Is. for *p.* treas.
*Ec.* 2:8 I gath. *p.* treas. of kings
*Tit.* 2:14 purify to himself *p.* people

**PEDIGREES.**

*Num.* 1:18 they declared their *p.*

**PEELED.**

*Is.* 18:2 nation scatter. and *p.* 7
*Ezek.* 29:18 every shoulder was *p.*

**PEEP, ED.**

*Is.* 8:19 wizards that *p.* and mut.
10:14 none opened mouth or *p.*

**PEKAH.**

2 *K.* 15:25 P. conspired again. 29
30 conspiracy against P. 16:5
2 *Chr.* 28:6 P. slew in Judah
*Is.* 7:1 Rezin and P. went tows.

PEKAHIAH. 2 *K.* 15:22, 23

**PELATIAH.**

1 *Chr.* 3:21 son of Hananiah P. 4:42; *Neh.* 10:22; *Ezek.* 11:13

**PELICAN.**

*Lev.* 11:18 *p.* uncl. *Deut.* 14:17
*Ps.* 102:6 I am like *p.* of wildern

**PEN.**

*Jud.* 5:14 they that handle *p.*
*Job* 19:24 graven with an iron *p.*
*Ps.* 45:1 tongue is *p.* of writer
*Is.* 8:1 write it with a man's *p.*
*Jer.* 8:8 *p.* of scribes is in vain
17:1 sin of Jud. written with *p.*
3 *John* 13 not with ink and *p.*

**PENCE.**

*Mat.* 18:28 one who owed 100 *p.*
*Mark* 14:5 have been sold for more than 300 *p. John* 12:5
*Luke* 7:41 the one owed 500 *p.*
10:35 on mo. he took out two *p.*

PENIEL. *Gen.* 32:30

**PENKNIFE.**

*Jer.* 36:23 Jehu. cut roll with *p.*

**PENNY.**

*Mat.* 20:2 ag. with laborers for *p.*
9 received every man a *p.* 13
22:19 they brought unto him *p.*
*Mark* 12:15 bring *p. Luke* 20:24
*Rev.* 6:6 meas. of wheat for a *p.* three meas. of barley for a *p.*

**PENNYWORTH.**

*Mark* 6:37 buy 200 *p.* of bread
*John* 6:7 200 *p.* is not sufficient

**PENTECOST.**

*Acts* 2:1 wh. day of P. was come
20:16 hasted to Jerus. day of P.
1 *Cor.* 16:8 tarry at Eph. until P.

**PENUEL.**

*Gen.* 32:31 as Ja. passed over P.
*Jud.* 8:8 Gid. went up to P. 17
1 *K.* 12:25 went and built P.

**PENURY.**

*Prov.* 14:23 talk of lips ten. to *p.*
*Luke* 21:4 she of her *p.* cast all

**PEOPLE.**

*Gen.* 27:29 let *p.* serve thee
48:19 he sh. become a *p.* great
*Ex.* 6:7 take you for a *p. Deut.* 4:20; 2 *Sam.* 7:24; *Jer.* 13:11
*Lev.* 20:24 separ. you from other *p.* 26
*Num* 22:5 *p.* come out fr. Eg. 11
*Deut.* 4:33 did *p.* hear voi. of G. ?
7:6 G. ha. chosen thee special *p.*
14:2 Lord hath cho. thee pec. *p.*
20:1 *p.* more than thou, be not
28:32 sons given to another *p.*
29:13 estab. thee for *p.* to hims.
32:21 move them wi. th. not a *p.*
33:29 who is like *p.* saved by L.?
1 *Sam.* 2:24 make L.'s *p.* transg.
5:10 to slay us and our *p.* 11
2 *Sam.* 7:23 wh. G. redeem for *p.*
22:28 afflicted *p.* thou wilt save, *Ps.* 18:27
44 *p.* I kn. not, serve, *Ps.* 18:43
1 *K.* 22:28 hearken, O *p.* ev. one
2 *K.* 11:17 be L.'s *p.* 2 *Chr.* 23:16
1 *Chr.* 16:20 went from one kin. to another *p. Ps.* 105:13
2 *Chr.* 1:9 made me king over *p.*
*Est.* 2:10 E. had not showed *p.*
3:8 a certain *p.* scattered abroad
*Job* 36:20 when *p.* are cut off
*Ps.* 62:8 *p.* pour out your hearts
66:8 bless God, *p.* 95:10 *p.* err
114:1 went out fr. *p.* of strange
144:15 happy *p.* 148:14 *p.* near
*Prov.* 14:34 sin is repro. to any *p.*
28:15 wicked ruler over poor *p.*
30:25 ants are a *p.* not strong
*Is.* 1:4 a *p.* laden with iniquity
10 give ear to law, *p.* of Gomo.
7:8 Ephraim broken, be not a *p.*
8:19 sho. not *p.* seek their God ?
27:11 a *p.* of no understanding
30:9 this is a rebellious *p.* 65:2
43:4 I will give *p.* for thy life
8 bring forth blind *p.* ha. eyes
65:3 a *p.* that provoketh me
18 Jerus. rejoicing, her *p.* a joy
*Jer.* 6:22 *p.* com. fr. north, 50:41
48:42 M. destroyed fr. being *p.*
*Lam.* 1:7 *p.* fell into hand of ene.
*Hos.* 4:9 sh. be like *p.* like priest
9:1 rejoice not, O Is. as other *p.*
*Jon.* 1:8 of what *p.* art thou ?
*Mic.* 4:1 *p.* shall flow unto it
*Zec.* 8:20 there shall come *p.*
*Luke* 1:17 ready *p.* prep. for L.
*Acts* 15:14 take out of them a *p.*
*Rom.* 10:19 them that are no *p.*
*Tit.* 2:14 purify to hims. pecu. *p.*
*Heb.* 8:10 shall be to me a *p.*
1 *Pet.* 2:9 ye are a peculiar *p.*
10 *p.* of G. in ti. past w. not *p.*
*Rev.* 5:9 redeem. us out of ev. *p.*

**All PEOPLE.**

*Ex.* 19:5 treas. above *all p. Deut.* 7:6, 14; 10:15; *Ps.* 99:2
*Deut.* 7:7 were fewest of *all p.*
1 *K.* 4:34 came of *all p.* to hear S.
8:43 *all p.* know name, 2 *Chr.* 6:33
*Est.* 9:2 fear of th. fell on *all p.*
*Ps.* 96:3 declare wond. am. *all p.*
117:1 praise L. *all* ye *p.* for his kindness, 148:11; *Rom.* 15:11
*Is.* 25:6 L. make to *all p.* a feast
56:7 house of prayer for *all p.*
*Lam.* 1:11 *all* her *p.* seek bread
18 hear, *a. p.* behold, *Mic.* 1:2
*Dan.* 5:19 *all p.* feared bef. him
7:14 *all p.* and nati. serve him
*Mic.* 4:5 *all p.* walk, ea. in name
*Zep.* 3:20 praise among *all p.*
*Luke* 2:10 tidings of joy to *all p.*
31 prepared before face of *a. p.*

**All the PEOPLE.**

*Ex.* 18:14 *all t. p.* stand by thee
19:8 *a. t. p.* answ. togeth. 24:3
11 L. come down in si. of *a. t. p.*
*Lev.* 10:3 bef. *a. t. p.* I will be glo.
*Num.* 11:29 *a. t.* L.'s *p.* prophets
*Deut.* 13:9 hand of *all t. p.* 17:7
27:15 *all t. p.* say, Amen, 16–21
28:10 *all t. p.* sh. see that thou
*Jos.* 4:24 *all the p.* might know
6:5 *all the p.* shall shout with
7:3 said, Let not *all t. p.* go up
*Jud.* 20:8 *all the p.* arose

1*Sa*. 10:24 none li. him am. *a. t. p.*
11:4 *all t. p.* wept; 12:18 feared
30:6 soul of *all the p.* grieved
2 *Sam.* 2:28 *a. t. p.* stood, pursu.
17:3 br. back *all the p.* unto th.
19:9 *all the p.* were at strife
20:22 woman went to *all the p.*
1 *K.* 8:53 separate th. fr. *all t. p.*
60 *a. t. p.* of earth may know
2 *K.* 23:3 *a. t. p.* stood to coven.
1 *Chr.* 16:36 *a. t. p.* said, Amen
2 *Chr.* 7:4 *a. t. p.* offer. sacrifices
*Ezr.* 7:25 wh. may judge *a. t. p.*
*Neh.* 8:5 in sight of *all the p.*
*Ps.* 67:3 let *a. t. p.* praise thee, 5
97:6 and *all the p.* see his glory
106:48 *all the p.* say, Amen
*Ec.* 4:16 th. is no end of *all t. p.*
*Jer.* 34:8 made cov. wi. *a. t. p.* 10
43:4 *all the p.* obeyed not the L.
*Ezek.* 31:12 *all the p.* are gone
*Dan.* 3:7 when *all t. p.* heard
*Zec.* 11:10 bre. cov. with *a. t. p.*
14:12 Lord will smite *all the p.*
*Mal.* 2:9 ma. you base bef. *a. t. p.*
*Luke* 13:17 *a. t. p.* rejoiced
18:43 *all the p.* gave praise to G.
20:6 *all the p.* will stone us
*Acts* 10:41 not *a. t. p.* but witn.
21:27 stirred up *all the p.*

**Among the PEOPLE.**

*Lev.* 18:29 cut off from *a. t. p.*
*Ezek.* 28:19 that know thee *a. p.*
*Dan.* 11:33 that unders. *a. the p.*
*Joel* 2:17 sho. they say *am. t. p.*
*Zec.* 10:9 sow them *a. the p.*
*John* 7:43 a division *am. the p.*
*Acts* 3:23 destroyed from *a. t. p.*
4:17 spread no further *a. t. p.*
14:14 Barnab. and P. ran *a. t. p.*

*See* COMMON, FOOLISH.

**PEOPLE of God.**

*Jud.* 20:2 assembly of *p. of God*
2 *Sam.* 14:13 such th. ag. *p. of G.*
*Ps.* 47:9 even *p. of G.* of Abrah.
*Heb.* 4:9 remain. rest to *p. of G.*
11:25 suf. affliction wi. *p. of G.*
1 *Pet.* 2:10 but now *p. of God*

*See* GREAT.

**His PEOPLE.**

*Gen.* 17:14 cut off from *his p. Ex.* 30:33, 38; 31:14; *Lev.* 7:20, 21, 25, 27; 17:4, 9; 19:8; 23:29; *Num.* 9:13; 15:30
49:16 Dan shall judge *his p.* 33
*Ex.* 18:1 for Moses and Is. *his p.*
*Lev.* 17:10 I will cut him off from among *his p.* 20:3, 6; 23:30
*Deut.* 26:18 L. avouch. thee *h. p.*
32:9 the Lord's portion is *his p.*
36 sh. judge *his p. Ps.* 135:14
43 rej. O ye nations, wi. *his p.* he will be merci. *Rom.* 15:10
33:7 L. and bring Jud. to *his p.*
*Ruth* 1:6 the Lord visited *his p.*
1 *Sam.* 12:22 L. not forsake *h. p.* pleased L. to make you *h. p.*
15:1 anoint thee king over *h. p.*
2 *Sam.* 8:15 David executed just. to all *his p.* 1 *Chr.* 18:14
1 *K.* 20:42 thy pe. sh. go for *h. p.*
1 *Chr.* 21:3 make *h. p.* 100 times
1 *Chr.* 22:18 sub. bef. L. and *h. p.*
23:25 G. of Is. given rest to *h. p.*
2 *Chr.* 2:11 L. hath loved *his p.*
31:10 Lord hath blessed *his p.*
32:14 who could deliv. *h. p.?* 15
36:15 had compassion on *his p.*
16 wrath of L. rose ag. *his p.*
23 who of all *his p. Ezr.* 1:3
*Job* 18:19 not have son am. *h. p.*
*Ps.* 14:7 captivity of *his p.* 53:6
29:11 strength to *his p.* L. will bl. *his p.* with peace, 68:35
50:4 that he may judge *his p.*
73:10 theref. *his p.* return hither
78:20 can he pro. flesh for *h. p.?*
62 he gave *his p.* over to swo.
71 bro. him to feed Jacob *h. p.*
85:8 will speak peace to *his p.*
94:14 Lord will not cast off *h. p.*
100:3 are *h. p.* 105:43 brought
105:24 increased *his p.* greatly
25 turn. th. heart to hate *h. p.*
111:6 he showed *his p.* power
9 he sent redemption to *his p.*
113:8 with princes of *his p.*
116:14 in presence of all *his p.*
125:2 so is L. round about *h. p.*
136:16 who led *his p.* thro' wild.
*Is.* 3:14 with ancients of *his p.*
7:2 moved, and heart of *his p.*
14:32 poor of *his p.* trust in him
25:8 rebuke of *his p.* sh. he take
30:26 L. bind. up breach of *h. p.*
49:13 hath comforted *h. p.* 52:9
51:22 God plead. cause of *h. p.*
56:3 L. separated me fr. *his p.*
63:11 remem. Moses and *his p.*
*Jer.* 27:12 serve him and *his p.*
50:16 return every one to *his p.*
*Ezek.* 18:18 did not good am. *h. p.*
30:11 he and *h. p.* sh. brought
*Joel* 2:18 L. jealous and pity *h. p.*
19 answer and say to *his p.*
3:16 Lord will be hope of *h. p.*
*Zec.* 9:16 L. save them as *his p.*
*Mat.* 1:21 he shall save *his p.*
*Luke* 1:68 and redeemed *h. p.*
7:16 that God hath visited *h. p.*
*Rom.* 11:1 ha. G. cast away *h. p.?*
2 God hath not cast away *h. p.*
*Heb.* 10:30 the L. sh. judge *h. p.*
*Rev.* 21:3 and they shall be *h. p.*

*See* HOLY, ISRAEL, MANY, MEN.

**PEOPLE of the land.**

*Gen.* 23:7 A. bow. to *p. of t. l.* 12
*Ex.* 5:5 the *p. of t. l.* are many
*Lev.* 20:2 *p. of t. l.* sh. stone him
4 if *p. of the l.* hide their eyes
*Num.* 14:9 nei. fear ye *p. of t. l.*
2 *K.* 11:14 all *p. of t.* rejoiced, 20
15:5 Joth. judged *p.* 2 *Chr.* 26:21
21:24 *p.* made J. ki. 2 *Chr.* 33:25
23:30 *p. of the l.* took Jehoahaz his son, 2 *Chr.* 36:1
25:3 no bre. for *p. of t. Jer.* 52:6
1 *Chr.* 5:25 after gods of *p. of t. l.*
*Ezr.* 10:2 stra. wives of *p. of t. l.*
11 separate from *p. of the land*
*Neh.* 10:30 not gi. dau. to *p. of l.*
31 if the *p. of the l.* bring ware
*Est.* 8:17 many *p. of t. l.* bec. J.
*Jer.* 34:19 *p. of t. l.* which passed
*Ezek.* 7:27 *p. of t. l.* be troubled
22:29 *p. of t. l.* used oppression
33:2 if *p. of the l.* take man
39:13 *p. of t. l.* shall bury them
45:16 *p. of t. l.* shall give obla.
22 sh. prince prepa. for *p. of l.*
46:3 *p. of t. l.* shall worship
9 *p. of t. l.* come in feasts
*Dan.* 9:6 proph. spa. to *p. of t. l.*
*Hag.* 2:4 be strong, ye *p. of t. l.*
*Zec.* 7:5 speak to all *p. of the l.*

**Much PEOPLE.**

*Num.* 20:20 E. came with *m. p.*
*Jos.* 11:4 they went with *m. p.*
2 *Chr.* 32:4 gath. *m. p.* together
*Ps.* 35:18 praise thee am. *m. p.*
*Mark* 5:21 *m. p.* gath. unto him
24 and *much p.* followed him
*John* 12:9 *m. p.* of Jews knew
*Acts* 5:37 drew away *m. p.* af. him
11:24 *m. p.* was added unto L.
18:10 I have *m. p.* in this city
19:26 P. hath turned away *m. p.*
*Rev.* 19:1 I heard a voice of *m. p.*

**My PEOPLE.**

*Gen.* 23:11 in presence of *my p.*
41:40 to thy word sh. all *my p.*
49:29 to be gathered to *my p.*
*Ex.* 3:7 I have seen affliction of *my p. Acts* 7:34
5:1 saith L. God, Let *my p.* go, 7:16; 8:1, 20; 9:1, 13; 10:3
8:22 land in wh. *my p.* are, 23
9:17 exaltest thyself ag. *my p.*
*Ex.* 9:27 L. righ. I and *my p.* wic.
12:31 get forth from am. *my p.*
22:25 if th. lend money to *my p*
*Lev.* 26:12 and ye shall be *my p. Jer.* 11:4; 30:22
*Num.* 24:14 I go unto *my p.*
*Jud.* 12:2 I and *my p.* at strife
14:3 never a wom. am. *my p.?*
*Ruth* 1:16 thy peo. shall be *my p.*
3:11 the city of *my p.* doth kn.
1 *Sam.* 9:16 to be cap. over *my p.*
2 *Sam.* 3:18 by D. wi. I save *my p.*
7:8 ruler over *my p.* 2 *Chr.* 6:5
1 *K.* 22:4 *my p.* as thy people, 2 *K.* 3:7; 2 *Chr.* 18:3
1 *Chr.* 17:6 I com. to feed *my p.*
28:2 Da. said, Hear me, *my p.*
29:14 and what *my p.?*
2 *Chr.* 1:11 mayest judge *my p.*
6:5 since day I bro. forth *my p.*
7:14 if *my p.* humb. themselves
*Est.* 7:3 let *my p.* be given me
4 I and *my p.* to be destroyed
*Ps.* 14:4 eat *my p.* as bread, 53:4
50:7 O *my p.* I will speak, 81:8
59:11 slay not, lest *my p.* forget
68:22 I will bring *my p.* fr. Bas.
78:1 give ear, O *my p.* to law
81:11 *my p.* would not hearken
144:2 subdueth *my p.* under me
*Is.* 1:3 *my p.* doth not consider
3:12 *my p.* child. are oppressors
15 that ye beat *my p.?*
10:2 take right fr. poor of *my p.*
24 O *my p.* that dwellest in Z.
19:25 blessed be Egypt, *my p.*
32:18 *my p.* sh. dwell in peace.
40:1 comfort ye, *my p.* saith G.
43:20 give drink to *my p.*
47:6 I was wroth with *my p.*
51:16 say to Z. Thou art *my p.*
52:4 *my p.* went down into Eg.
5 *my p.* is taken away
6 *my p.* shall know my name
58:1 show *my p.* th. transgres.
63:8 surely they are *my p.* chil.
65:10 Sharon a fold for *my p.*
19 rejoice in Jer. joy in *my p.*
22 as a tree, are days of *my p.*
*Jer.* 2:13 *my p.* have commit. ev.
31 say *my p.* we are lords?
32 *my p.* have forgot. me, 18:15
4:22 *my p.* is foolish, not kn. me
5:26 am. *my p.* are wicked men
31 *my p.* love, wh. will ye do?
7:23 obey my voice, be *my p.*
8:7 *my p.* kn. not judgm. of L.
9:2 that I might leave *my p.*
12:16 dilig. learn ways of *my p.*
15:7 destroy *my p.* th. retu. not
23:2 pastors that feed *my p.*
22 if they had caused *my p.*
27 think to cause *my p.* forget
24:7 they shall be *my p.* 31:1, 33; 32:38; *Ezek.* 11:20; 36:28; 37:23, 27; *Zec.* 8:8
29:32 nor good I will do *my p.*
31:14 *my p.* shall be satisfied
33:24 they have despised *my p.*
50:6 *my p.* hath been lost sheep
51:45 *my p.* go ye out of midst of her, *Rev.* 18:4
*Ezek.* 13:9 not in assem. of *my p.*
19 ye pollute me among *my p.* by lying to *my p.*
21 deliver *my p.* out of hand, 23
14:8 cut him off fr. midst *my p.*
11 but that they may be *my p.*
21:12 the sw. sh. be upon *my p.*
34:30 ev. house of Is. are *my p.*
37:12 O *m. p.* I will open gra. 13

38:16 thou shalt come ag. my p.
46:18 that my p. be not scatter.
Hos. 1:9 ye are not my p. 10
2:23 to them wh. were not my p.
4:6 my p. are destroyed for lack
8 they eat up the sin of my p.
6:11 return. captivity of my p.
Joel 2:26 my p. nev. be asha. 27
3:2 plead with them for my p.
3 they have cast lots for my p.
Amos 9:10 sinn. of my p. sh. die
Ob. 13 not enter. gate of my p.
Mic. 1:9 come to gate of my p.
2:8 my p. is risen as enemy
9 women of my p. ye cast out
3:3 who also eat flesh of my p.
5 proph. that make my p. err
6:3 O my p. wh. have I done? 5
16 shall bear reproach of my p.
Zep. 2:8 they reproached my p.
Zec. 2:11 many nations shall be my p.
8:7 save my p. from the east
13:9 it is my p. they shall say
Rom. 9:25 call them my p. which were not my p.
26 was said, Ye are not my p.
2 Cor. 6:16 they shall be my p.
See DAUGHTER.

### Of the PEOPLE.

Gen. 25:23 manner of p. be sep.
49:10 to him sh. gather. of p. be
Num. 26:4 take sum of t. p. fr. 20
Jos. 4:2 take 12 men of the p.
1 Sam. 9:2 higher than any of the p. 10:23
14:24 none of the p. tasted food
26:15 ca. one of t. p. destr. king
2 K. 13:7 nor did he leave of t. p.
Ezr. 3:3 of the p. of th. countries
Neh. 5:1 th. was a gre. cry of t. p.
7:73 some of the p. dw. in cities
Ps. 72:4 sh. judge poor of the p.
89:19 exalted one out of the p.
Is. 51:4 judg. for a light of t. p.
63:3 of the p. there was none
John 7:31 many of t. p. believed
11:42 bec. of t. p. that stand by
Acts 4:21 punish. beca. of the p.
Heb. 9:7 hims. and errors of t. p.
Rev. 11:9 they of p. see dead bod.
See EARS, ELDERS.

### One PEOPLE.

Gen. 25:23 one p. sh. be stronger
34:16 dwell wi. you, bec. one p.
22 dwell with us, to be one p.

### Own PEOPLE.

Ex. 5:16 the fault is in thi. o. p.
1 Chr. 17:21 went to redeem o. p.
2 Chr. 25:15 could not deli. o. p.
Ps. 45:10 forget also thy own p.
78:52 made his o. p. to go forth
Is. 13:14 ev. man turn to his o. p.
Jer. 46:16 let us go ag. to our o. p.

### The PEOPLE.

Gen. 11:6 L. said, Behold the p.
Ex. 5:4 why let t. p. from work?
5 the p. of land now are many
12:27 and t. p. bowed the head
14:31 the p. feared L. believed
15:14 the p. sh. hear and be afr.
16 the p. pass over wh. th. hast
24 the p. murmured, saying
16:30 the p. rest. on seventh day
17:1 th. was no water for the p.
2 t. p. did chide Mo. Num. 20:3
6 water out of it, the p. drink
18:19 be th. for the p. God-ward
19:9 t. p. may hear when I spe.
17 Moses brought forth the p.
20:18 when the p. saw it afar, 21
24:8 Moses sprinkled it on t. p.
Lev. 9:7 ato. for thyself and t. p.
15 sin-offer. for the p. 18; 16:15
Num. 11:2 the p. cried to Moses
13:18 see the p. that dwelleth
14:1 the p. wept; 39 t. p. mour.
21:5 the p. spake against God
23:9 lo, the p. shall dwell alone
24 the p. rise up as a great lion
Deut. 4:10 said, Gather me the p.
18:3 the priest's due from t. p.
33:3 loved the p. 17 push the p.
19 they shall call t. p. to moun.
Jos. 4:10 and the p. hasted over
6:20 t. p. shout. 24:28 t. p. dep.
Jud. 7:2 t. p. are with thee, 4
1 Sam. 2:13 priest's cust. wi. t. p.
4:4 t. p. sent to Sh. to bring ark
8:19 the p. ref. to obey Samuel
14:45 the p. said, Sh. Jonathan die? so the p. rescued Jona.
15:15 the p. spared best of sheep
21 the p. took of the spoil oxen
30:6 t. p. spake of stoning him
2 Sam. 1:4 t. p. fled from battle
15:12 the p. incre. with Absalom
1 K. 1:40 the p. piped with pipes
16:22 the p. that followed Omri prevailed against the p.
2 K. 4:41 pour out for the p.
43 give t. p. that they may eat
11:17 coven. bet. king and t. p.
18:36 but the p. held their peace
22:13 inquire of Lord for the p.
2 Chr. 12:3 the p. without numb.
20:33 the p. had not prepa. 30:3
27:2 and the p. did yet corruptly
30:20 and the Lord healed the p.
32:8 the p. rest. on words of H.
36:14 the p. transgr. very much
Ezr. 10:13 but the p. are many
Neh. 4:6 t. p. had mind to work
5:13 the p. did accord. to prom.
7:4 but the p. were few therein
8:16 the p. bro palm branches
11:2 t. p. blessed all that offered
Est. 3:6 showed him t. p. of Mo.
4:11 the p. of king's provinces
Job 12:2 no doubt but ye are t. p.
34:30 lest the p. be ensnared
Ps. 2:1 why do t. p. im. vain th.?
Ps. 33:12 bles. t. p. he hath cho.
44:2 how thou didst afflict t. p.
45:17 the p. praise thee for ever
56:7 in th. anger cast down t. p.
67:3 let the p. praise thee, O G. 5
89:15 blessed is t. p. that know
95:7 we are t. p. of his pasture
96:13 he sh. judge t. p. with tru.
98:9 he sh. judge t. p. with eq.
99:1 L. reign. let the p. tremble
105:1 make kno. deeds am. t. p.
Prov. 11:14 no coun. is, t. p. fall
29:2 the p. rejoiced, t. p. mourn
18 wh. is no vision, t. p. perish
Is. 9:2 t. p. that walked in dark.
13 t. p. turneth not to him sm.
14:2 and the p. shall take them
24:2 be with t. p. so with priest
30:19 the p. shall dwell in Zion
33:24 t. p. be forgiven th. iniq.
34:5 my sword sh. come on t. p.
40:7 t. p. is grass, grass wither.
51:7 the p. in wh. heart is my law
63:6 will tread t. p. in mi. anger
18 t. p. of thy holi. possess. it
Jer. 31:2 t. p. left of sw. found gr.
37:4 Jeremiah went amo. the p.
39:14 so he dwelt among the p.
40:5 go back and dw. with t. p. 6
51:58 the p. shall labor in vain
Ezek. 11:17 gather you from t. p.
20:34 br. you out from t. p. 34:13
25:7 I will cut thee off fr. the p.
26:20 bring thee down with t. p.
33:31 come to thee as t. p. com.
36:20 these are the p. of Lord
39:4 thou shalt fall, and the p.
42:14 approa. th. things for t. p.
44:19 shall not sanctify the p.
Dan. 9:26 the p. of the prince
11:32 the p. that know their G.
Hos. 4:14 t. p. doth not underst.
10:5 the p. thereof shall mourn
10 t. p. sh. be gath. aga. them
Joel 2:6 the p. sh. be much pain.
Amos 3:6 sh. t. p. not be afraid?
Jon. 3:5 t. p. of Nin. believ. God
Hab. 2:13 t. p. shall labor in fire, the p. shall weary themselv.
Zep. 2:10 magnifi. ag. t. p. of L.
Hag. 1:12 t. p. did fear the Lord
Mal. 1:4 the p. against whom L.
Mat. 4:16 t. p. in dark. saw light
21:26 we fear t. p. Mark 11:32
Luke 1:21 t. p. waited for Zacha.
3:15 as the p. were in expecta.
4:42 the p. sou. 5:1 t. p. pressed
8:40 the p. gladly received him
9:18 whom say t. p. that I am?
20:19 feared t. p. 22:2; 23:5 stir.
23:14 one that perverteth t. p.
John 7:12 he deceiveth the p.
11:50 man sho. die for t. p. 18:14
Acts 5:13 the p. magnified them
8:6 t. p. wi. one accord ga. heed
14:11 t. p. saw wh. P. had done
19 persuaded t. p. and ston. P.
26:17 delivering thee from t. p.
Heb. 5:3 as for t. p. so hims. 7:27
7:11 under it t. p. received law
13:12 he might sanctify the p.
Jude 5 Lord having saved the p.

### This PEOPLE.

Ex. 3:21 I will give t. p. favor
5:22 why hast evil entrea. t. p.?
17:4 cried, Wh. sh. I do to t. p.?
18:18 wear away, thou and t. p.
32:9 seen t. p. 21 what did t. p.
31 t. p. have sinned a great sin
33:12 sayest, Bring up this p.
Num. 11:11 burden of all t. p.
14 I am not able to bear all t. p.
14:11 how long will t. p. prov.?
15 if thou kill t. p. as one man
16 not able to br. t. p. into land
19 pardon t. p. hast forg. t. p.
22:6 I pray thee, curse t. p. 17
24:14 th. p. shall do to thy peo.
Deut. 5:28 heard voice of this p.
9:13 saying, I have seen this p.
27 look not to stubborn. of t. p.
31:7 for thou must go with t. p.
16 t. p. will go whor. after gods
Jud. 2:20 t. p. have transgressed
9:29 would to G. t. p. were und.
38 is not this the p. thou des.?
2 Sam. 16:18 wh. L. and t. p. ch.
1 K. 12:6 that I may answer this p. 9; 2 Chr. 10:6, 9
27 if t. p. do sacrifice at Jerusalem
14:2 I should be king over t. p.
18:37 that this p. may know
2 K. 6:18 smite t. p. wi. blindn.
2 Chr. 1:10 come in before th. p.
Neh. 5:19 all I have done for t. p.
Is. 6:9 go and tell t. p. hear ye
Is. 6:10 make the heart of t. p. fat, Mat. 13:15; Acts 28:26, 27
9:16 leaders of t. p. cause th. err
23:13 t. p. was not till A. found
28:14 scornful men that rule t. p.
29:13 t. p. dr. near me wi. mou.
14 a marv. work among t. p.
43:21 t. p. ha. I form. for myself
Jer. 4:10 thou hast deceived t. p.
5:14 my words fire, t. p. wood
6:19 I will bring evil on this p.
21 stumbling-blo. bef. this p.
7:16 therefore pray not thou for this p. 11:14; 14:11
8:5 why is this p. slidden back?
13:10 t. evil p. who ref. to hear
15:1 my mind co. not be to. t. p.
16:5 tak. away my peace fr. t. p.
19:11 even so will I break t. p.
23:32 they shall not profit t. p.

28:15 makest t. p. trust in a lie
29:32 a man to dwell amo. t. p.
32:42 bro. great evil upon t. p.
33:24 not what t. p. have spok.
35:16 t. p. have not hearkened
36:7 anger pronounced ag. t. p.
37:18 what have I offend. t. p.?
Mic. 2:11 sh. be prophet of t. p.
Hag. 2:14 so is this p. before me
Zec. 8:6 in eyes of remn. of t. p.
11 I will not be to this p.
12 cause rem. of t. p. possess
Mat. 15:8 t. p. draweth nigh
Mark 7:6 t. p. hon. me with lips
Luke 9:13 sho. buy meat for t. p.
21:23 th. sh. be wrath upon t. p.
John 7:49 t. p. knoweth not law
Acts 13:17 G. of t. p. chose our
1 Cor. 14:21 I will speak to t. p.

**Thy PEOPLE.**

Ex. 5:23 neither delivered t. p.
15:16 till t. p. pass over, O Lord
22:28 ca. ruler of t. p. Acts 23:5
23:11 poor of thy p. may eat
33:13 consider this nation t. p.
16 I and t. p. have found grace
Num. 5:21 make thee a curse and oath among thy p.
27:13 shalt be gathered to t. p. 31:2; Deut. 32:50
Deut. 9:12 t. p. corrupted thems.
26 O Lord, destroy not thy p.
29 yet are they t. p. Neh. 1:10
Ruth 1:10 return wi. thee to t. p.
16 thy p. shall be my people
2 Sam. 7:23 and what nation is like thy p.? 1 Chr. 17:21
23 bef. t. p. wh. thou redeeme.
1 K. 3:8 serv. is in midst of t. p.
8:44 if thy p. go out to battle
50 forgive t. p. 2 Chr. 6:34, 39
51 they be t. p. 20:42 thy p. his
22:4 my people as t. p. 2 K. 3:7
1 Chr. 21:17 not hand be on t. p.
29:18 thoughts of heart of t. p.
Ps. 3:8 blessing is upon thy p.
28:9 save t. p. bless, Jer. 31:7
44:12 sellest thy p. for naught
60:3 showed thy p. hard things
68:7 thou wentest before thy p.
72:2 judge t. p. with righteous.
77:20 leddest thy p. as flock
79:13 thy p. will give thee than.
80:4 angry aga. prayer of t. p.?
83:3 crafty counsel against t. p.
85:2 forgiven iniquity of thy p.
6 that t. p. may rejoice in thee
94:5 they break in pieces t. p.
106:4 favor th. thou bearest t. p.
110:3 thy p. shall be willing
Is. 2:6 thou hast forsaken thy p.
7:17 L. bring on thee and t. p.
14:20 destroyed land and thy p.
60:21 t. p. shall be all righteous
63:14 lead t. p. 64:9 are thy p.
Jer. 22:2 thou and t. p. that ent.
27:13 die, thou and t. p. by sw.?
Ezek. 3:11 get to t. p. and speak
13:17 against daughters of t. p.
26:11 he sh. slay t. p. by sword
33:2 speak to child. of t. p. 12
17 yet the children of t. p. say
30 chil. of t. p. still are talking
37:18 chil. of t. p. shall speak
Dan. 9:16 thy p. bec. a reproach
19 and thy p. are called by na.
12:1 standeth for chil. of thy p. at that time t. p. sh. be deli.
Hos. 4:4 t. p. as they that strive
10:14 a tumult arise among t. p.
Joel 2:17 spare t. p. O Lord
Mic. 7:14 feed t. p. with thy rod
Nah. 3:13 thy p. in midst of thee
18 t. p. scattered on mountain
Hab. 3:13 for salvation of thy p.

**To, or unto the PEOPLE.**

Ex. 4:16 be spokesman to t. p.
19:10 go to t. p. 12 bounds to p.
Deut. 20:2 priest speak to the p.
5 officers shall speak to the p.
Jud. 8:5 loaves of bread to the p.
Ruth 2:11 to t. p. th. knowest not
1 Sam. 26:7 Abishai came to t. p.
2 Sam. 24:3 L. thy G. add to t. p.
1 K. 12:15 king heark. not to p.
2 K. 4:42 give to p. they may eat
1 Chr. 10:9 carry tidings to t. p.
2 Chr. 35:8 gave willingly to t. p.
Neh. 4:22 said I to the p. lodge
5:15 govern. chargeable to t. p.
Ps. 9:8 minister judgm. to the p.
72:3 shall bring peace to the p.
Is. 42:5 giveth breath to the p.
49:22 set up my standard to t. p.
55:4 given him for witness to t. p. a leader and com. to t. p.
Ezek. 24:18 spake to t. p. in mor.
Dan. 7:27 kingdom given to t. p.
Joel 3:8 sell them to t. p. afar off
Hab. 3:16 cometh to t. p. will in.
Zep. 3:9 turn to t. p. pure langu.
Mat. 12:46 yet talked to the p.
Acts 5:20 speak in temple to t. p.
10:2 which gave alms to the p.
42 comma. us to preach to t. p.
13:31 seen of witnesses to the p.
17:5 J. sought to bring to the p.
19:33 made his defence to the p.
21:39 suffer me to speak to the p.
26:23 Christ show light to the p.

**PEOPLES.**

Rev. 10:11 prophesy bef. many p.
17:15 waters thou sawest are p.

PEOR. Num. 23:28; 25:18; Jos. 22:17

**PERADVENTURE.**

Gen. 18:24 p. there be 50 righte.
28 p. there lack five of the fifty
29 p. forty; 30 p. thirty; 31 p. twenty
32 this once, p. ten shall be
24:5 p. wom. not be willing, 39
27:12 my father p. will feel me
31:31 p. take by force thy daug.
32:20 p. he will accept of me
42:4 lest p. mischief befall him
43:12 p. it was an oversight
44:34 p. evil come on my father
50:15 Joseph will p. hate us
Ex. 13:17 lest p. people repent
32:30 p. I shall make atonement
Num. 22:6 p. I shall prevail, 11
23:3 p. L. will come to meet me
27 p. it please God thou curse
Jos. 9:7 p. ye dwell among us
1 Sam. 6:5 p. he will lighten ha.
9:6 p. he can show us our way
1 K. 18:5 p. we may find grass
27 p. sleep, must be awaked
20:31 p. he will save thy life
2 K. 2:16 p. Spirit hath cast him
Jer. 20:10 p. he will be enticed
Rom. 5:7 p. for good men so. die
2 Tim. 2:25 p. G. give them rep.

**PERCEIVE.**

Deut. 29:4 not given heart to p.
Jos. 22:31 we p. Lord is am. us
1 Sam. 12:17 p. your wickedness
2 Sam. 19:6 I p. if A. had lived
2 K. 4:9 I p. this is a holy man
Job 9:11 p. not; 28:3 cannot p.
Prov. 1:2 p. words of understan.
Ec. 3:22 p. there is noth. better
Is. 6:9 see ye indeed, but p. not
33:19 deeper speech th. canst p.
Mat. 13:14 shall see, and sh. not p. Mark 4:12; Acts 28:26
Mark 7:18 do ye not p. whatsoe.
8:17 p. ye not, neither unders.?
Luke 8:46 I p. virtue out of me
John 4:19 I p. thou art a prophet
12:19 p. ye how pre. nothing?
Acts 8:23 p. art in gall of bitter.
10:34 p. G. is no respect. of per.
17:22 I p. ye are too superstitio.
2 Cor. 7:8 I p. ep. made you sor.
1 John 3:16 here. p. we love of G.

**PERCEIVED.**

Gen. 19:33 p. not wh. she lay, 35
1 Sam. 28:14 S. p. it was Samuel
2 Sam. 5:12 D. p. Lord establish. him king over Is. 1 Chr. 14:2
1 K. 22:33 when captains p. it was not king. 2 Chr. 18:32
Neh. 6:12 p. G. had not sent him
16 p. this work was wro. of G.
13:10 p. portion of L. not given
Job 38:18 p. breadth of earth?
Ec. 1:17 I p. this also is vexat.
2:14 I p. one event happeneth
Is. 64:4 nor p. what God prep.
Jer. 23:18 who hath p. his word
Jer. 38:27 for matter was not p.
Mat. 21:45 p. he spa. Luke 20:19
22:18 Jesus p. their wickedness
Mark 2:8 Jesus p. they reasoned
Luke 1:22 p. he had seen vision
5:22 when Jesus p. th. thoughts
9:45 saying hid, they p. it not
20:23 but he p. their craftiness
John 6:15 J. p. would make him
Acts 4:13 p. they were unlearned
23:6 Paul p. part were Pharise.
Gal. 2:9 James p. grace giv. me

**PERCEIVEST, ETH.**

Job 14:21 low, but he p. it not
33:14 G. speaketh, man p. it not
Prov. 14:7 p. not in him knowl.
31:18 p. her merchandi. is good
Luke 6:41 p. not beam in own eye

**PERCEIVING.**

Mark 12:28 p. he answered well
Luke 9:47 Jesus p. the thought
Acts 14:9 p. he had faith to be

**PERDITION.**

John 17:12 no. lost but son of p.
Phil. 1:28 to them a token of p.
2 Thes. 2:3 be revealed, son of p.
1 Tim. 6:9 wh. drown men in p.
Heb. 10:39 who draw back to p.
2 Pet. 3:7 and p. of ungodly men
Rev. 17:8 beast goeth into p.
11 beast is eighth, goeth in. p.

**PERFECT, Adjective.**

Gen. 6:9 N. p. 17:1 be thou p.
Lev. 22:21 freewill-offering be p.
Deut. 18:13 thou shalt be p. with
25:15 have p. weight, p. measu.
1 Sam. 14:41 S. said, Give p. lot
2 Sam. 22:33 he maketh my way p. Ps. 18:32
Ezr. 7:12 Artax. to E. p. peace
Job 1:1 that man was p. 8; 2:3
8:20 G. not cast away a p. man
9:20 I am p. 21 tho' I were p.
22 he destroyeth p. and wicked
22:3 thou makest thy ways p.?
Ps. 37:37 p. man, end is peace
64:4 may shoot in secret at p.
101:2 behave myself in a p. way
6 he that walketh in a p. way
139:22 I hate th. with p. hatred
Prov. 2:21 p. shall remain in it
4:18 path of just shin. to p. day
11:5 righteousn. of p. sh. direct
Is. 26:3 keep him in p. peace
Ezek. 16:14 p. thro' my comelin.
27:3 thou said, I am of p. beauty
11 made thy beauty p. 28:12
28:15 thou was p. in thy ways
Mat. 5:48 be p. even as Fa. is p.
19:21 if thou wilt be p. go sell
Luke 1:3 hav. had p. understan.
John 17:23 be made p. in one
Acts 3:16 given him p. soundn.
22:3 taught accor. to p. manner
24:22 having more p. knowledge
Rom. 12:2 what is p. will of God

1 *Cor.* 2:6 among th. that are *p.*
2 *Cor.* 12:9 strength *p.* in weakn.
13:11 be *p.* be of good comfort
*Gal.* 3:3 are ye made *p.* by flesh?
*Eph.* 4:13 till we come to *p.* man
*Phil.* 3:12 not as tho' already *p.*
15 as many as be *p.*
*Col.* 1:28 present every man *p.* in
4:12 stand *p.* in will of God
1 *Thes.* 3:10 *p.* which is lacking
2 *Tim.* 3:17 man of G. may be *p.*
*Heb.* 2:10 Captain of salvation *p.*
5:9 being made *p.* beca. Author
7:19 for law made nothing *p.*
9:9 not make him did service *p.*
11 greater and more *p.* tabern.
10:1 law never make comers *p.*
11:40 without us not made *p.*
12:23 spirits of just men made *p.*
13:21 G. make you *p.* in every
*Jam.* 1:4 let patience have her *p.* work, that ye may be *p.*
17 every *p.* gift is from above
25 looketh into *p.* law of liber.
2:22 by works was faith ma. *p.*
3:2 offend not, same is *p.* man
1 *Pet.* 5:10 after suffer. make *p.*
1 *John* 4:17 herein is love made *p.*
18 *p.* love casteth out fear, he that feareth is not *p.* in love
*See* HEART.

**Is PERFECT.**

*Deut.* 32:4 his work *is p.*
2 *Sam.* 23:31 way *is p. Ps.* 18:30
*Job* 36:4 he that *is p.* in kn. 37:16
*Ps.* 19:7 law of L. *is p.* convert.
*Is.* 18:5 harvest when bud *is p.*
42:19 blind as he that *is p.*
*Mat.* 5:48 as Father in heaven *is p.*
*Luke* 6:40 every one that *is p.*
1 *Cor.* 13:10 that wh. *is p.* is co.

**PERFECT, Verb.**

*Ps.* 138:8 L. will *p.* wh. concern.

**PERFECTED.**

2 *Chr.* 8:16 so house of G. was *p.*
24:13 and work was *p.* by them
*Ezek.* 27:4 builders have *p.* bea.
*Mat.* 21:16 thou hast *p.* praise
*Luke* 13:32 third day I shall be *p.*
*Heb.* 10:14 by one offer he ha. *p.*
1 *John* 2:5 in him is love of G. *p.*
4:12 love one ano. his love is *p.*

**PERFECTING.**

2 *Cor.* 7:1 *p.* holin. in fear of G.
*Eph.* 4:12 for *p.* of the saints

**PERFECTION.**

*Job* 11:7 find Almighty to *p.*?
15:29 nor shall he prolong *p.*
28:3 he searcheth out all *p.*
*Ps.* 50:2 out of Zion, *p.* of beauty
119:96 I have seen an end of *p.*
*Is.* 47:9 come upon thee in th. *p.*
*Lam.* 2:15 men call *p.* of beauty
*Luke* 8:14 bring no fruit to *p.*
2 *Cor.* 13:9 we wish, even your *p.*
*Heb.* 6:1 let us go on to *p.*
7:11 if *p.* were by Levit. priest.

**PERFECTLY, NESS.**

*Jer.* 23:20 lat. days consider it *p.*
*Mat.* 14:36 touch. made *p.* whole
*Acts* 18:26 expound. way of G. *p.*
23:15 Inq. something more *p.* 20
1 *Cor.* 1:10 be *p.* joined together
*Col.* 3:14 charity is the bond of *p.*
1 *Thes.* 5:2 know *p.* that day of

**PERFORMANCE.**

*Luke* 1:45 shall be *p.* of th. thin.
2 *Cor.* 8:11 *p.* out of that ye have

**PERFORM.**

*Gen.* 26:3 I will *p.* oath, I sware to Ab. *Deut.* 9:5; *Luke* 1:72
*Ex.* 18:18 not able to *p.* it thys.
*Num.* 4:23 that enter to *p.* serv.
*Deut.* 4:13 commanded you to *p*
23:23 gone out of thy lips sh. *p.*
25:7 not *p.* duty of husband's brother
*Ruth* 3:13 *p.* part of kinsman
1 *Sam.* 3:12 I will *p.* against Eli
2 *Sam.* 14:15 king will *p.* requ.
1 *K.* 6:12 then I will *p.* my word
2 *K.* 23:3 to *p.* the words of this covenant. 24; 2 *Chr.* 34:31
*Est.* 5:8 if please king to *p.* req.
*Job* 5:12 cannot *p.* enterprise
*Ps.* 21:11 a device not able to *p.*
61:8 that I may daily *p.* vows
119:106 have sworn, I will *p.* it
112 inclined heart to *p.* statut.
*Is.* 9:7 zeal of Lord will *p.* this
19:21 pay a vow to L. and *p.* it
*Jer.* 1:12 for I will hasten to *p.* it
11:5 *p.* oath which I have sworn
28:6 L. *p.* words thou hast pro.
29:10 I will *p.* good word, 33:14
44:25 will surely *p.* your vows
*Ezek.* 12:25 word, and will *p.* it
*Mic.* 7:20 wilt *p.* truth to Jacob
*Nah.* 1:15 keep feasts, *p.* vows
*Mat.* 5:33 *p.* to Lord thine oaths
*Rom.* 4:21 prom. able also to *p.*
7:18 how to *p.* that wh. is good
2 *Cor.* 8:11 now *p.* the doing of
*Phil.* 1:6 *p.* it until day of J. Ch.

**PERFORMED.**

1 *Sam.* 15:11 S. hath not *p.* com.
13 I have *p.* commandm. of L.
2 *Sam.* 21:14 *p.* all th. king com.
1 *K.* 8:20 Lord hath *p.* his word, 2 *Chr.* 6:10; *Neh.* 9:8
*Est.* 1:15 Vashti not *p.* comma.
5:6 half of kingdom be *p.* 7:2
*Ps.* 65:1 unto thee sh. vow be *p.*
*Is.* 10:12 when L. hath *p.* work
*Jer.* 23:20 till *p.* thoughts, 30:24
34:18 not *p.* words of covenant
35:14 words of Jonad. are *p.* 16
51:29 purpose of Lord sh. be *p.*
*Ezek.* 37:14 spo. and *p.* it, saith Lord
*Luke* 1:20 these things be *p.*
2:39 wh. they had *p.* all things
*Rom.* 15:28 wh. I have *p.* all this

**PERFORMETH, ING.**

*Num.* 15:3 offering in *p.* vow, 8
*Neh.* 5:13 man *p.* not th. promise
*Job* 23:14 he *p.* thing appointed
*Ps.* 57:2 cry to G. that *p.* all thi.
*Is.* 44:26 *p.* counsel of messeng.

**PERFUME, S.**

*Ex.* 30:35 shalt make it a *p.* 37
*Prov.* 27:9 *p.* rejoice the heart
*Is.* 57:9 didst increase thy *p.*

**PERFUMED.**

*Prov.* 7:17 *p.* bed with myrrh
*Cant.* 3:6 who is this cometh *p.*?

PERGA. *Acts* 13:13; 14:25
PERGAMOS. *Rev.* 1:11; 2:12

**PERHAPS.**

*Phile.* 15 *p.* he depart. for season

**PERIL, S.**

*Lam.* 5:9 get our bread with *p.*
*Rom.* 8:35 shall *p.* separate us?
2 *Cor.* 11:26 *p.* of waters, of rob.

**PERILOUS.**

2 *Tim.* 3:1 *p.* times shall come

**PERISH.**

*Gen.* 41:36 *p.* not thro' famine
*Ex.* 19:21 and many of them *p.*
*Num.* 17:12 die, we *p.* we all *p.*
24:20 latter end be that *p.*
*Deut.* 11:17 lest ye *p.* quickly
26:5 ready to *p.* was my father
28:20 thou *p.* quick. 22; *Jo.* 23:13
*Jud.* 5:31 let enemies *p.* O Lord
1 *Sam.* 26:10 into battle and *p*
*Est.* 3:13 cause to *p.* all J. 7:4
4:16 if I *p.* I *p.* 8:11 *p.* power
9:28 nor memorial *p.* fr. th. seed
*Job* 3:3 let the day *p.* I was born
4:9 by the blast of God they *p.*
20 *p.* for ever, without any
6:18 paths go to nothing and *p.*
29:13 bless. of him ready to *p.*
31:19 *p.* for want of clothing
*Ps.* 2:12 lest he be angry, ye *p.*
9:18 expectation of poor not *p.*
49:10 fool and brutish person *p.*
12 like beasts that *p.* 20
68:2 let wicked *p.* 83:17
80:16 *p.* at the rebuke of thy
146:4 very day his thoughts *p.*
*Prov.* 11:10 wh. wicked *p.* 28:28
29:18 there is no vision, peo. *p.*
31:6 drink to him ready to *p.*
*Ec.* 5:14 those riches *p.* by evil
*Is.* 26:14 made th. memory to *p.*
27:13 which were ready to *p.*
*Jer.* 18:18 the law shall not *p.*
27:10 drive you out, ye *p.* 15
40:15 remnant in Judah sho. *p.*
*Ezek.* 25:7 I will cause thee to *p.*
*Dan.* 2:18 that D. should not *p.*
*Jon.* 1:6 that we *p.* not, 3:9
14 not *p.* for this man's life
*Mat.* 5:29 one of thy mem. *p.* 30
8:25 L. save us, we *p. Luke* 8:24
9:17 wine runneth out, bot. *p.*
18:14 one of little ones sho. *p.*
*Mark* 4:38 carest th. not we *p.*?
*Luke* 13:33 prophet *p.* out of J.
15:17 bread eno. I *p.* wi. hunger
21:18 not a hair of your head *p.*
*John* 3:15 whoso belie. not, *p.* 16
11:50 that whole nation *p.* not
*Acts* 8:20 thy money *p.* with th.
13:41 despisers, wonder and *p.*
2 *Cor.* 2:15 savor of C. in them *p.*
4:16 tho' outward man *p.* inwa.
*Col.* 2:22 which all are to *p.*
2 *Thes.* 2:10 unrig. in th. that *p.*
2 *Pet.* 3:9 not willing any sho. *p.*

**Shall PERISH.**

*Lev.* 26:38 ye *s. p.* among heath.
*Deut.* 4:26 ye *s.* soon utterly *p.* 8:19, 20; 30:18; *Jos.* 23:16
1 *Sam.* 27:1 I *s.* one day *p.* by S.
2 *K.* 9:8 whole house of A. *s. p.*
*Job* 8:13 hypocrite's hope *s. p.*
18:17 remem. *s. p.* 20:7; 36:12
34:15 all flesh *shall p.* together
*Ps.* 1:6 way of ungodly *shall p.*
37:20 wick. *s. p.* 92:9 enemies *p.*
73:27 that are far from thee *s. p.*
102:26 they *s. p.* thou endure
112:10 desire of wicked *shall p.*
*Prov.* 10:28 ex. of wick. *s. p.* 11:7
19:9 he that speaketh lies *s. p.*
21:28 a false witness *shall p.*
*Is.* 29:14 wisd. of wise men *s. p.*
41:11 that strive with thee *s. p.*
60:12 king. not serve thee *s. p.*
*Jer.* 4:9 heart of the king *s. p.*
6:21 neighbor and friend *s. p.*
10:11 the gods *s. p.* 15; 51:18
48:8 valley also *s. p.* and plain
*Ezek.* 7:26 law *s. p.* from priest
*Amos* 1:8 remnant of Phil. *s. p.*
2:14 therefore the flight *s. p.*
3:15 houses of ivory *shall p.*
*Zec.* 9:5 king *s. p.* from Gaza.
*Mat.* 26:52 *shall p.* with sword
*Luke* 5:37 wine spil. bottles *s. p.*
13:3 ye *shall* all likewise *p.* 5
*John* 10:28 the sheep *s.* never *p.* 5
*Rom.* 2:12 sinned with. law, *s. p.*
1 *Cor.* 8:11 *shall* weak brother *p.*
*Heb.* 1:11 they *s. p.* thou remai.
2 *Pet.* 2:12 *shall p.* in their cor.

**PERISHED.**

*Num.* 16:33 they *p.* fr. congreg.
*Jos.* 22:20 that man *p.* not alone
2 *Sam.* 1:27 weapons of war *p.*!
*Job* 4:7 who ev. *p.* being innoc.
30:2 in whom old age was *p.*

*Ps.* 9:6 memorial is *p.* with them
10:16 heathen are *p.* out of land
119:92 I sho. have *p.* in afflict.
*Ec.* 9:6 envy is *p.* *Jer.* 7:28 truth
*Jer.* 48:36 riches he hath got. *p.*
49:7 in counsel *p.* from prudent
*Lam.* 3:18 strength and hope *p.*
*Joel* 1:11 the harvest of field is *p.*
*Jon.* 4:10 which came up and *p.*
*Mic.* 4:9 why cry? is couns. *p.?*
7:2 good man is *p.* out of earth
*Mat.* 8:32 h. of swine ran and *p.*
*Lu.* 11:51 *p.* bet. altar and temp.
*Acts* 5:37 he also *p.* and as many
1 *Cor.* 15:18 fallen asleep in C. *p.*
*Heb.* 11:31 harlot Rahab *p.* not
2 *Pet.* 3:6 overflo. with water *p.*
*Jude* 11 *p.* in gainsaying of C.

**PERISHETH.**

*Job* 4:11 lion *p.* for lack of prey
*Prov.* 11:7 hope of unjust men *p.*
*Ec.* 7:15 th. is a just man that *p.*
*Is.* 57:1 righteous *p.* and no man
*Jer.* 9:12 land *p.* and is burnt up
*John* 6:27 labor not for meat *p.*
*Jam.* 1:11 grace of fashion of it *p.*
1 *Pet.* 1:7 more prec. than gold *p.*

**PERISHING.**

*Job* 33:18 his life fr. *p.* by sword

PERIZZITE. *Gen.* 13:7; *Ex.* 33:2; 34:11; *Jos.* 9:1; 11:3
PERIZZITES. *Gen.* 15:20; *Ex.* 3:8, 17; 23:23; *Jud.* 1:4, 5; 3:5; 2 *Chr.* 8:7; *Ezr.* 9:1

**PERJURED.**

1 *Tim.* 1:10 for liars *p.* persons

**PERMISSION.**

1 *Cor.* 7:6 I speak this by *p.*

**PERMIT.**

1 *Cor.* 16:7 tarry awhile, if L. *p.*
*Heb.* 6:3 this will we do, if G. *p*

**PERMITTED.**

*Acts* 26:1 thou art *p.* to speak
1 *Cor.* 14:34 not *p.* wo. to speak

**PERNICIOUS.**

2 *Pet.* 2:2 shall fol. their *p.* ways

**PERPETUAL.**

*Gen.* 9:12 cov. for *p.* generations
*Ex.* 29:9 priest's office be for *p.*
31:16 keep sab. for *p.* covenant
*Lev.* 3:17 a *p.* stat. not to eat fat
24:9 be Aaron's by a *p.* statute
25:34 it is their *p.* possession
*Num.* 19:21 a *p.* statute
*Ps.* 9:6 destruc. come to *p.* end
74:3 lift up feet to *p.* desolation
78:66 put them to a *p.* reproach
*Jer.* 5:22 by *p.* decree, it cannot
8:5 slid. back by *p.* backsliding?
15:18 why is my pain *p.* and my
18:16 land desolate, *p.* hissing
23:40 bring upon you *p.* shame
25:9 make them *p.* desolat. 12
49:13 cities thereof be *p.* wastes
50:5 join Lord in a *p.* covenant
51:39 may sleep a *p.* sleep, 57
*Ezek.* 35:5 hast had a *p.* hatred
9 *p.* desolations, *Zep.* 2:9
46:14 *p.* ordinance to the Lord
*Hab.* 3:6 and the *p.* hills did bow

**PERPETUALLY.**

1 *K.* 9:3 be there *p.* 2 *Chr.* 7:16
*Amos* 1:11 his anger did tear *p.*

**PERPLEXED.**

*Est.* 3:15 city Shushan was *p.*
*Joel* 1:18 herds of cattle are *p.*
*Luke* 9:7 H. was *p.* 24:4 they were
2 *Cor.* 4:8 *p.* but not in despair

**PERPLEXITY.**

*Is.* 22:5 it is a day of *p.* by Lord
*Mic.* 7:4 now shall be their *p.*
*Luke* 21:25 distress of nation, *p.*

**PERSECUTE.**

*Job* 19:22 why do ye *p.* me as G.
28 *p.* him, seeing root in me?
*Ps.* 7:1 save me fr. them that *p.*
5 let the enemy *p.* my soul
10:2 wicked in his pride doth *p.*
31:15 del. me from them that *p.*
35:3 stop way ag. them that *p.*
6 let angel of Lord *p.* them
69:26 they *p.* him thou hast sm.
71:11 *p.* and take him
83:15 so *p.* them with thy tem.
119:84 judgm. on them that *p.*
86 they *p.* me wrongfully, help
*Jer.* 17:18 confounded that *p.* me
*Jer.* 29:18 I will *p.* them wi. sw.
*Lam.* 3:66 *p.* and destroy them
*Mat.* 5:11 bles. when men *p.* you
44 pray for them which *p.* you
10:23 when they *p.* you in one
23:34 *p.* them from city to city
*Luke* 11:49 they shall *p.* 21:12
*John* 5:16 the Jews *p.* Jesus
15:20 they will also *p.* you
*Rom.* 12:14 bless them which *p.*

**PERSECUTED.**

*Deut.* 30:7 curses on them th. *p.*
*Ps.* 109:16 because he *p.* the poor
119:161 princes *p.* me wi. cause
143:3 enemy hath *p.* my soul
*Is.* 14:6 rul. nations in anger *p.*
*Lam.* 3:43 with anger, and *p.* us
*Mat.* 5:10 blessed which are *p.*
12 so *p.* they prophets bef. you
*John* 15:20 if they have *p.* me
*Acts* 7:52 have not your fath. *p.*
22:4 I *p.* this way unto death
26:11 I *p.* them to strange cities
1 *Cor.* 4:12 being *p.* we suffer it
15:9 I *p.* church of G. *Gal.* 1:13
2 *Cor.* 4:9 we are *p.* not forsaken
*Gal.* 1:23 *p.* us in times past
4:29 born after flesh *p.* him
1 *Thes.* 2:15 killed L. and *p.* us
*Rev.* 12:13 dragon *p.* woman that

**PERSECUTEST, ING.**

*Acts* 9:4 Saul, Saul, why *p.* thou me? 22:7; 26:14
5 I am Jesus, whom thou *p.* 22:8; 26:15
*Phil.* 3:6 concern. zeal, *p.* church

**PERSECUTION.**

*Lam.* 5:5 under *p.* have no rest
*Mat.* 13:21 wh. *p.* ari. *Mark* 4:17
*Acts* 8:1 great *p.* against church
11:19 were scatter. abroad on *p.*
13:50 and raised *p.* against Pa.
*Rom.* 8:35 sh. *p.* sep. us fr. C.?
*Gal.* 5:11 why do I yet suffer *p.?*
6:12 lest they should suffer *p.*
2 *Tim.* 3:12 godly shall suffer *p.*

**PERSECUTIONS.**

*Mark* 10:30 have lands with *p.*
2 *Cor.* 12:10 I take pleasure in *p.*
2 *Thes.* 1:4 faith in all your *p.*
2 *Tim.* 3:11 kn. my *p.* at Antioch

**PERSECUTOR, S.**

*Neh.* 9:11 their *p.* thou threwest
*Ps.* 7:13 ordaineth arrows ag. *p.*
119:157 many *p.* 142:6 del. from
*Jer.* 15:15 revenge me of my *p.*
20:11 theref. my *p.* sh. stumble
*Lam.* 1:3 all her *p.* overtook her
4:19 *p.* are swifter than eagles
1 *Tim.* 1:13 who was before a *p.*

**PERSEVERANCE.**

*Eph.* 6:18 watching with all *p.*

**PERSIA.**

2 *Chr.* 36:20 reign of king. of P.
*Est.* 1:3 to power of P. 14, 18
*Ezek.* 27:10 P. and Lud, 38:5
*Dan.* 8:20; 10:13, 20; 11:2

PERSIS. *Rom.* 16:12

**PERSON.**

*Lev.* 19:15 nor honor *p.* of mighty
*Num.* 35:30 one witness sh. not testify against any *p.*
*Deut.* 15:22 unc. and clean *p.* eat
27:25 reward to slay innocent *p.*
28:50 shall not regard *p.* of old
1 *Sam.* 16:18 David a comely *p.*
25:35 and have accepted thy *p.*
2 *Sam.* 4:11 have slain a righ. *p.*
14:14 nei. doth G. respect any *p.*
17:11 to battle in thine own *p.*
*Job* 22:29 shall save humble *p.*
*Ps.* 15:4 a vile *p.* is contemned
49:10 fool and brutish *p.* perish
101:4 I will not kn. a wicked *p.*
105:37 feeble *p.* am. their tribes
*Prov.* 28:17 to the blood of any *p.*
*Is.* 32:5 vile *p.* shall be no more
6 the vile *p.* will speak villany
*Jer.* 43:6 Johanan took ev. *p.* left
52:25 took seven near king's *p.*
*Ezek.* 16:5 to loathing of thy *p.*
33:6 if the sword take any *p.*
44:25 priests come at no dead *p.*
*Dan.* 11:21 sh. stand up. a vi. *p.*
*Mat.* 22:16 regardest not *p.* of men, *Mark* 12:14
27:24 inno. of blood of this *p.*
1 *Cor.* 5:13 put away wicked *p.*
2 *Cor.* 2:10 forgave I it in *p.* of C.
*Heb.* 1:3 express image of his *p.*
12:16 or profane *p.* as Esau
2 *Pet.* 2:5 saved Noah, eighth *p.*

**PERSONS.**

*Gen.* 14:21 give me *p.* take goods
*Lev.* 27:2 *p.* shall be for the L.
*Num.* 19:18 sh. sprinkle it up. *p.*
*Deut.* 10:17 regardeth not *p.*
22 fat. went into Eg. wi. 70 *p.*
*Jud.* 9:2 sons of J. were 70 *p.*
5 slew threescore and ten *p.* 18
1 *Sam.* 9:22 wh. were about 30 *p.*
22:18 Doeg slew eighty-five *p.*
22 occasion. death of all the *p.*
2 *K.* 10:6 king's sons being 70 *p.*
7 took king's sons, slew 70 *p.*
*Ps.* 26:4 ha. not sat with vain *p.*
*Prov.* 12:11 follow. vain *p.* 28:19
*Jer.* 52:29 carried from J. 832 *p.*
30 carried away of Jews 745 *p.*
*Ezek.* 17:17 to cut off many *p.*
27:13 traded the *p.* of men
*Jon.* 4:11 more than 120,000 *p.*
*Zep.* 3:4 her prophets treach. *p.*
*Luke* 15:7 ninety-nine just *p.*
*Acts* 17:17 disp. with devout *p.*
2 *Cor.* 1:11 by means of many *p.*
1 *Tim.* 1:10 law made for perj. *p.*
2 *Pet.* 3:11 what *p.* oug. ye to be
*Jude* 16 hav. men's *p.* in admir.

*See* RESPECT.

**PERSUADE.**

1 *K.* 22:20 who shall *p.* Ahab
21 I will *p.* him; 22 thou sh. *p.*
2 *Chr.* 32:11 doth not Hezek. *p.*
*Is.* 36:18 bew. lest Heze. *p.* you
*Mat.* 28:14 we will *p.* him, and
2 *Cor.* 5:11 terrors of L. *p.* men
*Gal.* 1:10 do I now *p.* men?

**PERSUADED.**

2 *Chr.* 18:2 Ahab *p.* Jehosaphat
*Prov.* 25:15 forbea. is a prince *p.*
*Mat.* 27:20 priests *p.* the multi.
*Luke* 16:31 will not be *p.* of one
20:6 be *p.* John was a prophet
*Acts* 13:43 *p.* them to continue
14:19 who *p.* the people
18:4 Paul *p.* Jews and Greeks
19:26 Paul hath *p.* much people
21:14 when he would not be *p.*
26:26 I am *p.* none of th. things
*Rom.* 4:21 *p.* that what he had
8:38 I am *p.* that nothing can
14:5 let every man be fully *p.*
14 I know and am *p.*
15:14 I myself also am *p.* of you
2 *Tim.* 1:5 I am *p.* that in thee

12 I am *p.* he is able to keep
*Heb.* 6:9 are *p.* bet. things of you
11:13 hav. seen afar off, were *p.*

**PERSUADETH, EST.**

2 *K.* 18:32 when Hezekiah *p.* you
*Acts* 18:13 P. *p.* men to worship
26:28 almost thou *p.* me to be

**PERSUADING.**

*Acts* 19:8 *p.* things concerning
28:23 *p.* them concerning Jesus

**PERSUASION.**

*Gal.* 5:8 *p.* cometh not of him

**PERTAIN.**

*Lev.* 7:20 peace-offerings *p.* to L.
1 *Sam.* 25:22 all that *p.* to him
*Rom.* 15:17 things which *p.* to G.
1 *Cor.* 6:3 things *p.* to this life
2 *Pet.* 1:3 all things that *p.* to life

**PERTAINED.**

*Num.* 31:43 half that *p.* to thee
*Jud.* 6:11 under oak that *p.* to J.
1 *Sam.* 25:21 of all that *p.* to N.
2 *Sam.* 2:15 which *p.* to Ish-bos.
6:12 G. blessed all that *p.* to O.
9:9 given all that *p.* to Saul
16:4 thine are all that *p.* to M.
1 *K.* 7:48 S. made vessels that *p.*
2 *K.* 24:7 that *p.* to king of E.
1 *Chr.* 9:27 opening ev. morn. *p.*
2 *Chr.* 12:4 took the cities wh. *p.*
34:33 Josiah took away abo. *p.*

**PERTAINETH.**

*Lev.* 14:32 that wh. *p.* to cleans.
*Num.* 4:16 office of Eleaz. *p.* oil
*Deut.* 22:5 wo. not wear what *p.*
2 *Chr.* 26:18 it *p.* not to Uzziah
*Rom.* 9:4 to whom *p.* adoption
*Heb.* 7:13 he *p.* to another tribe

**PERTAINING.**

1 *Chr.* 26:32 rulers *p.* to God
*Acts* 1:3 things *p.* to kingd. of G.
1 *Cor.* 6:4 judgm. of thi. *p.* to life
*Heb.* 2:17 H.-priest in thi. *p.* to G.
5:1 ordained in things *p.* to G.
9:9 not perf. as *p.* to conscience

**PERVERSE.**

*Num.* 22:32 thy way is *p.* bef. me
*Deut.* 32:5 they are a *p.* generat.
1 *Sam.* 20:30 son of *p.* woman
*Job* 6:30 cannot disc. *p.* things?
9:20 my mouth sh. prove me *p.*
*Prov.* 4:24 *p.* lips put from thee
*Prov.* 8:8 noth. fro. or *p.* in them
12:8 he of a *p.* heart sh. be desp.
14:2 he that is *p.* despiseth him
17:20 hath a *p.* tongue falleth
19:1 he that is *p.* in his lips
23:33 heart shall utter *p.* things
28:6 he that is *p.* in his ways
18 he that is *p.* in ways sh. fall
*Is.* 19:14 L. mingled a *p.* spirit
*Mat.* 17:17 O *p.* genera. *Luke* 9:41
*Acts* 20:30 men arise speaking *p.*
*Phil.* 2:15 blameless in *p.* nation
1 *Tim.* 6:5 *p.* disputings of men

**PERVERSELY.**

2 *Sam.* 19:19 what servant did *p.*
1 *K.* 8:47 have sin. and done *p.*
*Ps.* 119:78 they dealt *p.* with me

**PERVERSENESS.**

*Num.* 23:21 neither seen *p.* in Is.
*Prov.* 11:3 *p.* of trans. shall des.
15:4 *p.* therein as a breach in
*Is.* 30:12 ye trust in *p.* and stay
59:3 your tongues muttered *p.*
*Ezek.* 9:9 and the ci. is full of *p.*

**PERVERT.**

*Deut.* 16:19 a gift doth *p.* words
24:17 thou shalt not *p.* judgm.
*Job* 8:3 doth God *p.* judgment or
34:12 nor will the Al. *p.* judgm.
*Prov.* 17:23 to *p.* ways of judgm.
31:5 and *p.* the judgment of any
*Mic.* 3:9 hear this, ye that *p.* eq.
*Acts* 13:10 not cease to *p.* right
*Gal.* 1:7 would *p.* the gos. of C.

**PERVERTED.**

1 *Sam.* 8:3 Sa.'s sons *p.* judgm.
*Job* 33:27 have *p.* what was right
*Is.* 47:10 thy wisdom, it hath *p.*
*Jer.* 3:21 they have *p.* their way
23:36 ye have *p.* the words of G.

**PERVERTETH.**

*Ex.* 23:8 gift *p.* the righteous
*Deut.* 27:19 cursed be he that *p.*
*Prov.* 10:9 he that *p.* his ways
19:3 foolishness of a man *p.* way
*Luke* 23:14 man that *p.* people

**PERVERTING.**

*Ec.* 5:8 violent *p.* of judgment
*Luke* 23:2 this fellow *p.* nation

**PESTILENCE.**

*Ex.* 5:3 lest he fall on us wi. *p.*
9:15 I may smite thee with *p.*
*Lev.* 26:25 I will send *p.* among
*Num.* 14:12 will sm. th. with *p.*
*Deut.* 28:21 L. shall make *p.* cle.
2 *Sam.* 24:13 3 days' *p.* 1 *Chr.* 21:12
15 the Lord sent a *p.* on Israel, 1 *Chr.* 21:14
1 *K.* 8:37 if there be famine, *p.* 2 *Chr.* 6:28; 7:13; 20:9
*Ps.* 78:50 gave th. life over to *p.*
91:3 deli. thee from noisome *p.*
6 nor *p.* that walketh in dark.
*Jer.* 14:12 I will consume them by *p.* 24:10; 27:8
21:6 inhabitants shall die by *p.*
9 abideth in city die by *p.* 38:2
27:13 why will ye die by *p.*?
28:8 prophets of old prop. of *p.*
29:17 I will send upon th. *p.* 18
32:24 city is given bec. of *p.* 36
34:17 liberty for you to the *p.*
42:17 go to E. shall die by *p.* 22
44:13 as I punished Jeru. by *p.*
*Ezek.* 5:12 a third *p.* die with *p.*
17 *p.* and blood pass thro' thee
6:11 by sword, famine, and *p.* 12
7:15 sword without, *p.* within
12:16 I will leave a few from *p.*
14:19 if I send *p.* into land, 21
28:23 will send her *p.* and blood
33:27 be in caves shall die of *p.*
38:22 I will plead ag. him wi. *p.*
*Amos* 4:10 I have sent am. you *p.*
*Hab.* 3:5 before him went *p.* and

**PESTILENCES.**

*Mat.* 24:7 shall be *p.* *Luke* 21:11

**PESTILENT.**

*Acts* 24:5 found this man a *p.* fel.

**PESTLE.**

*Prov.* 27:22 bray a fool with a *p.*

**PETER.**

*Mat.* 14:29 when P. was come
16:18 I say to thee thou art P.
23 said to P. get th. *Mark* 8:33
17:1 taketh P. James and John, 26:27; *Mark* 5:37; 9:2; 14:33; *Luke* 8:51; 9:28
24 they rec. tribute, came to P.
26:58 P. follow. to H. P. palace
75 P. re. *Mark* 14:72; *Lu.* 22:61
*Mark* 16:7 disci. and P. *John* 1:44
*John* 18:26 ear P. cut off, 21:17
*Acts* 1:15 in those days P. stood
*Acts* 3:3 see. P. and John, 4:8, 13
5:15 shadow of P. 8:14; 9:40
10:13 P. kill and eat, 44; 11:7
12:3 to take P. also, 6, 7, 13, 18
*Gal.* 1:18 went to see P. 2:7, 8, 14

**Simon PETER.**

*Mat.* 4:18 Jesus saw S. called P.
10:2 the first S. who is called P.
*Mark* 3:16 S. he surnamed P.
*Luke* 5:8 S. P. fell at Jes. knees
6:14 Simon whom he named P.
*John* 13:6 cometh to S. P. 20:2
21:15 Jesus saith to Simon P.
*Acts* 10:5 call for one S. whose surname is P. 32; 11:13

**PETITION, S.**

1 *Sam.* 1:17 G. gr. thee thy *p.* 27
1 *K.* 2:16 ask one *p.* deny me not
20 I desire one small *p.* of thee
*Est.* 5:6 what is *p.*? 7:2; 9:12
8 if it please king to grant *p.*
7:3 let my life be given at my *p.*
*Ps.* 20:5 Lord fulfil all thy *p.*
*Dan.* 6:7 whoso. ask *p.* of any, 12
13 maketh *p.* three times a day
1 *John* 5:15 we have *p.* we desired

**PHALEC.**

*Luke* 3:35 Ragau was son of P.

**PHARAOH.**

*Gen.* 12:17 the Lord plagued P.
40:2 P. wroth against, 13, 14
41:1 P. dream. 4, 7, 16, 34, 55
*Ex.* 5:2 P. said, who is the L.?
14:4 will be honored upon P. 17
1 *K.* 3:1 made affinity with P.
7:8 Solo. made a house for P.
2 *K.* 17:7 br. th. out fr. under P.
18:21 P. to that trust, *Is.* 36:6
23:35 accor. to command. of P.
*Neh.* 9:10 wond. on P. *Ps.* 135:9
*Ps.* 136:15 overthrew P. in R. sea
*Is.* 19:11 say ye to P. 30:2, 3
*Jer.* 25:19 made P. drink, 37:11
46:17 P. a noise; 47:1 smote G.
*Ezek.* 29:2 face ag. P. 3; 30:22
30:21 brok. arm of P. 25; 31:18
*Acts* 7:13 kindred known to P. 21
*Rom.* 9:17 scripture saith to P.
*Heb.* 11:24 to be called son of P.

PHARAOH-HOPHRA. *Jer.* 44:30

**PHARAOH-NECHO.**

2 *K.* 23:29 P. N. went up, 33-35
*Jer.* 46:2 word came ag. P.-N.

**PHAREZ.**

*Gen.* 38:29 name was called P.
46:12 sons of Ju. P. 1 *Chr.* 2:4; *Mat.* 1:3; *Luke* 3:33; the sons of P. *Num.* 26:20, 21; *Ruth* 4:18; 1 *Chr.* 2:5; 9:4
*Ruth* 4:12 be like the house of P.

**PHARISEE.**

*Mat.* 23:26 thou blind P. cleanse
*Luke* 11:37 P. beso. him to dine
18:10 went to pray, one a P.
*Acts* 23:6 I am a P. son of a P.
26:5 after strict. sect I lived a P.
*Phil.* 3:5 touching the law a P.

**PHARISEES.**

*Mat.* 5:20 exceed righteou. of P.
9:14 why do P. fast? *Mark* 2:18
34 P. said, He cast. out devils
15:12 thou P. were offended
16:6 beware of leaven of the P. 11; *Mark* 8:15; *Luke* 12:1
19:3 P. also came to him
23:2 scribes and P. sit in M. seat
13 woe to scr. and P. 14, 15, 23, 25, 27, 29; *Luke* 11:42, 43, 44
*Luke* 5:30 P. murmured, 15:2
6:7 scribes and P. watched him
7:30 P. rejected counsel of God
11:39 P. make cl. outside of cup
16:14 P. who were covet. heard
*John* 1:24 were sent were of P.
3:1 a man of the P. named Nic.
7:32 P. sent officers to take him
48 any P. believed on him?
11:47 then P. gathered a council
57 P. had given a commandm.
*Acts* 15:5 rose certain sect of P.
23:7 dissension bet. P. and Sad.
8 no resur. P. but confess both

**PHARPAR.**

2 *K.* 5:12 Abana and P. better

**PHEBE.**

*Rom.* 16:1 I com. unto you P.

**PHENICE.**
Acts 11:19 travelled as far as P.
15:3 Paul and Barnabas passed through P.
21:2 find. ship sailing over to P.
27:12 they might attain to P.

**PHILADELPHIA.**
Rev. 1:11 write and send it to P.
3:7 angel of the church in P.

**PHILIP.**
Mat. 10:3 P. and Barthol. Mark 3:18; Luke 6:14; Acts 1:13
14:3 for his brother P. wife, Mark 6:17; Luke 3:19
Luke 3:1 his brother P. tetrarch
John 1:43 Jesus findeth P. 44, 45
12:21 the same came to P. 22
14:9 hast thou not kn. me, P.?
Acts 6:5 P. the deacon, 8:29
8:5 P. preached, 6, 12, 13, 30, 39
21:8 we enter. into house of P.

**PHILIPPI.**
Acts 16:12 Neapo. we came to P.
20:6 we sailed away from P.
1 Thes. 2:2 shamef. entreat at P.

**PHILISTIA.**
Ps. 60:8 P. triumph thou
87:4 Behold P. and Tyre, this
108:9 over P. will I triumph

**PHILISTIM.**
Gen. 10:14 came P. 1 Chr. 1:12

**PHILISTINE.**
1 Sam. 17:8 not I a P. 32, 43, 49
21:9 sw. of Goliath the P. 22:10
2 Sam. 21:17 Abishai smo. the P

**PHILISTINES.**
Gen. 21:34 Abraham in P. land
26:14 Isaac had flocks, P. env.
15 P. stopped wells Abrah. 18
Ex. 13:17 led th. not through P.
Ps. 83:7 the P. with the
Is. 2:6 soothsayers like the P.
9:12 before, and the P. behind
11:14 fly on shoulders of the P.
Zep. 2:5 land of P. I will destroy
Zec. 9:6 will cut off pride of P.

**PHILOLOGUS.**
Rom. 16:15 salute P. Julia, and

**PHILOSOPHY.**
Col. 2:8 lest any spoil you th. p.

**PHILOSOPHERS.**
Acts 17:18 cer. p. encounte. him

**PHINEHAS.**
Ex. 6:25 Eleazer's wife bare P.
Num. 25:11 P. hath turned wra.
Jos. 22:13 Israel sent P. 24:33
Jud. 20:28 P. stood before the
1 Sam. 1:3 Hophni and P. the
2:34 Hophni and P. sh. both die
4:17 Hophni and P. are dead, 19
14:3 the son of P. the Lord's
Ezr. 7:5 Abishua son of P. the
8:2 of the sons of P. Gersho. 33
Ps. 106:30 then stood up P.

**PHILEGON.**
Rom. 16:14 salute Asyncritus, P.

**PHRYGIA.**
Acts 16:6 had gone througho. P.
18:23 went over all count. of P.

**PHURAH.**
Jud. 7:11 he went down with P.

**PHYLACTERIES.**
Mat. 23:5 th. make broad th. p.

**PHYSICIAN.**
Jer. 8:22 is there no p. there?
Mat. 9:12 th. that be wh. need not a p. Mark 2:17; Luke 5:31
Luke 4:23 proverb, p. heal thys.
Col. 4:14 Luke, the beloved p.

**PHYSICIANS.**
Gen. 50:2 Joseph com. p. to embalm father; p. embalm. Is.
2 Chr. 16:12 Asa sou. not L. b. p.
Job 13:4 ye are all p. of no value
Mark 5:26 suffer many things of p. Luke 8:43

**PICK.**
Prov. 30:17 ravens shall p. it out

**PICTURES.**
Num. 33:52 shall destroy all p.
Prov. 25:11 apples of gold in p.
Is. 2:16 day of L. on pleasant p.

**PIECE.**
Gen. 15:10 one p. ag. another
Num. 10:2 trumpets of whole p.
1 Sam. 2:36 crouch to him for p.
2 Sam. 6:19 to every one a good p. of flesh, 1 Chr. 16:3
23:11 p. of grou. full of lentiles
2 K. 3:19 mar good p. of land, 25
Neh. 3:11 Has. repaired other p.
Job 41:24 hard as p. of millstone
42:11 ev. man gave p. of money
Prov. 6:26 brou. to a p. of bread
28:21 for p. bread man transgre.
Cant. 4:3 tem. p. of pomeg. 6:7
Jer. 37:21 give him daily p. bre.
Ezek. 24:4 every good p. the thi.
6 bring it out p. by p. let no
Amos 3:12 mouth of lion p. of e.
4:7 one p. was rained on, and p.
Mat. 9:16 no man putt. p. of new cloth, Mark 2:21; Luke 5:36
17:27 thou sh. find p. of money
Luke 14:18 I bought p. of grou.
15:8 lose one p. doth li. a cand.
24:42 ga. him p. of broiled fish

**PIECES.**
Gen. 15:17 lamp passed betw. p.
20:16 given bro. 1,000 p. of silv.
33:19 bou. for 100 p. Jos. 24:32
37:28 sold Jos. for 20 p. of silver
33 Joseph is rent in p. 44:28
45:22 gave to Benjamin thirty p.
Ex. 22:13 if it be torn in p.
Lev. 2:6 part meat-offering in p.
9:13 presented burnt-of. with p.
Jud. 9:4 gave A. 70 p. of silver
16:5 give thee 1,100 p. of silver
19:29 div. concubine into 12 p.
1 Sam. 11:7 S. hewed oxen in p.
15:33 Samuel hewed Agag in p.
1 K. 11:30 Ahij. rent garm. in p.
19:11 wind brake in p. the rocks
2 K. 2:12 Eli. rent clothes in p.
5:5 Nam. took 6,000 p. of gold
6:25 ass's head sold for eigh. p.
18:4 brake in p. brazen serpent
2 Chr. 23:17 brake the images in p. 31:1; 34:4; Mic. 1:7
Job 16:12 hath shaken me in p.
40:18 his bones are as p. of brass
Ps. 7:2 rending in p. none deliv.
50:22 lest I tear you in p.
68:30 till ev. one submit with p.
74:14 breakest heads of L. in p.
Cant. 8:11 for fruit bring 1,000 p.
Is. 3:15 beat my people to p.?
Jer. 5:6 goeth out be torn in p.?
23:29 hammer break. rock in p.
Lam. 3:11 he hath pull. me in p.
Ezek. 4:14 not eat. th. torn in p.
13:19 pollute me for p. of bread?
24:4 gather p. thereof into pot
Dan. 2:34 brake image in p. 45
6:24 lions brake th. bones in p.
7:7 iron teeth, and bra. in p. 19
Hos. 3:2 bought her for fifteen p.
Mic. 3:3 chop my people in p.
4:13 sh. beat in p. many people
5:8 as a lion teareth in p.
Nah. 2:12 lion did tear in p.
Zec. 11:12 th. weighed thirty p.
13 I took the 30 p. Mat. 27:6, 9
Luke 15:8 woman having ten p.
Acts 19:19 found price 50,000 p.
23:10 lest P. sho. be pulled in p.
27:44 and some on p. of the ship
See BREAK, BROKEN, CUT, DASH, DASHED.

**PIERCE.**
Num. 24:8 p. them with arrows
2 K. 18:21 hand, p. it, Is. 36:6
Luke 2:35 sword sh. p. thro' soul

**PIERCED.**
Job 30:17 my bones are p.
Ps. 22:16 p. my hands and feet
Zec. 12:10 they sh. look on me wh. they have p. John 19:37
John 19:34 one of soldiers p. side
1 Tim. 6:10 p. th. with sorrows
Rev. 1:7 they also which p. him

**PIERCETH, ING.**
Job 40:24 Behemoth's nose p.
Is. 27:1 L. shall punish p. serp.
Heb. 4:12 word of G. quick p.

**PIERCINGS.**
Prov. 12:18 speaketh like p. of a

**PIETY.**
1 Tim. 5:4 learn to show p.

PIGEON. See YOUNG.

**PILATE.**
Mat. 27:2 they delivered him to Pontius P. 24; Mark 15:1
Mark 15:5 so that P. marvel. 44
Luke 3:1 Pon. P. being governor
23:12 same day P. and Her. 52
John 18:33 P. entered judg. hall
19:8 when P. heard, 12, 19, 38
Acts 3:13 pres. of P. 4:27; 13:28
1 Tim. 6:13 before P. witnessed

**PILE.**
Is. 30:33 p. of it fire and wood
Ezek. 24:9 make p. for fire great

**PILGRIMAGE.**
Gen. 47:9 days of my p. 130 yea. not attain. to years of th. p.
Ex. 6:4 gi. them land of their p.
Ps. 119:54 my songs in the house of my p.

**PILGRIMS.**
Heb. 11:13 we. strangers and p.
1 Pet. 2:11 as p. abs. from lusts

**PILLAR.**
Gen. 19:26 became a p. of salt
28:18 J. set it for p. 22; 35:14
31:13 where thou anointedst p.
51 behold this p. 52 p. witn.
35:20 Jacob set p. on R.'s grave
Ex. 33:9 cloudy p. descended 10
Jud. 9:6 A. king by plain of p.
20:40 flame arose with p.
2 Sam. 18:18 Absa. reared up a p.
1 K. 7:21 set up right p. left p.
2 K. 11:14 the king stood by a p.
23:3; 2 Chr. 23:13
Neh. 9:12 led. them by cloudy p.
Ps. 99:7 spake to th. in cloud. p.
Is. 19:19 and a p. at the border
Jer 1:18 have made thee iron p.
52:21 p. was eighteen cubits
1 Tim. 3:15 p. and grou. of truth
Rev. 3:12 overcom. I make a p.
See CLOUD, FIRE.

**PILLARS.**
Ex. 24:4 M. built alt. and 12 p.
26:32 hang veil upon four p.
27:10 p. thereof brass hooks of p. 11; 38:10, 11, 12, 17
16 p. four; 38:17 sockets for p.
Jud. 16:25 Samson between p.
1 Sam. 2:8 p. of earth are Lord's
1 K. 7:15 he cast two p. of brass
10:12 made of almug-trees p.
2 K. 18:16 Hez. cut gold from p.
25:13 Chaldees brake in pieces p. 16; Jer. 52:17, 20
Est. 1:6 fast. to rings and p
Job 9:6 the p. tremble, 26:11

*Ps.* 75:3 I bear up the *p.* of it
*Prov.* 9:1 hath hewn her sev. *p.*
*Cant.* 3:6 com. like *p.* of smo.
10 make *p.* thereof of silver
5:15 *p.* of marble set on gold
*Joel* 2:30 will show *p.* of smoke
*Gal.* 2:9 J. and Cephas to be *p.*
*Rev.* 10:1 feet were as *p.* of fire

**PILLED.**

*Gen.* 30:37 J. *p.* whi. strakes, 38

**PILLOW, S.**

*Gen.* 28:11 Jac. put stones for *p.*
18 Jacob took the stone, his *p.*
1 *Sam.* 19:13 *p.* of goats'hair, 16
*Ezek.* 13:18 woe to women sew *p.*
20 behold, I am again. your *p.*
*Mark* 4:38 J. was asleep on a *p.*

**PILOTS.**

*Ezek.* 27:8 wise men were thy *p.*
28 shake at the sound of thy *p.*

**PIN.**

*Jud.* 16:14 Delil. fast. with a *p.*
*Ezek.* 15:3 take *p.* of vine-tree?

**PINE, ETH, ING.**

*Lev.* 26:39 shall *p.* away, in iniq. of their fathers shall they *p.*
*Is.* 38:12 cut me off with *p.* sick.
*Lam.* 4:9 these *p.* away, stricken
*Ezek.* 24:23 *p.* away for iniqu.
33:10 sins on us, we *p.* away
*Mark* 9:18 gnash. teeth, *p.* away

**PINE.**

*Neh.* 8:15 olive and *p.* branches

**PINE-TREE.**

*Is.* 41:19 plant *p.-t.* and box
60:13 *p.-t.* and box-trees sh. co.

**PINNACLE.**

*Mat.* 4:5 *p.* of temple, *Luke* 4:9

**PINS.**

*Ex.* 27:19 make *p.* of tabernacle, 35:18; 38:20, 31; 39:40
*Num.* 3:37 under Merari, *p.* 4:32

**PIPE, S.**

1 *Sam.* 10:5 com. of proph. wi. *p.*
1 *K.* 1:40 the people piped wi. *p.*
*Is.* 5:12 the *p.* are in their feasts
30:29 when one goeth with a *p.*
*Jer.* 48:36 heart sh. sound like *p.*
*Ezek.* 28:13 workmanship of *p.*
*Zec.* 4:2 seven *p.* to seven lamps
12 which through the gold. *p.*
1 *Cor.* 14:7 whether *p.* or harp

**PIPED.**

1 *K.* 1:40 people *p.* with pipes
*Mat.* 11:17 *p.* unto you, *Luke* 7:32
1 *Cor.* 14:7 how kno. wh. is *p.*?

**PIPERS.**

*Rev.* 18:22 voice of *p.* he. no mo.

**PISGAH.**

*Num.* 23:14 Balaam to top of P.
*Deut.* 3:27 up into top of P. 34:1
4:49 under the springs of P.

**PISIDIA.**

*Acts* 13:14 came to Antioch in P.
14:24 had passed throughout P.

**PISS.**

2 *K.* 18:27 drink own *p.* *Is.* 36:12

PISSETH. *See* WALL.

**PIT, S.**

*Gen.* 14:10 Siddim full of slime *p.*
37:20 cast him into some *p.* 24
*Ex.* 21:34 owner of *p.* ma. good
*Lev.* 11:36 a *p.* wherein is water
*Num.* 16:30 go down into *p.* 33
1 *Sam.* 13:6 Israelites hide in *p.*
2 *Sam.* 17:9 is now hid in so. *p.*
18:17 cast Absalom in great *p.*
23:20 sl. lion in *p.* 1 *Chr.* 11:22
2 *K.* 10:14 Jehu slew them at *p.*
*Job* 17:16 go down to bars of *p.*
33:18 keep. back soul from *p.* 30
24 deliver him from the *p.* 28
*Ps.* 9:15 heathen sunk into *p.*
28:1 like them that go into *p.*
30:3 I should not go down to *p.*
9 what profit in my blood, when I go down to the *p.*?
35:7 hid for me their net in *p.*?
40:2 br. me out of horrible *p.*
55:23 br. them to *p* of destruct.
69:15 let not *p.* shut her mouth
88:4 counted wi. th. go to *p.*
6 thou laid me in the lowest *p.*
119:85 proud digged *p.* for me
140:10 let th. be cast in. deep *p.*
143:7 go down to *p.* *Prov.* 1:12
*Prov.* 22:14 mouth of wo. deep *p.*
23:27 strange wo. is narrow *p.*
28:10 fall himself into own *p.*
17 he shall flee to the *p.*
*Is.* 14:15 brought to sides of *p.*
19 that go down to stones of *p.*
24:17 *p.* and snare are on thee
18 he that cometh out of midst of the *p.* *Jer.* 48:43, 44
22 prisoners are gathered in *p.*
30:14 water withal out of the *p.*
38:17 deli. from *p.* of corruption
18 go down to *p.* cannot hope
51:14 he should not die in the *p.*
*Jer.* 2:6 L. led us thro' a la. of *p.*
14:3 came to *p.* found no water
41:7 cast them into midst of *p.*
9 *p.* which Asa made for fear
*Lam.* 4:20 anoi. of L. taken in *p.*
*Ezek.* 19:4 he was taken in *p.* 8
26:20 descend into *p.* 28:8; 31:14, 16; 32:18, 24, 25, 29, 30
32:23 graves set in the side of *p.*
*Zep.* 2:9 of nettles and salt *p.*
*Zec.* 9:11 sent prisoners out of *p.*
*Mat.* 12:11 if it fall into a *p.* on the sabbath, *Luke* 14:5

*See* BOTTOMLESS, DIG, DIGGED.

**PITCH, Substantive.**

*Gen.* 6:14 pitch it within with *p.*
*Ex.* 2:3 she daubed it with *p.*
*Is.* 34:9 streams be turned to *p.* and the land bec. burning *p.*

**PITCH, Verb.**

*Num.* 1:52 Is. sh. *p.* by his camp
53 L. shall *p.* round tabernacle
2:2 ev. man shall *p.* by standard
*Deut.* 1:33 search out place to *p.*
*Jos.* 4:20 Joshua did *p.* 12 stones
*Is.* 13:20 neither sh. Arabian *p.*
*Jer.* 6:3 shepherds shall *p.* tents

**PITCHED.**

*Gen.* 12:8 Abram *p.* his tent, and
13:12 Lot *p.* his tent toward S.
26:17 I. *p.* in valley of Gerar, 25
31:25 Jacob *p.* tent in mount, Laban *p.* in Gilead
33:18 Jacob *p.* his tent before
*Ex.* 17:1 Israel *p.* in Rephidim
19:2 and had *p.* in wilderness
33:7 M. took tabernacle and *p.*
*Num.* 1:51 when tabernacle is *p.*
2:34 they *p.* by their standards
12:16 the peo. *p.* in wilderness
21:10 and Israel *p.* in Oboth
11 and *p.* in Ije-abarim, in the
33:5 and Israel *p.* in Succoth
6 *p.* in Etham, which is in the
*Jos.* 8:11 ambush *p.* on north
2 *Sam.* 17:26 Is. and Absalom *p.*
2 *K.* 25:1 Neb. *p.* ag. it, *Jer.* 52:4
1 *Chr.* 15:1 David prepared place for ark, *p.* tent, 16:1; 2 *Chr.* 1:4
*Heb.* 8:2 tabernacle which L. *p.*

**PITCHER, S.**

*Gen.* 24:14 let down *p.* I pray th.
15 Rebekah came with *p.* 45
*Jud.* 7:16 empty *p.* lamps in *p.*
19 brake *p.* that were in, 20
*Ec.* 12:6 or the *p.* be broken at
*Lam.* 4:2 esteemed as earthen *p.*
*Mark* 14:13 bear. a *p.* *Luke* 22:10

PITHOM. *Ex.* 1:11

**PITY, Substantive.**

*Deut.* 7:16 eye shall have no *p.*
2 *Sam.* 12:6 because he had no *p.*
*Job* 6:14 to the afflicted *p.* should
19:21 have *p.* on me, *p.* on me, O
*Ps.* 69:20 looked for some to *p.*
*Prov.* 19:17 that hath *p.* on poor
*Is.* 13:18 they shall have no *p.* on
63:9 in his *p.* he redeemed
*Jer.* 15:5 shall have *p.* on thee
21:7 shall not spare, nor have *p.*
*Ezek.* 5:11 nor will I have *p.* 7:4, 9; 8:18; 9:10
9:5 eye spare, neither have *p.*
36:21 but I had *p.* for my holy
*Amos* 1:11 Ed. did cast off all *p.*
*Jon.* 4:10 thou hast had *p.*
*Mat.* 18:33 as I had *p.* on thee

**PITY, Verb.**

*Deut.* 13:8 nor shall thine eye *p.* him, 19:13, 21
25:12 thine eye shall not *p.*
*Prov.* 28:8 him that will *p.* poor
*Jer.* 13:14 I will not *p.* nor spare
*Joel* 2:18 then the Lord will *p.*
*Zec.* 11:5 th. sheph. *p.* them not
6 I will no more *p.* inhabitants

**PITIED, ETH.**

*Ps.* 103:13 as a father *p.* his chil. so L. *p.* them th. fear him
106:46 he made them to be *p.*
*Lam.* 2:2 ha. not *p.* 17, 21; 3:43
*Ezek.* 16:5 none eye *p.* thee
24:21 profane what your soul *p.*

**PITIFUL.**

*Lam.* 4:10 hands of *p.* women
*Jam.* 5:11 that the L. is very *p.*
1 *Pet.* 3:8 love as brethren, be *p.*

**PLACE, Substantive.**

*Gen.* 13:14 L. said, Look from *p.*
18:24 destroy, and not spare *p.*
20:13 kindness show at every *p.*
22:4 third day Abraham saw *p.*
30:25 I may go to my own *p.*
*Ex.* 3:5 *p.* where thou standest is holy, *Jos.* 5:15
18:23 go to their *p.* in peace
23:20 to bring thee into the *p.*
*Lev.* 1:16 shall cast it by the *p.*
*Num.* 10:14 in first *p.* went out
*Deut.* 11:24 ev. *p.* whereon your feet tread, *Jos.* 1:3
12:5 *p.* L. sh. choose, 14; 16:16
21 if *p.* be too far from, 14:24
*Jud.* 11:19 pass land to my *p.*
20:36 men of Israel gave *p.* to
*Ruth* 3:4 mark *p.* where he lieth
1 *Sam.* 20:25 Da.'s *p.* empty, 27
2 *Sam.* 2:23 died in the same *p.*
15:21 what *p.* my lord the king
17:9 hid in some pit, or other *p.*
18:18 it is called Absalom's *p.*
1 *K.* 8:29 eyes be open toward *p.*
2 *K.* 5:11 strike hand over the *p.*
6:1 *p.* wh. we dwell is too strait
1 *Chr.* 21:25 Dav. gave for the *p.*
2 *Chr.* 30:16 pri. stood in *p.* 35:10
35:15 sons of Asaph, in their *p.*
*Neh.* 2:3 *p.* of my father's sepul.
14 there was no *p.* for beast
13:11 I set singers in their *p.*
*Est.* 2:9 Est. and maids best *p.*
4:14 deliverance fr. anoth. *p.*
*Job* 6:17 consumed out of the. *p.*
9:6 shake the earth out of *p.*
16:18 let my cry have no *p.*
28:12 where is *p.* of underst. 20
23 he knoweth the *p.* thereof
36:20 peo. are cut off in their *p.*
38:19 where is *p.* thereof?
40:12 tread wicked in their *p.*

*Ps.* 26:8 *p.* where thine honor
12 my foot standeth in even *p.*
32:7 art my hiding *p.* 119:114
33:14 the *p.* of his habitation
103:16 *p.* thereof shall know it
*Ec.* 3:16 the *p.* of judgment, the *p.* of righteousness
20 all go to one *p.* all are, 6:6
*Is.* 5:8 lay field, till th. be no *p.*
13:13 earth remove out of *p.*
14:2 and bring them to their *p.*
28:8 so that there is no *p.* clean
49:20 the *p.* is too strait for me
54:2 enlarge the *p.* of thy tent
60:13 will make *p.* of my feet
66:1 where is the *p.* of my rest?
*Jer.* 7:12 go to my *p.* in Shil. 32
17:12 glorious throne is the *p.*
18:14 waters come from anot. *p.*
19:11 till there be no *p.* to bury
*Ezek.* 6:13 th. slain be on the *p.*
43:7 *p.* of my throne shall Israel
*Dan.* 2:35 no *p.* was found for
8:11 the *p.* of his sanctuary was
*Hos.* 5:15 I will return to my *p.*
*Amos* 8:3 dead bodies in ev. *p.*
*Nah.* 3:17 their *p.* is not known
*Zec.* 10:10 *p.* shall not be found
12:6 inhabit. ag. in her *p.* 14:10
*Mal.* 1:11 inc. be offered in ev. *p.*
*Mat.* 28:6 see the *p.* where the Lord lay, *Mark* 16:6
*Mark* 6:10 in what *p.* soever ye
*Luke* 4:17 found the *p.* where it
10:1 sent two and two un. ev. *p.*
32 when he was at the *p.* pass.
14:9 and say, Give this man *p.*
*John* 4:20 Jerusalem is *p.* where
8:37 my word hath no *p.* in you
11:6 abode two days in same *p.*
48 Rom. shall take away our *p.*
18:2 Judas wh. betrayed, kn. *p.*
*Acts* 2:1 with one acco. in one *p.*
4:31 prayed, the *p.* was shaken
7:33 *p.* whereon thou standest
49 or what is the *p.* of my rest
8:32 the *p.* of scripture wh. he
*Rom.* 12:19 rather gi. *p.* to wrath
15:23 hav. no more *p.* in these
1 *Cor.* 1:2 in every *p.* call on J.
11:20 come together into one *p.*
14:23 church come into one *p.*
2 *Cor.* 2:14 knowledge in ev. *p.*
*Gal.* 2:5 to whom gave *p.* by sub.
*Eph.* 4:27 neither give *p.* to the
1 *Thes.* 1:8 in every *p.* your faith
*Heb.* 5:6 he saith also in ano. *p.*
8:7 no *p.* sho. have been sought
12:17 he found no *p.* of repent.
*Jam.* 3:11 at same *p.* sweet wat.
*Rev.* 12:8 nor was there *p.* found
20:11 for them was found no *p.*

**PLACE, Verb.**

*Ex.* 18:21 *p.* such to be rulers
*Deut.* 14:23 *p.* his name there, 16:2, 6, 11; 26:2
*Ezr.* 6:5 *p.* them in house of G.
*Is.* 46:13 I will *p.* salvation in Z.
*Ezek.* 37:14 *p.* you in yo. land, 26
*Dan.* 11:31 they sh. *p.* abomina.
*Hos.* 11:11 *p.* them in houses
*Zec.* 10:6 will bring them to *p.*

**A PLACE.**

*Ex.* 21:13 will appoint thee *a p.*
33:21 behold, th. is *a p.* by me
*Num.* 32:1 the place was *a p.* for
*Deut.* 23:12 thou shalt have *a p.*
*Jos.* 20:4 give him *a p.* in city
*Jud.* 18:10 *a p.* where is no want
1 *Sam.* 15:12 Saul set him up *a p.*
27:5 let them give me *a p.*
2 *Sam.* 7:10 I will appoint *a p.*
1 *K.* 8:21 I set there *a p.* for ark
2 *K.* 6:2 let us make *a p.* where
8 in such and such *a p.* sh. be
9 bew. thou pass not such *a p.*
1 *Chr.* 15:1 David prepared *a p.*
2 *Chr.* 6:2 I have built *a p.*
*Job* 28:1 there is *a p.* for gold
*Ps.* 132:5 until I find out *a p.*
*Prov.* 14:26 his childr. have *a p.*
*Is.* 4:6 shall be for *a p.* of refuge
33:21 the Lord will be to us *a p.*
34:14 find for herself *a p.* of rest
56:5 and within my walls *a p.*
65:10 Achor *a p.* for the herds
*Ezek.* 26:5 *a p.* for spread. nets, 14
*Zep.* 2:15 become *a p.* for beasts
*Mat.* 27:33 that is, *a p.* of a skull
*John* 14:2 I go to prepare *a p.* 3
19:17 into a *p.* called Golgotha
*Heb.* 2:6 one in *a* certain *p.* testi.
4:4 he spake in *a* certain *p.*
11:8 called to go out into *a p.*
*Rev.* 12:6 *a p.* prepared of God
16:16 *a p.* called Armageddon

*See* CHOOSE, DWELLING.

**High PLACE.**

*Num.* 23:3 Bal. went up to *a h. p.*
1 *Sam.* 9:12 sacri. to-day in *h. p.*
10:5 prophets coming from *h. p.*
1 *K.* 3:4 great *h. p.* 1 *Chr.* 16:39
11:7 Solomon built a *high p.*
2 *K.* 23:15 *high p.* that Jeroboam made, Josi. brake down the *h. p.* and burnt the *h. p.*
2 *Chr.* 1:3 Solomon went to *h. p.*
13 from his journey to *high p.*
*Is.* 16:12 Moab is weary on *h. p.*
*Ezek.* 16:24 *h. p.* in street, 25, 31
20:29 what is *h. p.* wher. ye go?

**His PLACE.**

*Gen.* 18:33 Ab. returned to *h. p.*
31:55 Laban returned to *his p.*
*Ex.* 10:23 neither rose from *h. p.*
16:29 abide every man in *his p.* none go out of *his p.*
*Num.* 2:17 in *his p.* by th. stan.
*Deut.* 21:19 br. him to gate of *h. p.*
*Ruth* 4:10 not cut off from *his p.*
1 *Sam.* 3:2 Eli was laid in *his p.*
9 Sam. went and lay in *his p.*
5:3 set Dagon in *his p.* again
23:22 *his p.* where his haunt is
2 *Sam.* 6:17 set ark of L. in *h. p.*
1 *K.* 8:6 the priests brought ark to *his p.* 2 *Chr.* 5:7
1 *Chr.* 15:3 br. ark of L. to *his p.*
16:27 and gladness are in *his p.*
2 *Chr.* 24:11 carried chest to *h. p.*
34:31 king stood in *his p.*
*Ezr.* 1:4 let men of *his p.* help
2:68 for the house of God set it in *his p.* 5:15; 6:7
*Job* 2:11 ev. one from *his* own *p.*
7:10 nei. shall *his p.* know him
8:18 if he destroy him fr. *his p.*
14:18 rock is remo. out of *his p.*
18:4 sh. rock be re. out of *h. p.?*
20:9 nor *h. p.* any more behold
27:21 hurleth him out of *his p.*
23 shall hiss him out of *his p.*
37:1 heart is remo. out of *his p.*
38:12 day-spring to know *h. p.*
*Ps.* 37:10 diligen. consider *his p.*
*Prov.* 27:8 wandereth from *his p.*
*Ec.* 1:5 sun hasteneth to *his p.*
*Is.* 26:21 Lord com. out of *his p.*
46:7 they set him in *his p.* from *h. p.* shall he not remove
*Jer.* 4:7 he is gone from *his p.*
6:3 feed every one from *his p.*
*Ezek.* 3:12 glory of L. from *h. p.*
*Mic.* 1:3 L. cometh out of *his p.*
*Zep.* 2:11 wors. ev. one fr. *his p.*
*Zec.* 6:12 shall grow out of *h. p.*
*Mat.* 26:52 put thy sw. into *h. p.*
*Acts* 1:25 might go to *his* own *p.*

*See* HOLY, *Most* HOLY.

**In the PLACE.**

*Gen* 50:19 I am *in the p.* of God
*Ex.* 15:17 plant them *in the p.*
*Jos.* 4:9 J. set 12 stones *in the p.*
1 *K.* 21:19 *in the p.* where dogs
2 *Chr.* 3:1 *in t. p.* D. had prepar.
*Prov.* 25:6 stand not *in t. p.*
*Ec.* 11:3 *in the p.* where tree
*Jer.* 22:12 die *in t. p.* 38:9; 42:22
*Ezek.* 17:16 *in the p.* where king
*Hos.* 13:13 not stay long *in the p.*
*John* 19:41 *in the p.* wh. crucified

**Of the PLACE.**

*Gen.* 26:7 men *of the p.* ask. him, lest men *of the p.* kill me
29:22 La. gathered men *of the p.*
32:30 name *of the p.* Peniel
2 *Sam.* 6:8 name *of t. p.* Perez-uz.
1 *Chr.* 28:11 *of t. p.* of mer.-seat
*Ezek.* 41:11 brea. *of the p.* 5 cub.
*Joel* 3:7 raise them out *of the p.*
*Nah.* 1:8 make utter end *of t. p.*

**That PLACE.**

*Deut.* 12:3 dest. names out *th. p.*
17:10 sentence they of *that p.*
*Mat.* 14:35 men of *that p.* had kn.
*Mark* 6:10 ye depart from *th. p.*
*John* 5:13 a multit. being in *t. p.*
11:30 in *t. p.* Martha met him
*Acts* 21:12 we and they of *th. p.*

**This PLACE.**

*Gen.* 19:12 bri. them out of *th. p.*
13 destroy *t. p.* 14 get out *t. p.*
20:11 fear of G. is not in *this p.*
28:16 L. is in *t. p.* 17 dreadful
38:21 no harlot in *this p.* 22
*Ex.* 13:3 L. brought you fr. *t. p.*
*Num.* 20:5 bri. us unto *t.* evil *p.*
*Deut.* 1:31 God bare thee till ye came to *this p.* 9:7; 11:5
*Jud.* 18:3 wh. mak. thou in *t. p.?*
1 *K.* 8:29 heark. to. *this p.* 30:35; 2 *Chr.* 6:20, 21, 26, 40; 7:15
2 *K.* 18:25 without L. ag. *this p.*
2 *Chr.* 7:12 chosen *t. p.* to myself
*Job* 18:21 *t. p.* of him knows not
*Jer.* 7:6 shed not in. blo. in *t. p.*
20 fury shall be poured on *t. p.*
14:13 give you peace in *this p.*
16:2 nei. sons nor daug. in *t. p.*
9 cause to cease out of *this p.*
19:3 bring evil upon *this p.*
12 thus will I do to *t. p.* 40:2
27:22 restore th. to *this p.* 32:37
28:3 bring to *t. p.* all vessels, 6
29:10 caus. you to return to *t. p.*
33:10 be heard in *this p.* joy
42:18 shall see *this p.* no more
44:29 I will punish you in *th. p.*
51:62 L. thou hast spo. ag. *t. p.*
*Zep.* 1:4 cut off remn. from *t. p.*
*Hag.* 2:9 in *t. p.* will I give peace
*Mat.* 12:6 in *this p.* one greater
*Luke* 16:28 lest come into *this p.*
*Acts* 6:14 J. shall destroy *th. p.*
*Acts* 7:7 shall serve me in *th. p.*
21:28 teacheth ag. law in *th. p.*
*Heb.* 4:5 and in *this p.* again

**Thy PLACE.**

*Gen.* 40:13 Pharaoh restore *t. p*
*Num.* 24:11 flee thou to *thy p.*
2 *Sam.* 15:19 return to *thy p.*
*Ec.* 10:4 ag. thee, leave not *t. p.*
*Ezek.* 12:3 remo. from *t. p.* 38:15

**To, *or* unto the PLACE.**

*Ex.* 3:8 bring you *u. p.* of Cana.
32:34 lead people *unto the p.*
*Num.* 10:29 journeying *to the p.*
1 *Sam.* 20:19 *to the p.* wh. th. hide
2 *Sam.* 2:23 many as came *to t. p.*
1 *Chr.* 15:12 bring ark *to the p.*
*Neh.* 1:9 I will bring th. *to the p.*
*Ps.* 104:8 *to the p.* thou founded
*Is.* 18:7 present brought *to t. p.*
*Jer.* 7:14 *to the p.* wh. I gave you
29:14 will bring you ag. *to t. p.*
*Acts* 25:23 ent. *into p.* of hearing

**PLACED.**

1 *K.* 12:32 Jeroboam *p.* priests

2 K. 17:6 and p. them in Halah
24 p. them in Samaria, 26
2 Chr. 1:14 wh. he p. in chariot
17:2 he p. forces in fenced cities
Job 20:4 si. man was p. on earth
Ps. 78:60 tent which he had p.
Is. 5:8 they may be p. alone
Jer. 5:22 wh. p. sand for bound
Ezek. 17:5 eagle p. it by waters

**PLACES.**

Gen. 28:15 keep thee in all p.
Ex. 20:24 p. wh. I rec. my name
Jas. 5:8 in p. till th. were whole
Jud. 5:11 deliv. from noise in p.
1 Sam. 7:16 judged Isr. in th. p.
30:31 Da. sent presents to all p.
2 K. 23:5 put down priests in p.
14 filled their p. with bones
Neh. 4:12 from p. whe. ye return
13 I set the people in lower p.
and on higher p.
Job 21:28 dwelling p. of wicked
37:8 beasts remain in their p.
Ps. 10:8 he sitteth in lurking p.
16:6 lines are fallen in pleas. p.
18:45 afraid out of their close p.
73:18 set them in slippery p.
74:20 dark p. of earth are full
103:22 bless the Lord in all p.
105:41 they ran in the dry p.
110:6 shall fill the p. with dead
Prov. 8:2 she standeth in the p.
Cant. 2:14 art in the secret p.
Is. 32:18 dw. in quiet resting p.
40:4 and rough p. plain
45:2 make crooked p. straight
Jer. 4:12 wind fr. those p. sh. co.
8:3 all p. whither driven, 29:14
17:26 come from p. about Jeru.
24:9 a taunt and curse in all p.
32:44 witnesses in p. about Jer.
40:12 Jews return. out of all p.
45:5 thy life for a prey in all p.
Lam. 2:6 he hath destroy. his p.
Ezek. 34:12 deliver th. out of p.
26 will make p. round my hill
47:11 miry p. sh. not be healed
Amos 4:6 want of bread in yo. p.
Zec. 3:7 give thee p. to walk
Mat. 12:43 thro' dry p. Lu. 11:24
13:5 some fell on stony p. 20
Acts 24:3 we accept it in all p.
Eph. 1:3 blessed us in heaven. p.
20 at right hand in heavenly p.
2:6 sit together in heavenly p.
3:10 to powers in heavenly p.
Phil. 1:13 bonds manif. in all p.
Rev. 6:14 island moved out th. p.
See DESOLATE, HOLY.

**High PLACES.**

Lev. 26:30 I will dest. your h. p.
Num. 21:28 consu. lords of h. p.
33:52 pluck down all their h. p.
Deut. 32:13 ma. him ride on h. p.
33:29 shalt tread on their h. p.
Jud. 5:18 jeop. lives in high p.
1 Sam. 13:6 people hide in h. p.
2 Sam. 1:19 Israel slain in h. p.
25 thou wast slain in thy h. p.
22:34 and setteth me on my high p. Ps. 18:33
1 K. 3:2 people sacrificed in h. p.
2 K. 17:32; 2 Chr. 33:17
3 burnt inc. in h. p. 22:43; 2 K. 12:3; 15:4, 35; 16:4; 17:11
12:31 Jerob. made house of h. p.
32 Beth-el priests of high p.
13:2 shall offer priests of h. p.
32 cried against houses of h. p.
33 Jeroboam made of the peo. priests of h. p. 2 K. 17:32
1 K. 15:14 h. p. were not remov.
22:43; 2 K. 12:3; 14:4; 15:4, 35
2 K. 17:29 gods in houses of h. p.
18:4 Hezekiah removed h. p. 22
23:8 defiled h. p. brake h. p. 13;
2 Chr. 31:1; 32:12; Is. 36:7
20 slew all the priests of h. p.
2 Chr. 11:15 ord. priests for h. p.
14:3 Asa took away high p. 5
15:17 h. p. not ta. away, 20:33
17:6 Jehosha. took away h. p.
21:11 J. made h. p. 28:25 Ahaz
34:3 purge Jerusalem from h. p.
Job 25:2 he maketh peace in h. p.
Ps. 78:58 provok. him with h. p.
Prov. 8:2 stand. on top of h. p.
9:14 sitteth on a seat in the h. p.
Is. 15:2 he is gone up to h. p.
41:18 I will open rivers in h. p.
49:9 pastures shall be in h. p.
58:14 cause thee to ride on h. p.
Jer. 3:2 lift up thine eyes to h. p.
21 a voice heard on high p.
4:11 dry wind in h. p. of wilder.
7:29 take up a lamenta. in h. p.
12:12 spoilers come on all h. p.
14:6 wild asses did stand in h. p.
17:3 I will give thy h. p. for sin
26:18 mountain shall become as h. p. of the forest, Mic. 3:12
48:35 him that offereth in h. p.
Ezek. 6:3 I will destroy your h. p.
16:16 deckedst h. p. divers colo.
39 shall break down thy h. p.
36:2 ancient high p. are ours
Hos. 10:8 h. p. of Aven destroyed
Amos 4:13 and treadeth upon the h. p. of the earth, Mic. 1:3
7:9 h. p. of Isaac sh. be desolate
Mic. 1:5 what are h. p. of Judah?
Hab. 3:19 make me walk on h. p.
Eph. 6:12 spiritual wick. in h. p.
See BUILT.

**Waste PLACES.**

Is. 5:17 waste p. of fat ones
51:3 L. will comfort her w. p.
52:9 ye waste p. of Jerusalem
58:12 shall build the old w. p.

**PLAGUE, Substantive.**

Ex. 11:1 bri. one p. on Pharaoh
12:13 the p. shall not be on you
Lev. 13:3 hair in p. turned wh. 17
5 if p. spr. not in skin, 6; 14:48
30 if man or wo. hath p. iest see p. 31, 32, 50, 51, 55; 4:37
44 lepr. man, p. is in his head
50 shut up it that hath the p.
58 if p. be departed from them
14:35 there is as it were a p. in
Num. 8:19 be no p. among Israel
11:33 L. smote people with a p.
16:46 wrath is out, p. begun, 47
48 the p. was stayed, 50; 25:8
Deut. 28:61 every p. not written
Jos. 22:17 although there was p.
1 Sam. 6:4 one p. was on you all
2 Sam. 24:21 that the p. may be stayed, 1 Chr. 21:22
1 K. 8:38 kn. ev. man p. of heart
2 Chr. 21:14 wi. p. will L. smite
Ps. 91:10 nor any p. come nigh
106:29 the p. brake upon them
30 judgm. so the p. was stayed
Zec. 14:12 be p. L. will smite, 18
Mark 5:29 she was healed of p.
34 and be whole of p.
Rev. 16:21 blasphemed p. of hail

**PLAGUE, Verb.**

Ps. 89:23 p. them that hate him

**PLAGUED.**

Gen. 12:17 the Lord p. Pharaoh
Ex. 32:35 the Lord p. the people
Jos. 24:5 and I p. Egypt
1 Chr. 21:17 that th. should be p.
Ps. 73:5 nor are p. like oth. men
14 all the day have I been p.

**PLAGUES.**

Gen. 12:17 L. plagued Ph. wi. p.
Ex. 9:14 I will send all my p.
Lev. 26:21 bring 7 times more p.
Deut. 28:59 L. will make thy p.
1 Sam. 4:8 gods smote Eg. wi. p.
Jer. 19:8 beca. of p. 49:17; 50:13
Hos. 13:14 I will be thy p.
Mark 3:10 as many as had p.
Luke 7:21 cured many of their p.
Rev. 9:20 rest not killed by th. p.
11:6 to smite earth with p.
16:9 G. hath power over th. p.
18:4 that ye recei. not of her p.
8 therefo. shall her p. come in
22:18 God sh. add to him the p.
See SEVEN.

**PLAIN, Adjective.**

Gen. 25:27 Jacob was a p. man
Ps. 27:11 lead me in a p. path
Prov. 8:9 th. are p. to him that
15:19 the way of righteous is p.
Is. 28:25 he made p. the face
40:4 and rough places made p.
Jer. 48:21 judgment come on p.
Hab. 2:2 make it p. upon tables
Mark 7:35 loosed, he spake p.

**PLAIN, Substantive.**

Gen. 11:2 p. in land of Shinar
13:10 Lot beheld all the p. 11
12 Lot dwelled in cities of p.
19:17 nor stay thou in all the p.
25 he overthr. cities in the p.
Jos. 11:16 Jos. took valley and p.
Jud. 9:6 made Ab. king by p.
1 Sam. 10:3 come to p. of Tabor
2 Sam. 2:29 Abner walked thr' p.
15:28 I will tarry in the p. until
18:23 Ahimaaz ran by the p.
1 K. 7:46 in p. of Jord. did king
20:23 fight ag. them in the p. 25
2 K. 25:4 went to p. Jer. 52:7
Neh. 3:22 after him priests of p.
Jer. 17:26 shall come from the p.
21:13 against thee, O rock of p.
48:8 p. shall be destroyed
Ezek. 3:22 go forth in the p. 23
8:4 the vision that I saw in p.

**PLAINS.**

Gen. 18:1 L. appeared in the p.
Num. 22:1 Is. pitched in p. 33:48
26:63 numbered Israel in the p.
31:12 spoil to camp in the p.
36:13 L. commanded in the p.
Deut. 34:1 Mo. went from the p.
2 Sam. 17:16 lodge not in the p.
2 K. 25:5 Chaldees overtook him in the p. Jer. 39:5; 52:8
1 Chr. 27:28 over trees in low p.
2 Chr. 9:27 cedar in lower p.
26:10 Uzziah had cattle in p.

**PLAINLY.**

Ex. 21:5 if the servant p. say
Deut. 27:8 write this law very p.
1 Sam. 2:27 p. appear to house
10:16 told us p. that the asses
Ezr. 4:18 let. hath been p. read
Is. 32:4 stammerer sh. speak p.
John 10:24 if thou be C. tell us p.
11:14 Jesus said to them p.
16:25 I shall show you p.
29 now speakest thou p. and
Heb. 11:14 such things declare p.

**PLAINNESS.**

2 Cor. 3:12 we use gr. p. of speech

**PLAITING.**

1 Pet. 3:3 let it not be p. of hair

**PLANES.**

Is. 44:13 fitteth image with p.

**PLANETS.**

2 K. 23:5 burnt incen. to sun, p.

**PLANKS.**

1 K. 6:15 covered floor with p.
Ezek. 41:25 were thick p. on face
26 side of house, and thick p.

**PLANT, Substantive.**

Gen. 2:5 God made every p.
Job 14:9 bring forth like the p.
Is. 5:7 men of Jud. his pleas. p.
17:11 shalt make thy p. grow
53:2 shall grow as a tender p.

*Jer.* 2:21 turned into degener. *p.*
*Ezek.* 34:29 raise for them a *p.*
*Mat.* 15:13 every *p.* my Father

**PLANTS.**

1 *Chr.* 4:23 that dwell among *p.*
*Ps.* 128:3 thy children like *p.*
144:12 our sons may be as *p.*
*Cant.* 4:13 thy *p.* as an orchard
*Is.* 16:8 have broken down *p.*
17:10 shalt thou plant pleas. *p.*
*Jer.* 48:32 thy *p.* are gone over
*Ezek.* 31:4 riv. run. about his *p.*

**PLANT, Verb.**

*Ex.* 15:17 *p.* them in mount of
*Deut.* 16:21 thou shalt not *p.*
28:30 thou shalt *p.* a viney. 39
2 *Sam.* 7:10 I will *p.* 1 *Chr.* 17:9
2 *K.* 19:29 *p.* vineyards, *Is.* 37:30
*Ps.* 107:37 sow the fields, and *p.*
*Is.* 17:10 thou shalt *p.* pleas.
41:19 I will *p.* in wilderness
51:16 that I may *p.* heavens
65:21 they shall *p.* vineyards
22 they sh. not *p.* and another
*Jer.* 1:10 to build and to *p.*
18:9 a kingdom, to build to *p.*
24:6 *p.* and not pluck, 42:10
29:5 *p.* gardens, and eat fruit
31:5 shall *p.* vines on mount.
28 I watch them to bu. and *p.*
32:41 I will *p.* them in this land
35:7 nor shall you sow, nor *p.*
*Ezek.* 17:22 *p.* it on a high, 23
28:26 they shall *p.* vineyards
36:36 L. build and *p.* that
*Dan.* 11:45 he sh. *p.* tabernacles
*Amos* 9:14 they sh. *p.* vineyards
15 I will *p.* them upon th. land
*Zep.* 1:13 they sh. *p.* vineyards

**PLANTATION.**

*Ezek.* 17:7 water it by fur. of *p.*

**PLANTED.**

*Gen.* 2:8 God *p.* a garden eastw.
9:20 Noah *p.* vine; 21:33 A. *p.*
*Num.* 24:6 trees which L. hath *p.*
*Jos.* 24:13 olive-yards ye *p.* not
*Ps.* 1:3 like a tree *p.* *Jer.* 17:8
80:8 cast out heathen, and *p.*
92:13 those that be *p.* in house
94:9 *p.* ear shall he not hear?
104:16 cedars which he hath *p.*
*Ec.* 2:4 I *p.* vine. 5 I *p.* trees
3:2 pluck up that which is *p.*
*Is.* 5:2 *p.* it with the choicest
40:24 yea, they shall not be *p.*
*Jer.* 2:21 I had *p.* thee a noble
11:17 Lord of hosts that *p.* thee
12:2 thou hast *p.* them, they
45:4 what I have *p.* I will pluck
*Ezek.* 17:5 *p.* it in a fruitful, 8
10 being *p.* shall it prosper?
19:10 *p.* by the waters, she was
*Hos.* 9:13 Ephr. is *p.* in a place
*Amos* 5:11 ye have *p.* vineyards
*Mat.* 15:13 heavenly Fath. not *p.*
21:33 householder *p.* *Mark* 12:1; *Luke* 20:9
*Luke* 17:6 and be thou *p.* in sea
28 they sold, they *p.* builded
*Rom.* 6:5 have been *p.* together
1 *Cor.* 3:6 have *p.* Apollos water.

**PLANTEDST, ETH.**

*Deut.* 6:11 trees which thou *p.*
*Ps.* 44:2 drive out heath. and *p.*
*Prov.* 31:16 fruit she *p.* vineyard
*Is.* 44:14 he *p.* ash, and the rain
1 *Cor.* 3:7 neither is he that *p.*
8 he that *p.* and he that wat.
9:7 who *p.* a viney. and eateth

**PLANTERS.**

*Jer.* 31:5 *p.* shall plant and eat

**PLANTING, S.**

*Is.* 60:21 branch of my *p.*
61:3 called the *p.* of the Lord
*Mic.* 1:6 make Samaria as *p.*

**PLASTER.**

*Is.* 38:21 lay it for a *p.* on boil

**PLASTER, ED.**

*Lev.* 14:42 and shall *p.* the house
48 plague, after house was *p.*
*Deut.* 27:2 *p.* them with *p.* 4
*Dan.* 5:5 wrote on *p.* of palace

**PLAT.**

2 *K.* 9:26 requite thee in this *p.* cast him into the *p.* of

**PLATE.**

*Ex.* 28:36 sh. make a *p.* of pure
39:30 they made the *p.* of holy
*Lev.* 8:9 on his forefront put *p.*

**PLATES.**

*Ex.* 39:3 beat gold into thin *p.*
*Num.* 16:38 ma. of censers *p.* 39
1 *K.* 7:30 every base had *p.* of
*Jer.* 10:9 silver spread into *p.* is

**PLATTED.**

*Mat.* 27:29 *p.* crown of thorns, *Mark* 15:17; *John* 19:2

**PLATTER.**

*Mat.* 23:25 cl. outs. *p.* *Luke* 11:39

**PLAY.**

*Ex.* 32:6 rose to *p.* 1 *Cor.* 10:7
*Deut.* 22:21 *p.* whore in fa. house
1 *Sam.* 16:16 that he shall *p.* wi.
17 now a man that can *p.* well
2 *Sam.* 2:14 y. men arise and *p.*
6:21 therefore will I *p.* bef. L.
10:12 and let us *p.* the men for
*Job* 40:20 where beasts of field *p.*
41:5 wilt thou *p.* with him
*Ps.* 33:3 *p.* skilfully with a loud
104:26 whom thou made to *p.*
*Is.* 11:8 sucking child shall *p.*
*Ezek.* 33:32 and can *p.* well on

**PLAYED.**

*Jud.* 19:2 concubine *p.* whore
1 *Sam.* 16:23 Da. *p.* 18:10; 19:9
26:21 I have *p.* fool, and have
2 *Sam.* 6:5 all Is. *p.* 1 *Chr.* 13:8
2 *K.* 3:15 when the minstrel *p.*
*Ezek.* 16:28 *p.* whore with Assy.
*See* HARLOT.

**PLAYER, S.**

1 *Sam.* 16:16 who is a cunning *p.*
*Ps.* 68:25 the *p.* on instruments
87:7 as well the singers as *p.* on

**PLAYETH, ING.**

1 *Sam.* 16:18 Jesse, cunning in *p.*
1 *Chr.* 15:29 Da. dancing and *p.*
*Ps.* 68:25 am. them damsels *p.*
*Ezek.* 23:44 as to woman that *p.*
*Zec.* 8:5 boys and girls *p.* in the

**PLEA.**

*Deut.* 17:8 hard betw. *p.* and *p.*

**PLEAD.**

*Jud.* 6:31 will ye *p.* for Baal?
*Job* 9:19 shall set me a time to *p.*
13:19 who is he that will *p.* wi.
16:21 O that one might *p.* for a
19:5 if he will *p.* against me my
23:6 will he *p.* against me pow.
*Is.* 1:17 judgment, *p.* for widow
3:13 Lord stand up to *p.* and
43:26 let us *p.* together, declare
66:16 by fire will the Lord *p.*
*Jer.* 2:9 will yet *p.* with you, 35
29 wheref. will ye *p.* with me?
12:1 righteous, when I *p.* with
25:31 Lord will *p.* with all flesh
*Ezek.* 17:20 I will *p.* with him
35 and will I *p.* with you
38:22 I will *p.* against him with
*Hos.* 2:2 *p.* with your mother, *p.*
*Joel* 3:2 and I will *p.* with them
*Mic.* 6:2 and the Lord will *p.*
*See* CAUSE.

**PLEADED, ETH.**

1 *Sam.* 25:39 blessed be L. th. *p.*
*Job* 16:21 as a man *p.* for neigh.
*Is.* 51:22 saith thy God that *p.*
59:4 justice, nor any *p.* for tru.
*Lam.* 3:58 O Lord, thou hast *p.*
*Ezek.* 20:36 as I *p.* with fathers

**PLEADING.**

*Job* 13:6 hearken to the *p.* of my

**PLEASANT.**

*Gen.* 2:9 ev. tree grow that is *p.*
3:6 *p.* to the eyes and a tree
49:15 Issachar saw that it was *p.*
2 *Sam.* 1:23 S. and Jon. were *p.*
26 *p.* hast thou been to me
1 *K.* 20:6 whatever is *p.* they
2 *K.* 2:19 situation of city is *p.*
*Ps.* 16:6 lines fallen in *p.* places
106:24 they despised *p.* land
133:1 how *p.* for breth. to dwell
135:3 sing praises, it is *p.* 147:1
*Prov.* 2:10 knowledge is *p.*
5:19 the loving hind and *p.* roe
9:17 bread eaten in secret is *p.*
15:26 words of the pure are *p.*
16:24 *p.* words as honey-comb
22:18 for it is *p.* if thou keep
24:4 chambers filled with all *p.*
*Ec.* 11:7 *p.* it is for the eyes to
*Cant.* 1:16 thou art fair, yea, *p.*
4:16 come and eat his *p.* fruits
7:6 how fair and *p.* art thou, O
13 at our gates are all *p.* fruits
*Is.* 5:7 men of Ju. his *p.* plant
13:22 dragons shall cry in th. *p.*
17:10 shalt thou plant *p.* plants
32:12 they lament for *p.* fields
54:12 thy borders of *p.* stones
64:11 and all our *p.* things are
*Jer.* 3:19 sh. I give th. a *p.* land?
12:10 made my *p.* portion a des.
23:10 *p.* places of wilderness
25:34 shall fall like a *p.* vessel
31:20 Ephr. is he a *p.* child?
*Lam.* 1:7 remembered all her *p.*
10 spread his hand on her *p.*
11 have given their *p.* things
2:4 slew all that were *p.* to eye
*Ezek.* 26:12 shall destroy thy *p.*
33:32 song of one that hath *p.*
*Dan.* 8:9 great toward *p.* land
10:3 I ate no *p.* bread
11:38 honor a god wi. *p.* things
*Hos.* 9:13 Ephr. is in a *p.* place
*Joel* 3:5 into your temple my *p.*
*Amos* 5:11 planted *p.* vineyards
*Mic.* 2:9 cast out from *p.* houses
*Nah.* 2:9 gl. out of *p.* furniture
*Zec.* 7:14 laid *p.* land desolate
*Mal.* 3:4 offering of J. be *p.* L.

**PLEASANTNESS.**

*Prov.* 3:17 her ways are w. of *p.*

**PLEASE.**

*Ex.* 21:8 if she *p.* not master
*Num.* 23:27 peradvent. it will *p.*
2 *Sam.* 7:29 let it *p.* 1 *Chr.* 17:27
*Job* 6:9 even *p.* G. to destroy me
20:10 shall seek to *p.* the poor
*Ps.* 69:31 this also shall *p.* Lord
*Prov.* 16:7 man's ways *p.* Lord
*Cant.* 2:7 love till he *p.* 3:5; 8:4
*Is.* 2:6 *p.* themselves in children
55:11 accomplish that wh. I *p.*
56:4 choose things that *p.* me
*John* 8:29 I do th. things that *p.*
*Rom.* 8:8 they in flesh cannot *p.*
15:1 bear and not *p.* ourselves
2 let every one *p.* his neighbor
*Cor.* 7:32 car. how he may *p.* L.
33 *p.* his wife; 34 she may *p.*
10:33 even as I *p.* all men
*Gal.* 1:10 do I seek to *p.* men?
1 *Thes.* 2:15 they *p.* not G.
4:1 ought to walk and to *p.* G.
2 *Tim.* 2:4 that ye may *p.* him
*Tit.* 2:9 to *p.* them well in all
*Heb.* 11:6 with. faith impos. *p.* G.

**PLEASED.**

*Gen.* 28:8 daugh. of Ca. *p.* not I.

45:16 it *p.* Pharaoh well
*Num.* 24:1 Balaam saw it *p.* L.
*Jud.* 13:23 if the Lord were *p.*
14:7 and she *p.* Samson well
1 *Sam.* 12:22 it *p.* L. to make you
18:26 it *p.* D. to be the king's
2 *Sam.* 3:36 what the king did *p.*
19:6 if we had died, it had *p.*
1 *K.* 3:10 Solomon's speech *p.* L.
2 *Chr.* 30:4 thing *p.* the king, *Neh.* 2:6; *Est.* 1:21; 2:4
*Est.* 2:9 the maiden *p.* the king
5:14 the thing *p.* Haman, he
*Ps.* 40:13 be *p.* O Lord, to deliver
51:19 then shalt thou be *p.* with
115:3 G. hath done whatsoever he *p.* 135:6; *Jon.* 1:14
*Is.* 53:10 it *p.* the Lord to bruise
*Mic.* 6:7 will the Lord be *p.* with
*Mal.* 1:8 will he be *p.* with thee?
*Acts* 6:5 saying *p.* the multitude
12:3 bec. Herod saw it *p.* Jews
*Rom.* 15:3 for even Christ *p.* not
26 for it hath *p.* them of, 27
1 *Cor.* 1:21 it *p.* G. by foolishness
7:12 she *p.* to dwell with him
12:18 God set members as it *p.*
15:38 G. giveth it a body as it *p.*
*Gal.* 1:10 for if I yet *p.* men, I
15 it *p.* God to reveal his Son
*Col.* 1:19 *p.* Father that in him
*Heb.* 11:5 had testimony he *p.* G.

**Well PLEASED.**

*Is.* 42:21 Lord is *well p.* for his
*Mat.* 3:17 in whom I am *well p.* 12:18; 17:5; *Mark* 1:11; *Luke* 3:22; 2 *Pet.* 1:17
1 *Cor.* 10:5 God was not *well p.*
*Heb.* 13:16 such sacri. G. is *w. p.*

**Men-PLEASERS.**

*Eph.* 6:6 eye-s. as *m.-p.* *Col.* 3:22

**PLEASETH.**

*Gen.* 16:6 do to her as it *p.* thee
*Jud.* 14:3 get her for me, she *p.*
*Est.* 2:4 maiden which *p.* king
*Ec.* 7:26 whoso *p.* G. sh. escape
8:3 he doeth whatsoever *p.* him

**PLEASING.**

*Est.* 8:5 if I be *p.* in his eyes
*Hos.* 9:4 neither shall they be *p.*
*Col.* 1:10 worthy of L. to all *p.*
1 *Thes.* 2:4 so we speak, not as *p.*
1 *John* 3:22 do things that are *p.*

**Well-PLEASING.**

*Phil.* 4:18 acceptable, *well-p.* to God
*Col.* 3:20 for this is *well-p.* to L.
*Heb.* 13:21 work. what is *well-p.*

**PLEASURE.**

*Gen.* 18:12 old, shall I have *p.*?
1 *Chr.* 29:17 I know thou hast *p.*
*Ezr.* 5:17 let king send his *p.*
*Neh.* 9:37 dom. over cattle at *p.*
*Est.* 1:8 drink to every man's *p.*
*Job* 21:21 what *p.* hath he in ho.?
25 and never eateth with *p.*
22:3 is it any *p.* to Almighty
*Ps.* 5:4 not a God that hath *p.*
35:27 which hath *p.* in prosper.
51:18 do good in good *p.* to Z.
102:14 servants take *p.* in her
103:21 bless L. ye that do his *p.*
105:22 bind his princes at his *p.*
111:2 sou. out of all that have *p.*
147:10 taketh not *p.* in the legs
11 the Lord taketh *p.* in them
149:4 the Lord taketh *p.* in his
*Prov.* 21:17 he that loveth *p.*
*Ec.* 2:1 enjoy *p.* 5:4 no *p.* in fools
12:1 say, I have no *p.* in them
*Is.* 21:4 night of my *p.* turned
44:28 Cyrus shall perform my *p.*
46:10 stand, I will do all my *p.*
48:14 will do his *p.* on Babylon
53:10 and *p.* of the Lord shall
58:3 in day of your fast find *p.*
13 doing thy *p.* not finding *p.*
*Jer.* 2:24 snuffeth wind at her *p.*
34:16 set at liberty at their *p.*
48:38 a vessel wherein is no *p.*
*Ezek.* 16:37 wh. thou hast tak. *p.*
*Ezek.* 18:23 have I any *p.* that wicked should die, 32; 33:11
*Hos.* 8:8 Is. vessel wherein no *p.*
*Hag.* 1:8 and I will take *p.* in it
*Mal.* 1:10 I have no *p.* in you
*Luke* 12:32 Father's good *p.* to
*Acts* 24:27 to do the Jews a *p.*
25:9 Festus to do the Jews a *p.*
*Rom.* 1:32 but have *p.* in them
2 *Cor.* 12:10 therefore I take *p.* in
*Eph.* 1:5 according to good *p.* 9
*Phil.* 2:13 to will and do his *p.*
2 *Thes.* 1:11 fulfil good *p.* of his
2:12 had *p.* in unrighteousness
1 *Tim.* 5:6 that liv. in *p.* is dead
*Heb.* 10:6 in sac. thou ha. no *p.* 8
38 my soul shall have no *p.* in
12:10 chastened us after own *p.*
*Jam.* 5:5 ye have lived in *p.* on
2 *Pet.* 2:13 as th. that count it *p.*
*Rev.* 4:11 for thy *p.* they are and

**PLEASURES.**

*Job* 36:11 spend their years in *p.*
*Ps.* 16:11 at thy right hand *p.*
36:8 drink of the river of thy *p.*
*Is.* 47:8 thou that art given to *p.*
*Luke* 8:14 are choked with the *p.*
2 *Tim.* 3:4 lovers of *p.* more than
*Tit.* 3:3 serv. divers lusts and *p.*
*Heb.* 11:25 enjoy the *p.* of sin

**PLEDGE.**

*Gen.* 38:17 wilt thou give *p.*?
18 what *p.*? 20 sent to rec. *p.*
*Ex.* 22:26 take raiment to *p.*
*Deut.* 24:6 no man take millst. to *p.* he taketh a man's life to *p.*
12 shalt not sleep with *p.* 13
17 not take widow's raim. to *p.*
1 *Sam.* 17:18 fare, take their *p.*
*Job* 22:6 tak. *p.* from thy broth.
24:3 take a widow's ox for a *p.*
9 and they take a *p.* of the poor
*Prov.* 20:16 take a *p.* of him for a strange woman, 27:13
*Ezek.* 18:7 to debtor his *p.* 12, 16
33:15 if wicked restore the *p.* he
*Amos* 2:8 on clothes laid to *p.* by

**PLEDGES.**

2 *K.* 18:23 give *p.* to, *Is.* 36:8

**PLEIADES.**

*Job* 9:9 wh. maketh Orion and P.
38:31 bind the influences of P.?

**PLENTEOUS.**

*Gen.* 41:34 fifth part in *p.* year
*Deut.* 28:11 L. make thee *p.* 30:9
2 *Chr.* 1:15 Solo. made gold *p.*
*Ps.* 86:5 art *p.* in mercy, 15
103:8 Lord is merciful, and *p.* in
130:7 with him is *p.* redemption
*Is.* 30:23 bread shall be fat and *p.*
*Hab.* 1:16 fat, and their meat *p.*
*Mat.* 9:37 the harvest truly is *p.*

**PLENTEOUSNESS.**

*Gen.* 41:53 seven years *p.* ended
*Prov.* 21:5 of diligent tend to *p.*

**PLENTIFUL.**

*Ps.* 68:9 thou didst send *p.* rain
*Is.* 16:10 joy is taken out of *p.*
*Jer.* 2:7 and I brought you to *p.*
48:33 gladness is taken from *p.*

**PLENTIFULLY.**

*Job* 26:3 hast *p.* declared thing
*Ps.* 31:23 *p.* rewardeth the proud
*Luke* 12:16 ground bro. forth *p.*

**PLENTY.**

*Gen.* 27:28 God give thee *p.* of
41:29 seven years of great *p.*
31 *p.* shall not be kno. in land
*Lev.* 11:36 wherein there is *p.*
2 *Chr.* 31:10 to eat have left *p.*
*Job* 22:25 shalt have *p.* of silver
37:23 in power and *p.* of justice
*Prov.* 3:10 barns be filled with *p.*
28:19 he that tilleth shall ha. *p.*
*Jer.* 44:17 then had we *p.* of vict.
*Joel* 2:26 sh. eat in *p.* and praise

**PLOTTETH.**

*Ps.* 37:12 wicked *p.* against just

**PLOUGH.**

*Luke* 9:62 having put hand to *p.*

**PLOUGH.**

*Deut.* 22:10 shalt not *p.* with ox
1 *Sam.* 14:14 yoke oxen might *p.*
*Job* 4:8 they that *p.* iniquity
*Prov.* 20:4 sluggard will not *p.*
*Is.* 28:24 doth the ploughman *p.*
*Hos.* 10:11 Judah sh. *p.* Jacob
*Amos* 6:12 will one *p.* there with
1 *Cor.* 9:10 he plougheth sho. *p.*

**PLOUGHED, ETH.**

*Jud.* 14:18 if ye had not *p.*
*Ps.* 129:3 ploughers *p.* on back
*Jer.* 26:18 shall be *p.* *Mic.* 3:12
*Hos.* 10:13 have *p.* wickedness
1 *Cor.* 9:10 that *p.* sh. pl. in hope

**PLOUGHING.**

1 *K.* 19:19 Elisha, who was *p.*
*Job* 1:14 oxen were *p.* and the
*Prov.* 21:4 the *p.* of the wicked
*Luke* 17:7 having a servant *p.*

**PLOUGHMAN, MEN.**

*Is.* 28:24 doth *p.* plough all day
61:5 sons of alien sh. be your *p.*
*Jer.* 14:4 the *p.* were ashamed
*Amos* 9:13 the *p.* shall overtake

**PLOUGHSHARES.**

*Is.* 2:4 beat sw. into *p.* *Mic.* 4:3
*Joel* 3:10 beat your *p.* into swo.

**PLUCK.**

*Lev.* 1:16 shall *p.* away his crop
*Num.* 33:52 *p.* down their high
*Deut.* 23:25 thou mayest *p.* ears
2 *Chr.* 7:20 then will I *p.* them up
*Job* 24:9 they *p.* fatherless from
*Ps.* 25:15 shall *p.* my feet out
52:5 *p.* thee out of thy place
74:11 thy right hand, *p.* it out
80:12 they which pass by *p.*
*Ec.* 3:2 and a time to *p.* up
*Jer.* 12:14 *p.* the house of Judah
17 utterly *p.* up and destroy
18:7 a kingdom, *p.* it up
22:24 would I *p.* thee thence
24:6 plant, and not *p.* 42:10
31:28 watched over th. to *p.* up
45:4 wh. I planted I will *p.* up
*Ezek.* 17:9 people, *p.* up by roots
23:34 thou sh. *p.* off thine own
*Mic.* 3:2 *p.* off the skin from
5:14 I will *p.* up thy groves
*Mat.* 5:29 if right eye offend thee *p.* it out, 18:9; *Mark* 9:47
12:1 beg. to *p.* corn, *Mark* 2:23
*John* 10:28 nor sh. any *p.* them
29 no man is able to *p.* them

**PLUCKED.**

*Gen.* 8:11 was an olive leaf *p.* off
*Ex.* 4:7 and he *p.* his hand out
*Deut.* 28:63 shall be *p.* from land
*Ruth* 4:7 a man *p.* off his shoe
2 *Sam.* 23:21 *p.* the spear out of Egyptian's hand, 1 *Chr.* 11:23
*Ezr.* 9:3 *p.* off hair of my head
*Neh.* 13:25 and *p.* off their hair
*Job* 29:17 *p.* spoil out of his teeth
*Is.* 50:6 them that *p.* off hair
*Jer.* 6:29 wicked are not *p.* away
12:15 after I have *p.* them out
31:40 it shall not be *p.* up
*Ezek.* 19:12 she was *p.* up in fury
*Dan.* 7:4 I beh. till wings we. *p.*
8 three of the first horns *p.* up
11:4 his kingdom sh. be *p.* up
*Amos.* 4:11 as a firebrand *p.* out
*Zec.* 3:2 not this *p.* out of fire?

*Mark* 5:4 chains *p.* asunder
*Luke* 6:1 disciples *p.* ears of corn
17:6 be thou *p.* up by the root
*Gal.* 4:15 *p.* out your own eyes
*Jude* 12 twice dead, *p.* up by ro.

**PLUCKETH.**

*Prov.* 14:1 the foolish *p.* it down

**PLUMB-LINE.**

*Amos.* 7:7 L. stood on wall made by a *p.-l.* wi. *p.-l.* in hand, 8

**PLUMMET.**

2 *K.* 21:13 stretch over Jerus. *p.*
*Is.* 28:17 lay righteousness to *p.*
*Zec.* 4:10 shall see *p.* in hand

**PLUNGE.**

*Job* 9:31 sh. thou *p.* me in ditch

**POETS.**

*Acts* 17:28 certain of your own *p.*

**POINT, S.**

*Gen.* 25:32 I am at the *p.* to die
*Ec.* 5:16 in all *p.* as he came
*Jer.* 17:1 writ. with *p.* of diamo.
*Mark* 5:23 daught. at *p.* of death
*John* 4:47 was at the *p.* of death
*Heb.* 4:15 was in all *p.* tempted
*Jam.* 2:10 offend in one *p.* is gu.

**POINT.**

*Num.* 34:7 *p.* out for you mount

**POINTED.**

*Job* 41:30 spread. sharp *p.* things

**POISON.**

*Deut.* 32:24 with *p.* of serpents
33 their wine is *p.* of dragons
*Job* 6:4 *p.* drinketh up my spirit
20:16 he shall suck *p.* of asps
*Ps.* 58:4 their *p.* like *p.* of serp.
140:3 adders' *p.* under their lips
*Rom.* 3:13 *p.* of asps under lips
*Jam.* 3:8 tongue is evil, full of *p.*

**POLE.**

*Num.* 21:8 set on *p.* 9 M. put it

**POLICY.**

*Dan.* 8:25 *p.* cause craft to pros.

**POLISHED.**

*Ps.* 144:12 *p.* after sim. of palace
*Is.* 49:2 hath made me *p.* shaft
*Dan.* 10:6 his feet like to *p.* brass

**POLISHING.**

*Lam.* 4:7 their *p.* was of sapph.

**POLL, S.**

*Num.* 1:2 every male by their *p.* 18:20, 22; 1 *Chr.* 23:3, 24
3:47 five shek. a piece by th. *p.*

**POLL, ED.**

2 *Sam.* 14:26 *p.* head, ye. end *p.*
*Ezek.* 44:20 they sh. *p.* th. heads
*Mic.* 1:16 and *p.* thee for children

**POLLUTE.**

*Num.* 18:32 neither *p.* holy thin.
35:33 so shall ye not *p.* the land
*Jer.* 7:30 in the house to *p.* it
*Ezek.* 7:21 *p.* my secret place, 22
13:19 will ye *p.* am. my people
20:31 ye *p.* yourselves with your idols, 23:30; 36:18
39 *p.* holy name no more, 39:7
44:7 in my sanctuary to *p.* it
*Dan.* 11:31 they sh. *p.* sanctuary

**POLLUTED.**

*Ex.* 20:25 lift tool. thou hast *p.*
2 *K.* 23:16 Josiah *p.* the altar
*Ps.* 106:38 land *p.* with blood
*Is.* 47:6 I have *p.* mine inherit.
48:11 how sho. my name be *p.*
*Jer.* 2:23 canst say, I am not *p.?*
3:1 not land be greatly *p.?* 2
34:16 ye turned and *p.* my name
*Lam.* 2:2 he hath *p.* the kingdom
4:14 *p.* themselves with blood
*Ezek.* 4:14 soul hath not been *p.*
14:11 nor be *p.* with transgres.
16:6 I saw thee *p.* in own bl. 22
20:9 it should not be *p.* 14, 22
13 sabbaths greatly *p.* 16, 21, 24
26 I *p.* them in their own gifts
30 are ye *p.* after your fath.?
23:17 was *p.* with Babylonians
*Hos.* 6:8 Gilead a city that is *p.*
9:4 all that eat thereof sh. be *p.*
*Amos* 7:17 thou sh. die in *p.* land
*Mic.* 2:10 not rest, because it is *p.*
*Zep.* 3:1 woe to her that is *p.*
4 her priests have *p.* sanctuary
*Mal.* 1:7 offered *p.* bread on altar
12 say, The ta. of the L. is *p.*
*Acts* 21:28 hath *p.* this holy place

**POLLUTING.**

*Is.* 56:2 keepeth sab. fr. *p.* it. 6

**POLLUTION, S.**

*Ezek.* 22:10 that was apart for *p.*
*Acts* 15:20 that they abs. from *p.*
2 *Pet.* 2:20 after having escap. *p.*

POLLUX. *Acts* 28:11

**POMEGRANATE.**

*Ex.* 28:34 gold. bell and *p.* 39:26
1 *Sam.* 14:2 S. tarried under a *p.*
*Cant.* 4:3 temp. like piece *p.* 6:7
8:2 cause th. to drink juice of *p.*
*Joel* 1:12 the *p.* trees are wither.
*Hag.* 2:19 *p.* hath not bro. forth

**POMEGRANATES.**

*Ex.* 28:33 make *p.* 39:24, 25
*Num.* 13:23 they brought of *p.*
20:5 no pla. of seed, vines, or *p.*
*Deut.* 8:8 into land of *p.* oil-olive
1 *K.* 7:18 chapiters with *p.* 2 *K.* 25:17; 2 *Chr.* 3:16; *Jer.* 52:22
*Cant.* 4:13 orch. of *p.* with fruits
6:11 see wheth. *p.* budded, 7:12

**POMMELS.**

2 *Chr.* 4:12 *p.* of the chapiters

**POMP.**

*Is.* 5:14 *p.* shall descend to hell
14:11 *p.* is brought to the grave
*Ezek.* 7:24 make *p.* of strong ce.
30:18 *p.* of strength cease, 33:28
32:12 shall spoil the *p.* of Egypt
*Acts* 25:23 A. and B. come wi. *p.*

**PONDER, ED, ETH.**

*Prov.* 4:26 *p.* the path of thy feet
5:6 lest thou *p.* the path of life
21 the Lord *p.* all his goings
21:2 L. *p.* heart; 24:12 he that
*Luke* 2:19 Mary *p.* them in her heart

**PONDS.**

*Ex.* 7:19 stretch hand on *p.* 8:5
*Is.* 19:10 purposes, that make *p.*

PONTUS. *Acts* 2:9; 18:2; 1 *Pet.* 1:1

**POOL.**

2 *Sam.* 2:13 on one side of the *p.*
4:12 they hanged them over *p.*
2 *K.* 18:17 by the conduit of the upper *p.* *Is.* 7:3; 36:2
*Neh.* 2:14 I went to the king's *p.*
*Is.* 22:9 waters of the lower *p.*
11 a ditch for wa. of the old *p.*
35:7 parched ground bec. a *p.*
41:18 I will make wilderness *p.*
*Nah.* 2:8 Nin. of old is like a *p.*
*John* 5:2 there is at Jerusal. a *p.*
7 no man to put me into *p.*
9:7 wash in *p.* of Siloam, 11

**POOLS.**

*Ex.* 7:19 stretch thy hand on *p.*
*Ps.* 84:6 rain also filleth the *p.*
*Ec.* 2:6 I made me *p.* of water
*Is.* 14:23 I will make it for *p.*
42:15 I will dry up *p.* and herbs

**POOR.**

*Ex.* 23:11 *p.* of thy people eat
30:15 the *p.* shall not give less
*Lev.* 14:21 if he be *p.* and cannot
19:10 shalt leave them for the *p.*
15 shalt not resp. person of *p.*
25:25 if brother be *p.* 35, 39, 47
*Deut.* 15:4 when there be no *p.*
11 the *p.* shall never cease out
*Ruth* 3:10 young men, *p.* or rich
1 *Sam.* 2:7 L. make. *p.* and rich
8 raiseth up the *p.* *Ps.* 113:7
2 *Sam.* 12:1 one rich, the oth. *p.*
2 *K.* 25:12 captain of guard left *p.* *Jer.* 39:10; 40:7; 52:15, 16
*Job* 5:15 he saveth *p.* from sword
16 *p.* hath hope, iniq. stoppeth
20:10 chil. sh. seek to please *p.*
19 because he oppressed the *p.*
24:4 *p.* of earth hide themselves
9 they take a pledge of the *p.*
14 murderer kill. *p.* and needy
29:12 because I delivered the *p.*
30:25 my soul grieved for *p.?*
31:16 if I withheld *p.* fr. desire
19 have seen *p.* without cover.
34:19 nor reg. rich more than *p.*
28 they cause cry of *p.* to come
36:15 deliver *p.* *Ps.* 72:12
*Ps.* 9:18 expecta. of *p.* not perish
10:2 wicked in pride do pers. *p.*
8 his eyes are set against *p.*
9 he lieth in wait to catch *p.*
10 *p.* may fall by strong ones
14 *p.* commit. himself to thee
12:5 for the oppression of the *p.*
14:6 shamed the counsel of *p.*
35:10 deliverest the *p.* from him
37:14 bent bow to cast down *p.*
40:17 but I am *p.* 69:29; 70:5; 86:1; 109:22
41:1 he that considereth *p.*
49:2 low and high, rich and *p.*
68:10 prepared goodness for *p.*
69:33 L. heareth *p.* and despis.
72:4 he shall judge *p.* of people
13 spare the *p.* 82:3 defend *p.*
74:21 let the *p.* praise thy name
82:4 deliver the *p.* and needy
107:41 yet setteth he *p.* on high
109:31 stand at right hand of *p.*
132:15 satisfy her *p.* with bread
140:12 maintain right of the *p.*
*Prov.* 10:4 becometh *p.* dealeth
15 destruction of *p.* is poverty
13:7 mak. himself *p.* hath riches
8 the *p.* heareth not rebuke
23 much food is in tillage of *p.*
14:20 *p.* is hated of neighbor
21 hath mercy on *p.* happy
31 oppres. *p.* reproach. Maker
17:5 mock. *p.* reproach. Maker
18:23 the *p.* useth entreaties
19:4 *p.* is separ. from neighbor
7 brethren of *p.* do hate him
21:13 stoppeth ears at cry of *p.*
22:2 rich and *p.* meet together
7 the rich ruleth over the *p.*
16 he that oppresseth the *p.*
28:8 for him that will pity *p.*
11 *p.* that hath understanding
15 so is wicked ruler over *p.*
29:7 considereth cause of *p.* 13
14 king faithfully judgeth *p.*
30:9 lest I be *p.* and steal
14 teeth as swords, to dev. *p.*
31:9 plead the cause of the *p.*
*Ec.* 4:14 his kingdom becom. *p.*
5:8 seest oppression of the *p.*
6:8 what hath the *p.* that kno.
*Is.* 3:14 the spoil of the *p.* is in
15 grind the faces of the *p.?*
10:2 take the right from the *p.*
30 to Laish, O *p.* Anathoth
11:4 with righ. sh. he judge *p*
14:30 the first-born of the *p.*
32 *p.* of his people shall trust
26:6 feet of the *p.* shall tread
29:19 even *p.* among men shall
32:7 destroy the *p.* with lying
*Is.* 41:17 the *p.* and needy seek
58:7 that thou bring the *p.*
*Jer.* 2:34 blood of *p.* innocents
5:4 I said, Surely these are *p.*
20:13 delivered soul of the *p.*

22:16 judge the cause of the p.
Ezek. 16:49 strength. hand of p.
18:12 oppressed p. and needy
17 taken off his hand fr. the p.
22:29 they have vexed the p.
Amos 2:6 sold the p. for shoes
7 dust on the head of the p.
4:1 oppress the p. and crush
5:11 your treading is on the p.
12 turn aside the p. in gate
8:4 make p. of the land to fail
6 we may buy p. for silver
Hab. 3:14 rejoicing to devour p.
Zep. 3:12 the p. shall trust in L.
Zec. 7:10 oppress not the p.
11:7 I will feed even you, O p.
11 p. of the flock waited on me
Mat. 5:3 blessed are p. in spirit
11:5 the p. have gospel preach.
26:11 ye have the p. always,
Mark 14:7; John 12:8
Mark 12:43 p. widow, Luke 21:3
Luke 6:20 blessed be ye p. yours
14:13 call the p. the maimed, 21
John 12:6 not that he car. for p.
Rom. 15:26 make contribu. for p.
2 Cor. 6:10 as p. yet making rich
8:9 for your sakes he became p.
Gal. 2:10 should remem. the p.
Jam. 2:5 hath not G. chos. the p.
6 but ye have despised the p.
Rev. 3:17 knowest not th. art p.
13:16 he causeth rich and p. to

**Is POOR.**

Ex. 22:25 of my peo. that *is* p.
Deut. 24:14 op. servant that *is* p.
15 for he *is* p. and setteth his
Jud. 6:15 my family *is* p.
Prov. 19:1 better *is* the p. 28:6
22:22 rob not poor bec. he *is* p.
Ec. 4:13 better *is* a p. and wise
Is. 66:2 to him that is p.

**POOR man.**

Ex. 23:3 nor countenance p. m.
Deut. 15:7 is a p. m. harden not
24:12 if a p. *man*, sleep not wi.
1 Sam. 18:23 seeing I am a p. m.
2 Sam. 12:3 p. *man* had nothing
Ps. 34:6 this p. m. cried, and the
109:16 persecu. p. and needy m.
Prov. 19:22 a p. *man* is better
21:17 loveth pleas. sh. be p. m.
28:3 a p. *man* that oppresseth
29:13 p. and deceitful m. meet
Ec. 9:15 found in it p. wise *man*
16 p. *man's* wisdom is despis.
Jam. 2:2 there come in a p. *man*

**To the POOR.**

Lev. 23:22 leave them *to the* p.
Est. 9:22 sending gifts *to the* p.
Job 29:16 I was a father *to the* p.
36:6 he giveth right *to the* p.
Ps. 112:9 giv. *to t.* p. 2 Cor. 9:9
Prov. 22:9 giveth bread *to the* p.
28:27 he that giveth *to the* p.
31:20 stretcheth hand *to the* p.
Is. 25:4 been a strength *to the* p.
Dan. 4:27 show. mercy *to the* p.
Mat. 19:21 gi. *to t.* p. Mark 10:21
Luke 4:18 preach *to the* p. 7:22
19:8 half of goods I give *to t.* p.
John 13:29 give somet. *to the* p.
1 Cor. 13:3 my goods to feed *t.* p.
Jam. 2:3 and say *to t.* p. Stand

**Thy POOR.**

Ex. 23:6 wrest judgment of *t.* p.
Deut. 15:7 hand fr. *thy* p. brother
11 open thy hand wide to *t.* p.
Ps. 72:2 he shall judge *thy* p.
74:19 forget not *thy* p. forever

**POORER, EST.**

Lev. 27:8 if he be p. than thy
2 K. 24:14 none remained save p.

**POPLAR, S.**

Gen. 30:37 Jacob took rods of p.
Hos. 4:13 burn incense under p.

**POPULOUS.**

Deut. 26:5 bec. a nation great, p.
Nah. 3:8 art thou better than p.

**PORCH.**

Jud. 3:23 Ehud went through p.
1 Chr. 28:11 D. gave So. patt. p.
2 Chr. 29:7 shut doors of the p.
Ezek. 8:16 between p. and altar
Joel 2:17 priests weep between p.
Mat. 26:71 was gone out into p.
Mark 14:68 into the p. the cock
John 10:23 Je. walked in S.'s p
Acts 3:11 toget. in Solomon's p.
5:12 with one accord in S.'s p.

**PORCHES.**

Ezek. 41:15 with temple and p.
John 5:2 Bethesda, having fi. p.

**PORCIUS.**

Acts 24:27 P. Festus came into

**PORTER, S.**

2 Sam. 18:26 watch. called to p.
2 K. 7:10 lepers called to the p.
1 Chr. 9:17 the p. were Shallum
23:5 four thousand were p.
2 Chr. 8:14 p. by their courses
35:15 the p. waited at ev. gate
Ezr. 7:7 p. and Nethinim went
Neh. 7:73 Levites and p. dwelt
Mark 13:34 commanded the p. to
John 10:3 to him the p. openeth

**PORTION.**

Gen. 14:24 let them take their p.
31:14 is there yet any p. for us?
48:22 given thee p. above breth.
Lev. 6:17 given them it for p.
Num. 31:47 M. took one p. of 50
Deut. 21:17 giv. him double p.
32:9 the Lord's p. is his people
33:21 in a p. of the lawgiver
Jos. 17:14 given me but one p.
1 Sam. 1:5 to Hannah he gave p.
1 K. 12:16 what p. have we in
David? 2 Chr. 10:16
2 K. 2:9 let a double p. of thy
9:10 eat Jez. in p. of Jez. 36, 37
21 Joram met him in p. of Na.
25 cast him in p. of Na.'s field
2 Chr. 28:21 Ahaz took p. out of
31:4 to give p. of the priests, 16
Ezr. 4:16 shalt have no p.
Neh. 2:20 no p. nor right in Jer.
11:23 a certain p. should be
Job 20:29 this is p. of a wicked
24:18 their p. is cursed in earth
26:14 lit. a p. is heard? 27:13
31:2 what p. of G. is fr. above?
Ps. 11:6 this shall be the p. of
16:5 L. is the p. of mine inher.
17:14 who have p. in this life
63:10 shall be a p. for foxes
73:26 God is my p. for ever
119:57 thou art my p. 142:5
Prov. 31:15 giv. a p. to maidens
Ec. 2:10 and this was my p.
21 shall he leave it for his p.
3:22 for that is his p. 5:18; 9:9
5:19 G. given power to take p.
9:6 nor have they any more p.
11:2 give a p. to seven, and also
Is. 17:14 this is the p. of them
53:12 I will divide him a p.
57:6 stones of stream is thy p.
61:7 they sh. rejoice in their p.
Jer. 10:16 the p. of Jacob, 51:19
12:10 they have tro. my p. made
my p. a desolate wilderness
13:25 this is p. of thy measures
52:34 every day a p. until death
Lam. 3:24 the Lord is my p.
Ezek. 45:1 shall offer a holy p. 4
Dan. 1:8 with p. of king's meat
4:15 let his p. be with beasts, 23
11:26 feed of the p. of his meat
Mic. 2:4 changed p. of my people
Hab. 1:16 by them their p. is fat
Zec. 2:12 Lord inherit Ju. his p.
Mat. 24:51 appoint him his p.
Luke 12:42 to give them their p.
46 his p. with unbelievers
15:12 give me the p. of goods

**PORTIONS.**

Deut. 18:8 they shall have like p.
Jos. 17:5 fell ten p. to Manasseh
1 Sam. 1:4 gave her daughters p.
2 Chr. 31:19 give p. to all males
Neh. 8:10 send p. to them, 12
12:44 p. priests; 47 p. of sing.
Est. 9:19 a day of sending p. 22
Ezek. 47:13 Jos. shall ha. two p.
Hos. 5:7 month shall de. their p.

**PORTRAY, ED.**

Ezek. 4:1 p. upon it city Jerusal.
8:10 all the idols of Israel p.
23:14 images of Chaldeans p.

**POSSESS.**

Gen. 22:17 seed p. gate, 24:60
Num. 13:30 and p. Deut. 1:21
27:11 next kinsman shall p. it
Deut. 1:39 they shall p. it
2:31 to p. that thou mayest
11:23 shall p. greater nations,
12:2, 29; 18:14; 31:3
Jos. 24:3 E. mount Seir to p. it
Jud. 11:23 shouldest thou p. it?
24 wilt not thou p. what Che.
1 K. 21:18 he is gone down to p.
Job 7:3 to p. months of vanity
13:26 mak. me to p. iniquities
Is. 34:11 bittern shall p. it, 17
Ezek. 7:24 they shall p. houses
Ezek. 35:10 be mine, we will p.
36:12 I will cause Is. to p. thee
Dan. 7:18 the saints shall p. the
Hos. 9:6 silver, nettles shall p.
Amos 9:12 they may p. Edom
Ob. 17 house of Jacob shall p.
19 sh. p. Esau, and Benj. p. G.
Hab. 1:6 Chaldeans to p. that is
Zep. 2:9 remnant shall p. them
Zec. 8:12 I will cause rem. to p.
Luke 18:12 give tithe of all I p.
21:19 in patience p. your souls
1 Thes. 4:4 know how to p. ves.

**POSSESS, *with* land.**

Lev. 20:24 give *l.* to p. Nu. 33:53;
Deut. 3:18; 5:31; 17:14
Num. 14:24 thy seed shall p. it, I
will bring them into this *l.*
Deut. 1:8 go in and p. the *land*,
4:1; 6:18; 8:1; 9:5, 23; 10:11;
11:31; Jos. 1:11
4:5 *land* whither ye go to p. it,
14, 26; 5:33; 6:1; 7:1; 11:10,
11, 29; 23:20
9:4 Lord brought me to p. th. *l.*
6 gives not this *l.* to p. for thy
11:8 be strong, and p. the *land*
28:21 consum. off *la.* goest to p.
63 plucked off the *l.* goest to p.
Jos. 23:5 ye shall p. their *land*
24:8 that ye might p. their *land*
Jud. 18:9 enter to p. the *land*
1 Chr. 28:8 ye may p. this good *l.*
Ezr. 9:11 ye go to p. an uncl. *l.*
Neh. 9:15 they should p. the *l.*
Is. 14:2 Is. sh. p. them in *l.* of L.
57:13 put. trust in me, shall p. *l.*
61:7 their *l.* sh. they p. double
Jer. 30:3 return to *l.* and p. it
Ezek. 33:25 shall ye p. *l.*? 26
Amos 2:10 I bro. you to p. *land*

**POSSESSED.**

Num. 21:24 Is. p. Sihon's land
Deut. 30:5 to land thy fathers p.
Jos. 13:1 much land to be p.
21:43 p. it and dw. therein, 22:9
Jud. 3:13 Eg. king of M. p. city
11:21 Is. p. land of Amorites, 22
2 K. 17:24 men of Ava p. Sam.
Ps. 139:13 thou hast p. my reins
Prov. 8:22 L. p. me in beginning
Is. 63:18 peo. of holiness hath p.

*Jer.* 32:15 vineyards shall be *p.*
23 and they came in and *p.* it
*Dan.* 7:22 saints *p.* the kingdom
*Luke* 8:36 he that was *p.* cured
*Acts* 4:32 none said aught he *p.*
16:16 a damsel *p.* with a spirit
1 *Cor.* 7:30 buy as tho' th. *p.* not
*See* DEVILS.

**POSSESSEST, ETH; ING.**

*Deut.* 26:1 come into land and *p.*
*Num.* 36:8 ev. daughter that *p.*
*Luke* 12:15 a man's life consists not in things which he *p.*
2 *Cor.* 6:16 noth. yet *p.* in all th.

**POSSESSION.**

*Gen.* 17:8 I will give land of Can., for everlasting *p.* 48:4
26:14 Isaac had *p.* of flocks
47:11 gave them *p.* in land of E.
*Lev.* 14:34 wh. I give to you for *p.*
25:25 if bro. sold some of his *p.*
33 the Levites' *p.* shall go out
45 strangers sh. be your *p.* 46
27:16 if man sanc. some of his *p.*
24 return to wh. *p.* did belong
*Num.* 24:18 Edom be *p.* S. be a *p.*
27:4 give us a *p.* among breth.
32:5 given to thy serv. for *p.*
22 this land shall be your *p.*
35:2 give to Levites their *p.* 8
28 slayer shall return to his *p.*
*Deut.* 2:5 mount Seir to E. for *p.*
9 have given Ar to L. for *p.* 19
12 as Isra. did in land of his *p.*
11:6 earth swallow. all in th. *p.*
32:49 which I gave Israel for *p.*
*Jos.* 12:6 Moses gave it for a *p.*
22:4 get ye unto land of your *p.*
19 if *p.* be unclean, take *p.*
1 *K.* 21:15 take *p.* of vineyard
19 hast thou killed, taken *p.*?
2 *Chr.* 20:11 cast us out of thy *p.*
*Neh.* 11:3 Ju. dwelt ev. one in *p.*
*Ps.* 2:8 uttern. parts for thy *p.*
44:3 got not land in *p.* by sword
69:35 dwell and have it in *p.*
83:12 take houses of God in *p.*
*Prov.* 28:10 upri. have good in *p.*
*Is.* 14:23 I will make it a *p.* for
*Ezek.* 11:15 this land given in *p.*
25:4 I will deliver thee for *p.*
36:2 high places are ours in *p.*
44:28 give them no *p.* in Israel
46:18 inherit. out of his own *p.*
*Acts* 5:1 An. with Sap. sold a *p.*
7:5 would give it to him for a *p.*
45 with Jesus into *p.* of Gent.
*Eph.* 1:14 redemption of the *p.*

**POSSESSIONS.**

*Gen.* 34:10 and get you *p.* therein
47:27 and Israel had *p.* therein
*Num.* 32:30 they shall have *p.*
*Jos.* 22:4 get to land of your *p.*
1 *Sam.* 25:2 whose *p.* were in C.
1 *Chr.* 9:2 inhabitants dw. in *p.*
2 *Chr.* 11:14 Levites left their *p.*
32:29 Hezeki. prov. *p.* of flocks
*Ec.* 2:7 I had great *p.* of great
*Ob.* 17 Jacob shall pos. their *p.*
*Mat.* 19:22 had *p.* *Mark* 10:22
*Acts* 2:45 sold *p.* and part. them
28:7 same quart. were *p.* of P.

**POSSESSOR, S.**

*Gen.* 14:19 high G. *p.* heaven, 22
*Zec.* 11:5 whose *p.* slay them
*Acts* 4:34 many as were *p.* lands

**POSSIBLE.**

*Mat.* 19:26 G. all *p.* *Mark* 10:27
24:24 if *p.* dec. elect, *Mar.* 13:22
26:39 if *p.* let this cup pass fr. me, *Mark* 14:35
*Mark* 9:23 all things *p.* to him
14:36 all things *p.* *Luke* 18:27
*Acts* 2:24 not *p.* he sho. be hold.
20:16 if *p.* at Jerusal. day of P.
*Rom.* 12:18 if *p.* live peaceably
*Gal.* 4:15 if *p.* ye would have
*Heb.* 10:4 not *p.* blood of bulls

**POST, S.**

2 *Chr.* 30:6 *p.* went with letters, *Est.* 3:13, 15; 8:10
*Est.* 8:14 *p.* rode on mules
*Job* 9:25 days are swifter than *p.*
*Jer.* 51:31 one *p.* run to meet an.

**POST.**

1 *Sam.* 1:9 E. sat on seat by a *p.*
*Ezek.* 40:16 on each *p.* palm-trees

**POSTS.**

*Deut.* 6:9 shalt write them on *p.*
*Jud.* 16:3 Samson took two *p.*
1 *K.* 7:5 doors and *p.* were square
*Prov.* 8:34 waiting at *p.* of doors
*Is.* 6:4 the *p.* of the door moved
57:8 behind the *p.* thou set up
*Ezek.* 40:10 *p.* had one measure
43:8 setting of their *p.* by my *p.*
*Amos* 9:1 that the *p.* may shake
*See* DOOR.

**Side-POSTS.**

*Ex.* 12:7 stri. blood on 2 *s.-p.* 22
1 *K.* 6:31 *s.-p.* were a fifth part

**POSTERITY.**

*Gen.* 45:7 preserve you a *p.*
*Num.* 9:10 any of yo. *p.* be uncl.
1 *K.* 16:3 take the *p.* of Baasha
21:21 take away the *p.* of Ahab
*Ps.* 49:13 *p.* approve th. sayings
109:13 let his *p.* be cut off
*Dan.* 11:4 not be divid. to his *p.*
*Amos* 4:2 your *p.* with fish-hooks

**POT.**

*Ex.* 16:33 take a *p.* put manna
*Jud.* 6:19 Gid. put broth in a *p.*
2 *K.* 4:2 not any thing, save a *p.*
38 on great *p.* 40 death in *p.*
*Job* 41:20 as out of a seething *p.*
31 maketh deep to boil like *p.*
*Prov.* 17:3 fining *p.* for sil. 27:21
*Jer.* 1:13 I see a seething *p.*
*Ezek.* 24:3 saith L. Set on a *p.*
6 woe to *p.* wh. scum is ther.
*Mic.* 3:3 chop in pieces, as for *p.*
*Zec.* 14:21 every *p.* in Jerusalem
*Heb.* 9:4 golden *p.* with manna

**Water-POT, S.**

*John* 2:6 there was set six *w.-p.*
4:28 woman then left her *w.-p.*

**POTS.**

*Ex.* 38:3 Bezaleel made the *p.*
*Lev.* 11:35 oven, or ranges for *p.*
1 *K.* 7:45 *p.* of brass, 2 *Chr.* 4:16
2 *Chr.* 4:11 Huram made the *p.*
*Ps.* 58:9 before your *p.* can feel
68:13 ye have lain among the *p.*
81:6 hands deliver. from the *p.*
*Jer.* 35:5 before Rech. *p.* of wine
*Mark* 7:4 wash. of cups and *p.* 8
*See* FLESH.

**POTENTATE.**

1 *Tim.* 6:15 blessed and only P.

**POTIPHAR.**

*Gen.* 37:36 sold Joseph to P. 39:1

**POTI-PHERAH.**

*Gen.* 41:45 the daughter of P. 50

**POTSHERD, S.**

*Job* 2:8 took *p.* to scrape himself
*Ps.* 22:15 stren. dried up like a *p.*
*Prov.* 26:23 are like a *p.* covered
*Is.* 45:9 let *p.* strive with the *p.*

**POTTAGE.**

*Gen.* 25:29 Jacob sod *p.* and Esau
30 feed me with *p.* 34 J. gave
2 *K.* 4:38 seethe *p.* for sons, 40
*Hag.* 2:12 if one touch bre. or *p.*

**POTTER, S.**

1 *Chr.* 4:23 these were the *p.*
*Ps.* 2:9 dash in pieces like *p.*'s
*Is.* 30:14 as breaking of a *p.*'s vessel, *Jer.* 19:11; *Rev.* 2:27
*Jer.* 18:2 go down to *p.*'s house
19:1 get a *p.*'s earthen bottle
*Lam.* 4:2 work of han. of the *p.*
*Zec.* 11:13 said, Cast it unto *p.*
*Mat.* 27:10 gave th. for *p.*'s field
*See* CLAY.

**POUND, S.**

1 *K.* 10:17 three *p.* of gold went
*Ezr.* 2:69 treas. 5,000 *p.* of silver
*Neh.* 7:71 treas. 2,200 *p.* of silver
72 rest gave 2,000 *p.* of silver
*Luke* 19:13 delivered to his servants ten *p.* 16, 18, 24
*John* 12:3 M. took *p.* of ointment
19:39 and of aloes about 100 *p.*

**POUR.**

*Ex.* 4:9 *p.* water on dry land
29:7 *p.* anointing oil on head
12 *p.* blood of bullock beside altar, *Lev.* 4:7, 18, 25, 30, 34
*Lev.* 2:1 *p.* oil on meat-offer. 6
14:15 *p.* it into palm of hand, 26
41 they shall *p.* out the dust
17:13 shall *p.* out blood thereof
*Num.* 24:7 he shall *p.* water out
*Deut.* 12:16 *p.* blood, 24; 15:23
1 *K.* 18:33 *p.* water on sacrifice
2 *K.* 4:4 *p.* oil into those vessels
41 *p.* out for the people
*Job* 36:27 *p.* rain accord. to vapor
*Ps.* 42:4 when I *p.* out my soul
62:8 *p.* out your heart bef. him
69:24 *p.* out thine indignation
79:6 *p.* out wrath on heathen
*Prov.* 1:23 will *p.* out my Sp. *Is.* 44:3; *Joel* 2:28, 29; *Ac.* 2:17,18
*Is.* 44:3 I will *p.* water on him
45:8 skies *p.* down righteousn.
*Jer.* 6:11 I will *p.* on children
7:18 to *p.* out drink-offerings
10:25 *p.* out fury on heathen
14:16 I will *p.* their wickedness
18:21 *p.* out their blood by swo.
44:17 *p.* out drink-off. 18, 19, 25
*Lam.* 2:19 *p.* out heart like wat.
*Ezek.* 7:8 now will I *p.* out fury, 14:19; 20:8, 13, 21; 30:15
21:31 *p.* out indignati. *Zep.* 3:8
24:3 set on pot and *p.* water in
*Hos.* 5:10 will *p.* out my wrath
*Mic.* 1:6 I will *p.* down stones
*Zec.* 12:10 *p.* on house of D.
*Mal.* 3:10 if I will not *p.* out
*Rev.* 16:1 *p.* out vials of wrath

**POURED.**

*Gen.* 28:18 Jacob *p.* oil on stone
35:14 Jacob *p.* a drink-offering
*Ex.* 9:33 rain not *p.* on earth
*Lev.* 4:12 ashes *p.* he sh. be burnt
8:12 Mo. *p.* oil on Aaron's head
21:10 on whose head oil was *p.*
*Num.* 28:7 *p.* to L. for drink-off.
*Deut.* 12:27 sacrifi. sh. be *p.* out
1 *Sam.* 1:15 I have *p.* out my soul
7:6 water, *p.* it out before Lord
10:1 Samuel *p.* oil on S.'s head
2 *Sam.* 23:16 Da. would not dri. but *p.* it, 1 *Chr.* 11:18
1 *K.* 13:3 and ashes *p.* out, 5
2 *K.* 3:11 *p.* wat. on hands of E.
4:5 ves. to her, and she *p.* out
16:13 Ahaz *p.* his drink-offering
2 *Chr.* 12:7 wrath not *p.* out on J.
34:21 wrath of Lord *p.* on us
25 there. wrath shall be *p.* out
*Job* 3:24 my roarings are *p.* out
10:10 thou *p.* me out as milk
29:6 rock *p.* me out rivers of oil
30:16 now my soul is *p.* out
*Ps.* 22:14 I am *p.* out like water
45:2 grace is *p.* into thy lips
77:17 clouds *p.* out water, skies
142:2 I *p.* out my complaint
*Cant.* 1:3 name is as ointment *p.*

*Is.* 26:16 *p.* out a prayer, when
29:10 Lord hath *p.* on you sleep
32:15 the Spirit be *p.* out on us
42:25 he hath *p.* on him the fury
53:12 *p.* out his soul to death
57:6 hast *p.* out a drink-offering
*Jer.* 7:20 my fury shall be *p.* out
19:13 *p.* out offerings, 32:29
*Jer.* 42:18 as fury, so sh. it be *p.*
44:6 mine anger was *p.* forth
19 wh. we *p.* drink-offerings
*Lam.* 2:4 *p.* fury like fire, 4:11
11 my liver is *p.* 12 soul *p.*
4:1 stones of sanctuary *p.* out
*Ezek.* 16:36 thy filthiness was *p.*
20:28 *p.* out their drink-offering
33 with fury *p.* out I rule, 34
22:22 I the Lord *p.* out my fury
31 therefore, I *p.* indignation
23:8 they *p.* their whoredom on
24:7 she *p.* it not on the ground
36:18 wherefore I *p.* out my fury
39:29 I *p.* out my Spirit on Isr.
*Dan.* 9:11 there. curse is *p.* on us
27 determ. sh. be *p.* on desol.
*Mic.* 1:4 waters *p.* down a steep
*Nah.* 1:6 fury is *p.* out like fire
*Zep.* 1:17 their blood be *p.* out
*Mat.* 26:7 *p.* oint. 12; *Mark* 14:3
*John* 2:15 he *p.* out the money
*Acts* 10:45 on Gentil. was *p.* gift
*Rev.* 14:10 wine of wrath of G. *p.*
16:2 *p.* out vial, 3, 4, 8, 10, 12

**POUREDST, ETH.**

*Job* 12:21 *p.* contempt on princes, *Ps.* 107:40
16:13 he *p.* out my gall on gro.
20 mine eye *p.* tears unto God
*Ps.* 75:8 wine is red, he *p.* out
*Prov.* 15:2 fools *p.* out foolishn.
28 the wicked *p.* out evil thi.
*Ezek.* 16:15 *p.* out thy fornicati.
*Amos* 5:8 *p.* out wat. on earth, 9:6
*John* 13:5 *p.* water into a basin

**POURING.**

*Ezek.* 9:8 destroy all in *p.* fury
*Luke* 10:34 his wounds, *p.* in oil

**POVERTY.**

*Gen.* 45:11 all th. hast come to *p.*
*Prov.* 6:11 *p.* co. as armed, 24:34
10:15 destruction of p. is th. *p.*
11:24 withhold. but tend. to *p.*
13:18 *p.* be to him that refuseth
20:13 not sleep, lest come to *p.*
23:21 drun. and glut. come to *p.*
28:19 vain persons, sh. have *p.*
22 considereth not *p.* sh. come
30:8 give me neit. *p.* nor riches
31:7 drink and forget his *p.*
2 *Cor.* 8:2 their deep *p.* abounded
9 ye thro' his *p.* might be rich
*Rev.* 2:9 I kn. thy works and *p.*

**POWDER, S.**

*Ex.* 32:20 Moses burnt calf to *p.*
*Deut.* 28:24 make rain of land *p.*
2 *K.* 23:6 stamped the grove to *p.*
15 stamp. alt. to *p.* 2 *Chr.* 34:7
*Cant.* 3:6 perfumed wi. all the *p.*
*Mat.* 21:44 grind to *p.* *Luke* 20:18

**POWER.**

*Gen.* 32:28 as a prince hast th. *p.*
49:3 dignity, excellency of *p.*
*Lev.* 26:19 I will break your *p.*
*Num.* 22:38 have I *p.* to say?
*Deut.* 4:37 bro. thee with his *p.*
8:18 it is he that giveth thee *p.*
32:36 wh. he seeth their *p.* gone
2 *Sam.* 22:33 my strength and *p.*
2 *K.* 19:26 inhabitan. of small *p.*
1 *Chr.* 20:1 Joab led forth the *p.*
29:11 thine is the *p.* *Mat.* 6:13
12 in thy hand is *p.* 2 *Chr.* 20:6
2 *Chr.* 25:8 God hath *p.* to help
32:9 and all his *p.* with him
*Ezr.* 4:23 made th. cease by *p.*
8:22 his *p.* ag. all that forsake
*Neh.* 5:5 nor is it in our *p.* to red.
*Est.* 1:3 feast to *p.* of Persia
8:11 cause to perish *p.* of people
9:1 the Jews hoped to have *p.*
*Job* 5:20 redeem in war from *p.*
24:22 draweth mighty with *p.*
26:2 him that is without *p.*?
12 divided the sea with his *p.*
14 his *p.* who can understand?
36:22 God exalteth by his *p.*
41:12 I will not conceal his *p.*
*Ps.* 22:20 darling from *p.* of dog
49:15 redeem soul fr. *p.* of grave
62:11 *p.* belongeth unto God
65:6 setteth fast mount. with *p.*
66:7 ruleth by his *p.* for ever
68:35 he giveth *p.* to his people
78:26 by *p.* he bro. south wind
90:11 who know. *p.* of th. ang.?
106:8 his mighty *p.* be known
111:6 showed people *p.* of works
150:1 praise in firma. of his *p.*
*Ec.* 4:1 side of oppressors was *p.*
5:19 hath given him *p.* to eat
6:2 God giveth him not *p.* to eat
8:4 word of a king is, there is *p.*
8 no man hath *p.* over spirit
*Is.* 37:27 inhabitants of small *p.*
*Is.* 40:29 he giv. *p.* to the faint
43:17 bring. forth army and *p.*
47:14 not deliver fr. *p.* of flame
*Jer.* 10:12 earth by his *p.* 51:15
*Ezek.* 22:6 their *p.* to shed blood
30:6 pride of her *p.* come down
*Dan.* 2:37 God hath given thee *p.*
6:27 delivered D. fr. *p.* of lions
8:6 fury of his *p.* 22 not in *p.*
24 his *p.* be mighty, not by *p.*
11:6 sh. not retain *p.* of his arm
25 shall stir up his *p.*
43 have *p.* over treas. of gold
12:7 scatter *p.* of the holy peop.
*Hos.* 12:3 by stren. had *p.* wi. G.
4 yea, he had *p.* over the angel
13:14 ransom th. from *p.* of gra.
*Mic.* 2:1 it is in *p.* of their hand
3:8 I am full of *p.* by the Spirit
*Hab.* 1:11 impu. his *p.* to his god
2:9 delivered from the *p.* of evil
3:4 there was hiding of his *p.*
*Zec.* 4:6 nor by *p.* but my Spirit
9:4 L. will smite her *p.* in sea
*Mat.* 9:6 hath *p.* to forgive sins, *Mark* 2:10; *Luke* 5:24
8 had given such *p.* to men
10:1 *p.* ag. uncl. spir. *Luke* 9:1
24:30 clouds with *p.* *Luke* 21:27
26:64 ri. hand of *p.* *Mark* 14:62
28:18 all *p.* is given me in heav.
*Mark* 3:15 *p.* to heal sickness.
9:1 kingd. of God come with *p.*
*Luke* 1:35 *p.* of Highest oversha.
4:6 said. All this *p.* will I give
32 for his word was with *p.*
36 with *p.* he command. spirits
5:17 *p.* of the Lord was present
10:19 I give you *p.* to tread on serp. and over *p.* of enemy
12:5 fear him that ha. *p.* to cast
20:20 deli. him to *p.* of governor
22:53 this is the *p.* of darkness
24:49 until ye be endued with *p.*
*John* 1:12 to them gave he *p.*
10:18 *p.* to lay it down, and *p.*
17:2 given him *p.* over all flesh
19:10 *p.* to crucify, *p.* to release
*Acts* 1:7 Fa. hath put in own *p.*
8 receive *p.* after Holy Ghost
3:12 by our own *p.* or holiness
4:7 by what *p.* ha. ye done this?
5:4 was it not in thine own *p.*?
6:8 Stephen full of faith and *p.*
8:19 say. Give me also this *p.*
10:38 anointed Jesus with *p.*
26:18 turn them fr. *p.* of Satan
*Rom.* 1:4 to be Son of G. wi. *p.*
20 his eternal *p.* and Godhead
9:21 hath not pot. *p.* over clay?
13:2 whosoever resisteth the *p.*
3 wilt thou not be afraid of *p.*?
15:13 through *p.* of Holy Ghost
19 by the *p.* of the Spi. of God
16:25 now to him that is of *p.*
1 *Cor.* 2:4 in demonstration of *p.*
4:19 not kn. speech, but the *p.*
5:4 with *p.* of our L. J. Christ
6:12 not be bro. under *p.* of any
14 raise us up by his own *p.*
7:4 wife and husb. have not *p.*
9:4 ha. we not *p.* to eat and dr.?
5 have not we *p.* to lead wife?
12 if oth. be partak. of this *p.* over you, we ha. not used *p.*
11:10 wom. ought to have *p.*
15:24 put down author. and *p.*
2 *Cor.* 4:7 excel. of *p.* be of God
8:3 to *p.* yea, beyond their *p.*
12:9 that the *p.* of Ch. may rest
13:10 according to *p.* G. given
*Eph.* 1:19 exceeding greatness of his *p.* work. of his mighty *p.*
21 above princi. *p.* and might
2:2 accord. to prince of *p.* of air
3:7 the effectual work of his *p.*
20 accord. to *p.* that worketh
*Phil.* 3:10 know the *p.* of resur.
*Col.* 1:11 accord. to his glori. *p.*
13 deliv. us from *p.* of darkn.
2:10 head of all princi. and *p.*
2 *Thes.* 1:9 pun. fr. glory of his *p.*
11 fulfil work of faith with *p.*
2:9 working of Satan wi. all *p.*
3:9 not because we have not *p.*
1 *Tim.* 6:16 wh. be honor and *p.*
2 *Tim.* 1:7 G. hath giv. sp. of *p.*
3:5 hav. godliness, denying *p.*
*Heb.* 1:3 by word of his *p.*
2:14 destroy him that had *p.*
7:16 after *p.* of an endless life
2 *Pet.* 1:3 *p.* given all things
16 made known *p.* of our Lord
*Jude* 25 to our Sav. glory and *p.*
*Rev.* 2:26 give *p.* over nations
4:11 worthy to receive *p.* 5:12
5:13 honor and *p.* be to him
6:4 *p.* was given to him
*Rev.* 6:8 *p.* giv. th. over 4th part
7:12 *p.* and might be giv. to G.
9:3 to them was given *p.*
10 their *p.* was to hurt men
19 their *p.* is in their mouth
11:3 give *p.* to my 2 witnesses
6 *p.* to shut heav. *p.* over wat.
12:10 now is *p.* of his Ch. come
13:2 the dragon gave him *p.* 4
5 *p.* was given to continue, 7
12 he exercis. *p.* of first beast
15 *p.* give life; 14:18 *p.* ov. fire
15:8 filled with smoke from *p.*
16:8 *p.* giv. him to scorch men
9 blasphemed G. who hath *p.*
17:12 receive *p.* as kings
13 give their *p.* and strength
19:1 glory, honor, and *p.* to L.

**POWER of God.**

*Mat.* 22:29 not know. scriptures nor *p. of God*, *Mark* 12:24
*Luke* 9:43 amazed at *p. of God*
22:69 sit on right of *p. of God*
*Acts* 8:10 man is great *p. of God*
*Rom.* 1:16 gospel is the *p. of God*
1 *Cor.* 1:18 saved, it is *p. of God*
24 Christ the *p. of God*
2:5 not stand but by *p. of God*
2 *Cor.* 6:7 of truth, by *p. of God*
13:4 he liveth by *p. of God*, we sh. live with him by *p. of G.*
2 *Tim.* 1:8 according to *p. of G.*
1 *Pet.* 1:5 by *p. of G.* thro' faith
*See* GREAT.

**In POWER.**

*Gen.* 31:29 *in p.* of my hand
*Ex.* 15:6 ri. hand glorious *in p.*
*Job* 21:7 why are wick. mi. *in p.*?
37:23 excellent *in p.* and judg.

Prov. 3:27 it is in p. of thy hand
18:21 and life in p. of tongue
Is. 40:26 that he is strong in p.
Nah. 1:3 slow to anger, gr. in p.
Luke 1:17 go before him in p.
4:14 Jesus returned in p. of Sp.
1 Cor. 4:20 not in word, but in p.
15:43 sown in weakn. rai. in p.
Eph. 6:10 strong in Lord and p.
1 Thes 1:5 in word and in p.
2 Pet. 2.11 angels greater in p.

**My POWER.**

Gen. 31:6 wi. all my p. I served
Ex. 9:16 to show in thee my p.
Deut. 8:17 my p. got. me wealth
Dan. 4:30 Babyl. built by my p.
Rom. 9:17 I might show my p.
1 Cor. 9:18 I abuse not my p.

**No POWER.**

Ex. 21:8 he shall have no p.
Lev. 26:37 have no p. to stand
1 Sam. 30:4 had no p. to weep
2 Chr. 14:11 help them ha. no p.
22:9 house of Ahaziah had no p.
Is. 50:2 have I no p. to deliver?
Dan. 3:27 on bodi. fire had no p.
8:7 there was no p. in the ram
John 19:11 ha. no p. against me
Rom. 13:1 th. is no p. but of God
Rev. 20:6 second death hath no p.

**Thy POWER.**

Deut. 9:29 brought. out by thy p.
Job 1:12 all th. he hath is in t. p.
Ps. 21:13 sing, and praise thy p.
59:11 scat. by t. p. 16 sing t. p.
63:2 to see t. p. and thy glory
66:5 through greatness of thy p.
71:18 t. p. to ev. one is to come
79:11 accord. to greatn. of t. p.
110:3 be willing in day of t. p.
145:11 they shall talk of thy p.
Nah. 2:1 fortify thy p. mightily

**POWERFUL.**

Ps. 29:4 the voice of the L. is p.
2 Cor. 10:10 for his letters are p.
Heb. 4:12 word of G. is quick, p.

**POWERS.**

Mat. 24:29 p. of heaven shall be sh. Mark 13:25; Luke 21:26
Luke 12:11 when brought bef. p.
Rom. 8:38 nor p. can sepa. fr. G.
13:1 p that be ordained of God
Eph. 3:10 p. in heavenly places
6:12 against principalit. and p.
Col. 1:16 p. were created by him
2:15 hav. spoiled p. made show
Tit. 3:1 to be subject to p.
Heb. 6:5 tasted p. of the world
1 Pet. 3:22 right hand of God p.

**PRACTICES.**

2 Pet. 2:14 exercised with cov. p.

**PRACTISE.**

Ps. 141:4 not to p. wicked works
Is. 32:6 the vile sh. p. hypocrisy
Dan. 8:24 shall destroy, and p.
Mic. 2:1 morning is light they p.

**PRACTISED.**

1 Sam. 23:9 S. secretly p. misc.
Dan. 8:12 lit. horn p. and prosp.

**PRAISE, Substantive.**

Deut. 10:21 thy p. and thy God
26:19 to make thee high in p.
Jud. 5:3 I will sing p. to the L. God of Israel, Ps. 7:17; 9:2; 57:7; 61:8; 104:33
1 Chr. 16:35 may glory in thy p.
2 Chr. 23:13 taught to sing p.
Neh. 9:5 who is exalted above p.
12:46 days of D. we. songs of p.
Ps. 9:14 I may show all thy p.
22:25 my p. shall be of thee
30:12 glory may sing p. to thee
33:1 for p. is comely for upright
34:1 his p. shall be in my mou.
35:28 shall speak of thy p.
40:3 p. to God, 42:4 voice of p.
48:10 thy p. to ends of earth
50:23 whoso offereth p. glorifie.
51:15 my mouth sh. show thy p.
65:1 p. waiteth for thee, O God
66:2 and make his p. glorious
8 make voice of his p. be hea.
71:6 my p. shall be continually
8 mouth be filled with thy p.
79:13 show thy p. 98:4 sing p.
100:4 enter his courts with p.
102:21 dec. his p. in Jerusalem
106:2 who can show all his p.?
12 sang p. 47 triumph in p.
108:1 I will sing, and give p.
109:1 G. of my p. 111:10 p. end.
119:171 my lips shall utter p.
138:1 before gods will I sing p.
145:21 mouth sh. speak p. of L.
147:1 p. is comely; 7 sing p. on
148:14 exalteth the p. of saints
149:1 sing his p. in congregati.
Prov. 27:21 so is man to p.
Is. 42:8 not give p. to images
10 sing his p. from end of ear.
12 declare his p. in the islands
43:21 they sh. show forth my p.
48:9 and for my p. will I refrain
60:18 thou shalt call thy gat. P.
61:3 garment of p. for heaviness
11 L. will cause p. to sp. forth
62:7 make Jerusa. a p. in earth
Jer. 13:11 might be to me a p.
17:14 O Lord, thou art my p.
26 bring. sacrifices of p. 33:11
33:9 shall be to me a joy, a p.
48:2 shall be no more p. of Mo.
51:41 how is p. of earth surpr.?
Hab. 3:3 earth was full of his p.
Zep. 3:19 get them p. and fame
20 make you a p. am. all peo.
Mat. 21:16 thou hast perfect. p.
Luke 18:43 they saw it, gave p.
John 9:24 give G. the p.
12:43 p. of men more than p. G.
Rom. 2:29 whose p. is not of m.
13:3 thou shalt have p. of same
1 Cor. 4:5 ev. man have p. of G.
2 Cor. 8:18 whose p. is in gospel
Eph. 1:6 predestinat. to p. of gl.
12 p. of gl. who trusted in C. 14
Phil. 1:11 J. C. to p. and gl. of G.
4:8 if any p. think on th. things
Heb. 2:12 in church will I sing p.
13:15 let us offer sacrifice of p.
1 Pet. 1:7 might be found to p.
2:14 for p. of them that do well
4:11 to whom be p. for ever

**PRAISE, Verb.**

Gen. 49:8 he whom breth. sh. p.
Lev. 19:24 fruit holy to p. Lord
1 Chr. 29:13 p. thy glorious name
2 Chr. 8:14 Lev. to p. bef. prie.
20:21 sho. p. beauty of holiness
31:2 p. in gates of tents of L.
Ps. 21:13 so will we sing and p.
22:23 ye that fear Lord p. him
30:9 shall the dust p. thee?
42:5 I shall yet p. him, 11; 43:5
44:8 in G. we boast, p. name
45:17 there. shall people p. thee
49:18 men p. thee, wh. doest w.
63:3 lips sh. p. thee; 5 mou. p.
67:3 let peop. praise th. 5 pe. p.
69:34 heaven and earth p. him
71:14 I will yet p. thee more
74:21 poor and needy p. name
76:10 wrath of man sh. p. thee
88:10 sh. dead arise and p. th.?
89:5 heavens sh. p. thy wonders
99:3 let them p. thy great name
107:32 p. him in assem. of elders
113:1 p. him, O serv. of L. 135:1
115:17 dead p. not the Lord
119:164 seven ti. a day I p. thee
175 let my soul live, it sh. p.
138:2 I will p. thy name for thy
4 kings of earth shall p. thee
Ps. 142:7 br. out of pris. that I p.
145:4 genera. sh. p. thy works
10 thy works shall p. thee, O
147:12 p. L. Jeru. p. G. O Zion
148:1 p. ye L. p. him in heights
2 p. him, angels, p. him, host
3 p. sun and moon, p. ye stars
4 p. him, ye heaven of heavens
149:3 let them p. name in dance
150:1 p. G. in sanctu. p. him in
2 p. him for his acts, p. him
3 p. with trump; 4 p. timbrel
5 p. him on sounding cymbals
Prov. 27:2 let anot. man p. thee
28:4 forsake the law p. wicked
31:31 let her own works p. her
Is. 38:18 grave cannot p. thee
19 the living he shall p. thee
Jer. 31:7 p. ye and say, O Lord
Dan. 2:23 I thank and p. thee
4:37 I p. and extol K. of heaven
Joel 2:26 p. the name of the Lord
Luke 19:37 disci. began to p. G.
1 Cor. 11:2 p. you, that ye reme.
17 in this I p. you not, 22
Rev. 19:5 saying, p. our God

**I will, or will I PRAISE.**

Gen. 29:35 Leah said, I will p.
Ps. 7:17 I will p. the Lord
9:1 I w. p. thee, 111:1; 138:1
22:22 in congrega. w. I p. thee
28:7 with my song w. I p. him
35:18 I w. p. am. much people, 57:9; 108:3; 109:30
43:4 on harp will I p. thee, O G.
52:9 I will p. thee for ever.
54:6 I w. p. thy name, O Lord
56:4 in G. w. I p. his word, 10
69:30 I w. p. the name of God
71:22 I w. p. thee with psaltery
86:12 I w. p. thee, O L. my God
118:19 I w. go into them, p. L.
21 I w. p. thee, thou heard me
28 thou art my God, I w. p. th.
119:7 I w. p. thee with uprigh.
139:14 I w. p. thee I am wond.
145:2 I w. p. thy name for ever
Is. 12:1 I w. p. thee though thou
25:1 I w. p. thy name

**PRAISE ye the Lord, or PRAISE the Lord.**

Jud. 5:2 p. ye t. L. for aven. Isr.
1 Chr. 16:4 appoi. Lev. to p. t. L.
25:3 with a harp to p. the L.
2 Chr. 20:21 p. t. L. for his mer.
Ezr. 3:10 cymbals to p. t. L.
Ps. 22:26 sh. p. t. L. seek him
32:2 p. t. L. with harp
102:18 peo. created shall p. t. L.
104:35 p. ye the L. 106:1. 48; 111:1; 112:1; 113:1. 9; 115:18; 116:19; 117:2; 135:1; 146:1, 10; 147:20; 148:1, 14; 149:1, 9; 150:1, 6; Jer. 20:13
107:8 O that men would p. t. L. 15, 21, 31
109:30 I will greatly p. t. Lord
118:19 I will p. L. 135:3 p. Lord
146:2 while I live will I p. t. L.
147:1 p. ye the L. for it is good
12 p. t. L. O Jerus. praise God
148:7 p. t. L. from the earth
Is. 12:4 p. t. L. call upon name
62:9 shall eat it, and p. t. L.
Jer. 33:11 p. the Lord of hosts
Rom. 15:11 p. t. L. all ye Gentil.

**PRAISED.**

Jud. 16:24 people p. Dagon
2 Sam. 14:25 none to be so m. p.
22:4 worthy to be p. Ps. 18:3
1 Chr. 16:25 L. is greatly to be p. Ps. 48:1; 96:4; 145:3
36 all the people p. the Lord
23:5 four thousand p. the Lord, 2 Chr. 7:3; Neh. 5:13

2 Chr. 5:13 with instrum. p. L.
7:6 David p. by their ministry
30:21 Levites and priests p. L.
Ezr. 3:11 shout when th. p. L.
Ps. 72:15 daily shall he be p.
113:3 from rising of sun L. be p.
Prov. 31:30 feareth L. sh. be p.
Ec. 4:2 I p. dead more than liv.
Cant. 6:9 queens and concu. p.
Is. 64:11 wh. our fathers p. thee
Dan. 4:34 I p. and honored him
5:4 they p. the gods of gold, 23
Luke 1:64 and Zacharias p. God

**PRAISES.**

Ex. 15:11 who is like th. in p.?
2 Sam. 22:50 sing p. to thy name,
Ps. 18:49; 92:1; 135:3
2 Chr. 29:30 commanded Lev. to
sing p. to Lord, they sang p.
Ps. 9:11 sing p. to the Lord in Z.
22:3 O thou that inhabitest p.
Ps. 27:6 yea, I will sing p. to G.
47:6; 68:32; 75:9; 108:3
47:7 sing p. with understanding
56:12 render p. to thee, 144:9
68:4 sing to G. p. to his name
78:4 to genera. to come p. of L.
146:2 I will sing p. to my God
147:1 good to sing p. to our G
149:3 sing p. to him with timb.
6 let p. of God be in mouths
Is. 60:6 show forth p. of the L.
63:7 I will mention p. of Lord
Acts 16:25 Paul and Silas sang p
1 Pet. 2:9 show forth p. of him

**PRAISETH.**

Prov. 31:28 her husb. also, p. her

**PRAISING.**

2 Chr. 5:13 sound heard in p. L.
23:12 Athaliah heard people p.
Ezr. 3:11 they sang in p. Lord
Ps. 84:4 will be still p. thee
Luke 2:13 heavenly host p. God
20 shepherds returned p. God
24:53 contin. in temple p. God
Acts 2:47 eat with gladn. p. G.
3:8 and leaping, and p. God, 9

**PRANCING, S.**

Jud. 5:22 broken by means of p.
Nah. 3:2 the noise of p. horses

**PRATING.**

Prov. 10:8 a p. fool shall fall, 10
3 John 10 p. ag. us with malicio.

**PRAY.**

Gen. 20:7 he shall p. for thee
1 Sam. 7:5 S. said, I will p. for y.
12:19 p. for thy servants to L.
23 I should sin in ceasing to p.
2 Sam. 7:27 in his heart to p.
1 K. 8:30 when they p. 35, 42, 44,
48; 2 Chr. 6:26, 34, 38
13:6 p. th. my hand be restored
2 Chr. 6:24 p. make supplica. 32
37 p. in land of their captivity
7:14 if my people shall p.
Ezr. 6:10 p. for life of the king
Neh. 1:6 hear prayer which I p.
Job 21:15 profit if we p. to him?
33:26 p. to G. he will be favor.
42:8 serv. Job shall p. for you
Ps. 5:2 my God, to thee will I p.
55:17 morn. and noon will I p.
122:6 p. for peace of Jerusalem
Is. 16:12 come to sanctuary to p.
45:20 p. to a god cannot save
Jer. 7:16 therefore p. not thou
for this people, 11:14; 14:11
29:7 peace of city, p. to Lord
12 p. to me, and I will hearken
37:3 p. now to the L. 42:2, 20
42:4 p. to the L. your God
Zec. 7:2 sent men to p. before L.
8:21 speedily p. before Lord, 22
Mat. 5:44 p. for them which de-
spitefully use, Luke 16:27
6:5 for they love to p. standing
6 p. to Father which is in sec.
9 after this manner p. ye
9:38 p. L. of harvest, Luke 10:2
14:23 he went to a mount. to p.
Mark 6:46; Luke 6:12; 9:28
19:13 put hands on them and p.
24:20 p. your flight be not in
winter, Mark 13:18
26:36 go p. yonder, Mark 14:32
41 watch and p. Mark 13:33.
14:38; Luke 21:36; 22:40, 46
53 think. thou that I cannot p.
Mark 5:17 and they began to p.
11:24 what ye desire when ye p.
Luke 11:1 Lord, teach us to p.
2 he said to them, When ye p.
18:1 men ought always to p.
10 two men went to tem. to p.
John 14:16 I will p. Fath. 16:26
17:9 I p. for th. p. not for world
15 I p. not that thou take them
20 nor p. I for these alone
Acts 8:22 p. God if perh. thought
24 Simon said, p. ye to the L.
10:9 P. went on house-top to p.
Rom. 8:26 kn. not what we p. for
1 Cor. 11:13 wom. p. uncovered?
14:13 let him p. that he interpr.
14 if I p. in unknown tongue
15 p. with sp. p. with underst.
2 Cor. 5:20 ambassa. for C. we p.
13:7 I p. to G. that ye do no ev.
Phil. 1:9 this I p. that your love
Col. 1:9 we do not cease to p.
1 Thes. 5:17 p. without ceasing
23 I p. G. your sp. be preserv.
25 brethren, p. for us, 2 Thes.
3:1; Heb. 13:18
2 Thes 1:11 we p. always for you
1 Tim. 2:8 I will that men p.
2 Tim. 4:16 I p. God it be not l.
Jam. 5:13 any afflicted? let hi. p.
14 and let them p. over him
16 confess your faults, and p.
1 John 5:16 I do not say he sh. p.

**PRAYED.**

Gen. 20:17 Abraham p. God
Num. 11:2 Mo. p. fire quenched
21:7 M. p. for people, Deut. 9:26
Deut. 9:20 I p. for Aa. same time
1 Sam. 1:10 Hannah p. to L. 21
27 for this child I p. 8:6 Sam.
2 K. 4:33 Elisha p. L. 6:17, 18
19:15 Hezekiah p. before Lord
20:2; 2 Chr. 30:18; 32:24
2 Chr. 32:20 Isaiah p. 33:13 Ma.
Job 42:10 captivity when Job p.
Jer. 32:16 Jeremiah p. unto L.
Dan. 6:10 D. p. 3 ti. a day, 9:4
Jon. 2:1 Jonah p. to L. 4:2
Mat. 26:39 Je. fell and p. 42:44;
Mark 14:35, 39; Luke 22:41
Mark 1:35 solitary place and p.
Luke 5:3 Jesus p. him he would
16 withdrew into wilde. and p.
9:29 as he p. countenance alter.
18:11 the Pharisee stood and p.
22:32 I p. that thy faith fail not
44 agony he p. more earnestly
John 4:31 his disciples p. him
Acts 1:24 the disciples p. and sa.
4:31 when they had p. the place
8:15 Peter and John p. for them
9:40 Peter p. 10:2 Cornel. p. 30
10:48 then they p. him to tarry
13:3 had fasted and p. 14:23
16:9 p. him, saying, Come to M.
25 at midnight Paul and S. p.
20:36 Paul kneeled down and p.
21:5 we kneeled on shore and p.
22:17 while I p. in the temple
28:8 to whom P. entered and p.
Jam. 5:17 E. p. it mi. not rain, 18

**PRAYER.**

2 Sam. 7:27 pray this p. to thee
1 K. 8:28 respect p. of thy serv.
45 hear thou in heaven their p.
49; 2 Chr. 6:35, 39, 40
54 made end of praying this p.
2 K. 19:4 p. for remnant, Is. 37:4
2 Chr. 7:15 ears be attent to p.
30:27 their p. came to dwelling
33:18 Manasseh's p. how G. 19
Neh. 1:6 thou mayest hear the p.
4:9 nevertheless we made our p.
Job 15:4 yea, thou restrainest p.
22:27 shalt make thy p. to him
Ps. 65:2 O thou that hearest p.
72:15 p. shall be made for him
80:4 how long be angry ag. p.?
102:17 he will regard p. of desti.
109:4 but I gave myself unto p.
7 and let his p. become sin
Prov. 15:8 p. of upri. is delight
29 heareth the p. of righteous
28:9 his p. shall be abomination
Is. 26:16 poured out a p.
56:7 joyfully in my house of p.
for my house shall be called
a house of p. Mat. 21:13;
Mark 11:17; Luke 19:46
Jer. 7:16 lift up cry nor p. 11:14
Lam. 3:44 p. should not pass
Dan. 9:3 set face to L. seek by p.
17 God, hear p. of thy servant
Hab. 3:1 a p. of Ha. the prophet
Mat. 17:21 not out but by p. and
fasting, Mark 9:29
Luke 1:13 Zacharias, thy p. hea.
Acts 3:1 temple at hour of p.
6:4 we will give ourselves to p.
10:31 Cornelius, thy p. is heard
12:5 p. made without ceasing
16:13 p. was wont be made
1 Cor. 7:5 give yourselves to p.
2 Cor. 1:11 helping by p. for us
9:14 by their p. for you, which
Eph. 6:18 praying with all p.
Phil. 1:4 in every p. of mine
19 turn to my salvat. thro' p.
4:6 by p. let requests be known
1 Tim. 4:5 it is sanctified by p.
Jam. 5:15 p. of faith shall save
16 p. of a righteous man avail.
1 Pet. 4:7 be sober, watch un. p.

See HEARD.

**In PRAYER.**

Neh. 11:17 Mattan. began in p.
Dan. 9:21 I was speaking in p.
Mat. 21:22 whate. ye ask in p.
Luke 6:12 contin. all night in p.
Acts 1:14 they continued in p.
Rom. 12:12 contin. instant in p.
Col. 4:2 continue in p. watch

**My PRAYER.**

Job 16:17 in mine hands: also
my p. is pure
Ps. 4:1 have mercy, hear my p.
17:1; 39:12; 54:2
5:3 in morn. will I direct my p.
6:9 the Lord will receive my p.
35:13 my p. returned to bosom
42:8 my p. to God of my life
55:1 give ear unto my p. O God
61:1 attend to my p. 64:1; 84:8;
86:6; 102:1; 143:1
66:19 attended to voice of my p.
20 God hath not turned my p.
69:13 my p. is to thee
88:2 let my p. come before th.
13 in morn. sh. my p. prev. th.
141:2 let my p. be set bef. thee
5 my p. shall be in their calam.
Lam. 3:8 he shutteth out my p.
Jon. 2:7 my p. came to thee
Rom. 10:1 my p. to G. for Is. is

**PRAYERS.**

Ps. 72:20 p. of David are ended
Is. 1:15 when ye make many p.
Mat. 23:14 for pretence making
long p. Mark 12:40; Luke
20:47

*Luke* 2:37 Anna continued in *p.*
5:33 disciples of John make *p.*?
*Acts* 2:42 breaking bread, and *p.*
10:4 thy *p.* are come up bef. G.
*Rom.* 1:9 I make mention of you
in my *p.* *Eph.* 1:16; 1 *Thes.*
1:2; 2 *Tim.* 1:3; *Phile.* 4.
15:30 strive with me in your *p.*
*Col.* 4:12 Epaphras labor. in *p.*
1 *Tim.* 2:1 I exh. that *p.* be made
5:5 widow indeed continu. in *p.*
*Phile.* 22 thro' your *p.* be given
*Heb.* 5:7 when he had offered *p.*
1 *Pet.* 3:7 that your *p.* be not
12 his ear is open to their *p.*
*Rev.* 5:8 which are *p.* of saints
8:3 offer it with *p.* of saints, 4

**PRAYEST.**

*Mat.* 6:5 when thou *p.* be not, 6.

**PRAYETH, ING.**

1 *Sam.* 1:12 as Hannah contin. *p.*
1 *K.* 8:28 hearken to prayer wh.
thy servant *p.* 2 *Chr.* 6:19, 20
*Is.* 44:17 he worshippeth it, *p.*
*Dan.* 6:11 these found Daniel *p.*
9:20 I was speaking, and *p.*
*Mark* 11:25 when ye stand *p.*
*Luke* 1:10 people were *p.* with.
3:21 Jes. *p.* the heaven opened
9:18 as he was alone *p.*
11:1 he was *p.* in certain place
*Acts* 9:11 beh. he *p.* 11:5 I was *p.*
12:12 many were together *p.*
1 *Cor.* 11:4 every man *p.* with his
14:14 my spirit *p.* but my und.
2 *Cor.* 8:4 *p.* us to rec. the gift
*Eph.* 6:18 *p.* always in the Spirit
*Col.* 1:3 *p.* for you; 4:3 *p.* for us
1 *Thes.* 3:10 night and day *p.*
*Jude* 20 ye *p.* in the Holy Ghost

**PREACH.**

*Neh.* 6:7 appoint. prophets to *p.*
*Is.* 61:1 hath anointed me to *p.*
*Jon.* 3:2 *p.* to it preaching I bid
*Mat.* 4:17 fr. that Je. began to *p.*
10:27 what ye hear, that *p.* upon
11:1 he departed thence to *p.*
*Mark* 1:4 John did *p.* baptism
3:14 send th. forth to *p.* *Luke* 9:2
*Luke* 4:18 to *p.* deliverance, 19
9:60 go and *p.* kingdom of God
*Acts* 5:42 ceased not to *p.* J. C.
10:42 he commanded us to *p.*
15:21 in every city them that *p.*
16:6 forbidden by H. Ghost to *p.*
17:3 Je. whom I *p.* to you is C.
*Rom.* 10:8 word of faith wh. we *p.*
15 how shall they *p.* exc. sent?
1 *Cor.* 1:23 we *p.* Christ crucified
9:16 tho' I *p.* the gospel, I have
noth. to glory, woe if I *p.* not
15:11 so we *p.* so ye believed
2 *Cor.* 4:5 we *p.* not ourselves
*Gal.* 2:2 the gospel which I *p.*
5:11 breth. if I yet *p.* circumci.
*Eph.* 3:8 I should *p.* am. Gent.
*Phil.* 1:15 some indeed *p.* Christ
16 one *p.* Christ of contention
*Col.* 1:28 we *p.* warning every
2 *Tim.* 4:2 *p.* the word, be inst.

**PREACHED.**

*Ps.* 40:9 I have *p.* righteousness
*Mat.* 11:5 poor have the gospel *p.*
*Mark* 1:7 John *p.* saying, There
39 he *p.* in their synagogues
2:2 he *p.* the word to them
6:12 *p.* that men should repent
16:20 went and *p.* every where
*Luke* 3:18 many others thi. *p.* he
16:16 the kingdom of God is *p.*
24:47 remission of sin sho. be *p.*
*Acts* 3:20 J. C. who before was *p.*
4:2 *p.* thro' J. the resurrection
8:5 *p.* C. to Samaria; 35 *p.* Jes.
25 *p.* the word of L. *p.* gospel
40 Philip *p.* in all cities till he
9:20 Saul *p.* C. in synagogues
10:37 baptism which John *p.*
13:5 they *p.* the word of God
24 when John had first *p.* bef.
38 *p.* to you forgiveness of sins
42 that th. words might be *p.*
15:36 let us visit wh. we ha. *p.*
17:13 word of G. was *p.* of Paul
18 he *p.* J. and the resurrect.
20:7 Paul *p.* ready to depart
1 *Cor.* 9:27 lest wh. I *p.* to others
15:2 keep in memory what I *p.*
12 if C. be *p.* that he rose
2 *Cor.* 1:19 J. who was *p.* am. you
11:4 Jes. whom we have not *p.*
*Gal.* 1:8 oth. gospel th. we ha. *p.*
*Eph.* 2:17 and *p.* peace to you
*Phil.* 1:18 Christ *p.* and I rejoice
*Col.* 1:23 was *p.* to every creature
1 *Tim.* 3:1 *p.* unto the Gentiles
*Heb.* 4:2 word *p.* did not profit
6 they to whom it was first *p.*
1 *Pet.* 3:19 *p.* to spirits in prison
*See* GOSPEL.

**PREACHER.**

*Ec.* 1:1 words of *p.* son of David
12 I the *p.* was king over Isr.
12:9 because *p.* was wise
10 the *p.* sought to find words
*Rom.* 10:14 hear without a *p.*?
1 *Tim.* 2:7 ord. a *p.* 2 *Tim.* 1:11
2 *Pet.* 2:5 Noah, *p.* of righteous.

**PREACHEST, ETH, ING.**

*Jon.* 3:2 preach to it the *p.* I bid
*Mat.* 3:1 came John *p.* *Luke* 3:3
12:41 at *p.* of Jonas, *Luke* 11:32
*Luke* 8:1 *p.* and showing tidings
9:6 through towns *p.* the gospel
*Acts* 8:4 went every where *p.*
12 *p.* concern. kingdom of G.
10:36 *p.* peace by Jesus Christ
11:19 *p.* word to none but Jews
19:13 by Jesus, whom Paul *p.*
20:9 as P. was long *p.* Eutychus
25 among wh. I have gone *p.*
28:31 *p.* the kingdom of God
*Rom.* 2:21 *p.* a man sho. not steal
16:25 according to *p.* of Jesus
1 *Cor.* 1:18 *p.* of cross is foolish.
21 by foolishness of *p.* to save
2:4 my *p.* was not with enticing
15:14 if C. not risen, our *p.* vain
2 *Cor.* 10:14 come to you *p.* gos.
11:4 cometh *p.* another Jesus
*Gal.* 1:23 he *p.* faith he destroyed
2 *Tim.* 4:17 by me *p.* might be
*Tit.* 1:3 manif. his word thro' *p.*

**PRECEPT, S.**

*Neh.* 9:14 commandedst them *p.*
*Ps.* 119:4 com. us to keep thy *p.*
15 I will meditate in thy *p.* 78
27 make me to understand *p.*
40 I have longed after thy *p.*
45 seek *p.* 87 forsook not *p.*
56 bec. I kept thy *p.* 100, 168
63 I will keep thy *p.* 69, 134
93 I will never forget thy *p*
94 I have sought thy *p.*
104 thro' thy *p.* I get underst.
110 yet I erred not from thy *p.*
128 theref. I esteem all thy *p.*
141 yet do not I forget thy *p.*
159 consider how I love thy *p.*
173 I have chosen thy *p.*
*Is.* 28:10 *p.* upon *p.* *p.* on *p.* 13
29:13 fear taught by *p.* of men
*Jer.* 35:18 ye kept all Jonad. *p.*
*Dan.* 9:5 rebelled, dep. fr. thy *p.*
*Mark* 10:5 he wrote you this *p.*
*Heb.* 9:19 Moses had spok. ev. *p.*

**PRECIOUS.**

*Gen.* 24:53 to R.'s mother *p.* thi.
*Deut.* 33:13 for *p.* things of heav.
14 for *p.* fruits brought forth
15 for the *p.* things of the hills
16 for *p.* things of the earth
1 *Sam.* 3:1 word of Lord was *p.*
26:21 my soul *p.* in thine eyes
2 *K.* 1:13 let my life be *p.* 14
20:13 Hezekiah showed them *p.*
things, *Is.* 39:2
2 *Chr.* 20:25 and *p.* jewels, which
21:3 Jehoshaphat gave *p.* thin
*Ezr.* 1:6 streng. with *p.* things
*Job* 28:10 seeth every *p.* thing
16 cannot be val. with *p.* onyx
*Ps.* 49:8 redemption of soul is *p.*
72:14 and *p.* shall their blood be
116:15 *p.* in sight of L. is death
126:6 goeth forth bear. *p.* seed
133:2 it is like the *p.* ointment
*Ps.* 139:17 how *p.* thy thoughts
*Prov.* 1:13 sh. find *p.* substance
3:15 wis. is more *p.* than rubies
6:26 adulteress hunt for *p.* life
12:27 subst. of a dili. man is *p.*
20:15 lips of knowl. a *p.* jewel
24:4 cham. filled with *p.* riches
*Ec.* 7:1 a g. name bet. th. *p.* oin.
*Is.* 13:12 man more *p.* than gold
28:16 I lay in Zion a *p.* corner-
stone, 1 *Pet.* 2:6
43:4 thou wast *p.* in my sight
*Jer.* 15:19 take *p.* from the vile
20:5 I will deliver the *p.* things
*Lam.* 4:2 the *p.* sons of Zion
*Ezek.* 22:25 ha. taken *p.* things
27:20 merchant in *p.* clothes
*Dan.* 11:8 carry away th. *p.* ves.
43 power over all *p.* things
*Jam.* 5:7 waiteth for the *p.* fruit
1 *Pet.* 1:7 more *p.* than gold
19 but with *p.* blood of Christ
2:4 stone chosen of God, and *p.*
7 to you which believe he is *p.*
2 *Pet.* 1:1 obtained like *p.* fruit
4 exceed. great and *p.* prom.
*Rev.* 18:12 no man buyeth *p.* ves.
21:11 light was like a stone *p.*

**PREDESTINATE, ED.**

*Rom.* 8:29 did foreknow. did *p.*
30 wh. he did *p.* them he call.
*Eph.* 1:5 hav. *p.* us to adoption
11 *p.* according to purpose

**PRE-EMINENCE.**

*Ec.* 3:19 man hath no *p.* above
*Col.* 1:18 that he might have *p.*
3 *John* 9 Diot. loveth to have *p.*

**PREFER, ED, ING.**

*Est.* 2:9 *p.* her and her maidens
*Ps.* 137:6 if I *p.* not J. above joy
*Dan.* 6:3 Daniel was *p.* ab. pres.
*John* 1:15 com. after me is *p.* 27
30 who is *p.* before me
*Rom.* 12:10 in honor *p.* one ano.
1 *Tim.* 5:21 without *p.* one bef.

**PREMEDITATE.**

*Mark* 13:11 neither *p.* whatsoev.

**PREPARATION, S.**

1 *Chr.* 22:5 I will make *p.* for it
*Prov.* 16:1 *p.* of heart of man
*Nah.* 2:3 torches in day of *p.*
*Mat.* 27:62 day that followed the
day of *p.* *Mark* 15:42; *Luke*
23:54; *John* 19:14, 31, 42
*Eph.* 6:15 shod with *p.* of gospel

**PREPARE.**

*Ex.* 15:2 I will *p.* him a habitat.
*Num.* 15:5 a drink-offering *p.*
12 accor. to number ye sh. *p.*
23:1 B. said, *p.* me seven oxen
29 build altars, *p.* 7 bullocks
*Deut.* 19:3 shalt *p.* thee a way
*Jos.* 1:11 *p.* your victuals
22:26 let us *p.* to build altar
1 *Sam.* 7:3 *p.* your hearts to L.
1 *Chr.* 9:32 to *p.* show-bread
29:18 O L. God, *p.* their heart
2 *Chr.* 2:9 *p.* timber in abund.
35:6 sanctify yourselves, and *p.*
*Job* 8:8 *p.* thyself to the search
11:13 *p.* thy heart toward him
27:16 *p.* raiment; 17 may *p.* it

Ps. 10:17 thou wilt p. their heart
59:4 p. themselves with. fault
61:7 O p. mercy and truth
107:36 that they may p. a city
Prov. 24:27 p. thy work without
30:25 p. their meat in summer
Is. 14:21 p. slaugh. for children
21:5 p. table, watch in tower
40:3 p. ye the way of the Lord; Mal. 3:1; Mat. 3:3; Mark 1:2, 3; Luke 1:76
20 workman to p. grav. image
57:14 say, Cast ye up, p. way
62:10 p. ye way of the people
65:11 p. a table for that troop
Jer. 6:4 p. ye war against her
12:3 p. them for day of slaugh.
22:7 I will p. destroyers
46:14 say ye, Stand fast and p.
51:12 set watchm. p. ambushes
Ezek. 4:15 th. shalt p. thy bread
12:3 p. thee stuff for removing
35:6 I will p. thee to blood
38:7 p. for thyself, thou and all
45:17 prince sh. p. sin-offering
24 p. a meat-offering, 46:7, 14
46:15 p. lamb and meat-offering
Joel 3:9 p. war; Amos 4:12 p. meet
Mic. 3:5 they p. war against him
Mat. 11:10 shall p. way bef. thee
26:17 where wilt thou th. we p. Mark 14:12; Luke 22:8, 9
Luke 3:4 p. ye way of L. 7:27
John 14:2 I go to p. place, 3
1 Cor. 14:8 who shall p. to bat.?
Phile. 22 p. me also a lodging

**PREPARED.**

Gen. 24:31 I p. house and room
Ex. 12:39 neither p. any victual
23:20 br. thee to place I have p.
Num. 23:4 I have p. seven altars
2 Sam. 15:1 Absalom p. chariots
1 K. 6:19 the oracle he p. in ho.
1 Chr. 15:1 Da. p. a place for ark of God, 3, 12; 2 Chr. 1:4; 3:1
22:3 David p. iron in abundance
5 Dav. p. abund. bef. 14; 29:2
2 Cor. 8:16 work of Solo. was p.
12:14 Reho. p. not his heart
19:3 Jehoshaphat p. his heart
20:33 peo. had not p. th. heart
26:14 Uz. p. shields and spears
27:6 Jotham p. his ways bef. L.
29:19 vessels A. cast away we p.
36 rejoiced G. had p. the peo.
31:11 p. chamb. in house of L.
35:20 when Josiah had p. tem.
Ezr. 7:10 Ezra had p. his heart
Neh. 5:18 which was p. for me
8:10 them for wh. nothing is p.
Est. 5:4 banq. I have p. 12; 6:14
6:4 Mordecai on gallows p. 7:10
Job 28:27 he p. it and searched it
29:7 when I p. my seat in street
Ps. 7:13 he p. instrum. of death
9:7 hath p. his throne for judg.
57:6 they p. a net for my steps
68:10 thou hast p. good. for poor
74:16 thou hast p. light and sun
103:19 the L. hath p. his throne
Prov. 8:27 when he p. heavens
19:29 judg. are p. for scorners
21:31 horse p. ag. day of battle
Is. 30:33 Tophet, for king it is p.
64:4 neit. eye seen what he p.
Ezek. 23:41 a table p. before it
28:13 workmanship of pipes p.
38:7 be thou p. and pre. thyself
Dan. 2:9 ye have p. lying words
Hos. 2:8 silver and gold they p.
6:3 going forth p. as morning
Jon. 1:17 the L. p. great fish
4:6 God p. a gourd; 7 p. worm
8 God p. a vehement east wind
Nah. 2:5 the defence shall be p.
Zep. 1:7 Lord hath p. a sacrifice
Mat. 20:23 it sh. be given to th. for whom it is p. Mark 10:40
22:4 I have p. my dinner
25:34 kingdom p. 41 into fire p.
Mark 14:15 a large upp. room p.
Luke 1:17 people p. for the Lord
2:31 p. before face of all people
12:47 knew L.'s will, but p. not
23:56 they p. spices, 24:1
Rom. 9:23 ves. of mercy afore p.
1 Cor. 2:9 things God p. for them
2 Tim. 2:21 p. to ev. good work
Heb. 10:5 a body hast thou p. me
11:7 Noah p. ark to the saving
16 he hath p. for them a city
Rev. 8:6 seven angels p. to sound
9:7 locusts like hors. p. for bat.
15 which were p. for an hour
12:6 the woman hath a place p.
16:12 kings of east may be p.
21:2 holy city p. as a bride

**PREPAREDST.**

Ps. 80:9 thou p. room before it

**PREPAREST, ETH.**

Num. 15:8 wh. thou p. a bullock
2 Chr. 30:19 p. heart to seek G.
Job 15:35 their belly p. deceit
Ps. 23:5 p. a table before me
65:9 thou p. them corn for it
147:8 who p. rain for the earth

**PREPARING.**

Neh. 13:7 p. him a chamber
1 Pet. 3:20 Noah, wh. ark was p.

**PRESBYTERY.**

1 Tim. 4:14 laying on hands of p.

**PRESCRIBED, ING.**

Ezr. 7:22 and salt without p.
Is. 10:1 grievousn. they have p.

**PRESENCE.**

Gen. 3:8 hid from p. of the Lord
4:16 Cain went from p. of Lord
27:30 Jacob was scarce from p.
45:3 Joseph's bret. troub. at p.
47:15 why sho. we die in thy p.
Ex. 10:11 driven from Phar. p.
33:14 my p. sh. go with thee, 15
35:20 Israel depart. fr. p. of M.
Lev. 22:3 shall be cut off fr. my p.
Num. 20:6 Moses went from p.
1 Sam. 18:11 David avoided p.
19:10 he slipped out of Saul's p.
2 Sam. 16:19 in thy father's p. so will I be in thy p.
1 K. 12:2 Jer. fled fr. p. of Solo.
2 K. 3:14 regard p. of Jehoshap.
5:27 and he went out fr. his p.
13:23 nei. cast he them fr. his p.
24:20 cast them out from his p.
1 Chr. 16:27 glory and honor in p.
33 shall trees sing at p. of G.
2 Chr. 9:23 kings sought p. of S.
20:9 stand bef. house in thy p.
Neh. 2:1 not been sad in his p.
Est. 7:6 Haman was afraid at p.
Job 1:12 Sa. went fr. p. of L. 2:7
23:15 I am troubled at his p.
Ps. 9:3 shall perish at thy p.
16:11 in thy p. fulness of joy
17:2 sentence come from thy p.
31:20 hide th. in secret of thy p.
51:11 cast me not away fr. thy p.
68:2 wicked perish at p. of G.
8 Sinai moved at the p. of G.
95:2 come bef. p. with thanks.
97:5 hills melted at the p. of G.
100:2 come bef. p. with singing
114:7 tremble at p. of the Lord
139:7 whither flee from thy p.?
140:13 upright sh. dw. in thy p.
Prov. 14:7 go fr. p. of a fool. man
Is. 1:7 strangers dev. land in p.
19:1 idols of Eg. be moved at p.
63:9 angel of his p. saved them
64:1 moun. might flow at thy p.
2 nations tremble at thy p.
3 mountains flowed at thy p.
Jer. 4:26 cities broken at p. of L.
5:22 will ye not tremble at p.
23:39 cast out of my p. 52:3
Ezek. 38:20 shall shake at my p.
Jon. 1:3 Jonah rose to flee fr. p.
10 men knew he fled fr. p. of L.
Nah. 1:5 earth is burnt at his p.
Zep. 1:7 hold peace at p. of Lord
Luke 13,26 eat. and drunk in p.
Acts 3:19 refreshing come fr. p.
5:41 departed from p. of council
1 Chr. 1:29 no flesh sho. gl. in p.
2 Cor. 10:1 who in p. am base
10 but his bodily p. is weak
Phil. 2:12 not as in my p. only
1 Thes. 2:17 taken from you in p.
2 Thes. 1:9 destruct. fr. p. of L.
Jude 24 faultless before p.

**In the PRESENCE.**

Gen. 16:12 dwell in t. p. of bret.
23:11 in the p. of my people
25:18 Ish. died in t. p. of breth.
2 Sam. 16:19 I not serve in the p.
1 K. 8:22 Solomon stood in the p.
1 Chr. 24:31 cast lots in t. p. of D.
Ps. 23:5 a table in t. p. of enem.
116:14 in the p. of all his peo. 18
Prov. 17:18 in the p. of friend
25:6 put not thyself in the p.
Jer. 28:1 Hanan. spake in the p.
Luke 1:19 stand in the p. of God
14:10 worship in the p. of them
15:10 joy in the p. of ang. of G.
John 20:30 signs did J. in the p.
Acts 3:13 deni. him in t. p. of P.
16 given him soundness in p.
27:35 gave thanks to G. in t. p.
1 Thes. 2:19 are not ye in the p.
Heb. 9:24 appear in the p. of G.
Rev. 14:10 in p. of ang. in p. of L.

**PRESENT, Substantive.**

Gen. 32:13 he took a p. for E. 18
21 so went p. over before him
33:10 receive my p. at my hand
43:11 said, Carry the man a p.
26 brought him the p. in hand
Jud. 3:15 Is. sent a p. to Eglon
6:18 depart not till I bring p.
1 Sam. 9:7 th. is not p. for man
30:26 a p. of spoil of enemies
1 K. 9:16 for a p. to his daughter
10:25 bro. ev. man p. 2 Chr. 9:24
15:19 I have sent thee a p.
2 K. 8:8 the king said, Take a p.
17:4 bro. no p. to king of Assyr.
18:31 agreem. by a p. Is. 36:16
20:12 sent a p. to Hez. Is. 39:1
Is. 18:7 a p. brought to the Lord
Ezek. 27:15 brought a p. horns
Hos. 10:6 for a p. to king Jareb

**PRESENT, Adjective.**

1 Sam. 13:15 S. numb. people p
2 Sam. 20:4 and be thou here p.
1 K. 20:27 Israel numbered all p.
1 Chr. 29:17 seen thy people p.
2 Chr. 30:21 Israel p. at Jerusal.
34:32 caused all p. to stand to it
Ezr. 8:25 all Israel p. offered
Est. 4:16 gather all the Jews p.
Ps. 46:1 G. is p. help in trouble
Luke 5:17 power of the L. was p.
13:1 were p. at that season
18:30 rec. more in this p. life
John 14:25 I have spok. being p.
Acts 10:33 are we all p. bef. God
21:18 all the elders were p.
Rom. 7:18 to will is p. with me
21 do good, evil is p. with me
8:18 sufferings of this p. time
38 nor things p. able to separ.
11:5 even at this p. time
1 Cor. 3:22 things p. or to come
4:11 to this p. hour we thirst
5:3 p. in spirit, as tho' I were p.
7:26 this is good for p. distress
15:6 greater part rem. to this p.

*Deut.* 2:35 cattle we took for a *p.*
3:7; *Jos.* 8:2, 27; 11:14
*Jud.* 5:30 div. *p.* a *p.* of divers
8:24 give me the ear-rings of his *p.*
2 *K.* 21:14 Judah sh. become a *p.*
*Neh.* 4:4 give them for a *p.*
*Est.* 3:13 spoil of th. for *p.* 8:11
9:15 on *p.* laid not hand, 16
*Job* 4:11 lion peris. for lack of *p.*
9:26 as eagle that hasteth to *p.*
24:5 as wild asses rising for *p.*
38:39 wilt th. hunt *p.* for lion?
39:29 from thence she seek. *p.*
*Ps.* 17:12 a lion greedy of *p.*
76:4 more ex. than mount. of *p.*
104:21 young lions roar after *p.*
124:6 hath not given us for *p.*
*Prov.* 23:28 lieth in wait as for *p.*
*Is.* 5:29 roar and lay hold of *p.*
10:2 widows may be their *p.*
6 take *p.* of a hypocrit. nation
31:4 young lion roaring on *p.*
33:23 the *p.* of a great spoil
42:22 for a *p.* none delivereth
49:24 sh. *p.* be taken fr. mighty?
59:15 from evil mak. hims. a *p.*
*Jer.* 21:9 his life shall be to him for a *p.* 38:2; 39:18; 45:5
30:16 and all that *p.* on thee will I give for a *p.*
*Ezek.* 7:21 give to stran. for a *p.*
19:3 yo. lion, learned to catch *p.*
22:27 princes like wol. raven. *p.*
26:12 make a *p.* of merchandise
29:19 shall take her spoil and *p.*
34:8 bec. my flock became a *p.*
22 flock sh. no more be a *p.* 28
36:4 to the cities that bec. a *p.*
38:12 go take spoil and *p.* 13
*Dan.* 11:24 scatter am. them *p.*
*Amos* 3:4 lion roar hath no *p.*?
*Nah.* 2:12 lions filled holes wi. *p.*
13 I will cut off thy *p.* fr. earth
3:1 bloody city, *p.* departeth not
*Zep.* 3:8 till day I rise up to *p.*

**PRICE, S.**

*Lev.* 25:16 according to years in. *p.* to fewness, diminish *p.* 50
52 shall give him again the *p.*
*Deut.* 23:18 not bring *p.* of a d.
2 *Sam.* 24:24 I will buy it of thee at a *p.* 1 *Chr.* 21:22, 24
*Job* 28:13 man knoweth not *p.* 15
18 *p.* of wisdom is above rubi.
*Ps.* 44:12 not incr. wealth by *p.*
*Prov.* 17:16 *p.* in hand of fool?
27:26 goats are the *p.* of field
31:10 her *p.* is far above rubies
*Is.* 45:13 shall let go not for *p.*
55:1 wine and milk without *p.*
*Jer.* 15:13 give to spoil witho. *p.*
*Zec.* 11:12 give me *p.* weighed
13 a goodly *p.* I was prized at
*Mat.* 13:46 found one pearl of *p.*
27:6 beca. it is the *p.* of blood
*Acts* 4:34 brought *p.* of the thin.
5:2 kept back part of the *p.* 3
19:19 counted *p.* of books burnt
1 *Cor.* 6:20 bought with a *p.* 7:23
1 *Pet.* 3:4 meek spirit of great *p.*

**PRICKED, ING.**

*Ps.* 73:21 I was *p.* in my reins
*Ezek.* 28:24 be no more a *p.* briar
*Acts* 2:37 th. were *p.* in th. heart

**PRICKS.**

*Num.* 33:55 th. that remain be *p.*
*Acts* 9:5 kick against the *p.* 26:14

**PRIDE.**

*Lev.* 26:19 break *p.* of your pow.
1 *Sam.* 17:28 *p.* and naughtiness
2 *Chr.* 32:26 Hez. humbled for *p.*
*Job* 33:17 he may hide *p.* fr. man
35:12 because of *p.* of evil men
41:15 scales are his *p.* shut up
34 king over all children of *p.*
*Ps.* 10:2 wicked in *p.* doth pers.
4 thro' *p.* of his countenance
31:20 hide them from *p.* of man
36:11 let not the foot of *p.* come
59:12 taken in their *p.*
73:6 theref. *p.* compasseth them
*Prov.* 8:13 *p.* I hate; 11:2 *p.* com.
13:10 by *p.* cometh contention
14:3 mouth of fool. is rod of *p.*
16:18 *p.* goeth before destructi.
29:23 a man's *p.* bring him low
*Is.* 9:9 say in *p.* of their hearts
16:6 have heard of *p.* of M. his haughtiness and *p.* *Jer.* 48:29
23:9 to stain *p.* of glory
25:11 shall bring down their *p.*
28:1 woe to the crown of *p.* 3
*Jer.* 13:9 I will mar *p.* of Judah
17 shall weep for your *p.*
49:16 *p.* of thy heart received
*Ezek.* 7:10 rod blos. *p.* budded
16:49 iniqu. of thy sister Sod. *p.*
56 not mentioned in day of *p.*
30:6 *p.* of power sh. come down
*Dan.* 4:37 those that walk in *p.*
5:20 mind was hardened in *p.*
*Hos.* 5:5 *p.* of Israel testify, 7:10
*Ob.* 3 *p.* of thy heart deceived
*Zep.* 2:10 shall they have for *p.*
3:11 take away th. rejoice in *p.*
*Zec.* 9:6 cut off *p.* of Philistines
10:11 *p.* of Assyria bro. down
11:3 the *p.* of Jordan is spoiled
*Mark* 7:22 out of heart proce. *p.*
1 *Tim.* 3:6 being lifted up wi. *p.*
1 *John* 2:16 *p.* of life, not of Fa.

**PRIEST.**

*Gen.* 14:18 *p.* of M. High, *Heb.* 7:1
*Ex.* 2:16 *p.* of M. had seven dau.
*Lev.* 1:9 *p.* sh. burn it all on the altar, 13, 17; 2:2, 9, 16; 3:11, 16; 4:10; 31:35; 7:5, 31
4:6 the *p.* shall dip his finger, 17
20 *p.* shall make atonement for them, 26; 5:6; 6:7; 12:8; 15:15, 30; 61:30; 19:22
7:8 *p.* shall have skin of offering
13:3 *p.* sh. look on plague, 5, 6, 17, 20, 21, 25, 26, 27, 30, 31, 32
14:16 *p.* dip his right finger in
21:9 if daughter of a *p.* profane
22:11 if *p.* buy any soul
23:11 *p.* shall wave it before L.
27:8 *p.* shall value him, accord.
*Num.* 5:8 tre. recompensed to *p.*
30 *p.* execute on her this law
35:32 not dw. till death of h.-*p.*
*Deut.* 20:2 the *p.* shall approach
*Jud.* 17:5 one of sons became *p.*
13 I have Levite to my *p.*
18:4 Micah hired me, am his *p.*
1 *Sam.* 2:14 the *p.* took himself
28 did I choose him to be *p.*?
35 raise me up a faithful *p.*
14:36 then said *p.* Draw to God
21:4 the *p.* answered, no bread
1 *Sam.* 21:6 *p.* gave him h. bread
1 *K.* 2:27 Abiathar from being *p.*
2 *Chr.* 13:9 the same may be a *p.*
15:3 Israel without teaching *p.*
*Ezr.* 2:63 stood up *p.* *Neh.* 7:65
*Ps.* 110:4 a *p.* for ever after order of Melch. *Heb.* 5:6; 7:17, 21
*Is.* 8:2 I took witnesses, Uriah *p.*
24:2 as with people, so with *p.*
28:7 the *p.* and prophet erred
*Jer.* 6:13 to the *p.* every one dealeth falsely, 8:10
14:18 *p.* go to a land they k. not
18:18 law sh. not perish from *p.*
23:11 prophet and *p.* are profa.
33 when a *p.* sh. ask thee, 34
29:26 Lord made thee *p.*
*Lam.* 2:6 despis. the king and *p.*
20 the *p.* and prophet be slain
*Ezek.* 7:26 law shall perish fr. *p.*
44:21 nor sh. any *p.* drink wine
31 *p.* sh. not eat any thing to.
*Hos.* 4:4 they that strive with *p.*
6 thou shalt be no *p.* to me
9 shall be like people like *p.*
*Amos* 7:10 the *p.* of Bethel sent
*Zec.* 6:13 shall be *p.* on throne
*Mal.* 2:7 *p.* lips sho. keep knowl.
*Mat.* 8:4 go, show thyself to the *p.* *Mark* 1:44: *Luke* 5:14
*Luke* 1:5 a certain *p.* Zacharias
10:31 came down a certain *p.*
*Acts* 14:13 *p.* of Jupiter br. oxen
*Heb.* 7:3 abideth a *p.* continually
11 what need another *p.* rise
15 after Melchizedek aris. a *p.*
20 without an oath was ma. *p.*
8:4 he should not be a *p.*
10:11 ev. *p.* standeth minister.
*See* CHIEF.

**High-PRIEST.**

*Lev.* 21:10 *h.-p.* not uncover head
*Num.* 35:25 in city of refuge till death of *h.-p.* *Jos.* 20:6
2 *K.* 12:10 money in chest, *h.-p.* put it in bags, 2 *Chr.* 24:11
*Zec.* 3:1 Joshua *h.-p.* 8; 6:11
*Mat.* 26:3 pal. of *h.-p.* *Luke* 22:54
57 led him to Caiaphas, the *h.-p.* *John* 18:24
26:65 *h.-p.* rent clothes, *Mark* 14:63
*Mark* 2:26 days of Abiathar, *h.-p.*
*John* 11:49 Caia. *h.-p.* 51; 18:13
18:15 disciple was kn. to *h.-p.*
*Acts* 4:6 were of kindred of *h.-p.*
9:1 Saul went to the *h.-p.*
22:5 also the *h.-p.* doth witness
23:4 revilest thou God's *h.-p.*?
*Heb.* 2:17 be a faithful *h.-p.*
3:1 consider apostle *h.-p.* of
4:14 have great *h.-p.* in heaven
15 *h.-p.* wh. cannot be touched
5:1 *h.-p.* taken from amo. men
5 C. glo. not himself to be *h.-p.*
10 called a *h.-p.* after Me. 6:20
7:26 such a *h.-p.* became us
8:1 we have such a *h.-p.* on thr.
3 every *h.-p.* ordained to offer
9:7 second, went *h.-p* alone
11 a *h.-p.* of good things
25 the *h.-p* entereth holy place
10:21 having a *h.-p.* over house
13:11 bro. into sanctu. by *h.-p*
*See* OFFICE.

**PRIESTS.**

*Gen.* 47:22 land of *p.* bought not
26 except land of the *p.* only
*Ex.* 19:6 to me a kingdom of *p.*
*Lev.* 1:11 *p.* sprinkle blood, 3:2
22:10 a sojourner of the *p.*
23:20 holy to the Lord for the *p.*
*Deut.* 18:3 this shall be *p.* due
*Jos.* 3:17 *p.* that bare the ark
6:4 *p.* bare seven trumpets, 13
*Jud.* 18:30 he and sons were *p.*
1 *Sam.* 5:5 nor the *p.* of Dagon
6:2 Philistines called for the *p.*
22:17 turn and slay *p.* of Lord
18 turn thou, and fall on the *p.*
1 *K.* 8:3 and *p.* took up the ark
12:31 Jeroboam made *p.* 13:33
13:2 on thee sh. he offer the *p.*
2 *K.* 10:11 Jehu slew Ahab's *p.*
19 call me all Baal's *p.*
12:6 *p.* had not repaired breach.
23:5 he put down idolatrous *p.*
2 *Chr.* 4:6 the sea was for the *p.*
5:12 120 *p.* sounding trumpets
14 *p.* could not min. for cloud
6:41 let *p.* be clothed with salv.
8:14 appointed courses of the *p.*
13:9 not cast out *p.* of Lord?
12 *p.* with trump. to cry alarm
23:6 came to house of L. save *p.*
26:19 Uzziah was wroth with *p.*
2 *Chr.* 29:34 but the *p.* were too
30:3 *p.* had not sancti. themsel.
34:5 Josiah burnt bones of *p.*
35:8 gave it to *p.* for offerings

*Ezr.* 6:18 set *p.* in divisions
20 *p.* killed the passover for *p.*
9:7 *p.* been delivered to kings
*Neh.* 2:16 nor had I told it to *p.*
3:22 after him repaired the *p.*
9:32 trouble that come on *p.*
34 we nor our *p.* kept thy law
*Ps.* 78:64 their *p.* fell by sword
99:6 Moses and Aaron among *p.*
132:9 let thy *p.* be clothed with
16 clothe her *p.* with salvation
*Is.* 37:2 he sent elders of *p.*
61:6 named the *p.* of the Lord
*Jer.* 1:18 against the *p.* thereof
2:8 *p.* said not, Where is Lord?
26 *p.* ashamed; 4:9 *p.* aston.
5:31 *p.* bare rule by th. means
8:1 bones of *p.* they shall bring
13:13 fill *p.* with drunkenness
31:14 satiate souls of *p.*
32:32 provoke to anger, their *p.*
48:7 into captivity with *p.* 49:3
*Lam.* 1:4 her *p.* sigh, her virgins
19 my *p.* gave up the ghost
4:13 iniq. of her *p.* shed blood
16 they respected not the *p.*
*Ezek.* 22:26 her *p.* viola. my law
40:45 this chamber is for *p.*
*Hos.* 5:1 hear this, O *p.* hearken
6:9 comp. of *p.* murder in way
*Joel* 1:9 the *p.* mourn, 13; 2:17
*Mic.* 3:11 the *p.* teach for hire
*Zep.* 1:4 cut off names of the *p.*
3:4 *p.* polluted the sanctuary
*Hag.* 2:11 as *p.* concerning law
*Mal.* 1:6 you, O *p.* that despise
2:1 *p.* this command. is for you
*Mat.* 12:4 lawf. only for *p.* to eat
5 *p.* profane sabbath, *Mark* 2:26; *Luke* 6:4
*Mark* 2:26 is not lawful but for *p.*
*Luke* 17:14 show yourselves to *p.*
*Acts* 4:1 the *p.* came upon them
6:7 a comp. of *p.* were obedient
*Heb.* 7:21 *p.* made without oath
23 *p.* not suffered to continue
8:4 seeing there are *p.* that offer
9:6 *p.* went into first tabernacle
*Rev.* 1:6 made us *p.* to God, 5:10
20:6 sh. be *p.* of God and Christ
*See* CHIEF, LEVITES, OFFICE.

**High-PRIESTS.**

*Luke* 3:2 An. and Ca. were *h.-p.*
*Heb.* 7:27 not daily as *h.-p.*
28 the law maketh men *h.-p.*

**PRIESTHOOD.**

*Ex.* 40:15 everl. *p.* throughout generations, *Num.* 25:13
*Num.* 16:10 and seek ye the *p.*
18:1 shall bear iniquity of *p.*
*Jos.* 18:7 *p.* of L. is their inherit.
*Ezr.* 2:62 pollu. fr. *p.* *Neh.* 7:64
*Neh.* 13:29 defiled *p.* coven. of *p.*
*Heb.* 7:5 Levi, who receive the *p.*
11 if perfection were by Le. *p.*
12 for the *p.* being changed
14 M. spake nothing conc. *p.*
24 hath an unchangeable *p.*
1 *Pet.* 2:5 a holy *p.* 9 a royal *p.*

**PRINCE.**

*Gen.* 23:6 thou art a mighty *p.*
32:28 as *p.* hast thou po. wi. G.
34:2 wh. Shechem *p.* of country
*Ex.* 2:14 who made thee a *p.*
*Num.* 16:13 make thyself *p.*
17:6 for each *p.* a rod, twelve
34:18 take one *p.* of every tribe
*Jos.* 22:14 each chief house a *p.*
2 *Sam.* 3:38 kn. ye not *p.* fallen?
1 *K.* 11:34 his days make him *p.*
14:7 made thee *p.* over peo. 16:2
*Job* 21:28 where is house of *p.*?
31:37 as a *p.* wo. I go near him
*Prov.* 14:28 want is dest. of a *p.*
17:7 less do lying lips bec. a *p.*
25:7 lower in presence of the *p.*
15 forbearing is a *p.* persuaded
28:16 *p.* that want. understand.
*Cant.* 7:1 beautif. thy feet, O *p.*
*Is.* 9:6 called the P. of peace
*Jer.* 51:59 Seraiah was a quiet *p.*
*Ezek.* 7:27 the *p.* shall be clothed
12:10 concerneth *p.* in Jerusal.
12 and *p.* shall bear on should.
21:25 profane, wicked *p.* of Is.
28:2 say to the *p.* of Tyrus
30:13 be no more a *p.* of Egypt
34:24 my servant David, a *p.*
37:25 David sh. be th. *p.* for ev.
38:2 the *p.* of Meshech, 3; 39:1
44:3 gate for *p.* *p.* shall sit in it
45:17 it sh. be the *p.* part to give
*Ezek.* 46:2 the *p.* sh. enter by por.
4 offering that the *p.* shall offer
12 when *p.* prepares an offeri.
16 if *p.* give a gift to any sons
18 *p.* shall not take people's in.
48:21 residue shall be for the *p.*
*Dan.* 1:7 to whom *p.* gave names
8 he requested of *p.* of eunuchs
9 Daniel in favor with the *p.*
8:11 magnifi. himself even to *p.*
25 shall stand up against the *p.*
9:25 build unto Messiah the P.
26 people of *p.* that shall come
10:13 the *p.* of Persia withstood
20 *p.* of Persia, *p.* of Gre. come
21 none hold. but Michael *p.*
11:18 but a *p.* for his own beha.
22 also the *p.* of the covenant
12:1 Michael stand up, great *p.*
*Hos.* 3:4 shall abide without a *p.*
*Mic.* 7:3 *p.* and judge ask reward
*Mat.* 9:34 casteth out dev. by *p.* of devils, 12:24; *Mark* 3:22
*John* 12:31 the *p.* of this world
14:30 for the *p.* of world cometh
16:11 *p.* of this world is judged
*Acts* 3:15 killed the P. of life
5:31 him God exalted to be a P.
*Eph.* 2:2 according to *p.* of air
*Rev.* 1:5 Jesus Christ P. of kings

**PRINCES.**

*Gen.* 12:15 *p.* also of Pharaoh
17:20 *p.* shall Ishm. beget, 25:16
*Num.* 7:3 for two *p.* 10 *p.* offer.
16:2 rose up 250 *p.* 21:18 *p.* dig.
22:8 and *p.* abode with Balaam
15 Ba. sent *p.* more honorable
*Jos.* 9:15 *p.* of congrega. sware
13:21 M. smote with *p.* of Mid.
22:14 P. ten *p.* sent to Reuben
*Jud.* 5:3 give ear, O ye *p.*
15 *p.* of Issachar were with D.
7:25 two *p.* of the Midianites
1 *Sam.* 2:8 to set them among *p.*
29:4 *p.* of Philisti. were wroth
1 *K.* 20:14 by young men of *p.*
1 *Chr.* 4:38 these *p.* in families
28:21 *p.* will be at thy command
2 *Chr.* 28:14 left spoil before *p.*
30:12 do commandments of *p.*
35:8 *p.* gave willingly to people
36:18 treas. of his *p.* to Babylon
*Ezr.* 7:28 bef. king's mighty *p.*
9:2 hand of *p.* hath been chief
10:8 according to counsel of *p.*
*Neh.* 9:34 nei. have *p.* kept law
*Est.* 1:3 feast to all his *p.* 2:18
6:9 of one of the king's noble *p.*
*Job* 3:15 had been at rest with *p.*
12:19 leadeth *p.* away spoiled
21 he poureth contempt on *p.*
29:9 the *p.* refrained talking
34:18 say to *p.* ye are ungodly?
19 him that accepteth not *p.*
*Ps.* 45:16 *p.* in all the earth
47:9 *p.* of people are gathered
68:27 *p.* of Zebulon, *p.* of Nap.
31 *p.* shall come out of Egypt
76:12 he shall cut off spirit of *p.*
82:7 and fall like one of the *p.*
105:22 bind his *p.* at his pleas.
107:40 poureth contempt on *p.*
113:8 set him wi. *p.* even wi. *p.*
118:9 tru. in L. than confi. in *p.*
119:23 *p.* also did speak ag. me
161 *p.* perse. me without cause
146:3 put not your trust in *p.*
148:11 *p.* and judges of earth
*Prov.* 8:15 *p.* decree; 16 *p.* rule
17:26 it is not good to strike *p.*
19:10 much less a ser. to rule *p.*
28:2 many are the *p.* thereof
31:4 not for *p.* to drink strong
*Ec.* 10:7 *p.* walking as servants
16 when thy *p.* eat in the mor.
17 blessed art thou, wh. *p.* eat
*Is.* 1:23 thy *p.* are rebellious
3:4 I will give children to th. *p.*
14 L. enter into judgm. wi. *p.*
10:8 are not my *p.* alto. kings?
19:11 *p.* of Zoan, *p.* of Noph, 13
21:5 ye *p.* anoint the shield
23:8 whose merchants are *p.*
30:4 his *p.* were at Zoan, amba.
31:9 *p.* shall be afraid of ensign
32:1 *p.* shall rule in judgment
34:12 all her *p.* shall be nothing
40:23 that bringeth *p.* to nothi.
41:25 and he shall come upon *p.*
43:28 I profaned *p.* of sanctuary
49:7 *p.* shall worship bec. of L.
*Jer.* 1:18 brazen walls ag. the *p.*
2:26 th. kings and *p.* ashamed
4:9 heart of *p.* sh. be astonish.
8:1 shall bring out bones of *p.*
17:25 *p.* sitting on throne of D.
26:16 *p.* said, This man is not
*Jer.* 32:32 kings and *p.* pro. me
34:21 *p.* I will give to enemies
38:17 if thou go to k. of B. *p.*
48:7 Ch. and *p.* go to capt. 49:3
49:38 I will destroy from the *p.*
50:35 sword on *p.* and wise men
51:57 I will make drunk her *p.*
*Lam.* 1:6 *p.* become like harts
2:9 kings and *p.* am. Gentiles
5:12 *p.* are hanged by th. hand
*Ezek.* 22:27 *p.* like wolves raven.
23:15 dyed attire, all of them *p.*
32:29 Edom and her *p.*
30 the *p.* of the north
39:18 ye shall drink blood of *p.*
45:8 my *p.* no more opp. people
*Dan.* 3:2 king sent to gather *p.*
6:1 to set over kingdom, 120 *p.*
4 *p.* sought occasion ag. Dani.
8:25 stand ag. the Prince of *p.*
9:8 confusion of face to our *p.*
10:13 Michael one of *p.* came
11:5 one of his *p.* sh. be strong
*Hos.* 7:3 they make *p.* glad
5 the *p.* have made him sick
16 their *p.* shall fall by sword
8:4 made *p.* and I knew it not
10 shall sorrow for king of *p.*
9:15 all their *p.* are revolters
13:10 Give me a king and *p.*
*Amos.* 1:15 into captiv. he and *p.*
*Mic.* 3:1 hear, *p.* of house of Is. 9
*Hab.* 1:10 the *p.* shall be a scorn
*Zep.* 1:8 I will punish the *p.*
3:3 *p.* within her are roar. lions
*Mat.* 20:25 *p.* of Gent. exercise
1 *Cor.* 2:6 nor wisdom of the *p.*
8 none of *p.* of this world

**All the PRINCES.**

2 *K.* 24:14 carried away *all the p.*
1 *Chr.* 29:24 *all p.* submit. them.
2 *Chr.* 24:23 destroyed *all the p.*
*Est.* 1:16 done wro. to *all the p.*
3:1 set his seat above *all the p.*
*Ps.* 83:11 *all* th. *p.* as Zebah and
*Jer.* 36:21 it in ears of *all the p.*
*Ezek.* 26:16 *all the p.* of the sea
*Amos* 2:3 will slay *all the p.*
*See* ISRAEL.

**PRINCES of Judah.**

*Neh.* 12:31 I brought up *p. of Ju.*
*Ps.* 68:27 there is *p. of Judah*

*Jer.* 52:10 slew all the *p. of Jud.*
*Mat.* 2:6 not least am. *p. of Jud.*

**PRINCESS, ES.**
1 *K.* 11:3 Solom. had 700 wiv. *p.*
*Lam.* 1:1 *p.* among provinces

**PRINCIPAL.**
*Ex.* 30:23 take th. also *p.* spices
*Lev.* 6:5 shall restore it in the *p.*
*Num.* 5:7 recomp. tresp. with *p.*
1 *K.* 4:5 son of Nathan *p.* officer
2 *K.* 25:19 the *p.* scribe of the host, *Jer.* 52:25
1 *Chr.* 24:6 one *p.* household
31 even *p.* fathers cast lots
*Neh.* 11:17 Mattaniah *p.* to begin
*Prov.* 4:7 wisdom is the *p.* thing
*Is.* 16:8 broken down *p.* plants
28:25 cast in *p.* wheat and barl.
*Jer.* 25:34 in ashes, *p.* of flock
35 nor the *p.* of the flock escape
*Mic.* 5:5 raise ag. him 8 *p.* me.
*Acts* 25:23 *p.* of the city entered

**PRINCIPALITY, IES.**
*Jer.* 13:18 your *p.* sh. come down
*Rom.* 8:38 *p.* nor powers able
*Eph.* 1:21 far above all *p.* power
3:10 to *p.* might be kn. wisdom
6:12 wrestle ag. *p.* and power
*Col.* 1:16 *p.* were created by him
2:10 head of all *p.* and power
15 having spoiled *p.* he made
*Tit.* 3:1 mind to be subject to *p.*

**PRINCIPLES.**
*Heb.* 5:12 one teach you first *p.*
6:1 *p.* of the doctrine of Chr.

**PRINT, ED.**
*Lev.* 19:28 shall not *p.* any mar.
*Job* 19:23 O that my words were *p.* in a book

**PRINT.**
*Job* 13:27 settest a *p.* on heels
*John* 20:25 exc. I see *p.* of nails, and put my finger into *p.*

PRISCA. 2 *Tim.* 4:19
PRISCILLA. *Acts* 18:2, 26; *Rom.* 16:3; 1 *Cor.* 16:19

**PRISON.**
*Gen.* 39:20 Potiph. put Jos. in *p.*
40:3 put butler and baker in *p.*
42:19 bound in house of your *p.*
1 *K.* 22:27 put this fellow in *p.* 2 *Chr.* 18:26
2 *K.* 17:4 bound Hoshea in *p.*
25:29 changed his *p.* garment, *Jer.* 52:31, 33
*Neh.* 3:25 Palal repaired by *p.*
*Ps.* 142:7 bring my soul out of *p.*
*Ec.* 4:14 for out of *p.* he cometh
*Is.* 24:22 they sh. be shut up in *p.*
42:7 bring out prisoners from *p.*
22 all of them hid in *p.*
53:8 he was taken from *p.*
61:1 proclaim opening of the *p.*
*Jer.* 32:2 Jeremiah was shut in *p.*
12 before Jews in court of *p.*
33:1 word came to Jerem. while in *p.* 37:21; 38:6, 28; 39:15
37:4 had not put him into *p.*
15 put him in *p.* in Jon. house
39:14 took Jeremiah out of *p.*
52:11 put Zedekiah in *p.*
*Mat.* 4:12 John was cast into *p.*
5:25 be cast into *p.* *Luke* 12:58
11:2 J. heard in *p.* works of C.
14:3 Herod put him in *p.*
18:30 he cast him into *p.*
25:36 I was in *p.* ye came to me
39 when saw we thee in *p.*? 44
*Mark* 1:14 after J. was put in *p.*
6:17 Her. had bound John in *p.*
*Luke* 3:20 he shut up John in *p.*
22:33 go with thee both into *p.*
23:19 for murder cast in *p.* 25
*John* 3:24 John not yet cast in *p.*
*Acts* 5:18 put apostles in com. *p.*
19 angel by night op. *p.* doors
8:3 men and women, com. to *p.*
12:4 Peter in *p.* 5 kept in *p.*
7 light in *p.* 17 L. br. out of *p.*
16:23 Paul and Silas cast in *p.*
24 inner *p.* 27 *p.* doors open
26:10 saints did I shut in *p.*
1 *Pet.* 3:19 preach. to spirits in *p.*
*Rev.* 2:10 shall cast some into *p.*
20:7 S. shall be loosed out his *p.*

*See* GATE.

**PRISON-HOUSE.**
*Jud.* 16:21 S. did grind in *p.-h.*
2 *Chr.* 16:10 Asa put H. in *p.-h.*
*Is.* 42:7 in darkness out of *p.-h.*

**PRISONER.**
*Ps.* 79:11 let sighing of *p.* come
102:20 hear groaning of the *p.*
*Mat.* 27:15 release to people a *p.*
*Acts* 23:18 P. *p.* called me to him
25:27 unreasonable to send a *p.*
28:17 yet was I delivered *p.*
*Eph.* 3:1 I P. the *p.* of Jesus, 4:1; *Phile.* 1:9
2 *Tim.* 1:8 not ashamed of his *p.*

*See* FELLOW.

**PRISONERS.**
*Gen.* 39:20 where king's *p.* were
*Num.* 21:1 took some of Israel *p.*
*Job* 3:18 there the *p.* rest toge.
*Ps.* 69:33 L. despiseth not his *p.*
146:7 the Lord looseth the *p.*
*Is.* 10:4 bow down under the *p.*
14:17 opened not house of *p.*
20:4 Assyria shall lead Egyp. *p.*
24:22 be gathered together as *p.*
42:7 bring out *p.* from prison
49:9 mayest say to *p.* Go forth
*Lam.* 3:34 crush under feet the *p.*
*Zec.* 9:11 have sent forth thy *p.*
12 turn to str.-hold, *p.* of hope
*Acts* 16:25 praises, *p.* heard them
27 supposing *p.* had been fled
27:1 delivered Paul and other *p.*
42 soldiers' coun. was to kill *p.*

**PRISONS.**
*Luke* 21:12 delivering you in. *p.*
*Acts* 22:4 del. in *p.* men and wo.
2 *Cor.* 11:23 in *p.* more frequent

**PRIVATE, LY.**
*Mat.* 24:3 disciples came to C. *p.*
*Mark* 6:32 Jesus went into a ship *p.* *Luke* 9:10
9:28 J. and And. ask him *p.* 13:3
*Luke* 10:23 turned to disciples *p.*
*Acts* 23:19 with Paul's kinsm. *p.*
*Gal.* 2:2 *p.* to them of reputation
2 *Pet.* 1:20 any *p.* interpretation

**PRIVILY.**
*Jud.* 9:31 he sent messengers *p.*
1 *Sam.* 24:4 Da. cut Saul's sk. *p.*
*Ps.* 10:8 eyes *p.* set against poor
11:2 may *p.* shoot at upright
31:4 out of net laid *p.* 142:3
64:5 commune of lay. snares *p.*
101:5 whoso *p.* slanders neighb.
*Prov.* 1:11 lurk *p.* for innocent
18 lurk *p.* for their own lives
*Mat.* 1:19 to put her away *p.*
2:7 Her. when he had *p.* called
*Acts* 16:37 now do they thrust us out *p.*?
*Gal.* 2:4 came in *p.* to spy out
2 *Pet.* 2:1 *p.* bring damna. here.

**PRIVY.**
*Deut.* 23:1 *p.* member cut off
1 *K.* 2:44 wickedness heart *p.* to
*Ezek.* 21:14 enters *p.* chamber
*Acts* 5:2 wife also being *p.* to it

**PRIZE.**
1 *Cor.* 9:24 but one receiveth *p.*
*Phil.* 3:14 I press toward the *p*

**PRIZED.**
*Zec.* 11:13 price that I was *p.* at

**PROCEED.**
*Jos.* 6:10 word *p.* out of mouth
2 *Sam.* 7:12 seed wh. shall *p.*
*Job* 40:5 but I will *p.* no further
*Is.* 29:14 I *p.* to do marvel. work
51:4 for a law shall *p.* from me
*Jer.* 9:3 they *p.* from evil to evil
30:21 governor shall *p.* fr. midst
*Hab.* 1:7 judgm. and dign. sh. *p.*
*Mat.* 15:18 *p.* out of mouth defile
19 heart *p.* murders, *Mark* 7:21
*Eph.* 4:29 no corrupt commu. *p.*
2 *Tim.* 3:9 they shall *p.* no furt.

**PROCEEDED.**
*Num.* 30:12 what. *p.* out of lips
*Jud.* 11:36 do that which *p.* out
*Job* 36:1 Elihu also *p.* and said
*Luke* 4:22 gracious words wh. *p.*
*John* 8:42 for I *p.* forth from God
*Acts* 12:3 he *p.* to take Peter also
*Rev.* 19:21 sword *p.* out of mouth

**PROCEEDETH, ING.**
*Gen.* 24:50 thing *p.* from the L.
*Num.* 30:2 according to all th. *p*
*Deut.* 8:3 by every word that *p* out of mouth of G. *Mat.* 4:4
1 *Sam.* 24:13 wick. *p.* fr. wicked
*Ec.* 10:5 error which *p.* fr. ruler
*Lam.* 3:38 out of M. High *p.* not
*Hab.* 1:4 wrong judgment *p.*
*John* 15:26 Spi. of truth *p.* fr. F.
*Jam.* 3:10 out of the same mo. *p.*
*Rev.* 11:5 fire *p.* out of th. mouth
22:1 water of life *p.* out of thr

**PROCESS.**
*Gen.* 4:3 in *p.* of time C. brought
38:12 in *p.* of time Shuah died
*Ex.* 2:23 in *p.* of time ki. of Eg.
*Jud.* 11:4 in *p.* chil. of Ammon
2 *Chr.* 21:19 in *p.* Jehor.'s bowe.

PROCHORUS. *Acts* 6:5

**PROCLAIM.**
*Ex.* 33:19 I will *p.* name of Lord
*Lev.* 23:2 feast of L. *p.* 4, 21, 37
25:10 *p.* lib. *Deut.* 20:10 *p.* peace
*Jud.* 7:3 to *p.* in ears of people
1 *K.* 21:9 *p.* a fast, set Naboth on
2 *K.* 10:20 Jehu said, *p.* assemb.
*Neh.* 8:15 *p.* they fetch branches
*Est.* 6:9 *p.* before him, Thus sh.
*Prov.* 20:6 men *p.* own goodness
*Is.* 61:1 he sent me to *p.* liberty
2 *p.* the acceptable year of L.
*Jer.* 3:12 *p.* th. words, 11:6; 19:2
7:2 stand in gate of L. *p.* there
34:8 made a coven. to *p.* liberty
17 I *p.* a liberty for you to sw.
*Joel* 3:9 *p.* this among the Gent.
*Amos* 4:5 *p.* the free-offerings

**PROCLAIMED.**
*Ex.* 34:5 *p.* name of Lord, 6
36:6 they caused it to be *p.*
1 *K.* 21:12 they *p.* a fast, set
2 *K.* 10:20 solemn assem. and *p.*
23:16 man of G. *p.* who *p.* 17
2 *Chr.* 20:3 Jehoshaphat *p.* a fast
*Ezr.* 8:21 I *p.* a fast at Ahava
*Est.* 6:11 Haman *p.* before him
*Is.* 62:11 hath *p.* Thy salvation
*Jer.* 36:9 they *p.* a fast before L.
*Jon.* 3:5 *p.* a fast, put on sackc.
7 caused it to be *p.* thro' Nine.
*Luke* 12:3 be *p.* on house-tops

**PROCLAIMETH, ING.**
*Prov.* 12:23 heart of fools *p.*
*Jer.* 34:15 *p.* liberty ev. man, 17
*Rev.* 5:2 I saw a strong angel *p.*

**PROCLAMATION.**
*Ex.* 32:5 Aaron made *p.*
1 *K.* 15:22 king Asa made a *p.*
22:36 went *p.* throughout host
2 *Chr.* 24:9 J. made a *p.* through
36:22 Cyrus made *p.* *Ezr.* 1:1
*Ezr.* 10:7 E. made *p.* thro' Judah
*Dan.* 5:29 Belshazzar made *p.*

**PROCURE, ED, ETH.**
*Prov.* 11:27 seek. good *p.* favor
*Jer.* 2:17 hast thou not *p.* this
4:18 thy doings *p.* th. things
26:19 might we *p.* great evil
33:9 for all posterity I *p.* to it

**PRODUCE.**
*Is.* 41:21 *p.* your cause, saith L.

**PROFANE, Adjective.**
*Lev.* 21:7 not ta. wife th. is *p.* 14
*Jer.* 23:11 proph. and priests *p.*
*Ezek.* 21:25 thus *p.* prince of I
28:16 cast as *p.* out of mount
42:20 sanctuary and *p.* place
44:23 differe. betw. holy and *p.*
48:15 sh. be a *p.* place for city
1 *Tim.* 1:9 law is made for *p.*
4:7 ref. *p.* and old wives' fables
6:20 avoid *p.* babbl. 2 *Tim.* 2:16
*Heb.* 12:16 lest th. be any *p.* per.

**PROFANE, Verb.**
*Lev.* 18:21 neit. shalt thou *p.* G.
19:12; 20:3; 21:6; 22:2, 32
21:12 shall not *p.* sanctuary, 23
15 nor shall *p.* his seed among
22:9 if they *p.* my ordinance
15 shall not *p.* holy things
*Neh.* 13:17 evil do, *p.* sabbath
*Ezek.* 23:39 came to sanctu. to *p.*
24:21 I will *p.* my sanctuary
*Amos* 2:7 to *p.* my holy name
*Mat.* 12:5 priests in temple *p.*
*Acts* 24:6 gone about to *p.* temp.

**PROFANED.**
*Lev.* 19:8 he *p.* hallowed things
*Ps.* 89:39 thou hast *p.* his crown
*Is.* 43:28 I have *p.* the princes of
*Ezek.* 22:8 thou *p.* my sab. 23:38
26 *p.* my holy things, I am *p.*
25:3 sanctuary when it was *p*
36:20 they *p.* my holy name
21 my name Is. had *p.* 22, 23
*Mal.* 1:12 ye have *p.* it, ye say
2:11 Jud. hath *p.* holiness of L.

**PROFANENESS.**
*Jer.* 23:15 prophets of Jeru. is *p.*

**PROFANETH, ING.**
*Lev.* 21:9 she *p.* her father, she
*Neh.* 13:18 bring wrath by *p.* sab.
*Mal.* 2:10 by *p.* covenant of fath.

**PROFESS.**
*Deut.* 26:3 I *p.* this day to the L.
*Mat.* 7:23 I *p.* I never knew you
*Tit.* 1:16 they *p.* they know God

**PROFESSED, ING.**
*Rom.* 1:22 *p.* themsel. to be wise
2 *Cor.* 9:13 glori. God for your *p.*
1 *Tim.* 2:10 becometh women *p.*
6:12 hast *p.* a good profession
21 some *p.* have erred

**PROFESSION.**
1 *Tim.* 6:12 professed a good *p*
*Heb.* 3:1 the High-priest of our *p.*
4:14 let us hold fast our *p.* 10:23

**PROFIT, Substantive.**
*Gen.* 25:32 what *p.* sh. birthright
37:26 what *p.* if we slay broth.?
*Est.* 3:8 it is not for king's *p.*
*Job* 21:15 what *p.* if we pray
30:2 whereto strength *p.* me?
35:3 what *p.* if I be cleansed
*Ps.* 30:9 what *p.* is in my blood?
*Prov.* 14:23 in all labor th. is *p.*
*Ec.* 1:3 what *p.* hath a man of all
his labor? 3:9; 5:16
2:11 there was no *p.* under sun
5:9 the *p.* of the earth is for all
7:11 by wisdom there is *p.* to
*Is.* 30:5 help nor *p.* but shame
*Jer.* 16:19 things where. is no *p.*
*Mal.* 3:14 what *p.* that we kept
*Rom.* 3:1 what *p.* of circumcis.?
1 *Cor.* 7:35 I sp. for your own *p.*
10:33 not seeking mine own *p.*

2 *Tim.* 2:14 about words to no *p.*
*Heb.* 12:10 chasteneth us for *p.*

**PROFIT, Verb.**
1 *Sam.* 12:21 thi. wh. cannot *p.*
*Job* 35:8 thy righteousn. may *p.*
*Prov.* 10:2 wickedness *p.* nothing
11:4 riches *p.* not in day of wra.
*Is.* 30:5 peo. that could not *p.* 6
44:9 delectable things sh. not *p.*
47:12 thou shalt be able to *p.*
57:12 works, shall not *p.* thee
*Jer.* 2:8 things that do not *p.*
11 for that which doth not *p.*
7:8 lying words that cannot *p.*
12:13 put to pain, but sh. not *p.*
23:32 they sh. not *p.* this peop.
*Mark* 8:36 what *p.* if gain world
1 *Cor.* 12:7 ev. man to *p.* withal
14:6 what shall I *p.* you?
*Gal.* 5:2 Ch. shall *p.* you nothing
*Heb.* 4:2 word preach. did not *p.*
*Jam.* 2:14 what doth it *p.* breth.
16 give not thi. needf. wh. *p.*?

**PROFITABLE.**
*Job* 22:2 can a man be *p.* to God?
*Ec.* 10:10 wisdom is *p.* to direct
*Is.* 44:10 image is *p.* for nothing
*Jer.* 13:7 girdle was *p.* for noth.
*Mat.* 5:29 *p.* members perish, 30
*Acts* 20:20 I kept noth. *p.* to you
1 *Tim.* 4:8 godliness is *p.* to all
2 *Tim.* 3:16 all Scripture is *p.*
4:11 M. is *p.* to me for ministry
*Tit.* 3:8 th. things are *p.* to men
*Phile.* 11 but now *p.* to thee

**PROFITED, ETH.**
*Job* 33:27 I have sinned, it *p.* not
34:9 it *p.* noth. to delight in G.
*Hab.* 2:18 what *p.* graven image
*Mat.* 15:5 it is a gift whatever
thou might. be *p.* *Mark* 7:11
16:26 what is man *p.* if he gain
*John* 6:63 quicken. flesh *p.* noth.
*Rom.* 2:25 circumcision *p.* if th.
1 *Cor.* 13:3 not char. it *p.* noth.
*Gal.* 1:14 I *p.* in Jews' religion
1 *Tim.* 4:8 bodily exerci. *p.* little
*Heb.* 13:9 not *p.* them that occu.

**PROFITING.**
1 *Tim.* 4:15 thy *p.* may appear

**PROFOUND.**
*Hos.* 5:2 the revolters are *p.*

**PROGENITORS.**
*Gen.* 49:26 above bless. of my *p.*

**PROGNOSTICATORS.**
*Is.* 47:13 let monthly *p.* stand up

**PROLONG, ED**
*Deut.* 4:26 not *p.* your days, 30:18
40 that thou mayest *p.* days on
earth, 5:16, 33; 6:2; 11:9;
17:20; 22:7
32:47 ye shall *p.* your days
*Job* 6:11 that I should *p.* life?
15:29 wicked sh. not *p.* perfect.
*Ps.* 61:6 thou will *p.* king's life
*Prov.* 28:2 by knowl. shall be *p.*
16 he that hateth covet. sh. *p.*
*Ec.* 8:12 a sinner's days be *p.*
13 nei. shall wicked *p.* his days
*Is.* 13:22 her days shall not be *p.*
53:10 seed, he shall *p.* his days
*Ezek.* 12:22 the days are *p.* and
25 to pass, it sh. be no more *p.*
28 none of my words be *p.* more
*Dan.* 7:12 their lives were *p.* for

**PROLONGETH.**
*Prov.* 10:27 fear of Lord *p.* days

**PROMISE, Substantive.**
*Num.* 14:34 kn. my breach of *p.*
1 *K.* 8:56 not failed of good *p.*
2 *Chr.* 1:9 let *p.* to David be esta.
*Neh.* 5:12 do according to this *p.*
13 perform. not *p.* accor. to *p.*

*Ps.* 77:8 doth *p.* fail evermore?
105:42 remembered his holy *p*
*Luke* 24:49 send *p.* of my Fath
*Acts* 1:4 wait for *p.* of the Father
2:33 received *p.* of Holy Ghost
39 the *p.* is to you and children
7:17 time of the *p.* drew nigh
13:23 his *p.* ha. raised a Saviour
32 *p.* made to fathers
23:21 looking for a *p.* from thee
26:6 hope of the *p.* made of G. 7
*Rom.* 4:13 *p.* that he sh. be heir
14 the *p.* is made of none effect
16 the *p.* might be sure to seed
20 he staggered not at the *p.*
9:8 chil. of *p.* counted for seed
9 this is word of *p.* I will come
*Gal.* 3:14 receive *p.* of the Spirit
17 sho. make *p.* of none effect
18 it is no more of *p.* but God
gave it to Abraham by *p.*
19 to whom the *p.* was made
22 that the *p.* by faith of J. C.
29 ye are heirs according to *p.*
4:23 he of free woman was by *p.*
28 we, as Isaac, children of *p.*
*Eph.* 1:13 with Holy Spirit of *p.*
2:12 strangers from coven. of *p.*
3:6 partakers of his *p.* in Christ
6:2 first commandment with *p.*
1 *Tim.* 4:8 hav. the *p* of the life
2 *Tim.* 1:1 according to *p.* of life
*Heb.* 4:1 fear, lest a *p.* being left
6:13 God made *p.* to Abraham
15 after he endured he obtai. *p.*
17 will. to show to heirs of *p.*
9:15 *p.* of eternal life, 10:36
11:9 sojourned in land of *p.*
heirs wi. him of the same *p.*
39 these all received not the *p.*
2 *Pet.* 3:4 wh. is *p.* of his coming
9 Lord not slack concer. his *p.*
13 according to his *p.* we look
1 *John* 2:25 this is the *p.* he hath

**PROMISE, Verb.**
2 *Pet.* 2:19 while they *p.* liberty,
they servants of corruption

**PROMISED.**
*Ex.* 12:25 give according as he *p.*
*Num.* 14:40 go to place Lord *p.*
*Deut.* 1:11 L. bless as he *p.* 15:6
6:3 increase as the Lord *p.* thee
10:9 L. is his inherit. as he *p.*
12:20 L. enlarge border, as he *p.*
19:8 give thee land he *p.* 27:3
26:18 to be his people as he *p.*
*Jos.* 23:5 possess th. land as L. *p.*
2 *Sam.* 7:28 *p.* goodness to serv.
1 *K.* 2:24 made me house he *p.*
5:12 L. gave S. wisdom as he *p.*
8:20 I sit on thro. of Is. as L. *p.*
56 given rest to people as he *p.*
9:5 as I *p.* to David, thy father
2 *K.* 8:19 *p.* to gi. light, 2 *Chr.* 21:7
1 *Chr.* 17:26 th. hast *p.* goodness
2 *Chr.* 6:10 set on throne as L. *p.*
*Neh.* 9:23 concern. whi. thou *p.*
*Jer.* 32:43 all good I *p.* 33:14
*Mat.* 14:7 Herod *p.* with oath
*Mark* 14:11 *p.* to give money
*Luke* 1:72 mercy *p.* to our fath.
22:6 he *p.* to betray him
*Acts* 7:5 he *p.* to give it to him
*Rom.* 1:2 gospel wh. he had *p.*
4:21 what he *p.* he was able
*Tit.* 1:2 *p.* before world began
*Heb.* 10:23 he is faithful that *p.*
11:11 him faithful that had *p.*
12:26 hath *p.* saying, Yet once
*Jam.* 1:12 L. *p.* to them love, 2:5
1 *John* 2:25 hath *p.* us eter. life

**PROMISEDST.**
1 *K.* 8:24 David that thou *p.* 25
*Neh.* 9:15 *p.* they sho. go to land

**PROMISES.**
*Rom.* 9:4 to whom pertain *p.*
15:8 to confirm *p.* made to fath.

2 *Cor.* 1:20 all *p.* of God in him
7:1 having therefore these *p.*
*Gal.* 3:16 to Abra. were *p.* made
21 is law against *p.* of God?
*Heb.* 6:12 thro' faith inherit *p.*
7:6 M. blessed him that had *p.*
8:6 established upon better *p.*
11:13 not having received *p.*
17 he that received *p.* off. son
33 through faith obtained *p.*
2 *Pet.* 1:4 given to us precious *p.*

**PROMISING.**

*Ezek.* 13:22 wick. way by *p.* life

**PROMOTE, ED.**

*Num.* 22:17 *p.* to honor, 24:11
37 am I not able to *p.* thee to
*Jud.* 9:9 go to be *p.* over, 11, 13
*Est.* 5:11 where. king had *p.* him
*Prov.* 4:8 exalt her, she sh. *p.* th.
*Dan.* 3:30 the king *p.* Shadrach

**PROMOTION.**

*Ps.* 75:6 *p.* cometh not from east
*Prov.* 3:35 shame be *p.* of fools

**PRONOUNCE.**

*Lev.* 5:4 man sh. *p.* with an oath
59 this is the law, *p.* it clean
*Jud.* 12:6 not frame to *p.* right

**PRONOUNCED.**

*Neh.* 6:12 he *p.* this prophecy
*Jer.* 11:17 the Lord hath *p.* evil
16:10 *p.* this great evil agai. us?
19:15; 35:17; 40:2
26:13 Lord will rep. of evil he *p.*
19 Lord repented of evil he *p.*
34:5 for I have *p.* the word
36:7 L. hath *p.* ag. this people

**PRONOUNCING.**

*Lev.* 5:4 if a soul sware, *p.* to do

**PROOF, S.**

*Acts* 1:3 hims. alive by many *p.*
2 *Cor.* 2:9 might know the *p.*
8:24 show to them the *p.* of love
13:3 since ye seek a *p.* of Christ
*Phil.* 2:22 ye know the *p.* of him
2 *Tim.* 4:5 *p.* of thy ministry

**PROPER.**

1 *Chr.* 29:3 mine own *p.* good
*Acts* 1:19 in *p.* tongue, Aceldama
1 *Cor.* 7:7 every man hath *p.* gift
*Heb.* 11:23 saw he was a *p.* child

**PROPHECY.**

2 *Chr.* 9:29 Sol.'s acts in *p.* of A.
15:8 when Asa heard *p.* of Oded
*Neh.* 6:12 he pronounced this *p.*
*Prov.* 30:1 *p.* man spake to Ithiel
31:1 *p.* that his mother tau. him
*Mat.* 13:14 fulfilled *p.* of Esaias
1 *Cor.* 12:10 ano. *p.* by same Sp.
13:2 though I have the gift of *p.*
1 *Tim.* 4:14 gift given thee by *p.*
2 *Pet.* 1:19 a more sure word of *p.*
20 no *p.* of script. is of private
21 *p.* came not by will of man
*Rev.* 1:3 bless. they that hear *p.*
*Rev.* 11:6 rain not in da. of th. *p.*
19:10 testimony of J. is sp. of *p*
22:7 blessed that keepeth th. *p.*
10 seal not the say. of the *p.*
19 if any man take from this *p.*

**PROPHECIES.**

1 *Cor.* 13:8 whether *p.* they cease
1 *Tim.* 1:18 according to *p.* befo.

**PROPHESY, Verb.**

*Num.* 11:27 Eldad and Me. do *p.*
1 *K.* 22:8 he doth not *p.* good
18 not *p.* good, 2 *Chr.* 18:17
1 *Chr.* 25:1 should *p.* with harps
*Is.* 30:10 *p.* not right, *p.* deceits
*Jer.* 5:31 the prophets *p.* falsely
11:21 *p.* not in name of the L.
14:14 prophets *p.* lies, *p.* false
16 people to whom they *p.* cast
23:16 heark. not to proph. th. *p.*
25 *p.* lies in my name, 26, 32;
27:10, 14, 15, 16; 29:9, 21
25:30 *p.* against inhab. of earth
26:12 Lord sent me to *p.* against
*Ezek.* 4:7 *p.* against Jerusalem
6:2 *p.* ag. mount. of Israel, 36:1
11:4 *p.* against Jaaz. and Pel. *p.*
13:2 *p.* against proph. that *p.* 17
20:46 *p.* aga. the forest of south
21:2 *p.* against Israel; 9 Jerusa.
14 Son of man *p.* smite hands
28 *p.* concerning Ammon. 25:2
28:21 Son of man *p.* against Zid.
29:2 *p.* aga. Pharaoh, king Eg.
30:2 *p.* against Egypt and say
34:2 *p.* against shepherds of Is.
35:2 *p.* against mount Seir
36:6 *p.* concerning land of Isra.
37:4 *p.* on th. bones; 9 *p.* wind
38:2 *p.* against Gog, 14; 39:1
*Joel* 2:28 sons sh. *p.* *Acts* 2:17, 18
*Amos* 2:12 say. *p.* not, *Mic.* 2:6
3:8 L. spoken, who can but *p.*?
7:12 eat bread, and *p.* there
13 *p.* not any more at Beth-el
15 L. said, Go, *p.* to my pe. Is.
16 *p.* not against house of Isa.
*Mic.* 2:11 I will *p.* to thee of wine
*Zec.* 13:3 when any sh. *p.* then
*Mat.* 15:7 well did Es. *p.* of you
26:68 *p.* unto us, thou Ch. *Mark*
14:65; *Luke* 22:64
*Acts* 21:9 had virgins wh. did *p.*
*Rom.* 12:6 whether *p.* let us *p.* to
1 *Cor.* 13:9 part. and *p.* in part
14:1 rather *p.* 39 covet to *p.*
24 if all *p.* 31 we may all *p.*
*Rev.* 10:11 thou must *p.* before
11:3 witnesses sh. *p.* 1,260 days

**PROPHESIED.**

*Num.* 11:25 they *p.* did not cease
1 *Sam.* 10:10 Spirit of God came
on Saul, and he did *p.* 11;
18:10; 19:23, 24
1 *K.* 18:29 they *p.* until evening
22:10 prophets *p.* 12; 2 *Chr.* 18:9
1 *Chr.* 25:2 the sons of Asaph *p.*
2 *Chr.* 20:37 Eliezer *p.* against J.
*Ezr.* 5:1 Zechariah *p.* to the J.
*Jer.* 2:8 the prophets *p.* by Baal
20:1 Pashur heard that Jere. *p.*
23:13 the prophets of Samar. *p.*
21 I have not spok. yet they *p.*
26:9 why hast thou *p.* in name
18 Micah *p.* in days of Hezek.
20 Urijah *p.* 28:8 *p.* against
29:31 Shem. hath *p.* to you a lie
37:19 where prophets which *p.*?
*Ezek.* 11:13 when I *p.* Pelat. died
37:7 I *p.* as I was com. I *p.* 10
38:17 who *p.* I would bring thee
*Zec.* 13:4 proph. asha. when *p.*
*Mat.* 7:22 Lord, have we not *p.*
11:13 the proph. *p.* until John
*Mark* 7:6 well hath Es. *p.* of you
*Luke* 1:67 his father Zacharias *p.*
*John* 11:51 Caiaphas *p.* that Jes.
*Acts* 19:6 sp. with tongues and *p.*
1 *Cor.* 14:5 I would rather ye *p.*
*Jude* 14 Enoch *p.* of these things

**PROPHESIETH.**

2 *Chr.* 18:7 he nev. *p.* good to me
*Jer.* 28:9 prophet wh. *p.* of peace
*Ezek.* 12:27 he *p.* of times far off
*Zec.* 13:3 thrust him when he *p.*
1 *Cor.* 11:5 *p.* with head uncov.
14:3 he that *p.* speak. unto men
4 he that *p.* edifieth church
5 greater he that *p.* than he

**PROPHESYING, S.**

1 *Sam.* 10:13 made an end of *p.*
19:20 saw comp. of prophets *p.*
*Ezr.* 6:14 they prospered thro' *p.*
1 *Cor.* 11:4 *p.* having head cover.
14:6 exce. I speak to you by *p.*
22 but *p.* serveth not for them
1 *Thes.* 5:20 desp. not *p.* prove all

**PROPHET.**

*Ex.* 7:1 Aaron shall be thy *p.*
1 *Sam.* 22:5 the *p.* Gad said to D.
1 *K.* 1:32 call me Nathan the *p.*
11:29 Ahijah the *p.* found Jero.
13:11 dwelt an old *p.* in B. 25
29 *p.* took up car. of man of G.
the old *p.* came to bury him
18:36 Elij. the *p.* came and said
2 *K.* 5:3 would G. my lord wi. *p.*
13 if *p.* had bid do some great
6:12 Elisha the *p.* telleth what
23:18 with bones of *p.* that came
2 *Chr.* 12:5 came Shemai. the *p.*
13:22 written in story of the *p.*
15:8 wh. Asa heard proph. of *p.*
21:12 a writing from Eli. the *p.*
32:20 *p.* Isaiah prayed to heaven
35:18 from days of Samu. the *p.*
36:12 humbl. not himself bef. *p.*
*Ezr.* 6:14 prophesying of Ha. *p.*
*Ps.* 74:9 there is no *p.* amo. you
*Is.* 3:2 Lord doth away the *p.*
9:15 the *p.* that teacheth lies
28:7 *p.* erred thro' strong drink
*Jer.* 6:13 from *p.* to priests, 8:10
18:18 nor sh. word perish fr. *p.*
23:11 *p.* and priests are profane
28 the *p.* that hath a dream.
28:6 the *p.* Jeremi. said, Amen
9 *p.* wh. prophesieth of peace,
word of *p.* co. to pass *p.* kn.
17 Hananiah *p.* died same year
37:2 nor servants hearken to *p.*
*Lam.* 2:20 shall *p.* be slain?
*Ezek.* 7:26 then seek a vis. of *p.*
14:4 come. to *p.* I will ans. him
9 if *p.* be deceived, I have dec.
10 punishm. of *p.* sh. be even
*Hos.* 4:5 the *p.* sh. fall with thee
9:7 the *p.* is a fool; 8 *p.* a snare
*Amos* 7:14 I was no *p.* nor *p.* son
*Zec.* 13:5 I am no *p.* husbandman
*Mal.* 4:5 I will send Elijah the *p.*
*Mat.* 1:22 which was spoken by
the *p.* Isaiah, 2:15; 3:3; 4:14
8:17; 21:4; *Luke* 3:4; *John*
1:23; 12:38; *Acts* 28:25
2:5 for thus it is written by *p.*
17 spoken by Jeremy *p.* 27:9
12:39 the sign of the *p.* Jonas,
*Luke* 11:29
13:35 spoken by the *p.* Da. 27:35
21:11 this is Jesus *p.* of Nazar.
24:15 sp. of by D. *p.* *Mark* 13:14
*Luke* 1:76 thou child be called *p.*
4:17 delivered book of *p.* Esai.
24 no *p.* is accept. in his coun.
7:28 not a greater *p.* than John
*John* 7:40 of a truth this is the *p.*
52 out of Galilee ariseth no *p.*
*Acts* 2:16 spoken by the *p.* Joel
8:28 he read Esaias the *p.* 30
34 of whom speaketh *p.* this?
13:20 gave judges until Sam. *p.*
2 *Pet.* 2:16 ass forb. madness of *p.*
*See* PRIEST.

**A PROPHET.**

*Gen.* 20:7 restore wife, he is *a p.*
*Deut.* 13:1 if there arise *a p.* or
18:15 I will raise *a p.* from am.
brethren, 18; *Acts* 3:22; 7:37
34:10 arose not *a p.* in Israel
*Jud.* 6:8 L. sent *a p.* to children
1 *Sam.* 3:20 Sam. esta. to be *a p.*
9:9 now called *a p.* called seer
1 *K.* 13:18 I am *a p.* as thou art
18:22 I only remain *a p.* of L.
22:7 is there not here *a p.* of
Lord? 2 *K.* 3:11; 2 *Chr.* 18:6
2 *K.* 5:8 know there is *a p.* in Is.
2 *Chr.* 25:15 L. sent *a p.* to Amaz.
28:9 *a p.* of the Lord was there
*Jer.* 1:5 I ordained thee *a p.*
29:26 maketh himself *a p.* 27
*Ezek.* 2:5 *a p.* among them, 33:33
14:7 cometh to *a p.* to inq. abo.

*Hos.* 12:13 by *a p.* L. brought Is.
out of Eg. by *a p.* preserved
*Mic.* 2:11 be *a p.* of his people
*Mat.* 10:41 he that receiv. *a p.* in
name of *a p.* rec. *a p.* reward
11:9 what went ye to see? *a p.*
13:57 *a p.* is not without honor,
*Mark* 6:4; *John* 4:44
14:5 accounted him *a p.* 21:26;
*Mark* 11:32; *Luke* 20:6
21:46 multi. took him for *a p.*
*Mark* 6:15 *a p.* or as one of pro.
*Luke* 7:16 *a* great *p.* among us
39 if he were *a p.* would have
13:33 it cannot be *a p.* perish
24:19 Je. who was *a p.* mighty
*John* 4:19 I perceive th. art *a p.*
9:17 blind man said, He is *a p.*
*Acts* 2:30 David *a p.* knowing G.
21:10 *a* cert. *p.* named Agabus
1 *Cor.* 14:37 man think to be *a p.*
*Tit.* 1:12 *a p.* of their own land

**False PROPHET.**

*Acts* 13:6 *f. p.* a Jew named Bar.
*Rev.* 16:13 like frogs out of *f. p.*
19:20 beast taken. wi. him *f. p.*
20:10 cast wh. beast and *f. p.* are

*See* LORD.

**That PROPHET.**

*Deut.* 13:5 *t. p.* shall die, 18:20
*Ezek.* 14:9 I the L. deceived *t. p.*
*John* 1:21 ask, Art thou *t. p.?* 25
6:14 this is of a truth *that p.*
*Acts* 3:23 wh. will not hear *t. p.*

**PROPHETS.**

*Num.* 11:29 L.'s people were *p.*
1 *Sam.* 10:5 meet a company of *p.*
12 is Saul among the *p.?* 19:24
28:6 L. answ. him not by *p.* 15
1 *K.* 18:4 Obad. hid 100 *p.* by 50
13 slew *p.* 19 *p.* of Baal 450, 22
40 take *p.* of B. let none esca.
19:10 Is. slain. *p.* 14; *Neh.* 9:26
22:22 lying spirit, in *p.* 2 *Chr.*
18:21
2 *K.* 3:13 *p.* of father, *p.* of mot.
2 *Chr.* 20:20 believe *p.* ye sh. pr.
24:19 sent *p.* 36:16 misused *p.*
*Ezr.* 5:2 with th. were *p.* of God
*Neh.* 6:7 appointed *p.* to preach
9:30 testifiedst by thy Spi. in *p.*
32 trouble that ha. come on *p.*
*Is.* 29:10 *p.* and seers he covered
30:10 *p.* proph. not, *Amos* 2:12
*Jer.* 2:8 *p.* prophesied by Baal
30 your sword devoured yo. *p.*
4:9 *p.* wonder; 5:13 *p.* bec. wind
5:31 *p.* prophesy falsely
8:1 bring out the bones of *p.*
13:13 fill *p.* with drunkenness
14:14 *p.* proph. lies in my name
15 by sword and famine sh. *p.*
23:13 I have seen folly in the *p.*
14 I have seen in *p.* horri. thi.
15 from *p.* is profaneness gone
21 I have not sent these *p.* yet
26 *p.* of deceit of th. own heart
30 I am against *p.* that steal, 31
26:11 then spake *p.* This man is
27:9 hearken not to your *p.* 16
18 *p.* and word of L. with the.
28:8 *p.* that have been before
29:1 letter Jeremiah sent to *p.*
8 let not your *p.* deceive you
15 the Lord hath rais. us up *p.*
32:32 and their *p.* provoke me
37:19 where are now your *p.*
*Lam.* 2:9 *p.* find no vision fr. L.
14 thy *p.* have seen vain thin.
4:13 sins of her *p.* th. shed blood
*Ezek.* 13:2 prophesy agai. the *p.*
3 saith L. Woe unto foolish *p.*
4 O Israel, thy *p.* are like fox.
9 my hand shall be upon the *p.*
22:25 a conspiracy of her *p.*
28 *p.* daubed them with mort.
*Hos.* 6:5 I have hewed th. by *p.*
12:10 spoken by *p.* multiplied
*Amos* 2:11 raised of your sons *p.*
*Mic.* 3:6 sun sh. go down over *p.*
11 and the *p.* divine for money
*Zep.* 3:4 her *p.* are light persons
*Zec.* 1:5 *p.* do they live for ever?
7:7 L. hath cried by former *p.*
12 L. sent in Sp. by former *p.*
13:2 I will cause *p.* to pass out
4 the *p.* shall be ashamed
*Mat.* 5:12 persecuted *p.* *Lu.* 6:23
17 think not I came to dest. *p.*
7:12 this is the law and the *p.*
13:17 *p.* desired to see, *Lu.* 10:24
22:40 on these hang law and *p.*
23:31 children of them killed *p.*
34 send unto you *p.* *Lu.* 11:49
37 O Jeru. thou that killest *p.*
*Mark* 1:2 as it is writ. in *p.* *Luke*
18:31; 24:25; *John* 6:45
*Luke* 1:70 spake by *p.* 2 *Pet.* 3:2
16:16 law and *p.* were until J.
29 said, They ha. M. and *p.* 31
24:25 slow to beli. wh. *p.* spok.
*John* 1:45 him of wh. *p.* did wri.
8:52 Abraham and *p.* dead, 53
*Acts* 3:18 showed by mo. of *p.* 21
11:27 *p.* came from Jerusalem
13:1 in church at Antioch cer. *p.*
15 reading of the law and *p.*
15:32 Judas and Silas being *p.*
24:14 believing all written in *p.*
26:22 none other th. than *p.* say
27 Agrippa, believ. thou *p.?*
*Rom.* 1:2 promis. afore by his *p.*
3:21 witness. by the law and *p.*
11:3 L. they have killed *p.*
1 *Cor.* 12:28 secondarily, *p.* thir.
29 are all *p.?* 14:29 let *p.* speak
*Eph.* 2:20 on the foundation of *p.*
3:5 as now revealed to his *p.*
4:11 gave some *p.* and teachers
1 *Thes.* 2:15 killed L. and the *p.*
*Heb.* 1:1 spake to fathers by *p.*
*Jam.* 5:10 take *p.* who have spo.
1 *Pet.* 1:10 of salvation *p.* inquir.
*Rev.* 11:10 th. *p.* tormented them
18:20 rejoice, ye apostles and *p.*
24 in her was found blood of *p.*
22:9 I am of thy brethren the *p.*

**All the PROPHETS.**

1 *K.* 19:1 how he had sla. *a. t. p.*
22:10 and *all the p.* prophesied,
12; 2 *Chr.* 18:9, 11
2 *K.* 10:19 call to me *a. t. p.* of B.
17:13 testified ag. Is. by *a. t. p.*
*Mat.* 11:13 *a. the p.* prophesied
*Luke* 11:50 blood of *a. t. p.* req.
13:28 wh. ye see *a. t. p.* in king.
24:27 and beginning at *a. t. p.*
*Acts* 3:24 *all the p.* from Samuel
10:43 to him give *all t. p.* witn.

**False PROPHETS.**

*Mat.* 7:15 beware of *false p.*
24:11 many *false p.* shall rise,
24; *Mark* 13:22
*Luke* 6:26 so did th. fath. to *f. p.*
2 *Pet.* 2:1 were *f. p.* among them
1 *John* 4:1 many *f. p.* gone out

**My PROPHETS.**

1 *Chr.* 16:22 do *my p.* no harm,
*Ps.* 105:15

**Of the PROPHETS.**

1 *Sam.* 10:10 comp. *of p.* met h.
1 *K.* 20:35 cert. men of sons *of p.*
41 king discern. he was *of t. p.*
22:13 words *of t. p.* decla. good.
2 *Chr.* 18:12
2 *K.* 2:3 sons *of t. p.* at Beth-el,
5 the sons *of the p.* at Jericho
15 sons *of t. p.* said, spirit of E.
4:38 pottage for sons *of the p.*
*Neh.* 6:14 thi. th. of rest *of t. p.*
*Jer.* 23:9 bec. *of the p.* bones sh.
16 hea. not to words *of p.* 27:14
26 sh. this be in heart *of t. p.?*
*Hos.* 12:10 simil. by minist. *of p.*
*Zec.* 8:9 hear by mouth *of the p.*
*Mat.* 16:14 Elias or one *of the p.*
*Mark* 6:15; 8:28
23:29 tombs *of t. p.* *Luke* 11:47
30 partakers in blood *of t. p.*
26:56 scrip. *of t. p.* be fulfilled
*Luke* 9:8 one *of the p.* risen, 19
*Acts* 3:25 ye are children *of t. p.*
7:52 wh. *of t. p.* not persecut.?
13:15 reading *of* law and *t. p.*
27 they know not voice *of t. p.*
15:15 to th. agree words *of t. p.*
28:23 persuad. them out *of t. p.*
*Rom.* 16:26 manif. by scrip. *of p.*
1 *Cor.* 14:32 spirits *of t. p.* subj.
*Eph.* 2:20 built on founda. *of p.*
*Heb.* 11:32 fail me to tell *of t. p.*
*Rev.* 16:6 shed the blood *of t. p.*
22:6 L. God *of t. p.* sent angel

**Servants the PROPHETS.**

2 *K.* 9:7 avenge blood of *s. t. p.*
17:13 law I sent by my *s. the p.*
23 Lord had said by his *s. t. p.*
21:10 L. spa. by his *s. t. p.* 24:2
*Ezr.* 9:11 commanded by *s. t. p.*
*Jer.* 7:25 sent you my *serv. the*
*p.* 25:4; 29:19; 35:15
*Ezek.* 38:17 in old tim. by *s. t. p.*
*Dan.* 9:6 nei. hearken. to *s. t. p.*
10 laws set be. us by his *s. t. p.*
*Amos* 3:7 reveal. secret to *s. t. p.*
*Zec.* 1:6 commanded my *s. t. p.*
*Rev.* 10:7 declared to his *s. t. p.*
11:18 give reward to *s. the p.*

**PROPHETESS.**

*Ex.* 15:20 Miriam *p.* took timb.
*Jud.* 4:4 Deborah a *p.* judged Is.
2 *K.* 22:14 went to Huldah a *p.*
2 *Chr.* 34:22
*Neh.* 6:14 think on *p.* Noadiah
*Is.* 8:3 went to *p.* she conceived
*Luke* 2:36 th. was one Anna a *p.*
*Rev.* 2:20 Jez. called herself a *p.*

**PROPITIATION.**

*Rom.* 3:25 God set to be a *p.*
1 *John* 2:2 *p.* for our sins, 4:10

**PROPORTION.**

1 *K.* 7:36 to the *p.* of every one
*Job* 41:12 not conceal comely *p.*
*Rom.* 12:6 accord. to *p.* of faith

**PROSELYTE, S.**

*Mat.* 23:15 sea and la. to ma. *p.*
*Acts* 2:10 Jews and *p.* we hear
6:5 Nicholas a *p.* of Antioch
13:43 Jews and religious *p.* followed Paul and Barnabas

**PROSPECT.**

*Ezek.* 40:44 *p.* was to the south
46 *p.* north; 42:15 *p.* east, 43:4

**PROSPER.**

*Gen.* 24:40 G. send angel, *p.* thee
42 if now thou do *p.* my way
39:3 Lord made Joseph to *p.* 23
*Num.* 14:41 transgress. not *p.*
*Deut.* 28:29 sh. not *p.* in thy wa.
29:9 that ye may *p.* in all ye do.
*Jos.* 1:7; 1 *K.* 2:3
1 *K.* 22:12 go to Ramoth-gilead
and *p.* 15; 2 *Chr.* 18:11, 14
1 *Chr.* 22:11 my son, L. *p.* thee
13 shalt *p.* if thou takest heed
2 *Chr.* 13:12 fight not, sh. not *p.*
20:20 believe proph. so sh. ye *p.*
24:20 why transg. ye can. *p.?*
26:5 Lord God made him to *p.*
*Neh.* 1:11 *p.* I pray thee, thy ser.
2:20 G. of heaven, he will *p.* us
*Job* 12:6 tabernac. of robbers *p.*
*Ps.* 1:3 what. he doeth shall *p.*
73:12 ungodly *p.* in the world
122:6 they sh. *p.* that love thee
*Prov.* 28:13 cover. his sins not *p.*

Ec. 11:6 know. not whether p.
Is. 53:10 pleas. of L. p. in hands
54:17 no weapon ag. thee sh. p.
55:11 it shall p. in thing I sent
Jer. 2:37 thou sh. not p. in them
5:28 th. p. 10:21 not p. 20:11
12:1 doth way of wicked p.?
22:30 man that sh. not p. in his days, man of his seed sh. p.
23:5 a king shall reign and p.
32:5 tho' ye fight, ye sh. not p.
Lam. 1:5 adversa. enemies p.
Ezek. 16:13 and thou didst p.
17:9 saith Lord, Shall it p.? 10
15 shall he p.? sh. he escape?
Dan. 8:24 he sh. destroy and p.
25 he shall cause craft to p.
11:27 speak lies, sh. not p. 36
3 John 2 I wish th. thou may p.

**PROSPERED, ETH.**

Gen. 24:56 seeing L. p. my way
Jud. 4:24 hand of Is. p. ag. Jab.
2 Sam. 11:7 deman. how war p.
2 K. 18:7 Hezek. p. 2 Chr. 31:21; 32:30; 2 Chr. 14:7 Asa p.
1 Chr. 29:23 Solomon p.
Ezr. 5:8 work p. in their hands
6:14 p. thro' prophesying of H.
Job 9:4 harden. ag. him and p.?
Ps. 37:7 because of him that p.
Prov. 17:8 whi. it turneth it p.
Dan. 6:28 Dan. p. in reign of D.
8:12 cast down truth, and it p.
1 Cor. 16:2 as God hath p. him
3 John 2 in health, ev. as soul p.

**PROSPERITY.**

Deut. 23:6 th. sh. not seek th. p.
1 Sam. 25:6 say to him liv. in p.
1 K. 10:7 thy wisdom and p.
Job 15:21 in p. destr. shall come
36:11 sh. spend their days in p.
Ps. 30:6 in my p. I said
35:27 L. hath plea. in p. of ser.
73:3 I saw the p. of the wicked
118:25 O L. I bes. thee, send p.
122:7 peace wi. walls, p. in pal.
Prov. 1:32 p. of fools destroy th.
Ec. 7:14 in day of p. be joyful
Jer. 22:21 I spake to th. in thy p.
33:9 the p. that I procure to it
Lam. 3:17 fr. peace, I forgat p.
Zec. 1:17 cit. thro' p. be spread
7:7 J. was inhabited and in p.

**PROSPEROUS, LY.**

Gen. 24:21 L. made his journ. p.
39:2 L. was with Jo. a p. man
Jos. 1:8 thou make thy way p.
Jud. 18:5 way we go sh. be p.
2 Chr. 7:11 Solomon p. effected
Ps. 45:4 in thy majesty ride p.
Job 8:6 habitation of righte. p.
Is. 48:15 shall make his way p.
Zec. 8:12 the seed shall be p.
Rom. 1:10 I mi. have p. journey

**PROSTITUTE.**

Lev. 19:29 do not p. thy daught.

**PROTECTION.**

Deut. 32:38 rise up and be yo. p.

**PROTEST, ED, ING.**

Gen. 43:3 man did solemnly p.
1 Sam. 8:9 p. solemnly unto th.
1 K. 2:42 and I p. unto thee
Jer. 11:7 I p. to your fathers, ris. early and p. saying, Obey
Zec. 3:6 the angel of the L. p.
1 Cor. 15:31 I p. by rejoic. in C.

**PROUD.**

Job 9:13 the p. helpers do stoop
26:12 smiteth through the p.
Job 38:11 thy p. waves be stayed
40:11 behold every one th. is p.
12 look on every one that is p.
Ps. 12:3 tongue speak p. things
31:23 and rewardeth the p. doer
40:4 blessed. respecteth not p.
86:14 p. are risen against me
94:2 render a reward to the p.
101:5 him that hath a p. heart
119:21 thou hast rebuked the p.
51 p. have had me in derision
69 p. have forged a lie ag. me
78 let p. be ashamed, they de.
85 the p. digged pits for me
122 let not the p. oppress me
123:4 filled with contempt of p.
124:5 p. waters had gone over
138:6 the p. he knoweth afar off
140:5 p. have hid a snare for me
Prov. 6:17 Lord hateth a p. look
15:25 L. will destroy house of p.
16:5 p. in heart abomina. to L.
19 to divide spoil with the p.
21:4 a p. heart is sin
24 p. scorner, deals in p. wra.
28:25 p. heart stirreth up strife
Ec. 7:8 better than p. in spirit
Is. 2:12 day of L. on ev. one p.
13:11 arrogancy of p. to cease
16:6 we heard of M. he is ve. p.
Jer. 13:15 be not p. L. hath spo.
43:2 all p. men answ. Jeremiah
48:29 pride of Moab exceed. p.
50:29 hath been p. 31 O most p.
32 most p. sh. stumble and fa.
Hab. 2:5 he is a p. man, neither
Mal. 3:15 p. happy; 4:1 p. stub.
Luke 1:51 hath scattered the p.
Rom. 1:30 unrighte. p. boasters
1 Tim. 6:4 he is p. know. noth.
2 Tim. 3:2 lov. of themselves, p.
Jam. 4:6 G. resisteth p. 1 Pet. 5:5

**PROUDLY.**

Ex. 18:11 p. he was above them
1 Sam. 2:3 talk no more so p.
Neh. 9:10 they dealt p. 16:29
Ps. 17:10 with mouth speak p.
31:18 speak grievous things p.
Is. 3:5 shall behave himself p.
Ob. 12 neither have spoken p.

**PROVE.**

Ex. 16:4 I may p. th. Deut. 8:16
20:20 for God is come to p. you
Deut. 8:2 humble thee, p. thee
33:8 holy one, wh. thou didst p.
Jud. 2:22 I may p. Isr. 3:1, 4
6:39 let me p. thee but th. once
1 K. 10:1 came to p. S. 2 Chr. 9:1
Job 9:20 it shall p. me perverse
Ps. 26:2 exam. me, O L. p. me
Ec. 2:1 I will p. th. with mirth
Dan. 1:12 p. thy serv. I beseech
Mal. 3:10 p. me now herewith
Luke 14:19 oxen, I go to p. them
John 6:6 this he said to p. him
Acts 24:13 nei. can they p. 25:7
Rom. 12:2 p. what is that good
2 Cor. 8:8 to p. sincerity of love
13:5 p. your own selves, know
Gal. 6:4 let ev. man p. his work
1 Thes. 5:21 p. all things

**PROVED.**

Gen. 42:15 sh. be p. by life of Ph.
16 that your words may be p.
Ex. 15:25 made stat. and p. them
1 Sam. 17:39 I have not p. them
Ps. 17:3 thou hast p. my heart
66:10 thou, O God, hast p. us
81:7 I p. thee at waters of M.
95:9 when your fathers p. me
Ec. 7:23 this have I p. by wisd.
Dan. 1:14 and p. them ten days
Rom. 3:9 we p. Jews and Genti.
2 Cor. 8:22 wh. we have often p.
1 Tim. 3:10 let th. also be first p.
Heb. 3:9 your fathers p. me

**PROVETH, ING.**

Deut. 13:3 Lord your G. p. you
Acts 9:22 Saul p. that this is Ch.
Eph. 5:10 p. what is accept. to L.

**PROVENDER.**

Gen. 24:25 we have straw and p.
32 gave straw and p. to cam.
42:27 opened sack to give ass p.
43:24 men gave their asses p.
Jud. 19:19 th. is straw and p. 21
Is. 30:24 asses shall eat clean p.

**PROVERB.**

Deut. 28:37 and ye shall be a p.
1 Sam. 10:12 p. is Saul am. prop.
24:13 as saith p. of the ancients
1 K. 9:7 Israel shall be a p.
2 Chr. 7:20 house will I ma. a p.
Ps. 69:11 I became a p. to them
Prov. 1:6 to understand a p. and
Is. 14:4 p. ag. king of Babylon
Jer. 24:9 to be a p. and a curse
Ezek. 12:23 I will make p. cease, no more use p. in Is. 18:2, 3
14:8 make him a sign and p.
Hab. 2:6 take up a p. ag. him
Luke 4:23 p. phys. heal thyself
John 16:29 spea. plain. and no p.
2 Pet. 2:22 happ. according to p.

**PROVERBS.**

Num. 21:27 they that speak in p.
1 K. 4:32 Solomon spake 3,000 p.
Prov. 1:1 p. of Solo. 10:1; 25:1
Ec. 12:9 preacher set in order p.
Ezek. 16:44 ev. one that useth p.
John 16:25 sp. in p. no more in p.

**PROVIDE.**

Gen. 22:8 G. will p. hims. lamb
30:30 shall I p. for own house?
Ex. 18:21 thou sh. p. able men
1 Sam. 16:17 p. me man can play
2 Chr. 2:7 men whom Da. did p.
Ps. 78:20 can he p. flesh for pe.?
Mat. 10:9 p. nei. gold nor silver
Luke 12:33 p. bags wax not old
Acts 23:24 p. beasts to set P. on
Rom. 12:17 p. things honest
1 Tim. 5:8 any p. not for house

**PROVIDED.**

Deut. 33:21 p. first part himself
1 Sam. 16:1 I have p. me a king
2 Sam. 19:32 p. king of susten.
1 K. 4:7 p. victuals for king, 27
Ps. 65:9 when thou hast p.
Luke 12:20 things th. hast p.?
Heb. 11:40 having p. bet. things

**PROVIDENCE.**

Acts 24:2 done to nation by p.

**PROVIDETH, ING.**

Job 38:41 p. for the raven food
Prov. 6:8 p. meat in summer
2 Cor. 8:21 p. for honest things

**PROVINCE, S.**

1 K. 20:14 princes of p. 15, 17, 19
Ezr. 4:15 this city hurtful to p.
6:2 found in p. of the Medes
7:16 gold thou canst find in p.
Neh. 11:3 the. are chief of the p.
Est. 1:1 Ahasu. reigned 127 p.
16 wrong to peo. in p. 22
2:3 king appoint officers in p.
3:8 people scattered in all p.
4:11 all peo. of king's p. know
9:4 Mord.'s fame went thro' p.
28 these days sh. be kept in p.
Ec. 2:8 I gathered treas. of p.
5:8 if thou seest oppres. in a p.
Lam. 1:1 she was princess am. p.
Ezek. 19:8 against him from p.
Dan. 2:48 made D. ruler over p.
3:30 promoted Shad. in the p.
8:2 Shushan, in p. of Elam
11:24 enter fattest places of p.
Acts 23:34 he asked of what p.
25:1 when Fes. was come to p.

**PROVISION.**

Gen. 42:25 give them p. for way
45:21 Jos. gave them p. for way
Jos. 9:5 bread of th. p. was dry
12 bread we took hot for our p.
1 K. 4:7 in his month made p.
22 Solomon's p. was 30 meas.

2 K. 6:23 he prepared great p.
1 Chr. 29:19 for which I made p.
Ps. 132:15 I will bless her p.
Dan. 1:5 king appoint. daily p.
Rom. 13:14 ma. not p. for flesh

**PROVOCATION.**
1 K. 15:30 Jer. made Is. sin by p.
21:22 for the p. wherewith Ah.
2 K. 23:26 bec. of p. Manasseh
Neh. 9:18 wrought great p. 26
Job 17:2 eye continue in th. p.?
Ps. 95:8 harden not your hearts as in p. Heb. 3:8, 15
Jer. 32:31 this city ha. been a p.
Ezek. 20:28 th. they presented p.

**PROVOKE.**
Ex. 23:21 obey and p. him not
Num. 14:11 how long people p.?
Deut. 31:20 if ye p. and break
Job 12:6 that p. God are secure
Ps. 78:40 how oft did th. p. him
Is. 3:8 doings against L. to p.
Jer. 7:19 they p. me to anger?
44:8 in that ye p. me to wrath
Luke 11:53 began to urge and p.
Rom. 10:19 I will p. to jealousy
11:11 to p. them to jealousy, 14
1 Cor. 10:22 do we p. L. to jeal.?
Eph. 6:4 p. not your chil. to wr.
Heb. 3:16 wh. they heard, did p.
10:24 p. to love and good works

**PROVOKED.**
Num. 14:23 nor sh. any that p.
Num. 16:30 these men have p. L.
Deut. 9:8 in Horeb ye p. the L.
22 at Tab. and Massah ye p. L.
1 Sam. 1:6 adversaries p. sore
7 so she p. her, theref. she we.
1 K. 14:22 Judah p. to jealousy
2 K. 23:26 Manasseh had p. him
1 Chr. 21:1 Satan p. David
Ezr. 5:12 our fathers had p. God
Ps. 78:56 tempted and p. God
106:7 but p. him at the sea
29 they p. him with invent.
33 they p. spirit of Moses, 43
Zec. 8:14 your fathers p. me
1 Cor. 13:5 char. is not easily p.
2 Cor. 9:2 your zeal p. very many

**PROVOKEDST, ETH.**
Deut. 9:7 forget not how p. Lord
Prov. 20:2 whoso p. him to ang.
Is. 65:3 peo. that p. me to anger
Ezek. 8:3 image which p. jeal.
See ANGER.

**PROVOKING.**
Deut. 32:19 because of p. sons
1 K. 14:15 made groves, p. Lord
16:7 ag. Baasha in p. Lord, 13
Ps. 78:17 by p. the Most H.
Gal. 5:26 vain glory, p. one ano.

**PRUDENCE.**
2 Chr. 2:12 son endued with p.
Prov. 8:12 I wisd. dwell with p.
Eph. 1:8 abound. in wisd. and p.

**PRUDENT.**
1 Sam. 16:18 Dav. p. in matters
Prov. 12:16 p. man cover. shame
23 a p. man conceal. knowl.
13:16 every p. man dealeth with
14:8 wisdom of p. to understand
15 the p. looketh to his goings
18 p. are crowned with knowl.
15:5 he that regar. p. repr. is p.
16:21 the wise shall be called p.
18:15 heart of p. getteth knowl.
19:14 a p. wife is from the Lord
22:3 a p. man foresc. evil, 27:12
Is. 3:2 take away p. and ancient
5:21 woe to p. in their own sig.
10:13 I have done it, for I am p.
29:14 understanding of p. men
Jer. 49:7 is counsel perish. fr. p.?
Hos. 14:9 who is p. and he shall?
Amos 5:13 p. shall keep silence
Mat. 11:25 hid these things from the wise and p. Luke 10:21
Acts 13:7 Serg. Paulus, a p. man
1 Cor. 1:19 understanding of p.

**PRUDENTLY.**
Is. 52:13 my servant sh. deal p.

**PRUNE, ED.**
Lev. 25:3 six years shalt thou p.
4 sev. year not sow field nor p.
Is. 5:6 it shall not be p.

**PRUNING.**
Is. 2:4 beat spears into p. hooks
18:5 cut off sprigs with p. hooks
Joel 3:10 beat p. hooks into spe.
Mic. 4:3 beat spears into p. hoo.

**PSALM.**
1 Chr. 16:7 David deliver. this p.
Ps. 81:2 take p. 98:5 voice of p.
Acts 13:33 as writ. in second p.
35 saith in ano. p. Thou shalt
1 Cor. 14:26 every one hath a p.?

**PSALMIST.**
2 Sam. 23:1 David sweet p. of Is

**PSALMS.**
1 Chr. 16:9 sing p. Ps. 105:2
Ps. 95:2 joyful noise with p.
Luke 20:42 D. saith in book of p.
24:44 which were written in p.
Acts 1:20 written in book of P.
Eph. 5:19 speak. to yours. in p.
Col. 3:16 admonish. other in p.
Jam. 5:13 is any merry? sing p.

**PSALTERY.**
1 Sam. 10:5 meet prop. with a p.
Ps. 33:2 sing with the p. 144:9
57:8 awake p. and harp, 108:2
71:22 I will praise with p. 92:3
81:2 bring hither harp with p.
150:3 praise him with p. harp
Dan. 3:5 sound of p. 7, 10, 15

PSALTERIES. See CYMBALS.

**PUBLIC, LY.**
Mat. 1:19 make her a p. example
Acts 18:28 p. convinced the Jews
20:20 but have taught you p.

**PUBLICAN, S.**
Mat. 5:46 do not p. same? 47
9:10 many p. sat with him, Mark 2:15; Luke 5:29
11 why eat. your master wi. p.
10:3 Thomas, and Matthew p.
Mat. 11:19 a friend of p. Lu 7:34
18:17 let him be as hea. and p.
21:31 p. go into kingdom of G.
32 p. and harlots beli. on him
Luke 3:12 came p. to be baptized
5:27 he saw a p. named Levi
7:29 p. justi. G. being baptized
15:1 then drew near to him p.
18:10 the one Pharisee, other p.
11 God, I thank thee, not as p.
13 p. standing afar off, said
19:2 Zaccheus chief among p.

**PUBLISH.**
Deut. 32:3 I will p. name of L.
1 Sam. 31:9 p. it in house of idols
2 Sam. 1:20 p. it not in Askelon
Neh. 8:15 p. that they bring pine
Ps. 26:7 may p. with the voice
Jer. 4:5 p. in Jeru. 16 p. against
5:20 declare this, p. it in Judah
31:7 p. ye and say, O Lord save
46:14 p. in Migdol, p. in Noph
50:2 p. and conceal not
Amos 3:9 p. in palaces of Ashdod
4:5 proclaim and p. fr. offerings
Mark 1:45 he began to p. it, 5:20

**PUBLISHED.**
Est. 1:20 dec. p. thro' empire, 22
3:14 Haman's decree p. 8:13
Ps. 68:11 great company p. it
Jon. 3:7 he caused it to be p.
Mark 7:36 more a gre. deal th. p.
13:10 the gospel must first be p.
Luke 8:39 p. through whole city
Acts 10:37 that word wh. was p.
13:49 word of the Lord was p.

**PUBLISHETH.**
Is. 52:7 that p. peace, p. salvat.
Jer. 4:15 voice p. affliction
Nah. 1:15 feet of him p. peace

**PUBLIUS.**
Acts 28:8 the father of P. lay sick

**PUDENS.**
2 Tim. 4:21 greeteth thee and P.

**PUFFED up.**
1 Cor. 4:6 no one of you be p. up
18 some are p. up, as though I
19 not speech of th. are p. up
5:2 are p. up and not mourned
13:4 charity is not p. up
Col. 2:18 vainly p. up

**PUFFETH at, up.**
Ps. 10:5 enemies, he p. at them
12:5 safety fr. him th. p. at him
1 Cor. 8:1 knowl. p. up, charity

**PUL.**
2 K. 15:19 P. king of Assyria
1 Chr. 5:26 stirred up spirit of P.
Is. 66:19 those that escape to P.

**PULL, ED.**
Gen. 8:9 Noah p. the dove to him
19:10 the men p. Lot into house
1 K. 13:4 Jerob. could not p. it
Ezr. 6:11 let timber be p. down
Ps. 31:4 p. me out of net
Is. 22:19 fr. thy state p. th. down
Jer. 1:10 set th. to p. down, 18:7
12:3 p. them like sheep for sla.
24:6 build, not p. down, 42:10
Lam. 3:11 p. me in pieces
Ezek. 17:9 sh. he not p. up roots?
Amos 9:15 shall no more be p. up
Mic. 2:8 p. off robe with garm.
Zec. 7:11 p. away shoulder
Mat. 7:4 p. out mote, Luke 6:42
Luke 12:18 p. down my barns
14:5 not p. him out on sab.?
Acts 23:10 lest Paul sho. been p.

**PULLING.**
2 Cor. 10:4 mighty to p. down
Jude 23 with fear p. out of fire

**PULPIT.**
Neh. 8:4 Ezra stood upon a p.

**PULSE.**
2 Sam. 17:28 and parched p.
Dan. 1:12 let them give p.

**PUNISH.**
Lev. 26:18 p. you sev. times, 24
Prov. 17:26 to p. just not good
Is. 10:12 p. stout heart of king
13:11 I will p. world for evil
24:21 Lord shall p. the host
26:21 L. cometh to p. inhabit.
27:1 L. with strong sw. sh. p.
Jer. 9:25 p. them are circumcised
11:22 p. men of Anathoth
13:21 what say when he sh. p.?
21:14 p. accord. to your doings
23:34 I will p. man; 25:12 p. king, 50:18
27:8 p. nation; 29:32 p. Shem.
30:20 I will p. all th. oppress th.
36:31 I will p. Jehoiakim
Jer. 44:13 p. them in E. as I p. J.
29 a sign that I will p. you
46:25 I will p. the multitude
51:44 I will p. Bel in Babylon
Hos. 4:9 p. them for their ways
14 I will not p. your daughters
12:2 p. J. according to his ways
Amos 3:2 I will p. you for iniq.
Zep. 1:8 in day I will p. princes
9 I will p. all those that leap
12 p. men that are settled
Zec. 8:14 as I thoug. to p. them
Acts 4:21 how th. might p. them

**PUNISHED.**
*Ex.* 21:20 shall surely be *p.* 22
21 not be *p.* he is his money
*Ezr.* 9:13 *p.* less than iniq. des.
*Job* 31:11 it is iniq. to be *p.* 28
*Prov.* 21:11 when scorner is *p.*
22:3 simple are *p.* 27:12
*Jer.* 44:13 as I have *p.* Jerusa.
50:18 punish as I have *p.* king
*Zep.* 3:7 not cut off, how I *p.*
*Zec.* 10:3 shepherds, I *p.* goats
*Acts* 22:5 br. them bou. to be *p.*
26:11 I *p.* them in every synag.
2 *Thes.* 1:9 *p.* with destruction
2 *Pet.* 2:9 day of judgm. to be *p.*

**PUNISHMENT.**
*Gen.* 4:13 *p.* great. th. I can bear
*Lev.* 26:41 accept *p.* of iniq. 43
1 *Sam.* 28:10 no *p.* shall hap. th.
*Job* 31:3 a strange *p.* to workers
*Prov.* 19:19 man of wrath suf. *p.*
*Lam.* 3:39 for *p.* of his sins
4:6 *p.* of my people is greater than the *p.* of Sodom
22 *p.* of thine iniq. is accomp.
*Ezek.* 14:10 bear *p.* of their iniq. *p.* of prophets as *p.* of him
*Amos* 1:3 I will not turn away *p.* thereof, 6, 9, 11, 13; 2:1, 4, 6
*Zec.* 14:19 this shall be *p.* of Eg.
*Mat.* 25:46 go into everlasting *p.*
2 *Cor.* 2:6 such a man is this *p.*
*Heb.* 10:29 how much sorer *p.*
1 *Pet.* 2:14 for *p.* of evil-doers

**PUNISHMENTS.**
*Job* 19:29 bringeth *p.* of sword
*Ps.* 149:7 execute *p.* upon people

PUNON *Num.* 33:42, 43

**PUR.**
*Est.* 3:7 cast P. that is, the lot
9:24 for Haman had cast P.
26 Purim, after the name of P.
*See* PURIM.

**PURCHASE, Substantive.**
*Gen.* 49:32 *p.* of field and cave
*Jer.* 32:11 I took evidence of *p.*
12 I gave evidence of *p.* 14, 16

**PURCHASE, ED.**
*Gen.* 25:10 Abra. *p.* of sons of H.
*Ex.* 15:16 over wh. thou hast *p.*
*Lev.* 25:33 if a man *p.* of Levites
*Ruth* 4:10 R. I *p.* to be my wife
*Ps.* 74:2 congregati. thou hast *p.*
78:54 wh. his right hand had *p.*
*Acts* 1:18 this man *p.* a field
8:20 gift of God may be *p.*
20:28 *p.* with his own blood
*Eph.* 1:14 redemption of *p.* pos.
1 *Tim.* 3:13 office of dea. well, *p.*

**PURE.**
*Ex.* 27:20 br. *p.* oil, *Lev.* 24:2
31:8 *p.* candles. 39:37; *Lev.* 24:4
*Deut.* 32:14 *p.* blood of grape
2 *Sam.* 22:27 with *p.* thou wilt show thyself *p.* *Ps.* 18:26
*Ezr.* 6:20 all *p.* killed passover
*Job* 4:17 shall a man be more *p.*?
8:6 thou wert *p.* and upright
11:4 thou said, My doctrine is *p.*
16:17 injustice, my prayer is *p.*
25:5 stars are not *p.* in his sight
*Ps.* 12:6 words of the Lord are *p.*
19:8 commandment of L. is *p.*
119:140 thy word is very *p.*
*Prov.* 15:26 words of *p.* are plea.
20:9 who can say, I am *p.* fr. sin?
11 whether his work be *p.*
21:8 as for *p.* his work is right
30:5 every word of God is *p.*
12 a generation *p.* in own eyes
*Dan.* 7:9 hair of head like *p.* wool
*Mic.* 6:11 shall I count them *p.*?
*Zep.* 3:9 turn to people *p.* langu.
*Mal.* 1:11 in ev. place a *p.* offer.
*Acts* 20:26 *p.* from blood of men
*Rom.* 14:20 all th. indeed are *p.*
*Phil.* 4:8 whatsoev. things are *p.*
1 *Tim.* 3:9 faith in a *p.* consci.
5:22 partak. of sins, keep thy. *p.*
2 *Tim.* 1:3 with *p.* conscience
*Tit.* 1:15 to the *p.* all thi. are *p.* to the defiled nothing is *p.*
*Heb.* 10:22 bodies washed with *p.*
*Jam.* 1:27 *p.* relig. and undefiled
3:17 wisdom fr. above is first *p.*
2 *Pet.* 3:1 I stir up your *p.* minds
1 *John* 3:3 purifieth as he is *p.*
*Rev.* 15:6 ang. clothed in *p.* linen
22:1 showed a *p.* river of water
*See* HEART, GOLD.

**PURELY.**
*Is.* 1:25 I will *p.* purge away

**PURENESS.**
*Job* 22:30 deliv. by *p.* of hands
*Prov.* 22:11 he loved *p.* of heart
2 *Cor.* 6:6 appro. ourselves by *p.*

**PURER.**
*Lam.* 4:7 Nazarites *p.* than snow
*Hab.* 1:13 thou art of *p.* eyes

**PURGE, ETH.**
2 *Chr.* 34:3 Josiah began to *p.* J.
*Ps.* 51:7 *p.* me with hyssop
65:3 transgressions thou sh. *p.*
*Is.* 1:25 *p.* away thy dross
*Ezek.* 20:38 I will *p.* fr. am. you
43:26 seven days shall they *p.*
*Dan.* 11:35 some of th. *p.* them
*Mal.* 3:3 *p.* as gold and silver
*Mat.* 3:12 *p.* his floor, *Luke* 3:17
*John* 15:2 branch that bea. he *p.*
1 *Cor.* 5:7 *p.* out the old leaven
2 *Tim.* 2:21 if a man *p.* himself
*Heb.* 9:14 *p.* your conscience

**PURGED.**
1 *Sam.* 3:14 Eli's house not be *p.*
2 *Chr.* 34:8 when he had *p.* land
*Prov.* 16:6 by mercy iniq. is *p.*
*Is.* 4:4 *p.* blood of Jerusalem
6:7 iniq. taken away, sin is *p.*
22:14 this iniq. shall not be *p.*
27:9 by this iniq. of Jacob be *p.*
*Ezek.* 24:13 beca. I have *p.* thee, and thou was not *p.*
*Heb.* 1:3 when he had *p.* our sins
9:22 almost all thi. are by law *p.*
10:2 bec. worshippers once *p.*
2 *Pet.* 1:9 forgotten he was *p.*

**PURGING.**
*Mark* 7:19 the draught, *p.* meats

**PURIFICATION, S.**
*Num.* 19:9 it is a *p.* for sin
17 ashes of burnt heifer *p.*
2 *Chr.* 30:19 *p.* of the sanctuary
*Neh.* 12:45 port. kept ward of *p.*
*Est.* 2:3 the things of their *p.*
12 so were the days of their *p.*
*Luke* 2:22 days of her *p.*
*Acts* 21:26 accomp. of days of *p.*

**PURIFY.**
*Num.* 19:12 shall *p.* himself, 19
20 unclean, and not *p.* himself
31:19 *p.* yourselves third day
20 *p.* all your raiment
*Job* 41:25 by rea. of break. th. *p.*
*Is.* 66:17 *p.* themselves in garden
*Ezek.* 43:26 seven days *p.* altar
*Mal.* 3:3 he shall *p.* sons of Levi
*John* 11:55 went to Jerus. to *p.*
*Acts* 21:24 take and *p.* thyself
*Tit.* 2:14 *p.* a peculiar people
*Jam.* 4:8 *p.* your hearts

**PURIFIED, ETH.**
*Lev.* 8:15 and *p.* the altar
*Num.* 8:21 Le. were *p.* *Ezek.* 6:20
19:13 touch dead body, *p.* not
31:23 *p.* with water of separat.
2 *Sam.* 11:4 Bathsheba was *p.*
*Ps.* 12:6 pure words, as silver *p.*
*Dan.* 12:10 many shall be *p.*
*Acts* 24:18 certain J. found me *p.*
*Heb.* 9:23 things in heavens *p.*
1 *Pet.* 1:22 ye *p.* your souls
1 *John* 3:3 this hope *p.* himself

**PURIFIER.**
*Mal.* 3:3 he shall sit as a *p.*

**PURIFYING.**
*Lev.* 12:4 continue in blood of *p.*
*Num.* 8:7 sprinkle water of *p.*
1 *Chr.* 23:28 in *p.* holy things
*Est.* 2:12 things for *p.* of women
*John* 2:6 manner of *p.* of Jews
3:25 th. arose question about *p.*
*Acts* 15:9 *p.* their hearts by faith
21:26 the next day *p.* himself
*Heb.* 9:13 sanctifi. to *p.* of flesh

**PURIM.**
*Est.* 9:26 called these days P.
28 days of P. sho. not fail, 29, 31
32 decree of Esther confirm. P.

**PURITY.**
1 *Tim.* 4:12 exam. in faith, in *p.*
5:2 rebuke younger with all *p.*

**PURLOINING.**
*Tit.* 2:10 not *p.* showing fidelity

**PURPLE.**
*Ex.* 25:4 the offering, *p.* 26:1
39:3 gold cut to work in the *p.*
*Num.* 4:13 take ashes, spread *p.*
*Jud.* 8:26 *p.* raiment on kings
2 *Chr.* 2:7 a man to work *p.* 14
3:14 made veil of blue, and *p.*
*Est.* 1:6 fast. with cords of *p.*
8:15 Mord. went with gar. of *p.*
*Prov.* 31:22 clothing is silk, *p.*
*Cant.* 3:10 made covering of *p.*
7:5 the hair of thy head like *p.*
*Jer.* 10:9 and *p.* is their clothing
*Ezek.* 27:7 *p.* which covered the
16 Syria occup. fairs with *p.*
*Mark* 15:17 clothed him with *p.*
20 they took off the *p.* fr. him
*Luke* 16:19 a rich man clo. in *p.*
*John* 19:2 soldiers put on him *p.*
5 then came Jesus, wearing *p.*
*Acts* 16:14 Lydia, a seller of *p.*
*Rev.* 17:4 woman arrayed in *p.*
18:12 buyeth merchandise of *p.*
16 great city, clothed in *p.*

**PURPOSE.**
*Ruth* 2:16 handfuls of *p.* for her
*Ezr.* 4:5 counsellors to frustr. *p.*
*Neh.* 8:4 a pulpit made for the *p.*
*Job* 33:17 withd. man from his *p.*
*Prov.* 20:18 ev. *p.* is established
*Ec.* 3:1 time to ev. *p.* 17; 8:6
*Is.* 1:11 to what *p.* sacrifices?
14:26 this is *p.* that is purposed
30:7 Egypti. shall help to no *p.*
*Jer.* 49:30 Nebu. conceived a *p.*
51:29 ev. *p.* of L. be performed
*Dan.* 6:17 that *p.* be not chang.
*Acts* 11:23 that with *p.* of heart
27:13 suppos. obtained their *p.*
43 centurion kept them fr. *p.*
*Rom.* 8:28 called according to *p.*
9:11 that the *p.* of God stand
17 for this *p.* I raised thee up
*Eph.* 1:11 according to *p.* of him
3:11 accord. to eternal *p.* in C.
6:22 for same *p.* *Col.* 4:8
2 *Tim.* 1:9 called us accor. to *p.*
3:10 hast fully known my *p.*
1 *John* 3:8 for this *p.* Son of God

**PURPOSES.**
*Job* 17:11 days past, *p.* broken
*Prov.* 15:22 with. counsel *p.* are
*Is.* 19:10 shall be broken in *p.*
*Jer.* 49:20 counsel of L. *p.* 50:45

**PURPOSE, ED.**
1 *K.* 5:5 I *p.* to build house to L.
2 *Chr.* 28:10 *p.* to keep under Ju.
32:2 Sennacherib *p.* to fight J.
*Ps.* 17:3 *p.* mouth sh. not trans.
140:4 who have *p.* to overthrow

*Is.* 14:24 I ha. *p.* so sh. it stand
26 the purpose *p.* on earth
27 L. hath *p.* who disannul it?
23:9 Lord hath *p.* to stain pride
46:11 I have *p.* it, will do it
*Jer.* 4:28 I *p.* it, will not repent
26:3 repent me of evil wh. I *p.*
36:3 will hear all evil wh. I *p.*
49:20 purposes that he *p.* 50:45
*Lam.* 2:8 Lord *p.* to destroy wall
*Dan.* 1:8 Daniel *p.* not to defile
*Acts* 19:21 Paul *p.* to go to Jeru.
20:3 Paul *p.* to return thro' M.
*Rom.* 1:13 oftent. I *p.* to come
2 *Cor.* 1:17 I *p.* accord. to flesh?
*Eph.* 1:9 his will wh. he hath *p.*
3:11 purp. which he *p.* in C. J.

**PURPOSETH, ING.**

*Gen.* 27:42 Esau *p.* to kill thee
2 *Cor.* 9:7 as he *p.* in heart

**PURSE, S.**

*Prov.* 1:14 let us have one *p.*
*Mat.* 10:9 silver nor brass in *p.*
*Mark* 6:8 no money in their *p.*
*Luke* 10:4 neither *p.* nor scrip
22:25 I sent you without *p.*
36 he that hath a *p.* let him

**PURSUE.**

*Gen.* 35:5 did not *p.* sons of J.
*Ex.* 15:9 enemy said, I will *p.*
*Deut.* 19:6 avenger *p. Jos.* 20:5
*Jos.* 2:5 *p.* them quickly, 10:19
1 *Sam.* 25:29 a man is risen to *p.*
30:8 shall I *p.*? he answered, *p.*
2 *Sam.* 17:1 arise and *p.* after D.
20:6 servants, *p.* after Sheba, 7
24:13 flee while enemies *p.*?
*Job* 13:25 wilt thou *p.* dry stub.?
30:15 ter. *p.* my soul as wind
*Ps.* 34:14 seek peace, and *p.* it
*Is.* 30:16 they that *p.* be swift
*Jer.* 48:2 Madmen, sword sh. *p.*
*Ezek.* 35:6 blood shall *p.* thee
*Hos.* 8:3 Israel, enemy shall *p.*
*Amos* 1:11 E. did *p.* his brother
*Nah.* 1:8 darkness *p.* his enemi.

**PURSUED.**

*Gen.* 14:14 Abram *p.* to Dan, 15
31:23 and Laban *p.* Jacob, 36
*Ex.* 14:8 Pharaoh *p.* Israel, 9, 23; *Deut.* 11:4; *Jos.* 24:6
*Jud.* 1:6 *p.* after Adoni-bezek
7:23 Gideon *p.* Mid. 25; 8:12
1 *Sam.* 7:11 Israel *p.* Phil. 17:52
2 *Sam.* 2:19 Asahel *p.* Abner
22:38 I *p.* enemies, *Ps.* 18:37
1 *K.* 20:20 Syrians fled, Israel *p.*
2 *K.* 25:5 army of Chaldees *p.* the king, *Jer.* 39:5; 52:8
2 *Chr.* 14:13 Asa *p.* Ethiop. to G.
*Is.* 41:3 he *p.* them and passed
*Lam.* 4:19 they *p.* us on mount.

**PURSUER, S.**

*Jos.* 2:16 mount. lest *p.* meet
8:20 people turned upon the *p.*
*Lam.* 1:6 are gone before the *p.*

**PURSUETH, ING.**

*Lev.* 26:17 shall flee wh. none *p.*
36 shall fall when none *p.* 37
*Jud.* 8:4 300 men, faint, yet *p.*
1 *Sam.* 23:28 S. returned from *p.*
2 *Sam.* 3:22 J. came from *p.* tro.
18:16 people returned from *p.* I.
1 *K.* 18:27 your god *p.* on jour.
*Prov.* 11:19 he th. *p.* evil, *p.* dea.
13:21 evil *p.* sinners, to righte.
19:7 he *p.* them with words
28:1 wick. flee when no man *p.*

**PURTENANCE.**

*Ex.* 12:9 roast wi. fire legs and *p.*

**PUSH.**

*Ex.* 21:29 if ox were to *p.* 36
*Deut.* 33:17 with them he shall *p.*
1 *K.* 22:11 with these shalt thou *p.* the Syrians, 2 *Chr.* 18:10
*Job* 30:12 they *p.* away my feet
*Ps.* 44:5 thro' thee we *p.* enem.
*Dan.* 11:40 shall king *p.* at him

**PUSHED, ING.**

*Ezek.* 34:21 *p.* diseased with hor.
*Dan.* 8:4 I saw ram *p.* westward

**PUT.**

*Gen.* 2:8 there G. *p.* the man, 15
3:15 I will *p.* enmity bet. thee
27:15 *p.* th. upon Jacob her son
29:3 *p.* stone ag. on well's mou.
30:42 feeble, he *p.* not the rods
32:16 *p.* space between drove
39:4 all he *p.* into Joseph's ha.
40:15 should *p.* me into dunge.
42:17 he *p.* altogether in ward
46:4 Joseph *p.* hand on th. eyes
48:18 *p.* right hand upon head
*Ex.* 3:22 shall *p.* them on sons
4:6 L. said, *p.* thy hand in bos.
15 *p.* words in his mouth
8:23 I will *p.* division bet. my
15:26 I will *p.* none of diseases
22:5 *p.* beast in ano. man's field
11 oath he hath not *p.* his ha.
23:1 *p.* not thy hand wi. wicked
29:24 shall *p.* all in hands of A.
33:5 now *p.* off thy ornaments
*Lev.* 8:27 he *p.* all on A.'s hands
26:8 *p.* 10,000 to fli. *Deut.* 32:30
*Num.* 6:27 sh. *p.* my name on Is.
11:17 spirit on thee, *p.* on them
29 L. would *p.* his Spi. on th.
23:5 L. *p.* word in Ba.'s mouth
*Deut.* 10:2 shalt *p.* them in ark
5 I *p.* tables in the ark I made
12:5 place he sh. *p.* his name, 21
7 rej. in all ye *p.* your hand to
18:18 *p.* my words in his mouth
*Jud.* 12:3 I *p.* my life in my ha.
1 *Sam.* 2:36 *p.* me in priest's offi.
14:26 no man *p.* hand to his m.
17:39 David *p.* them off him
19:5 did *p.* his life in his hand
28:21 I *p.* my life in my hand
1 *K.* 9:3 to *p.* my name there, 11:36; 14:21
12:29 other calves *p.* he in Dan
18:23 on wood, *p.* no fire under
22:27 king *p.* fellow in prison
2 *K.* 4:34 *p.* mouth upon mouth
11:12 they *p.* the crown on him
13:16 *p.* hand on bow, he *p.* ha.
21:7 in Jer. will I *p.* my name, 2 *Chr.* 6:20; 12:13; 33:7
1 *Chr.* 11:19 *p.* lives in jeopardy
13:10 because he *p.* hand to ark
2 *Chr.* 6:11 in house I *p.* the ark
*Ezr.* 7:27 *p.* thin. in king's heart
*Neh.* 2:12 what G. *p.* in my heart
3:5 nobles *p.* not necks to work
4:23 that every one *p.* them off
6:14 T. would *p.* me in fear, 19
*Job* 4:18 he *p.* no trust in his ser.
13:14 I *p.* my life in my hand?
19:13 *p.* my brethren far fr. me
23:6 he would *p.* strength in me
*Job* 41:2 can. *p.* hook in. his no.?
*Ps.* 4:7 *p.* gladness in my heart
8:6 thou hast *p.* all things under his feet, 1 *Cor.* 15:25, 27; *Eph.* 1:22; *Heb.* 2:8
9:20 *p.* in fear, O L. that nation
31:18 let lying lips be *p.* to sile.
40:3 *p.* new song in my mouth
14 let them be *p.* to shame that wish me evil, 44:7; 53:5
44:9 thou hast *p.* us to shame
78:66 *p.* them to perp. reproach
88:18 lover and friend *p.* fr. me
118:8 tr. L. than *p.* con. in man
9 tr. L. than put confi. in prin.
119:31 O L. *p.* me not to shame
*Prov.* 25:8 nei. *p.* thee to shame
10 heareth it *p.* thee to shame
*Ec.* 10:10 *p.* to more strength
*Cant.* 5:3 *p.* off coat, how *p.* on?
*Is.* 5:20 that *p.* darkn. for light
10:13 I ha. *p.* down inhabitants
42:1 I have *p.* my Spirit upon him, *Mat.* 12:18
47:11 not be able to *p.* it off
51:16 *p.* words in mou. *Jer.* 1:9
23 *p.* into hand that afflict th.
53:10 he hath *p.* him to grief
59:21 words I *p.* in thy mouth
63:11 where is he that *p.* his H. Spirit within him?
*Jer.* 3:19 how shall I *p.* thee am.
8:14 Lord our G. *p.* us to silence
12:13 they *p.* themselves to pain
31:33 *p.* my law in inward parts
32:40 will *p.* my fear in hearts
*Ezek.* 8:17 *p.* branch to th. nose
11:19 I will put a new spirit within you, 36:26, 27; 37:14
16:14 comel. I had *p.* upon thee
29:4 *p.* hooks in thy jaws, 38:4
30:13 *p.* a fear in land of Egypt
37:6 *p.* breath in you, ye shall
*Dan.* 5:19 and whom he *p.* down
*Mic.* 2:12 I will *p.* them together
7:5 *p.* not confidence in a guide
*Zep.* 3:19 ha. been *p.* to shame
*Mat.* 5:15 candle *p.* under bushel
19:6 no man *p.* asun. *Mark* 10:9
26:52 *p.* up thy swo. *John* 18:11
*Mark* 10:16 *p.* his hands on them
*Luke* 1:52 hath *p.* down mighty
15:22 *p.* it on him and *p.* a ring
*John* 5:7 none to *p.* me into pool
*Acts* 1:7 Fa. *p.* in his own power
4:3 they *p.* the apostles in hold
5:25 men whom ye *p.* in prison
13:46 *p.* word of God from you
15:9 *p.* no difference between us
1 *Cor.* 15:24 *p.* down authority
25 *p.* his enemies under his fe.
2 *Cor.* 8:16 G. *p.* same care in T.
*Eph.* 4:22 *p.* off old man, *Col.* 3:9
*Col.* 3:8 ye also *p.* off these, ang.
2 *Tim.* 1:6 I *p.* thee in remembr.
*Tit.* 3:1 *p.* them in mind to be subject
*Phile.* 18 *p.* that on my account
*Heb.* 2:5 hath he not *p.* in subj.
6:6 *p.* him to an open shame
8:10 I will *p.* my laws in mind
10:16 *p.* my laws into th. hearts
*Jam.* 3:3 *p.* bits in horses' mou.
1 *Pet.* 2:15 *p.* to silence ignoran.
2 *Pet.* 1:14 I must *p.* off this tab.
*Jude* 5 will *p.* you in remembr.
*Rev.* 2:24 *p.* on you none other
17:17 God hath *p.* in th. hearts

**PUT away.**

*Gen.* 35:2 *p. away* strange gods
*Lev.* 21:7 nor take a woman *p. a.*
*Deut.* 19:13 *p. a.* guilt of in. 21:9
22:19 he may not *p.* her *a.* 29
*Jos.* 24:14 *p. a.* strange gods, 23; *Jud.* 10:16; 1 *Sam.* 7:3
1 *Sam.* 1:14 Eli said, *p. a.* wine
2 *Sam.* 7:15 Saul whom I *p. a.*
12:13 Lord hath *p. a.* thy sin
2 *Chr.* 15:8 Asa *p. a.* abom. idols
*Rev.* 10:3 a cove. to *p. a.* wives
19 gave hands to *p. a.* wives
*Ps.* 18:22 I did not *p. away* his statutes
27:9 *p.* not thy serv. *a.* in anger
*Prov.* 4:24 *p. a.* a froward mou.
*Is.* 50:1 whom I have *p. away*
*Jer.* 3:1 if a man *p. a.* his wife
8 *p. a.* given her a bill of div.
*Ezek.* 44:22 nor pr. take her *p. a.*
*Hos.* 2:2 let her *p. a.* whoredoms
*Amos* 6:3 that *p.* far *a.* evil day
*Mat.* 1:19 J. minded to *p.* her *a.*
*Mark* 10:2 lawful to *p. a.* wife?
12 if a woman *p. a.* her husb.
1 *Cor.* 5:13 *p. a.* wicked person
7:11 let not husb. *p. a.* wife, 12
*Eph.* 4:31 evil speaking be *p. a.*
1 *Tim.* 1:19 some having *p. aw.*

*Heb.* 9:26 *p. a.* sin by sacrifice
*See* DEATH, EVIL.

**PUT forth.**

*Gen.* 3:22 lest he *p. f.* take tree
8:9 N. *p. f.* his hand and took
19:10 men *p. forth* their hand
*Ex.* 4:4 *p. f.* thy hand and take
*Deut.* 33:14 precious things *p. f.*
*Jud.* 15:15 Samson *p. f.* took
1 *Sam.* 14:27 Jonathan *p. f.* rod
22:17 servants not *p. f.* to slay
24:10 not *p. f.* my hand ag. L.
2 *Sam.* 6:6 Uzziah *p. forth* his hand to ark, 1 *Chr.* 13:9
18:12 not *p. f.* my hand against
1 *K.* 13:4 Jeroboam *p. f.* his ha.
*Job* 1:11 *p. f.* hand and tou. 2:5
12 on himself *p.* not *f.* hand
*Ps.* 55:20 *p. f.* his hands ag. him
125:3 lest righteous *p. f.* hands
*Prov.* 8:1 understan. *p. f.* voice?
25:6 *p.* not *f.* thyself in presen.
*Jer.* 1:9 Lord *p. f.* his hand
*Ezek.* 8:3 he *p. f.* form of a hand
*Mat.* 9:25 when peop. were *p. f.*
13:24 para. *p.* he *f.* 31; *Lu.* 14:7
*Acts* 5:34 to *p.* the apostles *forth*
9:40 but Peter *p.* them all *forth*

**PUT on.**

*Gen.* 28:20 raiment to *p. on*
*Lev.* 6:10 priest sh. *p. on* linen
11 he sh. *p. on* other garments
16:4 shall *p. on* holy linen coat
*Deut.* 22:5 nor man *p. on* wom.'s
2 *Sam.* 1:24 S. *p. on* ornaments
14:2 *p. on* mourning apparel
1 *K.* 22:30 but *p.* thou *on* thy robes, 2 *Chr.* 18:29
2 *K.* 3:21 all able to *p. on* armor
*Job* 27:17 the just shall *p.* it *on*
*Cant.* 5:3 how shall I *p.* it *on?*
*Is.* 51:9 *p. on* strength, 52:1
*Jer.* 13:1 take girdle, *p.* it *on*, 2
*Ezek.* 24:17 and *p. on* thy shoes
42:14 *p. on* other garm. 44:19
*Mat.* 6:25 nor what ye shall *p. on*, *Luke* 12:22
21:7 *p. on* the ass their clothes
*Mark* 6:9 not *p. on* two coats
*Luke* 15:22 *p. on* him best robe
*Rom.* 13:14 *p.* ye *on* the L. J. C.
*Gal.* 3:27 baptized, have *p. on* C.
*Eph.* 4:24 *p. on* new m. *Col.* 3:10
*Col.* 3:12 *p. on* bowels of mercies
14 *p. on* charity, which is bo.

**PUT out.**

*Gen.* 38:28 one *p. out* his hand
*Lev.* 6:12 fire of altar not be *p. o.*
*Num.* 5:2 *p. out* of camp leper, 4
3 male and fem. shall ye *p. o.*
16:14 wilt thou *p. out* the eyes?
*Deut.* 7:22 L. will *p. o.* tho. nati.
25:6 that his name be not *p. o.*
*Jud.* 16:21 Philis. *p. o.* S.'s eyes
2 *Sam.* 13:17 *p.* this woman *out*
2 *Chr.* 29:7 have *p. o.* lamps
*Job* 18:5 light of wicked be *p. o.*
6 his candle be *p. out*, 21:17; *Prov.* 13:9; 20:20; 24:20
*Ps.* 9:5 *p. o.* their name for ever
*Ezek.* 32:7 when I *p.* thee *out*
*Mark* 5:40 when he had *p.* them all *out*, *Luke* 8:54
*John* 9:22 be *p. o.* of synagogues
16:2 *p.* you *out* of synagogues

**PUT trust.**

*Jud.* 9:15 *p. t.* in my shadow
2 *K.* 18:24 *p. t.* on Eg. *Is.* 36:9
1 *Chr.* 5:20 they *p.* th. *t.* in him
*Ps.* 4:5 *p.* your *trust* in the Lord
5:11 all that *p. t.* in thee rejoice
7:1 O L. God in thee I *p. trust*, 16:1; 25:20; 71:1
9:10 know thy name, *p. trust* in them
11:1 in L. *p.* I my *t.* 31:1; 71:1
17:7 which *p.* their *t.* in thee
36:7 *p.* their *t.* under thy wings
56:4 in God I have *p.* my *trust*
73:28 I have *p.* my *t.* in the L.
146:3 *p.* not your *t.* in princes
*Prov.* 30:5 *p.* their *trust* in him
*Jer.* 39:18 hast *p.* thy *t.* in thee
1 *Thes.* 2:4 *p.* in *t.* with gospel
*Heb.* 2:13 I will *p.* my *t.* in him

**PUT, Participle.**

*Lev.* 11:38 if water be *p.* on seed
15:19 shall be *p.* apart sev. days
18:19 not as long as she is *p.*
1 *K.* 22:10 kings *p.* on their rob.
2 *K.* 14:12 Judah was *p.* to worse
1 *Chr.* 19:16 Syri. *p.* to worse, 19
2 *Chr.* 2:14 ev. device shall be *p.*
6:24 if Israel be *p.* to the worse
25:22 Jud. was *p.* to the worse
*Ps.* 35:4 be *p.* to shame, 83:17
71:1 let me never be *p.* to con.
*Prov.* 25:7 shouldest be *p.* lower
*Ec.* 3:14 nothing can be *p.* to it
*Is.* 54:4 shalt not be *p.* to shame
*Jer.* 50:42 every one *p.* in array
*Zep.* 3:19 have been *p.* to shame
*Mat.* 9:16 for that *p.* in to fill up
*Mark* 1:14 John was *p.* in prison
*John* 13:2 devil *p.* into hea. of J.
*Heb.* 2:8 noth. not *p.* under him
*Rev.* 11:9 not bo. be *p.* in graves

**PUTEOLI.**

*Acts* 28:13 came next day to P.

PUTIEL. *Ex.* 6:25

**PUTTEST.**

*Deut.* 12:18 *p.* thy hands, 15:10
2 *K.* 18:14 that thou *p.* on me
*Ps.* 119:119 thou *p.* away wicked

**PUTTETH.**

*Ex.* 30:33 *p.* any on a stranger
*Num.* 22:38 God *p.* in my mouth
*Deut.* 25:11 woman *p.* forth hand
*Job* 15:15 he *p.* no trust in saints
28:9 *p.* for. his hand upon rock
33:11 he *p.* my feet in the stoc.
*Ps.* 15:5 he that *p.* not his money
75:7 *p.* down one and set. up
*Prov.* 28:25 *p.* his trust in Lord
29:25 *p.* his trust in L. be safe
*Is.* 57:13 *p.* trust in me pos. land
*Lam.* 3:29 *p.* his mouth in dust
*Mic.* 3:5 *p.* not into their mouths
*Mat.* 9:16 *p.* new cloth, *Lu.* 5:36
*Luke* 8:16 no man *p.* ligh. candle
16:18 whoso *p.* away his wife
*John* 10:4 *p.* forth his own sheep

**PUTTING.**

*Lev.* 16:21 *p.* them upon head
*Jud.* 7:6 *p.* their hand to mouth
*Is.* 58:9 *p.* forth of the finger
*Mal.* 2:16 God hateth *p.* away
*Acts* 9:12 Anan. *p.* his hand, 17
19:33 Alex. J. *p.* him forward
*Rom.* 15:15 sort, as *p.* in mind
*Eph.* 4:25 *p.* away lying
*Col.* 2:11 in *p.* off body of sins
1 *Tim.* 1:12 *p.* me into ministry
2 *Tim.* 1:6 by *p.* on my hands
1 *Pet.* 3:21 not *p. a.* filth of flesh

**PUTREFYING.**

*Is.* 1:6 wounds, bruises, *p.* sores

# Q

**QUAILS.**

*Ex.* 16:13 at even *q.* came up.
*Num.* 11:31 a wind fr. L. bro. *q.*
32 the people stood, gather. *q.*
*Ps.* 105:40 asked, he brought *q.*

**QUAKE, ED.**

*Ex.* 19:18 the mount *q.* greatly
1 *Sam.* 14:15 trembled, earth *q.*
*Joel* 2:10 earth shall *q.* bef. them
*Nah.* 1:5 the mountains *q.* at hi.
*Mat.* 27:51 earth *q.* the rocks re.
*Heb.* 12:21 M. said, I fear and *q.*

**QUAKING.**

*Ezek.* 12:18 eat thy bread with *q.*
*Dan.* 10:7 great *q.* fell on them

**QUANTITY.**

*Is.* 22:24 hang vessels of small *q.*

**QUARREL.**

*Lev.* 26:25 a sword sh. avenge *q.*
2 *K.* 5:7 see how he seeketh a *q.*
*Mark* 6:19 Her. had *q.* ag. John
*Col.* 3:13 if any have *q.* ag. any

**QUARRIES.**

*Jud.* 3:19 Ehud turned from *q.*
26 Ehud escaped beyond the *q.*

**QUARTER.**

*Gen.* 19:4 peo. from ev. *q.* to Lo.
*Jos.* 18:14 Kirjath-jearim, we. *q.*
*Is.* 47:15 merchants wander to *q.*
56:11 every one for gain from *q.*
*Mark* 1:45 came to him fr. ev. *q.*
*See* SOUTH.

**QUARTERS.**

*Ex.* 13:7 no leav. seen in thy *q.*
*Deut.* 22:12 fringes on four *q.*
1 *Chr.* 9:24 in four *q.* were port.
*Jer.* 49:36 from four *q.* of heaven
*Acts* 9:32 Peter passed thr. all *q*
16:3 Jews which were in th. *q.*
28:7 in same *q.* were possessio.
*Rev.* 20:8 nations in 4 *q.* of earth

**QUATERNIONS.**

*Acts* 12:4 deliv. Peter to four *q.*

**QUARTUS.**

*Rom.* 16:23 Q. a brother, salute.

**QUEEN.**

1 *K.* 10:1 *q.* of Sheba heard of fame of Solomon, 2 *Chr.* 9:1
1 *K.* 10:4 wh. *q.* saw Solom.'s w.
10 spices *q.* of She. gave to S.
13 Solomon gave *q.* of Sheba all her desire, 2 *Chr.* 9:9, 12
11:19 gave Hadad sister of *q.*
15:13 Asa removed Maachah from being *q.* 2 *Chr.* 15:16
2 *K.* 10:13 salute children of *q.*
*Neh.* 2:6 king said, *q.* sitting by
*Est.* 1:9 Vashti *q.* made feast
11 bring the *q.* 12 *q.* refused
15 wh. sh. we do to *q.* Vashti?
16 the *q.* hath not done wrong
17 deed of *q.* sh. come abroad
2:4 maiden that pleaseth be *q.*
17 made Esther *q.* ins. of Vas.
4:4 *q.* grieved; 5:3 wilt, *q.* Est.
5:12 *q.* let no man to banquet
7:2 what is thy petition, *q.* Es.?
7 Haman made request to *q.*
8 will he force the *q.* befo. me
8:1 house of Haman to Esth. *q.*
9:31 Mordecai and Esth. the *q.*
*Ps.* 45:9 the *q.* in gold of Ophir
*Jer.* 13:18 say to king and *q.*
44:17 burn inc. to *q.* of heaven
25 vowed to burn incense to *q.*
*Dan.* 5:10 *q.* came to banq. house
*Mat.* 12:42 *q.* of south shall rise up in judgment, *Luke* 11:31
*Acts* 8:27 Candace, *q.* of Ethiop.
*Rev.* 18:7 I sit *q.* am no widow

**QUEENS.**
Cant. 6:8 there are threesc. q. 9
Is. 49:23 their q. nursing moth.

**QUENCH.**
2 Sam. 14:7 they shall q. my coal
21:17 thou q. not light of Israel
Ps. 104:11 wild asses q. thirst
Cant. 8:7 waters cannot q. love
Is. 1:31 both burn, none q. them
42:3 shall he not q. Mat. 12:20
Jer. 4:4 burn, none q. it, 21:12
Amos 5:6 none to q. it in Beth-el
Eph. 6:16 to q. darts of wicked
1 Thes. 5:19 q. not the Spirit

**QUENCHED.**
Num. 11:2 fire q. 2 Chr. 34:25
2 K. 22:17 wrath shall not be q.
Ps. 118:12 they are q. as thorns
Is. 34:10 not be q. night nor day
43:17 they are q. as tow
66:24 nor shall their fire be q.
Jer. 7:20 shall not be q. 17:27
Ezek. 20:47 fla. sh. not be q. 48
Mark 9:43 fire never be q. 45
44 where fire is not q. 46, 48
Heb. 11:34 q. the violence of fire

**QUESTION, Substantive.**
Mat. 22:35 lawyer asked him q.
Mark 11:29 I ask one q. ans. me
12:34 durst ask q. Luke 20:40
John 3:25 arose q. bet disciples
Acts 15:2 came to apos. about q.
18:15 if it be a q. of words
19:40 danger to be called in q.
23:6 of resur. called in q. 24:21
Cor. 10:25 asking no q. for, 27

**QUESTION, Verb.**
Mark 8:11 Phar. began to q. him
9:16 What q. ye with them?

**QUESTIONED, ING.**
2 Chr. 31:9 Heze. q. with priests
Mark 1:27 q. among themselves
9:10 q. what rising from dead
14 and scribes q. with them
Luke 23:9 Pilate q. with him

**QUESTIONS.**
1 K. 10:1 queen came to prove q.
3 Sol. told her q. 2 Chr. 9:1, 2
Mat. 22:46 nei. ask him more q.
Luke 2:46 hearing and asking q.
Acts 23:29 accused of q. of law.
25:19 certain q. against him
20 doubted such manner of q.
26:3 kn. thee to be expert in q.
1 Tim. 1:4 minister q. than edi.
6:4 doting about q. and strifes
2 Tim. 2:23 unlearned q. Tit. 3:9

**QUICK.**
Lev. 13:10 there be q. raw flesh
24 the q. flesh that burneth
Num. 16:30 go down q. into pit
Ps. 55:15 go down q. into hell
124:3 had swallowed us up q.
Is. 11:3 make him of q. underst.
Acts 10:42 orda. to be judge of q.
2 Tim. 4:1 sh. judge q. and dead
Heb. 4:12 the word of God is q.
1 Pet. 4:5 to judge q. and dead

**QUICKEN.**
Ps. 71:20 thou shalt q. me again
80:18 q. us, we will call on name
119:25 q. me according, 107, 154
37 q. me in thy way
Ps. 119:40 q. me in thy righteou.
88 q. me after thy kindn. 159
149 q. me accord. to judgment
143:11 q. me, L. for name's sake
Rom. 8:11 shall q. mortal bodies

**QUICKENED.**
Ps. 119:50 thy word hath q. me
93 with precepts th. hast q. me
1 Cor. 15:36 thou sowest is not q.
Eph. 2:1 you he q. who were de.
5 q. us toge. with C. Col. 2:13
1 Pet. 3:18 death in flesh, q. by S.

**QUICKENETH.**
John 5:21 Father q. them, Son q.
6:63 Sp. q. flesh profit. nothing
Rom. 4:17 God, who q. dead
1 Tim. 6:13 God, who q. all thi.

**QUICKENING.**
1 Cor. 15:45 Adam made q. spir.

**QUICKLY.**
Gen. 18:6 make ready q. meas.
27:20 hast thou found it so q.
Ex. 32:8 turned q. out of way,
Deut. 9:12, 16; Jud. 2:17
Num. 16:46 go q. to congregation
Deut. 9:12 down q. 11:17 per. q.
28:20 perish q. because of doin.
Jos. 2:5 pursue q. overtake them
10:6 come up to us q. save us
23:16 ye shall perish q. off land
1 Sam. 20:19 thou sh. go down q.
2 Sam. 17:16 send q. and tell D.
18 went both of them away q.
21 arise, pass q. over the wat.
2 K. 1:11 said, Come down q.
Ec. 4:12 threef. cord not q. bro.
Mat. 5:25 agree with adversa. q.
28:7 go q. tell discip. he is risen
8 they departed q. Mark 16:8
Luke 16:6 sit down q. write fifty
John 11:29 M. arose q. came to J.
13:27 J. That thou doest do q.
Acts 12:7 saying, Arise up q. P.
22:18 get thee q. out of Jerusal.
Rev. 2:5 repent, else I come q. 16
3:11 behold, I come q. 22:7, 12
11:14 third woe cometh q.
22:20 I come q. even so come

**QUICKSANDS.**
Acts 27:17 they should fall into q.

**QUIET.**
Jud. 16:2 Phil. laid wait were q.
18:7 after Zidonians, q. secure
2 K. 11:20 city q. 2 Chr. 23:21
1 Chr. 4:40 land was wide and q.
2 Chr. 14:1 in his days land q.
5 the kingdom was q. 20:30
Job 3:13 now sho. I have been q.
26 neit. was I q. trouble came
21:23 dieth, being at ease, q.
Ps. 35:20 devise ag. q. in land
107:30 glad, because they be q.
Prov. 1:33 whoso hearken. be q.
Ec. 9:17 wor. of wise heard in q.
Is. 7:4 take heed, and be q. fear
14:7 the earth is at rest, and q.
32:18 my peo. shall dwell in q.
33:20 see Jerusal. q. habitation
Jer. 30:10 Jacob return, be in q.
47:6 how long ere thou be q.?
7 be q. seeing L. given charge
49:23 sorrow on sea, can. be q.
51:59 Seraiah was a q. prince
Ezek. 16:42 fury rest, I will be q.
Nah. 1:12 though q. be cut down
Acts 19:36 ye ought to be q.
1 Thes. 4:11 that ye stu. to be q.
1 Tim. 2:2 we may lead a q. life
1 Pet. 3:4 ornament of a q. spirit

**QUIETED, ETH.**
Job 37:17 q. earth by south wind
Ps. 131:2 q. myself as a child
Zec. 6:8 q. my spirit in north

**QUIETLY.**
2 Sam. 3:27 Joab took Abner q.
Lam. 3:26 q. wait for salva. of L.

**QUIETNESS.**
Jud. 8:28 the country was in q.
1 Chr. 22:9 I will give q. to Isr.
Job 20:20 sh. not feel q. in belly
34:29 q. who can make trouble?
Prov. 17:1 bet. dry morsel and q.
Ec. 4:6 better is handful with q.
Is. 30:15 in q. be your strength
32:17 righte. q. and assurance
Acts 24:2 we enjoy great q.
2 Thes. 3:12 we ex. that with q.

**QUIT.**
Ex. 21:19 smote him be q. 28
Jos. 2:20 we will be q. of oath
1 Sam. 4:9 q. like men, 1 Cor. 16:13

**QUITE.**
Gen. 31:15 q. devoured our mon.
Ex. 23:24 q. break down images
Num. 17:10 q. take away murm.
33:52 q. pluck down high places
2 Sam. 3:24 Abner away, q. gone
Job 6:13 is wisdom q. from me?
Hab. 3:9 thy bow made q. naked

**QUIVER.**
Gen. 27:3 take thy q. and bow
Job 39:23 q. rattleth against him
Ps. 127:5 man that hath q. full
Is. 22:6 E. bare q. with chariots
49:2 polished shaft in his q.
Jer. 5:16 q. is as open sepulchre
Lam. 3:13 arrows of q. ent. reins

**QUIVERED.**
Hab. 3:16 my lips q. at the voice

# R

**RABBAH, *or* RABBATH.**
Deut. 3:11 is it not in R. of chil.
2 Sam. 11:1 J. besieged R. 12:26
17:27 Shobi of R. brought beds
1 Chr. 20:1 Joab smote R. and
Jer. 49:2 alarm heard in R. 3
Ezek. 21:20 sw. may come to R.
25:5 I will make R. a stable
Amos 1:14 a fire in wall of R.

**RABBI.**
Mat. 23:7 called of men, r. r.
8 be not ye called r. for one is
John 1:38 R. wh. dwellest thou?
49 R. thou art the Son of God
3:2 R. we know thou art teach.
26 R. he that was with thee
6:25 R. when cam. thou hither?

**RABBONI.**
John 20:16 M. turn. and saith, R.

**RAB-SHAKEH.**
2 K. 18:17 Assy. sent R. Is. 36:2
37 told words of R. Is. 36:22
19:4 hear words of R. 37:4

**RACA.**
Mat. 5:22 say r. sh. be in danger

**RACE.**
Ps. 19:5 strong man to run a r.
Ec. 9:11 r. is not to the swift
1 Cor. 9:24 they wh. run in a r.
Heb. 12:1 run with patience r.

**RACHEL.**
Gen. 29:12 Jacob told R. that he
30:1 R. bare no chil. R. 2, 22
2 anger was kindled ag. R. 22
31:19 R. had stolen imag. 34
35:19 R. died, 24; 46:22; 48:7
Ruth 4:11 make woman like R.
1 Sam. 10:2 men by R. sepulch.
Jer. 31:15 R. weeping, Mat. 2:18

**RAFTERS.**
Cant. 1:17 beams cedar r. of fir

**RAGAU.**
*Luke* 3:35 Saruch, the son of R.
**RAGE, Substantive.**
2 *K.* 5:12 Naaman turned in a *r.*
19:27 I know thy *r.* *Is.* 37:28
2 *Chr.* 16:10 A. in a *r.* with seer
28:9 ye have slain them in a *r.*
*Job* 39:24 swallow. ground wi. *r.*
40:11 cast abroad *r.* of wrath
*Ps.* 7:6 lift up thyself bec. of *r.*
*Prov.* 6:34 jeal. is *r.* of a man
*Dan.* 3:13 Neb. commanded in *r.*
*Hos.* 7:16 fall for *r.* of th. tongue
**RAGE, Verb.**
*Ps.* 2:1 heathen *r.*? *Acts* 4:25
*Prov.* 29:9 wheth. he *r.* or laugh
*Jer.* 46:9 come up *r.* ye chariots
*Nah.* 2:4 chariots sh. *r.* in stree.
**RAGED, ETH.**
*Ps.* 46:6 heath. *r.* kingd. moved
*Prov.* 14:16 fool *r.* is confident
**RAGGED.**
*Is.* 2:21 go into tops of *r.* rocks
**RAGING.**
*Ps.* 89:9 thou rulest *r.* of sea
*Prov.* 20:1 strong drink *r.*
*Jon.* 1:16 sea ceased from *r.*
*Luke* 8:24 rebuked *r.* of water
*Jude* 13 *r.* of waves of sea foam.
**RAGS.**
*Prov.* 23:21 clothe man with *r.*
*Is.* 64:6 righte. are as filthy *r.*
*Jer.* 38:11 Ebed. took rotten *r.*
12 *r.* under thine armholes
**RAHAB.**
*Jos.* 2:1 house of R. 6:17, 25
*Ps.* 87:4 I make mention of R.
89:10 thou hast broken R. in
*Is.* 51:9 not it that hath cut R.
*Mat.* 1:5 Salmon begat B. of R
*Heb.* 11:31 by faith harlot R
*Jam.* 2:25 was not R. justified?
**RAIL, ED.**
1 *Sam.* 25:14 Nabal *r.* on David's
2 *Chr.* 32:17 Sen. wrote let. to *r.*
*Mark.* 15:29 that passed *r.* on J.
*Luke* 23:39 one of malefactors *r.*
**RAILER.**
1 *Cor.* 5:11 keep not com. wi. *r.*
**RAILING.**
1 *Tim.* 6:4 whereof co. strife, *r.*
1 *Pet.* 3:9 not rendering *r.* for *r.*
2 *Pet.* 2:11 angels br. not *r.* accu.
*Jude* 9 durst not bring *r.* accus.
**RAIMENT.**
*Gen.* 24:53 serv. gave *r.* to Reb.
27:15 Rebekah took goodly *r.*
27 Isaac smelled *r.* and blessed
28:20 if L. give me *r.* to put on
41:14 Joseph shaved, chang. *r.*
45:22 each man changes of *r.*
*Ex.* 3:22 borrow of Eg. *r.* 12:35
21:10 her *r.* sh. he not diminish
22:9 trespass for sheep, for *r.*
26 thou take neighbor's *r.* 27
*Lev.* 11:32 uncl. beasts fall on *r.*
*Num.* 31:20 purify all your *r.*
*Deut.* 8:4 thy *r.* waxed not old
10:18 L. loveth stranger, giv. *r.*
21:13 put *r.* of captivity fr. her
22:3 lost *r.* restore
24:13 he may sleep in his *r.*
17 shalt not take a widow's *r.*
*Jos.* 22:8 return with much *r.*
*Jud.* 3:16 E. a dagger under *r.*
8:26 purple *r.* that was on kings
*Ruth* 3:3 and put thy *r.* on thee
1 *Sam.* 28:8 Saul disg. put on *r.*
2 *K.* 5:5 Naam. took chang. of *r.*
2 *Chr.* 9:24 Solomon, gold, and *r.*
*Est.* 4:4 sent *r.* to clothe Morde.
*Job* 27:16 tho' he prep. *r.* as clay
*Ps.* 45:11 brought to king in *r.*
*Is.* 14:19 cast out as *r.* of slain
63:3 and I will stain all my *r.*
*Ezek.* 16:13 *r.* was of fine linen
*Zec.* 3:4 clothe thee with *r.*
*Mat.* 3:4 J. had *r.* of camel's hair
6:25 body more th. *r.* *Luke* 12:23
28 why take ye thought for *r.*?
11:8 clothed in soft *r.* *Lu.* 7:25
17:2 his *r.* white as light, *Mark* 9:3; *Luke* 9:29
27:31 put his own *r.* on him
28:3 and his *r.* white as snow
*Luke* 10:30 thieves stri. him of *r.*
23:34 parted his *r.* *John* 19:24
*Acts* 18:6 Paul shook his *r.*
22:20 I kept *r.* of them that sle.
1 *Tim.* 6:8 having food and *r.*
*Jam.* 2:2 a poor man in vile *r.*
*Rev.* 3:5 be clothed in white *r.*
18 buy white *r.* that thou ma.
4:4 I saw 24 elders in white *r.*
**RAIN, Substantive.**
*Gen.* 7:12 *r.* was upon earth
8:2 *r.* from heaven was restrain.
*Ex.* 9:33 the *r.* was not poured
34 Pharaoh saw the *r.* ceased
*Lev.* 26:4 will give you *r.* in due season, *Deut.* 11:14; 28:12
*Deut.* 11 drink. of *r.* of heaven
17 shut heaven that th. be no *r.* 1 *K.* 8:35; 2 *Chr.* 6:26; 7:13
28:24 Lord shall make *r.* of land
32:2 my doctrine sh. drop as *r.*
1 *Sam.* 12:17 call on L. to send *r.*
18 Lord sent thunder and *r.*
2 *Sam.* 1:21 let there be no *r.*
23:4 by clear shining after *r.*
1 *K.* 8:36 hear, give *r.* 2 *Chr.* 6:27
17:1 th. shall be no dew nor *r.* 7
14 till day that Lord send *r.*
18:1 I will send *r.* upon earth
41 a sound of abundance of *r.*
44 *r.* stop thee not; 45 great *r.*
2 *K.* 3:17 not see wind, nor see *r.*
*Ezr.* 10:9 trembling for great *r.*
13 and it is a time of much *r.*
*Job* 5:10 giveth *r.* upon the earth
28:26 he made a decree for *r.*
29:23 waited for me as for the *r.*
36:27 clou. pour down *r.* accord.
37:6 to small *r.* and to great *r.*
38:28 hath *r.* a father?
*Ps.* 68:9 didst send plentiful *r.*
72:6 he shall come down like *r.*
84:6 the *r.* also filleth the pools
105:32 he gave them hail for *r.*
135:7 maketh lightnings for *r.*
147:8 L. prepareth *r.* for earth
*Prov.* 25:14 like clouds with. *r.*
23 north wind driveth away *r.*
26:1 snow in summer, and *r.* in
28:3 oppresseth poor is like a *r*
*Ec.* 11:3 if clouds be full of *r.*
12:2 nor clouds return after *r.*
*Cant.* 2:11 the *r.* is over and go.
*Is.* 4:6 covert from storm and *r.*
5:6 com. clouds they rain no *r.*
30:23 then shall he give the *r.*
44:14 an ash, *r.* doth nourish it
55:10 as *r.* cometh from heaven
*Jer.* 5:24 let us fear L. giveth *r.*
10:13 maketh lightn. wi. *r.* 51:16
14:4 ground chapt, th. was no *r.*
22 vanities of G. can cause *r.*?
*Ezek.* 1:28 as bow in cloud in *r.*
38:22 I will r. an overflowing *r.*
*Hos.* 6:3 shall make us as the *r.*
*Joel* 2:23 cause to come down *r.*
*Amos* 4:7 I have withholden *r.*
*Zec.* 14:17 upon th. be no *r.*
18 go not up, that have no *r.*
*Mat.* 5:45 he sendeth *r.* on just
7:25 and the *r.* descended, 27
*Acts* 14:17 did good, and gave *r*
28:2 because of the present *r.*
*Heb.* 6:7 earth drinketh in the *r.*
*Jam.* 5:18 and the heav. gave *r.*
*See* LATTER.
**RAIN, Verb.**
*Gen.* 2:5 L. not caused it to *r.*
7:4 cause to *r.* 40 days a. nights
*Ex.* 9:18 to-morrow cause it *r.*
16:4 I will *r.* bread from heaven
*Job* 20:23 G. shall *r.* his fury
38:26 cause it to *r.* on the earth
*Ps.* 11:6 on wicked he shall *r.*
*Is.* 5:6 that they *r.* no rain on it
*Ezek.* 38:22 I will *r.* overflow. ra.
*Hos.* 10:12 come and *r.* righteou.
*Amos.* 4:7 I caused it to *r.* on city
*Jam.* 5:17 E. pray it mig. not *r.*
*Rev.* 11:6 *r.* not in days of prop.
**RAINBOW.**
*Rev.* 4:3 th. was a *r.* round about
10:1 and a *r.* was upon his head
**RAINED.**
*Gen.* 19:24 L. *r.* upon S. and G.
*Ex.* 9:23 the L. *r.* hail on Egypt
*Ps.* 78:24 *r.* down manna, 27
*Ezek.* 22:24 the land not *r.* upon
*Amos* 4:7 one piece was *r.* upon
*Luke* 17:29 it *r.* fire from heaven
*Jam.* 5:17 it *r.* not for 3 y.'s 6 m.
**RAINY.**
*Prov.* 27:15 dropping in a *r.* day
**RAISE.**
*Gen.* 38:8 *r.* up seed to brother?
*Ex.* 23:1 shalt not *r.* false report
*Deut.* 18:15 L. thy God *r.* up a prophet, 18; *Acts* 3:22; 7:37
25:7 refuseth to *r.* up to brother
*Jos.* 8:29 *r.* ther. a heap stones
*Ruth* 4:5 *r.* up name of dead, 10
1 *Sam.* 2:35 *r.* faithful priest
2 *Sam.* 12:11 *r.* evil against thee
17 went to *r.* him from earth
1 *K.* 14:14 L. shall *r.* king in Is.
1 *Chr.* 17:11 I will *r.* up thy seed
*Job* 3:8 ready to *r.* up mourning
19:12 his troops *r.* up ag. thee
30:12 *r.* ways of destruction
*Ps.* 41:10 L. be merciful, *r.* me
*Is.* 15:5 *r.* cry of destruction
29:3 I will *r.* forts against thee
44:26 will *r.* up decayed places
49:6 servant to *r.* tribes of Jacob
58:12 *r.* foundations of genera.
61:4 sh. *r.* up former desolations
*Jer.* 23:5 will *r.* to Dav. a branch
50:9 *r.* ag. Babylon assembly
32 none *r.* him; 51:1 *r.* wind
*Ezek.* 23:22 will *r.* lovers ag. th.
34:29 will *r.* up plant of renown
*Hos.* 6:2 in third day he will *r.*
*Joel* 3:7 *r.* them whither ye driv.
*Amos* 5:2 virgin of Is. none to *r.*
6:14 I will *r.* a nation aga. you
9:11 I will *r.* tabernacle of Dav.
*Mic.* 5:5 *r.* against him 7 sheph.
*Hab.* 1:3 th. are that *r.* up strife
6 I will *r.* up Chaldeans
*Zec.* 11:16 *r.* shepherd in land
*Mat.* 3:9 *r.* children to A. *Lu.* 3:8
22:24 *r.* up seed to his brother, *Mark* 12:19; *Luke* 20:28
*John* 2:19 three days I will *r.* it
6:39 *r.* it at last day, 40, 44, 54
*Acts* 2:30 he *r.* C. to sit on thro.
26:8 why incredible G. *r.* dead?
1 *Cor.* 6:14 sh. *r.* up us by power
2 *Cor.* 4:14 sh. *r.* up us by Jesus
*Heb.* 11:19 God able to *r.* him.
*Jam.* 5:15 L. shall *r.* him up
**RAISED.**
*Ex.* 9:16 I *r.* thee up to show my power, *Rom.* 9:17
*Jos.* 5:7 chil. he *r.* up in stead
7:26 *r.* over him heap of stones
*Jud.* 2:16 L. *r.* up judges, 18
3:9 *r.* a deliverer to Israel, 15
2 *Sam.* 23:1 who was *r.* on high
1 *K.* 5:13 Sol. *r.* a levy of Is. 9:15
*Ezr.* 1:5 all whose spirit God *r.*
*Job* 14:12 nor *r.* out of their sleep

*Cant.* 8:5 r. th. under apple-tree
*Is.* 14:9 it r. up kings of nations
23:13 Assyrians r. palaces of C.
41:2 r. righteous man from east
25 I r. up one from the north
45:13 I r. him up in righteous.
*Jer.* 6:22 great nation r. fr. earth
29:15 L. r. proph. in Babylon
50:41 kings shall be r. fr. earth
51:11 L. r. spirit of kings of M.
*Dan.* 7:5 bear r. up on one side
*Amos* 2:11 I r. up sons for prop.
*Zec.* 2:13 r. out of holy habitati.
9:13 when I r. thy sons, O Zion
*Mat.* 11:5 dead r. up, *Luke* 7:22
16:21 r. again, 17:23; *Luke* 9:22
*Luke* 1:69 r. up horn of salvation
20:37 dead are r. Moses showed
*John* 12:1 Laz. whom he r. 9, 17
*Acts* 2:24 whom God hath r. up, 32; 3:15, 26; 4:10; 5:30; 10:40; 13:30, 33, 34; 17:31; *Rom.* 10:9; 1 *Cor.* 6:14; 2 *Cor.* 4:14; *Gal.* 1:1; *Eph.* 1:20
12:7 angel r. Peter; 13:22 r. Da.
13:23 G. r. Israel a Saviour J.
*Rom.* 4:24 bel. on him that r. J.
25 r. again for our justification
6:4 C. was r. fr. dead by Father
9 Ch. r. fr. dead, dieth no mo.
7:4 to him who is r. from dead
8:11 if Sp. of him that r. Jesus
1 *Cor.* 15:15 r. up C. wh. he r. n.
16 dead rise not, C. is not r.
17 if C. be not r. faith is vain
35 men say, How are dead r.?
42 sown in cor. r. in incorru. 52
43 it is r. in glory, r. in power
44 sown natu. body, r. spirit.
*Eph.* 2:6 r. us together in Ch. J.
*Col.* 2:12 through G. who r. him
1 *Thes.* 1:10 Son, he r. from dea.
2 *Tim.* 2:8 Je. seed of Da. was r.
*Heb.* 11:35 wom. received dead r.
1 *Pet.* 1:21 bel. in G. that r. him

**RAISER.**

*Dan.* 11:20 stand up r. of taxes

**RAISETH.**

1 *Sam.* 2:8 he r. poor, *Ps.* 113:7
*Job* 41:25 r. himself, mighty
*Ps.* 107:25 commands, r. winds
145:14 he r. those bowed, 146:8
*John* 5:21 the Father r. up dead
2 *Cor.* 1:9 trust in G. wh. r. dead

**RAISING.**

*Hos.* 7:4 baker who ceaseth fr. r.
*Acts* 24:12 found me r. up people

**RAISINS.**

1 *Sam.* 25:18 Ab. took 100 clus. r.
30:12 gave Egyp. two clusters r.
2 *Sam.* 16:1 met D. 100 bunch. r.
1 *Chr.* 12:40 brought bunch. of r.

**RAM.**

*Ruth* 4:19; 1 *Chr.* 2:9, 10, 25, 27
*Job* 32:2 Elihu of kindred of R.

**RAM.**

*Gen.* 15:9 take a r. 3 years old
22:13 a r. caught in a thicket
*Ex.* 29:15 take one r. 16 slay r.
22 r. of conse. 27, 31; *Lev.* 8:22
*Lev.* 9:2 take r. for burnt-offeri.
4 r. peace-offer. 19:21 trespass
*Num.* 5:8 besi. r. for atonement
*Ezr.* 10:19 they offered r.
*Ezek.* 43:23 they sh. offer a r. 25
45:24 ephah for a r. 46:5, 7, 11
46:6 in day of new moon a r.
*Dan.* 8:3 I saw r. had two horns
4 I saw r. pushing westward
6 goat ran to r. had two horns
7 no power in r. to deliver r.

**RAMS.**

*Gen.* 31:10 r. leaped ring-stre. 12
38 r. of flock have I not eaten
32:14 Jacob sent Esau twenty r.
*Deut.* 32:14 with r. breed of Bas.
1 *Sam.* 15:22 hearken th. fat of r.
2 *K.* 3:4 Moab rendered 100,000 r.
1 *Chr.* 29:21 sacrifi. to L. 1,000 r.
2 *Chr.* 17:11 Ar. brought 7,700 r.
*Ezr.* 6:17 off. at dedication 200 r.
7:17 buy with this money r.
8:35 offered ninety-six r. for sin
*Ps.* 66:15 with fat of r. *Is.* 34:6
114:4 mount. skipped like r. 6
*Is.* 1:11 full of burnt-offeri. of r.
34:6 filled with fat of kidn. of r.
60:7 r. of Nebaioth sh. minister
*Jer.* 51:40 br. to slaughter like r.
*Ezek.* 27:21 Kedar occupied in r.
34:17 I judge betw. r. and goats
*Ezek.* 39:18 ye sh. dr. blood of r.
*Mic.* 6:7 L. be pleased with r.?
*See* BATTERING, SEVEN.

**RAMS' horns.**

*Jos.* 6:4 seven priests shall bear before ark r. *horns*, 5, 6, 8, 13

**RAMS' skins.**

*Ex.* 25:5 r. *sk.* dyed red, 26:14; 35:7; 36:19; 39:34

**RAMAH, RAMA.**

*Jos.* 18:25 R. a city of tribe of
*Jud.* 4:5 Deborah dwelt betw. R.
1 *Sam.* 1:19 his house in R. 2:11
7:17 return to R. 15:34; 16:13
8:4 elders came to S. unto R.
19:18 Dav. came to Sa. to R. 22
25:1 buried in house at R. 28:3
1 *K.* 15:17 built R. 2 *Chr.* 16:1
2 *K.* 8:29 woun. at R. 2 *Chr.* 22:6
*Neh.* 11:33 chil. of B. dwell at R.
*Is.* 10:29 R. is afraid, Gibeah of
*Jer.* 31:15 heard in R. *Mat.* 2:18
*Ezek.* 27:22 the merchants of R.
*Hos.* 5:8 blow ye trumpet in R.

**RAMOTH-GILEAD.**

*Deut.* 4:43; *Jos.* 20:8; 21:38
1 *K.* 4:13 Geber officer in R.
22:3 that R. is ours, 4, 6, 12, 15
2 *K.* 8:28 against Hazael in R.
9:1 take box of oil, go to R. 14
2 *Chr.* 18:3, 11, 14; 22:5

**RAMPART.**

*Lam.* 2:8 he made r. to lament
*Nah.* 3:8 whose r. was the sea

**RAN.**

*Gen.* 18:2 Abr. r. from tent-door
7 r. to herd; 24:17 r. meet R.
24:20 Rebek. r. to well to draw
29:12 Rachel r. and told father
13 Laban r. to meet Jacob and
33:4 Esau r. and embraced him
*Ex.* 9:23 fire r. along the ground
*Num.* 11:27 r. man and told Mo.
16:47 Aaron r. into congregat.
*Jos.* 7:22 messen. r. to A.'s tent
*Jud.* 7:21 host of Midian r. fled
13:10 Manoah's wife r. showed
1 *Sam.* 3:5 Samuel r. to Eli, said
10:23 they r. and fetched Saul
17:22 D. r. and saluted brethren
51 D. r. stood upon Philistine
20:36 as lad r. he shot an arrow
2 *Sam.* 18:23 Ahimaaz r. by plain
1 *K.* 2:39 serv. of Shimei r. away
18:35 water r. about the altar
46 Elijah r. before Ahab to Je.
19:20 Elisha r. after Elijah
22:35 blood r. in midst of char.
*Ps.* 77:2 my sore r. in the night
105:41 waters r. in dry places
133:2 ointment r. down on bea.
*Jer.* 23:21 I have not sent, they r.
*Ezek.* 1:14 the living creatures r.
47:2 th. r. out waters on ri. side
*Dan.* 8:6 the goat r. to the ram
*Mat.* 8:32 herd of swine r. into sea, *Mark* 5:13; *Luke* 8:33
*Mark* 6:33 and r. afoot thither
*Luke* 15:20 father r. fell on neck
19:4 Zacch. r. and climbed tree
*John* 20:4 they r. both together
*Acts* 3:11 the people r. unto th.
7:57 they r. upon Stephen with
8:30 Philip r. to the chariot and
12:14 know Peter's voice she r.
14:14 Paul and Barnabas r. in
21:30 people r. and took Paul
32 captain took soldiers and r.
27:41 they r. the ship aground
*Jude* 11 r. after error of Balaam

**RANG.**

1 *Sam.* 4:5 shouted, the earth r.
1 *K.* 1:45 Is. shouted, the city r.

**RANGE.**

*Job* 39:8 r. of mountains pasture

**RANGES.**

*Lev.* 11:35 r. for pots, be broken
2 *K.* 11:8 cometh in r. be slain
15 ha. her forth, r. 2 *Chr.* 23:14

**RANGING.**

*Prov.* 28:15 roar. lion and r. bear

**RANK.**

*Gen.* 41:5 on one stock, r. good
7 seven thin ears dev. r. ears
*Num.* 2:16 set forth in second r.
24 shall go forward in third r.
1 *Chr.* 12:33 of Ze. 50,000 keep r.
38 men that keep r. came to H.

**RANKS.**

1 *K.* 7:4 against light three r. 5
*Joel* 2:7 shall not break their r.
*Mark* 6:40 sat down in r. by hundreds.

**RANSOM, Substantive.**

*Ex.* 21:30 shall give for r. of life
30:12 give ev. man r. for his so.
*Job* 33:24 del. from pit, I found r.
36:18 great r. cannot deliv. thee
*Ps.* 49:7 nor can they give G. a r.
*Prov.* 6:35 will not regard any r.
13:8 r. of man's life are riches
21:18 wicked be r. for righteous
*Is.* 43:3 I gave Egypt for thy r.
*Mat.* 20:28 even as the Son of man ga. life a r. *Mark* 10:45
1 *Tim.* 2:6 who gave himself r.

**RANSOM.**

*Hos.* 13:14 will r. them fr. grave

**RANSOMED.**

*Is.* 35:10 r. of the L. shall return
51:10 made sea a way for the r.
*Jer.* 31:11 L. redeemed J. and r.

**RAPHA *and* RAPHU.**

*Num.* 13:9 Benj. Palti, son of R.
1 *Chr.* 8:37 R. Eleasah, Azel

**RARE.**

*Dan.* 2:11 r. thing king requireth

**RASE.**

*Ps.* 137:7 r. it. r. it to foundat.

**RASH, LY.**

*Ec.* 5:2 be not r. with mouth
*Acts* 19:36 be quiet, do nothi. r.

**RATE.**

*Ex.* 16:4 peo. gather certain r.
1 *K.* 10:25 mules at r. 2 *Chr.* 9:24
2 *K.* 25:30 daily r. for every day
2 *Chr.* 8:13 even after a certain r.

**RATHER.**

*Jos.* 22:24 we have not r. done
2 *K.* 5:13 r. when he saith to th.
*Mat.* 25:9 go ye r. to th. th. sell
*Mark* 5:26 but r. grew worse
*Rom.* 8:34 yea, r. that is risen a.
1 *Cor.* 7:21 be made free, use it r.
*Gal.* 4:9 or r. known of God
*Heb.* 13:19 I beseech you r. do

**RATTLETH.**

*Job* 39:23 quiver r. against him

**RATTLING.**

*Nah.* 3:2 noise of r. of wheels

**RAVEN, S.**

*Gen.* 8:7 Noah sent forth a r.
*Lev.* 11:15 r. unclean, *Deut.* 14:14

1 *K.* 17:4 comma. *r.* to feed thee
6 the *r.* brought Elijah bread
*Job* 38:41 prov. *r.* food. *Ps.* 147:9
*Prov.* 30:17 *r.* of val. shall pick
*Cant.* 5:11 bushy, black as *r.*
*Is.* 34:11 the *r.* shall dwell in it
*Luke* 12:24 consider *r.* nei. sow

**RAVENING.**

*Ps.* 22:13 gaped as *r.* lion
*Ezek.* 22:25 like a roaring lion *r.*
27 princes are like wolves *r.*
*Mat.* 7:15 they are *r.* wolves
*Luke* 11:39 inw. part is full of *r.*

**RAVENOUS.**

*Ps.* 35:9 nor any *r.* beast sh. go
46:11 calling a *r.* bird from east
*Ezek.* 39:4 give thee to *r.* birds

**RAVIN, Verb.**

*Gen.* 49:27 Benjamin *r.* as wolf

**RAVIN.**

*Nah.* 2:12 lion filled dens with *r.*

**RAVISHED.**

*Prov.* 5:19 be thou *r.* with love
20 why be *r.* with st. woman?
*Cant.* 4:9 thou hast *r.* my heart
*Is.* 13:16 wives of Bab. sh. be *r.*
*Lam.* 5:11 *r.* the women in Zion
*Zec.* 14:2 women in Jerus. be *r.*

**RAW.**

*Ex.* 12:9 eat not it *r.* nor sodden
*Lev.* 13:10 if th. be quick *r.* flesh
15 priest see *r.* flesh, *r.* flesh
1 *Sam.* 2:15 not sod. flesh, but *r.*

**RAZOR.**

*Num.* 6:5 nor *r.* upon head, *Jud.* 13:5; 16:17; 1 *Sam.* 1:11
*Ps.* 52:2 tongue like a sharp *r.*
*Is.* 7:20 Lord shave with a *r.*
*Ezek.* 5:1 take thee a barber's *r.*

**REACH.**

*Gen.* 11:4 tower *r.* to heaven
*Ex.* 28:42 breeches *r.* to thighs
*Lev.* 26:5 threshing *r.* to vintage
*Num.* 34:11 border shall *r.* to sea
*Job* 20:6 his head *r.* unto clouds
*Is.* 8:8 he shall *r.* even to neck
30:28 breath *r.* to midst of neck
*Jer.* 48:32 thy plants *r.* to sea
*Zec.* 14:5 mountains sh. *r.* to A.
*John* 20:27 *r.* hither thy finger
2 *Cor.* 10:13 mea. to *r.* unto you

**REACHED.**

*Gen.* 28:12 ladder's top *r.* to hea.
*Ruth* 2:14 he *r.* her parched corn
*Dan.* 4:11 height *r.* to heaven, 20
2 *Cor.* 10:14 tho' we *r.* not to you
*Rev.* 18:5 Babyl.'s sins *r.* heaven

**REACHETH.**

2 *Chr.* 28:9 rage that *r.* to heav.
*Ps.* 36:5 faithfulness *r.* clouds
108:4 thy truth *r.* to the clouds
*Prov.* 31:20 *r.* hands to needy
*Jer.* 4:10 the sword *r.* to the soul
18 because it *r.* to thy heart
51:9 Bab.'s judgm. *r.* to heaven
*Dan.* 4:22 thy greatness *r.* heav.

**REACHING.**

*Phil.* 3:13 *r.* forth to th. things

**READ** (*short e*).

*Ex.* 24:7 *r.* in audience of people
*Jos.* 8:34 *r.* words of the law, 10
2 *K.* 5:7 king of Isr. *r.* the letter
22:8 Shaphan *r.* book of law, 10
23:2 Josiah *r.* in their ears book of the covenant, 2 *Chr.* 34:30
2 *Chr.* 34:24 bri. all the curses *r.*
*Ezr.* 4:18 letter been plainly *r.*
*Neh.* 8:3 he *r.* before all the book of the law, 8; 13:1
9:3 stood in their place and *r.*
*Est.* 6:1 book of records was *r.*
*Is.* 37:14 received let. and *r.* it
*Jer.* 29:29 Zephani. the priest *r.*
36:10 then *r.* Bar. words of Jer.
21 Jehudi *r.* it in ears of king
23 he *r.* three or four leaves
*Mat.* 12:3 have ye not *r.*? 19:4; 21:16; 22:31; *Mark* 2:25; 12:10, 26; *Luke* 6:3
*John* 19:20 this *r.* many of Jews
*Acts* 8:28 eunuch *r.* Esaias prop.
32 place of scripture wh. he *r.*
13:27 prophets *r.* ev. sab. 15:21
23:34 Governor had *r.* the letter
2 *Cor.* 3:2 epistle known and *r.*
15 when M. is *r.* the veil is on
*Col.* 4:16 when this epistle is *r.*
1 *Thes.* 5:27 that this epistle be *r.*

**READ** (*long e*).

*Deut.* 17:19 king shall *r.* therein
31:11 thou sh. *r.* this low before
*Is.* 29:11 *r.* this, I pray thee, 12
34:16 seek out book of L. and *r.*
*Jer.* 36:6 go and *r.* in the roll
15 sit do. and *r.* it in our ears
51:61 cometh to Babylon and *r.*
*Dan.* 5:7 whosoever shalt *r.* this
17 gifts be to thyself, I will *r.*
*Mat.* 21:42 did ye never *r.* in sc.?
*Luke* 4:16 Jesus went in for to *r.*
*Acts* 8:30 Philip heard him *r.* E.
2 *Cor.* 1:13 we write none other things than what ye *r.*
*Eph.* 3:4 wh. ye *r.* ye may und.
*Col.* 4:16 *r.* epistle fr. Laodicea.
*Rev.* 5:4 none worthy to *r.* book

**READEST.**

*Luke* 10:26 in law, how *r.* thou?
*Acts* 8:30 un. thou what thou *r.*?

**READETH.**

*Hab.* 2:2 he may run that *r.* it
*Mat.* 24:15 whoso *r.* let him understand, *Mark* 13:14
*Rev.* 1:3 blessed is he that *r.*

**READING.**

*Neh.* 8:8 caused to understand *r.*
*Jer.* 36:8 *r.* in the book of the L.
51:63 wh. hast ma. an end of *r.*
*Acts* 13:15 after the *r.* of the law
2 *Cor.* 3:14 untaken away in *r.*
1 *Tim.* 4:13 give attendance to *r.*

**READINESS.**

*Acts* 17:11 received word in *r.*
2 *Cor.* 8:11 as there was a *r.*
10:6 *r.* to revenge disobedience

**READY.**

*Ex.* 17:4 people *r.* to stone me
19:11 *r.* against third day, 15
34:2 *r.* in morning, and come
*Num.* 32:17 we will go *r.* armed
*Deut.* 26:5 a Syrian *r.* to perish
2 *Sam.* 15:15 thy servants are *r.*
18:22 hast no tidings *r.*?
*Ezr.* 7:6 Ezra was a *r.* scribe
*Neh.* 9:17 art a God *r.* to pardon
*Est.* 3:14 they should be *r.* 8:13
*Job* 3:8 *r.* to raise their mourning
15:23 day of darkn. is *r.* at hand
24 prevail as a king *r.* to battle
28 in houses *r.* to become hea.
18:12 destruction *r.* at his side
29:13 blessing of him *r.* to peri.
*Ps.* 38:17 for I am *r.* to halt
45:1 tongue pen of a *r.* writer
86:5 Lord art good, *r.* to forgive
88:15 *r.* to die from my youth
*Prov.* 24:11 those *r.* to be slain
31:6 stro. drink to him *r.* to pe.
*Ec.* 5:1 *r.* to hear th. give sacrif.
*Is.* 27:13 who were *r.* to perish
30:13 iniq. as breach *r.* to fall
32:4 tongue of stam. *r.* to speak
38:20 the L. was *r.* to save me
51:13 as if he were *r.* to destroy
*Dan.* 3:15 if ye be *r.* to worship
*Mat.* 22:4 fatlings killed, all *r.*
8 the wedding is *r.* *Luke* 14:17
24:44 be ye also *r.* *Luke* 12:40
25:10 they that were *r.* went in
*Mark* 14:38 spirit is *r.* flesh weak
*Luke* 7:2 servant sick, *r.* to die
22:33 L. I am *r.* to go with thee
*John* 7:6 your time is always *r.*
*Acts* 21:13 I am *r.* not to be bou.
23:21 are *r.* looking for promise
*Rom.* 1:15 I am *r.* to preach gos.
2 *Cor.* 8:19 declaration of *r.* mind
9:2 Achaia was *r.* a year ago
3 that, as I said, ye might be *r.*
5 that the same might be *r.*
12:14 third time I am *r.* to come
1 *Tim.* 6:18 ye be *r.* to distribute
2 *Tim.* 4:6 now *r.* to be offered
*Tit.* 3:1 be *r.* to every good work
*Heb.* 8:13 is *r.* to vanish away
1 *Pet.* 1:5 *r.* to be revealed
3:15 be *r.* always to give answer
4:5 give account to him th. is *r.*
5:2 not for lucre, of a *r.* mind
*Rev.* 3:2 things that are *r.* to die
12:4 wo. was *r.* to be delivered

*See* MADE, MAKE.

**REALM.**

2 *Chr.* 20:30 the *r.* of Jehoshaph.
*Ezr.* 7:13 they of my *r.* who go
23 why be wrath against *r.*?
*Dan.* 1:20 better th. all in his *r.*
6:3 king tho. to set him over *r.*
9:1 Darius, king over *r.* of Chal.
11:2 stir up all ag. *r.* of Grecia

**REAP.**

*Lev.* 19:9 when ye *r.* 23:10, 22
25:5 groweth of itself sh. not *r.*
11 ye shall neither sow nor *r.*
*Ruth* 2:9 eyes be on field they *r.*
1 *Sam.* 8:12 set your serva. to *r.*
2 *K.* 19:29 in the third year sow and *r.* *Is.* 37:30
*Job* 4:8 sow wickedness *r.* same
24:6 they *r.* every one his corn
*Ps.* 126:5 sow in tears *r.* in joy
*Prov.* 22:8 soweth iniq. *r.* vanity
*Ec.* 11:4 regard clouds sh. not *r.*
*Jer.* 12:13 sown wheat, *r.* thorns
*Hos.* 8:7 sown wind, *r.* whirlwind
10:12 sow in righte. *r.* in mercy
*Mic.* 6:15 th. sh. sow, but not *r.*
*Mat.* 6:26 fowls of the air *r.* not
25:26 I *r.* where I sowed not
*John* 4:38 to *r.* whereon no labor
1 *Cor.* 9:11 if we *r.* carnal things
2 *Cor.* 9:6 sow. sparingly *r.* spar.
*Gal.* 6:7 man sow. that sh. he *r.*
8 soweth to flesh shall *r.* cor.
9 we shall *r.* if faint not
*Rev.* 14:15 thrust in sickle and *r.*

**REAPED.**

*Hos.* 10:13 wickedness *r.* iniquity
*Jam.* 5:4 laborers which *r.* fields
*Rev.* 14:16 his sickle, ear. was *r.*

**REAPER, S.**

*Ruth* 2:3 Ruth gleaned after *r.*
7 I pray, let me glean after *r.*
2 *K.* 4:18 he went out to the *r.*
*Amos* 9:13 ploughm. overtake *r.*
*Mat.* 13:30 say to *r.* gather tares
39 enemy is devil, *r.* are angels

**REAPEST.**

*Lev.* 23:22 not cl. riddance wh. *r.*
*Luke* 19:21 thou *r.* didst not sow

**REAPETH.**

*Is.* 17:5 the harvest-man *r.* ears
*John* 4:36 he that *r.* recei. wages
37 one soweth, another *r.*

**REAPING.**

1 *Sam.* 6:13 Beth-shem. were *r.*
*Mat.* 25:24 man, *r.* *Luke* 19:22

REARWARD. *See* REREWARD.

**REASON, Substantive.**

1 *K.* 9:15 this is *r.* of the levy
*Prov.* 26:16 seven men render *r.*
*Ec.* 7:25 I applied to search *r.*
*Dan.* 4:36 at time my *r.* returned
*Acts* 6:2 not *r.* we leave word
18:14 O J. *r.* would I sho. bear

1 *Pet.* 3:15 ask. you a *r.* of hope

**By REASON.**

*Gen.* 41:31 plenty not kno. *by r.*
*Ex.* 2:23 Isr. sighed *by r.* bonda.
3:7 cry *by r.* of their taskmast.
*Num.* 9:10 uncl. *by r.* dead body
18:8 things given *by r.* of anoi.
*Deut.* 5:5 afraid *by r.* of the fire
1 *K.* 14:4 Ahijah's eyes *by r.* age
2 *Chr.* 5:14 not minister *by r.*
20:15 not afraid *by r.* of multit.
*Job* 17:7 eye dim *by r.* of sorrow
31:23 *by r.* of highness not end.
37:19 speech *by r.* of darkness
41:25 *by r.* of break. they purify
*Ps.* 78:65 man shout. *by r.* wine
90:10 if *by r.* of str. be fourscore
*Is.* 49:19 too nar. *by r.* of inhabi.
*Ezek.* 19:10 branches *by r.* of wa.
*Dan.* 8:12 given *by r.* of transgr.
*Jon.* 2:2 I cried *by r.* of affliction
*John* 12:11 *by r.* many beli. on J.
*Rom.* 8:20 *by r.* of him who subj.
*Heb.* 5:3 *by r.* hereof, off. for sins
7:23 not continue *by r.* death
2 *Pet.* 2:2 *by r.* of whom truth

**REASON, Verb.**

1 *Sam.* 12:7 I may *r.* with you
*Job* 9:14 ch. words to *r.* with you
13:3 and desire to *r.* with God
15:3 sh. he *r.* with unpro. talk?
*Is.* 1:18 now, let us *r.* together
*Mat.* 16:8 J. said, Why *r.* among yourselves, *Mark* 2:8; 8:17
*Luke* 5:21 scr. and Pha. began *r.*
22 what *r.* ye in your hearts?

**REASONABLE.**

*Rom.* 12:1 sacrifice, your *r.* serv.

**REASONED.**

*Mat.* 16:7 *r.* am. themselv. 21:15; *Mark* 8:16; 11:31; *Luke* 20:5
*Mark* 2:8 J. perceived they so *r.*
*Luke* 20:14 the husbandmen *r.*
24:15 while they *r.* J. drew near
*Acts* 17:2 three sabbaths Paul *r.*
18:4 he *r.* in synagogue ev. sab.
19 Paul *r.* with J. at Ephesus
24:25 as he *r.* of righteousness

**REASONING.**

*Job* 13:6 hear my *r.* and hearken
*Mark* 2:6 scribes *r.* in th. hearts
12:28 having heard them *r.* tog.
*Luke* 9:46 arose *r.* among them
*Acts* 28:29 J. departed, and had *r.*

**REASONS.**

*Job* 32:11 gave ear to your *r.*
*Is.* 41:21 br. *r.* saith king of Jac.

**REBEKAH.**

*Gen.* 22:23 Bethuel begat R.
24:15 R. ca. out. 51, 59, 60, 67
25:28 R. loved Jacob, 20
26:7 should kill me for R. 35
27:42 words of Es. were told R.
29:12 that he was R. son, 35:8
49:31 they buried Isaac and R.
*Rom.* 9:10 when R. conceived

**REBEL.**

*Num.* 14:9 only *r.* not aga. Lord
*Jos.* 1:18 whosoever *r.* shall die
22:16 builded altar ye might *r.*
19 *r.* not agai. L. *r.* not ag. us
29 God forbid we *r.* against L.
1 *Sam.* 12:14 ye obey and not *r.*
15 if ye will not obey L. but *r.*
*Neh.* 2:19 will ye *r.* aga. king?
6:6 thou and Jews think to *r.*
*Job* 24:13 those that *r.* aga. light
*Is.* 1:20 if ye *r.* ye sh. be devour.
*Hos.* 7:14 assemble for corn, *r.*

**REBELLED.**

*Gen.* 14:4 thirteenth year they *r.*
*Num.* 20:24 because ye *r.* ag. my word at Meribah, 27:14; *Deut.* 1:26, 43; 9:23
1 *K.* 12:19 Rehobo. fled, so Is. *r.* ag. house of Da. 2 *Chr.* 10:19
2 *K.* 1:1 Moab *r.* ag. Israel, 3, 5, 7
18:7 Hezek. *r.* ag. Assyria
24:1 Jehoiakim *r.* against Neb.
20 Ze. *r.* 2 *Chr.* 36:13; *Jer.* 52:3
2 *Chr.* 13:6 Jerob. *r.* ag. his lord
*Neh.* 9:26 disobe. and *r.* ag. thee
*Ps.* 5:10 for they *r.* against thee
105:28 they *r.* not against word
107:11 they *r.* ag. words of God
*Is.* 1:2 nourish. children, they *r.*
63:10 *r.* and vexed Holy Spirit
*Lam.* 1:18 have *r.* 20 griev. *r.*
3:42 we have *r.* has not pardon.
*Ezek.* 2:3 send th. to nation th. *r.*
17:15 he *r.* in sending to Egypt
20:8 they *r.* against me, 13, 21
*Dan.* 9:5 *r.* by departing fr. thee
9 to God mercy, though we have *r.*
*Hos.* 13:16 Samaria *r.* against G.

**REBELLEST.**

2 *K.* 18:20 on whom dost thou trust, that thou *r.*? *Is.* 36:5

**REBELLION.**

*Deut.* 31:27 know thy *r.* and stiff
*Jos.* 22:22 sh. know if it be in *r.*
1 *Sam.* 15:23 *r.* is as witchcraft
*Ezr.* 4:19 that *r.* made therein
*Neh.* 9:17 in *r.* appointed a capt.
*Job* 34:37 addeth *r.* unto his sin
*Prov.* 17:11 evil man seeketh *r.*
*Jer.* 28:16 hast taught *r.* 29:32

**REBELLIOUS.**

*Deut.* 9:7 *r.* against L. 24; 31:27
21:18 a stubborn and *r.* son
1 *Sam.* 20:30 son of the *r.* woman
*Ezr.* 4:12 building the *r.* city, 15
*Ps.* 66:7 let not *r.* exalt themsel.
68:6 the *r.* dwell in a dry land
18 for *r.* 78:8 *r.* generation
*Is.* 1:23 princes *r.* companions
30:1 woe to *r.* chil. saith Lord
9 a *r.* people; 50:5 I was not *r.*
65:2 spread hands to a *r.* people
*Jer.* 4:17 she ha. been *r.* saith L.
5:23 this people hath a *r.* heart
*Ezek.* 2:3 send thee to a *r.* nation
5 they are a *r.* house, 6, 7; 3:9, 26, 27; 12:2, 3
8 be not *r.* like that *r.* house
12:2 dwell. in midst of *r.* house
17:12 say to *r.* house, 44:6
24:3 utter parable to *r.* house

**REBELS.**

*Num.* 17:10 A. rod token ag. *r.*
20:10 M. and A. said, Hear, *r.*
*Ezek.* 20:38 I will purge out *r.*

**REBUKE, Substantive.**

*Deut.* 28:20 Lord send on thee *r.*
2 *K.* 19:3 this is day of *r.* *Is.* 37:3
*Ps.* 18:15 at thy *r.* blast of nost.
76:6 at *r.* horse cast into sleep
80:16 per. at *r.* of countenance
104:7 at thy *r.* they fled away
*Prov.* 13:1 a scorner hear. not *r.*
8 but the poor heareth not *r.*
27:5 open *r.* bet. than secret love
*Ec.* 7:5 better to hear *r.* of wise
*Is.* 25:8 *r.* of his peo. take away
30:17 thousand flee at *r.* of one at the *r.* of five shall ye flee
50:2 at thy *r.* I dry up the sea
51:20 thy sons lie full of *r.* of G.
66:15 render his *r.* with flames
*Jer.* 15:15 for thy sake I suff. *r.*
*Hos.* 5:9 Ep. sh. be des. day of *r.*
*Phil.* 2:15 without *r.* in per. nat.

**REBUKE, Verb.**

*Lev.* 19:17 in any wise *r.* neigh.
*Ruth* 2:16 glean them, *r.* her not
1 *Chr.* 12:17 God look thereon, *r.*
*Ps.* 6:1 O Lord, *r.* me not, 38:1
68:30 *r.* the spearmen, the bulls
*Prov.* 9:8 *r.* wise man
24:25 them that *r.* him
*Is.* 2:4 shall *r.* nations, *Mic.* 4:3
17:13 nations rush, G. *r.* them
54:9 I 'vou. not be wroth, nor *r.*
*Zec.* 3:2 Lord *r.* thee, even Lord that hath chosen Jer. *r.* thee
*Mal.* 3:11 *r.* devo. for your sakes
*Mat.* 16:22 P. *r.* him, *Mark* 8:32
*Luke* 17:3 if brot. trespass *r.* him
19:39 said, Master, *r.* thy disc.
1 *Tim.* 5:1 *r.* not elder, entreat
20 them that sin, *r.* before all
2 *Tim.* 4:2 *r.* with long-suffering
*Tit.* 1:13 wheref. *r.* sharply, 2:15
*Jude* 9 Mich. said, The L. *r.* thee
*Rev.* 3:19 as many as I love I *r.*

**REBUKED.**

*Gen.* 31:42 hath seen and *r.* thee
37:10 his father *r.* him, and said
*Neh.* 5:7 I *r.* the nobles and rul.
*Ps.* 9:5 hast *r.* the heathen, hast
106:9 he *r.* Red sea, it was dry
119:21 thou hast *r.* the proud
*Mat.* 8:26 he *r.* the wind and the sea, *Mark* 4:39; *Luke* 8:24
17:18 J. *r.* devil, and he depart.
19:13 his disci. *r.* them, *Mark* 10:13; *Luke* 18:15
20:31 multitude *r.* blind men
*Mark* 1:25 he *r.* the devil, 9:25; *Luke* 4:35; 9:42
8:33 Jesus *r.* Peter, Get behind
*Luke* 4:39 stood, and *r.* the fever
9:55 J. turned, *r.* James and J.
18:39 went before, *r.* blind man
23:40 thief answering, *r.* him
*Heb.* 12:5 nor faint wh. *r.* of him
2 *Pet.* 2:16 Balaam was *r.* for ini.

**REBUKER.**

*Hos.* 5:2 I have been a *r.* of all

**REBUKES.**

*Ps.* 39:11 with *r.* dost cor. man
*Ezek.* 5:15 execute judgment in *r.* 25:17

**REBUKETH, ING.**

2 *Sam.* 22:16 discover. at *r.* of L.
*Prov.* 9:7 he that *r.* wicked man
28:23 he that *r.* shall find favor
*Amos* 5:10 hate him that *r.* in
*Nah.* 1:4 he *r.* sea, and maketh
*Luke* 4:41 he *r.* th. suffered not

**RECALL.**

*Lam.* 3:21 this I *r.* to mind

**RECEIPT.**

*Mat.* 9:9 Mat. sitting at the *r.* of custom, *Mark* 2:14; *Lu.* 5:27

**RECEIVE.**

*Deut.* 33:3 ev. one *r.* thy words
1 *Sam.* 10:4 thou *r.* of their han.
*Job* 2:10 *r.* good at hand of G.?
27:13 shall *r.* of the Almighty
*Ps.* 6:9 Lord will *r.* my prayer
24:5 he shall *r.* blessing from L.
49:15 G. red. soul, he sh. *r.* me
73:24 afterward *r.* me to glory
75:2 when I *r.* congregation
*Prov.* 2:1 if th. wilt *r.* my words
10:8 wise will *r.* commandm.
*Is.* 57:6 sho. I *r.* comfort in these
*Ezek.* 16:61 asha. when *r.* sisters
*Dan.* 2:6 ye shall *r.* of me gifts
*Mic.* 1:11 shall *r.* of you standing
*Zep.* 3:7 thou wilt *r.* instruction
*Mat.* 10:41 *r.* a prophet's reward
11:5 the blind *r.* their sight
14 if ye *r.* it, this is E. to come
19:11 all men cannot *r.* saying
20:7 whatsoever is right that *r.*
21:22 believing, ye shall *r.*
34 that they might *r.* fruits
*Mark* 4:16 *r.* the word with gladness, *Luke* 8:13
20 hear the word, and *r.* it
10:51 Lord, that I might *r.* my sight, *Luke* 18:41
11:24 wh. ye pray, believe ye *r.*

*Luke* 10:8 city ye enter, they *r.*
16:9 *r.* into everlasting habita.
23:41 we *r.* reward of our deeds
*John* 5:43 own name, him ye *r.*
44 can ye believe, wh. *r.* honor
7:39 they that believe, *r.* H. G.
14:3 come again, and *r.* you
16:14 he shall *r.* of mine
24 ask and ye shall *r.*
*Acts* 1:8 but ye shall *r.* power
2:38 ye shall *r.* gift of Holy G.
8:15 pray. they might *r.* H. G.
19 on who. I lay hands may *r.*
9:12 that he might *r.* his sight
17 J. sent me, thou *r.* thy sig.
10:43 believeth, *r.* remis. of sins
26:18 may *r.* forgiveness of sins
*Rom.* 5:17 *r.* abundance of grace
16:2 that ye *r.* her in the Lord
1 *Cor.* 3:8 ev. man *r.* his reward
14 work abide, he *r.* reward
4:7 didst *r.* it, why glory?
2 *Cor.* 5:10 every one *r.* things
6:17 unclean thing, I will *r.* you
8:4 praying, we would *r.* gift
11:4 or if ye *r.* another spirit
*Gal.* 3:14 might *r.* promise of S.
*Eph.* 6:8 same shall he *r.* of L.
*Col.* 3:24 shall *r.* reward of inh.
25 he shall *r.* for wrong done
*Phile.* 15 should. *r.* him for ever
*Heb.* 7:8 men that die *r.* tithes
9:15 might *r.* promise, 10:36
*Jam.* 1:7 think he *r.* any thing
3:1 sh. *r.* greater condemnation
5:7 he *r.* early and latter rain
1 *Pet.* 5:4 shall *r.* crown of glory
1 *John* 3:22 whatso. we ask we *r.*
5:9 if we *r.* witness of men
2 *John* 8 that we *r.* a full reward
*Rev.* 14:9 if any man *r.* mark
17:12 *r.* powers as kings

**RECEIVE,** *imperatively.*

*Gen.* 33:10 *r.* pres. at my hand
*Job* 22:22 *r.* law from his mouth
*Prov.* 4:10 and *r.* my sayings
*Jer.* 9:20 let your ear *r.* the word
*Ezek.* 3:10 *r.* all my words
*Hos.* 14:2 say, *r.* us graciously
*Mat.* 19:12 is able let him *r.* it
*Luke* 18:42 *r.* sight, *Acts* 22:13
*John* 20:22 he saith, *r.* Holy Gh.
*Acts* 7:59 L. Jesus, *r.* my spirit
*Rom.* 14:1 him weak in faith *r.*
15:7 *r.* one ano. as Ch. received
2 *Cor.* 7:2 *r.* us, wronged no man
11:16 as a fool *r.* me, I boast
*Phil.* 2:29 *r.* him in L. with glad.
*Col.* 4:10 Mar. if he come, *r.* him
*Phile.* 12 *r.* him th. is mine own
17 count me partner, *r.* him

**RECEIVE,** *negatively.*

2 *K.* 5:16 Elisha said, I *r.* none
*Job* 2:10 we *r.* good, not *r.* evil?
*Jer.* 35:13 will ye not *r.* instruc.
*Ezek.* 36:30 ye shall *r.* no more
*Mark* 10:15 whosoever sh. not *r.* kingdom of G. *Luke* 18:17
*Luke* 9:53 they did not *r.* him
10:10 they *r.* you not, go into
18:30 who shall not *r.* manifold
*John* 3:11 ye *r.* not our witness
27 a man can *r.* noth. except
5:41 I *r.* not honor from men
43 come in F.'s na. ye *r.* me not
14:17 Sp. whom world cannot *r.*
*Acts* 22:18 will not *r.* testimony
1 *Cor.* 4:7 wh. hast thou, not *r.*?
2 *Cor.* 6:1 *r.* not grace of G. in v.
*Jam.* 4:3 ye ask and *r.* not
2 *John* 10 *r.* him not into house
3 *John* 10 nei. doth he *r.* breth.

**RECEIVE,** *infinitively.*

*Gen.* 4:11 earth op. mouth to *r.*
*Deut.* 9:9 gone up to *r.* tables
1 *K.* 8:64 braz. altar was too little to *r.* burnt-offer. 2 *Chr.* 7:7
2 *K.* 5:26 time to *r.* money, to *r.*
12:8 priest to *r.* no more money
*Prov.* 1:3 *r.* instruction of wisd.
*Jer.* 5:3 refused to *r.* correction
*Mal.* 3:10 not room enough to *r.*
*Mat.* 19:12 to *r.* it, let him *r.* it
*Mark* 2:2 no room to *r.* them
*Luke* 6:34 of whom ye hope to *r.*
*Acts* 8:27 ex. disciples to *r.* him
20:35 more bles. to give than *r.*
3 *John* 8 we ought to *r.* such
*Rev.* 4:11 thou worthy to *r.* glo.
5:12 worthy is L. to *r.* power
13:16 causeth to *r.* mark in ha.

**RECEIVED.**

*Gen.* 26:12 Isaac *r.* hundred-fold
*Ex.* 32:4 Aaron *r.* at th. hand
*Num.* 12:14 let Miriam be *r.* in
23:20 I *r.* commandm. to bless
*Jos.* 13:8 Gadites *r.* inheritance
1 *Sam.* 12:3 of wh. hand ha. I *r.*
2 *K.* 19:14 Hezekiah *r.* the letter, *Is.* 37:14
1 *Chr.* 12:18 David *r.* them
*Job* 4:12 mine ear *r.* little thereof
*Ps.* 68:18 hast *r.* gifts for men
*Prov.* 24:32 I looked and *r.* inst.
*Is.* 40:2 she hath *r.* of L.'s hand
*Ezek.* 18:17 hath not *r.* usury nor
*Zep.* 3:2 she *r.* not correction
*Mat.* 10:8 freely ye *r.* freely give
13:20 *r.* into stony gr. 22 thorns
23 *r.* seed into good ground
20:9 *r.* every man a penny, 10
34 immedi. their eyes *r.* sight
*Mark* 7:4 many things they *r.*
10:52 he immediately *r.* sight, *Luke* 18:43; *Acts* 9:18
16:19 was *r.* into heav. *Acts* 1:9
*Luke* 6:24 ye have *r.* consolation
8:40 the people gladly *r.* him
9:11 *r.* them, spake of kingdom
51 time come he sho. be *r.* up
10:38 Martha *r.* him into house
15:27 *r.* him safe and sound
19:6 Zaccheus *r.* him joyfully
15 returned, having *r.* kingd.
*John* 1:11 ca. to his own, own *r.*
12 as many as *r.* him he gave
16 of fulness *r.* grace for grace
3:33 he that hath *r.* testimony
4:45 when come, Galil. *r.* him
6:21 willingly *r.* him in ship
9:11 washed, and I *r.* sight
15 Pharis. asked how *r.* sight
10:18 comman. *r.* of my Father
17:8 given thy words, *r.* them
18:3 Ju. having *r.* band of men
*Acts* 1:9 cloud *r.* him out of sig.
2:33 hav. *r.* of Father promise
41 they *r.* word were baptized
7:53 who have *r.* law by angels
8:14 Samaria *r.* word of God
17 hands on them *r.* Holy Gh.
9:19 *r.* meat was strengthened
10:47 which have *r.* Holy Gh.
11:1 heard Genti. *r.* word of G.
15:4 they were *r.* of the church
17:7 whom Jason hath *r.*
11 Bereans *r.* word with readi.
19:2 have ye *r.* the Holy Ghost?
20:24 ministry which I *r.* of L.
21:17 the brethren *r.* us gladly
22:5 from whom I *r.* letters to
28:7 Publius *r.* us; Paul *r.* all
21 nei. *r.* letters out of Judea
*Rom.* 1:5 by whom we *r.* grace
5:11 by whom we *r.* atonement
8:15 have not *r.* spirit of bond.
14:3 him that eateth, G. *r.* him
15:7 rec. one another as C. *r.* us
1 *Cor.* 2:12 *r.* not spirit of world
4:7 glory, as if thou hadst not *r.*
11:23 I *r.* of Lord that which
1 *Cor.* 15:1 which ye *r.* 3 wh. I *r.*
2 *Cor.* 4:1 as we *r.* mercy
11:4 spirit which ye have not *r.*
*Gal.* 1:9 anot. gospel than ye *r.*
12 I *r.* it not of man, neither
3:2 *r.* ye Sp. by works of law?
4:14 *r.* me as an angel of God
*Phil.* 4:9 thi. ye have *r.* and seen
*Col.* 2:6 as ye *r.* Christ, so walk
4:10 whom ye *r.* commandm.
17 take heed to minis. thou *r.*
1 *Thes.* 1:6 *r.* word in affliction
2:13 when ye *r.* the word, ye *r.*
4:1 as ye *r.* of us how to walk
2 *Thes.* 2:10 they *r.* not the truth
1 *Tim.* 3:16 believed, *r.* into gl.
4:3 meats God created to be *r.*
4 crea. good, if *r.* with thanks.
*Heb.* 7:11 under it people *r.* law
10:26 if sin after *r.* knowledge
11:13 not having *r.* promises
17 *r.* promises offered only son
19 whence he *r.* him in a figure
35 women *r.* dead raised to life
39 these *r.* not the promise
1 *Pet.* 4:10 every one hath *r.* gift
2 *Pet.* 1:17 he *r.* from God honor
2 *John* 4 we have *r.* a command
*Rev.* 2:27 power, as *r.* of Father
3:3 remember how thou hast *r.*
19:20 that had *r.* mark of beast
20:4 nor *r.* mark reigned wi. C.

**RECEIVEDST.**

*Luke* 16:25 in lifetime *r.* good th.

**RECEIVER.**

*Is.* 33:18 scribe? where is *r.*?

**RECEIVETH.**

*Jud.* 19:18 no man *r.* to house
*Job* 35:7 what *r.* he of thy hand?
*Prov.* 21:11 when wise *r.* know.
29:4 he that *r.* gifts, overthr.
*Jer.* 7:28 nation *r.* not correction
*Mal.* 2:13 *r.* offer. with good-will
*Mat.* 7:8 that asketh *r.* *Luke* 11:10
10:40 that *r.* you, *r.* me; *r.* me, *r.* him sent me, *John* 13:20
41 he that *r.* a prophet, right.
13:20 heareth word, anon *r.* it
18:5 one such little child, *r.* me
*Mark* 9:37 *r.* not me, but him that sent me, *Luke* 9:48
*Luke* 15:2 this man *r.* sinners
*John* 3:32 no man *r.* his testim.
12:48 he that *r.* not my words
1 *Cor.* 9:24 run all, one *r.* prize
*Heb.* 6:7 earth *r.* blessing fr. God
7:9 L. who *r.* tithes, paid tithes
*Rev.* 2:17 know. saving he *r.* it
14:11 whoso. *r.* mark of name

**RECEIVETH not.**

1 *Cor.* 2:14 *r.* *not* things of God
3 *John* 9 but Diotrephes *r.* us *n.*

**RECEIVING.**

2 *K.* 5:20 in not *r.* at his hands
*Acts* 17:15 *r.* a comman. to Silas
*Rom.* 11:15 wh. sh. *r.* of th. be?
*Phil.* 4:15 concern. giving and *r.*
*Heb.* 12:28 wheref. we *r.* a king.
1 *Pet.* 1:9 *r.* the end of your faith

**RECHAB.**

2 *K.* 10:15 Jehonadab son of R.
1 *Chr.* 2:55 father of house of R.
*Jer.* 35:6 Jonadab the son of R.

**RECHABITES.**

*Jer.* 35:2 go to house of the R.

**RECKON, ETH.**

*Lev.* 25:50 he shall *r.* with him
27:18 priest shall *r.* to him, 23
*Num.* 4:32 by name *r.* instrum.
*Ezek.* 44:26 shall *r.* to him 7 days
*Mat.* 18:24 when he began to *r.*
25:19 lord of those servants *r.*
*Rom.* 6:11 *r.* yours. to be dead
8:18 I *r.* suffer. of present time

**RECKONED.**

*Num.* 23:9 people shall not be *r.*
2 *Sam.* 4:2 Beeroth *r.* to Benj.
2 *K.* 12:15 they *r.* not with men

1 *Chr*. 5:1 not be *r*. by birthrig.
7 genealogy of generations *r*.
17 *r*. by genealogies, 7:5, 7; 9:1, 22; 2 *Chr*. 31:19; *Ezr*. 2:62; 8:3; *Neh*. 7:5, 64
*Ps*. 40:5 thy tho' cannot be *r*.
*Is*. 38:13 I *r*. till morning
*Luke* 22:37 *r*. am. transgressors
*Rom*. 4:4 reward is not *r*. of gra.
9 *r*. to Abra. 10 how was it *r*.?

**RECKONING.**

2 *K*. 22:7 there was no *r*. made
1 *Chr*. 23:11 they were in one *r*.

**RECOMMENDED.**

*Acts* 14:26 whe. they had been *r*.
15:40 being *r*. to grace of God

**RECOMPENSE.**

*Deut*. 32:35 belong. veng. and *r*.
*Job* 15:31 vanity shall be his *r*.
*Prov*. 12:14 *r*. shall be rendered
*Is*. 35:4 God will come with a *r*.
59:18 repay *r*. to his enemies
66:6 voice of L. that render. *r*.
*Jer*. 51:6 will render to her a *r*.
*Lam*. 3:64 render to them a *r*.
*Hos*. 9:7 the days of *r*. are come
*Joel* 3:4 will ye render me *r*.?
7 I will return *r*. on your head
*Luke* 14:12 a *r*. be made thee
*Rom*. 1:27 rec. *r*. of their error
11:9 let their table be made a *r*.
2 *Cor*. 6:13 for a *r*. in the same
*Heb*. 2:2 trangr. received a *r*.
10:35 hath great *r*. of reward
11:26 he had respect to the *r*.

**RECOMPENSES.**

*Is*. 34:8 a year of *r*. for Zion
*Jer*. 51:56 L. God of *r*. sh. requ.

**RECOMPENSE, Verb.**

*Num*. 5:7 he shall *r*. his trespass
8 if he have no kinsman to *r*.
*Ruth* 2:12 the Lord *r*. thy work
2 *Sam*. 19:36 sho. king *r*. me?
*Job* 34:33 *r*. it whe. thou refuse
*Prov*. 20:22 say not, I wi. *r*. evil
*Is*. 65:6 I will *r*. into th. bosom
*Jer*. 16:18 I will *r*. their iniquity
25:14 I will *r*. them, *Hos*. 12:2
50:29 *r*. her according to work
*Ezek*. 7:3 will *r*. abominations, 8
4 will *r*. thy ways upon thee, 9; 9:10; 11:21; 16:43
17:19 my covenant I will *r*.
23:49 shall *r*. your lewdness
*Joel* 3:4 if ye *r*. me, will I return
*Luke* 14:14 they cannot *r*. thee
*Rom*. 12:17 *r*. no man evil for evil
2 *Thes*. 1:6 *r*. tribulation to them
*Heb*. 10:30 hath said, I will *r*.

**RECOMPENSED.**

*Num*. 5:8 let trespass be *r*. to L.
2 *Sam*. 22:21 accord. to cleanness hath he *r*. 25; *Ps*. 18:20, 24
*Prov*. 11:31 righteous shall be *r*.
*Jer*. 18:20 sh. evil be *r*. for good?
*Ezek*. 22:31 th. own way ha. I *r*.
*Luke* 14:14 be *r*. at resurrection
*Rom*. 11:35 it shall be *r*. to him

**RECOMPENSEST, ING.**

2 *Chr*. 6:23 *r*. way upon his head
*Jer*. 32:18 *r*. iniquity of fathers

**RECONCILE.**

*Lev*. 6:30 blood is brought to *r*.
1 *Sam*. 29:4 wherew. he *r*. hims.
*Ezek*. 45:20 so shall he *r*. house
*Eph*. 2:16 he might *r*. both to G.
*Col*. 1:20 to *r*. all things to him.

**RECONCILED.**

*Mat*. 5:24 first be *r*. to brother
*Rom*. 5:10 when enem. *r*. to God
1 *Cor*. 7:11 let her be *r*. to husb.
2 *Cor*. 5:18 hath *r*. us to himself
20 in Ch. stead, be ye *r*. to God
*Col*. 1:21 were enemies, yet he *r*.

**RECONCILIATION.**

*Lev*. 8:15 to make a *r*. upon it
2 *Chr*. 29:24 made *r*. with blood
*Ezek*. 45:15 make *r*. for them, 17
*Dan*. 9:24 to make *r*. for iniquity
2 *Cor*. 5:18 given us minist. of *r*.
19 committed to us word of *r*.
*Heb*. 2:17 *r*. for the sins of people

**RECONCILING.**

*Lev*. 16:20 he made end of *r*.
*Rom*. 11:15 if casting away be *r*.
2 *Cor*. 5:19 God in Chr. *r*. world

**RECORD, Substantive.**

*Ezr*. 6:2 therein was *r*. written
*Job* 16:19 behold, *r*. is on high
*John* 1:19 this is the *r*. of John
32 John bare *r*. saying, 34
8:13 thou bearest *r*. of thyself, thy *r*. is not true, 14
12:17 the peo. with him, bare *r*.
19:35 he saw bare *r*. his *r*. true
*Rom*. 10:2 bear *r*. they have zeal
2 *Cor*. 1:23 I call God for a *r*.
8:3 to their power I bear *r*.
*Gal*. 4:15 I bear you *r*.
*Phil*. 1:8 God is my *r*.
*Col*. 4:13 I bear *r*. he hath zeal
1 *John* 5:7 th. are 3 that bear *r*.
10 *r*. God gave of his Son, 11
3 *John* 12 we bear *r*. our *r*. is true
*Rev*. 1:2 who bare *r*. of word of G.

**RECORDS.**

*Ezr*. 4:15 search be made in *r*.
*Est*. 6:1 command. to bring *r*.

**RECORD, Verb.**

*Ex*. 20:24 where I *r*. my name
*Deut*. 30:19 I call heaven and earth to *r*. 31:28
1 *Chr*. 16:4 appoint. Levites to *r*.
*Is*. 8:2 took faithful witnes. to *r*.
*Acts* 20:26 I take you to *r*.

**RECORDED.**

*Neh*. 12:22 Levites were *r*. chief

**RECORDER.**

2 *Sam*. 8:16 Jehosh. was *r*. 20:24; 1 *K*. 4:3; 1 *Chr*. 18:15
2 *K*. 18:18 and Joah the son of Asaph *r*. *Is*. 36:3, 22
2 *Chr*. 34:8 Joah son of Joahaz *r*.

**RECOUNT.**

*Nah*. 2:5 he shall *r*. his worthies

**RECOVER.**

*Jud*. 11:26 did ye not *r*. them
1 *Sam*. 30:8 shalt without fail *r*.
2 *Sam*. 8:3 went to *r*. his border
2 *K*. 1:2 inquire whether I sh. *r*.
5:3 the prophet would *r*. him
11 strike his hand, and *r*. leper
8:8 shall I *r*. of this disease? 9
2 *Chr*. 13:20 nor did Jeroboam *r*.
14:13 could not *r*. themselves
*Ps*. 39:13 that I may *r*. strength
*Is*. 11:11 *r*. remn. of his people
38:16 *r*. me and make me live
21 for a plaster, and he shall *r*.
*Hos*. 2:9 and I will *r*. my wool
*Mark* 16:18 hands on sick, th. *r*.
2 *Tim*. 2:26 may *r*. themselves

**RECOVERED.**

1 *Sam*. 30:18 *r*. all Am. took, 19
22 not give aught of spoil we *r*.
2 *K*. 13:25 and *r*. cities of Israel
14:28 warred, and *r*. Damascus
16:6 Rez. king of Syria *r*. Elath
20:7 laid it on the boil, he *r*.
*Is*. 38:9 Hezekiah sick, *r*. 39:1
*Jer*. 8:22 why is not my peo. *r*.?
41:16 Johanan took people he *r*.

**RECOVERING.**

*Luke* 4:18 *r*. of sight to the blind

**RED.**

*Gen*. 25:25 came out *r*. all over
30 feed me with that *r*. pottage
49:12 eyes shall be *r*. with wine
*Ex*. 25:5 rams' skins dyed *r*. 26:14; 35:7; 36:19; 39:34
35:23 wi. wh. was found *r*. skins
*Num*. 19:2 bring thee a *r*. heifer
2 *K*. 3:22 Moabites saw water *r*.
*Est*. 1:6 a pavement of *r*. blue
*Ps*. 75:8 wine is *r*. full of mixtu.
*Prov*. 23:31 look not on wine *r*.
*Is*. 1:18 though your sins be *r*.
27:2 sing, a vineyard of *r*. wine
63:2 art thou *r*. in apparel?
*Nah*. 2:3 shield of mighty men *r*.
*Zec*. 1:8 a man on a *r*. horse
6:2 in first chariot we. *r*. horses
*Mat*. 16:2 fair weather, sky *r*. 3
*Rev*. 6:4 anot. horse that was *r*.
12:3 great *r*. dragon, sev. heads

**RED sea.**

*Ex*. 10:19 cast locusts into *R*. *s*.
13:18 G. led them by the *R*. *sea*
15:4 captains drowned in *R*. *s*.
22 Moses bro. Israel from *R*. *s*.
23:31 set thy bounds from *R*. *s*.
*Num*. 14:25 into wilder. by *R*. *s*.
21:14 what he did in the *R*. *s*.?
*Deut* 1:40 take journey by *R*. *s*.
11:4 he made *R*. *sea* overflow
*Jos*. 2:10 the L. dried up *R*. *sea*
4:23 as L. your G. did to *R*. *sea*
24:6 Egypt. pursu. after to *R*. *s*.
*Neh*. 9:9 heard. their cry by *R*. *s*.
*Ps*. 106:7 provoked him at *R*. *s*.
9 rebuked *R*. *s*. it was dried up
22 done terrible things by *R*. *s*.
136:13 him who divided *R*. *sea*
15 overthrew Pharaoh in *R*. *s*.
*Jer*. 49:21 noise was heard in *R*. *s*.
*Acts* 7:36 showed wond. in *R*. *sea*
*Heb*. 11:29 by faith passed *R*. *s*.

**REDDISH.**

*Lev*. 13:19 somewhat *r*. 24, 43
42 a white *r*. sore, a leprosy
49 if plague be *r*. in garment
14:37 if plag. be with streaks, *r*.

**REDEEM.**

*Ex*. 6:6 I will *r*. you with arm
13:13 firstl. of ass shalt *r*. 34:20
15 first-b. of my chil. *r*. 34:20
*Lev*. 25:25 if any of his kin *r*. it
32 the cities may the Levit. *r*.
49 or any of kin may *r*. him
27:15 house will *r*. it, 19, 20, 31
*Num*. 18:15 first-born sh. thou *r*.
17 firstling of a goat sh. not *r*.
*Ruth* 4:4 *r*. it, if not, I will *r*. it
6 I cannot *r*. it for mys. *r*. th.
2 *Sam*. 7:23 wh. nation is like Is. God went to *r*.? 1 *Chr*. 17:21
*Neh*. 5:5 is it in our power to *r*.
*Job* 5:20 in famine he sh. *r*. thee
6:23 *r*. me from hand of mighty
*Ps*. 25:22 *r*. Is. O G. out of troub.
26:11 *r*. me and be merciful
44:26 *r*. us for thy mercies' sake
49:7 none of th. can *r*. his brot.
15 G. will *r*. my soul fr. grave
69:18 draw ni. to my soul, *r*. it
72:14 *r*. their soul from deceit
130:8 *r*. Isr. from all iniquities
*Is*. 50:2 short. that it cannot *r*.?
*Jer*. 15:21 I will *r*. thee
*Hos*. 13:14 I will *r*. them fr. death
*Mic*. 4:10 L. sh. *r*. thee fr. Baby.
*Gal*. 4:5 *r*. them were under law
*Tit*. 2:14 he might *r*. us fr. iniq.

**REDEEMED.**

*Gen*. 48:16 the angel which *r*. me
*Ex*. 15:13 people whom thou *r*.
21:8 then shall he let her be *r*.
*Lev*. 19:20 with bondmaid not *r*.
25:30 if house in city be not *r*.
48 broth. sold may be *r*. again
54 if he be not *r*. then go out
27:20 sold field, it sh. not be *r*.
27 an uncl. beast not *r*. be sold
28 no devot. thing sh. be *r*. 29
33 tithe and change not be *r*.

*Num.* 3:46 those *r.* more th. Lev.
*Deut.* 7:8 L. hath *r.* you fr. king of Egypt. 15:15; 24:18
9:26 thy people thou hast *r.*
13:5 L. *r.* you out of bondage
21:8 merciful to Is. thou hast *r.*
2 *Sam.* 4:9 L. *r.* soul, 1 *K.* 1:29
1 *Chr.* 17:21 whom thou *r.* out of Egypt, *Neh.* 1:10; *Ps.* 77:15
*Neh.* 5:8 we have *r.* the Jews
*Ps.* 31:5 thou hast *r.* me, O L. G.
71:23 my soul rejo. thou hast *r.*
74:2 thine inherit. thou hast *r.*
106:10 he *r.* them from enemy
107:2 let *r.* of the Lord say so
136:24 hath *r.* us from enemies
*Is.* 1:27 Zion be *r.* with judgm.
29:22 saith L. who *r.* Abraham
35:9 but the *r.* shall walk there
43:1 fear not, I have *r.* thee
44:22 ret. to me, I have *r.* thee
23 Lord *r.* J. 48:20; *Jer.* 31:11
51:11 *r.* of the L. shall return
52:3 ye sh. be *r.* without money
9 *r.* Jer. 62:12 holy people *r.*
63:4 *r.* is come; 9 he *r.* them
*Lam.* 3:58 thou hast *r.* my life
*Hos.* 7:13 tho' I *r.* them, yet they
*Mic.* 6.4 I *r.* thee out of house
*Zec.* 10:8 hiss, I have *r.* them
*Luke* 1:68 visited and *r.* his peo.
24:21 who should have *r.* Israel
*Gal.* 3:13 Christ *r.* us from curse
1 *Pet.* 1:18 not *r.* with corrupti.
*Rev.* 5:9 thou hast *r.* us to God
14:3 the 144,000 which were *r.*
4 these were *r.* from am. men

**REDEEMEDST.**

2 *Sam.* 7:23 *r.* to thee from Egy.

**REDEEMER.**

*Job* 19:25 I know that my R. liv.
*Ps.* 19:14 O L. my stren. and R.
78:35 the high G. was their R.
*Prov.* 23:11 their R. is mighty
*Is.* 41:14 thy R. Holy One, 54:5
43:14 saith L. your R. H. One
44:6 saith L. his R. L. of hosts
24 sai. thy R. 48:17; 49:7; 54:8
47:4 as for our R. Lord of hosts
49:26 I the L. am thy R. 60:16
59:20 the R. shall come to Zion
63:16 art our Father, our R.
*Jer.* 50:34 their R. is strong

**REDEEMETH.**

*Ps.* 34:22 L. *r.* souls of his serv.
103:4 who *r.* life fr. destruction

**REDEEMING.**

*Ruth* 4:7 manner in Isr. conc. *r.*
*Eph.* 5:16 *r.* the time, *Col.* 4:5

**REDEMPTION.**

*Lev.* 25:24 ye shall grant a *r.*
51 he sh. give price of his *r.* 52
*Num.* 3:49 Moses took *r.* money
*Ps.* 49:8 *r.* of their soul is prec.
111:9 he sent *r.* to his people
130:7 with L. th. is plenteo. *r.*
*Jer.* 32:7 right of *r.* is thine, 8
*Luke* 2:38 that looked for *r.*
21:28 your *r.* draweth nigh
*Rom.* 3:24 justified thro' *r.* in C.
8:23 for adoption, *r.* of our body
1 *Cor.* 1:30 Chr. is made to us *r.*
*Eph.* 1:7 in whom we have *r.* thro' his blood, *Col.* 1:14
*Eph.* 1:14 *r.* of purchased poss.
4:30 sealed unto the day of *r.*
*Heb.* 9:12 obtai. eternal *r.* for us
15 the *r.* of the transgressions

**REDNESS.**

*Prov.* 23:29 who hath *r.* of eyes?

**REDOUND.**

2 *Cor.* 4:15 grace *r.* to glo. of G.

**REED.**

1 *K.* 14:15 L. sh. smite Isr. as *r.*
2 *K.* 18:21 thou trustest upon the staff of bruised *r.* *Is.* 36:6
*Is.* 42:3 a bruised *r.* shall he not break, *Mat.* 12:20
*Ezek.* 29:6 been staff of a *r.* to Is.
40:3 a man with a measuring *r.*
*Mat.* 11:7 a *r.* shaken *Luke* 7:24
27:29 put a *r.* in his right hand
30 sm. him with *r.* *Mark* 15:19
48 sponge on a *r.* *Mark* 15:36
*Rev.* 11:1 there was giv. me a *r.*
21:15 golden *r.* to meas. city, 16

**REEDS.**

*Job* 40:21 lieth in the covert of *r.*
*Is.* 19:6 *r.* and flags sh. wither, 7
35:7 in habita. of dragons be *r.*
*Jer.* 51:32 the *r.* they have burnt
*Ezek.* 42:16 measured east side, five hundred *r.* 17, 18, 19
45:1 shall be length of 25,000 *r.*

**REEL.**

*Ps.* 107:27 *r.* to and fro, and stag.
*Is.* 24:20 earth shall *r.* to and fro

**REFINE.**

*Zec.* 13:9 I will *r.* them as silver

**REFINED.**

1 *Chr.* 28:18 for the altar *r.* gold
29:4 7,000 talents of *r.* silver
*Is.* 25:6 wines on lees well *r.*
48:10 I have *r.* th. not with silv.
*Zec.* 13:9 refine th. as silver is *r.*

**REFINER.**

*Mal.* 3:2 for he is like a *r.*'s fire
3 he sh. sit as a *r.* and purifier

**REFORMATION.**

*Heb.* 9:10 on th. until time of *r.*

**REFORMED.**

*Lev.* 26:23 if ye will not be *r.*

**REFRAIN.**

*Gen.* 45:1 J. could not *r.* himself
*Job* 7:11 I will not *r.* my mouth
*Prov.* 1:15 *r.* thy foot from path
*Ec.* 3:5 a time to *r.* fr. embracing
*Is.* 48:9 for my praise I will *r.*
64:12 wilt thou *r.* thyself, O L.?
*Jer.* 31:16 *r.* voice from weeping
*Acts* 5:38 I say, *r.* from th. men
1 *Pet.* 3:10 *r.* his tong. from evil

**REFRAINED.**

*Gen.* 43:31 and Joseph *r* himself
*Est.* 5:10 Haman *r.* himself
*Job* 29:9 the princes *r.* talking
*Ps.* 40:9 I have not *r.* my lips
119:101 I have *r.* my feet fr. evil
*Is.* 42:14 been still, *r.* myself
*Jer.* 14:10 have not *r.* their feet

**REFRAINETH.**

*Prov.* 10:19 that *r.* lips is wise

**REFRESH.**

1 *K.* 13:7 come home *r.* thyself
*Acts* 27:3 J. suffered P. to *r.* him.
*Phile.* 20 *r.* my bowels in the L.

**REFRESHED, ETH.**

*Ex.* 23:12 stranger may be *r.*
31:17 sev. day rested and was *r.*
1 *Sam.* 16:23 so Saul was *r.*
2 *Sam.* 16:14 David and people *r.*
*Job* 32:20 speak that I may be *r.*
*Prov.* 25:13 he *r.* soul of masters
*Rom.* 15:32 I may with you be *r.*
1 *Cor.* 16:18 *r.* my spi. and yours
2 *Cor.* 7:13 Titus, his spir. was *r.*
2 *Tim.* 1:16 for he often *r.* me
*Phile.* 7 bow. of saints *r.* by th.

**REFRESHING.**

*Is.* 28:12 *r.* yet they wo. not hear
*Acts* 3:19 times of *r.* shall come

**REFUGE.**

*Num.* 35:13 six cit. ha. for *r.* 15
*Deut.* 33:27 eternal God is thy *r.*
*Jos.* 20:3 *r.* from aveng. of blood
2 *Sam.* 22:3 my high tower and *r.*
*Ps.* 9:9 L. be a *r.* for oppressed
14:6 because the Lord is his *r.*
46:1 G. is *r.* 7, 11; 48:3 G. know
57:1 thy wings will make my *r.*
59:16 my *r.* in day of trouble
62:7 my *r.* is God; 8 God is *r.*
71:7 thou art strong *r.* 142:5
91:2 is my *r.* 9; 94:22 G. is my
104:18 hills *r.* for wild goats
142:4 *r.* failed; 5 thou art my *r.*
*Prov.* 14:26 chil. have place of *r.*
*Is.* 4:6 place of *r.* 25:4 needy *r.*
28:15 we have made lies our *r.*
17 hail shall sweep away *r.*
*Jer.* 16:19 O L. my *r.* in affliction
*Heb.* 6:18 who have fled for *r.*

**REFUSE.**

1 *Sam.* 15:9 ev. thing that was *r.*
*Lam.* 3:45 hast made us as *r.*
*Amos* 8:6 may sell *r.* of wheat

**REFUSE, Verb.**

*Ex.* 4:23 if thou *r.* to let them go, 8:2; 9:2; 10:4
10:3 how long *r.* to humble thy.
16:28 *r.* ye to keep my com.?
22:17 if her father utterly *r.*
*Job* 34:33 whe. thou *r.* or choose
*Prov.* 8:33 be wise, and *r.* it not
21:7 because they *r.* to do judg.
25 his hands *r.* to labor
*Is.* 1:20 if ye *r.* sh. be devoured
7:15 he may know to *r.* evil, 16
*Jer.* 8:5 *r.* to return; 9:6 *r.* to kn.
13:10 peo. *r.* to hear my words
25:28 if they *r.* to take the cup
38:21 if thou *r.* to go forth
*Acts* 25:11 if offen. I *r.* not to die
1 *Tim.* 4:7 but *r.* profane fables
5:11 but the younger widows *r.*
*Heb.* 12:25 *r.* not him that speak.

**REFUSED.**

*Gen.* 37:35 Ja. *r.* to be comforted
39:8 J. *r.* to lie wi. master's wi.
48:19 Jacob *r.* to remove hand
*Num.* 20:21 Edom *r.* Is. passage
1 *Sam.* 8:19 people *r.* to obey S.
16:7 look not on him, I *r.* him
28:23 Saul *r.* said, I will not eat
2 *Sam.* 2:23 Asa. *r.* to turn aside
13:9 she poured, Amn. *r.* to eat
1 *K.* 20:35 man *r.* to smite him
21:15 vineyard he *r.* to give th.
2 *K.* 5:16 Naaman urged, he *r.*
*Neh.* 9:17 our fathers *r.* to obey
*Est.* 1:12 qu. Vashti *r.* to come
*Job* 6:7 things that my soul *r.*
*Ps.* 77:2 soul *r.* to be comforted
78:10 they *r.* to walk in his law
67 he *r.* tabernacle of Joseph
118:22 stone which builders *r.*
*Prov.* 1:24 I have called, ye *r.*
*Is.* 54:6 thou wast *r.* saith thy G.
*Jer.* 5:3 *r.* to receive correction
11:10 fath. *r.* to hear my words
31:15 Rachel *r.* to be comforted
50:33 took them *r.* to let th. go
*Ezek.* 5:6 they *r.* my judgments
*Hos.* 11:5 beca. they *r.* to return
*Zec.* 7:11 but they *r.* to hearken
*Acts* 7:35 Moses whom they *r.*
1 *Tim.* 4:4 and nothing to be *r.*
*Heb.* 11:24 Mo. *r.* to be called son
12:25 *r.* him th. spake on earth

**REFUSEDST.**

*Jer.* 3:3 thou *r.* to be ashamed

**REFUSETH.**

*Ex.* 7:14 Pharaoh *r.* to let people
*Num.* 22:13 L. *r.* to give me lea.
*Deut.* 25:7 bro. *r.* to raise name
*Prov.* 10:17 he that *r.* reproof
13:18 sha. to him that *r.* instru.
15:32 that *r.* instruction despis.
*Is.* 8:6 people *r.* wat. of Shiloah
*Jer.* 15:18 wound *r.* to be healed

**REGARD.**

*Ec.* 8:2 in *r.* of the oath of God

*Acts* 8:11 and to him they had *r*.

**REGARD, Verb.**

*Gen*. 45:20 *r*. not your stuff, for
*Ex*. 5:9 let not *r*. vain words
*Lev*. 19:31 *r*. not familiar spirits
*Deut*. 28:50 not *r*. person of aged
1 *Sam*. 25:25 *r*. not man of Belial
2 *Sam*. 13:20 *r*. not, he is broth.
2 *K*. 3:14 that I *r*. Jehoshaphat
*Job* 3:4 let not G. *r*. it fr. above
35:13 nor will Almighty *r*. it
36:21 take heed, *r*. not iniquity
*Ps*. 28:5 they *r*. not works of L.
31:6 hated that *r*. lying vanities
66:18 if I *r*. iniq. in my heart
94:7 neit. shall G. of Jacob *r*. it
102:17 will *r*. prayer of destitu.
*Prov*. 5:2 mayest *r*. discretion
6:35 he will not *r*. any ransom
*Is*. 5:12 they *r*. not work of L.
13:17 M. who will not *r*. silver
*Lam*. 4:16 L. will no more *r*. th.
*Dan*. 11:37 *r*. God, nor *r*. any god
*Amos* 5:22 nor *r*. peace-offerings
*Hab*. 1:5 *r*. wonder marvellously
*Mal*. 1:9 will he *r*. yo. persons?
*Luke* 18:4 fear not God nor *r*. man
*Rom*. 14:6 Lord he doth not *r*.

**REGARDED.**

*Ex*. 9:21 *r*. not the word of Lord
1 *K*. 18:29 no voice, nor any *r*.
1 *Chr*. 17:17 thou hast *r*. me
*Ps*. 106:44 he *r*. their affliction
*Prov*. 1:24 stret. hand, no man *r*.
*Dan*. 3:12 O king, have not *r*.
*Luke* 1:48 he *r*. his handmaid
18:2 feared not G. nei. *r*. man
*Heb*. 8:9 I *r*. them not, saith L.

**REGARDEST.**

2 *Sam*. 19:6 thou *r*. not princes
*Job* 30:20 I stand up, *r*. me not
*Mat*. 22:16 thou *r*. not the persons of men, *Mark* 12:14

**REGARDETH.**

*Deut*. 10:17 *r*. not persons
*Job* 34:19 nor *r*. rich mo. th. poor
39:7 neither *r*. crying of driver
*Prov*. 12:10 right. *r*. life of beast
13:18 that *r*. reproof be honored
15:5 that *r*. reproof is prudent
29:7 wicked *r*. not cause of poor
*Ec*. 5:8 higher than highest *r*.
11:4 he that *r*. clouds not reap
*Is*. 33:8 desp. cities, *r*. no man
*Dan*. 6:13 Daniel *r*. not thee
*Mal*. 2:13 *r*. not offer. any more
*Rom*. 14:6 that *r*. day, *r*. it to L.

**REGARDING.**

*Job* 4:20 perish without any *r*. it
*Phil*. 2:30 not *r*. life to sup. lack

REGEM-MELECH. *Zec*. 7:2

**REGENERATION.**

*Mat*. 19:28 wh. followed me in *r*.
*Tit*. 3:5 saved us by wash. of *r*.

**REGION.**

*Deut*. 3:4 all the *r*. of Argob, 13
1 *K*. 4:24 dominion over all the *r*.
*Mat*. 3:5 went to him *r*. round J.
4:16 which sat in *r*. of death
*Mark* 1:28 fame spread throughout *r*. of G. *Luke* 4:14; 7:17
6:55 ran thro' whole *r*. round
*Acts* 13:49 word of L. pub. thro' *r*.
14:6 they fled to *r* round about
16:6 gone thro' the *r*. of Galatia

**REGIONS.**

*Acts* 8:1 scattered thro' *r*. of Ju.
2 *Cor*. 10:16 preach in *r*. beyond
11:10 stop me in *r*. of Achaia
*Gal*. 1:21 I came into *r*. of Syria

**REGISTER.**

*Ezr*. 2:62 sought *r*. *Neh*. 7:64
*Neh*. 7:5 found a *r*. of genealogy

REHABIAH. 1 *Chr*. 23:17

**REHEARSE, ED.**

*Ex*. 17:14 *r*. in ears of Joshua
*Jud* 5:11 *r*. righteous acts of L.
1 *Sam*. 8:21 he *r*. in ears of Lord
17:31 *r*. David's words bef. Saul
*Acts* 11:4 Peter *r*. the matter
14:27 *r*. all G. done with them

**REHOBOAM.**

1 *K*. 11:43 R. son of Solo. 14:21
12:6 R. consulted men, 17, 21, 27
14:30 was war between R. 15:6
2 *Chr*. 9:31; 10:6, 17; 11:1
11:17 made R. strong, 21, 22
13:7 against R. when R. was

**REHOBOTH.**

*Gen*. 10:11 builded Nin. and R.
26:22 Isaac called the well R.
36:37 S. of R. reigned, 1 *Chr*. 1:48

**REHUM.**

*Ezr*. 2:2 R. came with, *Neh*. 12:3
4:8 R. the chancellor, 17, 23
*Neh* 3:17 R. the son of Bani
10:25 R. of chief of the people

**REIGN, Substantive.**

1 *K*. 6:1 Solomon's *r*. over Israel
1 *Chr*. 4:31 cities to *r*. of David
29:30 David's acts with *r*. writ.
2 *Chr*. 36:20 *r*. of king. Persia
*Luke* 3:1 year of *r*. of Tiberius

**REIGN, Verb.**

*Gen*. 37:8 shalt thou *r*. over us?
*Ex*. 15:18 the Lord shall *r*. for ever, *Ps*. 146:10
*Lev*. 26:17 they that hate shall *r*.
*Deut*. 15:6 *r*. over many nations
*Jud*. 9:2 seventy *r*. over you
8 *r*. thou over us, 10, 12, 14
1 *Sam*. 8:9 k. that shall *r*. 11
9:17 this same *r*. over my peop.
11:12 said, Shall S. *r*. over us?
12:12 a king shall *r*. over us
2 *Sam*. 3:21 thou mayest *r*. over
1 *K*. 1:11 heard th. Adonijah *r*.?
13 Sol. shall *r*. after me, 17, 30
2:15 set faces on me, I shou. *r*.
16:15 Zimri *r*. 7 days in Tirzah
2 *Chr*. 1:8 made me *r*. in his ste.
23:3 said, The king's son sh. *r*.
*Job* 34:30 the hypocrite *r*. not
*Prov*. 8:15 by me kings *r*.
*Ec*. 4:14 out prison he com. to *r*.
*Is*. 24:23 L. of hosts shall *r*. in Z.
32:1 king shall *r*. in righteous.
*Jer*. 22:15 shalt thou *r*. bec. thou
23:5 a king shall *r*. and prosper
33:21 D. sho. not have son to *r*.
*Mic*. 4:7 L. shall *r*. over th. in Z.
*Mat*. 2:22 heard Archelaus did *r*.
*Luke* 1:33 he shall *r*. over Jacob
19:14 not have this man to *r*.
27 enemies would not I sho. *r*.
*Rom*. 5:17 sh. *r*. in life by J. C.
21 so might grace *r*. by J. C.
6:12 let not sin *r*. in yo. bodies
15:12 shall rise to *r*. over Genti.
2 *Tim*. 2:12 if we suff. we sh. *r*.
*Rev*. 5:10 we shall *r*. on earth
11:15 he shall *r*. for ever
20:6 sh. *r*. wi. him 1,000 years
22:5 shall *r*. for ever and ever

*See* BEGAN.

**REIGNED.**

*Gen*. 36:31 the kings that *r*. in land of Edom, 1 *Chr*. 1:43
1 *Sam*. 13:1 Saul *r*. one yr. he *r*.
2 *Sam*. 2:10 Ish-bosh. *r*. two yea.
5:4 David *r*. 40 years over Jud.
5 Da. *r*. seven yea. in Hebron, thirty-three in Jerusa. 1 *K*. 2:11; 1 *Chr*. 3:4; 29:27
10:1 Ha. *r*. in stead, 1 *Chr*. 19:1
1 *K*. 4:21 and Solomon *r*. over all the kingd. 11:42; 1 *Chr*. 29:28; 2 *Chr*. 9:26, 30

*Est*. 1:1 Ahasuerus *r*. from Ind.
*Jer*. 22:11 Shall. *r*. instead of Jo.
*Rom*. 5:14 death *r*. fr. Ad. to M.
17 by one man's off. death *r*.
21 as sin *r*. to death, grace *r*.
1 *Cor*. 4:8 *r*. as kings without us
*Rev*. 11:17 great power and *r*.
20:4 *r*. with Ch. a thousand y.

**REIGNEST.**

1 *Chr*. 29:12 thou *r*. over all, and

**REIGNETH.**

1 *Sam*. 12:14 king that *r*. over y.
2 *Sam*. 15:10 Absalom *r*. in Heb.
1 *K*. 1:18 behold Adonijah *r*.
1 *Chr*. 16:31 the L. *r*. *Ps*. 96:10; 97:1; 99:1
*Ps*. 47:8 God *r*. over heathen
93:1 L. *r*. he is clothed wi. maj.
*Prov*. 30:22 a servant when he *r*.
*Is*. 52:7 saith unto Z. Thy G. *r*.
*Rev*. 17:18 *r*. over kings of earth
19:6 Lord God omnipotent *r*.

**REIGNING.**

1 *Sam*. 16:1 I rejected him fro. *r*.

**REINS.**

*Job* 16:13 he cleaveth my *r*. asu.
19:27 tho. my *r*. be consumed
*Ps*. 7:9 God trieth heart and *r*.
16:7 my *r*. also instr. me in ni.
26:2 O L. try my *r*. my heart
73:21 was I pricked in my *r*.
139:13 thou hast possess. my *r*.
*Prov*. 23:16 my *r*. shall rejoice
*Is*. 11:5 faithfuln. girdle of his *r*.
*Jer*. 11:20 O L. that triest the *r*.
12:2 thou art far from their *r*.
17:10 I try thy *r*. 20:12 seest *r*.
*Lam*. 3:13 arrows to enter my *r*.
*Rev*. 2:23 he who searcheth *r*.

**REJECT, ETH.**

*Hos*. 4:6 I will *r*. thee
*Mark* 6:26 oath's sake wo. not *r*.
7:9 ye *r*. commandment of G.
*John* 12:48 he that *r*. me, receiv.
*Tit*. 3:10 after second admoni. *r*.

**REJECTED.**

1 *Sam*. 8:7 they have not *r*. thee, but they have *r*. me
10:19 ye have this day *r*. your G.
15:23 thou hast *r*. word of L. he also *r*. thee fr. being kin. 26
16:1 I *r*. him from being king
2 *K*. 17:15 they *r*. his statutes
20 Lord *r*. all the seed of Isra.
*Is*. 53:3 he is despised, *r*. of men
*Jer*. 2:37 Lord *r*. thy confidence
6:19 *r*. my law; 30 L. *r*. them
7:29 Lord hath *r*. generation of
8:9 they have *r*. word of Lord
14:19 hast thou utterly *r*. Jud.?
*Lam*. 5:22 thou hast utterly *r*. us
*Hos*. 4:6 thou hast *r*. knowledge
*Mat*. 21:42 stone which builders *r*. *Mark* 12:10; *Luke* 20:17
*Mark* 8:31 and he shall be *r*. of the elders, *Luke* 9:22
*Luke* 7:30 law. *r*. counsel of God
*Luke* 17:25 be *r*. of this generat.
*Gal*. 4:14 tempt. in flesh *r*. not
*Heb*. 6:8 that beareth thorns is *r*.
12:17 have inherit. bless. was *r*.

**REJOICE.**

*Deut*. 12:7 ye sh. *r*. in all, 14:26
16:14 thou shalt *r*. in thy feast
15 God sh. bless thee, th. sh. *r*.
26:11 shalt *r*. in ev. good thing
28:63 L. will *r*. over you, 30:9
32:43 *r*. O nations, with his pe.
33:18 he said, *r*. Zebulun
*Jud*. 9:19 *r*. ye in Abimelech
1 *Sam*. 2:1 bec. I *r*. in thy salva.
19:5 thou sawest it, and didst *r*.
1 *Chr*. 16:10 let the heart of them *r*. that seek the L. *Ps*. 105:3
32 let fields *r*. and all therein

2 *Chr*. 6:41 and let thy saints *r*.
20:27 L. made th. *r*. *Neh*. 12:43
*Job* 20:18 he shall not *r*. therein
*Ps*. 2:11 serve L. *r*. with tremb.
5:11 all that put trust in thee *r*.
9:14 I will *r*. in thy salvation
13:4 those that trouble me *r*.
5 my heart shall *r*. in thy salv.
14:7 Ja. shall *r*. and Is. be glad
20:5 we will *r*. in thy salvation
21:1 in thy salvation shall he *r*.
30:1 made foes to *r*. over me
33:21 our heart shall *r*. in him
35:9 my soul sh. *r*. in his salva.
19 let not mine enemies *r*. ov.
24 O Lord, let them not *r*. over
26 let them be ashamed that *r*.
38:16 lest they sho. *r*. over me
48:11 let Zion *r*. let Jud. be glad
51:8 bones th. hast brok. may *r*.
58:10 righteous *r*. wh. he seeth
60:6 G. ha. spok. I will *r*. 108:7
63:7 in shad. of thy wings I *r*.
11 but the king shall *r*. in God
65:12 hills *r*. 66:6 did we *r*.
68:3 let righteous *r*. exceed. *r*.
4 *r*. bef. him; 71:23 lips sh. *r*.
85:6 that thy people may *r*.
86:4 *r*. the soul of thy servant
89:12 Tabor and Hermon sh. *r*.
16 in thy name shall they *r*.
42 hast made enemies to *r*.
96:11 let heavens *r*. 12 trees *r*.
97:1 let earth *r*. isles be glad
98:4 make noise, *r*. sing praise
104:31 L. shall *r*. in his works
106:5 that I may *r*. in gladness
107:42 righte. shall see it and *r*.
109:28 be ashamed, let serva. *r*.
119:162 I *r*. at thy word
149:2 let Is. *r*. in him that made
*Prov*. 2:14 who *r*. to do evil
5:18 *r*. wife of thy youth
23:15 my heart shall *r*.
16 yea, my reins shall *r*.
24 father of righteous shall *r*.
25 she that bare thee shall *r*.
24:17 *r*. not wh. enemy falleth
28:12 wh. righteous men do *r*.
29:2 right. in authority, peo. *r*.
6 righteous doth sing and *r*.
31:25 shall *r*. in time to come
*Ec*. 3:12 a man to *r*. do good
22 that a man should *r*. 5:19
4:16 that come after shall not *r*.
11:8 live many years, and *r*.
9 *r*. O you. man, in thy youth
*Is*. 8:6 *r*. in Rezin and R.'s son
9:3 as men *r*. when divide spoil
13:3 that *r*. in my highness
14:29 *r*. not thou, whole Pales.
23:12 thou shalt no more *r*.
24:8 noise of them that *r*.
29:19 poor among men shall *r*.
35:1 desert sh. *r*. 2 blosso. and *r*.
61:7 for confusion they shall *r*.
65:13 behold, my ser. shall *r*.
19 I will *r*. in Jerusalem
66:10 *r*. with Jerusalem
14 when ye see this, heart *r*.
*Jer*. 31:13 then shall virgin *r*.
32:41 will *r*. over them
51:39 they may *r*. and sleep
*Lam*. 2:17 caused enemy to *r*.
*Ezek*. 7:12 let not the buyer *r*.
35:15 *r*. at inheritance of Israel
*Hos*. 9:1 *r*. not, O Israel, for joy
*Amos* 6:13 ye wh. *r*. in naught
*Mic*. 7:8 *r*. not ag. me, O enemy
*Zep*. 3:11 take away th. that *r*.
17 the Lord will *r*. over thee
*Zec*. 2:10 sing and *r*. O daughter
9:9 *r*. greatly, O daughter of Z.
10:7 and their heart shall *r*.
*Luke* 1:14 shall *r*. at his birth
6:23 *r*. ye in that day, and leap
10:20 in this *r*. not, rather *r*.
15:6 *r*. with me, I have found
19:37 the disciples began to *r*.
*John* 4:36 he that reapeth may *r*.
5:35 willing for a sea. to *r*.
14:28 if ye loved me, ye wou. *r*.
16:20 weep, the world shall *r*.
22 see you, your heart shall *r*.
*Acts* 2:26 theref. did my heart *r*.
*Rom*. 5:2 *r*. in hope of gl. of God
12:15 *r*. with them that do *r*.
15:10 he saith, *r*. ye Gentiles
1 *Cor*. 7:30 *r*. as tho' they rej. n.
12:26 all the members *r*. with it
2 *Cor*. 2:3 of whom I ought to *r*.
7:9 I *r*. not that ye were sorry
16 I *r*. I have confidence in you
*Gal*. 4:27 *r*. barren that bear. not
*Phil*. 1:18 I do *r*. yea, and will *r*.
2:16 I may *r*. in day of Christ
17 I joy and *r*. with you all
18 for the same cause do ye *r*.
28 when see him ag. ye may *r*.
3:3 we worship God, *r*. in C. J
*Col*. 1:24 *r*. in my suffer. for you
1 *Thes*. 5:16 *r*. evermore, pray
*Jam*. 1:9 let broth. of low deg. *r*.
4:16 ye *r*. in your boastings
1 *Pet*. 1:6 wherein ye greatly *r*.
8 ye *r*. with joy unspeakable
4:13 *r*. inasm. as ye are partak.
*Rev*. 11:10 th. that dw. on ear. *r*.
12:12 therefore *r*. ye heavens.
18:20 *r*. over her, thou heaven
*See* GLAD.

**REJOICE before the Lord.**
*Lev*. 23:40 *r*. *bef. t. Lord* 7 days
*Deut*. 12:12 *r*. *bef. t. L.* your God
18 and thou shalt *r*. *before the L.* thy God, 16:11; 27:7

**REJOICE in the Lord.**
*Ps*. 33:1 *r*. *in the L.* righte. 97:12
*Is*. 41:16 *r*. *in L.* glory in H. One
61:10 I will greatly *r*. *in the L.*
*Joel* 2:23 chil. of Zion, *r*. *in t. L.*
*Hab*. 3:18 I will *r*. *in the Lord*
*Zec*. 10:7 heart shall *r*. *in the L.*
*Phil*. 3:1 brethren *r*. *in the Lord*
4:4 *r*. *in the Lord* alway

**REJOICED.**
*Ex*. 18:9 Jethro *r*. for goodness
*Deut*. 28:63 as Lord *r*. over you
30:9 as he *r*. over thy fathers
1 *Sam*. 11:15 S. and men of Is. *r*.
1 *K*. 1:40 people *r*. so earth rent
2 *K*. 11:14 the people *r*. and blew
1 *Chr*. 29:9 people *r*. and Dav. *r*.
2 *Chr*. 15:15 all Judah *r*. at oath
24:10 all princes and people *r*.
29:36 Hezekiah *r*. and all peop.
30:25 strangers of Is. and Ju. *r*.
*Neh*. 12:43 and *r*. the wives also, and the children *r*.
*Est*. 8:15 the city of Shushan *r*.
*Job* 31:25 if I *r*. bec. my wealth
29 if I *r*. at destruction of him
*Ps*. 35:15 in mine advers. they *r*.
97:8 the daughters of Judah *r*.
119:14 ha. *r*. in way of thy test.
*Ec*. 2:10 my heart *r*. in labor
*Jer*. 15:17 I *r*. not in assembly
50:11 ye *r*. O destroyers of my
*Ezek*. 25:6 Ammon. *r*. ag. Israel
*Hos*. 10:5 priests that *r*. mourn
*Ob*. 12 nor should. thou have *r*.
*Mat*. 2:10 saw star, they *r*.
*Luke* 1:47 my sp. hath *r*. in God
10:21 in that hour J. *r*. in spir.
13:17 people *r*. for the things
*John* 8:56 your father Abrah. *r*.
*Acts* 7:41 *r*. in works of th. hands
15:31 they *r*. for the consolation
16:34 jailer *r*. believing in God
1 *Cor*. 7:30 as though they *r*. not
2 *Cor*. 7:7 told us, so I *r*. the mo.
*Phil*. 4:10 I *r*. in the Lord great.
2 *John* 4 I *r*. greatly, 3 *John* 3

**REJOICETH.**
1 *Sam*. 2:1 Han. said, My hea. *r*.
*Job* 39:21 horse *r*. in strength
*Ps*. 16:9 heart is glad, glory *r*.
19:5 which *r*. as a strong man
28:7 theref. my heart greatly *r*.
*Prov*. 11:10 well wi. right. city *r*.
13:9 the light of the righteo. *r*.
15:30 light of the eyes *r*. heart
29:3 whoso loveth wisdom *r*.
*Is*. 5:14 he that *r*. shall descend
62:5 as bridegroom *r*. over bride
64:5 thou meetest him that *r*.
*Ezek*. 35:14 when whole earth *r*.
*Mat*. 18:13 *r*. more of that sheep
*John* 3:29 friend of bridegroom *r*.
1 *Cor*. 13:6 *r*. not in ini. *r*. in tr.
*Jam*. 2:13 mercy *r*. against judg.

**REJOICEST.**
*Jer*. 11:15 when thou doest evil, then thou *r*.

**REJOICING.**
1 *K*. 1:45 come up from thence *r*.
2 *Chr*. 23:18 burnt-offer. with *r*.
*Job* 8:21 he fill thy lips with *r*.
*Ps*. 19:8 statutes right, *r*. heart
45:15 with *r*. sh. they be broug.
107:22 declare his works with *r*.
118:15 voice of *r*. is in tabern.
119:111 they are *r*. of my heart
126:6 sh. come again with *r*.
*Prov*. 8:30 *r*. always before him
31 *r*. in habitable part of earth
*Is*. 65:18 I create Jerusalem a *r*.
*Jer*. 15:16 thy word was to me *r*.
*Hab*. 3:14 their *r*. was to devour
*Zep*. 2:15 this is *r*. city th. said
*Luke* 15:5 layeth it on should. *r*.
*Acts* 5:41 *r*. counted worthy to s.
8:39 eunuch went on his way *r*.
*Rom*. 12:12 *r*. in hope, patient in
1 *Cor*. 15:31 I protest by your *r*.
2 *Cor*. 1:12 our *r*. is testimony of
14 we are your *r*. ye are ours
6:10 as sorrowful, yet always *r*.
*Gal*. 6:4 sh. he have *r*. in himself
*Phil*. 1:26 your *r*. be more abun.
1 *Thes*. 2:19 wh. our crown of *r*.?
*Heb*. 3:6 *r*. of hope firm to end
*Jam*. 4:16 boastings, such *r*. evil

**RELEASE.**
*Deut*. 15:1 end of 7 years make *r*.
9 the year of *r*. is at hand
31:10 solemnity of year of *r*.
*Est*. 2:18 he made a *r*. to prov.

**RELEASE, Verb.**
*Deut*. 15:2 creditor that lend. *r*.
*Mat*. 27:15 gover. was wont to *r*. pris. *Luke* 23:17; *John* 18:39
17 w. will ye I *r*. 21; *Mark* 15:9
*Mark* 15:11 moved people, sho. rather *r*. Barab. *Lu*. 23:18
*Luke* 23:16 I will chastise and *r*.
20 Pilate willing to *r*. Jesus
*John* 19:10 I have power to *r*. 12

**RELEASED.**
*Mat*. 27:26 then *r*. he Barabbas *Mark* 15:15; *Luke* 23:25
*Mark* 15:6 at feast he *r*. prisoner

**RELIEF.**
*Acts* 11:29 determined to send *r*.

**RELIEVE.**
*Lev*. 25:35 if brother poor, *r*. him
*Is*. 1:17 and *r*. the oppressed
*Lam*. 1:11 thi. for meat to *r*. soul
16 comforter that should *r*. far
19 they sought meat to *r*. souls
1 *Tim*. 5:16 if any have wido. *r*.

**RELIEVED, ETH.**
*Ps*. 146:9 he *r*. fatherless, widow
1 *Tim*. 5:10 if she have *r*. afflict.

**RELIGION.**
*Acts* 26:5 straitest sect of our *r*.
*Gal*. 1:13 conversati. in Jews' *r*.
14 profited in the Jews' *r*.

Jam. 1:26 this man's r. is vain
27 pure r. and undefiled bef. G.

**RELIGIOUS.**

Acts 13:43 r. proselytes follow. P.
Jam. 1:26 if any am. you seem r.

**RELY, IED.**

2 Chr. 13:18 becau. they r. on L.
16:7 r. on Syr. hast not r. on L.
8 because thou didst r. on L.

**REMAIN.**

Ex. 12:10 let noth. r. till morn.
23:18 fat of sacri. r. till morni.
Lev. 19:6 if aught r. till 3d day
27:18 according to years that r.
Num. 33:55 those ye let r.
Deut. 2:34 destroyed all, none r.
16:4 nor any flesh r. till morn.
19:20 those which r. shall hear
21:23 his body sh. not r. on tree
Jos. 1:14 your little ones shall r.
8:22 let none of th. r. 10:28, 30
23:4 I divided nations that r.
Jud. 5:17 did Dan r. in ships?
21:7 wives for them that r. 16
1 K. 18:22 I only r. a proph. of L.
Ezr. 9:15 for we r. yet escaped
Job 21:32 shall he r. in the tomb
27:15 those that r. sh. be buried
Ps. 55:7 would I r. in wilderness
Prov. 2:21 perfect sh. r. in land
21:16 shall r. in congregation
Is. 10:32 yet shall he r. at Nob
32:16 righteousn. shall r. in fie.
65:4 which r. among the graves
66:22 heavens and new earth r.
Jer. 8:3 residue that r. of family
17:25 this city shall r. for ever
27:11 th. will I let r. in own la.
30:18 the palace shall r.
38:4 weak. hands of men that r.
Jer. 42:17 no. of th. r. 44:14; 51:62
44:7 com. evil, leave none to r.
Ezek. 7:11 violence risen, no. r.
17:21 they that r. shall be scat.
39:14 men to bury those that r.
Amos 6:9 if there r. ten men
Ob. 14 delivered those that r.
Zec. 12:14 families that r.
Luke 10:7 in same house r. eat.
John 6:12 gather fragm. that r.
15:11 my joy might r. in you
16 chosen that your fruit sh. r.
19:31 bodies sho. not r. on cross
1 Cor. 15:6 of wh. greater part r.
1 Thes. 4:15 r. till coming of L.
17 we which are alive and r.
Heb. 12:27 cannot be shaken r.
1 John 2:24 that ye have heard r.
Rev. 3:2 strengthen things wh. r.

**REMAINDER.**

Ex. 29:34 thou shalt burn the r.
Lev. 6:16 the r. shall Aaron eat
7:17 r. on third day sh. be bur.
2 Sam. 14:7 leave nei. name, r.
Ps. 76:10 r. of wrath sh. restrain

**REMAINED.**

Gen. 7:23 Noah only r. alive
14:10 they that r. fled to moun.
Ex. 14:28 th. r. not one chariot
Sam. 11:26 there r. two men
35:28 he should r. in city of ref.
36:12 inh. r. in house of father
Deut. 3:11 king of Bas. r. giants
Jos. 10:20 rest r. entered cities
11:22 in Ashdod there r. Anak.
18:2 there r. of Is. seven tribes
Jud. 7:3 there r. with G. 10,000
1 Sam. 11:11 they which r. scat.
2 K. 10:11 Jehu slew all that r. 17
25:22 people r. set G. over them
1 Chr. 13:14 ark r. in fami. of O.
Ec. 2:9 my wisdom r. with me
Jer. 37:10 there r. wounded men
21 r. in court of prison, 38:13
41:10 Ishm. carried capt. that r.
48:11 his taste r. in him
51:30 mighty men r. in th. holds
Lam. 2:22 L.'s anger none r.
Dan. 10:8 r. no stren. in me, 17
13 I r. there with kings of Pe.
Mat. 11:23 done in S. it would r.
14:20 took up fragments that r.
Luke 9:17; John 6:13
Luke 1:22 beckoned, r. speechl.
Acts 5:4 wh. it r. was it not thi.

**REMAINEST.**

Lam. 5:19 thou O L. r. Heb. 1:11

**REMAINETH.**

Gen. 8:22 while earth r. seed-ti. and harvest shall not cease
Ex. 12:10 which r. ye shall burn
Lev. 8:32 r. of flesh and bread
16:16 so do for taberna. that r.
Num. 24:19 destroy him that r.
Jos. 8:29 heap of stones that r.
13:1 there r. land to be possess.
Jud. 5:13 him that r. have dom.
1 Sam. 6:18 stone r. to this day
16:11 J. said, There r. youngest
Job 19:4 my error r. with myself
41:22 in his neck r. strength
Is. 4:3 he that r. in J. call. holy
Jer. 38:2 he that r. in city sh. die
Ezek. 6:12 he that r. besieged die
Hag. 2:5 so my Sp. r. am. them
Zec. 9:7 he that r. shall be for G.
John 9:41 therefore your sin r.
1 Cor. 7:29 it r. they that ha. wi.
2 Cor. 3:11 that which r. glorio.
9:9 his righteousness r. for ev.
Heb. 4:6 it r. some must enter in
9 there r. a rest to peop. of G.
10:26 there r. no sacrifice for sin
1 John 3:9 for seed r. in him

**REMAINING.**

Num. 9:22 cloud r. on tabernacle
Deut. 3:3 till none was left r.
Jos. 10:33 and he left none r. 37, 39, 40; 11:8
2 Sam. 21:5 dest. fr. r. in coasts
2 K. 10:11 Jehu left Ahab no. r.
1 Chr. 9:33 who r. in chambers
Job 18:19 nor any r. in dwelling
Ob. 18 shall not be any r. of Esau
John 1:33 on wh. shall see Sp. r.

**REMALIAH.**

Is. 7:4 anger of son of R. 5. 9
8:6 rejoice in Rezin and R. son

**REMEDY.**

2 Chr. 36:16 wrath arose, no r.
Prov. 6:15 be broken without r.
29:1 be destroyed, without r.

**REMEMBER.**

Gen. 40:23 did not butler r. Jos.
Ex. 13:3 Moses said to people r.
Ex. 20:8 r. sab.-day to keep holy
Num. 11:5 we r. fish eat in Egypt
15:39 r. all commandm. of Lord
Deut. 5:15 r. thou wast a serv. in Eg. 15:15; 16:12; 24:18, 22
7:18 r. what L. did to Pharaoh
8:18 r. L. gi. pow. to get wealth
9:7 r. thou provokest L. thy G.
16:3 r. day camest out of Egypt
24:9 r. what Lord did to Miriam
25:17 r. what Amal. did to thee
32:7 r. days of old, consider
Jos. 1:13 r. word wh. Moses com.
Jud. 9:2 r. I am your bone
1 Sam. 25:31 Ab. said, r. handm.
2 Sam. 14:11 let the king r. Lord
2 K. 9:25 r. when I rode after A.
20:3 r. I walk. bef. thee, Is. 38:3
1 Chr. 16:12 r. works, Ps. 105:5
2 Chr. 6:42 r. mercies of David
Neh. 1:8 r. word thou com. Mos.
4:14 r. L. wh. is great and terri
13:29 r. th. that defiled priesth.
Job 4:7 r. who perished
7:7 O r. my life is wind
10:9 r. thou hast made me
11:16 r. it as waters that pass
36:24 r. thou magnify his work
41:8 hand upon him, r. battle
Ps. 20:3 r. thy offerings, accept
7 we will r. name of the Lord
22:27 ends of world r. turn to L.
25:6 r. thy mercies ever of old
7 r. not sins of my you., r. me
74:2 r. congreg. thou purchased
18 r. this, enemy reproached
22 r. how foolish man reproa.
79:8 O r. not former iniquities
89:47 r. how short my time is
50 r. L. reproach of thy serv.
103:18 th. that r. his command.
119:49 r. word unto thy servant
132:1 L. r. D. and his afflictions
137:7 r. O Lord, child. of Edom
Prov. 31:7 r. misery no more
Ec. 5:20 he sh. not r. days of life
11:8 let him r. days of darkness
12:1 r. Creator in days of youth
Cant. 1:4 r. love more than wine
Is. 43:18 r. not former th.? 46:9
25 I will not r. sins
44:21 r. these, O Jacob, and Is.
46:8 r. this, show yoursel. men
47:7 neither didst r. latter end
54:4 not r. reproach of widowh.
64:5 meetest those that r. thee
9 neither r. iniquity for ever
Jam. 3:16 neither shall they r. it
14:10 he will now r. their iniq.
21 r. break not thy covenant
17:2 their children r. their altars
18:20 r. I stood to speak good
31:20 I do earnestly r. him still
44:21 did not the Lord r. them?
51:50 ye that have escaped, r. L.
Lam. 5:1 r. O L. what is come
Ezek. 16:61 then sh. r. thy ways, 20:43; 36:31
23:27 thou shalt not r. Egypt
Hos. 8:13 now will he r. th. iniq.
9:9 therefore he will r. iniquity
Mic. 6:5 r. now what Ba. consul.
Hab. 3:2 O L. in wrath r. mercy
Mal. 4:4 r. the law of Moses
Mat. 16:9 r. loaves, Mark 8:18
Luke 1:72 r. his holy covenant
16:25 r. that th. in thy lifetime
17:32 r. Lot's wife; 24:6 r. how
John 15:20 r. word that I said
16:4 time shall come, ye may r.
Acts 20:31 r. that by three years
35 r. words of the Lord Jesus
Gal. 2:10 we should r. the poor
Eph. 2:11 r. that in time past
Col. 4:18 r. my bonds
1 Thes. 2:9 ye r. breth. our labor
2 Thes. 2:5 r. ye not I told you?
2 Tim. 2:8 r. that J. Ch. raised
Heb. 13:3 r. them are in bonds
7 r. them which have the rule
Jude 17 r. words spoken of apos.
Rev. 2:5 r. fr. wh. thou art fallen
3:3 r. how thou hast received

**I REMEMBER.**

Gen. 41:9 I do r. my faults
1 Sam. 15:2 I r. that which Am.
Job 21:6 when I r. I am afraid
Ps. 42:4 when I r. these, I pour
63:6 wh. I r. thee upon my bed
137:6 if I do not r. thee, let my
143:5 I r. the days of old
Jer. 2:2 I r. thee, the kindness
Hos. 7:2 consider not that I r. all

**I will REMEMBER.**

Gen. 9:15 I will r. my coven. 16
Lev. 26:42 I w. r. coven. with A.
45 I w. for their sakes r. cove.
Ps. 42:6 therefore will I r. thee
77:10 I will r. the years of, 11
Jer. 31:34 I will r. their sin no more, Heb. 8:12; 10:17
Ezek. 16:60 I will r. my covenant
3 John 10 I will r. deeds he doeth

**REMEMBER me.**
*Jud.* 16:28 *r. me* that I may be
1 *Sam.* 1:11 look on hand. *r. me*
*Neh.* 13:14 *r. me*, O God, 22, 31
*Job* 14:13 appoint me, and *r. me*
*Ps.* 25:7 *r. me*, for thy sake, O L.
106:4 *r. me* with the favor that
*Jer.* 15:15 O L. thou know. *r. me*
*Ezek.* 6:9 escape of you sh. *r. me*
*Zec.* 10:9 sh. *r. me* in far countr.
*Luke* 23:42 L. *r. me* when comest
1 *Cor.* 11:2 ye *r. me* in all things

**REMEMBERED.**
*Gen.* 8:1 G. *r.* Noah; 19:29 Abr.
30:22 G. *r.* Rachel; 49:2 Jose. *r.*
*Ex.* 2:24 God *r.* his covenant, 6:5
*Num.* 10:9 ye shall be *r.* bef. L.
*Jud.* 8:34 child. of Isr. *r.* not L.
1 *Sam.* 1:19 the Lord *r.* Hannah
*Est.* 9:28 days of Pur. sho. be *r.*
*Job* 24:20 sin. shall be no more *r.*
*Ps.* 45:17 make thy name be *r.*
77:3 I *r.* God and was troubled
78:35 they *r.* G. was their Sav.
39 *r.* that they were but flesh
42 they *r.* not his hand, when
98:3 he *r.* his mercy tow. house
105:8 *r.* his covenant for ever
42 for he *r.* his holy promise
106:7 they *r.* not the multitude
45 he *r.* for them his covenant
109:14 iniq. of his fathers be *r.*
16 he *r.* not to show mercy
111:4 wonderful works to be *r.*
119:52 I *r.* thy judgments of old
55 I have *r.* thy name, O Lord
136:23 *r.* us in our low estate
137:1 we wept, when we *r.* Zion
*Ec.* 9:15 no man *r.* poor man
*Is.* 23:16 thou mayest be *r.*
57:11 thou hast not *r.* me
63:11 then he *r.* days of old
65:17 former heav. sh. not be *r.*
*Jer.* 11:19 may be no more *r.*
*Lam.* 1:7 Jerusalem *r.* in days
2:1 *r.* not his footstool in anger
*Ezek.* 3:20 his righteousness sh. not be *r.* 33:13
16:22 not *r.* days of youth, 43
21:24 made your iniq. to be *r.*
25:10 Ammonites may not be *r.*
*Hos.* 2:17 no more *r.* *Zec.* 13:2
*Amos* 1:9 *r.* not the covenant
*Jon.* 2:7 soul fainted I *r.* Lord
*Mat.* 26:75 Peter *r.* the words of Jesus, *Luke* 22:61
*Luke* 24:8 they *r.* his words
*John* 2:17 disciples *r.* it was wr.
22 when he was risen they *r.*
12:16 wh. J. was glorified th. *r.*
*Acts* 11:16 then *r.* I word of L.
*Rev.* 18:5 God hath *r.* her iniqui.

**REMEMBEREST, ETH.**
*Ps.* 9:12 mak. inquisition, he *r.*
88:5 like slain whom thou *r.*
103:14 he *r.* we are but dust
*Lam.* 1:9 she *r.* not her last end
*Mat.* 5:23 th. *r.* that thy brother
*John* 16:21 *r.* no more anguish
2 *Cor.* 7:15 whi. he *r.* obedience

**REMEMBERING.**
*Lam.* 3:19 *r.* mine affliction and
1 *Thes.* 1:3 *r.* your work of faith

**REMEMBRANCE.**
*Ex.* 17:14 put out *r.* of Amalek
*Num.* 5:15 bring iniquity to *r.*
*Dan.* 25:19 blot out *r.* of Amalek
32:26 make *r.* of them cease
2 *Sam.* 18:18 no son to keep *r.*
1 *K.* 17:18 to call my sin to *r.*?
*Job* 18:17 his *r.* perish fr. earth
*Ps.* 6:5 in death there is no *r.*
30:4 thanks at *r.* of holi. 97:12
34:16 to cut off the *r.* of them
38:1 psalm of Da. br. to *r.* 70:1
77:6 call to *r.* my song in night
83:4 Israel be no more in *r.*
102:12 *r.* unto all generations
112:6 righteous shall be in *r.*
*Ec.* 1:11 is no *r.* of former things
2:16 there is no *r.* of the wise
*Is.* 26:8 des. of our soul *r.* of thee
43:26 put me in *r.* let us plead
57:8 behind doors set up thy *r.*
*Lam.* 3:20 my soul hath th. in *r.*
*Ezek.* 21:23 call to *r.* the iniquity
24 bec. that ye are come to *r.*
23:19 to *r.* days of her youth, 21
29:16 bringeth their iniq. to *r.*
*Mal.* 3:16 book of *r.* was written
*Mark* 11:21 Peter calling to *r.*
*Luke* 1:54 hath holpen Is. in *r.*
22:19 do in *r.* of me, 1 *Cor.* 11:24
*John* 14:26 bring things to yo. *r.*
*Acts* 10:31 thine alms had in *r.*
1 *Cor.* 4:17 sh. bring you into *r.*
11:25 as ye dri. of it, in *r.* of me
*Phil.* 1:3 I thank God upon ev. *r.*
1 *Thes.* 3:6 that ye have good *r.*
1 *Tim.* 4:6 if thou put breth. in *r.*
2 *Tim.* 1:3 that I have *r.* of thee
5 I call to *r.* unfeigned faith
6 wherefore I put thee in *r.*
2:14 of th. things put them in *r.*
*Heb.* 10:3 there is a *r.* of sins
32 call to *r.* the former days
2 *Pet.* 1:12 always in *r.* *Jude* 5
13 putting you in *r.*
15 have th. things always in *r.*
3:1 pure minds by way of *r.*
*Rev.* 16:19 Babylon came in *r.*

**REMEMBRANCES.**
*Job* 13:12 your *r.* like to ashes

**REMISSION.**
*Mat.* 26:28 blo. shed for *r.* of sins
*Mark* 1:4 baptism of repentance for *r.* *Luke* 3:3
*Luke* 1:77 salvation by *r.* of sins
24:47 that *r.* should be preached
*Acts* 2:38 baptized for *r.* of sins
10:43 whoso belie. sh. receive *r.*
*Rom.* 3:25 *r.* of sins th. are past
*Heb.* 9:22 without shed bl. no *r.*
10:18 where *r.* is, th. is no offe.

**REMIT, TED.**
*John* 20:23 sins ye *r.* they are *r.*

**REMNANT.**
*Lev.* 2:3 the *r.* of meat-offering
5:13 *r.* sh. be priest's as offering
14:18 *r.* of oil in priest's hand
*Deut.* 28:54 eye evil toward the *r.*
*Jos.* 23:12 if ye cleave to the *r.*
2 *Sam.* 21:2 Gibeonites *r.* of Am.
1 *K.* 14:10 I will take away the *r.*
2 *K.* 19:4 lift up thy prayer for the *r.* *Is.* 37:4, 31, 32
30 *r.* escaped shall take root
31 out of Je. shall go forth a *r.*
21:14 forsa. *r.* of mine inherita.
25:11 *r.* did Nebuzar-adan carry
2 *Chr.* 30:6 retu. to the *r.* of you
*Ezr.* 3:8 the *r.* of their brethren
9:8 grace fr. L. to leave us a *r.*
14 so that there should be no *r.*
*Neh.* 1:3 *r.* left of the captivity
*Job* 22:20 *r.* of th. fire consumed
*Is.* 1:9 unless L. left us small *r.*
11:11 to recover *r.* of his people
16 there sh. be a highway for *r.*
14:22 cut off fr. Babylon the *r.*
30 kill thy root, he sh. sl. thy *r.*
15:9 I will bring lions on the *r.*
16:14 the *r.* shall be very small
17:3 kingdom shall cease from *r.*
46:3 hearken *r.* of house of Isr.
*Jer.* 6:9 they sh. glean *r.* of Isr.
11:23 there sh. be no *r.* of them
15:11 it shall be well with thy *r.*
23:3 I will gather *r.* of my flock
25:20 the *r.* of Ashdod did drink
31:7 O L. save thy peo. *r.* of Is.
40:11 king of Babylon left a *r.*
15 Jews scat. *r.* of Judah peri.
41:16 Joha. took *r.* of peo. 43:5
42:15 hear the Lord, ye *r.* of Ju.
19 O ye *r.* of Judah, go ye not
44:12 I will take the *r.* of Judah
28 *r.* sh. kn. wh. words stand
47:4 Lord will spoil *r.* of count.
*Ezek.* 5:10 whole *r.* will scatter
6:8 yet will I leave a *r.* that ye
11:13 L. wilt make end of *r.*?
14:22 behold, therein sh. be a *r.*
23:25 *r.* shall fall by the sword
25:16 destroy the *r.* of sea-coast
*Joel* 2:32 *r.* whom the L. sh. call
*Amos* 1:8 *r.* of Philist. sh. perish
5:15 God will be gracious to *r.*
9:12 that they may possess *r.*
*Mic.* 2:12 I will gather *r.* of Isra.
4:7 make her that halted, a *r.*
5:3 *r.* of brethren return to Isr.
7 *r.* of Ja. in midst of people, 8
7:18 transgres. of *r.* of heritage
*Hab.* 2:8 all the *r.* of the people
*Zep.* 1:4 I will cut off *r.* of Baal
2:7 coast for *r.* of house of Jud.
9 *r.* of people possess them
3:13 *r.* of Is. sh. not do iniquity
*Hag.* 1:12 *r.* of people obeyed L.
14 Lord stirred up spirit of *r.*
*Zec.* 8:6 marvellous in eyes of *r.*
12 I will cause *r.* of peo. to po.
*Mat.* 22:6 the *r.* took his servan.
*Rom.* 9:27 Es. crieth, *r.* be saved
*Rom.* 11:5 at present time there is a *r.*
*Rev.* 11:13 the *r.* were affrighted
12:17 dragon we. to war with *r.*
19:21 *r.* were slain with sword

**REMOVE.**
*Gen.* 48:17 father's hand to *r.* it
*Num.* 36:7 inheritance of Is. *r.* 9
*Deut.* 19:14 not *r.* neigh.'s land.
*Jos.* 3:3 ye sh. *r.* from your place
2 *Sam.* 6:10 Da. would not *r.* ark
2 *K.* 23:27 L. said, I will *r.* Judah
24:3 Ju. to *r.* them out of sight
2 *Chr.* 33:8 neither will I *r.* Isr.
*Job* 24:2 some *r.* landmarks, they
27:5 I will not *r.* mine integrity
*Ps.* 36:11 let not wicked *r.* me
39:10 *r.* thy stroke away fr. me
119:22 *r.* from me reproach and
29 *r.* from me the way of lying
*Prov.* 4:27 *r.* thy foot from evil
5:8 *r.* thy way far from her
22:28 *r.* not the landmarks, 23:10
30:8 *r.* from me vanity and lies
*Ec.* 11:10 *r.* sorrow from heart
*Is.* 13:13 earth *r.* out of her place
46:7 from his place sh. he not *r.*
*Jer.* 4:1 return, thou shalt not *r.*
27:10 prophesy lie, *r.* from land
50:3 they shall *r.* shall depart
8 *r.* out of the midst of Babyl.
*Ezek.* 12:3 *r.* by day, thou sh. *r.*
45:9 O princes, *r.* violence and
*Hos.* 5:10 like them that *r.* bound
*Joel* 2:20 I will *r.* northern army
3:6 ye might *r.* them from bor.
*Mic.* 2:3 fr. wh. sh. not *r.* necks
*Zec.* 3:9 I will *r.* iniquity of land
14:4 mountain *r.* toward north
*Mat.* 17:20 say, *r.* hence, sh. be *r.*
*Luke* 22:42 if willing, *r.* this cup
1 *Cor.* 13:2 that I could *r.* mount.
*Rev.* 2:5 else I will *r.* candlestick

**REMOVED.**
*Gen.* 8:13 Noah *r.* covering of ark
47:21 Joseph *r.* people to cities
*Ex.* 14:19 angel of God *r.* and
20:18 people saw it and *r.* afar
*Num.* 21:12 *r.* pitched, 33:7-21
*Deut.* 28:25 *r.* into all kingdoms
*Jos.* 3:1 they *r.* from Shittim
1 *Sam.* 6:3 why his ha. is not *r.*
2 *Sam.* 20:12 he *r.* Amasa out of

1 K. 15:12 Asa r. the idols
13 r. fr. bei. queen, 2 Chr. 15:16
14 high pla. not r. 2 K. 15:4, 35
2 K. 17:18 the Lord r. Israel out of his sight, 23; 23:27
26 nations wh. th. r. know not
18:4 Hezekiah r. the high places
2 Chr. 35:12 th. r. burnt-offerings
Job 14:18 rock is r. out of place
18:4 sh. rock be r. out of place?
19:10 hope hath he r. like a tree
36:16 would have r. out of stra.
Ps. 46:2 not fear tho' earth be r.
81:6 r. his shoulder from burden
103:12 so far he r. transgressions
104:5 earth, it should not be r.
125:1 as Zion which cannot be r.
Prov. 10:30 righteous never be r.
Is. 6:12 till L. hath r. men away
10:13 I have r. bounds of people
31 Madmenah is r. inhabitants
22:25 the sure place shall be r.
24:20 earth sh. be r. like cottage
26:15 hast r. it to ends of earth
29:13 r. their heart from me
30:20 yet sh. not teachers be r.
33:20 not one of stakes be r.
38:12 mine age r. fr. me as tent
54:10 the hills shall be r. coven. of my peace shall not be r.
Jer. 15:4 cause to be r. to kingd.
24:9 deliv. to be r. 29:18; 34:17
Lam. 1:8 Jerusalem sinned, is r.
3:17 thou hast r. my soul
Ezek. 7:19 their gold shall be r.
23:46 I will give them to be r.
36:17 way uncl. of a r. woman
Amos 6:7 banq. of them sh. be r.
Mic. 2:4 how hath he r. it fr. me
7:11 in that day sh. decree be r.
Mat. 21:21 Be r. Mark 11:23
Acts 7:4 he r. Abraham into land
13:22 he r. Saul, raised David
Gal. 1:6 marvel ye are so soon r.

### REMOVETH.

Deut. 27:17 cursed, th. r. landm.
Job 9:5 wh. r. the mountains
12:20 he r. speech of the trusty
Ec. 10:9 whoso r. stones be hurt
Dan. 2:21 chan. seasons, r. kings

### REMOVING.

Gen. 30:32 r. from flock speckled
Is. 49:21 I am a captive r. to and
Ezek. 12:3 prepare stuff for r. 4
Heb. 12:27 signifieth r. of things

### REMPHAN.

Acts 7:43 the star of your god R.

### REND.

Ex. 39:23 ephod should not r.
Lev. 10:6 neither r. your clothes
13:56 priest r. plague out of gar.
1 K. 11:11 I will r. kingd. 12, 31
13 I will not r. away kingdom
2 Chr. 24:27 didst r. clothes, we.
Ec. 3:7 a time to r. time to sew
Is. 64:1 thou wouldest r. heavens
Ezek. 13:11 stormy wind r. it, 13
29:7 and r. all their shoulder
Hos. 13:8 I will r. caul of heart
Joel 2:13 r. your heart, not gar.
Mat. 7:6 lest they turn and r.
John 19:24 not r. it, but cast lots

### RENDER.

Num. 18:9 offering they r. holy
Deut. 32:41 I will r. vengeance
43 r. vengeance to adversaries
Jud. 9:57 evil of men of S. G. r.
1 Sam. 26:23 L. r. to man faithf.
2 Chr. 6:30 r. to ev. man accord.
Job 33:26 will r. to man righte.
34:11 work of a man shall he r.
Ps. 28:4 r. to them their desert
38:20 they that r. evil for good
56:12 O God, I will r. praises to
79:12 r. to neighbor sevenfold
94:2 r. a word to the proud
116:12 what shall I r. to the L.?
Prov. 24:12 shall not he r. to ev. man ac. to words? Rom. 2:6
29 r. to man according to wo.
26:16 seven men can r. reason
Is. 66:15 Lord come to r. anger
Jer. 51:6 r. to Bab. recompen. 24
Lam. 3:64 r. to them recompense
Hos. 14:2 we r. calves of our lips
Joel 3:4 ye r. me a recompense?
Zec. 9:12 will r. double to thee
Mat. 21:41 r. him fruits in season
22:21 r. unto Cesar things are C.'s, Mark 12:17; Luke 20:25
Rom. 13:7 r. to all their dues
1 Cor. 7:3 husb. r. to wife bene.
1 Thes. 3:9 what thanks can we r.
5:15 see that none r. evil for ev.

### RENDERED.

Jud. 9:56 G. r. wickedness of A.
2 K. 3:4 king of M. r. king of Is.
2 Chr. 32:25 Heze. r. not accord.
Prov. 12:14 rec. of man's ha. r.

### RENDEREST, ETH, ING.

Ps. 62:12 r. to man acc. to work
Is. 66:6 voice of L. r. recomp.
1 Pet 3:9 not r. evil for evil

### RENDEST, ING.

Ps. 7:2 my soul r. it in pieces
Jer. 4:30 r. face with painting

### RENEW.

1 Sam. 11:14 go to G. r. kingd.
Ps. 51:10 r. right sp. within me
Is. 40:31 wait on L. r. strength
41:1 let people r. their stren.
Lam. 5:21 turn us, O L. r. days
Heb. 6:6 if fall, r. to repentance

### RENEWED, EST.

2 Chr. 15:8 Asa r. altar of Lord
Job 10:17 r. witnesses ag. me
29:20 my bow was r. in my ha.
Ps. 103:5 youth is r. like eagle's
104:30 thou r. face of the earth
2 Cor. 4:16 inw. man r. day by d.
Eph. 4:23 be r. in spirit of minds
Col. 3:10 man wh. is r. in know.

### RENEWING.

Rom. 12:2 transform. by r. mind
Tit. 3:5 he sav. us by r. of H. G.

### RENOUNCED.

2 Cor. 4:2 have r. hidden things

### RENOWN.

Gen. 6:4 giants of old, men of r.
Num. 16:2 fa. in cong. men of r.
Ezek. 16:14 r. went forth among
15 playedst harlot bec. of thy r.
34:29 raise for them a plant of r.
39:13 shall be to them r. sai. L.
Dan. 9:15 gotten thee r.

### RENOWNED.

Num. 1:16 these r. of congrega.
Is. 14:20 evil-doers never r.
Ezek. 23:23 captai. lords, and r.
26:17 r. city was strong in sea

### RENT, Substantive.

Is. 3:24 instead of girdle be a r.
Mat. 9:16 r. ma. worse, Mar. 2:21
Luke 5:36 then new maketh a r.

### RENT, Participle.

Gen. 37:33 Joseph is r. in pieces
Jos. 9:4 wine bot. old and r. 13
2 Sam. 15:32 H. with his coat r.
1 K. 13:3 altar be r. 5 altar r.
Ezr. 9:5 having r. my garment
Mat. 27:51 veil of temple r. in tw. Mark 15:28; Luke 23:45

See CLOTHES.

### RENT, Verb.

Jud. 14:6 Samson r. lion as he r.
1 Sam. 15:27 Saul r. Sam. man.
28 L. hath r. kingdom, 28:17
2 Sam. 13:19 Tamar r. her garm.
1 K. 1:40 earth r. with the sou.
11:30 Ahijah r. Jerob. garment
19:11 strong wind r. mountains
2 K. 17:21 he r. Israel from Dav.
Ezr. 9:3 when I heard I r. garm.
Job 1:20 Job arose, and r. mantle
2:12 Job's fr. r. ev. one mantle
26:8 cloud is not r. under them
Jer. 36:24 nor r. their garments
Ezek. 30:16 Sin have pain, No r.
Mat. 27:51 veil was r. rocks r.
Mark 9:26 spi. cried, and r. him

### REPAID.

Prov. 13:21 to right. good be r.

### REPAIR.

2 K. 12:5 let priests r. breaches of the house of God, 22:5, 6; 2 Chr. 24:4; 34:8, 10
7 why r. ye not house? 22:5, 6
2 Chr. 24:5 money to r. house
12 carpenters to r. house of L.
Ezr. 9:9 give reviv. to r. house
Is. 61:4 they shall r. waste cities

### REPAIRED.

Jud. 21:23 Benjamin r. cities
1 K. 11:27 Solomon r. breaches
18:30 Elijah r. altar of the Lord
2 K. 12:6 the priests had not r.
14 and r. the house of the L.
1 Chr. 11:8 Joab r. rest of the ci.
2 Chr. 29:3 Hezek. r. the doors
32:5 Hezekiah r. Millo in city
33:16 Manasseh r. altar of Lord
Neh. 3:4 next to them r. 5–19
6 and after him r. 17–24

### REPAIRER, ING.

2 Chr. 24:27 the r. of the house
Is. 58:12 shalt be called the r.

### REPAY.

Deut. 7:10 will r. him to his face
Job 21:31 r. him what ha. done?
41:11 that I should r. him?
Is. 59:18 accord. to their deeds r. fury, to islands r. recomp.
Luke 10:35 come again I will r.
Rom. 12:19 I will r. saith the L.
Phile. 19 I Paul, will r. it

### REPAYETH.

Deut. 7:10 r. them that hate him

### REPEATETH.

Prov. 17:9 but he that r. a mat.

### REPENT.

Ex. 13:17 lest peradv. people r.
32:12 turn from thy wrath, r.
Num. 23:19 nei. son of man, r.
Deut. 32:36 Lord r. for his serv.
1 Sam. 15:29 Strength of I. not r.
1 K. 8:47 if they r. in the land
Job 42:6 and r. in dust and ashes
Ps. 90:13 let it r. thee concern.
110:4 Lord will not r. Heb. 7:21
135:14 he will r. himself conc.
Jer. 4:28 I purp. it, will not r.
18:8 nation turn, r. of ev. 26:13
10 then I will r. of the good
26:3 that I may r. 42:10 for I r.
Ezek. 14:6 r. and turn yourselves, 18:30
24:14 neither spare, nei. will r.
Joel 2:14 if he will return and r. Jon. 3:9
Mat. 3:2 preach. saying r. 4:17
Mark 1:15 r. ye, and believe
6:12 preach. that men should r.
Luke 13:3 except ye r. perish, 5
16:30 if one we. fr. dead will r.
17:3 if thy brother r. forgive, 4
Acts 2:38 r. and be baptized ev.
3:19 r. ye theref. be converted
8:22 r. of this thy wickedness
17:30 commandeth all men to r.
26:20 they should r. turn to G.
2 Cor. 7:8 I do not r. tho' I did r.
Rev. 2:5 and r. except thou r.
16 r. else I will come unto th.
21 I gave her space to r. of her

3:3 how thou hast rec. and *r.*
19 be zealous therefore and *r.*

**REPENTANCE.**

*Hos.* 13:14 *r.* sh. be hid fr. eyes
*Mat.* 3:8 fru. meet for *r. Luke* 3:8
11 I indeed bapti. you unto *r.*
*Mat.* 9:13 to call sinners **to** *r.*
*Mark* 2:17; *Luke* 5:32
*Mark* 1:4 John did prea. bap. of *r. Luke* 3:3; *Acts* 13:24; 19:4
*Luke* 15:7 ninety-nine need no *r.*
24:47 *r.* and remission of sins
*Acts* 5:31 God exalted to give *r.*
11:18 to Gentiles granted *r.*
20:21 testifying to Greeks *r.*
26:20 works meet for *r.*
*Rom.* 2:4 good. of God lead. to *r.*
11:29 gifts of God without *r.*
2 *Cor.* 7:9 I rej. ye sorrowed to *r.*
10 godly sorrow worketh *r.*
2 *Tim.* 2:25 if G. will give th. *r.*
*Heb.* 6:1 laying again foun. of *r.*
6 to renew them again to *r.*
12:17 he found no place of *r.*
2 *Pet.* 3:9 perish, all come to *r.*

**REPENTED.**

*Gen.* 6:6 it *r.* Lord he made man
*Ex.* 32:14 *r.* of evil, 2 *Sam.* 24:16; 1 *Chr.* 21:15; *Jer.* 26:19
*Jud.* 2:18 it *r.* L. because of th.
21:6 the children of Israel, *r.* 15
1 *Sam.* 15:35 L. *r.* he made Saul
*Ps.* 106:45 L. *r.* acc. to mercies
*Jer.* 8:6 no man *r.* him of wick.
20:16 cities L. overthrew *r.* not
31:19 after I was turned, I *r.*
*Amos* 7:3 the Lord *r.* for this, 6
*Jon.* 3:10 God *r.* of the evil
*Zec.* 8:14 punish you, I *r.* not
*Mat.* 11:20 cities bec. they *r.* not
21 would have *r. Luke* 10:13
12:41 men of Nin. *r. Luke* 11:32
21:29 afterward he *r.* and went
32 when ye had seen it, *r.* not
27:3 Ju. *r.* himself, bro't silver
2 *Cor.* 7:10 repent. not to be *r.*
12:21 many that have not *r.*
*Rev.* 2:21 to repent, she *r.* not
9:20 were not killed, yet *r.* not
16:9 blasphemed G. *r.* not, 11

**REPENTEST, ETH.**

*Gen.* 6:7 it *r.* me I made them
1 *Sam.* 15:11 it *r.* me I set up S.
*Jon.* 4:2 gracious God *r.* of evil
*Joel* 2:13 slow to anger, *r.* him
*Luke* 15:7 one sinner *r.* 10

**REPENTING, S.**

*Jer.* 15:6 I am weary with *r.*
*Hos.* 11:8 *r.* are kindled together

**REPETITIONS.**

*Mat.* 6:7 use not vain *r.* as hea.

**REPHAIM.**

*Gen.* 14:5 smote R. in Ashteroth
15:20 have I given land of R.
2 *Sam.* 5:18 in valley of R. 22; 23:13; 1 *Chr.* 11:15; 14:9
*Is.* 17:5 gather. ears in val. of R.

**REPHIDIM.**

*Ex.* 17:1 pitch. in R. *Num.* 33:14
8 and fought with Israel in R.
19:2 dep. from R. *Num.* 33:15

**REPLENISH, ED.**

*Gen.* 1:28 mult. and *r.* earth, 9:1
*Is.* 2:6 bec. they be *r.* from east
23:2 merchants of Zidon have *r.*
*Jer.* 31:25 and I have *r.* every
*Ezek.* 26:2 I sh. be *r.* in waste pl.
27:25 thou wast *r.* made glori.

**REPLIEST.**

*Rom.* 9:20 thou that *r.* ag. God?

**REPORT, Substantive.**

*Gen.* 37:2 Jos. brought their *r.*
*Ex.* 23:1 shalt not raise false *r.*
*Num.* 13:32 brought up evil *r.*
14:37 men that bring up evil *r.*
*Deut.* 2:25 nations shall hear *r.*
1 *Sam.* 2:24 no good *r.* I hear
1 *K.* 10:6 it was true *r.* 2 *Chr.* 9:5
*Neh.* 6:13 matter for an evil *r.*
*Prov.* 15:30 a good *r.* maketh fat
*Is.* 23:5 at *r.* concerning Egypt, so at the *r.* of Tyre
28:19 vexation only to under. *r.*
53:1 who hath believed our *r.*? *John* 12:38; *Rom.* 10:16
*Jer.* 50:43 Babylon heard the *r.*
*Acts* 6:3 seven men of honest *r.*
10:22 Cornelius was of good *r.*
22:12 Ananias having a good *r.*
2 *Cor.* 6:8 by evil *r.* and good *r.*
*Phil.* 4:8 what. things of good *r.*
1 *Tim.* 3:7 bishop have good *r.*
*Heb.* 11:2 elders obt. a good *r.*
39 having obtained a good *r.*
2 *John* 12 Demetrius ha. good *r.*

**REPORT, Verb.**

*Jer.* 20:10 *r.* say they, will *r.* it
1 *Cor.* 14:25 will *r.* that God is in

**REPORTED.**

*Neh.* 6:6 it is *r.* among heathen
*Neh.* 6:7 sh. it be *r.* to king acc.
19 *r.* his good deeds before
*Est.* 1:17 husb. when it sh. be *r.*
*Ezek.* 9:11 man had inkhorn *r.*
*Mat.* 28:15 saying commonly *r.*
*Acts* 4:23 *r.* all chief priests said
16:2 Timotheus was well *r.*
*Rom.* 3:8 we be slanderously *r.*
1 *Cor.* 5:1 *r.* there is fornication
1 *Tim.* 5:10 *r.* for good works
1 *Pet.* 1:12 minis. things now *r.*

**REPROACH.**

*Jos.* 5:9 I rolled away *r.* of Eg.
1 *Sam.* 17:26 taketh away the *r.*
*Neh.* 1:3 remn. are afflic. and *r.*
4:4 and turn their *r.* upon head
5:9 because of the *r.* of heathen
*Ps.* 57:3 shall save me from *r.*
69:7 for thy sake I ha. borne *r.*
20 *r.* hath broken my heart
71:13 let them be cover. with *r.*
78:66 put them to perpetual *r.*
79:12 their *r.* wherewith they
89:50 remember *r.* of servants, I bear in my bosom the *r.*
119:22 remove from me *r.* and
*Prov.* 6:33 *r.* shall not be wiped
18:3 with ignominy cometh *r.*
19:26 that caus. shame and *r.*
22:10 strife and *r.* shall cease
*Is.* 4:1 name to take away our *r.*
51:7 fear ye not the *r.* of men
54:4 not remember the *r.* of thy
*Jer.* 23:40 I bring an everlast. *r.*
31:19 because I did bear the *r.*
51:51 confounded bec. heard *r.*
*Lam.* 3:30 he is fill. full with *r.*
61 thou hast heard their *r.* O L.
5:1 Lord consider and behold *r.*
*Ezek.* 16:57 discovered, time of *r.*
21:28 concerning *r.* of Ammon.
36:15 nor shalt thou bear *r.*
30 ye shall receive no more *r.*
*Dan.* 11:18 cause *r.* cease, his *r.*
*Hos.* 12:14 his *r.* shall L. return
*Joel* 2:17 give not heritage to *r.*
*Mic.* 6:16 ye shall bear *r.* of peo.
*Zep.* 2:8 I heard the *r.* of Moab
3:18 the *r.* of it was a burden
2 *Cor.* 11:21 I speak concern. *r.*
1 *Tim.* 3:7 report, lest fall into *r.*
4:10 we both labor and suffer *r.*
*Heb.* 11:26 esteeming *r.* of Christ
13:13 without camp, bearing *r.*

**A REPROACH.**

*Gen.* 34:14 do this, that were *a r.*
1 *Sam.* 11:2 lay it for *a r.* upon
*Neh.* 2:17 that be no more *a r.*
*Ps.* 15:3 not upon *a r.* ag. neigh.
22:6 *a r.* of men, and despised
31:11 I was *a r.* among enemies
39:8 make me not *r.* of foolish
44:13 thou makest us *a r.* to our
79:4 become *a r.* to neighbors
89:41 he is *a r.* to his neighbors
109:25 I became *a r.* to them
*Prov.* 14:34 sin is *a r.* to any pe.
*Is.* 30:5 a people that were *a r.*
*Jer.* 6:10 word of L. to them *a r.*
20:8 word of L. was made *a r.*
24:9 deliver for hurt to be *a r.* 29:18; 42:18; 44:8, 12
49:13 Bozrah shall become *a r.*
*Ezek.* 5:14 I will make thee *a r.*
15 Jeru. sh. be *a r.* and taunt
22:4 I made *a r.* unto heathen
*Dan.* 9:16 thy people become *a r.*
*Joel* 2:19 no more make you *a r.*

**My REPROACH.**

*Gen.* 30:23 God hath taken *my r.*
1 *Sam.* 25:39 ple. cause of *my r.*
*Job* 19:5 if plead ag. me *my r.*
20:3 I have heard check of *my r.*
*Ps.* 69:10 I wept, that was *my r.*
19 thou hast known *my r.*
119:39 turn away *my r.*
*Luke* 1:25 *my r.* among men

**REPROACH, Verb.**

*Ruth* 2:15 let her glean, *r.* not
2 *K.* 19:4 whom king of Assyria sent to *r.* G. 16; *Is.* 37:4, 17
*Neh.* 6:13 matter they might *r.*
*Job* 27:6 not *r.* long as I live
*Ps.* 42:10 mine enemies *r.* me
74:10 how long advers. *r.* me?
102:8 enemies *r.* me all day
*Luke* 6:22 *r.* you for my sake

**REPROACHED.**

2 *K.* 19:22 whom th. *r.*? *Is.* 37:23
23 messenger hast *r. Is.* 37:24
*Job* 19:3 ten times have ye *r.* me
*Ps.* 55:12 was not enemy that *r.*
69:9 they that *r.* thee are fallen upon me, *Rom.* 15:3
74:18 remember enemy hath *r.*
79:12 wherewith they *r.* thee
*Ps.* 89:51 wherew. thine enem. *r.* have *r.* footsteps of anointed
*Zep.* 2:8 whereby they *r.* people
10 bec. they *r.* and magnified
1 *Pet.* 4:14 if *r.* for C. hap. are ye

**REPROACHES.**

*Ps.* 69:9 the *r.* of them that repr. thee, *Rom.* 15:3
*Is.* 43:28 I have given Israel to *r.*
2 *Cor.* 12:10 pleas. in *r.* C.'s sake
*Heb.* 10:33 gazing-stock by *r.*

**REPROACHEST, ETH.**

*Num.* 15:30 doeth presump. *r.* L.
*Ps.* 44:16 voice of him that *r.*
74:22 remem. foolish man *r.* th.
119:42 to answer him that *r.* me, *Prov.* 27:11
*Prov.* 14:31 poor, *r.* Maker, 17:5
*Luke* 11:45 Master, thou *r.* us

**REPROACHFULLY.**

*Job* 16:10 smitten me on cheek *r.*
1 *Tim.* 5:14 none occa. to spe. *r.*

**REPROBATE.**

*Jer.* 6:30 *r.* silver men call them
*Rom.* 1:28 G. gave them to *r.*
2 *Tim.* 3:8 men *r.* concern. faith
*Tit.* 1:16 to every good work *r.*

**REPROBATES.**

2 *Cor.* 13:5 Chri. is in you, ex. *r.*
6 shall know that we are not *r.*
7 do that wh. is honest, tho' *r.*

**REPROOF.**

*Job* 26:11 they are astonish. at *r.*
*Prov.* 1:23 turn you at my *r.*
25 none of my *r.* 30 despised *r.*
5:11 and my heart despised *r.*
10:17 he that refuseth *r.* erreth
12:1 he that hateth *r.* is brutish
13:18 he that regardeth *r.*

15:5 he that regard. *r.* is prud.
10 he that hateth *r.* shall die
31 heareth of *r.* of life am. wise
32 he that hear. *r.* get. under.
17:10 a *r.* enter. more into wise
29:15 rod and *r.* give wisdom
2 *Tim.* 3:16 scri. profitable for *r.*

**REPROOFS.**

*Ps.* 38:14 in whose mouth no *r.*
*Prov.* 6:23 *r.* of instruc. are life

**REPROVE.**

2 *K.* 19:4 *r.* Rabshakeh, *Is.* 37:4
*Job* 6:25 doth your arguing *r.*?
26 do ye imagine to *r.* words
13:10 he will *r.* if ye accept
22:4 will he *r.* for fear of thee?
*Ps.* 50:8 will not *r.* for burnt-off.
21 I will *r.* thee, set in order
141:5 let him *r.* me, it sh. be oil
*Prov.* 9:8 *r.* not scorner
19:25 *r.* one that hath underst.
30:6 lest he *r.* thee, found liar
*Is.* 11:3 neit. *r.* hearing of ears
4 *r.* with equity for meek
37:4 will *r.* words wh. L. heard
*Jer.* 2:19 backslidings sh. *r.* thee
*Hos.* 4:4 let no man *r.* another
*John* 16:8 he will *r.* world of sin
*Eph.* 5:11 no fellowship, rather *r.*
2 *Tim.* 4:2 *r.* rebuke, exhort

**REPROVED.**

*Gen.* 20:16 thus she was *r.*
21:25 Abraham *r.* Abimelech
1 *Chr.* 16:21 yea, he *r.* kings for their sakes, *Ps.* 105:14
*Prov.* 29:1 often *r.* harden. neck
*Jer.* 29:27 why hast not *r.* Jer.?
*Hab.* 2:1 what answer, when *r.*?
*Luke* 3:19 Herod being *r.* by J.
*John* 3:20 lest deeds be *r.*
*Eph.* 5:13 things *r.* made manif.

**REPROVER.**

*Prov.* 25:12 so is a wise *r.* upon
*Ezek.* 3:26 not be to them a *r.*

**REPROVETH.**

*Job* 40:2 he that *r.* God
*Prov.* 9:7 *r.* scorner get. shame
15:12 scorner loveth not one *r.*
*Is.* 29:21 lay snare for him *r.*

**REPUTATION**

*Ec.* 10:1 him in *r.* for wisdom
*Acts* 5:34 Gamaliel in *r.* am. peo.
*Gal.* 2:2 privately to them of *r.*
*Phil.* 2:7 made himself of no *r.*
29 receive him, hold such in *r.*

**REPUTED.**

*Job* 18:3 *r.* vile in your sight?
*Dan.* 4:35 inhab. *r.* as nothing

**REQUEST, S.**

*Jud.* 8:24 Gid. said, I desire a *r.*
2 *Sam.* 14:15 king sh. perform *r.*
22 king hath fulfilled *r.* of ser.
*Ezr.* 7:6 granted him all his *r.*
*Neh.* 2:4 for wh. dost th. make *r.*
*Est.* 4:8 to king to make *r.*
5:3 what is thy *r.* 6; 7:2; 9:12
7:3 life given me, peo. at my *r.*
7 Haman stood up to *r.* for life
*Job* 6:8 I might have my *r.*!
*Ps.* 21:2 not withholden *r.*
106:15 gave th. *r.* sent leanness
*Rom.* 1:10 *r.* for prosper. journey
*Phil.* 1:4 in ev. prayer making *r.*
4:6 let your *r.* be known to God

**REQUESTED.**

*Jud.* 8:26 wei. of ear-rings he *r.*
1 *K.* 19:4 Elijah *r.* he might die
1 *Chr.* 4:10 G. granted Jab. he *r.*
*Dan.* 1:8 he *r.* of prince of eunu.
2:49 Dan. *r.* of king, he set Sh.

**REQUIRE.**

*Gen.* 9:5 blood I *r.* of every beast
31:39 my hand didst thou *r.* it
43:9 of my hand sh. thou *r.* him
*Deut.* 10:12 doth L. *r.*? *Mic.* 6:8
18:19 whoso not hear. I will *r.*
23:21 L. will surely *r.* it of thee
*Jos.* 22:23 let L. *r.* it, 1 *Sam.* 20:16
2 *Sam.* 3:13 one thing I *r.* of thee
4:11 shall I not *r.* his blood at?
19:38 thou sh. *r.* that will I do
1 *K.* 8:59 maintain as matter *r.*
1 *Chr.* 21:3 why doth my lord *r.*
2 *Chr.* 24:22 L. look on it, *r.* it
*Ezr.* 7:21 whatso. Ezra *r.* of you
8:22 asham. to *r.* of king a band
*Neh.* 5:12 restore, and *r.* nothing
*Ps.* 10:13 said, Thou wilt not *r.*
*Ezek.* 3:18 his blood will I *r.* at thy hand, 20; 33:6, 8
20:40 there will I *r.* your offer.
34:10 I will *r.* my flock at hand
1 *Cor.* 1:22 for the Jews *r.* a sign
7:36 *r.* let him do what he will

**REQUIRED.**

*Gen.* 42:22 behold, his blood is *r.*
*Ex.* 12:36 lent things as they *r.*
2 *Sam.* 12:20 he *r.* they set bread
1 *Chr.* 16:37 every day's work *r.*
2 *Chr.* 8:14 as the duty of every day *r.* *Ezr.* 3:4
*Neh.* 5:18 *r.* not I bread of gover.
*Est.* 2:15 *r.* nothing but what
*Ps.* 40:6 sin-offer. hast th. not *r.*
137:3 they that wasted *r.* mirth
*Prov.* 30:7 two things have I *r.*
*Is.* 1:12 who *r.* this at your hand
*Luke* 11:50 *r.* of this generati. 51
12:20 this night thy soul *r.*
48 much given, of him be m. *r.*
19:23 I might have *r.* mine own
23:24 gave sentence sho. be as *r.*
1 *Cor.* 4:2 *r.* of stew. be faithful

**REQUIREST, ETH, ING.**

*Ruth* 3:11 do all that thou *r.*
*Ec.* 3:15 God *r.* that whi. is past
*Dan.* 2:11 a rare thing king *r.*
*Luke* 23:23 *r.* he might be cruci.

**REQUITE.**

*Gen.* 50:15 Jos. will *r.* us the evil
*Deut.* 32:6 do ye thus *r.* Lord?
2 *Sam.* 2:6 I will *r.* you this kin.
16:12 L. will *r.* me good for this
2 *K.* 9:26 I will *r.* thee in plat
*Ps.* 10:14 behold. to *r.* with hand
41:10 that I may *r.* them
*Jer.* 51:56 G. of recomp. shall *r.*
1 *Tim.* 5:4 learn to *r.* th. parents

**REQUITED, ING.**

*Jud.* 1:7 as I done, so God *r.* me
1 *Sam.* 25:21 *r.* me evil for good
2 *Chr.* 6:23 judge serv. by *r.* wic.

**REREWARD,** *or* **REARWARD.**

*Num.* 10:25 stand. of Dan was *r.*
*Jos.* 6:9 *r.* came after ark, 13
1 *Sam.* 29:2 D. and men pass. *r.*
*Is.* 52:12 G. of Is. will be your *r.*
58:8 glory of Lord sh. be thy *r.*

**RESCUE, ETH.**

*Deut.* 28:31 shalt have none to *r.*
*Ps.* 35:17 *r.* my soul fr. destruc.
*Dan.* 6:27 he delivereth and *r.*
*Hos.* 5:14 I take, none shall *r.*

**RESCUED.**

1 *Sam.* 14:45 people *r.* Jonathan
30:18 David *r.* his two wives
*Acts* 23:27 came I with army, *r.*

**RESEMBLANCE.**

*Zec.* 5:6 their *r.* thro' all earth

**RESEMBLE, ED.**

*Jud.* 8:18 each *r.* childr. of king
*Luke* 13:18 shall *r.* kingd. of God

RESEN. *Gen.* 10:12

**RESERVE.**

*Jer.* 3:5 will he *r.* anger for ever?
50:20 I will pardon whom I *r.*
2 *Pet.* 2:9 *r.* unj. to day of judg.

**RESERVED.**

*Gen.* 27:36 hast thou not *r.* bles.
*Num.* 18:9 most holy things *r.*
*Jud.* 21:22 *r.* not each his wife
*Ruth* 2:18 gave moth. that she *r.*
2 *Sam.* 8:4 but *r.* for one hundred chariots, 1 *Chr.* 18:4
*Job* 21:30 wicked *r.* for destruc.
38:23 I *r.* agai. time of trouble
*Acts* 25:21 Paul appealed to be *r.*
*Rom.* 11:4 I have *r.* 7,000 men
1 *Pet.* 1:4 inheritance *r.* in heav.
2 *Pet.* 2:4 deliv. to be *r.* to judg.
17 mist of darkn. is *r.* for ever
3:7 heav. and earth *r.* unto fire
*Jude* 6 he hath *r.* in chains
13 to wh. is *r.* blackn. of dark.

**RESERVETH.**

*Jer.* 5:24 *r.* to us weeks of harv.
*Nah.* 1:2 L. *r.* wrath for enemi.

**RESIDUE.**

*Ex.* 10:5 locusts shall eat the *r.*
*Neh.* 11:20 *r.* of Is. were in cities
*Is.* 28:5 L. diadem to *r.* of people
38:10 deprived of *r.* of years
44:17 the *r.* he maketh a god
*Jer.* 8:3 chosen, by all the *r.* of
15:9 *r.* I deliver to the sword
29:1 Jeremiah sent to *r.* of eld.
39:3 *r.* of princes of Babylon
41:10 Ishm. carri. captive the *r.*
*Ezek.* 9:8 destroy the *r.* of Isr.?
23:25 thy *r.* shall be devoured
34:18 must tread *r.* of pastures
36:3 possession of *r.* to heathen
4 derision to *r.* of the heathen
5 have I spoken ag. *r.* of hea.
48:18 *r.* in length ag. oblation
21 the *r.* shall be for the prin.
*Dan.* 7:7 stamped *r.* with feet, 19
*Zep.* 2:9 *r.* of people shall spoil
*Hag.* 2:2 speak to Joshua and *r.*
*Zec.* 8:11 I will not be to the *r.*
14:2 *r.* of the people shall not
*Mal.* 2:15 had the *r.* of the Spir.
*Mark* 16:13 went and told it to *r.*
*Acts* 15:17 *r.* might seek the L.

**RESIST.**

*Zec.* 3:1 Satan at right hand to *r.*
*Mat.* 5:39 that ye *r.* not evil
*Luke* 21:15 adver. not able to *r.*
*Acts* 6:10 not able to *r.* wisdom
7:51 ye do always *r.* Holy Ghost
*Rom.* 13:2 *r.* shall receive damn.
2 *Tim.* 3:8 these also *r.* the truth
*Jam.* 4:7 *r.* devil and he will flee
5:6 killed just, doth not *r.* you
1 *Pet.* 5:9 wh. *r.* steadfast in fai.

**RESISTED, ETH.**

*Rom.* 9:19 who hath *r.* his will?
13:2 whoso *r.* power, *r.* ordin.
*Heb.* 12:4 have not *r.* unto blood
*Jam.* 4:6 God *r.* proud, 1 *Pet.* 5:5

**RESOLVED.**

*Luke* 16:4 I am *r.* what to do

**RESORT.**

*Neh.* 4:20 *r.* ye thither to us
*Ps.* 71:3 whereunto I may *r.*
*Mark* 10:1 the people *r.* to him
*John* 18:20 whi. Jews always *r.*

**RESORTED.**

2 *Chr.* 11:13 priests and Levit. *r.*
*Mark* 2:13 multitude *r.* to him
*John* 10:41 and many *r.* to him
18:2 Jesus ofttimes *r.* thither
*Acts* 16:13 spake to wom. who *r.*

**RESPECT.**

*Gen.* 4:4 the Lord had *r.* to Abel
*Ex.* 2:25 God looked and had *r.*
*Lev.* 26:9 I will have *r.* unto you
1 *K.* 8:28 have thou *r.* to prayer of thy servant, 2 *Chr.* 6:19
2 *K.* 13:23 the L. had *r.* to them
2 *Chr.* 19:7 *r.* of pers. with God, *Rom.* 2:11; *Eph.* 6:9; *Col.* 3:25
*Ps.* 74:20 have *r.* unto covenant

119:6 I have r. to all thy com.
15 I will have r. unto thy ways
117 have r. to thy statutes
138:6 hath he r. to the lowly
Prov. 24:23 not good to have r. of persons in judgm. 28:21
Is. 17:7 sh. have r. to Holy One
22:11 nor had r. to him that
2 Cor. 3:10 had no glory in th. r.
Phil. 4:11 I speak in r. of want
Col. 2:16 let none judge in r. of
Heb. 11:26 Mo. had r. to recomp
Jam. 2:1 not faith with r. of per.
3 have r. to him that weareth
9 if ye have r. to persons
1 Pet. 1:17 without r. of persons

### RESPECT, Verb.

Lev. 19:15 thou sh. not r. person
Num. 16:15 Moses said, r. not
Deut. 1:17 not r. persons, 16:19
2 Sam. 14:14 neither doth God r.
Is. 17:8 nor shall r. that which

### RESPECTED, ETH.

Job 37:24 he r. not wise of heart
Ps. 40:4 blessed is man that r.
Lam. 4:16 r. not pers. of priest

### RESPECTER.

Acts 10:34 God is no r. of persons

### RESPITE.

Ex. 8:15 Phar. saw there was r.
1 Sam. 11:3 said, Give 7 days r.

### REST, Substantive.

Gen. 49:15 Issa. saw r. was good
Ex. 16:23 to-morrow r. of sabb.
31:15 sev. is sabbath of r. 35:2; Lev. 16:31; 23:3, 32; 25:4
33:14 and I will give thee r.
Lev. 25:5 a year of r. to land
Deut. 3:20 L. given r. Jos. 1:13
12:9 ye are not yet come to r.
25:19 God hath given thee r.
28:65 neither sh. sole of foot r.
Jos. 1:15 L. hath given breth. r.
14:15 land had r. fr. war, Jud. 3:11; 5:31
21:44 the Lord gave them r.
22:4 God given r. 23:1 L. giv. r.
Jud. 3:30 land had r. 80 years
Ruth 1:9 L. grant you may find r.
3:18 the man will not be in r.
2 Sam. 7:1 L. had giv. him r. 1 K. 5:4; 8:56; 2 Chr. 14:6, 7
1 Chr. 6:31 after that ark had r.
22:9 man of r. I will gi. him r.
23:25 God hath given r. to peo.
28:2 I had to build house of r.
2 Chr. 15:15 L. gave them r.
20:30 G. gave him r. round ab.
Neh. 9:28 after they had r.
Est. 9:16 J. had r. from enemies
Job 3:13 slept, had been at r.
17 there the weary be at r.
26 not in safety, nei. had I r.
11:18 shalt take thy r. in safety
17:16 our r. together is in dust
Ps. 38:3 neither is there any r.
55:6 then wo. I fly and be at r.
94:13 thou mayest give him r.
116:7 ret. to thy r. O my soul
132:8 arise, O Lord, into thy r.
14 this is my r. for ever
Prov. 29:17 cor. son, he give r.
Ec. 2:23 his heart taketh not r.
6:5 this hath more r. than other
Is. 11:10 Gent. seek, r. be glor.
14:3 the Lord shall give thee r.
7 the earth is at r. Zec. 1:11
18:4 L. said, I will take my r.
28:12 this is r. wherew. weary r.
30:15 retur. and r. sh. ye be sav.
34:14 find for herself a pl. of r.
66:1 where is place of my r.?
Jer. 6:16 ye shall find r. for souls
30:10 Jacob shall be in r. 46:27
Ezek. 38:11 to them that are at r.
Dan. 4:4 I Nebuchad. was at r.
Mic. 2:10 this is not your r.
Zec. 9:1 Damascus shall be r.
Mat. 11:28 co. unto me, I give r.
29 ye sh. find r. to your souls
12:43 seek r. Luke 11:24
26:45 take your r. Mark 14:41
John 11:13 had spoken of tak. r.
Acts 7:49 what is place of my r.?
9:31 then had the churches r.
2 Thes. 1:7 are troub. r. with us
Heb. 3:11 not enter into r. 18
4:1 prom. left us of ent. into r.
3 wh. believed do enter into r.
8 if Jesus had given them r.
9 th. remaineth r. to peo. of G.
11 labor therefore to enter r.

See NO.

### RESTS.

1 K. 6:6 he made narrowed r.

### REST, Adjective.

Ex. 28:10 names of r. on stone
Num. 31:8 r. of them were slain
Deut. 3:13 the r. of Gilead gave I
Jud. 7:6 the r. bowed to drink
2 K. 4:7 live and childr. of the r.
1 Chr. 11:8 Joab repair. r. of city
2 Chr. 24:14 brought r. of money
Neh. 6:1 r. of enem. heard I built
11:1 r. of people also cast lots
Est. 9:12 wh. done in r. of prov.?
Ps. 17:14 leave r. to their babes
Is. 10:19 the r. of trees be few
Dan. 2:18 D. sh. not per. with r.
Zec. 11:9 r. eat flesh of another
Luke 12:26 why take tho. for r.?
24:9 told eleven and all the r.
Acts 2:37 to Pet. and r. of apost.
Acts 27:44 the r. esc. safe to land
1 Cor. 7:12 to the r. speak I
11:34 the r. will I set in order
1 Pet. 4:2 not live r. of his time
Rev. 2:24 to the r. in Thyatira
20:5 r. of dead lived not again

See ACTS.

### REST, Verb.

Gen. 18:4 wash feet, r. und. tree
Ex. 5:5 make th. r. fr. burdens
23:11 in seventh year let it r.
12 seventh day shalt r. 34:21
34:21 in harvest thou shalt r.
Lev. 26:35 not r. in sabbaths
Deut. 5:14 maid-serv. r. as thou
Jos. 3:13 feet of priests shall r.
2 Sam. 3:29 let it r. on head of J.
21:10 birds r. on them by day
2 K. 2:15 sp. of Elijah r. on Elis.
2 Chr. 14:11 we r. on thee
Job 3:18 the prisoners r. togeth.
14:6 may r. till he accomplish
Ps. 16:9 r. in hope, Acts 2:26
37:7 r. in the Lord, wait for him
125:3 rod of wick. not r. on rig.
Prov. 6:35 nor will he r. content
Cant. 1:7 makest flock r. at noon
Is. 7:19 shall r. in deso. valleys
11:2 Sp. of the Lord r. upon him
25:10 in moun. sh. hand of L. r.
28:12 ye cause the weary to r.
51:4 I will make judgment to r.
57:2 they shall r. in their beds
20 are like the sea, it cannot r.
62:1 for Jer.'s sake I will not r.
63:14 Sp. of L. caused him to r.
Jer. 31:2 to cause him to r.
Ezek. 5:13 my fury to r. upon th. 16:42; 21:17; 24:13
44:30 may cause blessing to r.
Dan. 12:13 th. shalt r. and stand
Hab. 3:16 I mi. r. day of trouble
Zep. 3:17 he will r. in love
Mark 6:31 come to desert and r.
Luke 10:6 your peace shall r.
2 Cor. 12:9 power of Chr. may r.
Heb. 4:4 God did r. seventh day
Rev. 4:8 r. not day and night
6:11 they should r. for a season
14:13 they may r. from labors

### RESTED.

Gen. 2:2 he r. on seventh day, 3; Ex. 20:11; 31:17
8:4 the ark r. in seventh month
Ex. 10:14 locusts r. in Egypt
16:30 people r. on seventh day
Num. 9:18 as cloud ab. they r. 23
10:12 cloud r. in wild. of Paran
36 when it r. he said, Ret. O L.
11:25 Spirit r. upon them, 26
Jos. 11:23 the land r. from war
1 K. 6:10 chambers r. on house
2 Chr. 32:8 r. on words of Hez.
Est. 9:17 on 14th day r. 18
Job 30:27 bow. boiled and r. not
Luke 23:56 they r. sabbath-day

### RESTEST, ETH.

Job 24:23 in safety, where. he r.
Prov. 14:33 wisdom r. in heart
Ec. 7:9 anger r. in bos. of fools
Rom. 2:17 thou art a J. r. in law
1 Pet. 4:14 Sp. of G. r. upon you

### RESTING-PLACE, S.

Num. 10:33 to search out a r.-pl.
2 Chr. 6:41 O Lord, into thy r.-p.
Prov. 24:15 spoil not his r.-place
Is. 32:18 my peo. dwell in r.-pl.
Jer. 50:6 forgotten their r.-place

### RESTITUTION.

Ex. 22:3 make full r. 5, 6, 12
Job 20:18 according to subs. r. be
Acts 3:21 until the times of r.

### RESTORE.

Gen. 20:7 r. the man his wife
40:13 Ph. will r. thee thy place
42:25 to r. every man's money
Ex. 22:1 r. five oxen for an ox
4 theft be found, he shall r.
Lev. 6:5 shall r. it in principal
24:21 killeth a beast, he sh. r. it
25:27 r. overpl. to wh. he sold it
Num. 35:25 congregation r. him
Deut. 22:2 things strayed r. aga.
Jud. 11:13 theref. r. those lands
17:3 I will r. it unto thee, 1 Sam. 12:3; 1 K. 20:34
2 Sam. 9:7 r. thee all land of Sa.
12:6 he shall r. lamb fourfold
16:3 to-day house of Isr. r. me
2 K. 8:6 r. all that was hers
Neh. 5:11 r. I pray you; 12 will r.
Job 20:10 his han. r. their goods
18 which he labored for, sh. r.
Ps. 51:12 r. to me joy of salvati.
Prov. 6:31 he shall r. sevenfold
Is. 1:26 I will r. thy judges
42:22 for spoil, and none sai. r.
49:6 to r. the preserved of Isr.
57:18 will r. comforts unto him
Jer. 27:22 r. them to this place
30:17 r. health to thee
Ezek. 33:15 if wicked r. pledge
Dan. 9:25 command to r. Jerus.
Joel 2:25 I will r. you the years
Mal. 17:11 Elias sh. r. all things
Luke 19:8 I r. him fourfold
Acts 1:6 Lord, wilt thou r. kingdom?
Gal. 6:1 r. such a one in meek.

### RESTORED.

Gen. 20:14 Abimelech r. Sarah
40:21 r. butler to his butlership
41:13 me he r. to mine office
42:28 money is r. in my sack
Deut. 28:31 thine ass sh. not be r.
Jud. 17:3 r. the 1,100 shekels, 4
1 Sam. 7:14 cities taken were r.
1 K. 13:6 the king's hand was r.
2 K. 8:1 whose son he r. 5
14:22 r. Elath to Jud. 2 Chr. 26:2
2 Chr. 8:2 the citi. Huram had r.
Ezr. 6:5 the vessels brought be r.
Ps. 69:4 I r. that which I took

*Ezek.* 18:7 *r.* to debtor his pledge
12 hath not *r.* pledge
*Mat.* 12:13 *r.* whole like as the other, *Mark* 3:5; *Luke* 6:10
*Mark* 8:25 sight *r.* saw clearly
*Heb.* 13:19 that I may be *r.*

**RESTORER.**

*Ruth* 4:15 shall be to thee a *r.*
*Is.* 58:12 sh. be called *r.* of paths

**RESTORETH.**

*Ps.* 23:3 he *r.* my soul
*Mark* 9:12 El. cometh first and *r.*

**RESTRAIN.**

*Job* 15:8 dost thou *r.* wisdom?
*Ps.* 76:10 the wrath shalt thou *r.*

**RESTRAINED.**

*Gen.* 8:2 rain from heaven was *r.*
11:6 nothing will be *r.* fr. them
16:2 Lord *r.* me from bearing
*Ex.* 36:6 peo. were *r.* fr. bring.
1 *Sam.* 3:13 Eli's sons vile, *r.* not
*Is.* 63:15 mercies, are they *r.*?
*Ezek.* 31:15 I *r.* the floods there.
*Acts* 14:18 sayings scarce *r.* peo.

**RESTRAINEST.**

*Job* 15:4 thou *r.* prayer before G.

**RESTRAINT.**

1 *Sam.* 14:6 there is no *r.* to L.

**RESURRECTION.**

*Mat.* 22:23 th. is no *r.* *Mark* 12:18; *Acts* 23:8; 1 *Cor.* 15:12
28 in *r.* whose wife sh. she be? *Mark* 12:23; *Luke* 20:33
30 in *r.* they neither marry, 31
27:53 came out of graves aft. *r.*
*Luke* 14:14 be recompensed at *r.*
20:27 deny any *r.* 36 child. of *r.*
*John* 5:29 done good, to *r.* of life, none evil, to *r.* of damnati.
11:25 J. said, I am the *r.* and life
*Acts* 1:22 witn. with us of his *r.*
2:31 David spake of *r.* of Christ
4:2 they preached thro' Jesus *r.*
33 witness of *r.* of Lord Jesus
17:18 preached Jesus and the *r.*
32 when they heard of the *r.*
23:6 of hope and *r.* I am called
24:15 there shall be a *r.* of dead
21 touching *r.* of the dead
*Rom.* 1:4 by *r.* from the dead
6:5 shall be in likeness of his *r.*
1 *Cor.* 15:13 but if there be no *r.*
21 by man came *r.* 42 so is *r.*
*Phil.* 3:10 know power of his *r.*
11 might attain to *r.* of dead
2 *Tim.* 2:18 *r.* is past already
*Heb.* 6:2 of *r.* from the dead
11:35 might obtain a better *r.*
1 *Pet.* 1:3 by *r.* of Jesus fr. dead
3:21 save us, by *r.* of Je. Christ
*Rev.* 20:5 this is the first *r.*
6 hath part in first *r.*

**RETAIN.**

*Job* 2:9 dost still *r.* integrity?
*Prov.* 4:4 thy heart *r.* my words
11:16 strong men *r.* riches
*Ec.* 8:8 no man power to *r.*
*Dan.* 11:6 she sh. not *r.* power
*John* 20:23 wh. soever sins ye *r.*
*Rom.* 1:28 did not like to *r.* God

**RETAINED.**

*Jud.* 7:8 Gideon *r.* those 300 men
19:4 damsel's father *r.* him
*Dan.* 10:8 I *r.* no strength, 16
*John* 20:23 sins ret. they are *r.*
*Phile.* 13 whom I would have *r.*

**RETAINETH.**

*Prov.* 3:18 happy ev. one *r.* her
11:16 a graci. woman *r.* honor
*Mic.* 7:18 *r.* not anger for ever

**RETIRE.**

2 *Sam.* 11:15 set in battle, and *r.*
*Jer.* 4:6 set up stand. *r.* stay not

**RETIRED.**

*Jud.* 20:39 when men of Israel *r.*
2 *Sam.* 20:22 they *r.* from city

**RETURN, Substantive.**

*Gen.* 14:17 meet Abram after *r.*
1 *Sam.* 7:17 Sam.'s *r.* was to Ra.
1 *K.* 20:22 at *r.* of the year the king of Syria will come, 26

**RETURN, Verb.**

*Gen.* 3:19 dust th. art, to dust *r.*
16:9 *r.* to mistress and submit
18:10 I will cert. *r.* to thee, 14
31:3 *r.* to land of kindred, 13
32:9 Lord which saidst to me, *r.*
*Ex.* 4:18 let me *r.* to breth. 19
13:17 people repent, *r.* to Egypt
*Lev.* 25:10 *r.* to posses. 13, 27, 28
41 shall *r.* unto his own family
27:24 the field shall *r.* unto him
*Num.* 10:36 *r.* L. to many of Is.
14:4 let us make a capt. and *r.*
23:5 L. said, *r.* unto Balak
35:28 slayer shall *r.* *Jos.* 20:6
*Deut.* 3:20 then shall ye *r.* every man to his posses. *Jos.* 1:15
17:16 nor cause people *r.* to Eg.
20:5 and *r.* to his house, 6, 7, 8
30:3 the Lord thy God will *r.*
8 thou shalt *r.* and obey the L.
*Jos.* 22:8 *r.* with much riches
*Jud.* 7:3 whos. afraid, let him *r.*
11:31 when I *r.* from children
*Ruth* 1:6 that she might *r.* fr. M.
8 go *r.* to her mother's house
15 *r.* thou after sister-in-law
1 *Sam.* 6:3 in any wise *r.* him
9:5 Saul said, Come, let us *r.*
26:21 then said Saul, I sinned, *r.*
29:4 said, Make this fellow *r.* 7
2 *Sam.* 2:26 ere thou bid peo. *r.*?
3:16 then said A. to him, Go. *r.*
10:5 beards grown, *r.* 1 *Chr.* 19:5
15:19 goest thou with us? *r.*
20 I go whither I may, *r.* thou
24:13 see what answer I sh. *r.*
1 *K.* 2:32 L. shall *r.* his blood, 33
44 Lord sh. *r.* thy wickedness
8:48 *r.* to thee with all th. heart
12:24 *r.* every man to his house
26 now shall kingd. *r.* to Dav.
19:15 *r.* on thy way to wildern.
22:17 *r.* every man to his house in peace, 2 *Chr.* 11:4; 18:16
28 if *r.* in peace, 2 *Chr.* 18:27
2 *K.* 18:14 I offended, *r.* from me
19:7 king of Assyria sh. *r.* to his own land, 33; *Is.* 37:7, 34
20:10 let shadow *r.* backward
2 *Chr.* 6:24 *r.* confess thy name
10:9 may *r.* answer to this peo.
18:26 fellow in prison until I *r.*
30:6 *r.* to you; 9 ye *r.* unto him
*Neh.* 2:6 said, When wilt th. *r.*?
4:12 whence ye shall *r.* to us
*Est.* 9:25 device of Haman sh. *r.*
*Job* 1:21 naked shall I *r.* thither
6:29 *r.* yea, *r.* ag. my righteous.
7:10 sh. *r.* no more to his house
15:22 believeth not he shall *r.*
17:10 but as for ye all, do ye *r.*
22:23 if thou *r.* to Almighty
33:25 shall *r.* to days of youth
36:10 that they *r.* from iniquity
*Ps.* 6:4 *r.* O L. deliver my soul
10 let mine enemies *r.* asham.
7:7 for their sakes therefore *r.*
16 mischief *r.* upon own head
59:6 *r.* at even. 14 let them *r.*
73:10 theref. his people *r.* hith.
74:21 let not oppress. *r.* asham.
80:14 *r.* we beseech thee, O G.
90:3 sayest, *r.* ye child. of men
13 *r.* O Lord? how long?
94:15 judgment *r.* to righteous.
104:29 they die, *r.* to their dust
116:7 *r.* to thy rest, O my soul
*Prov.* 2:19 no. th. go unto her *r.*
26:27 rolleth a stone, it will *r.*
*Ec.* 1:7 riv. come, thither they *r.*
5:15 naked sh. *r.* to go as he ca.
12:2 nor clouds *r.* after the rain
7 dust shall *r.* spirit *r.* to God
*Cant.* 6:13 *r.* *r.* O Shulami. *r.* *r.*
*Is.* 6:13 yet in it a tenth shall *r.*
10:21 remnant of Jacob sh. *r.* 22
21:12 if ye will, inqu. ye, *r.* co.
35:10 ransomed of L. sh. *r.* 51:11
44:22 *r.* unto me, I redeem. thee
63:17 *r.* for thy servant's sake
*Jer.* 3:1 shall he *r.* ag.? yet *r.* to
22 *r.* ye backsliding children
4:1 if thou *r.* saith L. *r.* unto
12:15 I will *r.* and have comps.
15:19 if thou wilt *r.* let them *r.* unto thee, *r.* not unto them
18:11 *r.* ev. one fr. evil way, 35:15
24:7 shall *r.* with whole heart
30:10 Jacob shall *r.* 46:27
31:8 great comp. shall *r.* thither
36:3 *r.* every man from evil
7 will *r.* ev. one from evil way
44:14 should *r.* into land of Ju.
50:9 none shall *r.* in vain
*Ezek.* 16:55 they desire to *r.* th. thou and thy daugh. shall *r.*
18:23 wicked *r.* fr. ways and live
*Dan.* 10:20 will *r.* to fight Persia
11:9 *r.* into his own land, 10, 28
13 the king of the north sh. *r.*
29 time appointed he shall *r.*
30 he shall be grieved, and *r.*
*Hos.* 2:7 and *r.* to first husband
9 I will *r.* take corn and wine
3:5 afterward chil. of Israel *r.*
7:16 they *r.* but not to M. High
8:13 they shall *r.* to Egypt, 9:3
12:14 reproach shall L. *r.* to hi.
14:7 they under shadow shall *r.*
*Joel* 2:14 know. he will *r.* repent
3:4 will *r.* recomp. on head, 7
*Ob.* 15 reward *r.* upon thy head
*Mic.* 5:3 remn. of brethren sh. *r.*
*Mal.* 1:4 Edom saith, We will *r.*
3:7 *r.* to me, and I will *r.* to y.
18 *r.* and discern between rig.
*Mat.* 10:13 let your peace *r.*
12:44 *r.* into house, *Luke* 11:24
24:18 nor let him in field *r.*
*Luke* 8:39 *r.* to thine own house
*Acts* 15:16 I will *r.* and build
18:21 I will *r.* to you, if G. will

**To RETURN.**

*Num.* 14:3 not better *to r.* to Eg.
*Deut.* 17:16 cause peo. *to r.* to E.
*Ruth* 1:16 not to leave th. or *to r.*
1 *Sam.* 29:11 David rose ear. *to r.*
2 *Chr.* 10:6 coun. give ye *to r.* 9
*Neh.* 9:17 captain *to r.* to bondage
*Jer.* 5:3 they have refused *to r.* 8:5; *Hos.* 11:5
22:27 they desire *to r.* 44:14
29:10 in causing you *to r.* to th. place, 30:3; 32:44; 33:7, 11, 26; 34:22; 42:12
34:11 caused servants *to r.* 16
*Ezek.* 21:30 cause *to r.* to sheath?
47:6 caused me *to r.* to the river
*Hos.* 11:5 bec. they refused *to r.*
*Luke* 19:12 rec. kingd. and *to r.*
*Acts* 13:34 no more *to r.* to corr.
20:3 pur. *to r.* thro' Macedonia

**RETURN to, *or* unto t. Lord.**

1 *Sam.* 7:3 ye *r. u. t. L.* wi. hea.
*Is.* 19:22 they shall *r. unto t. L.*
55:7 let him *r. u. t. L.* mercy
*Hos.* 6:1 let us *r. unto the Lord*
7:10 they do not *r. unto the L.*
14:1 O Is. *r. u. t. L.* hast fallen

**Not RETURN.**

*Num.* 32:18 will *not r.* to houses
1 *Sam.* 15:26 S. said, I will *not r.*
2 *Sam.* 12:23 go, he sh. *n. r.* to
1 *K.* 13:16 I may *not r.* with thee

*Job* 10:21 whe. I shall *not r*. 16:22
39:4 and *r*. *not* unto them
*Is*. 45:23 word gone out, sh. *n*. *r*.
55:11 it shall *not r*. to me void
*Jer*. 8:4 turn away, and *not r*.?
15:7 destroy, since they *r*. *not*
22:11 shall *not r*. any more, 27
23:20 anger of L. sh. *not r*. 30:24
*Ezek*. 7:13 for seller shall *not r*.
13:22 sho. *n*. *r*. fr. wicked ways
21:5 sw. shall *not r*. into sheath
35:9 thy cities shall *not r*.
46:9 he sh. *not r*. by way he ca.
*Hos*. 7:10 they do *not r*. to Lord
11:5 he sh. *not r*. to land of Eg.
9 I will *not r*. to destroy Ephr.
*Mat*. 2:12 warned sh. *not r*. to H.
*Luke* 16:31 let him likewise *n*. *r*.

**RETURNED.**

*Gen*. 8:3 waters *r*. from off earth
9 dove *r*. to him: 12 *r*. not ag.
43:18 because money *r*. in sacks
*Ex*. 14:27 sea *r*. to strength, 28
19:8 M. *r*. words of people to L.
*Lev*. 22:13 if she is *r*. to father's
*Num*. 24:25 Bal. rose, *r*. to place
*Jos*. 2:16 hide till pursu. be *r*. 22
4:18 waters of Jor. *r*. to th. pla.
*Jud*. 2:19 judge was dead th. *r*.
5:29 she *r*. answer to herself
11:39 Gid.'s daugh. *r*. to father
*Ruth* 1:22 so Naomi and Ruth *r*.
1 *Sam*. 17:57 D. *r*. from slaughter
25:39 Lord *r*. wickedness of Na.
2 *Sam*. 1:22 sw. of S. *r*. not emp.
3:16 said Ab. Return, and he *r*.
6:20 Da. *r*. to bless his housch.
16:8 L. *r*. on thee blood of house
19:15 king *r*. and came to Jord.
23:10 peo. *r*. after him to spoil
1 *K*. 13:10 *r*. not by way he came
33 after this Jer. *r*. not fr. evil
2 *K*. 4:35 Elisha *r*. and walked
2 *Chr*. 25:10 *r*. home in anger
32:21 Senn. *r*. with shame face
*Neh*. 9:28 when they *r*. and cried
*Ps*. 35:13 prayer *r*. into bosom
78:34 they *r*. inquired after G.
*Is*. 38:8 the sun *r*. ten degrees
*Jer*. 3:7 turn to me, she *r*. not
14:3 they *r*. wi. vessels empty
40:12 the Jews *r*. out of place
*Ezek*. 1:14 living creatures ran, *r*.
8:17 *r*. to provoke me to anger
47:7 I *r*. lo, at bank of river
*Dan*. 4:34 understanding *r*. 36
*Hos*. 6:11 I *r*. captivity of people
*Amos* 4:6 yet not *r*. to me, 8, 11
*Zec*. 1:6 they *r*. and said, As L.
16 I am *r*. to Jer. with mercies
7:14 no man passed thro' nor *r*.
8:3 I am *r*. to Zion, will dwell
*Mat*. 21:18 as he *r*. into city
*Mark* 14:40 *r*. found them asleep
*Luke* 2:20 sheph. *r*. glorifying G.
4:14 Jesus *r*. in power of Spirit
8:37 went into ship, and *r*. back
17:18 that *r*. to give glory to G.
19:15 *r*. having received kingd.
23:48 smote breasts, and *r*.
24:9 *r*. fr. sepulchre and told all
52 worshipped, *r*. to Jerusal.
*Acts* 8:25 apostles *r*. to Jerusal.
13:13 and John *r*. to Jerusalem
21:6 took ship, they *r*. home
*Gal*. 1:17 I *r*. ag. unto Damascus
*Heb*. 11:15 opportunity to have *r*.
1 *Pet*. 2:25 *r*. to Sheph. of souls

**RETURNETH.**

*Ps*. 146:4 breath goeth, *r*. to ear.
*Prov*. 26:11 as dog *r*. so a fool *r*.
*Ec*. 1:6 wind *r*. accord. to circu.
*Is*. 55:10 rain *r*. not thither, but
*Ezek*. 35:7 that *r*. I will cut off
*Zec*. 9:8 encamp bec. of him *r*.

**RETURNING.**

*Is*. 30:15 in *r*. rest ye be saved

*Luke* 7:10 *r*. found servant whole
*Acts* 8:28 *r*. sitting in chariot
*Heb*. 7:1 Abra. *r*. from slaughter

**REUBEN.**

*Gen*. 29:32 called his name R.
30:14 R. went in the days of
35:22 R. went and lay with Bil.
23 sons of Leah, R. Ja.'s 46:8; 49:3; *Num*. 26:5; 1 *Chr*. 5:1
37:22 R. said, Shed no blood, 29
46:9 sons of R. *Ex*. 6:14; *Num*. 16:1; 32:1, 37; *Deut*. 11:6; *Jos*. 4:12; 1 *Chr*. 5:3, 18
*Num*. 2:10 of camp of R. 10:18
7:30 prince of children of R.
32:33 child. of R. *Jos*. 13:23
*Deut*. 27:13 mount E. to curse, R.
33:6 let R. live, and let not his
*Jos*. 15:6 Boh. son of R. 18:17
22:13 Is. sent to children of R.
*Jud*. 5:15 divisions of R. 16
*Ezek*. 48:6 a portion for R. 31

**Tribe of REUBEN.**

*Num*. 1:5 of *t*. *of* R. Elizur, 21
13:4 of *tribe of* R. Shammua
34:14 *tribe of* R. have received
*Jos*. 20:8; 21:36; 1 *Chr*. 6:63, 78
*Rev*. 7:5 *tribe of* R. sealed 12,000

**REUBENITES.**

*Num*. 26:7 are the families of R.
*Deut*. 3:12, 16; 29:8; *Jos*. 12:6; 13:8
*Jos*. 1:12 Josh. spake to R. 22:1
2 *K*. 10:33 Hazael smote the R.

**REVEAL.**

*Job* 20:27 heaven sh. *r*. iniquity
*Jer*. 33:6 *r*. them abund. of peace
*Dan*. 2:47 couldest *r*. this secret
*Mat*. 11:27 he to whomsoever Son will *r*. him, *Lu*. 10:22
*Gal*. 1:16 called by grace to *r*. S.
*Phil*. 3:15 God sh. *r*. this unto y.

**REVEALED.**

*Deut*. 29:29 things *r*. to us
1 *Sam*. 3:7 word of Lord *r*. to h.
21 L. *r*. himself to Sam. in Sh.
2 *Sam*. 7:27 hast *r*. to thy serv.
*Is*. 22:14 *r*. in mine ears by L.
23:1 fr. Chittim it is *r*. to them
40:5 glory of the Lord sh. be *r*.
*Is*. 53:1 arm of L. *r*.? *John* 12:38
56:1 righteousness near to be *r*.
*Jer*. 11:20 unto thee I *r*. my cau.
*Dan*. 2:19 th. was secret *r*. to D.
10:1 a thing was *r*. to Daniel
*Mat*. 10:26 nothing covered that shall not be *r*. *Luke* 12:2
11:25 *r*. th. to babes, *Luke* 10:21
16:17 flesh and blood hath not *r*.
*Luke* 2:26 *r*. to Simeon by H. G.
35 thoughts of many hearts *r*.
17:30 day when Son of man is *r*.
*Rom*. 1:17 therein right. of G. *r*.
18 wrath of God is *r*. fr. heav.
8:18 glory which sh. be *r*. in us
1 *Cor*. 2:10 God *r*. them to us
3:13 bec. it shall be *r* by fire
14:30 if any thing be *r*. to ano.
*Gal*. 3:23 faith whi. should be *r*.
*Eph*. 3:5 now *r*. to holy apostles
2 *Thes*. 1:7 when L. J. shall be *r*.
2:3 and that man of sin be *r*.
6 he might be *r*. in his time
8 wick. one *r*. whom L. cons.
1 *Pet*. 1:5 to be *r*. in last time
12 unto whom it was *r*.
4:13 when his glory shall be *r*.
5:1 partaker of g. that sh. be *r*.

**REVEALER.**

*Dan*. 2:47 G. of gods, *r*. of secrets

**REVEALETH.**

*Prov*. 11:13 talebea. *r*. sec. 20:19
*Dan*. 2:22 *r*. deep and secret th.
28 G. in heaven that *r*. secrets
29 *r*. secrets maketh known

*Amos* 3:7 *r*. secrets to prophets

**REVELATION.**

*Rom*. 2:5 *r*. of judgment of God
16:25 according to *r*. of mystery
1 *Cor*. 14:6 sh. speak to you by *r*.
26 every one of you hath a *r*.
*Gal*. 1:12 by *r*. of Jesus Christ
2:2 went up by *r*. and commu.
*Eph*. 1:17 may give you sp. of *r*.
3:3 by *r*. he made known to me
1 *Pet*. 1:13 grace br. at *r*. of J. C.
*Rev*. 1:1 *r*. of J. C. wh. God gave

**REVELATIONS.**

2 *Cor*. 12:1 come to visions and *r*.
7 exalted thro. abundance of *r*.

**REVELLINGS.**

*Gal*. 5:21 works of the fle. are *r*.
1 *Pet*. 4:3 ye walked in lusts, *r*.

**REVENGE, ED, ETH.**

*Jer*. 20:10 we shall take *r*. on h.
*Ezek*. 25:12 Ed. *r*. himself on th.
15 Philistines have dealt by *r*.
*Nah*. 1:2 the Lord *r*. the Lord *r*.
2 *Cor*. 7:11 what *r*. is wr. in you

**REVENGER, S.**

*Num*. 35:19 *r*. sh. slay murde. 21
24 judge between slayer and *r*.
27 if *r*. find him and *r*. kill
2 *Sam*. 14:11 wouldest not suf. *r*.
*Rom*. 13:4 minister of God, a *r*.

**REVENGING.**

*Ps*. 79:10 by the *r*. of the blood

**REVENUE.**

*Ezr*. 4:13 thou sh. endamage *r*.
*Prov*. 8:19 my *r*. better than sil.
*Is*. 23:3 harvest of river is her *r*.

**REVENUES.**

*Prov*. 15:6 in *r*. of wick. is trou.
16:8 a little is better than gr. *r*.
*Jer*. 12:13 be ashamed of your *r*.

**REVERENCE, Verb.**

*Lev*. 19:30 *r*. sanct. I am L. 26:2
*Est*. 3:2 king's serv. *r*. Haman
*Mat*. 21:37 they will *r*. my son, *Mark* 12:6; *Luke* 20:13
*Eph*. 5:33 wife that she *r*. husb.

**REVERENCE.**

2 *Sam*. 9:6 Mephibosh. did *r*. Da.
1 *K*. 1:31 Bathsheba did *r*. king
*Est*. 3:2 Mord. did him not *r*. 5
*Ps*. 89:7 to be had in *r*. of all
*Heb*. 12:9 and we gave them *r*.
28 we may serve God with *r*.

**REVEREND.**

*Ps*. 111:9 holy and *r*. is his name

**REVERSE.**

*Num*. 23:20 be blessed, I can. *r*
*Est*. 8:5 let it be written to *r*.
8 with king's ring, no man *r*.

**REVILE.**

*Ex*. 22:28 thou shalt not *r*. gods
*Mat*. 5:11 blessed when men *r*.

**REVILED.**

*Mat*. 27:39 that passed by *r*. him
*Mark* 15:32 that were crucified *r*.
*John* 9:28 they *r*. him, and said
1 *Cor*. 4:12 being *r*. we bless
1 *Pet*. 2:23 when he was *r*. not

**REVILERS.**

1 *Cor*. 6:10 nor *r*. inh. king. of G.

**REVILEST.**

*Acts* 23:4 *r*. God's high-priest

**REVILINGS.**

*Is*. 51:7 neither afraid of their *r*.
*Zep*. 2:8 *r*. of child. of Ammon

**REVIVE.**

*Neh*. 4:2 will they *r*. the stones?
*Ps*. 85:6 wilt th. not *r*. us again
138:7 thou wilt *r*. me, th. shalt
*Is*. 57:15 *r*. spirit and to *r*. heart of contrite ones
*Hos*. 6:2 after days will he *r*. us
14:7 they shall *r*. as corn

*Hab.* 3:2 O Lord, *r.* thy work in

**REVIVED.**

*Gen.* 45:27 the spirit of Jacob *r.*
*Jud.* 15:19 spirit came ag. he *r.*
1 *K.* 17:22 soul of child ca. he *r.*
2 *K.* 13:21 touch. bones of Eli. *r.*
*Rom.* 7:9 command. came. sin *r.*
14:9 Ch. both died, rose, and *r.*

**REVIVING.**

*Ezr.* 9:8 to give us a little *r.* 9

**REVOLT.**

*Is.* 59:13 speaking oppres. and *r.*

**REVOLT, Verb.**

2 *Chr.* 21:10 same time did Li. *r.*
*Is.* 1:5 ye will *r.* more and more

**REVOLTED.**

2 *K.* 8:20 Edom *r.* 22: 2 *Chr.* 21:8
22 Libnah *r.* at the same time
*Is.* 31:6 Israel have deeply *r.*
*Jer.* 5:23 people are *r.* and gone

**REVOLTERS.**

*Jer.* 6:28 all grievous *r.* walking
*Hos.* 5:2 *r.* are profound to make
9:15 love no more, princes *r.*

**REVOLTING.**

*Jer.* 5:23 this peo. hath a *r.* hea.

**REWARD, Substantive.**

*Gen.* 15:1 Ab. I am thy great *r.*
*Num.* 18:31 it is your *r.* for serv.
*Deut.* 10:17 G. who taketh not *r.*
27:25 cursed that tak. *r.* to slay
*Ruth* 2:12 a full *r.* be given of L.
2 *Sam.* 4:10 wd. have giv. him *r.*
19:36 king recompense such a *r.*
1 *K.* 13:7 I will give thee a *r.*
*Job* 6:22 Bring me or give a *r.*
7:2 hireling look. for *r.* of work
*Ps.* 15:5 nor taketh *r.* ag. innoc.
19:11 keeping of them is gre. *r.*
40:15 let them be desolate for *r.*
58:11 there is a *r.* for righteous
70:3 let th. be turned back for *r.*
91:8 shalt see the *r.* of wicked
94:2 render a *r.* to the proud
119:20 let this be *r.* of adversa.
127:3 fruit of womb is his *r.*
*Prov.* 11:18 righteousn. a sure *r.*
21:14 a *r.* in bosom st. wrath
24:14 then there shall be a *r.*
20 shall be no *r.* to evil man
*Ec.* 4:9 they have a good *r.*
9:5 nei. have they any more *r.*
*Is.* 3:11 the *r.* of hands be given
5:23 which justify wicked for *r.*
40:10 his *r.* is with him, 62:11
45:13 go my captives, not for *r.*
*Jer.* 40:5 capt. gave Jeremiah *r.*
*Ezek.* 16:34 givest *r.* no *r.* given
*Hos.* 9:1 thou hast loved a *r.*
*Ob.* 15 thy *r.* shall return upon
*Mic.* 3:11 judge for *r.* priests
7:3 and judge asketh for a *r.*
*Mat.* 5:12 *r.* in heaven, *Luke* 6:23
46 love you, what *r.* have ye?
6:1 ye have no *r.* of your Father
2 they have their *r.* 5, 16
10:41 sh. receive a prophet's *r.*
sh. receive a right. man's *r.*
42 no wise lose *r.* *Mark* 9:41
*Luke* 6:35 your *r.* shall be great
23:41 we receive due *r.* of deeds
*Acts* 1:18 field with *r.* of iniqui.
*Rom* 4:4 to him that work. is *r.*
1 *Cor.* 3:8 man sh. receive his *r.*
14 abide, he shall receive a *r.*
9:17 if willingly, I have a *r.* 18
*Col.* 2:18 no man beg. you of *r.*
3:24 ye sh. receive *r.* of inherit.
1 *Tim.* 5:18 laborer worthy of *r.*
*Heb.* 2:2 recei. just recomp. of *r.*
10:35 great recompense of *r.*
11:26 he had respect to the *r.*
2 *Pet.* 2:13 shall receive the *r.* of
2 *John* 8 that we receive a full *r.*
*Jude* 11 after error of Bal. for *r.*
*Rev.* 11:18 thou shouldest give *r.*
22:12 I come quickly, my *r.* is

**REWARD, Verb.**

*Deut.* 32:41 and I will *r.* them
1 *Sam.* 24:19 Lord *r.* thee good
2 *Sam.* 3:39 L. sh. *r.* doer of evil
2 *Chr.* 20:11 behold how th. *r.* us
*Ps.* 54:5 shall *r.* evil to enemies
*Prov.* 25:22 the L. shall *r.* thee
*Hos.* 4:9 and I will *r.* them their
*Mat.* 6:4 Father sh. *r.* thee, 6:18
16:27 he shall *r.* every man
2 *Tim.* 4:14 Lord *r.* him accord.
*Rev.* 18:6 *r.* her, even as she rew.

**REWARDED.**

*Gen.* 44:4 wheref. have ye *r.* evil
1 *Sam.* 24:17 th. *r.* good, I *r.* evil
2 *Sam.* 22:21 L. *r.* me ac. *Ps.* 18:20
2 *Chr.* 15:7 your work shall be *r.*
*Ps.* 7:4 if I have *r.* evil to him
35:12 th. *r.* evil for good, 109:5
103:10 nor *r.* us accord. to iniq.
*Prov.* 13:13 feareth com. be *r.*
*Is.* 3:9 they have *r.* evil to them.
*Jer.* 31:16 work sh. be *r.* saith L.
*Rev.* 18:6 even as she *r.* you

**REWARDER.**

*Heb.* 11:6 a *r.* of them that seek

**REWARDETH.**

*Job* 21:19 he *r.* him, sh. know it
*Ps.* 31:23 plentifully *r.* proud
137:8 happy he that *r.* thee, as
*Prov.* 17:13 whoso *r.* evil for go.
6:10 both *r.* fool and *r.* transgr.

**REWARDS.**

*Num.* 22:7 with *r.* divination
*Is.* 1:23 every one followeth *r.*
*Dan.* 2:6 rec. of me gifts, and *r.*
5:17 said, give thy *r.* to another
*Hos.* 2:12 these are my *r.*

**REZIN.**

2 *K.* 15:37 R. the king, 16:5; *Is.* 7:1
16:6 R. recovered Elath to, 9
*Ezr.* 2:48 childr. of R. *Neh.* 7:50
*Is.* 7:4 the fierce anger of R. 8
8:6 as this people rejoice in R.
9:11 set up the adversaries of R.

**RHEGIUM.**

*Acts* 28:13 comp. and came to R.

**RHESA.**

*Luke* 3:27 who was the son of R.

**RHODA.**

*Acts* 12:13 to hearken named R.

**RHODES.**

*Acts* 21:1 we came unto R.

**RIB, S.**

*Gen.* 2:21 God took one of his *r.*
22 the *r.* which God had taken
2 *Sam.* 3:23 sm. A. under fifth *r.*
3:27 J. smote Ab. under fifth *r.*
4:6 smote Ishbosh. under fifth *r.*
20:10 J. smote Ama. un. fifth *r.*
*Dan.* 7:5 beast had *r.* in mouth

**RIBBAND.**

*Num.* 15:38 on fring. of bord. a *r.*

**RICH.**

*Gen.* 13:2 Abram was *r.* in cattle
14:23 lest say, I ha. made A. *r.*
*Ex.* 30:15 *r.* shall not give more
*Lev.* 25:47 if a stranger wax *r.*
*Ruth* 3:10 fol. not men poor or *r.*
1 *Sam.* 2:7 L. maketh poor and *r.*
2 *Sam.* 12:1 two men in city, 1 *r.*
*Job* 15:29 he shall not be *r.* nei.
34:19 nor regardeth the *r.* more
*Ps.* 45:12 *r.* shall entreat favor
49:2 hear this, both *r.* and poor
16 be not afraid when one is *r.*
*Prov.* 10:4 hand of dilig. mak. *r.*
22 blessing of Lord, maketh *r.*
13:7 there is that mak. hims. *r.*
14:20 the *r.* hath many friends
18:23 the *r.* answereth roughly
21:17 lov. wine and oil not *r.*
22:2 *r.* and poor meet together
7 the *r.* ruleth over the poor
16 giveth to *r.* shall come to
23:4 labor not to be *r.* cease
28:6 perverse, though he be *r.*
20 he maketh haste to be *r.* 22
*Ec.* 5:12 abund. of *r.* not suffer
10:6 and the *r.* sit in low place
20 curse not *r.* in thy bedcham.
*Is.* 53:9 and with *r.* in his death
*Jer.* 5:27 are great and waxen *r.*
*Hos.* 12:8 Ephraim said, I am *r.*
*Zec.* 11:5 bless. be L. for I am *r.*
*Mark* 12:41 many that were *r.*
*Luke* 1:53 the *r.* he sent away
6:24 woe unto you that are *r.*
12:21 that is not *r.* toward God
14:12 call not thy *r.* neighbors
18:23 sorrowful, he was very *r.*
*Rom.* 10:12 same Lord is *r.* to all
1 *Cor.* 4:8 are full, now ye are *r.*
2 *Cor.* 6:10 yet making many *r.*
8:9 *r.* yet poor, ye might be *r.*
*Eph.* 2:4 God who is *r.* in mercy
1 *Tim.* 6:9 they th. will be *r.* fall
17 charge th. that are *r.* in this
18 and be *r.* in good works
*Jam.* 1:10 let the *r.* rejoice in th.
2:5 G. chosen poor, *r.* in faith?
*Rev.* 2:9 I know pov. thou art *r.*
3:17 bec. thou sayest I am *r.* and
13:16 he causeth the *r.* and poor
18:19 made *r.* all that had ships

**RICH man, or men.**

2 *Sam.* 12:2 *r. man* had many fl.
*Job* 27:19 *r. man* shall lie down
*Prov.* 10:15 *r. man's* wealth is his strong city, 18:11
28:11 *r.* man is wise in his own
*Jer.* 9:23 let not the *r. man* glory
*Mic.* 6:12 *r. men* thereof are full
*Mat.* 19:23 *r. m.* sh. hardly enter
24 than a *r. m.* to enter kingd. of God, *Mark* 10:25; *Lu.* 18:25
27:57 a *r. man* of Arimathea
*Luke* 12:16 ground of *r. man* bro.
16:1 a certain *r. m.* had a stew.
19 a *r. man* was clo. in purple
21:1 and saw the *r. man* casting
*Jam.* 1:11 so shall the *r. m.* fade
2:6 do not *r. men* oppress you?
5:1 ye *r. men*, weep and howl
*Rev.* 6:15 *r. men* hid themselves

**RICHER.**

*Dan.* 11:2 the fourth sh. be far *r.*

**RICHES.**

*Gen.* 31:16 the *r.* G. hath taken
36:7 *r.* more than they might
*Jos.* 22:8 return with much *r.*
1 *Sam.* 17:25 enrich with great *r.*
1 *K.* 3:11 neither hast asked *r.* 2 *Chr.* 1:11
13 giv. thee both *r.* and honor
10:23 Solom. exceeded all kings of earth for *r.* 2 *Chr.* 9:22
1 *Chr.* 29:12 *r.* and honor come
28 David died full of days, *r.*
2 *Chr.* 17:5 *r.* and honor, 18:1
20:25 found *r.* with dead bodies
32:27 Hezek. had exceeding *r.*
*Est.* 1:4 showed *r.* of kingdom
5:11 Haman told them of his *r.*
*Job* 20:15 he swallowed down *r.*
36:19 will he esteem thy *r.*?
*Ps.* 37:16 bet. than *r.* of wicked
39:6 heapeth up *r.* knoweth not
49:6 boast themselves in th. *r.*
52:7 trusted in abund. of his *r.*
62:10 if *r.* increase, set not heart
73:12 ungodly prosper, incr. *r.*
104:24 O Lord, earth is full of *r.*
112:3 wealth and *r.* in his house
119:14 rejo. as much as in all *r.*
*Prov.* 3:16 in her left hand *r.*
8:18 *r.* and honor are with me

11:4 *r.* profit not in day of wra.
16 wom. honor, strong men *r.*
28 he that trust. in *r.* shall fall
13:7 himself poor, hath great *r*
8 ransom of man's life his *r.*
14:24 crown of wise is their *r.*
19:14 *r.* are inheritance of fath.
22:1 good name rather than *r.*
4 by the fear of the Lord are *r.*
16 oppres. poor to increase *r.*
23:5 for *r.* make themselves wi.
24:4 cham. be filled with all *r.*
27:24 for *r.* are not for ever
30:8 gi. me nei. poverty nor *r.*
*Ec.* 4:8 nor his eyes sati. with *r.*
5:13 even *r.* kept for owners
19 man whom G. given *r.* 6:2
9:11 nor yet *r.* to men of under.
*Is.* 8:4 *r.* of Damasc. taken away
10:14 hand found as a nest *r.*
30:6 carry their *r.* on yo. asses
45:3 I will give thee hidden *r.*
61:6 ye shall eat *r.* of Gentiles
*Jer.* 9:23 let not rich man gl. in *r.*
17:11 he that get. *r.* not by rig.
48:36 *r.* he hath gotten perished
*Ezek.* 26:12 make a spoil of thy *r.*
28:4 with understanding got. *r.*
5 by thy traffic increased *r.*
*Dan.* 11:2 thro' his *r.* sh. stir up
24 scat. am. prey, spoil and *r.*
28 then shall he return with *r.*
*Mat.* 13:22 deceitful. of *r.* choke
word, *Mark* 4:19; *Luke* 8:14
*Mark* 10:23 hardly th. that ha. *r.*
24 them that trust in *r.* to enter, *Luke* 18:24
*Luke* 16:11 who will commit *r.?*
*Rom.* 2:4 or despiseth thou *r.?*
9:23 make kn. *r.* of his glory
11:12 if fall of them be the *r.*
33 O the *r.* of the wisd. of God
2 *Cor.* 8:2 to *r.* of their liberality
*Eph.* 1:7 redemption accor. to *r.*
*Eph.* 1:18 *r.* of glory of inherita.
2:7 exceeding *r.* of his grace
3:8 I should preach unsearch. *r.*
16 grant you accord. to the *r.*
*Phil.* 4:19 accord. to *r.* in glory
*Col.* 1:27 what *r.* of the glory
1 *Tim.* 6:17 nor trust in uncer. *r.*
*Heb.* 11:26 repro. of C. greater *r.*
*Jam.* 5:2 your *r.* are corrupted
*Rev.* 5:12 worthy Lamb to rec. *r.*
18:17 great *r.* come to naught

**RICHLY.**

*Col.* 3:16 let word of C. dwell *r.*
1 *Tim.* 6:17 God who giveth *r.*

**RID.**

*Gen.* 37:22 that he might *r.* him
*Ex.* 6:6 *r.* you out of bondage
*Lev.* 26:6 *r.* evil beasts out land
*Ps.* 82:4 *r.* them out of wicked
144:7 *r.* me, and deliver me, 11

**RIDDANCE.**

*Lev.* 23:22 th. shalt not make *r.*
*Zep.* 1:18 shall make speedy *r.*

**RIDDEN.**

*Num.* 22:30 ass, wh. thou ha. *r.?*

**RIDDLE.**

*Jud.* 14:12 Sam. said, I will now put forth a *r.* to you, 13-19
*Ezek.* 17:2 put forth a *r.* speak.

**RIDE.**

*Gen.* 41:43 made him *r.* in char.
*Deut.* 32:13 made him *r.* on high
*Jud.* 5:10 that *r.* on white asses
2 *Sam.* 16:2 king's hous. to *r.* on
19:26 saddle ass that I may *r.*
1 *K.* 1:33 cause Solo. to *r.* 38, 44
2 *K.* 10:16 so th. made him to *r.*
*Job* 30:22 thou causest me to *r.*
*Ps.* 45:4 and in thy majesty *r.*
66:12 thou hast caused me to *r.*
*Is.* 30:16 we will *r.* upon swift
58:14 I will cause thee to *r.*
*Jer.* 6:23 *r.* on horses, 50:42
*Hos.* 10:11 will make Eph. to *r.*
14:3 we will not *r.* upon horses
*Hab.* 3:8 didst *r.* upon thy horses
*Hag.* 2:22 overthrow those th. *r.*

**RIDER.**

*Gen.* 49:17 so that *r.* shall fall
*Ex.* 15:1 horse and *r.* thrown, 21
*Job* 39:18 scorneth horse and *r.*
*Jer.* 51:21 *r.* break in pieces cha.
*Zec.* 12:4 smite *r.* with madness

**RIDERS.**

2 *K.* 18:23 if thou be able to set *r.* on them, *Is.* 36:8
*Est.* 8:10 he sent letters by *r.*
*Hag.* 2:22 horses and *r.* co. down
*Zec.* 10:5 *r.* shall be confounded

**RIDETH.**

*Deut.* 33:26 who *r.* upon heaven
*Est.* 6:8 horse king *r.* upon
*Ps.* 68:4 extol him that *r.* 23
*Is.* 19:1 the L. *r.* on a swift cloud
*Amos* 2:15 neither shall he that *r.*

**RIDING.**

2 *K.* 4:24 slack not thy *r.* for me
*Jer.* 17:25 kings enter *r.* 22:4
*Ezek.* 23:6 horsem. *r.* on hors. 12
23 all of them *r.* upon horses
38:15 thou and many people *r.*
*Zec.* 1:8 a man *r.* on a red horse
9:9 thy king com. unto thee *r.*

**RIDGES.**

*Ps.* 65:10 thou waterest *r.* thereof

**RIFLED.**

*Zec.* 14:2 houses *r.* wom. ravish.

**RIGHT, Substantive.**

*Gen.* 18:25 shall not the Judge of all the earth do *r.?*
*Deut.* 21:17 *r.* of first-born is his
*Ruth* 4:6 redeem thou my *r.*
2 *Sam.* 19:43 we ha. also more *r.*
*Neh.* 9:33 for thou hast done *r.*
*Job* 34:6 should I lie ag. my *r.?*
17 sh. he th. hateth *r.* govern?
36:6 he giveth *r.* to the poor
*Ps.* 9:4 hast maintained my *r.*
17:1 hear *r.* O Lo. attend to cry
140:12 L. maintain *r.* of poor
*Prov.* 16:8 great reve. without *r.*
13 they love him that speak. *r.*
*Is.* 10:2 to take away *r.* from
32:7 dest. when needy speak. *r.*
*Jer.* 5:28 *r.* of needy do not jud.
17:11 getteth riches not by *r.*
32:7 *r.* of redemption is thi. 8
*Lam.* 3:35 turn aside *r.* of man
*Ezek.* 21:27 he come whose *r.* it
*Amos* 5:12 turn poor from th. *r.*
*Mal.* 3:5 turn strang. from his *r.*
*Heb.* 13:10 they have no *r.* to eat
*Rev.* 22:14 have *r.* to tree of life

**RIGHT, Adjective.**

*Gen.* 24:48 L. led me in *r.* way
*Deut.* 32:4 G. of truth, just and *r.*
1 *Sam.* 12:23 teach you *r.* way
2 *Sam.* 15:3 matter good and *r.*
2 *K.* 10:15 is thy heart *r.* as my?
*Ezr.* 8:21 seek of him a *r.* way
*Neh.* 9:13 then gavest *r.* judgm.
*Job* 6:25 how forc. are *r.* words!
34:23 not lay on man mo. th. *r.*
35:2 thinkest thou th. to be *r.?*
*Ps.* 19:8 stat. of the Lord are *r.*
45:6 sceptre of thy king. *r.* sce.
51:10 O G. renew a *r.* sp. in me
107:7 led them forth by *r.* way
119:75 judgm. *r.* 128 precepts
*Prov.* 4:11 led thee in *r.* paths
8:6 opening of my lips sh. be *r.*
9 *r.* to them that find knowle.
12:5 thoughts of righteous are *r.*
14:12 way wh. seemeth *r.* 16:25
20:11 whether his work be *r.*
24:26 that giveth a *r.* answer
*Ec.* 4:4 I consid. every *r.* work
*Is.* 30:10 proph. not to us *r.* thin.
45:19 L. dec. things that are *r.*
*Jer.* 2:21 planted thee *r.* seed
23:10 and their force is not *r.*
34:15 had done *r.* in my sight
*Hos.* 14:9 ways of the Lord are *r.*
*Amos* 3:10 th. know not to do *r.*
*Mark* 5:15 his *r.* mind, *Luke* 8:35
*Acts* 4:19 whe. *r.* in sight of God
8:21 heart is not *r.* in sig. of G.
13:10 not cease to perv. *r.* ways

**Is RIGHT.**

*Ex.* 15:26 do that which *is r.*
*Deut.* 6:18 thou shalt do that *is r.* 12:25; 21:9
12:8 what *is r.* in own eyes
1 *K.* 11:33 walked to do that *r.* 38
2 *K.* 10:30 that *is r.* in my eyes
*Job* 42:7 not spoken that *is r.* 8
*Ps.* 33:4 word of the Lord *is r.*
*Prov.* 12:15 way of the fool *is r.*
21:2 way of man *is r.* in his eyes
8 for pure, his work *is r.*
*Ezek.* 18:5 if a man do that *is r.*
19 done that *is r.* and kept my stat. 21:27; 33:14, 16, 19
*Mat.* 20:4 what. *is r.* I will gi. 7.
*Luke* 12:57 judge ye not wh. *r.?*
*Eph.* 6:1 obey par. in L. this *is r.*

**Was RIGHT.**

*Jud* 17:6 ev. man did that which *was r.* in own eyes, 21:25
1 *K.* 15:11 Asa did *r.* 2 *Chr.* 14:2
22:43 Jehos. did *r.* 2 *Chr.* 20:32
2 *K.* 12:2 Jeh. did *r.* 2 *Chr.* 24:2
14:3 Amaziah did *r.* 2 *Chr.* 25:2
15:3 Azariah did *r.* 2 *Chr.* 26:4
34 Jotham did *r.* 2 *Chr.* 27:2
16:2 A. did not *r.* in sight of L.
18:3 Hezekiah did *r.* 2 *Chr.* 29:2
22:2 Josiah did *r.* 2 *Chr.* 34:2
1 *Chr.* 13:4 *was r.* in eyes of peo.
*Job* 33:27 pervert. that wh. *w. r.*
*Ps.* 78:37 heart *was* not *r.*
*Jer.* 17:16 came out of lips *w. r.*

**RIGHT.**

*Jos.* 3:16 people passed *r.* ag. J.

**RIGHT corner.**

2 *K.* 11:11 guard stood rou. *r. c.*

*See* FOOT, HAND.

**RIGHT forth.**

*Jer.* 49:5 be driven eve. man *r. f.*

**RIGHT well.**

*Ps.* 139:14 soul knoweth *r. well*

**RIGHTEOUS.**

*Gen.* 7:1 thee ha. I seen *r.* be. me
18:23 wilt destroy *r.* with wic.?
24 if th. be 50 *r.* wilt thou? 26
25 be far from thee to slay *r.*
20:4 L. wilt thou slay a *r.* natl.
38:26 said, She more *r.* than I
*Ex.* 23:7 innocent and *r.* sl. not
*Num.* 23:10 let me die death of *r.*
*Deut.* 4:8 nation ha. judg. so *r.*
25:1 shall justify *r.* 2 *Chr.* 6:23
*Jud.* 5:11 *r.* acts, 1 *Sam.* 12:7
1 *Sam.* 24:17 thou more *r.* than I
2 *Sam.* 4:11 wick. slain *r.* person
1 *K.* 2:32 fell on two men more *r.*
8:32 justifying *r.* to give him
2 *K.* 10:9 Jehu said to peo. Be *r.*
*Ezr.* 9:15 G. of Israel *r.* *Neh.* 9:8
*Job* 4:7 where were *r.* cut off?
9:15 tho' I we. *r.* would not an.
10:15 if I be *r.* not lift up head
15:14 what is man, he be *r.?*
17:9 *r.* also sh. hold on his w.
22:3 is it pleas. to A. th. art *r.?*
19 *r.* see it, glad, *Ps.* 107:42
23:7 *r.* might dispute with him
32:1 he was *r.* in his own eyes
*Job* 34:5 Job hath said, I am *r.*
35:7 if thou be *r.* what giv. thou
36:7 wit. not eyes fr. *r.* *Ps.* 34:15
40:8 cond. me that thou be *r.*

*Ps.* 1:5 nor sinners in cong. of *r.*
6 Lord knoweth way of the *r.*
5:12 wilt bless *r.* with favor
7:9 *r.* G. trieth hearts and reins
11 G. jud. *r.* angry wi. wicked
11:3 what can *r.* do? 5 L. tri. *r.*
14:5 God is in generation of *r.*
19:9 judgments of L. are true
and *r.* 119:7, 62, 106, 160, 164
31:18 lips speak against the *r.*
32:11 be glad in Lord, rej. ye *r.*
33:1 rejoice in L. O ye *r.* 97:12
34:17 *r.* cry, L. heareth them
19 ma. are the afflictions of *r.*
21 that hate *r.* sh. be desolate
35:27 glad that favor *r.* cause
37:17 but Lord upholdeth the *r.*
21 but the *r.* showeth mercy
25 have I not seen *r.* forsaken
30 mouth of *r.* speaketh wisd.
32 wicked watch *r.* to slay him
39 salvation of the *r.* is of Lo.
52:6 *r.* also shall see, fear, laugh
55:22 never suff. *r.* to be moved
58:10 *r.* rejoice, he seeth veng.
11 there is a reward for the *r.*
64:10 *r.* shall be glad in the L.
68:3 let *r.* be glad, let them rej.
69:28 let them not be wri. wi. *r.*
72:7 in his days sh. *r.* flourish
94:21 gather against soul of *r.*
112:4 L. full of compas. *r.* 116:5
6 *r.* be in everl. remembrance
118:15 rejoicing in tabern. of *r.*
20 gate, into which *r.* sh. ent.
119:106 keep thy *r.* judgments
137 *r.* art thou, O Lo. *Jer.* 12:1
138 thy testimonials are *r.*
125:3 rod of wicked sh. not rest
on *r.* lest *r.* put forth hands
140:13 *r.* give thanks to thy na.
141:5 let *r.* smite, kindness
142:7 *r.* shall compass me about
145:17 Lord *r.* in all his ways
146:8 Lord loveth *r.* preserveth
*Prov.* 2:7 layeth up wisd. for *r.*
20 mayest keep paths of *r.*
10:3 will not suffer *r.* to famish
16 labor of *r.* tendeth to life
21 the lips of the *r.* feed many
24 desire of *r.* shall be granted
25 *r.* is an everlasting founda.
28 hope of *r.* sh. be gladness
30 *r.* shall never be removed
32 lips of *r.* kn. what is accep.
11:8 *r.* is deliv. out of trouble.
10 well with *r.* city rejoiceth
21 seed of *r.* shall be delivered
23 desire of the *r.* is only good
28 *r.* shall flourish as a branch
31 *r.* be recompensed in earth
12:3 root of *r.* sh. not be moved
5 thoughts of the *r.* are right
7 house of the *r.* shall stand
12 root of the *r.* yieldeth fruit
26 *r.* is more excel. than neigh.
13:9 light of the *r.* rejoiceth
21 to *r.* good shall be repaid
25 *r.* eat. to satisfying of soul
14:9 among the *r.* there is favor
32 the *r.* hath hope in his dea.
15:6 in house of *r.* is much tre.
19 way of the *r.* is made plain
28 heart of *r.* studieth to ans.
29 he heareth the prayer of *r.*
18:5 not good to overthrow *r.*
10 *r.* runneth into it, is safe
21:18 shall be ransom for *r.*
26 *r.* giveth and spareth not
23:24 fath. of *r.* greatly rejoice
24:15 lay not wait ag. dwe. of *r.*
24 saith to wicked, Thou art *r.*
28:1 wicked flee, but *r.* bold
10 causeth *r.* to go astray
28 when wicked perish, *r.* inc.
29:2 *r.* in authority peo. rejoice
6 the *r.* doth sing and rejoice
7 *r.* considereth cause of poor

16 the *r.* shall see their fall
*Ec.* 3:17 G. judge *r.* and wicked
7:16 be not *r.* overmuch
9:1 *r.* and wise in hand of God
2 one event to *r.* and wicked
*Is.* 3:10 say to *r.* it be well
24:16 heard songs, glory to *r.*
26:2 open ye, that *r.* may enter
41:26 declared, we say, He is *r.*
53:11 *r.* serv. shall justify many
57:1 *r.* peri. *r.* taken from evil
60:21 people also shall be all *r.*
*Jer.* 12:1 *r.* art thou, O L. I plead
20:12 O Lord of hosts triest *r.*
*Ezek.* 13:22 with lies made *r.* sad
21:3 cut off *r.* and wicked, 4
*Ezek.* 21:13 wh. I say to *r.* he sh.
*Amos* 2:6 they sold *r.* for silver
*Hab.* 1:4 wicked comp. about *r.*
13 wicked devou. him more *r.*
*Mal.* 3:18 discern between *r.* and
*Mat.* 9:13 not come to call the *r.*
*Mark* 2:17; *Luke* 5:32
13:43 *r.* shine forth as sun
23:28 outwardly ap. *r.* to men
25:46 *r.* sh. go into life eternal
*Luke* 1:6 they were both *r.* bef. G.
18:9 trusted they were *r.*
*John* 7:24 judge not by ap. but *r.*
17:25 O *r.* F. world not known
*Rom.* 2:5 revel. of *r.* judg. of G.
3:10 there is none *r.* no not one
5:19 obed. of one, many made *r.*
2 *Tim.* 4:8 *r.* Judge shall give
*Heb.* 11:4 obt. witness he was *r.*
1 *Pet.* 3:12 eyes of L. are over *r.*
4:18 if *r.* scarcely be saved
2 *Pet.* 2:8 Lot vexed his *r.* soul
1 *John* 2:29 if ye know he is *r.*
3:7 doeth right. is *r.* as he is *r.*
12 his works evil, brother's *r.*
*Rev.* 16:5 angel say, Thou *r.*
7 O L. true and *r.* thy judgm.
22:11 that is *r.* let him be *r.* still
*See* LORD *is.*

**RIGHTEOUS man, *or* men.**

*Ps.* 37:16 lit. *r. m.* hath is better
*Prov.* 10:11 mo. of *r. m.* is a well
13:5 a *r. man* hateth lying
21:12 *r. m.* wisely consi. house
25:26 a *r. m.* falling bef. wicked
28:12 when *r. m.* rejoice, glory
*Is.* 41:2 raised *r. m.* from east
*Ezek.* 3:20 *r. m.* doth turn, 18:26
23:45 *r. m.* they sh. judge them
*Mat.* 10:41 that receiveth a *r. m.*
in name of *r. m.* rec. *r. m.'s*
13:17 *r. men* desi. to see things
*Luke* 23:47 cert. this was a *r. m.*
*Rom.* 5:7 for *r. m.* will one die
1 *Tim.* 1:9 law not made for *r. m.*
2 *Pet.* 2:8 *r. m.* dwelling am. th.

**RIGHTEOUSLY.**

*Deut.* 1:16 judge *r.* *Prov.* 31:9
*Ps.* 67:4 sh. judge peo. *r.* 96:10
*Is.* 33:15 walk. *r.* sh. dwell high
*Jer.* 11:20 O Lord that judgest *r.*
*Tit.* 2:12 should live soberly, *r.*
1 *Pet.* 2:23 to him that judgeth *r.*

**RIGHTEOUSNESS.**

*Deut.* 6:25 it shall be our *r.*
24:13 shall be *r.* to thee bef. L.
33:19 shall offer sacrifices of *r.*
*Job* 29:14 I put on *r.* clothed me
36:3 ascribe *r.* to my Maker
*Ps.* 4:5 offer the sacrifices of *r.*
11:7 right. Lord loveth *r.* 33:5
15:2 worketh *r.* never be moved
23:3 leadeth me in paths of *r.*
24:5 *r.* fr. God of his salvation
40:9 I preached *r.* in congrega.
45:4 bec. of truth, meekness, *r.*
7 lovest *r.* hatest, *Heb.* 1:9
48:10 r. hand, O G. is full of *r.*
51:19 pleased with sacrifi. of *r.*
52:3 lying, rather than speak *r.*
58:1 speak *r.* O congregation?

72:2 shall judge people with *r.*
3 moun. bring peace, hills *r.*
85:10 *r.* and peace kis. each oth.
13 *r.* go before him
94:15 judgment shall ret. unto *r.*
96:13 he judge world wi. *r.* 98:9
97:2 *r.* habitation of his throne
99:4 executest *r.* J. 103:6
106:3 blessed is he that doeth *r.*
118:19 open to me gates of *r.*
119:144 *r.* of thy testimonies
172 all thy commandm. are *r.*
132:9 priests be clothed with *r.*
*Prov.* 2:9 sh. thou understand *r.*
8:18 durable riches, *r.* with me
20 I lead in the way of *r.*
10:2 *r.* deliver. from death, 11:4
11:5 *r.* of perfect direct his way
6 *r.* of upright shall del. them
18 to him that soweth *r.* rew.
19 as *r.* tend. to life, so he that
12:17 speaketh truth, show. *r.*
28 the way of *r.* life, in path.
13:6 *r.* keepeth him that is upr.
14:34 *r.* exalteth a nation, sin
15:9 he loveth him that fol. *r.*
16:8 bet. is a little with *r.* than
12 throne is established by *r.*
31 glory, if found in way of *r.*
21:21 followeth *r.* find. life, *r.*
*Ec.* 3:16 place of *r.* iniq. there
*Is.* 1:21 *r.* lodged in it
26 city of *r.* 27 converts wi. *r.*
5:23 take away *r.* of righteous
10:22 consum. overflow with *r.*
11:4 with *r.* shall he judge poor
*Is.* 11:5 *r.* be the girdle of his lo.
16:5 judgment, and hasting *r.*
26:9 inhab. of world will learn *r.*
10 showed, he will not learn *r.*
28:17 *r.* will I lay to plummet
32:16 *r.* shall remain in fruitful
17 work of *r.* peace; of *r.* quie.
33:5 the Lord filled Zion with *r.*
45:8 skies pour *r.* let *r.* spring
19 I the L. speak *r.* I declare
24 in the Lord have I *r.*
46:12 ye that are far from *r.*
51:1 follow *r.* 7 ye that know *r.*
54:17 their *r.* is of me, saith L.
58:2 seek me as a nation did *r.*
59:17 he put on *r.* as breastpl.
60:17 officers peace, exactors *r.*
61:3 might be called trees of *r.*
10 covered me with robe of *r.*
11 Lord will cause *r.* and pra.
63:1 until the *r.* thereof go forth
64:5 rejoiceth and worketh *r.*
*Jer.* 9:24 I Lord wh. exercise *r.*
22:3 execute ye judgm. and *r.*
23:6 name, Lord our *r.* 33:16
33:15 branch of *r.* to execute *r.*
51:10 Lord brought forth our *r.*
*Ezek.* 14:14 deliver souls by *r.* 20
18:20 *r.* of the righteous sh. be
33:12 *r.* of right. sh. not deliver
*Dan.* 4:27 break off thy sins by *r.*
9:7 O Lord *r.* belongeth to thee
24 bring in everlasting *r.*
12:3 they that turn many to *r.*
*Hos.* 10:12 he come and rain *r.*
*Amos* 5:7 who will leave off *r.* in
24 let *r.* run down as a stream
6:12 have turned fruit of *r.* to
*Mic.* 6:5 may know the *r.* of L.
*Zep.* 2:3 meek of earth seek *r.*
*Mal.* 4:2 shall Sun of *r.* arise
*Mat.* 3:15 becometh us to fulfil *r.*
5:6 hunger and thirst after *r.*
20 except *r.* exc. *r.* of scribes
21:32 John came in way of *r.*
*Luke* 1:75 in *r.* bef. him all days
*John* 16:8 rep. world of sin and *r.*
*Acts* 10:35 he that worketh *r.* is
13:10 enemy of all *r.* wilt th.?
24:25 reasoned of *r.* and judgm.
*Rom.* 1:17 therein is the *r.* of G.
2:26 uncircum. keep *r.* of law

3:5 unright. commend *r.* of G.
21 *r.* of God without the law
22 even the *r.* of God which is
4:6 to whom God imputed *r.*
11 seal of *r.* of the faith, that *r.* might be imputed to them
13 promise was thro' *r.* of faith
5:17 which receive gift of *r.*
18 so by *r.* of one the free gift
21 grace reign thro' *r.* to eter.
6:13 instruments of *r.* to God
16 sin to death, obed. unto *r.*
18 ye became the servants of *r.*
19 yield memb. servants to *r.*
20 were serv. of sin, free fr. *r.*
8:4 *r.* of law might be fulfilled
10 Spirit is life because of *r.*
9:30 have attained to *r.* even *r.*
31 Israel followed after *r.* hath not attained to the law of *r.*
10:3 establish their own *r.* have not submitted to the *r.* of G.
5 Moses desc. the *r.* of law
6 *r.* which is of faith speaketh
10 with heart man believ. to *r.*
14:17 not meat and drink, *r.*
1 *Cor.* 1:30 of God who is made *r.*
15:34 awake to *r.* and sin not
2 *Cor.* 3:9 much more minis. of *r.*
5:21 might be made *r.* of God
6:7 armor of *r.* on right hand
14 what fellowship hath *r.* wi.
9:10 increase fruits of your *r.*
11:15 transformed as mini. of *r.*
*Gal.* 2:21 if *r.* come by law, Ch.
3:21 *r.* should have been by law
5:5 we thro' Spirit wait for *r.*
*Eph.* 5:9 fruit of Sp. is *r.* and tr.
6:14 having the breastplate of *r.*
*Phil.* 1:11 filled with fruits of *r.*
3:6 touching *r.* which is in law
9 the *r.* which is of G. by faith
1 *Tim.* 6:11 fol. aft. *r.* 2 *Tim.* 2:22
2 *Tim.* 4:8 laid up a crown of *r.*
*Tit.* 3:5 not by works of *r.*
*Heb.* 1:8 sceptre of *r.* is sceptre
5:13 is unskilful in word of *r.*
7:2 by interpretation king of *r.*
11:7 became heir of *r.* by faith
33 subdued kingd. wrought *r.*
12:11 yieldeth peace. fruit of *r.*
*Jam.* 1:20 worketh not *r.* of God
3:18 fruit of *r.* is sown in peace
1 *Pet.* 2:24 dead to sin live to *r.*
2 *Pet.* 1:1 faith through *r.* of God
2:5 save Noe a preacher of *r.*
2 *Pet.* 2:21 bet. not kn. way of *r.*
3:13 new earth, wherein dw. *r.*
1 *John* 2:29 doeth *r.* born of God
3:7 he that doeth *r.* is righteous
10 doeth not *r.* is not of God
*Rev.* 19:8 fine linen *r.* of saints

**For RIGHTEOUSNESS.**

*Gen.* 15:6 Ab. believ. L. counted to him *f. r.* *Ps.* 106:31; *Rom.* 4:3
*Ps.* 143:11 *for* thy *r.* sake bring
*Is.* 5:7 looked *for r.* but behold
*Mat.* 5:10 wh. are persecuted *f. r.*
*Rom.* 4:5 counted *f. r.* *Gal.* 3:6
9 reckoned to Abraham *for r.*
22 imp. to him *f. r.* *Jam.* 2:23
10:4 Ch. is the end of law *f. r.*
1 *Pet.* 3:14 if ye suffer *for r.* sake

**His RIGHTEOUSNESS.**

1 *Sam.* 26:23 L. render ev. *his r.*
1 *K.* 8:32 acc. to *h. r.* 2 *Chr.* 6:23
*Job* 33:26 will render man *his r.*
*Ps.* 7:17 praise L. acc. to *his r.*
22:31 they shall declare *his r.*
50:6 the heav. declare *his r.* 97:6
98:2 *his r.* hath openly showed
103:17 *h. r.* to children's child.
111:3 *h. r.* end. for ever, 112:3, 9
*Ec.* 7:15 just man perish in *his r.*
*Is.* 42:21 pleased for *his r.* sake
59:16 and *his r.* sustained him
*Ezek.* 3:20 turn fr. *h. r.* 18:24, 26
18:22 *his r.* that he hath done
33:12 not able to live for *his r.*
13 if he trust *his* own *r.* and commit iniq. *his r.* not rem.
*Mic.* 7:9 and I shall behold *his r.*
*Mat.* 6:33 seek king. of G. *h. r.*
*Rom.* 3:25 to declare *his r.* 26
2 *Cor.* 9:9 given to poor *his r.*

**In RIGHTEOUSNESS.**

*Lev.* 19:15 *in r.* shalt thou judge
1 *K.* 3:6 walk. in truth and *in r.*
*Ps.* 9:8 he shall judge world *in r.*
17:15 I will beh. thy face *in r.*
65:5 terrible things *in r.* wilt
*Prov.* 8:8 words of mouth *in r.*
25:5 throne shall be estab. *in r.*
*Is.* 5:16 G. shall be sanct. *in r.*
32:1 a king shall reign *in r.*
42:6 I the L. callde thee *in r.*
45:13 I have raised him *in r.*
23 word gone out of mou. *in r.*
48:1 mention G. of Isr. not *in r.*
54:14 *in r.* shalt thou be estab.
63:1 speak *in r.* mighty to save
*Jer.* 4:2 the Lord liveth *in r.*
*Hos.* 2:19 I will betroth thee *in r.*
10:12 sow *in r.* reap in mercy
*Zec.* 8:8 I will be their God *in r.*
*Mal.* 3:3 offer an offering *in r.*
*Acts* 17:31 will judge world *in r.*
*Rom.* 9:28 will cut it short *in r.*
*Eph.* 4:24 God is created *in r.*
2 *Tim.* 3:16 scrip. for instr. *in r.*
*Rev.* 19:11 *in r.* he doth judge

**My RIGHTEOUSNESS.**

*Gen.* 30:33 *my r.* answer for me
*Deut.* 9:4 for *my r.* Lord bro. me
2 *Sam.* 22:21 reward me accord. to *my r.* 25; *Ps.* 18:20, 24
*Job* 6:29 return ag. *my r.* is in it
27:6 *my r.* I hold fast
35:2 *my r.* more than God's
*Ps.* 4:1 I call, O God of *my r.*
7:8 judge me, O L. ac. to *my r.*
*Is.* 41:10 uph. with hand *my r.*
46:13 I bring *my r.* 51:5 *my r.* is
51:6 *my r.* sh. not be abolished
8 but *my r.* shall be for ever
56:1 come, *my r.* to be revealed
*Phil.* 3:9 not having *mine* own *r.*

**Thy RIGHTEOUSNESS.**

*Deut.* 9:5 for *thy r.* or upright. 6
*Job* 8:6 habi. of *t. r.* prosperous
35:8 *thy r.* may profit son of
*Ps.* 5:8 lead me, O Lord, in *t. r.*
31:1 deliver me in *thy r.* 71:2
35:24 judge me, O L. ac. to *t. r.*
28 shall speak of *thy r.* 71:24
36:6 *thy r.* is like great mount.
10 continue *thy r.* to upright
37:6 he shall bring forth *thy r.*
40:10 I have not hid *thy r.*
51:14 tongue shall sing of *thy r.*
69:27 let th. not come into *t. r.*
71:15 my mouth sh. show *thy r.*
16 I will make ment. of *thy r.*
19 *thy r.* O God, is very high
72:1 give *thy r.* unto king's son
88:12 *thy r.* be known in land
89:16 in *t. r.* sh. they be exalted
119:40 quicken *t. r.* 123 *thy r.*
142 *thy r.* is an everlast. right.
143:1 answer me, and in *thy r.*
11 for *t. r.* sake bring my soul
*Ps.* 145:7 they sh. sing of *thy r.*
*Is.* 48:18 *thy r.* as waves of sea
57:12 I will declare *thy r.*
58:8 *thy r.* shall go before thee
62:2 the Gentiles shall see *t. r.*
*Dan.* 9:16 O Lord, accord. to *t. r.*

**RIGHTEOUSNESSES.**

*Is.* 64:6 our *r.* are as filthy rags
*Ezek.* 33:13 his *r.* sh. not be rem.
*Dan.* 9:18 not for our *r.* but thy

**RIGHTLY.**

*Gen.* 27:36 is not he *r.* nam. J.?
*Luke* 7:43 Thou hast *r.* judged
20:21 we know thou teachest *r.*
2 *Tim.* 2:15 *r.* divid. word of tru.

**RIGOR.**

*Ex.* 1:13 made Is. serve wi. *r.* 14
*Lev.* 25:43 not r. with *r.* 46, 53

**RIMMON.**

*Jos.* 15:32 Ain, and R. cities of
*Jud.* 20:45 rock R. 47; 21:13
2 *Sam.* 4:2 Rec. sons of R. 5, 9
2 *K.* 5:18 goeth into house of R.
1 *Chr.* 4:32 villages of Simeon R.
6:77 was given to Merari, R.
*Zec.* 14:10 turn. as a plain to R.

**RING.**

*Gen.* 41:42 Phar. took off his *r.*
*Ex.* 26:24 coup. to one *r.* 36:29
*Est.* 3:10 Ahasuerus took his *r.*
8:2 the king took off *r.* gave it
*Luke* 15:22 said, Put a *r.* on hand
*Jam.* 2:2 came man with gold *r.*

**RINGLEADER.**

*Acts* 24:5 *r.* of sect of Nazarenes

**RINGS.**

*Ex.* 25:12 cast four *r.* of gold
14 put staves into the *r.* 15; 27:7; 37:5; 38:7
26:29 and make their *r.* of gold, 28:23, 26, 27; 30:4; 36:34; 37:3, 13; 39:16, 19, 20
*Est.* 1:6 hangings fastened to *r.*
*Cant.* 5:14 hands are as gold *r.*
*Is.* 3:21 take away *r.* jewels
*Ezek.* 1:18 *r.* so high were dread. *r.* were full of eyes

**RING-STREAKED.**

*Gen.* 30:35 he-goats were *r.-s.*
31:8 *r.-s.* sh. be thy hire, 10:12

**RINSED.**

*Lev.* 6:28 pot both scoured and *r.*
15:11 and hath not *r.* his hands
12 ev. vessel of wood sh. be *r.*

**RIOT, Substantive.**

*Tit.* 1:6 children not accus. of *r.*
1 *Pet.* 4:4 that you run not to *r.*

**RIOT, ING.**

*Rom.* 13:13 walk not in *r.*
2 *Pet.* 2:13 count it pleasure to *r.*

**RIOTOUS.**

*Prov.* 23:20 be not am. *r.* eaters
28:7 he that is companion of *r.*
*Luke* 15:13 wasted with *r.* living

**RIP, PED.**

2 *K.* 8:12 *r.* up women with chi.
15:16 women wi. child he *r.* up
*Hos.* 13:16 wo. wi. child be *r.* up
*Amos* 1:13 have *r.* up the women

**RIPE.**

*Gen.* 40:10 bro. forth *r.* grapes
*Ex.* 22:29 to offer thy *r.* fruits
*Num.* 13:20 time of first *r.* grap.
18:13 whatso. is first *r.* in land
*Jer.* 24:2 like figs that are first *r.* *Hos.* 9:10; *Nah.* 3:12
*Joel* 3:13 sickle, for harvest is *r.*
*Mic.* 7:1 my soul desired *r.* fruit
*Rev.* 14:15 harvest of earth is *r.*
18 gath. clusters, grapes are *r.*

**RIPENING.**

*Is.* 18:5 and the sour grape is *r.*

RIPHATH. *Gen.* 10:3

**RISE.**

*Num.* 24:17 sceptre *r.* out of Is.
*Deut.* 33:11 smite them that *r.* that they *r.* not again
*Jud.* 8:21 they said, *r.* thou
1 *Sam.* 24:7 suff. them not to *r.*
2 *Sam.* 12:21 child dead, didst *r.*
*Job* 30:12 upon my right hand *r.*

*Ps.* 18:38 were not able to *r.*
27:3 tho. war sho. *r.* against me
36:12 shall not be able to *r.*
140:10 that th. *r.* not up again
*Prov.* 28:12 when wicked *r.* 28
*Cant.* 3:2 *r.* now and go about
*Is.* 24:20 earth sh. fall and not *r.*
33:10 now will I *r.* saith the L.
43:17 lie together, shall not *r.*
*Amos* 5:2 virgin of Isr. no mo. *r.*
7:9 *r.* against house of Jerob.
*Mat.* 5:45 he maketh sun to *r.*
20:19 he shall *r.* ag. *Mark* 9:31; 10:34; *Luke* 18:33; 24:7
24:11 many false proph. shall *r.* *Mark* 13:22
27:63 3 days I will *r.* *Mark* 8:31
*Mark* 12:23 when they shall *r.* 25
*Luke* 11:7 I cannot *r.* and give
*John* 5:8 J. saith, *r.* take up bed
11:23 J. saith, Thy bro. sh. *r.*
*Acts* 10:13 came a voice, *r.* Peter
26:23 that should *r.* from dead
*Rom.* 15:12 he that sh. *r.* to reign
1 *Cor.* 15:15 dead *r.* not, 16, 29, 32
1 *Thes.* 4:16 dead in Christ sh. *r.*

**RISE up.**

*Ex.* 8:20 *r. up.* bef. Phar. 9:13
*Num.* 10:35 *r. up* L. let enemies
23:24 people shall *r. up* as lion
*Deut.* 19:15 one witness not *r. up*
28:7 L. cause enemies that *r. up*
31:16 this people will *r. up*
*Neh.* 2:18 let us *r. up* and build
*Job* 20:27 the earth shall *r. up*
*Ps.* 3:1 many are they *r. up*
17:7 save from those that *r. up*
18:48 liftest above th. that *r. up*
41:8 he shall *r. up* no more
44:5 tread them under th. *r. up*
92:11 desire of wicked *r. up*
94:16 who will *r. up* for me?
127:2 it is vain to *r. up* early
*Ec.* 12:4 *r. up* at voice of bird
*Cant.* 2:10 beloved said, *r. up*
*Is.* 5:11 woe unto them *r. up*
14:22 I will *r. up* against them
28:21 L. shall *r. up* as in Peraz.
*Jer.* 47:2 wat. *r. up* out of north
51:1 them that *r. up* against me
*Amos* 8:14 fall, never *r. up* again
*Ob.* 1 let us *r. up* against Edom
*Zep.* 3:8 until day that I *r. up*
*Zec.* 14:13 *r. up* against neighbor
*Mat.* 12:41 men of Nine. sh. *r. up*
42 qu. of so. *r. up*, *Lu.* 11:31, 32
*Mark* 3:26 Sat. *r. up* ag. himself
*Luke* 5:23 easier to say, *r. up*
*Acts* 3:6 in name of Jesus *r. up*

**RISEN.**

*Num.* 32:14 *r.* up in fath. stead
1 *Sam.* 25:29 man *r.* to pursue
1 *K.* 8:20 I am *r.* up in room of David, 2 *Chr.* 6:10
*Ps.* 20:8 we are *r.* and stand
54:3 strangers are *r.* against me
86:14 O G. proud are *r.* ag. me
*Is.* 60:1 glory of the Lord is *r.*
*Mic.* 2:8 of late my peo. is *r.* up
*Mat.* 11:11 not *r.* a greater th. J.
14:2 John the Baptist *r.* fr. dead, *Mark* 6:14, 16; *Luke* 9:7
17:9 Son of man be *r.* *Mark* 9:9
26:32 *r.* I will go bef. *Mark* 14:28
28:6 is *r.* as he said, *Mark* 16:6
*Mark* 16:9 J. *r.* early first day
*Luke* 7:16 a great prophet is *r.*
9:8 one of prophets was *r.* 19
24:34 the Lord is *r.* indeed
*Acts* 17:3 C. must needs have *r.*
*Rom.* 8:34 yea rather that is *r.*
1 *Cor.* 15:13 then is Christ not *r.*
*Col.* 3:1 if ye be *r.* with Christ

**RISEST.**

*Deut.* 6:7 talk of th. when thou *r.*

**RISETH.**

*Deut.* 22:26 man *r.* against neigh.
*Job* 9:7 com. sun and it *r.* not
14:12 man lieth down, *r.* not
24:22 *r.* up and no man is sure
27:7 he that *r.* up against me
31:14 wh. sh. I do wh. G. *r.* up?
*Prov.* 24:16 man fall. and *r.* ag.
*Is.* 47:11 know fr. whence it *r.*

**RISING, Substantive.**

*Lev.* 13:2 in skin of his flesh a *r.* or bright spot, 10, 19, 28, 43
14:56 this is the law for a *r.*
*Prov.* 30:31 ag. whom is no *r.*
*Is.* 60:3 to brightness of thy *r.*
*Mark* 9:10 what the *r.* from dead
*Luke* 2:34 fall and *r.* of many

**Sun-RISING.**

*Num.* 2:3 toward *r.* of the *sun*
21:11 bef. Moab tow. *s.-r.* 34:15; *Deut.* 4:41, 47; *Jos.* 12:1; 13:5; 19:12, 27, 34
*Ps.* 50:1 called earth fr. *r.* of *sun*
113:3 *r.* of *s.* L.'s name praised
*Is.* 41:25 fr. *r.* of *s.* shall he call
45:6 know from *r.* of the *sun*
59:19 fear his glory fr. *r.* of *sun*
*Mal.* 1:11 from *r.* of *sun* my name
*Mark* 16:2 to sepulc. at *r.* of *sun*

**RISING.**

*Job* 16:8 my leanness *r.* in me
*Job* 24:5 as wild asses go forth, *r.*
*Prov.* 27:14 bless. friend, *r.* early
*Jer.* 7:13 I spake unto you *r.* up early, 25:3; 35:14
25 I sent my servants prophets to you, *r.* up early, 25:4; 26:5; 29:19; 35:15; 44:4
11:7 *r.* early, and protesting
32:33 I taught them, *r.* up early
*Lam.* 3:63 sit. down and *r.* up
*Mark* 1:35 in morn. *r.* bef. day

**RITES.**

*Num.* 9:3 keep it according to *r.*

**RIVER.**

*Gen.* 31:21 Jacob passed over *r.*
41:1 behold, he stood by the *r.*
*Ex.* 1:22 every son cast into *r.*
2:5 daughter of Phar. came to *r.*
4:9 water of *r.* sh. become blood
8:3 the *r.* shall bring forth frogs
*Deut.* 2:24 journey, pass over *r.*
*Jos.* 13:9 the city in the midst of the *r.* 2 *Sam.* 24:5
*Jud.* 5:21 *r.* Kis. that ancient *r.*
2 *Sam.* 17:13 draw city into *r.*
1 *K.* 4:21 Solomon reigned fr. *r.*
*Ezr.* 4:10 rest on this side the *r.*
8:15 I gathered them to *r.*
*Job* 40:23 he drinketh up *r.*
*Ps.* 36:8 make them drink of *r.*
46:4 a *r.* streams sh. make glad
65:9 enrichest it with *r.* of God
72:8 have dominion from the *r.*
80:11 sent out branches unto *r.*
105:41 wat. ran in places like *r.*
*Is.* 8:7 bring. upon them the *r.*
11:15 shake his hand over the *r.*
19:5 and the *r.* shall be wasted
23:10 pass thro' thy land as a *r.*
48:18 had thy peace been as *r.*
66:12 ext. peace to her like a *r.*
*Jer.* 2:18 drink waters of the *r.*
17:8 spread. out her roots by *r.*
*Lam.* 2:18 tears run down like *r.*
*Ezek.* 29:3 My *r.* is my own, 9
47:5 it was *r.* I could not pass
*Amos* 6:14 *r.* of the wilderness
*Mic.* 7:12 come from fortr. to *r.*
*Zec.* 9:10 his dominion from *r.*
10:11 deeps of *r.* shall dry up
*Mark* 1:5 baptized in *r.* Jordan
*Acts* 16:13 on sab. we went by *r.*
*Rev.* 22:1 he showed me a pure *r.*
*See* BANK, BRINK, BEYOND, CHEBAR, EUPHRATES.

**RIVERS.**

*Ex.* 7:19 thy hand on the *r.* 8:5
*Lev.* 11:9 whatso. hath fins in *r.*
*Deut.* 10:7 a land of *r.* of waters
2 *K.* 5:12 are not *r.* of Damascus
19:24 I have dried up all the *r.*
*Job* 20:17 shall not see *r.* of hon.
28:10 cutteth out *r.* amo. rocks
29:6 rock poured me out *r.* of oil
*Ps.* 1:3 like a tree planted by *r.*
74:15 thou driedst up mighty *r.*
78:16 caused wat. to run like *r.*
89:25 set his right hand in *r.*
107:33 turneth *r.* into wildern.
119:136 *r.* of wat. run down eyes
137:1 by *r.* of Babylon we wept
*Prov.* 5:16 *r.* of waters in streets
21:1 in the hand of Lord, as *r.*
*Ec.* 1:7 all *r.* run into the sea
*Cant.* 5:12 as eyes of doves by *r.*
*Is.* 18:2 whose land *r.* spoiled, 7
19:6 they shall turn *r.* far away
30:25 on every high hill *r.*
32:2 be as *r.* in a dry place
33:21 L. be to us place of br. *r.*
37:25 all *r.* of besieged places
41:18 open *r.* in high places
42:15 I will make *r.* islands
43:2 passest thro' *r.* not overfl.
19 I will make *r.* in desert, 20
44:27 deep be dry, I wi. dry up *r.*
50:2 I make *r.* a wilderness
*Jer.* 31:9 I cau. th. to walk by *r.*
46:7 waters are moved as *r.* 8
*Lam.* 3:48 eye runneth *r.* of wat.
*Ezek.* 6:3 said L. to hills and *r.*
29:4 cause fish of thy *r.* to stick
10 I am against thee, again. *r.*
32:12 I will make *r.* dry
31:4 deep set him up with her *r.*
12 his boughs are broken by *r.*
32:2 camest forth with thy *r.*
14 cause their *r.* to run like oil
34:13 feed th. on mount. by *r.*
35:8 in *r.* sh. fall that are slain
36:6 say to hills, to *r.* valleys
47:9 whithersoever *r.* sh. come
*Joel* 1:20 *r.* of waters dried up
3:18 *r.* of Jud. sh. flow wi. wat.
*Mic.* 6:7 pleased with 10,000 *r.*
*Nah.* 1:4 rebuk. sea, drieth up *r.*
*Nah.* 2:6 gates of *r.* sh. be open.
*Hab.* 3:8 was L. displeas. ag. *r.*?
9 thou didst clea. earth wi. *r.*
*John* 7:38 out of belly sh. flow *r.*
*Rev.* 8:10 fell on third part of *r.*

**RIZPAH.**

2 *Sam.* 3:7 concub. name was R.
21:8 delivered two sons of R. 10

**ROAD.**

1 *Sam.* 27:10 ye made *r.* to-day

**ROAR.**

1 *Chr.* 16:32 sea *r.* *Ps.* 96:11; 98:7
*Ps.* 46:3 not fear, though wat. *r.*
74:4 enemies *r.* in thy congre.
104:21 young lions *r.* after prey
*Is.* 5:29 they sh. *r.* like lions, 30
42:13 L. sh. *r.* prevail ag. enem.
59:11 we *r.* all like bears, mou.
*Jer.* 5:22 they *r.* yet not pass ov.
25:30 Lord shall *r.* from on high
31:35 divideth sea, wh. waves *r.*
50:42 their voice sh. *r.* like sea
51:38 shall *r.* together like lions
55 her waves *r.* like great wat.
*Hos.* 11:10 *r.* like lion, wh. he *r.*
*Joel* 3:16 L. *r.* out of Z. *Amos* 1:2
*Amos* 3:4 will lion *r.* if no prey?

**ROARED.**

*Jud.* 14:5 lion *r.* against Samson
*Is.* 51:15 divided sea, waves *r.*
*Jer.* 2:15 young lions *r.* upon him
*Amos* 3:8 *r.* who will not fear?

**ROARETH.**

*Job* 37:4 after a voice *r.* thunder.
*Jer.* 6:23 their voice *r.* like sea

*Rev.* 10:3 angel cried, as a lion *r.*

**ROARING, Substantive.**

*Job* 4:10 *r.* teeth of lions broken
*Ps.* 22:1 why so far from my *r.?*
32:3 bones waxed old thr' my *r.*
*Prov.* 19:12 king's wr. as *r.* of lion
20:2 fear of king is as *r.* of lion
*Is.* 5:29 their *r.* sh. be like a lion
30 shall roar like *r.* of the sea
*Ezek.* 19:7 land desol. noise of *r.*
*Zec.* 11:3 *r.* of young lions

**ROARING, Adjective.**

*Ps.* 22:13 gaped up. me as *r.* lion
*Prov.* 28:15 *r.* lion, so is wicked
*Is.* 31:4 as young lion *r.* on prey
*Zep.* 3:3 her princes are *r.* lions
*Luke* 21:25 sea and waves *r.*
1 *Pet.* 5:8 devil as a *r.* lion walk.

**ROARINGS.**

*Job* 3:24 my *r.* poured like wat.

**ROAST, ED, ETH.**

*Ex.* 12:8 eat in that night flesh *r.* with fire, *Deut.* 16:7
1 *Sam.* 2:15 flesh to *r.* for priest
2 *Chr.* 35:13 they *r.* passover
*Prov.* 12:27 slothful man, *r.* not
*Is.* 44:16 roasteth *r.* is satisfied
*Jer.* 29:22 whom king of Bab. *r.*

**ROB, BETH.**

*Lev.* 19:13 shalt not *r.* neighbor
26:22 beasts shall *r.* you of chil.
1 *Sam.* 23:1 they *r.* thresh.-floors
*Prov.* 22:22 *r.* not poor
28:24 whoso *r.* his fath. or mot.
*Is.* 10:2 that they may *r.* fatherl.
17:14 this is lot of th. that *r.* us
*Ezek.* 39:10 spoil and *r.* those th.
*Mal.* 3:8 will a man *r.* God?

**ROBBED.**

*Jud.* 9:25 *r.* all came by them
2 *Sam.* 17:8 chafed as a bear *r.*
*Ps.* 119:61 bands of wick. *r.* me
*Prov.* 17:12 a bear *r.* of whelps
*Is.* 10:13 I have *r.* their treasures
42:22 a people *r.* and spoiled
*Jer.* 50:37 sword on treas. be *r.*
*Ezek.* 33:15 if wick. give th. he *r.*
39:10 rob those that *r.* them
*Mal.* 3:8 *r.* me, wh. have we *r.* 9
2 *Cor.* 11:8 I *r.* other churches

**ROBBER.**

*Job* 5:5 *r.* swallow. th. substance
18:9 *r.* shall prevail against him
*Ezek.* 18:10 beget son that is a *r.*
*John* 18:40 Barabbas was a *r.*

**ROBBERS.**

*Job* 12:6 tabernacles of *r.* prosp.
*Is.* 42:24 who gave Is. to the *r.?*
*Jer.* 7:11 house bec. den of *r.?*
*Ezek.* 7:22 *r.* sh. enter and defile
*Dan.* 11:14 *r.* of peo. exalt them.
*Hos.* 6:9 troops of *r.* wait for a man
7:1 troop of *r.* spoileth without
*Ob.* 5 if *r.* by night, would they
*John* 10:8 all came bef. me are *r.*
*Acts* 19:37 not *r.* of churches
2 *Cor.* 11:26 perils of water, of *r.*

**ROBBERY.**

*Ps.* 62:10 become not vain in *r.*
*Prov.* 21:7 *r.* of wick. dest. them
*Is.* 61:8 I hate *r.* for burnt-offer.
*Ezek.* 22:29 exerc. *r.* vexed poor
*Amos* 3:10 store *r.* in palaces
*Nah.* 3:1 city full of lies, *r.*
*Phil.* 2:6 thou. no *r.* to be equal

**ROBE.**

*Ex.* 28:4 make an ephod and *r.*
29:5 put on Aa. coat, *r.* *Lev.* 8:7
1 *Sam.* 18:4 Jona. stripped of *r.*
24:11 skirt of thy *r.* in my hand
1 *Chr.* 15:27 David clothed wi. *r.*
*Job* 29:14 my judgment was a *r.*
*Is.* 22:21 will clothe him with *r.*
61:10 cov. me with *r.* of righte.
*Jon.* 3:6 arose and laid *r.* fr. him
*Mic.* 2:8 ye pull off *r.* with garm.
*Mat.* 27:28 put on J. a scarlet *r.*
*Luke* 15:22 bri. best *r.* put it on
23:11 arrayed him in gorgeo. *r.*
*John* 19:2 put on Jes. a purple *r.*

**ROBES.**

2 *Sam.* 13:18 such *r.* we. virgins
1 *K.* 22:30 put thou on thy *r.*
*Ezek.* 26:16 princes lay away *r.*
*Luke* 20:46 scri. walk in long *r.*
*Rev.* 6:11 white *r.* given them
7:9 Lamb, clothed wi. white *r.*
13 in white *r.?* 14 washed th. *r.*

**ROCK.**

*Ex.* 17:6 will stand bef. thee on *r.*
33:21 L. Thou stand upon a *r.*
*Num.* 20:8 sp. to *r.* bef. th. eyes
11 Mo. with rod smote *r.* twice
24:21 puttest thy nest in a *r.*
*Deut.* 8:15 brought wat. out of *r.*
32:4 he is *r.* his work is perfect
15 lightly esteemed *r.* of salv.
18 *r.* begat thee art unmindful
30 except the *r.* had sold them
31 their *r.* is not as our *r.*
37 where *r.* wh. they trusted?
*Jud.* 6:21 fire of *r.* consu. flesh
7:25 slew Oreb on the *r.* Oreb
15:8 Sams. dwelt in top of *r.* E.
20:45 Benj. turned to *r.* of Rim.
1 *Sam.* 2:2 nei. any *r.* like our G.
14:4 sharp *r.* one side, sharp *r.*
2 *Sam.* 22:2 he said, Lord is my *r.* *Ps.* 18:2; 92:15
3 G. of my *r.* in wh. I will tru.
32 a *r.* save our G.? *Ps.* 18:31
47 blessed be my *r.* exalted be G. of *r.* of salvati. *Ps.* 18:46
23:3 God of Israel said, R. of Is.
1 *Chr.* 11:15 captains went to *r.*
2 *Chr.* 25:12 cast down fr. top of *r.*
*Neh.* 9:15 wat. out of *r.* for their thirst, *Ps.* 78:16; 105:41
*Job* 14:18 *r.* is remo. out of place
18:4 sh. *r.* be remo. out of pla.?
19:24 were graven in *r.* for ever
24:8 embr. *r.* for want of shelter
28:9 putteth forth hand upon *r.*
29:6 *r.* poured out rivers of oil
39:1 wild goats of *r.* bri. forth?
28 dwelleth on *r.* on crag of *r.*
*Ps.* 27:5 shall set me on *r.* 40:2
28:1 unto thee I cry, O L. my *r.*
31:2 be thou my strong *r.*
3 thou art my *r.* and fort. 71:3
42:9 my *r.* why ha. thou forg.?
61:2 lead me to *r.* higher than I
62:2 God is my *r.* 6; 7 *r.* of str.
78:20 smote *r.* waters gushed
89:26 *r.* of salva. 94:22 *r.* of ref.
95:1 joyful noise to *r.* of salva.
114:8 turned *r.* into stand. wat.
*Cant.* 2:14 art in clefts of *r.*
*Is.* 2:10 enter *r.* hide th. in dust
8:14 *r.* of offence to both houses
10:26 slaughter at *r.* of Oreb
17:10 not mindful of *r.* of stren.
22:16 habita. for himself in a *r.*
32:2 man be as shad. of great *r.*
42:11 let inhabitants of *r.* sing
48:21 caus. wat. to flow out of *r.*
51:1 look to *r.* ye are hewn
*Jer.* 5:3 made faces harder th. *r.*
18:14 snow which cometh fr. *r.*
21:13 I am ag. thee, inhab. of *r.*
23:29 hammer that breaketh *r.*
48:28 dwell in *r.* like the dove
49:16 thou dwell. in clefts of *r.*
*Ezek.* 24:7 set it upon top of *r.*
8 set her blood upon top of *r.*
26:4 make her like top of *r.* 14
*Amos* 6:12 sh. hors. run upon *r.?*
*Ob.* 3 thou dwell. in clefts of *r.*
*Mat.* 7:24 built house upon *r.*
16:18 upon th. *r.* I build church
27:60 new tomb wh. he had hewn out in the *r.* *Mar.* 15:46
*Luke* 8:6 some fell on *r.* 13 on *r.*
*Rom.* 9:33 I lay in Si. a stumb.-stone, *r.* of offence, 1 *Pet.* 2:8
1 *Cor.* 10:4 drank of spiritual *r.*

**ROCKS.**

*Num.* 23:9 top of *r.* I see him
1 *Sam.* 13:6 hid themselves in *r.*
1 *K.* 19:11 strong wind break *r.*
*Job* 28:10 cutteth rivers amo. *r.*
30:6 dwell in caves of earth, *r.*
*Ps.* 78:15 he clave *r.* in wildern.
104:18 *r.* are a refuge for conies
*Prov.* 30:26 make th. houses in *r.*
*Is.* 2:19 shall go into holes of *r.*
7:19 they sh. rest in holes of *r.*
57:5 slaying children under *r.*
*Jer.* 4:29 whole city climb on *r.*
16:16 hunt th. out of holes of *r.*
51:25 I will roll thee from the *r.*
*Nah.* 1:6 the *r.* are thrown down
*Mat.* 27:51 earth quake, *r.* rent
*Acts* 27:29 lest they sho. fal. on *r.*
*Rev.* 6:16 said to *r.* Fall on us

**ROD.**

*Ex.* 4:4 became a *r.* in his hand
20 Moses took *r.* of God, 17:9
7:9 say to Aa. Take th. *r.* 19
20 lifted up *r.* and smote, 14:16
21:20 man smite servant with *r.*
*Lev.* 27:32 whatso. pass. und. *r.*
*Num.* 17:2 wri. man's name on *r.*
8 *r.* of Aaron budded, *Heb.* 9:4
20:11 with his *r.* he smote rock
1 *Sam.* 14:27 Jona. put end of *r.*
2 *Sam.* 7:14 I will chasten with *r.*
*Job* 9:34 let him take his *r.* away
21:9 neither is *r.* of God upon
*Ps.* 2:9 shalt break them with *r.*
23:4 thy *r.* and staff comfort me
74:2 remem. *r.* of thine inherit.
89:32 I will visit transg. with *r.*
110:2 the Lord shall send the *r.*
125:3 *r.* of wicked shall not rest
*Prov.* 10:13 a *r.* for back of fools, 26:3
13:24 he that spar. *r.* hateth son
14:3 mouth of foolish is a *r.* of
22:8 *r.* of his anger shall fail
15 *r.* of correction shall drive
23:13 thou sh. beat him wi. *r.* 14
29:15 *r.* and reproof give wisd.
*Is.* 9:4 hast broken *r.* of oppres.
10:5 O Assyr. *r.* of mine anger
15 as if the *r.* sho. shake itself
24 he shall smite with a *r.* and
26 as his *r.* was on the sea, so
11:1 *r.* out of the stem of Jesse
4 shall smite earth with the *r.*
14:29 *r.* that smote is broken
30:31 Assyr. beat. smote with *r.*
*Jer.* 10:16 Is. the *r.* of his, 51:19
48:17 how is beauti. *r.* broken!
*Lam.* 3:1 affliction by *r.* of wra.
*Ezek.* 7:11 viol. is risen into a *r.*
19:14 fire is gone out of a *r.*
20:37 cause to pass under the *r.*
21:10 contemn. *r.* of my son, 13
*Mic.* 5:1 smite judge of Is. wi. *r.*
6:9 hear the *r.* who appoint. it
7:14 feed thy people with thy *r.*
1 *Cor.* 4:21 sh. I come with a *r.?*
*Rev.* 2:27 rule with *r.* of ir. 19:15
12:5 rule nations with *r.* of iron

**RODE.**

*Gen.* 24:61 Rebe. and damsels *r.*
*Jud.* 10:4 he had 30 sons that *r.*
1 *Sam.* 25:20 Abig. *r.* on ass, 42
30:17 400 which *r.* on camels
2 *Sam.* 22:11 he *r.* on a cherub, and did fly, *Ps.* 18:10
1 *K.* 13:13 old prophet *r.* on ass
2 *K.* 9:16 Jehu *r.* in a chariot
25 when I and thou *r.* togeth.
*Neh.* 2:12 beast that I *r.* upon
*Est.* 8:14 posts that *r.* on mules

**RODS.**

*Gen.* 30:37 Jac. took *r.* of poplar
*Ex.* 7:12 Aaron's rod swall. th. *r.*
*Num.* 17:6 princes ga. him 12 *r.*
*Ezek.* 19:11 she had strong *r.* for
12 her strong *r.* were broken
2 *Cor.* 11:25 thrice beaten wi. *r.*

**ROE, S.**

1 *Chr.* 12:8 swift as *r.* on mount.
*Prov.* 5:19 hind and pleasant *r.*
6:5 deli. thyself as *r.* fr. hunter
*Cant.* 2:7 I charge you by *r.* 3:5
9 my beloved is like a *r.* or a
17 be thou like *r.* or hart, 8:14
*Is.* 13:14 shall be as chased *r.*

*See* YOUNG.

**Wild ROE.**

2 *Sam.* 2:18 Asahel was as a *w. r.*

**ROEBUCK, S.**

*Deut.* 12:15 eat of the *r.* 22; 14:5; 15:22
1 *K.* 4:23 besides harts and *r.*

**ROLL, S, Substantive.**

*Ezr.* 6:1 sea. made in house of *r.*
2 was found at Achmetha a *r.*
*Is.* 8:1 take thee a great *r.* and
*Jer.* 36:2 take thee a *r.* of a book
23 till all the *r.* was consumed
29 saith L. Th. hast burnt th. *r.*
*Ezek.* 2:9 hand sent, and lo, a *r.*
3:1 eat this *r.* 2 caused me eat
*Zec.* 5:1 behold, a flying *r.* 2

**ROLL, Verb.**

*Gen.* 29:8 till they *r.* away
*Jos.* 10:18 Joshua said, *r.* stones
1 *Sam.* 14:33 *r.* a great stone
*Jer.* 51:25 I will *r.* thee down
*Mic.* 1:10 Aph. *r.* thyself in dust
*Mark* 16:3 who *r.* us away stone?

**ROLLED.**

*Gen.* 29:3 *r.* stone from well, 10
*Jos.* 5:9 I ha. *r.* away reproach
*Job* 30:14 *r.* themselves on me
*Is.* 9:5 garments *r.* in blood
34:4 heavens *r.* toget. *Rev.* 6:14
*Mat.* 27:60 he *r.* a great stone to door of sepulch. *Mark* 15:46
28:2 angel came *r.* back stone
*Mark* 16:4 stone was *r.* away
*Luke* 24:2 found stone *r.* away

**ROLLER.**

*Ezek.* 30:21 to put a *r.* to bind it

**ROLLETH.**

*Prov.* 26:27 he that *r.* a stone

**ROLLING.**

*Is.* 17:13 nations flee like *r.* thi.

**ROMAN.**

*Acts* 22:25 is a R. 26, 27, 29
23:27 unders. that he was a R.

**ROMANS.**

*John* 11:48 the R. shall come
*Acts* 16:21 obser. being R. 37, 38
28:17 prison. into hands of R.

**ROME.**

*Acts* 2:10 strangers of R. we do
18:2 Jews to depart from R.
19:21 there, I must also see R.
23:11 bear witness also at R.
28:16 when we came to R.
*Rom.* 1:7 all that be in R. 15
2 *Tim.* 1:17 when he was in R.

**ROOF, S.**

*Gen.* 19:8 under shadow of *r.*
*Deut.* 22:8 a battlement for *r.*
*Jos.* 2:6 brought them to the *r.*
*Jud.* 16:27 on *r.* were 3000 men
2 *Sam.* 11:2 David walked on *r.*
18:24 watchman went up to *r.*
*Jer.* 19:13 on wh. *r.* they, 32:29
*Ezek.* 40:13 measured gate fr. *r.*
*Mat.* 8:8 not worthy th. should. come under my *r.* *Luke* 7:6
*Mark* 2:4 they uncovered the *r.*

**ROOF, *with* mouth.**

*Job* 29:10 tongue clea. to *r.* of *m.*
*Ps.* 137:6 tong. cleave to *r.* of *m.*
*Cant.* 7:9 *r.* of *m.* like best wine
*Lam.* 4:4 cleaveth to *r.* of his *m.*
*Ezek.* 3:26 tong. clea. to *r.* of *m.*

**ROOM.**

*Gen.* 24:23 *r.* in father's house?
25 have straw, and *r.* to lodge
31 I have prepa. *r.* for camels
26:22 Lord hath made *r.* for us
1 *K.* 2:35 king put Benaiah in J.'s *r.* put Zad. in *r.* of Abi.
5:5 son wh. I will set in thy *r.*
8:20 I am risen in *r.* of David, 2 *Chr.* 6:10
19:16 Elis. shalt thou anoi. in *r.*
*Ps.* 31:8 set my feet in large *r*
80:9 thou preparedst *r.* before it
*Prov.* 18:16 a man's gift mak. *r.*
*Mal.* 3:10 shall not be *r.* enough
*Mark* 2:2 no *r.* to receive them
14:15 a large up. *r.* *Luke* 22:12
*Luke* 2:7 because th. was no *r.*
12:17 I have no *r.* to bestow
14:8 sit not down in highest *r.*
10 sit down in the lowest *r.*
22 it is done, and yet th. is *r.*
*Acts* 1:13 went up to an upper *r.*
24:27 Festus came in Felix's *r.*
1 *Cor.* 14:16 he that occupieth *r.*

**ROOMS.**

*Gen.* 6:14 *r.* sh. thou make in ark
1 *K.* 20:24 put captains in th. *r.*
1 *Chr.* 4:41 and dwelt in their *r.*
*Mat.* 23:6 uppermost *r.* at feasts, *Mark* 12:39; *Luke* 20:46
*Luke* 14:7 they chose out chief *r.*

**ROOT, Substantive.**

*Deut.* 29:18 among you a *r.* that
*Jud.* 5:14 out of Ephr. was a *r.*
2 *K.* 19:30 Judah shall take *r.*
*Job* 5:3 I have seen foolish ta. *r.*
14:8 though the *r.* thereof wax
19:28 seeing the *r.* of the matter
29:19 my *r.* spread out by wate.
*Ps.* 80:9 didst cause vine take *r.*
*Prov.* 12:3 *r.* of the righteous
12 *r.* of the righteous yieldeth
*Is.* 5:24 their *r.* shall be rotten.
11:10 a *r.* of Jesse, *Rom.* 15:12
14:30 I will kill thy *r.* with fam.
27:6 come of Jacob take *r.* 37:31
40:24 their stock sh. not take *r.*
53:2 he shall grow up as a *r.* out
*Jer.* 12:2 they have taken *r.* they
*Ezek.* 31:7 his *r.* was by waters
*Dan.* 11:7 out of branch of her *r.*
*Hos.* 9:16 Eph. is smit. their *r.*
*Mal.* 4:1 sh. leave neither *r.* nor
*Mat.* 3:10 axe laid to *r.* *Luke* 3:9
13:6 because they had not *r.* 21; *Mark* 4:6, 17; *Luke* 8:13
*Luke* 17:6 plucked up by the *r.*
*Rom.* 11:16 if the *r.* be holy
18 bearest not the *r.* but *r.* th.
1 *Tim.* 6:10 money is *r.* of all ev.
*Heb.* 12:15 lest any *r.* of bittern.
*Rev.* 5:5 *r.* of Da. hath prevailed
22:16 I am the *r.* of David

**ROOT, Verb.**

1 *K.* 14:15 he shall *r.* up Israel
*Job* 31:12 would *r.* all mine incr.
*Ps.* 52:5 and *r.* thee out of land
*Jer.* 1:10 I have set thee to *r.* out
*Mat.* 13:29 lest ye *r.* up wheat

**ROOTED.**

*Deut* 29:28 the Lord *r.* them out
*Job* 18:14 confidence sh. be *r.* out
31:8 let my offspring be *r.* out
*Prov.* 2:22 transgressors sh. be *r.*
*Zep.* 2:4 Ekron shall be *r.* up
*Mat.* 15:13 Fa. not planted, *r.* up
*Eph.* 3:17 being *r.* and grounded
*Col.* 2:7 *r.* and built up in him

**ROOTS.**

2 *Chr.* 7:20 pluck them up by *r.*
*Job* 8:17 his *r.* are wrapped about
18:16 his *r.* shall be dried up
28:9 overturn. mountains by *r.*
30:4 cut juniper *r.* for meat
*Is.* 11:1 bra. shall grow out of *r.*
*Jer.* 17:8 spreadeth out her *r.*
*Ezek.* 17:7 vine did bend her *r.*
*Dan.* 4:15 stump of his *r.* 23, 26
7:8 horns plucked up by the *r.*
*Hos.* 14:5 shall cast forth his *r.*
*Amos* 2:9 I destroyed his *r.* from
*Mark* 11:20 fig-tree dried from *r.*
*Jude* 12 trees, plucked up by *r.*

**ROPES.**

*Jud.* 16:11 bi. me wi. new *r.* 12
2 *Sam.* 17:13 Isr. bring *r.* to city
1 *K.* 20:31 put *r.* on heads, 32
*Acts* 27:32 soldiers cut off the *r.*

**ROSE, Substantive.**

*Cant.* 2:1 I am *r.* of Sharon
*Is.* 35:1 desert sh. blossom as *r.*

**ROSE, Verb.**

*Gen.* 4:8 Cain *r.* up against Abel
32:31 sun *r.* upon him
*Ex.* 10:23 nor *r.* any from place
12:30 Pharaoh *r.* up in night
33:10 and all the people *r.* up
*Num.* 25:7 Phinehas *r.* up from
*Deut.* 33:2 Lord *r.* up from Seir
*Jos.* 3:16 waters stood and *r.* up
*Jud.* 6:21 *r.* up fire out of rock
1 *K.* 2:19 king *r.* up to meet her
*Ps.* 124:2 on our side men *r.* up
*Cant.* 5:5 I *r.* up to open to my
*Lam.* 3:62 the lips of those th. *r.*
*Dan.* 8:27 I *r.* up did king's bus.
*Zep.* 3:7 *r.* early and corrupted
*Luke* 5:28 *r.* up and followed him
16:31 not be persua. tho' one *r.*
22:45 when he *r.* from prayer
*Acts* 5:36 bef. th. days *r.* Theud.
10:41 drink with him after he *r.*
*Rom.* 14:9 Christ bo. died and *r.*
1 *Cor.* 10:7 eat, and *r.* up to play
15:4 he was buried and *r.* again
2 *Cor.* 5:15 him who died and *r.*
1 *Thes.* 4:14 J. died and *r.* again

*See* MORNING.

**ROT.**

*Num.* 5:21 Lord ma. thigh *r.* 22, 27
*Prov.* 10:7 name of wicked sh. *r.*
*Is.* 40:20 choos. a tree will not *r.*

**ROTTEN.**

*Job* 13:28 and he, as a *r.* thing
41:27 esteemeth brass as *r.* wo.
*Jer.* 38:12 put these *r.* rags und.
*Joel* 1:17 seed is *r.* under their clods.

**ROTTENNESS.**

*Prov.* 12:4 maketh asha. is as *r.*
14:30 envy is *r.* of the bones
*Is.* 5:24 so their root sh. be as *r.*
*Hos.* 5:12 be to house of Ju. as *r.*
*Hab.* 3:16 wh. I heard *r.* entered

**ROUGH.**

*Deut.* 21:4 bring heifer to *r.* val.
*Is.* 27:8 he stayeth his *r.* wind
40:4 *r.* places sh. be made plain
*Jer.* 51:27 come as *r.* caterpillars
*Zec.* 13:4 neither wear *r.* garm.
*Luke* 3:5 *r.* ways be ma. smooth

**ROUGHLY.**

*Gen.* 42:7 Joseph spake *r.* 30
1 *Sam.* 20:10 fa. answer thee *r.*?
1 *K.* 12:13 the king answered the people *r.* 2 *Chr.* 10:13
*Prov.* 18:23 the rich answere. *r.*

**ROUND, Verb.**

*Lev.* 19:27 ye shall not *r.* corners

**ROUND.**

*Ex.* 16:14 there lay a *r.* thing

1 *K.* 7:35 *r.* comp. 10:19 throne
*Is.* 3:18 L. take away th. *r.* tires
*Luke* 19:43 enemies comp. thee *r.*

**ROUND about.**

*Num.* 16:34 all Is. *r. a.* them fled
*Jos.* 6:3 ye shall go *r. about* city
*Job* 37:12 turn. *r. a.* by counsels
*Ps.* 3:6 and set agai. me *r. about*
48:12 walk about Zion, go *r. a.*
59:6 and go *r. about* the city, 14
88:17 they came *r. ab.* me daily
*Rom.* 15:19 *r. about* to Illyricum
*See* CAMP.

**ROUSE.**

*Gen.* 49:9 who shall *r.* him up?

**ROVERS.**

1 *Chr.* 12:21 helped Da. agai. *r.*

**ROW, S.**

*Ex.* 28:17 four *r.* stones, 39:10
*Lev.* 24:6 six on a *r.* on table
1 *K.* 6:36 inner court wi. three *r.*
7:2 four *r.* of pillars; 3 fift. in *r.*
12 the great court with th. *r.*
2 *Chr.* 4:3 two *r.* of oxen cast
*Cant.* 1:10 with *r.* of jewels
*Ezek.* 46:23 boiling places und. *r.*

**ROWED, ING.**

*Jon.* 1:13 men *r.* hard to bring it
*Mark* 6:48 saw them toiling in *r.*
*John* 6:19 had *r.* 25 or 30 furlon.

**ROWERS.**

*Ezek.* 27:26 *r.* bro' thee into wa.

**ROYAL.**

*Gen.* 49:20 Ash. yield *r.* dainties
*Jos.* 10:2 Gib. as one of *r.* cities
1 *Sam.* 27:5 I dwell in *r.* city?
2 *Sam.* 12:26 Joab took the *r.* ci.
1 *K.* 10:13 Sol. gave of *r.* bounty
2 *K.* 11:1 Athaliah destroyed all the seed *r.* 2 *Chr.* 22:10
1 *Chr.* 29:25 on Solomon *r.* maj.
*Est.* 1:7 gave them *r.* wine
11 bring Vashti with crown *r.*
2:16 Es. taken into house *r.* 17
5:1 Esther put on *r.* apparel
6:8 let *r.* apparel be brought, and the crown *r.*
8:15 Mord. went in *r.* apparel
*Is.* 62:3 *r.* diadem in hand of G.
*Dan.* 6:7 to establish *r.* statute
*Acts* 12:21 Herod in *r.* apparel
*Jam.* 2:8 if ye fulfil the *r.* law
1 *Pet.* 2:9 ye are a *r.* priesthood

**RUBBING.**

*Luke* 6:1 *r.* them in their hands

**RUBBISH.**

*Neh.* 4:2 revive stones out of *r.*
10 decayed and th. is much *r.*

**RUBY, IES.**

*Job* 28:18 price of wisdom is ab. *r. Prov.* 8:11
*Prov.* 3:15 more precious than *r.*
20:15 and a multitude of *r.*
31:10 her price is far above *r.*
*Lam.* 4:7 N. more ruddy than *r.*

**RUDDER-BANDS.**

*Acts* 27:40 and loosed the *r.-b.*

**RUDDY.**

1 *Sam.* 16:12 David was *r.* 17:42
*Cant.* 5:10 beloved white and *r.*
*Lam.* 4:7 her Naz. were more *r.*

**RUDE.**

2 *Cor.* 11:6 tho' I be *r.* in speech

**RUDIMENTS.**

*Col.* 2:8 any spoil you after *r.*
20 if dead with Ch. from the *r.*

**RUE.**

*Luke* 11:42 mint, *r.* and herbs

**RUFUS.**

*Mark* 15:21 fa. of Alex. and R.
*Rom.* 16:13 salute R. chosen

**RUHAMAH.**

*Hos.* 2:1 say to your sisters, R.

**RUIN.**

2 *Chr.* 28:23 they were *r.* of him
*Ps.* 89:40 brought his holds to *r.*
*Prov.* 24:22 who knoweth the *r.*?
26:28 flatter. mouth worketh *r.*
*Is.* 3:6 let *r.* be under thy hand
23:13 land of Chaldeans to *r.*
25:2 made of a defen. city, a *r.*
*Ezek.* 18:30 iniq. not be your *r.*
27:27 comp. fall in day of thy *r.*
31:13 on his *r.* sha. fowls rema.
*Luke* 6:49 *r.* of that house great

**RUINS.**

*Ezek.* 21:15 *r.* may be multiplied
*Amos* 9:11 in day will I raise *r.*
*Acts* 15:16 build ag. the *r.* there.

**RUINED.**

*Is.* 3:8 Jerusalem is *r.* and Jud.
*Ezek.* 36:35 *r.* cities bec. fenced
36 I the L. build the *r.* places

**RUINOUS.**

2 *K.* 19:25 lay waste fenced cities into *r.* heaps, *Is.* 37:26
*Is.* 17:1 Damascus sh. be *r.* heap

**RULE, Substantive.**

1 *K.* 22:31 *r.* over Ahab's chario.
*Est.* 9:1 Jews had *r.* over them
*Prov.* 17:2 wise serv. *r.* over son
19:10 serv. have *r.* over princes
25:28 hath no *r.* ov. his own sp.
*Ec.* 2:19 yet shall he *r.* over all
*Is.* 44:13 as carpenter stretch. *r.*
63:19 never barest *r.* over th.
1 *Cor.* 15:24 have put down all *r.*
2 *Cor.* 10:13 to measure of the *r.*
15 enlarged according to our *r.*
*Gal.* 6:16 walk accord. to this *r.*
*Phil.* 3:16 let us walk by same *r.*
*Heb.* 13:7 that have *r.* over you
17 obey them that have *r.* 24
*See* BARE, BEAR.

**RULE, Verb.**

*Gen.* 1:16 greater light to *r.* day, lesser light to *r.* night, 18
3:16 thy husb. shall *r.* over thee
4:7 desire, th. shalt *r.* over him
*Lev.* 25:43 not *r.* wi. rigor, 46, 53
*Jud.* 8:22 *r.* thou over us, thou
23 I will not *r.* over you, nor shall my son *r.*
*Ps.* 110:2 *r.* in midst of enemies
136:8 sun to *r.* by day
*Prov.* 8:16 princes *r.* and nobles
*Is.* 3:4 babes shall *r.* over them
12 as for my peo. wom. *r.* over
14:2 sh. *r.* over their oppressors
19:4 fierce king sh. *r.* over them
28:14 *r.* this peo. in Jerusalem
32:1 princes sh. *r.* in judgment
40:10 his arm shall *r.* for him
41:2 made the righteous man *r.*
52:5 they that *r.* make th. howl
*Ezek.* 19:14 no strong rod to *r.*
20:33 wi. fury will I *r.* over you
29:15 no more *r.* over nations
*Dan.* 4:26 known that heavens *r.*
11:3 mighty kings that shall *r.*
*Joel* 2:17 heathen sho. *r.* over th.
*Zec.* 6:13 sit and *r.* on his throne
*Mat.* 2:6 a governor that shall *r.*
*Mark* 10:42 are accounted to *r.*
*Col.* 3:15 peace of G. *r.* in hearts
1 *Tim.* 3:5 kn. not how to *r.* ho.
5:17 elders that *r.* well, worthy
*Rev.* 2:27 *r.* with a rod of iron, 12:5; 19:15

**RULED.**

*Gen.* 24:2 his eld. servant that *r.*
41:40 at thy word my peo. be *r.*
1 *K.* 5:16 3,000 *r.* over the people
*Ezr.* 4:20 wh. *r.* over countries
*Ps.* 106:41 they that hated th. *r.*
*Is.* 14:6 that *r.* nations in anger
*Lam.* 5:8 servants ha. *r.* over us
*Ezek.* 34:4 wi. cruelty have ye *r.*
*Dan.* 5:21 till he knew that G. *r.*

**RULER.**

*Gen.* 41:43 Pharaoh made Joseph *r.* 45:8; *Ps.* 105:21
*Ex.* 22:28 thou shalt not curse *r.*
*Num.* 13:2 ev. one a *r.* am. them
1 *Sam.* 25:30 appointed thee *r.* over my peo. Is. 2 *Sam.* 6:21; 7:8; 1 *Chr.* 11:2; 17:7
2 *Sam.* 7:8 I took thee from fol. sheep to be *r.* 1 *Chr.* 17:7
1 *K.* 1:35 I appointed Solomon *r.*
1 *Chr.* 5:2 Jud. came the chief *r.*
9:11 A. *r.* of h. of G. 2 *Chr.* 31:13
2 *Chr.* 7:18 not fail a m. to be *r.*
*Ps.* 68:27 little Benja. wi. their *r.*
105:20 even the *r.* of the people
*Prov.* 23:1 sittest to eat with a *r.*
28:15 so is a wicked *r.* over poor
29:12 if a *r.* hearken to lies
26 many seek *r.* favor
*Ec.* 10:4 if spirit of the *r.* rise
5 error proceedeth from the *r.*
*Is.* 3:6 our *r.* 7 make me not *r.*
16:1 send ye the lamb to the *r.*
*Jer.* 51:46 viol. in land, *r.* ag. *r.*
*Dan.* 2:10 no *r.* ask. such things
5:7 third *r.* in kingdom, 16:29
*Mic.* 5:2 out of thee shall come *r.*
*Mat.* 9:18 there came a certain *r.*
24:45 hath made *r. Luke* 12:42
25:21 I will make thee *r.* ov. 23
*Luke* 13:14 *r.* of synagogue ans.
*John* 2:9 when *r.* of feast tasted
3:1 Nicodemus, a *r.* of the Jews
*Acts* 7:27 who made thee a *r.*? 35
35 same did G. send to be a *r.*
18:17 Greeks beat Sosthenes *r.*
23:5 shalt not spe. evil of the *r.*

**RULERS.**

*Gen.* 47:6 make th. *r.* over cattle
*Ex.* 18:21 *r.* of thou. *r.* of hun. 25
34:31 Moses called *r.* of congre.
*Deut.* 1:13 I will make them *r.*
2 *Sam.* 8:18 David's sons were *r.*
1 *K.* 9:22 were *r.* of his chariots
2 *K.* 11:4 Jehoiada set *r.* over, 19
1 *Chr.* 27:31 these were *r.* of sub.
2 *Chr.* 35:8 *r.* of the house of G.
*Ezr.* 9:2 hand of *r.* chief in this
*Neh.* 4:16 *r.* were behind house
12:40 half of the *r.* with me
13:11 then contended I with *r.*
*Est.* 9:3 of provinces helped
*Ps.* 2:2 *r.* take counsel ag. Lord
*Is.* 1:10 hear word of L. *r.* of S.
14:5 L. hath broken scept. of *r.*
22:3 all thy *r.* are fled together
29:10 your *r.* hath he covered
49:7 servant of *r.* kings sh. see
*Jer.* 33:26 not take of seed be *r.*
51:28 against *r.* 57 drunk *r.*
*Ezek.* 23:6 lov. were capts. and *r.*
23 I will raise up *r.* against th.
*Dan.* 3:3 all the *r.* were gather.
*Hos.* 4:18 *r.* with shame do love
*Mark* 5:22 one of *r.* of synagogue
13:9 brought bef. *r. Luke* 21:12
*Luke* 23:35 *r.* also derided him
24:20 priest and *r.* deliver him
*John* 7:26 do the *r.* know Chri.?
48 have any *r.* believ. on him?
12:42 chief *r.* believed on him
*Acts* 3:17 ye did it, as also did *r.*
4:26 *r.* gathered against Lord
13:15 *r.* of synagogue sent to P.
14:5 assault of Jews, with th. *r.*
16:19 damsel's mast. drew to *r.*
17:8 troubled the people and *r.*
*Rom.* 13:3 *r.* not a terror to good
*Eph.* 6:12 against *r.* of darkness

**RULEST.**

2 *Chr.* 20:6 *r.* thou over kingdo.

*Ps.* 89:9 thou *r.* raging of sea

**RULETH.**

2 *Sam.* 23:3 that *r.* over men
*Ps.* 59:13 know that G. *r.* in Ja.
66:7 he *r.* by his power for ever
103:19 his kingdom over all
*Prov.* 16:32 that *r.* his sp. is bet.
22:7 rich *r.* over the poor
*Ec.* 8:9 one man *r.* over another
9:17 him that *r.* among fools
*Dan.* 4:17 Most High *r.* 25, 32
*Hos.* 11:12 Judah yet *r.* with G.
*Rom.* 12:8 he that *r.* with dilig.
1 *Tim.* 3:4 one that *r.* his house

**RULING.**

2 *Sam.* 23:3 just, *r.* in fear of G.
*Jer.* 22:30 *r.* any more in Judah
1 *Tim.* 3:12 *r.* th. chil. and hou.

**RUMBLING.**

*Jer.* 47:3 at *r.* of his wheels

**RUMOR, S.**

2 *K.* 19:7 he shall hear *r.* *Is.* 37:7
*Jer.* 49:14 I have heard *r.* from L.
51:46 lest ye fear for *r.* in land,
a *r.* sh. co. one yea. ano. a *r.*
*Ezek.* 7:26 *r.* shall be upon *r.*
*Ob.* 1 we heard a *r.* from Lord
*Mat.* 24:6 wars and *r.* of wars
*Mark* 13:7 of wars and *r.* of wars
*Luke* 7:17 *r.* of him went forth

**RUMP.**

*Ex.* 29:22 the fat and the *r.* *Lev.* 3:9; 7:3; 8:25; 9:19

**RUN.**

*Gen.* 49:22 branches *r.* over wall
*Jud.* 18:25 angry fellows *r.* upon
1 *Sam.* 8:11 some shall *r.* before
20:36 *r.* find out now the arrows
2 *Sam.* 18:19 let me now *r.* 22, 23
22:30 ha. *r.* thro' troop, *Ps.* 18:29
2 *K.* 4:22 that I may *r.* to man
5:20 I will *r.* after Naaman
2 *Chr.* 16:9 ey. of L. *r.* to and fro
*Ps.* 19:5 strong man to *r.* race
58:7 wat. which *r.* continually
59:4 they *r.* and prep. themsel.
78:16 caused waters to *r.* down
104:10 springs which *r.* am. hil.
119:32 I will *r.* way of thy com.
136 riv. of waters *r.* down mine
*Prov.* 1:16 *r.* to evil, *Is.* 59:7
*Ec.* 1:7 all the rivers *r.* to sea
*Cant.* 1:4 we will *r.* after thee
*Is.* 40:31 shall *r.* not be weary
55:5 nations shall *r.* to thee
*Jer.* 5:1 *r.* to and fro thro' streets
9:18 eyes *r.* down with tears
12:5 thou hast *r.* wi. footmen
13:17 eyes *r.* do. wi. tears, 14:17
49:3 lament, and *r.* to and fro
19 I will make him *r.* 50:44
51:31 one post *r.* to meet anoth.
*Lam.* 2:18 let tears *r.* down
*Ezek.* 24:16 nei. shall thy tears *r.*
32:14 cause rivers to *r.* like oil
*Dan.* 12:4 many sh. *r.* to and fro
*Joel* 2:7 shall *r.* like mighty
9 shall *r.* in city, sh. *r.* on wall
*Amos* 5:24 let judgm. *r.* down
6:21 shall horses *r.* upon rock?
8:12 sh. *r.* to and fro to seek L.
*Hab.* 2:2 he may *r.* that readeth
*Hag.* 1:9 and ye *r.* every man to
*Zec.* 4:10 eyes of L. *r.* to and fro
*Mat.* 28:8 *r.* to bring disciples
1 *Cor.* 9:24 which *r.* in a race *r.* all, so *r.* that ye may obtain
26 I theref. so *r.* not uncertain.
*Gal.* 2:2 I should *r.* or had *r.* in
5:7 did *r.* well, who did hinder
*Phil.* 2:16 I have not *r.* in vain
*Heb.* 12:1 let us *r.* with patience
1 *Pet.* 4:4 that ye *r.* not to excess

**RUNNEST.**

*Prov.* 4:12 wh. thou *r.* thou shalt

**RUNNETH.**

*Job* 15:26 he *r.* upon him
16:14 *r.* upon me like a giant
*Ps.* 23:5 anoi. head, cup *r.* over
147:15 his word *r.* very swiftly
*Prov.* 18:18 righteous *r.* into it
*Lam.* 1:16 eyes *r.* do. wat. 3:48
*John* 20:2 *r.* and cometh to Sim.
*Rom.* 9:16 nor of him that *r.*

**RUNNING.**

*Lev.* 14:5 kill. over *r.* wat. 6. 50
15:2 man hath a *r.* issue, 22:4
*Num.* 19:17 person take *r.* water
2 *Sam.* 18:24 a man *r.* alone, 26
27 *r.* of forem. is like *r.* of Ah.
2 *K.* 5:21 Naaman saw him *r.*
2 *Chr.* 23:12 Athal. heard peo. *r.*
*Prov.* 5:15 *r.* waters out of well
6:18 swift in *r.* to mischief
*Is.* 33:4 *r.* to and fro of locusts
*Ezek.* 31:4 her rivers *r.* about
*Mark* 9:25 Jesus saw people *r.*
10:17 there came one *r.*
*Luke* 6:38 good meas. and *r.* ov.
*Rev.* 9:9 sound of char. *r.* to bat.

**RUSH, Substantive.**

*Job* 8:11 can *r.* grow with. mire?
*Is.* 9:14 will cut off branch and *r.*
19:15 whi. branch or *r.* may do

**RUSH, ETH.**

*Is.* 17:13 nations sh. *r.* like rush.
*Jer.* 8:6 as horse *r.* into battle

**RUSHED.**

*Jud.* 9:44 Abimelech *r.* forward
20:37 liers in wait *r.* upon Gib.
*Acts* 18:29 *r.* with one accord

**RUSHES.**

*Is.* 35:7 dragons lay shall be *r.*

**RUSHING.**

*Is.* 17:12 woe to multitude and *r.* of nations, *r.* like *r.* of wat.
*Jer.* 47:3 at *r.* of chariots fathers
*Ezek.* 3:12 I heard a great *r.* 13
*Acts* 2:2 sound as of *r.* mighty wind

**RUST.**

*Mat.* 6:19 moth and *r.* corrupt, 20
*Jam.* 5:3 *r.* of th. sh. be witness

**RUTH.**

*Ruth* 1:4 name of other R. 14
4:5 must buy it also of R. 10
*Mat.* 1:5 Booz beg. of Obed of R.

**RYE.**

*Ex.* 9:32 wheat and *r.* not smit.
*Is.* 28:25 barley and *r.* in place

# S

**SABAOTH.**

*Rom.* 9:29 except L. of *s.* had left
*Jam.* 5:4 into ears of the L. of *s.*

**SABBATH.**

*Ex.* 16:23 to-morrow is holy *s.*
25 to-day is a *s.* to the Lord
20:10 sev. day is *s.* of L. 31:15; 35:2; *Lev.* 23:3; *Deut.* 5:14
31:14 ye shall keep the *s.* 16
*Lev.* 16:31 *s.* of rest, 23:3, 32
23:11 after *s.* priest sh. wave it
16 after sev. *s.* shall ye number
24 first of month sh. ye have *s.*
32 from even to even your *s.*
39 first day a *s.* on eighth a *s.*
25:2 then sh. land keep a *s.* 4, 6
*Num.* 28:10 burnt-offering of *s.*
2 *K.* 4:23 neith. new moon nor *s.*
16:18 covert for *s.* turned Ahaz
1 *Chr.* 9:32 prep. show-br. ev. *s.*
2 *Chr.* 36:21 desolate she kept *s.*
*Neh.* 9:14 madest kn. thy holy *s.*
10:31 would not buy on the *s.*
13:15 tread wine-presses on *s.*
16 men of Tyre sold on the *s.*
21 came they no more on the *s.*
*Is.* 56:2 bles. man that keep *s.* 6
58:13 turn foot from *s.* call *s.*
66:23 from one *s.* to another
*Ezek.* 46:1 on *s.* it shall be open.
*Amos* 8:5 when will *s.* be gone?
*Mat.* 28:1 in end of *s.* came Mary
*Mark* 2:27 *s.* for m. not m. for *s.*
28 Son of m. is L. of *s.* *Lu.* 6:5
16:1 when *s.* was past M. Mag.
*Luke* 6:1 on second *s.* after first
13:15 doth not each on *s.* loose?
23:54 preparation, *s.* drew on
*John* 5:18 he not only had bro. *s.*
*Acts* 13:42 preached to th. next *s.*
16:13 on *s.* we went out of city
18:4 reasoned in syna. every *s.*

*See* DAY, DAYS.

**SABBATHS.**

*Ex.* 31:13 my *s.* ye shall keep, *Lev.* 19:3, 30; 26:2
*Lev.* 23:15 seven *s.* sh. be compl.
25:8 thou shalt number seven *s.*
26:34 then shall land enjoy *s.* 35, 43; 2 *Chr.* 36:21
1 *Chr.* 23:21 burnt-sa. in *s.* 2 *Chr.* 2:4; 8:13; 31:3; *Neh.* 10:33
*Is.* 1:13 new moons and *s.* I can.
56:4 eunuchs that keep my *s.*
*Lam.* 1:7 advers. did mock at *s.*
2:6 L. caused *s.* to be forgotten
*Ezek.* 20:12 I gave *s.* to be sign
13 my *s.* they polluted, 16, 24
22:8 hast profaned my *s.* 23:38
26 priests hid eyes from my *s.*
44:24 keep my laws, hallow *s.*
46:3 worship at this gate in *s.*
*Hos.* 2:11 make to cease her *s.*

**SABEANS.**

*Job* 1:15 the S. fell on the oxen
*Is.* 45:14 merchandise of the S.
*Ezek.* 23:42 common sort were S.
*Joel* 3:8 shall sell them to the S.

**SACK.**

*Gen.* 42:25 every man's money into *s.* 35; 43:21; 44:1
44:2 silver cup in *s.* mouth
12 cup was found in Benj.'s *s.*
*Lev.* 11:32 *s.* of uncle. put in wa.

**SACKBUT.**

*Dan.* 3:5 sound of *s.* 7, 10, 15

**SACKCLOTH.**

*Gen.* 37:34 Jac. put *s.* upon loins
2 *Sam.* 3:31 gird you with *s.*
21:10 Rizpah took *s.* and spread
1 *K.* 20:31 put *s.* on loins, 32
21:27 A. put *s.* on flesh, lay in *s.*
2 *K.* 6:30 looked, had *s.* within
19:1 H. cover. him wi. *s.* *Is.* 37:1
2 eld. of priests with *s.* *Is.* 37:2
1 *Chr.* 21:16 D. and elders clo. *s.*
*Est.* 4:2 none enter cloth. with *s.*
*Job* 16:15 sewed *s.* upon my skin
*Ps.* 30:11 put off *s.* girded with
35:13 sick, my clothing was *s.*
69:11 I made *s.* also my garm.
*Is.* 3:24 stomacher, girding of *s.*
15:3 in street gir. them. with *s.*
20:2 loose *s.* from off thy loins
22:12 day did L. call to girding *s.*

32:11 gird *s.* on loins, *Jer.* 4:8;
6:26; 48:37; 49:3
50:3 I make *s.* covering of hea.
*Lam.* 2:10 they girded themsel.
with *s.* *Ezek.* 7:18; 27:31
*Dan.* 9:3 seek L. with fast. and *s.*
*Joel* 1:8 lament like virgin wi. *s.*
13 lie all night in *s.*
*Amos* 8:10 I will bring *s.* on loins
*Jon.* 3:5 people of Nin. put on *s.*
6 king covered him with *s.*
8 man and beast be co. with *s.*
*Rev.* 6:12 sun became black as *c.*
11:3 proph. 1260 days, clo. in *s.*

**SACKCLOTHES.**

*Neh.* 9:1 Is. assembled with *s.* on

**SACKS.**

*Gen.* 42:25 fill *s.* with corn, 44:1
43:12 money brought again in *s.*
22 tell who put money in *s.*
*Jos.* 9:4 Gibeonites took old *s.*

**SACRIFICE.**

*Gen.* 31:54 J. offer. *s.* on mount
*Ex.* 5:17 let us do *s.* to Lord, 8:8
12:27 it is *s.* of Lord's passover
34:15 and thou eat of his *s.*
25 nor *s.* of passover be left
*Lev.* 7:12 shall offer *s.* of thanks.
16 if *s.* be vow, eaten same day
27:11 beast which they do not *s.*
*Num.* 15:3 *s.* in perform. vow, 8
28:6 *s.* made by fire unto Lord,
8, 13, 19, 24; 29:6, 13, 36
*Deut.* 18:3 from them th. offer *s.*
*Jud.* 16:23 offer great *s.* to Dagon
1 *Sam.* 1:21 to offer yearly *s.* 2:19
2:29 kick ye at my *s.* and offer.?
3:14 E.'s house not purged wi. *s.*
9:12 *s.* of my people to-day
15:22 to obey is better than *s.*
16:3 call Jesse to the *s.* and I, 5
20:6 is a yearly *s.* for family, 29
1 *K.* 12:27 people do *s.* at Jerus.
18:29 prophesied till evening *s.*
36 at evening *s.* E. drew near
2 *K.* 5:17 not offer *s.* to other go.
10:19 I have great *s.* to do to B.
17:36 him sh. ye fear, and do *s.*
2 *Chr.* 7:5 S. offered *s.* 22,000 ox.
12 chosen place for house of *s.*
*Ezr.* 9:4 sat aston. till evening *s.*
5 at even. *s.* I arose fr. heavin.
*Ps.* 40:6 *s.* didst not desire, 51:16
50:5 made coven. with me by *s.*
116:17 I offer *s.* of thanksgiving
118:27 bind *s.* to horns of altar
141:2 lifting up hands as eve. *s.*
*Prov.* 15:8 *s.* of wicked abomina.
21:3 justice more accep. than *s.*
*Ec.* 5:1 than give *s.* of fools
*Is.* 19:21 Eg. sh. do *s.* and oblat.
34:6 L. hath a *s.* in Boz. and Id.
57:7 thi. wentest thou to offer *s.*
*Jer.* 33:11 that bring *s.* of praise
18 nor want man to do *s.*
46:10 God a *s.* in north country
*Ezek.* 39:17 gath. to my *s.* gre. *s.*
19 drink blood till drunk of *s.*
44:11 they shall slay *s.* for peo.
46:24 ministers boil *s.* of people
*Dan.* 8:11 daily *s.* 9:27; 11:31
12 host given him ag. daily *s.*
12:11 daily *s.* sh. be taken away
*Hos.* 3:4 Is. sh. abide witho. a *s.*
6:6 I desired mercy and not *s.*
*Mat.* 9:13; 12:7
*Amos* 4:5 offer a *s.* of thanksgiv.
*Jon.* 1:16 men offered a *s.* to L.
*Zep.* 1:7 L. hath prepared a *s.* 8
*Mal.* 1:8 if ye offer blind for *s.*
*Mark* 9:49 every *s.* sh. be salted
*Luke* 2:24 offer a *s.* accor. to law
*Acts* 7:41 in those days off. *s.* to
14:13 would have done *s.* with
*Rom.* 12:1 present your bodies *s.*
1 *Cor.* 8:4 off. in *s.* idols, 10:19, 28
*Eph.* 5:2 *s.* to G. for sweet savor
*Phil.* 2:17 off. on *s.* of your faith
4:18 *s.* accep. well-pleas. to God
*Heb.* 7:27 daily as those to offer *s.*
9:26 put away sin by *s.* of him
10:5 *s.* and off. thou wou. not, 8
12 had offered one *s.* for sins
26 remain. no more *s.* for sins
11:4 Abel offered more excel. *s.*
13:15 let us offer *s.* of praise
*See* BURNT, PEACE-OFFERING.

**SACRIFICE, Verb.**

*Ex.* 3:18 go, *s.* to L. 5:3, 8; 8:27;
10:25; 8:25 go ye *s.*
8:26 *s.* abomina. of Egyptians?
13:15 I *s.* to L. openeth matrix
20:24 thou shalt *s.* burnt-offer.
*Deut.* 15:21 blem. not *s.* it, 17:1
1 *Sam.* 1:3 Elkan. went up to *s.*
15:15 peo. spared best to *s.* to L.
16:2 I am come to *s.* to Lord, 5.
2 *K.* 14:4 as yet the people did *s.*
2 *Chr.* 33:17
17:35 nor shall *s.* to other gods
2 *Chr.* 11:16 came to J. to *s.* to L.
*Ezr.* 4:2 seek your God and do *s.*
*Neh.* 4:2 will they *s.*?
*Ps.* 54:6 I will freely *s.* to thee.
*Ps.* 107:22 *s.* sacrifices of thanks.
*Ezek.* 39:17 gath. to my *s.* I do *s.*
*Hos.* 4:13 *s.* on tops of mountains
14 they *s.* with harlots, there.
8:13 th. *s.* but L. accepteth not
12:11 they *s.* bullocks in Gilgal
13:2 let men that *s.* kiss calves
*Jon.* 2:9 I will *s.* with thanksgi.
*Hab.* 1:16 they *s.* unto their net
*Zec.* 14:21 they that *s.* sh. seethe
1 *Cor.* 10:20 Gentiles *s.* to devils

**SACRIFICED.**

*Ex.* 32:8 made calf, *s.* thereunto
*Deut.* 32:17 *s.* to devils, not to G.
*Jos.* 8:31 *s.* thereon peace-offer.
*Jud.* 2:5 they *s.* there unto Lord
1 *Sam.* 11:15 pe. went to G. to *s.*
2 *Sam.* 6:13 Dav. *s.* ox. and fatl.
1 *K.* 3:2 only the people *s.* in the
high places, 3; 2 *K.* 12:3;
15:4, 35; 16:4; 2 *Chr.* 28:4
11:8 strange wives, *s.* to th. go.
2 *K.* 17:32 lowest priests wh. *s.*
1 *Chr.* 21:28 L. answ. then he *s.*
2 *Chr.* 5:6 assc. be. ark, *s.* sheep
28:23 A. *s.* to gods of Damascus
33:16 Manasseh *s.* on altar of L.
34:4 on graves of th. that had *s.*
*Ps.* 106:37 they *s.* sons to devils.
38 they *s.* to idols of Canaan
*Ezek.* 39:19 sacri. which I have *s.*
*Hos.* 11:2 they *s.* to Baalim
1 *Cor.* 5:7 Ch. our Pass. is *s.* for
*Rev.* 2:14 things *s.* to idols, 20

**SACRIFICEDST.**

*Deut.* 16:4 flesh *s.* rem. all night

**SACRIFICES.**

*Gen.* 46:1 Is. at Beer-sheba off. *s.*
*Ex.* 10:25 thou must give us *s.*
18:12 Jethro took *s.* for God
*Lev.* 10:13 *s.* of L. made by fire
17:7 sh. no more offer *s.* to dev.
*Num.* 25:2 called people to *s.*
28:2 *s.* observe to offer in season
*Deut.* 12:6 thither bring your *s.*
33:19 offer *s.* of righteousness
*Jos.* 13:14 *s.* of L. their inherita.
22:28 altar not for *s.* 29
1 *Sam.* 6:15 sacrificed *s.* to the L.
15:22 hath L. as great del. in *s.*
1 *Chr.* 29:21 sacrificed *s.* in abu.
2 *Chr.* 7:1 fire came and cons. *s.*
29:31 bring *s.* they brought in *s.*
*Ezr.* 6:3 place where he offer. *s.*
10 may offer *s.* to G. of heaven
*Neh.* 12:43 that day th. offered *s.*
*Ps.* 4:5 offer *s.* of righteousness
27:6 theref. will I offer *s.* of joy
50:8 not reprove thee for thy *s.*
51:17 *s.* of God are a broken sp.
19 pleased with *s.* of righteous.
106:28 joined to Baal-peor eat *s.*
107:22 sacrifice *s.* of thanksgivi.
*Prov.* 17:1 house full of *s.*
*Is.* 1:11 to what purpose your *s.*?
29:1 year to year, let th. kill *s.*
43:23 nor honor. me with thy *s.*
24 nor fill. me with fat of thy *s.*
56:7 their *s.* shall be accepted
*Jer.* 6:20 nor are your *s.* sweet
7:21 burnt offerings to your *s.*
17:26 bringing *s.* of praise to L.
*Ezek.* 20:28 saw hill, and offer. *s.*
*Hos.* 4:19 be ashamed, bec. of *s.*
9:4 *s.* be as bread of mourners
*Amos* 4:4 bring your *s.* ev. morn.
5:25 have ye offer. unto me *s.*?
*Mark* 12:33 love L. is more th. *s.*
*Luke* 13:1 blood Pi. mingl. wi. *s.*
*Acts* 7:42 offered *s.* forty years?
1 *Cor.* 10:18 eat *s.* partak. of altar
*Heb.* 5:1 offer gifts, *s.* for sins
8:3 high-pri. ordained to offer *s.*
9:9 were offered both gif. and *s.*
23 heav. things with better *s.*
10:3 in th. *s.* is a remembrance
11 off. same *s.* that never can
13:16 wi. such *s.* G. is well ple.
1 *Pet.* 2:5 priesthood to off. up *s.*
*See* BURNT.

**SACRIFICETH.**

*Ex.* 22:20 he that *s.* to any good
*Ec.* 9:2 that *s.* him that *s.* not
*Is.* 65:3 peo. that *s.* in gardens
66:3 he that *s.* a lamb
*Mal.* 1:14 and *s.* a corrupt thing

**SACRIFICING.**

1 *K.* 8:5 I. were wi. him *s.* sheep
12:32 *s.* to calves he had made

**SACRILEGE.**

*Rom.* 2:22 dost thou commit *s.*?

**SAD.**

*Gen.* 40:6 J. looked, they were *s.*
1 *Sam.* 1:18 counten. no more *s.*
1 *K.* 21:5 why is thy spirit so *s.*?
*Neh.* 2:2 why is thy counten. *s.*?
*Ezek.* 13:22 made heart of righte.
*s.* whom I have not made *s.*
*Mat.* 6:16 be not of a *s.* counten.
*Mark* 10:22 he was *s.* at saying
*Luke* 24:17 as ye walk, and are *s.*

**SADDLE.**

*Lev.* 15:9 what *s.* he rideth upon

**SADDLE, Verb.**

2 *Sam.* 19:26 I will *s.* me an ass
1 *K.* 13:13 said, *s.* me the ass, 27

**SADDLED.**

*Gen.* 22:3 Abrah. rose and *s.* ass
*Num.* 22:21 Balaam *s.* his ass
*Jud.* 19:10 with L. two asses *s.*
2 *Sam.* 16:1 met D. with asses *s.*
17:23 Ahithophel *s.* his ass
1 *K.* 2:40 Shimei *s.* and went
13:13 they *s.* him the ass, 23, 27
2 *K.* 4:24 the woman *s.* an ass

**SADDUCEES.**

*Mat.* 3:7 wh. he saw the S. come
16:1 S. came tempting Jesus
6 beware of leaven of S. 11, 12
22:23 the same day came the S.
34 he had put the S. to silence
*Acts* 4:1 the priests and S. came
5:17 S. laid hands on apostles
23:6 P. percei. one part were S.
8 S. say, There is no resurrect.

**SADLY.**

*Gen.* 40:7 why look ye so *s.*?

**SADNESS.**

*Ec.* 7:3 by *s.* of countenance

**SAFE.**

1 *Sam.* 12:11 and ye dwelled *s.*

2 Sam. 18:29 is Absalom s.? 32
Job 21:9 their houses s. from fear
Ps. 119:117 hold me up, I sh. be s.
Prov. 18:10 right. run in, are s.
29:25 whoso trusteth in L. be s.
Is. 5:29 carry the prey away s.
Ezek. 34:27 sh. be s. in th. land
Luke 15:27 had received him s.
Acts 23:24 may bring him s. to F.
27:44 they escaped all s. to land
Phil. 3:1 to write, for you it is s.

**SAFEGUARD.**

1 Sam. 22:23 thou shalt be in s.

**SAFELY.**

Ps. 78:53 he led them on s.
Prov. 1:33 heark. to me sh. dw. s.
3:23 shalt thou walk in way s.
31:11 husb. doth s. trust in her
Is. 41:3 pursued them, passed s.
Hos. 2:18 I will make them lie s.
Zec. 14:11 Jerusalem shall be s.
Mark 14:44 and lead him away s.
Acts 16:23 jailer to keep them s.
See DWELL.

**SAFETY.**

Job 3:26 not in s. nor had I rest
5:4 his children are far from s.
11 that th. may be exalted to s.
11:18 shalt take thy rest in s.
24:23 given him to be in s.
Ps. 12:5 I will set him in s.
33:17 horse is vain thing for s.
Prov. 11:14 in counsel. is s. 24:6
21:31 horse for battle, s. is of L.
Is. 14:30 shall lie down in s.
Acts 5:23 prison shut with all s.
1 Thes. 5:3 sh. say, Peace and s.
See DWELL.

**SAFFRON.**

Cant. 4:14 s. calamus and cinna.

**SAIL, Substantive.**

Is. 33:23 could not spread the s.
Ezek. 27:7 spreadest to be thy s.
Acts 27:17 strake s. so were driv.
40 hoised up main s. to wind

**SAIL.**

Acts 20:3 as he was about to s.
16 Paul had determined to s.
27:1 when we sho. s. into Italy
24 G. hath given thee th. th. s.

**SAILED.**

Luke 8:23 as th. s. he fell asleep
Acts 27:7 when we had s. slowly

**SAILING.**

Acts 21:2 finding a ship s. over
27:6 centurion found a ship s.
9 when s. was now dangerous

**SAILORS.**

Rev. 18:17 and s. stood afar off

**SAINT.**

Ps. 106:16 they envied Aa. the s.
Dan. 8:13 I heard one s. speak-
ing, another s. said to that
s. which
Phil. 4:21 Salute every s. in C. J.

**SAINTS.**

Deut. 33:2 came with 10,000 of s.
3 all his s. are in thy hand
1 Sam. 2:9 keep the feet of his s.
2 Chr. 6:41 let thy s. rejoice
Job 5:1 wh. of s. wilt thou turn?
15:15 putteth no trust in his s.
Ps. 16:3 to s. that are in earth
30:4 sing to Lord, O ye s. of his
31:23 O love the L. all ye his s.
34:9 fear the Lord, ye his s.
37:28 Lord forsaketh not his s.
50:5 gather my s. together to
52:9 for it is good before thy s.
79:2 flesh of thy s. to beasts
89:5 faithfulness in congre. of s.
7 God is feared in assem. of s.
97:10 preserveth souls of his s.
116:15 prec. to L. is death of s.
132:9 let thy s. shout for joy
16 s. shall shout aloud for joy
145:10 and s. shall bless thee
148:14 exalt. praise of all his s.
149:1 praise in congrega. of s.
5 let s. be joyful in glory
9 this honor have all his s.
Prov. 2:8 preserv. way of his s.
Dan. 7:18 s. sh. take king. 22, 27
21 same horn made war wi. s.
25 wear out the s. of M. High
Hos. 11:12 Ju. is faithful with s.
Zec. 14:5 G. sh. come and all s.
Mat. 27:52 bodies of s. that slept
Acts 9:13 evil hath done to thy s.
32 Peter came down also to s.
41 when he had called the s.
26:10 many of s. did I shut up
Rom. 1:7 belov. of G. called to s.
8:27 maketh intercession for s.
12:13 distributing to neces. of s.
15:25 go to Jer. to minister to s.
26 a contribution for poor s.
31 serv. may be accepted of s.
16:2 receive her as becometh s.
15 salute all the s. Heb. 13:24
1 Cor. 1:2 sanctif. called to be s.
6:2 know th. s. sh. jud. world?
14:33 as in all churches of s.
16:1 concern. collection for s.
15 addicted to ministry of s.
2 Cor. 1:1 with all s. in Achaia
8:4 take on us ministering to s.
9:1 touching ministering to s.
12 not only suppli. want of s.
13:13 s. salute you, Phil. 4:22
Eph. 1:1 to the s. at Ephesus
15 heard of your love to all s.
18 glo. of his inheritance in s.
2:19 fellow-citizens with s.
3:8 am less than least of all s.
18 able to comprehend with s.
4:12 for perfecting of the s.
5:3 not be named as becom. s.
6:18 pray. with prayer for all s.
Phil. 1:1 to all the s. in C. Jesus
Col. 1:2 to all the s. and faithful
4 the love ye have to all the s.
12 partak. of inheritance of s.
26 mystery made manif. to s.
1 Thes. 3:13 coming of L. with s.
2 Thes. 1:10 glorified in his s.
1 Tim. 5:10 washed the s. feet
Phile. 5 love thou hast to all s.
7 bowels of the s. are refreshed
Heb. 6:10 ye have minis. to s.
Jude 3 faith once delivered to s.
14 L. com. with 10,000 of his s.
Rev. 5:8 the prayers of s. 8:3, 4
11:18 should. give reward to s.
13:7 to make war with the s.
10 patience and faith of the s.
14:12 here is patience of the s.
15:3 just are thy ways, K. of s.
16:6 they shed blood of the s.
17:6 drunken with blood of s.
18:24 in her was blood of the s.
19:8 linen is righteousness of s.
20:9 compassed camp of the s.

**SAITH.**

See JESUS, LORD, etc.

**SAKE.**

Gen. 8:21 not curse gr. for m. s.
12:16 entreated Abram for her s.
18:29 not do it for forty's s.
31 not for tw.'s s. 32 ten's s.
20:11 slay me for my wife's s.
26:24 mult. thy seed for Ab.'s s.
39:5 bles. house for Joseph's s.
Ex. 18:8 to Egypt for Israel's s.
21:26 for eye's s. 27 tooth's s.
Num. 11:29 env. thou for my s.?
25:11 he was zealous for my s.
1 Sam. 12:22 fors. peo. for na. s.
23:10 destroy the city for my s.
2 Sam. 5:12 Lord exalted kingd.
for Israel's s.
7:21 for word's s. 1 Chr. 17:19
2 Sam. 9:1 kindness for Jon. s. 7
18:5 deal gently for my s.
1 K. 8:41 cometh out far country
for thy name's s. 2 Chr. 6:32
11:12 for Dav. thy father's s. 13,
32, 34; 15:4; 2 K. 8:19; 19:34;
20:6; Ps. 132:10
13 Jerusalem's s. I have chos.
Neh. 9:31 consume for mercies' s.
Job 19:17 entre. for children's s.
Ps. 6:4 save for mercies' s. 31:16
23:3 lead. me for name's s. 31:3
25:7 remem. me for goodness' s.
11 for name's s. pardon iniq.
44:26 redeem us for mercies' s.
69:6 not be confound. for my s.
79:9 purge sins for thy name's s.
106:8 saved th. for his name's s.
109:21 do for me, for name's s.
115:1 thy mercy and truth's s.
143:11 quick. me for name's s.
Is. 37:35 for own s. and Dav. s.
42:21 for righteousness' s.
43:14 for your s. sent to Baby.
25 our transgress. for own s.
45:4 for Jacob's s. I have called
48:9 for my name's s. I defer
11 for mine own s. will I do
62:1 for Zion's s. Jerusalem's s.
63:17 return for thy servant's s.
66:5 cast out for my name's s.
Jer. 14:7 do thou it for name's s.
21 do not abhor us for na. s.
Ezek. 20:9 but I wrought for my
name's s. 14, 22, 44; 36:22
Dan. 9:17 shine on, for L.'s s.
19 defer not for th. own s. O G.
Jon. 1:12 for my s. tempest is
Mic. 3:12 Z. for your s. be ploug.
Mat. 5:11 evil ag. you for my s.
10:22 hat. for my name's s. 24:9;
Mark 13:13; Luke 21:17
39 he that loseth life for my s.
16:25; Mark 8:35; Luke 9:24
14:3 Herod had bound John for
Herodias' s. Mark 6:17
19:12 eun. for kingd. heav.'s s.
29 left lands for my s. sh. rec.
Mark 10:29; Luke 18:29
Mark 4:17 persec. for word's s.
Luke 6:22 for Son of man's s.
John 12:9 came not for Jesus' s.
13:38 lay down life for my s.?
14:11 believe me for works' s.
15:21 do to you for my name's s.
Acts 9:16 suffer for my name's s.
26:7 hope's s. I am acc. of Jews
Rom. 4:23 written for his s. alone
11:28 are enemies for your s.
15:30 Lord's s. strive in prayers
1 Cor. 4:10 we are fools for C. s.
9:23 this I do for the gospel's s.
2 Cor. 4:5 your serv. for Jesus' s.
11 delivered to death for J. s.
12:10 pleas. in distress. for C. s.
Eph. 4:32 G. for C. s. forg. you
Phil. 1:29 to suffer for his s.
Col. 1:24 for his body's s. church
3:6 things' s. wrath of G. com.
1 Thes. 1:5 we were for your s.
5:13 esteem for their work's s.
Phile. 9 for love's s. I beseech
1 Pet. 2:13 submit to every ordi.
of man for Lord's s.
1 John 2:12 forgiv. for name's s.
2 John 2 for truth's s. that dwel.
3 John 7 for his name's s.
Rev. 2:3 for name's s. labored

**Thy SAKE.**

Gen. 3:17 cursed is gro. for thy s.
12:13 be well with me for thy s.
30:27 hath bless. me for thy s.
Ps. 44:22 for t. s. kill. Rom. 8:36
69:7 for t. s. I have borne repr.

*Is.* 54:15 shall fall for *thy s.*
*Jer.* 15:15 for *t. s.* I suff. rebuke
*John* 13:37 lay down life for *t. s.*

**SAKES.**

*Gen.* 18:26 spare place for th. *s.*
*Lev.* 26:45 for their *s.* rem. cov.
*Deut.* 1:37 Lord was angry with me for your *s.* 3:26; 4:21
*Jud.* 21:22 favorable for our *s.*
*Ruth* 1:13 grieveth me for your *s.*
1 *Chr.* 16:21 he reproved kings for their *s. Ps.* 105:14
*Ps.* 7:7 for th. *s.* return on high
106:32 went ill wi. Mo. for th. *s.*
*Is.* 65:8 so will I do for serv.'s *s.*
*Ezek.* 36:22 not for your *s.* Is. 32
*Dan.* 2:30 for th. *s.* make known
*Mark* 6:26 for their *s.* which sat
*John* 11:15 glad for your *s.*
12:30 this voice came for your *s.*
17:19 for their *s.* I sanct. myself
*Rom.* 11:28 belov. for fathers' *s.*
1 *Cor.* 9:10 saith he it for our *s.*?
2 *Cor.* 4:15 all things for your *s.*
8:9 for your *s.* he became poor
1 *Thes.* 3:9 joy for your *s.* bef. G.
2 *Tim.* 2:10 end. all for elect's *s.*

**SALAMIS.** *Acts* 13:5

**SALATHIEL.**

1 *Chr.* 3:17 S. son of, *Mat.* 1:12
*Luke* 3:27 which was son of S.

**SALE.**

*Lev.* 25:27 count years of *s.*
50 price of *s.* according to yea.
*Deut.* 18:8 that wh. cometh of *s.*

**SALEM.**

*Gen.* 14:18 Melchiz. king of S.
*Ps.* 76:2 in S. also his tabernacle
*Heb.* 7:1 Melchiz. king of S. 2

**SALMON.**

*Ruth* 4:20, 21; 1 *Chr.* 2:11; *Mat.* 1:4, 5
*Ps.* 68:14 white as snow in S.
*Luke* 3:32 wh. was the son of S.

**SALMONE.**

*Acts* 27:7 Crete, over against S.

**SALOME.** *Mark* 15:40; 16:1

**SALT.**

*Gen.* 19:26 Lot's wife became *s.*
*Lev.* 2:13 wi. all thy off. offer *s.*
*Deut.* 29:23 wh. land thereof is *s.*
*Jos.* 15:62 chil. of J. had city of *s.*
*Jud.* 9:45 and sowed it with *s.*
2 *Sam.* 8:13 Syrians in val. of *s.*
2 *K.* 2:20 cruse, put *s.* therein
21 went to spring, cast *s.* in
14:7 Amazi. slew in valley of *s.* 10,000, 1 *Chr.* 18:12; 2 *Chr.* 25:11
*Ezr.* 6:9 have need of, wheat, *s.*
7:22 *s.* without pres. how much
*Job* 6:6 unsav. eaten without *s.*?
*Jer.* 17:6 inh. places in a *s.* land
*Ezek.* 43:24 cast *s.* upon them
47:11 marshes shall be giv. to *s.*
*Zep.* 2:9 Moab shall be as *s.* pits
*Mat.* 5:13 ye are *s.* of earth, if *s.*
*Mark* 9:49 sacrifice salted wi. *s.*
50 *s.* is good, if *s.* have lost his saltness, ha. *s.* in yourselves
*Luke* 14:34 *s.* is good, but if *s.*
*Col.* 4:6 speech be season. wi. *s.*
*Jam.* 3:12 yield *s.* water and fre.

*See* COVENANT.

**SALT sea.**

*Gen.* 14:3 vale of Sid. wh. is *s. s.*
*Num.* 34:12 goings out be at *s. s.*
*Deut.* 3:17 *s. sea* under Ashdoth
*Jos.* 3:16 wat. came tow. *s. sea*
12:3 plain to *s. sea,* 15:2; 18:19

**SALTED.**

*Ezek.* 16:4 thou wast not *s.* at all
*Mat.* 5:13 wherew. shall it be *s.*?
*Mark* 9:49 ev. one sh. be *s.* with fire, ev. sacri. be *s.* with salt.

**SALTNESS.**

*Mark* 9:50 if salt have lost his *s.*

**SALUTATION, S.**

*Mark* 12:38 scribes who love *s.*
*Luke* 1:29 what manner of *s.*
41 at *s.* of M. babe leaped, 44
1 *Cor.* 16:21 greet you, the *s.* of me, *Col.* 4:18; 2 *Thes.* 3:17

**SALUTE.**

1 *Sam.* 10:4 they will *s.* thee and
13:10 meet S. they migh. *s.* him
25:14 Da. sent to *s.* our Master
2 *Sam.* 8:10 sent his son to *s.* D.
2 *K.* 4:29 *s.* him not, if any *s.* th.
10:13 we go to *s.* child. of king
*Mat.* 5:47 if ye *s.* brethren only
10:12 wh. ye come in house *s.* it
*Mark* 15:18 and began to *s.* him
*Luke* 10:4 *s.* no man by the way
*Acts* 25:13 came to *s.* Festus
*Rom.* 16:5 *s.* well-beloved Epe.
7 *s.* Andronicus; 9 *s.* Urbane
10 *s.* Apelles, *s.* Aristo. house
11 *s.* Herodian; 12 *s.* Persis
13 *s.* Rufus chosen in Lord
16 *s.* wi. holy kiss, churches *s.*
22 I Tertius, *s.* you in Lord
1 *Cor.* 16:19 churches of A. *s.* you, Aquila and Priscilla *s.* you
2 *Cor.* 13:13 sai. *s.* you, *Phil.* 4:22
*Phil.* 4:21 *s.* every saint in C. J.
*Col.* 4:15 *s.* brethren in Laodicea
2 *Tim.* 4:19 *s.* household of One.
*Tit.* 3:15 all that are with me *s.*
*Phile.* 23 there *s.* thee Epaphras
*Heb.* 13:24 *s.* them that have rule over you, they of Italy *s.*
3 *John* 14 our friends *s.* thee

**SALUTED.**

*Jud.* 18:15 the Danites *s.* Micah
1 *Sam.* 17:22 David *s.* his breth.
1 *Sam.* 30:21 David came to peo. *s.* them
*Mark* 9:15 peo. run. to J. *s.* him
*Luke* 1:40 M. entered, *s.* Elisab.
*Acts* 18:22 P. when he *s.* church
21:7 we came and *s.* brethren
19 when Paul had *s.* James

**SALUTETH.**

*Rom.* 16:23 and Erastus, *s.* you
*Col.* 4:10 fellow-prisoner, *s.* you
12 a servant of Christ, *s.* you
1 *Pet.* 5:13 church at Bab. *s.* you

**SALVATION.**

*Ex.* 14:13 and see the *s.* of the Lord, 2 *Chr.* 20:17
*Deut.* 32:15 esteemed rock of *s.*
1 *Sam.* 11:13 L. wrought *s.* in Is.
14:45 Jona. who wro. great *s.*
19:5 L. wrought great *s.* for Is.
2 *Sam.* 22:51 tower of *s.* for king
1 *Chr.* 16:23 show fr. day to d. *s.*
35 save us, O God of our *s.*
2 *Chr.* 6:41 priests be clo. with *s.*
*Ps.* 3:8 *s.* belongeth to the Lord
14:7 O th. *s.* of Is. we. come, 53:6
24:5 righteous. from G. of his *s.*
35:9 soul shall rejoice in his *s.*
37:39 *s.* of the righteous is of L.
50:23 to him will I show *s.* of G.
65:5 answer us O G. of our *s.*
68:19 blessed be L. G. of our *s.*
20 he that is our G. is G. of *s.*
74:12 work. *s.* in midst of earth
78:22 they trusted not in his *s.*
79:9 help us, O God of our *s.*
85:4 turn us, O God of our *s.*
9 his *s.* nigh them th. fear him
95:1 joyf. noise to rock of our *s.*
96:2 show his *s.* fr. day to day
98:2 Lord hath made kn. his *s.*
3 ends of earth seen *s.* of God
116:13 I will take cup of *s.*
118:15 voice of *s.* in tabernacle
119:155 *s.* is far from wicked
132:16 clothe her priests with *s.*
144:10 he that giv. *s.* unto kings
149:4 will beautify meek with *s.*
*Is.* 12:3 water out wells of *s.*
25:9 be glad and rejoice in his *s.*
26:1 *s.* will G. appoint for walls
33:2 our *s.* in time of trouble
6 knowledge, and stren. of *s.*
45:8 earth open, let th. bring *s.*
17 Is. be saved with everlas. *s.*
46:13 place *s.* in Zion, for Israel
49:8 in a day of *s.* I helped thee
52:7 feet of him that publish. *s.*
10 ends of earth sh. see *s.* of G.
59:11 we look for *s.* far from us
16 therefore his arm bro. *s.*
17 put on helmet of *s.* on head
60:18 thy walls *s.* gates praise
61:10 clo. me wi. garments of *s.*
62:1 *s.* thereof as lamp burneth
63:5 mine own arm brought *s.*
*Jer.* 3:23 in vain is *s.* hoped for fr. hills, truly in L. is *s.* of Isr.
*Lam.* 3:26 wait for *s.* of Lord
*Jon.* 2:9 that I vowed, *s.* of Lord
*Hab.* 3:8 didst ride on char. of *s.*
13 wentest for *s.* of thy people even for *s.* with th. anointed
*Zec.* 9:9 King, just, having *s.*
*Luke* 1:69 raised up horn of *s.*
77 to give knowl. of *s.* to peo.
3:6 all flesh shall see *s.* of God
19:9 *s.* is come to this house
*John* 4:22 worship, *s.* is of Jews
*Acts* 4:12 nei. is *s.* in any other
13:26 to you is word of *s.* sent
47 be for *s.* to ends of the earth
16:17 th. men show us way of *s.*
28:28 *s.* of G. is sent to Gentiles
*Rom.* 1:16 power of God to *s.*
10:10 confession is made to *s.*
11:11 *s.* is come to Gentiles
13:11 *s.* nearer th. wh. we beli.
2 *Cor.* 1:6 comfort. is for your *s.*
6:2 in day of *s.* I succored thee; now accepted time, day of *s.*
7:10 sorrow work. repent. to *s.*
*Eph.* 1:13 heard gospel of your *s.*
6:17 helmet of *s.* sword of Spirit
*Phil.* 1:28 evident token of *s.*
2:12 work out your *s.* with fear
1 *Thes.* 5:8 for a helm. hope of *s.*
9 appoi. us to obtain *s.* by L.
2 *Thes.* 2:13 G. chosen you to *s.*
2 *Tim.* 2:10 may obtain *s.* Christ
3:15 able to make wise to *s.*
*Tit.* 2:11 grace of G. bringeth *s.*
*Heb.* 1:14 who shall be heirs of *s.*
2:3 escape, if we neg. so great *s.*
10 Captain of their *s.* perfect
5:9 became Author of *s.* to all
6:9 things that accompany *s.*
9:28 sh. ap. without sin to *s.*
1 *Pet.* 1:5 kept thro' faith unto *s.*
9 your faith *s.* of your souls
10 of wh. *s.* prophets have inq.
2 *Pet.* 3:15 long-suffer. of L. is *s.*
*Jude* 3 to write to you of com. *s.*
*Rev.* 7:10 *s.* to G. 19:1 *s.* to Lord
12:10 now is come *s.* and stren.

**My SALVATION.**

*Ex.* 15:2 L. my song, bec. *my s.*
2 *Sam.* 22:3 shield, horn of *my s.*
47 be rock of *my s. Ps.* 18:46
23:5 all *my s.* all my desire
*Job* 13:16 he also shall be *my s.*
*Ps.* 25:5 thou art God of *my s.*
27:1 the Lord is my light and *my s.* 62:6; *Is.* 12:2
9 O God of *my s.* 51:14; 88:1
38:22 O L. *my s.* 62:2 is *my s.* 6
62:1 God, from him com. *my s.*
7 G. *my s.* 89:26 rock of *my s.*
91:16 and show him *my s.*
118:14 L. bec. *my s.* 21; *Is.* 12:2
140:7 Lord the strength of *my s.*

*Is.* 12:2 G. is *my s.* is bec. *my s.*
46:13 *my s.* shall not tarry
49:6 *my s.* to end of the earth
51:5 *my s.* gone for. 6 for ever
8 *my s.* fr. generation to gene.
56:1 *my s.* is near to come
*Mic.* 7:7 wait for God of *my s.*
*Heb.* 3:18 joy in God of *my s.*
*Phil.* 1:19 I kn. this turn to *my s.*

**Thy SALVATION.**

*Gen.* 49:18 I waited for *thy s.*
1 *Sam.* 2:1 bec. I rejoice in *t. s.*
2 *Sam.* 22:36 hast also given me the shield of *thy s.* *Ps.* 18:35
*Ps.* 9:14 I will rejoice in *thy s.*
13:5 my heart shall rej. in *thy s.*
20:5 we will rejoice in *thy s.*
21:1 in *t. s.* how shall he rej.!
5 his glory is great in *thy s.*
35:3 say unto soul, I am *thy s.*
40:10 declared faithful. and *t. s.*
16 let such as love *thy s.* say
51:12 rest. to me joy of *t. s.* 70:4
69:13 hear me in truth of *thy s.*
29 let *thy s.* set me up on high
71:15 mouth sh. show forth *t. s.*
85:7 O Lord, grant us *thy s.*
106:4 remember me with *thy s.*
119:41 let *t. s.* come ac. to word
81 my soul fainteth for *thy s.*
123 mine eyes fail for *thy s.*
166 Lord, I have hoped for *t. s.*
174 I have longed for *t. s.* O L.
*Is.* 17:10 hast forgot. God of *t. s.*
62:11 say to Zion, *t. s.* cometh
*Luke* 2:30 mine eyes ha. seen *t. s.*

**SAMARIA.**

1 *K.* 16:24 Omri bought hill S.
*Mic.* 1:6 will make S. as a heap
*Luke* 17:11 through midst of S.
*John* 4:4 must needs go thro' S.
*Acts* 8:1 thro' regions of S. 5, 14

**In SAMARIA.**

1 *K.* 16:28 O. buried *in* S. 22:37
29 Ahab reigned *in* S. 22:51
*Amos* 3:12 taken that dwell *in* S.
*Acts* 1:8 to me in Judea and *in* S.

**SAMARITAN.**

*Luke* 10:33 a certain S. came
17:16 giv. him thanks, was a S.
*John* 8:48 art a S. hast a devil

**SAMARITANS.**

2 *K.* 17:29 hi. places S. had made
*Mat.* 10:5 city of S. enter not
*Luke* 9:52 ent. into village of S.
*John* 4:9 J. have no deal. wi. S.
39 many of S. of that city bel.
40 the S. besought him to tarry
*Acts* 8:25 preached in vil. of S.

**SAME.**

*Jud.* 7:4 *s.* shall go, *s.* sh. not go
*Ps.* 102:27 but thou art the *s.*
113:3 to going do. of *s.* *Mal.* 1:11
*Acts* 24:20 or let these *s.* here say
*Heb.* 1:12 thou art *s.* thy years
2:14 he likewise took part of *s.*
13:8 J. Ch. *s.* yesterday, to-day

*See* DAY, HOUR.

SAMOS. *Acts* 20:15
SAMOTHRACIA. *Acts* 16:11

**SAMSON.**

*Jud.* 13:24 his name S. 16:29
*Heb.* 11:32 would fail to tell of S.

**SAMUEL.**

1 *Sam.* 1:20 son, called him S.
2:18 S. ministered bef. 21; 4:1
3:15 and S. feared to show Eli
10:1 S. took a vial of oil, 15, 25
15:11 it grieved S. 27, 33
16:13 S. took the horn of oil
19:18 Da. fled and came to S.

1 *Sam.* 28:11 wom. Bring me S.
2 *Chr.* 35:18 like that from S.
*Ps.* 99:6 S. among them that
*Jer.* 15:1 though Moses and S.
*Acts* 3:24 the prophets from S.
13:20 450 years till S. prophet
*Heb.* 11:32 would fail to tell of S.

**SANBALLAT.**

*Neh.* 2:10 when S. heard of it, 19
4:1 when S. heard we builded
6:2 S. and Ges. sent to me, 14
12 for Tobiah and S. had hired
13:28 Joiada son-in-law to S.

**SANCTIFICATION.**

1 *Cor.* 1:30 of G. is made to us *s.*
1 *Thes.* 4:3 will of G. even yo. *s.*
4 kn. how to possess ves. in *s.*
2 *Thes.* 2:13 *s.* of Sp. 1 *Pet.* 1:2

**SANCTIFY.**

*Ex.* 13:2 *s.* unto me first-born
19:10 go and *s.* them to-day
22 let the priests *s.* themselves
23 set bounds ab. mount, *s.* it
28:41 ano. and *s.* Aa. and sons, 29:33; 40:13; *Lev.* 8:12; 21:8
29:36 shalt *s.* altar, 37; 40:10
44 I will *s.* taberna. and altar
30:29 thou shalt *s.* the taberna. 40:10, 11; *Lev.* 8:11
31:13 I am L. that doth *s.* you, *Lev.* 20:8; 21:8; *Ezek.* 20:12
*Lev.* 11:44 ye shall *s.* yourselves, 20:7; *Num.* 11:18; *Jos.* 3:5; 7:13; 1 *Sam.* 16:5
21:15 seed, I the Lord do *s.* him
23 I the L. do *s.* them, 22:9, 16
27:14 when a man sh. *s.* house
*Num.* 20:12 believed me not, to *s.* me, 27:14
*Deut.* 5:12 keep the sabbath, to *s.* it, *Neh.* 13:22
15:19 firstling males thou sh. *s.*
*Jos.* 7:13 *s.* people, *s.* yourselves
1 *Chr.* 15:12 said, *s.* yourselves, 2 *Chr.* 29:5; 35:6
23:13 that he sho. *s.* holy things
2 *Chr.* 29:34 uprig. in heart to *s.*
30:17 every one not clean to *s.*
*Is.* 8:13 *s.* Lord of hosts himself
29:23 they sh. *s.* H. O. of Jacob
66:17 *s.* themselves in gardens
*Ezek.* 36:23 I will *s.* my gr. name
37:28 I the Lord do *s.* Israel
38:23 I magnify myself, *s.* mys.
44:19 *s.* peo. with garm. 46:20
*Joel* 1:14 *s.* ye a fast, 2:15
2:16 *s.* congregation, assemble
*John* 17:17 *s.* them thro' thy tru.
19 for their sakes I *s.* myself
*Eph.* 5:26 *s.* and cleanse church
1 *Thes.* 5:23 God of peace *s.* you
*Heb.* 13:12 that he might *s.* peo.
1 *Pet.* 3:15 but *s.* the Lord God

**SANCTIFIED.**

*Gen.* 2:3 G. blessed sev. day *s.* it
*Ex.* 19:14 Moses *s.* the people
29:43 the tabernacle shall be *s.*
*Lev.* 8:10 *s.* the tabernacle
15 *s.* the altar; 30 *s.* Aaron
10:3 I will be *s.* in th. that come
27:15 if he that *s.* it will redeem
19 if he that *s.* the field will
*Num.* 7:1 *s.* tabernacle instrum.
8:17 I *s.* the first-born of Isr.
*Deut.* 32:51 because ye *s.* me not
1 *Sam.* 7:1 and *s.* Eleazar his son
16:5 he *s.* Jesse and his sons
21:5 though it were *s.* this day
1 *Chr.* 15:14 priests and Levit. *s.*
2 *Chr.* 5:11 all the priests were *s.*
7:16 now I have *s.* this hou. 20
29:15 gather. and *s.* themselves
17 *s.* house of L. in eight days
19 all the vessels have we *s.*
30:3 priests had not *s.* themsel.
15 Lev. ashamed, *s.* themselv.
17 many in congregation not *s.*
31:18 set office they *s.* themsel.
*Neh.* 3:1 built and *s.* sheep-gate
12:47 *s.* holy things to Levites
*Job* 1:5 Job *s.* sons and daught.
*Is.* 5:16 holy God shall be *s.*
13:3 I have commanded *s.* ones
*Jer.* 1:5 I *s.* thee, ordained thee
*Ezek.* 20:41 be *s.* in you, 36:23
28:22 when I shall be *s.* in her
25 *s.* in sight of heathen, 39:27
38:16 when I shall be *s.* in thee
48:11 be for priests that are *s.*
*John* 10:36 him, whom the Fa. *s.*
17:19 that they also might be *s.*
*Acts* 20:32 an inheritance among them which are *s.* 26:18
*Rom.* 15:16 being *s.* by H. Ghost
1 *Cor.* 1:2 them th. are *s.* in C. J.
6:11 ye are *s.* in name of Lord
1 *Cor.* 7:14 husband is *s.* wife is *s.*
1 *Tim.* 4:5 it is *s.* by word of G.
2 *Tim.* 2:21 vessel *s.* for Master's
*Heb.* 2:11 they who are *s.* are all
10:10 by which will we are *s.*
14 he perfect. them that are *s.*
29 coven. wherewith he was *s.*
*Jude* 1 to them that are *s.* by G.

**SANCTIFIETH.**

*Mat.* 23:17 temple that *s.* gold?
19 or the altar that *s.* the gift?
*Heb.* 2:11 he that *s.* and they
9:13 if blood of bulls *s.* to puri.

**SANCTUARY.**

*Ex.* 15:17 plant them in the *s.*
25:8 and let them make me a *s.*
30:13 give every one after the *s.*
36:1 all man. of work for *s.* 3, 4
38:24 shek. after sh. of *s.* 25, 26; *Lev.* 5:15; 27:3, 25; *Num.* 3:47, 50; 7:13, 19, 25, 31, 37; 18:16
*Lev.* 4:6 sprinkle blood before *s.*
10:4 carry brethren fr. before *s.*
12:4 nor come into *s.* till her
16:33 make atonem. for holy *s.*
19:30 ye shall rever. my *s.* 26:2
21:12 nei. shall he go out of the *s.* nor prof. the *s.* of his God
*Num.* 3:28 keeping charge of *s.*
4:12 wherewith minister in *s.*
10:21 set forward, bearing the *s.*
18:1 bear the iniquity of the *s.*
3 not come nigh vessels of *s.*
5 ye shall keep charge of the *s.*
19:20 he hath defiled *s.* of the L.
*Jos.* 24:26 set up a stone by *s.*
1 *Chr.* 9:29 oversee instrum. of *s.*
22:19 build ye the *s.* of the Lord
24:5 divided for governors of *s.*
28:10 to build a house for the *s.*
2 *Chr.* 20:8 built thee a *s.* therein
26:18 go out of *s.* for thou hast
29:21 for a sin-offering for the *s.*
30:8 yield to L. enter into his *s.*
19 accord. to purification of *s.*
36:17 king of Bab. sl. men in *s.*
*Neh.* 10:39 where are vessels of *s.*
*Ps.* 20:2 L. send thee help fr. *s.*
63:2 I have seen thee in the *s.*
68:24 seen thy goings in the *s.*
73:17 till I went into *s.* of God
74:3 enemy done wickedly in *s.*
7 they have cast fire into thy *s.*
77:13 thy way, O G. is in the *s.*
78:54 brou. them to border of *s.*
69 built his *s.* like high palaces
96:6 stren. and beauty in his *s.*
102:19 looked fr. height of his *s.*
114:2 Jud. his *s.* Is. his domin.
134:2 lift up your hands in *s.*
150:1 praise L. praise God in *s.*
*Is.* 8:14 L. of hosts, sh. be for *s.*
16:12 he shall come to his *s.*
43:28 I have prof. princes of *s.*
60:13 beautify the place of my *s.*
63:18 our adversaries trodden *s.*
*Jer.* 17:12 from begin. is our *s.*
*Lam.* 1:10 heathen enter. her *s.*

2:7 the Lord hath abhor. his *s.*
20 shall prophet be slain in *s.?*
4:1 stones of *s.* are poured out
*Ezek.* 5:11 thou hast defil. my *s.*
11:16 be to them as a little *s.*
23:38 defiled my *s.* in same day
42:20 between *s.* and prof. place
44:5 with every going forth of *s.*
27 in day he goeth into *s.*
45:3 the *s.* and most holy place
47:12 their wat. issued out of *s.*
48:8 *s.* shall be in midst, 10, 21
*Dan.* 8:11 place of *s.* cast down
13 give *s.* to be trod. und. foot
14 then shall the *s.* be cleansed
9:17 cause face to shi. on thy *s.*
26 peo. shall destr. city and *s.*
11:31 sh. pollute *s.* of strength
*Zep.* 3:4 her priests polluted *s.*
*Heb.* 8:2 a minister of *s.* tabern.
9:1 first coven. had a worldly *s.*
2 tabernacle which is called *s.*
13:11 whose blood is bro. into *s.*

**SANCTUARIES.**

*Lev.* 21:23 that he prof. not my *s.*
26:31 I bring your *s.* to desolat.
*Jer.* 51:51 stran. are come into *s.*
*Ezek.* 28:18 defiled *s.* by iniqui.
*Amos* 7:9 *s.* of Is. sh. be laid wa.

**SAND.**

*Gen.* 22:17 multi. seed as *s.* 32:12
41:49 Joseph gathered corn as *s.*
*Ex.* 2:12 hid the Egyptian in *s.*
*Deut.* 33:19 suck of trea. hid in *s.*
*Jos.* 11:4 went much people as *s*
*Jud.* 7:12 their camels were as *s.*
1 *Sam.* 13:5 P. gath. to fight as *s.*
2 *Sam.* 17:11 all Is. be gath. as *s.*
1 *K.* 4:20 J. and Isr. are ma. as *s.*
29 G. gave S. larg. of hea. as *s.*
*Job* 6:3 it would be heavier th. *s.*
29:18 I shall mul. my days as *s.*
*Ps.* 78:27 feath. fowls like as *s.*
139:18 more in number than *s.*
*Prov.* 27:3 sto. heavy, *s.* weighty
*Is.* 10:22 tho' thy peo. Is. be as *s.*
48:19 seed also had been as *s.*
*Jer.* 5:22 plac. *s.* for bound of sea
15:8 widows increased above *s.*
33:22 *s.* of sea cannot be meas.
*Hos.* 1:10 Is. as *s.* *Rom.* 9:27
*Hab.* 1:9 gather captivity as *s.*
*Mat.* 7:26 man built house on *s.*
*Heb.* 11:12 spr. of one many as *s.*
*Rev.* 13:1 I stood upon *s.* of sea
20:8 number of whom is as *s.*

**SANDALS.**

*Mark* 6:9 but be shod with *s.* put
*Acts* 12:8 gird thyself, bind thy *s.*

**SANG.**

*Ex.* 15:1 then *s.* Moses this song
*Num.* 21:17 Isr. *s.* Spring O well
*Jud.* 5:1 then *s.* Debor. and Bar.
1 *Sam.* 29:5 not D. of wh. th. *s.?*
2 *Chr.* 29:28 singers *s.* trumpet.
30 they *s.* praises with gladn.
*Neh.* 12:42 the singers *s.* aloud
*Job* 38:7 morning stars *s.* togeth.
*Ps.* 106:12 belie. words *s.* praise
*Acts* 16:25 Pa. and Sil. *s.* praises

**SANK.**

*Ex.* 15:5 *s.* into the bottom
10 *s.* as lead in mighty waters

**SAP.**

*Ps.* 104:16 trees of L. full of *s.*

**SAPHIR.**

*Mic.* 1:11 thou inhabitant of S.

**SAPPHIRA.**

*Acts* 5:1 Ananias, with S. wife

**SAPPHIRE.**

*Ex.* 24:10 paved work of *s.* stone
28:18 second row a *s.* 39:11
*Job* 28:16 cannot be val. with *s.*
*Lam.* 4:7 th. polishing was of *s.*
*Ezek.* 1:26 thro. appearance of *s.*
10:1 over them as it were a *s.*
28:13 *s.* and emerald thy cover.
*Rev.* 21:19 founda. of wall was *s.*

**SAPPHIRES.**

*Job* 28:6 stones of it place of *s.*
*Cant.* 5:14 ivory, overlaid with *s.*
*Is.* 54:11 lay foundations with *s.*

**SARAH.**

*Gen.* 17:15 not Sar. but S. shall
18:9 where is S. 11, 12, 13, 14
20:2 Abraham said of S. She is
14 Abimelech restored S.
21:1 the Lord did unto S. as he
23:2 S. died in Kirjath-arba, 19
24:67 brought her into S. tent
25:10 Abra. buried and S. 49:31
*Num.* 26:46 daugh. of Asher S.
*Is.* 51:2 look to S. that bare you
*Rom.* 4:19 deadness of S. womb
9:9 will come, S. sh. have a son
*Heb.* 11:11 thro' faith S. receiv.
1 *Pet.* 3:6 as S. obeyed Abraham

**SARAI.**

*Gen.* 11:29 Ab.'s wife S. 30; 16:1
12:17 plagu. Pharaoh bec. of S.
16:6 S. dealt hardly with Ha. 8

**SARDINE.**

*Rev.* 4:3 to look upon like *s.* sto.

**SARDIS.**

*Rev.* 1:11 write and send it to S.
3:1 to the angel in S. write, 4

**SARDIUS.**

*Ex.* 28:17 first row be *s.* 39:10
*Ezek.* 28:13 *s.* and diam. thy cov.
*Rev.* 21:20 sixth founda. was *s.*

**SARDONYX.**

*Rev.* 21:20 fifth foundat. was a *s.*

**SAREPTA.**

*Luke* 4:26 S. a city of, 1 *K.* 17:9

SARGON. *Is.* 20:1

**SARON.**

*Acts* 9:35 all at S. saw him

**SARUCH.**

*Luke* 3:35 which was son of S.

**SAT.**

*Gen.* 31:34 Ra. *s.* upon images
*Ex.* 12:29 Pha. that *s.* on throne
18:13 Moses *s.* to judge people
*Jud.* 20:26 wept, and *s.* before L.
1 *Sam.* 1:9 E. *s.* by post of temp.
4:13 Eli *s.* by wayside
1 *K.* 16:11 soon as he *s.* on thro.
21:13 chil. of Belial *s.* before N.
1 *K.* 22:10 two kings *s.* on thro.
2 *K.* 6:32 Elisha *s.* in his house
1 *Chr.* 17:1 as Da. *s.* in his house
*Job* 29:25 I chose way, *s.* chief
*Ps.* 26:4 not *s.* with vain persons
*Jer.* 3:2 ways hast thou *s.* for th.
15:17 I *s.* not in assem. of mock.
36:22 king *s.* in winter-house
*Ezek.* 3:15 I *s.* where they *s.*
8:1 *s.* in my house, elders *s.* bef.
20:1 came to inqui. of L. and *s.*
*Dan.* 2:49 Da. *s.* in gate of king
*Mat.* 4:16 people who *s.* in dark.
14:9 wh. *s.* with him, *Mark* 6:26
26:55 I *s.* daily with you
58 Peter *s.* with servants
*Mark* 16:19 *s.* on right hand of G.
*Luke* 7:15 he that was dead *s.* up
10:39 Mary *s.* at Jesus' feet
19:30 a colt wher. never man *s.*
*John* 4:6 Je. wearied, *s.* on well
*Acts* 3:10 *s.* for alms at beau. gate
*Rev.* 4:3 he that *s.* on throne
14:14 one *s.* like Son of man
19:11 *s.* upon him called Faith.
19 war with him *s.* on horse

**SAT down.**

*Ex.* 32:6 people *s.* *down* to eat
*Deut.* 33:3 they *s.* *d.* at thy feet
*Ezr.* 9:3 *s.* *down* astonished
10:16 *s.* *down* to examine mat.
*Neh.* 1:4 I *s.* *d.* mourn. cer. days
*Est.* 3:15 king and Ham. *s.* *down*
*Job* 2:8 Job *s.* *down* am. the ash.
*Ps.* 137:1 we *s.* *down*, yea, wept
*Cant.* 2:3 I *s.* *down* under shad.
*Mat.* 9:10 sinners came, *s.* *down*
26:20 *s.* *d.* with 12, *Luke* 22:14
*Luke* 4:20 gave book to min. *s.* *d.*
5:3 *s.* *d.* taught peo. out of ship
*John* 8:2 *s.* *d.* and taught them
*Acts* 13:14 went into synag. *s.* *d.*
16:13 *s.* *d.* and spake to women
*Heb.* 1:3 *s.* *d.* ri. hand of G. 10:12

**SATAN.**

1 *Chr.* 21:1 S. provoked David to
*Job* 1:6 S. came among them, 2:1
12 S. went from presence of L.
*Ps.* 109:6 S. stand at his hand
*Zec.* 3:1 S. stand. at right hand
2 L. said to S. L. reb. thee, O S.
*Mat.* 4:10 Get thee hence, S.
12:26 if S. cast out S. *Mark* 3:23, 26; *Luke* 11:18
16:23 get thee behind me, S. *Mark* 8:33; *Luke* 4:8
*Mark* 4:15 S. taketh away word
*Luke* 10:18 beheld S. as lightning
13:16 S. hath bound eight. years
22:3 then entered S. into Ju. Is.
31 Simon, S. desired to ha. you
*John* 13:27 S. entered him
*Acts* 5:3 hath S. filled thy heart
26:18 turn fr. power of S. to God
*Rom.* 16:20 G. bruise S. und. feet
1 *Cor.* 5:5 deli. such an one to S.
7:5 S. tempt not for incontin.
2 *Cor.* 2:11 lest S. get advantage
11:14 S. transf. into angel of li.
12:7 messeng. of S. to buffet me
1 *Thes.* 2:18 come, but S. hinder.
2 *Thes.* 2:9 com. after work. of S.
1 *Tim.* 1:20 whom I deliv. to S.
5:15 some already turned aft. S.
*Rev.* 2:9 not J. but synag. of S.
13 Satan's seat where S. dwel.
24 have not kno. depths of S.
3:9 make th. of synagogue of S.
12:9 dragon cast out, called S.
20:2 laid hold on drag. wh. is S.
7 S. shall be loosed out of pris.

**SATIATE, ED.**

*Jer.* 31:14 *s.* soul of priests
25 I have *s.* weary soul
46:10 sw. shall be *s.* with blood

**SATISFACTION.**

*Num.* 35:31 no *s.* for life of mur.
32 no *s.* for him fled for refuge

**SATISFY.**

*Job* 38:27 *s.* deso. and waste gro.
*Ps.* 90:14 *s.* us early with mercy
91:16 wi. long life will I *s.* him
132:15 I will *s.* poor with bread
*Prov.* 5:19 let her breast *s.* thee
6:30 steal to *s.* soul wh. hungry
*Is.* 58:10 thou *s.* afflicted soul
11 L. sh. guide and *s.* thy soul
*Ezek.* 7:19 shall not *s.* their souls
*Mark* 8:4 man *s.* these wi. bread

**SATISFIED.**

*Ex.* 15:9 lust be *s.* upon them
*Lev.* 26:26 ye shall eat, not be *s.*
*Deut.* 14:29 fatherl. eat and be *s.*
33:23 O Naphtali, *s.* with favor
*Job* 19:22 are ye not *s.* wi. flesh?
*Job* 27:14 offsp. not be *s.* with br.
31:31 we cannot be *s.*
*Ps.* 17:15 be *s.* with thy likeness
22:26 meek shall eat and be *s.*
36:8 they sh. be *s.* with fatness
37:19 days of fam. they sh. be *s.*
59:15 let them grudge if not *s.*
63:5 my soul be *s.* with marrow
65:4 *s.* with goodn. of thy house

81:16 honey out of rock I *s.* thee
104:13 earth is *s.* with fruit
105:40 *s.* th. wi. bread of heaven
*Prov.* 12:11 tilleth land sh. be *s.*
14 man be *s.* wi. good by fruit
14:14 good man be *s.* fr. hims.
18:20 a man's belly be *s.*
19:23 he th. hath it sh. abide *s.*
20:13 open eyes, thou sh. be *s.*
30:15 three th. that are never *s.*
*Ec.* 1:8 eye is not *s.* wi. seeing
4:8 nei. is his eye *s.* with rich.
5:10 loveth silver shall not be *s.*
*Is.* 9:20 not be *s.* *Mic.* 6:14
44:16 he roasteth roast, and is *s.*
53:11 see of travail of soul, be *s.*
66:11 *s.* with breasts of consola.
*Jer.* 31:14 peo. be *s.* with goodn.
50:10 all th. spoil Chaldea be *s.*
19 soul be *s.* on mount Ephra.
*Lam.* 5:6 giv. hand to E. to be *s.*
*Ezek.* 16:28 couldest not be *s.* 29
*Amos* 4:8 drink wat. were not *s.*
*Hab.* 2:5 as death, cannot be *s.*

**SATISFIETH, EST.**

*Ps.* 103:5 *s.* mouth with good th.
107:9 he *s.* longing soul
145:16 and thou *s.* every thing
*Is.* 55:2 labor for that wh. *s.* not

**SATISFYING.**

*Prov.* 13:25 eateth to *s.* of soul
*Col.* 2:23 honor to the *s.* of flesh

**SATTEST.**

*Ps.* 9:4 th. *s.* in throne judging
*Ezek.* 23:41 *s.* upon stately bed

**SATYR, S.**

*Is.* 13:21 owls dwell, *s.* dance
34:14 *s.* shall cry to his fellow

**SAUL.**

*Gen.* 36:37 S. of Rehoboth, 38
1 *Sam.* 9:2 name was S. 14:51
17 when Samuel saw S. 18
10:11 is S. also among, 12; 19:24
21:11 S. hath sl. his thousands
*Is.* 10:29 Gibeah of S. is fled
*Acts* 7:58 man's feet name was S.
8:1 and S. was consenting to, 3
9:4 S. S. why perse. 22:7; 26:14
11 and inquire for one call. S.
17 S. the Lord hath sent, 22:13
22 but S. increased in strength
24 laying wait was kno. of S.
26 when S. was come to Jeru.
11:25 went to Tarsus to seek S.
30 by hands of Barnab. and S.
13:1 prophets brought up wi. S.
2 separate me Barnabas and S.
7 called for Barnabas and S.
9 S. set his eyes on him
21 G. gave unto th. S. son of C.

**SAVE,** *for except.*

2 *Sam.* 22:32 *s.* the L.? *Ps.* 18:31
*Mat.* 11:27 nor knoweth any the Father, *s.* Son
17:8 no man, *s.* J. *Mark* 9:8
*Luke* 18:19 none good, *s.* one, G.
*John* 6:46 seen Fa. *s.* he of God

**SAVE.**

*Gen.* 45:7 G. sent me to *s.* lives
*Deut.* 20:4 the Lord goeth to *s.*
22:27 there was none to *s.* her
28:29 and no man shall *s.* thee
*Jud.* 6:14 thou shalt *s.* Israel
15 wherewith shall I *s.* Israel?
31 plead for B.? will ye *s.* him
36 if thou *s.* Israel by my hand
37 I know thou wilt *s.* Israel
1 *Sam.* 9:16 th. he may *s.* my peo.
10:24 God *s.* king, 2 *Sam.* 16:16; 2 *K.* 11:12; 2 *Chr.* 23:11
14:6 no restraint, to *s.* by many
19:11 if thou *s.* not thy. this ni.
2 *Sam.* 3:18 by hand of Da. *s.* Is.
22:28 affli. peo. wilt *s.* *Ps.* 18:27
42 none to *s.* them, *Ps.* 18:41
1 *K.* 1:12 mayest *s.* thi. own life
25 say, God *s.* king Adonijah
34 God *s.* king Solomon, 39
20:31 peradvent. will *s.* thy life
2 *K.* 19:34 I will defend this city to *s.* it, *Is.* 37:35
*Neh.* 6:11 would go to *s.* his life
*Job* 2:6 in thy hand, *s.* his life
20:20 not *s.* that wh. he desired
22:29 he shall *s.* humble person
40:14 thine ri. hand can *s.* thee
*Ps.* 20:9 *s.* L. let king hear us
28:9 *s.* thy people, *Jer.* 31:7
37:40 he shall *s.* them
44:3 neit. did their arm *s.* them
60:5 *s.* with right hand, 108:6
69:35 God will *s.* Z. build Judah
72:4 he shall *s.* child. of needy
13 he shall *s.* souls of needy
76:9 when God arose to *s.* meek
86:2 O my God, *s.* thy servant
16 *s.* the son of thy handmaid
109:31 *s.* him fr. those that con.
118:25 *s.* I beseech thee, O Lord
145:19 hear their cry, *s.* them
*Prov.* 20:22 wait on L. sh. *s.* thee
*Is.* 35:4 your God will *s.* you
45:20 pray unto a god cannot *s.*
46:7 he cannot ans. nor *s.* him
47:15 none shall *s.* thee
49:25 saith L. I will *s.* thy chil.
59:1 not shortened, it cannot *s.*
63:1 in righteousn. mighty to *s.*
*Jer.* 2:28 arise, if th. can *s.* thee
11:12 not *s.* them at all
14:9 a mig. man that cannot *s.*
15:20 I am with thee to *s.* thee, saith L. 30:11; 42:11; 46:27
30:10 O Israel, I will *s.* thee
48:6 flee, *s.* your lives, be like
*Ezek.* 3:18 warn wicked, *s.* life
34:22 theref. will I *s.* my flock
36:29 will *s.* you; 37:23 *s.* them
*Hos.* 1:7 I will *s.* them by the L. and will not *s.* th. by sword
13:10 is there any may *s.* thee?
*Hab.* 1:2 cry to thee, wilt not *s.*
*Zep.* 3:17 he will *s.* will rejoice
19 I will *s.* her that halteth
*Zec.* 8:7 *s.* my people from east
9:16 L. their God shall *s.* them
10:6 I will *s.* house of Joseph
12:7 the Lord sh. *s.* tents of Ju.
*Mat.* 1:21 Je. shall *s.* his people
16:25 whosoever will *s.* his life, *Mark* 8:35; *Luke* 9:24; 17:33
18:11 Son of man come to *s.* th. wh. was lost, *Luke* 19:10
27:42 saved others, himself he cannot *s.* *Mark* 15:31
49 whether E. will come to *s.*
*Mark* 3:4 is it lawful to *s.* or kill? *Luke* 6:9
*Luke* 9:56 not to destroy, but *s.*
23:35 *s.* himself, if he be Christ
37 *s.* thyself; 39 if Ch. *s.* thys.
*John* 12:47 not to judge, to *s.*
*Acts* 2:40 *s.* yourselves fr. gener.
27:43 centurion, willing to *s.* P.
*Rom.* 11:14 if I might *s.* some of them, 1 *Cor.* 9:22
1 *Cor.* 1:21 preaching to *s.* them
7:16 shalt *s.* husband, *s.* wife
1 *Tim.* 1:15 Ch. came to *s.* sinn.
4:16 in doing this sh. *s.* thyself
*Heb.* 5:7 him that was able to *s.*
7:25 he is able also to *s.* them
*Jam.* 1:21 able to *s.* your souls
2:14 can faith *s.* him
4:12 able to *s.* and destroy
5:15 prayer of faith shall *s.* sick
20 shall *s.* a soul from death
*Jude* 23 and others *s.* with fear

*See* ALIVE.

**SAVE me.**

2 *K.* 16:7 *s.* *me* out of hand of k.
*Ps.* 3:7 arise, O L. *s.* *me*, O. G.
6:4 *s.* *me* for thy mercies' sake, 31:16; 109:26
7:1 *s.* *me* from them that perse.
31:2 house of defence to *s.* *me*
44:6 nor shall my sword *s.* *me*
54:1 *s.* *me*, O G. by thy name
55:16 and the Lord shall *s.* *me*
57:3 send from heav. and *s.* *me*
59:2 *s.* *me* from bloody men
69:1 *s.* *me*, for waters are come
71:2 incline thine ear, *s.* *me*
3 given commandment to *s.* *me*
119:94 *s.* *me*, I sou. thy precepts
146 I cried unto thee, *s.* *me*
138:7 thy right hand sh. *s.* *me*
*Is.* 38:20 L. was ready to *s.* *me*
*Jer.* 17:14 O Lord, *s.* *me*
*Mat.* 14:30 saying, Lord, *s.* *me*
*John* 12:27 Fa. *s.* *me* fr. this hour

**SAVE us.**

*Jos.* 10:6 come quickly, *s.* *us*
1 *Sam.* 4:3 may *s.* *us* fr. enemies
7:8 cry to the L. he will *s.* *us*
10:27 how shall this man *s.* *us*
11:3 if there be no man to *s.* *us*
2 *K.* 19:19 *s.* thou *us* out of his hand, *Is.* 37:20
1 *Chr.* 16:35 *s.* *us*, O God
*Ps.* 80:2 stir up strength, *s.* *us*
106:47 *s.* *us*, O Lord our God
*Is.* 25:9 wait. for him, will *s.* *us*
33:22 Lord is our king, will *s.* *us*
*Jer.* 2:27 in trouble say, *s.* *us*
*Lam.* 4:17 nation could not *s.* *us*
*Hos.* 14:3 Asshur shall not *s.* *us*
*Mat.* 8:25 awoke, saying, L. *s.* *us*
1 *Pet.* 3:21 bapt. doth also *s.* *us*

**SAVED.**

*Gen.* 47:25 hast *s.* our lives
*Ex.* 1:17 *s.* men-children, 18
*Num.* 22:33 *s.* her alive
31:15 have ye *s.* women alive?
*Jud.* 7:2 own hand hath *s.* me
8:19 if he had *s.* them alive
1 *Sam.* 27:11 Da. *s.* neither man
2 *Sam.* 19:5 serv. have *s.* thy life
2 *K.* 6:10 and *s.* himself there
*Neh.* 9:27 gavest saviors, who *s.*
*Ps.* 33:16 no king is *s.* by multi.
44:7 thou hast *s.* us fr. enemies
106:8 *s.* them for name's sake
10 *s.* fr. him that hated them
*Is.* 43:12 and have *s.* and showed
45:22 *s.* all ends of the earth
*Jer.* 4:14 wash heart may. be *s.*
8:20 summer ended, are not *s.*
*Mat.* 19:25 who then can be *s.*? *Mark* 10:26; *Luke* 18:26
24:22 no flesh be *s.* *Mark* 13:20
27:42 he *s.* others, *Mark* 15:31; *Luke* 23:35
*Luke* 1:71 *s.* from our enemies
7:50 faith hath *s.* thee, 18:42
8:12 lest they believe and be *s.*
13:23 L. are th. few that be *s.*?
*John* 3:17 that world might be *s.*
5:34 I say, that ye might be *s.*
*Acts* 2:47 L. ad. such as sh. be *s.*
4:12 no other na. whereby be *s.*
16:30 what must I do to be *s.*?
27:31 ex. abide in ship, not be *s.*
*Rom.* 8:24 we are *s.* by hope
10:1 for Is. that they may be *s.*
1 *Cor.* 1:18 to us who are *s.* of G.
5:5 that the spirit may be *s.*
10:33 that they may be *s.*
15:2 by which also ye are *s.*
2 *Cor.* 2:15 sweet savor in them *s.*
*Eph.* 2:5 by grace ye are *s.* 8
1 *Thes.* 2:16 Gent. that they be *s.*
2 *Thes.* 2:10 love of trut. th. be *s.*
1 *Tim.* 2:4 have all men to be *s.*
*Tit.* 3:5 accord. to mercy he *s.* us
1 *Pet.* 3:20 wherein 8 souls we. *s.*
4:18 if righteous scarcely be *s.*
2 *Pet.* 2:5 *s.* Noah, eighth person

Rev. 31:24 natio. s. walk in light

**God, or Lord SAVED.**

Ex. 14:30 L. s. Is. 1 Sam. 14:23
Deut. 33:29 who like th. s. by L.?
1 Sam. 10:19 reject. G. who s. y.
2 K. 14:27 L. s. them by Jerobo.
1 Chr. 11:14 L. s. them by deliv.
2 Chr. 32:22 thus L. s. Hezekiah
Ps. 34:6 L. s. him out of troubl.
107:13 L. s. them out of distres.
Is. 63:9 angel s. th. in his love
2 Tim. 1:9 God who hath s. us
Jude 5 the L. having s. people

**Shall, or shalt be SAVED.**

Num. 10:9 ye s. be s. fr. enemies
2 Sam. 22:4 I sh. be s. from mine enemies. Ps. 18:3
Ps. 80:3 face to shi. we s. be s.
Prov. 28:18 walk. uprigh. s. be s.
Is. 30:15 in returning s. ye be s.
45:17 but Israel s. be s. in Lord
Jer. 17:14 L. save me, I s. be s.
23:6 days Jud. s. be s. 33:16
30:7 Jacob's trouble, he s. be s.
Mat. 10:22 that endureth to end s. be s. 24:13; Mark 13:13
Mark 16:16 he that believ. s. be s.
John 10:9 by me he shall be s.
Acts 2:21 whosoever shall call on Lord, s. be s. Rom. 10:13
11:14 th. and thy house s. be s.
15:11 thro' grace we shall be s.
16:31 believe on L. Je. sh. be s.
Rom. 5:9 we sh. be s. from wrath
10 we shall be s. by his life
9:27 Is. as sand, remnant s. be s.
10:9 bel. God raised him, s. be s.
11:26 so all Israel shall be s.
1 Cor. 3:15 but he himself s. be s.
1 Tim. 2:15 s. be s. in child-bear.

**SAVEST.**

2 Sam. 22:3 th. s. me fr. violence
Job 26:2 how s. thou the arm?
Ps. 17:7 O thou that s. right hand

**SAVETH.**

1 Sam. 14:39 liveth, who s. Isra.
17:47 the L. s. not with sword
Job 5:15 s. poor from the sword
Ps. 7:10 God, who s. the upright
20:6 the Lord s. his anointed
Ps. 34:18 s. such as be of cont. sp.
107:19 he s. th. out of distresses

**SAVING.**

Gen. 19:19 mercy in s. my life
Neh. 4:23 s. that ev. one put off
Ps. 20:6 s. strength of ri. hand
28:8 s. strength of his anointed
67:2 s. health among all nations
Ec. 5:11 s. beholding of them
Amos 9:8 s. I will not destroy J.
Mat. 5:32 s. for cause of fornica.
Luke 4:27 none cleansed, s. Naa.
Heb. 10:39 believe to s. of soul
11:7 Noah prepared an ark to s.
Rev. 2:17 s. he that receiveth it

**SAVIOUR.**

2 Sam. 22:3 my refuge, my S.
2 K. 13:5 the L. gave Israel a s.
Ps. 106:21 forgat God their S.
Is. 19:20 shall send them a S.
43:3 I am H. O. of Is. thy S.
11 I am L. beside th. is no S.
45:15 hidest thyself, O God, S.
21 a just G. and a S. th. is no.
60:16 know I the L. am thy S.
63:8 my peo. so he was their S.
Jer. 14:8 S. of Israel in trouble
Hos. 13:4 th. is no S. beside me
Luke 1:47 sp. rejoic. in G. my S.
2:11 born in city of Da. a S.
John 4:42 this is Ch. S. of world
Acts 5:31 God exalted to be S.
13:23 God raised to Israel a S.
Eph. 5:23 Chr. is S. of the body
Phil. 3:20 whence we look for S.
1 Tim. 1:1 comm. of G. our S.
2:3 accept. in sight of G. our S.
4:10 trust in God who is S.
2 Tim. 1:10 appearing of our S.
Tit. 1:3 according to God our S.
4 peace from L. Jes. C. our S.
2:10 adorn doctr. of God our S.
13 glorious appearing of our S.
3:4 after kind. of G. S. appear.
6 shed on us through C. our S.
2 Pet. 1:1 righteous. of G. our S.
11 kingdom of our Lord and S.
2:20 knowledge of our L. and S.
2:2 apostles of the Lord and S.
18 grow in knowledge of our S.
1 John 4:14 Fa. sent Son to be S.
Jude 25 to only wise God our S.

**SAVIORS.**

Neh. 9:27 thou gavest them s.
Ob. 21 s. shall come up on Zion

**SAVOR.**

Ex. 5:21 made our s. be abhor.
Lev. 26:31 not s. of sweet odors
Ec. 10:1 ointm. send stinking s.
Cant. 1:3 s. of good ointment
Joel 2:20 his stink and his ill s.
Mat. 5:13 salt lost s. Luke 14:34
2 Cor. 2:14 maketh manifest s.
16 s. of death unto de. s. of life

**Sweet SAVOR.**

Gen. 8:21 Lord smelled a sw. s.
Ex. 29:18 it is s. s. Lev. 1:9, 13, 17; 2:9; 3:5; 8:21; Num. 15:14; 18:17; 28:8
25 for a s. s. an offer. to L. 41; Lev. 2:12; 3:16; 4:31; 6:15, 21; 8:28; 17:6; 23:13; Num. 15:7, 24; 28:2, 6, 13, 27; 29:2, 6, 8; Ezek. 16:19
Lev. 23:18 of a sweet s. unto the L. Num. 28:24; 29:13, 36
Num. 15:3 make a s. s. unto L.
28:13 offering of a s. s. to Lord
Ezek. 6:13 wh. they did offer s. s.
20:28 there th. made their s. s.
41 accept you with your s. s.
2 Cor. 2:15 we are to God a s. s.
Eph. 5:2 a sacrifice to God for a sweet smelling s.

**Sweet SAVORS.**

Ezr. 6:10 sacrifices of s. s. to G.

**SAVOREST.**

Mat. 16:23 th. s. not the things that be of God, Mark 8:33

**SAVORY.**

Gen. 27:4 ma. me s. meat, 7, 14
31 Esau had made s. meat

**SAW.**

Gen. 6:2 sons of G. s. daugh. of
9:23 they s. not; 22:4 Abrah. s.
26:28 we s. Lord was with thee
Ex. 2:12 he s. th. was no man
10:23 they s. not one ano. 3 days
24:10 they s. the G. of Isra. 11
Num. 25:7 when Phinehas s. it.
Jud. 19:30 all that s. it said, No
1 Sam. 10:14 s. they were no wh.
17:24 Is. when they s. the man
1 K. 19:3 wh. he s. that, he arose
2 K. 2:12 Elisha s. it, he s. him
2 K. 4:25 when man of God s. her
2 Chr. 15:9 s. Lord was with him
25:21 s. one another in the face
Neh. 6:16 when they s. th. thin.
Job 20:9 the eye which s. him
29:8 the young men s. me
11 when the eye s. me, it gave
Ps. 114:3 sea s. it, and fled,
Cant. 3:3 s. ye him my soul lo.?
Ezek. 8:10 so I went in, and s.
Hag. 2:3 who am. you s. house?
Mat. 2:9 the star which they s.
12:22 dumb both spake and s.
17:8 they s. no man, save Jesus
Mark 8:23 asked him, if he s.
Luke 8:34 they s. what was done
47 when the woman s. that she
9:32 awake, they s. his glory
24:24 even so, him they s. not
John 8:56 Abraham s. my day
12:41 Esaias, when he s. his gl.
19:35 he that s. it, bare record
Acts 9:8 eyes opened, s. no man
12:3 he s. it pleased the Jews

**SAW, with Lord or God.**

Gen. 1:4 G. s. light it was good
10 called dry land earth, G. s. it was good, 12, 18, 21, 25, 31
Ex. 3:4 L. s. that he turn. aside
2 K. 14:26 L. s. affliction of Isr.
2 Chr. 12:7 L. s. they humbled
Is. 59:15 L. s. it, it displeas. him
16 L. s. that there was no man
Jon. 3:10 God s. their works

**I SAW.**

Gen. 41:19 such as I never s.
44:28 and I s. him not since
Jud. 12:3 I s. he deliv. me not
1 Sam. 28:13 I s. gods ascending
1 K. 22:19 I s. the Lord on his throne, 2 Chr. 18:18
Job 31:21 when I s. my help
Prov. 24:32 I s. and considered it
Ec. 2:24 this I s. fr. hand of God
8:10 I s. the wicked buried
Ezek. 16:50 th. away as I s. good
Hos. 9:10 I s. your fath. as first
13 Ephraim, as I s. Tyrus
John 1:32 I s. Spirit descending
48 under the fig-tree, I s. thee
Acts 26:13 I s. a light fr. heaven
Gal. 1:19 other apostles s. I no.
2:14 when I s. that they walked
Rev. 1:17 when I s. him, I fell at

**SAW, S.**

2 Sam. 12:31 he put Ammonites under s. 1 Chr. 20:3
Is. 10:15 sh. s. magnify ag. him?

**SAWED, N.**

1 K. 7:9 costly stones s. wi. sta.
Heb. 11:37 they were s. asunder

**SAWEST.**

Gen. 20:10 s. th. done this thing?
1 Sam. 19:5 s. it and didst rejoice
28:13 be not afraid, for what s.
2 Sam. 18:11 J. said, thou s. him
Dan. 2:34 thou s. till a stone, 45

**SAY.**

Gen. 34:11 what ye s. to me, 12
37:20 s. some beast devour. him
44:16 what sh. we s. to my lord
Num. 22:19 know what L. will s.
Deut. 31:17 will s. in that day
Jos. 22:28 when they should s.
Jud. 7:11 sh. hear what they s.
2 Sam. 21:4 what you shall s.
1 K. 1:36 the L. G. of my lord s.
2:17 for he will not s. thee nay
Ezr. 9:10 O G. wh. shall we s.?
Job 9:12 who will s. to him, What doest thou? Ec. 8:4
37:19 teach us what we shall s.
Is. 44:5 one shall s. I am Lord's
58:9 and he shall s. Here I am
Jer. 14:17 therefore thou shalt s.
23:7 s. no more, The Lord liveth
39:12 as he shall s. unto thee
42:20 according to all L. shall s.
Ezek. 13:7 ye s. The L. saith it
Mic. 3:11 s. Is not Lord am. us?
Zec. 11:5 they s. I am rich
Mat. 3:9 think not to s. in yourselves, Luke 3:8
13:51 underst.? they s. Yea, L.
16:15 but wh. s. ye that I am? Mark 8:29; Luke 9:20
21:3 s. aug. to you, ye sh. s.
16 him, Hearest what these s.?
26 if we shall s. Of men, Mark 11:32; Luke 20:6
23:3 for they s. and do not
Mark 1:44 see thou s. nothi. to

*John* 8:26 many thi. to *s.* 16:12
54 whom ye *s.* he is your God
*Acts* 21:23 this that we *s.* to thee
23:18 something to *s.* unto thee
*Acts* 26:22 none but wh. M. did *s.*
1 *Thes.* 4:15 we *s.* to you by L.
*Heb.* 5:11 have many things to *s.*
*Jam.* 4:15 for that ye ought to *s.*
*See* BEGAN.

**SAY, *imperatively*.**
*Is.* 43:9 or hear, and *s.* it is truth
*Zec.* 1:3 *s.* unto them, Turn ye
*Mat.* 21:3 *s.* The Lord hath need of them, *Mark* 11:3
*Luke* 7:7 *s.* in a word, my serv.

**I SAY.**
*Ex.* 3:13 what sh. *I s.* to them?
4:23 *I s.* unto th. Let my son go
6:29 sp. all that *I s.* *Ezek.* 44:5
*Jud.* 7:4 *I s.* this shall go with
*Is.* 38:15 what shall *I s.?*
*Ezek* 2:8 hear wh. *I s.* unto thee
*Mat.* 8:9 *I s.* to th. man, *Lu.* 7:8
*Luke* 6:46 do not things wh. *I s.*
1 *Cor.* 9:8 *s. I* these thi. as man?
15:50 *I s.* brethren, 2 *Cor.* 9:6; *Gal.* 3:17; 5:16; *Eph.* 4:17; *Col.* 2:4
*Gal.* 1:9 before, so *s. I* now again
*Heb.* 11:32 what shall *I* more *s.?*

**I SAY unto you.**
2 *K.* 2:18 did *I* not *s. u. y.* go not
*Mark* 13:37 what *I. s. u. y.* I say
*Rev.* 2:24 *u. y. I s.* and to rest

**SAYEST.**
*Ex.* 33:12 *s.* to me, Bring people
*Num.* 22:17 do whatsoever th. *s.*
*Ruth* 3:5 all that thou *s.* unto me
1 *K.* 18:11 and now thou *s.* go, 14
*Neh.* 6:8 no such things as th. *s.*
*Job* 22:13 *s.* how doth G. know?
*Prov.* 24:12 if thou *s.* behold
*Is.* 40:27 why *s.* thou, O Jacob
47:8 that *s.* in thy heart, I am
*Mat.* 27:11 J. said unto him, th. *s.* *Mark* 15:2; *Luke* 23:3; *John* 18:37
*John* 1:22 what *s.* th. of thyself?

**SAYING, Participle.**
*Mat.* 26:44 prayed 3d time *s.* sa.
*Acts* 26:22 *s.* none other things

**SAYING, Substantive.**
*Deut.* 1:23 the *s.* pleased me well
1 *Sam.* 18:8 the *s.* displeased S.
2 *Sam.* 17:4 *s.* pleased Absalom
6 shall we do after his *s.?*
24:19 Da. accord. to *s.* of God
1 *K.* 2:38 Shimei said, *s.* is good
12:15 might perf. his *s.* by Ahij.
13:4 J. heard *s.* of man of God
15:29 acc. to *s.* of L. 2 *K.* 10:17
17:15 acc. to *s.* of Elij. 2 *K.* 2:22
2 *K.* 5:14 accor. to *s.* of man, 8:2
*Est.* 1:21 *s.* pleased the king
*Ps.* 49:4 open dark *s.* on harp
*Jon.* 4:2 my *s.* wh. in country
*Mat.* 15:12 offended after this *s.*
19:11 all men cannot rec. this *s.*
*Mark* 7:29 for this *s.* go thy way
9:10 kept that *s.* with themselv.
32 but they understood not that *s.* *Luke* 3:50; 9:45
10:22 he was sad at that *s.*
*Luke* 1:29 was troubled at his *s.*
2:17 they made known abroa. *s.*
9:45 feared to ask him of that *s.*
18:34 this *s.* was hid from them
*John* 4:37 herein *s.* true, one so.
39 many beli. for *s.* of wom. 42
6:60 hard *s.* who can hear?
7:36 what manner of *s.* he said?
8:51 if a man keep my *s.* 52
55 I know him, keep his *s.*
12:38 *s.* of Esaias be fulfilled
15:20 kept my *s.* will keep yours
18:9 *s.* of Je. might be fulfill. 32
19:8 Pilate heard *s.* was afraid
21:23 went *s.* abroad am. breth.
*Acts* 6:5 *s.* pleased the multitude
16:36 keeper told this *s.* to Paul
*Rom.* 13:9 comprehend. in this *s.*
1 *Cor.* 15:54 be brought to pass *s.*
1 *Tim.* 1:15 this is a faithful *s.* 4:9; 2 *Tim.* 2:11; *Tit.* 3:8
3:1 this is true *s.* if man desire

**SAYINGS.**
*Num.* 14:39 Mo. told th. *s.* to pe.
2 *Chr.* 13:22 Ahijah's *s.* are writ.
33:19 written am. *s.* of the seers
*Ps.* 78:2 I will utter dark *s.*
*Prov.* 1:6 underst. dark *s.* of wi.
4:10 O my son, receive my *s.*
20 incline thine ear to my *s.*
*Mat.* 7:24 whoso heareth these *s.* 26; *Luke* 6:47
*Luke* 1:65 these *s.* noised abroad
2:51 mother kept th. *s.* in heart
9:44 let th. *s.* sink into your ea.
*John* 14:24 lov. not, keep. not *s.*
*Acts* 14:18 *s.* scarce restrained
19:28 heard *s.* full of wrath
*Rom.* 3:4 might. be justi. in *s.*
*Rev.* 22:6 *s.* faithful and true
7 blessed that keep. *s.* of book
10 seal not *s.* of prophecy of this book

**SCAB.**
*Lev.* 13:2 in skin of flesh a *s.*
6 it is but a *s.* 7 if *s.* spread
14:56 this is the law for a *s.*
*Deut.* 28:27 L. smite thee with *s.*
*Is.* 3:17 L. will sm. thee wi. a *s.*

**SCABBARD.**
*Jer.* 47:6 put up thys. into thy *s.*

**SCABBED.**
*Lev.* 21:20 scurvy or *s.* not appr.
22:22 or *s.* he sh. not offer to L.

**SCAFFOLD.**
2 *Chr.* 6:13 S. had made braz. *s.*

**SCALES.**
*Lev.* 11:9 whatsoever have *s.* eat, *Deut.* 14:9
10 that have no *s.* not eat, 12; *Deut.* 14:10
*Job* 41:15 his *s.* are his pride
*Is.* 40:12 weighed mount. in *s.*
*Ezek.* 29:4 cause fish to stick to *s.*
*Acts* 9:18 fell from eyes as it had been *s.*

**SCALETH.**
*Prov.* 21:22 a wise man *s.* city

**SCALL.**
*Lev.* 13:30 it is a dry *s.* a lepr.
31 plague of *s.* not deeper than skin, shut him up th. h. *s.* 33
33 shav. but *s.* sh. be not shave
14:54 law of all leprosy and *s.*

**SCALP.**
*Ps.* 68:21 G. sh. wound hairy *s.*

**SCANT.**
*Mic.* 6:10 *s.* meas. is abominable

SCAPE-GOAT. *See* GOAT.

**SCARCE.**
*Gen.* 27:30 Ja. *s.* gone fr. father
*Acts* 14:18 sayings *s.* restrai. peo

**SCARCELY.**
*Rom.* 5:7 *s.* for right. man 1 die
1 *Pet.* 4:18 if righte. *s.* be saved

**SCARCENESS.**
*Deut.* 8:9 sh. eat bread witho. *s.*

**SCAREST.**
*Job* 7:14 thou *s.* me with dreams

**SCARLET.**
*Gen.* 38:38 bound a *s.* thread, 30
*Ex.* 25:4 and purple and *s.* 26:1, 31, 36; 27:16; 28:5, 6, 8, 15; 35:6, 23, 25; 38:18, 23
*Num.* 4:8 spr. on them cloth of *s.*
*Jos.* 2:18 bind *s.* thr. in window
2 *Sam.* 1:24 S. who clo. you in *s.*
*Prov.* 31:21 house. clothed wi. *s.*
*Cant.* 4:3 lips like a thread of *s.*
*Is.* 1:18 tho' your sins be as *s.*
*Lam.* 4:5 that were bro. up in *s.*
*Dan.* 5:7 clothed with *s.* 16, 29
*Nah.* 2:3 valiant men are in *s.*
*Mat.* 27:28 put on Jes. a *s.* robe
*Heb.* 9:19 took water, and *s.* wool
*Rev.* 17:3 woman sit on *s.* beast
18:12 no man buy. merch. of *s.*
16 great city that was cl. wi. *s.*

**SCATTER.**
*Gen.* 11:9 thence did L. *s.* them
49:7 divide in Ja. *s.* them in Is.
*Lev.* 26:33 I will *s.* you am. heat.
*Num.* 16:37 take censers, *s.* fire
*Deut.* 4:27 sh. *s.* you among hea. 28:64; *Jer.* 9:16; *Ezek.* 22:15
32:26 I would *s.* th. into corners
1 *K.* 14:15 *s.* them beyond river
*Neh.* 1:8 if ye transgress, I will *s.*
*Ps.* 59:11 *s.* by thy power, O L.
68:30 *s.* peo. that delight in war
106:27 lifted up hand to *s.* them
144:6 cast lightning, *s.* them
*Is.* 28:25 cast fitches, *s.* cummin
41:16 whirlwind shall *s.* them
*Jer.* 13:24 I will *s.* th. as stubble
18:17 I will *s.* th. as with wind
23:1 woe to pastors that *s.* sheep
49:32 I will *s.* them into all winds, 36; *Ezek.* 5:10, 12
*Ezek.* 5:2 third part thou shalt *s.*
6:5 *s.* your bones about altars
10:2 *s.* the coals over the city
12:14 *s.* tow. wind all that help
20:23 I would *s.* them am. heat.
29:12 I *s.* Egyptians, 30:23, 26
*Dan.* 4:14 hew down tree. *s.* fruit
11:24 he shall *s.* am. them prey
12:7 to *s.* power of holy people
*Hab.* 3:14 came as whirlw. to *s.*
*Zec.* 1:21 lift horn over Ju. *s.* it

**SCATTERED.**
*Gen.* 11:4 lest be *s.* upon earth
*Ex.* 5:12 peo. *s.* to gath. stubble
*Num.* 10:35 let all thine enemies be *s.* *Ps.* 68:1
*Deut.* 30:3 whither L. hath *s.* th.
1 *Sam.* 11:11 Ammonites were *s.*
13:8 people were *s.* from Saul
2 *Sam.* 18:8 bat. *s.* over country
22:15 and *s.* them, *Ps.* 18:14
1 *K.* 22:17 saw Is. *s.* 2 *Chr.* 18:16
2 *K.* 25:5 his army *s.* *Jer.* 52:8
*Est.* 3:8 certain people *s.* abroad
*Job* 4:11 stout lions' whe. are *s.*
18:15 brimstone be *s.* on habit.
*Ps.* 44:11 *s.* us am. heathen, 60:1
53:5 G. *s.* bones of him th. enc.
68:14 when Almighty *s.* kings
89:10 thou hast *s.* thine enemies
92:9 workers of iniqu. sh. be *s.*
141:7 bones *s.* at grave's mouth
*Is.* 18:2 go ye to a nation *s.*
7 present be brought of peo. *s.*
33:3 lifting thy. nations were *s.*
*Jer.* 3:13 *s.* ways to strangers
10:21 all their flocks shall be *s.*
23:2 ye have *s.* my flock, away
30:11 end of nations wh. I *s.* th.
31:10 he that *s.* Is. will gather
40:15 that Jews should be *s.*
50:17 Israel is a *s.* sheep, driven
*Ezek.* 6:8 ye be *s.* thro' countries
11:16 though I *s.* them
17:21 th. that remain shall be *s.*
29:13 Egyptians gath. whith. *s.*
34:5 flock *s.* because no sheph.
6 flock was *s.* on face of earth
12 have been *s.* in cloudy day
21 push. diseased till ye *s.* th.
36:19 I *s.* them among heathen
46:18 that my people be not *s.*

Joel 3:2 plead for pe. wh. they s.
Nah. 3:18 people is s. on mount.
Hab. 3:6 everlast. mountains s.
Zec. 1:19 horns wh. ha. s. Ju. 21
7:14 I s. them with whirlwind
13:7 smite Shepherd, the sheep be s. Mat. 26:31; Mark 14:27
Mat. 9:36 s. as sheep hav. no sh.
Luke 1:51 s. proud in imaginat.
John 11:52 gath. children were s.
16:32 hour cometh ye sh. be s.
Acts 5:36 obey. Theudas were s.
8:1 were s. thro' regions of Ju.
4 were s. went preaching, 11:19
Jam. 1:1 twelve tribes that are s.
1 Pet. 1:1 strangers s. thro' Pon.

**SCATTERETH.**

Job 37:11 the thick cloud he s.
38:24 wh. s. east wind on earth
Ps. 147:16 he s. the hoarfrost
Prov. 11:24 that s. yet increaseth
20:8 king s. away evil with eyes
26 a wise king s. the wicked
Is. 24:1 s. inhabitants of earth
Mat. 12:30 he that gath. not. wi. me, s. abroad, Luke 11:23
John 10:12 wolf catche. s. sheep

**SCATTERING.**

Is. 30:30 L. sh. show anger wi. s.

**SCENT.**

Job 14:9 through s. of water
Jer. 48:11 his s. is not changed
Hos. 14:7 s. thereof as wine of L.

**SCEPTRE.**

Gen. 49:10 s. not depart from Ju.
Num. 24:17 s. shall rise out of Is.
Est. 4:11 king shall hold out s.
5:2 held out to s. Es. golden s.
Ps. 45:6 s. of kingdom is right s.
Is. 14:5 Lord hath broken s.
Ezek. 19:11 had strong rods for s.
14 hath no strong rod to be s.
Amos 1:5 cut off him that hold. s.
8 him that holdeth s. from A.
Zec. 10:11 the s. of Egypt shall
Heb. 1:8 s. of righteous. is the s.

**SCEVA.**

Acts 19:14 seven sons of one S.

**SCHISM.**

Cor. 12:25 there should be no s.

**SCHOLAR.**

1 Chr. 25:8 the teacher as the s.
Mal. 2:12 L. cut off master and s.

**SCHOOL.**

Acts 19:9 disputing in s. of one

**SCHOOLMASTER.**

Gal. 3:24 the law was our s.
25 we are no longer under a s.

**SCIENCE.**

Dan. 1:4 in wisd. understand. s.
1 Tim. 6:20 avoi. babblings of s.

**SCOFF.**

Hab. 1:10 they sh. s. at kings

**SCOFFERS.**

2 Pet. 3:3 in last days s. walking

**SCORCH, ED.**

Mat. 13:6 they were s. Mark 4:6
Rev. 16:8 power was given to s.
9 men were s. with great heat

**SCORN, Substantive.**

Est. 3:6 s. to lay hands on Mord.
Ps. 44:13 makest us a s. 79:4
Hab. 1:10 princes shall be a s.
See LAUGHED.

**SCORN, Verb.**

Job 16:20 my friends s. me

**SCORNER.**

Prov. 9:7 that reproveth a s.
8 reprove not a s. lest he hate
13:1 but a s. heareth not rebuke
14:6 s. seeketh wis. findeth not
15:12 s. loveth not that reprov.
19:25 smite s. the simple will
21:11 when s. is punish. simple
24 s. is his name, deal. in wra.
22:10 cast out s. and contention
24:9 s. is abomination to men
Is. 29:20 the s. is consumed

**SCORNERS.**

Prov. 1:22 how long will s. deli.
3:34 surely he scorneth the s.
19:29 judgm. are prepared for s.
Hos. 7:5 stretched hand with s.

**SCORNEST, ETH.**

Job 39:7 he s. multitude of city
18 she s. horse and his rider
Prov. 3:34 surely he s. scorner
9:12 if s. thou alone sh. bear it.
19:28 ungodly witness s. judg.
Ezek. 16:31 harlot, in th. thou s.

**SCORNFUL.**

Ps. 1:1 nor sitteth in seat of s.
Prov. 29:8 s. bri. city into snare
Is. 28:14 hear word of Lord, ye s.

**SCORNING.**

Job 34:7 drinks s. like water?
Ps. 123:4 filled wi. s. of those at
Prov. 1:22 scorners delight in s.

**SCORPION.**

Luke 11:12 will he off. him a s.?
Rev. 9:5 torment was as of s.

**SCORPIONS.**

Deut. 8:15 thro' wilder. where s.
1 K. 12:11 I will chastise you with s. 14; 2 Chr. 10:11, 14
Ezek. 2:6 among s. be not afraid
Luke 10:19 power to tread on s.
Rev. 9:3 power, as s. have power
10 had tails like s. and stings

**SCOURED.**

Lev. 6:28 brazen pot, it sh. be s.

**SCOURGE, S.**

Jos. 23:13 s. in your sides
Job 5:21 thou sh. be hid from s.
9:23 if the s. slay suddenly
Is. 10:26 Lord shall stir up a s.
28:15 overflow. s. shall pass, 18
John 2:15 made s. of small cords

**SCOURGE, Verb.**

Mat. 10:17 they will s. in th. syn.
20:19 shall s. him, Mark 10:34; Luke 18:33
23:24 some of them ye shall s.
Acts 22:25 is it lawful to s. Ro.?

**SCOURGED, ETH**

Lev. 19:20 maid, she shall be s.
Mat. 27:26 wh. he had s. Jesus, Mark 15:15; John 19:1
Heb. 12:6 the Lord s. every son

**SCOURGING, S.**

Acts 22:24 sh. be examined by s.
Heb. 11:36 others had trial of s.

**SCRABBLED.**

1 Sam. 21:13 Da. feigned mad, s.

**SCRAPE, D.**

Lev. 14:41 cause house to be s. sh. pour out dust they s. off
43 if plague came after he s.
Job 2:8 Job took a potsherd to s.
Ezek. 26:4 I will also s. her dust

**SCREECHOWL.**

Is. 34:14 s. also shall rest there

**SCRIBE.**

2 Sam. 8:17 Seraiah was the s.
20:25 Sheva was s. and Zadok
2 K. 18:18 Shebna the s. 37; 19:2; Is. 36:3, 22; 37:2
22:3 Sha. the s. 8, 9, 10, 12; 2 Ch. 34:15, 18, 20; Jer. 36:10
25:15 princ. s. of host, Jer. 52:25
1 Chr. 24:6 Shemaiah s. wrote
27:32 Jona. a wise man and a s.
Ezr. 4:8 Shimshai the s. wrote a letter, 9, 17, 23
7:6 Ezra, a ready s. 11, 12; Neh. 8:4, 9, 13; 12:26, 36
Neh. 8:4 Ezra, s. stood on pulpit
Is. 33:18 where is the s.?
Jer. 36:12 Elishama the s. 20, 21
26 take Baruch the s. and Jer.
37:15 house of Jonath. the s. 20
Mat. 8:19 a s. said, Master, I will
13:52 s. instructed unto kingd.
Mark 12:32 s. said unto him
1 Cor. 1:20 where is the s.?

**SCRIBES.**

1 Chr. 2:55 the families of the s.
2 Chr. 34:13 of Lev. there were s.
Est. 3:12 king's s. called, 8:9
Jer. 8:8 pen of the s. is in vain
Mat. 5:20 ex. righteousness of s.
7:29 not as the s. Mark 1:22
16:21 suffer many things of s.
17:10 say s. E. must, Mark 9:11
20:18 betrayed to s. Mark 10:33
21:15 when the s. saw, they we.
23:2 s. and Phari. sit in M. seat
13 woe to y. s. 14:29; Lu. 11:44
Mark 2:6 went certain s. reason.
16 when the s. saw him eat wi.
8:31 be rejected of s. Luke 9:22
9:14 s. questioning with discip.
11:18 s. and c.-priests, Lu. 19:47
12:35 s. say Christ is son of D.?
38 said, Bew. of s. Luke 20:46
14:1 the s. sought to take him
Luke 5:30 s. and Pharisees, 15:2
6:7 s. and Pharis. watched him
11:23 s. began to urge vehem.
20:1 s. came upon him, elders
19 priests and s. sought to lay
22:2 and s. sought to kill him
23:10 s. stood and accused him
John 8:3 the s. brought a woman
Acts 4:5 s. gathered ag. apostles
6:12 s. brou. Stephen to council
23:9 s. of Pharisees' part arose

**SCRIP.**

1 Sam. 17:40 D. put stones in s.
Mat. 10:10 nor s. for your journ. Mark 6:8; Luke 9:3; 10:4
Luke 22:35 I sent you without s.
36 let him take his purse and s.

**SCRIPTURE.**

Dan. 10:21 what is noted in s.
Mark 12:10 ha. ye not read this s.
15:28 s. was fulfilled which saith
Luke 4:21 this day is s. fulfilled
John 2:22 they believed the s.
7:42 hath not s. said, Ch. com.?
10:35 the s. cannot be broken
19:35 another s. saith, They sh.
Acts 1:16 this s. must needs have
8:32 place of s. which he read
35 Philip began at the same s.
Rom. 4:3 what saith s.? 11:2; Gal. 4:30
9:17 s. saith, 10:11; 1 Tim. 5:18
Gal. 3:8 the s. foreseeing that G.
22 the s. hath concluded all
2 Tim. 3:16 s. is by inspi. of G.
Jam. 4:5 think s. saith in vain?
1 Pet. 2:6 it is contained in s.
2 Pet. 1:20 no s. is of priv. inter.

**SCRIPTURES.**

Mat. 21:42 ha. ye nev. read in s.
22:29 not know. s. Mark 12:24
26:54 how shall s. be fulfilled?
Mark 14:49 s. must be fulfilled
Luke 24:27 he expounded in all s.
32 while he opened to us the s.
45 that they mi. understand s.
John 5:39 search s. for in them
Acts 17:2 he reasoned out of s.
11 and searched the s. daily
18:24 Apollos, mighty in the s.
28 showing by s. Jesus was C.
Rom. 1:2 afore by prop. in ho. s.
15:4 thro' comf. of s. have hope
16:26 by the s. made known
1 Cor. 15:3 Christ died acc. to s.
4 Christ rose accordi. to the s.
2 Tim. 3:15 from child hast kn. s.

2 Pet. 3:16 as they do also oth. s.

**SCROLL.**

Is. 34:4 heav. sh. be rolled as s.
Rev. 6:14 heaven departed as a s.

**SCUM.**

Ezek. 24:6 woe to the pot wh. s.
11 that the s. may be consum.
12 her s. went out, her s. in fire

**SCURVY.**

Lev. 21:20 none sh. ap. that is s.
22:22 s. or scabbed sh. not offer

**SCYTHIAN.**

Col. 3:11 is neither barbarian, S.

**SEA.**

Ex. 14:16 stretch hand over s. 27
21 Lord caused the s. to go back, made the s. dry
15:10 blow, the s. covered them
20:11 L. made the s. Ps. 95:5; Jon. 1:9; Acts 4:24; 14:15
Deut. 30:13 nor is it beyond s.
Jos. 24:7 brought s. upon them
1 K. 7:23 a molten s. 2 Chr. 4:2
39 set s. on right side of house
10:22 king had at s. a navy
18:43 go up, look toward the s.
2 K. 14:25 he restored coast to s.
16:17 Ahaz took down the s.
25:13 s. did Chaldees break, 16
1 Chr. 16:32 let the s. roar, Ps. 96:11; 98:7
2 Chr. 4:6 s. for priests to wash
20:2 multit. against beyond s.
Neh. 9:11 thou didst div. s. went thro' the s. Job 26:12; Ps. 74:13; 78:13; Jer. 31:35
Job 7:12 am I a s.? 38:8 shut s.?
11:9 measure is broader than s.
14:11 as the waters fail from s.
28:14 s. saith, It is not with me
41:31 maketh the s. like a pot
Ps. 66:6 he turned s. to dry land
72:8 have dominion from s. to s.
78:53 s. overwhelmed th. enem.
104:25 this great and wide s.
107:23 go down to s. in ships
114:3 the s. saw it; 5 O thou s.
Prov. 8:29 gave to s. his decree
Is. 11:9 wat. cover s. Hab. 2:14
16:8 branches stretched over s.
19:5 waters shall fail from s.
23:2 merch. of Zid. pass over s.
4 be ashamed, s. hath spoken
11 he stretched his hand ov. s.
24:14 they shall cry aloud fr. s.
42:10 sing to L. ye that go to s.
50:2 at my rebuke I dry up s.
51:10 art thou w. hath dried s.?
57:20 wicked are like troubled s.
Jer. 6:23 their voice roar. like s.
27:19 saith L. the pillars and s.
48:32 plants are gone over s.
50:42 their voice sh. roar like s.
51:36 I will dry up her s.
42 s. is come up upon Babylon
Lam. 2:13 breach is great like s.
Ezek. 26:3 s. causeth his waves
Dan. 7:3 great beasts came fr. s.
Amos 8:12 wander from s. to s.
Jon. 1:11 that s. may be calm?
Mic. 7:12 shall come from s. to s.
Nah. 1:4 he rebuketh the s. and
Hab. 3:8 wrath ag. s. that didst
15 thou didst walk through s.
Hag. 2:6 I shake heav. earth, s.
Zec. 9:10 his domin. from s. to s.
10:11 he shall pass through s.
Mat. 8:26 he arose and rebuk. s.
27 s. obey him, Mark 4:39, 41
23:15 ye compass s. and land
Luke 21:25 s. and waves roaring
Acts 27:40 commit. themsel. to s.
28:4 tho' he hath escaped the s.
1 Cor. 10:1 fathers passed thro' s.
Rev. 4:6 before throne was s. of
7:2 given to hurt earth and s.
10:6 created s. things therein
14:7 worship him that made s.
15:2 I saw a s. of glass, mingled
20:13 the s. gave up the dead.
21:1 and there was no more s.

**By the SEA.**

Ex. 14:9 them encampi. by t. s.
2 Sam. 17:11 Is. as sand by the s.
1 K. 5:9 I will convey them by the s. 2 Chr. 2:16
Is. 18:2 sendeth ambassad. by s.
Jer. 46:18 as Carmel by the s.
Mark 4:1 multitude was by the s.
Rev. 18:17 many as trade by t. s.

See COAST, GREAT.

**In, and into the SEA.**

Ex. 15:1 horse and rider into t. s.
4 Pha.'s host he cast into the s.
Ps. 77:19 thy way in the s.
89:25 I will set his hand in t. s.
Ec. 1:7 all rivers run into the s.
Is. 43:16 L. mak. way in the s.
Ezek. 26:17 city strong in the s.
18 isles that are in the s.
47:8 waters go into the s. which brought forth into the s.
Jon. 1:4 a mighty tempest in t. s.
12 and cast me into the s. 15
Zec. 9:4 smite her power in t. s.
10:11 smite waves in the s.
Mat. 8:24 arose a temp. in the s.
13:47 kingdom of heaven is like a net cast into the s.
Mat. 21:21 cast into the s. Mark 11:23
Mark 9:42 we. cast i. s. Lu. 17:2
Luke 17:6 be thou plant. in t. s.
John 21:7 Pe. cast himself i. t. s.
Acts 27:38 cast out wheat i. t. s.
43 cast themselves into the s.
2 Cor. 11:26 in perils in the s.
Jam. 3:7 beasts and thi. in the s.
Rev. 5:13 ev. creature in the s.
16:3 ev. living soul died in t. s.
18:19 all that had ships in t. s.

**Of the SEA.**

Gen. 1:26 have dominion over the fish of the s. 28; Ps. 8:8
9:2 fear upon fishes of the s.
32:12 seed as sand of the s.
49:13 Z. dwell at haven of t. s.
Ex. 15:19 bro. ag. waters of t. s.
Num. 11:22 shall fish of the s. be
2 Sam. 22:16 channels of t. s. ap.
1 K. 18:44 aris. cloud out of t. s.
Job 6:3 heavier than sand of t. s.
9:8 tread. upon waves of the s.
12:8 fishes of the s. sh. declare
36:30 he covereth bot. of the s.
38:16 enter into springs of t. s.
Ps. 33:7 gathereth waters of t. s.
68:22 people fr. depths of the s.
89:9 rulest the raging of the s.
93:4 mightier th. waves of t. s.
139:9 dwell in utte. parts of t. s.
Is. 5:30 like roaring of the s.
9:1 afflict her by way of the s.
10:22 Is. be as sand of t. s. Hos. 1:10; Rom. 9:27
23:4 even strength of the s
51:10 made depths of the s.
60:5 abundance of the s. sh. be
63:11 bro. them up out of the s.
Jer. 5:22 sand for bound of the s.
33:22 nei. sand of t. s. be meas.
Ezek. 26:16 princes of the s.
27:3 Tyrus, at entry of the s.
9 ships of the s. were in thee
38:20 fishes of the s. sh. shake
Hos. 4:3 fishes of the s. be taken
Amos 5:8 call waters of t. s. 9:6
9:3 hid from sight in bot. of t. s.
Mic. 7:19 cast sins in. dep. of t. s.
Hab. 1:14 men as fishes of the s.
Zep. 1:3 I will con. fishes of s.
Mat. 4:15 by way of the s. bey. J.
18:6 drowned in depth of the s.
Jam. 1:6 wav. is like wave of s.
Jude 13 raging waves of the s.
Rev. 8:8 third part of the s. bec.
13:1 beast rise out of the s.
20:8 number is as sand of the s.

See MIDST.

**On, or upon the SEA.**

Ps. 65:5 afar off upon the s.
Jer. 49:23 faint-hearted, sor. on s.
Mat. 14:35 J. to them walking on the s. Mark 6:48; John 6:19
Rev. 7:1 wind sho. not blow o. s.
10:2 set his right foot upon t. s.
15:2 saw th. stand o. t. s. of gla.
16:3 poured out vial upon t. s.

**SEAFARING.**

Ezek. 26:17 was inhab. of s. men

**SEA-MONSTERS.**

Lam. 4:3 even the s.-m. draw out

See RED, SALT, SAND.

**SEA-SHORE.**

Gen. 22:17 seed as sand on s.-s.
Ex. 14:30 Egyp. dead upon s.-s.
Jos. 11:4 as sand upon s.-s.
Jud. 5:17 Asher contin. on s.-s.
1 Sam. 13:5 Phil. as sand on s.-s.
1 K. 4:29 heart as sand on s.-s.
Jer. 47:7 a charge against s.-s.
Heb. 11:12 as sand by s.-s.

**SEASIDE.**

Deut. 1:7 turn ye, and go by s.
Jud. 7:12 Midi. lay as sand by s.
2 Chr. 8:17 Solomon went to s.
Mat. 13:1 Jesus sat by the s.
Mark 2:13 he went again by s.
4:1 he began to teach by the s.
Acts 10:6 Sim. house is by s. 32

**SEAS.**

Gen. 1:10 gath. of wat. called s.
22 and fill the waters in the s.
Deut. 33:19 suck of abund. of s.
Neh. 9:6 thou hast made the s.
Ps. 8:8 passeth thro' paths of s.
24:2 he founded it upon the s.
65:7 stilleth the noise of the s.
69:34 let the s. praise him
135:6 Lord pleased, did he in s.
Is. 17:12 a noise like noise of s.
Jer. 15:8 wid. are abo. sand of s.
Ezek. 27:4 bor. are in midst of s.
25 made glorious in midst of s.
Ezek. 27:26 in the midst of s. 34
28:2 in seat of G. in midst of s.
8 slain in the midst of the s.
Dan. 11:45 taber. of palace bet. s.
Jon. 2:3 cast me into midst of s.
Acts 27:41 place wh. two s. met

**SEAL, Substantive.**

1 K. 21:8 Jez. sealed wi. Ah. s.
Job 38:14 turned as clay to the s.
41:15 scales shut with a close s.
Cant. 8:6 s. on heart, s. on arm
John 3:33 his s. that God is true
Rom. 4:11 circum. as s. of right.
1 Cor. 9:2 s. of mine apostleship
2 Tim 2:19 hav. this s. the Lord
Rev. 6:3 the sec. s. 5 the third s.
7 the fourth s. 9 the fifth s.
12 when he opened the sixth s.
7:2 having s. of the living God
8:1 when he opened seventh s.
9:4 hurt those that have not s.
20:3 shut him up, set a s. upon

**SEALS.**

Rev. 5:1 book sealed with 7 s.
5 lion of J. prevail. to loose s.
9 thou art worthy to open s.
6:1 the Lamb opened one of s.

**SEAL, Verb.**

Neh. 9:38 prin. and priests s. 10:1
Is. 8:16 s. law am. my disciples
Jer. 32:44 subs. evidences, s. th.

*Dan.* 9:24 70 weeks to *s.* vision
12:4 D. shut up words, *s.* book
*Rev.* 10:4 *s.* th. things 7 thunders
22:10 *s.* not sayings of prophecy

**SEALED.**

*Deut.* 32:34 is not this *s.* among?
1 *K.* 21:8 letters were *s.* wi. Ah.
*Est.* 3:12 *s.* wi. king's ring, 8:8
*Job* 14:17 transgres. *s.* in a bag
*Cant.* 4:12 my spouse is foun. *s.*
*Is.* 29:11 vis. as words of book *s.*
*Jer.* 32:10 I subscri. and *s.* evid.
*Dan.* 6:17 king *s.* it with a sign.
12:9 words are closed up, and *s.*
*John* 6:27 him hath G. the Fa. *s.*
*Rom.* 15:28 when I have *s.* to th.
2 *Cor.* 1:22 who hath *s.* and giv.
*Eph.* 1:13 ye were *s.* with H. Sp.
4:30 whereby ye are *s.* to-day
*Rev.* 5:1 book *s.* with sev. seals
7:3 hurt not earth, till *s.* serv.
4 I heard number of them *s.*
5 of Jud. were *s.* 12,000, 6, 7, 8

**SEALEST, ETH, ING.**

*Job* 9:7 sun, and *s.* up the stars
33:16 and *s.* their instruction
37:7 he *s.* up hand of ev. man
*Ezek.* 28:12 thou *s.* sum of wisd.
*Mat.* 27:66 *s.* stone and setting

**SEAM.**

*John* 19:23 coat was without *s.*

**SEARCH, Substantive.**

*Deut.* 13:14 inquire and make *s.*
*Ezr.* 4:15 that *s.* be made, 5:17
19 *s.* hath been ma. found, 6:1
*Job* 8:8 prepare thyself to the *s.*
38:16 hast th. walked in the *s.*?
*Ps.* 64:6 accomplish a diligent *s.*
77:6 my spirit made diligent *s.*
*Jer.* 2:34 not found it by secret *s.*

**SEARCH, Verb.**

*Lev.* 27:33 he sh. not *s.* whether
*Num.* 10:33 to *s.* out a resting-p.
13:2 that they may *s.* the land
14:7 land we passed to *s.* is good
*Deut.* 1:22 send men, they sh. *s.*
*Jos.* 2:2 men to *s.* country, 3
*Jud.* 18:2 Danites sent men to *s.*
1 *Sam.* 23:23 I will *s.* him out
2 *Sam.* 10:3 sent to *s.* 1 *Chr.* 19:3
1 *K.* 20:6 servants, they shall *s.*
2 *K.* 10:23 *s.* that none of serv.
*Job* 13:9 good that he should *s.*?
*Ps.* 44:21 sh. not G. *s.* this out?
139:23 *s.* me, O G. kn. my heart
*Prov.* 25:2 honor of kings to *s.*
27 men to *s.* their own glory
*Ec.* 1:13 heart to *s.* by wisd. 7:25
*Jer.* 17:10 I the Lord *s.* heart
29:13 shall *s.* for me with heart
*Lam.* 3:40 let us *s.* our ways
*Ezek.* 34:6 none did *s.* nor seek
8 neither did my shepherds *s.*
11 I will both *s.* my sheep
39:14 end of 7 months sh. they *s.*
*Amos* 9:3 will *s.* and take them
*Zep.* 1:12 *s.* Jerus. with candles
*Mat.* 2:8 *s.* dilig. for young child
*John* 5:39 *s.* scrip. they testify
7:52 *s.* out of G. aris. no proph.

**SEARCHED.**

*Gen.* 31:34 Lab. *s.* found not, 35
*Num.* 13:21 went up, and *s.* land
32 bro. evil report of land, *s.*
*Num.* 14:34 after number of days *s.* land
*Deut.* 1:24 came to Eshcol, *s.* it
*Job* 5:27 *s.* it, know it for good
28:27 he prepared it, *s.* it out
29:16 cause I knew not I *s.* out
32:11 whi. ye *s.* out what to say
36:26 number of his years *s.* out
*Ps.* 139:1 O L. thou hast *s.* me
*Jer.* 31:37 founda. of earth *s.* out
46:23 forest, tho' it cannot be *s.*
*Ob.* 6 how things of Esau *s.* out

*Acts* 17:11 Bereans *s.* scriptures
1 *Pet.* 1:10 prophets *s.* diligently

**SEARCHEST, ETH.**

1 *Chr.* 28:9 the Lord *s.* all hearts
*Job* 10:6 th. thou *s.* after my sin
28:3 and he *s.* out all perfection
39:8 he *s.* after ev. green thing
*Prov.* 2:4 if thou *s.* as for treas.
18:17 neighbor cometh, *s.* him
28:11 poor th. hath under. *s.* out
*Rom.* 8:27 *s.* knows mind of Sp.
1 *Cor.* 2:10 Spirit *s.* all things
*Rev.* 2:23 I am he wh. *s.* reins

**SEARCHING, S.**

*Num.* 13:25 ret. from *s.* of land
*Jud.* 5:16 divisions of Reuben *s.*
*Job* 11:7 canst thou by *s.* find G.?
*Prov.* 20:27 *s.* inw. parts of belly
*Is.* 40:28 no *s.* of his understand.
1 *Pet.* 1:11 *s.* what time Sp. of C.

**SEARED.**

1 *Tim.* 4:2 consc. *s.* wi. hot iron

**SEASON, Substantive.**

*Gen.* 40:4 continued a *s.* in ward
*Ex.* 13:10 keep ordin. in his *s.*
*Deut.* 16:6 *s.* th. comest out of E.
28:12 give rain unto land in *s.*
*Jos.* 24:7 dw. in wildern. long *s.*
2 *K.* 4:16 this *s.* embrace a son
1 *Chr.* 21:29 altar at that *s.* in G.
2 *Chr.* 15:3 for *s.* been with. God
*Job* 5:26 as corn cometh in his *s.*
38:32 bri. forth Mazzaroth in *s.*
*Ps.* 1:3 bringeth fruit in his *s.*
22:2 I cry in night *s.* not silent
*Prov.* 15:23 word in *s.* how good?
*Ec.* 3:1 to every thing th. is a *s.*
*Is.* 50:4 to speak a word in *s.*
*Jer.* 5:24 former and lat. rain in *s.*
33:20 not be day and ni. in th. *s.*
*Dan.* 7:12 lives prolong. for a *s.*
*Hos.* 2:9 take my wine in *s.*
*Mark* 12:2 at *s.* he sent to husb.
*Luke* 1:20 words fulfilled in *s.*
4:13 devil dep. from him for *s.*
13:1 present at that *s.* some
20:10 at the *s.* he sent servant
23:8 desir. to see him a long *s.*
*John* 5:4 angel went down at *s.*
35 willing for a *s.* to rejoice
*Acts* 13:11 not seeing sun for *s.*
19:22 himself stayed in A. a *s.*
24:25 convenient *s.* I will call
2 *Cor.* 7:8 though but for a *s.*
2 *Tim.* 4:2 instant in *s.* out of *s.*
*Phile.* 15 therefore departed a *s.*
*Heb.* 11:25 pleas. of sin for a *s.*
1 *Pet.* 1:6 tho' for a *s.* if need be
*Rev.* 6:11 sho. rest yet a little *s.*
20:3 after that loosed a little *s.*

*See* APPOINTED, DUE.

**SEASONS.**

*Gen.* 1:14 lights be for signs, *s.*
*Ex.* 18:22 judge peo. at all *s.* 26
*Lev.* 23:4 feasts proc. in their *s.*
*Ps.* 16:7 reins instr. in night *s.*
104:19 appointeth moon for *s.*
*Dan.* 2:21 changeth times and *s.*
*Mat.* 21:41 render fruits in th. *s.*
*Acts* 1:7 not for you to know *s.*
14:17 gave us rain and fruitful *s.*
20:18 I been with you at all *s.*
1 *Thes.* 5:1 of *s.* have no need

**SEASON, ED.**

*Lev.* 2:13 shalt thou *s.* with salt
*Mark* 9:50 wherew. will *s.* it?
*Luke* 14:34 wherew. sh. it be *s.*?
*Col.* 4:6 speech be with grace, *s.*

**SEAT.**

*Jud.* 3:20 Eg. rose out of his *s.*
1 *Sam.* 1:9 Eli sat upon *s.* 4:13
4:18 he fell from off *s.* backw.
20:18 bec. thy *s.* will be empty
25 sat on *s.* on a *s.* by wall
2 *Sam.* 23:8 Tachmon. sat in *s.*

1 *K.* 2:19 a *s.* for king's mother
*Est.* 3:1 Ha.'s *s.* above princes
*Job.* 23:3 O that I mi. come to *s.*
29:7 I prepared my *s.* in street
*Ps.* 1:1 sitteth in *s.* of scornful
*Prov.* 9:14 woman sitteth on *s.*
*Ezek.* 8:3 *s.* of image of jealousy
**28:2 I sit on *s.* of God in midst**
*Amos* 6:3 cause *s.* of viol. come
*Mat.* 23:2 Phar. sit in Moses' *s.*
*Rev.* 2:13 dwel. where Satan's *s.*

*See* JUDGMENT, MERCY.

**SEATED.**

*Deut.* 33:21 lawgiver was he *s.*

**SEATS.**

*Mat.* 21:12 *s.* of them that sold doves, *Mark* 11:15
23:6 chief *s.* in syn. *Mark* 12:39
*Luke* 1:52 put mighty fr. their *s.*
11:43 ye love uppermost *s.* 20:46
*Rev.* 4:4 four and twenty *s.* upon the *s.* twenty-four elders
11:16 elders sat before G. on *s.*

**SEBA.**

*Gen.* 10:7 sons of Cush, S. and
*Ps.* 72:10 kings of Sheba and S.
*Is.* 43:3 I gave Ethiopia and S.

SEBAT. *Zec.* 1:7

**SECOND.**

*Ex.* 26:4 the coupling of the *s.* 5:10; 36:11, 12, 17
28:18 *s.* row be emerald, 39:11
*Lev.* 5:10 offer *s.* for burnt offer.
*Num.* 2:16 set forth in *s.* rank
2 *K.* 9:19 he sent *s.* on horseback
1 *Chr.* 15:18 brethren of *s.* degree
*Ec.* 4:8 one alone, th. is not a *s.*
15 *s.* child stand up in stead
*Ezek.* 10:14 *s.* face was face of m.
*Dan.* 7:5 beast, *s.* like to a bear
*Mat.* 21:30 to *s.* said likewise
22:26 likewise the *s.* had her, *Mark* 12:21; *Luke* 20:30
*Luke* 19:18 *s.* came saying, Lord
*John* 4:54 *s.* miracle Jesus did
*Acts* 12:10 were past *s.* ward
1 *Cor.* 15:47 *s.* man L. fr. heaven
*Heb.* 10:9 aw. first, may estab. *s.*
2 *Pet.* 3:1 *s.* epistle I write you
*Rev.* 2:11 not hurt of *s.* dea. 20:6
20:14 hell, this is *s.* death, 21:8

*See* DAY, MONTH.

**SECOND time.**

*Gen.* 43:10 had returned *s. time*
*Lev.* 13:58 washed the *s. time*
1 *Sam.* 26:8 I will not smite *s. t.*
1 *K.* 18:34 do it *s. t.* did it *s. t.*
2 *K.* 10:6 Jehu wrote letter *s. t.*
*Is.* 11:11 L. set his hand *s. time*
*Jer.* 1:13 word of Lord came to me a *s. time*, 13:3; 33:1
*Jon.* 3:1 word came to Jon. *s. t.*
*Mat.* 26:42 he went *s. t.* prayed
*Mark* 14:72 *s. t.* the cock crew
*John* 3:4 enter *s. time* into womb
21:16 Jesus saith to Pe. *s. time*
*Acts* 10:15 voice spake to P. *s. t.*
2 *Cor.* 13:2 if I were present *s. t.*
*Heb.* 9:28 he shall appear *s. time*

**SECOND year.**

*Gen.* 47:18 they came the *s. y.* to Joseph, and said, *Num.* 1:1
*Num.* 9:1 first month of *s. y.* L.
10:11 *s. y.* cloud was taken up
2 *K.* 19:29 ye shall eat in *s. year*, springeth of same, *Is.* 37:30

**SECONDARILY.**

1 *Cor.* 12:28 God set *s.* prophets

**SECRET, Substantive.**

*Gen.* 49:6 come not into their *s.*
*Job* 15:8 hast th. heard *s.* of G.?
29:4 wh. *s.* of G. was upon tab.
40:13 and bind their faces in *s.*

*Ps.* 25:14 *s.* of Lord with them
27:5 in *s.* of tabernacle, 31:20
64:4 may shoot in *s.* at perfect
139:15 when I was made in *s.*
*Prov.* 3:32 *s.* is with righteous
9:17 bread eaten in *s.* pleasant
21:14 a gift in *s.* pacifieth anger
25:9 discover not a *s.* to another
*Is.* 45:19 not spoken in *s.* 48:16
*Ezek.* 28:3 no *s.* that th. can hide
*Dan.* 2:18 mercies of G. conc. *s.*
19 then was *s.* revealed to D.
30 *s.* not revealed to me
4:9 I know no *s.* troubleth thee
*Amos* 3:7 revealeth *s.* to his ser.
*Mat.* 6:4 alms may be in *s.* thy Father who seeth in *s.* 6, 18
6 pray to Father who is in *s.*
18 appear to fast to Fath. in *s.*
*John* 7:4 doeth any thing in *s.*
10 went to feast as it were in *s.*
18:20 openly, in *s.* I said noth.
*Eph.* 5:12 thi. done of them in *s.*

**SECRET, Adjective.**

*Deut.* 27:15 put. idol in *s.* place
29:29 *s.* things belong unto L.
*Jud.* 3:19 I have *s.* errand
13:18 askest my name, it is *s.* ?
1 *Sam.* 5:9 emerods in *s.* parts
1 *Sam.* 19:2 abide in *s.* place
*Job* 14:13 th. thou keep me in *s.*
15:11 is any *s.* thing with thee?
20:26 darkness be hid in *s.* pla.
*Ps.* 10:8 in *s.* places doth murder
17:12 lion lurking in *s.* places
18:11 made darkn. his *s.* place
19:12 cle. thou me from *s.* faults
64:2 hide me fr. *s.* counsel of wic.
81:7 I answered thee in *s.* place
90:8 *s.* sins in light of counten.
91:1 dwel. in *s.* place of Most H.
*Prov.* 27:5 rebuke bet. th. *s.* love
*Ec.* 12:14 to judgment ev. *s.* thi.
*Cant.* 2:14 that art in *s.* places
*Is.* 3:17 L. will discover *s.* parts
45:3 riches of *s.* places
*Jer.* 2:34 not found by *s.* search
13:17 soul sh. weep in *s.* places
23:24 hide himself in *s.* places
49:10 I have uncovered *s.* places
*Lam.* 3:10 as lion in *s.* places
*Ezek.* 7:22 pollute my *s.* place
*Dan.* 2:22 reveal. deep *s.* things
*Mat.* 13:35 kept *s.* from foundation of world, *Rom.* 16:25
24:26 behold, he is in *s.* chamb.
*Mark* 4:22 nor was any thi. kept *s.* *Luke* 8:17
*Luke* 11:33 put. candle in *s.* place

**SECRETS.**

*Deut.* 25:11 wife tak. him by *s.*
*Job* 11:6 shew thee *s.* of wisdom
*Ps.* 44:21 he knoweth *s.* of heart
*Prov.* 11:13 talebearer reveal. *s.*
20:19 as a talebearer, reveal. *s.*
*Dan.* 2:28 a God that revealeth *s.*
29 that revealeth *s.* make. kn.
47 your God is a revealer of *s.*
*Rom.* 2:16 God shall judge the *s.*
1 *Cor.* 14:25 thus are *s.* of heart

**SECRETLY.**

*Gen.* 31:27 wheref. didst flee *s.*?
*Deut.* 13:6 if bro. entice thee *s.*
27:24 smiteth his neighbor *s.*
28:57 eat for want of things *s.*
*Jos.* 2:1 sent two men to spy *s.*
1 *Sam.* 18:22 comm. with Dav. *s.*
23:9 Saul *s.* practised mischief
2 *Sam.* 12:12 for thou didst it *s.*
2 *K.* 17:9 did *s.* things not right
*Job* 4:12 a thing was *s.* bro. me
13:10 reprove, if you *s.* accept
31:27 heart hath been *s.* enticed
*Ps.* 10:9 lieth in wait *s.* as a lion
31:20 keep them *s.* in pavilion
*Jer.* 37:17 Zedekiah asked him *s.*
*Hab.* 3:14 to devour the poor *s.*
*John* 11:28 called M. her sister *s.*
19:38 Joseph was a disciple, *s.*

**SECT.**

*Acts* 5:17 wh. is *s.* of Sadducees
15:5 the *s.* of Pharisees believed
24:5 of the *s.* of the Nazarenes
26:5 straitest *s.* of our religion
28:22 *s.* everywhere spo. against

**SECURE.**

*Jud.* 8:11 smote host, it was *s.*
18:7 after manner of Zidoni. *s.*
*Job* 11:18 thou shalt be *s.*
12:6 they that provoke G. are *s.*
*Mat.* 28:14 persuade him, *s.* you

**SECURELY.**

*Prov.* 3:29 seeing he dwelleth *s.*
*Mic.* 2:8 them that pass by *s.*

**SECURITY.**

*Acts* 17:9 when they had taken *s.*

**SEDITION, S.**

*Ezr.* 4:15 moved *s.* in city, 19
*Luke* 23:19 for *s.* in prison, 25
*Acts* 24:5 this man mover of *s.*
*Gal.* 5:20 works of flesh are *s.*

**SEDUCE, ED.**

2 *K.* 21:9 Manasseh *s.* them to do
*Is.* 19:13 they have also *s.* Egypt
*Ezek.* 13:10 they have *s.* my peo.
*Mark* 13:22 signs and wonders *s.*
1 *John* 2:26 concern. them that *s.*
*Rev.* 2:20 Jezebel to *s.* my serv.

**SEDUCERS.**

2 *Tim.* 3:13 *s.* shall wax worse

**SEDUCETH, ING.**

*Prov.* 12:26 way of wicked *s.*
1 *Tim.* 4.1 giving heed to *s.* spi.

**SEE.**

*Gen.* 2:19 to *s.* what he wou. call
11:5 Lord came down to *s.* city
44:23 shall *s.* my face no more
45:12 your eyes *s.* the eyes of
28 will go and *s.* Joseph bef.
48:11 I had not tho. to *s.* face
*Ex.* 3:3 *s.* this great sight, 4
5:19 officers *s.* th. were in evil
6:1 shalt *s.* what I will do to P.
*Ex.* 10:5 cannot be able to *s.* ear.
28 ta. heed, *s.* my face no mo.
12:13 when I *s.* blood
33:20 no man *s.* me and live
23 thou shalt *s.* my back parts
34:10 people shall *s.* work of L.
*Lev.* 13:10 priest shall *s.* him, 17
*Num.* 22:41 thence he might *s.*
23:9 from top of rocks I *s.* him
13 whe. mayest *s.* them, sh. *s.*
24:17 I sh. *s.* him, but not now
32:11 none that came out of Eg. shall *s.* the land, *Deut.* 1:35
*Deut.* 1:36 save C. he sh. *s.* land
3:25 I pray thee, let me *s.* land
28:34 eyes wh. thou shalt *s.* 67
68 thou shalt *s.* it no more
29:4 hath not given eyes to *s.*
32:20 *s.* what their end will be
39 *s.* now, I, even I, am he
52 thou shalt *s.* land bef. thee
34:4 I have caused thee to *s.*
*Jos.* 22:10 built great altar to *s.*
1 *Sam.* 15:35 came no more to *s.*
19:3 what I *s.* that I will tell
2 *Sam.* 13:5 when fath. com. to *s.*
14:32 let me *s.* the king's face
1 *K.* 12:16 now *s.* to thine own house, David, 2 *Chr.* 10:16
22:25 *s.* that day, 2 *Chr.* 18:24
2 *K.* 2:10 *s.* when I am taken
6:17 open his eyes th. he may *s.*
20 open eyes that they may *s.*
7:2 shalt *s.* it with th. eyes, 19
13 send and *s.* 14 go and *s.*
10:16 *s.* my zeal for the Lord
19:16 open, Lord, thine eyes, and *s.* *Is.* 37:17
23:17 what title is that that I *s.*
2 *Chr.* 25:17 let us *s.* one another
*Job* 7:7 mine eye no more *s.* good
8 eye th. ha. seen me, *s.* no m.
9:25 days flee away, *s.* no good
17:15 my hope, who shall *s.* it?
19:26 in my flesh shall I *s.* God
27 whom I shall *s.* for myself
20:9 eye shall *s.* him no more
24:1 why do th. not *s.* his days?
15 adulterer sai. No eye sh. *s.*
31:4 doth not he *s.* my ways?
33:28 his life shall *s.* the light
36:25 every man may *s.* it
*Ps.* 10:11 God will never *s.* it
14:2 G. looked to *s.* if any, 53:2
31:11 they that did *s.* me
34:8 O taste and *s.* Lord is good
12 many days, he may *s.* good
37:34 wicked cut off, sh. *s.* it
40:3 shall *s.* it and trust in Lord
41:6 *s.* me, he speaketh vanity
49:19 they shall never *s.* light
64:5 say, Who shall *s.* them?
8 all that *s.* th. shall flee away
66:5 come and *s.* works of God
86:17 they wh. hate me may *s.*
112:8 *s.* his desire upon enemi.
10 wicked *s.* it and be grieved
119:74 be glad when they *s.* me
128:5 shalt *s.* the good of Jerus.
*Ec.* 1:10 be said, *s.* this is new
2:3 till I might *s.* wh. was good
3:22 to *s.* what sh. be after him
*Is.* 6:10 lest *s.* with their eyes
26:11 they shall *s.* and be asha.
30:20 th. eyes sh. *s.* thy teachers
32:3 the eyes of them that *s.*
33:17 thine eyes sh. *s.* the king
41:20 that th. may *s.* and know
48:6 *s.* this; 49:7 kings shall *s.*
52:8 for they shall *s.* eye to eye
15 not been told them sh. th. *s.*
53:2 when we shall *s.* him
10 he shall *s.* his seed
60:5 thou sh. *s.* and flow toget.
61:9 all that *s.* them acknowl.
64:9 behold, *s.* we beseech
*Jer.* 1:11 I *s.* rod; 13 *s.* seeth. pot
2:10 *s.* if there be such a thing
19 *s.* that it is an evil thing
23 *s.* thy way in the valley
3:2 *s.* where thou hast not been
5:1 *s.* now and know, and seek
6:16 stand ye in the ways and *s.*
7:12 go and *s.* what I did to it
51:61 and shalt *s.* and shalt read
*Ezek.* 39:21 all the heath. shall *s.*
*Dan.* 3:25 lo, I *s.* four men loose
*Joel* 2:28 your young men sh. *s.* visions, *Acts* 2:17
*Amos* 6:2 pass ye to Cal. and *s.*
*Mic.* 7:10 mine enemy shall *s.* it
*Hab.* 2:1 *s.* what he will say
*Zec.* 5:2 answer. I *s.* flying roll
5 lift your eyes, *s.* what is this
9:5 Ashkelon sh. *s.* it, and fear
10:7 their children shall *s.* it
*Mal.* 1:5 and your eyes shall *s.*
*Mat.* 5:8 pure in heart, sh. *s.* G.
*Mat.* 8:4 *s.* thou tell no man, 9:30; *Mark* 1:44; *Acts* 23:22
11:4 tell John th. ye hear and *s.*
12:38 would *s.* a sign from thee
13:14 seeing ye shall *s.* *Mark* 4:12; *Acts* 28:36
15 lest at any time they should *s.* with their eyes, *Acts* 28:27
16 bless. are your eyes, they *s.*
17 to *s.* those things wh. ye *s.*
15:31 when they saw the blind to *s.* *Luke* 7:22
16:28 *s.* Son of man coming
22:11 king came in to *s.* guests
24:6 wars, *s.* ye be not troubled
27:4 *s.* thou to that; 24 *s.* to it
28:6 come *s.* place where L. lay
10 Galilee, there shall *s.* me

*Mark* 5:14 to *s.* what was done
32 *s.* her had done this thing
6:38 go and *s.* 8:24 *s.* men
*Luke* 2:15 go to Bethleh. and *s.*
3:6 all flesh sh. *s.* salv. of God
8:16 who enter may *s.* 11:33
9:9 he desired to *s.* him, 23:8
27 not taste of death till th. *s.*
14:18 grou. I must go and *s.* it
17:22 when ye shall desire to *s.*
23 *s.* here, or *s.* there
19:3 Zaccheus sought to *s.* Jes.
*John* 1:39 come and *s.* 46; 11:34; *Rev.* 6:1, 3, 5, 7
50 thou shalt *s.* greater things
8:51 sayings, sh. never *s.* death
56 Abra. rejoiced to *s.* my day
9:15 do *s.* 25 blind, now I *s.*
39 th. who *s.* not might *s.* and th. they who *s.* mi. be blind
12:21 saying, Sir, we would *s.* J.
16:22 but I will *s.* you again
*Acts* 20:25 *s.* my face no more, 38
22:14 know and *s.* that Just One
28:20 I called you, to *s.* you
*Rom.* 15:21 not sp. of, they sh. *s.*
1 *Cor.* 8:10 if any man *s.* thee
*Phil.* 1:27 whether I come and *s.*
2:23 soon as I *s.* how it will go
1 *Thes.* 2:17 to *s.* your face with
3:6 desir. to *s.* us, we to *s.* you
1 *Tim.* 6:16 hath seen, nor can *s.*
*Heb.* 12:14 witho. holi. no man *s.*
13:23 come shortly, will *s.* you
1 *Pet.* 3:10 that will *s.* good days
1 *John* 5:16 if any man *s.* brother
3 *John* 14 I shall shortly *s.* thee
*Rev.* 1:7 every eye shall *s.* him
16:15 naked, they *s.* his shame
19:10 *s.* thou do it not, 22:9
22:4 and they shall *s.* his face

**SEE not, *or* not SEE.**

*Gen.* 21:16 *not s.* death of child
27:1 Is. old, that he could *not s.*
43:3 ye shall *not s.* my face, 5
44:26 we may *not s.* man's face
48:10 eyes of Is. dim, could *n. s.*
*Ex.* 33:20 canst *not s.* my face
*Num.* 14:23 they shall *not s.*
23:13 utmost part, shall *not s.*
1 *Sam.* 3:2 Eli could *not s.* 4:15
2 *Sam.* 3:13 *not s.* my face, exce.
14:24 let *not* Absal. *s.* my face
1 *K.* 14:4 Ahijah could *not s.*
2 *K.* 3:17 *n. s.* wind, nor sh. ye *s.*
22:20 thine eyes shall *n. s.* evil
*Job* 9:11 goeth by me, I *s.* him *n.*
20:17 *not s.* rivers of honey and
23:9 hideth that I *cannot s.* him
34:32 wh. I *s. not* teach thou me
35:14 thou shalt *not s.* him
37:21 men *s. not* bright light
*Ps.* 58:8 pass away, *not s.* sun
74:9 we *s. not* our signs, there is
89:48 liveth, shall *not s.* death
94:7 say, The Lord shall *not s.*
9 formed eye, shall he *not s.?*
115:5 eyes, they *s. not*, 135:16
*Is.* 26:11 is lifted up, will *not s.*
33:19 th. shalt *not s.* a fierce peo.
38:11 I shall *not s.* the Lord
44:9 they *s. not*, they be asha.
18 shut eyes, that th. *cannot s.*
*Jer.* 5:21 eyes, *s. not*, *Ezek.* 12:12
12:4 he shall *not s.* our last end
14:13 ye shall *not s.* the sword
17:6 shall *not s.* when good com.
8 sh. *not s.* when heat cometh
23:24 that I shall *not s.* him?
*Ezek.* 12:6 thou *s. not* ground, 12
13 shall he *not s.* it, tho' he die
*Dan.* 5:23 gods of gold, wh. *s. n.*
*Zep.* 3:15 thou shalt *not s.* evil
*Mat.* 13:13 seeing, *s. not*
23:39 shall *not s.* me, *Lu.* 13:35
24:2 *s.* ye *not* all these things?
*Mark* 8:18 hav. eyes, *s.* ye *not?*
*Luke* 2:26 *n. s.* dea. bef. seen C.
8:10 seeing, they might *not s.*
*Luke* 17:22 desi. to *s.* ye sh. *not s.*
*John* 3:3 *cannot s.* kingd. of G.
36 shall *not s.* life, wrath abid.
9:39 they who *s. not* might *s.*
12:40 that they should *not s.*
16:16 ye shall *not s.* me, 17, 19
18:26 did I *not s.* thee in gard.?
*Acts* 22:11 I could *not s.* for glory
*Rom.* 11:8 th. they should *not s.*
10 darkened that may *not s.*
1 *Cor.* 16:7 for I will *not s.* you
*Heb.* 2:8 we *s. not* yet all things
11:5 that he should *not s.* death
1 *Pet.* 1:8 tho' now ye *s.* him *not*
2 *Pet.* 1:9 blind, can *not s.* a far

**We SEE.**

*Ps.* 36:9 in thy light shall *we s.*
*Mark* 15:32 *we* may *s.* *John* 6:30
*John* 9:41 *we s.* your sin remain.
1 *Cor.* 13:12 *we s.* thro' a glass
1 *Thes.* 3:10 pray. *we* might *s.*
1 *John* 3:2 for *we* shall *s.* him

**Ye SEE, *or* SEE ye.**

*Ex.* 14:13 *ye* sh. *s.* them no more
16:7 *ye* shall *s.* glory of Lord
*Jos.* 3:3 when *ye s.* ark of coven.
1 *Sam.* 10:24 *s. ye* him L. chos.?
*Cant.* 6:13 what will *ye s.* in Sh.
*Is.* 6:9 *s. ye* indeed, perceive
42:18 blind, that *ye* may *s.*
66:14 wh. *ye s.* your hearts shall
*Jer.* 2:31 O generati. *s. ye* word
42:18 *ye* sh. *s.* th. place no more
*Ezek.* 13:23 *ye* sh. *s.* no more va.
14:22 *ye* shall *s.* their way
*Dan.* 2:8 *ye s.* thing is gone
*Mat.* 13:17 have desired to see th. things *ye s.* *Luke* 10:23
24:33 when *ye* shall *s.* these th. *Mark* 13:29; *Luke* 21:31
26:64 hereafter shall *ye s.* Son of man, *Mark* 14:62
27:24 *s. ye* to it, *Mark* 15:36
28:7 in Ga. shall *ye s.* *Mark* 16:7
*John* 14:19 but *ye s.* 16:10 *ye s.*
16:16 a lit. *ye* shall *s.* me, 17, 19
*Acts* 2:33 wh. *ye* now *s.* and hear
25:24 *ye s.* this man, about wh.
1 *Pet.* 1:8 tho' now *ye s.* him not

**SEEING.**

*Ex.* 4:11 maketh *s.* or blind?
22:10 driven away, no man *s.*
*Num.* 35:23 *s.* him not
1 *K.* 1:48 mine eyes even *s.* it
*Prov.* 20:12 Lord maketh *s.* eye
*Ec.* 1:8 eye not satisfied with *s.*
*Is.* 21:3 dismayed at the *s.* of it
33:15 shut. his eyes from *s.* evil
42:20 *s.* many things, but thou
*Mat.* 13:13 beca. they *s.* see not
14 *s.* ye shall see and shall not perc. *Mark* 4:12; *Acts* 28:26
*John* 9:7 washed and came *s.*
*Acts* 13:11 not *s.* sun for a season
2 *Pet.* 2:8 *s.* and hearing, vexed

**SEED.**

*Gen.* 1:11 herbs yield. *s.* 12, 29
47:19 give us *s.* 23 here is *s.*
24 four parts sh. be own for *s.*
*Lev.* 19:19 not sow with ming. *s.*
26:16 shall sow your *s.* in vain
27:16 estima. shall be acc. to *s.*
30 tithe of *s.* of land is Lord's
*Num.* 20:5 it is no place of *s.*
*Deut.* 11:10 Eg. where sowedst *s.*
28:38 carry much *s.* into field
1 *Sam.* 8:15 king take tenth of *s.*
1 *K.* 18:32 conta. 2 measures of *s.*
*Ps.* 126:6 bearing precious *s.*
*Ec.* 11:6 in morning sow thy *s.*
*Is.* 5:10 *s.* of homer sh. yield ep.
17:11 make thy *s.* to flourish
55:10 it may give *s.* to sower
*Jer.* 35:7 sow *s.* nor plant viney
*Ezek.* 17:5 he took of *s.* of land
*Joel* 1:17 *s.* is rotten under clods
*Amos* 9:13 overtake that sow. *s.*
*Hag.* 2:19 is the *s.* yet in barn?
*Zec.* 8:12 *s.* shall be prosperous
*Mal.* 2:3 I will corrupt your *s.*
*Mat.* 13:19 *s.* by way-side, 20, 22
23 receiv. *s.* into good ground
24 man sowed good *s.* in field
37 soweth good *s.* is S. of man
38 good *s.* are the children of
*Mark* 4:26 cast *s.* into ground
*Luke* 8:11 *s.* is the word of God
1 *Cor.* 15:38 ev. *s.* his own body
2 *Cor.* 9:10 minister. *s.* to sower
1 *Pet.* 1:23 born, not of corrup. *s.*
1 *John* 3:9 his *s.* remain. in him
*See* COPULATION.

**SEED, *for posterity.***

*Gen.* 4:25 G. appoint. me ano. *s.*
7:3 keep *s.* alive on fa. of earth
15:3 Ab. said, To me giv. no *s.*
*Gen.* 19:32 preser. *s.* of father, 34
38:8 raise *s.* to bro. *Mat.* 22:24; *Mark* 12:19; *Luke* 20:28
*Lev.* 21:21 a blemish of *s.* of Aa.
*Num.* 16:40 which is not *s.* of A.
*Deut.* 1:8 give it to their *s.* 11:9
4:37 chose *s.* after them, 10:15
31:21 out of mouths of their *s.*
*Ruth* 4:12 *s.* the Lord shall give
1 *Sam.* 2:20 L. give *s.* of this wo.
24:21 th. wilt not cut off my *s.*
1 *K.* 11:39 I will afflict *s.* of Dav.
2 *K.* 11:1 Athaliah destroyed all the *s.* royal, 2 *Chr.* 22:10
17:20 Lord rejected *s.* of Israel
25:25 Ishm. of *s.* royal, *Jer.* 41:1
1 *Chr.* 16:13 O ye *s.* of Israel
*Ezr.* 2:59 not show *s.* *Neh.* 7:61
9:2 holy *s.* have mingled them
*Neh.* 9:2 *s.* of Israel separated
*Est.* 9:27 J. took them and *s.* 31
*Job* 21:8 their *s.* is established in
*Ps.* 21:10 their *s.* sh. thou destr.
22:23 praise him, all ye *s.* of Jacob, all ye the *s.* of Israel
30 a *s.* shall serve him
37:28 *s.* of wicked shall be cut
69:36 the *s.* of his servants shall
102:28 their *s.* sh. be establish.
106:27 overthrow their *s.* among
*Prov.* 11:21 *s.* of righteous sh. be
*Is.* 1:4 nation, a *s.* of evil-doers
6:13 holy *s.* shall be substance
14:20 *s.* of evil-doers sh. never
45:19 I said not unto *s.* of Jacob
25 in L. all *s.* of Is. be justified
57:3 *s.* of adulterer and whore
4 transgres. a *s.* of falsehood
61:9 th. *s.* shall be among Gent.
65:9 I will bring a *s.* out of Ja.
23 *s.* of the blessed of the Lord
*Jer.* 2:21 I planted thee a right *s.*
7:15 I will cast out *s.* of Ephra.
31:27 *s.* of man and *s.* of beast
36 then *s.* of Is. also sh. cease
37 I cast off all *s.* of Is. 33:26
33:22 will I multiply *s.* of David
*Ezek.* 20:5 I lift. hand to *s.* of Ja.
43:19 give to be of *s.* of Zadok
*Dan.* 2:43 mingle with *s.* of men
9:1 Darius of *s.* of the Medes
*Mal.* 2:15 might seek a godly *s.*
*Mark* 12:20 left no *s.* 21, 22
*John* 7:42 Ch. cometh of *s.* of D.
*Acts* 13:23 of man's *s.* G. rais. J.
*Rom.* 1:3 of *s.* of D. 2 *Tim.* 2:8
4:16 promise might be to his *s.*
9:8 chil. of prom. counted for *s.*
29 except Lord had left us a *s.*
*Gal.* 3:19 was added, till *s.* come
*Rev.* 12:17 war with remn. of *s.*
*See* ABRAHAM.

**His SEED.**

*Gen.* 17:19 cov. wi. Is. and *h. s.*
48:19 *his s.* sh. become nations

Lev. 20:2 any of his s. to Mol. 3, 4
21:15 nor profane his s. am. pe.
Num. 14:24 Caleb and his s.
24:7 h. s. sh. be in many waters
Jos. 24:3 I multiplied his s.
2 Sam. 4:8 aveng. of S. and h. s.
Neh. 9:8 a coven. to give it h. s.
Est. 10:3 speaking peace to h. s.
Ps. 25:13 his s. sh. inherit earth
37:25 nor seen his s. beg. bread
26 merciful, his s. is blessed
89:29 his s. I make to end. 36
112:2 his s. shall be mighty
Is. 53:10 his s. sh. prolong days
Jer. 22:28 cast out, he and his s.
30 no man of his s. sh. prosper
33:26 not take of h. s. to be rul.
49:10 Esau, his s. is spoiled
Acts 7:5 give it to him and his s.

**Thy SEED.**

Gen. 3:15 enmi. bet. t. s. and her
12:7 to t. s. will I give th. land, 13:15; 15:18; 17:8; 24:7; 26:3; 28:4, 13; 35:12; 48:4; Ex. 33:1; Deut. 34:4
13:16 thy s. dust, 16:10; 28:14
15:5 so sh. thy s. be, Rom. 4:18
13 thy s. be a stranger in land
17:12 not of t. s. sh. be circum.
21:12 in Is. t. s. call. Heb. 11:18
13 Ish. a nation, bec. he is t. s.
22:17 thy s. possess gate, 24:60
18 in thy s. all nations be bles. 26:4; 28:14; Acts 3:25
26:24 mult. thy s. for Abraham's
32:12 I will make thy s. as sand
48:11 G. hath showed me thy s.
Lev. 18:21 not of t. s. pass thro'
Deut. 28:46 for a sign on thy s.
30:19 thou and thy s. may live
1 Sam. 20:42 bet. my s. and t. s.
2 Sam. 7:12 set up t. s. 1 Ch. 17:11
Job 5:25 shalt know that thy s.
Ps. 89:4 thy s. will I establish
Is. 43:5 I bring thy s. from east
44:3 I pour my Spirit on thy s.
48:19 thy s. had been as sand
54:3 thy s. sh. inherit Gentiles
59:21 Sp. not depart out of the mouth of t. s. nor t. seed's s.
Jer. 30:10 t. s. from land, 46:27
Gal. 3:16 to t. s. which is Christ

**Your SEED.**

Ex. 32:13 land I give to y. s.
Lev. 22:3 whoso. of your s. goeth
Is. 66:22 so y. s. and name rem.

**SEED-TIME.**

Gen. 8:22 s.-t. and harv. sh. not

**SEEDS.**

Deut. 22:9 not sow with divers s.
Mat. 13:4 so. s. fell by way-side
32 wh. is least of s. Mark 4:31
Gal. 3:16 saith not s. as of many

**SEEK.**

Gen. 37:16 I s. my brethren
43:18 that he may s. occasion
Deut. 4:29 s. him with thy heart
1 Sam. 9:3 said to S. Go s. asses
23:15 Saul come to s. his life, 25; 24:2; 26:2
25:26 th. that s. evil to my lord
29 risen to pursue and s. soul
27:1 Saul shall despair to s. me
1 K. 2:40 Shimei went to s. serv.
18:10 hath not sent to s. thee
19:10 s. my life to take it, 14
2 K. 2:16 go, and s. thy master
6:19 bring ye to man wh. ye s.
1 Chr. 28:8 s. commandm. of L.
9 if thou s. him, he will be found, 2 Chr. 15:2
2 Chr. 19:3 prep. heart to s. God
30:19 prep. his heart to s. God
31:21 to s. his God, he did it
34:3 Josiah began to s. after G.
Ezr. 4:2 we s. your God as ye do
7:10 prepared his heart to s. law
8:21 to s. him right way for us
22 G. is on them for good th. s.
Neh. 2:10 to s. welfare of Israel
Job 5:8 I would s. unto God
7:21 shalt s. me in the morning
8:5 if thou wouldst s. unto God
20:10 children shall s. to please
Ps. 4:2 vanity, s. after leasing
9:10 not forsaken th. that s. th.
10:15 s. out his wickedness
14:2 any that did s. God, 53:2
24:6 genera. of them that s. him
27:4 desired, that will I s. after
8 s. my face, thy fa. L. will I s.
34:14 s. peace, 1 Pet. 3:11
35:4 put to shame s. my soul
38:12 that s. my life, th. s. hurt
40:14 s. after my soul, 70:2
54:3 oppressors s. after my soul
63:1 my God, early will I s. th.
9 those that s. my soul go into
69:6 let not those that s. thee
32 heart shall live that s. God
70:4 let those that s. thee rejo.
71:13 with dishonor s. my hurt
24 bro. unto shame s. my hurt
83:16 they may s. thy name
104:21 yo. lions s. meat from G.
109:10 let his child. s. th. bread
119:2 s. him wi. th. whole heart
45 at liberty, for I s. thy prec.
176 as a sheep, s. thy servant
122:9 of God, I will s. thy good
Prov. 1:28 s. me, sh. not find me
8:17 and those that s. me early
23:35 I will s. it yet again
29:10 upright, just s. his soul
26 many s. the ruler's favor
Ec. 1:13 I gave my heart to s.
7:25 my heart to s. out wisdom
8:17 though man labor to s. it
Cant. 3:2 s. him my soul loveth
6:1 we may s. him with thee
Is. 1:17 s. judgment, relieve opp.
8:19 sho. not a people s. unto G.
11:10 to it shall Gentiles s.
26:9 wit. me will I s. thee early
34:16 s. ye out of book of Lord
41:12 thou shalt s. them
17 when the needy s. water
45:19 not to Ja. s. ye me in vain
58:2 yet they s. me daily, and
Jer. 2:24 s. her, in her mouth
4:30 thy lovers will s. thy life
11:21 men of Anath. s. thy life
19:7 th. that s. their lives, 21:7
9 that s. their lives sh. strait.
22:25 that s. thy life, 38:16
29:7 s. the peace of the city
13 shall s. me, and find me.
Jer. 34:20 them that s. th. life, 21
44:30 give Phar. to them that s.
46:26 Egyptians to those th. s.
49:37 dismayed bef. them th. s.
Lam. 1:11 people sigh, s. bread
Ezek. 7:25 they shall s. peace
26 then shall they s. a vision
34:11 sheep; and s. them out
12 so will I s. out my sheep
16 I will s. that wh. was lost
Dan. 9:3 God, to s. by prayer
Hos. 2:7 shall s. them, not find
Amos 5:4 saith the Lord, s. me
14 s. good and not evil
8:12 to s. the word of the Lord
Nah. 3:7 wh. sh. I s. comfort.?
11 thou shalt s. strength
Zep. 2:3 s. ye the Lord
Zec. 11:16 a sheph. shall not s.
12:9 in th. day I will s. to destr.
Mal. 2:7 they should s. the law
15 he might s. a godly seed
Mat. 6:32 th. things do Gent. s.
33 s. ye first the kingdom of God, Luke 12:31
7:7 s. and ye sh. find, Lu. 11:9
28:5 know ye s. J. Mark 16:6
Mark 1:37 All men s. for thee
3:32 thy brethren s. for thee
Luke 12:30 these thi. nations s.
13:24 many will s. to enter in
15:8 doth she not s. diligently?
17:33 whos. shall s. to save life
19:10 Son of man is come to s.
24:5 why s. living among dead?
John 1:38 Je. saith, What s. ye?
6:26 ye s. me, not beca. ye saw
7:25 he whom they s. to kill?
34 shall s. me, not find me, 36
8:21 ye shall s. me, die in sins
37 seed, but ye s. to kill me, 40
13:33 ye sh. s. me, whither I go
18:4 Jesus said, Whom s. ye? 7
8 ye s. me, let th. go their way
Acts 10:19 behold, 3 men s. thee
21 P. said, I am he whom ye s.
Rom. 2:7 to th. who s. for glory
11:3 I am alone, they s. my life
1 Cor. 10:24 let no man s. his own
Gal. 1:10 do I s. to please men?
Phil. 2:21 all s. their own things
Col. 3:1 s. those thi. that are ab.
Heb. 11:14 that they s. a country
13:14 have no city, we s. one
Rev. 9:6 in th. days men s. death

See FACE, LORD.

**Not SEEK, or SEEK not.**

Num. 15:39 s. n. after your heart
Deut. 23:6 thou shalt not s. their peace, Ezr. 9:12
Ruth 3:1 shall I not s. rest?
Ps. 10:4 wicked not s. after God
119:155 wicked s. not thy statu.
Jer. 30:14 lovers, they s. thee n.
45:5 great things? s. them not
Amos 5:5 but s. not Beth-el
Zec. 11:16 a shepherd shall not s.
Luke 12:29 s. n. what ye sh. eat
John 5:30 bec. I s. not mine own
8:50 I s. not mine own glory
1 Cor. 7:27 s. n. loosed, s. n. wife
2 Cor. 12:14 for I s. not yours

**SEEKEST.**

Gen. 37:15 asked, What s. thou?
Jud. 4:22 show thee man thou s.
2 Sam. 17:3 the man thou s.
20:19 s. to destroy a mother
1 K. 11:22 s. to go to thy country
Jer. 45:5 s. thou great things?
John 4:27 said, What s. thou?
20:15 saith, Woman, whom s. thou?

**SEEKETH.**

1 Sam. 19:2 Saul s. to kill thee
20:1 my sin, that he s. my life?
22:23 that s. my life, s. thy life
24:9 saying, David s. thy hurt?
Job 39:29 fr. thence she s. prey
Ps. 37:32 watch. s. to slay him
Prov. 11:27 s. good procur. favor, but he that s. mischief
14:6 scorner s. wisdom
18:1 separated himself, s. wisd.
15 the ear of wise s. knowledge
Ec. 7:28 which yet my soul s.
Jer. 5:1 any that s. the truth
30:17 Z. whom no man s. after
Lam. 3:25 L. good to soul s. him
Ezek. 34:12 shepherd s. out flock
Mat. 7:8 s. findeth, Luke 11:10
18:12 and s. that gone astray
John 4:23 Fa. s. such to worship
7:4 and s. to be known openly
18 s. his own glory; s. his glo.
8:50 there is one that s. and ju.
Rom. 3:11 none that s. after God
Rom. 11:7 Isr. not obt. that he s.
1 Cor. 13:5 charity s. not her own

**SEEKING.**

Mat. 12:43 s. rest, and findeth none, Luke 11:24

*Mark* 8:11 *s.* a sign from heaven
*Luke* 2:45 turned back *s.* him
11:54 *s.* to catch something
13:7 behold, I come *s.* fruit
*John* 6:24 to Capern. *s.* for Jesus
*Acts* 13:11 went *s.* some to lead
1 *Cor.* 10:33 not *s.* mine own pro.
1 *Pet.* 5:8 *s.* whom he may dev.

**SEEM.**

*Gen.* 27:12 I sh. *s.* as a deceiver
*Deut.* 15:18 not *s.* hard, wh. thou
25:3 thy brother should *s.* vile
*Jos.* 24:15 if it *s.* evil unto you
*Neh.* 9:32 let not trouble *s.* little
*Est.* 8:5 *s.* right before the king
1 *Cor.* 12:22 those members wh. *s.*
*Heb.* 4:1 lest any of you sho. *s.*
*Jam.* 1:26 if any *s.* to be religi.
*See* GOOD.

**SEEMED.**

*Gen.* 19:14 *s.* as one that mocked
29:20 *s.* to him but a few days
*Jer.* 27:5 unto whom it *s.* meet
*Luke* 24:11 th. words *s.* idle tales
*Gal.* 2:6 these who *s.* somewhat

**SEEMETH.**

*Num.* 16:9 *s.* it but a small thi.?
*Prov.* 14:12 which *s.* right, 16:25
18:17 first in own cause *s.* just
*Ezek.* 34:18 *s.* it a small thing
*Luke* 8:18 what he *s.* to have
1 *Cor.* 3:18 if *s.* to be wise
*See* GOOD.

**SEEMLY.**

*Prov.* 19:10 deli. is not *s.* for fool
26:1 so honor is not *s.* for a fool

**SEEN.**

*Num.* 14:22 have *s.* my glory
27:13 when thou hast *s.* it, thou
*Deut.* 1:28 we have *s.* sons of A.
31 *s.* how Lord bare thee
3:21 eyes have *s.* all Lord done
4:9 forget things eyes hath *s.*
5:24 *s.* th. G. doth talk wi. man
11:7 your eyes have *s.* acts of L.
21:7 nor have our eyes *s.* it
33:9 said, I have not *s.* him
*Jos.* 24:7 *s.* what I have done
*Jud.* 2:7 eld. who *s.* great works
13:22 because we have *s.* God
18:9 we have *s.* land, very good
1 *Sam.* 23:22 hath *s.* him there
24:10 this day thine eyes have *s.*
2 *Sam.* 18:21 tell king thou hast *s.*
1 *K.* 10:7 I came, mine eyes *s.*
13:12 *s.* way man of God went
20:13 *s.* this great multitude?
2 *K.* 20:15 what ha. they *s.*? all
in house ha. they *s. Is.* 39:4
23:29 slew J. wh. he had *s.* him
*Ezr.* 3:12 had *s.* first house
*Est.* 9:26 that they had *s.* conc.
*Job* 7:8 eye ha. *s.* me, see no mo.
8:18 pla. say, I have not *s.* thee
10:18 and no eye had *s.* me
13:1 mine eye hath *s.* all this
20:7 have *s.* him say, Wh. is he?
*Ps.* 10:14 thou hast *s.* it
35:21 eye *s.* it; 22 hast *s.* it
48:8 so have we *s.* city of Lord
68:24 have *s.* thy goings, O G.
*Prov.* 25:7 thine eyes have *s.*
*Ec.* 4:3 not *s.* evil work that is
6:5 not *s.* sun nor known any
6 I live, yet hath he *s.* no good
*Is.* 6:5 mine eyes have *s.* Lord
64:4 nor eye *s.* what he prepared
66:8 who hath *s.* such things?
*Jer.* 1:12 said L. thou hast well *s.*
3:6 *s.* what backsl. Isr. done?
12:3 hast *s.* me, tried heart
*Lam.* 2:14 prop. have *s.* vain thi.
have *s.* false burdens
16 enemies say, We have *s.* it
3:59 O L. thou hast *s.* my wrong
*Ezek.* 8:12 *s.* what ancients do
15 hast thou *s.* this? 17; 47:6
13:7 have ye not *s.* vain vision
*Mat.* 13:17 proph. desired to see
th. thi. not *s.* them, *Lu.* 10:24
21:32 ye had *s.* it, repented not
*Mark* 9:1 have *s.* kingd. of God
9 tell no man what they had *s.*
16:14 beli. not wh. had *s.* him
*Luke* 1:22 that he had *s.* a vision
2:20 praising G. for thi. had *s.*
26 death, bef. he had *s.* L.'s C.
5:26 we have *s.* strange things
9:36 told things wh. they had *s.*
19:37 mighty works they had *s.*
*Luke* 24:23 had *s.* vision of ang.
37 supposed they had *s.* a spirit
*John* 1:18 no man hath *s.* God at
any time, 1 *John* 4:12
3:11 we testify that we have *s.*
32 what he hath *s.* and heard
4:45 Galileans had *s.* all he did
5:37 not at any time *s.* shape
6:46 not that any man *s.* Father
8:57 hast thou *s.* Abraham?
9:8 neighbors which had *s.* him
37 hast *s.* it is he that talketh
11:45 had seen what J. did, bel.
14:9 *s.* me hath *s.* the Father
15:24 *s.* and hated both me
20:18 she had *s.* L. 25 *s.* Lord
29 bec. thou hast *s.* believed
*Acts* 4:20 speak things we ha. *s.*
9:27 declared how he had *s.* L.
10:17 vision he had *s.* sho. mean
11:23 he had *s.* grace of God
16:10 after he had *s.* vision
40 *s.* brethren, comforted them
1 *Cor.* 2:9 eye hath not *s.* nor ear
9:1 have I not *s.* Je. Ch. our L.?
*Phil.* 4:9 things ye heard and *s.*
*Col.* 2:1 many as have not *s.* face
1 *Tim.* 6:16 wh. no man hath *s.*
1 *John* 1:1 we have *s.* with eyes
3 have *s.* declare we unto you
3:6 whoso. sin. hath not *s.* him
4:14 we have *s.* and do testify
20 brot. whom he hath *s.* how
can he love G. he ha. not *s.*?
3 *John* 11 do. evil, hath not *s.* G.
*Rev.* 1:19 write thi. thou hast *s.*
22:8 heard and *s.* I fell down

**HAVE I seen.**

*Gen.* 7:1 thee *h. I s.* righteous
1 *Chr.* 29:17 now *h. I s.* people
*Ec.* 8:9 this *h. I s.* and applied
*Jer.* 46:5 wheref. *h. I s.* dismayed
*Zec.* 9:8 *h. I. s.* with mine eyes

**I have SEEN.**

*Gen.* 32:30 *I h. s.* G. face to face
33:10 *I have s.* thy face, 46:30
*Ex.* 3:9 *I h. s.* oppression, 16
32:9 *I h. s.* people, *Deut.* 9:13
*Jud.* 6:22 bec. *I h. s.* an angel
2 *K.* 20:5 thus saith the Lord, *I*
*have s.* thy tears, *Is.* 38:5
*Job* 15:17 that wh. *I h. s.* I decl.
31:19 if *I have s.* any perish
*Ps.* 37:35 *I h. s.* wicked in power
*Ec.* 1:14 *I h. s.* works under sun
5:13 evil wh. *I h. s.* under sun
18 that wh. *I h. s.* good to eat
6:1 evil which *I have s.* 10:5
*Is.* 57:18 *I have s.* his ways
*Jer.* 7:11 behold, *I h. s.* it, sai. L.
*Dan.* 2:26 make kn. dream *I h. s.*
*John* 8:38 I speak that *I have s.*
*Acts* 7:34 *I h. s.* affliction of peo.

**Ye have SEEN.**

*Ex.* 14:13 Egypt. wh. *ye have s.*
19:4 *ye h. s.* what I did to Egy.
20:22 *ye have s.* that I talked
*Deut.* 29:2 *ye have s.* all, *Jos.* 23:3
*Jud.* 9:48 what *ye have s.* me do
1 *Sam.* 17:25 *have ye s.* this man
*Job* 27:12 *ye* yourselves *h. s.* it
*Luke* 7:22 tell J. what *ye have s.*
*John* 6:36 *ye have s.* believe not
8:38 ye do that *ye h. s.* with fa.
14:7 *ye* know him, *have s.* him
*Acts* 1:11 come as *ye h. s.* him go
*Jam.* 5:11 *ye have s.* end of Lord

**SEEN,** *passively.*

*Gen.* 22:14 mount of L. sh. be *s.*
*Ex.* 33:23 my face sh. not be *s.*
34:3 any man be *s.* thro' mount
*Num.* 14:14 Lord *s.* face to face
*Jud.* 19:30 no deed done nor *s.*
2 *Sam.* 17:17 might not be *s.*
*Is.* 60:2 gl. shall be *s.* upon thee
*Zec.* 9:14 L. sh. be *s.* over them
*Mat.* 9:33 it was never so *s.* in I.
23:5 works do to be *s.* of men
*Mark* 16:11 he had been *s.* of her
*Acts* 1:3 *s.* of them 40 days, 13:31
*Rom.* 1:20 invis. things clearly *s.*
8:24 hope that is *s.* is not hope
1 *Cor.* 15:5 he was *s.* of Cephas
6 was *s.* of above 500 brethren
7 *s.* of James; 8 was *s.* of me
2 *Cor.* 4:18 look not at things *s.*
*Heb.* 11:1 evid. of things not *s.*
3 things which are *s.* not made
7 N. warned of G. things not *s.*
13 hav. *s.* them were persuad.
1 *Pet.* 1:8 having not *s.* ye love

**SEER.**

1 *Sam.* 9:9 let us go to *s.* proph.
was beforetime called a *s.*
11 is *s.* here? 18 where *s.* hou.
19 Samuel answer. I am the *s.*
2 *Sam.* 15:27 Art thou not a *s.*?
24:11 word came to Gad, D.'s *s.*
1 *Chr.* 9:22 Samuel the *s.* did ord.
25:5 Heman, king's *s.* in word
26:28 Samuel the *s.* had dedica.
29:29 acts of Da. writ. in book
of Sam. *s.* in book of Gad, *s.*
2 *Chr.* 9:29 in visions of Iddo, *s.*
12:15 Rehob. in book of Iddo, *s.*
16:7 Hanani the *s.* came to Asa
10 then Asa was wroth with *s.*
19:2 Je. son of *s.* went to meet
29:25 commandment of Gad, *s.*
30 words of Da. and Asaph, *s.*
35:15 command. of Jeduthun, *s.*
*Amos* 7:12 O thou *s.* flee away

**SEERS.**

2 *K.* 17:13 against Is. and J. by *s.*
2 *Chr.* 33:18 words of *s.* th. spake
19 written am. the sayings of *s.*
*Is.* 29:10 the *s.* hath he covered
30:10 who say to the *s.* see not
*Mic.* 3:7 then sh. *s.* be ashamed

**SEEST.**

*Gen.* 16:13 spake, Thou G. *s.* me
31:43 La. said, All thou *s.* is mi.
*Ex.* 10:28 day thou *s.* my face
*Deut.* 12:13 ev. place that thou *s.*
*Jud.* 9:36 *s.* shadow of mount.
1 *K.* 21:29 *s.* how Ahab humbleth
*Job* 10:4 *s.* thou as man seeth?
*Is.* 58:3 we fasted, thou *s.* not?
7 when *s.* naked, cover him
*Jer.* 1:11 word came to Jeremi.
What *s.* thou? 13; 24:3; *Amos*
7:8; 8:2; *Zec.* 4:2; 5:2
7:17 *s.* th. not what th. do in J.
32:24 come to pass, beh. th. *s.* it
*Ezek.* 8:6 *s.* thou what they do?
40:4 declare all thou *s.* to Israel
*Dan.* 1:13 as thou *s.* deal wi. ser.
*Luke* 7:44 Simon *s.* thou wom.?
*Jam.* 2:22 *s.* thou how faith wro.
*Rev.* 1:11 what *s.* write in a book

**SEETH.**

*Gen.* 16:13 looked after him *s.*?
*Ex.* 4:14 wh. he *s.* thee, be glad
1 *Sam.* 16:7 L. *s.* not as man *s.*
2 *K.* 2:19 city pleasant, as lord *s.*
*Job* 28:10 eye *s.* precious thing
24 he *s.* under whole heaven
34:21 eyes on man, *s.* all goings
42:5 but now mine eyes *s.* thee

*Ps.* 37:13 he *s.* his day is coming
40:10 he *s.* that wise men die
*Ec.* 8:16 day nor night *s.* sleep
*Is.* 28:4 that looked upon it, *s.* it
29:15 who *s.* us? 47:10 none *s.*
*Ezek.* 8:12 the Lord *s.* us not, 9:9
12:27 vision he *s.* for many days
18:14 son that *s.* father's sins
*Mat.* 6:4 Fa. who *s.* in sec. 6, 18
*John* 1:29 next day John *s.* Jesus
5:19 but what he *s.* Father do
6:40 who *s.* Son, and believeth
9:21 wh. means he *s.* we kn. not
12:45 *s.* me *s.* him sent me
14:18 because it *s.* him not, nor
19 world *s.* me no more
*Rom.* 8:24 what a man *s.*
2 *Cor.* 12:6 above what he *s.* me
1 *John* 3:17 *s.* brother have need

**SEETHE.**

*Ex.* 16:23 to-day *s.* that ye will *s.*
23:19 sh. not *s.* a kid in mother's milk, 34:26; *Deut.* 14:21
29:31 *s.* his flesh in holy place
2 *K.* 4:38 *s.* pottage for sons of
*Ezek.* 24:5 let them *s.* bones
*Zec.* 14:21 come and *s.* therein

**SEETHING.**

1 *Sam.* 2:13 while flesh was *s.*
*Job* 41:20 smoke as out of *s.* pot
*Jer.* 1:13 what seest thou? *s.* pot

SEGUB. 1 *K.* 16:34

**SEIR.**

*Gen.* 32:3 to the land of S. the
33:14 I come to my Lord to S.
36:20 sons of S. 21; 1 *Chr.* 1:38
*Num.* 24:18 S. sh. be a possessi.
*Deut.* 1:44 destroyed you in S.
33:2 Sinai and rose up from S.
*Jud.* 5:4 thou wentest out of S.
2 *Chr.* 20:23 of inhabitants of S.
25:11 smote of children of S.
14 the gods of the child. of S.
*Is.* 21:11 calleth to me out of S.
*Ezek.* 25:8 because Moab and S.

**Mount SEIR.**

*Gen.* 14:6 Horites in their *m.* S.
36:8 dwelt Esau in *mount* S. 9
*Deut.* 2:1 compassed *mount* S.
5 *mount* S. to Esau. *Jos.* 24:4
1 *Chr.* 4:42 500 went to *mount* S.
2 *Chr.* 20:10 children of *mount* S.
2 *Chr.* 20:22 ambushm. ag. *m.* S.
23 stood up against *mount* S.
*Ezek.* 35:2 thy face ag. *mount* S.
3 say to it, Behold, O *mount* S.
7 thus will I make *mount* S.

**SEIZE, ED.**

*Jos.* 8:7 rise up and *s.* upon city
*Job* 3:6 let darkness *s.* upon it
*Ps.* 55:15 let death *s.* upon them
*Jer.* 49:24 Damas. fear *s.* on her
*Mat.* 21:38 kill him, *s.* inherit.

**SELAH.**

*Ps.* 3:2 no help for him in God, *s.*
4 L. heard out of holy hill, *s.*
8 thy blessing upon people, *s.*
32:5 forgavest iniq. of my sin, *s.*
*See Ps.* 4:2, 4; 7:5; 9:16, 20; 20:3; 21:2; 24:6, 10; 32:4, 7; 39:5, 11; 44:8; 46:3, 7, 11; 47:4; 48:8; 49:13, 15; 50:6; 52:3, 5; 54:3; 55:7, 19; 57:3, 6; 59:5, 13; 60:4; 61:4; 62:4, 8; 66:4, 7, 15; 67:1, 4; 68:7, 19, 32; 75:3; 76:3, 9; 77:3, 9, 15; 81:7; 82:2; 83:8; 84:4, 8; 85:2; 87:3, 6; 88:7, 10; 89:4, 37, 45, 48; 140:3, 5, 8; 143:6; *Hab.* 3:3, 9, 13

**SELEUCIA.**

*Acts* 13:4 they departed unto S.

**Own SELF.**

*Ex.* 32:13 swarest by thine *o. s.*
*John* 5:30 can of *o. s.* do nothing
17:5 glorify me with thine *o. s.*
1 *Cor.* 4:3 I judge not mine *o. s.*
*Phile.* 19 even thine *own s.*
1 *Pet.* 2:24 his *o. s.* bare our sins

**SELFSAME.**

*Mat.* 8:13 servant healed *s.* hour
1 *Cor.* 12:11 worketh one *s.* Spirit
2 *Cor.* 5:5 wrought us for *s.* thing
7:11 *s.* thing, ye sorrowed after
*See* Same DAY.

**SELF-WILL.**

*Gen.* 49:6 in *s.-w.* dig. down wall
*See* FRET, HIDE.

**SELF-WILLED.**

*Tit.* 1:7 bishop must not be *s.-w.*
2 *Pet.* 2:10 presumptuous, *s.-w.*

**SELL.**

*Gen.* 25:31 *s.* me thy birthright
37:27 let us *s.* him to Ishmael.
*Ex.* 21:7 if a man *s.* his daughter
35 *s.* live ox, and divide money
22:1 if man steal ox, kill, or *s.*
*Lev.* 25:14 if thou *s.* to neighbor
29 if a man *s.* dwelling-house
47 if bro. *s.* himself to stranger
*Deut.* 2:28 sh. *s.* meat for money
14:21 *s.* that wh. dieth to alien
21:14 sh. not *s.* her for money
*Jud.* 4:9 *s.* Sisera into hand of
1 *K.* 21:25 Ahab did *s.* himself to
2 *K.* 4:7 go, *s.* oil, pay thy debt
*Neh.* 5:8 will ye *s.* your breth.?
10:31 victuals on sab.-day to *s.*
*Prov.* 23:23 buy truth, *s.* it not
*Ezek.* 30:12 *s.* land into hand of
48:14 not *s.* first-fruits of land
*Joel* 3:8 I will *s.* your sons and daugh. *s.* them to Sabeans
*Amos* 8:5 that we may *s.* corn
6 and *s.* refuse of the wheat
*Zec.* 11:5 that *s.* say, I am rich
*Mat.* 19:21 and *s.* that hast, *Mark* 10:21; *Luke* 12:33; 18:22
25:9 go ye to them that *s.* buy
*Luke* 22:36 *s.* garm. buy sword
*Jam.* 4:13 we will buy and *s.*
*Rev.* 13:17 no man mi. buy or *s.*

**SELLER, S.**

*Is.* 24:2 with buyer, so with *s.*
*Ezek.* 7:12 rejoice, nor *s.* mourn
13 *s.* not return to that sold
*Neh.* 13:20 *s.* lodged without Je.
*Acts* 16:14 Lydia, a *s.* of purple

**SELLEST, ETH.**

*Ex.* 21:16 he that stealeth a man and *s.* him, *Deut.* 24:7
*Ruth* 4:3 Naomi *s.* part of land
*Ps.* 44:12 *s.* thy peo. for naught
*Prov.* 11:26 blessing on him *s.*
31:24 maketh fine linen, *s.* it
*Nah.* 3:4 *s.* nations thro' whore.
*Mat.* 13:44 he *s.* all, buyeth field

**SELVEDGE.**

*Ex.* 26:4 fr. *s.* in coupling, 36:11

**Own SELVES.**

*Acts* 20:30 of *o. s.* shall men rise
2 *Cor.* 8:5 gave their *own s.* to L.
13:5 your *o. s.* know not *o. s.*
2 *Tim.* 3:2 lovers of their *own s.*
*Jam.* 1:22 deceiving your *own s.*
*See* ASSEMBLE, ED.

**SEMEI.**

*Luke* 3:26 Mattathias son of S.

**SENATE.**

*Acts* 5:21 called *s.* of Is. together

**SENATORS.**

*Ps.* 105:22 teach his *s.* wisdom

**SEND.**

*Gen.* 24:7 G. shall *s.* angel bef. 40
12 *s.* me good speed this day
54 *s.* me away unto master, 56
43:4 if thou wilt *s.* our brother
45:5 God did *s.* me to pres. life
*Ex.* 4:13 *s.* by him thou wilt *s.*
7:2 *s.* children of Is. out of land
12:33 *s.* them out in haste
33:12 know whom thou wilt *s.*
*Lev.* 16:21 *s.* him away
*Num.* 12:2 men to search land
31:4 every tribe *s.* thous. to war
*Deut.* 1:22 *s.* men bef. to search
19:12 elders *s.* fetch him thence
28:20 L. sh. *s.* upon thee cursing
48 enemies L. shall *s.* ag. thee
*Jud.* 13:8 man of God didst *s.*
1 *Sam.* 5:11 *s.* away ark, 6:8
6:3 *s.* ark, *s.* it not empty.
9:26 that I may *s.* thee away
11:3 that we may *s.* messengers
16:11 said to Jesse, *s.* fetch Da.
19 Saul said, *s.* me D. thy son
25:25 saw not men thou didst *s.*
2 *Sam.* 11:6 *s.* me U. the Hittite
14:32 that I may *s.* thee to king
15:36 ye sh. *s.* me every thing
17:16 now therefore *s.* quickly
1 *K.* 20:9 thou didst *s.* for serva.
2 *K.* 2:16 shall not *s.* 17 said *s.*
6:13 I may *s.* and fetch him
7:13 let us *s.* 9:17 *s.* meet Jehu
15:37 L. began to *s.* ag. Judah
1 *Chr.* 13:2 *s.* abroad unto breth.
2 *Chr.* 6:27 *s.* rain upon land
28:16 A. did *s.* to king of Assy.
32:9 Sennacherib did *s.* to Hez.
*Ezr.* 5:17 *s.* his pleasure to us
*Neh.* 2:5 wouldest *s.* me to Jud.
6 it pleased the king to *s.* me
8:10 *s.* portions unto them, 12
*Job* 21:11 they *s.* forth little ones
38:35 canst thou *s.* lightnings?
*Ps.* 43:3 *s.* out thy light
57:3 he sh. *s.* from heaven, and save fr. reproach; God sh. *s.*
68:3 he doth *s.* out his voice
110:2 *s.* rod of strength out of Z.
118:25 Lord, *s.* now prosperity
144:7 *s.* thy hand from above
*Prov.* 22:21 truth to them that *s.*
*Is.* 6:8 wh. shall I *s.*? I said, *s.*
10:16 Lord shall *s.* am. fat ones
16:1 *s.* ye lamb to ruler of land
19:20 shall *s.* them a Saviour
32:20 *s.* the feet of ox and ass
57:9 didst *s.* thy messengers
*Jer.* 1:7 go to all that I shall *s.*
2:10 *s.* to Kedar; 9:17 *s.* women
29:31 *s.* to all them of captivity
42:5 the L. shall *s.* thee to us
6 obey L. to whom we *s.* thee
*Mat.* 9:38 pray ye the Lord will *s.* forth laborers, *Luke* 10:2
10:34 th. not I come to *s.* peace
13:41 Son of man shall *s.* his angels, 24:31; *Mark* 13:27
15:23 *s.* her away, crieth after
21:3 he will *s.* them, *Mark* 11:3
*Mark* 3:14 *s.* to preach, 6:7
5:10 would not *s.* them away
12 saying, *s.* us into swine
*Luke* 16:24 *s.* Laz. 27 *s.* to house
*John* 14:26 Fa. will *s.* in name
17:8 belie. that thou didst *s.* me
*Acts* 3:20 he shall *s.* Jesus Christ
7:35 same did G. *s.* to be a ruler
10:5 *s.* men to Joppa, 32; 11:13
15:22 *s.* men of their compa. 25
25:3 would *s.* for him to Jerus.
*Phil.* 2:19 I trust to *s.* Timot. 23
25 necessary to *s.* Epaphrodit.
2 *Thes.* 2:11 G. shall *s.* delusions
*Tit.* 3:12 I shall *s.* Artemas unto
*Jam.* 3:11 fount. *s.* sweet water?
*Rev.* 1:11 and *s.* to sev. churches
11:10 *s.* gifts to one another

**I SEND.**

*Ex.* 23:20 behold, *I s.* an angel
*Num.* 22:37 did *I* not earne. *s.*?
1 *Sam.* 20:12 and *I s.* not to thee
*Is.* 6:8 saying, Whom shall *I s.*?
*Jer.* 25:15 all, to whom *I s.* thee
*Ezek.* 2:3 *I s.* thee to Israel, 4
14:21 *I s.* my four sore judgme.

Mat. 10:16 I s. you as sheep
11:10 behold, I s. my messenger, Mark 1:2; Luke 7:27
23:34 behold I s. you prophets
Mark 8:3 if I s. them away fast.
Luke 10:3 I s. you forth as lambs
24:49 I s. the promise of Father
John 13:20 whom I s. receiv. me
20:21 sent me, even so s. I you
Acts 25:21 kept till I s. to Cesar
26:17 unto whom now I s. thee

**I will SEND.**

Gen. 27:45 I w. s. and fetch thee
37:13 come, and I will s. thee
Ex. 3:10 I w. s. to Pha. Acts 7:34
Lev. 26:22 I will s. wild beasts
1 Sam. 9:16 I w. s. man of Benj.
16:1 I will s. thee to Jesse the
20:13 I will s. show it thee, s.
1 K. 18:1 I w. s. rain upon earth
20:6 I w. s. my serv. unto thee
34 I will s. thee away with co.
Is. 66:19 I will s. th. that escape
Jer. 43:10 I will s. Nebuchadne.
51:2 I w. s. unto Baby. fanners
Ezek. 5:16 I will s. famine, 17; 14:13; Amos 8:11
7:3 I will s. mine anger upon
Mal. 2:2 I w. s. cu. 4:5 I w. s. E.
3:1 I will s. my messenger
Mat. 15:32 I will not s. them
Luke 11:49 I will s. them proph.
20:13 I will s. my beloved son
John 15:26 Comfort. I w. s. 16:7
Acts 22:21 I w. s. thee far hence
1 Cor. 16:3 you approve, I will s.
See FIRE.

**SENDEST.**

Deut. 15:13 when s. him out, 18
Jos. 1:16 whithersoever thou s.
2 K. 1:6 thou s. to Baal-zebub
Job 14:20 chang. his countenance and s. him away
Ps. 104:30 thou s. thy Spirit

**SENDETH.**

Job 12:15 he s. them out
Ps. 147:15 s. forth his comm. 18
Mark 11:1 s. two disciples, 14:13
Luke 14:32 s. and desireth peace
Acts 23:26 Claud. Lys. to Felix s.

**SENDING.**

2 Sam. 13:16 evil in s. me away
2 Chr. 36:15 s. his messengers, Jer. 7:25; 25:4; 26:5; 29:19 35:15; 44:4
Est. 9:19 and of s. portions, 22
Ps. 78:49 s. evil angels among
Is. 7:25 s. forth of lesser cattle
Rom. 8:3 God s. his Son in like.

**SENNACHERIB.**

2 K. 18:13 S. came up, Is. 36:1
19:16 the words of S. Is. 37:17
20 prayed against S. Is. 37:21
36 S. dwelt at Ninev. Is. 37:37
2 Chr. 32:22 Hezekiah from S.

**SENSES.**

Heb. 5:14 have their s. exercised

**SENSUAL.**

Jam. 3:15 wisd. earthly, s. devil.
Jude 19 th. be s. having not Spi.

**SENT.**

Gen. 38:25 Ta. s. to her father-in.
41:14 Pharaoh s. and called Jos.
42:4 Benjamin Jacob s. not with
45:8 not you that s. me hither
50:16 s. a messenger unto Jos.
Ex. 3:14 I AM ha. s. me to you
5:22 why is it thou hast s. me?
Num. 13:16 men Moses s. 14:36
22:10 king of Moab hath s. to
Jos. 14:7 40 y.'s old wh. M. s. me
Jud. 20:6 I s. her through Israel
1 Sam. 31:9 s. into land of Philis.
2 Sam. 24:13 ans. him that s. me
1 K. 18:10 my lord hath not s. to
21:11 elders did as Jez. s. them
2 K. 1:6 return unto king that s.
6:10 king of Israel s. to place
19:4 master s. to reproach God
22:15 th. s. you, 18; 2 Chr. 34:23
Ezr. 4:11 copy of letter they s.
Neh. 6:4 s. unto me four times
Is. 48:16 God and his Spirit s. me
Jer. 14:3 nobles ha. s. little ones
23:21 I ha. not s. these prophets
37:7 say unto king that s. you
Ezek. 23:40 ye have s. for men to
Dan. 3:28 who had s. his angel
Hos. 5:13 Eph. s. to king Jareb
Zec. 7:2 s. unto house of God
Mat. 21:1 then s. Je. two discip.
27:19 Pilate's wife s. unto him
Luke 7:20 J. Baptist s. us to thee
10:1 Jesus s. them two and two
14:17 s. his servant at supper
23:11 s. him again to Pilate
John 1:22 ans. to them that s. us
4:34 to do will of him th. s. me
5:23 honoreth not F. wh. s. me
John 5:24 believeth him that s. me, 12:44
30 him who s. me, 6:38, 39, 40
33 ye s. un. John, and he bare
36 I bear witn. the Fath. hath s. me, 37; 6:57; 8:16, 18
6:44 except Father which s. me
7:16 not mine, his that s. me
18 seeketh his glory th. s. him
32 Phari. and priests s. officers
9:4 work the wor. of him s. me
10:36 of him whom Fa. hath s.
11:42 believe thou hast s. me
12:45 seeth me, seeth him s. me
49 Fa. who s. me gave me com.
14:24 not mine, Fa.'s who s. me
15:21 know not him that s. me
16:5 I go my way to him s. me
17:3 to know J. whom thou s.
18 s. me into the world, so I s.
21 may believe thou s. me
23 world may kn. thou s. me
25 these have kn. thou s. me
20:21 as my Father hath s. me
Acts 5:21 s. to prison to have
15:27 we have s. Jud. and Silas
19:31 Paul's friends s. unto him
2 Cor. 8:18 s. with him broth. 22
Phil. 4:16 in Thessalonica ye s.
1 John 4:14 testify Father s. Son

**SENT away.**

Gen. 12:20 Phara. s. a. Abraham
21:14 Abr. s. Ishm. and Hag. a.
25:6 Abr. s. Keturah's child. a.
26:27 hate me and hath s. me a.
29 we have s. thee a. in peace
28:6 Isaac blessed Ja. s. him a.
45:24 he s. his brethren away
Deut. 24:4 s. her a. not take her
1 Sam. 10:25 Samuel s. people a.
19:17 hast s. a. my enemy?
2 Sam. 3:21 Dav. s. Abner away
24 why is it th. hast s. him a.?
1 Chr. 12:19 Philistines s. Da. a.
Luke 8:38 Jesus s. him away
Acts 13:3 them, they s. them a.

**God SENT.**

Gen. 45:7 God s. me before you
Ex. 3:13 G. of your fathers s. me
15 God of Jacob hath s. me
Neh. 6:12 God had not s. him
Jer. 43:1 Lord their God s. him
2 G. hath not s. to thee to say
John 3:17 G. s. not Son to cond.
34 he whom God hath s. spea.
Acts 10:36 G. s. to child. of Israel
Gal. 4:4 G. s. Son made of wom.
6 G. s. forth Spirit of his Son
1 John 4:9 G. s. his only bego. S.
Rev. 22:6 God s. his angel

**He SENT.**

Gen. 45:23 he s. aft. this manner.
46:28 he s. Judah unto Joseph
Ex. 18:2 after he had s. her back
Jud. 11:28 Ammon hearkened not to words he s.
2 Sam. 10:5 he s. to meet them, 1 Chr. 19:5
14:29 when he s. aga. he would
22:17 he s. from above, Ps. 18:16
1 K. 20:7 he s. to me for my wives
2 Chr. 25:15 he s. unto Amaziah
Ps. 105:17 he s. a man bef. them
107:20 he s. his word and healed
Is. 61:1 he s. me to bind up the broken-hearted, Luke 4:18
Jer. 29:28 he s. unto us in Babyl.
42:21 he hath s. me unto you
Lam. 1:13 he s. fire into my bo.
Zec. 2:8 he s. me to nations
Mat. 21:36 ag. he s. other serva.
37 last of all he s. unto them his son, Mark 12:4
John 5:38 for wh. he hath s. him
6:29 believe on him he hath s.
7:28 he that s. me is true, 8:26
29 I know him, he hath s. me
8:29 he that s. me is with me
42 neither came I myself, he s.
Acts 24:26 wheref. he s. for Paul

**I SENT.**

Gen. 32:5 I have s. to tell my lord
Ex. 3:12 a token I have s. thee
Num. 32:8 your fathers when I s.
Jos. 24:5 I s. Moses, Mic. 6:4
Jud. 6:14 Is. have not I s. thee?
2 K. 5:6 I s. Naaman my servant
17:13 the law which I s. to you
Is. 43:14 for your sake I have s.
55:11 sh. prosper whereto I s.
Jer. 7:25 I s. unto you all my servants, 26:5; 35:15; 44:4
14:14 I s. them not, 15; 23:21, 32; 27:15; 29:9
29:31 I s. him not, caused you
Ezek. 3:6 surely had I s. thee
Dan. 10:11 O Dan. to thee am I s.
Joel 2:25 great army which I s.
Zec. 9:11 I s. forth thy prisoners
Mal. 2:4 ye know I have s. this
Luke 4:43 for therefore am I s.
John 17:18 I s. them into world
Acts 10:20 noth. I have s. them
1 Cor. 4:17 for this ha. I s. you T.
2 Cor. 12:17 did I make a gain of you by any whom I s.?
18 and with him I s. a brother
Eph. 6:22 whom I s. for same purpose, Col. 4:8
Phil. 2:28 I s. him more carefully
1 Thes. 3:5 I s. to kn. your faith
Phile. 12 whom I have s. again
See LORD.

**SENT forth.**

Mat. 10:5 these twelve Jesus s. f.
22:3 s. forth his servants to call
Mark 6:17 Herod s. f. laid hold
Acts 9:30 brethren s. him forth
11:22 they s. forth Barnabas

**SENT out.**

Job 39:5 who s. o. wild ass free?
Jer. 24:5 I have s. o. of this place
Ezek. 31:4 s. out her little rivers
Acts 7:12 Jacob s. out our fathers
Jam. 2:25 Rahab had s. them out

**SENT, *passive*.**

Gen. 32:18 present s. to lord Es.
1 K. 14:6 s. with heavy tidings
Ezr. 7:14 forasm. as thou art s.
Ezek. 2:9 a hand was s. unto me
Dan. 5:24 part of hand s. fr. him
Mat. 15:24 s. to lost sheep of Isr.
23:37 stonest them s. Luke 13:34
Luke 1:19 am s. to speak to thee
4:26 unto none was Elias s.
John 1:6 a man s. from God
8 John was s. to bear witness
24 they s. were of the Pharis.
3:28 not Christ, but s. bef. him

9:7 which is by interpretati. s.
13:16 nor he that s. greater than he that s. him
Acts 10:17 men s. made inquiry
29 came I as soon as s. for
13:4 s. forth by the Holy Ghost
26 to you is word of salvat. s.
28:28 salvation of G. s. to Gent.
Rom. 10:15 how preach, exc. s.?
Phil. 4:18 which were s. fr. you
1 Pet. 1:12 H. Ghost s. fr. heaven
Rev. 5:6 the seven spirits s. forth

**SENTEST.**

Ex. 15:7 s. forth thy wrath
Num. 13:27 whither thou s. us
1 K. 5:8 considered things th. s.

**SENTENCE, S.**

Deut. 17:9 they sh. show thee s.
10 shalt do according to s. 11
Ps. 17:2 let my s. come forth
Prov. 16:10 s. in lips of king
Ec. 8:11 s. is not executed
Jer. 4:12 now also will I give s.
Dan. 5:12 hard s. found in Dan.
8:23 a king understand. dark s.
Luke 23:34 Pilate gave s. that it
Acts 15:19 my s. is, that trouble
2 Cor. 1:9 we had the s. of death

**SEPARATE, Verb.**

Gen. 13:9 Abram said, s. thyself
30:40 Jacob did s. the lambs
Lev. 15:31 sh. ye s. children of I.
22:2 Aaron and sons that th. s.
Num. 6:2 when man or woman s.
3 the Nazarite shall s. himself
8:14 shall s. Levites from Israel
16:21 s. from this congregation
Deut. 19:2 shalt s. three cities, 7
29:21 Lord sh. s. him unto evil
1 K. 8:53 s. th. to be inheritance
Ezr. 10:11 s. yourselves fr. peop.
Jer. 37:12 Jerem. went to s. him.
Mal. 25:32 s. them as a shepherd
Luke 6:22 blessed when men s.
Acts 13:2 s. me Barnabas and S.
Rom. 8:35 who sh. s. us fr. Ch.?
39 noth. be able to s. us fr. G.
Jude 19 they who s. themselves

**SEPARATE.**

Gen. 49:26 him that was s. from his brethren, Deut. 33:16
Jos. 16:9 s. cities of Ephraim
Ezek. 41:12 build. before s. place
13 measured house and s. pla.
42:1 cham. ag. s. place, 10, 13
2 Cor. 6:17 fr. among them, be s.
Heb. 7:26 undefiled, s. fr. sinners

**SEPARATED.**

Gen. 13:11 Abram and Lot s.
25:23 two manner of peop. be s.
Ex. 33:16 so be s. from people
Lev. 20:24 I am L. who have s.
Lev. 20:25 I have s. from you as
Num. 16:9 God of Is. hath s. you
Deut. 10:8 Lord s. tribe of Levi
32:8 when he s. sons of Adam
1 Chr. 12:8 Gadites s. unto David
23:13 Aa. was s. that he should
Ezr. 6:21 such as had s. themse
8:24 I s. twelve chief of priests
9:1 priests and Lev. have not s.
10:8 be s. from congregation
16 all of th. by names were s.
Neh. 4:19 we are s. upon wall
9:2 Is. s. themselves fr. strang.
10:28 that s. clave to brethren
13:3 s. fr. Israel the multitude
Prov. 18:1 a man hav. s. himself
19:4 poor is s. from his neighb.
Is. 56:3 L. s. me from his people
59:2 iniq. s. betw. you and God
Hos. 4:14 for themselves are s.
9:10 went and s. themselves
Acts 19:9 Paul s. the disciples
Rom. 1:1 Paul s. to gospel of G.
Gal. 1:15 G. who s. me from my
2:12 P. withdrew and s. himself

**SEPARATETH.**

Num. 6:5 fulfilled in which he s.
Prov. 16:28 a whisper. s. friends
17:9 repeat. a matter s. friends
Ezek. 14:7 strang. wh. s. himself

**SEPARATION.**

Lev. 12:2 the s. for her infirmity
5 uncl. two weeks, as in her s.
15:20 bed she lieth up. in her s.
26 be to her as the bed of h. s.
Num. 6:4 days of s. eat nothing
8 days of s. is holy unto Lord
12 because his s. was defiled
18 Nazarite shave head of his s. and take the hair of his s.
21 offering for s. after law of s.
19:9 ashes be kept for wat. of s.
13 water of s. not sprinkled, 20
21 he that sprinkl. water of s. shall wash his clothes, that toucheth water of s. be unc.
31:23 purified with water of s.
Ezek. 42:20 had a wall to make s.

**SEPARATING.**

Zec. 7:3 I weep in 5th month, s.

**SEPHARVAIM.**

2 K. 17:24 brought men from S.
18:34 the gods of S.? Is. 36:19
19:13 king of S.? Is. 37:13

**SEPULCHRE.**

Gen. 23:6 none with. thee his s.
Deut. 34:6 no man kno. of his s.
Jud. 8:32 buried in father's s.
1 Sam. 10:2 two men by R.'s s.
2 Sam. 2:32 As. in his father's s.
4:12 Ishbosh. buried in Abn. s.
17:23 Ahithophel in s. of father
21:14 bones of Saul in s. of Kis.
1 K. 13:22 carcass not come to s.
31 bury me in s. w. man of G.
2 K. 9:28 Ahaziah in the s.
13:21 cast man into s. of Elish
21:26 Amon was buried in his s.
23:17 it is s. of the man of God
30 Josiah buried in his own s. 2 Chr. 35:24
Ps. 5:9 throat open s. Rom. 3:13
Is. 22:16 hewed out a s. here, as he that he. out a s. on high
Mat. 27:60 rol. stone to door of s.
64 that the s. be made sure, 66
28:1 other Mary came to see s.
Mark 15:46 laid him in a s. and rolled a stone to door of the s. Luke 23:53; Acts 13:29
16:2 came to s. at rising of sun
3 who sh. roll st. fr. door of s.?
5 entering s. 8 fled from s.
Luke 23:55 wom. also beheld s.
24:1 in morning they came to s.
2 stone rolled fr. s. John 20:1
9 returned fr. s. 12 Peter ran
22 women were early at the s.
John 19:41 in garden th. was a s.
42 for the s. was nigh at hand
20:1 com. Mary when dark to s.
2 taken away L. out of the s.
3 that disciple came to s. 4, 8
6 cometh Peter, went into s.
11 Mary stood at s. weeping
Acts 2:29 s. wi. us unto this day
7:16 Jacob laid in s. Abraham

**SEPULCHRES.**

Gen. 23:6 in the choice of our s.
2 K. 23:16 Josiah spied the s. and took the bones out of the s.
2 Chr. 21:20 Jeh. not buried in s.
24:25 Joash not; 28:27 A. not s.
32:33 Hezekiah buried in the s.
Neh. 2:3 place of my fathers' s.
5 send me to city of fathers' s.
Neh. 3:16 rep. to place over ag. s.
Mat. 23:27 are like to whited s.
29 because ye garnish the s.
Luke 11:47 s. of the prophets, 48

**SERAIAH.**

2 Sam. 8:17 S. was the scribe
2 K. 25:18 took S. Jer. 52:24
23 to Gedaliah, S. Jer. 40:8
1 Chr. 4:14 S. begat Joab, 35
6:14 Azariah begat S. and S.
Ezr. 7:1 E. son of S. Neh. 10:2
Neh. 11:11 S. was ruler of house
12:1 S. the priest went up
12 chief of the fathers of S.
Jer. 36:26 king commanded S.
51:59 S. was a quiet prince
61 Jeremiah said to S. when

**SERAPHIM.**

Is. 6:2 above it stood the s. each
6 one of the s. hav. a live coal

**SERGEANTS.**

Acts 16:35 sent the s. saying
38 s. told these words to mag.

**SERGIUS PAULUS.**

Acts 13:7 S. Paulus, a prudent

**SERPENT.**

Gen. 3:1 the s. was more subtle
13 s. beguiled me, 2 Cor. 11:3
49:17 Dan shall be a s. by way
Ex. 4:3 rod bec. a s. 7:9, 10, 15
Num. 21:8 said, Make thee a s.
9 Moses made a s. of brass
2 K. 18:4 Hezek. brake brazen s.
Job 26:13 hand formed crooked s.
Ps. 58:4 th. poison like pois. of s.
140:3 sharpen. tongues like a s.
Prov. 23:32 at last it bit. like a s.
30:19 way of a s. upon a rock
Ec. 10:8 whoso break. a hedge s. shall bite him
11 s. bite without enchantme.
Is. 14:29 of s. root come cockatrice; fruit be as fiery fly. s.
27:1 L. sh. punish s. crooked s.
30:6 viper and fiery flying s.
65:25 dust shall be the s. meat
Jer. 46:22 voice sh. go like a s.
Amos 5:19 and a s. bite him
Mic. 7:17 lick the dust like a s.
Mat. 7:10 will he give him a s.? Luke 11:11
John 3:14 as Moses lifted up s.
Rev. 12:9 old s. called devil, 20:2
14 nourished fr. face of the s.
15 the s. cast out of his mouth

**SERPENTS.**

Ex. 7:12 rods, they became s.
Num. 21:6 L. sent s. amo. them
7 pray to L. he take away s.
Deut. 8:15 wherein were fiery s.
32:24 send poi. of s. upon them
Jer. 8:17 I will send s. among y.
Mat. 10:16 be therefore wise as s.
23:33 ye s. how can ye escape?
Mark 16:18 they shall take up s.
Luke 10:19 power to tread on s.
1 Cor. 10:9 were destroyed of s.
Jam. 3:7 beasts and s. is tamed
Rev. 9:19 tails were like to s.

SERUG. Gen. 11:20–22

**SERVANT.**

Gen. 9:25 Canaan, a s. of servan.
24:34 said, I am Abraham's s.
49:15 Issa. bowed and bec. a s.
Ex. 21:5 if the s. plainly say
Deut. 5:15 remem. thou wast a s.
23:15 thou shalt not deliver s.
1 Sam. 2:13 priest's s. came, 15
9:27 bid the s. pass on before us
25:41 let thy handmaid be a s.
29:3 is not David the s. of Saul?
30:13 I am s. to an Amalekite
2 Sam. 9:2 s. named Ziba, 19:17
16:1 Ziba s. of Mephibosheth
18:29 wh. Joab sent sent k.'s s.
1 K. 11:26 Jeroboam Solom.'s s.
12:7 if thou wilt be a s. to peop.
Neh. 2:10 Tobi. s. Am. heard, 19

*Job* 3:19 there, and the *s.* is free
7:2 as a *s.* earne. desireth shad.
41:4 wilt take Leviathan for *s.?*
*Ps.* 105:17 Joseph, sold for a *s.*
*Prov.* 11:29 fool sh. be *s.* to wise
12:9 that is despi. and hath a *s.*
14:35 king's favor tow. a wise *s.*
17:2 wise *s.* shall rule over a son
19:10 much less a *s.* rule princes
22:7 the borrower is *s.* to lender
29:19 a *s.* not correct. with wor.
30:10 accuse not *s.* to master
22 not bear *s.* when reigneth
*Is.* 24:2 as with *s.* so with master
49:7 saith Lord to a *s.* of rulers
*Jer.* 2:14 is Israel a *s.?* a slave?
*Dan.* 6:20 O Daniel, *s.* of liv. G.
*Dan.* 10:17 can *s.* talk wi. my l.?
*Mal.* 1:6 *s.* honoreth his master
*Mat.* 10:24 nor *s.* above his lord
25 enough for *s.* to be as his lo.
18:27 lord of that *s.* was moved
32 O thou wicked *s.* I forg. th.
20:27 be chief, let him be your *s.* 23:11; *Mark* 10:44
24:45 is a faithful and wise *s.*
46 blessed is that *s.* *Luke* 12:43
48 evil *s.* shall say, *Luke* 12:45
50 lord of *s.* sh. come, *Lu.* 12:46
25:21 well done, th. good and faithful *s.* 23; *Luke* 19:17
26 thou wicked and slothful *s.* *Luke* 19:22
30 cast unprofit. *s.* into darkn.
26:51 P. struck *s.* of high-priest, *Mark* 14:47; *John* 18:10
*Mark* 12:2 sent to husband. a *s.*
*Luke* 12:47 *s.* knew lord's will
14:21 so that *s.* showed his lord
17:7 which having a *s.* plowing
9 doth thank th. *s.?* I trow not
20:10 at season he sent a *s.* 11
*John* 8:34 commit. sin, *s.* of sin
35 the *s.* abideth not in house
13:16 *s.* is not greater, 15:20
15:15 *s.* knoweth not what lord
*Rom.* 1:1 Paul a *s.* of Je. Christ
14:4 who judgest ano. man's *s.?*
16:1 Phebe. a *s.* of the church
1 *Cor.* 7:21 art called being a *s.?*
22 being a *s.* is L.'s freeman
9:19 I made myself a *s.*
*Gal.* 1:10 I sho. not be *s.* of Chr.
4:1 child differeth noth. from *s.*
7 art no more a *s.* but a son
*Phil.* 2:7 he took the form of a *s.*
*Col.* 4:12 Epaphras, a *s.* of Christ
2 *Tim.* 2:24 *s.* of Lord not strive
*Phile.* 16 not as a *s.* above a *s.*
*Heb.* 3:5 Mo. was faithful as a *s.*
2 *Pet.* 1:1 Peter, a *s.* of J. Christ
*Jude* 1 Jude the *s.* of Jesus Chr.
*See* DAVID.

**SERVANT, S. of God.**

*Gen.* 50:17 forgive *s. of God*
1 *Chr.* 6:49 Moses the *s. of God*
2 *Chr.* 24:9 Moses *s. of God* laid
*Neh.* 10:29 by Moses *s. of God*
*Dan.* 6:20 O Daniel *s. of* liv. *God*
9:11 in law of Mo. the *s. of God*
*Tit.* 1:1 P. a *s. of God*, an apost.
*Jam.* 1:1 Ja. a *s. of G.* and of L.
1 *Pet.* 2:16 liberty, as a *s. of G.*
*Rev.* 7:3 sealed the *s. of* our *God*
15:3 song of Moses the *s. of G.*
*See* HIRED.

**His SERVANT.**

*Gen.* 9:26 Can. shall be *his s.* 27
*Ex.* 14:31 believed L. and *his s.*
21:20 if a man smite *his s.*
26 if smite eye of *his s.*
*Jos.* 5:14 what saith L. to *h. s.?*
9:24 God commanded *his s.* Mo.
*Jud.* 7:11 Gi. went wi. Ph. *his s.*
19:3 Levite went, having *his s.*
1 *Sam.* 19:4 let not the king sin against *his s.*
12:15 let not king imp. to *his s.*
25:39 L. hath kept *h. s.* fr. evil
26:18 why doth my lo. pu. *h. s.?*
19 let lord hear words of *h. s.*
2 *Sam.* 9:11 my lord comm. *h. s.*
14:22 king fulfilled req. of *h. s,*
24:21 is my lord come to *h. s.?*
1 *K.* 1:51 that will not slay *h. s.*
8:56 prom. by hand of Mo. *h. s.*
59 maintain cause of *h. s.* Isr.
14:18 spake by *h. s.* Ahi. 15:29
19:3 Eli. left *h. s.* at Beer-sheba
2 *K.* 9:36 word he spake by *h. s.*
14:25 word he spake by *h. s.* Jo.
17:3 Hoshea bec. *his s.* and gave
24:1 Jehoiakim became *his s.*
1 *Chr.* 16:13 O ye seed of Is. *h. s.*
2 *Chr.* 32:16 spake ag. *his s.* Hez
*Neh.* 4:22 let ev. one with *h. s.*
*Ps.* 35:27 L. hath pleas. of *his s.*
105:6 O ye seed of Abra. *his s.*
26 he sent Moses *his s.* and A.
42 remembered Abraham *his s.*
136:22 a heritage unto Is. *his s.*
*Prov.* 29:21 delicately bring. *h. s.*
*Is.* 44:26 confirm. word of *his s.*
48:20 Lord redeemed *h. s.* Jacob
49:5 from the womb to be *his s.*
50:10 obeyeth voice of *his s.?*
*Jer.* 34:16 ev. man *h. s.* to return
*Mat.* 8:13 *his s.* was healed
*Luke* 1:54 hath holpen *his s.* Isr.
7:3 beseeching he wo. heal *h. s.*
14:17 sent *h. s.* at supper-time
*Rev.* 1:1 by his angel un. *h. s.* J.
*See* LORD, MAID.

**Man-SERVANT.**

*Ex.* 20:10 th. nor *m.-s.* *Deut.* 5:14
17 not cov. ne. *m.-s.* *Deut.* 5:21
21:27 smite out his *m.-s.* tooth
32 if the ox shall push a *m.-s.*
*Deut.* 12:18 eat, thou, and *m.-s.*
16:11 rejoice, th. and thy *m.-s.*
*Job* 31:13 if desp. cause of *m.-s.*
*Jer.* 34:9 let *m.-s.* go free, 10

**My SERVANT.**

*Gen.* 26:24 multi. seed for *my s.*
44:10 found he sh. be *my s.* 17
*Num.* 12:7 *my s.* Moses is not so
14:24 *my s.* Caleb had another
*Jos.* 1:2 Moses *my s.* is dead
1 *Sam.* 22:8 son stirred up *my s.*
27:12 he shall be *my s.* for ever
2 *Sam.* 19:26 O king, *my s.* decei.
2 *K.* 5:6 have sent Naaman *my s.*
21:8 according to law *my s.* M.
*Job* 1:8 consider. *my s.* Job? 2:3
19:16 I called *my s.* he gave me
42:7 not spok. right, as *my s.* J.
8 go to *my s.* J. he shall pray
*Is.* 20:3 like as *my s.* Isa. hath
22:20 I will call *my s.* Eliakim
41:8 Israel, *my s.* fear not, 9
42:1 behold *my s.* wh. I uphold
19 who is blind but *my s.?*
43:10 are witnesses and *my s.*
44:1 O Ja. *my s.* 2 fear not, *m. s.*
21 for thou art *my s.* 49:3
45:4 for Ja. *my s.* sake, and Isr.
49:6 thou shouldest be *my s.*
52:13 *my s.* deal prudently
65:8 so will I do for *my s.* sake
*Jer.* 25:9 Nebuchadnezzar *my s.* 27:6; 43:10
30:10 O *my s.* Jacob, 46:27, 28
*Ezek.* 28:25 given *my s.* J. 37:25
*Hag.* 2:23 O Zerubbabel *my s.*
*Zec.* 3:8 *my s.* the BRANCH
*Mal.* 4:4 law of Moses, *my s.*
*Mat.* 8:8 *my s.* be healed, *Lu.* 7:7
8 to *my s.* do this, *Luke* 7:8
12:18 *my s.* whom I ha. chosen
*John* 12:26 th. shall also *my s.* be

**Thy SERVANT.**

*Gen.* 18:3 pass, I pray, fr. *thy s.*
19:19 *thy s.* found gra. *Neh.* 2:5
32:10 mercies showed to *thy s.*
18 say, They be *thy s.* Jacob's
33:5 chil. God hath given *thy s.*
44:31 grey hairs of *thy s.* our fa.
*Ex.* 4:10 spoken unto *thy s.*
*Lev.* 25:6 for thee, and for *thy s.*
*Num.* 11:11 where. hast affl. *t. s.*
*Deut.* 3:24 show *thy s.* thy great.
15:17 he shall be *thy s.* for ever
*Jud.* 7:10 go down with Ph. *t. s.*
1 *Sam.* 3:9 Lord *thy s.* heareth, 10
20:7 *thy s.* shall have peace
22:15 *thy s.* knew noth. of this
23:11 I beseech thee tell *thy s.*
28:2 sh. know what *t. s.* can do
2 *Sam.* 7:19 hast spoken of *thy s.*
20 thou, L. G. knowest thy *s.*
39 bless the house of *thy s.*
13:35 came, as *thy s.* said
15:21 even there will *thy s.* be
24:10 take away iniq. of *thy s.*
1 *K.* 1:26 even me, *t. s.* and Zad. the priest, and *t. s.* Solomon
3:8 *thy s.* is in midst of thy peo.
9 give *thy s.* understand. heart
8:28 respect to prayer of *thy s.*
18:12 but I *thy s.* fear the Lord
20:40 as *thy s.* was busy here
2 *K.* 4:1 *thy s.* my husband dead, thou know. *thy s.* did fear L.
5:18 L. pardon *t. s.* in this thing
25 Ge. said, *thy s.* went no wh.
8:13 is *t. s.* a dog? 16:7 am *t s.*
*Neh.* 1:11 prosp. I pray thee, *t. s.*
*Ps.* 19:11 by th. is *thy s.* warned
27:9 put not *thy s.* away
31:16 face to shine upon *thy s.*
69:17 hide not thy face fr *thy s.*
86:2 O G. save *t. s.* that trusteth
16 give thy strength to *thy s.*
89:39 made void coven. of *thy s.*
116:16 am *t. s.* 119:125; 143:12
*Ec.* 7:21 hear *thy s.* curse thee
*Is.* 63:17 return, for *thy s.* sake
*Dan.* 9:17 hear prayer of *thy s.*
*Luke* 2:29 L. lettest *thy s.* depart

**SERVANTS.**

*Gen.* 9:25 a serv. of *s.* shall he be
27:37 breth. have I given for *s.*
*Lev.* 25:55 children of Is. are *s.*
1 *Sam.* 4:9 be not *s.* to Hebrews
7:8 Philist. and you *s.* of Saul
9 then will we be your *s.*
25:10 many *s.* break away from
41 wash feet of *s.* of my lord
2 *Sam.* 8:2 Moab. bec. David's *s.*
2 *Sam.* 8:6 Syrians bec. *s.* to D.
14 they of Edom be. David's *s.*
9:10 Ziba had 15 sons and 20 *s.*
11:11 *s.* of my lord are encamp.
1 *K.* 2:39 two *s.* of Shimei ran
2 *K.* 21:23 *s.* of Amon conspired
1 *Chr.* 21:3 are they not lord's *s.*
2 *Chr.* 8:9 of Israel S. made no *s.*
36:20 Babylon, wh. they were *s.*
*Ezr.* 5:11 we are the *s.* of God
*Neh.* 5:15 th. *s.* bare rule over p.
9:36 are *s.* this day, *s.* in land
*Job* 1:15 slain *s.* with sword, 17
*Ps.* 123:2 eyes of *s.* look to mast.
*Ec.* 2:7 I got me *s.* had *s.* born
10:7 I have seen *s.* on horses, and princes walking as *s.*
*Is.* 14:2 Israel possess them for *s.*
*Jer.* 34:11 caused the *s.* they had
*Lam.* 5:8 *s.* have ruled over us
*Dan.* 3:26 *s.* of the m. high God
*Joel* 2:29 upon *s.* will I pour Sp.
*Zec.* 2:9 shall be a spoil to *s.*
*Mat.* 22:13 said to *s.* Bind him
25:19 the lord of those *s.* come.
*Mark* 14:65 the *s.* did strike Jes.
*Luke* 12:37 blessed are those *s.* 38
17:10 unprofitable *s.* have done
*John* 15:15 I call you not *s.* for
*Acts* 16:17 these men are *s.* of G.

Rom. 6:16 yield yoursel. s. to ob.
17 that ye were the s. of sin
18 became s. of righteousness
19 yielded your mem. s. to sin
20 s. of sin, were free fr. right.
22 free from sin. bec. s. to God
1 Cor. 7:23 be not ye s. of men
2 Cor. 4:5 oursel. your s. for Jes.
Eph. 6:5 s. obedi. to mast. Col. 3:22; Tit. 2:9; 1 Pet. 2:18
6 eye service, but as s. of Chr.
Phil. 1:1 Paul and Tim. s. of Ch.
Col. 4:1 give your s. what is just
1 Tim. 6:1 as many s. as are un.
1 Pet. 2:16 liberty, but as s. of G.
2 Pet. 2:19 themselves are s. of c.
Rev. 7:3 we have sealed s. of G.
See HIRED.

**His SERVANTS.**

Ex. 12:30 Phar. rose, and his s.
Num. 22:22 Bala. rid. and h. 2 s.
Deut. 32:36 L. sh. repent for h. s.
43 he will avenge blood of h. s.
1 Sam. 8:14 best, give to h. s. 15.
19:1 S. spake to h. s. to kill Da.
22:6 h. s. standing about him
2 K. 5:13 h. s. came near, spake
1 Chr. 19:3 h. s. come to search?
2 Chr. 32:16 his s. spake ag. L.
Neh. 2:20 his s. will arise
Job 4:18 he put no trust in his s.
Ps. 69:36 seed of his s. inherit
135:14 repent himself conc. h. s.
Prov. 29:12 all his s. are wicked
Is. 56:6 love na. of L. to be h. s.
65:15 L. call h. s. by ano. name
66:14 L. be known toward his s.
Jer. 22:4 on horses, and his s.
36:31 punish him, seed, his s.
Ezek. 46:17 if p. give gift to h. s.
Dan. 3:28 deliver h. s. trusted
Mat. 18:23 king take acc. of h. s.
21:34 sent h. s. to husbandmen
Luke 19:13 he called his ten s.
Rom. 6:16 h. s. ye are wh. ye ob.
Rev. 1:1 h. s. things must come, 22:6
19:2 hath avenged blood of h. s.
5 praise God, ye h. s. fear him
22:3 and his s. shall serve him
See LORD, MAID, MEN.

**My SERVANTS.**

Lev. 25:42 my s. whom I bro. 55
1 Sam. 21:2 appoint. my s. a pl.
1 K. 5:6 my s. shall be with thy servants, 2 Chr. 2:8
22:49 let my s. go with thy serv.
2 K. 9:7 aven. the blood of my s.
Neh. 4:23 nor my s. put off clo.
5:10 I and my s. mig. exact mo.
16 my s. were gather. to work
13:19 my s. set I at gates
Is. 65:9 my s. shall dwell there
13 my s. eat; 14 my s. sing
Jer. 7:25 sent to you my s. 44:4
John 18:36 then wo. my s. fight
Acts 2:18 on my s. I will pour S.
Rev. 2:20 prophe. to seduce my s.
See PROPHETS.

**Thy SERVANTS.**

Gen. 44:16 G. found iniq. of t. s.
47:3 thy s. are shepherds
50:18 said, Behold, we be thy s.
Ex. 5:15 dealest thus with thy s.
11:8 these thy s. bow down
Ex. 32:13 remember Abraham, and Israel thy s. Deut. 9:27
Jos. 9:8 Gibeo. said, We are t. s.
10:6 slack not thy hand fr. t. s.
1 Sam. 12:19 pray for t. s. to L.
22:14 so faithf. am. t. s. as D.?
2 Sam. 19:7 speak comf. to thy s.
1 K. 2:39 told Shimei, t. s. in G.
5:6 my servants shall be with thy s. 2 Chr. 2:8
8:23 keepest mercy with thy s.
32 and judge t. s. 2 Chr. 6:23
10:8 happy th. t. s. 2 Chr. 9:7
12:7 thy s. for ever, 2 Chr. 10:7
2 K. 6:3 content, and go wi. t. s.
Neh. 1:10 these are thy s. and p.
11 attentive to prayer of thy s.
Ps. 79:2 bodies of thy s.
10 revenging of blood of t. s.
89:50 remem. reproach of thy s.
90:13 repent thee concern. t. s.
16 let thy work appear to t. s.
102:14 for thy s. take pleasure
28 child. of thy s. shall contin.
119:91 continue, for all are t. s.
Is. 37:24 by thy s. reproached L.
Dan. 1:12 prove thy s. ten days
13 as th. seest, deal with t. s.
Acts 4:29 grant unto thy s. that
See WOMEN.

**SERVE.**

Gen. 15:13 seed s. them 400 years
14 nation they s. I will judge
25:23 elder shall s. the younger
27:29 let people s. nations bow
40 by sw. live, and s. brother
29:18 I will s. 7 yrs. for Rachel
27 shalt s. seven other years
Ex. 1:13 made Is. s. with rigor
3:12 ye shall s. G. upon moun.
4:23 let my son go, he may s.
7:16 let my peo. go, that they may s. 8:1, 20; 9:1, 13; 10:3
14:12 alone, that we s. Egypt
20:5 bow down nor s. Deut. 5:9
21:6 he shall s. him for ever
Lev. 25:40 s. thee to year of jub.
Num. 4:24 family of Gers. to s.
8:25 age of fifty, sh. s. no more
18:21 to Levi. for serv. they s.
Deut. 6:13 fear the Lord and s. him, 10:12, 20; 11:13; 13:4; Jos. 22:5; 24:14, 15; 1 Sam. 7:3; 12:14; 20, 24
15:12 bro. be sold, s. six years
28:48 shalt thou s. thine enem.
Jos. 24:15 cho. whom ye will s.
Jud. 9:38 Ab. that we s. him?
1 Sam. 10:7 do as occasion sh. s.
11:1 make covenant, we will s.
12:10 deliver us, and we s. thee
17:9 be our servants, and s. us
2 Sam. 16:19 whom should I s.? should I not s.?
22:44 people I knew not shall s. me, Ps. 18:43
2 K. 10:18 but Jehu shall s. Baal
25:24 dwell in the land and s. the king of Babylon, Jer. 27:11, 12, 17; 28:14; 40:9
1 Chr. 28:9 s. him with perf. he.
2 Chr. 29:11 L. hath ch. you to s.
34:33 Josiah made all to s. Lord
Job 21:15 Almig. that we s. him?
36:11 if they obey, and s. him
39:9 unicorn be will. to s. thee?
Ps. 22:30 a seed shall s. him
72:11 all nations shall s. him
97:7 confounded that s. images
101:6 perfect way, he sh. s. me
Is. 14:3 bond. wast made to s.
19:23 Egyptians s. with Assyri.
43:23 ha. not caused thee to s.
24 made me to s. wi. thy sins
56:6 join themsel. to L. to s. h.
66:12 nation not s. thee sh. per.
Jer. 5:19 so shall ye s. strangers
17:4 cause thee to s. enemies
25:11 nations s. king of Babylon
14 nations s. themselves, 27:7
27:6 beasts have I given to s.
9 proph. say, Ye shall not s. 14
30:8 strang. no more s. themse.
34:9 none sho. s. himself of, 10
40:10 behold, I will s. Chaldea.
Ezek. 20:32 families to s. wood
39 s. ye every one his idols
40 all of th. in land sh. s. me
29:18 army s. against Tyrus
48:18 food to them that s. city
19 that s. city sh. s. of all trib.
Dan. 3:17 G. wh. we s. to deliver
28 not s. any, exc. th. own G.
7:27 dominions s. obey him
Zep. 3:9 s. him with consent
Mal. 3:14 it is in vain to s. God
Mat. 4:10 him only s. Luke 4:8
Mat. 6:24 no man can s. 2 mas. cannot s. G. and M. Lu. 16:13
Luke 1:74 we deliv. might s. him
10:40 sister left me to s. alone
12:37 will come forth s. them
15:29 these many years I s. thee
17:8 gird thyself and s. me
22:26 chief, as he that doth s.
John 12:26 if any man s. me
Acts 6:2 lea. word of G. s. tables
7:7 come, s. me in this place
27:23 angel of God whom I s.
Rom. 1:9 G. my witness, wh. I s.
6:6 that we should not s. sin.
7:6 should s. in newness of spi.
25 with mind I s. law of God
9:12 said, elder shall s. younger
16:18 th. that are such s. not L.
Gal. 5:13 by love s. one another
Col. 3:24 reward, ye s. Lord Ch.
1 Thes. 1:9 turned fr. id. to s. G.
2 Tim. 1:3 I thank G. whom I s.
Heb. 8:5 s. to exam. of heavenly
9:14 purge fr. dead wo. to s. G.
12:28 may s. God acceptably
13:10 right to eat wh. s. tabern.
Rev. 7:15 s. him in his temple
22:3 his servants shall s. him

**SERVED, with gods.**

Ex. 23:24 sh. not s. th. g. Deut. 6:14; 28:14; Jos. 23:7; 2 K. 17:35; Jer. 25:6; 35:15
33 if thou s. th. g. it be a snare
Deut. 4:28 there ye shall s. g. the work, 28:36, 64; Jer. 16:13
7:4 they may s. other g. 31:20
13:2 after, and s. other g. 6, 13
29:18 turneth from G. s. other g.
Jos. 24:16 G. forb. we s. other g.
Jud. 2:19 corrupted themsel. to s. other g. Jer. 11:10; 13:10
1 Sam. 26:19 saying, s. other g.
Jer. 44:3 prov. me, to s. other g.
Dan. 3:12 they s. not g. nor ima.
14 do ye not s. my g.? 18
See LORD.

**SERVED.**

Gen. 14:4 they s. Chedorlaomer.
29:20 Ja. s. 7 yrs. for Rachel, 30
30:29 know. how I have s. thee
31:41 s. 14 years for thy daught.
Deut. 17:3 hath gone, s. other gods, 29:26; Jos. 23:16
Jos. 24:2 fath. s. other gods, 15
31 Israel s. the Lord all the days of Joshua, Jud. 2:7
Jud. 2:11 s. Baa. 13; 3:7; 10:6
3:6 daught. to sons, s. th. gods
14 Is. s. Eglon, eighteen years
8:1 why hast thou s. us thus?
10:13 forsaken me, s. other gods
16 they put away th. gods, and s. the Lord, 1 Sam. 7:4
2 Sam. 10:19 the Syrians s. Israel
16:19 s. in thy fath.'s presence
1 K. 4:21 presents, and s. Solom.
9:9 s. other gods, 2 Chr. 7:22
2 K. 10:18 Jehu said, Ah. s. Baal
21:3 Manasseh s. the host of heaven, 2 Chr. 33:3
21 Amon s. idols, 2 Chr. 33:22
2 Chr. 24:18 princes of Ju. s. id.
Neh. 9:35 they have not s. thee
Ps. 106:36 and they s. their idols
137:8 reward. as thou hast s. us
Ec. 5:9 king him. is s. by field
Jer. 5:19 ye have s. strange gods
16:11 walk. after gods, s. them

34:14 *s.* six years, let him go
*Ezek.* 29:18 service he hath *s.* 20
34:27 out of hand of those th. *s.*
*Hos.* 12:12 Israel *s.* for wife
*Luke* 2:37 Anna *s.* G. in temple
*John* 12:2 ma. supper, Martha *s.*
*Acts* 13:36 Da. had *s.* generation
*Rom.* 1:25 worship. *s.* creature
*Phil.* 2:22 *s.* with me in gospel

**SERVEDST.**

*Deut.* 28:47 thou *s.* not the Lord

**SERVEST, ETH.**

*Num.* 3:36 under Mer. all that *s.*
*Dan.* 6:16 God thou *s.* wilt deli.
20 is God th. *s.* able to deliver?
*Mal.* 3:17 spareth son that *s.* him
18 him that *s.* G. him th. *s.* not
*Luke* 22:27 sit. at meat, or he that *s.*? I am as one that *s.*
*Rom.* 14:18 in these things *s.* Ch.
1 *Cor.* 14:22 prophesying *s.* not for them that believe not
*Gal.* 3:19 wherefore then *s.* law?

**SERVICE.**

*Gen.* 29:27 *s.* that th. shalt serve
*Ex.* 1:14 all *s.* in field; their *s.*
12:26 wh. mean you by this *s.*?
36:5 more than enough for *s.*
*Num.* 3:7 tribe of Levi to do *s.* 8
4:19 Aaron appoint them to *s.*
24 the *s.* of Gershonites, 27, 28
30 *s.* of the sons of Merari, 33, 43
8:11 Levites may execute *s.* of L.
25 50 years cease waiting on *s.*
16:9 small th. to bring you to *s.*
18:4 Levites be joined for all *s.*
1 *K.* 12:4 make grievous *s.* lighter
1 *Chr.* 6:31 whom Da. set over *s.*
9:13 men for work of *s.* 26:8
28:13 Levites for work of the *s.*
21 priests sh. be wi. thee for *s.*
29:5 who consecrate his *s.* to L.?
7 for *s.* of house of God silver
2 *Chr.* 8:14 courses of priests to *s.*
12:8 know my *s.* and *s.* of kingd.
31:2 ev. man according to his *s.*
35:2 encouraged them to *s.* of L.
10 so *s.* of L. was prepared, 16
*Ezr.* 6:18 in courses for *s.* 7:19
*Ps.* 104:14 herb to grow *s.* of man
*Jer.* 22:13 that useth neighb.'s *s.*
*Ezek.* 29:18 cau. army to serve *s.*
44:14 keepers of house for the *s.*
*John* 16:2 kill. think doeth G. *s.*
*Rom.* 9:4 wh. pertaineth *s.* of G.
12:1 which is your reasonable *s.*
15:31 *s.* be accepted of saints
2 *Cor.* 9:12 adminstra. of this *s.*
11:8 taking wages to do you *s.*
*Gal.* 4:8 did *s.* to th. are no gods
*Eph.* 6:7 good-will doing *s.* to L.
*Phil.* 2:17 offered upon *s.* of faith
30 to supply your lack of *s.*
1 *Tim.* 6:2 do *s.* because beloved
*Heb.* 9:1 ordinances of divine *s.*
6 priests accomplish *s.* of God
9 make him that did *s.* perfect
*Rev.* 2:19 know thy works and *s.*

**Bond-SERVICE.**

1 *K.* 9:21 Sol. levy tribute of *b.-s.*

**Eye-SERVICE.**

*Eph.* 6:6 not *e.-s.* as men-pleasers

**SERVILE.**

*Lev.* 23:7 ye shall do no *s.* work, 8, 21, 25, 35, 36: *Num.* 28:18, 25, 26; 29:1, 12, 35.

**SERVING.**

*Deut.* 15:18 hired serv. in *s.* thee
*Luke* 10:40 M. cumbered about *s.*
*Acts* 20:19 *s.* Lord with humility
26:7 twelve tribes *s.* G. day and
*Rom.* 12:11 fervent in spirit, *s.* L.
*Tit.* 3:3 sometimes fool. *s.* lusts

**SERVITOR.**

2 *K.* 4:43 *s.* said, set this bef. 100?

**SERVITUDE.**

2 *Chr.* 10:4 griev. *s.* of thy father
*Lam.* 1:3 Jud. gone because of *s.*

**SET.**

*Gen.* 4:15 L. *s.* mark upon Cain
9:13 I *s.* my bow in cloud
41:33 let Phar. *s.* him over Eg.
43:9 if I bring not and *s.* him
48:20 J. *s.* Eph. before Manass.
*Ex.* 7:23 nor *s.* his heart to this
19:12 *s.* bounds; 26:35 *s.* table
21:1 judgments *s.* before them
40:4 *s.* in order things to be *s.*
*Lev.* 24:8 ev. sabbath *s.* it in ord.
*Num.* 2:9 camp of J. first *s.* forth
8:13 *s.* the Levites bef. Aaron
27:16 let L. *s.* a man over cong.
*Deut.* 1:8 ha. *s.* land bef. you, 21
4:8 law which I *s.* bef. you, 44
7:7 L. did not *s.* his love on you
11:26 I *s.* before you blessing
14:24 cho. to *s.* name, *Neh.* 1:9
17:14 I will *s.* a king over me
28:1 L. G. will *s.* thee on high
30:15 I *s.* bef. you, life, death, 19
32:46 *s.* hearts to words I testify
*Jos.* 24:25 he *s.* a statute in Sh.
*Jud.* 6:18 *s.* my present bef. thee
7:19 had but newly *s.* watch
1 *Sam.* 2:8 rais. poor, to *s.* them am. princes, *s.* world on th.
10:19 said, Nay, *s.* king over us
12:13 L. hath *s.* a king over you
2 *Sam.* 19:28 *s.* thy serv. at table
1 *K.* 2:15 Is. *s.* their faces on me
5:5 I will *s.* on throne sh. build
21:9 *s.* Naboth high am. peo. 12
2 *K.* 4:4 *s.* aside that wh. is full
20:1 *s.* house in order, *Is.* 38:1
1 *Chr.* 16:1 *s.* ark in mid. of tent
22:19 *s.* your heart to seek Lord
2 *Chr.* 11:16 *s.* th. hea. to seek L.
20:3 *s.* himself to seek Lord.
24:13 *s.* house of G. in his state
*Neh.* 2:6 king, I *s.* him a time
9:37 incre. to kings *s.* over us
13:11 gather. *s.* them in place
*Job* 6:4 terrors of God *s.* ag. me
*Job* 7:17 should *s.* hea. upon him
20 why *s.* me a mark ag. thee?
9:19 who *s.* me a time to plead?
30:13 *s.* forward my calamity
33:5 *s.* thy words in order
*Ps.* 2:2 kings of earth *s.* themsel.
6 have I *s.* king on holy hill
3:6 not afraid if 10,000 *s.* them.
4:3 L. *s.* apart him that is godly
16:8 I *s.* Lord always bef. me
31:8 *s.* my feet in large room
40:2 *s.* my feet upon a rock
50:21 I *s.* them bef. thine eyes
54:3 have not *s.* God bef. them
62:10 riches, *s.* not yo. hearts on
73:18 didst *s.* th. in slip. places
78:7 might *s.* their hope in God
8 genera. *s.* not heart aright
85:13 *s.* us in way of his steps
86:14 viol. men have not *s.* thee
91:14 he hath *s.* his love upon me, theref. I *s.* him on high
101:3 *s.* no wicked thi. bef. eyes
104:9 *s.* bound th. may not pass
109:6 *s.* wicked man over him
113:8 may *s.* him with princes
118:5 *s.* me in a large place
141:3 *s.* a watch bef. my mouth
*Prov.* 1:25 *s.* at naught counsel
23:5 *s.* th. eyes on that is not?
*Ec.* 3:11 *s.* world in their heart
7:14 G. *s.* one against the other
12:9 *s.* in order many proverbs
*Is.* 7:6 *s.* a king in midst of it
14:1 L. *s.* th. in their own land
19:2 I will *s.* Egypti. ag. Egypt.
22:7 *s.* themsel. in array at gate
42:4 have *s.* judgm. in the earth
44:7 shall *s.* it in order for me?
46:7 and *s.* him in his place
66:19 I will *s.* a sign am. them
*Jer.* 1:10 I *s.* thee over nations
6:27 I have *s.* thee for a tower
7:12 place where I *s.* my name
9:13 forsaken law I *s.* bef. them
21:8 I *s.* before you way of life
24:6 *s.* eyes on them for good
26:4 walk in law I *s.* bef. you
34:16 serv. he had *s.* at liberty
38:22 friends have *s.* thee on
44:10 statutes wh. I *s.* bef. thee
*Lam.* 3:6 *s.* me in dark places
*Ezek.* 5:5 *s.* in midst of nations
7:20 theref. I *s.* it far from them
12:6 I *s.* thee for a sign unto Is.
17:22 highest branch, I will *s.* it
19:8 th. nations *s.* against him
22:7 *s.* light by fath. and moth.
24:2 king of Babylon *s.* ag. Jer.
7 she *s.* it upon top of a rock, 8
25 whereon they *s.* minds
26:20 *s.* glory in land of living
28:2 thou *s.* heart as heart of G.
40:4 *s.* heart upon all I sh. thee
44:8 *s.* keep. of charge in sanct.
*Dan.* 6:3 *s.* him over the realm
14 *s.* heart on Dan. to del. him
9:10 walk in laws he *s.* bef. us
10:12 *s.* thy heart to understand
*Hos.* 2:3 *s.* her as day was born
4:8 *s.* their heart on their iniq.
11:8 how sh. I *s.* th. as Zeboi.?
*Amos* 9:4 *s.* eyes on them for ev.
*Hab.* 2:9 may *s.* his nest on high
*Zec.* 5:11 be *s.* on her own base
8:10 *s.* every man ag. neighbor
*Mat.* 10:35 to *s.* man at variance
25:33 *s.* sheep on right hand
*Luke* 4:18 *s.* at liberty bruised
10:34 *s.* him on his own beast
11:6 have nothing to *s.* bef. thee
23:11 Herod *s.* him at naught
*John* 2:10 *s.* forth good wine
3:33 *s.* to his seal that G. is true
*Acts* 7:5 so much as to *s.* foot on
13:9 Paul *s.* his eyes on him
18:10 no man *s.* on thee to hurt
*Rom.* 14:10 *s.* at naught brother?
1 *Cor.* 4:9 God *s.* forth apostles
6:4 *s.* to judge least esteemed
12:28 G. hath *s.* some in church
*Eph.* 1:20 *s.* him at right hand
*Heb.* 2:7 *s.* over work of hands
*Rev.* 3:8 *s.* bef. thee an open door

**SET up.**

*Gen.* 28:18 Jacob took stone, and *s.* it *up,* 22; 31:45; 35:14
*Lev.* 26:1 nor *s.* *up* ima. of stone
*Num.* 10:21 other did *s.* it *up*
1 *Sam.* 15:11 repenteth I *s.* *up* S.
2 *Sam.* 3:10 to *s.* *up* throne of D.
7:12 I will *s.* *up* seed after thee
1 *K.* 15:4 to *s.* *up* son after him
2 *K.* 17:10 they *s.* th. *up* images
2 *Chr.* 25:14 Am. *s.* th. *up* gods
*Ezr.* 2:68 to *s.* *up* God's house
4:12 J. have *s.* *up* walls, 13, 16
*Ezr.* 5:11 house king of Is. *s.* *up*
*Neh.* 6:1 I had not *s.* *up* doors
*Job.* 5:11 *s.* *up* those that be low
16:12 and *s.* me *up* for his mark
*Ps.* 27:5 and *s.* me *up* upon rock
69:29 let thy salvation *s.* me *up*
89:42 *s.* *up* right hand of adver.
*Prov.* 8:23 was *s.* *up* everlasting
*Jer.* 11:13 *s.* *up* altars to thing?
*Ezek.* 14:3 men *s.* *up* their idols
31:4 the deep *s.* him *up* on high
*Dan.* 2:44 God sh. *s.* *up* a kingd.
5:19 whom he would he *s.* *up*
*Hos.* 8:4 they have *s.* *up* kings
*Mal.* 3:15 work wickedness *s.* *up*
*Acts* 6:13 *s.* *up* false witnesses
15:16 build ruins, and *s.* it *up*

**SET,** *passive.*

*Gen.* 24:33 th. was *s.* meat before

Ex. 32:22 th. are s. on mischief
1 Sam. 18:30 his name was s. by
26:24 thy life was much s. by
1 K. 14:4 for his eyes were s.
2 K. 12:4 money every man s. at
1 Chr. 19:10 J. saw battle was s.
2 Chr. 6:10 I am s. on thr. of Is.
29:35 house of Lord s. in order
31:15 in their s. office to give
Job 36:16 what sh. be s. on table
Ps. 10:8 privily s. against poor
141:2 let my prayer be s. forth
Ec. 8:11 heart is s. to do evil
10:6 folly is s. in great dignity
Is. 3:24 instead of well s. hair
Jer. 6:23 s. in array, Joel 2:5
31:29 teeth s. on edge, Ezek. 18:2
Dan. 7:10 judgment was s.
Mat. 5:14 a city s. on a hill
27:19 he was s. on judgm.-seat
Mark 1:32 when sun s. brought
9:12 things, he s. at naught
Luke 2:34 this child is s. for fall
7:8 a man s. under authority
10:8 eat such as are s. bef. you
Acts 4:11 the stone s. at naught
19:27 craft in danger to be s. at
26:32 man might ha. been s. at
1 Cor. 10:27 whatever is s. before you
Gal. 3:1 Ch. had been s. forth
Heb. 6:18 lay hold on hope s. bef.
8:1 is s. on right hand, 12:2
12:1 run the race s. before us
2 joy that was s. before him
13:23 brother Tim. s. at liberty
Jude 7 cities s. forth for examp.
Rev. 3:21 s. down with Father
4:2 a throne was s. in heaven

**SET day.**

Acts 12:21 on s. day He. arrayed

See FACE, FACES, FEASTS.

**SET time.**

Gen. 17:21 Sa. shall bear at s. t.
Ex. 9:5 Lord appointed a s. t.
Job 14:13 wouldest appoint a s. t.
Ps. 102:13 s. t. to favor is come

**SETH.**

Gen. 5:3 and called him S.
6 S. begat Enos, 1 Chr. 1:1; Luke 3:38

**SETTER.**

Acts 17:18 a s. forth of stra. gods

**SETTEST.**

Deut. 23:20 s. hand to, 28:8, 20
Job 7:12 that s. a watch over me?
Ps. 41:12 thou s. me before face

**SETTETH.**

Deut. 24:15 s. his heart on it
27:16 cursed that s. light by fa.
2 Sam. 22:34 s. me on hi. places, Ps. 18:33
Job 28:3 he s. an end to darkness
Ps. 36:4 he s. himself in a way
65:6 by strength s. fast mount.
75:7 put. down one, s. up ano.
107:41 s. poor on high
Jer. 5:26 as he that s. snares
43:3 Baruch s. thee on ag. us
Ezek. 14:4 th. s. idols in heart, 7
Dan. 2:21 remov. kings and s. up
4:17 s. up over it basest of men

**SETTING, S.**

Ex. 28:17 set in it s. of stones
Ezek. 43:8 in s. of their threshold
Mat. 27:66 seal. stone, s. a watch
Luke 4:40 when sun was s. they

**SETTLE.**

Ezek. 43:14 fr. ground to lower s.
17 s. shall be 14 cubits long
20 blood on corners of s. 45:19

**SETTLE, ST.**

1 Chr. 17:14 will s. him in house
Ps. 65:10 thou s. furrows thereof
Ezek. 36:11 I will s. you af. your

Luke 21:14 s. it in your hearts
1 Pet. 5:10 G. strengthen, s. you

**SETTLED.**

1 K. 8:13 built a s. place for thee
2 K. 8:11 he s. his countenance
Ps. 119:89 word is s. in heaven
Prov. 8:25 before mount. were s.
Jer. 48:11 he hath s. on lees
Zep. 1:12 are s. on their lees
Col. 1:23 faith, grounded and s.

**SEVEN.**

Gen. 46:25 Bil. all souls were s.
Ex. 2:16 priest of M. had s. dau.
Lev. 23:15 s. sab. shall be com.
25:8 number s. sabbaths of yrs.
Num. 23:1 build here s. altars, prep. s. oxen and s. rams, 29
Deut. 7:1 s. nations greater
16:9 s. weeks thou sh. number
28:7 L. cause ene. flee s. ways
25 shalt flee s. ways bef. them
Jos. 6:4 s. priests bearing s. trumpets, 6, 8, 13
18:2 remained of Is. s. tribes
1 Sam. 2:5 barren hath born s.
16:10 Jesse made s. of his sons
2 Sam. 21:9 they fell all s. toge.
Ezr. 7:14 king and his s. couns.
Est. 1:14 the s. princes wh. saw
Job 5:19 in s. troubles no evil
Prov. 9:1 wisd. hath hewn s. pil.
26:25 th. are s. abominations
Ec. 11:2 portion to s. also to 8
Is. 4:1 s. women take hold of 1
11:15 L. shall smite in s. strea.
Ezek. 39:12 s. months be burying
Dan. 9:25 Mes. sh. be s. weeks
Mic. 5:5 against him s. sheph.
Zec. 3:9 upon one stone s. eyes
Mark. 12:22 and s. had her, 23; Luke 20:31, 33
Rev. 1:4 John to s. churches in A.
10:3 when he cried, s. thunders
12:3 dragon, having s. heads and s. crowns, 13:1; 17:3, 7
15:1 I saw s. angels having the s. last plagues, 6
7 to s. angels s. golden vials
17:1 one of the s. angels which had the s. vials, 21:9
9 s. heads are s. mountains
11 beast is of the s. and goeth

See DAYS, HUNDRED.

**SEVEN bullocks, *or* rams.**

Num. 23:29 prepare s. bul. s. r.
29:32 seventh day s. b. two r.
1 Chr. 15:26 Lev. offered s. b. s. r.
2 Chr. 29:21 they brou. s. b. s. r.
Job 42:8 take you now s. b. s. r.
Ezek. 45:23 a burnt-offer. s. bul.

**SEVENFOLD.**

Gen. 4:15 venge. sh. be taken s.
24 if Cain shall be avenged s. Lamech seventy and s.
Ps. 79:12 render s. into bosom
Prov. 6:31 he shall restore s.
Is. 30:26 light of sun shall be s.

See LAMBS, LAMPS.

**SEVEN men.**

2 Sam. 21:6 let s. men of his sons
Prov. 26:16 that s. m. that can
Jer. 52:25 s. m. that were near
Acts 6:3 look out s. m. of honest

SEVEN *rams.* See SEVEN *bul.*

See SEALS.

**SEVEN sons.**

Ruth 4:15 dau. better than s. s.
Job 1:2 were born unto him s. s.
42:13 had s. s. and three daugh.
Acts 19:14 s. s. of Sceva a Jew

**SEVEN spirits.**

Mat. 12:45 then goeth he, and taketh s. s. Luke 11:26
Rev. 1:4 s. s. bef. throne of God

3:1 he that hath the s. s. of God
4:5 lamps, wh. are s. s. of God
5:6 seven eyes, are s. s. of God

**SEVEN stars.**

Amos 5:8 him that maketh s. s.
Rev. 1:16 in ri. hand s. s. 2:1; 3:1
20 myst. of s. s. thou sawest; s. s. are angels of s. churches

SEVEN and *Thirty.* See THIRTY.

See THOUSAND.

**SEVEN times.**

Gen. 33:3 Ja. bowed bef. Es. s. t.
Lev. 4:6 priests shall sprinkle of the blood s. t. 17; 8:11; 14:7; 16:14, 19; Num. 19:4
14:16 sprink. oil wi. fin. s. t. 27
51 sprinkle house s. t.
25:8 number s. t. seven years
Lev. 26:18 pu. s. t. more, 21, 24, 28
Ps. 119:164 s. t. a day do I praise
Prov. 24:16 a just man fall, s. t.
Dan. 4:16 s. t. pass, 23, 25, 32
Mat. 18:21 sh. I forgive? till s. t.
Luke 17:4 if brother tresp. s. t. a day, and s. *times* a day turn

SEVEN and *Twenty.* See TWENTY.

**SEVEN years.**

Gen. 29:18 serve s. y. for Rachel
20 Jac. served s. y. for Rachel
27 shalt serve me other s. y. 30
41:26 seven good kine are s. y. the seven good ears are s. y.
29 s. y. of plenty, 34, 47, 48
53 the s. y. of plenteousness

**SEVENS.**

Gen. 7:2 clean bea. sh. take by s.

**SEVENTEEN.**

Gen. 37:2 Jos. being s. years old
Jer. 32:9 Jer. weighed s. shekels

**SEVENTEENTH.**

Gen. 7:11 on s. day the fountains
8:4 ark rested on s. day in the

**SEVENTH.**

Ex. 21:2 in s. he sh. go out free
31:15 the s. is sabbath of rest
Lev. 23:16 morrow after s. sab.

See DAY.

**SEVENTH month.**

Gen. 8:4 ark rested in s. m. on
Lev. 16:29 in s. mon. afflict your souls, 23:27; 25:9
Num. 29:1 in s. m. holy conv. 12
1 K. 8:2 Isr. assembled at s. m.
Hag. 2:1 in s. m. the word came
Zec. 8:19 the fast of the s. month

**SEVENTH year.**

Ex. 23:11 s. y. thou sh. let it rest
Lev. 25:4 in s. y. shall be a sab.
Deut. 15:12 s. y. shalt let him go
2 K. 11:4 in s. y. Jehoiada sent rulers and capt. 2 Chr. 23:1
Est. 2:16 Esther taken in s. year
Jer. 52:28 carried captive in s. y.
Ezek. 20:1 in the s. y. eld came

**SEVENTY.**

Gen. 4:24 truly Lam. s. and sev.
Ex. 1:5 of loins of Jacob were s.
24:1 and s. elders of Israel, 9
Num. 11:16 ga. to me s. men, 24
25 gave of spirit unto s. elders
Jud. 9:56 slaying his s. brethren
2 K. 10:1 Ahab had s. sons in, 6
Is. 23:15 Tyre shall be forgot. s.
17 after end of s. years, the L.
Jer. 25:11 serve Babylon s. years
Ezek. 8:11 stood bef. them s. m.
Dan. 9:24 s. weeks are determin.
Zec. 7:5 even th. s. years did ye
Mat. 18:22 times, but until s. ti.
Luke 10:1 L. appointed other s.
17 the s. returned ag. with joy

**SEVER, ED.**
*Ex.* 8:22 I will *s.* in that day
9:4 L. shall *s.* bet. cattle of Isr.
*Lev.* 20:26 I *s.* you fr. other peo.
*Deut.* 4:41 Moses *s.* three cities
*Jud.* 4:11 Heber *s.* from Kenites
*Ezek.* 39:14 *s.* out men of employ
*Mat.* 13:49 *s.* wicked fr. the just

**SEVERAL, LY.**
*Num.* 28:13 and a *s.* tenth deal, 21, 29; 29:10, 15
2 *K.* 15:5 Azariah dwelt in *s.* house, 2 *Chr.* 26:21
2 *Chr.* 31:19 sons of A. in *s.* city
*Mat.* 25:15 accord. to *s.* ability
1 *Cor.* 12:11 to every man *s.*
*Rev.* 21:21 ev. *s.* ga. was of pearl

**SEVERITY.**
*Rom.* 11:22 behold goodn. and *s.*

**SEW.**
*Ec.* 3:7 time to rend, time to *s.*
*Ezek.* 13:18 woe to women, *s.* pil.

**SEWED, EST, ETH.**
*Gen.* 3:7 *s.* fig-leaves together
*Job* 14:17 thou *s.* up mine iniq.
16:15 I have *s.* sackcloth upon
*Mark* 2:21 no man *s.* new cloth

SHAALBIM. *Jud.* 1:35
SHAASHGAZ. *Est.* 2:14

**SHADE.**
*Ps.* 121:5 L. is thy *s.* upon right

**SHADOW.**
*Gen.* 19:8 under *s.* of my roof
*Jud.* 9:15 put yo. trust in my *s.*
36 thou seest the *s.* of mount.
2 *K.* 20:9 sh. the *s.* go forward?
10 light thing for *s.* to go down
1 *Chr.* 29:15 days as a *s.* *Job* 8:9
*Job* 7:2 as a serv. desireth the *s.*
14:2 he fleeth also as a *s.*
17:7 all my members are as a *s.*
40:22 trees cover him with th. *s.*
*Ps.* 17:8 hide me un. *s.* of wings
36:7 under *s.* of wings, 57:1
63:7 in *s.* of wings will I rejoice
80:10 hills were covered with *s.*
91:1 abide under *s.* of Almighty
102:11 my days are like a *s.*
109:23 I am gone like a *s.*
144:4 days are as a *s.* *Ec.* 8:13
*Ec.* 6:12 life he spendeth as a *s.*
*Cant.* 2:3 I sat under *s.* with del.
*Is.* 4:6 tabernacle for a *s.* in day
16:3 make thy *s.* as the night
25:4 hast been a *s.* from heat
5 bring heat with *s.* of a cloud
30:2 and trust in *s.* of Egypt
3 and the trust in *s.* of Egypt
32:2 as *s.* of a great rock
38:8 I will bring again *s.* of deg.
49:2 in *s.* of hand hid me, 51:16
*Jer.* 48:45 under *s.* of Heshbon
*Lam.* 4:20 und. his *s.* we sh. live
*Ezek.* 17:23 in *s.* thereof sh. they
31:6 und. his *s.* dw. all nations
12 peo. are gone down from *s.*
*Dan.* 4:12 beasts had *s.* under it
*Hos.* 4:13 bec. *s.* thereof is good
14:7 dwell under his *s.* sh. retu.
*Jon.* 4:5 and sat under in *s.*
6 it might be *s.* over his head
*Mark.* 4:32 fowls lodge under *s.*
*Acts* 5:15 th. *s.* of P. might over.
*Col.* 2:17 a *s.* of things to come
*Heb.* 8:5 serve unto *s.* of heaven
10:1 having a *s.* of good things
*Jam.* 1:17 with whom no *s.* of tu.
*See* DEATH.

**SHADOWS.**
*Cant.* 2:17 *s.* flee away, 4:6
*Jer.* 6:4 for *s.* of the evening are

**SHADOWING.**
*Is.* 18:1 to land *s.* with wings
*Ezek.* 31:3 a cedar with *s.* shroud
*Heb.* 9:5 cherubim of gl. *s.* mer.

SHADRACH. *Dan.* 1:7; 2:49; 3:23-30

**SHADY.**
*Job* 40:21 he lieth under *s.* trees
22 the *s.* trees cover him with

**SHAFT.**
*Ex.* 25:31 his *s.* and branches, his bowls, 37:17; *Num.* 8:4
*Is.* 49:2 made me a polished *s.*

**SHAKE.**
*Jud.* 16:20 I will go and *s.* mys.
*Neh.* 5:13 and said, So God *s.*
*Job* 4:14 made my bones to *s.*
15:33 shall *s.* off unripe grape
16:4 and *s.* my head at you
*Ps.* 46:3 tho' the mountains *s.*
69:23 make loins continu. to *s.*
72:16 fruit shall *s.* like Lebanon
*Is.* 2:19 he ariseth to *s.* earth, 21
10:15 as if rod should *s.* itself
32 he shall *s.* hand ag. mount
11:15 the Lord shall *s.* his hand
13:2 exalt the voice, *s.* the hand
13 I will *s.* heavens, *Joel* 3:16; *Hag.* 2:6, 21
24:18 foundations of earth do *s.*
33:9 Bashan and Carmel *s.* off
52:2 *s.* thyself from dust, O Jer.
*Jer.* 23:9 broken, all my bones *s.*
*Ezek.* 26:10 walls sh. *s.* at noise
15 shall not isles *s.* at sound?
27:28 suburbs shall *s.* at sound
31:16 I made nations *s.*
38:20 men shall *s.* at my pres.
*Dan.* 4:14 *s.* off his leaves
*Amos* 9:1 that the posts may *s.*
*Hag.* 2:7 I will *s.* all nations
*Zec.* 2:9 I will *s.* my hand on th.
*Mat.* 10:14 *s.* off dust of your feet, *Mark* 6:11; *Luke* 9:5
28:4 for fear the keepers did *s.*
*Luke* 6:48 beat house, co. not *s.*
*Heb.* 12:26 I *s.* not earth only

**SHAKED.**
*Ps.* 109:25 look. on me, *s.* heads

**SHAKEN.**
*Lev.* 26:36 sound of a *s.* leaf shall
1 *K.* 14:15 as a reed is *s.* in wat.
2 *K.* 19:21 daugh. of Jerus. hath *s.* head at thee, *Is.* 37:22
*Neh.* 5:13 even thus be he *s.* out
*Job* 16:12 neck, *s.* me to pieces
38:13 wicked mi. be *s.* out of it
*Ps.* 18:7 founda. of hills were *s.*
*Nah.* 2:3 fir-trees shall be ter. *s.*
3:12 if *s.* they fall into mouth
*Mat.* 11:7 *s.* with wind, *Lu.* 7:24
24:29 powers of heaven shall be *s.* *Mark* 13:25; *Luke* 21:26
*Luke* 6:38 good meas. pressed, *s.*
*Acts* 4:31 prayed, place was *s.*
16:26 founda. of prison were *s.*
2 *Thes.* 2:2 not soon *s.* in mind
*Heb.* 12:27 remov. things that are *s.* cannot be *s.* may remain
*Rev.* 6:13 fig-tree wh. *s.* of wind

**SHAKETH.**
*Job* 9:6 *s.* earth out of her place
*Ps.* 29:8 voice of L. *s.* wilderness
60:2 heal breaches, for it is *s.*
*Is.* 10:15 magnify ag. that *s.*?
19:16 hand of Lord be *s.* over it
33:15 *s.* his hand from holding

**SHAKING.**
*Job* 41:29 laugh. at *s.* of a spear
*Ps.* 44:14 the *s.* of head among
*Is.* 17:6 *s.* of olive-tree, 24:13
19:16 because of the *s.* of hand
30:32 in bat. of *s.* shall he fight
*Ezek.* 37:7 beh. a *s.* bones came
38:19 th. shall be great *s.* in Is.

**SHALIM.**
1 *Sam.* 9:4 passed thro' land of S.

**SHALISHA.**
1 *Sam.* 9:4 passed thro' land of S.

**SHALLUM.**
2 *K.* 15:10 S. son of Jabesh
14 Menahem slew S. son of
22:14 Huld. the prophetess, the wife of S. 2 *Chr.* 34:22
1 *Chr.* 2:40 of Judah, S. 4:25
6:12 of Levi, S. 7:13 S. the son
9:17 S. porter, 19; 31 S. the K.
2 *Chr.* 28:12 Jehizkiah son of S.
*Ezr.* 2:42 the child. of S. 10:24; *Neh.* 7:45; *Jer.* 35:4
7:2 S. the son of Zadok
10:42 S. and Amariah had taken
*Neh.* 3:12 next repaired S.
*Jer.* 22:11 saith L. touching S.
32:7 Hanameel the son of S.

SHALMAN. *Hos.* 10:14

**SHALMANESER.**
2 *K.* 17:3 S. came against, 18:9

**SHAMBLES.**
1 *Cor.* 10:25 whatso. is sold in *s.*

**SHAME.**
*Ex.* 32:25 made naked unto th. *s.*
*Jud.* 18:7 none to put them to *s.*
1 *Sam.* 20:34 father had done *s.*
2 *Sam.* 13:13 sh. I cause *s.* to go?
2 *Chr.* 32:21 return. with *s.* of fa.
*Job* 8:22 hate thee be clo. with *s.*
*Ps.* 4:2 how long turn gl. to *s.*?
35:4 put them to *s.* that seek my
26 let them be clothed with *s.*
40:14 let th. be put to *s.* 83:17
15 deso. for a reward of their *s.*
44:7 hast put them to *s.* 53:5
9 hast cast off and put us to *s.*
15 *s.* of face covered me, 69:7
69:19 known my reproach and *s.*
70:3 turned back reward of *s.*
71:24 let them be bro. unto *s.*
83:16 fill their faces with *s.* O L.
89:45 hast covered him with *s.*
109:29 adversaries clo. with *s.*
119:31 O Lord put me not to *s.*
132:18 enem. will I clothe wi. *s.*
*Prov.* 3:35 *s.* sh. be the promot.
9:7 reproveth scorner, getteth *s.*
10:5 is a son that causeth *s.*
11:2 pride cometh, then com. *s.*
12:16 a prudent man cover. *s.*
13:5 loathsome and cometh to *s.*
18 *s.* shall be to him that refu.
14:35 wrath ag. him that caus. *s.*
17:2 a son that causeth *s.*
18:13 answer. bef. heareth, is *s.*
19:26 mother, is a son causeth *s.*
25:8 neigh. hath put thee to *s.*
10 that heareth it put thee to *s.*
29:15 child left br. mother to *s.*
*Is.* 20:4 uncover. to *s.* of Egypt
22:18 chariots shall be the *s.* of
30:3 stren. of Phar. your *s.* 5
47:3 yea, thy strength sh. be *s.*
50:6 I hid my face from *s.* and
54:4 thou shalt not be put to *s.* for thou sh. forget *s.* of youth
61:7 *s.* you shall have double
*Jer.* 3:24 *s.* devoured the labor of
25 we lie down in *s.* and conf.
13:26 discover, that thy *s.* ap.
20:18 days be consumed with *s.*
23:40 a perpetual *s.* not forgot.
46:12 the nations heard of thy *s.*
48:39 Moab turned back with *s.*
51:51 *s.* hath covered our faces
*Ezek* 7:18 *s.* shall be on all faces
16:52 bear th. own *s.* for sins, 54
*Ezek.* 16:63 never open mouth because of *s.*
32:24 have they borne their *s.* 25
30 bear their *s.* with them
34:29 nor bear the *s.* of heathen
36:6 ye have borne *s.* of heathen
7 they shall bear their *s.* 44:13
15 hear in thee *s.* of heathen
39:26 they have borne their *s.*

Dan. 12:2 awake, some to s.
Hos. 4:7 change their gl. into s.
18 her rulers with s. do love
9:10 separated themsel. unto s.
10:6 Ephraim shall receive s. Is.
Ob. 10 for violence s. sh. cover
Mic. 1:11 pass away, having s.
2:6 prop. they shall not take s.
7:10 s. sh. cover her which said
Nah. 3:5 I will show king. thy s.
Hab. 2:10 thou hast consulted s.
16 thou art filled with s.
Zep. 3:5 unjust knoweth no s.
19 they have been put to s.
Luke 14:9 begin with s. to take
Acts 5:41 worthy to suffer s.
1 Cor. 6:5 speak to your s. 15:34
11:6 if it be a s. for a woman
14 man have long hair, is a s.
14:35 s. for wo. to sp. in church
Eph. 5:12 a s. to speak of things
Phil. 3:19 whose glory is their s.
Heb. 6:6 put him to an open s.
12:2 endured cross, despising s.
Jude 13 foaming out their own s.
Rev. 3:18 s. of thy nakedness
16:15 naked, and they see his s.

**SHAME, ED, ETH.**

2 Sam. 19:5 thou hast s. the faces
Ps. 14:6 have s. counsel of poor
Prov. 28:7 compan. of riotous s.
1 Cor. 4:14 I write not to s. you
11:22 church of God, s. them?

**SHAMEFACEDNESS.**

1 Tim. 2:9 women adorn with s.

**SHAMEFUL, LY.**

Jer. 11:13 set up altars to s. thi.
Hos. 2:5 conceived them, done s.
Hab. 2:16 s. spue. be on thy glo.
Mark 12:4 they sent him away s. handled, Luke 20:11
1 Thes. 2:2 and were s. entreated

**SHAMELESSLY.**

2 Sam. 6:20 fellows s. uncover.

**SHAMGAR.**

Jud. 3:31 after him was S. the
5:6 in the days of S. highways

**SHAMMAH.**

Gen. 36:13 Re. S. 17; 1 Chr. 1:37
1 Sam. 16:9 S. the son of Jesse, 13:13; 1 Chr. 2:13
2 Sam. 23:11 after him was S. 33
25 S. the Harodite, 1 Chr. 7:37

**SHAMMUAH.**

Num. 13:4 to spy land, S. son
2 Sam. 5:14 S. s. of D. 1 Chr. 14:4
Neh. 11:17 Abda, son of S. dwelt

**SHAPE, S.**

Luke 3:22 descended in bodily s.
John 5:37 voice, nor seen his s.
Rev. 9:7 s. of locusts like horses

**SHAPEN.**

Ps. 51:5 behold, I was s. in iniq.

**SHAPHAN.**

2 K. 22:3 king Josiah sent S. the scribe, 2 Chr. 34:8
8 gave book to S. 2 Chr. 34:15
12 king commanded Ahikam son of S. and S. the scribe
25:22 son of S. Jer. 39:14; 40:11
Jer. 26:24 the hand of son of S.
29:3 sent by Elasah son of S.
36:10 of Gemariah son of S.
Ezek. 8:11 Jaazaniah son of S.

**SHAPHAT.**

Num. 13:5 Sim. S. to spy land
1 K. 19:16 ano. Elisha, son of S.
2 K. 6:31 head of Elis. son of S.
1 Chr. 3:22 Shemaiah, Neari. S.
5:12 of Gadites, S. in Bashan
27:29 valleys was S. son of Ad.

**SHARE.**

1 Sam. 13:20 sharpen every man his s.

**SHAREZER.**

2 K. 19:37 S. his son, Is. 37:38

**SHARON.**

1 Chr. 5:16 in all suburbs of S.
27:29 over herds that fed in S.
Cant. 2:1 the rose of S. the lily
Is. 33:9 S. is like a wilderness
35:2 Carmel and S. given thee
65:10 S. shall be a fold of flocks

**SHARP.**

Ex. 4:25 Zippor. took a s. stone
Jos. 5:2 make thee s. knives
1 Sam. 14:4 bet. passa. a s. rock
Job 41:30 s. stones are under him, he spread. s. pointed things
Ps. 45:5 arrow s. in the heart
57:4 their tongue s. sword
Prov. 5:4 s. as two-edged sword
25:18 man bears false witn. is s.
Is. 5:28 whose arrows are s.
49:2 made my mouth like s. sw.
Acts 15:39 contention was so s.
Rev. 1:16 out of his mouth went a s. two-edged sword, 19:15
41:14 in his hand a s. sickle, 17
18 ang. cried to him had s. sic.

**SHARPEN, ED, ETH.**

1 Sam. 13:20 s. ev. man his share
21 a file for axes, to s. goads
Ps. 140:3 they s. their tongues
Prov. 27:17 iron s. iron, man s.
Job 16:9 mine enemy s. his eyes
Ezek. 21:9 a sword is s. 10, 11

**SHARPER.**

Mic. 7:4 upr. s. than thorn-hedge
Heb. 4:12 word of G. s. than sw.

**SHARPLY.**

Jud. 8:1 did chide with Gid. s.
Tit. 1:13 rebuke them s. that

**SHARPNESS.**

2 Cor. 13:10 present I sho. use s.

**SHAVE.**

Lev. 13:33 scall shall he not s.
14:8 unclean person sh. s. hair
21:5 nor s. corner of th. beard
Num. 6:9 he shall s. his head
18 Nazarite shall s. head of his
8:7 let them s. flesh, wash clo.
Deut. 21:12 captive, s. her head
Jud. 16:19 caus. him to s. locks
Is. 7:20 L. shall s. with a razor
Ezek. 44:20 neither s. their heads
Acts 21:24 that they s. th. heads

**SHAVED.**

Gen. 41:14 Jos. s. changed raim.
2 Sam. 10:4 and s. off half their beards, 1 Chr. 19:4
Job 1:20 J. rent mantle, s. head

SHAVEH. Gen. 14:5

**SHAVEN.**

Jud. 16:17 if I s. strength will
22 hair began to grow after s.
Jer. 41:5 fourscore men, bear. s.
1 Cor. 11:5 as if she were s.
6 if it be a shame to be s.

**SHEAF.**

Gen. 37:7 my s. arose, and stood
Lev. 23:11 wave s. bef. Lord, 12
Deut. 24:19 forgot s. not fetch it
Job 24:10 take away s. fr. hungry
Zec. 12:6 govern. like torch in s.

**SHEAR, ING.**

Gen. 31:19 La. went to s. sheep
38:13 Ju. goeth to s. his sheep
Deut. 15:19 nor s. firstl. of sheep
1 Sam. 25:2 Nabal s. sheep in C.
4 Da. heard Nabal did s. sheep

**SHEARER, S.**

Gen. 38:12 Ju. went to sheep-s.
1 Sam. 25:7 heard thou hast s.
11 flesh I killed for my s.
2 Sam. 13:23 Ab. had s. in B. 24
Is. 53:7 sheep before s. is dumb
Acts 8:32 lamb dumb before s.

**SHEARING-HOUSE.**

2 K. 10:12 brethren of Ahaziah at s.-h. 14

**SHEAR-JASHUB.**

Is. 7:3 to meet Ah. thou and S.

**SHEATH.**

1 Sam. 17:51 Da. d. sword out s.
2 Sam. 20:8 sword fastened in s.
1 Chr. 21:27 angel put sw. in s.
Ezek. 21:3 draw sw. out of s. 4, 5
30 cause it to return into s.?
John 18:11 put up thy sw. into s.

**SHEAVES.**

Gen. 37:7 binding s. in the field
Ruth 2:7 let me glean am. s. 15
Neh. 13:15 on sab. bringing in s.
Ps. 126:6 bringing s. with him.
129:7 that bindeth s. his bosom
Amos 2:13 as cart full of s.
Mic. 4:12 L. shall gather th. as s.

**SHEBA, SHEBAH.**

Gen. 10:7 son of Raamah S. 28
25:3 Joksh. begat S. 1 Chr. 1:32
26:33 Isaac called the well S.
Jos. 19:2 had S. in their inherit.
1 K. 10:1 when queen of S. heard of Solomon, 2 Chr. 9:1
1 Chr. 1:9 son of Raamah S. 22
1 Chr. 5:13 of the chil. of Gad, S.
Job 6:19 the companies of S.
Ps. 72:10 kings of S. and Seba
15 given of gold of S. Is. 60:6
Jer. 6:20 purp. is incense fr. S.?
Ezek. 27:22 merchants of S. 23
38:13 S. sh. say, Art thou come

**SHEBNA.**

2 K. 18:18 came to Rabshakeh S. the scribe, 37; Is. 36:3
19:2 sent S. to Isaiah, Is. 37:2
Is. 22:15 go to this treasurer, S.

**SHECHEM.**

Gen. 33:18 Ja. came to a ci. of S.
19 hand of Hamor S. father
34:2 S. lay with Di. 26 slew S.
35:4 under an oak by S.
37:12 feed father's flock in S.
14 Jos. came from Hebr. to S.
Num. 26:31 of S. family of the
Jos. 17:2 lot for children of S.
20:7 S. in mount Ephraim, a city, 21:21; 1 Chr. 6:67
24:1 all the tribes of Israel to S.
32 of Joseph buried they in S.
Jud. 8:31 Gid.'s concubine in S.
9:1 son of Jerubbaal went to S.
7 hearken to me, ye men of S.
20 fire come out fr. men of S.
28 who is S. 31 come to S.
41 should not dwell in S.
57 evil of men of S. did G. ren.
1 K. 12:1 went to S. 2 Chr. 10:1
25 Jeroboam built S. in mount
1 Chr. 7:19 Shemida, Ahian, S.
Ps. 60:6 I will divide S. 108:7
Jer. 41:5 th. came certain fr. S.

**SHED.**

2 Sam. 20:10 Jo. s. Am.'s bowels
Mat. 26:28 is s. for remis. of sins
Acts 2:33 he hath s. forth this
Rom. 5:5 love of G. s. in hearts
Tit. 3:6 wh. he s. on us thro' J. C.
See BLOOD.

**SHEDDER.**

Ezek. 18:10 beget son s. of blood

**SHEDDETH, ING.**

Gen. 9:6 whoso s. man s blood
Ezek. 22:3 city s. blood in midst
Heb. 9:22 without s. of blood

SHE-GOATS. See GOATS.

**SHEEP.**

Gen. 4:2 Abel was a keeper of s.
29:6 Rachel cometh with s. 5.
Ex. 9:3 hand of Lord is upon s.
20:24 sh. sacrifice thereon thy s.

22:10 give to neighbor *s.* keep
*Lev.* 1:10 if his offering be of *s.*
22:19 ye sh. offer a male of *s.* 21
27:26 sanctify firstling of a *s.*
*Num.* 18:17 firstl. of *s.* not rede.
*Deut.* 7:13 bless flocks of thy *s.*
18:3 due fr. them that offer *s.* 4
22:1 not see broth.'s *s.* go astray
28:4 blessed be flocks of thy *s.*
*Jos.* 6:21 destroyed at Jericho *s.*
*Jud.* 6:4 Midianites left nei. *s.*
1 *Sam.* 8:17 king take tenth of
14:34 bring every man ox and *s.*
15:3 slay *s.* 9 Saul spread *s.*
14 what meaneth bleating of *s.*
16:11 behold, youngest keep. *s.*
17:15 David returned to feed *s.*
20 rose early, left *s.* wi. keeper
27:9 Da. took away *s.* the oxen
2 *Sam.* 7:8 took from follow. *s.*
24:17 but these *s.* what have they done? 1 *Chr.* 21:17
1 *K.* 4:23 Sol.'s provision 100 *s.*
8:63 Solo. off. *s.* 2 *Chr.* 5:6; 7:5
2 *K.* 5:26 is it time to receive *s.*?
1 *Chr.* 5:21 took fr. H. 250,000 *s.*
2 *Chr.* 14:15 Asa carried fr. E. *s.*
15:11 offered of spoil 7,000 *s.*
18:2 A. killed *s.* for Jehoshaph.
30:24 Hezekiah did give 7,000 *s.*
31:6 brou. tithes of oxen and *s.*
*Neh.* 5:18 Nehem. one ox, six *s.*
*Job* 1:16 fire fallen, burnt up *s.*
31:20 not warm. wi. fleece of *s.*
42:12 had 14,000 *s.* 6,000 camels
*Ps.* 8:7 hast given him all *s.*
44:11 given us like *s.* for meat
49:14 like *s.* are laid in grave
74:1 why anger smo. ag. thy *s.*?
78:52 made peo. go forth like *s.*
95:7 we are *s.* of his hand, 100:3
119:176 astray like a lost *s.*
144:13 *s.* bring forth thousands
*Is.* 7:21 man sh. nourish two *s.*
22:13 joy and glad. killing of *s.*
53:6 we like *s.* are gone astray
*Jer.* 12:3 pull like *s.* for slaughter
50:6 my peo. hath been lost *s.*
17 Israel is as scattered *s.* lions
*Ezek.* 34:11 I will search my *s.* 12
*Hos.* 12:12 for a wife he kept *s.*
*Joel* 1:18 flock of *s.* made desol.
*Mic.* 5:8 a young lion among *s.*
*Zec.* 13:7 smite shepherd, and *s.* scat. *Mat.* 26:31; *Mark* 14:27
*Mat.* 7:15 false proph. in *s.* cloth.
10:6 go to lost *s.* of house of Is.
12:12 how much man bet. th. *s.*?
15:24 sent but to lost *s.* of Israel
18:12 man ha. 100 *s.* one be gone
13 he rejoiceth more of that *s.* *Luke* 15:4, 6
25:33 shall set *s.* on right hand
*John* 2:14 in tem. th. that sold *s.*
15 drove out of temple, and *s.*
10:2 entereth door sheph. of *s.*
3 *s.* hear voice, 27; 4 *s.* follow
7 said Jes. I am door of the *s.*
11 shepherd giv. life for his *s.*
12 a hireling leaveth the *s.* 13
14 I know *s.* 16 other *s.* I have
15 I lay down my life for the *s.*
26 ye are not of my *s.* as I said
21:16 saith to Peter, Feed my *s.* 17
*Heb.* 13:20 L. Jes Shepherd of *s.*
*Rev.* 18:13 none buyeth *s.* horses

**As SHEEP.**

*Num.* 27:17 *as s.* wh. ha. no shep.
1 *K.* 22:17 Israel *as s.* that have no shepherd, 2 *Chr.* 18:16
*Ps.* 44:22 we are counted *as s.* for the slaughter, *Rom.* 8:36
*Is.* 13:14 *as s.* that no man taketh
53:7 *as* a *s.* bef. shearers dumb
*Mic.* 2:12 put together *as s.* of B.
*Mat.* 9:36 scattered *as s.* having no shepherd, *Mark* 6:34
10:16 send *as s.* midst of wolves
*Acts* 8:32 led *as s.* to slaughter
1 *Pet.* 2:25 *as s.* going astray

**SHEEPCOTE, S.**

1 *Sam.* 24:3 Saul came to *s.*
2 *Sam.* 7:8 took fr. *s.* 1 *Chr.* 17:7

**SHEEPFOLD, S.**

*Num.* 32:16 we will build *s.*
*Jud.* 5:16 why abodest amo. *s.*?
*Ps.* 78:70 Dav. took him from *s.*
*John* 10:1 entereth not *s.* by

**SHEEP-GATE.**

*Neh.* 3:1 Eliashib built the *s.-g.*
32 going up of corner to *s.-g.*
12:39 they went on to the *s.-g.*

**SHEEP-MARKET.**

*John* 5:2 at Jerusalem by *s.-m.*

**SHEEP-MASTER.**

2 *K.* 3:4 Mesha was a *s.-m.*

*See* SHEARERS.

**SHEEPSKINS.**

*Heb.* 11:37 they wandered in *s.*

**SHEET.**

*Acts* 10:11 descending as *s.* 11:5

**SHEETS.**

*Jud.* 14:12 I will give you 30 *s.*

**SHEKEL.**

*Ex.* 30:13 *s.* after the *s.* of the sanctu. a *s.* is twenty gerahs. *Num.* 3:47; *Ezek.* 45:12
15 not give less than half *s.*
1 *Sam.* 9:8 ha. fourth part of a *s.*
2 *K.* 7:1 mea. of flour for *s.* 16, 18
*Neh.* 10:32 charged wi. third of *s.*
*Amos* 8:5 ephah small, *s.* great

**SHEKELS.**

*Gen.* 23:15 land worth 400 *s.* 16
*Ex.* 21:32 give her master 30 *s.*
*Lev.* 5:15 estima. by *s.* 27:3–16
*Deut.* 22:29 damsel's father 50 *s.*
*Jos.* 7:21 spoils, 200 *s.* silver
*Jud.* 8:26 weight of rings 1,700 *s.*
17:2 1,100 *s.* I took; 3 resto. *s.*
10 give thee ten *s.* silver
2 *Sam.* 14:26 Ab. wei. hair 200 *s.*
2 *K.* 15:20 exacted of each fifty *s.*
1 *Chr.* 21:25 David gave Ornan 600 *s.*
*Neh.* 5:15 gover. had taken 40 *s.*
*Jer.* 32:9 bou. field for 17 *s.* silver
*Ezek.* 4:10 be by weight 20 *s.*

*See* SANCTUARY.

**SHELAH.**

*Gen.* 38:5 Ju.'s son S. 11 till S.
26 I gave her not to S. my son
46:12 J. Er, Onan, and S. *Num.* 26:20; 1 *Chr.* 2:3; 4:21
1 *Chr.* 1:18 begat S. and S. E. 24

**SHELEMIAH.**

1 *Chr.* 26:14 lot eastw. fell to S.
*Ezr.* 10:39 S. and Nathan had
*Neh.* 13:13 I made S. treasurer
*Jer.* 36:14 S. son of Cushi, 26

**SHELTER.**

*Job* 24:8 emb. rock for want of *s.*
*Ps.* 61:3 hast been *s.* for me

**SHELUMIEL.**

*Num.* 1:6 S. son of Zurishaddai, 2:12; 7:36; 10:19

**SHEM.**

*Gen.* 5:32 Noah begat S. 6:10; 10:1; 1 *Chr.* 1:4
9:23 S. took a garm. and went
26 blessed be Lord God of S.
27 shall dwell in tents of S.
10:21 the children of S. 22, 31; 11:10; 1 *Chr.* 1:17
*Luke* 3:36 wh. was the son of S.

**SHEMAIAH.**

1 *K.* 12:22 word of the Lord came to S. 2 *Chr.* 11:2; 12:7
1 *Chr.* 4:37 Shimri the son of S.
5:4 Reuben, S. the son of Joel
9:14 of the Levit. S. 16; 15:8, 11; 24:6; 26:4, 6, 7; 2 *Chr.* 17:8; 29:14; 31:15; 35:9; *Ezr.* 8:16; 10:21, 31
*Ezr.* 8:13 S. son of Adonikam
*Neh.* 3:29 S. keeper of the east
6:10 I came to the house of S.
10:8 S. a priest, 12:34, 42
11:15 of Lev. S. 12:6, 18, 35, 36
*Jer.* 26:20 Urijah the son of S.
29:24 S. the Nehelamite, 31, 32
36:12 Delaiah son of S. prince

**SHEMINITH.**

1 *Chr.* 15:21 with harps on the S.

**SHENIR.**

*Deut.* 3:9 the Amorites call S.
*Cant.* 4:8 look from the top of S.

**SHEPHATIAH.**

2 *Sam.* 3:4 S. son of D. 1 *Chr.* 3:3
1 *Chr.* 9:8 Meshullam son of S.
12:5 S. the Haruphite came to
27:16 ruler of Simeonit. was S.
*Ezr.* 2:4 child. of S. 372, *Neh.* 7:9
*Jer.* 38:1 S. heard the words of

**SHEPHERD.**

*Gen.* 46:34 *s.* is abomina. to Eg.
49:24 thence is *s.* stone of Israel
1 *Sam.* 17:40 stones into *s.* bag
*Ps.* 23:1 the Lord is my *s.*
80:1 give ear, O *s.* of Israel
*Ec.* 12:11 words given fr. one *s.*
*Is.* 38:12 age departed as *s.* tent
40:11 feed his flock like a *s.*
44:28 L. saith of Cy. he is my *s.*
63:11 bro. up with *s.* of his flock
*Jer.* 31:10 keep him as *s.* flock
43:12 array himself as a *s.*
49:19 who is *s.* will stand, 50:44
51:23 I will break *s.* his flock
*Ezek.* 34:5 scatter. because no *s.*
8 beca. prey bec. th. was no *s.*
12 *s.* seek. out flock am. sheep
23 I will set up one *s.* over th. Da. feed them, be *s.* 37:24
*Amos* 3:12 as *s.* takes out mouth
*Zec.* 10:2 troubled, because no *s.*
11:15 instruments of a foolish *s.*
16 I will raise up a *s.* in land
17 woe to idle *s.* that leav. flo.
13:7 awake, O sword, ag. my *s.*
*John* 10:12 is hireling, not *s.*
14 a good *s.* know my sheep
16 shall be one fold, and one *s.*
*Heb.* 13:20 L. J. great *s.* of sheep
1 *Pet.* 2:25 now returned unto *s.*
5:4 when chief *s.* shall appear

*See* SHEEP.

**SHEPHERDS.**

*Gen.* 46:32 the men are *s.*
47:3 serv. are *s.* also our fathers
*Ex.* 2:17 *s.* came, dro. th. away
19 Eg. deliv. out of hand of *s.*
1 *Sam.* 25:7 now thy *s.* with us
*Cant.* 1:8 feed kids besi. *s.* tents
*Is.* 13:20 nor *s.* make folds there
31:4 multi. of *s.* called aga. him
56:11 *s.* that cannot understand
*Jer.* 6:3 *s.* shall come unto her
23:4 I will set up *s.* over them
25:34 howl, ye *s.* 35 *s.* no way
36 a voice of *s.* and a howling
33:12 cities be a habitation of *s.*
50:6 *s.* caused them to go astray
*Ezek.* 34:2 prophesy against *s.* of Is. should not *s.* feed flocks?
8 nor did *s.* search for flock, but the *s.* fed themselves
10 I am against *s.* neither shall *s.* feed themselves any more
*Amos* 1:2 habitations of *s.* mourn
*Mic.* 5:5 raise agai. him seven *s.*

Nah. 3:18 thy s. slumber, O king
Zep. 2:6 coasts be cottages for s.
Zec. 10:3 anger kindled again. s.
11:3 a voice of the howling of s.
Zec. 11:5 th. own s. pity th. not
8 3 s. I cut off in one month
Luke 2:8 in same country s.
20 s. returned, glorifying God

**SHERD, S.**

Is. 30:14 th. sh. not be found a s.
Ezek. 23:34 thou sh. break the s.

**SHERIFFS.**

Dan. 3:2 Nebuchadnezzar sent to gather the s. together, 3

**SHESHACH.**

Jer. 25:26 the king of S. shall
51:41 how is S. taken! how is

**SHESHBAZZAR.**

Ezr. 1:8 numbered them to S.
11 all these did S. bring up
5:14 delivered to S. wh. he had
16 S. laid foundation of the

SHEW, *see* SHOW.

**SHIBBOLETH.**

Jud. 12:6 say now S. he said

**SHIELD.**

Gen. 15:1 thy s. and reward
Deut. 33:29 Lord, the s. of help
Jud. 5:8 s. or spear amo. 40,000
1 Sam. 17:7 one bearing a s. 41
2 Sam. 1:21 the s. of mighty, s. of Saul as though not anoint.
22:3 he is my s. Ps. 3:3; 28:7; 119:114; 144:2
36 given me the s. of salvation, Ps. 18:35
1 K. 10:17 3 poun. of gold to 1 s.
2 K. 19:32 not come wi. s. Is. 37:33
1 Chr. 12:8 Gadites cou. handle s.
24 Jud. that bare s. and spear
34 Naph. wi. s. and spe. 37,000
2 Chr. 25:5 that could handle s.
Job 39:23 spear and s. rattleth
Ps. 5:12 compass him as with s.
33:20 Lord is our s. 59:11; 84:9
35:2 take hold of s. and buckler
76:3 brake arrows of bow, the s.
84:11 Lord God is sun and s.
91:4 his truth shall be thy s.
115:9 he is th. help and s. 10, 11
Prov. 30:5 s. to them that trust
Is. 21:5 arise, princes, anoint s.
22:6 Kir uncovered the s.
Jer. 46:3 order buckler and s.
9 come forth, that handle s.
Ezek. 23:24 ag. th. buckler and s.
27:10 hanged s. and helmet, 11
Nah. 2:3 s. of mighty made red
Eph. 6:16 taking s. of faith

**SHIELDS.**

2 Sam. 8:7 David took s. of gold, 1 Chr. 18:7
1 K. 10:17 Solomon made 300 s. of beaten gold, 2 Chr. 9:16
14:26 Shishak took away all s. of gold S. made, 2 Chr. 12:9
27 Rehoboam made in their stead brazen s. 2 Chr. 12:10
2 K. 11:10 gave Da. s. 2 Chr. 23:9
2 Chr. 11:12 in city put s. and sp.
14:8 of Benja. that bare s. 17:17
26:14 Uzziah pre. s. and spears
32:5 Hez. made darts and s. 27.
Neh. 4:16 half held spears and s.
Ps. 47:9 s. of earth belong to G.
Jer. 51:11 bright arrows, gath. s.
Ezek. 38:4 with bucklers and s. 5
39:9 shall burn s. and weapons

SHIGGAION. *See* Psalm VII.

**SHIGIONOTH.**

Hab. 3:1 prayer of prophet on S

**SHILOH.**

Gen. 49:10 nor scep. dep. till S.

**SHILOH.**

Jos. 18:1 assemb. together at S.
8 cast lots for you in S. 10
22:9 departed from Isr. out of S.
Jud. 18:31 house of G. was in S.
21:12 brou. young virgins to S.
19 is a feast of the Lord in S.
21 if the daughters of S. dance
1 Sam. 1:3 up to worship in S.
24 Samuel to house of L. in S.
2:14 so did priests in S. to all
3:21 Lord appeared again in S.
4:3 the ark of the Lord out of S.
12 a man came to S. with his
14:3 Ahitub, Lord's priest in S.
1 K. 2:27 aga. house of Eli in S.
14:2 got thee to S. to Ahijah
4 Jeroboam's wife went to S.
Ps. 78:60 forsook taberna. of S.
Jer. 7:12 place which was in S.
14 th. house as I ha. done to S.
26:6 I make this house like S.
41:5 there came certain from S.

**SHILOAH.**

Is. 8:6 refuseth the waters of S.

**SHIMEAH.**

2 Sam. 13:3 Jonadab son of S. 32; 21:21; 1 Chr. 20:7
1 Chr. 3:5 S. was born to David
6:39 Berachiah, the son of S.

**SHIMEI.**

2 Sam. 16:5 S. son of Gera, 19:16
13 S. went along on hill's side
1 K. 2:8 thou hast with thee S.
39 two of the servants of S.
4:18 S. the son of Elah
1 Chr. 3:19 S. son of Pedaiah, 5:4
4:26 Mish. Hamuel, Zaccur, S.
27 S. had sixteen sons and six
6:17 S. son of Ge. 42; 23:7, 29
23:9 s. of S. 10; 25:17 tenth to S.
27:27 over vineyards was S.
2 Chr. 29:14 Heman, Jeh. and S.
31:12 over dedicated thi. S. 13
Ezr. 10:23 S. taken strange wife
Est. 2:5 son of Jair, son of S.
Zec. 12:13 family of S. shall

**SHIMSHAI.**

Ezr. 4:8 S. the scribe wrote, 9
17 king sent an answer to S.

**SHINAR.**

Gen. 10:10 Calneh in land of S.
11:2 found a plain in land of S.
14:1 Amraphel king of S.
Is. 11:11 recover remna. from S.
Dan. 1:2 carried into land of S.
Zec. 5:11 a house in land of S.

**SHINE.**

Num. 6:25 L. make his face s.
Job 3:4 neither let light s. on it
10:3 thou should. s. on counsel
11:17 thou shalt s. forth
18:5 spark of his fire sh. not s.
22:28 light sh. s. upon thy ways
36:32 commandeth it not to s.
37:15 caused light of cloud to s.
41:32 mak. path to s. after him
Ps. 31:16 make thy face s.
67:1 cause face to s. 80:3, 7, 19
80:1 dwellest betw. cherubim s.
104:15 oil to make his face to s.
119:135 make face s. upon serv.
Ec. 8:1 man's wisd. mak. face s.
Is. 13:10 not cause light to s.
60:1 arise, s. thy light is come
Jer. 5:28 are waxen fat, they s.
Dan. 9:17 cause thy face to s.
12:3 that be wise, sh. s. as stars
Mat. 5:16 let your light s.
13:43 righteous s. forth as sun
17:2 his face did s. as sun
2 Cor. 4:4 lest light of Ch. sho. s.
6 G. commanded light to s.
Phil. 2:15 among whom ye s. as
Rev. 18:23 candle sh. s. no more
21:23 no need of sun or moon s.

**SHINED.**

Deut. 33:2 the L. s. forth fr. Par.
Job 29:3 candle s. upon my head
Ps. 50:2 perfect. of beauty G. s.
Is. 9:2 upon them hath light s.
Ezek. 43:2 the earth s. with glory
Acts 9:3 suddenly there s. about
12:7 and a light s. in the prison
2 Cor. 4:6 G. hath s. in our hearts

**SHINETH.**

Job 25:5 to the moon, it s. not
Ps. 139:12 night s. as the day
Prov. 4:18 shining light that s.
Mat. 24:27 lightning s. to west
John 1:5 the light s. in darkness
2 Pet. 1:19 light that s. in a dark
1 John 2:8 the true light now s.
Rev. 1:16 countenance as sun s.

**SHINING.**

2 Sam. 23:4 grass springing by s.
Prov. 4:18 the just is as s. light
Joel 2:10 stars sh. withd. s. 3:15
Mark 9:3 his raiment became s.
Luke 11:36 s. of a candle giveth
John 5:35 burning and s. light
Acts 26:13 above bright. of sun s.

**SHIP.**

Prov. 30:19 way of s. in the sea
Is. 33:21 no gallant s. shall pass
Jon. 1:3 Jonah found a s. going
Mat. 4:21 in a s. with Zebedee
8:24 s. was covered with waves
14:24 s. was tossed, Mark 4:37
Mark 1:19 in s. mending nets
4:38 in hinder part of s. asleep
8:14 had in the s. but one loaf
John 6:21 immediately the s. was
21:6 cast net on right side of s.
Acts 20:38 accompanied him to s.
21:2 a s. sailing over unto Phe.
27:2 entering a s. of Adramyt.

**SHIPS.**

Gen. 49:13 Zebul. a haven for s.
Num. 24:24 s. sh. come from Ch.
Deut. 28:68 L. sh. bring th. wi. s.
Jud. 5:17 did Dan remain in s.?
1 K. 9:26 Solo. made a navy of s.
22:48 Jehoshaph. made s. of T. s. were broken, 2 Chr. 20:37
2 Chr. 8:18 Hur. sent by serv. s.
9:21 king's s. went to Tarshish
Job 9:26 they pass. as the swift s.
Ps. 48:7 breakest s. of Tarshish
104:26 go s. th. is that leviathan
107:23 that go down to sea in s.
Prov. 31:14 is like merchant s.
Is. 2:16 day of L. on s. of Tarsh.
23:1 howl, ye s. of Tarshish, 14
43:14 Chal. whose cry is in s.
60:9 the s. of Tarshish first
Ezek. 27:9 all s. of sea with mar.
25 s. of Tarsh. did sing of thee
30:9 messengers go forth in s.
Dan. 11:30 s. of Chittim shall
40 king sh. come with many s.
Luke 5:7 filled s. began to sink
Jam. 3:4 s. though they be great
Rev. 8:9 third part of s. destroy.
18:17 compa. in s. stood afar off

**SHIP-BOARDS.**

Ezek. 27:5 thy s.-b. of fir-trees

**SHIPMASTER.**

Jon. 1:6 s. said, Wh. mean. thou?
Rev. 18:17 s. and sailors cried

**SHIPMEN.**

1 K. 9:27 Hiram sent s. that had
Acts 27:30 s. were about to flee

**SHIPPING.**

John 6:24 they took s. and came

SHIPHRAH. Ex. 1:15

**SHIPWRECK.**

2 Cor. 11:25 thrice suffered s.
1 Tim. 1:19 concer. faith made s.

**SHISHAK.**

1 *K.* 14:25 S. king of Egy. came against Jerusal. 2 *Chr.* 12:2
2 *Chr.* 12:5 gather. because of S. I left you in hand of S.
7 not poured out on Jer. by S.
9 S. took away treasures of

**SHITTAH-TREE.**

*Is.* 41:19 I will plant the *s.-t.*

**SHITTIM.**

*Num.* 25:1 Israel abode in S.
*Jos.* 2:1 sent out of S. two men
3:1 they removed from S. and
*Joel* 3:18 shall water valley of S.
*Mic.* 6:5 answered him from S.

**SHITTIM-WOOD.**

*Ex.* 25:10 make ark of *s.-w.* 35:7; 37:1; *Deut.* 10:3
13 staves of *s.-w.* 28; 27:6; 37:4, 15, 28; 38:6
23 make a table of *s.-w.* 37:10
26:15 tabernacle of *s.-w.* 36:20
32 pillows of *s.-w.* 37; 36:36
35:24 with wh. was found *s.-w.*

**SHIVERS.**

*Rev.* 2:27 ves. of potter bro. to *s.*

SHOBAB. 2 *Sam.* 5:14
SHOBACH. 2 *Sam.* 10:16

**SHOCK, S.**

*Jud.* 15:5 Samson burnt the *s.*
*Job* 5:26 like as *s.* of corn cometh

**SHOD.**

2 *Chr.* 28:15 took captives *s.* th.
*Ezek.* 16:10 I *s.* thee with badge.
*Mark* 6:9 be *s.* with sandals, put
*Eph.* 6:15 *s.* with prepar. of gos.

**SHOE.**

*Deut.* 25:9 bro.'s wife loose *s.* 10
29:5 thy *s.* is not waxen old
*Jos.* 5:15 put *s.* from off thy foot
*Ruth* 4:7 man plucked off his *s.*
*Ps.* 60:8 over Edom cast *s.* 108:9
*Is.* 20:2 put off thy *s* fr. thy foot

**SHOE-LATCHET.**

*Gen.* 14:23 from thread to *s.-l.*
*John* 1:27 *s.-l.* not worthy to lo.

**SHOES.**

*Ex.* 3:5 put off thy *s.* *Acts* 7:33
12:11 eat it, with *s.* on your feet
*Deut.* 33:25 *s.* shall be iron and brass
*Jos.* 9:5 old *s.* and clouted, 13
1 *K.* 2:5 put blood in *s.* on feet
*Cant.* 7:1 beautiful feet with *s.!*
*Is.* 5:27 nor latchet of *s.* be brok.
*Ezek.* 24:17 put on *s.* on feet, 23
*Amos* 2:6 th. sold the poor for *s.*
8:6 may buy needy for pair of *s.*
*Mat.* 3:11 *s.* not worthy to bear
10:10 carry neither *s.* *Luke* 10:4
*Mark* 1:7 latchet of whose *s.* *Luke* 3:16; *Acts* 13:25
*Luke* 15:22 ring on ha. *s.* on feet
22:35 I sent you with. purse, *s.*

**SHONE.**

*Ex.* 34:29 wist not that face *s.*
30 skin of his face *s.* afraid, 35
2 *K.* 3:22 rose early, the sun *s.*
*Luke* 2:9 glory of Lord *s.* round
*Acts* 22:6 *s.* fr. heaven gre. light
*Rev.* 8:12 day *s.* not for 3d part

**SHOOK.**

2 *Sam.* 6:6 hold, for oxen *s.* ark
22:8 and the earth *s.* *Ps.* 18:7; 68:8; 77:18
*Neh.* 5:13 *s.* my lap, so G. shake
*Is.* 23:11 stretched, *s.* kingdoms
*Acts* 13:51 *s.* off dust of their feet
28:5 he *s.* off beast into the fire
*Heb.* 12:26 whose voice *s.* earth

**SHOOT, ETH.**

*Ex.* 36:33 made middle bar to *s.*
1 *Sam.* 20:20 I will *s.* 3 arrows
2 *Sam.* 11:20 kn. ye not wo. *s.?*
2 *K.* 13:17 Elisha said, *s.* he shot
19:32 but he shall not *s.* an arrow there, *Is.* 37:33
1 *Chr.* 5:18 able to *s.* with bow
2 *Chr.* 26:15 engines to *s.* arrows
*Job* 8:16 branch *s.* in his garden
*Ps.* 11:2 privily *s.* at upright
22:7 they *s.* out lip, shake head
58:7 bendeth bow to *s.* arrows
64:3 to *s.* arrows, bitter words
7 God shall *s.* at them with ar.
144:6 *s.* out arrows, dest. them
*Is.* 27:8 measur. when it *s.* forth
*Jer.* 50:14 ye that bend bow, *s.*
*Ezek.* 31:14 nor *s.* among boughs
36:8 ye shall *s.* your branches
*Mark* 4:32 mustard-seed *s.* out
*Luke* 21:30 when they *s.* forth

**SHOOTERS.**

2 *Sam.* 11:24 *s.* shot on thy serv.

**SHOOTING.**

1 *Chr.* 12:2 ri. hand and left in *s.*
*Amos* 7:1 *s.* up of latter growth

**SHORE.**

*Mat.* 13:2 multitude stood on *s.*
48 when full, they drew to *s.*
*John* 21:4 morni. Je. stood on *s.*
*Acts* 21:5 kneeled on *s.* prayed
27:39 discove. a creek with a *s.*

*See* SEA.

**SHORN.**

*Cant.* 4:2 sheep that are even *s.*
*Acts* 18:18 hav. *s.* head in Cenc.
1 *Cor.* 11:6 wom. if not cov. be *s.*

**SHORT.**

*Num.* 11:23 L.'s hand waxen *s.?*
*Job* 17:12 light *s.* beca. of darkn.
20:5 triumphing of wicked is *s.*
*Ps.* 89:47 remem. how *s.* time is
*Rom.* 3:23 come *s.* of glory
9:28 a *s.* work L. make on earth
1 *Cor.* 7:29 brethren, time is *s.*
1 *Thes.* 2:17 tak. fr. you *s.* time
*Rev.* 12:12 know. he hath *s.* time
17:10 must continue a *s.* space

*See* COME, CUT.

**SHORTENED.**

*Ps.* 89:45 days of youth thou *s.*
102:23 weak. strength, *s.* days
*Prov.* 10:27 years of wick. be *s.*
*Is.* 50:2 is my hand *s.* at all
59:1 behold, L.'s hand is not *s.*
*Mat.* 24:22 ex. those days should be *s.* *Mark* 13:20

**SHORTER.**

*Is.* 28:20 bed *s.* th. a man stretch

**SHORTLY.**

*Ezek.* 7:8 now I *s.* pour out fury
1 *Cor.* 4:19 I will come to you *s.*
*Phil.* 2:19 trust to send Timo. *s.*
24 I trust I myself sh. come *s.*
*Heb.* 13:23 if he come *s.* I see
3 *John* 14 I trust I sh. *s.* see thee
*Rev.* 1:1 *s.* come to pass, 22:6

**SHOT, Verb.**

*Gen.* 49:23 the archers *s.* at him
*Ex.* 19:13 be stoned, or *s.* thro'
*Num.* 21:30 we have *s.* at them
2 *Sam.* 11:24 shooters *s.* fr. wall
2 *K.* 13:17 Elis. said, Shoot, he *s.*
2 *Chr.* 35:23 archers *s.* at Josiah
*Ps.* 18:14 *s.* out lightnings and
*Jer.* 9:8 tongue is an arrow *s.* out
*Ezek.* 17:6 beca. a vine, *s.* forth
31:10 *s.* up his top am. boughs

**SHOULDER.**

*Gen.* 21:14 putting bread H.'s *s.*
24:15 Reb. with pitcher on *s.* 45
49:15 Iss. bowed his *s.* to bear
*Ex.* 28:7 ephod ha. two *s.* pieces
29:27 sanctify *s.* of heave-offer.
*Ex.* 39:4 made *s.* pieces to coup.
*Num.* 6:19 *s.* of ram, *Deut.* 18:3
*Jos.* 4:5 take ev. man a st. on *s.*
*Jud.* 9:48 Abi. laid bow on his *s.*
1 *Sam.* 9:24 cook took up the *s.*
*Neh.* 9:29 withd. *s.* harden. neck
*Job* 31:36 I wou. take it on my *s.*
*Ps.* 81:6 I removed *s.* from burd.
*Is.* 9:4 hast broken staff of his *s.*
6 government sh. be on his *s.*
10:27 burden taken fr. off thy *s.*
22:22 key of D. will I lay on *s.*
46:7 they bear him upon the *s.*
*Ezek.* 12:7 I bare it on my *s.*
12 prince sh. bear upon his *s.*
24:4 gather pieces, thigh and *s.*
29:7 break and rent their *s.* 18
34:21 ye thrust with side and *s.*
*Zec.* 7:11 refused, pull. away *s.*
*Luke* 15:5 lay. it on *s.* rejoicing

**SHOULDER-BLADE.**

*Job* 31:22 arm fall from my *s.-b.*

**Heave-SHOULDER.**

*Lev.* 7:34 *h.-s* taken, *Num.* 6:20
10:14 *heave-s.* shall ye eat, 15

**Right SHOULDER.**

*Ex.* 29:22 take of ram *right s.*
*Lev.* 7:32 *r. s.* give unto priest
8:25 Moses took fat and *right s.*
9:21 *r. s.* waved is th. *Nu.* 18:18

**SHOULDERS.**

*Gen.* 9:23 laid garments upon *s.*
*Ex.* 12:34 troughs bound upon *s.*
*Num.* 7:9 sons of Ko. bear on *s.*
*Deut.* 33:12 shall dwell betw. *s.*
*Jud.* 16:3 Sam. took bar upon *s.*
1 *Sam.* 9:2 from *s.* upward, 10:23
17:6 had a target between his *s.*
2 *Chr.* 35:3 not be a bur. upon *s.*
*Is.* 11:14 sh. fly on *s.* of Philist.
14:25 burden depart fr. their *s.*
30:6 carry riches upon *s.* of ass.
49:22 daugh. be carried on th. *s.*
*Ezek.* 12:6 sight, bear it on thy *s.*
*Mat.* 23:4 bind burd. on men's *s.*

**SHOUT, Substantive.**

*Num.* 23:21 *s.* of king am. them
*Jos.* 6:5 shouted with great *s.* 20
1 *Sam.* 4:6 what mean. great *s.?*
2 *Chr.* 13:15 men of Ju. gave a *s.*
*Ezr.* 3:13 could not discern *s.*
*Ps.* 47:5 G. is gone up with a *s.*
*Jer.* 25:30 Lord shall give a *s.*
51:14 shall lift a *s.* ag. Babylon
*Acts* 12:22 peo. gave a *s.* saying
1 *Thes.* 4:16 L. descend with a *s.*

**SHOUT, ETH.**

*Ex.* 32:18 not voice of them th. *s.*
*Jos.* 6:5 hear trumpet, people *s.*
10 not *s.* till bid *s.* th. sh. ye *s.*
*Ps.* 47:1 *s.* to God with triumph
78:65 like a mighty man that *s.*
*Is.* 12:6 *s.* thou inhabitant of Zi.
42:11 let them *s.* from mountain
44:23 *s.* ye lower parts of earth
*Jer.* 31:7 *s.* amo. chief of nations
50:15 Babyl. sinned, *s.* aga. her
*Lam.* 3:8 when I *s.* he shutteth
*Zep.* 3:14 *s.* O Israel, be glad
*Zec.* 9:9 *s.* O daughter of Jerusa.

**SHOUTED.**

*Ex.* 32:17 they *s.* he said, Noise
*Lev.* 9:24 fire consumed, they *s.*
*Jos.* 6:20 *s.* when priests blew
*Jud.* 15:14 P. *s.* against Samson
1 *Sam.* 4:5 Is. *s.* because of ark
10:24 peo. *s.* said, G. save king
17:20 host going, *s.* for battle
2 *Chr.* 13:15 Jud. *s.* G. smote Je.
*Ezr.* 3:11 praised Lord, they *s.*
12 many of people *s.* aloud, 13

*See* JOY.

**SHOUTING, S.**

2 *Sam.* 6:15 and brought up ark with *s.* 1 *Chr.* 15:28
2 *Chr.* 15:14 sware to L. with *s.*
*Job* 39:25 smelleth battle, and *s.*

Prov. 11:10 when wick. per. is s.
Is. 16:9 s. sum.-fruits fallen, 10
Jer. 20:16 let th. hear s. noontide
48:33 one shall tread with s. th. s. shall be no s.
Ezek. 21:22 lift up voice with s.
Amos 1:14 a fire dev. Ra. with s.
2:2 M. shall die with tumult, s.
Zec. 4:7 forth head-stone with s.

**SHOVEL.**

Is. 30:24 been winnowed with s.

**SHOVELS.**

Ex. 27:3 shalt make pans and s.
38:3 he made the pots and the s.
Num. 4:14 put on purple cloth s.
1 K. 7:40 Hiram made lavers, s. 45; 2 Chr. 4:11, 16
2 K. 25:14 s. he took, and the snuffers, Jer. 52:18

**SHOW, Substantive.**

Ps. 39:6 ev. man walk. in vain s.
Is. 3:9 the s. of th. countenance
Luke 20:47 for s. make long pra.
Gal. 6:12 make a fair s. in flesh
Col. 2:15 made s. of them openly
23 which things have s. of wi.

**SHOW-BREAD.**

Ex. 25:30 set upon a table s.-b.
1 Sam. 21:6 no bread but s.-b.
1 K. 7:48 table whereon s.-b. was
1 Chr. 23:29 service for the s.-b.
28:16 gave gold for tables of s.-b.
2 Chr. 2:4 a house for the s.-b.
29:18 have cleansed s.-b. table
Neh. 10:33 charge oursel. for s.-b.
Mat. 12:4 David entered and did eat s.-b. Mark 2:26; Luke 6:4
Heb. 9:2 wherein was the s.-b.

**SHOW.**

Ex. 7:9 Ph. sh. speak, s. miracle
9:16 raised thee to s. my power
10:1 that I might s. my signs
14:13 see the salva. Lord will s.
18:20 shalt s. the way they must walk, Deut. 1:33
25:9 accord. to all that I s. thee
33:13 s. me now thy way
18 I beseech thee s. me thy glory
Deut. 5:5 s. you word of the Lo.
7:2 nor s. mercy unto them
17:9 s. thee sentence of judgm.
28:50 old, nor s. favor to young
32:7 thy father, he will s. thee
1 Sam. 3:15 Sam. feared to s. Eli
8:9 s. them manner of the king
9:27 may s. thee the word of G.
14:12 and we will s. you a thing
25:8 ask, and they will s. thee
2 Sam. 15:25 he will s. me
1 K. 2:2 strong, s. thyself a man
18:1 go, s. thyself to Ahab, 2
2 Chr. 16:9 to s. himself strong
Ezr. 2:59 th. could not s. fathers' house, Neh. 7:61
Est. 4:8 the writing to s. Esther
Job 11:6 he would s. thee secrets
Ps. 4:6 who will s. us any good?
9:14 s. forth all thy praise
16:11 wilt s. me the path of life
25:4 s. me thy ways, O Lord
14 L. will s. them his covenant
51:15 my mouth sh. s. thy praise
71:15 my mouth s. thy righte.
79:13 thy people s. thy praise
85:7 s. us mercy, O Lord
92:15 to s. that the L. is upright
106:2 who can s. all his praise
Prov. 18:24 must s. himself
Is. 27:11 form. them. s. no favor
30:30 L. sh. s. lightning of arm
41:22 s. us what shalt happen, let them s. the former thin.
43:9 who can s. us former thi.?
21 peo. shall s. forth my praise
44:7 things coming let them s.
46:8 remem. s. yourselves men
49:9 in darkness s. yourselves
60:6 s. forth praises of the Lord
Jer. 16:10 s. them all these words
42:3 thy God may s. us the way
51:31 to s. the king of Babylon
Ezek. 33:31 wi. mouth th. s. love
37:18 s. us what thou meanest?
43:10 s. the house to house of I.
Dan. 9:23 I am come to s. thee
Hab. 1:3 dost s. me iniquity?
Mat. 8:4 s. thys. to priest, Mark 1:44; Luke 5:14; 17:14
11:4 s. John the things ye hear
14:2 mighty works s. Mark 6:14
16:1 desired he would s. a sign
24:24 and shall s. great signs and wonders, Mark 13:22
Luke 1:19 sent to s. glad tidings
8:39 s. great thi. God hath done
John 5:20 will s. greater works
7:4 if thou do th. things s. thy.
11:57 if any kn. they shou. s. it
16:13 will s. you things to come
14 receive of mine, and s. it, 15
25 I sh. s. you plainly of Fath.
Acts 1:24 Lord s. whether of th.
7:3 come into land I sh. s. thee
12:17 s. these things to James
16:17 s. us way of salvation
26:23 should s. light to the peo.
Rom. 2:15 s. work of law written
9:17 that I might s. my power
22 if G. willing to s. his wrath
1 Cor. 11:26 ye do s. Lord's dea.
2 Cor. 8:24 s. proof of your love
1 Thes. 1:9 for they themselves s.
1 Tim. 6:15 in his times he sh. s.
2 Tim. 2:15 s. thyself appr. to G.
Heb. 6:11 that every one s. dilig.
Jam. 2:18 s. me thy faith witho.
3:13 s. works out of good conv.
1 Pet. 2:9 s. forth praises of him
1 John 1:2 s. unto you etern. life
Rev. 1:1 angel to s. servants, 22:6

**I will SHOW.**

Gen. 12:1 land that I w. s. thee
Ex. 33:19 I w. s. mercy on whom I will s. mercy
Jud. 4:22 I will s. thee the man
1 Sam. 16:3 I w. s. what shalt do
20:13 then I will s. it thee
1 K. 18:15 I w. surely s. myself
2 K. 7:12 I w. s. you what Syria.
Job 15:17 I w. s. thee that which
Ps. 50:23 I will s. the salvation of God, 91:16
Jer. 18:17 I will s. them the back
33:3 I w. s. thee mighty things
42:12 I w. s. mercies unto you
Dan. 11:2 I w. s. thee the truth
Joel 2:30 I will s. wonders in heaven, Acts 2:19
Mic. 7:15 I will s. marvel. things
Zec. 1:9 I will s. thee what these
Luke 6:47 I will s. wh. he is like
Acts 9:16 I will s. how great thi.
Jam. 2:18 I will s. thee my faith
Rev. 4:1 I will s. thee things wh.
See KINDNESS.

**SHOWED.**

Num. 13:26 s. them fruit of land
Deut. 34:12 Mo. s. in sight of Is.
Jud. 1:25 he s. them entrance
13:10 woman s. her husband
16:18 he hath s. me his heart
Ruth 2:11 s. me all th. hast done
1 Sam. 11:9 s. it to men of Jab.
24:18 Saul said, Thou hast s.
2 Sam. 11:22 messenger s. David
1 K. 1:27 not s. it to thy servant
16:27 his might that he s. 22:45
2 K. 6:6 he s. him the place
20:15 there is nothing I have not s. them, Is. 39:4
Est. 1:4 s. riches of his kingdom
3:6 s. him the people of Morde.
Job 6:14 to afflicted pity sh. be s.
Ps. 71:18 until I ha. s. thy stren.
Prov. 26:26 wickedness sh. be s.
Ec. 2:19 I have s. myself wise
Is. 40:14 s. him way of understa.
Mat. 28:11 s. to chief priests
Luke 4:5 devil s. him all kingdo.
7:18 disciples of John s. him
14:21 serv. came and s. his lord
John 10:32 good works have I s.
21:1 Jesus s. himself again to disciples, 14; Acts 1:3
Acts 7:26 Mo. s. himself to them
52 which s. bef. of the coming
20:20 s. taught you publicly
23:22 tell no man hast s. these
26:20 P. s. to them of Damascus
1 Cor. 10:28 for his sake that s.
Heb. 6:10 love which ye have s.

**God, or Lord SHOWED.**

Gen. 19:19 thy mercy s. to me
32:10 not worthy of mercies s.
39:21 the Lord s. Joseph mercy
41:25 God s. P. what he is about
39 foras. as God hath s. thee
48:11 G. ha. s. me also thy seed
Lev. 24:12 mind of L. might be s.
Num. 14:11 all signs I have s. among them, Deut. 6:22
Deut. 4:36 upon earth he s. thee
5:24 L. our God s. us his glory
34:1 Lord s. him the land of G.
Jud. 13:23 nor would he have s.
2 K. 8:10 L. hath s. me, he shall
13 the L. s. me thou sh. be ki.
Ezr. 9:8 grace s. fr. L. our God
Ps. 60:3 thou hast s. thy people
71:20 hast s. me great troubles
111:6 s. the power of his works
118:27 God the L. s. us light
Is. 26:10 let favor be s. to wick.
43:12 s. when no strange God
48:3 I s. th. I did them sudden.
5 bef. it came to pass I s. thee
Jer. 38:21 word Lord hath s. me
Ezek. 11:25 thi. Lord hath s. me
Amos 7:1 Lord s. me, 4, 7; 8:1
Mic. 6:8 he hath s. thee, O man
Luke 1:58 Lord hath s. mercy
Acts 3:18 things which G. had s.
10:40 G. raised him and s. him
Rom. 1:19 G. hath s. it to them
2 Pet. 1:14 L. Jesus hath s. me

**SHOWEDST, EST.**

Neh. 9:10 s. signs upon Pharaoh
Jer. 11:18 thou s. me their doin.
Jer. 32:18 that s. loving-kind. to
John 2:18 what sign s. thou? 6:30

**SHOWETH.**

Gen. 41:28 God is about to do, s.
Num. 23:3 whatsoever he s. me
Job 36:9 he s. them their work
Ps. 19:2 night unto night s. kno.
112:5 good man s. favor
147:19 he s. his word unto Jac.
Prov. 12:17 speaks tru. s. right.
Is. 41:26 no. that s. your words
Mat. 4:8 s. him all kingdoms
John 5:20 Father s. Son all thin.

**SHOWING.**

Ex. 20:6 and s. mercy unto thousands, Deut. 5:10
Dan. 5:12 s. of hard sentences
Luke 1:80 in deserts till his s.
8:1 s. glad tidings of kingdom
2 Thes. 2:4 as G. s. himself
Tit. 2:7 in all things s. a pattern

**SHOWER.**

Ezek. 13:11 be overflowing s. 13
34:26 cause s. to come in season
Luke 12:54 say, There cometh s.

**SHOWERS.**

Deut. 32:2 my speech dist'l as s.
Job 24:8 the poor are wet with s.

Ps. 65:10 mak. earth soft with s.
72:6 king shall come like s.
Jer. 3:3 s. have been withholden
14:22 can the heavens give s.?
Ezek. 34:26 his season s. of bles.
Mic. 5:7 Jac. shall be as s. on gr.
Zec. 10:1 Lord shall give them s.

**SHRANK.**

Gen. 32:32 Is. not eat of sinew s.

**SHRED.**

2 K. 4:39 came and s. wild gour.

**SHRINES.**

Acts 19:24 Demet. made silver s.

**SHROUD.**

Ezek. 31:3 Assyr. a cedar with s.

**SHRUBS.**

Gen. 21:15 Ha. cast child und. s.

**SHUAH.**

Gen. 25:2 Ishbak, S. 1 Chr. 1:32
38:2 married daugh. of a Canaanite, nam. S. 12; 1 Chr. 2:3

**SHUAL.**

1 Sam. 13:17 turned to land of S.

**SHULAMITE.**

Cant. 6:13 O S. what see in S.?

**SHUN, NED.**

Acts 20:27 not s. to decl. counsel
2 Tim. 2:16 s. profane babblings

**SHUNAMMITE.**

1 K. 1:3 they found Abishag a S.
2:17 he gave me Abishag the S.
22 why dost ask Abishag S.
2 K. 4:12 call this S. 36; 25

SHUNEM. 1 Sam. 28:4
SHUR. Gen. 16:7

**SHUSHAN.**

Neh. 1:1 I was in S. the palace
Est. 2:8 maidens gathered to S.
3:15 the city S. was perplexed
4:16 gather all the Jews in S.
8:15 the city of S. rejoiced and
9:11 number slain in S. was
15 Jews slew in S. three hund.

**SHUT.**

Gen. 7:16 the Lord s. him in
Ex. 14:3 wilderness s. them in
Num. 12:14 let her be s. out
15 Miriam was s. out fr. camp
Deut. 15:7 nor s. hand from poor
Jos. 2:7 they s. gate of Jericho
Jud. 9:51 they s. tower to them
1 Sam. 23:7 he is s. in, by enter.
Ps. 69:15 let not pit s. mouth
Is. 6:10 s. eyes lest they see
22:22 open and none shall s. he shall s. none open
44:18 he hath s. their eyes
45:1 and gates shall not be s.
52:15 kings sh. s. their mouths
60:11 gates shall not be s. day
66:9 shall I s. womb, saith G.?
Ezek. 3:24 go s. thys. with. hou.
44:2 G. hath entered, it sh. be s.
46:1 gate shall be s. six days
12 going forth, one sh. s. gate
Dan. 6:22 God hath s. lion's mo.
Acts 5:23 the prison found we s.
Rev. 11:6 have power to s. heav.
21:25 gates sh. not be s. by day
See DOOR.

**SHUT up.**

Lev. 13:11 shall not s. him up
14:38 priest shall s. up house
Deut. 11:17 and he s. up heaven
32:30 the Lord had s. them up
36 seeth there is none s. up
1 Sam. 1:5 L. s. up Han.'s womb
6 the Lord had s. up her womb
6:10 s. up their calves at home
1 K. 8:35 when heaven is s. up, 2 Chr. 6:26; 7:13
14:10 from Jeroboam him that is s. up, 21:21; 2 K. 9:8
2 K. 14:26 th. was not any s. up
17:4 king of Assyria s. him up
2 Chr. 28:24 A. s. up doors, 29:7
Neh. 6:10 house of Sh. was s. up
Job 3:10 because it s. not up
11:10 s. up, who can hinder?
38:8 who hath s. up the sea?
Ps. 31:8 hast not s. me up into
77:9 ha. he s. up tender merc.?
88:8 I am s. up, I cannot come
Is. 24:10 every house is s. up
22 they shall be s. up in prison
Jer. 13:19 cities of south be s. up
32:2 prophet was s. up by Z. 3
33:1 while he was s. up, 39:15
36:5 I am s. up, I cannot go
Dan. 8:26 s. thou up the vision
12:4 O Daniel, s. up the words
Mat. 23:13 s. up kingd. of heav.
Luke 3:20 s. up John in prison
4:25 heaven was s. up three yrs.
Acts 26:10 many did I s. up
Gal. 3:23 s. up to faith
Rev. 20:3 s. up devil, set a seal

**SHUTTETH.**

Job 12:14 he s. up a man
Prov. 17:28 that s. lips is a man
Is. 33:15 s. eyes from seeing
Lam. 3:8 when I cry he s. out
1 John 3:17 s. up bow. of compa.
Rev. 3:7 no m. s. and s. no m. op.

**SHUTTING.**

Jos. 2:5 about time of s. gate

**SHUTTLE.**

Job 7:6 swifter than a weaver's s.

**SICK.**

Gen. 48:1 behold, thy father is s.
Lev. 15:33 is s. of her flowers
1 Sam. 19:14 she said, He is s.
30:13 three days ago I fell s.
2 Sam. 12:15 L. struck ch. was s.
13:2 Amnon was vexed, fell s.
5 Jonadab said, Make thys. s.
6 Am. lay down made hims. s.
1 K. 14:1 the son of Jerob. fell s.
5 cometh to ask for son, is s.
17:17 son of the woman fell s.
2 K. 1:2 Ahaz. fell down, was s.
8:7 Benha. king of Syria was s.
29 Joram son of Ahab, bec. he was s. 2 Chr. 22:6
13:14 Elisha was fallen s. died
20:1 Hezekiah s. unto death, 2 Chr. 32:24; Is. 38:1
Neh. 2:2 why sad, art not s.?
Ps. 35:13 when they were s.
Prov. 13:12 hope deferred make. the heart s.
23:35 stricken me, I was not s.
Cant. 5:8 I am s. of love
Is. 1:5 wh. head s. heart faint
33:24 inhab. not say, I am s.
38:9 Hezekiah had been s.
Jer. 14:18 art s. with famine
Ezek. 34:4 nor heal. that was s.
16 strengthen that wh. was s.
Hos. 7:5 princes made him s.
Mic. 6:13 I make thee s. in smi.
Mal. 1:8 offer s. is it not evil?
Mat. 4:24 brou. to him s. people
8:14 Pet.'s wife's moth. s. of fe.
16 healed all th. were s. 14:14
9:12 but they that are s. Mark 2:17; Luke 5:31
10:8 heal the s. cleanse the lepers, Luke 9:2; 10:9
25:36 I was s. and ye visited me
Mark 6:5 laid hands on a few s.
13 anoint. many that were s.
56 laid s. in streets, Acts 5:15
16:18 lay hands on the s.
Luke 7:2 centurion's serv. was s.
10 serv. whole that had been s.
John 4:46 a nobleman's son s.
11:1 Laz. of Bethany was s. 2
3 L. he whom thou lovest is s.
Acts 9:37 Dorcas was s. and died
19:12 brou. the s. handkerchiefs
28:8 father of Publius lay s.
Phil. 2:26 heard he had been s.
2 Tim. 4:20 Tro. I left at Mil. s.
Jam. 5:14 s. let him call elders

See PALSY.

**SICKLE.**

Deut. 16:9 beg. to put s. to corn
23:25 not move s. unto neigh.'s
Jer. 50:16 cut off that handl. s.
Joel 3:13 put ye in s. harv. ripe
Mark 4:29 immedi. he put. in s.
Rev. 14:14 in his hand sharp s.
15 thrust in thy s. 16, 18, 19

**SICKLY.**

1 Cor. 11:30 for this cause ma. s.

**SICKNESS.**

Ex. 23:25 I will take s. away
Lev. 20:18 if lie wi. wom. hav. s.
Deut 7:15 L. will take fr. thee s.
28:61 ev. s. not written in law
1 K. 8:37 whatsoever s. there be, 2 Chr. 6:28
17:17 his s. was so sore
2 K. 13:14 Elisha was sick of s.
2 Chr. 21:15 shalt have great s.
19 bow. fell out by rea. of s.
Ps. 41:3 wilt make his bed in s.
Ec. 5:17 sor. and wrath with s.
Is. 38:9 Hez. recovered of his s.
12 pining s. from day to night
Hos. 5:13 when Ephr. saw his s.
Mat. 4:23 Je. went healing all s.
9:35 Jesus went about heali. s.
10:1 to heal. s. Mark 3:15
John 11:4 s. is not unto death

**SICKNESSES.**

Deut. 28:59 sore s. of long conti.
29:22 when they see s. L. laid
Mat. 8:17 sa. Himself bare our s.

**SIDE.**

Gen. 6:16 do. of the ark in the s.
Ex. 12:7 stri. blood on s. pos. 22
17:12 stayed Moses' hands, one on one s. the other on oth. s.
32:26 who is on the Lord's s. let
27 put ev. man his sword by s.
Lev. 1:15 blood wru. at s. of alt.
Num. 22:24 on this and that s.
32:19 not inh. yonder s. Jordan
Deut. 4:32 ask from one s. heav.
31:26 book of law in s. of ark
1 Sam. 4:18 fell by the s. of gate
20:25 and Abner sat by Saul's s.
2 Sam. 2:16 thrust sw. into his s.
13:34 king's sons came by hill s.
16:13 Shimei went on hill's s.
2 K. 9:32 who is on my s. who?
1 Chr. 12:18 David, and on thy s.
2 Chr. 11:12 Ju. and Benj. on s.
Job 18:12 destruc. ready at his s.
Ps. 91:7 thousand shall fall at s.
118:6 the Lord is on my s. I will
124:1 if it had not be. L. on s. 2
Is. 60:4 daughte. be nursed at s.
Ezek. 4:8 not turn from one s. to
9 days thou sh. lie upon thy s.
25:9 I will open the s. of Moab
34:21 thrust with s. and should.
Dan. 7:5 rais. up itself on one s.
11:17 she sh. not stand on his s.
John 19:34 wi. a spear pierced s.
20:20 showed his hands and s.
25 except I thrust hand into s.
27 hand, and thrust into my s.
Acts 16:13 on sab. went by riv. s.
Rev. 22:2 on either s. of river

See CHAMBERS.

**Every SIDE.**

1 Sam. 14:47 Saul fought on e. s.
1 K. 5:4 L. hath giv. rest on e. s.
1 Chr. 22:18 not giv. rest on e. s.
2 Chr. 14:7 hath giv. rest on e. s.
Ps. 12:8 the wicked walk on e. s.
31:13 fear was on every s.

*Jer.* 6:25 fear *e. s.* 20:10; 42:29
*Ezek.* 16:33 come to thee on *e. s.*
19:8 nations set ag. him on *e. s.*
23:22 bring th. ag. thee on *e. s.*
37:21 I will gather them on *e. s.*
2 *Cor.* 4:8 are troubled on *e. s.* 7:5

**Farther SIDE.**

*Mark* 10:1 J. came by *f. s.* Jord.

*See* LEFT.

**On this SIDE.**

*Jos.* 8:33 I. and jud. stood *on t. s.*
1 *Sam.* 23:26 Saul went *on this s.*
*Ezr.* 4:16 no portion *on this s.*
*Ezek.* 1:23 had two wings, *on t. s.*
40:39 were two tables *on this s.*
*Dan.* 12:5 stood two, one *on t. s.*

**On other SIDE.**

*Jos.* 24:2 fathers dwelt *on o. s.*
1 *Sam.* 14:40 I and Jona. *on o. s.*
*Ob.* 11 day thou stood. *on o. s.*
*John* 6:25 found him *on o. s.*

**Right SIDE.**

*Ezek.* 4:6 lie again on thy *r. s.*
47:1 from und. *r. s.* of house, 2

*See* SEA, SOUTH, WAY, WEST.

**SIDES.**

1 *Sam.* 24:3 David in *s.* of cave
1 *K.* 4:24 Sol. had peace on all *s.*
*Ps.* 48:2 Zion on *s.* of the north
*Is.* 14:13 I will sit on *s.* of north
15 brought down to *s.* of pit
*Jer.* 6:22 raised from *s.* of earth
49:32 bring calamity from all *s.*
*Ezek* 1:17 went on four *s.* 10:11
48:1 th. are his *s.* east and west
*Amos.* 6:10 say to him by *s.* of h.
*Jon.* 1:5 gone down to *s.* of ship

**SIDON.**

*Gen.* 10:5 Canaan begat S. his
19 border of Canaan. was fr. S.
*Jud.* 18:28 Laish was far fr. S.
*Mat.* 11:21 done in Tyre and S.
22 tolera. for S. *Luke* 10:13, 14
15:21 Jesus departed into coasts of Tyre and S. *Mark* 7:24
*Mark* 3:8 they about Tyre and S. came, *Luke* 6:17
7:31 from coasts of Tyre and S.
*Luke* 4:26 to Sarepta, a city of S.
*Acts* 12:20 displea. wi. them of S.
27:3 next day we touched at S.

**SIEGE.**

*Deut.* 20:19 to employ them in *s.*
28:53 sh. eat thy children in *s.*
2 *Chr.* 32:10 that ye abide in *s.*?
*Is.* 29:3 I will lay *s.* against thee
*Jer.* 19:9 eat flesh of friend in *s.*
*Ezek.* 4:2 lay *s.* ag. it, a fort, 3
*Mic.* 5:1 hath laid *s.* against us
*Nah.* 3:14 draw thee waters for *s.*
*Zec.* 12:2 cup of trembling in *s.*

**SIEVE.**

*Is.* 30:28 sift nations with the *s.*
*Amos* 9:9 as corn sifted in a *s*

**SIFT.**

*Is.* 30:28 *s.* nations with sieve
*Amos* 9:9 I will *s.* Israel as corn
*Luke* 22:31 Sat. desired to *s.* you

**SIGH.**

*Is.* 24:7 all merry-hearted do *s.*
*Lam.* 1:4 priests *s.* 11 people *s.*
*Ezek.* 9:4 foreheads of men th. *s.*
21:6 *s.* with break. of thy loins

**SIGHED, EST, ETH.**

*Ex.* 2:23 Is. *s.* by reason of bon.
*Lam.* 1:8 she *s.* turneth backw.
*Ezek.* 21:7 say, Whereof *s.* thou?
*Mark* 7:34 look. to heaven he *s.*
8:12 *s.* deeply in his spirit

**SIGHING.**

*Job* 3:24 my *s.* cometh bef. I eat
*Ps.* 12:5 *s.* of needy will I arise
31:10 spent with grief, years *s.*
79:11 let *s.* of the prisoner come
*Is.* 21:2 *s.* thereof I ma. to cease
35:10 sorrow and *s.* flee away
*Jer.* 45:3 I fainted in my *s.*

**SIGHS.**

*Lam.* 1:22 *s.* many, heart faint

**SIGHT.**

*Gen.* 2:9 every tree pleasant to *s.*
*Ex.* 3:3 turn and see th. great *s.*
24:17 *s.* of glory of L. like fire
*Lev.* 13:4 in *s.* not deep. th. skin
14:37 if plague in *s.* lower
*Num.* 13:33 in their *s.* as grassh.
27:19 give him charge in th. *s.*
*Deut.* 28:34 mad for *s.* of eyes, 67
*Jos.* 23:5 G. drive them out of *s.*
24:17 did great signs in our *s.*
*Job* 18:3 why rep. vile in your *s.*?
21:8 seed established in their *s.*
34:26 striketh them in *s.* of oth.
41:9 not cast down at *s.* of him?
*Ps.* 79:10 am. heathen in our *s.*
*Ec.* 6:9 better *s.* of eyes than
*Is.* 5:21 prudent in their own *s.*
11:3 not judge after *s.* of eyes
*Jer.* 51:24 evil in Zion in your *s.*
*Ezek.* 12:3 remo. by day in th. *s.*
20:9 in whose *s.* I made known
14 in who. *s.* I brought out, 22
43:11 show forms, write in th. *s.*
*Dan.* 4:11 *s.* thereof to end of, 20
*Mat.* 11:5 the blind receive their *s.* 20:34; *Luke* 7:21
*Luke* 4:18 preach *s.* to the blind
23:48 came to *s.* smote breasts
24:31 he vanished out of their *s.*
*John* 9:11 washed and I recei. *s.*
*Acts* 1:9 received him out of *s.*
7:31 Mo. saw, he wondered at *s.*
9:9 three days with. *s.* nor eat
18 he received *s.* forthwith
2 *Cor.* 5:7 we walk by fai. not *s.*

**SIGHT of God.**

*Prov.* 3:4 understand. in *s. of G.*
*Acts* 4:19 whe. right in *s. of G.*
8:21 heart not right in *s. of G.*
2 *Cor.* 2:17 in *s. of G.* speak we
7:12 care for you in *s. of God*
1 *Tim.* 2:3 acceptable in *s. of G.*
1 *Tim.* 6:13 I gi. th. ch. in *s. of G.*
1 *Pet.* 3:4 in *s. of G.* of great pri.

**His SIGHT.**

*Ex.* 15:26 wh. is right in *his s.*
*Deut.* 4:37 bro. thee out in *his s.*
*Jud.* 6:21 angel dep. out of *his s.*
2 *Sam.* 12:9 L. to do evil in *his s.*
2 *K.* 17:18 th. o. of *h. s.* 20, 23; 24:3
1 *Chr.* 19:13 L. do good in *his s.*
*Job* 25:5 stars not pure in *his s.*
*Ps.* 10:5 judgments out of *his s.*
72:14 preci. their blood in *his s.*
*Ec.* 2:26 giv. man good in *his s.*
8:3 not hasty to go out of *his s.*
*Hos.* 6:2 we shall live in *his s.*
*Mark* 10:52 Bartim. immediately received *his s. Luke* 18:43
*John* 9:15 how he receiv. *his s.* 18
*Acts* 9:12 he might receive *his s.*
*Col.* 1:22 pres. you holy in *his s.*
*Heb.* 13:21 well-pleasing in *h. s.*
1 *John* 3:22 things pleas. in *h. s.*

**In the SIGHT.**

*Gen.* 47:18 left *in the s.* of lord
*Ex.* 4:30 signs *in the s.* of people
11:3 Mo. great *in the s.* of serv.
19:11 L. come down *in the s.* of
*Lev.* 20:17 cut off *in the s.* of peo.
26:45 out of Eg. *in the s.* of hea.
*Num.* 25:6 wom. *in the s.* of Mo.
33:3 *in the s.* of Egyptians
*Deut.* 31:7 M. said, *in the s.* of Is.
*Jos.* 10:12 *in the s.* of Israel
1 *Chr.* 28:8 *in the s.* of Is. keep
29:25 magni. Sol. *in the s.* of Is.
2 *Chr.* 32:23 Hez. magnifi. *in t. s.*
*Ezr.* 9:9 mercy *in the s.* of kings
*Neh.* 1:11 mercy *in the s.* of man
*Ps.* 78:12 thi. did he *in s.* of fath.
98:2 showed *in the s.* of heathen
*Prov.* 1:17 net spr. *in the s.* of b.
*Ec.* 11:9 walk *in the s.* of eyes
*Jer.* 43:9 hid stones *in t. s.* of Ju.
*Ezek.* 5:8 *in the s.* of nations
16:41 judgm. *in the s.* of women
28:25 sa. in th. *in t. s.* of h. 39:27
*Acts* 7:10 wisdom *in the s.* of Ph.
*Rom.* 12:17 hon. *in the s.* of men
*Rev.* 13:14 *in the s.* of beast

*See* LORD.

**My SIGHT.**

*Gen.* 23:4 dead out of *my s.* 8
*Ex.* 33:12 found gra. in *my s.* 17
1 *Sam.* 29:6 coming good in *my s.*
9 I kn. thou art good in *my s.*
1 *K.* 8:25 not fail thee a man in *my s.* 2 *Chr.* 6:16
11:38 that wh. is right in *my s.*
2 *K.* 21:15 done evil in *my s.*
23:27 remove Jud. out of *my s.*
*Is.* 43:4 wast precious in *my s.*
*Jer.* 7:15 cast you out of *my s.*
30 chil. of Ju. done ev. in *m. s.*
15:1 cast them out of *my s.*
18:10 if it do evil in *my s.*
34:15 had done right in *my s.*
*Ezek.* 10:2 went in *my s.* to fill
*Amos* 9:3 hid from *my s.* in sea
*Mark* 10:51 L. that I might rec. *my s. Luke* 18:41

**Thy SIGHT.**

*Gen.* 19:19 found grace in *thy s.*
21:12 let it not be griev. in *t. s.*
33:10 Ja. said, If I have found grace in *thy s.* 47:29; *Ex.* 33:13, 16; 34:9; *Jud.* 6:17
1 *Sam.* 15:17 little in *th.* own *s.*
2 *Sam.* 7:9 enemies out of *thy s.*
19 a small thing in *thy s.*
14:22 I have found grace in *t. s.*
2 *K.* 1:13 life precious in *t. s.* 14
20:3 done good in *t. s. Is.* 38:3
*Ps.* 5:5 fool. not stand in *thy s.*
9:19 let heath. be judged in *t. s.*
51:4 I sinned, done evil in *t. s.*
76:7 who may stand in *thy s.*?
143:2 in *thy s.* no man justified
*Is.* 26:17 so ha. we been in *thy s.*
*Jer.* 18:23 blot out sin from *t. s.*
*Jon.* 2:4 I am cast out of *thy s.*
*Mat.* 11:26 so it seemed good in *thy s. Luke* 10:21
*Luke* 15:21 sin. ag. heav. in *t. s.*
18:42 Jesus said, Receive *thy s.*
*Acts* 9:17 mightest receive *thy s.*
22:13 brother Saul, receive *t. s.*

*See* FAVOR, FIND.

**SIGHTS.**

*Luke* 21:11 fearful *s.* sh. there be

**SIGN, Substantive.**

*Ex.* 4:8 first *s.* believe latter *s.*
8:23 to-morrow shall this *s.* be
31:13 my sabbaths, a *s.* bet. me and you, 17; *Ezek.* 20:12, 20
*Num.* 16:38 they sh. be a *s.* to Is.
*Deut.* 6:8 for *s.* on hand, 11:18
13:1 arise a prophet, giveth a *s.*
28:46 on thee for *s.* and wonder
*Jos.* 4:6 this be a *s.* among you
*Jud.* 6:17 show me *s.* thou talk.
20:38 *s.* betw. Israel and liers in
1 *Sam.* 2:34 this shall be *s.* to thee, 2 *K.* 19:29
14:10 this shall be a *s.* unto us
1 *K.* 13:3 *s.* Lord hath spoken
2 *K.* 20:8 what shall be the *s.*
9 this *s.* shall they have of the Lord, *Is.* 37:30; 38:7, 22
2 *Chr.* 32:24 and he gave him a *s.*
*Is.* 7:11 ask thee a *s.* of the Lord
14 L. himself shall give you a *s.*
19:20 it shall be for a *s.* to Lord
20:3 Is. walked barefoot for a *s.*
55:13 for an everlasting *s.*

66:19 I will set a *s.* among them
*Jer.* 6:1 set up *s.* in Beth-haccer.
44:29 this be *s.* to you, *Lu.* 2:12
*Ezek.* 4:3 this be *s.* to house of I.
12:6 I set thee for a *s.* to Is. 11
14:8 make him a *s.* and a prov.
24:24 Ezek. is a *s.* 27 thou be *s.*
39:15 th. sh. he set up a *s.* by it
*Mat.* 12:38 Master, we wo. see a *s.*
16:1; *Mark* 8:11; *Luke* 11:16
39 seek. af. a *s.* no *s.* be given,
but *s.* of Jonas, 16:4; *Mark*
8:12; *Luke* 11:29, 30
24:3 what the *s.* of thy coming?
30 then appear *s.* of Son of man
26:48 betrayed him gave them *s.*
*Mark* 13:4 what *s.* when things
*Luke* 2:34 *s.* which be spoken
*John* 2:18 wh. *s.* show. th.? 6:30
*Acts* 28:11 whose *s.* was Castor
*Rom.* 4:11 received *s.* of circum.
1 *Cor.* 1:22 for Jews require a *s.*
14:22 wherefore tongues are *s.*
*Rev.* 15:1 I saw ano. *s.* in heaven

**SIGN.**

*Dan.* 6:8 establish decree, and *s.*

**SIGNED.**

*Dan.* 6:9 Darius *s.* the writing, 10

**SIGNS.**

*Gen.* 1:14 let them be for *s.*
*Ex.* 4:9 if they will not believe *s.*
17 with this rod th. shalt do *s.*
7:3 I will multiply my *s.* in Eg.
10:2 mayest tell thy son my *s.*
*Num.* 14:11 for all *s.* I showed
*Deut.* 4:34 take nation by *s.* 26:8
6:22 Lord showed *s.* on Egypt,
*Neh.* 9:10; *Ps.* 78:43
7:19 great *s.* thi. eyes saw, 29:3
34:11 in all *s.* L. sent him to do
1 *Sam.* 10:7 when th. *s.* are come
9 and all those *s.* came to pass
*Ps.* 74:4 th. set up ensigns for *s.*
9 we see not our *s.* there is no
105:27 showed his *s.* amo. them
*Is.* 8:18 I and children are for *s.*
*Jer.* 10:2 be not dismayed at *s.*
32:20 set *s.* and wonders in E.
*Dan.* 4:2 I thou. good to show *s.*
3 how great his *s.*! mighty
6:27 he worketh *s.* in heaven
*Mat.* 16:3 not discern *s.* of times?
24:24 th. shall arise false Christs
and show *s.* *Mark* 13:22
*Mark* 16:17 these *s.* follow them
20 confirming the word with *s.*
*Luke* 1:62 they made *s.* to Zacha.
21:11 and great *s.* shall there be
25 *s.* in sun, moon and stars
*John* 4:48 except ye see *s.* ye will
20:30 other *s.* truly did Jesus
*Acts* 2:19 I will show *s.* in earth
22 a man approved of G. by *s.*
43 *s.* were done by apost. 5:12
4:30 *s.* may be done by name
7:36 had showed *s.* and wonders
8:13 Simon wond. beholding *s.*
14:3 granted *s.* and wond. to be
*Rom.* 15:19 through mighty *s.*
and wonders, 2 *Cor.* 12:12
2 *Thes.* 2:9 work. of Satan, wi. *s.*
*Heb.* 2:4 G. bearing wit. with *s.*

**SIGNET, S.**

*Gen.* 38:18 thy *s.* and staff, 25
*Ex.* 28:11 like engravings of a *s.*
21, 36; 39:14, 30
39:6 onyx-stones graven as *s.*
*Jer.* 22:24 though Coniah were *s.*
*Dan.* 6:17 king sealed it with *s.*
*Hag.* 2:23 I will make th. as a *s.*

**SIGNIFICATION.**

1 *Cor.* 14:10 none of th. with. *s.*

**SIGNIFY.**

*Acts* 21:26 to *s.* accomplishment
23:15 *s.* to capt. that he bring P.
25:27 not to *s.* the crimes laid
1 *Pet.* 1:11 search. what Sp. did *s.*

**SIGNIFIED, ETH.**

*Acts* 11:28 Agab. *s.* there should
*Heb.* 12:27 *s.* removing those thi.
*Rev.* 1:1 *s.* it by his angel to Jo.

**SIGNIFYING.**

*John* 12:33 *s.* by what death sho.
glorify God 18:32; 21:19
*Heb.* 9:8 H. Gh. *s.* that the way

**SIHON.**

*Num.* 21:23 S. would not suffer
Is. to pass, *Jud.* 11:20
27 let the city of S. be built
28 flame gone out fr. city of S.
34 as didst to S. *Deut.* 3:2, 6
*Deut.* 2:30 S. king of Heshbon
21 I have begun to give S. and
32 S. ca. out, 29:7; *Jud.* 11:20
31:4 do to them as he did to S.
*Jos.* 9:10 all that he did to S.
*Jud.* 11:21 God delivered S. into
*Neh.* 9:22 possessed land of S.
*Jer.* 48:45 flame com. fr. mi. of S.

**SIHON, king of the Amorites.**

*Num.* 21:21 messeng. to S. *k. of*
*A.* *Deut.* 2:26; *Jud.* 11:19
26 city of S. *k. of A.* *Jos.* 12:2
29 into captiv. to S. *k. of Am.*
34 to S. *ki. of A.* *Deut.* 3:2
*Deut.* 1:4 slain S. *k. of A.* king
of Bashan, *Ps.* 135:11; 136:19
*Jos.* 13:10 cities of S. *ki. of A.*

**SIHOR.**

*Jos.* 13:3 S. which is before
*Jer.* 2:18 to drink waters of S.

**SILAS.**

*Acts* 15:22 S. chief among, 27
34 it pleased S. to abide there
40 Pa. chose S. 16:19 caught S.
16:25 at midnight Paul and S.
29 fell down bef. Paul and S.
17:4 consorted with Paul and S.
10 sent away S. by night
15 commandm. to S. to come
18:5 S. and Timoth. were come

**SILENCE.**

*Job* 4:16 image before me, was *s.*
29:21 men gave ear, and kept *s.*
*Ps.* 31:18 lying lips be put to *s.*
39:2 I was dumb with *s.* I held
94:17 my soul almost dw. in *s.*
115:17 nei. any that go into *s.*
*Is.* 15:1 Moab bro. to *s.* Kir to *s.*
*Jer.* 8:14 our G. hath put us to *s.*
*Lam.* 3:28 sitteth alone, keep. *s.*
*Amos* 8:3 cast them forth with *s.*
*Mat.* 22:34 put Sadducees to *s.*
*Acts* 21:40 th. was made great *s.*
22:2 spake in Heb. they kept *s.*
1 *Tim.* 2:11 let wom. learn in *s.*
12 nor to usurp but to be in *s.*
1 *Pet.* 2:15 may put to *s.* ignor.
*Rev.* 8:1 there was *s.* in heaven

*See* KEEP, KEPT.

**SILENT.**

1 *Sam.* 2:9 wicked shall be *s.*
*Ps.* 22:2 I cry in night, not *s.*
28:1 not *s.* to me, if thou be *s.*
30:12 sing praise to th. not be *s.*
31:17 let wicked be *s.* in grave
*Is.* 47:5 sit thou *s.* and get thee
*Jer.* 8:14 defenced ci. let us be *s.*
*Zec.* 2:13 be *s.* O all flesh, bef. L.

**SILK.**

*Prov.* 31:22 her clothing is *s.*
*Ezek.* 16:10 I covered thee wi. *s.*
13 thy raiment was *s.*
*Rev.* 18:12 no man buyeth her *s.*

**SILLY.**

*Job* 5:2 envy slayeth the *s.* one
*Hos.* 7:11 Ephr. is like a *s.* dove
2 *Tim.* 3:6 lead captive *s.* wom.

**SILOAH, SILOAM.**

*Neh.* 3:15 repai. wall of pool of S.
*Luke* 13:4 on wh. tower in S. fell
*John* 9:7 wash in pool of S. 11

**SILVANUS.**

2 *Cor.* 1:19 preach. am. you by S.
1 *Thes.* 1:1 Paul, S. and Timoth.
to the church, 2 *Thes.* 1:1
1 *Pet.* 5:12 by S. a faithful broth.

**SILVER.**

*Gen.* 23:15 worth 400 shek. of *s.*
*Ex.* 20:23 not make gods of *s.*
26:19 sockets of *s.* 21, 25, 32;
36:24, 26, 30, 36
27:17 hooks shall be of *s.* 38:19
38:25 *s.* of th. that were numb.
*Lev.* 5:15 ram with estima. of *s.*
27:3 esti. of male 50 shek. of *s.*
6 of female three shekels of *s.*
16 hom. of bar. seed 50 shek. *s.*
*Num.* 7:13 offer. one *s.* charger,
*s.* bowl of 70 shekels, 19–79
*Num.* 7:84 12 cha. of *s.* 12 *s.* bowls
10:2 make two trumpets of *s.*
*Deut.* 22:19 amerce in 100 she. *s.*
29 give damsel's fa. 50 shek. *s.*
*Jos.* 7:21 I saw 200 shekels of *s.*
*Jud.* 17:2 1,100 shekels of *s.*
10 I will give ten shekels of *s.*
1 *Sam.* 9:8 fourth part of shek. *s.*
2 *Sam.* 18:11 I wo. given 10 sh. *s.*
12 should re. 1,000 shek. of *s.*
24:24 oxen for 50 shekels of *s.*
1 *K.* 10:21 none *s.* 2 *Chr.* 9:20
27 king made *s.* to be as stones
20:39 thou sh. pay a talent of *s.*
2 *K.* 5:22 give them a talent of *s.*
15:20 exacted of each 50 she. *s.*
18:15 Hezek. gave him all the *s.*
22:4 Hilk. may sum *s.* brought
1 *Chr.* 28:14 instruments of *s.*
29:2, 5
15 for the candlesticks of *s.*
17 by weight for ev. basin of *s.*
2 *Chr.* 17:11 Jehosha. presents *s.*
*Neh.* 5:15 gover. had 40 she. of *s.*
*Job* 3:15 filled houses with *s.*
22:25 thou sh. have plenty of *s.*
27:16 th. he heap up *s.* as dust
17 innocent shall divide the *s.*
28:15 nor shall *s.* be weighed for
*Ps.* 12:6 words of L. pure, as *s.*
66:10 hast tried us, as *s.* is tried
*Prov.* 2:4 if thou seekest her as *s.*
3:14 of wisd. is better than of *s.*
8:10 receive instruction, not *s.*
10:20 tongue of just is choice *s.*
16:16 get underst. rath. than *s.*
17:3 fining-pot is for *s.* and the
25:4 take away dross from the *s.*
*Ec.* 5:10 he that loveth *s.* shall
not be satisfied with *s.*
*Cant.* 8:9 will build a palace of *s.*
*Is.* 1:22 thy *s.* is become dross
30:22 sh. defile thy images of *s.*
48:10 I refined thee, not with *s.*
60:17 for iron I will bring *s.* and
*Jer.* 6:30 reproba. *s.* sh. men call
10:9 *s.* spr. in. plates is brought
32:9 I weighed him 17 she. of *s.*
*Ezek.* 22:18 they are dross of *s.*
20 they gather *s.* brass and iron
22 *s.* is melted in the furnace
27:12 with *s.* Tarshish traded in
*Dan.* 2:32 breast and arms were *s.*
*Hos.* 9:6 pleasant places for *s.*
13:2 made molten images of *s.*
*Amos* 2:6 they sold righte. for *s.*
8:6 that we may buy poor for *s.*
*Zep.* 1:11 howl, all that bear *s.*
*Zec.* 9:3 Tyrus heaped *s.* as dust
13:9 I will refine them as *s.*
*Mal.* 3:3 refiner and purifier of *s.*

*See* FILLETS, GOLD, PIECES.

**SILVER, Adjective.**

*Gen.* 44:2 put *s.* cup in sack's
*Prov.* 26:23 potsherd cov. with *s.*
*Ec.* 12:6 ever *s.* cord be loosed

*Mat.* 27:6 chief priests took *s.*
*Acts* 19:24 Dem. made *s.* shrines
*See* VESSELS.

**SILVERLINGS.**

*Is.* 7:23 thous. vines at thous. *s.*

**SILVERSMITH.**

*Acts* 19:24 Demetrius a *s.* made

**Talents of SILVER.**

1 *K.* 16:24 bought hill for 2 *t. o. s.*
2 *K.* 5:5 Naam. took ten *t. of s.*
23 two *tal. of s.* in two bags
15:19 M. gave Pul 1,000 *t. of s.*
1 *Chr.* 19:6 Ha. sent 1,000 *t. of s.*
22:14 a thous. thousand *t. of s.*
29:4 seven thou. *t. of* refined *s.*
2 *Chr.* 25:6 hir. men for 100 *t. of s.*
27:5 Am. gave Joth. 100 *t. of s.*
36:3 condem. land in 100 *t. of s.*
*Ezr.* 7:22 I decr. it to 100 *t. of s.*
8:26 I weigh. to hand 650 *t. of s.*
*Est.* 3:9 will pay 10,000 *t. of s.*

**Vessels of SILVER.**

*Num.* 7:85 *s. v.* weigh. 2,400 she.
2 *Sam.* 8:10 Jor. brought *v. of s.*
1 *K.* 10:25 man his pres. *ves. of s.*
2 *K.* 12:13 not made *ves. of s.*
1 *Chr.* 18:10 all manner of *v. of s.* gold and brass, 2 *Chr.* 24:14
*Ezr.* 1:6 strength. with *v. of s.* 11
5:14 *v. of* gold and *s.* of house
8:26 I weighed *s. v.* hundred ta.
*Dan.* 5:2 bring golden and *s. v.*
11:8 carry their precious *v. of s.*

**SIMEON.**

*Gen.* 29:33 and called name S.
34:25 S. and Levi took each sw.
35:23 S. son of Leah, *Ex.* 1:2
42:24 Joseph took fr. them S. 36
43:23 he brought S. out unto
*Gen.* 46:10 sons of S. *Ex.* 6:15; *Num.* 1:22; 26:12; 1 *Chr.* 4:24, 42; 12:25
48:5 Reuben and S. they shall
49:5 S. and Levi are brethren
*Num.* 1:6 prince of S. 2:12; 7:36
*Deut.* 27:12 S. Levi, and Judah
*Jos.* 19:1 second lot came to S. 9
*Jud.* 1:3 S. went with Judah, 17
2 *Chr.* 15:9 the strange. out of S.
34:6 so did Josiah in S.
*Ezek.* 48:24 S. have a portion, 33
*Luke* 2:25 whose name was S. 34
3:30 Levi, which was son of S.
*Acts* 13:1 at Antioch S. that was
15:14 S. hath declared how God

**Tribe of SIMEON.**

*Num.* 1:23 *t. of* S. numb. 59,300
2:12 *t. of* S. sh. pitch by Reuben
10:19 over the host of *tribe of* S.
13:5 *t. of* S. Shaph. to spy land
34:20 *t. of* S. Shemuel to divide
*Jos.* 19:1 second lot for *tr. of* S.
8 the inheritance of *tribe of* S.
21:4 of *tr. of* S. 9; 1 *Chr.* 6:65
*Rev.* 7:7 of *t. of* S. sealed 12,000

**SIMILITUDE.**

*Num.* 12:8 *s.* of the Lord shall
*Deut.* 4:12 but saw no *s.* 15, 16
2 *Chr.* 4:3 under it was *s.* of oxen
*Ps.* 106:20 changed glory into *s.*
144:12 stones polished after *s.*
*Dan.* 10:16 one like *s.* of sons of
*Rom.* 5:14 after *s.* of Ad.'s trans.
*Heb.* 7:15 after *s.* of Melchisedek
*Jam.* 3:9 men made after *s.* of G.

**SIMILITUDES.**

*Hos.* 12:10 I have used *s.*

**SIMON.**

*Mat.* 10:4 S. Canaan. *Mark* 3:18
13:55 James, Jos. S. *Mark* 6:3
16:17 blessed art th. S. Bar-jona
17:25 what thinkest thou S.?
26:6 of S. the leper, *Mark* 14:3
27:32 man of Cyre. S. by name, *Mark* 15:21; *Luke* 23:26
*Mark* 1:29 house of S. *Luke* 4:38
14:37 S. sleepest thou? couldest
*Luke* 5:3 one of ships wh. was S.
4 he said unto S. Launch out
10 who were partners with S.
6:15 S. called Zelotes, *Acts* 1:13
7:40 S. I have somewhat to say
22:31 S. S. Satan hath desired to
24:34 risen, and appeared to S.
*John* 1:41 findeth his brother S.
42 Jesus said, Thou art S.
6:71 Ju. son of S. 12:4; 13:2, 26
21:15 S. son of Jo. lovest? 16, 17
*Acts* 8:9 man S. who beforetime
13 then S. himself believed also
9:43 Peter tarried many days at Joppa wi. one S. 10:6, 17, 32
*See* PETER.

**SIMPLE.**

*Ps.* 19:7 Lord maketh wise the *s.*
116:6 the Lord preserveth the *s.*
119:130 giv. understanding to *s.*
*Prov.* 1:4 to give subtilty to *s.*
22 how long, ye *s.* ones, will
32 turning away of *s.* shall slay
7:7 among *s.* ones a young man
8:5 O ye *s.* understand wisdom
9:4 whoso is *s.* let him turn, 16
13 a foolish woman is *s.*
14:15 *s.* believeth every word
18 *s.* inh. folly; 19:25 *s.* beware
21:11 punished, *s.* made wise
22:3 *s.* pass on are punish. 27:12
*Ezek.* 45:20 do for him that is *s.*
*Rom.* 16:18 fair speeches dec. *s.*
19 wise to good, *s.* concer. evil

**SIMPLICITY.**

2 *Sam.* 15:11 th. went in their *s.*
*Prov.* 1:22 how lo. wi. ye love *s.*?
2 *Cor.* 1:12 in *s.* had conversation
11:3 corrupted from *s.* in Christ

**SIN.**

*Ex.* 16:1 I came to wildern. of S.
17:1 journey. fr. S. *Num.* 33:12
*Ezek.* 30:15 pour my fury up. S.
16 S. shall have great pain

**SIN.**

*Gen.* 4:7 not well, *s.* lie. at door
*Ex.* 34:7 forgiv. iniquity, and *s.*
*Lev.* 4:3 if priest *s.* accord. to *s.*
14 wh. *s.* is known, cong. offer
6:26 priest offereth it for *s.* 9:15
19:17 not suffer *s.* on neighbor
*Num.* 5:6 when man or wom. *s.*
12:11 I beseech, lay not *s.* upon
19:9 it is a purification for *s.* 17
27:3 father died in his own *s.*
*Deut.* 15:9 cry to L. it be *s.* 24:15
19:15 witness sh. not rise for *s.*
*Deut.* 21:22 if a man have com. *s.*
22:26 in damsel no *s.* wor. death
23:21 it would be *s.* in thee
24:16 put to death for his own *s.* 2 *K.* 14:6; 2 *Chr.* 25:4
1 *Sam.* 15:23 rebel. as *s.* of witch.
1 *K.* 8:34 forgive *s.* of thy people
36 forgive the *s.* of thy servants, 2 *Chr.* 6:25, 27
12:30 this thing bec. a *s.* 13:34
2 *K.* 12:16 *s.* money was priests'
*Job* 20:11 his bones are full of *s.*
*Ps.* 32:1 blessed whose *s.* cover.
51:5 in *s.* did mother con. me
59:12 for *s.* of their mouth
109:7 let his prayer become *s.*
14 let not *s.* of mother be blot.
*Prov.* 10:16 wicked tendeth to *s.*
19 in words there want. not *s.*
14:9 fools make a mock at *s.*
34 *s.* is a reproach to any peo.
21:4 plowing of wicked is *s.*
24:9 thought of foolishness is *s.*
*Is.* 5:18 woe to th. who draw *s.*
30:1 that they may add *s.* to *s.*
31:7 idols your hands ma. for *s.*
53:10 make soul an offer. for *s.*
12 he bare *s.* of many
*Jer.* 17:1 *s.* of Ju. writ. with pen
3 I will give high place for *s.*
51:5 th. land was filled with *s.*
*Lam.* 4:6 punishm. of *s.* of Sod.
*Hos.* 4:8 eat up *s.* of people
10:8 *s.* of Is. shall be destroyed
12:8 no iniq. in me that were *s.*
*Amos* 8:14 sw. by *s.* of Samaria
*Mic.* 1:13 beginning of *s.* to Zion
6:7 fruit of body for *s.* of soul
*Zec.* 13:1 a fount. opened for *s.*
*Mat.* 12:31 all *s.* sh. be forgiven
*John* 1:29 tak. away *s.* of world
8:7 that is without *s.* am. you
34 whoso commit. *s.* serv. of *s.*
9:41 if blind, should have no *s.*
15:22 not come, had not *s.* 24
16:8 Comfor. will reprove of *s.* 9
19:11 deliv. me hath greater *s.*
*Acts* 7:60 lay not *s.* to th. charge
*Rom.* 3:9 J. and Gentil. under *s.*
20 by law is knowledge of *s.*
4:7 blessed whose *s.* is covered
5:12 *s.* ent. world, death by *s.*
13 till the law *s.* was in world
20 where *s.* abounded, grace
21 as *s.* reigned unto death
6:1 shall we continue in *s.*?
2 sh. we th. are dead to *s.* live?
7 he that is dead is freed fr. *s.*
10 he died, he died to *s.* once
11 reck. yourselves dead to *s.*
12 let not *s.* reign in yo. body
13 nor yield your memb. to *s.*
14 *s.* shall not have dominion
16 serv. ye are, whether of *s.*
17 G. thanked, were serv. of *s.*
18 being made free from *s.* 22
20 wh. ye were servants of *s.*
23 for the wages of *s.* is death
7:7 is law *s.*? G. forbid; kn. *s.*
8 *s.* tak. occasion wro. in me; without law *s.* is dead
9 commandm. came, *s.* revived
11 *s.* by commandm. slew me
17 *s.* that dwelleth in me, 20
23 bring. me into captiv. to *s.*
25 but with flesh, the law of *s.*
8:3 *s.* condemned *s.* in the flesh
10 body dead because of *s.*
14:23 whats. is not of faith is *s.*
1 *Cor.* 6:18 every *s.* a man doeth
15:56 the sting of death is *s.* and the strength of *s.* is the law
2 *Cor.* 5:21 made him be *s.* for us
*Gal.* 2:17 Ch. the minister of *s.*?
3:22 scrip. conclu. all under *s.*
2 *Thes.* 2:3 man of *s.* be revealed
*Heb.* 3:13 be hardened through *s.*
4:15 tempted, yet without *s.*
9:26 he appeared to put away *s.*
28 appear without *s.* to salvat.
10:6 in sacrifices for *s.* no pleas.
8 off. for *s.* thou wouldest not
18 remission, no offering for *s.*
11:25 enjoy the pleasures of *s.*
12:1 lay aside *s.* doth beset us
4 not resisted, striv. against *s.*
13:11 bod. of beasts for *s.* burnt
*Jam.* 1:15 it bring. forth *s.* and *s.* when finished, bring. death
2:9 if have respect to per. ye *s.*
4:17 not good, to him it is *s.*
1 *Pet.* 2:22 did no *s.* nor guile
4:1 suff. in flesh, ceased from *s.*
2 *Pet.* 2:14 eyes can. cease fr. *s.*
1 *John* 1:7 the blood of Jesus Christ his Son cleanseth us from all *s.*
8 say, We have no *s.* we dece.
1 *John* 3:4 whoso comm. *s.* transgresseth; *s.* is transgression
5 manifested, in him is no *s.*
8 committeth *s.* is of the devil
9 born of G. doth not commit *s.*

5:16 *s.* wh. is not to death, *s.*
17 all unrighteousn. is *s.* and there is a *s.* not unto death
*See* BEAR.

**Great SIN.**

*Gen.* 20:9 brought on me *great s.*
*Ex.* 32:21 bro. *g. s.* on them
30 M. said, Ye sinned a *g. s.* 31
1 *Sam.* 2:17 *s.* of young men *g.*
2 *K.* 17:21 Jeroboam made them sin a *great s.*

**His SIN.**

*Lev.* 4:3 bring for *his s.* a bullock
23 if *h. s.* come to knowl. 28
5:6 bring trespass-offer. for *h. s.*
1 *K.* 15:26 Nadab walked in *h. s.*
34 Baa. walked in way of *h. s.*
16:19 Zimri walked in *his s.*
26 Omri in *his s.*
2 *K.* 21:16 beside *h. s.* wherewith made Judah
17 acts of Manasseh, and *h. s.*
2 *Chr.* 33:19 all *h. s.* bef. humbl.
*Job* 34:37 addeth rebellion to *h. s.*
*Is.* 27:9 fruit to take away *his s.*
*Ezek.* 3:20 shall die in *h. s.* 18:24
33:14 if he turn from *his s.*
*Hos.* 13:12 bound up, *h. s.* is hid
*Mic.* 3:8 full to declare to Is. *h. s.*

**My SIN.**

*Gen.* 31:36 what is *my s.* that th.
*Ex.* 10:17 forg. *my s.* this once
1 *Sam.* 15:25 I pray, pardon *my s.*
20:1 what *my s.* bef. thy father
1 *K.* 17:18 to call *my s.* to rem.
*Job* 10:6 thou search. after *my s.*
13:23 make me to know *my s.*
14:16 dost thou not watch *my s.*
35:3 if I be cleansed from *my s.*
*Ps.* 32:5 I acknowledged *my s.* and thou forgavest *my s.*
38:3 nor rest because of *my s.*
18 iniqu. I be sorry for *my s.*
51:2 cleanse me from *my s.*
3 *my s.* bef. 59:3 not for *my s.*
*Prov.* 20:9 I am pure from *my s.*
*Dan.* 9:20 I was confessing *my s.*
*See* OFFERING.

**Our SIN.**

*Ex.* 34:9 pardon iniq. and *our s.*
*Jer.* 16:10 what *o. s.* we commit.

**Their SIN.**

*Gen.* 18:20 because *t. s.* is griev.
50:17 forgive *their s.* 2 *Chr.* 7:14
*Ex.* 32:32 if thou forgive *their s.*
34 when I visit, I will visit *t. s.*
*Num.* 5:7 they shall confess *t. s.*
*Deut.* 9:27 stubbornness, nor *t. s.*
1 *K.* 8:35 if they turn from *their s.* 2 *Chr.* 6:26
*Neh.* 4:5 let not *t. s.* be blotted
*Ps.* 85:2 thou hast covered *t. s.*
*Is.* 3:9 they declare *t. s.* as Sod.
*Jer.* 16:18 recompense *t. s.* doub.
18:23 neither blot out *their s.*
31:34 rememb. *their s.* no more
36:3 that I may forgive *their s.*
*John* 15:22 have no cloak for *t. s.*

**Thy SIN.**

2 *Sam.* 12:13 Lord put away *t. s.*
*Is.* 6:7 taken away, *t. s.* purged

**Your SIN.**

*Ex.* 32:30 atonement for *your s.*
*Num.* 32:23 *y. s.* wi. find you out
*Deut.* 9:21 I took *y. s.* the calf
*John* 9:41 theref. *y. s.* remaineth

**SIN, Verb.**

*Gen.* 39:9 do this, and *s.* ag. G.?
42:22 do not *s.* ag. the child
*Ex.* 20:20 fear, that thou *s.* not
23:33 lest make thee *s.* ag. me
*Lev.* 4:2 if soul *s.* thro' ignorance
3 if priest *s.* 13 if congregat. *s.*
27 if people *s.* thro' ignorance
5:1 if a soul *s.* and hear swear.
6:2 if a soul *s.* lie unto neighbor
*Num.* 16:22 *s.* wroth with all?
*Deut.* 20:18 should you *s.* ag. L.
24:4 shalt not cause land to *s.*
1 *Sam.* 2:25 if one man *s.* against another; *s.* against the Lord
12:23 God forbid I should *s.*
14:33 people *s.* against Lord
34 *s.* not in eating with blood
19:4 let not king *s.* ag. servant
5 why *s.* ag. innocent blood?
1 *K.* 8:46 if they shall *s.* against thee, 2 *Chr.* 6:36
2 *K.* 21:11 Man. made Judah *s.*
2 *Chr.* 6:22 if man *s.* ag. neighbor
*Neh.* 6:13 and do so, and *s.*
13:26 did not Solo. *s.* by these
*Job* 2:10 did not J. *s.* wi. his lips
5:24 visit habitation, and not *s.*
10:14 if I *s.* thou markest me
31:30 nei. suffered mouth to *s.*
*Ps.* 4:4 stand in awe, and *s.* not
39:1 take heed I *s.* not
119:11 I might not *s.* ag. thee
*Ec.* 5:6 mouth cause flesh to *s.*
*Jer.* 32:35 do this to cau. J. to *s.*
*Ezek.* 3:21 rig. *s.* not, doth not *s.*
*Hos.* 8:11 Ephraim hath made altars to *s.* altars to him to *s.*
13:2 now they *s.* more and more
*Mat.* 18:21 L. how oft brot. *s.*?
*John* 5:14 *s.* no more, lest worse
8:11 nei. do I cond. *s.* no more
9:2 who did *s.* man or parents?
*Rom.* 6:15 *s.* bec. not under law?
1 *Cor.* 8:12 *s.* ag. breth. *s.* ag. C.
15:34 awake to righteous. *s.* not
*Eph.* 4:26 be ye angry and *s.* not
1 *Tim.* 5:20 them that *s.* rebuke
*Heb.* 10:26 if we *s.* wilfully after
1 *John* 2:1 I write unto you that ye *s.* not, and if any man *s.*
3:9 can. *s.* bec. he is born of G.
5:16 any man see his brother *s.*
*See* ISRAEL.

**SINAI.**

*Deut.* 33:2 Lord came from S.
*Jud.* 5:5 melted, even that S.
*Ps.* 68:8 S. moved at presence
17 Lord is among th. as in S.
*See* MOUNT.

**SINCERE.**

*Phil.* 1:10 be *s.* till day of Ch.
1 *Pet.* 2:2 as babes desire *s.* milk

**SINCERELY.**

*Jud.* 9:16 if ye have done *s.* 19
*Phil.* 1:16 one preach Ch. not *s.*

**SINCERITY.**

*Jos.* 24:14 serve the Lord in *s.*
1 *Cor.* 5:8 unleavened bread of *s.*
2 *Cor.* 1:12 in godly *s.* we have
2:17 as of *s.* in the sight of God
8:8 to prove the *s.* of your love
*Eph.* 6:24 that love Lord J. in *s.*
*Tit.* 2:7 in doc. show. gravity, *s.*

**SINEW.**

*Gen.* 32:32 Israel eat not of the *s.* touched J. in *s.* that shrank
*Is.* 48:4 thy neck is an iron *s.*

**SINEWS.**

*Job* 10:11 with bones and *s.*
30:17 bones are pierced, *s.* take
40:17 *s.* of his stones are wrap.
*Ezek.* 37:6 I will lay *s.* upon you
6 the *s.* and flesh came upon

**SINFUL.**

*Num.* 32:14 increase of *s.* men
*Is.* 1:4 ah *s.* nation, a peo. laden
*Amos* 9:8 eyes of L. on *s.* kingd.
*Mark* 8:38 ashamed in *s.* genera.
*Luke* 5:8 for I am a *s.* man, O L.
24:7 deliv. into hands of *s.* men
*Rom.* 7:13 sin bec. exceeding *s.*
8:3 send. S. in liken. of *s.* flesh

**SING.**

*Ex.* 15:21 *s.* to the Lord, 1 *Chr.* 16:23; *Ps.* 30:4; 95:1; 96:1, 2; 98:1; 147:7; 149:1; *Is.* 12:5
32:18 noise of them that *s.*
*Num.* 21:17 spring up, O well, *s.*
1 *Sam.* 21:11 did they not *s.* one
1 *Chr.* 16:9 *s.* unto him, *s.* psalms
33 the trees of the wood *s.* out
2 *Chr.* 20:22 they began to *s.* and
29:30 Hez. command. Lev. to *s.*
*Job* 29:13 I caused wid. heart *s.*
*Ps.* 21:13 so will we *s.* praise
33:2 praise the Lord, *s.* to him
3 *s.* to him a new so. *Is.* 42:10
51:14 *s.* of thy righteousn. 145:7
65:13 valleys shout, they also *s.*
66:2 *s.* forth honor of his name
4 earth *s.* to thee, they shall *s.*
67:4 let nations be glad and *s.*
68:32 *s.* to God, ye kingdoms
71:22 to thee will I *s.* 98:5
81:1 *s.* aloud to G. our strength
104:12 fowls *s.* among branches
105:2 *s.* to him, *s.* psal. unto him
137:3 *s.* us one of the songs of Z.
4 how shall we *s.* L. song in?
138:5 they shall *s.* in ways of L.
149:5 *s.* aloud upon their beds
*Prov.* 29:6 righteous *s.* and rej.
*Is.* 23:15 after 70 years sh. T. *s.*
24:14 they shall *s.* for maj. of L.
26:19 *s.* ye that dwell in dust
27:2 in that day *s.* ye to her
35:6 then sh. tongue of dumb *s.*
*Is.* 38:20 we will *s.* my songs
42:11 let inhabitants of rock *s.*
44:23 *s.* O ye heav. for L. 49:13
52:8 with the voice shall they *s.*
9 *s.* to the L. ye waste places
54:1 *s.* O barren, didst not bear
65:14 my servants sh. *s.* for joy
*Jer.* 31:7 *s.* with gladness for Ja.
12 they shall *s.* in height of Z.
51:48 all that is therein shall *s.*
*Ezek.* 27:25 ships of Tarsh. did *s.*
*Hos.* 2:15 sh. *s.* in days of youth
*Zep.* 2:14 their voice shall *s.*
3:14 *s.* daugh. of Zion, *Zec.* 2:10
*Jam.* 5:13 any merry? let him *s.*
*Rev.* 15:3 they *s.* song of Moses

**I will SING.**

*Ex.* 15:1 *I will s.* to the Lord, *Jud.* 5:3; *Ps.* 13:6
*Ps.* 57:7 fixed, O God, *I will s.*
9 *I will s.* to thee am. nations
59:16 *I w. s.* of thy power, 89:1
17 unto thee, O my stre. *w. I s.*
101:1 *I will s.* of mercy and jud.
104:33 *I will s.* to the L. as long
144:9 *I will s.* a new song
*Is.* 5:1 now *will I s.* to well-belo.
*Rom.* 15:9 for this cause *will I s.*
1 *Cor.* 14:15 *I will s.* with the sp. *I will s.* with understanding
*See* PRAISE, PRAISES.

**SINGED.**

*Dan.* 3:27 nor w. hair of head *s.*

**SINGER.**

1 *Chr.* 6:33 Heman a *s.* son of J.
*Hab.* 3:19 to chief *s.* on instrum.

**SINGERS.**

1 *K.* 10:12 made psalteries for *s.* 2 *Chr.* 9:11
1 *Chr.* 9:33 these are the *s.* 15:16
15:19 *s.* were appoint. to sound
27 Levites and *s.* had fine lin.
2 *Chr.* 5:13 trumpet. and *s.* were
20:21 Jehoshaphat appointed *s.*
23:13 peo. rejoiced also *s.* 29:28
35:15 the *s.* the sons of Asaph
*Ezr.* 2:41 *s.* childr. of Asaph 128
70 *s.* dwelt in cities, *Neh.* 7:73
7:7 some *s.* went up to Jerusa.

*Neh.* 7:1 the *s.* were appointed
10:29 the *s.* clave to their bret.
11:22 *s.* were over bus. of house
23 portion for *s.* 12:47; 13:5
12:28 sons of *s.* gathered thems.
29 the *s.* builded them villages
42 *s.* sang; 45 *s.* kept ward of G.
46 in days of Da. there were *s.*
13:10 Levites and *s.* were fled
*Ps.* 68:25 *s.* went before
87:7 as well *s.* as players
*Ezek.* 40:44 chamb. of *s.* in court

**Men-SINGERS, women-SINGERS.**

*Ec.* 2:8 I gat *men-s.* and *wo.-s.*

**SINGETH.**

*Prov.* 25:20 so is he that *s.* songs

**SINGING.**

1 *Sam.* 18:6 wo. came out of Is. *s.*
1 *Chr.* 6:32 ministered with *s.*
13:8 Dav. and Is. played with *s.*
2 *Chr.* 23:18 offer burnt-off. wi. *s.*
30:21 *s.* with loud instru. to L.
*Neh.* 12:27 kept dedication wi. *s.*
*Ps.* 100:2 bef. presence with *s.*
126:2 our tongue filled with *s.*
*Cant.* 2:12 time of the *s.* of birds
*Is.* 14:7 they break forth into *s.*
16:10 in vineyards shall be no *s.*
35:2 sh. blossom with joy and *s.*
44:23 break into *s.* ye mount.
48:20 flee from Chaldeans wi. *s.*
49:13 break forth into *s.*
51:11 redeemed sh. come wi. *s.*
54:1 break forth into *s.* O bar.
55:12 mount. shall break into *s.*
*Zep.* 3:17 joy over thee with *s.*
*Eph.* 5:19 *s.* in y. heart, *Col.* 3:16

**SINGING-MEN, SINGING-WOMEN.**

2 *Sam.* 19:35 I hear *s.-m. s.-w.*
2 *Chr.* 35:25 the *s.-m.* spake of J.
*Ezr.* 2:65 200 *s.-m.* 200 *s.-women*
*Neh.* 7:67 245 *s.-m.* and *s.-women*

**SINGLE.**

*Mat.* 6:22 if eye *s.* whole body
full of light, *Luke* 11:34

**SINGLENESS.**

*Acts* 2:46 eat meat wi. *s.* of heart
*Eph.* 6:5 in *s.* of heart, *Col.* 3:22

**SINGULAR.**

*Lev.* 27:2 man shall make *s.* vow

**SINK.**

*Ps.* 69:2 I *s.* in deep mire where
*Jer.* 51:64 Baby. *s.* and not rise
*Mat.* 14:30 beginning to *s.* cried
*Luke* 5:7 so that they began to *s.*
9:44 sayings *s.* into your ears

**SINNED.**

*Ex.* 9:34 Pharaoh *s.* yet more
32:30 ye have *s.* a great sin, 31
33 whosoever hath *s.* him will
*Lev.* 4:3 for sin he hath *s.* a bul.
22 ruler *s.* 23; 28 one of peo. *s.*
5:5 confess he hath *s.*
6:4 bec. he hath *s.* shall restore
*Num.* 12:11 lay not *s.* wher. we *s.*
32:23 ye have *s.* against the L.
*Deut.* 9:16 behold, ye had *s.* ag. L.
18 your sins wh. ye *s.* in doing
*Jos.* 7:11 Isr. hath *s.* and trangr.
*Jud.* 11:27 I have not *s.* ag. thee
1 *Sam.* 19:4 he hath not *s.* ag th.
24:11 I have not *s.* against thee
1 *K.* 8:33 they have *s.* against
thee, 35; 2 *Chr.* 6:24, 26
50 forgive peo. th. *s.* 2 *Chr.* 6:39
15:30 Jer. which he *s.* 16:13, 19
18:9 what have I *s.* that thou
2 *K.* 17:7 Israel had *s.* against L.
21:17 sin th. Manas. *s.* is writ.
*Neh.* 9:29 *s.* against thy judgm.
*Job* 1:5 Job said, My sons ha. *s.*
22 in this J. *s.* not, nor charg.
8:4 if chil. have *s.* against him
24:19 so doth grave who have *s.*
*Ps.* 78:17 they *s.* yet more, 32
*Is.* 43:27 thy first father hath *s.*
*Jer.* 2:35 sayest, I have not *s.*
40:3 because ye have *s.* 44:23
50:14 Babylon hath *s.* ag. Lord
*Lam.* 1:8 Jer. hath grievously *s.*
5:7 fathers have *s.* and are not
*Ezek.* 18:24 sin he hath *s.* in th.
28:16 violence, and thou hast *s.*
37:23 dwelling-p. wherein th. *s.*
*Hos.* 4:7 as they increased they *s.*
10:9 thou hast *s.* fr. days of G.
*Hab.* 2:10 thou hast *s.* ag. soul
*John* 9:3 neither this man *s.* nor
*Rom.* 2:12 as have *s.* with. law,
as have *s.* in the law
3:23 all have *s.* and come. 5:12
5:14 death over them had not *s.*
16 not as it was by one that *s.*
1 *Cor.* 7:28 if marry, hast not *s.*
2 *Cor.* 12:21 I bewail many that *s.*
13:2 I write to them wh. have *s.*
*Heb.* 3:17 was it not wi. them *s.?*
2 *Pet.* 2:4 G. spared not angels *s.*
1 *John* 1:10 if say, We have not *s.*

**I have SINNED.**

*Ex.* 9:27 Phar. said, *I h. s.* 10:16
*Num.* 22:34 Balaam said, *I h. s.*
*Jos.* 7:20 indeed, *I h. s.* ag. God
1 *Sam.* 15:24 Saul said, *I have s.*
30; 26:21
2 *Sam.* 12:13 Da. said to Na. *I h. s.* 24:10, 17; 1 *Chr.* 21:8, 17
19:20 thy serv. doth know *I h. s.*
*Job* 7:20 *I h. s.* 33:27 say, *I h. s.*
*Ps.* 41:4 heal my soul, *I have s.*
51:4 against thee only *have I s.*
*Mic.* 7:9 *I have s.* against him
*Mat.* 27:4 Judas said, *I have s.*
*Luke* 15:18 prodi. said, *I h. s.* 21

**We have SINNED.**

*Num.* 12:11 sin, wherein *we h. s.*
14:40 for *we have s.* *Deut.* 1:41
21:7 *we h. s.* have spoken ag. L.
*Jud.* 10:10 *we h. s.* bec. we have
forsaken God, 1 *Sam.* 12:10
15 *we h. s.* do what seem. good
1 *Sam.* 7:6 and said, *we have s.*
1 *K.* 8:47 *we h. s.* done perversely
2 *Chr.* 6:37 *we h. s.* done amiss
*Neh.* 1:6 confess sins *we have s.*
*Ps.* 106:6 *we h. s.* with our fath.
*Is.* 42:24 L. ag. whom *we have s.*
64:5 thou art wroth, for *we h. s.*
*Jer.* 3:25 lie down in sh. *we h. s.*
8:14 given us gall, for *we h. s.*
14:20 acknow. wick. *we have s.*
*Dan.* 9:5 *we h. s.* committed ini.
15 *we have s.* done wickedly

**SINNER.**

*Prov.* 11:31 more wicked and *s.*
13:6 wickedn. overthroweth *s.*
22 wealth of *s.* laid up for just
*Ec.* 2:26 the *s.* he giveth travail
7:26 *s.* shall be taken by her
8:12 thro' *s.* do evil 100 times
9:2 so is *s.* and he that sweareth
18 one *s.* destroy. much good
*Is.* 65:20 *s.* being 100 years old
*Lu.* 7:37 wo. in city who was *s.*
15:7 joy in heaven over one *s.*
18:13 G. be merciful to me a *s.*
19:7 guest with man a *s.*
*John* 9:16 can *s.* do miracles?
*John* 9:24 gi. G. praise, man is *s.*
25 whe. he be a *s.* I know not
*Rom.* 3:7 yet judged as a *s.?*
*Jam.* 5:20 convert. *s.* save a soul
1 *Pet.* 4:18 where ungodly *s.* ap.

**SINNERS.**

*Gen.* 13:13 men of Sod. were *s.*
1 *Sam.* 15:18 utterly destroy *s.*
*Ps.* 1:1 stand. not in way of *s.*
5 nor *s.* in congre. of righteous
25:8 theref. will he teach *s.* way
26:9 gather not my soul with *s.*
51:13 *s.* sh. be converted to thee
104:35 let the *s.* be consumed
*Prov.* 1:10 if *s.* ent. consent not
13:21 evil pursueth *s.* to right.
23:17 let not thy heart envy *s.*
*Is.* 1:28 destr. of *s.* be together
13:9 destroy *s.* thereof out of it
33:14 the *s.* in Z. are afraid
*Amos* 9:10 *s.* shall die by sword
*Mat.* 9:10 many *s.* sat at meat
with Jesus, *Mark* 2:15
13 call right. but *s.* to repentance, *Mark* 2:17; *Luke* 5:32
11:19 fri. of pub. and *s.* *Lu.* 7:34
*Luke* 6:32 *s.* love those love them
33 what tha. ha. ye? *s.* do same
34 *s.* lend to *s.* to receive again
13:2 suppose th. these were *s.* 4
15:1 publicans and *s.* to hear
*John* 9:31 kn. G. heareth not *s.*
*Rom.* 5:8 wh. we were *s.* C. died
*Gal.* 2:15 Jews, not *s.* of Gentiles
17 if we ourselves are found *s.*
1 *Tim.* 1:9 the law is made for *s.*
15 Ch. Jesus came to save *s.*
*Jam.* 4:8 ye *s.* purify hearts
*Jude* 15 speeches *s.* have spoken

**SINNEST.**

*Job* 35:6 if thou *s.* what do. thou

**SINNETH.**

*Num.* 15:28 soul that *s.* ignoran.
29 law for him *s.* thro' ignor.
*Deut.* 19:15 not rise in sin he *s.*
1 *K.* 8:46 is no man that *s.* not
2 *Chr.* 6:36; *Ec.* 7:20
*Prov.* 8:36 he that *s.* wrong. soul
14:21 that despiseth neighbor *s.*
19:2 that hasteth with feet *s.*
20:2 whoso provoketh a king *s.*
*Ezek.* 14:13 wh. land *s.* I stretch
18:4 soul that *s.* it shall die, 20
33:12 for righteous. in day he *s.*
1 *Cor.* 6:18 fornicator *s.* ag. body
7:36 do what he will, *s.* not
*Tit.* 3:11 such is subverted and *s.*
1 *John* 3:6 whoso. abid. in him *s.*
not, whoso. *s.* hath not seen
8 devil *s.* from the beginning
5:18 whoso. is born of G. *s.* not

**SINNING.**

*Gen.* 20:6 I withheld thee fr. *s.*
*Lev.* 6:3 man does, *s.* therein

**SINS.**

1 *K.* 14:16 give Is. up bec. of *s.*
15:3 Abij. walked in *s.* of Reho.
30 smote N. bec. of *s.* of Jero.
16:13 *s.* of Baasha, and *s.* of El.
31 light thing to wa. in *s.* of J.
2 *K.* 3:3 Jeho. cleaved to *s.* of J.
10:29 from *s.* of Jeroboam Jehu
13:6 Is. departed not fr. *s.* of J.
17:22 Is. walked in *s.* of Jerob.
24:3 remove Ju. for *s.* of Mana.
2 *Chr.* 28:10 are th. not wi. y. *s.?*
*Neh.* 1:6 confess the *s.* of Israel
*Job* 13:23 how many are my *s.?*
*Ps.* 19:13 keep thy servant fr. *s.*
25:7 remem. not *s.* of my youth
*Prov.* 5:22 hold. with cords of *s.*
10:12 strifes, love covereth all *s.*
28:13 that covereth *s.* not prosp.
*Is.* 40:2 received double for her *s.*
43:24 ma. me to serve wi. thy *s.*
25 blot out, not remem. thy *s.*
44:22 blot. out as a cloud thy *s.*
*Jer.* 15:13 I give to spoil for *s.*
30:14 bec. thy *s.* increased, 15
50:20 *s.* of Judah sought
*Lam.* 3:39 for punishm. of his *s.*
4:13 *s.* of her proph. and priests
22 Edom, he will discov. thy *s.*
*Ezek.* 16:51 S. committed thy *s.*
52 bear thine own shame for *s.*
18:14 that seeth his father's *s.*
21 if wicked turn from his *s.*

23:49 shall bear *s.* of your idols
33:16 none of his *s.* be mention.
*Dan.* 9:24 make end of *s.*
*Mic.* 1:5 for *s.* of house of Israel
6:13 making desol. bec. of thy *s.*
*Mat.* 26:28 shed for remissi. of *s.*
*Luke* 24:47 remis. of *s.* preached
*John* 9:34 altogether born in *s.*
20:23 *s.* ye remit, whose *s.* reta.
*Acts* 22:16 wash away thy *s.*
*Rom.* 7:5 *s.* did work in members
*Eph.* 2:1 who were dead in *s.* 5
*Col.* 2:11 putti. off the body of *s.*
1 *Tim.* 5:22 partakers of men's *s.*
24 men's *s.* opened beforehand
*Heb.* 2:17 reconcilia. for *s.* of pe.
5:1 gifts and sacrifices for *s.*
7:27 for his own *s.* for people's
9:28 Ch. off. to bear *s.* of many
10:4 blood of goats take away *s.*
12 offered one sacrifice for *s.*
*Jam.* 5:20 and hide multit. of *s.*
1 *Pet.* 2:24 dead to *s.* live to righ.
3:18 Christ once suffered for *s.*
4:8 charity cover multitude of *s.*
2 *Pet.* 1:9 was purged from his *s.*
1 *John* 2:2 the *s.* of whole world
*Rev.* 18:4 be not partak. of her *s.*
5 her *s.* have reach. unto heav.

*See* FORGIVE, FORGIVEN.

**My SINS.**

*Ps.* 51:9 hide thy face from *my s.*
69:5 O G. *my s.* not hid fr. thee
*Is.* 38:17 cast *my s.* behind back

**Our SINS.**

1 *Sam.* 12:19 added to *our s.*
2 *Chr.* 28:13 int. to add to *our s.*
*Neh.* 9:37 ki. over us bec. of *o. s.*
*Ps.* 79:9 purge away *our s.*
90:8 *o.s.* in light of countenance
103:10 not dealt accord. to *o. s.*
*Is.* 59:12 *our s.* testify against us
*Ezek.* 33:10 if *our s.* be on us
*Dan.* 9:16 bec. of *o. s.* peo. beco.
1 *Cor.* 15:3 Christ died for *our s.*
*Gal.* 1:4 gave himself for *our s.*
*Heb.* 1:3 himself purged *our s.*
1 *Pet.* 2:24 his own self bare *o. s.*
1 *John* 1:9 if we confess *our s.*
3:5 manifest. to take away *o. s.*
*Rev.* 1:5 washed us from *our s.*

**Their SINS.**

*Lev.* 16:16 transgression in *th. s.*
*Num.* 16:26 consumed in all *t. s.*
1 *K.* 14:22 provoked with *their s.*
16:2 prov. me to anger with *t. s.*
*Neh.* 9:2 Israel confessed *their s.*
*Is.* 58:1 show house of Jacob *t. s.*
*Jer.* 14:10 vis. *t. s.* *Hos.* 8:13; 9:9
*Mic.* 7:19 cast all *t. s.* into sea
*Mat.* 1:21 save his peo. from *t. s.*
3:6 bapt. confes. *t. s.* *Mark* 1:5
*Mark* 4:12 *t. s.* should be forgiv.
*Luke* 1:77 salva. by remis. of *t. s.*
*Rom.* 11:27 shall take away *t. s.*
1 *Thes.* 2:16 to fill up *t. s.* alway
*Heb.* 8:12 I w. be merciful to *t. s.*
10:17 *th. s.* remember no more

**Your SINS.**

*Lev.* 16:30 may be clean fr. *y. s.*
26:18 punish you for *y. s.* 24, 28
*Deut.* 9:18 nor drink, bec. of *y. s.*
*Jos.* 24:19 G. will not forgi. *y. s.*
*Is.* 1:18 tho' *your s.* be as scarlet
59:2 *your s.* have hid his face
*Jer.* 5:25 *y. s.* withholden good
*Ezek.* 21:24 in doings *y. s.* appe.
*Amos* 5:12 know *y.* trans. and *s.*
*John* 8:21 seek me, die in *y. s.* 24
*Acts* 3:19 repent, that *y. s.* may
1 *Cor.* 15:17 raised, ye are in *y. s.*
*Col.* 2:13 you being dead in *y. s.*
1 *John* 2:12 *y. s.* are forgiven you

SION. *Deut.* 4:48
*See* ZION.

**SIR, S.**

*Gen.* 43:20 *s.* we ca. to buy food
*Mat.* 21:30 I go *s.* and went not
*John* 4:11 *s.* thou hast nothi. to
49 *s.* come ere my child die
5:7 *s.* I ha. no man to put me in
12:21 saying, *s.* we would see J.
*Acts* 7:26 *s.* ye are brethren, why
16:30 *s.* wh. mu. I do to be sa.?
27:25 where. *s.* be of good cheer
*Rev.* 7:14 said to him, *s.* th. kno.

**SIRION.**

*Deut.* 3:9 which Sidonians call S.
*Ps.* 29:6 Lebanon and S. like a

**SISERA.**

*Jud.* 4:2 captain of host was S.
17 S. fled away on his feet, 22
5:20 the stars fought against S.
26 with hammer she smote S.
28 the mother of S. looked out
1 *Sam.* 12:9 sold into hand of S.
*Ezr.* 2:53 children of S. Nethi-
nim went up, *Neh.* 7:55
*Ps.* 83:9 do unto them as to S.

**SISTER.**

*Gen.* 24:60 our *s.* be thou mother
34:13 defiled Dinah their *s.* 27
31 deal with our *s.* as a harlot?
*Ex.* 2:4 his *s.* stood afar off
*Lev.* 18:9 shalt not uncover *s.*
11 thy *s.* 18 a wife to her *s.*
20:17 if a man take *s.* see nake.
21:3 his *s.* a virgin, be defiled
*Num.* 6:7 not defiled for his *s.*
*Deut.* 27:22 curs. that lieth wi. *s.*
*Jud.* 15:2 youn. *s.* fairer th. she?
2 *Sam.* 13:1 Ab. had fair *s.* Tamar
22 had forced his *s.* Tamar, 32
*Cant.* 8:8 lit. *s.* hath no breasts
*Jer.* 3:7 treacherous *s.* Ju. saw it
8 *s.* feared not; 10 *s.* not turn.
22:18 lament, saying, Ah, my *s.*
*Ezek.* 16:45 thou art *s.* of sisters
46 elder *s.* Samaria, youn. *s.* S.
48 So. thy *s.* not done as thou
22:11 ano. hath humbled his *s.*
23:4 Ah. elder, Aholibah her *s.*
18 mind was alienated from *s.*
31 thou walk. in way of thy *s.*
32 drink of thy *s.* cup deep, 33
44:25 *s.* that hath no hus. defile
*Mat.* 12:50 same is brother, *s.*
*Luke* 10:39 had a *s.* *John* 11:1, 5
*John* 19:25 stood by cross m.'s *s.*
*Acts* 23:16 Paul's *s.* son heard of
*Rom.* 16:1 Phebe our *s.* servant
1 *Cor.* 7:15 *s.* is not under bond.
9:5 we not power to lead a *s.*?
*Col.* 4:10 Marcus *s.* son to Barna.
*Jam.* 2:15 if a bro. or *s.* be naked
2 *John* 13 children of thy elect *s.*

**SISTER-IN-LAW.**

*Ruth* 1:15 *s.-i.-l.* is gone back

**My SISTER.**

*Gen.* 12:13 say, thou art *my s.*
19 why saidst thou, She is *my*
*s.* 20:2, 5, 12; 26:7, 9
30:8 I have wrestled with *my s.*
2 *Sam.* 13:5 let *my s.* Ta. come, 6
20 hold thou thy peace, *my s.*
*Job* 17:14 said to worm, art *my s.*
*Prov.* 7:4 thou art *my s.*
*Cant.* 4:9 ravi. my heart, *my s.*
10 how fair is thy love, *my s.*
5:1 am come into my gar. *my s.*
2 open to me, *my s.* my love
*Mark* 3:35 same my bro. *my s.*
*Luke* 10:40 do. th. not care *my s.*?

**SISTERS.**

*Jos.* 2:13 swe. ye will save my *s.*
*Job* 1:4 called for three *s.* to eat
42:11 came his brethren and *s.*
*Ezek.* 16:45 th. art sister of thy *s.*
51 thou hast justified thy *s.* 52
61 asha. when thou receive *s.*
*Hos.* 2:1 say unto your *s.* Ruha.
*Mat.* 13:56 *s.* with us? *Mark* 6:3
1 *Tim.* 5:2 int. as *s.* with purity

**SIT.**

*Num.* 32:6 go to war ye *s.* here
*Jud.* 5:10 ye that *s.* in judgment
*Ruth* 4:1 ho, *s.* down here, 2
1 *Sam.* 9:22 *s.* in chiefest place
16:11 will not *s.* down till he co.
20:5 not fail to *s.* with king
2 *Sam.* 19:8 king doth *s.* in gate
1 *K.* 1:13 Solomon shall *s.* 17
8:25 not fail man to *s.* on thr. of
Is. 2 *Chr.* 6:16; *Jer.* 33:17
2 *K.* 7:3 *s.* here till we die? 4
10:30 sons *s.* on throne, 15:12
18:27 to men who *s.* *Is.* 36:12
*Ps.* 26:5 will not *s.* with wicked
69:12 *s.* in gate speak aga. me
110:1 *s.* thou at my right hand
119:23 princes also did *s.*
127:2 vain for you to *s.* up late
*Ec.* 10:6 rich *s.* in low place
*Is.* 3:26 desolate *s.* on ground
16:5 *s.* upon the throne in truth
30:7 their strength is to *s.* still
42:7 bring them that *s.* in dark.
47:1 *s.* in dust, *s.* on grou. 52:2
5 *s.* thou silent, O daughter
14 not be a fire to *s.* before it
*Jer.* 8:14 why do we *s.* still?
13:13 I will fill them that *s.*
18 say unto king, *s.* down 36:15
36:30 none to *s.* on throne of D.
48:18 come fr. glory, *s.* in thirst
*Lam.* 2:10 elders of Z. *s.* on gro.
*Ezek.* 26:16 *s.* upon the ground
28:2 said, I *s.* in seat of God
33:31 *s.* before thee as my peop.
44:3 prince shall *s.* in it to eat
*Dan.* 7:26 the judgment shall *s.*
*Joel* 3:12 *s.* to judge the heathen
*Mic.* 4:4 *s.* every man under vine
*Zec.* 3:8 thou and thy fellows *s.*
6:13 *s.* and rule upon his throne
*Mat.* 8:11 many sh. *s.* with Abr.
20:21 sons *s.* one on thy ri. hand
23 but to *s.* on my right hand,
*Mark* 10:37, 40
*Mat.* 23:2 Phar. *s.* in Moses' seat
26:36 *s.* ye here, *Mark* 14:32
*Luke* 9:14 *s.* by fifties in a comp.
12:37 make them to *s.* down
13:29 shall *s.* in kingdom of G.
14:8 *s.* not down in high. room
17:7 go, and *s.* down to meat
*John* 6:10 Je. said, Make men *s.*
*Acts* 2:30 Ch. to *s.* on his throne
8:31 come up and *s.* with him
1 *Cor.* 8:10 to see thee *s.* at meat
*Jam.* 2:3 *s.* th. here in good pla.
*Rev.* 3:21 *s.* with me in my thro.
18:7 for she saith, I *s.* a queen

**SITTEST.**

*Ex.* 18:14 why *s.* thou thyself?
*Deut.* 6:7 talk of th. when thou *s.*
*Ps.* 50:20 thou *s.* and speakest
*Prov.* 23:1 *s.* to eat with a ruler
*Jer.* 22:2 that *s.* on the throne
*Acts* 23:3 *s.* thou to judge me?

**SITTETH.**

*Ex.* 11:5 from first-born that *s.*
*Lev.* 15:4 ev. thing whereon he *s.*
*Deut.* 17:18 when he *s.* on throne
1 *K.* 1:46 Solomon *s.* on throne
*Est.* 6:10 Mordecai *s.* at gate
*Ps.* 1:1 nor *s.* in seat of scornful
10:8 he *s.* in the lurking places
29:10 *s.* on flood; Lord *s.* king
47:8 G. *s.* on throne of holiness
99:1 L. *s.* betw. the cherubim
*Prov.* 9:14 for she *s.* at the door
20:8 king *s.* in throne of judgm.
*Is.* 28:6 to him that *s.* in judgm.
40:22 he that *s.* on the heavens
*Jer.* 29:16 saith of king that *s.*

*Lam.* 3:28 *s.* and keepeth silence
*Zec.* 1:11 behold, earth *s.* still
*Mat.* 23:22 swear by him that *s.*
*Luke* 14:28 *s.* not down first, 31
22:27 is not he that *s.* at meat?
1 *Cor.* 14:30 if any thing be revealed to another that *s.* by
*Col.* 3:1 C. *s.* on right hand of G.
2 *Thes.* 2:4 G. *s.* in temp. of God
*Rev.* 5:13 power to him that *s.*
6:16 from face of him that *s.*
7:10 salva. to our God which *s.*

**SITTING.**

1 *K.* 10:5 *s.* of serv. 2 *Chr.* 9:4
13:14 man of God *s.* under oak
22:19 I saw L. *s.* upon his thro. 2 *Chr.* 18:18; *Is.* 6:1
2 *K.* 4:38 sons of proph. were *s.*
9:5 captains of the host were *s.*
*Neh.* 2:6 queen also *s.* by him
*Est.* 5:13 Mordecai the Jew *s.*
*Ps.* 139:2 knowest my down-*s.*
*Jer.* 17:25 king *s.* on thr. 22:4, 30
38:7 king *s.* in gate of Benjamin
*Lam.* 3:63 behold their *s.* down
*Mat.* 20:30 blind men *s.* by way
26:64 Son of man *s.* on right hand of God, *Mark* 14:62
27:36 *s.* down, watched him
*Mark* 5:15 him that was poss. *s.*
16:5 they saw a young man *s.*
*Luke* 2:46 *s.* in midst of doctors
8:35 and found him *s.* clothed
*John* 2:14 changers of money *s.*
*Acts* 2:2 house where th. were *s.*
*Rev.* 4:4 I saw twenty-four elders *s.*

**SITTING-PLACE.**

2 *Chr.* 9:18 stays each side *s.-p.*

**SITUATE.**

*Ezek.* 27:3 art *s.* at entry of sea
*Nah.* 3:8 populous No th. was *s.*

**SITUATION.**

2 *K.* 2:19 *s.* of the city is pleasa.
*Ps.* 48:2 beauti. for *s.* joy of earth

**SIVAN.**

*Est.* 8:9 3d month, month of S.

SIX. *See* BRANCHES.

**SIX cities.**

*Num.* 35:6 be *s. c.* for ref. 13, 15

**SIX cubits.**

1 *Sam.* 17:4 Goliah's height *s. c.*
*Ezek.* 40:5 measuring-reed of *s. c.*
41:1 measured posts *s. c.* broad
8 foundations were *s.* great *c.*
*Dan.* 3:1 breadth of image *s. c.*

**SIX months.**

*Luke* 4:25 heav. was shut three years and *s. m.* *Jam.* 5:17

**SIX sheep.**

*Neh.* 5:18 prep. daily *s.* choice *s.*

**SIX sons.**

*Gen.* 30:20 I have borne *s. s.*
1 *Chr.* 8:38 Azel had *s. s.* 9:44

**SIX things.**

*Prov.* 6:16 *s. t.* doth Lord hate

**SIX times.**

2 *K.* 13:19 ha. smitten five or *s. t.*

**SIX troubles.**

*Job* 5:19 sh. deliver thee in *s. tr.*

**SIX water-pots.**

*John* 2:6 were set there *s. wa.-p.*

**SIX wings.**

*Is.* 6:2 seraphim, each had *s. w.*
*Rev.* 4:8 4 beasts had each *s. w.*

**SIX years.**

*Ex.* 21:2 *s. y.* shall serve, seventh go fr. *Deut.* 15:12; *Jer.* 34:14

**SIXTH.**

*Lev.* 25:21 bless. on you *s.* year
*Ezr.* 6:15 house finish. in *s.* year
*Ezek.* 4:11 drink water, *s.* part of
39:2 leave but the *s.* part of th.
*Mat.* 27:45 darkn. over land fr. *s.* to ninth hour, *Mark* 15:33; *Luke* 23:44
*John* 19:44 crucified about *s.* ho.
*Rev.* 21:20 *s.* founda. was sardius

**SIXTY.**

*Gen.* 5:15 Mahalal. lived *s.* years
21 Enoch lived *s.*-five years
*Lev.* 27:3 estimation fr. 20 to *s.*
*Mat.* 13:8 brought forth *s.* fold, 23; *Mark* 4:8, 20

**SIZE.**

*Ex.* 36:9 curtains were one *s.* 15
1 *K.* 7:37 bases one meas. and *s.*
1 *Chr.* 23:29 all manner of *s.* Da.

**SKILL, Verb.**

1 *K.* 5:6 *s.* to hew tim. 2 *Chr.* 2:8
2 *Chr.* 2:7 m. that can *s.* to grave
34:12 all that could *s.* of music

**SKILL.**

*Ec.* 9:11 nor favor to men of *s.*
*Dan.* 1:17 God gave them *s.*
9:22 come to give thee *s.* under.

**SKILFUL.**

1 *Chr.* 5:18 sons of Re. *s.* in war
15:22 instructed, bec. he was *s.*
28:21 be with thee every *s.* man
2 *Chr.* 2:14 a cunning man, *s.*
*Ezek.* 21:31 gi. you into ha. of *s.*
*Dan.* 1:4 children *s.* in all wisd.
*Amos* 5:16 *s.* of lamentation

**SKILFULLY, NESS.**

*Ps.* 33:3 sing new song, play *s.*
78:72 guided them by *s.* of hand

**SKIN.**

*Ex.* 22:27 his raiment for *s.*
29:14 bullock's flesh, *s.* *Lev.* 4:11
34:29 wist not that *s.* sho. 30, 35
*Lev.* 7:8 priest that offer. have *s.*
13:2 in *s.* a rising like plague
4 bright spot, white in the *s.*
11 old leprosy in *s.* of his flesh
56 sh. rend it out of gar. or *s.*
15:17 every *s.* whereon is seed
*Num.* 19:5 burn heifer, *s.* flesh
*Job* 2:4 *s.* for *s.* for all a man hath
7:5 *s.* broken, and loathsome
10:11 clo. me with *s.* and flesh
16:15 sewed sackcl. on *s.* defiled
18:13 it shall dev. strength of *s.*
19:20 bone cleaveth to my *s.* I am esca. with *s.* of my teeth
26 after my *s.* worms des. body
30:30 *s.* black, bones are burnt
41:7 canst fill his *s.* with irons?
*Ps.* 102:5 my bones cleave to *s.*
*Jer.* 13:23 can Ethiop. change *s.*?
*Lam.* 3:4 flesh and *s.* made old
4:8 *s.* cleaveth to their bones
5:10 our *s.* was black like oven
*Ezek.* 37:6 cover you with *s.* 8
*Mic.* 3:2 pluck off their *s.*
3 flay their *s.* from off them
*Mark* 1:6 John had a girdle of *s.*

**SKINS.**

*Gen.* 3:21 Lord made coats of *s.*
27:16 put *s.* of goats on hands
*Ex.* 35:23 *s.* of rams, badgers' *s.*
*Lev.* 13:59 law of plague of *s.*
16:27 burn in fire their *s.*
*Num.* 31:20 purify. rai. ma. of *s.*
*Heb.* 11:37 wandered in sheep *s.*

**SKIP, PED, EDST.**

*Ps.* 29:6 maketh them also to *s.*
114:4 mountains *s.* like rams, 6
*Jer.* 48:27 spakest, thou *s.* for joy

**SKIPPING.**

*Cant.* 2:8 cometh *s.* upon hills

**SKIRT.**

*Deut.* 22:30 not unco. father's *s.*
*Ruth* 3:9 spread *s.* over handma.
1 *Sam.* 15:27 he laid hold on *s.*
24:4 Da. cut off *s.* of Saul's robe
11 *s.* of thy robe in my hand
*Ezek.* 16:8 I sp. my *s.* over thee
*Hag.* 2:12 if one bear holy flesh in *s.* and with *s.* touch bread
*Zec.* 8:23 10 men take hold of *s.*

**SKIRTS.**

*Ps.* 133:2 down to *s.* of garments
*Jer.* 2:34 in *s.* is found blood of
13:22 are thy *s.* discov. *Nah.* 3:5
*Lam.* 1:9 filthiness is in her *s.*
*Ezek.* 5:3 bind a few hairs in *s.*

**SKULL.**

*Jud.* 9:53 millsto. to break his *s.*
2 *K.* 9:35 no more of Jez. than *s.*
*Mat.* 27:33 Golgotha, place of a *s.* *Mark* 15:22; *John* 19:17

**SKY.**

*Deut.* 33:26 rideth in excell. on *s.*
*Job* 37:18 hast th. spread out *s.*?
*Mat.* 16:2 fair weather, *s.* red, 3
*Luke* 12:56 can discern face of *s.*
*Heb.* 11:12 many as stars of *s.*

**SKIES.**

2 *Sam.* 22:12 clou. of *s.* *Ps.* 18:11
*Ps.* 77:17 *s.* sent out a sound
*Is.* 45:8 let *s.* pour down righte.
*Jer.* 51:9 her judgm. lifted to *s.*

**SLACK.**

*Deut.* 7:10 he will be *s.* to him
*Jos.* 18:3 how long are ye *s.*
*Prov.* 10:4 poor deal. with *s.* ha.
*Zep.* 3:16 Z. let not hands be *s.*
2 *Pet.* 3:9 L. not *s.* concer. prom.

**SLACK, ED.**

*Deut.* 23:21 vow th. shalt not *s.*
*Jos.* 10:6 *s.* not hand from serva.
2 *K.* 4:24 *s.* not riding for me
*Hab.* 1:4 law *s.* judgm. never go.

**SLACKNESS.**

2 *Pet.* 3:9 as some men count *s.*

**SLAIN,** *active.*

*Gen.* 4:23 *s.* a man to my wound.
*Num.* 14:16 hath *s.* them in wil.
22:33 surely now I had *s.* thee
*Deut.* 21:1 not kno. who hath *s.*
*Jud.* 9:18 ha. *s.* sons upon stones
15:16 bone of an ass *s.* 1,000
1 *Sam.* 18:7 Saul *s.* thous. 21:11
22:21 Saul had *s.* Lord's priests
2 *Sam.* 1:16 I have *s.* Lord's ano.
4:11 wicked men have *s.* righte
13:30 A. hath *s.* all king's sons
21:12 Philist. had *s.* Saul in Gil.
1 *K.* 13:26 lion ha. to. and *s.* him
16:16 say, Zimri hath *s.* king
19:1 Ah. told he had *s.* prophets
10 Is. have *s.* thy prophets, 14
2 *K.* 14:5 servants who had *s.* ki.
2 *Chr.* 21:13 hast *s.* thy brethren
22:1 band of men had *s.* eldest
*Est.* 9:12 Jews have *s.* 500 men
*Job* 1:15 Sabeans have *s.* serv. 17
*Prov.* 7:26 strong men been *s.*
*Is.* 14:20 destroyed and *s.* people
*Jer.* 33:5 bod. of men *s.* in anger
41:4 had *s.* Gedaliah, 9, 16, 18
*Lam.* 2:21 *s.* th. in anger, 3:43
*Ezek.* 16:21 hast *s.* my children
23:39 *s.* their children to idols
*Hos.* 6:5 *s.* th. by words of mouth
*Amos* 4:10 young men have I *s.*
*Acts* 2:23 by wick. hands have *s.*
7:52 *s.* them th. showed coming
23:14 eat noth. till we have *s.* P.

**SLAIN,** *passive.*

*Gen.* 34:27 sons of Ja. came on *s.*
*Lev.* 26:17 be *s.* before your ene.
*Num.* 11:22 and the herds be *s.*?
23:24 eat prey, drink blood of *s.*
25:14 Israelite that was *s.* Zimri
*Deut.* 21:1 if one be found *s.*
28:31 thine ox *s.* bef. thine eyes
*Jos.* 11:6 deli. them *s.* before Is.

13:22 Balaam also was among s.
Jud. 20:4 husband of the woman that was s.
1 Sam. 19:6 as L. liv. not be s.
20:32 wherefore shall he be s.
31:1 fell s. in Gilboa, 1 Chr. 10:1
2 Sam. 1:19 beauty of Israel is s.
22 bl. of s. from fat of mighty
25 O Jonathan, thou wast s. in
1 K. 11:15 Joab gone to bury s.
2 K. 3:23 the kings are surely s.
11:8 cometh with. ranges, be s.
1 Chr. 5:22 fell down many s.
2 Chr. 13:17 fell s. of Isr. 500,000
Est. 7:4 for we are sold to be s.
Job 39:30 where s. are, th. is she
Ps. 62:3 ye shall be s. all of you
88:5 like s. that lie in the grave
89:10 hast broken Rah. as one s.
Prov. 22:13 sloth. sai. I sh. be s.
24:11 deliv. those ready to be s.
Is. 10:4 they shall fall under s.
22:2 thy s. men not s. with sw.
Is. 26:21 earth no more cov. her s.
27:7 s. accord. to slaughter of s.
34:3 their s. also sh. be cast out
66:16 s. of Lord shall be many
Jer. 9:1 might weep for s. of peo.
14:18 go into field, beho. s. with
18:21 let their young men be s.
25:33 s. of L. be fr. end of earth
41:9 Ishmael filled the pit wi. s.
51:47 her s. shall fall in midst
49 Bab. caused s. of Is. to fall
Lam. 2:20 priest and proph. be s.
4:9 s. wi. sw. better than s. with
Ezek. 6:7 s. shall fall in midst
9:7 fill courts with s.
21:14 sw. of s. is of great men s.
29 bring thee upon necks of s.
26:6 her daugh. in field sh. be s.
28:8 die deaths of th. that are s.
30:11 shall fill land with the s.
31:18 sh. lie with them s. 32:29
32:20 fall in midst of the s. 25
21 lie s. by sword, 22, 23, 24
35:8 fill his mount. with s. men
37:9 O breath. breathe on th. s.
Dan. 2:13 wise men should be s.
5:30 in that night was Belsh. s.
11:26 many shall fall down s.
Zep. 2:12 ye Ethiopi. shall be s.
Luke 9:22 Son of man must be s.
Acts 5:36 Theud. s. and as many
7:42 ye offered to me s. beasts?
Eph. 2:16 cross, having s. enmity
Heb. 11:37 were s. with sword
Rev. 2:13 Antipas who was s.
5:6 stood Lamb, as had been s.
9 wast s. 12 Lamb s. 13:8
6:9 souls of them that were s.

**SLANDER, S.**

Num. 14:36 by bring. a s. on land
Ps. 31:13 I ha. heard s. of many
Prov. 10:18 uttereth s. is a fool
Jer. 6:28 revolt. walking with s.
9:4 every neighbor walk with s.

**SLANDERED, EST, ETH.**

2 Sam. 19:27 he hath s. thy serv.
Ps. 50:20 thou s. mother's son
101:5 s. neighbor, him cut off

**SLANDERERS.**

1 Tim. 3:11 wives be grave, not s.

**SLANDEROUSLY.**

Rom. 3:8 not rather, as s. report.

**SLANG.**

1 Sam. 17:49 D. took sto. and s.

**SLAUGHTER.**

1 Sam. 14:14 first s. Jona. made
30 had there not been great. s.
17:57 D. returned fr. s. of Phili.
2 Sam. 17:9 is s. among people
Ps. 44:22 counted as sheep for s.
Prov. 7:22 after her, as ox to s.
Is. 10:26 accord. to s. of Midian
14:21 prepare s. for his children
27:7 accord. to s. of them slain
34:2 delivered them to s.
53:7 bro. as lamb to s. Jer. 11:19
65:12 ye shall bow down to s.
Jer. 7:32 Toph. but val. of s. 19:6
12:3 like sheep for s. prep. for s.
25:34 days of s. are accomplish.
48:15 young men are gone to s.
50:27 let them go down to the s.
51:40 bri. down like lambs to s.
Ezek. 9:2 every man a s. weapon
21:10 sharpened to make sore s.
28 sw. is drawn, for s. furbish.
26:15 when s. is made in midst
Hos. 5:2 revolters profound to s.
Ob. 9 mount E. be cut off by s.
Zec. 11:4 sai. L. Feed flock of s.
7 I will feed flock of s.
Acts 8:32 was led as a sheep to s.
9:1 Saul yet breathing out s.
Rom. 8:36 counted as sheep to s.
Heb. 7:1 Abra. returning from s.
Jam. 5:5 hearts as in days of s.
See GREAT.

**SLAVE, S.**

Jer. 2:14 a serv.? a home-born s.?
Rev. 18:13 buy. merchandise of s.

**SLAY.**

Gen. 4:14 every one shall s. me
20:4 wilt thou s. right. nation?
27:41 then will I s. brother Ja.
34:30 gather ag. me and s. me
37:20 come now, let us s. him
42:37 s. my two sons if I bring
43:16 bring men, s. make ready
Ex. 4:23 s. thy son first-born
32:12 bring them out to s. them
Lev. 4:29 s. sin-off. 14:13 s. lamb
Num. 25:5 s. ye ev. one his men
Deut. 19:6 avenger pursue and s.
Jos. 13:22 Israel did s. Balaam
Jud. 8:20 said to J. Up, s. them
9:54 s. me, that men say not
1 Sam. 2:25 bec. L. would s. them
14:34 bring ev. man ox, s. here
19:15 bri. him that I may s. him
20:8 if in me iniq. s. me thyself
22:17 said. Turn and s. priests
2 Sam. 1:9 Sa. said, Stand and s.
1 K. 1:51 swear he will not s.
18:12 cannot find thee, sh. s. me
20:36 departed, lion s. thee
2 K. 8:12 young men wilt thou s.
10:25 go in and s. them
17:26 God sent lions, they s.
2 Chr. 23:14 s. her not in ho. of L.
Neh. 4:11 we will s. them, cause
Job 9:23 if scourge s. suddenly
13:15 though he s. me yet will I
Ps. 34:21 evil shall s. wicked
59:11 s. them not, lest my peop.
94:6 they s. widow and stranger
109:16 might s. broken in heart
139:19 thou wilt s. wick. O God
Prov. 1:32 turn. of simple sh. s.
Is. 11:4 with breath shall he s.
14:30 he shall s. thy remnant
27:1 Lord shall s. the dragon
65:15 for Lord God shall s. thee
Jer. 5:6 lion of forest sh. s. them
20:4 carry Judah capti. s. them
29:21 shall s. Ahab and Zedek.
41:8 men fo. that said, s. us not
Ezek. 9:6 s. utter. old and young
23:47 sh. s. sons and daughters
26:8 he shall s. thy daughters
Hos. 2:3 s. her with thirst
9:16 yet will I s. the fruit
Amos 2:3 I will s. all princes
9:1 I will s. the last of them
4 comm. sword, it sh. s. them
Zec. 11:5 whose posses. s. them
Luke 11:49 some they shall s.
19:27 bring hither, and s. them

**To SLAY.**

Gen. 18:25 far fr. thee to s. right.
22:10 Abra. stretched hand to s.
37:18 they conspired to s. him
Ex. 2:15 Ph. sought to s. Moses
21:14 if come on neighbor to s
Deut. 9:28 brou. out to s. them
27:25 taketh reward to s. inno.
1 Sam. 5:10 brou. the ark to s. us
19:5 why then sin, to s. David?
11 S. went to watch and s. him
2 Sam. 3:37 not of king to s. Ab.
21:2 Saul sought to s. them
1 K. 17:18 art come to s. my son?
18:9 deliv. me to Ahab to s. me
2 Chr. 20:23 utterly to s. and des.
Neh. 6:10 to s. th. in night to s.
Ps. 37:14 to s. such as be upright
32 watcheth righte. seek. to s.
Jer. 15:3 appoint sw. to s. dogs
18:23 know. their counsel to s.
Ezek. 13:19 to s. souls th. should
John 5:16 Jews, sou. to s. him
Acts 5:33 took counsel to s. apos.
9:29 they went about to s. him
Rev. 9:15 prep. to s. third part

**SLAYER.**

Num. 35:11 cities of refuge th. s.
Deut. 4:42; 19:3, 4; Jos. 20:3
28 after death of high-priest s. shall return, Jos. 20:6
Deut. 19:6 lest avenger pursue s.
Jos. 20:5 shall not deliver the s
21:13 Hebron city of ref. for s.
21 Shech. 27 Golan a ref. for s.
32 Kedesh in Galilee for the s.
38 Ramoth in Gil. refuge for s.
Ezek. 21:11 sw. to be given to s.

**SLAYETH.**

Gen. 4:15 Lord said, Whoso. s. C.
Deut. 22:26 neighbor, and s. him
Job 5:2 wrath killeth, envy s.
Ezek. 28:9 bef. him that s. thee, I am G.? in hand of him th. s.

**SLAYING.**

Jos. 8:24 Is. made end of s. 10:20
Jud. 9:56 G. rendered wick. in s.
1 K. 17:20 evil on wid. by s. son
Is. 57:5 s. children in the valleys
Ezek. 9:8 while th. were s. them

**SLEEP, Substantive.**

Gen. 2:21 God caused a s. on Ad.
15:12 a deep s. fell on Abram
28:16 Jacob awaked out of s.
31:40 s. departed fr. mine eyes
Jud. 16:14 S. awaked out of s. 20
1 Sam. 26:12 a deep s. from God
Job 4:13 when deep s. fall. 33:15
14:12 nor raised out of their s.
Ps. 13:3 lest I s. the s. of death
76:5 stout-hearted slept their s.
6 chari. and horse cast into s.
78:65 Lord awaked us out of s.
Ps. 90:5 them away, th. are as a s.
127:2 so he giveth his belov. s.
132:4 I will not give s. to eyes
Prov. 3:24 lie down, s. be sweet
4:16 their s. is taken away
6:4 give not s. to thine eyes
9 wh. wilt thou arise out of s.?
10 a little more s. 24:33
19:15 slothfuln. casteth into s.
20:13 love not s. lest co. to pov.
Ec. 5:12 the s. of laboring man
8:16 nei. day nor night seeth s.
Is. 29:10 L. pour. on you deep s.
Jer. 31:26 my s. was sweet to me
51:39 may sleep a perpet. s. 57
Dan. 2:1 his s. brake from him
6:18 passed night his s. went fr.
8:18 I was in deep s. 10:9
Zec. 4:1 man wakened out of s.
Mat. 1:24 J. being raised from s.
Luke 9:32 were heavy with s.
John 11:11 awake him out of s.
13 spoken of taking rest in s.
Acts 16:27 keeper awak. out of s.
20:9 Euty. being fallen into s.
Rom. 13:11 to awake out of s.

**SLEEP, Verb.**

*Gen.* 28:11 Jacob lay down to *s.*
*Ex.* 22:27 wherein shall he *s.?*
*Deut.* 24:12 not *s.* with his pledge
31:16 *s.* with fath. 2 *Sam.* 7:12
*Jud.* 16:19 ma. him *s.* on her kn.
1 *Sam.* 3:3 Sam. laid down to *s.*
1 *K.* 1:21 lord the king shall *s.*
*Est.* 6:1 night could not king *s.*
*Job* 7:21 now sh. I *s.* in the dust
*Ps.* 4:8 will lay me down and *s.*
121:4 shall nei. slumber nor *s.*
*Prov.* 4:16 they *s.* not except
6:9 how long wilt th. *s.* O slug.?
10 folding of hands to *s.* 24:33
*Ec.* 5:12 *s.* of lab. man is sweet,
abund. of rich not suffer *s.*
*Cant.* 5:2 I *s.* but my heart wak.
*Is.* 5:27 none sh. slumber nor *s.*
*Jer.* 51:39 may *s.* perp. sleep, 57
*Ezek.* 34:25 they shall *s.* in woods
*Dan.* 12:2 many that *s.* in dust
*Mat.* 26:45 *s.* on now, *Mark* 14:41
*Mark* 4:27 sho. *s.* and seed spri.
*Luke* 22:46 why *s.* ye? rise
*John* 11:12 if he *s.* he sh. do well
1 *Cor.* 11:30 for th. cause many *s.*
15:51 we shall not all *s.*
1 *Thes.* 4:14 who *s.* in Je. will G.
5:6 let us not *s.* as do others
7 they that *s.* *s.* in the night
10 that whether we wake or *s.*

**SLEEPER.**

*Jon.* 1:6 what mean. thou, O *s.*

**SLEEPEST.**

*Ps.* 44:23 why *s.* thou, O Lord
*Prov.* 6:22 wh. thou *s.* it sh. keep
*Mark* 14:37 Simon, *s.* thou?
*Eph.* 5:14 awake, thou that *s.*

**SLEEPETH.**

1 *K.* 18:27 said. Peradvent. he *s.*
*Prov.* 10:5 he that *s.* in harvest.
*Hos.* 7:6 their baker *s.* all night
*Mat.* 9:24 maid is not dead but *s.* *Mark* 5:39; *Luke* 8:52
*John* 11:11 our friend Lazarus *s.*

**SLEEPING.**

1 *Sam.* 26:7 S. lay *s.* with. trench
*Is.* 56:10 blind, *s.* loving slumber
*Mark* 13:36 lest com. find you *s.*
14:37 cometh and find. them *s.*
*Acts* 12:6 Peter was *s.* betw. two

**SLEIGHT.**

*Eph.* 4:14 carried by *s.* of men

**SLEPT.**

*Gen.* 2:21 Adam *s.* 41:5 Phara. *s.*
2 *Sam.* 11:9 Uriah *s.* at door of
1 *K.* 3:20 while thy handmaid *s.*
19:5 as he lay and *s.* an angel
*Job* 3:13 ha. been quiet and ha. *s.*
*Ps.* 3:5 I laid me down and *s.*
*Mat.* 13:25 while men *s.* his ene.
25:5 bridegroom tarried, they *s.*
27:52 bod. of saints wh. *s.* arose
28:13 disciples stole while we *s.*
1 *Cor.* 15:20 first-fruits of that *s.*

*See* FATHERS.

**SLEW.**

*Gen.* 34:25 *s.* males; 26 *s.* Hamor
49:6 in their anger th. *s.* a man
*Ex.* 2:12 Moses *s.* the Egyptian
13:15 Lord *s.* all first-born in E.
*Num.* 31:7 they *s.* males of Mid.
8 *s.* kings of Mid. Bala. they *s.*
*Jud.* 1:4 they *s.* in Bezek 10,000
3:29 they *s.* of Moab 10,000 men
31 Shamgar *s.* of Phil. 600 men
7:25 they *s.* Oreb and Zeeb two
*Jud.* 9:5 Abim. *s.* breth. 70 pers.
14:19 Samson *s.* 30 men of As.
15:15 jaw-bone Samson *s.* 1,000
16:30 dead which he *s.* at death
1 *Sam.* 14:34 brou. his ox and *s.*
17:36 thy servant *s.* both lion
19:5 life in hand and *s.* Philist.
22:18 Doeg *s.* 85 persons that
29:5 sang, Saul *s.* thousands
2 *Sam.* 4:12 Da. *s.* them and cut
8:5 David *s.* of Syrians 22,000
21:1 because he *s.* Gibeonites
23:20 *s.* two lion-like men of M. he *s.* a lion, 1 *Chr.* 11:22
1 *K.* 18:13 Jeze. *s.* prophets of L.
40 Elijah *s.* prophets of Baal
2 *K.* 9:31 peace, who *s.* master?
10:9 I *s.* him, but who *s.* these?
11:18 people *s.* Mat. priest of B.
14:6 chil. he *s.* not, 2 *Chr.* 25:4
7 he *s.* of Edom, 1 *Chr.* 18:12
17:25 L. sent lions wh. *s.* some
23:20 Jos. *s.* all the priests of
1 *Chr.* 7:21 men of Ga. in land *s.*
2 *Chr.* 21:4 Jehoram *s.* his breth.
*Neh.* 9:26 they *s.* thy prophets
*Est.* 9:16 Jews *s.* of foes 75,000
*Ps.* 78:31 God *s.* fattest of them
34 when he *s.* them, then they
105:29 into blood, *s.* their fish
135:10 *s.* great; 136:18 *s.* kings
*Is.* 66:3 an ox as if he *s.* a man
*Jer.* 20:17 because he *s.* me not
41:3 Ishmael *s.* all the Jews
8 *s.* them not among brethren
*Lam.* 2:4 *s.* all that were pleas.
*Dan.* 3:22 fire *s.* men that took
5:19 whom he would he *s.*
*Mat.* 2:16 Herod sent, *s.* children
22:6 took his serv. and *s.* them
23:35 whom ye *s.* betw. temple
*Luke* 13:4 tower in Sil. fell and *s.*
*Acts* 5:30 Je. whom *s.* and hang.
10:39 Je. whom they *s.* and han.
*Rom.* 7:11 commandment *s.* me
1 *John* 3:12 C. who *s.* his brother

**SLEW him.**

*Gen.* 4:8 C. rose ag. Abel and *s. h.*
38:7 Er was wicked, Lord *s. h.*
*Jud.* 9:54 say not, A wom. *s. him*
12:6 took and *s. h.* at passages
1 *Sam.* 17:35 I cau. him and *s. h.*
2 *Sam.* 1:10 stood upon and *s. h.*
4:7 smote Ish-bosheth and *s. h.*
18:15 compassed Absalom *s. h.*
1 *K.* 13:24 lion met and *s. h.* 20:36
2 *K.* 10:9 I conspired and *s. him*
15:10 Shall. conspired and *s. h.*
1 *Chr.* 10:14 therefore *s.* he *him*
2 *Chr.* 22:11 Athaliah *s. him* not
24:25 his own servants *s. him*
32:21 came of his bowels *s. h.*
33:24 his serv. *s. him* in house
*Jer.* 41:2 Ishm. *s. h.* whom king
*Mat.* 21:39 cast out of vine. *s. h.*
*Acts* 22:20 raim. of th. that *s. h.*

**SLEWEST.**

1 *Sam.* 21:9 sword of Goli. th. *s.*

**SLIDE, ETH.**

*Deut.* 32:35 foot sh. *s.* in due time
*Ps.* 26:1 trusted in L. I sh. not *s.*
37:31 none of his steps shall *s.*
*Hos.* 4:16 Is. *s.* as backslid. heifer

**SLIDDEN.**

*Jer.* 8:5 why peo. of Jer. *s.* back

**SLIGHTLY.**

*Jer.* 6:14 healed my peo. *s.* 8:11

**SLIME.**

*Gen.* 11:3 brick for st. *s.* for mor.
*Ex.* 2:3 she daubed ark with *s.*

**SLIME-PITS.**

*Gen.* 14:10 Sid. was full of *s.-p.*

**SLING, Verb.**

*Jud.* 20:16 ev. one could *s.* stones
1 *Sam.* 25:29 them shall he *s.* out
*Jer.* 10:18 *s.* out inhabit. at once

**SLING, S.**

1 *Sam.* 17:40 Da. had *s.* in hand
50 David prevailed with a *s.*
25:29 sling enem. as out of a *s.*
2 *Chr.* 26:14 Uzziah prepared *s.*
*Prov.* 26:8 bindeth stone in a *s.*

**SLINGERS.**

2 *K.* 3:25 *s.* went about it, smote

**SLING-STONES.**

*Job* 41:28 *s.* turned into stubble

**SLIP, PETH.**

*Deut.* 19:5 head *s.* from helve
2 *Sam.* 22:37 feet not *s.* *Ps.* 18:36
*Job* 12:5 he that is ready to *s.*
*Ps.* 17:5 that my footst. *s.* nor
38:16 wh. foot *s.* they magnify
94:18 foot *s.* mercy held me up
*Heb.* 2:1 lest we sho. let them *s.*

**SLIPPED.**

1 *Sam.* 19:10 D. *s.* out of S.'s pre.
*Ps.* 73:2 steps had well nigh *s.*

**SLIPPERY.**

*Ps.* 35:6 let their way be dark, *s.*
73:18 didst set them in *s.* places
*Jer.* 23:12 th. way be to them *s.*

**SLIPS.**

*Is.* 17:10 thou shalt set it with *s.*

**SLOTHFUL.**

*Jud.* 18:9 be not *s.* to poss. land
*Prov.* 12:24 *s.* shall be under tri.
27 *s.* roast. not he took hunti.
15:19 way of *s.* is as a hedge
18:9 *s.* is broth. to great waster
19:24 *s.* hid. hand in bos. 26:15
21:25 desire of *s.* killeth him
22:13 *s.* saith, Th. is a lion, 26:13
24:30 went by field of *s.* viney.
*Mat.* 25:26 wicked and *s.* servant
*Rom.* 12:11 not *s.* in business
*Heb.* 6:12 ye be not *s.* but follow.

**SLOTHFULNESS.**

*Prov.* 19:15 *s.* cast. into deep sle.
*Ec.* 10:18 by *s.* building decayeth

**SLOW.**

*Ex.* 4:10 *s.* of speech, of *s.* tong.
*Neh.* 9:17 thou art G. *s.* to anger
*Prov.* 14:29 *s.* to wrath, of great
*Luke* 24:25 O fools, *s.* of heart
*Tit.* 1:12 Cretians liars, *s.* bellies
*Jam.* 1:19 *s.* to speak, *s.* to wrath

*See* ANGER.

**SLOWLY.**

*Acts* 27:7 had sailed *s.* many days

**SLUGGARD.**

*Prov.* 6:6 go to the ant, thou *s.*
9 how long wilt th. sleep, O *s.*
10:26 smoke to eyes, so *s.* to th.
13:4 the soul of *s.* desireth
20:4 the *s.* will not plough
26:16 *s.* wiser in own conceit

**SLUICES.**

*Is.* 19:10 th. make *s.* and ponds

**SLUMBER, Substantive.**

*Ps.* 132:4 not give *s.* to eyelids
*Prov.* 6:4 eyes, nor *s.* to eyelids
10 a little sleep, little *s.* 24:33
*Rom.* 11:8 G. hath given them *s.*

**SLUMBER, ED, ETH.**

*Ps.* 121:3 that keep. will not *s.* 4
*Is.* 5:27 none shall *s.* nor sleep
56:10 watchm. lying, lov. to *s.*
*Nah.* 3:18 thy shepherds *s.* O king
*Mat.* 25:5 bridegroom tar. th. *s.*
2 *Pet.* 2:3 their damnation *s.* not

**SLUMBERINGS.**

*Job* 33:15 God speak. in *s.* on bed

**SMALL.**

*Gen.* 30:15 is it *s.* matter that th.
*Ex.* 16:14 *s.* thi. *s.* as hoarfrost
*Num.* 16:13 is it *s.* thing th. hast
2 *Sam.* 7:19 a *s.* thing in thy sight, O Lord, 1 *Chr.* 17:17
22:43 beat. *s.* as dust, *Ps.* 18:42
1 *K.* 19:12 after fire, still *s.* voice
*Is.* 7:13 is it *s.* th. to weary men?
60:22 a *s.* one sh. bec. a nation

*Jer.* 30:19 and they sh. not be *s.*
49:15 make thee *s.* am. heathen
*Amos.* 7:2 Ja. arise? for he is *s.* 5
*Ob.* 2 made thee *s.* am. heathen
*Zec.* 4:10 desp. day of *s.* things?
*See* GREAT.

**SMALLEST.**
1 *Sam.* 9:21 Benja. of *s.* tribes?

**SMART.**
*Prov.* 11:15 surety for str. sh. *s.*

**SMELL, Substantive.**
*Gen.* 27:27 Is. smelled *s.* of raim.
*s.* of my son is as *s.* of a field
*Cant.* 2:13 tender grape give *s.*
4:10 *s.* of oint. better th. spices
11 *s.* of garm. like *s.* of Leban.
7:8 *s.* of thy nose like apples
*Is.* 3:24 instead of sweet *s.* stink
*Dan.* 3:27 nor *s.* of fire passed on
*Hos.* 14:6 his *s.* as Lebanon
*Phil.* 4:18 sent an od. of sweet *s.*

**SMELL, Verb.**
*Ex.* 30:38 make like to that to *s.*
*Lev.* 26:31 will not *s.* your odors
*Deut.* 4:28 wh. neither see nor *s.*
*Ps.* 45:8 garments *s.* of myrrh
115:6 noses have they, *s.* not
*Amos* 5:21 not *s.* in your assem.

**SMELLED, ETH.**
*Gen.* 8:21 Lord *s.* a sweet savor
27:27 Isaac *s.* raim. blessed him
*Job* 39:25 he *s.* the battle afar off

**SMELLING.**
*Cant.* 5:5 fing. with *s.* myrrh, 13
*Eph.* 5:2 sacrifi. to G. for *s.* sav.

**SMELLING, Substantive**
1 *Cor.* 12:17 hear. where were *s.*?

**SMITE.**
*Gen.* 32:8 to one comp. and *s.* it
*Ex.* 7:17 I will *s.* upon waters
12:23 not suffer destroyer to *s.*
17:6 thou shalt *s.* rock in Horeb
21:18 if men strive, one *s.* ano.
26 if a man *s.* eye of servant
*Num.* 22:6 prev. that we *s.* them
24:17 sceptre out of Is. *s.* Moab
25:17 vex Midianites, *s.* them
35:16 if he *s.* him with instrum.
18 if he *s.* him wi. hand-weap.
*Deut.* 7:2 shalt *s.* Canaanites
13:15 shalt surely *s.* inhabitants
20:13 thou shalt *s.* every male
*Jud.* 6:16 thou sh. *s.* Midianites
20:31 then Benj. began to *s.* 39
1 *Sam.* 17:46 I will *s.* thee
18:11 Saul said, I will *s.* David
20:33 Saul cast javelin to *s.* him
23:2 *s.* Philistines? Go, *s.* Phil.
26:8 let me *s.* him to earth
2 *Sam.* 2:22 why sho. I *s.* thee?
13:28 when I say, *s.* Amnon
15:14 lest he *s.* city with sword
17:2 and I will *s.* the king only
18:11 said, Why not *s.* him th.?
1 *K.* 20:35 in word of the L. *s.* me
2 *K.* 3:19 shall *s.* ev. fenced city
6:21 sh. I *s.* them? sh. I *s.* th.?
9:7 thou shalt *s.* house of Ahab
27 Jehu said, *s.* him in the
13:17 sh. *s.* Syri. till consumed
18 said to king, *s.* upon ground
*Ps.* 121:6 sun not *s.* thee by day
141:5 let righte. *s.* it be kindn.
*Prov.* 19:25 *s.* a scorner
*Is.* 10:24 shall *s.* thee with rod
49:10 nei. heat nor sun *s.* them
58:4 fast to *s.* with fist of wick.
*Jer.* 18:18 let us *s.* him wi. tong.
43:11 shall *s.* land of Eg. 46:13
*Ezek.* 5:2 part of hair, *s.* about
6:11 *s.* wi. hand. stamp wi. foot
21:12 son of man, *s.* on thy thi.
14 prophesy, *s.* hands together
*Amos* 9:1 he said, *s.* lintel of do.
*Mic.* 5:1 they shall *s.* judge of Is.
*Nah.* 2:10 the knees *s.* together
*Zec.* 10:11 *s.* the waves in sea
11:6 deliv. men, they shall *s.* la.
*Mat.* 5:39 wh. sh. *s.* th. on cheek
24:49 begin to *s.* his fellow-serv.
*Luke* 22:49 Lord, shall we *s.* with the sword?
*Acts* 23:2 commanded to *s.* Paul
2 *Cor.* 11:20 man *s.* you on face
*Rev.* 11:6 witne. hav. pow. to *s.*

**SMITE, *referred to God.***
*Gen.* 8:21 nor will I *s.* any more
*Ex.* 3:20 stretch hand, and *s.* E.
9:15 I may *s.* thee and people
12:12 I will *s.* first-born in Eg.
*Num.* 14:12 *s.* them with pestil.
*Deut.* 28:35 L. *s.* thee in knees
33:11 *s.* through loins
1 *Sam.* 26:10 Da. said, L. shall *s.*
2 *Sam.* 5:24 shall Lord go to *s.* Philistines, 1 *Chr.* 14:15
1 *K.* 14:15 L. shall *s.* Is. as a reed
2 *K.* 6:18 *s.* this people wi. blin.
2 *Chr.* 21:14 wi. plague will L. *s.*
*Is.* 11:4 *s.* earth with rod of mou.
15 the Lord shall *s.* Egypt in the seven streams, 19:22
*Jer.* 21:6 I will *s.* inhabit. of city
*Ezek.* 21:17 I will *s.* hands toge.
32:15 I *s.* th. that dwell in Egy.
39:3 *s.* thy bow out of hand
*Amos* 3:15 I will *s.* winter-house
6:11 Lord will *s.* great house
*Zec.* 9:4 L. will *s.* her power
12:4 I will *s.* ev. horse and rider
13:7 awake, O sword, *s.* Sheph. *Mat.* 26:31; *Mark* 14:27
14:12 plague wherewith L. *s.* 18
*Mal.* 4:6 lest I *s.* earth wi. a cur.
*Rev.* 19:15 with it sho. *s.* nations

**SMITERS.**
*Is.* 50:6 I gave my back to the *s.*

**SMITEST, ETH.**
*Ex.* 2:13 wheref. *s.* thy fellow?
21:12 *s.* man so he die
15 *s.* fath. or moth. put to dea.
*Deut.* 25:11 wife to deliver husb. out of hand of him th. *s.* him
27:24 cursed that *s.* his neighb.
*Job* 26:12 by understanding he *s.*
*Is.* 9:13 turn not to him that *s.*
*Lam.* 3:30 cheek to him that *s.*
*Ezek.* 7:9 kn. that I am L. that *s.*
*Luke* 6:29 *s.* thee on one cheek
*John* 18:23 why *s.* thou me?

**SMITH.**
1 *Sam.* 13:19 no *s.* found in Isra.
*Is.* 44:12 *s.* with tongs worketh
54:16 I created *s.* bloweth coals

**SMITHS.**
2 *K.* 24:14 Nebuchadnez. carried away *s.* 16; *Jer.* 24:1
*Jer.* 29:2 *s.* were departed fr. Jer.

**SMITING.**
*Ex.* 2:11 Egyptian *s.* a Hebrew
1 *K.* 20:37 so in *s.* wounded him
2 *K.* 3:24 went forward *s.* Moab
*Mic.* 6:13 make thee sick in *s.*

**SMITTEN.**
*Ex.* 7:25 after Lord had *s.* river
22:2 if thief be found, and be *s.*
*Num.* 14:42 go not up that ye be not *s.* *Deut.* 1:42
22:32 wherefore hast th. *s.* ass
33:4 buried first-born L. had *s.*
*Deut.* 28:7 cause enemies be *s.*
25 L. cause th. be *s.* bef. enem.
*Jud.* 20:36 were *s.* 39 they are *s.*
1 *Sam.* 4:2 Is. *s.* bef. Philist. 10
3 why hath L. *s.* us bef. Phil.?
6:19 lamented bec. L. *s.* many
30:1 Amalek had *s.* Ziklag
2 *Sam.* 2:31 had *s.* of Ab.'s men
11:15 that ye may be *s.*
1 *K.* 8:33 when people of Is. be *s.*
11:15 after he had *s.* ev. male
2 *K.* 2:14 when he had *s.* waters
3:23 kings have *s.* one another
14:10 hast *s.* Ed. 2 *Chr.* 25:19
2 *Chr.* 20:22 M. and Seir were *s.*
25:16 why should. thou be *s.*?
26:20 because L. had *s.* him
*Job* 16:10 have *s.* me on cheek
*Ps.* 3:7 hast *s.* mine enemies
69:26 persec. him thou hast *s.*
102:4 my heart is *s.* withered
143:3 hath *s.* my life to ground
*Is.* 5:25 the L. hath *s.* his people
24:12 gate is *s.* with destruction
27:7 hath he *s.* him, as smo. th.
53:4 est. him stricken, *s.* of God
*Jer.* 2:30 in vain ha. I *s.* children
14:19 why hast thou *s.* us
*Ezek.* 22:13 I have *s.* my hand at
33:21 came, saying, City is *s.*
*Hos.* 6:1 he hath *s.* will bind up
9:16 Ephraim is *s.* root dried
*Amos* 4:9 *s.* you, ha. not return.
*Acts* 23:3 commanded me to be *s.*
*Rev.* 8:12 third part of sun was *s.*

**SMOKE, Substantive.**
*Gen.* 19:28 *s.* of co. went up as *s.*
*Ex.* 19:18 mount Sin. was on *s.*
*Jos.* 8:20 *s.* of Ai ascended up, 21
*Jud.* 20:38 ma. *s.* rise out of city
2 *Sam.* 22:9 there went up a *s.* out of his nostrils, *Ps.* 18:8
*Job* 41:20 out of his nostr. go. *s.*
*Ps.* 37:20 wicked consu. into *s.*
68:2 as *s.* is driven away
102:3 my days are consu. like *s.*
119:83 I am bec. like bottle in *s.*
*Prov.* 10:26 as *s.* to eyes, so slug.
*Cant.* 3:6 com. like pillars of *s.*
*Is.* 4:5 on her assemb. *s.* by day
6:4 the house was filled with *s.*
9:18 mount like lifting up of *s.*
14:31 shall come from north *s.*
34:10 *s.* thereof shall go up
51:6 heavens sh. vanish like *s.*
65:5 th. are as *s.* in my nose
*Hos.* 13:3 as *s.* out of chimney
*Joel* 2:30 fire, and pillars of *s.*
*Nah.* 2:13 burn her chariots in *s.*
*Acts* 2:19 fire, and vapor of *s.*
*Rev.* 8:4 *s.* of incense ascended
9:2 arose *s.* out of bottoml. pit
3 came out of *s.* locu. on earth
17 out of mouth iss. fire and *s.*
18 3d part of men killed by *s.*
14:11 *s.* of their torment ascend.
15:8 temple was filled with *s.*
18:9 lament for her when see *s.*
18 they saw *s.* of her burning
19:3 and her *s.* rose up for ever

**SMOKE.**
*Deut.* 29:20 anger of Lord sh. *s.*
*Ps.* 74:1 G. why thine anger *s.*?
104:32 toucheth hills, they *s.*
144:5 touch mountains, they *s.*

**SMOKING.**
*Gen.* 15:17 behold, a *s.* furnace
*Ex.* 20:18 peo. saw mountain *s.*
*Is.* 7:4 tails of th. *s.* firebrands
42:3 *s.* flax not que. *Mat.* 12:20

**SMOOTH, ER.**
*Gen.* 27:11 E. hairy, I am *s.* man
16 skins of kids on *s.* of neck
1 *Sam.* 17:40 Da. chose 5 *s.* ston.
*Ps.* 55:21 words were *s.* th. butter
*Prov.* 5:3 her mouth is *s.* th. oil
*Is.* 30:10 speak unto us *s.* things
57:6 among *s.* stones of stream
*Luke* 3:5 rough ways be made *s.*

**SMOOTHETH.**
*Is.* 41:7 he that *s.* with hammer

**SMOTE.**
*Gen.* 19:11 *s.* men with blindness

Ex. 7:20 lift up rod, s. waters
12:27 when he s. the Egyptians
29 L. s. first-born in land of Egypt, Num. 3:13; 8:17; Ps. 78:51; 105:36; 135:8
Num. 11:33 L. s. peo. wi. plague
20:11 Moses s. rock, Ps. 78:20
22:23 Balaam s. the ass, 25, 27
24:10 Balak s. his hands togeth.
32:4 the country the Lord s.
Jos. 9:18 s. th. not, bec. princes
11:12 s. all kings with sword, 17
20:5 s. his neighbor unwittingly
Jud. 4:21 J. s. nail into temples
5:26 s. Sisera, s. off his head
7:13 came and s. it that it fell
20:35 L. s. Benjamin before Isr.
1 Sam. 4:8 gods th. s. Egyptians
6:9 it is not his hand that s. us
17:49 Da. s. Philist. in forehead
25:38 Lord s. Nabal that he died
2 Sam. 14:7 him that s. his brot.
2 K. 2:8 Eli. s. waters; 14 Elis. s.
6:18 he s. them with blindness
15:5 L. s. king, he was a leper
19:35 angel s. 185,000, Is. 37:36
2 Chr. 14:12 L. s. Ethiopians
Neh. 13:25 s. certain of them
Ps. 78:31 s. down chosen of Isra.
66 s. enemies in hinder parts
Cant. 5:7 watchmen, they s. me
Is. 10:20 no more stay on him s.
14:6 who s. people is persecut.
29 rod of him that s. thee is b.
30:31 Assyr. beaten down wh. s.
41:7 encoura. him that s. anvil
60:10 in my wrath I s. thee
Jer. 20:2 Pashur s. Jeremiah
31:19 after I was instructed I s.
Dan. 2:34 which s. the image, 35
5:6 Belshazzar's knees s. one a.
Hag. 2:17 I s. you with blasting
Mat. 26:51 Peter s. off his ear
68 who is he s. thee, Lu. 22:64
Luke 18:13 publican s. his breast
23:48 beholding Je. s. th. brea.
Acts 12:7 angel s. Peter on side

**SMOTE him.**

Ex. 21:19 he that s. h. be quit
Num. 35:21 he that s. h. sh. die
1 Sam. 24:5 David's heart s. h.
2 Sam. 2:23 s. him under fifth rib, 3:27; 4:6
6:7 God s. him there for his error, 1 Chr. 13:10
1 K. 20:37 s. h. he wounded him
2 K. 19:37 his sons s. him with sword, Is. 37:38
Is. 27:7 smote those that s. h.?
57:17 for his coveteousn. I s. h
Jer. 37:15 wroth with J. and s. h.
Mat. 26:67 s. h. with th. hands
27:30 s. h. on head, Mark 15:19; Luke 22:63; John 19:3
Acts 12:23 angel of Lord s. him

**SMOTEST.**

Ex. 17:5 wherew. thou s. river

**SMYRNA.**

Rev. 1:11 send to church in S.
2:8 to angel of church in S.

**SNAIL.**

Lev. 11:30 s. and mole unclean
Ps. 58:8 as a s. let ev. one pass

**SNARE.**

Ex. 10:7 how long th. man be s.?
23:33 it will surely be s. unto thee, Deut. 7:16; Jud. 2:3
34:12 no covenant, lest it be a s.
Jud. 8:27 bec. a s. unto Gideon
1 Sam. 18:21 that she may be a s.
28:9 layest thou a s. for my life?
Job 18:8 a net, he walketh on a s.
10 the s. is laid for him in a tr.
Ps. 69:22 let their table become a s. unto them, Rom. 11:9
91:3 deliver thee fr. s. of fowler
106:36 idols, wh. were s. to th.
119:110 wicked have laid s.
124:7 escaped as a bird out of s. of fowler; s. is broken
140:5 proud have hid a s. for me
141:9 keep me from the s. laid
142:3 they privily laid s. for me
Prov. 7:23 as a bird hasteth to s.
18:7 fool's lips are s. of his soul
Prov. 20:25 s. to man who devo.
22:25 and get a s. to thy soul
29:6 transgress. of evil man is s.
8 scorn. men br. a city into s.
25 fear of man bringeth a s.
Ec. 9:12 as birds caught in the s.
Is. 8:14 for a s. to inhabitants
24:17 pit, and the s. are upon thee, 18; Jer. 48:43, 44
29:21 s. for him that reproveth
Jer. 50:24 I ha. laid a s. for thee
Lam. 3:47 a s. is come upon us
Ezek. 12:13 taken in my s. 17:20
Hos. 5:1 bec. ye have been a s.
9:8 the prophet is s. of fowler
Amos 3:5 can bird fall in a s. wh. no gin is? sh. one take up s.?
Luke 21:35 as a s. shall it come
1 Cor. 7:35 not th. I may cast s.
1 Tim. 3:7 lest he fall in s.
6:8 rich, fall into a s. and lusts
2 Tim. 2:26 may recover out of s.

**SNARED.**

Deut. 7:25 not take idols, lest s.
12:30 take heed thou be not s.
Ps. 9:16 s. in work of hands
Prov. 6:2 s. with words, 12:13
Ec. 9:12 so are sons of men s.
Is. 8:15 many shall fall and be s.
28:13 they might fall, and be s.
42:22 they are all of them s.

**SNARES.**

Jos. 23:13 s. and traps unto you
2 Sam. 22:6 s. of death prevented me, Ps. 18:5
Job 22:10 s. are round about thee
40:24 Behemoth's nose pierc. s.
Ps. 11:6 on wicked he sh. rain s.
38:12 seek my life, lay s. for me
64:5 commune of laying s. priv.
Prov. 13:14 s. of death, 14:27
22:5 thorns and s. are in way
Ec. 7:26 woman wh. heart is s.
Jer. 5:26 as he that setteth s.
18:22 for they hid s. for my feet

**SNATCH.**

Is. 9:20 he shall s. on right hand

**SNEEZED.**

2 K. 4:35 child s. seven times

**SNORTING.**

Jer. 8:16 s. of horses was heard

**SNOUT.**

Prov. 11:22 jewel in swine's s.

**SNOW.**

Ex. 4:6 hand was leprous as s.
Num. 12:10 Miriam became as s.
2 Sam. 23:20 sl. lion in time of s.
2 K. 5:27 Gehazi went whi. as s.
Job 6:16 and wherein the s. is hid
9:30 if I wash myself in s. water
24:19 heat consumeth s. waters
37:6 saith to s. Be thou on earth
38:22 entered into treasures of s.
Ps. 51:7 I shall be whiter than s.
68:14 it was white as s. in Sal.
147:16 he giveth s. like wool
148:8 fire, hail, s. and vapor
Prov. 25:13 as cold of s. in harv.
26:1 as s. in summer, so honor
31:21 she is not afraid of the s.
Is. 1:18 sins as scar. white as s.
55:10 s. fr. heaven returneth not
Jer. 18:14 will a man leave s.?
Lam. 4:7 her Nazar. purer th. s.
Dan. 7:9 garm. was white as s.
Mat. 28:3 raim. as s. Mark 9:3
Rev. 1:14 his hairs white as s.

**SNOWY.**

1 Chr. 11:22 slew a lion in s. day

**SNUFFED.**

Jer. 14:6 wild asses s. up wind
Mal. 1:13 ye have s. at it

**SNUFF-DISHES.**

Ex. 25:38 s.-d. of gold, 37:23
Num. 4:9 and cover his s.-d.

**SNUFFERS.**

Ex. 37:23 made his s. of pure gold, 1 K. 7:50; 2 Chr. 4:22
2 K. 12:13 s. made of money
25:14 s. took th. away, Jer. 52:18

**SNUFFETH.**

Jer. 2:24 a wild ass s. up wind

**SO.**

2 K. 17:4 sent messengers to S.

**Not SO.**

Job 9:35 but it is not s. with me
Mat. 20:26 it sh. n. be s. am. you
John 14:2 if it were not s. I wou.
Acts 10:14 P. said, not s. L. 11:8
Jam. 3:10 these things ought not s.

**SOAKED.**

Is. 34:7 land sh. be s. with blood

**SOAP.**

Jer. 2:22 wash, and take much s.
Mal. 3:2 for he is like fuller's s.

**SOBER.**

2 Cor. 5:13 whether we be s. it is
1 Thes. 5:6 let us watch and be s.
8 let us who are of day be s.
1 Tim. 3:2 bis. mu. be s. Tit. 1:8
11 deacons' wives must be s.
Tit. 2:2 that aged men be s.
4 teach young women to be s.
1 Pet. 1:13 gird loi. of mind, be s.
4:7 be ye s. watch unto prayer
5:8 be s. be vigilant, bec. your

**SOBERLY.**

Rom. 12:3 think s. acc. to faith
Tit. 2:12 teach. we should live s.

**SOBER-MINDED.**

Tit. 2:6 exh. yo. men to be s.-m.

**SOBERNESS.**

Acts 26:25 speak forth words of s.

**SOBRIETY.**

1 Tim. 2:9 adorn themse. with s.
15 continue in holiness with s.

SOCHO. Jos. 15:48

**SOCKET.**

Ex. 38:27 100 talents, talent for s.

**SOCKETS.**

Ex. 26:19 make forty s. of silver, 21; 36:24, 26
21 two s. 25; 36:24, 26
25 s. of silver, sixt. s. 36:30, 36
37 cast five s. of brass, 36:38
27:10 20 s. be of brass, 38:10, 11
12 west side pill. s. ten, 38:12
14 hangings on side, s. three
16 pillars sh. be 4, their s. four
17 hooks of sil. and s. brass, 18
35:11 pillars s. of tabernacle
38:27 s. of sanctu. s. veil, 100 s.
31 s. court, s. of court-gate
40:18 reared taberna. fastened s.
Num. 3:36 under custody sons of Merari sh. be s. 37; 4:31, 32
Cant. 5:15 as pillars on s. of gold

**SOD.**

Gen. 25:29 Jacob s. pottage
2 Chr. 35:13 holy offerings s. they

**SODDEN.**

Ex. 12:9 raw, nor s. with water
Lev. 6:28 earthen ves. wherein is s. be bro. if s. in brazen pot
Num. 6:19 priest sh. take s. sho.
1 Sam. 2:15 not have s. flesh
Lam. 4:10 women have s. child.

**SODOM.**
Gen. 13:10 bef. Lord destroy. S.
13 the men of S. were wicked
14:11 took all the goods of S.
12 took Lot who dwelt in S.
17 the king of S. went out to
18:20 because cry of S. is great
26 if I find in S. fifty righteous
19:24 Lord rained upon S. fire
Deut. 29:23 like overthrow of S.
Is. 13:19; Jer 49:18; 50:40
32:32 their vine is of vine of S.
Is. 1:9 should have been as S.
10 hear Lord, ye rulers of S.
3:9 shall declare their sin as S.
Jer. 23:14 are all unto me as S.
Lam. 4:6 punishm. of sin of S.
Ezek. 16:46 sister is S. 48, 49, 55
53 when I bring captivity of S.
Amos 4:11 as God overthrew S.
Zep. 2:9 surely M. shall be as S.
Mat. 10:15 for land of S. 11:24; Mark 6:11; Luke 10:12
Luke 17:29 Lot went out of S.
Rom. 9:29 we had been as S.
2 Pet. 2:6 turn. S. and Go. to as.
Jude 7 even as S. and Gomorrah
Rev. 11:8 spiritually called S.

**SODOMITE.**
Deut. 23:17 there shall be no S.

**SODOMITES.**
1 K. 14:24 there were also S. in
15:12 Asa took away S. 22:46
2 K. 23:7 bra. down houses of S.

**SOFT.**
Job 23:16 G. maketh my heart s.
41:3 will he speak s. words?
Ps. 65:10 thou makest it s.
Prov. 15:1 a s. answer turn. wra.
25:15 a s. tongue breaketh bone
Mat. 11:8 man clothed in s. rai. that wear s. cloth. Luke 7:25

**SOFTER.**
Ps. 55:21 words were s. than oil

**SOFTLY.**
Gen. 33:14 I will lead s. as cattle
Jud. 4:21 Jael went s. to him
Ruth 3:7 came s. and uncovered
1 K. 21:27 A. in sackcl. went s.
Is. 8:6 waters of Shil. that go s.
38:15 I shall go s. all my years
Acts 27:13 south wind blew s.

**SOIL.**
Ezek. 17:8 planted in good s.

**SOJOURN.**
Gen. 12:10 Ab. went to Eg. to s.
19:9 This fellow came in to s.
26:3 s. in this land, I will be
47:4 to s. in land are we come
Ex. 12:48 stran. s. wi. thee, Lev. 19:33; Num. 9:14; 15:14
Lev. 17:8 strang. who s. th. offer
25:45 strangers that s. of them
Jud. 17:8 Levite went to s.
Ruth 1:1 Elimel. went to s. in M.
1 K. 17:20 widow wi. whom I s.
2 K. 8:1 s. wheres. thou canst s.
Ps. 120:5 woe is me, I s. in Mes.
Is. 23:7 her feet carry her to s.
52:4 my peo. went to Eg. to s.
Jer. 42:15 into Egypt, and go to s. there, 17; 44:12, 14, 28
42:22 die in place whither ye s.
Lam. 4:15 they shall no more s.
Ezek. 20:38 bring fr. where th. s.
47:22 you and strangers who s.
Acts 7:6 seed should s. in a stra.

**SOJOURNED.**
Gen. 20:1 Abraham s. in Gerar
21:34 and s. in Philistines' land
32:4 I s. with Laban, and stayed
35:27 where Abra. and Isaac s.
Deut. 18:6 Le. come fr. wh. he s.
26:5 s. in Egypt with a few
Jud. 17:7 a Lev. s. in Bethlehem
19:16 an old man s. in Gibeah
2 K. 8:2 she s. in land of Philist.
Ps. 105:23 Jac. s. in land of Ham
Heb. 11:9 by faith he s. in land

**SOJOURNER.**
Gen. 23:4 I am a s. with you
Lev. 22:10 s. of priest sh. not eat
25:35 s. fallen in decay
40 thy brother shall be as a s.
47 s. wax rich, brother sell to s.
Num. 35:15 six cities a ref. for s.
Ps. 39:12 stranger, s. as my fath

**SOJOURNERS.**
Lev. 25:23 ye are strangers and s
2 Sam. 4:3 Beerothites were s.
1 Chr. 29:15 we are s. as our fat.

**SOJOURNETH.**
Ex. 3:22 woman borrow of th. s.
12:49 one law to stranger th. s. Lev. 16:29
Lev. 17:12 nor stranger that s.
18:26 that s. am. you shall keep
25:6 meat for stranger that s.
Num. 15:15 one ordi. for you and stranger that s. 16:29; 19:10
Jos. 20:9 cit. for strangers that s.
Ezr. 1:4 remaineth where he s.
Ezek. 14:7 every one that s. in Is.

**SOJOURNING.**
Ex. 12:40 the s. of Is. 430 years
Jud. 19:1 a Lev. s. on mount E.
1 Pet. 1:17 pass time of s. in fear

**SOLACE.**
Prov. 7:18 let us s. ourselves

**SOLD.**
Gen. 25:33 Esau s. his birthright
31:15 our father hath s. us
37:28 they s. Jos. to Ishmaelites
36 Midianites s. him into Eg.
41:56 Jos. s. corn to Egyptians
42:6 he it was that s. to people
45:4 I am Joseph whom ye s.
47:20 Egyptians s. every man
22 priests s. not their lands
Ex. 22:3 then shall he be s.
Lev. 25:23 land shall not be s.
33 house that was s. sh. go out
42 breth. sh. not be s. as bond
27:28 no devoted thing sh. be s.
Deut. 15:12 if thy brother be s.
32:30 except their Rock s. them
Jud. 2:14 he s. th. into enemies
10:7 s. them into hands of Phil.
1 Sam. 12:9 s. them into hand of
1 K. 21:20 thou hast s. thyself to
2 K. 6:25 ass's head s. for 80 pie.
7:1 mea. of flour be s. for she. 16
17:17 Is. s. themselves to do ev.
Neh. 5:8 brethren who were s.
13:15 day wherein they s. vict.
16 bought and s. on sabbath
Est. 7:4 we are s. I and people
Ps. 105:17 Jos. was s. for serv.
Is. 50:1 which is it to whom I s. you? have ye s. yourselves
52:3 ye s. yourselves for naught
Jer. 34:14 let go who hath been s.
Lam. 5:4 our wood is s. unto us
Ezek. 7:13 seller not retu. that s.
Joel 3:3 have s. a girl for wine
6 children of Judah have ye s.
7 out of place whit. ye s. them
Amos 2:6 they s. right. for silver
Mat. 10:29 not two sparrows s.
13:46 and s. all that he had
18:25 commanded him to be s.
21:12 cast out th. that s. of them s. Mark 11:15; Luke 19:45
26:9 this ointm. might ha. been s. Mark 14:5; John 12:5
Luke 12:6 five sparrows s.
17:28 they s. they planted
John 2:14 in temple that s. oxen
16 said to them that s. doves
Acts 2:45 s. their possessi. 4:34
4:37 Joses having land s. it
5:1 Ananias s. 8 ye s. land for
4 after it was s. was it not in
Rom. 7:14 carnal, s. under sin
1 Cor. 10:25 whats. is s. in sham.
Heb. 12:16 for one morsel s. birt.

**SOLDERING.**
Is. 41:7 ready for s. he fastened

**SOLDIER.**
John 19:23 to every s. a part
Acts 10:7 Cornelius called a s.
28:16 suff. Paul to dwell with s.
2 Tim. 2:3 end. as a good s. of C.
4 hath chosen him to be a s.

**SOLDIERS.**
2 Chr. 25:13 s. fell upon cities
Ezr. 8:22 I ashamed to requ. s.
Is. 15:4 armed s. of Moab cry
Mat. 8:9 having s. und. Luke 7:8
27:27 the s. took J. and gathered to him s.
28:12 they gave money to s.
Luke 3:14 s. demanded, saying
John 19:23 the s. took his garm.
24 these things theref. s. did
32 then came s. and bra. legs
34 one of the s. with a spear
Acts 12:4 delivered Peter to s.
6 Pe. was sleeping bet. two s.
18 no small stir among the s.
21:35 he was borne of the s.
23:23 make ready 200 s.
27:31 P. said to the s. Except
32 then the s. cut off the ropes
42 s. counsel was to kill pris.

**SOLE.**
Gen. 8:9 dove found no rest for s.
Deut. 28:35 wi. botch from s. of
56 not set s. of foot upon gro.
65 nei. shall s. of thy foot rest
Jos. 1:3 place s. of foot tread
2 Sam. 14:25 from s. of foot to cr.
Job 2:7 Satan smote Job fr. s. of
Is. 1:6 from s. of foot to head
Ezek. 1:7 s. of feet li. s. of calf's
See FEET.

**SOLEMN.**
Num. 10:10 in your s. days ye sh.
Ps. 92:3 praise with s. sound
Is. 1:13 iniq. even the s. meet.
Lam. 2:22 called as in a s. day
Hos. 9:5 will ye do in s. day?
See ASSEMBLY, FEAST, FEASTS.

**SOLEMNITY, IES.**
Deut. 31:10 in the s. of the year
Is. 30:29 as wh. a holy s. is kept
33:20 upon Z. the city of our s.
Ezek. 45:17 burnt-offerings in s.
46:11 in s. meat-offering shall

**SOLEMNLY.**
Gen. 43:3 the man did s. protest
1 Sam. 8:9 yet protest s. to them

**SOLITARY.**
Job 3:7 let that night be s.
30:3 for famine they were s.
Ps. 68:6 G. setteth s. in families
107:4 wandered in a s. way
Is. 35:1 wilderness and s. place
Lam. 1:1 how doth city sit s.
Mark 1:35 Je. departed to s. pl.

**SOLITARILY.**
Mic. 7:14 feed peo. which dw. s.

**SOLOMON.**
2 Sam. 5:14 there was born to David S. 1 Chr. 3:5; 14:4
12:24 he called his name S. and
1 K. 1:10 S. his brother, 19, 26
13 S. sh. reign after me, 17, 30
21 I and my son S. shall be
34 God save king S. 39, 43
37 wi. D. even so be he wi. S.
47 God make name of S. better
51 S. swear to me that he will
2:1 David charged S. his son, 23

3:1 S. made affinity with Phar.
3 S. loved Lord; 10 S. asked
1 *K.* 3:5 Lord appear to S. 9:2;
2 *Chr.* 1:7; 7:12
4:22 S. provision for one day
29 God gave S. wisdom, 5:12
34 hear wis. of S. from all the
kings, *Mat.* 12:42; *Luke* 11:31
5:1 Hiram sent servants to S.
13 king S. raised a levy out of
6:14 S. built house and finished
it, 2 *Chr.* 7:11; *Acts* 7:47
7:51 so ended the work S. made
8:1 S. assemb. elders, 2 *Chr.* 5:2
22 S. spread forth his hands to
54 S. made an end, 2 *Chr.* 7:1
65 S. held a feast; 9:26 S. ma.
10:1 when queen of Sheba heard
of fame of S. 2 *Chr.* 9:1
24 all sought to S. 2 *Chr.* 9:23
11:1 king S. loved many wom.
2 S. clave to these in love, 4
5 S. went after Ashtoreth and
6 S. did evil; 7 S. built for C.
9 Lord was angry with S. 27
14 Hadad, an adversary to S.
28 S. made Jeroboam ruler
40 S. sought therefore to kill
43 S. slept with his fathers
12:2 fled from the presence of S.
14:26 shields S. ma. 2 *Chr.* 12:9
2 *K.* 21:7 the Lord said to David
and to S. 2 *Chr.* 33:7
1 *Chr.* 22:5 S. my son, is young
9 for his name shall be S. 17
28:6 S. thy son he shall build
9 thou S. my son, know the G.
11 David gave to S. pattern
29:1 S. my son, whom G. alone
19 give to S. my son a perfect
23 S. sat on the throne of the
25 L. magnified S. exceedingly
2 *Chr.* 2:17 S. number. strangers
3:3 things wherein S. was inst.
30:26 since time of S. not such
*Ezr.* 2:55 the children of S. serv.
58; *Neh.* 7:57, 60; 11:3
*Neh.* 12:45 commandment of S.
13:26 did not king S. sin by th.?
*Prov.* 1:1 prov. of S. 10:1; 25:1
*Cant.* 1:1 Song of songs wh. is S.
5 comely, as the curtains of S.
3:7 behold, his bed which is S.
11 behold king S. 8:12 S. must
8:11 S. had vineyard at Baal-h.
*Jer.* 52:20 sea S. ma. was carried
*Mat.* 1:6 Da. begat S. 7 S. begat
6:29 S. in all his gl. *Luke* 12:27
12:42 greater than S. *Luke* 11:31
*John* 10:23 Je. walked in S. por.
*Acts* 3:11 ran to them to S. porch
5:12 with one accord in S. por.

**SOMEBODY.**

*Luke* 8:46 Jesus said, *s.* touched
*Acts* 5:36 Theu. boasting to be *s.*

**SOMETHING.**

*Mark* 5:43 that *s.* should be giv.
*Luke* 11:54 seeking to catch *s.*
*John* 13:29 he sh. give *s.* to poor
*Acts* 3:5 expecting to receive *s.*
23:15 would inquire *s.* more per.
18 young man hath *s.* to say
*Gal.* 6:3 man think him. to be *s.*

**SOMETIMES.**

*Eph.* 2:13 ye who were *s.* afar off
*Col.* 3:7 in which ye walked *s.*

**SOMEWHAT.**

*Lev.* 4:22 wh. ruler hath done *s.*
1 *K.* 2:14 he said, I have *s.* to say
2 *K.* 5:20 I will run and take *s.*
*Luke* 7:40 have *s.* to say unto th.
*Acts* 23:20 inq. *s.* more perfectly
25:26 I might have *s.* to write
*Rom.* 15:24 if first I be *s.* filled
2 *Cor.* 5:12 may have *s.* to answer
10:8 tho' I should boast *s.* more
*Gal.* 2:6 th. who seemed to be *s.*
*Heb.* 8:3 this man have *s.* to offer
*Rev.* 2:4 I have *s.* against thee

**SON.**

*Gen.* 17:16 I will give thee a *s.* of
Sarah, 19; 18:10, 14
21:2 Sarah bare Abraham a *s.* 7
24:36 my master's wife bare a *s.*
51 let her be master's *s.* wife
29:33 he hath given me this *s.*
30:6 G. heard me, given me *s.*
24 Lord shall add to me ano. *s.*
35:17 thou shalt have this *s.*
37:3 bec. he was *s.* of old age
*Ex.* 1:16 if *s.* then ye kill him
22 every *s.* born cast into river
2:10 child grew, and bec. her *s.*
*Lev.* 12:6 days of purify. for a *s.*
24:10 *s.* of an Israelitish woman
25:49 his uncle's *s.* may redeem
*Num.* 23:18 hearken, *s.* of Zip.
27:4 hath no *s.* 8 and have no *s.*
*Deut.* 13:6 if *s.* of mo. ent. thee.
21:16 not make *s.* of belov. first-
born before *s.* of hated, 17
20 our *s.* is stubborn, rebellious
28:56 eye sh. be evil tow. her *s.*
*Jos.* 6:26 in young. *s.* set up gat.
*Jud.* 5:12 lead captive *s.* of Ab.
9:18 made *s.* of his servant king
11:2 thou art *s.* of strange wo.
34 he had nei. *s.* nor daughter
13:3 conceive and bear a *s.* 5, 7
*Ruth* 4:13 Ruth bare a *s.*
17 a *s.* born to Naomi
1 *Sam.* 1:23 Hannah gave *s.* suck
4:20 fear not, th. hast borne a *s.*
10:11 wh. is come to *s.* of Kish?
16:18 I have seen a *s.* of Jesse
17:55 whose *s.*? 58 whose *s.* art
20:27 wheref. com. not *s.* of J.?
31 as long as *s.* of Jesse liveth
22:7 will *s.* of Jesse give fields?
9 I saw *s.* of Jesse com. to N.
12 hear, now, thou *s.* of Ahit.
25:10 who is the *s.* of Jesse?
17 he is such a *s.* of Belial
2 *Sam.* 1:13 I am *s.* of a stranger
9:9 give. *s.* all that pertain. to S.
10:2 show kindness to *s.* of Na.
16:3 where is thy master's *s.*
18:12 put forth ha. ag. king's *s.*
18 have no *s.* to keep my name
20 because the king's *s.* is dead
1 *K.* 3:6 thou hast given him a *s.*
5:7 hath given David a wise *s.*
12:16 no inheritance in *s.* of
Jesse, 2 *Chr.* 10:16
14:5 cometh to ask of thee for *s.*
22:26 Joa. king's *s.* 2 *Chr.* 18:25
2 *K.* 1:17 because he had no *s.*
4:16 season th. sh. embrace a *s.*
28 did I desire a *s.* 37 took *s.*
6:29 give *s.* to eat him, hid *s.*
32 *s.* of a murderer hath sent
8:1 whose *s.* he restored to life
11:1 *s.* was dead, 2 *Chr.* 22:9
4 Jehoiada sho. them king's *s.*
1 *Chr.* 12:18 side, thou *s.* of Jesse
22:9 behold, a *s.* shall be born
2 *Chr.* 21:17 never a *s.* left him
23:3 behold, king's *s.* shall rei.
*Job* 18:19 nei. have *s.* nor neph.
*Ps.* 2:12 kiss *s.* lest he be angry
72:1 righteousn. unto king's *s.*
86:16 save *s.* of thy handmaid
89:22 nor *s.* of wicked. afflict h.
116:16 I am *s.* of thy hand-ma.
*Prov.* 3:12 *s.* in whom he deligh.
4:3 I was my father's *s.* belov.
10:1 a wise *s.* mak. glad fa. 15:20
5 gath. is wise *s.* sleep. in har.
*s.* caus. shame, 17:2; 19:26
13:1 a wise *s.* heareth instruc.
17:25 foolish *s.* is a grief to fat.
19:13 foolish *s.* calamity of fath.
28:7 whoso keep. law is wise *s.*
31:2 *s.* of womb, *s.* of vows?
*Ec.* 5:14 begetteth a *s.* nothing
10:17 when king is *s.* of nobles
*Is.* 7:14 virgin conc. and bear *s.*
9:6 ch. born, unto us *s.* is given
14:12 O Lucifer, *s.* of morning
22 I will cut off fr. Babylon *s.*
19:11 *s.* of wise, *s.* of kings
49:15 compassion on *s.* of womb
56:3 nei. *s.* of stranger speak
*Jer.* 6:26 mourn. as for only *s.*
33:21 sho. not have a *s.* to reign
*Ezek.* 14:20 deliv. nei. *s.* nor dau.
18:4 soul of *s.* is mine
14 a *s.* that seeth his fa.'s sins
19 why doth not *s.* bear iniq.
20 *s.* not bear iniq. of father
44:25 for *s.* or daugh. they may
*Hos.* 13:13 he is an unwise *s.*
*Amos* 7:14 nor was I proph.'s *s.*
8:10 as mourning of an only *s.*
*Mic.* 7:6 *s.* dishonoreth father
*Mal.* 1:6 *s.* honoreth his father
*Mat.* 1:21 bring forth *s.* *Luke* 1:31
9:2 *s.* be of go. cheer, *Mark* 2:5
10:37 he that loveth *s.* or daug.
11:27 know. *S.* but Father, nor
Father save *S.* *Luke* 10:22
13:55 the carpen.'s *s.* *Mark* 6:3;
*Luke* 4:22
16:16 thou art Christ, *S.* of God
21:28 *s.* go work in my viney.
22:42 of Christ? whose *s.* is he?
*Mark* 12:6 having one *s.* beloved
13:32 hour knoweth not the *S.*
14:61 Christ, *S.* of the Blessed?
*Luke* 1:13 Elisab. shall bear a *s.*
32 be called *S.* of the Highest
3:23 Jesus *s.* of Joseph, *s.* of H.
7:12 only *s.* of his mother
10:6 if *s.* of peace be there
11:11 if a *s.* ask bread of any
12:53 father divided against *s.*
*Luke* 15:13 younger *s.* gathered
16:25 *s.* remember, in thy lifet.
19:9 forasmuch as he is *s.* of A.
*John* 1:18 only *S.* in bosom of F.
3:35 Father loveth the *S.* 5:20
36 beli. on *S.* believeth not *S.*
5:19 *S.* can do noth. of himself
21 *S.* quicken. whom he will
22 committed all judgm. to *S.*
23 men should honor *S.* he th.
honor. not *S.* honor. not F.
26 given to *S.* to have life
6:40 ev. one who seeth the *S.*
42 is not this Jes. *s.* of Joseph
8:35 *s.* abideth; 9:19 is this *s.*?
36 if *S.* shall make you free
9:20 we kn. that this is our *s.*
14:13 Fa. may be glorified in *S.*
17:12 none lost but *s.* of perdit.
*Acts* 4:36 Barnabas, *s.* of consol.
23:6 Pharisee, *s.* of a Pharisee
16 Paul's sister's *s.* heard of
*Rom.* 9:9 Sarah shall have a *s.*
1 *Cor.* 15:28 then *S.* himself sub.
*Gal.* 4:7 no more serv. but a *s.*
*Phil.* 2:22 as *s.* he serv. in gospel
*Col.* 4:10 Marcus sister's *s.* to B.
2 *Thes.* 2:3 man of sin, *s.* of per.
1 *Tim.* 1:18 commit to thee *s.* T.
*Heb.* 1:5 he shall be to me a *s.*
8 to *S.* he saith, Thy throne
3:6 Christ as a *s.* over his own
5:8 tho' he were a *s.* yet learned
7:28 word of the oath maketh *s.*
11:24 refu. to be called *s.* of Ph.
12:6 scourg. every *s.* he receiv.
1 *John* 2:22 antic. deni. F. and *S.*
23 whosoever denieth the *S.*
the same hath not the Fath.
24 continue in *S.* and in Fath.
4:14 Father sent *S.* to be Savi.
5:12 he that hath *S.* hath life
2 *John* 3 L. Je. Ch. *S.* of Father
9 hath both the Father and *S.*
*See* DAVID.

**SON of God.**

Dan. 3:25 fourth is like s. of G.
Mat. 8:29 thou S. of G. Luke 8:28
14:33 of a truth th. art S. of G.
26:63 whether he be Ch. S. of G.
27:43 he said, I am the S. of G.
54 was S. of G. Mark 15:39
Mark 3:11 art S. of G. John 1:49
Luke 1:35 sh. be called S. of G.
3:38 s. of Adam, was s. of G.
4:41 crying, Thou art Christ the S. of G. John 6:69; 11:27
22:70 art th. then the S. of G.?
John 1:34 this is the S. of God
3:18 the only begotten S. of G.
5:25 shall hear voice of S. of G.
9:35 dost thou beli. on S. of G.?
10:36 I said, I am the S. of God
11:4 that S. of G. might be glo.
19:7 he made himself S. of God
20:31 beli. Je. is C. the S. of G.
Acts 8:37 J. Christ is the S. of G.
9:20 Christ, that he is S. of G.
Rom. 1:4 declared to be S. of G.
2 Cor. 1:19 the S. of G. was not
Gal. 2:20 by faith of S. of God
Eph. 4:13 knowledge of S. of G
Heb. 4:14 high-pr. J. the S. of G
6:6 crucify to themsel. S. of G
7:3 made like to the S. of God
10:29 trod. under foot S. of God
1 John 3:8 for this purp. S. of G.
4:15 shall confess Je. is S. of G.
5:5 believeth Jesus is S. of God
10 that believeth on S. of God
13 believe on name of S. of G.
20 know that S. of G. is come
Rev. 2:18 write, saith S. of God

**His SON.**

Gen. 22:13 bu.-off. in stead of h. s.
25:11 Abraham, G. blessed h. s.
37:34 Jacob mourned for his s.
Ex. 32:29 every man upon his s.
Lev. 21:2 for his s. he may be
Num. 20:26 put on Elea. h. s. 28
Deut. 1:31 man doth bear his s.
7:3 thy daugh. not give to his s.
8:5 as a man chasteneth his s.
18:10 not any mak. h. s. to pass
2 Sam. 16:19 serve in pres. of h. s.
1 K. 11:36 and to h. s. will I give
2 K. 3:27 Moab took his eldest s.
16:3 A. made his s. to pass thro'
21:6 Manas. made his s. to pass
23:10 no man mi. make h. s. pass
2 Chr. 24:22 Jo. the ki. slew h. s.
Prov. 13:24 spareth rod, hat. h. s.
29:21 shall have him bec. his s.
30:4 what is his s. name?
Jer. 27:7 his s. and his son's s.
Mal. 3:17 as a man spareth h. s.
Mat. 21:37 last of all sent his s.
Mat. 22:2 made a marr. for his s.
45 how is he then h. s.? Mark 12:37; Luke 20:44
John 3:16 gave h. only begot. S.
17 God sent not his S. to con.
Acts 3:13 God hath glori. h. S. J.
26 God having raised up h. S.
Rom. 1:9 serve in gospel of h. S.
8:3 God sending his own S. in
32 that spared not his own S.
Gal. 1:16 it pleas. G. to rev. h. S.
4:4 God sent forth his S.
1 Thes. 1:10 to wait for his S.
Heb. 1:2 spoken to us by his S.
Jam. 2:21 had offered Isaac his s.
1 John 1:3 fel. is with F. and h. S.
7 blood of Jes. Ch. h. S. clea.
3:23 believe on name of h. S.
5:9 he hath testified of h. S.
10 beli. not rec. G. gave of h. S.
11 this life is in his S.
20 we are in him, even his S.

**SON-IN-LAW.**

Gen. 19:12 hast thou any s.-i.-l.?
Jud. 15:6 Samson the s.-i.-l. of
19:5 damsel's fa. said to s.-i.-l.
1 Sam. 18:18 should be s.-i.-l. 23
22:14 faithful as king's s.-i.-l.?
2 K. 8:27 Jehoram was s.-i.-l.
Neh. 6:18 Tobiah was s.-i.-l. to
13:28 was s.-i.-l. to Sanballat

See BELOVED.

**My SON.**

Gen. 21:23 not deal fal. wi. my s.
22:7 he said, Here am I, my s.
24:3 not take wife to my s. 37
6 bring not my s. thither ag. 8
27:8 now theref. my s. obey, 43
18 am I, who art thou, my s.?
21 whe. thou be my very s. 24
37 what shall I do now, my s.?
37:33 and said, It is my s. coat
35 will go into grave to my s.
42:38 he said, my s. shall not go
45:28 Joseph my s. is yet alive
Ex. 4:22 Is. is my s. even my
Jud. 8:23 neith. shall my s. rule
1 Sam. 3:6 I called not my s. lie
4:16 what is there done, my s.?
10:2 what shall I do for my s.?
24:16 voice, my s. David? 26:17
26:21 sinned, return, my s. Dav.
2 Sam. 7:14 he shall be my s.
13:25 my s. let us not all go
14:16 dest. me and my s. out of
16:11 my s. who came forth
18:33 king said, O my s. Absal. my s. my s. Absalom, 19:4
1 K. 3:20 took my s. from, 22, 23
17:12 dress it for me and my s.
2 K. 6:29 we boiled my s. and eat
14:9 dau. to my s. 2 Chr. 25:18
1 Chr. 17:13 shall be my s. 22:10
22:11 my s. Lord will be with
28:6 ha. chosen him to be my s.
29:1 Sol. my s. whom God hath
Ps. 2:7 thou art my s. Acts 13:33; Heb. 1:5; 5:5
Prov. 6:3 do this now, my s.
23:26 my s. give me thy heart
24:21 my s. fear thou the Lord
27:11 my s. be wise and make
31:2 what, my s. and what, son
Jer. 31:20 is Ephra. my dear s.?
Hos. 11:1 called my s. Mat. 2:15
Mat. 3:17 my beloved S. 17:5
Mark 9:17 I have brought my s.
Luke 9:38 Mast. look upon my s.
15:24 for this my s. was dead
1 Tim. 1:2 to Timothy my own s.
2 Tim. 2:1 my s. be stro. in grace
Tit. 1:4 to Titus mine own s.
Phile. 10 I beseech th. for my s.
Rev. 21:7 his God, he sh. be my s.

**Thy SON.**

Gen. 22:2 take t. s. thine only s.
24:5 must I needs bring thy s.?
37:32 know whe. it be t. s. coat
48:2 behold, thy s. Jos. cometh
Ex. 10:2 tell in the ears of thy s.
13:8 thou shalt show thy s.
14 wh. t. s. asketh, Deut. 6:20
Deut. 6:21 shalt say unto thy s.
7:3 nor daughter take unto t. s.
4 they will turn away thy s.
Jud. 6:30 bring out t. s. that he
8:22 rule over us, thou, thy s.
1 Sam. 16:19 send me David t. s.
1 K. 1:12 save life of thy s. Solo.
3:22 dead is t. s. 23 and thy s.
5:5 thy s. whom I will set upon
11:12 rend it out of hand of t. s.
17:13 for thee and for thy s.
19 give me t. s. 23 t. s. liveth
2 K. 4:36 he said, Take up thy s.
6:28 gi. t. s. that we may eat, 29
2 K. 16:7 I am thy ser. and thy s.
Prov. 19:18 chasten thy s. while
29:17 correct thy s. and he shall
Luke 9:41 Je. said, Bring thy s.
15:19 no more wor. to be t. s. 21
30 soon as this t. s. was come
John 4:50 thy s. liveth, 51, 53
17:1 glorify t. S. that t. S. may
19:26 saith, Woman, beh. thy s.

**SON of man.**

Ezekiel—above ninety times.

**SONG.**

Ex. 15:1 then sang Moses this s. unto the Lord, Num. 21:17
2 the Lord is my strength and s. Ps. 118:14; Is. 12:2
Deut. 31:19 wri. this s. th. th. s.
21 this s. sh. testify aga. them
22 Moses theref. wrote this s.
30 Mo. spake words of s. 32:44
Jud. 5:12 awake, Debor. utter s.
2 Sam. 22:1 Da. spa. words of s.
1 Chr. 6:31 D. set over serv. of s.
15:22 chief of Lev. was for s. 27
25:6 under their father for s.
2 Chr. 29:27 s. of the Lord began
Job 30:9 I am their s. by-word
Ps. 28:7 with my s. will I praise
33:3 sing a new s. Is. 42:10
40:3 put a new s. in my mouth
42:8 in night his s. sh. be wi. me
69:12 I was s. of the drunkards
30 I will praise God with a s.
77:6 I call to remembra. my s.
96:1 O sing to the Lord a new s. 98:1; 149:1
137:3 they required of us a s.
4 how sh. we sing Lord's s.?
144:9 I will sing a new s.
Ec. 7:5 man to hear s. of fools
Cant. 1:1 s. of songs which is S.
Is. 5:1 now will I sing a s.
24:9 sh. not drink wine wi. a s.
26:1 in th. day sh. th. s. be sung
30:29 shall have a s. as in night
Lam. 3:14 I was their s. all day
Ezek. 33:32 to them as a lovely s.
Rev. 5:9 they sung a new s. 14:3
14:3 no man could learn that s.
15:3 the s. of Moses and s. of L.

**SONGS.**

Gen. 31:27 sent thee away wi. s.
1 K. 4:32 s. a thousand and five
1 Chr. 25:7 were instructed in s.
Neh. 12:46 in days of D. were s.
Job 35:10 G. who giv. s. in night
Ps. 32:7 comp. wi. s. of deliver
119:54 have been my s. in house
137:3 sing us one of the s. of Z.
Prov. 25:20 singeth s. to heavy
Cant. 1:1 song of s. which is Sol.
Is. 23:16 melody, sing many s.
24:16 part of earth we heard s.
35:10 ranso. come to Z. with s.
38:20 we will sing my s.
Ezek. 26:13 noise of s. to cease
Amos 5:23 take away noise of s.
8:3 s. of temple shall be howl.
10 turn your s. into lamentati.
Eph. 5:19 in psalms, spiritual s.
Col. 3:16 hymns, and spiritual s.

**SONS.**

Gen. 9:19 the three s. of Noah
10:1 and to them were s. born
23:11 in pres. of s. of my people
27:29 let mother's s. bow down
42:5 s. of Is. came to buy corn
11 we are all one man's s. 32
46:5 s. of Israel carried Jacob
Lev. 26:29 eat flesh of your s.
Num. 27:3 father died, had no s.
36:3 married to s. of oth. tribes
Deut. 32:8 separated s. of Adam
Jud. 8:19 the s. of my mother
30 Gideon had 70 s. 10:4 Jair
12:14 Abdon had 40 s. 30 neph.
19:22 cert. s. of Bel. beset house
Ruth 1:11 are there any more s.?
1 Sam. 1:8 am not I bet. th. 10 s.?
2:12 s. of Eli were s. of Belial
8:11 take your s. appoint them

2 *Sam.* 2:18 three *s.* of Zeruiah
3:39 *s.* of Zeruiah be too hard
9:11 eat as one of king's *s.*
13:30 Absa. hath slain king's *s.*
16:10 what to do, *s.* of Z.? 19:22
23:6 *s.* of Bel. shall be as thorns
1 *K.* 20:35 the *s.* of the prophets
21:10 set two men, *s.* of Belial
2 *K.* 10:8 heads of the king's *s.*
1 *Chr.* 21:20 Orn. and his four *s.*
28:4 among the *s.* of my fathers
2 *Chr.* 23:3 Lord said of *s.* of Da.
24:25 blood of the *s.* of Jehoiada
*Est.* 9:10 ten *s.* of Ha. slew they
13 Ha.'s ten *s.* be hanged, 14
*Ps.* 89:6 who amo. *s.* of mighty?
144:12 our *s.* may be as plants
*Is.* 51:18 no. to guide her amo. *s.*
56:6 *s.* of strang. that join Lord
60:10 *s.* of stranger build walls
14 *s.* of them th. afflicted thee
*Jer.* 6:21 *s.* shall fall upon them
13:14 fathers and *s.* together
29:6 beget *s.* ta. wives for yo. *s.*
35:6 drink no wine, ye, nor *s.*
49:1 hath Israel no *s.*? no heir?
*Lam.* 4:2 precious *s.* of Zion
*Ezek.* 5:10 fathers eat *s.* *s.* fathers
20:31 your *s.* pass thro' the fire
23:37 caused *s.* to pass thro' fire
*Hos.* 1:10 ye are *s.* of living God
*Amos* 2:11 I raised up of your *s.*
*Mal.* 3:3 he shall purify *s.* of Le.
*Mark* 3:17 Boanerges, *s.* of thun.
*Luke* 11:19 your *s.* cast th. out?
1 *Cor.* 4:14 but as my beloved *s.*
*Gal.* 4:5 receive the adopti. of *s.*
6 bec. ye are *s.* God hath sent
*Heb.* 2:10 bring. many *s.* to glory
11:21 Jacob blessed *s.* of Joseph
12:7 G. deal. with you as wi. *s.*

*See* AARON, DAUGHTER.

**SONS of God.**

*Gen.* 6:2 *s. of G.* saw daughters
*Job* 1:6 *s. of G.* came to pres. 2:1
38:7 *s. of G.* shouted for joy
*Hos.* 1:10 ye are *s.* of living *God*
*John* 1:12 power to bec. *s. of G.*
*Rom.* 8:14 Sp. of God, are *s. of G.*
19 manifestation of *s. of God*
*Phil.* 2:15 be harmless, *s. of God*
1 *John* 3:1 we be called *s. of G.*
2 beloved, now are we *s. of G.*

**His SONS.**

*Gen.* 9:1 God blessed N. and *h. s.*
30:35 gave th. into hands of *h. s.*
50:12 *his s.* did unto him as he
*Ex.* 18:5 Jethro came with *h. s.*
28:1 take Aa. and *h. s.* to mini.
*Lev.* 6:22 priest of *his s.* is anoi.
*Deut.* 18:5 chosen him and *h. s.*
21:16 he maketh *h. s.* inherit
*Jud.* 9:18 slain *h. s.* 70 persons
17:11 Levite was as one of *his s.*
1 *Sam.* 2:22 heard all *his s.* did
8:1 S. when old made *h. s.* jud.
3 *his s.* walk. not in his ways
16:1 provided a king am. *his s.*
30:6 grieved, ev. man for *his s.*
2 *Sam.* 21:6 let 7 of *h. s.* be deli.
1 *K.* 13:11 *h. s.* came and to. him
12 *h. s.* seen way man of God
21:29 in *h. s.* days will I bring
2 *K.* 19:37 *his s.* smote him with sword, *Is.* 37:38
2 *Chr.* 11:14 Jeroboam and *his s.*
21:7 give light to him and *h. s.*
17 carried away *his s.* save the youngest of *his s.*
36:20 serv. to him and *his s.*
*Ezr.* 6:10 life of king and *his s.*
*Est.* 9:25 and *his s.* be hanged
*Job* 1:4 *his s.* went and feasted
14:21 *his s.* came to honor
38:32 canst guide A. with *h. s.*?
42:16 J. saw *h. s.* and *h. s.* sons
*Ezek.* 46:16 a gift to any of *h. s.*

*Dan.* 11:10 *h. s.* sh. be stirred up

*See* MAN.

**My SONS.**

*Gen.* 48:9 J. said, They are *my s.*
1 *Sam.* 2:24 *my s.* it is no good
12:2 S. said, *my s.* are with you
1 *Chr.* 28:5 of all *my s.* chosen S.
*Job* 1:5 it may be *my s.* have sin.
*Is.* 45:11 to come concern. *my s.*
1 *Cor.* 4:14 but as *my* beloved *s.*

*See* SEVEN.

**Thy SONS.**

*Ex.* 12:24 th. and *t. s.* *Num.* 18:8
22:29 first-born of *thy s.* sh. give
34:20 first-born of *t. s.* shalt red.
*Lev.* 10:14 thy due, and *t. s.* due
*Num.* 18:1 *t. s.* sh. bear iniquity
11 I have given them to *thy s.*
*Deut.* 4:9 teach *t. s.* and *t. s.* sons
1 *Sam.* 2:29 and honorest *thy s.*
8:5 *thy s.* walk not in thy ways
28:19 to-mor. *thy s.* be with me
2 *Sam.* 9:10 *t. s.* shall till land
2 *K.* 20:18 *thy s.* shall be eunuchs in Babylon, *Is.* 39:7
*Is.* 49:22 they shall bring *thy s.*
51:20 *thy s.* have fainted
60:4 *thy s.* sh. come from far, 9
*Jer.* 48:46 *t. s.* are taken captives
*Zec.* 9:13 *t. s.* O Zi. against *t. s.*

**Two SONS.**

*Gen.* 10:25 to E. *t. s.* 1 *Chr.* 1:19
34:25 *two* of *s.* of Ja. slew males
*Gen.* 41:50 to Jos. were born *t. s.*
42:37 slay my *t. s.* if I bri. him
44:27 kn. my wife bare me *t. s.*
48:1 he took with him his *t. s.*
*Ex.* 18:3 Zipporah and her *t. s.*
*Lev.* 16:1 death of *t. s.* of Aaron
*Ruth* 1:1 *t. s.* Mahlon and Chil. 2
1 *Sam.* 2:34 come upon thy *t. s.*
4:4 the *two s.* of Eli were there
2 *Sam.* 14:6 handmaid had *two s.*
15:36 they had with them *t. s.*
21:8 king took *two s.* of Rizpah
*Mat.* 20:21 grant that th. my *t. s.*
21:28 a man had *t. s.* *Lu.* 15:11
26:37 Peter and *t. s.* of Zebedee
*Acts* 7:29 in Midi. he begat *t. s.*
*Gal.* 4:22 Abraham had *two s.*

**SOON.**

*Ex.* 2:18 ye are come so *s.* to-day?
*Deut.* 4:26 ye shall *s.* utt. perish
*Job* 32:22 Maker *s.* take me away
*Ps.* 90:10 for it is *s.* cut off
106:13 they *s.* forgat his works
*Tit.* 1:7 not self-wil. not *s.* angry

**SOONER.**

*Heb.* 13:19 restored to you the *s.*
*Jam.* 1:11 the sun is no *s.* risen

**SOOTHSAYER, S.**

*Jos.* 13:22 Balaam son of Beor *s.*
*Is.* 2:6 peo. because they are *s.*
*Dan.* 2:27 secret cannot *s.* show
5:7 king cried aloud to bring *s.*
11 whom king made mas. of *s.*
*Mic.* 5:12 shalt have no more *s.*

**SOOTHSAYING.**

*Acts* 16:16 mast. much gain by *s.*

**SOP.**

*John* 13:26 to wh. I shall give a *s.*
27 after the *s.* Satan enter. 30

SOPATER. *Acts* 20:4

**SORCERER, ESS.**

*Is.* 57:3 draw hither, sons of *s.*
*Acts* 13:6 certain *s.* a false proph.
8 Elym. the *s.* withstood them

**SORCERERS.**

*Ex.* 7:11 called wise men and *s.*
*Jer.* 27:9 hearken not to your *s.*
*Dan.* 2:2 N. command. to call *s.*
*Mal.* 3:5 be a witn. against the *s.*
*Rev.* 21:8 *s.* sh. have part in lake

22:15 without are dogs and *s.*

**SORCERY.**

*Acts* 8:9 who beforetime used *s.*

**SORCERIES.**

*Is.* 47:9 come on thee for thy *s.*
12 stand with multi. of thy *s.*
*Acts* 8:11 long ti. bewitch. wi. *s.*
*Rev.* 9:21 nei. repented of th. *s.*
18:23 by *s.* were nations deceiv.

**SORE, Adj.** *or* **Adv.**

*Gen.* 19:9 pressed *s.* upon man
31:30 bec. thou *s.* longedst after
34:25 day, when they were *s.*
41:56 famine waxed *s.* in land
57 famine was so *s.* in all lands
43:1 famine *s.* in land, 47:4, 13
*Deut.* 6:22 Lord showed signs *s.*
*Jud.* 10:9 Israel was *s.* distress.
14:17 bec. she lay *s.* upon him
20:34 battle was *s.* 1 *Sam.* 31:3
2 *Sam.* 2:17; 2 *K.* 3:26
21:2 lifted their voices, wept *s.*
1 *Sam.* 1:10 Han. prayed, wept *s*
5:7 his hand is *s.* on us, and on
14:52 *s.* war against Philistines
2 *Sam.* 13:36 and servant wept *s.*
1 *K.* 17:17 sickn. so *s.* no breath
2 *K.* 6:11 king of Syria *s.* troub.
20:3 Hezekiah wept *s.* *Is.* 38:3
2 *Chr.* 21:19 Jeho. died of *s.* dis.
28:19 Ahaz transgress. *s.* ag. L.
*Ezr.* 10:1 people wept very *s.*
*Neh.* 13:8 it grieved me *s.* theref.
*Job* 5:18 maketh *s.* bindeth up
*Ps.* 6:3 my soul is *s.* vexed
38:2 thy hand presseth me *s.*
44:19 thou hast *s.* broken us
55:4 my heart is *s.* pained
118:13 thou hast thrust *s.* at me
*Is.* 27:1 with *s.* and great sword
64:9 be not wroth very *s.* O Lo.
12 wilt thou afflict us very *s.*?
*Lam.* 1:2 she weepeth *s.* in night
*Ezek.* 14:21 my four *s.* judgm.
*Dan.* 6:14 king was *s.* displeased
*Mat.* 21:15 th. were *s.* displeased
*Mark* 9:26 sp. cried, rent him *s.*
*Acts* 20:37 wept *s.* and kissed P.

*See* AFRAID.

**SORE, Substantive.**

*Lev.* 13:42 if a white reddish *s.*
2 *Chr.* 6:29 know his own *s.* gri.
*Ps.* 38:11 friends stand aloof fr. *s.*
*Ps.* 77:2 my *s.* ran in the night
*Rev.* 16:2 there fell a grievous *s.*

**SOREK.**

*Jud.* 16:4 a woman in vall. of S.

**SORES.**

*Is.* 1:6 bruises and putrefying *s.*
*Luke* 16:20 Lazarus full of *s.* 21
*Rev.* 16:11 blasphemed bec. of *s.*

**SORELY.**

*Is.* 23:5 *s.* pained at report of T.

**SORER.**

*Heb.* 10:29 how much *s.* punish.

**SORROW.**

*Gen.* 3:16 greatly multi. thy *s.* in *s.* thou shalt bring forth ch.
17 in *s.* shalt thou eat of it
42:38 bring my gray hairs with *s.* to the grave, 44:29, 31
*Ex.* 15:14 *s.* take hold of inhab.
*Lev.* 26:16 terror cause *s.* of heart
*Deut.* 28:65 L. sh. give *s.* of mind
1 *Chr.* 4:9 bec. I bare him wi. *s.*
*Neh.* 2:2 noth. else but *s.* of hea.
*Est.* 9:22 turned from *s.* to joy
*Job* 3:10 hid not *s.* fr. mine eyes
6:10 I would harden myself in *s.*
17:7 eye dim by reason of *s.*
41:22 *s.* is turned into joy
*Ps.* 13:2 having *s.* in my heart
38:17 my *s.* continually bef. me
39:2 held peace, my *s.* stirred
55:10 and *s.* in the midst of it

90:10 their strength labor and *s.*
107:39 brought low through *s.*
116:3 I found trouble and *s.*
*Prov.* 10:10 that winketh caus. *s.*
22 L. mak. rich, addeth no *s.*
15:13 by *s.* of heart spirit is bro.
17:21 begetteth fool, doeth to *s.*
23:29 who ha. woe? who hath *s.*
*Ec.* 1:18 knowledge, increaseth *s.*
5:17 hath much *s.* and wrath
7:3 *s.* is better than laughter
11:10 remove *s.* from thy heart
*Is.* 5:30 look to land, behold *s.*
14:3 L. shall give thee rest fr. *s.*
17:11 heap in day of desperate *s.*
29:2 distress Ariel, th. sh. be *s.*
35:10 *s.* and sighing shall flee
50:11 ye shall lie down in *s.*
51:11 *s.* and mourning flee away
65:14 sing, but ye sh. cry for *s.*
*Jer.* 8:18 comf. myself against *s.*
20:18 womb, see labor and *s.*?
30:15 why criest thou? *s.* incu.
31:13 make them rej. fr. their *s.*
45:3 L. hath add. grief to my *s.*
49:23 there is *s.* on the sea
*Lam.* 1:12 any *s.* like unto my *s.*
18 behold *s.* 3:65 give them *s.*
*Ezek.* 23:33 fill. wi. drunk. and *s.*
*Luke* 22:45 found th. sleep. for *s.*
*John* 16:6 *s.* ha. fill. your hearts
20 your *s.* shall be turn. to joy
21 wo. when in travail hath *s.*
22 and ye now therefore ha. *s.*
*Rom.* 9:2 I have *s.* in my heart
2 *Cor.* 2:3 I sho. have *s.* from th.
7 swallo. up with overmuch *s.*
7:10 godly *s.* work. repentance,
but *s.* of world worke. death
*Phil.* 2:27 lest I have *s.* upon *s.*
*Rev.* 18:7 *s.* give her, see no *s.*
21:4 be no more death, neith. *s.*

**SORROW, Verb.**

*Jer.* 31:12 shall not *s.* any more
51:29 land shall tremble and *s.*
*Hos.* 8:10 they shall *s.* for burden
1 *Thes.* 4:13 *s.* not as others

**SORROWS.**

*Ex.* 3:7 cry, for I know their *s.*
2 *Sam.* 22:6 *s.* of hell compassed
me about, *Ps.* 18:4, 5; 116:3
*Job* 9:28 I afraid of *s.*
21:17 God distribut. *s.* in anger
39:3 bow themselves, cast out *s.*
*Ps.* 16:4 *s.* shall be multiplied
32:10 many *s.* shall be to wick.
127:2 rise up, to eat bread of *s.*
*Ec.* 2:23 his days *s.* travail grief
*Is.* 13:8 and *s.* take hold of them
53:3 man of *s.* acquainted with
4 borne our griefs carri. our *s.*
*Jer.* 13:21 shall not *s.* take as wo.
49:24 *s.* taken her as a woman
*Dan.* 10:16 by visions *s.* turned
*Hos.* 13:13 *s.* of travailing wom.
*Mat.* 24:8 begin. of *s.* *Mark* 13:8
1 *Tim.* 6:10 pierced with many *s.*

**SORROWED, ETH.**

1 *Sam.* 10:2 thy father *s.* for you
2 *Cor.* 7:9 I rejoice ye *s.* to repe.
11 that ye *s.* after a godly sort

**SORROWFUL.**

1 *Sam.* 1:15 woman of a *s.* spirit
*Job* 6:7 refus. are as my *s.* meat
*Ps.* 69:29 I am poor and *s.* let
*Prov.* 14:13 in laugh. heart is *s.*
*Jer.* 31:25 replenis. every *s.* soul
*Zep.* 3:18 gather them that are *s.*
*Zec.* 9:5 Gaza see it, be very *s.*
*Mat.* 19:22 that saying, he went
away *s.* *Luke* 18:23, 24
26:22 were exc. *s.* *Mark* 14:19
37 began to be *s.* very heavy
38 soul exceed. *s.* *Mark* 14:34
*John* 16:20 shall be *s.* but sorrow
2 *Cor.* 6:10 *s.* yet always rejoici.
*Phil.* 2:28 I may be the less *s.*

**SORROWING.**

*Luke* 2:48 father and I so. thee *s.*
*Acts* 20:38 *s.* th. see face no more

**SORRY.**

1 *Sam.* 22:8 none of you that is *s.*
*Neh.* 8:10 holy to L. nei. be ye *s.*
*Ps.* 38:18 I will be *s.* for my sin
*Is.* 51:19 who shall be *s.* for thee
*Mat.* 14:9 king was *s.* *Mark* 6:26
17:23 and they were exceedi. *s.*
2 *Cor.* 2:2 if I ma. you *s.* sa. is *s.*
7:8 *s.* same epistle made you *s.*
9 rejoice not ye we. *s.* for ye *s.*

**SORT.**

*Gen.* 6:19 two of ev. *s.* in ark, 20
1 *Chr.* 24:5 divid. one *s.* wi. ano.
29:14 able to offer after this *s.*
*Ezr.* 4:8 wrote to Ar. after th. *s.*
*Neh.* 6:4 sent 4 times after this *s.*
*Ezek.* 23:42 men of the comm. *s.*
*Dan.* 1:10 worse th. chil. of yo. *s.*
3:29 no god can del. after this *s.*
*Acts* 17:5 lewd fellows of baser *s.*
*Rom.* 15:15 wri. boldly in some *s.*
1 *Cor.* 3:13 man's work of wh. *s.*
2 *Cor.* 7:11 sorrow. after godly *s.*
2 *Tim.* 3:6 of this *s.* who creep
3 *John* 6 journey after a godly *s.*

**SORTS.**

*Deut.* 22:11 garment of divers *s.*
*Neh.* 5:18 store of all *s.* of wine
*Ps.* 78:45 divers *s.* of flies, 105:31
*Ezek.* 27:24 merch. in all *s.* of th.
38:4 clothed with all *s.* of armor

**SOSIPATER.**

*Rom.* 16:21 Ja. and S. my kins.

**SOSTHENES.**

*Acts* 18:17 the Greeks took S.
1 *Cor.* 1:1 Paul and S. to church

**SOTTISH.**

*Jer.* 4:22 foolish. th. are *s.* child.

**SOUGHT.**

*Gen.* 43:30 he *s.* where to weep
*Ex.* 4:19 men dead wh. *s.* life
24 L. met him, *s.* to kill him
33:7 that *s.* L. went to taberna.
*Num.* 35:23 ene. nor *s.* his harm
*Jud.* 14:4 Samson *s.* occasion
1 *Sam.* 27:4 S. *s.* no more for him
2 *Sam.* 3:17 *s.* for Da. to be king
4:8 head of ene. that *s.* thy life
21:2 Saul *s.* to slay them in zeal
1 *K.* 10:24 earth *s.* to Sol. to hear
2 *K.* 2:17 *s.* three days for Elijah
1 *Chr.* 26:31 among Heb. were *s.*
*Chr.* 14:7 because we have *s.* L.
17:4 *s.* to Lord God of his father
25:15 *s.* after gods of Ed.? 20
26:5 *s.* G. in days of Zechariah,
as long as he *s.* the Lord
*Neh.* 12:27 they *s.* the Levit. out
*Est.* 9:2 hand on such as *s.* hurt
*Ps.* 34:4 I *s.* Lord, he heard, 77:2
111:2 *s.* out of all that have ple.
119:10 with wh. heart I *s.* thee
94 I have *s.* thy precepts
*Ec.* 7:29 *s.* many inventions
12:9 preacher *s.* out many prov.
*Is.* 62:12 shalt be called *s.* out
65:1 *s.* of them asked not, found
of th. that *s.* not, *Rom.* 10:20
10 place for my peo. that *s.* me
*Jer.* 8:2 moon, whom they ha. *s.*
10:21 the pastors have not *s.* L.
26:21 king *s.* put him to death
50:20 iniquity of Israel sh. be *s.*
*Lam.* 1:19 they *s.* meat to relieve
*Ezek.* 22:30 I *s.* a man am. them
26:21 tho' *s.* yet never be found
34:4 nei. *s.* that which was lost
*Dan.* 8:15 I had *s.* for meaning
*Ob.* 6 Esau's hidden things *s.* up
*Zep.* 1:6 those that have not *s.*
*Mat.* 2:20 dead wh. *s.* child's life
21:46 *s.* to lay hands upon him,
*Mark* 12:12; *Luke* 20:19
*Luke* 2:48 I *s.* thee sorrowing
49 how is it that ye *s.* me?
11:16 others *s.* a sign fr. heaven
13:6 *s.* fru. thereon, found none
19:3 Zaccheus *s.* to see Jesus

*John* 7:11 J. *s.* him at feast, 11:56
30 they *s.* to take him, 10:39
*Acts* 12:19 when Herod *s.* for Pe.
17:5 they *s.* to bring them out
*Rom.* 9:32 bec. *s.* it not by faith
1 *Thes.* 2:6 nor of men *s.* we glo.
2 *Tim.* 1:17 in Rome he *s.* me
*Heb.* 8:7 place shou. have been *s.*
12:17 he *s.* carefully with tears

**SOUGHT him.**

1 *Sam.* 10:21 *s. h.* could not be f.
13:14 L. *s. h.* a man to be capt.
23:14 Saul *s. him* every day
1 *Chr.* 15:13 *s.* not after order
2 *Chr.* 14:7 *s. h.* he hath giv. rest
15:4 when th. *s. h.* he was found
15 they *s. h.* with their desire
*Ps.* 37:36 I *s. h.* could not be fou.
78:34 slew them then they *s. h.*
*Cant.* 3:1 by night I *s. h.* I *s. h.*
but I found him not, 2; 5:6
*Luke* 2:44 they *s. h.* among kins.
4:42 people *s. h.* came to him

**SOUL.**

*Gen.* 2:7 man became a living *s.*
34:8 *s.* of son longeth for daugh.
35:18 as her *s.* was in departing
*Lev.* 4:2 if a *s.* sin thro' ignoran.
5:1 if a *s.* sin, and hear sweari.
6:2 if *s.* lie; 17:12 no *s.* eat blood
17:11 blood mak. atonem. for *s.*
22:11 if priest buy *s.*
23:30 whatso. *s.* doeth any work
*Num.* 21:4 *s.* of peo. discouraged
30:4 every bond she hath bound
her *s.* 5, 6, 7, 8, 9, 10, 11, 12, 13
31:28 one *s.* of five hund. for L.
*Deut.* 11:13 serve him with yo. *s.*
18 lay up th. words in your *s.*
13:3 wheth. you love L. with all
your *s.* *Jos.* 22:5; 1 *K.* 2:4
1 *Sam.* 18:1 *s.* of Jonathan knit
to *s.* of David
30:6 *s.* of the people was griev.
2 *Sam.* 5:8 blind hated of D.'s *s.*
13:39 *s.* of D. longed to go to A.
1 *K.* 8:48 return to thee with *s.*
17:21 let this child's *s.* come
2 *K.* 4:27 let alone, her *s.* is vex.
23:3 keep commandm. with *s.*
1 *Chr.* 22:19 set yo. *s.* to seek L.
2 *Chr.* 6:38 if they return with *s.*
15:12 seek the L. with their *s.*
*Job* 3:20 life giv. to bitter in *s.*?
12:10 hand is *s.* of every thing
16:4 if yo. *s.* were in my soul's
24:12 *s.* of the wounded crieth
*Ps.* 19:7 law perfect converting *s.*
33:19 deliver their *s.* from death
34:22 L. redeem. *s.* of his serva.
49:8 redemption of *s.* precious
72:14 he shall redeem their *s.*
78:50 spared not th. *s.* fr. death
86:4 rejoice *s.* of thy serv. O L.
94:21 gather against *s.* of right.
106:15 sent leanness to their *s.*
107:18 their *s.* abhorreth all me.
26 th. *s.* melted bec. of trouble
*Prov.* 10:3 not suff. *s.* of righteo.
11:25 liberal *s.* shall be made fat
13:2 *s.* of transgressors sh. eat
19 desire accom. is sweet to *s.*
16:24 pleasant words sweet to *s.*
19:2 *s.* without knowl. not good
15 idle *s.* shall suffer hunger
21:10 *s.* of wicked desireth evil
22:23 Lord will spoil *s.* of those
25:13 he refresheth *s.* of masters
27:7 full *s.* loathe. honey-comb,
to hungry *s.* bitter is sweet

*Is.* 3:9 woe to their *s.* they have
32:6 make empty *s.* of hungry
55:2 let yo. *s.* delight in fatness
3 hear, and your *s.* shall live
58:10 if thou satisfy afflicted *s.*
66:3 th. *s.* delighteth in abomi.
*Jer.* 4:10 the swo. reacheth the *s.*
20:13 he delivered *s.* of the poor
31:12 their *s.* shall be as a gard.
38:16 L. liveth, made us this *s.*
*Lam.* 1:11 for meat to relieve *s.*
2:12 wh. their *s.* was poured out
3:25 the Lord is good to the *s.*
*Ezek.* 18:4 as *s.* of father, so *s.* of
son, the *s.* that sinneth, 20
24:21 what your *s.* pitieth shall
*Hos.* 9:4 *s.* shall not come into
*Mat.* 10:28 fear th. can destroy *s.*
*Mark* 12:33 lo. him wi. he. and *s.*
*Acts* 2:43 fear came on every *s.*
3:23 eve. *s.* which will not hear
4:32 multitude believ. of one *s.*
*Rom.* 13:1 let every *s.* be subject
1 *Thes.* 5:23 that your *s.* and bo.
*Heb.* 10:39 believe to saving of *s.*
*Jam.* 5:20 he sh. save a *s.* fr. dea.
1 *Pet.* 2:11 lusts war agai. the *s.*
2 *Pet.* 2:8 Lot vexed righteous *s.*
*Rev.* 16:3 ev. living *s.* died in sea

*See* AFFLICTED, BITTERNESS.

**His SOUL.**

*Gen.* 34:3 *his s.* clave to Dinah
*Ex.* 30:12 give ransom for *his s.*
*Num.* 30:2 sw. oath to bind *h. s*
*Jud.* 10:16 *his s.* was grieved for
16:16 so that *his s.* was vexed
2 *K.* 23:25 Josiah turned to Lord
with all *his s.* 2 *Chr.* 34:31
*Job* 14:22 *his s.* within him
21:25 dieth in bitterness of *h. s.*
23:13 what *his s.* desireth, even
27:8 when God tak. away *his s.*
31:30 sin, by wish. curse to *h. s.*
33:18 keepeth back *h. s.* fr. pit
22 *his s.* draw. near unto grave
28 will deliver *his s.* from, 30
*Ps.* 11:5 violence, *his s.* hateth
24:4 who had not lifted up *his s.*
25:13 *his s.* shall dwell at ease
49:18 wh. he lived he bless. *h. s.*
89:48 sh. he deliver *his s.* from?
109:31 save fr. th. condemn *h. s.*
*Prov.* 6:30 if steal to satisfy *h. s.*
16:17 his way, preserveth *h. s.*
21:23 his mouth, keepeth *his s.*
22:5 that doth keep *his s.* shall
23:14 shalt deliver *his s.* fr. hell
29:10 but the just seek *his s.*
*Ec.* 2:24 shou. make *his s.* enjoy
6:2 wanteth nothing for *his s.*
3 *his s.* be not filled with good
*Is.* 29:8 awak. and *his s.* empty
44:20 he cannot deliver *his s.*
53:10 ma. *his s.* an offer. for sin
11 see of travail of *his s.*
12 poured out *h. s.* unto death
*Jer.* 50:19 *his s.* shall be satisfied
51:6 deliver every man *his s.* 45
*Ezek.* 18:27 right. he sh. sa. *h. s.*
33:5 warning, shall deliver *h. s.*
*Hab.* 2:4 *his s.* that is lifted up
*Mat.* 16:26 lose *h.* own *s.* give in
exchange for *s.*? *Mark* 8:37
*Acts* 2:31 *his s.* not left in hell.

**My SOUL.**

*Gen.* 12:13 *my s.* sh. live because
19:20 let me escape, *my s.* shall
27:4 *my s.* may bless thee, 25
49:6 O *my s.* come not into their
*Lev.* 26:11 *my s.* sh. not abh. 30
1 *Sam.* 1:15 poured out *my s.* be.
24:11 thou huntest *my s.* to
26:21 beca. *my s.* was precious
2 *Sam.* 4:9 Lord who hath redeemed *my s.* 1 *K.* 1:29
*Job* 6:7 the things *my s.* refused
9:21 yet would I not kn. *my s.*
10:1 *my s.* is weary of life, I will
speak bitterness of *my s.*
19:2 how lo. will ye vex *my s.*
27:2 Alm. who hath vexed *my s.*
30:15 they pursue *my s.* as wind
16 *my s.* is poured out upon
25 was not *my s.* gri. for poor?
*Ps.* 3:2 who say of *my s.* There is
6:3 *my s.* is sore vex. but, O L.
4 deliver *my s.* 17:13; 22:20;
116:4; 120:2
13:2 sh. I take couns. in *my s.*?
16:10 not leave *my s.* *Acts* 2:27
23:3 he restoreth *my s.* he lead.
25:1 unto th. O L. do I lift *my s.*
20 O keep *my s.* and deliver me
26:9 gather not *my s.* with sin.
30:3 brought *my s.* from grave
31:7 hast known *my s.* in adver.
34:2 *my s.* sh. make boast in L.
35:3 say unto *my s.* I am thy sa.
4 put to shame that seek *my s.*
7 have digged a pit for *my s.*
9 *my s.* shall be joyful in Lord
13 I humbled *my s.* with fast.
41:4 heal *my s.* I have sinned
42:4 I pour out *my s.* in me
5 cast down O *my s.*? 11; 43:5
6 O my G. *my s.* is cast down
54:4 L. is with that upho. *my s.*
55:18 delivered *my s.* in peace
56:6 when they wait for *my s.*
13 thou hast delivered *my s.*
57:1 be merciful, *my s.* trusteth
4 *my s.* is amo. lions and I lie
6 *my s.* is bowed down
59:3 they lie in wait for *my s.*
62:1 *my s.* waiteth upon God
5 *my s.* wait thou only upon G.
63:8 *my s.* followeth hard after
9 that seek *my s.* to destroy it
66:16 what G. ha. done for *my s.*
69:1 wa. are come in unto *my s.*
18 draw nigh to *my s.*
71:23 *my s.* shall rejoice
77:2 my sore ran, my *s.* refused
*Ps.* 84:2 *my s.* longeth for the L.
86:2 preserve *my s.* I am holy
4 O Lord, do I lift *my s.* 143:8
13 thou hast deliv. *my s.* from
88:3 *my s.* is full of troubles
14 why castest thou off *my s.*?
94:17 *my s.* had dwelt in silence
103:1 bless the Lord, O *my s.* 2,
22; 104:1, 35
109:20 them th. speak ag. *my s.*
116:7 ret. unto thy rest, O *my s.*
8 thou hast delivered *my s.*
119:20 *my s.* break. for longing
109 *my s.* is continu. in hand
129 therefore doth *my s.* keep
175 let *my s.* live and it shall
120:2 deliver *my s.* O Lord
6 *my s.* dw. wi. him that hate.
130:5 wait for the Lord, *my s.* 6
138:3 strengthen me in *my s.*
139:14 that *my s.* knoweth well
142:4 no man cared for *my s.*
7 bring *my s.* out of prison
143:11 bring *my s.* out of troub.
146:1 praise the Lord, O *my s.*
*Ec.* 7:28 which yet *my s.* seeketh
*Cant.* 1:7 wh. *my s.* lo. 3:1, 2, 3, 4
5:6 *my s.* failed when he spake
*Is.* 1:14 new moons *my s.* hateth
26:9 with *my s.* have I desired
38:17 in love to *my s.* deliv. it
61:10 my *s.* sh. be joyful in God
*Jer.* 4:19 hast heard, O *my s.*
5:9 *my s.* be avenged? 29; 9:9
6:8 instructed, lest *my s.* depart
12:7 beloved of *my s.* into hand
18:20 they dig. a pit for *my s.*
32:41 rej. over them *my* whole *s.*
*Lam.* 3:24 L. my por. saith *my s.*
58 pleased the causes of *my s.*
*Mic.* 6:7 body for sin of *my s.*?
7:1 *my s.* desired first ripe fruit
*Mat.* 12:18 in wh. *my s.* is pleas.
26:38 *my s.* is sor. *Mark* 14:34
*Luke* 1:46 *my s.* doth magnify L.
12:19 I will say to *my s.*
*John* 12:27 is *my s.* troubled
2 *Cor.* 1:23 for record upon *my s.*
*Heb.* 10:38 *my s.* sh. have no ple.

**Our SOUL.**

*Num.* 11:6 *our s.* is dried away
*Ps.* 33:20 *our s.* waiteth for Lord
44:25 *our s.* is bowed down
66:9 God who holdeth *our s.*
124:4 stre. had gone over *our s.*
*Is.* 26:8 the desire of *our s.* is

**Own SOUL.**

*Deut.* 13:6 friend as thine *o. s.*
*Ps.* 22:29 none can keep his *o. s.*
*Prov.* 6:32 destroyeth his *own s.*
8:36 sinneth, wrongeth his *o. s.*
19:16 commandm. keep. his *o. s.*
20:2 king, sinneth aga. his *o. s*
29:24 partner with thief ha. *o. s.*
*Mat.* 16:26 if he shall gain world
and lose his *o. s.*? *Mark* 8:36
*Luke* 2:35 sword pierce thy *o. s.*

**That SOUL.**

*Lev.* 17:10 set face ag. *t. s.* 20:6
22:3 *that s.* shall be cut off from
23:30 *that s.* will I destroy from
*Num.* 15:31 *t. s.* sh. utter. be cut

**Thy SOUL.**

*Gen.* 26:19 *thy s.* may bless, 31
*Deut.* 4:9 keep *thy s.* diligently
29 if seek him with all *thy s.*
6:5 L. thy G. with all *t. s.* 30:6
10:12 serve Lord with all *t. s.*
12:15 whatso. *t. s.* lusteth, 14:26
26:16 do with *t. s.* 30:2 obey
with *thy s.*
30:2 obey wi. thy heart and *t. s.*
10 turn to Lord with all *thy s.*
1 *Sam.* 2:16 as much as *t. s.* desi.
20:4 whatsoever *t. s.* desireth
23:20 according to desire of *t. s.*
25:29 man risen to pursue *t. s.*
1 *K.* 11:37 reign according *t. s.*
*Ps.* 121:7 L. shall preserve *thy s.*
*Prov.* 2:10 know. is pleas. to *t. s.*
3:22 shall be life to *thy s.*
19:18 let not *thy s.* spare
22:25 and get a snare to *thy s.*
24:12 he that keepeth *t. s.* doth
14 knowl. of wisdom be to *t. s.*
29:17 he sh. give delight to *t. s.*
*Is.* 51:23 have said to *t. s.* Bow
58:10 draw out *thy s.* to hungry
11 Lord shall satisfy *thy s.*
*Jer.* 14:19 hath *thy s.* loathed Z.?
38:17 forth, *thy s.* shall live, 20
*Ezek.* 3:19 deliv. *thy s.* 21; 33:9
*Hab.* 2:10 hast sinned ag. *thy s.*
*Mat.* 22:37 love L. with all *thy s.*
*Mark* 12:30; *Luke* 10:27
*Luke* 12:20 *thy s.* be requ. of thee
3 *John* 2 even as *thy s.* prospere.
*Rev.* 18:14 fruits *t. s.* lust. after

*See* LIVETH.

**SOULS.**

*Gen.* 12:5 A. took *s.* th. had got
46:26 *s.* that came into Egypt
27 sons of Joseph in Egy. were
two *s.* all the *s.* of the house
of Jacob were 70 *s.* *Ex.* 1:5
*Ex.* 12:4 a lamb according to *s.*
30:15 atonement for your *s.* 16;
*Lev.* 17:11; *Num.* 31:50
*Lev.* 18:29 *s.* that commit them
20:25 not make your *s.* abomin.
*Num.* 16:38 sin. ag. their own *s.*
30:9 wherewith ha. bound th. *s.*
*Jos.* 23:14 know in all your *s.*
1 *Sam.* 25:29 *s.* of ene. shall sling
*Ps.* 72:13 shall save *s.* of needy
97:10 preserveth *s.* of his saints

*Prov.* 11:30 that win. *s.* is wise
14:25 a true witness deliver. *s.*
*Is.* 57:16 spi. should fail, and *s.*
*Jer.* 2:34 in thy skirts is bl. of *s.*
6:16 rest for your *s.* *Mat.* 11:29
26:19 procure evil against our *s.*
44:7 why com. evil ag. your *s.*?
*Lam.* 1:19 sought meat to th. *s.*
*Ezek.* 7:19 sh. not satisfy their *s.*
13:18 hunt *s.* hunt *s.* of peo. 20
19 slay *s.* that should not die
14:14 should deliver their own *s.*
18:4 *s.* are mine; 22:25 devou. *s.*
*Acts* 2:41 added to them 3,000 *s.*
7:14 Jacob and his kindred 75 *s.*
14:22 confirming *s.* of disciples
15:24 troubled you, subvert. *s.*
27:37 we. in all in the ship 276 *s.*
1 *Thes.* 2:8 imparted our *s.* to you
*Heb.* 13:17 they watch for your *s.*
*Jam.* 1:21 word able to save yo. *s.*
1 *Pet.* 1:22 have purified your *s.*
3:20 that is, eight *s.* were saved
4:19 commit keep. of *s.* to him
*Rev.* 6:9 I saw *s.* of them slain
18:13 no man buyeth *s.* of men
20:4 I saw *s.* of them beheaded
*See* AFFLICT.

**SOUND, Substantive.**

*Ex.* 28:35 his *s.* shall be heard
*Lev.* 26:36 *s.* of a shaken leaf
*Jos.* 6:5 hear *s.* of trumpet, 20
2 *Sam.* 5:24 *s.* of going in tops of mulberry-trees, 1 *Chr.* 14:15
1 *K.* 1:40 earth rent with the *s.*
14:6 Ahijah heard *s.* of her feet
18:41 *s.* of abundance of rain
2 *K.* 6:32 is not *s.* of mas.'s feet?
1 *Chr.* 16:42 with trum. make *s.*
2 *Chr* 5:13 one *s.* to be heard
*Neh.* 4:20 in wh. place ye hear *s.*
*Job* 15:21 dreadful *s.* in his ears
21:12 rejoice at *s.* of the organ
37:2 *s.* that go. out of his mouth
39:24 not believ. he it is the *s.*
*Ps.* 47:5 gone up with *s.* of trum.
77:17 water, skies sent out a *s.*
89:15 people that know joyful *s.*
92:3 sing upon harp with sol. *s.*
150:3 praise him wi. *s.* of trum.
*Ec.* 12:4 *s.* of grinding is low
*Jer.* 4:19 hast heard *s.* of trum.
6:17 hearken to *s.* of trumpet?
42:14 where we shall hear no *s.*
50:22 *s.* of battle is in the land
51:54 a *s.* of a cry from Babylon
*Ezek.* 10:5 *s.* of cherubim's wings
26:13 *s.* of thy harps be no more
15 sh. not the isles sha. at *s.*?
27:28 suburbs shall shake at *s.*
31:16 made nati. to shake at *s.*
33:5 he heard *s.* of the trumpet
*Dan.* 3:5 ye hear the *s.* 7, 10, 15
*Amos* 2:2 Moab shall die with *s.*
*Mat.* 24:31 angels with great *s.*
*John* 3:8 hearest *s.* canst not tell
*Acts* 2:2 there came *s.* from hea.
*Rom.* 10:18 *s.* went into all earth
1 *Cor.* 14:7 thin. with. life giv. *s.* 8
*Heb.* 12:19 not come to *s.* of tru.
*Rev.* 1:15 as *s.* of many waters
9:9 *s.* of wings as *s.* of chariots

**SOUND, Adjective.**

*Ps.* 119:80 let my heart be *s.*
*Prov.* 2:7 he layeth up *s.* wisdom
8:14 counsel is mine and *s.* wis.
14:30 a *s.* heart is life of flesh
*Luke* 15:27 rec. him safe and *s.*
1 *Tim* 1:10 contrary to *s.* doctri.
2 *Tim.* 1:7 G. hath giv. us *s.* mi.
13 hold fast form of *s.* words
4:3 will not endure *s.* doctrine
*Tit.* 1:9 be able by *s.* doctrine
13 that they may be *s.* in faith
2:1 things which become *s.* doctrine
*Tit.* 2:2 th. aged men be *s.* in fa.
8 *s.* speech cannot be condem.

**SOUND, Verb.**

*Num.* 10:7 shall not *s.* an alarm
1 *Chr.* 15:19 were appointed to *s.*
*Is.* 16:11 my bowels sh. *s.* for M.
*Jer.* 48:36 my heart sh. *s.* for M.
*Joel* 2:1 *s.* alarm in holy mount.
*Mat.* 6:2 do not *s.* trumpet bef.
1 *Cor.* 15:52 the trumpet shall *s.*
*Rev.* 8:6 prep. themselves to *s.*
10:7 sev. angel shall begin to *s.*

**SOUNDED.**

*Ex.* 19:19 the trumpet *s.* long
1 *Sam.* 20:12 wh. I have *s.* father
*Neh.* 4:18 he that *s.* the trumpet
*Luke* 1:44 saluta. *s.* in my ears
*Acts* 27:28 *s.* found 20 fathoms
1 *Thes.* 1:8 fr. you *s.* word of L.
*Rev.* 8:7 first angel *s.* and there
8 second *s.* 10 third; 12 fourth
9:1 fifth *s.* 13 sixth; 11:15 sev.

**SOUNDETH.**

*Ex.* 19:13 when trumpet *s.* long

**SOUNDING.**

2 *Chr.* 5:12 with th. 120 priests *s.*
13:12 his priests with *s.* trum.
*Is.* 63:15 wh. is thy zeal and *s.*?
*Ezek.* 7:7 not the *s.* of mountains
1 *Cor.* 13:1 not charity, as *s.* brass

**SOUNDNESS.**

*Ps.* 38:3 th. is no *s.* in my flesh, 7
*Is.* 1:6 no *s.* in it, but wounds
*Acts* 3:16 given him this perf. *s.*

**SOUNDS.**

1 *Cor.* 14:7 give a distinct. in *s.*

**SOUR.**

*Is.* 18:5 when *s.* grape is ripen.
*Jer.* 31:29 the fathers have eaten a *s.* grape, *Ezek.* 18:2
30 ev. man that eateth *s.* grape
*Hos.* 4:18 their drink is *s.*

**SOUTH.**

*Gen.* 12:9 Abr. journeyed tow. *s.*
13:1 A. went into *s.* 3 went fr. *s.*
28:14 spr. abroad to north and *s.*
*Num.* 13:29 Amalekites dw. in *s.*
*Deut.* 33:23 pos. thou west and *s.*
1 *Sam.* 20:41 Dav. arose out of *s.*
1 *K.* 7:25 three looking towards the *s.* 2 *Chr.* 4:4
*Job* 9:9 mak. chambers of the *s.*
39:26 stretch wings toward *s.*
*Ps.* 75:6 com. not fr. east not *s.*
89:12 north and *s.* thou created
107:3 gathered fr. north and *s.*
*Ec.* 1:6 wind goeth toward *s.*
11:3 if the tree falleth toward *s.*
*Is.* 30:6 burden of beasts of *s.*
43:6 say to *s.* Keep not back
*Jer.* 13:19 cit. of *s.* shall be shut
32:44 buy fields in cities of *s.*
33:13 in cit. of *s.* shall flocks pa.
*Ezek.* 21:4 sword ag. all from *s.*
40:2 as the frame of a city on *s.*
*Dan.* 11:5 and the king of the *s.*
*Ob.* 19 they of *s.* sh. pos mount
20 captivity sh. poss. cit. of *s.*
*Zec.* 7:7 when men inhabited *s.*
14:4 mountain remove toward *s.*
*Mat.* 12:42 queen of *s.* shall rise
*Luke* 13:29 come fr. *s.* to sit do.
*Acts* 8:26 arise, and go toward *s.*
*Rev.* 21:13 on the *s.* three gates

**SOUTH border.**

*Num.* 34:3 *s. b.* the outmost coa.
*Jos.* 15:2 the *s. border* of Judah

**SOUTH country.**

*Gen.* 20:1 Abrah. sojourned *s. c.*
24:62 for Isaac dwelt in the *s. c.*

**SOUTH land.**

*Jos.* 15:19 given me *s. l.* *Jud.* 1:15

**SOUTH quarter.**

*Num.* 34:3 *s. q.* fr. Zin by coast
*Jos.* 18:15 *s. q.* fr. end of Kirjath.

**SOUTH Ramoth.**

1 *Sam.* 30:27 which were in *s. R.*

**SOUTH side.**

*Ex.* 26:18 boards on *s. s.* 36:23
*Num.* 2:10 on *s. s.* shall be stan.
*Ezek.* 48:16 *s. s.* 4,500 meas. 33

**SOUTHWARD.**

*Gen.* 13:14 L. said to A. Look *s.*
*Num.* 13:17 get ye up this way *s.*

**SOUTH-WEST.**

*Acts* 27:12 lying toward *s.-w.*

**SOUTH wind.**

*Job* 37:17 quieteth earth by *s. w.*
*Ps.* 78:26 he brought in *s. w.*
*Cant.* 4:16 *s. w.* blow on my gar.
*Luke* 12:55 *s. w.* bl. will be heat
*Acts* 27:13 wh. *s. w.* blew softly

**SOW, Substantive.**

2 *Pet.* 2:22 the *s.* washed, to her

**SOW, Verb.**

*Gen.* 47:23 ye shall *s.* the land
*Ex.* 23:10 *s.* the land, *Lev.* 25:3
*Lev.* 19:19 sh. not *s.* wi. mingled
25:4 in sev. year shalt not *s.* 11
20 we shall not *s.* nor gather
26:16 shall *s.* your seed in vain
2 *K.* 19:29 in the third year *s.* ye. *Is.* 37:30
*Job* 4:8 *s.* wickedness reap same
31:8 let me *s.* let another eat
*Ps.* 107:37 *s.* fields and vineyards
126:5 *s.* in tears sh. reap in joy
*Ec.* 11:4 observ. wind, sh. not *s.*
6 in the morning *s.* thy seed
*Is.* 28:24 ploughman pl. to *s.*?
30:23 rain of seed thou shalt *s.*
32:20 blessed that *s.* beside wat.
*Jer.* 4:3 *s.* not among thorns
31:27 I will *s.* the house of Isr.
35:7 nei. build house nor *s.* seed
*Hos.* 2:23 I will *s.* her unto me
10:12 *s.* to yourselves in right.
*Mic.* 6:15 thou shalt *s.* not reap
*Zec.* 10:9 *s.* them among people
*Mat.* 6:26 fowls of the air *s.* not
13:3 a sower went forth to *s.* *Mark* 4:3; *Luke* 8:5
27 didst thou *s.* good seed
*Luke* 12:24 ravens nei. *s.* nor reap
19:21 reap. thou didst not *s.* 22

**SOWED, EDST.**

*Gen.* 26:12 Is. *s.* in land sa. year
*Deut.* 11:10 wh. thou *s.* thy seed
*Jud.* 9:45 Abimelech *s.* Shechem
*Mat.* 13:24 man which *s.* good seed; 25 *s.* tares, 39

**SOWER.**

*Is.* 55:10 it may give seed to *s.*
*Jer.* 50:16 cut off *s.* from Baby.
*Mat.* 13:18 hear ye parable of *s.*
*Mark* 4:14 *s.* soweth word
2 *Cor* 9:10 ministereth seed to *s.*

**SOWEST.**

1 *Cor.* 15:36 thou *s.* not quicken.
37 *s.* not body that shall be

**SOWETH.**

*Prov.* 6:14 *s.* discord; 19 *s.* disc.
11:18 that *s.* righteousn. a rew.
16:28 a froward man *s.* strife
22:8 *s.* iniquity, reap vanity
*Amos* 9:13 overtake him that *s.*
*Mat.* 13:37 that *s.* good seed is S.
*Mark* 4:14 sower *s.* the word
*John* 4:36 he that *s.* and reapeth
37 true, one *s.* another reapeth
2 *Cor.* 9:6 *s.* sparingly, *s.* bounti.
*Gal.* 6:7 whatsoever a man *s.*
8 that *s.* to flesh, reap corrup.

**SOWING.**

*Lev.* 11:37 if carc. fall on any *s.*
26:5 vint. shall reach to *s.* time

**SOWN.**

*Deut.* 21:4 val. nei. eared nor *s.*
22:9 lest fruit of seed *s.* be defi.
29:23 generation see land not *s.*
*Jud.* 6:3 Israel had *s.* Mid. came
*Ps.* 97:11 light is *s.* for righteous
*Is.* 19:7 thing *s.* by brook wither
40:24 plant. yea, shall not be *s.*
61:11 caus. things *s.* to spring
*Jer.* 2:2 after me in a land not *s.*
12:13 they have *s.* wheat, thorns
*Ezek.* 36:9 ye sh. be tilled and *s.*
*Hos.* 8:7 *s.* wind, reap whirlwind
*Nah.* 1:14 no more of thy name *s.*
*Hag.* 1:6 *s.* much, bring little
*Mat.* 13:19 catcheth away that which was *s.* *Mark* 4:15
25:24 reaping wh. th. hast not *s.*
*Mark* 4:16 wh. *s.* on stony grou.
18 *s.* am. thorns; 20 *s.* on gro.
31 wh. *s.* is less than all seeds
1 *Cor.* 9:11 *s.* to you spir. things
15:42 *s.* in cor. 43 *s.* in dishonor
44 it is *s.* a natural body, raised
2 *Cor.* 9:10 multiply your seed *s.*
*Jam.* 3:18 righteousn. *s.* in peace

**SPACE.**

*Gen.* 32:16 put a *s.* betwixt drove
*Lev.* 25:8 *s.* of 7 sabbaths of yea.
*Jos.* 3:4 a *s.* between you and it
1 *Sam.* 26:13 *s.* betw. D.'s comp.
*Ezr.* 9:8 *s.* grace sh. be showed
*Luke* 22:59 about *s.* of one hour
*Acts* 5:34 put apostles forth lit. *s.*
13:20 about *s.* of 450 years
19:8 spake boldly *s.* of 3 months
10 continued by *s.* of 2 years
34 about *s.* of two hours
20:21 *s.* of 3 years I ceased not
*Rev.* 2:21 I gave her *s.* to repent
8:1 silence about *s.* of half hour
*Rev.* 14:20 blood by *s.* of 1,600 fur.
17:10 must continue a short *s.*

**SPAIN.**

*Rom.* 15:24 whenso. I jour. to S.
28 I will come by you into S.

**SPAKE.**

*Gen.* 29:9 wh. he *s.* Rachel came
*Deut.* 1:43 I *s.* ye would not hear
28:68 L. br. thee by whereof I *s.*
1 *Sam.* 1:13 Han. *s.* in her heart
2 *K.* 9:12 and thus *s.* he to him
2 *Chr.* 18:19 one *s.* after manner
32:19 they *s.* ag. God of Jerusa.
*Neh.* 13:24 *s.* half in speech of A.
*Job* 2:13 sat down, none *s.* a word
19:18 I arose, they *s.* against me
29:22 after my words they *s.* not
32:16 they *s.* not, but stood still
*Ps.* 78:19 they *s.* against God
*Prov.* 30:1 the man *s.* unto Ithiel and Ucal
*Jer.* 20:8 for since I *s.* I cried out
*Ezek.* 24:18 so I *s.* to the people
*Mal.* 3:16 feared L. *s.* one to ano.
*Mat.* 9:33 devil cast out dumb *s.*
12:22; *Luke* 11:14
21:45 perceived he *s.* of them
*Luke* 1:55 as he *s.* to our fathers
2:50 understood not say. he *s.*
24:6 remember how he *s.* to you
36 as they thus *s.* Jesus stood
*John* 1:15 this was he of wh. I *s.*
7:13 no man *s.* openly of him
46 Never man *s.* like this man
8:27 understood not that he *s.*
10:6 wh. things they were he *s.*
41 things John *s.* of this man
12:38 saying fulfil. he *s.* 18:9, 32
13:22 look. doubt. of who. he *s.*
24 who it sho. be of who. he *s.*
*Acts* 13:45 Jews *s.* ag. things sp.
22:9 heard not voice of him *s.*
26:24 as he *s.* for himself, Fest.
1 *Cor.* 13:11 wh. child *s.* as child
14:5 I would ye *s.* with tongues
*Heb.* 12:25 refus. him *s.* on earth
2 *Pet.* 1:21 men of G. *s.* as moved
*Rev.* 1:12 turn. to see voice th. *s.*

**God SPAKE.**

*Gen.* 35:15 place where *God s.*
*Deut.* 1:6 L. *God s.* to us in Hor.
*Jos.* 23:14 of good things *God s.*
*John* 9:29 we know *G. s.* to Mo.
*Acts* 7:6 and *God s.* on this wise
*Heb.* 1:1 *God* who *s.* in time past
*See* LORD, *expressly*.

**Lord** *or* **God SPAKE,** *implicitly.*

1 *Sam.* 9:17 which I *s.* to thee of
28:17 *Lord* hath done as he *s.*
1 *K.* 6:12 word I *s.* unto David
2 *Chr.* 6:4 who fulfilled that he *s.*
*Ps.* 33:9 he *s.* and it was done
*Is.* 65:12 I *s.* did not hear, 66:4
*Jer.* 7:13 I *s.* to you, rising up
22 I *s.* not to fathers, I broug.
14:14 I sent them not, neither *s.*
31:20 since I *s.* ag. him I rem.
*Lam.* 1:28 heard one that *s.* 2:2
*Luke* 24:44 these are words I *s.*
*Heb.* 4:4 he *s.* in a certain place

**SPAKEST.**

*Jud.* 13:11 man *s.* to woman?
*Neh.* 9:13 *s.* with them fr. heaven
*Jer.* 48:27 since thou *s.* skippedst

**SPAN.**

*Ex.* 28:16 *s.* length, *s.* brea. 39:9
1 *Sam.* 17:4 G. height, 6 cu. a *s.*
*Is.* 40:12 meted heaven with *s.*?
*Lam.* 2:20 wom. eat chil. *s.* long
*Ezek.* 43:13 bord. of altar be a *s.*

**SPANNED.**

*Is.* 48:13 right hand *s.* heavens

**SPARE.**

*Gen.* 18:24 not *s.* pl. for 50 right.
*Deut.* 13:8 sh. not *s.* nor conceal
29:20 Lord will not *s.* him
1 *Sam.* 15:3 destroy Amal. *s.* not
*Neh.* 13:22 *s.* me accor. to mercy
*Job* 6:10 let him not *s.* I have not
20:13 he *s.* and forsake it not
27:22 sh. cast upon him, not *s.*
30:10 *s.* not to spit in my face
*Ps.* 39:13 O *s.* that I may recover
72:13 he shall *s.* poor and needy
*Prov.* 6:34 not *s.* in day of veng.
19:18 let not soul *s.* for crying
*Is.* 9:19 no man shall *s.* brother
13:18 their eye shall not *s.* chil.
30:14 shall break it, shall not *s.*
54:2 *s.* lengthen cords
58:1 *s.* not, lift voice like trum.
*Jer.* 13:14 will not *s.* *Ezek.* 24:14
21:7 not *s.* th. 50:14 *s.* no arro.
51:3 *s.* ye not her young men
*Ezek.* 5:11 nor mine eyes *s.* 7:4, 9; 8:18; 9:10
9:5 let not your eyes *s.*
*Joel* 2:17 say, *s.* thy people, O L.
*Jon.* 4:11 should not I *s.* Nine.?
*Hab.* 1:17 not *s.* to slay nations
*Mal.* 3:17 *s.* th. as man spar. son
*Luke* 15:17 bread enough to *s.*
*Rom.* 11:21 lest he also *s.* not
1 *Cor.* 7:28 have trouble, I *s.* you
2 *Cor.* 1:23 to *s.* you I came not
13:2 if I come again, will not *s.*

**SPARED.**

1 *Sam.* 15:9 Saul and people *s.*
24:10 kill thee, but mine eye *s.*
2 *Sam.* 12:4 *s.* to take of his flock
21:7 the king *s.* Mephibosheth
2 *K.* 5:20 master hath *s.* Naaman
*Ps.* 78:50 he *s.* not soul fr. death
*Ezek.* 20:17 mi. eye *s.* them from
*Rom.* 8:32 he that *s.* not his Son
11:21 if God *s.* not nat. branches
2 *Pet.* 2:4 if God *s.* not angels
5 *s.* not old world, saved Noah

**SPARETH, ING.**

*Prov.* 13:24 that *s.* rod, hat. son
17:27 hath knowledge *s.* words
21:26 righteous giveth, *s.* not
*Mal.* 3:17 as a man *s.* his son
*Acts* 20:29 wolves enter, not *s.*

**SPARINGLY.**

2 *Cor.* 9:6 he who sow. *s.* reap *s.*

**SPARK.**

*Job* 18:5 *s.* of his fire not shine
*Is.* 1:31 maker of it be as a *s.*

**SPARKS.**

*Job* 5:7 trouble as *s.* fly upward
41:19 burning lamps, *s.* of fire
*Is.* 50:11 comp. yourselves wi. *s.*

**SPARKLED.**

*Ezek.* 1:7 *s.* like color of brass

**SPARROW.**

*Ps.* 84:3 *s.* hath found a house
102:7 as a *s.* upon house-top

**SPARROWS.**

*Mat.* 10:29 two *s.* sold for farth.?
31 more value th. *s.* *Luke* 12:7
*Luke* 12:6 5 *s.* sold for 2 farth.?

**SPAT.**

*John* 9:6 spok. he *s.* on ground

**SPEAK.**

*Gen.* 18:27 ta. on me to *s.* to G. 31
24:50 we cannot *s.* bad or good
31:24 take heed thou *s.* not to J.
44:16 what shall we *s.*?
*Ex.* 4:14 I kn. that he can *s.* well
29:42 wh. I will meet you to *s.*
34:35 he went in to *s.* with Lord
*Num.* 12:8 not afraid to *s.* ag. M.
22:35 word I *s.* that thou shalt *s.*
23:12 must I not *s.* which the L.
*Deut.* 18:19 words *s.* in my name
20 presume to *s.* in my name
2 *Sam.* 19:10 *s.* ye not a word
1 *K.* 12:7 *s.* go. words, 2 *Chr.* 10:7
22:24 spirit from me to *s.* to th. 2 *Chr.* 18:23
*Job* 8:2 how long *s.* these thi.?
11:5 oh that G. would *s.* ag. th.
13:7 will ye *s.* wickedly for G.?
18:2 afterwards we will *s.*
36:2 ha. yet to *s.* on G.'s behalf
41:3 will he *s.* soft words?
*Ps.* 2:5 them sh. he *s.* in wrath
28:3 which *s.* peace to neigh.
40:5 if I would declare and *s.* of
69:12 that sit in gate *s.* ag. me
71:10 mine enemies *s.* ag me
85:8 I will hear what L. will *s.*
94:4 how long they *s.* hard thi.?
119:172 my tongue shall *s.* of
139:20 *s.* against thee wickedly
145:6 shall *s.* of might of thy
21 my mouth sh. *s.* praise of L.
*Ec.* 3:7 to be silent, time to *s.*
*Is.* 8:20 if they *s.* not accord. to
28:11 with ano. tongue sh. he *s.*
29:4 thou shalt *s.* out of ground
52:6 I am he that doth *s.*
*Jer.* 5:14 saith L. Bec. ye *s.* this
7:27 thou sh. *s.* all these words
13:12 thou shalt *s.* this word to
18:7 I shall *s.* about a nation, 9
20:9 I will not *s.* any more
26:2 *s.* words I command to *s.* 8
32:4 shall *s.* with him mouth to mouth
34:3 he shall *s.* with thee
*Ezek.* 2:7 thou shalt *s.* my words
24:27 shalt *s.* be no more dumb
*Hab.* 2:3 at the end it shall *s.*
*Mat.* 10:19 ye shall *s.* *Mark* 13:11
20 not ye that *s.* *Mark* 13:11
12:34 can ye being evil *s.* good?
*Mark* 14:71 kn. not of wh. ye *s.*
*Luke* 1:19 I am sent to *s.* to thee
20 not able to *s.* till th. sh. be
22 wh. he came he could not *s.*
6:26 when men *s.* well of you
12:10 whosoever shall *s.* a word
*John* 3:11 verily we *s.* th. we kn.

9:21 of age, he shall *s.* for hims.
16:13 *s.* of himself, that shall he
*Acts* 2:11 hear them *s.* in tongu.
26:1 P. thou art permitted to *s.*
*Rom.* 15:18 I will not dare to *s.*
1 *Cor.* 3:1 I could not *s.* to you as
12:30 do all *s.* with ? 14:23 all *s.*
14:35 sha. for women to *s.* in ch.
2 *Cor.* 2:17 in sight of God *s.* we
4:13 we believe and therefore *s.*
12:19 we *s.* before God in Christ
*Col.* 4:4 manifest, as I ought to *s.*
1 *Thes.* 1:8 so that we need not *s.*
2:4 so we *s.* not as pleasing men
*Tit.* 3:2 put th. in mind to *s.* evil
*Heb.* 6:9 we thus *s.* 9:5 cannot *s.*
*Jam.* 1:19 let ev. man be sl. to *s.*
1 *John* 4:5 theref. *s.* they of world

**SPEAK,** *imperatively.*

*Ex.* 20:19 *s.* thou, we will hear
*Deut.* 3:26 Lord said, *s.* no more
5:27 *s.* to us that L. sh. *s.* to th.
1 *Sam.* 3:9 *s.* L. servant hear. 10
2 *Sam.* 17:6 his say. ? if not *s.*
1 *K.* 22:13 *s.* that which is good,
2 *Chr.* 18:12
*Est.* 5:14 to-morrow *s.* to king
*Job* 13:22 let me *s.* and answer
33:32 *s.* for I desire to justify th.
34:33 theref. *s.* what thou know.
*Prov.* 23:9 *s.* not in ears of a fool
*Is.* 8:10 *s.* word, it sh. not stand
30:10 who say, *s.* to us smooth
41:1 come near, then let them *s.*
*Jer.* 1:17 *s.* to them that I comm.
*Dan.* 10:19 I said, Let my lord *s.*
*Zec.* 8:16 *s.* the truth, *Eph.* 4:25
*Mark* 13:11 given in that hour, *s.*
*Acts* 18:9 *s.* hold not thy peace
1 *Cor.* 14:28 let him *s.* to himself
29 let prophets *s.* two or three
*Jam.* 2:12 so *s.* ye and do, as th.

**I SPEAK.**

*Ex.* 19:9 peo. may hear, wh. *I s.*
*Deut.* 11:2 *I s.* not wi. your chil.
1 *K.* 22:14 L. saith, that will *I s.*
*Job* 9:35 then would *I s.* and not
13:3 *I* would *s.* to Almighty
16:4 *I* also could *s.* as ye do
37:20 shall it be told him *I s.* ?
*Ps.* 45:1 *I s.* of things that I have
120:7 when *I s.* they are for war
*Jer.* 1:6 L. *I* cannot *s.* I am a ch.
6:10 sh. *I s.* and give warning ?
28:7 hear this word that *I s.* in
38:20 voice of the L. which *I s.*
*Ezek.* 3:27 when *I s.* with thee, I
*John* 4:26 Jesus saith, *I* that *s.*
6:63 the words that *I s.* to you
7:17 or whether *I s.* of myself
8:28 as Father taught me, *I s.*
38 *I s.* that which I have seen
12:49 gave com. what *I* should *s.*
50 *I s.* as Father said, so *I s.*
13:18 *I s.* not of all, I know
14:10 words *I s. I s.* not of mys.
17:13 these things *I s.* in world
*Acts* 21:37 P. said, May *I s.* to th.
26:26 bef. whom *I* also *s.* freely
*Rom.* 3:5 God unrighte. ? *I s.* as
6:19 *I s.* after manner, *Gal.* 3:15
1 *Cor.* 14:18 *I s.* with tongues
19 *I* had rather *s.* five words
2 *Cor.* 11:17 that wh. *I s. I s.* not
*Eph.* 6:20 that therein *I* may *s.*

**I will SPEAK,** *or* **will I.**

*Gen.* 18:30 L. angry, *I will s.* 32
*Num.* 12:8 with him *will I s.*
24:13 what L. sai. that *will I s.*
1 *K.* 22:14; 2 *Chr.* 18:13
*Deut.* 32:1 give ear, and *I will s.*
*Jud.* 6:39 Gideon said, *I will s.*
1 *K.* 2:18 well, *I will s.* for thee
*Job* 32:20 *I w. s.* th. I be refresh.
33:31 hold thy peace, *I will s.*
42:4 I beseech thee, and *I w. s.*
*Ps.* 50:7 hear, my peo. *I will s.*
73:15 if I say, *I will s.* thus
145:5 *I w. s.* of the honor of thy
*Jer.* 5:5 to great men, and *I w. s.*
*Ezek.* 2:1 stand on feet and *I w. s.*
12:25 *I will s.* and word I speak
1 *Cor.* 14:21 wi. other lips *w. I s.*

**SPEAKER.**

*Ps.* 140:11 let not evil *s.* be esta.
*Acts* 14:12 because he was chi. *s.*

**SPEAKEST.**

1 *Sam.* 9:21 wheref. then *s.* th. ?
*Job* 2:10 *s.* as one of foolish wom.
*Is.* 40:27 why *s.* thou, O Israel
*Jer.* 43:2 thou *s.* falsely, the Lord
*Zec.* 13:3 *s.* lies in name of Lord
*John* 16:29 now *s.* thou plainly
19:10 Pi. saith, *s.* thou not unto
*Acts* 17:19 know whereof th. *s.* ?

**SPEAKETH.**

*Gen.* 45:12 it is my mouth that *s.*
*Ex.* 33:11 spa. to M. as man *s.*
*Num.* 23:26 all that Lord *s.*
*Job* 33:14 G. *s.* once, yea, twice
*Prov.* 6:13 he *s.* with his feet
16:13 they love him that *s.* right
26:25 wh. he *s.* fair, believe not
*Jer.* 10:1 word which L. *s.* to you
28:2 thus *s.* L. G. 29:25; 30:2;
*Hag.* 1:2; *Zec.* 6:12; 7:9
*Ezek.* 10:5 voice of G. when he *s.*
*Mat.* 10:20 S. of Father *s.* in you
*John* 3:31 of earth, *s.* of the earth
34 wh. God sent, *s.* words of G.
7:18 he that *s.* of himself, seek.
26 but lo, he *s.* boldly, they say
8:44 wh. he *s.* a lie, he *s.* of own
*Acts* 8:34 of wh. *s.* the pro. this ?
*Heb.* 11:4 he being dead yet *s.*
12:24 that *s.* better things than
25 th. ye refuse not him that *s.*

**SPEAKING.**

*Gen.* 24:15 before he had done *s.*
45 before I had done *s.* in hea.
*Deut.* 11:19 *s.* of them when thou
*Est.* 10:3 *s.* peace to his seed
*Job* 1:16 wh. he was yet *s.* 17, 18
4:2 who can withhold from *s.* ?
32:15 no more, they left off *s.*
*Is.* 58:13 nor *s.* thine own words
65:24 while they are yet *s.* I
*Jer.* 7:13 early, *s.* 25:3; 34:14
*Dan.* 8:13 I heard one saint *s.*
*Acts* 14:3 they abode, *s.* boldly in
2 *Cor.* 13:3 a proof of Ch. *s.* in me
*See* END.

**SPEAKINGS, S.**

*Mat.* 6:7 th. be heard for much *s.*
*Eph.* 4:31 let evil *s.* be put away
1 *Pet.* 2:1 laying aside all evil *s.*

**SPEAR.**

*Jos.* 8:18 stretch out thy *s.* 26
*Jud.* 5:8 a *s.* seen among 40,000
1 *Sam.* 13:22 *s.* with any but wi.
17:7 staff of *s.* like weaver's bea.
2 *Sam.* 21:19; 1 *Chr.* 20:5
45 comest with a sword and *s.*
21:8 under thy hand a *s.*
26:7 S.'s *s.* stuck at bolster, 11
16 now see where king's *s.* is
2 *Sam.* 1:6 Saul lean. upon his *s.*
2:23 Abner with *s.* smote Asahel
23:7 with iron and staff of a *s.*
8 he lifted up his *s.* against 800
18 lifted up his *s.* against 300,
1 *Chr.* 11:11, 20
21 he slew the Egyptian with
his own *s.* 1 *Chr.* 11:23
*Job* 39:23 qui. rattleth, glitter. *s.*
41:26 *s.* of him that lay. at him
29 Leviathan laugheth at a *s.*
*Ps.* 35:3 draw out *s.* stop way
46:9 breake. bow and cutteth *s.*
*Jer.* 6:23 lay hold on bow and *s.*
*Nah.* 3:3 lifteth up sword and *s.*
*Hab.* 3:11 at shining of glitter. *s.*
*John* 19:34 one of the soldiers
with a *s.* pierced his side

**SPEARS.**

1 *Sam.* 13:19 Heb. make sw. or *s.*
2 *K.* 11:10 king David's *s.* that
were in temple. 2 *Chr.* 23:9
2 *Chr.* 11:12 in ev. city he put *s.*
26:14 Uzziah prep. for them *s.*
*Neh.* 4:13 I set the people with *s.*
16 the other half held the *s.* 21
*Ps.* 57:4 whose teeth are *s.* and
*Is.* 2:4 *s.* into hooks, *Mic.* 4:3
*Jer.* 46:4 furbish *s.* and put on
*Ezek.* 39:9 shall burn *s.* with fire
*Joel* 3:10 pruning-hooks into *s.*

**SPEARMEN.**

*Ps.* 68:30 rebuke company of *s.*
*Acts* 23:23 make ready 200 *s.*

**SPECIAL.**

*Deut.* 7:6 L. chosen thee, a *s.* pe.
*Acts* 19:11 *s.* miracles done by P.
*See* ESPECIALLY.

**SPECKLED.**

*Gen.* 30:32 removing the *s.* cattle
31:8 *s.* thy wages, cattle bare *s.*
*Jer.* 12:9 heritage is as *s.* bird
*Zec.* 1:8 red horses, *s.* and white

**SPECTACLE.**

1 *Cor.* 4:9 made a *s.* to the world

**SPED.**

*Jud.* 5:30 have they not *s.* ?

**SPEECH.**

*Gen.* 4:23 hearken to my *s.*
11:1 whole earth was of one *s.*
*Ex.* 4:10 M. said, I am slow of *s.*
*Deut.* 22:14 give occas. of *s.* aga.
32:2 my *s.* shall distil as dew
2 *Sam.* 14:20 fetch ab. form of *s.*
19:11 the *s.* of Is. come to king
1 *K.* 3:10 Solomon's *s.* pleased L.
*Neh.* 13:24 chil. spake half in *s.*
*Job* 12:20 removeth *s.* of trusty
13:17 my *s.* and declara. 21:2;
*Ps.* 17:16; *Is.* 28:23; 32:9
24:25 make *s.* nothing worth ?
29:22 my *s.* dropped upon them
37:19 we cannot order our *s.* by
*Ps.* 19:2 day unto day uttereth *s.*
3 there is no *s.* wh. voice is not
*Prov.* 7:21 fair *s.* cau. him to yie.
17:7 excel. *s.* becom. not a fool
*Cant.* 4:3 lips like scarl. *s.* come.
*Is.* 29:4 thy *s.* sh. be low out of
the dust; thy *s.* sh. whisper
33:19 deeper *s.* th. thou perceive
*Jer.* 31:23 shall use this *s.* in Ju.
*Ezek.* 1:24 voi. of *s.* as noise of h.
3:5 sent to a peo. of strange *s.* 6
*Hab.* 3:2 O L. I ha. heard thy *s.*
*Mat.* 26:73 thy *s.* bewrayeth th.
*Mark* 7:32 impediment in his *s.*
14:70 thy *s.* agreeth thereto
*John* 8:43 not underst. my *s.* ?
*Acts* 14:11 in *s.* of Lycaonia
20:7 continued his *s.* till midni.
1 *Cor.* 2:1 not with excelle. of *s.*
4 *s.* was not with entic. words
4:19 not the *s.* but the power
2 *Cor.* 3:12 great plainness of *s.*
7:4 great my boldness of *s.* tow.
10:10 his *s.* is contemptible
11:6 rude in *s.* not in knowled.
*Col.* 4:6 let *s.* be alw. with grace
*Tit.* 2:8 sound *s.* cannot be cond.

**SPEECHES.**

*Num.* 12:8 speak not in dark *s.*
*Job* 6:26 *s.* of one that is despe.
15:3 with *s.* he can do no good ?
32:14 nei. will I answer with *s.*
*Rom.* 16:18 by fair *s.* dec. hearts
*Jude* 15 convince them of hard *s.*

**SPEECHLESS.**

*Mat.* 22:12 garm. and he was *s.*
*Luke* 1:22 Zacharias remained *s.*
*Acts* 9:7 men with him stood *s.*

**SPEED.**
*Gen.* 24:12 O L. send me good *s.*
*Ezr.* 6:12 let it be done with *s.*
*Is.* 5:26 they shall come with *s.*
*Acts* 17:15 come to him wi. all *s.*
2 *John* 10 rec. not, nor bid G. *s.*
11 that biddeth him God *s.*

*See* MAKE, MADE.

**SPEEDY.**
*Zep.* 1:18 make a *s.* riddance

**SPEEDILY.**
2 *Sam.* 17:16 not in plains, *s.* pa.
*Ezr.* 6:13 king sent, they did *s.*
7:17 may. buy *s.* with this mon.
21 E. shall requi. it be done *s.*
26 let judgment be executed *s.*
*Ps.* 31:2 bow thine ear; deliv. *s.*
69:17 in trou. hear me *s.* 143:7
79:8 let thy mercies *s.* prev. us
102:2 in day when I call, ans. *s.*
*Ec.* 8:11 sent. not executed *s.*
*Is.* 58:8 health sh. spring forth *s.*
*Zec.* 8:21 let us go *s.* and pray

**SPEND.**
*Deut.* 32:23 I will *s.* mine arrows
*Job* 21:13 *s.* their days in wealth
36:11 *s.* their days in prosperity
*Ps.* 90:9 we *s.* our years as a tale
*Is.* 55:2 why *s.* money for that?
*Acts* 20:16 wou. not *s.* time in A.
2 *Cor.* 12:15 I will very gladly *s.*

**SPENDEST, ETH.**
*Prov.* 21:20 a foolish man *s.* it up
29:3 with harlots, *s.* substance
*Ec.* 6:12 whi. he *s.* as a shadow
*Luke* 10:35 whatsoever thou *s.*

**SPENT.**
*Gen.* 21:15 and the water was *s.*
47:18 not hide how money is *s.*
*Lev.* 26:20 strength be *s.* in vain
*Jud.* 19:11 by Jeb. day was far *s.*
1 *Sam.* 9:7 the bread is *s.* in our
*Job* 7:6 days are *s.* without hope
*Ps.* 31:10 my life is *s.* with grief
*Is.* 49:4 I have *s.* my strength
*Jer.* 37:21 the bread in city was *s.*
*Mark* 5:26 and had *s.* all that she had, *Luke* 8:43
6:35 day was far *s.* *Luke* 24:29
*Luke* 15:14 prodigal had *s.* all
*Acts* 17:21 *s.* their time to tell
*Rom.* 13:12 the night is far *s.*
2 *Cor.* 12:15 I will gladly be *s.*
SPEW, SPEWING. *See* SPUE.

**SPICE, Substantive.**
*Ex.* 35:28 rulers brought *s.* and
*Cant.* 5:1 gath. myrrh wi. my *s.*

**SPICES.**
*Gen.* 43:11 carry a pres. balm, *s.*
*Ex.* 25:6 *s.* for anointing, 35:8
30:23 take thou *s.* of myrrh, 34
37:29 pure incense of sweet *s.*
1 *K.* 10:2 camels that bare *s.* 10; 2 *Chr.* 9:1
25 brought to Sol. *s.* 2 *Chr.* 9:24
2 *K.* 20:13 Hezekiah showed th. *s.* ointment, *Is.* 39:2
1 *Chr.* 9:29 appoint. to oversee *s.*
30 sons of the priests made *s.*
2 *Chr.* 9:9 queen of Sh. gave S. *s.*
16:14 divers *s.* prep. for burial
32:27 He. made treasuries for *s.*
*Cant.* 4:10 thine ointments th. *s.*
14 myrrh and aloes, chief *s.*
16 blow upon my gard. that *s.*
5:13 his cheeks are as a bed of *s.*
6:2 my belo. is gone to bed of *s.*
8:14 to a hart upon mount. of *s.*
*Ezek.* 27:22 in fairs wi. chief of *s.*
*Mark* 16:1 M. had bought sweet *s.* *Luke* 24:1
*Luke* 23:56 prepared *s.* and oint.
*John* 19:40 they wound it in *s.*

**SPICE, Verb.**
*Ezek.* 24:10 consume flesh and *s.*

**SPICE-MERCHANTS.**
1 *K.* 10:15 the traffic of the *s.-m.*

**SPICED.**
*Cant.* 8:2 cau. thee drink *s.* wine

**SPICERY.**
*Gen.* 37:25 Ishmael. bear. *s.* balm

**SPIDER.**
*Job* 8:14 wh. trust sh. be a *s.* web
*Prov.* 30:28 *s.* tak. hold wi. hands
*Is.* 59:5 eggs, and weave *s.* web

**SPIKENARD.**
*Cant.* 1:12 *s.* sendeth the smell
4:13 fruits, camphire with *s.* 14
*Mark* 14:3 alabaster box of ointment of *s.* *John* 12:3

**SPILLED.**
*Gen.* 38:9 On. *s.* seed on ground
*Mark* 2:22 wine is *s.* *Luke* 5:37

**SPILT.**
2 *Sam.* 14:14 water *s.* on ground

**SPIN.**
*Ex.* 35:25 wise-hearted, did *s.*
*Mat.* 6:28 neither *s.* *Luke* 12:27

**SPINDLE.**
*Prov.* 31:19 lay. her hands to *s.*

**SPIRIT.**
*Gen.* 41:8 Phar.'s *s.* was troubled
45:27 the *s.* of Jacob their fath.
*Ex.* 6:9 heark. not for angu. of *s.*
35:21 whom his *s.* made willing
*Num.* 11:17 I will take of *s.* 25
26 the *s.* rested on them
29 L. wo. put his *S.* upon them
14:24 he had ano. *s.* with him
27:18 Jos. a man in whom is *s.*
*Deut.* 2:30 L. G. hardened his *s.*
*Jos.* 5:1 nor was th. *s.* in them
*Jud.* 15:19 drunk his *s.* came
1 *Sam.* 30:12 eaten his *s.* came
1 *K.* 10:5 no *s.* in her, 2 *Chr.* 9:4
21:5 said, Why is thy *s.* so sad?
22:21 th. came a *s.* 2 *Chr.* 18:20
2 *K.* 2:9 double portion of *s.* on
15 *s.* of Elijah doth rest on El.
1 *Chr.* 5:26 Lord stirr. up *s.* of P.
12:18 *s.* came upon Amasai
28:12 pattern of all he had by *s.*
*Ezr.* 1:5 wh. *s.* G. raised to go up
*Neh.* 9:30 by *S.* in thy prophets
*Job* 4:15 a *s.* passed bef. my face
15:13 thou turnest thy *s.* ag. G.
20:3 *s.* of my understanding
26:4 whose *s.* came from thee?
13 by his *S.* he garnished hea.
32:8 there is a *s.* in man
18 *s.* within me constraineth
34:14 if he gather to hims. his *s.*
*Ps.* 32:2 in wh. *s.* there is no gu.
51:10 renew right *s.* within me
12 uphold me with thy free *S.*
76:12 shall cut off *s.* of princes
78:8 whose *s.* not stead. with G.
104:30 thou sendest forth thy *S.*
106:33 so they provoked his *S.*
139:7 whit. sh. I go fr. thy *S.*?
143:10 *S.* good, lead me to upr.
*Prov.* 14:29 he that is hasty of *s.*
15:4 perversen. is a breach in *s.*
16:18 haughty *s.* goeth bef. a fall
*Prov.* 16:32 that rul. *s.* bet. th. he
18:14 *s.* of a man sust. infirmity
20:27 *s.* of a man is candle of L.
25:28 hath no rule over his *s.*
*Ec.* 3:21 *s.* of man, *s.* of beast
7:9 not hasty in *s.* to be angry
8:8 no power over *s.* to retain *s.*
10:4 if *s.* of ruler rise ag. thee
11:5 kno. not what is way of *s.*
12:7 the *s.* shall return to God
*Is.* 19:3 *s.* of Egypt shall fail
29:10 L. pour. on you *s.* of sleep
24 they th. erred in *s.* sh. come
31:3 their horses flesh and not *s.*
32:15 till *S.* be poured upon us
34:16 his *s.* it hath gathe. them
42:5 giveth *s.* to them that walk
48:16 L. G. and his *S.* hath sent
54:6 forsak. and grieved in *s.*
57:16 *s.* shall fail before me
61:1 *S.* of L. G. on me, *Lu.* 4:18
3 garment of praise for the *s.*
*Jer.* 51:11 L. raised *s.* of the king
*Ezek.* 1:12 whit. *S.* was to go, 20
2:2 the *s.* entered into me, 3:24
3:12 the *s.* took me up, 11:24
14 *s.* lifted me up, and I went in heat of my *s.* 8:3; 11:1
13:3 proph. that follow own *s.*
21:7 every *s.* shall faint
*Dan.* 2:1 Nebuc. *s.* was troubled
4:8 in whom is *S.* of the holy gods, 9, 18; 5:11, 14
5:12 excellent *s.* in Daniel, 6:3
*Mic.* 2:11 if man in *s.* and falseh.
*Hag.* 1:14 L. stirred *s.* of Zerub.
*Zec.* 7:12 sent his *S.* by prophets
12:1 form. *s.* of man within him
*Mal.* 2:15 had residue of *S.* 16
*Mat.* 4:1 Je. led up of *S.* *Luke* 4:1
14:26 say, It is a *s.* *Mark* 6:49
22:43 David in *s.* call him Lord?
26:41 *s.* is willing, *Mark* 14:38
*Mark* 1:10 *S.* descend. *John* 1:32
12 *S.* driveth him into wilder.
8:12 he sighed deeply in his *s.*
9:20 *s.* tare him; 26 *s.* cried
*Luke* 1:17 go before him in *s.*
80 child waxed st. in *s.* 2:40
2:27 he came by *S.* into temple
4:14 Je. returned in power of *S.*
8:55 her *s.* came ag. she arose
9:55 know not what *s.* ye are
10:21 in that hour J. rejoi. in *s.*
13:11 wom. had *s.* of infirmity
24:37 supp. they had seen a *s.*
39 *s.* ha. not flesh and bones
*John* 1:33 on wh. thou sh. see *S.*
3:34 G. giveth not *S.* by meas.
4:23 worship the Father in *s.*
24 G. is a *S.* worship him in *s.*
6:63 it is *s.* that quickeneth; words I speak, they are *s.*
7:39 spake of *S.* 11:33 groan. in
13:21 he was troubled in *s.*
*Acts* 2:4 spake as *S.* gave them
6:10 were not able to resist *s.*
8:29 the *S.* said to Philip, Go
10:19 *S.* said unto Peter, 11:12
11:28 Agabus signified by *S.*
16:7 the *S.* suffered them not
17:16 his *s.* was stir. within him
18:5 Paul was pressed in *s.*
25 and being fervent in the *s.*
20:22 bound in the *S.* to Jerusa.
21:4 said to Saul through the *S.*
23:8 Sadducees say th. is no *s.*
9 if a *s.* hath spoken to him
*Rom.* 1:4 Son of God accord. to *s.*
2:29 circumcis. is of heart in *s.*
8:1 walk not aft. flesh, but *s.* 4
2 law of *s.* of life made me free
5 after the *S.* things of the *S.*
9 flesh but *s.* if so be that *S.*
10 *s.* is life bec. of righteousn.
11 quick. your bodies by his *S.*
13 if ye through the *S.* mortify
16 *S.* beareth witn. with our *s.*
23 ourse. who have fruits of *S.*
26 *S.* also help. our infirmities; but the *S.* maketh interces.
27 kno. what is the mind of *S.*
1 *Cor.* 2:4 in demonstration of *S.*
10 G. hath revealed th. unto us by *S.* for *S.* searcheth all th.
11 *s.* of man which is in him
12 not *s.* of world, but *s.* of G.
5:3 absent in body, present in *s.*
5 *s.* be saved in day of Lord J.
6:17 joined to the Lord is one *s.*
20 glori. G. in your body and *s.*
7:34 may be holy in body and *s.*
12:4 gifts, but same *S.* 8, 9, 11

8 given by *S.* word of wisdom
13 by one *S.* we are all baptiz. been made to drink into *S.*
14:2 in *s.* he speaketh mysteries
15 sing with *s.* 16 bless with *s.*
1 *Cor.* 15:45 A. was ma. a quick. *s.*
2 *Cor.* 3:6 but of the *s.* letter killeth, but the *s.* giveth life
8 ministrations of *s.* be glorio.
17 L. is that *S.* where *S.* of L.
4:13 we having same *s.* of faith
7:1 from filthiness of flesh and *s.*
13 because his *s.* was refreshed
11:4 *s.* which ye have not recei.
12:18 walk. we not in same *s.?*
*Gal.* 3:2 receiv. ye *S.* by works?
3 foolish, having begun in *s.?*
5 he that ministereth to you *S.*
14 might receive promise of *S.*
4:6 G. sent forth *S.* of his Son
5:5 we thro' *S.* wait for hope
16 walk in *S.* 18 if led by *S.*
17 flesh lusteth against the *S.* and the *S.* against the flesh
25 if we live in *S.* walk in *S.*
6:8 soweth to *S.* shall of *S.* reap
18 grace of our Lord be with your *s.* *Phile.* 25
*Eph.* 2:2 *s.* that work. in child.
18 have access by one *S.* to F.
22 habitation of G. through *S.*
3:5 revealed to apostles by *S.*
16 strength. with might by *S.*
4:3 unity of *s.* in bond of peace
4 th. is one *S.* as ye are called
23 renewed in *s.* of your mind
5:18 not drunk, but filled wi. *s.*
6:17 sw. of *S.* is the word of God
18 praying with prayer in *S.*
*Phil.* 1:19 supply of *s.* of Je. Ch
27 that ye stand fast in one *s.*
2:1 any fellowship of the *S.*
3:3 which worship God in the *s.*
*Col.* 1:8 declared your love in *s.*
2:5 yet am I with you in the *s.*
1 *Thes.* 5:19 quench not *S.* despise
23 I pray G. your *s.* soul, body
2 *Thes.* 2:2 neith. by *s.* nor word
8 L. shall consume with the *s.*
13 chosen thro' sanctific. of *S.*
1 *Tim.* 3:16 God justified in *S.*
4:1 the *S.* speaketh expressly
12 be thou an example in *s.*
2 *Tim.* 4:22 L. J. C. be wi. thy *s.*
*Heb.* 4:12 dividing of soul and *s.*
9:14 who through the eternal *S.*
*Jam.* 2:26 body witho. *s.* is dead
4:5 the *s.* in us lusteth to envy
1 *Pet.* 1:2 thro' sanctification of *s.*
22 in obeying truth through *S.*
3:4 the ornament of a meek *s.*
18 but quickened by *S.*
4:6 live accord. to God in the *S.*
1 *John* 3:24 *s.* he hath given us
4:1 beloved, believe not every *s.*
2 ev. *s.* that confesseth Je. Ch.
3 ev. *s.* that confesseth not Je.
13 bec. hath given us of his *S.*
5:6 *S.* beareth witn. *S.* is truth
8 wit. in earth, *S.* water, blood
*Jude* 19 sensual, not having *S.*
*Rev.* 1:10 I was in *S.* on L.'s day
2:7 what *S.* saith to churches, 11, 17, 29; 3:6, 13, 22
4:2 immediately I was in the *S.*
11:11 *S.* of life from G. entered
14:13 blessed are dead, saith *S.*
17:3 carried me in the *S.* 21:10
22:17 *S.* and bride say, Come

**SPIRIT of adoption.**

*Rom.* 8:15 ye have recei. *s. of a.*

**SPIRIT of antichrist.**

1 *John* 4:3 this is that *s. of anti.*

**SPIRIT of bondage.**

*Rom.* 8:15 have not rece. *s. of b.*

**Born of the SPIRIT.**

*John* 3:5 ex. man be *b. of the S.*
6 that which is *born of the S.*
8 so is ev. one that is *b. of S.*
*Gal.* 4:29 persec. him *b.* after *S.*

**Broken SPIRIT.**

*Ps.* 51:17 sacri. of G. are a *b. s.*
*Prov.* 15:13 sorrow of heart *s.* is *b.*
17:22 a *b. s.* drieth the bones

*See* CONTRITE.

**SPIRIT of burning.**

*Is.* 4:4 blood of Jer. by *s. of b.*

**SPIRIT of Christ.**

*Rom.* 8:9 if man ha. not *S. of C.*
1 *Pet.* 1:11 *S. of Ch.* did signify

**SPIRIT of counsel.**

*Is.* 11:2 *s. of c.* rest upon him

**SPIRIT of divination.**

*Acts* 16:16 possess. with *s. of di.*

**Dumb SPIRIT.**

*Mark* 9:17 son. who hath a *d. s.*
25 thou *dumb s.* I charge thee

**Earnest of the SPIRIT.**

2 *Cor.* 1:22 given us *e. of t. S.* 5:5

**SPIRIT of error.**

1 *John* 4:6 kn. we *s. of* tru. and *e.*

*See* EVIL.

**Faithful SPIRIT.**

*Prov.* 11:13 he that is of *faith. s.*

*See* FAMILIAR.

**SPIRIT of fear.**

2 *Tim.* 1:7 ha. not giv. us *s. of f.*

**Foul SPIRIT.**

*Mark* 9:25 he rebuked the *foul s.*
*Rev.* 18:2 become hold of ev. *f. s.*

**Fruit of the SPIRIT.**

*Gal.* 5:22 *f. of the S.* is love, joy
*Eph.* 5:9 *f. of t. S.* is in all good.

**Good SPIRIT.**

*Neh.* 9:20 th. gavest thy *good S.*
*Ps.* 143:10 thy *S.* is *g.* lead me

**SPIRIT of God.**

*Gen.* 1:2 *S. of G.* moved on wat.
41:38 a man in wh. *S. of God* is
*Ex.* 31:3 Bez. wi. *S. of G.* 35:31
*Num.* 24:2 *S. of G.* came on Bal.
1 *Sam.* 10:10 the *S. of God* came on Saul, 11:6; 19:23
19:20 *S. of G.* came on messen.
2 *Chr.* 15:1 *S. of G.* came on Aza.
*Job* 27:3 *S. of G.* is in my nost.
33:4 *S. of God* hath made me
*Ezek.* 11:24 in vision by *S. of G.*
*Mat.* 3:16 saw *S. of G.* descend.
12:28 cast out devils by *S. of G.*
*Rom.* 8:9 *S. of God* dwell in you
14 many as are led by *S. of G.*
15:19 by the power of *S. of G.*
1 *Cor.* 2:11 no man, but *S. of G.*
14 recei. not things of *S. of G.*
3:16 *S. of God* dwelleth in you
6:11 sanctified by the *S. of God*
7:40 I think I have *S. of God*
12:3 no man speak. by *S. of G.*
2 *Cor.* 3:3 written with *S. of G.*
*Eph.* 4:30 grie. not holy *S. of G.*
1 *Pet.* 4:14 *S. of God* rest. on you
1 *John* 4:2 hereby kn. ye *S. of G.*

**SPIRIT of glory.**

1 *Pet.* 4:14 *S. of g.* resteth on you

**SPIRIT of grace.**

*Zec.* 12:10 house of Da. *S. of g.*
*Heb.* 10:29 done desp. to *S. of g.*

*See* HOLY.

**Humble SPIRIT.**

*Prov.* 16:19 bet. to be of an *h. s.*
29:23 honor sh. uphold the *h. s.*
*Is.* 57:15 with him that is of *h. s.*

**SPIRIT of jealousy.**

*Num.* 5:14 *s. of j.* co. on him, 30

**SPIRIT of judgment.**

*Is.* 4:4 purged Jerusa. by *s. of j.*
28:6 L. shall be for a *s. of jud.*

**SPIRIT of knowledge.**

*Is.* 11:2 *s. of k.* sh. rest upon him

*See* LORD, LYING.

**SPIRIT of meekness.**

1 *Cor.* 4:21 come in *s. of m.?*
*Gal.* 6:1 such a one in *s. of m.*

**My SPIRIT.**

*Gen.* 6:3 *my S.* sh. not always
*Job* 6:4 poison drinketh up *my s.*
7:11 speak in anguish of *my s.*
10:12 visita. hath preserv. *m. s.*
21:4 sho. not *my s.* be troubled
*Ps.* 31:5 into hand I com. *my s.*
77:3 *my s.* was overwhelmed
6 *my s.* made diligent search
142:3 *my s.* overwhelmed in me
143:4 theref. is *my s.* overwhel.
7 hear me, O L. *my s.* faileth
*Prov.* 1:23 I will pour out *my s.*
*Is.* 26:9 with *my s.* will I seek
30:1 covering, but not of *my s.*
38:16 in th. things is life of *m. s.*
42:1 I ha. put *my S.* upon him
44:3 pour *my S.* upon thy seed
59:21 *my S.* that is upon thee
*Ezek.* 3:14 went in heat of *my s.*
36:27 *my S.* within you, 37:14
39:29 pour. *my S.* on house of I.
*Dan.* 2:3 and *my s.* was troubled
7:15 I Dan. was griev. in *my s.*
*Joel* 2:28 I will pour out *my S.* on all flesh, 29; *Acts* 2:17, 18
*Hag.* 2:5 *my S.* remain. am. you
*Zec.* 4:6 by power, but by *my S.*
6:8 quiet. *my s.* in north count.
*Mat.* 12:18 I will put *my S.* on
*Luke* 1:47 *my s.* hate rejoi. in G.
23:46 in thy hands I com. *my s.*
*Acts* 7:59 Lord Je. receive *my s.*
*Rom.* 1:9 wh. I serve with *my s.*
1 *Cor.* 5:4 when gath. and *my s.*
14:14 *my s.* prayeth, but my
16:18 they have refresh. *my s.*
2 *Cor.* 2:13 had no rest in *my s.*

**New SPIRIT.**

*Ezek.* 11:19 a *n. s.* in you, 36:26
18:31 a new heart and *new s.*

**Newness of SPIRIT.**

*Rom.* 7:6 we sho. serve in *n. of s.*

**Patient SPIRIT.**

*Ec.* 7:8 *p.* in *s.* bet. than proud

**Perverse SPIRIT.**

*Is.* 19:14 L. hath mingled a *p. s.*

**Poor SPIRIT.**

*Mat.* 5:3 blessed are *poor* in *s.*

**SPIRIT of promise.**

*Eph.* 1:13 sealed with H. *S. of p.*

**SPIRIT of prophecy.**

*Rev.* 19:10 testim. of J. is *s. of p.*

**SPIRIT of slumber.**

*Rom.* 11:8 G. given them *s. of s.*

**Sorrowful SPIRIT.**

1 *Sam.* 1:15 a woman of a *s. s.*

**SPIRIT of truth.**

*John* 14:17 *S. of t.* whom world
15:26 *S. of t.* which proceedeth
16:13 when *S. of truth* is come
1 *John* 4:6 hereby kn. we *S. of t.*

*See* VEXATION.

**Unclean SPIRIT.**

*Zec.* 13:2 cause *uncl. s.* to pass
*Mat.* 12:43 when the *u. s.* is gone out of a man, *Luke* 11:24
*Mark* 1:23 synag. a man wi. *u. s.*
26 when *u. s.* had torn him
3:30 they said, He hath an *u. s.*
5:2 met him a man with *u. s.*
8 come out, th. *u. s.* *Luke* 8:29
7:25 whose daugh. had an *u. s.*
*Luke* 9:42 Jesus rebuked *u. s.*

**SPIRIT of understanding.**

*Is.* 11:2 the *s. of u.* sh. rest upon

**SPIRIT of whoredoms.**
*Hos.* 4:12 *s. of w.* caused to err
5:4 *s. of w.* is in midst of them
**SPIRIT of wisdom.**
*Ex.* 28:3 wh. I filled wi. *s. of w.*
*Deut.* 34:9 Joshua full of *s. of w.*
*Is.* 11:2 *s. of w.* sh. rest up. him
*Eph.* 1:17 G. may give *s. of w.*
**Wounded SPIRIT.**
*Prov.* 18:14 *w. s.* who can bear?
**SPIRITS.**
*Num.* 16:22 O God, the God of *s.* 27:16
*Ps.* 104:4 mak. angels *s. Heb.* 1:7
*Prov.* 16:2 Lord weighed the *s.*
*Zec.* 6:5 th. are four *s.* of heaven
*Mat.* 8:16 cast out *s.* with word
10:1 power ag. uncl. *s. Mark* 6:7
*Mark* 1:27 commandeth he the unclean *s. Luke* 4:36
3:11 uncl. *s.* fell down bef. him
5:13 unclean *s.* entered swine
*Luke* 10:20 rejoice not that *s.* are
*Acts* 5:16 vexed with unclean *s.*
8:7 *s.* crying, came out of many
1 *Cor.* 12:10 to ano. discern. of *s.*
14:32 *s.* of proph. are subject to
1 *Tim.* 4:1 giv. heed to seduc. *s.*
*Heb.* 1:14 not all ministering *s.*
12:9 in subjection to Fath. of *s.*
23 to *s.* of just men made per.
1 *Pet.* 3:19 preach. to *s.* in prison
1 *John* 4:1 try *s.* wheth. they are
*Rev.* 16:13 I saw 3 unclean *s.* like
14 they are the *s.* of devils

*See* EVIL, FAMILIAR, SEVEN.

**SPIRITUAL.**
*Hos.* 9:7 the *s.* man is mad
*Rom.* 1:11 impart to you *s.* gift
7:14 we know that the law is *s.*
15:27 partak. of their *s.* things
1 *Cor.* 2:13 comparing *s.* things with *s.*
15 he that is *s.* judgeth all thi.
3:1 could not spe. to you as to *s.*
9:11 have sown unto you *s.*
10:3 did all eat same *s.* meat
4 same *s.* dri. drank of *s.* rock
12:1 concern. *s.* gifts, brethren
14:1 desire *s.* gifts; 12 zeal. of *s.*
37 if any man think himself *s.*
15:44 *s.* body, there is a *s.* body
46 that was not first whi. is *s.* afterwards that which is *s.*
*Gal.* 6:1 ye which are *s.* restore
*Eph.* 1:3 blessed us with *s.* bless.
5:19 speak. to yours. in *s.* songs
6:12 wrestle against *s.* wickedn.
*Col.* 1:9 filled with *s.* understand.
3:16 admon. in psa. and *s.* songs
1 *Pet.* 2:5 built up a *s.* house, to offer *s.* sacrifices
**SPIRITUALLY.**
*Rom.* 8:6 to be *s.* minded is life
1 *Cor.* 2:14 because are *s.* discer.
*Rev.* 11:8 whi. *s.* is called Sodom
**SPIT, TED.**
*Lev.* 15:8 *s.* on him that is clean
*Num.* 12:14 if fath. had *s.* in face
*Deut.* 25:9 she shall *s.* in his face
*Job* 30:10 sp. not to *s.* in my face
*Mat.* 26:67 they did *s.* in his face
27:30 and they *s.* upon him and
*Mark* 7:33 he *s.* touched tongue
8:23 when he had *s.* on his eyes
10:34 they shall *s.* upon him
14:65 began to *s.* on him, 15:19
*Luke* 18:32 spitef. entreated *s.* on
**SPITE.**
*Ps.* 10:14 for thou beholdest *s.* to
**SPITEFULLY.**
*Mat.* 22:6 they entreated them *s.*
*Luke* 18:32 shall be *s.* entreated
**SPITTING.**
*Is.* 50:6 I hid not my face from *s.*

**SPITTLE.**
1 *Sam.* 21:13 let his *s.* fall down
*Job* 7:19 alone, till I swallow *s.*
*John* 9:6 he made clay of *s.* and

**SPOIL, Substantive.**
*Gen.* 49:27 at night he divide *s.*
*Ex.* 15:9 enemy said, I divide *s.*
*Num.* 31:9 Is. took *s.* of cattle, 11
*Deut.* 2:35 *s.* of cities we took, 3:7; *Jos.* 8:27; 11:14
13:16 thou sh. gather all the *s.*
20:14 *s.* thou shalt take, *Jos.* 8:2
*Jud.* 5:30 necks of th. that take *s.*
14:19 Sam. slew 30 men, took *s.*
1 *Sam.* 14:30 eaten freely of *s.*
32 the people flew upon the *s.*
15:19 but didst fly upon the *s.*
30:16 because the great *s.* that
19 neither *s.* nor any thing was
20 and said, This is David's *s.*
22 we will not give them of *s.*
26 he sent of *s.* to elders of Ju.
2 *Sam.* 3:22 Joab bro. in great *s.*
12:30 he brought *s.* of Rabbah
2 *K.* 3:23 now, theref. M. to the *s.*
21:14 they sh. bec. *s.* to enemies
1 *Chr.* 20:2 fr. Rab. he brought *s.*
2 *Chr.* 14:13 carried away *s.* 14
15:11 they offered to Lord of *s.*
20:25 were 3 days gathering *s.*
24:23 Syri. sent *s.* to king of D.
28:8 took *s.* brou. *s.* to Samaria
14 armed men left capti. and *s.*
*Ezr.* 9:7 kings ha. been deli. to *s.*
*Est.* 3:13 take *s.* of them, 8:11
9:10 on *s.* laid they not th. hand
*Job* 29:17 I plucked *s.* out of teeth
*Ps.* 68:12 tarried at home divi. *s.*
119:162 rejoice, as one findeth *s.*
*Prov.* 1:13 sh. fill houses with *s.*
16:19 to divide *s.* with proud
31:11 he shall have no need of *s.*
*Is.* 3:14 *s.* of poor is in houses
8:4 *s.* of Samaria shall be taken
9:3 rejoice when they divide *s.*
10:6 give him charge to take *s.*
33:4 your *s.* shall be gathered
23 prey of a great *s.* divided
42:22 they are for a *s.* and none
24 who gave Jacob for a *s.*?
53:12 he sh. divide *s.* wi. strong
*Jer.* 6:7 violence and *s.* is heard
15:13 thy subst. will I give to *s.*
17:3 I will give thy substa. to *s.*
20:8 I cried violence and *s.*
30:16 they that *s.* thee sh. be a *s.*
49:32 their cattle shall be a *s.*
50:10 Chaldea shall be a *s.*
*Ezek.* 7:21 I will give it for a *s.*
25:7 deliver Ammonite for a *s.*
26:5 Tyr. for a *s.* to nations, 12
29:19 Nebuch. take *s.* of Egypt
38:12 I will go up to take a *s.*
13 art thou come to take a *s.*
45:9 Is. remove violence and *s.*
*Dan.* 11:24 he shall scatter the *s.*
33 shall fall by *s.* many days
*Nah.* 2:9 *s.* of silver, *s.* of gold
*Hab.* 2:17 *s.* of beasts shall cover
*Zec.* 2:9 as *s.* to their servants
14:1 *s.* shall be divided in midst
**SPOIL, Verb.**
*Ex.* 3:22 ye shall *s.* Egyptians
1 *Sam.* 14:36 *s.* them until morn.
2 *Sam.* 23:10 people return. to *s.*
*Ps.* 44:10 they who hate us *s.*
89:41 all that pass by way *s.*
109:11 let strangers *s.* his labor
*Prov.* 22:23 will *s.* soul of those
24:15 O man, *s.* not resting-pla.
*Cant.* 2:15 foxes that *s.* vines
*Is.* 11:14 they sh. *s.* them of east
*Is.* 17:14 portion of th. that *s.* us
33:1 when shalt cease to *s.* thou
*Jer.* 5:6 wolf of even. sh. *s.* them
20:5 I will give Jerusal. to *s.* it.
30:16 they that *s.* thee sh. be a *s.*

47:4 day cometh to *s.* Philistines
49:28 Kedar, *s.* men of the east
50:10 all that *s.* shall be satisfied
*Ezek.* 14:15 they *s.* it so that it be
32:12 they shall *s.* pomp of Egy.
39:10 they shall *s.* those that
*Hos.* 10:2 break altars, *s.* images
13:15 he shall *s.* treasure of all
*Hab.* 2:8 remn. of peo. sh. *s.* thee
*Zep.* 2:9 residue of people shall *s.*
*Mat.* 12:29 *s.* goods? *Mark* 3:27
*Col.* 2:8 lest any man *s.* you
**SPOILED.**
*Gen.* 34:27 sons of Jacob *s.* city
*Ex.* 12:36 they *s.* the Egyptians
*Deut.* 28:29 sh. be oppress. and *s.*
*Jud.* 2:14 hand of spoilers that *s.*
1 *Sam.* 14:48 Is. fr. them that *s.*
2 *K.* 7:16 Is. *s.* tents of Syrians
2 *Chr.* 14:14 A. *s.* cities of Gerar
*Job* 12:17 leadeth coun. away *s.*
19 leads princes away *s.*
*Ps.* 76:5 the stout-hearted are *s.*
*Prov.* 22:23 spoil soul of th. that *s.*
*Is.* 13:16 their houses shall be *s.*
18:2 whose land rivers have *s.* 7
24:3 land shall be utterly *s.*
33:1 spoilest, and wast not *s.*
42:22 this is a people rob. and *s.*
*Jer.* 2:14 a serv. why is he *s.*?
4:13 woe unto us, for we are *s.*
20 whole land is *s.* tents are *s.*
30 wh. thou art *s.* wh. wilt do?
9:19 are we *s.*! 10:20 taber. is *s.*
21:12 deliver him that is *s.* 22:3
25:36 L. hath *s.* their pasture
48:1 Nebo is *s.* 15 Moab is *s.* 20
49:3 Ai is *s.* 10 E. his seed is *s.*
51:55 Lord hath *s.* Babylon
*Ezek.* 18:7 *s.* none by violence, 16
12 hath oppressed, hath *s.* 18
23:46 I will give them to be *s.*
39:10 shall spoil those that *s.*
*Hos.* 10:14 fortresses shall be *s.*
*Amos* 3:11 thy palaces shall be *s.*
5:9 strengtheneth *s.* ag. strong
*Mic.* 2:4 say, We be utterly *s.*
*Hab.* 2:8 hast *s.* many nations
*Zec.* 2:8 sent to nations wh. *s.*
11:2 because mighty are *s.*
3 glory *s.* for pride of Jor. is *s.*
*Col.* 2:15 having *s.* principalities
**SPOILER.**
*Is.* 16:4 fr. face of *s.* the *s.* cease
21:2 *s.* spoileth, go up, O Elam
*Jer.* 6:26 *s.* suddenly come on us
15:8 I brought upon them a *s.*
48:8 *s.* sh. come upon every city
18 *s.* of M. shall come on thee
32 *s.* is fallen upon thy fruits
51:56 bec. *s.* is come on Babylon
**SPOILERS.**
*Jud.* 2:14 he delivered them into hand of *s.* 2 *K.* 17:20
1 *Sam.* 13:17 *s.* out of camp of P.
14:15 the *s.* they also trembled
*Jer.* 12:12 *s.* are come upon high
51:48 *s.* come to her from north
53 from me sh. *s.* come to her
**SPOILEST, ETH.**
*Ps.* 35:10 needy from him that *s.*
*Is.* 21:2 spoiler *s. Hos.* 7:1 rob. *s.*
33:1 woe to thee that *s.*
*Nah.* 3:16 canker-worm *s.* flieth
**SPOILING.**
*Ps.* 35:12 good, to *s.* of my soul
*Is.* 22:4 *s.* of daught. of my peo.
*Jer.* 48:3 voice from Horonaim *s.*
*Hab.* 1:3 *s.* and violence bef. me
*Heb.* 10:34 joyf. *s.* of your goods
**SPOILS.**
*Jos.* 7:21 saw among *s.* a garment
1 *Chr.* 26:27 out of *s.* did dedic.
*Is.* 25:11 bri. down pride with *s.*
*Luke* 11:22 and divideth his *s.*
*Heb.* 7:4 Abrah. gave tenth of *s.*

**SPOKEN.**
*Gen.* 18:19 L. br. what he hath *s.*
*Num.* 14:28 as ye have *s.* so will
21:7 we have *s.* ag. L. and thee
23:19 he *s.* not make it good?
*Deut.* 18:17 well *s.* that th. ha. *s.*
1 *Sam.* 25:30 L. done all he ha. *s.*
2 *Sam.* 2:27 *s.* people had gone up
1 *K.* 18:24 peo. said, It is well *s.*
2 *K.* 4:13 thou be *s.* for to king?
*Ps.* 87:3 glorious things are *s.* of
*Ec.* 7:21 ta. heed to all words *s.*
*Cant.* 8:8 in the day wh. she be *s.*
*Jer.* 26:16 *s.* to us in name of L.
*Mal.* 3:13 wh. ha. we *s.* ag. thee?
*Luke* 18:34 nor kn. they things *s.*
*John* 15:22 if I had not co. and *s.*
*Acts* 8:24 none of things *s.* come
13:46 word sho. first ha. been *s.*
19:36 these things cannot be *s.*
*Rom.* 15:21 to wh. he was not *s.*
1 *Cor.* 10:30 why am I evil *s.* of
14:9 shall it be kno. what is *s.*?
1 *Pet.* 4:14 on their part evil *s.* of
2 *Pet.* 2:2 way of truth evil *s.* of

**SPOKEN, *with* God.**
*Gen.* 21:2 time of wh. *God* had *s.*
*Ps.* 62:11 *G.* hath *s.* once, twice
*Mat.* 22:31 that wh. was *s.* by *G.*
*See* LORD.

**I have, *or* have I SPOKEN.**
*Gen.* 28:15 done what *I h. s.*
*Ex.* 32:13 land *I have s.* of
1 *Sam.* 20:23 matter wh. *I h. s.* of
*Job* 40:5 once *h. I s.* will not ans.
*Ps.* 116:10 therefore *have I s.* 2 *Cor.* 4:13
*Is.* 45:19 *I h.* not *s.* in sec. 48:16
46:11 *I h. s.* it, bring it to pass
48:15 *I,* even *I h. s.* I called
*Jer.* 35:17 *I h. s.* have not heard
*Ezek.* 12:28 word *I h. s.* be done
13:7 L. saith, Albeit *I h.* not *s.*
26:5 *I h. s.* it, saith Lord, 28:10
38:17 art thou he of wh. *I h. s.*
*John* 12:49 *I h.* not *s.* of myself
14:25 *have I s.* 15:11; 16:1, 25, 33

**SPOKEN, *with* prophet.**
*Mat.* 2:23 fulfilled which was *s.* by the *prophet,* 13:35; 27:35
3:3 that was *s.* of by the *p.* Es.
4:14 *s.* by Es. *p.* 8:17; 12:17; 21:4

**Thou hast SPOKEN.**
*Ex.* 4:10 nor since *thou h. s.*
10:29 Moses said, *T. h. s.* well
33:17 I will do this thing *t. h. s.*
*Deut.* 1:14 thing which *t. h. s.*
2 *K.* 20:19 good is word of Lord which *thou hast s. Is.* 39:8
*Est.* 6:10 let nothing fail *t. h. s.*
*Jer.* 3:5 *t. h. s.* done evil things
32:24 that *t. h. s* is come to pass
44:16 as for word *t. h. s.* unto us
51:62 O L. *t. h. s.* ag. this place

**SPOKES.**
1 *K.* 7:33 felloes and *s.* all molten

**SPOKESMAN.**
*Ex.* 4:16 he sh. be thy *s.* to peo.

**SPONGE.**
*Mat.* 27:48 one of them took a *s.* *Mark* 15:36; *John* 19:29

**SPOON.**
*Num.* 7:14 one *s.* of ten shekels, 20, 26, 32, 38, 44, 50, 56, 62

**SPOONS.**
*Ex.* 25:29 make dishes and *s.*
*Num.* 4:7 put there. dishes and *s.*
7:84 silver bowls, twelve *s.* 86
1 *K.* 7:50 *s.* we. gold, 2 *Chr.* 4:22
2 *K.* 25:14 *s.* took, *Jer.* 52:18, 19
2 *Chr.* 24:14 rest of money *s.* ma.

**SPORT, Substantive.**
*Jud.* 16:25 Sam. make *s.* made *s.*
27 beheld while Sams. made *s.*
*Prov.* 10:23 *s.* to fool to do misc.
26:19 saith, Am not I in *s.*?

**SPORT, ING.**
*Gen.* 26:8 Isa. was *s.* wi. Rebek.
*Is.* 57:4 ag. whom *s.* yourselves?
2 *Pet.* 2:13 *s.* themsel. with dec.

**SPOT.**
*Num.* 19:2 br. heifer without *s.*
28:3 two lambs without *s.* 9, 11; 29:17, 26
*Deut.* 32:5 *s.* is not *s.* of his chil.
*Job* 11:15 thy face without *s.*
*Cant.* 4:7 there is no *s.* in thee
*Eph.* 5:27 glori. church, not ha. *s.*
1 *Tim.* 6:14 keep com. without *s.*
*Heb.* 9:14 off. himself without *s.*
1 *Pet.* 1:19 as a lamb without *s.*
2 *Pet.* 3:14 be found without *s.*
*See* BRIGHT.

**SPOTS.**
*Jer.* 13:23 can leopard change *s.*?
2 *Pet.* 2:13 *s.* they are and blemi.
*Jude* 12 the. are *s.* in your feasts

**SPOTTED.**
*Gen.* 30:32 removing *s.* cattle
39 brou. cattle, speckled and *s.*
*Jude* 23 hating garm. *s.* by flesh

**SPOUSE, S.**
*Cant.* 4:8 come from Leb. my *s.*
9 ravi. my heart, my sister, *s.*
10 fair thy love, my sister, *s.*
11 lips, O my *s.* drop as honey
*Cant.* 4:12 garden inc. is my sis. *s.*
5:1 into my garden, my sister, *s.*
*Hos.* 4:13 your *s.* commit adult.
14 I will not punish your *s.*

SPOUTS. *See* WATER-SPOUTS.

**SPRANG.**
*Mark* 4:8 fruit th. *s.* up, *Luke* 8:8
*Acts* 16:29 call. for light and *s.* in
*Heb.* 7:14 evident L. *s.* out of J.
11:12 there *s.* of one many
*See* SPRUNG.

**SPREAD.**
*Gen.* 33:19 wh. J. *s.* tent, 35:21
*Lev.* 13:5 plague *s.* not, 6, 23, 28
*Num.* 4:7 on table *s.* cloth, 11
*Deut.* 22:17 *s.* cloth before elders
*Jud.* 8:25 they *s.* a garment
15:9 Philistines *s.* thems. in L.
2 *Sam.* 5:18 Philist. also came and *s.* thems. 22; 1 *Chr.* 14:9, 13
16:22 they *s.* Absal. tent on roof
17:19 wom. *s.* covering on well
21:10 Rizpah *s.* sackclo. for her
1 *K.* 8:54 with hands *s.* to heaven
2 *K.* 8:15 Hazael *s.* cloth on face
19:14 *s.* letter bef. L. *Is.* 37:14
*Ps.* 105:39 he *s.* a cloud for cov.
140:5 *s.* a net by the way-side
*Prov.* 1:17 net *s.* in sight of bird
*Is.* 14:11 worm is *s.* under thee
19:8 *s.* nets on water languish
33:23 they could not *s.* the sail
*Jer.* 8:2 they sh. *s.* them bef. sun
10:9 silv. *s.* into plates brought
*Lam.* 1:13 hath *s.* net for my feet
*Ezek.* 2:10 he *s.* the roll before me
12:13 my net also will I *s.* 17:20
26:14 be a place to *s.* nets upon
*Hos.* 5:1 have been a net *s.* on T.
7:12 when they go, I will *s.* net
14:6 branches sh. *s.* his beauty
*Joel* 2:2 as morn. *s.* upon mount
*Mal.* 2:3 I will *s.* dung on your fa.
*Mat.* 21:8 multit. *s.* garments in way, *Mark* 11:8; *Luke* 19:36
*Acts* 4:17 but that it *s.* no further

**SPREAD abroad.**
*Gen.* 10:18 Canaanites were *s. a.*
28:14 thou shalt *s. a.* to west
*Ex.* 9:29 I will *s. a.* hand to L.
33 Moses *s. a.* his hands to L.
1 *Sam.* 30:16 th. were *s. a.* earth
2 *Sam.* 22:43 *s. a.* mine enemies
2 *Chr.* 26:8 Uzziah's name *s. a.* 15
*Zec.* 1:17 cities thro' prosp. *s. a.*
2:6 I *s.* you *a.* as the four winds
1 *Thes.* 1:8 faith to God-w. is *s. a.*

**SPREAD forth.**
*Num.* 24:6 as valleys are th. *s. f.*
1 *K.* 8:7 cherubim *s. f.* 2 wings
22 S. *s. f.* hands, 2 *Chr.* 6:12, 13
*Is.* 1:15 wh. ye *s. f.* your hands
25:11 he shall *s. f.* hands, swim.
42:5 saith G. he that *s. f.* earth
*Ezek.* 47:10 a place to *s. f.* nets

**SPREAD over.**
*Num.* 4:6 shall *s. o.* cloth of blue
*Is.* 25:7 that is *s. o.* all nations
*Jer.* 48:40 shall *s.* wings *o.* Moab
49:22 he sh. *s.* his wings *o.* Boz.
*Ezek.* 16:8 I *s.* my skirt *over* thee
19:8 nations *s.* their net *o.* him

**SPREAD out.**
*Ex.* 37:9 cherubim *s. o.* wings, 1 *Chr.* 28:18
*Ezr.* 9:5 *s. out* my hands to L.
*Job* 29:19 my root *s. o.* by water
37:18 hast th. wi. him *s. o.* sky?
*Is.* 65:2 *s. o.* hands to a rebelli.
*Lam.* 1:10 advers. *s. o.* his hand
*Ezek.* 32:3 will *s. o.* net over thee

**SPREADEST, ETH.**
*Lev.* 13:8 if priest see that scab *s.*
*Deut.* 32:11 as eagle *s.* her wings
*Job* 9:8 G. who alone *s.* out heav.
26:9 and he *s.* his cloud upon it
36:30 he *s.* his light upon it
*Prov.* 29:5 flatter. neighb. *s.* a net
*Is.* 25:11 he that swim. *s.* hands
40:22 that *s.* heavens as a tent
44:24 I the L. that *s.* abroad
*Jer.* 4:31 daughter of Z. *s.* hands
17:8 a tree that *s.* out her roots
*Ezek.* 27:7 linen th. *s.* for thy sail
*Lam.* 1:17 Z. *s.* forth her hands

**SPREADING.**
*Ps.* 37:35 I have seen wicked *s.*
*Ezek.* 17:6 and became a *s.* vine

**SPREADING, S.**
*Job* 36:29 underst. *s.* of clouds?
*Ezek.* 26:5 a place for *s.* of nets

**SPRIGS.**
*Is.* 18:5 afore harvest cut off *s.*
*Ezek.* 17:6 a vine, shot forth *s.*

**SPRING, Substantive.**
2 *K.* 2:21 he went forth to the *s.*
*Prov.* 25:26 troub. and corrupt *s.*
*Cant.* 4:12 spouse, is *s.* shut up
*Is.* 58:11 sh. be like *s.* of water
*Hos.* 13:15 his *s.* sh. become dry

**SPRINGS.**
*Deut.* 4:49 under *s.* of Pisgah
*Jos.* 10:40 smote country of *s.*
12:8 kings in plains and in *s.*
15:19 give me *s.* of water, gave upper *s. Jud.* 1:15
*Job* 38:16 hast entered into *s.*?
*Ps.* 87:7 all my *s.* are in thee
104:10 he sendeth *s.* into valleys
107:33 turn. water *s.* into dry
35 turn. dry ground to water *s.*
*Is.* 35:7 land become *s.* of water
41:18 I will make dry land *s.*
49:10 by *s.* of water guide them
*Jer.* 51:36 I will make her *s.* dry

**SPRING.**
1 *Sam.* 9:26 about *s.* of day Sam.
*See* DAYSPRING.

**SPRING.**
*Ezek.* 17:9 in all leaves of her *s.*

**SPRING, Verb.**
*Num.* 21:17 Is. sang, *s.* up, O w.
*Deut.* 8:7 and depths that *s.* out
*Jud.* 19:25 when day began to *s.*
*Job* 5:6 nei. doth trouble *s.* out
38:27 bud of tender herb to *s.*

*Ps.* 85:11 truth sh. s. out of earth
92:7 wh. wicked s. as the grass
*Is.* 42:9 bef. they s. forth I tell
43:19 now it shall s. forth
44:4 they sh. s. up as am. grass
45:8 righteousness s. up togeth.
58:8 thy health shall s. forth
61:11 gard. causeth things to s.
*Joel* 2:22 for the pastures do s.
*Mark* 4:27 seed s. he kn. not how

**SPRINGETH.**

2 *K.* 19:29 eat in second year that which s. of same, *Is.* 37:30
*Hos.* 10:4 thus judgment s. up

**SPRINGING.**

*Gen.* 26:19 found well of s. water
2 *Sam.* 23:4 as tender grass s. out
*Ps.* 65:10 thou blessedst the s.
*John* 4:14 a well of water s. up
*Heb.* 12:15 any root s. trouble you

**SPRINKLE.**

*Ex.* 9:8 let Moses s. the ashes
*Lev.* 14:7 s. on him to be cleansed
51 s. the house seven times
16:14 shall s. on mercy-seat, 15
*Num.* 8:7 s. water of purifying
19:18 shall s. it upon the tent
19 the clean person shall s. it
*Is.* 52:15 sh. he s. many nations
*Ezek.* 36:25 s. clean wa. upon you

**SPRINKLED, ETH.**

*Ex.* 9:10 s. ashes toward heaven
*Lev.* 7:14 priest's that s. blood
*Num.* 19:13 wa. not s. on him, 20
*Job* 2:12 s. dust on their heads
*Heb.* 9:19 he s. the book and peo.
10:22 hearts s. from evil conscie.
*See* BLOOD.

**SPRINKLING.**

*Heb.* 9:13 the ashes of a heifer s.
11:28 thro' faith kept s. of blood
12:24 we are come to blood of s.
1 *Pet.* 1:2 s. of blood of Jesus Ch.

**SPROUT.**

*Job* 14:7 tree that it will s. again

**SPRUNG.**

*Mat.* 4:16 shad. of death, light s.
13:5 and they s. up, *Mark* 4:5
26 but when blade was s. up
*Luke* 8:6 as soon as it was s. up

**SPUE, ED.**

*Lev.* 18:28 th. land s. you, 20:22
28 as it s. out nations th. were
*Jer.* 25:27 s. fall, rise no more
*Rev.* 3:16 then I will s. thee out

**SPEWING.**

*Hab.* 2:16 s. shall be on thy glory

**SPUN.**

*Ex.* 35:25 th. which they had s.

**SPY.**

*Num.* 13:16 M. sent to s. land, 17
21:32 Mo. sent to s. out Jaazer
*Jos.* 2:1 sent 2 men to s. 6:23, 25
*Jud.* 18:2 Dani. sent to s. 14, 17
2 *Sam.* 10:3 David sent serv. to s. out the city, 1 *Chr.* 19:3
2 *K.* 6:13 go and s. where he is
*Gal.* 2:4 came in privily to s.

**SPIED.**

*Ex.* 2:11 s. Egyptian smiting
2 *K.* 9:17 a watchman s. company
13:21 they s. a band of men
23:16 he s. sepulchres that were
*See* ESPY, ESPIED.

**SPIES.**

*Gen.* 42:9 said, Ye are s. 14, 16
34 then sh. I know ye are no s.
*Num.* 21:1 Is. came by way of s.
*Jos.* 6:23 young men that were s.
1 *Sam.* 26:4 David sent out s.
2 *Sam.* 15:10 Absalom sent s.
*Luke* 20:20 they sent forth s.
*Heb.* 11:31 Rahab had received s.

**SQUARE.**

1 *K.* 7:5 doors and posts were s.
*Ezek.* 45:2 s. round about, 50 cub.
*See* FOUR-SQUARE.

**SQUARED.**

*Ezek.* 41:21 posts of temp. were s.

**SQUARES.**

*Ezek.* 43:16 square in 4 s. thereof

**STABLE, Substantive.**

*Ezek.* 25:5 I will make Rab. a s.

**STABLE.**

1 *Chr.* 16:30 world also sh. be s

**STABILITY.**

*Is.* 33:6 knowl. s. of thy times

STABLISH. *See* ESTABLISH.

**STACHYS.**

*Rom.* 16:9 salute Urbane and S.

**STACKS.**

*Ex.* 22:6 s. of corn be consumed

**STACTE.**

*Ex.* 30:34 take to th. s. onycha

**STAFF.**

*Gen.* 32:10 with my s. I passed
38:18 give me thy sig. and s. 25
*Ex.* 12:11 with s. in your hand
21:19 and walk abroad on his s.
*Num.* 13:23 between two on a s.
22:27 Balaam sm. ass with a s.
*Jud.* 6:21 put forth end of s.
1 *Sam.* 17:7 s. of his spear like weav.'s beam, 2 *Sam.* 21:19
40 Dav. took his s. in his hand
2 *Sam.* 3:29 one that leaneth on a s.
23:7 fenced with s. of a spear
21 he went down to him with a s. 1 *Chr.* 11:23
2 *K.* 4:29 take my s. lay my s. on
31 Geh. laid s. on face of child
18:21 thou trust. on s. *Is.* 36:6
*Ps.* 23:4 thy rod and s. comf. me
*Is.* 3:1 L. will take fr. Ju. the s.
9:4 hast brok. s. of his shoulder
10:5 and the s. in their hand is
15 or as if s. should lift itself
24 lift up his s. against thee
14:5 L. hath broken s. of wicked
28:27 fitches beaten out wi. a s.
30:32 wh. grounded s. shall pass
*Jer.* 48:17 how is strong s. broken
*Ezek.* 29:6 have been a s. to Isr.
*Hos.* 4:12 their s. declar. to them
*Zec.* 8:4 every man with his s.
11:10 I took my s. even beauty
14 I cut asunder my other s.
*Mark* 6:8 take nothing, save a s.
*Heb.* 11:21 lean. on top of his s.
*See* BREAD.

**STAGGER.**

*Job* 12:25 s. like a drunken man, *Ps.* 107:27
*Is.* 29:9 they s. not with strong

**STAGGERED, ETH.**

*Is.* 19:14 as a drunken man s.
*Rom.* 4:20 s. not at promise of G.

**STAIN.**

*Job* 3:5 and shadow of death s. it
*Is.* 23:9 L. purposed to s. pride
63:3 sprinkled, I will s. my raim.

**STAIRS.**

1 *K.* 6:8 went up with winding s.
2 *K.* 9:13 under him on top of s.
*Neh.* 9:4 then stood on s. Jeshua
*Cant.* 2:14 in secret places of s.
*Ezek.* 43:17 s. look towards east
*Acts* 21:40 Paul stood on the s.

**STAKES.**

*Is.* 33:20 not one of s. removed
54:2 cords and strengthen thy s.

**STALK, S.**

*Gen.* 41:5 seven ears on one s. 22
*Jos.* 2:6 hid them with s. of flax
*Hos.* 8:7 no s. bud yield no meal

**STALL.**

*Amos* 6:4 out of midst of the s.
*Mal.* 4:2 grow up as calves of s.
*Luke* 13:15 loose his ox from the s.

**STALLS.**

1 *K.* 4:26 Solomon had forty thousand s. 2 *Chr.* 9:25
2 *Chr.* 32:28 Hezek. had s. for all
*Hab.* 3:17 there be no herd in s.

**STALLED.**

*Prov.* 15:17 th. a s. ox. and hatr.

**STAMMERERS.**

*Is.* 32:4 tongue of s. shall speak

**STAMMERING.**

*Is.* 28:11 s. lips and anoth. tongue
33:19 not see a peo. of s. tongue

**STAMP.**

2 *Sam.* 22:43 did s. them as mire
*Ezek.* 6:11 smite s. with thy foot

**STAMPED.**

*Deut.* 9:21 I s. calf and ground
2 *K.* 23:6 Josiah s. the grove
15 s. high pla. small to powder
2 *Chr.* 15:16 A. cut her idol and s.
*Ezek.* 25:6 thou hast s. with feet
*Dan.* 7:7 a fourth beast s. 19
8:7 he-goat cast down and s. 10

**STAMPING.**

*Jer.* 47:3 at noise of s. of hoofs

**STANCHED.**

*Luke* 8:44 wo.'s issue of blood s.

**STAND.**

*Ezek.* 29:7 their loins to be at a s.

**STAND, Verb.**

*Lev.* 27:14 priest, so shall it s. 17
*Deut.* 25:8 if he s. to it and say
*Jos.* 20:4 s. at enter. gate of city
1 *Sam.* 12:16 s. see this thing
19:3 s. beside my father in field
1 *K.* 17:1 as L. liveth bef. whom I s. 18:15; 2 *K.* 3:14; 5:16
2 *K.* 5:11 I thought he will s.
10:4 not, how then shall we s.?
1 *Chr.* 23:30 to s. every morning
2 *Chr.* 34:32 caused all pres. to s.
*Ezr.* 10:14 let rulers of congreg. s.
*Est.* 8:11 and to s. for their life
*Job* 8:15 lean on house, sh. not s.
19:25 s. at latter day on earth
*Ps.* 38:11 my kinsm. s. afar off
45:9 on right hand did s. queen
78:13 made waters to s. as heap
109:6 let Sa. s. at his right hand
31 shall s. at right hand of poor
122:2 our feet s. with. thy gates
130:3 mark iniqui. O L. who s.?
*Prov.* 19:21 counsel of L. shall s.
25:6 s. not in pl. of great men
*Ec.* 8:3 s. not in an evil thing
*Is.* 7:7 saith L. It sh. not s. 8:10
14:24 as I purposed, so it sh. s.
40:8 word of our G. sh. s. for ever
46:10 counsel shall s. I do pleas.
61:5 strangers s. and feed flocks
*Jer.* 6:16 s. ye in the ways
44:28 know whose word shall s.
46:21 did not s. bec. day came
*Ezek.* 17:14 keeping cov. might s.
*Dan.* 2:44 kingd. shall s. for ever
11:6 king of the north sh. not s.
*Mic.* 5:4 s. and feed in strength
*Nah.* 2:8 s. s. shall they cry
*Mal.* 3:2 who s. when he appear.
*Mark* 11:25 when ye s. praying
*Acts* 1:11 why s. gaz. to heaven?
5:20 go, s. and speak in temple
26:6 I s. and judged for hope
*Rom.* 14:4 G. able to ma. him. s
2 *Cor.* 1:24 joy, for by faith ye s
*Eph.* 6:13 having done all to s.
*Pet.* 5:12 grace of G. wherein s.

*Rev.* 3:20 I *s.* at door and knock
6:17 who shall be able to *s.?*
18:15 merchants *s.* afar off

**STAND abroad.**

*Deut.* 24:11 *s. a.* man br. pledge

**STAND against.**

*Lev.* 19:16 nor *s. a.* blood of thy neighbor
*Jer.* 44:29 my words sh. *s. a.* you

**STAND aloof.**

*Ps.* 38:11 my friends *s. aloof*

**STAND back.**

*Gen.* 19:9 *s. b.* this fellow came

**STAND before.**

*Ex.* 8:20 *s. before* Pharaoh, 9:13
17:6 I will *s. before* thee on rock
*Lev.* 26:37 power to *s. b.* enem. *Jos.* 7:12, 13; *Jud.* 2:14
*Num.* 27:21 he sh. *s. b.* Eleazar
35:12 till *s. b.* congre. *Jos.* 20:6
*Deut.* 7:24 no man able to *s. b.* th. 11:25; *Jos.* 1:5; 10:8; 23:9
9:2 who *s. b.* children of Anak?
19:17 both men shall *s. b.* Lord
29:10 *s.* this day all of you *b.* L.
1 *Sam.* 6:20 who able to *s. b.* L.?
1 *Sam.* 16:22 let David, I pray, *s. b.* me
1 *K.* 10:8 happy are thy servants who *s. b.* thee, 2 *Chr.* 9:7
2 *Chr.* 20:9 we *s. b.* house
*Ezr.* 9:15 we cannot *s. b.* thee
*Job* 41:10 who is able to *s. b.* me?
*Prov.* 22:29 a man diligent sh. *s. b.* kings, shall not *s. b.* mean
27:4 who is able to *s. b.* envy?
*Jer.* 7:10 *s. b.* me in this house
15:19 if th. ret. th. shalt *s. b.* me
35:19 Jo. not want man to *s. b.*
49:19 shepherd *s. b.* me? 50:44
*Dan.* 1:5 at end might *s. b.* king
8:4 no beast might *s. b.* him
11:16 none shall *s. b.* him
*Nah.* 1:6 who can *s. b.* his indi.?
*Luke* 21:36 worthy to *s. b.* Son
*Rom.* 14:10 all *s. b.* judgm.-seat
*Rev.* 20:12 small and gr. *s. b.* G.

**STAND by.**

*Ex.* 18:14 peo. *s. by* thee to even
*Neh.* 7:3 they *s. by* shut doors
*Is.* 65:5 *s. by,* I am ho. th. thou
*Jer.* 48:19 *s. by,* ask, What done
*Zec.* 3:7 walk am. th. that *s. by*
4:14 anointed ones that *s. by* L.
*John* 11:42 bec. of peo. wh. *s. by*

**STAND fast.**

*Jer.* 46:14 say ye, *s. f.* and prep.
1 *Cor.* 16:13 wat. ye, *s. f.* in faith
*Gal.* 5:1 *s. f.* in liberty Ch. made
*Phil.* 1:27 *s. f.* in sp. 4:1 *s. f.* in L.
1 *Thes.* 3:8 live, if ye *s. f.* in L.
2 *Thes.* 2:15 *s. f.* and hold trad.

**STAND forth.**

*Mark* 3:3 sa. to man, *s. f. Lu.* 6:8

**STAND here.**

*Deut.* 5:31 *s.* thou *here* by me
2 *Sam.* 18:30 turn aside, and *s. h.*
*Mat.* 20:6 why *s.* ye *h.* all day?
*Acts* 4:10 doth this man *s. here*

**STAND in.**

*Ps.* 4:4 *s. in* awe, and sin not
5:5 foolish sh. not *s. in* thy sig.
24:3 who sh. *s. in* his holy pl.?
76:7 *s. in* thy sight wh. angry?
89:43 not made him to *s. in* bat.
134:1 by night *s. in* house, 135:2
*Jer.* 26:2 *s. in* court of L.'s house
*Ezek.* 13:5 not gone to *s. in* bat.
*Dan.* 12:13 *s. in* lot end of days
*Zec.* 14:4 feet *s. in* that day
*Mat.* 24:15 abomin. *s. in* holy pl.
*Gal.* 4:20 for I *s. in* doubt of you

**STAND on.**

*Ex.* 17:9 to-morrow I *s. on* hill
2 *K.* 6:31 if head of Eli. *s. on* him
*Dan.* 11:17 sh. not *s. on* his side

**STAND out.**

*Ps.* 73:7 eyes *s. out* with fatness

**STAND perfect.**

*Col.* 4:12 may *s. p.* and complete

**STAND still.**

*Ex.* 14:13 fear ye not, *s. s.* and see salv. of L. 2 *Chr.* 20:17
*Num.* 9:8 *s. s.* I will hear wh. L.
*Jos.* 3:8 ye shall *s. s.* in Jordan
10:12 sun *s. s.* upon Gibeon
1 *Sam.* 9:27 *s.* thou *s.* that I show
12:7 *s. s.* that I may reason
14:9 we will *s. s.* in our place
*Job* 37:14 *s. s.* consi. works of G.
*Jer.* 51:50 escaped sword *s.* not *s.*

**STAND strong.**

*Ps.* 30:7 made mountain to *s. s.*

**STAND there.**

*Num.* 11:16 may *s. t.* with thee
*Deut.* 18:7 Levites who *s. there*
*Jam.* 2:3 say to the poor, *s.* th. *t.*

**STAND together.**

*Is.* 50:8 let us *s. t.* who advers.

**STAND up.**

*Neh.* 9:5 *s. up,* bless L. your G.
*Job* 30:20 I *s. up,* thou regar. not
33:5 set words in order, *s. up*
*Ps.* 35:2 shield, *s. up* for my help
94:16 who will *s. up* for me ag.
*Ec.* 4:15 shall *s. up* in stead
*Is.* 27:9 images shall not *s. up*
44:11 let them *s. up,* yet they
48:13 call to th. they *s. up* tog.
51:17 awake, *s. up,* O Jerusa.
*Dan.* 8:22 4 kingd. *s. up* of nati.
11:2 sh. *s. up* 3 kings in Persia
3 a mighty king shall *s. up,* 4
14 many *s. up* ag. king of sou.
12:1 that time sh. Michael *s. up*
*Acts* 10:26 Peter said, *s. up,* I am

**STAND upon.**

*Ex.* 33:21 thou shalt *s. u.* rock
*Deut.* 27:12 shall *s. u.* mount Ge.
*Jos.* 3:13 shall *s. upon* a heap
2 *Sam.* 1:9 Saul said, *s. upon* me
1 *K.* 19:11 *s. u.* mount before L.
*Ezek.* 2:1 *s. u.* thy feet, *Acts* 26:16
33:26 *s. u.* sword, work abomi.
*Dan.* 7:4 made *s. upon* feet
*Hab.* 2:1 I will *s. u.* my watch
*Zec.* 14:12 while they *s. u.* feet

**STAND upright.**

*Ps.* 20:8 we are risen, and *s. u.*
*Dan.* 10:11 underst. words, *s. u.*
*Acts* 14:10 he said to cripple, *s. u.*

**STAND with.**

*Num.* 1:5 men that sh. *s. w.* you

**STAND without.**

*Ezr.* 10:13 are not able to *s. w.*
*Mat.* 12:47 *s. w.* to sp. *Luke* 8:20
*Luke* 13:25 ye begin to *s. with.*

**STANDARD.**

*Num.* 2:3 on east side sh. *s.* of J.
10 on south side be *s.* of Reu.
18 on west side be *s.* of Ephr.
25 on north side be the *s.* of D.
10:14 in first place went *s.* of J.
*Is.* 49:22 I will set up *s.* to peo.
59:19 L. sh. lift up a *s.* ag. him
62:10 lift up a *s.* for the people
*Jer.* 4:6 set up *s.* toward Zion
21 how long see *s.* hear trum.
50:2 set ye up *s.* 51:12, 27

**STANDARD-BEARER.**

*Is.* 10:18 as when *s.-b.* fainteth

**STANDARDS.**

*Num.* 2:31 Dan go hindm. wi. *s.*

**STANDEST.**

*Gen.* 24:31 wheref. *s.* thou with.?
*Ex.* 3:5 place wher. th. *s.* is holy ground, *Jos.* 5:15; *Acts* 7:33
*Ps.* 10:1 why *s.* afar off, O Lord?
*Rom.* 11:20 bro. thou *s.* by faith

**STANDETH.**

*Deut.* 1:38 Jos. who *s.* bef. thee
29:15 with him that *s.* with us
*Jud.* 16:26 pillars wher. house *s.*
*Ps.* 1:1 nor *s.* in way of sinners
26:12 my feet *s.* in even place
33:11 counsel of Lord *s.* for ever
119:161 my heart *s.* in awe
*Prov.* 8:2 wisdom *s.* in high pl.
*Cant.* 2:9 behold, he *s.* beh. wall
*Is.* 3:13 *s.* to plead, *s.* to judge
46:7 set him in his place, he *s.*
*Dan.* 12:1 prince who *s.* for peo.
*Zec.* 11:16 nor feed that that *s.*
*John* 1:26 *s.* one among you
*Rom.* 14:4 to his own mas. he *s.*
1 *Cor.* 7:37 that *s.* steadf. in heart
8:13 eat no flesh while world *s.*
10:12 that thinketh he *s.* take heed lest he fall
*Heb.* 10:11 every priest *s.* daily
*Jam.* 5:9 judge *s.* before door
*Rev.* 10:8 angel who *s.* on sea

**STANDING, Substantive.**

*Ps.* 69:2 sink in mire whe. no *s.*
*Mic.* 1:11 shall rec. of you his *s.*

**STANDING.**

*Lev.* 26:1 nor rear ye up a *s.* im.
1 *Sam.* 19:20 S. *s.* appointed over
22:6 servants were *s.* about him
1 *K.* 22:19 h. of hea. *s.* 2 *Chr.* 18:18
*Ps.* 107:35 wildern. into *s.* water
*Amos* 9:1 I saw L. *s.* upon altar
*Mic.* 5:13 I will cut off thy *s.* im.
*Zec.* 3:1 Sa. *s.* at his right hand
6:5 go forth from *s.* before Lord
*Mat.* 6:5 love to pray *s.* in syna.
20:3 saw others *s.* idle in mark.
*Luke* 1:11 angel *s.* on side of alt.
*John* 8:9 and woman *s.* in midst
20:14 she saw Je. *s.* knew not
*Acts* 2:14 Peter *s.* up with eleven
5:25 men are *s.* in temple
7:55 J. *s.* on right hand of G. 56
22:20 I was *s.* by and consent.
*Heb.* 9:8 while taber. was yet *s.*
2 *Pet.* 3:5 earth *s.* out of water
*Rev.* 7:1 four angels *s.* on earth
18:10 *s.* off for fear of her torm.
19:17 an angel *s.* in the sun

*See* CORN.

**STANK.**

*Ex.* 7:21 the fish in the river *s.*
8:14 th. gathered frogs, land *s.*
16:20 manna bred worms and *s.*
2 *Sam.* 10:6 Ammon saw they *s.*

**STARE.**

*Ps.* 22:17 bones, Look and *s.*

**STAR.**

*Num.* 24:17 sh. co. a *s.* out of J.
*Amos* 5:26 ye have borne *s.*
*Mat.* 2:2 have seen his *s.* in east
9 lo, *s.* which they saw in east
*Mat.* 2:10 wh. they saw *s.* th. rej.
*Acts* 7:43 took up *s.* of your god
1 *Cor.* 15:41 *s.* differ. from ano. *s.*
*Rev.* 8:10 there fell a great *s.* 11
9:1 a *s.* fell from heaven to ear.

DAYSTAR. *See* DAY.

**Morning STAR.**

*Rev.* 2:28 I will give him *m. s.*
22:16 I am the bright and *m s.*

**STAR-GAZERS.**

*Is.* 47:13 let the *s.-g.* stand up

**STARS.**

*Gen.* 1:16 G. made lights, ma. *s.*
15:5 tell the *s.* if thou be able
37:9 sun, moon, and eleven *s.*
*Deut.* 4:19 when seest *s.* sho. be
*Jud.* 5:20 *s.* in their courses

Neh. 4:21 fr. morn. till s. appear.
Job 3:9 let s. of twilight be dark
9:7 sun, and sealeth up the s.
22:12 behold height of s.
25:5 s. are not pure in his sight
38:7 morning s. sang together
Ps. 8:3 moon and s. which thou
136:9 moon and s. to rule by ni.
147:4 telleth number of the s.
148:3 praise him, ye s. of light
Ec. 12:2 while sun or s. be not
Is. 14:13 ex. my throne above s.
Jer. 31:35 giveth s. for a light
Ezek. 32:7 I will make s. dark
Dan. 8:10 cast down some of s.
12:3 shall shine as s. for ever
Joel 2:10 s. withdraw shin. 3:15
Ob. 4 tho' set thy nest among s.
Luke 21:25 th. sh. be signs in s.
Acts 27:20 nei. sun nor s. appear
1 Cor. 15:41 another glory of s.
Heb. 11:12 so many as s. of sky
Jude 13 rag. waves, wandering s.
Rev. 8:12 third part of s. was
12:1 upon head a crown of 12 s.

See HEAVEN, SEVEN.

### STATE.

Ps. 39:5 man at best s. is vanity
Mat. 12:45 last s. is worse than the first, Luke 11:26

See ESTATE.

### STATELY.

Ezek. 23:41 sattest upon a s. bed

### STATION.

Is. 22:19 I will drive thee from s

### STATURE.

Num. 13:32 saw, men of great s.
1 Sam. 16:7 look not on hei. of s.
2 Sam. 21:20 a man of great s. 1 Chr. 11:23; 20:6
Cant. 7:7 thy s. is like a pa.-tree
Is. 10:33 high one of s. be hewn
45:14 men of s. shall come over
Ezek. 13:18 kerchi. on head of s.
17:6 it became a vine of low s.
19:11 her s. was exalted among
31:3 Assy. was cedar of high s.
Mat. 6:27 not add one cubit to his s. Luke 12:25
Luke 2:52 Jesus increased in s.
19:3 Zaccheus little of s. climb.
Eph. 4:13 measure of s. of Christ

### STATUTE.

Ex. 15:25 he made a s. and ordi.
29:9 priests' office for perpet. s.
Lev. 3:17 a perpetual s. 16:34; 24:9; Num. 19:21
Num. 27:11 sh. be for a s. 35:29
Jos. 24:25 he set a s. in Shechem
1 Sam. 30:25 David made it a s.
Ps. 81:4 this was a s. for Israel
Dan. 6:7 consulted to estab. a s.
15 that no s. king establisheth

### STATUTE for ever.

Ex. 27:21 it shall be a s. for ever, 28:43; 29:28; Lev. 6:18; 7:34; 10:9; 16:31; 23:21; Num. 18:23
Lev. 6:22 it is a s. for e. to the L.
Num. 19:10 to stran. for a s. f. e.

### STATUTES.

Ex. 18:26 make them know s.
Lev. 10:11 teach Israel all the s.
Num. 30:16 these are s. the L.
Deut. 4:6 which shall hear th. s.
6:24 L. commanded to do th. s.
16:12 shall observe and do th. s.
17:19 may learn to keep these s.
1 K. 3:3 walking in the s. of Da.
2 K. 17:8 walked in s. of hea. 19
34 neither do they after th. s.
37 s. he wrote, ye sh. observe
2 Chr. 33:8 take heed to do the s.
Neh. 9:14 commandedst them s.
Ps. 19:8 s. of Lord are right
Ezek. 20:25 I gave th. s. not good
33:15 if wicked walk in s. of life
Mic. 6:16 for s. of Omri are kept

### His STATUTES.

Ex. 15:26 if thou wilt keep his s. Deut. 6:17; 10:13; 11:1
Deut. 27:10 thou shalt do his s.
2 Sam. 22:23 h. s. I did not dep.
1 K. 8:61 perfect, to walk in h. s.
2 K. 17:15 they rejected h. s. and
23:3 made a covenant to keep his s. 2 Chr. 34:31
Ezr. 7:11 Ezra a scribe of his s.
Ps. 18:22 did not put away his s.
105:45 they might observe h. s.
Jer. 44:23 in his law, nor in h. s.

See JUDGMENTS.

### My STATUTES.

Gen. 26:5 Abraham kept my s.
Lev. 18:5 keep my s. 26; 19:19
25:18 wherefore ye sh. do my s.
26:3 if walk in my s. and keep
15 and if ye despise my s. or if
43 their soul abhorred my s.
1 K. 3:14 if thou wilt keep my s.
11:34 because he kept my s.
2 K. 17:13 keep my com. my s.
2 Chr. 7:19 if ye forsake my s.
Ps. 50:16 hast thou to decl. my s.
89:31 if they break my s.
Jer. 44:10 neither walk. in my s.
Ezek. 5:6 hath changed my s.
7 ye have not walked in my s.
11:20 they may walk in my s.
18:19 when son hath kept my s.
36:27 cau. you to walk in my s.
Zec. 1:6 my s. did take hold of

### Thy STATUTES.

1 Chr. 29:19 heart to keep thy s.
Ps. 119:12 O Lord, teach me t. s. 26, 33, 64, 68, 124, 135
16 I will delight my. in thy s.
23 thy servant did med. in t. s.
48 and I will meditate in thy s.
54 thy s. have been my songs
71 that I might learn thy s.
80 let my heart be sou. in t. s.
83 yet do I not forget thy s.
112 inclined my heart to t. s.
117 I will have respect to t. s.
118 hast trod. that err fr. t. s.
155 the wicked seek not t. s.
171 thou hast taught thy s.

### STAVES.

Ex. 25:13 makes s. of shittim-w. 28; 27:6; 30:5; 37:4
14 put s. into rings, 15; 27:7; 37:5; 38:7
40:20 he set s. on ark and put
Num. 4:6 put in s. ther. 8, 11, 14
21:18 nobles digged with their s.
1 Sam. 17:43 com. to me wi. s.?
1 Chr. 15:15 L. carried ark wi. s.
Hab. 3:14 didst strike with his s.
Zec. 11:7 I took unto me two s.
Mat. 10:10 coats nor s. Luke 9:3
26:47 Judas, with him a multitude with s. Mark 14:43

### STAY, Substantive.

Lev. 13:5 if plague in si. be at s.
2 Sam. 22:19 L. my s. Ps. 18:18
Is. 3:1 L. doth take away the s.
19:13 they that are s. of tribes

### STAYS.

1 K. 10:19 s. on either side thro. 2 Chr. 9:18

### STAY, Verb.

Gen. 19:17 nei. s. thou in plain
Ex. 9:28 ye shall s. no longer
Jos. 10:19 s. not, pursue after
Ruth 1:13 would ye s. for them?
1 Sam. 15:16 s. I will tell thee
20:38 make speed, haste, s. not
2 Sam. 24:16 s. hand, 1 Chr. 21:15
Job 37:4 he will not s. them
38:37 can s. bottles of heaven
Prov. 28:17 let no man s. him
Cant. 2:5 s. me with flagons
Is. 10:20 sh. no more s. on him
29:9 s. yourselves and wonder
30:12 and s. on oppression
31:1 woe to th. that s. on hors.
48:2 s. themselves on God of Is.
50:10 trust in L. s. on his God
Jer. 4:6 s. not for I will bri. evil
20:9 I was weary, I could not s.
Dan. 4:35 none can s. his hand
Hos. 13:13 not s. in place

### STAYED.

Gen. 8:10 Noah s. seven days, 12
32:4 I have s. there until now
Ex. 10:24 flocks and herds be s.
17:12 Aa. and Hur s. up Moses'
Num. 16:48 plague s. 50; 25:8: 2 Sam. 24:25; Ps. 106:30
Jos. 10:13 stood still, moon s.
1 Sam. 20:19 thou hast s. 3 days
24:7 Da. s. servants with words
1 Sam. 30:9 those that were left behind s.
2 Sam. 17:17 Jon. s. by En-rogel
24:21 that plague may be s. fr. people, 1 Chr. 21:22
1 K. 22:35 king was s. in chariot, 2 Chr. 18:34
2 K. 4:6 not a vessel more, oil s.
13:18 he smote thrice, and s.
15:20 king of Assyria s. not
Job 38:11 shall thy waves be s.
Is. 26:3 keep him wh. mind is s.
Lam. 4:6 overthro. no hands s.
Ezek. 31:15 great waters were s.
Hag. 1:10 heav. is s. earth is s.
Luke 4:42 peo. came and s. him
Acts 19:22 he himself s. in Asia

### STAYETH.

Is. 27:8 he s. his rough wind

### STEAD.

Gen. 30:2 Ja. said, Am I in G. s.?
44:33 let serv. abide in s. of lad
Ex. 29:30 priest in s. Lev. 16:32
Num. 10:31 to us in s. of eyes
32:14 risen in your fathers' s.
Jos. 5:7 wh. he raised in their s.
Job 16:4 in my soul's s.
33:6 acc. to thy wish in G.'s s.
34:24 sh. set others in their s.
2 Cor. 5:20 pray you in Ch.'s s.

See REIGNED.

### STEADFAST.

Job 11:15 yea, thou shalt be s.
Ps. 78:8 spirit was not s. with G.
37 neither were s. in his covenant
Dan. 6:26 living God s. for ever
1 Cor. 7:37 stand. in his heart s.
15:58 beloved brethren, be s.
2 Cor. 1:7 our hope of you is s.
Heb. 2:2 spok. by angels was s.
3:14 if we hold our confid. s.
6:19 an anchor sure and s.
1 Pet. 5:9 whom resist s. in faith

### STEADFASTLY.

2 K. 8:11 settled countenance s.
Luke 9:51 he s. set fa. to go to J.
Acts 1:10 while they looked s.
2:42 s. in the apostles' doctrine
6:15 they all looking s. on him
7:55 Step. looked s. into heav.
14:9 who s. beholding him, and
2 Cor. 3:7 Is. could not s. behold
13 could not s. look to the end

### STEADFASTNESS.

Col. 2:5 s. of your faith in Christ
2 Pet. 3:17 lest ye fall fr. your s.

### STEADS.

1 Chr. 5:22 they dwelt in their s.

### STEADY.

Ex. 17:12 Moses' hands were s.

**STEAL.**
Gen. 31:27 wheref. didst s. away
44:8 how should we s. silver?
Ex. 20:15 shalt not s. Lev. 19:11; Deut. 5:19; Mat. 19:18; Rom. 13:9
22:1 if a man s. an ox, he shall
2 Sam. 19:3 as people s. away
Prov. 6:30 if he s. to satisfy soul
30:9 or lest I be poor and s.
Jer. 7:9 will ye s. murder, and
23:30 I am ag. prophets that s.
Mat. 6:19 thi. break thro' and s.
20 thieves do not break nor s.
27:64 lest his disc. s. him away
Mark 10:19 do not s. Luke 18:20
John 10:10 thief com. but to s.
Rom. 2:21 sho. not s. dost thou s.
Eph. 4:28 that stole s. no more
STEALERS. See MENSTEALERS.

**STEALETH.**
Ex. 21:16 he that s. a man
Job 27:20 tempest s. him away
Zec. 5:3 for every one that s.

**STEALING.**
Deut. 24:7 if a man be found s.
Hos. 4:2 by swearing and s.

**STEALTH.**
2 Sam. 19:3 peo. gat them by s.

**STEEL.**
2 Sam. 22:35 s. is brok. Ps. 18:34
Job 20:24 bow of s. strike him
Jer. 15:12 shall iron break s.?

**STEEP.**
Ezek. 38:20 s. places shall fall
Mic. 1:4 poured down s. place
Mat. 8:32 the swine ran violent. down a s. place, Mark 5:13; Luke 8:33

**STEM.**
Is. 11:1 a rod out of s. of Jesse

**STEP.**
1 Sam. 20:3 th. is but s. between
Job 31:7 if my s. hath turned out

**STEPHANAS.**
1 Cor. 1:16 baptiz. househ. of S.
16:15 house of S. the first-fruits
17 I am glad of coming of S.

**STEPHEN.**
Acts 6:5 chose S. a man full, 8
7:59 they stoned S. calling on
8:2 devout men carried S. to his
11:19 abroad on perse. about S.
22:20 blood of thy martyr S.

**STEPPED, ETH.**
John 5:4 whosoev. first s. in was
7 another s. down before me

**STEPS.**
Ex. 20:26 neither go up by s.
2 Sam. 22:37 thou hast enlarged my s. Ps. 18:36
1 K. 10:19 the throne had six s.
20 twelve lions on s. 2 Chr. 9:19
Job 14:16 thou numberest my s.
18:7 s. of his strength be strait.
23:11 my foot hath held his s.
29:6 I washed my s. with butter
31:4 see my ways and count s.
37 decl. to him numb. of my s.
Ps. 17:11 compassed us in our s.
37:23 s. of a good man ordered
31 none of his s. shall slide
44:18 nor have our s. declined
56:6 mark my s. when th. wait
57:6 prepared a net for my s.
73:2 my s. had well nigh slipped
85:13 set us in the way of his s.
119:133 order my s. in thy word
Prov. 4:12 thy s. not be straiten.
5:5 her s. take hold on hell
16:9 the Lord directeth his s.
Is. 26:6 s. of the needy sh. tread.
Jer. 10:23 not in man to dir. his s.
Lam. 4:18 they hunt our s. we
Ezek. 40:22 went to it by 7 s. 26
49 brought me by s. whereby
Dan. 11:43 Ethiopi. be at his s.
Rom. 4:12 walk in s. of that faith
2 Cor. 12:18 walked we not in s.?
1 Pet. 2:21 that ye sho. fol. his s.

**STERN.**
Acts 27:29 cast 4 ancho. out of s.

**STEWARD.**
Gen. 15:2 and the s. of my house
43:19 they came near to the s.
1 K. 16:9 drunk in house of his s.
Mat. 20:8 L. of viney. saith to s.
Luke 8:3 wife of Chu. Herod's s.
12:42 who th. is that faithful s.
16:1 rich man who had a s.
2 thou mayest be no longer s.
8 L. commended the unjust s.
Tit. 1:7 bishop blameless s. of G.

**STEWARDS.**
1 Chr. 28:1 David assembled s.
1 Cor. 4:1 s. of mysteries of God
2 required in s. that a man
1 Pet. 4:10 good s. of grace of G.

**STEWARDSHIP.**
Luke 16:2 give account of thy s.
3 my lord taketh fr. me the s. 4

**STICK, Verb.**
Job 33:21 bones not seen, s. out
41:17 scales are joined, they s.
Ps. 38:2 thi. arrows s. fast in me
Ezek. 29:4 cau. fish to s. to scales

**STICKETH.**
Prov. 18:24 friend s. closer than

**STICK.**
2 K. 6:6 cut down a s. and cast it
Lam. 4:8 skin withered like a s.
Ezek. 37:16 one s. another s. 17

**STICKS.**
Num. 15:32 gath. s. on sabbath
1 K. 17:10 woman was gather. s.
12 behold, I am gather. two s.
Ezek. 37:20 s. whereon thou wri.
Acts 28:3 Paul gath. bundle of s.

**STIFF.**
Jer. 17:23 but made their neck s.

**STIFF-HEARTED.**
Ezek. 2:4 impud. child. and s.-h.

**STIFF neck.**
Deut. 31:27 I know thy s. neck
Ps. 75:5 speak not with a s. neck

**STIFF-NECKED.**
Ex. 32:9 this peo. is a s.-n. peo.
33:3 art a s.-n. people, Deut. 9:6
5 say to Is. Ye are a s.-n. peo.
34:9 a s.-n. people, Deut. 9:13
Deut. 10:16 be no more s.-n.
2 Chr. 30:8 not s.-n. as your fath.
Acts 7:51 s.-n. ye resist H. Ghost

**STIFFENED.**
2 Chr. 36:13 s. his neck and har.

**STILL, Adverb.**
Ex. 9:2 and wilt hold them s.
Num. 14:38 Josh. and C. lived s.
2 Sam. 14:32 to have been th. s.
2 K. 7:4 and if we sit s. here
Job 2:9 dost s. retain th. integ.?
3:13 now should I have lain s.
20:13 tho' he keep it s. within
Ps. 49:9 that he should s. live
Jer. 8:14 why do we sit s.?
Rev. 22:11 unj. s. filthy s. holy s.
See STAND, STOOD.

**STILL, Adjective and Verb.**
Ex. 15:16 sh. be as s. as a stone
Jud. 18:9 land good, are ye s.?
1 K. 19:12 after fire s. small voice
22:3 Ram. is ours, and we be s.
Ps. 4:4 commu. with heart, be s.
8:2 thou mightest s. the enemy
23:2 leadeth me beside s. waters
46:10 be s. and kn. that I am G.
76:8 the earth feared, and was s.
83:1 hold not, and be not s. O G.
107:29 so that waves ther. are s.
Is. 23:2 be s. ye inhabit. of isle
30:7 their strength is to sit s.
42:14 been s. and refrai. myself
Jer. 47:6 sw. of L. rest and be s.
Mark 4:39 to sea, Peace, be s.

**STILLED.**
Num. 13:30 Caleb s. the people
Neh. 8:11 the Levites s. the peo.

**STILLEST, ETH.**
Ps. 65:7 who s. noise of the seas
89:9 when waves ari. thou s. th.

**STING, S.**
1 Cor. 15:55 where is s.? 56 s. of
Rev. 9:10 were s. in their tails

**STINGETH.**
Prov. 23:32 it s. like an adder

**STINK, Substantive.**
Is. 3:24 instead smell, shall be s.
34:3 s. come out of their carcas.
Joel 2:20 his s. shall come up
Amos 4:10 made s. of your camps

**STINK, Verb.**
Gen. 34:30 ye have made me to s.
Ex. 7:18 and the river shall s.
16:24 manna laid up, did not s.
Ps. 38:5 wounds s. and corrupt

**STINKETH, ING.**
Ec. 10:1 send forth a s. savor
Is. 50:2 fish s. there is no water
John 11:39 L. by this time he s.

**STIR, Verb.**
Num. 24:9 who shall s. him up?
Job 17:8 innocent s. himself ag.
41:10 no. is so fierce th. dare s.
Ps. 35:23 s. up thyself, awake
78:38 did not s. up all his wrath
80:2 s. up thy strength, come
Prov. 15:1 griev. words s. anger
Cant. 2:7 that ye s. not up my love, 3:5; 8:4
Is. 10:26 L. shall s. up a scourge
13:17 behold, I will s. up Medes
42:13 he shall s. up jealousy
Dan. 11:2 shall s. up agai. realm
25 s. up his power agai. king
2 Tim. 1:6 thou s. up gift of God
2 Pet. 1:13 meet to s. you up, 3:1

**STIR, S.**
Is. 22:2 full of s. a tumultu. city
Acts 12:18 s. among the soldiers
19:23 no small s. about way

**STIRRED.**
Ex. 35:21 s. him up, 26; 36:2
1 Sam. 22:8 my son hath s. up
26:19 L ha. s. thee up agai. me
1 K. 11:14 L. s. up an adversary
23 G. s. him up ano. adversary
21:25 whom Jez. his wife s. up
1 Chr. 5:26 G. s. up spirit of Pul
2 Chr. 21:16 L. s. up Philistines
36:22 the Lord s. up the spirit of Cyrus, Ezr. 1:1
Ps. 39:2 and my sorrow was s.
Dan. 11:10 his sons shall be s. up
25 king of south be s. up
Hag. 1:14 L. s. spirit of Zerubb.
Acts 6:12 they s. up the people, 17:13; 21:27
13:50 Jews s. up devout women
14:2 unbelieving Jews s. Genti.
17:16 P. his spirit was s. in him

**STIRRETH.**
Deut. 32:11 as eagle s. her nest
Prov. 10:12 hatred s. up strifes
15:18 wrath. man s. strife, 29:22
28:25 he of proud heart s. strife
Is. 14:9 hell fr. ben. s. up dead
Is. 64:7 none s. up hims. to take
Luke 23:5 he s. up peo. teaching

**STOCK.**
Lev. 25:47 to the s. of stranger's
Job 14:8 though s. thereof die

*Is.* 40:24 their *s.* not take root
44:19 sh. I fall down to the *s.*?
*Jer.* 2:27 saying to a *s.* Thou art
10:8 *s.* is a doctrine of vanities
*Acts* 13:26 chil. of *s.* of Abraham
*Phil.* 3:5 of the *s.* of Is. a Hebr.

**STOCKS.**

*Job* 13:27 puttest my feet in *s.*
33:11 he putteth my feet in *s.*
*Prov.* 7:22 as fool to correct. of *s.*
*Jer.* 3:9 committed adul. with *s.*
20:2 Pashur put Jerem. in *s.* 3
29:26 put him in prison and *s.*
*Hos.* 4:12 peo. ask counsel at *s.*
*Acts* 16:24 their feet fast in *s.*

**Gazing-STOCK.**

*Nah.* 3:6 I will set th. as a *g.-s.*
*Heb.* 10:33 ye were made a *g.-s.*

**STOICS.**

*Acts* 17:18 cer. philosophers of *s.*

**STOLE.**

*Gen.* 31:20 Ja. *s.* away unawares
2 *Sam.* 15:6 Absa. *s.* hearts of Is.
2 *K.* 11:2 Jehosheba *s.* Joash fr. king's sons, 2 *Chr.* 22:11
*Mat.* 28:13 disciples *s.* him while
*Eph.* 4:28 let him th. *s.* steal no

**STOLEN.**

*Gen.* 30:33 shall be counted *s.*
31:19 Rachel has *s.* images, 32
30 wherefore hast *s.* my gods?
40:15 ind. I was *s.* away out of
*Ex.* 22:7 if the stuff be *s.* out of
12 if it be *s.* from him, he shall
*Jos.* 7:11 they have *s.* and disse.
2 *Sam.* 19:41 have men of Jud. *s.*
21:12 men of Jab. had *s.* bones
*Prov.* 9:17 *s.* waters are sweet
*Ob.* 5 would they not have *s.*?

**STOMACH.**

1 *Tim.* 5:23 use wine for *s.* sake

**STOMACHER.**

*Is.* 3:24 inst. of *s.* gird. of sack.

**STONE.**

*Gen.* 11:3 they had brick for *s.*
28:18 Jacob set up a *s.* 22; 31:45
29:3 rolled *s.* from well's, 8, 10
35:14 Jacob set up a pillar of *s.*
49:24 the sheph. the *s.* of Israel
*Ex.* 4:25 Zippor. took a sharp *s.*
15:5 they sank to bottom as a *s.*
16 they shall be still as a *s.*
17:12 they took a *s.* and put it
21:18 if one smite ano. with a *s.*
28:10 six on 1 *s.* six on other *s.*
*Lev.* 26:1 nor set up image of *s.*
*Num.* 35:17 if smite with a *s.* 23
*Jos.* 4:5 take eve. man of you *s.*
15:6 border went to *s.* of Bohan
18:17 border descend. to *s.* of B.
24:27 this *s.* shall be a witness
*Jud.* 9:5 slew 70 persons on *s.* 18
1 *Sam.* 6:18 *s.* remain. to this day
7:12 Samuel set up a *s.*
17:49 Da. took from his bag a *s.*
50 David prevailed with a *s.*
20:19 remain by the *s.* Ezel
25:37 Nab.'s hea. died, bec. as *s.*
2 *Sam.* 17:13 not one sm. *s.* found
1 *K.* 6:7 house was built of *s.*
18 cedar, there was no *s.* seen
2 *K.* 3:25 on land cast ev. man *s.*
1 *Chr.* 22:15 there are hew. of *s.*
2 *Chr.* 2:14 skilful to work in *s.*
*Neh.* 9:11 thou threwest as a *s.*
*Job* 28:2 brass is molten out of *s.*
38:30 waters are hid as with a *s.*
41:24 his heart is as firm as a *s.*
*Ps.* 91:12 lest thou dash foot ag. a *s.* *Mat.* 4:6; *Luke* 4:11
118:22 *s.* wh. build. ref. is head *s.* *Mat.* 21:42; *Mark* 12:10
*Prov.* 26:8 as he that bindeth a *s.*
27 as he that rolleth a *s.* it will
27:3 a *s.* is heavy, a fool's wrath
*Jer.* 2:27 to a *s.* Th. hast brought
51:26 shall not take of thee a *s.*
*Lam.* 3:58 they cast a *s.* upon me
*Dan.* 2:34 a *s.* was cut out of, 45
6:17 a *s.* laid on mouth of den
*Hab.* 2:11 *s.* shall cry out of wall
19 woe to him saith to dumb *s.*
*Hag.* 2:15 *s.* was laid upon a *s.*
*Zec.* 3:9 upon one *s.* seven eyes
4:7 sh. bri. forth head *s.* thereof
7:12 made hearts as adamant *s.*
*Mat.* 7:9 will give *s.*? *Luke* 11:11
21:44 whoso. shall fall on this *s.* shall be brok. *Luke* 20:18
*Mat.* 24:2 not be left one *s.* *Mark* 13:2; *Luke* 19:44; 21:6
27:66 sealing *s.* setting a watch
28:2 angel came and rol. back *s.*
*Luke* 4:3 command this *s.* th. it
20:17 *s.* which builders reject. *Acts* 4:11; 1 *Pet.* 2:7
22:41 withdr. fr. them a *s.* cast
24:2 fou. *s.* rolled away, *Mark* 16:4; *John* 20:1
*John* 1:42 Cephas, by inter. a *s.*
2:6 were set six water-pots of *s.*
8:7 let him first cast *s.* at her
11:38 a cave, a *s.* lay upon it
39 take away *s.* 41 they took *s.*
*Acts* 17:29 Godhead is like *s.* gra.
*Rev.* 16:21 hail fell ev. *s.* wei. of
18:21 angel took up *s.*

**Burdensome STONE.**

*Zec.* 12:3 I will make Jer. a *b. s.*

*See* CORNER, GREAT, HEWED.

**Hewn STONE.**

*Ex.* 20:25 not build altar of *h. s.*
2 *K.* 22:6 timber and *h. s.* to repair house, 2 *Chr.* 34:11
*Lam.* 3:9 encl. my ways wi. *h. s.*
*Ezek.* 40:42 four tables of *h. s.*
*Amos* 5:11 built houses of *h. s.*
*Luke* 23:53 sepulchre was *h.* in *s.*

**Living STONE.**

1 *Pet.* 2:4 coming as to *l. s.* chos.

**Precious STONE.**

*Prov.* 17:8 a gift is a *p. s.* to him
*Is.* 28:16 in Zion a *p. s.* 1 *Pet.* 2:6
*Ezek.* 28:13 *p. s.* was thy cover.
*Rev.* 17:4 with gold and *p. s.*
21:11 was like to a *s.* most *p.*

*See* STUMBLING.

**STONE-SQUARERS.**

1 *K.* 5:18 builders and *s.-s.* did

**Tables of STONE.**

*Ex.* 24:12 I give th. *t. of s.* 31:18
34:1 hew two *t. of s.* *Deut.* 10:1
*Deut.* 4:13 wrote on *t. of s.* 5:22
9:9 I was up to receive *t. of s.*
10 L. deliv. to me two *t. of s.*
1 *K.* 8:9 in ark save two *t. of s.*
2 *Cor.* 3:3 not in *t. of s.* in fleshly

**Tried STONE.**

*Is.* 28:16 I lay in Zion a *tried s.*

**White STONE.**

*Rev.* 2:17 I will give him a *wh. s.*

**STONE, *joined with* wood.**

*Ex.* 7:19 in vessels of *w.* and *s.*
*Deut.* 4:28 work of men's han. *w.* and *s.* 28:36, 64; 29:17; 2 *K.* 19:18; *Is.* 37:19; *Ezek.* 20:32
*Dan.* 5:4 gods of *wood* and *s.* 23
*Rev.* 9:20 wor. idols of *w.* and *s.*

**STONE of Zoheleth.**

1 *K.* 1:9 Adonij. slew sheep by *s.*

*See* WALL.

**STONE, Verb.**

*Ex.* 8:26 will they not *s.* us?
17:4 almost ready to *s.* me
*Lev.* 20:2 people shall *s.* him
27 shall *s.* wizards with stones
24:14 let congreg. *s.* him, 16, 23
*Num.* 14:10 congre. bade *s.* them
15:35 sh. *s.* sabbath-breaker, 36
*Deut.* 13:10 *s.* with stones entic.
17:5 *s.* idolat. 21:21 *s.* rebellious
22:21 *s.* her that playeth whore
24 sh. *s.* adulterers with stones
1 *K.* 21:10 car. Nab. out, *s.* him
*Ezek.* 16:40 shall *s.* thee with st.
23:47 company shall *s.* them
*Luke* 20:6 the people will *s.* us
*John* 10:31 Jews took ston. to *s.*
32 for wh. of works do *s.* me?
11:8 Jews of late sou. to *s.* thee
*Acts* 14:5 assault made to *s.* th.

**STONED.**

*Ex.* 19:13 he shall be *s.* or shot
21:28 ox shall be surely *s.* 29, 32
*Jos.* 7:25 all Israel *s.* Achan
1 *K.* 12:18 all Israel *s.* Adoram, 2 *Chr.* 10:18
21:13 they *s.* Naboth, 14, 15
2 *Chr.* 24:21 they *s.* Zechariah in
*Mat.* 21:35 husband. beat one, *s.*
*John* 8:5 Moses com. such be *s.*
*Acts* 5:26 lest should have been *s.*
7:58 they *s.* Stephen, calling, 59
14:19 having *s.* Paul, drew him
2 *Cor.* 11:25 beaten, once was I *s.*
*Heb.* 11:37 they were *s.* th. were
12:20 touch mount it shall be *s.*

**STONES.**

*Gen.* 31:46 Jacob said, Gather *s.*
*Ex.* 28:11 engrave two *s.* 12
17 of *s.* even four rows of *s.*
*Ex.* 28:21 *s.* sh. be wi. names of Is.
39:7 that th. be *s.* for memorial
*Lev.* 14:42 *s.* in place of those *s.*
45 break down house, *s.* of it
21:20 or hath his *s.* broken
*Deut.* 8:9 a land wh. *s.* are iron
23:1 wound. in *s.* sh. not enter
27:4 set up these *s.* in mount E.
5 altar of *s.* 8 write on *s.*
*Jos.* 4:6 what mean these *s.*? 21
8 took twelve *s.* out of Jordan
8:32 wrote on *s.* a copy of law
*Jud.* 20:16 sli. *s.* at hair-breadth
1 *Sam.* 17:40 David chose five *s.*
2 *Sam.* 16:6 Shimei cast *s.* 13
1 *K.* 5:18 prepared timber and *s.*
10:27 king made silver to be as *s.* 2 *Chr.* 1:15; 9:27
15:22 took away *s.* 2 *Chr.* 16:6
18:31 Elijah took twelve *s.*
2 *K.* 3:19 good piece land with *s.*
25 Kir-haraseth left th. the *s.*
1 *Chr.* 12:2 hurling *s.* shooting
2 *Chr.* 26:14 pre. slings to cast *s.*
*Neh.* 4:2 will they revive the *s.*?
*Job* 5:23 in league with *s.* of field
6:12 is strength the stren. of *s.*?
8:17 wrapped, seeth place of *s.*
14:19 the waters wear the *s.*
22:24 gold of O. as *s.* of brooks
28:6 the *s.* of it are place of
40:17 sinews of his *s.* are wrap.
*Ps.* 102:14 serv. take pleas. in *s.*
137:9 dasheth little ones aga. *s.*
*Ec.* 3:5 cast *s.* time to gather *s.*
10:9 whoso removeth *s.* be hurt
*Is.* 5:2 gathered out *s.* thereof
14:19 that go down to *s.* of pit
27:9 the *s.* of altar as chalk *s.*
54:11 I will lay *s.* with fair col.
12 I make bord. of pleasant *s.*
57:6 amo. smooth *s.* of stream
60:17 for *s.* iron; 62:10 gather *s.*
*Jer.* 3:9 commit. adultery with *s.*
43:10 I will set his throne on *s.*
*Lam.* 4:1 *s.* of sanct. poured out
*Ezek.* 26:12 lay thy *s.* in water
28:14 walked in midst of *s.*
*Mic.* 1:6 pour down *s.* in valley
*Zec.* 5:4 consu. it with *s.* thereof
9:16 shall be as *s.* of a crown
*Mat.* 3:9 of these *s.* to raise up children, *Luke* 3:8
4:3 command *s.* be made bread

*Mark* 12:4 at him they cast *s.*
13:1 see what manner of *s.* here
*Luke* 19:40 *s.* would immedi. cry
*John* 8:59 took *s.* to cast, 10:31
1 *Pet.* 2:5 as lively *s.* are built
*See* STONE, *Verb.*

**Corner STONES.**
*Ps.* 144:12 daughters be as *c. s.*
*See* COSTLY.

**STONES of darkness.**
*Job* 28:3 searcheth out *s. of d.*

**STONES of emptiness.**
*Is.* 34:11 stret. out upon *s. of e.*

**Glistering STONES.**
1 *Chr.* 29:2 I have prepared *g. s.*

**Gravel STONES.**
*Lam.* 3:16 bro. my teeth wi. *g. s.*
*See* GREAT.

**Heap of STONES.**
*Jos.* 7:26 raised a *h. of s.* on Ac.
8:29 a *h. of s.* on king of Ai
2 *Sam.* 18:17 laid *h. of s.* on Abs.

**Hewed STONES.**
1 *K.* 5:17 brought *h. s.* foundati.
7:9 according to meas. of *h. s.* 11

**Hewn STONES.**
*Is.* 9:10 we will build with *h. s.*

**Marble STONES.**
1 *Chr.* 29:2 I have prepared *m. s.*

**Precious STONES.**
2 *Sam.* 12:30 tal. of gold wi. *p. s.*
1 *K.* 10:2 queen of S. ca. wi. *p. s.*
11 navy brou. *p. s.* 2 *Chr.* 9:10
1 *Chr.* 29:2 I prepared all *p. s.*
8 with whom *p. s.* were found
2 *Chr.* 3:6 garnis. house wi. *p. s.*
32:27 made treasuries for *p. s.*
*Ezek.* 27:22 occupied in fairs *p. s.*
*Dan.* 11:38 a god honor with *p. s.*
1 *Cor.* 3:12 build on founda. *p. s.*
*Rev.* 18:12 no man buyeth *p. s.*
21:19 founda. garnish. with *p. s.*

**Whole STONES.**
*Deut.* 27:6 al. of *w. s. Jos.* 8:31

**Wrought STONES.**
1 *Chr.* 22:2 masons to hew *w. s.*

**STONEST, ING.**
1 *Sam.* 30:6 people spake of *s.* D.
*Mat.* 23:37 *s.* th. sent, *Luke* 13:34

**STONY.**
*Ps.* 141:6 overthrown in *s.* places
*Ezek.* 11:19 I take *s.* heart, 36:26
*Mat.* 13:5 some fell on *s.* places, 20; *Mark* 4:5, 16

**STOOD.**
*Gen.* 18:22 Abraham *s.* before L.
*Num.* 16:48 *s.* bet. dead and liv.
*Deut.* 5:5 I *s.* bet. Lord and you
*Jos.* 3:16 waters *s.* and rose up
*Est.* 9:16 other Jews *s.* for lives
*Ps.* 33:9 command. and it *s.* fast
*Jer.* 46:15 they *s.* not because L.
*Ezek.* 1:21 those *s.* these *s.* 10:17
24 when they *s.* let down win.
*Dan.* 12:5 behold, there *s.* other
*Mat.* 12:46 brethren *s.* without
*Acts* 16:9 there *s.* man of Maced.
27:21 Paul *s.* forth in the midst

**STOOD above.**
*Gen.* 28:13 Lord *s. a.* the ladder
2 *Chr.* 24:20 Zechariah *s. a.* peo
*Ps.* 104:6 waters *s. a.* mountains

**STOOD afar.**
*Ex.* 20:18 people *s. afar* off, 21
*Luke* 17:12 ten lepers, *s. a.* off
*Rev.* 18:17 trade by sea *s. a.* off

**STOOD before.**
*Gen.* 19:27 place where he *s. b.* L.
43:15 went to Egy. *s. b.* Joseph
*Lev.* 9:5 congregation *s. b.* Lord
*Jos.* 20:9 until he *s. b.* congrega.
*Jud.* 20:28 Phinehas *s. b.* ark
1 *K.* 12:6 old men that *s. b.* Solomon, 2 *Chr.* 10:6
8 young men *s. b.* 2 *Chr.* 10:8
22:21 spirit *s. b.* L. 2 *Chr.* 18:20
2 *K.* 10:4 two kings *s.* not *b.* him
*Ps.* 106:23 had not Mo. *s. b.* him
*Jer.* 18:20 I *s. b.* th. to spe. good
*Ezek.* 8:11 th. *s. b.* them 70 men
*Dan.* 1:19 th. *s. b.* the king, 2:2
*Zec.* 3:4 spake to those *s. b.* him

**STOOD by.**
*Ex.* 18:13 the people *s. by* Moses
*Jud.* 3:19 that *s. by* went fr. him
18:16 men *s. by* entering of gate
1 *Sam.* 1:26 wom. that *s. by* thee
1 *K.* 13:1 Jeroboam *s. by* altar
2 *K.* 2:7 they two *s. by* Jord. 13
*Ezek.* 43:6 man *s. by* me, and sa.
*Dan.* 7:16 near to one that *s. by*
*Zec.* 3:5 an angel of Lord *s. by*
*Mark* 14:37 one th. *s. by* drew sw.
15:35 some that *s. by,* wh. they
*Luke* 19:24 said to them th. *s. by*
*Acts* 23:11 night fol. L. *s. by* him
27:23 there *s. by* me angel of G.

**STOOD in.**
*Ex.* 5:20 Mo. and Aa. *s. in* way
*Num.* 12:5 L. *s. in* door of taber.
16:27 Dath. and Abir. *s. in* door
22:22 angel of L. *s. in* way. 24
*Jos.* 3:17 priest *s. in* Jordan, 4:10
2 *Sam.* 23:12 *s. in* midst ground
2 *Chr.* 30:16 th. *s. in* place, 35:10
34:31 king *s. in* his place
*Neh.* 8:7 people *s. in* their place
*Jer.* 23:18 who *s. in* counsel of L.
*Ob.* 14 nor *s. in* cross-way
*Luke* 24:36 Jesus *s. in* the midst of them, *John* 20:19, 26
*Rev.* 5:6 *in* midst of elders *s.* a L.

**STOOD on.**
1 *Sam.* 17:3 Philist. *s. on* mountain, Israel *s. on* a mountain
26:13 David *s. on* top of a hill
1 *Chr.* 6:39 Asaph *s. on* ri. hand
*Rev.* 14:1 a Lamb *s. on* mount S.

**STOOD over.**
*Deut.* 31:15 pillar of cloud *s. o.*
*Jos.* 5:13 a man *s. o.* against him
*Ezek.* 10:4 glory of L. *s. o.* thres.
*Mat.* 2:9 star *s. o.* wh. child was
*Luke* 4:39 *s. o.* her, rebuked fever

**STOOD round.**
*Acts* 14:20 disciples *s. round* him
*Rev.* 7:11 angels *s. r.* about thro.

**STOOD still.**
*Jos.* 10:13 sun *s. s.* moon stayed
11:13 cities that *s. s.* in strength
2 *Sam.* 2:23 as many as came *s. s.*
20:12 when man saw people *s. s.*
*Job* 4:16 spirit *s. s.* I could not discern.
32:16 they spake not, but *s. s.*
*Hab.* 3:11 sun and moon *s. still*
*Mat.* 20:32 Jesus *s. s.* called them
*Mark* 10:49 Je. *s. s.* commanded
*Luke* 7:14 th. that bare him *s. s.*

**STOOD there.**
*Ex.* 34:5 L. descended, and *s. t.*
*Ezek.* 3:23 behold, glo. of L. *s. t.*
*Mat.* 27:47 some *s. t. Mark* 11:5

**STOOD up.**
*Gen.* 23:3 Abr. *s. up* fr. bef. dead
*Ex.* 2:17 M. *s. up,* helped them
*Num.* 11:32 peo. *s. up* all night
1 *Chr.* 21:1 Sat. *s. up* against Is.
2 *Chr.* 13:4 Abijah *s. up* and said
20:19 Levites *s. up* to praise Lc.
*Neh.* 8:5 opened book, peo. *s. up*
9:3 they *s. up* in their place
*Job* 4:15 hair of my flesh *s. up*
29:8 yo. men saw me, aged *s. up*
30:28 I *s. up* and cried in cong.
*Acts* 4:26 kings of earth *s. up* ag.

**STOOD upon.**
*Gen.* 41:17 I *s. u.* bank of river
1 *Sam.* 17:51 David *s. u.* Philist.
2 *Sam.* 1:10 so I *s. u.* S. slew him
2 *K.* 13:21 and *s. upon* his feet
*Amos* 7:7 *s. u.* wall made by line
*Rev.* 11:11 two proph. *s. u.* feet

**STOOD with.**
*Gen.* 45:1 th. *s. with* him no man
*Lam.* 2:4 *s. with* right hand
*Luke* 9:32 two men th. *s. w.* him
*John* 18:18 Peter *s. with* them
2 *Tim.* 4:16 no man *s. with* me
17 L. *s. w.* me, strengthen. me

**STOODEST.**
*Num.* 22:34 kn. not thou *s.* in w.
*Deut.* 4:10 day that thou *s.* be. L.
*Ob.* 11 day thou *s.* on other side

**STOOL, S.**
*Ex.* 1:16 wh. ye see them on *s.*
2 *K.* 4:10 set for him bed, and *s.*

**STOOP.**
*Job* 9:13 proud hel. *s.* under him
*Prov.* 12:25 mak. heart of man *s.*
*Is.* 46:2 they *s.* they bow down
*Mark* 1:7 I am not worthy to *s.*

**STOOPED.**
*Gen.* 49:9 Jud. *s.* down, couched
1 *Sam.* 24:8 David *s.* 28:14 Saul *s.*
2 *Chr.* 36:17 no co. on him th. *s.*
*John* 8:6 Jesus *s.* down, wrote, 8
20:11 she *s.* down, and looked

**STOOPETH, ING.**
*Is.* 46:1 Nebo *s.* their idols
*Luke* 24:12 *s.* down, *John* 20:5

**STOP.**
1 *K.* 18:44 that rain *s.* thee not
2 *K.* 3:19 *s.* all wells of water, 25
2 *Chr.* 32:3 took coun. to *s.* wat.
*Ps.* 35:12 *s.* way ag. that persec.
107:42 iniquity sh. *s.* her mouth
*Ezek.* 39:11 *s.* noses of passenge.
2 *Cor.* 11:10 no man *s.* me

**STOPPED.**
*Gen.* 8:2 wind. of heaven were *s.*
26:15 Philistin. had *s.* wells, 18
*Lev.* 15:3 flesh be *s.* fr. his issue
2 *Chr.* 32:4 who *s.* all fountains
30 Hezekiah *s.* water-course
*Neh.* 4:7 breaches began to be *s.*
*Ps.* 63:11 that speake. lies, be *s.*
*Jer.* 51:32 passages are *s.* reeds
*Zec.* 7:11 refused, *s.* their ears
*Acts* 7:57 they *s.* their ears, ran
*Rom.* 3:19 ev. mouth may be *s.*
*Tit.* 1:11 wh. mouths must be *s.*
*Heb.* 11:33 *s.* mouths of lions

**STOPPETH.**
*Job* 5:16 iniquity *s.* her mouth
*Ps.* 58:4 like adder that *s.* ears
*Prov.* 21:13 whoso *s.* his ears
*Is.* 33:15 *s.* ears fr. hearing blood

**STORE, Verb.**
*Amos* 3:10 who *s.* up violence

**STORE, Substantive.**
*Gen.* 26:14 Isaac had *s.* of serva.
41:36 that food shall be for *s.*
*Lev.* 25:22 eat of old *s.* 26:10
*Deut.* 28:5 bles. be basket and *s.*
17 cursed sh. be basket and *s.*
32:34 is not this laid up in *s.*
1 *K.* 10:10 gave of spices great *s.*
2 *K.* 20:17 fathers laid up in *s.* to
1 *Chr.* 29:16 this *s.* com. of thine
2 *Chr.* 11:11 he put *s.* of victuals
31:10 that is left is this great *s.*
*Neh.* 5:18 *s.* of all sorts of wine
*Ps.* 144:13 our garners afford. *s.*
*Is.* 39:6 fathers laid up in *s.*
*Nah.* 2:9 there is none end of *s.*
1 *Cor.* 16:2 let ev. one lay by in *s.*
1 *Tim.* 6:19 laying in *s.* a good
2 *Pet.* 3:7 by word are kept in *s.*

**STORE-CITIES.**
1 *K.* 9:19 *cities* of *s.* Solomon had
2 *Chr.* 8:4 *s.-c* which he built, 6
16:4 th. smote *s.-c* of Naphtali
17:12 Jehosha. built *s.-c.* in Ju.

**STOREHOUSE.**
*Mal.* 3:10 bring tithes into the *s.*
*Luke* 12:24 the ravens have no *s.* nor barn

**STOREHOUSES.**
*Gen.* 41:56 Joseph opened the *s.*
*Deut.* 28:8 command bless. on *s.*
1 *Chr.* 27:25 over *s.* was Jehona.
2 *Chr.* 32:28 Hezekiah made *s.*
*Ps.* 33:7 layeth up depth in *s.*
*Jer.* 50:26 open her *s.* cast her

**STORK.**
*Lev.* 11:19 *s.* not eat, *Deut.* 14:18
*Ps.* 104:17 for *s.* the fir-trees
*Jer.* 8:7 *s.* knoweth her times
*Zec.* 5:9 had wings like a *s.*

**STORM.**
*Job* 21:18 as chaff that *s.* carrieth
27:21 *s.* hurl. him out of place
*Ps.* 55:8 I hasten my escape fr. *s.*
83:15 make them af. with thy *s.*
107:29 he maketh the *s.* a calm
*Is.* 4:6 and for a covert from *s.*
25:4 hast been a refuge from *s.*
28:2 wh. as destroying *s.* shall
29:6 shalt be visited with *s.*
*Ezek.* 38:9 shalt come like a *s.*
*Nah.* 1:3 Lord hath his way in *s.*
*Mark* 4:37 there arose a great *s.*
*Luke* 8:23 there came down a *s.*

**STORMY.**
*Ps.* 107:25 raiseth the *s.* wind
148:8 *s.* wind fulfilling his word
*Ezek.* 13:11 *s.* wind shall rend, 13

**STORY.**
2 *Chr.* 13:22 acts of Abijah in *s.*
24:27 in the *s.* of book of kings

**STORIES.**
*Gen.* 6:16 with sec. and third *s.*
*Ezek.* 41:16 galleries three *s.* over
42:3 against gallery in three *s.* 5
*Amos* 9:6 build. his *s.* in heaven

**STOUT.**
*Job* 4:11 *s.* lion's whelps are sca.
*Is.* 10:12 I punish fruit of *s.* heart
*Dan.* 7:20 who. look was more *s.*
*Mal.* 3:13 your words ha. been *s.*

**STOUT-HEARTED.**
*Ps.* 76:5 *s.-h.* are spoiled, they
*Is.* 46:12 heark. unto me, ye *s.-h.*

**STOUTNESS.**
*Is.* 9:9 they say in the *s.* of heart

**STRAIGHT.**
*Jos.* 6:5 ascend *s.* before him, 20
*Ps.* 5:8 make thy way *s.* before
*Ec.* 1:15 crooked can. be made *s.*
7:13 for who can make that *s.?*
*Is.* 40:3 make *s.* in desert a high.
4 the crooked shall be made *s.*
42:16; 45:2; *Luke* 3:5
*Jer.* 31:9 cause to walk in *s.* way
*Ezek.* 1:7 their feet were *s.* feet
9 they went *s.* forw. 12; 10:22
*Mat.* 3:3 make his paths *s.* *Mark* 1:3; *Luke* 3:4; *John* 1:23
*Luke* 13:13 she was made *s.* and
*Acts* 9:11 go into street called *S.*
*Heb.* 12:13 made *s.* paths for feet

**STRAIGHTWAY.**
1 *Sam.* 9:13 ye shall *s.* find him
28:20 Saul fell *s.* along on earth
*Prov.* 7:22 goeth after her *s.*
*Mat.* 4:20 *s.* left nets, *Mark* 1:18
21:3 *s.* will send th. *Mark* 11:3
*Mark* 6:54 and *s.* they knew him
*Luke* 5:39 no man *s.* desire. new
*John* 13:32 God shall *s.* glorify
*Acts* 5:10 then fell she down *s.* at
22:29 then *s.* they departed from
23:30 when told me, I sent *s.* to

**STRAIN.**
*Mat.* 23:24 guides *s.* at a gnat

**STRAIT, S.**
1 *Sam.* 13:6 saw they were in a *s.*
2 *Sam.* 24:14 in a *s.* 1 *Chr.* 21:13
*Job* 20:22 sufficiency sh. be in *s.*
36:16 removed thee out of *s.*
*Lam.* 1:3 overtook her betwe. *s.*
*Phil.* 1:23 I am in *s.* betwixt two

**STRAIT.**
2 *K.* 6:1 place we dwell is two *s.*
*Is.* 49:20 place is too *s.* for me
*Mat.* 7:13 enter ye in at *s.* gate
14 bec. *s.* is gate, *Luke* 13:24

**STRAITEN, ETH.**
*Job* 12:23 he enlar. nations and *s.*
*Jer.* 19:9 seek lives shall *s.* them

**STRAITENED.**
*Job* 18:7 steps of stre. shall be *s.*
37:10 breadth of the waters is *s.*
*Prov.* 4:12 thy steps sh. not be *s.*
*Ezek.* 42:6 building was *s.* more
*Mic.* 2:7 is Spirit of Lord *s.?*
*Luke* 12:50 how am I *s.* till it be
2 *Cor.* 6:12 not *s.* in us, *s.* in your

**STRAITEST.**
*Acts* 26:5 after most *s.* sect

**STRAITLY.**
*Gen.* 43:7 asked *s.* of our state
*Jos.* 6:1 Jericho was *s.* shut up.
*Mark* 1:43 he *s.* charged him and
*Acts* 4:17 let us *s.* threaten them
5:28 did not we *s.* comma. you?

**STRAITNESS.**
*Deut.* 28:53 eat child. in *s.* 55, 57
*Job* 36:16 place wh. there is no *s.*
*Jer.* 19:9 eat flesh of friend in *s.*

**STRAKE.**
*Acts* 27:17 they fearing *s.* sail
*See* STRUCK.

STRAKES. *See* STREAKS.

**STRANGE.**
*Gen.* 42:7 Joseph made himself *s.*
*Ex.* 2:22 stranger in *s.* land, 18:3
21:8 sell her to a *s.* nation
30:9 ye shall offer no *s.* incense
*Lev.* 10:1 Nadab and Abihu offered *s.* fire, *Num.* 3:4; 26:61
2 *K.* 19:24 I have drunk *s.* waters
*Job* 19:3 not asha. make your. *s.*
17 my breath is *s.* to my wife
31:3 a *s.* punishment to workers
*Ps.* 114:1 went fr. peo. of *s.* lang.
137:4 sing L.'s song in *s.* land
*Prov.* 21:8 the way of man is *s.*
*Is.* 17:10 shalt set it with *s.* lips
28:21 he may do his *s.* work, bring to pass his *s.* act
*Jer.* 2:21 how turned into *s.* vine
8:19 provoked with *s.* vanities
*Ezek.* 3:5 sent to peo. of *s.* spee.
*Hos.* 8:12 counted a *s.* thing
*Zep.* 1:8 clothed with *s.* apparel
*Luke* 5:26 have seen *s.* things
*Acts* 7:6 sojourn in a *s.* land
17:20 bringest *s.* things to ears
26:11 I persecuted to *s.* cities
*Heb.* 11:9 sojou. as in *s.* country
13:9 be not carried with *s.* doct.
1 *Pet.* 4:4 they think it *s.* ye run
12 think it not *s.* concerning trial, as though *s.* thing
*Jude* 7 as So. going after *s.* flesh
*See* CHILDREN, GOD, GODS.

**STRANGE wives.**
1 *K.* 11:8 likewi. did he for *s. w.*
*Ezr.* 10:2 tak. *s. w.* 10, 14, 17, 44
11 separ. yourselves from *s. w.*
18 were found to have *s. w.*
*Neh.* 13:27 trans. in marry. *s. w.*

**STRANGE woman.**
*Jud.* 11:2 thou art son of a *s. w.*
*Prov.* 2:16 deliv. thee from *s. w.*
5:3 lips of *s. w.* drop as honey-c.
20 wilt th. be ravis. with *s. w.*
6:24 from flattery of *s. w.* 7:5
20:16 pledge for a *s. w.* 27:13
23:27 and a *s. w.* is a narrow pit

**STRANGE women.**
1 *K.* 11:1 king loved many *s. w.*
*Prov.* 22:14 mouth of *s. w.* is pit
23:33 th. eyes shall behold *s. w.*

**STRANGELY.**
*Deut.* 32:27 lest advers. behave *s.*

**STRANGER.**
*Gen.* 15:13 thy seed shall be a *s.*
17:8 I will give thee land wherein thou art a *s.* 28:4; 37:1
27 bought with money of the *s.*
23:4 I am *s.* *Ps.* 39:12; 119:19
*Ex.* 2:22 I ha. been a *s.* in land
12:19 cut off, whether a *s.* *Lev.* 16:29; 17:15; *Num.* 15:30
43 sh. no *s.* eat thereof, 29:33
49 homeborn and *s.* *Lev.* 24:22; *Num.* 9:14; 15:15, 16, 29
20:10 nor *s.* that is within thy gates, *Deut.* 5:14
22:21 thou shalt not oppress a *s.*
23:9 ye know heart of a *s.* seei.
12 that the *s.* may be refreshed
30:33 whoso. putteth it upon *s.*
*Lev.* 17:12 neither sh. any *s.* eat
19:10 sh. leave for *s.* 23:22; 25:6
33 if a *s.* sojourn in the land
22:10 no *s.* eat holy thing, 13
22:25 neither from a *s.* hand
24:16 as well *s.* when blasphem.
25:35 tho' he be a *s.* thou shalt
47 if a *s.* wax rich by thee
*Num.* 1:51 *s.* th. cometh nigh sh. be put to death, 3:10, 38
15:14 if a *s.* sojo. and will offer
16:40 that no *s.* offer incense
18:7 the *s.* that cometh nigh
19:10 to Israel and *s.* a statute
35:15 cit. of ref. for *s.* *Jos.* 20:9
*Deut.* 1:16 judge righte. betw. *s.*
10:18 L. loveth the *s.* in giving
*Deut.* 10:19 love *s.* ye were stran.
14:21 give that wh. dieth to *s.*
17:15 not set a *s.* over thee
23:20 unto a *s.* thou may. lend
28:43 *s.* shall get above thee
29:11 *s.* to enter in cove. wi. G.
31:12 gather thy *s.* that he may
*Jos.* 8:33 *s.* stood to hear words
*Jud.* 19:12 not turn to city of *s.*
*Ruth* 2:10 seeing I am a *s.?*
2 *Sam.* 1:13 I am the son of a *s.*
15:19 thou art a *s.* and an exile
1 *K.* 3:18 there was no *s.* with us
8:43 do all *s.* calleth, 2 *Chr.* 6:33
*Job* 15:19 no *s.* passed am. them
19:15 maids count me for a *s.*
31:32 *s.* did not lodge in street
*Ps.* 69:8 I am become a *s.* to my
94:6 they slay the widow and *s*
109:11 let the *s.* spoil his labor
*Prov.* 2:16 to deliver thee from *s.*
5:10 thy labors in house of a *s.*
20 wilt thou emb. bosom of *s.?*
6:1 if hast stricken hand with *s.*
7:5 they may keep thee from *s.*
11:15 he that is surety for a *s.*
14:10 a *s.* doth not intermeddle
20:16 is surety for a *s.* 27:13
27:2 let a *s.* praise thee
*Ec.* 6:2 not power to eat, a *s.*
*Is.* 56:3 neith. let son of *s.* speak
6 the sons of *s.* that join them
62:8 sons of *s.* not drink thy w.
*Jer.* 14:8 why be as a *s.* in land
*Ezek.* 14:7 ev. *s.* setteth up idols
22:7 dealt by oppress. with *s.* 29
44:9 no *s.* uncircumci. sh. enter
*Ob.* 12 in day he became a *s.*
*Mal.* 3:5 that turn aside *s.* from
*Mat.* 25:35 was *s.* took me in, 43

38 when saw we thee a *s.*? 44
*Luke* 17:18 not found save this *s.*
24:18 art thou only *s.* in Jeru.?
*John* 10:5 *s.* will they not follow
*Acts* 7:29 Mo. was a *s.* in Midian
*See* FATHERLESS.

**STRANGERS.**

*Gen.* 31:15 are we not count. *s.*?
36:7 land where. were *s.* *Ex.* 6:4
*Ex.* 22:21 *s.* in Egypt, 23:9; *Lev.* 19:34; 25:23; *Deut.* 10:19
*Lev.* 17:10 whatsoever of *s.* that
20:2 of *s.* that give seed to Mol.
25:45 children of *s.* shall ye buy
*Jos.* 8:35 *s.* that were conversing
2 *Sam.* 22:45 *s.* sh. submit them.
46 *s.* sh. fade away. *Ps.* 18:44,45
1 *Chr.* 16:19 ye were *s.* *Ps.* 105:12
22:2 D. commanded to gather *s.*
29:15 we are *s.* as were our fath.
2 *Chr.* 2:17 Solomon numbered *s.*
30:25 *s.* of Is. and Judah rejoic.
*Neh.* 9:2 seeds of Is. sepa. from *s.*
13:30 cleansed I them from all *s.*
*Ps.* 54:3 *s.* are risen up aga. me
146:9 the Lord preserveth the *s.*
*Prov.* 5:10 *s.* be filled wi. wealth
17 let be only thine own, not *s.*
*Is.* 1:7 your land *s.* devour it in
2:6 they please themselves in *s.*
5:17 places of fat ones sh. *s.* eat
14:1 *s.* sh. be joined with them
25:2 made a palace of *s.* no city
5 shalt bring down noise of *s.*
29:5 multitude of thy *s.* shall be
60:10 sons of *s.* sh. build walls
61:5 *s.* shall feed your flocks
*Jer.* 2:25 I have loved *s.* after th.
3:13 hast scatter. thy ways to *s.*
5:19 so sh. ye serve *s.* in a land
30:8 *s.* sh. no more serve thems.
35:7 live in land where ye be *s.*
51:51 *s.* are come into sanctuar.
*Lam.* 5:2 inher. is turn. *s.* houses
*Ezek.* 7:21 I give it in. hand of *s.*
11:9 deliver you into hands of *s.*
16:32 wife taketh *s.* inst. of hus.
28:10 die deaths by hands of *s.*
30:12 make land waste by *s.*
31:12 *s.* have cut him off
44:7 brou. into my sanctuary *s.*
47:22 for an inheritance to the *s.*
*Hos.* 7:9 *s.* devoured his strength
8:7 the *s.* shall swallow it up
*Joel* 3:17 th. shall no *s.* pass thro'
*Ob.* 11 in the day that *s.* carried
*Mat.* 17:25 tribute? of chil. or *s.*
26 P. saith, Of *s.* 27:7 bury *s.*
*John* 10:5 they kn. not voice of *s.*
*Acts* 2:10 and *s.* of Rome, Jews
13:17 wh. th. dwelt as *s.* in Eg.
*Eph.* 2:12 were *s.* from the cove.
19 therefore ye are no more *s.*
1 *Tim.* 5:10 if she have lodged *s.*
*Heb.* 11:13 confessed they were *s.*
13:2 not forgetful to entertain *s.*
1 *Pet.* 1:1 to *s.* scat. thro' Pontus
1 *Pet.* 2:11 beseech you as *s.* pil.
3 *John* 5 whatso. thou doest to *s.*

**STRANGLED.**

*Nah.* 2:12 the lion did tear and *s.*
*Acts* 15:20 abst. from *s.* 29; 21:25

**STRANGLING.**

*Job* 7:15 my soul chooseth *s.* and

**STRAW.**

*Gen.* 24:25 we have *s.* and prove.
32 he gave *s.* and provender for
*Ex.* 5:7 no more give *s.* 10, 16, 18
11 get *s.* where you can find it
*Jud.* 19:19 there is *s.* and proven.
1 *K.* 4:28 barley, and *s.* for horses
*Job* 41:27 esteem. iron as *s.* brass
*Is.* 11:7 lion eat *s.* like ox, 65:25
25:10 Moab sh. be trodden as *s.*

**STREAKS.**

*Gen.* 30:37 Jacob pilled white *s.*
*Lev.* 14:37 if plague be wi. hol. *s.*

**STREAM.**

*Num.* 21:15 what he did at the *s.*
*Job* 6:15 as *s.* of brooks they pass
*Ps.* 124:4 the *s.* had gone over
*Is.* 27:12 L. shall beat off to the *s.*
30:28 breath as an overflowing *s.*
33 like a *s.* of brimstone
57:6 among smooth stones of *s.*
66:12 glory of G. like flowing *s.*
*Dan.* 7:10 fiery *s.* issu. and came
*Amos* 5:24 righteo. as mighty *s.*
*Luke* 6:48 *s.* beat vehemently, 49

**STREAMS.**

*Ex.* 7:19 stretch hand on *s.* 8:5
*Ps.* 46:4 *s.* make glad city of God
78:16 he brought *s.* out of rock
20 waters gushed, *s.* overflow.
126:4 turn ag. our captivi. as *s.*
*Cant.* 4:15 living waters, *s.* fr. L.
*Is.* 11:15 L. shall smite in sev. *s.*
30:25 on ev. high hill *s.* of wat.
33:21 place of broad rivers and *s.*
34:9 *s.* shall be turned into pitch
35:6 waters break out *s.* in desert

**STREET.**

*Gen.* 19:2 abide in *s.* all night
*Deut.* 13:16 gather spoil into *s.*
*Jos.* 2:19 go out of house into *s.*
*Jud.* 19:15 he sat down in a *s.* 17
2 *Sam.* 21:12 had stolen fr. the *s.*
22:43 stamp them as mire of *s.*
2 *Chr.* 29:4 gather. in east *s.* 32:6
*Ezr.* 10:9 peo. sat in *s.* of house
*Neh.* 8:1 people gathered into *s.*
8:3 he read therein before *s.*
*Est.* 6:9 on horseback thro. *s.* 11
*Job* 18:17 sh. have no name in *s.*
29:7 I prepared my seat in the *s.*
31:32 strang. did not lodge in *s.*
*Prov.* 7:8 pass. thro' the *s.* near
*Is.* 42:2 not hea. in *s.* *Mat.* 12:19
51:23 hast laid thy body as *s.*
59:14 truth is fallen in the *s.*
*Jer.* 37:21 bread out of bakers' *s.*
*Lam.* 2:19 faint for hun. is ev. *s.*
4:1 stones poured out in ev. *s.*
*Ezek.* 16:24 high place in *s.* 31
*Dan.* 9:25 the *s.* shall be built ag.
*Acts* 9:11 go into *s.* call. Straight
12:10 Peter pass. through one *s.*
*Rev.* 11:8 dead bodies sh. lie in *s.*
21:21 *s.* of city was pure gold
22:2 in midst of *s.* tree of life

**STREETS.**

2 *Sam.* 1:20 publish it not in *s.* of
1 *K.* 20:34 shalt make *s.* in Dam.
*Ps.* 18:42 I cast them as dirt in *s.*
55:11 guile depart not fr. her *s.*
144:13 sheep br. forth 10,000 in *s.*
14 be no complaining in our *s.*
*Prov.* 1:20 wisd. utter. voice in *s.*
5:16 rivers of waters in the *s.*
7:12 now is she in the *s.* lieth
22:13 lion, I shall be slain in *s.*
26:13 slothful sai. A lion is in *s.*
*Ec.* 12:4 doors shall be shut in *s.*
5 the mourners go about the *s.*
*Cant.* 3:2 I will go about in the *s.*
*Is.* 5:25 carcasses were torn in *s.*
10:6 tread them like mire of *s.*
15:3 in th. *s.* they sh. gird them
24:11 a crying for wine in the *s.*
51:20 thy sons lie at head of *s.*
*Jer.* 5:1 run through *s.* of Jerus.
7:17 seest th. what they do in *s.*
34 cause to cease from *s.* of Je.
9:21 cut off young men from *s.*
11:6 proclaim words in *s.* of Je.
13 accord. to number of *s.* of J.
14:16 people be cast out in the *s.*
33:10 mirth shall be heard in *s.*
44:6 anger was kind. in *s.* of J.
9 wickedness they commi. in *s.*
48:38 shall be lamentation in *s.*
49:26 men shall fall in *s.* 50:30
*Jer.* 51:4 are thrust through in *s.*
*Lam.* 2:11 suckli. swoon in *s.* 12
21 young and old lie in the *s.*
4:5 delicately, are desolate in *s.*
8 Nazarit. are not known in *s.*
14 wandered as blind men in *s.*
18 th. hunt our steps in our *s.*
*Ezek.* 7:19 sh. cast silver in the *s.*
11:6 ye have filled *s.* with slain
26:11 hoofs of horses tread thy *s.*
28:23 will send blood into her *s.*
*Amos* 5:16 wailing in all *s.*
*Mic.* 7:10 trodden as mire of *s.*
*Nah.* 2:4 chariots shall rage in *s.*
3:10 dashed in pieces at top of *s.*
*Zep.* 3:6 I made their *s.* waste
*Zec.* 8:4 old women sh. dw. in *s.*
5 *s.* sh. be full of boys and gir.
9:3 heaped up gold as mire in *s.*
10:5 who tread down ene. in *s.*
*Mat.* 6:2 not sound a trum. in *s.*
5 pray standing in corners of *s.*
*Mark* 6:56 sick in *s.* *Acts* 5:15
*Luke* 10:10 go into the *s.* of same
13:26 thou hast taught in our *s.*
14:21 go into *s.* and lanes of city

**STRENGTH.**

*Gen.* 4:12 ground sh. not yield *s.*
*Ex.* 13:3 by *s.* L. brought, 14, 16
*Num.* 23:22 *s.* of unicorn, 24:8
*Jud.* 5:21 O my soul, hast trod. *s.*
1 *Sam.* 2:4 stumbl. are girt wi. *s.*
9 for by *s.* shall no man prevail
10 he shall give *s.* un. his king
15:29 the *S.* of Israel will not lie
28:22 that thou mayest have *s.*
2 *Sam.* 22:40 thou hast girded me with *s.* *Ps.* 18:32, 39
2 *K.* 18:20 and *s.* for war, *Is.* 36:5
19:3 and there is no *s.* *Is.* 37:3
1 *Chr.* 16:27 *s.* and gladn. are in
28 give to the Lord glory and *s.* *Ps.* 29:1; 96:7
26:8 their sons, able men for *s.*
29:12 in thy hand it is to give *s.*
2 *Chr.* 13:20 nei. did Jer. reco. *s.*
*Neh.* 4:10 *s.* of bearers of burdens
*Job* 9:19 if I speak of *s.* he is str.
12:13 wi. him is wisdom and *s.*
21 weakeneth *s.* of the mighty
18:13 it sh. devour *s.* of his skin
23:6 he would put *s.* in me
30:2 wher. might their *s.* profit
36:19 not esteem forces of *s.*
39:19 hast thou given horse *s.*?
41:22 in his neck remaineth *s.*
*Ps.* 8:2 out of babes ordained *s.*
20:6 with saving *s.* of rig. hand
27:1 Lord is the *s.* of my life
28:8 he is saving *s.* of his anoi.
29:11 L. will give *s.* to his peo.
33:16 mighty is not deliv. by *s.*
39:13 that I may recover *s.*
46:1 God is our *s.* a help, 81:1
60:7 Ephrai. is *s.* of head, 108:8
68:34 ascribe *s.* unto God, his *s.*
35 God of Israel that giveth *s.*
73:26 God is the *s.* of my heart
81:1 sing aloud unto God our *s.*
84:5 blessed is man whose *s.* is
7 they go from *s.* to *s.* ev. one
90:10 by rea. of *s.* be fourscore
93:1 the Lord is clothed with *s.*
95:4 *s.* of the hills is his also
96:6 *s.* and beauty are in his sa.
99:4 the king's *s.* loveth judgm.
138:3 strengthenedst me with *s.*
140:7 O God, *s.* of my salvation
*Prov.* 8:14 I have *s.* 10:29 L. is *s.*
14:4 increase is by the *s.* of ox
21:22 a wise man cast. down *s.*
24:5 man of knowledge incr. *s.*
31:17 girdeth her loins with *s.*
25 *s.* and honor are her cloth.
*Ec.* 9:16 wisdom is better than *s.*
10:10 if iron blunt, put more *s.*
17 princes eat for *s.* not for dr.

Is. 5:22 men of s. to mingle dri.
10:13 by the s. of my hand
23:4 spoken, even the s. of sea
25:4 s. to the poor, s. to needy
26:4 L. JEHOVAH is everlast. s.
28:6 s. to them that turn battle
30:3 s. of Pharaoh sh. be shame
33:6 wisd. sh. be stability and s.
40:9 O Je. lift up voice with s.
29 no might, he increaseth s.
42:25 poured on him s. of battle
44:12 worketh it with s. of arms
45:24 in L. have I righte. and s.
51:9 awake, put on s. O Lord
Jer. 20:5 I will deli. all s. of city
51:53 tho' she fortify height of s.
Lam. 1:6 are gone without s.
Ezek. 30:15 fury on Sin, s. of Eg.
18 pomp of s. sh. cease, 33:28
Dan. 2:37 G. hath given thee s.
Dan. 2:41 th. sh. be in it s. of iron
11:15 neit. shall there be any s.
17 enter wi. s. of his kingdom
31 shall pollute sanctuary of s.
Joel 3:16 Lord the s. of Israel
Amos 6:13 not ta. horns by our s.
Nah. 3:9 E. and Eg were her s.
11 thou also shalt seek s.
Hag. 2:22 will destr. s. of kingd.
Luke 1:51 he showed s. with arm
Acts 3:7 his ancle bones recei. s.
Rom. 5:6 wh. without s. Ch. died
1 Cor. 15:56 s. of sin is the law
2 Cor. 1:8 we were pressed ab. s.
Heb. 11:11 Sarah herself recei. s.
Rev. 3:8 for thou hast a little s.
5:12 worthy is La. to receive s.
12:10 now is salvation and s.
17:13 these shall give s. to beast

**His STRENGTH.**

Ex. 14:27 sea returned to his s.
Deut. 21:17 he is begin. of his s.
Jud. 8:21 as man is, so is his s.
16:5 see wher. his great s. lieth
9 his s. not kn. 19 his s. went
2 K. 9:24 Jehu drew bow wi. h. s.
1 Chr. 16:11 seek the Lord and his s. Ps. 105:4
Job 18:7 steps of h. s. sh. be stra.
12 his s. shall be hunger-bitten
13 first-born of death de. his s.
21:23 one dieth in his full s.
37:6 saith to great rain of his s.
39:11 trust bec. h. s. is great?
21 rejoice. in h. s. 40:16 h. s. is
Ps. 33:17 nor deli. by h. great s.
52:7 this man made not G. h. s.
59:9 because of h. s. will I wait
65:6 by h. s. setteth fast mount.
68:34 ascribe s. to G. his s. is in
78:4 showing to generation h. s.
61 delive. his s. into captivity
Is. 44:12 he is hungry, h. s. fail.
62:8 the L. ha. sw. by arm of h. s.
63:1 travel. in greatness of h. s.
Dan. 11:2 by h. s. sh. stir up all
Hos. 7:9 strangers devoured h. s.
12:3 by h. s. he had power wi. G.
Rev. 1:16 count. as son in his s.

**In STRENGTH.**

Gen. 49:24 his bow abode in s.
1 K. 19:8 went in the s. of meat
Job 9:4 and mighty in s. 36:5
Ps. 71:16 I will go in the s. of L.
103:20 bless L. ye that excel in s.
147:10 delight not in s. of horse
Is. 30:2 strengthen in s. of Phar.
Mic. 5:4 he shall feed in s. of L.
Acts 9:22 S. increased more in s.

**My STRENGTH.**

Gen. 49:3 R. beginning of my s.
Ex. 15:2 the Lord is my s. 2 Sam. 22:33; Ps. 18:2; 28:7; 118:14; Is. 12:2
Jos. 14:11 as my s. was then, so is my s. now
Jud. 16:17 if I be shav. my s. will
Job 6:11 what is my s. that I sh.?
12 is my s. of stones?
Ps. 18:1 I love thee, O L. my s.
19:14 O L. my s. 22:15 my s. dr.
31:4 the net, for thou art my s.
10 my s. fails bec. 38:10; 71:9
43:2 thou art the God of my s.
59:17 to th. O my s. will I sing
62:7 art my s. 102:23 my s.
144:1 blessed be Lord, my s.
Is. 27:5 take hold of my s.
49:4 I have spent my s. for nau.
5 glorious, my G. sh. be my s.
Jer. 16:19 O L. my s. and fortress
Lam. 1:14 he made my s. to fall
3:18 my s. and hope perished
Hab. 3:19 the Lord God is my s.
Zec. 12:5 be my s. in L. of hosts
2 Cor. 12:9 my s. is made perfect

**Their STRENGTH.**

Jos. 11:13 cit. that stood in t. s.
Ps. 37:39 he is their s. in trouble
73:4 no ba. in death, t. s. is firm
78:51 he smote their s. 105:36
89:17 thou art the glory of t. s.
90:10 yet is t. s. labor and sor.
Prov. 20:29 glory of men is t. s.
Is. 30:7 I cried, t. s. is to sit still
40:31 that wait on L. renew t. s.
41:1 let the people renew their s.
63:6 I will bring down their s.
Ezek. 24:25 I take from them t. s,
Joel 2:22 fig-t. and vine yield t. s.

**Thy STRENGTH.**

Ex. 15:13 hast guid. them in t. s.
Deut. 33:25 as days, so sh. t. s. be
Jud. 16:6 tell wher. t. s. lieth, 15
2 Chr. 6:41 ark of t. s. Ps. 132:8
Ps. 21:1 king shall joy in thy s.
Ps. 21:13 be ex. O L. in . own s.
54:1 name, judge me by thy s.
68:28 G. hath commanded thy s.
71:18 until I have showed thy s.
74:13 didst divide sea by thy s.
77:14 hast declared t. s. am. pe.
80:2 stir up thy s. and save us
86:16 give thy s. to thy servant
110:2 L. shall send rod of t. s.
Prov. 24:10 faint, thy s. is small
31:3 give not t. s. unto women
Is. 17:10 not mind. of rock of t. s.
52:1 awake, put on t. s. O Zion
63:15 wh. is thy zeal and thy s.
Amos 3:11 he sh. bring down t. s.
Mark 12:30 love the Lord with all thy s. 33; Luke 10:27

**Your STRENGTH.**

Lev. 26:20 y. s. be spent in vain
Neh. 8:10 joy of the Lord is y. s.
Is. 23:14 ships, your s. is waste
30:15 in confidence shall be y. s.
Ezek. 24:21 my sanct. ex. of y. s.

**STRENGTHEN.**

Deut. 3:28 charge Joshua, s. him
Jud. 16:28 s. me, I pray thee
1 K. 20:22 s. thys. mark and see
Ezr. 6:22 s. their hands in work
Neh. 6:9 O God, s. my hands
Job 16:5 I wo. s. you with mouth
Ps. 20:2 Lord s. thee out of Zion
27:14 L. shall s. thy heart, 31:24
41:3 Lord will s. him on the bed
68:28 s. whi. thou hast wrought
89:21 mine arm also shall s. him
119:28 s. me accord. to thy word
Is. 22:21 I will s. him wi. girdle
30:2 to s. themselves in strength
33:23 they could not s. th. mast
35:3 s. we. hands; 41:10 I will s.
54:2 length. cords, s. thy stakes
Jer. 23:14 s. hands of evil doers
Ezek. 7:13 nor sh. any s. himself
16:49 neither did she s. hand of
30:24 I will s. arms of king, 25
34:16 I will s. that wh. was sick
Dan. 11:1 stood to confirm and s.
Amos 2:14 strong sh. not s. force
Zec. 10:6 I will s. house of Judah
12 I will s. them in the Lord
Luke 22:32 when convert. s. bre.
1 Pet. 5:10 God stablish, s. you
Rev. 3:2 be watchful and s. thi.

**STRENGTHENED.**

Gen. 48:2 Israel s. himself
Jud. 3:12 Lord s. Eglon against
7:11 afterwards shall hands be s.
1 Sam. 23:16 Jona. s. hand in G.
2 Sam. 2:7 let your hands be s.
1 Chr. 11:10 who s. themselves
2 Chr. 1:1 Solom. was s. in king.
11:17 they s. kingdom of Judah
12:1 when Reho. had s. himself
24:13 set house of God and s. it
25:11 Amaziah s. himself
28:20 distressed Ahaz, but s. not
32:5 Hezek. s. himself, and built
Ezr. 1:6 that were about them s.
7:28 I was s. as hand of God was
Neh. 2:18 they s. their hands for
Job 4:3 thou hast s. weak hands
4 thou hast s. the feeble knees
Ps. 52:7 s. himself in wickedness
147:13 hath s. bars of thy gates
Prov. 8:28 when he s. fountains
Ezek. 13:22 ye s. hands of wicked
34:4 the diseased have ye not s.
Dan. 10:18 touched and s. me, 19
11:6 he that begat her and s. her
12 cast down many, not be s.
Hos. 7:15 ha. bound and s. arms
Acts 9:19 received meat, S. was s.
Eph. 3:16 to be s. with might
Col. 1:11 s. with all might accor.
2 Tim. 4:17 Lord stood and s. me

**STRENGTHENEDST, ETH.**

Job 15:25 he s. himself again. Al.
Ps. 104:15 which s. man's heart
138:3 and s. me with strength
Prov. 31:17 gird. loins, s. arms
Ec. 7:19 wisdom s. the wise
Is. 44:14 cypress and oak he s.
Amos 5:9 s. spoiled ag. strong
Phil. 4:13 all thro' C. who s. me

**STRENGTHENING.**

Luke 22:43 appe. an angel s. him
Acts 18:23 Paul s. all the discipl.

**STRETCH**

Ex. 7:19 s. out hand on waters
8:5 s. forth hand over streams
25:20 cherub. sh. s. their wings
Jos. 8:18 s. out the spear to Ai
2 K. 21:13 I will s. over Jerusal.
Job 11:13 if thou s. out tow. him
39:26 doth hawk s. her wings?
Ps. 68:31 soon s. her hands to G.
Is. 28:20 shorter th. a man can s.
34:11 s. upon it line of confusion
54:2 s. curtains of thy habitation
Jer. 10:20 none to s. forth tent
Ezek. 30:25 king of Bab. s. sword
Amos 6:4 s. themsel. on couches
Mat. 12:13 Je. said, s. thy hand
John 21:18 shalt s. forth hands
2 Cor. 10:14 s. not beyond meas.

**STRETCHED**

Gen. 22:10 A. s. hand to slay son
48:14 Israel s. out right hand
Ex. 8:6 Aa. s. out his hand, 17
9:23 Mo. s. forth his rod, 10:13
Jos. 8:18 Joshua s. out spear, 26
19 ran as he s. out his hand
1 K. 6:27 cherub. s. forth wings
17:21 and he s. himself on the child, 2 K. 4:34, 35
1 Chr. 21:16 angel with a swo. s.
Job 38:5 who hath s. line up. it?
Ps. 44:20 or s. to a strange god
88:9 I have s. my hands unto th.
136:6 to him that s. out earth
Prov. 1:24 bec. I s. out my hand
Is. 3:16 walk with s. forth necks

5:25 he *s.* forth hand ag. them,
*s.* out still, 9:12, 17. 21; 10:4
14:26 this is hand that is *s.* out
27 hand *s.* who sh. turn it back?
16:8 her branches are *s.* out
23:11 *s.* out his hand over sea
42:5 *s.* out heavens, 45:12; 51:13
*Jer.* 6:4 shadows of even. *s.* out
10:12 *s.* out heavens by discreti.
51:15 he *s.* heaven by understa.
*Lam.* 2:8 Lord hath *s.* out a line
*Ezek.* 1:11 wings were *s.* upward
10:7 cherub *s.* forth his hand
16:27 I have *s.* my hand over th.
*Hos.* 7:5 *s.* hand with scorners
*Amos* 6:7 that *s.* sh. be removed
*Zec.* 1:16 line be *s.* forth on Jer.
*Mat.* 12:13 *s.* hand, *Mark* 3:5
*Luke* 22:53 *s.* no hands aga. me
*Acts* 12:1 Her. *s.* hand to vex chu.
*Rom.* 10:21 all day I *s.* my hands
*See* ARM.

### STRETCHEDST.
*Ex.* 15:12 thou *s.* thy right hand

### STRETCHEST, ETH.
*Job* 15:25 *s.* his hand against God
26:7 *s.* north over empty place
*Ps.* 104:2 who *s.* out the heavens
*Prov.* 31:20 *s.* her hand to poor
*Is.* 40:22 that *s.* out the heavens
44:13 the carpen. *s.* out his rule
24 *s.* forth heavens, *Zec.* 12:1

### STRETCHING.
*Is.* 8:8 *s.* of his wings fill land
*Acts* 4:30 by *s.* forth hand to heal

### STREWED.
*Ex.* 32:20 he ground calf, *s.* it
2 *Chr.* 34:4 he *s.* upon the graves
*Mat.* 21:8 cut do. branches and *s.*
25:24 gath. where hast not *s.* 25

### STRICKEN.
*Gen.* 18:11 well *s.* in age, 24:1
*Jos.* 13:1 J. was *s.* in yrs. 23:1, 2
*Jud.* 5:26 Jael had *s.* his temples
1 *K.* 1:1 David was *s.* in years
*Prov.* 6:1 *s.* thy hand with stran.
23:35 they have *s.* me, I was
*Is.* 1:5 sho. ye be *s.* any more?
16:7 they are *s.* 53:4 est. him *s.*
53:8 for transgression was he *s.*
*Jer.* 5:3 thou hast *s.* them, they
*Lam.* 4:9 *s.* for want of fruits
*Luke* 1:7 Elizab. *s.* in years, 18

### STRIFE.
*Gen.* 13:7 a *s.* bet. the herdmen
8 Abra. said, Let there be no *s.*
*Num.* 27:14 rebell. in *s.* of cong.
*Deut.* 1:12 can I bear your *s.*?
*Jud.* 12:2 I and peo. were at *s.*
2 *Sam.* 19:9 people were at *s.*
*Ps.* 31:20 keep fr. *s.* of tongues
55:9 I have seen *s.* in the city
80:6 makest us a *s.* to neighbors
106:32 ang. him at waters of *s.*
*Prov.* 15:18 a wrathful man stir.
*s.* slow to anger app. *s.* 29:22
16:28 a froward man soweth *s.*
17:1 house full of sacrifi. with *s.*
14 begin. of *s.* one letteth out
19 loveth transg. that loveth *s.*
20:3 honor for man to cease fr. *s.*
22:10 cast out scorner, *s.* cease
26:17 he that meddleth with *s.*
20 no talebearer, the *s.* ceaseth
21 so is contentious to kind. *s.*
28:25 proud heart stirreth up *s.*
30:33 forcing of wrath bring. *s.*
*Is.* 58:4 ye fast for *s.* and debate
*Jer.* 15:10 borne me a man of *s.*
*Ezek.* 47:19 to waters of *s.* 48:28
*Hab.* 1:3 there are th. raise up *s.*
*Luke* 22:24 a *s.* among disciples
*Rom.* 13:13 honestly, not in *s.*
1 *Cor.* 3:3 there is among you *s.*
*Gal.* 5:20 works of the flesh are *s.*
*Phil.* 1:15 some preach Chr. of *s.*
2:3 let nothing be done thro' *s.*
1 *Tim.* 6:4 wher. cometh envy, *s.*
*Heb.* 6:16 an oath is end of all *s.*
*Jam.* 3:14 bitter envying and *s.*
16 where *s.* is, there is confus.

### STRIFES.
*Prov.* 10:12 hatred stirreth up *s.*
2 *Cor.* 12:20 envyings, wraths, *s.*
1 *Tim.* 6:4 quest. and *s.* of words
2 *Tim.* 2:23 knowing that they
gender *s.*

### STRIKE.
*Deut.* 21:4 *s.* off heifer's neck
2 *K.* 5:11 come and *s.* his hands
*Job* 17:3 who will *s.* ha. wi. me?
20:24 bow of steel *s.* him thro'
*Ps.* 110:5 *s.* thro' kings in wrath
*Prov.* 7:23 till a dart *s.* thro' liver
17:26 it is not good to *s.* princes
22:26 be not th. one th. *s.* hands
*Hab.* 3:14 *s.* thro' with his staves
*Mark* 14:65 did *s.* Je. with hands

### STRIKER.
1 *Tim.* 3:3 bishop no *s.* *Tit.* 1:7

### STRIKETH.
*Job* 34:26 he *s.* th. as wicked men
*Prov.* 17:18 void of understand. *s.*
*Rev.* 9:5 scorp. when he *s.* a man

### STRING, S.
*Ps.* 11:2 make ready arrow on *s.*
21:12 make thine arrows on *s.*
33:2 instrum. of 10 *s.* 92:3; 144:9
*Mark* 7:35 *s.* of tongue loosed

### STRINGED.
*Ps.* 150:4 praise him wi. *s.* instr.
*Is.* 38:20 sing songs to *s.* instru.
*Hab.* 3:19 singer on *s.* instrume.

### STRIPE.
*Ex.* 21:25 for wound, *s.* for *s*

### STRIPES.
*Deut.* 25:3 forty *s.* he may give
2 *Sam.* 7:14 with *s.* of children
*Ps.* 89:32 visit iniquity with *s.*
*Prov.* 17:10 hundred *s.* into a fool
19:29 *s.* are prepared for fools
20:30 so do *s.* the inward parts
*Is.* 53:5 with his *s.* we are healed,
1 *Pet.* 2:24
*Luke* 12:47 beaten with many *s.*
48 knew not, beaten wi. few *s.*
*Acts* 16:23 laid many *s.* upon th.
33 same hour, washed their *s.*
2 *Cor.* 6:5 in *s.* in imprisonments
11:23 in *s.* above measure
24 of Jews received I forty *s.*

### STRIP.
*Num.* 20:26 *s.* Aaron of garments
1 *Sam.* 31:8 Philistines came to
*s.* slain, 1 *Chr.* 10:8
*Is.* 32:11 *s.* ye, make ye bare
*Ezek.* 16:39 they sh. *s.* thee, 23:26
*Hos.* 2:3 I *s.* her naked, set her

### STRIPPED.
*Gen.* 37:23 they *s.* Joseph of coat
*Ex.* 33:6 Israel *s.* themselves
*Num.* 20:28 Moses *s.* Aa. of gar.
1 *Sam.* 18:4 Jonathan *s.* himself
19:24 Saul *s.* off his clothes also
31:9 Philist. *s.* Saul of his armor
2 *Chr.* 20:25 jewels wh. th. *s.* off
*Job* 19:9 *s.* me of glory and crown
22:6 for thou hast *s.* of clothing
*Mic.* 1:8 therefore I will go *s.*
*Mat.* 27:28 they *s.* Jesus, put on
*Luke* 10:30 which *s.* him of raim.

### STRIPLING.
1 *Sam.* 17:56 inq. whose son *s.* is

### STRIVE.
*Gen.* 6:3 Spi. not always *s.* with
26:20 herdmen of Gerar did *s.*
*Ex.* 21:18 if men *s.* together
22 *s.* and hurt wo. *Deut.* 25:11
*Deut.* 33:8 with wh. thou didst *s.*
*Jud.* 11:25 did he ever *s.* aga. Is.
*Job* 33:13 why *s.* against him?
*Ps.* 35:1 plead with them that *s.*
*Prov.* 3:30 *s.* not without cause
25:8 go not forth hastily to *s.*
*Is.* 41:11 they that *s.* shall perish
45:9 let potsherd *s.* wi. potsherd
*Hos.* 4:4 let no man *s.* thy people are as they that *s.*
*Mat.* 12:19 he shall not *s.*
*Luke* 13:24 *s.* to enter strait gate
*Rom.* 15:30 *s.* wi. me in prayers
2 *Tim.* 2:5 if a man *s.* for maste.
2 *Tim.* 2:14 th. th. *s.* not ab. wor.
24 servant of Lord must not *s.*

### STRIVED, ETH.
*Is.* 45:9 woe to him that *s.* wi. M.
*Rom.* 15:20 I *s.* to preach gospel
1 *Cor.* 9:25 *s.* for mastery is tem.

### STRIVEN.
*Jer.* 50:24 bec. th. hast *s.* ag. L.

### STRIVING.
*Phil.* 1:27 with mind *s.* for gospel
*Col.* 1:29 *s.* according to working
*Heb.* 12:4 not resisted, *s.* aga. sin

### STRIVINGS.
2 *Sam.* 22:44 hast deliv. me from
*s.* of the people, *Ps.* 18:43
*Tit.* 3:9 avoid contentions and *s.*

### STROKE, S.
*Deut.* 17:8 hard betwe. *s.* and *s.*
19:5 hand fetcheth a *s.* wi. axe
21:5 by word every *s.* be tried
*Est.* 9:5 J. smote enem. with *s.*
*Job* 23:2 my *s.* is heavier th. my
36:18 lest he take th. with his *s.*
*Ps.* 39:10 remove thy *s.* from me
*Prov.* 18:6 fool's mouth call. for *s.*
*Is.* 14:6 smote with a contin. *s.*
30:26 the Lord healeth the *s.* of
*Ezek.* 24:16 desi. of eyes with a *s.*

### STRONG.
*Gen.* 49:14 Issachar is a *s.* ass
24 arms of hands were made *s.*
*Ex.* 6:1 with a *s.* hand shall, 13:9
*Num.* 20:20 Ed. came wi. *s.* hand
21:24 border of Ammon was *s.*
28:7 *s.* wine poured out to Lord
*Deut.* 2:36 not one city too *s.* for
*Jos.* 14:11 I am as *s.* this day
17:13 Is. were wax. *s.* *Jud.* 1:28
23:9 great nations and *s.*
*Jud.* 14:14 out of *s.* came sweet.
18:26 Mic. saw they were too *s.*
1 *Sam.* 14:52 when S. saw *s.* man
2 *Sam.* 3:6 Abner made hims. *s.*
10:11 if Syri. be too *s.* for me, if
Am. be too *s.* 1 *Chr.* 19:12
1 *K.* 8:42 sh. hear of thy *s.* hand
2 *Chr.* 11:12 he made the cities *s.*
17 made Rehoboam *s.* 3 years
16:9 eyes run to show himself *s.*
26:16 Uzziah was *s.* was lifted
*Neh.* 9:25 they took *s.* cities
*Job* 8:2 words be like a *s.* wind
9:19 if I speak of stren. he is *s.*
37:18 spread out sky that is *s.*
*Ps.* 19:5 rejoiceth as a *s.* man
24:8 Lord *s.* and mighty
30:7 made my mount. stand *s.*
31:2 be thou my *s.* rock
35:10 from him that is too *s.* for
38:19 enemies are lively and *s.*
60:9 who br. into *s.* city? 108:10
71:3 my *s.* habita. 7 my *s.* refuge
80:15 branch thou madest *s.* 17
89:8 who is a *s.* Lord like thee?
13 *s.* is thy hand, high is thy
136:12 a *s.* hand, *Jer.* 32:21
*Prov.* 7:26 *s.* men have been
11:16 wom. retai. honor, *s.* men
18:19 harder to be won th. *s.* ci.
24:5 wise *s.* 30:25 ants not *s.*
*Ec.* 9:11 battle is not to the *s.*
12:3 *s.* men shall bow thems.
*Cant.* 8:6 for love is *s.* as death

Is. 8:7 L. bringeth waters, s. and
11 L. spake to me with s. hand
17:9 s. cities sh. be as forsaken
25:3 theref. shall s. glorify thee
26:1 be sung, we have a s. city
28:2 hath a mighty and s. one
40:10 will come with a s. hand
26 for that he is s. in power
53:12 shall divide spoil with s.
60:22 one shall bec. a s. nation
Jer. 21:5 will fight wi. a s. arm
48:14 mighty, s. men for war
49:19 come ag. habita. of the s.
50:34 th. Redeemer is s. the L.
44 sh. come unto habita. of s.
Ezek. 3:14 hand of the L. was s.
26:17 city which wast s. in sea
30:21 make it s. to hold sword
22 I will break s. arms of Pha.
32:21 s. shall speak to him
34:16 I will destroy fat and s.
Dan. 4:11 grew and was s. 20
22 thou, O king, art become s.
7:7 fourth beast terrible, s. exc.
11:23 he shall bec. s. wi. small
Joel 1:6 nation is come up, s. 2:2
2:11 he is s. that execut. word
3:10 let the weak say, I am s.
Amos 2:14 s. sh. not strengthen
5:9 strengtheneth spoiled ag. s.
Mic. 4:3 shall rebuke s. nations
7 I will make her a s. nation
Nah. 2:1 make thy loins s.
Zec. 8:22 s. nations sh. seek L.
Mat. 12:29 how ent. s. man s ho.
exc. bind s. man? Mark 3:27
Luke 1:80 child waxed s. 2:40
11:21 a s. man armed keepeth
Acts 3:16 thro' faith made man s.
Rom. 4:20 was s. in faith
15:1 we th. are s. ought to bear
1 Cor. 4:10 are weak, ye are s.
2 Cor. 12:10 weak, then am I s.
13:9 we are weak, and ye are s.
Heb. 5:12 milk, not s. meat
11:34 out of weak. were made s.
1 John 2:14 ye are s. word of God
Rev. 5:2 I saw a s. angel proclai.
18:2 he cried with a s. voice
8 s. is the Lord God who judg.

**Be STRONG.**

Num. 13:18 see wheth. they be s.
28 people be s. that dwell in
Deut. 11:18 keep co. that ye be s.
Jos. 17:18 drive Canaa. tho' be s.
1 Sam. 4:9 be s. quit yourselves
2 Sam. 16:21 han. of all shall be s.
1 K. 2:2 be thou s. show thyself a
1 Chr. 28:10 L. chosen thee, be s.
2 Chr. 15:7 be s. work sh. be re.
25:8 do it, be s. for the battle
Ezr. 9:12 that ye may be s.
Ps. 144:14 that oxen be s. to lab.
Is. 35:4 th. of fearful heart, be s.
Ezek. 22:14 can thy hands be s.
Dan. 2:42 kingd. sh. be partly s.
10:19 peace to th. be s. yea, be s.
11:5 king of the south shall be s.
and he sh. be s. above him
32 pe. that know G. shall be s.
Hag. 2:4 be s. O Zerubabbel, be
s. O Joshua, be s. ye people
Zec. 8:19 let hands be s. ye that
13 but let your hands be s.
1 Cor. 16:13 quit you li. m. be s.
Eph. 16:10 brethr. be s. in the L.
2 Tim. 2:1 my son, be s. in grace
See COURAGE, DRINK.

**STRONG ones.**

Ps. 10:10 may fall by his s. ones
Jer. 8:16 sound of neigh. of s. on.

**STRONGER.**

Gen. 25:23 one people shall be s.
30:42 feebler were L.'s s. Jac.'s
Num. 13:31 not able, they are s.
Jud. 14:18 what is s. th. a lion?
2 Sam. 3:1 David waxed s. and s.
13:14 Amnon being s. than she
1 K. 20:23 s. we shall be s. 25
Job 17:9 cl. hands sh. be s. and s.
Ps. 105:24 he made them s. than
142:6 deli. me, they are s. th. I
Jer. 20:7 thou art s. than I, and
Luke 11:22 wh. a s. th. he come
1 Cor. 1:25 weak. of G. is s. than
10:22 do we pro. L.? are we s.?

**STRONGEST.**

Prov. 30:30 wh. is s. am. beasts

**STRONG-HOLD, S.**

Num. 13:19 whe. in tents or s.-h.
Jud. 6:2 Is. ma. caves and s.-h.
1 Sam. 23:14 David abode in s.-h.
29 D. dwelt in s.-h. at En-gedi
2 Sam. 5:7 David took s.-h. of Z.
24:7 came to the s.-h. of Tyre
2 K. 8:12 their s.-h. set on fire
2 Chr. 11:11 Rehob. fortified s.-h.
Ps. 89:40 broug. his s.-h. to ruin
Is. 23:11 destroy s.-h. thereof
31:9 shall pass over to his s.-h.
Jer. 48:18 spoiler sh. destroy s.-h.
41 the s.-holds are surprised
Lam. 2:2 he hath thr. down s.-h.
5 Lord destroyed his s.-holds
Dan. 11:24 his devices aga. s.-h.
39 thus sh. he go in most s.-h.
Mic. 4:8 s.-h. of the daugh. of Z.
Nah. 1:7 L. a s.-h. in day of trou.
3:12 thy s.-h. shall be like fig-t.
14 draw waters, forti. thy s.-h.
Hab. 1:10 shall deride every s.-h.
Zec. 9:3 Tyrus did build a s.-h.
12 turn to the s.-h. ye prisone.
2 Cor. 10:14 mig. to pull. do. s.-h.

**STRONGLY.**

Ezr. 6:3 let foundation be s. laid

**STROVE.**

Gen. 26:20 they s. with him, 21
22 another well, and s. not
Ex. 2:13 two men of Hebrews s.
Lev. 24:10 man of Is. s. in camp
Num. 20:13 chil. of Is. s. with L.
26:9 Dathan, who s. against M.
2 Sam. 14:6 they two s. together
Dan. 7:2 four winds s. upon sea
John 6:52 the Jews s. am. them.
Acts 7:26 M. show. him. as th. s.
23:9 s. saying, We find no evil

**STRUCK.**

1 Sam. 2:14 he s. it into the pan
2 Sam. 12:15 the Lord s. the ch.
20:10 Jo. s. him not again, and
2 Chr. 13:20 the Lord s. Jerobo.
Mat. 26:51 one of them s. a serv.
Luke 22:64 they s. Jesus, John
18:22

**STRUGGLED.**

Gen. 25:22 children s. together

**STUBBLE.**

Ex. 5:12 gath. s. instead of straw
15:7 wrath consumed them as s.
Job 13:25 wilt th. pursue dry s.?
21:18 they are as s. before wind
41:28 stones are turned into s.
29 darts are counted as s. he
Ps. 83:13 make them as s. before
Is. 5:24 as fire devoureth the s.
33:11 conceive chaff br. forth s.
40:24 whirlwind take away as s.
41:2 he gave them as driven s.
47:14 they shall be as s. the fire
Jer. 13:24 I will scatter th. as s.
Joel 2:5 flame, that devou. the s.
Ob. 18 house of E. sh. be for s.
Nah. 1:10 they sh. be devo. as s.
Mal. 4:1 wicked, and proud be s.
1 Cor. 3:12 on the found. hay, s.

**STUBBORN.**

Deut. 21:18 if a man ha. a s. son
20 say to eld. This our son is s.
Jud. 2:19 ceased not from s. way
Ps. 78:8 not as fath. a s. gener.
Prov. 7:11 she is loud and s. her

**STUBBORNNESS.**

Deut. 9:27 look not to s. of peop.
1 Sam. 15:23 and s. is as iniquity

**STUCK.**

1 Sam. 26:7 spear s. in ground
Ps. 119:31 I ha. s. unto testimo.
Acts 27:41 part of the ship s. fast

**STUDS.**

Cant. 1:11 borders of gold wi. s.

**STUDY.**

Ec. 12:12 much s. is a weariness
1 Thes. 4:11 s. to be quiet
2 Tim. 2:15 s. to show thys. app.

**STUDIETH.**

Prov. 15:28 heart of righteous s.
24:2 their heart s. destruction

**STUFF.**

Gen. 31:37 th. hast search. my s.
45:20 regard not your s.
Ex. 22:7 if man deliv. s. to keep
36:7 the s. they had was suffici.
Jos. 7:11 they put it amo. their s.
1 Sam. 10:22 he hath hid amo. s.
25:13 two hund. abode by the s.
30:24 his part be that tarr. by s.
Ezek. 12:3 prepare s. for removi.
4 bring forth thy s. by day, 7
Luke 17:31 house-top, s. in hou.

**STUMBLE.**

Prov. 3:23 walk, foot not s. 4:12
4:19 know not at what they s.
Is. 5:27 none sh. be weary nor s.
8:15 many among them shall s.
28:7 err in vision, s. in judgme.
59:10 we s. at noonday as night
63:13 led th. that th. sho. not s.
Jer. 13:16 before your feet s. on
18:15 caused them to s. in ways
20:11 therefore persecuto. sh. s.
31:9 in a way they shall not s.
46:6 they shall s. and fall
50:32 proud shall s. and fall
Dan. 11:19 he shall s. and fall
Nah. 2:5 shall s. in their walk
3:3 they shall s. on corpses
Mal. 2:8 have caused many to s.
1 Pet. 2:8 offence to them that s.

**STUMBLED.**

1 Sam. 2:4 that s. girt with stre.
1 Chr. 13:9 hold ark, for oxen s.
Ps. 27:2 came to eat flesh, th. s.
Jer. 46:12 mighty s. ag. mighty
Rom. 9:32 th. s. at stumb.-stone
11:11 have s. that they sho. fall

**STUMBLETH.**

Prov. 24:17 heart glad wh. he s.
John 11:9 walk in day, s. not
10 if man walk in night he s.
Rom. 14:21 whereby thy bro. s.

**STUMBLING.**

John 2:10 is none occasion of s.

**STUMBLING-BLOCK.**

Lev. 19:14 nor put s.-b. bef. blind
Is. 57:14 take s.-b. out of way
Ezek. 3:20 I lay s.-b. before him
7:19 bec. it is s.-b. of their iniq.
14:3 they put s.-b. of iniqu. 4, 7
Rom. 11:9 made a trap, a s.-b.
Rom. 14:13 put s.-b. in br. way
1 Cor. 1:23 C. cruci. to Jews s.-b.
8:9 lest liber. of yours bec. s.-b.
Rev. 2:14 Bal. to cast s.-b. bef. Is.

**STUMBLING-BLOCKS.**

Jer. 6:21 I will lay s.-b. bef. peo.
Zep. 1:3 I will consume s.-b.

**STUMBLING, with stone.**

Is. 8:14 be for a s. of s. to Israel
Rom. 9:32 stumbled at th. s.-s.
33 behold, I lay in Sion a s.-st.
1 Pet. 2:8 s. of s. to th. that stum.

**STUMP.**
1 *Sam.* 5:4 only *s.* of Da. was left
*Dan.* 4:15 leave *s.* in earth, 23, 26

**SUBDUE.**
*Gen.* 1:28 replenish earth, *s.* it
1 *Chr.* 17:10 I will *s.* thi. enemi.
*Ps.* 47:3 he shall *s.* peo. under
*Is.* 45:1 to *s.* nations before him
*Dan.* 7:24 he shall *s.* three kings
*Mic.* 7:19 will *s.* our iniquities
*Zec.* 9:15 *s.* with sling-stones
*Phil.* 3:21 he is able to *s.* all thi.

**SUBDUED, EST.**
*Num.* 32:22 land be *s.* before L.
29 land shall be *s.* before you
*Deut.* 20:20 bulwarks, until be *s.*
*Jos.* 18:1 land was *s.* before th.
1 *Sam.* 7:13 Phili. were *s.* 2 *Sam.* 8:1; 1 *Chr.* 18:1; 20:4
2 *Sam.* 8:11 gold of nations he *s.*
22:40 th. *s.* under me, *Ps.* 18:39
1 *Chr.* 22:18 land is *s.* before Lord
*Neh.* 9:24 thou *s.* inhabi. of land
*Ps.* 81:14 soon have *s.* enemies
1 *Cor.* 15:28 all be *s.* unto him
*Heb.* 11:33 thro' faith *s.* kingdo.

**SUBDUETH.**
*Ps.* 18:47 it is G. *s.* peo. 144:2
*Dan.* 2:40 iron breaks and *s.* all

**SUBJECT.**
*Luke* 2:51 Jesus was *s.* to them
10:17 L. even devils are *s.* to us
20 rejo. not spirits are *s.* to you
*Rom.* 8:7 it is not *s.* to law of G.
20 creature was *s.* to vanity
13:1 let eve. soul be *s.* to powers
5 wherefo. ye must needs be *s.*
1 *Cor.* 14:32 spirits of prophets
15:28 then sh. Son hims. be *s.*
*Eph.* 5:24 as church is *s.* to Chr.
*Col.* 2:20 are ye *s.* to ordinances
*Tit.* 3:1 put in mind to *s.* to pow.
*Heb.* 2:15 lifetime *s.* to bondage
*Jam.* 5:17 Elias was *s.* to passio.
1 *Pet.* 2:18 serv. be *s.* to masters
3:22 pow. being made *s.* to him
5:5 all of you be *s.* one to ano.

**SUBJECTED.**
*Rom.* 8:20 who *s.* same in hope

**SUBJECTION.**
*Ps.* 106:42 enemies brou. into *s.*
*Jer.* 34:11 brought th. into *s.* 16
1 *Cor.* 9:27 br. my body into *s.*
2 *Cor.* 9:13 glorify G. for your *s.*
*Gal.* 2:5 we gave place by *s.* not
1 *Tim.* 2:11 wom. learn with all *s.*
3:4 having his children in *s.*
*Heb.* 2:5 put in *s.* world to come
8 put all things in *s.* under feet
12:9 rather be in *s.* to Father
1 *Pet.* 3:1 be in *s.* to husbands, 5

**SUBMIT.**
*Gen.* 16:9 *s.* thyself under her ha.
2 *Sam.* 22:45 strang. sh. *s.* themselves to me, *Ps.* 18:44
*Ps.* 66:3 enemies shall *s.* to thee
68:30 till every one *s.* with silv.
1 *Cor.* 16:16 that ye *s.* yourselves
*Eph.* 5:22 *s.* to husb. *Col.* 3:18
*Heb.* 13:17 *s.* th. watch for souls
*Jas.* 4:7 *s.* yourselves theref. to G.
1 *Pet.* 2:13 *s.* to every ordinance
5:5 younger *s.* yourselv. to elder

**SUBMITTED, ING.**
1 *Chr.* 29:24 sons of Da. *s.* to Sol.
*Ps.* 81:15 haters of L. *s.* to him.
*Rom.* 10:3 not *s.* to righteousness
*Eph.* 5:21 *s.* yours. one to anoth.

**SUBORNED.**
*Acts* 6:11 then they *s.* men who

**SUBSCRIBE, ED.**
*Is.* 44:5 another shall *s.* unto L.
*Jer.* 32:10 I *s.* evidence, sealed it
12 in pres. of witnesses that *s.*
44 men shall *s.* evidences

**SUBSTANCE.**
*Gen.* 7:4 I will destroy ev. liv. *s.*
23 every living *s.* was destroyed
12:5 Abraham took *s.* they gath.
13:6 their *s.* was great, so they
15:14 shall come with great *s.*
*Gen.* 34:23 sh. not th. *s.* be ours?
36:6 E. took his cattle and his *s.*
*Deut.* 11:6 swallow. them and *s.*
33:11 bless, L. his *s.* accept work
*Jos.* 14:4 gave Lev. cities for *s.*
1 *Chr.* 27:31 th. were rulers of *s.*
28:1 stewards over all *s.* of king
2 *Chr.* 21:17 carried away all *s.*
31:3 appoint. king's portion of *s.*
32:29 God had given Hez. *s.*
35:7 bullocks. th. were king's *s.*
*Ezr.* 8:21 seek ri. way for our *s.*
10:8 come, *s.* should be forfeited
*Job* 1:3 Job's *s.* was 7,000 sheep
10 his *s.* increased in the land
5:5 robber swallow. up their *s.*
6:22 Give a reward of your *s.*?
15:29 nor shall his *s.* continue
20:18 according to *s.* restitution
22:20 whereas our *s.* is not cut
30:22 liftest, and dissolv. my *s.*
*Ps.* 17:14 leave their *s.* to babes
105:21 made Joseph ruler over *s.*
139:15 my *s.* was not hid fr. thee
16 thine eyes did see my *s.*
*Prov.* 1:13 sh. find all precious *s.*
3:9 honor L. with *s.* first fruits
6:31 he shall give *s.* of house
8:21 cause th. love me inherit *s.*
10:3 he casteth away *s.* of wick.
12:27 *s.* of a diligent man preci.
28:8 he that by usury increas. *s.*
29:3 with harlots, spend. his *s.*
*Cant.* 8:7 if a man give *s.* for love
*Is.* 6:13 as an oak wh. *s.* is in th. so holy seed be *s.* thereof
*Jer.* 15:13 *s.* give to spoil, 17:3
*Hos.* 12:8 I have found me out *s.*
*Ob.* 13 nor laid hands on their *s.*
*Mic.* 4:13 I will consecrate th. *s.*
*Luke* 8:3 minister. to him th. *s.*
15:13 prodigal wasted his *s.*
*Heb.* 10:34 ye have in heaven a *s.*
11:1 faith is *s.* of thi. hoped for

**SUBTILE.**
*Gen.* 3:1 serpent more *s.* than any
2 *Sam.* 13:3 Jonadab was a *s.* man
*Prov.* 7:10 harlot. and *s.* of heart

**SUBTILELY.**
1 *Sam.* 23:22 told me, he deal. *s.*
*Ps.* 105:25 to deal *s.* with serv.
*Acts* 7:19 dealt *s.* with our kindr.

**SUBTILTY.**
*Gen.* 27:35 thy bro. came with *s.*
2 *K.* 10:19 Jehu did it in *s.* that
*Prov.* 1:4 to give *s.* to the simple
*Mat.* 26:4 might take Jesus by *s.*
*Acts* 13:10 O full of *s.* and mischi.
2 *Cor.* 11:3 beguiled Eve thro' *s.*

**SUBURBS.**
*Lev.* 25:34 field of *s.* not be sold
*Num.* 35:3 *s.* sh. be for th. cattle
7, 48 cit. sh. ye give wi. th. *s.*
*Jos.* 14:4 save cities wi. *s.* 21:2
2 *K.* 23:11 took by chamber in *s.*
2 *Chr.* 11:14 Levites left their *s.*
*Ezek.* 27:28 *s.* sh. shake at sound
48:15 place for dwelli. and for *s.*
*See* CITIES.

**SUBVERT, ED, ING.**
*Lam.* 3:36 to *s.* a man L. approv.
*Acts* 15:24 troubled you, *s.* souls
2 *Tim.* 2:14 to the *s.* of hearers
*Tit.* 1:11 who *s.* whole houses
3:11 th. is such is *s.* and sinneth

**SUCCEED, EST.**
*Deut.* 12:29 when thou *s.* 19:1
25:6 first-born *s.* his broth. dead

**SUCCEEDED.**
*Deut.* 2:12 children of Es. *s.* 22
21 Ammonites *s.* them

**SUCCESS.**
*Jos.* 1:8 prosper and have good *s.*

**SUCCOTH.**
*Gen.* 33:17 Jacob journeyed to S. therefore it is called S.
*Ex.* 12:37 jour. fr. Rameses to S.
13:20 journ. fr. S. *Num.* 33:5, 6
*Jos.* 13:27 Gad had in valley S.
*Jud.* 8:5 Gid. said to men of S.
8 Penuel answ. as men of S.
16 he taught men of S.
1 *K.* 7:46 clay-ground between S. and Zarthan, 2 *Cor.* 4:17
*Ps.* 60:6 mete valley of S. 108:7

**SUCCOTH-BENOTH.**
2 *K.* 17:30 men of Bab. made S.

**SUCCOR, ED.**
2 *Sam.* 8:5 Syri. came to *s.* Had.
18:3 better thou *s.* us out of city
21:17 Abishai *s.* him, smote Ph.
2 *Cor.* 6:2 day of salva. I *s.* thee
*Heb.* 2:18 able to *s.* them tempted

**SUCCORER.**
*Rom.* 16:2 she hath been *s.*

**SUCH.**
*Ex.* 34:10 *s.* as ha. not been done
*Rev.* 20:6 on *s.* death ha. no pow.

**SUCH a one.**
*Gen.* 41:38 can we find *s. a one*
*Ruth* 4:1 ho, *s. a one*, turn aside

**SUCH things.**
*Neh.* 6:8 no *s. t.* done as thou say.

**SUCK, Substantive.**
*Gen.* 21:7 Sarah given children *s.*
1 *Sam.* 1:23 Han. gave her son *s.*
1 *K.* 3:21 I rose to give child *s.*
*Lam.* 4:3 sea-monsters give *s.*
*Mat.* 24:19 them that gave *s.* *Mark* 13:17; *Luke* 21:23
*Luke* 23:29 paps that never ga. *s.*

**SUCK, Verb.**
*Deut.* 32:13 made him to *s.* honey
33:19 they shall *s.* of abund. of
*Job* 3:12 or breast I should *s.*?
20:16 he shall *s.* poison of asps
39:30 young ones *s.* up blood
*Is.* 60:16 thou shalt *s.* milk of G. and shalt *s.* breast of kings
66:11 that ye may *s.* and be satis.
12 then shall ye *s.* sh. be borne
*Ezek.* 23:34 thou sh. even *s.* it out
*Joel* 2:16 gath. th. that *s.* breasts

**SUCKED.**
*Cant.* 8:1 *s.* breasts of mother
*Luke* 11:27 blessed are paps th. *s.*

**SUCKING.**
*Num.* 11:12 as fa. beareth *s.* child
1 *Sam.* 7:9 Samuel took a *s.* lamb
*Is.* 11:8 *s.* ch. play on hole of asp
49:15 can a wom. forget *s.* child
*Lam.* 4:4 tongue of *s.* child cleav.

**SUCKLING, S.**
*Deut.* 32:35 *s.* wi. man of gr. hairs
1 *Sam.* 15:3 slay man, inf. and *s.*
22:19 Doeg smo. children and *s.*
*Ps.* 8:2 out of mouth of babes and *s.* *Mat.* 21:16
*Jer.* 44:7 cut off fr. you ch. and *s.*
*Lam.* 2:11 *s.* swoon in streets

**SUDDEN.**
*Job* 22:10 *s.* fear troubleth thee
*Prov.* 3:25 not afraid of *s.* fear
1 *Thes.* 5:3 then *s.* destruct. com.

**SUDDENLY.**
*Num.* 6:9 if any man die *s.*
12:4 the Lord spake *s.* unto Mo.
*Jos.* 10:9 Joshua came *s.* 11:7
2 *Sam.* 15:14 lest he overt. us *s.*
*Job* 5:3 *s.* I cursed his habitat.
9:23 if scourge by day slay *s.*

Ps. 6:10 let them be ashamed s.
64:4 s. do they shoot at him
Prov. 6:15 he shall be broken s.
24:22 their calamity sh. rise s.
29:1 shall s. be destroyed,
Ec. 9:12 it falleth s. upon them
Is. 29:5 it shall be at an inst. s.
47:11 desolation shall come s.
48:3 I did them s. they came
Jer. 6:26 spoiler shall s. come
15:8 have caused him to fall s.
49:19 will s. ma. him run, 50:44
51:8 Babylon is s. destroyed
Hab. 2:7 sh. they not rise up s.
Mal. 3:1 the Lord shall s. come
Mark 13:36 lest com. s. he find
Luke 9:39 and he s. crieth out
Acts 28:6 fallen down dead s.
1 Tim. 5:22 lay hands s. on no m.

**SUE.**

Mat. 5:40 if any man s. thee

**SUFFER.**

Ex. 22:18 sh. not s. witch to live
Lev. 19:17 not s. sin upon him
22:16 or s. th. to bear iniquity
Num. 21:23 Sih. would not s. Is.
Jos. 10:19 s. not to enter cities
Jud. 1:34 not s. th. to come down
15:1 her fath. would not s. him.
1 K. 15:17 that might not s. any
Est. 3:8 not king's profit to s.
Job 9:18 not s. me to take breath
21:3 s. me that I may speak
36:2 s. me a little, I will show
Ps. 9:13 consider trouble I s. of
55:22 nev. s. right. to be moved
88:15 while I s. terrors, I am
89:33 nor will I s. faithful. fail
101:5 proud heart, will not I s.
121:3 not s. foot to be moved
Prov. 10:3 L. not s. righte. fam.
19:15 idle soul shall s. hunger
19 man of wrath sh. s. punish.
Ec. 5:6 s. not mouth to cause
12 abund. of rich not s. to sleep
Ezek. 44:20 nor s. locks to grow
Mat. 3:15 Jesus said, s. it to be
8:21 s. me to bury, Luke 9:59
16:21 he must s. many things
17:12; Mark 8:31; 9:12; Lu. 9:22; 17:25
17:17 how long shall I s. you? Mark 9:19; Luke 9:41
19:14 s. little children, Mark 10:14; Luke 18:16
23:13 neither s. ye them th. are
Mark 7:12 s. him no more to do
11:16 Je. would not s. any man
Luke 22:51 s. ye thus far,
24:46 it behooved Christ to s. Acts 3:18; 26:23
Acts 3:18 G. showed Ch. should s.
5:41 counted worthy to s. shame
7:24 seeing one s. wrong
9:16 must s. for my name's sake
21:39 s. me to speak to people
Rom. 8:17 if so be we s. wi. him
1 Cor. 3:15 if work be burnt sh. s.
9:12 used power but s. all thi.
10:13 will not s. to be tempted
12:26 if one mem. s. all mem. s.
2 Cor. 1:6 same suffer, wh. we s.
11:20 ye s. if a man bring you
Gal. 6:12 lest they sh. s. persec.
Phil. 1:29 given to believe and s.
1 Thes. 3:4 told you, we should s.
2 Thes. 1:5 kingd. of G. for wh. s.
1 Tim. 4:10 we both labor and s.
2 Tim. 1:12 for wh. cause I also s.
2:9 wherein I s. as an evil doer
12 if we s. we shall also reign
Heb. 11:25 choosing to s. afflicti.
13:22 s. the word of exhortation
1 Pet. 2:20 if ye do well, and s.
3:14 if ye s. for righteousn. sake
17 it is bet. ye s. for well-doing
4:15 let none s. as a murderer
16 if any man s. as a Christian
19 let them that s. according to
Rev. 2:10 those things thou sh. s.
11:9 not s. dead bodies to be put

**SUFFERED.**

Gen. 20:6 therefore s. I thee not
31:7 God s. him not to hurt me
Deut. 8:3 he s. thee to hunger.
18:14 G. ha. not s. thee so to do
Jud. 3:28 s. not a man to pass
1 Sam. 24:7 D. s. them not to rise
1 Chr. 16:21 he s. no man to do them wrong, Ps. 105:14
Job 31:30 neither have I s. mouth
Jer. 15:15 for thy sake I s. rebuke
Mat. 3:15 suf. it to be so, he s.
24:43 nor s. his hou. Lu. 12:39
27:19 I have s. many things this
Mark 1:34 he s. not dev. Lu. 4:41
5:19 Jesus s. him not, but said
26 s. many things of physici.
Luke 8:32 s. them to enter swine
51 he s. no man to go in,
13:2 because they s. such things
24:26 ought not Ch. to have s.?
Acts 13:18 about 40 years s. he
14:16 who s. all nations to walk
16:7 but the Spirit s. them not
19:30 discip. s. him not to enter
28:16 P. was s. to dwell by hims.
2 Cor. 7:12 not for his cau. th. s.
Gal. 3:4 have ye s. th. in vain?
Phil. 3:8 for whom I s. loss of all
1 Thes. 2:2 after that we had s.
14 have s. like things of your
Heb. 2:18 hath s. being tempted
5:8 learn. obed. by things he s.
7:23 they were not s. to continue
9:26 then must he often have s.
13:12 Jesus s. without the gate
1 Pet. 2:21 Christ s. for us, leav.
23 when he s. he threaten. not
3:18 Christ hath once s. for sins
4:1 Christ hath s. for us in flesh, he that hath s. in the flesh
5:10 after ye have s. a while

**SUFFEREST.**

Rev. 2:20 bec. thou s. that wom.

**SUFFERETH.**

Ps. 66:9 bless G. who s. not our
107:38 s. not cattle to decrease
Acts 28:4 vengeance s. him not
1 Cor. 13:4 charity s. long, is kind

**SUFFERING.**

Acts 27:7 wind not s. us, we sail.
Jas. 5:10 an exam. of s. affliction
1 Pet. 2:19 if a man end. grief, s.
Jude 7 example, s. vengeance of

**SUFFERING.**

Heb. 2:9 for s. of death, crown.

**SUFFERINGS.**

Rom. 8:18 I reckon that the s of
2 Cor. 1:5 for as the s. of Christ
2 Cor. 1:6 endur. same s. wh. we
7 ye are partakers of the s.
Phil. 3:10 fellowship of his s.
Col. 1:24 who now rejo. in my s.
Heb. 2:10 Captain perfect thro' s.
1 Pet. 1:11 it testified the s. of Ch.
4:13 ye are partakers of Ch.'s s.
5:1 I am a witn. of the s. of Ch.

**SUFFICE.**

Num. 11:22 sh. herds be sl. to s.?
Deut. 3:26 let it s. thee, speak no
1 K. 20:10 if dust of Samar. sh. s.
Ezek. 44:6 let it s. you of all, 45:9
1 Pet. 4:3 for the time past may s.

**SUFFICED, ETH.**

Jud. 21:14 wives, so they s. not
Ruth 2:14 she did eat, and was s.
18 gave her, after she was s.
John 14:8 L. show Fath. it s. us

**SUFFICIENCY.**

Job 20:22 in fulness of his s.
2 Cor. 3:5 but our s. is of God
9:8 s. in all thi. ye may abound

**SUFFICIENT.**

Ex. 36:7 the stuff th. had was s.
Deut. 15:8 thou shalt lend him s.
33:7 let his hand be s. for him
Prov. 25:16 so much honey as s.
Is. 40:16 Leban. is not s. to burn
Mat. 6:34 s. to the day is the evil
Luke 14:28 whether he have s.
John 6:7 200 pennyworth is not s.
2 Cor. 2:6 s. to such a man is this
16 who is s. for these things?
3:5 not that we are s. of oursel.
12:9 he said, My grace is s.

**SUFFICIENTLY.**

Is. 23:18 bef. the Lord to eat s.

**SUIT, S.**

Jud. 17:10 I will give thee a s.
2 Sam. 15:4 man who ha. any s.
Job 11:19 many sh. make s. unto
Is. 3:22 changeable s. of apparel

**SUM, Substantive.**

Ex. 21:30 if laid on him a s. of
38:21 this is the s. of tabernacle
Num. 1:2 take s. of congre. 26:2
26:4 take the s. of the people
31:26 take the s. of the prey
2 Sam. 24:9 Joab gave up s. to king, 1 Chr. 21:5
Est. 4:7 the s. of money Haman
Ps. 139:17 great is the s. of th.
Ezek. 28:12 thou sealest up the s.
Dan. 7:1 Daniel told s. of dream
Acts 7:16 Abraham bought for s.
22:28 with a great s. obtained I
Heb. 8:1 of the things th. is the s.

**SUM.**

2 K. 22:4 that he may s. the silver

**SUMMER.**

Gen. 8:22 s. and winter, day and
Ps. 32:4 turned into drought of s.
74:17 thou hast made s. and
Prov. 6:8 provid. meat in s. 30:25
10:5 gathereth in s. is wise son
26:1 snow in s. rain in harvest
Is. 28:4 as hasty fruit before s.
Jer. 8:20 harv. is past, s. is end.
Dan. 2:35 chaff of s. threshing-fl.
Zec. 14:8 in s. and winter
Mat. 24:32 ye kn. that s. is nigh, Mark 13:28; Luke 21:30

**SUMMER chamber.**

Jud. 3:24 he cov. his feet in s. c.

**SUMMER fruit.**

2 Sam. 16:2 s. f. for young men
Amos 8:1 a basket of s. fruit, 2

**SUMMER fruits.**

2 Sam. 17:1 bro. 100 bun. of s. f.
Is. 16:9 shouting for s. fruits
Jer. 40:10 ga. wine and s. f. 12
48:32 spoiler is fallen on s. f.
Mic. 7:1 as wh. they gather s. f.

**SUMMER-HOUSE.**

Amos 3:15 smite winter-ho. s.-h.

**SUMMER parlor.**

Jud. 3:20 Eg. was sitting in s. p.

**SUMMER.**

Is. 18:6 fowls sh. s. upon them

**SUMPTUOUSLY.**

Luke 16:19 rich man fared s.

**SUN.**

Gen. 15:17 when s. went down
19:23 s. risen when Lot entered
28:11 Jacob tarried, bec. s. set
32:31 as he passed Pen. s. rose
37:9 s. moon, stars, made obeis.
Ex. 16:21 when s. waxed hot
22:3 if s. be risen, blood be shed
Lev. 22:7 when s. is down, he shall be clean, Deut. 23:11
Num. 25:4 hang them ag. the s.
Deut. 4:19 lest wh. thou seest s.

17:3 hath worshipped either *s.*
24:15 nor sh. *s.* go down upon it
33:14 precious fruits brou. by *s.*
*Jos.* 1:4 tow. going down of *s.*
10:12 *s.* stand still upon Gibeon
13 *s.* stood still, moon stayed
*Jud.* 5:31 that love him be as *s.*
8:13 G. return. before *s.* was up
9:33 soon as *s.* is up, rise early
14:18 said, before *s.* went down
19:14 *s.* went down, they were
1 *Sam.* 11:9 *s.* be hot have help
2 *Sam.* 3:35 aught till *s.* be down
12:11 lie with wives in si. of *s.*
12 I will do this bef. Is. and *s.*
23:4 light of morn. when *s.* ris.
2 *K.* 3:22 and *s.* shone on water
23:5 them that burn ince. to *s.*
11 burnt chari. of *s.* with fire
*Neh.* 7:3 gates be ope. till *s.* hot
*Job* 8:16 hypocrite green bef. *s.*
9:7 commandeth *s.* riseth not
30:28 I went mourn. without *s.*
31:26 if I beheld *s.* when it shi.
*Ps.* 19:4 set a tabernacle for *s.*
58:8 pass aw. th. they see not *s.*
72:5 fear thee as long as *s.* end.
17 name contin. as long as *s.*
74:16 prepared light and *s.*
84:11 L. God is a *s.* and shield
89:36 his throne sh. endure as *s.*
104:22 *s.* aris. they gath. thems.
121:6 *s.* shall not smite by day
136:8 him that made *s.* to rule
148:3 praise him, *s.* and moon
*Ec.* 1:5 *s.* riseth, *s.* goeth down
6:5 moreo. he hath not seen *s.*
11:7 pleas. for eyes to behold *s.*
12:2 wh. *s.* or stars be not dark.
*Cant.* 1:6 bec. *s.* looked on me
6:10 fair as moon, clear as *s.*
*Is.* 24:23 then *s.* sh. be ashamed
30:26 light of moon as *s.* light
49:10 nor heat nor *s.* smite th.
60:19 *s.* be no more li. by day
20 *s.* shall no more go down
*Jer.* 15:9 *s.* down while yet day
31:35 wh. giveth the *s.* for light
*Ezek.* 8:16 they worshipp. the *s.*
32:7 I will cover *s.* with cloud
*Joel* 2:10 *s.* be dark. 3:15; *Mat.* 24:29; *Mark* 13:24; *Luke* 23:45
31 *s.* sh. be turned to darkness
*Amos* 8:9 cause *s.* to go down
*Jon.* 4:8 wh. *s.* did arise, *s.* beat
*Mic.* 3:6 *s.* go down over proph.
*Nah.* 3:17 when *s.* aris. they flee
*Hab.* 3:11 *s.* and moon stood still
*Mal.* 4:2 to you *s.* of right. arise
*Mat.* 5:45 maketh his *s.* to rise
13:43 then sh. right. shine as *s.*
17:2 his face did shine as the *s.* *Rev.* 1:16; 10:1
*Mark* 1:32 *s.* set, they bro. sick
*Luke* 4:40 when *s.* was setting
21:25 there shall be signs in *s.*
*Acts* 2:20 the *s* into darkness
13:11 not seeing *s.* for a season
26:13 light above brightn. of *s.*
27:20 nei. *s.* nor stars appeared
1 *Cor.* 15:41 th. is one glory of *s.*
*Eph.* 4:26 let not *s.* go down
*Jam.* 1:11 *s.* is no sooner risen
*Rev.* 6:12 *s.* became as sackcloth
7:16 nor shall *s.* light on them
8:12 third part of *s.* was smit.
9:2 *s.* and the air were darken.
12:1 appeared wom. clo. with *s.*
16:8 angel poured out vial on *s.*
19:17 I saw angel standing on *s.*
21:23 city had no need of *s.* 22:5

*See* GOETH, GOING, RISING.

**Under the SUN.**

*Ec.* 1:3 what profit *under the s.?* 2:18, 19, 20, 22; 5:18; 9:9
9 there is no new thing *u. t. s.*
14 I have seen all works done *u. t. s.* 2:17: 4:3; 8:17; 9:3
2:11 there was no profit *u. t. s.*
3:16 I saw *u. t. s.* place of judg.
4:7 returned, I saw vanity *u. s.*
5:13 evil I seen *u. t. s.* 6:1; 10:5
6:12 tell what shall be *u. the s.*
8:9 ap. heart to every work *u. s.*
15 hath no better thing *u. t. s.*
9:6 portion in any thing *u. t. s.*
9 days he hath given th. *u. t. s.*
11 I saw *u. t. s.* race not to sw.
13 wisdom have I seen *u. t. s.*

**SUNDER.**

*Ps.* 46:9 cutteth the spear in *s.*
107:14 he brake their bands in *s.*
16 he hath cut bars of iron in *s.*
*Is.* 27:9 chalk stones beaten in *s.*
*Is.* 45:2 I will cut in *s.* bars of ir.
*Nah.* 1:13 I will burst bonds in *s.*
*Luke* 12:46 and cut him in *s.*

**SUNDERED.**

*Job* 41:17 stick, they cannot be *s.*

**SUNDRY.**

*Heb.* 1:1 God who at *s.* times

**SUNG.**

*Ezr.* 3:11 *s.* together by course
*Is.* 26:1 this song be *s.* in Judah
*Mat.* 26:30 *s.* hymn, *Mark* 14:26
*Rev.* 5:9 they *s.* a new song
14:3 *s.* as it were a new song

**SUNK.**

1 *Sam.* 17:49 stone *s.* into foreh.
2 *K.* 9:24 Jehoram *s.* in chariot
*Ps.* 9:15 heath. are *s.* in the pit
*Jer.* 38:6 down, so Jer. *s.* in mire
22 thy feet are *s.* in the mire
*Lam.* 2:9 her gates are *s.* in gro.
*Acts* 20:9 Eutychus *s.* down with

**SUP, PED.**

*Hab.* 1:9 their faces shall *s.* up
*Luke* 17:8 make ready, I may *s.*
1 *Cor.* 11:25 took cup, when he *s.*
*Rev.* 3:20 I will *s.* with him, he

**SUPERFLUITY.**

*Jam.* 1:21 filthiness *s.* of naugh.

**SUPERFLUOUS.**

*Lev.* 21:18 man hath any thing *s.*
22:23 lamb, th. hath any thi. *s.*
2 *Cor.* 9:1 it is *s.* to write to you

**SUPERSCRIPTION.**

*Mat.* 22:20 wh. is image and *s.?* *Mark* 12:16; *Luke* 20:24
*Mark* 15:26 *s.* of accu. *Luke* 23:38

**SUPERSTITION.**

*Acts* 25:19 questi. ag. him of *s.*

**SUPERSTITIOUS.**

*Acts* 17:22 in all thi. ye are too *s.*

**SUPPER.**

*Mark* 6:21 Herod made *s.* to lords
*Luke* 14:12 makest a dinner or *s.*
16 a cert. man made a great *s.*
24 none bid. shall taste of my *s.*
22:20 likewise also cup after *s.*
*John* 12:2 there they made Je. *s.*
13:2 *s.* ended; 3 Je. ris. from *s.*
21:20 disc. lean. on breast at *s.*
1 *Cor.* 11:20 not to eat Lord's *s.*
21 taketh bef. other his own *s.*
*Rev.* 19:9 that are called to the *s.*
17 come to *s.* of the great God

**SUPPLANT, ED.**

*Gen.* 27:36 hath *s.* me two times
*Jer.* 9:4 every bro. will utterly *s.*

**SUPPLE.**

*Ezek.* 16:4 nei. washed to *s.* thee

**SUPPLIANTS.**

*Zep.* 3:10 my *s.* shall bring offer.

**SUPPLICATION.**

1 *Sam.* 13:12 I have not made *s.*
1 *K.* 8:28 respect to *s.* 2 *Chr.* 6:19
30 hearken thou to the *s.* 45, 49
52 eyes open to *s.* of thy serv.
54 made end of praying and *s.*
59 words wherewith I made *s.*
9:3 I heard thy *s.* th. hast made
2 *Chr.* 6:29 what *s.* shall be made
33:13 Lord heard Manasseh's *s.*
*Est.* 4:8 make *s.* for her people
*Job* 8:5 wouldest make *s.* to Al.
9:15 I wo. make my *s.* to judge
*Ps.* 6:9 Lord hath heard my *s.*
30:8 unto L. I made my *s.* 142:1
55:1 hide not thyself from my *s.*
119:170 let my *s.* come bef. thee
*Is.* 45:14 they sh. make *s.* to thee
*Jer.* 36:7 th. will present their *s.*
37:20 let my *s.* be accepted bef.
38:26 present. my *s.* bef. king
42:2 let our *s.* be accepted bef.
9 ye sent me to present your *s.*
*Dan.* 6:11 men and D. making *s.*
9:20 I was present. *s.* before G.
*Hos.* 12:4 and made *s.* to him
*Acts* 1:14 accord in prayer and *s.*
*Eph.* 6:18 with all prayer and *s.*
*Phil.* 4:6 but in every thing by *s.*

**SUPPLICATIONS.**

2 *Chr.* 6:21 hearken to *s.* of serv.
39 hear th. their prayer and *s.*
*Job* 41:3 will leviathan make *s.?*
*Ps.* 28:2 voice of my *s.* 140:6
6 he heard my *s.* 31:22; 116:1
86:6 attend to the voice of my *s.*
130:2 be attent. to my *s.* 143:1
*Jer.* 3:21 weeping and *s.* of Isr.
31:9 with *s.* will I lead them
*Dan.* 9:3 I set face to seek by *s.*
17 hear prayer of serv. and *s.*
18 we do not pres. *s.* for right.
*Dan.* 9:23 begin. of *s.* com. came
*Zec.* 12:10 pour out Spirit of *s.*
1 *Tim.* 2:1 *s.* be made for all men
5:5 continueth in *s.* and prayer
*Heb.* 5:7 he offered prayers and *s.*

**SUPPLY, Substantive.**

2 *Cor.* 8:14 abund. may be a *s.*
*Phil.* 1:19 through prayer and *s.*

**SUPPLY, Verb.**

*Phil.* 2:30 not regard. to *s.* lack
4:19 God shall *s.* all your need

**SUPPLIED, ETH.**

1 *Cor.* 16:17 what lack. they *s.*
2 *Cor.* 9:12 not only *s.* want of
11:9 what lacking, brethren *s.*
*Eph.* 4:16 that wh. every joint *s.*

**SUPPORT.**

*Acts* 20:35 ought to *s.* the weak, 1 *Thes.* 5:14

**SUPPOSE.**

2 *Sam.* 13:32 let not my lord *s.*
*Luke* 7:43 I *s.* that he to whom
12:51 *s.* I am co. to give peace
13:2 *s.* ye these Galileans were
*John* 21:25 I *s.* world could not
1 *Cor.* 7:26 I *s.* that this is good
2 *Cor.* 11:5 I *s.* I was not behind
1 *Pet.* 5:12 a faithful bro. as I *s.*

**SUPPOSED.**

*Mat.* 20:10 they *s.* they sho. have
*Mark* 6:49 *s.* it had been a spirit
*Luke* 3:23 Je. as was *s.* son of J.
*Acts* 7:25 *s.* his brethren would
25:18 none accus. of thi. as I *s.*
*Phil.* 2:25 I *s.* it neces. to send

**SUPPOSING.**

*Luke* 2:44 *s.* him to have been
*Acts* 14:19 drew P. out, *s.* he had
16:27 jailer *s.* prisoners had fled
27:13 *s.* they had obt. purpose
*Phil.* 1:16 *s.* to add affliction
1 *Tim.* 6:5 corrupt minds *s.* gain

**SUPREME.**

1 *Pet.* 2:13 whether to king as *s.*

**SURE.**

*Ex.* 3:19 I am *s.* king will not

Num. 32:23 be s. sin will find
1 Sam. 2:35 build a s. house
2 Sam. 23:5 cove. ordered and s.
1 K. 11:38 I build thee a s. house
Job 24:22 no man is s. of life
Ps. 111:7 his commandm. are s.
Prov. 6:3 make s. thy friend
Is. 33:16 bread given, waters s.
55:3 s. mercies of D. Acts 13:34
John 6:69 are s. thou art Christ
16:30 are we s. thou knowest
Rom. 15:29 I am s. when I come

**SURELY.**

Ec. 8:12 s. it sh. be well with th.
Is. 45:14 s. G. is in th. and there
Mat. 26:73 s. thou art one of th. Mark 14:70
Rev. 22:20 s. I come quickly
See DIE.

**SURELY be put to death.**

Gen. 26:11 man, s. be put to d.
Ex. 19:12 tou. mount, s. p. to d.
21:12 killeth, sh. s. be put to d.
15 smiteth fa. sh. s. be put to d.
16 steal. a man, sh. s. be p. to d.
17 curseth his father, shall s. be put to death, Lev. 20:9
22:19 lieth with beast, sh. s. be put to death, Lev. 20:15, 16
31:14 defileth sab. s. p. to d. 15
Lev. 20:2 giveth to M. s. p. to d.
10 adulteress sh. s. be put to d.
11 lieth wi. fa. wife, bo..s. p. d.
12 daughter-in-l. both s. p. to d.
13 lie wi. mank. bo. s. p. to d.
24:16 blasphem. sh. s. be p. to d.
17 killeth man, sh. s. be put to d. Num. 35:16, 17, 18, 21, 31
27:29 but shall s. be put to death
Jud. 21:5 ca. not, s. be put to d.
Jer. 38:15 w. not s. p. me to d.?

**SURETY.**

Gen. 43:9 I will be s. for him
44:32 thy serv. bec. s. for lad
Job 17:3 put me in a s. with th.
Ps. 119:122 be s. for thy serv.
Prov. 6:1 if thou be s. for friend
11:15 he that is s. for stranger
17:18 becometh s. in presence
20:16 s. for stranger, 27:13
Heb. 7:22 Je. made s. of a better

**SURETIES.**

Prov. 22:26 not of th. that are s.

**Of a SURETY.**

Gen. 15:13 know of a s. thy seed
18:13 sh. I of a s. bear a child?
Gen. 26:9 of a s. she is thy wife
Acts 12:11 of a s. Lord sent ang.

**SURETYSHIP.**

Prov. 11:15 he that hateth s.

**SURFEITING.**

Luke 21:34 overcharged with s.

**SURMISINGS.**

1 Tim. 6:4 whereof com. evil s.

**SURNAME, Substantive.**

Mat. 10:3 Lebbeus, s. was Thad.
Acts 10:5 Sim. s. is P. 32; 11:13
12:12 John, s. was M. 25; 15:37

**SURNAME, Verb.**

Is. 44:5 s. hims. by name of Isr.

**SURNAMED.**

Is. 45:4 s. thee, tho' not kn. me
Mark 3:16 Si. he s. P. Acts 10:18
17 he s. th. Boanerges, sons of
Acts 1:23 Barsabas, who was s. J.
4:36 by apostles was s. Barnab.

**SURPRISED.**

Is. 33:14 fearfuln. s. hypocrites
Jer. 48:41 the strong-holds are s.
51:41 how is praise of earth s.!

**SUSANNA.**

Luke 8:3 Joanna and S. minist.

**SUSTAIN, ED.**

Gen. 27:37 wi. corn and wi. I s.
1 K. 17:9 comman. a widow to s.
Neh. 9:21 forty years didst s. th.
Ps. 3:5 I awaked, the Lord s. me
55:22 burden on L. he sh. s. th.
Prov. 18:14 spirit of man will s.
Is. 59:16 his righteous. it s. him

**SUSTENANCE.**

Jud. 6:4 Midian. left no s. for Is.
2 Sam. 19:32 Barzillai provid. s.
Acts 7:11 our fathers found no s.

**SWADDLED.**

Lam. 2:22 tho. I s. hath my ene.
Ezek. 16:4 not salt. not s. at all

**SWADDLING.**

Job 38:9 I made darkn. a s. band
Luke 2:7 wrap. him in s. clo. 12

**SWALLOW.**

Ps. 84:3 the s. hath found a nest
Prov. 26:2 as s. by flying, so the
Is. 38:14 like a crane or a s. did I
Jer. 8:7 crane and s. observe ti.

**SWALLOW, Verb.**

Num. 16:30 if earth open and s.
34 lest the earth s. us up also
2 Sam. 20:19 why wilt thou s. up
20 that I should s. up or destr.
Job 7:19 alone till I s. my spittle
20:18 shall restore, and not s. it
Ps. 21:9 the L. shall s. them up
56:1 O G. man would s. me up
2 mine ene. would s. me up
57:3 repr. of him that would s.
69:15 nei. let the deep s. me up
Prov. 1:12 let us s. them up alive
Ec. 10:12 lips of fool s. up hims.
Is. 25:8 will s. up death in vict.
Hos. 8:7 strangers shall s. it up
Amos 8:4 ye that s. needy
Ob. 16 and they shall s. down
Jon. 1:17 Lord prep. a fish to s.
Mat. 23:24 stra. at gnat, s. camel

**SWALLOWED.**

Ex. 7:12 Aaron's rod s. th. rods
15:12 stretch. thy hand, earth s.
Num. 16:32 earth opened and s. 26:10; Deut. 11:6
2 Sam. 17:16 lest king be s. up
Job 6:3 theref. my words are s.
20:15 he hath s. down riches
37:20 if speak, he sh. be s. up
Ps. 35:25 not say, we s. him up
106:17 the earth s. up Dathan
124:3 they had s. us up quick
Is. 28:7 priest and prophet are s.
49:19 they that s. thee up, shall
Jer. 51:34 s. me up like a dragon
44 br. out mouth that he ha. s.
Lam. 2:2 Lord hath s. up inhab.
5 he hath s. up Israel, hath s.
16 they say, We have s. her up
Ezek. 36:3 they have s. you up
Hos. 8:8 Israel is s. up am. Gent.
1 Cor. 15:54 death is s. up in vic.
2 Cor. 2:7 lest such a one be s. up
5:4 that mortal. might be s. up
Rev. 12:16 earth s. up the flood

**SWALLOWETH.**

Job 5:5 robber s. their substance
39:24 he s. ground with fiercen.

**SWAN.**

Lev. 11:18 s. uncl. Deut. 14:16

**SWARE.**

Gen. 21:31 because th. s. both of
24:7 L. God of heaven s. to me
Gen. 24:9 servant s. to him conc.
25:33 Ja. said, Sw. to me, he s.
26:3 oath which I s. to Abrah.
31 Abimel. and Isaac s. to one
31:53 Jacob s. by fear of Isaac
47:31 Jos. s. to Jacob his father
50:24 G. will br. to land he s. to
Ex. 13:5 land the Lord s. to thy fathers, 11; 33:1; Num. 14:16, 30; 32:11; Deut. 1:8, 35; 6:10, 18, 23; 7:13; 8:1; 11:9, 21; 26:3; 28:11; 30:20; 31:21, 23; 34:4; Jos. 1:6; 5:6; 21:43
Num. 32:10 L.'s anger was kind. and he s. Deut. 1:34
Deut. 2:14 were wasted, as L. s.
4:21 Lord s. that I should not
31 not forget the coven. he s.
7:12 wh. he s. to thy salvation
8:18 covenant which he s. 9:5
Jos. 6:22 br. out Rahab as ye s.
9:15 princes s. to Gibeonites
20 because of oath we s. to th.
14:9 M. s. on that day, saying
21:44 according to all that he s.
Jud. 2:1 bro. to land which I s.
1 Sam. 19:6 Saul s. Da. shall not
24:22 David s. to Saul
2 Sam. 3:35 Da. s. he would not
19:23 D. s. to Shimei, 1 K. 2:8
1 K. 2:23 S. s. to A. he sho. die
2 K. 25:24 Gedaliah s. Jer. 40:9
2 Chr. 15:14 they s. to the Lord
Ezr. 10:5 they s. to put away
Ps. 95:11 I s. in wrath, Heb. 3:11
132:2 how he s. to L. and vowed
Jer. 38:16 king s. secretly to Jer.
Ezek. 16:8 I s. and entered cove.
Dan. 12:7 s. by him, Rev. 10:6
Mark 6:23 Herod s. to daughter
Luke 1:73 oath which he s. to A.
Heb. 3:18 to whom s. he that th.
6:13 no greater, he s. by himself
7:21 Lord s. and will not repent
See Their FATHERS.

**SWAREST.**

Ex. 32:13 to whom thou s. by
Num. 11:12 carry them to land s.
Deut. 26:15 as thou s. to our fat.
1 K. 1:17 thou s. that Solomon
Ps. 89:49 kindnesses th. s. to D.

**SWARM, S.**

Ex. 8:21 I will send s. of flies
22 no s. of flies shall be in Go.
24 there came a grie. s. of flies
29 that s. of flies may depart
Jud. 14:8 a s. of bees and honey

**SWEAR.**

Gen. 21:23 Abim. said to Abr. s.
24 and Abraham said, I will s.
24:3 I will make thee s. by L.
37 my master made me s.
25:33 Jacob said, s. to me
47:31 Jacob said to Joseph, s.
50:5 father made me s. saying
Ex. 6:8 land concerning wh. I s.
Lev. 5:4 if a soul s. pronouncing
19:12 ye shall not s. by name
Num. 30:2 if a man s. to bind
Deut. 6:13 s. by his name, 10:20
Jos. 2:12 Rahab said to spies, s.
23:7 nor cause to s. by th. gods
Jud. 15:12 s. ye will not fall
1 Sam. 20:17 Jon. caused D. to s.
24:21 s. th. wilt not cut off seed
30:15 s. thou wilt nei. kill me
2 Sam. 19:7 s. by L. if th. go not
1 K. 1:13 didst th. s. S. sh. reign
51 let Solo. s. unto me to-day
2:42 did I not ma. thee s. by L.?
8:31 oath laid on him to cause him to s. 2 Chr. 6:22
2 Chr. 36:13 Nebuc. made him s.
Ezr. 10:5 Ezra, Lev. and Isr. s.
Neh. 13:25 I made them s. by G.
Is. 3:7 in that day shall he s.
19:18 five cities in Egypt sh. s.
45:23 to me ev. tongue shall s.
48:1 wh. s. by L. not in truth
65:16 that swear. shall s. by G.
Jer. 4:2 thou shalt s. Lord liveth
5:2 Lord liveth, they s. falsely
7:9 murder, commit adultery, s.

12:16 *s.* by my name, as peo. *s.*
22:5 I *s.* saith Lord, this house
32:22 giv. them land th. didst *s.*
*Hos.* 4:15 not go to Beth-a. nor *s.*
*Amos* 8:14 *s.* by sin of Samaria
*Zep.* 1:5 that *s.* by L. *s.* by Mal.
*Mat.* 5:34 *s.* not: 36 *s.* not by h.
23:16 *s.* by temple, *s.* by gold
18 whoso shall *s.* by altar
20 whoso theref. sh. *s.* by altar
21 *s.* by temple; 22 *s.* by heav.
26:74 be. to curse, *s.* *Mark* 14:71
*Heb.* 6:13 *s.* by no greater, he *s.*
*Heb.* 6:16 men verily *s.* by the gr.
*Jam.* 5:12 my brethren *s.* not

**SWEARERS.**

*Mal.* 3:5 a swift witness ag. *s.*

**SWEARETH.**

*Lev.* 6:3 was lost, and *s.* falsely
*Ps.* 15:4 that *s.* to his hurt
63:11 every one that *s.* by him
*Ec.* 9:2 he that *s.* as he feareth
*Is.* 65:16 he that *s.* swear by G.
*Zec.* 5:3 every one that *s.* cut off
4 enter house of him that *s.*
*Mat.* 23:18 whosoever *s.* by gift
20 *s.* by altar; 21 *s.* by temple
22 *s.* by throne of God

**SWEARING.**

*Lev.* 5:1 soul sin, hear voice of *s.*
*Jer.* 23:10 bec. of *s.* land mourn.
*Hos.* 4:2 by *s.* lying, and steal.
10:4 *s.* falsely in making coven.

**SWEAT.**

*Gen.* 3:19 in *s.* of face eat bread
*Ezek.* 44:18 any thing causeth *s.*
*Luke* 22:44 *s.* as drops of blood

**SWEEP.**

*Is.* 14:23 *s.* it wi. besom of dest.
28:17 hail sh. *s.* refuge of lies
*Luke* 15:8 doth not *s.* house

**SWEEPING.**

*Prov.* 28:3 is like *s.* rain which

**SWEET.**

*Ex.* 15:25 tree into wat. made *s.*
30:23 *s.* cinna. and *s.* calamus
2 *Sam.* 23:1 D. *s.* psalmist of Isr.
*Neh.* 8:10 eat fat, drink the *s.*
*Job* 20:12 wickedness *s.* in mouth
21:33 clods of valley shall be *s.*
38:31 bind *s.* influ. of Pleiades?
*Ps.* 55:14 we took *s.* counsel
104:34 medita. of him sh. be *s.*
119:103 *s.* thy words to taste
141:6 hear my words, they are *s.*
*Prov.* 3:24 thy sleep shall be *s.*
9:17 stolen waters are *s.* bread
13:19 desire accomplished is *s.*
16:24 pleasant words are *s.*
20:17 bread of dec. *s.* to a man
23:8 and lose thy *s.* words
24:13 eat honey-comb wh. is *s.*
27:7 to hun. soul bitter thing *s.*
*Ec.* 5:12 sleep of laboring man *s.*
11:7 truly light is *s.* a pl. thing
*Cant.* 2:3 fruit *s.* 14 *s.* is voice
5:5 fingers drop. with *s.* myrrh
13 as *s.* flowers, drop. *s.* myrrh
16 his mouth is most *s.* lovely
*Is.* 3:24 inst. of *s.* smell, stink
5:20 that put bitter for *s.* and *s.*
23:16 make *s.* melody, si. songs
*Jer.* 6:20 nor your sacri. *s.* to me
31:26 my sleep was *s.* to me
*Jam.* 3:11 pl. *s.* water and bitter?
*Rev.* 10:9 in mouth *s.* as hon. 10

*See* INCENSE, ODORS, SAVOR.

**SWEET cane.**

*Is.* 43:24 thou brou. me no *s. c.*
*Jer.* 6:20 *s. c.* came fr. a far coun.

**SWEET spices.**

*Ex.* 30:34 take *s. s.* frankincense
37:29 he made pure inc. of *s. s.*
*Mark* 16:1 brou. *s. s.* anoint him

**SWEET wine.**

*Is.* 49:26 drun. wi. blood as *s. w.*
*Amos* 9:13 moun. shall drop *s. w.*
*Mic.* 6:15 *s. w.* not drink wine

**SWEETER.**

*Jud.* 14:18 what is *s.* th. honey?
*Ps.* 19:12 thy word *s.* th. honey
119:103 words *s.* than honey

**SWEETLY.**

*Job* 24:20 worms shall feed *s.*
*Cant.* 7:9 best wi. goeth down *s.*

**SWEETNESS.**

*Jud.* 9:11 sho. I forsake my *s.*?
14:14 out of strong came forth *s.*
*Prov.* 16:21 *s.* of lips incr. learn.
27:9 so doth *s.* of a man's friend
*Ezek.* 3:3 in mouth as hon. for *s.*

**SWELL, ED.**

*Num.* 5:21 th. rot, belly to *s.* 22
27 belly shall *s.* thigh shall rot
*Deut.* 8:4 nor thy foot *s.* 40 years
*Neh.* 9:21 forty years feet *s.* not

**SWELLING, S.**

*Ps.* 46:3 tho' mount. shake wi. *s.*
*Is.* 30:13 as a breach *s.* in a wall
*Jer.* 12:5 how do in *s.* of Jordan?
49:19 lion from *s.* of Jord. 50:44
2 *Cor.* 12:20 lest there be *s.* tum.
2 *Pet.* 2:18 speak *s.* words of van.
*Jude* 16 their mouth speaketh *s.* words

**SWEPT.**

*Jud.* 5:21 riv. of Kishon *s.* them
*Jer.* 46:15 why valiant *s.* away?
*Mat.* 12:44 find. it *s.* *Luke* 11:25

**SWERVED.**

1 *Tim.* 1:6 having *s.* turned aside

**SWIFT.**

*Deut.* 28:49 nation *s.* as eagle
1 *Chr.* 12:8 *s.* as roes on mount.
*Job* 9:26 passed away as *s.* ships
24:18 he is *s.* as waters, behold.
*Prov.* 6:18 feet *s.* run. to mischi.
*Ec.* 9:11 the race is not to *s.*
*Is.* 18:2 go, ye *s.* messengers
19:1 behold, L. rid. on *s.* cloud
30:16 ride on *s.* th. pursue be *s.*
66:20 bring brethr. on *s.* beasts
*Jer.* 46:6 let not *s.* flee away, nor
*Amos* 2:14 flight sh. perish fr. *s.*
15 *s.* of foot sh. not deli. hims.
*Mic.* 1:13 bind chariot to *s.* beast
*Mal.* 3:5 a *s.* witn. ag. sorcerers
*Rom.* 3:15 feet *s.* to shed blood
*Jam.* 1:19 let every man be *s.*
2 *Pet.* 2:1 sh. bring *s.* destruction

**SWIFTER.**

2 *Sam.* 1:23 were *s.* than eagles
*Job* 7:6 days are *s.* than shuttle
9:25 my days are *s.* than a post
*Jer.* 4:13 his horses *s.* than eagles
*Lam.* 4:19 persecut. *s.* th. eagles
*Hab.* 1:8 horses *s.* than leopards

**SWIFTLY.**

*Ps.* 147:15 his word runneth *s.*
*Is.* 5:26 behold, they sh. come *s.*
*Dan.* 9:21 Gabriel caused to fly *s.*
*Joel* 3:4 if ye recompense me *s.*

**SWIM.**

2 *K.* 6:6 and the iron did *s.*
*Ps.* 6:6 night ma. I my bed to *s.*
*Is.* 25:11 sprea. forth hands to *s.*
*Ezek.* 47:5 risen, waters to *s.* in
*Acts* 27:42 lest any should *s.* out
43 comman. they that could *s.*

**SWIMMEST, ETH.**

*Is.* 25:11 as he that *s.* spreadeth
*Ezek.* 32:6 water land wher. th. *s.*

**SWINE.**

*Lev.* 11:7 *s.* is unclean, *Deut.* 14:8
*Prov.* 11:22 a jewel in a *s.* snout
*Is.* 65:4 which *s.* flesh and broth
66:3 as if he offered *s.* blood
17 eating *s.* flesh and abomin.

*Mat.* 7:6 nei. cast pearls befo. *s.*
8:30 herd of *s.* feeding, *Mark* 5:11; *Luke* 8:32
31 go into herd of *s.* *Mark* 5:12
32 went into *s.* the herd of *s.* ran, *Mark* 5:13; *Luke* 8:33
*Mark* 5:14 they that fed *s.* fled
*Luke* 15:15 he sent him to feed *s.*
16 filled belly with husks *s.* eat

**SWOLLEN.**

*Acts* 28:6 look. he should have *s.*

**SWOON, ED.**

*Lam.* 2:11 children *s.* in street
12 wh. they *s.* as the wounded

**SWORD.**

*Gen.* 3:24 cherubim and flam. *s.*
34:25 took each man his *s.*
*Ex.* 5:21 put a *s.* in their hand
32:27 put ev. man his *s.* by side
*Lev.* 26:6 nor *s.* go through land
25 br. *s.* upon you, *Ezek.* 5:17; 6:3; 14:17; 29:8; 33:2
33 I will draw out *s.* after you
37 they sh. fall as were bef. *s.*
*Num.* 22:23 angel's *s.* drawn, 31
29 there was a *s.* in my hand
*Deut.* 32:25 *s.* without, terror
33:29 is *s.* of thy excellency
*Jos.* 5:13 stood with his *s.* drawn
24:12 not with thy *s.* nor bow
*Jud.* 7:18 *s.* of L. and Gideon, 20
8:20 youth drew not his *s.*
9:54 draw thy *s.* and slay me
20:35 destr. 25,100 that drew *s.*
46 fell were 25,000 that drew *s.*
1 *Sam.* 13:22 neither *s.* nor spear
15:33 *s.* as made wom. childless
17:39 David girded *s.* on, 25:13
50 th. was no *s.* in hand of Da.
51 D. took his *s.* and slew him
21:8 not und. hand spear or *s.*?
9 *s.* of Goli. is wrapt in a cloth
22:10 he gave him *s.* of Goliath
13 given him bread and a *s.*
25:13 gird ye on ev. man his *s.*
31:4 Saul took a *s.* fell upon it
5 armor-bearer fell upon his *s.*
2 *Sam.* 1:22 *s.* of S. returned not
2:16 thrust *s.* into fellow's side
26 said, Sh. *s.* devour for ever?
3:29 not fail one that fall. on *s.*
2 *Sam.* 11:25 *s.* devo. one as ano.
12:10 *s.* sh. never dep. fr. house
18:8 wood devour. more than *s.*
20:10 Amasa took no heed to *s.*
23:10 his hand clave unto *s.*
24:9 in Is. 800,000 men drew *s.*
1 *K.* 3:24 bring *s.* they broug. *s.*
19:17 that escapeth *s.* of Hazael
1 *Chr.* 5:18 men able to bear *s.*
10:4 Saul took a *s.* fell upon it
5 his armor-bear. fell on the *s.*
21:5 a 100,000 that drew *s.*
12 or 3 days the *s.* of the Lord
16 the angel having a *s.* drawn
27 he put up his *s.* again
30 he was afraid of *s.* of angel
2 *Chr.* 20:9 wh. *s.* of judgm. com.
*Ezr.* 9:7 kings are delivered to *s.*
*Neh.* 4:18 ev. one had his *s.* gird.
*Est.* 9:5 Jews smote ene. with *s.*
*Job* 5:20 deliver from power of *s.*
15:22 he is waited for of the *s.*
19:29 *s.* for wrath, punish. of *s.*
20:25 glittering *s.* cometh out
27:14 if be multiplied it is for *s.*
40:19 make his *s.* to approach
41:26 *s.* of him that layeth at
*Ps.* 7:12 if turn not will whet *s.*
17:13 deliv. from wicked, thy *s.*
37:14 wicked have drawn *s.*
15 *s.* shall enter their heart
45:3 gird thy *s.* on thy thigh
57:4 their tongue is a sharp *s.*
64:3 whet th. tongue like a *s.*
76:3 brake he the shield and *s.*
78:62 he gave his people to *s.*
149:6 a two-edged *s.* in th. hand

*Prov.* 5:4 her end as a two-edg. *s.*
12:18 speaketh like pierc. of *s.*
25:18 bear. false witness is a *s.*
*Cant.* 3:8 every man hath his *s.*
*Is.* 2:4 nation not lift *s.* ag. nati.
31:8 the *s.* not of a mean man
34:6 *s.* of L. is filled with blood
41:2 he gave th. as dust to his *s.*
49:2 made mouth like sharp *s.*
51:19 famine and *s.* are come
65:12 I will number you to *s.*
66:16 by his *s.* will Lord plead
*Jer.* 2:30 your *s.* devoured proph.
4:10 *s.* reacheth unto the soul
5:12 neith. shall we see *s.* 14:13
6:25 *s.* of enemy is on ev. side
9:16 I will send a *s.* after them, 24:10; 25:27; 29:17; 49:37
12:12 *s.* of the L. shall devour
14:13 peo. say, Ye sh. not see *s.*
15 say *s.* and famine shall not
15:2 for the *s.* to the *s.* 43:11
3 I will appoint the *s.* to slay
9 residue will I deliver to *s.*
18:21 pour out th. blood by *s.*
25:16 they sh. be mad bec. of *s.*
29 call for a *s.* *Ezek.* 38:21
31 he will give wicked to *s.*
31:2 peo. left of *s.* found grace
32:24 city given because of *s.*
34:17 I proclaim a liberty to *s.*
42:16 *s.* ye feared sh. overtake
44:28 a small number esc. the *s.*
47:6 O thou *s.* of the Lord, how
48:2 O Madmen, *s.* shall pursue
10 curs. that keep. back his *s.*
50:16 fear of the oppressing *s.*
35 a *s.* is on Chaldea, saith L.
36 a *s.* on liars, *s.* on mighty
37 a *s.* on horses, *s.* on treasu.
51:50 ye that have escaped *s.*
*Lam.* 5:9 bre. by peril bec. of *s.*
*Ezek.* 5:2 I will draw out *s.* 12
17 I will bri. *s.* upon thee, 6:3
6:8 some that shall escape *s.*
7:15 *s.* is without, pestilence
11:8 ye feared *s.* I will bring a *s.*
14:17 if I bring a *s.* and say, *s.*
21 my four sore judgm. the *s.*
21:9 a *s.* a *s.* is sharpened, 11
12 terrors, by reason of the *s.*
13 what if *s.* contemn the rod?
14 let *s.* be doubled, *s.* of great
15 set point of the *s.* against
19 appoint 2 ways, that *s.* may
20 appoint a way that *s.*
28 the *s.* the *s.* is drawn for the
30:4 *s.* shall come upon Egypt
21 to make it strong to hold *s.*
22 I will cause the *s.* to fall out
32:11 *s.* of the king of Babylon
33:3 when he seeth *s.* come on
4 if *s.* come and take him, 6
6 if watchmen see the *s.* come
26 ye stand upon your *s.*
35:5 thou hast shed blood by *s.*
*Hos.* 2:18 I will break bow and *s.*
11:6 *s.* shall abide on his cities
*Amos* 9:4 thence will I com. *s.*
*Mic.* 4:3 nation not lift *s.* ag. na.
6:14 deliverest, will I give to *s.*
*Nah.* 2:13 *s.* shall devour lions
3:3 horseman lift. up bright *s.*
15 there the *s.* sh. cut thee off
*Zec.* 9:13 made thee as *s.* of mi.
11:17 *s.* shall be upon his arm
13:7 awake, O *s.* ag. my sheph.
*Mat.* 10:34 not send peace, but *s.*
26:51 drew his *s.* struck serv. *Mark* 14:47; *John* 18:10
52 put up ag. thy *s.* *John* 18:11
*Luke* 2:35 a *s.* sh. pierce thy soul
22:36 he that hath no *s.* let him
*Acts* 16:27 he drew his *s.* and wo.
*Rom.* 8:35 shall *s.* separate us from the love of Christ?
13:4 he beareth not *s.* in vain
*Eph.* 6:17 *s.* of Sp. which is word
*Heb.* 4:12 sharp. th. two-edged *s.*
*Rev.* 1:16 out of mouth went a *s.*
2:12 the sharp *s.* with two edges
6:4 was given to him a great *s.*
19:15 out of his mou. goeth *s.* 21

**By the SWORD.**

*Gen.* 27:40 *by thy s.* thou sh. live
*Lev.* 26:7 they sh. fall *by the s.* 8
2 *Chr.* 29:9 fath. ha. fallen *b. t. s.*
*Job* 33:18 from perish. *by the s.*
36:12 they shall perish *by the s.*
*Ps.* 44:3 got not land *by their s.*
78:64 their priests fell *by the s.*
*Jer.* 11:22 young men shall die *by the s.* 18:21; *Lam.* 2:21
14:12 I will consu. them *by t. s.*
15 *by s.* and famine shall pro.
16:4 shall be consumed *by the s.* 44:12, 18, 27
19:7 cause them to fall *by the s.*
21:9 abideth, shall die *by the s.* 38:2; 42:17, 22
27:13 why will ye die *by the s.?*
32:36 city sh. be deliver. *by t. s.*
33:4 houses thro. down *by the s.*
34:4 Zedek. sh. not die *by the s.*
44:13 I punished Jerusal. *by t. s.*
*Ezek.* 26:6 daugh. be slain *by t. s.*
11 he sh. slay thy peo. *by t. s.*
28:23 be judged in her *by the s.*
31:18 th. that be slain *by the s.* 32:20, 21, 22, 25, 30; 33:27
39:23 so they fell all *by the s.*
*Hos.* 1:7 will not save them *by s.*
*Amos* 7:11 Jerobo. sh. die *by t. s.*
9:10 my people sh. die *by the s.*
*Hag.* 2:22 ev. one *by the s.* of his
*Rev.* 13:14 had the wound *by a s.*

*See* EDGE, FALL.

**From the SWORD.**

*Ex.* 18:4 delivered me *fr. the s.*
*Lev.* 26:36 they sh. flee as *f. a s.*
1 *K.* 19:17 him that escap. *f. t. s.*
2 *Chr.* 36:20 escaped *from the s.*
*Job* 5:15 he saveth poor *fr. the s.*
39:22 neither turneth he *f. t. s.*
*Ps.* 22:20 deliver my soul *fr. t. s.*
144:10 delivereth David *fr. t. s.*
*Is.* 21:15 they fled *f. t.* drawn *s.*
31:8 but he shall flee *from the s.*
*Jer.* 21:7 such as are left *fr. t. s.*
46:16 let us go *fr. the* oppress. *s.*
*Ezek.* 12:16 I'll leave a few *fr. s.*
38:8 land that is brou. *fr. the s.*

**My SWORD.**

*Gen.* 48:22 I took fr. A. wi. *m. s.*
*Ex.* 15:9 I will draw *my s.* my
*Deut.* 32:41 whet *my* glit. *s.* 42
1 *Sam.* 21:8 neith. brought *my s.*
*Ps.* 44:6 neither shall *my s.* save
*Is.* 34:5 *my s.* shall be bathed in
*Ezek.* 21:3 I will draw *my s.*
5 I the Lord have drawn *my s.*
30:24 I have put *my s.* in ha. 25
32:10 when I sh. brandish *my s.*
*Zec.* 2:12 shall be slain by *my s.*

**With the SWORD.**

*Gen.* 31:26 as capti. taken *w. t. s.*
*Ex.* 5:3 lest he fall on us *w. t. s.*
22:24 I will kill you *w. the s.*
*Num.* 19:16 touch. slain *w. t. s.*
20:18 lest I come out *w. the s.*
31:8 Balaam they slew *w. the s.*
*Deut.* 28:22 L. sh. smi. th. *w. t. s.*
*Jos.* 10:11 Is. slew *w. t. s.* 13:22
11:10 smote king of Ha. *w. t. s.*
1 *Sam.* 17:45 thou comest *w. t. s.*
47 the Lord saveth not *w. s.*
2 *Sam.* 20:8 girdle *w. a s.* fasten.
1 *K.* 1:51 not slay serv. *w. the s.*
2:8 not put th. to death *w. t. s.*
19:1 had slain prophets *w. t. s.*
2 *K.* 8:12 wilt thou slay *w. the s.*
11:20 they slew Athaliah *with the s.* 2 *Chr.* 23:21
2 *Chr.* 21:4 slew breth. *w. the s.*
36:17 slew young men *w. the s.*
*Ps.* 42:10 as *w. a s.* in my bones
*Is.* 1:20 sh. be devoured *w. the s.*
*Is.* 14:19 slain, thr. thro' *w. a s.*
22:2 thy men not slain *w. the s.*
27:1 Lord *w. his* strong *s.* shall
*Jer.* 5:17 impover. cities *w. t. s.*
14:18 behold the slain *w. the s.*
20:4 he sh. slay Judah *w. the s.*
27:8 nati. will I punish *w. t. s.*
29:18 I will persecute *w. the s.*
*Lam.* 4:9 that be slain *w. the s.*
*Ezek.* 7:15 in field sh. die *w. t. s.*
26:8 sh. slay daughters *w. the s.*
31:17 to hell with them that be slain *w. the s.* 32:28, 32; 35:8
*Amos* 1:11 did pursue bro. *w. t. s.*
4:10 men have I slain *w. the s.*
9:1 I will slay last of th. *w. t. s.*
*Mic.* 5:6 waste Assyria *w. the s.*
*Mat.* 26:52 that take the *s.* shall perish *with the s.*
*Luke* 22:49 sh. we smite *w. t. s.?*
*Acts* 12:2 Her. killed Jas. *w. t. s.*
*Heb.* 11:37 tempt. slain *w. the s.*
*Rev.* 2:16 I will fight th. *w. the s.*
6:8 and power to kill *w. s.* and
13:10 killeth *w. s.* be kill. *w. s.*
19:21 remnant were slain *with the s.*

**SWORDS.**

1 *Sam.* 13:19 lest Hebr. make *s.*
2 *K.* 3:26 took 700 men drew *s.*
*Neh.* 4:13 I set the people wi. *s.*
*Ps.* 55:21 words were drawn *s.*
59:7 belch out, *s.* are in th. lips
*Prov.* 30:14 gener. teeth are as *s.*
*Cant.* 3:8 hold *s.* expert in war
*Is.* 2:4 beat their *s.* into ploughshares, *Mic.* 4:3
21:15 they fled from the *s.*
*Ezek.* 16:40 thrust through wi. *s.*
23:47 dispatch them with th. *s.*
28:7 strangers sh. draw their *s.*
30:11 they shall draw their *s.*
32:12 by *s.* of the mighty will I
27 they have laid their *s.* und.
*Joel* 3:10 beat ploughsh. into *s.*
*Mat.* 26:47 with Ju. great multitude with *s.* *Mark* 14:43
*Luke* 22:38 beho. here are two *s.*

**SWORN.**

*Gen.* 22:16 by myself have I *s.* saith L. *Is.* 45:23; *Jer.* 49:13; 51:14; *Amos* 6:8
*Ex.* 13:19 Joseph had straitly *s.*
17:16 Lord hath *s.* that he will
*Lev.* 6:5 about wh. had *s.* falsely
*Deut.* 7:8 keep oath *s.* *Jer.* 11:5
13:17 as he hath *s.* to thy fath.
28:9 estab. th. as he hath *s.* 29:13
31:7 bri. to land L. *s.* *Neh.* 9:15
*Jos.* 9:18 because princes had *s.*
19 we have *s.* to th. 2 *Sam.* 21:2
*Jud.* 21:1 men of Is. had *s.* to M.
7 have *s.* not to give wives, 18
1 *Sam.* 3:14 I ha. *s.* to hou. of E.
2 *Sam.* 21:2 Is. had *s.* to Gibeon.
2 *Chr.* 15:15 had *s.* with hearts
*Neh.* 9:15 land th. badst *s.* to give
*Ps.* 24:4 hath not *s.* deceitfully
89:3 I have *s.* to David my serv.
35 *s.* by my holiness, *Amos* 4:2
102:8 mad ag. me, are *s.* ag. me
110:4 L. hath *s.* will not repent
119:106 I have *s.* will perform
132:11 L. hath *s.* in truth to D.
*Is.* 14:24 Lord of hosts hath *s.*
45:23 I have *s.* by myself, word
54:9 I have *s.* wat. no more go over earth, I have *s.*
62:8 L. hath *s.* by his ri. hand
*Jer.* 5:7 *s.* by th. that are no gods
44:26 I ha. *s.* by my great name
*Ezek.* 21:23 them that have *s.*
*Amos* 8:7 Lord hath *s.* by Jacob
*Mic.* 7:20 perf. mercy th. hast *s.*

*Acts* 2:30 know. God hath *s.* oath
7:17 pro. drew nigh God had *s.*
*Heb.* 4:3 I have *s.* in my wrath

**SYCAMINE.**

*Luke* 17:6 to *s.* tr. Be plucked

**SYCAMORE fruit.**

*Amos* 7:14 and gather of *s. fruit*

**SYCAMORE-TREE.**

*Luke* 19:4 Zaccheus climbed *s.-t.*

**SYCAMORE-TREES.**

1 *K.* 10:27 Solomon made cedars as *s.-trees*, 2 *Chr.* 1:15; 9:27
1 *Chr.* 27:28 over *s.-t.* Baal-hanan
*Ps.* 78:47 he destroyed their *s.-t.*

**SYCAMORES.**

*Is.* 9:10 the *s.* are cut down

SYCHAR. *John* 4:5
SYENE. *Ezek.* 29:10

**SYNAGOGUE.**

*Mat.* 12:9 he went into their *s.*
13:54 tau. in their *s.* *Mark* 6:2
*Mark* 5:22 Jairus, one of the rul. of the *s.* 36, 38; *Luke* 8:41, 49
*Luke* 4:16 custom, went into *s.*
20 eyes of all in *s.* fast. on him
7:5 loveth nation, built us a *s.*
*John* 9:22 he sho. be put out of *s.*
12:42 lest they be put out of *s.*
18:20 I ever taught in *s.* temple
*Acts* 6:9 then arose cert. of the *s.* called *s.* of the Libertines
13:14 they went into *s.* on sab.
14:1 P. and Barna. went into *s.*
17:1 Thessalonica, wh. was a *s.*
17 he disputed in *s.* with Jews
18:4 reasoned in *s.* ev. sabbath
7 Justus, whose house join. *s.*
8 Crispus, chief ruler of the *s.*
17 Sosthenes, chief ruler of *s.*
26 Apollos began to speak in *s.*
22:19 beat. in *s.* such beli. 26:11
*Rev.* 2:9 but are the *s.* of Satan
3:9 I will make them of *s.* of Sa.

**SYNAGOGUES.**

*Ps.* 74:8 they burned all *s.* of G.
*Mat.* 4:23 Je. went teaching in *s.* 9:35; *Mark* 1:39; *Luke* 13:10
6:2 as hypocrites do in the *s.*
5 love to pray standing in *s.*
10:17 scourge you in *s.* 23:34
23:6 love chief seats in *s.* *Mark* 12:39; *Luke* 11:43; 20:46
*Mark* 13:9 in *s.* ye sh. be beaten
*Luke* 4:15 taught in *s.* glorified
44 he preached in *s.* of Galilee
12:11 they bring you unto *s.*
21:12 delivering you up to the *s.*
*John* 16:2 shall put you out *s.*
*Acts* 9:2 Saul desired letters to *s.*
20 he preached Christ in the *s.*
13:5 P. and Barn. preached in *s.*
15:21 being read in *s.* every sa.
24:12 neither raising people in *s.*

**SYNTYCHE.**

*Phil.* 4:2 I beseech Euod. and S.

**SYRACUSE.**

*Acts* 28:12 landing at S. tarried three days

**SYRIA.**

*Jud.* 10:6 Is. served gods of S.
2 *Sam.* 8:6 David put garrisons in S. 1 *Chr.* 18:6
15:8 I abode at Geshur in S.
1 *K.* 10:29 kings of S. did th. br.
11:25 Rezon reigned over S.
19:15 Haz. king of S. 2 *K.* 13:3
22:1 without war betw. S. and
2 *K.* 5:1 deliverance given to S.
6:23 bands of S. came no more
7:5 no man in the camp of S.
8:13 that thou sh. be king of S.
13:7 for the king of S. destroy.
17 arrow of deliveran. from S.
19 thou sh. smite S. but thrice
16:6 king of S. recove. El. to S.
2 *Chr.* 18:10 thou shalt push S.
24:23 host of S. came against
28:23 gods of kings of S. help
*Is.* 7:2 saying S. is confederate
8 for head of S. is Damascus
*Ezek.* 16:57 of the daughters of S.
27:16 S. was thy merchant
*Hos.* 12:12 fled into country of S.
*Amos* 1:5 S. shall go into captiv.
*Mat.* 4:24 went throughout all S.
*Luke* 2:2 Cyrenius governor of S.
*Acts* 15:23 to the brethren in S.
41 he went through S. and
18:18 sailed thence into S. 21:3; *Gal.* 1:21

**SYRIAC.**

*Dan.* 2:4 spake to the king in S.

**SYRIAN.**

*Gen.* 25:20 daugh. of Bethuel S. Lab. the S. 28:5; 31:20, 24
*Deut.* 26:5 a S. ready to perish
2 *K.* 5:20 spared Naaman this S.
18:26 speak in the S. *Is.* 36:11
*Ezr.* 4:7 written in S. tongue and interpreted in S. tongue
*Luke* 4:27 saving Naaman the S.

**SYRIANS.**

2 *Sam.* 8:5 when S. of Da. came, David slew of S. 22,000
6 the S. became David's servants, 1 *Chr.* 18:5, 6
13 returned from smiting of S.
10:6 Ammonites hired the S.
11 if S. be too str. 1 *Chr.* 19:12
19 the S. feared to help children of Ammon, 1 *Chr.* 19:19
1 *K.* 20:20 the S. fled, and Israel
27 flocks, but S. filled country
29 Israel slew of the S. 100,000
22:11 th. shalt thou push the S.
2 *K.* 5:2 the S. had taken a maid
2 *K.* 6:9 thith. S. are come down
7:4 let us fall unto host of S.
6 Lord made the host of the S.
10 we came to camp of the S.
8:28 S. wounded Joram, 29; 9:15; 2 *Chr.* 22:5
13:5 from under the hand of S.
17 for thou shalt smite the S.
16:6 the S. came to Elath and
*Is.* 9:12 S. bef. and Philistines
*Jer.* 35:11 for fear of army of S.
*Amos* 9:7 brou. the S. from Kir?

**SYROPHENICIAN.**

*Mark* 7:26 a Greek, a S. by. nat.

# T

**TABEAL.**

*Is.* 7:6 a king, even the son of T.

**TABERAH.**

*Num.* 11:3 he called the place T.
*Deut.* 9:22 at T. he provoked L.

TAANACH. 1 *K.* 4:12

**TABERING.**

*Nah.* 2:7 vo. of doves *t.* on brea.

**TABERNACLE.**

*Ex.* 25:9 make after pattern of *t.*
27:9 thou shalt make court of *t.*
19 vessels of *t.* of brass, 39:40
29:43 *t.* be sanctif. by my glory
33:7 Mo. pitch. *t.* without camp
11 Josh. departed not out of *t.*
36:8 them that wrou. work of *t.*
39:32 th. was work of *t.* finished
33 they brought the *t.* to Mo.
40:2 set up the *t.* 9 anoint *t.*
17 on first day the *t.* was reared up, 18; *Num.* 7:1
33 reared court round about *t.*
34 glory of Lord filled the *t.* 35
36 cloud was taken from over *t.* *Num.* 9:17; 10:11; 12:10
38 the cloud of Lord was on the *t.* *Num.* 9:18, 19, 22
*Lev.* 8:10 Mo. anointed *t.* and all
15:31 die not when they defile *t.*
17:4 bringeth not offering bef. *t.*
26:11 will set my *t.* among you
*Num.* 1:50 appoint Levites over *t.* bear *t.* sh. encamp ro. *t.* 53
51 when *t.* setteth forward, and when *t.* is to be pitched
53 Levites sh. keep charge of *t.* 3:7, 25; 18:3; 31:30, 47
4:16 oversi. of *t.* pertain. to E.
5:17 priest sh. take of dust of *t.*
7:3 they brou. offering before *t.*
9:15 on day that *t.* was reared, cloud cov. *t.* tent of testimo.
10:21 Kohathites did set up *t.*
11:24 Mos. set 70 elders round *t.*
26 they went not out unto *t.*
16:9 seem. small to do ser. of *t.*
24 get from about *t.* of Ko. 27
17:13 whos. com. near *t.* sh. die
*Deut.* 31:15 appeared in *t.* in clo.
*Jos.* 22:19 wherein L.'s *t.* dwell.
2 *Sam.* 6:17 set ark in midst *t.*
7:6 ha. walked in tent and in *t.*
1 *K.* 2:28 Joab fled to *t.* of Lord
8:4 vessels in *t.* bro. 2 *Chr.* 5:5
1 *Chr.* 6:48 Levites for serv. of *t.*
9:23 they had oversight of the *t.*
16:39 priests before *t.* of Lord
17:5 ha. gone from one *t.* to ano.
21:29 *t.* M. made in wilderness
23:26 they sh. no more carry *t.*
2 *Chr.* 1:5 put brazen altar bef. *t.*
*Job* 5:24 kn. thy *t.* sh. be in pea.
18:6 light shall be dark in his *t.*
14 confidence be rooted out *t.*
15 destruc. shall dwell in his *t.*
19:12 his troops encamp rou. *t.*
20:26 ill with him th. is left in *t.*
29:4 wh. secret of G. was up. *t.*
31:31 if men of my *t.* said not
36:29 can any und. noise of *t.*?
*Ps.* 15:1 L. who sh. abide in *t.*?
19:4 in them he set a *t.* for sun
27:5 in secret of his *t.* hide me
6 I will offer in his *t.* sacrifices
61:4 I will abide in thy *t.*
76:2 in Salem is his *t.* dwell.-pl.
78:60 so he forsook *t.* of Shiloh
67 moreo. he refused *t.* of Jos.
132:3 I will not come into *t.* 7
*Prov.* 14:11 *t.* of upright flourish
*Is.* 4:6 *t.* for shadow from heat
16:5 he sh. sit on it in *t.* of Da.
33:20 *t.* th. sh. not be ta. down
*Jer.* 10:20 my *t.* is spoiled, cords
*Lam.* 2:4 slew all pleasant in *t.*
6 he hath violently ta. away *t.*
*Ezek.* 37:27 my *t.* sh. be with th.
41:1 which was breadth of *t.*
*Amos* 5:26 have borne *t.* of Mol.
*Amos* 9:11 will I raise up *t.* of D.
*Acts* 7:43 ye took up *t.* of Moloch
46 desired to find a *t.* for God
15:16 will build again *t.* of Dav.
2 *Cor.* 5:1 if house of *t.* be disso.
4 we th. are in th. *t.* do groan
*Heb.* 8:2 true *t.* which L. pitched
5 when Moses was to make *t.*

9:2 there was a *t.* made, sanctu.
3 *t.* which is called holiest
6 priests went alw. into first *t.*
8 while as first *t.* was yet stan.
11 priest by greater and per. *t.*
21 sprinkled with blood the *t.*
13:10 no right to eat wh. ser. *t.*
2 *Pet.* 1:13 as long as I am in *t.*
14 shortly I must put off my *t.*
*Rev.* 13:6 blasp. his name and *t.*
15:5 behold temple of *t.* opened
*See* CONGREGATION, DOOR.

**TABERNACLE of witness.**
*Num.* 17:7 M. la. rods in *t. of w.*
8 on mor. M. went into *t. of w.*
2 *Chr.* 24:6 br. colle. for *t. of w.*
*Acts* 7:44 our fathers had *t. of w.*

**TABERNACLES.**
*Num.* 24:5 how goodly thy *t.*
*Job* 11:14 let not wic. dwell in *t.*
12:6 *t.* of robbers prosper, they
15:34 fire sh. cons. *t.* of bribery
22:23 put away iniq. from thy *t.*
*Ps.* 43:3 let them bring me to *t.*
46:4 make glad holy place of *t.*
78:51 smote their strength in *t.*
83:6 *t.* of E. consulted together
84:1 how amiable are thy *t.*
118:15 salvation in *t.* of righte.
132:7 we will go into *t.* worship
*Dan.* 11:45 he sh. plant *t.* of pal.
*Hos.* 9:6 thorns sh. be in their *t.*
12:9 make thee to dwell in *t.*
*Mal.* 2:12 L. cut off man out of *t.*
*Mat.* 17:4 let us make here three *t.* *Mark* 9:5; *Luke* 9:33
*Heb.* 11:9 Abrah. dwelling in *t.*
*See* FEAST.

**TABITHA.**
*Acts* 9:36 a disciple named T.
40 turn. to body said, T. arise

**TABLE.**
*Ex.* 25:23 thou sh. also make a *t.*
27 staves to bear *t.* 28; 37:14
31:8 Beza. sh. make *t.* and altar
37:10 made *t.* 16 vessels on *t.*
40:22 put *t.* in tent of congreg.
*Lev.* 24:6 six on a row on pure *t.*
*Num.* 3:31 Kohathites' charge *t.*
*Jud.* 1:7 gath. meat under my *t.*
1 *Sam.* 20:29 co. not to king's *t.*
34 Jona. arose from *t.* in anger
2 *Sam.* 9:7 Mephibosheth sh. eat at my *t.* 10, 11, 13; 19:28
1 *K.* 2:7 be th. that eat at my *t.*
4:27 all that came to Solo.'s *t.*
10:5 queen of Sheba saw meat of his *t.* 2 *Chr.* 9:4
13:20 as th. sat at *t.* word of L.
18:19 proph. eat at Jezebel's *t.*
2 *K.* 4:10 let us set for him a *t.*
*Neh.* 5:17 we. at my *t.* 150 Jews
*Job* 36:16 wh. should be set on *t.*
*Ps.* 23:5 thou preparest *t.* be. me
69:22 let th. *t.* become a snare
78:19 can G. furn. *t.* in wildern.
128:3 child. like plants about *t.*
*Prov.* 3:3 wri. on *t.* of heart, 7:3
9:2 wisd. hath furnished her *t.*
*Cant.* 1:12 wh. king sitteth at *t.*
*Is.* 21:5 prepare the *t.* eat
30:8 write before them in *t.*
65:11 prepare *t.* for that troop
*Jer.* 17:1 it is graven on *t.* of he.
*Ezek.* 23:41 prepar. a *t.* before it
39:20 ye shall be filled at my *t.*
41:22 this is *t.* that is bef. Lord
44:16 shall come near to my *t.*
*Dan.* 11:27 shall speak lies at *t.*
*Mal.* 1:7 *t.* of L. is contemptible
12 ye say, *t.* of Lord is pollut.
*Mat.* 15:27 dogs eat crumbs from their master's *t.* *Mark* 7:28
*Luke* 16:21 crn. fr. rich man's *t.*
22:21 betrayeth, is wi. me on *t.*
30 may eat and drink at my *t.*
*John* 12:2 L. was one th. sat at *t.*
13:28 no man at *t.* knew wh. in.
*Rom.* 11:9 let their *t.* be a snare
1 *Cor.* 10:21 ye cannot be partakers of Lord's *t.* and *t.* of dev.
*See* SHOW-BREAD.

**Writing TABLE.**
*Luke* 1:63 Zacha. asked for *w. t.*

**TABLES.**
*Ex.* 32:15 *t.* were writ. on sides
16 *t.* were work of G. gra. on *t.*
*Ex.* 32:19 cast the *t.* out of his h.
34:1 write on *t.* words in first *t.*
*Deut.* 10:4 he wr. on *t.* acco. to *t.*
5 put *t.* in the ark, *Heb.* 9:4
1 *Chr.* 28:16 David ga. gold for *t.*
2 *Chr.* 4:8 Solo. also made ten *t.*
*Is.* 28:8 all *t.* are full of vomit
*Ezek.* 40:41 8 *t.* whereon slew sa.
42 four *t.* were of hewn stone
*Hab.* 2:2 write vision, plain on *t.*
*Mat.* 21:12 he overthrew *t.* of the money-changers, *Mark* 11:15
*Mark* 7:4 wash. of cups, pots, *t.*
*John* 2:15 dro. out, overthrew *t.*
*Acts* 6:2 leave word of G. serve *t.*
2 *Chr.* 3:3 not in *t.* of st. fleshly *t.*
*See* STONE, TWO.

**TABLETS.**
*Ex.* 35:22 brought *t.* of jewels
*Num.* 31:50 brought *t.* atonement
*Is.* 3:20 I will take away the *t.*

**TABOR.**
*Jud.* 4:6 draw toward mount T.
12 Barak was gone to mount T.
8:18 they whom ye slew at T.?
1 *Sam.* 10:3 come to plain of T.
*Ps.* 89:12 T. and Hermon shall
*Jer.* 46:18 surely, as T. is among
*Hos.* 5:1 a net spread upon T.

**TABRET.**
*Gen.* 31:27 have sent thee with *t.*
1 *Sam.* 10:5 fr. high place with *t.*
*Job* 17:6 aforetime I was as a *t.*
*Is.* 5:12 *t.* and wine are in feasts

**TABRETS.**
1 *Sam.* 18:6 ca. to meet S. wi. *t.*
*Is.* 24:8 mirth of *t.* ceaseth, joy
30:32 it sh. be with *t.* and harps
*Jer.* 31:4 again be adorn. with *t.*
*Ezek.* 28:13 workmansh. of thy *t.*

**TACHES.**
*Ex.* 26:6 thou shalt make fifty *t.*
11 thou sh. make fifty *t.* 35:11
36:13 he made fifty *t.* of gold, 18
39:33 they brought his *t.* boards

**TACKLING, S.**
*Is.* 33:23 thy *t.* are loosed, could
*Acts* 27:19 third day cast out *t.*

**TADMOR.**
2 *Chr.* 8:4 Solomon built T.

**TAHAPANES, *or* TEHAPHNEHES,**
*Jer.* 2:16 the children of T. have
43:7 thus came they even to T.
46:14 punish in Noph and T.
*Ezek.* 30:18 at T. also the day sh.

**TAHPHENES.**
1 *K.* 11:19 gave him sister of T.

**TAIL.**
*Ex.* 4:4 put out hand, ta. it by *t.*
*Deut.* 28:13 make head, not *t.* 44
*Jud.* 15:4 foxes, turned *t.* to *t.*
*Job* 40:17 behemoth mov. his *t.*
*Is.* 9:14 cut off fr. Is. head and *t.*
15 prophet teache. lies, he is *t.*
19:15 wo. wh. head or *t.* may do
*Rev.* 12:4 his *t.* dr. third of stars

**TAILS.**
*Jud.* 15:4 firebrand betw. two *t.*
*Is.* 7:4 two *t.* of these firebrands
*Rev.* 9:10 *t.* like scor. stings in *t.*
19 power in *t.* their *t.* like ser.

**TAKE.**
*Gen.* 13:9 if thou *t.* left hand
14:21 give me persons, *t.* goods
22:2 *t.* now thy son, th. only s.
24:3 shalt not *t.* wife to son, 37
31:32 discern what is thine, *t.* it
38:23 let her *t.* it to her, lest we
*Ex.* 6:7 I will *t.* you for a people
10:26 thereof must we *t.* serve L.
17:5 and thy rod *t.* in thy hand
20:7 not *t.* na. L. vain, *Deut.* 5:11
21:14 *t.* him from mine altar
23:8 sh. *t.* no gift, *Deut.* 16:19
34:9 *t.* us for inheritance
*Lev.* 25:46 ye sh. *t.* them for chil.
*Num.* 8:6 *t.* Levites from am. Is.
11:17 I will *t.* of spirit on thee
16:3 ye *t.* too much upon you, 7
*Deut.* 1:13 *t.* ye wise men
4:34 *t.* him a nation, fr. nation
25:8 if say, I like not to *t.* her
*Jos.* 10:42 their land did Josh. *t.*
20:4 they shall *t.* him into city
*Jud.* 14:15 called to *t.* th. we ha.
*Ruth* 2:10 should. *t.* knowledge
1 *Sam.* 2:16 then *t.* as soul desir.
17:46 and *t.* thy head from thee
19:14 S. sent messengers to *t.* D.
21:9 if thou wilt *t.* that, *t.* it
25:11 sh. I then *t.* bread and w.
2 *Sam.* 12:4 spared to *t.* his flock
2 *Sam.* 12:28 *t.* it, lest I *t.* city
16:9 go over, and *t.* off his head
19:19 king sh. *t.* to heart, 13:33
30 Mephibosh. said, Let him *t.*
1 *K.* 11:31 said to Jer. *t.* 10 piec.
14:3 *t.* ten loaves; 18:40 *t.* prop.
20:18 war or peace, *t.* th. alive
22:26 *t.* Micaiah, car. him back
2 *K.* 5:16 urged to *t.* 20 I will *t.*
23 *t.* 2 talents; 8:8 *t.* a present
10:14 *t.* th. alive; 12:5 priests *t.*
19:30 *t.* root downward, *Is.* 37:31
1 *Chr.* 21:24 I will not *t.* that is
*Ezr.* 5:14 those did Cyrus *t.*
15 *t.* vessels, carry into temple
*Job* 23:10 he know. way that I *t.*
31:36 I wo. *t.* it on my shoulder
41:4 wilt thou *t.* him for serv.?
*Ps.* 7:5 persecute my soul, and *t.*
51:11 *t.* not thy Holy Sp. fr. me
71:11 *t.* him, none to deliv. him
81:2 *t.* psalm; 83:12 *t.* houses
89:33 kind. will I not *t.* fr. him
109:8 let another *t.* his office
119:43 *t.* not word of truth out
139:20 ene. *t.* thy name in vain
*Prov.* 6:25 neither let her *t.* thee
7:18 let us *t.* our fill of love
30:9 *t.* name of my God in vain
*Ec.* 5:15 shall *t.* nothing of labor
19 *t.* his portion, rejo. in labor
*Is.* 27:6 cause th. of J. to *t.* root
28:19 fr. time it goeth, sh. *t.* you
33:23 prey is divi. lame *t.* prey
40:24 their stock sh. not *t.* root
44:15 he will *t.* thereof
58:2 they *t.* deli. in approac. G.
66:21 I will *t.* of th. for priests
*Jer.* 2:22 *t.* soap; 3:14 *t.* 1 of city
13:21 sh. not sorrows *t.* th. as?
15:19 if thou *t.* precious fr. vile
18:22 have digged pit to *t.* me
19:1 *t.* of ancients of the people
25:9 I will *t.* families of north
10 will *t.* fr. th. voice of mirth
32:24 th. are come to city to *t.*
28 Nebu. king of Bab. sh. *t.* it
39:12 *t.* Jeremiah, look to him
50:15 *t.* vengeance upon her
51:26 shall not *t.* of thee stone
*Lam.* 2:13 wh. *t.* to wit. for th.?
*Ezek.* 11:19 I will *t.* stony heart
24:5 *t.* choice of flock
25 when I *t.* fr. their strength
33:2 if peo. *t.* man of their coast
36:24 I will *t.* you from heathen
46:18 prince not *t.* peo.'s inher.

*Dan.* 7:18 saints shall *t.* kingd.
11:18 turn to isles, shall *t.* many
*Hos.* 14:2 *t.* with you words
*Amos* 5:12 afflict just, *t.* bribe
9:2 shall my hand *t.* them, 3
*Jon.* 4:3 *t.* I beseech th. my life
*Mic.* 2:2 covet fields, *t.* by viole.
*Nah.* 1:2 L. *t.* venge. on advers.
*Hab.* 1:10 th. sh. heap dust, *t.* it
*Hag.* 1:8 build house, I *t.* pleas.
2:23 will I *t.* thee, O Zerubbab.
*Zec.* 6:10 *t.* of them of captivity
*Mat.* 1:20 fear not to *t.* to th. M.
2:13 *t.* yo. child and its mother
6:25 *t.* no thought for your life, 28, 31, 34; 10:19; *Mark* 13:11; *Luke* 12:11, 22, 26
15:26 it is not meet to *t.* children's bread, *Mark* 7:27
16:5 forg. to *t.* bread, *Mark* 8:14
18:16 *t.* with thee one or two
20:14 *t.* that thine is, go thy w.
24:17 let him on house-top not co. to *t.* any th. *Mark* 13:15
26:4 that they might *t.* Jesus by subtilty, *Mark* 14:1, 44
26 Je. took bread, said *t.* eat, *Mark* 14:22; 1 *Cor.* 11:24
52 they that *t.* sword sh. peri.
*Mark* 6:8 *t.* nothing for their journey, *Luke* 9:3
12:19 his br. *t.* wife, *Luke* 20:28
15:36 whether E. come to *t.* him
*Luke* 10:35 *t.* care of him; 2:19 *t.* ease
14:9 begin with shame to *t.* low.
22:36 that hath purse let him *t.*
*John* 2:16 J. said, *t.* things hence
6:7 every one may *t.* a little
15 th. would come, *t.* by force
7:30 sou. to *t.* 32; 10:39; 11:57
10:17 lay down life, *t.* it aga. 18
16:15 sh. *t.* of mine and show it
17:15 shouldest *t.* th. out world
18:31 *t.* ye him, and judge him
19:6 *t.* him and crucify him
*Acts* 12:3 H. proceeded to *t.* Pet.
15:14 to *t.* of them a people
37 Barnab. determined to *t.* J.
38 P. thoug. not good to *t.* him
20:13 there intending to *t.* Paul
*Acts* 20:26 wherefore I *t.* you to
27:33 besou. them to *t.* meat, 34
1 *Cor.* 6:7 why not ra. *t.* wrong?
9:9 doth God *t.* care for oxen?
2 *Cor.* 11:20 if a man *t.* of you
1 *Tim.* 3:5 how *t.* care of church
2 *Tim.* 4:11 *t.* Mark, bring him
1 *Pet.* 2:20 if ye *t.* it patiently
*Rev.* 3:11 that no man *t.* thy cro.
5:9 thou art worthy to *t.* book
6:4 power to *t.* peace fr. earth
22:17 let him *t.* water of life

**TAKE away.**

*Gen.* 42:36 ye will *t.* Benjamin *a.*
*Ex.* 2:9 *t.* this child *a.* and nurse
10:17 may *t. a.* from me death
33:23 I will *t. away* my hand
*Lev.* 3:4 he *t. a.* 10, 15; 4:9; 7:4
4:31 *t. a.* all the fat thereof, 35
*Num.* 17:10 quite *t. a.* th. murm.
2 *Sam.* 4:11 shall I not *t.* you *a.*
5:6 except thou *t. a.* the blind
24:10 *t. a.* iniq. of thy servant
1 *K.* 2:31 *t. away* innocent blood
19:4 enough, O L. *t. a.* my life
10 seek my life to *t.* it *a.* 14
20:6 pleasant sh. servant *t. a.*
20:24 *t.* kings *a.* put captains
2 *K.* 2:3 Lord will *t. a.* master, 5
6:32 hath sent to *t. a.* my head
18:62 I come *t.* you *a. Is.* 36:17
1 *Chr.* 17:13 I wi. not *t.* mercy *a.*
*Job* 7:21 why dost not *t. a.* iniq.
24:2 they violently *t. a.* flocks
32:22 my Maker would *t.* me *a.*
36:18 beware, lest he *t.* thee *a.*
*Ps.* 31:13 devised to *t. a.* my life
52:5 he sh. *t.* thee *a.* and pluck
58:9 he sh. *t.* them *a.* as with a
102:24 *t.* me not *a.* in midst of
*Prov.* 22:27 why should he *t. a.*
25:4 *t. a.* the dross from silver
5 *t. a.* wicked from before king
*Is.* 1:25 will *t. away* all thy tin
10:2 to *t. a.* right from the poor
25:8 rebu. of his peo. sh. he *t. a.*
27:9 all fruit to *t. away* his sin
39:7 of thy sons shall they *t. a.*
58:9 if thou *t. away* from midst
*Jer.* 15:15 *t.* me not *a.* in long-s.
*Ezek.* 24:16 I *t. a.* desire of eyes
33:4 if sword come and *t. a.* 6
36:26 I will *t. a.* stony heart
*Hos.* 1:6 will utterly *t.* them *a.*
2:17 I will *t. a.* name of Baalim
5:14 *t. a.* none sh. rescue them
14:2 say unto him, *t. a.* iniquity
*Amos* 4:2 he will *t.* you *away*
*Mic.* 2:2 covet houses, *t.* them *a.*
*Zep.* 3:11 will *t. a.* out of midst
*Zec.* 9:7 *t. a.* blood out of mouth
*Mal.* 2:3 sh. *t.* you *a.* with dung
*Mat.* 5:40 *t. away* thy coat
*Mark* 14:36 Father, *t. a.* this cup
*Luke* 1:25 to *t. aw.* my reproach
17:31 not come down to *t.* it *a.*
*John* 11:39 Jesus said, *t. a.* stone
*Rom.* 11:27 when I sh. *t. a.* sins
1 *John* 3:5 manifest. to *t. a.* sins
*Rev.* 22:19 if any man *t. a.* from
*See* COUNSEL.

**TAKE heed.**

*Gen.* 31:24 *t. h.* th. speak not, 29
*Ex.* 10:28 *t. h.* to thyself, 34:12; *Deut.* 4:9; 12:13, 19, 30; 1 *Sam.* 19:2; 1 *Tim.* 4:16
19:12 *t. h.* to yourselves, *Deut.* 2:4; 4:15, 23; 11:16; *Jos.* 23:11; *Jer.* 17:21
*Num.* 23:12 must I not *t. h.* to s.
*Deut.* 27:9 *t. h.* and heark. O Isr.
*Jos.* 22:5 *t. h.* to do commandm.
1 *K.* 2:4 if thy children *t. heed* to their way, 8:25; 2 *Chr.* 6:16
1 *Chr.* 28:10 *t. h.* for L. hath ch.
2 *Chr.* 19:6 *t. heed* what ye do
7 let fear of L. be on you, *t. h.*
33:8 so that th. *t. h. Ezr.* 4:22
*Job* 36:21 *t. h.* reg. not iniquity
*Ps.* 39:1 I will *t. h.* to my ways
*Ec.* 7:21 *t.* no *h.* to words spoken
*Is.* 7:4 say unto him, *t. heed*
*Jer.* 9:4 *t. h.* every one of neigh.
*Hos.* 4:10 left off to *t. h.* to Lord
*Mal.* 2:15 *t. heed* to your spir. 16
*Mat.* 6:1 *t. h.* do not alms bef. m.
18:10 *t. h.* that ye despise not
24:4 *t. h.* lest any man deceive you, *Mark* 13:5
*Mark* 4:24 *t. h.* what you hear
13:9 *t. h.* to yoursel. *Luke* 17:3; 21:34; *Acts* 5:35; 20:28
23 *t. h.* I foreto. 33 *t. h.* watch
*Luke* 8:18 *t. h.* the. how ye hear
11:35 *t. h.* that lig. be not dark.
21:8 *t. h.* ye be not deceived
*Acts* 22:26 *t. heed* wh. thou doest
*Rom.* 11:21 *t. h.* lest he spare not
1 *Cor.* 3:10 man *t. h.* how he bui.
10:12 standeth *t. h.* lest he fall
*Gal.* 5:15 *t. h.* ye be not consum.
*Heb.* 3:12 *t. h.* lest heart of unbe.
2 *Pet.* 1:19 ye do well to *t. heed*

**TAKE hold.**

*Ex.* 15:14 sorrow *t. h.* of inhabi.
*Deut.* 32:41 if hand *t. h.* of judg.
*Job* 27:20 terrors *t. h.* on him as
36:17 justice *t. hold* on thee
38:13 mi. *t. h.* on ends of earth
*Ps.* 69:24 let anger *t. h.* of them
*Prov.* 2:19 nor *t. h.* of pa. of life
5:5 down, her steps *t. h.* on hell
*Ec.* 7:18 good that th. *t. h.* of
*Is.* 3:6 when a man *t. h.* of brot.
4:1 sev. wom. *t. h.* of one man
27:5 let him *t. h.* of my strength
64:7 stir. himself to *t. h.* of thee
*Mic.* 6:14 *t. h.* but sh. not deliver
*Zec.* 1:6 not *t. h.* of your fathe.?
8:23 ten men *t. hold* of him
*Luke* 20:20 mi. *t. h.* of his words

**TAKE up.**

*Gen.* 41:34 *t. up* 5th part of land
*Jos.* 4:5 *t. up* every man a stone
2 *K.* 2:1 when L. would *t. up* El.
4:36 *t. up* son; 6:7 *t. up* iron
9:25 *t. up* cast him into field
*Ps.* 16:4 nor *t. up* names
27:10 then the L. will *t.* me *up*
*Jer.* 9:10 mountains *t. up* weep.
18 *t. up* wail. 38:10 *t. up* Jer.
*Ezek.* 19:1 *t. up* lam. for princes
*Amos* 3:5 *t. up* snare from earth
5:1 hear word I *t. up* aga. you
*Jon.* 1:12 *t.* me *up* and cast me
*Mat.* 9:6 *t. up* bed, *Mark* 2:9, 11; *Luke* 5:24; *John* 5:8, 11, 12
16:24 *t. up* cross, *Mark* 8:34; 10:21; *Luke* 9:23
17:27 *t. up* fish that first cometh

**TAKEN.**

*Gen.* 2:23 she was *t.* out of man
12:15 wo. was *t.* into P.'s house
19 I might have *t.* her to wife
14:14 Abr. heard brother was *t.*
18:27 I have *t.* upon me to speak
20:3 woman, thou hast *t.* is a w.
31:16 riches G. hath *t.* fr. father
*Num.* 3:12 *t.* Lev. 8:16, 18; 18:6
5:13 nei. she be *t.* with manner
31:49 ha. *t.* sum of men of war
*Deut.* 20:7 wife, and hath not *t.*
24:1 when a man hath *t.* wife
*Jos.* 7:15 he that is *t.* be burnt
16 the tribe of Judah was *t.*
17 Zabdi was *t.* 18 Ac. was *t.*
*Jud.* 15:6 because he had *t.* wife
17:2 1,100 shekels that were *t.*
1 *Sam.* 4:11 ark *t.* 17, 19, 21, 22
7:14 cities wh. Philistines had *t.*
10:21 S. *t.* 12:3 ox have I *t.*?
12:4 nor *t.* aught of man's hand
14:41 Saul and Jonathan were *t.*
42 cast lots, Jonathan was *t.*
30:19 noth. lacking they had *t.*
2 *Sam.* 12:9 hast *t.* his wife, 10
16:8 thou art *t.* in mischief
23:6 because they cannot be *t.*
1 *K.* 16:18 Zimri saw city was *t.*
2 *K.* 2:10 if thou see me when *t.*
18:10 ninth year of Ho. Sama. *t.*
*Ezr.* 9:2 they have *t.* of daught.
10:2 *t.* strange wives, 14, 17, 18
*Neh.* 5:15 hand *t.* of them bread
*Est.* 2:15 *t.* Esther for daughter
*Job* 16:12 hath *t.* me by my neck
24:24 they are *t.* out of the way
*Ps.* 9:15 in net hid is their foot *t.*
10:2 let them be *t.* in devices
59:12 let th. be *t.* in their pride
119:111 thy testimonies have I *t.*
*Prov.* 3:26 keep foot fr. being *t.*
6:2 art *t.* with words of mouth
11:6 transgressors shall be *t.*
*Ec.* 3:14 nor any thing *t.* from it
7:26 sinner shall be *t.* by her
*Is.* 7:5 have *t.* evil counsel agai.
8:15 many be broken, snared, *t.*
23:8 who hath *t.* coun. ag. T.?
24:18 be *t.* in snare, *Jer.* 48:44
28:13 mi. be broken, snared, *t.*
33:20 tabernacle not be *t.* down
41:9 wh. I ha. *t.* fr. ends of earth
53:8 he was *t.* from prison and
*Jer.* 6:11 husband with wife be *t.*
12:2 planted, they have *t.* root
34:3 thou sh. surely be *t.* 38:23
38:28 till day that Jerus. was *t.*
39:5 when they had *t.* him

40:1 when he had *t.* him, being
48:1 Kiriath. is *t.* 7 thou sh. be *t.*
41 Kerioth is *t.* 46 sons are *t.*
49:20 hear counsel *t.* against Ed.
50:2 Babylon is *t.* 24 ; 51:31, 41
*Lam.* 4:20 anointed of L. was *t.*
*Ezek.* 12:13 prince of Israel be *t.*
16:20 hast *t.* sons and daughte.
17:12 hath *t.* the king thereof
13 *t.* of king's seed, *t.* oath
20 he shall be *t.* in my snare
18:17 hath *t.* off his hand fr. po.
19:4 he was *t.* in their pit, 8
21:23 remembra. that they be *t.*
*Dan.* 5:2 whi. his father had *t.* 3
*Amos* 3:4 if ye have *t.* nothing, 5
12 so sh. I. be *t.* that dw. in S.
*Mat.* 9:15 bridegroom be *t.* fr. th.
21:43 kingd. of God be *t.* fr. you
24:40 one *t.* *Luke* 17:34, 35, 36
28:12 had *t.* counsel
*Mark* 4:25 fr. him *t.* that which
9:36 he had *t.* him in arms
*Luke* 5:5 toiled, have *t.* nothing
19:8 if I have *t.* any thing from
*John* 7:44 some wo. have *t.* him
*Acts* 2:23 have *t.* by wick. hands
8:33 for his life is *t.* from earth
23:27 this man was *t.* of Jews
*Rom.* 9:6 word ha. *t.* none effect
1 *Thes.* 2:17 *t.* from you a sh. ti.
2 *Thes.* 2:7 until he be *t.*
2 *Tim.* 2:26 who are *t.* captive
2 *Pet.* 2:12 made to be destroyed
*Rev.* 11:17 th. hast *t.* great power
19:20 beast was *t.* and wi. him

**TAKEN away.**

*Gen.* 21:25 Abim.'s ser. had *t. a.*
27:36 he hath *t. a.* my blessing
31:1 J. hath *t. a.* all that is our
*Ex.* 14:11 hast *t.* us *away* to die
*Lev.* 14:43 he hath *t. a.* stones
*Deut.* 26:14 nor *t. away* aught
*Jud.* 18:24 have *t. a.* my gods
1 *Sam.* 21:6 day when it was *t. a.*
1 *K.* 22:43 high places were not
*t. away*, 2 *K.* 12:3; 14:4;
2 *Chr.* 15:17 ; 20:33
2 *K.* 2:9 bef. I be *t. a.* from thee
*Job* 1:21 L. gave, L. hath *t. aw.*
20:19 hath violently *t. a.* house
27:2 who hath *t. a.* my judgme.
34:5 God hath *t. a.* my judgm.
20 mighty be *t. a.* with. hand
*Ps.* 85:3 th. hast *t. a.* thy wrath
*Prov.* 4:16 their sleep is *t. away*
*Is.* 6:7 thine iniquity is *t. away*
8:4 spoil of Samaria sh. be *t. a.*
16:10 glad. *t. a.* 17:1 Da. *t. a.*
52:5 my peo. is *t. a.* for naught
57:1 merciful *t. a.* righteo. *t. a.*
64:6 our iniquities have *t.* us *a.*
*Jer.* 16:5 I have *t. aw.* my peace
*Ezek.* 33:6 he is *t. a.* in his iniq.
*Amos* 4:10 I ha. *t. a.* your horses
*Mic.* 2:9 ye have *t. aw.* my glory
*Zep.* 3:15 L. ha. *t. a.* thy judgm.
*Mat.* 13:12 fr. him *t. a.* that he
hath, 25:29 ; *Luke* 8:18 ; 19:26
*Luke* 10:42 good part not be *t. a.*
*John* 19:31 that th. might be *t. a.*
*Acts* 27:20 sho. be saved was *t. a.*
1 *Cor.* 5:2 done th. might be *t. a.*

**TAKEN hold.**

1 *K.* 9:9 have *t. h.* on other gods
*Job* 30:16 days of afflic. have *t. h.*
*Ps.* 40:12 iniquities have *t. hold*
*Is.* 21:3 pangs have *t. h.* on me

**TAKEN up.**

*Ex.* 40:36 cloud was *t. up* from
*Num.* 9:17 w. cloud was *t. up*, 21
2 *Sam.* 18:9 Absalom was *t. up*
*Jer.* 29:22 of th. sh. be *t. up* curse
*Ezek.* 36:3 ye are *t. up* in the lips
*Luke* 9:17 *t. up* of fragments
*Acts* 1:9 he was *t. up*, a cloud
11 Jesus which is *t. up* fr. you
22 unto day he was *t. up* fr. us
20:9 Eutychus fell, *t. up* dead

**TAKEST.**

*Ps.* 144:3 that *t.* knowl. of him?
*Is.* 58:3 thou *t.* no knowledge
*Luke* 19:21 *t.* up thou layedst not

**TAKEST heed.**

1 *Chr.* 22:13 if *t. h.* to fulfil statu.

**TAKETH.**

*Ex.* 20:7 that *t.* his name in vain,
*Deut.* 5:11
32:11 an eagle *t.* them, beareth
*Jos.* 7:14 tribe L. *t.* shall come
*Job* 5:13 he *t.* wise in their crafti-
ness, 1 *Cor.* 3:19
9:12 *t.* away, who can hinder?
12:20 and *t.* away understand.
27:8 what is hope when God *t.*?
*Ps.* 118:7 L. *t.* my part with th.
149:4 L. *t.* pleasure in his people
*Prov.* 1:19 which *t.* away life of
16:32 better than he that *t.* city
26:17 one that *t.* a dog by ears
*Ec.* 1:3 of his labor which he *t.*
*Ec.* 2:23 heart *t.* not rest in nig.
*Is.* 40:15 he *t.* up isles as a little
51:18 nor is there that *t.* her by
*Ezek.* 16:32 wh. *t.* strangers inst.
33:4 *t.* not warning ; 5 *t.* warn.
*Mat.* 4:5 devil *t.* him up into ho.
10:38 that *t.* not his cross, and
12:45 *t.* sev. spirits, *Luke* 11:26
*Mark* 4:15 Satan cometh, and *t.*
away word, *Luke* 8:12
5:40 he *t.* father and mother of
9:18 wher. he *t.* him, he teareth
*Luke* 6:30 that *t.* goods, ask not
9:39 a spirit *t.* him, he suddenly
*John* 1:29 Lamb of G. *t.* away sin
10:18 no man *t.* it from me
16:22 your joy no man *t.* fr. you
21:13 Je. then cometh, *t.* bread
1 *Cor.* 11:21 every one *t.* bef. an.
*Heb.* 10:9 he *t.* away the first

**TAKETH hold.**

*Job* 21:6 tremb. *t. h.* on my flesh
*Prov.* 30:28 spider *t. h.* wi. hands
*Is.* 56:6 that *t. h.* of my covenant

**TAKING.**

2 *Chr.* 19:7 with God no *t.* of gif.
*Job* 5:3 I have seen foolish *t.* root
*Ps.* 119:9 by *t.* heed thereto
*Jer.* 50:46 at noise of *t.* of Babyl.
*Hos.* 11:3 I taught Ephraim also
to go, *t.* them by their arms
*Mat.* 6:27 by *t.* tho. *Luke* 12:25
*Luke* 19:22 *t.* up I laid not down
*John* 11:13 he had spok. of *t.* rest
2 *Cor.* 2:13 *t.* my leave of them, I
3 *John* 7 th. went forth *t.* nothi.

**TALE, S.**

*Ps.* 90:9 we spend years as a *t.*
*Ezek.* 22:9 carry *t.* to shed blood
*Luke* 24:11 th. words seemed as *t.*

**TALEBEARER.**

*Lev.* 19:16 shalt not go as a *t.*
*Prov.* 11:13 *t.* rev. secrets, 20:19
18:8 words *t.* are wounds, 26:22
26:20 where is no *t.* strife

**TALE,** *reckoning.*

*Ex.* 5:8 the *t.* of bricks which
18 yet shall he deliver the *t.* of
1 *Sam.* 18:27 foreski. in *t.* to king
1 *Chr.* 9:28 bring vessels in by *t.*

**TALENT.**

*Ex.* 25:39 *t.* of pure gold, 37:24
38:27 sockets, a *t.* for a socket
2 *Sam.* 12:30 weight of crown a *t.*
1 *K.* 20:39 shalt pay a *t.* of silver
2 *K.* 5:22 give them a *t.* of silver
23:33 of *t.* of gold, 2 *Chr.* 36:3
*Zec.* 5:7 th. was lifted a *t.* of lead
*Mat.* 25:25 I went and hid thy *t.*
28 take therefore the *t.* fr. him
*Rev.* 16:21 sto. about weight of *t.*

**TALENTS.**

*Ex.* 38:24 gold of off. was 29 *t.*
27 100 *t.* of silver were cast
1 *K.* 16:24 bought hill for two *t.*
2 *K.* 5:5 Naaman took ten *t.*
23 said, Be content, take two *t.*
15:19 Menahem gave P. 1,000 *t.*
18:14 appointed to Hezek. 300 *t.*
23:33 trib. of 100 *t.* 2 *Chr.* 36:3
1 *Chr.* 19:6 Ammon. sent 1,000 *t.*
29:4 David gave 3,000 *t.* of gold
7 gold 5,000 *t.* of silver 10,000 *t.*
2 *Chr.* 25:9 what do for 100 *t.*?
27:5 child. of Ammon gave 100 *t.*
*Mat.* 18:24 one ow. him 10,000 *t.*
25:15 to one he gave five *t.*

*See* GOLD, SILVER.

**TALITHA cumi.**

*Mark* 5:41 he said unto her, *t. c.*

**TALK, Substantive.**

*Job* 11:2 man full of *t.* be justi.?
15:3 reason wi. unprofitable *t.*?
*Prov.* 14:23 *t.* of lips tendeth to
*Ec.* 10:13 end of *t.* is mischievo.
*Mat.* 22:15 mi. entangle him in *t.*

**TALK, Verb.**

*Num.* 11:17 I will come and *t.*
*Deut.* 5:24 seen that God doth *t.*
6:7 shall *t.* of them when thou
1 *Sam.* 2:3 *t.* no more so proudly
2 *K.* 18:26 *t.* not with us in the
1 *Chr.* 16:9 *t.* ye of all his won-
drous works, *Ps.* 105:2
*Job* 13:7 will ye *t.* deceitfully?
*Ps.* 69:26 they *t.* to the grief of
71:24 my tongue shall *t.* of thy
77:12 I will *t.* of thy doings
119:27 so shall I *t.* of thy works
145:11 speak of thy king. and *t.*
*Prov.* 6:22 when th. awa. it sh. *t.*
24:2 and their lips *t.* of mischi.
*Jer.* 12:1 let me *t.* with th. of thy
*Ezek.* 3:22 arise, I will *t.* wi. thee
*Dan.* 10:17 how can thy serv. *t.*
*John* 14:30 I will not *t.* much

**TALKED.**

*Gen.* 45:15 his breth. *t.* with him
*Ex.* 20:22 I *t.* with you, *Deut.* 5:4
33:9 and the Lord *t.* with Moses
34:29 his face shone while he *t.*
1 *Sam.* 14:19 Saul *t.* unto priest
2 *Chr.* 25:16 it ca. to pass as he *t.*
*Jer.* 38:25 if princes hear I ha. *t.*
*Luke* 9:30 *t.* with him two men
24:32 heart burn while he *t.*
*John* 4:27 marvelled that he *t.*
*Acts* 10:27 as P. *t.* with Cornelius
20:11 *t.* long, till break of day
26:31 th. *t.* between themselves
*Rev.* 21:15 he th. *t.* with me had

**TALKERS.**

*Ezek.* 36:3 taken up in lips of *t.*
*Tit.* 1:10 there are many vain *t.*

**TALKEST, ETH.**

*Jud.* 6:17 show me a sign thou *t.*
1 *K.* 1:14 while thou *t.* with king
*Ps.* 37:30 his tongue *t.* of judgm.
*John* 4:27 why *t.* thou with her?
9:37 it is he that *t.* with thee

**TALKING.**

*Gen.* 17:22 he left off *t.* with him
1 *K.* 18:27 he is *t.* or pursuing
*Est.* 6:14 while they were *t.* wi.
*Ezek.* 33:30 people are *t.* ag. thee
*Mat.* 17:3 Mo. and Elias *t.* with
him, *Mark* 9:4
*Rev.* 4:1 voice of a trumpet *t.*

**TALKING.**

*Job* 29:9 the princes refrained *t.*
*Eph.* 5:4 filthiness, nor foolish *t.*

**TALL.**

*Deut.* 2:10 *t.* as Anak. 21 ; 9:2
1 *K.* 19:23 will cut down *t.* cedar-
trees, *Is.* 37:24

**TALLER.**
Deut. 1:28 people is t. than we

**TAMAR.**
Gen. 38:6 a wife, wh. na. was T.
24 was told Judah, T. hath
Ruth 4:12 Pharez, wh. T. bare to Judah, 1 Chr. 2:4; Mat. 1:3
2 Sam. 13:1 a fair sister, na. T.
2 Amn. fell sick for T. 22, 32
14:27 daugh. wh. name was T.
Ezek. 47:19 side southward fr. T.

**TAME, ED.**
Mark 5:4 neith. could man t. him
Jam. 3:7 of sea is t. hath been t.
8 the tongue can no man t.

**TAMMUZ.**
Ezek. 8:14 wom. weeping for T.

**TANNER.**
Acts. 9:43 Pe. tarried wi. Si. a t.
10:6 lodged with Simon a t. 32

TAPESTRY. *See* COVERINGS.

**TARE.**
2 Sam. 13:31 king t. his garmen.
2 K. 2:24 two she-bears t. 42 chil.
Mark 9:20 spi. t. him, Luke 9:42

**TARES.**
Mat. 13:25 his enemy sowed t.
26 then appeared the t. also
29 lest while you gather up t.

**TARGET, S.**
1 Sam. 17:6 Goli. had a t. of brass
1 K. 10:16 Solom. made 200 t. 600 shekels to one t. 2 Chr. 9:15
2 Chr. 14:8 army that bare t.

**TARRY.**
Gen. 19:2 t. all night, and wash
27:44 t. with Laban a few days
30:27 if I found favor in eyes t.
45:9 come down to me, t. not
Ex. 12:39 thrust out, cou. not t.
24:14 t. ye here till we come
Num. 22:19 I pray you, t. here
Jud. 5:28 why t. wheels of ch.?
6:18 I will t. until thou come
Ruth 1:13 would ye t. for them
1 Sam. 1:23 t. until th. ha. wea.
10:8 seven days shalt thou t.
2 Sam. 10:5 at Jeri. till beards be grown, 1 Chr. 19:5
11:12 t. to-day; 15:28 I will t.
18:14 Joab said, I may not t.
19:7 th. will not t. one with th.
2 K. 2:2 t. here, L. sent me, 4, 6
7:9 if we t. till morning light
14:10 gl. of this, and t. at home
Ps. 101:7 liar not t. in my sight
Prov. 23:30 that t. long at wine
Is. 46:13 my salvation sh. not t.
Jer. 14:8 turneth to t. for night
Hab. 2:3 though it t. wait for it, for it will not t.
Mat. 26:38 t. and wa. Mark 14:34
Luke 24:29 he went to t. with th.
49 t. ye in city of Jerusalem
John 4:40 besought that he w. t.
21:22 if I will that he t. 23
Acts 10:48 th. prayed Peter to t.
18:20 they desired Paul to t.
28:14 were desired to t. 7 days
1 Cor. 11:33 wheref. t. one for a.
16:7 I tr. to t. a while with you
8 I will t. at Ephesus until P.
1 Tim. 3:15 if I t. long thou may.
Heb. 10:37 will come, and not t.

**TARRIED.**
Gen. 24:54 Abraham's servant t.
28:11 Jacob t. there all night
31:54 J. and Leb. t. all night
Num. 9:19 wh. cloud t. long, 22
Jud. 3:25 t. they were ashamed
19:8 they t. till the afternoon
Ruth 2:7 save that she t. a little
1 Sam. 13:8 he t. 7 days accord.
2 Sam. 15:17 king t. in place
20:5 he t. longer than set time
Ps. 68:12 she that t. divid. spoil
Mat. 25:5 bridegroom t. th. slept
Luke 1:21 people marvelled he t.
2:43 child Jesus t. in Jerusalem
John 3:22 he t. and baptized
Acts 9:43 P. t. many days in Jop.
18:18 Paul t. a good while at C.
20:5 going befo. t. for us at Tr.
21:4 finding disci. we t. 7 days
10 as we t. many days at Cesa.
25:6 Festus t. at Jerus. ten days
27:33 fourteenth day ye t. fast.
28:12 at Syracuse, we t. 3 days

**TARRIEST, ETH.**
1 Sam. 30:24 part that t. by stuff
Mic. 5:7 that t. not for a man,
Acts 22:16 and now why t. thou?

**TARRYING.**
Ps. 40:17 make no t. O G. 70:5

**TARSHISH.**
Gen. 10:4 Elisha, T. 1 Chr. 1:7
1 K. 10:22 for the king had at sea a navy of T. 2 Chr. 9:21
2 Chr. 20:36 make ships go to T.
37 broken, not able to go to T.
Ps. 48:7 th. breakest ships of T.
72:10 the kings of T. shall bring
Is. 2:16 Lord on all ships of T.
23:1 howl, ye ships of T. 14
6 pass over to T. howl, ye
10 thy land, O daughter of T.
60:9 the ships of T. shall wait
66:19 those that escape to T.
Jer. 10:9 silver is brought fr. T.
Ezek. 27:12 T. was thy merchant
25 ships of T. did sing of thee
38:13 the merchants of T. shall
Jon. 1:3 rose up to flee unto T.
4:2 I fled before unto T. for I

**TARSUS.**
Acts 9:11 inq. for one Saul of T.
30 the brethren sent him to T.
11:25 Barnabas departed to T.
21:39 who am a Jew of T. 22:3

**TARTAK.**
2 K. 17:31 made T. their god

TARTAN. 2 K. 18:17

**TASK, S.**
Ex. 5:13 fulfil works, daily t.
14 why not fulfilled t. in mak.
19 not minish fr. your daily t.

**TASKMASTERS.**
Ex. 1:11 they set over them t.
3:7 cry by reason of their t.
5:10 t. told people; 13 t. hasted

**TASTE, Substantive.**
Ex. 16:31 t. of manna like wafers
Num. 11:8 t. was as t. of fresh oil
Job 6:6 any t. in white of an egg?
30 my t. disc. perverse things
Ps. 119:103 sw. thy word to t.!
Prov. 24:13 honey-co. sweet to t.
Cant. 2:3 fruit sweet to my t.
Jer. 48:11 his t. remained in him

**TASTE, Verb.**
1 Sam. 14:43 but t. a little honey
2 Sam. 3:35 if I t. bread or aught
19:35 can servant t. what I eat?
Job 12:11 doth not mouth t. meat
Ps. 34:8 O t. and see L. is good
Jon. 3:7 nor flock t. any thing
Mat. 16:28 so. stand. here not t. of death, Mark 9:1; Lu. 9:27
Luke 14:24 none bidden t. of sup.
John 8:52 keep say. nev. t. death
Col. 2:21 touch not, t. not,
Heb. 2:9 sho. t. death for ev. man

**TASTED, ETH.**
1 Sam. 14:24 none t. 29 I t. hon.
Job 34:3 words as mouth t. meat
Dan. 5:2 Belshaz. while he t. wi.
Mat. 27:34 wh. he had t. thereof
John 2:9 ruler t. wat. made wine
Heb. 6:4 have t. of heavenly gift
1 Pet. 2:3 t. that L. is gracious

**TATTLERS.**
1 Tim. 5:13 not only idle, but t.

TATNAI. Ezr. 5:3, 6

**TAUGHT.**
Deut. 4:5 I have t. you statutes
31:22 Moses t. the children of Is.
Jud. 8:16 he t. men of Succoth
2 K. 17:28 t. them how to fear L.
2 Chr. 6:27 ha. t. them good way
17:9 Levites t. people in Judah
23:13 rejoiced, t. to sing praise
30:22 that t. knowledge of L.
35:3 Josiah said to L. that t. Is.
Neh. 8:9 Levites that t. people
Ps. 71:17 hast t. me, 119:102
119:171 hast t. me thy statutes
Prov. 4:4 he t. me also, and said
11 I t. thee in way of wisdom
31:1 prophecy his moth. t. him
Ec. 12:9 he t. people knowledge
Is. 29:13 fear t. by prec. of men
40:13 being counsel. t. him, 14
54:13 thy child. shall be t. of G.
Jer. 2:33 theref. hast th. t. wick.
9:5 they t. tongues to speak lies
14 after Baalim, whi. fathers t.
12:16 t. my peo. to swear by B.
13:21 t. them to be captains
28:16 t. them rebellion ag. Lord
29:32 he hath t. rebellion ag. L.
32:33 tho' I t. them, rising early
Ezek. 23:48 women t. not lewdn.
Hos. 10:11 Ephr. is as a heifer t.
11:3 I t. Ephraim to go, taking
Zec. 13:5 t. me to keep cattle
Mat. 7:29 he t. them as one having authority, Mark 1:22
28:15 th. took money, did as t.
Mark 6:30 told things done and t.
10:1 as he wont he t. th. again
Luke 11:1 as John t. his disciples
13:26 thou hast t. in our streets
John 6:45 they sh. be all t. of G.
7:14 Je. went into temple, t. 28; Mark 12:35; Lu. 19:47; 20:1
8:2 peo. came, he sat and t. th.
28 as my Father hath t. me, I
18:20 I ever t. in the synagogue
Acts 4:2 grieved that they t. peo.
5:21 entered temple early and t.
11:26 P. and Barn. t. peo. 14:21
15:1 certain men t. the brethren
18:25 Apollos t. dilig. thi. of L.
20:20 I showed you and t. pub.
22:3 t. accord. to manner of law
Gal. 1:12 nor t. but by revelation
6:6 let him that is t. communi.
Eph. 4:21 if ye have been t.
Col. 2:7 faith, as ye have been t.
1 Thes. 4:9 ye are t. of G. to love
2 Thes. 2:15 hold tradi. ye have t.
Tit. 1:9 word, as he hath been t.
1 John 2:27 as anoint. ha. t. you
Rev. 2:14 t. Bal. to cast stum.-bl.

**TAUNT, ING.**
Jer. 24:9 I deliver them to be a t.
Ezek. 5:15 so it be repro. and t.
Hab. 2:6 these take up a t. prov.

**TAXATION.**
2 K. 23:35 exacted of every one t.

**TAXED.**
2 K. 23:35 Jehoiakim t. the land
Luke 2:1 a decree world sho. be t.
3 all went to be t. 5 J. to be t.

**TAXES, ING.**
Dan. 11:20 stand up a raiser of t.
Luke 2:2 t. first made when Cy.
Acts 5:37 rose up J in days of t.

**TEACH.**
Ex. 4:15 I will t. wh. ye sh. do
35:34 G. put in his heart he t.
Lev. 10:11 may t. Is. all statutes
14:57 to t. when uncl. and clean

*Deut.* 4:1 hearken to judgm. I t.
10 that they may t. their child.
14 L. commanded me to t. 6:1
31:19 write and t. child. of Is.
33:10 they sh. t. Ja. judgments
*Jud.* 13:8 t. us what we shall do
1 *Sam.* 12:23 wi. t. you good way
2 *Sam.* 1:18 bade th. t. use of bow
2 *Chr.* 17:7 t. in cities of Judah.
*Ezr.* 7:10 to t. in Israel statutes
*Job* 21:22 shall any t. G. knowl.
27:11 will t. you by hand of G.
32:7 multitude of years t. wisd.
37:19 t. us what we shall say
*Ps.* 25:8 he will t. sinners
9 meek will he guide and t.
*Ps.* 25:12 him th. fear. L. sh. he t.
34:11 I will t. you fear of the L.
51:13 I t. transgress. thy ways
90:12 t. us to number our days
105:22 and t. his senators wisd.
*Prov.* 9:9 t. a just man, he incre.
*Is.* 2:3 t. us his ways, *Mic.* 4:2
28:9 whom sh. he t. knowledge
26 G. doth instruct and t. him
*Jer.* 9:20 t. your daught. wailing
31:34 t. no more nei. *Heb.* 8:11
*Ezek.* 44:23 t. my peo. difference
*Dan.* 1:4 whom they might t.
*Mic.* 3:11 priests ther. t. for hire
*Hab.* 2:19 saith to stone, it sh. t.
*Mat.* 5:19 t. men so; 28:19 t. na.
*Luke* 11:1 Lord, t. us to pray
12:12 Holy Gh. t. what to say
*John* 7:35 t. Gent. 9:34 dost t.?
14:26 Holy Gh. t. you all things
*Acts* 1:1 Jesus began to do and t.
4:18 nor t. in name of Je. 5:28
5:42 ceased not to t. Jesus Chr.
16:21 t. customs wh. not lawful
1 *Cor.* 4:17 as I t. every where in
11:14 doth not nature itself t.
14:19 by voice I might t. others
1 *Tim.* 1:3 charge t. no oth. doc.
2:12 I suffer not a woman to t.
3:2 bish. apt to t. 2 *Tim.* 2:24
4:11 these thi. command and t.
6:2 these things t. and exhort
3 if any t. otherw. he is proud
2 *Tim.* 2:2 men able to t. others
*Tit.* 2:4 t. yo. women to be sober
*Heb.* 5:12 need that one t. you
1 *John* 2:27 need not that any t.
*Rev.* 2:20 sufferest Jezebel to t.
*See* BEGAN.

### TEACH me.

*Job* 6:24 t. *me*, will hold tongue
34:32 wh. I see not, t. thou *me*
*Ps.* 25:4 t. *me* paths; 5 le. and t.
27:11 t. *me* thy way, O L. 86:11
119:12 t. *me* thy statutes, 26, 33, 64, 68, 124, 135
66 t. *me* judgm. 108 t. m. thy j.
143:10 t. *me* to do thy will

### TEACH thee.

*Ex.* 4:12 I t. t. what th. sh. say
*Deut.* 17:11 sentence they sh. t. t.
*Job* 8:10 fath. sh. they not t. t.?
12:7 ask beasts, they shall t. t.
8 speak to earth, it shall t. t.
33:33 hold peace, I sh. t. t. wisd.
*Ps.* 32:8 will t. t. in way sh. go.
45:4 ri. hand sh. t. t. ter. things

### TEACH them.

*Ex.* 18:20 shalt t. t. ordinances
24:12 writ. th. thou mayest t. t.
*Deut.* 4:9 t. *them* thy son's sons
5:31 judgments thou shalt t. t.
6:7 t. *them* to thy children, 11:19
*Jud.* 3:2 Is. might know to t. t.
1 *K.* 8:36 thou t. *them* good way
2 *K.* 17:27 let him t. t. manner of
*Ezr.* 7:25 t. ye t. that know not
*Ps.* 132:12 keep testimony I t. t.
*Mat.* 5:19 whoso shall do and t. t.
*Mark* 6:34 began t. t. many thi.
8:31 to t. t. Son of man suffer

### TEACHER.

1 *Chr.* 25:8 as well t. as scholar
*Hab.* 2:18 profit. image, t. of lies
*John* 3:2 thou art a t. come fr. G.
*Rom.* 2:20 confident thou art a t.
1 *Tim.* 2:7 t. of Gent. 2 *Tim.* 1:11

### TEACHERS.

*Ps.* 119:99 more underst. than t.
*Prov.* 5:13 not obeyed voice of t.
*Is.* 30:20 yet sh. not t. be remov. but thine eyes sh. see thy t.
43:27 thy t. have transgressed
*Acts* 13:1 at Anti. were certain t.
1 *Cor.* 12:28 proph. t. 29 all t.?
*Eph.* 4:11 evangelists, pastors, t.
1 *Tim.* 1:7 desir. to be t. of law
2 *Tim.* 4:3 heap to themselves t.
*Tit.* 2:3 women be t. of good thi.
*Heb.* 5:12 time ye ought to be t.
2 *Pet.* 2:1 sh. be false t. am. you

### TEACHEST.

*Ps.* 94:12 blessed is man thou t.
*Mat.* 22:16 t. way of G. in truth, *Mark* 12:14; *Luke* 20:21
*Acts* 21:21 t. Jews to forsake M.
*Rom.* 2:21 t. ano. t. not thyself?

### TEACHETH.

2 *Sam.* 22:35 he t. my hands to war, *Ps.* 18:34
*Job* 35:11 who t. more th. beasts
36:22 G. exalt. who t. like him?
*Ps.* 94:10 that t. man knowledge
144:1 which t. my hands to war
*Prov.* 6:13 wick. man t. wi. fing.
*Prov.* 16:23 hea. of wise t. his m.
*Is.* 9:15 the prophet that t. lies
48:17 I am thy G. which t. thee
*Acts* 21:28 man that t. all men
*Rom.* 12:7 he that t. on teaching
1 *Cor.* 2:13 wis. t. but wh. H. G. t.
*Gal.* 6:6 communi. to him th. t.
1 *John* 2:27 same anointing t. you

### TEACHING.

2 *Chr.* 15:3 Is. without t. priest
*Jer.* 32:33 rising early and t. th.
*Mat.* 4:23 Jesus went about Galilee, t. 9:35; *Luke* 13:10
15:9 t. for doctrines commandments of men, *Mark* 7:7
26:55 I sat daily t. in temple
28:20 t. them to observe all thi.
*Luke* 23:5 t. throughout all Jewry
*Acts* 5:25 the apostles t. the peo.
15:35 Paul and B. in Antioch t.
*Rom.* 12:7 he that teacheth on t.
*Col.* 1:28 warning and t. ev. man
3:16 t. and admonish. one ano.
*Tit.* 1:11 t. things they ought not
2:12 t. us, denying ungodliness

### TEAR, Verb.

*Jud.* 8:7 then will I t. your flesh
*Ps.* 7:2 lest t. my soul like lion
35:15 they did t. me, ceased not
50:22 consider this, lest I t. you
*Jer.* 15:3 I will appoint dogs to t.
16:7 nor shall men t. themselves
*Ezek.* 13:20 your pillows I will t.
*Hos.* 5:14 I will t. and go away
13:8 the wild beast shall t. them
*Amos* 1:11 his anger did t. perp.
*Nah.* 2:12 the lion did t. enough
*Zec.* 11:16 shepherd sh. t. claws

### TEARETH.

*Deut.* 33:20 as a lion, and t. arm
*Job* 16:9 he t. me in his wrath
18:4 he t. himself in his anger
*Mic.* 5:8 young lion t. in pieces
*Mark* 9:18 he t. him, *Luke* 9:39

### TEARS.

2 *K.* 20:5 I have seen t. *Is.* 38:5
*Job* 16:20 mine eye pour. out t.
*Ps.* 6:6 I water my couch with t.
39:12 hold not peace at my t.
42:3 my t. have been my meat
56:8 put th. my t. in thy bottle
80:5 wi. bread of t. giv. t. to dr.
116:8 hast delivered eyes from t.
126:5 th. sow in t. sh. reap in joy
*Ec.* 4:1 behold the t. of such as
*Is.* 16:9 I will water thee with t.
25:8 the Lord will wipe away t.
*Jer.* 9:1 O that mi. eyes were t.!
18 our eyes run down with t.
13:17 eyes sh. run down with t.
14:17 let mine eyes run with t.
31:16 weeping, thine eyes fr. t.
*Lam.* 1:2 t. are on her cheeks
2:11 mine eyes do fail with t.
18 let t. run down like a river
*Ezek.* 24:16 neither sh. thy t. run
*Mal.* 2:13 cover. altar of L. wi. t.
*Mark* 9:24 father said with t. L.
*Luke* 7:38 to wash feet with t.
44 she washed my feet with t.
*Acts* 20:19 serving the L. with t.
31 cease not to warn with t.
2 *Cor.* 2:4 I wrote to you with t.
2 *Tim.* 1:4 mindful of thy t.
*Heb.* 5:7 offered supplica. with t.
12:17 he sought it caref. with t.
*Rev.* 7:17 G. sh. wipe away t. 21:4

### TEATS.

*Is.* 32:12 they shall lament for t.
*Ezek.* 23:3 they bruised the t. 21

### TEBETH.

*Est.* 2:16 tenth month, wh. is T.

### TEDIOUS.

*Acts* 24:4 that I be not t. to thee

### TEETH.

*Gen.* 49:12 his t. shall be white
*Num.* 11:33 wh. flesh was bet. t.
*Deut.* 32:24 will send t. of beasts
1 *Sam.* 2:13 flesh-hook of three t.
*Job* 4:10 t. of lions are broken
13:14 wherefore take flesh in t.?
19:20 I escap. with skin of my t.
29:17 plucked spoil out of t. of
41:14 Leviathan's t. are terrible
*Ps.* 3:7 hast broken t. of ungodly
57:4 who. t. are spe. and arrows
58:6 break th. t. O G. in mouth
124:6 not given us as prey to t.
*Prov.* 10:26 as vinegar to the t.
30:14 wh. t. are swords. jaw-t.
*Cant.* 4:2 thy t. like a flock, 6:6
*Is.* 41:15 make instrum. hav. t.
*Jer.* 31:29 children's t. are set on edge, *Ezek.* 18:2
*Lam.* 3:16 hath broken my t.
*Dan.* 7:7 4th beast had iron t. 19
*Joel* 1:6 cheek t. of a great lion
*Amos* 4:6 have given clean. of t.
*Mic.* 3:5 bite with t. cry peace
*Zec.* 9:7 abominations from his t.
*Mat.* 27:44 cast the same in his t.
*Rev.* 9:8 their t. as the t. of lions
*See* GNASH.

### TEIL-TREE.

*Is.* 6:13 as a t.-t. and as an oak

### TEKEL.

*Dan.* 5:25 writ. Mene, Mene, *T.*
27 *T.* thou art weighed in the

### TEKOAH, *or* TEKOA.

2 *Sam.* 14:2 Joab sent to T. to
4 when the woman of T. spake
1 *Chr.* 2:24 Asher father of T.
4:5 Asher the father of T. had
2 *Chr.* 11:6 built Etam and T.
20:20 into the wilderness of T.
*Jer.* 6:1 blow the trumpet in T.
*Amos* 1:1 among herdmen of T.

### TELL.

*Gen.* 15:5 t. stars if thou be able
32:5 I have sent to t. my lord
45:13 t. my father of my glory
*Ex.* 10:2 may. t. in ears of son
*Num.* 14:14 they will t. inhabita.
1 *Sam.* 6:2 t. us wherewith we
9:8 man of God, to t. us way
17:55 as liv. O king, I cannot t.

22:22 I knew he would t. Saul
27:11 lest they t. on us, saying
2 Sam. 1:20 t. it not in Gath
1 K. 1:20 that thou shouldest t.
18:12 when I come and t. Ahab
2 K. 7:9 th. we may t. the king's
9:12 said, It is false; t. us now
15 let none escape to go to t. it
Ps. 22:17 I may t. my bones
26:7 t. of thy wondrous works
48:13 that ye may t. the genera.
Prov. 30:4 na. if thou canst t.?
Ec. 6:12 who can t. what, 10:14
8:7 who can t. when it sh. be?
10:20 that hath wings sh. t. mat.
Is. 6:9 t. this peo.; 48:20 t. this
Jer. 15:2 t. such as are for death
23:27 dreams wh. they t. 28:32
36:16 we will t. king of th. words
17 t. us how thou didst write
Ezek. 24:19 not t. us what thi.?
Dan. 2:4 O king, t. thy serv. 7
Joel 1:3 t. your child. let child. t.
Jon. 3:9 who can t. if God will
Mat. 8:4 see thou t. no man, Mark 8:26, 30; 9:9; Lu. 5:14; 8:56; Acts 23:22
17:9 t. the vision to no man
18:15 t. him his fault alone
17 if he negl. to hear t. church
21:5 t. ye the daughter of Sion
24:3 t. us when shall these things be, Mark, 13:4
26:63 t. us whether thou be C. Luke 22:67; John 10:24
28:7 go and t. that he is risen
9 went to t. discip. Mark 16:7
Mark 1:30 they t. him of her
5:19 t. them how great things
11:33 we cannot t. Mat. 21:27; Luke 20:7
Luke 7:22 t. J. what ye have seen
John 3:8 canst not t. whence
4:25 wh. he is come, he will t.
8:14 cannot t. whence I come
16:18 a little while? cannot t.
18:34 or did others t. it of me?
Acts 15:27 shall t. same things
17:21 either to t. or hear some
2 Cor. 12:2 out of body I can. t. 3
Heb. 11:32 time would fail to t.

**TELL me.**

Gen. 12:18 why didst not t. me?
24:49 t. me, if not, t. me that
31:27 steal aw. didst not t. me
32:29 Ja. said, t. me thy name
37:16 t. me wh. they feed flocks
Jos. 7:19 t. me what hast done
Ruth 4:4 if not redeem it, t. me
1 Sam. 14:43 S. said, t. me what
20:10 D. said, Who shall t. me?
2 Sam. 1:4 how went mat. t. me
1 K. 22:16 t. me noth. but truth
2 K. 4:2 what do for thee, t. me
Job 34:34 men of underst. t. me
Cant. 1:7 t. me, O th. whom my
Mat. 21:24 th. which if you t. me
Luke 7:42 t. me wh. of them will
John 20:15 t. me wh. ha. laid him
Acts 23:19 what hast to t. me?
Gal. 4:21 t. me ye that desire to

**TELL thee.**

Ex. 14:12 the word we did t. t.
Num. 23:3 showeth me, I will t. t.
Deut. 17:11 the judgm. they t. t.
Jud. 14:16 told it and sh. I t. it t.
Ruth 3:4 he will t. thee what th.
1 Sam. 9:19 t. t. that is in heart
15:16 will t. thee what L. said
19:3 and what I see, I will t. t.
20:9 then would not I t. it t.?
1 Chr. 17:10 I t. thee that the L.
Job 1:15 escap. to t. t. 16, 17, 19
Is. 19:12 let thy wise men t. thee
Luke 12:59 I t. t. sh. not depart
Acts 10:6 t. t. what to do, 11:14

**I TELL you.**

Gen. 49:1 that I may t. you what
Is. 42:9 forth I t. you of them
Mat. 10:27 what I t. you in dark.
Mark 11:29 I t. y. by wh. author.
Luke 4:25 I t. y. of a truth, 9:27
13:27 I t. you I know you not
19:40 I t. y. if these hold peace
22:67 said, If I t. you, not belie.
John 3:12 beli. if I t. you of heav.
8:45 I t. y. the truth, Gal. 4:16
13:19 now I t. you befo. it come
16:7 I t. you truth, it is expedi.
Gal. 5:21 of which I t. y. before
Phil. 3:18 of whom I now t. you

**TELLEST.**

Ps. 56:8 thou t. my wanderings

**TELLETH.**

2 Sam. 7:11 the L. t. thee that he
2 K. 6:12 Elisha t. the king of Is.
Ps. 41:6 when he goeth he t. it
101:7 he th. t. lies sh. not tarry
147:4 he t. number of the stars
Jer. 33:13 hands of him that t. th.
John 12:22 Philip cometh t. And.

**TELLING.**

Jud. 7:15 Gid. heard t. of dream
2 Sam. 11:19 made an end of t.
2 K. 8:5 as he was t. the king

**TEMA.**

Gen. 25:15 Hadar, T. 1 Chr. 1:30
Job 6:19 troops of T. looked for
Is. 21:14 the inhabitants of T.
Jer. 25:23 I made T. to drink the

**TEMAN.**

Gen. 36:11 sons of Eliphaz, T.
15 duke T. 42; 1 Chr. 1:53
Jer. 49:7 is wisd. no more in T.?
20 hath purposed against T.
Ezek. 25:13 make desolate fr. T.
Amos 1:12 send a fire upon T.
Ob. 9 thy mighty men, O T.
Hab. 3:3 God came from T. Holy

**TEMPERANCE.**

Acts 24:25 as he reasoned of t.
Gal. 5:23 t. ag. such th. no law
2 Pet. 1:6 add to know. t. and to t.

**TEMPERATE.**

1 Cor. 9:25 striv. for mastery is t.
Tit. 1:8 bishop be t. 2:2 aged t.

**TEMPER.**

Ezek. 46:14 oil to t. wi. fine flour

**TEMPERED.**

Ex. 29:2 unleavened t. with oil
30:35 a perfume t. together
1 Cor. 12:24 God hath t. body

**TEMPEST.**

Job 9:17 he breaketh me with a t.
27:20 a t. stealeth him away in
Ps. 11:6 on wicked sh. he rain t.
55:8 I hasten from storm and t.
83:15 so persecute them with t.
Is. 28:2 which as a t. of hail
29:6 visited with storm and t.
30:30 Assyr. be beaten with a t.
32:2 man shall be a covert fr. t.
54:11 O afflicted, tossed with t.
Amos 1:14 t. in day of whirlw.
Jon. 1:4 was a mighty t. in sea
12 for my sake great t. is come
Mat. 8:24 there arose a t. in sea
Acts 27:18 exceed. tossed with t.
20 no small t. lay on us, hope
Heb. 12:18 not co. to darkn. and t.
2 Pet. 2:17 clouds carried with a t.

**TEMPESTUOUS.**

Ps. 50:3 be very t. round him
Jon. 1:11 sea wrought and t. 13
Acts 27:14 arose ag. it t. wind

**TEMPLE.**

2 Sam. 22:7 he did hear my voice out of his t. Ps. 18:6
1 K. 6:17 t. before 40 cubits long
2 Chr. 36:7 put vessels in t. at B.
Ezr. 4:1 they builded t. unto L.
5:14 took out t. brought to t. 6:5
Neh. 6:10 hid in t. shut doors of t.
Ps. 27:4 beauty of L. inq. in t.
29:9 in t. ev. one speak of glory
48:9 kindness in midst of thy t.
68:29 because of thy t. at Jerus.
Is. 6:1 and his train filled the t.
Is. 44:28 to t. thy founda. be laid
66:6 a voice from t. voice of L.
Jer. 50:28 decl. veng. of t. 51:11
Ezek. 41:1 afterw. brou. me to t.
Dan. 5:2 vessels taken out of t. 3
Amos 8:3 songs of t. be howlings
Zec. 8:9 strong, that t. be built
Mal. 3:1 L. come sudd. to his t.
Mat. 4:5 set him on a pinnacle of t. Luke 4:9
12:6 place is one greater than t.
23:16 sw. by t. or gold of t. 17, 21
35 wh. ye slew bet. t. and altar
24:1 show build. of t. Luke 21:5
26:61 I am able to dest. t. of G.
27:40 destroyest t. Mark 15:29
51 veil of t. rent in twain, Mark 15:38; Luke 23:45
Mark 11:16 carry vessels thro' t.
14:58 destroy t. ma. with hands
Luke 2:37 An. departed not fr. t.
John 2:15 he drove them out of t.
19 destroy t. 21 spake of t. of
20 forty and six years t. build.
Acts 3:2 laid daily at gate of t. to ask alms of them ent. t. 10
19:27 t. of Diana sho. be despis.
21:30 took Paul, drew him out t.
24:6 hath gone about to prof. t.
25:8 neither against t. nor Cesar
1 Cor. 3:16 that ye are t. of God
17 if any man defile t. of G. him G. dest. t. holy, wh. t. ye are
6:19 your body is t. of H. Ghost
8:10 these sit at meat in idol's t.
9:13 they who minister live of t.
2 Cor. 6:16 hath t. of G. wi. idols
Rev. 7:15 serve day and ni. in t.
11:1 rise and measure t. of God
19 t. of G. was open. in heaven
14:15 ano. angel came out of t.
15:5 t. of tabernacle was opened
8 t. was filled with smoke from
16:1 I heard a voice out of t. 17
21:22 no t. Almig. and Lamb t.
See HOLY, LORD.

**In, or into the TEMPLE.**

1 Chr. 6:10 priest's office in the t.
Ezr. 5:15 carry these ves. i. t. t.
Neh. 6:11 go i. the t. to save life
Mat. 12:5 priests in t. prof. sabb.
21:12 went into the t. to cast out them that sold in t. Mark 11:15; Luke 19:45
14 and lame came to him i. t. t.
15 child. crying in t. Hosanna
26:55 teaching in t. Luke 21:37
27:5 cast down pieces of sil. i. t.
Mark 14:49 I was daily teaching in the t. Luke 22:53
Luke 1:21 tarried so long in t. t.
2:27 he came by Spirit into t. t.
46 found him in the t. sitting
18:10 two men went into the t.
24:53 continu. in t. praising G.
Acts 2:46 with one accord in t. t.
3:1 Peter and John went i. the t.
3 to go into t. 5:20 speak in t.
5:25 men are standing in t.
21:26 P. entered t. 27 saw in t.
28 brought Greeks i. the t. 29
24:12 neither found me in the t.
18 J. found me purified in t. t.
26:21 causes J. caught me in t.
2 Thes. 2:4 as G. sitteth i. t. of G.
Rev. 3:12 I make a pillar in t.
15:8 no man able to enter i. t. t.

**TEMPLES, of the head.**

Jud. 4:21 sm. nail into his t. 22

5:26 she had stricken thro' his *t.*
*Cant.* 4:3 thy *t.* like pomegr. 6:7

**TEMPLES.**

*Hos.* 8:14 forgot Maker, build. *t.*
*Joel* 3:5 into *t.* my goodly things
*Acts* 7:48 the M. H. dwelleth not in *t.* made with hands, 17:24

**TEMPORAL.**

2 *Cor.* 4:18 for things seen are *t.*

**TEMPT.**

*Gen.* 22:1 God did *t.* Abraham
*Ex.* 17:2 wheref. do ye *t.* Lord?
*Deut.* 6:16 ye shall not *t.* the L.
*Is.* 7:12 not ask, nor will I *t.* L.
*Mal.* 3:15 that *t.* God are deliv.
*Mat.* 4:7 shalt not *t.* L. *Luke* 4:12
22:18 why *t.* ye me? *Mark* 12:15; *Luke* 20:23
*Acts* 5:9 ye have agreed to *t.* Sp.
15:10 therefore why *t.* ye God?
1 *Cor.* 7:5 Sa. *t.* you not for your
10:9 neither let us *t.* Christ

**TEMPTATION.**

*Ps.* 95:8 as in *t.* in wild. *Heb.* 3:8
*Mat.* 6:13 and lead us not into *t.* *Luke* 11:4
*Mat.* 26:41 that ye enter not into *t.* *Mark* 14:38; *Luke* 22:40, 46
*Luke* 4:13 wh. devil ended his *t.*
8:13 in a time of *t.* fall away
1 *Cor.* 10:13 no *t.* tak. you, wi. *t.*
*Gal.* 4:14 *t.* in flesh despised not
1 *Tim.* 6:9 that be rich fall into *t.*
*Jam.* 1:12 bless. that endureth *t.*
*Rev.* 3:10 keep thee fr. hour of *t.*

**TEMPTATIONS.**

*Deut.* 4:34 natl. out of nat. by *t.*
7:19 great *t.* th. eyes saw, 29:3
*Luke* 22:28 contin. with me in *t.*
*Acts* 20:19 serv. G. with many *t.*
*Jam.* 1:2 joy when ye fall into *t.*
1 *Pet.* 1:6 are in heaviness thro' *t.*
2 *Pet.* 2:9 L. deli. godly out of *t.*

**TEMPTED.**

*Ex.* 17:7 because they *t.* Lord
*Num.* 14:22 ha. *t.* me ten times
*Deut.* 6:16 tempt G. ye *t.* in Ma.
*Ps.* 78:18 they *t.* G. in heart, 41
56 *t.* and provo. most high God
95:9 when fath. *t.* me, *Heb.* 3:9
106:14 lusted, *t.* God in desert
*Mal.* 4:1 wildern. to be *t.* of the devil, *Mark* 1:13; *Luke* 4:2
*Luke* 10:25 a lawyer *t.* him
1 *Cor.* 10:9 some *t.* were destroy.
13 not suffer you to be *t.* above
*Gal.* 6:1 lest thou also be *t.*
1 *Thes.* 3:5 by means tempter *t.*
*Heb.* 2:18 himself suff. being *t.*
4:15 in all points *t.* like as we
11:37 were sawn asun. were *t.*
*Jam.* 1:13 say wh. he is *t.* I am *t.* of God, for God cannot be *t.*
14 ev. man *t.* wh. drawn of lust

**TEMPTER.**

*Mat.* 4:3 when *t.* came to him
1 *Thes.* 3:5 by means *t.* tempted

**TEMPTETH.**

*Jam.* 1:13 tempt. neither *t.* any

**TEMPTING.**

*Mat.* 16:1 the Pharisees *t.* Christ, *Mark* 8:11; *Luke* 11:16
19:3 Pharis. came to him *t.* him
22:35 lawyer asked quest. *t.* him
*Mark* 10:2 put away wife, *t.* him
*John* 8:6 this they said, *t.* him

**TEN.**

*Gen.* 16:3 Ab. dw. *t.* years in C.
18:32 I will not dest. for *t.* sake
42:3 Jos.'s *t.* breth. went to buy
*Ex.* 34:28 wrote *t.* commandm. *Deut.* 4:13; 10:4
*Lev.* 26:26 *t.* women bake bread
*Jos.* 17:5 fell *t.* portions to Man.
*Jud.* 12:11 E. judged Is. *t.* years
20:10 take *t.* men of a hundred
*Ruth* 1:4 dwelt in Moab *t.* years
1 *Sam.* 1:8 not better th. *t.* sons?
2 *Sam.* 19:43 ha. *t.* parts in king
1 *K.* 11:31 *t.* piec. give *t.* trib. 35
14:3 take *t.* loaves to Ahijah
2 *K.* 15:17 Mena. reigned *t.* years
*Neh.* 11:1 one of *t.* to dw. at Jer.
*Est.* 9:10 *t.* sons of Ham. slew, 12
*Ps.* 33:2 instrument of *t.* strings, 92:3; 144:9
*Ec.* 7:19 more than *t.* mighty men
*Ezek.* 45:14 homer of *t.* baths, *t.*
*Amos* 5:3 leave *t.* to house of Is.
6:9 if *t.* remain in one house
*Zec.* 8:23 *t.* men take hold of Jew
*Mat.* 25:1 kingdom likened to *t.* virgins
*Luke* 15:8 wom. having *t.* pieces
17:17 were th. not *t.* cleansed?
19:13 delivered them *t.* pounds
*Rev.* 12:3 a dragon hav. *t.* horns, 13:1; 17:3
17:12 the *t.* horns are *t.* kings
*See* CUBITS, DAYS, DEGREES, THOUSAND, THOUSANDS.

**TEN times.**

*Gen.* 31:7 changed wages *t. t.* 41
*Num.* 14:22 have tempt. me *t. t.*
*Neh.* 4:12 J. came, said to us *t. t.*
*Job* 19:3 *t. t.* ye reproached me
*Dan.* 1:20 found them *t. t.* better

**TENS.**

*Ex.* 18:21 over them rul. of *t.* 25
*Deut.* 1:15 heads, captains over *t.*

**TENTH.**

*Gen.* 28:22 surely give *t.* to thee
*Lev.* 27:32 *t.* shall be holy to L.
*Num.* 18:21 given child. of L. *t.*
1 *Sam.* 8:15 king take *t.* of seed
*Is.* 6:13 yet in it shall be a *t.*
*John* 1:39 it was about *t.* hour
*See* DAY, DEAL, MONTH, PART.

**TEND.**

*Prov.* 21:5 diligent *t.* to plente

**TENDETH.**

*Prov.* 10:16 labor of righteous *t.*
11:19 as righteousness *t.* to life
24 withholdeth, it *t.* to poverty
14:23 talk of lips *t.* to penury
19:23 fear of the Lord *t.* to life

**TENDER.**

*Gen.* 18:7 Abra. fetched a calf *t.*
33:13 lord know. children are *t.*
*Deut.* 28:54 man that is *t.* among
56 the *t.* and delicate woman
32:2 small rain on the *t.* herb
2 *Sam.* 23:4 as *t.* grass springing
2 *K.* 22:19 heart *t.* 2 *Chr.* 34:27
1 *Chr.* 22:5 Sol. young and *t.* 29:1
*Job* 14:7 *t.* branch will not cease
38:27 cause the *t.* herb to spring
*Prov.* 4:3 *t.* and belov. in sight of
27:25 the *t.* grass showeth itself
*Cant.* 2:13 the vines with *t.* grape
7:12 see whether *t.* grape appear
*Is.* 47:1 no more be called *t.* and
53:2 shall grow up as a *t.* plant
*Ezek.* 17:22 I will crop off a *t.* one
*Dan.* 1:9 G. brought Dan. into *t.*
4:15 in earth, in the *t.* grass, 23
*Mat.* 24:32 bra. is *t.* *Mark* 13:28
*Luke* 1:78 thro' *t.* mercy of God
*Jam.* 5:11 L. is pitiful, of *t.* mercy

**TENDER-HEARTED.**

2 *Chr.* 13:7 Reh. young and *t.-h.*
*Eph.* 4:32 be kind and *t.-h.*
*See* MERCIES.

**TENDERNESS.**

*Deut.* 28:56 set foot on gro. for *t.*

**TENONS.**

*Ex.* 26:17 two *t.* in one board, 19; 36:22, 24

**TENOR.**

*Gen.* 43:7 according to *t.* of words
*Ex.* 34:27 after *t.* of these words

**TENT.**

*Gen.* 9:21 Noah was uncov. in *t.*
12:8 Abra. pitched his *t.* 13:3
13:12 Lot pitched his *t.* tow. S.
18:1 sat in *t.* 6 hastened into *t.*
9 where is Sa. he said, In the *t.*
24:67 brought her to Sarah's *t.*
26:17 Isaac pitched his *t.* in val.
25 pitched his *t.* at Beer-sheba
31:25 Jacob had pitched his *t.*
33:18 Ja. pitched his *t.* before, 19
35:21 Is. pitched his *t.* beyond
*Ex.* 18:7 M. and Jeth. came to *t.*
33:8 stood every man at *t.* door
10 they worshipped in *t.* door
39:33 they brought the *t.* to Mo.
40:19 he spread *t.* over taberna.
*Lev.* 14:8 tarry out of *t.* sev. days
*Num.* 9:15 cloud cov. *t.* of testi.
11:10 heard people weep in *t.*
19:14 when a man dieth in a *t.*
18 a clean person sh. sprinkle *t.*
25:8 went aft. man of Is. into *t.*
*Jos.* 7:21 hid in midst of my *t.*
23 took them out of midst of *t.*
24 Israel burnt his *t.* and all he
*Jud.* 4:17 Sisera fled to *t.* of Jael
20 said, Stand in door of the *t.*
21 Jael took a nail of the *t.* and
5:24 blessed above women in *t.*
7:8 he sent rest of Israel to his *t.*
20:8 not any of us go to *t.*
1 *Sam.* 4:10 fled every man into his *t.* 2 *Sam.* 18:17; 19:8
13:2 rest of people he sent to *t.*
17:54 put Goliath's armor into *t.*
2 *Sam.* 7:6 walk. in a *t.* 1 *Chr.* 17:5
16:22 they spread Absalom a *t.*
20:22 retired every man to his *t.*
2 *K.* 7:8 lepers went into one *t.*
1 *Chr.* 15:1 Da. pitched a *t.* for ark
2 *Chr.* 25:22 fled ev. man to his *t.*
*Ps.* 78:60 the *t.* which he placed
*Is.* 13:20 nor Arabian pitch *t.* th.
38:12 age removed as a shep.'s *t.*
40:22 spreadeth them out as a *t.*
54:2 enlarge the place of thy *t.*
*Jer.* 10:20 none to stretch forth *t.*
37:10 rise up every man in his *t.*

**TENT-MAKERS.**

*Acts* 18:3 by occupation *t.-m.*

**TENTS.**

*Gen.* 4:20 such as dwell in *t.*
9:27 Japheth shall dwell in *t.*
13:5 Lot also had herds and *t.*
25:27 a plain man, dwelling in *t.*
31:33 L. went into maid-serv. *t.*
*Ex.* 16:16 gather for them in *t.*
*Num.* 1:52 Is. shall pitch their *t.*
9:17 cloud abode, they pitched *t.*
18 rested in their *t.* 20, 22, 23
13:19 whether th. dwell in *t.* or
16:26 depart from the *t.* of these
27 stood in the door of their *t.*
*Num.* 24:2 Bal. saw Is. abid. in *t.*
5 how goodly are thy *t.* O Jac.
*Deut.* 1:27 ye murmur. in your *t.*
33 search a pla. to pitch your *t.*
5:30 get you into your *t.* again
11:6 earth swallowed up their *t.*
33:18 rejoice, Issachar, in thy *t.*
*Jos.* 22:4 get you unto your *t.* 6.
8 return wi. riches unto your *t.*
*Jud.* 6:5 Midianites came with *t.*
8:11 way of them th. dwelt in *t.*
1 *Sam.* 17:53 spoil. Philistines' *t.*
2 *Sam.* 11:11 Is. and J. abide in *t.*
20:1 every man to his *t.* 1 *K.* 12:16; 2 *Chr.* 10:16
1 *K.* 8:66 I. we. to th. *t.* 2 *Chr.* 7:10
2 *K.* 7:7 Syrians left their *t.* 10
8:21 peo. fled into their *t.* 14:12
13:5 children of Israel dwelt in *t.*
1 *Chr.* 4:41 they smote *t.* of Ham

5:10 they dwelt in Hagarites' *t.*
2 *Chr.* 14:15 smote *t.* of cattle
31:2 to praise in *t.* of the Lord
*Ezr.* 8:15 we abode in *t.* 3 days
*Ps.* 69:25 let none dw. in their *t.*
78:55 made Israel to dwell in *t.*
84:10 th. dwell in *t.* of wickedn.
106:25 murmured in their *t.* and
120:5 I dwell in the *t.* of Kedar
*Cant.* 1:5 comely as *t.* of Kedar
*Jer.* 4:20 sudd. are my *t.* spoiled
6:3 they shall pitch their *t.*
30:18 bring captiv. of Jacob's *t.*
35:7 days ye shall dwell in *t.*
10 but we have dwelt in *t.*
49:29 th. *t.* and flocks shall they
*Hab.* 3:7 I saw the *t.* of Cushan
*Zec.* 12:7 L. shall save *t.* of Jud.
14:15 plague of all in these *t.*

**TERAH.**

*Gen.* 11:24 begat T. 1 *Chr.* 1:26
26 T. begat Abr. 27; *Jos.* 24:2
31 T. took Abram his son, and

**TERAPHIM.**

*Jud.* 17:5 made an ephod and *t.*
18:14 in these houses is *t.* 20
*Hos.* 3:4 many days without *t.*

**TERMED.**

*Is.* 62:4 sh. no more be *t.* forsak.

**TERRACES.**

2 *Chr.* 9:11 ma. of algum-trees *t.*

**TERRESTRIAL.**

1 *Cor.* 15:40 bodies *t.* glory of *t.*

**TERRIBLE.**

*Ex.* 34:10 for it is a *t.* thing
*Deut.* 1:19 went thro' *t.* wild. 8:15
7:21 Lord is a mighty God and *t.*
10:17; *Neh.* 1:5; 4:14; 9:32
10:21 done *t.* thi. 2 *Sam.* 7:23
*Jud.* 13:6 angel of God, very *t.*
*Job* 37:22 with God is *t.* majesty
39:20 glory of his nostrils is *t.*
41:14 teeth are *t.* round about
*Ps.* 45:4 hand sh. teach *t.* things
47:2 the Lord most high is *t.* he
65:5 by *t.* things in righteousn.
66:3 *t.* art thou in thy works
5 *t.* in his doing towards men
68:35 thou art *t.* out of thy holy
76:12 he is *t.* to the kings of
99:3 prai. thy great and *t.* name
106:22 done *t.* things by R. sea
145:6 shall speak of thy *t.* acts
*Cant.* 6:4 art *t.* as an army, 10
*Is.* 13:11 lay low haughtin. of *t.*
18:2 to a peo. *t.* 7 fr. a people *t.*
21:1 from desert, from a *t.* land
25:3 the city of the *t.* nations
4 blast of *t.* ones is as a storm
5 branch of *t.* shall be bro. low
29:5 mult. of *t.* ones be as chaff
20 *t.* one is brought to naught
49:25 prey of *t.* sh. be delivered
64:3 when thou didst *t.* things
*Jer.* 15:21 red. out of hand of *t.*
20:11 L. is as a mighty *t.* one
*Lam.* 5:10 because of *t.* famine
*Ezek.* 1:22 color of the *t.* crystal
28:7 will bring the *t.* of nations
upon thee, 30:11; 31:12
32:12 cause to fall *t.* of nations
*Dan.* 2:31 form of image was *t.*
7:7 fourth beast dreadf. and *t.*
*Joel* 2:11 L. is great and very *t.*
31 before the great and *t.* day
*Hab.* 1:7 Chaldeans are *t.* and
*Zep.* 2:11 L. will be *t.* unto M.
*Heb.* 12:21 so *t.* was sight that

**TERRIBLENESS.**

*Deut.* 26:8 L. brought us with *t.*
1 *Chr.* 17:21 make thee a name *t.*
*Jer.* 49:16 thy *t.* hath deceived th.

**TERRIBLY.**

*Is.* 2:19 to shake *t.* the earth, 21
*Nah.* 2:3 fir-trees sh. be *t.* shak.

**TERRIFY.**

*Job* 3:5 let blackness of day *t.* it
9:34 his rod, let not his fear *t.*
31:34 did contempt of famil. *t.*?
2 *Cor.* 10:9 seem as if I wo. *t.* you

**TERRIFIED, EST.**

*Deut.* 20:3 fear not nor be *t.*
*Job* 7:14 thou *t.* me thro' visions
*Luke* 21:9 hear of wars, be not *t.*
24:37 they were *t.* and affrighted
*Phil.* 1:28 in nothing *t.* by adv.

**TERROR.**

*Gen.* 35:5 the *t.* of God was upon
*Lev.* 26:16 will ap. over you *t.*
*Deut.* 32:25 sw. without, *t.* with.
34:12 in the *t.* which M. showed
*Jos.* 2:9 *t.* is fallen upon us
*Job* 31:23 destruc. fr. G. was a *t.*
33:7 my *t.* not make thee afraid
*Ps.* 91:5 not afr. for *t.* by night
*Is.* 10:33 L. will lop bough wi. *t.*
19:17 Ju. shall be a *t.* to Egypt
33:18 thy heart shall meditate *t.*
54:14 thou shalt be far from *t.*
*Jer.* 17:17 not a *t.* 20:4 *t.* to thys.
32:21 brought forth Isr. with *t.*
*Ezek.* 26:17 cause *t.* to be on all
21 I make th. a *t.* 27:36; 28:19
32:23 wh. caused *t.* 24, 25, 26, 27
30 with their *t.* they are asha.
32 I have caused my *t.* in land
*Rom.* 13:3 rulers not *t.* to good
2 *Cor.* 5:11 knowing the *t.* of L.
1 *Pet.* 3:14 be not afraid of th. *t.*

**TERRORS.**

*Deut.* 4:34 assa. to take nat. by *t.*
*Job* 6:4 *t.* of God set themselves
18:11 *t.* shall make him afraid
14 sh. bring him to king of *t.*
20:25 sword cometh, *t.* are upon
24:17 they are in the *t.* of death
27:20 *t.* take hold on him
30:15 *t.* are turned upon me
*Ps.* 55:4 *t.* of death are fallen on
73:19 utterly consumed with *t.*
88:15 while I suff. *t.* I am distr.
16 thy *t.* have cut me off
*Jer.* 15:8 caused *t.* to fall on city
*Lam.* 2:22 hast called my *t.*
*Ezek.* 21:12 *t.* by reason of sword

**TERTIUS.**

*Rom.* 16:22 I T. who wrote this

**TERTULLUS.**

*Acts* 24:1 certain orator nam. T.
2 T. began to accuse Paul

**TESTAMENT.**

*Mat.* 26:28 this is my blood in
new *t.* *Mark* 14:24
*Luke* 22:20 this cup is the new *t.*
1 *Cor.* 11:25
2 *Cor.* 3:6 made minis. of new *t.*
14 remains veil, in read. old *t.*
*Heb.* 7:22 surety of a better *t.*
9:15 he is mediator of new *t.* for
redemption under first *t.*
16 where a *t.* is, th. must death
17 *t.* is of force after men dead
20 this is blood of *t.* G. enjoin.
*Rev.* 11:19 in temple ark of *t.*

**TESTATOR.**

*Heb.* 9:16 of neces. be death of *t.*
17 no strength while *t.* liveth

**TESTIFY.**

*Num.* 35:30 one witness not *t.*
*Deut.* 8:19 I *t.* that ye sh. perish
19:16 if a false wit. *t.* against
31:21 song *t.* ag. them as witn.
32:46 set yo. hearts to wor. I *t.*
*Neh.* 9:34 wherew. thou didst *t.*
*Job* 15:6 thine own lips *t.* ag. th.
*Ps.* 50:7 O Is. I *t.* ag. thee, 81:8
*Is.* 59:12 our sins *t.* against us
*Jer.* 14:7 our iniquities *t.* ag. us
*Hos.* 5:5 pride of Israel doth *t.*
*Amos* 3:13 *t.* in house of Jacob

*Mic.* 6:3 what have I done? *t.* ag.
*Luke* 16:28 send Laza. that he *t.*
*John* 2:25 that any sho. *t.* of man
3:11 *t.* have seen; 5:39 *t.* of me
7:7 bec. I *t.* of it; 15:26 *t.* of me
*Acts* 2:40 wi. oth. words did he *t.*
10:42 *t.* it is he was ordai. of G.
20:24 to *t.* gospel of grace of G.
26:5 know they, if th. would *t.*
*Gal.* 5:3 I *t.* to ev. man circum.
*Eph.* 4:17 this I say, and *t.* in L.
1 *John* 4:14 we ha. seen and do *t.*
*Rev.* 22:16 I Jesus sent ang. to *t.*
18 I *t.* to ev. man that heareth

**TESTIFIED.**

*Ex.* 21:29 it ha. been *t.* to owner
*Deut.* 19:18 *t.* falsely ag. brother
*Ruth* 1:21 see. L. hath *t.* ag. me
2 *Sam.* 1:16 thy mouth *t.* ag. th.
2 *K.* 17:13 yet L. *t.* against Israel
2 *K.* 17:15 testim. he *t.* ag. them
2 *Chr.* 24:19 prophets *t.* against
them, *Neh.* 9:26
*Neh.* 13:15 I *t.* against them, 21
*John* 4:39 for saying wh. wo. *t.*
44 Je. himself *t.* a proph. 13:21
*Acts* 8:25 wh. they *t.* and preach
18:5 P. *t.* to Jews that J. was C.
23:11 as thou hast *t.* of me at J.
28:23 to whom he *t.* king. of G.
1 *Cor.* 15:15 bec. we ha. *t.* of G.
1 *Thes.* 4:6 we forewarned you, *t.*
1 *Tim.* 2:6 gave himself to be *t.*
*Heb.* 2:6 one in a certain place *t.*
1 *Pet.* 1:11 *t.* beforeh. sufferings
1 *John* 5:9 witness G. *t.* of his S.
3 *John* 3 *t.* of truth that is in th.

**TESTIFIEDST, ETH.**

*Neh.* 9:29 *t.* ag. them by Sp. 30
*Hos.* 7:10 pride of Is. *t.* his face
*John* 3:32 wh. he ha. seen, he *t.*
21:24 disciple wh. *t.* of these thi.
*Heb.* 7:17 he *t.* thou art a priest
*Rev.* 22:20 which *t.* these things

**TESTIFYING.**

*Acts* 20:21 *t.* both to Jews and G.
*Heb.* 11:4 witn. G. *t.* of his gifts
1 *Pet.* 5:12 *t.* this is grace of God

**TESTIMONY.**

*Ex.* 16:34 pot of manna bef. *t.*
25:16 sh. put into ark the *t.* 21
27:21 without vail before *t.*
30:6 mercy-s. over *t.* *Lev.* 16:13
31:18 gave M. two tables of *t.*
32:15 tables of *t.* in hand, 34:29
38:21 this is sum of tabern. of *t.*
*Num.* 1:50 Lev. over taber. of *t.*
53 Lev. pitch about taber. of *t.*
9:15 cloud covered the tent of *t.*
10:11 cloud taken off taber. of *t.*
17:4 thou sh. lay up rods bef. *t.*
10 bring Aa. rod again bef. *t.*
*Ruth* 4:7 and this was a *t.* in Is.
2 *K.* 11:12 gave the king the *t.*
2 *Chr.* 23:11
*Ps.* 78:5 he established a *t.* in J.
81:5 this he orda. in Jos. for *t.*
119:88 so sh. I keep *t.* of mouth
122:4 tribes go up to the *t.* of I.
132:12 if thy children keep my *t.*
*Is.* 8:16 bind up *t.* 20 law and *t.*
*Mat.* 8:4 gift M. commanded for
a *t.* *Mark* 1:44; *Luke* 5:44
10:18 *t.* against them, *Mark* 13:9
*Mark* 6:11 sh. dust for *t.* *Luke* 9:5
*Luke* 21:13 sh. turn to you for *t.*
*John* 3:32 no man receiv. his *t.*
33 he that receiv. *t.* set to seal
8:17 writ. *t.* of two men is true
21:24 know that his *t.* is true
*Acts* 13:22 to wh. also he gave *t.*
14:3 gave *t.* to word of his grace
22:18 they will not recei. thy *t.*
1 *Cor.* 1:6 as *t.* of C. was confir.
2:1 declaring unto you *t.* of God
2 *Cor.* 1:12 *t.* of our conscience

2 *Thes.* 1:10 bec. our *t.* was beli.
2 *Tim.* 1:8 not asham. of *t.* of L.
*Heb.* 3:5 *t.* of things which were
11:5 Enoch had *t.* he pleased G.
*Rev.* 1:2 bare record of *t.* of J. C.
9 I was in Patmos for *t.* of Je.
6:9 souls of th. were slain for *t.*
11:7 when they have finished *t.*
12:11 overca. by word of th. *t.*
17 war with them wh. have *t.*
15:5 tabernacle of *t.* in heaven
19:10 *t.* of J. is spirit of proph.
*See* ARK.

**TESTIMONIES.**
*Deut.* 4:45 these are *t.* M. spake
6:17 sh. diligently keep *t.* of G.
20 wh. mean *t.* G. commanded
1 *K.* 2:3 to keep his statutes and his *t.* 2 *K.* 23:3; 1 *Chr.* 29:19; 2 *Chr.* 34:31
2 *K.* 17:15 rejected *t.* followed
*Neh.* 9:34 nor kings heark. to *t.*
*Ps.* 25:10 keep coven. and his *t.*
78:56 keep not *t.* 93:5 *t.* sure
99:7 th. kept *t.* and ordinances
119:2 bles. are they th. keep *t.*
14 I rejoiced in way of thy *t.*
22 I have kept thy *t.* 167, 168
24 thy *t.* deli. 31 I stuck to *t.*
36 incline my heart to thy *t.*
46 I will speak of *t.* bef. kings
59 I turned my feet to thy *t.*
79 have known *t.* turn to me
95 wick. waited, I consider *t.*
99 thy *t.* are my meditation
111 thy *t.* have I taken
119 I love thy *t.* 125 know *t.*
129 thy *t.* are wonderful
138 thy *t.* are righte. faithful
144 righteous. of *t.* everlasting
*Ps.* 119:146 save me, and I shall keep *t.*
152 concerning *t.* I have kno.
157 yet do I not decline fr. *t.*
*Jer.* 44:23 have not walked in *t.*

THADDEUS. *Mark* 3:18

**THANK.**
*Luke* 6:32 those that love you what *t.* have ye? 33:34

**THANK, Verb.**
1 *Chr.* 16:4 appoint. Lev. to *t.* L.
7 Da. delivered psalm to *t.* L.
23:30 stand ev. morning to *t.* L.
29:13 we *t.* thee, praise name
*Dan.* 2:23 I *t.* thee, praise thee
*Mat.* 11:25 Je. said, I *t.* thee, O Fa. L. of heaven, *Luke* 10:21
*Luke* 17:9 doth he *t.* that serv.?
18:11 G. I *t.* th. not as oth. men
*John* 11:41 Father, I *t.* thee
*Rom.* 1:8 I *t.* my God, 7:25
1 *Cor.* 1:4 I *t.* G. on your behalf
14 I *t.* G. I bapt. none of you
14:18 I *t.* G. I speak with tong.
*Phil.* 1:3 I *t.* G. on rem. of you
1 *Thes.* 2:13 for this cau. *t.* we G.
2 *Thes.* 1:3 are bound to *t.* God
1 *Tim.* 1:12 I *t.* Jesus Christ
2 *Tim.* 1:3 I *t.* G. whom I serve
*Phile.* 4 I *t.* God, mak. mention
*See* OFFERING.

**THANKED.**
2 *Sam.* 14:22 J. bowed, *t.* king
*Acts* 28:15 P. *t.* G. took courage
*Rom.* 6:17 G. be *t.* ye were serv.

**THANKFUL.**
*Ps.* 100:4 *t.* to him *Col.* 3:15
*Rom.* 1:21 glori. not, nor we. *t.*

**THANKFULNESS.**
*Acts* 24:3 we accept it with all *t.*

**THANKING.**
2 *Chr.* 5:13 singers were one *t.* L.

**THANKWORTHY.**
1 *Pet.* 2:19 *t.* if man endure grief

**THANKS.**
*Neh.* 12:31 companies th. gave *t.*
*Dan.* 6:10 he prayed, and gave *t.*
*Mat.* 26:27 he took the cup, and gave *t.* *Luke* 22:17
*Mark* 8:6 seven loaves and ga. *t.*
14:23 when he had given *t.* he
*Luke* 2:38 Anna gave *t.* to Lord
22:19 and gave *t.* and brake it
*John* 6:11 when he had given *t.*
23 after Lord had given *t.*
*Acts* 27:35 bread, and ga. *t.* to G.
*Rom.* 14:6 for he giveth G. *t.* he eateth not, and giveth G. *t.*
1 *Cor.* 11:24 had given *t.* he bra.
14:17 thou verily givest *t.* well
15:57 *t.* be to G. who giv. vict.
2 *Cor.* 1:11 *t.* may be given
2:14 *t.* to G. who caus. triumph
8:16 *t.* to G. who put care in T.
9:15 *t.* to G. for unspeak. gift
*Eph.* 5:20 giving *t.* always for all
1 *Thes.* 3:9 what *t.* can we render
*Heb.* 13:15 offer praise, giving *t.*
*Rev.* 4:9 give *t.* to him on throne
*See* GIVE, GIVING.

**THANKSGIVING.**
*Lev.* 7:12 if he offer it for a *t.* 13:15; 22:29
*Neh.* 11:17 to begin *t.* in prayer
12:8 which was over the *t.*
46 th. were songs of praise, *t.*
*Ps.* 26:7 publish with voice of *t.*
50:14 offer unto God *t.* pay vows
69:30 I will mag. him with *t.*
95:2 come before his face wi. *t.*
100:4 enter into his gates wi. *t.*
107:22 let sacrifice sacri. of *t.*
116:17 offer to thee sacri. of *t.*
147:7 sing to the L. with *t.* sing
*Is.* 51:3 *t.* and melo. found there
*Jer.* 30:19 out of them shall proceed *t.*
*Amos* 4:5 offer a sacrifice of *t.*
*Jon.* 2:9 sacrifice with voice of *t.*
2 *Cor.* 4:15 thro' *t.* grace redound
9:11 causeth thro' us *t.* to God
*Phil.* 4:6 wi. *t.* let your requests
*Col.* 2:7 abounding therein wi. *t.*
4:2 watch in the same with *t.*
1 *Tim.* 4:3 God to be rece. wi. *t.*
4 creature good if rece. with *t.*
*Rev.* 7:12 *t.* and hon. be to our G.

**THANKSGIVINGS.**
*Neh.* 12:27 keep dedication wi. *t.*
2 *Cor.* 9:12 abundant by many *t.*

**THEATRE.**
*Acts* 19:29 they rush. into the *t.*
31 would not adventure into *t.*

**THEBEZ.**
*Jud.* 9:50 went Abimelech to T.
2 *Sam.* 11:21 that he died in T.

**THEFT, S.**
*Ex.* 22:3 he sh. be sold for his *t.*
4 if the *t.* be found in his hand
*Mat.* 15:19 out of the heart proceed *t.* *Mark* 7:22
*Rev.* 9:21 nei. repented they of *t.*

THELASAR. 2 *K.* 19:12

**THENCE.**
*Num.* 23:13 curse me th. fr. *t.* 27
*Deut.* 4:29 if from *t.* thou seek L.
5:15 the Lord brought thee out *t.* 6:23; 24:18
1 *K.* 2:36 go not forth from *t.*
2 *K.* 2:21 shall not be from *t.* any
*Ezr.* 6:6 theref. be ye far from *t.*
*Is.* 65:20 no more *t.* an infant of
*Jer.* 5:6 every one that goes *t.*
43:12 he shall go forth from *t.* in
*Luke* 16:26 that would come fr. *t.*

**THEOPHILUS.**
*Luke* 1:3 to write to thee, T.
*Acts* 1:1 treatise have I ma. O T.

**THERE.**
*John* 12:26 where I am. *t.* sh. my
14:3 where I am, *t.* ye may be

**THEREAT.**
*Ex.* 30:19 wash th. feet *t.* 40:31
*Mat.* 7:13 many th. be wh. go in *t.*

**THEREBY.**
*Gen.* 24:14 *t.* shall I know thou
*Job* 22:21 with G. *t.* good will co.

**THEREON.**
*Mat.* 21:7 they set him *t.* *Luke* 19:35; *John* 12:14
19 found nothing *t.* but leaves, *Mark* 11:13; *Luke* 13:6

**THERETO.**
*Ps.* 119:9 by taking heed *t.*

**THEREUNTO.**
1 *Pet.* 3:9 knowing ye are *t.* call.

**THESSALONICA.**
*Acts* 17:1 at T. was a synagogue
11 more noble than those of T.
27:2 one Aristarchus of T. being
*Phil.* 4:16 in T. ye sent once and
2 *Tim.* 4:10 Demas depart. to T.

**THEUDAS.**
*Acts* 5:36 bef. th. days rose up T.

**THICK.**
*Deut.* 32:15 waxen fat, grown *t.*
2 *Sam.* 18:9 mule we. unto *t.* bo.
2 *K.* 8:15 he took a *t.* cloth, and
*Neh.* 8:15 branches of *t.* trees
*Job* 15:26 runneth on *t.* bosses
*Ps.* 74:5 lift. up axes on *t.* trees
*Ezek.* 6:13 slain under ev. *t.* oak
19:11 stat. was am. *t.* branches
31:3 among *t.* boughs, 10, 14
*Hab.* 2:6 lad. himself with *t.* clay
*Luke* 11:29 peo. gathered *t.* tog.
*See* CLOUDS, DARKNESS.

**THICKER.**
1 *K.* 12:10 my little finger sh. be *t.* than, 2 *Chr.* 10:10

**THICKET, S.**
*Gen.* 22:13 a ram caught in a *t.*
1 *Sam.* 13:6 Israel did hide in *t.*
*Is.* 9:18 wickedn. sh. kindle in *t.*
10:34 cut down *t.* of the forest
*Jer.* 4:7 lion is come up fr. his *t.*
29 city sh. flee and go into *t.*

**THICKNESS.**
2 *Chr.* 4:5 *t.* of sea a handbreadth
*Jer.* 52:21 *t.* of pillars four fingers
*Ezek.* 41:9 *t.* of wall five cubits
42:10 chamb. were in *t.* of wall

**THIEF.**
*Ex.* 22:2 if *t.* be found break. 7
*Deut.* 24:7 stealing, th. *t.* sh. die
*Job* 24:14 the murderer is as a *t.*
30:5 cried after them as after *t.*
*Ps.* 50:18 when thou sawest a *t.*
*Prov.* 6:30 not desp. *t.* if he steal
29:24 partner with *t.* hateth soul
*Jer.* 2:26 as a *t.* is ashamed when
*Hos.* 7:1 *t.* cometh in, robbers
*Joel* 2:9 enter at windows like *t.*
*Zec.* 5:4 shall enter house of *t.*
*Mat.* 24:43 *t.* wo. come, *Lu.* 12:39
26:55 are ye come as ag. a *t.*? *Mark* 14:48; *Luke* 22:52
*Luke* 12:33 wh. no *t.* approacheth
*John* 10:1 same is a *t.* and robber
10 *t.* cometh not but to steal
12:6 bec. he was a *t.* and had
1 *Thes.* 5:2 day of the L. cometh as a *t.* 2 *Pet.* 3:10
4 day sho. overtake you as a *t.*
1 *Pet.* 4:15 let none suffer as a *t.*
*Rev.* 3:3 I will come as a *t.* 16:15

**THIEVES.**
*Is.* 1:23 princes are compan. of *t.*
*Jer.* 48:27 was not Is. among *t.*?
49:9 if *t.* by night, *Ob.* 5

*Mat.* 6:19 where *t.* break through
20 wh. *t.* do not break through
21:13 made it a den of *t.* *Mark* 11:17; *Luke* 19:46
27:38 two *t.* cruci. *Mark* 15:27
44 the *t.* cast same in his teeth
*Luke* 10:30 went and fell am. *t.*
*John* 10:8 that ca. bef. me are *t.*
1 *Cor.* 6:10 nor *t.* inh. king. of G.

**THIGH.**

*Gen.* 24:2 hand under *t.* 9; 47:29
32:25 touched hollow of Ja.'s *t.*
*Num.* 5:21 L. mak. *t.* rot, 22, 27
*Jud.* 3:16 E. did gird dag. on *t.*
21 E. took dagger fr. right *t.*
15:8 Samson smote hip and *t.*
*Ps.* 45:3 gird sword on thy *t.*
*Cant.* 3:8 ev. man hath sw. on *t.*
*Is.* 47:2 uncover the *t.* pass over
*Jer.* 31:19 I smote upon my *t.*
*Ezek.* 21:12 smite theref. upon *t.*
24:4 gather the *t.* and shoulder
*Rev.* 19:16 hath on his *t.* a name

**THIGHS.**

*Ex.* 28:42 breeches reach to *t.*
*Cant.* 7:1 joints of *t.* like jewels
*Dan.* 2:32 belly and *t.* of brass

**THIN.**

*Gen.* 41:6 7 *t.* ears, 7, 23, 24, 27
*Ex.* 39:3 beat gold into *t.* plates
*Lev.* 13:30 in it a yellow *t.* hair
1 *K.* 7:29 additi. made of *t.* work
*Is.* 17:4 glory of Ja. be made *t.*

**THINE.**

*Gen.* 14:23 any thing that is *t.*
*Lev.* 10:15 it sh. be *t.* thy sons, *Num.* 18:9, 11, 13, 14, 15, 18
1 *K.* 3:26 let nei. be mine nor *t.*
20:4 O king, I am *t.* all I have
1 *Chr.* 12:18 *t.* are we, Dav. and
21:24 will not take that wh. is *t.*
*Ps.* 119:94 I am *t.* save me, I
*John* 17:6 *t.* they were; 9 are *t.*
10 all mine are *t.* and *t.* mine

**THING.**

*Gen.* 24:50 *t.* proceedeth from L.
34:7 *t.* ought not, 2 *Sam.* 13:12
41:32 *t.* is established by God
*Ex.* 18:11 *t.* wherein they dealt
17 *t.* that th. doest is not good
22:9 for any manner of lost *t.*
*Lev.* 4:13 the thing be hid fr. eyes
20:17 it is a wicked *t.* they sh.
*Num.* 16:30 if L. make a new *t.*
*Deut.* 1:14 *t.* thou hast spoken
12:32 what *t.* soever I command
13:14 truth, and *t.* certain, 17:4
18:22 if *t.* follow not, nor come
32:47 it is not a vain *t.* for you
*Jud.* 19:24 do not so vile a *t.*
*Ruth* 3:18 till he have finished *t.*
1 *Sam.* 3:11 I will do a *t.* in Isr.
17 what is the *t.* L. hath said?
4:7 not been such a *t.* heretof.
14:12 and we will show you a *t.*
18:20 told Saul, *t.* pleased him
2 *Sam.* 13:33 let not lord take *t.*
14:13 wheref. thought such *t.*?
18 hide not *t.* I shall ask thee
15:35 what *t.* shalt hear, tell Za.
1 *K.* 14:5 Jerob. cometh to ask *t.*
2 *K.* 20:9 the Lord will do the *t.*
1 *Chr.* 13:4 *t.* right in eyes of
17:23 let *t.* hast spok. be estab.
2 *Chr.* 29:36 *t.* done suddenly
*Ezr.* 7:27 a *t.* in king's heart
*Est.* 2:4 the *t.* pleased the king
*Job* 3:25 the *t.* I feared is come
6:8 th. G. wo. grant *t.* I long for
14:4 who can br. clean *t.* out of?
26:3 how hast decl. *t.* as it is?
42:7 not spo. *t.* that is right, 8
*Ps.* 2:1 why imagine a vain *t.*?
38:20 I follow *t.* that good is
89:34 nor alter *t.* that is gone
101:3 I set no wicked *t.* bef. eyes

*Prov.* 22:18 it is a pleasant *t.*
*Ec.* 7:8 better end of *t.* th. begin.
8:15 no better *t.* than to eat
11:7 pleas. *t.* for eyes to behold
*Is.* 29:16 sh. the *t.* framed say?
21 turn aside for *t.* of naught
40:15 tak. isles as a very little *t.*
43:19 I will do a new *t.* it shall
55:11 sh. prosper in *t.* where. I
66:8 who hath heard such a *t.*
*Jer.* 2:10 see if there be such a *t.*
18:13 Is. hath done a horrible *t.*
31:22 Lord hath created a new *t.*
*Jer.* 38:14 I will ask a *t.* hide not.
42:3 G. may show us *t.* we do
44:17 will do what *t.* goeth out
*Lam.* 2:13 what *t.* sh. I take to witness? wh. *t.* liken to th.?
*Ezek.* 16:47 as if it were a little *t.*
*Dan.* 2:5 king said, *t.* is gone, 8
11 it is a rare *t.* king requireth
5:15 show interpreta. of the *t.*
6:12 *t.* is true, according to law
10:1 a *t.* was revealed to Daniel
*Hos.* 6:10 I ha. seen a horrible *t.*
8:12 were counted a strange *t.*
*Amos* 6:13 rejoi. in a *t.* of naught
*Mark* 1:27 what *t.* is this? what
*Luke* 12:11 what *t.* ye sh. answ.
*John* 5:14 lest a worse *t.* come to
*Acts* 17:21 or hear some new *t.*
23:17 he hath a certain *t.* to tell
25:26 I have no cert. *t.* to write
*Rom.* 9:20 sh. *t.* form. say to him
1 *Cor.* 1:10 I beseech sp. same *t.*
2 *Cor.* 5:5 wro. us for self-same *t.*
*Phil.* 3:16 let us mind same *t.*
1 *Pet.* 4:12 as some stran. *t.* hap.
1 *John* 2:8 which *t.* is true in him

*See* ACCURSED.

**Any THING.**

*Gen.* 14:23 I will not take *any t.*
18:14 is *any t.* too hard for L.?
19:22 cannot do *any t.* till thou be come
22:12 nei. do thou *any t.* to lad
30:31 Ja. said, Not give me *a. t.*
39:9 nei. hath he kept back *a. t.*
*Ex.* 20:17 nor *any t.* that is thy neighbor's, *Deut.* 5:21
*Lev.* 15:6 sitteth on *a. t.* wher. 23
*Num.* 20:19 without doing *any t.*
22:38 have I power to say *a. t.*?
35:22 cast upon him *any t.*
*Deut.* 4:32 if hath been *a.* such *t.*
24:10 when dost lend bro. *a. t.*
31:13 who have known *any t.*
*Jos.* 21:45 failed not of *a. t.* spo.
*Jud.* 11:25 art *a. t.* better th. B.?
18:10 wh. no want of *a. t.* 19:19
1 *Sam.* 3:17 G. do so, if hide *a. t.*
20:26 S. spake not *a. t.* that day
21:2 let no man know *any t.* of
2 *Sam.* 13:2 tho. it hard to do *a. t.*
1 *K.* 10:3 was not *any t.* hid from
20:33 whether *a. t.* would come
2 *Chr.* 9:20 silv. not *a. t.* accoun.
*Job* 33:32 if thou hast *a. t.* to say
*Ec.* 1:10 *a. t.* whereof it may be
5:2 heart not hasty to utter *a. t.*
9:5 dead kn. not *a. t.* nor have
*Jer.* 32:27 *a. t.* too hard for me?
38:5 king not he th. can do *a. t.*
42:21 nor *a. t.* for wh. he sent me
*Dan.* 3:29 spe. *a. t.* amiss ag. G.
*Mat.* 18:19 agree touching *any t.*
24:17 take *any t.* out of his house, *Mark* 13:15
*Mark* 4:22 *a. t.* secret, *Luke* 8:17
11:13 if he might find *any t.*
16:8 neither said they *any t.*
*Luke* 19:8 taken *a. t.* fr. any man
22:35 lacked ye *any t.*? nothing
*John* 1:3 with. him not *a. t.* ma.
7:4 no man doeth *a. t.* in secret
14:14 if ask *any t.* in my name
*Acts* 17:25 as tho' he needed *a. t.*

1 *Cor.* 10:19 that the idol is *a. t.*
2 *Cor.* 2:10 if I forgive *any t.*
1 *Thes.* 1:8 need not to spe. *a. t.*
1 *Tim.* 1:10 if th. be *a. t.* contra.
*Rev.* 21:27 *any t.* that defileth

**Every THING.**

*Gen.* 6:17 *ev. t.* in earth shall die
*Lev.* 23:37 offer *e. t.* upon his day
2 *Sam.* 15:36 send to me *every t.*

*See* CREEPETH, CREEPING, EVIL, GOOD, GREAT, HOLY, LIGHT, LIVING, ONE, SMALL.

**That THING.**

*Gen.* 18:17 hide fr. Abr. *t. t.* I do
*Ex.* 9:6 L. did *that t.* on morrow
*Luke* 9:21 to tell no man *that t.*
12:26 not able to do *t. t.* is least
*Rom.* 14:22 not himself in *that t.*

**This THING.**

*Gen.* 19:21 accep. th. concer. *t. t.*
20:10 that thou hast done *th. t.*
34:14 we cannot do *this t.*
41:28 *t.* is *t.* I have spoken to P.
44:7 we should do accor. to *t. t.*
*Ex.* 1:18 why have ye done *t. t.*
2:14 M. said, Surely *t. t.* is kno.
9:5 to-morrow L. shall do *t. t.*
16:16 *t.* is *t.* which Lord commanded. 32; 35:4; *Lev.* 8:5; 9:6; 17:2; *Num.* 30:1; 36:6; *Deut.* 15:15; 24:18, 22
*Ex.* 18:14 wh. is *t. t.* doest to pe.?
29:1 *t.* is *t.* thou sh. do to them
33:17 I will do *t. t.* thou ha. spo.
*Jos.* 22:24 done it for fear of *t. t.*
*Jud.* 6:29 said, Who hath done *t. t.*? Gideon hath done *this t.*
11:37 let *this t.* be done for me
20:9 *this* shall be *t.* we will do
21:11 *this* is the *t.* ye shall do
1 *Sam.* 24:6 L. forbid I sh. do *t. t.*
26:16 *t. t.* is not good hast done
28:18 L. ha. done *t. t.* unto thee
2 *Sam.* 11:11 I do not *this t.*
12:5 man hath done *t. t.* sh. die
6 bec. he did *t. t.* had no pity
12 I will do *t. t.* before Israel
13:20 brother, regard not *this t.*
14:15 to speak of *this t.* to king
24:3 why doth lord del. in *t. t.*?
1 *K.* 1:27 is *this t.* done by king?
3:10 pleased L. S. asked *t. t.* 11
12:24 return, for *t. t.* is from me
13:34 *t. t.* bec. sin to house of J.
20:9 tell king, *t. t.* I may not do
2 *K.* 5:18 in *t. t.* L. pardon serv.
11:5 *this* is the *t.* that ye shall do, 2 *Chr.* 23:4
17:12 L. said, Ye sh. not do *t. t.*
1 *Chr.* 11:19 G. forb. I sh. do *t. t.*
21:3 why doth my lord req. *t. t.*
8 sinned, bec. I have done *t. t.*
*Ezr.* 10:2 hope in Is. concer. *t. t.*
*Neh.* 2:19 wh. is *t. t.* that ye do.?
*Is.* 38:7 L. will do *t. t.* he ha. spo.
*Jer.* 22:4 if do *t. t.* enter in kings
40:3 theref. *t. t.* is come on you
*Mark* 5:32 her that done *this t.*
*Luke* 2:15 see *this t.* come to pass
22:23 which that should do *t. t.*
*John* 18:34 sayest *t. t.* of thyself?
2 *Cor.* 12:8 for *t. t.* I besought L.
*Phil.* 3:13 *t. t.* I do, press toward

**Unclean THING.**

*Lev.* 5:2 if a soul touch *u. t.* 7:21
7:19 flesh touch. *u. t.* not eaten
20:21 take bro.'s wife, it is *u. t.*
*Deut.* 23:14 see no *u. t.* in thee
*Jud.* 13:4 eat not any *u. t.* 7, 14
*Is.* 52:11 tou. no *u. t.* 2 *Cor.* 6:17
64:6 we are all as an *unclean t.*
*Acts* 10:14 never eaten any *t. u.*

**THINGS.**

*Lev.* 4:2 sin thro' ignor. conc. *t.*

Deut. 4:9 forget t. eyes have seen
29:29 secret t. belong unto Lord
32:35 t. th. come on them haste
1 Sam. 12:21 ye go after vain t.
2 Sam. 24:12 I offer thee three t.
1 Chr. 21:10
1 K. 15:15 Asa brought in t. his father dedicated, 2 Chr. 15:18
1 Chr. 4:22 these are ancient t.
2 Chr. 12:12 in Jud. t. went well
Job 12:22 deep t. out of darkness
13:20 only do not two t. to me
41:34 behold. high t. king over
42:3 uttered t. too wonderful
Ps. 12:3 that speaketh proud t.
35:11 laid to charge t. I kn. not
45:1 I speak of t. I have made
60:3 showed thy people hard t.
65:5 by terrible t. wilt answer
72:18 G. who doeth wondrous t.
86:10 and doest wondrous t.
87:3 glorious t. are spo. of thee
94:4 how long utter hard t.?
113:6 to behold t. in heaven
119:18 behold wondr. t. out law
131:1 or in t. too high for me
Prov. 8:6 speak of ex. t. right t.
22:20 written to th. excellent t.
23:33 thy heart utter perverse t.
30:7 two t. have I requ. of thee
15 three t. that are never satis.
18 three t. be too wonderful
21 for 3 t. earth is disquieted
24 four t. wh. are lit. on earth
29 there be three t. wh. go well
Ec. 7:25 wisdom and reason of t.
Is. 12:5 he hath done excellent t.
25:6 make to peo. feast of fat t.
41:23 show t. to come hereafter
42:9 t. come to pass, new t. dec.
44:7 t. that are com. shall come
45:11 ask me of t. to come
19 I declare t. that are right
48:6 showed thee new t. hid. t.
64:3 thou didst terrible t. we
Jer. 2:8 t. do not profit, 16:19
8:13 t. I hav. giv. them sh. pass
Lam. 1:7 J. rememb. pleasant t.
2:14 proph. have seen foolish t.
Ezek. 11:5 I kn. t. come in mind
16:16 like t. shall not come
Joel 3:5 into temp. my goodly t.
Ob. 6 how are t. of Es. searched
Mic. 7:15 sh. unto him marv. t.
Zec. 4:10 desp. day of small t.
Mat. 6:34 thought for t. of itself
13:52 out of treas. t. new and old
22:21 render to Cesar t. that are C.'s, to God t. that are God's, Mark 12:17; Luke 20:25
Luke 5:26 seen strange t. to-day
6:46 and do not t. which I say
10:23 blessed eyes which see t.
18:27 t. impossible with men
19:42 known t. belong to peace
22:37 t. concer. me have an end
23:48 peo. behold t. were done
24:18 not kno. t. come to pass
John 1:50 greater t. than these
3:12 told earthly t. heavenly t.
16:13 will show you t. to come
Acts 4:20 cannot but spe. t. seen
32 aught of t. he possessed
20:22 not know. t. sh. befall me
24:13 nei. can they prove the t.
Rom. 2:1 that judg. doest same t.
14 by nat. t. contained in law
8:5 mind t. of flesh, mi. t. of S.
38 nor t. present, nor t. to come, 1 Cor. 3:22
12:16 not high t. 17 t. honest
14:19 fol. t. that make for peace
1 Cor. 1:27 G. hath chosen fool. t. of world to confo. t. mighty
2:9 t. God hath prep. for them
10 Spirit search. deep t. of G.
11 what man know. t. of man
12 might know t. freely given
14 man receiveth not t. of Spi.
6:3 more t. that pert. to life, 4
10:20 t. which Gentiles sacrifice
14:37 acknowledge t. I write to
2 Cor. 1:13 write none other t. to
17 or t. I purpose, do I purpo.
4:18 look not at t. wh. are seen
5:10 receive t. done in his body
18 old t. passed, all t. bec. new
10:7 ye look on t. after outward
13 boast of t. without meas. 15
16 not boast in anoth. man's t.
11:30 glo. of t. wh. concern mine
Gal. 2:18 build ag. t. I destroyed
5:17 cannot do t. that ye would
Eph. 6:9 do same t. to them
Phil. 1:12 t. whi. happen. to me
2:4 lo. not ev. man on his own t.
10 t. in hea. t. on earth, t. und.
21 seek not t. which are J. C.'s
3:1 write same t. 19 earthly t.
4:8 whatso. t. are true, honest
18 received t. sent from you
Col. 1:20 t. in earth, t. in heaven
2:23 which t. ha. show of wisd.
3:6 for wh. t. wrath of G. come.
1 Thes. 2:14 ye ha. suffer. like t.
2 Thes. 3:4 do t. wh. we comma.
1 Tim. 5:13 speak. t. ought not
2 Tim. 2:2 t. th. hast heard of me
3:14 continue in t. th. hast lear.
Tit. 2:1 spe. t. wh. become doc.
Heb. 2:1 heed to t. we have heard
6:9 we are persuaded better t.
11:1 faith substance of t. hoped, the evidence of t. not seen
3 t. seen not made of t. wh. ap.
12:24 speak. better t. than Abel
1 Pet. 1:12 did minister t. report.
2 Pet. 2:12 evil of t. th. under. not
1 John 2:15 neither t. in the wor.
Rev. 1:19 write t. whi. thou hast seen, t. which are, t. sh. be
2:14 I have a few t. against thee
4:1 show thee t. must be hereaf.
21:4 former t. are passed away

See CREEPING, DEDICATE, DETESTABLE, EVIL, FORMER, HOLY, MANY. PRECIOUS, SUCH.

**All THINGS.**

Gen. 9:3 have I given you all t.
24:1 L. hath blessed Ab. in all t.
Ex. 29:35 do according to all t. I have commanded thee
Num. 1:50 Levites over a. t. that
Deut. 1:18 com. a. t. ye shou. do
4:7 our God is in a. t. we call for
12:8 not do after a. t. we do here
Jos. 1:17 hearken. to M. in all t.
Ruth 4:7 manner, to confirm a. t.
1 Sam. 3:17 hide any of all t.
19:7 Jonath. showed Dav. all t.
2 Sam. 11:18 Joab told Dav. a. t.
14:20 kn. all t. that are in earth
23:5 a covenant ordered in all t.
1 K. 21:26 he did all t. as Amori.
2 K. 20:15 they have seen all t.
1 Chr. 29:14 all t. come of thee
Neh. 9:6 thou, Lord, made all t. Acts 14:15; 17:24, 25; Col. 1:16; Rev. 4:11
Job 41:34 he beholdeth all high t.
Ps. 8:6 hast put all t. under his feet, 1 Cor. 15:27; Eph. 1:22
57:2 God that performeth all t.
119:128 precepts concern. all t.
Prov. 3:15 more prec. th. a. t. 8:11
16:4 the Lord hath made all t.
28:5 seek L. understand all t.
Ec. 7:15 all t. have I seen
9:2 all t. come alike to all
10:19 but money answer. all t.
Is. 44:24 L. that mak. all t. 66:2
Jer. 10:16 is former of all t. 51:19
44:18 we wanted all t. and have
Ezek. 11:25 I spa. a. t. L. showed
Zep. 1:2 I will consume all t.
Mat. 7:12 all t. ye would men sh.
11:27 a. t. deli. to me, Lu. 10:22
19:26 with God all t. are possible, Mark 10:27; 14:36
21:22 all t. whatsoever ye ask
28:20 teaching to observe all t.
Mark 6:30 they told him all t.
7:37 he hath done all t. well
13:23 I have foretold you all t.
Luke 2:20 praising God for all t.
9:43 wondered at all t. Jesus did
11:41 all t. are clean unto you
John 1:3 all t. were made by him
3:35 gi. all t. into his hand, 13:3
4:25 he will tell us all t.
29 see a man who told me a. t.
5:20 Father showeth Son all t.
10:41 a. t. John spake were true
15:15 all t. I heard, I made kno.
16:15 all t. Fath. hath are mine
30 we are sure thou know. a. t.
17:7 all t. thou hast given me
18:4 Jesus knowing all t. 19:28
21:17 P. said, L. thou know. a. t.
Acts 3:22 him sh. ye hear in a. t.
10:33 hear all t. command. of G.
39 we are witnesses of all t. he
14:15 who made earth and all t.
20:35 I have showed you all t.
22:10 there it sh. be told th. a. t.
Rom. 8:28 we kn. all t. work for
32 sh. he not free. gi. us a. t.?
11:36 thro' him and to him a. t.
14:20 all t. indeed are pure
1 Cor. 2:10 Spirit searcheth a. t.
3:21 in men, for all t. are yours
6:12 all t. are not expedi. 10:23
8:6 one G. the F. of wh. are a. t. one L. J. C. by wh. are all t.
10:33 as I please men in all t.
11:12 all t. are of G. 2 Cor. 5:18
15:28 when all t. sh. be subdued
2 Cor. 4:15 all t. for your sakes
5:17 are away, a. t. become new
6:10 nothing, yet possess. all t.
7:14 spake all t. to you in truth
11:6 manifest to you in all t.
Eph. 1:10 gath. toge. in one a. t.
22 to be head over all t.
3:9 in God, who created all t.
5:20 giv. thanks always for a. t.
6:21 make known all t. Col. 4:9
Phil. 3:8 I count all t. but loss
4:12 and in all t. I am instruct.
13 I can do all t. through Chr.
Col. 1:17 before all t. by him a. t.
1 Thes. 5:21 prove all t. hold fast
3 John 2 I wish above all t. that
Rev. 21:5 beh. I make all t. new
7 that overcometh sh. inh. a. t.

**These THINGS.**

Gen. 42:36 J. said, t. t. are ag. me
Num. 15:13 all born shall do t. t.
Deut. 30:1 t. t. are come upon
Jos. 2:11 heard t. t. our hearts
2 Sam. 23:17 t. t. did these three mighty men, 1 Chr. 11:19
Neh. 13:26 did not So. sin by t. t.
Job 8:2 how long wilt speak t. t.?
10:13 t. t. hast thou hid in heart
33:29 t. t. worketh G. with man
Ps. 15:5 he that doeth t. t. shall
50:21 t. t. hast thou done and I
Prov. 6:16 t. six t. doth L. hate
24:23 t. t. also belong to wise
Ec. 11:9 for t. t. will G. br. thee
Is. 38:16 O L. by t. t. men live, in t. t. is the life of my spir.
42:16 t. t. will I do, not forsake
51:19 t. two t. are come unto th.
Jer. 3:7 aft. she had done all t. t.
5:9 sh. I not vi. for t. t.? 29; 9:9
9:24 for in t. t. do I delight
13:22 wheref. come t. t. on me?
14:22 thou hast made all th. t.
30:15 for thy sins ha. I done t. t.

*Ezek.* 16:30 doest all *t. t.* 17:18
17:12 kn. ye not what *t. t.* mean
23:30 I will do *th. t.* unto thee
24:19 wilt not tell wh. *t. t.* are?
*Dan.* 12:8 what be end of *t. t.?*
*Zec.* 8:16 *t.* are the *t.* whi. ye sh.
*Zec.* 8:17 all *t.* are *t.* that I hate
*Mat.* 6:33 all *th. t.* shall be added unto you, *Luke* 12:31
13:56 whence then hath this man *these t. Mark* 6:2
19:20 all *t. t.* have I kept fr. my
23:36 *t. t.* sh. come on this gen.
24:2 J. said, See ye not all *t. t.?*
3 tell us when shall *these t.* be? *Mark* 13:4; *Luke* 21:7
34 till *t. t.* be fulfil. *Mark* 13:30
*Luke* 15:26 ask. wh. *t. t.* meant?
24:21 third day since *th. t.* were
*John* 2:16 said, Take *t. t.* hence
18 seeing that thou doest *t. t.*
3:9 Nic. said, How can *t. t.* be?
13:17 if ye kn. *t. t.* happy are ye
15:21 all *t. t.* will they do, 16:3
*Acts* 7:1 are *these t.* so? 14:15 do ye *these t.?*
15:17 the L. who doeth all *t. t.*
17:20 wo. know what *t. t.* mean
20:24 none of *these t.* move me
26:26 king knoweth of *these t.*
*Rom.* 8:31 what shall we say to *these t.?*
14:18 he that in *th. t.* serv. Chr.
*Jam.* 3:10 breth. *t. t.* ought not
2 *Pet.* 1:10 if ye do *these t.*
3:17 seeing ye know *t. t.* before

**Those THINGS.**

*Lev.* 22:2 in *t. t.* whi. they allow
*Ps.* 107:43 whoso will obser. *t. t.*
*Is.* 66:2 all *th. t.* hath my hand
*Mat.* 13:17 desired to see *t. t.* wh.
*John* 8:29 *t. t.* that please him
*Acts* 3:18 *t. t.* he hath fulfilled
13:45 spake ag. *those t.* which
26:16 of *t. t.* in wh. I will appe.
*Col.* 3:1 seek *t. t.* whi. are above
*Jam.* 2:16 give not *t. t.* wh. are

**Unclean THINGS.**

*Hos.* 9:3 they sh. eat *u. t.* in Assy.

**What THINGS.**

*Ex.* 10:2 tell son *w. t.* I wrought
*Mat.* 6:8 F. knows *w. t.* ye need
*Mark* 9:9 tell no man *w. t.* they
11:24 *w. t.* soever ye desire
*Luke* 7:22 tell J. *w. t.* have seen
24:35 they told *w. t.* were done
*John* 5:19 *what t.* he doeth
10:6 unders. not *w. t.* they were
11:46 told *w. t.* Jesus had done
*Phil.* 3:7 *w. t.* were gain to me

**THINK.**

*Gen.* 40:14 *t.* on me wh. it be well
*Num.* 36:6 marry to wh. *t.* best
2 *Sam.* 13:33 to *t.* king's sons are
2 *Chr.* 13:8 ye *t.* to withsta. king
*Neh.* 5:19 *t.* on me, my God
6:6 thou and Jews *t.* to rebel
14 God *t.* on Tobiah and Sanb.
*Est.* 4:13 *t.* not thou shalt escape
*Job* 31:1 why should I *t.* upon a maid?
41:32 would *t.* deep be hoary
*Ec.* 8:17 though a wise man *t.*
*Is.* 10:7 nor doth his heart *t.* so
*Jer.* 23:27 *t.* cause my peo. forget
29:11 thoughts I *t.* toward you
*Ezek.* 38:10 sh. *t.* an evil thought
*Dan.* 7:25 shall *t.* to change tim.
*Jon.* 1:6 if God will *t.* upon us
*Zec.* 11:12 if ye *t.* good give me
*Mat.* 3:9 and *t.* not to say within
5:17 *t.* not I am come to destroy
6:7 *t.* they sh. be heard for spe.
9:4 why *t.* ye evil in yo. hearts
10:34 *t.* not I co. to send peace
18:12 how *t.* ye? if ha. hundred
22:42 what *t.* ye of Chr.? 26:66; *Mark* 14:64
24:44 as ye *t.* not, *Luke* 12:40
*Luke* 13:4 *t.* ye th. were sinners
*John* 5:39 ye *t.* ye have eter. life
45 do not *t.* I will accuse you
11:56 wh. *t.* ye, th. he will not?
16:2 will *t.* that he doth G. ser.
*Acts* 13:25 whom *t.* ye th. I am?
17:29 not to *t.* that Godhead
26:2 I *t.* myself happy, king Ag.
*Rom.* 12:3 not to *t.* of hims. more than he ought to *t.* but to *t.*
1 *Cor.* 4:6 learn in us not to *t.* of
9 I *t.* G. hath set forth us apo.
7:40 I *t.* also I have Spirit of G.
8:2 if any man *t.* he knoweth
12:23 we *t.* to be less honorable
14:37 if any *t.* himself a prophet
2 *Cor.* 3:5 to *t.* any thing of our.
10:2 I *t.* to be bold against some which *t.* of us
7 Ch. let him *t.* this again, 11
11:16 let no man *t.* me a fool
12:6 lest any *t.* of me above wh.
*Gal.* 6:3 if a man *t.* himself to be
*Eph.* 3:20 above all we ask or *t.*
*Phil.* 4:8 if any praise, *t.* on these
*Jam.* 1:7 let not man *t.* he sh. re.
4:5 do ye *t.* that scripture saith
1 *Pet.* 4:4 wherein they *t.* strange
12 *t.* it not strange concerning
2 *Pet.* 1:13 I *t.* it meet as long as

**THINKEST.**

2 *Sam.* 10:3 *t.* thou David doth honor thy fath.? 1 *Chr.* 19:3
*Job* 35:2 *t.* thou this right, that
*Mat.* 17:25 What *t.* thou? 22:17
26:53 *t.* th. I cannot pray to my
*Luke* 10:36 wh. *t.* th. was neigh.
*Acts* 28:22 de. to hear what th. *t.*
*Rom.* 2:3 *t.* thou this, O man

**THINKETH.**

2 *Sam.* 18:27 *t.* running of fore.
*Ps.* 40:17 poor, yet Lord *t.* on me
*Prov.* 23:7 as he *t.* in his heart
1 *Cor.* 10:12 let him that *t.* he st.
13:5 charity seek. not, *t.* no evil
*Phil.* 3:4 if any *t.* he hath where.

**THINKING.**

2 *Sam.* 4:10 *t.* to have bro. good
5:6 *t.* Da. cannot come in hither

**THIRD.**

*Gen.* 32:19 so commanded he *t.*
2 *K.* 1:13 he sent capt. of *t.* fifty
*Is.* 19:24 Is. sh. be *t.* with Egypt
*Dan.* 2:39 ano. *t.* kingd. of brass
5:7 *t.* ruler in kingdom, 16, 29
*Zec.* 6:3 in *t.* chariot white hors.
*Mat.* 20:3 went out about *t.* hour
22:26 likew. the *t.* died, *Mark* 12:21; *Luke* 20:31
*Luke* 20:12 sent *t.* wounded him
*Acts* 2:15 seei. it is *t.* hour of day
23:23 ready at *t.* hour of night
2 *Cor.* 12:2 caught up to *t.* heav.
*Rev.* 4:7 *t.* beast h. face as a man
6:5 opened *t.* seal, heard *t.* beast
8:10 *t.* angel sounded, fell a star
11:14 be. *t.* woe cometh quickly
14:9 *t.* angel followed them
16:4 *t.* angel poured vial on riv.
*See* DAY, MONTH, PART.

**THIRD time.**

1 *Sam.* 3:8 L. called Samuel *t. t.*
19:21 Saul sent messenger *t. t.*
1 *K.* 18:34 do it *t. t.* th. did it *t. t.*
*Ezek.* 21:14 sword be doubled *t. t.*
*Mat.* 26:44 prayed *t. t. Ma.* 14:41
*John* 21:14 *t. t.* Je. showed hims.
17 saith *t. t.* Lovest thou me? P. grieved, bec. he said *t. t.*
2 *Cor.* 12:14 *t. t.* ready to co. 13:1

**THIRD year.**

*Deut.* 26:12 *t. y.* year of tithing
2 *K.* 19:29 in *t. y.* sow, *Is.* 37:30

**THIRDLY.**

1 *Cor.* 12:28 *t.* teachers, miracles

**THIRST, Substantive.**

*Ex.* 17:3 kill us and chil. with *t.*
*Deut.* 28:48 serve enemies in *t.*
29:19 to add drunkenness to *t.*
*Jud.* 15:18 now I shall die for *t.*
2 *Chr.* 32:11 persuade to die by *t.*
*Neh.* 9:15 brought. water for *t.* 20
*Job* 24:11 wine-presses and suf. *t.*
*Ps.* 69:21 in *t.* gave me vinegar
104:11 wild asses quench th. *t.*
*Is.* 5:13 multil. dried up with *t.*
41:17 when tongue faileth for *t.*
50:2 fish stinketh, dieth for *t.*
*Jer.* 2:25 withh. thy throat fr. *t.*
48:18 come fr. thy glory, sit in *t.*
*Lam.* 4:4 cleaveth to mou. for *t.*
*Hos.* 2:3 naked, slay her with *t.*
*Amos* 8:11 not *t.* for water
13 young men shall faint for *t.*
2 *Cor.* 11:27 in hunger and *t.*

**THIRST, Verb.**

*Is.* 49:10 shall not hunger, nor *t.*
*Mat.* 5:6 hung. and *t.* after right.
*John* 4:13 drink. of this water *t.*
14 drinketh, shall never *t.* 6:35
15 give me this wa. th. I *t.* not
7:37 any *t.* let him come to me
19:28 after this, Jesus saith, I *t.*
*Rom.* 12:20 if enemy *t.* gi. drink
1 *Cor.* 4:11 to present hour we *t.*
*Rev.* 7:16 th. sh. not *t.* any more

**THIRSTED, ETH.**

*Ex.* 17:3 peo. *t.* there for water
*Ps.* 42:2 my soul *t.* for God, 63:1; 143:6
*Is.* 48:21 they *t.* not when he led
55:1 ev. one that *t.* come to wa.

**THIRSTY**

*Jud.* 4:19 give me water, I am *t.*
2 *Sam.* 17:29 peo. is *t.* in wilder.
*Ps.* 63:1 longeth in *t.* land, 143:6
107:5 hungry and *t.* soul fainted
*Prov.* 25:21 if enemy *t.* gi. drink
25 as cold waters to a *t.* soul, so good news
*Is.* 21:14 wat. to him that was *t.*
29:8 be as when *t.* man dream.
32:6 cause drink of the *t.* to fail
35:7 *t.* land bec. springs of wat.
44:3 pour wat. on him that is *t.*
65:13 serva. drink, but ye be *t.*
*Ezek.* 19:13 she is plan. in *t.* gro.
*Mat.* 25:35 I was *t.* ye gave drink
37 when saw we thee *t.?*
42 I was *t.* ye gave no drink

**THIRTEEN.**

*Gen.* 17:25 Ish. was *t.* years old
*Num.* 29:13 offer *t.* bullocks, 14
1 *K.* 7:1 building house *t.* years

**THIRTEENTH.**

*Gen.* 14:4 in *t.* year they rebelled
*See* DAY.

**THIRTIETH.**

2 *K.* 15:13 reign in nine and *t. y.*
17 nine and *t.* year of Azariah
25:27 seven and *t.* year of the captivity of Jehoi. *Jer.* 52:31
2 *Chr.* 15:19 five and *t.* year of A.
16:1 in six and *t.* year of Asa
*Neh.* 5:14 two and *t. y.* of A. 13:6

**THIRTY.**

*Gen.* 6:15 height of ark *t.* cubits
11:14 Salah lived *t.* years, begat
18:30 th. sh. be *t.* found, he sa. I will not do it if I find *t.*
41:46 Joseph was *t.* years old
*Num.* 4:3 from *t.* years old and up, 23, 47; 1 *Chr.* 23:3
*Jud.* 14:12 give you *t.* sheets
20:31 smite abo. *t.* men of Is. 39
1 *Sam.* 9:22 Saul sat amo. *t.* per.
2 *Sam.* 5:4 Dav. was *t.* years old
1 *K.* 4:22 provision was *t.* meas.

*Jer.* 38:10 take from hen. *t.* men
*Ezek.* 41:6 side chambers were *t.*
*Zec.* 11:12 weigh. for my price *t.*
13 *t.* pieces of silver, *Mat.* 27:9
*Mat.* 13:8 brought forth some *t.* fold, 23; *Mark* 4:8, 20
26:15 covenanted for *t.* pieces
27:3 Judas brought ag. *t.* pieces
*Luke* 3:23 began to be *t.* yea. old
*John* 6:19 rowed 25 or *t.* furlongs
*See* DAYS.

**THIRTY-ONE.**

*Jos.* 12:24 kings J. subdu. *t.-one*
1 *K.* 16:23 in *t.* and *o.* year of A.

**THIRTY-TWO.**

*Num.* 31:40 L.'s tribu. *t.-t.* pers.

**THIRTY-THREE.**

*Gen.* 46:15 sons and daugh. *t.-t.*
*Lev.* 12:4 bl. of purify. *t.-t.* days

**THIRTY-FOUR.**

*Gen.* 11:16 Eber lived *t.-f* years

**THIRTY-FIVE.**

2 *Chr.* 3:15 pillars *t.-f.* cubits

**THIRTY-SIX.**

*Jos.* 7:5 men of Ai sm. *t.-s.* of Is.

**THIRTY-SEVEN.**

2 *Sam.* 23:39 Uriah, *t.-s.* in all

**THIRTY-EIGHT.**

*Deut.* 2:14 over Zered *t.-e.* years
*John* 5:5 had infirmity *t.-e.* years

**THIRTY-NINE.**

2 *Chr.* 16:12 A. in *t.-n.* year dis.
*See* THOUSAND.

**THISTLE, S.**

*Gen.* 3:18 *t.* shall it bring forth
2 *K.* 14:9 *t.* was in Leban. wild beast trod *t.* 2 *Chr.* 25:18
*Job* 31:40 let *t.* grow inst. wheat
*Hos.* 10:8 *t.* come up on th. altars
*Mat.* 7:16 do men ga. figs of *t.*?

**THITHER.**

*Gen.* 19:22 esca. *t.* tell be come *t.*
*Num.* 35:6 that the slayer may flee *t.* 11, 15; *Deut.* 4:42; 19:3, 4; *Jos.* 20:3, 9
*Deut.* 1:37 sh. not go in *t.* 38, 39
2 *K.* 2:8 divided hither and *t.* 14
*Luke* 17:37 where carcass is, *t.* will the eagles be gathered
*John* 7:34 *t.* cannot come, 36
11:8 and goeth thou *t.* again?

**THITHERWARD.**

*Jer.* 50:5 to Z. with their faces *t.*

**THOMAS.**

*Mat.* 10:3 T. and Matthew, *Mark* 3:18; *Luke* 6:15; *Acts* 1:13
*John* 11:16 T. said, Let us go
20:24 T. was not with them
26 T. with them, then came Jesus
*John* 20:27 to T. reach hith. fin.
21:2 together Si Peter and T.

**THONGS.**

*Acts* 22:25 bound him with *t.*

**THORN.**

*Job* 41:2 canst bore jaw with *t.*?
*Prov.* 26:9 as *t.* goeth into hand
*Is.* 55:13 instead of *t.* fir-tree
*Ezek.* 28:24 no more any grie. *t.*
*Hos.* 10:8 *t.* come up on th. alta.
*Mic.* 7:4 upri. sharper than *t.* he.
2 *Cor.* 12:7 gi. to me a *t.* in flesh

**THORNS.**

*Gen.* 3:18 *t.* and thistles br. forth
*Ex.* 22:6 break out, catch in *t.*
*Num.* 33:55 they sh. be *t.* in your sides, *Jud.* 2:3
*Jos.* 23:13 they shall be *t.* in eyes
2 *Sam.* 23:6 sons of Bel. be as *t.*
2 *Chr.* 33:11 took Man. among *t.*
*Ps.* 58:9 bef. pots feel *t.* take th.
118:12 quenched as a fire of *t.*
*Prov.* 15:19 slothf. as hedge of *t.*
22:5 *t.* are in way of froward
24:31 it was grown over with *t.*
*Ec.* 7:6 as crackling of *t.* under
*Cant.* 2:2 lily am. *t.* so my love
*Is.* 7:19 they shall rest upon *t.*
32:13 sh. come up *t.* and briers
34:13 *t.* sh. come up in palaces
*Jer.* 4:3 and sow not among *t.*
12:13 sown wheat, shall reap *t.*
*Hos.* 2:6 I will hedge way with *t.*
9:6 *t.* sh. be in th. tabernacles
*Nah.* 1:10 be folden togeth. as *t.*
*Mat.* 7:16 do men gather grapes of *t.*? *Luke* 6:44
13:7 fell among *t.* 22; *Mark* 4:7, 18; *Luke* 8:7, 14
27:29 platted crown of *t.* put it on, *Mark* 15:17; *John* 19:2

THOROUGHLY. *See* THROUGHLY.

**THOUGHT, Verb.**

*Gen.* 20:11 I *t.* fear of God not in
38:15 he *t.* her to be a harlot
48:11 had not *t.* to see thy face
50:20 ye *t.* evil against me
*Ex.* 32:14 repented of evil he *t.*
*Num.* 24:11 I *t.* to promote thee
33:56 you, as I *t.* to do to them
*Deut.* 19:19 as he *t.* to have done
*Jud.* 15:2 I *t.* th. hadst hated her
1 *Sam.* 1:13 Eli *t.* she been drun.
18:25 Saul *t.* to make David fall
2 *Sam.* 4:10 who *t.* I give reward
13:2 Ammon *t.* it hard to do any
21:16 Ishbi-be. *t.* to ha. slain D.
2 *K.* 5:11 I *t.* he will come out
2 *Chr.* 11:22 Reho. *t.* to make A.
32:1 Sennacherib *t.* to win them
*Neh.* 6:2 th. *t.* to do me mischief
*Est.* 3:6 he *t.* scorn to lay hands
6:6 Haman *t.* in his heart
*Ps.* 48:9 we *t.* of thy loving-kind.
73:16 when I *t.* to know this it
119:59 I *t.* on my ways, turned
*Prov.* 30:32 thou hast *t.* lay hand
*Is.* 14:24 *t.* so sh. it come to pass
*Jer.* 18:8 repent of evil I *t.* to do
*Zec.* 1:6 like as Lord of hosts *t.*
8:14 *t.* to punish; 15 *t.* do dwell
*Mal.* 3:16 for th. that *t.* on name
*Mat.* 1:20 while he *t.* on th. thin.
*Mark* 14:72 when he *t.* he wept
*Luke* 7:7 nor *t.* myself worthy to
12:17 he *t.* within himself
19:11 they *t.* kingd. of G. appear
*John* 11:13 *t.* he had spok. of rest
*Acts* 8:20 *t.* gift of G. be purcha.
10:19 while Peter *t.* on vision
12:9 but *t.* he saw a vision
15:38 P. *t.* not good to take him
26:8 why be *t.* a thi. incredible?
9 *t.* I ought to do many things
1 *Cor.* 13:11 child, I *t.* as a child
*Phil.* 2:6 *t.* it not robbery to eq.
*Heb.* 10:29 pun. he be *t.* worthy

**THOUGHTEST.**

*Ps.* 50:21 thou *t.* I was as thyself

**THOUGHT.**

*Deut.* 15:9 not a *t.* in thy heart
1 *Sam.* 9:5 lest my father take *t.*
*Job* 12:5 is despised in *t.* of him
42:2 that no *t.* can be withhold.
*Ps.* 49:11 their *t.* is, their houses
64:6 the inward *t.* of every one
139:2 thou understandest my *t.*
*Prov.* 24:9 *t.* of foolishness is sin
*Ec.* 10:20 curse not king in *t.*
*Ezek.* 38:10 thou sh. think evil *t.*
*Amos* 4:13 declare, to man his *t.*
*Mat.* 6:25 take no *t.* for your life, 31:34; 10:19; *Mark* 13:11; *Luke* 12:11. 22
*Mat.* 6:27 which of you by taking *t.* can add unto stature? *Luke* 12:25
28 take *t.* for rai.? *Luke* 12:26
*Acts* 8:22 if *t.* of thy heart may
2 *Cor.* 10:5 bri. into captiv. ev. *t.*

**THOUGHTS.**

*Gen.* 6:5 imagination of *t.* of his
*Jud.* 5:15 for Reub. were great *t.*
1 *Chr.* 28:9 L. understandeth *t.*
29:18 keep in imaginat. of the *t.*
*Job* 4:13 in *t.* fr. visions of night
17:11 purpos. are broken, my *t.*
20:2 my *t.* cause me to answer
21:27 I know your *t.* and devic.
*Ps.* 10:4 God is not in all his *t.*
33:11 the *t.* of his heart to all
40:5 thy *t.* cannot be reckoned
56:5 all their *t.* are against me
92:5 how gre. thy works! thy *t.*
94:11 L. knoweth the *t.* of man
19 in multitude of *t.* within me
119:113 I hate vain *t.* thy law
139:17 how precious are thy *t.*
23 O God, try me, know my *t.*
146:4 in that very day his *t.* pe.
*Prov.* 12:5 the *t.* of the righteous
15:26 the *t.* of wicked are abom.
16:3 thy *t.* shall be established
21:5 *t.* of the diligent tend to
*Is.* 55:7 let unrighteous forsake *t.*
8 my *t.* are not your *t.* saith L.
9 so are my *t.* higher th. yo. *t.*
59:7 their *t.* are *t.* of iniquity
65:2 peo. walketh after their *t.*
66:18 I know their works and *t.*
*Jer.* 4:14 how long shall vain *t.*?
6:19 even the fruit of their *t.*
23:20 till he have performed *t.*
29:11 I know the *t.* I think towards you, *t.* of peace
*Dan.* 2:30 migh. know *t.* of heart
4:5 Nebuchadnez.'s *t.* trou. him
19 D. was astonish. *t.* troubled
5:6 Belshazzar's *t.* troubled him
10 Let not thy *t.* trouble thee
*Mic.* 4:12 they know not *t.* of L.
*Mat.* 9:4 J. knowi. their *t.* 12:25; *Luke* 5:22; 6:8; 9:47; 11:17
15:19 out of heart proceed evil *t.* *Mark* 7:21
*Luke* 2:35 the *t.* of many hearts
24:38 why do *t.* arise in hearts?
*Rom.* 2:15 their *t.* accusing
1 *Cor.* 3:20 the Lord knoweth *t.*
*Heb.* 4:12 God is a discerner of *t.*
*Jam.* 2:4 become judges of evil *t.*

**THOUSAND.**

*Gen.* 20:16 given bro. a *t.* pieces
*Num.* 31:4 of every tribe a *t.* 5, 6
35:4 suburbs of cities are *t.* cub.
*Deut.* 1:11 L. ma. you a *t.* times
7:9 G. keepeth cove. to *t.* gene.
32:30 one chase a *t.*? *Jos.* 23:10
*Jud.* 9:49 of Shec. died, about *t.*
15:15 Samson slew a *t.* men, 16
20:10 hundred of a *t.* a *t.* out of
1 *Sam.* 18:13 Dav. capt. over a *t.*
2 *Sam.* 19:17 there were a *t.* men
1 *Chr.* 12:14 great. was over a *t.*
16:15 commanded to a *t.* gener.
*Job* 9:3 cannot answer one of a *t.*
33:23 an interpreter, one of a *t.*
42:12 Job had a *t.* yoke of oxen, a *t.* she-asses
*Ps.* 50:10 cattle on a *t.* hills are
84:10 day in courts be. than a *t.*
90:4 *t.* years in thy sight are but
91:7 a *t.* shall fall at thy side
*Ec.* 6:6 though he live a *t.* years
7:28 one man a among *t.* have I
*Cant.* 8:11 fruit was to bring a *t.*
*Is.* 7:23 a *t.* vines at a *t.* silverli.
30:17 one *t.* shall flee at rebuke
60:22 a little one shall beco. a *t.*
*Ezek.* 47:3 man measur. *t.* cubits
*Amos* 5:3 city went out by a *t.*
2 *Pet.* 3:8 one day wi. L. is as a *t.* years, a *t.* years as one day

*Rev.* 20:2 he bound Sa. a *t.* years
3 deceive no more, till *t.* years
4 they reigned with C. a *t.* yrs.
7 when the *t.* years are expired

**One THOUSAND two hundred sixty.**
*Rev.* 11:3 proph. *o. t. t. h. s.* days
12:6 feed her *o. t. t. h. s.* days

**One THOUSAND two hundred ninety.**
*Dan.* 12:11 shall be *o. t. t. h. n.*

**THOUSAND three hundred thirty-five.**
*Dan.* 12:12 co. to *t. t. h. t.-f.* days

**One THOUSAND six hundred.**
*Rev.* 14:20 space of *o. t. s. h.* fur.

**Two THOUSAND.**
*Num.* 35:5 mea. on east side *t. t.*
1 *K.* 7:26 sea contain. *t. t.* baths
2 *K.* 18:23 I will deliver thee *two t.* horses, *Is.* 36:8
*Neh.* 7:72 peo. gave *t. t.* pounds
*Mark* 5:13 about *two t.* swine

**Two THOUSAND two hundred.**
*Neh.* 7:71 *t. t. t. h.* pounds silver

**Two THOUSAND three hundred.**
*Dan.* 8:14 *t. t. t. h.* days, sanctu.

**Two hundred THOUSAND.**
2 *Chr.* 28:8 carried capt. *two h. t.*

**Two hundred eighty THOUSAND.**
2 *Chr.* 14:8 out of Benj. *t. h. e. t.*

**Three THOUSAND.**
*Ex.* 32:28 fell of people *three t.*
*Jud.* 15:11 *t. t.* went to bind S.
16:27 were upon roof *t. t.* men
1 *Sam.* 24:2 S. took *t. t.* men, 26:2
1 *K.* 4:32 So. spake *t. t.* proverbs
*Job* 1:3 substa. was *t. t.* camels
*Jer.* 52:28 carried capt. *t. t.* Jews
*Acts* 2:41 were added *t. t.* souls

**Four THOUSAND.**
1 *Sam.* 4:2 slew of Is. about *f. t.*
2 *Chr.* 9:25 Sol. had *f. t.* stalls
*Mat.* 15:38 th. that eat were *f. t.* *Mark* 8:9
16:10 seven loaves among *four t.* *Mark* 8:20
*Acts* 21:38 leddest into wild. *f. t.*

**Five THOUSAND.**
*Jos.* 8:12 he took about *f. t* men
*Jud.* 20:45 they gleaned *f. t.* men
*Ezr.* 2:69 they gave *f. t.* pounds
*Mat.* 14:21 had eat. were ab. *f. t.*
16:9 five loaves of *five t. Mark* 6:44; 8:19; *Luke* 9:14; *John* 6:10
*Acts* 4:4 that believed were *f. t.*

**Six THOUSAND.**
1 *Sam.* 13:5 against Is. with *s. t.*
2 *K.* 5:5 Naaman took *s. t.* piec.
1 *Chr.* 23:4 *six t.* were officers
*Job* 42:12 Job had *six t.* camels

**Seven THOUSAND.**
1 *K.* 19:8 I ha. left *s. t. Rom.* 11:4
1 *Chr.* 12:25 of Simeon, *seven t.*
29:4 I prep. *s. t.* talents of silver
2 *Chr.* 15:11 th. offer. *s. t.* sheep
30:24 Hezek. gave *seven t.* sheep
*Job* 1:3 his subst. was *s. t.* sheep
*Rev.* 11:13 were slain *s. t.* men

**Ten THOUSAND.**
*Lev.* 26:8 hundred sh. put *t. t.* to
*Deut.* 32:30 2 put *t. t.* to flight?
33:2 L. came with *t. t. Jude* 14
*Jud.* 1:4 they slew in Bezek *t. t.*
3:29 they slew of M. *t. t.* men
4:10 went up with *t. t.* men, 14
7:3 there remained to Gid. *t. t.*
2 *Sam.* 18:3 thou art worth *t. t.*
1 *K.* 5:14 sent to Lebanon *ten t.*
2 *K.* 14:7 Amaziah slew of E. *t. t.*
2 *Chr.* 25:11 smote of Seir *ten t.*
12 other *t. t.* left alive, did Ju.
30:24 Hezek. gave *ten t.* sheep
*Est.* 3:9 I will pay *t. t.* talents
*Ps.* 91:7 *t. t.* sh. fall at thy right
*Cant.* 5:10 is chiefest among *t. t.*
*Dan.* 7:10 *t. t.* times *t. t.* stood
*Mat.* 18:24 wh. owed *t. t.* talents
*Luke* 14:31 wheth. able with *t. t.*
1 *Cor.* 4:15 though you have *t. t.*
14:19 then *ten t.* words in an unknown tongue
*Rev.* 5:11 num. was *t. t.* time *t. t.*

**Ten THOUSANDS.**
*Deut.* 33:17 they are *t. t.* of Eph.
1 *Sam.* 18:7 Da. hath slain his *t. t.* 8; 21:11; 29:5
*Ps.* 3:6 I will not be afra. of *t. t.*
144:13 our sheep may bri. *t. t.*
*Dan.* 11:12 cast down many *t. t.*
*Mic.* 6:7 pleas. wi. *t. t.* riv. of oil

**Twelve THOUSAND.**
*Jos.* 8:25 th. fell of Ai were *t. t.*
*Jud.* 21:10 sent *t. t.* to Jabesh-g.
*Rev.* 7:5 tribe of Juda, Gad, *t. t.*
6 of Aser, Napht. Manas. *t. t.*
7 Simeon, Levi, Issachar, *t. t.*
8 Zabulon, Joseph, Benja. *t. t.*
21:16 measu. city *t. t.* furlongs

**Fourteen THOUSAND.**
*Job* 42:12 Job had *fourt. t.* sheep

**Sixteen THOUSAND.**
*Num.* 31:40 persons were *s. t.* 46

**Eighteen THOUSAND.**
*Jud.* 20:25 destroy. of Israel *e. t.*
1 *Chr.* 18:12 Abis. slew of E. *e. t.*
29:7 gave of brass *e. t.* talents

**Twenty THOUSAND.**
1 *K.* 5:11 Solomon gave Hiram *t. t.* measures, 2 *Chr.* 2:10
*Neh.* 7:71 fath. gave *t. t.* dr. 72
*Ps.* 68:17 chariots of G. are *t. t.*
*Luke* 14:31 him that com. wi. *t. t.*

**Twenty-two THOUSAND.**
*Num.* 3:39 number of Lev. *t.-t. t.*
43 first-born males were *t.-t. t.*

**Twenty-three THOUSAND.**
1 *Cor.* 10:8 fell in one day *t.-t. t.*

**Twenty-four THOUSAND.**
*Num.* 25:9 died in plague *t.-f. t.*

**Twenty-five THOUSAND.**
*Jud.* 20:35 destroyed of B. *t.-f. t.*

**Twenty-six THOUSAND.**
*Jud.* 20:15 Benja. numb. *t.-s. t.*

**Twenty-seven THOUSAND.**
1 *K.* 20:30 wall fell on *t.-s. t.* men

**Twenty-eight THOUSAND.**
1 *Chr.* 12:35 expert in war, *t.-e. t.*

**Thirty THOUSAND.**
*Num.* 31:39 asses were *t. t.* 45
1 *K.* 5:13 the levy was *t. t.* men

**Thirty-two THOUSAND.**
*Num.* 31:35 *t.-t. t.* wo. tak. cap.

**Thirty-three THOUSAND.**
2 *Chr.* 35:7 gave *t.-t. t.* bullocks

**Thirty-five THOUSAND.**
*Num.* 1:37 of Benja. were *t.-f. t.*

**Thirty-six THOUSAND.**
*Num.* 31:38 beev. we. *t.* and *s. t.*

**Thirty-seven THOUSAND.**
1 *Chr.* 12:34 of Naph. *t.* and *s. t.*

**Thirty-eight THOUSAND.**
1 *Chr.* 23:3 Lev. fr. 30 years *t.-e. t.*

**Forty THOUSAND.**
*Jos.* 4:13 *f. t.* prepared for war
*Jud.* 5:8 shield seen am. *f. t.*?

**Forty-two THOUSAND.**
*Ezr.* 2:64 cong. *f.-t. t. Neh.* 7:66

**Fifty THOUSAND.**
1 *Sam.* 6:19 Lord smote *f. t.* men
1 *Chr.* 5:21 Hagarites sheep *f. t.*
12:33 of Zebulon *f. t.* keep rank
*Acts* 19:19 price of books *f. t.* pie.

**Sixty THOUSAND.**
2 *Chr.* 12:3 Shish. came with *s. t.*

**Sixty-one THOUSAND.**
*Num.* 31:34 booty was *s.-o. t.*
*Ezr.* 2:69 *s.-o. t.* drams of gold

**Seventy THOUSAND.**
2 *Sam.* 24:15 died of people *s. t.*
1 *K.* 5:15 Sol. had *seventy t.* that bare burdens, 2 *Chr.* 2:2, 18

**Seventy-two THOUSAND.**
*Num.* 31:33 of beeves *s.-t. t.*

**Seventy-five THOUSAND.**
*Num.* 31:32 booty was *s.-f. t.* sh.
*Est.* 9:16 J. slew of foes *s.-f. t.*

**Seventy-six THOUSAND five hundred.**
*Num.* 26:22 num. of J. *s.-s. t. f. h.*

**Eighty THOUSAND.**
1 *K.* 5:15 Solomon had *eighty t.* hewers, 2 *Chr.* 2:2, 18

**Eighty-seven THOUSAND.**
1 *Chr.* 7:5 Issachar reckon. *e.-s. t.*

**THOUSAND THOUSAND.**
1 *Chr.* 21:5 they of Is. were *t. t.*
22:14 I prepared a *t. t.* of talents
2 *Chr.* 14:9 Eth. came with *t. t.*

**Two hundred THOUSAND THOUSAND.**
*Rev.* 9:16 army of horse. *t. h. t. t.*

**THOUSANDS.**
*Gen.* 24:60 moth. of *t.* of millions
*Ex.* 18:21 place ov. rul. of *t.* 25
20:6 sh. mercy to *t. Deut.* 5:10
34:7 keeping mercy for *t.* forgiv.
*Num.* 1:16 princes of trib. heads of *t.* 10:4; *Jos.* 22:14, 21, 30
10:36 return, O L. to *t.* of Israel
31:5 were deliver. out of *t.* of Is.
*Deut.* 1:15 I made captains ov. *t.*
33:17 they are *t.* of Manasseh
1 *Sam.* 8:12 appoint capt. over *t.*
10:19 present yourselves by *t.*
18:8 to me th. have ascri. but *t.*
22:7 son of J. make capt. of *t.*?
23:23 search throughout *t.* of J.
29:2 lords of Phil. passed by *t.*
2 *Sam.* 18:4 peo. came out by *t.*
*Ps.* 119:72 law better th. *t.* gold
*Jer.* 32:18 showest loving-k. to *t.*
*Dan.* 7:10 *t.* minister. unto him
*Mic.* 5:2 tho' little among *t.* of J.
6:7 will L. be plea. wi. *t.* rams?
*Acts* 21:20 *t.* of Jews which belie.
*Rev.* 5:11 number of them *t.* of *t.*
*See* CAPTAINS.

**THREAD.**
*Gen.* 14:23 not take fr. *t.* to latch.
38:28 bound on hand scarl. *t.* 30
*Jos.* 2:18 bind scar. *t.* in window
*Jud.* 16:9 bra. withs as *t.* of tow
12 be brake ropes fr. arms as *t.*
*Cant.* 4:3 lips like *t.* of scarlet

**THREATEN, ED.**
*Acts* 4:17 let us straitly *t.* th. 21
1 *Pet.* 2:23 wh. he suff. he *t.* not

**THREATENING, S.**
*Acts* 4:29 Lord, behold their *t.*
9:1 Saul yet breathing out *t.*
*Eph.* 6:9 same to th. forbearing *t.*

**THREE.**
*Gen.* 18:2 and lo, *t.* men stood by
*Ex.* 21:11 do not th. *t.* unto her
*Deut.* 4:41 Moses served *t.* cities, 19:2, 3, 7, 9
17:6 mouth of *t.* witnes. 19:15
2 *Sam.* 24:12 I offer thee *t.* things, 1 *Chr.* 21:10

Prov. 30:15 t. things never satis.
18 t. thi. too wonderf. for me
21 for t. thi. earth is disquieted
29 t. things which go well,
Ezek. 14:14 t. men were in, 16, 18
Acts 10:19 t. men seek thee, 11:11
1 Cor. 13:13 now abideth these t.
14:27 by two, or at most by t.
29 let prophets speak two or t.
1 Tim. 5:19 before two or t. wit.
Heb. 10:28 died un. two or t. wit.
1 John 5:7 t. bear record in heaven, and these t. agree
See DAYS.

**THREE months.**

Gen. 38:24 about t. m. after it
Ex. 2:2 child, she hid him t. m.
2 Sam. 6:11 ark of L. continued in ho. of O. t. m. 1 Chr. 13:14
24:13 wilt thou flee t. m. before thine enemies? 1 Chr. 21:12
Amos 4:7 were yet t. m. to harv.
Acts 7:20 M. was nourished t. m.
19:8 P. spake the space of t. m.
28 Paul abode in Greece t. m.
Heb. 11:23 Mo. was hid t. months

THREE-TAVERNS. Acts 28:15

**THREE times.**

Ex. 23:14 t. t. keep a feast to me
17 t. t. in year all males shall appear bef. L. Deut. 16:16
Num. 22:28 smitten me t. t. 32
1 K. 17:21 stretched on child t. t.
2 K. 13:25 t. t. did Joash beat H.
2 Chr. 8:13 offering t. t. in year
Dan. 6:10 he kneeled t. t. a day
13 D. maketh his petition t. t.
Acts 11:10 this was done t. times

**THREE years.**

Gen. 15:9 take heifer t. y. old
Lev. 25:21 br. forth fruits for t. y.
Deut. 14:28 end of t. y. br. tithe
1 K. 2:39 end of t. y. S.'s servant
10:22 once in t. years came navy of Tarshish, 2 Chr. 9:21
2 K. 17:5 Assyr. besieged S. t. y.
18:10 at end of t. y. th. took it
1 Chr. 21:12 cho. either t. y. fam.
2 Chr. 11:17 made R. strong t. y. t. y. th. walked in way of D.
31:16 fr. t. y. old and upwards
Is. 16:14 within t. y. as of hirel.
20:3 as Isa. walked barefoot t. y.
Jer. 48:34 as a heifer of t. y. old
Dan. 1:5 nourishing them t. y.
Amos 4:4 br. your tithes aft. t. y.
Luke 4:25 shut t. y. Jam. 5:17
13:7 th. t. y. I come seek. fruit
Acts 20:31 t. y. I ceased not to
Gal. 1:18 after t. y. I went to J.
See HUNDRED.

**THREEFOLD.**

Ec. 4:12 t. cord not quic. brok.

**THREESCORE.**

Gen. 25:26 Isaac t. wh. she bare
Deut. 3:4 took fr. them t. cities, Jos. 13:30
2 Sam. 2:31 thr. hund. and t. died
1 K. 4:13 to him pertain. t. cities
6:2 length of L.'s house t. cub.
2 K. 25:19 he took t. men of peo.
1 Chr. 2:21 Hezron married t. old
2 Chr. 11:21 Rehob. took t. concu.
Ezr. 6:3 height of temple t. cub.
Cant. 3:7 t. vali. men are about
6:8 t. queens, fourscore concu.
Jer. 52:25 put to death t. men
Dan. 3:1 wh. height was t. cubits
Luke 24:13 fr. Jerus. t. furlongs
1 Tim. 5:9 widow be tak. und. t.
See SIXTY.

**THREESCORE and one.**

Num. 31:39 trib. of asses t. a. o.

**THREESCORE and two.**

Dan. 5:31 Dar. t. a. t. years old
9:25 in t. a. t. weeks street built
26 after t. a. t. weeks Messiah

**THREESCORE and five.**

Is. 7:8 within t. a. f. years Eph.

**THREESCORE and six.**

Gen. 46:26 came with Ja. t. a. s.

**THREESCORE and ten.**

Gen. 46:27 house of Ja. which ca. into E. t. a. t. Deut. 10:22
50:3 mourned for Is. t. a. t. days
Ex. 15:27 t. a. t. tr. Num. 33:9
Jud. 1:7 t. a. t. kings, thum. cut
9:5 slew t. and t. persons, 18, 24
12:14 that rode on t. and t. asses
2 Chr. 29:32 bro. t. a. t. bullocks
36:21 to fulfil t. and ten years
Ps. 90:10 days of our y. t. a. t.
Zec. 1:12 indigna. t. a. t. years
Acts 23:23 ready t. a. t. horsem.
See SEVENTY.

**THREESCORE and twelve.**

Num. 31:38 trib. t. and t. beeves

**THREESCORE and fifteen.**

Acts 7:14 Jos.'s kindr. t. and f.

**THRESH.**

Is. 41:15 th. sh. t. mountains
Jer. 51:33 floor it is time to t. her
Mic. 4:13 and t. O daughter of Zi.
Hab. 3:12 didst t. heath. in anger

**THRESHED, ETH.**

Jud. 6:11 Gid. t. wheat by the
Is. 28:27 fitches not t. with inst.
Amos 1:3 because they t. Gilead
1 Cor. 9:10 t. in hope, be partaker

**THRESHING.**

Lev. 26:5 t. reach to vintage
2 Sam. 24:22 here be t. instruments, 1 Cor. 21:23
2 K. 13:7 made th. like dust by t.
1 Chr. 21:20 Ornan was t. wheat
Is. 21:10 my t. and corn of floor
28:28 he will not ever be t. it
41:15 make sharp t. instrument
See FLOOR, FLOORS.

**THRESHOLD.**

Jud. 19:27 her hands were on t.
1 Sam. 5:4 hands cut off on the t.
5 tread not on t. of Dagon
1 K. 14:17 came to t. child died
Ezek. 9:3 glory of G. on t. 10:4
10:18 glory of G. departed fr. t.
43:8 in their sitting of their t.
46:2 prince shall worship at t.
47:1 waters issued from under t.
Zep. 1:9 pun. all that leap on t.

**THRESHOLDS.**

Neh. 12:25 keeping ward at the t.
Ezek. 43:8 setting threshold by t.
Zep. 2:14 desolation shall be t.

**THREW.**

2 Sam. 16:13 Shi. t. stones at Da.
2 K. 9:33 they t. Jezebel down
2 Chr. 31:1 t. down high places
Mark 12:42 she t. in two mites
Luke 9:42 the devil t. him down
Acts 22:23 cried, t. dust in air

**THREWEST.**

Neh. 9:11 persecu. t. into deeps

**THRICE.**

Ex. 34:23 t. in year sh. app. 24
2 K. 13:18 Joash smote t. stayed
19 shalt smite Syria but t.
Mat. 26:34 thou shalt deny me t. 75; Mark 14:30, 72; Luke 22:34, 61; John 13:38
Acts 10:16 this was done t. vessel
2 Cor. 11:25 t. was I beaten with rods, t. I suffered shipwreck
12:8 for this I besought the L. t.

**THROAT.**

Ps. 5:9 t. is sepulch. Rom. 3:13
69:3 weary of crying, t. is dried
115:7 neither speak thro' their t.
Prov. 23:2 put a knife to t. if giv.
Jer. 2:25 withh. thy t. fr. thirst
Mat. 18:28 servant took him by t.

**THRONE.**

Gen. 41:40 in t. will I be greater
Deut. 17:18 sitteth on t. of king.
1 Sam. 2:8 make them inherit t.
2 Sam. 3:10 to set up t. of David
7:13 stablish t. of kingdom, 16
1 K. 1:13 Solomon shall sit on my t. 17, 24, 30, 35
48 given one to sit on my t.
2:4 not fail thee a man on the t. of Israel, 8:25; 9:5; 2 Chr. 6:16; Jer. 33:17
12 Sol. sat on t. of David, 24; 8:20; 10:9; 1 Chr. 29:23; 2 Chr. 6:10
10:18 king made a t. 2 Chr. 9:17
2 K. 10:3 set him on his fath. s t.
30 fourth gener. sit on t. 15:12
11:19 Joa. sat on t. 2 Chr. 23:20
Neh. 3:7 repair. to t. of governor
Job 36:7 with kings are th. on t.
Ps. 9:4 thou satest in t. judging
11:4 the Lord's t. is in heaven
45:6 thy t. O God, is for ever, Lam. 5:19; Heb. 1:8
47:8 G. sitteth on t. of his holi.
89:4 will build thy t. to all gen.
14 jus. and judgm. are of thy t.
94:20 sh. t. of iniq. ha. fellow.?
132:11 fr. of body will I set on t.
12 chil. shall sit on t. for ever
Prov. 20:8 king that sit. in t. of
Is. 6:1 I saw L. sitting upon a t.
9:7 on t. of Da. and his kingdom
14:13 I will exalt my t. ab. stars
22:23 Eliakim sh. be for glori. t.
47:1 there is no t. O daughter of
66:1 heaven is my t. Acts 7:49
Jer. 3:17 call Jerusalem t. of L.
13:13 kings th. sit on David's t.
14:21 do not disgrace t. of glory
17:12 a glori. high t. from begin.
25 sitting on t. of Da. 22:4, 30
22:2 sittest upon the t. 29:16
36:30 none to sit on t. of David
49:38 I will set my t. in Elam
Ezek. 1:26 likeness of a t. 10:1
43:7 place of my t. shall Is. no
Hag. 2:22 I will overthrow the t.
Mat. 5:34 heaven, G.'s t. 23:22
19:28 Son shall sit in t. 25:31
Luke 1:32 L. sh. give him t. of D.
Heb. 4:16 come boldly to t. of gr.
8:1 on ri. hand of t. of God, 12:2
Rev. 3:21 will I grant to sit in t.
4:2 a t. was set, one sat on the t.
3 was a rainbow round about t.
5 out of t. proceed. lightnings, were seven lamps before t.
6 bef. t. was a sea of glass, in t. and about t. were 4 beasts
10 bef. him that sat on t. 7:11
5:1 in hand of him that sat on t.
6 in the midst of the t. a Lamb
7 out of hand of him sat on t.
13 glory to him that sit. on t.
6:16 hide fr. him that sit. on t.
7:9 a multitude stood before t.
10 our God which sitteth on t.
15 they are bef. t. of God, that sitteth on t. shall dwell
17 the Lamb in midst of t. shall
8:3 golden altar was before t.
14:3 sung a new song before t.
5 without fault before t. of G.
19:4 worshipped G. that sat on t.
20:11 I saw a great white t. and
21:5 he that sat on t. said, Beh.
22:1 a river proceeding out of t.
3 t. of God and of the Lamb

**His THRONE.**

Ex. 11:5 that sits on h. t. 12:29
2 Sam. 14:9 king and h. t. guiltl.

1 *K.* 1:37 L. make *h. t.* greater, 47
2:19 he bowed, and sat on *his t.*
33 and on *his t.* shall be peace
16:11 as Zi. sat on *his t.* he slew
22:10 king of Is. and Jehoshaphat, king of Judah, sat each on *his t.* 2 *Chr.* 18:9
19 L. sit. on *his t.* 2 *Chr.* 18:18
2 *K.* 13:13 Jerob. sat upon *his t.*
25:28 set *his t.* above the throne of kings, *Jer.* 52:32
*Job* 26:9 hold. back face of *his t.*
*Ps.* 9:7 prepared *h. t.* for judgm.
89:29 *his t.* to endure as days
36 *his t.* shall endure as sun
44 th. hast cast *his t.* to ground
97:2 judgment habita. of *his t.*
103:19 L. prep. *his t.* in heaven
*Prov.* 29:28 *h. t.* is upholden
*Jer.* 1:15 set each *his t.* at gates
33:21 D. not have a son on *h. t.*
43:10 I will set *his t.* on stones
*Dan.* 5:20 was deposed from *h. t.*
7:9 *his t.* was like fiery flame
*Jon.* 3:6 king of N. rose fr. *h. t.*
*Zec.* 6:13 he shall rule upon *his t.* and be a priest on *his t.*
*Acts* 2:30 raise C. to sit on *his t.*
*Rev.* 1:4 from seven spi. bef. *h. t.*
3:21 set down wi. my F. in *h. t.*
*Rev.* 12:5 child was cau. up to *h. t.*
*See* ESTABLISH, ESTABLISHED.

**THRONES.**

*Ps.* 122:5 are set *t.* of judgment
*Is.* 14:9 raised up from their *t.*
*Ezek.* 26:16 princes sh. come fr. *t.*
*Dan.* 7:9 till *t.* were cast down
*Mat.* 19:28 sh. sit on 12 *t. Lu.* 22:30
*Col.* 1:16 whether they be *t.*
*Rev.* 20:4 I saw *t.* and they sat

**THRONG, ED, ING.**

*Mark* 3:9 lest they should *t.* him
5:24 much peo. *t.* him, *Luke* 8:42
31 thou seest multitude *t.* thee
*Luke* 8:45 the multitude *t.* thee

**THROUGH.**

*Rom.* 11:36 *t.* him, to him,
*Eph.* 4:6 one God who is *t.* all

**THROUGHLY.**

*Job* 6:2 my grief were *t.* weighed
*Ps.* 51:2 wash me *t.* from iniq.
*Jer.* 7:5 if ye *t.* amend yo. ways
*Ezek.* 16:9 I *t.* wash. away blood
*Mat.* 3:12 *t.* purge, *Luke* 3:17

**THROUGHOUT.**

*Mark* 14:9 gosp. preach. *t.* world
*John* 19:23 woven from the top *t.*
*Rom.* 1:8 faith is spo. of *t.* world
*See* GENERATIONS.

**THROW.**

*Jud.* 2:2 sh. *t.* down their altars
6:25 *t.* down the altar of Baal
2 *K.* 9:33 *t.* her down, so they
*Jer.* 1:10 over nations *t.* down
31:28 I watched over them, to *t.*
*Ezek.* 16:39 th sh. *t.* down thine
*Mic.* 5:11 I will *t.* down thy stro.
*Mal.* 1:4 build, I will *t.* down

**THROWING.**

*Num.* 35:17 smite with *t.* stone

**THROWN.**

*Ex.* 15:1 horse and rider *t.* 21
*Jud.* 6:32 he hath *t.* down altar
2 *Sam.* 20:21 his head shall be *t.*
1 *K.* 19:10 Isr. have *t.* down, 14
*Jer.* 31:40 it shall not be *t.* down
50:15 her walls are *t.* down
*Lam.* 2:2 L. ha. *t.* down in wrath
17 hath *t.* down, not pitied
*Ezek.* 29:5 I will leave th. *t.* into
38:20 mount. shall be *t.* down
*Nah.* 1:6 the rocks are *t.* down
*Mat.* 24:2 stone th. shall not be *t.* down, *Mark* 13:2; *Lu.* 21:6

*Luke* 4:35 when devil had *t.* him
*Rev.* 18:21 Babyl. sh. be *t.* down

**THRUST.**

*Ex.* 11:1 sh. surely *t.* you out
12:39 they were *t.* out of Egypt
*Num.* 22:25 Bala.'s ass *t.* herself
25:8 Phinehas *t.* them through
35:20 but if he *t.* him of hatred
22 if he *t.* him suddenly with
*Deut.* 13:5 to *t.* thee out of way
10 he sought to *t.* thee from L.
15:17 *t.* the awl through his ear
33:27 he shall *t.* out the enemy
*Jud.* 3:21 Eh. *t.* dagger into his
6:38 he *t.* fleece together, and
9:41 Ze. *t.* out Gaal and breth.
54 young man *t.* Ab. through
11:2 and they *t.* out Jephthah
1 *Sam.* 11:2 I may *t.* out yo. eyes
31:4 S. said, *t.* me through, lest uncircumcised *t.* 1 *Chr.* 10:4
2 *Sam.* 2:16 *t.* sw. in his fellow's
18:14 J. *t.* three darts thro' Abs.
23:6 Belial shall be as thorns *t.*
1 *K.* 2:27 Solom. *t.* out Abiathar
2 *K.* 4:27 Gehazi came to *t.* her
2 *Chr.* 26:20 they *t.* Uzziah out fr.
*Ps.* 118:13 thou hast *t.* at me
*Is.* 13:15 every one sh. be *t.* thro'
14:19 raiment of those th. are *t.*
*Jer.* 51:4 they that are *t.* through
*Ezek.* 16:40 they shall *t.* thee thro'
34:21 have *t.* wi. side and shoul.
46:18 *t.* them out of possessions
*Joel* 2:8 neither shall one *t.* ano.
*Zec.* 13:3 shall *t.* him through
*Luke* 4:29 rose and *t.* him out
5:3 prayed he would *t.* out a lit
10:15 shall be *t.* down to hell
13:28 and you yourselves *t.* out
*John* 20:25 *t.* my ha. into his, 27
*Acts* 7:27 did wrong *t.* him away
39 our fath. *t.* him from them
16:24 *t.* them into inner prison
37 now do th. *t.* us out privily?
27:39 if it were possi. to *t.* ship
*Heb.* 12:20 stoned or *t.* through
*Rev.* 14:15 *t.* in thy sickle, harv.
16 *t.* in his sickle on the earth
18 *t.* in thy sharp sickle

**THRUSTETH.**

*Job* 32:13 God *t.* him down

**THUMB, S.**

*Ex.* 29:20 put it on *t.* of right hand, *Lev.* 8:23; 14:14-28
*Jud.* 1:6 cau. him and cut off *t.*
7 seventy kings hav. *t.* cut off

**THUMMIM.**

*Ex.* 28:30 put on breastplate, the urim and the *t. Lev.* 8:8
*Deut.* 33:8 let thy *t.* and urim be
*Ezr.* 2:63 priest with urim and *t.* *Neh.* 7:65

**THUNDER.**

*Ex.* 9:23 the L. sent *t.* and hail
29 the *t.* shall cease, nor shall
1 *Sam.* 7:10 L. thundered with *t.*
12:17 send *t.* 18 the Lord sent *t.*
*Job* 26:14 *t.* of power who und.?
28:26 way for light. of *t.* 38:25
39:19 clothed neck with *t.*?
25 smelleth *t.* of captains afar
*Ps.* 77:18 voice of thy *t.* in heav.
81:7 I answ. thee in place of *t.*
104:7 at voice of thy *t.* th. hasted
*Is.* 29:6 sh. be visited of L. wi. *t.*
*Mark* 3:17 Boanerges, is sons of *t.*
*Rev.* 6:1 as it were the noise of *t.*
14:2 as the voice of a great *t.*

**THUNDER, Verb.**

1 *Sam.* 2:10 out of heav. sh. he *t.*
*Job* 40:9 canst thou *t.* like him?

**THUNDERS.**

*Ex.* 9:33 *t.* and hail ceased, 34
19:16 *t.* and lightni. *Rev.* 16:18
*See* SEVEN.

**THUNDERBOLTS.**

*Ps.* 78:48 gave their flocks to *t.*

**THUNDERED, ETH.**

1 *Sam.* 7:10 Lord *t.* with thunder
2 *Sam.* 22:14 the L. *t. Ps.* 18:13
*Job* 37:4 he *t.* with his excellency
5 G. *t.* marvellously with voice
*Ps.* 29:3 God of glory *t.* the Lord
*John* 12:29 heard it, said that it *t.*

**THUNDERINGS.**

*Ex.* 9:28 be no more mighty *t.*
20:18 all the people saw the *t.*
*Rev.* 4:5 out throne proc. *t.* 19:6
8:5 th. were voices and *t.* 11:19

**THUS and THUS.**

*Jos.* 7:20 *t. and t.* have I done
*Jud.* 18:4 *t. and t.* dealeth Micah
2 *Sam.* 17:15 *t. a. t.* did Ahithop. counsel A. and *t. a. t.* have I
1 *K.* 14:15 *t. and t.* say to Jero.'s
2 *K.* 5:4 *t. and t.* said maid of Is.
9:12 *t. and t.* spake he to me

**THYATIRA.**

*Acts* 16:14 of city of T. worship.
*Rev.* 1:11 wh. th. seest send to T.
2:18 to angel of church in T.
24 to you and to the rest in T.

**THYSELF.**

*Gen.* 13:9 separate *t.* I pray thee
14:21 give persons, take goods *t.*
33:9 keep that thou hast unto *t.*
*Ex.* 10:3 refuse to humble *t.*?
28 take heed to *t.* see my face no more, 34:12; *Deut.* 4:9; 12:13, 19:30; 1 *Sam.* 19:2
18:22 shall it be easier for *t.*
*Est.* 4:13 think not with *t.* thou
*Ps.* 49:18 thou doest well to *t.*
*John* 1:22 what sayest thou of *t.*?
18:34 sayest thou this of *t.*?
*Rom.* 14:22 hast faith? have to *t.*

**THYINE.**

*Rev.* 18:12 merchant of *t.* wood

**TIBERIAS.**

*John* 6:1 Galilee, wh. is sea of T.
23 came other boats from T.

**TIBNI.**

1 *K.* 16:21 half people followed T.
22 ag. those that followed T.

TIDAL. *Gen.* 14:1, 9

**TIDINGS.**

*Ex.* 33:4 when peo. heard evil *t.*
1 *Sam.* 4:19 Phine. wife heard *t.*
11:4 told *t.* of men of Jabesh, 5
27:11 none alive to bring *t.* to G.
2 *Sam.* 4:4 when *t.* came of Saul
13:30 *t.* came, Absa. hath slain
18:19 run and bear king *t.*
20 thou sh. not bear *t.* this day
22 why run? hast no *t.* ready
31 C. said, *t.* my lord the king
1 *K.* 2:28 then *t.* came to Joab
14:6 I am sent to thee with *t.*
1 *Chr.* 10:9 to carry *t.* to idols
*Ps.* 112:7 not be afraid of evil *t.*
*Jer.* 20:15 cursed that brought *t.*
49:23 for they have heard evil *t.*
*Ezek.* 21:7 thou shalt answ. for *t.*
*Dan.* 11:44 *t.* out of east trouble
*Luke* 1:19 show thee glad *t.* 2:10
8:1 showing glad *t.* kingd. of G.
*Acts* 11:22 *t.* of th. things came
13:32 declare unto you glad *t.*
21:31 *t.* came to chief captain
*Rom.* 10:15 bring glad *t.* of good
*See* GOOD.

**TIE.**

1 *Sam.* 6:7 *t.* kine to the cart, 10
*Prov.* 6:21 and *t.* about thy neck

**TIED.**

*Ex.* 39:31 *t.* to it a lace of blue
2 *K.* 7:10 horses *t.* and asses *t.*
*Mat.* 21:2 ye shall find an ass *t.* *Mark* 11:2, 4; *Luke* 19:30

**TIGLATH-PILESER.**
2 *K.* 15:29 T. took Ij. and Kedesh
16:7 Ah. sent messengers to T.
1 *Chr.* 5:6 T. carried Bee. captive
26 God stirred up spirit of T.
2 *Chr.* 28:20 T. distressed Ahaz

**TILE, ING.**
*Ezek.* 4:1 son of man, take th. a *t.*
*Luke* 5:19 let him down thro' *t.*

**TILL, Conjunctive.**
*Dan.* 4:23 *t.* sev. times pass over
12:13 go thy way *t.* the end be
*John* 21:22 he tarry *t.* I come, 23
*See* CONSUMED, MORNING.

**TILL, ED, EST, ETH.**
*Gen.* 2:5 not a man to *t.* 3:23
4:12 when thou *t.* ground, it
2 *Sam.* 9:10 servants shall *t.* land
*Prov.* 12:11 that *t.* sh. be satisfied
28:19 th. *t.* land sh. have plenty
*Jer.* 27:11 they that *t.* it, and dw.
*Ezek.* 36:9 ye sh. be *t.* and sown
34 desolate land shall be *t.*

**TILLAGE.**
1 *Chr.* 27:26 them that were for *t.*
*Neh.* 10:37 Lev. have tithes of *t.*
*Prov.* 13:23 much food in *t.*

**TILLER.**
*Gen.* 4:2 Cain was *t.* of ground

**TIMBER.**
*Lev.* 14:45 sh. break down the *t.*
1 *K.* 5:18 so they prepared *t.* 1 *Chr.* 22:14; 2 *Chr.* 2:9
15:22 they took away *t.* of Ra.
*Ezr.* 5:8 *t.* is laid in walls
6:11 let *t.* be pulled fr. his house
*Neh.* 2:8 give me *t.* to ma. beams
*Ezek.* 26:12 lay thy *t.* in water
*Hab.* 2:11 beam out of *t.* answer
*Zec.* 5:4 shall consume it with *t.*

**TIMBREL.**
*Ex.* 15:20 Miri. took *t.* in hand
*Job* 21:12 they take *t.* and harp
*Ps.* 81:2 take psalm, bring *t.*
149:3 sing praises to him with *t.*
150:4 praise him with *t.*

**TIMBRELS.**
*Ex.* 15:20 wom. went out with *t.*
*Jud.* 11:34 daught. came with *t.*
2 *Sam.* 6:5 house of Is. played before Lord on *t.* 1 *Chr.* 13:8
*Ps.* 68:25 damsels play. with *t.*

**TIME.**
*Gen.* 18:10 accord. to *t.* of life, 14
24:11 *t.* women go to draw wat.
39:5 fr. *t.* he made him overseer
47:29 *t.* drew nigh Is. must die
*Ex.* 21:19 shall pay for loss of *t.*
*Lev.* 15:25 beyond *t.* of separa.
18:18 besides other in her life-*t.*
*Num.* 13:20 *t.* was *t.* of ripe gra.
26:10 wh. *t.* fire devou. 250 men
*Deut.* 16:9 *t.* thou put sickle
*Jos.* 10:27 at *t.* of going down of sun, 2 *Chr.* 18:31
42 land did Josh. take at one *t.*
*Jud.* 18:31 *t.* house of G. in Shi.
2 *Sam.* 7:11 since *t.* I command.
11:1 *t.* when kings go to battle
23:8 eight hund. slew at one *t.*
2 *K.* 5:26 is it *t.* to receive money
1 *Chr.* 9:25 to come from *t.* to *t.*
*Ezr.* 4:10 at such a *t.* 17; 7:12
10:13 and it is a *t.* of rain.
*Neh.* 2:6 return? I set him a *t.*
*Job* 6:17 *t.* they wax warm
9:19 who shall set me a *t.*
15:32 accomplished before his *t.*
22:16 were cut down out of *t.*
38:23 preserved ag. *t.* of trouble
39:1 knoweth. th. *t.* br. forth? 2
*Ps.* 32:6 *t.* thou mayest be found
37:19 not be ashamed in evil *t.*
41:1 L. deli. him in *t.* of trouble
56:3 *t.* I am afraid, I trust in th.
69:13 prayer to thee in accept. *t.*
*Ps.* 81:15 their *t.* should have endured
89:47 remember how short *t.* is
105:19 until *t.* his word came
*Ec.* 3:1 *t.* to ev. purpose, 17; 8:6
2 a *t.* to be born, a *t.* to die, a *t.* to plant
7:17 why should thou die before thy *t.*?
8:5 wise man's heart discern. *t.*
9:11 *t.* and chance happen. to all
12 so are men snared in evil *t.*
*Is.* 26:17 near *t.* of her delivery
28:19 from *t.* it goeth forth
45:21 decla. this from ancient *t.*
48:16 from *t.* it was, there am I
49:8 in an acceptable *t.* I heard
60:22 L. will hasten it in his *t.*
*Jer.* 6:15 at *t.* I visit, cast down
8:7 swallow observe *t.* of com.
15 looked for *t.* of health
14:8 Saviour the. in *t.* of trouble
19 *t.* of healing, behold trouble
30:7 it is *t.* of Jacob's trouble
46:21 *t.* of their visitation 50:27
49:8 *t.* I will visit him, 50:31
19 who will app. me *t.*? 50:44
51:33 floor, it is *t.* to thresh her
*Ezek.* 4:10 fr. *t.* to *t.* sh. thou eat
16:8 thy *t.* was the *t.* of love
57 as *t.* of thy reproach of dau.
30:3 it shall be the *t.* of heathen
*Dan.* 2:8 I know ye would gain *t.*
9 speak, till the *t.* be changed
16 desired he would give him *t.*
3:5 at wh. *t.* ye hear cornet, 15
7:12 lives were prolong. for a *t.*
22 *t.* came saints posses. kingd.
25 until *t.* and divid. of *t.* 12:7
8:17 at *t.* of end shall be vision
9:21 touched *t.* of evening obla.
11:24 forecast his devices for a *t.*
35 to make th. white, *t.* of end
40 at *t.* of end king of south
12:1 there shall be a *t.* of trouble
4 seal book, even to *t.* of end, 9
11 fr. *t.* sacrifice be taken away
*Hos.* 10:12 is it *t.* to seek the L.
*Mic.* 5:3 till *t.* she which travail.
*Hag.* 1:4 is it *t.* to dw. in houses?
*Zec.* 14:7 evening *t.* sh. be light
*Mal.* 3:11 cast her fruit before *t.*
*Mat.* 1:11 *t.* they were car. away
2:7 H. inquired *t.* star appeared
8:29 come to torment us bef. *t.*?
21:34 when *t.* of fruit drew near
26:18 master saith, *t.* is at hand
*Mark* 1:15 *t.* is fulfilled, repent
4:17 and so endure but for a *t.*
6:35 and now the *t.* is far passed
11:13 for *t.* of figs was not yet
13:33 ye know not wh. the *t.* is
*Luke* 1:57 Elisabeth's full *t.*
4:5 showed kingd. in mom. of *t.*
7:45 this woman, since *t.* I came
8:13 in *t.* of tempta. fall away
13:35 not see me till *t.* came
19:44 knew. not *t.* of visitation
*John* 7:6 my *t.* is not co. your *t.*
16:2 *t.* cometh, whosoev. killeth
25 *t.* com. I sh. no more speak
*Acts* 1:21 *t.* L. went in and out
7:17 when *t.* of prom. drew nigh
20 in what *t.* Moses was born
17:21 spent their *t.* in noth. else
*Rom.* 13:11 it is high *t.* to awake
1 *Cor.* 4:5 judge nothing before *t.*
7:5 except with consent for a *t.*
29 I say, brethren, *t.* is short
*Eph.* 5:16 redeeming *t.* *Col.* 4:5
1 *Thes.* 2:17 taken fr. you short *t.*
2 *Thes.* 2:6 might be revealed in *t.*
2 *Tim.* 4:3 *t.* come, will not end.
6 *t.* of my departure is at hand
*Heb.* 4:16 to help in *t.* of need
5:12 for *t.* ye ought to be teach.
9:9 figure for the *t.* then present
10 impos. till *t.* of reformation
11:32 *t.* would fail to tell of G.
*Jam.* 4:14 that appeareth little *t.*
1 *Pet.* 1:11 what manner of *t.* Sp.
17 pass *t.* of sojourning in fear
4:2 no longer live rest of his *t.*
*Rev.* 1:3 for *t.* is at hand, 22:10
10:3 there should be *t.* no longer
11:18 *t.* of dead, who. be judged
12:12 knoweth he hath a short *t.*
14 she is nourished for a *t.* and

**Any TIME.**
*Lev.* 25:32 Lev. redeem at *any t.*
*Luke* 21:34 *a. t.* hearts overchar.
*John* 1:18 no man seen G. at *a. t.*
5:37 nor heard his voice at *a. t.*
*Heb.* 2:1 lest at *any t.* we should
1 *John* 4:12 no man se. G. at *a. t.*
*See* APPOINTED, BEFORE, COME, DAY, DUE.

**In the TIME.**
*Gen.* 38:27 came to pass *in the t.*
1 *K.* 15:23 *in the t.* of old age he
2 *Chr.* 28:22 *in the t.* of distress
*Neh.* 9:27 *in the t.* of trouble thou
*Ps.* 4:7 *in t. t.* when corn increa.
27:5 *in the t.* of trouble sh. hide
71:9 cast not off *in the t.* of age
*Is.* 33:2 salva. *in t. t.* of trouble
*Jer.* 2:27 *in the t.* of trouble they
28 save thee *in t. t.* of trouble
11:12 not save th. *in t. t.* of tro.
14 not hear th. *in t. t.* they cry
18:23 deal thus with th. *in the t.*
*Ezek.* 27:34 *in t. t.* when thou sh.
*Hos.* 2:9 take corn *in the t.* ther.
*Zec.* 10:1 rain *in the t.* of rain
*Mat.* 13:30 *in the t.* of harvest
*See* LAST, LONG, MANY, OLD, PAST, PROCESS, SET.

**That TIME.**
*Neh.* 4:16 from *t. t.* forth, 13:21
*Is.* 16:13 concern. M. since *t. t.*
18:7 in *that t.* shall the pres. be
45:21 who hath told it fr. *t. t.*?
*Mat.* 4:17 from *t. t.* Je. began to
16:21 from *that t.* began to show
26:16 from *t. t.* J. sought oppor.

**At that TIME.**
*Deut.* 5:5 I stood between the Lord and you *at that t.*
9:19 L. hearkened *at t. t.* 10:10
2 *Chr.* 30:3 not keep passo. *at t. t.*
35:17 Is. kept passover *at t. t.*
*Zep.* 3:20 *at that t.* will I br. you
*Eph.* 2:12 *at t. t.* we. without Ch.
*See* THIRD.

**This TIME.**
*Ex.* 9:14 *t. t.* send my plagues
18 to-morrow about *t. t.* I will
*Num.* 23:23 according to *t. t.*
*Jud.* 13:23 nor would at *t. t.* ha.
1 *Sam.* 9:13 ab. *t. t.* ye shall find
2 *Sam.* 17:7 coun. not good at *t. t.*
1 *K.* 2:26 not at *t. t.* put to death
19:2 to-morrow *t. t.* 20:6; 2 *K.* 7:1, 18; 10:6
*Neh.* 13:6 all *t. t.* was not I at J.
*Est.* 4:14 hold. thy peace at *t. t.*
*Ps.* 113:2 blessed be L. from *t. t.*
115:18 we will bless L. from *t. t.*
121:8 he will pres. thee from *t. t.*
*Is.* 48:6 showed new thi. fr. *t. t.*
*Jer.* 3:4 wilt thou not fr. *t. t.* cry?
*Acts* 1:6 wilt thou at *t. t.* restore?
24:25 answ. Go thy way for *t. t.*
*Rom.* 3:26 decl. at *t. t.* his right.
9:9 at *t. t.* will I come, S. shall
11:5 so at *t.* present *t.* there is a
1 *Cor.* 16:12 not to come at *t. t.*

**TIMES.**
*Gen.* 27:36 supplanted me two *t.*
*Lev.* 19:26 ye shall not observe *t.* *Deut.* 18:10, 14

*Deut.* 4:42 hated not in *t.* past
*Jud.* 13:25 S. began to move at *t.*
16:20 I will go out as at other *t.*
20:31 began to kill as at other *t.*
1 *Sam.* 3:10 L. call. as at other *t.*
20:25 sat on seat as at other *t.*
2 *K.* 21:6 Manasseh observed *t.* 2 *Chr.* 33:6
1 *Chr.* 12:32 had understand. of *t.*
29:30 the *t.* that went over him
2 *Chr.* 15:5 in those *t.* no peace
*Est.* 1:13 men which knew the *t.*
*Job* 24:1 *t.* are not hid. fr. Almi.
*Ps.* 9:9 L. a ref. in *t.* of trouble
10:1 why hid. in *t.* of trouble?
31:15 my *t.* are in thy hand
44:1 works th. didst in *t.* of old
77:5 consider. years of ancient *t.*
*Is.* 33:6 knowledge stability of *t.*
46:10 from ancient *t.* things not
*Ezek.* 12:27 he prophesied of *t.*
*Dan.* 2:21 he changeth *t.*
7:25 think to change *t.* and laws
9:25 streets sh. be built in tro. *t.*
11:14 in th. *t.* shall many stand
12:7 for a time, *t. Rev.* 12:14
*Mat.* 16:3 not discern signs of *t.*?
*Luke* 21:24 till *t.* of the Gentiles
*Acts* 1:7 not for you to kn. the *t*
3:19 *t.* of refreshing shall come
21 the *t.* of restitution of all
14:16 who in *t.* past suffered all
17:26 hath determined the *t.* be.
30 *t.* of ignorance God winked
*Rom.* 11:30 ye in *t.* past have not
2 *Cor.* 11:24 five *t.* rece. I stripes
*Gal.* 1:23 persecuted in *t.* past
4:10 days and months, *t.* years
*Eph.* 1:10 dispensa. of fuln. of *t.*
1 *Thes.* 5:1 of *t.* ye have no need
1 *Tim.* 4:1 in latter *t.* some shall
6:15 in his *t.* he sh. show who is
2 *Tim.* 3:1 in last days perilous *t.*
*Tit.* 1:3 in *t.* manifest. his word
*Heb.* 1:1 God who at sundry *t.*

### All TIMES.

*Lev.* 16:2 come not at *all t.*
*Ps.* 34:1 I will bless Lord at *all t.*
62:8 trust in him at *all t.* ye peo.
119:20 to thy judgments at *all t.*
*Prov.* 5:19 breasts satisfy at *a. t.*
17:17 a friend loveth at *all t.*

*See* APPOINTED, MANY, SEVEN, TEN, THREE.

### TIMNATH.

*Gen.* 38:12 to his shearers in T.
*Jud.* 14:1 Samson went to T.

TIMON. *Acts* 6:5

### TIMOTHEUS.

*Acts* 16:1 cert. disciple named T.
*Rom.* 16:21 T. my work-fellow
1 *Cor.* 16:10 if T. come, see that
2 *Cor.* 1:19 was preach. ev. by T.
*Phil.* 2:19 trust in L. to send T.
1 *Thes.* 3:2 we sent T. to comfort

### TIMOTHY.

2 *Cor.* 1:1 and T. our brother
1 *Tim.* 1:2 T. my son, 2 *Tim.* 1:2
*Heb.* 13:23 bro. T. set at liberty

### TIN.

*Num.* 31:22 *t.* that may abide fire
*Is.* 1:25 will take away all thy *t.*
*Ezek.* 22:18 they are brass, and *t.*
20 as they gather lead and *t.*
27:12 Tarshish was merch. in *t.*

### TINGLE.

1 *Sam.* 3:11 ears of ev. one shall *t.* 2 *K.* 21:12; *Jer.* 19:3

### TINKLING.

*Is.* 3:16 mincing and making a *t.*
18 take away their *t.* ornam.
1 *Cor.* 13:1 I am bec. *t.* cymbal

### TIP.

*Luke* 16:24 may dip *t.* of finger

*See Right* EAR.

TIPHSAH. 1 *K.* 4:24

### TIRE, ED.

2 *K.* 9:30 Jezebel *t.* her head and
*Ezek.* 24:17 bind *t.* of thy head

### TIRES.

*Is.* 3:18 L. will take away their *t.*
*Ezek.* 24:23 your *t.* sh. be on hea.

TIRHAKAH. 2 *K.* 19:9

### TIRSHATHA.

*Ezr.* 2:63 T. said th. *Neh.* 7:65
*Neh.* 7:70 T. gave gold to the
10:1 sealed were Nehem. the T.

### TIRZAH.

*Num.* 26:33 and T. daughters of Zeloph. 36:11; *Jos.* 17:3
27:1 Hoglah, and Melc. and T.
*Jos.* 12:24 Joshua sm. king of T.
1 *K.* 14:17 Jeroboam's wife to T.
15:21 Baasha reigned in T. 33
16:8 Elah reigned in T. 15 Zi.
17 O. besieged in T. 23 reigned
2 *K.* 15:16 smote coasts from T.
*Cant.* 6:4 th. art beautiful as T.

### TITHE.

*Lev.* 27:30 the *t.* of land is L.'s
*Num.* 18:26 off. a tenth part of *t.*
*Deut.* 12:17 not eat the *t.* of corn
14:23 eat *t.* in place the Lord
28 at end of three years bring *t.*
2 *Chr.* 31:5 they brought the *t.* of all thin. 6, 12; *Neh.* 13:12
*Neh.* 10:38 Levites shall bring *t.*
*Mat.* 23:23 pay *t.* of mint, anise

### TITHE, Verb.

*Deut.* 14:22 thou sh. *t.* increase.
*Luke* 11:42 ye *t.* mint and rue

### TITHES.

*Gen.* 14:20 Abr. gave Melchi. *t.*
*Lev.* 27:31 man redeem of his *t.*
*Num.* 18:24 *t.* I have given to L.
28 heave-off. to Lord of your *t.*
*Deut.* 12:6 ye sh. bring your *t.* 11
26:12 made end of tithing the *t.*
*Neh.* 10:37 Levites might have *t.*
12:44 some were appointed for *t.*
13:5 aforetime they laid *t.* of
*Amos* 4:4 bring your *t. Mal.* 3:10
*Mal.* 3:8 ye have robbed me of *t.*
*Luke* 18:12 I give *t.* of all I poss.
*Heb.* 7:5 have command. to ta. *t.*
6 he received *t.* of Abraham
8 here men that die receive *t.*
9 Levi who received *t.* paid *t.*

### TITHING.

*Deut.* 26:12 end of *t.* 3d year is *t.*

### TITLE.

2 *K.* 23:17 wh. *t.* is that that I s.
*John* 19:19 P. wrote a *t.* and put
20 this *t.* read many of the Je.

### TITLES.

*Job* 32:21 nor give flat. *t.* to man
22 I kn. not to give flattering *t.*

### TITTLE.

*Mat.* 5:18 one *t.* shall in no wise
*Luke* 16:17 one *t.* of law to fail

### TITUS.

2 *Cor.* 2:13 bec. I found not T.
7:6 comforted us by com. of T.
13 more joyed we for joy of T.
14 which I made before T.
8:6 desired T. *Gal.* 2:1 took T.
16 earnest care into heart of T.
23 whether any inquire of T.
12:18 T. made a gain of you?
*Gal.* 2:3 nor was T. comp. to be
2 *Tim.* 4:10 T. is departed to D.

TO AND FRO. *See* FRO.
TOB. *Jud.* 11:3, 5

### TOBIAH.

*Ezr.* 2:60 children of T. not sho.
*Neh.* 2:10 T. heard, 19; 4:7; 6:1
6:12 T. hired him; 14 thi. of T.
19 T. sent let. put me in fear
13:4 Eliashib was allied to T.
8 cast forth house. stuff of T.

### TOE.

*Ex.* 29:20 upon great *t.* of their right foot, *Lev.* 8:23, 24; 14:14, 17, 25, 28

### TOES.

*Jud.* 1:6 cut off thumbs and *t.*
7 seventy kings hav. *t.* cut off
1 *Chr.* 20:6 fingers and *t.* were 2
*Dan.* 2:41 thou sawest the *t.* 42

### TOGARMAH.

*Gen.* 10:3 Riphath, T. 1 *Chr.* 1:6
*Ezek.* 27:14 of house of T. traded

### TOGETHER.

*Ezr.* 4:3 ourselves *t.* will build
*Prov.* 22:2 rich and poor meet *t.*
*Ec.* 4:11 if two lie *t.* then they
*Is.* 65:25 wolf and lamb sh. feed *t.*
*Mat.* 18:20 two or three gath. *t.*
19:6 what God hath joined *t.* let not man put, *Mark* 10:9

*See* DWELL.

TOI. 2 *Sam.* 8:9, 10

### TOIL.

*Gen.* 5:29 conc. our work and *t.*
41:51 God made me forget my *t.*

### TOIL, ED, ING.

*Mat.* 6:28 they *t.* not, neither do they spin, *Luke* 12:27
*Mark* 6:48 saw them *t.* in rowing
*Luke* 5:5 Mast. we ha. *t.* all nig.

### TOKEN.

*Gen.* 9:12 this is the *t.* of, 13, 17
*Ex.* 3:12 shall be a *t.* I sent thee
12:13 the blood shall be for a *t.*
13:16 for a *t.* upon thy hand
*Num.* 17:10 kept for *t.* ag. rebels
*Jos.* 2:12 and give me a true *t.*
*Ps.* 86:17 show me a *t.* for good
*Mark* 14:44 Ju. had given th. a *t.*
*Phil.* 1:28 evident *t.* of perdition
2 *Thes.* 1:5 *t.* of righteous judg.
3:17 which is the *t.* in ev. epist.

### TOKENS.

*Deut.* 22:15 br. *t.* of virgin. 17, 20
*Job* 21:29 do ye not know th. *t.*?
*Ps.* 65:8 they also are afraid at *t.*
135:9 sent *t.* in midst of thee
*Is.* 44:25 frustrateth *t.* of liars

### TOLA.

*Gen.* 46:13 T. son of I. 1 *Chr.* 7:1
*Jud.* 10:1 T. son of Puah, arose

### TOLD.

*Gen.* 37:10 he *t.* it to his father
*Num.* 23:26 *t.* not I thee, all that
*Deut.* 17:4 it be *t.* thee, behold
*Jud.* 6:13 his miracles fathers *t.*
13:6 neither *t.* he me his name
23 nor would have *t.* such thi.
14:2 he came up, *t.* his father
6 *t.* not fath. 9, 16; 1 *Sam.* 14:1
16:17 he *t.* her all his heart, 18
1 *K.* 8:5 and oxen could not be *t.*
13:11 they *t.* to their father
18:13 was it not *t.* my lord
2 *K.* 12:11 gave money, being *t.*
*Est.* 8:1 Est. had *t.* what he was
*Job* 15:18 which wise men have *t.*
*Ps.* 90:9 spend years as a tale *t.*
*Is.* 44:8 have not I *t.* thee from?
45:21 who ha. *t.* it fr. that time?
52:15 what had not been *t.* them
*Dan.* 8:26 vision which is *t.* true
*Jon.* 1:10 because he had *t.* them
*Mat.* 8:33 they went and *t.* every
*Mat.* 14:12 took the bo. and *t.* J.
*Luke* 1:45 performance of thin. *t.*
2:18 wondered at things *t.* by

John 5:15 man t. Jews it was J.
Acts 9:6 be t. thee what do, 22:10

**TOLD him.**

Gen. 22:3 place of wh. G. t. h. 9
1 Sam. 3:13 t. h. I will jud. hou.
25:36 she t. h. nothing till mor.
2 K. 6:10 place man of God t. h.
Job 37:20 it be t. h. that I speak
Mark 5:33 woman t. h. all truth

**TOLD me.**

2 Sam. 4:10 when one t. me
1 K. 10:7 the half was not t. me, 2 Chr. 9:6
14:2 t. me I should be king over
2 K. 4:27 hid, and hath not t. me
8:14 he t. me th. should. recover
John 4:29 which t. me all thi. 39
Acts 27:25 sh. be as it was t. me

**TOLD you.**

Is. 40:21 t. y. from beginning?
Hab. 1:5 not beli. tho' it be t. y.
Mat. 24:25 behold, I t. y. before
28:7 ye shall see him, lo, I t. y.
John 3:12 if I t. y. earthly things
8:40 a man that hath t. y. truth
9:27 I have t. y. already, and ye did not hear, 10:25
14:2 not so, I would have t. y.
29 I have t. you before it come
16:4 have I t. you, that wh. time come, ye may remem. I t. y.
18:8 said, I have t. you I am he
Gal. 5:21 have t. y. in time past
Phil. 3:18 walk of whom I t. you
1 Thes. 3:4 we t. you we sh. suff.
2 Thes. 2:5 I t. you these things

**TOLERABLE.**

Mat. 10:15 more t. for Sodo. and Gomorrah, 11:24; Mark 6:11; Luke 10:12
11:22 more t. for Tyre, Lu. 10:14

**TOLL.**

Ezr. 4:13 th. will th. not pay t.
20 t. trib. and custom was paid
7:24 not be lawful to impose t.

**TOMB.**

Job 21:32 he shall remain in t.
Mat. 27:60 Joseph laid body in t.
Mark 6:29 laid John's corpse in t.

**TOMBS.**

Mat. 8:28 with devils com. out t. Mark 5:2, 3, 5; Luke 8:27
23:29 ye build t. of the prophets

**TONGS.**

Ex. 25:38 ma. t. thereof of gold
Num. 4:9 cov. t. wi. cloth of blue
1 K. 7:49 t. of gold, 2 Chr. 4:21
Is. 6:6 coal he had taken with t.
44:12 smith with t. work. coals

**TONGUE.**

Ex. 11:7 not a dog move his t.
Jos. 10:21 none moved t. ag. Isr.
Jud. 7:5 lappeth of water wi. t.
Job 5:21 he hid from scourge of t.
15:5 thou choosest t. of crafty
20:12 hide wickedn. under his t.
16 the viper's t. shall slay him
29:10 t. cleav. to roof of mouth
Ps. 5:9 they flatter with their t.
10:7 under his t. is mischief
12:3 cut off t. speak. proud thi.
4 with our t. will we prevail
15:3 backbiteth not with his t.
34:13 keep t. fr. evil, 1 Pet. 3:10
37:30 his t. talketh of judgment
50:19 and thy t. frameth deceit
52:2 thy t. deviseth mischiefs
57:4 their t. is a sharp sword
64:3 whet their t. like sword
8 make t. fall on themselves
68:23 t. of thy dogs may be dip.
73:9 their t. walketh thro' earth
109:2 spo. ag. me with lying t.
120:3 done to th. thou false t.?
126:2 our t. filled with singing
Prov. 6:17 hateth proud, lying t.
24 flattery of t. of stra. woman
10:20 t. of just as choice silver
31 froward t. shall be cut out
12:18 t. of the wise is health
19 a lying t. is but for a mom.
15:2 t. of wise useth knowledge
4 a wholes. t. is a tree of life
16:1 answer of t. is from the L.
17:4 liar giv. ear to naughty t.
20 perv. t. falls into mischief
18:21 dea. and life in pow. of t.
21:6 treasu. by lying t. is vanity
23 whoso keepeth t. keep. soul
25:15 soft t. breaketh the bone
23 angry counten. a backbit. t.
26:28 lying t. hateth th. afflicted
Prov. 28:23 he that flat. with t.
31:26 in her t. is law of kindne.
Cant. 4:11 milk are under thy t.
Is. 3:8 because their t. is ag. L.
11:15 destroy t. of Egyptian sea
30:27 his t. is as a devour. fire
32:4 t. of stammer. speak plain.
33:19 not see peo. of stammer. t.
35:6 then shall t. of dumb sing
41:17 when th. t. fail. for thirst
45:23 unto me ev. t. shall swear
50:4 L. ha. giv. me t. of learned
54:17 every t. that shall rise
57:4 ag. whom draw ye out t.?
59:3 your t. muttered perverse.
Jer. 9:3 bend their t. like bow
5 taught their t. to speak lies
8 t. is an arrow shot out
18:18 let us smite him with t.
Lam. 4:4 t. of sucking child cle.
Ezek. 3:26 make t. cleave to mo.
Hos. 7:16 princes fall for ra. of t.
Hab. 1:13 holdest t. when wicked
Zec. 14:12 t. consume in mouth
Mark 7:33 spit, and touch. his t.
35 his t. was loosed, Luke 1:64
Jam. 1:26 and bridleth not his t.
3:5 so the t. is a little member
6 t. is fire; 8 t. no man tame
1 John 3:18 nor love in t. in tru.

See DECEITFUL, HOLD.

**My TONGUE.**

2 Sam. 23:2 his wo. was in my t.
Est. 7:4 if sold, I had held my t.
Job 6:30 is there iniqui. in my t.
27:4 nor shall my t. utter deceit
33:2 my t. hath spok. in mouth
Ps. 22:15 my t. cleaveth to jaws
35:28 my t. shall speak of thy righteousness, 51:14; 71:24
39:1 heed th. I sin not wi. my t.
3 hot, then spake I with my t.
45:1 my t. is pen of ready writ.
66:17 G. was extolled with my t.
119:172 my t. speak of thy word
137:6 let my t. cleave to mouth
139:4 not a word in my t. but
Luke 16:24 dip finger, cool my t.
Acts 2:26 heart rejoice, my t. gl.

**TONGUE, *for language, speech.***

Gen. 10:5 every one after his t.
Ex. 4:10 slow of speech, slow t.
Deut. 28:49 whose t. not unders.
Ezr. 4:7 letter written in Syr. t.
Is. 28:11 anoth. t. will he speak
Dan. 1:4 might teach t. of Chal.
John 5:2 call. in Hebrew t. Beth.
Acts 1:19 in proper t. Aceldama
2:8 how hear we in our own t.?
26:14 saying in Hebrew t. Saul
Rom. 14:11 every t. confess to G.
1 Cor. 14:2 speak in unkn. t. 4:27
9 by t. words easy understood
26 every one hath a psalm, a t.
Phil. 2:11 ev. t. confess. J. is L.
Rev. 5:9 redeemed out of every t.
9:11 in Hebrew t. is Abaddon
14:6 gospel to preach unto ev. t.
16:16 in Hebrew t. Armageddon

**TONGUED.**

1 Tim. 3:8 be gra. not double-t.

**TONGUES.**

Gen. 10:20 sons of H. after th. t.
31 sons of Shem, after their t.
Ps. 31:20 keep th. fr. strife of t.
55:9 O Lord, and divide their t.
78:36 lied to him with their t.
140:3 sharpened t. like a serpe.
Is. 66:18 gath. all nations and t.
Jer. 23:31 use their t. and say
Mark 16:17 sh. speak wi. new t.
Acts 2:3 th. appeared cloven t. 4
11 hear in our t. works of God
10:46 heard them speak with t.
19:6 spake with t. prophesied
Rom. 3:13 with t. th. used dece.
1 Cor. 12:10 divers kinds of t. 28
30 do all speak with t.? do all
13:1 tho' I speak with t. of men
8 whether t. they shall cease
14:5 I would ye all spake wi. t.
6 if I come to you speak. wi. t.
18 I speak with t. more than
21 with men of other t. I speak
22 t. for a sign; 23 speak wi. t.
39 forbid not to speak with t.
Rev. 7:9 peo. and t. stood before
10:11 prophesy before natio. t.
11:9 t. and natio. see dead bod.
13:7 power given him over t.
16:10 gnawed their t. for pain
17:15 thou sawe. are nations, t.

**TOOK.**

Gen. 5:24 En. was not, G. t. him
Num. 11:25 L. t. of Spirit on him
1 Sam. 14:47 so Saul t. kingdom
2 Sam. 7:15 depart, as I t. fr. S.
Ps. 22:9 t. me out of womb, 71:6
48:6 fear t. hold on them there
55:14 t. sweet counsel together
Amos 7:15 L. t. me as I followed
Mat. 8:17 himself t. our infirmit.
25:43 stranger, ye t. me not in
Mark 12:20 the first t. a wife
21 second t. her, Luke 20:29, 30
14:49 teaching, and ye t. me not
John 19:27 t. her to his home
Acts 1:16 guide to th. who t. Je.
Phil. 2:7 t. on him form of serva.
Col. 2:14 t. it out of way

**TOOK away.**

Ps. 69:4 that which I t. not aw.
Cant. 5:7 keepers t. aw. my veil
Ezek. 16:50 I t. them a. as I saw
Hos. 13:11 t. king a. in my wra.
Mat. 24:39 flood came, t. them a.
John 11:41 they t. aw. the stone

**He TOOK.**

Gen. 34:2 Sh. saw her, he t. her
Ex. 4:6 when he t. it out, hand
2 Sam. 13:11 he t. hold of her
22:17 above he t. me, Ps. 18:16
1 K. 17:19 he t. her son out bos.
2 K. 5:24 he t. them fr. their ha.
Acts 16:33 he t. them same hour
21:11 he t. Paul's girdle, bound
Heb. 2:16 he t. not nat. of angels

**They TOOK.**

Gen. 6:2 t. t. wives they chose
14:11 they t. all goods of Sodom
12 t. t. Lot, Abram's brother's
Deut. 1:25 t. t. of the fruit of land
Jos. 6:20 peo. went, and t. t. city
11:19 all other they t. in battle
Jud. 3:6 t. t. their daught. to be
2 K. 10:14 t. t. them alive, and
Ezek. 23:13 I saw th. t. one way
Dan. 5:20 t. t. his glory from him
Mat. 21:46 t. t. him for a prophet
28:15 t. t. the money, and did as
Mark 12:8 t. t. him, killed him
Luke 22:54 t. t. him, John 19:16
Acts 13:29 t. t. him down fr. tree

**TOOK up.**

Num. 23:7 Balaam t. up his parable, 18; 24:3, 15, 20, 21, 23

*Jos.* 3:6 the priests *t.* *up* the ark, 6:12; 1 *K.* 8:3
2 *K.* 2:13 he *t.* *up* mantle of Elij.
10:15 *t.* him *up* into the chariot
*Neh.* 2:1 I *t.* *up* wine and gave
*Ezek.* 3:12 then the Spirit *t.* me *up*, 11:24; 43:5
*Mat.* 14:12 they *t.* *up* body of John, *Mark* 6:29
16:9 many baskets ye *t.* *up*, 10
*Mark* 10:16 he *t.* them *up* in arms
*Luke* 2:28 *t.* him *up* in his arms
*Acts* 10:26 Pet. *t.* him *up*, saying
*Rev.* 18:21 mig. angel *t.* *up* stone

**TOOKEST.**

*Ps.* 99:8 tho. thou *t.* vengeance
*Ezek.* 16:18 *t.* thy broid. garmen.

**TOOL.**

*Ex.* 20:25 if lift up thy *t.* thou
32:4 fashioned it with a grav. *t.*
*Deut.* 27:5 sh. not lift any iron *t.*
1 *K.* 6:7 nor any *t.* of iron heard

**TOOTH.**

*Ex.* 21:24 give *t.* for *t.* *Lev.* 24:20; *Deut.* 19:21; *Mat.* 5:38
27 if he smite man-servant's *t.* he shall go free for *t.* sake
*Prov.* 25:19 a broken *t.* a foot out

**TOP**

*Gen.* 11:4 tower wh. *t.* may reach
28:12 *t.* of ladder reached heav.
18 Ja. poured oil on *t.* of stone
*Ex.* 19:20 L. came on *t.* of Sinai
24:17 like fire on *t.* of mount
28:32 there shall be a hole in *t.*
30:3 overlay *t.* with gold, 37:26
*Num.* 14:40 gat into *t.* of mount.
20:28 Aaron died on *t.* of mount
23:9 from *t.* of rocks I see him
*Deut.* 3:27 get into *t.* of Pis. 34:1
28:35 fr. foot to *t.* of thy head
33:16 on *t.* of him that was sep.
*Jud.* 6:26 build alt. on *t.* of rock
9:51 peo. gat up to *t.* of tower
15:8 Samson dwelt on *t.* of E.
1 *Sam.* 9:25 commun. on *t.* of, 26
2 *Sam.* 16:22 tent on *t.* of house
1 *K.* 10:19 the *t.* of throne round
2 *K.* 9:13 under him on *t.* of sta.
2 *Chr.* 25:12 cast from *t.* of rock
*Est.* 5:2 Esth. touch. *t.* of scept.
*Ps.* 72:16 corn on *t.* of mountains
102:7 a sparrow on the house-*t.*
*Prov.* 8:2 she stand. in *t.* of high
21:9 in corner of house-*t.* 25:24
*Prov.* 23:34 lie. on the *t.* of a ma.
*Cant.* 4:8 the *t.* of Amana, fr. *t.*
*Is.* 2:2 L.'s house sh. be establis. in *t.* of mountains, *Mic.* 4:1
17:6 berries in *t.* of the bough
30:17 a beacon on *t.* of mount.
42:11 shout fr. the *t.* of mount.
*Lam.* 2:19 faint for hunger in *t.*
4:1 stones poured in *t.* of street
*Ezek.* 17:4 he cropt off *t.* of twigs
22 crop off *t.* of young twigs
24:7 she set it on *t.* of a rock
8 I set her blood on *t.* of rock
26:4 ma. her like *t.* of rock, 14
31:3 *t.* was am. boughs, 10, 14
43:12 house on *t.* of mountains
*Nah.* 3:10 dashed at *t.* of streets
*Mat.* 24:17 on house-*t.* *Mark* 13:15; *Luke* 17:31
27:51 veil rent fr. *t.* to bottom, *Mark* 15:38
*Luke* 5:19 they went on house-*t.*
*John* 19:23 woven fr. *t.* through.
*Heb.* 11:21 leaning on *t.* of staff
*See* HILL.

**TOPS.**

*Gen.* 8:5 *t.* of mounta. were seen
2 *Sam.* 5:24 when hearest so. on *t.* of trees, 1 *Chr.* 14:15
2 *K.* 19:26 as grass upon house-*t.* *Ps.* 129:6; *Is.* 37:27
*Job* 24:24 cut off as the *t.* of ears
*Is.* 2:21 into *t.* of ragged rocks
15:3 on *t.* of houses every one
22:1 wholly gone up to house-*t.*
*Jer.* 48:38 lamenta. on house-*t.*
*Ezek.* 6:13 slain in *t.* of mounta.
*Hos.* 4:13 sacrifi. on *t.* of mount.
*Zep.* 1:5 worsh. host on house-*t.*
*Mat.* 10:27 preach upon house-*t.*
*Luke* 12:3 proclaim. on house-*t.*

**TOPAZ.**

*Ex.* 28:17 a sardius, a *t.* 39:10
*Job* 28:19 the *t.* of Ethiopia shall
*Ezek.* 28:13 *t.* was thy covering
*Rev.* 21:20 beryl, the ninth a *t.*

**TOPHET.**

2 *K.* 23:10 Josiah defiled T. in v.
*Is.* 30:33 for T. is ordained of old
*Jer.* 7:31 built high places of T.
32 no more be called T. 19:6
19:11 they shall bury in T.
12 even make this city as T.
13 Jerusa. shall be defiled as T.
14 then came Jeremiah from T.

**TORCH.**

*Zec.* 12:6 make govern. like a *t.*

**TORCHES.**

*Nah.* 2:3 chariots sh. be with *t.*
4 chariots shall seem like *t.*
*John* 18:3 Judas cometh with *t.*

**TORMENT, S.**

*Mat.* 4:24 tak. wi. disease and *t.*
*Luke* 16:23 lift up eyes bei. in *t.*
28 lest th. come into place of *t.*
1 *John* 4:18 because fear hath *t.*
*Rev.* 9:5 *t.* was *t.* of a scorpion
14:11 smoke of their *t.* ascend.
18:7 so much *t.* and sorrow give
10 afar off for fear of her *t.* 15

**TORMENT, Verb.**

*Mat.* 8:29 art thou come to *t.* us?
*Mark* 5:7 *t.* me not, *Luke* 8:28

**TORMENTED.**

*Mat.* 8:6 serv. lieth grievously *t.*
*Luke* 16:24 I am *t.* in this flame
25 he is comforted, thou art *t.*
*Heb.* 11:37 destitute, afflicted, *t.*
*Rev.* 9:5 should be *t.* five months
11:10 two prophets *t.* them
14:10 he sh. be *t.* with fire and
20:10 shall be *t.* day and night

**TORMENTORS.**

*Mat.* 18:34 lord deliver. him to *t.*

**TORN.**

*Gen.* 31:39 which was *t.* of beasts
44:28 Surely he is *t.* in pieces
*Ex.* 22:13 not make good what *t.*
31 nor shall eat any flesh *t.* of
*Lev.* 7:24 fat of *t.* may be used
17:15 if any eat that wh. was *t.*
22:8 dieth itself, or *t.* of beasts
1 *K.* 13:26 lion, which hath *t.* him
28 eaten carcass nor *t.* the ass
*Is.* 5:25 carcasses *t.* in streets
*Jer.* 5:6 that goeth out shall be *t.*
*Ezek.* 4:14 not eaten of that is *t.*
44:31 priests sh. not eat th. is *t.*
*Hos.* 6:1 he hath *t.* he will heal
*Mal.* 1:13 bro. that which was *t.*
*Mark* 1:26 uncl. spirit had *t.* him

**TORTOISE.**

*Lev.* 11:29 the *t.* shall be unclean

**TORTURED.**

*Heb.* 11:35 oth. were *t.* not acce.

**TOSS.**

*Is.* 22:18 he will turn and *t.* thee
*Jer.* 5:22 tho' waves *t.* themselv.

**TOSSED.**

*Ps.* 109:23 I am *t.* up and down
*Prov.* 21:6 a vanity, *t.* to and fro
*Is.* 54:11 O thou afflicted, *t.* with
*Mat.* 14:24 ship was *t.* wi. waves
*Acts* 28:17 exceedi. *t.* with tem.
*Eph.* 4:14 children *t.* to and fro
*Jam.* 1:6 waver. is like wave *t.*

**TOSSINGS.**

*Job* 7:4 I am full of *t.* till dawn.

**TOTTERING.**

*Ps.* 62:3 ye shall be as a *t.* fence

**TOUCH.**

*Gen.* 3:3 nor shall ye *t.* it lest die
20:6 suffered I thee not to *t.* her
*Ex.* 19:12 that ye *t.* not border
13 shall not a hand *t.* it
*Lev.* 5:2 if a soul *t.* unclean thi.
6:27 whatsoever sh. *t.* the flesh
11:8 carcass sh. not *t.* *Deut.* 14:8
31 whosoe. doth *t.* them when
12:4 he sh. *t.* no hallowed thing
*Num.* 4:15 sh. not *t.* any holy th.
16:26 and *t.* nothing of theirs
*Jos.* 9:19 theref. we may not *t.*
*Ruth* 2:9 they should not *t.* thee
2 *Sam.* 14:10 he shall not *t.* thee
18:12 none *t.* the young man
23:7 that shall *t.* them must be
1 *Chr.* 16:22 *t.* not mine anointed, *Ps.* 105:15
*Job* 1:11 *t.* all he hath, and he
2:5 *t.* his bone and his flesh, he
5:19 in seven sh. no evil *t.* thee
6:7 that my soul refused to *t.*
*Ps.* 144:5 *t.* the mountains, and
*Is.* 52:11 *t.* no uncl. 2 *Cor.* 6:17
*Jer.* 12:14 that *t.* the inheritance
*Lam.* 4:14 men could not *t.* gar.
15 it is unclean, depart, *t.* not
*Hag.* 2:12 if one with skirt *t.* br.
13 if one that is unclean *t.*
*Mat.* 9:21 if I but *t.* *Mark* 5:28
14:36 that they might *t.* the hem, *Mark* 6:56; 8:22
*Mark* 3:10 to *t.* him, *Luke* 6:19
8:22 besou. him to *t.* blind man
*Luke* 11:46 ye *t.* not the burdens
18:15 infants, that he would *t.*
*John* 20:17 Jesus saith, *t.* me not
1 *Cor.* 7:1 good not to *t.* a wom.
*Col.* 2:21 *t.* not, taste not, handle
*Heb.* 11:28 first-born, sho. *t.* th.
12:20 if so much as beast *t.* mo.

**TOUCHED.**

*Gen.* 26:29 as we have not *t.* thee
32:25 he *t.* Jacob's thigh, 32
*Lev.* 22:6 soul which hath *t.* any
*Num.* 31:19 whoso. hath *t.* any
*Jud.* 6:21 angel of L. *t.* the flesh
1 *Sam.* 10:26 wh. hearts G. ha. *t.*
1 *K.* 6:27 wings of cherubim *t.*
19:5 an angel *t.* him, and said, 7
2 *K.* 13:21 when the man *t.* bon.
*Est.* 5:2 Esther *t.* top of sceptre
*Job* 19:21 hand of G. hath *t.* me
*Is.* 6:7 lo, this hath *t.* thy lips
*Jer.* 1:9 the Lord *t.* my mouth
*Dan.* 8:5 he-goat *t.* not ground
18 *t.* me, and set me upright, 9:21; 10:10, 16, 18
*Mat.* 8:3 and Jesus *t.* him, *Mark* 1:41; *Luke* 5:13
15 he *t.* her hand, the fever left
9:20 diseased with an issue *t.* garm. *Mark* 5:27; *Luke* 8:44
29 then *t.* he their eyes, 20:34
14:36 many as *t.* him were made whole, *Mark* 6:56
*Mark* 5:30 *t.* clothes, *Lu.* 8:45, 47
7:33 he spit, and *t.* his tongue
*Luke* 7:14 he came and *t.* the bier
8:47 declared cause she *t.* him
22:51 J. *t.* his ear, healed him
*Acts* 27:3 next day we *t.* at Zid.
*Heb.* 4:15 not priest wh. can. be *t.*
12:18 to mount that might be *t.*

**TOUCHETH.**

*Gen.* 26:11 *t.* this man shall die
*Ex.* 19:12 whos. *t.* mount sh. die
29:37 whatsoever *t.* altar be holy
30:29 that *t.* them, *Lev.* 6:18

*Lev.* 7:19 flesh that *t.* uncl. thing
11:26 every one that *t.* be uncl.
15:5 whoso *t.* his bed, sh. wash
11 whomsoever he *t.* hath iss.
12 vessel of earth he *t.* broken
23 if on her bed wh. he *t.* it, be uncl. 27; 22:4, 5; *Num.* 19:22
*Num.* 19:11 *t.* dead body, 13, 16
*Num.* 19:18 *t.* a bone; 21 *t.* water of separation
*Jud.* 16:9 broken when it *t.* fire
*Job* 4:5 it *t.* thee, th. art troubl.
*Ps.* 104:32 he *t.* hills, th. smoke
*Prov.* 6:29 whoso *t.* her, not inn.
*Ezek.* 17:10 when east wind *t.* it
*Hos.* 4:2 break, blood *t.* blood
*Amos* 9:5 L. of hosts that *t.* land
*Zec.* 2:8 *t.* you *t.* apple of eye
*Luke* 7:39 what wom. that *t.* him
1 *John* 5:18 wick. one *t.* him not

**TOUCHING.**

*Lev.* 5:13 as *t.* his sin he sinned
1 *Sam.* 20:23 *t.* matter thou and I
2 *K.* 22:18 *t.* words thou heard
*Job* 37:23 *t.* Almig. not find out
*Ps.* 45:1 things I made *t.* king
*Ezek.* 7:13 vision is *t.* multitude
*Mat.* 18:19 *t.* any thing they ask
*Rom.* 11:28 as *t.* elect. they are
1 *Cor.* 8:1 as *t.* things offer. idols
16:12 *t.* our brother Apollos
*Col.* 4:10 *t.* whom ye received
2 *Thes.* 3:4 confidence in L. *t.* you

**TOW.**

*Jud.* 16:9 as a thread of *t.* brok.
*Is.* 1:31 the strong shall be as *t.*
43:17 extinct, are quenched as *t.*

**TOWARD, *or* TOWARDS.**

*Deut.* 28:54 eye evil *t.* his broth.
56 shall be evil *t.* her husband
2 *Chr.* 24:16 bec. Jeho. had done good in Is. *t.* G. *t.* his house
*Ezr.* 3:11 his mercy endur. *t.* Is.
*Ps.* 5:7 worship *t.* temple, 138:2
25:15 mine eyes are ever *t.* L.
28:2 I lift hands *t.* thy oracle
*Is.* 63:7 goodness *t.* house of Is.
*Jer.* 15:1 mind not be *t.* this peo.
*Jon.* 2:4 look *t.* thy holy temple
*Luke* 2:14 pea. good will *t.* men

*See* HEAVEN.

**TOWEL.**

*John* 13:4 he riseth, and took a *t.*

**TOWER.**

*Gen.* 11:4 let us build city and *t.*
5 Lord came to see city and *t.*
35:21 spread tent beyo. *t.* of E.
*Jud.* 8:9 I will break this *t.* 17
9:46 men of *t.* of Shech. entered
51 there was a strong *t.* in city
2 *Sam.* 22:51 he is *t.* of salvation
2 *K.* 5:24 came to *t.* he took th.
*Ps.* 61:3 a strong *t.* from enemy
*Prov.* 18:10 name of L. strong *t.*
*Cant.* 4:4 thy neck like *t.* of Da.
7:4 thy neck is as a *t.* of ivory
*Is.* 5:2 built *t.* in midst of viney.
*Jer.* 6:27 I have set thee for a *t.*
31:38 city built from *t.* of Han.
*Ezek.* 29:10 desolate fr. *t.* of Sy.
30:6 fr. *t.* of Syene sh. they fall
*Mic.* 4:8 O *t.* of flock
*Hab.* 2:1 I will set me upon *t.*
*Zec.* 14:10 inhabited fr. *t.* of H.
*Mat.* 21:33 built a *t.* *Mark* 12:1
*Luke* 13:4 on whom *t.* of Sil. fell
14:28 you intending to build a *t.*

**High TOWER.**

2 *Sam.* 22:3 God is my *high t.* *Ps.* 18:2; 144:2
*Is.* 2:15 day of L. on every *h. t.*

**TOWERS.**

2 *Chr.* 14:7 build cit. and make *t.*
26:9 Uzziah built *t.* in Jerusa.
10 he built *t.* in desert
27:4 Jotham built castles and *t.*
32:5 Hezek. raised up wall to *t.*
*Ps.* 48:12 Zion, and tell her *t.*
*Cant.* 8:10 my breasts like *t.*
*Is.* 23:13 Assy. set up *t.* thereof
30:25 high hill riv. when *t.* fall
32:14 forts and *t.* sh. be for dens
33:18 wh. is he that counted *t.*?
*Ezek.* 26:4 sh. break do. her *t.* 9
27:11 Gammad. were in thy *t.*
*Zep.* 3:6 their *t.* are desolate

**TOWN.**

*Jos.* 2:15 Ra.'s house on *t.* wall
1 *Sam.* 16:4 elders of *t.* trembled
23:7 by entering into a *t.* that
27:5 give me a place in some *t.*
*Hab.* 2:12 woe to him builds a *t.*
*Mat.* 10:11 whatso. *t.* ye enter
*Mark* 8:23 led bli. man out of *t.*
26 neither go into *t.* nor tell any in *t.*
*John* 7:42 C. com. out of *t.* of B.
11:1 *t.* of Mary and sis. Martha
30 J. was not yet come into *t.*

**TOWNS.**

*Est.* 9:19 J. dwelt in unwalled *t.*
*Jer.* 19:15 bring on her *t.* the evil
*Zec.* 2:4 inhab. as *t.* with. walls
*Luke* 9:6 and went thro' the *t.*
12 that th. go into *t.* and lodge

**TOWN-CLERK.**

*Acts* 19:35 when *t.-c.* appeas. peo.

**TRADE.**

*Gen.* 46:32 *t.* about cattle, 34

**TRADE, Verb.**

*Gen.* 34:10 and *t.* you therein, 21
*Rev.* 18:17 as *t.* by sea stood afar

**TRADED.**

*Ezek.* 27:12 Tarsh. *t.* in thy fairs
13 Meshech *t.* persons of men
14 they of Togar. *t.* wi. horses
17 Ju. and Is. *t.* in thy market
*Mat.* 25:16 five tal. went and *t.*

**TRADING.**

*Luke* 19:15 ev. man gained by *t.*

**TRADITION.**

*Mat.* 15:2 why do disci. transgr. *t.* of the elders? *Mark* 7:5
3 why do you transgr. comma. of God by *t.*? *Mark* 7:9
6 made commandment of G. of none effect by *t.* *Mark* 7:13
*Mark* 7:3 hold. *t.* of elders, 8, 9
*Col.* 2:8 spoil you after *t.* of men
2 *Thes.* 3:6 *t.* wh. he recei. of us
1 *Pet.* 1:18 received by *t.* fr. fa.

**TRADITIONS.**

*Gal.* 1:14 zealous of *t.* of my fa.
2 *Thes.* 2:15 hold *t.* ye been tau.

**TRAFFIC.**

*Gen.* 42:34 and ye shall *t.* in land

**TRAFFIC, Substantive.**

1 *K.* 10:15 had of *t.* of merchants
*Ezek.* 17:4 car. it into land of *t.*
28:5 by *t.* hast thou increased
18 defiled sanct. by iniq. of *t.*

**TRAFFICKERS.**

*Is.* 23:8 whose *t.* are honorable

**TRAIN.**

1 *K.* 10:2 to Jerus. with great *t.*
*Is.* 6:1 his *t.* filled the temple

**TRAIN, Verb.**

*Prov.* 22:6 *t.* ch. in way he sh. go

**TRAINED.**

*Gen.* 14:14 Abram armed *t.* serv.

**TRAITOR, S.**

*Luke* 6:16 Iscariot which was *t.*
2 *Tim.* 3:4 in last days men be *t.*

**TRAMPLE.**

*Ps.* 91:13 dragon *t.* under foot
*Is.* 63:3 I will *t.* them in my fury
*Mat.* 7:6 lest th. *t.* th. und. foot

**TRANCE.**

*Num.* 24:4 falling into *t.* 16
*Acts* 10:10 he fell into a *t.*
11:5 and in a *t.* I saw a vision
22:17 in temple I was in a *t.*

**TRANQUILLITY.**

*Dan.* 4:27 be a length. of thy *t.*

**TRANSFERRED.**

1 *Cor.* 4:6 I ha. in figure *t.* to my

**TRANSFIGURED.**

*Mat.* 17:2 *t.* bef. them, *Mark* 9:2

**TRANSFORMED, ING.**

*Rom.* 12:2 be ye *t.* by renewing
2 *Cor.* 11:13 *t.* thems. into apost.
14 Sat. is *t.* into angel of light
15 no great thing if min. be *t.*

**TRANSGRESS.**

*Num.* 14:41 where. do ye *t.* commandm. of L.? 2 *Chr.* 24:20
1 *Sam.* 2:24 make L.'s peo. to *t.*
*Neh.* 1:8 if ye *t.* I will scat. you
13:27 heark. to you to *t.* ag. G.?
*Ps.* 17:3 purp. mouth sh. not *t.*
25:3 ash. who *t.* without cause
*Prov.* 28:21 for bread that man *t.*
*Jer.* 2:20 thou saidst, I will not *t.*
*Ezek.* 20:38 purge out them th. *t.*
*Amos* 4:4 come to Beth-el and *t.*
*Mat.* 15:2 do disciples *t.* tradit.?
3 why do ye *t.* comm. of God?
*Rom.* 2:27 by circumcis. *t.* law

**TRANGRESSED.**

*Deut.* 26:13 I have not *t.* com.
*Jos.* 7:11 they *t.* my covenant, 15
23:16 when ye have *t.* covenant
1 *Sam.* 14:33 have *t.* roll a stone
15:24 I have *t.* command. of L.
1 *K.* 8:50 wherein they have *t.*
1 *Chr.* 2:7 *t.* in thing accursed
5:25 they *t.* ag. G. of their fath.
2 *Chr.* 12:2 because they *t.* ag. L.
26:16 Uzziah *t.* against the L.
28:19 Ahaz *t.* sore against Lord
36:14 priests and peo. *t.* much
*Ezr.* 10:10 ye ha. *t.* taken wives
*Ezr.* 10:13 many th. *t.* in this th.
*Is.* 24:5 bec. they have *t.* laws
43:27 thy teachers ha. *t.* ag. me
66:24 look at men's carc. that *t.*
*Jer.* 2:8 the pastors *t.* against me
29 ye all have *t.* against me
3:13 acknowledge thou hast *t.*
33:8 iniquities whereby they *t.*
34:18 give men that *t.* covenant
*Lam.* 3:42 we ha. *t.* and rebelled
*Ezek.* 2:3 they and fath. *t.* ag. me
18:31 trangres. whereby ye *t.*
*Dan.* 9:11 all Is. have *t.* thy law
*Hos.* 7:13 destruction, bec. they *t.*
*Zep.* 3:11 doings wherein thou *t.*
*Luke* 15:29 nor *t.* thy command.

*See* COVENANT.

**TRANSGRESSEST, ETH.**

*Est.* 3:3 why *t.* king's com.?
*Prov.* 16:10 mouth *t.* not in judg.
*Hab.* 2:5 because he *t.* by wine
1 *John* 3:4 committeth sin, *t.* law
2 *John* 9 whoso *t.* and abid. not

**TRANSGRESSING.**

*Deut.* 17:2 wickedn. in *t.* coven.
*Is.* 59:13 in *t.* and lying ag. Lord

**TRANSGRESSION.**

*Ex.* 34:7 forgiving *t.* *Num.* 14:18
*Jos.* 22:22 if it be in *t.* ag. Lord
1 *Sam.* 24:11 no *t.* in my hand
1 *Chr.* 9:1 carried to Babyl. for *t.*
10:13 Saul died for *t.* committed
2 *Chr.* 29:19 Ahaz cast away in *t.*
*Ezr.* 9:4 bec. of *t.* of those car.
10:6 he mourned bec. of their *t.*
*Job* 7:21 why not pardon my *t.*
8:4 cast them away for their *t.*
13:23 make me to know my *t.*
14:17 my *t.* is sealed up in a bag

33:9 I am without t. I am inno.
34:6 wound is incurable with. t.
Ps. 19:13 innocent from great t.
32:1 blessed he wh. t. is forgiven
36:1 t. of wicked saith within
59:3 wait for soul, not for my t.
89:32 then will I visit their t.
107:17 fools bec. of t. are afflict.
Prov. 12:13 wick. is snared by t.
17:9 covereth t. seeketh love
19 loveth t. that loveth strife
19:11 his glory to pass over t.
28:2 for t. of land many princes
24 robbeth, saith, It is no t.
29:6 in t. of evil man is a snare
16 wicked multiplied, t. incre.
22 a furious man abound. in t.
Is. 24:20 t. thereof be heavy
53:8 for t. of peo. was he strick.
57:4 are ye not children of t.?
58:1 show my people their t.
59:20 to them that turn from t.
Ezek. 33:12 deliver in day of his t.
Dan. 8:12 ag. sacri. by reas. of t.
13 sacrifice, and t. of desolat.
9:24 seventy weeks to finish t.
Amos 4:4 at Gilgal multiply t.
Mic. 1:5 for t. of Jacob is all this;
what is the t. of Jacob?
3:8 full of power to dec. to J. t.
6:7 first-born for my t. and sin?
7:18 passeth by t. of remnant
Acts 1:25 from which J. by t. fell
Rom. 4:15 wh. no law is, is no t.
5:14 after similit. of Adam's t.
1 Tim. 2:14 being dece. was in t.
Heb. 2:2 every t. receiv. recomp.
1 John 3:4 for sin is t. of the law

**TRANSGRESSIONS.**

Ex. 23:21 will not pard. your t.
Lev. 16:16 atonement bec. of t.
21 Aa. confess over goat th. t.
Jos. 24:19 will not forg. your t.
1 K. 8:50 forgive people their t.
Job 31:33 I covered my t. as Ad.
35:6 if thy t. be multiplied
36:9 showeth their work and t.
Ps. 5:10 cast them out in their t.
25:7 sins of my youth, my t.
32:5 I will confess my t. unto L.
39:8 deliver me from all my t.
51:1 mercy, blot out all my t.
3 for I acknowl. my t. my sin
65:3 as for our t. purge th. away
103:12 so far hath he removed t.
Is. 43:25 he that blotteth out t.
44:22 blot. as a thi. cloud thy t.
50:1 for your t. is your mother
53:5 he was wounded for our t.
59:12 our t. are multiplied bef.
thee, for our t. are with us
Jer. 5:6 because th. t. are many
Lam. 1:5 multitu. of her t. gone
14 yoke of my t. bound by his
22 do to th. as to me for my t.
Ezek. 14:11 nor polluted wi. th. t.
18:22 his t. not be mentioned
Ezek. 18:28 he turn. away from
all his t.
30 turn yourselves fr. your t.
31 cast away all your t.
21:24 your t. are discovered
33:10 if our t. be upon us
37:23 nor defile thems. with t.
39:24 according to their t. have
Amos 1:3 for three t. of Damas.
6 t. of Gaza; 9 Tyrus; 11 Ed.
13 t. of Am. 2:1 Moab; 4 Ju.
2:6 Isr. 3:14 visit t. of Israel
5:12 I know your manifold t.
Mic. 1:13 t. of Is. found in thee
Gal. 3:19 law was add. bec. of t.
Heb. 9.15 for redemption of t.

**TRANSGRESSOR.**

Prov. 21:18 t. be ransom for upr.
22:12 he overthrow. words of t.
Is. 48:8 called a t. from womb
Gal. 2:18 I make myself a t.
Jam. 2:11 kill, th. art become t.

**TRANSGRESSORS.**

Ps. 37:38 t. be destroyed togeth.
51:13 will I teach t. thy ways
59:5 be not merciful to wick. t.
Prov. 2:22 t. shall be rooted out
11:3 perversen. of t. destr. them
6 t. be taken in their naughti.
13:2 soul of t. shall eat violence
15 favor, but way of t. is hard
23:28 she increaseth t. am. men
26:10 God rewardeth fool and t.
Is. 1:28 destruction of t. together
46:8 bring it ag. to mind, ye t.
53:12 he was numbered with t.
and made intercession for t.
Dan. 8:23 when t. are come
Hos. 14:9 but t. sh. fall therein
Mark 15:28 he was numbered
with t. Luke 22:37
Jam. 2:9 are convin. of law as t.

**TRANSLATE, D.**

2 Sam. 3:10 t. kingdom fr. Saul
Col. 1:13 t. us into kingd. of Son
Heb. 11:5 Enoch was t. that he

**TRANSLATION.**

Heb. 11:5 bef. t. he had testim.

**TRANSPARENT.**

Rev. 21:21 str. of city was t. glass

**TRAP, S.**

Jos. 23:13 shall be t. and snares
Job 18:10 and a t. is laid for him
Ps. 69:22 welfare, let become t.
Jer. 5:26 wait, set a t. catch men
Rom. 11:9 let their table be made
a snare, a t.

**TRAVAIL.**

Gen. 38:27 in time of her t.
Ex. 18:8 told Jethro t. by way
Num. 20:14 know. t. ha. befallen
Ps. 48:6 pain as woman in t.
Jer. 6:24; 13:21; 22:23; 49:24;
50:43; Mic. 4:9, 10
Ec. 1:13 sore t. G. given to men
2:23 days are sorrows, t. grief
26 to sinner he giveth t.
3:10 seen t. G. hath giv. to men
4:4 I considered all t. ev. work
6 than both hands full with t.
8 is vanity, yea, it is a sore t.
5:14 riches perish by evil t.
Is. 23:4 I t. not; 53:11 t. of soul
54:1 that didst not t. with child
Jer. 4:31 voice as of woman in t.
30:6 see whether man doth t.
Lam. 3:5 compas. wi. gall and t.
John 16:21 woman in t. hath sor.
Gal. 4:19 my chil. of whom I t.
1 Thes. 2:9 for ye rememb. our t.
5:3 destruction cometh as t.
2 Thes. 3:8 wrought with t. night

**TRAVAILED.**

Gen. 35:16 Rach. t. 38:28 Tam. t.
1 Sam. 4:19 Phinehas' wife t.
Is. 66:7 bef. she t. brought forth
8 as soon as Zion t. brou. forth

**TRAVAILEST, ETH.**

Job 15:20 wick. man t. wi. pain
Ps. 7:14 behold, he t. with iniq.
Is. 13:8 in pain as a woman t.
21:3 pangs of a woman that t.
Jer. 31:8 her that t. with child
Mic. 5:3 till she who t. br. forth
Rom. 8:22 creation t. in pain
Gal. 4:27 break forth thou th. t.

**TRAVAILING.**

Is. 42:14 I cry like woman in t.
Hos. 13:13 sorrows of t. woman
Rev. 12:2 t. in birth, and pained

**TRAVEL.**

Acts 19:29 Paul's companion in t.
2 Cor. 8:19 chosen of churches
to t.

**TRAVELLED, ETH.**

Prov. 6:11 as one that t. 24:34
Acts 11:19 t. as far as Phenice

**TRAVELLER, S.**

2 Sam. 12:4 came t. to rich man
Jud. 5:6 t. walk. thro' by-ways
Job 31:32 I open. my doors to t.

**TRAVELLING.**

Is. 21:13 O ye t. companies
63:1 who is this t. in his stren.?
Mat. 25:14 heaven is as a man t.

**TRAVERSING.**

Jer. 2:23 dromedary t. her ways

**TREACHEROUS.**

Is. 21:2 t. dealeth treach. 24:16
Jer. 3:7 her t. sister Jud. saw it
8 her t. sister Jud. fear. not, 10
11 justi. herself more than t. J
9:2 an assembly of t. men
Zep. 3:4 proph. are light and t.

**TREACHEROUSLY.**

Jud. 9:23 dealt t. with Abimel.
Is. 33:1 deal. t. they dealt not t.
48:8 thou wouldest deal very t.
Jer. 3:20 as a wife t. departeth
5:11 of Judah dealt t. Mal. 2:11
12:1 why hap. th. deal very t.?
6 they have dealt t. with thee
Lam. 1:2 her friends ha. dealt t.
Hos. 5:7 they dealt t. against L.
6:7 there they dealt t. agai. me
Mal. 2:10 why do we deal t. eve.
14 wife aga. whom th. dealt t.
15 let none deal t. against wife
16 take heed, th. ye deal not t.

**TREACHERY.**

2 K. 9:23 there is t. O Ahaziah

**TREAD.**

Deut. 11:24 whereon your feet t.
25 dre. of you on all land ye t.
33:29 thou sh. t. on high places
1 Sam. 5:5 none t. on thresho. of
Job 24:11 t. their wine-presses
40:12 t. down wick. in th. place
Ps. 7:5 let him t. down my life
44:5 thro' thy name we t. them
60:12 t. down our enemi. 108:13
91:13 thou shalt t. upon the lion
Is. 1:12 requir. to t. my courts?
10:6 to t. them down like mire
14:25 mountains t. him under
16:10 tread. shall t. out no wine
26:6 the foot shall t. it down
63:3 I will t. them in anger, 6
Jer. 25:30 as they that t. grapes
48:33 wine fail, none t. shout.
Ezek. 26:11 with horses sh. he t.
34:18 must t. residue with feet
Dan. 7:23 fourth beast t. it down
Hos. 10:11 Eph. loveth to t. corn
Mic. 1:3 L. will t. on high places
5:5 wh. Assyrian t. our palaces
6:15 thou shalt t. olives
Nah. 3:14 t. mortar, make brick.
Zec. 10:5 which t. their enemies
Mal. 4:3 ye shall t. down wicked
Luke 10:19 power to t. on scorp.
Rev. 11:2 city they t. under foot

**TREADER, S.**

Is. 16:10 t. shall tread no wine
Amos 9:13 t. of grapes sh. over.

**TREADETH.**

Deut. 25:4 not muz. ox wh. he t.
corn, 1 Cor. 9:9; 1 Tim. 5:18
Job 9:8 t. upon waves of the sea
Is. 41:25 come as potter t. clay
63:2 garme. like him th. t. wine
Amos 4:13 that t. on high places
Mic. 5:6 wh. he t. within borders
8 he both t. down and teareth
Rev. 19:15 he t. wine-press of wr.

**TREADING.**

Neh. 13:15 some t. wine-presses

*Is.* 7:25 be for *t.* of lesser cattle
22:5 a day of trou. and *t.* down
*Amos* 5:11 forasmuch as your *t.*

**TREASON.**

1 *K.* 16:20 acts of Zim. and his *t.*
2 *K.* 11:14 cried *t. t.* 2 *Chr.* 23:13,

**TREASURE.**

*Gen.* 43:23 God hath given you *t.*
*Ex.* 19:5 a peculiar *t.* *Ps.* 135:4
*Deut.* 28:12 L. shall open good *t.*
1 *Chr.* 29:8 the *t.* of house of L.
*Ezr.* 2:69 ability to *t.* of work
*Neh.* 7:70 Tirsh. gave to *t.* 1,000
71 fath. gave to the *t.* of work
*Ps.* 17:14 belly th. fillest with *t.*
135:4 chosen Is. for his pecu. *t.*
*Prov.* 15:6 in house of right. is *t.*
16 than great *t.* and trouble
21:20 there is a *t.* to be desired
*Ec.* 2:8 I gathered *t.* of kings
*Is.* 33:6 fear of the Lord is his *t.*
*Ezek.* 22:25 taken *t.* and precious
*Hos.* 13:15 spoil *t.* of pleas. ves.
*Mat.* 6:21 where *t.* is, *Lu.* 12:34
12:35 a good man out of good *t.*
evil man of evil *t.* *Luke* 6:45
13:44 kingd. of heav. is like a *t.*
52 bring. out of *t.* new and old
19:21 thou sh. have *t.* in heaven,
*Mark* 10:21; *Luke* 18:22
*Luke* 12:21 so is he that lay. up *t.*
33 provide *t.* in the heavens
*Acts* 8:27 eunu. had charge of *t.*
2 *Cor.* 4:7 *t.* in earthen vessels
*Jam.* 5:3 heaped *t.* for last days

**TREASURE-CITIES.**

*Ex.* 1:11 built for Pharaoh *t.-c.*

**TREASURE-HOUSE.**

*Ezr.* 5:17 search be made in *t.-h.*
7:20 bestow it out of king's *t.-h.*
*Neh.* 10:38 L. bring tithe to *t.-h.*
*Dan.* 1:2 brou. vessels into *t.-h.*

**TREASURED, EST.**

*Is.* 23:18 sh. not be *t.* nor laid up
*Rom.* 2:5 *t.* up wrath ag. day of

**TREASURER, S.**

*Ezr.* 1:8 Cyr. brou. vessels by *t.*
7:21 I Artax. make decree to *t.*
*Neh.* 13:13 I made *t.* over treas.
*Is.* 22:15 get thee unto this *t.*
*Dan.* 3:2 Nebuch. gathered *t.* 3

**TREASURES.**

*Deut.* 32:34 sealed up am. my *t.*
33:19 sh. suck of *t.* hid in sand
1 *K.* 7:51 put dedicated among *t.*
14:26 Shishak took away the *t.*
15:18 Asa took gold left in the
*t.* 2 *Chr.* 16:2
2 *K.* 12:18 Jehoa. took gold fou.
in *t.* 14:14; 16:8 Ahaz took
18:15 Hez. gave silv. found in *t.*
20:13 Hezek. showed silver and
gold in his *t.* 15; *Is.* 39:2, 4
24:13 Nebuchad. carried out the
*t.* of house of Lord and *t.* of
king's house, 2 *Chr.* 36:18
1 *Chr.* 26:26 brethr. were over *t.*
27:25 over king's *t.* was Azmav.
2 *Chr.* 8:15 command. concer. *t.*
*Neh.* 12:44 some appointed for *t.*
*Job* 3:21 dig more than for hid *t.*
38:22 *t.* of snow? *t.* of hail?
*Prov.* 2:4 if search. as for hid *t.*
8:21 I will fill *t.* of those that
10:2 *t.* of wickedn. profit noth.
21:6 get. of *t.* by lying tongue
*Is.* 2:7 neith. any end of their *t.*
10:13 I have robbed their *t.*
30:6 carry *t.* on bunches of cam.
45:3 I will give thee *t.* of dark.
*Jer.* 10:13 wind out of *t.* 51:16
15:13 *t.* to spoil, 17:3; 20:5
41:8 for we have *t.* in the field
48:7 bec. thou trusted in thy *t.*
49:4 daughter, trusted in her *t.*
50:37 a sword is on her *t.*
51:13 dwe. on waters abun. in *t.*
*Ezek.* 28:4 silver and gold in *t.*
*Dan.* 11:43 have power over *t.*
*Mic.* 6:10 are yet *t.* of wickedn.?
*Mat.* 2:11 wh. th. had opened *t.*
6:19 lay not up for yourselves *t.*
20 lay up for yoursel. *t.* in hea.
*Col.* 2:3 in wh. are hid *t.* of wis.
*Heb.* 11:26 greater riches than *t.*

**TREASURY.**

*Jos.* 6:19 sil. sh. come into *t.* 24
*Jer.* 38:11 went into hou. und. *t.*
*Mat.* 27:6 not lawful to put in *t.*
*Mark* 12:41 Je. sat against *t.* and
beheld peo. cast mon. into *t.*
*Luke* 21:1 rich cast. gifts into *t.*
*John* 8:20 words spake Je. in *t.*

**TREASURIES.**

1 *Chr.* 9:26 Levites were over *t.*
28:11 gave Sol. pattern of *t.* 12
2 *Chr.* 32:27 Hez. made *t.* for sil.
*Neh.* 13:12 brought tithe into *t.*
*Est.* 3:9 bring it into king's *t.*
4:7 H. prom. to pay to king's *t.*
*Ps.* 135:7 bringeth wind out of *t.*

**TREATISE.**

*Acts* 1:1 former *t.* have I made

**TREE.**

*Gen.* 1:29 I have given you ev. *t.*
2:9 G. made ev. *t.* to grow, the *t.*
of life and *t.* of knowledge
16 of every *t.* of the garden
2:17 of *t.* of knowl. not eat, 3:3
3:6 woman saw the *t.* was good
11 hast thou eaten of *t.*? 17
12 woman gave me of the *t.*
22 lest he take also of *t.* of life
24 to keep the way of *t.* of life
*Gen.* 18:4 rest yoursel. under *t.*
8 he stood by them und. the *t.*
40:19 Phara. sh. hang thee on *t.*
*Ex.* 9:25 the hail brake every *t.*
15:25 the Lord showed him a *t.*
*Deut.* 19:5 fetch. stroke to cut *t.*
20:19 *t.* of the field is man's life
21:23 body sh. not remain on *t.*
*Jos.* 8:29 take king of Ai from *t.*
1 *Sam.* 22:6 Saul abode under *t.*
31:13 they buried th. under a *t.*
2 *K.* 3:19 and shall fell ev. good *t.*
*Est.* 2:23 were hanged on a *t.*
*Job* 14:7 hope of a *t.* if cut down
19:10 hope hath he remo. like *t.*
24:20 wicked. sh. be brok. as *t.*
*Ps.* 1:3 like a *t.* plant by rivers
*Prov.* 3:18 she is a *t.* of life to th.
11:30 fr. of righte. is a *t.* of life
13:12 desire com. it is a *t.* of life
15:4 a wholes. tongue is a *t.* of
*Ec.* 11:3 if *t.* fall to the south or
north; where the *t.* fall.
*Isa.* 40:20 chooseth a *t.* that will
44:19 sh. I fall d. to stock of *t.*?
56:3 nei. eunu. say, I am dry *t.*
65:22 as days of a *t.* are days of
66:17 purify themsel. behind *t.*
*Jer.* 10:3 one cutteth a *t.*
11:19 let us destroy the *t.*
17:8 as a *t.* planted by waters
*Ezek.* 15:2 vine *t.* more th. any *t.*
17:24 brought down high *t.* exalted low *t.* dried up green *t.*
made dry *t.* to flourish
21:10 contemneth rod, as ev. *t.*
31:8 nor any *t.* in garden of G.
34:27 *t.* of field shall yield fruit
36:30 I will multiply fruit of *t.*
*Dan.* 4:10 beh. a *t.* 11, 14, 20, 23
*Joel* 2:22 fear not *t.* beareth fruit
*Mat.* 3:10 ev. *t.* that bringeth not
good fruit, 7:19; *Luke* 3:9
7:17 good *t.* bring. good fruit,
cor. *t.* evil fruit, *Luke* 6:43
18 good *t.* cannot bri. evil fruit
12:33 make *t.* good and fr. good,
*t.* is kno. by fruit, *Luke* 6:44
*Luke* 17:6 mi. say to sycamine *t.*
*Acts* 5:30 wh. ye hanged on a *t.*
10:39 Je. wh. they hanged on *t.*
*Gal.* 3:13 cursed is th. hang. on *t.*
1 *Pet.* 2:24 bare sins in body on *t.*
*Rev.* 2:7 I will give to eat of *t.*
7:1 wind sh. not blow on any *t.*
9:4 not hurt green thing, nor *t.*
22:2 in midst was the *t.* of life
14 may have right to *t.* of life

*See* GREEN.

**TREES.**

*Gen.* 3:8 hid amongst *t.* of gard.
23:17 *t.* were made sure to Abr.
*Ex.* 10:15 locusts did eat fr. of *t.*
*Lev.* 19:23 planted all man. of *t.*
23:40 take boughs of goodly *t.*
26:4 *t.* of the field shall yield
*Num.* 24:6 as *t.* of lign-aloes wh.
L. planted, and as cedar *t.*
*Deut.* 16:21 not plant grove of *t.*
20:19 sh. not destroy *t.* thereof
20 *t.* th. know. not *t.* for meat
*Jos.* 10:26 J. hang. them on 5 *t.*
*Jud.* 9:8 *t.* went to anoint king
9 to be promoted over *t.* 11, 13
10 *t.* said to the fig-tree reign
12 *t.* said to vine; 14 *t.* to bra.
1 *K.* 4:33 he spake of *t.* fr. cedar
2 *K.* 3:25 they felled the good *t.*
1 *Chr.* 16:33 th. shall *t.* of wood
sing, *Ps.* 96:12
*Neh.* 10:35 bring first-fr. of *t.* 37
*Job* 40:21 lieth under shady *t.* 22
*Ps.* 74:5 lifted axes on thick *t.*
78:47 destroyed th. sycamore *t.*
104:16 *t.* of Lord are full of sap
105:33 brake *t.* of their coasts
148:9 fruitf. *t.* and cedars praise
*Ec.* 2:5 I planted *t.* of all kinds
*Cant.* 2:3 as apple-tree am. the *t.*
4:14 all *t.* of frankincense
*Is.* 7:2 moved as the *t.* of wood
10:19 the rest of the *t.* of forest
44:14 he strengthen. among *t.*
55:12 *t.* of the fields shall clap
61:3 be called *t.* of righteousn.
*Jer.* 6:6 Lord said, Hew down *t.*
7:20 my fury sh. be poured on *t.*
*Ezek.* 17:24 the *t.* of field shall
know
20:28 they saw all the thick *t.*
31:5 height was exalted above *t.*
9 all the *t.* of Eden envied him
47:7 many *t.* on the one side and
12 by the riv. shall grow all *t.*
*Joel* 1:12 *t.* of field are withered
19 flame hath burnt all the *t.*
*Mat.* 3:10 axe laid to *t.* *Luke* 3:9
*Mat.* 21:8 others cut down bran.
of *t.* and strewed, *Mark* 11:8
*Mark* 8:24 I see men as *t.* walk.
*Luke* 21:29 beh. fig-tree and all *t.*
*Jude* 12 *t.* whose fruit withereth
*Rev.* 7:3 hurt not *t.* till we have
8:7 third part of *t.* was burnt up

*See* PALM.

**TREMBLE.**

*Deut.* 2:25 nations sh. *t.* because
20:3 do not *t.* because of them
*Ezr.* 10:3 that *t.* at commandm.
*Job* 9:6 the pillars thereof *t.*
26:11 the pillars of heaven *t.*
*Ps.* 60:2 hast made earth to *t.*
99:1 L. reigneth, let the peo. *t.*
114:7 *t.* earth, at presence of L.
*Ec.* 12:3 keepers of house sh. *t.*
*Is.* 5:25 hills did *t.* th. carcasses
14:16 man that made earth *t.*
32:11 *t.* ye wom. th. are at ease
64:2 nati. may *t.* at thy presence
66:5 hear word of L. ye that *t.*
*Jer.* 5:22 will ye not *t.* at my pre.
10:10 at his wrath earth shall *t.*
33:9 they sh. *t.* for the goodness
51:29 land of Babylon shall *t.*

*Ezek.* 26:16 *t.* at ev. mom. 32:10
18 now shall the isles *t.* in day
*Dan.* 6:26 men *t.* bef. G. of Dan.
*Hos.* 11:10 chil. sh. *t.* from west
11 th. sh. *t.* as a bird out of E.
*Joel* 2:1 let inhabitants of land *t.*
10 quake, the heavens shall *t.*
*Amos* 8:8 sh. not land *t.* for this?
*Hab.* 3:7 captains of Midi. did *t.*
*Jam.* 2:19 the devils beli. and *t.*

**TREMBLED.**

*Gen.* 27:33 I. *t.* very exceedingly
*Ex.* 19:16 peo. th. was in camp *t.*
*Jud.* 5:4 earth *t.* heavens dropped, 2 *Sam.* 22:8; *Ps.* 18:7; 77:18; 97:4
1 *Sam.* 4:13 Eli's heart *t.* for ark
14:15 spoilers *t.* 16:4 elders *t.*
28:5 Saul was afraid, heart *t.*
*Ezr.* 9:4 assemb. ev. one that *t.*
*Jer.* 4:24 mountains *t.* *Hab.* 3:10
8:16 land *t.* at sound of neighi.
*Dan.* 5:19 all peo. and nations *t.*
*Hab.* 3:16 my belly *t.* and I *t.* in
*Mark* 16:8 fled fr. sepulch. th. *t.*
*Acts* 7:32 Moses *t.* 24:25 Felix *t.*

**TREMBLETH.**

*Job* 37:1 at this also my heart *t.*
*Ps.* 104:32 looketh on earth it *t.*
119:120 my flesh *t.* for fear
*Is.* 66:2 I will look to him that *t.*

**TREMBLING.**

*Ex.* 15:15 *t.* take hold on mighty
*Deut.* 28:65 L. sh. give *t.* heart
1 *Sam.* 13:7 people followed *t.*
14:15 in the host was a great *t.*
*Ezr.* 10:9 peo. sat *t.* because of
*Job* 4:14 fear ca. upon me and *t.*
21:6 *t.* taketh hold on my flesh
*Ps.* 2:11 serve L. rejoice with *t.*
55:5 fearfulness and *t.* are come
*Is.* 51:17 dregs of the cup of *t.* 22
*Jer.* 30:5 we heard a voice of *t.*
*Ezek.* 12:18 drink thy wat. wi. *t.*
26:16 clothe themselves with *t.*
*Dan.* 10:11 had spoken, I stood *t.*
*Hos.* 13:1 Eph. spake *t.* he exalt.
*Zec.* 12:2 make Jeru. a cup of *t.*
*Mark* 5:33 woman *t.* *Luke* 8:47
*Acts* 9:6 S. *t.* said, What wilt th.?
16:29 keeper came *t.* fell down
1 *Cor.* 2:3 with you in much *t.*
2 *Cor.* 7:15 wi. fear and *t.* ye rec.
*Eph.* 6:5 serv. be obed. with *t.*
*Phil.* 2:12 work out salva. with *t.*

**TRENCH.**

1 *Sam.* 17:20 Dav. came to the *t.*
26:5 S. lay sleeping in the *t.* 7
1 *K.* 18:32 Elijah made a *t.* about
35 filled the *t.* with water, 38
*Luke* 19:43 enemies sh. cast a *t.*

**TRESPASS, Substantive.**

*Gen.* 31:36 wh. is my *t.* that thou
50:17 forgive *t.* of thy servants
*Ex.* 22:9 manner of *t.* whether
*Lev.* 5:15 for his *t.* to L. a ram
26:40 conf. their *t.* th. trespass.
*Num.* 5:6 when any do *t.* ag. L.
7 he shall recompense his *t.*
27 if she *t.* against husband
1 *Sam.* 25:28 forg. *t.* of handm.
1 *Chr.* 21:3 be cause of *t.* to Is.?
2 *Chr.* 24:18 wr. come on J. for *t.*
28:13 ye intend to add to our *t.*
33:19 Manasseh's prayer and *t.*
*Ezr.* 9:2 rul. been chief in this *t.*
6 our *t.* is grown unto heavens
7 in great *t.* to this day, 13
*Ezr.* 10:10 wives, to incr. *t.* of Is.
19 th. offered a ram for their *t.*
*Ezek.* 17:20 I will plead for his *t.*
18:24 in his *t.* he hath trespass.
*Dan.* 9:7 bec. of *t.* they trespas.

**TRESPASSES.**

*Ezr.* 9:15 before thee in our *t.*
*Ps.* 68:21 one as goeth on in *t.*
*Ezek.* 39:26 they have borne th. *t.*
*Mat.* 6:14 if ye forg. men their *t.*
15 if forgive not *t.* neither will your Fa. forgive yo. *t.* 18:35
*Mark* 11:25 Fath. may forgive *t.*
26 nei. will F. forgive your *t.*
2 *Cor.* 5:19 not imputing their *t.*
*Eph.* 2:1 who were dead in *t.*
*Col.* 2:13 having forg. you all *t.*
*See* COMMIT, COMMITTED, OFFERING.

**TRESPASS-MONEY.**

2 *K.* 12:16 *t.-m.* was not brought

**TRESPASS, Verb.**

1 *K.* 8:31 man *t.* ag. his neighb.
2 *Chr.* 19:10 that they *t.* not
28:22 Ahaz did *t.* yet more
*Mat.* 18:15 if brother *t.* tell fault
*Luke* 17:3 if bro. *t.* rebuke him
4 if he *t.* ag. thee seven times

**TRESPASSED.**

*Lev.* 5:19 he hath *t.* against L.
26:40 if confess trespass they *t.*
*Num.* 5:7 recompensed ag. wh. *t.*
*Deut.* 32:51 bec. ye *t.* against me
2 *Chr.* 26:18 sanct. for th. hast *t.*
29:6 our fathers have *t.*
30:7 not like fath. who *t.* ag. L.
33:23 Amon *t.* more and more
*Ezr.* 10:2 we have *t.* ag. our God
*Ezek.* 17:20 trespass that he *t.*
39:23 they *t.* against me, 26
*Dan.* 9:7 trespass that they *t.*
*Hos.* 8:1 they *t.* against my law

**TRESPASSING.**

*Lev.* 6:7 any t. he hath done in *t.*
*Ezek.* 14:13 land sinneth by *t.*

**TRIAL.**

*Job* 9:23 laugh at *t.* of innocent
*Ezek.* 21:13 it is a *t.* what if swo.
2 *Cor.* 8:2 how in *t.* of affliction
*Heb.* 11:36 others had *t.* of mock.
1 *Pet.* 1:7 *t.* of your faith might
4:12 not strange concerning *t.*

**TRIBE.**

*Num.* 1:4 man of every *t.* 13:2; 34:18
4:18 cut not off *t.* of Kohathites
18:2 *t.* of thy father bring thou
31:4 of every *t.* a thousand, 5, 6
36:6 marry to the family of *t.* 8
9 inherit. from one *t.* to ano. *t.*
*Deut.* 1:23 I took twelve, one of a *t.* *Jos.* 3:12; 4:2, 4
29:18 *t.* whose heart turneth
*Jos.* 7:14 *t.* which Lord taketh
18:4 give out 3 men for each *t.*
*Jud.* 21:3 one *t.* lacking in Is. 6
1 *K.* 11:13 one *t.* to son, 32, 36
1 *Chr.* 6:61 of family of that *t.*
*Ezek.* 47:23 in what *t.* the stran.
*Heb.* 7:13 he pertain. to anoth. *t.*
14 of wh. *t.* Mo. spake nothing
*See* REUBEN, SIMEON, *and the rest.*

**TRIBES.**

*Ex.* 28:21 according to 12 *t.* 39:14
*Num.* 24:2 in tents accord. to *t.*
33:54 according to *t.* of fathers
34:13 give to the nine *t.* *Jos.* 13:7; 14:2
15 two *t.* and the half have received inheritance, *Jos.* 14:3
*Deut.* 1:13 wise men, am. your *t.*
18:5 G. hath cho. him out of *t.*
*Jos.* 7:14 brought according to *t.*
1 *Sam.* 10:19 present your. by *t.*
1 *K.* 11:31 I will give ten *t.* to
18:31 according to number of *t.*
*Ps.* 105:37 not one feeble amo. *t.*
122:4 the *t.* go up, *t.* of the Lord
*Is.* 19:13 that are stay of *t.*
49:6 to raise up the *t.* of Jacob
63:17 for *t.* of thine inheritance
*Ezek.* 45:8 to Isr. according to *t.*
*Hab.* 3:9 according to oaths of *t.*
*Mat.* 24:30 th. *t.* of earth mourn
*Acts* 26:7 promise our 12 *t.* hope
*Jam.* 1:1 the twelve *t.* scattered
*Rev.* 7:4 sealed 144,000 of all *t.*
*See* ISRAEL.

**TRIBULATION.**

*Deut.* 4:30 wh. in *t.* if thou turn
*Jud.* 10:14 let th. deliv. you in *t.*
1 *Sam.* 26:24 deli. me out of all *t.*
*Mat.* 13:21 when *t.* ariseth, he is
*Mat.* 24:21 then shall be great *t.*
29 immed. after *t.* *Mark* 13:24
*John* 16:33 ye shall have *t.*
*Acts* 14:22 we must thro' *t.* enter
*Rom.* 2:9 *t.* and ang. on eve. soul
5:3 know. *t.* worketh patience
8:35 shall *t.* separate us fr. Ch.?
12:12 rejo. in hope, patient in *t.*
2 *Cor.* 1:4 who comforte. us in *t.*
7:4 I am exceeding joyful in *t.*
1 *Thes.* 3:4 we should suffer *t.*
2 *Thes.* 1:6 recompense *t.* to th.
*Rev.* 1:9 John your compan. in *t.*
2:9 I know thy works, and *t.*
10 ye shall have *t.* ten days
22 I will cast th. into great *t.*
7:14 they which came of great *t.*

**TRIBULATIONS.**

1 *Sam.* 10:19 saved you out of *t.*
*Rom.* 5:3 but we glory in *t.* also
*Eph.* 3:13 faint not at *t.*
2 *Thes.* 1:4 for your faith in all *t.*

**TRIBUTARY.**

*Lam.* 1:1 how is she become *t.*

**TRIBUTARIES.**

*Deut.* 20:11 the people shall be *t.*
*Jud.* 1:30 Canaani. bec. *t.* 33, 35

**TRIBUTE.**

*Gen.* 49:15 Issa. bec. servant to *t.*
*Num.* 31:28 levy a *t.* to the Lord
37 Lord's *t.* of sheep was 675
38 L.'s *t.* of the beeves was 72
39 Lord's *t.* threescore and one
40 16,000 the Lord's *t.* 32 pers.
*Deut.* 16:10 with *t.* of a freewill
*Jos.* 16:10 Canaan. under *t.* 17:13
2 *Sam.* 20:24 Ad. was over *t.* 1 *K.* 4:6; 12:18; 2 *Chr.* 10:18
1 *K.* 9:21 on these did Sol. levy *t.*
2 *K.* 23:33 Pharaoh put land to *t.*
2 *Chr.* 8:8 did Solo. make pay *t.*
17:11 Philistines brou. *t.* silver
*Ezr.* 4:13 will they not pay *t.*
20 *t.* and custom paid to them
6:8 *t.* expenses be given to men
7:24 not lawful to imp. *t.* on Le.
*Neh.* 5:4 bor. money for king's *t.*
*Prov.* 12:24 slothful be under *t.*
*Mat.* 17:24 doth not mas. pay *t.*?
25 of whom do kings take *t.*?
22:17 is it lawf. to give *t.* to Ce.? *Mark* 12:14; *Luke* 20:22
19 show me the *t.* money, they
*Luke* 23:2 forbidding *t.* to Cesar
*Rom.* 13:6 for this cau. pay ye *t.*
7 render *t.* to whom *t.* is due

**TRICKLETH.**

*Lam.* 3:49 mine eye *t.* down, and

**TRIMMED, EST.**

2 *Sam.* 19:24 M. had not *t.* beard
*Jer.* 2:33 *t.* way to seek love?
*Mat.* 25:7 arose, *t.* their lamps

**TRIUMPH, ED, ING.**

*Ex.* 15:1 he hath *t.* gloriously, 21
2 *Sam.* 1:20 lest uncircumcised *t.*
*Ps.* 25:2 let not enemies *t.* over
41:11 mine enemy doth not *t.*
60:8 Philistia, *t.* th. bec. of me
92:4 *t.* in works of thy hands
94:3 L. how long sh. wicked *t.*?
106:47 gi. thanks, *t.* in thy pra.
108:9 over Philistia will I *t.*?
2 *Cor.* 2:14 causeth us to *t.* in C.

Col. 2:15 show of them t. over

**TRIUMPH, ING.**

Job 20:5 that t. of wicked is short
Ps. 47:1 shout unto God with t.

**TROAS.**

Acts 16:8 by M. they came to T.
11 loosing from T. 20:5 at T.
2 Cor. 2:12 when I came to T. to
2 Tim. 4:13 the cloak I left at T.

**TRODE.**

Jud. 9:27 t. grapes, cursed Abi.
20:43 Is. t. Benjamites wi. ease
2 K. 7:17 people t. upon him, 20
9:33 Jehu t. Jezebel under foot
14:9 beast t. thist. 2 Chr. 25:18
Luke 12:1 they t. one on another

**TRODDEN.**

Deut. 1:36 land t. on, Jos. 14:9
Jud. 5:21 hast t. down strength
Job 22:15 old way wicked have t.
28:8 lion's whelps have not t. it
Ps. 119:118 th. hast t. all that err
Is. 5:5 vineyard shall be t. down
14:19 as a carcass t. under foot
18:2 to nation meted, t. down
25:10 M. t. under as straw is t.
28:3 drunkards of Eph. sh. be t.
18 scourge pass, then be t. do.
63:3 I have t. wine-press alone
18 adversaries have t. sanctua.
Jer. 12:10 th. have t. my portion
Lam. 1:15 L. hath t. under foot
mighty men, hath t. virgin
Ezek. 34:19 flock eat ye have t.
Dan. 8:13 sanctu. and host be t.
Mic. 7:10 now shall she be t.
Mat. 5:13 salt unsavory to be t.
Luke 8:5 fell by way-side, was t.
21:24 Jerus. sh. be t. of Gentil.
Heb. 10:29 t. under foot Son of G.
Rev. 14:20 wine-p. t. witho. city

TROGYLLIUM. Acts 20:15

**TROOP.**

Gen. 30:11 a t. cometh; 49:19 a t.
shall overcome him
1 Sam. 30:8 sh. I pursue this t.?
2 Sam. 2:25 Benjamin bec. one t.
3:22 Joab came from pursu. a t.
22:30 I run through t. Ps. 18:29
23:11 Phil. were gath. into a t.
13 t. pitched in valley of Rep.
Is. 65:11 prep. a table for that t.
Jer. 18:22 sh. bring a t. suddenly
Hos. 7:1 t. of rob. spoileth with.
Amos 9:6 founded his t. in earth

**TROOPS.**

Job 6:19 the t. of Tema looked
19:12 his t. come together, and
Jer. 5:7 they assembled by t. in
Hos. 6:9 as t. of robbers wait for
Mic. 5:1 gath. in t. O daug. of t.
Hab. 3:16 invade them wi. his t.

**TROUBLE, Substantive.**

1 Chr. 22:14 in my t. I prepared
2 Chr. 15:4 when they in t. did
turn and sought L. Neh. 9:27
Neh. 9:32 let not all t. seem lit.
Job 3:26 nei. quiet, yet t. came
5:6 neither doth t. spring out of
7 man born to t. as sparks fly
14:1 is of few days, full of t.
15:24 t. shall make him afraid
27:9 will G. hear wh. t. cometh?
30:25 I weep for him in t.
34:29 quietn. who can make t.?
38:23 I reserved aga. time of t.
Ps. 9:9 L. will be a refuge in t.
13 consider my t. wh. I suffer
10:1 why hid. th. thyself in t.?
22:11 be not far fr. me, t. is near
27:5 in time of t. he sh. hide me
31:7 thou hast considered my t.
9 mercy, O Lord, for I am in t.
32:7 thou shalt pres. me from t.
37:39 strength in time of t.
41:1 L. will deli. him in ti. of t.
46:1 God is our ref. a help in t.
54:7 he hath deliv. me out of t.
60:11 give us help from t.
66:14 my mouth hath spo. in t.
69:17 hide not face, I am in t.
73:5 they are not in t. as other
78:33 years did he consu. in t.
49 cast on them indign. and t.
81:7 calledst in t. I deliv. thee
91:15 I will be with him in t.
102:2 hide not face fr. me in t.
107:6 cried to Lord in t. 13, 19
26 soul is melted because of t.
28 they cry to Lord in their t.
116:3 pains gat hold, I found t.
119:143 t. and angu. have taken
138:7 tho' I walk in midst of t.
142:2 I showed before him my t.
143:11 bring my soul out of t.
Prov. 11:8 right. del. out t. 12:13
15:6 in revenues of wicked is t.
16 than treas. and t. therewith
25:19 unfaithful man in t.
Is. 1:14 new-moons, they are a t.
8:22 look to earth and behold t.
17:14 behold at evening tide t.
26:16 L. in t. they visited thee
30:6 into land of t. carry riches
33:2 be our salvat. in time of t.
46:7 not save him out of t.
65:23 shall not bring forth for t.
Jer. 2:27 in t. will say, Save us
28 if they can save th. in thy t.
8:15 looked for health, behold t.
11:12 shall not save them in t.
14 in time th. cried for their t.
14:8 Saviour of Is. in time of t.
19 looked for healing, beho. t.
30:7 it is time of Jacob's t.
Lam. 1:21 enem. heard of my t.
Dan. 12:1 there sh. be time of t.
1 Cor. 7:28 shall have t. in flesh
2 Cor. 1:4 able to com. them in t.
8 not have you ignor. of our t.
2 Tim. 2:9 I suffer t. as evil-doer
See DAY.

**TROUBLES.**

Deut. 31:17 t. sh. befall them, 21
Job 5:19 he sh. del. thee in six t.
Ps. 25:17 t. of heart are enlarged
22 redeem Is. O God, out of t.
Ps. 34:6 L. saved him out of t. 17
71:20 wh. hast show. me sore t.
88:3 ear, for my soul is full of t.
Prov. 21:23 he keepeth soul fr. t.
Is. 65:16 former t. are forgotten
Mark 13:8 shall be famine and t.

**TROUBLE, Verb.**

Jos. 6:18 lest ye t. camp of Israel
7:25 Lord shall t. thee this day
Jud. 11:35 one of th. that t. me
2 Chr. 32:18 they cried to t. th.
Ps. 3:1 how increas. that t. me?
13:4 those that t. me rejoice
Ezek. 32:13 nei. foot of man t. th.
nor hoofs of beasts t. them
Dan. 4:19 let not interpr. t. thee
5:10 let not thy thoughts t. thee
11:44 tidings out of north t. him
Mat. 26:10 why t. ye the woman?
Mark 14:6
Luke 7:6 Lord, t. not thyself
11:7 say, t. me not, door is shut
Acts 15:19 t. not G. turned to G.
16:20 th. do exceedingly t. city
20:10 t. not yoursel. his life is
Gal. 1:7 there be some th. t. you
5:12 th. were cut off who t. you
6:17 hencefor. let no man t. me
2 Thes. 1:6 trib. to th. that t. you
Heb. 12:15 lest bitterness t. you

**TROUBLED.**

Gen. 34:30 ye ha. t. me, to make
41:8 in morn. Ph.'s spirit was t.
45:3 his brethren t. at his pres.
Ex. 14:24 L. t. host of Egyptians
Jos. 7:25 why hast thou t. us?
1 Sam. 14:29 father hath t. land
16:14 evil spirit fr. Lord t. him
28:21 woman saw that S. was t.
2 Sam. 4:1 Abner dead, all Is. t.
1 K. 18:18 I have not t. Israel
2 K. 6:11 king of Syria was t.
Ezr. 4:4 peo. t. them in building
Job 4:5 toucheth thee, thou art t.
21:4 why shou. not spirit be t.?
23:15 theref. am I t. at his pres.
34:20 peo. sh. be t. at midnight
Ps. 30:7 hide thy face, I was t.
38:6 I am t. 77:4 I am so t. I
46:3 tho' waters roar and be t.
48:5 kings were t. hasted away
77:3 I remember. G. and was t.
16 the depths also were t.
83:17 let them be comfo. and t.
90:7 by thy wrath are we t.
104:29 hidest thy face, th. are t.
Prov. 25:26 is as a t. fountain
Is. 32:10 and years shall ye be t.
11 wom. be t. ye careless ones
57:20 wicked are like the t. sea
Jer. 31:20 my bowels are t.
Lam. 1:20 my bowels are t. 2:11
Ezek. 7:27 hands of peo. sh. be t.
26:18 isles in sea shall be t.
27:35 their kings be t. in count.
Dan. 2:1 Neb.'s spirit was t. 3
4:5 visions of my head t. 7:15
19 his thoughts t. him
5:6 Belsha.'s thoughts t. him, 9
7:28 my cogitations much t. me
Zec. 10:2 t. because no shepherd
Mat. 2:3 Herod was t. and Jerus.
14:26 they were t. Mark 6:50
24:6 not t. thi. must co. to pass,
Mark 13:7; John 14:1, 27
Luke 1:12 Zac. was t. 29 Mary t.
10:41 Martha t. about many thi.
24:38 why are t. and why do
John 5:4 angel went and t. water
7 no man wh. water is t. to put
11:33 and wast t. 12:27; 13:21
Acts 15:24 some fr. us have t. y.
17:8 they t. people and rulers
2 Cor. 4:8 are t. on ev. side, 7:5
2 Thes. 1:7 to you that are t. rest
2:2 that ye be not t. nei. by sp.
1 Pet. 3:14 not af. of terror, nor t.

**TROUBLEDST.**

Ezek. 32:2 thou t. waters wi. feet

**TROUBLER.**

1 Chr. 2:7 Achar, the t. of Israel

**TROUBLEST, ETH.**

1 Sam. 16:15 an evil spirit t. thee
1 K. 18:17 art thou he that t. Is.?
Job 22:10 sudden fear t. thee
23:16 heart soft, Almighty t. me
Prov. 11:17 that is cruel t. flesh
29 that t. his house, inh. wind
15:27 that is greedy of gain t.
Dan. 4:9 I know no secret t. th.
Mark 5:35 why t. thou Master?
Luke 18:5 bec. this widow t. me
Gal. 5:10 he th. t. you shall bear

**TROUBLING.**

Job 3:17 there wicked cease fr. t.
John 5:4 step. in after t. of water

**TROUBLOUS.**

Dan. 9:25 sh. be built in t. times

**TROUGH, S.**

Gen. 24:20 empt. pitcher into t.
30:38 J. set rods in watering t.
Ex. 2:16 they filled t. to water
8:3 frogs sh. go into kneading t.
12:34 th. kneading t. bound up

**TROW.**

Luke 17:9 thank serva.? I t. not

**TRUCE-BREAKERS.**

1 Tim. 3:3 last days shall be t.-b.

**TRUE.**

Gen. 42:11 we are t. men, 31
19 if ye be t. men let one of y.

Deut. 17:4 if ye be t. and, 22:20
2 Sam. 7:28 God, thy words be t.
1 K. 10:6 it was a t. report I heard, 2 Chr. 9:5
22:16 tell me noth. but that is t.
Neh. 9:13 gavest them t. laws
Ps. 19:9 judgments of Lord are t.
119:160 thy word is t. fr. begin.
Jer. 42:5 the Lord be a t. witness
Dan. 3:14 is it t. O Shadrach, do
24 t. O king; 6:12 thing is t.
10:1 revealed and thing was t.
Mat. 22:16 thou art t. Mark 12:14
Luke 16:11 com. to trust t. riches
John 1:9 that was the t. light
4:37 herein is saying t. 1 soweth
5:31 of myself, my wit. is not t.
6:32 Father giveth the t. bread
7:18 same is t. 8:13 reco. not t.
28 he that sent me is t. 8:26
8:14 record is t. 16 judgm. is t.
17 testimony of two men is t.
10:41 all things J. spake were t.
9:35 and his record is t. 21:24
Acts 12:9 wist not that it was t.
2 Cor. 1:18 as God is t. our word
6:8 as deceivers, and yet t.
Phil. 4:8 whatsoev. things are t.
1 Tim. 3:1 this is a t. saying
Tit. 1:13 this witness is t. wher.
Heb. 8:2 t. tabernacle which L.
9:24 which are figures of the t.
10:22 draw near with a t. heart
1 Pet. 5:12 this is t. grace of God
2 Pet. 2:22 accordi. to t. proverb
1 John 2:8 which thing is t.
5:20 may kn. him that is t. and we are in him that is t.
3 John 12 we know our rec. is t.
Rev. 3:7 saith holy, he that is t.
14 saith faithful and t. witness
6:10 long, O Lord, holy and t.?
15:3 just and t. are thy ways
16:7 t. are thy judgments, 19:2
19:9 these are t. say. of G. 22:6
11 he th. sat was Faith. and T.
21:5 write, for these words are t.

**TRUE God.**

2 Chr. 15:3 Is. ha. been wi. t. G.
Jer. 10:10 Lord is the t. God
John 17:3 eternal life to kn. t. G.
1 Thes. 1:9 turn fr. idols to t. G.
1 John 5:20 this is the t. God

**TRULY.**

Num. 14:21 t. as I live, saith L.
Ps. 116:16 t. I am thy servant
Prov. 12:22 deal t. are his delight
Mat. 27:54 t. this was Son of G.
Luke 20:21 teachest way of G. t.
John 4:18 no husb. saidst thou t.

**TRUMP.**

1 Cor. 15:52 at last t. dead shall
1 Thes. 4:16 L. shall des. with t.

**TRUMPET.**

Ex. 19:16 voice of t. excee. loud
20:18 people heard noise of t.
Num. 10:4 if th. blow wi. one t.
Jud. 7:16 put a t. in every man's
Ps. 81:3 blow t. in new moon
Is. 18:3 when he bloweth t. hear
27:13 great t. shall be blown
58:1 lift up thy voice like a t.
Jer. 4:5 blow ye the t. in land
6:1 blow the t. in Tekoah
51:27 blow t. among nations
Ezek. 7:14 they have blown t.
33:3 if ye blow t. and warn, 6
Hos. 5:8 blow ye the t. in Ramah
8:1 set the t. to thy mouth
Joel 2:1 blow the t. in Zion, 15
Amos 3:6 sh. t. be blo. not afra.?
Zep. 1:16 day of t. ag. fenced cit.
Zec. 9:14 Lord God shall blow t.
Rev. 1:10 heard voice as of t. 4:1
9:14 sixth angel which had t.

See BLEW, SOUND, SOUNDED.

**TRUMPETS.**

Lev. 23:24 a memorial of blow. t.
Num. 10:2 make two t. of silver

Num. 10:8 sons of Aa. bl. with t.
10 blow with t. over burnt-off.
29:1 day of blowing t. unto you
31:6 wi. t. to blow in his hand
Jos. 6:4 priests sh. blow with t.
8 bearing seven t. of rams'
Jud. 7:8 300 men took t. 16
19 they blew the t. 20, 22
2 K. 9:13 they blew with t. sayi.
11:14 trumpeters blew with t.
1 Chr. 13:8 with cymbals and t.
15:24 the priests did blow wi. t. before ark of God, 16:6, 42; 2 Chr. 5:12; 7:6; 13:12, 14
28 Israel brought up ark wi. t.
2 Chr. 5:13 they lift voice with t.
29:27 song of L. began with t.
Job 39:25 horse say. am. t. Ha, ha
Ps. 98:6 wi. t. make joyful noise

See SEVEN.

**TRUMPETERS.**

2 K. 11:14 and t. stood by king
2 Chr. 5:13 t. and singers were
29:28 singers sang, and t. sound.
Rev. 18:22 voi. of t. heard no mo.

**TRUST.**

Job 8:14 wh. t. sh. be a spider's
15:15 putteth no t. in his saints
Ps. 40:4 that maketh Lord his t.
71:5 O Lord God, thou art my t.
141:8 in thee is my t. leave not
Prov. 22:19 thy t. may be in Lord
28:25 that puts his t. in Lord
29:25 who putteth his t. in Lord
Is. 30:3 t. in Egypt shall be conf.
57:13 that putteth t. in me shall
Luke 16:11 com. to t. true riches
2 Cor. 3:4 such t. ha. we thro' C.
1 Tim. 1:11 gospel, com. to my t.
6:20 keep that commi. to thy t.

See PUT.

**TRUST, Verb.**

Ruth 2:12 thou art come to t.
2 Sam. 22:3 in him will I t. Ps. 18:2; 91:2
31 a buckler to all that t. in him, Ps. 18:30
1 K. 18:20 on whom dost thou t.? 2 Chr. 32:10; Is. 36:5
21 so is Pharaoh to all that t. in him, Is. 36:6
22 we t. in L. our God, Is. 36:7
30 neither let Hezekiah make you t. in the Lord, Is. 36:15
Job 13:15 yet will I t. in him
15:31 let not him th. is decei. t.
35:14 judg. bef. him, t. in him
39:11 wilt t. him bec. strong?
Ps. 20:7 some t. in chariots
25:2 I t. in thee, 31:6; 55:23; 56:3; 143:8
31:19 hast wrou. for them th. t.
34:22 none th. t. in him sh. be
37:3 t. in the Lord, and do good, 5; 40:3; 62:8; 115:9, 10, 11; Prov. 3:5; Is. 26:4
40 he sh. save, because they t.
44:6 I will not t. in my bow
49:6 they that t. in their wealth
52:8 I t. in the mercy of God
61:4 I will t. in cov. of thy wings
62:10 t. not in oppression
64:10 righte. shall be glad, and t.
91:4 under his wings sh. thou t.
118:8 it is better to t. in Lord, 9
119:42 answer, I t. in thy word
125:1 that t. in the Lord sh. be
144:2 shield, and he in wh. I t.
Prov. 31:11 her husband doth t.
Is. 12:2 I will t. not be afraid
14:32 poor of his people shall t.
30:2 to t. in shadow of Egypt
12 because ye t. in oppression

31:1 and t. in chariots because
42:17 ashamed th. t. in images
50:10 let him t. in name of L.
51:5 on mine arm shall they t.
59:4 they t. in vanity and speak
Jer. 7:4 t. ye not in lying words
8 ye t. in lying words
14 by name, wherein ye t.
9:4 and t. ye not in any brother
28:15 makest peo. to t. in, 29:31
46:25 punish Ph. and all that t.
49:11 let thy widows t. in me
Ezek. 16:15 th. didst t. in beauty
33:13 if he t. to his own righte.
Hos. 10:13 thou didst t. in way
Amos 6:1 that t. in mount. of Sa.
Mic. 7:5 t. ye not in a friend
Nah. 1:7 L. knoweth them th. t.
Zep. 3:12 shall t. in name of L.
Mat. 12:21 in his name shall Gentiles t. Rom. 15:12
Mark 10:24 them that t. in riches
John 5:45 Moses in whom ye t.
Rom. 15:24 I t. to see you in my
1 Cor. 16:7 I t. to tarry a while
2 Cor. 1:9 sho. not t. in ourselves
10 in whom we t. that he will
10:7 if any man t. to himself
Phil. 3:4 if any think. hath to t.
1 Tim. 4:10 we t. in living God
6:17 they t. not in uncertain
2 John 12 I t. to come unto you
3 John 14 I t. I shall shortly see thee

**TRUSTED.**

Deut. 32:37 rock in wh. they t.?
Jud. 11:20 Sih. t. not Is. to pass
20:36 they t. to the liers in wait
2 K. 18:5 he t. in the Lord God
Ps. 13:5 I have t. in thy mercy
22:4 our fathers t. th. have t. 5
8 he t. on Lord that he would
26:1 I have t. in L. 28:7; 31:14
33:21 have t. in his holy name
41:9 familiar friend in wh. I t.
52:7 t. in abund. of his riches
78:22 t. not in his salvation
Is. 47:10 th. hast t. in thy wick.
Jer. 13:25 thou hast t. in falseh.
48:7 thou hast t. in thy works
49:4 daugh. that t. in her treas.
Dan. 3:28 God delivereth that t.
Zep. 3:2 she t. not in the Lord
Mat. 27:43 he t. in God, let him
Luke 11:22 armor wherein he t.
18:9 cer. which t. in themselves
24:21 we t. it had been he that
Eph. 1:12 who first t. in Christ
13 in whom ye also t. after ye
1 Pet. 3:5 holy wom. who t. in G.

**TRUSTEDST.**

Deut. 28:52 walls down thou t.
Jer. 5:17 cities wherein thou t.
12:5 land of peace wher. thou t.

**TRUSTEST.**

2 K. 18:19 what confidence is this wherein thou t.? Is. 36:4
21 t. on bruised reed, Is. 36:6
19:10 G. in wh. thou t. Is. 37:10

**TRUSTETH.**

Job 40:23 he t. that he can draw
Ps. 21:7 the king t. in the Lord
32:10 that t. in L. mercy shall
34:8 blessed is man th. t. 84:12; Prov. 16:20; Jer. 17:7
57:1 be merci. my soul t. in thee
86:2 save thy serv. that t. in thee
115:8 so is ev. one that t. 135:18
Prov. 11:28 he that t. in riches
28:26 that t. his heart is a fool
Is. 26:3 peace bec. he t. in thee
Jer. 17:5 cursed be man t. man
Hab. 2:18 maker of work t. ther.
1 Tim. 5:5 th. is a widow, t. in G.

**TRUSTING.**

Ps. 112:7 heart is fixed, t. in L.

**TRUSTY.**

*Job* 12:20 removeth speech of *t.*

**TRUTH.**

*Gen.* 24:27 not left dest. mas. of *t.*
32:10 not worthy of least of *t.*
42:16 be proved, whether any *t.*
*Ex.* 18:21 men of *t.* hating cov.
34:6 abundant in goodn. and *t.*
*Deut.* 13:14 if it be *t.* 32:4 G. of *t.*
2 *Sam.* 2:6 L. show kindn. and *t.*
15:20 mercy and *t.* be with thee
1 *K.* 17:24 word of the Lord is *t.*
2 *K.* 20:19 if *t.* be in my, *Is.* 39:8
2 *Chr.* 18:15 say nothing but *t.*
31:20 Hez. wrought that was *t.*
*Est.* 9:30 letters with words of *t.*
*Ps.* 15:2 speaketh *t.* in heart
25:10 paths of L. mercy and *t.*
31:5 redeemed me, O L. G. of *t.*
45:4 ride prosperously bec. of *t.*
51:6 thou desirest *t.* in inward
57:3 God shall send forth his *t.*
60:4 ban. be displayed bec. of *t.*
61:7 O prepare mercy and *t.*
85:10 mercy and *t.* met togeth.
11 *t.* shall spring out of earth
86:15 plenteous in mercy and *t.*
89:14 mercy and *t.* sh. go before
91:4 his *t.* shall be thy shield
96:13 he shall judge peo. with *t.*
98:3 he hath remembered his *t.*
100:5 his *t.* endur. to all, 117:2
119:30 I have chosen way of *t.*
142 and thy law is the *t.* 151
146:6 L. is God who keepeth *t.*
*Prov.* 3:3 let not *t.* forsake thee
8:7 for my mouth shall speak *t.*
12:17 he that speaks *t.* showeth
19 lip of *t.* shall be established
14:22 mercy and *t.* be to them
16:6 by mercy and *t.* iniquity is
20:28 mercy and *t.* preserve king
*Prov.* 22:21 kn. certain. of words of *t.* answer the words of *t.*
23:23 buy the *t.* and sell it not
*Ec.* 12:10 writ. were words of *t.*
*Is.* 25:1 couns. are faithf. and *t.*
26:2 nation which keepeth *t.*
42:3 bring forth judgm. unto *t.*
43:9 let th. hear, and say, it is *t.*
59:4 nor any pleadeth for *t.*
14 for *t.* is fallen in the street
15 yea, *t.* faileth, and he
*Jer.* 5:1 if th. be that seeketh *t.*
3 O L. are not th. eyes upon *t.?*
7:28 *t.* is perished and cut off
9:3 they are not valiant for *t.*
5 deceive and will not speak *t.*
33:6 revealed abundance of *t.*
*Dan.* 4:37 all whose works are *t.*
7:16 I asked him *t.* of this, 19
8:12 it cast down *t.* to ground
10:21 is noted in scriptures of *t.*
11:2 now will I show thee the *t.*
*Hos.* 4:1 no *t.* nor mercy in land
*Mic.* 7:20 wilt perform *t.* to Jac.
*Zec.* 8:3 Jer. be called city of *t.*
16 speak ye every man *t.* execute judgment of *t.* *Eph.* 4:25
19 theref. love the *t.* and peace
*Mal.* 2:6 law of *t.* in his mouth
*Mat.* 15:27 she said, *t.* Lord, yet
*Mark* 5:33 woman told him *t.*
12:32 Master, thou hast said *t.*
*John* 1:14 full of grace and *t.*
17 grace and *t.* came by J. C.
5:33 J. bare witness unto the *t.*
8:32 kn. *t.* and *t.* make you free
40 seek to kill me, that told *t.*
44 abode not in *t.* because no *t.* in him.
45 I tell *t.* ye believe me not
46 if I say *t.* why not believe?
14:6 I am the way, *t.* the life
16:7 I tell you *t.* it is expedient
13 Sp. of *t.* guide you into all *t.*
17:19 be sanctified through *t.*
18:37 th. I should bear witness to *t.* every one that is of *t.*
38 Pil. saith to him, what is *t.?*
*Acts* 26:25 I spe. forth words of *t.*
*Rom.* 1:18 hold *t.* in unrighteous.
25 changed *t.* of God into a lie
2:2 judgm. of G. according to *t.*
8 to them that do not obey *t.*
20 whi. hast form of *t.* in law
3:7 if *t.* of G. ha. more abound.
9:1 I say *t.* in Christ, I lie not
15:8 minister of circumci. for *t.*
1 *Cor.* 5:8 unleavened bread of *t.*
2 *Cor.* 4:2 by manifestation of *t.*
7:14 boast. I made is found a *t.*
11:10 as *t.* of Ch. is in me none
12:6 for I will say the *t.*
13:8 we can do nothing ag. *t.*
*Gal.* 2:5 *t.* of gospel might conti.
14 walked not according to *t.*
3:1 ye should not obey *t.* 5:7
4:16 enemy bec. I tell you *t.?*
*Eph.* 4:15 speak. the *t.* in love
21 taught by him as *t.* is in J.
5:9 fruit of Spirit is in all *t.*
6:14 hav. your loins girt with *t.*
2 *Thes.* 2:10 recei. not love of *t.*
12 damned who believe not *t.*
13 salvation thro' belief of *t.*
1 *Tim.* 2:4 come to knowl. of *t.*
7 I speak *t.* in Christ, lie not
3:15 the pillar and ground of *t.*
4:3 received of them wh. kn. *t.*
6:5 corrupt minds, destitu. of *t.*
2 *Tim.* 2:18 concern. *t.* ha. erred
25 repent. to acknowledg. of *t.*
3:7 to come to knowledge of *t.*
8 Jambres, so do these resist *t.*
4:4 turn away their ears from *t.*
*Tit.* 1:1 to acknowledging of *t.*
14 commandm. that turn fr. *t.*
*Heb.* 10:26 received knowl. of *t.*
*Jam.* 3:14 lie not against the *t.*
5:19 if any of you err fr. the *t.*
1 *Pet.* 1:22 purified in obeying *t.*
2 *Pet.* 2:2 way of *t.* evil spok. of
1 *John* 1:6 we lie, do not the *t.*
8 dec. ourselves, *t.* is not in us
2:4 *t.* not in him; 27 *t.* is no lie
21 because ye know not *t.* and no lie is of the *t.*
3:19 we know that we are of *t.*
5:6 witness, because Spirit is *t.*
2 *John* 1 they that have known *t.*
2 for *t.* sake that dwell. in us
3 *John* 3 tes. of *t.* that is in thee
8 might be fellow-helpers to *t.*
12 good report of men and of *t.*

**In TRUTH.**

*Jos.* 24:14 serve Lord *in t.* 1 *Sam.* 12:24
*Jud.* 9:15 if *in t.* ye anoint me
1 *K.* 2:4 if my children walk *in t.*
3:6 as Da. walked bef. thee *in t.*
2 *K.* 20:3 I have walked *in t.*
*Ps.* 33:4 works done *in t.* 111:8
132:11 L. hath sworn *in t.* to D.
145:18 L. nigh to all call *in t.*
*Is.* 10:20 stay on Holy One *in t.*
16:5 he shall sit upon it *in t.*
48:1 mention of G. but not *in t.*
61:8 I will direct th. work *in t.*
*Jer.* 4:2 swear, the L. liveth *in t.*
*Zec.* 8:8 I will be their God *in t.*
*Mat.* 22:16 teachest the way of God *in t.* *Mark* 12:14
*John* 4:23 in spirit and *in t.* 24
2 *Cor.* 7:14 speak all things *in t.*
*Phil.* 1:18 whe. *in t.* C. preached
*Col.* 1:6 ye knew grace of G. *in t.*
1 *Thes.* 2:13 it is *in t.* word of G.
1 *John* 3:18 love in tongue, *in t.*
2 *John* 3 Son of the Father *in t.*
4 I found of thy children walking *in t.* 3 *John* 4

**In the TRUTH.**

*Ps.* 69:13 hear *in t. t.* of salva.
*John* 8:44 mur. abode not *in t. t.*
1 *Cor.* 13:6 charity rejoic. *in t. t.*
2 *Pet.* 1:12 be established *in t. t.*
2 *John* 1 I love *in t. t.* 3 *John* 1
3 *John* 3 as thou walkest *in t. t.*

**Of a TRUTH.**

*Job* 9:2 I know it is so *of a t.*
*Jer.* 26:15 *of a t.* Lord sent me
*Dan.* 2:47 *of a t.* it is, your G. is
*Mat.* 14:33 *of a t.* thou art Son
*Luke* 4:25 I tell you *of a t.* 9:27
12:44 *of a t.* I say unto, 21:3
*John* 6:14 *of a t.* th. proph. 7:40
*Acts* 4:27 *of a t.* ag. holy child J.
1 *Cor.* 14:25 God is in you *of a t.*
*See* SPIRIT.

**Thy TRUTH.**

*Ps.* 25:5 lead me in *thy t.* teach
26:3 and I have walked in *thy t.*
30:9 shall dust declare *thy t.?*
40:10 *thy t.* from great congreg.
11 *thy t.* continu. preserve me
43:3 send out thy light and *t. t.*
54:5 enemies, cut th. off in *t. t.*
57:10 *thy t.* unto clouds, 108:4
71:22 praise *thy t.* 86:11 in *t. t.*
89:49 swarest to David in *thy t.*
115:1 glory for *t. t.* sake, 138:2
*Is.* 38:18 cannot hope for *thy t.*
19 chil. shall make known *t. t.*
*Dan.* 9:13 might understand *t. t.*
*John* 17:17 sanctify th. thro' *t. t.*

**Word of TRUTH.**

*Ps.* 119:43 take not *w. of t.* out
2 *Cor.* 6:7 appr. ours. by *w. of t.*
*Eph.* 1:13 that ye heard *w. of t.*
*Col.* 1:5 ye heard bef. in *w. of t.*
2 *Tim.* 2:15 dividing *word of t.*
*Jam.* 1:18 begat he us by *w. of t.*

**TRY.**

*Jud.* 7:4 I will *t.* them for thee
2 *Chr.* 32:31 G. left him to *t.* him
*Job* 7:18 that thou should. *t.* him
12:11 doth not the ear *t.* words
*Ps.* 11:4 eyelids *t.* chil. of men
26:2 *t.* my reins; 139:23 *t.* me
*Jer.* 6:27 mayest kn. and *t.* way
9:7 melt and *t.* them, *Zec.* 13:9
17:10 Lord search heart, *t.* reins
*Lam.* 3:40 let us search and *t.*
*Dan.* 11:35 some fall to *t.* them
1 *Cor.* 3:13 fire *t.* ev. man's work
1 *Pet.* 4:12 trial wh. is to *t.* you
1 *John* 4:1 *t.* spirits whether of G.
*Rev.* 3:10 temptation to *t.* them

**TRIED.**

*Deut.* 21:5 by Lev. ev. stroke be *t.*
2 *Sam.* 22:31 the word of the Lord is *t.* *Ps.* 18:30
*Job* 23:10 when he hath *t.* me
34:36 desire is that J. may be *t.*
*Ps.* 12:6 as silver is *t.* in furnace
17:3 th. hast *t.* me, find nothing
66:10 hast *t.* us as silver is *t.*
105:19 word of the Lord *t.* him
*Is.* 28:16 I lay in Z. a *t.* stone
*Jer.* 12:3 thou hast *t.* my heart
*Dan.* 12:10 many be puri. and *t.*
*Zec.* 13:9 try them as gold *t.*
*Heb.* 11:17 Abra. when he was *t.*
*Jam.* 1:12 when *t.* receive crown
1 *Pet.* 1:7 tho' it be *t.* with fire
*Rev.* 2:2 hast *t.* them which say
10 into prison, ye may be *t.*
3:18 buy of me gold *t.* in the fire

**TRIEST, ETH.**

1 *Chr.* 29:17 I know thou *t.* heart
*Job* 34:3 ear *t.* words as mouth
*Ps.* 7:9 righteous God *t.* hearts
11:5 the Lord *t.* the righteous
*Prov.* 17:3 but Lord *t.* the hearts
*Jer.* 11:20 O L. that *t.* the reins
20:12 L. of hosts that *t.* righte.
1 *Thes.* 2:4 but God who *t.* hearts

**TRYING.**

*Jam.* 1:3 *t.* of faith work. patien.

**TRYPHENA, TRYPHOSA.**
Rom. 16:12 salute T. and T. who

**TUBAL.**
Gen. 10:2 Ja. Javan, T. 1 Ch. 1:5
Is. 66:19 those that escape to T.
Ezek. 27:13 Javan T. thy merch.
32:26 Meshech, T. and multit.
38:2 of Meshech and T. 3; 39:1

**TUMBLED.**
Jud. 7:13 a cake t. into the host

**TUMULT.**
1 Sam. 4:14 wh. noise of this t.?
2 Sam. 18:29 I saw a t. but knew
2 K. 19:28 thy t. come unto mine ears, Is. 37:29
Ps. 65:7 stilleth t. of the people
74:23 t. of th. that rise ag. thee
83:2 lo, thine enemies make a t.
Is. 33:3 at noise of t. people fled
Jer. 11:16 with noise of a great t.
Hos. 10:14 t. rise among people
Amos 2:2 Moab shall die with t.
Zec. 14:13 a t. fr. Lord am. them
Mat. 27:24 rather a t. was made
Mark 5:38 he seeth t. and them
Acts 21:34 could not know for t.
24:18 with multitude, nor wi. t.

**TUMULTS.**
Amos 3:9 behold gre. t. in midst
2 Cor. 6:5 ourselves as min. in t.
12:20 whisperings, swellings, t.

**TUMULTUOUS.**
Is. 13:4 a t. noise of kingdoms
22:2 thou that art a t. city
Jer. 48:45 devour head of t. ones

**TURN.**
Est. 2:11 ev. maid's t. was come
15 when t. of Esther was come

**TURN, Verb.**
Gen. 24:49 that I may t. to right
Ex. 23:27 make thine enemies t.
32:12 t. from thy fierce wrath
Num. 14:25 to-morrow t. you
20:17 will not t. to right hand
22:23 he smote the ass to t. her
26 wh. was no way to t. right
Deut. 1:40 t. ye, take journey
30:3 Lord will t. their captivity
31:20 th. will th. t. to oth. gods
Jos. 1:7 t. not from it to right or
22:23 to t. from following L. 29
24:20 then he will t. and do
Jud. 20:8 nor any t. into house
1 Sam. 14:7 t. I am with thee
22:17 t. and slay priests of L. 18
2 Sam. 14:19 none can t. to ri. or
24 said, Let him t. to house
1 K. 8:35 t. from their sin, 2 Chr. 6:26, 37; 7:14
9:6 if you t. from following me
17:3 t. eastward, hide thyself
22:34 t. thy hand, 2 Chr. 18:33
2 K. 9:18 t. thee behind me, 19
17:13 t. ye from your evil ways, Jer. 18:8; 26:3; Zec. 1:3, 4
1 Chr. 12:23 to t. kingd. of Saul
2 Chr. 35:22 J. would not t. face
Neh. 1:9 t. and keep com. Ezek. 3:20; 18:21; 33:11, 14, 19
9:26 testified to t. them to thee
Job 5:1 wh. of saints wilt th. t.?
14:6 t. fr. him that he may rest
23:13 who can t. him?
24:4 they t. needy out of way
Ps. 4:2 how long will ye t. glory?
7:12 if he t. not, will whet sw.
21:12 make them t. their back
25:16 t. unto me, 69:16; 86:16
85:4 t. us, O God of our salva.
119:79 let those th. fear thee t.
132:11 sworn to D. he will not t.
Prov. 1:23 t. you at my reproof
4:15 t. from it and pass away
27 t. not to right hand nor left
Ec. 3:20 and all t. to dust again
Cant. 2:17 t. my beloved, and
Is. 1:25 I will t. my hand on thee
13:14 every man t. to his people
19:6 shall t. rivers far away
22:18 he will t. and toss thee
23:17 she shall t. to her hire
28:6 strength to them t. battle
30:21 ye t. to right and left
31:6 t. ye to him fr. whom Is.
59:20 to them that t. fr. transg.
Jer. 2:35 his anger shall t. fr. me
3:7 and I said, t. unto me, 14
13:16 before he t. it into death
Jer. 31:18 t. th. me, I sh. be turn.
44:5 hearken. not to t. fr. wick.
50:16 t. every one to his people
Lam. 5:21 t. us unto thee, O L.
Ezek. 3:19 he t. not fr. wick. 33:9
4:8 sh. not t. from one side to
7:22 my face will I t. fr. them
14:6 t. fr. idols, 18:30, 32; 33:9, 11; Hos. 12:6; Joel 2:12
36:9 I will t. unto you, and ye
38:12 to t. hand on desol. places
Dan. 9:13 might t. fr. iniquities
11:18 shall he t. face unto isles
19 shall t. his face toward fort
12:3 that t. many to righteous.
Hos. 5:4 frame their doings to t.
12:6 therefore t. thou to thy G.
Amos 1:8 t. my hand ag. Ekron
8:10 I will t. feasts into mourn.
Jon. 3:8 t. ev. one from evil way
Zep. 3:9 t. to people pure langu.
Zec. 9:12 t. you to strong-hold
13:7 t. my hand upon little ones
Mal. 4:6 he sh. t. heart of fathers
Mat. 5:39 cheek, t. to him other
Luke 1:17 to t. hearts of fathers
21:13 sh. t. to you for a testim.
Acts 13:46 we t. to the Gentiles
14:15 sho. t. from these vanities
26:18 to t. them from darkn. to
20 should repent and t. to God
Phil. 1:19 this sh. t. to my salva.
Tit. 1:14 comm. that t. fr. truth
Jam. 3:3 we t. about their body
2 Pet. 2:21 to t. from command.
Rev. 11:6 to t. waters to blood

**TURN again.**
Jud. 11:8 we t. a. to thee now
Ruth 1:11 t. a. my daughters, 12
1 Sam. 15:25 t. a. with me, 30
1 K. 8:33 when Israel shall t. a.
12:27 heart of people t. again
13:9 nor t. a. by same way, 17
2 K. 1:6 go t. again to the king
2 Chr. 30:6 t. a. to L. 9 if ye t. a.
Job 34:15 man sh. t. a. into dust
Ps. 18:37 nor did I t. a. till they
60:1 displeas. O t. thys. to us a.
80:3 t. us a. O L. of hosts, 7, 19,
85:8 let them not t. a. to folly
104:9 th. t. not a. to cover earth
126:4 t. again our captivity
Jer. 25:5 t. ye a. from evil way
31:21 t. a. O virgin, t. a. to cit.
Lam. 3:40 try our ways, t. again
Ezek. 8:6 t. a. thou sh. see, 13, 15
Mic. 7:19 will t. a. have compas.
Zec. 10:9 live with child. t. again
Mat. 7:6 lest they t. a. and rend
Luke 10:6 it shall t. to you again
17:4 seven times in a day t. a.
Gal. 4:9 t. a. to weak elements

**TURN aside.**
Ex. 3:3 I will t. a. and see this
Deut. 5:32 not t. a. to right hand
17:20 t. not a. from command.
31:29 after my death ye will t. a.
Jos. 23:6 that ye t. not a. therefrom, 1 Sam. 12:20, 21
Ruth 4:1 ho, such a one, t. aside
2 Sam. 2:21 t. a. and take armor
23 he refused to t. aside
18:30 king said, t. a. stand here
Ps. 40:4 respect. not such as t. a.
101:3 work of them that t. a.
125:5 for such as t. a. to crooked
Is. 10:2 t. a. needy from judgm.
29:21 t. a. just for thing of nau.
30:11 t. aside out of path
Lam. 3:35 to t. a. right of a man
Amos 2:7 that t. a. way of meek
5:12 they t. a. poor in the gate
Mal. 3:5 t. a. stranger from right

**TURN away.**
Gen. 27:44 till brother's fury t. a.
45 till thy broth.'s anger t. a.
Num. 32:15 if ye t. a. from after him, Deut. 30:17; Jos. 22:16; 2 Chr. 7:19
Deut. 7:4 they will t. a. thy son
13:5 he hath spoken to t. you a.
1 K. 11:2 th. will t. a. your heart
1 Chr. 14:14 go not, t. a. fr. thence
2 Chr. 25:27 Amaziah did t. a.
29:10 that wrath may t. a. 30:8; Ps. 106:23; Prov. 24:18
30:9 L. will not t. a. his face
Ps. 119:37 t. a. mine eyes from
39 t. a. my reproach wh. I fear
Prov. 29:8 wise men t. a. wrath
Cant. 6:5 t. a. thine eyes fr. me
Is. 58:13 if t. a. foot from sabbath
Jer. 3:19 thou sh. not t. a. fr. me
8:4 sh. he t. a. and not return?
18:20 I stood to t. a. thy wrath
32:40 I will not t. a. from them
Ezek. 14:6 t. a. faces from abom.
Jon. 3:9 God will t. a. from his
Mal. 2:6 did t. many a. from ini.
2 Tim. 3:5 traitors, fr. such t. a.
4:4 sh. t. a. their ears fr. truth
Heb. 12:25 how esca. if we t. a.?

**TURN back.**
Deut. 23:13 t. b. and cover that
Ps. 44:10 makest us to t. b. from
56:9 then sh. mine enemies t. b.
Is. 14:27 hand stretc. who t. b.?
Jer. 4:28 nei. will I t. b. from it
21:4 I will t. b. weapons of war
49:8 flee ye, t. back, dwell deep
Ezek. 38:4 I will t. thee b. 39:2
Mark 13:16 not t. b. to take gar.

**TURN in.**
Gen. 19:2 lords, t. in, I pray you
Jud. 4:18 t. in, my lord, t. in
19:11 let us t. in to this city of
2 K. 4:10 the man of God sh. t. in
Prov. 9:4 wh. is simple, t. in, 16

**TURN to the Lord.**
Deut. 4:30 if th. t. to the L. 30:10
2 Sam. 15:4 in trou. did t. to t. L.
Ps. 22:27 world shall t. to the L.
Lam. 3:40 try ways, t. to the L.
Hos. 14:2 take words, t. to the L.
Joel 2:13 rend heart, t. to the L.
Luke 1:16 many sh. he t. to the L.
2 Cor. 3:16 when it sh. t. to the L.

**TURNED.**
Gen. 3:24 a flaming sword wh. t.
42:24 Joseph t. about from them
Ex. 7:15 rod was t. to a serpent
14:5 heart of Pharaoh was t. ag.
Num. 21:33 t. and went by B.
Deut. 23:5 t. the curse, Neh. 13:2
31:18 are t. unto other gods
Jud. 2:17 they t. out of the way
15:4 S. took firebra. and t. tail
1 Sam. 10:6 sh. be t. to ano. man
14:21 they also t. to be with Is.
47 whithersoever he t. himself
15:27 Sam. t. about to go away
17:30 Dav. t. from him towards
2 Sam. 2:19 Asahel t. not fr. fol.
1 K. 2:15 the kingdom is t. about
28 Joab t. after Adonijah
8:14 the king t. his face about
11:9 his heart was t. fr. the L.

2 K. 5:12 Naaman t. went away
20:2 t. his face to wall, Is. 38:2
23:25 no king t. to L. like him
26 L. t. not fierce. of his wrath
1 Chr. 10:14 t. kingd. unto David
2 Chr. 12:12 wrath of L. t. fr. him
20:10 t. fr. them destroyed not
29:6 fathers have t. their backs
Ezr. 6:22 t. heart of the king
Neh. 9:35 nei. t. fr. wick. works
Est. 9:1 tho' t. to the contrary
Job 16:11 G. t. me into hands of
19:19 wh. I loved are t. ag. me
28:5 it is t. up as it were fire
30:15 terrors are t. upon me
31:7 if my step t. out of the way
38:14 it is t. as clay to the seal
42:10 L. t. the captivity of Job
Ps. 9:17 wick. sh. be t. into hell
30:11 thou hast t. my mourning
81:14 t. my hand ag. adversar.
105:25 he t. their heart to hate
119:59 I t. my feet unto testim.
Ec. 2:12 I t. mys. to behold wis.
Is. 21:4 pleasure he t. into fear
53:6 we have t. every one to his
63:10 was t. to be their enemy
Jer. 2:21 how t. into degenerate?
27 they ha. t. their back to me
3:10 Judah hath not t. to me
6:12 their houses sh. be t. unto
8:6 every one t. to his course
23:22 they should have t. fr. evil
31:18 I shall be t. 19 I was t.
32:33 they t. unto me the back
34:15 were now t. done right
16 ye t. and polluted my name
48:39 how hath M. t. thee back?
Lam. 1:20 heart is t. within me
3:3 surely against me is he t.
5:2 our inheri. is t. to strangers
21 turn us, O L. we sh. be t.
Ezek. 1:9 they t. not, 12; 10:11
17:6 a vine, whose branches t.
Dan. 10:16 my sorrows t. upon
Hos. 7:8 Ephraim is a cake not t.
11:8 my heart is t. within me
Joel 2:31 sun shall be t. Acts 2:20
Amos 6:12 ye have t. judg. into
Jon. 3:10 they t. from their evil
Hab. 2:16 cup of L.'s hand be t.
Zec. 14:10 land be t. into plain
Mark 5:30 Jes. t. about in press
Luke 22:61 L. t. looked upon Pe.
John 16:20 sor. shall t. into joy
Acts 7:42 God t. gave them up
9:35 all at Lyd. saw and t. to L.
11:21 a great number t. to Lord
15:19 the Gentiles are t. to God
17:6 ha. t. the world upside do.
1 Thes. 1:9 show how ye t. to G.
Heb. 11:34 t. to flight armies of
12:13 lest lame be t. out of way
Jam. 3:4 t. with a very sm. helm
2 Pet. 2:22 dog is t. to his vomit

**TURNED again.**

Ex. 4:7 it was t. a. as his flesh
Jud. 20:41 Is. t. a. Benjamites
1 Sam. 15:31 Samuel t. a. after S.
2 Sam. 22:38 I t. not a. till I had
Ps. 126:1 L. t. a. captivity of Zi.

**TURNED aside.**

Ex. 3:4 Lord saw that he t. a.
32:8 have t. a. Deut. 9:12, 16
1 K. 15:5 David t. not aside from
20:39 a man t. a. brought man
2 K. 22:2 Josiah t. not a. to right
Job 6:18 paths of their way t. a.
Cant. 6:1 is thy beloved t. a.?
Is. 44:20 deceived heart t. him a.
Lam. 3:11 hath t. aside my ways
1 Tim. 5:15 some already t. aside

**TURNED away.**

Num. 14:43 ye are t. a. from L.
20:21 Israel t. away from him
25:4 anger of Lord may be t. a.
11 Phine. hath t. my wrath a.
1 K. 11:3 wives t. a. his heart, 4
2 Chr. 29:6 our fathers t. a. faces
Ps. 66:20 not t. away my prayer
78:38 many time t. he anger a.
Is. 5:25 for all this his anger is
not t. a. 9:12, 17, 21; 10:4
12:1 anger t. a. 50:5 nor t. I a.
Jer. 5:25 your iniq. have t. away
46:5 have I seen th. t. a. back?
50:6 shepherds have t. them a.
Dan. 9:16 let thy fury be t. a.
Hos. 14:4 mine anger is t. away
Nah. 2:2 L. hath t. a. excellency
Acts 19:26 P. ha. t. a. much peo.
2 Tim. 1:15 they in Asia be t. a.

**TURNED back.**

Jos. 8:20 peo. t. b. upon pursuers
11:10 Joshua at that time t. b.
1 Sam. 15:11 Saul t. b. from fol.
2 Sam. 1:22 bow of Jon. t. not b.
1 K. 18:37 hast t. their heart b.
22:33 not king of Is. they t. b.
2 K. 1:5 messengers t. b. why t. b.
2:24 t. b. and looked on them
15:20 king of Assyria t. b. stay.
1 Chr. 21:20 Orn. t. b. saw angel
Job 34:27 bec. they t. b. from him
Ps. 9:3 mine enemies are t. back
35:4 let them be t. back, 70:2, 3
44:18 our heart is not t. b. from
78:9 Ephr. t. b. in day of battle
41 t. b. and tempted God, 57
129:5 let th. be t. b. that hate Z.
Is. 42:17 t. back trust in images
Jer. 4:8 anger of Lord is not t. b.
11:10 they are t. b. to iniquities
46:21 they are t. b. fled away
Lam. 1:13 he hath t. me b. made
Zep. 1:6 that are t. b. from Lord
Luke 2:45 t. b. again to Jerusa.
John 20:14 she t. herself b. saw
Acts 7:39 in hea. t. b. ag. into E.

**TURNED in.**

Gen. 19:32 angels t. in unto Lot
38:1 Ju. t. in to Hirah the Adu.
Jud. 4:18 Sisera t. in unto Jael
18:3 the Danites t. in thither
2 K. 4:8 Elisha t. in thither
11 he t. into the chamber

**TURNEST.**

1 K. 2:3 prosper whither. thou t.
Job 15:13 t. thy spirit ag. God
Ps. 90:3 thou t. man to destruct.

**TURNETH.**

Lev. 20:6 soul th. t. after wizards
Deut. 29:18 whose heart t. away
Jos. 7:8 when Is. t. their backs?
Job 39:22 the horse t. not back
Ps. 107:33 t. rivers into a wilder.
35 he t. wilderness into water
146:9 wicked he t. upside down
Prov. 15:1 soft ans. t. away wra.
21:1 t. king's heart whithersoe.
26:14 as door t. upon his hinges
28:9 t. away his ear fr. hearing
30:30 a lion t. not away for any
Ec. 1:6 wind t. about unto the
Cant. 1:7 sho. I be as one that t.?
Is. 9:13 the people t. not to him
24:1 Lord t. earth upside down
44:25 t. wise men backward
Jer. 14:8 that t. aside to tarry
49:24 Damascus t. herself to flee
Lam. 1:8 she sigheth and t. bac.
3:3 he t. his hand against me
Ezek. 18:24 righteous t. away fr.
his righteousness, 26; 33:18
27 wick. man t. aw. 28; 33:12
Amos 5:8 t. shadow of death into

**TURNING.**

2 K. 21:13 wipe Jer. as a dish, t.
2 Chr. 36:13 hardened heart fr. t.
Prov. 1:32 the t. away of simple
Is. 29:16 your t. of things upside
Mic. 2:4 t. away he hath divided
Acts 3:26 to bless you in t. you
Jam. 1:17 wi. wh. is no sha. of t.
Jude 4 t. grace of G. into lasciv.

**TURTLE, S.**

Gen. 15:9 take a t. dove and a yo.
Lev. 5:7 he sh. bri. two t. doves,
12:8; 14:22, 30; 15:14, 29
11 if not able to br. two t. dov.
12:6 she shall bring a t. dove
Num. 6:10 on 8th day sh. bri. 2 t.
Ps. 74:19 deliver not soul of t. d.
Cant. 2:12 voice of the t. is hea.
Jer. 8:7 t. and crane observe time
Luke 2:24 sacri. pair of t. doves

**TUTORS.**

Gal. 4:2 a child is under t. and

**TWAIN.**

1 Sam. 18:21 son-in-law one of t.
2 K. 4:33 shut the door on th. t.
Is. 6:2 with t. he cover. his face,
with t. he cover. feet, with t.
Jer. 34:18 they cut the calf in t.
Ezek. 21:19 both t. sh. come out
Mat. 5:41 a mile, go with him t.
19:5 they t. shall be one flesh
6 are no more t. Mark 10:8
21:31 whe. of t. did will of fath.?
27:21 whe. of t. will I release?
51 veil rent in t. Mark 15:38
Eph. 2:15 make in himself of t.

**TWELFTH.**

1 K. 19:19 oxen, he with the t.
Rev. 21:20 t. founda. was ameth.

See MONTH.

**TWELVE.**

Gen. 14:4 t. years they served C.
17:20 t. princes sh. Ishm. 25:16
35:22 the sons of Jacob were t.
42:13 thy serv. are t. breth. 32
49:28 these are t. tribes of Isr.
Ex. 15:27 Elim, where were t.
24:4 t. pillars acc. to t. tribes
28:21 t. precious stones, 39:14
Lev. 24:5 thou sh. bake t. cakes
Deut. 1:23 I took t. men of you
Jos. 3:12 take ye t. men, 4:2
4:3 t. stones out of Jor. 8, 9, 20
2 Sam. 2:15 th. arose t. of Benja-
min, and t. servants of Dav.
1 K. 7:25 the sea stood on t. oxen,
44; 2 Chr. 4:15
10:20 t. lions on side, 2 Chr. 9:19
11:30 Ah. rent garm. in t. pieces
Neh. 5:14 t. years not eat. bread
Mat. 9:20 a wom. was diseased t.
years, Mark 5:25; Luke 8:43
10:2 names of t. apos. Luke 6:13
26:20 he sat down with the t.
Mark 14:17; Luke 22:14
Mark 5:42 age of t. yrs. Luke 8:42
14:20 it is one of t. that dippeth
Luke 2:42 when Je. was t. years
John 6:70 have I not cho. you t.?
11:9 are th. not t. hours in day
1 Cor. 15:5 seen of Cep. th. of t.
Rev. 12:1 on head cro. of t. stars
21:12 city had t. gates, at gat. t.
14 wall of city had t. foundat.
in them names of t. apostles
21 the t. gates were t. pearls
22:2 tr. bare t. manner of fruits

See HUNDRED, THOUSAND.

**TWENTY.**

Gen. 18:31 be found t. there, I
will not destroy it for t. sake
31:38 t. ye. I have been with, 41
37:28 sold J. for t. pieces silver
Ex. 30:14 fr. t. old, 38:26; Num.
1:3, etc.
Lev. 27:3 estim. of males fr. t. y.
2 K. 4:42 brought man t. loaves
Ezr. 8:27 weighed t. bas. of gold
Zec. 5:2 length of roll t. cubits

**TWENTY-TWO.**

Jud. 10:3 Jair judged Is. t.-t. ye.

# U

Mark 4:12 hear. they may hear,
not u. Luke 8:10; Acts 28:26
14:68 nor u. I what thou sayest
Luke 24:45 might u. scriptures
John 8:43 why not u. my speech ?
Rom. 15:21 have not heard sh. u.
1 Cor. 13:2 tho' I u. all mysteries
Heb. 11:3 u. worlds were framed
2 Pet. 2:12 evil of thi. they u. not

**UNDERSTANDEST.**

Job 15:9 what u. thou, which is
Ps. 139:2 thou u. my thoughts
Jer. 5:15 neither u. what th. say
Acts 8:30 u. thou wh. th. readest ?

**UNDERSTANDETH.**

1 Chr. 28:9 Lord u. imaginations
Job 28:23 God u. the way thereof
Ps. 49:20 man in honor u. not
Prov. 8:9 all plain to him that u.
14:6 knowl. easy to him that u.
Jer. 9:24 glory in this, that he u.
Mat. 13:19 hear. word, u. it not
23 that heareth word, and u. it
Rom. 3:11 there is none that u.
1 Cor. 14:2 to men, for no man u.
16 he u. not what thou sayest

**UNDERSTANDING.**

Ex. 31:3 I have filled Bezaleel
with u. 35:31; 36:1
Deut. 4:6 this is your wis. and u.
32:28 neither is any u. in them
1 K. 3:11 hast asked u. to disce.
4:29 God gave Solomon u.
7:14 Hiram was filled with u.
1 Chr. 12:32 were men th. had u.
22:12 L. give thee wisd. and u.
2 Chr. 2:12 a wise son end. wi. u.
26:5 Zechari. had u. in visions
Ezr. 8:16 Joi. and El. men of u.
Neh. 8:2 that could hear with u.
10:28 ev. one hav. know. and u.
Job 12:3 I have u. as well as you
12 length of days u. 13 hath u.
20 he taketh away u. of aged
17:4 hast hid their heart from u.
20:3 my u. caus. me to answer
26:12 by his u. he smiteth thro'
28:12 where is place of u. ? 20
28 said, To depart fr. evil is u.
32:8 Almighty giveth them u.
34:10 hearken to me, men of u.
16 if now th. hast u. hear this
34 let men of u. tell me
38:4 declare, if thou hast u.
36 who hath given u. to heart ?
39:17 neither imparted to her u.
Ps. 32:9 as mule that hath no u.
47:7 King, sing praises with u.
49:3 medita. of heart shall be u.
119:34 give u. 73, 125, 144, 169
99 I have u. 130 word giveth u.
104 thro' thy precepts I get u.
147:5 great our L. u. is infinite
Prov. 1:2 to perceive words of u.
2:2 thou apply th. heart to u.
3 if thou liftest up voice for u.
6 out of his mouth cometh u.
11 discretion pres. thee, u. sh.
3:5 lean not to thine own u.
13 happy is man th. getteth u.
19 by u. he establish. heavens
4:1 attend to kn. u. 5 get u. 7
5:1 bow thine ear to my u.
6:32 commit. adult. lacketh u.
7:4 and call u. thy kinswoman
8:1 doth not u. put forth voice ?
14 I am u. 9:6 in way of u.
9:4 him that wanteth u. 16
10 knowledge of the holy is u.
10:13 that hath u. wisd. is found
14:29 is slow to wrath is of u.
33 wisdom in him that hath u.
15:14 heart of him that hath u.
32 that heareth reproof get. u.
16:16 better to get u. than silv.
22 u. is a well-spring of life to
17:24 wisd. bef. him that ha. u.
18:2 fool hath no delight in u.
19:8 he that keepeth u. sh. find
25 reprove one that hath u.
21:16 wander. out of way of u.
30 there is no u. nor counsel
23:23 buy also instruct. and u.
24:3 by u. house is established
28:11 poor that hath u. search.
16 prince that wanteth u.
30:2 have not the u. of a matter
Ec. 9:11 nor rich. to men of u.
Is. 11:2 sp. of u. shall rest upon
3 make him of quick u.
27:11 for it is a people of no u.
29:14 u. of their prudent men
16 framed it, he had no u. ?
24 erred in spir. sh. come to u.
40:14 showed him way of u. ?
28 there is no search. of his u.
44:19 neither knowledge nor u.
Jer. 3:15 past. sh. feed you wi. u.
4:22 people foolish, have no u.
5:21 O foolish peo. without u.
51:15 stretched out heaven by u.
Ezek. 28:4 wi. thy u. thou hast
Dan. 1:17 Dan. had u. in visions
20 in matters of u. he found
2:21 giv. to them that know u.
4:34 mine u. returned to me
5:11 and u. was found, 12, 14
9:22 I am come to give thee u.
10:1 Daniel had u. of vision
11:35 some of th. of u. shall fall
Hos. 13:2 made idols ac. to th. u.
Ob. 7 there is no u. in him
8 sh. I not destroy u. out of E.?
Mat. 15:16 ye wi. u. ? Mark 7:18
Mark 12:33 to love him with u.
Luke 1:3 having had perfect u.
2:47 were astonished at his u.
24:45 then opened he their u.
Rom. 1:31 without u. coven.-br.
1 Cor. 1:19 bring to noth. the u.
14:14 sp. prayeth, u. is unfruit.
15 pray with u. sing with u.
19 ra. speak five words with u.
20 not child. in u. in u. be men
Eph. 1:18 eyes of u. being enlig.
4:18 having the u. darkened
Phil. 4:7 peace of G. pass. all u.
Col. 1:9 filled with all spiritu. u.
2:2 rich. of full assurance of u.
2 Tim. 2:7 the Lord give thee u.
1 John 5:20 G. hath giv. us an u.
Rev. 13:18 him that hath u.

See GOOD.

**Man of UNDERSTANDING.**

Ezr. 8:18 they broug. a m. of u.
Prov. 1:5 a m. of u. shall attain
10:23 a m. of u. hath wisdom
11:12 a m. of u. hold. his peace
15:21 a m. of u. walk. uprightly
17:27 a m. of u. is of an excell.
28 shutteth lips is a m. of u.
20:5 a m. of u. will dr. counsel
28:2 by a m. of u. state shall be

**Void of UNDERSTANDING.**

Prov. 7:7 a young man v. of u.
10:13 a rod for him th. is v. of u.
12:11 follow vain per. is v. of u.
17:18 a man v. of u. strik. han.
24:30 vineyard of man v. of u.

**UNDERSTANDING, Adj.**

Deut. 1:13 take wise men and u.
4:6 this nation is an u. people
1 K. 3:9 give servant an u. heart
12 lo, I have given thee an u.
Prov. 8:5 be of an u. heart
Dan. 1:4 u. science; 8:23 u. dark
Eph. 5:17 u. what will of L. is
1 Tim. 1:7 u. neit. what they say

**UNDERSTOOD.**

Gen. 42:23 knew not Jos. u. th.
Deut. 32:29 were wise, they u.
1 Sam. 4:6 they u. ark of L. was
26:4 Da. u. that Saul was come
2 Sam. 3:37 u. it was not of D.
Neh. 8:12 had u. words that were
13:7 I u. of the evil Eliashib did
Job 13:1 mine ear heard and u. it
42:3 I uttered that I u. not
Ps. 73:17 then u. I their end
81:5 heard langu. that I u. not
106:7 our fath. u. not thy wond.
Is. 40:21 ha. ye not u. fr. founda.
44:18 nor u. for he shut th. eyes
Dan. 8:27 astonished, but none u.
9:2 Dan. u. by books; 10:1 he u.
12:8 I heard, but I u. not, then
Mat. 13:51 have ye u. these thi. ?
16:12 then u. they how he bade
17:13 they u. that he spake of J.
Mark 9:32 u. not that sayi. Luke
2:50; 9:45; John 8:27; 10:6
Luke 18:34 they u. none of these
John 12:16 thi. u. not his discip.
Acts 7:25 he supposed they u. G.
would deliver th. they u. not
23:27 hav. u. he was a Roman
34 when I u. he was of Cilicia
Rom. 1:20 being u. by the things
1 Cor. 13:11 I u. as a child
14:9 ut. by tongue wor. to be u.
2 Pet. 3:16 some thi. hard to be u.

**UNDERTAKE.**

Is. 38:14 I am oppress. u. for me

**UNDERTOOK.**

Est. 9:23 Jews u. to do as they

**UNDO.**

Is. 58:6 the fast ? to u. burdens
Zep. 3:19 I will u. all that afflict

**UNDONE.**

Num. 21:29 thou art u. O people
Jos. 11:15 Joshua left nothing u.
Is. 6:5 woe is me, for I am u.
Mat. 23:23 lea. oth. u. Lu. 11:42

**UNDRESSED.**

Lev. 25:5 grapes of thy vine u. 11

**UNEQUAL, LY.**

Ezek. 18:25 are not y. ways u. ? 29
2 Cor. 6:14 be not u. yoked with

**UNFAITHFUL, LY.**

Ps. 78:57 they dealt u. like fath.
Prov. 25:19 confid. in an u. man

**UNFEIGNED.**

2 Cor. 6:6 by H. Ghost, by love u.
1 Tim. 1:5 pure heart, faith u.
2 Tim. 1:5 I call to remembr. u.
1 Pet. 1:22 thro' Spi. unto u. love

**UNFRUITFUL.**

Mat. 13:22 becom. u. Mark 4:19
1 Cor. 14:14 my understand. is u.
Eph. 5:11 no fellowship with u.
Tit. 3:14 that they be not u.
2 Pet. 1:8 neith. be barren nor u.

**UNGIRDED.**

Gen. 24:32 man u. the camels

**UNGODLINESS.**

Rom. 1:18 wrath of God agai. u.
11:26 he sh. turn away u. fr. Ja.
2 Tim. 2:16 will increase unto u.
Tit. 2:12 denying u. and worldly

**UNGODLY.**

2 Sam. 22:5 floods of u. men ma.
me afraid, Ps. 18:4
2 Chr. 19:2 shouldest thou help u.
Job 16:11 G. deliver. me to the u.
34:18 is it fit to say, Ye are u. ?
Ps. 1:1 walk. not in coun. of u.
Ps. 1:4 u. are not so; 5 u. not sta.
6 the way of the u. shall perish
3:7 hast broken the teeth of u.
43:1 pl. my cause ag. u. nation
73:12 these are u. who prosper
Prov. 16:27 u. man dig. up evil
19:28 u. witness scorneth judg.
Rom. 4:5 him that justifieth u.
5:6 in due time Chr. died for u.
1 Tim. 1:9 the law is for the u.
1 Pet. 4:18 where shall u. appear ?

2 *Pet.* 2:5 bringing the flood on *u.*
6 those who after should live *u.*
3:7 judgment and perdi. of *u.*
*Jude* 4 *u.* men turn. grace of God
15 convince *u.* of th. *u.* deeds
18 who walk after th. *u.* lusts

**UNHOLY.**
*Lev.* 10:10 differ. bet. holy and *u.*
1 *Tim.* 1:9 law was made for *u.*
2 *Tim.* 3:2 men be unthankful, *u.*
*Heb.* 10:29 counted blood of *u.*

**UNICORN.**
*Num.* 23:22 strength of *u.* 24:8
*Job* 39:9 will the *u.* serve thee?
10 canst bind *u.* in the furrow?
*Ps.* 29:6 Leb. and Sirion like *u.*
92:10 shall exalt like horn of *u.*

**UNICORNS.**
*Deut.* 33:17 horns like horns of *u.*
*Ps.* 22:21 heard from horns of *u.*
*Is.* 34:7 the *u.* shall come down

**UNITE, D.**
*Gen.* 49:6 mine honor be not *u.*
*Ps.* 86:11 *u.* my heart to fear

**UNITY.**
*Ps.* 133:1 for bre. to dwell in *u.*
*Eph.* 4:3 endeavoring to keep *u.*
13 till we come in the *u.* of

**UNJUST.**
*Ps.* 43:1 deliv. me from *u.* man
*Prov.* 11:7 hope of *u.* men peris.
28:8 who by *u.* gain increaseth
29:27 an *u.* man is an abomina.
*Zep.* 3:5 *u.* knoweth no shame
*Mat.* 5:45 sen. rai. on just and *u.*
*Luke* 16:8 L. commend. *u.* stew.
10 is *u.* in least, is *u.* in much
18:6 hear what *u.* judge saith
11 I am not as oth. men are, *u.*
*Acts* 24:15 resurrec. of just and *u.*
1 *Cor.* 6:1 any go to law bef. *u.*?
1 *Pet.* 3:18 Christ suf. just for *u.*
2 *Pet.* 2:9 res. *u.* to day of judg.
*Rev.* 22:11 th. is *u.* let him be *u.* st.

**UNJUSTLY.**
*Ps.* 82:2 how lo. will ye judge *u.*
*Is.* 26:10 in land of upri. deal *u.*

**UNKNOWN.**
*Acts* 17:23 inscript. To the *u.* G.
1 *Cor.* 14:2 sp. in *u.* tong. 4, 13, 27
14 if I pray in *u.* tongue
19 10,000 words in *u.* tongue
2 *Cor.* 6:9 as *u.* yet well known
*Gal.* 1:22 *u.* by face unto the

**UNLADE.**
*Acts* 21:3 ship was to *u.* burden

**UNLAWFUL.**
*Acts* 10:28 an *u.* thing for a man
2 *Pet.* 2:8 vexed his soul with *u.*

**UNLEARNED.**
*Acts* 4:13 perceived they were *u.*
1 *Cor.* 14:16 occupieth room of *u.*
23 come in those that are *u.* 24
2 *Tim.* 2:23 foolish and *u.* quest.
2 *Pet.* 3:16 they that are *u.* wrest

**UNLEAVENED.**
*Ex.* 12:39 they baked *u.* cakes
*Lev.* 2:4 an *u.* cake of fine flour
7:12 *u.* cakes mingled with oil
8:26 Moses took one *u.* cake
*Num.* 6:19 priest take one *u.* cake
*Jos.* 5:11 eat old corn of land *u.*
*Jud.* 6:19 Gid. made rea. *u.* cakes
20 take the flesh and *u.* cakes
21 ang. touc. flesh and *u.* cakes
1 *Chr.* 23:29 flour and *u.* cakes
1 *Cor.* 5:7 new lump, as ye are *u.*
*See* BREAD.

**UNLOOSE.**
*Mark* 1:7 shoes I am not worthy
to *u.* *Luke* 3:16; *John* 1:27

**UNMARRIED.**
1 *Cor.* 7:8 the *u.* 11 remain *u.*
32 he that is *u.* 34 *u.* woman

**UNMERCIFUL.**
*Rom.* 1:31 without affection, *u.*

**UNMINDFUL.**
*Deut.* 32:18 rock th. begat th. *u.*

**UNMOVABLE.**
*Acts* 27:41 forep. of ship rema. *u.*
1 *Cor.* 15:58 bret. be steadfast, *u.*

**UNOCCUPIED.**
*Jud.* 5:6 Sha. highways were *u.*

**UNPERFECT.**
*Ps.* 139:16 substan. yet being *u.*

**UNPREPARED.**
2 *Cor.* 9:4 if come and find you *u.*

**UNPROFITABLE.**
*Job* 15:3 sh. reason with *u.* talk
*Mat.* 25:30 cast *u.* ser. into dark.
*Luke* 17:10 say, We are *u.* serv.
*Rom.* 3:12 are altogether bec. *u.*
*Tit.* 3:9 genealogies, *u.* and vain
*Phile.* 11 in time past was *u.*
*Heb.* 13:17 not wi. grief, th. is *u.*

**UNPROFITABLENESS.**
*Heb.* 7:18 the weakness and *u.*

**UNPUNISHED.**
*Prov.* 11:21 wicked sh. not be *u.*
16:5 the proud shall not be *u.*
17:5 glad at calamities not be *u.*
19:5 false witness not be *u.* 9
*Jer.* 25:29 utterly *u.* sh. not be *u.*
30:11 not leave thee altoget. *u.*
46:28 not leave thee wholly *u.*
49:12 sh. thou go *u.*? not go *u.*

**UNQUENCHABLE.**
*Mat.* 3:12 but burn the chaff with
*u.* fire, *Luke* 3:17

**UNREASONABLE.**
*Acts* 25:27 it seemeth *u.* to send
2 *Thes.* 3:2 delivered fr. *u.* men

**UNREBUKABLE.**
1 *Tim.* 6:14 keep this comm. *u.*

**UNREPROVABLE.**
*Col.* 1:22 to present you holy, *u.*

**UNRIGHTEOUS.**
*Ex.* 23:1 put not hand to be *u.*
*Job* 27:7 riseth ag. me be as *u.*
*Ps.* 71:4 deli. out of hand of *u.*
*Is.* 10:1 woe to th. that decree *u.*
55:7 *u.* man forsake thoughts
*Luke* 16:11 not faithful in *u.* ma.
*Rom.* 3:5 is G. *u.* who tak. ven.?
1 *Cor.* 6:9 the *u.* shall not inherit
*Heb.* 6:10 God is not *u.* to forget

**UNRIGHTEOUSLY.**
*Deut.* 25:16 all that do *u.* are ab.

**UNRIGHTEOUSNESS.**
*Lev.* 19:15 do no *u.* in judgm. 35
*Ps.* 92:15 there is no *u.* in him
*Jer.* 22:13 buildeth house by *u.*
*Luke* 16:19 friends of mam. of *u.*
*John* 7:18 true, no *u.* in him
*Rom.* 1:18 *u.* of men who hold
the truth in *u.*
29 filled with all *u.* fornication
2:8 them that obey *u.* indigna.
3:5 if our *u.* commend righte.
6:13 yield mem. as instru. of *u.*
9:14 is there *u.* with God?
2 *Cor.* 6:14 wh. fellow. with *u.*?
2 *Thes.* 2:10 wi. deceivab. of *u.*
12 beli. not, had pleasure in *u.*
*Heb.* 8:12 be merciful to their *u.*
2 *Pet.* 2:13 shall receive rew. of *u.*
15 Bal. who loved wages of *u.*
1 *John* 1:9 cleanse us from all *u.*
5:17 all *u.* is sin; th. is a sin not

**UNRIPE.**
*Job* 15:33 shall shake off *u.* grape

**UNRULY.**
1 *Thes.* 5:14 warn th. that are *u.*
*Tit.* 1:6 not accused of riot, or *u.*
10 there are many *u.* and vain
*Jam.* 3:8 the tongue is an *u.* evil

**UNSATIABLE.**
*Ezek.* 16:28 because thou wast *u.*

**UNSAVORY.**
*Job* 6:6 *u.* be eaten with. salt?

**UNSEARCHABLE.**
*Job* 5:9 G. doeth great th. and *u.*
*Ps.* 145:3 L. his greatness is *u.*
*Prov.* 25:3 heart of kings is *u.*
*Rom.* 11:33 how *u.* are his judg.
*Eph.* 3:8 preach *u.* riches of Ch.

**UNSEEMLY.**
*Rom.* 1:27 work. that which is *u.*
1 *Cor.* 13:5 doth not behave *u.*

**UNSHOD.**
*Jer.* 2:25 withhold from being *u.*

**UNSKILFUL.**
*Heb.* 5:13 babe is *u.* in the word

**UNSPEAKABLE.**
2 *Cor.* 9:15 thanks to G. for his *u.*
12:4 cau. up and heard *u.* words
1 *Pet.* 1:8 rejoice with joy *u.* full

**UNSPOTTED.**
*Jam.* 1:27 to keep himself *u.* from

**UNSTABLE.**
*Gen.* 49:4 *u.* as water, not excel
*Jam.* 1:8 doublemind. man is *u.*
2 *Pet.* 2:14 beguiling *u.* souls
3:16 are unlearned and *u.* wrest

**UNSTOPPED.**
*Is.* 35:7 ears of the deaf sh. be *u.*

**UNTAKEN.**
2 *Cor.* 3:14 remain. veil *u.* away

**UNTEMPERED.**
*Ezek.* 13:10 others daubed it with
*u.* mortar, 11, 14, 15; 22:28

**UNTHANKFUL.**
*Luke* 6:35 he is kind to the *u.*
2 *Tim.* 3:2 blasphem. *u.* unholy

**UNTIMELY.**
*Job* 3:16 or as a hidden *u.* birth
*Ps.* 58:8 like *u.* birth of a woman
*Ec.* 6:3 an *u.* birth is better than
*Rev.* 6:13 as fig-trees cast. *u.* figs

**UNTOWARD.**
*Acts* 2:40 save from *u.* generation

**UNWALLED.**
*Deut.* 3:5 cities, beside *u.* towns
*Est.* 9:19 Jews dw. in *u.* towns
*Ezek.* 38:11 I will go to land of *u.*

**UNWASHEN.**
*Mat.* 15:20 to eat with *u.* hands,
*Mark* 7:2, 5

**UNWEIGHED.**
1 *K.* 7:47 Solomon left vessels *u.*

**UNWISE.**
*Deut.* 32:6 thus requi. L. *u.* peo.
*Hos.* 13:13 *u.* son, sh. not stay
*Rom.* 1:14 debtor to wise and *u.*
*Eph.* 5:17 be not *u.* but underst.

**UNWITTINGLY.**
*Lev.* 22:14 if eat of holy things *u.*
*Jos.* 20:3 that killeth person *u.* 5

**UNWORTHY, ILY.**
*Acts* 13:46 judge yourselves *u.* of
1 *Cor.* 6:2 are ye *u.* to judge the?
11:27 drink this cup of the L. *u.*
29 he that eateth and drink. *u.*

**UP,** *interjectional.*
*Gen.* 19:14 L. said, *u.* get ye out
44:4 Joseph said, *u.* follow after
*Ex.* 32:1 *u.* make us gods that
*Jos.* 7:13 *u.* sanctify the people
*Jud.* 4:14 *u.* for this is the day
8:20 to first-born, *u.* slay them
9:32 *u.* thou and the people that
19:28 *u.* and let us be going
1 *Sam.* 9:26 *u.* that I may send

**UP.**
*Ps.* 88:15 rea. to die fr. youth *u.*
*Mat.* 19:20 I kept fr. my youth *u.*

*Luke* 18:21 I kept fr. my youth *u.*
*See* DOWN.

**UPBRAID, ED, ETH.**
*Jud.* 8:15 with wh. ye did *u.* me
*Mat.* 11:20 then began he to *u.*
*Mark* 16:14 he *u.* th. with unbel.
*Jam.* 1:5 giveth liberally, *u.* not

**UPHARSIN.**
*Dan.* 5:25 Mene, Mene, Tekel, *U.*

**UPHAZ.**
*Jer.* 10:9 gold is brought from U.
*Dan.* 10:5 girded with gold of U.

**UPHELD.**
*Is.* 63:5 and my fury it *u.* me

**UPHOLD.**
*Ps.* 51:12 *u.* me with thy free Sp.
54:4 L. with th. that *u.* my soul
119:116 *u.* me according to word
*Prov.* 29:23 honor sh. *u.* humble
*Is.* 41:10 I will *u.* thee wi. right
42:1 my servant whom I *u.*
63:5 I wondered was none to *u.*
*Ezek.* 30:6 that *u.* Egypt sh. fall

**UPHOLDEN.**
*Job* 4:4 thy words have *u.* him
*Prov.* 20:28 throne is *u.* by mercy

**UPHOLDEST, ETH.**
*Ps.* 37:17 Lord *u.* the righteous
24 Lord *u.* him with his hand
41:12 thou *u.* me in mine integ.
63:8 follow. thy right hand *u.*
145:14 the Lord *u.* all that fall

**UPHOLDING.**
*Heb.* 1:3 *u.* all things by word of

**UPPER.**
*Ex.* 12:7 blood on *u.* door-posts
*Lev.* 13:45 put a cover. on *u.* lip
*Deut.* 24:6 no man take *u.* millst.
*Jos.* 15:19 gave *u.* spri. *Jud.* 1:15
*Zep.* 2:14 lodge in the *u.* lintels
*Mark* 14:15 will show you an *u.* room, *Luke* 22:12
*Acts* 1:13 went up into *u.* room
19:1 P. passed through *u.* coasts
*See* CHAMBER.

**UPPERMOST.**
*Gen.* 40:17 *u.* basket bakemeats
*Is.* 17:6 in top of the *u.* bough
9 cities sh. be as an *u.* branch
*Mat.* 23:6 they love the *u.* rooms, *Mark* 12:39; *Luke* 11:43

**UPRIGHT.**
*Gen.* 37:7 my sheaf. arose, sto. *u.*
*Lev.* 26:13 and made you go *u.*
1 *Sam.* 29:6 thou hast been *u.* with me, 2 *Chr.* 29:34
2 *Sam.* 22:24 I was also *u.* before him, *Ps.* 18:23
26 wi. *u.* show thy. *u.* *Ps.* 18:25
2 *Chr.* 29:34 Levites were more *u.*
*Job* 1:1 perf. and *u.* man, 8; 2:3
8:6 if *u.* he wou. awake for thee
12:4 *u.* man is laughed to scorn
17:8 *u.* men shall be astonished
*Ps.* 11:7 countenance behold *u.*
19:13 then sh. I be *u.* innocent
25:8 Lord is good and *u.* 92:15
33:1 for praise is comely for *u.*
37:14 as be of *u.* conversation
18 Lord knoweth days of the *u.*
37 perfect man, behold the *u.*
49:14 *u.* sh. have dominion over
111:1 praise L. in assemb. of *u.*
112:2 generation of *u.* be bless.
4 to *u.* ariseth light in darkn.
119:137 *u.* are thy judgments
125:4 do good to the *u.* in heart
140:13 *u.* shall dwell in thy presence
*Prov.* 2:21 *u.* shall dwell in land
10:29 way of L. is strength to *u.*
11:3 integ. of *u.* sh. guide them
6 righteousness of *u.* deli. them
11 by bless. of *u.* city exalted
20 *u.* in their way are his deli.
12:6 mouth of *u.* shall deli. them
13:6 righteousness keep. the *u.*
14:11 taberna. of *u.* sh. flourish
15:8 prayer of *u.* is his delight
16:17 way of *u.* to dep. fr. evil
21:18 transg. be ransom for *u.*
29 as for *u.* he direct his way
28:10 *u.* ha. good in possession
29:10 bloodthirsty hate the *u.*
27 *u.* is an abomina. to wicked
*Ec.* 7:29 found G. made man *u.*
12:10 written *u.* words of truth
*Cant.* 1:4 rememb. *u.* love thee
*Is.* 26:7 *u.* weigh path of just
*Jer.* 10:5 they are *u.* as palm-tr.
*Dan.* 8:18 touched and set me *u.*
11:17 enter and *u.* ones wi. him
*Mic.* 7:2 is none *u.* among men
4 *u.* sharper th. a thorn hedge
*Hab.* 2:4 lifted, not *u.* in him
*See* HEART, STAND, STOOD.

**UPRIGHTLY.**
*Ps.* 15:2 walketh *u.* shall abide
58:1 ye judge *u.?* 75:2 judge *u.*
84:11 good fr. them that walk *u.*
*Prov.* 2:7 buckler to th. walk *u.*
10:9 walketh *u.* walketh surely
15:21 man of underst. walk. *u.*
28:18 whoso walk. *u.* be saved
*Is.* 33:15 speak. *u.* sh. dwell high
*Amos* 5:10 him that speaketh *u.*
*Mic.* 2:7 to him that walketh *u.*
*Gal.* 2:14 that th. walked not *u.*

**UPRIGHTNESS.**
1 *K.* 3:6 walked before thee in *u.*
1 *Chr.* 29:17 hast pleasure in *u.*
*Job* 4:6 and the *u.* of thy ways?
33:23 to show unto man his *u.*
*Ps.* 9:8 judgment to people in *u.*
25:21 and *u.* preserve me
111:8 st. fast and are done in *u.*
143:10 lead me into land of *u.*
*Prov.* 2:13 who leave paths of *u.*
14:2 walketh in *u.* feareth Lord
28:6 better is poor walketh in *u.*
*Is.* 26:7 way of the just is *u.*
10 in land of *u.* deal unjustly
57:2 each one walking in his *u.*
*See* HEART.

**UPRISING.**
*Ps.* 139:2 my down-sitt. and *u.*

**UPROAR.**
1 *K.* 1:41 city being in an *u.*
*Mat.* 26:5 lest th. be *u.* *Mark* 14:2
*Acts* 17:5 Jews set city on an *u.*
19:40 question for this day's *u.*
20:1 after *u.* was ceased, Paul
21:31 Jerusalem was in an *u.*
38 Egypt. who madest an *u.?*

**UPSIDE down.**
2 *K.* 21:13 dish, turning it *u. d.*
*Ps.* 146:9 wicked he turn. *u. d.*
*Is.* 24:1 L. turneth earth *u. d.*
29:16 your turning of th. *u. d.*
*Acts* 17:6 have turn. world *u. d.*

**UPWARD.**
*Num.* 8:24 from 25 years old and *u.* 1 *Chr.* 23:3
1 *Sam.* 9:2 from should. *u.* 10:23
2 *K.* 19:30 bear fruit *u.* *Is.* 37:31
2 *Chr.* 31:16 fr. 3 years old and *u.*
*Job* 5:7 to trouble as sparks fly *u.*
*Ec.* 3:21 spirit of man goeth *u.*
*Is.* 8:21 curse God, and look *u.*
38:14 mine eyes fail looking *u.*
*Ezek.* 1:27 app. of loins *u.* 8:2
41:7 a winding about still *u.*
*Hag.* 2:15 fr. this day and *u.* 18

**UR.**
*Gen.* 11:28 before his father in U.
15:7 bro. thee out of U. *Neh.* 9:7
1 *Chr.* 11:35 Eliphal the son of U.

**URGE, D.**
*Gen.* 33:11 Jacob *u.* Esau, and he
*Jud.* 16:16 Delilah *u.* Samson
19:7 depart, his father-in-law *u.*
2 *K.* 2:17 *u.* him till ashamed
5:16 *u.* Elisha; 23 he *u.* Gehazi
*Luke* 11:53 Pharisees began to *u.*

**URGENT.**
*Ex.* 12:33 Egypt. were *u.* on peo.
*Dan.* 3:22 king's commmand. *u.*

**URI.**
*Ex.* 31:2 B. son of U. 35:30; 38:22; 1 *Chr.* 2:20; 2 *Chr.* 1:5
1 *K.* 4:19 son of U. was in Gile.
*Ezr.* 10:24 Telem, and U. porters

**URIAH, *or* URIJAH.**
2 *Sam.* 11:3 Bath-sh. wife of U.?
6 say. Send me U. the Hittite
14 sent it by U. 21 U. is dead
12:9 hast killed U. with sword
23:39 U. one of David's worthies
1 *K.* 15:5 only in matter of U.
1 *Chr.* 11:41 U. the Hittite
*Ezr.* 8:33 weighed by son of U.
*Neh.* 3:4 next repaired son of U.
21 Meremoth, son of U.
8:4 U. on his right hand
*Is.* 8:2 I took faithful witnes. U.
*Mat.* 1:6 Solomon of wife of U.

**URIJAH.**
2 *K.* 16:10 sent U. fashion of alt.
16 did U. as king A. comman.
*Jer.* 26:20 U. prophesied against
21 U. fled into Egypt

**URIM.**
*Ex.* 28:30 *u.* and thum. *Lev.* 8:8
*Num.* 27:21 coun. aft. judg. of *u.*
*Deut.* 33:8 let *u.* be with holy O.
1 *Sam.* 28:6 by *u.* nor prophets
*Ezr.* 2:63 pric. with *u.* *Neh.* 7:65

**Against US.**
*Mark* 9:40 he that is not *a. u.* is on our part, *Luke* 9:50
*Rom.* 8:31 G. for us, who *a. u.?*

**For US.**
2 *Chr.* 13:10 as *f. u.* L. is our G.
*Mat.* 17:4 L. it is good *for u.* to be here, *Mark* 9:5; *Lu.* 9:33

**From US.**
1 *John* 2:19 they went out *fr. u.*
*See* DEPART.

**Of US.**
1 *John* 2:19 th. were not *of u.* for if they had been *of u.* they

**To US-WARD.**
*Ps.* 40:5 though. wh. are *to u.-w.*
*Eph.* 1:19 gre. of power *to u.-w.*
2 *Pet.* 3:9 long suffering *to u.-w.*

**With US.**
*Mat.* 1:23 interpret. is, G. *w. u.*

**USE, Substantive.**
*Lev.* 7:24 be used in any other *u.*
*Deut.* 26:14 aught for unclean *u.*
2 *Sam.* 1:18 teach Ju. *u.* of bow
1 *Chr.* 28:15 to *u.* of candlestick
*Rom.* 1:26 did change natural *u.*
*Eph.* 4:29 good to *u.* of edifying
2 *Tim.* 2:21 meet for master's *u.*
*Heb.* 5:14 by *u.* ha. senses exer.

**USES.**
*Tit.* 3:14 works for necessary *u.*

**USE, Verb.**
*Lev.* 19:26 neither *u.* enchantm.
*Num.* 10:2 *u.* trumpe. for calling
15:39 ye *u.* to go a whoring
1 *Chr.* 12:2 could *u.* right hand
*Jer.* 23:31 *u.* th. tongues and say
31:23 shall *u.* this speech in J.
46:11 vain *u.* many medicines
*Ezek.* 12:23 no more *u.* it a prov.
16:44 shall *u.* proverb ag. thee
18:2 that ye *u.* this proverb?
3 not have occasion to use pro.
21:21 stood to *u.* divination
*Mat.* 6:7 *u.* not vain repetitions

*Acts* 14:5 to *u.* apostles despitef·
1 *Cor.* 7:21 made free, *u.* it rath·
31 *u.* this world as not abus. it
2 *Cor.* 1:17 did I *u.* lightness
3:12 we *u.* great plai. of speech
13:10 present, I should *u.* sharp
*Gal.* 5:13 *u.* not liberty for occa.
1 *Tim.* 1:8 if a man *u.* it lawfully
3:10 let th. *u.* office of a deacon
5:23 *u.* wine for stomach's sake
1 *Pet.* 4:9 *u.* hospitality one to

**USED.**

*Ex.* 21:36 if ox hath *u.* to push
*Lev.* 7:24 may be *u.* in any use
*Jud.* 14:10 so *u.* you. men to do
20 wh. Samson *u.* as his friend
2 *K.* 17:17 *u.* enchantments, 21:6
*Jer.* 2:24 ass *u.* to the wilderness
*Ezek.* 22:29 people *u.* oppression
35:11 envy which thou hast *u.*
*Hos.* 12:10 *u.* similitud. by prop.
*Mark* 2:18 disc. of John *u.* to fa.
*Acts* 19:19 which *u.* curious arts
*Rom.* 3:13 with tongues *u.* deceit
1 *Cor.* 9:12 have not *u.* this pow.
15 I ha. *u.* none of these things
1 *Thes.* 2:5 *u.* we flattering wor.
1 *Tim.* 3:13 ha. *u.* office of deac.
*Heb.* 10:33 companio. were so *u.*

**USEST.**

*Ps.* 119:132 *u.* to those that love

**USETH.**

*Deut.* 18:10 any th. *u.* divination
*Est.* 6:8 apparel king *u.* to wear
*Prov.* 15:2 the wise *u.* knowled.
18:23 the poor *u.* entreati. rich
*Jer.* 22:13 *u.* service with. wages
*Ezek.* 16:44 that *u.* proverbs shall
*Heb.* 5:13 every one that *u.* milk

**USING.**

*Col.* 2:22 wh. are to perish wi. *u.*
1 *Pet.* 2:16 not *u.* liberty for clo.

**USURP.**

1 *Tim.* 2:12 wom. to *u.* authority

**USURER.**

*Ex.* 22:22 shalt not be as a *u.*

**USURY.**

*Ex.* 22:25 thou lay upon him *u.*
*Lev.* 25:36 take no *u.* of him, 37
*Deut.* 23:19 lend on *u.* to brother
20 thou mayest lend upon *u.*
*Neh.* 5:7 exact *u.* 10 leave off *u.*
*Ps.* 15:5 putteth his money to *u.*
*Prov.* 28:8 *u.* increas. substance
*Is.* 24:2 tak. of *u.* so wi. gi. of *u.*
*Jer.* 15:10 neither lent on *u.* nor
have men lent to me on *u.*
*Ezek.* 18:8 not giv. forth on *u.* 17
13 given on *u.* 22:12 taken *u.*
*Mat.* 25:27 own wi. *u.* *Luke* 19:23

**UTMOST OUTMOST.**

*Gen.* 49:26 *u.* bound of the hills
*Num.* 22:41 see *u.* of peop. 23:13
*Deut.* 30:4 driven to *u.* parts
*Jer.* 9:26 *u.* corners, 25:23; 49:32
*Luke* 11:31 she came fr. *u.* parts

**UTTER, Verb.**

*Lev.* 5:1 if he do not *u.* it bear
*Jos.* 2:14 our life if ye *u.* not this
20 if thou *u.* it we will be quit
*Jud.* 5:12 Debor. *u.* song. Arise
*Job* 8:10 shall th. not *u.* words?
15:2 wise man *u.* vain knowl.?
27:4 nor shall tongue *u.* deceit
33:3 my lips shall *u.* knowledge
*Ps.* 78:2 I will *u.* dark sayings
94:4 long shall *u.* hard things?
106:2 who can *u.* mighty acts?
119:171 my lips shall *u.* praise
145:7 shall *u.* memory of goodn.
*Prov.* 14:5 false witn. will *u.* lies
23:33 heart shall *u.* perv. things
*Ec.* 1:8 labor, man cannot *u.* it
5:2 not hasty to *u.* before God
*Is.* 32:6 vile person will *u.* error
48:20 *u.* it even to end of earth
*Jer.* 1:16 I will *u.* my judgments
25:30 *u.* voice from holy habita.
*Ezek.* 24:3 *u.* a parab. unto rebel.
*Joel* 2:11 Lord shall *u.* his voice
3:16 *u.* voice fr. Jeru. *Amos* 1:2
*Mat.* 13:35 I will *u.* things kept
1 *Cor.* 14:9 *u.* words easy under.
2 *Cor.* 12:4 not law. for man to *u.*

**UTTER, Adjective.**

1 *K.* 20:42 I appointed to *u.* des.
*Nah.* 1:8 make *u.* end of place
*Zec.* 14:11 no more *u.* destructi.

**UTTERANCE.**

*Acts* 2:4 spake as Spirit gave *u.*
1 *Cor.* 1:5 are enriched in all *u.*
2 *Cor.* 8:7 as ye abound in *u.* and
*Eph.* 6:19 pray. that *u.* be given
*Col.* 4:3 G. wo. open a door of *u.*

**UTTERED.**

*Num.* 30:6 husba. when she *u.* 8
*Jud.* 11:11 Jephthah *u.* his words
2 *Sam.* 22:14 Most High *u.* his
voice, *Ps.* 46:6
*Job* 26:4 to whom hast *u.* words?
42:3 I *u.* that I understood not
*Ps.* 66:14 lips *u.* when in trouble
*Hab.* 3:10 deep *u.* his voice and
*Rom.* 8:26 groan. wh. can. be *u.*
*Heb.* 5:11 many th. hard to be *u.*
*Rev.* 10:3 seven thun. *u.* voices
4 when seven thunders had *u.*

**UTTERETH.**

*Job* 15:5 thy mouth *u.* iniquities
*Ps.* 19:2 day unto day *u.* speech
*Prov.* 1:20 wisdom *u.* her voice
21 she *u.* her words, saying
10:18 that *u.* slander is a fool
29:11 a fool *u.* all his mind, but
*Jer.* 10:13 wh. he *u.* voice, 51:16
*Mic.* 7:3 great man *u.* his desire

**UTTERING.**

*Is.* 59:13 *u.* from heart words

**UTTERLY.**

*Ex.* 17:14 *u.* put out remembra.
*Jud.* 15:2 I thou. hadst *u.* hated
21:11 shall *u.* destroy eve. male
1 *Sam.* 15:3 *u.* dest. Amalekites
*Is.* 2:18 idols he shall *u.* abolish
6:11 until land be *u.* desolate
24:3 *u.* emptied; 19 *u.* broken
*Hos.* 1:6 I will *u.* take th. away
10:15 king of Israel *u.* cut off

*See* DESTROYED.

**UTTERMOST.**

2 *K.* 7:5 lep. came to *u.* part, 8
*Neh.* 1:9 were cast to *u.* part
*Ps.* 2:8 give *u.* parts for possess.
*Mat.* 5:26 till hast paid *u.* farth.
12:42 ca. from *u.* parts to hear
*Mark* 13:27 gath. elect fr. *u.* part
*Acts* 24:22 I will kn. *u.* of your
1 *Thes.* 2:16 wrath is come to *u.*
*Heb.* 7:25 save them to *u.*

*See* UTMOST.

**UZ.**

*Gen.* 10:23 children of Aram; U.
36:28 of Dishan; U. 1 *Chr.* 1:42
1 *Chr.* 1:17 Sh. Lud, Ara. and U.
*Job* 1:1 man in land of U. Job
*Jer.* 25:20 made king of U. drink
*Lam.* 4:21 O daught. of E. in U.

**UZZA, UZZAH.**

2 *Sam.* 6:3 U. drave, 1 *Chr.* 13:7, 9
6 U. put forth his hand to ark
8 L. had made breach upon U.
2 *K.* 21:18 buried in garden of U.
26 Am. 1 *Chr.* 6:29 Mahli, U.
1 *Chr.* 8:7 remo. them, begat U.
*Ezr.* 2:49 childr. of U. *Neh.* 7:51

**UZZIAH,** *called* **AZARIAH, OZIAS.**

2 *K.* 15:13 in 39th year of U.
34 Jotham did as his father U.
1 *Chr.* 6:24 a son of Kohath, U.
11:44 U. the Ashterathite, vali.
27:25 over storehouses son of U.
2 *Chr.* 26:1 all pe. made U. king
8 Ammonites gave gifts to U.
18 pertaineth not to thee, U. to
21 U. a leper to day of death
*Ezr.* 10:21 U. son of Harim had
*Neh.* 11:4 dw. Athaiah son of U.
*Is.* 1:1 in the days of U. *Hos.* 1:1;
*Amos* 1:1
6:1 in year king U. died, I saw
*Zec.* 14:5 earthqu. in days of U.
*Mat.* 1:8 Joram begat O.
9 O. begat Joatham

**UZIEL.**

*Ex.* 6:18 sons of Ko. Iz. U. *Num.*
3:19; 1 *Chr.* 6:2, 18; 23:12
22 and the sons of U. *Lev.* 10:4;
*Num.* 3:30; 1 *Chr.* 15:10;
23:20; 24:24
1 *Chr.* 4:42 of Simeon had U. for
7:7 U. son of Bela; 25:4 U. son
2 *Chr.* 29:14 Jeduthun; She. U.
*Neh.* 3:8 U. of goldsmiths repair.

# V

**VAGABOND, S.**

*Gen.* 4:12 a fugitive and *v.* shalt
14 I shall be fugitive and *v.* in
*Ps.* 109:10 let his children be *v.*
*Acts* 19:13 certain *v.* Jews took

**VAIN.**

*Ex.* 5:9 let not regard *v.* words
*Deut.* 32:47 it is not a *v.* thing
*Jud.* 9:4 Abimelech hired *v.* per.
11:3 gathered *v.* men to Jephth.
1 *Sam.* 12:21 shou. ye go after *v.*
2 *Sam.* 6:20 one of the *v.* fellows
2 *K.* 17:15 became *v.* and went
18:20 are but *v.* words, *Is.* 36:5
2 *Chr.* 13:7 gath. to Jero. *v.* men
*Job* 11:11 he knoweth *v.* men
12 for *v.* man would be wise
15:2 wise man utter *v.* knowl.?
16:3 sh. *v.* words have an end?
27:12 are ye thus altogether *v.*?
*Ps.* 2:1 imag. a *v.* thing, *Acts* 4:25
26:4 I have not sat with *v.* per.
33:17 horse *v.* thing for safety
39:6 eve. man walk. in *v.* show
60:11 *v.* is help of man, 108:12
62:10 become not *v.* in robbery
119:113 I hate *v.* thoughts
127:2 *v.* for you to rise early
*Prov.* 12:11 followeth *v.* persons
28:19 followeth *v.* persons shall
31:30 favor deceitful, beauty *v.*
*Ec.* 6:12 all days of his *v.* life
*Is.* 1:13 br. no more *v.* oblations
36:5 they are but *v.* words
*Jer.* 2:5 vanity, are become *v.*
4:14 how long thy *v.* thoughts?
10:3 customs of the peop. are *v.*
23:16 prophets make you *v.* th.
*Lam.* 2:14 prophets have seen *v.*
4:17 our eyes failed for *v.* help
*Ezek.* 12:24 no more any *v.* vision
13:7 have ye not seen *v.* vision

*Mal.* 3:14 it is *v.* to serve God
*Mat.* 6:7 use not *v.* repetitions
*Rom.* 1:21 bec. *v.* in imaginatio.
1 *Cor.* 3:20 thoug. of wise are *v.*
15:14 is our preaching *v.* and your faith is also *v.* 17
*Eph.* 5:6 decei. you. wi. *v.* words
*Col.* 2:8 spoil you thro' *v.* deceit
1 *Tim.* 1:6 turn. aside to *v.* jang.
6:20 *v.* babblings, 2 *Tim.* 2:16
*Tit.* 1:10 unruly and *v.* talkers
3:9 they are unprofitable and *v.*
*Jas.* 1:26 this man's religion is *v.*
2:20 know, O *v.* man, that faith
1 *Pet.* 1:18 redeemed fr. *v.* conv.

### In VAIN.

*Ex.* 20:7 not take name of Lord *in v.* *Deut.* 5:11
*Lev.* 26:16 ye shall sow seed *in v.*
*Job* 9:29 why then labor I *in v.?*
35:16 doth Job open mouth *in v.*
39:16 her labor is *in v.* without
41:9 behold, ho. of him is *in v.*
*Ps.* 89:47 hast th. m. men *in v.?*
127:1 la. *in v.* watch. wak. *in v.*
*Prov.* 30:9 take name of G. *in. v.*
*Is.* 45:19 seed of Jac. seek *in v.*
49:4 I have labored *in v.* spent strength for naught *in v.*
*Jer.* 2:30 *in v.* have I smit. chil.
4:30 *in v.* sh. make thyself fair
8:8 are wise, lo, certainly *in v.*
46:11 *in v.* sh. thou use medici.
51:58 people shall labor *in v.*
*Ezek.* 6:10 kn. have not said *in v.*
*Rom.* 13:4 bear. not sword *in v.*
1 *Cor.* 15:2 unless ye belie. *in v.*
2 *Cor.* 6:1 not grace of G. *in v.*
*Gal.* 2:2 lest I should run *in v.*
21 then Christ is dead *in v.*
1 *Thes.* 3:5 and our labor be *in v.*
*Jam.* 4:5 think scri. saith *in v.?*

### VAIN-GLORY.

*Gal.* 5:26 not be desirous of *v.-g.*
*Phil.* 2:3 noth. be done thro' *v.-g.*

### VAINLY.

*Col.* 2:18 *v.* puffed up by fleshly

### VALE.

*Gen.* 14:3 kings in *v.* of Sidd. 8
10 *v.* of Siddim was full of pits
37:14 he sent Joseph out of *v.*
*Deut.* 1:7 in hills and in the *v.*
*Jos.* 10:40 J. smote country of *v.*
1 *K.* 10:27 cedars as sycamore-trees in *v.* 2 *Chr.* 1:15
*Jer.* 33:13 in cit. of *v.* sh. flocks

### VALIANT.

1 *Sam.* 14:52 when S. saw *v.* man
16:18 son of J. a mighty *v.* man
18:17 be *v.* for me, and fight
26:15 Art not thou a *v.* man?
31:12 the *v.* men took body of S.
2 *Sam.* 2:7 be *v.* 13:28; 17:10 is *v.*
11:16 he knew that *v.* men were
23:20 Benaiah, son of a *v.* man of Kabzeel, 1 *Chr.* 11:22
1 *K.* 1:42 for thou art a *v.* man
1 *Chr.* 7:2 sons of T. we. *v.* men
11:26 *v.* men of the armies were
*Cant.* 3:7 threescore *v.* men about it, of the *v.* of Israel
*Is.* 10:13 put down inhab. like *v.*
33:7 th. *v.* ones sh. cry without
*Jer.* 9:3 are not *v.* for the truth
46:15 are thy *v.* men. sw. away?
*Nah.* 2:3 *v.* men are in scarlet
*Heb.* 11:34 through faith wax. *v.*

### VALIANTEST.

*Jud.* 21:10 12,000 men of the *v.*

### VALIANTLY.

*Num.* 24:18 and Israel shall do *v.*
1 *Chr.* 19:13 and let us behave *v.*
*Ps.* 60:12 we shall do *v.* 108:13
118:15 hand of Lord doeth *v.* 16

### VALLEY.

*Gen.* 14:17 king of Sod. met at *v.*
*Num.* 32:9 went to *v.* of Eshcol
*Deut.* 1:24 came to *v.* of Eshcol
21:4 bring heifer to a rough *v.*
34:3 the plain of *v.* of Jericho
6 he buried Moses in a *v.* in
*Jos.* 7:24 broug. them to *v.* of A.
10:12 moon, in *v.* of Aijalon
15:8 which is at end of the *v.*
*Jud.* 1:19 drive out inhabit. of *v.*
7:8 host of Midian was in *v.* 12
16:4 a woman in the *v.* of Sorek
1 *Sam.* 6:13 reap. wheat-ha. in *v.*
21:9 whom th. slewest in the *v.*
2 *Sam.* 5:18 spread themselves in *v.* of Rephaim, 22; 23:13
8:13 smi. Syrians in *v.* of salt
2 *K.* 2:16 Spirit cast him into *v.*
3:16 make this *v.* full of ditches
14:7 he slew of Edom in *v.* of salt, 1 *Chr.* 18:12
2 *Chr.* 35:22 fight in *v.* of Megid.
*Job* 21:33 clods of *v.* sh. be sweet
39:21 paweth in *v.* and rejoiceth
*Ps.* 23:4 I walk thro' *v.* of death
60:6 mete *v.* of Succoth, 108:7
84:6 passing through *v.* of Baca
*Prov.* 30:17 ravens of *v.* pick out
*Cant.* 6:11 went to see frui. of *v.*
*Is.* 17:5 gathereth in *v.* of Reph.
22:1 burden of the *v.* of vision
5 day of trouble in *v.* of vision
28:4 beauty on head of fat *v.*
21 sh. be wroth as in *v.* of Gi.
40:4 every *v.* shall be exalted
65:10 *v.* of Ac. a place of herds
*Jer.* 2:23 see thy way in the *v.*
7:32 *v.* of H. *v.* of slaught. 19:6
21:13 ag. thee, O inhabita. of *v.*
48:8 *v.* perish, plain destroyed
49:4 why gloriest in flowi. *v.?*
*Ezek.* 37:1 in *v.* full of bones
*Hos.* 1:5 bow of Is. in *v.* of Jezr.
2:15 give *v.* of A. door of hope
*Joel* 3:2 br. into *v.* of Jehoshap.
14 multitudes in the *v.* of dec.
18 fountain shall water *v.* of S.
*Zec.* 12:11 mourning in *v.* of M.
14:4 there shall be a great *v.*
5 shall flee to *v.* of mountains
*Luke* 3:5 every *v.* shall be filled

*See* GATE.

### VALLEYS.

*Num.* 24:6 as *v.* are they spread
*Deut.* 8:7 depths spring out of *v.*
11:11 a land of hills and *v.*
1 *K.* 20:28 but he is not G. of *v.*
*Job* 30:6 to dwell in clifts of *v.*
39:10 he harrow *v.* after thee?
*Ps.* 65:13 *v.* covered with corn
104:8 go down by *v.* unto place
10 sendeth springs into the *v.*
*Cant.* 2:1 rose of Shar. lily of *v.*
*Is.* 22:7 thy *v.* full of chariots
28:1 which are on head of fat *v.*
41:18 open fount. in midst of *v.*
57:5 slaying the children in *v.*
*Jer.* 49:4 wheref. glori. thou in *v.*
*Ezek.* 6:3 saith L. to *v.* 36:4, 6
7:16 on mount. like doves of *v.*

### VALOR.

*Jud.* 3:29 slew 10,000 men of *v.*
6:12 with th. mighty man of *v.*
11:1 Jephth. mighty man of *v.*
1 *K.* 11:28 Jeroboam, a man of *v.*
2 *K.* 5:1 Naa. mighty man in *v.*
1 *Chr.* 12:28 Zadok, a man of *v.*
2 *Chr.* 17:17 Eliada, a man of *v.*

*See Mighty* MEN.

### VALUE.

*Job* 13:4 ye are physici. of no *v.*
*Mat.* 10:31 ye are of more *v.* than many sparrows, *Luke* 12:7

### VALUE, ST.

*Lev.* 27:8 the priest shall *v.* him
12 as thou *v.* it who art priest
*Mat.* 27:9 whom they of I. did *v.*

### VALUED.

*Lev.* 27:16 barley *v.* at 50 shekels
*Job* 28:16 wisdom cannot be *v.*
19 nei. shall it be *v.* with gold
*Mat.* 27:9 pri. of him that was *v.*

### VANISH, ED, ETH.

*Job* 6:17 they wax warm, they *v.*
*Job.* 7:9 as cloud is consumed, *v.*
*Is.* 51:6 heavens shall *v.* away
*Jer.* 49:7 is their wisdom *v.?*
*Luke* 24:31 *v.* out of their sight
1 *Cor.* 13:8 knowledge, it shall *v.*
*Heb.* 8:13 wax. old, ready to *v.*
*Jam.* 4:14 life is a vapor that *v.*

### VANITY.

2 *K.* 17:15 followed *v.* beca. vain
*Job* 7:3 ma. possess months of *v.*
16 let me alone, days are *v.*
15:31 let not him that is deceiv. trust in *v.* *v.* sh. be recomp.
35 mischief, and bring forth *v.*
31:5 if I walked with *v.* or hast.
35:13 sure G. will not hear *v.*
*Ps.* 4:2 how long will ye love *v.?*
10:7 under his tongue misc. *v.*
12:2 they speak *v.* every one to
24:4 hath not lifted up soul to *v.*
39:5 best estate is altogether *v.*
11 man is *v.* 94:11 thoughts *v.*
41:6 he speaketh *v.* 144:8, 11
62:9 are *v.* and lighter than *v.*
78:33 days did he consume in *v.*
119:37 turn eyes from behold. *v.*
144:4 man is like to *v.* a shadow
*Prov.* 13:11 wealth gotten by *v.*
21:6 treas. by lying tong. is *v.*
22:8 soweth iniq. shall reap *v.*
30:8 remove from me *v.* and lies
*Ec.* 1:2 *v.* of vanities, saith the preacher, all is *v.* 14; 3:19; 11:8; 12:8
2:1 this is also *v.* 15, 19, 21, 23; 4:8, 16; 5:10; 6:2, 9; 7:6; 8:10, 14
11 beh. all was *v.* 17, 26; 4:4
4:7 I saw *v.* 6:4 cometh with *v.*
6:11 many things that incre. *v.*
7:15 thi. I ha. seen in days of *v.*
8:14 a *v.* that is done on earth
9:9 with wife all the days of *v.*
11:10 childhood and youth are *v.*
*Is.* 5:18 dr. iniq. with cords of *v.*
30:28 sift nations wi. sieve of *v.*
40:17 nations to him counted *v.*
23 maketh judges of earth as *v.*
41:29 behold, they are all *v.* 44:9
57:13 wind carry, *v.* take them
58:9 take away *v.* 59:4 tru. in *v.*
*Jer.* 2:5 th. have walked after *v.*
10:15 they are *v.* errors, 51:18
16:19 fathers have inherited *v.*
18:15 people burnt incense to *v.*
*Ezek.* 13:6 th. have seen *v.* 22:28
8 because ye have spoken *v.*
9 prophets that see *v.* 21:29
23 sh. see no more *v.* nor div.
*Hos.* 12:11 *v.* they sacri. bullocks
*Hab.* 2:13 weary themsel. for *v.*
*Zec.* 10:2 for idols have spok. *v.*
*Rom.* 8:20 creature subject to *v.*
*Eph.* 4:17 as Gentiles walk, in *v.*
2 *Pet.* 2:18 speak gre. words of *v.*

### VANITIES.

*Deut.* 32:21 provo. me with their *v.* 1 *K.* 16:13,26; *Jer.* 8:19
*Ps.* 31:6 that regard lying *v.*
*Ec.* 1:2 vanity of *v.* saith, 12:8
5:7 in multi. of dreams are *v.*
*Jer.* 10:8 stock is doctrine of *v.*
14:22 any am. *v.* can cause rain?
*Jon.* 2:8 that observe lying *v.*
*Acts* 14:15 ye should turn from *v.*

### VAPOR, S.

*Job* 36:27 pour rain accord. to *v.*
33 cattle also concerning the *v.*

*Ps.* 135:7 causeth *v.* to ascend
148:8 and *v.* fulfilling his word
*Acts* 2:19 signs in earth, *v.*
*Jam.* 4:14 what is your life? a *v.*

**VARIABLENESS.**

*Jam.* 1:17 lights, wi. wh. is no *v.*

**VARIANCE.**

*Mat.* 10:35 set a man at *v.* ag. fa.
*Col.* 5:20 works of flesh, hat. *v.*

**VASHTI.**

*Est.* 1:9 V. queen made a feast
12 queen V. refused to come at
19 V. come no more bef. king
2:17 made her queen inst. of V.

**VAUNT, ETH.**

*Jud.* 7:2 lest Isr. *v.* against me
1 *Cor.* 13:4 charity *v.* not itself

**VEHEMENT.**

*Cant.* 8:6 love, th. ha. a *v.* flame
*Jon.* 4:8 G. prepared a *v.* wind
2 *Cor.* 7:11 *v.* desire it wrought

**VEHEMENTLY.**

*Mark* 14:31 Peter spake more *v.*
*Luke* 6:48 beat *v.* on house, 49
11:53 Pha. began to urge him *v.*
23:10 stood and *v.* accused him

**VEIL.**

*Gen.* 24:65 Rebekah took a *v.*
38:14 Tam. covered hers. with *v.*
*Ex.* 26:31 sh. make a *v.* of blue
34:33 Moses put a *v.* on face, 35
36:35 *v.* of blue, 2 *Chr.* 3:14
*Lev.* 16:2 come not within the *v.*
15 bring his blood within *v.*
24:3 without *v.* sh. Aaron order
*Ruth* 3:15 bring *v.* th. hast upon
*Cant.* 5:7 keep. took away my *v.*
*Is.* 25:7 destroy *v.* spread over
*Mat.* 27:51 *v.* of temple was rent, *Mark* 15:38; *Luke* 23:45
2 *Cor.* 3:13 M. put a *v.* over face
14 same *v.* untaken away, wh *v.* is done away in Christ
15 to this day *v.* is upon heart
16 the *v.* shall be taken away
*Heb.* 6:19 wh. entereth within *v.*
9:3 aft. second *v.* the tabernacle
10:20 thro' the *v.* that is to say

**VEILS.**

*Is.* 3:23 L. will take away the *v.*

**VEIN.**

*Job* 28:1 there is a *v.* for silver

**VENGEANCE.**

*Gen.* 4:15 *v.* sh. be taken on him
*Deut.* 32:35 to me belongeth *v.* and, *Ps.* 94:1; *Heb.* 10:30
41 render *v.* to mine enemies
43 will render *v.* to adversaries
*Jud.* 11:36 Lord hath taken *v.*
*Ps.* 58:10 rejoice wh. he seeth *v.*
99:8 took. *v.* of their inventions
149:7 execute *v.* upon heathen
*Prov.* 6:34 not spare in day of *v.*
*Is.* 34:8 day of *v.* 61:2; *Jer.* 51:6
35:4 your God will come with *v.*
47:3 I will take *v.* *Jer.* 51:36
59:17 he put on garments of *v.*
63:4 for day of *v.* is in my heart
*Jer.* 11:20 let see thy *v.* 20:12
46:10 day of *v.* 50:15 *v.* of the Lord, 28
50:28 *v.* of L. *v.* of temp. 51:11
*Lam.* 3:60 hast seen all their *v.*
*Ezek.* 24:8 cause fury to take *v.*
25:12 by taking *v.* hath offended
14 *v.* on Edom by hand of Isr.
15 bec. Philistines have tak. *v.*
17 when I lay *v.* on Philistines
*Mic.* 5:15 execute *v.* *Ezek.* 25:17
*Nah.* 1:2 Lord will take *v.* on his adversaries
*Luke* 21:22 for these be days of *v.*
*Acts* 28:4 *v.* suffereth not to live
*Rom.* 3:5 unright. who tak. *v.*?
12:19 *v.* is mine, saith the Lord
2 *Thes.* 1:8 flaming fire, taking *v.*
*Jude* 7 suffering *v.* of eternal fire

**VENISON.**

*Gen.* 25:28 because he eat of *v.*
27:3 go to field, take some *v.* 7
19 arise, and eat of my *v.* 31

**VENOM.**

*Deut.* 32:33 wine is *v.* of asps

**VENOMOUS.**

*Acts* 28:4 barbarians saw *v.* beast

**VENT.**

*Job* 32:19 as wine wh. hath no *v.*

**VENTURE.**

1 *K.* 22:34 a certain man drew a bow at a *v.* 2 *Chr.* 18:33

**VERIFIED.**

*Gen.* 42:20 so sh. your words be *v.*
1 *K.* 8:26 and let thy word be *v.* 2 *Chr.* 6:17

**VERILY.**

*Gen.* 42:21 we are *v.* guilty
*Mat.* 5:38 *v.* I say unto you, 6:2, 5, 16; 8:10; 10:15, 23, 42; 11:11; 13:17; 16:28; 17:20; 18:3, 13, 18; 19:23, 28; 21:21, 31; 23:36; 24:2, 34, 47; 25:12, 40, 45; 26:13; *Mark* 3:28; 6:11; 8:12; 9:1, 41; 10:15, 29; 11:23; 12:43; 13:30; 14:9, 18, 25; *Luke* 4:24; 11:51; 12:37; 13:35; 18:17, 29; 21:32
26 *v.* I say unto thee, 26:34; *Mark* 14:30; *Luke* 23:43
*Acts* 22:3 am *v.* a Jew born in T.
1 *Cor.* 5:3 I *v.* as absent in body
*Heb.* 2:16 *v.* he took not nature
1 *John* 2:5 in him *v.* is love of G.

**VERILY, VERILY.**

*John* 1:51 *v. v.* I say unto you, 5:19, 24, 25; 6:26, 32, 47, 53; 8:34, 51, 58; 10:1, 7; 12:24; 13:16, 20, 21; 14:12; 16:20, 23
*John* 3:3 *v. v.* I say unto thee, 5:11; 13:38; 21:18

**VERITY.**

*Ps.* 111:7 works of hands are *v.*
1 *Tim.* 2:7 teach. in faith and *v.*

**VERMILION.**

*Jer.* 22:14 and painted with *v.*
*Ezek.* 23:14 C. portrayed with *v.*

**VERY.**

*Gen.* 27:21 thou be my *v.* son E.
*Ex.* 9:16 in *v.* deed for this I
*Deut.* 30:14 word is *v.* nigh to th.
1 *Sam.* 25:34 in *v.* deed exc. thou
26:4 Saul was come in *v.* deed
*Prov.* 17:9 he separat. *v.* friends
*John* 7:26 this is *v.* Ch. *Acts* 9:22
8:4 taken in adultery, in *v.* act
1 *Thes.* 5:23 *v.* G. of peace sanc.

**VESSEL.**

*Deut.* 23:24 not put any in thy *v.*
1 *Sam.* 21:5 sancti. this day in *v.*
1 *K.* 17:10 fetch me water in *v.*
2 *K.* 4:6 bring *v.* not a *v.* more
*Ps.* 2:9 pieces like a potter's *v.*
31:12 I am like a broken *v.*
*Prov.* 25:4 come forth *v.* for finer
*Is.* 66:20 bring offer. in clean *v.*
*Jer.* 18:4 *v.* mar. in hand of pot.
22:28 *v.* wher. is no pleasure?
25:34 ye sh. fall like a pleas. *v.*
48:11 M. not emptied fr. *v.* to *v.*
38 I have broken M. like a *v.*
51:34 Neb. made me empty *v.*
*Ezek.* 4:9 put them in one *v.* and
15:3 a pin of it to hang any *v.*?
*Hos.* 8:8 *v.* wherein is no pleas.
*Mark* 11:16 carry *v.* thro' temple
*Luke* 8:16 covereth candle wi. *v.*
*Acts* 9:15 a chosen *v.* unto me
10:11 Pe. saw a certain *v.* 11:5
*Rom.* 9:21 make one *v.* to honor
1 *Thes.* 4:4 his *v.* in sanctificati.
2 *Tim.* 2:21 sh. be *v.* to honor
1 *Pet.* 3:7 to wife as to weaker *v.*

**VESSELS.**

*Gen.* 43:11 best fruits in your *v.*
*Ex.* 40:10 anoint *v.* *Lev.* 8:11
*Num.* 18:3 nigh *v.* of sanctuary
1 *Sam.* 9:7 bread spent in our *v.*
21:5 *v.* of young men are holy
2 *K.* 4:3 go, borrow *v.* abroad
2 *Chr.* 29:19 *v.* A. did cast away
*Ezr.* 1:7 Cyrus brought forth *v.*
5:15 take *v.* 7:19 *v.* given thee
*Neh.* 13:9 thither brought I *v.*
*Is.* 18:2 in *v.* of bulrushes
22:24 *v.* of small quantity, *v.* of
52:11 be clean that bear *v.* of L.
65:4 abominable things is in *v.*
*Jer.* 14:3 returned with *v.* empty
27:16 *v.* of L.'s house, 28:3
*Dan.* 5:23 brought *v.* of house
*Hos.* 13:15 treasure of pleas. *v.*
*Hag.* 2:16 dr. fifty *v.* out of press
*Mat.* 13:48 gathered good into *v.*
25:4 but wise took oil in their *v.*
*Rom.* 9:22 *v.* of wr. 23 *v.* of mercy
*Rev.* 2:27 as *v.* of potter be brok.
*See* BRASS, EARTHEN, GOLD, SILVER.

**VESTMENTS.**

2 *K.* 10:22 *v.* for worshippers

**VESTRY.**

2 *K.* 10:22 said to him over *v.*

**VESTURE, S.**

*Gen.* 41:42 arrayed Joseph in *v.*
*Deut.* 22:12 ma. fringe on thy *v.*
*Ps.* 22:18 they cast lots upon my *v.* *Mat.* 27:35; *John* 19:24
102:26 as a *v.* sh. thou change th.
*Heb.* 1:12 as a *v.* sh. thou fold th.
*Rev.* 19:13 clothed with *v.* dipt
16 on his *v.* and thigh a name

**VEX.**

*Ex.* 22:21 and thou shalt not *v.* a stranger, *Lev.* 19:33
*Lev.* 18:18 wife to sister to *v.* her
*Num.* 25:17 *v.* the Midianites
18 they *v.* you with their wiles
33:55 ye let remain sh. *v.* you
2 *Sam.* 12:18 how will he *v.* him.
2 *Chr.* 15:6 God did *v.* them
*Job* 19:2 how long will ye *v.* soul
*Ps.* 2:5 *v.* th. in his displeasure
*Is.* 7:6 let us go ag. J. and *v.* it
11:13 Judah shall not *v.* Ephr.
*Ezek.* 32:9 I will *v.* hearts of peo.
*Hab.* 2:7 not awake that *v.* thee?
*Acts* 12:1 Herod did *v.* the church

**VEXATION, S.**

*Deut.* 28:20 L. sh. send on thee *v.*
2 *Chr.* 15:5 *v.* were on inhabit.
*Ec.* 1:14 *v.* of spirit, 2:11, 17
17 *v.* of spi. 2:26; 4:4, 16; 6:9
2:22 ha. man of *v.* of his heart?
4:6 hands full with *v.* of spirit
*Is.* 9:1 not such as was in her *v.*
28:19 a *v.* to understand report
65:14 ye sh. howl for *v.* of spirit

**VEXED.**

*Num.* 20:15 Egyptians *v.* us and
*Jud.* 2:18 of them that *v.* them
10:8 that year Ammonites *v.* Is.
16:16 his soul was *v.* unto death
1 *Sam.* 14:47 Saul *v.* his enemies
2 *Sam.* 13:2 Amnon *v.* fell sick
2 *K.* 4:27 alone, for his soul is *v.*
*Neh.* 9:27 enemies who *v.* them
*Job* 27:2 Almighty *v.* my soul
*Ps.* 6:2 my bones *v.* 3 soul *v.*
10 let enemies be asha. and *v.*
*Is.* 63:10 they rebelled and *v.* Sp.
*Ezek.* 22:5 infamous and much *v.*
7 *v.* fatherless: 29 *v.* the poor

*Mat.* 15:22 daugh. is *v.* wi. devil
17:15 he is lunatic and sore *v.*
*Luke* 6:18 they that were *v.* with unclean spirits. *Acts* 5:16
2 *Pet.* 2:7 Lot *v.* with conversat.
8 *v.* his righteous soul fr. day

**VIAL.**

1 *Sam.* 10:1 Sam. took a *v.* of oil
*Rev.* 16:2 first angel pour. his *v.*
3 second *v.* on sea; 4 third *v.*
8 fourth *v.* 10 fifth *v.* on beast
12 sixth *v.* 17 sev. *v.* into air

**VIALS.**

*Rev.* 5:8 golden *v.* full of odors
15:7 gave seven angels seven *v.*
16:1 pour out *v.* of wrath of G.
17:1 angels wh. had 7 *v.* 21:9

**VICTORY.**

2 *Sam.* 19:2 *v.* th. day was turn.
23:10 L. wrought a great *v.* 12
1 *Chr.* 29:11 thine, O L. is the *v.*
*Ps.* 98:1 arm hath gotten him *v.*
*Is.* 25:8 will swallow up death in *v.* 1 *Cor.* 15:54
*Mat.* 12:20 send judgm. unto *v.*
1 *Cor.* 15:55 O gra. where thy *v.*?
57 to God, who giv. us the *v.*
1 *John* 5:4 this is the *v.* even fai.
*Rev.* 15:2 had got. *v.* over beast

**VICTUAL, S.**

*Gen.* 14:11 goods of Sod. and *v.*
*Ex.* 12:39 nei. had prepared *v.*
*Lev.* 25:37 nor lend him thy *v.*
*Deut.* 23:19 usury of *v.* of any th.
*Jos.* 1:11 prepare *v.* 9:11 take *v.*
9:14 the men took of their *v.*
*Jud.* 17:10 will gi. apparel and *v.*
1 *Sam.* 22:10 gave *v.* and sword
1 *K.* 4:7 provided *v.* for king, 27
11:18 Pharaoh appointed him *v.*
*Neh.* 10:31 peo. bring *v.* on sab.
13:15 ag. th. in day they sold *v.*
*Jer.* 40:5 capt. gave Jeremiah *v.*
44:17 then had we plenty of *v.*
*Mat.* 14:15 to buy *v.* *Luke* 9:12

**VIEW, ED.**

*Jos.* 2:7 *v.* land; 7:2 *v.* country
7:2 *v.* Ai; *Ezr.* 8:15 *v.* people
2 *K.* 2:7 prophets stood to *v.* 15
*Neh.* 2:13 I *v.* walls of Jerus. 15

**VIGILANT.**

1 *Tim.* 3:2 a bishop must be *v.*
1 *Pet.* 5:8 be *v.* bec. your advers.

**VILE.**

*Deut.* 25:3 lest thy brot. seem *v.*
*Jud.* 19:24 do not so *v.* a thing
1 *Sam.* 3:13 sons made thems. *v.*
15:9 every thing that was *v.*
2 *Sam.* 6:22 I will yet be more *v.*
*Job* 18:3 why are we reputed *v.*?
40:4 I am *v.* what shall I ans.?
*Ps.* 15:4 *v.* person is contemned
*Is.* 32:5 *v.* person be no more
6 *v.* person will speak villany
*Jer.* 15:19 take prec. from the *v.*
29:17 I will make them *v.* figs
*Lam.* 1:11 O L. for I am bec. *v.*
*Dan.* 11:21 sh. stand a *v.* person
*Nah.* 1:14 make grave, th. art *v.*
3:6 cast filth on th. make thee *v.*
*Rom.* 1:26 G. gave them up to *v.*
*Phil.* 3:21 shall change *v.* body
*Jam.* 2:2 a poor man in *v.* raim.

**VILELY.**

2 *Sam.* 1:21 shield *v.* cast away

**VILER, VILEST.**

*Job* 30:8 they were *v.* than earth
*Ps.* 12:8 when *v.* men are exalted

**VILLAGE.**

*Mat.* 21:2 go into *v.* over ag. you, *Mark* 11:2; *Luke* 19:30
*Luke* 24:13 two of th. went to *v.*

**VILLAGES.**

*Lev.* 25:31 houses of *v.* counted
*Jud.* 5:7 inhabitants of *v.* ceased
*Neh.* 6:2 meet in one of the *v.*
*Est.* 9:19 J. of *v.* made 14th day
*Cant.* 7:11 let us lodge in *v.*
*Ezek.* 38:11 to land of unwall. *v.*
*Hab.* 3:14 strike head of his *v.*
*Mat.* 14:15 they may go into the the *v.* and buy, *Mark* 6:36
*See* CITIES.

**VILLANY.**

*Is.* 32:6 vile person will speak *v.*
*Jer.* 29:23 committed *v.* in Israel

**VINE.**

*Gen.* 40:9 a *v.* was before me
10 in *v.* were three branches
49:11 Judah binding his foal to *v.* his ass's colt to choice *v.*
*Lev.* 25:5 nor ga. grapes of *v.* 11
*Num.* 6:4 eat nothing made of *v.*
*Deut.* 32:32 their *v.* is *v.* of Sod.
*Jud.* 9:12 trees said to *v.* reign
13:14 not eat that cometh of *v.*
1 *K.* 4:25 ev. man under his *v.*
2 *K.* 4:39 found a wild *v.* gather.
18:31 eat of own *v.* *Is.* 36:16
*Job* 15:33 sha. off grape as the *v.*
*Ps.* 80:8 hast bro. *v.* out of Eg.
14 look down, and visit this *v.*
128:3 wife sh. be as a fruitful *v.*
*Cant.* 6:11 whe. *v.* flourish. 7:12
7:8 breasts as clusters of the *v.*
*Is.* 5:2 plant. it with choicest *v.*
16:8 *v.* of Sibmah languisheth
9 bewail *v.* of Sib. *Jer.* 48:32
24:7 wine mourneth, *v.* languis.
32:12 sh. lament for fruitful *v.*
34:4 as leaf falleth from the *v.*
*Jer.* 2:21 I planted th. a noble *v.* how turned into strange *v.*?
6:9 glean remnant of Is. as a *v.*
8:13 no grapes on *v.* nor figs
*Ezek.* 15:2 *v.* more th. any tree?
6 *v.* which I have given for fuel
17:6 it became a spreading *v.*
7 *v.* did bend roots towards
19:10 moth. is like *v.* in blood
*Hos.* 10:1 Israel is an empty *v.*
14:7 revive as corn, grow as *v.*
*Joel* 1:7 he laid my *v.* waste
12 *v.* is dried up, the fig-tree
2:22 fig-tree and *v.* yield stren.
*Mic.* 4:4 sit ev. man under his *v.*
*Hag.* 2:19 *v.* hath not bro. forth
*Zec.* 3:10 call ev. man under *v.*
8:12 the *v.* shall give her fruit
*Mal.* 3:11 nei. *v.* cast her fruit
*Mat.* 26:29 not drink of fruit of *v.* *Mark* 14:25; *Luke* 22:18
*John* 15:1 I am the true *v.* 5
4 bear fruit, exc. it abide in *v.*
*Jam.* 3:12 can a *v.* bear figs?
*Rev.* 14:18 ga. clusters of *v.* 19

**VINES.**

*Num.* 20:5 no pl. of *v.* or pomeg.
*Deut.* 8:8 a land of wheat and *v.*
*Ps.* 78:47 he destroyed their *v.*
105:33 smote th. *v.* and fig-trees
*Cant.* 2:13 *v.* give a good smell
15 foxes, that spoil the *v.* our *v.* have tender grapes
*Is.* 7:23 th. were a thousand *v.*
*Jer.* 5:17 they shall eat up thy *v.*
31:5 plant *v.* on mountains
*Hos.* 2:12 I will destroy her *v.*
*Hab.* 3:17 nei. fruit be in the *v.*

**VINE-DRESSERS.**

2 *K.* 25:12 left the poor of land to be *v.-d.* *Jer.* 52:16
2 *Chr.* 26:10 Uzziah had *v.-d.*
*Is.* 61:5 sons of alien your *v.-d.*
*Joel* 1:11 be ashamed, O ye *v.-d.*

**VINEGAR.**

*Num.* 6:3 Naz. shall drink no *v.*
*Ruth* 2:14 dip thy morsel in *v.*
*Ps.* 69:21 gave *v.* *Mat.* 27:34
*Prov.* 10:26 as *v.* to the teeth
25:20 as *v.* upon nitre, so is he
*Mat.* 27:48 took a sponge and filled it with *v.* *Mark* 15:36; *Luke* 23:36; *John* 19:29, 30

**VINEYARD.**

*Gen.* 9:20 Noah planted a *v.* and
*Ex.* 22:5 if cause *v.* to be eaten
23:11 thou sh. deal with thy *v.*
*Lev.* 19:10 shalt not glean thy *v.*
25:3 six years sh. prune thy *v.*
4 nei. sow field, nor prune *v.*
*Deut.* 20:6 what man planted *v.*?
22:9 not sow *v.* with div. seeds
23:24 comest into neighbor's *v.*
24:21 when gather. grapes of *v.*
28:30 plant *v.* not gath. grapes
1 *K.* 21:1 Nabo. had a *v.* hard by
2 give me thy *v.* I will give thee a better *v.* 6
7 I will give thee *v.* of Naboth
*Ps.* 80:15 *v.* thy ri. hand planted
*Prov.* 24:30 I went by *v.* of man
31:16 hand she planteth a *v.*
*Cant.* 1:6 own *v.* have I not kept
8:11 Solomon had a *v.* he let *v.*
12 my *v.* is bef. me, O Solom.
*Is.* 1:8 Z. is left as cottage in *v.*
3:14 for ye have eaten up the *v.*
5:1 my beloved touching his *v.*
7 *v.* of L. of hosts is hou. of Is.
10 ten acres of *v.* yi. one bath
27:2 sing to her, *v.* of red wine
*Jer.* 12:10 pastors destroy. my *v.*
35:7 Rechab. sh. not plant *v.* 9
*Mic.* 1:6 Samaria as plant. of *v.*
*Mat.* 20:1 hire labor. into his *v.*
4 he said, Go ye also into *v.* 7
21:28 go work to-day in my *v.*
33 certain householder planted *v.* *Mark* 12:1; *Luke* 20:9
*Luke* 13:6 fig-tree planted in *v.*
7 said unto dresser of *v.*
1 *Cor.* 9:7 planteth *v.* eat. not?

**VINEYARDS.**

*Num.* 16:14 not giv. inher. of *v.*
20:17 not pass through *v.* 21:22
22:24 angel stood in path of *v.*
*Deut.* 6:11 he swore to give thee *v.* *Jos.* 24:13; *Neh.* 9:25
28:39 shalt plant *v.* dress them
*Jud.* 15:5 the foxes burnt up *v.*
21:20 go and lie in wait in *v.*
1 *Sam.* 8:14 take yo. fields and *v.*
22:7 will son of J. give you *v.*?
2 *K.* 5:26 is it time to receive *v.*?
18:32 I take you to a land of *v.*
19:29 in the third year plant *v.*
1 *Chr.* 27:27 over *v.* was Shimei
*Neh.* 5:3 have mortgaged our *v.*
11 restore *v.* and olive-yards
*Job* 24:18 behold. not way of *v.*
*Ps.* 107:37 sow fields, plant *v.*
*Ec.* 2:4 houses, I planted me *v.*
*Cant.* 1:6 made me keeper of *v.*
14 as cluster of camphire in *v.*
7:12 let us get up early to the *v.*
*Is.* 16:10 in *v.* sh. be no singing
65:21 shall plant *v.* and eat the fruit of them, *Amos* 9:14
*Jer.* 32:15 *v.* sh. be possessed ag.
39:10 Nebuzar-ad. gave poor *v.*
*Ezek.* 28:26 build hous. and pl. *v.*
*Hos.* 2:15 I will give her her *v.*
*Amos* 4:9 palmer-worm devo. *v.*
5:11 ye have planted *v.*
17 in all *v.* shall be wailing
*Zep.* 1:13 sh. plant *v.* not drink

**VINTAGE.**

*Lev.* 26:5 thresh. shall reach to the *v.* the *v.* reach to sowi. time
*Jud.* 8:2 better than *v.* of Abi.?
*Job* 24:6 they gather *v.* of wick.
*Is.* 16:10 made *v.* shout. to cease
24:13 gleaning when *v.* is done
32:10 the *v.* shall fail, gathering
*Jer.* 48:32 spoiler is fallen up. *v.*
*Mic.* 7:1 as grape-gleanings of *v.*

*Zec.* 11:2 for. of *v.* is come down

**VIOL, S.**

*Is.* 5:12 harp and *v.* and wine
14:11 noise of *v.* brought down
*Amos* 5:23 not hear melody of *v.*
6:5 that chant to sound of *v.*

**VIOLATED.**

*Ezek.* 22:26 priests ha. *v.* my law

**VIOLENCE.**

*Gen.* 6:11 earth filled with *v.* 12
*Lev.* 6:2 if lie in thi. taken by *v.*
2 *Sam.* 22:3 savest me from *v.*
*Ps.* 11:5 loveth *v.* his soul hateth
55:9 I have seen *v.* and strife in
58:2 weigh the *v.* of your hands
72:14 shall redeem th. soul fr. *v.*
73:6 *v.* covereth them as a gar.
*Prov.* 4:17 they drink wine of *v.*
10:6 *v.* covereth the mouth, 11
13:2 transgressors shall eat *v.*
28:17 man that doeth *v.* to blood
*Is.* 53:9 he had done no *v.*
59:6 act of *v.* is in their hands
60:18 *v.* shall no more be heard
*Jer.* 6:7 *v.* and spoil heard in her
20:8 I spake, I cried *v.* and spoil
22:3 do no *v.* to the stranger
17 th. eyes, thy heart are for *v.*
51:35 *v.* done to me and flesh
46 *v.* in the land, ruler ag. rul.
*Ezek.* 7:11 *v.* risen up into a rod
23 for the city is full of *v.*
8:17 filled land with *v.* 28:16
12:19 because of the *v.* of them
18:7 spoiled none by *v.* 16, 18
45:9 Israel, remove *v.* and spoil
*Joel* 3:19 Edom a wildern. for *v.*
*Amos* 3:10 store *v.* in palaces
6:3 cause seat of *v.* to come
*Ob.* 10 for *v.* shame shall cover
*Jon.* 3:8 turn every one from *v.*
*Mic.* 2:2 covet fields, take by *v.*
6:12 the rich men are full of *v.*
*Hab.* 1:2 I cry out to thee of *v.*?
3 *v.* bef. me; 9 come all for *v.*
2:8 and for the *v.* of the land
17 *v.* of Leba. cover thee, *v.* of
*Zep.* 1:9 fill mast. houses with *v.*
3:4 her priests have done *v.*
*Mal.* 2:16 covereth *v.* with garm.
*Mat.* 11:12 kingd. of hea. suff. *v.*
*Luke* 3:14 do *v.* to no man, nor
*Acts* 5:26 capt. bro. them with. *v.*
21:35 P. borne of soldiers for *v.*
27:41 was brok. for *v.* of waves
*Heb.* 11:34 quenched *v.* of fire
*Rev.* 18:21 with *v.* shall Babylon

**VIOLENT.**

2 *Sam.* 22:49 hast delivered me from the *v.* man, *Ps.* 18:48
*Ps.* 7:16 his *v.* dealing come on
86:14 assemb. of *v.* men sought
140:1 preserve me fr. *v.* man, 4
11 evil shall hunt the *v.* man
*Prov.* 16:29 *v.* man enticeth neighbor
*Ec.* 5:8 if thou seest *v.* pervert.
*Mat.* 11:12 the *v.* take it by force

**VIOLENTLY.**

*Lev.* 6:4 sh. rest. that he took *v.*
*Deut.* 28:31 ass shall be *v.* taken
*Job* 20:19 hath *v.* taken a house
24:2 they *v.* take away flocks
*Is.* 22:18 will *v.* turn and toss
*Lam.* 2:6 hath *v.* taken away tab.

**VIPER.**

*Job* 20:16 *v.* tongue sh. slay him
*Is.* 30:6 when. come *v.* and serp.
59:5 that is crushed br. into *v.*
*Acts* 28:3 *v.* fasten. on P.'s hand

**VIPERS.**

*Mat.* 3:7 O generation of *v.* 12:34; 23:33; *Luke* 3:7

**VIRGIN.**

*Gen.* 24:16 Rebekah was fair, *v.*
43 when the *v.* cometh to draw
*Lev.* 21:3 a *v.* he may be defiled
14 he shall take a *v.* to wife
*Deut.* 22:19 evil name upon a *v.*
23 *v.* betroth. 28 *v.* not betro.
32:25 destroy young man and *v.*
2 *Sam.* 13:2 sick for Ta. was a *v.*
2 *K.* 19:21 the *v.* the daughter of Zi. laughed to scorn, *Is.* 37:22
*Is.* 7:14 *v.* sh. concei. *Mat.* 1:23
23:12 rejoice, O th. oppressed *v.*
47:1 sit in the dust, O *v.* of Ba.
62:5 as a yo. man marrieth a *v.*
*Jer.* 14:17 the *v.* dau. is broken
18:13 *v.* of Is. ha. done horrible
31:4 shalt be built, O *v.* of Israel
13 then sh. *v.* rejoice in dance
21 turn, O *v.* of Is. to thy citi.
46:11 O *v.* daughter of Egypt
*Lam.* 1:15 L. hath trod. *v.* of Ju.
2:13 comfort thee, O *v.* of Zion
*Joel* 1:8 lament like a *v.* girded
*Amos* 5:2 *v.* of Israel is fallen
*Luke* 1:27 angel was sent to a *v.*
1 *Cor.* 7:28 if a *v.* marry, not sin.
34 difference betw. wife and *v.*
37 that he will keep his *v.*
2 *Cor.* 11:2 pres. you as chaste *v.*

**VIRGINS.**

2 *Sam.* 13:18 were king's dau. *v.*
*Ps.* 45:14 *v.* her companions
*Cant.* 1:3 theref. do *v.* love thee
6:8 queens, *v.* without number
*Is.* 23:4 nor do I bring up *v.*
*Lam.* 1:4 her *v.* are afflicted
18 *v.* are gone into captivity
2:10 *v.* of Jer. hang their heads
21 *v.* and yo. men are fallen
*Amos* 8:13 that day shall *v.* faint
*Mat.* 25:1 heaven is lik. to ten *v.*
*Acts* 21:9 daught. *v.* prophesied
1 *Cor.* 7:25 concern. *v.* I have not
*Rev.* 14:4 not defiled, they are *v.*

**Young VIRGINS.**

*Jud.* 21:12 were four hund. *y. v.*
1 *K.* 1:2 sought for king a *y. v.*
*Est.* 2:2 fair *y. v.* sou. for king
3 gather together the fair *y. v.*

**VIRGINITY.**

*Lev.* 21:13 take a wife in her *v.*
*Deut.* 22:15 bring tok. of *v.* 17, 20
*Jud.* 11:37 may bewail my *v.* 38
*Ezek.* 23:3 bruised teats of *v.* 8
*Luke* 2:36 A. lived 7 years fr. *v.*

**VIRTUE.**

*Mark* 5:30 *v.* had gone out of him, *Luke* 6:19; 8:46
*Phil.* 4:8 if there be any *v.*
2 *Pet.* 1:3 called us to glo. and *v.*
5 add to faith *v.* to *v.* knowl.

**VIRTUOUS, LY.**

*Ruth* 3:11 thou art a *v.* woman
*Prov.* 12:4 a *v.* wom. is a crown
31:10 who can find a *v.* wom.?
29 many daugh. have done *v.*

**VISAGE.**

*Is.* 52:14 his *v.* was marred
*Lam.* 4:8 *v.* is blacker th. a coal
*Dan.* 3:19 form of *v.* changed

**VISIBLE.**

*Col.* 1:16 all things created, *v.*

**VISION.**

*Num.* 24:4 *v.* of Almighty, 16
1 *Sam.* 3:1 there was no open *v.*
15 S. feared to show Eli the *v.*
2 *Sam.* 7:17 accord. to this *v.* did Nathan speak, 1 *Chr.* 17:15
2 *Chr.* 32:32 written in *v.* of Isa.
*Job* 20:8 be chased away as a *v.*
*Ps.* 89:19 spakest in *v.* to H. O.
*Prov.* 29:18 wh. no *v.* peo. perish
*Is.* 1:1 the *v.* of Isa. son of Amoz
21:2 a grievous *v.* is declared
22:1 burden of valley of *v.* 5
28:7 they err in *v.* stumble in
29:7 be as a dream of a night *v.*
11 *v.* is become as a book seal.
*Jer.* 14:14 they proph. a false *v.*
23:16 sp. a *v.* of their own heart
*Lam.* 2:9 proph. find no *v.* fr. L.
*Ezek.* 7:13 *v.* is touching whole
26 they seek a *v.* of prophet
8:4 according to *v.* 11:24; 43:3
12:22 days are prolonged *v.* fail.
23 the effect of ev. *v.* is at hand
24 no more vain *v.* nor divina.
27 *v.* he seeth is for days
13:7 ha. ye not seen a vain *v.*?
*Dan.* 2:19 revealed to D. in a *v.*
7:2 in my *v.* four winds strove
8:1 a *v.* appeared unto me
16 make this man understa. *v.*
26 shut up *v.* 27 astonish. at *v.*
9:21 whom I had seen in *v.* 23
10:1 he had understanding of *v.*
7 I saw *v.* men saw not *v.* 8
14 yet the *v.* is for many days
16 by *v.* my sorrows are turn.
11:14 exalt themsel. to estab. *v.*
*Ob.* 1 the *v.* of Obadiah
*Mic.* 3:6 ye shall not have a *v.*
*Nah.* 1:1 book of *v.* of Nahum
*Hab.* 2:2 write *v.* make it plain
3 *v.* is for an appointed time
*Zec.* 13:4 prophets asha. of his *v.*
*Mat.* 17:9 tell the *v.* to no man
*Luke* 1:22 perc. he had seen a *v.*
24:23 had seen a *v.* of angels
*Acts* 10:17 Peter doubted of *v.* 19
11:5 I saw a *v.* a vessel descend
12:9 but thought he saw a *v.*
16:9 *v.* appeared to Paul, 18:9
26:19 I was not disobedi. to *v.*
*Rev.* 9:17 I saw horses in the *v.*

**In a VISION.**

*Gen.* 15:1 L. came to Ab. *in a v.*
*Num.* 12:6 make myself kn. *in v.*
*Ezek.* 11:24 brought me *in a v.*
*Dan.* 8:2 I saw *in a v.* by river
*Acts* 9:10 to An. said L. *in a v.*
12 S. hath seen *in a v.* a man
10:3 Cor. saw *in a v.* an angel

**VISIONS.**

*Gen.* 46:2 God spake to Is. in *v.*
2 *Chr.* 9:29 written in *v.* of Iddo
26:5 Z. had understanding in *v.*
*Job* 4:13 thoughts fr. *v.* of night
7:14 thou terrifiest me thro' *v.*
*Ezek.* 1:1 I saw the *v.* of God
8:3 he bro. me in *v.* of G. to J.
13:16 which see *v.* of peace
40:2 in *v.* bro. he me to land of
*Dan.* 1:17 D. had underst. in *v.*
2:28 *v.* of thy head on thy bed
4:5 *v.* of my head troubled me
7:1 D. had *v.* of his head upon
7 I saw in night *v.* behold, 13
15 *v.* of my head troubled me
*Hos.* 12:10 I have multiplied *v.*
*Joel* 2:28 shall see *v.* *Acts* 2:17
2 *Cor.* 12:1 come to *v.* and revela.

**VISIT.**

*Gen.* 50:24 will *v.* 25; *Ex.* 13:19
*Ex.* 32:34 when I *v.* I will *v.* sin
*Lev.* 18:25 I do *v.* iniq. thereof
*Job* 5:24 shalt *v.* thy habitation
7:18 that thou shouldest *v.* him
*Ps.* 59:5 awake, to *v.* the heath.
80:14 look down and *v.* this vine
89:32 th. will I *v.* transgression
106:4 O *v.* me wi. thy salvation
*Is.* 23:17 the Lord will *v.* Tyre
*Jer.* 3:16 they shall *v.* ark of L.
*Jer.* 5:9 shall I not *v.*? 29; 9:9
6:15 *v.* them, shall be cast down
14:10 rememb. iniq. and *v.* sins
15:15 thou kno. remem. and *v.*
23:2 *v.* on you evil of doings
27:22 there sh. they be till I *v.*
29:10 *v.* you and perf. my word

32:5 th. shall he be till I *v.* him
49:8 will *v.* Esau; 50:31 *v.* Baby.
*Lam.* 4:22 he will *v.* thine iniq.
*Hos.* 2:13 *v.* on her days of Baal.
8:13 now will he *v.* th. sins, 9:9
*Amos* 3:14 I will *v.* alt. of Beth-el
*Zep.* 2:7 L. shall *v.* turn captiv.
*Zec.* 11:16 not *v.* th. that be cut
*Acts* 7:23 into heart to *v.* his br.
15:14 decla. how G. did *v.* Gent.
36 let us go and *v.* our breth.
*Jam.* 1:27 *v.* fatherl. and widows

**VISITATION.**

*Num.* 16:29 if visi. aft. *v.* of men
*Job* 10:12 thy *v.* preser. my spir.
*Is.* 10:3 what do in day of *v.*?
*Jer.* 8:12 in time of *v.* cast down
10:15 in time of *v.* perish, 51:18
11:23 in year of *v.* 23:12; 48:44
46:21 time of th. *v.* come, 50:27
*Hos.* 9:7 the days of *v.* are come
*Mic.* 7:4 thy *v.* cometh, perplex.
*Luke* 19:44 knew. not time of *v.*
1 *Pet.* 2:12 glorify G. in day of *v.*

**VISITED.**

*Gen.* 21:1 Lord *v.* Sar. as he said
*Ex.* 3:16 I have surely *v.* you
4:31 heard that Lord had *v.* Is.
*Num.* 16:29 if th. be *v.* aft. visit.
*Ruth* 1:6 heard how L. *v.* people
1 *Sam.* 2:21 the Lord *v.* Hannah
*Job* 35:15 he hath *v.* in his anger
*Ps.* 17:3 thou hast *v.* me, thou
*Prov.* 19:23 sh. not be *v.* wi. evil
*Is.* 24:22 after many days be *v.*
26:14 theref. hast thou *v.* them
16 Lord in trouble have they *v.*
29:6 thou sh. be *v.* with thund.
*Jer.* 6:6 Jerusal. is city to be *v.*
23:2 scattered flock, not *v.* th.
*Ezek.* 38:8 after many days be *v.*
*Zec.* 10:3 L. of hosts *v.* his flock
*Mat.* 25:36 *v.* me; 43 *v.* me not
*Luke* 1:68 *v.* and redeemed peop.
78 the day-spring hath *v.* us
7:16 God hath *v.* his people

**VISITEST, ETH, ING.**

*Ex.* 20:5 *v.* iniquity of fathers, 34:7; *Num.* 14:18; *Deut.* 5:9
*Job* 31:14 *v.* what sh. I answer?
*Ps.* 8:4 thou *v.* him, *Heb.* 2:6
65:9 thou *v.* earth, waterest it

**VOCATION.**

*Eph.* 4:1 walk worthy of the *v.*

**VOICE.**

*Gen.* 4:10 *v.* of thy broth.'s blood
27:22 *v.* is Jacob's *v.* but hands
39:15 heard that I lift. up my *v.*
*Ex.* 4:8 believe *v.* of latter sign
19:19 God answered him by a *v.*
23:21 bewa. of him, obey his *v.*
24:3 people answer. with one *v.*
32:18 is not *v.* of th. that shout
*Lev.* 5:1 if soul hear *v.* of swear.
*Num.* 14:1 congr. lifted their *v.*
*Deut.* 4:30 if thou be obedi. to *v.*
8:20 would not be obedi. to *v.*
*Jos.* 6:10 nor make noise wi. *v.*
*Jud.* 18:3 they knew *v.* of Levite
1 *Sam.* 24:16 is this thy *v.* my son David? 26:17
2 *Sam.* 22:14 M. High uttered *v.*
1 *K.* 18:26 was no *v.* nor any, 29
19:12 after fire a still small *v.*
2 *K.* 4:31 neither *v.* nor hearing
7:10 there was no *v.* of man
19:22 ag. wh. exalt. *v.*? *Is.* 37:23
1 *Chr.* 15:16 lifting up *v.* wi. joy
*Job* 2:12 Job's friends lift. up *v.*
3:7 let no joyful *v.* come there
30:31 the *v.* of them that weep
37:4 a *v.* roareth, he thundereth
5 God thundereth with his *v.*
40:9 thund. with a *v.* like him?
*Ps.* 18:13 the Highest gave his *v.*
26:7 publish with *v.* of thanksg.
31:22 heardest *v.* of supplicati.
42:4 went to house of G. wi. *v.*
44:16 *v.* of him th. reproacheth
46:6 uttered his *v.* earth melted
47:1 shout to G. wi. *v.* of trium.
66:19 attend. to *v.* of my prayer
68:33 send. out *v.* th. a mighty *v.*
74:23 forget not *v.* of enemies
77:1 cried unto L. with *v.* 142:1
18 *v.* of thy thunder in heaven
86:6 attend to *v.* of my suppli.
93:3 floods have lifted up th. *v.*
98:5 sing to L. with *v.* of psalm
*Ps.* 102:5 by reas. of *v.* of groan.
103:20 hearkening to *v.* of word
104:7 at *v.* of thund. th. hasted
118:15 *v.* of rejoic. in tabernac.
141:1 give ear to my *v.*
*Prov.* 1:20 uttereth *v.* in streets
2:3 if liftest up *v.* for understa.
5:13 not obeyed *v.* of my teach.
8:1 understand. put forth her *v.*
4 my *v.* is to sons of men
*Ec.* 5:3 a fool's *v.* is known by
6 sho. G. be angry at thy *v.*?
10:20 bird of air sh. carry the *v.*
12:4 he shall rise at *v.* of bird
*Cant.* 2:8 the *v.* of my beloved
12 *v.* of turtle is heard in land
5:2 it is *v.* of beloved knocketh
*Is.* 6:4 posts moved at *v.* of him
13:2 exalt the *v.* shake the hand
29:4 *v.* as one that hath a spirit
30:19 graci. to thee at *v.* of cry
31:4 lion not afraid of their *v.*
40:3 *v.* th. crieth in wilder. *Mat.* 3:3; *Mark* 1:3; *Luke* 3:4.
6 *v.* said, Cry; 48:20 *v.* of sing.
50:10 obeyeth *v.* of his servant
51:3 thanksgiving, *v.* of melody
52:8 wi. *v.* together sh. th. sing
65:19 *v.* of weeping shall be no more heard, nor *v.* of crying
66:6 a *v.* of noise, a *v.* fr. temp.
*Jer.* 4:15 *v.* declareth from Dan
16 give their *v.* ag. cities of J.
6:23 *v.* roareth like sea, 50:42
7:34 *v.* of mirth, *v.* of gladness, *v.* of the bridegroom, 16:9; 25:10; 33:11
8:19 *v.* of cry of dau. of people
10:13 when he uttereth *v.* 51:16
25:36 a *v.* of cry of shepherds
30:19 *v.* of th. that make merry
31:15 a *v.* was heard in Ram. 16
46:22 *v.* thereof go like a serp.
48:3 a *v.* of crying from Horon.
50:28 *v.* of them that flee
51:55 destro. out of her great *v.*
*Ezek.* 1:24 I heard *v.* of Almighty
10:5 as the *v.* of Almighty God
23:42 a *v.* of multitude at ease
33:32 one that hath a pleas. *v.*
43:2 *v.* li. noise of wat. *Rev.* 1:15
*Dan.* 4:31 there fell *v.* fr. heaven
6:20 cried with a lamentable *v.*
10:6 *v.* of words like *v.* of mult.
*Joel* 2:11 L. utter *v.* before army
3:16 utter *v.* from J. *Amos* 1:2
*Jon.* 2:9 with *v.* of thanksgiving
*Nah.* 2:7 lead as with *v.* of doves
*Mat.* 3:17 a *v.* fr. heaven, *Mark* 1:11; *Luke* 3:22
17:5 a *v.* out of cloud, this is my S. *Mark* 9:7; *Lu.* 9:35, 36
*Luke* 1:44 *v.* of saluta. sounded
*John* 1:23 *v.* of one cry. in wild.
10:4 follow, for they kn. his *v.*
5 know not *v.* of strangers
12:28 then came a *v.* saying, I
30 *v.* came not because of me
18:37 that is of truth hear. my *v.*
*Acts* 9:7 hear. *v.* seeing no man
10:13 a *v.* say. Rise, 15; 11:9
12:14 when she knew Peter's *v.*
22 it is *v.* of a god, not of man
19:34 with *v.* cried, Great is Di.
24:21 exc. it be for this one *v.*
26:10 I gave my *v.* again. them
1 *Cor.* 14:11 know not mean of *v.*
19 by my *v.* I might teach oth.
*Gal.* 4:20 I des. to change my *v.*
1 *Thes.* 4:16 with *v.* of archangel
*Heb.* 12:26 whose *v.* shook earth
2 *Pet.* 1:17 *v.* fr. excellent glory
2:16 ass speaking with man's *v.*
*Rev.* 1:12 I turned to see the *v.*
16:17 there came a great *v.*

**VOICE,** *with* **hear.**

*Gen.* 4:23 *hear* my *v.* ye wives
*Deut.* 4:33 did people *h.* *v.* of G.
36 he made thee to *hear* his *v.*
5:25 if we *h.* *v.* of God, we die
33:7 *hear*, Lord, the *v.* of Judah
2 *Sam.* 19:35 I *h.* *v.* of singing?
22:7 did *h.* my *v.* out of temple
*Job* 3:18 *h.* not *v.* of oppressor
37:2 *h.* attentive. noise of his *v.*
*Ps.* 5:3 my *v.* shalt thou *hear*
27:7 *hear*, O Lord, when I cry wi. my *v.* 28:2; 64:1; 119:149; 130:2; 140:6
55:3 *h.* because of *v.* of enemy
17 cry aloud, he shall *h.* my *v.*
95:7 to-day if ye will *hear* his *v.* *Heb.* 3:7, 15; 4:7
*Cant.* 2:14 let me *h.* *v.* sweet *v.*
*Is.* 32:9 *h.* my *v.* ye careless dau.
*Jer.* 9:10 can men *h.* *v.* of cattle
*Mat.* 12:19 neither any *h.* his *v.*
*John* 5:25 dead *h.* *v.* of Son, 28
10:3 sheep *hear* his *v.* 16, 27
*Acts* 22:14 should. *h.* *v.* of mouth
*Rev.* 3:29 if any man *hear* my *v.*
*See* HEARD.

**VOICE,** *with* **hearken, ed.**

*Gen.* 3:17 hast *h.* to *v.* of wife
16:2 Abram *h.* to the *v.* of Sarai
*Ex.* 3:18 they shall *h.* to thy *v.*
4:8 nor *h.* to *v.* of the first sign
15:26 if diligently *h.* to *v.* of L.
18:19 *h.* to my *v.* I give counsel
24 and Moses *h.* to *v.* of Jethro
*Num.* 14:22 they have not *h.* to my *v.* *Deut.* 9:23; 28:45
21:3 Lord *h.* to the *v.* of Israel
*Deut.* 1:45 L. would not *h.* to *v.*
15:5 if thou carefully *h.* to *v.* of L. 26:17; 28:1, 2; 30:10
28:15 if th. wilt not *h.* to *v.* of L.
*Jos.* 10:14 L. *h.* to *v.* of a man
*Jud.* 2:20 people not *h.* to my *v.*
13:9 God *h.* to *v.* of Manoah
20:13 B. would not *h.* to *v.* of Is.
1 *Sam.* 2:25 *h.* not to *v.* of father
8:7 *h.* to the *v.* of people, 9:22
12:1 I have *h.* to your *v.* in all
25:35 go in peace, I *h.* to thy *v.*
28:22 *h.* thou to *v.* of thy hand.
2 *Sam.* 12:18 wo. not *h.* to our *v*
2 *K.* 10:6 if ye will *h.* to my *v.*
*Job* 9:16 beli. he had *h.* to my *v.*
34:16 *hearken* to *v.* of my words
*Ps.* 5:2 *h.* to the *v.* of my cry
58:5 not *h.* to *v.* of charmers
81:11 peo. would not *h.* to my *v.*
*Cant.* 8:13 compan. *h.* to thy *v.*
*Jer.* 18:19 *h.* to *v.* of them that
*See* LIFT, LORD, LOUD, OBEY, OBEYED.

**VOICES.**

*Luke* 17:13 lepers lifted up th. *v.*
23:23 the *v.* of priests prevailed
*Acts* 13:27 knew not *v.* of proph.
22:22 lift up their *v.* and said
1 *Cor.* 14:10 so many *v.* in world
*Rev.* 4:5 throne proceed. *v.* 16:18
8:5 into earth, and there were *v.*
13 by rea. of other *v.* of trump.
10:3 seven thunders uttered *v.* 4
11:15 there were *v.* in heaven
19 temple opened, th. were *v.*

**VOID.**
*Gen.* 1:2 earth with. form and *v.*
*Num.* 30:12 husb. made th. *v.* 15
*Deut.* 32:28 people *v.* of counsel
1 *K.* 22:10 in *v.* place. 2 *Chr.* 18:9
*Ps.* 89:39 made *v.* the covenant
119:126 have made *v.* thy law
*Prov.* 11:12 *v.* of wisd. despiseth
*Is.* 55:11 word not ret. to me *v.*
*Jer.* 4:23 earth with. form and *v.*
19:7 I will make *v.* counsel of J.
*Nah.* 2:10 Nineveh is empty, *v.*
*Acts* 24:16 conscien. *v.* of offence
*Rom.* 3:31 do we make *v.* law?
4:14 be heirs, faith is made *v.*
1 *Cor.* 9:15 make my glorying *v.*
*See* UNDERSTANDING.

**VOLUME.**
*Ps.* 40:7 in *v.* is writ. *Heb.* 10:7

**VOLUNTARY.**
*Lev.* 1:3 off. it of his own *v.* will
7:16 a *v.* offering shall be eaten
*Ezek.* 46:12 prepare *v.* burnt-off.
*Col.* 2:18 a *v.* humility, worship

**VOLUNTARILY.**
*Ezek.* 46:12 prepare offerings *v.*

**VOMIT, ED, ETH.**
*Lev.* 18:25 land *v.* inhabitants
*Job* 20:15 swallo. riches, *v.* them
*Prov.* 23:8 morsel eaten shalt *v.*
25:16 filled with honey and *v.* it
*Jon.* 2:10 the fish *v.* out Jonah

**VOMIT, Substantive.**
*Prov.* 26:11 dog return. to his *v.*
*Is.* 19:14 man stagger. in his *v.*
28:8 tables are full of *v.* filthin.
*Jer.* 48:26 Moab sh. wallow in *v.*
2 *Pet.* 2:22 dog is turned to his *v.*

**VOW.**
*Gen.* 28:20 Ja. vowed a *v.* 31:13
*Lev.* 7:16 sacri. be a *v.* 22:18, 21
27:2 wh. man make singular *v.*
*Num.* 6:2 when a man vow a *v.*
5 days of *v.* 21 according to *v.*
21:2 Israel vowed a *v.* to Lord
30:2 if man vow *v.* 3 wo. vow *v.*
9 every *v.* of widow shall stand
13 every *v.* her husband may
*Deut.* 23:18 br. price of dog for *v.*
21 when thou shalt vow a *v.*
*Jud.* 11:30 Jephthah vowed a *v.*
39 did wi. her according to *v.*
1 *Sam.* 1:11 Hannah vowed a *v.*
21 Elka. went to offer L. his *v.*
2 *Sam.* 15:7 let go and pay my *v.*
8 thy servant vowed a *v.* at G.
*Ps.* 65:1 to thee *v.* be performed
*Ec.* 5:4 when thou vowest a *v.*
*Is.* 19:21 they sh. vow a *v.* to L.
*Acts* 18:18 head, for he had a *v.*
21:23 which have a *v.* on them

**VOWS.**
*Lev.* 22:18 off. oblation for his *v.*
23:38 and beside all your *v.*
*Num.* 29:39 th. do beside your *v.*
30:5 not any of *v.* stand, 8, 12
*Deut.* 12:6 thi. bring *v.* 11, 17, 26
*Job* 22:27 thou shalt pay thy *v.*
*Ps.* 22:25 I will pay my *v.* 66:13; 116:14, 18
50:14 pay *v.* 56:12 *v.* are on me
61:5 th. O G. hast heard my *v.*
8 that I may daily perf. my *v.*
*Prov.* 7:14 this day I paid my *v.*
20:25 snare after *v.* to make inq.
31:2 what the son of my *v.*?
*Jer.* 44:25 will surely perf. our *v.*
*Jon.* 1:16 men fear. L. made *v.*
*Nah.* 1:15 keep feasts, perform *v.*

**VOW, EST, ETH.**
*Num.* 6:2 sepa. themselves to *v.*
*Deut.* 23:22 if forbear to *v.* no sin
*Ps.* 76:11 *v.* and pay to the Lord
*Ec.* 5:4 when thou *v.* a vow
5 better thou shouldest not *v.*
*Mal.* 1:14 *v.* to L. corrupt thing

**VOWED.**
*Gen.* 28:20 Jacob *v.* a vow, 31:13
*Lev.* 27:8 accord. to ability th. *v.*
*Num.* 6:21 law of N. who hath *v.*
21:2 Is. *v.* a vow to L. and said
30:6 a husband when she *v.* 10
*Deut.* 23:23 accord. as th. hast *v.*
*Jud.* 11:30 Jephthah *v.* a vow
*Ps.* 132:2 *v.* to the mighty God
*Ec.* 5:4 pay th. wh. thou hast *v.*
*Jon.* 2:9 I will pay that that I *v.*

**VOYAGE.**
*Acts* 27:10 *v.* will be with hurt

**VULTURE.**
*Lev.* 11:14 the *v.* and kite, *Deut.* 14:13
*Job* 28:7 path *v.* eye ha. not seen
*Is.* 34:15 there sh. *v.* be gathered

# W

**WAFER, S.**
*Ex.* 16:31 the taste was like *w.*
29:2 *w.* unleav. anoint. with oil
23 *w.* out of basket, *Lev.* 8:26
*Lev.* 2:4 *w.* anointed with oil, 7:12; *Num.* 6:15
*Num.* 6:19 one *w.* on hands of N.

**WAG.**
*Jer.* 18:16 passeth sh. *w.* head
*Lam.* 2:15 *w.* heads at dau. of J.
*Zep.* 2:15 ev. one passeth sh. *w.*

**WAGES.**
*Gen.* 29:15 wh. shall thy *w.* be?
30:28 app. thy *w.* I will give it
31:7 changed my *w.* ten tim. 41
8 the speckled shall be thy *w.*
*Ex.* 2:9 child, I will gi. thee *w.*
*Lev.* 19:13 *w.* of hired not abide
*Jer.* 22:13 neigh.'s serv. with. *w.*
*Ezek.* 29:18 had no *w.* nor army
19 her spoil sh. be *w.* for army
*Hag.* 1:6 earn. *w.* to put into bag
*Mal.* 3:5 oppress hireling in *w.*
*Luke* 3:14 be cont. with your *w.*
*John* 4:36 that reapeth receiv. *w.*
*Rom.* 6:23 the *w.* of sin is death
2 *Cor.* 11:8 taking *w.* of them
2 *Pet.* 2:15 B. lov. *w.* of unright.

**WAGGING.**
*Mat.* 27:39 th. passed by reviled him, *w.* heads, *Mark* 15:29

**WAGON, S.**
*Gen.* 45:19 take *w.* out of Eg. 21
27 Jacob saw *w.* Jos. had sent
*Num.* 7:3 *w.* for two of princes
7 two *w.* 4 oxen to sons of G. 8
*Ezek.* 23:24 come ag. th. with *w.*

**WAIL, ED.**
*Ezek.* 32:18 *w.* for multit. of Eg.
*Mic.* 1:8 I will *w.* and howl
*Mark* 5:38 he seeth them th. *w.*
*Rev.* 1:7 kindr. of earth shall *w.*

**WAILING.**
*Est.* 4:3 whi. decree came was *w.*
*Jer.* 9:10 for mount. will I ta. *w.*
18 let them take up *w.* for us
19 a voice of *w.* heard out of Z.
20 teach your daughters *w.*
*Ezek.* 7:11 neither be *w.* for them
*Ezek.* 27:31 they sh. weep wi. *w.*
*Amos* 5:16 *w.* sh. be in all streets
17 in all vineyards shall be *w.*
*Mic.* 1:8 I will make *w.* like dra.
*Mat.* 13:42 *w.* and gna. teeth, 50
*Rev.* 18:15 merchants stand *w.* 19

**WAIT, Noun.**
*Num.* 35:20 if hurl by lay. of *w.*
22 cast on him with. laying *w.*
*Jer.* 9:8 in his heart he lay. his *w.*

**WAIT, Verb.**
*Num.* 3:10 Aa. and sons shall *w.* on priest's office, 8:24; 1 *Chr.* 23:28; 2 *Chr.* 5:11; 13:10
2 *K.* 6:33 sho. I *w.* for the L.?
*Job* 14:14 I will *w.* till change
17:13 if I *w.* grave is my house
*Ps.* 25:3 let none that *w.* 69:6
5 on thee do I *w.* all the day
21 preserve me, for I *w.* on th.
27:14 *w.* on the Lord, 37:34; *Prov.* 20:22
37:7 *w.* patiently; 52:9 will *w.*
9 that *w.* on Lord shall inherit
39:7 *w.* I for; 62:5 *w.* on God
56:6 when they *w.* for my soul
59:9 bec. of strength will I *w.*
69:3 mine eyes fail while I *w.*
104:27 th. *w.* upon thee, 145:15
123:2 our eyes *w.* on the L. God
130:5 I *w.* for Lord, soul doth *w.*
*Is.* 8:17 I will *w.* on the Lord
30:18 L. *w.* to be graci. blessed are they that *w.* for him
40:31 th. *w.* on L. shall renew
42:4 isles shall *w.* for his law
49:23 not asham. that *w.* for me
51:5 the isles shall *w.* upon me
59:9 we *w.* for light, but behold
60:9 the isles shall *w.* for me
*Jer.* 14:22 we will *w.* upon thee
*Lam.* 3:25 L. good to them th. *w.*
26 a man hope and quietly *w.*
*Hos.* 6:9 as troops of robbers *w.*
12:6 keep mercy and *w.* on God
*Mic.* 7:7 I will *w.* for God
*Hab.* 2:3 tarry, *w.* for it, it will
*Zep.* 3:8 *w.* upon me, saith Lord
*Mark* 3:9 small ship would *w.*
*Luke* 12:36 like men that *w.*
*Acts* 1:4 *w.* for promise of Father
*Rom.* 8:25 we with patience *w.*
12:7 let us *w.* on our ministeri.
1 *Cor.* 9:13 which *w.* at the altar
*Gal.* 5:5 we through the Sp. *w.*
1 *Thes.* 1:10 and to *w.* for his Son
*See* LAY, LAID, LYING.

**WAITED.**
*Gen.* 49:18 I ha. *w.* for thy salva.
1 *K.* 20:38 prophet *w.* for king
2 *K.* 5:2 maid *w.* on Naa.'s wife
1 *Chr.* 6:32 they *w.* on office, 33
*Neh.* 12:44 priests and L. that *w.*
*Job* 6:19 companies of Sheba *w.*
15:22 he is *w.* for of the sword
29:21 to me men gave ear, *w.*
23 *w.* for me as for the rain
30:26 I *w.* for light, dark. came
32:4 Elihu *w.* till J. had spoken
*Ps.* 40:1 I *w.* patiently for Lord
106:13 they *w.* not for counsel
119:95 wicked have *w.* for me
*Is.* 25:9 our God, we *w.* for him
26:8 in way of judg. have we *w.*
33:2 be gracious, we *w.* for thee
*Ezek.* 19:5 saw that she had *w.*
*Mic.* 1:12 inhabit. of Maroth *w.*
*Zec.* 11:11 poor of flock that *w.*
*Luke* 1:21 peo. *w.* for Zacharias
*Acts* 10:7 Corn. called sol. th. *w.*
17:16 while P. *w.* his spirit was

*1 Pet.* 3:20 long-suffer. of G. *w.*

**WAITETH.**

*Job* 24:15 eye of the adulterer *w.*
*Ps.* 33:20 our soul *w.* for Lord
62:1 my soul *w.* upon G. 130:6
65:1 praise *w.* for thee, O God
*Prov.* 27:18 he that *w.* on master
*Is.* 64:4 prepared for him that *w.*
*Dan.* 12:12 blessed is he that *w.*
*Mic.* 5:7 as showers that *w.* not
*Rom.* 8:19 *w.* for manifestation
*Jam.* 5:7 husbandman *w.* for fru.

**WAITING.**

*Num.* 8:25 fr. age of 50 cease *w.*
*Prov.* 8:34 *w.* at gates, *w.* posts
*Luke* 2:25 Simeon *w.* for consol.
*John* 5:3 *w.* for moving of water
*Rom.* 8:23 we ourselv. groan, *w.*
*1 Cor.* 1:7 *w.* for coming of our L.
*2 Thes.* 3:5 into patient *w.* for C.

**WAKE, ED.**

*Ps.* 139:18 when I *w.* I am still
*Jer.* 51:39 perp. sleep and not *w.*
*Joel* 3:9 *w.* up the mighty men
*Zec.* 4:1 angel came and *w.* me
*1 Thes.* 5:10 whether *w.* or sleep

**WAKENED, ETH.**

*Is.* 50:4 *w.* morning by morning, he *w.* mine ear to hear
*Joel* 3:12 let heathen be *w.* and
*Zec.* 4:1 as a man that is *w.*

**WAKETH, ING.**

*Ps.* 77:4 th. holdest mine eyes *w.*
127:1 watchman *w.* in vain
*Cant.* 5:2 I sleep but my hea. *w.*

**WALK, Verb.**

*Gen.* 24:40 L. before whom I *w.*
48:15 bef. wh. my fathers did *w.*
*Ex.* 16:4 wheth. *w.* in law or no
18:20 way wherein th. must *w.*
21:19 if he *w.* abroad, that smote
*Lev.* 18:3 nor *w.* in ordin. 20:23
26:3 if ye *w.* in my statut. 1 *K.* 6:12; *Ezek.* 33:15; *Zec.* 3:7
12 I will *w.* am. you, be yo. G.
21 if *w.* contrary to me, 23, 27
24 I *w.* contrary to you, 28
*Deut.* 5:33 shall *w.* in ways of L. 13:4; 28:9; *Ezek.* 37:24
8:19 if ye *w.* after other gods ye
29:19 I *w.* in imagina. of heart
*Jos.* 22:5 take heed *w.* in ways
*Jud.* 5:10 ye that *w.* by the way
*1 Sam.* 2:30 house sh. *w.* bef. me
35 sh. *w.* before mine anointed
8:5 thy sons *w.* not in thy ways
*1 K.* 3:14 if wilt *w.* to keep my comman. as Da. did *w.* 8.25; 9:4; 11:38; 2 *Chr.* 7:17
8:23 servants that *w.* before thee, 2 *Chr.* 6:14
36 teach them way wherein they should *w.* 2 *Chr.* 6:27
*Ps.* 12:8 wicked *w.* on every side
23:4 though I *w.* thro' the val.
26:11 will *w.* in mine integrity
56:13 may *w.* before G. in light
82:5 they *w.* on in darkness
84:11 no good fr. th. th. *w.* upr.
86:11 L. I will *w.* in thy truth
89:15 sh. *w.* in light of counten.
30 child. *w.* not in my judgm.
101:2 will *w.* in house with per.
115:7 feet have they, but *w.* not
116:9 I will *w.* before the Lord
119:3 do no iniquity, *w.* in ways
45 I will *w.* at liberty, I seek
138:7 I walk in midst of trouble
143:8 cause me kn. way I sh. *w.*
*Prov.* 2:7 buckler to th. that *w.*
20 may. *w.* in way of good men
3:23 then sh. thou *w.* in thy way
*Is.* 2:3 *w.* in his paths; *Mic.* 4:2
5 let us *w.* in light of the Lord
3:16 *w.* with stretched necks
8:11 not *w.* in way of this peo.
35:9 the redeemed sh. *w.* there
40:31 that wait on L. shall *w.*
42:5 giv. spirit to them that *w.*
24 would not *w.* in his ways
59:9 but we *w.* in darkness
*Jer.* 3:17 nor *w.* aft. imagination
18 Judah shall *w.* with Israel
6:16 said, We will not *w.* there.
7:6 if ye *w.* not after other gods
9 will ye *w.* after other gods?
9:4 neighb. will *w.* wi. slanders
13:10 peo. which *w.* in imagina. of heart, *w.* 16:12; 18:12
23:14 commit adult. *w.* in lies
42:3 G. may show wher. may *w.*
*Lam.* 5:8 Z. desolate, foxes *w.*
*Ezek.* 11:20 they *w.* in my statu.
37:24 they sh. *w.* in my judgm.
*Dan.* 4:37 *w.* in pride he is able
*Hos.* 11:10 shall *w.* after the Lord
14:9 the just shall *w.* in them
*Joel* 2:8 *w.* ev. one in his path
*Amos* 3:3 can two *w.* ex. agreed?
*Mic.* 4:5 ev. one *w.* in name of G.
6:16 ye *w.* in counsels of Omri
*Hab.* 3:15 thou didst *w.* thro' sea
*Zep.* 1:17 they sh. *w.* like blind
*Zec.* 6:7 th. might *w.* to and fro
10:12 th. shall *w.* up and down
*Mat.* 11:5 the lame *w.* *Luke* 7:22
*Mark* 7:5 why *w.* not thy discip.
*Luke* 11:44 men that *w.* over th.
13:33 must *w.* to-day and to-mo.
24:17 commune as *w.* are sad?
*John* 7:1 Je. wo. not *w.* in Jewry
8:12 not *w.* in darkness but lig.
11:9 if any *w.* in day, stum. not
10 man *w.* in night, stumbleth
*Rom.* 4:12. *w.* in steps of faith
6:4 sho. *w.* in newness of life
8:1 who *w.* not after the flesh, 4
*2 Cor.* 5:7 we *w.* by faith
6:16 dw. in them and *w.* in th.
10:3 tho' we *w.* in flesh, not war
*Gal.* 6:16 as many as *w.* accord.
*Eph.* 2:10 we should *w.* in them
4:1 *w.* worthy of the vocation
17 ye *w.* not as other Gentiles
5:15 see ye *w.* circumspectly
*Phil.* 3:17 mark them which *w.*
18 many *w.* of wh. I told you
*Col.* 1:10 that ye mi. *w.* worthy of Lord, 1 *Thes.* 2:12
*1 Thes.* 4:12 ye may *w.* honestly
*2 Thes.* 3:11 which *w.* disorderly
*2 Pet.* 2:10 th. that *w.* after flesh
*1 John* 1:6 and *w.* in darkness
7 if *w.* in light as he in light
*2 John* 6 *w.* after his commandm.
*3 John* 4 children *w.* in the truth
*Jude* 18 mock. *w.* after their lus.
*Rev.* 3:4 they shall *w.* with me
9:20 cannot see, hear, nor *w.*
16:15 watch. lest he *w.* naked
21:24 nations *w.* in light of city

**WALK,** *imperatively.*

*Gen.* 13:17 *w.* thro. land, *Jos.* 18:8
17:1 *w.* before me, be perfect
*Ps.* 48:12 *w.* about Z. go round
*Prov.* 1:15 *w.* not in way wi. th.
*Ec.* 11:9 *w.* in ways of thy heart
*Is.* 2:5 let us *w.* in sight of Lord
30:21 this is the way, *w.* in it
50:11 *w.* in light of your fire
*Jer.* 6:16 good way, *w.* therein
25 go not into fields, nor *w.* by
7:23 *w.* in ways I command. you
*Ezek.* 20:18 *w.* ye not in stat. of
*Zec.* 6:7 might *w.* to and fro
*Mat.* 9:5 say, Rise, and *w.* *Mark* 2:9; *Luke* 5:23; *John* 5:8, 11, 12; *Acts* 3:6
*John* 12:35 *w.* wh. ye have light
*Rom.* 13:13 let us *w.* honestly
*1 Cor.* 7:17 ev. one, so let him *w.*
*Gal.* 5:16 *w.* in the Spirit, 25
*Eph.* 5:2 *w.* in love, C. loved us
8 *w.* as children of light
*Phil.* 3:16 let us *w.* by same rule
*Col.* 2:6 received C. so *w.* in him
4:5 *w.* in wisdom toward them

**To WALK.**

*Lev.* 18:4 *to w.* in my ordinances
*Deut.* 8:6 *to w.* in his ways, 10:12; 11:22; 13:5; 19:9; 26:17; 30:16; *Jos.* 22:5; *Jud.* 2:22; 1 *K.* 2:3; 8:58; 2 *Chr.* 6:31
*1 K.* 2:4 take heed *to w.* in truth
8:61 *to w.* in statut. *Ezek.* 36:27
16:31 *to w.* in sins of Jeroboam
*2 K.* 10:31 no heed *to w.* in law
23:3 Josiah made a coven. *to w.* after the Lord, 2 *Chr.* 34:31
*2 Chr.* 6:16 ta. heed *to w.* in law
*Neh.* 5:9 not *to w.* in fear of G.?
10:29 an oath to *w.* in G.'s law
*Ps.* 78:10 refu. *to w.* in his law
*Prov.* 2:13 *to w.* in ways of dark.
*Ec.* 6:8 know. *to w.* bef. living
*Jer.* 18:15 *to w.* in paths
26:4 not hearken *to w.*
31:9 cause th. to *w.* in strai. way
*Ezek.* 36:12 men *to w.* upon you
*Dan.* 9:10 nor obeyed *to w.*
*Mic.* 6:8 *to w.* humb. with thy G.
*Hab.* 3:19 make me *to w.* on high
*Zec.* 1:10 sent *to w.* to and fro
3:7 *to w.* am. these th. stand by
*Mat.* 15:31 saw the lame *to w.*
*Luke* 20:46 desire *to w.* in robes
*Acts* 3:12 made this man *to w.*
14:16 nations *to w.* in th. ways
21:21 nor *to w.* after customs
*1 Thes.* 4:1 how you ought to *w.*
*1 John* 2:6 *to w.* as he walked

**WALKED.**

*Gen.* 5:22 Enoch *w.* wi. God, 24
6:9 a just man, and *w.* with G.
*Ex.* 14:29 Is. *w.* upon dry land
*Lev.* 26:40 th. *w.* contrary to me
*Jos.*. 5:6 Is. *w.* 40 years in wild.
*Jud.* 2:17 way their fathers *w.*
5:6 travellers *w.* thro' by-paths
11:16 when Is. *w.* thro' wilder.
*1 Sam.* 8:3 *w.* not in his ways
*2 Sam.* 2:29 men *w.* all night
11:2 David *w.* on roof of house
1 K. 9:4 as David thy father *w.* 2 *Chr.* 6:16; 7:17
11:33 not *w.* in my ways, *Ezek.* 5:6, 7; 11:12; 20:13, 16, 21
15:26 *w.* in way of father, 22:52
34 Baasha *w.* in way of Jerob. 16:2; 2 *K.* 13:6; 17:22
*2 K.* 4:35 *w.* in house to and fro
17:8 H. *w.* in statutes of heath.
19 Judah *w.* in statutes of Isr. which th. made, 2 *Chr.* 21:13
21:22 *w.* not in way of L. *Jer.* 9:13; 32:23; 44:10, 23
*2 K.* 22:2 Josiah *w.* in ways of David, 2 *Chr.* 34:2
*2 Chr.* 11:17 *w.* in way of David
17:4 Je. *w.* in G.'s commandm.
21:12 not *w.* in ways of Jehosh.
*Job* 29:3 I *w.* through darkness
31:7 if my heart *w.* after eyes
*Ps.* 55:14 we *w.* to house of God
81:12 *w.* in their own counsels
13 O th. I. had *w.* in my ways!
142:3 in way I *w.* th. laid snare
*Is.* 9:2 people th. *w.* in darkness
20:3 Isaiah *w.* naked for a sign
*Jer.* 2:5 they *w.* after vanity, 8
7:24 *w.* in couns. of heart, 11:8
8:2 after wh. th. *w.* 9:14; 16:11
*Ezek.* 16:47 not *w.* after th. ways
18:9 hath *w.* in my statutes, 17
23:31 *w.* in way of thy sister
28:14 hast *w.* in midst of stones
*Amos* 2:4 which their fathers *w.*
*Nah.* 2:11 even the old lion *w.*
*Zec.* 1:11 we *w.* to and fro, 6:7

*Mal.* 3:14 what profit we *w.* mournfully?
*Mark* 16:12 J. appear. as they *w.*
*John* 6:66 disciples *w.* no more
11:54 Jesus *w.* no more openly
*Acts* 3:8 leap. stood and *w.* 14:10
14:8 cripple, who never had *w.*
2 *Cor.* 10:2 we *w.* accord. to flesh
12:18 *w.* we not in same spirit?
*w.* we not in same steps?
*Gal.* 2:14 they *w.* not uprightly
*Eph.* 2:2 time past ye *w.* *Col.* 3:7
1 *Pet.* 4:3 we *w.* in lasciviousness

**He WALKED.**

1 *K.* 3:6 as *he w.* before thee
15:3 Abijam *w.* in all sins of his father, 2 *K.* 21:21
16:26 *he w.* in ways of Jeroboam
22:43 for *he w.* in all ways of Asa, 2 *Chr.* 20:32
2 *K.* 8:18 *he w.* in ways of kings of Is. 16:3; 2 *Chr.* 21:6; 28:2
27 *he w.* in way of kings, as did house of A. 2 *Chr.* 22:3, 5
2 *Chr.* 17:3 *he w.* in ways of Da.
*Dan.* 4:29 Nebuch. *w.* in palace
*Hos.* 5:11 *he w.* aft. commandm.
*Mal.* 2:6 *he w.* with me in peace
*Mat.* 14:29 Peter *w.* on the water
1 *John* 2:6 ought to walk as *he w.*

**I have WALKED.**

*Lev.* 26:41 *I h. w.* contr. to them
1 *Sam.* 12:2 *I have w.* before you
2 *Sam.* 7:6 *I have w.* in a tent
7 places wher. *I h. w.* with Is.
2 *K.* 20:3 how *I h. w.* befo. thee
*Job* 31:5 if *I have w.* with vanity
*Ps.* 26:1 for *I h. w.* in integrity
3 *I h. w.* in thy truth, *Is.* 38:3

**WALKEDST.**

*John* 21:18 *w.* whit. th. wouldest

**WALKEST.**

*Deut.* 6:7 talk wh. thou *w.* 11:19
1 *K.* 2:42 day thou *w.* abroad
*Is.* 43:2 when thou *w.* thro' fire
*Acts* 21:24 thou thyself *w.* orderly
*Rom.* 14:15 *w.* not charitably
3 *John* 3 even as thou *w.* in truth

**WALKETH.**

*Gen.* 24:65 wh. man *w.* in field?
*Deut.* 23:14 *w.* in midst of camp
1 *Sam.* 12:2 king *w.* before you
*Job* 18:8 and he *w.* on a snare
22:14 he *w.* in circuit of heaven
34:8 and *w.* with wicked men
*Ps.* 1:1 *w.* not in couns. of ungo.
15:2 he that *w.* uprightly shall
39:6 ev. man *w.* in a vain show
73:9 their tongue *w.* thro' earth
91:6 pestilence that *w.* in dark.
101:6 *w.* in perf. way serve me
104:3 *w.* upon wings of wind
128:1 bles. ev. one th. *w.* in ways
*Prov.* 6:12 *w.* with frow. mouth
10:9 *w.* uprigh. *w.* surely, 28:18
13:20 that *w.* with wise be wise
14:2 *w.* in uprightn. feareth L.
15:21 understand. *w.* uprightly
19:1 poor *w.* in integrity, 28:6
20:7 just man *w.* in his integr.
28:26 whoso *w.* wisely be deliv.
*Ec.* 2:14 but fool *w.* in darkness
10:3 he that is a fool *w.* by way
*Is.* 33:15 *w.* right. dw. on high
50:10 *w.* in dark. hath no light
65:2 which *w.* in way not good
*Jer.* 10:23 *w.* to direct his steps
23:17 *w.* after imagina. of heart
*Ezek.* 11:21 heart *w.* after det. th.
*Mic.* 2:7 to him that *w.* upright.
*Mat.* 12:43 spirit is gone out, *w.* thro' dry places, *Luke* 11:24
*John* 12:35 that *w.* in darkness
2 *Thes.* 3:6 brother *w.* disorderly
1 *Pet.* 5:8 devil *w.* about seeking
1 *John* 2:11 hate. bro. *w.* in dark.
*Rev.* 2:1 *w.* in midst of candlest.

**WALKING.**

*Gen.* 3:8 voice of L. *w.* in garden
*Deut.* 2:7 Lord knoweth thy *w.*
1 *K.* 3:3 Sol. loved L. *w.* as Dav.
16:19 Zimri *w.* in way of Jerob.
*Job* 1:7 fr. *w.* up and down, 2:2
31:26 beheld moon *w.* in bright.
*Ec.* 10:7 princes *w.* as servants
*Is.* 3:16 *w.* and minc. as they go
20:2 so, *w.* naked and barefoot
57:2 each *w.* in his uprightness
*Jer.* 6:28 revolters, *w.* with sland.
*Dan.* 3:25 men loose, *w.* in fire
*Mic.* 2:11 if a man *w.* in spirit
*Mat.* 14:25 Jesus went *w.* on sea
26 saw him *w.* *Mark* 6:48
*Mark* 8:24 I see men as trees *w.*
*Luke* 1:6 *w.* in all commandm.
*Acts* 3:8 lame man *w.* leaping, 9
9:31 *w.* in the fear of the Lord
2 *Cor.* 4:2 not *w.* in craftiness
2 *Pet* 3:3 *w.* after lusts, *Jude* 16
2 *John* 4 thy children *w.* in truth

**WALL.**

*Gen.* 49:6 they digged down a *w.*
22 whose branches run over *w.*
*Ex.* 14:22 waters were a *w.* to
*Lev.* 14:37 if plague lower th. *w.*
*Num.* 22:24 *w.* on th. side, a *w.*
25 ass crushed B.'s foot ag. *w.*
*Jos.* 2:15 Rah. dwelt on town-*w.*
6:5 *w.* of city shall fall flat, 20
1 *Sam.* 18:11 smi. D. to *w.* 19:10
20:25 king sat on seat by the *w.*
25:16 they were a *w.* by night
22 if I leave any th. pisseth ag. the *w.* 34; 1 *K.* 14:10; 16:11; 21:21; 2 *K.* 9:8
31:10 fastened Saul's body to *w.*
2 *Sam.* 11:20 they wo. shoot fr. *w.*
21 fr. *w.* why went ye nigh *w.*?
20:15 the people battered the *w.*
21 head sh. be thrown over *w.*
22:30 I have leaped *w.* *Ps.* 18:29
1 *K.* 4:33 hyssop th. springs of *w.*
20:30 a *w.* fell on 27,000 men
21:23 dogs shall eat Jez. by *w.*
2 *K.* 3:27 for burnt-offering on *w.*
4:10 a little chamber on *w.*
6:26 king of Isr. pass. by on *w.*
9:33 Jezebel's blood was on *w.*
18:26 people on the *w.* *Is.* 36:11
20:2 Hezekiah turned his face to the *w.* *Is.* 38:2
2 *Chr.* 25:23 Joash brake down *w.*
36:19 Nebuchad. brake down *w.*
*Ezr.* 5:3 who com. to make *w.*?
9:9 give us a *w.* in Ju. and Jer.
*Neh.* 1:3 *w.* of J. is broken down
2:15 I viewed *w.* 17 build *w.*
4:3 fox sh. break their stone *w.*
6 so built we *w.* all *w.* joined
15 we returned all of us to *w.*
6:6 for wh. cause th. build. *w.*
15 *w.* was finished in month E.
12:27 dedication of *w.* of Jerus.
13:21 why lodge ye about *w.*?
*Ps.* 62:3 a bowing *w.* shall ye be
*Prov.* 18:11 as high *w.* in conceit
24:31 stone *w.* was broken down
*Cant.* 2:9 belov. stand. behind *w.*
8:9 if she be a *w.* 10 I am a *w.*
*Is.* 2:15 day of L. on fenced *w.*
5:5 I will break down the *w.*
25:4 as a storm against the *w.*
30:13 as a breach in a high *w.*
59:10 grope for the *w.* like blind
*Jer.* 15:20 make thee a fenced *w.*
49:27 I will kindle a fire in *w.*
51:44 *w.* of Babylon shall fall
*Lam.* 2:8 to destroy *w.* of Zion
18 O *w.* of daughter of Zion
*Ezek.* 4:3 for *w.* of iron between
8:7 hole in *w.* 8 dig in *w.* 12:5
10 idols of Is. portrayed on *w.*
13:12 *w.* is fall. 15; 38:20 ev. *w.*
15 accomplish my wrath on *w.*
41:5 measured *w.* of the house
43:8 setting *w.* betw. me and th.
*Dan.* 5:5 fingers wrote on the *w.*
9:25 street sh. be built, and *w.*
*Hos.* 2:6 I will make a *w.*
*Joel* 2:7 they shall climb the *w.*
9 they shall run upon the *w.*
*Amos* 1:7 I will send a fire on *w.*
10 *w.* of Tyrus; 14 *w.* of Rab.
5:19 leaned his hand on the *w.*
7:7 Lord stood upon a *w.* made
*Nah.* 2:5 shall make haste to *w.*
*Hab.* 2:11 stone sh. cry out of *w.*
*Acts* 9:25 let Saul down by the *w.* in a basket, 2 *Cor.* 11:33
23:3 G. sh. smite thee, whited *w.*
*Eph.* 2:14 Ch. ha. brok. down *w.*
*Rev.* 21:14 *w.* of city had 12 fou.
18 the *w.* of it was of jasper
*See* BUILT.

**WALLED.**

*Lev.* 25:29 sell house in *w.* city
30 *w.* city shall be established
*Num.* 13:28 *w.* great, *Deut.* 1:28

**WALLOW, ED.**

2 *Sam.* 20:12 Amasa *w.* in blood
*Jer.* 6:26 gird with sackcloth, *w.*
25:34 *w.* yourselves in ashes
48:26 M. shall *w.* in his vomit
*Ezek.* 27:30 they sh. *w.* in ashes
*Mark* 9:20 he fell on ground, *w.*

**WALLOWING.**

2 *Pet.* 2:22 sow washed to *w.*

**WALLS.**

*Lev.* 14:37 if plague be in *w.* 39
25:31 the villages having no *w.*
*Deut.* 3:5 cit. fenced with high *w.*
28:52 till high *w.* come down
2 *K.* 25:4 men fled between 2 *w.*
10 Chaldees brake down the *w.* of Jerusalem, *Jer.* 39:8
*Ezr.* 4:13 if city be built, *w.* 16
5:8 timb. in *w.* work goeth fast
*Neh.* 4:7 *w.* of Jer. were made up
*Job* 24:11 make oil within th. *w.*
*Ps.* 51:18 build the *w.* of Jerus.
55:10 they go about on *w.*
122:7 peace be within thy *w.*
*Prov.* 25:28 city broken, with. *w.*
*Cant.* 5:7 keepers of *w.* took veil
*Is.* 22:5 a day of break. down *w.*
25:12 thy *w.* sh. he bring down
26:1 salvati. will G. app. for *w.*
49:16 thy *w.* are continu. bef. me
56:5 within my *w.* a place
60:10 strang. shall build thy *w.*
18 thou shalt call thy *w.* salva.
62:6 I have set watchmen on *w.*
*Jer.* 1:15 set thrones ag. *w.* of J.
5:10 go upon her *w.* destroy
50:15 Bab.'s *w.* are down, 51:58
*Ezek.* 26:4 destroy *w.* Tyrus, 12
27:11 men of Arv. were upon *w.*
33:30 talking against thee by *w.*
38:11 all dwelling without *w.* or
*Mic.* 7:11 in day thy *w.* are built
*Zec.* 2:4 inhabit. towns with. *w.*
*Heb.* 11:30 *w.* of Jeri. fell down

**WANDER.**

*Gen.* 20:13 God caused me to *w.*
*Num.* 14:33 your chil. shall *w.* in wilderness 32:13; *Ps.* 107:40
*Deut.* 27:18 causeth blind to *w.*
*Job* 12:24 he causeth them to *w.*
38:41 ravens *w.* for lack of meat
*Ps.* 55:7 then would I *w.* far off
59:15 let them *w.* up and down
119:10 let me not *w.* fr. comm.
*Is.* 47:15 they shall *w.* every one
*Jer.* 14:10 thus they loved to *w.*
48:12 wanderers th. cause to *w.*
*Amos* 8:12 shall *w.* fr. sea to sea

**WANDERERS.**

*Jer.* 48:12 I will send to him *w.*

*Hos.* 9:17 be *w.* am. the nations

**WANDERED.**

*Gen.* 21:14 Hagar *w.* in wildern.
*Ps.* 107:4 *w.* in wildern. *Is.* 16:8
*Lam.* 4:14 have *w.* as blind men
*Ezek.* 34:6 my sheep *w.* through
*Amos* 4:8 three cities *w.* to 1 city
*Heb.* 11:37 *w.* about in sheep-sk.
38 they *w.* in deserts, in moun.

**WANDEREST, ETH.**

*Job* 15:23 he *w.* abroad for bread
*Prov.* 21:16 *w.* out of way
27:8 as a bird that *w.* from nest, so is a man that *w.*
*Is.* 16:3 bewray not him that *w.*
*Jer.* 2:20 under ev. green tree *w.*
49:5 none sh. gather him that *w.*

**WANDERING.**

*Gen.* 37:15 he was *w.* in the field
*Prov.* 26:2 *w.* as swallow by fly.
*Ec.* 6:9 bet. sight of eyes th. *w.*
*Is.* 16:2 it shall be as a *w.* bird
1 *Tim.* 5:13 *w.* fr. house to house
*Jude* 13 *w.* stars to wh. is reser.

**WANDERINGS.**

*Ps.* 56:8 thou tellest my *w.* put

**WANT, Substantive.**

*Deut.* 28:48 serve thy ene. in *w.*
57 she shall eat them for *w.*
*Jud.* 18:10 where is no *w.* 19:19
*Job* 24:8 they embrace rock for *w.*
30:3 for *w.* they were solitary
31:19 seen any perish for *w.*
*Ps.* 34:9 no *w.* to them that fear
*Prov.* 6:11 *w.* as arm. man, 24:34
10:21 fools die for *w.* of wisdom
*Prov.* 13:23 destr. for *w.* of judg.
14:28 in *w.* of people is destruc.
21:5 that is hasty only to *w.*
22:16 giv. to rich sh. come to *w.*
*Lam.* 4:9 stric. thro' *w.* of fruits
*Amos* 4:6 I have giv. *w.* of bread
*Mark* 12:44 of her *w.* cast in all
*Luke* 15:14 he began to be in *w.*
2 *Cor.* 8:14 abundance for th. *w.*
9:12 supplieth *w.* of the saints
*Phil.* 4:11 not that I speak of *w.*

**WANTS.**

*Jud.* 19:20 all thy *w.* lie on me
*Phil.* 2:25 Ep. ministered to *w.*

**WANT, Verb.**

*Ps.* 23:1 shepherd, I shall not *w.*
34:10 that seek Lord shall not *w.*
*Prov.* 13:25 belly of wicked sh. *w.*
*Is.* 34:16 none shall *w.* her mate
*Jer.* 33:17 D. not *w.* a man to sit
18 Lev. not *w.* 35:19 J. not *w.*
*Ezek.* 4:17 th. they may *w.* bread

**WANTED.**

*Jer.* 44:18 we have *w.* all things
*John* 2:3 *w.* wine, mother of Je.
2 *Cor.* 11:9 wh. I *w.* I was charg.

**WANTETH.**

*Deut.* 15:8 lend him in th. he *w.*
*Prov.* 9:4 th. *w.* understand. 16
10:19 in words there *w.* not sin
28:16 prince that *w.* understand.
*Ec.* 6:2 he *w.* noth. for his soul
*Cant.* 7:2 like goblet that *w.* not

**WANTING.**

2 *K.* 10:19 proph. of B. let none be *w.* whoso be *w.* not live
*Prov.* 19:7 pursu. wi. wor. yet *w.*
*Ec.* 1:15 *w.* cannot be numbered
*Dan.* 5:27 weighed and found *w.*
*Tit.* 1:5 set in order the things *w.*
3:13 that noth. be *w.* unto them
*Jam.* 1:4 and entire, *w.* nothing

**WANTON.**

*Is.* 3:16 daught. walk wi. *w.* eyes
1 *Tim.* 5:11 wax *w.* ag. Christ
*Jam.* 5:5 have lived and been *w.*

**WANTONNESS.**

*Rom.* 13:13 not in chamb. and *w*
2 *Pet.* 2:18 allure thro' much *w.*

**WAR.**

*Ex.* 1:10 when there is *w.* they
13:17 lest peo. rep. when see *w.*
17:16 L. will have *w.* with Ama.
32:17 a noise of *w.* in the camp
*Num.* 1:3 all th. are able to go to *w.* 20:22; 26:2; *Deut.* 3:18
10:9 if ye go to *w.* ye shall blow
31:3 arm some of yoursel. to *w.*
32:6 shall your breth. go to *w.?*
20 go before the Lord to *w.* 27
*Deut.* 4:34 G. assa. by *w.* to take
21:10 wh. thou goest forth to *w.*
*Jos.* 11:23 land rest. fr. *w.* 14:15
14:11 so is my strength for *w.*
*Jud.* 3:2 Is. might teach th. *w.*
5:8 then was *w.* in the gates
21:22 reserved not his wife in *w.*
1 *Sam.* 14:52 *w.* ag. Philist. 19:8
2 *Sam.* 3:1 *w.* bet. house of S. and
11:7 Da. demand. how *w.* prosp.
1 *K.* 2:5 shed the blood of *w.* put the blood of *w.*
14:30 *w.* bet. Re. and Jer. 15:6
15:7 *w.* bet. Abijam and Jerob.
16 *w.* bet. Asa and Baasha, 32
20:18 come for *w.* take th. alive
22:1 contin. 3 years without *w.*
2 *K.* 18:20 and strength for *w.*
1 *Chr.* 5:10 made *w.* with H. 19
22 slain, bec. *w.* was of God
2 *Chr.* 15:19 no *w.* till 35th year
35:21 house wherewith I ha. *w.*
*Job* 5:20 in *w.* redeem fr. sword
10:17 changes and *w.* are ag. me
38:23 reserved against day of *w.*
*Ps.* 27:3 tho' *w.* rise against me
55:21 but *w.* was in his heart
68:30 scatter peo. th. deli. in *w.*
120:7 wh. I speak th. are for *w.*
140:2 continual. are gath. for *w.*
*Prov.* 20:18 with advice make *w.*
24:6 by counsel th. sh. make *w.*
*Ec.* 3:8 time of *w.* time of peace
8:8 th. is no discharge in th. *w.*
*Is.* 2:4 nor learn *w.* *Mic.* 4:3
3:25 mighty shall fall in the *w.*
21:15 fled fr. grievousness of *w.*
36:5 counsel and strength for *w.*
*Jer.* 4:19 hast heard alarm of *w.*
6:4 prepare ye *w.* against her
23 as men for *w.* against thee
21:2 Nebuch. maketh *w.* ag. us
42:14 where we shall see no *w.*
48:14 are mighty men for *w.?*
*Ezek.* 17:17 nor Phar. make in *w.*
*Dan.* 7:21 made *w.* with saints
9:26 to end of *w.* are desolation
*Joel* 3:9 prepare *w.* wake up men
*Mic.* 2:8 as men averse from *w.*
3:5 even prepare *w.* against him
*Luke* 14:31 king going to ma. *w.?*
*Rev.* 11:7 beast made *w.* ag. th.
12:7 *w.* in heaven ag. dragon
17 make *w.* with rem. of seed
13:4 able to make *w.* wi. beast?
7 to make *w.* wi. saints, 17:14
19:11 in righteousness make *w.*
19 kings gathered to make *w.*

*See* EXPERT, MAN, MEN.

**Weapons of WAR.**

*Deut.* 1:41 ye girded on *w. of w.*
*Jud.* 18:11 600 wi. *w. of w.* 16, 17
2 *Sam.* 1:27 how are *w. of w.* per.
*Ec.* 9:18 wisd. bet. than *w. of w.*
*Jer.* 21:4 turn back *w. of w.*
51:20 battle-axe and *w. of w.*
*Ezek.* 32:27 do. to hell wi. *w. of w.*

**WAR, Verb.**

2 *Sam.* 22:35 Lord teacheth my hands to *w.* *Ps.* 18:34; 144:1
2 *K.* 16:5 to *w.* against it, *Is.* 7:1
2 *Chr.* 6:34 if peo. *w.* ag. enemy
*Is.* 41:12 *w.* ag. thee be as noth.
2 *Cor.* 10:3 do not *w.* after flesh
1 *Tim.* 1:18 mightest *w.* a warf.
*Jam.* 4:1 lusts that *w.* in memb.
2 fight and *w.* yet ye have not
1 *Pet.* 2:11 lusts wh. *w.* ag. soul

**WARRED, ETH.**

*Num.* 31:7 *w.* against Midianites
*Jos.* 24:9 Balak *w.* against Israel
1 *K.* 14:19 how he *w.* and reigned
22:45 Jehosh. how he *w.* writ.
2 *K.* 6:8 king of Syria *w.* ag. Is.
2 *Chr.* 26:6 Uzziah *w.* ag. Philist.
2 *Tim.* 2:4 *w.* entangl. himself

**WARRING.**

2 *K.* 19:8 *w.* ag. Libnah, *Is.* 37:8
*Rom.* 7:23 a law in my memb. *w.*

**WARRIOR, S.**

1 *K.* 12:21 who were *w.* 2 *Ch.* 11:1
*Is.* 9:5 battle of *w.* is with noise

**WARS.**

*Num.* 21:14 in book of *w.* of Lord
*Jud.* 3:1 not known *w.* of Canaan
1 *Chr.* 22:8 great *w.* sh. not build
2 *Chr.* 16:9 hencef. shalt have *w.*
*Ps.* 46:9 he maketh *w.* to cease
*Mat.* 24:6 hear of *w.* and rumors of *w.* *Mark* 13:7; *Luke* 21:9
*Jam.* 4:1 from whence come *w.?*

**WARD.**

*Gen.* 40:3 put in *w.* 4, 7; 41:10
42:7 Joseph put brethren in *w.*
*Lev.* 24:12 put blasphemer in *w.*
*Num.* 15:34 gath. of sticks in *w.*
2 *Sam.* 20:3 ten concubin. in *w.*
1 *Chr.* 12:29 had kept *w.* of Saul
25:8 cast lots, *w.* against *w.*
26:16 by cause of *w.* goi. ag. *w.*
*Neh.* 12:24 thanks *w.* against *w.*
25 porters keep. *w.* at gates, 45
*Is.* 21:8 I am set in my *w.*
*Jer.* 37:13 capt. of *w.* was there
*Ezek.* 19:9 they put Zedek. in *w.*
*Acts* 12:10 first and second *w.*

**WARDS.**

1 *Chr.* 9:23 house of taber. by *w.*
26:12 hav. *w.* one ag. another
*Neh.* 13:30 appoint. *w.* of priests

**WARDROBE.**

2 *K.* 22:14 Shallum the keeper of the *w.* 2 *Chr.* 34:22

**WARE.**

*Luke* 8:27 man *w.* no clothes

**WARE.**

*Acts* 14:6 *w.* of it, fled to Lys.
2 *Tim.* 4:15 of coppersmith be *w.*

**WARE, S.**

*Neh.* 10:31 if peo. bri. *w.* on sab.
13:16 men of Tyre brought *w.*
20 merchants and sellers of *w.*
*Jer.* 10:17 gath. up *w.* out of land
*Ezek.* 27:16 by reas. of *w.* 18, 33
*Jon.* 1:5 mariners cast forth *w.*

**WARFARE.**

1 *Sam.* 28:1 gath. armies for *w.*
*Is.* 40:2 her *w.* is accomplished
1 *Cor.* 9:7 goeth a *w.* any time
2 *Cor.* 10:4 weap. of *w.* not carnal
1 *Tim.* 1:18 might. war a good *w.*

**WARM.**

2 *K.* 4:34 flesh of child waxed *w.*
*Job* 6:17 th. wax *w.* they vanish
37:17 how garm. are *w.* when
*Ec.* 4:11 how can one be *w.* al.?
*Is.* 44:15 take ther. and *w.* hims.
*Is.* 47:14 sh. not be a coal to *w.*
*Hag.* 1:6 but there is none *w.*

**WARMED, ETH, ING.**

*Job* 31:20 were not *w.* wi. fleece
39:14 ostrich *w.* eggs in dust
*Is.* 44:16 *w.* himself, and saith
*Mark* 14:54 and Pet. *w.* himself, *John* 18:18, 25
67 when she saw P. *w.* himself
*Jam.* 2:16 depart in peace, be *w.*

**WARN.**

*2 Chr.* 19:10 sh. *w.* they tresp. not
*Ezek.* 3:18 to *w.* the wicked, 33:8
19 yet if thou *w.* wicked, 33:9
21 *w.* righteous; 33:3 *w.* peo. 7
*Acts* 20:31 I ceased not to *w.* ev.
1 *Cor.* 4:14 beloved sons I *w.* you
1 *Thes.* 5:14 *w.* that are unruly

**WARNED.**

2 *K.* 6:10 man of God *w.* him
*Ps.* 19:11 by them is servant *w.*
*Ezek.* 3:21 live, because he is *w.*
33:6 and the people be not *w.*
*Mat.* 2:12 Joseph being *w.* of G.
3:7 O generation of vipers, who hath *w.* you? *Luke* 3:7
*Acts* 10:22 Cornelius *w.* from G.
*Heb.* 11:7 Noah *w.* prepared ark

**WARNING.**

*Jer.* 6:10 to whom sh. I give *w.?*
*Ezek.* 3:17 and give them *w.*
18 thou givest him not *w.* 20
33:4 tak. not *w.* 5 took not *w.*
*Col.* 1:28 *w.* every man, teaching

**WARP.**

*Lev.* 13:48 pla. in *w.* 49, 51, 57, 59
52 burn *w.* 56 rend *w.* 58 wash.

**WAS.**

*Gen.* 5:24 walked with G. *w.* not
*Rev.* 1:4 is and which *w.* 8; 4:8
17:8 beast th. saw. *w.* is not, 11

**It WAS.**

*Ex.* 16:15 wist not what *it w.*
*Is.* 48:16 from time that *it w.*
*Ezek.* 16:15 his *it w.* 19 thus *it w.*

**WASH.**

*Gen.* 18:4 *w.* y. feet, 19:2; 24:32
*Ex.* 2:5 daught. of P. came to *w.*
29:4 Aa. *w.* 30:19, 20, 21; 40:12
*Lev.* 6:27 shalt *w.* that whereon
13:54 *w.* thi. wherein plague is
14:8 *w.* himself, *Deut.* 23:11
9 *w.* his flesh in water, 15:16; 16:4, 24; 22:6
17:16 if he *w.* not sh. bear iniq.
*Deut.* 21:6 *w.* hands over heifer
*Ruth* 3:3 *w.* thyself, and anoint
1 *Sam.* 25:41 servant to *w.* feet
2 *Sam.* 11:8 go down and *w.* feet
2 *K.* 5:10 go *w.* in Jordan 7 times
12 may I not *w.* and be clean?
13 saith to thee, *w.* be clean?
2 *Chr.* 4:6 lavers to *w.* in, sea for
*Job* 9:30 if I *w.* myself wi. water
*Ps.* 26:6 I will *w.* my hands in
51:2 *w.* me from mine iniquity
7 *w.* me and I sh. be whiter th.
58:10 *w.* feet in blood of wicked
*Is.* 1:16 *w.* ye, make you clean
*Jer.* 2:22 tho' thou *w.* with nitre
4:14 *w.* thy heart from wickedn.
*Ezek.* 23:40 thou didst *w.* thyself
*Mat.* 6:17 when fastest, *w.* face
15:2 they *w.* not when they eat
*Mark* 7:3 exc. they *w.* eat not, 4
*Luke* 7:38 began to *w.* his feet
*John* 9:7 *w.* in pool of Siloam, 11
13:5 began to *w.* disciples' feet
6 Lord, dost thou *w.* my feet?
8 never *w.* my feet, if I *w.* not
14 ought to *w.* one ano.'s feet
*Acts* 22:16 and *w.* away thy sins
*See* CLOTHES, FEET.

**WASHED.**

*Gen.* 43:24 water, they *w.* feet
31 Joseph *w.* face and went out
49:11 Ju. *w.* garments in wine
*Ex.* 40:32 *w.* as L. commanded
*Lev.* 13:55 plague aft. it is *w.* 58
*Jud.* 19:21 concub. *w.* their feet
2 *Sam.* 12:20 David arose and *w.*
1 *K.* 22:38 one *w.* chariot in pool
*Job* 29:6 I *w.* steps with butter
*Ps.* 73:13 I *w.* hands in innocen.
*Prov.* 30:12 not *w.* fr. filthiness
*Cant.* 5:3 I have *w.* my feet
12 his eyes are *w.* with milk
*Is.* 4:4 *w.* away filth of daughters
*Ezek* 16:4 nor wast *w.* in water
9 I thorou. *w.* away thy blood
*Mat.* 27:24 Pilate *w.* his hands
*Luke* 7:44 she hath *w.* my feet
11:38 marvelled he had not *w.*
*John* 9:7 he went and *w.* 11, 15
*John* 13:10 is *w.* need. not save to
14 Master have *w.* your feet
*Acts* 9:37 wh. when they had *w.*
16:33 he took them, *w.* stripes
1 *Cor.* 6:11 ye are *w.* sanctified
1 *Tim.* 5:10 if she *w.* saints' feet
*Heb.* 10:22 having our bodies *w.*
2 *Pet.* 2:22 sow *w.* to wallowing
*Rev.* 1:5 that *w.* us fr. our sins
7:14 have *w.* their robes white
*See* CLOTHES.

**WASHEST, ING.**

2 *Sam.* 11:2 Da. saw a woman *w.*
*Job* 14:19 *w.* away thi. wh. grow
*Luke* 5:2 fishermen were *w.* nets

**WASHING, S.**

*Lev.* 13:56 plague dark after *w.*
*Neh.* 4:23 ev. one put off for *w.*
*Cant.* 4:2 sheep came fr. *w.* 6:6
*Mark* 7:4 *w.* of cups and tables, 8
*Eph.* 5:26 cleanse wi. *w.* of wat.
*Tit.* 3:5 saved us by *w.* of regen.
*Heb.* 9:10 stood in meats and *w.*

**WASHPOT.**

*Ps.* 60:8 Moab is my *w.* 108:9

**WAST.**

*Ob.* 11 thou *w.* as one of them
*Rev.* 11:17 who art, and *w.* art

**WASTE, Substantive.**

*Jer.* 49:13 Bozrah shall bec. a *w.*
*Mat.* 26:8 to what purpose is this *w.?* *Mark* 14:4

**WASTE, Adjective.**

*Deut.* 32:10 found him in *w.* wil.
*Job* 30:3 fleeing into the *w.* wil.
38:27 to satisfy desol. *w.* ground
*Is.* 24:1 Lord maketh earth *w.*
42:15 I will make *w.* mountains
49:17 that made *w.* sh. go forth
*Jer.* 2:15 lions made his land *w.*
46:19 Noph shall be *w.* and des.
*Ezek.* 5:14 I will make Jerusal. *w.*
29:9 Eg. shall be *w.* 10; 30:12
38:8 mountains been always *w.*
*Nah.* 2:10 Ninev. is void and *w.*
*Zep.* 3:6 I have made streets *w.*
*Hag.* 1:9 because my house is *w.*
*See* CITIES, LAY, LAID, PLACES.

**WASTE, Verb.**

1 *K.* 17:14 barrel of meal not *w.*
1 *Chr.* 17:9 no childr. of wick. *w.*
*Ps.* 80:13 boar of wood doth *w.*
*Jer.* 50:21 *w.* inhabitants of Pek.
*Mic.* 5:6 they sh. *w.* land of Assy.

**WASTED.**

*Num.* 14:33 till carcasses be *w.*
24:22 the Kenite shall be *w.*
*Deut.* 2:14 men of war were *w.*
1 *K.* 17:16 barrel of meal *w.* not
1 *Chr.* 20:1 J. *w.* country of Am.
*Ps.* 137:3 that *w.* required mirth
*Is.* 6:11 till cities be *w.* without
19:5 river sh. be *w.* dried up
60:12 nations sh. be utterly *w.*
*Jer.* 44:6 are *w.* and desolate as
*Joel* 1:10 field is *w.* corn is *w.*
*Luke* 15:13 prodig. *w.* substance
16:1 accused that he *w.* goods
*Gal.* 1:13 persecu. church and *w.*

**WASTENESS.**

*Zep.* 1:15 day of *w.* desolation

**WASTER.**

*Prov.* 18:9 brother to a great *w.*
*Is.* 54:16 created *w.* to destroy

**WASTES.**

*Is.* 61:4 they shall build old *w.*
*Jer.* 49:13 Boz. sh. be perpet. *w.*
*Ezek.* 33:24 that inhab. *w.* of Is.
27 they in the *w.* shall fall
36:4 thus saith L. to desolate *w.*
10 the *w.* shall be builded, 33

**WASTETH.**

*Job* 14:10 man dieth, *w.* away
*Ps.* 91:6 nor destruction that *w.*
*Prov.* 19:26 he that *w.* father

**WASTING.**

*Is.* 59:7 *w.* and destruction are in
60:18 not heard *w.* nor destruc.

**WATCH, Substantive.**

*Ex.* 14:24 in morn. *w.* L. looked
*Jud.* 7:19 middle *w.* had set *w.*
1 *Sam.* 11:11 S. came in morn. *w.*
2 *K.* 11:6 so shall ye keep the *w.* of house, 7; 2 *Chr.* 23:6
*Neh.* 4:9 prayed to God set a *w.*
7:3 every one in his *w.* and
*Job* 7:12 am I a sea, that set. *w.?*
*Ps.* 90:4 a thous. years as a *w.*
141:3 set a *w.* before my mouth
*Jer.* 51:12 make the *w.* strong
*Hab.* 2:1 I will sta. upon my *w.*
*Mat.* 14:25 in 4th *w.* *Mark* 6:48
*Mat.* 24:43 wh. *w.* thief wo. come
27:65 ye have a *w.* go your way
66 seal. stone and setting a *w.*
28:11 some of *w.* came into city
*Luke* 2:8 shepherds keeping *w.*
12:38 if he come in second *w.*

**WATCHES.**

*Neh.* 12:9 over against th. in *w.*
*Ps.* 63:6 when I meditate in *w.*
119:148 mine eyes prev. night *w.*
*Lam.* 2:19 in beginning of the *w.*

**WATCH, Verb.**

*Gen.* 31:49 Lord *w.* between me
1 *Sam.* 19:11 Saul sent to *w.* Da.
*Ezr.* 8:29 *w.* ye, keep vessels till
*Job* 14:16 not *w.* over my sin?
*Ps.* 102:7 I *w.* am as sparrow
130:6 more than they that *w.*
*Is.* 21:5 *w.* in the watch-tower
29:20 all that *w.* for iniquity
*Jer.* 5:6 a leop. sh. *w.* over cities
31:28 so will I *w.* over them
44:27 I will *w.* over them
*Nah.* 2:1 keep munit. *w.* way
*Hab.* 2:1 I will *w.* to see what he
*Mat.* 24:42 *w.* therefore, 25:13; *Mark* 13:35; *Luke* 21:36; *Acts* 20:31
26:38 Jesus said, *w.* with me
40 could ye not *w.?* *Mark* 14:34, 37
41 *w.* and pray, *Mark* 13:33; 14:38; *Col.* 4:2
*Mark* 13:34 command. porter to *w.* 37 I say unto all, *w.*
1 *Cor.* 16:13 *w.* stand in faith
1 *Thes.* 5:6 let us *w.* 1 *Pet.* 4:7
2 *Tim.* 4:5 *w.* th. in all things
*Heb.* 13:17 th. *w.* for your souls

**WATCHED.**

*Jer.* 20:10 familiars *w.* for halt.
31:28 as I have *w.* over them
*Lam.* 4:17 *w.* for a nation that
*Dan.* 9:14 Lord *w.* on evil
*Mat.* 24:43 man of house would have *w.* *Luke* 12:39
27:36 sitting down they *w.* him
*Mark* 3:2 *w.* whether he would heal on sab. *Luke* 6:7; 14:1
*Luke* 20:20 th. *w.* and sent spies
*Acts* 9:24 *w.* gates day and night

**WATCHER, S.**

*Jer.* 4:16 published that *w.* come
*Dan.* 4:13 *w.* and holy one came
17 degree of *w.* 23 king saw *w.*

**WATCHETH.**

*Ps.* 37:32 wicked *w.* righteous

Ezek. 7:6 it w. for th. it is come
Rev. 16:15 blessed is he that w.

**WATCHFUL.**

Rev. 3:2 be w. strengthen things

**WATCHING, S.**

1 Sam. 4:13 E. sat by way-si. w.
Prov. 8:34 heareth me, w. daily
Lam. 4:17 in w. we ha. watched
Mat. 27:54 centurion w. Jesus
Luke 12:37 L. when com. find w.
2 Cor. 6:5 in labors, in w. in fast.
11:27 w. often, in hunger, thirst
Eph. 6:18 w. with perseverance

**WATCHMAN.**

2 Sam. 18:25 w. cried, told king
26 w. saw anoth. man running
2 K. 9:18 w. told, cometh not, 20
Ps. 127:1 w. waketh but in vain
Is. 21:6 set w. 11 w. what of the night?
Jer. 51:12 set up the w. prepare
Ezek. 3:17 made thee a w. 33:7
33:2 if peo. set him up for th. w.
Hos. 9:8 w. of Ephr. was with G.

**WATCHMEN.**

Cant. 3:3 w. go about city, 5:7
Is. 52:8 thy w. shall lift voice
56:10 his w. are blind, ignorant
62:6 I have set w. on thy walls
Jer. 6:17 set w. over you, saying
31:6 w. on mount Ephr. sh. cry
Mic. 7:4 day of thy w cometh

**WATCH-TOWER.**

2 Chr. 20:24 Ju. came toward w.
Is. 21:5 watch in w. eat, drink
8 I stand continually on the w.

**WATER, Substantive.**

Gen. 16:7 angel found Ha. by w
18:4 let a little w. be fetched
21:14 Abra. took a bottle of w.
24:32 Laban gave the man w.
43 give me w. to drink
26:20 w. is ours; 32 found w.
43:24 the steward gave them w.
49:4 unstable as w. sh. not excel
Ex. 12:9 nor sodden with w.
17:6 shall come w. out of rock
Ex. 20:4 any likeness th. is in w.
23:25 L. bless thy bread and w.
29:4 Aaron and his sons shall wash them with w. 30:20; 40:12; Lev. 8:6; 16:4, 24
Lev. 6:28 be scoured in w. 15:12
11:32 it must be put into w.
Num. 5:22 w. that causeth curse
8:7 sprinkle w. of purification
19:9 for a w. of separation, 13, 20, 21; 31:23
20:8 w. out of the rock, 10, 11; Neh. 9:15; Ps. 114:8
13 w. of Meribah, 24; 27:14
21:5 th. is no bread, nor any w.
16 gather peo. I will give th. w.
24:7 shall pour w. out of bucket
31:23 make go through the w.
Deut. 8:7 L. bri. to brooks of w.
11:11 land drinketh w. of rain
12:16 on earth as w. 24; 15:23
23:4 with w. in way, Neh. 13:2
Jos. 7:5 melted and became w.
Jud. 5:25 he asked w. gave milk
7:4 bring th. down to the w. 5
15:19 w. came out of the jaw
1 Sam. 7:6 gathered and drew w.
25:11 I take my bread and w.
26:11 take now the cruse of w.
30:12 nor drunk any w. 3 days
2 Sam. 14:14 are as w. on ground
17:21 arise and pass over the w.
21:10 till w. dropped on them
1 K. 13:19 did eat bread drank w.
22 eaten bread and drunk w.
14:15 smite Is. as a reed in w.
17:10 fetch, I pray, a little w.
18:4 fed them with bread and w.
35 w. ran, filled trench wi. w.
38 fire of Lord licked up the w.
22:27 feed him with bread and w. of affliction, 2 Chr. 18:26
2 K. 2:19 the w. is naught, the
3:11 Eli. poured w. on Elijah's
17 valley shall be filled with w.
22 and the sun shone on the w.
6:5 the ax-head fell into w.
22 set bread and w. bef. them
8:15 dipped a thick cloth in w.
20:20 brought w. into the city
2 Chr. 32:4 king of Assy. find w.
Job 8:11 can flag grow with. w.?
14:9 yet through the scent of w.
15:16 who drink. iniq. like w.
22:7 hast not given w. to weary
34:7 drinketh scorning like w.
Ps. 22:14 I am poured out like w.
65:9 river of God is full of w.
66:12 went through fire and w.
79:3 blood have th. shed like w.
88:17 came about me like w.
109:18 come into bowels like w.
Prov. 17:14 when one let. out w.
20:5 coun. of man like deep w.
27:19 as in w. face answereth
30:16 that is not filled with w.
Is. 1:22 thy wine mixed with w.
3:1 doth take away stay of w.
21:14 land of Tema brought w.
30:14 found a sherd to take w.
20 L. gave you w. of affliction
41:17 when the poor seek w.
44:3 I will pour w. on thirsty
63:12 dividing w. before them
Jer. 13:1 girdle, put it not in w.
23:15 make th. drink w. of gall
Lam. 1:16 eyes ru.. with w. 3:48
2:19 pour out thy heart like w.
5:4 we have drunken our w. for
Ezek. 4:17 want bread and w.
7:17 knees be weak as w. 21:7
16:4 nor wast thou washed in w.
9 then washed I thee with w.
36:25 sprinkle cle. w. upon you
Hos. 2:5 lov. that gave me my w.
5:10 pour wrath on them like w.
10:7 king cut off as foam on w.
Amos 8:11 not fam. nor thi. of w.
Nah. 2:8 Nineveh like pool of w.
Hab. 3:10 overflow. of w. passed
Mat. 3:11 bapt. you wi. w. Mark 1:8; Luke 3:16: John 1:26
16 J. went out of w. Mark 1:10
10:42 giv. cup of w. Mark 9:41
14:28 bid me come to thee on w.
17:15 falleth oft into fire and w.
27:24 Pilate took w. and washed
Mark 14:13 bearing pitcher of w. Luke 22:10
Luke 8:23 ship was filled with w.
24 rebuked w. 25 w. obeyed
16:24 may dip his finger in w.
John 2:7 fill water-pots with w.
3:5 except a man be born of w.
23 because there was much w.
4:10 living w. 11; 15 give me w.
46 came wh. he made w. wine
5:3 waiting for moving of w.
John 5:4 ang. went down, tro. w.
7:38 out of his belly flow liv. w.
13:5 he poureth w. into a basin
19:34 came thereout blo. and w.
Acts 1:5 J. bapt. with w. 11:16
8:36 here is w. 38 went into w.
10:47 can any forbid w. th. be
Eph. 5:26 cle. it wi. wash. of w.
Heb. 9:19 blood of calves wi. w.
10:22 bod. washed with pure w.
Jam. 3:12 yield salt w. and fresh
1 Pet. 3:20 8 souls saved by w.
2 Pet. 2:17 th. are wells witho. w.
3:6 world bei. overflowed wi. w.
Jude 12 clouds they are with. w.
1 John 5:6 came by w. and blood
8 three witn. Spirit, w. blood
Rev. 12:15 serpent cast out w.
16:12 Euphrates, w. dried up
21:6 give of fount. of w. of life
22:1 show. me a pure river of w.
17 let take w. of life freely

See BITTER, DRAW, DREW, DRINK, WELL.

**No WATER.**

Gen. 37:24 there was no w. in it
Ex. 15:22 fou. no w. 17:1; Num. 20:2; 33:14; Deut. 8:15
1 K. 13:22 bread, and drink no w.
2 K. 3:9 there was no w. for host
Ps. 63:1 thirsty la. wh. no w. is
Is. 1:30 as garden that ha. no w.
44:12 smith drinketh no w.
50:2 stinketh bec. there is no w.
Jer. 2:13 cist. that can hold no w.
14:3 came to pits found no w.
38:6 in dungeon th. was no w.
Zec. 9:11 out of pit wher. no w.
Luke 7:44 thou gavest me no w.

**WATER, Verb.**

Gen. 2:10 out of E. to w. garden
29:7 w. sheep and feed them, 8
Ps. 6:6 I w. couch with my tears
72:6 as showers that w. earth
Ec. 2:6 pools of wa. to w. wood
Is. 16:9 I will w. thee with tears
27:3 I will w. it every moment
Ezek. 17:7 mi. w. it by furrows
32:6 I will w. with my blood
Joel 3:18 fountain w. valley of S.

**WATERED, ST.**

Gen. 2:6 mist th. w. face of gro.
13:10 Jord. that it was well w.
29:2 w. flocks, 3; 10 J. w. flocks
Ex. 2:17 and w. their flocks, 19
Deut 11:10 w. it with thy foot
Prov. 11:25 water. be w. himself
Is. 58:11 sh. be like a w. garden
Jer. 31:12 soul sh. be a w. garden
1 Cor. 3:6 I planted, Apollos w.

**WATEREST, ETH.**

Ps. 65:9 visitest earth and w. it
10 thou w. the ridges thereof
104:13 w. hills from chambers
Prov. 11:25 th. w. sh. be watered
Is. 55:10 returneth not, w. earth
1 Cor. 3:7 nor w. any thing, 8

**WATERING.**

Gen. 30:38 rods in w. troughs
Job 37:11 by w. he weari. clouds
Luke 13:15 lead his ass to w.?

**WATER-BROOKS.**

Ps. 42:1 hart panteth after w.-b.

**WATER-COURSE, S.**

2 Chr. 32:30 stopped upper w.-c.
Job 38:25 who hath divid. w.-c.?
Is. 44:4 spri. as willows by w.-c.

**WATER-FLOOD.**

Ps. 69:15 let not w.-f. overfl. me

**WATER-POT, S.**

John 2:6 set there six w.-p. of st.
7 J. saith, Fill w.-p. wi. water
4:28 wo. left w.-p. went to city

**WATER-SPOUTS.**

Ps. 42:7 deep at noise of w.-s.

**WATER-SPRINGS.**

Ps. 107:33 he turneth the w.-s.
35 turneth dry grou. into w.-s.

**WATERS.**

Gen. 1:2 moved upon face of w.
6 divide the w. from the w. 7
9 let w. be gather. 20 w. bring
6:17 I br. a flood of w. on earth
7:17 w. increased, 18, 19, 20, 24
8:1 w. decrea. 3, 5; 13 w. dried
9:11 not cut off any more by w.
Ex. 7:17 smite w. 20 w. blood
8:6 stretched out hand over w.
14:21 by east wind the w. divid.
22 w. a wall, 29; 28 w. returned, 15:19

15:8 w. were gathered together
23 could not drink of w. of M.
27 they encamped there by w.
Num. 24:6 cedar-trees beside w.
Deut. 10:7 to Jotbath, riv. of w.
32:51 trespass. at w. of Meribah
33:8 didst str. at w. of Meribah
Jos. 3:16 w. which came down
4:7 w. of Jordan were cut off
23 L. dried up w. of Jord. 5:1
11:5 pitched at w. of Merom
Jud. 5:19 kings by w. of Megid.
7:24 take the w. before them
2 Sam. 5:20 br. of w. 1 Chr. 14:11
12:27 I have tak. the city of w.
2 K. 2:8 smote w. 14 Elisha
21 went forth unto spring of w.
5:12 Damascus bet. th. w. of Is.
2 Chr. 32:3 took coun. to stop w.
Job 3:24 roarings poured like w.
5:10 who sendeth w. upon fields
11:16 remem. thy misery as w.
12:15 he withholdeth w. th. dry
14:11 as the w. fail from the sea
19 the w. wear the stones, thou
22:11 abunda. of w. cover, 38:34
24:18 he is swift as the w. thou
26:5 things formed fr. under w.
8 bindeth up w. in thick clou.
10 he compassed w. wi. clouds
27:20 ter. take ho. on him as w.
28:4 even w. forgotten of foot
25 he weigheth w. by measure
29:19 my root was spread by w.
30:14 came on me as brea. of w.
37:10 breadth of w. is straitened
38:30 w. are hid as with a stone
Ps. 23:2 lead. me beside still w.
33:7 he gathereth w. of the sea
46:3 though the w. thereof roar
58:7 let them melt away as w.
69:1 w. come in unto my soul
73:10 w. of a full cup are wrung
77:16 w. saw thee, O G. w. saw
78:13 made w. stand as a heap
16 caused w. to run like rivers
20 smote rock that w. gushed, 105:41; 114:8; Is. 48:21
81:7 I proved thee at w. 106:32
104:6 w. stood above mountains
105:29 he turned w. into blood
106:11 w. covered their enemies
119:136 rivers of w. run down
124:4 w. had overwhelmed us
5 proud w. gone over our soul
136:6 stretched earth above w.
147:18 wind to blow and w. flow
148:4 ye w. above the heavens
Prov. 5:15 drink w. out of cistern
16 let rivers of w. be dispersed
8:29 that the w. should not pass
9:17 stolen w. are sweet, bread
25:25 as cold w. to thirsty soul
30:4 who bound w. in a garment
Ec. 11:1 cast thy bread upon w.
Cant. 4:15 a well of w. streams
Is. 8:6 people refused w. of Shil.
7 the Lord bringeth on th. w.
11:9 as w. cover seas, Hab. 2:14
15:6 w. of Nimrim sh. be deso.
9 w. of Dimon be full of blood
17:12 like rushing of mighty w.
19:5 w. shall fail from the sea
22:9 gathered w. of lower pool
28:17 w. overflow hiding-place
32:20 bless th. sow beside all w.
33:16 bread given him, w. sure
35:6 in wildern. w. break forth
40:12 who hath measured w.?
43:2 thro' w. I will be with thee
16 maketh a path in mighty w.
10 I give w. in the wilderness
48:1 are come out of w. of Jud.
21 caused w. flow out of rock
51:10 which dri. w. of the deep
54:9 w. of Noah to me, w. not
55:1 th. thirsteth, come ye to w.
57:20 whose w. cast up mire
58:11 spring, whose w. fail not
Jer. 2:13 fountain of living w.
18 to do, to drink w. of Sihor?
6:7 as a fountain casteth out w.
8:14 G. hath given us w. of gall
9:1 O that my head were w.!
13 our eyelids gush out wi. w.
10:13 mult. of w. in heav. 51:16
14:3 nobles sent little ones to w.
15:18 as a liar, as w. that fail
17:8 as a tree planted by the w.
13 forsak. Lord, fountain of w.
18:14 shall cold w. be forsaken?
46:7 whose w. are moved, 8
47:2 w. rise up out of the north
48:34 w. of Nimrim be desolate
50:38 a drought is upon her w.
Lam. 3:54 w. flowed overhead
Ezek. 19:10 moth. like vine by w.
31:4 w. made him great
14 trees by w. exalt themselv.
32:2 troublest w. with thy feet
47:1 w. issu. fr. under threshold
Ezek. 47:3 brought me thro' w. the w. 4
5 w. were risen, w. to swim in
8 w. issued out toward east, 12
19 w. of strife in Kadesh, 48:28
Dan. 12:6 said to man upon w. 7
Amos 5:8 call. for w. of sea, 9:6
24 let judgm. run down as w.
Jon. 2:5 w. compassed me about
Mic. 1:4 as w. pour. down steep
Nah. 3:8 had w. round about it
14 draw w. for siege, fortify
Zec. 14:8 living w. sh. go fr. Jer.
2 Cor. 11:26 in perils of w.
Rev. 7:17 lead th. to fount. of w.
8:11 w. became wormwood and
11:6 have power over w. to turn
14:7 that made fountain of w.
16:4 angel poured his vial on w.
5 I heard ang. of w. say, Thou
17:15 the w. where whore sits

See DEEP, GREAT.

**In, or into WATERS.**

Ex. 15:10 th. sank as lead in w.
25 a tree when cast into w.
Lev. 11:9 shall eat what hath fins and scales in w. 10, 46; Deut. 14:9
Deut. 4:18 liken. of fish in w. 5:8
Jos. 3:13 feet of priests rest in w.
Neh. 9:11 threwest a stone in. w.
Ps. 74:13 heads of dragons in w.
104:3 beams of his chamb. in w.
Mat. 8:32 sw. ran, perished in w.
Mark 9:22 cast into fire, into w.

**Many WATERS.**

Num. 24:7 seed shall be in m. w.
2 Sam. 22:17 drew me out of m. w. Ps. 18:16
Ps. 29:3 voice of L. upon m. w.
93:4 might. than noise of m. w.
Cant. 8:7 m. w. cannot qu. love
Is. 17:13 like rushing of m. w.
Jer. 51:13 dwellest upon m. w.
Ezek. 19:10 fruit. by rea. of m. w.
43:2 his voice was like noise of m. w. Rev. 1:15; 14:2; 19:6
Rev. 17:1 whore sitteth on m. w.

**WAVE.**

Jam. 1:6 waver. is like w. of sea

**WAVE, Verb.**

Ex. 29:24 w. them for wave-offer. Lev. 8:27; 23:20; Num. 6:20
26 shalt w. breast; 27 w. sho. Lev. 7:30; 8:29; 9:21; 10:15
Lev. 23:11 w. sheaf before L. 12
Num. 5:25 w. jealousy-offering

**WAVED.**

Lev. 14:21 take 1 lamb to be w.

See OFFERING.

**WAVERETH.**

Jam. 1:6 he that w. is like wave

**WAVERING.**

Heb. 10:23 hold faith without w.
Jam. 1:6 ask in faith, nothi. w.

**WAVES.**

Ps. 42:7 w. are gone over me
65:7 stilleth w. 89:9; 107:29
88:7 th. afflicted me with thy w.
93:3 floods lift up their w.
4 L. is mightier th. mighty w.
107:25 wind which lifteth up w.
Is. 48:18 righteous. as w. of sea
51:15 whose w. roared, Jer. 31:35
Jer. 5:22 tho' w. tossed, not pre.
51:42 Babyl. is covered with w.
55 Babylon where her w. roar
Ezek. 26:3 as sea causeth his w.
Jon. 2:3 thy w. passed over me
Zec. 10:11 shall smite w. in sea
Mat. 8:24 ship covered with w.
14:24 tossed with w. Mark 4:37
Luke 21:25 sea and w. roaring
Acts 27:41 part was bro. with w.
Jude 13 raging w. of sea, foami.

**WAX.**

Ps. 22:14 my heart is like w.
68:2 as w. melt. wicked perish
97:5 hills melted like w.
Mic. 1:4 cleft as w. before fire

**WAX, Verb.**

Ex. 22:24 wrath w. hot, 32:10
32:11 why doth thy wra. w. hot
22 let not anger of my lord w.
Lev. 25:47 or stranger w. rich
1 Sam. 3:2 eyes began to w. dim
Job 6:17 they w. warm, they van.
14:8 root thereof w. old in earth
Ps. 102:26 w. old as garment, Is. 50:9; 51:6; Heb. 1:11
Is. 17:4 fatness of flesh w. lean
29:22 nei. shall his face w. pale
Jer. 6:24 our hands w. feeble
Mat. 24:12 love of many w. cold
Luke 12:33 bags wh. w. not old
1 Tim. 5:11 begun to w. wanton
2 Tim. 3:13 seduc. sh. w. worse

**WAXED.**

Gen. 26:13 Isaac w. great
41:56 famine w. sore in Egypt
Ex. 1:7 Israel w. mighty, 20
16:21 when sun w. hot
32:19 Moses' anger w. hot
Num. 11:23 L.'s hand w. short?
Deut. 8:4 their raiment w. not old, 29:5; Neh. 9:21
32:15 Jeshur. w. fat and kicked
Jos. 23:1 Joshua w. old, stricken
1 Sam. 2:5 had child. is w. feeble
2 Sam. 3:1 but Dav. w. stronger, 1 Chr. 11:9
21:15 David fought, w. faint
2 K. 4:34 flesh of child w. warm
2 Chr. 13:21 Abijah w. mighty
17:12 Jehoshaphat w. great
24:15 Jehoi. w. old full of days
Est. 9:4 Mordecai w. greater
Ps. 32:3 silence my bones w. old
Jer. 49:24 Damascus w. feeble
50:43 king of Baby.'s hands w.
Dan. 8:8 he-goat w. very great
9 lit. horn w. exceed. great, 10
Mat. 13:15 this people's heart w. gross, Acts 28:27
Luke 1:80 child w. strong, 2:40
13:19 mustard seed w. great tree
Acts 13:46 P. and Barn. w. bold
Heb. 11:34 w. valiant in fight
Rev. 18:3 merchants w. rich

**WAXEN, WAXED.**

Gen. 18:12 after I am w. old
19:13 cry of Sod. was w. great
Lev. 25:25 bro. be w. poor, 35, 39
Deut. 31:20 w. fat, turn to other
Jos. 17:13 child. of Is. w. strong
Jer. 5:27 bec. great and w. rich
28 they are w. fat, they shine
Ezek. 16:7 increased and w. great

**WAXETH, ING.**
Ps. 6:7 mine eye w. old because
Heb. 8:13 w. old, ready to vanish
Phil. 1:14 brethren w. confident

**WAY.**
Gen. 24:42 if thou prosper my w.
Ex. 13:17 through w. of Philist.
18 led people thro' w. of wild.
21 pillar of cloud to lead the w.
18:20 thou shalt show them the w. Neh. 9:19; Ps. 107:4
Num. 21:4 discouraged be. of w.
22:26 there was no w. to turn
Deut. 1:22 by what w. Jos. 3:4
8:2 remember w. Lord led you
14:24 if w. be too long for thee
17:16 return no more that w.
19:3 prepare a w. 6 w. is long
28:25 shalt go out one w. ag. th.
31:29 turn from w. I command
Jos. 23:14 I am going w. of earth
24:17 preser. us in w. we went
Jud. 2:19 ceased not fr. their w.
9:25 they rob. all came that w.
18:5 whether w. be prosperous
6 Lord is your w. wher. ye go
19:9 to-morrow get on your w.
1 Sam. 9:6 he can show us our w.
8 man of God to tell us w.
12:23 I will teach you good w.
15:20 have gone w. L. sent me
2 Sam. 19:36 go little w. over J.
1 K. 2:2 I will go w. of all earth
8:36 teach th. good way to walk
13:9 turn ag. by w. thou camest
10 another w. 12 what w.?
18:6 Ahab went one w. Obadi.
22:24 which w. went Spirit of Lord? 2 Chr. 18:23
2 K. 3:8 which w. shall we go?
5:19 departed fr. him a little w.
2 Chr. 6:27 taught them good w.
Ezr. 8:21 seek of him w. for us
Job 3:23 a man whose w. is hid
12:24 wander in a wilderness wh. there is no w. Ps. 107:40
16:22 go w. whence not return
22:15 hast thou marked old w.
23:10 he knoweth w. that I take
28:23 G. understands w. thereof
38:19 wh. is w. light dwelleth?
Ps. 1:6 L. knoweth w. of righte
2:12 kiss Son, lest perish fr. w.
36:4 set. himself in w. not good
78:50 he made a w. to his anger
101:2 behave wisely in per. w. 6
119:27 underst. w. of precepts
29 remove from me w. of lying
30 I have chosen w. of truth
32 I will run w. of thy comma.
33 teach me w. of statu. 143:8
104 I hate every false w. 128
Ps. 139:24 if there be wicked w.
146:9 w. of the wicked he turns
Prov. 2:8 preserveth w. of saints
12 deliv. thee fr. w. of evil man
4:19 w. of wicked is as darkness
6:23 w. of life, 15:24; Jer. 21:8
7:8 he went the w. to her house
27 her house is the w. to hell
12:15 w. of fool rig. in own eyes
26 w. of wick. seduceth them
13:15 w. of transgressors hard
14:12 w. whi. seem. right, 16:25
15:9 w. of wicked is abominati.
10 griev. to him th. forsak. w.
19 w. of slothf. man is a hedge
16:29 lead. him into w. not good
21:8 w. of man is froward and
30:19 w. of eagle, of serpent
20 such w. of adulterous wom.
Ec. 11:5 knowest not w. of Spirit
Is. 3:12 to err and destroy the w.
26:7 w. of just is uprightness
35:8 a w. called w. of holiness
40:14 who show. w. of unders.?
43:16 L. mak. a w. in sea, 51:10
19 I will make w. in wildern.
49:11 make my mountains a w.
57:14 prepare w. 62:10 high w.
59:8 w. of peace they know not, Rom. 3:17
Jer. 6:16 where is the good w.
10:2 learn not w. of the heathen
23 w. of man is not in himself
12:1 doth w. of wicked prosp.?
18:15 paths, in a w. not cast up
32:39 give th. one heart, one w.
42:3 L. thy G. may show us w.
50:5 they shall ask the w. to Z.
Ezek. 21:20 appoint w. swo. may
23:13 I saw th. both took one w.
43:2 glory came from w. of east
Amos 2:7 turn aside w. of meek
Mal. 3:1 prepare w. before me
Mat. 7:13 broad is w. to destruc.
14 narrow is w. lead. unto life
8:28 no man mi. pass by that w.
10:5 go not into w. of Gentiles
22:16 teach. w. of God in truth, Mark 12:14; Luke 20:21
Luke 5:19 by what w. bring him
10:31 there came a priest th. w.
15:20 wh. he was a great w. off
19:4 Z. to see him, pass that w.
John 10:1 climb. up some oth. w.
14:4 w. ye know; 6 I am the w.
5 Lord, how can we know w.?
Acts 16:17 show us w. of salvati.
18:26 expound. to him w. of G.
19:9 but spake evil of that w.
23 arose no small stir about w.
24:14 after w. they call heresy
Rom. 14:13 to fall in brother's w.
1 Cor. 10:13 make a w. to escape
12:31 a more excellent w.
1 Thes. 3:11 L. Je. direct our w.
Heb. 9:8 the w. into the holiest
10:20 living w. he consecrated
Jam. 2:25 sent them out ano. w.
2 Pet. 2:2 w. of truth evil spo. of
15 have forsaken right w. and are following w. of Balaam
21 not known w. of righteous.
Rev. 16:12 w. of kings be prepar.

**By the WAY.**
Gen. 42:38 if misch. befall by t. w.
45:24 fall not out by the w.
Num. 14:25 by t. w. of Red sea, 21:4; Deut. 1:2, 40; 21:1
Deut. 6:7 walkest by t. w. 11:19
25:18 met by t. w. 1 Sam. 15:2
28:68 L. sh. bring thee by t. w.
Jos. 5:7 not circum. them by t. w.
1 K. 13:9 not turn ag. by t. w. 17
20:28 prophet waited by the w.
2 K. 3:20 came water by the w.
19:28 I will turn th. back by the w. thou camest, Is. 37:29, 34
Ezr. 8:31 lay in wait by the w.
Job 21:29 not ask. th. go by w.?
Ps. 80:12 th. who pass by the w.
89:41 that pass by the w. spoil
Ec. 10:3 fools walk by the w.
Is. 42:16 bring blind by the w.
48:17 God leadeth thee by t. w.
Jer. 2:17 he led thee by the w.
6:25 walk not by t. w. for sword
Ezek. 43:4 glory of L. came by w.
44:3 shall enter by t. w. 46:2, 8
46:9 he that entereth by the w.
Hos. 13:7 as a leopard by the w.
Mark 8:3 they faint by the w.
27 by the w. he asked his disc.
9:33 that ye disputed by w.? 34
Luke 24:32 talked wi. us by t. w.
1 Cor. 16:7 not see you by the w.

**Every WAY.**
Ps. 119:101 refrain fr. e. evil w.
Ps. 119:104 I hate e. false w. 128
Prov. 21:2 every w. of man right
Ezek. 16:31 build. place in e. w.
Rom. 3:2 much e. w. bec. to th.
Phil. 1:18 e w. whe. in pretence
See EVIL.

**His WAY.**
Gen. 6:12 flesh had corrup. h. w.
2 Sam. 22:31 as for God, his w. is perfect, Ps. 18:30
1 K. 8:32 to bring his w. on his own head, 2 Chr. 6:23
Job 8:19 this is the joy of his w.
17:9 righte. shall hold on his w.
21:31 who shall declare his w.?
23:11 his w. have I kept
36:23 who enjoined him his w.?
Ps. 25:9 meek will he teach h. w.
37:7 him who prosper. in his w.
23 and he delighteth in his w.
34 wait on L. and keep his w.
119:9 sh. young man clea. h. w.
Prov. 8:22 in beginning of h. w.
11:5 righ. of perfect direct h. w.
14:8 prudent is to unders. h. w.
16:9 a man's heart devis. his w.
17 that keepeth his w. preser.
19:3 foolish. of man perv. h. w.
20:14 when he is gone his w.
21:29 upright, directeth his w.
Is. 48:15 make his w. prospero.
55:7 let wicked forsake his w.
Jer. 4:7 destroyer of G. on h. w.
Ezek. 3:18 warn wicked fr. h. w.
19 turn not from h. w. 33:8, 9
13:22 sho. not return fr. his w.
Nah. 1:3 L. hath h. w. in whirl.
Jam. 1:24 beholdeth, goeth h. w.

**In the WAY.**
Gen. 24:27 I being in the w.
48 who led me in the right w.
35:3 L. was with me in the w.
Ex. 5:20 M. and A. stood in t. w.
23:20 to keep thee in the w.
Deut. 1:33 who went in the w.
1 K. 11:29 Ahijah found J. in w.
13:24 carc. was cast in w. 25:28
15:26 walked in w. of fath. 22:52
18:7 as Obadiah was in the w.
2 K. 8:18 he walked in the w. of the kings of Israel, 16:3; 2 Chr. 21:6, 13
27 he walked in the w. of Aha.
2 Chr. 11:17 three years in t. w.
20:32 he walked in the w. of A.
Ezr. 8:22 the enemy in the w.
Neh. 9:12 to give th. light in w.
19 depart. not to lead in t. w.
Job 18:10 snare and trap in t. w.
Ps. 1:1 nor standeth in the w.
25:8 teach sinners in the w.
12 shall he teach in the w. 32:8
85:13 set us in the w. of steps
102:23 weak. strength in the w.
110:7 drink of brook in the w.
119:1 bless. are undefiled in w.
14 I have rejoiced in the w. of
139:24 lead me in the w. everla.
142:3 in the w. they laid a snare
Prov. 1:15 walk not thou in t. w.
2:20 thou mayest walk in t. w.
4:11 I ha. taught thee in the w.
14 go not in t. w. of evil men
8:20 I lead in t. w. of righteous.
9:6 go in the w. of understand.
10:17 he is in the w. of life
12:28 in the w. of righteousness
13:6 him that is upright in t. w.
16:31 if it be found in the w. of
22:5 thorns and snares in the w.
6 train up a child in the w. he
23:19 guide thy heart in the w.
26:13 slothf. saith a lion in t. w.
29:27 upright in the w. is abom.
Ec. 12:5 fears shall be in the w.
Is. 8:11 not walk in t. w. of peo.
26:8 in the w. of thy judgments
57:17 went on in the w. of heart
65:2 walked in the w. not good
Jer. 2:18 wh. to do in t. w. of E.? what to do in t. w. of Assy.?

*Ezek.* 23:31 walk. *in t. w.* of sis.
*Hos.* 6:9 priests murder *in t. w.*
*Mat.* 5:25 agree whil. art *in t. w.*
21:32 J. came *in the w.* of right.
*Mark* 11:8 spread garments *in t. w.* oth. strewed branches *in the w. Mat.* 21:8; *Lu.* 19:36
*Luke* 1:79 guide our feet *in t. w.*
12:58 as thou art *in the w.* give
*Acts* 9:17 J. that appeared *in w.*
27 he had seen the Lord *in w.*
*Jude* 11 have gone *in the w.* of C.
*See* LORD.

**My WAY.**

*Gen.* 24:56 Lord prospered *my w.*
2 *Sam.* 22:33 maketh *my w.* perfect, *Ps.* 18:32
*Job* 19:8 fenced *my w.* that I can
*Is.* 40:27 sayest *my w.* is hid?
*Ezek.* 18:25 is not *my w.* equal?
*John* 8:21 I go *my w.* ye sh. seek
*Rom.* 15:24 brought on *my w.*
2 *Cor.* 1:16 be brought on *my w.*

**Out of the WAY**

*Ex.* 32:8 turned aside *o. of the w.* *Deut.* 9:12, 16; *Jud.* 2:17
*Deut.* 11:28 if ye turn *o. of the w.*
13:5 thrust thee *out of the w.*
27:18 blind wander *out of the w.*
*Job* 24:4 turn needy *out of the w.*
24 they are taken *out of the w.*
31:7 if my step turned *o. of t. w.*
*Prov.* 21:16 wand. *out of the w.*
*Is.* 28:7 thro' drink are *o. of t. w.*
30:11 get you *o. of the w.* turn
57:14 take stumbling-bl. *o. of w.*
*Mal.* 2:8 departed *out of the w.*
*Rom.* 3:12 all gone *out of the w.*
*Col.* 2:14 took handwri. *o. of w.*
2 *Thes.* 2:7 be taken *out of the w.*
*Heb.* 5:2 comp. on them *o. of w.*
12:13 lame be turned *o. of t. w*

**Own WAY.**

*Prov.* 1:31 eat fruit of their *o. w.*
20:24 can man unders. his *o w.*?
*Is.* 53:6 turn. every one to *o. w.*
56:11 they all look to their *o. w.*
*Ezek.* 22:31 *o. w.* have I recomp.
36:17 defiled Isr. by their *o. w*

**WAY-SIDE.**

*Gen.* 38:21 har. th. was by *w.-s.*?
1 *Sam.* 4:13 Eli sat by *w.-s.*
*Ps.* 140:5 proud spr. net by *w.-s.*
*Mat.* 13:4 seeds fell by *w.-s.* 19; *Mark* 4:4, 15; *Luke* 8:5, 12
20:30 blind men sitting by *w.-s.*
*Mark* 10:46 blind Bartimeus sat by *w.-s.* begging, *Luke* 18:35

**Their WAY.**

1 *K.* 2:4 if children take heed to *t. w.* 8:25; 2 *Chr.* 6:16
*Job* 6:18 paths of *t. w.* are turned
19:12 troops raise up *t. w.* ag.
29:25 I chose out *t. w.* sat chief
*Ps.* 35:6 let *their w.* be dark
49:13 this *their w.* is their folly
*Jer.* 3:21 they have pervert. *t. w.*
6:27 mayest know and try *t. w.*
*Ezek.* 7:27 I will do to them after *their w.* 9:10; 11:21
14:22 ye sh. see *t. w.* and doings
33:7 as for th. *t. w.* is not equal
36:17 *t. w.* was bef. me as uncl.
19 accord. to *t. w.* and doings
*Acts* 15:3 bro. on *t. w.* by church
*See* WENT.

**This WAY.**

*Gen.* 28:20 will keep me in *t. w.*
*Ex.* 2:12 Moses looked *t. w.* and
*Jos.* 8:20 no power to flee *t. w.*
2 *K.* 6:19 Elisha said, *t.* is not *w.*
*Is.* 30:21 *this* is *w.* walk ye in it
*Acts* 9:2 if he found any of *t. w.*
22:4 I persecu. *t. w.* unto death

**Thy WAY.**

*Gen.* 24:40 L. will prosper *t. w.*
*Ex.* 33:13 I pray, show me *t. w.*
*Num.* 22:32 bec. *t. w.* is perverse
*Jos.* 1:8 sh. make *t. w.* prosper.
1 *K.* 19:15 return on *t. w.* to wil.
*Ps.* 5:8 make *t. w.* straight bef.
27:11 teach me *t. w.* O L. 86:11
37:5 commit *t. w.* unto the L.
44:18 neit. declined from *t. w.*
67:2 that *thy w.* may be known
77:13 *t. w.* O G. is in sanctuary
19 *t. w.* is in the sea, thy path
119:37 and quicken me in *t. w.*
*Prov.* 3:23 sh. thou walk in *t. w.*
5:8 remove *thy w.* far from her
*Is.* 57:10 in greatness of *thy w.*
*Jer.* 2:23 see *thy w.* in the valley
33 why trim. thou *t. w.* to seek
36 why gad. to change *thy w.*?
4:18 *thy w.* have procured these
*Ezek.* 16:43 I will recomp. *thy w.*
*Hos.* 2:6 I will hedge up *thy w.*
10:13 bec. thou didst trust *t. w.*
*Mat.* 11:10 prepare *t. w.* before thee, *Mark* 1:2; *Luke* 7:27

**WAYS.**

*Gen.* 19:2 early, go on your *w.*
*Deut.* 5:33 walk in *w.* Lord com.
1 *K.* 22:43 he walked in *w.* of A.
2 *K.* 21:21 walked in *w.* of Man.
22:2 he walked in *w.* of David, 2 *Chr.* 17:3; 34:2
2 *Chr.* 21:12 walk. not in *w.* of J.
22:3 he walked in *w.* of Ahab
28:2 walked in *w.* of kings of Is.
*Job* 24:13 they kn. not *w.* of light
30:12 raise up *w.* of destruction
34:21 eyes are upon *w.* of man
40:19 Behe. is chief of *w.* of G.
*Ps.* 84:5 in heart are *w.* of them
*Prov.* 1:19 so *w.* of ev. one greedy
2:13 to walk in *w.* of darkness
15 whose *w.* are crooked, fro.
3:17 wisd.'s *w.* are *w.* of pleas.
5:6 her *w.* are movable
21 *w.* of man are bef. eyes of L.
6:6 go to ant, consider her *w.*
7:25 let not heart decl. to her *w.*
14:12 end the. *w.* of death, 16:25
16:2 *w.* of a man cl. in his eyes
7 when a man's *w.* please L.
17:23 gift to perv. *w.* of judgm.
31:27 looketh to *w.* of househ.
*Ec.* 11:9 walk in *w.* of thy heart
*Is.* 49:9 feed in *w.* and pastures
*Jer.* 2:23 dromedary travers. *w.*
3:2 in *w.* hast thou sat as Arab.
6:16 stand in *w.* and see, ask
7:3 amend your *w.* 5; 26:13
23 walk in *w.* I command. you
12:16 diligently learn *w.* of peo.
18:11 make *w.* and doings good
32:19 eyes open on *w.* of men
*Lam.* 1:4 *w.* of Zion do mourn
3:40 let us search and try our *w.*
*Ezek.* 18:25 are not *w.* uneq.? 29
20:43 remember your *w.* doings
44 not acc. to your wicked *w.*
21:19 son of man appoi. two *w.*
21 stood at head of two *w.*
*Hag.* 1:5 consider your *w.* 7
*Zec.* 1:6 do according to our *w.*
*Luke* 3:5 rough *w.* made smooth
*Acts* 2:28 known to me *w.* of life

**Any WAYS.**

*Lev.* 20:4 do *a. w.* hide their eyes
*Num.* 30:15 *any w.* make void
2 *Chr.* 32:13 *a. w.* able to deliver
*See* BY-WAYS, EVIL, HIGH.

**His WAYS.**

*Deut.* 8:6 to walk in *h. w.* 26:17; 28:9; 30:16; 1 *K.* 2:3
10:12 walk in all *his w.* 11:22; *Jos.* 22:5; 1 *K.* 8:58
19:9 love L. walk ever in *his w.*
32:4 *h. w.* are judgm. *Dan.* 4:37
1 *Sam.* 8:3 walked not in *his w.*
18:14 D. behav. wisely in *his w.*
1 *K.* 8:39 give every man according to *his w.* 2 *Chr.* 6:30
2 *Chr.* 13:22 *his w.* are written
27:6 Jotham prepared *his w.*
7 *h. w.* are writ. in book, 28:26
*Job* 26:14 these are parts of *h. w.*
34:11 man find accord. to *h. w.*
27 would not cons. any of *h. w.*
*Ps.* 10:5 *his w.* always grievous
103:7 made known *h. w.* to Mo.
119:3 iniq. they walk in *his w.*
128:1 blessed that walk. in *h. w.*
145:17 Lord is right. in all *h. w.*
*Prov.* 3:31 choose none of *his w.*
10:9 perverteth *h. w.* be known
14:2 perverse in *h. w.* despi. L.
19:16 despiseth *his w.* shall die
22:25 lest thou learn *his w.*
28:6 he that is perverse in *h. w.*
18 perverse in *his w.* shall fall
*Is.* 2:3 teach us *his w. Mic.* 4:2
42:24 would not walk in *his w.*
45:13 I will direct *h. w.* saith L.
57:18 I have seen *his w.*
*Jer.* 17:10 accord. to *his w.* 32:19
*Ezek.* 18:23 sho. return fr. *his w.*
30 judge Is. acc. to *h. w.* 33:20
*Hos.* 9:8 snare of fowler in *h. w.*
12:2 punish Jac. accord. to *h. w.*
*Joel* 2:7 march ev. one in *his w.*
*Hab.* 3:6 *his w.* are everlasting
*Luke* 1:76 bef. L. to prep. *his w.*
*Rom.* 11:33 *his w.* past finding
*Jam.* 1:8 is unstable in all *his w.*
11 rich man fade aw. in *his w.*
*See* LORD.

**My WAYS.**

1 *K.* 3:14 if thou wilt walk in *my w.* 11:38; *Zec.* 3:7
*Job* 31:4 doth not he see *my w.*
*Ps.* 39:1 will take heed to *my w.*
81:13 O th. Is. walk. in *my w.*!
95:10 not kno. *my w. Heb.* 3:10
119:5 O that *my w.* were direct.
26 I have declared *my w.* and
59 I thought on *my w.* turned
168 all *my w.* are before thee
139:3 acquainted wi. all *my w.*
*Prov.* 8:32 bles. that keep *my w.*
23:26 let thine eyes obs. *my w.*
*Is.* 55:8 neit. your ways *my w.*
9 *my w.* higher th. your ways
58:2 delight to know *my w.*
*Lam.* 3:9 hath inclosed *my w.*
11 he turned aside *my w.*
*Ezek.* 18:29 are not *my w.* equ.?
*Zec.* 3:7 if wilt walk in *my w.*
*Mal.* 2:9 have not kept *my w.*
1 *Cor.* 4:17 remembr. of *my w.*

**Own WAYS.**

*Job* 13:15 I will maint. my *o. w.*
*Prov.* 14:14 filled with his *o. w.*
*Is.* 58:13 not doing thine *o. w.*
66:3 th. have chosen their *o. w.*
*Ezek.* 36:31 remember your *o. w.*
32 be ashamed for your *o. w.*
*Acts* 14:16 nati. to walk in *o. w.*

**Their WAYS.**

2 *Chr.* 7:14 turn fr. *t.* wicked *w.*
*Job* 24:23 his eyes are upon *t. w.*
*Ps.* 125:5 turn to *t.* crooked *w.*
*Prov.* 9:15 who go right on *t. w.*
*Jer.* 15:7 return not from *t. w.*
16:17 mine eyes upon all *t. w.*
18:15 caused to stumble in *t. w.*
*Ezek.* 14:23 when ye see *t. w.*
16:47 hast not walk. after *t. w.*
*Hos.* 4:9 punish them for *t. w.*
*Rom.* 3:16 misery are in *their w.*
2 *Pet.* 2:2 follow *t.* pernicious *w.*

**Thy WAYS.**

*Deut.* 28:29 not prosper in *thy w.*
1 *Sam.* 8:5 walk not in *thy w.*

2 Chr. 6:31 fear to walk in thy w.
Job 4:6 the uprightness of thy w.
21:14 not knowledge of thy w.
22:3 gain that mak. t. w. perf.?
28 light sh. shine upon thy w.
Ps. 25:4 show me thy w. O Lord
51:13 teach transgressors t. w.
91:11 to keep thee in all thy w.
119:15 will ha. respect to thy w.
Prov. 3:6 in t. w. acknowl. him
4:26 let all t. w. be established
31:3 not t. w. to that wh. destr.
Is. 63:17 made us err from t. w.
64:5 that rememb. thee in t. w.
Jer. 2:33 hast taught wick. t. w.
3:13 thou hast scattered thy w.
Ezek. 7:3 accord. to thy w. 4, 8, 9
16:47 corrupted more in thy w.
61 remember t. w. be ashamed
24:14 according to t. w. judge
28:15 thou wast perfect in t. w.
Dan. 5:23 in wh. hand are t. w.
Rev. 15:3 just and true are t. w.

### WAYFARING.

Jud. 19:17 a w. man in street
2 Sam. 12:4 flock to dress for w.
Is. 33:8 the w. man ceaseth
35:8 w. men sh. not err therein
Jer. 9:2 a lodg.-place of w. men
14:8 why should. be as w. man?

### WAY-MARKS.

Jer. 31:21 set thee up w.-m. make

### WEAK.

Num. 13:18 whether strong or w.
Jud. 16:7 w. as oth. men, 11, 17
2 Sam. 3:39 I am w. tho' anoint.
2 Chr. 15:7 let not hands be w.
Job 4:3 strengthened w. hands
Ps. 6:2 I am w. 109:24 knees w.
Is. 14:10 art thou bec. w. as we?
35:3 strengthen ye the w. hands
Ezek. 7:17 knees w. as wat. 21:7
16:30 w. is thy heart, saith Lord
Joel 3:10 let w. say, I am strong
Mat. 26:41 flesh w. Mark 14:38
Acts 20:35 ye ought to supp. w.
Rom. 4:19 being not w. in faith
8:3 law was w. through flesh
14:1 that is w. in faith recei. ye
2 another who is w. eat. herbs
21 broth. stumb. or is made w.
15:1 ought to bear infirm. of w.
1 Cor. 1:27 w. things to confound
4:10 we are w. 8:7 being w. 10
8:12 wound their w. conscience
9:22 to the w. I became w. that
11:30 for this cause many are w.
2 Cor. 10:10 bodily presence is w.
11:21 I speak as we had been w.
29 who is w. and I am not w.?
12:10 when I am w. then strong
13:3 wh. to you-ward in not w.
4 we are w. in him, but sh. live
9 wh. we are w. and ye strong
Gal. 4:9 turn ye to w. elements?
1 Thes. 5:14 support w. be pati.

### WEAK-HANDED.

2 Sam. 17:2 come wh. he is w.-h.

### WEAKEN.

Is. 14:12 wh. didst w. nations?

### WEAKENED, ETH.

Ezr. 4:4 people of land w. Judah
Neh. 6:9 their hands shall be w.
Job 12:21 he w. stren. of mighty
Ps. 102:23 w. my strength in way
Jer. 38:4 w. hands of men of war

### WEAKER.

2 Sam. 3:1 S.'s house w. and w.
1 Pet. 3:7 honor wife as w. vessel

### WEAKNESS.

1 Cor. 1:25 w. of God is stronger
2:3 I was with you in w.
15:43 sown in w. raised in pow.
2 Cor. 12:9 strength is perf. in w.
13:4 though crucified thro' w.
Heb. 7:18 going before for the w.
11:34 out of w. were made stro.

### WEALTH.

Gen. 34:29 sons of Ja. took th. w.
Deut. 8:17 hand got me this w.
18 L. giv. thee power to get w.
Ruth 2:1 a kinsman, man of w.
1 Sam. 2:32 see enemy in all w.
2 K. 15:20 exacted of men of w.
2 Chr. 1:11 th. hast not asked w.
12 I will give th. riches and w.
Ezr. 9:12 nor seek peace or w.
Est. 10:3 M. seeking w. of peo.
Job 21:13 spend their days in w.
31:25 if I rejoiced bec. w. great
Ps. 44:12 dost not increase w.
49:6 trust in w. boast in riches
10 and leave their w. to others
112:3 w. and riches in his house
Prov. 5:19 lest stra. be fill. wi. w.
10:15 man's w. is his city, 18:11
13:11 w. gotten by vanity sh. be
22 w. of sinner is laid up
19:4 w. maketh many friends
Ec. 5:19 God hath given w. 6:2
Zec. 14:14 w. of heathen shall
Acts 19:25 by this craft have w.
1 Cor. 10:24 seek every man another's w.

### WEALTHY.

Ps. 66:12 thou bro. us into w.
Jer. 49:31 get up unto w. nation

### WEANED.

Gen. 21:8 Isaac grew and was w.
1 Sam. 1:22 not go till chi. be w.
1 K. 11:20 whom Taphenes w.
Ps. 131:2 w. of moth. soul as w.
Is. 11:8 w. child put his hand
28:9 them th. are w. from milk
Hos. 1:8 wh. she w. Lo-ruhama

### WEAPON.

Deut. 23:13 a paddle upon w.
Neh. 4:17 other hand held a w.
Job 20:24 shall flee from iron w.
Is. 54:17 no w. form. sh. prosper
Ezek. 9:1 with his destroy. w. 2

### WEAPONS.

Gen. 27:3 take, I pray, thy w.
1 Sam. 21:8 neither sword nor w.
2 K. 11:8 every man with his w. in hand, 11; 2 Chr. 23:7, 10
Is. 13:5 L. cometh and the w. of his indignation, Jer. 50:25
Jer. 22:7 prepare ev. one with w.
Ezek. 39:9 set on fire, burn w. 10
John 18:3 Judas cometh with w.
2 Cor. 10:4 w. of warf. not carnal

See WAR.

### WEAR.

Ex. 18:18 wilt surely w. away
Deut. 22:5 woman not w. what
11 not w. garm. of divers sorts
1 Sam. 2:28 w. an ephod before
22:18 pers. that did w. an ephod
Job 14:19 waters w. the stones
Is. 4:1 eat our bread, w. apparel
Dan. 7:25 w. out saints of M. H.
Zec. 13:4 nor w. a rough garm.
Mat. 11:8 that w. soft clothing
Luke 9:12 day began to w. away

### WEARETH, ING.

1 Sam. 14:3 priest w. an ephod
John 19:5 Jesus came w. purple
1 Pet. 3:3 let it not be w. of gold
Jam. 2:3 him that w. gay cloth.

### WEARY.

Gen. 27:46 Rebek. said, I am w.
Deut. 25:18 Amalek sm. when w.
Jud. 4:21 J. smote Sis. when w.
8:15 bread to men that are w.
2 Sam. 16:14 and people came w.
17:2 come upon him while w.
23:10 smote Philist. till was w.
Job 3:17 wicked cease, w. at rest
10:1 my soul is w. of my life
16:7 he hath made me w. deso.
22:7 not given wat. to w. to dr.
Ps. 6:6 I am w. with groaning
68:9 confirm thine inh. when w.
69:3 I am w. of my crying
Prov. 3:11 be not w. of L.'s cor.
25:17 lest he be w. of thee
Is. 1:14 feasts are trouble, am w.
Is. 5:27 none sh. be w. nor stum.
7:13 is it small thing to w. men
16:12 when it is seen M. is w.
28:12 wherewi. cause w. to rest
32:2 shadow of rock in w. land
40:28 G. fainteth not, nei. is w.
30 youths shall faint and be w.
31 that wait on L. sh. not be w.
43:22 thou hast been w. of me
46:1 a burden to the w. beast
50:4 spe. a word to him th. is w.
Jer. 2:24 th. seek her will not w.
6:11 I am w. with holding in
9:5 they w. thems. to commit
15:6 I am w. with repenting
20:9 I was w. with forbearing
31:25 I have satiated w. soul
51:58 folk shall labor and be w.
64 B. sink and they shall be w.
Hab. 2:13 peo. sh. w. themselves
Luke 18:5 by contin. com. she w.
Gal. 6:9 let us not be w. in well-doing. 2 Thes. 3:13

### WEARIED.

Gen. 19:11 w. themselves to find
Is. 43:23 nor have I w. thee
24 hast w. me with thine iniq.
47:13 art w. in multitude
57:10 w. in greatness of way
Jer. 4:31 soul is w. bec. of murd.
12:5 if run and they w. thee, if in land of peace they w. th.
Ezek. 24:12 w. herself with lies
Mic. 6:3 wherein have I w. thee
Mal. 2:17 w. Lord, wherein have we w. him?
John 4:6 J. being w. sat on well
Heb. 12:3 lest ye be w. and faint

### WEARIETH.

Job 37:11 he w. the thick cloud
Ec. 10:15 labor of foolish w.

### WEARINESS.

Ec. 12:12 study is a w. of the flesh
Mal. 1:13 said, What a w. is it!
2 Cor. 11:27 w. and painfulness

### WEARISOME.

Job 7:3 w. nights are appointed

### WEASEL.

Lev. 11:29 w. and mouse, uncl.

### WEATHER.

Job 37:22 fair w. com. out of nor.
Prov. 25:20 tak. a gar. in cold w.
Mat. 16:2 fair w. for sky is red
3 in morning it will be foul w.

### WEAVE, EST.

Jud. 16:13 if th. w. seven locks
Is. 19:9 they that w. net-works
59:5 they w. a spider's web

### WEAVER.

Ex. 35:35 work the work of w.
1 Sam. 17:7 staff of Goli.'s spear like a w. beam, 2 Sam. 21:19; 1 Chr. 11:23; 20:5
Job 7:6 days swift. th. w. shuttle
Is. 38:12 I have cut off like a w.

### WEB, S.

Jud. 16:13 if thou weavest seven locks with the w. 14
Job 8:14 shall be a spider's w.
Is. 59:5 they weave spider's w.
6 w. sh. not become garments

### WEDDING.

Mat. 22:3 were bidden to w. 8, 10
11 man had not on a w. garm.
Luke 12:36 will return from w.
14:8 when th. art bidden to a w.

**WEDGE.**

*Jos.* 7:21 Achan saw a *w.* of gold
24 Joshua took Achan and *w.*
*Is.* 13:12 more precious than golden *w.* of Ophir

**WEDLOCK.**

*Ezek.* 16:38 as women th. br. *w.*

**WEEDS.**

*Jon.* 2:5 *w.* were about my head

**WEEK.**

*Gen.* 29:27 fulfil her *w.* we will
28 Jacob did so, fulfill. her *w.*
*Dan.* 9:27 one *w.* in midst of *w.*
*Mat.* 28:1 1st day of *w. Mark* 16:2, 9; *Luke* 24:1; *John* 20:1, 19
*Luke* 18:12 I fast twice in the *w.*
*Acts* 20:7 first day of *w.* Paul preached
1 *Cor.* 16:2 on first day of *w.* let

**WEEKS.**

*Lev.* 12:5 child, be unclean 2 *w.*
*Num.* 28:26 bri. offering after *w.*
*Jer.* 5:24 reserveth *w.* of harvest
*Dan.* 9:24 seventy *w.* are deter.
25 after threescore and 2 *w.* 26
10:2 I Dan. was mourning 3 *w.*
*Dan.* 10:3 nor ano. thys. till 3 *w.*
*See* FEAST, SEVEN.

**WEEP.**

*Gen.* 23:2 A. ca. to mourn and *w.*
43:30 Jos. sought where to *w.*
*Num.* 11:10 Moses heard peo. *w.*
13 they *w.* unto me, saying
1 *Sam.* 11:5 what ail. peo. th. *w.*?
30:4 had no more power to *w.*
2 *Sam.* 1:24 daugh. of Is. *w.* over
12:21 thou didst *w.* for the child
2 *Chr.* 34:27 rend thy clothes, *w.*
*Neh.* 8:9 holy, mourn not, nor *w.*
*Job* 27:15 his widows sh. not *w.*
30:25 did I not *w.* for him
31 into voice of them that *w.*
*Ec.* 3:4 a time to *w.* a time to
*Is.* 15:2 gone to high places to *w.*
22:4 I will *w.* bitterly, labor not
30:19 thou shalt *w.* no more
33:7 ambassad. of peace sh. *w.*
*Jer.* 9:1 that I might *w.* day and
13:17 my soul shall *w.* in secret places, mine eyes shall *w.*
22:10 *w.* not for the dead, nor bemo. him, *w.* sore for him
48:32 O vine, I will *w.* for thee
*Lam.* 1:16 for these things I *w.*
*Ezek.* 24:16 thou mou. nor *w.* 23
27:31 sh. *w.* for thee with bitter.
*Joel* 1:5 drunkards, *w.* and howl
2:17 priests *w.* between porch
*Mic.* 1:10 declare it not, *w.* not
*Zec.* 7:3 sho. I *w.* in 5th month
*Mark* 5:39 why make ado and *w.*
*Luke* 6:21 blessed are ye that *w.*
25 woe to you th. laugh, sh. *w.*
7:13 *w.* not, 8:52; *Rev.* 5:5
23:28 *w.* not for me, *w.* for you.
*John* 11:31 goeth to grave to *w.*
16:20 ye sh. *w.* world sh. rejoice
*Acts* 21:13 what mean ye to *w.*
*Rom.* 12:15 *w.* wi. them that *w.*
1 *Cor.* 7:30 th. *w.* as though they
*Jam.* 4:9 afflicted, mourn, and *w.*
5:1 ye rich men, *w.* and howl
*Rev.* 18:11 merchants shall *w.*

**WEEPEST.**

1 *Sam.* 1:8 Han. why *w.* thou?
*John* 20:13 wom. why *w.* th.? 15

**WEEPETH.**

2 *Sam.* 19:1 behold the king *w.*
2 *K.* 8:12 Hazael said, Why *w.*?
*Ps.* 126:6 goeth forth and *w.*
*Lam.* 1:2 she *w.* sore in the night

**WEEPING.**

*Num.* 25:6 *w.* bef. door of taber.
*Deut.* 34:8 days of *w.* for Moses
2 *Sam.* 3:16 husband with her *w.*
15:30 *w.* as they went up
*Ezr.* 3:13 not discern joy fr. *w.*
10:1 E. prayed and confess. *w.*
*Est.* 4:3 in ev. province was *w.*
*Job* 16:16 my face is foul with *w.*
*Ps.* 6:8 L. heard voice of my *w.*
30:5 *w.* may endure for a night
102:9 I mingl. my drink wi. *w.*
*Is.* 15:3 in their streets howl, *w.*
16:9 I will bewail with *w.* of Ja. vine of Sibmah, *Jer.* 48:32
22:12 did L. of hosts call to *w.*
65:19 voice of *w.* no more heard
*Jer.* 3:21 *w.* of Is. heard on high
9:10 for mountains I take up *w.*
31:9 they shall come with *w.*
15 lamentation and *w.* Rachel *w.* for her childr. *Mat.* 2:18
16 restrain thy voice from *w.*
41:6 Ish. went to meet them *w.*
48:5 continual *w.* shall go up
50:4 Judah going *w.* to seek L.
*Ezek.* 8:14 wom. *w.* for Tammuz
*Joel* 2:12 turn wi. fasting and *w.*
*Mal.* 2:13 covering altar with *w.*
*Mat.* 8:12 there sh. be *w.* 22:13; 24:51; 25:30; *Luke* 13:28
*Luke* 7:38 wom. stood at feet *w.*
*John* 11:33 when Je. saw her *w.*
20:11 Mary stood without *w.*
*Acts* 9:39 wido. stood by him *w.*
*Phil.* 3:18 told you often, now *w.*
*Rev.* 18:15 merch. shall stand *w.*
19 shipmaster and sailors, *w.*

**WEIGH.**

1 *Chr.* 20:2 crown to *w.* a talent
*Ezr.* 8:29 keep until ye *w.* them
*Ps.* 58:2 *w.* violence of hands
*Is.* 26:7 thou dost *w.* path of just

**WEIGHED.**

*Gen.* 23:16 *w.* to Ephron silver
1 *Sam.* 2:3 by L. actions are *w.*
17:7 his spear's head *w.* 600 shekels, 2 *Sam.* 21:16
2 *Sam.* 14:26 Ab. *w.* hair of head
*Ezr.* 8:25 priests *w.* sil. and gold
*Ezr.* 8:26 *w.* into han. silver, 33
*Job* 6:2 oh that my grief were *w.*
28:15 nor shall silver be *w.* for
31:6 let me be *w.* in even bala.
*Is.* 40:12 who hath *w.* mount.?
*Jer.* 32:9 Jeremi. *w.* him money
*Dan.* 5:27 thou art *w.* in balance
*Zec.* 11:12 they *w* thirty pieces

**WEIGHETH.**

*Job* 28:25 he *w.* waters by meas.
*Prov.* 16:2 the Lord *w.* spirits

**WEIGHING.**

*Num.* 7:85 each *w.* 86 spoons *w.*

**WEIGHT.**

*Gen.* 43:21 money in sack full *w.*
*Ex.* 30:34 of each a like *w.*
*Lev.* 19:35 do no unright. in *w.*
26:26 deliver your bread by *w.*
*Deut.* 25:15 thou sh. have just *w.*
*Jud.* 8:26 *w.* of golden ear-rings
2 *Sam.* 12:30 *w.* of king's crown
1 *K.* 7:47 was *w.* of brass found out, 2 *K.* 25:16
1 *Chr.* 28:14 he gave gold by *w.*
*Job* 28:25 make *w.* for the winds
*Prov.* 11:1 a just *w.* is his delight
16:11 a just *w.* and bal. are L.'s
*Ezek.* 4:10 thy meat sh. be by *w.*
16 they shall eat bread by *w.*
*Zec.* 5:8 *w.* of lead on mouth
2 *Cor.* 4:17 a more exceeding *w.*
*Heb.* 12:1 let us lay aside ev. *w.*
*Rev.* 16:21 stone of hail *w.* of tal.

**WEIGHTS.**

*Lev.* 19:36 just *w.* shall ye have
*Deut.* 25:13 sh. not ha. divers *w.*
*Prov.* 16:11 *w.* of bag his work
20:10 divers *w.* are abomina. 23
*Mic.* 6:11 wi. bag of deceitful *w.*

**WEIGHTY.**

*Prov.* 27:3 stone heavy, sand *w.*
2 *Cor.* 10:10 let. say they, are *w.*

**WEIGHTIER.**

*Mat.* 23:23 omitted *w.* matters

**WELFARE.**

*Gen.* 43:27 asked th. of their *w.*
*Ex.* 18:7 asked each other of *w.*
1 *Chr.* 18:10 sent to inq. of his *w.*
*Neh.* 2:10 man to seek *w.* of Is.
*Job* 30:15 my *w.* passeth away
*Ps.* 69:22 sho. have been for *w.*
*Jer.* 38:4 seeketh not *w.* of peo.

**WELL, Substantive.**

*Gen.* 21:19 she saw a *w.* of water
30 witness I have dig. this *w.*
24:13 I stand here by *w.* 43
*Num.* 21:16 *w.* whereof L. spake
17 spring up, O *w.* 18 dig. *w.*
2 *Sam.* 17:18 man that had *w.*
23:15 give me drink of water of *w.* of Beth. 1 *Chr.* 11:17, 18
*Ps.* 84:6 passing Baca make it *w.*
*Prov.* 5:15 wat. of thine own *w.*
10:11 a righte. man is *w.* of life
*Cant.* 4:15 a *w.* of waters fr. L.
*John* 4:6 Jacob's *w.* was there
11 *w.* is deep; 12 J. gave us *w.*
14 sh. be in him a *w.* of water

**WELLS.**

*Gen.* 26:15 *w.* Abr.'s serv. digg.
18 Isaac digged ag. *w.* of water
*Ex.* 15:27 where were twelve *w.*
*Num.* 20:17 drink of water of *w.*
*Deut.* 6:11 *w.* thou diggedst not
2 *K.* 3:19 ye sh. stop *w.* of water
25 they stopped all *w.* of wat.
2 *Chr.* 26:10 towers and dig. *w.*
*Is.* 12:3 draw out of *w.* of salvat.
2 *Pet.* 2:17 are *w.* without water

**WELL-SPRING.**

*Prov.* 16:22 und. is a *w.-s.* of life
18:4 *w.-s.* of wisdom as a brook

**WELL, Adverb.**

*Gen.* 4:7 if thou dost not *w.* sin
12:13 that it may be *w.* wi. me
29:6 Ja. said, Is he *w.*? he is *w.*
40:14 it shall be *w.* with thee
43:27 is your father *w.*? is he
*Ex.* 4:14 I kn. he can speak *w.*
*Num.* 36:5 sons of Joseph said *w.*
*Deut.* 1:23 saying pleased me *w.*
3:20 rest to breth. as *w.* as you,
4:40 that it may go *w.* with th. 5:16; 6:3, 18; 12:25, 28; 19:13; 22:7; *Ruth* 3:1; *Eph.* 6:3
5:29 it might be *w.* with them
33 that it may be *w.* *Jer.* 7:23
15:16 because he is *w.* wi. thee
*Jud.* 14:3 she pleaseth me *w.* 7
1 *Sam.* 16:16 and thou sh. be *w.*
2 *Sam.* 18:28 and said, All is *w.*
1 *K.* 18:24 answered, *w.* spoken
2 *K.* 4:26 is it *w.* with thee?
5:21 all *w.* 9:11; 7:9 do not *w.*
2 *Chr.* 12:12 in J. things went *w.*
*Ps.* 49:18 th. doest *w.* to thyself
*Ec.* 8:12 *w.* with them fear God
*Is.* 3:10 it shall be *w.* with him
*Jer.* 22:15 it was *w.* with him, 16
40:4 and I will look *w.* to thee
42:6 that it may be *w.* with us
*Ezek.* 33:32 one that can play *w.*
*Mat.* 25:21 *w.* done, th. good and faithful serv. 23; *Luke* 19:17
*Luke* 20:39 Master, thou hast *w.* said, *John* 4:17
1 *Tim.* 5:17 elders that rule *w.* be counted worthy
*See* DO, FAVORED, PLEASED.

**WELL-BELOVED.**

*Cant.* 1:13 myrrh is my *w.-b.*
*Is.* 5:1 will I sing to my *w.-b.*
*Mark* 12:6 he sent his *w.-b.* son
*Rom.* 16:5 salute *w.-b.* Epenetus

3 *John* 1 elder to the *w.-b.* Gaius

**Very WELL.**

*Acts* 25:10 as thou *v. w.* knowest
2 *Tim.* 1:18 thou knowest *v. w.*

**WELL-NIGH.**

*Ps.* 73:2 steps had *w.-n.* slipped

**WEN.**

*Lev.* 22:22 having a *w.* or scurvy

**WENCH.**

2 *Sam.* 17:17 a *w.* told Jonathan

**WENT.**

*Gen.* 35:3 L. wi. me in way I *w.*
*Deut.* 1:31 bare th. in way ye *w.*
*Jos.* 24:17 preser. in way we *w.*
*Jud.* 1:17 Judah *w.* wi. Simeon
1 *Sam.* 10:14 said, Whi. *w.* ye?
1 *K.* 13:12 said, What way *w.* he?
*Mat.* 21:30 I go, sir, but *w.* not

**WENT about.**

*Num.* 11:8 people *w. a.* gath. it
2 *K.* 3:25 slinger *w. a.* smote it
2 *Chr.* 17:9 they *w. about*, taught
*Ec.* 2:20 I *w. a.* to cause my hea.
*Cant.* 5:7 watchmen that *w. a.*
*Mat.* 4:23 Jesus *w. about* teaching, 9:35; *Mark* 6:6
*Acts* 9:29 they *w. a.* to slay him, 21:31; 26:21
10:38 Jesus *w. about* doing good
13:11 he *w. a.* seeking some to

**WENT aside.**

*Luke* 9:10 and *w. aside* privately
*Acts* 23:19 chief captain *w. aside*

**WENT astray.**

*Ps.* 119:67 before afflicted I *w. a.*
*Ezek.* 44:10 when Israel *w. a.* 15
48:11 priests wh. *w.* not *astray*
*Mat.* 18:13 which *w.* not *astray*

**WENT away.**

*Mat.* 19:22 he *w. away* sorrowful, *Mark* 10:22
26:42 he *w. away* second time
44 *w. a.* third time, *Mark* 14:39

**WENT back.**

1 *K.* 13:19 so he *w. back* and eat
*John* 6:66 many disciples *w. back*

**WENT before.**

*Ex.* 13:21 L. *w. b.* them in cloud
1 *Tim.* 1:18 prophecies wh. *w. b.*

**WENT down.**

*Num.* 16:33 *w. d.* alive into pit
*Acts* 8:38 th. both *w. d.* into wat.

**WENT forth.**

2 *Sam.* 20:8 as he *w. f.* it fell out

**WENT out.**

*Gen.* 44:28 one *w. out* from me
2 *Sam.* 13:9 they *w. o.* from him
*John* 13:30 received sop, *w. out*
1 *John* 2:19 they *w. out* from us

**WENT over.**

2 *K.* 2:14 smote waters, *w. over*

**WENT their way.**

*Neh.* 8:12 people *w. t. way* to eat
*Zec.* 10:2 *w. t. way* as a flock
*Mat.* 8:33 fled, and *w. their way*
20:4 you, and they *w. th. way*
22:5 light of it, and *w. th. way*
22 heard words they *w. t. way*

**WENT up.**

*Gen.* 17:22 God *w. up* from Abr.
49:4 *w. up* to his father's bed
*Ex.* 19:3 Moses *w. up* to G. 20:; 24:13, 15; 34:4; *Deut.* 10:3

**WENT a whoring.**

*Jud.* 2:17 Isr. *w. a whoring*, 8:33
*Ps.* 106:39 *w. a w.* with inventi.

**WENTEST.**

*Jud.* 5:4 when thou *w.* out of S.
2 *Sam.* 16:17 why *w.* thou not
19:25 wheref. *w.* thou not with

**WEPT.**

*Gen.* 21:16 Hag. *w.* 27:38 Es. *w.*
29:11 and Jacob *w.* 33:4; 37:35; *Hos.* 12:4
42:24 Joseph *w.* 43:30; 45:2, 14, 15; 46:29; 50:1, 17
*Ex.* 2:6 behold, the babe *w.*
*Num.* 11:4 child. of Is. *w.* 18, 20; 14:1; *Deut.* 1:45; 34:8; *Jud.* 2:4; 20:23, 26; 21:2
*Jud.* 14:16 Samson's wife *w.*
*Ruth* 1:9 kissed daughters, *w.* 14
1 *Sam.* 1:7 Hannah *w.* not eat, 10
11:4 people *w.* 2 *Sam.* 3:32, 34
20:41 Jonathan and David *w.*
24:16 S. lifted up his v. and *w.*
30:4 and David *w.* 2 *Sam.* 1:12
2 *Sam.* 3:32 Da. *w.* at grave of A.
12:22 child alive, I fast. and *w.*
13:36 servants *w.* for Amnon
15:23 country *w.* 30 *w.* as he w.
18:33 moved, and *w.* for Absal.
2 *K.* 8:11 the man of God *w.*
13:14 Joash *w.* over Elisha
20:3 Hezekiah *w.* sore, *Is.* 38:3
22:19 king of Judah *w.* bef. me
*Ezr.* 3:12 priests seen 1st ho. *w.*
10:1 peo. *w.* very sore, *Neh.* 8:9
*Neh.* 1:4 wh. I heard words I *w.*
*Job* 2:12 friends lift. voice and *w.*
*Ps.* 69:10 when I *w.* and chasten.
137:1 by rivers of Babyl. we *w.*
*Mat.* 26:75 P. *w.* bitterly, *Mark* 14:72; *Luke* 22:62
*Mark* 5:38 them th. *w.* *Luke* 8:52
16:10 Mary told them as th. *w.*
*Luke* 7:32 mourned ye ha. not *w.*
19:41 beheld city and *w.* over it
*John* 11:35 Jesus *w.* 20:11 M. *w.*
*Acts* 20:37 *w.* fell on P.'s neck
1 *Cor.* 7:30 weep as tho' *w.* not
*Rev.* 5:4 *w.* because no man was

**As it WERE.**

*Is.* 53:3 we hid *as it w.* our faces
*Luke* 22:44 *as it w.* drops of blo.
*John* 7:10 but *as it w.* in secret
*Rev.* 10:1 his face *as it w.* sun
13:3 one of heads *as it w.* woun.
14:3 sung *as it w.* a new song
15:2 I saw *as it w.* a sea of glass

**WEST.**

*Gen.* 28:14 shalt spread abroad to *w.*
*Deut.* 33:23 possess *w.* and south
1 *K.* 7:25 three oxen towards *w.*
1 *Chr.* 9:24 porters tow. east, *w.* north and south, 2 *Chr.* 4:4
12:15 to flight tow. east and *w.*
*Ps.* 75:6 promot. not from the *w.*
103:12 as far as east is from *w.*
107:3 gath. them fr. east and *w.*
*Is.* 11:14 fly on Philist. tow. *w.*
43:5 gather thee from the *w.*
45:6 that they may know fr. *w.*
49:12 come from north and *w.*
59:19 shall fear the L. from *w.*
*Ezek.* 48:1 his sides east and *w.*
*Dan.* 8:5 a he-goat came from *w.*
*Hos.* 11:10 children tremb. fr. *w.*
*Zec.* 8:7 I will save peo. from *w.*
14:4 mount of O. cleave tow. *w.*
*Mat.* 8:11 many shall come from east and *w.* *Luke* 13:29
24:27 as lightning shineth to *w.*
*Luke* 12:54 cloud rise out of *w.*
*Rev.* 21:13 and on *w.* three gates

**WEST border.**

*Num.* 34:6 this shall be *w. bord.*
*Jos.* 15:12 *w. b.* was to great sea
*Ezek.* 45:7 to the *w. b.* a portion

**WESTERN.**

*Num.* 34:6 as for the *w.* border

**WEST quarter.**

*Jos.* 18:14 this was *w. quarter*

**WEST side.**

*Ex.* 27:12 *w. s.* 50 cubits, 38:12
*Num.* 2:18 on *w. s.* stand. of Ep.
35:5 meas. on *w. s.* Lev.'s cities
*Ezek.* 48:3 to *w. s.* a portion for Naphtali, 4, 5, 6, 7, 8, 23, 24

**WESTWARD.**

*Gen.* 13:14 A. looked east. and *w.*
*Num.* 3:23 behind tabernacle *w.*
*Deut.* 3:27 lift up thine eyes *w.*
*Ezek.* 48:18 resi. sh. be 10,000 *w.*
*Dan.* 8:4 I saw ram pushing *w.*

**WEST wind.**

*Ex.* 10:19 *w. w.* took away locu.

**WET.**

*Job* 24:8 th. are *w.* with showers
*Dan.* 4:15 let it be *w.* with dew of heaven, 23, 25, 33; 5:21

**WHALE.**

*Job* 7:12 am I a sea or a *w.* that
*Ezek.* 32:2 Phar. thou art as a *w.*
*Mat.* 12:40 Jo. was 3 days in *w.*

**WHALES.**

*Gen.* 1:21 God created great *w.*

**WHAT.**

*Ex.* 13:14 wh. son ask, *w.* this?
16:7 *w.* are we that ye murm.?
15 they wist not *w.* it was
*Deut.* 20:5 *w.* man is th.? 6, 7, 8
*Jud.* 18:8 *w.* say ye? 18 *w.* do?
24 *w.* have I more? *w.* is this? *w.* aileth thee?

**WHATSOEVER.**

*Gen.* 31:16 *w.* G. said unto thee
*Num.* 22:17 I will do *w.* th. say.
*Deut.* 12:32 *w.* I command, obs.
*Jud.* 10:15 do th. *w.* 1 *Sam.* 14:36
*Ps.* 115:3 God hath done *w.* he pleased, 135:6; *Ec.* 8:3
*Ec.* 3:14 *w.* God doeth, it sh. be
*Mat.* 5:37 *w.* is more than these
7:12 *w.* ye would men sho. do
17:12 done *w.* listed, *Mark* 9:13
20:4 *w.* right I will give you, 7
*John* 15:16 *w.* ye shall ask, 16:23

**WHEAT.**

*Gen.* 30:14 R. found mand. in *w.*
*Ex.* 9:32 *w.* and rye were not
34:22 first-fr. of *w.* *Num.* 18:12
*Deut.* 32:14 fat of kidneys of *w.*
*Jud.* 6:11 Gideon threshed *w.*
15:1 time of *w.* harvest Samson
*Ruth* 2:23 to end of *w.* harvest
1 *Sam.* 6:13 Beth-she. reaping *w.*
12:17 is it not *w.* harv. to-day?
2 *Sam.* 4:6 they wo. ha. fetch. *w.*
1 *K.* 5:11 Solom. gave Hiram *w.*
1 *Chr.* 21:23 *w.* for meat-offering
*Ezr.* 6:9 need of, *w.* salt, wine
7:22 a hundred measures of *w.*
*Job* 31:40 thistles grow ins. of *w.*
*Ps.* 81:16 fed th. wi. finest of *w.*
147:14 fill. thee with finest of *w.*
*Prov.* 27:22 bray a fool among *w.*
*Cant.* 7:2 belly like a heap of *w.*
*Jer.* 12:13 they have sown *w.*
23:28 what is chaff to the *w.*
31:12 flow together for *w.*
*Ezek.* 27:17 Judah traded in *w.*
*Joel* 2:24 floors shall be full of *w.*
*Amos* 5:11 take fr. him bur. of *w.*
8:5 that we may set forth *w.*
6 buy poor, sell refuse of *w.*
*Mat.* 3:12 gath. his *w.* *Luke* 3:17
13:25 enemy sowed tares am. *w.*
29 lest ye root up *w.* wi. them
30 gather the *w.* into my barn
*Luke* 16:7 said 100 measu. of *w.*
22:31 Satan may sift you as *w.*
*John* 12:24 exc. *w.* fall to ground
*Acts* 27:38 cast *w.* into the sea
1 *Cor.* 15:37 it may chance of *w.*
*Rev.* 6:6 meas. of *w.* for a penny
18:13 merchand. of *w.* is depart.
*See* BARLEY.

**WHEATEN.**

*Ex.* 29:2 wafers make of *w.* flour

**WHEEL.**

Ps. 83:13 O G. make th. like w.
Prov. 20:26 king bringeth w. ov.
Ec. 12:6 or w. broken at cistern
Is. 28:28 nor break with w.
Ezek. 1:15 one w. upon the earth
16 a w. in midst of a w. 10:10
10:13 cried to the wheels, O w.

**WHEELS.**

Ex. 14:25 took off th. chariot w.
Jud. 5:28 why tarry w. of chari.
Is. 5:28 their w. like a whirlwind
Jer. 18:3 he wrought work on w.
47:3 at the rumbling of his w.
Ezek. 1:16 appearance of the w.
3:13 at noise of w. over against
10:19 w. were beside th. 11:22
23:24 B. come ag. thee with w.
26:10 walls shake at noise of w.
Dan. 7:9 his w. a burning fire
Nah. 3:2 noise of rattling of w.

**WHELP, S.**

2 Sam. 17:8 as bear robbed of w.
Prov. 17:12 a bear robbed of w.
Ezek. 19:2 nourish. w. am. lions
3 she brought up one of her w.
Hos. 13:8 a bear bereaved of w.
Nah. 2:12 lion did tear for his w.
See LIONS.

**WHEN.**

Ps. 94:8 w. will ye be wise?
Ec. 8:7 who can tell w. it be?

**WHENCE.**

Gen. 42:7 w. come ye? Jos. 9:8
Jud. 17:9 M. said, w. comest th.?
19:17; 2 Sam. 1:3; 2 K. 5:25;
Job 1:7; 2:2; Jon. 1:8
Job 10:21 I go w. not ret. 16:22
John 7:28 and ye know w. I am
8:14 ye cannot tell w. I come
9:29 know not from w. he is, 30

**WHENSOEVER.**

Mark 14:7 w. ye may do th. good

**WHERE.**

Gen. 3:9 Lord said, w. art thou?
Ex. 2:20 w. is he? 2 Sam. 9:4
Job 9:24 if not, w. who is he?
14:10 the ghost, and w. is he?
38:4 w. wast thou wh. I laid.?
Luke 17:37 w. Lord?
John 7:11 w. is he? 9:12
34 w. I am, 12:26; 14:3; 17:24

**WHEREABOUT.**

1 Sam. 21:2 let no man know w.

**WHEREAS.**

1 K. 8:18 w. it was in thy heart
Ezek. 13:7 w. ye say, L. saith it

**WHEREFORE.**

2 Sam. 16:10 say, w. done so?
Mat. 26:50 w. art thou come?

**WHERETO.**

Is. 55:11 sh. prosper w. I sent it

**WHEREWITH.**

Jud. 6:15 w. shall I save Israel?
1 K. 22:22 Lord said, w. 2 Chr. 18:20
Mic. 6:6 w. come before Lord?

**WHEREWITHAL.**

Mat. 6:31 w. shall we be clothed?

**WHET.**

Deut. 32:41 I w. my glit. sword
Ps. 7:12 he will w. his sword
64:3 who w. tongue like sword
Ec. 10:10 and he w. not edge

**WHILE.**

Ps. 49:18 w. he lived, he blessed
63:4 bless thee w. I live, 146:2
Jer. 40:5 w. he was not go. back

**A WHILE.**

Gen. 46:29 Jos. wept a good w.
1 Sam. 9:27 S. said to S. st. a. w.
2 Sam. 7:19 hast spok. a great w.
Mat. 13:21 root, dureth for a. w.
Luke 8:13 which for a w. believe
18:4 he would not for a w.
1 Pet. 5:10 after suffered a w.

**All the WHILE.**

1 Sam. 22:4 a. t. w. Da. was in
25:7 none missing all the w. 16
27:11 will be his man. all the w.
Job 27:3 all t. w. breath is in me

**Long WHILE.**

Acts 20:11 had talked a long w.

**WHIP.**

Prov. 26:3 a w. for the horse
Nah. 3:2 noise of a w. noise of

**WHIPS.**

1 K. 12:11 my fath. chastis. you with w. 14; 2 Chr. 10:11, 14

**WHIRLETH.**

Ec. 1:6 wind w. continually

**WHIRLWIND.**

2 K. 2:1 take up Elijah by a w. 11
Job 37:9 out of south cometh w.
38:1 L. answ. Job out of w. 40:6
Ps. 58:9 take th. away as in a w.
Prov. 10:25; Hos. 13:3
Prov. 1:27 destruction com. as w.
Is. 5:28 their wheels like a w.
17:13 like a rolling thing bef. w.
40:24 w. shall take them away
41:16 the w. shall scatter them
66:15 chariots like w. Jer. 4:13
Jer. 23:19 a w. of L. is gone forth
25:32 a w. great w. sh. be raised
30:23 a w. shall fall on wicked
Ezek. 1:4 a w. came out of north
Dan. 11:40 come aga. him like w.
Hos. 8:7 sown wind, shall reap w.
Amos 1:14 devour in day of w.
Nah. 1:3 L. hath his way in w.
Hab. 3:14 they came out as a w.
Zec. 7:14 I scattered th. with w.

**WHIRLWINDS.**

Is. 21:1 as w. in south pass thro'
Zec. 9:14 Lord go forth with w.

**WHISPER, ED.**

2 Sam. 12:19 Da. saw servants w.
Ps. 41:7 all that hate me w.
Is. 29:4 speech w. out of dust

**WHISPERER, S.**

Prov. 16:28 a w. separat. friends
Rom. 1:29 debate, deceit, w.

**WHISPERINGS.**

2 Cor. 12:20 lest there be w.

**WHIT.**

1 Sam. 3:18 S. told Eli every w.
John 7:23 man every w. whole
John 13:10 but is clean every w.
2 Cor. 11:5 not a w. behind apo.

**WHITE.**

Gen. 30:37 Jacob made w. appear
49:12 his teeth be w. with milk
Ex. 16:31 like coriander-seed, w.
Lev. 13:3 turned w. 4, 20, 21, 25
Num. 12:10 leprous, w. as snow
Jud. 5:10 that ride on w. asses
2 K. 5:27 went out a leper, w.
2 Chr. 5:12 Levites arrayed in w.
Est. 8:15 Mord. went out in w.
Job 6:6 any taste in w. of egg?
Ps. 68:14 it was w. as snow in
Ec. 9:8 let thy garments be w.
Cant. 5:10 beloved is w. ruddy
Is. 1:18 sins sh. be w. as snow
Ezek. 27:18 D. traded in w. wool
Dan. 7:9 garm. was w. as snow
11:35 some fall to make them w.
12:10 many purifi. and made w.
Joel 1:7 branches thereof are w.
Zec. 1:8 horses speckled and w.
Mat. 5:36 make hair w. or black
17:2 his raim. was w. Luke 9:29
28:3 raim. w. as snow, Acts 1:10
Mark 16:5 a man clothed in w.
John 4:35 fields are w. to harvest
Rev. 1:14 head and hairs were w.
2:17 give him a w. stone, name
3:4 shall walk with me in w.
5 clothed in w. raiment, 4:4;
7:9, 13; 15:6; 19:8, 14
18 buy w. raiment, be clothed
6:2 behold, a w. horse, 19:11
7:14 made them w. in blood
14:14 w. cloud; 20:11 w. throne

**WHITE, D.**

Mat. 23:27 scribes like w. sepul.
Mark 9:3 no fuller can w. them
Acts 23:3 smite thee, thou w. wall

**WHITER.**

Ps. 51:7 I shall be w. than snow
Lam. 4:7 Nazarites w. th. milk

**WHITHER.**

1 Sam. 10:14 said, w. went ye?
2 K. 5:25 thy servant went no w.
Heb. 11:8 went, not knowing w.
See GO, GOEST, GOETH.

**WHITHERSOEVER.**

Prov. 17:8 w. it turn. it prosper.
21:1 king's heart w. he will
Mat 8:19 fol. w. goest, Luke 9:57
Rev. 14:4 follow L. w. he goeth

**WHOLE.**

2 Sam. 1:9 my life is yet w.
2 Chr. 15:15 sou. with w. desire
1 Cor. 12:17 if w. body were eye
See CONGREGATION, HEART.

**WHOLE, for sound.**

Jos. 5:8 abode in camp till w.
Job 5:18 and his hands make w.
Mat. 9:12 th. that be w. need not a physic. Mark 2:17; Lu. 5:31
21 I shall be w. Mark 5:28
12:13 and his hand was made w.
Mark 3:5; Luke 6:10
15:28 her daugh. was made w.
31 wond. saw maimed to be w.
Mark 5:34 faith hath made th. w.
go, be w. Luke 8:48; 17:19
Luke 7:10 found the servant w.
John 5:6 wilt th. be made w.? 14
7:23 made a man every whit w.
Acts 4:9 by what means he is w.
9:34 J. Christ maketh thee w.

**WHOLLY.**

Num. 32:11 not w. followed me
Deut. 1:36 bec. Caleb w. followed Lord, Jos. 14:8, 9, 14
Jer. 46:28 leave thee w. unpunis.
1 Thes. 5:23 God sanctify you w.
1 Tim. 4:15 give thy. w. to them

**WHOLESOME.**

Prov. 15:4 w. tongue tree of life
1 Tim. 6:3 cons. not to w. words

**WHOM.**

1 K. 20:14 Ahab said, By w.? 22:8
Ezr. 10:44; Rom. 1:5; 5:2, 11
Gal. 6:14
See BEFORE.

**WHOMSOEVER.**

Dan. 4:17 he giveth to w. he will, 25:32; 5:21

**WHORE.**

Lev. 19:29 not cause to be a w.
21:7 not take wife that is a w.
Deut. 22:21 play w. in father's
23:17 there shall be no w. of Is.
18 not bring hire of a w.
Jud. 19:2 concubine played w.
Prov. 23:27 a w. is a deep ditch
Is. 57:3 seed of adulterer and w.
Jer. 3:3 thou hast a w. forehead
Ezek. 16:28 thou hast played w.
Rev. 17:1 judgm. of great w. 19:2
15 waters where w. sitteth, 16

**WHORES.**

Ezek. 16:33 they give gifts to w.
Hos. 4:14 are separated with w.

**WHOREDOM.**

Gen. 38:24 Ta. is wi. child by w.

*Lev.* 19:29 lest land fall to *w.*
*Jer.* 3:9 thro' lightness of her *w.*
13:27 seen lewdness of thy *w.*
*Ezek.* 16:33 may come for thy *w.*
23:8 they pour. their *w.* on her
17 Babylon defiled her with *w.*
43:7 not defile my holy n. by *w.*
9 let them put their *w.* fr. me
*Hos.* 4:11 *w.* and wine take heart
5:3 O Ephraim, th. commit. *w.*
6:10 there is the *w.* of Ephraim

**WHOREDOMS.**

*Num.* 14:33 wander and bear *w.*
2 *K.* 9:22 *w.* of thy mother Jezeb.
2 *Chr.* 21:13 *w.* of house of Ahab
*Jer.* 3:2 polluted land with *w.*
*Ezek.* 16:20 is *w.* a small matter?
22 in *w.* not remember. youth
25 multiplied *w.* 26 increas. *w.*
34 contrary from women in *w.*
23:35 bear thy lewdness and *w.*
*Hos.* 1:2 wife and children of *w.*
2:2 let her put away her *w.*
4 for they be children of *w.*
4:12 *w.* caused them to err, 5:4
*Nah.* 3:4 *w.* selleth nat. thro' *w.*
*See* COMMIT.

**WHOREMONGER, S.**

*Eph.* 5:5 no *w.* hath any inherit.
1 *Tim.* 1:10 law made for *w.* liars
*Heb.* 13:4 *w.* and adulterers God
*Rev.* 21:8 *w.* have th. part in lake
22:15 without are *w.* murderers

WHORING. *See* GO, GONE, WENT.

**WHORISH.**

*Prov.* 6:26 by means of *w.* wom.
*Ezek.* 6:9 brok. with her *w.* heart
16:30 an imperious *w.* woman

WHOSE. *See* HEART.

**WHOSESOEVER.**

*John* 20:23 *w.* sin remit, *w.* sins

**WHOSOEVER.**

*Mat.* 11:6 bles. *w.* not be offend.
13:12 *w.* hath, to him be given
*Gal.* 5:10 bear judgm. *w.* he be
*Rev.* 22:17 *w.* will, let him take

**WHY.**

*Jer.* 25:13 turn ye, *w.* will ye die? *Ezek.* 18:31; 33:11
*Luke* 2:48 *w.* thus dealt with us?
*Acts* 14:15 *w.* do ye these things?

**WICKED.**

*Gen.* 18:23 righteous wi. *w.*? 25
38:7 Er was *w.* *Ex.* 9:27 people are *w.*
*Ex.* 23:7 I will not justify *w.*
*Lev.* 20:17 it is a *w.* thing
*Deut.* 15:9 not thou. in *w.* heart
17:5 committed that *w.* thing
23:9 keep thee from ev. *w.* thing
25:1 condemn *w.* 1 *K.* 8:32
1 *Sam.* 2:9 *w.* be silent in darkn.
24:13 wick. proceedeth from *w.*
2 *K.* 17:11 Is. wrought *w.* things
2 *Chr.* 6:23 judge by requiti. *w.*
7:14 if my peo. turn fr. th. *w.* ways, *Ezek.* 18:21; 33:11, 19
24:7 Athaliah that *w.* woman
*Neh.* 9:35 nor turned fr. *w.* ways, *Ezek.* 3:19; 13:22
*Est.* 7:6 adversary is *w.* Haman
9:25 Haman's *w.* device sh. ret.
*Job* 3:17 *w.* cease from troubling
9:22 destroyeth perfect and *w.*
29 if I be *w.* why labor, 10:15
10:7 knowest that I am not *w.*
21:7 wherefore do the *w.* live?
30 *w.* reserv. to-day of destru.
27:7 let mine enemy be as *w.*
34:18 say to king, Thou art *w.*?
38:13 *w.* might be shaken out of
15 from *w.* light is withholden
40:12 tread down *w.* in th. place
*Ps.* 7:11 God is angry with *w.*
9:5 thou hast destroyed the *w.*
16 *w.* snared in work of hands
17 *w.* shall be turned into hell
10:2 *w.* in pride persecute poor
3 *w.* boasteth; 4 *w.* not seek G.
13 wherefore doth *w.* cont. G.?
11:2 *w.* bend their bow, make
5 but the *w.* his soul hateth
6 upon *w.* he shall rain snares
12:8 *w.* walk on every side
17:9 keep me fr. *w.* that oppress
*Ps.* 17:13 deli. my soul fr. the *w.*
26:5 I will not sit with the *w.*
27:2 when *w.* came upon me
28:3 draw me not away with *w.*
31:17 let the *w.* be ashamed
34:21 evil sh. slay *w.* hate right.
37:7 bringeth *w.* devices to pass
10 *w.* shall not be, *Prov.* 10:25
12 *w.* plotteth; 20 *w.* sh. perish
14 *w.* have drawn out sword
16 better th. riches of many *w.*
21 *w.* borroweth, payeth not
32 *w.* watcheth the righteous
34 when *w.* are cut off, see it
35 I have seen *w.* in power
40 he sh. deliver them from *w.*
39:1 while the *w.* is before me
58:3 *w.* are estranged fr. womb
59:5 be not merciful to any *w.*
68:2 let *w.* perish at presence of
75:8 *w.* earth shall wring th. out
92:7 when *w.* spring as grass
94:3 how long sh. *w.* triumph?
13 until pit be digged for *w.*
101:3 I will set no *w.* thing bef.
4 I will not know a *w.* person
8 I will destroy all *w.* of land
104:35 let the *w.* be no more
106:18 flame burnt up the *w.*
112:10 *w.* see it and be grieved
119:95 *w.* have waited to destroy
110 the *w.* laid a snare for me
119 thou puttest away all *w.*
155 salvation is far fr. the *w.*
139:19 surely thou wilt slay *w.*
21 if th. be any *w.* way in me
140:8 further not his *w.* device
141:4 to practice *w.* works with
10 let *w.* fall into th. own nets
145:20 all the *w.* will he destroy
147:6 casteth *w.* down to ground
*Prov.* 2:22 the *w.* shall be cut off
5:22 his iniquities shall take *w.*
6:18 heart that deviseth *w.* im.
10:30 *w.* shall not inhabit earth
11:5 *w.* shall fall by his wicked.
7 when a *w.* man dieth, expe.
8 the *w.* cometh in his stead
10 wh. *w.* perish th. is shouting
18 *w.* worketh a deceitful work
21 *w.* sh. not be unpunish. 31
12:2 *w.* devices will he condemn
7 the *w.* are overthrown, 21:12
12 *w.* desireth net of evil men
13 *w.* snared by transgression
21 *w.* sh. be filled wi. mischief
13:17 *w.* messenger falleth into
14:17 man of *w.* devices is hated
19 *w.* bow at gates of righteous
32 *w.* driven away in wickedn.
15:29 Lord is far from the *w.*
16:4 even *w.* for the day of evil
17:4 *w.* doer giv. heed to false
15 th. justifieth *w.* is abomin.
18:3 when *w.* cometh
20:26 a wise king scattereth *w.*
21:18 *w.* sh. be ransom for right.
27 bringeth it with a *w.* mind
24:16 *w.* shall fall into mischief
19 nei. be thou envious at *w.*
25:5 take *w.* from before king
26 righteous man fall. bef. *w.*
26:23 a *w.* heart like a potsherd
28:1 *w.* flee when no man purs.
4 th. that forsake law praise *w.*
12 wh. *w.* rise, 28; 15 *w.* ruler
29:2 when the *w.* beareth rule
7 *w.* regardeth not to know it
12 servants *w.* 16 *w.* multitude
*Ec.* 3:17 God shall judge the *w.*
7:17 be not overmuch *w.*
8:10 I saw the *w.* buried, they
13 it shall not be well with *w.*
*Is.* 5:23 justify *w.* for reward
11:4 with breath sh. he slay *w.*
13:11 I will punish *w.* for iniq.
32:7 he deviseth *w.* devices
53:9 he made his grave with *w.*
55:7 let the *w.* forsake his way
57:20 *w.* are like troubled sea
*Jer.* 2:33 taught *w.* thy ways
6:29 *w.* are not plucked away
17:9 heart deceitf. and desp. *w.*
25:31 he will give *w.* to sword
*Ezek.* 3:18 warn *w.* 19; 33:8, 9
8:9 behold the *w.* abominations
11:2 these men give *w.* counsel
18:23 have I pleas. that *w.* die?
20:44 not according to *w.* ways
21:3 cut off from thee the *w.* 4
25 profane *w.* prince of Israel
33:15 if the *w.* restore pledge
*Dan.* 12:10 *w.* shall do wickedly
*Mic.* 6:11 shall I count them pure with *w.* balances?
*Nah.* 1:3 L. shall not acquit *w.*
11 there is come a *w.* counsel.
15 the *w.* shall no more pass
*Hab.* 1:4 *w.* doth compass right.
13 *w.* devour. man more right.
*Zep.* 1:3 consu. blocks with *w.*
*Mal.* 3:18 discern between righteous and *w.*
4:3 tread down *w.* as ashes
*Mat.* 12:45 more *w.* than himself, so to this *w.* gen. *Luke* 11:26
13:49 angels sh. sever *w.* fr. just
16:4 *w.* generation seek. a sign
18:32 *w.* serv. 25:26; *Luke* 19:22
*Acts* 2:23 by *w.* hands ha. slain
18:14 if it were matter of *w.*
1 *Cor.* 5:13 put away *w.* person
*Col.* 1:21 enemies by *w.* works
2 *Thes.* 2:8 th. sh. *w.* be revealed
*See* MAN, MEN.

**Of the WICKED.**

*Job* 8:22 place *of w.* come to nau.
9:24 earth giv. into hand *of w.*
10:3 shine upon couns. *of t. w.*
11:20 eyes *of the w.* shall fail
16:11 into hands *of the w.*
18:5 light *of the w.* be put out
21 such are dwellings *of t. w.*
20:5 triumphing *of the w.* short
22 hand *of t. w.* sh. come upon
21:16 counsel *of the w.* 22:18
17 how oft is candle *of the w.* put out? *Prov.* 13:9; 24:20
28 where dwelling-pl. *of t. w.*?
24:6 they gath. vintage *of t. w.*
29:17 I brake the jaws *of t. w.*
36:6 preserveth not life *of t. w.*
17 fulfilled judgment *of the w.*
*Ps.* 7:9 let wickedness *of the w.*
10:15 break arm *of the w.* man
22:16 assembly *of the w.*
36:1 transgression *of the w.*
11 let not hand *of the w.* rem.
37:17 arms *of t. w.* sh. be brok.
28 seed *of the w.* sh. be cut off
38 end *of the w.* sh. be cut off
55:3 bec. of oppression *of t. w.*
58:10 wash feet in bl. *of the w.*
64:2 hide me fr. counsel *of t. w.*
71:4 deliver me out of hand *of the w.* 74:19; 82:4; 97:10
73:3 I saw prosperity *of the w.*
75:10 horns *of w.* will I cut off
82:2 will ye accept pers. *of w.*?
91:8 see the reward *of the w.*
92:11 sh. hear my desire *of t. w.*
109:2 mouth *of t. w.* is opened
112:10 desi. *of t. w.* *Prov.* 10:28
119:53 bec. *of the w.* th. forsake
61 hands *of t. w.* have rob. me

125:3 rod *of the w.* sh. not rest
129:4 L. cut asun. cords *of t. w.*
140:4 keep me fr. hands *of the w.*
8 grant not, O L. desi. *of t. w.*
146:9 way *of the w.* turns
*Prov.* 2:14 in forwardn. *of the w.*
3:25 not afra. of desola. *of t. w.*
33 curse of L. in house *of t. w.*
4:14 ent. not into path *of t. w.*
19 way *of t. w.* is as darkness
10:3 casteth away substa. *of w.*
6 viole. cover. mouth *of w.* 11
7 the name *of the w.* shall rot
16 fruit *of t. w.* tendeth to sin
20 heart *of t. w.* is little worth
24 fear *of t. w.* sh. come upon
27 years *of the w.* sh. be short.
32 mouth *of t. w.* speak. frow.
11:11 overthrew by mouth *of w.*
23 expecta. *of the w.* is wrath
12:5 counsels *of t. w.* are deceit
6 words *of w.* are to lie in wait
10 tender mercies *of t. w.* cruel
26 way *of the w.* seduceth
13:25 belly *of the w.* shall want
14:11 house *of w.* sh. be overth.
15:6 revenues *of t. w.* is trouble
8 sacrifi. *of w.* is abomin. 21:27
9 way *of the w.* is an abomina.
26 thou. *of the w.* are abomin.
28 mouth *of w.* pour. out evil
18:5 not good to acce. per. *of w.*
19:28 mouth *of t. w.* devoureth
21:4 plowing *of the w.* is sin
7 robbery *of t. w.* shall destroy
10 soul *of the w.* desireth evil
12 he consider. house *of the w.*
*Is.* 14:5 L. hath brok. staff *of w.*
*Jer.* 5:28 overpass deeds *of t. w.*
12:1 doth way *of t. w.* prosper?
15:21 deliv. out of hand *of t. w.*
23:19 whirlw. on he. *of w.* 30:23
*Ezek* 13:22 strength. hands *of w.*
18:20 wickedness *of the w.*
21:29 br. thee upon necks *of w.*
30:12 land into hand *of the w.*
33:11 no pleas. in death *of t. w.*
12 as for the wickedn. *of t. w.*
*Dan.* 12:10 none *of w.* sh. under.
*Mic.* 6:10 wicked. in house *of w.*
*Hab.* 3:13 wound. head *of the w.*
*Eph.* 6:16 qu. fiery darts *of t. w.*
2 *Pet.* 2:7 wi. conversation *of w.*
3:17 led away with error *of t. w.*
*See* ONE.

**To, *or* unto the WICKED.**

*Job* 31:3 is not destr. *to the w.?*
*Ps.* 32:10 many sorrows *to t. w.*
50:16 *u. the w.* God saith, What
*Prov.* 24:24 that saith *u. the w.*
29:27 upright is abomi. *to t. w.*
*Ec.* 9:2 event to right. and *to w.*
*Is.* 3:11 woe *u. the w.* sh. be ill
26:10 let favor be showed *to w.*
48:22 no peace, saith the Lord, *unto the w.* 57:21
*Ezek.* 3:18 I say *unto w.* 33:8, 14
7:21 give it *to t. w.* of the earth

**WICKEDLY.**

*Gen.* 19:7 not so *w.* *Jud.* 19:23
*Deut.* 9:18 ye sinned in doing *w.*
1 *Sam.* 12:25 if ye sh. still do *w.*
2 *Sam.* 22:22 I ha. not *w.* departed from my God, *Ps.* 18:21
24:17 I have sinned and done *w.*
2 *K.* 21:11 Manasseh done *w.*
2 *Chr.* 6:37 we have dealt *w.* *Neh.* 9:33; *Ps.* 106:6; *Dan.* 9:5, 15
20:35 Ahaziah did very *w.*
22:3 mother was couns. to do *w.*
*Job* 13:7 will you spe. *w.* for G.?
34:12 surely God will not do *w.*
*Ps.* 73:8 they speak *w.* concern.
74:3 the enemy hath done *w.*
139:20 they speak ag. thee *w.*
*Dan.* 11:32 such as do *w.* against
12:10 but the wicked shall do *w.*
*Mal.* 4:1 that do *w.* be as stubble

**WICKEDNESS.**

*Gen.* 6:5 God saw *w.* was great
39:9 how can I do th. great *w.?*
*Lev.* 18:17 not unco. it is *w.* 20:14
19:29 land become full of *w.*
20:14 that there be no *w.* among
*Deut.* 9:4 *w.* of these nations, 5
13:11 Israel shall do no more *w.*
17:2 if any that hath wrou. *w.*
28:20 bec. of *w.* of thy doings
*Jud.* 9:56 G. rendered *w.* of Abi.
20:3 tell us, how was this *w.?*
12 what *w.* is this th. is done?
1 *Sam.* 12:17 see your *w.* is great
20 ye have done all this *w.*
24:13 *w.* proceed. from wicked
25:39 returned the *w.* of Nabal
2 *Sam.* 3:39 reward acc. to his *w.*
7:10 children of *w.* *Ps.* 89:22
1 *K.* 1:52 if *w.* be found in him
2:44 the *w.* thy heart is privy to
8:47 we have committed *w.*
21:25 Ahab sold him to work *w.*
2 *K.* 21:16 Manasseh wrought *w.*
1 *Chr.* 17:9 nor the children of *w.*
*Job* 4:8 that sow *w.* reap same
11:11 seeth *w.* 24:20 *w.* be brok.
14 let not *w.* dwell in taberna.
20:12 tho' *w.* be sweet in mouth
27:4 my lips shall not speak *w.*
34:10 far fr. G. he should do *w.*
*Ps.* 5:4 that hath pleasure in *w.*
9 their inward part is very *w.*
7:9 let *w.* of wick. come to end
10:15 seek out *w.* 45:7 hatest *w.*
28:4 according to *w.* of endeav.
52:7 he strength. himself in *w.*
55:11 *w.* is in the midst thereof
15 *w.* is in their dwellings
58:2 yea, in heart you work *w.*
84:10 th. to dwell in tents of *w.*
107:34 for *w.* them that dwell therein, *Jer.* 12:4
*Prov.* 4:17 they eat bread of *w.*
8:7 *w.* is abomina. to my lips
10:2 treasures of *w.* profit noth.
11:5 wicked shall fall by his *w.*
12:3 man not be establish. by *w.*
13:6 *w.* overthroweth the sinner
14:32 wicked is driven aw. in *w.*
16:12 abomination to commit *w.*
21:12 overthroweth wick. for *w.*
26:26 his *w.* shall be shown bef.
30:20 saith, I have done no *w.*
*Ec.* 3:16 judgment, *w.* was there
7:15 wicked prolong. life in *w.*
25 I applied to know *w.* of folly
8:8 nor *w.* deliver th. given to
*Is.* 9:18 for *w.* burneth as a fire
58:4 ye smite with the fist of *w.*
6 chosen, to loose bands of *w.*
*Jer.* 2:19 own *w.* sh. correct thee
4:14 wash thy heart from *w.*
6:7 casteth out *w.* continually
7:12 see wh. I did for *w.* of peo.
8:6 no man repented of his *w.*
14:20 we acknowledge, our *w.*
23:14 none doth ret. from his *w.*
33:5 whose *w.* I hid face fr. city
*Jer.* 44:9 ha. ye forg. *w.* of kings?
*Ezek.* 3:19 if he turn not from *w.*
5:6 changed my judgm. into *w.*
7:11 violence risen into rod of *w.*
18:20 *w.* of wicked sh. be on him
27 turn. from *w.* he committed
31:11 driven him out for his *w.*
33:12 day he turneth from *w.* 19
*Hos.* 7:1 *w.* of S. was discovered
9:15 for *w.* of doings drive out
10:13 ploughed *w.* reaped iniq.
15 do to you beca. of your *w.*
*Joel* 3:13 overflow for *w.* is great
*Mic.* 6:10 treasures of *w.* in house
*Zec.* 5:8 and he said, This is *w.*
*Mal.* 1:4 call them border of *w.*
3:15 th. that work *w.* are set up
*Mark* 7:22 out heart proceed. *w.*
*Luke* 11:39 inw. part is full of *w.*
*Acts* 25:5 man, if any *w.* in him
*Rom.* 1:29 being filled wi. all *w.*
1 *Cor.* 5:8 leav. of malice and *w.*
*Eph.* 6:12 ag. *w.* in high places
1 *John* 5:19 wh. world lieth in *w.*

**Their WICKEDNESS.**

*Deut.* 9:27 look not to *their w.*
*Ps.* 94:23 cut them off in *their w.*
*Prov.* 21:12 overth. wick. for *t. w.*
*Jer.* 1:16 judgm. touching *t. w.*
14:16 pour *their w.* upon them
23:11 in house ha. I found *t. w.*
44:3 desolation because of *t. w.*
5 inclined ear to turn fr. *t. w.*
*Lam.* 1:22 let *t. w.* come before
*Hos.* 7:2 I remember all *their w.*
3 make king glad wi. *their w.*
9:15 *their w.* is in Gilgal
*Jon.* 1:2 *their w.* is come up
*Mat.* 22:18 Jesus perceived *t. w.*

**Thy WICKEDNESS.**

1 *K.* 2:44 L. return *thy w.* upon
*Job* 22:5 is not *thy w.* great?
35:8 *thy w.* may hurt a man as
*Is.* 47:10 hast trusted in *thy w.*
*Jer.* 3:2 polluted land with *t. w.*
4:18 this is *t. w.* for it is bitter
22:22 be confounded for *thy w.*
*Ezek.* 16:23 ca. to pass after *t. w.*
57 bef. *thy w.* was discovered
*Nah.* 3:19 on whom hath not *thy w.* passed
*Acts* 8:22 repent of this *thy w.*

**WIDE.**

*Deut.* 15:8 shalt open hand *w.* 11
1 *Chr.* 4:40 land was *w.* quiet
*Job* 29:23 opened their mouth *w.*
30:14 came as *w.* breaking wat.
*Ps.* 35:21 opened their mouth *w.*
81:10 open thy mouth *w.*
104:25 this great and *w.* sea
*Prov.* 13:3 openeth *w.* his lips
21:9 wom. in a *w.* house, 25:24
*Is.* 57:4 make ye a *w.* mouth?
*Jer.* 22:14 will build a *w.* house
*Nah.* 3:13 set *w.* op. to enemies
*Mat.* 7:13 *w.* gate to destruction

**WIDENESS.**

*Ezek.* 41:10 chambers *w.* 20 cub.

**WIDOW.**

*Gen.* 38:11 a *w.* in fath.'s house
14 put her *w.* garments off
*Ex.* 22:22 sh. not afflict any *w.*
*Lev.* 21:14 *w.* or harlot not take
22:13 if priest's daugh. be a *w.*
*Num.* 30:9 vow of *w.* stand ag.
*Deut.* 10:18 judgment of a *w.*
14:29 and *w.* shall come and eat, 16:11, 14; 26:12
24:17 nor take *w.* rai. to pledge
19 sheaf for *w.* 20, 21; 26:13
27:19 perverteth judgm. of *w.*
2 *Sam.* 14:5 I am a *w.* woman
1 *K.* 7:14 he was a *w.* son of
11:26 Zeruah was a *w.* woman
17:9 com. a *w.* to sustain thee
*Job* 24:3 take *w.* ox for a pledge
21 and doeth not good to *w.*
29:13 I caused *w.* heart to sing
31:16 caused eyes of *w.* to fail
*Ps.* 94:6 th. slay *w.* and stranger
109:9 child. be fatherl. wife a *w.*
146:9 reliev. fatherless and *w.*
*Prov.* 15:25 establ. border of *w.*
*Is.* 1:17 fatherless, plead for *w.*
23 nei. doth cause of *w.* come
47:8 I shall not sit as a *w.*
*Jer.* 7:6 if ye oppress not the *w.* 22:3; *Zec.* 7:10
*Lam.* 1:1 how is she bec. as a *w.*
*Ezek.* 22:7 have th. vexed the *w.*
44:22 take *w.* that had a priest
*Mal.* 3:5 those that oppress *w.*
*Mark* 12:42 *w.* threw in 2 mites

Deut. 8:2 forty years in the w.
29:5; Jos. 5:6; 14:10
16 fed thee in t. w. wi. manna?
Neh. 9:21 didst sust. them in t. w.
Ps. 95:8 day of tempta. in t. w.
Prov. 21:19 better dwell in t. w.
Is. 32:16 judgm. sh. dwell in w.
35:6 in w. shall wat. break out
40:3 voice of him that crieth in the w. Mat. 3:3; Mark 1:3; Luke 3:4; John 1:23
41:19 I will plant in t. w. cedar
43:19 will make a way in the w.
Jer. 2:2 went, after me in the w.
9:2 oh that I had in t. w. a lodg.
31:2 peo. found grace in the w.
48:6 be like the heath. in the w.
Lam. 4:19 laid wait for us in t. w.
Ezek. 19:13 she is planted in w.
20:13 Is. rebelled ag. me in t. w.
15 lifted my hand in the w. 23
34:25 shall dwell safely in t. w.
Hos. 9:10 I found Israel in the w.
13:5 I did know thee in the w.
Mat. 3:1 John preaching in t. w.
15:33 whe. so much bread in w. to fill multitude? Mark 8:4
Luke 15:4 leave 99 sheep in t. w.
Acts 7:30 angel appear. in w. 38
2 Cor. 11:26 in perils in the w.

**Into the WILDERNESS.**

Lev. 16:21 by a fit man i. the w.
22 sh. let go the goat i. the w.
Ezek. 20:10 I bro. them i. the w.
35 I will bring you into the w.
Hos. 2:14 I will bri. her in the w.
Mat. 11:7 what went ye out in the w. to see? Luke 7:24
Luke 8:29 driven of devil i. the w.
Acts 21:38 led. into w. 4,000 men
Rev. 12:6 woman fled i. t. w. 14
17:3 so he carried me into t. w.

**WILES.**

Num. 25:18 th. vex you with w.
Eph. 6:11 able to stand ag. w.

**WILILY.**

Jos. 9:4 Gibeonites did work w.

**WILL.**

Deut. 33:16 for good w. of him
Ps. 27:12 deliver me not to w. of
41:2 not deliver to w. of enem.
Ezek. 16:27 delivered thee to w.
Mal. 2:13 recei. it with good w.
Mat. 7:21 doeth w. of Fath. 12:50
18:14 it is not w. of your Father
21:32 whether did w. of father?
Luke 2:14 good w. toward men
23:25 delivered Jesus to their w.
John 1:13 not of w. of the flesh
4:34 my meat is to do w. of him
5:30 I seek the w. of my Father
6:39 this is the Father's w. 40
Acts 21:14 w. of the L. be done
Eph. 5:17 what the w. of Lord is
6:7 with good w. doing service
Phil. 1:15 preach C. of good w.
Heb. 10:10 by wh. w. are sancti.
1 Pet. 4:3 suffice to have wro. w.
2 Pet. 1:21 proph. came not by w.

**WILL of God.**

Ezr. 7:18 do after w. of your G.
Mark 3:35 whoso sh. do w. of G.
John 1:13 not of w. of man, of G.
Acts 13:36 generation by w. of G.
Rom. 1:10 pros. jour. by w. of G.
8:27 interces. accor. to w. of G.
12:2 accepta. and perf. w. of G.
15:32 come with joy by w. of G.
1 Cor. 1:1 Paul an apostle by w. of G. 2 Cor. 1:1; Eph. 1:1; Col. 1:1; 2 Tim. 1:1
2 Cor. 8:5 ga. thems. by w. of G.
Gal. 1:4 deli. fr. evil by w. of G.
Eph. 6:6 doing the w. of God
Col. 4:12 complete in w. of God
1 Thes. 4:3 this is w. of God, 5:18
Heb. 10:36 have done w. of God
1 Pet. 2:15 so is the w. of God
3:17 better if w. of God be so
4:2 live not to lusts, to w. of G.
19 suffer according to w. of G.
1 John 2:17 he that doeth w. of G.

**His WILL.**

Dan. 4:35 doeth accord. to his w.
8:4 he did according to his w.
11:3 do accord. to his w. 16, 36
Luke 12:47 nei. accord. to his w.
John 7:17 if any do h. w. sh. kn.
Acts 22:14 shouldest know his w.
Rom. 2:18 and knowest his w.
9:19 who hath resisted his w.?
1 Cor. 7:37 hath power over h. w.
16:12 his w. not at all to come
Eph. 1:5 good pleasure of his w.
9 kn. to us mystery of his w.
Col. 1:9 with knowledge of h. w.
2 Tim. 2:26 taken capt. at his w.
Heb. 13:21 good work to do h. w.
1 John 5:14 ask accord. to his w.
Rev. 17:17 hearts to fulfil his w.

**My WILL.**

Luke 22:42 not my w. but thine
Acts 13:22 shall fulfil all my w.
1 Cor. 9:17 if I do this ag. my w.

**Own WILL.**

Lev. 1:3 shall offer it of his o. w.
19:5 as your own w. 22:19, 29
Dan. 11:16 according to his o. w.
John 5:30 I seek not mine o. w.
6:38 not to do mine own w.
Eph. 1:11 counsel of his own w.
Heb. 2:4 according to his own w.
Jam. 1:18 of his o. w. begat he us

**Thy WILL.**

Ps. 40:8 I delight to do thy w.
143:10 teach me to do thy w.
Mat. 6:10 t. w. be done, Luke 11:2
26:42 not pass, thy w. be done
Heb. 10:7 I come to do thy w. 9

**WILL, Verb.**

Job 13:13 let come on me what w.
Prov. 21:1 heart whither. he w.
Dan. 4:17 giveth it to whomsoever he w. 25, 32; 5:21
Mat. 8:3 and said, I w. be thou clean, Mark 1:41; Luke 5:13
20:15 do wh. I w. wi. my own?
26:39 not as I w. Mark 14:36
Mark 14:7 when. w. may do good
15:12 what w. ye I should do?
Luke 4:6 to whomsoever I w.
12:49 what w. I, if it be kindl.?
John 15:7 ask what ye w.
17:24 I w. that they be with me
21:22 if I w. that he tarry, 23
Rom. 7:18 to w. is pres. with me
Phil. 2:13 G. worketh both to w.
1 Tim. 5:14 I w. women marry
Jam. 4:15 if L. w. we sh. do this

**WILL not.**

Ezek. 20:3 I w. n. be inquired of
Amos 7:8 I w. not ag. pass, 8:2
Mat. 21:29 he answered, I w. not
John 5:40 ye w. not come to me

**WILLETH.**

Rom. 9:16 it is not of him th. w.

**WILFULLY.**

Heb. 10:26 if we sin w. after we

**WILLING.**

Gen. 24:5 wom. not w. to follow
Ex. 35:5 whosoever is of a w. heart, 21, 22, 29
1 Chr. 28:9 serve G. wi. w. mind
29:5 who is w. to consecrate his
Ps. 110:3 thy people shall be w.
Is. 1:19 if w. sh. eat good of land
Mat. 1:19 not w. to make her a
26:41 spirit is w. flesh is weak
Luke 10:29 w. to justify himself
22:42 if thou be w. remove cup
John 5:35 ye were w. to rejoice
Rom. 9:22 if G. w. to show wrath
2 Cor. 5:8 w. rather to be absent
8:3 they were w. of themselves
12 if there be first a w. mind
1 Thes. 2:8 w. to have imparted
Heb. 6:17 w. to show heirs of pro.
2 Pet. 3:9 not w. any sho. perish

**WILLINGLY.**

Ex. 25:2 ev. man that gives w.
Jud. 5:2 people w. offered, 9
1 Chr. 29:6 rulers off. w. 9, 14, 17; 2 Chr. 35:8; Ezr. 1:6; 3:5
2 Chr. 17:16 Amaziah w. himself
Neh. 11:2 that w. offered thems.
Prov. 31:13 work. w. with hands
Lam. 3:33 he doth not afflict w.
Hos. 5:11 Ephr. w. walked after
John 6:21 they w. received him
Rom. 8:20 subj. to vanity not w.
2 Cor. 9:17 if I do this w. a rew.
Phile. 14 not as of necessity, but w. 1 Pet. 5:2
2 Pet. 3:5 they are w. ignorant

**WILLOWS.**

Lev. 23:40 shall take w. of brook
Job 40:22 w. of brook comp. him
Ps. 137:2 hanged harps on w.
Is. 15:7 car. riches to brook of w.
44:4 they shall spring up as w.

**WILLOW-TREE**

Ezek. 17:5 he has set it as a w.-t.

**WILL-WORSHIP.**

Col. 2:23 show of wisd. in w.-w.

**WILT.**

Jud. 1:14 wh. w. thou? Est. 5:3; Mat. 20:21; Mark 10:51; Lu. 18:41
Ps. 60:10 w. not thou, O God? 108:11
Mat. 15:28 be it to th. as thou w.
17:4 if th. w. let us make taber.
26:39 not as I will, but as thou w. Mark 14:36

**WIMPLES.**

Is. 3:22 take aw. mantles and w.

**WIN, NETH.**

2 Chr. 32:1 he thought to w. th.
Prov. 11:30 he that w. souls
Phil. 3:8 that I may w. Christ

**WIND.**

Gen. 8:1 God made a w. to pass
Ex. 15:10 didst blow with thy w.
Num. 11:31 w. brought quails
2 Sam. 22:11 was seen on wings of w. Ps. 18:10; 104:3
1 K. 18:45 heaven black with w.
19:11 strong w. rent mountains
2 K. 3:17 shall not see w. nor rain
Job 1:19 came w. from wildern.
6:26 speeches which are as w.
7:7 O remem. that my life is w.
8:2 words of thy mouth like w.
21:18 they are as stubble bef. w.
30:15 ter. pursue my soul as w.
22 thou liftest me up to the w.
37:21 w. passeth, Ps. 103:16
Ps. 1:4 which w. driveth away
78:39 w. that passeth away
135:7 bringeth w. out of treas.
147:18 causeth his w. to blow
Prov. 11:29 he shall inherit w.
25:14 clouds and w. with. rain
23 north w. driveth away rain
27:16 whoso hid. her, hideth w.
30:4 who gath. wind in his fists
Ec. 1:6 w. goeth toward south
5:16 what profit, labored for w.
11:4 he that observ. w. not sow
Cant. 4:16 awake, O north w.
Is. 7:2 trees are moved with w.
11:15 with w. shake his hand
26:18 as it were brou. forth w.
27:8 he stayeth his rough w.
32:2 as a hiding-place from w.

41:16 w. carry them away, 57:13
29 their molten images are w.
64:6 like w. have taken us away
Jer. 4:12 a w. from those places
5:13 prophets shall become w.
10:13 w. out of his treas. 51:16
22:22 w. shall eat up thy past.
Ezek 5:2 thou shalt scatter in w.
12:14 scatter tow. w. about him
37:9 prophesy to w. say to w.
Dan. 2:35 w. carried them away
Hos. 4:19 w. hath bound her up
8:7 sown w. shall reap whirlw.
12:1 Ephraim feedeth on w.
Amos 4:13 he that createth w.
Jon. 1:4 L. sent a great w. to sea
Zec. 5:9 w. was in their wings
Mat. 11:7 a reed shaken with the w. Luke 7:24
14:24 w. was contrary, Mark 6:48; Acts 27:4
32 w. ceased, Mark 4:39; 6:51
John 3:8 w. blow. where it listeth
Acts 2:2 sound as of a mighty w.
Eph. 4:14 car. about with ev. w.
Jam. 1:6 like wave driven wi. w.
Rev. 6:13 wh. she is shaken of w.
7:1 w. should not blow on earth

### WINDS.

Job 28:25 to make weight for w.
Ezek. 37:9 come from the four w.
Mat. 7:25 w. blew, beat house, 27
8:26 rebuked the w. Luke 8:24
27 even the w. and sea obey him? Mark 4:41; Luke 8:25
Jam. 3:4 ships driven of fierce w.
Jude 12 clouds carri. about of w.
See EAST, FOUR, SCATTER, STORMY.

### WINDY.

Ps. 55:8 hasten from w. storm

### WINDOW.

Gen. 6:16 a w. shalt thou make
8:6 Noah opened w. of the ark
26:8 king of Gerar looked out w.
Jos. 2:15 Rah. let spies thro' w.
21 she bound scarlet line in w.
Jud. 5:28 moth. looked out of w.
2 Sam. 6:16 Mi. looked thro' w.
2 K. 9:30 and look out at a w.
13:17 he said, Open w. eastward
Prov. 7:6 at w. I looked through
Acts 20:9 sat in w. a young man
2 Cor. 11:33 thro' a w. let down

### WINDOWS.

Gen. 7:11 w. of heav. were open.
8:2 w. of heaven were stopped
2 K. 7:2 if L. make w. in hea. 19
Ec. 12:3 that look out of w.
Cant. 2:9 my beloved look. at w.
Is. 24:18 w. fr. on high are open
54:12 I will ma. thy w. of agates
60:8 flee as doves to their w.
Jer. 9:21 death is co. into our w.
22:14 that cutteth him out w.
Dan. 6:10 his w. being open
Joel 2:9 enter in at w. like thief
Zep. 2:14 voice shall sing in w.
Mal. 3:10 if I will not open w. of

### WINE.

Gen. 9:24 Noah awoke fr. his w.
14:18 Melchisedek brought w.
49:11 washed his garments in w.
12 his eyes were red with w.
Ex. 29:40 fourth part of a hin of w. Lev. 23:13; Num. 15:5
Num. 6:3 separate himself fr. w.
28:7 cause strong w. to be pour.
Deut. 32:33 w. is poison of drag.
Jud. 9:13 leave w. wh. cheereth
19:19 th. is bread and w. for me
1 Sam. 1:14 put away w. fr. thee
25:37 when w. gone out of Nab.
2 Sam. 6:19 flesh, and a flagon of w. 1 Chr. 16:3
13:28 Am. heart merry with w.
16:2 w. such as faint may drink
Neh. 2:1 the w. was before him
5:15 gover. taken bread and w.
18 once in ten days st. of all w.
13:15 lad. asses with w. grapes
Est. 1:7 they gave them royal w.
10 heart of king merry with w.
5:6 king said to Esth. at w. 7:2
7:7 arising from banquet of w.
Job 1:13 w. in th. bro. house, 18
32:19 my belly is as w. no vent
Ps. 75:8 w. is red, full of mixture
78:65 shouteth by reason of w.
104:15 w. that mak. glad heart
Prov. 9:2 hath mingled her w.
20:1 w. is a mocker, str. drink
23:30 they that tarry long at w.
31 look not on w. wh. it is red
31:6 gi. w. to th. of heavy heart
Ec. 2:3 to give myself to w.
10:19 w. maketh merry, money
Cant. 1:2 love better th. w. 4:10
5:1 I have drunk my w.
7:9 roof of thy mou. like best w.
Is. 1:22 thy w. mixed with water
5:11 night, till w. inflame them
12 pipe and w. are in th. feasts
22:13 eating flesh and drink. w.
24:11 there is a crying for w.
27:2 red w. 55:1 come, buy w.
28:1 that are overcome with w.
7 they have also erred thro' w.
29:9 drunken, not wi. w. 51:21
56:12 come, say I will fetch w.
Jer. 23:9 man whom w. overcome
Jer. 25:15 take w. of fury at my hand
35:5 full of w. 40:12 gathered w.
48:33 I have caused w. to fail
51:7 nations drunken of her w.
Ezek. 27:18 Damascus trad. in w.
Dan. 1:5 king gave of w.
8 not to defile himself with w.
5:1 Belshazzar drank w. bef. 4
2 he tasted w. 23 drunk w.
10:3 neither came w. nor flesh
Hos. 2:9 take away my w. in sea.
3:1 gods, and love flagons of w.
14:7 scent be as w. of Lebanon
Joel 1:5 howl, ye drinkers of w.
Mic. 2:11 I will prophesy of w.
Hab. 2:5 he transgresseth by w.
Zec. 9:15 make noise, as thro' w.
10:7 hearts rejoice, as thro' w.
Luke 7:33 J. neither drinking w.
John 2:3 saith, They have no w.
9 tasted water made w. 4:46
10 at begin. set forth good w.
Eph. 5:18 be not drunk with w.
1 Tim. 3:3 and not given to w. 8; Tit. 1:7; 2:3
5:23 use w. for stomach's sake
1 Pet. 4:3 walked in excess of w.
Rev. 16:19 give cup of w. of wrath
17:2 drunk with w. of forni. 18:3
See BOTTLE, CORN, DRINK, NEW, OFFERINGS, OIL, SWEET.

### WINE-BIBBER, S.

Prov. 23:20 be not with w.-b.
Mat. 11:19 man a w.-b. Luke 7:34

### WINE-BOTTLES.

Jos. 9:4 Gibeonites took w.-bot.
13 b. of w. which we filled

### WINE-CELLARS.

1 Chr. 27:27 over w.-c. was Zabdi

### WINE-FAT.

Is. 63:2 like him treadeth w.-f.
Mark 12:1 dig. a place for w.-f.

### WINE-PRESS.

Num. 18:27 fulness of w.-p. 30
Deut. 15:14 furnish out of w.-p.
Jud. 6:11 thres. wheat by w.-p.
7:25 they slew at w.-p. of Zeeb
2 K. 6:27 help thee out of w.-p.?
Is. 5:2 made a w.-p. therein
63:3 I have trodden w.-p. alone
Lam. 1:15 trodden Jud. as w.-p.
Hos. 9:2 w.-p. sh. not feed them
Mat. 21:33 digged a w.-p. in it
Rev. 14:19 cast it into gr. w.-p.
20 w.-p. trodden without city
19:15 he treadeth w.-p. of wrath

### WINE-PRESSES.

Neh. 13:15 treading w.-p. on sab.
Job 24:11 tread their w.-p.
Jer. 48:33 wine to fail from w.-p.
Zec. 14:10 upon king's w.-p.

### WINES.

Is. 25:6 make feast of w. on lees

### WING.

2 K. 6:24 w. of cherub. 5 cubits other w. 27; 2 Chr. 3:11, 12
Is. 10:14 none that moved the w.
Ezek. 17:23 dw. fowl of every w.

### WINGS.

Ex. 19:4 bare you on eagle's w.
25:20 covering mercy-seat with their w. 37:9; 1 K. 8:7
Lev. 1:17 cleave it with w. ther.
Deut. 32:11 eagle spread. her w.
Ruth 2:12 under wh. w. thou art
2 Sam. 22:11 upon w. of wind
Job 39:13 gavest w. to peacock?
Ps. 17:8 hide me under thy w.
18:10 fly on w. of wind, 104:3
36:7 put th. trust under shadow of thy w. 57:1; 61:4; 91:4
55:6 O that I had w. like a dove
63:7 in shadow of w. will I rej.
68:13 sh. ye be as w. of a dove
139:9 if I take w. of morning
Prov. 23:5 riches make thems. w.
Ec. 10:20 whi. hath w. shall tell
Is. 6:2 each one had six w.
8:8 stretch. out his w. fill land
18:1 woe to land shadow. wi. w.
40:31 mount up with w. eagles
Jer. 48:9 give w. to M. may fly
40 he sh. spread his w. over M.
49:22 he sh. spread w. over Boz.
Ezek. 1:6 every one had four w.
9 w. were joined; 10:12 w. full of eyes
24 I heard the noise of their w. 3:13; 10:5, 25
17:3 a great eagle with great w.
7 another great eagle with w.
Dan. 7:4 like lion, had eagles' w.
6 ano. having on back four w.
Hos. 4:19 bou. her up in her w.
Zec. 5:9 wind was in their w.
Mal. 4:2 with healing in his w.
Mat. 23:37 as a hen gathereth her chick. under w. Luke 13:34
Rev. 9:9 sound of th. w. as horses
12:14 to wom. were giv. two w.

### WINGED.

Gen. 1:21 G. created ev. w. fowl
Deut. 4:17 liken. of any w. fowl
Ezek. 17:3 great eagle, long-w.

### WINK, ED, ETH.

Job 15:12 wh. do thi. eyes w. at?
Ps. 35:19 neither let them w.
Prov. 6:13 a wicked man w.
10:10 he th. w. causeth sorrow
Acts 17:30 ignorance God w. at

### WINNOWED, ETH.

Ruth 3:2 Bo. w. barley to-night
Is. 30:24 hath been w. wi. shovel

### WINTER.

Gen. 8:22 and w. shall not cease
Ps. 74:17 made summer and w.
Cant. 2:11 for lo, the w. is past
Zec. 14:8 in summer and w.
Mat. 24:20 pray that your flight be not in w. Mark 13:18
John 10:22 feast of dedicat. in w.
2 Tim. 4:21 to come before w.

### WINTER-HOUSE.

Jer. 36:22 the king sat in w.-h.

*Amos* 3:15 I will smite *w.-h.*

**WINTER, Verb.**

*Is.* 18:6 beasts shall *w.* on them
*Acts* 27:12 not commod. to *w.* in
1 *Cor.* 16:6 abide, *w.* with you
*Tit.* 3:12 I determin. there to *w.*

**WINTERED.**

*Acts* 28:11 ship which *w.* in isle

**WIPE.**

2 *K.* 21:13 *w.* Jerusalem as a dish
*Neh.* 13:14 *w.* not out good deeds
*Is.* 25:8 Lord will *w.* away tears fr. all faces, *Rev.* 7:17; 21:4
*Luke* 7:38 woman did *w.* th. with hairs, 44; *John* 11:2; 12:3
*John* 13:5 began to *w.* them with

**WIPED, ETH, ING.**

2 *K.* 21:13 *w.* it as a man *w.* dish
*Prov.* 6:33 reproach not *w.* way
30:20 she eateth, *w.* her mouth

**WIRES.**

*Ex.* 39:3 cut gold plates into *w.*

**WISDOM.**

*Ex.* 31:3 I have filled him wi. Sp. of God in *w.* 6; 35:31, 35
35:26 stirred them in *w.* 36:1, 2
*Deut.* 4:6 for this is your *w.* and
2 *Sam.* 14:20 acco. to *w.* of angel
20:22 woman went to peo. in *w.*
1 *K.* 3:28 saw *w.* of G. was in h.
4:29 God gave Solomon *w.* 5:12; 2 *Chr.* 1:12
30 Solomon's *w.* excelled *w.* of Egypt, 34; 7:14; 10:4, 23, 24; 2 *Chr.* 9:3, 22, 23
1 *Chr.* 22:12 Lord give thee *w.*
2 *Chr.* 1:10 give *w.* 11 asked *w.*
*Ezr.* 7:25 after the *w.* of thy God
*Job* 4:21 die, even without *w.*
12:2 peo. *w.* shall die with you
13:5 and it should be your *w.*
15:8 dost thou restr. *w.* to thy. ?
26:3 coun. him th. hath no *w.* ?
28:12 where shall *w.* be found ?
20 whence cometh *w.* where
32:7 multitude of years teach *w.*
13 say, We have found out *w.*
33:33 and I shall teach thee *w.*
34:35 Job's words were with. *w.*
36:5 G. mighty in stren. and *w.*
38:37 who can num. clou. in *w.* ?
39:17 G. hath deprived her of *w.*
*Ps.* 37:30 mouth of righ. speak *w.*
51:6 shalt make me to know *w.*
90:12 apply our hearts to *w.*
104:24 in *w.* hast th. made wor.
105:22 and teach his senators *w.*
136:5 him th. by *w.* made heav.
*Prov.* 1:2 kn. *w.* 7 fools desp. *w.*
20 *w.* crieth, 8:1; 2:2 ear to *w.*
2:6 Lord giveth *w.* 3:21 keep *w.*
7 he layeth up *w.* for righteous
10 when *w.* entereth into heart
3:13 happy man that findeth *w.*
19 Lord by *w.* founded earth
4:5 get *w.* 7; 5:1 atte. to my *w.*
7:4 say to *w.* Thou art my sister
8:5 unders. *w.* 9:1 *w.* buildeth
12 I *w.* dwell with prudence
14 counsel is mine, sound *w.*
10:23 man of understan. hath *w.*
31 mouth of just brin. forth *w.*
12:8 commend. according to *w.*
*Prov.* 14:6 scorner seeketh *w.* fin.
8 *w.* of prudent is to understa.
33 *w.* resteth in heart of him
16:16 better to get *w.* than gold
17:16 in hand of fool to get *w.*
18:1 man intermeddleth with *w.*
19:8 that getteth *w.* loveth soul
21:30 there is no *w.* against L.
23:4 rich, cea. from thy own *w.*
9 a fool will despise *w.* of wor.
23 buy *w.* 24:3 thro' *w.* house
29:3 whoso loveth *w.* rejoiceth
15 the rod and reproof give *w.*
30:3 I nei. learned *w.* nor have
31:26 openeth her mouth wi. *w.*
*Ec.* 1:13 I gave my heart to *w.*
16 I have more *w.* than all
17 I gave my heart to know *w.*
18 for much *w.* is much grief
2:3 acquaint. my heart with *w.*
9 my *w.* remained with me
12 I turned myself to beho. *w.*
13 *w.* excel. folly; 21 lab. in *w.*
26 G. give. *w.* 7:12 *w.* giv. life
7:19 *w.* strengtheneth the wise
23 all this I have proved by *w.*
25 I applied heart to seek *w.*
8:1 man's *w.* mak. face to shine
16 I appli. my heart to kn. *w.*
9:10 there is no *w.* in the grave
13 *w.* have I seen under sun
15 poor man by *w.* deliv. city
10:1 that is in reputation for *w.*
3 *w.* faileth him, he is a fool
*Is.* 10:13 by my *w.* I have done it
29:14 *w.* of their wise sh. perish
33:6 *w.* be stability of thy times
*Jer.* 9:23 let not wise glory in *w.*
10:12 establi. world by *w.* 51:15
*Dan.* 1:4 chil. skilful in all *w.*
2:14 answ. with counsel and *w.*
20 blessed be G. *w.* and might
21 he giveth *w.* to the wise
23 God, who hast given me *w.*
30 not revealed for any *w.*
5:11 *w.* of gods found in him
*Mat.* 12:42 came fr. utterm. parts to hear *w.* of Sol. *Luke* 11:31
13:54 whence ha. this man *w.* ?
*Luke* 1:17 turn disobedient to *w.*
2:40 Jesus filled with *w.*
52 increased in *w.* and stature
11:49 also said the *w.* of God
21:15 give you a mouth and *w.*
*Acts* 6:3 seven men full of *w.*
10 we. not able to resist the *w.*
7:10 God gave Joseph *w.* in the
22 learned in *w.* of the Egypt.
1 *Cor.* 1:17 not with *w.* of words
19 destroy the *w.* of the wise
20 God made foolish the *w.* of
21 in the *w.* of God the world by *w.* knew not G. it pleas.
22 and Greeks seek after *w.*
24 C. power of G. and *w.* of G.
30 God is made to us *w.* and
2:4 not with words of man's *w.*
5 not stand in the *w.* of men
6 speak *w.* 7 speak *w.* of God
13 which man's *w.* teacheth
3:19 for the *w.* of this world is
2 *Cor.* 1:12 not with fleshly *w.*
*Eph.* 1:8 aboun. toward us in *w.*
3:10 the manifold *w.* of God
*Col.* 1:9 mi. be filled with all *w.*
28 teaching eve. man in all *w.*
3:16 words dw. in you in all *w.*
4:5 walk in *w.* tow. them that
*Jam.* 1:5 any lack *w.* let him ask
3:15 this *w.* descendeth not from
2 *Pet.* 3:15 according to *w.* given
*Rev.* 5:12 the Lamb to receive *w.*
7:12 glory, and *w.* be to our God
17:9 the mind which hath *w.*

**WISDOM,** *joined with* **is.**

*Job* 6:13 and *is w.* driven quite
12:12 with ancient *is w.* 13:16
28:18 *w. is* abo. rubi. *Prov.* 8:11
28 fear of the Lord that *is w.*
*Prov.* 4:7 *w. is* principal thing
10:13 with him that hath understanding *w. is* found
11:2 but with the lowly *is w.*
13:10 with well-advised *is w.*
14:8 the *w.* of the prudent *is* to
17:24 *w. is* before him that hath
24:7 *w. is* too high for a fool, he
*Ec.* 1:18 in much *w. is* much
7:11 *w. is* good with an inherit.
12 *w. is* a defence, and money
9:16 *w. is* better than strength; the poor man's *w. is* despis.
18 *w. is* better than weapons
10:10 *w. is* profitable to direct
*Jer.* 8:9 lo, th. have rejected the word, what *w. is* in them?
49:7 *is w.* no more in Teman?
*Dan.* 5:14 excellent *w. is* found
*Mat.* 11:19 but *w. is* justified of her children, *Luke* 7:35
*Mark* 6:2 wh. *w. is* giv. to him?
*Jam.* 3:17 *w.* from above *is* pure
*Rev.* 13:18 here *is w.* let him that

**Of WISDOM.**

*Job* 11:6 show thee secrets *of w.*
28:18 price *of w.* is above rubies
*Ps.* 49:3 speak *of w.* and meditа.
111:10 fear of the Lord is the beginning *of w. Prov.* 9:10
*Prov.* 1:3 instruct. *of w.* justice
4:11 in the way *of w.* have led
10:21 fools die for want *of w.*
11:12 he that is void *of w.* des.
15:21 to him that is desti. *of w.*
33 fear of L. is instruct. *of w.*
18:4 spring *of w.* as flow. brook
24:14 knowle. *of w.* to thy soul
*Ec.* 1:16 great experience *of w.*
*Ezek.* 28:12 the sum full *of w.*
*Dan.* 1:20 matters *of w.* be fou.
*Mic.* 6:9 the man *of w.* shall see
*Rom.* 11:33 depth *of w.* of God!
1 *Cor.* 2:1 of speech or *of w.*
12:8 by Spirit the word *of w.*
*Col.* 2:3 are hid all treasu. *of w.*
23 have indeed a show *of w.*
*Jam.* 3:13 show with meek. *of w.*
*See* SPIRIT.

**Thy WISDOM.**

1 *K.* 2:6 according to *thy w.*
10:6 true report I heard of *t. w.*
7 *thy w.* and prosperity exce.
8 hear *thy w.* 2 *Chr.* 9:5, 7
2 *Chr.* 9:6 *t. w.* was not told me
*Job* 39:26 th hawk fly by *t. w.*
*Is.* 47:10 *thy w.* perverted thee
*Ezek.* 28:4 *t. w.* and understanding hast got. thee riches, 5
17 corrupted *thy w.* by bright.

**WISE.**

*Gen.* 3:6 a tree to make one *w.*
41:39 none discreet and *w.* as
*Ex.* 23:8 for the gift blindeth the *w. Deut.* 16:19
*Deut.* 4:6 this nation is a *w.* peo.
32:29 O that they were *w.*
*Jud.* 5:29 her *w.* ladies answered
2 *Sam.* 14:20 my lord is *w.* accor.
1 *K.* 3:12 given thee a *w.* heart
5:7 blessed L. that hath given David a *w.* son. 2 *Chr.* 2:12
1 *Chr.* 26:14 Zec. a *w.* counsellor
*Job* 5:13 taketh *w.* in own crafti.
9:4 he is *w.* in heart and stren.
11:12 vain man would be *w.*
22:2 he that is *w.* may be profi.
32:9 great men are not alw. *w.*
37:24 he respecteth not any that are *w.* of heart
*Ps.* 2:10 be *w.* now, O ye kings
19:7 making *w.* the simple
36:3 left off to be *w.* do good
94:8 fools, when will ye be *w.* ?
107:43 whoso is *w.* and will ob.
*Prov.* 1:5 *w.* man at. *w.* counsel
6 understand *w.* and sayings
3:7 be not *w.* in thine own eyes
35 the *w.* shall inherit glory
6:6 be *w.* 8:33; 23:19; 27:11
9:12 be *w.* thou shall be *w.* for
10:1 a *w.* son maketh a glad father, 15:20
5 gathereth in summer is *w.*
8 *w.* receive commandments
19 he that refrai. his lips is *w.*
11:29 servant to the *w.* in heart
30 he that winneth souls is *w.*

12:15 hearken. to counsel is *w.*
18 tongue of the *w.* is health
13:1 a *w.* son heareth instruct.
14 law of *w.* is a founta. of life
20 walk. with *w.* men sh. be *w.*
14:3 lips of the *w.* preserve th.
24 crown of the *w.* is th. riches
35 favor is toward *w.* servant
15:2 the tongue of the *w.* useth knowledge aright.
7 lips of *w.* dispe. knowledge
12 a scorner will not go to *w.*
24 way of life is above to *w.*
31 reproof abideth among *w.*
16:21 *w.* in heart called prudent
23 heart of *w.* teach. his mouth
17:2 *w.* serv. shall rule over son
28 hol. his peace is counted *w.*
18:15 the *w.* seeketh knowledge
19:20 be *w.* in thy latter end
20:1 deceived thereby, is not *w.*
26 *w.* king scattereth wicked
21:11 simple is made *w.* when *w.* is instructed he rec. kno.
20 oil in the dwelling of the *w.*
22:17 hear the words of the *w.*

*Prov.* 23:15 be *w.* my hea. sh. rej.
24 begetteth a *w.* son have joy
24:6 by *w.* coun. make thy war
23 these things belong to *w.*
25:12 *w.* reprover on obedi. ear
26:5 answer a fool, lest he be *w.*
12 a man *w.* in his own conceit
28:7 whoso keep. law is *w.* son
11 rich is *w.* in his own conceit
30:24 be four things that are *w.*
*Ec.* 2:15 why was I more *w.*?
16 th. is no remembrance of *w.*
19 wherein I show. myself *w.*
4:13 better *w.* child than foolish
6:8 wh. hath *w.* more th. fool?
7:4 heart of *w.* house of mourn.
5 better to hear rebuke of *w.*
16 neither make thys. over *w.*
19 wisd. strengtheneth the *w.*
23 I will be *w.* far from me
9:1 *w.* are in the hand of God
11 I saw that bre. is not to *w.*
12:9 preacher was *w.* he taught
11 words of *w.* are as goads

*Is.* 5:21 woe to them that are *w.*
19:11 say ye, I am son of *w.*?
31:2 yet he is also *w.* bring evil
*Jer.* 4:22 they are *w.* to do evil
8:8 how do ye say, We are *w.*
18:18 nor counsel perish fr. *w.*
*Dan.* 2:21 God giv. wisdom to *w.*
12:3 they that be *w.* shall shine
10 but the *w.* shall understand
*Hos.* 14:9 *w.* underst. th. things
*Zec.* 9:2 Tyrus and Zidon be *w.*
*Mat.* 10:16 be ye *w.* as serpents
11:25 because th. hast hid these things from *w.* *Luke* 10:21
24:45 who is faith. and *w.* ser.?
25:2 five virgins *w.* five foolish
4 *w.* took oil in their vessels
*Luke* 12:42 who is that *w.* stew.
*Rom.* 1:14 I am debtor to the *w.*
22 profess. thems. *w.* be. fools
11:25 lest ye be *w.* in your conc.
12:16 be not *w.* in your conceits
16:19 *w.* to that which is good
27 to God only *w.* be glory, 1 *Tim.* 1:17; *Jude* 25
1 *Cor.* 1:19 destroy wisdom of *w.*
20 where is the *w.*?
27 chosen foolish th. to con. *w.*
3:10 as *w.* master-builder I lay
18 be *w.* let him become a fool
19 taketh *w.* in their craftiness
20 L. knows thoughts of the *w.*
4:10 but ye are *w.* in Christ
2 *Cor.* 10:12 compar. are not *w.*
11:19 fools, seeing ye are *w.*
*Eph.* 5:15 not as fools, but *w.*
2 *Tim.* 3:15 scrip. able to ma. *w.*

**Any WISE.**
*Lev.* 19:17 shall in *a. w.* rebuke
*See* MAN, MEN.

**WISE-HEARTED.**
*Ex.* 28:3 speak to all *w.-hearted*
31:6 I put wisdom in *w.-hearted*
35:10 every *w.-hearted* am. you
25 women *w.-hearted* did spin
36:1 wrought every *w.-h.* man
8 ev. *w.-h.* man made 10 curta.

**WISE men.**
*Gen.* 41:8 Phar. called for magicians and *w. men*, *Ex.* 7:11

**In no WISE.**
*Mat.* 5:18 shall *in no w.* pass
10:42 he shall *in no w.* lose rew.
*Luke* 18:17 he shall *in no w.* enter therein, *Rev.* 21:27
*John* 6:37 will *in no w.* cast out
*Rom.* 3:9 are we bet.? *in no w.*

**On this WISE.**
*Mat.* 1:18 birth of C. was *on t. w.*
*Acts* 13:34 he said *on t. w.* I will
*Heb.* 4:4 spake of 7th day *on t. w.*

**WISE woman.**
2 *Sam.* 14:2 Joab fetched *w. w.*
20:16 cried a *w. w.* out of city
*Prov.* 14:1 ev. *w. w.* buil. house

**WISELY.**
*Ex.* 1:10 let us deal *w.* with them
1 *Sam.* 18:5 behav. *w.* 14, 15, 30
2 *Chr.* 11:23 Rehoboam dealt *w.*
*Ps.* 58:5 charming never so *w.*
64:9 shall *w.* cons. of his doings
101:2 I will behave myself *w.*
*Prov.* 16:20 handleth a matter *w.*
21:12 he *w.* considereth wicked
28:26 who walk. *w.* sh. be deliv.
*Ec.* 7:10 thou dost not inquire *w.*
*Luke* 16:8 becau. he had done *w.*

**WISER.**
1 *K.* 4:31 Sol. was *w.* th. all men
*Job* 35:11 mak. us *w.* than fowls
*Ps.* 119:98 made me *w.* th. enem.
*Prov.* 9:9 and he will be yet *w.*
26:16 slug. is *w.* in his conceit
*Ezek.* 28:3 thou art *w.* th. Daniel
*Luke* 16:8 in their generation *w.*
1 *Cor.* 1:25 fool. of G. *w.* th. men

**WISH.**
*Job* 33:6 to thy *w* in God's stead
*Ps.* 40:14 put to sha. that *w.* evil
73:7 more than heart could *w.*
*Rom.* 9:3 co. *w.* myself accursed
2 *Cor.* 13:9 we *w.* even your per.
3 *John* 2 I *w.* th. mayest prosper

**WISHED.**
*Jon.* 4:8 and *w.* himself to die
*Acts* 27:29 cast anch. *w.* for day

**WISHING.**
*Job* 31:30 *w.* a curse to his soul

**WIST.**
*Ex.* 16:15 th. *w.* not what it was
34:29 Mo. *w.* not his face shone
*Jud.* 16:20 *w.* not Lord departed
*Mark* 9:6 he *w.* not what to say
*Luke* 2:49 *w.* ye not I must be about my Father's business
*Acts* 12:9 *w.* it not true wh. was
23:5 *w.* not he was high-priest

**To WIT.**
*Gen.* 24:21 *to w.* wheth. L. made
*Ex.* 2:4 *to w.* what wou. be done
2 *Cor.* 5:19 *to w.* th. G. in C. rec.
8:1 we do you *to w.* of gr. of G.

**WITCH.**
*Ex.* 22:18 not suffer a *w.* to live
*Deut.* 18:10 not be am. you a *w.*

**WITCHCRAFT.**
1 *Sam.* 15:23 rebelli. as sin of *w.*
2 *Chr.* 33:6 Manasseh used *w.*
*Gal.* 5:20 works of flesh are *w.*

**WICTHCRAFTS.**
2 *K.* 9:22 Jezebel's *w.* are many
*Mic.* 5:12 cut off *w.* out of hand
*Nah.* 3:4 mist. of *w.* selleth nati.

**WITHAL.**
1 *K.* 19:1 *w.* Elij. slain prophets
*Acts* 25:27 not *w.* to signi. crimes

**WITHDRAW.**
1 *Sam.* 14:19 S. said to priest *w.*
*Job* 9:13 if God will not *w.* anger
13:21 *w.* thy hand far from me
33:17 that he may *w.* hand from
*Prov.* 25:17 *w.* fr. neigh.'s house
*Ec.* 7:18 fr. this *w.* not thy hand
*Is.* 60:20 neit. thy moon *w.* itself
*Joel* 2:10 stars *w.* shining, 3:15
2 *Thes.* 3:6 *w.* from every brother
1 *Tim.* 6:5 cor. minds *w.* thyself

**WITHDRAWN.**
*Deut.* 13:13 have *w.* inhabitants
*Cant.* 5:6 my beloved had *w.*
*Lam.* 2:8 hath not *w.* his hand
*Ezek.* 18:8 *w.* his hand from iniq.
*Hos.* 5:6 L. *w.* himself from them
*Luke* 22:41 was *w.* a stone's cast

**WITHDRAWEST, ETH.**
*Ps.* 74:11 why *w.* thy rig. hand?
*Job* 36:7 *w.* not from righteous

**WITHDREW.**
*Neh.* 9:29 *w.* and would not hear
*Ezek.* 20:22 I *w.* my hand
*Mat.* 12:15 Je. knew, *w.* himself
*Mark* 3:7 J. *w.* fr. then. *Lu.* 5:16
*Gal.* 2:12 when they come, he *w.*

**WITHER.**
*Ps.* 1:3 his leaf also shall not *w.*
37:2 shall *w.* as the green herb
*Is.* 19:6 reeds and flags shall *w.*
7 thing sown by brooks sh. *w.*
40:24 blow upon them, shall *w.*
*Jer.* 12:4 shall herbs of field *w.*?
*Ezek.* 17:9 cut off fruit that it *w.*
10 shall it not utterly *w.*?
*Amos* 1:2 top of Carmel shall *w.*

**WITHERED.**
*Gen.* 41:23 seven ears *w.*
*Ps.* 102:4 heart is *w.* 11 I am *w.*
*Is.* 15:6 the hay is *w.* away
27:11 boughs are *w.* broken off
*Lam.* 4:8 Nazarite's skin is *w.*
*Ezek.* 19:12 rods *w.* and consum.
*Joel* 1:12 trees of the field are *w.*
17 barns broken down, corn *w.*
*Amos* 4:7 where it rained not *w.*
*Jon.* 4:7 smote gourd that it *w.*
*Mat.* 12:10 man wh. had his hand *w.* *Mark* 3:1, 3; *Luke* 6:6, 8
13:6 hav. no root, *w.* *Mark* 4:6
21:19 fig-tree *w.* 20; *Mark* 11:21
*Luke* 8:6 it *w.* bec. lacked moist.
*John* 5:3 *w.* folk wait. mov. wat.
15:6 cast fo. as a branch and *w.*

**WITHERETH.**
*Job* 8:12 flag *w.* before any herb
*Ps.* 90:6 even. cut down and *w.*
*Ps.* 129:6 gra. *w.* bef. groweth up
*Is.* 40:7 grass *w.* the flower fadeth, 8; 1 *Pet.* 1:24
*Jam.* 1:11 the sun *w.* the grass
*Jude* 12 trees *w.* without fruit

**WITHHELD, EST.**
*Gen.* 20:6 I *w.* thee from sinning
22:12 thou hast not *w.* son
30:2 *w.* fr. thee, fruit of womb?
*Neh.* 9:20 *w.* not manna
*Job* 31:16 have *w.* poor fr. desire
*Ec.* 2:10 I *w.* not my heart

**WITHHOLD.**
*Gen.* 23:6 none sh. *w.* his sepulc.
2 *Sam.* 13:13 he will not *w.* me
*Job* 4:2 who can *w.* himself from
*Ps.* 40:11 *w.* not thy mercies
84:11 no good thing will he *w.*
*Prov.* 3:27 *w.* not good
23:13 *w.* not correct. from child

*Ec.* 11:6 even. *w.* not thy hand
*Jer.* 2:25 *w.* foot fr. being unsh.

**WITHHOLDEN.**

1 *Sam.* 25:26 *w.* th. from reveng.
*Job* 22:7 *w.* bread from hungry
38:15 from wicked light is *w.*
42:2 no thought *w.* from thee
*Ps.* 21:2 hast not *w.* request
*Jer.* 3:3 showers have been *w.*
5:25 sins have *w.* good things
*Ezek.* 18:16 hath not *w.* pledge
*Joel* 1:13 drink-off. *w.* from God
*Amos* 4:7 I have *w.* rain from you

**WITHHOLDETH.**

*Job* 12 15 behold he *w.* waters
*Prov.* 11 24 *w.* more than meet
26 he that *w.* corn, peo. curse
2 *Thes.* 2:6 now ye kn. what *w.*

**WITHIN.**

*Ec.* 9:14 little city, few men *w.*
*Luke* 11:7 he from *w.* sh. answer

**WITHOUT.**

*Gen.* 24:31 wheref. stan. th. *w.?*
*Prov.* 7:12 now she is *w.*
22:13 there is a lion *w.*
1 *Cor.* 5:13 but them that are *w.*

**WITHOUT, *with* within.**

*Lev.* 13:55 if garm. bare *w.* or *w.*
*Ezek.* 2:10 was written *w.* and *w.*

**WITHS.**

*Jud.* 16:7 bind with 7 green *w.*
8 brought *w.* 9 brake the *w.*

**WITHSTAND.**

*Num.* 22:32 angel went to *w.* Ba.
2 *Chr.* 13:7 R. could not *w.* them
8 ye think to *w.* kingdom of L.
20:6 none is able to *w.* thee
*Est.* 9:2 no man can co. *w.* Jews
*Ec.* 4:12 one prevail, two sh. *w.*
*Dan.* 11:15 his people sh. not *w.*
*Acts* 11:17 that I could *w.* God?
*Eph.* 6:13 able to *w.* in evil day

**WITHSTOOD.**

2 *Chr.* 26:18 *w.* Uzziah the king
*Dan.* 10:13 prince of Pers. *w.* me
*Acts* 13:8 Elymas sorcerer *w.* th.
*Gal.* 2:11 I *w.* Peter to the face
2 *Tim.* 3:8 Jannes and J. *w.* Mo.
4:15 hath greatly *w.* our words

**WITNESS.**

*Gen.* 21:30 a *w.* that I dig. well
31:44 covenant be a *w.* betw. us
48 this heap a *w.* pillar a *w.* 52
50 God is *w.* between me and thee, 1 *Thes.* 2:5
*Ex.* 22:13 if torn br. it for a *w.*
23:1 be not an unrighteous *w.*
*Lev.* 5:1 a soul sin and *w.* of sw.
*Num.* 5:13 if th. be no *w.* ag. her
35:30 one *w.* shall not testify, *Deut.* 17:6; 19:15
*Deut.* 31:19 song be a *w.* 21, 26
*Jos.* 22:27 altar *w.* bet. us, 28, 34
24:27 this stone shall be a *w.*
*Jud.* 11:10 L. *w.* bet. us, *Jer.* 42:5
1 *Sam.* 12:5 L. *w.* against you
*Job* 16:8 my wrinkles *w.* ag. me
19 *w.* in heaven record on high
29:11 eye saw me it gave *w.*
*Ps.* 89:37 a faithful *w.* in heaven
*Prov.* 14:5 faithf. *w.* will not lie
25 a true *w.* delivereth souls
19:28 ungodly *w.* scorn. judgm.
24:28 be not *w.* ag. thy neighb.
*Is.* 19:20 a *w.* to the L. of hosts
55:4 given him for *w.* to people
*Jer.* 29:23 and am a *w.* saith L.
42:5 L. faithful *w.* between us
*Mic.* 1:2 let L. G. be *w.* ag. you
*Mal.* 2:14 L. *w.* bet. thee and wi.
3:5 swift *w.* against sorcerers
*Mat.* 24:14 preached for *w.* to na.
*Mark* 14:55 sought for *w.* ag. Je.
56 *w.* agreed not together, 59
*Luke* 22:71 need we further *w.?*
*John* 1:7 came for a *w.* to bear *w.*
3:11 ye receive not our *w.*
26 whom bear. *w.* same bapti.
5:31 if bear *w.* mys. *w.* not true
32 *w.* he witness. of me is true
36 I have greater *w.* than John
37 Father hath borne *w.* of me
*Acts* 1:22 one ordained to be *w.*
4:33 gave *w.* of resurrect. of L.
10:43 all proph. *w.* whoso beli.
14:17 left not himself without *w.*
22:15 thou shalt be his *w.* to all
26:16 make thee minister and *w.*
*Rom.* 1:9 God is my *w.* I serve
2:15 conscience bearing *w.* 9:1
*Tit.* 1:13 this *w.* is true, rebuke
*Heb.* 2:4 God bear. *w.* with signs
10:15 the Holy Ghost is *w.* to us
11:4 Abel obtained *w.* righteous
*Jam.* 5:3 rust shall be *w.* ag. you
1 *Pet.* 5:1 P. a *w.* of suffer. of C.
1 *John* 5:9 if we receive *w.* of m.
10 he th. beli. hath *w.* in hims.
3 *John* 6 borne *w.* of thy charity
*Rev.* 1:5 Jesus Ch. the faithf. *w.*
3:14 write th. thi. saith true *w.*
20:4 were beheaded for *w.* of J.

*See* BARE, BEAR, BEARETH, FALSE, TABERNACLE.

**WITNESSES.**

*Num.* 35:30 put to death by *w.*
*Deut.* 17:6 at mouth of two or three *w.* shall he be put to death, 19:15; 2 *Cor.* 13:1
7 hands of *w.* be first on him
*Jos.* 24:22 Josh. said, Ye are *w.*
*Ruth* 4:9 ye are *w.* I have bou. 10
*Job* 10:17 renew. thy *w.* ag. me
*Is.* 8:2 I took faithful *w.* to rec.
43:9 all nations bring their *w.*
10 my *w.* saith the L. 12; 44:8
44:9 they are their own *w.*
*Jer.* 32:10 I seal. evid. took *w.* 12
25 buy field, take *w.* 44
*Mat.* 18:16 mou. of two or th. *w.*
23:31 ye be *w.* to yourselves
26:65 need of *w.?* *Mark* 14:63
*Luke* 24:48 ye are *w.* of th. thin.
*Acts* 1:8 ye sh. be *w.* in Jerusal.
2:32 Jesus G. raised up, whereof we are *w.* 3:15
5:32 *w.* of these things, 10:39
7:58 *w.* laid th. clothes at S.'s f.
10:41 unto *w.* chosen of G. to us
13:31 are his *w.* unto the people
1 *Thes.* 2:10 ye are *w.* God also
1 *Tim.* 5:19 no ac. but bef. 2 *w.*
6:12 good profes. bef. many *w.*
2 *Tim.* 2:2 thi. heard among *w.*
*Heb.* 10:28 died under 2 or 3 *w.*
12:1 compassed wi. cloud of *w.*
*Rev.* 11:3 give power to my *w.*

*See* FALSE

**WITNESS, Verb.**

*Deut.* 4:26 I call heaven and earth to *w.* against you
1 *Sam.* 12:3 here I am, *w.* ag. me
*Is.* 3:9 countenance *w.* ag. them
*Lam.* 2:13 what sh. I take to *w.?*
*Mat.* 26:62 what is it wh. these *w.* against thee? *Mark* 14:60
27:13 how many things they *w.* against thee? *Mark* 15:4

**WITNESSED, ETH, ING.**

1 *K.* 21:13 men of B. *w.* ag. Nab.
*John* 5:32 witness *w.* of me
*Acts* 20:23 H. G. *w.* in every city
26:22 *w.* both to small and great
*Rom.* 3:21 being *w.* by law and
1 *Tim.* 6:13 bef. P. *w.* good conf.
*Heb.* 7:8 of whom it is *w.* he liv.

**WITS.**

*Ps.* 107:27 stag. at their *w.* end

**WITTY.**

*Prov.* 8:12 I find out *w.* inventi.

**WITTINGLY.**

*Gen.* 48:14 Is. guid. his hands *w.*

**WIVES.**

*Gen.* 4:19 Lamech took two *w.*
6:2 took them *w.* wh. they cho.
30:26 give me my *w.* and child.
31:50 if thou take other *w.*
*Num.* 14:3 *w.* and chil. be a prey
*Deut.* 17:17 nor multi. *w.* to him.
21:15 if a man have two *w.*
*Jud.* 8:30 Gideon had many *w.*
21:7 how do for *w.* for them? 16
18 not give them *w.* of our da.
1 *Sam.* 25:43 they were Da.'s *w.*
2 *Sam.* 5:13 Da. took *w.* out of J.
12:8 gave master's *w.* into thy
1 *K.* 11:3 Solomon had 700 *w.*
4 his *w.* turn. his heart wh. old
20:7 sent for my *w.* and childr.
2 *Chr.* 11:21 Ma. above all his *w.*
23 he desired many *w.*
24:3 Jehoi. took for him two *w.*
29:9 our *w.* in captivity for this
*Ezr.* 10:3 a cov. to put aw. *w.* 44
*Neh.* 12:43 *w.* and chil. rejoiced
13:23 Jews married *w.* of Ashd.
*Est.* 1:20 *w.* give husbands hon.
*Jer.* 29:6 take *w.* and *w.* for sons
35:8 d. no wine, nor *w.* nor sons
*Dan.* 5:2 his *w.* drink therein, 3
*Luke* 17:27 eat, drank, marri. *w.*
*Acts* 21:5 on our way, with *w.*
1 *Cor.* 7:29 ha. *w.* be as had none
*Eph.* 5:22 *w.* submit to your husbands as unto the Lord, *Col.* 3:18; 1 *Pet.* 3:1
24 so let *w.* be to th. husbands
1 *Tim.* 4:7 refuse old *w.* fables
1 *Pet.* 2:1 won by conversa. of *w.*

*See* STRANGE.

**Their WIVES.**

*Gen.* 34:29 *t. w.* capt. 1 *Sam.* 30:3
*Jud.* 3:6 took daught. to be *t. w.*
2 *Chr.* 20:13 Ju. with *t. w.* stood
*Ezr.* 10:19 put away *their w.*
*Neh.* 5:1 cry of people and *th. w.*
10:28 *t. w.* entered into an oath
*Is.* 13:16 houses spoil. *w.* ravish.
*Jer.* 6:12 *t. w.* turned to oth. 8:10
14:16 none to bury *their w.*
18:21 *t. w.* be bereaved of child.
44:9 forgotten wicked. of *t. w.*
15 men knew *t. w.* burnt ince.
*Ezek.* 44:22 nor take for *t. w.* wi.
*Dan.* 6:24 cast *t. w.* into den of l.
*Zec.* 12:12 *t. w.* mourn, 13, 14
*Eph.* 5:28 love *t. w.* as th. bodies
1 *Tim.* 3:11 so must *t. w.* be gr.

**Thy WIVES.**

2 *Sam.* 12:11 take *t. w.* bef. eyes
19:5 who saved lives of *t. w.*
1 *K.* 20:3 gold is mine and *t. w.*
5 deliver me *thy w.* and child.
2 *Chr.* 21:14 L. will smite *t. w.*
*Jer.* 38:23 bring *thy w.* and chil.
*Dan.* 5:23 *thy w.* have dru. wine

**Your WIVES.**

*Ex.* 19:15 come not at *your w.*
22:24 *your w.* shall be widows
32:2 break ear-rings of *your w.*
*Deut.* 3:19 *y. w.* and little ones remain in cities, *Jos.* 1:14
29:11 *y. w.* enter coven. with L.
*Neh.* 4:14 fight for *y. w.* and hou.
*Jer.* 44:9 forgot. wicked. of *y. w.*
25 ye and *your w.* have spoken
*Mat.* 19:8 suff. to put away *y. w.*
*Eph.* 5:25 love *your w.* *Col.* 3:19

**WIZARD, S.**

*Lev.* 19:31 nor seek after *w.*
20:6 turns after *w.* I will cut off
27 a *w.* shall be put to death
*Deut.* 18:11 sh. not be am. you *w.*
1 *Sam.* 28:3 Saul put *w.* out, 9
2 *K.* 21:6 dealt with *w.* 2 *Chr.* 33:6

23:24 Josiah put *w.* out of land
*Is.* 8:19 *w.* that peep and mutter
19:3 shall seek to idols and *w.*

**WOE.**

*Num.* 21:29 *w.* to M. *Jer.* 48:46
1 *Sam.* 4:7 *w.* unto us, 8; *Jer.* 4:13; 6:4; *Lam.* 5:16
*Prov.* 23:29 hath *w.?* hath sor.?
*Ec.* 4:10 *w.* to him that falls
10:16 *w.* to th. wh. king is a ch.
*Is.* 3:9 *w.* to their soul
11 *w.* to wick. sh. be ill wi. h.
17:12 *w.* to multi. of many peo.
18:1 *w.* to the land with wings
28:1 *w.* to pride, to drunkards
29:1 *w.* to Ariel; 33:1 *w.* to them
30:1 *w.* to rebellious children
45:9 *w.* to him striv. wi. Maker
10 *w.* to him saith to father
*Jer.* 13:27 *w.* unto thee, O Jerus.
22:13 *w.* to him that builds
23:1 *w.* to pastors destroy sheep
48:1 *w.* to Nebo
*Ezek.* 2:10 written mour. and *w.*
13:3 *w.* to foolish prophets
18 *w.* to wom. th. sew pillows
16:23 *w. w.* unto thee, saith L.
24:6 *w.* to bloody city, *Nah.* 3:1
30:2 howl, *w.* worth the day
34:2 *w.* be to the shepherds
*Amos* 5:18 *w.* to you de. day of L.
*Hab.* 2:6 *w.* to him that increas.
9 *w.* to him that coveteth
12 *w.* to him that build. a town
15 *w.* to him giv. neigh. drink
19 *w.* to him saith wood awake
*Zep.* 2:5 *w.* to inh. of sea-coasts
3:1 *w.* to her that is polluted
*Zec.* 11:17 *w.* to idol shepherd
*Mat.* 11:21 *w.* to thee, Chora. *w.* to thee, Bethsaida, *Lu.* 10:13
18:7 *w.* to the world because of offences, *Luke* 17:1
23:13 *w.* unto you scribes and Pharisees, 14, 15, 23, 25, 27, 29; *Luke* 11:44
16 *w.* unto you, blind guides
26:24 *w.* to man by whom Son of man is betrayed, *Mark* 14:21; *Luke* 22:22
*Luke* 6:24 *w.* unto you are rich
25 *w.* to you that are full
26 *w.* to you wh. all speak well
11:42 *w.* unto you, Pharisees, 43
46 *w.* to you, ye lawyers, 47, 52
*Rev.* 8:13 *w. w. w.* to the inhabiters of the earth, 12:12
9:12 one *w.* past; 11:14 sec. *w.*

**WOE is me.**

*Ps.* 120:5 *w. is me* th. I sojourn
*Is.* 6:5 *w. is me*, I am undone
*Jer.* 4:31 *w. is me*, soul wearied
10:19 *w. is me*, for my hurt
15:10 *w. is me*, moth. hast borne
45:3 *w. is me*, for L. added grief
*Mic.* 7:1 *w. is me*, I am as fruit

**WOE unto me.**

*Job* 10:15 if I be wicked, *w. u. me*
*Is.* 24:16 my leanness, *w. u. me*
1 *Cor.* 9:16 *w. u. me* if I preach

**WOE to them.**

*Is.* 5:8 *w. to them* that join house
11 *w. to t.* that rise in morning
18 *w. to them* that draw iniqu.
20 *w. to t.* that call evil good
21 *w. to them* wise in own eyes
22 *w. to them* that drink wine
10:1 *w. to t.* decree unrigh. dec.
29:15 *w. to t.* that seek counsel
31:1 *w. to t.* th. go down to Eg.
*Jer.* 50:27 *w. to t.* their day come
*Hos.* 7:13 *w. to t.* have fled fr. me
9:12 *w. to t.* I depart from them
*Amos* 6:1 *w. to t.* at ease in Zion
*Mic.* 2:1 *w. to t.* devise iniquity
*Mat.* 24:19 *w. to t.* wh. are with chi. *Mark* 13:17; *Luke* 21:23
*Jude* 11 *w. to t.* gone way of Cain

**WOES.**

*Rev.* 9:12 two *w.* more hereafter

**WOFUL.**

*Jer.* 17:16 neither desired *w.* day

**WOLF.**

*Gen.* 49:27 Benja. ravin as a *w.*
*Is.* 11:6 *w.* sh. dwell with lamb
65:25 *w.* and lamb feed together
*Jer.* 5:6 *w.* of evening spoil them
*John* 10:12 hirel. seeth *w.* coming

**WOLVES.**

*Ezek.* 22:27 her princ. are like *w.*
*Hab.* 1:8 horses fiercer than *w.*
*Zep.* 3:3 her judges evening *w.*
*Mat.* 7:15 inwardly they are *w.*
10:16 as sheep in midst of *w.*
*Luke* 10:3 send you forth am. *w.*
*Acts* 20:29 *w.* sh. ent. among you

**WOMAN.**

*Gen.* 2:22 rib of man made he *w.*
23 she shall be called *w.*
3:15 enmity between th. and *w.*
24:5 peradven. *w.* not come, 39
44 let same be *w.* L. appointed
*Ex.* 21:22 hurt a *w.* with child
*Lev.* 18:23 nor *w.* stand bef. beast
20:13 lie with mank. as with *w.*
*Num.* 5:18 set *w.* before Lord, 30
27 *w.* be curse among her peo.
25:6 brought Midianitish *w.*
8 Phineh. thrust *w.* thro' belly
31:17 kill ev. *w.* hath kno. man
*Deut.* 22:14 I took *w.* not a maid
*Jos.* 2:4 *w.* took men, hid them
6:22 bring out thence *w.* Rahab
*Jud.* 4:9 Sisera into hand of *w.*
9:53 *w.* cast millsto. on Abimelech's head, 2 *Sam.* 11:21
54 say not of me, *w.* slew him
14:3 never *w.* am. my people?
19:26 came *w.* in dawni. of day
*Ruth* 1:5 *w.* was left of her sons
3:11 kn. thou art a virtuous *w.*
4:11 L. make *w.* like Rachel
1 *Sam.* 1:15 *w.* of sorrowful spi.
26 I am *w.* stood by thee here
2:20 L. give thee seed of this *w.*
28:7 *w.* that hath a familiar spi.
2 *Sam.* 11:2 Da. saw *w.* washing
13:17 put this *w.* out, bolt door
17:19 *w.* spread cover. ov. well
20:22 then *w.* went to the peo.
1 *K.* 3:17 I and *w.* dwell in house
14:5 feign herself to be ano. *w.*
17:17 son of *w.* fell sick, died
2 *K.* 4:8 where was a great *w.*
2 *K.* 6:26 there cried a *w.* saying
8:5 this is *w.* 9:34 see cursed *w.*
2 *Chr.* 24:7 Athal. that wick. *w.*
*Job* 31:9 if heart deceiv. by a *w.*
*Ps.* 48:6 pain as of a *w.* in travail, *Is.* 13:8; 21:3; 26:17; *Jer.* 4:31; 6:24; 13:21; 22:23; 30:6; 31:8; 48:41; 49:22, 24; 50:43
*Prov.* 6:24 keep thee fr. evil *w.*
7:10 there met him a *w.* subtile
9:13 a foolish *w.* is clamorous
12:4 virtu. *w.* is a crown, 31:10
14:1 ev. wise *w.* buildeth house
21:9 brawling *w.* in house, 19
31:10 who can find a virtu. *w.?*
30 *w.* that fears L. be praised
*Ec.* 7:26 *w.* wh. heart is snares
28 *w.* am. th. I have not found
*Is.* 42:14 I cry like travailing *w.*
45:10 to *w.* what hast th. bro.?
49:15 can *w.* forget suck. child?
54:6 L. called thee as *w.* forsak.
*Jer.* 6:2 daughter of Zion to a *w.*
31:22 a *w.* compass a man
*Lam.* 1:17 J. is a menstruous *w.*
*Ezek.* 16:30 work of a whorish *w.*
23:44 went as they go in to *w.*
36:17 unclean. of a removed *w.*
*Hos.* 3:1 love *w.* beloved of friend
13:13 source of a travailing *w.* sh. come on him, *Mic.* 4:9, 10
*Zec.* 5:7 a *w.* that sit. in ephah.
*Mat.* 5:28 whoso looketh on a *w.*
9:20 a *w.* whi. was diseased 12 years, *Mark* 5:25; *Luke* 8:43
13:33 which a *w.* took and hid
15:28 O *w.* great is thy faith
22:27 last of all *w.* died also, *Mark* 12:22; *Luke* 20:32
26:10 said, Why trouble ye *w.*
13 that *w.* hath done sh. be to.
*Mark* 10:12 if *w.* put away husb.
*Luke* 7:39 what man. of *w.* this?
44 Simon, seest thou this *w.?*
13:16 ought not this *w.* daught.
*John* 2:4 *w.* wh. have I to do wi.
4:9 askest of me, a *w.* of Sama.
39 many belie. for saying of *w.*
8:3 brought *w.* taken in adult. 4
10 when Jesus saw none but *w.*
19:26 mother, *w.* behold thy son
*Acts* 9:36 *w.* was full of works
17:34 a *w.* named Damaris beli.
*Rom.* 1:27 men leaving use of *w.*
7:2 *w.* that hath husb. is bound
1 *Cor.* 7:1 good not to touch a *w.*
2 every *w.* have her own husb.
11:5 *w.* th. prayeth uncovered, 6
7 *w.* is glory of the man, 8, 9
10 *w.* ought to have power, 11
12 as *w.* is of man, so m. by *w.*
13 is it comely for *w.* to pray
15 if a *w.* have long hair
*Gal.* 4:4 sent his S. made of a *w.*
1 *Thes.* 5:3 com. as travail on *w.*
1 *Tim.* 2:12 suff. not *w.* to teach
14 *w.* being deceiv. in transgr.
*Rev.* 2:20 suff. *w.* Jezeb. to teach
12:1 appear. *w.* cloth. with sun
6 *w.* fled; 16 earth helped *w.*
17 dragon was wroth with *w.*
17:3 I saw a *w.* sit on a beast
6 *w.* drunken; 7 mystery of *w.*

*See* BORN, MAN, STRANGE.

**Young WOMAN.**

*Ruth* 4:12 seed L. give th. of *y. w.*

**WOMANKIND.**

*Lev.* 18:22 not lie wi. man. as *w.*

**WOMB.**

*Gen.* 25:23 two nations in thy *w.*
24 were twins in her *w.* 38:27
29:31 Leah's *w.* 30:22 Rach.'s *w.*
49:25 bless. of breasts and of *w.*
*Ex.* 13:2 whatso. open. *w.* mine
*Num.* 8:16 such as open ev. *w.*
*Jud.* 13:5 be a Nazarite fr. *w.* 7.
*Ruth* 1:11 any more sons in *w.?*
1 *Sam.* 1:5 L. had shut up *w.* 6
*Job* 3:11 why died I not fr. *w.?*
10:18 why brou. me forth of *w.?*
24:20 the *w.* shall forget him
31:15 made th. in *w.* make him?
38:8 as if it had issu. out of *w.*
29 out of whose *w.* came ice?
*Ps.* 22:9 who took me out of *w.*
10 I was cast upon thee fr. *w.*
58:3 wick. are estranged fr. *w.*
71:6 been upholden from *w.*
110:3 willing, from *w.* of morn.
*Prov.* 30:16 barren *w.* says not
31:2 what, the son of my *w.?*
*Ec.* 11:5 how bones grow in *w.*
*Is.* 44:2 Lord formed thee from the *w.* 24; 49:5
46:3 which are carried from *w.*
48:8 called a transgressor fr. *w.*
*Is.* 49:1 Lord called me from *w.*
15 have compas. on son of *w.*
66:9 bring forth, and shut *w.?*
*Jer.* 1:5 bef. th. camest out of *w.*
20:17 he slew me not from *w.*
18 why ca. I forth out of *w.?*
*Ezek.* 20:26 fire that openeth *w.*

*Hos.* 9:11 gl. flee fr. birth and *w.*
14 give them a miscarrying *w.*
12:3 took brother by heel in *w.*
*Luke* 1:31 sh. conceive in thy *w.*
41 babe leaped in her *w.* 44
2:21 bef. he was conceiv. in *w.*
23 male that open. *w.* be holy
*See* FRUIT, MOTHER.

**WOMBS.**

*Gen.* 20:18 L. had closed all *w.*
*Luke* 23:29 bless. *w.* never bare

**WOMEN.**

*Gen.* 24:11 *w.* go to draw water
*Ex.* 15:20 *w.* went after Miriam
35:25 *w.* wise-hearted spin, 26
*Lev.* 26:26 ten *w.* sh. bake bread
*Num.* 31:15 have saved *w.* alive
*Jos.* 8:35 Jos. read law before *w.*
*Jud.* 5:24 blessed above *w.* Jael
21:14 saved *w.* of Jabesh-Gilead
1 *Sam.* 2:22 Eli heard lay wi. *w.*
15:33 thy sword made *w.* child.
18:7 *w.* answered one another
21:5 *w.* have been kept from us three days
30:2 Amalek. had taken *w.* cap.
2 *Sam.* 1:26 passing love of *w.*
15:16 left ten *w.* to keep house
1 *K.* 3:16 came *w.* were harlots
2 *K.* 8:12 rip *w.* with child, 15:16
*Neh.* 13:26 outland. *w.* cause sin
*Est.* 1:9 made a feast for the *w.*
2:17 A. loved Esther above *w.*
3:13 little children and *w.* 8:11
*Job* 42:15 no *w.* fair as Job's dau.
*Ps.* 45:9 among thy honorable *w.*
*Prov.* 31:3 give not stren. to *w.*
*Cant.* 1:8 fair. among *w.* 5:9; 6:1
*Is.* 3:12 peo. *w.* rule over them
4:1 sev. *w.* ta. hold of one man
19:16 Egypt shall be like to *w.*
27:11 *w.* come, set them on fire
32:9 ye *w.* that are at ease
10 careless *w.* 11 *w.* be troub.
*Jer.* 7:18 *w.* knead their dough
9:17 mourning and cunning *w.*
20 yet hear word of L. O ye *w.*
38:22 *w.* left be brought to king
44:24 Jer. said to *w.* Hear word
50:37 they sh. become *w.* robbed
51:30 men of Ba. became as *w.*
*Lam.* 2:20 shall *w.* eat children?
4:10 *w.* have sodden th. children
5:11 they ravished *w.* in Zion
*Ezek.* 8:14 *w.* weeping for Tam.
9:6 slay maids, children, and *w.*
13:18 woe to *w.* that sew pillows
16:34 contrary from other *w.*
38 judge thee, as *w.* break wedlock
23:2 two *w.* daughters of one
45 after man. of *w.* shed blood
48 *w.* tau. not to do after lewd.
*Dan.* 11:17 give him dau. of *w.*
37 nor sh. he regard des. of *w.*
*Hos.* 13:16 *w.* with child be rip.
*Amos* 1:13 ripped *w.* with child
*Mic.* 2:9 *w.* of people ye cast out
*Nah.* 3:13 people in midst are *w.*
*Zec.* 5:9 there came out two *w.*
8:4 old *w.* shall dwell in Jerus.
14:2 houses rifled, *w.* ravished
*Mat.* 11:11 th. are born of *w.* not greater than Bapt. *Luke* 7:28
14:21 5,000 men, besi. *w.* 15:38
24:41 two *w.* grind. *Luke* 17:35
27:55 *w.* were beholding afar off
*Luke* 1:28 blessed among *w.* 42
24:22 *w.* made us astonish. 24
*Acts* 1:14 conti. in prayer wi. *w.*
13:50 Jews stirred up devout *w.*
16:13 speak to *w.* wh. resorted
17:4 of *w.* not a few believ. 12
*Rom.* 1:26 th. *w.* did change use
1 *Cor.* 14:34 let *w.* keep silence
35 shame for *w.* to speak in ch.
*Phil.* 4:3 help *w.* which labored
1 *Tim.* 2:9 *w.* adorn in mod. ap.
10 becom. *w.* professing godli.
11 let *w.* learn with subjection
5:2 entreat elder *w.* as mothers
14 I will that young. *w.* marry
2 *Tim.* 3:6 captive *w.* laden with sins
*Tit.* 2:3 aged *w.* behave as beco.
4 teach younger *w.* to be sober
*Heb.* 11:35 *w.* receiv. dead raised
1 *Pet.* 3:5 manner holy *w.* adorn.
*Rev.* 9:8 had hair as hair of *w.*
*Rev.* 14:4 that are not defil. wi. *w.*
*See* CHILDREN, MEN, STRANGE, SINGING.

**WOMEN-SERVANTS.**

*Gen.* 20:14 Abimelech gave *w.-s.*
32:5 Jacob had men-serv. *w.-s.*

**WON.**

1 *Chr.* 26:27 spoils *w.* in battles
*Prov.* 18:19 offend. bar. to be *w.*
1 *Pet.* 3:1 *w.* by conver. of wives

**WONDER.**

*Deut.* 13:1 give thee a sign or *w.*
2 sign of the *w.* come to pass
28:46 on thee for a sign and *w.*
2 *Chr.* 32:31 sent to inquire of *w.*
*Ps.* 71:7 I am as a *w.* to many
*Is.* 20:3 walked barefoot for a *w.*
29:14 marvellous work and *w.*
*Acts* 3:10 they were filled wi. *w.*
*Rev.* 12:1 appear. a *w.* in heav. 3

**WONDER, Verb.**

*Is.* 29:9 stay yourselves and *w.*
*Jer.* 4:9 priests and proph. sh. *w.*
*Hab.* 1:5 regard, *w.* marvellously
*Acts* 13:41 despisers, *w.* and per.
*Rev.* 17:8 dwell on earth sh. *w.*

**WONDERFUL.**

*Deut.* 28:59 will ma. plagues *w.*
2 *Sam.* 1:26 love to me was *w.*
2 *Chr.* 2:9 house I am to build *w.*
*Job* 42:3 uttered things too *w.* for
*Ps.* 119:129 thy testimoni. are *w.*
139:6 knowledge too *w.* for me
*Prov.* 30:18 three thi. are too *w.*
*Is.* 9:6 his name sh. be called *W.*
25:1 thou hast done *w.* things
28:29 Lord, who is *w.* in coun.
*Jer.* 5:30 a *w.* thing is committed
*Mat.* 21:15 saw *w.* things he did
*See* WORKS.

**WONDERFULLY.**

1 *Sam.* 6:6 when he wrought *w.*
*Ps.* 139:14 for I am *w.* made
*Lam.* 1:9 Jerusal. came down *w.*
*Dan.* 8:24 he shall destroy *w.*

**WONDERS.**

*Ex.* 3:20 and smite Egypt with my *w.* 7:3; 11:9; *Deut.* 6:22; 7:19; 26:8; 34:11
4:21 do those *w.* 11:10 did *w.*
15:11 fearf. in praises, doing *w.*
*Deut.* 4:34 to take a nation by *w.*
*Jos.* 3:5 to-morrow L. will do *w.*
1 *Chr.* 16:12 rem. his *w.* *Ps.* 105:5
*Neh.* 9:10 showedst *w.* on Phara.
17 nor were mindful of thy *w.* *Ps.* 78:11, 43
*Job* 9:10 G. doeth *w.* with. num.
*Ps.* 77:11 I remember *w.* of old
14 thou art God that doest *w.*
88:10 wilt th. show *w.* to dead?
12 shall thy *w.* be kn. in dark?
89:5 heavens shall praise thy *w.*
96:3 declare his *w.* among peo.
105:27 showed his *w.* in land of
106:7 underst. not thy *w.* in Eg.
107:24 see works and *w.* in deep
135:9 sent *w.* in midst of Egypt
136:4 who alone doeth great *w.*
*Is.* 8:18 children are for *w.* in Is.
*Jer.* 32:20 set signs and *w.* in Eg.
21 brought forth people wi. *w.*
*Dan.* 4:2 to show signs and *w.*
3 great signs! mighty his *w.!*
6:27 he worketh *w.* in heaven
12:6 how long to end of th. *w.?*
*Joel* 2:30 I will sh. *w.* *Acts* 2:19
*Mat.* 24:24 show *w.* *Mark* 13:22
*John* 4:48 except ye see signs, *w.*
*Acts* 2:22 approved of God by *w.*
43 ma. signs and *w.* were done
4:30 *w.* done by name of Je. by apostles, 5:12; 14:3; 15:12
6:8 Stephen did *w.* among peo.
7:36 after he had sh. *w.* in Eg.
*Rom.* 15:19 Gent. obed. thro' *w.*
2 *Cor.* 12:12 signs of apost. in *w.*
2 *Thes.* 2:9 com. in signs and *w.*
*Heb.* 2:4 witn. with signs and *w.*
*Rev.* 13:13 *w.* in sight of men

**WONDERED.**

*Is.* 59:16 *w.* was no intercessor
63:5 I *w.* th. was none to uphold
*Zec.* 3:8 hear, for they are *w.* at
*Luke* 2:18 they that heard it *w.*
4:22 they *w.* at gracious words
24:41 believed not for joy, *w.*
*Acts* 7:31 Mos. *w.* 8:13 Magus *w.*
*Rev.* 13:3 world *w.* after beast
17:6 I *w.* with great admiration

**WONDERING.**

*Gen.* 24:21 *w.* at her, held peace
*Luke* 24:12 Pe. *w.* at that which
*Acts* 3:11 people ran together *w.*

**WONDROUS.**

1 *Chr.* 16:9 talk of his *w.* wo. *Ps.* 26:7; 105:2; 119:27; 145:5
*Job* 37:14 consid. *w.* works of G.
16 dost kn. *w.* works of him?
*Ps.* 71:17 I declar. thy *w.* works
72:18 G. doeth *w.* things, 86:10
75:1 near, thy *w.* works declare
78:32 believed not for *w.* works
106:22 who had done *w.* works
119:18 behold *w.* thi. out of law
*Jer.* 21:2 accord. to his *w.* works

**WONDROUSLY.**

*Jud.* 13:19 the angel did *w.*
*Joel* 2:26 Lord dealt *w.* with you

**WONT.**

*Num.* 22:30 was I ever *w.* to do so to thee?
2 *Sam.* 20:18 th. were *w.* to spe.
*Mark* 10:1 as he was *w.* he tau.
*Luke* 22:39 he was *w.* to mount

**WOOD.**

*Gen.* 22:6 Abraham took *w.*
7 Isa. said, Behold fire and *w.*
*Num.* 13:20 wheth. be *w.* or not
31:20 purify things made of *w.*
*Deut.* 10:1 make th. an ark of *w.*
19:5 when man goeth into *w.*
29:11 hewer of thy *w.* *Jos.* 9:21, 23, 27; *Jer.* 46:22
*Jos.* 17:18 mountain is a *w.*
1 *Sam.* 6:14 th. clave *w.* of cart
14:25 they of land came to a *w.*
23:16 Jonath. went to Da. in *w.*
2 *Sam.* 18:8 *w.* devoured people
1 *K.* 18:23 lay the bullock on *w.*
2 *K.* 2:24 two she-bears out of *w.*
1 *Chr.* 29:2 I have prepared *w.*
*Ps.* 80:13 boar of *w.* doth waste
132:6 found it in fields of *w.*
141:7 when one cleaveth *w.*
*Prov.* 26:20 no *w.* fire goeth out
21 as *w.* to fire, so is contenti.
*Ec.* 10:9 he that cleaveth *w.*
*Is.* 10:15 lift itself as if no *w.*
30:33 pile thereof is fire and *w.*
45:20 set up *w.* of their image
60:17 for iron silv. for *w.* brass
*Jer.* 5:14 make words fire, peo. *w.*
7:18 children gather *w.* the fa.
28:13 hast broken yokes of *w.*
*Ezek.* 15:3 sh. *w.* thereof be tak.
24:10 heap on *w.* 39:10 no *w.*

*Mic.* 7:14 flock whi. dwell in *w.*
*Hab.* 2:19 saith to *w.* Awake
*Hag.* 1:8 bring *w.* build house
*Zec.* 12:6 like a hearth among *w.*
1 *Cor.* 3:12 this founda. *w.* hay
2 *Tim.* 2:20 also vessels of *w.*
*See* OFFERING, STONE.

**WOODS.**

*Ezek.* 34:25 sleep safely in *w.*

**WOOF.**

*Lev.* 13:48 plague be in *w.* 51-59

**WOOL.**

*Jud.* 6:37 fleece of *w.* in floor
2 *K.* 3:4 100,000 rams with *w.*
*Ps.* 147:16 L. giveth snow like *w*
*Prov.* 31:13 seeketh *w.* and flax
*Is.* 1:18 sins like crim. be as *w.*
51:8 worm sh. eat them like *w.*
*Ezek.* 27:18 was merchant in *w.*
34:3 eat fat, clothe you with *w.*
44:17 no *w.* sh. come upon them
*Dan.* 7:9 hair like *w.* *Rev.* 1:14
*Hos.* 2:5 lovers that give me *w.*
9 I will recover my *w.* and flax

**WOOLLEN.**

*Lev.* 13:47 wheth. *w.* or linen, 59
48 in warp or woof of *w.* 52
19:19 a garment mingled of linen and *w.* *Deut.* 22:11

**WORD.**

*Gen.* 37:14 br. me *w.* ag. *Mat.* 2:8
44:18 let me sp. a *w.* 2 *Sam.* 14:12
*Ex.* 12:35 according to *w.* of Mo.
32:28 Levi did according to the *w.* *Lev.* 10:7
*Num.* 22:8 bri. you *w.* *Deut.* 1:22
20 the *w.* I say to thee, that do
35 *w.* I speak; 38 *w.* God put.
23:5 L. put *w.* in Bala.'s mouth
*Deut.* 1:25 brought us *w.* again
4:2 not add to *w.* I comm. you
8:3 by *w.* that proceed. out of mouth of God, *Mat.* 4:4
18:20 prophet pres. to speak *w.*
21 how know the *w.*? *Jer.* 28:9
21:5 by *w.* controversy be tried
30:14 *w.* is nigh thee, *Rom.* 10:8
*Jos.* 1:13 remember *w.* Moses
14:7 I brought *w.* 22:32 them *w.*
1 *Sam.* 4:1 *w.* of Sa. came to Is.
2 *Sam.* 3:11 not answer Ab. a *w.*
2 *Sam.* 7:7 and in all places spake I a *w.* 1 *Chr.* 17:6
25 *w.* thou hast spoken conce.
15:28 till there come *w.* fr. you
19:10 not a *w.* of bringing king
24:4 and the king's *w.* prevailed, 1 *Chr.* 21:4
1 *K.* 2:30 Ben. bro. king *w.* 2 *K.* 22:9, 20; 2 *Chr.* 34:16, 28
42 *w.* that I have heard is good
8:56 not failed one *w.* of prom.
18:21 answer. not a *w.* *Is.* 36:21
2 *K.* 18:28 hear *w.* of king of As.
1 *Chr.* 16:15 be ye mindful of *w.* *Ps.* 105:8
21:12 advise *w.* I sh. bring him
*Neh.* 1:8 remember *w.* thou com.
*Est.* 1:21 according to *w.* of Me.
7:8 *w.* went out of king's mouth
*Job* 2:13 none spake a *w.* to Job
*Ps.* 17:4 by *w.* of thy lips I kept
68:11 L. gave *w.* many publish.
119:49 rememb. *w.* to thy serv.
123 eyes fail for *w.* of righteo.
139:4 there is not *w.* in tongue
*Prov.* 12:25 a good *w.* mak. glad
13:13 despiseth *w* be destroyed
14:15 simple believeth every *w.*
15:23 *w.* spoken in season good
25:11 *w.* fitly spo. is like apples
*Ec.* 8:4 where *w.* of king, power
*Is.* 5:24 despised *w.* of Holy One
8:10 speak *w.* it shall not stand
9:8 the Lord sent a *w.* to Jacob
29:21 make man offend. for a *w.*
30:21 ears sh. hear *w.* behind th.
41:28 no counsel. could ans. *w.*
44:26 confirmeth *w.* of his serv.
45:23 *w.* is gone out of mouth
50:4 to speak a *w.* in season
*Jer.* 5:13 the *w.* is not in them
9:20 rec. *w.* of his mouth, 10:1
18:18 nor *w.* perish from proph.
23:36 every man's *w.* his burden
26:2 speak, diminish not a *w.*
34:5 I have pronounced the *w.*
37:17 king said, any *w.* fr. L.?
44:16 for the *w.* spoken unto us
*Ezek.* 3:17 hear *w.* at mouth, 33:7
12:25 the *w.* shall come to pass
28 *w.* I have spok. sh. be done
13:6 they would confirm the *w.*
*Dan.* 3:28 ha. changed king's *w.*
4:17 demand by *w.* of holy ones
31 the *w.* in the king's mouth
*Jon.* 3:6 *w.* came to king of Nin.
*Hag.* 2:5 acco. to *w.* I covenant.
*Mat.* 8:8 speak the *w.* only
12:32 whoso speak. a *w.* against the Son of man, *Luke* 12:10
36 idle *w.* men sh. give accou.
13:21 because of the *w.* he is offended, *Mark* 4:17
15:23 Je. ans. woman not a *w.*
18:16 *w.* be establ. 2 *Cor.* 13:1
22:46 no man able to answ. a *w.*
27:14 Jesus answer. never a *w.*
28:8 run to bring disciples *w.*
*Mark* 4:14 sower soweth the *w.*
14:72 Pe. called to mind the *w.*
16:20 confirming *w.* with signs
*Luke* 4:36 amaz. what *w.* is this!
7:7 say in a *w.* my serv. healed
24:19 Je. mighty in *w.* and deed
*John* 1:1 in beginn. was the *W.*
14 the *W.* was made flesh
2:22 believed *w.* Jesus said, 4:50
12:48 *w.* I have spok. judge him
14:24 *w.* you hear is not mine
15:3 through *w.* I spake to you
20 rememb. *w.* I said unto you
25 that *w.* might be fulfilled
17:20 sh. believe me through *w.*
*Acts* 10:36 *w.* God sent to Israel
13:15 any *w.* of exhortation
26 to you is *w.* of salva. sent
15:7 th. Gentiles should hear *w.*
17:11 receiv. *w.* with readiness
20:32 I commend *w.* of his grace
28:25 Paul had spoken one *w.*
*Rom.* 10:8 that is the *w.* of faith
15:18 Gent. obe. by *w.* and deed
1 *Cor.* 4:20 not in *w.* but in power
12:8 *w.* of wisdom, *w.* of know.
2 *Cor.* 1:18 our *w.* to you was not
5:19 to us *w.* of reconciliation
10:11 as we are in *w.* by letters
*Gal.* 5:14 law is fulfill. in one *w.*
6:6 taught in *w.* communicate
*Eph.* 5:26 clea. with water by *w.*
*Phil.* 1:14 speak *w.* without fear
2:16 holding forth the *w.* of life
*Col.* 1:5 heard in *w.* of the truth
3:16 *w.* of C. dwell in you richly
17 do in *w.* or deed, do in name
1 *Thes.* 1:5 gospel came not in *w.*
6 received the *w.* in affliction
2:13 receive it not as *w.* of men
2 *Thes.* 2:2 not by Spi. nor by *w.*
15 wheth. by *w.* or our epistle
17 stablish you in ev. good *w.*
3:14 man obey not *w.* by epistle
1 *Tim.* 4:12 exam. of belie. in *w.*
5:17 labor in *w.* and doctrine
2 *Tim.* 2:17 *w.* eat as a canker
4:2 preach *w.* instant in season
*Tit.* 1:9 holding fast *w.* as taught
*Heb.* 1:3 all things by *w.* of pow.
2:2 if *w.* spoken by angels stea.
4:2 *w.* preached did not profit
5:13 unskilful in *w.* of righteo.
7:28 but the *w.* of the oath.
12:19 entreat. *w.* sh. not be spo.
13:22 suffer *w.* of exhortation
*Jam.* 1:21 receive the ingraft. *w.*
22 doers of *w.* not hearers only
23 if any be a hearer of the *w.*
3:2 if any man offend not in *w.*
1 *Pet.* 2:2 babes desire milk of *w.*
8 to them who stumble at *w.*
3:1 if any obey not *w.* they may
2 *Pet.* 1:19 more sure *w.* of pro.
3:7 heav. by *w.* are kept in store
1 *John* 1:1 handled *w.* of life
3:18 not love in *w.* but in deed
5:7 Father, *W.* and Holy G. one
*Rev.* 3:10 kept *w.* of my patience
12:11 overcome by *w.* of testi.

**WORD of God.**

1 *Sam.* 9:27 I show thee *w. of G.*
1 *K.* 12:22 *w. of G.* came to She.
1 *Chr.* 17:3 *w. of G.* came to Na.
*Prov.* 30:5 every *w. of G.* is pure
*Is.* 40:8 *w. of G.* stand for ever
*Mark* 7:13 *w. of God* of no effect
*Luke* 3:2 *w. of G.* came unto J.
4:4 not by bread but by *w. of G.*
5:1 pressed to hear *w. of God*
8:11 the seed is the *w. of God*
21 breth. th. wh. hear *w. of G.*
11:28 they that hear *w. of God*
*John* 10:35 gods to wh. *w. of G.*
*Acts* 4:31 sp. *w. of G.* wi. boldn.
6:2 not leave the *w. of God*
7 *w. of G.* increas. in Jer. 12:24
8:14 Samaria receiv. *w. of God*
11:1 Gentiles received *w. of G.*
13:7 desired to hear *w. of God*
44 city came to hear *w. of God*
46 *w. of G.* first spoken to you
19:20 mightily grew *w. of God*
*Rom.* 9:6 not as though *w. of God* hath taken none effect
10:17 hearing by the *w. of God*
1 *Cor.* 14:36 ca. *w. of G.* fr. you?
2 *Cor.* 2:17 many corr. *w. of God*
4:2 not handl. *w. of G.* deceitf.
*Eph.* 6:17 helmet of sal. *w. of G.*
*Col.* 1:25 given to fulfil *w. of G.*
1 *Thes.* 2:13 received *w. of God*
1 *Tim.* 4:5 sanctified by *w. of G.*
2 *Tim.* 2:9 *w. of G.* is not bound
*Tit.* 2:5 *w. of G.* be not blasph.
*Heb.* 4:12 *w. of G.* qui. and pow.
6:5 tasted the good *w. of God*
11:3 worlds framed by *w. of G.*
13:7 spoken to you *w. of God*
1 *Pet.* 1:23 born ag. by *w. of God*
2 *Pet.* 3:5 by *w. of G.* heav. were
1 *John* 2:14 *w. of G.* abid. in you
*Rev.* 1:2 bare record of *w. of G.*
9 in isle of Patmos for *w. of G.*
6:9 were slain for *w. of God*
19:13 name is called *W. of God*
20:4 were beheaded for *w. of G.*
*See* HEARD.

**His WORD.**

*Num.* 27:21 at *his w.* they go out
30:2 a man vow not break *h. w.*
1 *Sam.* 1:23 the Lord estab. *h. w.*
2 *Sam.* 23:2 *h. w.* in my tongue
1 *K.* 2:4 the Lord continue *h. w.*
8:20 L. perfor. *h. w.* 2 *Chr.* 6:10
2 *K.* 1:16 no G. in Is. to inq. *h. w.*
2 *Chr.* 10:15 L. might perf. *h. w.*
*Ps.* 56:4 in G. will I prai. *h. w.* 10
103:20 unto the voice of *his w.*
105:19 time that *his w.* came
28 rebelled not against *his w.*
106:24 believed not *his w.*
107:20 sent *his w.* healed them
130:5 L. and in *h. w.* do I hope
147:15 *his w.* run. very swiftly
18 sendeth *h. w.* melteth them
19 he showeth *his w.* unto Ja.
148:8 stormy wind fulfill. *h. w.*
*Is.* 66:5 ye that tremble at *h. w.*
*Jer.* 20:9 *his w.* was in my heart
*Lam.* 2:17 hath fulfilled *his w.*
*Joel* 2:11 strong th. execut. *h. w.*

Mat. 8:16 cast out spi. with h. w.
Luke 4:32 his w. was with power
John 4:41 many beli. his own w.
5:38 not his w. abiding in you
Acts 2:41 that gladly rec. his w.
Tit. 1:3 hath manifested his w.
1 John 2:5 whoso keepeth his w.
See LORD.

**My WORD.**

Num. 11:23 my w. come to pass
20:24 rebelled against my w.
1 K. 6:12 perfor. my w. with th.
17:1 but according to my w.
Is. 55:11 so sh. my w. that goeth
66:2 to him that trem. at my w.
Jer. 1:12 hasten my w. to perf. it
23:28 hath my w. speak my w.
29 not my w. as a fire, sai. L.?
30 ag. proph. that steal my w.
29:10 perf. my good w. to. you
Mat. 24:35 my w. not pass away
John 5:24 he that heareth my w.
8:31 continue in my w. dis. ind.
37 my w. hath no place in you
43 bec. ye cannot hear my w.
Rev. 3:8 kept my w. not den. na.

**This WORD.**

Ex. 14:12 is not t. w. we tell th.?
Jos. 14:10 L. spake t. w. to Mos.
2 Sam. 19:14 sent this w. to king
1 K. 2:23 not spok. t. w. against his own life
2 K. 19:21 this is the w. spoken of him, Is. 16:13; 24:3; 37:22
Ezr. 6:11 whoso. shall alter t. w.
10:5 should do accord. to this w.
Is. 8:20 if speak not acc. to t. w.
30:12 because ye despise this w.
Jer. 5:14 bec. ye spe. t. w. 23:38
7:2 proclaim there t. w. and say
13:12 speak unto them this w.
14:17 therefore say t. w. to them
22:1 L. said, Go and speak t. w.
26:1 t. w. came from the Lord, saying, 27:1; 34:8; 36:1
28:7 hear thou now this w. Amos 3:1; 4:1; 5:1
Dan. 10:11 wh. he had spok. t. w.
Zec. 4:6 t. is w. of L. to Zerub.
Acts 22:22 gave audience to t. w.
Rom. 9:9 this is w. of promise
Heb. 12:27 t. w. once more signi.
1 Pet. 1:25 t. w. preached to you

**Thy WORD.**

Gen. 30:34 might be acc. to t. w.
41:40 acc. to t. w. peo. be ruled
Ex. 8:10 be it according to t. w.
Num. 14:20 pardoned acc. to t. w.
Deut. 33:9 observed t. w. and cov.
1 K. 3:12 done accord. to thy w.
8:26 let thy w. be verified
18:36 done all th. things at t. w.
22:13 let thy w. speak what is good, 2 Chr. 18:12
Ps. 119:9 by taking heed to t. w.
11 thy w. ha. I hid in my heart
16 I will not forget thy w.
17 may live and keep t. w. 101
25 quick. acco. to t. w. 107, 154
28 strengthen me according to thy w. 116
38 stablish t. w. 42 I tr. in t. w.
41 salvation according to t. w.
50 for thy w. quickened me
58 be merciful ac. to t. w. 65, 76
67 but now have I kept thy w.
74 because I hoped in t. w. 147
81 but I hope in t. w. 114; 140 thy w. is very pure
82 fail for t. w. 105 t. w. lamp
89 O L. t. w. is settled in heav.
133 order my steps in thy w.
148 that I mi. meditate in t. w.
158 bec. they kept not thy w.
160 t. w. true; 162 rej. at t. w.
161 heart stand. in awe of t. w.
169 give me under. ac. to t. w.
170 deliver me accord. to t. w.
172 my tong. sh. speak of t. w.
138:2 thou hast magnified t. w.
Jer. 15:16 t. w. to me joy of heart
Ezek. 20:46 drop t. w. tow. south
21:2 drop t. w. tow. holy places
Amos 7:16 drop not t. w. ag. Isa.
Hab. 3:9 bow naked, even t. w.
Luke 1:38 be it to me ac. to t. w.
2:29 depart in peace, ac. to t. w.
5:5 at t. w. I will let down net
John 17:6 they have kept thy w.
14 given thy w. 17 thy w. truth
Acts 4:29 with boldn. speak t. w.
See TRUTH.

**WORDS.**

Ex. 4:15 shalt put w. in mouth
5:9 let them not regard vain w.
19:8 Moses returned w. of peo.
23:8 gift perverteth w. of righteous, Deut. 16:19
34:1 w. whi. were in first tables
28 Moses wrote the w. of the covenant, Deut. 10:2
Deut. 2:26 Sihon wi. w. of peace
28:14 not go aside fr. any of w.
29:9 keep w. of this covenant, 2 K. 23:3, 24; 2 Chr. 34:31
32:1 hear, O earth, w. of my mo. Ps. 54:2; 78:1; Prov. 7:24
2 Sam. 19:43 w. of men fiercer
1 K. 22:13 behold, w. of proph. declare good, 2 Chr. 18:12
2 K. 6:13 Elisha telleth the w.
18:20 they are vain w. Is. 36:5
2 Chr. 29:30 sing prais. wi. w. of
32:8 people rested on w. of Hez.
Est. 9:30 letters with w. of peace
Job 6:26 ye imagine to reprove w.
8:2 w. of mouth be like wind?
12:11 doth not ear try w.? 34:3
15:13 lettest w. go out of mouth
16:3 shall vain w. have an end?
4 I could heap up w. ag. you
18:2 how long ere make end w.?
19:2 how long bre. me wi. w.?
23:5 I would know w. he answ.
12 I esteemed w. of his mouth
35:16 multi. w. without knowl.
38:2 who dark. counsel by w.?
Ps. 19:14 let w. of my mouth be
22:1 why far fr. w. of my roar.?
36:3 w. of his mouth are iniq.
52:4 th. lovest all devouring w.
55:21 w. of his mouth smoother
59:12 w. of their lips let them
Prov. 1:6 understand w. of wise
4:5 decline not from w. of, 5:7
6:2 art snared with w. of mouth
10:19 in w. wanteth not sin
12:16 w. of wick. to lie in wait
15:26 w. of pure are pleasant w.
18:4 w. of mouth are as waters
8 w. of talebea. wounds, 26:22
19:7 he pursueth them with w.
27 he causeth thee to err fr. w.
22:12 overthrows w. of transg.
17 bow ear, hear w. of the wise
21 make thee know w. of truth
23:8 thou sh. lose thy sweet w.
29:19 serv. not be correct. by w.
Ec. 5:3 voice known by w. 10:14
10:12 w. of wise are gracious
12:10 sought out acceptable w.
11 w. of wise as goads, nails
Is. 29:11 bec. as w. of book seal.
37:4 God will hear w. of Rabsh.
59:13 uttering w. of falsehood
Jer. 11:2 hear w. of covenant, 6
23:9 bec. of L. and w. of holin.
44:28 remnant kn. wh. w. stand
Ezek. 3:6 w. th. canst not unders.
Dan. 7:25 speak w. ag. Most H.
12:4 shut up w. 9 w. are closed
Hos. 6:5 slain th. by w. of mouth
14:2 take with you w. and turn
Zec. 1:13 answered with good w.
7:7 should ye not hear the w.?
Mat. 26:44 prayed, saying same w. Mark 14:39
Luke 4:22 wondered at graci. w.
John 6:63 w. I speak to you
68 thou hast w. of eternal life
17:8 given them w. gavest me
Acts 2:40 with w. did he testify
7:22 Moses was mighty in w.
10:22 Cornel. warned to hear w.
11:14 Peter, who sh. tell the w.
15:15 to this agree w. of proph.
24 certain troubled you wi. w.
18:15 if it be a question of w.
20:35 to remember w. of L. J.
38 sorrowing for w. he spake
26:25 I speak forth w. of truth
Rom. 16:18 by w. deceive hearts
1 Cor. 1:17 not wisd. of w. 2:4, 13
14:9 except ye utter w. easy
19 ra. speak 5 w. with underst.
Eph. 5:6 let no man dec. wi. w.
1 Tim. 4:6 nouri. in w. of faith
2 Tim. 2:14 strive not about w.
4:15 he hath withstood our w.
2 Pet. 3:2 mindful of w. spoken
Rev. 1:3 hear w. of proph. 22:18
22:19 take from w. of prophecy

**All the WORDS.**

Ex. 4:28 told Aar. a. t. w. of L.
24:3 Moses told people all the w. Num. 11:24
Deut. 9:10 on tables writ. a. t. w.
17:19 keep a. w. 29:29 do a. w.
27:3 write on stones all the w. 8
26 that confirmeth not all t. w.
28:58 not observe to do a. t. w.
31:12 observe to do all the w.
32:44 Mo. spake all t. w. of song
46 set hearts to a. t. w. I testi.
Jos. 8:34 read all the w. of law
1 Sam. 8:10 Samuel told a. t. w.
2 K. 23:2 Josiah read all t. w. of covenant, 2 Chr. 34:30
Prov. 8:8 all the w. of mouth
Ec. 7:21 no heed to a. t. w. spo.
Jer. 11:8 bring all t. w. of coven.
26:2 speak all t. w. I command
30:2 write all t. w. spoken, 36:2
36:4 Ba. wrote a. t. w. of L. 32
43:1 J. had ended all t. w. of L.
Acts 5:20 speak to peo. all the w.

**WORDS of God.**

Num. 24:4 wh. heard w. of G. 16
1 Chr. 25:5 ki.'s seer in w. of G.
Ezr. 9:4 trembleth at w. of God
Ps. 107:11 rebelled ag. w. of God
John 3:34 G. sent speak. w. of G.
8:47 that is of G. hear. w. of G.
Rev. 17:17 until w. of G. be fulf.
See HEARD.

**His WORDS.**

Gen. 37:8 th. hated him for h. w.
Deut. 4:36 heard. h. w. out of fire
Jud. 11:11 Jephth. uttered h. w.
1 Sam. 3:19 let none of h. w. fall
2 Chr. 36:16 they despised his w.
Job 22:22 lay up his w. in heart
32:14 not directed h. w. ag. me
34:35 his w. were without wisd.
37 he multiplieth his w. ag. G.
Ps. 55:21 his w. softer than oil
106:12 then believed they his w.
Prov. 17:27 knowl. spareth his w.
29:20 man th. is hasty in h. w.?
30:6 add thou not unto his w.
Is. 31:2 Lord not call back his w.
Jer. 18:18 not give heed to h. w.
Dan. 9:12 he hath confirm. h. w.
Amos 7:10 not able to bear h. w.
Mark 10:24 astonished at his w.
12:13 to catch him in his w. Luke 20:20
Luke 20:26 not take hold of h. w.
24:8 they remembered his w.
See LORD.

**My WORDS.**

*Num.* 12:6 hear *my w.* *Job* 34:2
*Deut.* 4:10 make th. hear *my w.*
11:18 lay up *my w.* in yo. heart
18:18 I will put *my w.* in mouth
19 whoso. will not heark. to *my w.* I requ. *Jer.* 29:19; 35:13
*Neh.* 6:19 uttered *my w.* to him
*Job* 6:3 *my w.* are swallowed up
19:23 O that *my w.* were written
29:22 *my w.* they spake not
33:1 hearken to all *my w.* 34:16 *Acts* 2:14
3 *my w.* shall be of upri. 36:4
*Ps.* 5:1 give ear to *my w.* O Lord
50:17 casteth *my w.* behind th.
56:5 every day th. wrest *my w.*
141:6 they shall hear *my w.*
*Prov.* 1:23 make kn. *m. w.* to you
2:1 if thou wilt receive *my w.*
4:4 let thy heart retain my *w.*
20 my son, attend to *my w.*
7:1 my son, keep *my w.*
*Is.* 51:16 I have put *my w.* in thy mouth, *Jer.* 1:9
59:21 *my w.* wh. I put in mouth
*Jer.* 5:14 *my w.* in thy mouth
6:19 not hearkened to *my w.*
11:10 refused to hear *my w.*
18:2 cause thee to hear *my w.*
19:15 they mi. not hear *my w.*
23:22 caused peo. to hear *my w.*
25:8 ye have not heard *my w.*
13 bring upon that land *my w.*
39:16 bring *my w.* on this city
44:29 you may know *my w.*
*Ezek.* 2:7 speak *my w.* 3:4, 10
12:28 none of *my w.* be prolon.
*Mic.* 2:7 do not *my w.* do good to
*Zec.* 1:6 *my w.* did they not take
*Mark* 8:38 ashamed of *my w.* of him Son be asha. *Luke* 9:26
13:31 *my w.* shall not pass away, *Luke* 21:33
*Luke* 1:20 thou believ. not *my w.*
*John* 5:47 how believe *my w.?*
12:47 if any man hear *my w.*
48 he that receiveth not *my w.*
14:23 keep *my w.* 15:7 abide

**Their WORDS.**

*Gen.* 34:18 *t. w.* pleased Hamor
2 *Chr.* 9:6 I believed not *their w.*
*Ps.* 19:4 *their w.* to the end of the world, *Rom.* 10:18
*Ezek.* 2:6 be not afraid of *their w.*
*Luke* 24:11 *t. w.* seemed as tales

**These WORDS.**

*Ex.* 19:6 *t. w.* th. shalt speak, 7
20:1 God spake *t. w.* *Deut.* 5:22
34:27 write *these w.* *Jer.* 36:17
35:1 *these* are the *w.* which Lord commanded, *Deut.* 6:6; 29:1
*Num.* 16:31 end of *these w.* *Deut.* 32:45; 1 *Sam.* 24:16
*Deut.* 12:28 all *these w.* *Zec.* 8:9
1 *Sam.* 21:12 David laid up *t. w.*
2 *K.* 23:16 man proclaimed *t. w.*
*Jer.* 3:12 procl. *t. w.* tow. north
7:27 speak *t. w.* unto th. 26:15
16:10 sh. *t. w.* 25:30 proph. *t. w.*
38:24 let no man know of *t. w.*
45:1 wh. he had writ. *t. w.* 51:60
51:61 when thou shalt read *t. w.*
*Luke* 24:44 *t.* are the *w.* I spake
*John* 9:22 *t. w.* spake his parents
10:21 *these* are not *w.* of a devil
*Acts* 2:22 men of Israel hear *t. w.*
10:44 while Pet. yet spake *t. w.*
13:42 *t. w.* might be preached
28:29 said *t. w.* Jews departed
1 *Thes.* 4:18 comfort one another with *these w.*
*Rev.* 21:5 *t. w.* true and faithful

**Thy WORDS.**

*Deut.* 33:3 ev. one sh. rec. of *t. w.*
*Jos.* 1:18 wh. not heark. to *t. w.*
*Jud.* 11:10 if do not acc. to *t. w.*
13:12 let *thy w.* come to pass
1 *Sam.* 15:24 I have transg. *t. w.*
28:21 I have hearkened to *t. w.*
2 *Sam.* 7:21 for *thy w.* sake
28 that God and *thy w.* be true
1 *K.* 1:14 come and confirm *t. w.*
*Neh.* 9:8 th. hast performed *t. w.*
*Job* 4:4 *t. w.* upheld him th. was
*Ps.* 119:57 said I wo. keep *t. w.*
103 sweet *t. w.* to my taste!
130 entrance of *t. w.* giv. light
139 enemies ha. forgotten *t. w.*
*Prov.* 23:8 shalt lose *t.* sweet *w.*
9 he will despise wisd. of *t. w.*
*Ec.* 5:2 not rash, let *t. w.* be few
*Jer.* 15:16 *thy w.* were found
*Ezek.* 33:31 hear *thy w.* 32
*Dan.* 10:12 Daniel, *thy w.* heard
*Mat.* 12:37 by *t. w.* shalt be justi.

**Your WORDS.**

*Gen.* 42:16 in prison *y. w.* be pro.
44:10 accord. to *y. w.* *Jos.* 2:21
*Deut.* 1:34 Lord heard *y. w.* 5:28
*Job* 32:11 I waited for *your w.*
*Is.* 41:26 none heareth *your w.*
*Jer.* 42:4 I will pray acc. to *y. w.*
*Ezek.* 35:13 have multiplied *y. w.*
*Mal.* 2:17 wearied L. with *y. w.*
3:13 *y. w.* been ag. me, saith L.
*Mat.* 10:14 not rec. nor hear *y. w.*

**WORK.**

*Ex.* 5:9 more *w.* laid on the men
12:16 no manner of *w.* shall be done, 20:10; *Lev.* 16:29, 23:3, 28, 31; *Num.* 29:7
18:20 show the *w.* they must do
31:14 whoso doeth any *w.* ther. sh. be cut off, 15; *Lev.* 23:30
35:2 six days *w.* be done, 20:9
36:7 sufficient for all the *w.*
*Lev.* 23:7 do no servile *w.* therein, 8, 21, 25, 35, 36; *Num.* 28:18, 25, 26; 29:1, 12, 35
*Deut.* 4:28 *w.* of men's hands, 27:15; 2 *K.* 19:18; 2 *Chr.* 32:19; *Ps.* 115:4; 135:15
5:14 sabbath, in it thou shalt not *w.* 16:8; *Jer.* 17:22, 24
31:29 to provoke him thro' *w.* of hands, 1 *K.* 16:7; *Jer.* 32:30
33:11 bless L. acc. *w.* of his han.
1 *K.* 5:16 officers over *w.* 9:23
7:8 house had court of like *w.*
2 *K.* 12:11 into han. did *w.* 22:5, 9
1 *Chr.* 9:33 in that *w.* day and ni.
16:37 minister as day's *w.* requ.
29:1 the *w.* is great, *Neh.* 4:19
2 *Chr.* 31:21 ev. *w.* he began did it
34:12 men did the *w.* faithfully
*Ezr.* 4:24 then ceased the *w.*
5:8 this *w.* goeth fast on
6:7 let *w.* of house of G. alone
22 stren. hands in *w.* of house
10:13 nei. a *w.* of one day or two
*Neh.* 3:5 nob. put not necks to *w.*
4:11 slay th. cause *w.* to cease
6:3 why should the *w.* cease
16 they perc. this *w.* was of G.
7:70 the fathers gave to the *w.*
*Job* 1:10 blessed *w.* of his hands
10:3 despise *w.* of thy hands
14:15 desire to *w.* of thy hands
24:5 as asses go they to their *w.*
34:11 for *w.* of a man shall he render to him, 1 *Pet.* 1:17
19 they are all *w.* of his hands
36:9 he showeth *w.* and transg.
*Ps.* 8:3 I consi. *w.* of th. fingers
9:16 snared in *w.* of his hands
19:1 firmament show. handy *w.*
28:4 after the *w.* of their hands
44:1 heard what *w.* thou didst
90:17 establish *w.* of our hands
*Ps.* 95:9 fa. proved me, saw my *w.*
101:3 I hate the *w.* of them that
102:25 heav. are *w.* of thy hands
143:5 I muse on *w.* of thy hands
*Prov.* 11:18 worketh deceitful *w.*
*Ec.* 3:17 a time for every *w.*
5:6 sh. G. destroy *w.* of hands?
8:9 I applied my heart to ev. *w.*
14 happen acc. to *w.* of wicked
9:10 there is no *w.* in grave
12:14 G. will bri. *w.* into judg.
*Cant.* 7:1 *w.* of a cun. workman
*Is.* 2:8 they worship *w.* of their own hands, 37:19; *Jer.* 1:16; 10:3, 9, 15; 51:18
17:8 not look to *w.* of his hands
19:15 nei. be any *w.* for Egypt
25 Assyria the *w.* of my hands
28:21 that he may do his *w.*
29:16 sh. *w.* say of him made it
23 children, the *w.* of my hands
32:17 *w.* of righteousness, peace
45:11 concerni. *w.* of my hands
49:4 surely my *w.* is with my G.
60:21 inherit *w.* of my hands
61:8 I will direct th. *w.* in truth
64:8 we are the *w.* of thy hands
65:22 elect enjoy *w.* of thy hands
*Jer.* 32:19 great and mighty in *w.*
50:29 recompense her according to *w.* *Lam.* 3:64
*Ezek.* 15:3 shall wood do any *w.?*
4 is it meet for *w.?* 5 no *w.*
16:30 *w.* of a whorish woman
*Hos.* 13:2 the *w.* of craftsman
14:3 say no more to *w.* of hands
*Mic.* 5:13 no more w. *w.* of hands
*Hab.* 1:5 work a *w.* in your days
*Hag.* 2:14 so is ev. *w.* of hands
*Mark* 6:5 there do no mighty *w.*
*John* 7:21 done one *w.* ye marvel.
17:4 finished the *w.* thou gavest
*Acts* 5:38 if this *w.* be of men
13:2 *w.* whereunto I called them
41 I work a *w.* in your day
14:26 *w.* which they fulfilled
15:38 went not with them to *w.*
*Rom.* 2:15 show *w.* of law writ.
9:28 short *w.* L. make up. earth
11:6 otherwise *w.* is no more *w.*
1 *Cor.* 3:13 ev. man's *w.* be manif.
14 if *w.* abide; 15 if *w.* burnt
9:1 are not ye my *w.* in Lord?
*Eph.* 4:12 some for *w.* of minis.
*Phil.* 2:30 *w.* of C. was nigh death
2 *Thes.* 1:11 God fulfil *w.* of faith
2:17 stablish you in ev. good *w.*
2 *Tim.* 4:5 *w.* of an evangelist
*Jam.* 1:4 let patience ha. perf. *w.*
25 a doer of *w.* sh. be blessed

*See* EVIL.

**WORK, S of God.**

*Ex.* 32:16 tables were *w. of God*
*Job* 37:14 wondrous *w. of God*
*Ps.* 64:9 all declare the *w. of G.*
66:5 come and see *w. of God*
78:7 might not forget *w. of God*
*Ec.* 7:13 consider the *w. of God*
8:17 I beheld all the *w. of God*
11:5 thou knowest not *w. of G.*
*John* 6:28 might work *w. of God*
29 this is *w. of God* that ye
9:3 that *w. of God* be manifest
*Acts* 2:11 hear th. speak *w. of G.*
*Rom.* 14:20 for meat destroy not the *w. of God*

*See* GOOD, GREAT.

**His WORK.**

*Gen.* 2:2 G. ended *h. w.* 3 rested
*Ex.* 36:4 every man from *his w.*
*Deut.* 32:4 *his w.* is perfect
*Jud.* 19:16 old man ca. fr. *his w.*
1 *Sam.* 8:16 take asses to *his w.*
1 *K.* 7:14 Hiram wrought *his w.*
1 *Chr.* 4:23 dw. wi. king for *h. w.*
2 *Chr.* 8:9 made no serv. for *h. w.*
16:5 Baasha let *his w.* cease
*Neh.* 4:15 return. ev. man to *h. w.*

*Job* 7:2 looketh for rew. of *h. w.*
36:24 rem. thou magnify *his w.*
37:7 all men may know *his w.*
*Ps.* 62:12 renderest to ev. man according to *h. w. Prov.* 24:29
104:23 man goeth to *his w.*
111:3 *h. w.* is honorable,glorious
*Prov.* 16:11 weights of bag *h. w.*
20:11 whether *his w.* be pure
21:8 for the pure *h. w.* is right
*Is.* 5:19 let him hasten *his w.*
10:12 L. performed *h.* whole *w.*
28:21 that he may do *his w.*
40:10 *his w.* is before him, 62:11
54:16 bring. an instru. for *h. w.*
*Jer.* 22:13 giveth not for *his w.*
*Hab.* 2:18 maker of *h. w.* trusteth
*Mark* 13:34 gave ev man *his w.*
*John* 4:34 my meat is to fin. *h. w.*
*Gal.* 6:4 every man prove *his w.*
*Rev.* 22:12 to every man as *h. w.*

*See* LORD, NEEDLE.

### Our WORK.

*Gen.* 5:29 this sh. comfort *our w.*

### Thy WORK.

*Ex.* 20:9 six days do all *thy w.* 23:12; *Deut.* 5:13
*Ruth* 2:12 L. recompense *thy w.*
*Ps.* 77:12 I will meditate *thy w.*
90:16 let *t. w.* ap. unto thy serv.
92:4 made me glad thro' *thy w.*
*Prov.* 24:27 prep. *thy w.* without
*Is.* 45:9 or *t. w.* hath no hands?
*Jer.* 31:16 *thy w.* sh. be rewarded
*Hab.* 3:2 revive *thy w.* in years

### Your WORK.

*Ex.* 5:11 not aught of *y. w.* dim.
2 *Chr.* 15:7 *y. w.* sh. be rewarded
*Is.* 41:24 *your w.* is of naught
1 *Thes.* 1:3 remember *y. w.* faith
*Heb.* 6:10 to forget *y. w.* of faith

### WORK-FELLOW.

*Rom.* 16:21 my *w.-f.* salute you

### WORK, Verb.

*Ex.* 5:18 go therefore now and *w.*
34:21 six days thou shalt *w.*
35:2 whoso *w.* ther. put to death
1 *Sam.* 14:6 may be Lord will *w.*
1 *K.* 21:20 sold thys. to *w.* evil, 25
*Neh.* 4:6 people had a mind to *w.*
*Job* 23:9 on left hand wh. he *w.*
*Ps.* 58:2 in heart you *w.* wicked.
119:126 it is time for Lord to *w.*
*Prov.* 11:18 wick. *w.* decei. work
*Is.* 19:9 they that *w.* in flax
43:13 I will *w.* who shall let it
*Ezek.* 33:26 ye *w.* abomination
*Dan.* 11:23 he sh. *w.* deceitfully
*Mic.* 2:1 woe to them that *w.* evil
*Hab.* 1:5 I will *w.* a work in your days, *Acts* 13:41
*Hag.* 2:4 *w.* for I am with you
*Mal.* 3:15 *w.* wicked. are set up
*Mat.* 21:28 go *w.* in my vineyard
*Luke* 13:14 wh. men ought to *w.*
*John* 5:17 Father worketh, I *w.*
6:28 might *w.* the works of God
30 said, What dost thou *w.*?
9:4 I must *w.* the works of him
*Rom.* 7:5 sin did *w.* in our mem.
8:28 all thi. *w.* togeth. for good
*Eph.* 4:19 to *w.* uncleanness with
*Phil.* 2:12 *w.* out your salvation
1 *Thes.* 4:11 to *w.* with hands
2 *Thes.* 2:7 mys. of iniq. doth *w.*
3:10 not *w.* neit. should he eat
12 that with quietness they *w.*

*See* INIQUITY.

### WORKER.

1 *K.* 7:14 was a *w.* in brass

### WORKERS.

2 *K.* 23:24 *w.* wi. familiar spirits
2 *Cor.* 6:1 *w.* together with him
11:13 false apostles, deceitful *w.*
*Phil.* 3:2 dogs, beware of evil *w.*

*See* INIQUITY.

### WORKS.

*Ex.* 5:13 fulfil your *w.* and tasks
*Num.* 16:28 sent me to do th. *w.*
*Deut.* 2:7 bles. thee in *w.* 16:15
*Jud.* 2:10 which knew not *w.*
1 *Sam.* 8:8 acc. to *w.* they done
1 *K.* 13:11 told *w.* man of G. did
2 *K.* 22:17 provoked me to anger with *w.* of hands, 2 *Chr.* 34:25
*Neh.* 9:35 nor turned fr. wick. *w.*
*Ps.* 14:1 done abominable *w.*
17:4 concerning the *w.* of men
92:4 triumph in *w.* of thy hands
111:2 *w.* of the Lord are great
7 *w.* of hands, verity and jud.
138:8 forsake not *w.* of own ha.
141:4 to practise wicked *w.*
*Prov.* 31:31 let her *w.* praise her
*Ec.* 1:14 I have seen *w.* done, 2:11
*Is.* 26:12 wrought our *w.* in us
*Jer.* 7:13 bec. ye have done th. *w.*
25:6 provo. not with *w.* 7; 44:8
14 recompense them according to *w.* of hands, *Rev.* 2:23
*Ezek.* 6:6 your *w.* be abolished
*Dan.* 4:37 him wh. *w.* are truth
*Mic.* 6:16 *w.* of house of A. kept
*Mat.* 11:2 John heard *w.* of Chr.
*John* 5:20 show him greater *w.*
36 *w.* Father hath given me
7:3 may see the *w.* thou doest
7 I testify *w.* thereof are evil
8:39 would do *w.* of Abraham
9:4 I must work the *w.* of him
10:25 *w.* I do in Father's name
32 for wh. of *w.* do ye sto. me?
*John* 10:37 if I do not *w.* 38 believe *w.*
14:10 doeth *w.* 11 believe for *w.*
12 *w.* that I do, shall he do, gr.
15:24 if I had not done the *w.*
*Acts* 7:41 rejoiced in *w.* of hands
26:20 do *w.* meet for repentance
*Rom.* 3:27 by what law? of *w.*?
4:2 if Abr. were justified by *w.*
6 G. imputeth right. with. *w.*
9:11 not of *w.* but of him that
32 but as it were by *w.* of law
11:6 if by grace, no more of *w.*
13:12 cast off *w.* of darkness
*Gal.* 2:16 man is not justi. by *w.*
3:2 receiv. ye Sp. by *w.* of law?
5 doeth he it by *w.* of the law
10 as many as are of *w.* of law
5:19 *w.* of the flesh are manifest
*Eph.* 2:9 not of *w.* lest any boast
5:11 wi. unfruitful *w.* of darkn.
*Col.* 1:21 enemies by wicked *w.*
1 *Thes.* 5:13 esteem for *w.* sake
2 *Tim.* 1:9 saved us, not according to our *w.* *Tit.* 3:5
*Tit.* 1:16 but in *w.* they deny G.
*Heb.* 1:10 heav. *w.* of thy hands
2:7 set him ov. *w.* of thy hands
3:9 your fathers saw my *w.*
4:3 although *w.* were finished
6:1 repentance from dead *w.*
9:14 purge consc. from dead *w.*
*Jam.* 2:14 not *w.* can faith save?
17 faith with. *w.* is dead, 20:26
18 show me thy faith with. *w.*
21 was not Abr. justi. by *w.*?
22 by *w.* was faith made perf.
24 by *w.* a man is justified
25 was not R. justified by *w.*?
2 *Pet.* 3:10 *w.* therein burnt up
1 *John* 3:8 mi. destroy *w.* of devil
*Rev.* 2:26 that keepeth *w.* to end
9:20 repented not of *w.* of hands
18:6 double, according to her *w.*

*See* EVIL, GOOD, WORK *of God.*

### His WORKS.

1 *Sam.* 19:4 *his w.* to thee good
2 *Chr.* 32:30 Hez. prosp. in *h. w.*
*Ps.* 33:4 *h. w.* are done in truth
78:11 forget *his w.* wond. 106:13
103:22 bless the Lord, all *his w.*
104:31 L. shall rejoice in *his w.*
107:22 declare *h. w.* with rejoic.
111:6 show. peo. power of *h. w.*
145:9 his mercies are over *h. w.*
17 Lord is holy in all *his w.*
*Prov.* 8:22 pos. me before *his w.*
24:12 render to ev. man ac. to *h. w.*? *Mat.* 16:27; 2 *Tim.* 4:14
*Ec.* 3:22 man sh. rejoice in *h. w.*
*Dan.* 9:14 G. is right. in *his w.*
*Acts* 15:18 known to G. are *h. w.*
*Heb.* 4:4 rest. on 7th day fr. *h. w.*
10 hath ceased from *h.* own *w.*
*Jam.* 2:22 faith wro. with *h. w.*?
3:13 of a good conversat. *his w.*

*See* LORD, MARVELLOUS, MIGHTY.

### Their WORKS.

*Ex.* 5:4 let people from *their w.*
23:24 shalt not do after *their w.*
*Neh.* 6:14 accord. to these *t. w.*
*Job* 34:25 therof. he know. *t. w.*
*Ps.* 33:15 he considereth *their w.*
106:35 they learned *their w.*
39 thus defiled with *t.* own *w.*
*Ec.* 9:1 *t. w.* are in hand of God
*Is.* 29:15 *t. w.* are in the dark
41:29 vanity, *t. w.* are nothing
59:6 nor cover thems. wi. *t. w.*
66:18 I kn. *t. w.* and thoughts
*Amos* 8:7 nev. forg. any of *t. w.*
*Jon.* 3:10 G. saw *t. w.* th. turned
*Mat.* 23:3 do not ye after *t. w.*
5 *t. w.* do to be seen of men
2 *Cor.* 11:15 end accord. to *t. w.*
*Rev.* 14:13 *t. w.* do follow them
20:12 judged accord. to *t. w.* 13

### Thy WORKS.

*Deut.* 3:24 according to *thy w.*?
15:10 L. sh. bless thee in *t. w.*
2 *Chr.* 20:37 L. hath broken *t. w.*
*Ps.* 26:7 tell of *t.* wond. *w.* 145:4
66:3 how terri. art thou in *t. w.*
73:28 that I may declare *thy w.*
86:8 neither are any works like unto *thy w.*
92:5 O L. how great are *thy w.*
104:13 earth satisfied with the fruit of *thy w.*
24 how manifold are *thy w.*!
143:5 remem. I meditate on *t. w.*
145:10 *thy w.* shall praise thee
*Prov.* 16:3 commit *t. w.* to Lord
*Ec.* 9:7 God accepteth *thy w.*
*Is.* 57:12 I will declare *thy w.*
*Jer.* 48:7 thou trusted in *thy w.*
*Jam.* 2:18 sh. faith without *t. w.*
*Rev.* 2:2 I know *thy w.* 9, 13, 19; 3:1, 8, 15
3:2 I have not found *t. w.* perf.

### Wonderful WORKS.

*Ps.* 40:5 many are thy *wond. w.*
78:4 showing his *wonderful w.*
107:8 praise L. for his *w. w.* to children of men, 15, 21, 31
111:4 made his *w. w.* rememb.
*Mat.* 7:22 in thy na. done *w. w.*
*Acts* 2:11 hear in tongues *w. w.*

*See* WONDROUS.

### WORKETH.

*Job* 33:29 these *w.* God for man
*Ps.* 15:2 *w.* righteousness, dwell
101:7 *w.* deceit shall not dwell
*Prov.* 11:18 wicked *w.* deceitful
26:28 flattering mouth *w.* ruin
31:13 she *w.* with her hands
*Ec.* 3:9 what profit he that *w.*?
*Is.* 44:12 the smith *w.* in coals
64:5 meetest him th. *w.* right.
*Dan.* 6:27 *w.* signs and wonders
*John* 5:17 my Fath. *w.* hitherto
*Acts* 10:35 he that *w.* righteous.
*Rom.* 2:10 to every one *w.* good
4:4 to him that *w.* is reward

5 him that w. not, but believ.
15 because the law w. wrath
5:3 tribulation w. patience
13:10 love w. no ill to neighbor
1 Cor. 12:6 it is same G. that w.
11 these w. that one and same
16:10 for he w. the work of L.
2 Cor. 4:12 then death w. in us
17 w. for us more weight of gl.
7:10 godly sor. w. repentance
Gal. 3:5 he that w. miracles
5:6 but faith which w. by love.
Eph. 1:11 who w. all things
2:2 spirit that w. in disobed.
3:20 according to power w. in us
Phil. 2:13 it is God w. in you
Col. 1:29 wh. w. in me mightily
1 Thes. 2:13 effectually w. in you
Jam. 1:3 try. of faith w. patience
20 wrath of man w. not right.
Rev. 21:27 whosoe. w. abomina.

**WORKING, Participle.**

Ps. 52:2 like a razor w. deceit.
74:12 w. salvation in the earth
Ezek. 46:1 gate shut six w. days
Mark 16:20 Lord w. with them
Rom. 1:27 w. that is unseemly
7:13 sin w. death in me by good
1 Cor. 4:12 w. with our hands
Eph. 4:28 w. thing that is good
2 Thes. 3:11 w. not, busybodies
Heb. 13:21 w. th. wh. is pleasing
Rev. 16:14 spir. of devils w. mira.

**WORKING, Substantive.**

Is. 28:29 Lord excellent in w.
1 Cor. 9:6 power to forbear w.?
12:10 another the w. of miracles
Eph. 1:19 accord. to w. of power
3:7 giv. me by w. of his power
4:16 accord. to w. in measure
Phil. 3:21 accord. to w. thereby
Col. 1:29 his w. wh. work. in me
2 Thes. 2:9 after the w. of Satan

**WORKMAN.**

Ex. 35:35 work of cun. w. 38:23
Cant. 7:1 work of a cunning w.
Is. 40:19 w. melteth an image
20 seeketh to him a cun. w.
Jer. 10:3 work of w. with axe
Hos. 8:6 w. made it, not of God
Mat. 10:10 w. is worthy of meat
2 Tim. 2:15 a w. not to be asha.

**WORKMANSHIP.**

Ex. 31:3 and in all manner of w. 5; 35:31
2 K. 16:10 accord. to w. thereof
Ezek. 28:13 w. of tabrets prepar.
Eph. 2:10 we are his w. in C. Je.

**WORKMEN.**

2 K. 12:14 they gave that to the w. 15; 2 Chr. 34:10, 17
1 Chr. 22:15 w. with th. in abun.
25:1 the number of the w.
2 Chr. 24:13 so the w. wrought
Ezr. 3:9 set w. in house of God
Is. 44:11 the w. they are of men
Acts 19:25 with w. of like occup.

**WORLD.**

1 Sam. 2:8 he set w. upon them
2 Sam. 22:16 the foundations of the w. appeared, Ps. 18:15
1 Chr. 16:30 w. sh. not be moved
Job 18:18 sh. be chased out of w.
34:13 who hath disposed the w.
37:12 may do on the face of w.
Ps. 9:8 he shall judge the w. in righteousness, 96:13; 98:9
Ps. 17:14 deliver from men of the w.
19:4 to end of w. Rom. 10:18
22:27 ends of w. shall remember
24:1 the earth and the w. is the Lord's, 98:7; Nah. 1:5
33:8 inhabit. of w. stand in awe
49:1 give ear, inhabitants of w.
50:12 for the w. is mine
77:18 lightnings light. w. 97:4
89:11 founded w. and its fulness
90:2 form. the earth and the w.
93:1 the w. also is established
96:10 w. also sh. be established
Prov. 8:26 not made dust of w.
Ec. 3:11 set w. in their heart
Is. 13:11 I will punish w. for evil
14:17 is this he made w. wild.?
21 nor fill face of w. wi. cities
24:4 the w. languisheth away
27:6 Is. sh. fill the w. with fruit
34:1 let world hear, and all that
45:17 not confoun. w. with. end
Mat. 4:8 the devil showeth him all kingd. of the w. Luke 4:5
5:14 ye are the light of the w.
13:38 field is w. good seed chil.
40 so shall it be in end of w. 49
16:26 what profit. gain w. lose soul? Mark 8:36; Luke 9:25
18:7 woe to w. bec. of offences
24:14 sh. be preached in all the w. for witness, Mark 14:9
Luke 1:70 who ha. been since w. began, Acts 3:21
2:1 decree that w. sh. be taxed
20:35 worthy to obtain that w.
John 1:10 he was in w. the w. was made by him, Acts 17:24
29 L. of G. takes away sin of w.
3:16 God so loved the w. that
17 w. thro' him might be sav.
4:42 C. Savi. of w. 1 John 4:14
6:33 bread of G. giv. life to w.
51 my flesh, I give for life of w.
7:4 these th. show thyself to w.
7 w. cannot hate you
8:12 said, I am light of w. 9:5
12:19 the w. is gone after him
47 I co. not to jud. but save w.
14:17 Sp. wh. w. cannot receive
19 the w. seeth me no more
22 how manifest thyself unto us and not unto the w.?
27 I give, not as the w. giveth
31 the w. may know I love Fa.
15:18 w. hate you, 1 John 3:13
19 of w. the w. love his own
16:20 but the w. shall rejoice
28 I leave w. and go to Father
33 I have overcome the w.
17:5 glory I had before w. was
6 name to men gav. out of w.
9 I pray not for w. but for them
14 w. hated th. bec. not of w.
15 not take them out of w.
16 not of w. as I am not of w.
21 that the w. may believe th. hast sent me, 23
25 the w. hath not known me
18:20 I spake openly to w.
21:25 w. could not cont. books
Acts 17:6 turned w. upside down
19:27 Diana, Asia and w. worsh.
24:5 a mover of sedit. thro' w.
Rom. 1:8 faith is spo. of thro' w.
3:6 for how shall G. judge w.?
18 w. may bec. guilty bef. G.
4:13 he should be heir of w.
11:12 fall of th. be riches of w.
15 if casting away of them be reconciling of w.
1 Cor. 1:21 w. by wis. kn. not G.
2:7 wisdom G. ordained bef. w.
12 not received spirit of w.
3:22 w. or life, or death, yours
4:9 are made a spectacle to w.
13 we are made as filth of w.
5:10 then must ye go out of w.
6:2 kn. th. saints sh. judge w.?
7:33 careth for things in w. 34
8:13 eat no flesh wh. w. stand.
11:32 not be condemned with w.
2 Cor. 5:19 C. reconc. w. to hims.
Gal. 6:14 by wh. w. is crucified
2 Tim. 1:9 in Christ before w. began, Tit. 1:2
Heb. 2:5 in subjection w. to come
6:5 tasted powers of w. to come
11:38 of wh. w. was not worthy
Jam. 1:27 unspotted from the w.
3:6 tongue is a w. of iniquity
4:4 friend. of w. enmity with G.
2 Pet. 2:5 God spared not old w.
3:6 whereby w. that then was
1 John 2:2 propitia. for sins of w.
15 love not w. 16 is of the w.
17 the w. passeth away
1 John 3:1 the w. knoweth us not
4:5 they are of the w.
5:4 born of G. overcometh w.
19 whole w. lieth in wickedn.
Rev. 3:10 temptation come on w.
12:9 Satan, deceiveth whole w.
13:3 w. wondered after the beast

See FOUNDATION.

**In, or into the WORLD.**

Ps. 73:12 ungod. wh. pros. i. t. w.
Mat. 26:13 this gospel be preached in the whole w.
Mark 10:30 and in the w. to come eternal life, Luke 18:30
John 1:9 man that comes i. the w.
10 he was in the w.
3:17 sent not his Son into the w.
19 light is come into the w.
6:14 should come i. t. w. 11:27
9:5 as long as I am in the w.
12:46 I am come a light i. t. w.
16:33 in w. ye sh. have tribula.
17:11 I am no more in the w.
12 while I was in w. I kept th.
18:37 for this came I into the w.
Rom. 5:12 sin entered into the w.
13 until law, sin was in the w.
1 Cor. 8:4 an idol is noth. in t. w.
Eph. 2:12 without God in the w.
Col. 1:6 as it is in all the w.
1 Tim. 1:15 Christ Jesus came into the w. to save sinners
3:16 and believed on in the w.
Heb. 10:5 when he cometh i. t. w.
1 Pet. 5:9 afflict. that are in t. w.
1 John 2:15 love not thi. in t. w.
4:1 false prophets gone i. t. w.
3 now already is it in the w.
4 greater th. he that is in t. w.
9 sent his Son into the w. that
2 John 7 many deceivers i. t. w.

**This WORLD.**

Mat. 12:32 not forgi. him in t. w.
13:22 cares of this w. choke the word, Mark 4:19
Luke 16:8 children of this w. are
20:34 children of this w. marry
John 8:23 ye are of this w.
9:39 for judg. I come into t. w.
12:25 that hateth life in this w
31 now is judgment of this w.
13:1 should depart out of t. w.
14:30 prince of this w. cometh
16:11 prince of this w. is judged
18:36 kingdom is not of this w
Rom. 12:2 not conformed to t. w
1 Cor. 1:20 wh. is disp. of t. w.
2:6 speak not wisdom of this w.
3:18 if man seem. wise in t. w.
19 wisd. of t. w. foolish. wi. G.
5:10 not with fornicat. of t. w.
7:31 use t. w. as not abusing it
2 Cor. 4:4 god of t. w. blinded
Gal. 1:4 deli. us fr. t. present w.
Eph. 1:21 not only in t. w. but
2:2 according to course of t. w.
6:12 against rulers of this w.
1 Tim. 6:7 brou. nothing in t. w.
17 those that are rich in t. w.
2 Tim. 4:10 De. loved t. pres. w.
Tit. 2:12 live godly in t. pres. w.
Jam. 2:5 chosen poor of this w.
1 John 3:17 wh. hath t. w. good
4:17 as he is, so are we in t. w.

**WORLDLY.**

Tit. 2:12 ungodlin. and w. lusts

*Heb.* 9:1 first cov. had *w.* sanct.

**WORLDS.**

*Heb.* 1:2 by whom he made *w.*
11:3 *w.* were fram. by word of G.

**WORM.**

*Ex.* 16:24 neither any *w.* therein
*Job* 17:14 said to *w.* my mother
24:20 *w.* feed sweetly on him
25:6 man is a *w.* son of man
*Ps.* 22:6 I am a *w.* and no man
*Is.* 14:11 *w.* is spread under thee
41:14 fear not thou *w.* Jacob
51:8 *w.* sh. eat them like wool
66:24 their *w.* sh. not die. *Mark* 9:44, 46, 48
*Jon.* 4:7 a *w.* smote the gourd

**WORMS.**

*Ex.* 16:20 bred *w.* and stank
*Deut.* 28:39 the *w.* shall eat them
*Job* 7:5 clothed with *w.* and dust
19:26 tho' *w.* destroy this body
21:26 and *w.* shall cover them
*Is.* 14:11 and the *w.* cover thee
*Mic.* 7:17 out of holes like *w.*
*Acts* 12:23 Herod was eaten of *w.*

**WORMWOOD.**

*Deut.* 29:18 a root that beareth *w.*
*Prov.* 5:4 her end is bitter as *w.*
*Jer.* 9:15 feed them with *w.* 23:15
*Lam.* 3:15 made drunken with *w.*
19 my misery, the *w.* and gall
*Amos* 5:7 who turn judgm. to *w.*
*Rev.* 8:11 name of star called *W.*

**WORSE.**

*Gen.* 19:9 deal *w.* with thee than
2 *Sam.* 19:7 *w.* th. all that befell
2 *K.* 14:12 Judah was put to the *w.* 2 *Chr.* 25:22
1 *Chr.* 19:16 Syrians put to *w.* 19
2 *Chr.* 6:24 if people be put to *w.*
33:9 Manasseh made Jer. do *w.*
*Jer.* 7:26 *w.* th. their fath. 16:12
*Dan.* 1:10 see faces *w.* liking?
*Mat.* 12:45 last state of that man is *w.* than first. *Luke* 11:26
27:64 last error *w.* than the first
*John* 5:14 a *w.* thi. come unto th.
1 *Cor.* 8:8 if eat not are we *w.*
11:17 not for better but for *w.*
2 *Tim.* 3:13 seducers sh. wax *w.*
2 *Pet.* 2:20 latter end is *w.* with

**WORSHIP.**

*Gen.* 22:5 I and the lad will go and *w.*
*Ex.* 24:1 and *w.* ye afar off
34:14 thou shalt *w.* no other G.
*Deut.* 4:19 lest th. be driven to *w.*
8:19 if thou *w.* other gods, 11:16; 30:17
26:10 and *w.* before the L. thy God, *Ps.* 22:27, 29; 86:9
1 *Sam.* 1:3 man went up to *w.*
15:25 that I may *w.* Lord, 30
1 *K.* 12:30 the people went to *w.*
2 *K.* 5:18 *w.* in house of Rimmon
17:36 L. ye fear, him sh. ye *w.*
18:22 shall *w.* bef. this altar in Jeru. 2 *Chr.* 32:12; *Is.* 36:7
1 *Chr.* 16:29 *w.* L. in the beauty of holiness, *Ps.* 29:2; 66:4; 96:9; *Mat.* 4:10; *Luke* 4:8
*Ps.* 5:7 *w.* tow. thy temple 138:2
45:11 he is thy L. *w.* thou him
81:9 neither *w.* any strange god
95:6 let us *w.* and bow down
97:7 *w.* him all ye gods
99:5 *w.* at his footstool, 132:7
9 and *w.* at his holy hill
*Is.* 2:8 *w.* work of han. 20; 46:6
27:13 *w.* Lord in holy mount
49:7 princes also shall *w.*
66:23 all flesh *w.* before me
*Jer.* 7:2 enter th. gates to *w.* 26:2
13:10 *w.* other gods be as girdle
25:6 go not after oth. gods to *w.*
44:19 did we *w.* her with. men?
*Ezek.* 46:2 he sh. *w.* at threshold
3 people of land sh. *w.* at door
9 entereth to *w.* by north gate
*Dan.* 3:5 *w.* golden image, 10, 15
12 not *w.* im. 18:28; 15 if ye *w.*
14 do not ye *w.* ima. I set up?
*Mic.* 5:13 thou shalt no more *w.* work of thine hands
*Zep.* 1:5 that *w.* host of heaven
2:11 men sh. *w.* him, every one
*Zec.* 14:16 *w.* Lord of hosts, 17
*Mat.* 2:2 and come to *w.* him
8 that I may come and *w.* him
4:9 if thou wilt *w.* me, *Lu.* 4:7
15:9 but in vain they do *w.* me
*John* 4:20 in Jerusal. is the place wh. men oug. to *w. Mark* 7:7
22 ye *w.* ye know not what
23 *w.* the Father in spirit, 24
12:20 Greeks ca. to *w.* at feast
*Acts* 7:42 gave th. to *w.* host, 43
8:27 eunuch came to Jer. to *w.*
17:23 whom ye ignorantly *w.*
18:13 persuaded men to *w.* God
24:11 Paul came to Jerus. to *w.*
14 so *w.* I God of my fathers
1 *Cor.* 14:25 he will *w.* God
*Phil.* 3:3 which *w.* God in spirit
*Heb.* 1:6 let angels of G. *w.* him
*Rev.* 3:9 and *w.* before thy feet
4:10 *w.* him that liveth for ever
9:20 they should not *w.* devils
11:1 and them that *w.* therein
13:8 all that dwell on earth shall *w.* beast, 12
15 th. would not *w.* the image
14:7 *w.* him that made heaven
9 if any man *w.* beast and im.
11 who *w.* beast, have no rest
15:4 nations come, *w.* bef. him
19:10 I fell at his feet to *w.* 22:8; 22:9 *w.* God

**WORSHIPPED.**

*Gen.* 24:26 Abraham *w.* Lord, 48
52 Abraham's servant *w.* Lord
*Ex.* 4:31 Israel *w.* 12:27; 33:10
32:8 they made a calf, and *w.* it, *Ps.* 106:19
34:8 Mos. *w. Jud.* 7:15 Gid. *w.*
*Deut.* 17:3 served other gods, and *w.* 29:26; 1 *K.* 9:9; 2 *K.* 21:21; 2 *Chr.* 7:22; *Jer.* 1:16; 8:2; 16:11; 22:9
1 *Sam.* 1:19 Hannah *w.* before L.
28 Samuel *w.* 15:31; S. *w.* Lord
2 *Sam.* 12:20 D. arose *w.* 15:32
1 *K.* 11:33 forsaken me, *w.* Ash.
16:31 served Baal, *w.* him, 22:53
2 *K.* 17:16 they *w.* host of heaven, 21:3, 2 *Chr.* 33:3
1 *Chr.* 29:20 cong. bowed, and *w.* L. 2 *Chr.* 7:3; 29:28, 29, 30
*Neh.* 8:6 all people *w.* Lord, 9:3
*Job* 1:20 Job *w. Ezek.* 8:16 *w.* sun
*Dan.* 2:46 king *w.* 3:7 *w.* image
*Mat.* 2:11 wise men fell, *w.* Christ
8:2 leper *w.* him, 9:18 a ruler *w.*
14:33 that were in ship *w.* him
15:25 woman of Canaan *w.* him
18:26 servant fell, *w.* his lord
28:9 held him by feet, *w.* him
17 disciples *w.* him, *Lu.* 24:52
*Mark* 5:6 ran out of tombs, *w.*
15:19 spit on him, bowing, *w.*
*John* 4:20 our fath. *w.* in mount.
9:38 man believed, and *w.* him
*Acts* 10:25 Cornelius *w.* Peter
16:14 Ly. *w.* God; 18:7 Justus *w.*
17:25 neither is *w.* with hands
*Rom.* 1:25 *w.* creature more than
2 *Thes.* 2:4 exalteth above all *w.*
*Heb.* 11:21 Jacob *w. Rev.* 7:11 *w.* God
*Rev.* 5:14 twenty-four elders *w.* 11:16; 19:4
13:4 they *w.* dragon, *w.* beast
16:2 sore fell on them *w.* image
19:20 deceiv. that *w.* his image
20:4 souls that had not *w.* beast

**WORSHIPPER, S.**

2 *K.* 10:19 destroy *w.* of Baal
21 all *w.* of B. came, none left
23 none but the *w.* of Baal only
*John* 4:23 *w.* sh. worship in spirit
9:31 if any man be a *w.* of God
*Acts* 19:35 Ephesus is a *w.* of D.
*Heb.* 10:2 because *w.* once purged

**WORSHIPPETH.**

*Neh.* 9:6 host of heaven *w.* thee
*Is.* 44:15 maketh god, *w.* it, 17
*Dan.* 3:6 falleth not and *w.* 11
*Acts* 19:27 Asia and the world *w.*

**WORSHIPPING.**

2 *K.* 19:37 as he was *w.* in house of Nisroch, *Is.* 37:38
2 *Chr.* 20:18 Ju. fell down, *w.* L.
*Mat.* 20:20 Zeb's chil. came *w.*
*Col.* 2:18 begu. you in *w.* of ang.

**WORST.**

*Ezek.* 7:24 bri. *w.* of the heathen

**WORTH.**

*Gen.* 23:9 for as much money as it is *w.*
*Job* 24:25 make speech noth. *w.*
*Prov.* 10:20 heart of wick. lit. *w.*
*Ezek.* 30:2 say, howl, woe *w.* day

**WORTHY.**

*Gen.* 32:10 I am not *w.* of merci.
1 *Sam.* 1:5 he gave a *w.* portion
26:16 as L. liv. ye are *w.* to die
2 *Sam.* 22:4 who is *w.* to be praised, *Ps.* 18:3
1 *K.* 1:52 show himself a *w.* man
*Jer.* 26:11 *w.* to die; 16 is not *w.*
*Mat.* 3:11 I am not *w.* to bear
8:8 Lord, I am not *w. Luke* 7:6
10:11 inquire who in it is *w.* 13
37 loveth more, he is not *w.* 38
22:8 which were bidden not *w.*
*Mark* 1:7 not *w.* to unloose, *Lu.* 3:16; *John* 1:27; *Acts* 13:25
*Luke* 3:8 fruits *w.* of repentance
7:4 *w.* for whom he sho. do this
7 nor thought I myself *w.*
10:7 laborer is *w.* of his hire
15:19 no more *w.* to be son, 21
*Acts* 24:2 *w.* deeds done to nati.
*Rom.* 8:18 not *w.* to be compared
*Eph.* 4:1 th. ye walk *w.* of voca.
*Col.* 1:10 ye might walk *w.* of L.
1 *Thes.* 2:12 ye would walk *w.*
1 *Tim.* 1:15 *w.* of acceptati. 4:9
5:18 laborer is *w.* of his reward
*Heb.* 11:38 world was not *w.*
*Jam.* 2:7 blasph. that *w.* name?
*Rev.* 3:4 walk in white, are *w.*
4:11 *w.* to receive glory, 5:12
5:2 who is *w.* to open the book
4 no man fo. *w.* to open book
9 thou art *w.* to take book
16:6 to drink, for they are *w.*

*See* COUNT, COUNTED, DEATH.

**WORTHIES.**

*Nah.* 2:5 he shall recount his *w.*

**WORTHILY.**

*Ruth* 4:11 do thou *w.* in Ephrat.

**WOT, TETH.**

*Gen.* 21:26 I *w.* not who done
39:8 *w.* not what is with me
44:15 *w.* ye not I can divine?
*Ex.* 32:1 we *w.* not what is become of him, 23; *Acts* 7:40
*Num.* 22:6 *w.* he wh. thou bless.
*Jos.* 2:5 whither the men went I *w.* not
*Acts* 3:17 I *w.* thro' ignor. ye did
*Rom.* 11:2 *w.* ye not what scrip.
*Phil.* 1:22 what choose I *w.* not

**WOVE.**

2 *K.* 23:7 women wove hangings

**WOVEN.**
Ex. 28:32 bin. of w. work, 39:22
39:27 linen, w. work for Aaron
John 19:23 coat without seam, w.

**WOULD.**
Neh. 9:24 do with th. as they w.
Ps. 81:11 Israel w. none of me
Prov. 1:25 ye w. none of reproof
Mark 10:36 what w. ye I sho. do
Rom. 7:15 what w. that I do not
19 the good that I w. I do not

**WOULD God.**
Ex. 16:3 w. God we had died in Egypt, Num. 14:2
Num. 11:29 w. G. people proph.
20:3 w. God we died wh. breth.
Deut. 28:67 w. God it were even
Jos. 7:7 w. God we dw. on side
Jud. 9:29 w. G. peo. under hand
2 Sam. 18:33 w. G. I died for th.
2 K. 5:3 w. G. lord with prophet
Acts 26:29 w. G. all such as I am
1 Cor. 4:8 I w. God ye did reign
2 Cor. 11:1 w. to G. bear wi. me

**WOULD not.**
1 Sam. 20:9 w. not I tell thee?
Is. 30:15 and ye w. not, Mat. 23:37; Luke 13:34
Rom. 7:16 do that whi. I w. not
19 evil that I w. not that I do
2 Cor. 12:20 such as ye w. not

**WOULDEST.**
Jos. 15:18 and Caleb said, What w. thou? 1 K. 1:16

**WOULDEST not.**
John 21:18 carry whi. thou w. n.

**WOUND.**
Ex. 21:25 give w. for w. stripe
1 K. 22:35 blood ran out of w.
Job 34:6 my w. is incurable
Prov. 6:33 a w. and dishonor
20:30 blueness of a w. cleanseth
Is. 30:26 heal. stroke of their w.
Jer. 10:19 for my w. is grievous
15:18 why is my w. incurable?
30:12 w. is grievous, Nah. 3:19
14 I wounded thee with w.
Hos. 5:13 Jud. saw his w. could
Ob. 7 have laid a w. under thee
Mic. 1:9 her w. is incurable
Rev. 13:3 w. was healed, 12, 14

**WOUNDS.**
2 K. 8:29 king J. went to be heal. of the w. 9:15; 2 Chr. 22:6
Job 9:17 he multiplied my w.
Ps. 38:5 my w. stink, corrupt
147:3 and bindeth up their w.
Prov. 18:8 talebearer as w. 26:22
23:29 hath w. without cause?
27:6 faithful are w. of a friend
Is. 1:6 no soundness in it, but w.
Jer. 6:7 before me is grief and w.
30:17 I will heal thee of thy w.
Zec. 13:6 are th. w. in thy hands?
Luke 10:34 Samari. bound up w.

**WOUND, Verb.**
Deut. 32:39 I w. and I heal
Ps. 68:21 God sh. w. his enemies
110:6 w. heads ov. many countr.
1 Cor. 8:12 ye w. their conscience

**WOUND.**
John 19:40 th. w. body of Jesus
Acts 5:6 yo. men w. up Ananias

**WOUNDED.**
Deut. 23:1 he that is w. in stones
1 Sam. 17:52 w. of Philistines
2 Sam. 22:39 I have w. mine enemies, Ps. 18:38
1 K. 20:37 in smiting he w. him
22:34 for I am w. 2 Chr. 18:33
2 Chr. 35:23 for I am sore w.
Job 24:12 soul of w. crieth out
Ps. 64:7 suddenly sh. they be w.
69:26 grief of those th. hast w.
109:22 my heart is w. within me
Prov. 7:26 cast down many w.
18:14 a w. spirit who can bear?
Cant. 5:7 found me, they w. me
Is. 51:9 art not it that w. drag.?
53:5 he was w. for our transgr.
Jer. 30:14 I w. thee with wound
37:10 th. remained but w. men
51:52 thro' land w. shall groan
Lam. 2:12 they swooned as w.
Ezek. 26:15 when the w. cry
28:23 w. be judged in the midst
30:24 groanings of a w. man
Joel 2:8 fall on sword, not be w.
Zec. 13:6 w. in house of my frie.
Mark 12:4 w. him, Luke 20:12
Luke 10:30 am. thieves, w. him
Acts 19:16 fled out house nak. w.
Rev. 13:3 his heads as it were w.

**WOUNDEDST, ETH.**
Job 5:18 w. hands make whole
Hab. 3:13 thou w. head of wick.

**WOUNDING.**
Gen. 4:23 slain a man to my w.

**WRAP.**
Is. 28:20 he can w. himself in it
Mic. 7:3 reward, so they w. it up

**WRAPPED, or WRAPT.**
Gen. 38:14 Tamar w. herself
1 Sam. 21:9 sword is w. in cloth
1 K. 19:13 Elijah w. his face
2 K. 2:8 mantle, w. it together
Job 8:17 roots are w. about heap
40:17 sinews of stones w. togeth.
Ezek. 21:15 swo. is w. for slaug.
Jon. 2:5 weeds w. about head
Mat. 27:59 Jos. w. body in linen, Mark 15:46; Luke 23:53
Luke 2:7 Mary w. him in clothes
12 babe w. in swaddl. clothes
John 20:7 napkin w. together

**WRATH.**
Gen. 49:7 cursed be their w.
Lev. 10:6 lest w. come upon peo.
Num. 1:53 no w. be on cong. 18:5
16:46 there is w. gone out fr. L.
Deut. 9:7 provokedst L. to w. 22
29:28 rooted them out in w.
32:27 were it not I feared w.
Jos. 9:20 lest w. be upon us
22:20 w. fell on all the congre.
2 Sam. 11:20 if king's w. arise
2 K. 23:26 L. turned not from w
1 Chr. 27:24 because th. fell w.
2 Chr. 19:2 theref. is w. on thee
10 and so w. come upon you
24:18 w. came on Ju. for tresp.
28:13 there is fierce w. ag. Isr.
29:10 his w. may turn away
32:25 theref. th. was w. on him
Ezr. 5:12 had provoked G. to w.
7:23 why sho. be w. ag. realm?
Neh. 13:18 bri. more w. upon Is.
Est. 1:18 th. arise too much w.
2:1 w. of king was appeased
3:5 bowed not, Ham. full of w.
7:10 then was king's w. pacified
Job 5:2 for w. killeth foolish man
19:29 for w. brings punishments
21:20 drink of w. of Almighty
36:13 hypocri. in heart heap w.
18 because there is w. beware
Ps. 37:8 forsake w. 55:3 w. hate
76:10 w. of man sh. praise thee
138:7 stre. hand ag. w. of ene.
Prov. 11:23 exp. of wicked is w
12:16 fool's w. presently known
14:29 slow to w. of great under.
15:1 soft answer turn. away w.
16:14 w. of king as messeng. of
19:12 king's w. as roar. of lion
19 man of w. suffer punishm.
21:14 rew. in bosom pacifieth w.
24 scorner, who dealeth in w.
27:3 fool's w. heavier than both
4 w. is cruel, anger is outrage.
29:8 wise men turn away w.
30:33 forcing of w. bring. strife
Ec. 5:17 much w. with sickness
Is. 13:9 day of L. cometh with w.
14:6 who smote the people in w.
54:8 in a little w. I hid my face
Jer. 21:5 fight against you in w.
32:37 driven them in great w.
44:8 provoke me to w. wi. idols
Ezek. 7:12 w. is on all multitude
Nah. 1:2 reserv. w. for enemies
Hab. 3:2 in w. remember mercy
Zep. 1:18 gold not deliver in w.
Zec. 7:12 a great w. from Lord
8:14 fathers provoked me to w.
Mat. 3:7 flee from w. to come, Luke 3:7
Luke 4:28 fill. wi. w. Acts 19:28
21:23 th. sh. be w. on this peo.
Rom. 2:5 treasurest up w. agai.
8 to them th. obey unright. w.
4:15 because law worketh w.
5:9 be saved from w. thro' him
Rom. 9:22 ves. of w. fit. to destr.
12:19 rather give place to w.
13:4 minister of G. to execu. w.
5 ye be subject, not only for w.
Gal. 5:20 works of flesh are w.
Eph. 2:3 by nature childr. of w.
4:26 let not sun go do. upon w.
31 let all w. anger, and clamor
6:4 provoke not your chil. to w.
Col. 3:8 put off these, w. malice
1 Thes. 1:10 delivered us from w.
2:16 for w. is come on them
5:9 G. hath not appoi. us to w.
1 Tim. 2:8 lift. hands without w.
Heb 11:27 not fearing w. of king
Jam. 1:19 slow to spe. slow to w.
20 w. of man work. not right.
Rev. 6:16 hide us fr. w. of Lamb
12:12 devil come, hav. great w.
14:8 nations drink of w. 18:3

**Day of WRATH.**
Job 20:28 flow away in d. of w.
21:30 wicked brou. to day of w.
Ps. 110:5 strike kings in d. of w.
Prov. 11:4 riches profit not in the day of w.
Zep. 1:15 that day is a day of w.
Rom. 2:5 treasu. w. ag. d. of w.
Rev. 6:17 great d. of w. is come

**WRATH of God.**
2 Chr. 28:11 w. of God upon you
Ezr. 10:14 w. of God be turned
Ps. 78:31 w. of God ca. on them
John 3:36 w. of G. abid. on him
Rom. 1:18 w. of God is revealed
Eph. 5:6 w. of God com. Col. 3:6
Rev. 14:10 dr. wine of w. of God
19 into wine-press of w. of G.
15:1 for th. is filled up w. of G.
7 seven vials full of w. of God
Rev. 16:1 pour vial of w. of God
19:15 tread. wine-pr. of w. of G.

**His WRATH.**
Deut. 29:23 L. overthr. in his w.
1 Sam. 28:18 execu. h. w. on A.
2 K. 23:26 L. turned not fr. h. w.
2 Chr. 29:10 his fierce w. may turn from us, 30:8
Ezr. 8:22 his w. is against them
Est. 7:7 from banquet in his w.
Job 16:9 he teareth me in his w.
20:23 cast fury of his w. on him
Ps. 2:5 speak to them in his w.
21:9 swallow them up in his w.
58:9 take them away in his w.
78:38 did not stir up all his w.
49 cast on th. fierceness of h. w.
106:23 Mo. stood to turn his w.
Prov. 14:35 his w. ag. him that
24:18 lest L. turn his w. fr. him
Is. 16:6 Moab's pride and his w.
Jer. 7:29 L. forsak. gen. of h. w.
10:10 at his w. earth sh. tremble
48:30 I know his w. saith Lord

Lam. 2:2 thrown down in his w.
3:1 affliction by rod of his w.
Amos 1:11 kept his w. for ever
Rom. 9:22 G. will. to show h. w.
Rev. 16:19 cup of wine of his w.
See KINDLED, Wrath of the LORD.

### My WRATH.

Ex. 22:24 my w. shall wax hot
32:10 that my w. may wax hot
Num. 25:11 hath turned my w.
2 Chr. 12:7 my w. shall not be poured out
Ps. 95:11 I sware in my w.
Is. 10:6 against people of my w.
60:10 for in my w. I smote thee
Ezek. 7:14 my w. is on multitude
13:15 thus will I accomp. my w.
21:31 in fire of my w. 22:21
22:31 I consu. them with my w.
38:19 in fire of my w. ha. I spo.
Hos. 5:10 I will pour my w. on
13:11 I took him away in my w.
Heb. 3:11 I sware in my w. they
4:3 as I have sworn in my w.

### Thy WRATH.

Ex. 15:7 thou sentest thy w.
32:11 why doth t. w. wax hot?
12 turn from t. w. and repent
Job 14:13 until thy w. be past
40:11 cast abroad rage of thy w.
Ps. 38:1 rebuke me not in t. w.
79:6 pour out t. w. on heathen
85:3 thou hast taken away t. w.
88:7 thy w. lieth hard on me
16 thy fierce w. goeth over me
89:46 how long shall thy w. burn like fire?
90:7 by thy w. are we troubled
9 days are passed away in t. w.
11 acc. to thy fear, so is t. w.
102:10 bec. of indigna. and t. w.
Jer. 18:20 to turn thy w. fr. them
Hab. 3:8 was thy w. ag. the sea
Rev. 11:18 t. w. is come, time of

### WRATHFUL.

Ps. 69:24 let w. anger take hold
Prov. 15:18 a w. man stir. strife

### WRATHS.

2 Cor. 12:20 envyings, w. strifes

### WREATH, S.

1 K. 7:17 w. for the chapiters
2 Chr. 4:2 two w. to cover the two pommels
13 400 pomegranates on two w. two rows of pomeg. on w.

### WREATHED, EN.

Ex. 28:14 two chains at ends of w. work, 22, 24, 25; 39:15-18
2 K. 25:17 pillar of w. work he
Lam. 1:14 my transgres. are w.

### WREST.

Ex. 23:2 many, to w. judgment
6 not w. judgment of thy poor
Deut. 16:19 shalt not w. judgm.
Ps. 56:5 ev. day th. w. thy words
2 Pet. 3:16 that are unstable w.

### WRESTLE.

Eph. 6:12 we w. not against flesh

### WRESTLED.

Gen. 30:8 have I w. with sister
32:24 there w. a man with him
25 thigh out of joint as he w.

### WRESTLINGS.

Gen. 30:8 wi. w. have I wrestled

### WRETCHED.

Rom. 7:24 O w. man that I am
Rev. 3:17 know. not thou art w.

### WRETCHEDNESS.

Num. 11:15 let me not see my w.

### WRING, ED.

Lev. 1:15 priest w. off head, 5:8
Jud. 6:38 Gide. w. dew of fleece
Ps. 75:8 wicked sh. w. them out

### WRINGING.

Prov. 30:33 w. of nose bri. blood

### WRINKLE, S.

Job 16:8 hast filled me with w.
Eph. 5:27 not having spot or w.

### WRITE.

Ex. 34:1 will w. on ta. Deut. 10:2
27 L. said to Mo. w. th. words
Num. 17:2 w. every man's name
3 w. Aaron's name on rod of L.
Deut. 6:9 w. them on posts, 11:20
24:1 let him w. her a bill of divorcement, 3; Mark 10:4
27:3 w. the words of this law, 8
31:19 w. ye this song for you
2 Chr. 26:22 acts of U. did Is. w.
Ezr. 5:10 w. the names of men
Neh. 9:38 sure coven. and w. it
Est. 8:8 w. ye also for the Jews
Prov. 3:3 w. on tab. of heart, 7:3
Is. 8:1 w. in great roll wi. a pen
10:1 w. grievousness prescribed
19 that a child may w. them
30:8 w. it before them in a table
Jer. 22:30 w. ye this man childl.
30:2 w. the words I have spoken, 36:2, 17, 28
31:33 w. in th. hearts, Heb. 8:10
Ezek. 24:2 w. the na. of the day
37:16 w. for Judah and Israel
43:11 w. it in their sight
Hab. 2:2 w. the vision on tables
Luke 1:3 it seem. good to w. th.
16:6 w. fifty; 7 w. fourscore
John 1:45 Mos. and prop. did w.
19:21 w. not, king of the Jews
Acts 15:20 w. that th. abstain fr.
25:26 no cert. thi. to w. my lord
1 Cor. 4:14 I w. not to sha. you
14:37 things I w. are command.
2 Cor. 1:13 we w. none other thi.
2:9 I w. that I might know
9:1 it is superfluous to w. you
13:2 I w. to th. wh. have sinned
10 I w. these thi. being absent
Gal. 1:20 things I w. unto you
Phil. 3:1 to w. the same things
1 Thes. 4:9 not that I w. 5:1
2 Thes. 3:17 is the token; so I w.
1 Tim. 3:14 these w. I unto thee
Heb. 10:16 in minds will I w.
2 Pet. 3:1 I w. to you, 1 John 2:1
1 John 1:4 th. thi. w. we to you
2:7 I w. no new commandment
8 a new commandm. I w. you
12 I w. to you, lit. children, 13
13 I w. to you, fathers
2 John 12 many th. to w. to you
3 John 13 not wi. ink and pen w.
Jude 3 it was needful to w.
Rev. 1:11 what seest w. 19
Rev. 2:1 angel of ch. of Ephe. w.
8 angel of chur. of Smyrna w.
12 angel of chu. in Pergam. w.
18 angel of chu. in Thyatira w.
3:1 angel of church in Sardis w.
7 angel of chu. in Philadel. w.
12 I will w. on him new name
14 angel in ch. of Laodicea w.
10:4 abo. to w. voice said w. not
14:13 w. bles. are dead die in L.
19:9 w. bless. are called to sup.
21:5 w. words true and faithful
See BOOK.

### WRITER.

Jud. 5:14 that handle pen of w.
Ps. 45:1 tong. is pen of ready w.
Ezek. 9:2 w. inkhorn by his si. 3

### WRITEST, ETH.

Job 13:26 thou w. bitter things
Ps. 87:6 shall count wh. he w. up
Ezek. 37:20 sticks whereon th. w.

### WRITING.

Ex. 32:16 the w. was w. of God
39:30 on plate of holy cro. a w.
Deut. 10:4 wrote acco. to first w.
31:24 wh. Mos. made end of w.
1 Chr. 28:19 L. made me und. w.
2 Chr. 2:11 Hur. answered in w.
21:12 a w. from Elij. to Jehoram
35:4 prepare accord. to w. of D.
36:22 Cyrus put the proclamation in w. Ezr. 1:1
Ezr. 4:7 w. of letter in Sy. tong.
Est. 1:22 sent letters accordi. to w. whereof, 3:12; 8:9; 9:27
3:14 copy of w. published to all
4:8 Mord. gave Hata. copy of w.
8:8 the w. in the king's name
Is. 38:9 the w. of Hezekiah
Ezek. 13:9 not in w. of ho. of Is.
Dan. 5:7 whoso sh. read this w.
8 they could not read the w.
15 th. they should read this w.
16 if thou canst read the w.
17 I will read w. to the king
24 this is w. that was writ. 25
6:8 establ. decree, and sign w.
9 Darius signed w. and decree
10 Daniel knew w. was signed
Mat. 5:31 let him give her a w. of divorcement, 19:7
John 19:19 w. was, Jesus of Naz.

### WRITING-TABLE.

Luke 1:63 Zacha. asked for w.-t.

### WRITINGS.

John 5:47 if ye believe not his w.

### WRITTEN.

Ex. 31:18 w. with the finger of God, Deut. 9:19
1 K. 21:11 elders did as it was w.
1 Chr. 4:41 w. by name sm. tents
2 Chr. 30:5 not kept passo. as w.
Ezr. 8:34 weight of ves. was w.
Neh. 6:6 sent letter wh. was w.
8:14 found w. in law to dwell
Est. 1:19 w. amo. laws of Medes
3:9 let it be w. that they may be
12 name of Ahasue. was it w.
8:5 w. to reverse Ham.'s letters
Ps. 69:28 not w. with righteous
102:18 w. for generati. to come
149:9 to execute judgment w.
Prov. 22:20 have not I w. to thee
Ec. 12:10 which was w. was upright
Jer. 17:13 depart from me be w.
36:29 w. king of Baby. sh. come
Ezek. 2:10 w. within and witho.
13:9 w. in writ. of house of Ju.
Dan. 5:24 the writing was w. 25
Mat. 27:37 set up his accusat. w.
Mark 11:17 w. my hou. be called
15:26 his accusation was w. K. of J. Luke 23:38; John 19:20
Luke 4:17 place where it was w.
10:20 your names are w. in hea.
18:31 thi. w. be accompli. 21:22
John 2:17 remembered it was w.
10:34 is it not w. in your law
20:31 w. that ye might believe
21:25 if should be w. every one
Acts 13:29 fulfill. all that was w.
21:25 touching Ge. we have w.
Rom. 2:15 work of the law w.
4:23 not w. for his sake alone
1 Cor. 10:11 w. for our admonit.
2 Cor. 3:2 epistle w. in hearts
3 w. not with ink, but S. of G.
7 minis. of death w. in stones
Phile. 19 I Paul have w.
Heb. 12:23 church of first-born w.
Rev. 1:3 things wh. are w. ther.
2:17 in stone a new name w.
13:8 whose names are not w.
14:1 Fa.'s name w. in foreheads
Rev. 17:5 up. head was w. Myst.
19:12 name w. on his thigh, 16
21:12 names w. on the gates

### Is WRITTEN.

Jos. 1:8 do all that is w. therein
2 K. 22:13 wh. is w. concern. us

Est. 8:8 is w. in king's name
Is. 4:3 that is w. among living
Jer. 17:1 sin of Judah is w.
Dan. 9:11 curse that is w. in law
Luke 10:26 what is w. in law ?
20:17 what is this that is w. ?
22:37 is w. must be accomplish.
John 15:25 be fulfilled that is w.
1 Cor. 4:6 to think ab. that is w.
9:10 for our sakes this is w.
15:54 he bro. to pass that is w.

**It is WRITTEN.**

Jos. 8:31 as it is w. in the law of Moses, 1 K. 2:3; 2 Chr. 23:18; 25:4; 31:3; 35:12 Ezr. 3:2, 4; 6:18; Neh. 8:15; 10:34, 36; Dan. 9:13
Ps. 40:7 in book it is w. of me, Heb. 10:7
Is. 65:6 it is w. before me
Mat. 2:5 thus it is w. Luke 24:46
11:10 of whom it is w. Luke 7:27
26:24 as it is w. of him, Mark 9:13; 14:21, 27
31 it is w. Luke 4:8; Acts 23:5
Mark 9:12 it is w. of Son of man
Luke 2:23 it is w. in law of Lord
Rom. 11:8 according as it is w
1 Cor. 1:31; 2 Cor. 4:13
12:19 it is w. 14:11; Gal. 3:10
15:3 pleas. not himself, it is w.
1 Cor. 15:45 it is w. first man A.
1 Pet. 1:16 it is w. be ye holy

**I have, or have I WRITTEN.**

Hos. 8:12 I have w. of my law
John 19:22 what I ha. w. I h. w.
1 John 2:14 I h. w. to you fath.
26 these things have I w. 5:13

**Were WRITTEN.**

Num. 11:26 they were of them that were w.
Job 19:23 O that my words w. w.
Luke 24:44 be fulfilled wh. w. w.
John 12:16 th. thi. w. w. of him
Rom. 15:4 whatsoever thi. w. w.
See BOOK.

**WRONG.**

Gen. 16:5 my w. be upon thee
Ex. 2:13 to him that did the w.
Deut. 19:16 to testify what is w.
Jud. 11:27 w. to war against me
1 Chr. 12:17 no w. in my hands
16:21 he suffered no man to do them w. Ps. 105:14
Est. 1:16 not done w. to king
Job 19:7 cry out of w. not heard
Jer. 22:3 do no w. no violence
13 that buildeth chambers w.
Lam. 3:59 thou hast seen my w.
Hab. 1:4 w. judgment proceed.
Mat. 20:13 frie. I do thee no w.
Acts 7:24 see. one of th. suffer w.
26 why do ye w. one to anot. ?
27 he that did his neighbor w.
18:14 a matter of w. or lewdness
25:10 P. said, Have I done no w.
1 Cor. 6:7 why do ye not rather take w. ?
8 ye do w. defraud brethren
2 Cor. 7:12 his cause th. done w.
12:13 burdensome, forg. this w.
Col. 3:25 doth w. receive for w.

**WRONGED, ETH.**

Prov. 8:36 sinneth w. own soul
2 Cor. 7:2 we have w. no man
Phile. 18 if he hath w. thee

**WRONGFULLY.**

Job 21:27 devices ye w. imagine
Ps. 35:19 let not enemi. w. rejoi.
38:19 that hate me w. multipli.
69:4 being mine enemies w.
119:86 they persecute me w.
Ezek. 22:29 oppressed strang. w.
1 Pet. 2:19 grief, suffering w.

**WROTE.**

Ex. 24:4 Moses w. all the words of the Lord, Deut. 31:9
34:28 L. w. on tables words of coven. Deut. 4:13; 5:22; 10:4
Num. 33:2 Moses w. their goings
Deut. 31:22 Moses w. this song
1 Sam. 10:25 Sam. w. manner of
2 Sam. 11:14 Dav. w. a letter, 15
1 K. 21:8 Jezebel w. letters, 9
2 K. 10:1 and Jehu w. letters, 6
Chr. 24:6 Shemaiah w. bef. king
2 Chr. 30:1 Hezekiah w. to Eph.
Ezr. 4:6 w. accusation aga. Jud.
8 Rehum w. a letter ag. Jer. 9
Est. 8:5 Haman w. to destroy J.
Jer. 51:60 Jerem. w. all the evil
Dan. 5:5 man's hand w. on wall
7:1 dream, and he w. the dream
Mark 10:5 Moses w. this precept
12:19 Moses w. to us, Luke 20:28
Luke 1:63 Zacharias w. saying
John 5:46 for Moses w. of me
8:6 wi. his fing. w. on ground, 8
19:19 Pilate w. title, and put it
21:24 John w. of these things
Acts 15:23 apostles w. let. by th.
18:27 brethren w. exhorting
23:25 Lysias w. after this man.
Rom. 16:22 I Terti. who w. this
1 Cor. 5:9 Paul w. in an epistle, 2 Cor. 2:3, 4; 7:12; Eph. 3:3; Phile. 21
7:1 things whereof ye w. to me
2 John 5 not as th. I w. new com.
3 John 9 I w. to the church

**WROTH.**

Gen. 4:5 and Cain was very w.
6 L. sa. to C. Why art th. w. ?
31:36 Jacob was w. 34:7 sons w.
40:2 Pharaoh was w. 41:10
Ex. 16:20 and Moses was very w. Num. 16:15; 31:14
Num. 16:22 wilt thou be w. with
Deut. 1:34 L. heard, was w. 3:26; 9:19; 2 Sam. 22:8; 2 Chr. 28:9; Ps. 18:7; 78:21, 59, 62
1 Sam. 18:8 S. was very w. 20:7
29:4 prince of Ph. w. with him
2 Sam. 3:8 Abner w. 13:21 D. w.
2 K. 5:11 but Naaman was w.
13:19 man of God w. with him
2 Chr. 16:10 Asa w. 26:19 Uz. w.
Neh. 4:1 Sanballat was w. took
Est. 1:12 theref. the king was w.
2:21 Bigthan and Teresh w.
Ps. 89:38 been w. with anointed
Is. 28:21 w. as in val. of of Gibe.
47:6 I was w. with my people
54:9 I would not be w. with th.
57:16 nor will I be always w.
17 for iniquity of his covetousness was I w.
64:5 thou art w. we have sinned
9 be not w. very sore, O Lord
Jer. 37:15 the princes were w.
Lam. 5:22 th. art very w. ag. us
Mat. 2:16 Her. was exceeding w.
18:34 his lord was w. and deliv.
22:7 and the king was very w.
Rev. 12:17 the dragon was w.

**WROUGHT, *actively*.**

Gen. 34:7 Shechem w. folly in Is.
Ex. 10:2 what things I w. in E.
36:1 then w. Bezaleel and Ahol.
4 wise men w. work, 8; 39:6
Num. 23:23 what hath God w. ?
Deut. 17:2 hath w. wickedness
22:21 hath w. folly in Israel, Jos. 7:15; Jud. 20:10
31:18 for evils they sh. have w.
Ruth 2:19 show. with wh. she w.
1 Sam. 6:6 L. had w. wonderful.
11:13 hath w. salva. in Isr. 19:5
14:45 Jonathan hath w. with G.
2 Sam. 23:10 L. w. great vict. 12
1 K. 5:16 ov. people that w. 9:23
2 K. 17:11 Is. w. wick. Neh. 9:18
21:6 Manasseh w. much wickedness, 2 Chr. 33:6
2 Chr. 24:12 hir. such as w. iron
13 workmen w. work, 34:10, 13
Neh. 4:16 my serv. w. in work
17 every one with hand w.
Job 12:9 hand of L. hath w. this
36:23 say, thou hast w. iniqu. ?
Ps. 31:19 hast w. for them that
68:28 strength. th. thou hast w.
78:43 had w. his signs in Egypt
Ec. 2:11 works my hands w.
Is. 26:12 th. hast w. works in us
18 ha. not w. any deliverance
41:4 who hath w. and done it ?
Jer. 18:3 he w. a work on wheels
Ezek. 20:9 I w. for my name's sake, 14, 22, 44
29:20 because they w. for me
Dan. 4:2 won. that God hath w.
Jon. 1:11 sea w. tempestuous, 13
Zep. 2:3 who w. his judgment
Mat. 20:12 have w. but one hour
26:10 she hath w. a good work on me, Mark 14:6
Acts 15:12 wonders God w. 21:19
18:3 abode with Aquila and w.
Rom. 15:18 Ch. ha. not w. by me
2 Cor. 5:5 w. us for same thi. G.
Gal. 2:8 th. w. effectually in Pet.
Eph. 1:20 which he w. in Christ
Jam. 2:22 faith w. with works ?
1 Pet. 4:3 to have w. will of Gen.
2 John 8 lose not thi. we have w.

**WROUGHT, *passively*.**

Num. 31:51 took of them w. jew.
Deut. 21:3 heifer ha. not been w.
Neh. 6:16 this work was w. of G.
Ps. 45:13 her clothing of w. gold
139:15 in secret, curiously w.
Ec. 2:17 work w. under sun
John 3:21 manif. th. are w. in G.
Acts 5:12 wonders w. am. people

**WROUGHTEST.**

Ruth 2:19 sa. to her, wh. w. th. ?

**WRUNG.**

Lev. 1:15 blood sh. be w. out, 5:9
Ps. 73:10 wat. of cup w. to them
Is. 51:17 ha. w. out dregs of cup

# Y

**YARN.**

1 K. 10:28 Solomon had linen y. out of Egypt, 2 Chr. 1:16

**YEA.**

Mat. 5:37 conve. be y. Jam. 5:12
2 Cor. 1:17 sho. be y. y. and nay
18 word toward you was not y.
19 for Son of God was not y.
20 promises of G. in him are y.

**YEAR.**

Gen. 17:21 Sar. shall bear next y.
Ex. 12:2 first month of the y.
23:14 keep feast in y. Lev. 23:41
29 not drive them out in one y.
Lev. 16:34 atonement once a y.
25:5 a y. of rest; 29 within a y.
Num. 9:22 if y. that cloud tarried
14:34 for a y. sh. ye bear iniqu.
Jos. 5:12 eat fruit of Can. that y.
Jud. 10:8 that y. Am. vexed Isr.
11:40 to lament four days in y.

17:10 give thee ten shek. by y.
1 Sam. 27:7 David dwelt y. and
1 K. 9:25 in a y. did Solom. offer
2 K. 19:29 eat this y. such things as grow of themsel. Is. 37:30
Est. 9:27 keep two days every y.
Ps. 65:11 crowned y. with goodn.
Is. 6:1 in y. that Uzziah died
21:16 in a y. glory of Kedar fail
61:2 procl. acc. y. of L. Lu. 4:19
63:4 y. of my redeemed is come
Jer. 11:23 y. of visit. 23:12; 48:44
17:8 not careful in y. of drought
28:16 saith L. th. y. th. shalt die
51:46 rumor both come in one y.
Ezek. 4:6 appoin. each day for y.
46:17 be his to the y. of liberty
Luke 2:41 went to Jerusal. ev. y.
13:8 Lord, let it alone this y.
Acts 11:26 whole y. they assem.
2 Cor. 8:10 to be forward a y. ago
9:2 Achaia was ready a y. ago
Heb. 9:7 pri. went in once a y. 25
10:3 remembrance of sins ev. y.
Jam. 4:13 continue there a y.
Rev. 9:15 prepare for month, a y.

**YEAR after YEAR.**

2 Sam. 21:1 fam. 3 years y. a. y.

**YEAR by YEAR.**

Deut. 14:22 tithe inc. of thy seed field bringeth forth y. by y.
15:20 eat before Lord y. by y.
1 Sam. 1:7 as he did so y. by y.
1 K. 10:25 they brought a rate y. by y. 2 Chr. 9:24
2 K. 17:4 as he had done y. by y.
Neh. 10:34 wood-offering y. by y.
Heb. 10:1 they offered y. by y.

**YEAR to YEAR.**

Ex. 13:10 ordinance from y. to y.
1 Sam. 2:19 brou. coat fr. y. to y.
7:16 Samuel went from y. to y.
2 Chr. 24:5 rep. house fr. y. to y.
Is. 29:1 add ye y. to y. let them
Zec. 14:16 fr. y. to y. to worship

See SECOND, THIRD, SEVENTH.

**YEARLY.**

Lev. 25:53 a y. serv. shall he be
Jud. 11:40 went y. to lament
21:19 a feast of L. in Shiloh y.
1 Sam. 1:3 E. went y. to worship
21 went to offer y. sacrifi. 2:19
20:6 a y. sacrifice for family
Est. 9:21 keep 15th of same y.

**YEARS.**

Gen. 1:14 for seasons, days, y.
25:7 days of the y. of Abraham
8 Abraham died full of y.
47:9 evil have y. of my life been
Ex. 34:22 feast at the y. end
Lev. 25:15 accord. to y. 16, 50, 52
27:18 accord. to y. that remain
Deut. 32:7 y. of many generations
Jos. 13:1 Jos. was stricken in y.
1 Sam. 29:3 Da. been with th. y.
1 K. 1:1 David was stricken in y.
1 K. 17:1 not dew nor rain th. y.
2 Chr. 14:6 and Asa had no war in those y.
Job 10:5 thy y. as man's days
15:20 num. of y. hid. to oppres.
16:22 when a few y. are come
32:7 multit. of y. teach wisdom
36:11 spend their y. in pleasure
26 nor can his y. be searched
Ps. 31:10 my y. spent with sigh.
61:6 prol. y. as many generatio.
77:5 the y. of ancient times
10 the y. of the right hand
78:33 their y. did he consume
90:4 a thous. y. in thy sight are but as yesterday, 2 Pet. 3:8
9 sp. our y. as a tale th. is told
10 y. are threescore y. and ten
15 y. wherein we ha. seen evil
102:24 y. throughout all genera.
27 thy y. shall have no end
Prov. 4:10 y. of life many, 9:11
5:9 lest thou give y. unto cruel
10:27 y. of wicked sh. be short.
Ec. 12:1 nor y. draw nigh
Is. 21:16 accord. to y. of hireling
38:10 I am deprived of my y.
15 I shall go softly all my y.
Ezek. 4:5 on thee y. of th. iniq.
22:4 thou art come unto thy y.
38:8 latter y. th. come into land
Dan. 9:2 I underst. number of y.
11:6 end of y. they join togeth.
8 more y. than king of north
13 king of north shall come after certain y.
Joel 2:2 y. of many generations
25 restore y. locust hath eaten
Hab. 3:2 thy work in midst of y.
Mal. 3:4 offerings as in former y.
Luke 1:7 both were stri. in y. 18
Gal. 4:10 ye obse. months and y.
Heb. 1:12 thy u. shall not fail
11:24 M. wh. come to y. refused
Rev. 20:2 bound Satan a thou. y.
3 till thousand y. be fulfilled, 4
7 when thousand y. are expir.

See Numeral words in their places, as HUNDRED, MANY, TWO, THREE, SIX, OLD.

**YELL, ED**

Jer. 51:38 like lions, they sh. y.
2:15 lions roared and y. on him

**YELLOW.**

Lev. 13:30 if th. be in it a y. hair
32 if th. be in it no y. hair, 36
Ps. 68:13 covered with y. gold

**YEARN, ED.**

Gen. 43:30 for his bowels did y.
1 K. 3:26 her bowels y. upon son

**YESTERDAY.**

Ex. 5:14 why not fulfill. task y.?
1 Sam. 20:27 son of J. to meat y.
2 Sam. 15:20 thou camest but y.
2 K. 9:26 seen y. blood of Naboth
Job 8:9 we are of y. know noth.
Ps. 90:4 a thous. years, but as y.
John 4:52 y. the fever left him
Acts 7:28 kill me as Egyptian y.
Heb. 13:8 same y. and for ever

**YESTERNIGHT.**

Gen. 19:34 I lay y. with my fath.
31:29 G. of your father spake y.
42 affliction, rebuked thee y.

**YIELD.**

Gen. 4:12 earth not y. her stren.
49:20 shall y. royal dainties
Lev. 19:25 y. to you the increase
26:4 land shall y. her increase
20 your land not y. her increa.
2 Chr. 30:8 y. yoursel. to the L.
Ps. 67:6 land y. her incre. 85:12
107:37 may y. fruits of increase
Prov. 7:21 fair speech cau. him y.
Is. 5:10 ten acres sh. y. one bath
Hos. 8:7 the bud shall y. no meal
Joel 2:22 fig-tree y. strength
Hab. 3:17 altho' fields y. no meat
Acts 23:21 do not th. y. unto th.
Rom. 6:13 y. yourselves to God
16 that to whom ye y. yoursel.
19 y. members to righteousn.
Jam. 3:12 no fount. y. salt water

**YIELDED.**

Gen. 49:33 Jacob y. up the ghost
Num. 17:8 rod of Aa. y. almonds
Dan. 3:28 y. th. bodies that they
Mat. 27:50 Jesus y. up the ghost
Rom. 6:19 ye have y. your mem.

**YIELDETH.**

Neh. 9:37 y. increase to kings
Job 24:5 wildern. y. food for th.
Heb. 12:11 y. fruit of righteousness

**YIELDING.**

Gen. 1:11 forth herb y. seed 12
29 given you every tree y. seed
Ec. 10:4 y. pacifie. great offences

See FRUIT.

**YOKE.**

Gen. 27:40 break his y. Jer. 30:8
Lev. 26:13 I have broken the bands of your y. Ezek. 34:27
Num. 19:2 heif. on which never came y. Deut. 21:3; 1 Sa. 6:7
Deut. 28:48 he sh. put a y. of iron upon thy neck, Jer. 28:14
1 Sam. 11:7 S. took a y. of oxen
14:14 wh. a y. of oxen mi. plow
1 K. 12:14 thy father made our y. griev. 10, 11, 14; 2 Chr. 10:4
19:19 plowing wi. 12 y. of oxen
21 took a y. of oxen, slew them
Job 1:3 Job had 500 y. of oxen
42:12 had a thousand y. of oxen
Is. 9:4 thou hast broken the y. of his burden, 10:27; 14:25
47:6 hast very heavi. laid thy y.
58:6 and that ye break every y.
Jer. 2:20 of old time brok. thy y.
5:5 these have broken thy y.
27:8 will not put neck under y.
11 bring their neck under y. 12
28:2 broken y. of king of B. 4, 11
12 H. had broken y. from Jer.
31:18 bullock unaccustom. to y.
51:23 break husband. and his y.
Lam. 1:14 y. of my transgressions is bound
3:27 good for a man to bear y.
Hos. 11:4 as they that take off y.
Nah. 1:13 now will I break his y.
Mat. 11:29 take my y. upon you
30 my y. is easy, burden light
Luke 14:19 I bought 5 y. of oxen
Acts 15:10 put y. on disciples' neck
Gal. 5:1 be not entangled with y.
1 Tim. 6:1 as many as under y.

**YOKES.**

Jer. 27:2 make bonds and y.
28:13 hast broken y. of wood
Ezek. 30:18 when I break y. of E

**YOKED.**

2 Cor. 6:14 be not unequally y.

**YOKE-FELLOW.**

Phil. 4:3 I entreat thee, true y.-f.

**YONDER.**

Gen. 22:5 I and the lad will go y.
Num. 16:37 scatter th. the fire y.
23:15 stand here, I meet Lord y.
Mat. 17:20 say, Rem. to y. place

**YOUNG.**

Gen. 31:38 she-goats not cast y.
33:13 flocks with y. are with me
Ex. 23:26 nothing cast their y.
Lev. 22:28 shall not kill it and y.
Deut. 22:6 not take dam with y.
7 let the dam go and take the y.
28:50 not show favor to the y.
32:11 as the eagle over her y.
1 Chr. 22:5 S. my son is y. 29:1
2 Chr. 13:6 when Rehob. was y.
34:3 Josiah, while he was yet y.
Ps. 78:71 ewes great with y.
84:3 where she may lay her y.
Is. 40:11 those that are with y.
Jer. 31:12 together for y. of flock
Ezek. 17:4 cropped y. twigs, 22
Mark 7:25 y. dau. unclean spirit
John 21:18 y. thou gird. thyself

See OLD.

**YOUNG ass, or asses.**

Is. 30:6 carry riches on y. asses
24 y. a. sh. eat clean provender
John 12:14 when he found a y. a.

See BULLOCK.

**YOUNG bullocks.**
*Num.* 28:11 offer two *y. b.* 19, 27
*Ezr.* 6:9 gi. what th. need, *y. b.*

**YOUNG calf.**
*Lev.* 9:2 take *y. c.* for sin-offering
*See* CHILD, CHILDREN.

**YOUNG cow.**
*Is.* 7:21 man sh. nourish a *y. cow*

**YOUNG dromedaries.**
*Est.* 8:10 lett. by riders on *y. d.*

**YOUNG eagles.**
*Prov.* 30:17 *y. eagles* shall eat it

**YOUNG hart.**
*Cant.* 2:9 belo. like *y. h.* 17; 8:14
*See* LION, LIONS, MAN, MEN.

**YOUNG one.**
*Deut.* 28:57 evil toward her *y. o.*
*Zec.* 11:16 neither seek *y. one*

**YOUNG ones.**
*Deut.* 22:6 whether *y. o.* or eggs
*Job* 38:41 when his *y. o.* cry to G.
39:3 they bring forth their *y. o.*
4 their *y. o.* are in good liking
16 ostrich is harden. aga. *y. o.*
30 eagles' *y. o.* suck up blood
*Is.* 11:7 *y. o.* lie down together
*Lam.* 4:3 give suck to their *y. o.*

**YOUNG pigeon.**
*Gen.* 15:9 turtle-dove and *y. p.*
*Lev.* 12:6 bring *y. p.* for sin-offer.

**YOUNG pigeons.**
*Lev.* 1:14 bring his offer. of *y. p.*
5:7 he sh. bring two *y. pigeons*, 12:8; 14:22, 30; 15:14, 29; *Num.* 6:10; *Luke* 2:24
11 if not able to bring 2 *y. p.*

**YOUNG ravens.**
*Ps.* 147:9 he giveth food to *y. r.*

**YOUNG roes.**
*Cant.* 4:5 breasts like *y. roes*, 7:3

**YOUNG virgin.**
1 *K.* 1:2 let there be sought *y. v.*

**YOUNG virgins.**
*Jud.* 21:12 were found 400 *y. v.*
*Est.* 2:2 let *y. v.* be sou. for king
3 may gather together *y. v.*

**YOUNG unicorn.**
*Ps.* 29:6 and Sirion like a *y. u.*

**YOUNG woman.**
*Ruth* 4:12 L. give th. of this *y. w.*

**YOUNG women.**
*Tit.* 2:4 teach *y. w.* to be sober

**YOUNGER.**
*Gen.* 9:24 knew what *y.* son done
19:31 first-born said to the *y.* 34
38 the *y.* bare a son Ben-ammi
25:23 elder serve *y. Rom.* 9:12
29:18 I will serve 7 years for *y.*
26 it must not be so, to give *y.*
43:29 is this your *y.* brother of
48:14 Is. laid right ha. on the *y.*
19 *y.* brother be greater th. he
*Jud.* 1:13 *y.* brother took it, 3:9
15:2 is not her *y.* sister fairer?
1 *Sam.* 14:49 Saul's *y.* daughter
1 *Chr.* 24:31 against *y.* brethren
*Job* 30:1 that are *y.* than I, have
*Ezek.* 16:46 thy *y.* sister is Sodom
*Luke* 15:12 *y.* said, Gi. me portion
13 *y.* gathered all, took journ.
22:26 greatest, let him be as *y.*
1 *Tim.* 5:1 entreat *y.* as brethren
2 the *y.* women as sisters, with
11 *y.* widows refuse, for when
14 I will that *y.* women marry
1 *Pet.* 5:5 *y.* submit to the elder

**YOUNGEST.**
*Gen.* 42:13 *y.* is with our fath. 32
15 except your *y.* brother com. 20, 34; 44:23, 26
43:33 *y.* according to his youth
44:2 cup in sack's mouth of *y.*
*Jos.* 6:26 in his *y.* son set up gates, 1 *K.* 16:34
*Jud.* 9:5 Jotham, *y.* son, was left
1 *Sam.* 16:11 there remains yet *y.*
17:14 David was *y.* the eldest
2 *Chr.* 21:17 none left save the *y.*
22:1 made Ahaz. his *y.* son king

**YOURS.**
2 *Chr.* 20:15 battle not *y.* God's
2 *Cor.* 12:14 I seek not *y.* but you

**YOUTH.**
*Gen.* 8:21 imagina. evil fr. his *y.*
43:33 youngest accord. to his *y.*
46:34 from our *y.* even till now
*Lev.* 22:13 in fa.'s house as in *y.*
*Num.* 30:3 in fa.'s house in *y.* 16
*Jud.* 8:20 the *y.* drew not sword
1 *Sam.* 17:33 a man of war fr. *y.*
42 a *y.* of fair countenance
55 said, Whose son is this *y.*?
2 *Sam.* 19:7 evil befell thee fr. *y.*
1 *K.* 18:12 I fear Lord from *y.*
*Job* 13:26 possess iniqu. of my *y.*
20:11 bones full of sins of his *y.*
29:4 as I was in days of my *y.*
30:12 on my right hand rise *y.*
31:18 fr. *y.* he was brought up
33:25 shall return to days of *y.*
36:14 hypocrites die in *y.* and
*Ps.* 25:7 remember not sins of *y.*
71:5 art my trust from my *y.*
17 hast taught me from my *y.*
88:15 ready to die from my *y.*
89:45 days of his *y.* thou short.
103:5 thy *y.* renew. like eagle's
110:3 th. hast the dew of thy *y.*
127:4 so are children of thy *y.*
129:1 have afflicted me fr. my *y.*
144:12 as plants grown up in *y.*
*Prov.* 2:17 forsak. guide of her *y.*
5:18 rejoice with wife of thy *y.*
*Ec.* 11:9 rejoi. O man, in thy *y.*
10 childhood and *y.* are vanity
12:1 remember thy Creator in *y.*
*Is.* 47:12 has labored from *y.*
15 thy merchants fr. *y.* wander
54:4 sh. forget shame of thy *y.*
6 Lord called thee as wife of *y.*
*Jer.* 2:2 I remember kindn. of *y.*
3:4 thou art the guide of my *y.*
24 labor of our fathers from *y.*
25 our fathers from *y.* sinned
22:21 thy manner from thy *y.*
31:19 I did bear reproa. of my *y.*
32:30 only done evil fr. their *y.*
48:11 Moab been at ease from *y.*
*Lam.* 3:27 he bear yoke in his *y.*
*Ezek.* 4:14 not polluted fr. my *y.*
16:22 not remem. days of *y.* 43
60 rememb. my covenant in *y.*
23:3 committed whored. in *y.*
8 in *y.* they lay with her
19 call to remembra. her *y.* 21
*Hos.* 2:15 sing as in days of *y.*
*Joel* 1:8 as virgin for husb. of *y.*
*Zec.* 13:5 to keep cattle fr. my *y.*
*Mal.* 2:14 and the wife of thy *y.*
15 treach. again. wife of his *y.*
*Mat.* 19:20 th. have I kept fr. my *y. Mark* 10:20; *Luke* 18:21
*Acts* 26:4 manner of life fr. my *y.*
1 *Tim.* 4:12 no man desp. thy *y.*

**YOUTHS.**
*Prov.* 7:7 among *y.* a young man
*Is.* 40:30 even the *y.* shall faint

**YOUTHFUL.**
2 *Tim.* 2:22 flee also *y.* lusts, but

# Z

**ZACCHEUS.**
*Luke* 19:5 Z. haste, come down

**ZACHARIAH, ZECHARIAH.**
2 *K.* 14:29 Z. reigned, 15:8, 11
18:2 Abi dau. of Z. 2 *Chr.* 29:1
1 *Chr.* 5:7 of Reubeni. Jeiel, Z.
9:21 Z. of Levit. 15:18, 24; 26:2
37 Geder, Ahio, Z. and Mickl.
16:5 to Asaph, Z. 24:25 Issh. Z.
26:11 Z. the 4th son of Hosah
14 Z. son of Shelemiah, wise
27:21 ruler was Iddo son of Z.
2 *Chr.* 17:7 Jehoshap. sent to Z.
20:14 Jahaziel son of Z. came
21:2 Jehiel and Z. sons of Jeho.
24:20 Spirit of G. came upon Z.
26:5 sought G. in the days of Z.
29:13 Asaph, Z. sancti. himself
34:12 Z. of the Kohathites was
35:8 Hilkiah, Z. rulers of house
*Ezr.* 5:1 Z. son of Iddo prophes. to J. in Jud. 6:14; *Neh.* 12:16
8:3 of Pharo. Z. 11 of Bebai, Z.
10:26 Elam, Z. *Neh.* 11:4 Z. son
*Neh.* 8:4 Ezra's left ha. stood Z.
11:5 Z. son of Shiloni; 12 Pash.
12:35 Z. son of Jonathan, 41
*Is.* 8:2 Z. the son of Jeberechiah
*Zec.* 1:1 Z. son of Barachiah, 7:1; *Mat.* 23:35: *Luke* 11:51
*Luke* 1:5 Z. a priest of the course
13 fear not, Z. 59 called him Z.

**ZADOK.**
2 *Sam.* 8:17 Z. and Abim. priests
15:29 Z. carried the ark of God
35 hast not with thee Z.?
20:25 Z. and Abiathar, 1 *K.* 4:4
1 *K.* 1:8 but Z. was not with, 26
45 Z. and Nathan have anoint.
2:35 Z. the priest, 1 *Chr.* 29:22
4:2 Azariah son of Z. the priest
2 *K.* 15:33 dau. of Z. 2 *Chr.* 27:1
1 *Chr.* 6:8 Ahitub begat Z. 12, 53
12:28 Z. a yo. man, mighty man
24:3 both Z. sons of El. and Ah.
27:17 of Aaronites Z. was capt.
2 *Chr.* 31:10 priest of house of Z.
*Ezr.* 7:2 son of Shall. son of Z.
*Neh.* 3:4 Z. repaired, 29; 10:21
11:11 the son of Z. Meshullam
13:13 I made Z. scribe treasurer
*Ezek.* 40:46 the sons of Z. 43:19: 44:15
48:11 priests sanc. of sons of Z.

**ZALMUNNA.**
*Jud.* 8:5 pursu. aft. Zeba and Z.
6 hands of Zeba and Z. in, 15
21 Gideon slew Zeba and Z.
*Ps.* 83:11 princes as Zeba and Z.

**ZARAH.**
*Gen.* 38:30 son called Z. 46:12
1 *Chr.* 2:4 Pharez and Z. *Mat.* 1:3
6 sons of Z. Zimri, and Ethan
*See* ZERAH.

**ZAREPHATH.**
1 *K.* 17:9 get thee to Z. 10
*Ob.* 20 of Israel sh. possess to Z.

**ZEAL.**
2 *Sam.* 21:2 slay them in his *z.*
2 *K.* 10:16 see my *z.* for the Lord
19:31 *z.* of L. do this, *Is.* 37:32
*Ps.* 69:9 the *z.* of thy house hath eaten me up, *John* 2:17

119:139 my z. hath consum. me
Is. 9:7 z. of L. will perform this
59:17 was clad wi. z. as a cloak
63:15 wh. is thy z. and stren.?
Ezek. 5:13 I have spoken it in z.
Rom. 10:2 they have a z. of God
2 Cor. 7:11 what z.? 9:2 your z.
Phil. 3:6 concerning z. persecut.
Col. 4:13 hath a great z. for you

**ZEALOUS.**

Num. 25:11 was z. for my sake
13 he was z. for his God, made
Acts 21:20 they are all z. of law
22:3 z. towards God, Gal. 1:14
1 Cor. 14:12 z. of spiritual gifts
Tit. 2:14 people, z. of good works
Rev. 3:19 be z. theref. and repent

**ZEALOUSLY.**

Gal. 4:17 they z. affect you, not
18 it is good to be z. affected

ZEBAH. See ZALMUNNA.

**ZEBEDEE.**

Mat. 4:21 in ship with Z. father
10:2 James and John sons of Z.
26:37; Mark 1:19; 3:17; 10:35; Luke 5:10; John 21:2
20:20 mother of Z. childr. 27:56
Mark 1:20 their father Z. in ship

**ZEBOIM.**

Gen. 14:2 king of Z. Deut. 29:23
1 Sam. 13:18 valley of Z. to the
Neh. 11:34 of Benja. dwelt at Z.
Hos. 11:8 shall I set thee as Z.?

**ZEBUL.**

Jud. 9:28 Jerubba. Z. his officer
41 Z. thrust out Baal and bre.

**ZEBULUN.**

Gen. 30:20 L. called his name Z.
35:23 Reuben, Simeon, Jud. Z.
46:14 the sons of Z. Num. 1:30; 26:26
49:13 Z. shall dwell at haven
Num. 1:9 of Z. 2:7; 7:24; 10:16
Deut. 27:13 curse; Reu. Gad, Z.
33:18 of Z. he said, Rejoice Z.
Jos. 19:10 lot came up for Z.
Jud. 1:30 Z. drive out inhabita.
4:10 Barak called Z. and Naphtali
5:14 out of Z. that handle pen
18 Z. and Naphtali jeoparded
6:35 he sent messengers to Z.
12:12 E. buried in country of Z.
Ps. 68:27 the princes of Z. and
Is. 9:1 lightly afflicted land of Z.
Ezek. 48:26 Z. a portion; 33 gate
Mat. 4:13 in the borders of Z.
15 land of Z. and Nephthalim

**Tribe of ZEBULUN.**

Num. 1:31 numbered of t. of Z.
2:7 t. of Z. Eliab captain, 10:16
13:10 of t. of Z. Gaddiel to spy
34:25 prince of t. of Z. to divide
Jos. 21:7 t. of Z. 34; 1 Chr. 6:77
Rev. 7:8 of t. of Z. sealed 12,000

**ZEDEKIAH.**

1 K. 22:11 Z. made, 2 Chr. 18:10
24 Z. smote Mic. 2 Chr. 18:23
2 K. 24:17 changed name to Z.
25:7 of Z. Jer. 39:6, 7; 52:11
1 Chr. 3:15 son of Josiah, Z. 16
2 Chr. 36:10 made Z. his br. king
Jer. 21:7 deliver Z. and his peo.
29:22 Lord make thee like Z.
32:4 Z. shall not escape from
5 shall lead Z. to Babylon
Jer. 39:5 army overtook Z. 52:8

**ZELOPHEHAD.**

Num. 26:33 Z. had no sons, Jos. 17:3
27:7 daught. of Z. speak right
36:11 daughters of Z. married

**ZELZAH.**

1 Sam. 10:2 men by sepulc. at Z.

**ZENAS.**

Tit. 3:13 bring Z. on his journey

**ZEPHANIAH.**

2 K. 25:18 took Z. Jer. 52:24
1 Chr. 6:36 Z. of sons of Kohath.
Jer. 21:1 when Zedekiah sent Z.
29:25 letters in thy name to Z.
29 Z. read this letter in ears
37:3 Z. son of Maaseiah priest
Zep. 1:1 the word came to Z.
Zec. 6:10 house of Jos. son of Z.
14 sh. be to Hen the son of Z.

**ZERAH.**

Gen. 36:13 sons of Reuel, Z. 1 Chr. 1:37, 44
33 Johab the son of Z. reigned
Num. 26:13 of Z. family of, 20
Jos. 7:1 son of Zabdi, son of Z.
22:20 son of Z. commit a tresp.
1 Chr. 4:24 sons of Sim. were Z.
6:21 Z. son of Iddo, 41 son of Z.
9:6 of sons of Z. Jeuel dwelt in
2 Chr. 14:9 Z. Ethiopian came
Neh. 11:24 Pethah. of chil. of Z.

**ZERESH.**

Est. 5:10 called for Z. his wife

**ZERUBBABEL.**

1 Chr. 3:19 son of Pedaiah, Z.
Ezr. 2:2 ca. up wi. Z. Neh. 12:1
3:2 Z. son of Shealtiel, 8; 5:2
Neh. 12:47 days of Z. gave port.
Hag. 1:1 word of the Lord to Z.
12 then Z. obeyed the voice of
14 Lord stirred up spirit of Z.
2:4 yet now be strong, O Z. 21
Zec. 4:6 word of Lord unto Z.
7 before Z. sh. become a plain
9 the hands of Z. have laid the

**ZERUIAH.**

2 Sam. 2:18 three sons of Z.
3:39 sons of Z. too hard for me
8:16 Joab son of Z. 1 Chr. 18:15
16:10 what have I to do with you, ye sons of Z.? 19:22
1 Chr. 2:16 whose sisters were Z.

**ZIBA.**

2 Sam. 9:2 art thou Z.? 10 Z. had
16:4 Z. thine are all that pertain
19:29 thou and Z. divide land

**ZIBEON.**

Gen. 36:2 Anah daugh. of Z. 14
24 these are the children of Z.
1 Chr. 1:40 fed asses of Z. 29

**ZIDON.**

Gen. 49:13 border shall be to Z.
Jos. 11:8 chased th. to great Z.
19:28 Kanah, even unto great Z.
Jud. 10:6 and served gods of Z.
18:28 because it was far from Z.
1 K. 17:9 which belongeth to Z.
Ezr. 3:7 drink unto them of Z.
Is. 23:2 merch. of Z. replenished
4 O Z. the sea hath spoken
12 O thou virgin, daught. of Z.
Jer. 25:22 kings of Z. shall drink
27:3 and yokes to king of Z.
47:4 Tyre and Z. every helper
Ezek. 27:8 the inhabitants of Z.
28:21 set thy face against Z.
22 behold, I am ag. thee, O Z.
Joel 3:4 with me, O Tyre and Z.
Zec. 9:2 Tyrus and Z. though it

**ZIDONIANS.**

Jud. 10:12 Z. and Amalekites
18:7 careless, after manner of Z.
1 K. 11:1 Sol. loved women of Z.
33 Ashtoreth, goddess of Z.
Ezek. 32:30 Z. th. are gone down

**ZIF.**

1 K. 6:1 month of Z. is second
37 foundation laid in month Z.

**ZIKLAG.**

1 Sam. 27:6 Achish gave Z. to D.
30:14 we burnt Z. with fire
2 Sam. 1:1 D. abode 2 days in Z.
4:10 I slew them in Z.
1 Chr. 4:30 dw. at Z. Neh. 11:28
12:1 came to David to Z. 20

**ZILPAH.**

Gen. 29:24 Lab. gave to Leah Z.
30:9 Leah gaze Z. her maid to
10 Z. bare Jacob a son, 12
35:26 sons of Z. Gad, A. 46:18
37:2 lad was with the sons of Z.

**ZIMRI.**

Num. 25:14 th. was slain was Z.
1 K. 16:9 Z. conspired against, 16
15 Z. reigned 7 days in Tirzah
2 K. 9:31 had Z. peace, who?
1 Chr. 2:6 sons of Zerah, Z. and
8:36 Z. son of Jehoadah, 9:42
Jer. 25:25 I made kings of Z. dr.

**ZIN.**

Num. 13:21 from wildern. of Z.
20:1 I came to desert of Z. 33:36
27:14 in desert of Z. Deut. 32:51

**ZION.**

2 Sam. 5:7 David took strong-hold of Z. 1 Chr. 11:5
1 K. 8:1 which is Z. 2 Chr. 5:2
Ps. 2:6 on my holy hill of Z.
48:12 walk about Z. go round about her

Ps. 51:18 thy good pleas. unto Z.
69:35 for God will save Z. and
87:2 the Lord loveth gates of Z.
5 said of Z. this and that man
97:8 Z. heard and was glad
102:13 and have mercy on Z.
16 when Lord shall build up Z.
126:1 L. turned captivity of Z.
129:5 be turned back th. hate Z.
132:13 the Lord hath chosen Z.
133:3 as dew on mountains of Z.
137:1 when we remembered Z.
3 sing us one of the son. of Z.
146:10 the Lord shall reign, O Z.
147:12 praise thy God, O Z.
149:2 let children of Z. be joyful
Is. 1:27 Z. shall be redeemed
12:6 shout, th. inhabitant of Z.
14:32 that Lord hath founded Z.
33:5 hath filled Z. with judgm.
20 look on Z. 35:10 come to Z.
34:8 for controversy of Z.
40:9 O Z. bringest good tidings
41:27 sh. say to Z. behold them
49:14 Z. said, L. hath forsaken
51:3 the Lord shall comfort Z.
11 sh. come with singing to Z.
16 say unto Z. Th. art my peo.
52:1 put on thy strength, O Z.
7 saith unto Z. Thy G. reigneth
8 Lord shall bring again Z.
59:20 Redeemer sh. come to Z.
60:14 Z. of the Holy One of Is.
62:1 for Z. sake will I not hold
64:10 Z. is a wilderness, Jerusa.
66:8 as soon as Z. travailed, she
Jer. 3:14 I will bring you to Z.
4:6 set up standard towards Z.
14:19 hath thy soul loathed Z.?
26:18 Z. shall be plow. Mic 3:12
Jer. 30:17 Z. whom no man seek.
31:6 let us go up to Z. to the
12 and sing in height of Z.
50:5 they sh. ask the way to Z.
51:35 shall the inhabitant of Z.
Lam. 1:4 ways of Z. do mourn
17 Z. spreads forth her hands
4:2 sons of Z. compara. to gold
5:18 mountain of Z. is desolate
Joel 2:23 be glad, ye child. of Z.
Amos 1:2 Lord will roar from Z.
Mic. 3:10 th. build Z. with blood
4:2 for law shall go forth of Z.
11 let our eye look upon Z.